ADVANCED ORGANIC CHEMISTRY

Louis F. Fieser
*Sheldon Emery Professor
of Organic Chemistry
Harvard University*

Mary Fieser
*Research Fellow in Chemistry
Harvard University*

REINHOLD BOOK CORPORATION
A Subsidiary of Chapman-Reinhold, Inc.
NEW YORK   AMSTERDAM   LONDON

Second printing, 1962
Third printing, 1963
Fourth printing, 1964
Fifth printing, 1965
Sixth printing, 1968

PRINTED IN THE UNITED STATES OF AMERICA
PRINTED BY THE GUINN COMPANY

PREFACE

In this book we have attempted to present a reasonably up-to-date and complete account of fundamental organic chemistry as interpreted by modern theory. A perhaps novel plan of organization involves inclusion in the first three chapters of the following topics: Kekulé structures; the covalent bond; the hydrogen bond; Lewis acids and bases; activation energy; transition states and intermediates; orbital theory (CH_4, C_2H_6); structures and names of hydrocarbons, alcohols, amines, acids, carbonyl compounds; conformational stability of derivatives of ethane and of cyclohexane; resonance in the acetate ion; aromatic types and resonance stabilization; inductive effects from pK_a values; and stereochemistry. Development of the chemistry of the alkanes, alkenes, etc. is then possible on a comprehensive scale and at a mature level. Where possible, we have adopted a topical presentation and have selected material that fits into a narrative account of developments in a given area. Some of the accounts are very new, others have been gleaned from the literature by restudy of early papers. We have tried to do full justice to history, to modern theory, and to details of experimentation.

The subjects selected include many exciting developments that highlight current research. Special fields that are, on the whole, less active are covered adequately in our *Organic Chemistry, 3rd edition,* and are omitted from this already lengthy book. However, standard reactions are often illustrated with examples taken from a special field: use of three types of OH-protective groups in the synthesis of UDPG; use of the Wittig reaction in the total synthesis of lycopene, vitamin D_3, and quinquephenyl; cortisol, to exemplify the behavior of alcoholic hydroxyl group of three types; mechanism of *vic*-glycol cleavage of stereoisomeric steroid diols.

A book needs a name, and we have used about the only one which is at least partly descriptive and which distinguishes this book from the one published in 1956. Our book differs from others of the same title in developing the subject from the beginning. The book certainly is not advanced in the sense of being difficult, and we have tried to make it understandable and interesting to students at all levels.

Documentation of the book with full references to the literature would have defeated the objective of presenting a volume of reasonable size and price. However, guidance to the original literature is provided by name-and-date references and by biographies. Identification of at least one member of a research group not only pinpoints a reference but, we think, adds interest to the account of the work. Our selections are based in part upon entries in *American Men of Science*. Unfortunately no comparable guide is available with respect to chemists of other countries and we apologize for omissions arising from lack of information or from

iii

oversight. Academic chemists are favored over those in the industry partly because their records are available in the A.C.S. Directory of Graduate Research
and partly in the interest of student readers. Thus a chemist of the industry is
often identified merely by citation of his company.

It is a pleasure to identify and thank most cordially five outstanding advisers
who read the entire galley proof, noted corrections, and suggested significant
changes and improvements; they are Gilbert Stork of Columbia, Alfred T. Blomquist of Cornell, Theodore L. Cairns of the du Pont Company, and Paul Stecher
and Barbara M. Szafranski, Editor and Assistant Editor of the *Merck Index*. For
long hours of careful proofreading and checking, we thank our research associates
Amareshwar Chatterjee, Musa Z. Nazer, and Vivian Viegas. Of a number of
chemists who kindly checked chapters or sections, we wish to mention particularly
Charles K. Bradsher, Albert W. Burgstahler, Gerhard L. Closs, Hyp J. Dauben,
Jr., William S. Dauben, Ernest L. Eliel, Theodora W. Greene, Jack Hine, Thomas
L. Jacobs, E. R. H. Jones, Charles N. Kimberlin, Jerrold Meinwald, Melvin S.
Newman, Alex Nickson, Gaston L. Schmir, Edward C. Taylor, Harry H. Wasserman, Mark C. Whiting, Saul Winstein. We acknowledge helpful suggestions on
the carbohydrate chapter from Nelson K. Richtmyer and Melville L. Wolfrom
but must state that these gentlemen protested vigorously our failure to adhere to
all rules of the American and British committees on carbohydrate nomenclature.

A grant from Research Corporation has been of assistance in various ways. Our
publisher contributed significantly by letting us adopt unorthodox devices for reducing to a few months the gap between publication and literature coverage (to
July 1, 1961). The photographs of models are by Frank White; the photograph
of Tio and Shio Pooh is by Walter Kray.

We welcome corrections and criticisms, and also suggestions of topics and
biographies for inclusion in a future edition or supplement.

Cambridge, Massachusetts   Louis F. Fieser
July 1, 1961   Mary Fieser

GLOSSARY

TABLES AT END OF BOOK

Section 31.1: Bond Distances	Section 31.3: Resonance Energies, Properties of Solvents; Inductive Effects; Electronegativity Values
Section 31.2: Bond Energies	

SOLVENTS

Al	Methanol or ethanol	Di	Dioxane	AcOH	Acetic Acid
An	Acetone	DMF	Dimethylformamide	H_2O	Water
Chf	Chloroform	EtOH	Ethanol	MeOH	Methanol
C_6H_6	Benzene	Hex	Hexane	Py	Pyridine

REAGENTS, REACTIONS

NBA	N-Bromoacetamide	TNM	Tetranitromethane
NBS	N-Bromosuccinimide	TsCl	*p*-Toluenesulfonyl chloride
DNF	2,4-Dinitrofluorobenzene	TsOH	*p*-Toluenesulfonic acid
OH^+	$ArCO_3H$	W.-K.	Wolff-Kishner reduction

GROUPS

Ac	Acetyl	Cb	Carbobenzoxy	Phth	Phthaloyl
t-Bu	*t*-Butyl	Et	Ethyl	Ph_3C	Trityl, $(C_6H_5)_3C$-
Bz	Benzoyl	Me	Methyl	Pr	Propyl
Cathyl	Carbethoxyl	Ms	Mesyl, CH_3SO_2	Ts	Tosyl, *p*-$CH_3C_6H_5SO_2$-
		Ph	Phenyl		

CONSTANTS

α_D	Specific rotation for sodium D line at or near 25°, conventionally reported as $[\alpha]_D^{t°}$.
M_D	Molecular rotation (units, not degrees) $= \alpha_D \times$ mol. wt./100.
λ	(a) Ultraviolet (UV) absorption maximum in $m\mu$ determined in ethanol or valid for an ethanolic solution. The molecular extinction coefficient, ϵ, or log ϵ, is given in parentheses. (b) Infrared (IR) absorption maximum in μ.
cm^{-1}	Frequency, or wave number, of an IR absorption band.
cps	Cycles per sec. (nuclear magnetic resonance spectra).
kcal./mole	Kilogram calories per mole.

BONDS

Full line	up, or to the front	Wavy	ξ, configuration unknown
Dotted line	down, or to the rear	No bond	epimer mixture

SYSTEMATIC NAMES

A chemical name is divided only when each part is a correctly pronounceable word in its own right. Examples:

1. Δ^2-Octene (or 2-octene or octene-2). *Not* oct-5-ene (oct is not a word).
2. Δ^5-Cholestene-3β-ol (or 5-cholestene-3β-ol). *Not* cholest-5-en-3β-ol (en is not a word, as is ene, and is pronounced differently; ol is a word. Other endings used as words: diene, triene, diol, polyol).
3. Cholestanyl acetate. *Not* cholestan-3β-yl acetate (cholestan is not a word, yl is not a word).

Also correct: cholestane-3β-ol acetate (to be read in the sense "cholestane-3β-ol, acetate of". The same form is appropriate for estrone acetate, cholic acid triacetate, cortisol 21-acetate.

DEVIATIONS FROM USUAL STRUCTURE

2-Desoxo-	Lacking a 2-keto group
3-Desoxy-	Lacking a 3-hydroxyl group
Homo- (acid)	$-CO_2H$ extended to $-CH_2CO_2H$
Nor- (acid)	$-CH_2CH_2CO_2H$ shortened to $-CH_2CO_2H$
Bisnor- (acid)	$-CH_2CH_2CO_2H$ shortened to $-CO_2H$

SPECIFIC TO STEROIDS

7-Dehydro-	7,8-Olefinic derivative
D-Homo-	Ring D expanded to a six-membered ring
A-Nor-	Ring A contracted to a five-membered ring
18-Nor-	Lacking the methyl group at C_{13}
19-Nor-	Lacking the methyl group at C_{10}
2,3-Seco-	2,3-Bond severed and hydrogen added at C_2 and C_3
2,3-Seco-2,3-dioic	2,3-Bond severed, C_2 and C_3 converted to CO_2H groups

NOTE ON SPELLING

Since chemical names should be and usually are pronounced as they are spelled, we prefer use of dioxāne, furāne, tryptophāne, and urethāne, since the pronunciation is stronger than with the -ăn equivalents. For the same reason we favor desoxo- and desoxy- over deoxo- and deoxy-.

EUROPEAN TERMS

ETH	Eidgenössische Technische Hochschule, Zürich (Swiss Federal Institute of Technology)
MPI	Max-Planck-Institut für Biochemie (Medizinische Forschung)
KWI	Kaiser-Wilhelm-Institut (before World War II; now MPI)
Geheimrat	Title of special academic distinction in Germany
Habilitationsschrift	Independent postdoctoral research publication required for appointment as Privatdozent
Privatdozent	Post equivalent to that of an assistant or associate professor
AG.	Aktiengesellschaft (Company)
BASF	Badische Anilin-und Soda-Fabrik (Germany)
Ciba	Gesellschaft für Chemische Industrie, Basel, Switzerland
SASM	Société applications scientifique et méchanique
UCLAF	Usines chimiques des Laboratoires Francaise

JOURNALS

Journal of the **American** Chemical **Society**
Angewandte **Chem**ie
Annalen der Chemie
Annales de **chim**ie (Paris)
Chemische **Berichte** (formerly **Ber**ichte der deutschen chemischen Gesellschaft)
Bulletin de la **société** chimique de France
Acta **Chem**ica **Scand**inavia
Collection of **Czech**oslovak Chemical Communications
Comptes **rend**us hebdomadaires des séances de l'académie des sciences
Gazzetta chimica italiana
Helvetica Chimica Acta
Journal of the **Chem**ical **Society** (London)
Journal of **Org**anic Chemistry
Monatshefte für Chemie
Recueil des **trav**aux chimique des Pays-Bas (The Netherlands)

BIOCHEMISTRY

Adenosine	9-β-D-Ribofuranosyladenine, a nucleoside
AMP	Adenosine-5'-monophosphate, adenylic acid, a mononucleotide
ADP	Adenosine-5'-diphosphate, a dinucleotide
ATP	Adenosine-5'-triphosphate, the principal biological phosphorylating agent and repository for chemical energy
DPN	Diphosphopyridine nucleotide (formerly called coenzyme I), a dinucleotide composed of AMP joined through a diphosphate linkage to 1-β-D-ribofuranosylnicotinamide-5'-phosphate·
DNPH	Reduced DPN
TPN	Triphosphopyridine nucleotide (formerly called Coenzyme II), DPN with an additional phosphate ester group at the 2'-position in the adenosine unit
FAD	Flavin adenine dinucleotide, a dinucleotide composed of AMP joined through a diphosphate linkage to riboflavin-5'-phosphate
FADH	Reduced FAD
RNA	Ribonucleic acid, a polymer of ribose nucleotide monophosphates joined together by phosphate linkages between 3'- and 5'-hydroxyl groups
DNA	Desoxyribonucleic acid, a polymer of 2-desoxyribose nucleotide monophosphates joined together by phosphate linkages between 3'- and 5'-hydroxyl groups
CoASH	Coenzyme A, adenylic acid joined through a pyrophosphate linkage to pantothenic acid, which is joined by a peptide link to β-mercaptoethanol
UDPG	Uridinediphosphoglucose

Pyrimidines:

C   Cytosine
T   Thymine
U   Uracil

Purines:

A   Adenine
G   Guanine

CONTENTS

Chapter 1

THE NATURE OF ORGANIC COMPOUNDS

1.1 **Early History.** — Some organic compounds have been known since earliest antiquity. Prehistoric peoples knew sugar ($C_{12}H_{22}O_{11}$) as the sweet principle of sugar cane, and some may have recognized that fermentation of grape juice involves conversion of a sugar of the juice into alcohol (C_2H_6O). Wine on exposure to air turns sour with formation of vinegar, a dilute solution of acetic acid (L. *acetum*, vinegar); the chemical change is oxidation of alcohol to acetic acid ($C_2H_4O_2$) under catalysis of the microorganism *Acetobacter* of mother of vinegar. Vegetable oils and animal fats are available in abundance, and the process of making soap from fat was known centuries ago. Ancient Egyptians and Romans dyed cotton, wool, and silk blue with indigo ($C_{16}H_{10}O_2N_2$) from the root of one plant, and they dyed cotton in beautiful shades of red with a substance present in madder root and later identified as alizarin ($C_{14}H_8O_4$). The Phoenicians prized the dye Tyrian purple ($C_{16}H_8Br_2O_4N_2$) from a rare species of mollusk.

A crude technique of distillation first employed for the production of oil of turpentine from pine rosin was adapted about 900 A.D. to the distillation of wine for the purpose of increasing the content of alcohol. Destructive distillation of plant products was explored in the 16th and 17th centuries. Pyrolysis of wood in a closed container without access of enough air to permit free combustion was observed (1661) to afford both charcoal and a distillate named pyroligneous acid (Gr. *pyro*, fire + L. *lignum*, wood); the volatile liquid produced is a solution in water of acetic acid, methyl alcohol (CH_4O), and acetone (C_3H_6O). Destructive distillation of amber gave succinic acid ($C_4H_6O_4$; L. *succinum*, amber); pyrolysis of gum benzoin (1608) gave products which were named benzoic acid ($C_7H_6O_2$) and benzyl alcohol (C_7H_8O). The organic compounds produced in the manner described do not occur as such in nature but are fragments split off in the decomposition of true natural products. Investigation of organic compounds in their

1

native forms was initiated in 1769–86 by German born Carl Wilhelm Scheele,[1] who made a career in Sweden as an apothecary. Self-taught in science and conducting chemical investigations as a side issue, Scheele acquired a rare mastery of techniques for the manipulation of sensitive organic compounds. He found that acid components of mixtures of substances in plant or animal extracts often can be isolated by forming an insoluble calcium or lead salt and subsequently liberating the organic acid by treatment of the salt with a mineral acid. He isolated tartaric acid ($C_4H_6O_6$) as the sour principle of the grape, citric acid ($C_6H_8O_7$) from lemon, malic acid ($C_4H_6O_5$) from apples, gallic acid ($C_7H_6O_5$) from nut galls, lactic acid ($C_3H_6O_3$) from sour milk, uric acid ($C_5H_4O_3N_4$) from urine, and oxalic acid ($C_2H_2O_4$) from wood sorrel. Scheele also prepared oxalic acid by oxidizing sugar with nitric acid; he discovered glycerol ($C_3H_8O_3$) as a component common to all animal fats and vegetable oils. Other early chemists isolated urea (CH_4ON_2) from human urine (Rouelle, 1773), hippuric acid ($C_9H_9O_3N$) from horse urine (Liebig, 1829), cholesterol ($C_{27}H_{46}O$) from animal tissues (Chevreul,[2] 1815), morphine ($C_{17}H_{19}O_3N$) from opium (Sertürner,[3] 1805), and the alkaloidal (alkali-like, *i.e.* basic) drugs quinine, strychnine, brucine, and cinchonine (Pelletier and Caventou, 1820).

The classical investigations of combustion conducted by Lavoisier[4] in 1772–77 provided the first evidence of the chemical nature of substances derived from living organisms. Oxygen was discovered independently by Scheele and by Priestley.[5] Lavoisier established that air is composed of oxygen and an inert gas which he named azote (nitrogen), and he was the first to recognize combustion as an interaction of the burning substance with oxygen of the air. He proved that sulfur, phosphorus, and carbon on burning form acidic oxides, that is, oxides which in the presence of water appear as sulfuric, phosphoric, and carbonic acid. Metals on burning form basic oxides. Lavoisier devised a method for burning a sample of an organic compound in a small lamp floating on mercury under a bell jar containing oxygen or air. All compounds examined yielded carbon dioxide and water and hence must contain carbon and hydrogen. The amount of carbon dioxide formed was determined by absorption in potassium hydroxide solution and afforded a measure of the carbon content of the sample burned. The amount of water formed indicated the percentage of hydrogen present. Thus a method was available for identifying the elements present in compounds of organic origin and for gaining a rough indication of their relative amounts.

Application of Lavoisier's method of approximate analysis established that some organic compounds are composed of carbon and hydrogen alone; they are called hydrocarbons. Thus the main constituents of oil of turpentine are hydrocarbons of the formula $C_{10}H_{16}$; petroleum is a complex mixture of a large number of hydro-

[1] Carl Wilhelm Scheele, 1742–86; b. Stalsund; apothecary in Stockholm, Uppsala, Köping

[2] Michel Eugène Chevreul, 1786–1889; b. Angers; Paris

[3] Friedrich W. Sertürner, 1783–1841; b. Paderborn; apothecary in Hameln

[4] Antoine Lavoisier, 1743–94; b. Paris; guillotined; see D. McKie, "Antoine Lavoisier" (Lippincott)

[5] Joseph Priestley, 1733–1804; b. Yorkshire, England

carbons.   Other compounds on combustion yielded only carbon dioxide and water, but the combined carbon and hydrogen content did not account for the whole; these compounds must be composed of carbon, hydrogen, and oxygen (sugar, alcohol, acetic acid).   A few of the organic compounds known at the time when burned in an atmosphere of oxygen afforded carbon dioxide, water, and nitrogen (unabsorbed by alkali), and were thus recognized as containing nitrogen (urea, uric acid, indigo).   Investigation of an expanding list of products of plant or animal origin led to the surprising conclusion that these compounds of widely diversified types and properties are made up of combination of the same small group of elements: C, H, O, and N.   All the substances thus far mentioned (except Tyrian purple) conform to this pattern.   Different combinations of the four elements give rise to solids, liquids, and gases, to principles that are sour and to those that are sweet, to blue and to red dyes, and to substances essential to the human diet as well as to plant products poisonous to animals.

Parallel investigations of inorganic substances of mineral origin presented a contrasting picture.   Discoveries in this field were abundant in the early part of the 19th century, particularly by able Swedish and Finnish chemists and mineralogists investigating rare ores found in Sweden.   Here diversification in elementary composition prevailed, and the first investigator to analyze a given mineral was often rewarded with the discovery of a new element.   By 1807 thirty-six elements had been identified; by 1830 the list had mounted to fifty-three.

The Swedish chemist Berzelius[1] was the first to describe substances derived from living organisms as organic compounds (1807).   That they are composed of a selected few elements set organic compounds apart from inorganic ones.   Organic compounds are also combustible, and many of them are sensitive to moderate heat or damaged by strong acids or bases.   Since all organic compounds known at the beginning of the 19th century had been isolated as products of the life process, Berzelius, Gerhardt,[2] and other leaders of the period believed that organic compounds can arise only through operation of a vital force inherent in living cells. Although inorganic compounds had been prepared artificially in the laboratory, the chemical synthesis of organic compounds seemed beyond the realm of possibility.   However, in 1828 the German Wöhler[3] discovered that evaporation of an aqueous solution of the inorganic salt ammonium cyanate results in the production of urea, identical with material isolated from urine.   Wöhler repeated the experi-

$$NH_4OCN \longrightarrow CO(NH_2)_2$$
$$\text{Ammonium cyanate} \qquad \text{Urea}$$

ment many times until fully satisfied that the evidence refuted the postulated requirement of a vital force and addressed a letter to Berzelius: "I must tell you that I can prepare urea without requiring a kidney or an animal, either man or dog."

The synthetic preparation of organic compounds presents no mystery but is

[1] Jöns Jacob Freiherr von Berzelius, 1779–1848; Stockholm

[2] Charles Frédéric Gerhardt, 1816–56; b. France; Strasbourg

[3] Friedrich Wöhler, 1800–82; b. Strasbourg; Göttingen; *Ber.*, **23,** 829 (1890)

merely a matter of knowledge, skill and imagination. Most natural products now known have been prepared synthetically, and purely synthetic organic compounds exceed by far those found in nature. The designation organic has persisted for the convenient classification of a group of compounds having some features in common. Most of them contain carbon and hydrogen, a larger number contain oxygen as well, many contain nitrogen, and some contain halogen, sulfur, phosphorus, and other elements. Since they all contain carbon, organic chemistry is **the chemistry of carbon compounds.**

1.2   **Combustion Analysis.** — Lavoisier's technique of burning a compound in oxygen sufficed for establishment of the nature of the elements present but was not sufficiently accurate for determination of the relative atomic proportions. Modified procedures all suffered from the difficulty that if the ratio of oxygen to sample is high the burning mixture may explode, and that reduction in the proportion of oxygen may result in incomplete combustion. In 1831 Liebig[1] devised a method of combustion analysis which gave good service from the start and which was the forerunner of the methods in use today. Liebig took advantage of an earlier observation that organic vapors are burned efficiently on contact with red-hot copper oxide, for example:

$$C_2H_6 + 7 \, CuO \rightarrow 2 \, CO_2 + 3 \, H_2O + 7 \, Cu$$
$$C_4H_{10}O + 12 \, CuO \rightarrow 4 \, CO_2 + 5 \, H_2O + 12 \, Cu$$

In Liebig's method the sample is burned in oxygen in a glass tube packed with copper oxide as an auxiliary source of oxygen to insure complete combustion. The tube is swept with a slow stream of oxygen which effects direct combustion of a part of the sample and eventually oxidizes any metallic copper formed. The original supply of copper oxide is thus replenished. The stream of oxygen, which is freed from traces of moisture and carbon dioxide before entering the combustion tube, carries the products of combustion into a calcium chloride tube, which retains the water formed, and then into a bubbler containing potassium hydroxide solution to absorb the carbon dioxide. Prior to analysis each absorption unit is weighed separately and then mounted in position. The sample is weighed into a small porcelain or platinum boat inserted with a wire hook into a rear position in the combustion tube before this has been heated. The front section, packed with copper oxide wire, is brought to a red glow before introducing the sample. When the boat is in place, burners under the rear part of the tube are lighted progressively, and eventually the whole tube is brought to a dull red heat. Oxygen is passed through the hot tube for a sufficient period to sweep the products of combustion into the absorption train.

At the end of the combustion the absorption tubes are weighed; the gain in weight of the calcium chloride tube gives the amount of water produced and that of the potassium hydroxide bubbler the weight of carbon dioxide. Calculation of the percentage composition then follows from the proportion of hydrogen in

[1] Justus von Liebig, 1803–73; b. Darmstadt, Germany; Univ. Giessen, Munich; *Ber.*, **R. 23**, 785 (1890); A. W. von Hofmann, Faraday Lecture for 1875, "The Life and Work of Liebig," Macmillan, London (1876)

water and of carbon in carbon dioxide, using the atomic weights H = 1.008 and
C = 12.01.

$$\text{Wt. of hydrogen} = \text{Wt. of water} \times \frac{2.016 \ (H_2)}{18.016 \ (H_2O)}$$

$$\% \ H = \frac{\text{Wt. of hydrogen}}{\text{Wt. of sample}} \times 100$$

$$\text{Wt. of carbon} = \text{Wt. of carbon dioxide} \times \frac{12.01 \ (C)}{44.01 \ (CO_2)}$$

$$\% \ C = \frac{\text{Wt. of carbon}}{\text{Wt. of sample}} \times 100$$

If the percentages of carbon and hydrogen do not add up to 100 and no other
element is detected, the difference is taken as the percentage of oxygen.

For interpretation of the results of an analysis, the first step is to divide the
percentage of each element by its atomic weight; the next is to divide the resulting
numbers by the smallest one of the group and so ascertain the atomic ratios. An
ideal analysis for ethyl alcohol would give 52.14% C and 13.13% H, whence the
oxygen content by difference is 34.73%. The calculations are then:

	Percent		Atomic weight				Atomic ratio
C	52.14	÷	12.01	=	4.3		2
H	13.13	÷	1.008	=	13.03	$\times \dfrac{1}{2.17} =$	6
O	34.73	÷	16	=	2.17		1

Ethyl alcohol contains two carbon and six hydrogen atoms for every oxygen atom
A molecule cannot contain less than one of the least abundant species of atom
which in this case is oxygen, but it might contain two or more such atoms. From
the analysis alone, ethyl alcohol might be C_2H_6O or $C_4H_{12}O_2$ or $(C_2H_6O)_n$, where
n is any integer, for these formulas all have the same percentage composition. A
choice between the different possibilities is made possible by knowledge of the
molecular weight; even an experimental value recognized as only a rough approximation may suffice. Thus the unit C_2H_6O has the molecular weight (rounded) of
46, and a choice would be required between 46, 92, 138, etc. Molecular weight
determinations accurate to no better than 20% and falling in the range from 37
to 55 units would suffice to show that n = 1; the empirical formula of ethyl alcohol
is thus C_2H_6O. The molecular weight of a gas or of an easily vaporized substance
can be determined by the vapor density method, which consists in weighing a
measured volume of the gaseous substance and calculating the number of grams
that would occupy a volume of 22.4 liters at standard conditions (N.P.T.).
Methods applicable to solid compounds utilize the fact that a dissolved substance
raises the boiling point or lowers the freezing point of a solvent to an extent
directly dependent on the proportion of the dissolved to the total molecules. These ebullioscopic and cryoscopic methods are widely applicable and are
precise. Organic chemists frequently use a rapid, approximate cryoscopic method
(Rast), in which the solid substance camphor is used as solvent and determination
of the lowering of the melting point is made with use of only a few milligrams of the
mixture and an ordinary thermometer. The method succeeds because the melting
or freezing point of camphor is lowered to an extraordinary extent by a small

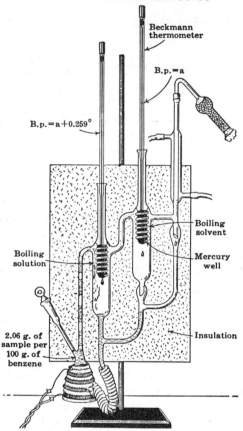

FIG. 1.1.— Ebullioscopic Determination of the Molecular Weight of a Nonvolatile Solid
This determination is made by direct measurement of the difference in the boiling point of a
solution of the substance in benzene and of pure benzene (Swietoslawski apparatus).

$$\text{Mol. wt.} = \frac{\text{Wt. of sample} \times 1000 \times k}{\text{Wt. of solvent} \times \Delta t}$$

where the constant k is the elevation in boiling point produced by 1 mole of substance in 1000 g.
of solvent (for benzene, k = 2.53°), and Δt is the observed elevation in boiling point.

amount of a dissolved substance. A rapid boiling point method which gives
reasonably accurate results is illustrated in Fig. 1.1.

Because of experimental error associated with an actual analysis, the atomic
ratios calculated may deviate appreciably from integral values; therefore careful
judgment must be exercised to decide which of possibly two or three of the nearest
sets of integral values is the most likely. The best way of making such a decision
is to calculate the theoretical percentages of carbon and hydrogen for each possible
formula and see how closely they correspond to the experimentally determined
values. An illustrative example is taken from a series of analyses carried out by
Liebig in 1838 and interpreted by him on the basis of the atomic weights accepted
at the time. Since the same values figure in the calculation of both experimental

and theoretical percentages, the inaccuracy in early atomic weights did not seriously distort the picture, and Liebig usually arrived at formulas that have stood the test of time.   In the following example the results are recalculated on the basis of modern atomic weights.   Liebig's combustion of a 0.533-g. sample of gallic acid afforded 0.969 g. of carbon dioxide and 0.172 g. of water, and calculations of the percentage composition and the ratio of carbon, hydrogen, and oxygen are as follows:

	Percent		Atomic weight					Atomic ratio
C	49.61	÷	12.01	=	4.13			1.41
H	3.61	÷	1.008	=	3.58	$\times \dfrac{1}{2.92} =$		1.22
O	46.78	÷	16	=	2.92			1

The result indicates that the compound contains approximately 1.4 carbon atoms and 1.2 hydrogen atoms for every oxygen atom.   If 2 oxygen atoms were present there would be 2.4 hydrogen atoms, but this figure is too far from an integral value for serious consideration.   Multiplication of the atomic ratio values by 3 and 5, however, gives figures not far from integral, namely $C_{4.2}H_{3.7}O_3$, and $C_{7.1}H_{6.1}O_5$. It would seem possible, then, that the substance is either $C_4H_4O_3$ or $C_7H_6O_5$, or a higher multiple of one of these formulas, and although the second appears to be a better fit than the first, a decision can be made from comparison of the experimentally determined values for carbon and hydrogen with those calculated for the possible alternative formulas:

	% C	% H
Found..........................	49.61	3.61
Calculated for $C_4H_4O_3$............	48.01	4.03
Calculated for $C_7H_6O_5$............	49.42	3.56

The percentage of hydrogen found is in fair agreement with that required for the first formula, but the carbon value is 1.6% too high, and this deviation is considerably greater than the experimental error of some 0.3–.4%.   The analytical values check well, however, with the calculated percentages for $C_7H_6O_5$, and hence this minimal formula is correct for gallic acid.   Liebig interpreted the analysis in this way and his formula was substantiated in subsequent work.

Research chemists can save time by use of two books of computations.   One, by Gysel,[1] gives the percentage composition of compounds containing the following combinations of elements: CH, CHO, CHN, and CHON.   The other,[2] applicable to the combinations CH, CHO, CHS, and CHOS, permits one to determine quickly all possible empirical formulas which fit the analytical data within the estimated limit of accuracy.   For example, if the tolerance is ±0.3% and the analysis of a CHO compound is: C, 48.0%; H, 8.0%, the composition is fixed

[1] H. Gysel, "Tables of Percentage Composition of Organic Compounds," Birkhäuser, Basel, 1951

[2] H. H. Hatt, T. Pearcey, and A. Z. Szumer, "Anti-Composition Tables for Carbon Compounds," Commonwealth Scientific and Industrial Research Organization, Australia

within the range C, 48.0 ± 0.3%; H, 8.0 ± 0.3%.   Reference to the appropriate table shows 52 empirical formulas containing 50 or fewer carbon atoms which satisfy these requirements.

In this book an **empirical formula** is defined as the formula determined by experimentation (empirically) which indicates the ratio of atoms present and the molecular weight.   The empirical formula of ethyl alcohol is C_2H_6O; at a time when the molecular weight had not been established, the formula $(C_2H_6O)_2$ would be merely a step toward determination of the complete empirical formula.   Determination of the molecular weight of a new compound is often unnecessary, for usually the order of magnitude of the molecular weight can be inferred from that of the starting material.   The preceding paragraph cites an analysis consistent with 52 empirical formulas containing up to 50 carbon atoms.   If the starting material contained 27 carbon atoms and the reaction involved could not decrease or increase the number of carbons, the product must also contain 27 carbon atoms and all but a few empirical formulas would be eliminated.

1.3   **Microanalysis.** — That Liebig was able to obtain remarkably accurate results with the comparatively crude laboratory equipment and analytical balances of the day is attributable both to his skill and to his use of a sample sufficiently large to offset error (0.5–.9 g.).   Improvements in the instrumental facilities in the ensuing hundred-year period made it possible to reduce the size of the sample to 100–120 mg. and still maintain an adequate degree of accuracy. Although this would appear to be a trivial amount of an abundantly available material such as sugar, acetic acid, or alcohol, many interesting organic compounds of both natural and synthetic origin have been encountered that, initially at least, were obtainable in only minute amounts. Butenandt's[1] discovery in 1931 of the male sex hormone androsterone, for example, was the result of the processing of 15,000 liters of urine, which afforded a total of 15 mg. of the physiologically active principle.   This difficult feat of isolation would have been rather pointless, and might not have been undertaken, had there not been available a modification of Liebig's method of analysis applicable to such minute quantities of material.   The procedure of microanalysis was introduced in 1911 by Pregl,[2] whose own research experience had convinced him of the serious limitations to a method of analysis requiring for a single combustion an amount of sample considerably greater than that which the chemist may be able to secure.   With the aid of special manipulative techniques, a skilled chemist can carry out a reaction with no more than 5–10 mg. of material and can purify the product for analysis by crystallization or, in some instances, even by distillation.   Pregl reinvestigated and refined every detail of the existing analytical method.   The chief determining factor was the accuracy of the balance, and under Pregl's leadership a microbalance was developed with which minute samples can be weighed with extraordinary precision. Microbalances now available, when operated in an air-conditioned room on a vibra-

---

[1] Adolf Butenandt, b. 1903 Wesermünde-Lehe; Ph.D. Göttingen (Windaus); Danzig; Kaiser Wilhelm Inst. Biochem., Berlin; Tübingen; Univ. Munich; Nobel Prize, 1939

[2] Fritz Pregl, 1869–1930; b. Laibach, Austria; Ph.D. Graz; Innsbruck, Graz; Nobel Prize 1923; *Ber.*, **64A**, 113 (1931)

tion-free mounting, can weigh to a precision of about 1 microgram (0.001 mg., or 0.000001 g.). With the aid of a precision instrument and by redesigning the combustion tube, absorption train, and all accessories, Pregl was able to work out a scheme of microanalysis by which the carbon and hydrogen content of a 3–4 mg. sample of material can be determined accurately. By application of the micro method, which was duly recognized as one of the achievements of modern science by the award to Pregl of the Nobel Prize, Butenandt's 15-mg. sample of androsterone sufficed for two analyses and for preparation and analysis of a derivative. The analytical results, coupled with keen observations and inferences, led in 1932 to an initial postulate of the chemical nature of the hormone that proved to be correct.

A compromise method requiring a less elaborate outlay of equipment but employing several of the refinements introduced by Pregl, known as semimicroanalysis, is often employed. Adequate precision in the determination of carbon and hydrogen is achieved with a sample weighing from 10 to 50 mg. A typical assembly of apparatus is illustrated in Fig. 1.2.

1.4   **Determination of Nitrogen.** — The most widely used method of determining nitrogen in organic compounds was introduced in 1830 by Dumas.[1] The sample is mixed with fine copper oxide and placed in a tube packed with coarse copper oxide. The tube is swept with a stream of carbon dioxide until all the air has been displaced, and then gradually brought to a dull red heat, when the sample is oxidized by the copper oxide to carbon dioxide, water, and elementary nitrogen containing oxides of nitrogen. The gaseous products are swept by a slow stream of carbon dioxide over a roll of hot copper gauze at the end of the tube which reduces oxides of nitrogen to nitrogen. The effluent gas passes into the base of an inverted, graduated glass tube filled with potassium hydroxide solution, which absorbs the carbon dioxide. The volume of the residual nitrogen is measured after adjustment of the pressure to that of the atmosphere with a leveling bulb.

A second method of analysis was introduced in 1883 by Kjeldahl.[2] The sample is digested with concentrated sulfuric acid, usually with addition of an oxidizing agent ($KMnO_4$, $HClO_4$), to decompose the substance and convert the nitrogen into ammonium sulfate. The solution is diluted, excess alkali is added, and the ammonia is distilled with steam into a known amount of standard acid and estimated by titration of the excess acid. The Kjeldahl method is less general than that of Dumas, but it is useful for the rapid analysis of specific groups of compounds of low nitrogen content, for example proteins.

1.5   **Apparatus.** — No less important to the advancement of the science than the analytical methods described was the development of laboratory equipment adapted to chemical experimentation. Four major inventions were made by professors in German Universities. Nowadays only professional analysts have a first-hand experience with the Liebig combustion analysis, but all

[1] Jean Baptiste André Dumas, 1800–84; b. Alais; Paris; *Ber.*, **17**, 629 (1884)
[2] Johan Kjeldahl, 1849–1900; b. Denmark; Carlsberg Laborat., Copenhagen; *Ber.*, **33**, 3881 (1900)

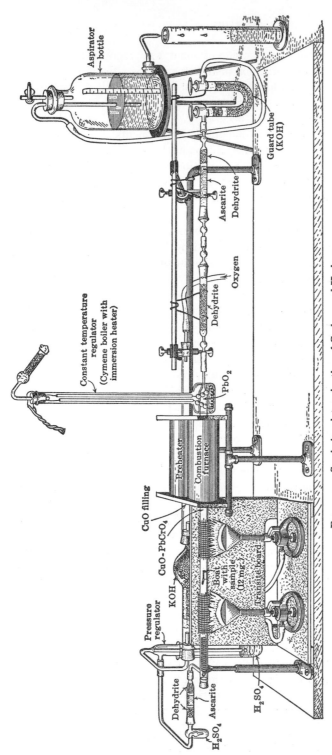

FIG. 1.2. — Semimicrodetermination of Carbon and Hydrogen

Oxygen from a low-pressure tank passes first through a preheater to burn any traces of organic matter, and then through a large tube of solid potassium hydroxide to absorb water and carbon dioxide, and a small unit to condition the gas exactly as it will be discharged from the absorption train. The first tube in this train contains solid Dehydrite (magnesium perchlorate trihydrate) to absorb water, and the second is filled with Ascarite (sodium hydroxide on asbestos) for the absorption of carbon dioxide and with an end section of Dehydrite to maintain the same condition of the gas on exit as on entrance. The oxygen is delivered to the combustion tube at a slight positive pressure and is drawn through the system at an adjustable, measured rate by the aspirator. The combustion furnace and preheater are heated with electric resistance units connected in series. The part of the combustion tube heated in the furnace is filled largely with copper oxide, but contains, at the exit end, a charge of lead chromate to combine with and retain oxides of sulfur. The end section of the tube contains lead peroxide to combine with oxides of nitrogen; this reagent must be maintained at a critical temperature different from that of the furnace, provided by the use of a boiler containing liquid of proper boiling point (cymene, $C_{10}H_{14}$). Silver wool or wire is introduced at the extreme end of the tube to retain halogen.

10

organic chemists make constant use of one or another modification of the Liebig condenser, introduced at Giessen in 1832. The familiar Bunsen burner was developed at Heidelberg (1855) where Bunsen[1] in lecturing on the burner amazed his audience by holding a finger of his powerful, thick-skinned hand in the non-luminous flame until the smell of burning flesh was perceptible. The Erlenmeyer flask was invented by another Heidelberg professor (1859; for biography, see section 8.2). The Claisen flask for vacuum distillation originated at the University of Aachen (1893, see 13.7). The Büchner funnel was first described in 1888 by Ernst Büchner, a German of now unidentifiable professional connection. No one name is associated with the separatory funnel, which evolved through a succession of crude precursors.

1.6   Complexity of Organic Compounds. — The substances of natural origin analyzed by Liebig, Dumas, Chevreul, Pelletier and Caventou, Robiquet, and contemporaries were mainly compounds of a complex character, and some of the problems uncovered in these pioneer investigations were eventually solved only in extended researches by succeeding generations of chemists. Thus Liebig in 1831 analyzed such compounds as the following series of physiologically active alkaloids:

Morphine.....................	$C_{17}H_{19}O_3N$
Cinchonine...................	$C_{19}H_{22}ON_2$
Quinine......................	$C_{20}H_{24}O_2N_2$
Strychnine...................	$C_{21}H_{22}O_2N_2$
Brucine......................	$C_{23}H_{26}O_4N_2$

In this series the molecules are made up of as many as 55 atoms, of which the majority are carbon and hydrogen in varying numbers. The oxygen content varies from one to four atoms, and one substance contains a single atom of nitrogen whereas the others contain two. No regularity is discernible, and the formulas alone reveal little concerning the chemical individualities of the compounds or the nature of their divergent action on the animal organism. Why does $C_{17}H_{19}O_3N$ represent an alkali-soluble base that is a powerful analgesic agent of great use in medicine (alleviation of pain)? Why is the compound $C_{20}H_{24}O_2N_2$ an alkali-insoluble base of value as an antimalarial drug? The early chemists were confronted with particularly complicated problems. Wöhler, in a letter written to Berzelius in 1835, said: "Organic chemistry just now is enough to drive one mad. It gives me an impression of a primeval tropical forest, full of the most remarkable things, a monstrous and boundless thicket, with no way to escape, into which one may well dread to enter."

Another complication in the interpretation of analytical data had been encountered in 1823 by Liebig, who discovered that silver fulminate has the same composition as silver cyanate, characterized previously by Wöhler. The substances are different chemical entities possessing distinctive properties; for example, the fulminate is a powerful explosive and the cyanate is not. Yet both compounds have the same empirical formula, AgCNO. This observation proved to be no

---

[1] Robert W. Bunsen, 1811–99; b. Göttingen, Germany; Ph.D. Marburg; Univ. Marburg, Breslau, Heidelberg

isolated case but merely the first established example of a phenomenon that was soon to be regarded as general.   Berzelius found that tartaric acid and racemic acid have the formula $C_4H_6O_6$, and he introduced the term isomerism for the phenomenon (Greek *isos*, the same; *meros*, parts).   Silver fulminate and silver cyanate are isomers.   Many other pairs of isomers exist, and numerous instances of isomerism of a much higher degree can be cited.   There are four isomers of the formula $C_3H_6Br_2$, four corresponding to $C_4H_{10}O$, and seven represented by $C_5H_{12}O$. As many as 150 isomers of the formula $C_{10}H_{12}O_2$ are known, and more may be discoverable.

Comparable difficulties are almost never encountered in the inorganic field. There is only one compound of the formula $KMnO_4$ and only one corresponding to $K_2Cr_2O_7$, and generally no thought need be given to the phenomenon of isomerism. Furthermore, once the empirical formula is established, it is an essentially complete chemical characterization.   When qualitative and quantitative analyses have established the formula for potassium permanganate as $KMnO_4$, it is evident that the manganese atom is utilizing eight negative valences of oxygen and one positive valence of the potassium atom and hence is exhibiting a positive valence of seven corresponding to its position in the periodic table.

With even simple organic compounds, the valence balance is not always clear from the formulas.   The first few members of the series of hydrocarbons are as follows:

$$
\begin{array}{ll}
\text{Methane.....................} & CH_4 \\
\text{Ethane.......................} & C_2H_6 \\
\text{Propane.....................} & C_3H_8 \\
\text{Two isomers} \left\{ \begin{array}{l} \text{Butane......................} \\ \text{Isobutane....................} \end{array} \right\} & C_4H_{10}
\end{array}
$$

The carbon atom of methane obviously has a valence of four, but with ethane the usual method of dividing the number of attached atoms by the number of carbon atoms would seem to indicate a valence of three, which, however, is inconsistent with the fact that ethane exhibits almost exactly the same chemical properties as methane.   Application of the same system of calculation would indicate a fractional carbon valence for propane, which again closely resembles the other two hydrocarbons.   With an increase in carbon content, the phenomenon of isomerism is encountered, for C_4H_{10} describes two chemical individuals, butane and isobutane.   That the combination of four carbon and ten hydrogen atoms can give rise to two different hydrocarbons, differing in boiling point, density, and other properties, must mean that two modes of combination between these fourteen atoms are possible.   Isomerism must result from a difference in the arrangement of atoms within the molecule.

1.7   **Kekulé Theory of Structure.** — Chemists of the early analytical period appreciated the importance of discovering the manner in which atoms are arranged in individual molecules, that is, of determining the structures, but they saw no way of doing it.   The problem remained at a standstill for a number of years, but in 1859 a simple solution was conceived by Kekulé,[1] a German

---

[1] August Kekulé, 1829–96; b. Darmstadt, Germany; Bonn; *Ber.*, **23**, 1265 (1890); **29**, 1971 (1896); *J. Chem. Soc.*, **73**, 97–138 (1898)

chemist of keen intuitive faculties and endowed with such a combination of energy and personal charm that he became a leading and dominant figure in the rationalization of existing empirical data. Kekulé deduced that carbon has the same normal valence of four in complicated organic compounds as it has in simple compounds (CH_4, CCl_4, CO_2), and that it is joined to other elements by four chemical bonds, represented by lines. Hydrogen and chlorine, of valence 1, have one such

$$-\overset{\textstyle |}{\underset{\textstyle |}{C}}- \qquad H- \qquad Cl- \qquad -O- \qquad -\overset{\textstyle |}{N}-$$

bond, oxygen has two, and trivalent nitrogen has three. Carbon can thus join with four hydrogens to form the molecule methane. In ethane two carbon atoms are bonded by utilization of one bond of each, and each is further bonded to three

$$\begin{array}{ccc}
\text{H} & & \\
| & & \\
\text{H}-\text{C}-\text{H} & & \\
| & & \\
\text{H} & & \\
\text{Methane} & &
\end{array}
\qquad
\begin{array}{ccc}
\text{H} & \text{H} & \\
| & | & \\
\text{H}-\text{C}-\text{C}-\text{H} & & \\
| & | & \\
\text{H} & \text{H} & \\
\text{Ethane} & &
\end{array}
\qquad
\begin{array}{ccc}
\text{H} & \text{H} & \text{H} \\
| & | & | \\
\text{H}-\text{C}-\text{C}-\text{C}-\text{H} \\
| & | & | \\
\text{H} & \text{H} & \text{H} \\
\text{Propane} & &
\end{array}$$

$$\begin{array}{c}
\text{Cl} \\
| \\
\text{Cl}-\text{C}-\text{Cl} \\
| \\
\text{Cl} \\
\text{Carbon tetrachloride}
\end{array}
\qquad
\begin{array}{c}
\text{O}=\text{C}=\text{O} \\
\text{Carbon dioxide}
\end{array}
\qquad
\begin{array}{c}
\text{H}-\text{C}\equiv\text{N} \\
\text{Hydrogen cyanide}
\end{array}$$

hydrogen atoms. A third carbon in the chain gives propane, which corresponds to the empirical formula C_3H_8. That the three hydrocarbons are similar in structure accords with the fact that they are similar in properties. Carbon tetrachloride is similar in structure to methane. Carbon dioxide has two double bonds, which utilize the four valences of carbon and the two valences of each oxygen. In hydrogen cyanide, carbon is singly bonded to hydrogen and triply bonded to trivalent nitrogen. Organic compounds containing trivalent nitrogen are illustrated by the formulas of ethyl cyanide, methylamine, and dimethylamine. Double and

$$\begin{array}{cccc}
\text{H} & \text{H} & & \\
| & | & & \\
\text{H} & \text{C} & \text{C} & \text{C}=\text{N} \\
| & | & & \\
\text{H} & \text{H} & & \\
& \text{Ethyl cyanide} & &
\end{array}
\qquad
\begin{array}{ccc}
\text{H} & \text{H} & \\
| & | & \\
\text{II} & \text{C}-\text{N}-\text{II} & \\
| & & \\
\text{H} & & \\
\text{Methylamine} & &
\end{array}
\qquad
\begin{array}{ccc}
\text{H} & \text{H} & \text{H} \\
| & | & | \\
\text{II}-\text{C}-\text{N}-\text{C}-\text{H} \\
| & & | \\
\text{H} & & \text{H} \\
\text{Dimethylamine} & &
\end{array}$$

$$\begin{array}{c}
\text{H} \quad \text{H} \\
| \quad | \\
\text{H}-\text{C}=\text{C}-\text{H} \\
\text{Ethylene}
\end{array}
\qquad\qquad
\begin{array}{c}
\text{H}-\text{C}\equiv\text{C}-\text{H} \\
\text{Acetylene}
\end{array}$$

triple bonds between carbon atoms are shown in the formulas of ethylene and acetylene; in each case the number of bonds extending to carbon is four, the valence of carbon.

1.8 **Rule of Valence Summation.** — The number of hydrogen atoms in an organic compound is even if the sum of the valences of the other elements present is even; the number is odd if the summation is odd. Thus hydrocarbons all contain an even number of hydrogens to match tetravalent carbon, for example, ethane, C_2H_6 ; propane, C_3H_8 ; ethylene, C_2H_4 . Since the valence of oxygen is even, CHO compounds all have even numbers of hydrogen atoms: C_2H_6O ; $C_{10}H_8O_3$; $C_{27}H_{46}O$. Thus the formulas C_6H_{11} , $C_7H_7O_5$, $C_{27}H_{47}O$ are at once recognized as fallacious. The combinations CHS and CHOS also must have an even number of hydrogens; $C_{21}H_{32}O_3S_2$ is possible, $C_{21}H_{31}O_3S_2$ is impossible. Nitrogen has a valence of three in typical organic compounds, for example: methylamine, CH_5N; dimethylamine, C_2H_7N. Thus compounds containing C, H, O and an odd number of nitrogens always have an odd number of hydrogens; if two or four nitrogens are present the number of hydrogens is even. In mono and di halogen derivatives containing C, H, O, or S, the number of hydrogens is odd and even, respectively.

1.9   **Determination of Structure.** — Kekulé introduced in 1859 a basic principle for determination of structure which has been used ever since. One considers all possible structures corresponding to the empirical formula and selects the one which alone is consistent with the properties and reactions of the compound and (or) with methods for its synthesis. The empirical formula C_4H_{10} allows of two structural formulas, that of the straight-chain, or normal (*n*-), hydrocarbon *n*-butane and that of the branched-chain isomer isobutane. Consideration of properties is not easy in this case because the hydrocarbons are relatively inert, particularly *n*-butane, but the problem can be resolved

$$
\begin{array}{cccc}
H & H & H & H \\
| & | & | & | \\
H-C-C-C-C-H \\
| & | & | & | \\
H & H & H & H
\end{array}
= CH_3CH_2CH_2CH_3
\qquad
\begin{array}{ccc}
H & H & H \\
| & | & | \\
H-C-C-C-H \\
| & | & | \\
H & | & H \\
 & H-C-H \\
 & | \\
 & H
\end{array}
= CH_3CHCH_3 \atop \hspace{1em} | \atop \hspace{1em} CH_3
$$

$$n\text{-Butane} \hspace{8em} \text{Isobutane}$$

by synthesis. Treatment of ethyl bromide with sodium couples two ethyl groups together to produce a hydrocarbon which can only be *n*-butane. Methods for the

$$
\begin{array}{cc}
H & H \\
| & | \\
H-C-C-Br \\
| & | \\
H & H
\end{array}
+ 2Na +
\begin{array}{cc}
H & H \\
| & | \\
Br-C-C-H \\
| & | \\
H & H
\end{array}
\rightarrow
\begin{array}{cccc}
H & H & H & H \\
| & | & | & | \\
H-C-C-C-C-H \\
| & | & | & | \\
H & H & H & H
\end{array}
+ 2NaBr
$$

synthesis of isobutane will become apparent later.

Deduction of structure from consideration of properties is illustrated by the case of two isomers of the formula C_2H_6O, characterized by their boiling points, 78° and −25°. Two structures are possible, I and II, and the problem is to

$$
\begin{array}{cc}
H & H \\
| & | \\
H-C-C-OH \\
| & | \\
H & H
\end{array}
= CH_3CH_2OH
\qquad
\begin{array}{cc}
H & H \\
| & | \\
H-C-O-C-H \\
| & | \\
H & H
\end{array}
= CH_3OCH_3
$$

$$\text{I} \hspace{12em} \text{II}$$

distinguish between them. Experiment shows that the isomers react differently with hydriodic acid, namely:

$$\text{C}_2\text{H}_6\text{O}(\text{b.p. }78°) \;+\; \text{HI} \;\rightarrow\; \overset{\displaystyle H\ \ H}{\underset{\displaystyle H\ \ H}{H-C-C-I}} \;+\; \text{HOH}$$

Ethyl iodide

$$\text{C}_2\text{H}_6\text{O}(\text{b.p. }-25°) \;+\; 2\text{HI} \;\rightarrow\; 2\overset{\displaystyle H}{\underset{\displaystyle H}{H-C-I}} \;+\; \text{HOH}$$

Methyl iodide

The higher boiling isomer reacts with one equivalent of acid to give a molecule each of water and $\text{C}_2\text{H}_5\text{I}$, for which only one formula is possible, that of ethyl iodide. Iodine, entering the molecule, displaces the hydroxyl group (OH), which combines with H of HI to form HOH. Structure I contains a hydroxyl group whereas II does not, and hence the observation is consistent only with the structure I for the isomer b.p. 78°. The evidence would be incomplete if the behavior of the isomer b.p. $-25°$ were not considered as well. This isomer reacts with hydriodic acid at a higher temperature, consumes two moles of reagent, and gives two moles of methyl iodide and one of water. This behavior is consistent alone with formula II, in which two methyl groups are joined through an intervening oxygen. When the central oxygen is abstracted by two hydrogen atoms, the molecule is disrupted and each methyl group combines with an atom of iodine.

$$\overset{\displaystyle H\qquad H}{\underset{\displaystyle \underset{I+H\ \ H+I}{H\ \ \ \ H}}{H-C+O+C-H}} \longrightarrow \overset{\displaystyle H}{\underset{\displaystyle H}{H-C-I}} \;+\; \text{H}_2\text{O} \;+\; \overset{\displaystyle H}{\underset{\displaystyle H}{I-C-H}}$$

Both reactions with hydriodic acid thus lead to the conclusion that the isomer b.p. 78° is ethyl alcohol, $\text{CH}_3\text{CH}_2\text{OH}$ (I), and the isomer b.p. $-25°$ dimethyl ether, CH_3OCH_3 (II). Confirmatory evidence is that ethyl alcohol reacts with metallic sodium with displacement of one hydrogen by sodium, whereas dimethyl ether is inert to the metal. In structure I one hydrogen is attached to oxygen and therefore is different from the other five, which are linked to carbon; in structure II all six hydrogens are carbon-bonded, like those of ethane, which is inert to sodium. Hence the differing behavior is consistent with the formulas:

$$\overset{\displaystyle H\ \ H}{\underset{\displaystyle H\ \ H}{H-C-C-OH}} \;+\; \text{Na} \longrightarrow \overset{\displaystyle H\ \ H}{\underset{\displaystyle H\ \ H}{H-C-C-ONa}} \;+\; \tfrac{1}{2}\text{H}_2$$

$$\overset{\displaystyle H\qquad H}{\underset{\displaystyle H\qquad H}{H-C-O-C-H}} \quad\text{and}\quad \overset{\displaystyle H\ \ H}{\underset{\displaystyle H\ \ H}{H-C-C-H}}$$

inert to Na

TABLE 1.1. PERIODIC TABLE (atomic numbers under symbols)

O	I	II	III	IV	V	VI	VII	O
	H 1							
He 2	Li 3	Be 4	B 5	C 6	N 7	O 8	F 9	Ne 10
Ne 10	Na 11	Mg 12	Al 13	Si 14	P 15	S 16	Cl 17	A 18

The structures assigned from chemical properties and reactions can be confirmed by synthesis. In the present example, ethyl alcohol can be synthesized as in (1) by the action of silver hydroxide on ethyl iodide; the reaction is just the reverse of that mentioned above and reformulated in (2). The structure of ethyl

1. $CH_3CH_2\overline{|I + Ag|}OH \longrightarrow CH_3CH_2OH + Ag^+I^-$

2. $CH_3CH_2\overline{|OH + H|}I \longrightarrow CH_3CH_2I + H_2O$

3. $CH_3OH + Na \longrightarrow CH_3ONa + \frac{1}{2}H_2$

4. $CH_3\overline{|I + Na|}OCH_3 \longrightarrow CH_3OCH_3 + Na^+I^-$

alcohol is established unambiguously by this synthesis because only one structure is possible for CH_3CH_2I and there can be no doubt that OH of AgOH replaces the iodine atom. Dimethyl ether can be synthesized by the equally unequivocal two-step process involving reactions (3) and (4). Reaction (3) is analogous to the reaction of ethyl alcohol with sodium cited above. Reaction (4) is analogous to reaction (1); in each case an organic halide reacts with a metal-containing compound, and the driving force is the tendency of the metal and the halogen to split out to form an ionic salt, Ag^+I^- and Na^+I^-.

1.10   **The Covalent Bond.** — Many inorganic compounds contain ionic (electrostatic) bonds. In sodium chloride, the valence electron of the sodium atom, a donor element, has been transferred to chlorine; sodium thereby acquires a positive charge and the stable eight-electron configuration of neon, and the chlorine atom becomes negatively charged and completes an octet comparable to that of argon. The formula Na^+Cl^- appropriately identifies the salt as ionic, as demonstrated by the fact that it is an electrolyte. The acid H^+Cl^- is ionic, but the molecules H_2 and Cl_2 are nonionic and are represented by the Kekulé formulas, H—H and Cl—Cl. The bond must be of the same type as those in typical organic compounds, which likewise are nonionic; thus CCl_4 gives no precipitate on treatment with $Ag^+NO_3^-$. Carbon, at the top center of the periodic table, has little tendency either to gain or to lose electrons.

The Kekulé theory of structure performed valuable service for half a century before the nature of the Kekulé bond became understood. Finally in 1916 G. N. Lewis,[1] professor of physical chemistry at the University of California,

---

[1] Gilbert N. Lewis, 1875–1946; b. Weymouth, Mass.; Ph.D. Harvard (Richards); Univ. Calif., Berkeley

introduced the concept of a bond formed by electron sharing. Each of two hydrogen atoms can share an electron to form the hydrogen molecule, in which each atom has the stable two-electron configuration of helium. A chlorine atom, by sharing

$$\text{H·} \; + \; \text{H·} \; \longrightarrow \; \text{H:H} \qquad \text{:}\overset{..}{\underset{..}{\text{Cl}}}\text{·} \; + \; \text{·}\overset{..}{\underset{..}{\text{Cl}}}\text{:} \; \longrightarrow \; \text{:}\overset{..}{\underset{..}{\text{Cl}}}\text{:}\overset{..}{\underset{..}{\text{Cl}}}\text{:}$$

its one unpaired electron with a second atom, gives a molecule in which each atom is surrounded by an eight-electron shell, as in argon. A pair of shared electrons is called a covalent bond. Carbon, with its four valence electrons (dots), can form a stable compound with four hydrogen atoms, each of which brings one external electron (cross) into the molecular sphere of the resulting methane, CH_4. The carbon atom is thereby surrounded by four electrons of its own and four derived from the hydrogens; the resultant stable octet conforms to the neon pattern. Each hydrogen atom now is associated with two electrons, and hence is electronically comparable to helium. Since every atom conforms in electron arrangement to a noble gas, the union affords a stable molecule. Since all the electrons are

$$\overset{.}{\underset{.}{\text{C}}}\text{·} \; + \; 4\overset{\times}{\text{H}} \; = \; \begin{matrix} \text{H} \\ \text{H:}\overset{\times}{\underset{\times}{\text{C}}}\text{:H} \\ \text{H} \end{matrix}$$

Methane

still within the original atomic spheres and are still neutralized by the respective atomic nuclei, the molecule is nonionic. The pair of shared electrons linking each hydrogen to carbon is a covalent bond. Methane is a union of carbon with an element that in many of its other compounds is an electron donor. Electron-acceptor atoms can also form stable carbon compounds. In carbon tetrachloride (CCl_4), for example, each of the four electrons of carbon fills a gap in the nearly complete external shell of a chlorine atom and gives a cluster of eight around the

$$\overset{.}{\underset{.}{\text{C}}}\text{·} \; + \; 4\overset{\times\times}{\underset{\times\times}{\times\text{Cl}\times}} \; = \; \begin{matrix} \times\text{Cl}\times \\ \times\text{Cl}\times\text{C}\times\text{Cl}\times \\ \times\text{Cl}\times \end{matrix}$$

halogen. Electron sharing results also in surrounding of the carbon atom with an octet of electrons without electron transfer and consequent development of an ionic charge.

The Kekulé bond is thus identified as a pair of shared electrons. A double bond is then two pairs of shared electrons, as in ethylene, and the triple bond of acety-

$$\begin{matrix} \text{H} \quad \text{H} \\ \text{H:}\overset{..}{\text{C}}\text{::}\overset{..}{\text{C}}\text{:H} \end{matrix} \qquad\qquad \text{H:C:::C:H}$$

Ethylene   Acetylene

lene consists of three shared electron pairs. Each carbon atom of acetylene has associated with it eight electrons: its original four electrons plus one shared with hydrogen and three shared with the second carbon.

Kekulé formulas are so easy to write, particularly abbreviated ones such as CH_2=CH_2 and CH≡CH, that they are commonly used for convenience. However, an electronic formula sometimes discloses a property not evident from the Kekulé formula. For example, the Kekulé formulas of ammonia and of methane suggest no difference between the two compounds. Nitrogen, with five valence electrons, forms with hydrogen the covalently bonded ammonia in which, unlike methane, the octet surrounding the central atom includes a pair of unshared elec-

$$\cdot \ddot{N} \cdot \; + \; 3\,H \cdot \; \longrightarrow \; H\!:\!\ddot{N}\!:\!H \; \xrightarrow{H^+} \; H\!:\!\overset{+}{\underset{\displaystyle H}{\overset{\displaystyle H}{\ddot{N}}}}\!:\!H$$

$$\underset{\text{Ammonia}}{} \qquad \underset{\text{Ammonium ion}}{}$$

trons, often called a lone pair. Because of the presence of this lone pair, ammonia can combine with a proton (hydrogen ion) by sharing the extra electron pair with hydrogen to give an ammonium ion, which carries the charge derived from the proton. Oxygen (6 electrons) forms compounds containing two pairs of unshared electrons, for example water, and water likewise combines with a proton to form a

$$H\!:\!\ddot{O}\!:\!H \; + \; H^+ \; \longrightarrow \; H\!:\!\overset{\displaystyle +}{\underset{\displaystyle H}{\ddot{O}}}\!:\!H$$

$$\underset{\text{Water}}{} \qquad\qquad \underset{\text{Hydronium ion}}{}$$

hydrated proton or hydronium ion, and this ion or a hydrate of it is present in an aqueous solution of a mineral acid. Methyl alcohol likewise can combine with a proton by utilization of its unshared electrons. Thus the oxygen is basic, al-

$$H\!:\!\overset{\displaystyle H}{\underset{\displaystyle H}{\ddot{C}}}\!:\!\ddot{O}\!:\!H \xrightarrow{H^+} H\!:\!\overset{\displaystyle H}{\underset{\displaystyle H}{\ddot{C}}}\!:\!\overset{\displaystyle +}{\underset{\displaystyle H}{\ddot{O}}}\!:\!H \qquad H\!:\!\overset{\displaystyle H}{\underset{\displaystyle H}{\ddot{C}}}\!:\!\overset{\displaystyle H}{\underset{}{\ddot{N}}}\!:\!H \xrightarrow{H^+} H\!:\!\overset{\displaystyle H}{\underset{\displaystyle H}{\ddot{C}}}\!:\!\overset{\displaystyle H}{\underset{\displaystyle H}{\overset{+}{N}}}\!:\!H$$

$$\underset{\text{Methyl alcohol}}{} \qquad \underset{\text{Oxonium ion}}{} \quad \underset{\text{Methylamine}}{} \qquad \underset{\text{Methylammonium ion}}{}$$

though not so strongly basic as the nitrogen in ammonia or in methylamine, and oxonium salts are hence not so stable as ammonium salts. Cations such as those from methyl alcohol, however, exist in solution and participate in certain reactions of alcohols. It should be noted in passing that methyl alcohol and methylamine can be regarded as derived from methane by replacement of one hydrogen by OH, a hydroxyl group, or by NH_2, an amino group. They can also be regarded as derived from water and from ammonia, respectively, by replacement of one hydrogen by the methyl group.

The basicity of elements decreases from left to right across the periodic table because the increasing positive charge on the central nucleus exerts an increasingly stronger pull on the electrons and holds them more strongly. Thus the lone pair on the oxygen atom of water is less available for sharing than that on the nitrogen atom of ammonia; ammonia added to a solution of hydronium ion abstracts the proton and liberates water. The chlorine atom of methyl chloride carries three pairs of unshared electrons, but the pull from the nucleus is so strong that basicity is completely lacking and a proton cannot be bound, even that of concentrated sulfuric acid.

1.11   **Lewis Acids and Bases.** — G. N. Lewis in 1923 introduced the useful concept that any acceptor of an electron pair is an acid and any electron donor is a base. The reactions pictured in the preceding section illustrate the idea. Water, an electron donor and hence a Lewis base, reacts with a proton, a Lewis acid, to form the hydronium ion. Methyl alcohol functions also as a Lewis base in its combination with a proton to form an oxonium ion. Methylamine combines with a proton in the same way, and it is also a base in the ordinary sense in that an aqueous solution when tested with indicator paper is found to be basic. Methyl alcohol and water are not basic in the same sense, but since they combine with a proton just as ammonia and methylamine do they are appropriately described as Lewis bases. The reaction of neutralization involves combination of an electron acceptor with an electron donor:

$$H^+ \ + \ :\!\overset{\cdot\cdot}{\underset{\cdot\cdot}{O}}\!:\!H \ \longrightarrow \ H\!:\!\overset{\cdot\cdot}{\underset{\cdot\cdot}{O}}\!:\!H$$

Lewis acid   Lewis base

The members of an acid-base pair are said to be conjugate with respect to each other. Thus water is the conjugate acid of the hydroxide ion, the hydronium ion is the conjugate acid of water, and the ammonium ion is the conjugate acid of ammonia.

1.12   **Characteristic Properties.** — Almost all organic compounds are combustible. Carbon tetrachloride, CCl_4, one of the very few exceptions to the rule, is used as a fire extinguisher (Pyrene). Liquid sprayed on a fire volatilizes (b.p. 76.8°) and the heavy vapor blankets the flame and smothers it by excluding oxygen. Carbon tetrachloride is exceptional because it contains no hydrogen atoms. Inorganic salts, as a rule, do not burn. Furthermore, inorganic salts are mainly solids, and most of them are either infusible or difficultly fusible, whereas at ordinary temperature organic compounds are gases, liquids, or low-melting solids. Nearly all solid organic compounds melt at temperatures in the range 25–400°, and the easily determined **melting point** of a compound is a characteristic property distinctive of that compound. Determination of the melting point of a sample gives a convenient index of purity, for as a sample is put through successive stages of purification by crystallization, chromatography, or distillation[1] (*e.g.* vacuum distillation of a solid), the melting point rises and reaches a constant level and a sharp range (*e.g.* over no more than 0.5–1.0°). Identity or nonidentity of two samples of the same melting point is established by a mixed melting point determination, that is, observation of the melting point of a mixture of the two substances. If the sample being tested is not identical with the authentic reference sample it depresses the melting point and the mixture melts low and over a range.

A useful rule of **solubility** is that like dissolves like. Solubility in water requires resemblance to water, of which an important structural feature is the presence of a

[1] L. F. Fieser, "Experiments in Organic Chemistry," 3rd Ed. revised, D. C. Heath, 1957

hydroxyl group (OH). Hydrocarbons, which are nonhydroxylic and wholly unlike water, are insoluble in water; hydrocarbon solvents such as hexane (C_6H_{14}), ligroin (mixture, *e.g.* of C_6H_{14}, C_7H_{16}, C_8H_{18}), benzene (C_6H_6) are immiscible with water and when shaken with an aqueous solution in a separatory funnel separate as an upper layer, since they are lighter than water. Carbon tetrachloride, also structurally unlike water, is a water-immiscible solvent heavier than water. The common solvent ether, $CH_3CH_2OCH_2CH_3$, contains an atom of oxygen but is predominantly hydrocarbon in composition and when shaken with water separates as an upper layer. Fats of plants and animals are mixtures of several constituents having the same structural pattern and differing in the length and nature of three long hydrocarbon chains, as illustrated in the formula. Since these hydrocarbon chains dominate the structure, the oily or solid fats are all insoluble in water.

$$
\begin{array}{l}
\overset{\displaystyle O}{\underset{|}{CH_2-O-\overset{\|}{C}}-CH_2CH_2CH_2CH_2CH_2CH_2\,CH_2CH_2CH_2CH_2CH_2CH_2CH_2CH_2CH_2CH_3} \\[4pt]
\overset{\displaystyle O}{\underset{|}{CH-O-\overset{\|}{C}}-CH_2CH_2CH_2CH_2CH_2CH_2CH_2CH_2CH_2CH_2CH_2CH_2CH_3} \\[4pt]
\overset{\displaystyle O}{CH_2-O-\overset{\|}{C}-CH_2CH_2CH_2CH_2CH_2CH_2CH_2CH=CHCH_2CH_2CH_2CH_2CH_2CH_2CH_2CH_3}
\end{array}
$$

Constituent of a fat

Fats resemble hexane, benzene, and ether in composition and they dissolve freely in these solvents. Fats and all other constituents of plant and animal tissues which are insoluble in water and soluble in ether or hexane are called **lipids,** and lipids are commonly isolated by extraction of a tissue with such a solvent. Structural material, for example cellulose, is undissolved by either solvent, and nonlipid organic constituents are retained in the aqueous phase. Low-boiling ether (b.p. 34.6°) as well as hexane (*n*-hexane, b.p. 68.7°) is removed by distillation of the dried extract on the steam bath (temperature about 87°), and the lipid or lipid mixture is left as a residue.

Cholesterol, an abundant lipid of the animal organism is an alcohol of the formula $C_{27}H_{45}OH$. It contains a hydroxyl group, but this functional group accounts for only 4.4% of the molecular weight and is overwhelmed by the hydrocarbon part; cholesterol is soluble in ether or hexane and insoluble in water. Small molecules are rendered water-soluble by a single hydroxyl function, since they are predominantly hydroxylic: methyl alcohol (CH_3OH), ethyl alcohol (C_2H_5OH), acetic acid (abbreviation: AcOH). Sucrose from cane sugar has the empirical formula $C_{12}H_{22}O_{11}$, and since it contains eight hydroxyl groups, the formula can be written as $C_{12}H_{14}O_3(OH)_8$. Although the molecule is large (mol. wt. 342), the hydroxyl functions account for 40% of the total, and sucrose is abundantly soluble in water (1 g. in 0.5 ml. at 25°) and completely insoluble in ether or hexane. One would expect these organic solvents to be surpassed by hydroxylic ones in ability to dissolve the sugar, and indeed 1 g. of sucrose dissolves in 170 ml. of ethyl alcohol (25°) or in about 100 ml. of methyl alcohol.

That many inorganic acids, bases, and salts dissolve in water is attributable to their ionic character. Water molecules in an electric field acquire an orientation disclosing the presence of a negative end and a positive end that together form a

dipole. No polarization could result if the water molecule were linear, but physical evidence shows that it is not linear but that the two O—H bonds are at an angle of 105° to each other. Polarization occurs because oxygen is more electronegative than hydrogen (see Table, 32.3) and tends to draw the bonding electrons closer to it than they are to the hydrogen atoms. The electron displacement produces a fractional negative charge (δ^-) at the oxygen end of the dipole balanced by

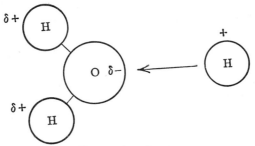

Protonation of water

an equal fractional positive charge distributed between the two hydrogens at the other end. When hydrogen chloride dissolves in water the proton (hydrogen ion) is attracted to the negative oxygen and forms the hydronium ion, H_3O^+. A larger cation, for example Na^+, can attract and hold many molecules of water to form a polyhydrate ion. Anions are solvated by attraction of the positive end of the water molecule.

1.13   Hydrogen Bonding. — A phenomenon of a different type is responsible for the fact that hydroxylic compounds are associated in the liquid state and consequently much less volatile than unassociated liquids of comparable molecular weight. Thus the molecular weights of ethyl alcohol and of propane are about the same, 46 and 44, but the alcohol boils at 78.3° and the hydrocarbon at −42.2°.

The low volatility of alcohols is due to the fact that in the liquid state the molecules are associated. Liquid water is also associated, and contrasts with unassociated hydrogen compounds of comparable molecular weight that are gases at ordinary temperature: H_2, H_2S, HCl, NH_3; water vapor is monomeric. The association of alcohol and water molecules is due to the phenomenon of hydrogen bonding. The electronic formulation of an alcohol dimer shows that the hydroxylic hydrogen atom of one monomer molecule is attracted by the strongly electronegative oxygen of a second molecule with the result that the

$$\underbrace{:\overset{..}{O}:H \quad + \quad :\overset{..}{O}:H}_{R \qquad\qquad R} \;\rightleftharpoons\; \underbrace{:\overset{..}{O}:H \;\; :\overset{..}{O}:H \quad \text{or} \quad \begin{array}{c} O-H \\ | \\ R \end{array} \!\!\leftarrow\!\! \begin{array}{c} -O-H \\ | \\ R \end{array}}_{}$$

Alcohol monomer (vapor)   Alcohol dimer (liquid)

hydrogen forms a bridge, or hydrogen bond, linking the two oxygen atoms. The bonding of oxygen to hydrogen through an unshared pair of electrons is often represented by an arrow pointing to hydrogen, as in the alternative formula for the alcohol dimer.   In electronegativity, defined as the tendency of an atom to gain electrons, fluorine surpasses oxygen and all other atoms, and hydrogen fluoride dimer contains a particularly stable hydrogen bond (for Table of electronegativities, see 32.3).   The boiling point of methanol (64.7°) is lower than that of water, even though it has a higher molecular weight, because it is not so highly associated as water.

The presence in a compound of an unbonded hydroxyl group can be recognized by the appearance in the infrared spectrum of an absorption band of characteristic wave length, and the disappearance of this band is evidence of hydrogen bonding. The high boiling points of water and of alcohols are attributable to the fact that heat energy is required to break the hydrogen bonds.   Energy required to dissociate a given covalent bond in a gaseous molecule is the bond energy of that linkage and is determinable by experimentation or by calculation (see Table, 32.2).   Typical values are: C—H, 87; C—C, 59; C=C, 100 kcal./mole.   The hydrogen bond energy is in the range 2–10 kcal./mole; the energy is distinctly less than that of covalent single and double bonds but is still appreciable.

1.14   **Organic Reactions.** — Reactions of inorganic compounds in aqueous solution are very rapid because they involve union of oppositely charged ions which are drawn together by electrostatic attraction.   Reactions such as the neutralization of an acid with a base, an oxidation-reduction reaction, or the precipitation of silver chloride or barium sulfate are also quantitative and form the basis of inorganic quantitative analysis.   Organic compounds being nonionic react much more slowly; for example, a reaction conducted at room temperature may reach completion only after several hours or even days.   That reactions occur at all is ascribed to random **collisions**, a certain fraction of which are fruitful.   Thus some collisions may involve inert sites of one or both molecules, whereas reaction occurs only when a collision brings two reactive sites together. The random motion of neutral molecules in solution or in the gas phase, and hence the number of effective collisions, should and does increase with increasing temperature.   However, calculation has shown that the observed increase in reaction rate with temperature is greater than can be accounted for by an increase in the number of collisions.

Recognition of a second controlling factor has resulted from theoretical concepts of reaction mechanisms.   The mechanism of a reaction is a series of postulated steps by which reactants A and B become transformed into products C and D. Sometimes it is possible, perhaps by conducting the reaction at a low temperature or by using an insufficient amount of one reactant, to isolate as an intermediate (X) a fully formed molecule; one then wonders about the steps by which A and B give X and about the mechanism of the conversion of X into C and D.   We lose sight of the reactants as they pass through a curtain into a mechanistic box, and what we see next are the emergent products.   What has happened in the box, what transient and unisolable complexes appear and disappear, may be undeterminable by present techniques.   Nevertheless, sound theories have been developed which make many known reactions more readily understandable and which sometimes help forecast the outcome of an untried reaction.   All postulated reaction mechanisms invoke an intermediate called a **transition state** (or **activated complex**), formed by combination of the reactants and synchronously

$$A + B \longrightarrow \boxed{\text{Complex} = A \cdots B \text{ or } C \cdots D} \longrightarrow C + D$$

Reactants   Transition state   Products

converted into the products. The transition state complex resembles both the two reactants and the two products; it may be a little more like one pair than the other, but it partakes of the nature of both. The transition state is the arrangement of maximum energy content through which the reactants must pass on the way to products; the complex is unisolable because the energy content is higher than that of either reactants or products; it has the least stable arrangement of the sequence. The energy that must be supplied to the reactants for formation of the transition state is the **activation energy** for the reaction ($\Delta H\ddagger$). An energy profile is a curve showing the postulated relative energy levels at various stages from reactants to products. In the profile curve of Fig. 1.3a the activation energy is the difference between the energy of the initial state and that of the transition state. If the energy of the final system is less than that of the starting system, energy is released as heat during the reaction; the reaction is exothermic; the **heat of reaction, ΔH,** has a negative sign. Fig. 1.3b is a schematic representation of an endothermic reaction, that is, one which requires energy input; the heat of reaction, ΔH, is of positive sign. Fig. 1.3c is the energy profile of a two-stage reaction proceeding through an intermediate. In the example pictured the first step requires a higher activation energy than the second step and hence the first step is the slower process of the two and the rate in this step determines the overall rate of reaction.

The foregoing analysis suggests that an increase in temperature speeds up a reaction not only by increasing the frequency of collisions but also by increasing the proportion of collisions which have the energy required to reach the activation energy. If the activation energy ($\Delta H\ddagger$) is about 11 kcal./mole, a 10° rise in temperature doubles the reaction rate; if $\Delta H\ddagger = 20$ kcal./mole, a more usual value, a 10° rise in temperature triples the reaction rate. Thus reactions are speeded up enormously on raising the temperature from 20°, room temperature in some laboratories, to 90°, about the maximum temperature attainable by heating the reaction mixture on the steam bath. If the rate of a reaction in which $\Delta H\ddagger = 11$ kcal./mole is 1 at 20°, the rate is 128 at 90°; in a reaction in which $\Delta H\ddagger = 20$ kcal./mole, the change in reaction rate over the same temperature interval is from 1 to 6561. Steam heating provides a safe way of accelerating reactions of flammable reactants or of solutions of reactants in flammable organic solvents. If a reagent or solvent is volatile at 90°, the mixture is boiled briskly in a flask fitted with a vertical condenser which condenses the vapors and returns the material to the refluxing mixture.

If a reaction is reversible, the equilibrium often can be shifted to favor a desired product by use of a large excess of the less expensive reactant. A catalyst, usually a mineral acid or a base, often accelerates a reaction, reversible or ir-

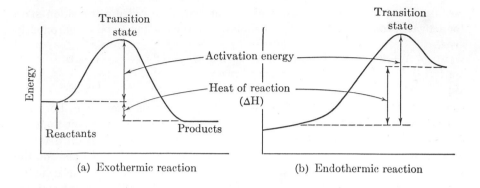

(a) Exothermic reaction   (b) Endothermic reaction

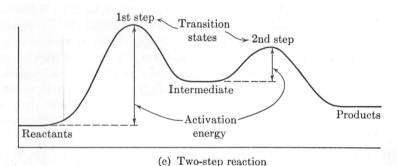

(c) Two-step reaction

FIG. 1.3. — Energy Profiles

reversible, by lowering the activation energy.   In a reversible process the forward and reverse reactions both involve the same transition state and require the same activation energy, and hence a catalyst speeds attainment of equilibrium but does not alter the position of equilibrium.   After a reaction has reached equilibrium the operator may be able to isolate not only the product but a certain amount of starting material; if this is of quality satisfactory for recycling in a subsequent run, the calculation of the theoretical yield is based upon the weight of starting material taken less that recovered.

Organic compounds as a rule are delicate and easily decomposed.   Thus acceleration of a reaction by heat or by acidic or basic catalysis is liable to damage reactants or products, or both, with decrease in yield and formation of brown tars or gums.   Formation of by-products may reduce the yield still further.   The reaction of A with B to form C may be accompanied by an inevitable side-reaction to form D.   A slow main reaction affords opportunity for formation of by-products AA and BB, or for interaction of either reactants or products with the solvent, with a catalyst, or with oxygen of the air.

Several factors thus conspire to decrease the yields of organic reactions, and in a first trial of a new reaction the yield may be discouragingly low.   Expedients that can be explored include a change in the reaction temperature, use of a different solvent or a milder catalyst, variation of the proportion of the reagents, exclusion of air. In the industry, where a difference of a few percent in the yield may spell the success or the failure of a process, developmental research teams study exhaustively each reaction involved in an effort to increase the yield. In a multi-step synthesis a loss anywhere along the line hurts, because the effect is cumulative. A yield of 80% of the theoretical amount would appear good, but a yield of 80% in each step would, in a two-step synthesis, amount to an overall yield of 64%; in a 10-step synthesis the overall yield would be 10.6%.

Because a given product often is accompanied in the reaction mixture by by-products of side reactions and by gummy and pigmented contaminants resulting from decomposition, and because it may contain solvent and catalyst, a large part of preparative work may involve processing the mixture for separation and purification of the desired product. Isolation of a natural product from a plant or animal tissue presents the further difficulty that the substance may be present in only minute amount and may be accompanied by an array of related compounds of nearly the same chemical and physical properties.

1.15   **Stereochemistry.** — Stereochemistry deals with the arrangement of atoms in space. In 1874 van't Hoff and LeBel independently deduced that the **carbon atom is tetrahedral** (a), that is, that its four bonds are directed at equal angles to one another in three-dimensional space. Their inference was later abundantly confirmed by chemical and physical evidence. The methane molecule is three-dimensional and symmetrical, with carbon at the center and the four hydrogens attached symmetrically, as at the corners of a regular tetrahedron. The arrangement is shown schematically in the ball-and-stick model (b), in which

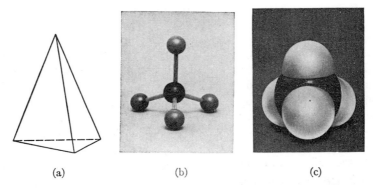

(a)   (b)   (c)

the central carbon is black and the attached hydrogens are gray. The model shows that the angle between any pair of valence bonds, the tetrahedral angle, is 109° 28′. The model lacks reality in some respects because the balls are of arbitrary size and do not reflect the relative size of carbon and hydrogen atoms. The Stuart model (c) gives an accurate conception of the actual shape of the methane molecule because the atoms are represented by spheres of appropriate relative diameters, and because the spheres have facings to accord with the fact that the merging of atoms to form a molecule is attended with some compression or flattening of the original spheres. The radius of the carbon atom is 0.77 Å and that of the hydrogen atom is 0.32 Å; the black and white balls are cut accurately to this proportion. The distance from the center of the carbon atom of methane to the center of any hydrogen atom is thus the sum of the radii, or 1.09 Å; this center-to-center distance is the length of the C—H bond (see Table of Bond Distances, 32.1). In ethane the six C—H bond distances are also 1.09 Å and the C—C bond distance is 1.54 Å; this internuclear distance is the sum of the two radii: 0.77 + 0.77 = 1.54 Å.

van't Hoff and LeBel arrived at the conception of the tetrahedral carbon atom in seeking an explanation of the phenomena of optical activity. Certain organic compounds are described as optically active because they rotate the plane of plane polarized light. If the rotation is to the right, the compound is dextrorotatory, if to the left it is levorotatory. Some of the natural products already mentioned which are optically active are sucrose, tartaric acid, malic acid, lactic acid; some that are optically inactive are ethyl alcohol, acetic acid, urea, benzoic acid. Since compounds exhibit optical activity in solution, the phenomenon is associated with the architecture of individual molecules. The requirement for optical activity is simply a tetrahedral carbon with four different attached atoms or groups. The alcohol I meets the requirement, for the four valences of carbon are

$$CH_3CH_2-\underset{\underset{\displaystyle OH}{|}}{\overset{\overset{\displaystyle H}{|}}{C}}-CH_3$$

I

II

III

occupied by a hydrogen atom, a methyl group, an ethyl group, and a hydroxyl group. The four groups can be attached to a tetrahedron as in II, but they can also be attached in the alternative way shown in III. The two formulas are very similar but one is not superimposable on the other. They are different, and they differ in the same way that the right hand differs from the left. The formulas represent actual compounds, each of which is optically active. One is dextrorotatory; it rotates plane polarized light a certain number of degrees to the right. The other is levorotatory; the angle of rotation is exactly the same but rotation is in the opposite direction.

If the hydroxyl group (OH) of II were replaced by a second methyl group, a plane bisecting the hydrogen and the ethyl groups and passing midway between the two methyl groups would divide the model into identical halves. But a plane bisecting the original model would not give identical halves. In short neither II nor III possesses a plane of symmetry; each is asymmetric. Thus optical activity arises from the presence of an **asymmetric carbon**: one in which the four attached atoms or groups are all different. The phenomenon is general; the four groups may be very similar, but if they differ in any detail then two optically active isomers are possible. The photograph shows models of a pair of

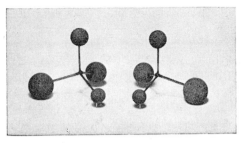

optical isomers containing an asymmetric carbon with attached balls of four sizes, representing four different groups. Notice that the models are symmetrical with respect to a plane passed between them. If the one on the left faced a mirror instead of the second model, the image seen would be identical with the model to the right. Thus these substances are **mirror-image isomers, or enantiomers.** One represents a dextrorotatory enantiomer, or *d*-form, the other its levorotatory optical opposite, or *l*-form. A mixture of equal parts of the two would be an optically inactive *dl*-mixture.

Natural products that contain one or more asymmetric carbon atoms almost always occur in optically active forms rather than as *dl*-mixtures, probably because they are produced by biosynthesis in the organism under the influence of enzymes, natural catalytic agents which themselves are optically active. The optically inactive natural products mentioned above contain no asymmetric carbon atoms.

Further principles of stereochemistry and of its interesting history are included in Chapter 3. Those compounds discussed in the next chapter which contain an asymmetric carbon atom are mainly optically inactive *dl*-forms which behave as single chemical entities and which are resolvable into optically active enantiomers only by special techniques to be described later.

ORBITAL THEORY

1.16   **Atomic Orbitals.** — The orbital concept for describing molecular structure, which is based on quantum mechanics, was developed in 1925 in different forms by Heisenberg and by Schrödinger. In contrast to the older quantum theory of Bohr in which the orbit of an electron about a nucleus appeared as simple as the orbit of a planet around the sun, quantum mechanics, more realistically, provides a method for calculation of the probable position of an electron in relation to the nucleus from consideration of the energy relationships. It describes statistically the behavior of an electron in terms of a wave function, ψ, which defines the region, or orbit, within which the electron is, in probability, largely located. In the case of the hydrogen atom, with one electron, the orbit is spherically symmetrical and is called a 1*s* orbital (1 = quantum number, *s* = orbital type). The 1*s* orbital can be represented (Fig. 1.4) as a cloud, or charge-cloud, where most of the negative charge resides; the density at any point in this cloud is proportional to ψ^2. The charge-cloud is symmetrical with respect to the x, y, and z axes in both the 1*s* orbital and when a 1*s* orbital is surrounded by a 2*s* orbital (Fig. 1.4). The 2*s* state contains an interior spherical node in which $\psi = 0$, that is, the probability of finding an electron at this site is zero.

A second type of orbital, the p type, is not spherical but directional. Here the electron is practically confined to two contiguous regions or clouds that, together, form a sort of dumbbell (Fig. 1.5). A $2p$ orbital is oriented along a particular axis and is defined as a $2p_x$, $2p_y$, or $2p_z$ orbital. In one half of the dumbbell the sign of ψ is positive and in the other half it is negative, and hence the two regions are separated by a nodal plane, represented in Fig. 1.5 by a disc, over which $\psi = 0$. For brevity, the dumbbell is sometimes represented by two balls (Fig. 1.6a) or by a symbol (Fig 1.6b) that does not even depict the three-dimensional character of the region defining the probable location of the electron.

An orbital can be occupied by one electron or by two, but no more. The pairing of two electrons in a single orbital is possible only if the electron spins are suitably aligned. The property of spin (Uhlenbeck and Goudsmit, 1925) gives to an electron angular momentum and a magnetic moment such that, in a magnetic field, the orientation is either with or against the field. According to the Pauli exclusion principle (1925), two electrons can occupy the same orbital only if their magnetic moments of spin are opposed. The helium atom in the normal

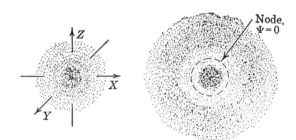

Fig. 1.4. — Atomic $1s$ and $2s$ Orbitals

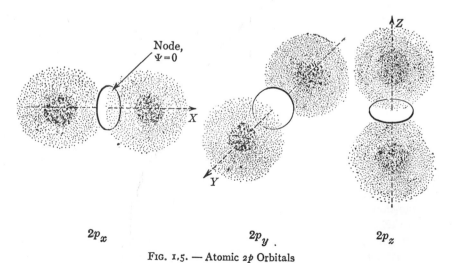

$2p_x$ $2p_y$ $2p_z$

Fig. 1.5. — Atomic $2p$ Orbitals

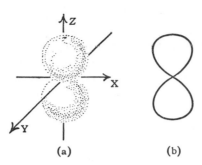

(a)   (b)

Fig. 1.6 — Atomic $2p_z$ Orbitals

TABLE 1.2. ELECTRONIC CONFIGURATIONS OF THE K AND L SHELLS
(An arrow designates an electron and indicates the sense of spin)

ELEMENT	K SHELL	L SHELL			
	1s	2s	$2p_x$	$2p_y$	$2p_z$
H	↓				
He	↑ ↓				
Li	↑ ↓	↓			
Be	↑ ↓	↑ ↓			
B	↑ ↓	↑ ↓	↓		
C	↑ ↓	↑ ↓	↓	↓	
N	↑ ↓	↑ ↓	↓	↓	↓
O	↑ ↓	↑ ↓	↑ ↓	↓	↓
F	↑ ↓	↑ ↓	↑ ↓	↑ ↓	↓
Ne	↑ ↓	↑ ↓	↑ ↓	↑ ↓	↑ ↓

state contains two electrons in the s orbital. The L-shell of other elements, when completely filled with 8 electrons, consists of four orbitals each containing two electrons. One of these is the spherical $2s$ orbital, and the others are dumbell-type orbitals, $2p_x$, $2p_y$, and $2p_z$. Because of the attraction of the positively charged nucleus, the $1s$ orbital is filled before a $2s$ orbital, which in turn is filled before a $2p$ orbital. The order for filling the three $2p$ orbitals is further deter-mined by the rule (F. Hund) that two electrons do not occupy any p orbital of the shell until all p orbitals of the shell have one electron. The normal electronic configurations of the first ten atoms of the periodic series are shown in Table 1.2 (each doublet contains electrons of opposed spins).

It will be noted from the table that application of the Hund rule implies that carbon, with two unpaired electrons in the $2p$ orbitals, should be bivalent. However, for purposes of bond formation, atoms tend to make use of all possible orbitals by a process of mixing that results in hybridization. In the case of carbon it is postulated that the $2s$ orbital mixes with the two $2p$ orbitals to form four equivalent hybrid orbitals (Fig. 1.7) called sp^3 hybrid orbitals (the superscript indicates that three original p orbitals are utilized). The hybrid sp^3 orbitals are directional and resemble the p orbital components more than the s. The four species together comprise an electron cloud that is directed tetrahedrally and permits utilization of four, now equivalent, valence electrons (Fig. 1.8). Through hybridization, the carbon atom is thus prepared for symmetrical bonding through four equivalent t orbitals (t = tetrahedral).

1.17   Molecular Orbitals. — The electronic distribution in a molecule is described by an extension of the principles used in the case of atoms. Thus each molecular orbital is compounded out of atomic orbitals and retains the characteristics of the components. When two hydrogen atoms bond to form a hydrogen molecule the two $1s$ orbitals coalesce to form a molecular orbital occupied by two electrons of opposed spins and encompassing the two nuclei (Fig. 1.9). This orbital is symmetrical about a line connecting the two nuclei, and hence has the same symmetrical character as an atomic s orbital and is known as a σ (sigma) molecular orbital. The energy of a molecular orbital is lowest, and consequently the binding energy is highest, when the component atomic orbitals overlap to the highest degree, since overlapping facilitates electron exchange. Two s orbitals overlap efficiently, and hence the covalent bond, or σ-bonded link, of the hydrogen molecule is strong. The same is true of the C—H bonds of methane, in which, according to the theory, four σ molecular orbitals are formed, with maximum overlapping, by linear combination of each of the four carbon t orbitals with a hydrogen $1s$ orbital; it is described as $[C(t) + H(1s), \sigma]^8$, where 8 is the number of electrons involved. Methane thus should

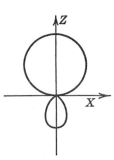

FIG. 1.7. — Cross Section of a
Single sp^3 Hybrid Orbital

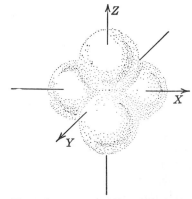

FIG. 1.8. — Four sp^3 Hybrid Orbitals

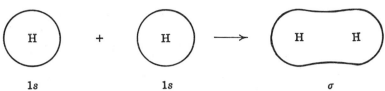

| 1s | 1s | σ |

FIG. 1.9. — Atomic and Molecular Orbitals (Cross Sections)

have a tetrahedral configuration with valence angles of 109° 28′. The covalent carbon–carbon bond of ethane is similarly characterized by a σ orbital.

PROBLEMS

(Answers in back of book)

1. Write the Kekulé formulas for the following compounds (only one formula is possible for each): hydrazine, N_2H_4 (trivalent nitrogen); formic acid, CH_2O_2.

2. There are two isomers of the formula $C_2H_4Br_2$ and two of the formula $C_2H_3Br_3$. Write the four structural formulas.

3. Write an electronic formulation for the reaction of ammonia with hydrogen chloride.

4. Write electronic formulas for $CHBr_3$, CH_3OH, and C_2H_4.

5. A semimicroanalysis of an 11.25-mg. sample of an unknown substance gave 26.99 mg. of CO_2 and 6.77 mg. of H_2O. Calculate the percentage composition.

6. The following two compounds containing only C, H, and O were analyzed and the molecular weights determined, with the results recorded. Calculate the empirical formulas.

   (a) % C = 65.55; 65.25   (b) % C = 70.31; 69.95
       % H = 5.65; 5.35   % H = 4.08; 4.18
       Mol. wt. = 111; 115   Mol. wt. = 185, 187

7. Which of the following formulas represent possible compounds and which are false: $C_{10}H_{22}O$, $C_{20}H_{41}$, $C_{14}H_8O_4$, $C_{21}H_{31}O_3$, $C_{21}H_{31}O_3N$, $C_8H_{14}ON$, $C_{20}H_{32}OSN_2$, $C_{10}H_{20}Br_3$?

8. An analysis of a substance that is a gas at room temperature gave the results 83.06% C, 16.85% H; 1 liter of gas at N.P.T. was found to weigh 3.20 g. What is the most likely empirical formula?

9. A crystalline yellow substance occurring in the grain of certain tropical woods and found to be composed of C, H, and O gave the analysis: C, 74.11%; H, 5.90%. Determinations of the molecular weight by the Rast method gave the results 240 and 255. Calculate the empirical formula and the theoretical percentage composition.

10. A liquid vitamin factor extracted from green plants gave no test for nitrogen or sulfur, and the results of a microanalysis were: 82.64% C, 10.20% H. Calculate the minimal empirical formula.

11. A derivative of morphine contains 72.27% C, 7.13% H, and 4.60% N. No other element except oxygen is present, and the molecular weight is in the range 250–350. Calculate the empirical formula.

12. The determination of molecular weight illustrated in Fig. 1.1 was carried out with the substance benzil, $C_6H_5COCOC_6H_5$. Calculate the result of the determination and compare it with the theoretical value.

13. The synthesis of ethyl alcohol from C_2H_5I and AgOH proves the structure. Would the synthesis of a propyl alcohol from C_3H_7I prove the structure?

14. Write structural formulas of all possible isomers of the formula C_3H_8O. One isomer is inert to sodium, and when heated with HI it yields a mixture of methyl and ethyl iodide. What is the structure?

15. Which of the following natural products would you expect to occur in optically active forms?

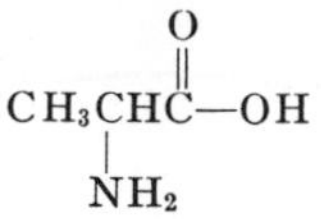

$$CH_3CH\overset{\overset{O}{\|}}{C}-OH$$
$$\underset{NH_2}{|}$$

Alanine
(a)

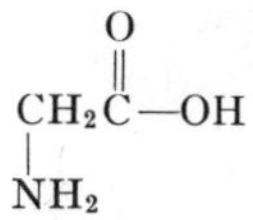

$$CH_2\overset{\overset{O}{\|}}{C}-OH$$
$$\underset{NH_2}{|}$$

Glycine
(b)

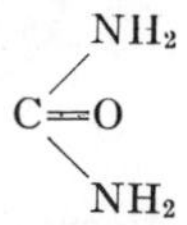

$$\underset{NH_2}{\overset{NH_2}{C=O}}$$

Urea
(c)

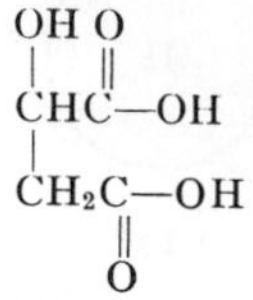

$$\overset{OH\ O}{\underset{|}{CH}}\overset{|\ \|}{C}-OH$$
$$CH_2\overset{\overset{|}{C}}{C}-OH$$
$$\underset{O}{\|}$$

Malic acid
(d)

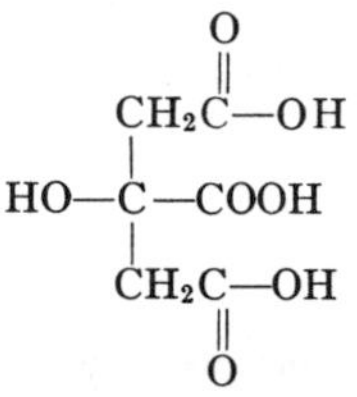

$$CH_2\overset{\overset{O}{\|}}{C}-OH$$
$$HO-\overset{|}{C}-COOH$$
$$CH_2\overset{|}{C}-OH$$
$$\underset{O}{\|}$$

Citric acid
(e)

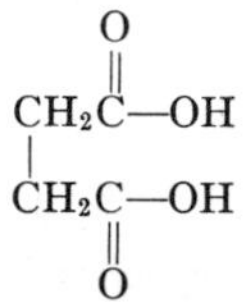

$$CH_2\overset{\overset{O}{\|}}{C}-OH$$
$$CH_2\overset{|}{C}-OH$$
$$\underset{O}{\|}$$

Succinic acid
(f)

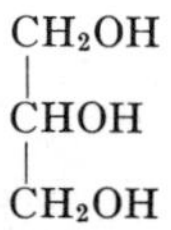

$$CH_2OH$$
$$\overset{|}{C}HOH$$
$$\overset{|}{C}H_2OH$$

Glycerol
(g)

$$CH_3CHCH\overset{\overset{O}{\|}}{C}-OH$$
$$\underset{OH\ NH_2}{|\ |}$$

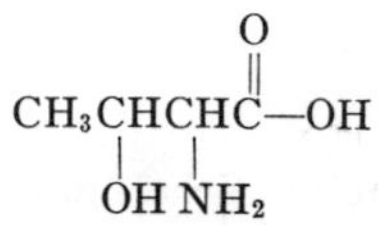

Threonine
(h)

16. Would you expect the fat constituent formulated in Section 1.12 to be optically active or inactive?

17. Tartaric acid exists in a *d*-form, an *l*-form, a *dl*-form, and a second optically inactive form. See if you can account for the four forms.

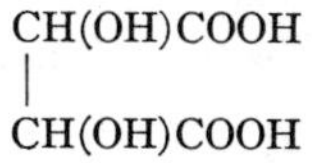

$$CH(OH)COOH$$
$$|$$
$$CH(OH)COOH$$

Tartaric acid

Chapter 2

STRUCTURAL TYPES

2.1   **Classification of Types.** — Methyl iodide, CH_3I, and ethyl iodide, C_2H_5I, are representatives of a group of compounds that includes bromides (CH_3Br, C_2H_5Br), chlorides, and fluorides, and also similar halides derived from propane (C_3H_8) and hydrocarbons still higher in the series. Early chemists saw a formal analogy between alkali halides, such as $NaCl$, KBr, KI, and organic halides of the type CH_3Cl, C_2H_5Br, and C_2H_5I, and named the latter "alkali-like" halides or **alkyl** (al̲k̲ali + y̲l) **halides.** The name has been retained, and the symbol RX is used as a general formula for any alkyl halide; X stands for any halogen (F, Cl, Br, I), and R represents any hydrocarbon group such as methyl, ethyl, or propyl. If RX represents any alkyl halide, then ROH represents any alcohol, for example, methyl alcohol, CH_3OH, or ethyl alcohol, C_2H_5OH. The reaction of ethyl alcohol with hydriodic acid is an example of a reaction which can be formulated in general terms as follows:

$$\underset{\text{Alcohol}}{ROH} + \underset{\text{Hydrogen halide}}{HX} \longrightarrow \underset{\text{Alkyl halide}}{RX} + H_2O$$

Methane and ethane can be thought of as combinations of the methyl and ethyl group with hydrogen, CH_3—H and C_2H_5—H, and the general formula for such a hydrocarbon is RH, whence the generic name (class name) **alkane.** Ethylene and acetylene are the common names of the first members of series of hydrocarbons characterized by having double and triple bonds, respectively, and hence, in a systematic nomenclature worked out at an international congress at Geneva in 1890, these series are designated **alkenes** (from ethyl̲e̲n̲e) and **alkynes** (from acety̲l̲e̲ne). Alkenes are also known as **olefins** (see section 5.1).

A generalized formula of another type is derived as follows. The simplest alkane is methane, CH_4, and the next member is ethane, C_2H_6, and in each case

33

the number of hydrogen atoms is twice the number of carbon atoms plus 2. If n stands for the number of carbons, the number of hydrogens is $(2n + 2)$, and hence the general formula for these alkanes is C_nH_{2n+2}. This fits the empirical formulas of propane (C_3H_8) and of butane (C_4H_{10}), which are described as the next two members of the **homologous series** of alkanes. Succeeding homologs differ in composition by one carbon and two hydrogen atoms, or by the increment of CH_2, a methylene group. The alkane having 10 carbon atoms, or the C_{10}-alkane, is a higher homolog of methane, and the formula, easily derivable from the type formula, is $C_{10}H_{22}$. Ethylene, $CH_2{=}CH_2$, has two hydrogens less than ethane, and any alkene must have two hydrogens less than the alkane of the same number of carbon atoms; hence the type for alkenes is C_nH_{2n}. Acetylene, C_2H_2, and homologous acetylenes, such as C_3H_4, C_4H_6, conform to the type C_nH_{2n-2}.

The compounds listed in the first row below can be imagined as derived from methane by replacement of one of the four hydrogens by one of the groups: —OH (hydroxyl group), —Cl, —NH$_2$ (amino group), —OCH$_3$ (methoxyl group).

	H	H	H	H
	|	|	|	|
Derivatives of methane:	H—C—OH	H—C—Cl	H—C—NH₂	H—C—OCH₃
	|	|	|	|
	H	H	H	H
Alkane derivatives:	ROH	RCl	RNH₂	ROCH₃
	Alcohol	Alkyl chloride	Amine	Methoxyalkane

$$R = C_nH_{2n+1}$$

Each compound is the first member of a homologous series of the type listed in the second row. Since the alkyl group R has one hydrogen less than the corresponding alkane, the general formula for it is C_nH_{2n+1}.

The compound types listed and a few additional ones belong to one of two broad groups of organic compounds. Compounds of the first group, identifiable as being derived from methane or other alkane, are called **aliphatic**. The word is derived from the Greek word *aleiphar*, meaning fat, and the connection is that animal and vegetable fats, with which early chemists were familiar, are made up of molecules in which large alkyl groups such as $C_{15}H_{31}$— and $C_{17}H_{35}$— determine the predominating characteristics (see formula of a fat, section 1.12). All other compounds which have an alkane part, or which are alkanes, alkenes, and alkynes, are now classified as aliphatic. The second group is composed of compounds derived from or related to benzene, C_6H_6. It includes, for example, compounds analogous to the derivatives of methane listed above; the corresponding derivatives of benzene are C_6H_5OH, C_6H_5Cl, $C_6H_5NH_2$, and $C_6H_5OCH_3$. Because the first-known derivatives of benzene were natural products extracted from balsams and impressed the discoverers because of their fragrant aromas, the group as a whole came to be known as **aromatic** compounds.

The group C_6H_5— in the above compounds is called a phenyl group; the corresponding group derived from naphthalene, $C_{10}H_8$, is called a naphthyl group, $C_{10}H_7$—. The general name for groups of this type is **aryl**, from aromatic, and the symbol is Ar. Thus ArCl is an aryl chloride, just as RCl is an alkyl chloride.

As will be seen presently, benzene is a cyclic compound; it consists of a ring of six carbon atoms. Nonbenzenoid compounds containing rings of carbon atoms are called **alicyclic**. Ring compounds containing one or more atoms of nitrogen, oxygen, or sulfur are described as **heterocyclic**.

2.2   **Derivatives of Methane.** — Since the carbon atom is tetrahedral and the methane molecule symmetrical in space, as shown in the Stuart model (a), the four hydrogen atoms are equivalent, and if one of them is imagined to be

(a)   (b)   (c)

replaced by chlorine it is immaterial which one is selected. Replacement of the uppermost hydrogen of (a) gives (b); note that, in this model, made to scale, chlorine (radius 1.00 Å) is the largest atom, carbon (radius 0.77) is next, and hydrogen (radius 0.32) is the smallest. If the hydrogen shown in (a) to the right rear is replaced by chlorine, the result is (c), but this is the same as (b), only oriented in a different way. It is evident that only one monochloro derivative of methane is theoretically possible, and indeed only one substance of the formula CH_3Cl has been discovered; it is correctly defined as monochloromethane but is known by the simpler name methyl chloride.

If any second hydrogen atom of either (b) or (c) is replaced by chlorine, the result is (d), which is the only possible spatial arrangement for CH_2Cl_2, called

(d)

methylene chloride. The model can be oriented in various positions, but there is no way in which switching of any pair of atoms gives rise to a different model. When a Kekulé formula is used, the corresponding model should be kept in mind. Thus formula I for methylene chloride appears different from II, but since they

represent one and the same compound of space formula (d) they are understood
to be equivalent representations. The flat Kekulé formula shows merely which
atoms are joined together, and not how the atoms are arranged in space. Formulas I and II indicate merely that the molecule is made up of a carbon atom to

$$\begin{array}{ccc}
\text{H} & \text{H} & \\
| & | & \\
\text{H--C--Cl} & \text{Cl--C--Cl} & \text{CH}_2\text{Cl}_2 \\
| & | & \\
\text{Cl} & \text{H} & \\
\text{I} & \text{II} & \text{III} \\
& \text{Methylene chloride} &
\end{array}$$

which two hydrogen and two chlorine atoms are attached. The formulas of
trichloromethane (chloroform) and of tetrachloromethane (carbon tetrachloride)
likewise represent one compound each:

$$\begin{array}{cc}
\text{Cl} & \text{Cl} \\
| & | \\
\text{H--C--Cl} \quad \text{or} \quad \text{CHCl}_3 & \text{Cl--C--Cl} \quad \text{or} \quad \text{CCl}_4 \\
| & | \\
\text{Cl} & \text{Cl} \\
\text{Chloroform} & \text{Carbon tetrachloride}
\end{array}$$

2.3   Monochloro and Dichloro Derivatives of Ethane. — In ethane all
six hydrogen atoms are identically situated and hence equivalent,
and only one monosubstitution product is possible. The monochloro derivative,
which can be described as monochloroethane but which is more generally known
as ethyl chloride, is represented correctly by any one of the formulas shown, for
each conveys the same information.

$$\begin{array}{ccc}
\text{H} \quad \text{H} & \text{H} \quad \text{H} & \\
| \quad \ | & | \quad \ | & \\
\text{H--C--C--Cl} & \text{H--C--C--H} & \text{CH}_3\text{CH}_2\text{Cl} \\
| \quad \ | & | \quad \ | & \\
\text{H} \quad \text{H} & \text{Cl} \quad \text{H} & \\
\end{array}$$

Ethyl chloride

Isomerism becomes possible whenever two substituents are introduced into the
ethane molecule, for these can either be located on the same carbon atom or
distributed between the two carbon atoms. If two chlorine atoms are linked to
one carbon atom, as in the formula below on the left, the compound represented
can be distinguished from the isomer on the right by numbering the carbon atoms
and indicating the position of each chlorine atom by citing the number of the

$$\begin{array}{cc}
\text{H} \quad \text{H} & \text{H} \quad \text{H} \\
|2 \quad |1 & |2 \quad |1 \\
\text{H--C--C--Cl} \quad (\text{CH}_3\text{CHCl}_2) & \text{H--C--C--H} \quad (\text{ClCH}_2\text{CH}_2\text{Cl}) \\
| \quad \ | & | \quad \ | \\
\text{H} \quad \text{Cl} & \text{Cl} \quad \text{Cl} \\
\text{1,1-Dichloroethane} & \text{1,2-Dichloroethane}
\end{array}$$

carbon atom to which it is joined. In the first compound both chlorines are
attached to carbon atom No. 1 (or C_1), and hence the compound is 1,1-dichloro-

ethane. The name 1-dichloroethane is incomplete and therefore incorrect; it would leave unspecified the location of one of the chlorine atoms. The name 1,1-chloroethane is incorrect because it implies 1-monochloroethane. The second dichloroethane is the 1,2-derivative. In this case the molecule is symmetrical and it makes no difference whether the carbon atoms are numbered from right to left, as shown, or in the reverse order. In the case of the isomer, left-to-right counting would give the name, 2,2-dichloroethane, but a choice between the prefixes 1,1- and 2,2- is afforded by the rule that numbers be kept as low as possible. However a formula is written, one should try all possible methods of counting the carbon atoms and select the name which gives the smallest numbers for the positions of substituent groups.

In the model (a) for 1,2-dichloroethane the balls are not of accurate relative sizes, but the two large balls attached to carbon represent chlorine atoms and the four smaller balls stand for hydrogen atoms. If the lower carbon atom of the model is held stationary, the upper one can be rotated about the single bond connecting the two through an angle of 180°, and the result is (b). Models (a)

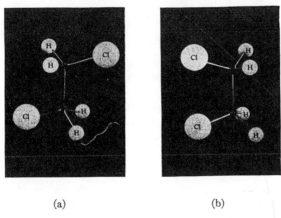

(a)   (b)

and (b) represent two extremes, one (a) in which the chlorine atoms are maximally distant, and the other (b) in which the same atoms are as close as possible. Rotation to smaller angles theoretically could give an infinite number of other forms intermediate between (a) and (b). Experimentation shows that 1,2-dichloroethane exists in only one form, and from this fact it is concluded that in the molecule itself the carbon atoms are as free to rotate about a single connecting bond, or pair of shared electrons, as are the balls in the models.

2.4   Conformation. — The 1,2-dichloroethane molecule is able, by rotation about the single bond, to assume the shape, or conformation, of greatest stability. Stability, in such a molecule, is determined by repulsive effects between nearby atoms. Two atoms of a molecule which are not bonded together but which are close to each other in space tend to repel each other. The repulsive effect, described as a **nonbonded interaction**, introduces a factor of instability. Such interactions become increasingly severe with increasing size of the two atoms concerned, but even hydrogen:hydrogen interactions can be of significant magnitude because the severity of repulsion increases exponentially with decreasing separation distance. Since chlorine atoms are much larger than hydrogen atoms, the dominant factor in determination of the preferred conformation of 1,2-dichloroethane is the strong repulsion of chlorine-to-chlorine. Hence 1,2-dichloroethane exists predominantly in the conformation (a), in which the large chlorine atoms are as distant from each other as possible. Thus (a) is the form of maximal stability, and (b) is the form of minimal stability. The relationship is shown better in the Stuart models (a') and (b'). Model (a') has

(a')   (b')

the greater symmetry, or balance, in that the large chlorine atoms are on opposite sides. In (b') the two large halogen atoms are bunched on one side of the molecule, and the repulsion of one large chlorine for another chlorine in close proximity renders (b') considerably less stable.

2.5   Polychloroethanes. — Three chlorine atoms can be introduced into the ethane molecule in the following two ways:

$$
\begin{array}{ccc}
& H & Cl \\
& | & | \\
H - & C - C & - Cl \quad (CH_3CCl_3) \\
& | & | \\
& H & Cl
\end{array}
\qquad
\begin{array}{ccc}
& H & H \\
& | & | \\
H - & C - C & - Cl \quad (ClCH_2CHCl_2) \\
& | & | \\
& Cl & Cl
\end{array}
$$

1,1,1-Trichloroethane   1,1,2-Trichloroethane

Note that with the second isomer the numbering of the carbon atoms from right to left, as the formula is written, gives smaller numbers (1,1,2-) than the alternative counting (1,2,2-). The two possible types of tetrasubstitution products are illustrated as follows:

CH_2ClCCl_3   CHCl_2CHCl_2
(1, 1, 1, 2-)   (1, 1, 2, 2-)

Only one pentachloro and one hexachloro derivative are possible, for the situation is the same as with the penta- and hexahydrogen compounds.

2.6   Derivatives of Propane. — The propane molecule presents a different situation because the eight hydrogen atoms are not all similarly

located. The six hydrogens attached to the two terminal carbon atoms are equivalent (dotted lines), but the environment is different from that of the two hydrogens located on the central carbon atom of the chain.

$$
\begin{array}{ccccc}
& H & H & H \\
& | & | & | \\
H - & C - C - C & - H \\
& | & | & | \\
& H & H & H
\end{array}
$$

There is thus a differentiation between end and middle positions in the molecule; one result is that two isomeric monosubstitution products are possible, as exemplified by the monochloro derivatives:

$$\begin{array}{c} \text{H} \ \ \text{H} \ \ \text{H} \\ | \ \ \ \ | \ \ \ \ | \\ \text{H}-\text{C}-\text{C}-\text{C}-\text{Cl} \\ | \ \ \ \ | \ \ \ \ | \\ \text{H} \ \ \text{H} \ \ \text{H} \end{array}$$

(CH₃CH₂CH₂Cl)
1-Chloropropane, or
n-propyl chloride

$$\begin{array}{c} \text{H} \ \ \text{H} \ \ \text{H} \\ | \ \ \ \ | \ \ \ \ | \\ \text{H}-\text{C}-\text{C}-\text{C}-\text{H} \\ | \ \ \ \ | \ \ \ \ | \\ \text{H} \ \ \text{Cl} \ \ \text{H} \end{array}$$

(CH₃CHClCH₃)
2-Chloropropane, or
isopropyl chloride

These can be described as the 1-chloro and 2-chloro derivatives of propane but are more commonly called normal (*n*-) propyl chloride and isopropyl chloride. Although there is only one form of a methyl (CH_3—) or ethyl (C_2H_5—) group, the next higher hydrocarbon radical exists as either the *n*-propyl group, $CH_3CH_2CH_2$—, or the isopropyl group, $(CH_3)_2CH$—.

Polysubstitution in propane presents opportunity for isomerism of a still higher degree, as can be seen from the following tabulation:

Dichloropropanes:		Trichloropropanes:	
$CH_3CH_2CHCl_2$	1,1-	$CH_3CH_2CCl_3$	1,1,1-
$CH_3CHClCH_2Cl$	1,2-	$CH_3CHClCHCl_2$	1,1,2-
$ClCH_2CH_2CH_2Cl$	1,3-	$ClCH_2CH_2CHCl_2$	1,1,3-
$CH_3C(Cl_2)CH_3$	2,2-	$CH_3CCl_2CH_2Cl$	1,2,2-
		$ClCH_2CHClCH_2Cl$	1,2,3-

2.7   Butanes. — The formula of ethane can be derived from that of methane by replacing one hydrogen atom by a methyl group, and the propane formula can be built up similarly. This systematic method of derivation serves a useful purpose, for if all modes of substitution are considered, no isomers can be missed. Propane has two different types of hydrogen atoms, the type on the ends (*a*) and that in the middle (*b*), and hence in the derivation of butanes substitution of each by methyl must be tried:

$$\overset{a}{} \ \ \overset{b}{} \ \ \overset{a}{}$$
Methyl substitution in propane, $CH_3CH_2CH_3$, gives:

a. CH₃CH₂CH₂CH₃
n-Butane
(b.p. −0.5°)

b. CH₃CHCH₃
|
CH₃
Isobutane
(b.p. −12°)

Replacement of any one of the terminal hydrogens by a methyl group gives a straight-chain hydrocarbon of the formula C_4H_{10}, namely, normal butane. A similar operation on a centrally located hydrogen affords the isomeric, branched-chain hydrocarbon isobutane. The formula shown can be simplified by pooling the three methyl groups attached to the central carbon atom: $(CH_3)_3CH$. This formula suggests an alternative and descriptive name. The substance is seen to be a derivative of methane in which only one of the original hydrogens remains and the other three have been replaced by methyl groups; isobutane therefore can be defined as trimethylmethane, just as $CHCl_3$ is described as trichloro-methane.

The spatial characteristics of *n*-butane and of isobutane are illustrated with photographs of two types of models. Note the zig-zag arrangement of the

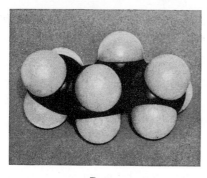

n-Butane   Isobutane

methylene groups (CH_2) in *n*-butane, occasioned by the tetrahedral configuration of the carbon atoms. A long chain of the same type is kept from coiling back on itself by hydrogen : hydrogen repulsions. Isobutane, which has a branched-chain structure, has the lower boiling point, and is thus more volatile than the straight-chain isomer.

2.8   **Pentanes.** — Structural formulas of the C_5-hydrocarbons can be derived by the same systematic procedure of making all possible methyl substitutions in both butanes, and the only added operation necessary is to inspect the resulting formulas and eliminate duplicates:

From the butanes,
$$\overset{a}{C}H_3\overset{b}{C}H_2\overset{b}{C}H_2\overset{a}{C}H_3, \qquad \overset{c}{C}H_3\overset{d}{C}H\overset{c}{C}H_3,$$
$$\underset{c}{|}\atop CH_3$$

are derived:

a. $CH_3CH_2CH_2CH_2CH_3$

b. $CH_3CH_2CHCH_3$
$\qquad\qquad\quad |$
$\qquad\qquad\ CH_3$

$\left[\begin{array}{l} c.\ CH_3CHCH_2CH_3 \quad \text{same as } b \\ \qquad\quad | \\ \qquad\ CH_3 \end{array}\right]$

d. $\quad CH_3$
$\qquad\ |$
$\quad CH_3CCH_3$
$\qquad\ |$
$\qquad CH_3$

TABLE 2.1. HEXANES, C_6H_{14}

ISOMER	FORMULA	NAME	M.P., °C.	B.P., °C.
I	$CH_3CH_2CH_2CH_2CH_2CH_3$	n-Hexane	−94.0	68.7
II	$CH_3CH_2CH_2CHCH_3$ $\quad\quad\quad\quad\vert$ $\quad\quad\quad\quad CH_3$	2-Methylpentane	−153.7	60.3
III	$CH_3CH_2CHCH_2CH_3$ $\quad\quad\quad\vert$ $\quad\quad\quad CH_3$	3-Methylpentane	(−118)	63.3
IV	$\quad\quad\; CH_3$ $\quad\quad\;\vert$ $CH_3CH_2CCH_3$ $\quad\quad\;\vert$ $\quad\quad\; CH_3$	2,2-Dimethylbutane	−98.2	49.7
V	$CH_3CH—CHCH_3$ $\quad\;\vert\quad\quad\vert$ $\quad CH_3\;\; CH_3$	2,3-Dimethylbutane	−128.8	58.0

It is seen that the third substitution tried (*c*) gives a formula identical with the second (*b*) but merely written in a different manner. Three distinct formulas remain and, since all possibilities have been investigated, the conclusion is reached that three pentanes can exist. The branched-chain isomers can be represented by simplified formulas and named as derivatives of methane; the three pentanes are as follows:

	B.P.	NAME
$CH_3CH_2CH_2CH_2CH_3$	36.1°	n-Pentane
$CH_3CH_2CH(CH_3)_2$	27.9°	Dimethylethylmethane (Isopentane)
$(CH_3)_4C$	9.5°	Tetramethylmethane (Neopentane)

Again, the most highly branched isomer is the most volatile. Boiling points in a given series are dependent chiefly on molecular weight. Melting points are more sensitive to differences in structure and the more symmetrical isomers tend to have the higher melting points. n-Pentane melts at −129.7°, isopentane (2-methylbutane) at −159.6°, and the symmetrical tetramethylmethane at the much higher temperature of −16.6°.

2.9   Hexanes. — The five hexanes are listed in the table along with their Geneva names. In the Geneva system the basic name is that of the parent hydrocarbon corresponding to the longest chain of carbons present: pentane (C_5), hexane (C_6), heptane (C_7), etc. Methyl groups are regarded as substituents and their positions in the chain are indicated by numbers; counting is done from whichever direction gives the smaller numbers. It is also proper and

ISOMER	FORMULA	METHANE DERIVATIVE
II	$CH_3CH_2CH_2CH(CH_3)_2$	Dimethyl-n-propylmethane
III	$(CH_3CH_2)_2CHCH_3$	Methyldiethylmethane
IV	$CH_3CH_2C(CH_3)_3$	Trimethylethylmethane
V	$(CH_3)_2CHCH(CH_3)_2$	Dimethylisopropylmethane

for some purposes desirable to employ the methane-derivative system, illustrated
in the above list in which simplified formulas are employed.   Melting points
are scattered and irregular in the hexane series.   There is less spread in boiling
points than in the pentane series of lower molecular weight, and *n*-hexane is less
volatile than the branched-chain isomers.

2.10   **Heptanes.** — The formulas and Geneva-system names of the nine known
                isomers are given in Table 2.2.   Again, the straight-chain hydrocarbon
boils at a slightly higher temperature than branched-chain isomers, but differences between isomers have become progressively less as the molecular weight has
increased.   The highly branched isomer IX, of tightly knit structure, has the
highest melting point.

Heptanes can be named as derivatives of methane, but this method of nomenclature is scarcely practical for hydrocarbons containing more than seven carbon
atoms.   The point of greatest branching ordinarily is taken as the focus of the
substituted   methane   molecule.   Isomer   II   can   be   described   as   dimethyl-*n*-

TABLE 2.2.   HEPTANES, C_7H_{16}

ISOMER	FORMULA	NAME	M.P., °C.	B.P., °C.
I	$CH_3(CH_2)_5CH_3$	*n*-Heptane	-90.5	98.4
II	$CH_3CH_2CH_2CH_2CHCH_3$ $\mid$ CH_3	2-Methylhexane	-118.2	90.0
III	$CH_3CH_2CH_2CHCH_2CH_3$ $\mid$ CH_3	3-Methylhexane	-119	92.0
IV	CH_3 $\mid$ $CH_3CH_2CH_2CCH_3$ $\mid$ CH_3	2,2-Dimethylpentane	-125.0	78.9
V	$CH_3CH_2CH{-}CHCH_3$ $\mid\quad\mid$ $CH_3\ \ CH_3$	2,3-Dimethylpentane	. . . .	89.7
VI	$CH_3CHCH_2CHCH_3$ $\mid\quad\quad\mid$ $CH_3\quad CH_3$	2,4-Dimethylpentane	-119.3	80.8
VII	CH_3 $\mid$ $CH_3CH_2CCH_2CH_3$ $\mid$ CH_3	3,3-Dimethylpentane	-134.9	86.0
VIII	$CH_3CH_2CHCH_2CH_3$ $\mid$ CH_2 $\mid$ CH_3	3-Ethylpentane	-119	93.3
IX	CH_3 $\mid$ $CH_3CH{-}CCH_3$ $\mid\quad\ \mid$ $CH_3\ \ CH_3$	2,2,3-Trimethylbutane	-25.0	80.8

butylmethane, III as methylethyl-*n*-propylmethane, IV as trimethyl-*n*-propyl-methane. Isomer VI cannot be named according to this scheme on the basis of the information at hand, but can be called diisopropylmethane. Similarly, the hexane listed in Table 2.1 as isomer V can be described adequately as diisopropyl. The heptane V (Table 2.2) can be named methylethylisopropylmethane.

2.11 **Further Notes on Names.** — Note that the name 1,1,2-trimethyl-pentane for the hydrocarbon is seen at once to be incorrect, for attachment of a methyl group at C_1 of *n*-pentane makes it a hexane, not a pentane. The correct name is 2,3-dimethylhexane. "Heptamethylethane" is an ob-

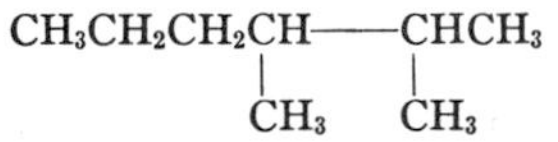

$$CH_3CH_2CH_2CH\underset{\underset{CH_3}{|}}{}\underset{\underset{CH_3}{|}}{}CHCH_3$$

viously erroneous name, because ethane has only six positions for attachment of methyl groups.

A formula often can be arranged in various ways, and sometimes the arrangement obscures the derivation of the Geneva name. Formula (1) is confusing because of the bracketing of the four methyl groups. Actually one of the methyl

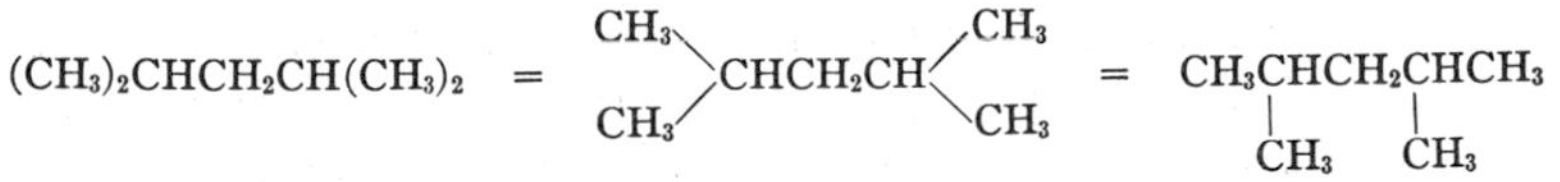

$$(CH_3)_2CHCH_2CH(CH_3)_2 \quad = \quad \underset{CH_3}{\overset{CH_3}{>}}CHCH_2CH\underset{CH_3}{\overset{CH_3}{<}} \quad = \quad CH_3CHCH_2CHCH_3$$

(1) (2) (3)

groups at each end is part of the longest carbon chain, which is C_5, and the other is a substituent attached to this chain. The true situation is seen better in the arrangement (2) and most clearly when the formula is written as in (3); the hydrocarbon is 2,4-dimethylpentane. Another example, formula (4), is written in a way that tends to suggest that the substance is a methyl-ethyl derivative of

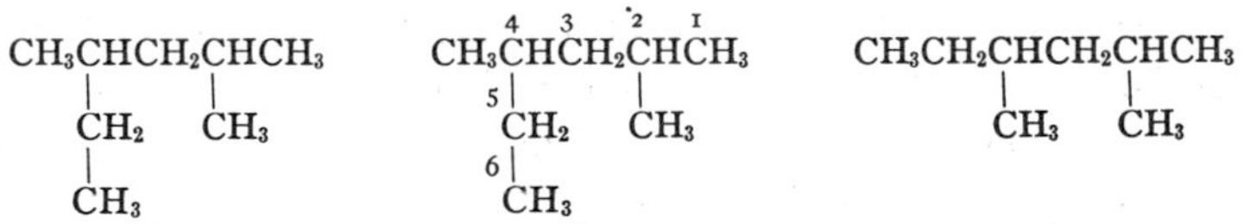

CH₃CHCH₂CHCH₃   CH₃CHCH₂CHCH₃   CH₃CH₂CHCH₂CHCH₃
   CH₂   CH₃   CH₂   CH₃   CH₃   CH₃
   CH₃   CH₃
   (4)   (5)   (6)

pentane, since the carbon atoms written in a row form a chain of five. However, in selecting the longest chain one must consider all possible chains, including those that go around corners. The ethyl group at a right angle to the horizontal chain extends the chain to six, as shown by the numbers in (5). Had the formula been arranged as in (6), the correct name would have been obvious from the start: 2,4-dimethylhexane.

COMPOUNDS WITH FUNCTIONAL GROUPS

2.12 **Butyl Alcohols.** — In an earlier section the formulas of the pentanes were derived by substitution of methyl for each of the four types of hydrogen atoms in the two butanes:

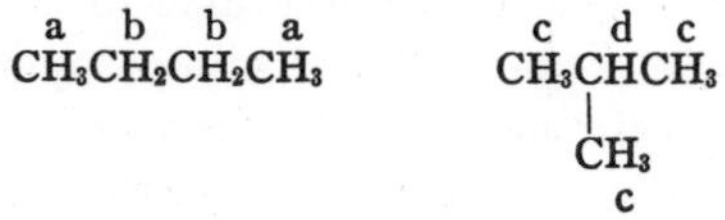

$$\underset{\text{a}\quad\text{b}\quad\text{b}\quad\text{a}}{CH_3CH_2CH_2CH_3} \qquad \underset{\text{c}\quad\text{d}\quad\text{c}}{CH_3CHCH_3}$$
$$\underset{\text{c}}{|CH_3}$$

Substitution of methyl at (b) and at (c) gives the same hydrocarbon, and there are only three pentanes. If the group substituted for hydrogen in the butanes is anything other than methyl there are no duplicates and the number of isomeric derivatives is four. Thus systematic substitution of the hydroxyl group gives formulas for the four butyl alcohols:

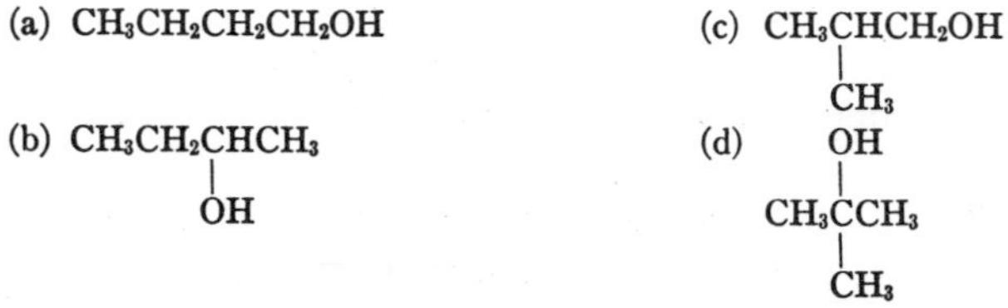

(a) $CH_3CH_2CH_2CH_2OH$

(b) $CH_3CH_2CHCH_3$
$\qquad\quad |$
$\qquad\quad OH$

(c) CH_3CHCH_2OH
$\qquad\quad |$
$\qquad\quad CH_3$

(d) $\quad OH$
$\qquad |$
$\quad CH_3CCH_3$
$\qquad\quad |$
$\qquad\quad CH_3$

These isomers are usually known by common names assigned in part according to the alcohol types which they represent. An alcohol having just one alkyl group attached to the carbon carrying the hydroxyl is a primary alcohol. Secondary and tertiary alcohols have two and three alkyl groups, respectively, at

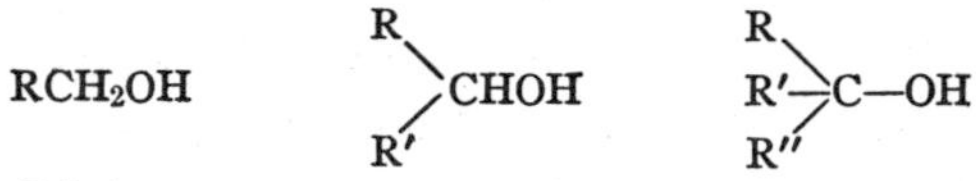

$$RCH_2OH \qquad \underset{R'}{\overset{R}{\diagdown}}CHOH \qquad \underset{R''}{\overset{R}{\underset{|}{R'-C-OH}}}$$

Primary $\qquad\qquad$ Secondary $\qquad\qquad$ Tertiary

the position indicated. Alcohols (a) and (c) are both primary; (a) has an *n*-propyl group linked to —CH_2OH, and in (c) the corresponding group is isopropyl. Isomer (a) is adequately described as *n*-butyl alcohol, and its isomer (c) is known as isobutyl alcohol. Alcohol (b), which has a methyl and an ethyl group linked to the hydroxylated carbon, is the only secondary alcohol of the series, and (d) is the only tertiary alcohol, and hence they are distinguished by prefixes which indicate the alcohol type: *sec-* (secondary) and *t-* (tertiary). The four alcohols are summarized as follows:

n-Butyl alcohol $\qquad CH_3CH_2CH_2CH_2OH$

Isobutyl alcohol $\qquad \underset{CH_3\diagup}{\overset{CH_3\diagdown}{}}CHCH_2OH$

sec-Butyl alcohol $\qquad CH_3CH_2CHCH_3$
$\qquad\qquad\qquad\qquad\qquad |$
$\qquad\qquad\qquad\qquad\quad OH$

t-Butyl alcohol $\qquad \underset{CH_3}{\overset{CH_3}{\underset{|}{\overset{|}{CH_3-C-OH}}}}$

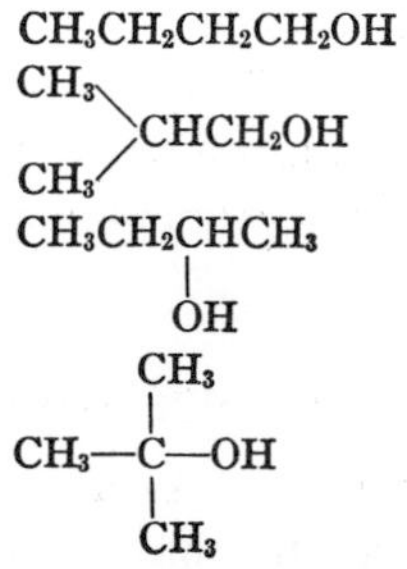

Alcohols are also named as derivatives of carbinol, that is, CH_3OH. Thus *sec*-butyl alcohol is methylethylcarbinol and *t*-butyl alcohol is trimethylcarbinol.

2.13   Amine Types. — Amines are derivatives of ammonia in which hydrocarbon groups replace one, two, or three hydrogens, and they are described as primary, secondary, or tertiary according to the number of such groups: RNH_2, R_2NH, R_3N. An alkyl group may be primary (a), secondary (b), or tertiary (c), but as long as only one group is linked to nitrogen the substance is a primary amine; it has the $—NH_2$ group. Secondary amines are exemplified

$$CH_3CH_2NH_2 \qquad \overset{\displaystyle CH_3}{\underset{\displaystyle CH_3}{\diagdown\!\diagup}}CHNH_2 \qquad CH_3\!-\!\overset{\displaystyle CH_3}{\underset{\displaystyle CH_3}{\overset{|}{\underset{|}{C}}}}\!-\!NH_2$$

(a) Ethylamine	(b) Isopropylamine	(c) *t*-Butylamine

Primary amines

in (d) and (e), tertiary amines in (f) and (g). The amines are all basic and form salts similar to ammonium chloride.

$$(CH_3CH_2)_2NH \qquad\qquad \overset{\displaystyle CH_3\ \ H\ \ CH_3}{\underset{}{\overset{|\ \ \ \ |\ \ \ \ |}{CH_3CH\!-\!N\!-\!CH\!-\!CH_3}}}$$

(d) Diethylamine   (e) Diisopropylamine

$$(CH_3CH_2)_3N \qquad\qquad \overset{\displaystyle CH_2CH_3}{\underset{}{\overset{|}{CH_3\!-\!N\!-\!CH_2CH_2CH_3}}}$$

(f) Triethylamine   (g) Methylethyl-*n*-propylamine

2.14   Amyl and Higher Alcohols. — *n*-Butyl alcohol takes its name from the name of the parent hydrocarbon, *n*-butane. The next normal hydrocarbon is *n*-pentane, C_5H_{12}, but the corresponding normal alcohol, $CH_3(CH_2)_3CH_2OH$, is called *n*-amyl alcohol. The name arose because the first known alcohol of the formula $C_5H_{11}OH$ was discovered as a by-product of the fermentation of crude potato starch (L. *amylum*, starch).

2.15   Geneva Names of Alcohols. — Alcohols and amines of more complicated structure are usually known by their Geneva names. Just as hydrocarbons having a double or a triple bond are named alkenes (from ethyl<u>ene</u>) or alkynes (from acetyl<u>ene</u>), alcohols are designated by changing the ending of the basic alkane from -**ane** to -**anol** (-ol from alcohol). Thus the Geneva name for methyl alcohol is methanol, and that for ethyl alcohol is ethanol. The hydroxyl group, or "ol" group, confers upon a molecule specific properties or functions; it is called a functional group, since it causes the compound to function in specific ways. Ethyl alcohol has the ability to react with sodium and with hydriodic acid because it contains the alcohol functional group. Alkenes and alkynes similarly have specific reaction characteristics because of their functional groups: the double-bond, or ene group, and the triple-bond, or yne group.

In order to apply Geneva names to the butyl alcohols, it is necessary first to select the **longest chain of carbon atoms that includes the maximum number of functional groups. The position of the functional group is then indicated by a**

number placed at the end of the name. Isobutyl alcohol has one three-carbon chain which includes the two methyl groups, and another which includes one of these groups and the carbon carrying the hydroxyl group; the latter is selected and the compound is named 2-methylpropanol-1. *n*-Butyl alcohol is butanol-1, and *sec*-butyl alcohol is butanol-2. In case of a conflict, **functional group numbers take precedence over substituent group numbers.** Thus the basic name is decided upon first, that is, the substance is a butanol, a pentanol, etc., the carbon carrying the functional group is assigned the smallest possible number, and there is then no choice in numbers indicating the positions of substituent groups. Compound I is a dimethylhexanol, specifically 5,5-dimethylhexanol-1. Halogen

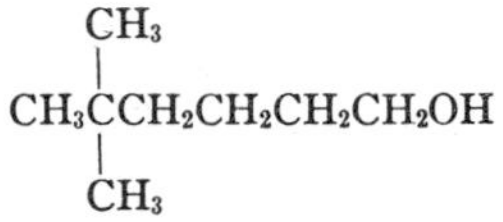

$$CH_3$$
$$CH_3CCH_2CH_2CH_2CH_2OH \qquad ClCH_2CH_2CH_2CH_2CH_2OH$$
$$CH_3$$

I   II

in the Geneva system, is treated as a substituent, and hence II is 5-chloropentanol-1 (not 1-chloropentanol-5). If two alcoholic hydroxyl groups are present, the substance is a diol; if three, it is a triol. Thus III is butanediol-1,4, and IV is 2,3,4-trimethylpentanetriol-2,3,4. Compound V has one chain of seven

$$HOCH_2CH_2CH_2CH_2OH \qquad\qquad CH_3-\overset{CH_3}{\underset{OH}{C}}-\overset{CH_3}{\underset{OH}{C}}-\overset{CH_3}{\underset{OH}{C}}-CH_3$$

III   IV

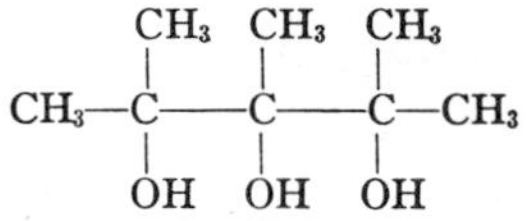

carbon atoms, but since this includes only one of the two alcoholic groups it is

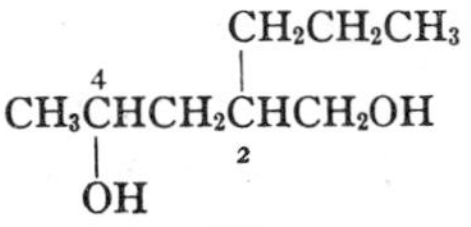

$$CH_2CH_2CH_3$$
$$\overset{4}{CH_3}\underset{OH}{CHCH_2}\overset{}{\underset{2}{CH}}CH_2OH$$

V

not selected as the basis for the name. Instead, the five-carbon chain including both groups is selected, for the basic name pentanediol shows that the compound is a diol and should function like other diols and not like monohydroxy alcohols. Attached to the pentanediol unit is a substituent group identified as an *n*-propyl group. Use of just the name propyl would be ambiguous, for it then would not be clear whether the group has the straight-chain structure of an *n*-propyl compound or is a branched-chain isopropyl derivative. The name of V is thus 2-*n*-propylpentanediol-1,4.

2.16 **Alkenes.** — The first two hydrocarbons of this series are usually referred to by their common names: ethylene, $CH_2\!\!=\!\!CH_2$; propylene, $CH_3CH\!\!=\!\!CH_2$. The Geneva system is used for higher alkenes, including the two butenes. In one of these the double-bond function is at the end of the chain and in the other it is at the middle. The terminal number indicating the position of the functional group gives the position of just the first of the doubly bonded

$$CH_3CH_2CH=CH_2 \qquad\qquad CH_3CH=CHCH_3$$
Butene-1 Butene-2

carbons. The other principles of naming are as outlined in the preceding section. Examples (1) and (2) require no comment. Examples (3) and (4) show that the

$$CH_3CHCH_2CH_2CH=CH_2 \qquad CH_3CH_2CH_2CH=CHCH_2CH_3$$
$$\qquad| \qquad\qquad\qquad\qquad\qquad\quad \text{Heptene-3 (not 4)}$$
$$CH_3 \qquad\qquad\qquad\qquad\qquad\qquad\qquad (2)$$
5-Methylhexene-1
(1)

$$CH_2=CHCH=CH_2 \qquad\qquad CH_2=CHCH=CHCH=CH_2$$
Butadiene-1,3 Hexatriene-1,3,5
(3) (4)

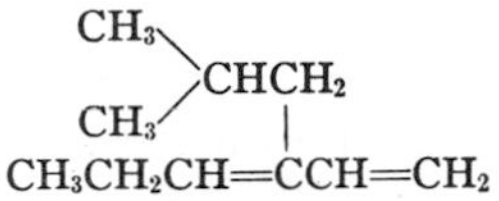

$$CH_3$$
$$\qquad\qquad\qquad\quad \searrow CHCH_2$$
$$CH_3 \qquad\qquad |$$
$$CH_3CH_2CH=CCH=CH_2$$
3-Isobutylhexadiene-1,3
(5)

system provides the convenient names diene and triene for compounds having two and three double bonds, respectively. Example (5) is a case where the basic name, hexadiene, is that including both functional groups, even though the six-carbon chain is not so long as that extending from the left-hand terminus and out along the branching group. Note that.this four-carbon group is specifically the isobutyl group.

Usage varies in application of the Geneva system of naming, and this term now refers to what is actually a system modified by the International Union of Pure and Applied Chemistry. Thus "hexane" is used by some instead of "*n*-hexane"; some prefer "1-butanol" and "2-pentene" to "butanol-1" and "pentene-2"; "hexane-1,2,3-triol" rather commonly replaces "hexanetriol-1,2,3." Another useful variation is to indicate the presence of one or more double bonds by a Greek delta and to indicate the positions of the first unsaturated carbon of each pair by a superscript number:

$$CH_3 \qquad\qquad CH_3$$
$$\qquad\qquad\qquad\qquad\qquad | \qquad\qquad\quad |$$
$$CH_2=CHCH=CHCH=CH_2 \qquad CH_3C=CHCH_2CH_2C=CHCH_2OH$$
$$\Delta^{1,3,5}\text{-Hexatriene} \qquad\qquad 3,7\text{-Dimethyl-}\Delta^{2,6}\text{-octadiene-1-ol}$$

2.17   Space Models of Alkenes. — To make a model of ethylene from two tetrahedra, some way has to be found for connecting the bonds of the two methylene groups (a). One way is to use sections of tubing (b), and another is to represent bonds by steel springs (c). The connectors of (b) or the springs of (c) are under tension, which suggests that the double bond is under strain and hence prone to open to produce a strain-free ethane derivative.

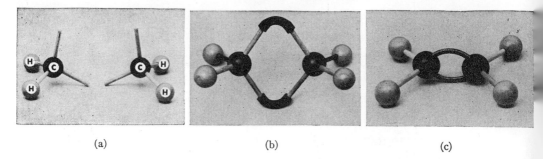

     (a)   (b)   (c)

Hence the model leads to the expectation that ethylene and other alkenes are reactive compounds, which indeed is the case. Both alkenes and alkynes have potentialities for reaction not shared by alkanes. Since in alkanes all valences not involved in covalent C—C bonds are saturated with hydrogen, alkanes are described as saturated hydrocarbons. Alkenes and alkynes are unsaturated hydrocarbons.

2.18   **Geometrical Isomerism.** — It will be noted from the model (b) above, or from the same model arranged as in (d), that the four hydrogen and two carbon atoms of ethylene all lie in the same plane. The molecule is symmetrical, or balanced, since the two hydrogens on the right-hand side are

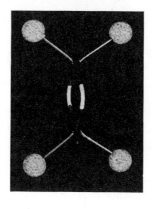

(d)

matched by two on the left-hand side. Inspection of the formula for butene-2, $CH_3CH{=}CHCH_3$, shows that here the situation is different. Each doubly bonded carbon has attached to it two atoms or groups which are different, methyl and hydrogen, and hence two arrangements in space are possible. In one arrangement (e) the two methyl groups are on the same side of the molecule, and in the other (f) they are across from each other, or on opposite sides; the double bond prevents conversion of one form to the other by rotation of one carbon atom. Butene-2 indeed exists in two isomeric forms, and these have the same structure, represented in the formula $CH_3CH{=}CHCH_3$, but differ in the orientation of their atoms in space, or in configuration. Any isomers which differ only in configura-

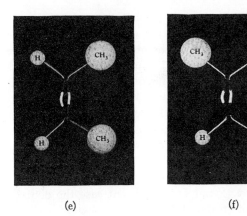

(e)   (f)

tion, or spatial arrangement, are called stereoisomers, and the particular kind of stereoisomerism illustrated by the butenes is known as geometrical isomerism. Form (e) is called *cis*-butene-2, and form (f) is *trans*-butene-2. The prefixes come from the Latin prepositions *cis* and *trans*, meaning "on this side" and "across."

In models (e) and (f) the balls representing methyl are larger than those representing hydrogen, although the difference is not fully in accord with the difference in volume of the groups.[1] The bonds connecting CH_3 to carbon should be longer than the carbon–hydrogen bonds, corresponding to the actual bond distances, which are: C—C, 1.54 Å; and C—H, 1.09 Å. Because of the difference in the

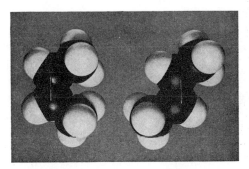

cis-Butene-2   *trans*-Butene-2

size of the attached groups, model (f), with the two large groups on opposite sides of the molecule, has greater balance, or symmetry, than model (e), with the two bulky groups bunched on the same side. The actual shapes of the molecules are seen better in the Stuart models, which show more clearly the greater

[1] The tetrahedral models were designed by André Dreiding, are manufactured by W. Büchi, Switzerland, and are distributed by Schaar and Co. (Chicago). Two bonds of each tetrahedron are tubes and two are rods, which snap-fit into tubes of other tetrahedra. Cork balls are supplied by Armstrong Cork Co. The double bond is formed by joining tetrahedra with plastic tubing. The models were leveled for photography by needles thrust into the cork balls.

symmetry of the *trans* stereoisomer. *trans*-Butene-2 is significantly more stable than the *cis* isomer. Under the influence of an appropriate catalyst, each compound can be isomerized in part to the other until equilibrium is reached, and the equilibrium mixture is found to be composed preponderantly of the *trans* isomer and to contain only a minor amount of the *cis* form. The relationship is the usual one: *trans* isomers are almost invariably more stable than their *cis* isomers. The greater stability is partly due to the greater symmetry, or better balance, of the *trans* form, and partly to a repulsive effect. The Stuart models show that the two large methyl groups of *cis*-butene-2 are very close to each other, and hence repulsion of these groups must contribute to the instability of this isomer. The repulsive effect is analogous to that in the unstable form of 1,2-dichloroethane (section 2.3), but in the present case the double bond prevents rotation to a condition of greater stability.

For convenience in writing, models such as (e) and (f), above, are represented by the projection formulas (e') and (f'). The methyl groups and hydrogen atoms,

$$
\begin{array}{cc}
\text{H—C—CH}_3 & \text{CH}_3\text{—C—H} \\
(1)|\vdots(2) & (1)|\vdots(2) \\
\text{H—C—CH}_3 & \text{H—C—CH}_3 \\
\text{(e')} & \text{(f')}
\end{array}
$$

which in the models are at an angle of 109° 28', the normal tetrahedral angle, are written for simplicity on a line. One member of the double bond (1) is represented by a full line, to indicate that it extends above, or in front of, the plane of the paper or blackboard, and the other is represented by a dotted line, which is intended to indicate that this bond is below the plane of the paper, or to the rear. Inspection of models (e) and (f) will serve to identify these front and rear bonds, which lie in a plane at right angles to the plane of the six atoms.

Geometrical isomerism, or *cis-trans* isomerism, is possible whenever each of two doubly bound carbons carries two different atoms or groups, whether the groups attached to the first carbon are the same as those attached to the other or different. In pentene-2, $CH_3CH_2CH{=}CHCH_3$, the two pairs of groups are

$$
\begin{array}{cccc}
\text{CH}_3\text{—C—H} & \text{CH}_3\text{—C—H} & \text{CH}_3\text{—C—H} & \text{CH}_3\text{—C—H} \\
|\vdots & |\vdots & |\vdots & |\vdots \\
\text{CH}_3\text{CH}_2\text{—C—H} & \text{H—C—CH}_2\text{CH}_3 & \text{CH}_3\text{CH}_2\text{—C—CH}_3 & \text{CH}_3\text{—C—CH}_2\text{CH}_3 \\
\textit{cis-} & \textit{trans-} & \textit{cis-} & \textit{trans-} \\
\multicolumn{2}{c}{\text{Pentene-2}} & \multicolumn{2}{c}{\text{3-Methylpentene-2}}
\end{array}
$$

different, in contrast to butene-2, but *cis* and *trans* forms are possible. It is not necessary that each doubly bonded carbon carry a hydrogen atom, and 3-methylpentene-2 is a typical case where one carbon carries two alkyl groups, but two that are different; the *cis* isomer is identified as that in which hydrogen is *cis* to the smaller of the two groups. Geometrical isomerism is not possible if either carbon of an ene group carries two of the same atoms or groups, as in the examples listed:

$$
\begin{array}{ccc}
\text{CH}_3\text{—C—H} & \text{CH}_3\text{—C—CH}_3 & \text{H—C—Cl} \\
|\vdots & |\vdots & |\vdots \\
\text{H—C—H} & \text{CH}_3\text{—C—H} & \text{Cl—C—Cl}
\end{array}
$$

2.19   **Alkynes.** — The model of acetylene (a) shows that the four atoms are in a line and hence that no opportunity exists for geometrical

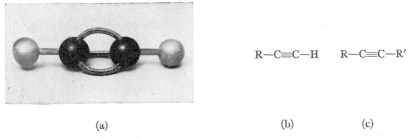

$$R—C≡C—H \qquad R—C≡C—R'$$

(a)   (b)   (c)

isomerism in alkynes describable as either monosubstituted acetylenes (b) or disubstituted acetylenes (c).

2.20   **Cycloalkanes.** — Examination of tetrahedral models with steel-spring bonds leads to the expectation that a hydrocarbon should be possible having three carbons joined in a ring and each saturated with hydrogen.

Cyclopropane   Cyclobutane   Cyclopentane

The hydrocarbon is indeed known, and since it has the same number of carbon atoms as propane but is cyclic it is called cyclopropane. It is the first member of a series known as cycloalkanes. Cycloalkanes have the same type formula as alkenes, C_nH_{2n}. The formulas can be written in the manner shown, or abbreviated by writing just the connecting lines. Cyclohexane derivatives are

$$CH_2——CH_2 \qquad CH_2——CH_2 \qquad CH_2——CH_2 \qquad \overset{CH_2}{CH_2 \quad CH_2}$$

particularly common and are conveniently represented with abbreviated formulas, as illustrated in the examples. The names cyclohexene and cyclohexanol require no number for indication of the position of the functional groups, since all six

Cyclohexane   Cyclohexene   Cyclohexanol   1,1,4-Tetramethyl-cyclohexane positions in cyclohexane are identical. The last example shows what is done when numbers (in this case substituent group numbers) are required.

In the models shown of cyclopropane and cyclobutane the spring bonds are distorted and the ring carbon atoms lie in a plane. In the wooden ball-and-stick model of cyclopentane the ring appears also to be planar, but actually all the wooden sticks are bent slightly.

2.21   Conformation of Cyclohexane. — Construction of a model of cyclohexane shows that the six carbon atoms fit together, without any bending of bonds or distortion of angles, to form a puckered ring, as illustrated in model (1) made of wooden parts;[1] hydrogen atoms are assumed to be at the ends of the bonds extending from the carbon atoms. The molecule depicted is called the chair-form of cyclohexane: atoms 6, 1, 2 lie in a plane forming the back rest;

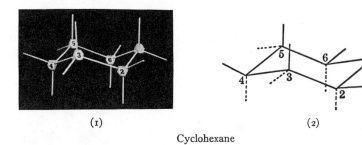

(1)   (2)

Cyclohexane

the plane including carbons 2, 3, 5, 6 forms the seat; carbons 3, 4, 5 form the leg rest. The angle between all pairs of valences is the normal tetrahedral angle of 109° 28′, and the molecule is completely free from bond strain. The perspective representation of (1) used in writing is (2). Note that at each carbon atom one

Axial bonds (a)   Equatorial bonds (e)

Cyclohexane bonds (chair)

hydrogen is up or directed upwards, and the other is down or directed downwards. The six hydrogens that are up are called β-hydrogens and are represented by full-line bonds. The hydrogens that are down are α-hydrogens and are represented by dotted bonds. Note further that the 1β-, 3β-, and 5β-hydrogens are parallel to the axis of symmetry of the ring and that the 2α-, 4α-, and 6α-hydrogens also are parallel to this axis. These six hydrogens are described as axial (a). The remaining six hydrogens radiate equatorially and are called equatorial (e).

[1] Supplier: Bennett Lumber Co., Zeeland, Mich.

The contrast is evident from formulas showing the axial and equatorial bonds separately.

Two practical consequences of the axial or equatorial orientation of bonds can be appreciated best from inspection of Stuart models. In model (3) of cyclohexane the three white balls on the top side represent axial β-hydrogens and

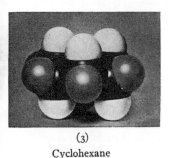

(3)	(4)	(5)
Cyclohexane	Methylcyclohexane	

the three on the underside axial α-hydrogens; equatorial hydrogens, represented in gray, are radial and almost coplanar. These equatorial hydrogens alternate between the β (up) and α (down) orientation. It is evident that the three axial hydrogens on each side of the plane are close to one another, close enough for slight hydrogen:hydrogen repulsive interaction. If an axial hydrogen is replaced by a methyl group (4), axial methyl is so close to the two axial β-hydrogens that repulsive forces decrease the stability. If, on the other hand, an equatorial hydrogen of cyclohexane is replaced by a methyl group (5), no comparable interactions are set up and the molecule should be more stable than (4). Thus theory predicts that (4) is destabilized by repulsion between the axial methyl group and the two axial hydrogens, each of which is in a $1:3$ position with respect to methyl. Another statement of the case is that (4) acquires instability from two $1:3$ $CH_3:H$ interactions. Evidence abundantly supports the prediction. Thus **conformational analysis**, or reasoning from inspection of models, permits accurate prediction of relative stability. Conformational analysis also permits prediction of relative reactivity. Suppose a hydroxyl or other functional group can occupy either an axial or an equatorial position. If it is axial, the group is shielded from attack by two axial hydrogens; if equatorial, the group is not shielded and its peripheral position makes it vulnerable to attack.

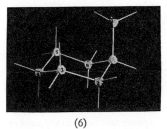
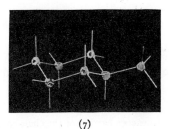

(6)	(7)
Methylcyclohexane	

If methylcyclohexane were generated by a reaction which could give only the less stable conformation (4), the substance would tend to change into the more stable form (5). The change occurs by a simple mechanism described as a ring flip and illustrated in models (6) and (7). There is little energy barrier to the flip of one chair form (6) into another (7), and in a proper model the transformation is accomplished easily by rotations about single bonds.[1] Axial 1-methyl at an uptilted corner (6) becomes equatorial 1-methyl at a downtilted corner (7)

(8)   (9)

without losing its identity as β-oriented. Perspective formulas (8) and (9) show the flip depicted in the models.

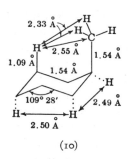

(10)

The relative magnitude of the repulsive effects in the unstable form of methylcyclohexane can be judged from the separation distances given in diagram (10). Interaction of 1:3 axial hydrogens produces little strain, for the separation distance is 2.50 Å. On the β-side, however, each of two axial hydrogens (only one of which is shown) is only 2.33 Å distant from two hydrogens of the methyl group, and the cumulative effect of all interactions involved must be substantial. If two axial methyl groups were present, the conformation obviously would be highly unstable. Since the hydroxyl group is also large, diaxial cyclohexane-1β,3β-diol is much less stable than the diequatorial form.

CARBONYL COMPOUNDS

2.22   **Compound Types.** — A carbon atom doubly bound to oxygen constitutes a carbonyl group, and simple compounds containing this group are illustrated in the formulas. The carbon–oxygen double bond is made up of two pairs of shared electrons, but, since oxygen is significantly

$>C=O$ $O=C=O$

Carbonyl   Carbon
group   dioxide

Formaldehyde   Acetone

more electronegative than carbon (see table, 32.3), carbonyl compounds have properties considerably different from those of carbon–carbon double-bonded compounds. Differences of only a quantitative nature distinguish

---

[1] Study of the nuclear magnetic resonance spectrum of cyclohexane at low temperatures indicates that the energy barrier for the chair-chair interconversion is 9.7 kcal./mole (F. R. Jensen, 1960).

the main types of carbonyl compounds, which are identifiable from the nature of the two groups attached to carbon. If one is an alkyl group and the other hydrogen, the compound is an aldehyde; formaldehyde is the only aldehyde having two hydrogens and no alkyl group. A ketone contains two alkyl groups joined to the carbonyl carbon, and an ester contains one alkyl group and one alkoxyl group (RO—). The carbonyl group is a functional group, and Geneva

$$\begin{array}{ccc} \underset{\text{H}}{\overset{\text{R}}{\diagdown}}C{=}O & \underset{\text{R}'}{\overset{\text{R}}{\diagdown}}C{=}O & \underset{\text{R}'O}{\overset{\text{R}}{\diagdown}}C{=}O \\ \text{Aldehyde} & \text{Ketone} & \text{Ester} \end{array}$$

names are derived by adding to the basic name the suffix -**al** to indicate an aldehyde and -**one** to indicate a ketone as shown in the examples below. A number after the name indicates the position of the ketone or "one" group of a ketone; in an aldehyde the carbonyl group has to occupy a terminal C_1 position and hence a number is superfluous.

$$\begin{array}{ccc} \underset{\text{CH}_3}{\overset{\text{CH}_3}{\diagdown}}\text{CHCH}_2\text{C}\underset{\text{O}}{\overset{\text{H}}{\diagup}} & \overset{\text{O}}{\overset{\|}{\underset{\underset{\text{CH}_3}{|}}{\text{CH}_3\text{CHCCH}_3}}} & \text{CH}_3\text{COCH}_2\text{COCH}_3 \\ \text{3-Methylbutanal} & \text{3-Methylbutanone-2} & \text{Pentanedione-2,4} \end{array}$$

An ester is a derivative of an alcohol precursor, which furnishes the alkoxyl

$$\begin{array}{ccc} \text{R}-\text{C}\underset{\text{OR}'}{\overset{\text{O}}{\diagup}} & \text{R}-\text{C}\underset{\text{OH}}{\overset{\text{O}}{\diagup}} & \text{HOR}' \\ \text{Ester} & \text{Carboxylic acid} & \text{Alcohol} \end{array}$$

group, and of a carboxylic acid, so called because the group is a combination carbonyl-hydroxyl function. Ethyl acetate is the ethyl ester of acetic acid,

$$\underset{\underset{\text{Acetic acid} \quad\quad \text{Ethanol}}{}}{\text{CH}_3-\text{C}\overset{\text{O}}{\underset{\text{OH} + \text{H}\,\text{OCH}_2\text{CH}_3}{\diagup}}} \longrightarrow \text{CH}_3\text{C}\underset{\text{OCH}_2\text{CH}_3}{\overset{\text{O}}{\diagup}} + \text{H}_2\text{O}$$

$$\text{Ethyl acetate}$$

derived by elimination of water between the molecules of the two components. If the formula is abbreviated to $CH_3COOC_2H_5$, one should remember that a double-bonded carbonyl group is present. Esters of valuable acids are generally made by heating the acid with a large excess of the alcohol and a trace of hydrogen chloride as catalyst. The reaction eventually reaches equilibrium; the catalyst greatly increases the speed with which equilibrium is reached but does not alter the position of equilibrium. A large excess of the alcoholic component, by the mass-action effect, shifts the equilibrium in favor of the ester and hence improves the efficiency of conversion of acid to ester. This procedure for formation of an ester was developed by E. Fischer and is known as the **Fischer method of esterification.** A catalyst accelerates the reverse reaction of an equi-

$$R-C\overset{O}{\underset{OH}{\big<}} \quad + \quad CH_3OH \quad \xrightarrow[\text{HCl (catalyst)}]{} \quad R-C\overset{O}{\underset{OCH_3}{\big<}} \quad + \quad H_2O$$

Carboxylic acid   (large excess)   Methyl ester

librium just as it accelerates the forward reaction, and hence an ester is hydrolyzed to the components when heated with a large excess of water and a catalytic amount of hydrochloric acid:

$$R-C\overset{O}{\underset{OCH_3}{\big<}} \quad + \quad H_2O \quad \xrightarrow[\text{HCl (catalyst)}]{} \quad R-C\overset{O}{\underset{OH}{\big<}} \quad + \quad CH_3OH$$

(large excess)

A strong base also catalyzes hydrolysis of an ester and is particularly effective because it combines with the acid liberated to form a salt and so displaces the equilibrium.

Fats are mixtures of esters of glycerol (propane-1,2,3-triol) and higher fatty acids. Since alkaline hydrolysis of a fat liberates glycerol and gives a mixture

$$
\begin{array}{c}
CH_2O-\overset{O}{\overset{\|}{C}}(CH_2)_{16}CH_3 \\
CHO-\overset{O}{\overset{\|}{C}}(CH_2)_{16}CH_3 \\
CH_2O-\overset{O}{\overset{\|}{C}}(CH_2)_7\underset{H\ \ H}{C{=}C}(CH_2)_7CH_3
\end{array}
\quad \xrightarrow{\text{NaOH}} \quad
\begin{array}{c}
CH_2OH \\
CHOH \\
CH_2OH
\end{array}
\quad + \quad
\left\{
\begin{array}{l}
2\,CH_3(CH_2)_{16}COONa \\
\text{Sodium stearate} \\
CH_3(CH_2)_7\underset{H\ \ H}{C{=}C}(CH_2)_7COONa
\end{array}
\right\} \text{Soap}
$$

     Glyceride   Glycerol   Sodium oleate

of sodium salts which is a soap (L. *sapo*, soap), this long-known process of soap fabrication is called saponification. By extension of meaning, the hydrolysis of any ester with alkali is described as a saponification. The glyceride formulated is the ester of the triol with two molecules of stearic acid and one of oleic acid. Note that each of these natural higher fatty acids has a straight chain with an even number of carbon atoms (C_{18}); all acidic components of fats conform to this pattern. Note also that oleic acid has the *cis*-configuration.

2.23   **Carboxylic Acids.** — Esters display at least some of the chemical properties characteristic of aldehydes and ketones, the typical carbonyl compounds, but carboxylic acids do not. The reason for this divergence is bound up with the acidic character of the carboxylic compounds. Acetic acid

$$CH_3C\overset{O}{\underset{OH}{\big<}} \quad + \quad NaOH \quad \longrightarrow \quad CH_3C\overset{O}{\underset{O^-Na^+}{\big<}} \quad + \quad H_2O$$

Sodium acetate

combines with sodium hydroxide in water solution to form a salt, sodium acetate, a polar compound containing sodium ions and acetate ions comparable to sodium chloride, Na^+Cl^-. These salts are stable to water and merely dissociate to the component ions. Sodium acetate is entirely different in behavior from sodium methoxide, the compound resulting from the action of sodium on methanol, for this is destroyed by water and converted into methanol and sodium hydroxide:

$$CH_3OH + Na \rightarrow CH_3ONa + \tfrac{1}{2}H_2$$
Sodium
methoxide

$$CH_3ONa + H_2O \rightleftharpoons CH_3OH + Na^+OH^-$$

Methanol contains a hydroxyl group, as does acetic acid, but this is not an acidic hydroxyl. Tested with indicator paper in water solution, methanol is neutral, whereas acetic acid shows a pH of about 3.

2.24   Resonance. — A simple and convincing explanation of why the one hydroxy compound is acidic whereas the other is neutral is afforded by the theory of resonance, a concept of very general application and usefulness introduced around 1930, largely by Linus Pauling[1] of the California Institute of Technology. According to the resonance theory, when a substance can have two or more structures that are comparable in energy to one another and that are interconvertible by redistribution of valence electrons of either unsaturated or ionized centers, the actual molecule does not conform to any one of these structures but is a hybrid of them all, a resonance hybrid. Each resonance structure contributes to the character of the hybrid, and the greater the number of contributing structures the greater is the stability of the hybrid. Inspection of the electronic formula (a) for the acetate ion shows that the situation is favorable for electron

$$CH_3 : \overset{\overset{\cdot\cdot}{:\underset{}{O}:}}{\underset{\cdot\cdot}{C}} : \overset{\cdot\cdot}{\underset{\cdot\cdot}{O}} :^- \quad \longleftrightarrow \quad CH_3 : \overset{\overset{\cdot\cdot}{:\overset{-}{O}:}}{\underset{}{C}} :: \overset{}{\underset{\cdot\cdot}{O}} :$$

(a)   (b)

Acetate anion

redistribution. Carbon is joined to the upper oxygen by two pairs of shared electrons and to the oxygen at the right by one pair, and the latter oxygen carries the negative charge of the ion. If an electron pair originally shared with the upper oxygen moves entirely into the sphere of this oxygen (arrow) and a pair originally associated with the oxygen to the right moves into a shared position (arrow), the result is (b). The ionic charge is now on the upper oxygen because one of the two electrons that this atom has gained originally belonged to carbon and has been donated by carbon to oxygen, giving the oxygen a negative charge.

That the structures such as (a) and (b) are in resonance is indicated by a double-headed arrow; this means that the components are contributors to the hybrid that constitutes the actual entity, in this case an ion. The formation of a resonant hybrid acetate ion on dissociation of acetic acid can be represented with

---

[1] Linus Pauling, b. 1901 Portland, Oregon; Ph.D. Calif. Inst. Techn. (R. Dickinson); Calif. Inst. Techn.; Nobel Prize 1954

Kekulé formulas, as follows:

$$CH_3C\!\!\begin{array}{c}{}^{\displaystyle O}\\[-2pt]\diagdown{}\\OH\end{array} \rightleftharpoons CH_3C\!\!\begin{array}{c}{}^{\displaystyle O}\\[-2pt]\diagdown{}\\O^-\end{array} \longleftrightarrow CH_3C\!\!\begin{array}{c}{}^{\displaystyle O^-}\\[-2pt]\diagdown{}\\O\end{array} + H^+$$

$$\underbrace{\qquad(a')\qquad\qquad\qquad(b')\qquad}_{\text{Hybrid ion}}$$

The negative charge and the double bond can be located either as in (a′) or as in (b′), and these are identical resonance structures. The formulas meet the general requirement for resonance that electrons assume new orientations without any movement of atoms. It is important to avoid the misconception that the acetate ion has the structure (a′) one moment and (b′) the next and that the bonds are thrashing back and forth between the two positions. A mule does not alternate between being a horse and being an ass but is a hybrid having characteristics intermediate between those of its parents, a mare and a male ass.

As stated above, resonance is attended with stabilization. The acetate ion is stabilized by hybridization between two resonance structures and this stabilization provides a driving force promoting dissociation of acetic acid to a hybrid ion. Thus carboxylic acids owe their acidic character, or their ability to dissociate to give hydrogen ions, to the opportunity which the structure provides for formation of a resonance-stabilized hybrid carboxylate ion. Alcohols present no comparable opportunity for resonance stabilization of an ion and have only the low acidity inherent in the hydroxyl group.

A further consequence of the resonance effect is that the carboxylate ion has no true carbonyl group. Each of the carbon–oxygen links is a double bond in one structure and a single bond in the other, and hence each is a hybrid bond of character intermediate between a double and a single bond. That carboxylic acids, unlike esters, do not enter into reactions characteristic of carbonyl compounds is thus understandable, since the usual reaction conditions are such that the acid is present in the form of its resonant ion.

2.25   Acidity Constant. — In pure water the concentration of hydrogen ions, or $[H^+]$, is equal to that of hydroxide ions, $[OH^-]$, and both quantities have the numerical value 1×10^{-7}. The equilibrium constant for the slight dissociation of water, k, is 10^{-14}, that is, $[H^+] \times [OH^-] = 10^{-14}$. In a weakly acidic solution where $[H^+] = 10^{-6}$, the value of $[OH^-]$ is then $10^{-14}/10^{-6} = 10^{-8}$; in a strongly alkaline solution where $[OH^-] = 10^{-2}$, the value of $[H^+]$ is 10^{-12}. The exponential expression of ion concentrations is awkward and is now generally replaced by logarithmic expression pH, defined by the equation

$$pH = -\log[H^+]$$

Thus a neutral solution has the pH 7, a slightly acidic one may have the pH 6, a slightly alkaline one the pH 8, a strongly acidic solution the pH 2, etc. In the same way, the dissociation constant of an acid, k_a, is translated into an acidity

TABLE 2.3.   DIPOLE MOMENTS OF COVALENT LINKAGES IN SATURATED COMPOUNDS

LINKAGE $+\rightarrow$	MOMENT (DEBYE UNITS)	LINKAGE $+\rightarrow$	MOMENT (DEBYE UNITS)
C—H*	0.4	H—N	1.31
C—N	1.25	H—O	1.51
C—O	1.6	H—S	0.68
C—Cl	2.3	H—Cl	1.08
C—Br	2.2	H—Br	0.78
C—I	2.0	H—I	0.38

* C. A. Coulson, *Trans. Faraday Soc.*, **38**, 433 (1942); in acetylene the direction of the moment is reversed.

constant pK_a, defined as the negative logarithm of the dissociation constant, or

$$pK_a = -\log k_a$$

Acetic acid, a weak acid, has the acidic dissociation constant (k_a) of 1.75×10^{-5} and hence:

$$pK_a \text{ (acetic acid)} = -(-5 + 0.24) = 4.76$$

Carbonic acid is more weakly acidic than acetic acid; for separation of the first hydrogen as proton, $pK_{a_1} = 6.5$.   Mineral acids are so highly dissociated that pK_a is not accurately measurable; presumably $pK_a = 1$ or less.

2.26   Inductive Effects; Mesomerism. — Many organic molecules when placed in an electric field show definite orientation, which must be the result of positive and negative electrical charges in the molecule.   If the center of the positive charge is at a position different from that of the negative charge, the molecule possesses a dipole moment, the magnitude of which can be measured with precision (and expressed in Debye units).   Methane and carbon tetrachloride, being symmetrical, have no dipole moment, but alkyl halides and alcohols, for example, have dipole moments indicative of a certain degree of polarity.   The direction of the moment can be ascertained by an indirect method and in methyl chloride the negative pole lies toward the chlorine atom ($H_3\overset{+\rightarrow}{C}$—Cl), which means that the chlorine atom is more electron-attracting than carbon. The value and direction of the moments associated with groups commonly encountered are shown in Table 2.3.   The permanent electron displacement revealed by the dipole moment corresponds to the inductive effect postulated somewhat earlier by G. N. Lewis as responsible for the effect of various substituents on the strength of organic aliphatic acids and bases.

In the period 1925–30, Lapworth,[1] Robinson,[2] Ingold,[3] and other chemists

[1] Arthur Lapworth, 1872–1941; b. Galoshiels, Scotland; Ph.D. Birmingham; Univ. Manchester; *J. Chem. Soc.*, 989 (1947)

[2] Sir Robert Robinson, b. 1886 Rufford/Chesterfield, England; Ph.D. Manchester (Perkin); Liverpool, Manchester, Oxford Univ.; Nobel Prize 1947

[3] Sir Christopher Ingold, b. 1893 Ilford, England; D.Sc. London (Thorpe); Univ. College, London

of the English school applied the idea of inductive effects with some success to interpretation of an array of perplexing facts about aromatic substitutions. Seeing, however, that inductive effects alone did not provide a complete explanation of the facts, Ingold introduced an intuitively conceived second factor termed mesomerism (between the parts). In an unsaturated system such as that of an α,β-unsaturated ketone the relative electronegativity of the oxygen atom induces a partial displacement ($\frown$) of an electron pair from the 3,4-position in the direction of the 2,3-position, as in (a); complete displacement would result in separa-

$$\underset{4 \quad 3 \quad 2 \quad \text{I}}{C=\overset{\frown}{C}-\overset{\longrightarrow}{C=O}} \qquad\qquad \overset{+}{C}-C=C-\overset{-}{O}$$

$$\text{(a)} \qquad\qquad\qquad\qquad \text{(b)}$$

tion of charges to give the excited form (b). Electronic displacements can originate in a pair of unshared electrons of a hydroxyl group ($-\overset{..}{O}H$), an amino group ($-\overset{..}{N}H_2$), or a halogen atom ($-\overset{..}{\underset{..}{C}l}:$). Thus the molecule of vinyl chloride is not represented accurately by either the completely covalent formula (c) or the completely ionic structure (e), but rather by the intermediate mesomeric state (d),

$$\underset{(c)}{CH_2{=}CH{-}\overset{..}{\underset{..}{C}l}:} \qquad\qquad \underset{(d)}{\overset{\delta-}{CH_2}{=}CH{\frown}\overset{\delta+}{Cl}} \qquad\qquad \underset{(e)}{\overset{-}{CH_2}{-}CH{=}\overset{+}{Cl}}$$

in which, in consequence of displacement of an electron pair from the chlorine atom, chlorine bears a fractional positive charge ($\delta+$) and the terminal carbon atom a fractional negative charge ($\delta-$).

The idea of an intermediate mesomeric state arrived at intuitively by the English school represented an initial expression of the concept of resonance derived in mathematical form by Pauling by application of the principles of quantum mechanics. The particular contribution of the resonance concept was in accounting for striking stabilization effects associated with resonating systems and attributable in exact terms to resonance energy. Vinyl chloride is described as a resonance hybrid partaking of the character of both form (c) and form (e); it is not a mixture of the two forms, but a separate entity that combines the properties of the two forms and possesses resonance stabilization that decreases the reactivity of the system. That the hybrid partakes in part of the form (e), in which chlorine is doubly bonded to carbon, is shown by the fact that the C—Cl bond distance is 0.08 Å shorter in vinyl chloride (1.69 Å) than in ethyl chloride (1.77 Å). By comparison with dimensions of reference molecules, this bond shortening is found to correspond to about 33% double-bond character, and consequently the chlorine is more firmly bound than when attached to a saturated carbon atom. Although the earlier concept of mesomerism is less definitive than that of resonance, a formulation such as (d), which indicates the direction of electronic displacements, affords a convenient expression of the idea of an intermediate state in a single formulation.

ALIPHATIC TYPES

2.27   **Summary.** — The preceding pages have included at least some reference to the structures and names of nearly all the important classes of aliphatic compounds. These fall into groups, as summarized below.

HYDROCARBONS

Alkanes	RH	C_nH_{2n+2}
Alkenes	$>C{=}C<$	C_nH_{2n}
Alkynes	$-C{\equiv}C-$	C_nH_{2n-2}
Cycloalkanes	$(CH_2)_n$	C_nH_{2n}

ALCOHOLS AND DERIVATIVES

Alcohols	ROH	$C_nH_{2n+1}OH$

(primary, RCH_2OH; secondary, $RR'CHOH$; tertiary, $RR'R''COH$)

Alkyl halides	RX	$C_nH_{2n+1}X$
Methyl ethers	$ROCH_3$	$C_nH_{2n+1}OCH_3$
Amines	RNH_2	$C_nH_{2n+1}NH_2$

CARBONYL COMPOUNDS

Aldehydes	$RCH{=}O$	$C_nH_{2n+1}CHO$
Ketones	$RR'C{=}O$	$C_nH_{2n+1}COC_mH_{2m+1}$
Methyl esters	$RC\overset{\displaystyle O}{\underset{\displaystyle OCH_3}{\diagup\!\!\!\diagdown}}$	$C_nH_{2n+1}C\overset{\displaystyle O}{\underset{\displaystyle OCH_3}{\diagup\!\!\!\diagdown}}$

HYBRID-CARBONYL COMPOUNDS

Carboxylic acids	$RC\overset{\displaystyle O}{\underset{\displaystyle OH}{\diagup\!\!\!\diagdown}}$	$C_nH_{2n+1}C\overset{\displaystyle O}{\underset{\displaystyle OH}{\diagup\!\!\!\diagdown}}$

As a preview of later discussions of methodology, we may mention a few reactions for interconversion of compound types. Thus a primary alcohol can be oxidized first to an aldehyde and then to an acid (1). The aldehyde can be reduced

1. $RCH_2OH \xrightarrow{[O]} RCH{=}O \xrightarrow{[O]} RCOOH$

2. $RCH{=}O \xrightarrow{NaBH_4} RCH_2OH$

3. $RCOOH \xrightarrow{LiAlH_4} RCH_2OH$

4. $R_2CHOH \xrightarrow{[O]} R_2C{=}O$

5. $R_2C{=}O \xrightarrow{H_2,\ Pt} R_2CHOH$

6. $R_2C{=}CR_2 \xrightarrow{H_2,\ Pt} R_2CHCHR_2$

with sodium borohydride in alcohol (2); reduction of a carboxylic acid can be accomplished with lithium aluminum hydride in ether (3). The product of oxidation of a secondary alcohol is a ketone (4); the reverse change can be accomplished by reduction with sodium borohydride or lithium aluminum hydride and also by hydrogenation of the ketone in the presence of platinum catalyst (5). Catalytic hydrogenation also affords a route to alkanes from alkenes (6).

Only a few additions are needed to complete the list of aliphatic types. Formally analogous to the derivatives of alcohols, RX, RNH_2, and ROR, are the following derivatives of acids:

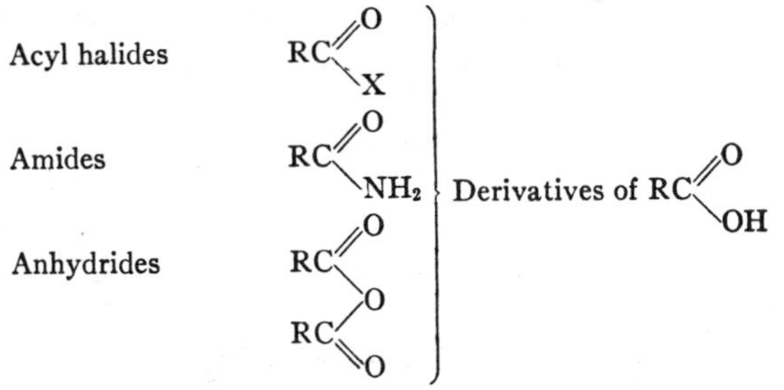

Acyl halides $RC\!\!\begin{array}{c}\nearrow O \\ \searrow X\end{array}$

Amides $RC\!\!\begin{array}{c}\nearrow O \\ \searrow NH_2\end{array}$ Derivatives of $RC\!\!\begin{array}{c}\nearrow O \\ \searrow OH\end{array}$

Anhydrides $\begin{array}{c}RC\!\!\nwarrow^{\nearrow O}\!\!{}_{O} \\ RC\!\!\searrow_{O}\end{array}$

A nitrile, $RC\!\!\equiv\!\!N$, also can be regarded as a derivative of an acid and is convertible into the acid on hydrolysis. A carboxylic acid having an alcoholic group not too distant from the carboxyl group may be convertible into an internal ester, called a lactone. γ-Lactones are particularly stable and easily formed.

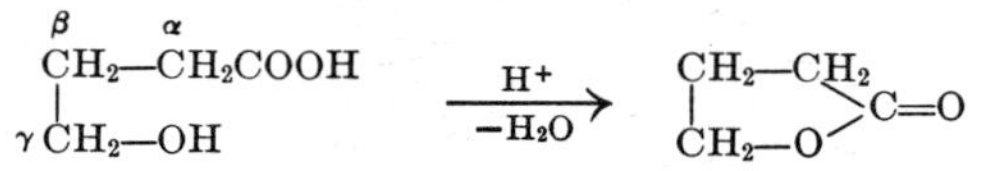

$$\begin{array}{c}{}^{\beta}{}^{\alpha} \\ CH_2\!\!-\!\!CH_2COOH \\ | \\ {}_{\gamma}CH_2\!\!-\!\!OH\end{array} \quad \xrightarrow[-H_2O]{H^+} \quad \begin{array}{c}CH_2\!\!-\!\!CH_2 \\ | \quad\quad\;\; \searrow\!C\!\!=\!\!O \\ CH_2\!\!-\!\!O\nearrow\end{array}$$

γ-Hydroxy acid   γ-Lactone

AROMATIC COMPOUNDS

2.28   **Benzene.** — This second broad group of organic compounds includes all substances derived from or related to benzene. The structure of benzene for many years presented a perplexing problem. The empirical formula C_6H_6 indicated a degree of unsaturation comparable to that of acetylene (C_2H_2) and yet benzene does not show chemical properties comparable to acetylene, or to alkenes or polyenes; it is much more stable and far less reactive. The nature of the problem and the history of early attempts to resolve it are reserved for later discussion, but it will be helpful to the reader at this stage to have a preview of the eventual solution. Kekulé proposed (1865) the formula (a) or (b) of cyclohexatriene, but the formula was contested for many years because benzene is

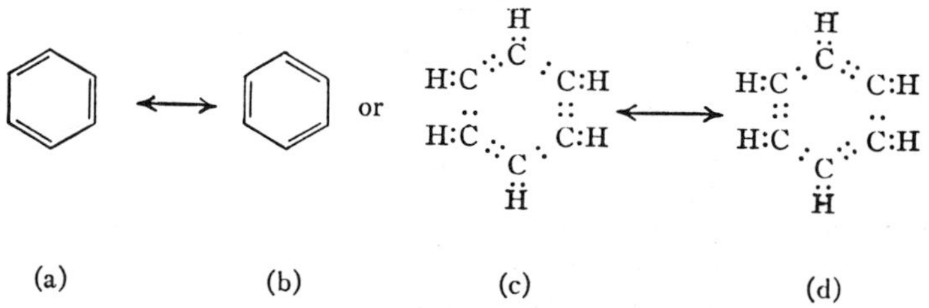

(a)   (b)   (c)   (d)

peculiarly inert. However, the resonance theory provides a simple explanation. The Kekulé formulas (a) and (b), or the electronic counterparts (c) and (d), are identical resonance structures which contribute equally to the resonance hybrid. Change of (c) to (d) involves redistribution of three electron pairs, and the six bonds linking the carbon atoms are neither single nor double bonds but hybrid bonds, each identical with the others.   X-ray analysis has established that the six carbon and six hydrogen atoms all lie in a plane and that the six carbon–carbon bonds all have the identical length, 1.40 Å.   The aromatic bond is thus shorter than the average of 1.44 Å for three single bonds (1.54 Å) and three nonresonant double bonds (1.33 Å).   Model sets include special pieces to represent aromatic

Stuart model   SASM model

Benzene

carbon atoms.   The Stuart model shows the flat, discuslike contour of the compact model and reveals the point that the six-membered ring of identical carbons is unique; comparable rings of smaller or of larger size are impossible.   In the SASM model set[1] each aromatic bond has a flattened end so that when secured

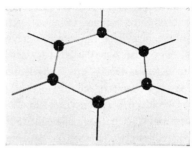

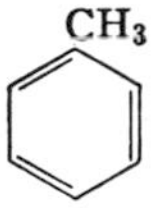

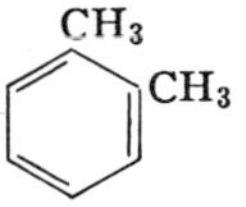

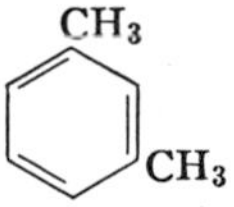

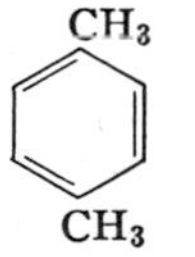

Toluene   o-   m-   p-

Xylene

(b. p. 111°)   (b. p. 144°)   (b. p. 139°)   (b. p. 138°)

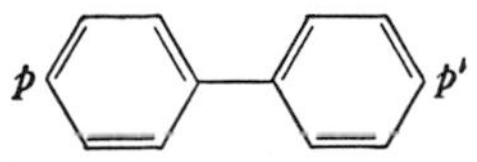

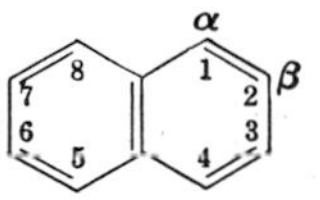

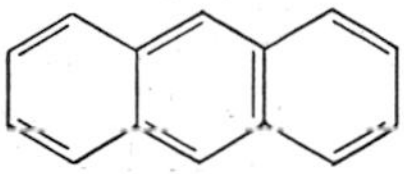

Diphenyl   Naphthalene   Anthracene
(m. p. 69°)   (m. p. 80°)   (m. p. 216°)

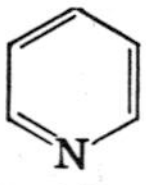

Pyridine 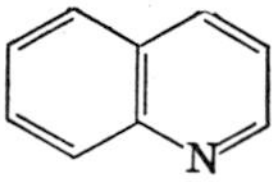   Quinoline    Thiophene

into a trigonal carbon rotation about the bond is prevented.   The trigonal angle is 120°.   The C—C and C—H bonds are made to the scale 1.40 Å and 1.09 Å; the C—H bond length is thus the same as in aliphatic compounds.   The SASM model emphasizes the radial character of the aromatic C—H bonds and shows

[1] Supplier: SASM, 99 rue Oberkampf, Par s XIᵉ

that bonds directly across the molecule point in opposite directions and are in a line.

Benzene is thus unique in having a ring of a particular size in which double and single bonds alternating in a closed system lose identity and become hybrid bonds. The resonance effect produces uniquely developed resonance stabilization. The phenyl group, C_6H_5—, is so stable that compounds such as allylbenzene, $C_6H_5CH_2CH=CH_2$, and styrene, $C_6H_5CH=CH_2$, can be put through all reactions characteristic of alkenes without alteration of the phenyl group.

Toluene is the monomethyl derivative of benzene. The three dimethylbenzenes, or xylenes, have substituents in the 1,2-, 1,3-, and 1,4-positions and are known as *ortho*-, *meta*-, and *para*-isomers, from the Greek prefixes meaning straight, regular (*o*-), between, after (*m*-), and beside, beyond (*p*-). Naphthalene is made up of two fused benzene rings and anthracene of three. Pyridine and thiophene are heterocyclic analogs of benzene; quinoline is the analog of naphthalene. The heterocyclic nitrogen atom of pyridine and quinoline is trisubstituted and the two aromatic bases are tertiary amines.

PROBLEMS

1. Formulate and name all possible dibromo derivatives of isobutane (3 isomers) and *n*-butane (6 isomers).
2. Write formulas for all heptanes derived from $CH_3CH(CH_3)CH_2CH_2CH_3$ and name them as derivatives of methane.
3. Write structural formulas for:
   - (a) 1-Bromo-2-chlorononane
   - (b) 2,2,3-Trichloroheptane
   - (c) 2-Methylbutanol-2
   - (d) Dimethylisopropylmethane
   - (e) Tetraethylmethane
4. Name the following compounds as derivatives of methane:
   - (a) CCl_2F_2
   - (b) $(CH_3)_2C(CH_2CH_3)_2$
   - (c) $(CH_3)_3CCH_2CH_2CH_2CH_3$
   - (d) $(CH_3CH_2CH_2)_2CHCH(CH_3)_2$
5. Give Geneva names for:
   - (a) $CH_3CH(CH_3)CH_2CH_2CH(CH_3)CH_2CH_3$
   - (b) Isobutane
   - (c) $CH_3CH_2CH_2CH(C_2H_5)CH_3$
   - (d) $(CH_3)_2CHCH(C_2H_5)CH_2CH(CH_3)_2$
6. What octanes can be derived from the heptane $CH_3CH_2CH_2C(CH_3)_3$? Give the Geneva names.
7. Give the Geneva names for:

(a) CH_2CHCH_2 (Glycerol)
    | | |
   OH OHOH

(b) $(CH_3)_2CCH_2CHCH_2CH_3$
       | |
      OH   CH_3

(c) $CH_3CH_2CHCH=CHCH(CH_3)_2$
        |
        CH_3

(d) $CH\equiv CCH_2CHCH_3$
         |
         CH_2CH_3

(e) $(CH_3)_2C=CHCH=C(CH_3)_2$

(f) $(CH_3)_2CHCHCH(CH_3)CH_2OH$
        |
        CH_2CH=CH_2

(g) $CH_3CHCH_2CHCH_2CH_3$
    | |
   CH_3CHCH_2CH_2

(h) $CH_2CH_2C=O$
    | |
   CH_2CH_2C=O

8. Write formulas for:
   (a) 2-Methyl-3-ethylpentanol-1
   (b) 1,4-Diphenylbutadiene-1,3
   (c) Trimethylethylene
   (d) Butanediol-2,3
   (e) 5-Chloro-4-methylpentene-1

9. Give the Geneva names of all alcohols that are monohydroxy derivatives of

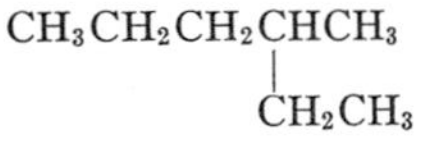

$$CH_3CH_2CH_2CHCH_3$$
$$|$$
$$CH_2CH_3$$

10. Propionic acid has the formula $C_3H_6O_2$. Write formulas showing the structures of the following derivatives:
    (a) Methyl propionate
    (b) Isopropyl propionate
    (c) Propionyl chloride
    (d) Propionic acid anhydride

11. Ethanol has a hydroxyl group, like acetic acid; why is it neutral and not acidic?

12. In the carbonate ion, $CO_3^{=}$, the three oxygens are symmetrically spaced and equidistant. Write all possible resonance structures.

13. From the formulas of the three pentanes, derive the formulas for all possible monohydroxy derivatives (8 isomers). These are called amyl alcohols ($C_5H_{11}OH$).

14. Which of the following formulas represent possible compounds and which compounds that probably are incapable of existence?

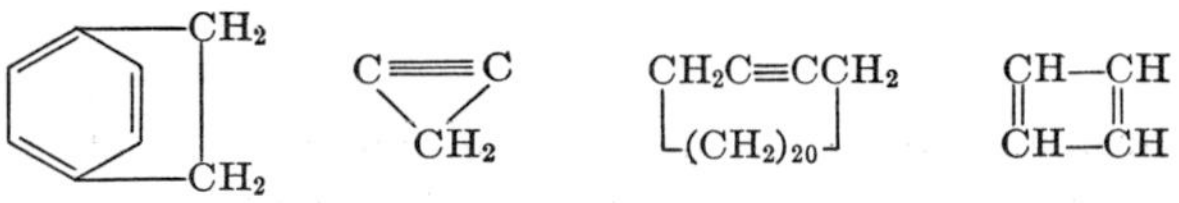

(a)   (b)   (c)   (d)

Chapter 3

STEREOCHEMISTRY

3.1   **Optical Activity.** — Ordinary white light consists of rays of different wave length vibrating in many different planes, and if selection is made of light of a single wave length, either with a special light source, such as a sodium lamp, or with filters, the resulting monochromatic light likewise consists of waves vibrating in many planes at right angles to the direction of propagation. In 1908 Etienne Louis Malus discovered that light transmitted by a crystal of Iceland spar, a transparent variety of the doubly refractive mineral calcite ($CaCO_3$) found in Iceland, differs from normal light in being polarized in a single plane determined by the orientation of the crystal, or polarizer. The character of the crystal is such that it permits passage of only those light waves vibrating in a specific plane and transmits two rays, ordinary and extraordinary, which are polarized in planes at right angles to each other. Experimentation with plane polarized light is simplified by use of the Nicol prism (William Nicol, Edinburgh), a device made by bisecting a rhombohedron of Iceland spar obliquely through the obtuse corners and uniting the parts with a cement (Canada balsam) of an index that allows complete reflection of the ordinary ray at the interface; this is thereby rejected from the field of vision, and the extraordinary ray of plane polarized light alone is transmitted. A rough analogy to the operation of a Nicol prism is that a closed book will permit easy insertion of a table knife between the pages only when the knife is held in a specific plane.

    Although Malus' experiments were terminated by his death at the age of 37, investigation of the interesting phenomenon was actively pursued by the French physicists D. F. Arago and J. B. Biot.[1] A quartz crystal cut parallel to the axis and traversed by plane polarized light normal to the surface was found to rotate the plane of polarization, and Biot ascertained that some quartz crystals turn the

---

[1] Jean Baptiste Biot, 1774–1862; b. Paris; physicist, Collège de France

66

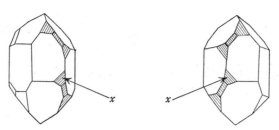

FIG. 3.1. — Hemihedral Quartz Crystals

beam of light to the right whereas others turn it to the left. A few years later the mineralogist Haüy noticed that some specimens of quartz crystals exist in two hemihedral forms, each characterized by the presence of a set of faces arranged in either a right-handed or left-handed sense and having just half of the faces required to give a symmetrical crystal. Such crystals, illustrated in Fig. 3.1 are enantiomorphous, that is, related to each other as the right hand is to the left hand. The examples illustrated represent rare specimens; ordinarily evidence of hemihedry is discernible in but a small portion of the quartz crystals examined, and then only on careful scrutiny. Sir John Herschel in 1820 suggested a possible relationship between the crystallographic and optical properties of quartz, and experiment established that crystals with the faces inclined to the right and to the left rotate the plane of polarized light in opposite directions.

Biot in 1815 discovered that certain naturally occurring organic compounds rotate plane polarized light in either the liquid or the dissolved state. Oil of turpentine, solutions of sugar, of camphor, and of tartaric acid were found to exhibit this property; they are optically active. The importance of the discovery was apparent to Biot, who pointed out that, whereas in the previously observed phenomena the optical activity was associated with a specific crystalline structure and disappeared with destruction of the crystalline form by either melting or dissolving the solid, the ability of the organic substances to rotate the plane of polarization in the noncrystalline state must be inherent in the molecules.

3.2 **Polarimeter.** — The extent of rotation for a given amount of material can be determined with a polarimeter (Fig. 3.2), which contains two Nicol prisms traversed by a beam of monochromatic light. One, the polarizer, is mounted in a fixed position and transmits plane polarized light to a tube of known length with glass windows at the two ends, in which the solution to be examined is placed. The second Nicol prism, the analyzer, is mounted on a movable axis and can be rotated as desired; the angle of rotation is measured on a circular scale. The zero point on the scale is that which, with the polarimeter tube either empty or containing a solvent devoid of optical activity, permits maximum transmission of light, an indication that the analyzer has been oriented in the same optical plane as the polarizer; if the analyzer is now turned through an angle of 90°, a point of minimum light transmission is reached, and the Nicols are crossed. When a solution of an optically active substance is placed in the polarimeter tube, light transmitted by the polarizer is rotated to a certain extent either to the right or to

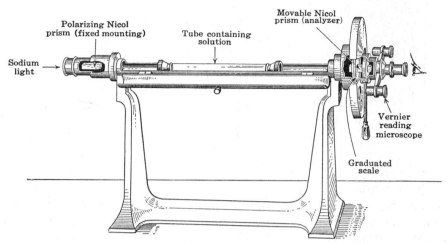

Sodium
light

Polarizing Nicol
prism (fixed mounting)

Tube containing
solution

Movable Nicol
prism (analyzer)

Vernier
reading
microscope

Graduated
scale

FIG. 3.2. — Polarimeter

the left; light reaching the eyepiece is thus diminished in intensity, but by rotating the analyzer a point can be found where the original intensity is restored and at which the analyzer is aligned with the plane of light emerging from the polarimeter tube; the angle of rotation in either the dextro or levo sense is then read from the scale. The optical system shown in the illustration is of a simplified form; instruments ordinarily used contain two additional small Nicol prisms that provide segments in the light field permitting exact matching of light intensities and obviate necessity of estimating relative brightness.

Rotatory power of a given substance in the dissolved state is dependent on the concentration of the solution, the length of the polarimeter tube, the temperature of measurement, the wave length of light used, and the solvent. Results are reported in terms of the specific rotation, α, defined as the rotation in degrees due to a solution containing 1 g. of substance in 1 ml. of solution as examined in a 1-decimeter polarimeter tube. The rotation value, which may be to the right

$$\alpha = \frac{\text{Observed rotation}}{\text{Length of tube in dm.} \times \text{concentration (g. per ml.)}}$$

(positive) or to the left (negative), is reported with a notation of the temperature of measurement and either the nature or wave length of the light source. Sodium light of wave length 589 mμ is usually employed and is indicated by the letter D (D line of the spectrum). Thus a specific rotation at 25° based on this light source can be reported as $[\alpha]_{589}^{25}$ or, for simplicity, as αD^{25}; when the green light of mercury of wave length 546 mμ is used the symbol is $[\alpha]_{546}^{25}$. Since specific rotation may vary from solvent to solvent and also with the concentration in a given solvent, one must report both the solvent used and the concentration ($c = $ g./100 ml.), for example:

$$\alpha D^{22} = +66.5° \text{ CHCl}_3 \ (c \ 1.06)$$

Abbreviations for common solvents are: Chf (chloroform), EtOH (ethanol), An (acetone), Di (dioxane), AcOH (acetic acid), Hex (hexane), Py (pyridine).

Comparisons of compounds of different molecular weight are based on molecular rotations, M_D, calculated as follows:

$$M_D = \frac{\alpha_D \times \text{Mol. Wt.}}{100}$$

The M_D values are numbers, not degrees.

That optical activity varies with the wave length of the light source was recognized by Biot in 1817. The phenomenon is known as rotatory dispersion. Thus values for the specific rotation of cholesterol (sodium lamp and mercury lamp) are: $[\alpha]_{589} -39°$, $[\alpha]_{578} -41.7°$, $[\alpha]_{546} -48°$, $[\alpha]_{436} -83°$. A photoelectric spectropolarimeter with a mechanically oscillating polarizer developed in 1954 can be operated over the range 270–700 mμ and has been employed extensively for determination of rotatory dispersion curves, particularly of optically active ketones (C. Djerassi[1]). Since specific rotation varies inversely with the wave length of the light, values determined around a wave length of 300 mμ are often in the thousands of degrees.

3.3　　　　**Work of Pasteur.** — One naturally occurring substance found by Biot to be optically active is tartaric acid, available from the wine industry. Now known to be a dibasic acid of the structure shown, the substance is present in grape juice as the potassium acid salt, and as the sugar in the juice ferments to

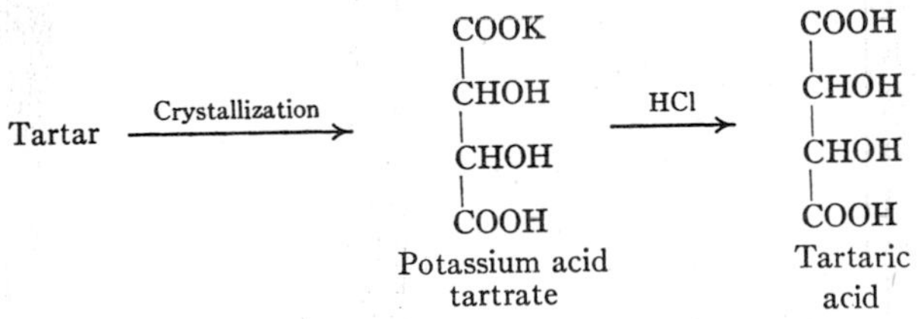

$$
\text{Tartar} \xrightarrow{\text{Crystallization}}
\begin{array}{c}
\text{COOK} \\
| \\
\text{CHOH} \\
| \\
\text{CHOH} \\
| \\
\text{COOH} \\
\text{Potassium acid} \\
\text{tartrate}
\end{array}
\xrightarrow{\text{HCl}}
\begin{array}{c}
\text{COOH} \\
| \\
\text{CHOH} \\
| \\
\text{CHOH} \\
| \\
\text{COOH} \\
\text{Tartaric} \\
\text{acid}
\end{array}
$$

alcohol the alcohol decreases the solubility of the salt and causes it to separate as a sludgy precipitate called tartar. Purification of the salt by crystallization and acidification gives tartaric acid. A by-product of the crystallization was studied in 1831 by Berzelius and named racemic acid (L. *racemus*, grape). Berzelius recognized that both tartaric and racemic acid have the formula $C_4H_6O_6$ (and coined the name isomer to describe them), but no other relationship between the two substances had been established or suspected. Indeed, Biot had found tartaric acid and its salts to be dextrorotatory and racemic acid to be optically inactive.

Louis Pasteur,[2] on completion of the curriculum at the École Normale in Paris, sought to strengthen himself in the knowledge of crystallography by repeating a series of careful measurements published a few years earlier (1841) by de la Provostaye on the crystalline forms of various salts of tartaric acid. Pasteur's determinations agreed substantially with those reported previously, but as the work proceeded he noticed a very interesting fact that had escaped his predecessor, namely, that all tartrates show undoubted evidence of hemihedral faces. The phenomenon is frequently obscured by irregular development of the crystals, by

---

[1] Carl Djerassi, b. 1923 Vienna, Austria; Ph.D. Wisconsin (Wilds); Ciba N. J.; Syntex; Wayne State Univ.; Stanford Univ.

[2] Louis Pasteur, 1822–95; b. Dôle, Dept. Jura; Dijon, Strasbourg, Lille, Paris (Sorbonne)

chance deformations, or by arrestment of the development of faces, but nevertheless Pasteur, by repeating crystallizations where necessary under modified conditions, established that every one of nineteen different tartrates investigated exhibits hemihedral faces. A further observation that seemed significant was that the tartrates are all hemihedral in the same sense. Since Biot had found the tartrates to be optically active in the same sense, and Herschel had suggested a correlation between the hemihedral and optical characteristics of quartz crystals, Pasteur was led to think that a relation might exist between the hemihedry of the tartrates and the property of rotating the plane of polarized light in the dissolved state.

This hypothesis, however, appeared to be invalidated by an observation reported in 1844 by the chemist and crystallographer Mitscherlich[1] concerning racemic acid. Mitscherlich made a crystallographic comparison of the sodium ammonium salts of optically active tartaric acid and of optically inactive racemic acid and reported that these two salts of the same chemical composition have the same crystalline form, the same double refraction, and consequently the same inclination of their optical axes, and in short differ only in that one is dextrorotatory and the other optically inactive. Since the existence of optically active and inactive isomers of identical crystalline form would be contradictory to the relationship tentatively postulated, Pasteur had the audacity to think that Mitscherlich might have overlooked the existence of hemihedry in the tartrate, and he reinvestigated the two salts in the hope of finding the tartarate hemihedral and the inactive racemate symmetrical. He found that sodium ammonium tartrate affords hemihedral crystals, like all other tartrates previously studied, but discovered to his great surprise and in apparent contradiction to his hypothesis, that sodium ammonium racemate is hemihedral also. He then observed that "the hemihedral faces which in the tartrate were all turned the same way were in the racemate inclined sometimes to the right and sometimes to the left." Pasteur carefully picked out a quantity of crystals that were hemihedral to the right and a further quantity of those hemihedral to the left and examined their solutions separately in the polarimeter; he thereupon made the exciting observation that the former material rotated the plane of polarized light to the right and the latter to the left. When equal weights of the two kinds of crystals were dissolved in water, the solution of the mixture, like the starting material, was indifferent to polarized light. In this experiment, conducted in 1848, Pasteur had for the first time achieved the resolution of an optically inactive compound into the component, optically active parts. By precipitation of the lead or barium salts of each substance and digestion of these with sulfuric acid, the free acids were obtained. One proved identical with the natural, dextrorotatory tartaric acid, or d-tartaric acid, whereas the other was a heretofore unknown substance exhibiting rotation to the same extent in the opposite direction and hence called the *levo* acid, or l-tartaric acid.

Pasteur's striking discovery was referred to Biot for review before presentation to the Academy of Sciences, and this veteran worker required the young investi-

[1] Eilhard A. Mitscherlich, 1794–1863; b. Neuerde, Ostfriedland; Univ. Berlin

gator to repeat the experiment before his eyes with a sample of racemic acid that he himself had studied and found to be optically inactive. Pasteur prepared a solution of the sodium ammonium salt with reagents that Biot likewise provided, and the solution was set aside for slow evaporation in one of the rooms at the Collège de France. In due course Pasteur was called in to collect and separate the crystals. Biot prepared the solutions and examined first the more interesting solution, that which Pasteur declared should show levorotation, and the discoverer of the phenomenon of optical activity in organic compounds was immensely impressed on observing that it was indeed levorotatory.

It was recognized only some time later that the resolution achieved by Pasteur is dependent upon a critical temperature factor. If sodium ammonium racemate is crystallized from a hot concentrated solution, the crystals have the same form and are symmetrical; they show no sign of hemihedrism. In this case each crystal contains equal parts of the *dextro* and the *levo* form and is optically inactive; the racemate salt is a molecular compound having the analysis of a monohydrate, $Na(NH_4)C_4H_4O_6 \cdot H_2O$. It is only when the crystals separate at a temperature below a critical transition point of 28° that hemihedral crystals composed respectively of molecules of the *dextro* and the *levo* salt separate to give a crystal mixture known as a conglomerate; this consists of crystals of sodium ammonium d-tartrate and sodium ammonium l-tartrate, both of which are tetrahydrates of the formula $Na(NH_4)C_4H_4O_6 \cdot 4H_2O$. Transition temperatures are often observed in inorganic chemistry between different hydrates of a given salt or between double and single salts. For example, a solution of sodium and magnesium sulfate deposits crystals of $Na_2SO_4 \cdot 10H_2O$ and $MgSO_4 \cdot 7H_2O$ at temperatures below 22°, but yields the double salt $Na_2SO_4 \cdot MgSO_4 \cdot 4H_2O$ at higher temperatures. Pasteur adopted a technique of slow crystallization from a very dilute solution and thereby had the good fortune to operate at a temperature below the transition point, whereas previous investigators evidently had conducted crystallization at higher temperatures and had obtained only the inactive racemate. The initial resolution accomplished in 1848 is particularly remarkable because such instances are rare; in a century of subsequent research, only nine other examples have been encountered in which crystallization at any temperature affords a conglomerate of sufficiently large crystals displaying hemihedry to permit their segregation by hand picking under a lens. Fortunately, two other methods are now known for resolution of inactive molecular compounds composed of dextro- and levorotatory component parts, described as *dl*-compounds, or racemates, or racemic forms. Both of these methods were discovered by Pasteur in the period 1848–54, before he turned his attention to fermentation. He also discovered a fourth form of tartaric acid that is optically inactive and is called mesotartaric acid. These developments are discussed later.

Dextro- and *levo*-tartaric acid have the same melting point, solubility in a given solvent, dissociation constant, and density, and they exhibit the same chemical behavior. In fact the two substances are identical except that they rotate the plane of polarized light in opposite directions (but to the same extent) and that they form crystals that are hemihedral in the opposite sense. Pasteur, in view of the hypothesis that he had entertained on first examining the racemate, thought there must be a connection between the optical activity of the substances in solution and the hemihedral forms of the crystals. The relationship between the crystals of *d*- and *l*-tartaric acid is the same as that illustrated in Fig. 3.1 for right- and left-handed quartz crystals. The two are similar but not superposable, and the one is to the other as an object is to its mirror image; the crystals are thus asymmetric, for they possess no plane of symmetry. In a remarkably lucid interpretation of the new phenomenon, Pasteur concluded that tartaric acid must possess asymmetry within the molecule itself. Although the concept of structural formulas was developed many years later, Pasteur had the vision to foresee the need of something beyond structural formulas for full understanding of organic compounds. He recognized that two substances identical in the nature and number of elements may differ in arrangement of the atoms in space and envisioned arrangements showing asymmetry in opposite senses. "Are the atoms of the *dextro* acid grouped on the spirals of a right-handed helix," questioned Pasteur in 1860, "or situated at the corners of an irregular tetrahedron, or have they some other asymmetric grouping? We cannot answer these questions. But it cannot be a subject of doubt that there exists an asymmetric arrangement having a non-superposable image. It is not less certain that the atoms of the *levo* acid possess precisely the inverse asymmetric arrangement."

3.4　　　　Isomerism of the Lactic Acids. — Pasteur's deductions were so far ahead of the thought of the time that many years elapsed before any substantial advance was made in the understanding of optical isomerism. Although other optically active compounds were examined from time to time, the only investigations other than those of Pasteur that proved fruitful were those on the lactic acids. Scheele (1780) had discovered in sour milk a substance which he called lactic acid and which was subsequently found to arise as a product of bacterial fermentation of milk sugar (lactose). The structure is now known to be that of α-hydroxypropionic acid. Berzelius (1807) discovered a similar acidic substance as a constituent of muscle tissue extractable with water, and the substance was characterized by Liebig (1832) as having the same composition as the fermentation lactic acid. The acids have properties unfavorable for purposes of identification and comparison, for they are very soluble both in water and in organic solvents and are obtained only with considerable difficulty as low-melting, highly hygroscopic, and generally ill-defined solids (m.p. 26°). Thus a reliable conclusion regarding the relationship of the two acids was first reached by Engelhardt (1848) on the basis of a comparison of a series of salts with respect to solubility, crystalline form, amount of water of crystallization, and course of dehydration.

$$CH_3-\overset{\overset{\displaystyle H}{|}}{\underset{\underset{\displaystyle OH}{|}}{C}}-COOH$$

Lactic acid

The comparison established that the lactic acids are two distinct chemical entities but have the same composition. The acid from muscle is dextrorotatory and can be referred to as *d*-lactic acid; fermentation lactic acid, at least as originally obtained, is optically inactive.

After the advent of the structural theory of Kekulé (1859), the problem of the structures of the interesting lactic acids received considerable attention, particularly in the hands of Wislicenus.[1]   In a series of researches initiated at Zurich in 1863, Wislicenus applied the methods both of synthesis and of degradation and, though he encountered early difficulties and uncertainties in identification of materials of different origin, he eventually secured unequivocal evidence that the two natural acids have the same structure (1873).   Thus they are both decom-

$$CH_3-\underset{\underset{OH}{|}}{\overset{\overset{H}{|}}{C}}-COOH \quad \underset{Oxid.}{\overset{H_2SO_4,\,130°}{\diagup\!\!\!\diagdown}} \quad \begin{array}{l} CH_3CHO \ + \ HCOOH \\[1em] CH_3COOH \ + \ CO_2 \ + \ H_2O \end{array}$$

posed by hot sulfuric acid to acetaldehyde and formic acid, and they both yield acetic acid on oxidation.   The alternate structure $HOCH_2CH_2COOH$ was thereby excluded, for this could not yield products with an intact methyl group.   Indeed Wislicenus synthesized this structural isomer from ethylene chlorohydrin through the nitrile, $HOCH_2CH_2CN$, and proved that it differs from either lactic acid. Synthesis of α-hydroxypropionic acid from acetaldehyde gave a product identical with the optically inactive fermentation lactic acid.   At the conclusion of his

$$CH_3C\!\!\diagup^{\!H}_{\diagdown O} \quad \xrightarrow{HCN} \quad CH_3-\underset{\underset{OH}{|}}{\overset{\overset{H}{|}}{C}}-CN \quad \xrightarrow{Hydrol.} \quad CH_3-\underset{\underset{OH}{|}}{\overset{\overset{H}{|}}{C}}-COOH$$

experiments of 1873 which had established the identity of the structures, Wislicenus wrote: "If molecules can be structurally identical and yet possess dissimilar properties, this difference can be explained only on the ground that it is due to a different arrangement of the atoms in space."

3.5   Theory of van't Hoff and Le Bel. — The concept of the tetrahedral carbon atom was deduced independently in 1874 by van't Hoff[2] in The Netherlands (September) and by Le Bel[3] in France (November).   The young chemists had met as students of Wurtz in Paris but had not discussed the problem of optical isomerism.   Le Bel, impressed by the correlation suggested by Pasteur between the rotatory power of the tartrates and the hemihedral character of the crystals, saw that molecular asymmetry can exist if four different groups are joined to a nonplanar carbon atom, regardless of the exact geometry.   van't Hoff, inspired by the publications of Wislicenus, reasoned that the four valences of carbon cannot lie in a plane or isomerism would be encountered in CH_2RR and $CH_2R_1R_2$, and proposed the tetrahedral arrangement as an explanation for both the nonexistence of such isomerism and the existence of optical isomers of the formula $CR_1R_2R_3R_4$ or C_{abcd}.   The two forms, which are optical opposites

[1] Johannes Wislicenus, 1835–1902; b. Germany; Univ. Zurich, Würzburg, Leipzig; *Ber.*, **37**, 4861 (1904)

[2] Jacobus Hendricus van't Hoff, 1852–1911; b. Rotterdam; Ph.D. Utrecht; Univ. Amsterdam; Nobel Prize 1901; *J. Chem. Soc.*, 1127 (1913)

[3] Joseph Achille Le Bel, 1847–1930; b. Péchelbronn, France; *J. Chem. Soc.*, 2789 (1930)

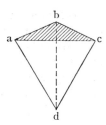 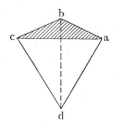

or mirror-image isomers, are called enantiomers (Gr. *enantio-*, opposite). That they are different is apparent from observation that one model is not superimposable on the other.

At the time the van't Hoff-Le Bel theory was announced only meager evidence was available for its evaluation. Thirteen optically active compounds of established structure were known and they all contained at least one asymmetric carbon atom, designated C* in the following examples:

Lactic acid,	$CH_3C^*H(OH)COOH$
Aspartic acid,	$HOOCC^*H(NH_2)CH_2COOH$
Asparagine,	$HOOCC^*H(NH_2)CH_2CONH_2$
Malic acid,	$HOOCC^*H(OH)CH_2COOH$
Active amyl alcohol,	$CH_3CH_2C^*H(CH_3)CH_2OH$

Wislicenus welcomed the theory as an answer to the problem that his own experiments had raised, and he sponsored van't Hoff's work to the extent of writing a supporting introduction to a German translation of the original Dutch pamphlet. Kolbe, who was reaching the end of his career, took an opposite view and wrote a scathing criticism of the "fanciful nonsense" and "supernatural explanations" of the two "unknown" chemists. Within a decade, however, those few observations that had appeared contradictory to the theory were shown to be in error (*e.g.*, supposed activity of propyl alcohol, due to contamination with amyl alcohol), abundant new evidence was accumulated in substantiation of the concept, and the interpretation of optical activity in the dissolved state as due to the asymmetric character of the carbon atom gained general acceptance. Kolbe had died, and Wislicenus had been appointed to his post at Leipzig.

The conventional ball and stick models of the lactic acids shown in the upper part of Fig. 3.3 are not so realistic as those (1.15) in which the four groups are represented by balls of four sizes; Stuart models (Fig. 3.3, lower part) show the actual shape of the molecules. Any one of these models is seen to be asymmetric from the fact that it possesses no plane of symmetry that will bisect the molecule into identical halves.

The data of Table 3.1 for the optically active mandelic acids show that, within the limit of experimental error, the *d*- and *l*-acids are identical in melting point and solubility, a relationship which obviously follows from the identity of the groups and the fact that all nonbonded interactions in one enantiomer are exactly matched in the other. Although the enantiomers melt at the same temperature, a small amount of the *d*-acid depresses the melting point of the *l*-form, and vice versa; a mixed melting-point determination thus detects the subtle difference between

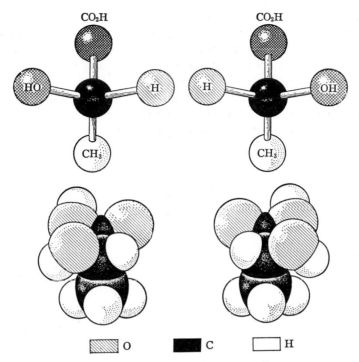

Fig. 3.3. — Enantiomeric Lactic Acids

TABLE 3.1.   THE MANDELIC ACIDS, $C_6H_5CH(OH)COOH$

	M.P., °C.	SOLUBILITY, G./100 G. $H_2O^{20°}$	ACIDIC DISSOCIATION, $pK_a^{25°}$	SPECIFIC ROTATION, $[\alpha]_D^{20°}$ 2% IN H_2O
d-Acid	132.8	8.54 g.		+ 155.5°
l-Acid	132.8	8.64 g.	3.37	− 154.4°
dl-Acid	118.5	15.97 g.	3.38	inactive

them. That the melting point of the *dl*-acid, or racemic form, is below the melting points of the component acids is purely fortuitous, for such molecular compounds can have properties not predictable from those of the component parts. Relative solubilities are likewise unforetellable. The acidic dissociation constant is a property of the dissolved molecules and the fact that the *dl*-acid has the same value as that found for the *l*-acid is evidence that the enantiomers correspond in acidity. Chemical properties are also independent of the physical form, and the *d*-, *l*-, and *dl*-acids exhibit the same chemical characteristics; they react in the same way with the same reagents, and the reactions proceed at the identical rate in the three cases. That one acid rotates the plane of polarized light to the right is a phenomenon associated with asymmetry of the molecule in a manner not as yet fully interpretable, but it is understandable that the mirror-image counterpart shows an equal rotatory power in the opposite sense.

The lactic acid obtained from acetaldehyde by the hydrogen cyanide synthesis is the optically inactive *dl*-modification. Indeed any synthesis of a compound having a single asymmetric carbon atom yields a *dl*-form or racemate; that is, it affords exactly the same number of molecules of the *d*- and of the *l*-forms. A simple explanation of this observation is found in the van't Hoff-Le Bel theory. If acetaldehyde is represented by a space formula in which the carbon atom of the carbonyl group is indicated by a tetrahedron with methyl at one corner and hydrogen at another and with the other two corners united to oxygen by a double link, the molecule has a plane of symmetry bisecting the oxygen atom and the

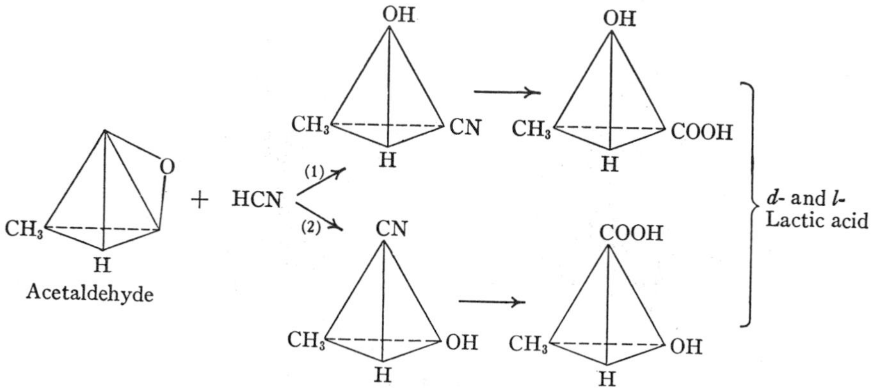

hydrogen and methyl substituents. This symmetry means that there is no difference in the two linkages of the carbonyl group, and hence that in the reaction with hydrogen cyanide, the same opportunity exists for opening of the one linkage as of the other, (1) and (2). Since an experiment on even a microscale involves many million molecules, the law of the probability of occurrence of two equally likely events is applicable with accuracy, and the carbonyl group must open, on the average, to an equal extent in the two possible directions. Asymmetry is established in the initial addition; the two enantiomeric cyanohydrins are formed in equal amounts, and equal amounts of the *d*- and *l*-acids result on hydrolysis.

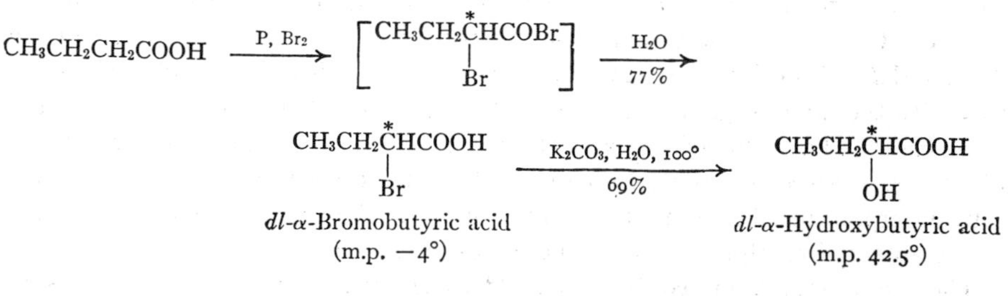

Another reaction leading to production of an asymmetric center is the synthesis of α-hydroxybutyric acid starting with the α-bromination of butyric acid by the action of bromine and red phosphorus (Hell-Volhard-Zelinsky method); the initial reaction product is the acid bromide, which undergoes halogenation in the α-position more readily than the free acid. The crude α-bromo acid bromide is not isolated, but is poured slowly into hot water to hydrolyze the more reactive halogen atom. The resulting α-bromo acid is then hydrolyzed to the hydroxy acid by boiling with water containing one molecular equivalent of potassium carbonate. Asymmetry is established with replacement of one of the two α-hydrogen atoms by bromine, and a space model shows that there is exactly the same opportunity

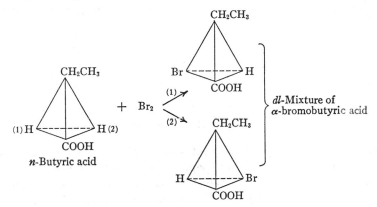

for replacement of the one as of the other. Again the law of chance dictates formation of equal amounts of the two possible products, and hence a dl-mixture results. These two examples typify the general situation in the synthesis of compounds that can exist in mirror-image forms, for the production of an asymmetric carbon atom is invariably accomplished by either an addition reaction, in which either of two linkages of a double bond is utilized, or the substitution or replacement of one of two identical atoms or groups.

3.6　　Correlations and Conventions. — The dextrorotatory lactic acid from muscle forms metallic salts that are all levorotatory. Actually both the acid and its salts are so weakly rotatory that the absolute difference in rotation between them is slight and the reversal in the sign of rotation therefore of little significance (see formulas). The salts, as well as the likewise weakly levorotatory

CH_3CHCO_2H	$(CH_3CHCO_2)_2Zn$	$CH_3CHCO_2CH_3$	CH_3CHCO_2H	CH_3CHCO_2H
$\overset{\mid}{O}H$	$\overset{\mid}{O}H$	$\overset{\mid}{O}H$	$\overset{\mid}{O}CH_3$	$\overset{\mid}{O}C_2H_5$
$+3.3°$	$-6.0°$	$-8.2°$	$-75.5°$	$-66.4°$

$[\alpha]_D$ of d-lactic acid and derivatives

methyl ester, are reconvertible into the weakly dextrorotatory free acid; these substances all have the same configuration, or orientation of groups in space. The methyl and ethyl ethers of dextrorotatory lactic acid also belong to the same configurational series, even though they are relatively strongly levorotatory. Thus the magnitude and even the direction of rotation in a given stereochemical series is subject to considerable variation according to the groups attached to the asymmetric center. Therefore the sign of rotation of one member of the series, for example free d-lactic acid, is not a satisfactory characterization of the configurational feature common to all members of the series.

The accepted convention for designation of configurational relationships was introduced by Emil Fischer[1] (1891), slightly modified by M. A. Rosanoff (1906), and fully interpreted by C. S. Hudson (1949). Dextrorotatory glyceraldehyde, $HOCH_2CH(OH)CHO$, was taken as the reference standard and arbitrarily assigned a configuration that is defined in terms of the perspective tetrahedral model (a) or the equivalent, symmetrically oriented model (b). In both (a) and (b) the

D-(+)-Glyceraldehyde

solid line connecting H and OH represents an edge of the tetrahedron that projects in front of or above the plane of the paper, and the dotted line connecting CHO and CH_2OH is an edge of the tetrahedron that would be unseen in an opaque mechanical model. For convenience in writing and printing, Fischer defined the following convention for planar projection of the three-dimensional model; the model is oriented as in (b) with the carbon chain vertical and to the rear and the hydrogen and hydroxyl standing out in front; the model is then imagined to be flattened and the groups are laid on the plane of the paper in the order that they appear in the model, as in (c). The planar projection (c) must be thought of in terms of the actual model that it represents (H and OH extending toward the front); it can be turned around in the plane of the paper, but must not be imagined to be lifted and inverted. If the carbon chain contains two or more adjacent asymmetric carbon atoms (see tartaric acid, below), the projection is made in the same way from a model oriented with CHO or equivalent group at the top, CH_2OH or equivalent at the bottom, the carbon chain vertical and to the rear, and H and OH groups extending to the front.

The second convention is that the configuration of dextrorotatory glyceraldehyde is designated by the small capital Roman D; the opposite configuration is designated L. The reference substance is thus D-glyceraldehyde; a fuller description is given by the name D-(d)-glyceraldehyde, in which D indicates the configuration and d records the incidental fact that the substance is dextrorotatory. The same information is given by the name D-(+)-glyceraldehyde, which is less confusing and therefore preferable.

Any compound that has been shown experimentally to contain an asymmetric carbon atom of the same configuration as that of D-glyceraldehyde belongs to the D-series. This is true of the acid resulting from oxidation of the aldehydic function; the substance is levorotatory and is therefore fully described by the name D-(−)-glyceric acid. If the CHO group of glyceraldehyde is oxidized and the CH_2OH group is reduced, the resulting substance is lactic acid. Experimental correlation has established the fact that levorotatory lactic acid, or l-lactic acid

[1] Emil Fischer, 1852–1919; b. Euskirchen, Germany; Ph.D. Strasbourg (Baeyer); Univ. Erlangen, Würzburg, Berlin; Nobel Prize 1902; *Ber.* **52A**, 129 (1919)

$$
\begin{array}{ccc}
\text{COOH} & \text{COOH} & \text{COOH} \\
| & | & | \\
\text{HCOH} & \text{HCOH} & \text{HOCH} \\
| & | & | \\
\text{CH}_2\text{OH} & \text{CH}_3 & \text{CH}_2\text{COOH} \\
\text{D-(−)-Glyceric acid} & \text{D-(−)-Lactic acid} & \text{L-(−)-Malic acid}
\end{array}
$$

or (−)-lactic acid, corresponds in configuration to the reference standard and therefore is D-(−)-lactic acid. In the projection formula, hydroxyl is thus to the right and hydrogen to the left; this formula corresponds to the models shown at the right-hand side in Fig. 3.3 and in the corresponding tetrahedral diagrams. The designation of configuration eliminates confusion associated with the opposite sign of rotation of the lactic acids and their derivatives. Thus the statement that esterification of L-(+)-lactic acid gives the L-(−)-ester indicates that the direction of rotation changes but the configuration remains the same. Natural malic acid has been demonstrated to belong to the L-series; it is weakly levorotatory in dilute aqueous solution and becomes weakly dextrorotatory as the concentration is increased.

D-Glyceraldehyde was chosen as reference standard because it is the simplest member of the sugar series and corresponds in configuration to one of four asymmetric carbon atoms in the key sugar glucose. The complete series of related

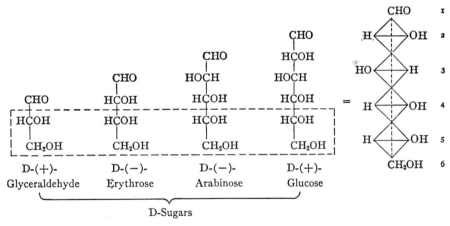

D-Sugars

sugars includes the further members arabinose and erythrose, of projection formulas shown. The lowermost asymmetric center of each of the higher sugars (C_5 in glucose) has the configuration of D-glyceraldehye, and hence the substances all belong to the D-series; it is incidental that D-glucose is dextrorotatory and the others levorotatory.

Fischer's decision to call the series of natural (+)-glyceraldehyde the D-series was purely arbitrary. It was not until sixty years later that a special technique of X-ray analysis was devised by which it became possible to determine whether compounds of Fischer's D-series actually have the configurations assigned or the opposite configurations (J. M. Bijvoet, 1951). The results showed Fischer's choice to have been correct. Thus configurations established relative to that of the standard are now absolute configurations.

3.7 **Compounds with Two Dissimilar Asymmetric Carbons.** — Application of the typical addition reactions of alkenes frequently gives rise to substances having two asymmetric carbon atoms, for example:

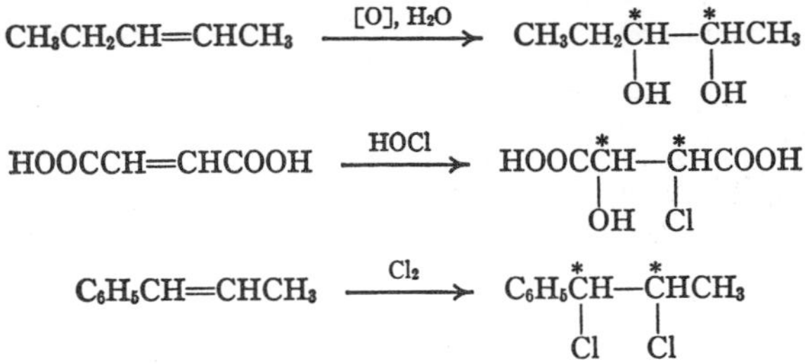

CH₃CH₂CH=CHCH₃ [O], H₂O → CH₃CH₂C*H—C*HCH₃ (OH, OH)
HOOCCH=CHCOOH HOCl → HOOCC*H—C*HCOOH (OH, Cl)
C₆H₅CH=CHCH₃ Cl₂ → C₆H₅C*H—C*HCH₃ (Cl, Cl)

In each of these examples the two asymmetric centers are dissimilar, and each therefore can contribute to a certain different extent to the rotatory power of the molecule as a whole in either a dextro or levo sense. If the contribution of one center of asymmetry is designated as $\pm a$ and the other as $\pm b$, then the possible combinations are:

$+a$	$-a$	$+a$	$-a$
$+b$	$-b$	$-b$	$+b$
dl-Form		*d'l'*-Form	

The theory therefore predicts existence of four isomers, grouped in two pairs of enantiomeric modifications, or *dl*-mixtures, and this prediction has been verified. For example, two substances corresponding to the formula $C_6H_5\overset{*}{C}HBr\overset{*}{C}HBrCOOH$ are known; both are optically inactive but distinguished from each other by a profound difference in melting point, and both have been shown to be racemic mixtures. One, cinnamic acid dibromide, m.p. 201°, has been resolved into the active components of specific rotations +67.5° and −68.3°, and the other, allo-cinnamic acid dibromide, m.p. 90°, is also resolvable. Space formulas can be written to represent the four isomers, but since the configurations relative to glyceraldehyde are not known, a given formula cannot be identified as attributable to a particular isomer. A first formula is constructed by joining two tetrahedrons together and affixing appropriate groups to the free corners in an arbitrary manner, for example, as in I. This arbitrary formula can be taken as representing

Mirror
Mirror
C₆H₅
H Br
Br H
COOH
(+a, +b)
I
C₆H₅
Br H
H Br
COOH
(−a, −b)
II
dl
C₆H₅
H Br
H Br
COOH
(+a, −b)
III
C₆H₅
Br H
Br H
COOH
(−a, +b)
IV
d'l'

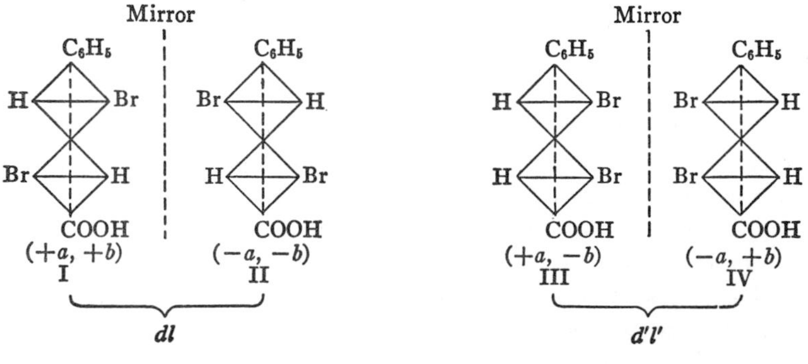

a *d*-acid, in which the upper half of the molecule is a $+a$ part and the lower half a $+b$ part. Formula II, representing the enantiomer of I, is constructed by visualizing the image of I in a mirror, and the upper and lower halves are, by definition, $-a$ and $-b$ parts. Formula III is made up of the upper half of I $(+a)$ and the lower half of II $(-b)$, and IV is its mirror image. Projection formulas utilizing the simplification that the asymmetric carbons are represented merely as the intersections of the lines connecting substituents are as follows:

	C_6H_5			C_6H_5			C_6H_5			C_6H_5	
H—		—Br	Br—		—H	H—		—Br	Br—		—H
Br—		—H	H—		—Br	H—		—Br	Br—		—H
	COOH			COOH			COOH			COOH	

The two racemates are appropriately designated as *dl-* and *d'l'*-forms, and it is understandable that they should differ in melting point and other physical properties and indeed even in the rates at which they undergo reactions. The *d*-acid I is composed of two different asymmetric molecular halves $(+a, +b)$, and the combination is neither duplicated nor mirrored in either the *d'*-acid III $(+a, -b)$ or the *l'*-acid IV $(-a, +b)$. Stereoisomers that, like the *d-*, *d'-*, and *l'*-acids, are not identical and yet are not mirror images, are defined as **diastereoisomers** (Gr. *dia*, apart). The *l*-acid II is the enantiomer of I, but is a diastereoisomer of III and IV. Note the enantiomers have the same melting point, solubility, and angle of rotation (of opposite sign); diastereoisomers differ in all physical properties and sometimes are very dissimilar.

Orientation of the two tetrahedrons as shown in formula I does not permit easy visualization of the effect of rotation of the two asymmetric carbon atoms about the single bond connecting them. Formula Ia is another orientation that is equivalent to formula I; in Ia the corner of the upper tetrahedron that projects to the front carries hydrogen, and the projecting corner of the lower tetrahedron carries the carboxyl group. If the upper tetrahedron of Ia is rotated 120° clockwise, the bromine atom appears at the projecting position and formula Ib is obtained. This, like Ia, is made up of $+a$ and $+b$ halves and has a mirror-image

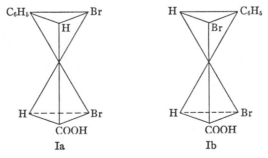

Ia   Ib

counterpart, and is a satisfactory *alternative* to Ia. It does not, however, represent an *additional* isomer; if this were the case an infinite number of isomers could exist corresponding to the setting of the upper tetrahedron at any of an infinite number of angles from the original position. Furthermore, if the phenyl and carboxyl groups in Ia and Ib were replaced by hydrogen the formulas would stand for two stereoisomeric dibromoethanes, but no such isomerism exists. These facts indicate that carbon atoms ordinarily are free to rotate about a single bond. Exceptions to the principle of free rotation are known where molecules contain ring systems or bulky groups so situated as to prevent or restrict normal rotation.

3.8 **Compounds with Several Dissimilar Asymmetric Carbons.** — If three centers of asymmetry in a given molecule can contribute in either a positive or negative sense to the extent of a, b, and c to the rotatory power as a whole, then the possible combinations are:

$$
\begin{array}{cc}
+a & -a \\
+b & -b \\
+c & -c \\
\end{array}
\qquad
\begin{array}{cc}
-a & +a \\
+b & -b \\
+c & -c \\
\end{array}
\qquad
\begin{array}{cc}
+a & -a \\
-b & +b \\
+c & -c \\
\end{array}
\qquad
\begin{array}{cc}
+a & -a \\
+b & -b \\
-c & +c \\
\end{array}
$$

$$
\quad\quad dl \quad\quad\quad\quad\quad d'l' \quad\quad\quad\quad\quad d''l'' \quad\quad\quad\quad\quad d'''l'''
$$

Eight different optically active forms are possible, falling into four pairs of mirror image isomers. A general relationship by which the number of isomers can be calculated is: number of optically active forms = 2^n (where n is the number of dissimilar asymmetric carbon atoms). When n = 4 the number of optically active forms possible is sixteen, and indeed an instance is known in the sugar series in which all sixteen isomers predicted by the van't Hoff-Le Bel theory have been obtained.

3.9 **Tartaric Acids.** — The tartaric acid series is the classical example of compounds possessing two similar asymmetric carbon atoms. Pasteur had established that the inactive racemic acid can be resolved into d- and l-forms and is in fact dl-tartaric acid, and he had discovered another inactive isomer, mesotartaric acid. This isomer, typical of other substances

*CH(OH)COOH which are therefore described as *meso* modifications, is pro-
|
*CH(OH)COOH duced along with the dl-acid by heating d-tartaric acid with water at 165° and can be isolated from the mixture in the form of the sparingly soluble acid potassium salt. The existence of two active and two inactive tartaric acids is readily explained. Since the rotatory contribution of each of two similar centers of asymmetry can be represented as $\pm a$, the following forms are predicted:

$$
\begin{array}{cc}
+a & -a \\
+a & -a \\
\end{array}
\qquad\qquad
\begin{array}{c}
+a \\
-a \\
\end{array}
$$

$$
\quad dl\text{-Form} \quad\quad\quad\quad meso \text{ Form}
$$

The combination of equal parts of the d- and the l-acid is one inactive form, and the second, or *meso* form is inactive because the molecule has a plane of symmetry. Pasteur's own researches afforded a proof that mesotartaric acid consists of symmetrical molecules, for he encountered evidence that this substance, unlike the dl-acid, is incapable of resolution into component, optically active forms (3.10).

Natural dextrorotatory tartaric acid, or $(+)$-tartaric acid, can be reduced to a substance identified as D-$(+)$-malic acid because it has been degraded in a series of steps to the reference substance D-$(-)$-lactic acid. It is immaterial whether

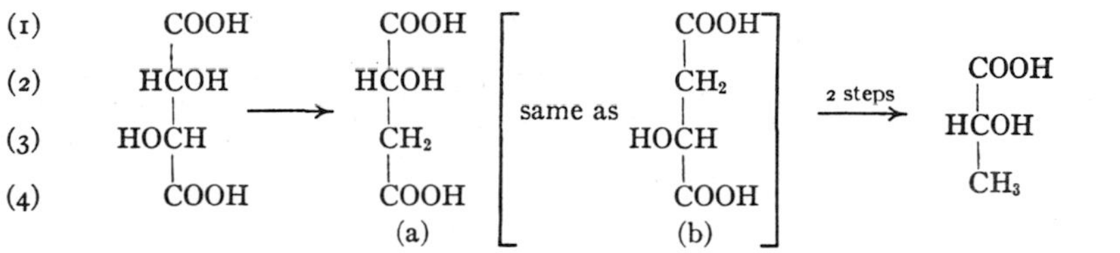

(1)   COOH   COOH   COOH

The scheme shows structures:

(1) COOH	COOH	COOH
(2) HCOH	HCOH	CH$_2$
(3) HOCH	CH$_2$	HOCH
(4) COOH	COOH	COOH
D-(+)-Tartaric acid	(a) D-(+)-Malic acid	(b)

$\xrightarrow{\text{same as}}$ ... $\xrightarrow{\text{2 steps}}$

COOH
HCOH
CH$_3$

D-(−)-Lactic acid

reduction occurs at position 3 to give (a), or at position 2 to give (b), for when formula (b) is inverted it is seen to be identical with (a). Thus both asymmetric centers of natural tartaric acid have the D-configuration, and the substance is fully described as D-(+)-tartaric acid. The complete series of tartaric acids is represented in tetrahedral formulas and projections. The two asymmetric carbon atoms of *d*-tartaric acid make equal dextrorotatory contributions, and, as the formulas are written, the arrangement of the groups COOH, OH, and H (listed in order of decreasing size) is clockwise, or right-handed, in both the upper and lower centers. In *l*-tartaric acid the arrangement is counterclockwise throughout, and

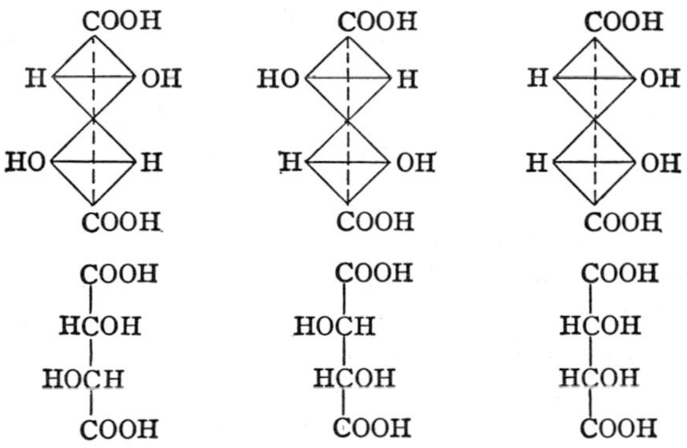

COOH   COOH   COOH

H — OH   HO — H   H — OH

HO — H   H — OH   H — OH

COOH   COOH   COOH

COOH	COOH	COOH
HCOH	HOCH	HCOH
HOCH	HCOH	HCOH
COOH	COOH	COOH
dextro (D)	*levo* (L)	*meso*

Tartaric acids

in the *meso* acid the upper and lower centers are right- and left-handed, respectively. Note that the projection formula for mesotartaric acid is derived from a model by tilting each asymmetric carbon atom to the front and hence that viewing both carbons in projection from the front is the equivalent, in the model, of inspecting the upper carbon from above and the lower one from below, to determine whether the group order is clockwise or counterclockwise.

Properties of the two active and two inactive forms of tartaric acid are given in Table 3.2. A noteworthy point is that the *dl*-form, racemic acid, melts at a higher temperature than the optically active components. This property is not inconsistent with the observation, already noted, that the melting point of the *d*-acid is depressed by admixture with a *small* amount of the *l*-acid, and vice versa, for racemic acid is not a mixture of the active forms but a molecular compound having its own characteristics. The situation can be appreciated by consideration of diagrams giving the melting points (or freezing points) of mixtures of the *d*- and

TABLE 3.2.   PROPERTIES OF THE TARTARIC ACIDS

ACID	M.P., °C.	$[\alpha]_D^{25°}$, 20% AQ. SOLUTION	SOLUBILITY, G. PER 100 G. H_2O	ACIDIC DISSOCIATION	
				pK_{a_1}	pK_{a_2}
dextro	170	$+12°$	139	2.93	4.23
levo	170	$-12°$	139	2.93	4.23
dl (racemic)	206	inactive	20.6	2.96	4.24
meso	140	inactive	125	3.11	4.80

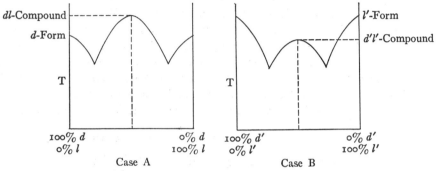

FIG. 3.4. — Melting Point — Composition Diagrams of Enantiomers Which Form
Racemic Compounds

acids of compositions varying from 100 percent of the one to 100 percent of the
other (Roozeboom,[1] 1899).   Figure 3.4, case A, gives the typical relationship to
which the tartaric acids conform.   The melting point of the *d*-acid is depressed by
successive additions of the *l*-form till a eutectic point is reached; the curve then
rises to a maximum at the 50:50 point, corresponding to the melting point of the
molecular (*dl*-) compound, which in this instance is higher than that of either
component.   An equally characteristic relationship is shown in case B as exemplified by the mandelic acids; here the diagram again consists of two complementary
halves, each having a eutectic point, but the *dl*-compound has a lower melting
point than the active forms.   In either case A or B, addition of a small amount
of one of the active forms to the *dl*-compound depresses the melting point.   In
those instances where equal parts of two enantiomers fail to combine to a molecular compound but afford a racemic mixture or conglomerate, this 50:50 mixture
melts lower than mixtures of any other composition melt, and addition of an active
isomer to the inactive form raises the melting point.   This difference provides a
method of distinguishing racemic compounds from racemic mixtures.

3.10   **Enzymic Resolution of *dl*-Mixtures.** — The resolution of racemic
              acid into *d*- and *l*-tartaric acid achieved in the classical experiment of
Pasteur by crystallization and mechanical separation is an example of a method
which is applicable only in very rare instances.   However, Pasteur discovered two
other more practical methods of resolution.   While on a visit to the wine-making

[1] Hendrick W. Bakhuis Roozeboom, 1854–1907; b. Alkman, Netherlands; Ph.D. Leiden;
Univ. Amsterdam

region of Bavaria, he acquired from an apothecary an old bottle of racemic acid on which a green mold had appeared. On returning to his laboratory he examined the remaining acid and found it to be levorotatory. The green mold was identified as the microorganism *Penicillium glaucum;* it is the mold found on aging cheese. When the microbes grow in a dilute aqueous solution containing racemic acid and nutrient salts, the originally optically inactive solution slowly becomes levorotatory because the microorganism preferentially assimilates natural *d*-tartaric acid.

Many instances are known of the preferential utilization of one of two enantiomers by microorganisms, and the action has been found due to enzymes necessary to growth. Enzymes, catalysts of biological reactions, are proteins, and like all proteins are made up of α-amino acids condensed together to form long chains.

$$\overset{*}{R}\overset{O}{\overset{\|}{CH}}\overset{}{C}-(NH\overset{*}{C}H\overset{O}{\overset{\|}{C}})_n-(NH\overset{*}{C}H\overset{O}{\overset{\|}{C}})_m-etc. \longrightarrow R\overset{*}{C}HCOOH, etc.$$

$$\underset{NH_2}{|} \qquad \underset{R'}{|} \qquad \underset{R''}{|} \qquad\qquad\qquad \underset{NH_2}{|}$$

Protein $\qquad\qquad\qquad\qquad\qquad$ α-Amino acid

Proteins on hydrolysis yield mixtures of the component acids. Most of the natural α-amino acids are optically active, and hence the proteinoid enzyme is optically active. Hence the preferential attack of a natural, optically active enzyme on the natural component of a *dl*-mixture is understandable. The enzymatic method for many years was used mainly to determine whether or not an optically inactive substance is resolvable. Thus mesotartaric acid develops no optical activity when acted on by *Penicillium glaucum*. Preparative use of the method ordinarily is limited by the fact that the more interesting natural enantiomer is the one sacrificed. Eventually, however, methods were found for utilizing enzymes not for destruction of a natural substrate but for merely altering the nature of a specific functional group to an extent sufficient for separation from the unaltered isomer. Thus an efficient enzymic method is available for the resolution of *dl*-α-amino acids (31.7).

3.11 **General Method of Resolution.** — After Pasteur had isolated unnatural *l*-tartaric acid for the first time, he prepared numerous salts of the new acid with inorganic and organic bases and compared them with the corresponding *d*-tartrates. The salts of *d*- and *l*-tartaric acid with metals, ammonia, and aniline were identical in solubility and other physical properties; but Pasteur observed that with salts derived from asymmetric, optically active natural bases such as quinine or strychnine "all is changed in an instant. The solubility is no longer the same and the properties all differ as much as in the case of the most distantly related isomers." The reason is apparent from consideration of an example. If a *dl*-acid is neutralized with a dextrorotatory (*d'*) base, one of the two salts produced is composed of two right-handed parts (*dd'*), and the other is made up of right- and

$$\text{Enantiomers}\begin{cases} d\text{-Acid} \\ \quad + d'\text{-Base} \longrightarrow \\ l\text{-Acid} \end{cases} \begin{cases} dd'\text{-Salt} \\ \\ ld'\text{-Salt} \end{cases}\text{Diastereoisomers}$$

left-handed components (*ld'*). The two salts obviously differ in rotatory power and are in fact diastereoisomers. If the acidic and basic components are strongly rotatory, the *dd'*-salt probably will be dextrorotatory; the *ld'*-salt is composed of oppositely acting but unbalanced parts and may show either positive or negative rotation. In any case, the two salts have different rotatory values, different solubilities, and different melting points; they therefore are separable by fractional crystallization, and the course of separation can be followed by determination of appropriate physical constants. Once one salt has been secured pure, it can be treated with sodium hydroxide, the resolving *d'*-base recovered, and the optically active acid liberated by acidification of the alkaline solution.

The method is equally applicable to resolution of a synthetic *dl*-amine with an optically active acid. Sometimes resolution of a neutral compound is accomplished most advantageously by conversion into a derivative capable of salt formation. An often efficient modification in the procedure of resolution consists in treating a *dl*-base with half the amount of a resolving organic acid required for neutralization, together with a further half equivalent of hydrochloric acid (Pope,[1] 1912). Equilibrium is set up among the two pairs of salts, but those derived from the organic acid are distinctly less soluble than the hydrochlorides. Thus the less soluble of the two diastereoisomeric organic salts tends to crystallize, and the solution contains chiefly the hydrochloric acid salt of the enantiomeric amine. Typical relationships between pairs of salts encountered in resolutions are given in Table 3.3 for the case of cinchonine ($+223°$) combined with the mandelic acids ($\pm154°$) and for that of *l*-menthylamine ($-36°$) combined with the tartaric acids ($\pm12°$). Rotatory values of the salts fall roughly in the order expected. The salt of *l*-menthylamine with the optically inactive mesotartaric acid has a specific rotation not far from that of the free base but falling between those of the other isomers. Of greatest practical significance is the fact that solubilities of the diastereoisomeric salts differ considerably; one of the mandelic acid salts is twice as soluble as the other.

When a pair of diastereoisomeric salts is fractionated, the less soluble isomer often can be obtained relatively easily, but isolation of the more soluble salt in pure form may present difficulties. Change to another resolving agent is sometimes advantageous, for with another pair of salts the solubility relationships may be reversed.

TABLE 3.3. OPTICALLY ACTIVE SALTS

		M.P., °C.	SOLUBILITY IN 100 G. H₂O AT 21.6°	$[\alpha]_D$
d-Cinchonine {	*d*-mandelate	80	1.08 g.	+152.4
	l-mandelate	165	2.05 g.	+92.1
l-Menthylamine {	*d*-tartrate	198		−12.6
	l-tartrate	194		−42.0
l-Menthylamine mesotartrate		218		−32.1

[1] Sir William J. Pope, 1870–1939; b. London; Univ. Manchester; Cambridge; *Nature*, **144**, 810 (1935)

TABLE 3.4. RESOLVING AGENTS

NAME	FORMULA	M.P., ° C.	$[\alpha]_D$
	Bases		
Cinchonine	$C_{19}H_{21}N_2(OH)$	264	$+223$
Cinchonidine	$C_{19}H_{21}N_2(OH)$	207	-111
Quinine	$C_{19}H_{20}N_2(OH)OCH_3$	175	-158
Quinidine	$C_{19}H_{20}N_2(OH)OCH_3$	173	$+243$
Strychnine	$C_{21}H_{22}O_2N_2$	290	-110
Brucine	$C_{21}H_{20}O_2N_2(OCH_3)_2$	178	-80
Morphine	$C_{16}H_{14}ON(OH)_?CH_3$	254	-133
l-Menthylamine	$C_{10}H_{19}NH_2$	liq.	-36
d- and l-α-Phenylethylamine	$C_6H_5CH(NH_2)CH_3$	liq.	±39
d-2-Amino-1-hydroxyhydrindene	$C_9H_8(OH)NH_2$	142	$+23$
L-Arginine	$C_6H_{14}O_2N_4$	238° dec.	$+12.5$
	Acids		
d-Tartaric acid	HOOCCHOHCHOHCOOH	170	$+12$
l-Malic acid	HOOCCHOHCH$_2$COOH	100	-2.3^1
l-Mandelic acid	$C_6H_5CHOHCOOH$	133	-154
d-Camphorsulfonic acid	$C_{10}H_{15}OSO_3H$	196	$+24$
α-Bromocamphor-π-sulfonic acid	$C_{10}H_{14}OBrSO_3H$		$+85^2$
l-Quinic acid	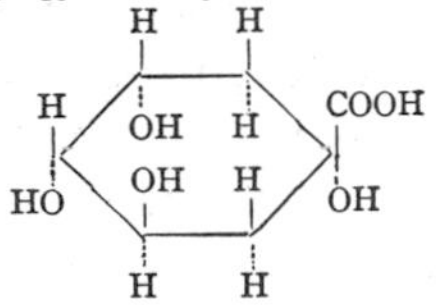 (structure)	162	-44
d- and l-6,6'-Dinitrodiphenic acid		231	±127

[1] The substance is levorotatory only in dilute aqueous solutions, and becomes dextrorotatory as the concentration is increased; thus the following specific rotations are noted at the concentrations indicated: 8.4%, $-2.3°$; 34%, $\pm0°$; 70%, $+3.3°$.

[2] As the ammonium salt.

Thus in an efficient procedure for resolution of dl-α-phenylethylamine, the d-form is obtained by fractionally crystallizing the salt formed with l-malic acid, treating the purified, less soluble salt with alkali, and isolating the free d-amine by steam distillation and extraction with benzene; yield 58–65%. The crude malate salt from the mother liquors is then converted into the free amine and this is crystallized with d-tartaric acid; l-α-phenylethylamine is obtained from the pure l-base-d-tartrate in overall yield of 53–70%.

The method of resolution by conversion into diastereoisomers has been applied in only a few instances involving formation of derivatives other than salts. Sometimes resolution of a neutral compound is accomplished most advantageously by conversion into a derivative capable of salt formation. For example, octanol-2 (capryl alcohol) is converted by treatment with phthalic anhydride into the acid

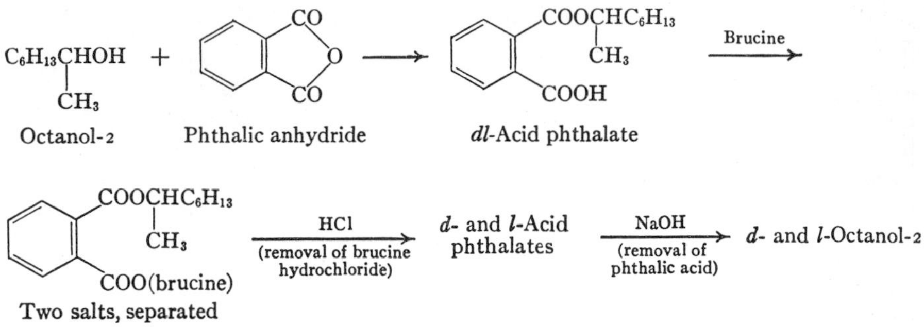

$C_6H_{13}CHOH$ + Phthalic anhydride $\longrightarrow$ dl-Acid phthalate $\xrightarrow{\text{Brucine}}$

Octanol-2   Phthalic anhydride dl-Acid phthalate

Two salts, separated $\xrightarrow[\substack{\text{(removal of brucine} \\ \text{hydrochloride)}}]{\text{HCl}}$ d- and l-Acid phthalates $\xrightarrow[\substack{\text{(removal of} \\ \text{phthalic acid)}}]{\text{NaOH}}$ d- and l-Octanol-2

phthalate, which is resolved by crystallization of the brucine salts.   The separated salts are decomposed with hydrochloric acid and the brucine is recovered, and the two acid phthalates are then hydrolyzed with alkali; the d- and l-forms of the alcohol are thereby obtained in yields of about 65% in each case.

3.12   Special Methods of Resolution. — Examples cited later include resolution by stereospecific dehydration of an alcohol by reaction with an optically active acid (3.23), resolution by chromatography on an optically active adsorbent (14.1), and resolution by crystallization of urea complexes (4.18) and clathrates (22.23).   A method introduced by Velluz[1] (U. S. patent, 1957) involves seeding of a supersaturated solution of a racemic mixture with crystals of the optically active isomer sought.   The method is particularly useful as applied to an acidic or basic DL-mixture, for partial neutralization with alkali or with hydrochloric acid permits substantial reduction of the volume of solvent required.   An example is the resolution of synthetic DL-glutamic acid.   Dextrorotatory L-glutamic acid, a component of many proteins, is used extensively in the form of

$$NaO_2CCH_2CH_2CHCO_2H \;=\; Na^+O_2^-CCH_2CH_2CHCO_2^-$$

with NH_2 below the first and NH_3^+ below the second.

Monosodium L-(+)-glutamate

the monosodium salt as a flavor enhancing agent for nonacidic foods.   It imparts a meat flavor to foods; the unnatural D-acid is without effect.   DL-Glutamic acid monohydrate (127 g.) and L-glutamic acid (5.8 g.) are dissolved in hot water containing an amount of potassium hydroxide sufficient to convert 80–85% of the DL-acid into the monopotassium salt and the solution is cooled to 75° and seeded with 16.9 g. of L-glutamic acid.   On cooling to 30° the solution deposits L-glutamic acid (34.5 g.) of high purity, αD + 32° (du Pont patent, 1958).

Chloramphenicol, an antibiotic drug, is the N-dichloroacetyl derivative of the amine known as chloramphenicol base.   Resolution of the dl-base by seeding a

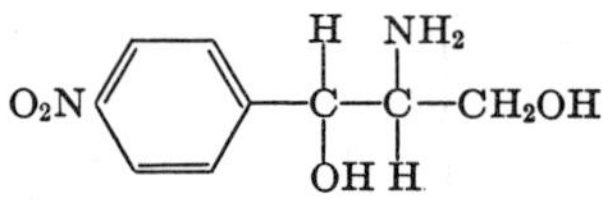

Chloramphenicol base

[1] Léon Velluz, b. 1904 Bourg (Ain); Dr. Sc. phys.; Dir. gén. recherches Roussel-Uclaf, Paris

saturated solution partially neutralized with hydrochloric acid (Velluz) is particularly interesting because it is necessary to seed only once with one optically pure enantiomer. Thereafter, the two enantiomers crystallize alternatively in successive crops, because only the isomer of the greater degree of supersaturation will crystallize.

3.13 **Asymmetric Synthesis.** — A phenomenon related to that just discussed is illustrated by the following typical experiments on the reduction of esters of pyruvic acid, $CH_3COCOOH$ (McKenzie,[1] 1904–09). Reduction of the carbonyl group of the methyl or ethyl ester of this α-keto acid can proceed equally well in opposite steric directions and affords the methyl or ethyl ester of *dl*-lactic acid, $CH_3CHOHCOOH$. When, however, the acid is esterified with the optically active natural alcohol *l*-menthol, reduction does not proceed to an equal extent in the two possible ways but gives a mixture containing an excess of the ester of *l*-lactic acid; the product resulting on hydrolysis and removal of the *l*-menthol is optically active and consists of a mixture of *dl*- and *l*-lactic acid. The

$$CH_3-\overset{O}{\overset{\|}{C}}-COOH \; + \; \text{HOHC}^* \quad \longrightarrow \quad CH_3-\overset{O}{\overset{\|}{C}}-COOC_{10}H_{19} \xrightarrow{\text{Al(Hg)}}$$

Pyruvic acid   *l*-Menthol $(C_{10}H_{19}OH)$ *l*-Menthyl pyruvate

$$CH_3-\overset{H}{\underset{OH}{C}}-COOC_{10}H_{19} \xrightarrow{\text{KOH}} CH_3-\overset{H}{\underset{OH}{C}}-COOH$$

{ *l*-Menthyl-*d*-lactate
{ *l*-Menthyl-*l*-lactate (excess)

{ *d*-Lactic acid
{ *l*-Lactic acid (excess)

reduction proceeds to a greater degree in one steric sense than in the other. The reason is that the two esters produced on reduction are diastereoisomers, one made of *l*- and *d'*-parts, the other of *l*- and *l'*-parts. The two products thus differ in rotation, and they differ in energy and rate of formation. The production of a new center of asymmetry is thus under control by the asymmetric centers already present. When any optically active compound enters into a reaction that can proceed in opposite steric directions, one of the two products invariably is favored over the other. Some reactions are highly stereospecific; some reagents effect a given result with higher stereoselectivity than others. As examples to follow will show, it is sometimes possible to define steric factors responsible for the course of an asymmetric synthesis.

3.14 **Racemization.** — Conversion of half of a given quantity of an optically active compound into the enantiomer, with resultant formation of the

[1] Alexander McKenzie, 1869–1951; b. Dundee, Scotland; Ph.D. St. Andrews (Purdie); Univ. London, Dundee; *J. Chem. Soc.*, 270 (1952)

dl-modification, is defined as racemization. The experiment by Pasteur in which *d*-tartaric acid was converted by the action of water at 165° into a mixture of the *meso* and *dl*-acids involved racemization of a part of the material. The racemic (*dl*) acid occurring as a by-product of the production of *d*-tartaric acid in the wine industry probably arises by partial racemization of the *d*-acid during processing.

Racemization occurs especially readily with compounds having a carbonyl group adjacent to an asymmetric carbon carrying a hydrogen atom, for example tartaric acid, lactic acid, and glyceraldehyde. Where the specific grouping indicated is lacking, racemization usually proceeds with difficulty. Thus, in contrast with mandelic acid, $C_6H_5CHOHCOOH$, the C-methyl derivative atrolactic acid, $C_6H_5C(CH_3)OHCOOH$, does not undergo racemization. The easily racemized compounds contain the group (a), which by a shift of hydrogen from carbon to

oxygen can afford the structure (b), described as an enol because of the combination of an ene (double bond) and an ol (OH) group. If one optically active form of mandelic acid (c) is converted in an equilibrium process into the enolic form (d), the production of a double bond temporarily destroys asymmetry and when the hydrogen migrates back to carbon the process can involve opening of either of the two linkages of the symmetrical double bond and hence can afford either the original configuration (c) or the opposite configuration (e); the chances being equal, a mixture of equal parts of (c) and (e) must result. Since all the transformations are reversible, formation of only a minute amount of the enol (d) would result in eventual racemization of the entire material. The interpretation is strengthened by the fact that racemization is promoted by acids and bases, reagents which catalyze enolization.

3.15   Epimerization. — The sugar D-glucose has four dissimilar asymmetric carbon atoms and is thus one of sixteen stereoisomers. The sugar has a carbonyl group adjacent to a carbon carrying a hydrogen atom and hence is capable of enolization; shift of hydrogen from carbon to oxygen in this case can produce the enediol formulated. The enolic hydrogen can then return to the original position to give D-glucose, but preference is for its return in the alternative direction to give D-mannose. Thus treatment of D-glucose with alkali gives an equilibrium mixture in which D-mannose predominates. The result is a selective inversion at one of four centers of asymmetry and is described as an epimerization. D-Mannose is one of several diastereoisomers of D-glucose and, specifically, it is

1	$\overset{H}{\underset{\|}{C}}=O$		$\begin{bmatrix}\\ \overset{H}{\underset{\|}{C}}\!-\!OH \end{bmatrix}$		$\overset{H}{\underset{\|}{C}}=O$	1
2	H—C—OH		C—OH		HO—C—H	2
3	HO—C—H	$\underset{\rightleftharpoons}{\longrightarrow}$	HO—C—H	$\underset{\rightleftharpoons}{\longrightarrow}$	HO—C—H	3
4	H—C—OH		H—C—OH		H—C—OH	4
5	H—C—OH		H—C—OH		H—C—OH	5
6	CH₂OH		CH₂OH		CH₂OH	6
	D-Glucose		Enediol		D-Mannose	

the 2-epimer of D-glucose. Epimers thus differ in having the opposite configuration at one of several centers of asymmetry.

3.16   **Quasi-Racemates.** — The formation of a molecular compound from two closely related compounds of opposite configuration was first observed in the case of (+)-chlorosuccinic acid and (−)-bromosuccinic acid (M. Centnerszwer, 1899). Substances of this type are known as quasi-racemates. They display optical activity, except in the rare case when the two components have identical but opposite molecular rotations, but in any case they are recognizable as quasi-racemates from melting point-composition diagrams. Whereas with a true racemate the first half of the diagram giving melting points of mixtures of from 0%A and 100%B to the 50:50 mixture is exactly matched by the second half extending to 100%A and 0%B, with a quasi-racemate the two halves of the curve are similar but not identical. Fredga[1] (1934–47) used this method for correlation of configuration. The substance under investigation and the comparison compound of known configurations must be very similar in structure; in some cases it is necessary to compare both substances with a suitably chosen third substance. Another expedient is to introduce a common large substituent into both compounds and thus decrease the structural difference. The method is limited by the fact that formation of quasi-racemates is not general.

3.17   **Walden Inversion.** — In 1896 Walden,[2] at the Technical Institute, Riga, discovered a phenomenon which presented a most baffling problem. On heating levorotatory malic acid with phosphorus pentachloride to replace the hydroxyl group by chlorine, he obtained a dextrorotatory product. Direction of rotation, of course, does not indicate the configurational series of the chloro compound. However, on transforming the chloro compound back to an alcohol by reaction with silver oxide in moist ether, Walden found the product to be dextrorotatory malic acid. Therefore an inversion of configuration, a Walden inversion, occurs in one reaction or the other. The reactions described, and others that complete the cycle, are shown in the chart with formulas representing the now known absolute configurations. Inversions occur in the reactions with phosphorus

[1] Arne Fredga, b. 1902 Uppsala, Sweden; Ph.D. Uppsala (L. Ramberg); Univ. Uppsala

[2] Paul von Walden, 1863–1957; b. Latvia; stud. Riga; Univ. Riga, Russia; Univ. Rostock Tübingen, Germany; *Proc. Chem. Soc.*, 186 (1960)

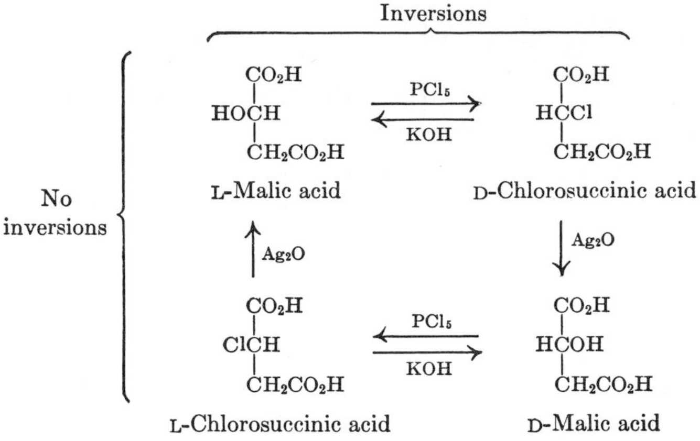

Inversions

CO$_2$H   CO$_2$H

HOCH $\xrightarrow[\text{KOH}]{\text{PCl}_5}$ HCCl

CH$_2$CO$_2$H   CH$_2$CO$_2$H

No inversions {   L-Malic acid   D-Chlorosuccinic acid

↑ Ag$_2$O   ↓ Ag$_2$O

CO$_2$H   CO$_2$H

ClCH $\xleftarrow[\text{KOH}]{\text{PCl}_5}$ HCOH

CH$_2$CO$_2$H   CH$_2$CO$_2$H

L-Chlorosuccinic acid   D-Malic acid

pentachloride and with potassium hydroxide; hydrolysis with silver oxide proceeds with retention of configuration.

Many subsequent observations showed that Walden inversion occurs only when the group displaced is attached to an asymmetric carbon. When such is the case, a displacement may proceed with inversion, with retention of configuration, or with racemization, and the result is dependent upon the reagent, the conditions, and the special characteristics of the substance undergoing reaction. The nature of the reaction in which one optically active compound is converted into another of the opposite configuration remained a mystery for many years. How kinetic studies of the mechanisms of displacement reactions eventually led to an understanding of the phenomenon will be described at an appropriate point.

GEOMETRICAL ISOMERISM

3.18   **van't Hoff's Prediction.** — In his classical paper of 1874, van't Hoff not only developed the fundamental theory of optical isomerism but deduced all essential principles of geometrical isomerism. Although his conception of the double bond as being formed by a pair of tetrahedrons joined at two corners has given place to the theory that the double bond consists of one σ and one π bond and that restriction of rotation is the result of overlap of p-atomic orbitals in formation of the π orbital (section 5.9), the orbital theory has not extended the interpretations of the original mechanical concept. van't Hoff's theoretical analysis of *cis-trans* isomerism was advanced as a prediction, for at the time no instance of such isomerism was on record. It had long been known that malic acid loses water readily when heated and affords two substances, maleic acid and fumaric acid, and Liebig in 1838 established that these have the same composition

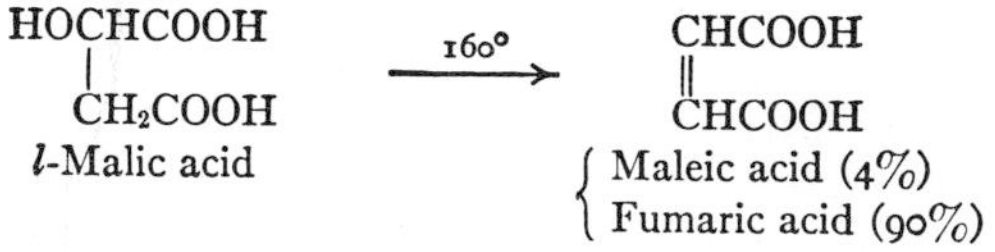

HOCHCOOH   CHCOOH

CH$_2$COOH $\xrightarrow{160°}$ CHCOOH

l-Malic acid   { Maleic acid (4%)

                                       { Fumaric acid (90%)

and are both dibasic acids. Since maleic acid (m.p. 130°) can be converted in part into the much higher-melting fumaric acid (m.p. 287°) when heated at a temperature slightly above the melting point, Liebig and, later, Erlenmeyer (1870, 1886) considered fumaric acid to be a polymer of maleic acid, or a molecular compound containing units of this substance. The relationship of these acids remained unsettled for some time after van't Hoff's publication, but eventually the acids were shown to be monomeric isomers of identical structure. Recognition of the existence of this pair of geometrical isomers as postulated by van't Hoff was due particularly to experimentation by Wislicenus (1887).

3.19   Configuration of Maleic and Fumaric Acids. — Differentiation between a pair of geometrical isomers can be achieved chemically by relating one of the isomers to a ring compound into which it can be converted or from which it can be derived. Maleic and fumaric acids have the same skeletal structure as succinic acid, and they both yield this substance on catalytic hydrogenation. Since succinic acid readily forms a cyclic anhydride, similar cyclization to

$$\begin{array}{ccc}
\text{CHCOOH} & \xrightarrow{\text{Na(Hg)}} & \text{CH}_2\text{COOH} \\
\| & & | \\
\text{CHCOOH} & & \text{CH}_2\text{COOH} \\
\left\{\begin{array}{l}\text{Maleic acid}\\\text{Fumaric acid}\end{array}\right. & & \text{Succinic acid}
\end{array} \xrightarrow{-\text{H}_2\text{O}} \begin{array}{c}
\text{CH}_2\text{CO} \\
| \quad \diagup \\
\quad\diagdown\text{O} \\
\text{CH}_2\text{CO} \\
\text{Succinic anhydride}
\end{array}$$

an anhydride would appear possible in the case of the *cis* isomer, where the carboxyl groups are on the same side of the molecule but not in the *trans* form. Ex-

$$\begin{array}{cc}
\text{H---C---CO}\overline{\text{OH}} & \text{H---C---COOH} \\
\| \qquad\qquad | & \| \\
\text{H---C---COO}\underline{\text{H}} & \text{HOOC---C---H} \\
\textit{cis} & \textit{trans}
\end{array}$$

periment shows that maleic acid readily affords a crystalline anhydride (m.p 57°), for example, when warmed on the steam bath with acetyl chloride. However, fumaric acid also can be converted into the identical anhydride. One or the other acid therefore must undergo molecular rearrangement in the course of its transformation to the derivative. The acids, to be sure, differ considerably in the ease with which they are converted into the common anhydride. Thus fumaric acid remains largely unchanged when heated with pure acetyl chloride in a sealed tube at 100°, although it affords the anhydride if the temperature is raised to 140°. When maleic acid is heated alone at 160°, it is converted in part into the anhydride and in part into fumaric acid; the latter substance evidently arises as the result of rearrangement, and indeed when maleic acid is heated at 200° in a sealed tube to prevent escape of water, it yields fumaric acid as the chief product, along with some *dl*-malic acid. On the other hand, if pyrolysis is conducted in vacuum to promote elimination of water, the anhydride can be prepared at temperatures as low as 100°. Fumaric acid affords the anhydride only at much higher temperatures. This isomer melts at 287° when heated in a sealed capillary tube, but when heated in an open flask it begins to sublime at about 200°, and at 250–300° is in part carbonized and in part converted into the anhydride.

TABLE 3.5. PHYSICAL PROPERTIES OF MALEIC AND FUMARIC ACIDS

	MALEIC ACID *cis*	FUMARIC ACID *trans*
Melting point	130°	287°
Solubility in water, g. per 100 cc. at 25°	78.8	0.7
Density	1.590	1.635
Heat of combustion, kcal. per mole	327	320
pK_{a_1}	1.9	3.0
pK_{a_2}	6.5	4.5

The greater ease of anhydride formation suggests but does not prove that maleic acid is the *cis* isomer. However the matter is settled unambiguously by the observation that the anhydride can be hydrolyzed with cold water, that is, under conditions where rearrangement is excluded, and yields maleic acid as the sole product. Therefore maleic acid has the *cis* configuration, and the product of dehydration is maleic anhydride. Fumaric acid is the *trans* isomer, and when heated strongly or treated with chemical dehydrating agents under special conditions, rearranges into maleic acid, which then yields the anhydride. That the more symmetrical *trans* structure is more stable than the *cis* is shown by the higher melting point of fumaric acid, the greater density and lesser solubility (Table 3.5)

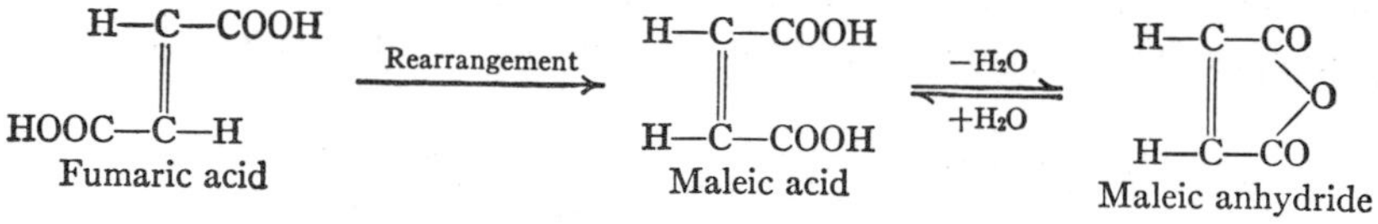

$$
\begin{array}{ccccc}
\text{H—C—COOH} & & \text{H—C—COOH} & & \text{H—C—CO} \\
\| & \xrightarrow{\text{Rearrangement}} & \| & \underset{+\text{H}_2\text{O}}{\overset{-\text{H}_2\text{O}}{\rightleftharpoons}} & \| \quad \diagdown\text{O} \\
\text{HOOC—C—H} & & \text{H—C—COOH} & & \text{H—C—CO} \\
\text{Fumaric acid} & & \text{Maleic acid} & & \text{Maleic anhydride}
\end{array}
$$

and by the maleic → fumaric rearrangement. The heats of combustion show that maleic acid has an energy content 7 kcal. higher than that of fumaric acid and

 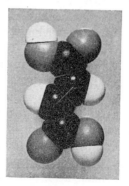

Maleic acid Fumaric acid

therefore has a greater tendency to undergo change. That the *cis* isomer is the more strongly acidic, as judged by comparison of the constants for the first dissociation, pK_{a_1}, means that the ionizing tendency of one carboxyl group is enhanced by the second unsaturated group in a near-by position. The greater spread between the first and second dissociation constants observed with maleic acid is also understandable. Once a proton has separated from the *cis* dibasic acid, the negatively charged group exerts an attractive force on the second hydrogen atom in the neighboring position and opposes its liberation as a proton.

The energy-richer *cis* isomer is convertible into fumaric acid at room temperature under the catalytic influence of hydrochloric or hydrobromic acid. The halogens as well as the halogen acids are effective catalysts for the rearrangement; for example, diethyl maleate is transformed rapidly into the ester of fumaric acid by a trace of iodine. The transformations represent the reversion of a labile isomer to a more stable form under the driving force of higher energy content. The reverse change is brought about by irradiation of an aqueous solution of fumaric acid with ultraviolet light at 45–50°; within a few hours, a condition of equilibrium is reached corresponding to isomerization of 75% of the material. Here the *trans* isomer acquires radiant energy by absorption, and the energy level is built up to that of the *cis* isomer. A more practical preparation of maleic acid consists in warming malic acid with acetyl chloride, distilling the mixture, and hydrolyzing the resulting maleic anhydride. An industrial process for the preparation of maleic anhydride consists in catalytic vapor-phase oxidation of benzene with atmospheric oxygen over vanadium pentoxide on alumina at 400°.

$$
\underset{\substack{HC\\ \| \\ HC \\ \diagdown CH}}{\overset{\substack{CH \\ \diagup\diagdown CH \\ |}}{}} \xrightarrow{[O]} \underset{\substack{CH \\ \| \\ CH \\ \diagdown CO}}{\overset{\substack{CO \\ \diagdown \\ }}{}} O \;+\; CO_2,\ H_2O
$$

3.20   Other *cis-trans* Isomers. — Citraconic acid and mesaconic acid, the methyl derivatives of maleic and fumaric acids, show the same relationships in physical properties; the configurations are similarly known from correlation of the lower-melting isomer and the cyclic anhydride.

$$
\begin{array}{cc}
\underset{\substack{\| \\ H-C-COOH}}{CH_3-C-COOH} & \underset{\substack{\| \\ H-C-COOH}}{HOOC-C-CH_3} \\[1em]
\text{Citraconic acid} & \text{Mesaconic acid} \\
(\text{m.p. } 91°,\ pK_{a_1}\ 2.42, & (\text{m.p. } 202°,\ pK_{a_1}\ 3.10, \\
\text{kcal./mole } 482) & \text{kcal./mole } 478)
\end{array}
$$

Crotonic and isocrotonic acid, geometrical isomers of the structure $CH_3CH=$ CHCOOH, represent a typical case where the method of determining configuration by correlation with a ring compound is not applicable. The problem, however, was solved by von Auwers[1] (1923) by relating one of the isomers to fumaric acid by the preparation of each substance from a common intermediate under conditions shown not to permit rearrangements. The product of stepwise

[1] Karl von Auwers, 1863–1939; b. Gotha, Germany; Ph.D. Berlin (Hofmann); Univ. Marburg; *Ber.*, **72A**, 111 (1939)

$$\underset{\gamma,\gamma,\gamma\text{-Trichlorocrotonic acid}}{\underset{\text{H}-\text{C}-\text{COOH}}{\text{CCl}_3-\text{C}-\text{H}}} \xrightarrow[60\%]{\text{Zn, HOAc}} \underset{\text{H}-\text{C}-\text{COOH}}{\text{CHCl}_2-\text{C}-\text{H}} \xrightarrow[74\%]{\text{Na(Hg)}} \underset{\text{Crotonic acid}}{\underset{\text{H}-\text{C}-\text{COOH}}{\text{CH}_3-\text{C}-\text{H}}}$$

$$\xrightarrow[66\%]{\text{concd. H}_2\text{SO}_4 \text{ at } 30°} \underset{\text{Fumaric acid}}{\underset{\text{H}-\text{C}-\text{COOH}}{\text{HOOC}-\text{C}-\text{H}}}$$

reduction of the trichloro compound proved to be the higher-melting (solid) crotonic acid, and therefore this has the *trans* configuration. From the properties of the two unsaturated acids, listed under the formulas, it is seen that the rela-

$$\underset{\text{H}-\text{C}-\text{COOH}}{\text{H}-\text{C}-\text{CH}_3}$$
Isocrotonic acid (*cis*)
(m.p. 15.5°, pK$_a$ 4.44, kcal./mole 486,
g./100 ml. H$_2$O$^{25°}$ 40.0)

$$\underset{\text{H}-\text{C}-\text{COOH}}{\text{CH}_3-\text{C}-\text{H}}$$
Crotonic acid (*trans*)
(m.p. 72°, pK$_a$ 4.70, kcal./mole 478,
g./100 ml. H$_2$O$^{25°}$ 8.3)

tionships are the same as those of the dibasic acids. The *trans* isomer, with the relatively large methyl and carboxyl groups balanced on the two sides of the molecule, has the more symmetrical structure, and it has the higher melting point, is less soluble, and has a lower energy content; this form also is produced readily by catalyzed rearrangement of the liquid *cis* isomer.

Those instances in which physical properties have been correlated with chemically established configurations provide a rational, but not infallible, basis on which to deduce the probable configurations of other pairs of isomers. Thus the unsaturated fatty acids oleic and elaidic are regarded as having the *cis* and *trans* configurations, respectively, because the former has the lower melting point and the higher heat of combustion and is convertible into the more stable isomer under the catalytic influence of nitric or nitrous acid. In the case of the isomeric

$$\underset{\text{H}-\text{C}-(\text{CH}_2)_7\text{COOH}}{\text{H}-\text{C}-(\text{CH}_2)_7\text{CH}_3}$$
Oleic acid
(**m.p. 13°, 16°; kcal./mole 2682**)

$$\underset{\text{H}-\text{C}-(\text{CH}_2)_7\text{COOH}}{\text{CH}_3(\text{CH}_2)_7\text{C}-\text{H}}$$
Elaidic acid
(**m.p. 44°, kcal./mole 2664**)

cinnamic acids, assignment of configuration on the basis of physical properties has been verified by a series of reactions by which the *cis* isomer is obtained from a cyclic derivative where a ring extends from the carboxyl group to the benzene ring. Allocinnamic acid is the most stable of three polymorphic forms of *cis*-cinnamic acid; the less stable forms melt at 58° and at 42°. Liebermann[1] (1889) first isolated the 58°-form as a degradation product of an alkaloid accompanying cocaine in coca leaves and found it to change to a more stable crystalline modification, m.p. 68° (*allo* form). Once the laboratory was seeded with the higher-melting material, Liebermann was unable to secure further lots of the 58°-form; eventually Biilmann[2] (1909) worked out special methods of crystallization by which the three known polymorphic forms can be interconverted. The

[1] Carl Liebermann, 1842–1914; b. Berlin; Ph.D. Berlin; Univ. Berlin; *Ber.*, **48**, 4 (1915)
[2] Einar Biilmann, 1873–1946; b. Copenhagen; Ph.D. Copenhagen; Univ. Copenhagen; *J. Chem. Soc.*, 534 (1949)

$$C_6H_5—C—H$$
$$\|$$
$$HOOC—C—H$$

Allocinnamic acid

(m.p. 68°, pK_a 3.96, kcal./mole 1047,
g./100 ml. $H_2O^{25°}$ 14.4)

$$C_6H_5—C—H$$
$$\|$$
$$H—C—COOH$$

Cinnamic acid

(m.p. 133°, pK_a 4.44, kcal./mole 1040,
g./100 ml. $H_2O^{25°}$ 0.1)

greater energy content associated with the *cis* configuration is illustrated by the fact that when a solution of allocinnamic acid in methanol is saturated with hydrogen chloride in the cold, the substance is converted into the methyl ester of cinnamic acid.   An interesting relationship is exhibited by the isomeric α,β-dibromocinnamic acids of the formula $C_6H_5CBr=CBrCOOH$.   The more stable form, m.p. 138°, is colorless, whereas the lower-melting isomer, m.p. 100°, presumably *cis*, is yellow; the color apparently is an outward mark of higher energy content.

With the isomers angelic acid and tiglic acid, $CH_3CH=C(CH_3)COOH$, the designations *cis* and *trans* have only arbitrary significance, and there is no obvious decision as to which configuration is the more symmetrical.   The configurations formulated are assigned partly on the basis of the dissociation constants.   Angelic acid is the more strongly acidic of the two isomers, just as isocrotonic acid is more strongly acidic than crotonic acid.   Further evidence is that the rate of esterifica-

$$CH_3—C—H$$
$$\|$$
$$HOOC—C—CH_3$$

Angelic acid
(m.p. 45°, pK_a 4.30,
kcal./mole 635)

$$CH_3—C—H$$
$$\|$$
$$CH_3—C—COOH$$

Tiglic acid
(m.p. 64.5°, pK_a 5.02
kcal./mole 627)

tion of tiglic acid with methanol is greater than that of the more hindered angelic acid.   These configurations have been confirmed by X-ray analysis.

3.21   **Steric Course of Additions.** — Kekulé and Anschütz[1] (1880–81) established that, on controlled oxidation with alkaline permanganate at a low temperature, maleic acid yields mesotartaric acid and fumaric acid yields *dl*-tartaric acid.   Reference to models, or to perspective formulas, shows that the

$$H—C—COOH \quad \xrightarrow{KMnO_4} \quad H—C—OH$$
$$\|$$
$$H—C—COOH \qquad\qquad\qquad H—C—OH$$

with COOH above and COOH below on the mesotartaric product

Maleic acid   Mesotartaric acid

$$H—C—COOH \quad \xrightarrow{KMnO_4} \quad H—C—OH \quad + \quad HO—C—H$$
$$\|$$
$$HOOC—C—H \qquad\qquad\qquad HO—C—H \qquad\qquad H—C—OH$$

Fumaric acid   *dl*-Tartaric acid

reactions are *cis* hydroxylations.   The members of the double bond of (I) are perpendicular to the plane in which the atoms lie and one (1) extends to the front

[1] Richard Anschütz, 1852–1937; b. Darmstadt, Germany; Ph.D. Univ. Heidelberg, Bonn; *Ber.*, **74A**, 29 (1941)

(solid line) and the other (2) to the rear (dotted line). If the hydroxyls approach from the rear and open the rear bond (2), the product is II, in which the hydroxyls

$$
\begin{array}{c}
\text{HOOC—C—H} \\
{\scriptstyle 1|{:}2} \\
\text{HOOC—C—H}
\end{array}
\xrightarrow{\text{2 OH}}
\begin{array}{c}
\text{OH} \\
{:} \\
\text{HOOC—C—H} \\
{\scriptstyle 1|} \\
\text{HOOC—C—H} \\
{:} \\
\text{OH}
\end{array}
=
\begin{array}{c}
\text{OH} \\
\text{HOOC} \diamondsuit \text{H} \\
\\
\text{HOOC} \diamondsuit \text{H} \\
\text{OH}
\end{array}
=
\begin{array}{c}
\text{COOH} \\
\text{H} \diamondsuit \text{OH} \\
\\
\text{H} \diamondsuit \text{OH} \\
\text{COOH}
\end{array}
$$

| I | II | III | IV |

are to the rear and which is therefore equivalent to the tetrahedral model III, arranged as in the Fischer convention. According to the convention that the order COOH → OH → H is right-handed, the upper carbon in III is right-handed and the lower one left-handed; the clockwise and counterclockwise nature can be inferred equally well from II. If each carbon of III is turned in the direction COOH → OH → H until carboxyls are at top and bottom, the conventional formula IV of mesotartaric acid is obtained. *cis* Hydroxylation of fumaric acid gives different products, according to the bond opened. Rear attack of V by opening of bond 2 gives VI, in which both carbon atoms are seen to be left-handed. Since frontal attack is not easily represented, alternative opening of bond 1 can

$$
\begin{array}{c}
\text{H—C—COOH} \\
{\scriptstyle 1|{:}2} \\
\text{HOOC—C—H}
\end{array}
\xrightarrow{\text{2 OH}}
\begin{array}{c}
\text{OH} \\
{:} \\
\text{H—C—COOH} \\
{\scriptstyle 1|} \\
\text{HOOC—C—H} \\
{:} \\
\text{OH}
\end{array}
\qquad
\begin{array}{c}
\text{HOOC—C—H} \\
{\scriptstyle 2|{:}1} \\
\text{H—C—COOH}
\end{array}
\xrightarrow{\text{2 OH}}
\begin{array}{c}
\text{OH} \\
{:} \\
\text{HOOC—C—H} \\
{\scriptstyle 2|} \\
\text{H—C—COOH} \\
{:} \\
\text{OH}
\end{array}
$$

| V | VI | VII | VIII |

be considered by turning V upside down as in VII, in which bond 1 is to the rear and can be opened as before by rear attack. The product VIII contains two right-handed carbons. Thus VI and VIII represent *l-* and *d-*tartaric acid; the probability of opening being the same for each bond, the *dl-*product results.

To the early chemists *cis* addition appeared to be the normal, expected mode of reaction. Hence reactions that seemed to proceed in the opposite sense were viewed with suspicion and regarded as abnormal. Thus on addition of bromine maleic acid gives the *dl-*product and fumaric acid gives the *meso-*dibromide. van't Hoff noted that halogens and halogen acids are effective catalysts for inter-conversion of *cis-trans* isomers and postulated that the unexpected additions are attended with catalyzed rearrangement of the olefinic starting materials.

$$
\begin{array}{c}
\text{COOH} \\
| \\
\text{C} \\
||| \\
\text{C} \\
| \\
\text{COOH}
\end{array}
\xrightarrow{\text{aq. Br}_2}
\begin{array}{c}
\text{Br—C—COOH} \\
|| \\
\text{Br—C—COOH} \\
30\%
\end{array}
\quad + \quad
\begin{array}{c}
\text{Br—C—COOH} \\
|| \\
\text{HOOC—C—Br} \\
70\%
\end{array}
$$

Michael,[1] however, in a series of investigations of the addition of bromine and hydrogen halides to maleic and fumaric acid and to acetylenedicarboxylic acid (1892–95) demonstrated beyond question that *trans* addition can be accomplished under conditions such that interconversions do not occur, and his work led to eventual acceptance of *trans* addition. Michael found further that addition of hydrochloric or hydrobromic acid to acetylenedicarboxylic acid leads exclusively to bromo- or chlorofumaric acid.

Actually, contrary to the initial supposition, *trans* addition is the rule and *cis* addition the exception. As will be evident in due course, inquiry into the mechanisms of the reactions has made available rational interpretations of both phenomena.

3.22   **Stereoisomerism of Cyclic Compounds.** — The opportunity for a *cis* and a *trans* arrangement of groups characteristic of the structure HOOCCH=CHCOOH is encountered in the ring structure of cyclopropane-1,2-dicarboxylic acid. The carbon atoms of the cyclopropane ring lie in a plane, and the two carboxyl groups can either project on the same side or on opposite sides of this plane. The three-membered ring, however, lacks the symmetry of a double bond, and models of all possible forms of the cyclopropanedicarboxylic acids, as shown in Fig. 3.5, show that three configurations are possible. One is the *cis* form

HOOCCH—CHCOOH
$\diagdown\diagup$
CH$_2$

I, and as long as the two carboxyl groups are represented as being on the same side of the molecule it makes no difference whether these are represented as

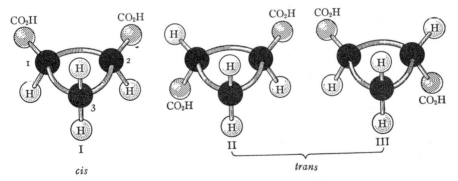

FIG. 3.5. — Cyclopropanedicarboxylic Acids

being above or below the plane of the ring or whether they are affixed to carbon atoms 1 and 2 or 1 and 3. The molecule as written has a plane of symmetry passing through carbon atom 3 and the two attached hydrogen atoms. When the carboxyl groups are placed on opposite sides of the plane of the ring, two arrangements are possible, II and III. These possess no plane of symmetry and are asymmetric; they are not superposable and are mirror images of each other. Theory thus predicts existence of one *cis* form and of two enantiomeric *trans* forms, and the prediction has been verified by experiment. One isomeric cyclopropane-

---

[1] Arthur Michael, 1853–1942; b. Buffalo, N. Y.; stud. Heidelberg, Berlin, École de Médecine, Paris; Tufts; Harvard Univ.

dicarboxylic acid, m.p. 139°, is nonresolvable and readily forms an anhydride from which it can be regenerated on hydrolysis; it therefore has the *cis* configuration. Another isomer, m.p. 175°, yields no anhydride and is the *dl-trans* form, resolvable into optically active components.

The relationships can be summarized with a conventional representation in which the ring system is imagined to be in a plane at right angles to the paper with the attached groups either above (full lines) or below (dotted lines) this plane. Paralleling the relationship between maleic and fumaric acid, the *cis* form is the more labile and is converted into the *dl-trans* form on being heated

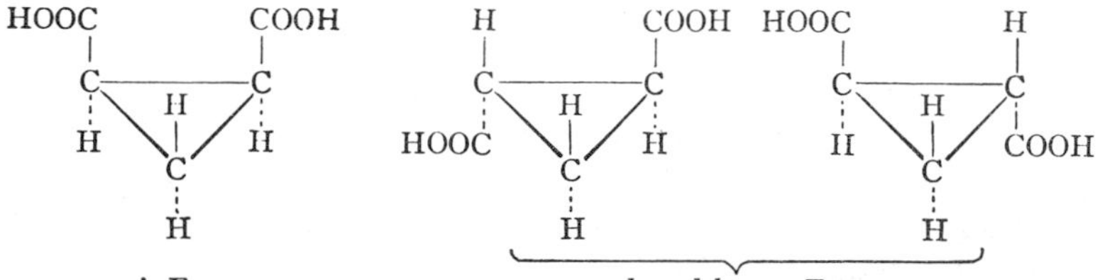

cis Form

(m.p. 139°, pK$_{a_1}$ 3.40,
g./100 g. H$_2$O 112)

d- and *l-trans* Forms

(*dl*-acid: m.p. 175°, pK$_{a_1}$ 3.68, g./100 g.
H$_2$O$^{20°}$ 19.1; *d*- and *l*-acids, m.p. 175°,
[α]$_D$ ± 84.4°)

with 50% sulfuric acid at 150°. The higher melting point, lower solubility, and weaker acidic strength of the *trans* form are further marks of this configuration, and thus the relationships in both chemical and physical properties correspond to those noted in ethylenic compounds. Thus assignment of configurations on the basis of anhydride formation and physical properties is confirmed independently by the observation that one acid is resolvable whereas the other is not.

The example cited is typical only of those cyclic compounds in which the two parts of the ring extending between the unsymmetrically substituted carbon atoms are different, for, if they are the same, the situation is exactly like that of the maleic-fumaric type of isomers. Thus cyclohexane-1,4-dicarboxylic acid presents merely the same opportunity for geometrical isomerism found in ethylenic compounds:

compare

Of the two modifications of the acid that have been isolated, neither forms an anhydride and neither is resolvable. The *trans* form is the more stable because both carboxyl groups are equatorial.

If the two carboxyl groups are located at the 1,2- or 1,3-positions in the cyclohexane ring, the ring system becomes unsymmetrical, and the same opportunity exists for both geometrical and optical isomerism as in the cyclopropane series.

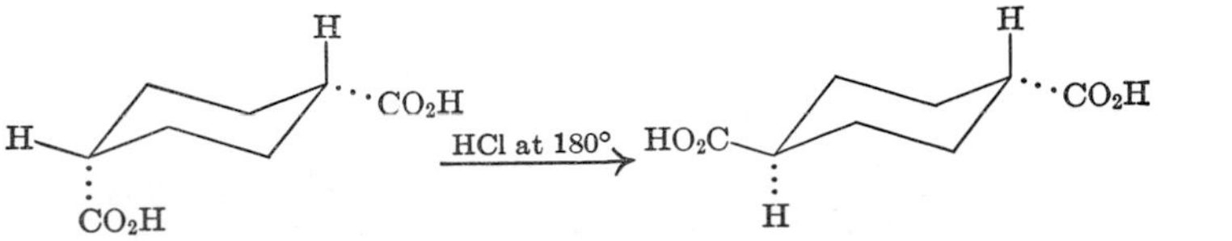

M. p. 161°, pKa₁ 4.52, pKa₂ 5.52
928.6 kcal./mole, v. sol. H₂O

M. p. 300°, pKa₁ 5.34, pKa₂ 5.60
929.5 kcal./mole, 0.09 g./100 g. H₂O 16.5°

The isomeric cyclohexane-1,2-dicarboxylic acids (hexahydrophthalic acids), for example, are represented in the following formulations:

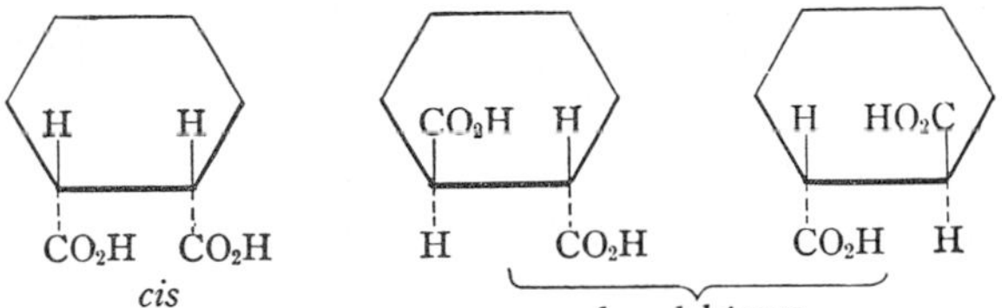

cis   *d*- and *l-trans*

ASYMMETRIC MOLECULES

3.23   **Diphenyl Isomerism.** — In 1922 G. H. Christie and J. Kenner re-ported the resolution of o,o'-dinitrodiphenic acid, a diphenyl deriva-tive which contains no asymmetric carbon atoms.   Many similar and related compounds were later investigated in several laboratories and the phenomenon interpreted as due to restriction of rotation about the single bond by bulky *ortho*

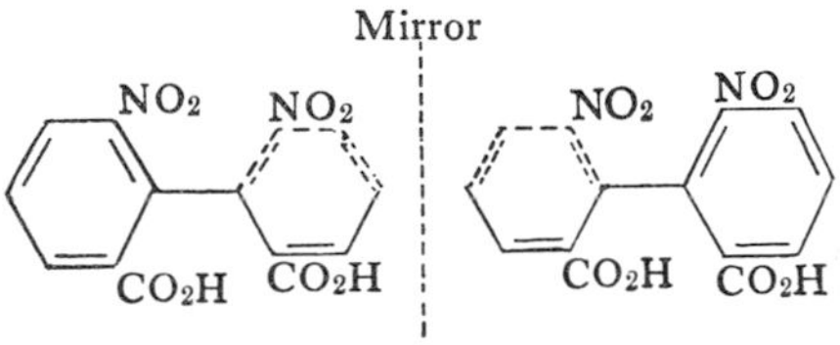

substituents.   The two rings are held in approximately perpendicular planes and hence two mirror-image forms are possible.   Optical isomerism is observed principally in diphenyl derivatives having at least three *ortho* substituents, and the ease of racemization is correlated with the number and size of *ortho* groups.

3.24   **Allene Isomerism.** — Another prediction made by van't Hoff in 1874 was that suitably substituted derivatives of allene, $CH_2=C=CH_2$, should be resolvable.   In an allene of type (1) the two double bonds lie in planes perpendicular to each other, and the groups *a* and *b* lie in a plane perpendicular

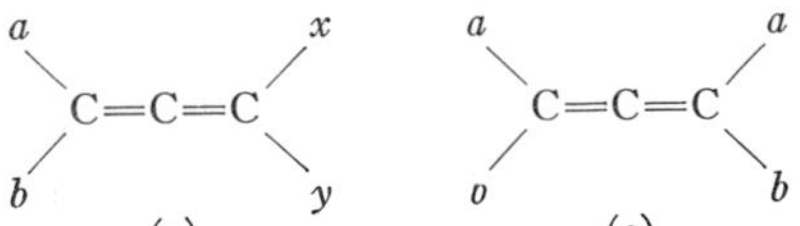

to that of the groups *x* and *y*; hence the molecule is asymmetric and should be capable of existing in nonsuperposable mirror-image forms.   Even an allene of type (2) should be resolvable, and the photograph shows a pair of such enantiomers. Several attempts to synthesize allenes of type (1) or (2) having groups suitable

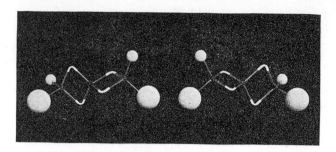

for resolution were unsuccessful, but in 1935 van't Hoff's prediction was verified independently by two groups. P. Maitland and W. H. Mills[1] effected asymmetric dehydration of the alcohol (3) with d-camphorsulfonic acid and obtained an optically active form of the hydrocarbon (4), $[\alpha]_{546°} + 437$; dehydration with l-camphor-

$$
\begin{array}{ccc}
\underset{\alpha\text{-}C_{10}H_7}{\overset{C_6H_5}{>}}C=CH-\underset{\underset{OH}{|}}{\overset{C_6H_5}{C}}<C_{10}H_7\text{-}\alpha & \xrightarrow{\text{H}^+} & \underset{\alpha\text{-}C_{10}H_7}{\overset{C_6H_5}{>}}C=C=\underset{}{\overset{C_6H_5}{C}}<C_{10}H_7\text{-}\alpha \\
(3) & & (4)
\end{array}
$$

sulfonic acid gave the enantiomer ($-438°$). E. P. Kohler, J. T. Walker, and M. Tishler synthesized the allenic acid (5) and resolved it by fractional crystalli-

$$
\underset{\alpha\text{-}C_{10}H_7}{\overset{C_6H_5}{>}}C=C=\underset{\overset{}{C_6H_5}}{\overset{COOCH_2CO_2H}{C}}<
$$
$$
(5)
$$

zation of the brucine salts. The two forms melted at 146° and had specific rotations in ethyl acetate of $+29.5°$ and $-28.4°$. (For another synthesis see 6.22.)

PROBLEMS

1. Write projection formulas for all the stereoisomeric forms of

$$\text{HOOCCH(CH}_3)\text{CHBrCOOH}$$

Which are enantiomers and which diastereoisomers?

2. How many optically active forms corresponding to the following formulas are possible?

  (a) $CH_3CH_2CH(OH)CHClCH_3$
  (b) $(CH_3)_2CHCH_2CH(CH_3)COOH$

---

[1] William Hobson Mills, 1873–1959; b. London; Ph.D. Tübingen (v. Pechmann); Cambridge Univ.

(c) $C_6H_5CHBrCH_2CH(OH)CH_2CH(NH_2)COOH$

(d) $CH_2(OH)CH(OH)CH(OH)CH(OH)CH(OH)CHO$

3. An acid of the formula $C_5H_{10}O_2$ is optically active. What is its structure?

4. A derivative of one of the tartaric acids is optically active but gives optically inactive products when esterified with diazomethane or when hydrolyzed. What is it?

5. Give the number and nature of the possible stereoisomers, if any, corresponding to each of the following formulas:

(a) $(CH_3)_2CHCH(NH_2)CH_2CH(CH_3)_2$

(b) $CH_3CH_2C(CH_3)=C(CH_3)_2$

(c) $C_6H_5CH=CHCOC_6H_5$

(d) $CH_2=CHCH_2CH(NH_2)COOH$

(e) $C_6H_5CHBrCHBrCOC_6H_5$

(f) $(C_6H_5)_2C=CHCH_2CH_2CH=C(C_6H_5)_2$

(g) $CH_3CH(OH)CH(OH)CH_3$

(h) $HOCH_2CH(OH)CH(OH)CH(OH)CHO$

6. When a dextrorotatory isomer of the formula $HOCH_2CH(OH)CH(OH)CHO$ is boiled with dilute hydrochloric acid the rotatory power increases for a time and then becomes constant. What is the nature of the change?

7. Formulate all possible stereoisomeric forms of cyclobutane-1,2-dicarboxylic acid and cyclobutane-1,3-dicarboxylic acid.

8. What are the possibilities for stereoisomerism in menthol (3.13)?

9. Certain substances of the types $R_1R_2R_3R_4N^+X^-$ have been resolved into optically active components. What inference can be drawn regarding the spatial character of the nitrogen atom?

10. The compound formulated below, which exhibits brilliant blue fluorescence in dilute aqueous solution and which has affinity for cotton fabric, is employed, in its most stable steric form, as a brightening agent, or colorless dye added to soap to increase whiteness of washed goods. What change would you expect to occur when the washed material is exposed to sunlight?

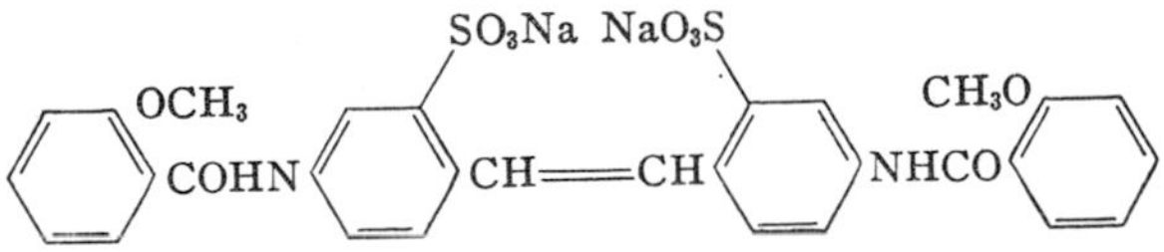

11. Account for the existence of two forms of oxalacetic acid, $HOOCCH_2COCOOH$.

12. Which of the following pairs of diastereoisomers are epimers, and which epimer pairs offer prospect for easy interconversion?

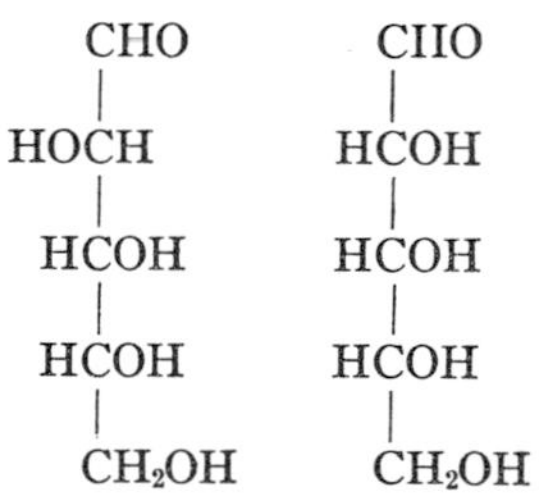

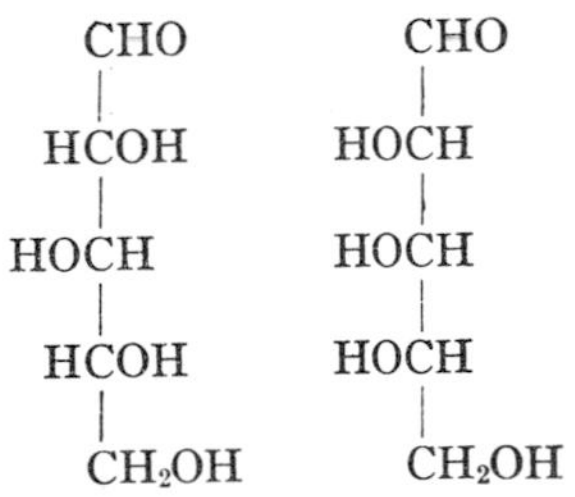

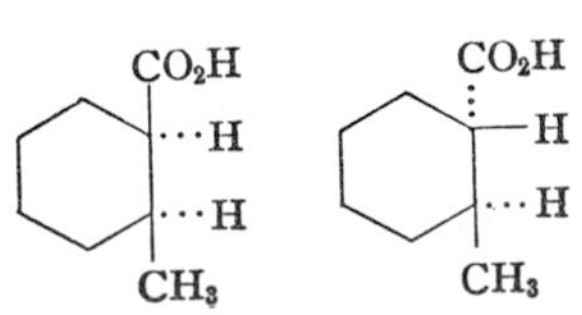

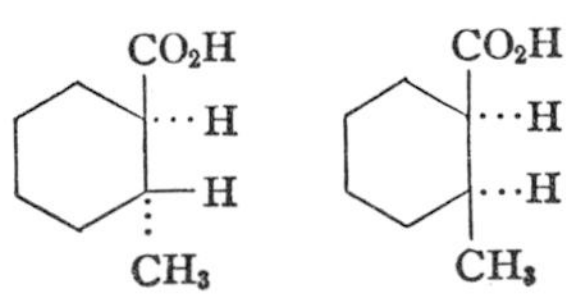

13. Identify the following isomer pairs. (1) Are they enantiomers, epimers, diastereoisomers, geometrical isomers, structural isomers, or identical? (2) Which members are optically active?

(a)   C₆H₅   C₆H₅   (b)   CH₃   CO₂H
        | | | |
      HCBr   HCBr   HCNH₂   H₂NCH
        | | | |
      BrCH   HCBr   HCNH₂   H₂NCH
        | | | |
      C₆H₅   C₆H₅   CO₂H   CH₃

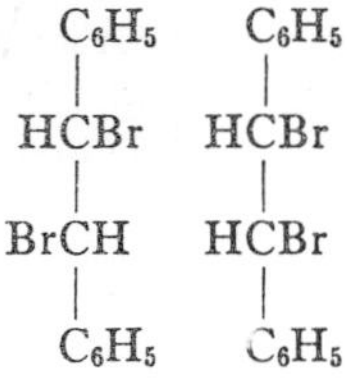

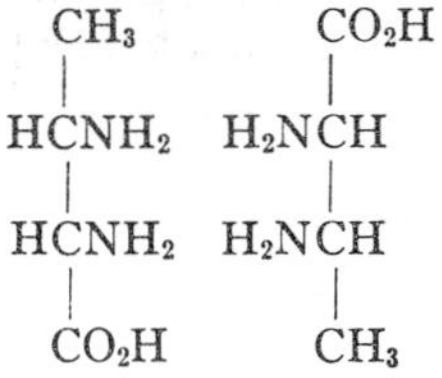

(c)   CH≡C—C≡C—C≡C—CH=CH₂
      CH≡C—C≡C—CH=C=C=CH₂

(d)   CO₂H   CO₂H
                | |
             H₂NCH   HCNH₂
                | |
              HCOH   HOCH
                | |
              CH₃   CH₃

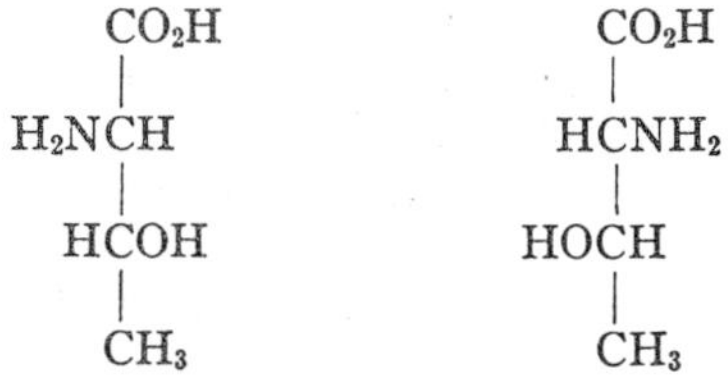

(e) *l*-Quinine *d*-tartrate   *l*-Quinine *l*-tartrate

Chapter 4

ALKANES

4.1   **Number of Isomers.** — The compounds now assigned the generic name alkane are also referred to as saturated hydrocarbons and as paraffin hydrocarbons. The word paraffin, from the Latin *parum affinis* (slight affinity) refers to the inert chemical nature of the substances and is applied also to the wax obtainable from petroleum and consisting of a mixture of higher alkanes.

Derivation of the formulas of the pentanes (3 isomers), hexanes (5), and heptanes (9) in Chapter 2 has already demonstrated the sharp rise in diversity with increasing carbon content. Table 4.1 shows that there are 18 octanes, 35 nonanes, and 75 decanes. The figures through C_{14} were obtained by writing the formulas; the other figures were calculated from a finite recursive formula (H. R. Henze and C. M. Blair, 1931). The table refers only to structural isomers; if stereoisomers were included as well the figures would be astronomical.

TABLE 4.1. NUMBER OF ISOMERS

CARBON CONTENT	ISOMERS
C_8	18
C_9	35
C_{10}	75
C_{11}	159
C_{12}	355
C_{13}	802
C_{14}	1,858
C_{15}	4,347
C_{20}	366,319
C_{25}	36,797,588
C_{30}	4,111,846,763
C_{40}	62,491,178,805,831

4.2   **Normal Alkanes.** — Successive members of the series (Table 4.2) differ in composition by the increment CH_2 and form a homologous series. Thus heptane and octane are homologous hydrocarbons; eicosane is a higher homolog of methane. Names of the hydrocarbons beyond butane are derived largely from the Greek numerals, although Latin prefixes are used in some instances (undecane).

105

TABLE 4.2. NORMAL ALKANES

NAME	FORMULA, C_nH_{2n+2}	M.P., °C.	B.P., °C.	SP. GR. (AS LIQUIDS) [1]	
Methane	CH_4	−182.6	−161.7	0.4240	⎫
Ethane	C_2H_6	−172.0	−88.6	.5462	⎪
Propane	C_3H_8	−187.1	−42.2	.5824	⎬ gases
n-Butane	C_4H_{10}	−135.0	−0.5	.5788	⎭
n-Pentane	C_5H_{12}	−129.7	36.1	.6264	⎫
n-Hexane	C_6H_{14}	−94.0	68.7	.6594	⎪
n-Heptane	C_7H_{16}	−90.5	98.4	.6837	⎪
n-Octane	C_8H_{18}	−56.8	125.6	.7028	⎪
n-Nonane	C_9H_{20}	−53.7	150.7	.7179	⎪
n-Decane	$C_{10}H_{22}$	−29.7	174.0	.7298	⎪
n-Undecane	$C_{11}H_{24}$	−25.6	195.8	.7404	⎬ liquids
n-Dodecane	$C_{12}H_{26}$	−9.6	216.3	.7493	⎪
n-Tridecane	$C_{13}H_{28}$	−6	(230)	.7568	⎪
n-Tetradecane	$C_{14}H_{30}$	5.5	251	.7636	⎪
n-Pentadecane	$C_{15}H_{32}$	10	268	.7688	⎪
n-Hexadecane	$C_{16}H_{34}$	18.1	280	.7749	⎪
n-Heptadecane	$C_{17}H_{36}$	22.0	303	.7767	⎭
n-Octadecane	$C_{18}H_{38}$	28.0	308	.7767	⎫
n-Nonadecane	$C_{19}H_{40}$	32	330	.7776	⎪
n-Eicosane	$C_{20}H_{42}$	36.4		.7777	⎪
n-Heneicosane	$C_{21}H_{44}$	40.4		.7782	⎪
n-Docosane	$C_{22}H_{46}$	44.4		.7778	⎪
n-Tricosane	$C_{23}H_{48}$	47.4		.7797	⎪
n-Tetracosane	$C_{24}H_{50}$	51.1		.7786	⎪
n-Pentacosane	$C_{25}H_{52}$	53.3			⎬ solids
n-Triacontane	$C_{30}H_{62}$	66			⎪
n-Pentatriacontane	$C_{35}H_{72}$	74.6		.7814	⎪
n-Tetracontane	$C_{40}H_{82}$	81			⎪
n-Pentacontane	$C_{50}H_{102}$	92		.7940	⎪
n-Hexacontane	$C_{60}H_{122}$	99			⎪
n-Dohexacontane	$C_{62}H_{126}$	101			⎪
n-Tetrahexacontane	$C_{64}H_{130}$	102			⎪
n-Heptacontane	$C_{70}H_{142}$	105	300 at 0.00001 mm.		⎭

[1] Specific gravities reported in this and subsequent tables refer to the liquid state. With substances liquid at 20°, values for this temperature are given where available. The data given for more volatile substances are for temperatures close to the boiling point, those for less volatile compounds for temperatures just above the melting points.

The hydrocarbons having from one to four carbon atoms are gases, the C_5 to C_{17} homologs are liquids, and the higher members of the series are solids. A similar relationship in a series of progressively increasing molecular weight is found in the halogens: chlorine, bromine, and iodine. Melting points of the hydrocarbons show an initial irregularity but tend to rise as the molecules become larger; melting points rise also with increasing symmetry of structure. In Fig. 4.1 the boiling points of the first ten n-alkanes are plotted against their molecular weights. The curve rises steeply at first, for the increase of molecular weight of 14 units for each CH_2 represents a large proportional change when the molecular weight

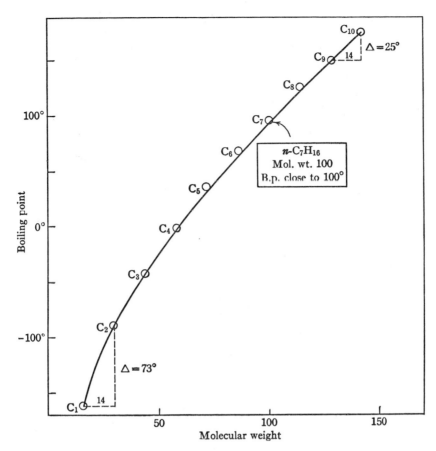

FIG. 4.1. — Boiling Points of *n*-Alkanes

is small. Thus the C_1 and C_2 homologs differ in boiling points by 73°, but the C_9 and C_{10} homologs differ by only 25°. The chart brings out a point of reference useful to remember: the *n*-alkane of molecular weight 100 has a boiling point close to 100°. The chart for *n*-alkanes typifies the relationship generally found for other compounds which, in the liquid phase, are unassociated and not bound together in aggregates. If a straight-chain aliphatic compound is known to belong to one of the unassociated types, the boiling point can be inferred with at least a fair degree of approximation from Fig. 4.1. In the case of a branched-chain compound, allowance can be made for the fact that branching produces some increase in volatility (2.7, 2.8). The degree of accuracy of the generalization that unassociated liquids of molecular weight of about 100 boil at about 100° can be seen from Table 4.3.

The relationship shown in the chart means that lower alkanes are more easily separable by fractional distillation than higher alkanes. The still shown in Fig. 4.2 is useful in general laboratory practice; it is shown in use for distillation at atmospheric pressure, but with a suitable adapter it can be employed for distil-

TABLE 4.3.

Correlation of Molecular Weight and Boiling Point

Compound	Mol. Wt.	B.P.	Type
$CH_3CH_2CH_2CH_2CH_2CH_2CH_3$	100.20	98.4°	Alkane
$CH_3CH_2CH_2CH_2CH_2CH\!=\!CH_2$	98.18	93.1°	Alkene
$CH_3CH_2CH_2CH_2CH_2C\!\equiv\!CH$	96.17	99.6°	Alkyne
$CH_3CH_2CH_2OCH_2CH_2CH_3$	102.17	90.5°	Ether
$CH_3CH_2CH_2CH_2CH_2Cl$	106.60	105.7°	Alkyl halide
$CH_3C\!\!\overset{O}{\underset{OCH_2CH_2CH_3}{\diagdown}}$	102.13	101.7°	Ester
$CH_3CH_2CH_2C\!\!\overset{O}{\underset{Cl}{\diagdown}}$	106.55	102°	Acid chloride

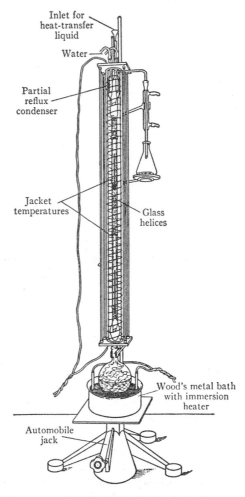

Inlet for
heat-transfer
liquid

Water

Partial
reflux
condenser

Jacket
temperatures

Glass
helices

Wood's metal bath
with immersion
heater

Automobile
jack

FIG. 4.2. — Distillation at Atmospheric Pressure

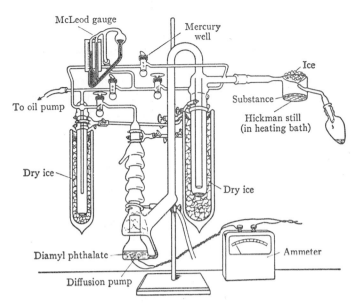

FIG. 4.3. — High-Vacuum Distillation

lation at the pressure of an oil pump (1–2 mm.). Substances of very low vapor pressure can be purified by high-vacuum distillation at the pressure of a mercury-diffusion pump, or of a pump operating on the diffusion principle but employing a high-boiling organic liquid for expulsion of gas molecules (Fig. 4.3). In the chemical industry techniques of fractional distillation refined to a state of almost miraculous effectiveness are applicable to substances of all ranges of volatility. Gaseous hydrocarbons are liquefied and then fractionated at temperatures far below 0°.

Specific gravities of the hydrocarbons in the liquid phase are given in the last column of Table 4.2. The hydrocarbons are all lighter than water and, being insoluble, float on water. Methane is less than half as heavy as water; with succeeding members the density increases rapidly for a time and then, in $C_{15}H_{32}$, reaches a limiting value of 0.77–0.78.

4.3 **Occurrence.** — Natural gas and petroleum are made up in large part of mixtures of saturated hydrocarbons. The only abundant sources of natural gas for industrial utilization are in the United States, and the gas from these wells contains chiefly methane. Petroleum consists chiefly of a mixture of homologs of methane ranging in carbon content from C_1 to C_{30}–C_{40} (Chapter 7).

Methane occurs as the sole hydrocarbon constituent of marsh gas, which is formed by anaerobic (absence of oxygen) fermentation of cellulose by microorganisms. In swamps and marshlands where plant parts have become covered with water, bacterial fermentation of cellulose constituents $(C_6H_{10}O_5)_n$ of the vegetation results in production of a flammable gas which rises to the surface and which consists principally of methane, together with small amounts of hydrogen, carbon dioxide, and nitrogen. Sewage sludge on fermentation affords a similar gas, which has been utilized in some cities as a fuel.

Saturated hydrocarbons have been isolated in small amounts from the waxy constituents of certain plants. *n*-Heptane occurs in the wood turpentine of two pines found in the western part of the United States, *Pinus jeffreyi* and *P. sabiniani*, and can be extracted easily. All natural wax paraffins contain an odd number of carbon atoms ranging from 27 to 37. They probably arise through decarboxylation of higher fatty acids, since the natural acids all have an even number of carbon atoms. *n*-Nonacosane ($C_{29}H_{60}$), m.p. 62.7–62.8°, has been extracted from cabbage leaves (1.5 g. from 220 kg.), and the cuticle of the apple contains C_{27}- and C_{29}-paraffin hydrocarbons. Beeswax contains heptacosane ($C_{27}H_{56}$) and hentriacontane ($C_{31}H_{64}$).

SYNTHETIC PREPARATION

4.4   **Kolbe Synthesis.** — The first general hydrocarbon synthesis was discovered prior to the Kekulé structure theory in work aimed at clarifying the relationship of ethyl alcohol to diethyl ether. In the face of opposition from Dumas, Liebig regarded the ether as the oxide of the ethyl radical and ethyl alcohol as the hydrate of this oxide. The ethyl radical, then, should bear the same relationship to its oxide as a metal (Na) does to a metal oxide (Na_2O). Since sodium and other metals were known as such, isolation of ethyl and other alkyl radicals seemed a possible and worthwhile objective for research. In 1849 the German chemist Kolbe[1] found that electrolysis of an aqueous solution of a salt of the acid C_4H_9COOH gave a hydrocarbon assumed to have the formula C_4H_9 and to be the butyl radical. In the same year Frankland[2] in England treated ethyl iodide with zinc to abstract the halogen and obtained a hydrocarbon which he assumed to be the ethyl radical, C_2H_5 (but which was later recognized as ethane). Kolbe's supposed butyl radical, and others made in the same way, were surprisingly inert, and not highly reactive like metallic sodium. Furthermore, molecular weight determinations by gas density measurement gave values about twice those expected, and the boiling points also seemed suspiciously high. Describing the position of uncertainty of the period, von Hofmann,[3] one-time president of both the Chemical Society (London) and the German Chemical Society, said "One could feel the ground shaking under his feet." Then, in 1850, Sir Benjamin Brodie resolved the issue by pointing out that a differentiation must exist between a free radical and a combined radical, that is, that Kolbe's supposed C_4H_9 is C_4H_9—C_4H_9. If a butyl radical had indeed been formed, it had combined with a second radical to form a stable molecule of twice the size.

[1] Herman Kolbe, 1818–84; b. Germany; Ph.D. Göttingen; Univ. Marburg, Leipzig

[2] Edward Frankland, 1825–99; b. England; successor to A. W. von Hofmann at the Royal School of Mines (previously the Royal College of Chemistry), London

[3] August Wilhelm von Hofmann, 1818–92; b. Giessen, Germany; Professor at Bonn, at the Royal College of Chemistry, London (1845–64), and at Berlin. See Lord Playfair, Sir F. A. Abel, W. H. Perkin, and H. E. Armstrong, "Hofmann Memorial Lecture," *J. Chem. Soc.* **69**, 575–732 (1896); *Ber.*, **25**, 3369 (1892); **35**, 4503 (1902)

The Kolbe synthesis thus can be formulated as follows:

$$2\ CH_3COO^-Na^+ + 2\ H_2O \xrightarrow{\text{Electrolysis}} \underbrace{C_2H_6 + 2\ CO_2}_{\text{Anode}} + \underbrace{2\ NaOH + H_2}_{\text{Cathode}}$$

Under the electric current, sodium ions migrate to the cathode, pick up electrons from the inflowing stream, and yield sodium hydroxide and hydrogen. The acetate anion travels to the anode, gives up its charge, probably with formation of a transient acetate free radical, with an unpaired electron on oxygen. The radical at once loses carbon dioxide to form a transient methyl radical, with an

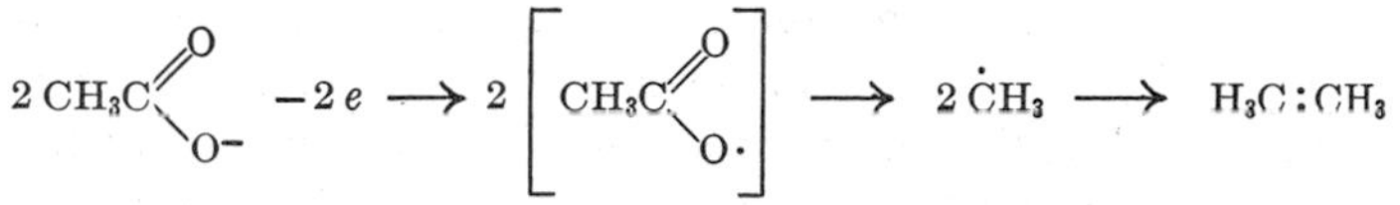

$$2\ CH_3C\overset{O}{\underset{O^-}{\diagdown}} \quad -2e \longrightarrow 2\left[CH_3C\overset{O}{\underset{O\cdot}{\diagdown}}\right] \longrightarrow 2\ \dot{C}H_3 \longrightarrow H_3C:CH_3$$

Acetate ion   Acetate radical   Methyl radical

odd electron, which achieves stabilization by doubling up to form ethane.

Sodium propionate on electrolysis affords *n*-butane, and sodium or potassium *n*-butyrate yields *n*-hexane:

$$\begin{array}{l} CH_3CH_2CH_2COOK \\ CH_3CH_2CH_2COOK \\ \text{Potassium } \textit{n}\text{-butyrate} \end{array} \xrightarrow{\text{Electrolysis}} \begin{array}{l} CH_3CH_2CH_2 \\ | \\ CH_3CH_2CH_2 \\ \textit{n}\text{-Hexane} \end{array}$$

Acids derived from fats provide starting materials for synthesis of higher homologs:

$$\begin{array}{l} C_{11}H_{23}COO \\ \phantom{C_{11}H_{23}COO}\diagdown Ca \\ C_{11}H_{23}COO\diagup \\ \text{Calcium laurate} \end{array} \xrightarrow[86\%]{\text{0.8 Amp., 45}^\circ} \begin{array}{l} C_{22}H_{46} \\ \textit{n}\text{-Docosane} \end{array}$$

Electrolysis of a mixture of the acid salts RCOOK and R'COOK yields not only the unsymmetrical product RR' but also the two symmetrical hydrocarbons RR and R'R'. The hydrocarbon mixtures usually are separable only with difficulty and the yield of the RR' product is of necessity low. However, a modern adaptation of a crossed Kolbe reaction of different components provided an effective method for the synthesis of compounds otherwise difficultly accessible

$$\begin{array}{c} CH_3 \\ | \\ CH_3(CH_2)_7CHCH_2COONa \end{array} + \ NaOOC(CH_2)_7COOCH_3 \xrightarrow{\text{Electrolysis}}$$
$$\text{I} \text{II}$$

$$\begin{array}{c} CH_3 \\ | \\ CH_3(CH_2)_7CH(CH_2)_8COOCH_3 \end{array} + \begin{array}{c} CH_3 CH_3 \\ | | \\ CH_3(CH_2)_7CHCH_2CH_2CH(CH_2)_7CH_3 \end{array}$$
$$\text{III} \text{IV}$$

$$+ \ CH_3OOC(CH_2)_{14}COOCH_3$$
$$\text{V}$$

TABLE 4.4. CONSTANT BOILING MIXTURES

	HX	MOLES/L.	B.P.
	%		
Hydriodic acid	57	6.1	127°
Hydrobromic acid	47.5	8.8	126°
Hydrochloric acid	20.2	7.6	110°

(R. P. Linstead[1] and B. C. L. Weedon, 1950). One component is the salt of a monocarboxylic acid, for example, I, and the second the salt of the half-ester of a diacid, II. Electrolysis of a solution of the two salts in methanol gives a mixture of three products, but these are of different types and are easily separated. The desired product III is the ester of a mono acid, one by-product is a hydrocarbon (IV), and the other, V, is the diester of a diacid. Saponification of the mixture with alkali converts III and V into ether-insoluble salts from which the hydrocarbon can be separated by extraction with ether. Acidification of the sodium salt mixture gives a mixture of the monoacid from III, m.p. 18°, and the diacid from IV, m.p. 122°; the two differ markedly in solubility as well as in melting point and are easily separated. Variations in this anodic synthesis have afforded a number of interesting acids.

4.5   From Alcohols via Alkyl Halides. — The methods for conversion of alcohols into alkanes to be discussed in this chapter involve initial conversion to an alkyl halide. In one procedure the alcohol is heated with an aqueous solution of hydrogen halide, if necessary at the reflux temperature. Since the reaction rate decreases with decreasing concentration of acid, both the compositions and boiling points of the constant-boiling mixtures (Table 4.4) place the acids in the following order of decreasing effectiveness: HI > HBr > HCl. Hydrochloric acid clearly can operate only at a concentration and a temperature much lower than those attainable with the other two acids. Furthermore, the relative reactivity at equivalent concentrations is in the same order. Note that the order of reactivity can be inferred from the bond energies, that is, the energy in kcal./mole required to break the H—X bond (see Table, 32.2): HCl, 103; HBr, 87.5; HI, 71. Thus ordinary alcohols are convertible into the corresponding iodides or bromides by the HX-method but not into the chlorides.

4.6   Wurtz and Wurtz-Fittig Syntheses. — Whatever doubts remained about the validity of Brodie's suggestion that the reaction described by Kolbe had involved the doubling up of two alkyl radicals were dispelled by the work of the French chemist Adolphe Wurtz[2] in 1855. If the reactions described had afforded compounds of the types C_2H_5—C_2H_5 and C_5H_{11}—C_5H_{11}, it should be possible to prepare a hydrocarbon of mixed type, namely C_2H_5—C_5H_{11}. As a modification of the reaction studied by Frankland, Wurtz investigated the

[1] Sir Patrick Linstead, b. 1902 London; Ph.D. and D.Sc. London (Thorpe); Univ. Sheffield; Harvard Univ.; Imperial College (London)

[2] Adolphe Wurtz, 1817-84; b. Strasbourg; Paris; see biography by A. W. von Hofmann, *Ber.*, **20**, 815-996 (1887)

reaction of a mixture of two alkyl halides with metallic sodium and succeeded in synthesizing a number of new hydrocarbons of the types sought, for example:

$$C_2H_5I + C_5H_{11}I + 2 Na \longrightarrow C_2H_5—C_5H_{11} + 2 NaI$$

Wurtz succeeded in establishing the point at issue at the time because he was an able and hard-working experimentalist. The crossed reaction of halides RI and R'I inevitably gives a mixture of RR', RR, and R'R', and the hydrocarbon RR' is isolable only by laborious fractionation and the yield is low. The reaction now affords a practical method of synthesis only for the coupling of two identical groups. With halides of high molecular weight the yields are often good, and the reaction has served well in the synthesis of higher hydrocarbons starting with alcohols found in nature, for example:

$$2 C_{20}H_{41}Br \xrightarrow[\text{31\% yield}]{Na} C_{40}H_{82}$$
Dihydrophytyl bromide   Perhydrolycopene

$$2\,n\text{-}C_{16}H_{33}I \xrightarrow[\text{70–80\% yield}]{Mg \text{ (ether)}} C_{32}H_{66}$$
Cetyl iodide   n-Dotriacontane

Cetyl iodide (from the alcohol of spermaceti wax) has been converted into the C_{32}-hydrocarbon both by the action of sodium amalgam in alcohol—ether and, as shown in the equation, with use of magnesium in place of sodium.

The Wurtz reaction probably does not follow a free-radical course like the Kolbe synthesis but rather involves formation of an alkylsodium, for example methylsodium (1), which then reacts with a second molecule of alkyl halide (2). That

1. $CH_3I + 2 Na \rightarrow CH_3Na + NaI$
2. $CH_3Na + ICH_3 \rightarrow CH_3CH_3 + NaI$
3. $CH_3CH_2ONa + BrCH_2CH_3 \rightarrow CH_3CH_2OCH_2CH_3 + NaBr$

the intermediate has not been isolated means that the activation energy of the second step is less than that of the first step. The reaction is analogous to the **Williamson synthesis** (3), in which a sodium alkoxide reacts with an alkyl halide to form an ether. Williamson,[1] who had studied with Liebig at Giessen, devised this synthesis (1850) in order to establish the relationship between ethyl alcohol and diethyl ether postulated by Liebig. The reaction involves a stable sodio derivative and hence is as satisfactory for the preparation of mixed ethers as in the synthesis of those of symmetrical structure.

Wurtz had also worked with Liebig after his first indoctrination into chemistry at his birthplace, Strasbourg. Strasbourg was temporarily lost by France in the Franco-Prussian war, and German professors replaced the French staff. Rudolph Fittig,[2] who succeeded the German Baeyer to the "Strassburg" chair in 1876, devised a modification of the Wurtz reaction which became known as the Wurtz-

[1] Alexander W. Williamson, 1824–1904; b. Wandsworth, England; Ph.D. Giessen (Liebig); University College, London

[2] Rudolph Fittig, 1835–1910; b. Hamburg, Germany; Ph.D. Göttingen; Univ. Strasbourg

Fittig synthesis. Fittig found that unsymmetrical coupling is practicable between an alkyl halide and an aryl halide (4). The reaction succeeds because the

$$\text{4.} \quad ArX + RX + 2\,Na \rightarrow ArR + ArAr + RR + 2\,NaX$$

three products are of different types, and hence are easily separated. For example, if methyl bromide is condensed with bromobenzene in the presence of two equivalents of sodium with the object of preparing toluene (b.p. 111°), the by-products are ethane (a gas) and diphenyl (b.p. 254°). The reaction is illustrated (5) by the synthesis of *p*-xylene from either *p*-dibromobenzene or *p*-bromotoluene, and (6) by a particularly favorable synthesis of a mixed alkyl-aryl hydrocarbon requiring little excess alkyl halide.

5.

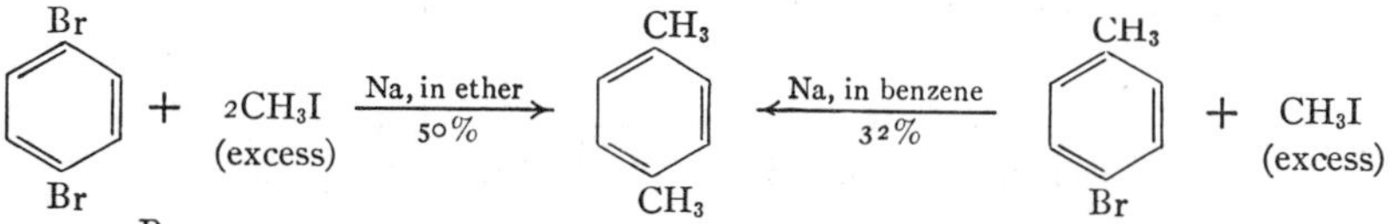

6.

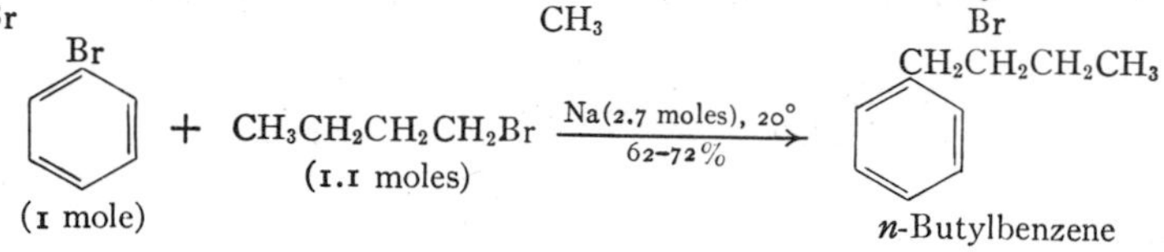

4.7   Reduction; the Grignard Reaction.

— Alkyl halides in some instances can be reduced directly to hydrocarbons:

$$RX + 2\,H \text{ (reducing agent)} \longrightarrow RH + HX$$

Reductions have been accomplished with zinc and hydrochloric acid, with the zinc—copper couple in alcohol, with magnesium amalgam and water, with hydrogen in the presence of palladium catalyst, and by heating the iodide with hydriodic acid in a sealed tube. Examples are as follows:

$$C_2H_5I + HI \xrightarrow{\text{High temp.}} C_2H_6 + I_2$$

$$CH_3CH_2CH_2CH_2I \xrightarrow[\text{nearly quantitative}]{Mg(Hg),\ ROH} CH_3CH_2CH_2CH_3$$

$$\underset{\substack{\text{Ceryl iodide}\\ \text{(alcohol from Chinese wax)}}}{C_{26}H_{53}I} \xrightarrow[68\%]{Zn-HCl} \underset{\text{Cerane}}{C_{26}H_{54}}$$

Some bromides and iodides can be reduced with lithium aluminum hydride; 1-bromodecane affords *n*-decane in 72% yield.

An efficient method for the indirect reduction of an alkyl halide consists in reaction of the halide in ether with magnesium to form an alkylmagnesium halide, which on treatment with water affords the alkane. The first reaction usually

$$RI + Mg \longrightarrow \underset{\substack{\text{Alkylmagnesium iodide}\\ \text{(Grignard reagent)}}}{RMgI} \xrightarrow{H_2O} RH + HOMgI$$

proceeds in high yield; the decomposition of the alkylmagnesium halide is quantitative. The reaction with water is only one of a large number of reactions exhibited by the versatile alkylmagnesium halides. These organometallic compounds were discovered by Victor Grignard[1] in 1901 at the University of Lyon, France, and they proved so extraordinarily useful in synthesis that the Nobel Prize of 1912 was awarded to Grignard. Readily prepared in ethereal solution, the compounds are called **Grignard reagents.**

Ether is not merely a convenient solvent but forms a dietherate essential to the reaction. The electronic formulation shows that a Grignard reagent func-

$$\text{R:Mg:X:} \quad + \quad 2\text{C}_2\text{H}_5\text{:O:C}_2\text{H}_5 \quad \rightarrow \quad \begin{array}{c} \overset{..+}{\text{C}_2\text{H}_5\text{:O:C}_2\text{H}_5} \\ \text{R:Mg}^{=}\text{:X:} \\ \overset{..+}{\text{C}_2\text{H}_5\text{:O:C}_2\text{H}_5} \end{array}$$

Diethyl ether

Grignard reagent dietherate

tions as a Lewis acid in combining with two electron-donor ether molecules to form a complex in which magnesium is surrounded by an electron octet. Since each oxygen has donated one electron to magnesium for sharing, each oxygen acquires a positive charge and magnesium acquires a negative charge of two. Magnesium is bonded to each oxygen by the combination of a shared electron pair, a covalent bond, and also by a polar bond. The part polar part nonpolar link is called a **coordinate covalent bond** or a **semipolar bond.**

Alkyl iodides, bromides, and chlorides, whether primary, secondary, or tertiary, are convertible into Grignard reagents. Bromobenzene reacts satisfactorily to give phenylmagnesium bromide, but chlorobenzene lacks adequate reactivity. The magnesium, as either thin turnings or granules, is covered with absolute

$$\underset{\text{Bromobenzene}}{\text{C}_6\text{H}_5\text{Br}} \quad + \quad \text{Mg} \quad \longrightarrow \quad \underset{\text{Phenylmagnesium bromide}}{\text{C}_6\text{H}_5\text{MgBr}}$$

ether in a flask fitted with a reflux condenser, and about one tenth of the total amount of halide is added. If reaction does not start promptly, the mixture is heated briefly on the steam bath, a trace of iodine is added as catalyst, or a piece of metal is crushed against the bottom of the flask with a flattened stirring rod. Once the reaction starts, the ether refluxes so briskly without application of heat that cooling in ice may be necessary. When the reaction has started and is under control, the remainder of the halide is dropped in from a separatory funnel. A trace of water in the ether or a film of moisture in the flask not only destroys an equivalent amount of Grignard reagent but also may prevent the reaction from starting.

A variation is required in the synthesis of n-pentane (b.p. 36.1°) from 2-bromopentane because the boiling point is close to that of diethyl ether (b.p. 34.6°). A satisfactory procedure utilizes di-n-butyl ether (b.p. 141°). Alkylation of a Grignard reagent extends the scope of the synthesis. In example (1) the alkylat-

[1] Victor Grignard, 1871–1935; b. Cherbourg; Univ. Nancy, Lyon; Nobel Prize 1912; *J. Chem. Soc.*, 171 (1937)

ing agent is diethyl sulfate, in (2) it is dimethyl sulfate.   At the end of the reaction, excess sulfate ester and magnesium salts are hydrolyzed by refluxing with

1. $C_6H_5CH_2Cl$ $\xrightarrow[\text{Ether}]{\text{Mg}}$ $C_6H_5CH_2MgCl$ $\xrightarrow[70\text{-}75\%]{2 \ (CH_3CH_2O)_2SO_2}$ $C_6H_5CH_2CH_2CH_3$

n-Propylbenzene

$+ \begin{cases} CH_3CH_2Cl \\ (CH_3CH_2OSO_2O)_2Mg \end{cases}$

2.

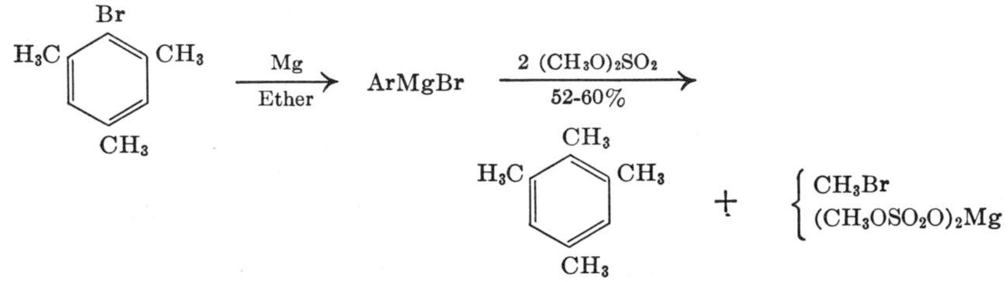

Isodurene
m. p. $-24°$

aqueous alkali (1) or sodium ethoxide (2).

Methylmagnesium iodide not only reacts with water with quantitative liberation of methane, but it reacts in the same way with organic compounds containing
an OH or NH group or other group having an active hydrogen.   Added to a solution of excess methylmagnesium iodide, a primary, secondary, or tertiary alcohol
liberates an equivalent amount of methane; so does a carboxylic acid, a primary

$$CH_3MgI + \begin{cases} H_2O \\ ROH \\ RCOOH \\ RNH_2 \\ R_2NH \\ RC\equiv CH \end{cases} \rightarrow CH_4 + \begin{cases} HOMgI \\ ROMgI \\ RCOOMgI \\ RNHMgI \\ R_2NMgI \\ RC\equiv CMgI \end{cases}$$

amine, or a secondary amine.   Tertiary amines, ethers, and esters have no active
hydrogen.   Only one of the two hydrogens of water or of a primary amine reacts;
the hydrogen in the MgI-compound produced is inert.   Alkanes and alkenes are
inert to methylmagnesium iodide; an alkyne of the type $RC\equiv CR$ is also inert,
but one of the type $RC\equiv CH$ liberates one mole of methane.   Since the volume
of methane produced is easily measured, the reaction affords a useful analytical
method for determination of the number of active hydrogens present in a compound (Zerewitinoff determination, 12.26).

W. Schlenk[1] and W. Schlenk, Jr.[2] (1929) postulated that in an ethereal solution
of a Grignard reagent the species RMgX is in equilibrium with the dialkylmag-

[1] Wilhelm Schlenk, Sr., 1879–1943; b. Munich; Ph.D. Munich; Univ. Jena, Vienna, Berlin,
Tübingen
[2] Wilhelm Schlenk, Jr., b. 1907 Munich; Ph.D. Techn. Hochschule Berlin (Pschorr); BASF
Ludwigshafen/Rhine

nesium and magnesium bromide, and indeed a solution of these components behaves like a Grignard reagent prepared in the usual way. Diethylmagnesium is

$$2 \ C_2H_5MgBr \rightleftharpoons (C_2H_5)_2Mg + MgBr_2$$

prepared by treating an ethereal solution of the ethyl Grignard reagent with dioxane, which precipitates virtually all the halogen and part of the magnesium; after centrifugation, the clear supernatant liquid is evaporated in vacuum and the residue is baked in vacuum at 150° for removal of dioxane bound as a complex. Diethylmagnesium so prepared is a solid, soluble in ether and of reactivity comparable to that of a Grignard reagent. Magnesium bromide, as well as ethylmagnesium bromide, forms an ether-soluble coordinate covalent complex with ether; since dioxane

Dioxane
(b. p. 101.3°)

has two oxygen atoms to function as Lewis bases, it forms complexes which are insoluble in ether. If ethylmagnesium bromide is indeed the initial product of reaction of ethyl bromide with magnesium, the forward reaction in the equilibrium postulated has thus been demonstrated. The reverse reaction, however, is not so clear. R. E. Dessy[1] (1957) added radioactive $Mg^{28}Br_2$ to a solution of nonisotopic diethylmagnesium and found that even after 36 hrs. the extent of exchange was only about one tenth that expected on the basis of the postulated equilibrium. The observation suggests that the reactants participate in a more important equilibrium which does not necessitate exchange of metal atoms, namely, combination to form a complex:

$$(C_2H_5)_2Mg + MgBr_2 \rightleftharpoons (C_2H_5)_2Mg(MgBr_2)$$

Conductivity data indicate that magnesium bromide is a Lewis base, and diethylmagnesium obviously can function as a Lewis acid. Since the complex should be more stable and less reactive than unbound diethylmagnesium, an explanation is at hand for the observation that the reaction of hexyne-1 with diethylmagnesium is about three times as fast as the reaction under comparable conditions with ethyl Grignard reagent. Although the complex $R_2Mg(MgBr_2)$ thus appears to be the chief species present in a solution of a Grignard reagent, the formula RMgX will be used in this book for simplicity. Thus the reaction of hexyne-1 can be represented as proceeding through the transition state formulated:

$$n\text{-}C_4H_9C{\equiv}C{-}H \qquad n\text{-}C_4H_9C{\equiv}C \cdots H \qquad n\text{-}C_4H_9C{\equiv}C \ + \ H$$
$$Br{-}Mg{-}C_2H_5 \quad \longrightarrow \quad Br{-}Mg \cdots C_2H_5 \quad \longrightarrow \quad Br{-}Mg \qquad C_2H_5$$

Transition state

The dotted lines represent bonds that are in the process of forming or in the process of breaking, and each one represents half a valence; thus each atom participating in a transition state retains its normal valence.

4.8   **Calculation of Formal Charge.** — The validity of an electronic formula containing charged atoms, for example, that of the Grignard reagent dietherate, can be checked by calculation of the formal charge on each atom from

[1] Raymond E. Dessy, b. 1931 Reynoldsville, Pa.; Ph.D. Pittsburgh (Hollingsworth); Univ. Cincinnati

the following equation:

$$F \text{ (formal charge)} = \text{Valence electrons} - \frac{\text{Shared electrons}}{2} - \text{Unshared electrons}$$

In the true meaning of the expression the first term on the right is actually the positive charge on the nucleus, which is numerically equivalent to the number of valence electrons. Calculations for the Grignard reagent dietherate are as follows: for Mg, $F = 2 - 8/2 - 0 = -2$; for each oxygen, $F = 6 - 6/2 - 2 = +1$.

4.9　　　　Decarboxylation. — When solid sodium acetate is fused with sodium hydroxide (m. p. 318°) or heated with the less fusible soda lime [NaOH–Ca(OH)₂], the salt decomposes with liberation of methane and formation of sodium carbonate. The reaction demonstrates that the acetate ion of the one

$$\overset{\displaystyle O}{\underset{\displaystyle}{CH_3\overset{\parallel}{C}}}-O^-Na^+ + Na^+O^-H \xrightarrow{\text{Fuse}} CH_4 + O{=}C\overset{\displaystyle O^-Na^+}{\underset{\displaystyle O^-Na^+}{\Big\langle}}$$

salt is less stable than the carbonate ion of the other, and the resonance theory accounts for the difference: the acetate ion is stabilized by resonance between two structures (2.24), whereas the carbonate ion is stabilized by resonance among three. X-ray analysis of crystalline carbonates shows that the three oxygens

$$O{=}C\overset{O^-}{\underset{O^-}{\Big\langle}} \longleftrightarrow {}^-O{-}C\overset{O}{\underset{O^-}{\Big\langle}} \longleftrightarrow {}^-O{-}C\overset{O^-}{\underset{O}{\Big\langle}}$$

lie in a plane with the carbon atom and are equidistant from the carbon atom and from one another. The interatomic distance between carbon and each oxygen is 1.30 Å, whereas in a nonresonating system the average distance of one C=O link (1.21 Å) and two C—O links (1.42 Å) would be 1.35 Å.

Decarboxylation of ordinary aliphatic acids has little preparative value because high temperatures are required and the yields are low, particularly with the long-chain acids available from fats. Certain other acids, however, have structural features which markedly facilitate decarboxylation. Thus salts of trichloroacetic acid undergo decarboxylation in aqueous solution at temperatures as low as 50°. Since the free acid itself is much more stable in solution, the reaction must involve the anion. A mechanistic interpretation (F. H. Verhoek, 1934–47) is based upon the well-established fact that a chlorine atom linked to carbon is electron-attracting. The three chlorine atoms of the anion put an inductive pull on the electron pair shared by the two carbon atoms to the extent that this pair is captured by the chlorinated carbon, as a lone pair on the ionic oxygen moves in to be shared

$$\begin{array}{c} \overset{Cl}{\underset{Cl}{Cl\!:\!C\!:}} \overset{O}{\underset{}{C\!:\!O\!:}} \longrightarrow \overset{Cl}{\underset{Cl}{Cl\!:\!C\!:}} + \overset{O}{\underset{}{C\!::\!O}} \end{array}$$

$$\text{Anion} \qquad\qquad \text{Carbanion}$$

$$\underset{}{\Big\lfloor} \xrightarrow{H^+} Cl_3CH$$

with the oxygenated carbon. The result is liberation of carbon dioxide and formation of a transient carbanion, which combines with a proton to form chloroform. Calculation of the formal charge on carbon validates the structure
attributed to the carbanion: $4 - 3 - 2 = -1$.

The case cited involves three powerfully electron-attracting groups, but even
one group having a mild inductive effect in the same direction may make decarboxylation a practical preparative reaction. The phenyl group is electron
attracting, and the first fully pure sample of benzene was made by decarboxylation
of benzoic acid by heating it with soda lime. Aromatic acids can generally be
decarboxylated in satisfactory yield. Since the vinyl group (CH_2=CH—) is
also electron-attracting, a carboxyl group linked to an olefinic carbon usually can
be eliminated as carbon dioxide. The preferred procedure uses the tertiary
heterocyclic amine quinoline (2.28) as the base for production of the required
anion and employs a trace of copper chromite as catalyst; the copper salt of the
acid to be decarboxylated also serves as a satisfactory catalyst. An example is
the preparation of cis-stilbene by decarboxylation of cis-α-phenylcinnamic acid.
A solution of the acid in quinoline containing a suspension of copper chromite is

$$
\begin{array}{ccc}
C_6H_5-C-COOH & & C_6H_5-C-H \\
\parallel & \xrightarrow[\substack{Cu-Cr \\ Quinoline \\ 75\%}]{} & \parallel \quad + \quad CO_2 \\
C_6H_5-C-H & & C_6H_5-C-H \\
\end{array}
$$

cis-α-Phenylcinnamic   cis-Stilbene (m. p. 6°)
    acid (m. p. 174°)

kept just below the boiling point of the solvent (238°) until decarboxylation is
complete, and the hydrocarbon is isolated by extracting the cooled mixture with
ether and removal of the quinoline by extraction with dilute mineral acid. Evaporation of the dried ethereal solution affords a residue consisting of the hydrocarbon (75% yield).

REACTIONS OF ALKANES

4.10   Stability. — Alkanes are relatively inert, chemically, since they are
indifferent to reagents which react readily with alkenes or with
alkynes. n-Hexane, for example, is not attacked by concentrated sulfuric acid,
boiling nitric acid, molten sodium hydroxide, potassium permanganate, or chromic
acid; with the exception of sodium hydroxide, these reagents all attack alkenes at
room temperature. The few reactions of which alkanes are capable require a
high temperature or special catalysis.

4.11   Halogenation. — If a test tube containing n-hexane is put in a dark
place and treated with a drop of bromine, the original color will remain
undiminished in intensity for days. If the solution is exposed to sunlight, the
color fades in a few minutes, and breathing across the mouth of the tube produces
a cloud of condensate revealing hydrogen bromide as one reaction product. The
reaction is a photochemical substitution:

$$C_6H_{14} + Br_2 \xrightarrow{Light} C_6H_{13}Br + HBr$$

Chlorination of alkanes is more general and more useful than bromination and
can be effected not only photochemically but also by other methods.

Light initiates chlorination of an alkane by converting chlorine molecules into chlorine atoms by a process of **homolysis** (Gr. *homos*, same; *lysis*, loosing), in which a covalent bond is severed and one electron is retained by each of the atoms forming the bond: $Cl:Cl \rightarrow Cl\cdot + \cdot Cl$. A chlorine atom has an odd, or unpaired, electron and is a free radical. Because of the tendency of atoms to attain their normal valence shells, any free radical is a highly reactive species. Photochemical chlorination proceeds through a succession of free radicals; it is a **free radical chain reaction**. The chain initiating step (1), homolytic fission of chlorine molecules, produces chlorine free radicals; in chain propagating steps, a chlorine

Initiation:

Heat of reaction, kcal./mole

1. $Cl:Cl \xrightarrow{\text{Light energy}} Cl\cdot + \cdot Cl$ $\Delta H = +58$

Propagation:

2. $Cl\cdot + R:H \rightarrow R\cdot + HCl$ $\Delta H = +87 - 103 = -16$
3. $R\cdot + Cl:Cl \rightarrow RCl + \cdot Cl$ $\Delta H = +58 - 70 = -12$

Termination:

4. $Cl\cdot + Cl\cdot \rightarrow Cl:Cl$
5. $R\cdot + Cl\cdot \rightarrow R:Cl$

radical attacks a molecule of alkane to produce hydrogen chloride and an alkyl radical (2), which in turn attacks a chlorine molecule to produce a chloroalkane and a chlorine radical (3). Since chlorine radicals required in step (2) are regenerated in step (3), the two reactions together constitute a chain which, if both reactions proceeded with perfect efficiency, would be self-propagating without further requirement of light energy. The efficiency, however, is not perfect, for chlorine radicals can recombine (4), combine with alkyl radicals (5), or dissipate energy by collision with the flask walls. Hence continued radiation is required to maintain an adequate supply of initiating radicals. The chain initiating step requires input of light energy amounting to $+58$ kcal./mole (see table of bond energies, 32.2). Step (2), however, is exothermic, since the energy required to break the C—H bond is less than the bond energy of H—Cl. The second chain propagating step (3) is likewise exothermic, and indeed chlorination of an alkane can proceed explosively.

Photochemical chlorination of methane with a limited amount of chlorine gives a mixture of methyl chloride, methylene chloride (CH_2Cl_2), chloroform ($CHCl_3$), and carbon tetrachloride even though considerable methane is still present. The susceptibility of hydrogen to substitution thus increases in the order: $ClCH_3$ (primary H), Cl_2CH_2 (secondary), Cl_3CH (tertiary). In the light-

$$22\%$$

$$34\% \left\langle \begin{array}{c} H_3C \\ \\ H_3C \end{array} \right\rangle CHCH_2CH_3 \longleftarrow 16\%$$

$$28\%$$

Photochemical chlorination

induced chlorination of isopentane the three types of C—H bonds compete with one another. Four monochloro derivatives are formed in relative amounts indicated in the diagram (H. B. Hass, 1935–36). Two arise from replacement of primary methyl-group hydrogens, and account for 50% of the total, a third from attack of a secondary hydrogen (28%), and a fourth from replacement of a tertiary hydrogen (22%). However, the starting material contains 9 primary hydrogens, two secondary, and only one tertiary hydrogen atom, and in consideration of this statistical factor the results show that the order of reactivity is tertiary > secondary > primary.

Free-radical reactions can be induced to occur in one or all of three ways: by light, by heat, and under catalysis by a peroxide capable of ready homolytic decomposition to free radicals: $RO:OR' \rightarrow RO\cdot + \cdot OR'$. Kharasch[1] developed a method for the low-temperature chlorination of alkanes utilizing sulfuryl chloride catalyzed by dibenzoyl peroxide (1939):

$$RH + SO_2Cl_2 \xrightarrow[40\text{-}80°]{\text{Peroxide}} RCl + HCl + SO_2$$

In the initiating steps the peroxide dissociates to two benzoate radicals (1), these lose carbon dioxide to give the phenyl radical (2), which attacks sulfuryl chloride with formation of the radical $\cdot SO_2Cl$ (3). In a chain propagating process, a

1. $C_6H_5\overset{O}{\underset{\|}{C}}{-}O{:}O{-}\overset{O}{\underset{\|}{C}}C_6H_5 \longrightarrow 2\ C_6H_5\overset{O}{\underset{\|}{C}}{-}O\cdot$

2. $C_6H_5\overset{O}{\underset{\|}{C}}{-}O\cdot \longrightarrow C_6H_5\cdot + CO_2$

3. $C_6H_5\cdot + SO_2Cl_2 \longrightarrow C_6H_5Cl + \cdot SO_2Cl$

4. $\cdot SO_2Cl \longrightarrow SO_2 + Cl\cdot$

5. $Cl\cdot + RH \longrightarrow HCl + R\cdot$

6. $R\cdot + SO_2Cl_2 \longrightarrow RCl + \cdot SO_2Cl$

chlorine radical is formed (4) and attacks the alkane to give the alkyl radical (5); this attacks the reagent to produce the chlorinated hydrocarbon with regeneration of $\cdot SO_2Cl$ for recycling (6). The results summarized for the reaction of n-heptane show a pattern of distribution similar to photochemical chlorination: the ratio

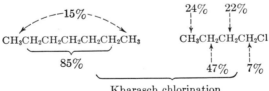

Kharasch chlorination

of secondary:primary hydrogens is 5:3, but the ratio of attack is 6:1. In the chlorination of 1-chlorobutane a second chlorine prefers a position remote from the first. Of the two unchlorinated CH₂ groups available, the more distant one is

[1] Morris S. Kharasch, 1895–1957; b. Kremenetz, Ukraine; Ph.D. Chicago (Piccard); Univ. Chicago; Proc. Chem. Soc., 361 (1958)

favored by a factor of about 2:1; these secondary positions are more reactive than the primary methyl group even though this group is still more distant. Attack at the chlorine-containing position is minor, even though methyl chloride, which offers no alternative site, reacts 4.4 times as fast as methane.

Thermal halogenation is illustrated by the Sharples Co. process for chlorination of a petroleum fraction (b.p. 29–39°) containing *n*-pentane and isopentane. The reaction is conducted in the vapor phase at 200° in the dark and without catalyst; initiating chlorine radicals are produced thermally. Chlorine is fed continuously at the rate of 22 tons per day into a 60-mile an hour stream of hot pentane vapor. The percentages of the monochloropentanes formed, considered with allowance

41%
33%

$$CH_3CH_2CH_2CH_2CH_3 \qquad 34\% \quad \begin{array}{c} H_3C \\ \\ H_3C \end{array}\!\!> CHCH_2CH_3 \longleftarrow 45\%$$

26%
10%
11%

n-Pentane   Isopentane

for the statistical factor, show a preference for tertiary over secondary hydrogen atoms but not for secondary over primary, as in the photochemical reaction. To be sure, the reactions are conducted at widely different temperatures.

Photochemical bromination follows the same pattern as chlorination except that the reaction is usually endothermic, since a C—H bond is generally stronger than the H—Br bond:

$$\cdot Br + CH_3\!-\!H \longrightarrow H\!-\!Br + \cdot CH_3$$
$$\Delta H = 91 - 87.5 = +3.5 \text{ kcal./mole}$$

Bromine radicals are so much more selective than chlorine radicals that tertiary halides are often obtainable in high yield; for example, $(CH_3)_3CCH(CH_3)_2$ affords $(CH_3)_3CCBr(CH_3)_2$ in 96% yield. Iodine is too inert to effect substitution, and indeed the reverse reaction can be realized: $RI + HI \rightarrow RH + I_2$. Fluorine attacks alkanes with explosive violence.

4.12   **Conversion to Acid Chlorides.** — In the presence of actinic radiation (hν) in a weakly basic medium the reaction of an alkane with sulfuryl chloride results in introduction of the chlorosulfonyl group:

$$RH + SO_2Cl_2 \xrightarrow[50\%]{h\nu \text{ (pyridine)}} RSO_2Cl + HCl$$

The same reaction can be accomplished by use of sulfur dioxide and chlorine under illumination, when presumably the steps are as shown in equations 1–4. Propane affords about equal amounts of the two possible isomers. Cyclohexane

$$\begin{array}{ll} \text{1. } Cl_2 & \longrightarrow \quad 2 \cdot Cl \\ \text{2. } RH + \cdot Cl & \longrightarrow \quad R\cdot + HCl \\ \text{3. } R\cdot + SO_2 & \longrightarrow \quad RSO_2\cdot \\ \text{4. } RSO_2\cdot + Cl_2 & \longrightarrow \quad RSO_2Cl + Cl\cdot \end{array}$$

yields a single product. The products of the formula RSO_2Cl are the acid chlorides of alkylsulfonic acids, RSO_2OH, and they are called alkylsulfonyl chlorides.

$$CH_3CH_2CH_3 \xrightarrow{SO_2,\ Cl_2,\ h\nu,\ 50°} CH_3CH_2CH_2SO_2Cl + (CH_3)_2CHSO_2Cl$$
$$\qquad\qquad\qquad\qquad\qquad\quad 48\% \qquad\qquad\qquad 52\%$$

They are hydrolyzed readily to the alkylsulfonic acids, which are water-soluble and strongly acidic like sulfuric acid. The sodium salts are sodium alkylsulfonates, $RSO_3^-Na^+$, and if the alkyl group is of the proper size such a substance has properties similar to those of a soap and may have application as a detergent or other surface-active agent. A large alkyl group confers lipophilic, or lipidlike properties, and the ionic sodium sulfonate group is hydrophilic, or water-seeking. With an alkyl group having 10–14 carbon atoms, the substance has the proper balance between lipophilic and hydrophilic properties to produce an emulsion of fat or oil in water. Thus synthetic detergents are prepared by chlorosulfonation of a suitable hydrocarbon fraction from petroleum, followed by saponification.

A related reaction, introduction of the —COCl group by reaction of an alkane with phosgene, $COCl_2$, or with oxalyl chloride, $(COCl)_2$, is induced by either light or a peroxide. The products are acid chlorides of carboxylic acids. The reaction proceeds more readily with cycloparaffins, for example cyclohexane, than with

Cyclohexane   Cyclohexanecarboxylic acid chloride

straight-chain paraffins. The process likewise involves a chain mechanism and is formulated as in 1–4.

1. $(COCl)_2 \longrightarrow 2\,CO + 2\,Cl\cdot$
2. $RH + Cl\cdot \longrightarrow R\cdot + HCl$
3. $R\cdot + (COCl)_2 \longrightarrow RCOCl + \cdot COCl$
4. $\cdot COCl \longrightarrow CO + Cl\cdot$

4.13   **Cracking.** — Heated to temperatures in the range 500–700°, higher alkanes undergo pyrolytic rupture or cracking to mixtures of smaller molecules, some saturated and some unsaturated.

The type of reactions involved in thermal cracking are shown in the formulation. Homolysis of a covalent bond (1) produces two free radicals, each of which reacts further in various ways. For example, a radical (2) may abstract hydrogen

1. $CH_3CH_2CH_2\overset{\text{H H}}{\underset{\text{H H}}{C:C}}CH_2CH_2CH_3 \longrightarrow CH_3CH_2CH_2\dot{C}H_2 + \dot{C}H_2CH_2CH_2CH_3$

2. $CH_3CH_2CH_2\dot{C}H_2 + CH_3CH_2CH_2CH_2CH_2CH_2CH_2CH_3 \longrightarrow$
$$\qquad\qquad CH_3CH_2CH_2CH_3 + CH_3CH_2CH_2CH_2\dot{C}HCH_2CH_3$$

3. $CH_3CH_2CH_2CH_2CH_2\dot{C}HCH_2CH_3 \longrightarrow CH_3CH_2CH_2\dot{C}H_2 + CH_2{=}CHCH_2CH_3$

TABLE 4.5. HEATS OF COMBUSTION

HYDROCARBON		KCAL. PER MOLE	KCAL. PER GRAM	%H	KCAL. PER ML.
NAME	FORMULA				
Methane	CH_4	212.8	13.3	25.1	5.6
Ethane	C_2H_6	372.8	12.4	20.1	6.7
Propane	C_3H_8	530.6	12.2	18.3	6.9
Isobutane	C_4H_{10}	688.0	11.9	17.3	6.8
n-Pentane	C_5H_{12}	845.2	11.6	16.8	7.3
n-Hexane	C_6H_{14}	995.0	11.6	16.4	7.6
n-Heptane	C_7H_{16}	1151.3	11.5	16.1	7.8
n-Octane	C_8H_{18}	1307.5	11.5	15.9	8.0
n-Decane	$C_{10}H_{22}$	1620.1	11.4	15.6	8.3
n-Hexadecane	$C_{16}H_{34}$	2559	11.3	15.1	8.8
n-Eicosane	$C_{20}H_{42}$	3183	11.3	15.0	8.8

from an alkane to produce a small alkane and a new large radical; the large radical may then suffer fission to a smaller radical and an alkene (3). By these and other reactions discussed in Chapter 7, large molecules are converted into mixtures of smaller alkanes and alkenes, and hence petroleum fractions of boiling point too high for use as motor fuels are converted by cracking into lower boiling liquids which can be so used. Unsaturated hydrocarbons produced by selective cracking of specific petroleum fractions are useful in chemical synthesis. Cracking ruptures carbon–carbon rather than carbon–hydrogen bonds because the energy required to break the C—C bond is 59 kcal./mole, whereas the C—H bond energy is 87 kcal./mole.

4.14   **Oxidation.** — The reaction of hydrocarbons with oxygen with the output of energy is the basis for use of gasoline as fuel in internal combustion engines. The energy release on burning a given hydrocarbon is expressed as the heat of combustion in terms of kcal.[1]/mole, as in the third column of Table 4.5. The heat release per mole increases regularly with increasing size of the molecule, and in the series shown the average increment is 156 kcal. per methylene group. The fourth column of the table gives a comparison on the basis of equal weights of fuel; methane has the highest heat of combustion per gram and the value falls off fairly sharply at first and then becomes essentially constant starting with the C_8-hydrocarbon. This relationship is correlated with the hydrogen content (fifth column), which is also greatest with methane and then drops to a fairly constant value. The explanation is that the heat of combustion of hydrogen is 33.9 kcal./g., whereas the value for carbon is only 8.08 kcal./g.; hydrocarbons of highest hydrogen content therefore have the advantage. If the weight of a given fuel charge were the only consideration, liquid methane or ethane would appear to represent more efficient fuels than higher hydrocarbons. The volume capacity of a fuel tank, however, is usually a more important limiting factor than the weight, and low molecular weight sub-

[1] One kcal. = 1000 calories = 3,968 B.T.U. (British thermal units).

stances are light and bulky.   Figures for the heats of combustion per ml. (last column) show that in the higher members of the series the increased density more than compensates for a somewhat lower heat value on the weight basis.   The homologous hydrocarbons containing sixteen to twenty carbon atoms release 57% more heat per ml. than methane does.   A fuel tank or an incendiary bomb of a given volume capacity obviously will carry a greater fuel load if charged with higher hydrocarbons than with the lighter members of the series, though a balance must be struck between the fuel load and the particular ignition characteristics required.

Cycloalkanes boil 10–20° higher than normal alkanes of the same carbon content (and of only slightly higher molecular weight).   The most noteworthy contrast in physical properties between the cyclic and noncyclic alkanes is that the former have densities some 20% greater than the latter.   The heat of combustion of cyclohexane on a weight basis is slightly lower than that of n-hexane, namely 939 kcal./mole, or 11.2 kcal./g.; owing to the distinctly greater density, the heat of combustion on a volume basis, 8.7 kcal./ml., is considerably higher than the value (7.6) for the straight-chain hydrocarbon.

Incomplete combustion of gaseous hydrocarbons is important in the manufacture of carbon blacks, particularly lampblack, a pigment for ink, and channel black, used as a filler in rubber compounding.   Natural gas is used because of its cheapness and availability; the yield of black varies with the type of gas and the manufacturing process but usually is in the range of 2–6% of the theoretical amount.

4.15   **Partial air oxidation** of a more limited extent is a means for production of specific oxygenated substances.   Controlled air oxidation of high-boiling mineral oils and waxes from petroleum affords mixtures of higher carboxylic acids similar to those derived from fats and suitable for use in making soaps: $RCH_2CH_2R' \xrightarrow{O_2} RCO_2H + HO_2CR'$.

4.16   **Hydroperoxides.** — The burning of gasoline in an automobile engine is a high-temperature reaction which undoubtedly involves cracking of hydrocarbons to radicals and combination of these radicals with molecular oxygen, which is a diradical (odd electron on each oxygen).   The steps leading eventually to carbon dioxide and water have not been traced in detail.

Study of alkanes of various types at noncracking temperatures has shown that those having a tertiary hydrogen (R_3CH) are the most susceptible to air oxidation.   Furthermore, the reaction is catalyzed by peroxides and sometimes can be conducted at a temperature sufficiently moderate for isolation of the initial product, a highly sensitive **hydroperoxide:** ROOH.   In the initiation step the alkane reacts with oxygen (1a) or, more satisfactorily, with an odd-electron initiator (1b), to produce an alkyl radical; the chain is then propagated by combination with oxy-

$\cdot \ddot{O} \colon \ddot{O} \cdot$

Molecular oxygen

1a. $R_3CH + \cdot O{-}O\cdot \longrightarrow R_3C\cdot + \cdot OOH$

1b. (Initiator)$\cdot + R_3CH \longrightarrow R_3C\cdot + $ (Initiator)$-$H

2. $R_3C\cdot + \cdot O{-}O\cdot \longrightarrow R_3C{:}O{-}O\cdot$

3. $R_3C{:}O{-}O\cdot + R_3CH \longrightarrow R_3COOH + R_3C\cdot$

gen (2) and conversion to the hydroperoxide with regeneration of the alkyl radical (3).   In some cases the reaction is autocatalytic, since hydroperoxides, like peroxides, are free-radical initiators, albeit less effective ones.   A few nontertiary alkane hydroperoxides have been isolated in low yield, but they decompose readily and have no preparative use.

However, a hydrocarbon of mixed aliphatic-aromatic type is the starting material for a commercial process involving a hydroperoxide intermediate.   The hydrocarbon is cumene, or isopropylbenzene, $C_6H_5CH(CH_3)_2$; since the hydrocarbon is now available by synthesis from petroleum, cumene and the products derived from it are petrochemicals.   Cumene has a hydrogen atom which is not only tertiary but which is activated by the unsaturated benzene ring.   If this hydrogen is identified by the number 1, it can be described as activated by a

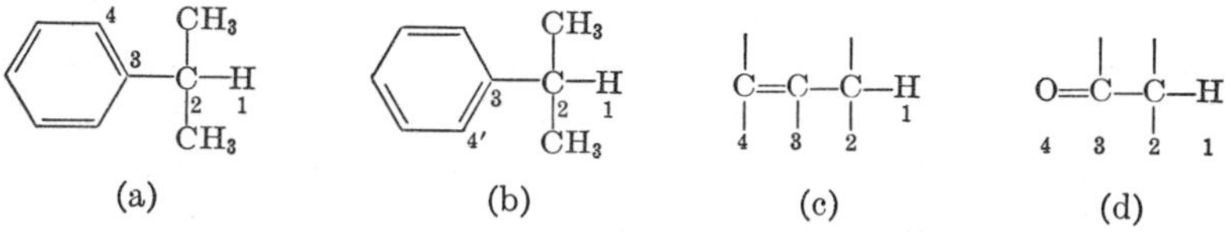

(a)   (b)   (c)   (d)

hybrid unsaturated bond in the 3,4-position of one resonance structure (a) or in the 3,4′-position of the other (b).   Any 3,4-unsaturated group activates an atom or group occupying position 1.   Thus in (c) the 1-hydrogen is activated by a 3,4-ene group, and in (d) the activation is by a carbonyl group.   Activation is manifested in various ways.   Acetic acid has a 1,2,3=4 system and the acti-

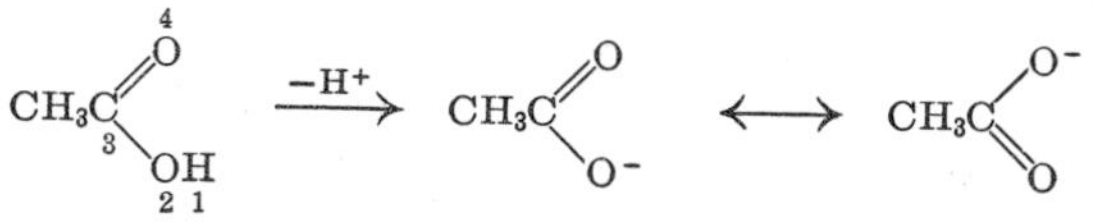

vated 1-hydrogen separates as a proton to give the resonance stabilized, hybrid acetate ion.   In allyl bromide activation of the bromine atom by the 3,4-double bond is demonstrated by the fact that alkaline hydrolysis and similar reactions are 50–100 times faster than the same reactions of n-propyl bromide.   The prob-

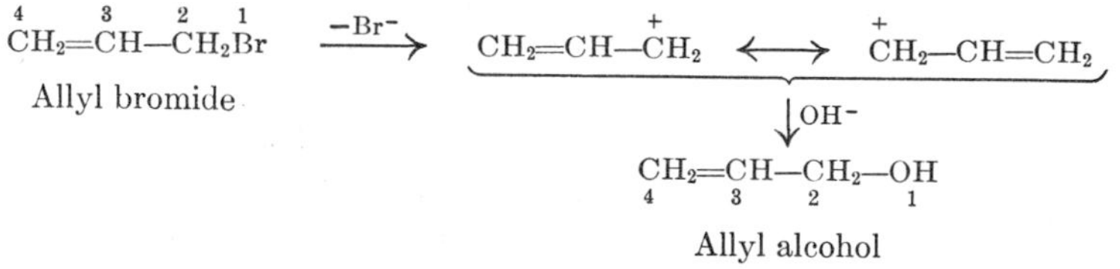

Allyl bromide

Allyl alcohol

able mechanism of the hydrolysis is separation of bromine as bromide ion to produce the allyl **carbonium ion** with a positive charge on carbon.   By migration of the double bond, the positive charge can be shifted to the other terminal carbon and hence the two bonds connecting the carbon atoms are hybrid in character and the charge is distributed over the two terminal carbon atoms.   The opportunity for formation of a resonance-stabilized hybrid carbonium ion provides driving force for the hydrolysis and is responsible for the high rate of reaction.

Dissociation is the rate-controlling step; it is followed immediately by the faster combination with hydroxide ion to form allyl alcohol. In allyl alcohol the whole hydroxyl group occupies position 1 and is activated by the 3,4-double bond; the alcohol is highly reactive and combines rapidly with hydrobromic acid with reformation of allyl bromide.

Activation of the tertiary hydrogen atom of cumene promotes attack by molecular oxygen at or below the reflux temperature of the hydrocarbon (b.p. 152°). Air is blown into the hot liquid in the presence of a trace of sodium hydroxide to inhibit premature decomposition of the sensitive hydroperoxide, which is formed in yield of 89%. The hydroperoxide is then decomposed under catalysis by acid

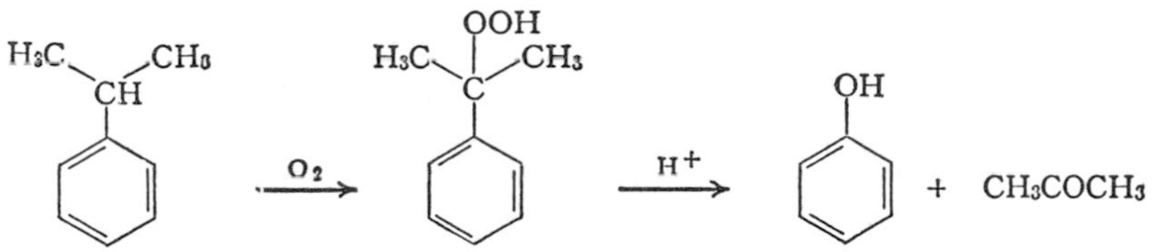

| Cumene | Hydroperoxide | Phenol |

to phenol and acetone; the manufacturing process thus affords two useful petrochemicals. The reaction is a rearrangement, since it involves rupture of a carbon–carbon bond, and consideration of the mechanism will be reserved for discussion along with consideration of related rearrangements.

Conversion of tetralin (1,2,3,4-tetrahydronaphthalene) into the α-hydroperoxide and alkaline decomposition of this intermediate affords a useful preparative route to α-tetralone (*Org. Syn.*[1]). The hydrogen atom displaced is secondary, but it is activated by the adjacent benzene ring. Air is drawn into the hot hydrocarbon at a temperature of 70° until about one tenth of the material

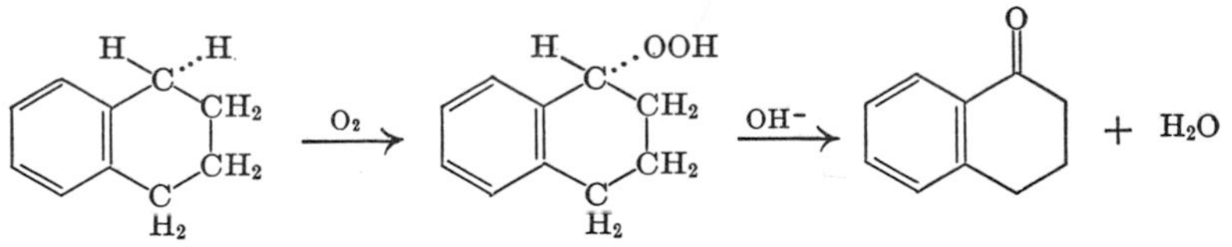

| Tetralin | d- or l- | α-Tetralone |

is converted into the hydroperoxide (for 500 g., about 50 hrs.; mildly exothermic reaction). When stirred with sodium hydroxide solution, the hydroperoxide breaks down to α-tetralone and water; the mixture is dried and fractionated, and considerable hydrocarbon is recovered in usable form. The yield of ketone is about 50% (calculated with allowance for recovered tetralin). The base-catalyzed reaction can be represented as proceeding through the concerted production and destruction of an intermediate transition state. The dotted lines in the formula represent bonds that are in the course of forming or in the course of breaking. Thus the attacking hydroxyl group is partially bonded to hydrogen and the

[1] Procedure of *Organic Syntheses*.

$$\overset{-}{HO} + H-\underset{\underset{R'}{|}}{\overset{\overset{R}{|}}{C}}-O-OH \rightarrow \overset{\delta-}{HO}\cdots H\cdots\underset{\underset{R'}{|}}{\overset{\overset{R}{|}}{C}}\overset{\delta-}{\cdots O\cdots OH} \rightarrow HOH + \underset{\underset{R'}{|}}{\overset{\overset{R}{|}}{C}}=O + \overset{-}{OH}$$

Transition state

charge is distributed over this group and the leaving hydroxyl group, already partially separated from oxygen. The formation and collapse of the transition states are synchronous; the reaction sequence is concerted.

Tetralin-α-hydroperoxide (m.p. 56°) is reduced to the alcohol α-tetralol by a variety of reducing agents including potassium iodide in aqueous acetic acid. Thus its hydroperoxidic character is revealed by a test with starch-iodide paper moistened with dilute acetic acid. When shaken with 22% aqueous sodium hydroxide, tetralin-α-hydroperoxide forms a sodium salt; this salt dissolves in water with hydrolysis.

Notice that tetralin α-hydroperoxide has an asymmetric carbon, whereas the starting material does not. The reaction product is the optically inactive *dl*-mixture.

4.17 **Nitroalkanes.** — The first methods for the preparation of nitroalkanes were introduced by German workers in 1872. Victor Meyer[1] utilized the reaction of an alkyl halide with silver nitrite (1); later investigations showed that the reaction is useful only for the synthesis of primary nitroalkanes (nitroparaffins). Kolbe added one equivalent of sodium nitrite to an aqueous solution

1. $RBr + AgNO_2 \rightarrow RNO_2 + AgBr$

2. $\underset{\underset{Cl}{|}}{CH_2COO^-Na^+} \xrightarrow{NaNO_2} \underset{\underset{O=N^+-O^-}{|}}{CH_2COO^-Na^+} \rightarrow \overset{-}{C}H_2NO_2 + CO_2 + Na^+$

$$\downarrow H_2O$$

$$CH_3NO_2 + NaHCO_3$$
Nitromethane
(b. p. 120°)

of sodium chloroacetate (2) and heated the mixture at 80–85°. Nitromethane is recovered from the mixture by steam distillation and is obtained in yield of 35–38% (*Org. Syn.*). The nitro group contains a semipolar or coordinate covalent bond and hence the nitrogen atom is positively charged and the group is strongly electron-attracting. The inductive effect of the nitro group of nitroacetic acid is comparable to that of the halo substituents in trichloroacetic acid (section 4.9), and hence the nitroacetate ion undergoes ready decarboxylation to the carbanion ($\overset{-}{C}H_2NO_2$), which then affords nitromethane. The yield of nitromethane is low and the method is worthless for the preparation of higher nitroparaffins. An improved laboratory procedure (3) is due to N. Kornblum[2] (1955). A primary

3. $RBr + NaNO_2 \xrightarrow[25°]{\overset{O}{\overset{\|}{H-C-N(CH_3)_2}}} RNO_2 + NaBr$

[1] Victor Meyer, 1848–97; b. Berlin; Univ. Geneva; Zurich ETH; Univ. Heidelberg; *Ber.*, **30**; 2157 (1897); *Proc. Chem. Soc.*, 137 (1959)

[2] Nathan Kornblum, b. 1914 New York; Ph.D. Illinois (Adams); Purdue Univ.

or secondary bromide or iodide is treated with sodium nitrite in solution in dimethylformamide, a liquid of superior solvent power. Urea is sometimes added to increase the solubility of sodium nitrite; dimethylsulfoxide, $(CH_5)_2S^+\!\!-\!\!O^-$, is a more powerful solvent requiring no additive. Yields of 50–60% are realized and the chief by-product is the nitrite ester $(RON\!\!=\!\!O)$. Alkyl chlorides react too slowly to be useful: *t*-butyl bromide is converted into isobutylene.

Tetranitromethane (m.p. 13.8°) is useful as a test reagent because it forms yellow complexes with alkenes (5.11). The preparation (4) requires caution, for the volatile product is toxic and the liquid is liable to explode if overheated.

$$4.\ \ 4(CH_3CO)_2O + 4HNO_3 \rightarrow C(NO_2)_4 + 7CH_3COOH + CO_2$$

The method of F. D. Chattaway (1910) involves nitration of acetic anhydride with an equivalent amount of anhydrous nitric acid (concd. HNO_3 is distilled from a mixture with concd. H_2SO_4), and recovery of the product by addition of water and steam distillation; yield 57–65% (*Org. Syn.*).

Nitromethane, nitroethane, and the two nitrobutanes are produced commercially by vapor-phase nitration (H. B. Hass,[1] 1936). When a gaseous mixture of two moles of hydrocarbon and one mole of nitric acid vapor is passed through a narrow reactor tube at 420° (760 mm. pressure), ethane, propane, and *n*-butane react rapidly. Methane is attacked only slowly at this temperature, but at 475° some 13% of the material is converted in each pass through the reactor into nitromethane, and the recovered hydrocarbon can be recycled. Ethane and the higher homologs behave abnormally in that they afford mixtures containing nitro compounds having fewer carbon atoms than the original hydrocarbon. Ethane yields not only nitroethane (9 parts, b.p. 114.5°) but nitromethane (1 part, b.p. 102°), and propane affords a complex mixture also containing nitromethane:

$$CH_3CH_2CH_3 \xrightarrow{\ HNO_3,\ 420°\ } \begin{cases} CH_3CH_2CH_2NO_2\ (32\ parts) \\ \underset{\underset{NO_2}{|}}{CH_3CHCH_3}\ (33\ parts) \\ CH_3CH_2NO_2\ (26\ parts) \\ CH_3NO_2\ (9\ parts) \end{cases} \begin{array}{l} total \\ yield, \\ 21\% \end{array}$$

The degradative reaction doubtless involves cracking at the elevated temperatures. The nitroalkanes, being nontoxic, noncorrosive, and stable, are useful as solvents, primary fuels, and starting materials in synthesis.

In an investigation of phenylnitromethane, $C_6H_5CH_2NO_2$, Hantzsch[2] (1896) discovered an interesting type of isomerism. The nitro compound, a light yellow oil, gives a neutral test with indicator paper but when shaken with aqueous alkali it slowly dissolves. Careful acidification of the solution at 0° with dilute acetic acid gives a colorless solid, m.p. 84°. This isomeric white substance, which behaves like a true acid (immediately soluble in cold bicarbonate solution), is called the aci-form; on standing it slowly reverts to the more stable nitro-form,

[1] Henry B. Hass, b. 1902 Huntington, Ohio; Ph.D. Ohio State (Evans); Purdue Univ.; Sugar Res. Found.

[2] Arthur Hantzsch, 1857–1935; b. Dresden; Ph.D. Würzburg (R. Schmitt); Univ. Leipzig; *J. Chem. Soc.*, 1451 (1936).

a pseudo acid. The facts are accounted for as follows. The nitro-form is stabilized by resonance in the nitro group (a, b) and it has no ionizable hydrogen. The two hydrogens on carbon, however, are activated by both the phenyl group and the unsaturated nitro group, and migration of an activated hydrogen in the 1—2—3=4 system gives the aci-form (c). This substance is similar to acetic acid, for it has a hydroxyl group on an unsaturated atom; in the presence of base,

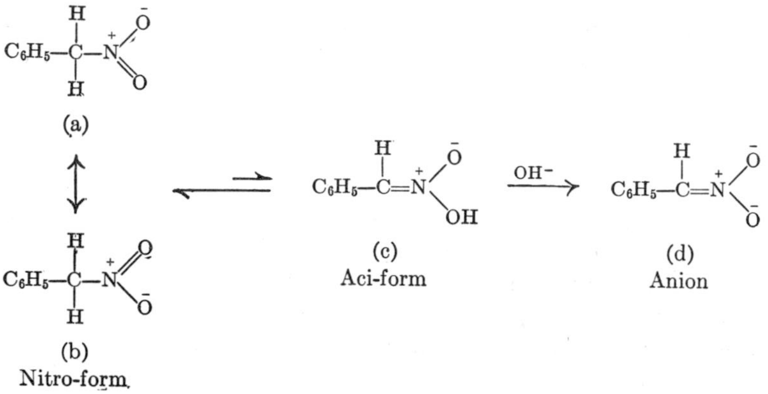

(a)

(c)
Aci-form

(d)
Anion

(b)
Nitro-form.

hydrogen separates as a proton from the new 1—2—3=4 system with formation of the anion (d).

Isomers of this type, which differ in the relative position of a hydrogen atom, are known as **tautomers** (Gr. *tauto-*, the same + *meros*, part); the alternative name **prototropy** is sometimes applied to the phenomenon (proton shift). In the strict sense a tautomeric substance such as phenylnitromethane is a mixture, even though the aci-form is present in only traces. The content of aci-form depends upon the structure; because of the activating effect of the phenyl group, the aci-content of phenylnitromethane exceeds by far that of nitromethane. Tertiary nitro compounds, such as $(CH_3)_3CNO_2$, are incapable of existing in aci-forms.

The standard method for the preparation of phenylnitromethane (*Org. Syn.*) is that of Hantzsch. In the first step (5) benzyl cyanide (e), which has a doubly activated hydrogen, is condensed with methyl nitrate in the presence of sodium

5. $C_6H_5CH—H$ + CH_3ONO_2 ⇌ $C_6H_5CH—N^+=O$ + CH_3OH

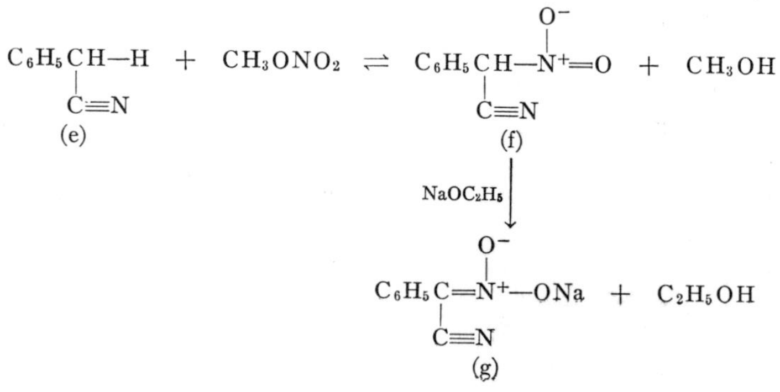

(e)

(f)

NaOC₂H₅

$C_6H_5C=N^+—ONa$ + C_2H_5OH

(g)

$$
\text{6. } \underset{\underset{C\equiv N}{|}}{C_6H_5\,C}\!\!=\!\!\overset{\overset{O^-}{|}}{N^+}\!\!-\!ONa \xrightarrow{\ \text{NaOH, H}_2\text{O}\ } \underset{\underset{COONa}{|}}{C_6H_5\,C}\!\!=\!\!\overset{\overset{O^-}{|}}{N^+}\!\!-\!ONa \ +\ NH_3
$$

(h)

$$
\Big\downarrow\ -CO_2 \ \Big|\ HCl\ (-5°)
$$

$$
C_6H_5\,CH\!\!=\!\!\overset{\overset{O^-}{|}}{N^+}\!\!-\!OH \ \rightarrow\ C_6H_5\,CH_2\overset{\overset{O^-}{|}}{N^+}\!\!=\!O
$$

ethoxide; the splitting out of methyl alcohol is an equilibrium, but the equilibrium is displaced by conversion of the product (f) to the aci-form sodium salt (g). The crude white solid (g) is then added to boiling aqueous alkali (6) to hydrolyze the cyanide group with liberation of ammonia. On cooling, the resulting disodio salt (h) separates as a solid and this is stirred with ice, with external cooling in an ice-salt bath, and carefully acidified (HCl). The carboxyl group liberated is on an unsaturated carbon atom and undergoes decarboxylation even at −5°. Ether extraction gives an only faintly yellow product evidently consisting largely of the aci-form; distillation at 3 mm. gives the yellow nitro-form in overall yield of 56%.

4.18   **Urea Inclusion Compounds.** — A German patent of 1941 (M. F. Bengen) reported that normal alkanes containing seven or more carbon atoms combine with urea to form stable, crystalline complexes. The mode of combination presented a problem. Urea is very soluble in water and insoluble in ether and hence wholly unlike a lipid hydrocarbon. An inert paraffin surely

$$
O\!\!=\!\!C\underset{NH_2}{\overset{NH_2}{<}} \qquad\qquad S\!\!=\!\!C\underset{NH_2}{\overset{NH_2}{<}}
$$

Urea   Thiourea
m. p. 132.7°   m. p. 182°

cannot combine chemically with the amide. The failure of highly branched hydrocarbons to form urea complexes added to the mystery. Research at the ammonia laboratory of the Badische Anilin und Soda Fabrik (W. Schlenk, Jr.) and in various laboratories in the U.S.A. finally clarified the problem in 1949. The complexes are inclusion compounds. X-ray analysis shows that urea molecules in the complex are oriented in the crystal lattice in such a way as to leave a cylindrical channel in which a hydrocarbon such as cetane fits. The guest component (cetane) is not bonded to the host (urea) but merely trapped in the channel. The hydrocarbon can be recovered either by stirring the complex with water to dissolve the urea or by treatment with ether to dissolve the n-cetane and leave a residue of urea. Slow heating in a melting-point capillary drives off the hydrocarbon, and the melting point is that of urea.

The molar proportion of urea in the complex increases with increasing chain length, but the ratio is not necessarily an integral number. Thus n-C_7H_{16} combines with 6 moles of urea, n-$C_{10}H_{22}$ with 8.3 moles, n-$C_{16}H_{34}$ with 12 moles, and

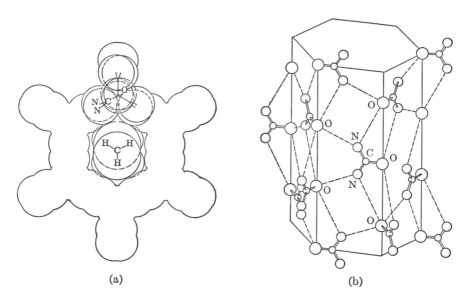

Fɪɢ. 4.4. — *n*-Alkane–Urea Complex.   (a) Cross Section; (b) Hydrogen Bonding
(Courtesy of A. E. Smith)

n-$C_{28}H_{58}$ with 21 moles.   The hole is of such a diameter (5.3 Å) as to accommodate a zig-zag normal alkane molecule but not a thick branched-chain hydrocarbon. Since a terminal functional group does not appreciably alter the space requirement, urea forms inclusion compounds with alcohols, aldehydes, carboxylic acids, and amines derived from *n*-C_7 and higher hydrocarbons.

X-ray analysis reveals the orientation of molecules shown in Fig. 4.4 (A. E. Smith,[1] 1950–52).   Stabilization of the lattice is the result of hydrogen bonding between urea molecules and van der Waals forces between urea molecules themselves and between urea and hydrocarbon molecules.   Three interpenetrating spirals of urea molecules are hydrogen bonded together and form the walls of the channel.   Each oxygen is hydrogen bonded to four nitrogen atoms, and each nitrogen to two oxygen atoms; the hydrogen bonds are of two types, of lengths about 2.93 and 3.04 Å.   The hexagonal arrangement evident from the diagrams accounts for the fact that the channel inclusion compounds all crystallize in hexagonal needles or in hexagonal plates.

Urea complexes are useful for separation of straight-chain from branched-chain hydrocarbons.   The complex of a liquid hydrocarbon (*n*-heptane) can be prepared by shaking a suspension of finely powdered urea for several hours.   A solid hydrocarbon can be converted into its inclusion compound in a solution in 2,2,4-trimethylpentane (isooctane), which forms no complex.   In another procedure an alkane, alcohol, or acid is stirred into a saturated solution of urea in methanol.   In the petroleum industry the urea process is used for improvement of fuels for spe-

[1] Albert E. Smith, b. 1908 Elmira, N. Y.; M.S. Univ. Calif., Berkeley; Shell Development Co.

cific purposes. Treatment of gasoline improves the quality because the straight-chain components cause engine knocking. Removal of n-alkanes from fuel for jet planes lowers the freezing point, since branched-chain hydrocarbons melt considerably lower than straight-chain ones (compare Tables 2.2 and 4.2).

Schlenk, Jr. succeeded (1952) in resolving racemates, for example dl-2-chlorooctane, via the urea complexes. The hexagonal urea lattice can assume either a right-handed or a left-handed form, and the complex of right-handed urea with (+)-2-chlorooctane and that of left-handed urea with (−)-2-chlorooctane have the character of diastereoisomers. When a solution saturated with urea and the racemate is seeded with the (+)-guest component, the crystallizate is enriched in this enantiomer. Thus one crystallization of the diheptyl ester of dl-malic acid, n-$C_7H_{15}O_2CCH_2CH(OH)CO_2C_7H_{15}$-$n$, with urea gave material of 16.3% optical activity and six recrystallizations gave an optically pure product.

Among acetylenic hydrocarbons that form urea inclusion compounds are 1-, 2-, and 3-nonyne and 2-, and 3-decyne; among those that do not are 4-nonyne, 1,8-nonadiyne, and 5-decyne (L. D. Yuhas, 1960).

Thiourea also forms inclusion compounds, but the channel diameter is somewhat larger (about 6.5 Å) and the structural requirements of the guest molecule less specific. Thus 2,2,4-trimethylpentane fits into the channel, but cyclopentane and decahydronaphthalene (decalin) do not. Normal hydrocarbons do not fill the available space to an extent sufficient for stability and hence do not form complexes.

PROBLEMS

1. Suppose you have available all normal acids in the range CH_3CO_2H to n-$C_{12}H_{25}CO_2H$ and wish to synthesize n-$C_{15}H_{31}CO_2H$ by a crossed Kolbe electrolysis. What would be the most favorable and the least favorable combinations?

2. Suppose you had carried out a Wurtz synthesis with a mixture of $CH_3(CH_2)_5Br$ and $(CH_3)_2CHCH_2CH_2Br$ with the view to obtaining $CH_3(CH_2)_5CH_2CH_2CH(CH_3)_2$. What technique might you use to simplify the working up of the reaction mixture?

3. Suggest an explanation for the fact that chloroacetic acid and nitroacetic acid are more strongly acidic than acetic acid.

4. Write electronic formulas for the following species and check them by calculation of formal charges: Cl_3C^-, $CH_2{=}CH{-}C^+H_2$, O_2, $C_6H_5CH{=}N^+{-}O^-$.
$$\underset{\underset{\displaystyle OH}{|}}{}$$

5. Diethylmagnesium reacts with excess methanol with liberation of two equivalents of ethane. Formulate the reactions involved.

6. From consideration of the bond energies involved (see Table 22.2), explain why the following reaction can be realized: $RI + HI \rightarrow RH + I_2$.

7. What significant inference can be drawn from the fact that $C_6H_5CH{=}CHCH_2Br$ reacts with potassium acetate (KOAc) to give a mixture of $C_6H_5CH{=}CHCH_2OAc$ and $C_6H_5CH(OAc)CH{=}CH_2$?

8. Is nitromethane associated or unassociated in the liquid phase?

9. An explosive is a substance capable of suddenly decomposing with liberation of a large volume of gas in the space initially occupied by the liquid or solid substance. Explain why tetranitromethane is an explosive whereas nitromethane is not.

10. Why does thiourea accommodate thicker guest molecules than urea?

Chapter 5

ALKENES

5.1   **Physical Properties.** — Alkenes are known also as ethylenic hydrocarbons and as **olefins.**   The term olefin, meaning oil-forming, was applied by early chemists because the gaseous members of the series combine with
chlorine and bromine to form oily addition products.

In the three physical properties listed in Table 5.1 alkenes are hardly distinguishable from the corresponding saturated hydrocarbons.   The boiling points are
no more than a few degrees below those of alkanes of slightly higher molecular
weight, and the densities are a few percent higher; in the first few members of the
two series there is even a marked correspondence in the melting points.   Cycloalkanes differ more from alkanes than alkenes do, and hence ring formation influences physical properties more than introduction of an ethylene linkage.   The
heat of combustion of hexene-1 is practically the same as that of *n*-hexane on
either a weight or volume basis: 952.6 kcal./mole, 11.32 kcal./g., 7.64 kcal./ml.

SYNTHETIC PREPARATION

5.2   **Pyrolytic Dehydration.** — Elimination of water from alcohols is a useful method for the preparation of alkenes; thus on elimination of OH
from one carbon atom and of H from another, ethanol yields ethylene.

One of several experimental procedures is catalytic dehydration.   The alcohol

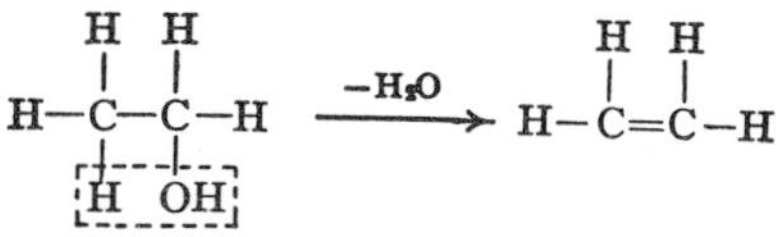

$$\underset{\substack{\lfloor\text{H} \quad \text{OH}\rfloor}}{\overset{\displaystyle \text{H} \quad \text{H}}{\text{H}-\overset{|}{\underset{|}{\text{C}}}-\overset{|}{\underset{|}{\text{C}}}-\text{H}}} \quad \xrightarrow{\;-\text{H}_2\text{O}\;} \quad \overset{\displaystyle \text{H} \quad \text{H}}{\text{H}-\overset{|}{\text{C}}=\overset{|}{\text{C}}-\text{H}}$$

is distilled through a tube packed with granules of alumina and maintained at a
temperature of 350–400° in an electrically heated furnace.   The reaction resembles

134

TABLE 5.1.　PHYSICAL CONSTANTS OF ALKENES

NAME	FORMULA C_nH_{2n}	CARBON STRUCTURE	M.P., °C.	B.P., °C.	SP. GR., LIQUID
Ethylene	C_2H_4	C=C	−169.4	−102.4	0.6100
Propylene	C_3H_6	C·C=C	−185	−47.7	.6104
Butene-1	C_4H_8	C·C·C=C		−6.5	.6255
Butene-2 (*cis*)	C_4H_8	C·C=C·C	−139.3	−3.7	
Isobutylene	C_4H_8	C·C=C C	−140.7	−6.6	.6266
Pentene-1	C_5H_{10}	C·C·C·C=C		30.1	.6429
2-Methylbutene-1	C_5H_{10}	C·C·C=C C		31	.6501
3-Methylbutene-1	C_5H_{10}	C·C·C=C C		20.1	.6340
Hexene-1	C_6H_{12}	C·C·C·C·C=C	−138	63.5	.6747
Heptene-1	C_7H_{14}	C·C·C·C·C·C=C	−119	93.1	.6976
Octene-1	C_8H_{16}	C·C·C·C·C·C·C=C	(−104)	122.5	.7159

pyrolysis of an alkane, since it involves production of an unsaturated product from a saturated one at an elevated temperature, but the pyrolysis temperature for an alcohol is distinctly lower, and the process is simpler and more uniform. A partial vacuum is sometimes advantageous for removal of the alkene before secondary changes can occur, as in the apparatus shown in Fig. 5.1.

Examples illustrating results obtainable by catalytic dehydration are as follows:

1. $$CH_3CH_2OH \xrightarrow[\text{98\%}]{\text{Kaolin or alumina, 350-360°}} CH_2{=}CH_2$$

(Used during the first World War as a source of ethylene for mustard gas)

2. 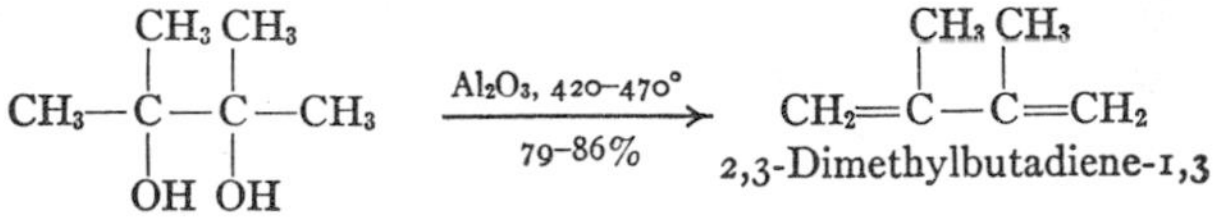
$$\underset{\text{Pinacol}}{\overset{\displaystyle CH_3\ CH_3}{CH_3-\underset{\underset{OH}{|}}{C}-\underset{\underset{OH}{|}}{C}-CH_3}} \xrightarrow[\text{79-86\%}]{Al_2O_3,\ 420\text{-}470°} \underset{\text{2,3-Dimethylbutadiene-1,3}}{\overset{\displaystyle CH_3\ CH_3}{CH_2{=}C-C{=}CH_2}}$$

3.

Cyclohexanol　$\xrightarrow[\text{89\%}]{Al_2O_3,\ 380\text{-}450°}$　Cyclohexene

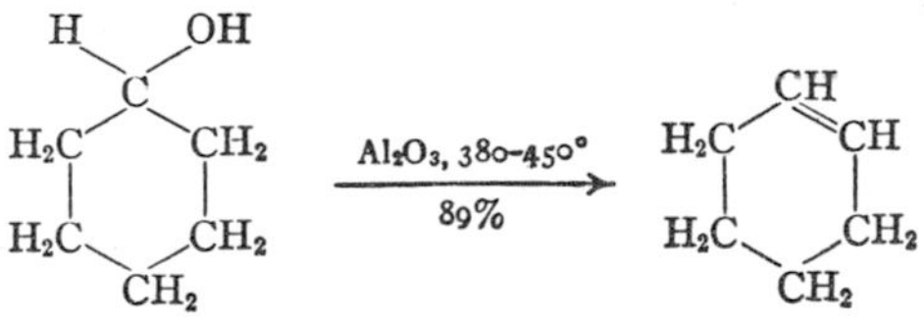

5.3　Sulfuric Acid Method. — Sulfuric acid is a dihydroxy acid represented for simplicity by formula I. The substance may have one semipolar

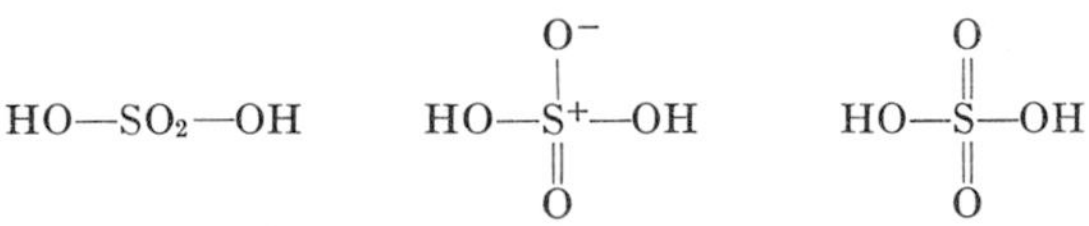

$$HO{-}SO_2{-}OH \qquad HO{-}\overset{\displaystyle O^-}{\underset{\displaystyle \underset{O}{\|}}{S^+}}{-}OH \qquad HO{-}\overset{\displaystyle O}{\underset{\displaystyle \underset{O}{\|}}{\overset{\|}{S}}}{-}OH$$

I　　　　　　II　　　　　　III

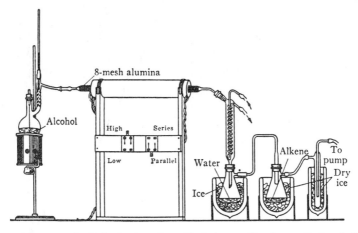

Fɪɢ. 5.ɪ. — Apparatus for Dehydration of an Alcohol over Alumina at Reduced Pressure

bond as in II, in which case sulfur has expanded its shell to accommodate twelve electrons, or it may have two double bonds (III).

When concentrated sulfuric acid is added gradually to ethanol with ice cooling, water is eliminated from the two components and ethylsulfuric acid is formed. The reaction proceeds to completion because the water formed is absorbed by the

$$CH_3CH_2OH \ + \ HOSO_2OH \ \underset{\text{Excess } H_2O}{\overset{\text{Concd. } H_2SO_4 \ (0°)}{\rightleftarrows}} \ CH_3CH_2OSO_2OH \ + \ H_2O$$

$$\text{Ethylsulfuric acid}$$

concentrated acid; the process, however, is an equilibrium, and can be reversed by treatment of the product with a large excess of water. Ethylsulfuric acid is the mono ester of the inorganic diacid; it is a strong acid soluble in sulfuric acid as well as in water. It is stable at a low temperature but decomposes when heated. The chief organic product of the decomposition is ethylene, formed by loss of

$$\begin{array}{cc} H & H \\ | & | \\ H-C-C-OSO_2OH \\ | & | \\ H & H \end{array} \xrightarrow{170°} CH_2{=}CH_2 \ + \ HOSO_2OH$$

OSO₂OH from one carbon atom and of hydrogen from the adjacent position to produce sulfuric acid. A side reaction consists in formation of diethyl ether (ordinary ether) by the action of alcohol on ethylsulfuric acid. This reaction can

$$\begin{array}{c} CH_3CH_2OSO_2OH \\ \xrightarrow{140°} \\ CH_3CH_2OH \end{array} \qquad \begin{array}{c} CH_3CH_2 \\ \diagdown \\ \diagup \\ CH_3CH_2 \end{array} O \ + \ HOSO_2OH$$

$$\text{Diethyl ether}$$
$$\text{b.p. 34.6°}$$

be operated for preparation of ether by adjusting the proportions of reagents and maintaining a temperature of 140°. The difference in the optimum temperatures for ethylene and ether formation is so slight that each product is a by-product of the production of the other. A third product, diethyl sulfate, can be prepared by heating ethylsulfuric acid at a temperature below 140° at a pressure sufficiently reduced to cause diethyl sulfate to distill from the nonvolatile acids. Diethyl sul-

$$CH_3CH_2O|SO_2OH \atop CH_3CH_2OSO_2|OH \qquad \xrightarrow{-H_2SO_4} \qquad {CH_3CH_2O \atop CH_3CH_2O} \!\!\searrow\!\!\nearrow SO_2$$

Diethyl sulfate

fate is the normal ester, or di-ester, of sulfuric acid. It is useful as an ethylating reagent, sometimes as an alternative to an ethyl halide. Dimethyl sulfate (b.p. 188.5°) is used similarly.

5.4   Acid-Catalyzed Dehydration. — Dehydration can be effected also with hydrochloric acid, phosphoric acid, potassium bisulfate, or oxalic acid, $(COOH)_2$. These are strong acids capable of effecting elimination in catalytic amounts, and some are incapable of forming intermediate esters. Hence the following mechanism applies to the more general case of acid-catalyzed dehydration. In the first step the alcohol functions as a Lewis base and accepts a proton to form an oxonium ion (a). In a second step (b), the bond between carbon and oxygen is

$$\underset{\overset{|}{R}}{RCH_2CHOH} \quad \xrightarrow{H^+} \quad \underset{\overset{|}{R} \atop (a)}{RCH_2\overset{+}{C}HOH_2} \quad \longrightarrow \quad \underset{\overset{|}{R} \atop (b)}{RCH_2\overset{\delta+}{C}H \cdots \overset{\delta+}{O}H_2} \quad \xrightarrow{-H_2O}$$

$$\underset{\overset{|}{R} \atop (c)}{R\overset{+}{C}H_2CH} \;=\; \underset{\overset{|}{\ddot{R}} \atop (c')}{RCH_2\!:\!\overset{+}{C}} \quad \longrightarrow \quad \underset{\overset{|}{R} \atop (d)}{RCH\overset{\overset{\displaystyle H}{\displaystyle :}}{\cdots}\overset{+}{C}H} \quad \xrightarrow{-H^+} \quad \underset{\overset{|}{R} \atop (e)}{RCH\!=\!CH}$$

weakened and the positive charge is distributed equally between carbon and oxygen. At this stage there is equal probability that product or reactant will result. The terminal group then separates with the bonding electrons as a neutral water molecule to give the carbonium ion (c). The electronic formula (c′) shows that one carbon atom is surrounded by only six electrons. This electron-deficient species is thus highly reactive and it achieves stability by expulsion of a proton and formation of the alkene (e); the reaction may involve a transition state (d) in which the electron pair bonding the departing hydrogen is partly bonded to

$$RCH_2CH_2CH_2\overset{+}{O}H_2 \quad \longrightarrow \quad \underset{\overset{\displaystyle :}{\displaystyle H} \atop (2)}{RCH_2\overset{+}{C}H\overline{\cdots}CH_2\cdots\overset{+}{O}H_2} \quad \xrightarrow{-\overset{+}{O}H_3} \quad RCH_2CH\!=\!CH_2$$

$$(1) \hspace{9cm} (3)$$

$$\underset{\substack{-\overset{+}{O}H_3}}{\Big\downarrow} \;\; \overset{\displaystyle ROH}{\underset{\displaystyle }{\rule{4cm}{0.4pt}}} \Big| \Big\downarrow {-H_2O}$$

$$\underset{(4)}{RCH_2CH_2CH_2OR} \qquad\qquad \underset{(5)}{RCH_2\overset{+}{C}HCH_3} \quad \xrightarrow{-H^+} \quad \underset{(6)}{RCH\!=\!CHCH_3}$$

the adjacent carbon. The formation of the unstable carbonium ion requires the highest activation energy and hence is the rate-determining step. Acid-catalyzed dehydration is described as an E_1 reaction (unimolecular elimination). The carbonium ion mechanism probably applies to dehydration with sulfuric acid; the formation of an alkylsulfuric acid in an equilibrium reaction thus may be an incidental process not essential to the actual dehydration. A primary carbonium ion is so very unstable (see below) that in the dehydration of a primary alcohol the transition state (2) probably collapses to give the alkene (3) directly, without formation of an intermediate carbonium ion. A Δ^1-alkene (3) is often accompanied by some of the Δ^2-alkene (6), formed from (2) by expulsion of water and shift of a hydride ion (H:) to give the secondary carbonium ion (5), which loses a proton to form (6). Another by-product is the ether (4), formed by attack of the alcohol on the transition state (2).

5.5   **Ease of Dehydration.** — Among alcohols having no activating group, the ease of dehydration depends upon the alcohol type and is in the following order: tertiary > secondary > primary. The differences are illustrated in the accompanying examples. The case of ethanol (1), a primary alcohol, has been cited; the acid strength is 96% and the temperature 170°. The secondary

1. $CH_3CH_2OH \xrightarrow{\text{96\% } H_2SO_4,\ 170°} CH_2{=}CH_2$

2. $CH_3CH_2CH_2\underset{\underset{OH}{|}}{C}HCH_3 \xrightarrow[80\%]{\text{62\% } H_2SO_4,\ 87°} CH_3CH_2CH{=}CHCH_3$

   Pentanol-2   Pentene-2

3. $CH_3CH_2\underset{\underset{OH}{|}}{\overset{\overset{CH_3}{|}}{C}}CH_3 \xrightarrow[84\%]{\text{46\% } H_2SO_4,\ 87°} CH_3CH{=}\overset{\overset{CH_3}{|}}{C}CH_3$

   2-Methyl-   2-Methyl-
   butanol-2   butene-2

alcohol of example 2 is dehydrated by 62% acid at the temperature of the steam bath, whereas the tertiary alcohol (3) affords an alkene at the same temperature on reaction with acid of only 46% strength. Tertiary alcohols are dehydrated with such ease that selective elimination of one mole of water from a tertiary-primary or tertiary-secondary diol can be realized (4, 5). It is necessary merely to find conditions just sufficient for elimination of the more labile group.

4. $(CH_3)_2\underset{\underset{OH}{|}}{C}CH_2CH_2CH_2OH \xrightarrow[-H_2O]{H^+} (CH_3)_2C{=}CHCH_2CH_2OH$

5. $\xrightarrow[-H_2O]{H^+}$

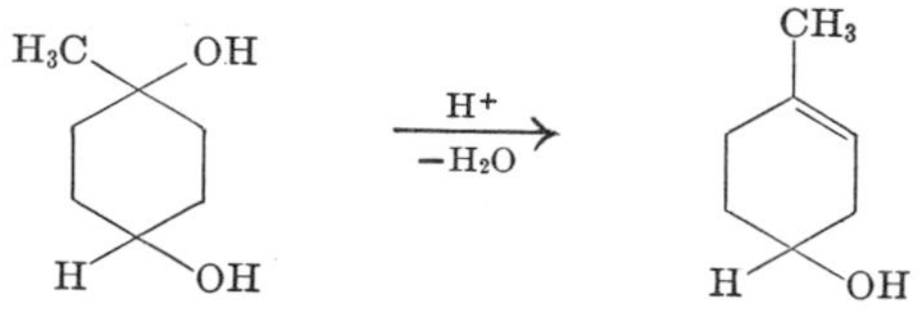

An interpretation of the marked difference between the alcohol types requires knowledge of the inductive effect of alkyl groups in comparison with that of the hydrogen atom. One method of evaluation is by comparison of the acidic strength of formic and acetic acid. If the methyl group were more electron-attracting than

$$\underset{\text{Formic acid}}{H-\overset{\displaystyle O}{\overset{\|}{C}}-O-H} \xrightarrow{-H^+} H-\overset{\displaystyle O}{\overset{\|}{C}}-O^- \qquad \underset{\text{Acetic acid}}{CH_3-\overset{\displaystyle O}{\overset{\|}{C}}-O-H} \xrightarrow{-H^+} CH_3-\overset{\displaystyle O}{\overset{\|}{C}}-O^-$$

hydrogen, as a chlorine atom or nitro group is, acetic acid should be the stronger acid, but it is considerably weaker than formic acid. Therefore the methyl group is electron-repelling; it induces a drift of electrons along the chain which renders the oxygen atom more negative and less prone to allow hydrogen to separate as a proton. That the acids $C_2H_5CO_2H$, $C_3H_7CO_2H$, etc. are of nearly the same acidic strength as acetic acid means that ethyl and higher alkyl groups have essentially the same electron-repelling inductive effect as methyl.

Formulation of the reactions of alcohols of the three types (with omission of the transition states) reveals significant differences. A primary alcohol forms a carbonium ion with great difficulty because the positive charge is partially neu-

$$(prim)\ RCH_2CH_2OH \xrightarrow{H^+} RCH_2CH_2\overset{+}{\underset{H}{O}H} \xrightarrow{-H_2O} RCH_2\overset{+}{C}H_2 \xrightarrow{-H^+} RCH=CH_2$$

$$(sec)\ RCH_2\underset{R}{CHOH} \xrightarrow{H^+} RCH_2\underset{R}{\overset{+}{C}H}\overset{|}{\underset{}{O}H} \xrightarrow{-H_2O} RCH_2\underset{R}{\overset{+}{C}H} \xrightarrow{-H^+} RCH=\underset{R}{CH}$$

$$(tert)\ RCH_2\underset{R}{\overset{R}{C}OH} \xrightarrow{H^+} RCH_2\underset{R}{\overset{R}{\overset{+}{C}}}\overset{|}{\underset{}{O}H} \xrightarrow{-H_2O} RCH_2\underset{R}{\overset{R}{C^+}} \xrightarrow{-H^+} RCH=\underset{R}{\overset{R}{C}}$$

tralized by electron release from only one alkyl group (RCH_2). An intermediate secondary carbonium ion is stabilized by two groups (RCH_2 and R), and a tertiary alcohol gives a tertiary carbonium ion stabilized by the neutralizing effect of three electron-repelling alkyl groups. The order of reactivity in dehydration thus follows the order of stability of the intermediate carbonium ions. Stabilization of an essential intermediate provides driving force for its formation.

The presence of a carbonyl group in a compound containing an alcoholic function may influence the ease of elimination of the hydroxyl group. In the β-hydroxyaldehyde (6) an α-hydrogen is activated by the adjacent carbonyl group (1—2—3=4 system) and water is eliminated very easily under acid or base catalysis to form crotonaldehyde. This aldehyde, described as an α,β-unsaturated

$$6.\ CH_3\overset{\beta}{C}H\overset{\alpha}{C}H_2CH=O \xrightarrow[-H_2O]{H^+\ or\ HO^-} \underset{\text{Crotonaldehyde}}{CH_3\overset{\beta}{C}H=\overset{\alpha}{C}HCH-O}$$

$$\underset{OH}{\overset{}{}}$$

$$7.\ CH_3\overset{\beta}{C}H\overset{\alpha}{C}H_2\overset{OH}{\overset{|}{C}}=O \xrightarrow[-H_2O]{H^+} \underset{\text{Crotonic acid}}{CH_3\overset{\beta}{C}H=\overset{\alpha}{C}H\overset{OH}{\overset{|}{C}}=O}$$

aldehyde, has a system of **conjugated double bonds**: C=C—C=O. Such a system has special stability and special properties. Conjugated dienes, as exemplified by butadiene-1,3, CH_2=CH—CH=CH_2, are unusually stable, and the system of conjugated double bonds functions as a unit. The β-hydroxy acid (7) is easily converted into an α,β-unsaturated acid, which likewise has a conjugated system of double bonds.

In the instances cited a carbonyl group promotes dehydration by activation of an α-hydrogen atom adjacent to the hydroxylated carbon. A different situation exists in an α-ketol, that is, a compound having a keto group adjacent to an alcoholic function, as in (8); α-ketols are very resistant to acid-catalyzed dehydration. The reason is clear. Since oxygen is a more electronegative atom than carbon

$$
\text{8.} \quad \overset{\delta+}{R}\!\!-\!\!\overset{\delta-}{\underset{\alpha\,\text{CHOH}}{\underset{|}{\overset{|}{C}}}}\!\!=\!\!O \quad \xrightarrow{\;H^+\;} \quad R\!\!-\!\!\overset{+}{\underset{\underset{CH_2R'}{|}}{\underset{CHOH}{\overset{|}{C}}}}\!\!=\!\!\overset{+}{O}H
$$

(see Table, 32.2), the carbonyl group is partially polarized in the sense that carbon carries a partial positive charge and oxygen a partial negative charge. The result is that the carbonyl oxygen is a more inviting site for acceptance of a proton than the hydroxylic oxygen, and the charge on this atom inhibits attack by a proton on the nearby oxygen of the hydroxyl group. An α-ketol of sufficient volatility usually can be converted into the α,β-unsaturated ketone efficiently by catalytic dehydration over alumina.

5.6   Direction of Dehydration. — The structure of an alcohol may be such that two routes of dehydration are open. Pentanol-2 offers the possibility for elimination of hydrogen from either the 1- or the 3-position, along with the adjacent hydroxyl group, but the 3-hydrogen is utilized almost exclusively and the product is pentene-2. Two routes of elimination are open in 2-methylpentanol-3, but one is preferred. Where no special features intervene, these examples

$$
CH_3CH_2\overset{3}{C}H_2\overset{1}{C}H\underset{\underset{OH}{|}}{}CH_3 \quad \xrightarrow{-H_2O} \quad CH_3CH_2CH\!\!=\!\!CHCH_3
$$

Pentanol-2   Pentene-2

$$
(CH_3)_2\overset{2}{C}H\overset{4}{C}H\underset{\underset{OH}{|}}{}CH_2CH_3 \quad \xrightarrow{-H_2O} \quad (CH_3)_2C\!\!=\!\!CHCH_2CH_3
$$

2-Methylpentanol-3   2-Methylpentene-2

are representative of a general pattern summarized by Saytzeff[1] in the form of an empirical rule: in the dehydration of alcohols, hydrogen is eliminated preferentially from the adjacent carbon atom that is poorer in hydrogen.[2] In pentanol-2 a secondary hydrogen at C_3 reacts in preference to a primary hydrogen at C_1; in

[1] Alexander M. Saytzeff, 1841–1910; b. Kasan; stud. Marburg, Paris; Kasan

[2] S. Matthew, XXV, 29, "... but from him that hath not shall be taken away even that which he hath."

2-methylpentanol-3 a tertiary hydrogen at C_2 surpasses in reactivity a secondary hydrogen at C_4. Thus the order of reactivity is the same as in the reaction of alkanes with chlorine and with oxygen.

A theoretical interpretation advanced for the Saytzeff rule is based on the concept of **hyperconjugation**, a low-order resonance effect (J. W. Baker[1] and W. S. Nathan, 1935). This effect is considered to be due to the ability of the electron pair of the C—H bond to undergo conjugation with an adjacent center of unsatu-

$$
\begin{array}{cc}
\underset{\substack{|\\ \text{H}}}{\overset{\text{H}}{\text{H}-\text{C}-\text{CH}=\text{CH}_2}} & \longleftrightarrow & \text{H}-\text{C}-\text{CH}=\text{CH}_2 \\
\text{(a)} & & \text{(b)}
\end{array}
$$

ration, much as one double bond becomes conjugated with another, but to a more limited extent. Thus in propene (a) some displacement of the electron pair in each of three C—H bonds of the methyl group produces a structure (b) in which a partial positive charge distributed among the three hydrogens is balanced by a partial negative charge on the terminal carbon. In a dehydration, for example of butanol-2, hyperconjugation may favor stabilization of one of the two possible transition states and hence favor formation of one of the products. In transition state (c) the incipient double bond is stabilized by hyperconjugation with six C—H bonds, whereas that in the alternative transition state (d) is stabilized by

$$
\text{(c)} \quad \xleftarrow[-\text{H}_2\text{O}]{\text{H}^+} \quad \underset{\substack{|\\ \text{OH}}}{\text{CH}_3\text{CH}_2\text{CHCH}_3} \quad \dashrightarrow \quad \text{(d)}
$$

Butanol-2

$$\Big\downarrow -\text{H}^+$$

hyperconjugation with only two C—H bonds. Hence (c) should be formed the more readily and butene-2 is the expected product.

An activating group may overshadow the Saytzeff effect. Thus the β-hydroxy-ketone I has an α-hydrogen atom activated by the carbonyl group and loses water readily to give conjugated α,β-unsaturated ketone II, rather than the nonconjugated ketone. Another example is the allylic alcohol III, in which the hydroxyl

$$
\underset{\substack{|\\ \text{OH}}}{(\text{CH}_3)_2\text{CH}\overset{\beta}{\text{C}}\text{H}\overset{\alpha}{\text{C}}\text{H}_2\overset{\text{CH}_3}{\text{C}}=\text{O}} \quad \xrightarrow[-\text{H}_2\text{O}]{\text{H}^+} \quad (\text{CH}_3)_2\text{CH}\overset{\beta}{\text{CH}}=\overset{\alpha}{\text{CH}}\overset{\text{CH}_3}{\text{C}}=\text{O}
$$

$$\text{I} \qquad\qquad\qquad \text{II}$$

[1] John W. Baker, b. 1898 London; Ph.D. University College, London (Ingold); D.Sc. London; Univ. Leeds

group is activated by the double bond and which loses water readily in the direction shown because the product (IV) has a conjugated system further stabilized

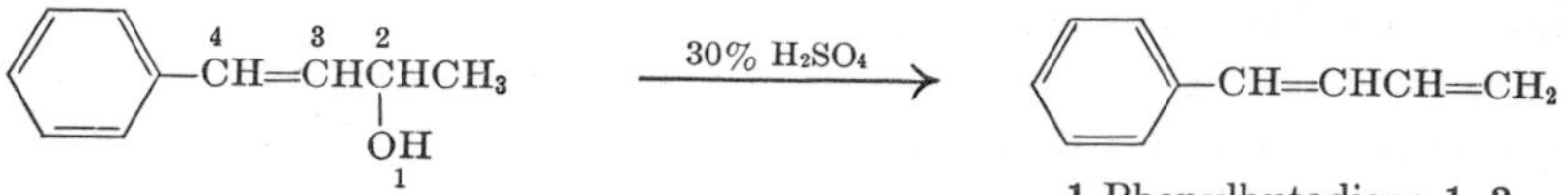

$$\underset{\text{III}}{\underset{\overset{4\quad 3\quad 2}{\bigcirc}}{-\text{CH}=\text{CH}\underset{\overset{|}{\text{OH}}}{\text{CH}}\overset{2}{\text{CH}}\text{CH}_3}} \xrightarrow{\quad 30\% \text{ H}_2\text{SO}_4 \quad} \underset{\underset{\text{IV}}{\text{1-Phenylbutadiene-1, 3}}}{\bigcirc-\text{CH}=\text{CHCH}=\text{CH}_2}$$

by conjugation with the benzene ring.

5.7   **Other Methods of Dehydration** (see also 5.20). — Secondary and tertiary alcohols are often dehydrated most successfully by the action of phosphorus oxychloride (POCl₃) in pyridine; the method is particularly useful with substances sensitive to acids.   Thionyl chloride, SOCl₂, is a still more powerful reagent and often effects dehydration of secondary alcohols in pyridine solution even at $-5°$.   In at least some instances the reaction appears to involve conversion of the alcohol to the corresponding phosphorus or sulfurester, followed by elimination.

The **Tschugaeff[1] reaction** involves in the key step a nonionic, pyrolytic elimination.   An alcohol is condensed with carbon disulfide and alkali to produce a xanthate, the solid is methylated to form the corresponding methyl ester, and the latter is pyrolyzed.   The thermal decomposition is unimolecular (Nace,[2] 1952–53)

$$\text{RCH}_2\text{CH}_2\text{OH} \;+\; \text{CS}_2 \;+\; \text{NaOH} \;\rightarrow\; \text{RCH}_2\text{CH}_2\text{O}-\overset{\overset{\text{S}}{\|}}{\text{C}}-\text{S}^-\text{Na}^+ \xrightarrow{\quad \text{CH}_3\text{I} \quad}$$

Sodium xanthate

$$\underset{\text{Methyl xanthate}}{\text{RCH}_2\text{CH}_2\text{O}-\overset{\overset{\text{S}}{\|}}{\text{C}}-\text{SCH}_3} \xrightarrow{\quad \text{Pyrolysis} \quad} \text{RCH}=\text{CH}_2 \;+\; \text{O}=\overset{\overset{\text{SH}}{|}}{\text{C}}-\text{SCH}_3$$

and probably is a concerted process involving a cyclic transition state:

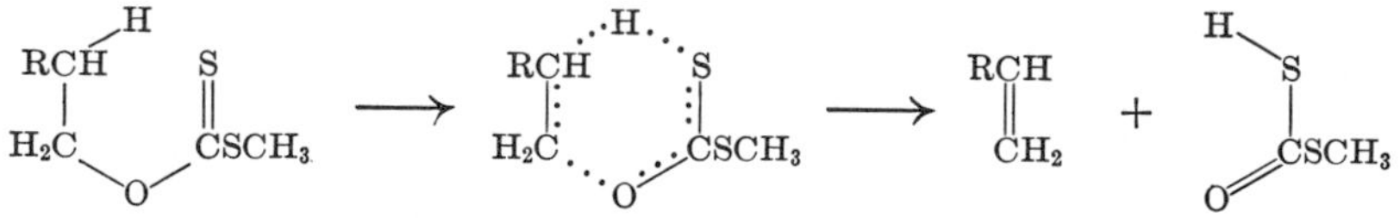

A study of the isotope effects of the carbonyl carbon and the two sulfur atoms has substantiated this mechanism (Bourns,[3] 1961).   Another method involves heating an alcohol with dimethyl sulfoxide at 160°; the alcohol cited in the example is stable at 160° in the absence of the reagent (V. J. Traynelis,[4] 1960).

$$\underset{\overset{|}{\text{OH}}}{\text{C}_6\text{H}_5\text{CHCH}_2\text{CH}_3} \xrightarrow[79\%]{\text{CH}_3\text{SOCH}_3 \ (160°)} \text{C}_6\text{H}_5\text{CH}=\text{CHCH}_3$$

---

[1] Lev A. Tschugaeff, 1873–1922; b. Moscow; Ph.D. St. Petersburg; St. Petersburg
[2] Harold R. Nace, b. 1921 Camden, N. J.; Ph.D. Mass. Inst. Techn. (Cope); Brown Univ.
[3] Arthur Newcombe Bourns, b. 1919 Petitcodiac, New Brunswick, Canada; Ph.D. McGill (R. V. V. Nicholls); McMaster Univ., Canada
[4] Vincent J. Traynelis, b. 1928; Ph.D. Wayne State Univ.; Univ. Notre Dame

5.8　　　　**Dehydrohalogenation.** — Elimination of the elements of hydrogen
halide by the action of a base on a halogen-containing compound is
another useful method for introduction of a double bond. Dehydrohalogenation
of an alkyl halide can be accomplished with a solution of alcoholic potassium hy-

$$-\underset{\underset{H}{|}}{\overset{|}{C}}-\underset{\underset{X}{|}}{\overset{|}{C}}- \; + \; \text{Base} \;\longrightarrow\; -\overset{|}{C}{=}\overset{|}{C}- \; + \; \text{Salt}$$

droxide prepared by dissolving the alkali in the minimum amount of water and
adding alcohol; a water-insoluble alkyl halide may be sufficiently soluble in alcohol
for efficient reaction. Dehydrohalogenation of a halogen compound of slight
solubility or of low reactivity can be accomplished by refluxing the substance
in pyridine (b.p. 115°) or its higher-boiling 2,4-dimethyl derivative, lutidine
(b.p. 158°).

　　Kinetic studies of Ingold indicate that dehydrohalogenation of a primary alkyl
halide is a bimolecular reaction; that is, the reaction rate is proportional to the
concentration of both the alkyl halide and the basic reagent. The reaction is
classified as an E_2-reaction (elimination-bimolecular), and regarded as proceeding
through the transition state shown in the formulation. The order of reactivity
is the same as with alcohols: tertiary > secondary > primary. The Saytzeff

$$\text{OH}^- \; + \; \text{RCH}_2\text{CH}_2\text{Br} \;\xrightarrow{\;E_2\;}\; \left[\begin{array}{c} \overset{\displaystyle Br^{\delta-}}{\underset{\displaystyle \vdots}{}} \\ \text{RCH}\cdots\text{CH}_2 \\ \overset{\displaystyle \delta-}{}\;\;\vdots \\ \text{HO}\cdots\text{H} \end{array}\right] \;\longrightarrow\; \text{H}_2\text{O} \; + \; \text{RCH}{=}\text{CH}_2 \; + \; \text{Br}^-$$

rule for the direction of dehydration of alcohols applies as well to the dehydrohalogenation of halogen compounds.

　　The occasion for introduction of a double bond arises in other series; for example,
a double bond can be introduced into isobutyric acid by bromination, followed by
elimination of hydrogen bromide.

$$\begin{array}{c}\text{CH}_3\\ \diagdown\\ \text{CH}_3{\diagup}\;\underset{\underset{\text{Br}}{|}}{\text{C}}{-}\text{COOH}\end{array} \xrightarrow[\;78\text{--}80\%\;]{\;25\%\text{ aq. NaOH}\;} \begin{array}{c}\overset{\text{CH}_3}{\overset{|}{}}\\ \text{CH}_2{=}\text{C}{-}\text{COOH}\\ \text{Methacrylic acid}\\ \text{(m.p. 15°)}\end{array}$$

α-Bromoisobutyric acid

　　Dehydrobromination of an acid of the type $\text{RCH}_2\text{CH}_2\text{CHBrCO}_2\text{H}$ to the Δ^2-
alkenoic acid is conducted efficiently with potassium t-butoxide in t-butyl alcohol;
potassium hydroxide in methanol, ethanol, or propanol gives mixtures of the Δ^2-
and Δ^3-acids (Cason,[1] 1953).

ELECTRONS OF THE DOUBLE BOND

5.9　　　　**Sigma (σ) and Pi (π) Bonds.** — The molecular orbital theory provides
a concept of the nature of the two pairs of electrons constituting a

---

[1] James Cason, b. 1912 Murfreesboro, Tenn.; Ph.D. Yale (R. J. Anderson); Vanderbilt Univ.;
Univ. Calif., Berkeley

double bond which is of aid in understanding the reactions involving this functional group. The orbital treatment of methane and ethane developed in Chapter 1 involves some simplifying assumptions but leads to a plausible interpretation of the properties of molecules containing tetrahedral carbon. A further plausible interpretation applies to ethylene. A form of hybridization different from the tetrahedral type (Fig. 1.8) is postulated, namely sp^2 or trigonal hybridization (Fig. 5.2). Each carbon atom has available four electrons: a $2s$ pair, and two other electrons listed in Table 1.2 as a $2p_x$ and a $2p_y$, but actually $2p_x$, $2p_y$, and $2p_z$ are all equivalent. The three orbitals comprising these four electrons are hybridized to give three equivalent trigonal orbitals and one undistributed $2p$ orbital, described as a $2p_z$ orbital for simplification of formulation (Fig. 1.6). One hybrid trigonal orbital merges with that of the second carbon atom to form a σ orbital linking the two carbon atoms together by a covalent, σ bond, comparable to that of ethane. The other two form σ orbitals with two hydrogen atoms. The six atoms of the ethylene molecule thus all lie in the same plane, and the σ bonds linking each carbon with two hydrogens are at angles of 120° from each other. In Fig. 5.3 the five σ bonds are indicated by conventional bars. The $2p_z$ orbitals of the two carbon atoms merge to form a molecular orbital which is not spherically symmetrical but has a dumbbell-like character resembling an atomic p orbital and therefore is described as a π (pi) molecular orbital, represented in Fig. 5.3 for hypothetical unsaturated atoms A and B. The dumbbell arrangement here consists in one cloud structure (a) overlying another (b); these structures have the shape of holeless doughnuts. The most stable state, or ground state (π_1), is that in which the nodal planes (low electron density) of the atomic orbital contributors are aligned with the σ bond linking A to B. In consequence of the Pauli exclusion principle, only two electrons can occupy a given π orbital such as that pictured (π_1), but in case additional electrons require accommodation the cloud-charge can take the form π_2 (Fig. 5.3), in which a new nodal plane perpendicular to the A—B σ bond separates the cloud into two vertically oriented doughnut-like areas (c and d) that, together, form a dumbbell. Since stability is greatest when the number of nodular planes is at a minimum, the π_1 orbital is more stable than the π_2 orbital. The π_2 orbital, in fact, can be occupied only in an excited state such as is produced by light absorption.

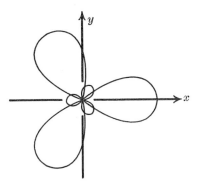

FIG. 5.2. — Trigonal Orbitals (sp^2 Hybridization)

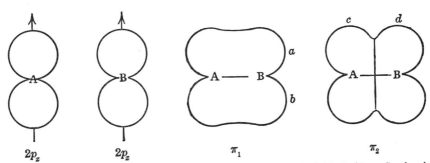

FIG. 5.3. — Formation of π Molecular Orbitals from $2p_z$ Atomic Orbitals (Cross Sections)

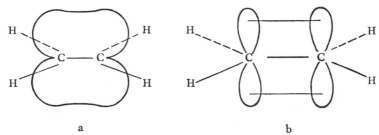

FIG. 5.4. — Ethylene (Cross Section of π Orbital)

In the case of ethylene (Fig. 5.4), the π molecular orbital can be represented as a two-doughnut cloud (a) or by two figure eight loops (b) corresponding to the original atomic p orbitals, but with lines joining them to indicate the overlapping involved in the formation of the molecular orbital. The concept of a double bond as two pairs of shared electrons is thus extended, in the orbital theory, to the concept of two kinds of two-electron bonds: a σ bond, stabilized by efficient overlapping of symmetrical atomic orbitals, and a π bond, compounded with poor overlapping and hence of higher energy content and greater reactivity. The loop representation (Fig. 5.4b) has the advantage of emphasizing the point that π electrons, that is, the two electrons occupying the π orbital, retain some character of the original p orbitals and that the plane of vibration of a π electron is perpendicular to the plane of the σ bond. The reactivity of ethylene, particularly in additions, is thus attributable to lack of stability of the π electrons and hence their availability for formation of more stable σ bonds with other atoms. The overlap in formation of the π orbital although weak is not without significant consequence. Thus the carbon–carbon bond distance in ethane of 1.54 Å is, in ethylene, shortened to 1.33 Å, evidently because the additional π orbital surrounding the two nuclei draws them together more strongly.

5.10   **Inorganic π-Complexes.** — Loose addition compounds of ethylene with $PtCl_2$ and with $KPtCl_3$ were described as early as 1831. Ethylene and propylene combine with hydrobromic acid at room temperature to form covalently bonded addition products, but at a very low temperature these olefins when introduced into liquid hydrogen bromide lower the freezing point by forming coordinate compounds of low-order stability which easily revert to the components.   Noting that silver salts added to aqueous acids increase the capacity for absorption of olefins, Lucas[1] (1938–) investigated the complexes of olefins with silver ions in aqueous solution.   Thus on distribution of an olefin between carbon tetrachloride and aqueous silver nitrate a certain amount of hydrocarbon passes into the aqueous phase due to formation of a 1:1 complex with silver ion.   Such a complex is called a π-complex because the metallic ion is regarded as imbedded in the π-electron cloud of the double bond.   The silver is not covalently bonded to either carbon atom but is equidistant from the two carbon atoms and situated on the lobes of the two π-electrons.   Since the three atoms form a ring, the complex is described as a three-membered cyclic positive ion.

Formula (a) is a symbolic representation of an olefin-silver ion complex.   The

(a)   (b)   (c)

corresponding approximate formulation of an olefin-hydrogen bromide π-complex is shown in (b); the more specific representation (c) assumes that the π-electrons of the double bond combine with a proton derived from the acid.   Such π-complexes are probably involved in alkene addition reactions.

5.11   Organic π-Complexes. — Alfred Werner[2] (Switzerland, 1910) and I. Ostromisslensky· (Russia) independently discovered that olefins form colored complexes with tetranitromethane of value for detection of carbon–carbon unsaturation.   Since the reagent is costly ($4 per 10 g.), tests for unsaturation are advisedly made in melting point capillaries; since it is very volatile but freezes in the refrigerator (m.p. 13.8°, b.p. 126°), the reagent is mixed with an equal volume of solvent chloroform and stored in the cold.   The color of the complex increases in intensity (yellow to dark red) with increasing unsaturation. Since chemically inert double bonds give a normal response, the test is useful for their detection.   Alkyl groups on the double bond progressively increase intensity of light absorption.   The test is feeble with α,β-unsaturated ketones and negative with allylic alcohols.   Benzene forms a yellow complex; naphthalene, which is more reactive, forms an orange complex.   The test is positive with cyclopropane and negative with all other cycloalkanes and with alkynes.   The colored products are now regarded as π-complexes similar to those formed with hydrogen bromide and with metallic compounds or ions.

π-Complexes of aromatic hydrocarbons have been investigated particularly extensively for the case of tetracyanoethylene (T. L. Cairns[3] et al., 1958).   The reagent is a colorless solid which melts at 200° in a sealed capillary; heated in an

---

[1] Howard J. Lucas, b. 1885 Marietta, Ohio; M.A. Ohio State (W. L. Evans); Calif. Inst. Techn.

[2] Alfred Werner, 1866–1919; b. Mülhausen; Ph.D. ETH Zurich; Univ. Zurich; Nobel Prize 1913.

[3] Theodore L. Cairns, b. 1914 Edmonton, Alberta, Canada; Ph.D. Illinois (R. Adams); du Pont Co.

open tube, it sublimes. It is made by the action of copper powder on dibromo-malononitrile in refluxing benzene (yield, 60%); the reaction may involve an inter-

$$Br_2C(CN)_2 \xrightarrow{Cu} [C(CN)_2] \xrightarrow{Dimerization} (N\equiv C)_2C=C(C\equiv N)_2$$

| Dibromomalono-nitrile | Dicyano-carbene | Tetracyanoethylene |

mediate carbene having bivalent carbon (see 15.4). The four strongly electron-attracting cyano groups so decrease the electron density around the double bond that tetracyanoethylene functions as an electron acceptor (Lewis acid), or π-acid. Benzene, which combines reversibly with the reagent to give a yellow π-complex, functions as an electron donor or π-base, and the complex results from partial transfer of a π-electron from the π-base to orbitals of the π-acid. Tetracyano-ethylene forms a π-complex with cyclohexene, but the association constant (K) is only about one tenth that of the benzene π-complex. The yellow complex with benzene absorbs light in the ultraviolet region with a maximum at a wave length of 384 mμ. The intensity of absorption at a particular wave length is expressed by citation of the molecular extinction coefficient, ϵ. In the present case $\epsilon = 3,570$, and the combined data are summarized thus: λ_{max} 384 mμ ($\epsilon = 3,570$). Electron-releasing methyl groups attached to the benzene ring should enhance the electron-donating power of the π-base and hence increase the association constant, shift the absorption band to higher wave length, and increase intensity of absorption. The data of Table 5.2 strikingly verify these expectations. Note that hexamethylbenzene is an enormously more powerful π-base than benzene. The two partners of the complex probably lie parallel to each other, for such an arrangement would allow maximum overlap between the π-molecular orbitals of the components. Since all twelve carbon atoms of hexamethylbenzene lie in a plane, the methyl groups do not interfere with close approach of the π-acid (about 3.5 Å). In hexaethylbenzene, however, the six terminal methyl groups are above or below the plane of the other twelve carbons and limit the approach of the second component to about 5 Å. Since bonding energy falls off abruptly with separation

TABLE 5.2. π-COMPLEXES OF TETRACYANOETHYLENE IN CH_2Cl_2

	K	λ_{max}, mμ	ϵ
Benzene	2.00	384	3,570
Toluene (Methylbenzene)	3.70	406	3,330
o-Xylene	6.97	430	3,860
m-Xylene	6.00	440	3,300
p-Xylene	7.64	460	2,650
1,3,5-Trimethylbenzene	17.3	461	3,120
1,2,4,5-Tetramethylbenzene	54.2	480	2,075
Pentamethylbenzene	123	520	3,270
Hexamethylbenzene	263	545	4,390
Hexaethylbenzene	5.11	550	56
Naphthalene	11.7	550	1,240
Pyrene	29.5	724	1,137

distance, the complex has little stability, and shows only feeble light absorption. The π-complex of benzene is yellow; that of naphthalene is red; and that of anthracene is brilliant green.

Maleic anhydride and *p*-benzoquinone are somewhat similar in structure to tetracyanoethylene in that each has an olefinic linkage flanked by two electron-attracting carbonyl groups. Comparison of complexes with the tetracyclic hydro-

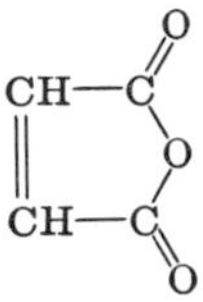

| Maleic anhydride | *p*-Benzoquinone (yellow) | Pyrene |

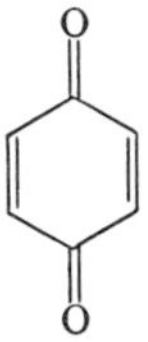

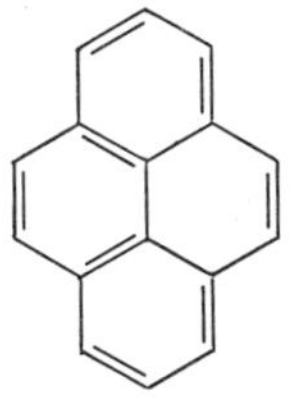

carbon pyrene showed these substances to be considerably weaker π-acids than tetracyanoethylene. Thus the equilibrium constants are: tetracyanoethylene, 29.5; maleic anhydride, 17.6; *p*-benzoquinone, 14.4.

Tetranitromethane functions as an electron-acceptor or π-acid because in the four semipolar bonds of the nitro groups the atom adjacent to carbon carries a positive charge.

REACTIONS

5.12 Halogen Addition. — The double bond of an alkene makes the molecule far more reactive than an alkane and capable of undergoing addition reactions, rather than substitutions, because the π electrons can bind other atoms. Addition of bromine to a double bond gives a product described as a vicinal (*vic*-) dibromide because the halogen atoms are in the same vicinity. The

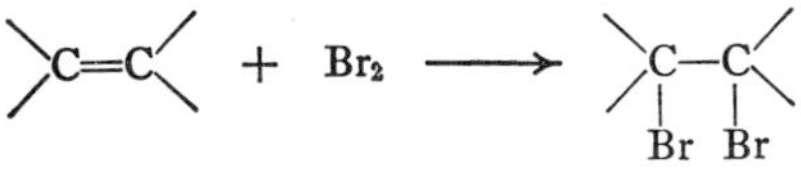

$$\text{\Large $>$C=C$\Large $<$} + Br_2 \longrightarrow \text{\Large $>$C--C$\Large $<$}$$
$$\underset{Br \quad Br}{}$$
vic-Dibromide

reaction is used as a test for unsaturation: an unsaturated compound discharges the color of a dilute solution of bromine in carbon tetrachloride or chloroform. Tetraphenylethylene is one of the few unsaturated compounds that fails to add bromine; it adds chlorine only to a small extent in an equilibrium reaction:

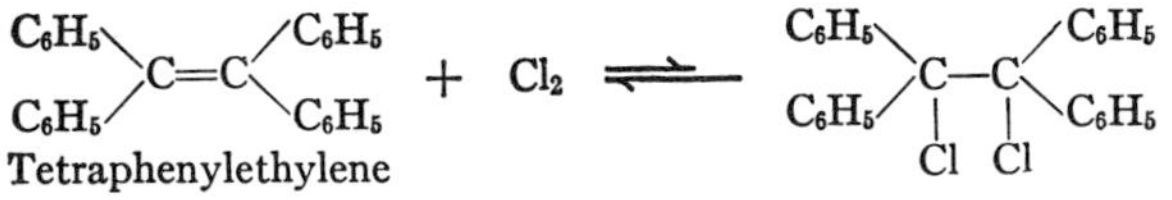

$$\underset{C_6H_5}{\overset{C_6H_5}{>}}C=C\underset{C_6H_5}{\overset{C_6H_5}{<}} + Cl_2 \rightleftharpoons \underset{C_6H_5}{\overset{C_6H_5}{>}}\underset{Cl \quad Cl}{C-C}\underset{C_6H_5}{\overset{C_6H_5}{<}}$$

Tetraphenylethylene

Chlorine is more reactive than bromine, and the smaller size of the chlorine atom means that there is less steric interference with the phenyl groups. Iodine, less reactive than bromine and also larger, can be added to olefinic compounds best by use of iodine monochloride, iodine monobromide, or iodomercuric chloride.

Halogen addition is not dependent upon conditions favoring formation of free radicals but is often catalyzed by a trace of hydrogen bromide. That the catalyst is ionic, H^+Br^-, suggests that addition proceeds by an ionic mechanism. The concept developed by Ingold, Bartlett[1] and others is that halogen addition does not involve the opening of a double bond and simultaneous joining of halogen atoms to adjacent carbon atoms but that the halogens are attached one at a time. The initial step is an attack by an **electrophile**, a cation or other positively charged fragment that is electron-seeking and can bond with π-electrons of the olefin. If the bromine molecule is considered to be an ion pair, Br^+Br^-, the electrophile is the cation Br^+ and attack of the unsaturated center gives an intermediate carbonium ion (a), which then combines with Br^- with neutralization of the charge

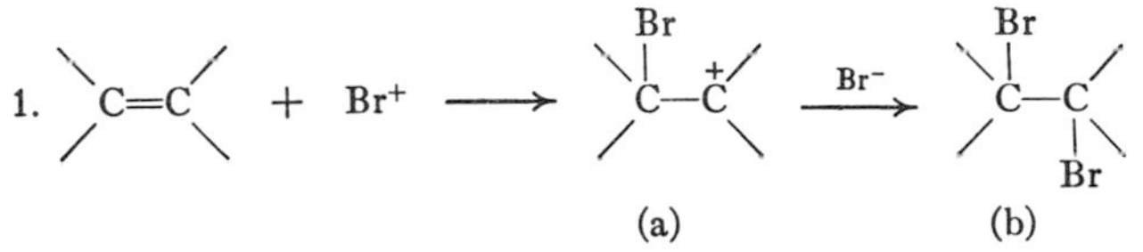

and formation of the dibromide (b).

The concept of the two-step reaction mechanism can be expressed alternatively in the electronic formulation 2. Here the same result is achieved without assump-

tion of an initial ionization of the bromine molecule. Instead, one atom of this molecule retains the covalent pair of electrons and becomes a bromide ion, Br^-, and the other accepts a pair of electrons from the double bond and becomes bonded to one of the carbon atoms. The electronic formula (a′) for the carbonium ion intermediate shows that the charged carbon is surrounded by only an electron sextet. The ion is thus a highly reactive species of only fleeting existence; it combines with bromide ion at a rate greater than the rate at which it is formed.

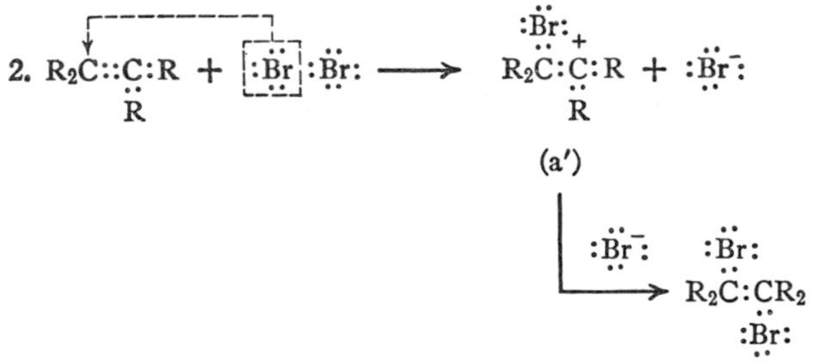

In both formulations 1 and 2 the two bromine atoms of the final product are represented as being on opposite sides of the molecule. The fact is that the two bromines do approach from opposite sides; one comes in from the front (or above) and the other from the rear (or below). The addition is, specifically, a *trans* addition. In an open-chain dibromide where free rotation about the single connecting bond is possible, *cis* and *trans* addition may give the identical product (although it will be evident later that this is not always the case). If the olefinic bond is a member of a ring, however, rotation is restricted and *cis* and *trans* products are possible. Cyclohexene presents such a situation and the product of bromine

[1] Paul D. Bartlett, b. 1907 Ann Arbor, Mich.; Ph.D. Harvard (Conant); Harvard Univ.

addition is the *trans*-dibromide, $1\alpha, 2\beta$-dibromocyclohexane. Two conformations for this substance are possible, one in which the two bromines are axial, and one in which they are equatorial. The diaxial form is destabilized by $1:3$ interactions of the 2β-bromine atom with axial 4β-H and 6β-H and of the 1α-bromine atom

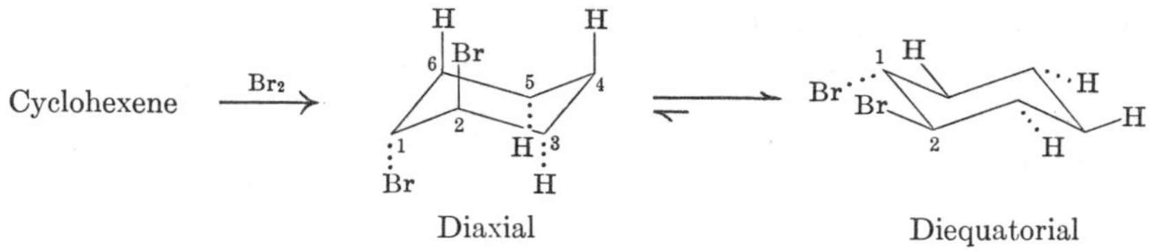

Diaxial   Diequatorial

$1\alpha, 2\beta$-Dibromocyclohexane

with axial 3α-H and 5α-H. This obviously unstable form, in case it is the initial product of the reaction, would be expected to undergo a ring flip to the diequatorial form in which the steric strain is completely relieved. An isolated cyclohexane ring is so labile that no means exists for determining the nature of the actual product initially formed. Identification can be made, however, with the dibromide of a compound having a cyclohexene ring linked to other rings in such a way that a flip is impossible. Cholesterol is such a compound; since it is

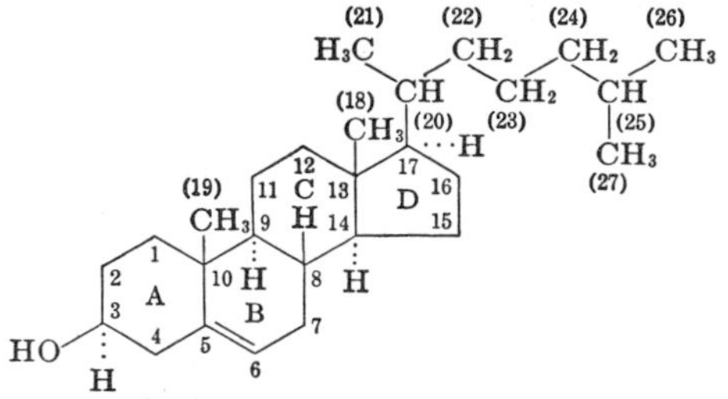

Cholesterol

the most abundant nonsaponifiable lipid of animal tissue, this crystalline secondary alcohol is a readily available starting material (it is manufactured from brain and spinal cord of cattle). The formula shows that cholesterol is made of three cyclohexane rings (A, B, C) and one cyclopentane ring (D) carrying a side chain. Angular methyl groups at C_{10} and C_{13} are β-oriented (to the front), as is the 3-hydroxyl, the 8-H, and the side chain at C_{17}. The double bond in ring B is at the 5,6-position; the conformational formula[1] shows that the molecule is rigid. Cholesterol adds bromine to give in high yield a product shown by unequivocal evidence to be the diaxial cholesterol-$5\alpha, 6\beta$-dibromide. This substance is destabilized even more than the diaxial cyclohexene *trans*-dibromide because of strong repulsion of the large methyl group and the bromine atom, but ring B is restricted from undergoing a flip because it is locked in place by rings A and C. The initially formed dibromide is thus isolable without difficulty and its configura-

---

[1] Ring B is represented for simplification as a regular chair form; actually the ring is slightly distorted by the double bond to what is known as a half-chair conformation (see 15.14).

tion shows that the addition is *trans*.   Note also that the bromines are maximally separated, that the four atoms Br—C_5—C_6—Br all lie in a plane, and that the bonds extending to bromine are *trans* antiparallel.

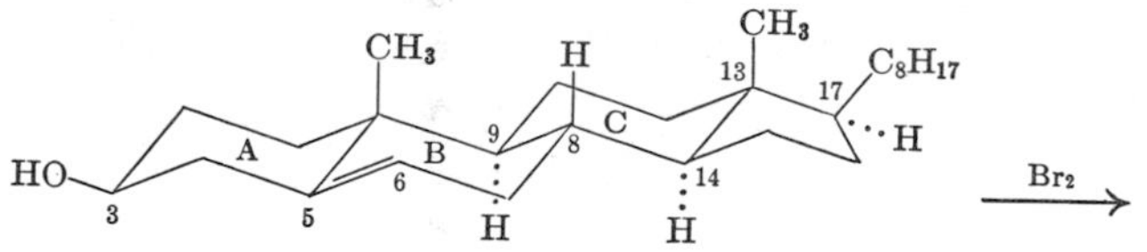

Cholesterol

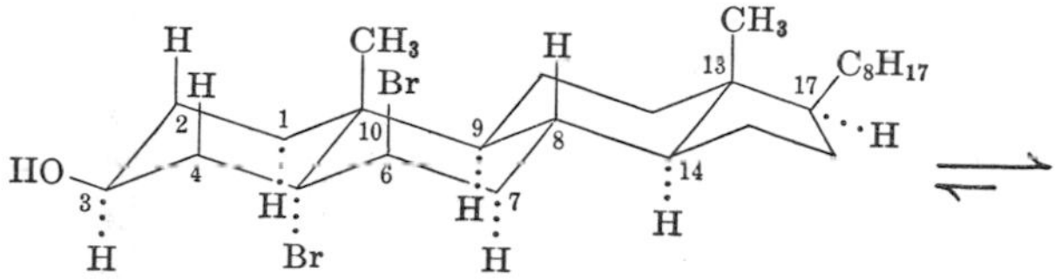

$5\alpha,6\beta$-Dibromide

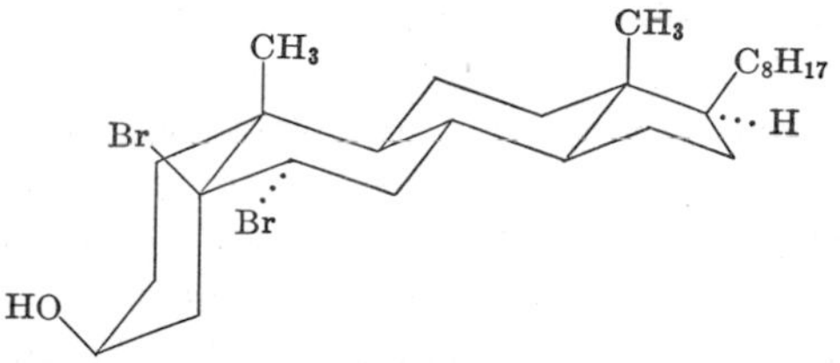

$5\beta,6\alpha$-Dibromide

The diaxial cholesterol-$5\alpha,6\beta$-dibromide is under considerable steric strain from the following 1:3 interactions: CH_3:Br (severe); CH_3:H (β-H at C_2, C_4, C_8, C_{11}); 6β-Br:H (β-H at C_4, C_8); 5α-Br:H (α-H at C_1, C_3, C_7, C_9).   The substance is stable as a crystalline solid but when a solution in chloroform is let stand for a few weeks an equilibrium mixture is formed of which the chief component is the iso-meric $5\beta,6\alpha$-dibromide formulated.   This product arises not from a ring flip, but by a molecular rearrangement involving Walden inversion at the asymmetric centers C_5 and C_6.   The original strain is relieved, for both bromines are now equatorial.   Since inversion occurs at both centers, the bromine atoms are still *trans*; they are now $5\beta,6\alpha$ rather than $5\alpha,6\beta$.   The behavior of the two dibro-mides on debromination will be of interest for later consideration.   A point for emphasis at this stage is that the relative stability of a given structure under equi-librium conditions, that is, the thermodynamic stability, does not determine whether or not it will be the product of an addition.   The *trans* diaxial dibromide is labile with respect to the *trans* diequatorial isomer, but it is nevertheless the primary reaction product; the addition by which it is formed is a faster reaction than that leading to its isomerization.   Halogen addition is not under thermo-dynamic control but under kinetic control (determined by relative reaction rates).

I. Roberts and G. E. Kimball (1937) postulated that the ionic species resulting from attack by Br^+ on a double bond is not a simple carbonium ion, as pictured above, but a resonance hybrid of the two possible carbonium ions (a) and (c) and the **cyclic bromonium ion** (b). However, one carbonium ion may be so stabilized by electron-releasing alkyl groups as to be favored to the practical exclusion of the other. Furthermore, the evidence seems to show that if there is no restriction to rotation about the connecting covalent bond the preferred species is the carbo-

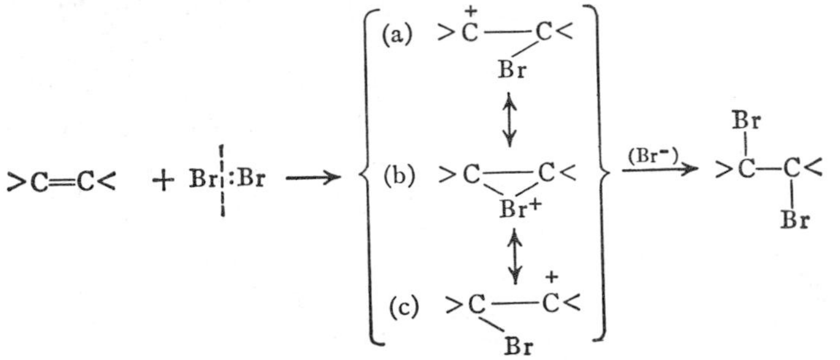

nium ion of greater stability, but that in a compound in which rotation is restricted by a ring system the cyclic bromonium ion is the key intermediate. The first situation is illustrated in section 5.16; the second by the case of cholesterol. The conformational formula of cholesterol shows that the β-face, or front side, is shielded by the two angular methyl groups and the side chain, whereas the α-face, or rear side, is relatively flat and unshielded. This spatial difference accounts for a general tendency for a reagent to attack from the rear to produce an α-linked product. This rule of rear attack, although not infallible, holds for the majority of reactions involving functional groups at various positions in the steroid structure. If cholesterol, shown in the partial formula I, were to suffer rear attack by

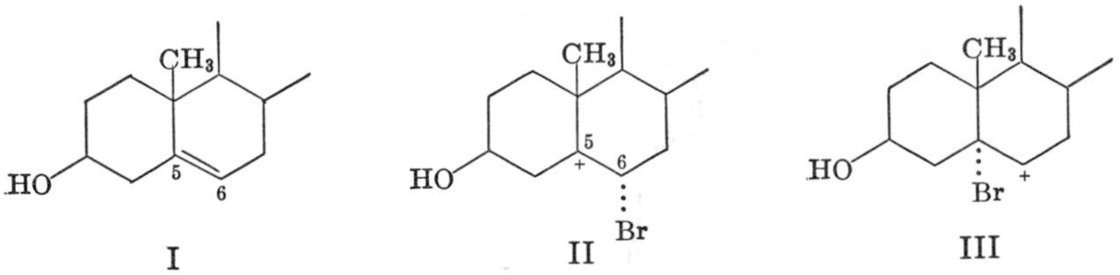

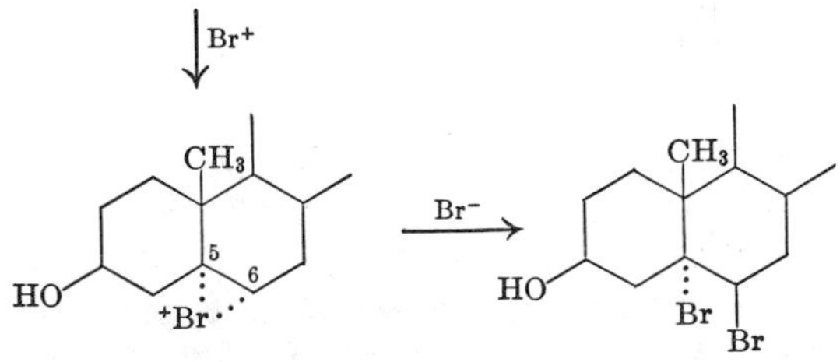

Br^+ to form a carbonium ion, the ion II, being tertiary, would have preference over the secondary carbonium ion III. The *trans* reaction product would then be the 5β,6α-dibromide, whereas the actual product is the 5α,6β-dibromide V.

On the other hand, formation of $5\alpha,6\alpha$-cyclic bromonium ion IV follows the rule of the rear, and attack of this ion by Br⁻ on the side opposite the three-membered ring with inversion at C_6, the site of bond cleavage, would account for the formation of the known product V. The mode of cleavage is exactly analogous to cleavage reactions of cholesterol α-oxide, a substance of unambiguous structure having a three-membered oxide ring in the α-orientation. This substance is cleaved by hydrogen chloride to the 5α-hydroxy-6β-chloro derivative, a chloro-

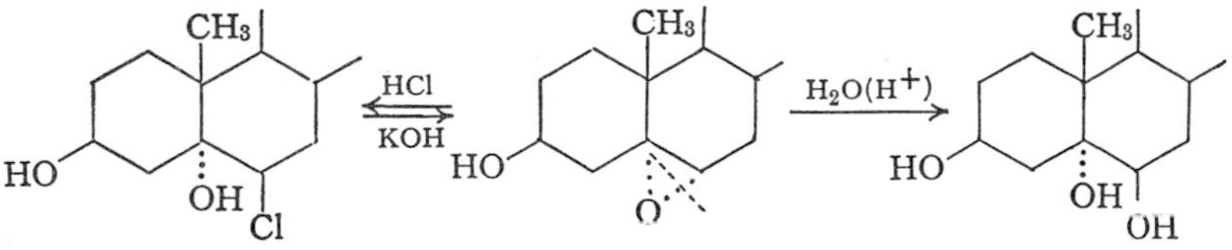

α-Oxide

hydrin; inversion occurs at C_6 because the bond cleaved is that extending from oxygen to C_6. Treatment of the chlorohydrin with alkali eliminates hydrogen chloride and reforms the oxide ring, again with inversion at C_6 from β to α because the C_6–Cl bond is severed. Acid-catalyzed hydrolysis of the α-oxide again cleaves the C_6–oxygen bond with inversion and affords cholestane-$3\beta,5\alpha,6\beta$-triol.

Initial formation of a cyclic bromonium ion also accounts for the reaction of cholesterol with a combination of reagents that generates Br⁺Cl⁻, for the product is the 5α-bromo-6β-chloro derivative, not a 5-chloro-6-bromo compound as expected if the carbonium ion II were involved.

To account for the double inversion involved in the isomerization of diaxial cholesterol-$5\alpha,6\beta$-dibromide into the diequatorial $5\beta,6\alpha$-dibromide formulated above, Grob[1] and Winstein[2] (1952) postulated that the reaction involves the intermediate bromonium-bromide ion pair formulated. This mechanism implies that

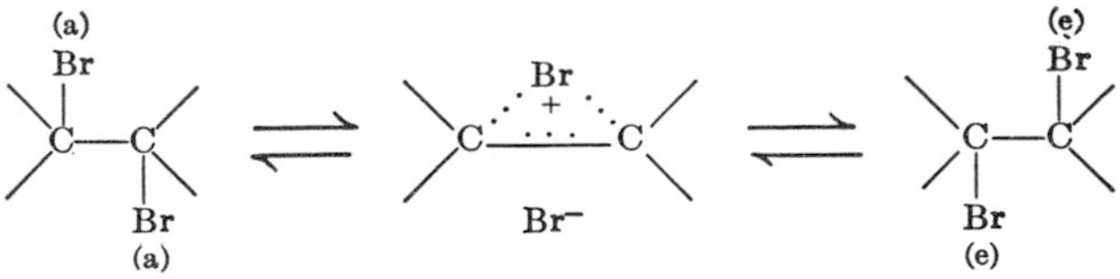

Diaxial   Ion pair   Diequatorial

each bromine atom is retained on the original side of the molecule and becomes bonded to the carbon atom adjacent to the original site. In neat confirmation of

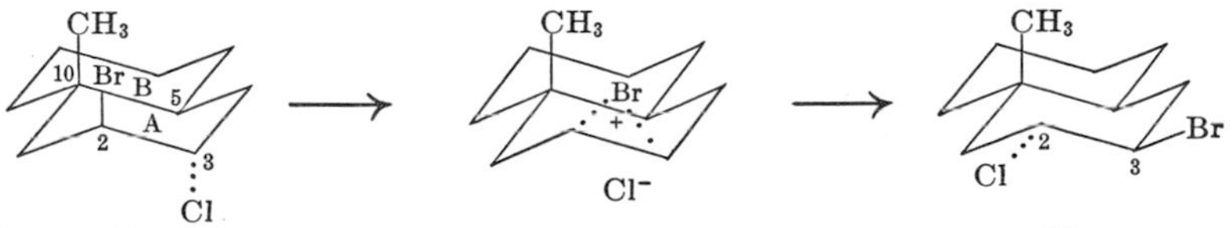

[1] Cyril A. Grob, b. 1917 London; Ph.D. ETH Zurich (Ruzicka, Reichstein); Univ. Basel
[2] Saul Winstein, b. 1912 Montreal; Ph.D. Calif. Inst. Techn. (Lucas); Univ. Calif. Los Angeles

TABLE 5.3. RATES OF BROMINATION OF OLEFINIC DOUBLE BONDS

COMPOUNDS	FORMULA	RELATIVE RATE
Ethylene	CH_2=CH_2	1
Propylene	CH_3CH=CH_2	2.0
as-Dimethylethylene	$(CH_3)_2C$=CH_2	5.5
Tetramethylethylene	$(CH_3)_2C$=$C(CH_3)_2$	14.0
Acrylic acid	CH_2=$CHCO_2H$	<0.03
Crotonic acid	CH_3CH=$CHCO_2H$	0.26
Vinyl bromide	CH_2=$CHBr$	<0.03

the postulate, Barton[1] (1951) found that diaxial 2β-bromo-3α-cholorocholestane (1) rearranges on heating to diequatorial 2α-chloro-3β-bromocholestane (2); the perspective formulas show only rings A and B, viewed from the side.

5.13   Rates of Bromination. — Table 5.3 shows that olefinic compounds vary considerably in the rate at which they add bromine (or chlorine or iodine). Propylene adds bromine twice as fast as ethylene; tetramethylethylene adds fourteen times as fast. A methyl group on an unsaturated carbon thus increases the electron-availability, or negativity, of the atom and so makes it a more attractive site for attack by the electrophile Br^+. The methyl group is identified as electron-releasing, or electron-repelling, and the present evidence confirms an independent inference based upon comparison of the acidic strength of acids (11.3). The four methyl groups of tetramethylethylene all contribute to an increased electron density of the unsaturated center. The carboxyl group of acrylic acid decreases the rate of bromine addition and hence is strongly electron-attracting; crotonic acid is intermediate between acrylic acid and ethylene. The inductive effect of bromine in vinyl bromide is likewise one of strong electron attraction.

5.14   Halogenation with Bond Migration. — M. Sheshukov (1884) and later workers found that chlorination of isobutene at 0° affords in 83 % yield a product which is not the expected dichloride but methallyl chloride (c). W. Reeve (1952) investigated the course of the reaction with synthetic isobutene

$$\overset{3}{C}H_3-\overset{2}{C}=\overset{1}{C}H_2-|\!|\!\rightarrow \left[Cl\overset{3}{C}H_2-\overset{2}{C}=\overset{1}{C}H_2 \right]$$
$$\qquad\quad | \qquad\qquad\qquad\qquad\quad |$$
$$\qquad\quad CH_3 \qquad\qquad\qquad\qquad CH_3$$

Isobutene (a)

$$\downarrow Cl^+$$

$$CH_3-\overset{+}{C}-CH_2Cl \xrightarrow{-H^+} CH_2=C-CH_2Cl$$
$$\qquad\; | \qquad\qquad\qquad\qquad\qquad |$$
$$\qquad CH_3 \qquad\qquad\qquad\qquad\quad CH_3$$

(b)   (c) Methallyl chloride

having radioactive C^{14} at position 1. If attack by chlorine involved substitution of a hydrogen of the C_3-methyl group (a), ozonization (5.31) of the methallyl

[1] Derek H. R. Barton, b. 1918 Gravesend, Kent; Ph.D. and D.Sc. London (Heilbron, E. R. H. Jones); Birkbeck College, Harvard, Glasgow, Imperial College, London

chloride formed would give radioactive formaldehyde. Since the formaldehyde formed was not isotopic, and since isobutene dichloride once formed is stable, the reaction must involve attack by Cl^+ to produce the tertiary carbonium ion (b), which expels a proton to form methallyl chloride (c), rather than to combine with chloride ion. The location of the double bond in the product is thus different from that in the starting material. A free radical mechanism is ruled out by the lack of effect on the liquid phase reaction of light or oxygen and by the fact that no reaction occurs in the vapor phase in the temperature range 70 to 150°.

5.15   HX-Addition. — Hydrogen halides add to alkenes, and the order of reactivity is the same as in their reaction with alcohols: $HI > HBr >$ HCl. Ethylene itself adds the first two reagents but not the less reactive hydrogen chloride. Propylene adds hydrogen chloride and the reaction product is isopropyl chloride, rather than *n*-propyl chloride. These facts are explained very simply by a two-step process of *trans* addition (1) analogous to bromine addition. Initial

$$1.\ CH_3CH{=}CH_2 \xrightarrow{H^+} CH_3\overset{+}{C}HCH_2 \xrightarrow{Cl^-} \overset{\overset{\displaystyle H}{|}}{CH_3CHCH_2} \ \underset{\underset{\displaystyle Cl}{|}}{}$$

$$2.\ (CH_3)_2C{=}CH_2 \xrightarrow{H^+} (CH_3)_2\overset{+}{C}{-}CH_3 \xrightarrow{Br^-} (CH_3)_2CBrCH_3$$

$$3.\ (CH_3)_2C{=}CHCH_3 \xrightarrow{H^+} (CH_3)_2\overset{+}{C}{-}CH_2CH_3 \xrightarrow{Br^-} (CH_3)_2CBrCH_2CH_3$$

$$4.\ CH_3CH{=}CH_2 \xrightarrow{H^+} CH_3\overset{+}{C}HCH_3 \xrightarrow{^-OSO_2OH} \underset{\underset{\displaystyle OSO_2OH}{|}}{CH_3CHCH_3}$$

attack of propylene by a proton as electrophile gives the secondary carbonium ion rather than the less stable primary one and hence the product formed on combination with a chloride ion is isopropyl chloride. Where *cis* and *trans* addition could lead to different products, the product formed invariably is that requiring *trans* addition. Propylene is more reactive than ethylene because electron-release by the methyl group enhances susceptibility to attack by the electrophile. In example (2) a tertiary carbonium ion is formed in preference to a primary ion, and in (3) a tertiary ion is formed in preference to a secondary carbonium ion. Sulfuric acid, that is, concentrated sulfuric acid at 0°, adds readily to olefins in the same way (4). It is easy to infer the direction of addition from knowledge of the mechanism of the reaction. In 1869, long before the mechanism was understood, Markownikoff[1] formulated an empirical rule which summarized the facts known at the time and all those discovered since. The **Markownikoff rule** states that, in the addition of H^+X^- or Br^+OH^-, the positive ion becomes attached to the unsaturated carbon carrying the smaller number of alkyl groups; we now know that this is the point of attachment because the more highly alkylated site will then acquire the positive charge.

[1] Vladimir W. Markownikoff, 1838–1904; b. Russia; Kasan, Odessa, Moscow; *Ber.*, **38,** 4249 (1905); *J. Chem. Soc.*, **87,** 597 (1905)

The reaction of acrylic acid with hydrogen bromide to give β-bromopropionic acid (5) can be explained as involving initial attack by a proton and distribution

$$5.\ CH_2=CHC\overset{\displaystyle OH}{\underset{\displaystyle O}{\Big\langle}} \quad \xrightarrow{H^+} \quad CH_2=CHC\overset{\displaystyle OH}{\underset{\displaystyle OH}{\Big\langle}}{}^+ \quad \longleftrightarrow$$

$$\overset{+}{C}H_2-CH=C\overset{\displaystyle OH}{\underset{\displaystyle OH}{\Big\langle}} \quad \xrightarrow{Br^-} \quad BrCH_2CH_2COOH$$

of the positive charge from one resonance structure to another. In the addition of iodine chloride to crotonic acid (6) the more positive iodine atom (less electron-attracting) becomes attached to the more negatively polarized α-carbon atom (the straight arrows show inductive effects).

$$6.\quad CH_3{\rightarrow}CH{=}CH{\rightarrow}CO_2H + \overset{+-}{I}Cl \xrightarrow[92\%]{} CH_3CHClCHICO_2H$$

The addition of hydrogen bromide to vinyl bromide (7) takes a course opposite to that expected on the basis of the strong electron-attracting effect of the bromine atom, evident in the slowness of bromine addition (Table 5.3). In this instance

$$7.\ CH_2{=}CH{\rightarrow}Br \xrightarrow{H^+} CH_3\overset{+}{C}HBr \xrightarrow{Br^-} CH_3CHBr_2$$

addition seems to be controlled by a shift of an electron pair from bromine in the direction opposite to that of the inductive effect. Neither inductive nor resonance polarization effects are necessarily permanent, and there is some variation with the polarity of the reagent or of the solvent; in view of such complications predictions are particularly difficult where two effects operate in opposite directions. In allyl bromide (8) an electron displacement, similar to that in (7), initiated by the

$$8.\ CH_2{=}CH{\rightarrow}CH_2{\rightarrow}Br \xrightarrow{HBr} CH_3CHBrCH_2Br$$
$$(not\ BrCH_2CH_2CH_2Br)$$

unshared electrons of bromine is not possible because of the absence of a double bond capable of transmitting the effect, and the addition proceeds as usual through the more stable intermediate carbonium ion.

5.16   Halohydrins. — Ethylene reacts with bromine in the presence of water or methanol to give ethylene bromohydrin, $HOCH_2CH_2Br$, or its methyl ether, $CH_3OCH_2CH_2Br$. The reactions were once regarded as additions of hypobromous acid or methyl hypobromite, formed in the equilibrium process (1). This interpretation was ruled out by the results of a kinetic study of the

$$1.\ Br_2 + HOH(R) \leftrightarrows BrOH(R) + HBr$$

bromination of stilbene in methanol (Bartlett and Tarbell, 1936), which results in formation of the methoxy bromide 2a in 99% yield. If the reaction involved methyl hypobromite, the rate of formation of the ether (a) would be decreased by addition of acid, which would suppress formation of methyl hypobromite according to (1). Actually, increase in the hydrogen-ion concentration was without effect; on the other hand, formation of the methoxy bromide was suppressed by added bromide ion. A rational explanation is that the initial product is a car-

2. $C_6H_5CH=CHC_6H_5$ $\xrightarrow{Br^+}$ $C_6H_5\overset{+}{C}HCHC_6H_5$
    Stilbene |
                                                          Br

CH₃O⁻ ↗ $C_6H_5CHCHC_6H_5$
                  | |
                  Br OCH₃
                    (a)

Br⁻ ↘ $C_6H_5CHCHC_6H_5$
                  | |
                  Br Br
                    (b)

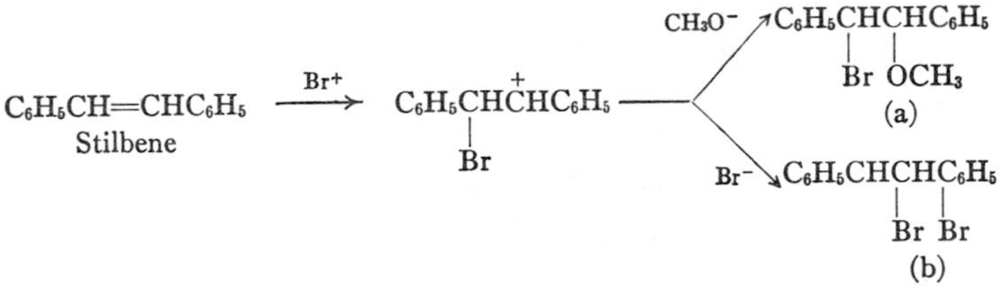

bonium ion that can react with either methoxide ion (a) or with bromide ion (b). From the reaction of bromine in aqueous solution with the anion of dimethylmaleic acid (3), Tarbell and Bartlett isolated a β-lactone which on hydrolysis yielded the

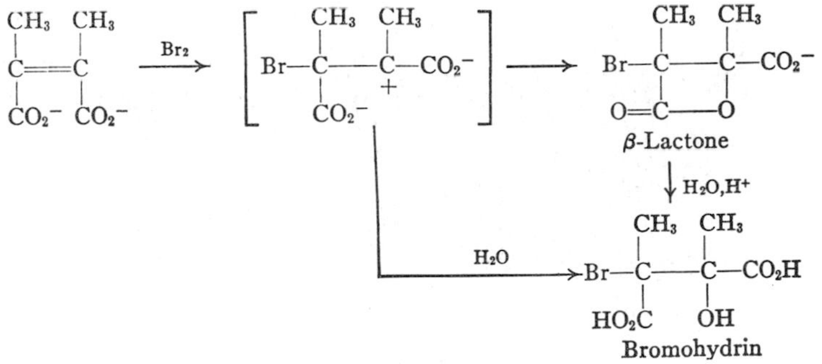

corresponding bromohydrin. The β-lactone was found not to arise from the bromo-hydrin, and it evidently is formed from an intermediate carbonium ion by intra-molecular attack of the anionic carboxylate group on the electron-deficient carbon atom.

The two-step mechanism accounts for the direction of addition to unsymmetrical olefins as defined empirically in the Markownikoff rule. In example (4) the electro-phile attacks in such a way as to produce the carbonium ion of greater stability

4. $(CH_3)_2C=CH_2$ $\xrightarrow{Br^+}$ $(CH_3)_2\overset{+}{C}-CH_2$ $\xrightarrow{OH^-}$ $(CH_3)_2\overset{\overset{\displaystyle OH}{|}}{C}-CH_2$
                                                          | |
                                                          Br   Br

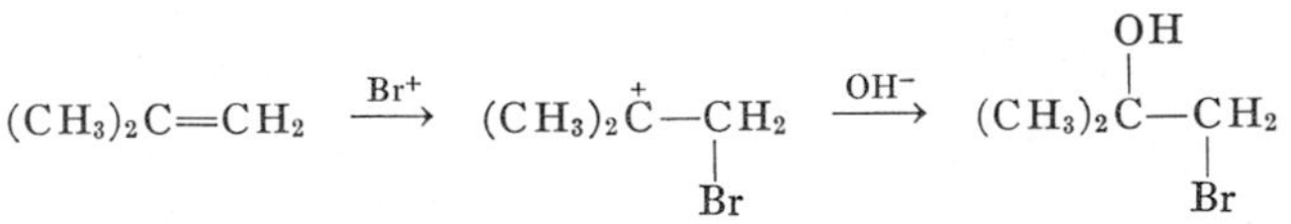

Notice that this interpretation of the reaction adequately explains the facts and is simpler than one invoking a cyclic bromonium ion.

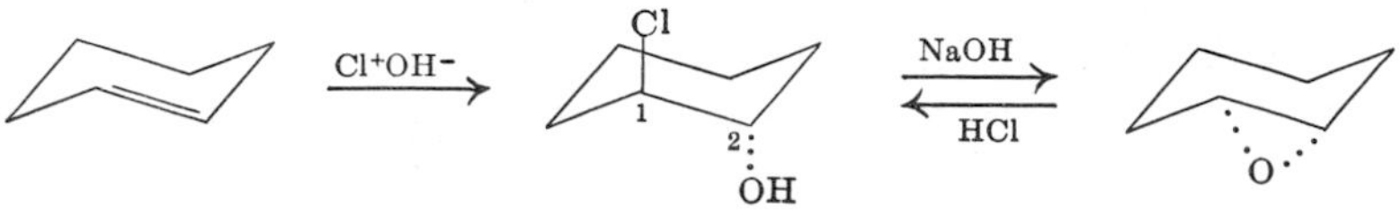

The initial product of hypochlorite addition to cyclohexene undoubtedly is the diaxial chlorohydrin, 1β-chloro-2α-cyclohexanol (5). Although the diequatorial form is more stable, the conversion of the substance to the oxide by reaction with base must proceed by reversion to the diaxial form and elimination of hydrogen chloride from the antiparallel groups. The standard procedure (*Org. Syn.*) calls for adding sodium hydroxide solution to ice and water containing a small amount of mercuric chloride, and yellow mercuric oxide precipitates, when passing in chlorine at 0–5° until the precipitate just dissolves. Nitric acid is added to produce an approximately neutral solution, cyclohexene is added, and the mixture is stirred and kept at 15–20° by cooling. The mixture is saturated with salt and the product separated by steam distillation and then distilled at 20 mm. pressure; yield 72%. Conversion to cyclohexane-1α,2α-oxide, which involves inversion at C_1, is effected by stirring the chlorohydrin with aqueous sodium hydroxide at 40–45°; yield 72%. The reverse reaction, cleavage of the oxide to the chlorohydrin, gives initially the diaxial product.

Conversion of a solid unsaturated compound insoluble in water into a bromohydrin can be done with N-bromoacetamide in aqueous dioxane or acetone. Like other reagents of similar structure, this bromoamide has a bromine atom described

$$CH_3\overset{\overset{O}{\|}}{C}-N\overset{\diagup H}{\diagdown Br} \quad + \quad H_2O \quad \rightleftharpoons \quad CH_3\overset{\overset{O}{\|}}{C}-N\overset{\diagup H}{\diagdown H} \quad + \quad Br^+OH^-$$

N-Bromoacetamide
m.p. 102–105°

as positive because in the presence of water it is in equilibrium with hypobromous acid.

5.17   **Reaction with Peracids (Epoxidation[1]).** — **Perbenzoic acid** is a rather unstable reagent which is prepared as required from dibenzoyl peroxide, a crystalline solid (dec. 105°) of reasonable shelf stability prepared by dropwise addition of benzoyl chloride with stirring to an ice-cold 5–7% solution of sodium peroxide (1). Treatment of dibenzoyl peroxide at 0° with a methanolic solution

$$1. \ 2\ C_6H_5\overset{\overset{O}{\|}}{C}Cl + NaOONa \rightarrow C_6H_5\overset{\overset{O}{\|}}{C}-O-O-\overset{\overset{O}{\|}}{C}C_6H_5 + 2\ NaCl$$

Dibenzoyl peroxide

$$2. \ C_6H_5\overset{\overset{O}{\|}}{C}-O-O-\overset{\overset{O}{\|}}{C}-C_6H_5 \xrightarrow{CH_3ONa} C_6H_5\overset{\overset{O}{\|}}{C}OONa + C_6H_5\overset{\overset{O}{\|}}{C}OCH_3$$

$$3. \ C_6H_5\overset{\overset{O}{\|}}{C}OONa \xrightarrow[CHCl_3]{H_2SO_4} C_6H_5\overset{\overset{O}{\|}}{C}OOH$$

Perbenzoic acid

of sodium methoxide in the presence of chloroform to extract the methyl benzoate produces (2), careful addition of sulfuric acid at 0° (3) and extraction with chloroform gives a solution which when separated and dried is ready for use. Such a so-

---

[1] Some chemists prefer the name epoxide or epoxy derivative (from *epi-*, on, upon) to describe a 1,2- or *vic*-oxide resulting from addition of oxygen to the two carbons of a double bond. Description of the process as an epoxidation is particularly convenient.

lution usually contains a trace of sulfuric acid, which in certain instances introduces a complication. Chloroform exposed to air may contain a trace of phosgene ($O{=}CCl_2$, see 10.5), which may inhibit reaction. An alternative reagent free from these disadvantages is **monoperphthalic acid,** prepared by stirring a suspension of phthalic anhydride and sodium perborate in water at 0° (4). A solution

4.

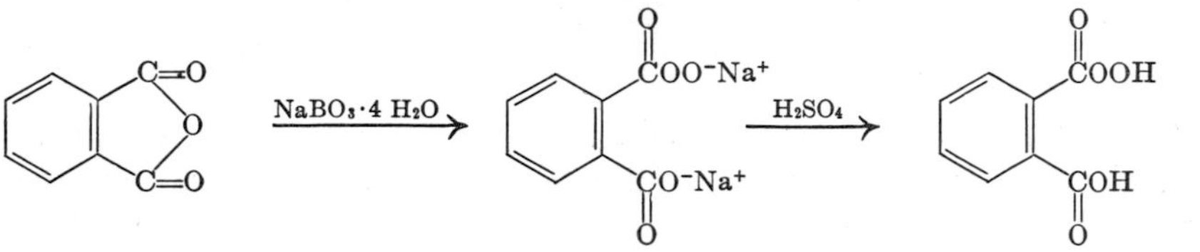

Phthalic anhydride   Monoperphthalic acid

of the sodium salt results, and this is acidified and extracted with ether. The ethereal solution can be kept for long periods at 0°. The peracid reacts with an alkene to give up the extra oxygen with formation of phthalic acid, which is insoluble in ether, and hence the progress of the reaction can be followed roughly from the amount of crystalline phthalic acid that separates. When perbenzoic acid is used the benzoic acid formed remains in solution in chloroform and there is no visual evidence of reaction. In either case the peracid content of the solution is determined by titration with thiosulfate and the alkene is treated with 1.1–1.2 equivalents of reagent in ether or chloroform. The solution is let stand for several days and tested with starch-iodide paper to make sure that excess reagent is still present; the rate of consumption of reagent can be followed by titration of an aliquot portion of the solution.

Either peracid reacts with an alkene to produce an oxide. Since the three-membered oxide ring can only have the *cis* configuration, oxide formation is an instance of *cis* addition, the first yet considered. Two mechanisms can be formulated; probably instances exist in which one is to be preferred to the other. In (5) the reaction is pictured as an electrophilic attack by OH^+ with formation of the oxide oxonium ion and the benzoate ion; the latter ion then acquires the proton to

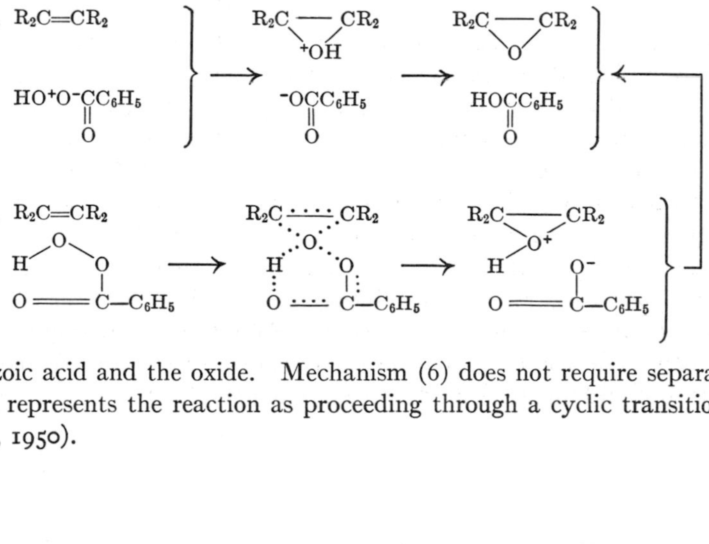

give benzoic acid and the oxide. Mechanism (6) does not require separation of OH^+ but represents the reaction as proceeding through a cyclic transition state (Bartlett, 1950).

The cleavage of an oxide with hydrogen chloride to give a *trans* diaxial chlorohydrin is illustrated in the preceding section. Two other typical cleavage reactions are shown in (7) for cholestane-$3\alpha,4\alpha$-oxide, which is the product of reaction

7.

of Δ^3-cholestene with monoperphthalic acid (rear attack). Reduction with lithium aluminum hydride cleaves the oxide bond extending to C_4 and gives the axial 3α-ol; note that cleavage of the other bond would lead to the 4α-ol, which is equatorial. The O—C_4 bond is cleaved in all other reactions, for example, in the reaction with acetic acid (acetolysis). Inversion occurs at the site of attack, C_4, and the product is the diaxial $3\alpha,4\beta$-diol 4-acetate. Oxide rings in all parts of the steroid structure have been investigated and found to conform to the pattern illustrated: reductive cleavage gives the axial alcohol, and acid cleavage gives a diaxial halohydrin or diol derivative. Hydrolytic cleavage of an oxide to a free diol is done most efficiently by using a water-containing solvent and an acid catalyst incapable of forming an ester. Thus in one procedure a solution of the oxide in aqueous tetrahydrofurane is treated with a little perchloric acid and let stand at room temperature for several hours and then diluted with water.

$$
\begin{array}{c}
CH_2\text{—}CH_2\\
CH_2 \quad CH_2\\
O
\end{array}
$$

Tetrahydrofurane
B. p. 65.4°, miscible
with water

Ordinarily an oxide formed by reaction with perbenzoic acid in chloroform solution is not cleaved by the benzoic acid formed. However, a conjugated diene

8. $R_2C{=}CH{-}CH{=}CR'_2 \longrightarrow \left[R_2C\underset{\ddot{O}}{\text{——}}\overset{H}{\underset{|}{C}}{-}CH{=}CR'_2 \right] \xrightarrow{C_6H_5CO_2H}$

$$
\begin{array}{c}
OCOC_6H_5\\
R_2C{-}\underset{|}{C}{-}CH{=}CR'_2\\
HO \;\; H
\end{array}
$$

(8) is attacked by one mole of perbenzoic acid at the more reactive double bond to give an allylic oxide with an activated oxide linkage and this substance is cleaved by benzoic acid under the mild conditions to give a diol monobenzoate.

Peracetic acid and **performic acid** usually are not employed as preformed reagents but are generated *in situ* when a solution of an alkene in acetic or formic acid is treated with 30% hydrogen peroxide and maintained at a temperature in the range 40–90°. Performic acid is the more reactive of the two reagents. Since the temperature is higher than in a reaction with an aromatic peracid, and particularly since the concentration of acid is very much higher, the oxide is cleaved as it is formed to an ester or mixture of esters. Formic acid, not only more strongly acidic than acetic acid but also more reactive, reacts with primary and secondary alcohols to yield formate esters at moderate temperatures. Thus a disubstituted olefin (9) may give either a monoformate or a diformate, or a mixture, and usually the crude product is saponified for isolation of the free diol (*trans*, if isomerism is possible). Nonaqueous solutions of pure peracetic acid are made (Union Car-

9. 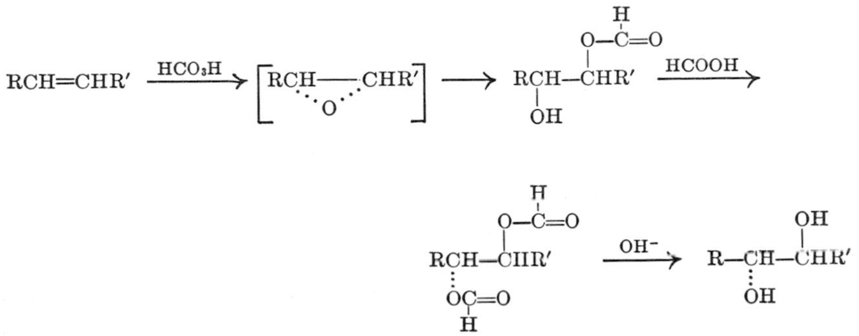 $RCH{=}CHR' \xrightarrow{HCO_3H} \left[RCH{-}CHR' \text{ (O)} \right] \longrightarrow \underset{\underset{OH}{|}}{RCH{-}CHR'} \overset{\overset{O-C=O}{|}\overset{H}{}}{} \xrightarrow{HCOOH}$

$\underset{\underset{H}{\overset{|}{OC=O}}}{RCH{-}CHR'} \overset{\overset{O-C=O}{|}\overset{H}{}}{} \xrightarrow{OH^-} \underset{\underset{OH}{|}}{R{-}CH{-}CHR'} \overset{OH}{\overset{|}{}}$

bide, 1957) by low-temperature oxygenation of acetaldehyde to a peroxide of the composition $(CH_3CHO)_2(O_2)$, which at temperatures above $0°$ decomposes to acetaldehyde and peracetic acid. Still more reactive is **pertrifluoroacetic acid** (W. D. Emmons, 1954). The anhydrous reagent is particularly effective; it is made by adding trifluoroacetic anhydride with ice cooling to a suspension of 90% hydrogen peroxide in methylene chloride. The resulting solution of peracid is then added to a solution of the olefin in methylene chloride containing the trimethylamine salt of trifluoroacetic acid (to inhibit polycondensation). The mono ester formed on cleavage of the oxide (10) is converted to the free glycol when refluxed with methanolic hydrogen chloride. The reaction is very rapid and yields are excellent.

10. 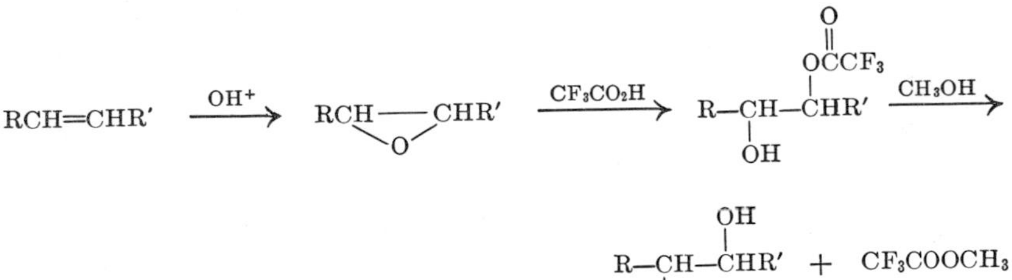 $RCH{=}CHR' \xrightarrow{OH^+} RCH{-}CHR' \text{(O)} \xrightarrow{CF_3CO_2H} \underset{\underset{OH}{|}}{R{-}CH{-}CHR'} \overset{\overset{OCCF_3}{|}\overset{O}{\|}}{} \xrightarrow{CH_3OH}$

$\underset{\underset{OH}{|}}{R{-}CH{-}CHR'} \overset{OH}{\overset{|}{}} + CF_3COOCH_3$

A more easily prepared and highly reactive reagent is **p-nitroperbenzoic acid** (Vilkas,[1] 1959). It is made by gradual addition of p-nitrobenzoyl chloride to a stirred suspension of sodium peroxide in tetrahydrofurane at $-20°$ to $-5°$ in the

$$p\text{-}O_2NC_6H_4COCl + Na_2O_2 \xrightarrow[84\text{-}87\%]{\substack{\text{Tetrahydrofurane (H}_2\text{O);}\\ \text{HCl}}} p\text{-}O_2NC_6H_4CO_3H$$

M.p. 137°

[1] Michel Vilkas, b. 1923; Ph.D. Paris (Dupont); École Normal Supérieure, Paris

presence of a catalytic amount of frozen water. The catalytic effect of water is accounted for as follows:

$$NaOONa + H_2O \rightarrow HO\bar{O} + O\bar{H} + 2\overset{+}{Na}$$

$$\underset{\substack{\|\\O}}{ArCCl} + HO\bar{O} \rightarrow \underset{\substack{|\\OOH}}{Ar\overset{\overset{\bar{O}}{|}}{C}-Cl} \rightarrow \underset{\substack{\|\\O}}{ArCOOH} + \bar{Cl}$$

$$ArCO_3H + O\bar{H} \rightarrow ArCO_3^- + H_2O$$

p-Nitroperbenzoic acid has the advantage of being a crystalline solid which is completely stable at room temperature. Rate constants show the reagent to be 7–20 times as reactive as perbenzoic acid.

5.18   **Peroxide Effect.** — Prior to 1933 a number of investigators had studied the addition of hydrogen bromide, usually liquid hydrogen bromide, to allyl bromide, but with highly variable results. The 1,2- and 1,3-dibromides were both obtained, but sometimes one product predominated and sometimes the

$$CH_2=CHCH_2Br + HBr \rightarrow CH_3CHBrCH_2Br + BrCH_2CH_2CH_2Br$$
Allyl bromide   1,2-   1,3-

other. In a careful reinvestigation of the reaction reported in 1933, Kharasch and Mayo[1] developed special techniques for purification of the allyl bromide, for removing unchanged starting material from the reaction mixture, and for analysis of mixtures of the two products (b.p. difference about 24°). But the results were variable and not reproducible; in experiments conducted under apparently identical conditions, the ratio of products varied from run to run. Eventually the Chicago workers recognized a trend in the ratio depending upon the length of time a sample of allyl bromide had been exposed to the air. They then found that this particular unsaturated compound absorbs oxygen with great avidity and that a sample on even brief exposure may contain a percent or two of peroxide, determinable by titration. Furthermore, this or other peroxide catalyzes an abnormal reaction which does not occur in its absence. The normal reaction can be caused

$$CH_2=CHCH_2Br + HBr \begin{cases} \xrightarrow{\text{Antioxidant}} CH_3CHBrCH_2Br \text{ (normal)} \\ \xrightarrow{\text{Peroxide}} BrCH_2CH_2CH_2Br \text{ (abnormal)} \end{cases}$$

to take precedence by addition of a small amount of hydroquinone, an antioxidant which breaks a free radical chain reaction induced by a peroxide. The abnormal reaction becomes the predominant reaction when dibenzoyl peroxide is added as initiator.

Application of the two procedures to a number of alkenes showed that the products predicted from the Markownikoff rule are the normal products of addition conducted with elimination of the peroxide effect by use of an antioxidant.

[1] Frank R. Mayo, b. 1908 Chicago; Ph.D. Chicago (Kharasch); U. S. Rubber Co.; General Electric Research Lab.; Stanford Research Inst.

Normal addition follows the ionic mechanism outlined above; peroxide-catalyzed addition evidently is a free-radical reaction. In the usual case, for example propylene, normal addition gives the Markownikoff product $CH_3CHBrCH_3$. In the case of allyl bromide and vinyl bromide, where the empirical rule seems inapplicable and the interpretation not too certain (see p. 156), addition in the presence of peroxide takes a direction opposite to that followed in the absence of peroxide.

Hydroquinone
m. p. 170°

In explanation of the abnormal reaction, Kharasch, Engelmann, and Mayo (1937) suggested that a radical formed by homolysis of the peroxide (1) attacks hydrogen bromide to produce a bromine radical (2), which in turn attacks the alkene (3) to give a bromine-containing fragment with an odd electron. This radical abstracts hydrogen from hydrogen bromide (4) to give the addition product with regeneration of a bromine radical. Presumably in the reaction of the alkene with a bromine radical the more stable radical is that having the greater number of carbon substituents; in the case formulated, it

1. $RO:OR \rightarrow 2\ RO\cdot$
2. $RO\cdot + HBr \rightarrow ROH + \cdot Br$
3. $CH_3CH{=}CH_2 + \cdot Br \rightarrow CH_3\dot{C}HCH_2Br$ (not $CH_3CHBr\dot{C}H_2$)
4. $CH_3\dot{C}HCH_2Br + HBr \rightarrow CH_3CH_2CH_2Br + \cdot Br$

is secondary rather than primary. The order of stability thus parallels the order in carbonium ions (compare 5.6). Stabilization may result from hyperconjugation of an odd electron with electrons on an adjacent carbon atom:

$$H:\overset{\overset{H}{\cdot\cdot}}{\underset{\underset{H}{\cdot\cdot}}{C}}:\overset{\overset{H}{\cdot\cdot}}{\underset{\underset{H}{}}{C}}:\overset{\overset{}{\cdot\cdot}}{\underset{\underset{H}{}}{C}}:Br \longrightarrow H:\overset{\overset{H\cdot}{}}{\underset{\underset{H}{\cdot\cdot}}{C}}::\overset{}{\underset{\underset{H}{\cdot\cdot}}{C}}:\overset{\overset{H}{\cdot\cdot}}{\underset{\underset{H}{\cdot\cdot}}{C}}:Br$$

Radical addition differs from ionic addition in that the bond first formed is C—Br rather than C—H. The steric requirements appear to be the same, for free radical addition of hydrogen bromide has been shown to be stereospecific and to occur by *trans* addition (H. L. Goering, 1952).

Radical chain addition makes available products otherwise difficultly accessible, for example, the bromo acid formulated in (5). Note that the peroxide effect is

5. $CH_2{=}CH(CH_2)_8CO_2H\ +\ HBr\ \xrightarrow{\text{Peroxide}}\ Br(CH_2)_{10}CO_2H$
    Undecylenic acid   ω-Bromoundecylic acid
    (from castor oil)

specific to hydrogen bromide. Hydrogen iodide is oxidized by peroxides. Additions of hydrogen chloride and of sulfuric acid proceed the same way in the presence of a peroxide as in its absence.

5.19   **Debromination and Related Eliminations.** — A *vic*-dibromide resulting from addition of bromine to an olefinic product can be reconverted into the olefin (1) by the action of zinc dust in acetic acid, or of zinc dust in an ethereal solution containing a little acetic acid, or with zinc dust in boiling ethanol. An alternative method is to reflux the dibromide in acetone with an equivalent amount

of sodium iodide (2), which is readily soluble in the organic solvent; the iodine
formed can be reduced with sodium bisulfite prior to recovery of the organic
product.　Compounds containing an olefinic double bond often can be purified

$$1.\ R_2CBrCBrR_2' + Zn \rightarrow R_2C{=}CR_2' + ZnBr_2$$
$$2.\ R_2CBrCBrR_2' + 2\,NaI \rightarrow R_2C{=}CR_2' + 2\,NaBr + I_2$$

efficiently by conversion to the *vic*-dibromide and debromination.　Thus a sample
of trimethylethylene contaminated with the corresponding saturated hydrocarbon,
2-methylbutane (isopentane), could not be separated effectively from this substance by distillation because the boiling points lie too close together.　If the
mixture is treated with bromine without undue exposure to light, the alkene reacts
selectively and is converted into a derivative heavier by some 160 units of molecular weight and consequently having a much higher boiling point.　Trimethyl-

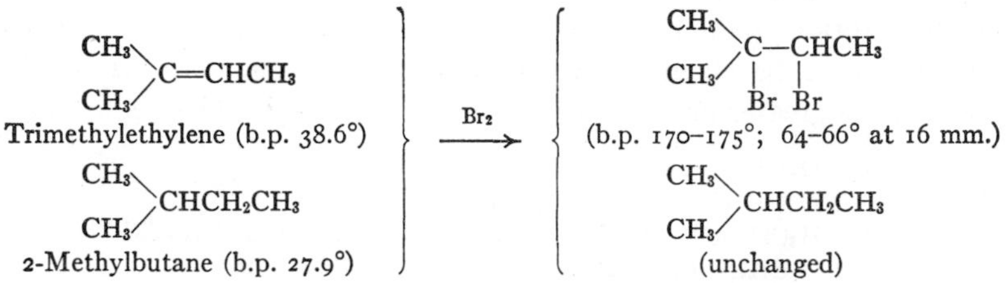

Trimethylethylene (b.p. 38.6°)

2-Methylbutane (b.p. 27.9°)

(b.p. 170–175°; 64–66° at 16 mm.)

(unchanged)

ethylene dibromide boils at a temperature 140–145° higher than 2-methylbutane,
and can be separated easily by distillation; the distillation is conducted in vacuum,
for slight decomposition of the halide at the higher temperature is thereby obviated.　By treatment of the distilled addition product with zinc dust in alcoholic
solution, pure trimethylethylene is regenerated.

The cholesterol isolated from animal lipids or from gall stones can be purified
by treatment of a solution of the solid in ether with a solution of bromine in acetic
acid.　Cholesterol-$5\alpha,6\beta$-dibromide crystallizes at once and leaves companion
steroids in the mother liquor.　A suspension of the sparingly soluble dibromide in
ether containing a little acetic acid reacts rapidly with zinc dust with formation
of pure cholesterol in 93% yield.　It was noted earlier (5.12) that this dibromide
is *trans* diaxial and that it rearranges to the more stable *trans* diequatorial dibromide.　Both dibromides when treated with sodium iodide in acetone undergo
trans elimination with regeneration of cholesterol, but the labile $5\alpha,6\beta$-dibromide

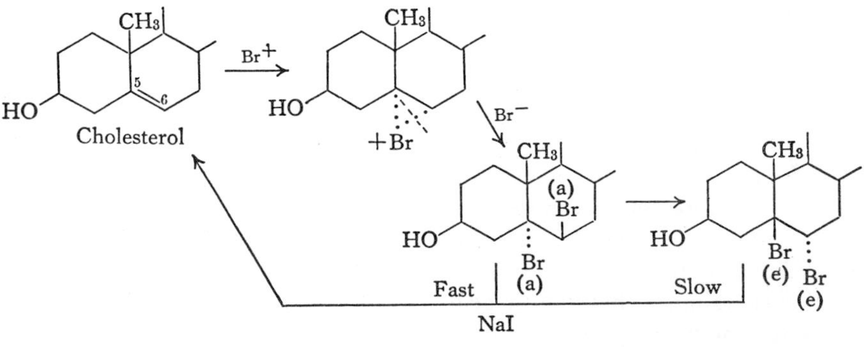

Cholesterol

reacts much faster because the bromine and carbon atoms concerned all lie in a plane and hence are ideally oriented for a four-center transition state (a) requiring

| (a) | (b) | (c) |

minimum activation energy. Formulations (b) and (c) depict the views obtained on looking along the C_5–C_6 axis from C_5 to C_6 in the labile (b) and in the stable (c) dibromide (Newman projections, see p. 168); the planarity of the bromines and carbons in the first and lack of planarity in the second is evident. A similar planar transition state in the reverse reaction of bromination accounts for the formation of the diaxial $5\alpha,6\beta$-dibromide. Probably the *trans* diaxial dibromide alone is capable of undergoing debromination and the slow reaction of the more stable isomer proceeds through reversion to the less favored equilibrium partner.

Young[1] (1939) studied the debromination of dibromides with iodide ion in homogeneous solution and found that the rate of reaction is proportional to the concentration of both the dibromide and the iodide ion. The reaction is believed to take place in two steps, the first of which (a) is the slower. Iodide ion abstracts

(a) $I^- + Br{-}CH_2{-}CH_2{-}Br \longrightarrow IBr + CH_2{=}CH_2 + Br^-$

(b) $I^- + IBr \longrightarrow I_2 + Br^-$

Br^+ with simultaneous shift of electrons, as shown by the curved arrows, with elimination of Br^-. The process is described as an E_2 reaction (elimination, second order).

A related elimination reaction of preparative value consists in formation of an ethylenic double bond by the action of zinc and acetic acid on a bromohydrin or chlorohydrin, or the corresponding acetate. Use of the reaction is illustrated by

$$R_2C{-}CR_2 \quad \xrightarrow{Zn,\ HOAc} \quad R_2C{=}CR_2 \quad \xleftarrow{Zn,\ HOAc} \quad R_2C{-}CR_2$$
$$\;\;|\;\;\;\;|\qquad\qquad\qquad\qquad\qquad\qquad\qquad\;\;|\;\;\;\;\;\;\;|$$
$$Br\ OH \qquad\qquad\qquad\qquad\qquad\qquad\qquad Br\ OCOCH_3$$

the synthesis of *trans*-stilbene from benzoin, a readily available starting material (25.11). Reaction with thionyl chloride replaces the hydroxyl group by chlorine and the resulting desyl chloride is reduced with sodium borohydride in ethanol to a chlorohydrin mixture. Zinc dust and a little acetic acid are added to the alcoholic solution and the mixture is refluxed for 1 hr. to effect elimination. Crystallization of the recovered product affords diamond-shaped irridescent plates of *trans*-stilbene in overall yield of 65%. *cis*-Stilbene, a liquid (m.p. 6°), is formed as a minor product and can be isolated from the mother liquid as the crystalline di-

[1] William G. Young, b. 1902 Colorado Springs, Colo.; Ph.D. Calif. Inst. Techn. (Lucas); Univ. Calif. Los Angeles

bromide. Notice that desyl chloride has one asymmetric carbon atom; since the starting material is *dl*-benzoin, the chloride is likewise composed of equal parts of the *d*- and *l*-forms. Reduction of the carbonyl group generates a second center of asymmetry and the product is a mixture of two chlorohydrins which can be described as *dl*- and *d'l'*-forms. Because of a relationship to the sugars erythrose

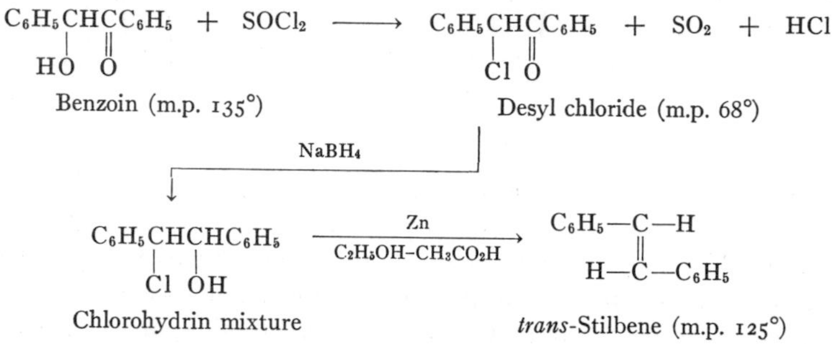

$$C_6H_5CHCC_6H_5 \; + \; SOCl_2 \; \longrightarrow \; C_6H_5CHCC_6H_5 \; + \; SO_2 \; + \; HCl$$
$$\quad | \quad || \qquad\qquad\qquad\qquad | \quad ||$$
$$\quad HO \quad O \qquad\qquad\qquad\qquad\; Cl \quad O$$

Benzoin (m.p. 135°)   Desyl chloride (m.p. 68°)

NaBH₄

$$C_6H_5CHCHC_6H_5 \; \xrightarrow[\;C_2H_5OH-CH_3CO_2H\;]{Zn} \; C_6H_5-C-H$$
$$\quad | \quad | \qquad\qquad\qquad\qquad\qquad\qquad ||$$
$$\quad Cl \; OH \qquad\qquad\qquad\qquad\qquad\; H-C-C_6H_5$$

Chlorohydrin mixture   *trans*-Stilbene (m.p. 125°)

and threose, the predominant product is called the *erythro* chlorohydrin and the minor product is called the *threo* chlorohydrin. The convention for formulation of a *dl*-compound is to show just one of the two forms, either *d*- or *l*-; the enantiomer not shown is the mirror image isomer. In one space formula (1) for the *erythro* chlorohydrin the phenyl groups are swung to the rear (dotted lines), hydrogen appears at the left front corner of each carbon, and hydroxyl and chlorine

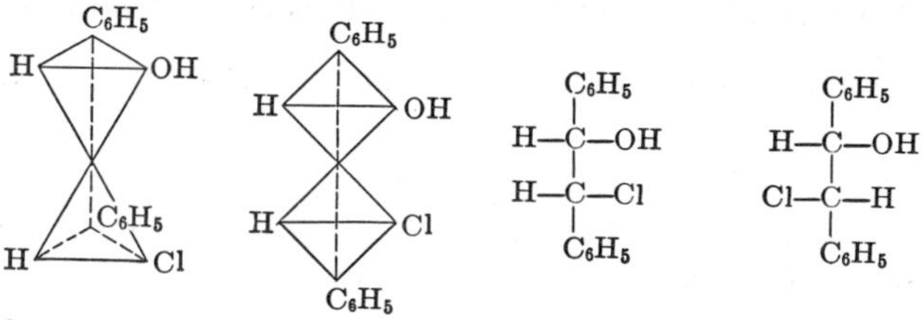

| (1) | (2) | (3) | (4) |

Erythro (d- or l-)   *Threo (d'- or l'-)*

are at the right front corners. Formula (2) is a diagrammatic representation of (1) in which both tetrahedra have been tilted forward until they are both viewed in the same way; the dotted base line extends to the rear. Formula (3) is a planar projection of (2); in using this simplified formula, one must remember that the phenyl groups are to the rear and the other four groups are to the front. Formula (4) is the planar projection of one member of the *dl-threo* pair. Note that formulas (1)–(4) show only the respective arrangement of groups on the two carbon atoms and that the placing of the phenyl groups to the rear is a purely arbitrary convention and is not intended to imply that this is the most stable conformation of the molecule. The latter problem will be discussed presently. Formulas (3) and (4) are conventional representations of two of four optically active isomers. The *d*- and *l-erythro* forms are enantiomers, as are the *d'*- and *l'-threo* forms. The *d*- and *l-erythro* forms are described as **diastereoisomers** of the *d*- and *l-threo* forms. Enantiomers rotate to the same degree but in opposite direction; diastereoisomers are almost like unrelated compounds and usually differ in magnitude of rotation, in melting point, and other properties.

That the *erythro* chlorohydrin is the main reduction product and that it affords only *trans*-stilbene is interpreted as follows. The steric course of the reduction of desyl chloride is determined by the relative size of the three groups on the asymmetric carbon atom (Prelog[1]-Cram[2] rule, 1952–53): phenyl is large (L), chlorine is medium (M), and hydrogen is small (S). The most stable conformation of desyl chloride may be that shown in model (5), in which the large phenyl groups are on opposite sides of the molecule, but in this form the carbonyl group is too

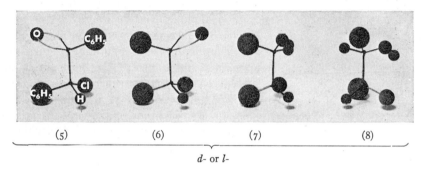

(5)   (6)   (7)   (8)

d- or *l-*

hindered by the nearby phenyl group below it for ready reaction. Thus the conformation assumed for reduction is (6), in which the carbonyl group points away from the large group (phenyl) and is flanked by the medium (Cl) and small group (H). The carbonyl group is then accessible to attack by the borohydride, which approaches on the side of the small group and opens the double bond to give the *erythro* product (7). If model (7) is turned 90° to the right, the result is a model (8) which corresponds to formulas (1)–(3) for the *erythro* chlorohydrin. That the carbonyl group in (5) is hindered is particularly evident in the Stuart model (5a);

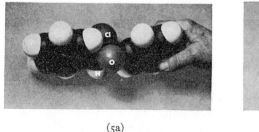

(5a)   (5b)

rotation of both phenyl groups as in (5b) produces a very congested situation. In the Stuart model (6a), corresponding to (6) above, the carbonyl group becomes much more accessible. Reduction in the specific steric direction expected is the major reaction, but the reaction is not 100 % **stereospecific** and a certain amount

---

[1] Vladimir Prelog, b. 1906 Sarajevo, Jugoslavia; Dr. Ing. Prague (Votoček); ETH Zurich
[2] Donald J. Cram, b. 1919 Chester, Vt.; Ph.D. Harvard (Fieser); Univ. Calif. Los Angeles

of *threo* product is formed as well. Notice that if the lower carbon atom were not asymmetric, for example, if it carried a phenyl group and two hydrogens, no preference would exist for the opening of one or the other member of the double bond; the chances of opening in the two directions would be equal, and a 50:50 mixture would result. The reduction of desyl chloride

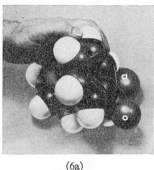

(6a)

with preferential formation of the *erythro* chlorohydrin is an **asymmetric synthesis;** that is, a synthesis in which a center of asymmetry already present exerts a steric control over the formation of a further center of asymmetry and gives preference to one product over the other.

Model (8) shows merely the conformation of the *erythro* chlorohydrin as it is initially produced, but not the most stable form. The most stable conformation must be that in which steric strain from nonbonded interactions is at a minimum. Since repulsive effects are dependent upon the size of interacting groups, severity of interaction must decrease in the order phenyl:phenyl, hydroxyl:chlorine, hydrogen:hydrogen. Hence the most stable conformation is that (9) in which

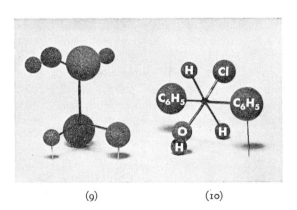

(9)   (10)

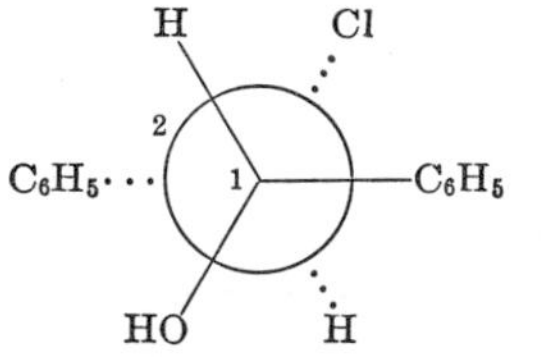

(11, most stable)
Erythro (*d-* or *l-*)
M. p. of *dl* 77°

the two phenyls are maximally separated and in which hydroxyl and chlorine are also on opposite sides of the molecule. This arrangement is known as a **staggered conformation,** in which steric strain is at a minimum. The diagrammatic representation (11) is a Newman[1] projection derived by viewing model (9) along the axis of the bond connecting the asymmetric centers as shown by placing model (9) as in (10). The carbon atom nearest the eye is

(12, least stable)

numbered C_1 and its other three valence bonds are represented by full lines; the carbon atom to the rear (C_2) is represented by a circle and its valences by dotted lines. Diagram (11) emphasizes the point that the large phenyl groups are as

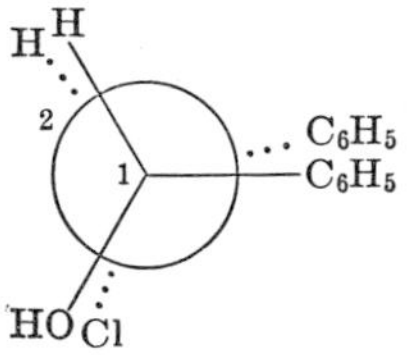

[1] Melvin S. Newman, b. 1908 New York; Ph.D. Yale (R. J. Anderson); Ohio State Univ.

far apart as possible and that OH:Cl and H:H interactions are also at a minimum; all three pairs are in the favorable staggered arrangement. The least stable conformation for the *erythro* form is that (12) in which carbon 1 is rotated until phenyl eclipses phenyl and hydroxyl eclipses chlorine; two severe eclipsed interactions would contribute to instability. In the *threo* isomer (13) the two large phenyls assume a staggered orientation and force hydroxyl and chlorine

d- and *l-Threo*
M. p. of *dl* 47°
(13)

into an arrangement described as **skew.** A skew interaction is intermediate in severity of strain between an eclipsed and a staggered interaction. The *threo* form is not so symmetrical as the *erythro* form in which the large and medium groups on one side of the molecule are balanced by groups of the same or of comparable size on the opposite side. The *erythro* compound, as expected, has the higher melting point.

The staggered conformation of the *erythro* chlorohydrin (11) is ideal for *trans* elimination of HOCl, since the groups eliminated and carbons to which they are attached all lie in a plane; the phenyl groups retain essentially the original staggered arrangement in the product, *trans*-stilbene. The reaction of the *threo* chlorohydrin (13) with zinc and acetic acid must involve rotation about the connecting bond until hydroxyl and chlorine are staggered; the phenyl groups are then skew and in positions appropriate for formation of *cis*-stilbene. Since an energy barrier must be overcome to effect the necessary rotation, the reaction rate should be lower than with the isomer. Reaction rates have been compared in related reactions and found to bear the expected relationship. Thus on treatment with potassium hydroxide the *erythro* chlorohydrin yields *trans*-stilbene oxide and the *threo* isomer yields *cis*-stilbene oxide (both with inversion at the chlorinated center), and the former reaction is considerably faster than the latter.

Addition of bromine (*trans*) to *cis*-stilbene gives a dibromide (14, 15) analogous to the *threo* chlorohydrin but in which the two asymmetric carbon atoms have the same substituents and are hence similar rather than dissimilar. Each asymmetric center or rotophore makes the same contribution to rotatory power, but the effect is in either a dextro- or levorotatory sense. In isomer (14) both rotophores operate in one sense, and in (15) they both operate in the opposite sense. In formula (14), viewed from the front, the order of the groups C_6H_5, Br, H is clockwise, and if C_2 is viewed from the rear the order is also clockwise; both rotophores contribute to the same extent to rotation in the same direction, dextro or levo. In (15) the order in each case is counterclockwise and hence (15) is the enantiomer of (14), and the two together form a *dl*-pair. If C_1 of (14) is combined with C_2 of (15), the result is (16). In this substance the clockwise rotophoric effect of C_1 is exactly balanced by the counterclockwise effect of C_2, and the substance is optically inactive and is described as a *meso* compound, *meso*-stilbene dibromide. In the

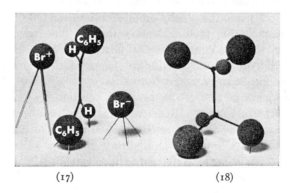

$$\underbrace{\text{(14)} \qquad\qquad\qquad \text{(15)}}_{dl\text{-Dibromide}} \qquad \begin{array}{c}\text{(16)}\\ meso\text{-Dibromide}\end{array}$$

meso-dibromide the two strongly repelling phenyl groups are on opposite sides of the molecule, as are the two large bromine atoms, and hence the conformation is more symmetrical, or better balanced, than that of the *dl*-dibromide. The differ-

	dl-Dibromide	*meso*-Dibromide
Melting point	114°	237°
Solubility in ether	1 part in 3.7 parts	1 part in 1025 parts
Br–Br distance	3.85 Å	4.50 Å

ence in symmetry of the two optically inactive isomers accounts for the marked contrast in melting point and solubility. X-ray diffraction measurements of distances between bromine atoms confirm the conformations assigned.

(17)   (18)

The products of *trans* addition to *cis*- and to *trans*-stilbene are the *dl*-dibromide and the *meso*-dibromide, respectively. The processes are difficult to formulate but can be appreciated from inspection of models. Thus (17) represents the

cis-Stilbene $\longrightarrow$ (19) $\longrightarrow$ (14)

transition state in the addition of bromine to *trans*-stilbene. The planar hydrocarbon is attacked by Br^+ on one side and by Br^- on the other, with establishment of asymmetry at the two sites. Model (18) of the *meso*-dibromide represents the most stable conformation and corresponds to (16), above. Attacked in the same way, *cis*-stilbene gives initially a *d*- or *l*-product with staggered bromines (19), which by bond rotation acquires the more stable conformation (14) with staggered phenyl groups.

5.20   **Steric Effects in HA-Eliminations.** — In an ionic elimination of water from an open chain alcohol, free rotation about a single bond permits the hydrogen and hydroxyl eliminated to assume a *trans*-like orientation favorable for the elimination. In cyclic structures in which rotation is not possible, ionic dehydration can be effected smoothly, if at all, only if the groups to be eliminated

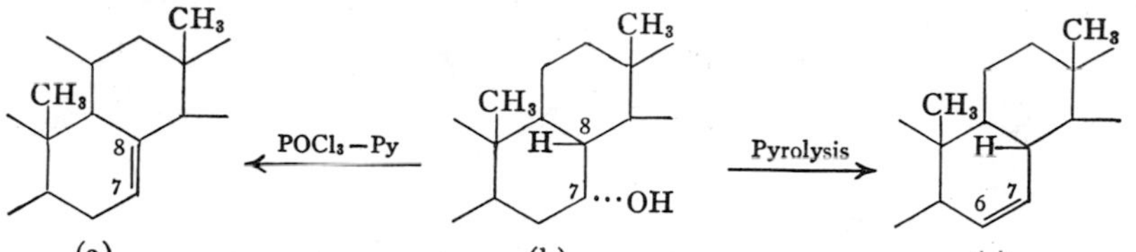

CH₃   CH₃   CH₃

CH₃   CH₃   CH₃

POCl₃—Py   Pyrolysis

(a)   (b)   (c)

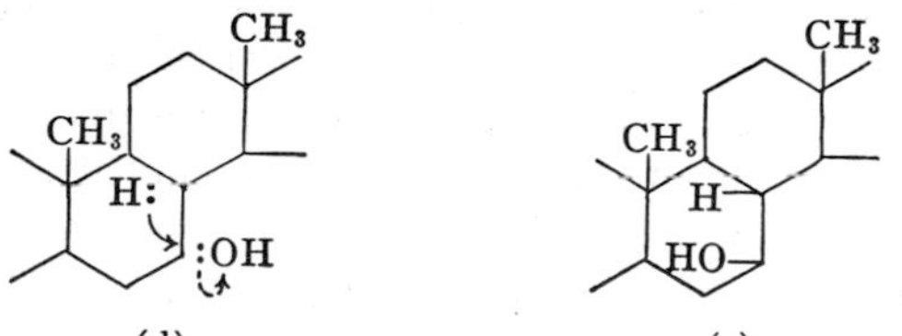

(d)   (e)

are *trans*. Thus in the steroid alcohol (b) the 7α-hydroxyl group is *trans* to the 8β-hydrogen and *trans* elimination to the 7,8-unsaturated derivative (a) occurs readily. The reaction possibly involves the transition state pictured in (d): the electron pair of the C₈—H bond enters the C₇-octet from the front (β) as the hy-

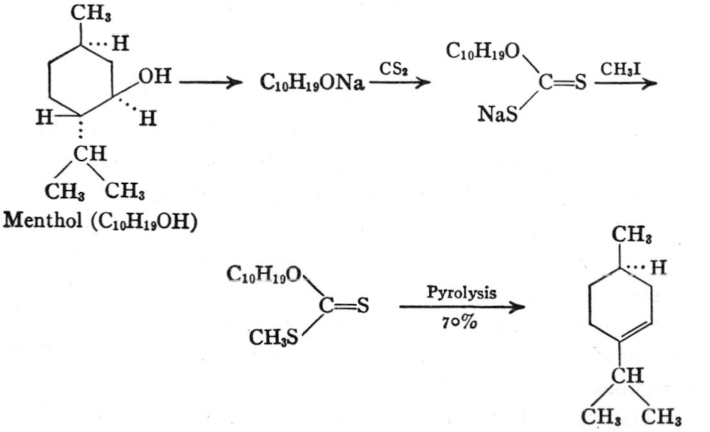

CH₃

OH ⟶ $C_{10}H_{19}ONa$ —CS₂→ $C_{10}H_{19}O$\C=S —CH₃I→ NaS/

Menthol ($C_{10}H_{19}OH$)

$C_{10}H_{19}O$\C=S —Pyrolysis 70%→ CH₃S/

CH₃ ···H

CH

CH₃ CH₃

Δ³-*p*-Menthene

droxyl group departs from the rear (α) with the shared electron pair. Since the hydrogen at C_8 is tertiary, it is eliminated in preference to the 6β-hydrogen. However, the 7β-hydroxy isomer (e) has the same structural feature but, since the hydrogen and hydroxyl are *cis*, it is resistant to dehydration; on treatment with phosphorus oxychloride in pyridine it yields the corresponding chloride and not the ethylene. Dehydrohalogenation of halogen compounds with bases follow the same pattern: *trans* elimination, if possible, occurs readily; *cis* elimination occurs with difficulty if at all.

Pyrolytic dehydration of alcohols follows the opposite pattern: *cis* elimination is the rule and *trans* elimination the exception. Thus pyrolysis of the 7α-hydroxy-steroid (b), best as the benzoate, does not proceed by a *trans* elimination involving

(a)   (b)

the tertiary 8β-hydrogen atom but gives the 6,7-olefinic product (c). The Tschu-gaeff method of dehydration involves a pyrolytic step and the example formulated shows that the elimination is *cis*. Note that the mechanism suggested for the Tschugaeff reaction (5.7) postulates a cyclic transition state and that, in the rigid menthol structure, transient ring formation is possible only if the groups eliminated are *cis*. Pyrolysis of an ester (a) has been shown to be a unimolecular *cis* elimination and probably proceeds through a cyclic transition state (b) in which bond formation and bond cleavage occur simultaneously.

5.21   Hydration. — Hydration of a double bond can be effected by addition of concentrated sulfuric acid to an alkene and hydrolysis of the result-ing alkylsulfuric acid. If the alkene is unsymmetrical, the structure of the alcohol

can be inferred from the Markownikoff rule; thus propylene affords isopropyl alcohol. Production of ethanol by the hydration of ethylene derived from petro-leum by cracking has almost completely supplanted fermentation as a source of industrial alcohol. The operation involves absorption of the olefin in sulfuric acid followed by hydrolysis and stripping of the alcohol (fractionation). Actual oper-ating conditions vary widely with respect to acid concentration, mole ratio, and temperature, since each plant adjusts its process in accordance with local avail-ability of acid and olefin (are they long or short?) and facilities for disposal of spent acid. Considerable ether is produced as a by-product of the manufacture of synthetic alcohol.

Olefins can also be hydrated catalytically in aqueous solutions of sulfuric or nitric acid of such low concentration that esters are not intermediates. The reaction lends itself to kinetic studies aimed at elucidation of the reaction mechanism. One possibility is that the adding proton must first free itself from the hydronium ion before it can enter into a rate-determining step affording a carbonium ion (Ingold, 1954). Another (Taft,[1] 1952) is that the first step is a rapid and reversible formation of a π-complex, which then slowly isomerizes to a carbonium ion, which reacts rapidly with water to form the alcohol with regeneration of the hydronium ion. This postulate was suggested by an observation concerning the hydration of trimethylethylene and of methylethylethylene with dilute nitric acid; both olefins give t-amyl alcohol as the product. If either reaction is stopped at

$$
\underset{\text{Trimethylethylene}}{CH_3-\overset{\overset{\displaystyle CH_3}{|}}{C}=CHCH_3} \longrightarrow \underset{t\text{-Amyl alcohol}}{CH_3-\overset{\overset{\displaystyle CH_3}{|}}{\underset{\underset{\displaystyle OH}{|}}{C}}-CH_2CH_3} \longleftarrow \underset{\text{Methylethylethylene}}{CH_2=\overset{\overset{\displaystyle CH_3}{|}}{C}-CH_2CH_3}
$$

the point of 50% conversion, the original olefin is recovered. Therefore there is no interconversion of olefins through a rapid and reversible formation of a common carbonium ion.

5.22   **Hydroboration.** — H. C. Brown[2] and B. C. Subba Rao (1959) discovered an indirect method for hydration of a double bond involving in the first step treatment of an olefinic reactant with a clear solution of sodium borohydride and aluminum chloride in diethylene glycol dimethyl ether, $(CH_3OCH_2CH_2)_2O$, to form a trialkylborane (1). Alternatively (1a), hydroboration is accomplished by

1. 9 $RCH{=}CH_2$ + 3 $NaBH_4$ + $AlCl_3$ → 3 $(RCH_2CH_2)_3B$ + 3 $NaCl\downarrow$ + $AlH_3\downarrow$
1a. 6 $RCH{=}CH_2$ + B_2H_6 → 2 $(RCH_2CH_2)_3B$

2. $(RCH_2CH_2)_3B \xrightarrow{H_2O_2} (RCH_2CH_2O)_3B \xrightarrow{OH^-}$ 3 RCH_2CH_2OH

reaction with diborane (B_2H_6) generated from sodium borohydride and boron trifluoride. The trialkylborane is then oxidized with alkaline hydrogen peroxide to the borate ester, which is hydrolyzed in the alkaline medium to give the alcohol in high yield (2). Alkenes with a terminal double bond yield almost exclusively the corresponding primary alcohols; for example, 1-octene gives a mixture of 1-octanol and 2-octanol in the ratio 9:1. Addition is thus as expected: the electron-deficient Lewis acid BH_3 becomes linked to the carbon richer in hydrogen atoms. 2-Hexene gives about equal parts of the two possible borane derivatives, but if the reaction mixture is refluxed for several hours in a high-boiling solvent and then oxidized, 1-hexanol is obtained in high yield. The addition is thus reversible, and boron shifts from an internal position in the carbon chain to a terminal position. Isomerization of an internal olefin, for example 3-ethyl-2-pentene, to a thermodynamically less stable terminal olefin (see 5.24) can be accomplished by hydroboration, equilibration, addition of 1-decene as boron acceptor, and slow distillation of the more volatile 3-ethyl-1-pentene resulting by elimination (H. C. Brown, 1960).

---

[1] Robert W. Taft, Jr., b. 1922 Lawrence, Kans.; Ph.D. Ohio State (Newman); Penn. State Univ.

[2] Herbert C. Brown, b. 1922 London, England; Ph.D. Chicago (Schlesinger); Purdue Univ.

Application to cholesterol (I) shows that hydroboration involves *cis* addition; for the two *cis* products II and III are formed, again in the counter-Markownikoff sense (R. Pappo,[1] 1959). The departure from the usual rule of *trans* addition in

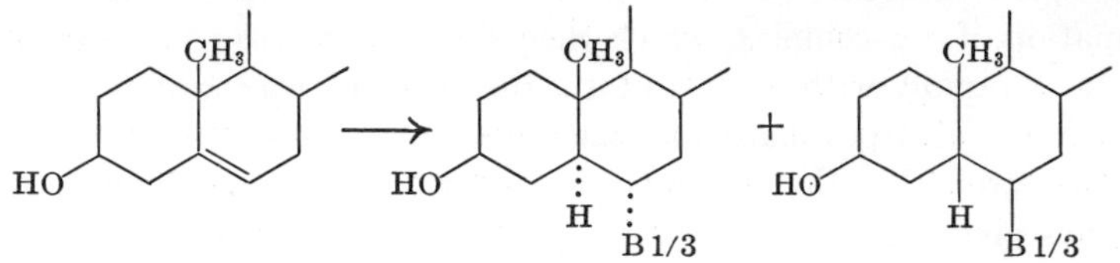

ionic reactions suggests that the addition proceeds through a cyclic transition state:

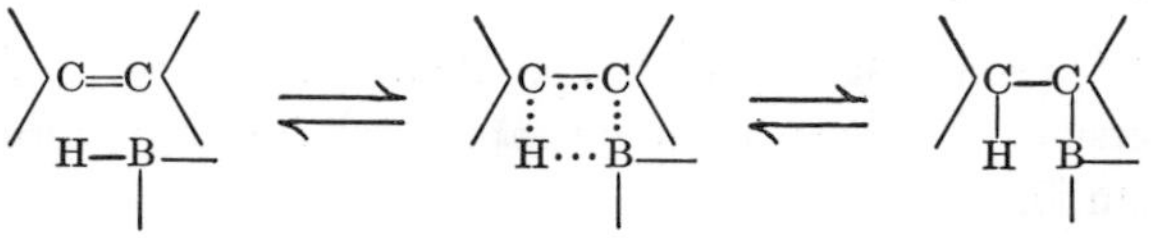

Since the reaction is reversible at elevated temperatures, a series of eliminations and additions would account for the shift of boron from an internal to a terminal position, as cited above. The direction of addition would appear to be determined by a preference of the boron for the least hindered position (*e.g.*, in cholesterol) or for the terminal position in a chain, where steric interactions are at a minimum.

Bis-3-methyl-2-butylborane (BMB), obtained as in (1) even in the presence of excess olefin, gives increased yields of the less hindered products and permits selective reductions not otherwise possible (H. C. Brown, 1961). Since it does not reduce the carboxyl group, the reagent can be used for hydroboration of an unprotected acid (2). γ-Lactones react with only one mole of reagent, even when the latter is in excess (3).

1. $2\ CH_3\overset{\overset{\displaystyle CH_3}{|}}{C}{=}CHCH_3\ +\ BH_3\ \xrightarrow{\ o^0\ }\ [(CH_3)_2\overset{\overset{\displaystyle CH_3}{|}}{C}HCH]_2BH$
                                                                       BMB

2. $CH_2{=}CH(CH_2)_8CO_2H\ \xrightarrow[82\%]{BMB;\ alk.\ H_2O_2}\ CH_2(CH_2)_9CO_2H$
                                                                                 OH

            Δ¹⁰-Undecanoic acid   11-Hydroxyundecanoic acid (m. p. 69⁰)

3. 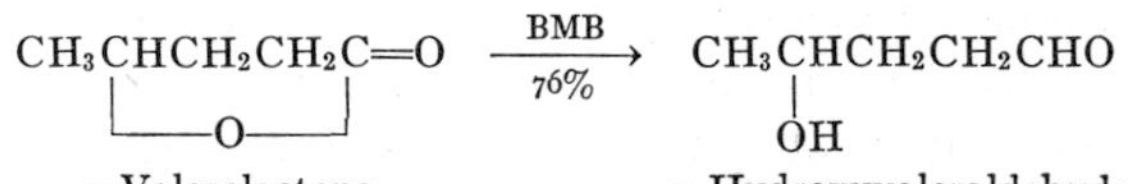 $CH_3CHCH_2CH_2C{=}O\ \xrightarrow[76\%]{BMB}\ CH_3CHCH_2CH_2CHO$
              └——O——┘   OH

             γ-Valerolactone   γ-Hydroxyvaleraldehyde

Hydroboration of a hindered, optically active olefin (*e. g.* a terpene or a steroid) proceeds rapidly to give a dialkylborane which can be used for conversion of a

---

[1] Raphael Pappo, b. 1922 Cairo, Egypt; Ph.D. Hebrew University (E. D. Bergmann, Weizmann Inst. Sci.); G. D. Searle and Co.

suitable olefin, for example cis-2-butene, to an optically active alcohol: $(-)$2-butanol; yield 90%, optical purity 87% (H. C. Brown, 1961).

Cyclopentadiene undergoes a double hydroboration-oxidation to give cis-cyclopentane-1,3-diol (K. A. Saegebarth, 1960). The infrared spectrum shows the presence of a free hydroxyl group (3620 cm^{-1}) and a bonded one (3450 cm^{-1}), and the diol reacts with p-nitrobenzaldehyde (boiling xylene, trace of TsOH) to form a cyclic acetal.

5.23   **Allylic Bromination.** — In 1942 K. Ziegler[1] discovered that N-bromosuccinimide reacts with a number of olefinic compounds with replacement of an allylic hydrogen by bromine. For example, cyclohexene (a) affords 3-bromocyclohexene-1 (b) in about 80% yield. Since the reaction is often cata-

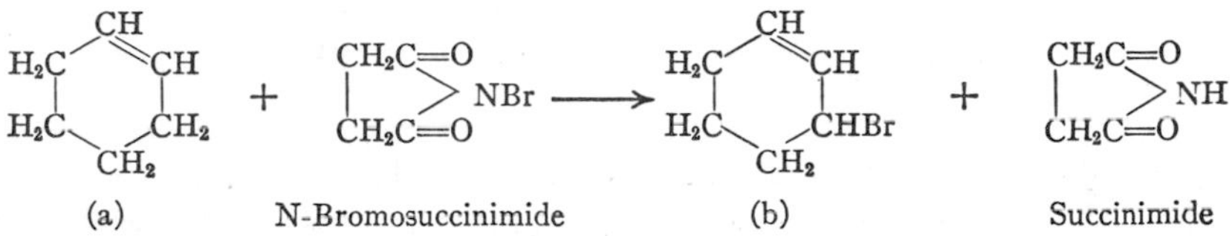

(a)   N-Bromosuccinimide   (b)   Succinimide

lyzed by light, or by a peroxide, it probably involves free radicals. Kinetic studies (Dauben,[2] 1959) support a mechanism (G. F. Bloomfield, 1944) according to which an initiating radical removes bromine to form the succinimido radical, which abstracts an allylic hydrogen to give an allylic radical (1) and this then

    1. $(CH_2CO)_2N\cdot + RH \rightarrow (CH_2CO)_2NH + R\cdot$
    2. $R\cdot + (CH_2CO)_2NBr \rightarrow RBr + (CH_2CO)_2N\cdot$

propagates the chain (2).

Allylic bromination with N-bromosuccinimide is particularly useful for conversion of monounsaturated compounds into dienes, and of dienes into trienes. Thus the allylic bromide (b) derived from cyclohexene is convertible by dehydro-

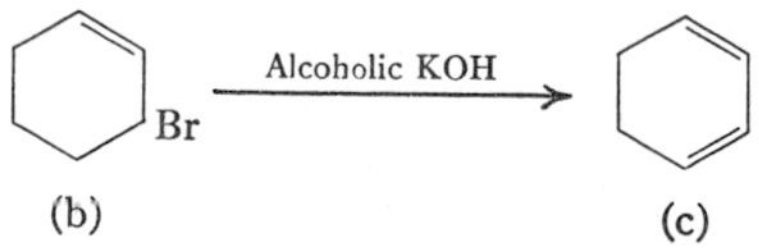

(b)   (c)

halogenation into cyclohexadiene-1,3 (c). A benzyl group has an allyl-type hydrogen capable of reaction with N-bromosuccinimide; thus dibenzyl is convertible

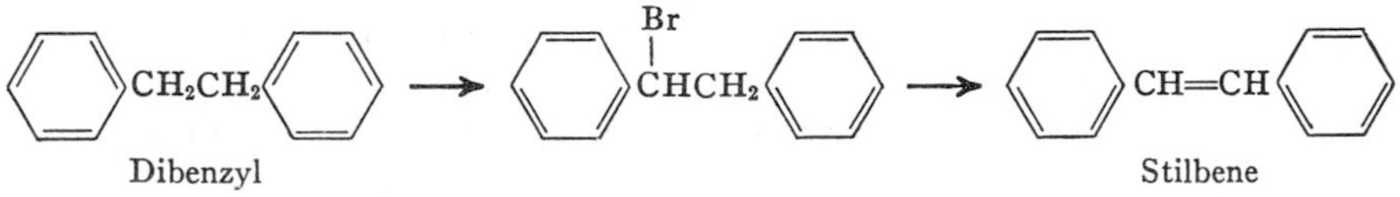

Dibenzyl   Stilbene

into trans-stilbene in about 50% yield by reaction with N-bromosuccinimide followed by dehydrobromination with potassium acetate. The bromination prod-

[1] Karl Ziegler, b. 1898 Kassel, Germany; Ph.D. Marburg (von Auwers); Univ. Heidelberg, Max Planck Inst. for Coal Res., Mülheim/Ruhr

[2] Hyp J. Dauben, Jr., b. 1915 Marion, Ohio; Ph.D. Harvard (Bartlett); Washington State Univ.

ucts possess the high reactivity characteristic of allylic bromides and are often useful synthetic reagents. An example is methyl γ-bromocrotonate, prepared as follows:

$$CH_3CH{=}CHCOOCH_3 \;+\; \text{N-Bromosuccinimide} \xrightarrow[86\%]{\text{Boiling } CCl_4}$$
Methyl crotonate

$$BrCH_2CH{=}CHCOOCH_3 \;+\; \text{Succinimide}$$
Methyl γ-bromocrotonate

5.24   Hydrogenation. — In the presence of specific metal catalysts, alkenes and alkynes are able to add hydrogen, or undergo catalytic hydrogenation. Thus an alkene on hydrogenation affords an alkane. Essentially quantita-

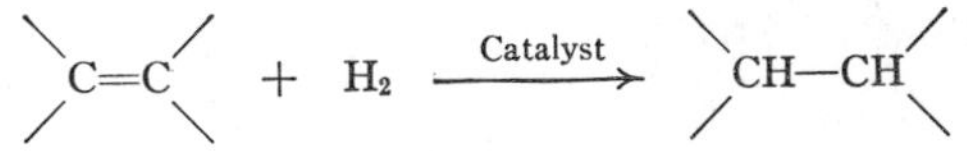

$$\diagup C{=}C \diagdown \;+\; H_2 \xrightarrow{\text{Catalyst}} \diagup CH{-}CH \diagdown$$

tive and widely applicable, catalytic hydrogenation has numerous uses. It is possible by this method to transform unsaturated alcohols, acids, esters, and amines into the corresponding saturated compounds, for example, as in (1). A complication arises with an allylic alcohol (2), for normal hydrogenation (a) is

1. $RCH{=}CHCH_2CHR'$ $\xrightarrow{H_2,\,Pt}$ $RCH_2CH_2CH_2CHR'$
            $\overset{|}{O}H$ $\overset{|}{O}H$

2. 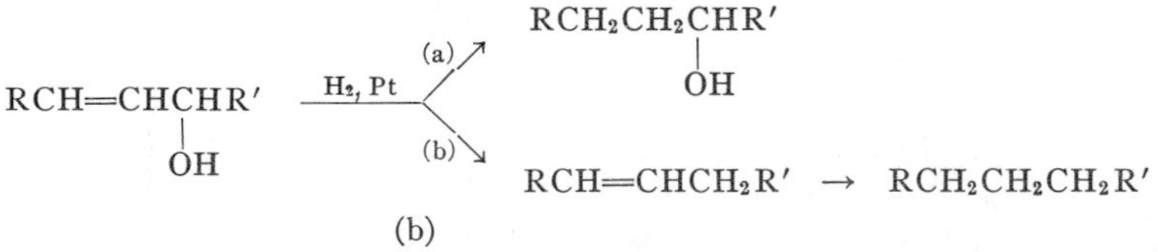 $RCH{=}CHCHR'$ $\xrightarrow{H_2,\,Pt}$
            $\overset{|}{O}H$

    (a)↗ RCH_2CH_2CHR'
                 $\overset{|}{O}H$

    (b)↘ $RCH{=}CHCH_2R' \;\rightarrow\; RCH_2CH_2CH_2R'$

accompanied by hydrogenolysis (b), with reductive replacement of the activated hydroxyl group. Aldehydes and ketones can be reduced to alcohols by catalytic hydrogenation, but since somewhat different conditions are required it is often possible to selectively hydrogenate the ethylenic bond of an unsaturated carbonyl compound without attack of the carbonyl group. Benzene can be hydrogenated to cyclohexane and phenol to cyclohexanol, but the conditions are considerably more severe than required for hydrogenation of an olefin and there is no difficulty in hydrogenating the double bond of allylbenzene ($C_6H_5CH_2CH{=}CH_2$) without attack of the phenyl group. A halogen substituent in a saturated aliphatic or an aromatic compound sometimes can be replaced by hydrogen by hydrogenolysis usually in a basic medium.

The most active, and also the most expensive, catalysts are of platinum, palladium, or ruthenium. The metal must be so finely divided that it is black and has a very large surface area capable of adsorbing both hydrogen and the substrate. Adams[1] platinum or palladium catalyst is made by fusing chloroplatinic

---

[1] Roger Adams, b. 1889 Boston; Ph.D. Harvard (Torrey, Richards); Univ. Illinois

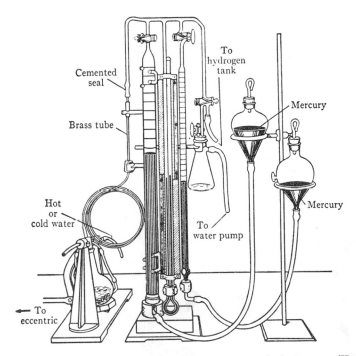

FIG. 5.5. — Apparatus for Catalytic Hydrogenation at Atmospheric Pressure (Hershberg) Hydrogen, introduced to the shaker flask through a flexible tube, is taken from either the large or the small burette; the volume of reserve gas present at any time is read on the burette after adjusting the appropriate leveling bulb to a point where the mercury is at the same level in the two arms of the central manometer tube.

acid or palladium chloride with sodium nitrite to produce a brown metal oxide, which is washed with water, dried and stored. A small charge of oxide is added to a solution of the compound to be hydrogenated and when the mixture is shaken with hydrogen a small amount of the gas is consumed with reduction of the oxide to a black suspension of finely divided metal, which then catalyzes addition of hydrogen to a double bond. In another method a reducing agent is added to an aqueous solution of platinum or palladium chloride in which finely divided charcoal is suspended; the metal is precipitated in an active condition on the surface of the charcoal particles. Platinum and palladium catalysts are sufficiently active to promote hydrogenation in solution at temperatures of 25–90° and with a hydrogen pressure only slightly above one atmosphere. The reaction is conducted in a shaking apparatus capable of maintaining intimate contact between the gas, liquid, and solid phases (Fig. 5.5).

Sabatier[1] and Senderens (1897) were the first to utilize base-metal catalysts (Ni, Cu, Co, Fe); the lower activity of the catalyst was compensated for by conducting the hydrogenation in the vapor phase at a high temperature (300°). The tech-

[1] Paul Sabatier, 1854–1941; Ph.D. Paris; Toulouse; Nobel Prize 1912; *J. Am. Chem. Soc.*, **66**, 1615 (1944)

nique is favored in the industry because it lends itself to continuous processes. Ipatieff[1] introduced high-pressure liquid-phase hydrogenation. The efficient Adkins[2] copper–chromium oxide catalyst is widely used in high-pressure hydrogenations conducted in a special alloy-steel, electrically heated bomb mounted in a mechanical rocker; hydrogenations ordinarily are conducted at temperatures of 150 to 250° and pressures of 3000 to 5000 lbs. per sq. in. A special nickel catalyst discovered by the American M. Raney (1927) possesses such remarkable activity that it will promote many hydrogenations at room temperature and at pressures of no more than 50–100 lbs. per sq. in. Raney nickel catalyst is prepared by treating a nickel–aluminum alloy with warm sodium hydroxide solution which dissolves the aluminum and leaves the nickel as a black pyrophoric suspension saturated with hydrogen.

Quantitative microhydrogenation is useful in the investigation of new compounds since it provides a means for determining the number of double bonds present. From the results of such an analysis and from the empirical formula, one can calculate the number of rings present. If a hydrocarbon of the empirical formula C_nH_m contains X double bonds, the number of rings is given by the following expression:

$$\text{Number of rings} = n - \frac{m}{2} - X + 1$$

For example, cyclohexene is C_6H_{10} and has one double bond, hence $6 - 5 - 1 + 1 = 1$ ring. Cyclohexadiene is C_6H_8, and the number of rings is $6 - 4 - 2 + 1 = 1$. If the compound contains one or more oxygen or nitrogen functions, the formula is first reduced to that of the parent hydrocarbon. Measurement of heats of hydrogenation of a number of alkenes by Kistiakowsky[3] showed that reaction is exothermic and that for alkenes of the type $RCH{=}CH_2$ the average heat evolved amounts to 30 kcal. This experimentally determined value figures in the calculation of some of the bond energies given in the table section 32.2, and hence the following "calculation" of the heat of hydrogenation is a mere statement of the case in reverse. The difference in the bond energy of C=C (100) and C—C (59), or 41 kcal., can be described as the energy required for breaking the π-bond of the alkene, and to this must be added the energy required for breaking the H—H bond (103), a total input of 144 kcal. The formation of two C—H bonds, how-

$$\underset{\text{(100-59)}}{>\!C{=}C\!<} \;+\; \underset{103}{H{-}H} \;\rightarrow\; \underset{2 \times 87 \qquad \Delta H \,=\, -30 \text{ kcal.}}{>\!\underset{H}{\overset{|}{C}}{-}\underset{H}{\overset{|}{C}}\!<}$$

ever, represents an energy gain of 174 kcal., and hence the heat of hydrogenation is −30 kcal. Although the reaction is exothermic, ΔH is small relative to the

[1] Vladimir N. Ipatieff, 1867–1952; b. Moscow; St. Petersburg, Northwestern Univ.; *Nature*, **171**, 151 (1953)

[2] Homer Adkins, 1892–1949; b. Newport, Ohio; Ph.D. Ohio State Univ. (Evans); Univ. Wisconsin

[3] George B. Kistiakowsky, b. 1900 Kiev, Russia; Ph.D. Berlin (Bodenstein); Harvard Univ.

energy required to break the π-bond of the alkene and the σ-bond of the hydrogen molecule. Addition of hydrogen thus does not occur spontaneously because the activation energy is too high. A metal catalyst lowers the activation energy and permits hydrogen to add in a series of steps, the activation energy for each of which is lower than that required for breaking of a π- or σ-bond.

The heat of hydrogenation of an alkene measures the energy content of the alkene, and hence ΔH values for a pair of isomeric olefins which yield the same product on hydrogenation provide an accurate index of the relative thermodynamic stability of the two compounds. That *cis*-butene-2 (1) has a higher heat of hydrogenation than the *trans* isomer (2) means that it has the higher energy content, a conclusion which agrees with the fact that catalytic equilibration of the isomers

$$
\begin{array}{cccc}
\mathrm{CH_3-C-H} & \mathrm{CH_3-C-H} & \mathrm{CH_3-C-H} & \mathrm{CH_3-C-H} \\
\| & \| & \| & \| \\
\mathrm{CH_3-C-H} & \mathrm{H-C-CH_3} & \mathrm{CH_3CH_2-C-H} & \mathrm{H-C-CH_2CH_3} \\
\text{(1) 28.6} & \text{(2) 27.6} & \text{(3) 28.6} & \text{(4) 27.6}
\end{array}
$$

$$\Delta H \text{ in kcal./mole}$$

gives a mixture in which the *trans* form predominates (2.18). The same relationship holds for the *cis* and *trans* forms of pentene-2 (3, 4). Compounds (1)–(4) all have internal double bonds; they are all more stable than alkenes with a terminal double bond, $RCH{=}CH_2$, for which ΔH is close to 30 kcal. The types $RCH{=}CHR'$ and $RCH{=}CH_2$ differ, of course, in that the double bond is disubstituted in the first case (more stable) and monosubstituted in the second; in general stability tends to increase with increasing number of alkyl groups. For ethylene, with no substituents, $\Delta H = 32.8$ kcal.

Methylenecyclohexane (5) has a terminal double bond and 1-methylcyclohexene (6) has an internal one, but it is more significant that the double bond is external to the ring in one case and internal in the other; these isomers, which

$$
\begin{array}{cccc}
\mathrm{CH_2} & \mathrm{CH_3} & \mathrm{CHCH_3} & \mathrm{CH_2CH_3} \\
\text{(5) 27.8} & \text{(6) 25.7} & \text{(7) 26.3} & \text{(8) 25.1}
\end{array}
$$

$$\Delta H \text{ in kcal./mole}$$

yield the same product on hydrogenation are thus described as having an exocyclic and an endocyclic double bond, respectively. Turner[1] (1957–58) measured the heats of hydrogenation and his results, recorded under the formulas, show that the endocyclic isomer (6) had the greater stability and hence that the relationship is the same as with open chain olefins. Since (5) and (6) differ in the number of alkyl groups or ring residues joined to the unsaturated carbon atoms, Turner compared the exo-endo pair (7) and (8), in each of which the double bond is trisubstituted. The difference in ΔH is not so large as before, but again the endocyclic isomer is the more stable. The modern measurements account for an

[1] Richard B. Turner, b. 1916 Minneapolis; Ph.D. Harvard (Fieser); Rice Univ.

early observation of Wallach[1] (1906–08) that ethylidenecyclohexane (7) undergoes acid-catalyzed isomerization to 1-ethylcyclohexene (8). For isomerizations conducted in a mixture of benzene and tetramethylene sulfone, the catalytic effectiveness is in the following order (J. W. Powell, 1960):

$$HBF_4 \; > \; BF_3 \; > \; H_2SO_4 \; > \; CF_3CO_2H$$

Isolated examples in the early literature suggested that hydrogenation proceeds by *cis* addition, and this point was firmly established by Linstead (1942) in a stereochemical study of the hydrogenation of polycyclic compounds. Selective hydrogenation of disubstituted acetylenes are particularly pertinent because the two possible products are *cis* and *trans* isomers. If the conditions are sufficiently mild to prevent isomerization subsequent to reduction, the *cis* isomer is the sole product. Thus acetylenedicarboxylic acid on hydrogenation affords maleic acid,

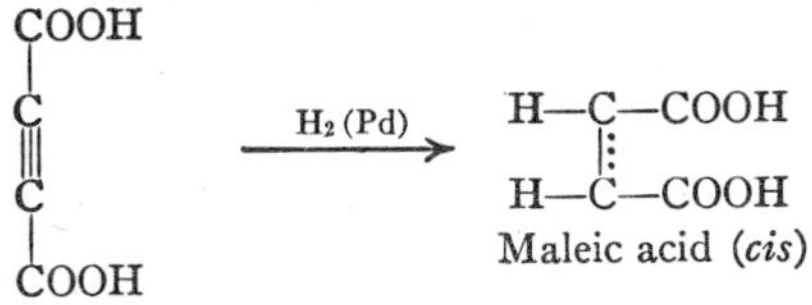

Acetylenedicarboxylic acid → Maleic acid (*cis*)

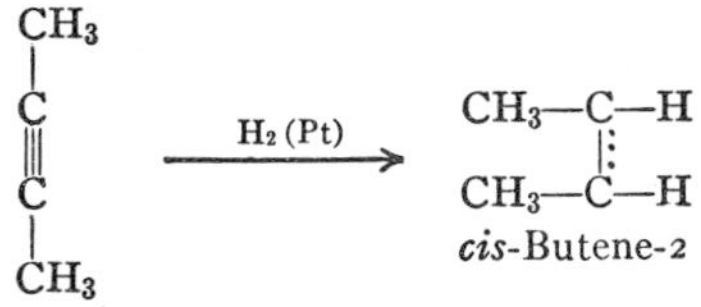

Butyne-2 → *cis*-Butene-2

in which the two carboxyl groups have been shown to be on the same side of the molecule, and butyne-2 affords *cis*-butene-2.

Where catalytic hydrogenation of an ethylenic compound can afford isomeric products, the product formed is likewise that resulting from *cis* addition, as in the example of 1,2-dimethylcyclohexene. Since all other instances of *cis* addition are

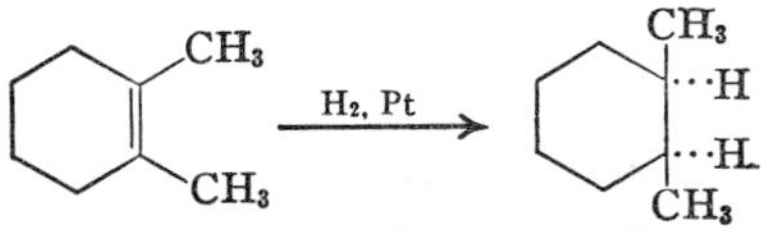

known to follow this course because they proceed through cyclic intermediates, it seems likely that hydrogenation also involves what amounts to a cyclic intermediate. Linstead suggested that the substance undergoing hydrogenation lies, on its flattest side, on the catalyst surface, and that two active sites of the surface form a quasi-ring with the unsaturated carbon atoms and two hydrogens initially dissolved in the catalyst (9). The two hydrogens thus both approach from the

[1] Otto Wallach, 1847–1931; b. Königsberg; Ph.D. Göttingen; Univ. Göttingen; Nobel Prize 1910; *J. Chem. Soc.*, 1582 (1932)

under side and so give a *cis* product.   Inspection of the conformational formula for cholesterol on page 151 shows that the front or β-side is shielded by the two angular methyl groups and the side chain but that the rear or α-side presents a flat

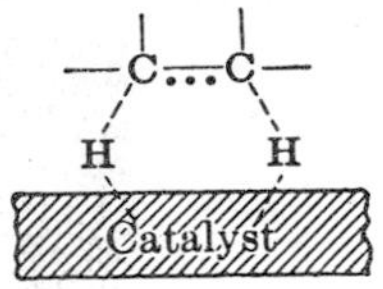

(9)

surface suitable for adsorption on a catalyst.   The formation on hydrogenation of the 5α,6-dihydride (rather than the 5β,6-product) shows that attack has occurred from the rear as expected.

Compounds with an unhydrogenable double bond are rare, but a few are known.

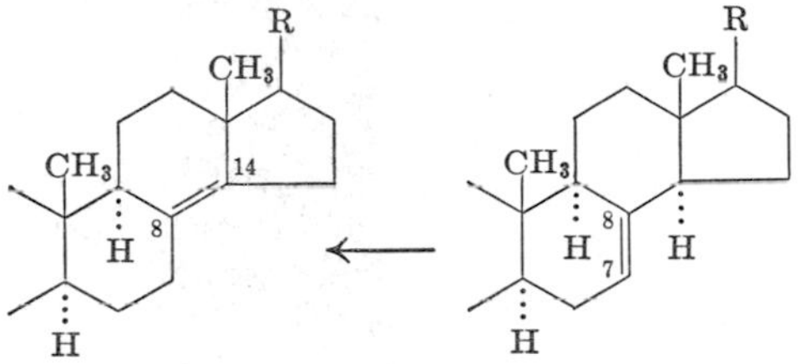

(10)   (11)

Thus steroids having a double bond in the 8,14-position (10) are resistant to hydrogenation by all known methods.   The two unsaturated carbon atoms are in connected rings and the unhydrogenable tetrasubstituted double bond lies between bridgehead positions.   The $\Delta^{8(14)}$-enes, though inert to catalytic hydrogenation, give a positive test with tetranitromethane and are capable of forming oxides.   A steroid Δ^7-ene (11) is likewise unhydrogenable, but when shaken with a sufficiently active catalyst saturated with hydrogen it undergoes isomerization to the $\Delta^{8(14)}$-ene (10).   Palladium catalyst is effective with ether as solvent; platinum is less effective and operates only with assistance of solvent acetic acid to promote isomerization.   Since isomerization occurs only if the catalyst is saturated with hydrogen,

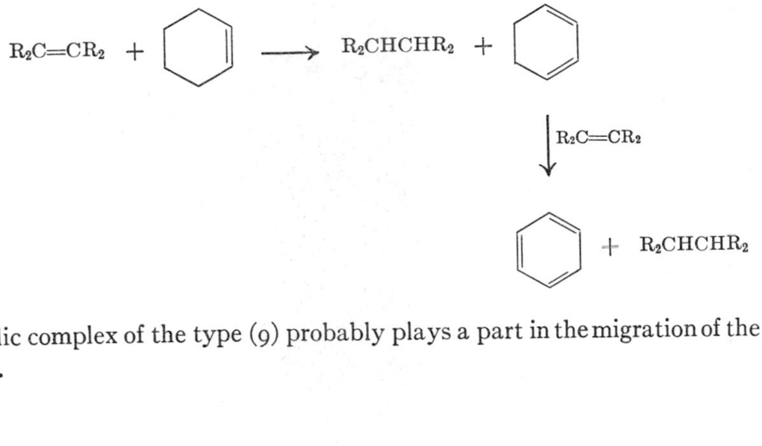

a cyclic complex of the type (9) probably plays a part in the migration of the double bond.

Conversion of an alkene into an alkane can be effected also by transfer hydrogenation (Linstead, 1954). Hydrogen is not used as such but is transferred catalytically from a donor, usually cyclohexene. Thus an alkene heated in refluxing cyclohexene in the presence of palladium catalyst is converted into the corresponding alkane. Dehydrogenation of cyclohexene gives initially $\Delta^{1,3}$-cyclohexadiene, which can also be described as 1,2-dihydrobenzene. This substance is a highly effective hydrogen donor because by loss of two hydrogens it affords resonance-stabilized benzene. The method offers no advantage over ordinary hydrogenation except that no special apparatus is required.

OXIDATION

5.25 **Permanganate Test.**—A useful test for distinguishing between liquid alkenes and alkanes consists in shaking a sample with a dilute aqueous solution of potassium permanganate acidified with sulfuric acid: an alkene discharges the color within a few seconds; a pure alkane is without effect. The acid permanganate test also shows whether or not a sample of petroleum ether or ligroin solvent mixture is free from unsaturated contaminants. Primary and secondary alcohols give a positive response in the acid permanganate test but can be distinguished from unsaturated hydrocarbons by a second test conducted after acetylation; the alcohols are converted into oxidation-resistant acetates, whereas alkenes are unaffected. Permanganate oxidation of an alkene can proceed to various stages, depending upon the amount of reagent used and the conditions, but the reagent is so powerful that differentiation between successive steps is difficult. The permanganate reaction sequence will thus be deferred for discussion after consideration of reagents which effect the first and second steps of oxidation and nothing more.

5.26 **Osmium Tetroxide Hydroxylation.** — Osmium tetroxide, OsO_4, is a colorless crystalline solid melting at 40° and readily soluble in ether. On addition of cyclohexene to an ethereal solution of the reagent, a reaction product separates as a black precipitate. This substance is a cyclic osmate ester of the

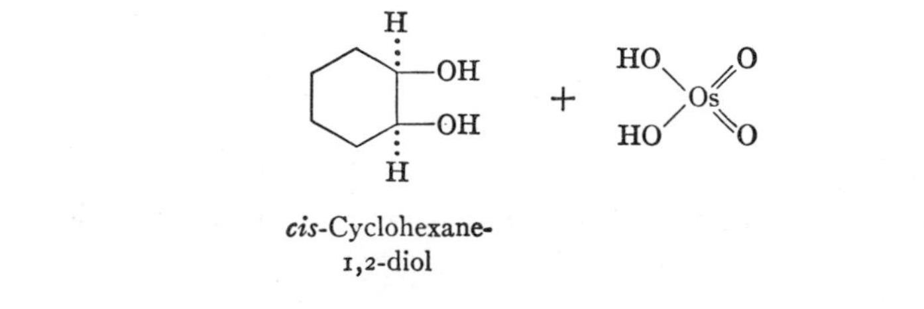

Osmate ester

cis-Cyclohexane-
1,2-diol

structure shown; it arises from simultaneous opening of the carbon–carbon double bond of the alkene and of two double bonds of the metal oxide. The black ester is then hydrolyzed, with use of sodium sulfite as catalyst, and the product is *cis*-cyclohexane-1,2-diol (the hydroxyls are β, or to the front, and the hydrogens α, or to the rear). The five-membered ring of the osmate ester can be formed only in the *cis* orientation and hence the reaction product is necessarily the *cis* diol. Thus the ultimate result of osmium tetroxide hydroxylation is a *cis* addition. Whenever a reaction is free to follow either a *cis* or *trans* course, the course normally taken is *trans* addition. *cis* Addition occurs only when the reaction involves a cyclic intermediate, which is of necessity *cis* oriented, as in the example cited.

Practical aspects of the reaction are interesting. Osmium tetroxide costs over ten dollars per gram. Furthermore, the molecular weight is so high (254.20) in comparison to that of cyclohexene (82.14) that 1 g. of osmium tetroxide is equiva-

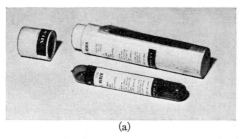

(a)

(b)

lent to only 0.32 g. of cyclohexene. Osmium tetroxide is supplied in sealed glass ampoules (a); each contains 1.0 g. and is packed in a wooden case with a taped-on steel scorer with a filing edge. The ampoule is scored in the middle, broken (b), and the crystals of oxide are scraped out into a flask and dissolved in ether. On addition of cyclohexene a black precipitate forms at once but remains partly in suspension, even during several hours while the mixture is let stand to ensure complete reaction. The ether and excess cyclohexene are removed by evaporation on the steam bath and the black osmate ester is heated for several hours with aqueous-alcoholic sodium sulfite to effect hydrolysis to *cis*-cyclo-

(c)

hexane-1,2-diol. An efficient procedure applicable to solids of low solubility in ether consists in osmylation in dioxane solution (*e.g.*, for 2 days) and decomposition of the osmate ester by saturation of the solution with hydrogen sulfide; the dioxane solution of diol is filtered from a black precipitate and evaporated at reduced pressure. Addition can also be carried out in pyridine, which catalyzes the reaction; the osmate ester is then precipitated with petroleum ether and decomposed with hydrogen sulfide in dioxane.

The melting point of *cis*-cyclohexane-1,2-diol (98°) is nearly as high as that of the *trans* isomer (104°); the relationship between *cis*-cyclopentane-1,2-diol (30°) and the *trans* isomer (55°) is more typical.

5.27   *vic*-Glycol Cleavage. — Among diols, or glycols, those in which the hydroxyl groups are vicinal undergo ready oxidative fission of the carbon–carbon bond between the two hydroxylated carbon atoms. To effect glycol cleavage without further oxidation of the initial products, it is necessary to use one of three specific oxidizing agents, lead tetraacetate, periodic acid, or phenyliodoso diacetate. Lead tetraacetate, introduced by R. Criegee[1] (1933), is used in acetic acid solution at room temperature. A disecondary glycol gives two

$$
\begin{array}{c}
RCHOH \\
| \\
R'CHOH
\end{array}
\xrightarrow{Pb(OAc)_4}
RCH{=}O \ + \ R'CH{=}O
$$

$$
\begin{array}{c}
(CH_3)_2C\text{——}C(CH_3)_2 \\
| \qquad\quad | \\
OH \quad\ OH \\
\text{Pinacol}
\end{array}
\xrightarrow{Pb(OAc)_4}
2(CH_3)_2C{=}O
$$

moles of aldehyde; pinacol, a ditertiary diol, gives two moles of acetone. Phenyliodoso diacetate [$C_6H_5I(OAc)_2$, m.p. 158°], also employed in acetic acid solution, reacts in the same way but much more slowly; the rate constant (k^{20} in l. mole^{-1} min.$^{-1}$) is about one hundredth that of lead tetraacetate (Criegee, 1939). Cleavage with periodic acid (H_5IO_6) is done in aqueous solution or in a solvent mixture containing water, and the active species is the ion II. The intermediate is regarded as either the hydrated ion III or the dehydrated ion IV (C. C. Price,[2] 1942; G. J.

$$
\underset{I}{\begin{array}{c}RCH{-}OH \\ | \\ R'CH{-}OH\end{array}}
+
\underset{II}{\begin{array}{c}HO \ \overset{OH}{\underset{\underset{O}{\|}}{|}} \ OH \\ HO \quad\quad O^-\end{array}}
\longrightarrow
\underset{III}{\begin{array}{c}RCH{-}O \ \overset{OH}{\underset{\underset{O}{\|}}{|}} \ OH \\ R'CH{-}O \quad\quad O^-\end{array}}
\longrightarrow
\underset{IV}{\begin{array}{c}RCH{-}O \ \overset{O}{\underset{\underset{O}{\|}}{\|}} \\ R'CH{-}O \ \ I{-}O^- \ + \ H_2O\end{array}}
$$

$$
\begin{array}{c}
RCH{=}O \\
R'CH{=}O
\end{array}
+
\overset{O}{\underset{\underset{O}{\|}}{\|}}I{-}O^-
$$

Buist and C. A. Bunton, 1954).

The most fully studied reaction is that with lead tetraacetate. With cyclic *cis-trans* isomers, the *cis* diol usually is cleaved faster than the *trans*. Thus k^{20} for *cis*-cyclohexane-1,2-diol is 8.1 and k^{20} for the *trans* isomer is 0.3. That ring size and conformation are of influence is evident from data for the cyclopentane-1,2-diols; *cis*, 40,000; *trans*, 21.4.

[1] Rudolf Criegee, b. 1902 Düsseldorf; Ph.D. Würzburg (K. Dimroth); Univ. Düsseldorf, Karlsruhe

[2] Charles C. Price, b. 1913 Passaic, N. J.; Ph.D. Harvard (Fieser); Univ. Notre Dame, Univ. Pennsylvania

One factor of importance in determining rates of cleavage is the distance separating the two hydroxyl groups, determinable by infrared spectroscopy (L. P. Kuhn,[1] 1954). In dilute solution in carbon tetrachloride, a *vic*-diol gives rise to two bands in the three-micron region; one, at higher frequency, due to the free OH group and the other due to the bonded OH. The spread between the two bands, $\Delta \nu$, increases

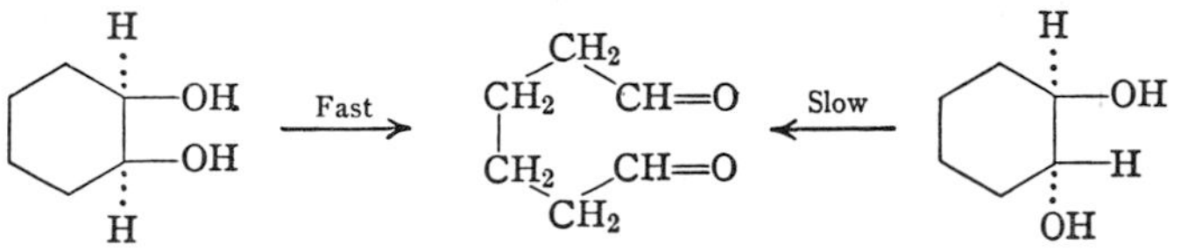

as the length of the hydrogen bond decreases and hence, with related diols, the observed values of $\Delta \nu$ provide a measure of the relative proximity of the hydroxyl groups. In cyclohexane all adjacent hydrogen pairs are equidistant, but with the 1,2-diols the $\Delta \nu$ values of 38 and 33 cm^{-1} for the *cis* and *trans* isomers show that the hydroxyls are closer together in the *cis* than in the *trans* diol. The situation is shown in Newman projections in which the observer looks down the axis of the C_1—C_2 bond. The angle ϕ formed by the exocyclic bonds to the hydroxyl

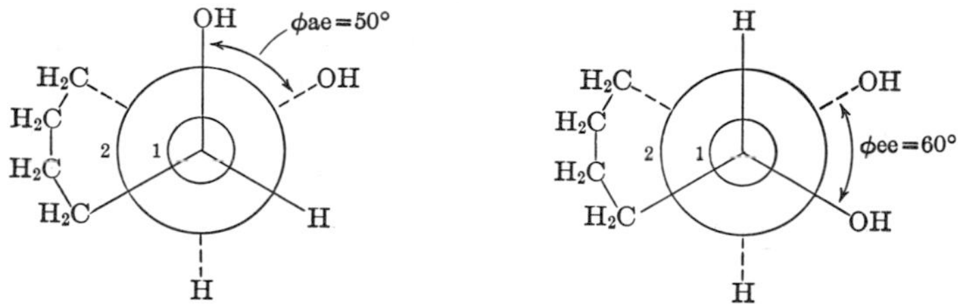

groups is, in the *cis*-diol (1), defined as ϕ_{ae}, since one bond is axial and the other equatorial. This angle is smaller than the angle ϕ_{ee} between the two equatorial groups of the *trans* diol (2). Calculations by trigonometry indicate that the separation distances in (1) and (2) are 2.22 and 2.37 Å. A possible reason for the difference is that an axial hydroxyl is assisted in bonding with an adjacent equatorial hydroxyl by 1:3 interactions with the two axial hydrogen atoms.

The $\Delta \nu$ values listed in Table 5.4 show that in rings containing less than 10 carbon atoms the *cis* hydroxyls are closer than the *trans*, but that the situation is reversed in rings containing more than 10 carbons. That in the larger rings the distance is greater for the *cis* diols than for the *trans* is explained as follows. The attractive force between the hydroxyl groups that decreases ϕ_{ae} in the *cis* diols brings the methylene groups closer together (see 1), whereas in decreasing ϕ_{ee} in the *trans* diols it brings the methylene groups closer to a hydrogen atom. Since repulsion between methylene groups is stronger than repulsion between a methyl-

[1] Lester P. Kuhn, b. 1913 Brooklyn, N. Y.; Ph.D. Johns Hopkins (Corwin); Ballistics Res. Labs., Aberdeen Proving Ground

TABLE 5.4. BOND SEPARATION AND RATES OF Pb(OAc)$_4$ CLEAVAGE

CYCLIC I, 2-DIOL		$\Delta\nu$, CM^{-1}	ϕ_{ae}	ϕ_{ee}	k^{20}(CRIEGEE)
C$_5$-cis		61	0°		40,000
	C$_5$-trans	0		120°	21.4
C$_6$-cis		38	50°		8.1
	C$_6$-trans	33		60°	0.3
C$_7$-cis		44	42°		
	C$_7$-trans	37		51°	
C$_8$-cis		51	33°		
	C$_8$-trans	43		44°	
C$_9$-cis		49	36°		2.9
	C$_9$-trans	45		41°	20.7
C$_{10}$-cis		44	42°		2.6
	C$_{10}$-trans	45		41°	100
C$_{12}$-cis		38	50°		1.3
	C$_{12}$-trans	51		33°	73.6
C$_{16}$-cis		—			7.8
	C$_{16}$-trans	50		34°	91.2

ene group and hydrogen, a given expenditure of energy makes ϕ_{ee} smaller than ϕ_{ae}.

The $\Delta\nu$ values fall into line with the relative rates of glycol cleavage with the C$_5$-, C$_6$-, and C$_{12}$-isomer pairs but not with the C$_9$- and C$_{10}$-diols. A rough parallelism is evident also in results for a series of bicyclic pinacols (Criegee). However, a glaring discrepancy emerged from a study of the isomeric 9,10-dimethyl-

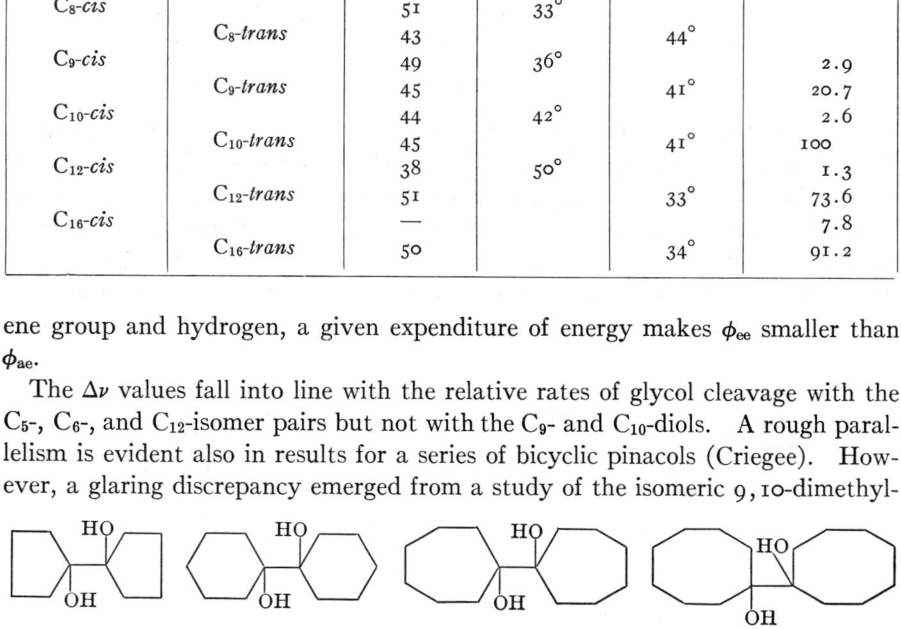

k^{20} 0.04	11.8	2,390	3,000
$\Delta\nu$ 36	46	60	65

dihydrophenanthrene-9,10-diols. At a time when only the 164° isomer derived from phenanthrenequinone was known (1940), the substance was thought to be

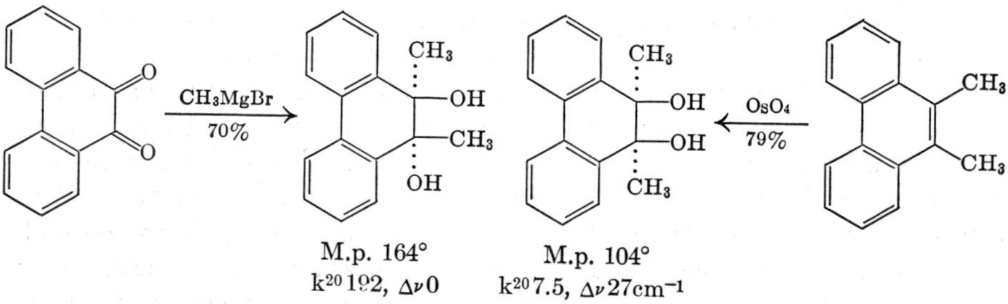

M.p. 164°
k^{20} 192, $\Delta\nu$ 0

M.p. 104°
k^{20} 7.5, $\Delta\nu$ 27cm^{-1}

the cis isomer because of the high rate of cleavage, k^{20} 192. Later, tests with reagents described below prompted synthesis, by osmylation of 9,10-dimethyl-phenanthrene, of a second isomer (104°) and this reacted at a lower rate (7.5) even though, from the method of preparation, it must be the cis isomer.

One reagent for characterizing diols is dipotassium tetramethylosmate (1), a crystalline green solid readily made from osmium tetroxide and methanolic potassium hydroxide (Criegee, 1941). It reacts in methanol with *cis* diols and also with sufficiently flexible *trans* diols. *trans*-Cyclohexane-1,2-diol, for example,

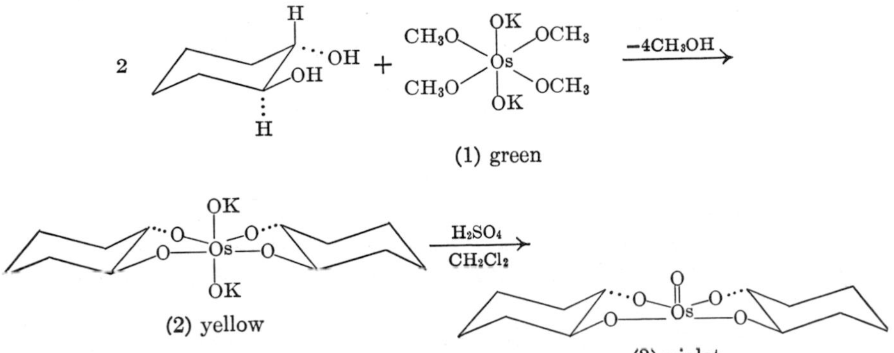

(1) green

(2) yellow   (3) violet

dissolves in a solution of the reagent in methanol (KOH) with a color change, and the sparingly soluble salt (2) separates in high yield. The substance is very sensitive to water, but on acidification of a suspension of the salt in methylene chloride the diester (3) passes into the organic phase and is recoverable as a crystalline solid. A second reagent, monopotassium triacetylosmate (6), is made by dissolv-

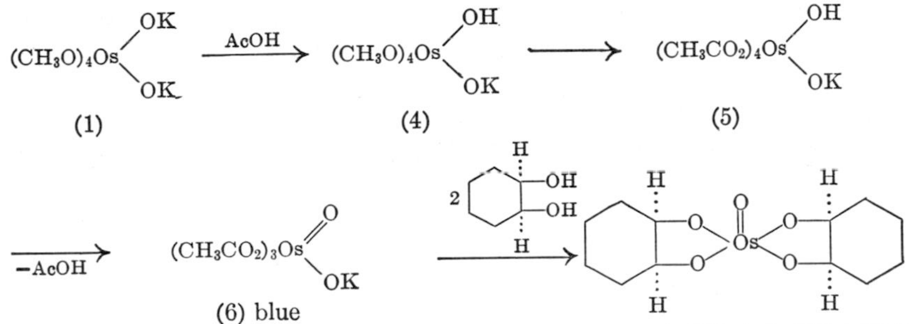

$(CH_3O)_4Os$ (1) $\xrightarrow{AcOH}$ $(CH_3O)_4Os$ (4) $\longrightarrow$ $(CH_3CO_2)_4Os$ (5)

$\xrightarrow{-AcOH}$ $(CH_3CO_2)_3Os$ (6) blue

(7) + 2 AcOH + AcOK + H$_2$O

ing the tetramethylosmate (1) in acetic acid; at a suitable concentration, the cobalt-blue solution deposits crystals of (6). This substance reacts in acetic acid with *cis* diols irreversibly, with discharge of the blue color and formation of the diester (7). It also reacts with a number of *trans* diols, but the reaction can be reversed: addition of potassium acetate to a solution of a *trans* diol diester is attended with appearance of the blue color of the salt (6); the diester of a *cis* diol is unaffected under the same conditions.

By application of these tests, Criegee (1956) established beyond question that the fast-acting dimethyldihydrophenanthrenediol is *trans* and the slow-acting one *cis*. The rate relationship is the same with the two 9,10-dihydrophenanthrene-9,10-diols; E. Boyland (1949) proved the isomer obtained by reduction of phenanthrenequinone to be *trans* by resolving it, and he found that the other isomer alone forms an acetonide; J. Böeseken (1921) showed that *cis*-cyclohexane-1,2-diols form acetonides, whereas the *trans* isomers do not. The first eleven diols in Table 5.4 have been tested and all form acetonides except *trans*-cyclopentane-1,2-diol and *trans*-cyclohexane-1,2-diol; hence it would appear that diols of $\Delta\nu$ greater than 36 react with acetone and those of $\Delta\nu$ less than 34 do not react.

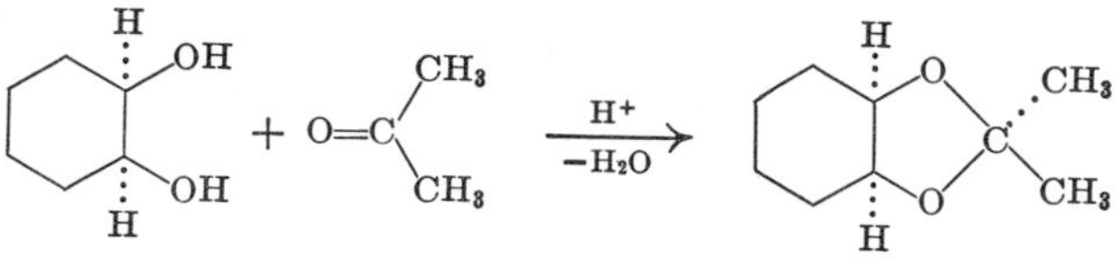

Acetonide

The work cited shows that relative rates of cleavage do not provide a secure basis for establishment of configuration, even when both isomers are available for study, and also that proximity of the two hydroxyl groups is not a necessary requirement for rapid cleavage.

Lead tetraacetate cleavage is a bimolecular reaction, and Criegee originally suggested that it proceeds through an intermediate cyclic ester. Such a substance,

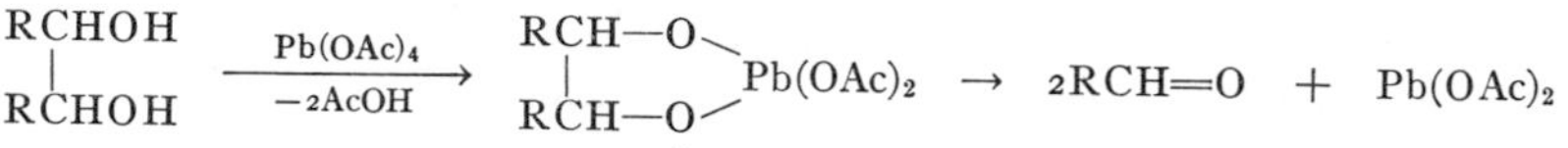

however, could hardly be formed from a *trans*-dihydrophenanthrenediol, in which the hydroxyl groups are held rigidly in the diaxial, antiparallel orientation. Furthermore, the mechanism gives no account of a striking basic catalysis by water or methanol. Thus the rate constant for *cis*-dimethyldihydrophenanthrene-9,10-diol rises from 7.5 in acetic acid to 202 in 75:25 AcOH–CH$_3$OH and to 2430 in 25:75 AcOH–CH$_3$OH. A concerted reaction (Criegee, 1950) involving participation of a Lewis base (HO$^-$, CH$_3$O$^-$) in formation of the transition state II ac-

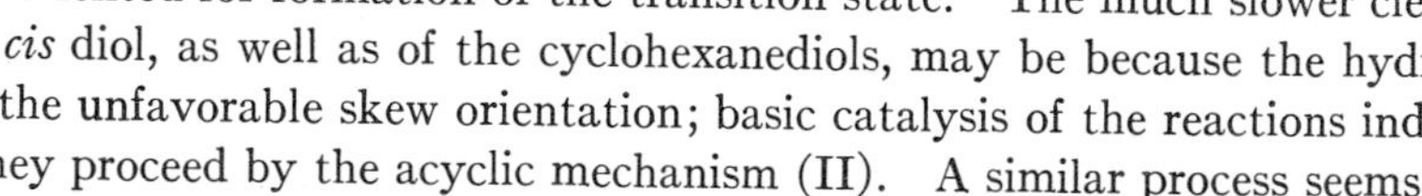

counts for both the catalytic effect and for the rapid cleavage of the *trans*-dihydro-phenanthrenediols, since the diaxial antiparallel hydroxyls are coplanar and hence ideally oriented for formation of the transition state. The much slower cleavage of the *cis* diol, as well as of the cyclohexanediols, may be because the hydroxyls are in the unfavorable skew orientation; basic catalysis of the reactions indicates that they proceed by the acyclic mechanism (II). A similar process seems to be involved in the reaction of lead tetraacetate with dienes to give 1,4-diacetoxy derivatives, since in acetic acid solution the reaction is markedly catalyzed by water, methanol, or potassium acetate. Anthracene, in which the reactive diene system extends across the central ring, reacts with lead tetraacetate in benzene to give a mixture of *cis*- and *trans*-9,10-diacetoxy-9,10-dihydroanthracene (S. T. Putnam,[1] 1947); the occurrence of *trans* addition rules out a cyclic intermediate.

---

[1] Stearns T. Putnam, b. 1917 Springfield, Vt.; Ph.D. Harvard (Fieser); Hercules Powder Co.

R. P. Bell (1958) found that glycol cleavage by lead tetraacetate is markedly catalyzed by trichloroacetic acid; the acid catalysis is accounted for by the transition state III. A practical application of acid-catalyzed glycol cleavage is

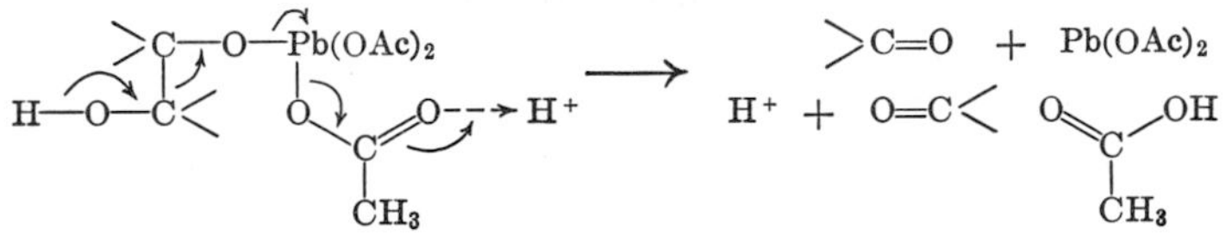

III

reported by C. A. Grob (1960). The diaxial diol IV could not be cleaved satisfactorily under ordinary conditions to $1,6$-dioxo-$\Delta^{3,8}$-decadiene (V) but reacted in

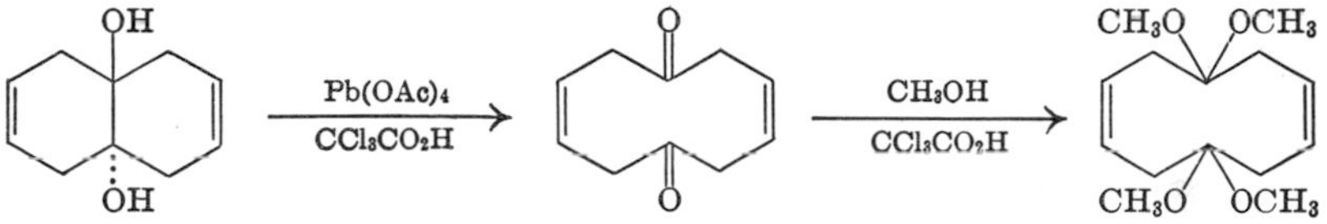

IV m.p. 83°   V m.p. 185°   VI m.p. 202°

methanol in the presence of trichloroacetic acid as catalyst to give the high-melting tetramethyl ketal VI in 75 % yield.

The interesting case of four stereoisomeric ring B vic-diols derived from cholesterol has been explored by S. J. Angyal[1] and R. J. Young (1959). Ring B, being locked between two other rings, is rigid and not free to flip. Rate constants for

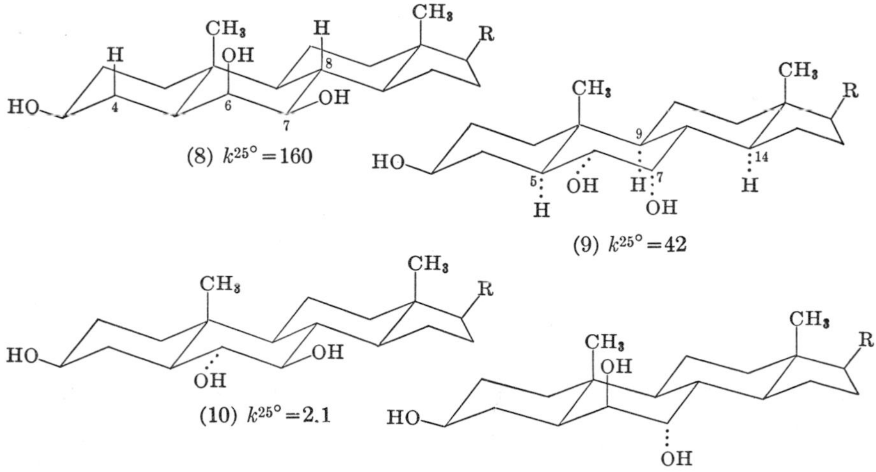

(8) $k^{25°} = 160$

(9) $k^{25°} = 42$

(10) $k^{25°} = 2.1$

(11) $k^{25°} = 0$

glycol cleavage with lead tetraacetate are given under the formulas. The greater reactivity of the $6\beta,7\beta$-diol (8) over the $6\alpha,7\alpha$-diol (9) may be in part because the repulsion of the axial 6β-hydroxyl group by the axial methyl group at C_{10} facilitates

[1] S. J. Angyal, b. 1914 Budapest; Ph.D. Budapest (Zemplén); Univ. New South Wales, Sydney, Australia

stronger bonding with the equatorial OH and in part because cleavage of (8) relieves the steric strain imposed by the CH_3:OH interaction. The diaxial diol was resistant to attack under the conditions tried, but acid catalysis was not investigated.[1] Parallel results were obtained with the less powerful phenyliodoso diacetate at 50–80°. Periodic acid in 80% ethanol failed to cleave the diaxial diol (11) but, as had been found before in comparable studies, the rates for the other diols were in an order opposite to that found with the other two glycol-splitting reagents: the *trans* diol (10) reacts considerably faster than the *cis* compounds, with which the order is (9) > (8). If the reaction involves a cyclic intermediate in which the large iodine atom forms part of a five-membered ring, as formulated above, perhaps this ring can form most easily when the hydroxyl groups are both equatorial (10). A ring involving one axial oxygen would be more stable on the α-side (9), where it is hindered by axial hydrogens at C_5, C_9, and C_{14}, than on the β-side (8), where hindrance arises from the axial C_{10}-methyl group, along with axial hydrogens at C_4 and C_8.

5.28   Potassium Permanganate. — Potassium permanganate is a powerful oxidizing agent capable not only of hydroxylating a double bond and of cleaving the resulting *vic*-glycol but also of oxidizing an aldehyde to an acid. Control of the reaction to the stage of *vic*-glycol formation presents difficulties but under controlled conditions glycols can sometimes be prepared in low or moderate yield. When the reaction can afford geometrical isomers, or isomers of the *erythro-threo* type, the product is exclusively the *cis* or *threo* diol. Since the products are those of *cis* addition, the reaction probably involves a cyclic intermediate (1) comparable to an osmate ester. However, the oxidation is conducted in water solution and the postulated manganate ester, being a salt, is soluble in

Manganate ester

water and evidently undergoes immediate hydrolysis, since isolation of an intermediate has not been accomplished. Unlike an osmate ester, the intermediate thus affords no protection to the *cis*-glycol. The balanced equation (2) appears to represent the ideal reaction. Potassium hydroxide is a reaction product and

$$2. \ 3 \ C_6H_{10} + 2 \ KMnO_4 + 4 \ H_2O \longrightarrow 3 \ C_6H_{10}(OH)_2 + 2 \ KOH + 2 \ MnO_2$$

hence in an oxidation commenced in neutral solution the mixture becomes increasingly alkaline as the reaction proceeds. If this effect slows down the reaction, it can be counteracted by addition of acetic acid.

[1] Dr. F. Mukawa of our group has found that cholestane-3β,5α,6β-triol is oxidized rapidly by the Grob procedure with formation of the 6,6-dimethoxy derivative of the 5-keto-6-aldehyde.

cis-Cyclohexane-1,2-diol was prepared for the first time in 1878 by Markowni-koff by the reaction formulated. A modern procedure calls for vigorous mechanical stirring of a mixture of 16.4 g. of cyclohexene and 700 ml. of water to produce a near-emulsion. The flask is cooled in an ice bath kept at about −10° in order to counteract a mild exothermic effect and maintain a reaction temperature close to 0°. A solution of 21.2 g. of permanganate in 300 ml. of water is run in from a separatory funnel over a period of one hour. Each drop produces a fleeting purple coloration with rapid change to brown manganese dioxide. The mixture is then heated to coagulate the precipitate and filtered by suction. The filtrate is an alkaline solution of the desired diol and the mono- or di-potassium salt of adipic acid, $HO_2C(CH_2)_4CO_2H$, an inevitable by-product. Acidification with hydrochloric acid would liberate adipic acid which would then be extracted along with the *cis* diol, but addition of pieces of dry ice until the pH is reduced from 12 to about 8 leaves the by-product in the form of its salt, since carbonic acid is less acidic than a carboxylic acid. The neutralized filtrate is evaporated to a small volume and the diol is recovered by repeated extraction with chloroform (12 times). Colored impurities are left in the upper aqueous layer, and evaporation of the dried extract and crystallization from benzene-

Piperidine
b. p. 106°

hexane affords 7.0 g. (30%) of pure cyclohexane-1,2-diol. Adipic acid can be isolated by acidification (HCl) of the aqueous layer.

The only high-yield permanganate hydroxylation on record is one in which the initially formed *cis*-glycol (II) loses hydrogen cyanide as soon as formed and

$$\underset{\text{I}}{RR'C{=}C{-}CN} \ \overset{KMnO_4}{\longrightarrow} \ \underset{\text{II}}{\left[\begin{array}{c} CH_2OAc \\ | \\ RR'C{-}C{-}CN \\ | \ | \\ OHOH \end{array} \right]} \ \overset{-HCN}{\longrightarrow} \ \underset{\text{III}}{RR'C{-}C{-}CH_2OAc}$$

with CH₂OAc above the first carbon.

affords the α-ketol III (M. Tishler,[1] 1955). The reaction is carried out with a solution of I and potassium permanganate in acetone containing piperidine as catalyst. The yield of the α-ketol III is 98%.

5.29   Exhaustive Oxidation. — When an alkene is oxidized without cooling with all the alkaline permanganate that it will consume or when it is oxidized exhaustively with acidified permanganate, with chromic acid in acetic acid solution, or with potassium dichromate and sulfuric acid, the intermediary glycol is destroyed, and the end result is severance of the carbon chain at the point of the original double bond with production of two oxidized fragments. A symmetrical alkene (I) affords two identical fragments having a carboxyl group, for the limit of oxidation of the group —C(H)= is —C(OH)=O. If the alkene has a terminal double bond (II), exhaustive oxidation of the end unit containing a lone carbon atom gives carbon dioxide. A third structural type is that in which one or both of the unsaturated carbon atoms are substituted by two alkyl groups and carry no hydrogen, as in III. Here a terminal point in the oxidation is

[1] Max Tishler, b. 1908 Boston; Ph.D. Harvard (Kohler); Merck and Co.

reached with cleavage of the double bond and production of a substance having double-bonded oxygen attached to the originally ethylenic carbon, a ketone.

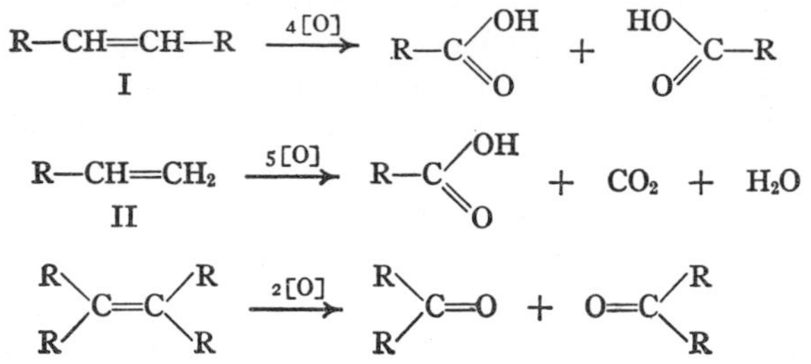

$$R-CH{=}CH-R \xrightarrow{\ 4\,[O]\ } R-C\overset{\diagup OH}{\diagdown_{O}} + \overset{HO\diagdown}{\underset{O\diagup}{}}C-R$$

I

$$R-CH{=}CH_2 \xrightarrow{\ 5\,[O]\ } R-C\overset{\diagup OH}{\diagdown_{O}} + CO_2 + H_2O$$

II

$$\overset{R\diagdown}{\underset{R\diagup}{}}C{=}C\overset{\diagup R}{\diagdown R} \xrightarrow{\ 2\,[O]\ } \overset{R\diagdown}{\underset{R\diagup}{}}C{=}O + O{=}C\overset{\diagup R}{\diagdown R}$$

III

Exhaustive oxidation, involving as it does fission of an unsaturated compound between the unsaturated centers, provides an experimental method of locating these centers and hence of determining the structures of unsaturated substances. The three butylenes IV–VI, for example, give characteristic oxidation products that not only locate the positions of the double bonds but also fix the nature of the carbon chains. The first isomer (IV) yields a three-carbon acid and carbon dioxide, a result indicative of a chain of four carbons with a terminal double bond,

$$CH_3CH_2CH{=}CH_2 \xrightarrow{\ [O]\ } CH_3CH_2COOH + CO_2$$

IV

$$CH_3CH{=}CHCH_3 \xrightarrow{\ [O]\ } 2\,CH_3COOH$$

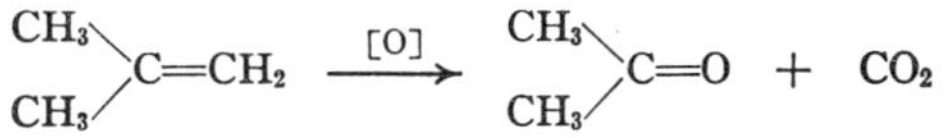

V

$$\overset{CH_3\diagdown}{\underset{CH_3\diagup}{}}C{=}CH_2 \xrightarrow{\ [O]\ } \overset{CH_3\diagdown}{\underset{CH_3\diagup}{}}C{=}O + CO_2$$

VI

C·C·C:C. Production of a single two-carbon acid identifies the structure V, and formation, in the last instance, of the three-carbon ketone acetone along with carbon dioxide fixes the structure as having a branched chain and a terminal double-bonded methylene group.

5.30   **Catalytic Oxidation.** — An aqueous solution 0.019 M in sodium meta-periodate ($NaIO_4$) and 0.0034 M in potassium permanganate (pH 7–8) cleaves an olefinic double bond rapidly at 25° (Lemieux,[1] 1955). The permanganate is reduced only to the manganate stage, from which it is regenerated by the periodate, which by itself does not attack the olefin. A symmetrically disubstituted olefin (1) or a trisubstituted olefin (2) is converted initially to an α-ketol, which sometimes can be isolated; further oxidation gives acids or ketones. An olefin with a terminal double bond (3) yields formaldehyde as one product. Water-insoluble compounds can be oxidized in aqueous dioxane or aqueous t-butyl alcohol.

[1] Raymond U. Lemieux, b. 1920 Lac la Biche, Alberta, Canada; Ph.D. McGill (Purves); Univ. Ottawa

In another method sodium metaperiodate is the primary oxidant and osmium tetroxide the catalyst (R. Pappo, 1956). The particular value of the method is that it permits oxidation to the stage of an aldehyde but no further. Oxidation of *trans*-stilbene to benzaldehyde (4) illustrates the procedure. A solution of 0.5 g.

1. $\begin{array}{c} RCH \\ \parallel \\ R'CH \end{array} \xrightarrow[\text{NaIO}_4]{\text{KMnO}_4} \begin{array}{c} RCHOH \\ \mid \\ R'C{=}O \end{array} \rightarrow \begin{array}{c} RCO_2H \\ R'CO_2H \end{array}$

2. $R_2C{=}CHR' \xrightarrow{[O]} \begin{array}{c} R_2C{-}CHR' \\ \mid \ \ \mid \\ OH \ OH \end{array} \rightarrow \begin{array}{c} R_2C{-}CR' \\ \mid \ \ \parallel \\ OH \ O \end{array} \rightarrow R_2C{=}O + HO_2CR'$

3. $RCH{=}CH_2 \xrightarrow{[O]} RCH{=}O + CH_2{=}O$

of hydrocarbon in 15 ml. of dioxane and 5 ml. of water is treated at 25° with 15.4 mg. of osmium tetroxide and 1.25 g. of sodium metaperiodate; benzaldehyde is isolated as a derivative in 85% yield. Osmium tetroxide effects hydroxylation;

4. $\begin{array}{c} H \\ \mid \\ C_6H_5C{=}C{-}C_6H_5 \\ \mid \\ H \end{array} \xrightarrow[85\%]{\text{NaIO}_4(\text{OsO}_4)} 2C_6H_5CHO$

the periodate oxidizes osmium in lower valence forms to osmium tetroxide and also effects glycol cleavage.

A technical process used for the manufacture of ethylene oxide consists in catalytic air oxidation of ethylene:

$$CH_2{=}CH_2 + O_2 \xrightarrow{\text{Catalyst}} \begin{array}{c} CH_2{-}CH_2 \\ \diagdown \diagup \\ O \end{array}$$

Ethylene oxide
(b.p. 13.5°)

5.31 Ozonization. — Ozone, produced in concentrations up to 6–8% by passing a stream of oxygen through a generator in which it is submitted to an electric discharge (Fig. 5.6), adds rapidly to the double bond of an alkene to give an ozonide. Since ozonides usually are viscous oils or glasses,

$$RCH{=}CR_2 \xrightarrow{O_3} \begin{array}{c} O \\ \diagup \diagdown \\ RCH \ \ CR_2 \\ \mid \ \ \ \ \mid \\ O{-}O \end{array} \xrightarrow[\text{b. Pt, H}_2]{\text{a. H}_2O} RCH{=}O + O{=}CR_2 + \begin{array}{c} \text{a. H}_2O_2 \\ \text{b. 2H}_2O \end{array}$$

sometimes of explosive properties, they usually are not isolated but converted into cleavage products, aldehydes or ketones, or both. Decomposition with water liberates the third oxygen in part as hydrogen peroxide and in part as peroxidic derivatives of the carbonyl compounds formed. Formation of troublesome mixtures is avoided by decomposing the ozonide with hydrogen in the presence of platinum catalyst or by reduction with zinc and acetic acid; in either case peroxides are destroyed as formed. The reaction is of value for preparation of aldehydes and was used in France for the commercial production of vanillin

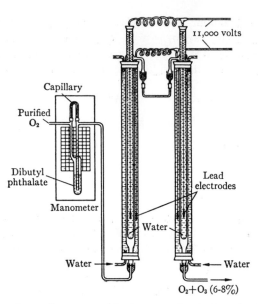

FIG. 5.6. — Ozone Generator, with Flowmeter for the Entering Oxygen

before Harries[1] investigated the reaction as a possible tool for attacking the problem of the structure of rubber, a polymeric unsaturated hydrocarbon. With the aid of the firm Siemens and Halske, he developed the first practical laboratory generator and soon established ozonolysis, the complete process of forming and cleaving an ozonide, as a reaction of wide application for investigation of structure, including the structure of rubber.

In spite of the experimental difficulties of characterizing highly sensitive compounds of unfavorable properties, R. Criegee (1954–56) was able to unravel details of a complicated chain of events. Ozone itself is a resonance hybrid of four structures, in which two terminal oxygens are bonded to a central atom at an

angle of about 116°; the two bonds are of equal length, 1.29 Å. The reaction with an olefin is considered to involve electrophilic attack by one of the oxygen atoms of ozone to form an "initial" ozonide (2), which is very unstable and rear-

---

[1] Carl Dietrich Harries, 1866–1923; b. Luckenwalde; Ph.D. Berlin (Tiemann); Univ. Berlin; *Ber.*, **59A**, 123 (1926)

ranges to the true ozonide (5). Criegee presented evidence that the isomerization of (2) to (5) involves decomposition to a peroxidic dipolar ion (3) and a ketone (4, or an aldehyde), followed by addition of (3) to (4).

$$\overset{\delta^+ \;\; \delta^-}{R_2C{=}CR_2} \;+\; {}^-O\diagup{}^O\diagdown O^+ \;\longrightarrow\; \left[\,\bar{O}\diagup{}^O\diagdown \overset{+}{O} \atop R_2C{-\!\!-\!\!-}CR_2 \right] \;\longrightarrow$$

$$\text{(1)}$$

$$\underset{\text{(2)}}{R_2C{-\!\!-\!\!-}CR_2 \atop O\diagup{}^O\diagdown O} \;\longrightarrow\; \underset{\text{(3)}}{R_2\overset{+}{C}{\diagup}^O{\diagdown}O^-} \;+\; \underset{\text{(4)}}{\overset{\delta^- \;\; \delta^+}{O{=}CR_2}}$$

$$\longrightarrow \quad \underset{\text{(5)}}{R_2C\diagdown_O\diagup CR_2 \atop O{-\!\!-\!\!-}O}$$

Aliphatic tetrasubstituted olefins fail to form monomeric ozonides (5) because the carbonyl group in the ketonic component (4) is not sufficiently reactive. Ozonides result, however, from compounds carrying electron attracting groups: $BrCH_2(CH_3)C{=}C(CH_3)CH_2Br$, $(CH_3)_2C{=}C(CH_3)CO_2CH_3$ (Criegee, 1960). Trimethylacrolein (6) yields the same ozonide (7) as mesityl oxide (8), probably

$$\underset{\text{(6)}}{\overset{H_3C}{}\overset{}{\underset{H_3C}{}}{>}C{=}C{<}\overset{CH_3}{\underset{CHO}{}}} \xrightarrow{O_3} \underset{\text{(7)}}{\overset{H_3C}{\underset{H_3C}{>}}C\overset{OO}{\underset{O}{}}C{<}\overset{COCH_3}{\underset{H}{}}} \xleftarrow{O_3} \underset{\text{(8)}}{\overset{H_3C}{\underset{HC_3}{>}}C{=}C{<}\overset{COCH_3}{\underset{H}{}}}$$

through formation of methylglyoxal, CH_3COCHO, as the intermediate of type (4) and participation of the more reactive aldehyde function in combination with (3).

5.32   **Allylic Oxidation.** — Alkenes react with molecular oxygen to form hydroperoxides more readily than alkanes react. The attack is at an activated allylic position, and may result in the production of a mixture of allylic hydroperoxides:

$$-CH_2-CH{=}CH- \xrightarrow{O_2} -\underset{OOH}{\overset{|}{C}H}-CH{=}CH- \;+\; -CH{=}CH-\underset{OOH}{\overset{|}{C}H}-$$

The products derived from unsaturated fatty acids or other aliphatic compounds are highly sensitive, difficult to isolate, and unstable on storage.

Whereas t-butyl perbenzoate on thermal decomposition gives a complex mixture of products, Kharasch and co-workers found (1959) that in the presence of a catalytic amount of a copper or cobalt salt it decomposes to give methyl benzoate (34%) by a chain reaction:

$$C_6H_5CO_3C(CH_3)_3 + Cu^+ \to C_6H_5CO_2Cu^+ + \cdot OC(CH_3)_3$$

$$(CH_3)_3CO\cdot \to (CH_3)_2CO + \cdot CH_3$$

$$C_6H_5CO_3C(CH_3)_3 + \cdot CH_3 \to C_6H_5CO_2CH_3 + \cdot OC(CH_3)_3$$

When the decomposition is carried out in the presence of an olefin, the hydrocarbon is converted into an allylic benzoate; yields are in the range 30–80%. A noteworthy feature is the absence of allylic rearrangement. Thus terminal olefins such as allylbenzene, 1-octene, and 1-hexene yield allylic benzoates with terminal

$$C_6H_5CO_3C(CH_3)_3 + Cu^+ \longrightarrow C_6H_5CO_2Cu^+ + \cdot OC(CH_3)_3$$

$$(CH_3)_3CO\cdot + C_6H_5CH_2CH{=}CH_2 \longrightarrow (CH_3)_3COH + C_6H_5\overset{\cdot}{C}HCH{=}CH_2$$

$$C_6H_5\overset{\cdot}{C}HCH{=}CH_2 + C_6H_5CO_2Cu^+ \xrightarrow[55\%]{} \underset{\underset{OCOC_6H_5}{|}}{C_6H_5CHCH{=}CH_2} + Cu^+$$

double bonds. *t*-Butyl peracetate reacts similarly but yields are lower.

5.33   **Mustard Gas.** — Di-(β-chloroethyl) sulfide is a high-boiling vesicant liquid of low vapor pressure, b.p. 217.5°, m.p. 14.4°, sp. gr. 1.27. The substance is called a poisonous gas because in low concentration in the air over a combat area it can take a high toll of casualties of unprotected enemy troops (artillery bombardments against the British front at Ypres, Flanders, July, 1917). The vesicant penetrates the skin without causing immediate pain but soon forms deep blisters over the exposed area. Since the liquid evaporates only slowly a section subjected to mustard gas attack remains hazardous for many days. The Levinstein process of manufacture involves reaction of ethylene with sulfur chloride and affords di-(β-chloroethyl) sulfide and free sulfur, which is

$$\begin{matrix} CH_2{=}CH_2 \\ + \; S_2Cl_2 \; \to \\ CH_2{=}CH_2 \end{matrix} \qquad S \overset{\textstyle CH_2CH_2Cl}{\underset{\textstyle CH_2CH_2Cl}{<}} \qquad + \; S$$

Di-(β-chloroethyl) sulfide
Mustard gas

retained in the crude reaction product in the colloidal state. The name arose from the fact that the crude Levinstein product in high concentrations has an odor resembling mustard. A possible mechanism suggested by Conant[1] (1920) is as follows:

$$ClSSCl \rightleftharpoons S + SCl_2$$
$$SCl_2 + CH_2{=}CH_2 \to CH_2ClCH_2SCl$$
$$CH_2ClCH_2SCl + CH_2{=}CH_2 \to (ClCH_2CH_2)_2S$$

A second process gives a purer product that is less easily detected. Ethylene is converted by addition of hypochlorous acid into ethylene chlorohydrin, which on reaction with sodium sulfide yields di-(β-hydroxyethyl) sulfide (also called β-thiodiglycol). This nontoxic intermediate reacts with hydrogen chloride gas in a final step to give mustard gas.

$$\begin{matrix} HOCH_2CH_2Cl \\ + \; Na_2S \longrightarrow \\ HOCH_2CH_2Cl \end{matrix} \qquad \overset{\textstyle HOCH_2CH_2}{\underset{\textstyle HOCH_2CH_2}{>}}S \xrightarrow{HCl} \text{Mustard gas}$$

β-Thiodiglycol

[1] James B. Conant, b. 1893 Boston; Ph.D. Harvard (Kohler); Harvard Univ.

CONJUGATED DIENES

5.34   Special Properties. — Hydrocarbons having two double bonds separated by one or more saturated carbon atoms present no novel features and behave as expected from analogy with monounsaturated alkenes. The hydrocarbons (1) and (2) have identical double bonds at the ends of the carbon

$$CH_2\!\!=\!\!CHCH_2CH\!\!=\!\!CH_2 \qquad\qquad CH_2\!\!=\!\!CHCH_2CH_2CH\!\!=\!\!CH_2$$
(1) Pentadiene-1,4   (2) Hexadiene-1,5

chains, and these absorb bromine, hydrogen bromide, and hydrogen (in the presence of a catalyst) at the same rate and in the manner expected from the behavior of the monounsaturated analog propylene, $CH_3CH\!\!=\!\!CH_2$. The two double bonds thus function independently of each other and are described as isolated double bonds.

A different situation is encountered in butadiene-1,3, a hydrocarbon usually referred to as butadiene and available as a petrochemical by dehydrogenation of the mixture of butene-1 and butene-2 produced by cracking. Butadiene has a pair of double bonds adjacent to each other. It is a conjugated diene, and the

$$CH_3CH_2CH\!\!=\!\!CH_2 \xrightarrow{\;-\,2H\;} CH_2\!\!=\!\!\overset{3}{C}HCH\!\!=\!\!\overset{1}{C}H_2 \xleftarrow{\;-\,2H\;} CH_3CH\!\!=\!\!CHCH_3$$
Butene-1   Butadiene   Butene-2

system $C\!\!=\!\!C\!\!-\!\!C\!\!=\!\!C$ is a conjugated system. The significance of the term is that when a conjugated diene participates in an addition reaction the two centers of unsaturation often function as a unit rather than as isolated double bonds.

Addition of one mole of bromine to butadiene in various solvents at $-15°$ gives a mixture of about equal parts of 3,4-dibromo-1-butene and *trans*-1,4-dibromo-2-butene. The first product results from 1,2-addition to one of the two double

$$\overset{4}{C}H_2\!\!=\!\!\overset{3}{C}H\!\!-\!\!\overset{2}{C}H\!\!=\!\!\overset{1}{C}H_2 \xrightarrow{\;Br_2\;} CH_2\!\!=\!\!CHCHBrCH_2Br \; + \;$$

(1,2-addition)

$$\begin{array}{cc} H & CH_2Br \\ \diagdown & \diagup \\ & C\!\!=\!\!C \\ \diagup & \diagdown \\ BrCH_2 & H \end{array}$$
(1,4-addition)

bonds and the second results from addition to the terminal positions 1 and 4, with establishment of a new double bond at the 2,3-position. In the 1,4-addition the conjugated system participates as an entity.

The special mode of addition of butadiene is associated with special characteristics of the molecule disclosed by physical measurements. Thermochemical data show that butadiene is significantly more stable, in the sense of having a lower energy content, than dienes with isolated (nonconjugated) double bonds; and electron-diffraction measurements reveal abnormality in bond length, defined as the distance between atomic centers. The normal bond length for the $C\!\!-\!\!C$ link is 1.54 Å and for the isolated $C\!\!=\!\!C$ link the distance is 1.33 Å. In butadiene the central bond in the molecule, represented in the ordinary formula as a single link, actually has a bond distance of 1.46 Å, intermediate between a double and a single bond; the two terminal bonds (1.35 Å) are slightly longer than an isolated double bond.   The evidence suggests that the three bonds linking the carbon atoms are neither true double nor true single bonds but something of an intermediate character.

The resonance theory accounts for the facts cited on the postulate of redistribution of electrons.   Thus redistribution of the electrons in formula (a) in the direc-

$$CH_2:\overset{\frown}{CH:CH::}CH_2 \longleftrightarrow \overset{\frown}{CH_2:CH::CH:}CH_2 \longleftrightarrow \overset{+}{CH_2}:CH::CH:\overset{-}{CH_2} \longleftrightarrow \overset{-}{CH_2}:CH::CH:\overset{+}{CH_2}$$
$$\quad\;(a)\qquad\qquad\qquad (b)\qquad\qquad\qquad (c)\qquad\qquad\qquad (d)$$

tions indicated by the dotted lines (one electron of each double bond moved to the center) would give structure (b), which has a central double bond, two terminal single bonds, and terminal carbon atoms each having an unpaired electron.   An electron transfer in (b) from one terminal carbon atom to the other could give a polarized species, (c) or (d), depending upon the direction of transfer.   These four structures differ merely in the positions of the electrons.   According to the resonance theory, when a substance can have two or more equivalent or nearly equivalent structures, the actual molecule does not conform to any one of the structures but exists as a resonance hybrid of the principal contributing structures.

The diradical (b) is probably a minor contributor, an excited state, and hence butadiene can be regarded as a resonance hybrid of (a), (c), and (d).   The equivalent Kekulé formulation is:

$$CH_2{=}CH{-}CH{=}CH_2 \longleftrightarrow \overset{+}{CH_2}{-}CH{=}CH{-}\overset{-}{CH_2} \longleftrightarrow \overset{-}{CH_2}{-}CH{=}CH{-}\overset{+}{CH_2}$$
$$\quad\;(a')\qquad\qquad\qquad\;\; (c')\qquad\qquad\qquad\;\; (d')$$

The resonance concept explains why the central linkage partakes of the character of both a single and a double bond.   Bond shortening is a necessary consequence of such a resonance effect, as is the lengthening of the terminal linkages in consequence of their partial single-bond character.

A further consequence of resonance is dissipation of energy, or thermodynamic stabilization.   Conversely, thermodynamic data afford a measure of the magnitude of resonance stabilization.   The average heat of hydrogenation of propylene, butene-1, and other alkenes having the terminal-bond structure of butadiene is 30.3 kcal./mole.   The heats of hydrogenation of the nonconjugated pentadiene-1,4 and hexadiene-1,5, namely 60.8 and 60.5 kcal./mole, are almost twice this value.   The value observed for butadiene, however, is only 57.1 kcal./mole, and hence this hydrocarbon has a lower energy content than that corresponding to two isolated double bonds.   The difference of 3.5 kcal./mole represents the resonance stabilization, or resonance energy, of butadiene.

Any structure contributing to a resonance hybrid may participate in a reaction such as bromination.   If structure (a') of butadiene is attacked by Br^+, the resulting carbonium ion would be a resonant hybrid of structures (e') and (f'); attack of the polarized structure (c') would afford the same hybrid ion.   The combination of this hybrid with bromide ion can give either the 1,2- or the 1,4-addition product.

$$
\left.\begin{array}{c}
CH_2=CHCH=CH_2 \\
(a') \\
\uparrow\downarrow \\
\overset{+}{C}H_2CH=CH\overset{-}{C}H_2 \\
(c')
\end{array}\right\}
\xrightarrow{Br^+}
\left\{\begin{array}{c}
CH_2=CH-\overset{+}{C}HCH_2Br \\
(e') \\
\uparrow\downarrow \\
\overset{+}{C}H_2-CH=CHCH_2Br \\
(f')
\end{array}\right\}
\xrightarrow{Br^-}
\left\{\begin{array}{l}
CH_2=CHCHBrCH_2Br \\
\quad (1,2\text{-product}) \\
\\
BrCH_2CH=CHCH_2Br \\
\quad (1,4\text{-product})
\end{array}\right.
$$

In the addition of a hydrogen halide to a symmetrical diene the electron displacements, shown in (1) for one of the two identical structures, cause the initial proton uptake to occur at one of the terminal atoms. The resulting carbonium ion is a resonance hybrid (a ↔ b), and the proportion of 1,2- and 1,4-addition products formed on combination with halide ion is dependent upon the relative rates of reactions leading from the hybrid to the products. Thus addition of

1. $CH_2\!=\!CH\!-\!CH\!=\!CH_2 \xrightarrow{H^+} CH_2\!=\!CHCHCH_3 \longleftrightarrow \overset{+}{C}H_2CH\!=\!CHCH_3$
    $\qquad\qquad\qquad\qquad\quad (a\!:\!1,2\text{-addition}) \qquad\qquad (b\!:\!1,4\text{-addition})$

hydrogen chloride to butadiene under various experimental conditions (2) gives mixtures of two products in which crotyl chloride, the product of 1,4-addition, invariably predominates, even though it is thermodynamically less stable than

2. $CH_2\!=\!CHCH\!=\!CH_2$ $\xrightarrow[\displaystyle HCl]{}$
    $\begin{array}{l}
    \overset{75\text{-}80\%}{\nearrow} CH_3CH=CHCH_2Cl \;\;(1,4\text{-addition}) \\
    \qquad\qquad\quad \text{Crotyl chloride} \\
    \\
    \underset{20\text{-}25\%}{\searrow} CH_2=CHCHClCH_3 \;\;(1,2\text{-addition}) \\
    \qquad\qquad\quad \alpha\text{-Methylallyl chloride}
    \end{array}$

α-methylallyl chloride and can be converted by prolonged treatment with hydrogen chloride into an equilibrium mixture containing 80% of α-methylallyl chloride. The complete absence of the third possible product, 4-chlorobutene-1, conforms to the prediction that neither nonterminal carbon atom can become a center of negative polarity. In an unsymmetrical diene the point of initial attack is again one of the terminal carbon atoms, but the choice is determined by the

3. $\overset{\cdot}{C}H_2\!=\!CCH\!=\!CH_2 \xrightarrow{HCl} CH_3C\!=\!CHCH_2Cl$
    $\quad\;\; \underset{\displaystyle CH_3}{\uparrow} \qquad\qquad\qquad \underset{\displaystyle CH_3}{|}$
    $\qquad\qquad\qquad\qquad (1,4\text{-addition})$

4. $\overset{\cdot}{C}H\!=\!CHCH\!=\!\overset{\cdot}{C}H \xrightarrow{HBr} CH_2CHBrCH\!=\!CH \;+\; CH_2CH\!=\!CHCHBr$
    $\;\; \underset{\displaystyle CH_3}{\uparrow} \qquad \underset{\displaystyle CH_3}{\uparrow} \qquad\quad \underset{\displaystyle CH_3}{|} \qquad\quad \underset{\displaystyle CH_3}{|} \qquad\quad \underset{\displaystyle CH_3}{|} \qquad\quad \underset{\displaystyle CH_3}{|}$
    $\qquad\qquad\qquad\qquad\quad \underset{(1,2\text{-addition})}{90\%} \qquad\quad \underset{(1,4\text{-addition})}{10\%}$

5. $CH\!=\!CH\!-\!CH\!=\!\overset{\cdot}{C}H_2 \xrightarrow{HCl} CH\!=\!CHCHClCH_3$
    $\;\; \underset{\displaystyle C_6H_5}{\uparrow} \qquad\qquad\qquad\qquad \underset{\displaystyle C_6H_5}{|}$
    $\qquad\qquad\qquad\qquad\quad (1,2\text{-addition})$

polarity of substituent groups. Typical examples are shown in formulations (3)–(5); the starred carbon atoms represent the point of attack by the proton. Reaction (5) gives exclusively the 1,2-addition product, probably because this isomer retains the double bond conjugated with the ring.

An interesting 1,4-addition occurs in the reaction of a diene with liquid sulfur dioxide to form a cyclic sulfone, such as that from isoprene (Staudinger, 1935).

$$
\begin{array}{c}
\underset{\substack{|| \\ CH_2 \quad\quad CH_2}}{CH\text{------}CCH_3} + SO_2 \xrightarrow[\substack{78\text{-}82\%}]{\text{Hydroquinone (85°)}} \underset{\substack{| \quad\quad | \\ CH_2 \quad CH_2 \\ \diagdown SO_2 \diagup}}{CH\text{====}CCH_3}
\end{array}
$$

Isoprene   Isoprene cyclic sulfone
                                                m. p. 64°

The reaction is conducted in a pressure vessel in the presence of a little hydroquinone to inhibit polymerization and the product is crystallized from methanol. Since the crystalline sulfones decompose to the components when heated to 100°, they afford a means of purification of dienes.

Tetrafluorobutadiene can be prepared in high yield by reaction of tetrafluoroethylene with acetylene at 225° and pyrolysis of the resulting 3,3,4,4-tetrafluorocyclobutene (W. H. Sharkey,[1] du Pont, 1961). The high reactivity of the

$$
\begin{array}{c}
\underset{\substack{+ \\ HC \equiv CH}}{F_2C = CF_2} \xrightarrow{225°} \underset{\substack{| \quad | \\ HC = CH}}{F_2C - CF_2} \xrightarrow{200°} F_2C = CHCH = CF_2
\end{array}
$$

                                        b.p. 55°

                                        $\big|$ NaOC$_2$H$_5$; H$_2$O

                        $C_2H_5O_2CCH_2CH_2CO_2C_2H_5$
                                Diethyl succinate

diene is illustrated by its reaction with sodium ethoxide to give a product hydrolyzed by water to diethyl succinate.

5.35   Orbital Theory. — The case of butadiene is an extension of that of ethylene but presents an additional feature. In a polyatomic molecule such as methane the bonds are all localized, that is, each separately resembles the bond in the diatomic hydrogen molecule, since the tetrahedral arrangement isolates each molecular orbital present from the others and so prevents them from interacting. The π orbital of ethylene is also isolated and localized. In butadiene, however, a molecular orbital is compounded out of four $2p_z$ orbitals on four adjacent and coplanar carbon atoms, and these orbitals are parallel to one another and at right angles to the common nuclear axis (Fig. 5.7a). Hence it is clear that C_2 and C_3 overlap each other as much as they overlap C_1 and C_4 and hence that formation of two localized π orbitals is impossible. Instead, all four wave functions coalesce to form a π orbital that encompasses all four nuclei (b). This initial orbital (b), designated π_1, is particularly stable because it possesses

---

[1] William H. Sharkey, b. 1916 Vinita, Okla.; Ph.D. Illinois (Marvel); du Pont Co.

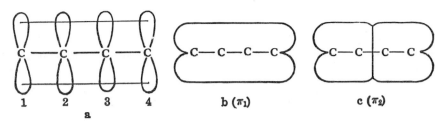

FIG. 5.7 — Butadiene (Carbon Skeleton)

only one nodal plane, but, in accordance with the Pauli exclusion principle, only two of the four electrons can occupy it. The second pair of electrons is accommodated in a further orbital, π_2 (c), having a second nodal plane perpendicular to the first and hence less stable than π_1. The electrons thus swarm over the complete molecule, and hence an electrical influence at one part of the molecule is transmitted throughout the system. The electrons have more room in which to move and have lower total energy and therefore greater binding energy than when paired in localized double bonds. Energy postulated in the orbital theory to be derived from delocalization is quantitatively identical with energy postulated in the resonance theory to be derived from resonance. It is obvious from the orbital theory that the stability and other special properties of conjugated systems requires coplanarity of the unsaturated centers but not colinearity. Thus one could expect even more delocalization in cyclohexatriene (benzene) than in butadiene.

5.36　　　Light Absorption. — In the absence of light, electrons of butadiene travel in orbitals of the lowest possible energy, the ground state. On irradiation with ultraviolet light specific light waves are destroyed in causing transition of appropriate electrons of the diene from the ground state to orbitals of higher energy level. Hence a part of the light passing through the hydrocarbon is not transmitted but absorbed, and butadiene exhibits an intense ab-

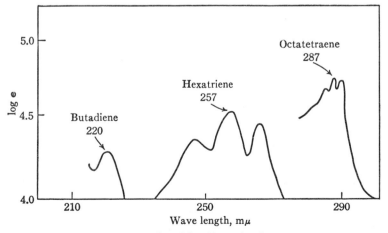

FIG. 5.8. — Ultraviolet Absorption Spectra

sorption band in the region 215–225 mμ with a maximum at 220 mμ, or λ_{max} = 220 mμ. The absorption spectrum is shown in the chart, Fig. 5.8, in which wave length is plotted against intensity of absorption expressed as the logarithm of the extinction coefficient (ϵ). Extension of the conjugated system shifts the absorption band in the direction of longer wave length, and also increases intensity of absorption. Both relationships are evident from the graph and from the following summary:

	λ_{max}	log ϵ
CH_2=CHCH=CH_2 Butadiene	220	4.32
CH_2=CHCH=CHCH=CH_2 Hexatriene-1,3,5	257	4.54
CH_2=CHCH=CHCH=CHCH=CH_2 Octatetraene-1,3,5,7	287	4.72

The determinations were made at sufficiently high dilution for resolution of the bands for the triene and tetraene into three separate peaks; the lower-intensity band of butadiene shows no comparable fine structure. Alkyl substituents or ring residues attached to a conjugated system shift the position of an absorption band to progressively higher wave length, depending upon their number. Thus in the dienes listed below the absorption band is shifted about 5 mμ to longer wave length for each alkyl group joined to the diene system:

		λ_{max}, mμ
Piperylene	CH_3CH=CHCH=CH_2	224

2,3-Dimethylbutadiene-1,3	CH_2=C——C=CH_2
	        $\mid$ $\mid$
	       CH_3 CH_3
		230

1,1,4,4-Tetramethylbutadiene-1,3	CH_3\ /CH_3 C=CHCH=C CH_3/ \\CH_3	240

The unsubstituted straight-chain conjugated pentaene that would extend the above series is not known, but vitamin A has been characterized as having a

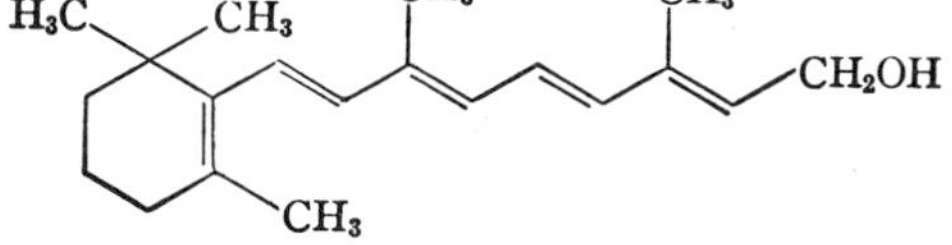

Vitamin A

system of five conjugated double bonds. It not only absorbs ultraviolet light, with λ_{max} 326 mμ, but also absorbs in the visible region of the spectrum (400–700 mμ) and is a crystalline yellow substance. As compared with the conjugated octatetraene (λ_{max} 287 mμ), vitamin A has one more double bond extending the conjugation and the polyene system contains six carbon substituents.

The deduction from the molecular orbital theory that the four unsaturated centers of butadiene are coplanar means that two conformations are possible, and since these are related to geometrical isomers they are named cisoid (1) and transoid (2) forms. The terms s-*cis* and s-*trans* are sometimes used, the letter s

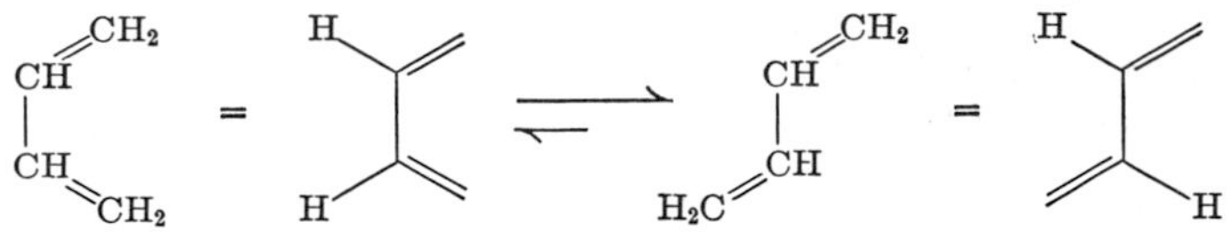

cisoid
(1)

transoid
(2)

referring to a single bond which, because of resonance, has some double bond character. Calculation from colorimetric data indicates that butadiene itself exists mainly in the transoid form and that this form is more stable than the cisoid form by an energy factor of 2.3 kcal./mole (J. G. Aston,[1] 1946). Abundant evidence shows that a cisoid diene absorbs ultraviolet light at a higher wave length but at lower intensity than a comparable transoid diene. The bridging methylene group of cyclopentadiene (3) forces the conjugated system to assume

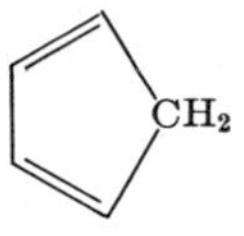

λ238.5 mμ (3,400)
(3)

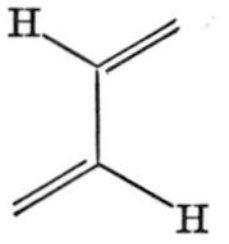

λ220 mμ (20,900)
(4)

the less stable cisoid configuration, and the relationship to a transoid diene (4) is that outlined.

In a polycyclic system a cisoid diene (5) can also be described as homoannular and a transoid one (6) as heteroannular. Examples (5) and (6) are steroids, and

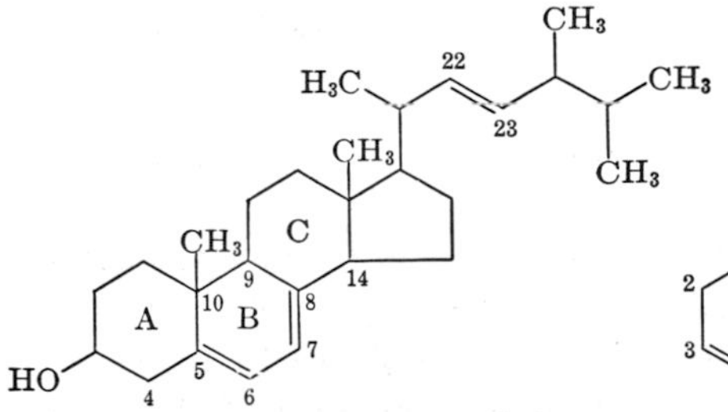

(5) Ergosterol (from yeast)
λ282 (11,900)

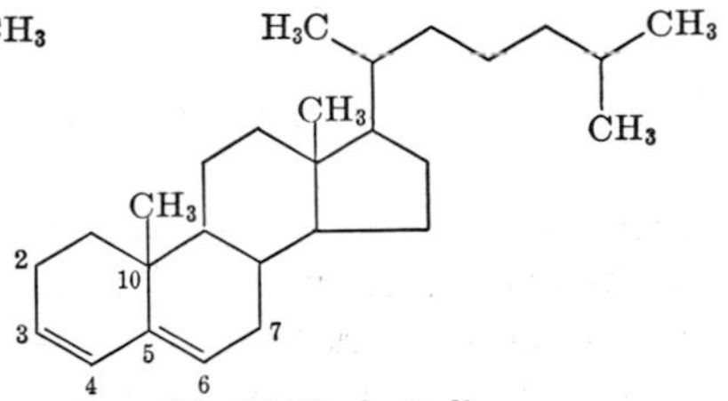

(6) Δ[3,5]-Cholestadiene
λ234 (20,000)

in this series correlation of structure and ultraviolet absorption follows a pattern so regular that the positions of absorption maxima can be calculated with reason-

[1] J. G. Aston, b. 1902 Barrow-in-Furness, England; Ph.D. Univ. California, Berkeley (T. D. Stewart); Penn. State Univ.

TABLE 5.5. CALCULATION OF λ_{max} FOR STEROID POLYENES

	Increment $m\mu$
Parent diene (hypothetical)..	214
Cisoid diene system..	39
Double bond extending the conjugation...	30
Exocyclic location of double bond..	5
Alkyl substituent or ring residue...	5
OR, OAc substituent..	0
	λ_{max} = Total

able accuracy from the data of Table 5.5. In the homoannular diene (5), ring residues extend to C_5 from C_4 and C_{10} and to C_8 from C_9 and C_{14}; the 5,6-double bond is exocyclic to ring A and the 7,8-double bond is exocyclic to ring C; the calculated λ_{max} is thus $253 + 4 \times 5 + 2 \times 5 = 283$ mμ (found, 283 mμ). For the heteroannular diene (6), $\lambda_{max}^{caled} = 214 + 3 \times 5 + 5 = 234$ mμ (found, 234 mμ). Notice that the cisoid diene (5) absorbs at higher wave length and lower intensity than the transoid diene (6). Ergosterol (5) contains an isolated double bond at the 22,23-position in the side chain. This disubstituted double bond, which gives rise to only weak ultraviolet absorption in the range 205–210 mμ, was characterized as *trans* by X-ray analysis (Dorothy Crowfoot, 1948). An infrared absorption band at 960–970 cm^{-1} distinguishes a *trans* double bond from a *cis* one, which gives rise to a band at 660–700 cm^{-1}. Examples of steroids containing triene and tetraene systems are shown in partial formulas (7)–(9); the calculated maxima are given in parentheses. In (9) the acetoxy group (AcO)

(7)
324 (11,800)
(323)

(8)
315 (19,800)
(313)

(9)
355 (19,700)
(353)

is without influence on the ultraviolet absorption of the conjugated system to which it is linked.

Homocyclic and heterocyclic dienes differ markedly in chemical properties, as well as in light absorption. The contrast between ergosterol (5, homo) and $\Delta^{3,5}$-cholestadiene (6, hetero) is typical. Ergosterol is reduced by sodium and alcohol to 5,6-dihydroergosterol and the remaining two isolated double bonds are untouched. On treatment of ergosterol with hydrogen chloride in chloroform the double bonds remain conjugated but migrate to heteroannular positions. $\Delta^{3,5}$-Cholestadiene is not reduced by sodium and alcohol and it is not isomerized by hydrogen chloride.

The conjugated system of an α,β-unsaturated ketone, aldehyde, or acid also gives rise to a strong absorption band in the region 220–260 mμ, and extension of

TABLE 5.6. CALCULATION OF λ_{max}^{EtOH} FOR CONJUGATED STEROID KETONES

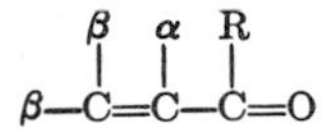

$$\overset{\beta}{\underset{|}{}}\overset{\alpha}{\underset{|}{}}\overset{R}{\underset{|}{}} \qquad \overset{\delta}{\underset{|}{}}\overset{\gamma}{\underset{|}{}}\overset{\beta}{\underset{|}{}}\overset{\alpha}{\underset{|}{}}\overset{R}{\underset{|}{}}$$

$$\beta-C{=}C{-}C{=}O \qquad \text{and} \qquad \delta-C{=}C{-}C{=}C{-}C{=}O$$

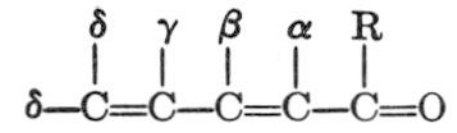

	Increment, $m\mu$
Parent α,β-unsaturated ketone (hypothetical)	215
Cisoid diene system	39
Double bond extending the conjugation	30
Exocyclic location of double bond	5
R (alkyl or ring residue), OR, OAc α	10
β	12
γ (and higher)	18

$$\lambda_{max}^{EtOH} = \text{Total}$$

the conjugated system shifts the band to higher wave lengths. Constants for calculation of maxima (Table 5.6) are in part the same, or nearly the same, as for polyenes; substituents produce a larger bathochromic effect in the ketone series and the effect increases with increasing distance from the carbonyl group. Another difference is that the wave length of absorption of polyenones varies with the solvent by as much as 19 $m\mu$, whereas with polyenes no solvent effects have been noticed. The data for steroid enones (10)–(13) are for solutions in ethanol; calculated values are given in parentheses. Notice that the transoid

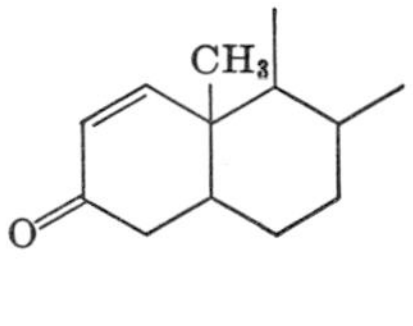

(10)
$\lambda 230$ (10,700)
β (227)

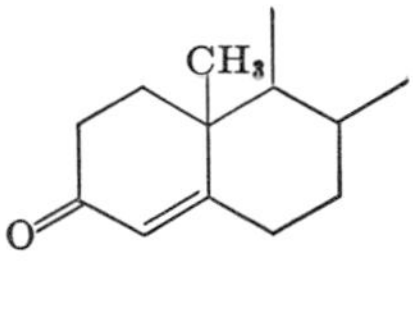

(11)
$\lambda 241$ (16,600)
$\beta, \beta,$ exo (244)

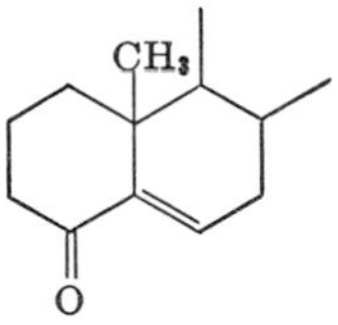

(12)
$\lambda 241$ (5,200)
$\alpha, \beta,$ exo (242)

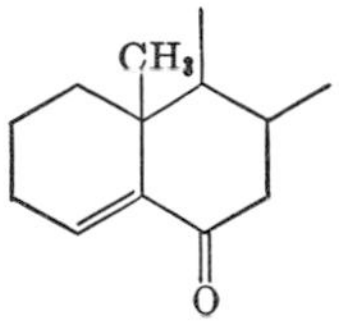

(13)
$\lambda 244$ (6,300)
$\alpha, \beta,$ exo (242)

enones (10) and (11) have extinction coefficients much higher than the cisoid enones (12) and (13). In dienone (14) the enone and diene systems are both

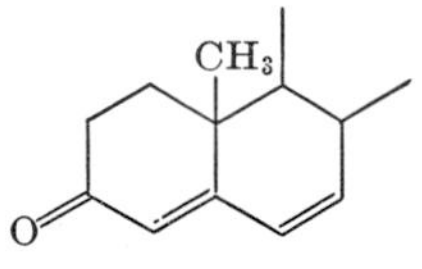

(14)
$\lambda 284$ (28,000)
(280)

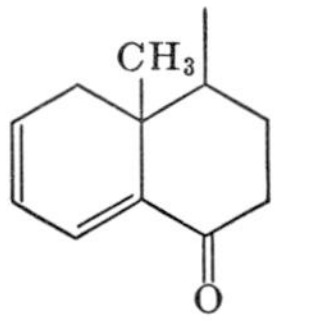

(15)
$\lambda 315$ (7,000)
(317)

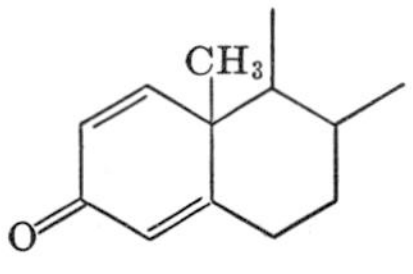

(16)
$\lambda 244$ (15,000)
(244)

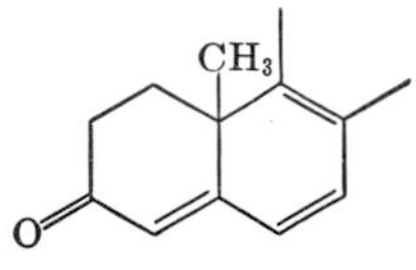

(17)
$\lambda 388$ (12,300)
(385)

transoid; in (15) both systems are cisoid and a marked increase in λ and decrease in extinction coefficient is evident. The dienone (16) has a crossed-conjugated system of linkages, and in this case calculation is based upon the more powerful of the two chromophoric systems, namely that extending to C_5 and having two β-substituents and one exo bond; the secondary system extending to C_1 makes no contribution. The positions of absorption bands for the enone (10) and the trienone (17), 230 and 388 mμ, illustrate the wide range of spectrum over which the highly characteristic constants are distributed.

5.37   Diels-Alder Reaction. — The synthetic reaction discovered by Diels[1] and Alder[2] (1928) consists in 1,4-addition of a diene to a second component, a dienophile, of the type represented by maleic anhydride. The reaction is a stereospecific *cis* addition. Yields are high, and the Diels-Alder reaction

Butadiene   Maleic anhydride   *cis*-Δ[4]-Tetrahydrophthalic anhydride (m.p. 104°)

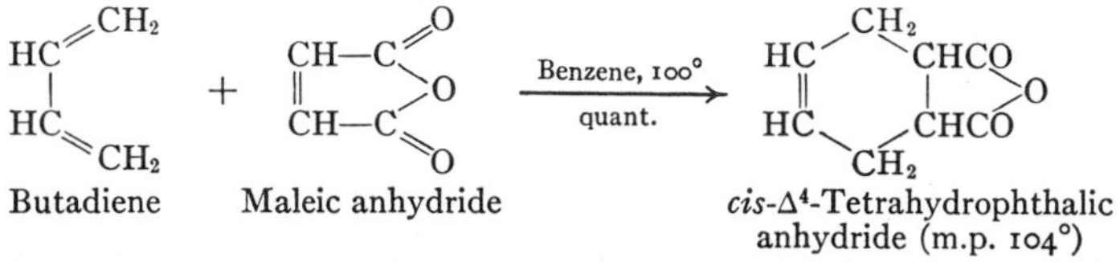

is applicable to a variety of dienes and dienophiles. 2,3-Dimethylbutadiene (b.p. 69°) is a more conveniently manipulated reagent than butadiene (b.p. −4°) and it is also more reactive. In general, alkyl substituents increase reactivity if located at C_2 or C_3 but decrease reactivity if they are on the terminal carbon atoms (hindrance). Sorbic acid, $CH_3CH{=}CHCH{=}CHCO_2H$, from unripe berries of the mountain ash (*Sorbus aucuparia*) forms typical adducts at a higher reaction temperature than required for butadiene. The Diels-Alder reaction can be reversed by heating an adduct in high vacuum for removal of the more volatile component.

One factor determining the reactivity of dienes is conformation. Thus *trans*-piperylene is most stable in the transoid form I, but reacts with maleic anhydride in the cisoid form Ia. The same is true of *cis*-piperylene (III), which, however, is so much less reactive that for purification it is refluxed with maleic anhydride

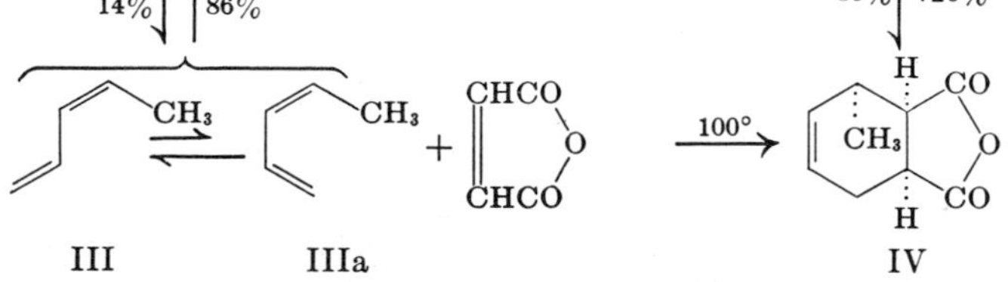

for removal of the *trans* isomer. The *cis*-methyl group in the cisoid diene IIIa thus exerts a marked blocking effect. The adduct IV is obtained on reaction at

[1] Otto Diels, 1876–1954; b. Hamburg; Ph.D. Berlin (E. Fischer); Kiel; Nobel Prize 1950
[2] Kurt Alder, 1902–58; b. Königshütte; Ph.D. Kiel (Diels); Cologne; Nobel Prize 1950

100° only in low yield, although it is more stable than II and predominates in the mixture resulting from equilibration in the presence of a trace of dibutylaniline at 280° (D. Craig, 1950). *trans,trans*-Diphenylbutadiene, V, evidently can exist in the cisoid form Va, for it adds maleic anhydride readily at the boiling point of xylene (K. Alder, 1951). The *trans,cis* and *cis,cis* isomers react only at a temperature at which they are isomerized to the *trans,trans* hydrocarbon, and hence

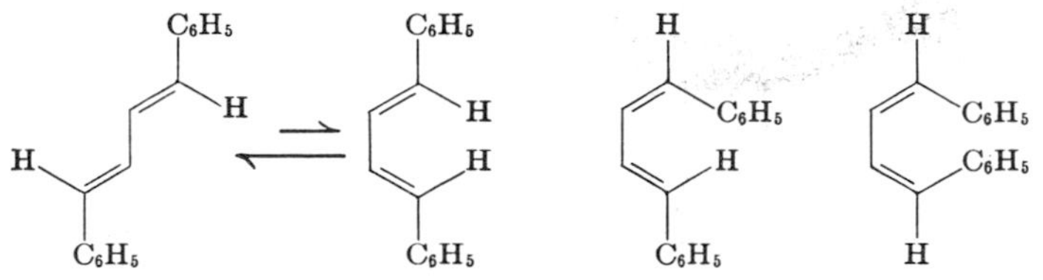

| V | Va | VIa | VIIa |

the cisoid forms VIa and VIIa are either nonexistent or very unreactive. The homoannular diene ergosterol (VIII) is necessarily 100% cisoid and it adds maleic anhydride fairly readily in spite of the fact that the carbon atoms at the ends of the diene system are both disubstituted.

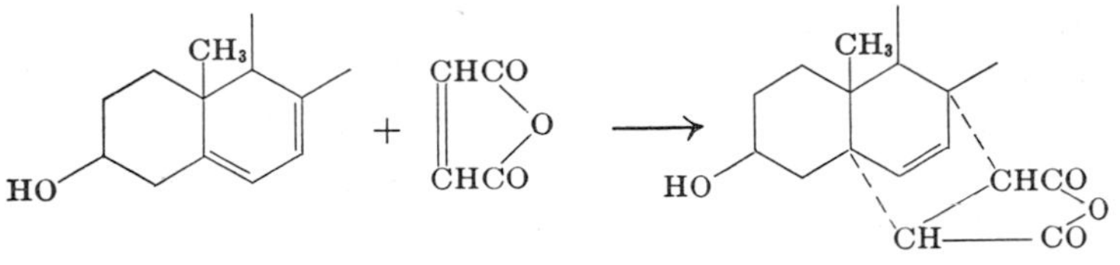

| VIII | IX |

The addition of cyclopentadiene to maleic anhydride produces an interesting ring system in which the methylene bridge across a cyclohexane ring produces

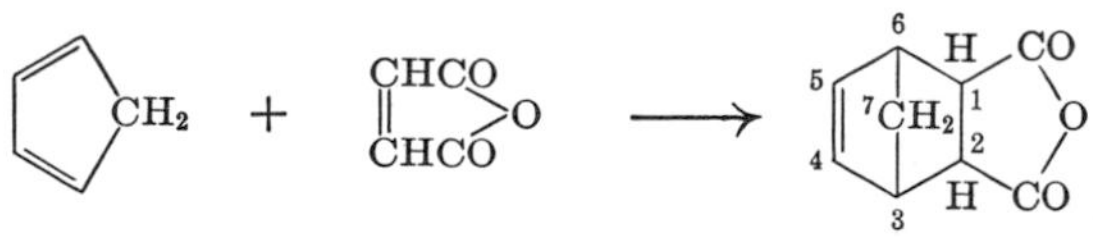

two five-membered rings. Two steric forms are possible, as shown in the models and they are described as endo and exo. The perspective formulas are best interpreted by reference to the models. The cyclohexane ring cannot assume the usual chair conformation but is forced by the methylene bridge into the somewhat strained boat form, in which C_3 is the prow and C_6 the stern. Additions are usually carried out at the lowest practical temperature and for a short time, and under these conditions the product is the endo adduct. The exo form, however, is thermodynamically the more stable, and under equilibrating conditions or at temperatures sufficiently high to overcome the unfavorable activation energy for its formation it accumulates at the expense of the endo product.

Maleic anhydride is perhaps the most widely used dienophile, and diesters of maleic acid are also employed. Citraconic anhydride, because of the presence of

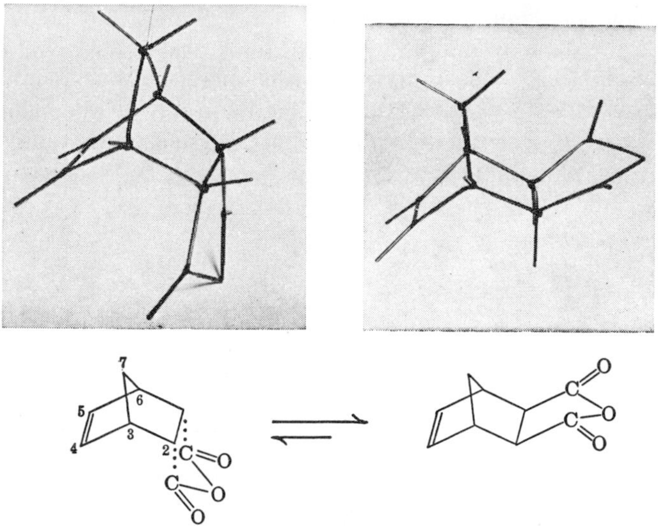

Endo   Exo

a blocking methyl group, reacts less readily than maleic anhydride and has been used for selective removal of a highly reactive component of a diene mixture. Acetylenedicarboxylic acid and its esters function as dienophiles and give derivatives of 1,4-dihydrophthalic acid. Acrolein, with only one carbonyl group adjacent to the double bond, adds dienes only at higher temperatures than required with maleic anhydride and yields are lower.

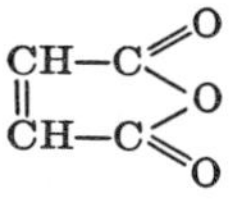

Maleic	Citraconic	Acetylenedicarboxylic	Acrolein
anhydride	anhydride	acid	b. p. 52.5°
m. p. 53°	m. p. 8°	m. p. 180°	

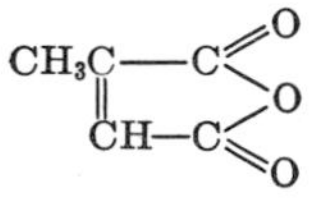

Quinone (*p*-benzoquinone), a yellow substance of extraordinary reactivity to a variety of reagents, adds either one or two moles of butadiene depending upon the conditions. The reaction sequence formulated can be effected as follows. A

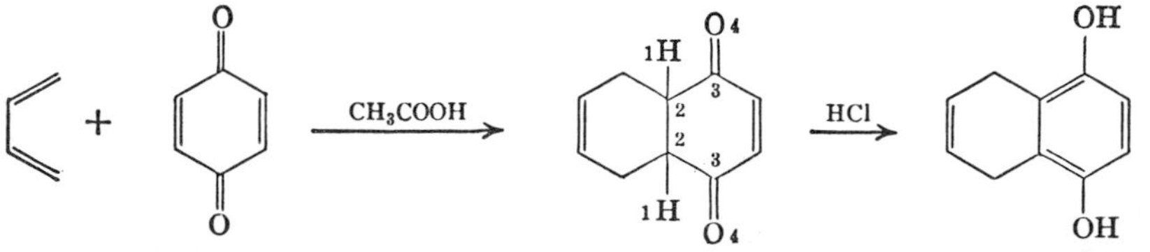

| Butadiene   Quinone | | Adduct | Dihydronaphtho-
hydroquinone |

suspension of 1 mole (108 g.) of pure, bright yellow quinone in acetic acid (500 ml.) is chilled until the solvent begins to crystallize (m.p. 16.7°). Butadiene gas is run from a steel cylinder and condensed in a calibrated tube cooled in dry ice; 1.1 mole is added to the chilled suspension of quinone and the flask is closed with a wired-on rubber stopper and placed in a cooling bath maintained for a few hours at 10–15°. In 40–48 hrs. the yellow solid has dissolved and a nearly color-less solution of adduct results. After addition of a hot solution of concentrated hydrochloric acid (100 ml.) in water (500 ml.), the solution is heated to effect isomerization to 5,8-dihydro-1,4-naphthohydroquinone, which soon begins to separate in colorless crystals; the yield is 143 g. (88%). Isomerization occurs readily because shift of the two activated hydrogens of the adduct from carbon to oxygen produces a resonance stabilized benzenoid ring. The butadiene–maleic anhydride adduct under comparable conditions does not undergo acid-catalyzed isomerization.

A dienophile useful for characterizing dienes and for investigations of diene mixtures is *p*-phenylazomaleinanil (M. C. Whiting, 1955). The adducts from

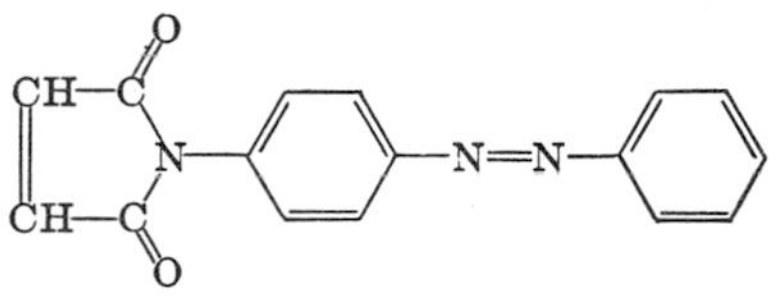

p-Phenylazomaleinanil
(orange needles, m.p. 162°)

butadiene, cyclopentadiene, $\Delta^{1,3}$-cyclohexadiene, and cosmene (8.6) are obtain-able under mild conditions (20–50°), and they are high-melting and crystallize well. They can be separated readily by chromatography and have identifying ultraviolet and infrared spectra.

A comparison cited earlier (5.11) shows that maleic anhydride and quinone form colored π-complexes but that they are surpassed as π-acids by tetracyanoethylene. That a π-complex is an intermediate in the Diels-Alder reaction is suggested by the fact that tetracyanoethylene functions as a dienophile and is considerably more reactive than the other two compounds. When butadiene is added in slight excess to an ice-cold solution of tetracyanoethylene in tetrahydrofurane, the solution first takes on the bright yellow color of a π-complex of the components and within a few minutes the colorless adduct begins to separate. Under the

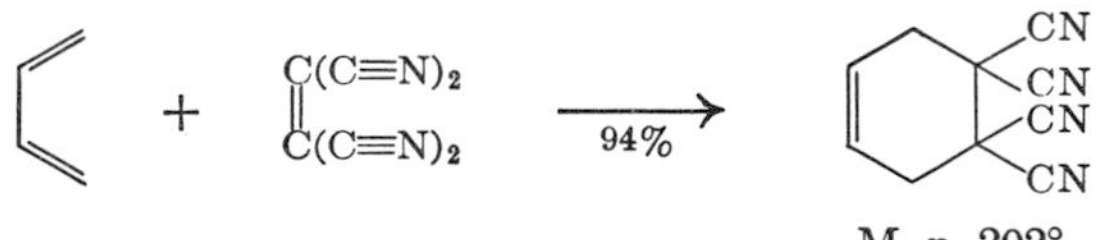

M. p. 202°

same conditions the reaction of maleic anhydride with butadiene requires many hours for completion. Transient colors have been noted with other dienophiles, but none are as striking as those characteristic of the tetracyanoethylene deriva-tive.

Adducts of cyclic dienes with quinones or dimethyl acetylenedicarboxylate which contain an endocyclic ethylene bridge decompose smoothly on pyrolysis to an aromatic compound, with liberation of the endo bridge.

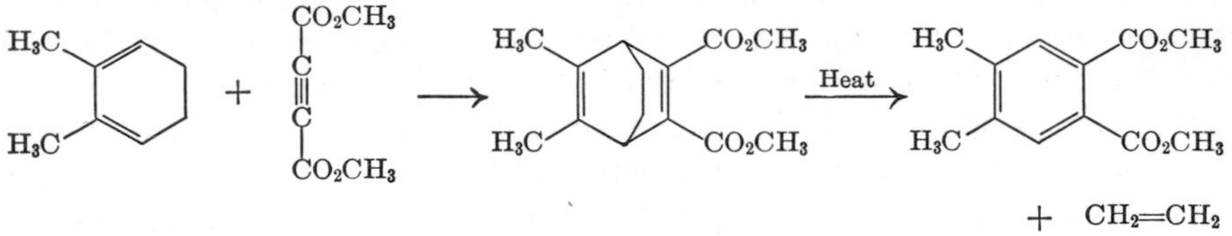

$$+ \quad CH_2{=}CH_2$$

Whereas catalysts had been generally thought to have little or no effect on diene additions, Yates[1] (1960) and G. I. Fray (1961) found that the presence of one or more equivalents of aluminum chloride can bring about remarkable acceleration of certain Diels-Alder reactions. The 1,4-diene system in 2,3-dimethyl-

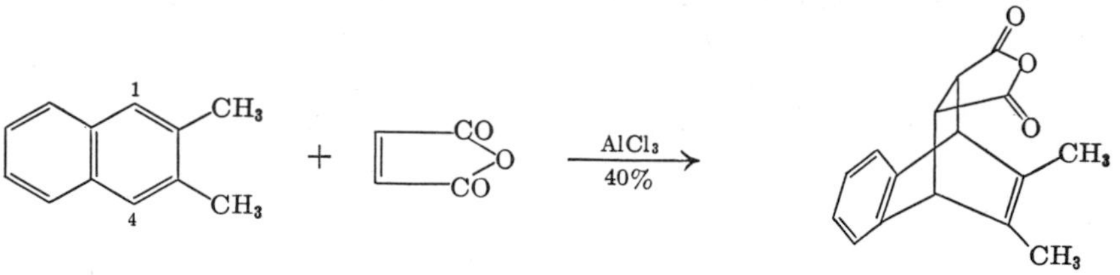

naphthalene is not very reactive, and Kloetzel[2] (1950) had obtained the maleic anhydride adduct only by heating the hydrocarbon with 30 equivalents of anhydride in a sealed tube at 100° for 24 hrs. Reaction of equivalent amounts of 2,3-dimethylnaphthalene, maleic anhydride, and aluminum chloride in methylene chloride at room temperature was complete in 4 hrs. and the yield was comparable to that obtained by Kloetzel. Striking catalysis of the addition of the more reactive anthracene to maleic anhydride, quinone, and dimethyl fumarate is reported.

5.38   Chlorinated Adducts.—K. Alder and G. Stein demonstrated (1931) that certain norbornene derivatives enter into the Diels-Alder reaction with dienes, but this was regarded as a special case attributable to exceptional reactivity due to ring strain. However, L. M. Joshel and L. W. Butz found (1941) that the simplest olefin, ethylene, can function as a dienophile. At 200° and 200–400 atmospheres, ethylene reacts with butadiene, 2,3-dimethylbutadiene, and cyclopentadiene to form cyclohexene, 1,2-dimethylcyclohexene, and norbornene-bicyclo [2,2,1]-2-heptene.

Variations of the basic reaction are now operated on a large scale for the production of insecticides, two of which appropriately bear the trade names Dieldrin and Aldrin. A key reaction, the condensation of cyclopentadiene (1) with acetylene to give norbornadiene (5) was discovered by Julius Hyman (patent of 1951). The reaction is carried out as a continuous process in a tube and shell reactor with diphenyl–diphenyl ether as solvent. The yield per pass is not high, but the yield based on consumption of reactants is good. The route to the insecticide chlordane

---

[1] Peter Yates, b. 1924 Wanstead, England; Ph.D. Yale (W. Bergmann); Harvard Univ.; Univ. Toronto

[2] Milton C. Kloetzel, b. Detroit 1913; Ph.D. Michigan (Bachmann); Univ. Southern Calif.

(4) requires preparation of hexachlorocyclopentadiene (2); this was at first done commercially by reaction of cyclopentadiene with aqueous sodium hypochlorite,

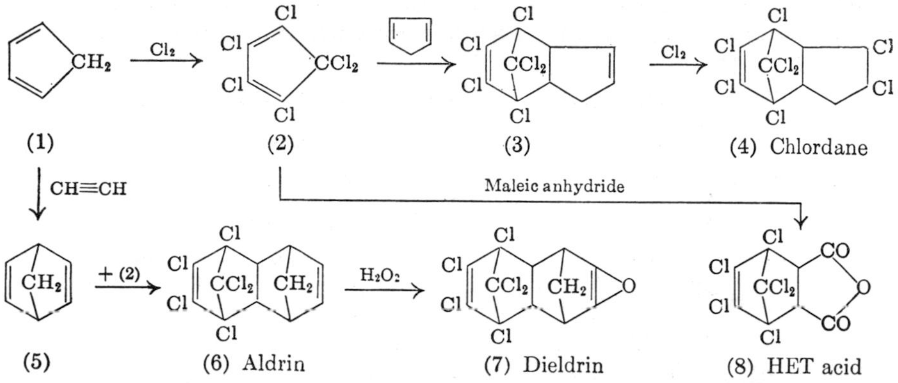

(1)   (2)   (3)   (4) Chlordane

CH≡CH   Maleic anhydride

(5)   (6) Aldrin   (7) Dieldrin   (8) HET acid

but direct high temperature chlorination gives a better product in higher yield. The maleic anhydride adduct, HET Acid, is converted into fire-retarding polymers for use in paints.

PROBLEMS

1. Predict the relative ease of dehydration of the following compounds and indicate methods by which each can be dehydrated.
   (a) $(CH_3)_2CHCH(OH)CH_2CH_2COCH_3$
   (b) $CH_3CH_2CH_2CH(OH)COCH_2CH_3$
   (c) $CH_3CH_2CH_2CH(OH)CH_2COCH_3$
   (d) $CH_3CH_2CHCH_2CH_2COCH_3$
            OH

2. Predict the products resulting from treatment of each of the following compounds with base under conditions sufficient for elimination of just one mole of hydrogen halide.
   (a) $(CH_3)_2CBrCH_2CH_2CH_2Br$
   (b) $CHCl_2CHCl_2$
   (c) $BrCH_2CHBrCH_2Br$
   (d) $C_6H_5CHBrCHBrCO_2H$

3. When heated with ethanolic potassium hydroxide at 175°, the allene $CH_3CH_2CH=C=CH_2$ is largely isomerized to the acetylenes $CH_3CH_2CH_2C≡CH$ and $CH_3CH_2C≡CCH_3$. (a) Account for the formation of these products on the assumption that in the initial step OH⁻ abstracts a proton from an unsaturated carbon atom to form a transient carbanion. (b) Predict the relative stability of the two alkynes on the assumption that stability is determined by degree of hyperconjugation.

4. Added to test solutions of tetracyanoethylene in ethyl acetate, *trans*-stilbene gives a violet solution and diphenylacetylene gives a cherry red complex. Which hydrocarbon would you expect to be the more reactive to bromine?

5. Cholesterol β-oxide on hydrolysis yields cholestane-3β,5α,6β-triol. What are the expected products of (a) cleavage with HCl and (b) reduction with lithium aluminum hydride?

6. Predict the products of the selective addition of one equivalent of bromine to:
   (a) $CH_3CH=CHCH_2CH=CHBr$
   (b) $(CH_3)_2C=CHCH_2CH=CH_2$
   (c) $CH_2=CHCOOCH=CH_2$

7. Why is peracetic acid less reactive to olefins than performic acid?

8. Suggest a mechanism for the acid-catalyzed isomerization of ethylidenecyclohexane (7, 5.24).

9. Note the structure and ultraviolet absorption maximum of vitamin A (or A₁, 5.36). This substance occurs in halibut liver oil and in most marine fish oils. Fresh-water fish oils contain a companion substance, vitamin A₂, which is similar in chemical behavior but which

is distinguished by a markedly shifted absorption maximum, λ_{max} 351 mμ. The structure was established by synthesis, and A_2 is now known to have the same skeletal structure as A_1 and to have two hydrogen atoms less than A_1. From this information you should be able to deduce the structure of A_2 and to suggest a method for its synthesis from A_1.

10. What products would you expect to result from acid-catalyzed dehydration of each of the following alcohols?

(a) $C_6H_5CH_2CH_2CHCH(CH_3)_2$
     |
     OH

(b) $CH_3CH_2CHCH=CHCH_3$
     |
     OH

(c) CH_3 CH_3
     \\   /
        CHCHCH
     / | \\
     CH_3 OH C_6H_5

(d) CH_3CH——$CHOH$
     | |
     CH_2 CH_2
     | |
     CH_2——CH_2

(e) CH_2——$CHCH_2OH$
     | |
     CH_2 $CHCH_3$ (on loss of one
     \\   /   mole of water)
        C
     /   \\
     CH_3 OH

11. By what methods can each of the following hydrocarbon samples be purified?
    (a) n-Hexane, contaminated with hexene-3
    (b) n-Hexane, contaminated with hexanol-1
    (c) Hexene-3, contaminated with n-hexane

12. In what way can the following isomers be distinguished?

$$CH_3CH_2CH=C(CH_3)_2 \quad \text{and} \quad CH_3CH_2C(CH_3)=CHCH_3$$

13. A hydrocarbon C_7H_{10} on drastic oxidation gives the products O=CCH$_2$C=O and HOOC—
                                                                              | |
                                                                              CH$_3$ CH$_3$
COOH. What is its structure?

14. A pure hydrocarbon of the formula C_6H_{12} decolorizes bromine solution, dissolves in concentrated sulfuric acid, yields n-hexane on hydrogenation, and on oxidation with excess potassium permanganate affords a mixture of two acids of the type RCOOH. What is the structure?

15. A hydrocarbon $C_{11}H_{20}$, which on catalytic hydrogenation absorbs two moles of hydrogen, gives on oxidation the products

$$CH_3CH_2COCH_3, \quad HOOCCH_2CH_2COOH, \quad \text{and} \quad CH_3CH_2COOH$$

What is its structure?

16. (a) A hydrocarbon of the formula $C_{10}H_{14}$ absorbs two moles of hydrogen on catalytic hydrogenation and gives a product inert to acid permanganate. How many rings does it contain?
    (b) If a compound with the formula $C_{27}H_{46}$ absorbs just one mole of hydrogen, how many rings are present?

17. A hydrocarbon $C_{10}H_{16}$ absorbs one mole of hydrogen, is known to contain no methyl, ethyl, or other alkyl groups, and on ozonization gives a symmetrical diketone of the formula $C_{10}H_{16}O_2$. What is its structure?

Chapter 6

ACETYLENIC AND RELATED COMPOUNDS

6.1   **Introduction.** — Acetylene chemistry has grown rapidly in importance in recent years for a number of reasons. That the hydrocarbon is abundantly available from both coal and petroleum makes acetylene an attractive starting material for industrial chemical synthesis. Where the same chemical can be made from either acetylene or ethylene, the choice falls on ethylene since it is cheaper, but acetylenic compounds offer a possibility for polyfunctionality not realizable with olefins. The triple bond enters not only into electrophilic additions, but also into nucleophilic, or anionic additions. The $\equiv$C—H group presents the possibility for replacement of hydrogen by metals and then by alkyl groups, and also the potentiality for oxidation to $\equiv$C—C$\equiv$. Thus several industrially important intermediates are derived uniquely from acetylene itself. Because of the special properties associated with the triple bond, acetylenes have proved valuable as intermediates in the synthesis of triterpenoid and steroid vitamins and hormones. Development of new methods of synthesis in the field has been spurred by an enormous expansion in the number of acetylenes known to occur in nature.

6.2   **Properties.** — The physical properties of several alkynes are listed in Table 6.1. Acetylene itself boils at a temperature close to the melting point. In general, alkynes distil at temperatures 10–20° higher than the corresponding alkenes, and the boiling points are closer to those of the alkanes of the same number of carbons than to those of the alkenes. Alkynes are slightly denser in the liquid state than alkenes.

PREPARATION

6.3   **Acetylene.** — In consequence of certain unique chemical properties, acetylene can be converted into a host of interesting and useful products and is a starting material of key importance in the chemical industry. Two abundant sources are available: coal and petroleum. In the older process

TABLE 6.1. PROPERTIES OF ALKYNES

NAME	FORMULA C_nH_{2n-2}	CARBON SKELETON	M.P., °C.	B.P., °C.	SP. GR. (LIQ.)
Acetylene	C_2H_2	C≡C	−81.8*	−83.4	0.6179
Methylacetylene	C_3H_4	C·C≡C	−101.5	−23.3	.6714
Ethylacetylene	C_4H_6	C·C·C≡C	−122.5	8.6	.6682
Dimethylacetylene	C_4H_6	C·C≡C·C	−28	27.2	.6937
Pentyne-1	C_5H_8	C·C·C·C≡C	−98	39.7	.695
Pentyne-2	C_5H_8	C·C·C≡C·C	−101	55.5	.7127
3-Methylbutyne-1	C_5H_8	C·C·C≡C · C		28	.665
Hexyne-1	C_6H_{10}	C·C·C·C·C≡C	−124	71	.7195
Hexyne-2	C_6H_{10}	C·C·C·C≡C·C	−92	84	.7305
Hexyne-3	C_6H_{10}	C·C·C≡C·C·C	−51	82	.7255
3,3-Dimethylbutyne-1	C_6H_{10}	C · C·C·C≡C · C	−81	38	.6686
Octadecyne-1	$C_{18}H_{34}$	C·(C)₁₅·C≡C	28	180 at 15 mm.	.8025

* At 891 mm.

coke is fused with quicklime in an electric furnace to produce calcium carbide; the crude product, which consists of hard gray lumps with a crystalline fracture,

$$CaO \ + \ 3C \ \xrightarrow{2500-3000°} \ CaC_2 \ + \ CO$$

Quicklime   Coke   Calcium carbide

$$CaC_2 \ + \ 2H_2O \ \longrightarrow \ Ca(OH)_2 \ + \ HC≡CH$$

reacts exothermally with water with liberation of acetylene. The acetylene made by this method has a characteristic odor due to traces of hydrogen sulfide and phosphine, which can be removed by passage of the gas through a solution of mercuric chloride in dilute hydrochloric acid; pure acetylene is practically odorless. Processes for the production of acetylene as a petrochemical for the most part involve partial oxidation, with formation of carbon monoxide and hydrogen as by-products. Both methane and higher hydrocarbons can be used. Energy required for cracking is supplied by burning part of the feed or by burning a lean gas taken off in the recovery process and consisting largely of hydrogen. Quenching is vital.

Acetylene burns with a highly luminous flame, probably because at the combustion temperature the hydrocarbon is in part broken down to finely divided carbon particles that become incandescent. Because of this luminosity, acetylene was once employed as an illuminating gas, particularly for transportation vehicles. A few decades ago the usual bicycle lamp was a small acetylene generator consisting of a calcium carbide canister into which water could be dripped as desired through a setscrew valve. A still important use is in the oxyacetylene torch for the welding and cutting of metals. That acetylene gives a hotter flame (about 2700°) than ethylene or ethane is because less oxygen is required for combustion and hence less heat is dissipated for raising the gases to flame temperature. Acetylene cannot be liquefied safely for transportation because in this condition it is sensitive to shock and may explode, since the substance is endothermic (in contrast to ethane):

$$2\ C + H_2 \rightarrow C_2H_2 - 55\ \text{kcal.}$$

Acetylene is only sparingly soluble in water or in most common organic solvents, but acetone has considerable solvent capacity for the gas. Thus acetone dissolves 25 volumes of acetylene at 15° and 760 mm., and at 12 atmospheres pressure 300 volumes of acetylene dissolve in 1 volume of acetone. The solution is stable and can be transported when prepared in a steel cylinder containing asbestos or other porous solid to prevent slushing about in transit.

6.4   **By Dehydrohalogenation.** — One useful route to acetylenic compounds involves bromination of the corresponding olefin and dehydrobromination of the resulting *vic*-dibromide. *trans* Addition of bromine to fumaric acid gives the *meso*-dibromide, which on reaction with methanolic potassium hydroxide

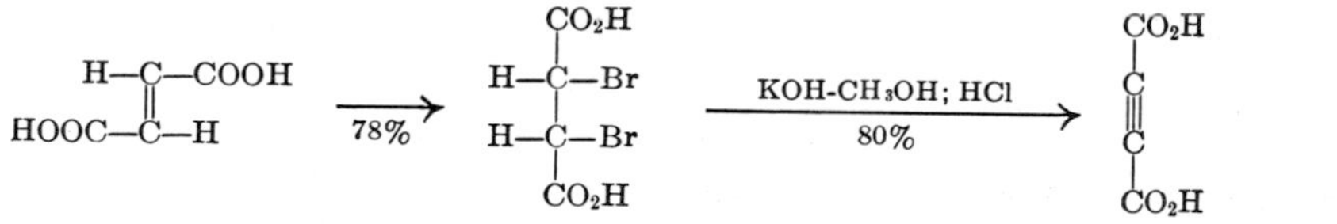

Fumaric acid   *meso*-Dibromo-   Acetylenedicarboxylic
                    succinic acid   acid
                    m. p. 256°, dec.

and acidification affords acetylenedicarboxylic acid. In an analogous sequence *trans*-stilbene is converted into diphenylacetylene. An early procedure called for refluxing the dibromide with 43% alcoholic potassium hydroxide in an oil bath

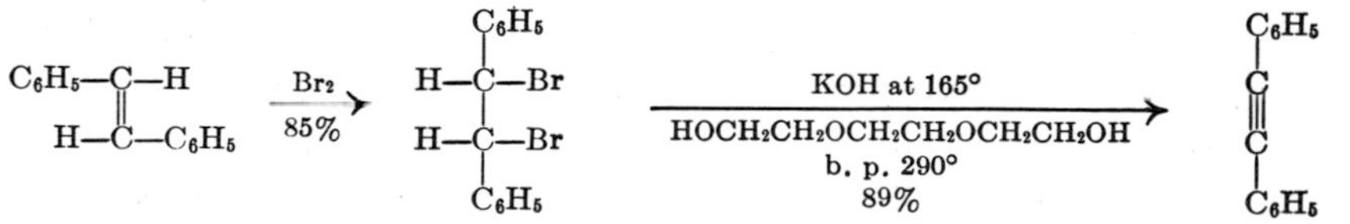

                                                      m. p. 61°

at 140° for 24 hrs. (yield 68%); in the procedure formulated the reaction is conducted in an open vessel in high-boiling triethylene glycol, which permits operation at such a temperature that the reaction is complete in a few minutes.

In an investigation conducted at Bonn in 1869, Carl Glaser[1] developed methods for the conversion of cinnamic acid into two interesting new acetylenes, phenylpropiolic acid and phenylacetylene. The procedures were later improved by

[1] Carl Glaser, 1841–1935; b. Kirchheimbolanden (Rheinpfalz), Germany; Ph.D. Tübingen (Strecher); Bonn; Badische Anilin und Soda Fabrik

others, particularly by Nef,[1] and the stereochemistry is now evident. *trans* Bromination of the acid (*trans*) gives a crystalline *dl*-dibromide (m.p. 202°), which when warmed with methanolic potassium hydroxide loses two equivalents of hydrogen bromide and gives the potassium salt of phenylpropiolic acid. The salt is collected, dissolved in ice water, and iced hydrochloric acid is added cau-

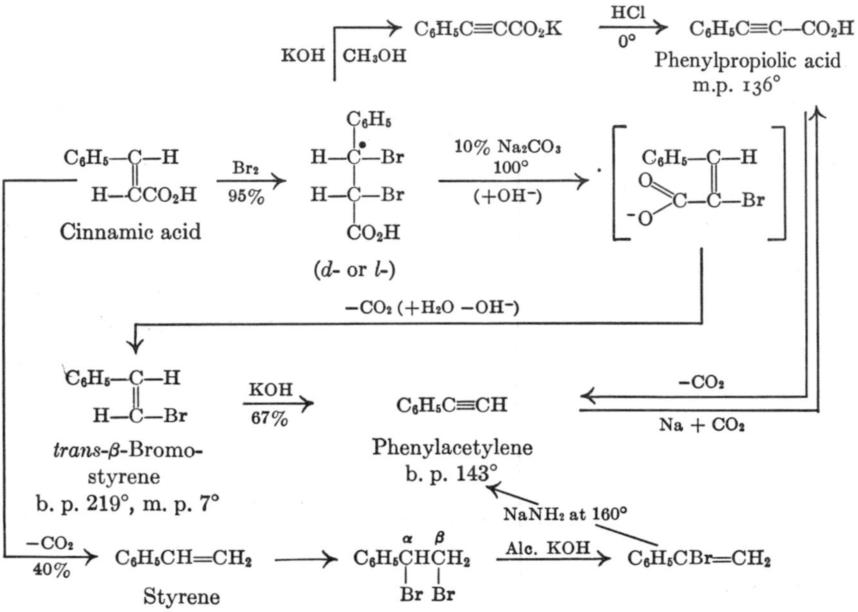

tiously to precipitate phenylpropiolic acid without damaging the product. This acid when heated loses carbon dioxide and gives phenylacetylene, but the hydrocarbon can be prepared in better yield by another process starting with cinnamic acid *dl*-dibromide. A weak base such as aqueous soda solution is able to eliminate only one mole of HBr and affords initially a solution of the anion of *trans-α*-bromocinnamic acid. The combined effect of the unsaturation and the electron-attracting bromine atom causes this ion to lose carbon dioxide in the alkaline medium, and the carbanion formed abstracts a proton from water and affords *trans-β*-bromostyrene in good yield. This substance is a vinyl bromide (=CHBr), and, since such halides are characteristically unreactive, vigorous conditions are required for the completing step. For dehydrobromination the unsaturated bromide is heated with molten potassium hydroxide at 200–220°; phenylacetylene distills as formed and the higher boiling bromide is retained until it reacts.

Glaser found a further route to phenylacetylene by decarboxylation of cinnamic acid to styrene, bromination, and dehydrobromination. Alcoholic alkali suffices for removal of the first mole of HBr, but elimination of bromine from the initially formed vinyl-type halide requires the more powerful sodamide suspended in mineral oil at 160°. Styrene dibromide loses HBr in the direction opposite to that

[1] John Ulric Nef, 1862–1915; b. Herisau, Switzerland; Ph.D. Munich (Königs); Purdue Univ.; Clark Univ.; Univ. Chicago

in the reaction $CH_3CHBrCH_2Br \rightarrow CH_3CH{=}CHBr$, where the bromine lost is secondary rather than primary; the hydrogen eliminated from styrene dibromide is α to the phenyl group and hence activated by it. In cinnamic acid dibromide the hydrogen eliminated is that α to the more powerful of the two activating groups (COOH). The route to phenylacetylene via styrene suffered initially from a low yield in the decarboxylation step (40%, *Org. Syn.*). Now, however, styrene is available as a low-cost petrochemical; the commercial material is stabilized with *t*-butylcatechol as antioxidant to inhibit polymerization.

t-Butylcatechol
m. p. 57°

Glaser discovered two further interesting routes to phenylpropiolic acid. He treated an ethereal solution of *trans-β*-bromostyrene with sodium, followed by carbon dioxide, and obtained the sodium salt of phenylpropiolic acid. The same salt resulted when phenylacetylene in ether was treated in succession with sodium and with carbon dioxide. The second reaction was understandable because the acetylenic hydrogen, $\equiv C{-}H$, was known to be acidic. The first reaction was clarified only later when Nef showed that sodium in ether is a powerful agent for dehydrohalogenation and converts the unsaturated bromine initially into phenylacetylene, which is then transformed through the sodio derivative to sodium phenylpropiolate.

$$C_6H_5C{\equiv}CH \xrightarrow{\text{Na, Ether}} C_6H_5C{\equiv}CNa \xrightarrow{CO_2} C_6H_5C{\equiv}CCOONa$$

$$\Big\uparrow \text{Na, Ether}$$

$$C_6H_5CH{=}CHBr$$

Oleic acid, a *cis* acid abundantly available from fats, is a convenient starting material for the synthesis of stearolic acid. In an early procedure methyl oleate was brominated and the product heated with potassium hydroxide in *n*-amyl alcohol at 150°; the yield is 38%. The yield was raised to 56% by brominating

$$CH_3(CH_2)_7 \quad (CH_2)_7CO_2H$$
$$\underset{H}{\overset{}{C}}{=}\underset{H}{\overset{}{C}} \xrightarrow[\text{Ether}]{Br_2} CH_3(CH_2)_7{-}\overset{Br\ H}{\underset{H\ Br}{C{-}C}}{-}(CH_2)_7CO_2H$$

Oleic acid   (*d* or *l*)

$$\xrightarrow[\text{56\% overall}]{\text{NaNH}_2,\ \text{Ether, NH}_3;\ \text{HCl}} CH_3(CH_2)_7C{\equiv}C(CH_2)_7CO_2H$$

Stearolic acid (m. p. 46°)

oleic acid in ether and adding the solution to a solution of sodamide in liquid ammonia (N. A. Khan, 1951). The sodamide method has the advantage that the reaction mixture need contain no water, which can be destructive to an acetylenic product:

$$-CHBrCHBr- + 2\ NaNH_2 \rightarrow -C{\equiv}C- + 2\ NaBr + 2\ NH_3$$

The acetylenic acid is isolated by crystallization from petroleum ether and the product or products remaining in the mother liquor have not been identified.

Unlike the high-yield examples cited above, the dehydrobromination of oleic acid dibromide conceivably can yield three products, the acetylene (a), a diene (b), or an allene (c), and possibly the mother liquor contains products of types (b)

$$-CH_2-\underset{\underset{H}{|}}{\overset{\overset{Br}{|}}{C}}-\underset{\underset{Br}{|}}{\overset{\overset{H}{|}}{C}}-CH_2- \rightarrow \quad -C\equiv C- \qquad -CH=CH-CH=CH- \qquad -CH=C=CH-$$

Acetylene	Diene	Allene
(a)	(b)	(c)

and (c). Dienes and allenes have never been isolated as major reaction products, but it is possible that an acetylenic product isolated in low yield is merely the component that crystallizes most readily; acetylenic compounds often crystallize unusually well. Thus application of the superior sodamide process to the conversion of undecylenic acid (from castor oil) into 10-undecynoic acid improved the yield by some 10–15% over that obtained by the KOH–ethanol method, but the

$$CH_2=CH(CH_2)_8CO_2H \xrightarrow[\underset{44\%}{2.NaNH_2}]{1.Br_2} CH\equiv C(CH_2)_8CO_2H$$

Undecylenic acid   10-Undecynoic acid
                                           m.p. 43°

bulk of the material was unaccounted for; the low-melting acid again was isolated (after distillation) by crystallization.

In another route to acetylenes an aldehyde or ketone is treated with a phosphorus pentahalide to produce a *gem*-dihalide, which is then dehydrohalogenated: $RCH_2CH=O \rightarrow RCH_2CHBr_2 \rightarrow RC\equiv CH$. Thus the best route to *t*-butylacetylene involves reaction of pinacolone with phosphorus pentachloride and

$$(CH_3)_3CCCH_3 \xrightarrow[\underset{0-5°}{}]{PCl_5} \left\{ \begin{matrix} (CH_3)_3CCCl_2CH_3 \\ (CH_3)_3CCCl=CH_2 \end{matrix} \right\} \xrightarrow{KOH} (CH_3)_3CC\equiv CH$$

Pinacolone   *t*-Butylacetylene

treatment of the resulting mixture of products with powdered potassium hydroxide. Note that this hydrocarbon is not available by the alkylation of acetylene because of the ready conversion of tertiary halides to olefins.

A few of over 80 acetylenic compounds available from Farchan Research Laboratories (Cleveland, Ohio) are listed below:[1]

$CH\equiv CCH_2OH$	$CH\equiv CHCH_2Br$	$CH\equiv CCH_2CH_2OH$
Propargyl alcohol	Propargyl bromide	3-Butyne-1-ol
b.p. 115°	b.p. 89°	b.p. 103°
$CH\equiv CCO_2H$	$CH_3CH_2CH_2C\equiv CH$	$CH\equiv C(CH_2)_5C\equiv CH$
Propiolic acid	1-Pentyne	1,8-Nonadiyne
m.p. 18°	b.p. 40°	b.p. 55°/13 mm.

---

[1] Some of these chemicals are available at lower cost from primary manufacturers.

6.5   **Bishydrazone Method.** — Acetylenic derivatives of cycloalkanes are easily formed only if the ring contains thirteen or more carbon atoms, for then the linear system —C≡C— can be accommodated without strain.   Introduction of a triple bond into a ring of intermediate size, C_8 to C_{12}, produces such strain that attempts to prepare the hydrocarbons by dehydrohalogenation procedures either afford no acetylenic products or give mixtures of the acetylene and the allene.   Fortunately an alternative method for introduction of a triple bond due to Curtius[1] is applicable (Blomquist,[2] Prelog, 1952).   Cyclooctane-1,2-dione, an α-diketone, is condensed with two equivalents of hydrazine to form the bis-

$$
(CH_2)_6
\begin{array}{c} C=O \\ C=O \end{array}
\xrightarrow[93\%]{2\ H_2NNH_2}
(CH_2)_6
\begin{array}{c} C=NNH_2 \\ C=NNH_2 \end{array}
\xrightarrow{HgO,\ C_6H_6,\ KOH}
$$

Cyclooctane-   Bishydrazone
1,2-dione

$$
(CH_2)_6
\begin{array}{c} C=\overset{+}{N}=\bar{N} \\ C=N=N \\ {\scriptstyle +\quad -} \end{array}
\xrightarrow[9\%]{Heat}
(CH_2)_6
\begin{array}{c} C \\ \| \\ C \end{array}
$$

                                                              Cyclooctyne

hydrazone, which is then oxidized by stirring a solution of the substance in benzene under reflux with mercuric oxide, with addition of ethanolic potassium hydroxide as catalyst (70 hrs.).   Bisdiazo derivatives, usually yellow solids, can be isolated by operating at a lower temperature with ether as solvent, but at the boiling point of benzene the derivative loses nitrogen as formed with conversion to the acetylene, which is isolated, after removal of the benzene, by distillation, and purified by chromatography on silica gel.   The yield is low, for cyclooctyne is highly strained and represents the lower limit of hydrocarbons of its type that have been shown capable of existing.   Cyclodecyne was obtained by the same procedure in 36% yield.   The Curtius method is of distinct service in this special case but lacks appeal for general use because it is lengthy and the yields are not high (yield of diphenylacetylene, 75%).

6.6   **Metal Derivatives.** — Acetylene and monoalkylacetylenes (RC≡CH) are unique among hydrocarbons in that the lone hydrogen attached to triply bound carbon is acidic and · replaceable by metals. Acetylene (H—C≡CH) is thus analogous to hydrogen cyanide (H—C≡N).   When acetylene gas is passed into a solution of cuprous ammonium hydroxide, a reddish brown precipitate of cuprous acetylide is produced.   Both acetylenic hydrogens are replaced by univalent copper atoms; an alkyne of the type RC≡CH gives a monocopper derivative.   Silver acetylides are similarly precipitated from an ammoniacal solution of silver nitrate.   Since formation of a heavy metal derivative is specific to compounds containing an acetylenic hydrogen but is not shown

[1] Theodor Curtius, 1857–1928; Ph.D. Leipzig (Kolbe); successor (1902) to Victor Meyer at Heidelberg

[2] Alfred T. Blomquist, b. 1906 Chicago; Ph.D. Illinois (Marvel); Cornell Univ.

by alkanes, alkenes, or alkynes of the type $RC\equiv CR'$, the reaction is used as a diagnostic test for recognition of the group $\equiv CH$. A very sensitive test reagent is a 5% solution of silver nitrate in 95% ethanol. Even a trace of a 1-alkyne is

$$HC\equiv CH + 2\,Cu(NH_3)_2OH \longrightarrow CuC\equiv CCu + 4\,NH_3 + 2\,H_2O$$
$$\text{Cuprous acetylide}$$

precipitated quantitatively as the silver acetylide–silver nitrate complex. A 1-alkyne can be determined quantitatively by titration of the nitric acid generated in the reaction. Purification of a 1-alkyne is achieved by precipitation of the silver complex and regeneration of the hydrocarbon by reaction with aqueous

$$RC\equiv CH + 2\,AgNO_3 \rightarrow RC\equiv CAg(AgNO_3) + HNO_3$$

sodium cyanide. Silver acetylide in the dry state is sensitive to shock and on explosion produces silver and carbon and no gaseous products. Although copper acetylide is capable of being exploded, it can be used in chemical reactions without hazard.

Acetylene (3 moles) when passed into the deep blue solution of sodium (2 moles) in liquid ammonia is converted into the monosodio derivative, sodium acetylide,

$$3\,HC\equiv CH + 2\,Na \xrightarrow{\text{liq. NH}_3} HC\equiv CNa + H_2C=CH_2$$

with reduction of one mole of acetylene to ethylene. In a laboratory preparation the ethylene escapes and does no harm. It is more economical to convert the sodium into sodamide and use this for conversion of acetylene into sodium acetylide. Lithium amide, often the reagent of choice, is made in the same way.

$$Na + NH_3 \xrightarrow{\text{Fe}} NaNH_2 + \tfrac{1}{2}\,H_2$$
$$HC\equiv CH + NaNH_2 \rightarrow HC\equiv CNa + NH_3$$

Sodamide and lithium amide are used also for replacement of the lone hydrogen of a monoalkylacetylene ($RC\equiv CH$). Disodium acetylide is easily obtained by passing a limited amount of acetylene into a suspension of sodamide in liquid ammonia. Sodium acetylide and disodium acetylide are hydrolyzed by water with regeneration of the hydrocarbon. The sodio derivatives are useful in synthesis because they provide a means for alkylation of the group $\equiv CH$. A methyl group is introduced readily by reaction with methyl iodide (1). Higher primary iodides are liable to suffer conversion in part to the alkene; the primary alkyl

1. $CH\equiv CNa + CH_3I \rightarrow CH\equiv CCH_3 + NaI$
2. $CH_3(CH_2)_{10}Br + NaC\equiv CH \rightarrow CH_3(CH_2)_{10}C\equiv CH$
3. $CH_3C\equiv CNa + [(CH_3)_2CH]_2SO_4 \rightarrow CH_3C\equiv CCH(CH_3)_2 + (CH_3)_2CHOSO_2ONa$

bromide of formulation (2) was selected for the synthesis of undecylacetylene. Secondary and tertiary alkyl halides are too subject to dehydrohalogenation under alkylating conditions to be useful as alkylating agents. However, secondary alkyl sulfates react normally, as in example (3). That t-butylacetylene is not available by alkylation lends importance to the alternative preparative method described in the preceding section.

2-Butyne-1,4-diol, prepared as described in section 6.18, affords a ready source of 1,4-dichlorobutyne-2, which undergoes smooth dehydrochlorination in an alkaline medium to diacetylene (4). Either the mono- or the disodio derivative

$$4.\ ClCH_2C{\equiv}CCH_2Cl \xrightarrow[60\%]{10\%\ NaOH} CH{\equiv}CC{\equiv}CH$$

1,4-Dichlorobutyne-2   Diacetylene

$$NaC{\equiv}CC{\equiv}CH \qquad\qquad NaC{\equiv}CC{\equiv}CNa$$

$$RX\downarrow \qquad\qquad\qquad 2\ RX\downarrow$$

$$RC{\equiv}CC{\equiv}CH \qquad\qquad RC{\equiv}CC{\equiv}CR$$

of this hydrocarbon can be obtained conveniently without isolation of the hydrocarbon itself by treatment of 1,4-dichlorobutyne-2 with either 3 or 4 equivalents of sodamide in liquid ammonia. Alkylation then affords a mono or dialkyl conjugated diyne.

A possible mechanism for the interesting course of dehydrohalogenation of 1,4-dichlorobutyne-2 is initial formation of a dicarbene (5); the same interpretation applies to the related reaction (6) leading to dimethylpentaacetylene (Jones,[1]

$$5.\ Cl{:}\overset{H}{\underset{H}{\ddot{C}}}{:}C{:}{:}{:}C{:}\overset{H}{\underset{H}{\ddot{C}}}{:}Cl \xrightarrow{-2\ HCl} :\ddot{C}{:}\ddot{C}{:}{:}{:}\ddot{C}{:}\ddot{C}: \longrightarrow H{:}C{:}{:}{:}C{:}\overset{H}{C}{:}{:}{:}C{:}\overset{H}{C}{:}H$$

$$6.\ CH_3\underset{Cl}{CH}(C{\equiv}C)_4\underset{Cl}{CH}CH_3 \xrightarrow{NaNH_2} CH_3(C{\equiv}C)_5CH_3$$

$$7.\ CH_3\underset{Cl}{CH}CH{=}CH(C{\equiv}C)_2CH{=}CH\underset{Cl}{CH}CH_3 \xrightarrow{NaNH_2} CH_3(CH{=}CH)_2(C{\equiv}C)_3CH_3$$

Whiting,[2] 1952). The reaction of the symmetrical dichloride (7) to give an unsymmetrical product (Bohlmann, 1958) presents a different situation, for the structure permits an initial 1,2-elimination to give either the allene ($CH_3CH{=}C{=}CH{-}$) or the diene ($CH_2{=}CHCH{=}CH{-}$).

The acetylenic hydrogen ($\equiv C{-}H$) is sufficiently acidic to react with an alkylmagnesium halide with liberation of the alkane and formation of the acetylenic Grignard derivative (8). Since derivatives of the type $RCH(OMgBr)C{\equiv}CMgBr$ are generally insoluble in ether, tetrahydrofurane is preferred as the solvent. The

$$8.\ RC{\equiv}CH\ +\ C_2H_5MgBr \to RC{\equiv}CMgBr\ +\ C_2H_6$$

Grignard reagents react as usual with active-hydrogen reagents and they enter into a variety of useful synthetic reactions to be discussed later; they are appreciably less reactive than alkylmagnesium halides. Ethynylmagnesium bromide, the mono-Grignard derivative of acetylene, is particularly useful, but a

[1] Ewart Ray Herbert Jones, b. 1911 Wrexham, Denbighshire; Ph.D. Univ. Wales (Simonsen); D.Sc. Manchester (Heilbron); Imperial College London; Manchester; Oxford Univ.

[2] Mark C. Whiting, b. 1925 Jarrow, England; Ph.D. London (E. R. H. Jones); Manchester, Oxford Univ.

practical method for its preparation only became available in 1956 (Jones and Whiting). The difficulty is that when acetylene is passed into an ethereal solution of ethylmagnesium bromide the formation of the mono-derivative (9) is followed by the equally rapid reaction (10) leading to the di-Grignard derivative,

9. $CH{\equiv}CH + C_2H_5MgBr \rightarrow CH{\equiv}CMgBr + C_2H_6$

10. $CH{\equiv}CMgBr + C_2H_5MgBr \rightarrow BrMgC{\equiv}CMgBr + C_2H_6$

which separates and does not redissolve. Maintenance of a constant excess of acetylene minimizes the undesired reaction. Thus a solution of ethylmagnesium bromide in tetrahydrofurane is prepared in a nitrogen atmosphere and run slowly into stirred solution of tetrahydrofurane kept saturated with acetylene; ethynyl-magnesium bromide is produced in solution in about 85% yield.

6.7   Oxidative Coupling. — As noted above, phenylacetylene was prepared for the first time by Glaser in 1869. In characterizing experiments aimed at establishing the structure of the new hydrocarbon, Glaser treated a dilute ethanolic solution of the substance with an ammoniacal solution of cuprous chloride and obtained a bright yellow precipitate. Analysis, completed successfully in the face of a tendency of the compound to explode, established the substance to be of the expected type: $C_6H_5C{\equiv}C{-}Cu$. Glaser then discovered that when a suspension of the yellow derivative in alcoholic ammonia is shaken with air the solid gradually dissolves with formation of a new hydrocarbon and cuprous oxide. He characterized the organic product as diphenyldiacetylene, which

$$2\ C_6H_5C{\equiv}CCu \xrightarrow{1/2\ O_2} C_6H_5C{\equiv}C{-}C{\equiv}CC_6H_5 + Cu_2O$$

Diphenyldiacetylene, m. p. 87°

crystallizes in long, well-formed needles. Subsequent investigation confirmed the observation and showed that the oxidative coupling proceeds smoothly and in much higher yield than the Kolbe or Wurtz coupling reactions. The reaction evidently involves formation and dimerization of the free radical $C_6H_5C{\equiv}C\cdot$.

Baeyer employed the Glaser reaction in 1882 in an early synthesis of indigo, but it was not until some seventy years after Glaser's discovery that a general synthetic use for the reaction arose from the discovery of natural products containing the

$$CH_2{=}CH(CH_2)_4C{\equiv}CC{\equiv}C(CH_2)_7CO_2H \xrightarrow{5\ H_2(Pt)} n\text{-}C_{17}H_{35}CO_2H$$

Erythrogenic acid, m.p. 39°   Stearic acid

$\lambda\ 227,\ 237,\ 254\ m\mu$

$\downarrow O_3$

$$CH_2{=}O + HO_2C(CH_2)_4CO_2H + HO_2CCO_2H + HO_2C(CH_2)_7CO_2H$$

Adipic acid   Oxalic acid   Azelaic acid

conjugated diyne unit $-C{\equiv}C-C{\equiv}C-$. The natural products are not symmetrical, like diphenyldiacetylene, but they nevertheless can be synthesized readily by oxidative crossed coupling. The reaction gives a mixture of three products, but if these are of different types the mixture can be separated readily.

An example is the synthesis of erythrogenic acid, so called (Gr. *erythro-*, red) because on exposure to light it is converted into a vivid red polymer.   Hydrogenation to stearic acid established the presence of a normal C_{18}-chain, but the results of ozonization experiments did not distinguish between the *vic*-diacetylene structure eventually established and the alternative structure $CH_2\!\!=\!\!CHC\!\!\equiv\!\!C\!\!-\!\!(CH_2)_4C\!\!\equiv\!\!C(CH_2)_7CO_2H$.   Ultraviolet absorption characteristics of synthetic model compounds seemed to the E. R. H. Jones group to exclude the alternative structure, and the *vic*-diacetylenic formula was established by the following synthesis carried out by H. K. Black and B. C. L. Weedon[1] (1953).   A mixture of octene-1-yne-7 and Δ^9-decynoic acid in alcohol and hydrochloric acid containing cuprous am-

$$CH_2\!\!=\!\!CH(CH_2)_4C\!\!\equiv\!\!CH \;+\; HC\!\!\equiv\!\!C(CH_2)_7CO_2H \xrightarrow{Cu^+\text{-}O_2}$$

Octene-1-yne-7 Δ^9-Decynoic acid

$$CH_2\!\!=\!\!CH(CH_2)_4C\!\!\equiv\!\!CC\!\!\equiv\!\!C(CH_2)_7CO_2H$$
Erythrogenic acid

monium chloride (from Cu_2Cl_2 and NH_4Cl) was shaken with oxygen in a hydrogenation apparatus.   Removal of the hydrocarbon fraction left a mixture of diacid (m.p. 120°) and the much more volatile monoacid from which the latter component was easily separated by distillation.   This acid, obtained in yield of about 30%, proved to be identical with a sample of natural erythrogenic acid purified through the urea inclusion complex.

A modification of the Glaser reaction introduced by W. Chodkiewicz in Paris (1957) greatly increases the efficiency and scope of the synthetic method.   One component is a 1-alkyne and the other the bromo derivative of a 1-alkyne, and condensation is effected in an aqueous solution of ethylamine in the presence of a

$$C_6C_5C\!\!\equiv\!\!CBr \;+\; HC\!\!\equiv\!\!CC(C_6H_5)_2 \xrightarrow[87\%]{\substack{Cu^+ \\ aq.\ C_2H_5NH_2}} C_6H_5C\!\!\equiv\!\!CC\!\!\equiv\!\!CC(C_6H_5)_2$$

$$\overset{|}{OH} \qquad\qquad\qquad\qquad\qquad\qquad\qquad \overset{|}{OH}$$

M. p. 86°

$$(CH_3)_2CC\!\!\equiv\!\!CBr \;+\; HC\!\!\equiv\!\!C(CH_2)_8CO_2H \xrightarrow[98\%]{\substack{Cu^+ \\ aq.\ C_2H_5NH_2}}$$

$$\overset{|}{OH}$$

$$(CH_3)_2CC\!\!\equiv\!\!CC\!\!\equiv\!\!C(CH_2)_8CO_2H$$
$$\overset{|}{OH}$$
M. p. 46°

catalytic amount of a cuprous salt.   There is very little coupling of the 1-alkyne component, and yields are high.   The required bromides are readily available by reaction of the parent acetylene with sodium hypobromite.

6.8   Strauss Reaction. — A coupling reaction somewhat similar to that discovered by Glaser was described in 1905 by F. Strauss, who found that copper phenylacetylide when heated in acetic acid solution in the presence of air

[1] Basil C. L. Weedon, b. 1923 London; Ph.D. and D.Sc. London (Heilbron, E. R. H. Jones); Imperial College (London); Queen Mary College, Univ. London

is converted into 1,4-diphenylbuteneyne (II). The same hydrocarbon was obtained by prolonged refluxing of diphenyldiacetylene (III) in ethanol with zinc dust activated with copper. No further examples of the reaction were observed

$$2\ C_6H_5C{\equiv}CCu\ \rightarrow\ C_6H_5CH{=}CHC{\equiv}CC_6H_5\ \xleftarrow[\text{C}_2\text{H}_8\text{OH}]{\text{Zn(Cu)}}\ C_6H_5C{\equiv}CC{\equiv}CC_6H_5$$
$$\text{I}\qquad\qquad\qquad\text{II}\qquad\qquad\qquad\qquad\qquad\qquad\text{III}$$

until 1958, when M. Akhtar and B. C. L. Weedon reported that the reaction is applicable to a variety of monosubstituted acetylenes, for example: $n\text{-}C_8H_{17}C{\equiv}CH$, $CH_3O_2C(CH_2)_8C{\equiv}CH$, $CH_3COOCH_2C{\equiv}CH$, $C_6H_5CH{=}CHC{\equiv}CH$, 1-ethynylcyclohexanol. The initial products are mixtures of *cis* and *trans* enes. The reaction consists in heating a copper acetylide in acetic acid in the presence of either air or chloroacetic acid; the mechanism is still obscure.[1]

6.9   Ethoxyacetylene (b.p. 51°). — The starting material for preparation of this useful reagent is chloroacetaldehyde diethylacetal (5, b.p. 157°), which is made in one step by passing chlorine into cooled 96% ethanol

$$CH_3CH_2OH\ \xrightarrow{\text{Cl}_2}\ CH_3CH{=}O\ \xrightarrow{\text{Cl}_2}\ ClCH_2CH{=}O\ \xrightarrow[\text{(HCl)}]{\text{HOC}_2\text{H}_5}$$
$$\text{(1)}\qquad\qquad\qquad\text{(2)}\qquad\qquad\qquad\text{(3)}$$

$$ClCH_2CH\!\!\begin{array}{l}\diagup OH\\ \diagdown OC_2H_5\end{array}\ \xrightarrow[\text{(HCl)}]{\text{HOC}_2\text{H}_5}\ ClCH_2CH\!\!\begin{array}{l}\diagup OC_2H_5\\ \diagdown OC_2H_5\end{array}\ \xrightarrow[\text{NH}_2]{\text{NaNH}_2}$$
$$\text{(4)}\qquad\qquad\qquad\qquad\qquad\text{(5)}$$

$$NaC{\equiv}C{-}OC_2H_5\ \xrightarrow{\text{H}_2\text{O}}\ HC{\equiv}C{-}OC_2H_5$$
$$\text{(6)}\qquad\qquad\qquad\qquad\text{(7)}$$

(1 l.) until the specific gravity has increased from 0.789 to 1.025 and adding a further quantity of alcohol (0.5 l.). The steps are: oxidation (2), chlorination (3), addition of ethanol under catalysis by the hydrogen chloride produced to give the hemiacetal (4), and conversion of this to the acetal (5). Elimination of hydrogen chloride and ethanol to give ethoxyacetylene (7) is effected with sodamide (*Org. Syn.*; for improvements, see H. H. Wasserman, 1960). Liquid ammonia (500 ml.) is stirred at −35°, hydrated ferric nitrate (0.5 g.) is added, followed by enough sodium (1 g.) to reduce it to a black suspension of finely divided metal catalyst, with discharge of the blue color. When more sodium (37 g.) is added in portions it is converted rapidly into a pale gray suspension of sodamide with evolution of hydrogen. Chloroacetaldehyde diethylacetal (76.5 g.) is run in during 15 min., the ammonia is evaporated in a stream of nitrogen, and the mixture is treated at −70° with cold saturated sodium chloride solution for hydrolysis of the pyrophoric sodio derivative (6). The flask is fitted with a still head connected to a trap cooled to −70° and the condensate allowed to warm up to 0° and freed of ammonia by addition of an aqueous slurry of sodium dihydrogen phosphate. The neutral aqueous layer is frozen and the supernatant liquid is decanted, dried, and distilled; yield 21 g. (60%).

[1] Private communication from Professor Weedon.

Treatment of ethoxyacetylene with ethylmagnesium bromide affords ethoxy-acetylenemagnesium bromide (8), a powerful reagent for addition to a carbonyl group to produce acetylenic carbinols of the type (9). Semihydrogenation of the triple bond gives a product (10) which is an enol ether and which consequently is

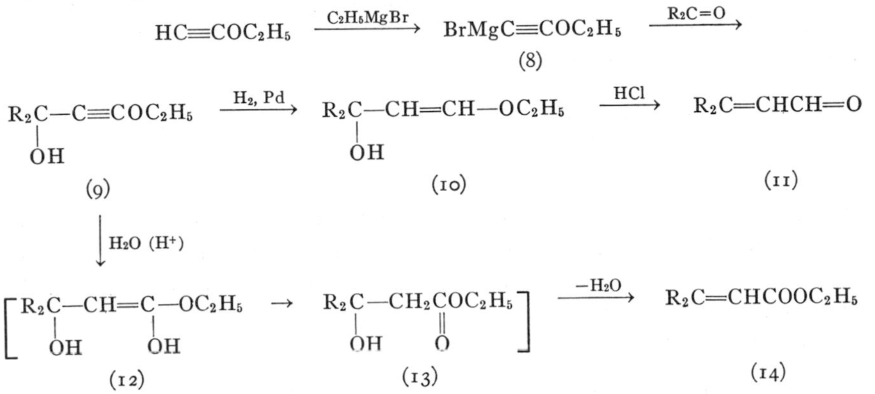

$$HC\equiv COC_2H_5 \xrightarrow{C_2H_5MgBr} BrMgC\equiv COC_2H_5 \xrightarrow{R_2C=0}$$
$$(8)$$

$$R_2C-C\equiv COC_2H_5 \xrightarrow{H_2,\ Pd} R_2C-CH=CH-OC_2H_5 \xrightarrow{HCl} R_2C=CHCH=0$$
$$\underset{OH}{|} \qquad\qquad\qquad \underset{OH}{|}$$
$$(9) \qquad\qquad\qquad (10) \qquad\qquad\qquad (11)$$

$$\downarrow H_2O\ (H^+)$$

$$\left[R_2C-CH=C-OC_2H_5 \;\rightarrow\; R_2C-CH_2COC_2H_5 \right] \xrightarrow{-H_2O} R_2C=CHCOOC_2H_5$$
$$\left[\underset{OH}{|}\ \ \underset{OH}{|} \qquad\quad \underset{OH}{|}\ \ \underset{O}{\|} \right]$$
$$(12) \qquad\qquad\qquad (13) \qquad\qquad\qquad (14)$$

split easily by dilute mineral acid to the enolic form of a β-hydroxyaldehyde, and the latter loses water with efficient conversion to the α,β-unsaturated aldehyde (11). Another synthesis arises from the fact that the acetylenic carbinol (9) undergoes ready hydration with formation, via (12) and (13), of the α,β-unsaturated ester (14); possibly (9) yields (14) by allylic rearrangement.

1-Methoxybutene-1-yne-3 (2), obtained by smooth base-catalyzed addition of methanol to diacetylene (1) is a vinylog of methoxyacetylene, that is, it is a deriva-

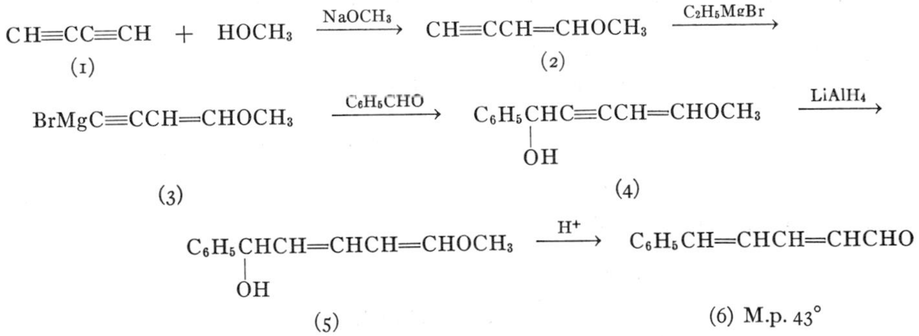

$$CH\equiv CC\equiv CH\ +\ HOCH_3 \xrightarrow{NaOCH_3} CH\equiv CCH=CHOCH_3 \xrightarrow{C_2H_5MgBr}$$
$$(1) \qquad\qquad\qquad\qquad\qquad (2)$$

$$BrMgC\equiv CCH=CHOCH_3 \xrightarrow{C_6H_5CHO} C_6H_5CHC\equiv CCH=CHOCH_3 \xrightarrow{LiAlH_4}$$
$$\underset{OH}{|}$$
$$(3) \qquad\qquad\qquad\qquad\qquad (4)$$

$$C_6H_5CHCH=CHCH=CHOCH_3 \xrightarrow{H^+} C_6H_5CH=CHCH=CHCHO$$
$$\underset{OH}{|}$$
$$(5) \qquad\qquad\qquad\qquad\qquad (6)\ M.p.\ 43°$$

tive of the acetylenic ether in which the two functions are connected by a con-jugated vinyl group. The substance is used in the same way that an alkoxyacetylene is used but for the synthesis of conjugated dienic aldehydes. For example, benzaldehyde reacts with the Grignard derivative (3) to give the carbinol (4). This substance has a triple bond flanked by a carbinol group, and a special mechanism applicable to such a structure (6.16) makes possible reduction of (4) to the diene (5) with lithium aluminum hydride. Hydrolysis of the enol ether (5) is attended with dehydration, with production of the dienic aldehyde (6) in 75% overall yield (Whiting, 1956).

REACTIONS

6.10   **Electrophilic Additions.** — Alkynes, like alkenes, add halogens and hydrogen halides in reactions that initiate in attack by an electrophilic agent. For example, acetylene reacts with chlorine by the usual two-step mechanism (1) to form acetylene dichloride, which in turn adds a further mole of chlorine to form s-tetrachloroethane (s stands for *symmetrical*), a useful solvent. Com-

1. $CH{\equiv}CH \xrightarrow{Cl^+} \overset{+}{C}H{=}CHCl \xrightarrow{Cl^-} ClCH{=}CHCl \xrightarrow{Cl_2} Cl_2CHCHCl_2$

                                           Acetylene s-Tetrachloro-
                                           dichloride   ethane

parison of the rate of addition of the first mole of halogen to an alkyne with the rate of addition of the halogen to an alkene of comparable structure reveals the fact that the triple bond is considerably less susceptible to electrophilic attack than the double bond. The difference is so great that selective addition to an eneyne is easily accomplished (2).

2. $CH_2{=}CHCH_2C{\equiv}CH \xrightarrow{Br_2} CH_2BrCHBrCH_2C{\equiv}CH$

A triple bond lacks the activating power of a double bond responsible for allylic bromination. Whereas methyl crotonate reacts readily with N-bromosuccinimide to give the γ-bromo derivative: $CH_3CH{=}CHCO_2CH_3 \rightarrow BrCH_2CH{=}CHCO_2CH_3$, no comparable product is obtained from methyl tetrolate, $CH_3C{\equiv}CCO_2CH_3$.

Hydrogen iodide adds to acetylene in the manner shown in formulation (3). Hydrogen bromide adds in the same sense in the absence of a peroxide (4), but

3. $CH{\equiv}CH \xrightarrow{HI} CH_2{=}CHI \xrightarrow{HI} CH_3CHI_2$

                                Vinyl icdide   Ethylidene
                                                      iodide

                                       n-$C_4H_9CBr{=}CH_2 \rightarrow n$-$C_4H_9CBr_2CH_3$

                             (normal)

4. n-$C_4H_9C{\equiv}CH + HBr$

                           (peroxide)

                                   n $C_4H_9CH{=}CHBr \rightarrow n$-$C_4H_9CH_2CHBr_2$

5. $CH_3C{\equiv}CH \xrightarrow{2\ HF} CH_3CF_2CH_3$

the direction of addition is reversed if a peroxide is present. Slow addition of an alkyne to liquid hydrogen fluoride at $-20°$ results in normal reaction (5) in about 80% yield. Hypobromous acid, generated from aqueous N-bromoacetamide, reacts to give a dibromoketone (6); sodium hypobromite, however, replaces the acetylenic hydrogen by bromine (7).

                                             O
                                            ‖

6. $RC{\equiv}CH + 2\ HOBr \rightarrow R\overset{O}{\underset{}{C}}CHBr_2 + H_2O$

7. $RC{\equiv}CH + NaOBr \rightarrow RC{\equiv}CBr + NaBr + \frac{1}{2} H_2O$

6.11   **Oxidation.** — The triple bond is also less subject to oxidation than a double bond. Thus the Δ^9-decynoic acid required for the synthesis of erythrogenic acid was obtained readily by oxidation of the corresponding diphenyleneyne (1). The acid has been obtained also by oxidation of the

1. $CH\equiv C(CH_2)_7CH = C(C_6H_5)_2 \xrightarrow[58\%]{CrO_3} CH\equiv C(CH_2)_7CO_2H$

                                               Δ^9-Decynoic acid

2. $CH\equiv C(CH_2)_7CH = C(CH_3)_2 \xrightarrow[40\%]{CrO_3}$ ↑

dimethyleneyne (2). Rate measurements for the reaction with a peracid, which involves electrophilic attack (OH^+), show a striking difference; if the rate of reaction with ethylene is taken as unity, typical relative rates are: $CH\equiv CH$, immeasurably slow; $RC\equiv CH$, 0.1; $RCH = CH_2$, 20; $RC\equiv CR$, 0.5; $RCH = CHR$, 500; $C_6H_5C\equiv CH$, 0.02. Thus selective attack of the double bond of an eneyne is a simple matter, as in reactions 3 and 4.

3. $C_6H_5C\equiv CCH = CHC_5H_{11}\text{-}n \xrightarrow{C_6H_5CO_3H} C_6H_5C\equiv CCH \overset{\diagdown}{\underset{O}{\diagup}} CHC_5H_{11}\text{-}n$

4. $CH_2 = CHC\equiv CH \xrightarrow{HCO_3H;\ hydrol.} \underset{OH\ \ OH}{CH_2CHC\equiv CH}$

6.12   **Nucleophilic Addition.** — A nucleophile is an anion or other negative fragment capable of attacking a positive center, or a positively polarized site in a molecule. The carbon atom of a carbonyl group is positively polarized because oxygen is more electronegative than carbon and the partial positive charge at this site invites attack by a nucleophile, for example the anion of H^+CN^-. The addition of hydrogen cyanide to a ketone (1), a typical nucleophilic addition, involves attack by cyanide ion with acceptance of the charge by

1. $\overset{\delta^+\ \ \delta^-}{R_2C = O} \xrightarrow{CN^-} R_2C \overset{\diagup O^-}{\underset{\diagdown CN}{}} \xrightarrow{H^+} R_2C \overset{\diagup OH}{\underset{\diagdown CN}{}}$

                                      Cyanohydrin

oxygen; capture of a proton completes the sequence.

     In line with the decreased reactivity of the triple bond to attack by electrophiles is the fact that alkynes show susceptibility to nucleophilic attack not shared by alkenes. Thus hydrogen cyanide adds to acetylene, as it does to aldehydes and ketones, but it does not add to alkenes. This nucleophilic addition (2) is conducted in the industry in either the liquid phase or the vapor phase. Acrylonitrile

2. $CH\equiv CH \xrightarrow{CN^-} \overset{-}{C}H = CHCN \xrightarrow{H^+} CH_2 = CHCN$

                                        Acrylonitrile
                                        b.p. 78.5°

is a valuable monomer for the production of polymeric plastics.

6.13   **Hydration.** — Alkynes undergo catalytic hydration much more readily
than alkenes, and the reaction finds use in the industry for the production of acetaldehyde from acetylene.   The addition is effectively catalyzed by a
mercuric salt and can be conducted in 10% aqueous sulfuric acid containing 5%
of mercuric sulfate.   An intermediate mercury complex appears to be involved,

$$CH\equiv CH \ + \ HOH \ \xrightarrow{(Hg^{++},\ H_2SO_4)} \ [CH_2=CH-OH] \ \rightarrow \ CH_3CH=O$$
$$\qquad\qquad\qquad\qquad\qquad\qquad\qquad\quad \text{Vinyl alcohol} \qquad \text{Acetaldehyde}$$

but the mechanism is not clear.   The initial product of hydration, vinyl alcohol, is
an unstable enol which at once isomerizes by shift of the activated hydrogen from
oxygen to carbon to give acetaldehyde.   An interesting variation in the procedure
employs as catalyst a sulfonated polystyrene ion exchange resin (Dowex-50)
impregnated with mercuric sulfate (M. S. Newman, 1953).   When a suspension of
the resin in an aqueous solution of propargyl alcohol was stirred at 23°, the temperature soon rose to 55° from the heat of the reaction; filtration from the resin
gave a solution from which hydroxyacetone was easily isolated as a derivative.

$$\cdots CHCH_2\!\!-\!\!-\!\!-\!\!CHCH_2\!\!-\!\!-\!\!-\!\!CH\!\!-\!\!CH_2 \cdots$$
$$\qquad\qquad\qquad | \qquad\qquad\quad | \qquad\qquad\quad | \qquad\qquad (HgSO_4)$$
$$\qquad\qquad\qquad C_6H_4SO_3H \quad\ C_6H_4SO_3H \quad\ C_6H_4SO_3H$$
$$CH\equiv CCH_2OH \ + \ H_2O \ \xrightarrow{\qquad\qquad\qquad\qquad\qquad\qquad\qquad}$$

Propargyl alcohol

$$\begin{bmatrix} CH_2=CCH_2OH \\ \quad | \\ \quad OH \end{bmatrix} \ \xrightarrow[87\%]{} \ CH_3CCH_2OH$$
$$\qquad\qquad\qquad\qquad\qquad\qquad\qquad\qquad\quad \overset{\|}{O}$$

$$\qquad\qquad\qquad\qquad\qquad\qquad\qquad\qquad\qquad \text{Hydroxyacetone}$$

The structure of the product shows that addition of water follows the
Markownikoff rule.   The point is illustrated also by the hydration of vinylacetylene to methyl vinyl ketone, a reaction which also demonstrates the selective

$$\qquad\qquad\qquad\qquad\qquad\qquad\qquad\qquad\qquad\qquad\qquad \overset{O}{\|}$$
$$CH_2=CH-C\equiv CH \ + \ H_2O \ \xrightarrow{(H^+,\ Hg^{++})} \ CH_2=CH-C-CH_3$$
$$\quad \text{Vinylacetylene} \qquad\qquad\qquad\qquad \text{Methyl vinyl ketone (b. p. 80°)}$$

reaction of a triple bond when a double bond is also available.
     Acetic acid adds to acetylene in the presence of mercuric salts or acetylsulfuric
acid as catalyst to give vinyl acetate, which does not isomerize because the mobile

$$\quad\ \overset{O}{\|} \qquad\qquad\qquad\qquad\qquad\qquad\qquad\qquad\qquad\quad \overset{O}{\|}$$
$$CH_3-C-OH \ + \ CH\equiv CH \ \xrightarrow[80\%]{\text{Acetylsulfuric acid}} \ CH_3-C-O-CH=CH_2$$
$$\qquad\qquad\qquad\qquad\qquad\qquad\qquad\qquad\qquad\qquad \text{Vinyl acetate}$$

hydrogen atom of vinyl alcohol is replaced by an acetyl group.   Vinyl acetate is
made on a very large scale for polymerization to vinyl plastics.
     Vinyl esters are obtainable in practically quantitative yield by heating a
carboxylic acid such as acetic or benzoic acid with divinylmercury without solvent
(D. J. Foster and E. Tobler, Union Carbide, 1960).   When the reaction is carried

out in a suitable solvent (hexane, heptane, benzene, toluene, etc.) the intermediate vinylmercuric ester usually crystallizes from the reaction mixture. Stronger acids such as *p*-toluenesulfonic acid and the chloroacetic acids are added portionwise to

$$RCO_2H + (CH_2{=}CH)_2Hg \rightarrow RCO_2CH_2CH_2HgCH{=}CH_2$$
$$RCO_2CH_2CH_2HgCH{=}CH_2 \rightarrow RCO_2CH{=}CH_2 + Hg + CH_2{=}CH_2$$

divinylmercury at room temperature, since the reaction is strongly exothermic. Phenols react to give vinyl aryl ethers. Divinylmercury is made from vinylmagnesium chloride or bromide and mercuric chloride in tetrahydrofurane.

6.14   Free Radical Addition. — An interesting addition to the triple bond involves thiols, particularly thiolacetic acid (b.p. 93°). The reaction is

$$\textit{n-}C_4H_9C{\equiv}CH + CH_3COSH \rightarrow \textit{n-}C_4H_9CH{=}CHSCOCH_3 \rightarrow \textit{n-}C_4H_9CH_2CH{=}O$$

catalyzed by ultraviolet irradiation or by peroxides and, like other free radical additions, follows the counter-Markownikoff course (compare the addition of HBr, 5.12). The unsaturated product, for example, that resulting from addition of thiolacetic acid to hexyne-1 in the presence of ascaridole,[1] is convertible into a derivative of the corresponding aldehyde by reaction with a suitable carbonyl reagent. The two-step process provides a useful technique for reverse hydration (I. M. Heilbron,[2] H. Behringer, 1949). The conversion of phenylacetylene into phenylacetaldehyde has been effected in 70 % yield by conducting the addition in the presence of dibenzoyl peroxide; in the absence of a peroxide the yield was only 25 %.

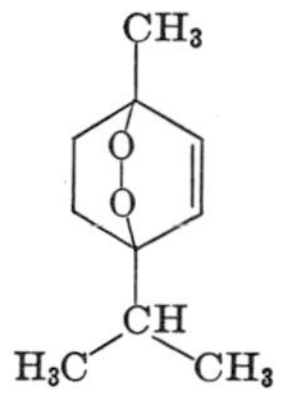

Ascaridole

$$C_6H_5C{\equiv}CH + CH_3COSH \rightarrow C_6H_5CH{=}CHSCOCH_3 \rightarrow C_6H_5CH_2CH{=}O$$

6.15   Reduction. — Comparison of the conditions required for catalytic hydrogenation of alkynes and alkenes of analogous structure shows that a triple bond is significantly more reactive than a double bond. The relative reactivities are such that an alkyne can be selectively hydrogenated to an alkene in high yield, and that a compound containing both a triple bond and a double bond can be transformed to the corresponding diene. The most generally successful procedure utilizes the Lindlar catalyst, a palladium-on-calcium carbonate catalyst partially inactivated with lead acetate (H. Lindlar, 1952); Raney nickel also finds some use. Catalytic hydrogenation of the triple bond proceeds by *cis* addition and gives 90–98 % *cis* olefinic products. The reaction is of particular importance because the thermodynamically more stable *trans* olefins are the products of most synthetic reactions. Most olefinic acids of natural occurrence have been found to have the *cis* configuration, and several have been synthesized by catalytic hydrogenation of the corresponding acetylenes. For example, selec-

---

[1] Ascaridole, a liquid, is the active principle of chenopodium oil, formerly used as an anthelmintic (Gr. *askaris*, an intestinal worm). The transannular peroxide has been synthesized by Diels-Alder addition of oxygen to α-terpinene (1-methyl-4-isopropyl-Δ[1,4]-cyclohexadiene).

[2] Sir Ian Heilbron, b. 1886 Glasgow; Ph.D. Leipzig (Hantzsch); D.Sc. Glasgow (Henderson); Manchester: Imperial College (London); Brewing Industrial Research Foundation

tive hydrogenation of stearolic acid (6.4) affords a product identical with natural oleic acid from olive oil.

$$CH_3(CH_2)_7C{\equiv}C(CH_2)_7CO_2H \xrightarrow{\text{H}_2,\ \text{Ni}} \begin{array}{l} CH_3(CH_2)_7-C-H \\ \ \ \ \ \ \ \ \ \ \ \ \ \ \ \ \| \\ HO_2C(CH_2)_7-C-H \end{array}$$

Stearolic acid   Oleic acid

cis Hydrogenation of an alkyne presumably involves a cyclic transition state in which the unsaturated carbon atoms are partially bonded through hydrogen to the catalyst. Since a triple bond is more reactive than a double bond, and since in other reactions a triple bond is reactive specifically to nucleophilic attack, it would appear that hydrogenation involves nucleophilic hydride attack (H^-), followed by acquisition of a proton. Alkynes also can be reduced to alkenes with sodium or lithium in liquid ammonia, and in this case there is no difficulty in avoiding over-reaction because alkenes are completely resistant to chemical reduction under these conditions. The products are predominantly *trans* olefins.

Use of the two methods is illustrated by the preparation of a series of *cis-trans* isomer pairs for quantitative study of their relative thermodynamic stability (Cope,[1] 1960). Hydrogenation of cyclononyne in methanol containing a little

$$(\text{CH}_2)_7 \left[\begin{array}{c} C \\ \| \\ C \end{array} \right. \begin{array}{c} \xrightarrow{\text{10\% Pd-C, H}_2} \text{\textit{cis}-Cyclononene} (\lambda 697\ \text{cm}^{-1}) \\ \xrightarrow{\text{Na, NH}_3} \text{\textit{trans}-Cyclononene} (\lambda 980\ \text{cm}^{-1}) \end{array}$$

Cyclononyne

pyridine in the presence of palladium-on-Norit gave a product which on gas chromatography in a column containing silicone oil or tetraethylene glycol supported on 50–100 mesh firebrick afforded about 93% of pure *cis*-cyclononene and 7% of the *trans* isomer. Reduction of the acetylene with sodium in refluxing ammonia gave 71% of *trans*-cyclononene, 19% of *cis*-cyclononene, and 10% of unchanged acetylene.

6.16   **Reduction of Allylic and Propargylic Alcohols.** — Lithium aluminum hydride, LiAlH$_4$ or Li$^+$[AlH$_4$]$^-$ is a powerful reagent for the reduction of carbonyl compounds and acids in ethereal solution, for example, $R_2C{=}O \rightarrow R_2CHOH$; $RCOOH \rightarrow RCH_2OH$. The reagent does not attack ethylenic or acetylenic hydrocarbons, but it reduces allylic alcohols and their acetylenic counterparts. The reaction was first encountered by W. G. Brown[2] (1947–48) in the reduction of cinnamyl alcohol to dihydrocinnamyl alcohol. Experimentation eliminated alternative pathways and indicated that the unusual reaction probably proceeds as follows. The hydride first reacts rapidly with the alcohol with liberation of hydrogen and formation of the lithium aluminum alcoholate. Reduction

[1] Arthur C. Cope, b. 1909 Dunreith, Indiana; Ph.D. Wisconsin (McElvain); Bryn Mawr College; Columbia Univ.; Mass. Inst. Techn.

[2] Weldon G. Brown, b. 1908 Saskatoon, Saskatchewan, Canada; Ph.D. California, Berkeley; Univ. Chicago

then occurs at a moderate rate with formation of a bicyclic complex in which hydrogen has become bonded to one originally unsaturated carbon and aluminum to the other. The second hydrogen atom required for saturation of the original double bond is supplied in the terminal step of hydrolysis of the complex, when

$$4 \; C_6H_5CH{=}CHCH_2OH \; + \; LiAlH_4 \; \longrightarrow \; (C_6H_5CH{=}CHCH_2O)_4AlLi \; + \; 4 \; H_2$$

Cinnamyl alcohol

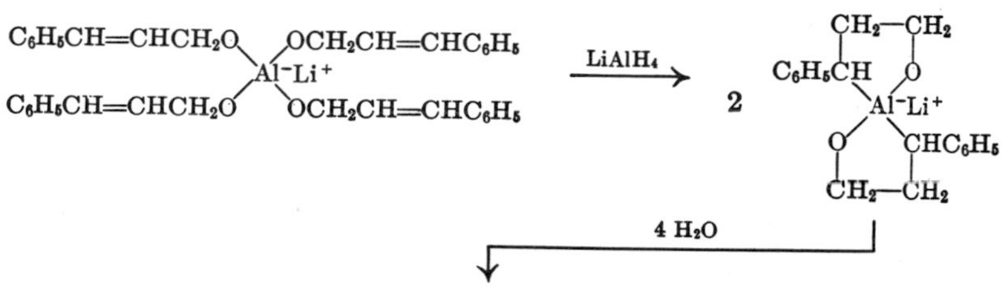

4 H₂O

$$4 \; C_6H_5CH_2CH_2CH_2OH \; + \; Al(OH)_3 \; + \; LiOH$$

Hydrocinnamyl alcohol

water cleaves the carbon–aluminum bond. Actually the complexes formed in this reaction and those described below usually separate as insoluble precipitates and are probably polymeric equivalents of the cyclic monomers here formulated for simplification.

Glaxo Laboratories found the reaction applicable to acetylenic alcohols and

1. $C_6H_5C{\equiv}CCO_2H \; \xrightarrow[-70°]{LiAlH_4} \; C_6H_5C{\equiv}CCH_2OH \; \xrightarrow{LiAlH_4} \; C_6H_5CH{=}CHCH_2OH$

   Phenylpropiolic acid   Phenylpropargyl alcohol   Cinnamyl alcohol

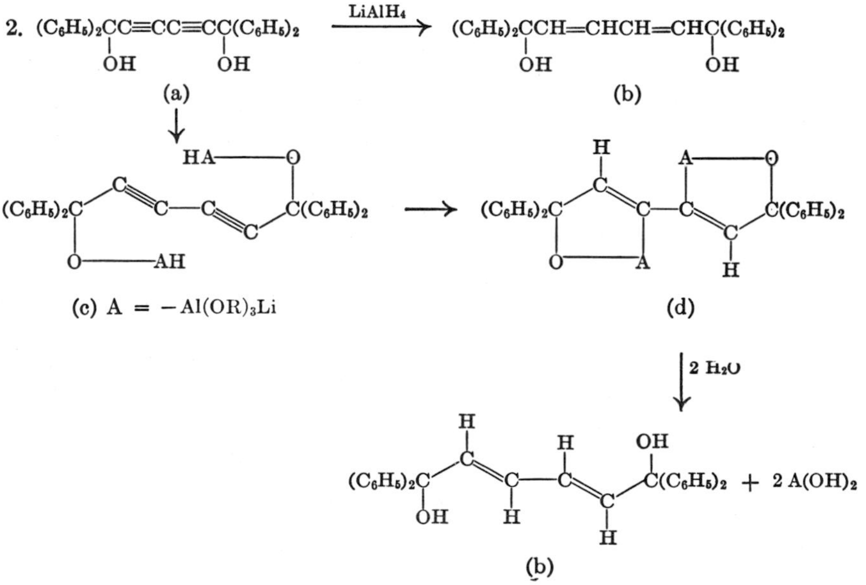

2.

(c) A = $-Al(OR)_3Li$

2 H₂O

(b)

employed it in a synthesis of vitamin A (J. Attenburrow, J. Elks,[1] *et al.*, 1952), and further examples were explored by E. R. H. Jones and M. C. Whiting (1954). Phenylpropiolic acid (1) is reduced first to phenylpropargyl alcohol, which then affords a complex which on decomposition with water affords cinnamyl alcohol. In example 2 a diacetylenic glycol (a) is reduced to a diethylenic glycol (b) in which the double bonds are both *trans*. Possibly the intermediate glycolate (c) cyclizes by *trans* additions to the triple bonds with establishment of carbon–aluminum bonds (d), the cleavage of which introduces a second pair of hydrogens *trans* to those introduced in the first step. The monoacetylenic glycol (3e) presents a different situation, for reduction results in elimination of both hydroxyl

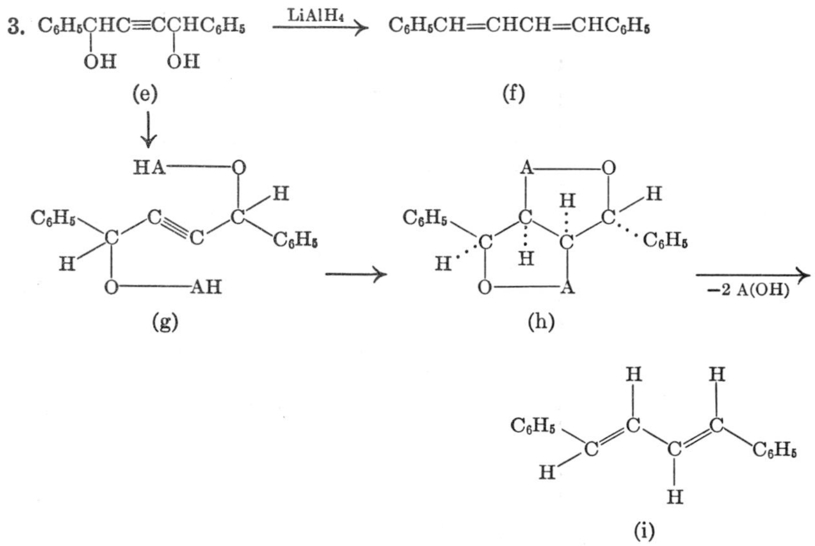

3. $C_6H_5\overset{|}{\underset{OH}{C}}HC{\equiv}C\overset{|}{\underset{OH}{C}}HC_6H_5$ $\xrightarrow{\text{LiAlH}_4}$ $C_6H_5CH{=}CHCH{=}CHC_6H_5$

     (e)   (f)

functions and formation of a *trans, trans* diene (i). The interpretation suggested in the formulas is that intramolecular *trans* addition of the glycolate (g) gives an intermediate (h) of stereochemistry favorable for *trans* eliminations involving the first pair of hydrogen atoms as another pair become attached on severance of the carbon–aluminum bonds. This variation of the reduction reaction has been of considerable value in the synthesis of naturally occurring polyenes.

6.17   **Vinylacetylene.** — In some reactions acetylene functions as the entity H—A in additions to unsaturated compounds. One is addition of acetylene to itself to form vinylacetylene, a dimerization. The addition is effected by absorption of acetylene in a solution of cuprous chloride and ammonium chloride in hydrochloric acid. This addition of H—C≡CH is analogous to the nucleophilic addition of H—C≡N and may involve attack by ⁻C≡CH. Adjustment of conditions makes possible the addition of one more mole of acetylene

[1] Joseph Elks, b. 1920 London; Ph.D. Imperial College, Univ. London (Hey); Glaxo Laboratories

to produce divinylacetylene. Vinylacetylene is employed in the synthesis of Neoprene rubber; divinylacetylene is manufactured on a more limited scale for use as a synthetic drying oil for paints. The sodium derivative of vinylacetylene has synthetic uses, but its preparation from the hydrocarbon presents the difficulty

$$CH\equiv CH \ + \ H{-}C\equiv CH \ \xrightarrow{\text{Cu}_2\text{Cl}_2-\text{NH}_4\text{Cl}} \ CH_2{=}CHC\equiv CH \ \xrightarrow{HC\equiv CH}$$
$$\underset{\text{Vinylacetylene}}{}$$

$$CH_2{=}CHC\equiv CCH{=}CH_2$$
$$\underset{\text{Divinylacetylene}}{}$$

that vinylacetylene is difficult to store and to handle. A convenient laboratory preparation consists in treatment of 1,4-dichloro-2-butene (next section) with sodamide in liquid ammonia. An allene may result initially, but the acetylene

$$ClCH_2CH{=}CHCH_2Cl \ \xrightarrow{\text{3 NaNH}_2} \ CH_2{=}CHC\equiv CNa$$
$$\underset{\text{1,4-Dichloro-2-butene}}{} \qquad \underset{\text{Sodium vinylacetylide}}{}$$

alone can afford a sodio derivative.

6.18   Addition to the Carbonyl Group. — A further analogy between acetylene and hydrogen cyanide is that both reagents enter into nucleophilic addition to carbonyl compounds. A basic catalyst abstracts a proton and the carbanion attacks the polarized carbon of the carbonyl group. Development

$$HC\equiv CH \ \xrightarrow{OH^-} \ {}^-C\equiv CH \ \xrightarrow[R_2C=O]{\overset{\delta^+ \ \delta^-}{}} \ R_2C\!\!\begin{smallmatrix} O^- \\ \\ C\equiv CH \end{smallmatrix} \ \xrightarrow{H_2O} \ R_2C\!\!\begin{smallmatrix} OH \\ \\ C\equiv CH \end{smallmatrix} \ + \ OH^-$$
$$\underset{\text{Ethynylcarbinol}}{}$$

of a technical process for addition of acetylene to formaldehyde was one of a series of triumphs achieved by Reppe[1] of the I. G. Farbenindustrie in the period 1925–45. The key to the success of the processes lay in the devising of techniques for manipulating acetylene with safety at the high pressures (up to 100 atmospheres) required for efficient reaction. The reaction of acetylene with formaldehyde is conducted under pressure in the presence of copper acetylide and affords the useful products propargyl alcohol and 2-butyne-1,4-diol. These, in turn, are

$$CH\equiv CH \ + \ CH_2{=}O \ \rightarrow \ CH\equiv CCH_2OH \ + \ HOCH_2C\equiv CCH_2OH$$
$$\underset{\text{Propargyl alcohol}}{} \qquad \underset{\text{2-Butyne-1,4-diol}}{}$$
$$\text{(a)} \qquad\qquad\qquad \text{(b)}$$

$$\text{(a)} \rightarrow \begin{cases} CH\equiv CCH_2Cl \\ CH_2{=}CHCH_2OH \\ CH_2{=}CHCH_2Cl \end{cases} \qquad \text{(b)} \rightarrow \begin{cases} ClCH_2C\equiv CCH_2Cl \\ HOCH_2CH{=}CHCH_2OH \\ ClCH_2CH{=}CHCH_2Cl \end{cases}$$

convertible into the corresponding chlorides and into the ethylenic alcohols and their chlorides. The triple bond is sufficiently resistant to oxidative attack that the oxidation of propargyl alcohol is a practical method for production of propiolic

---

[1] Walter Reppe, b. 1892 Föringen, Germany; Ph.D. Munich (K. H. Meyer); BASF Ludwigshafen

acid, formerly prepared by heating sodium acetylide with carbon dioxide under pressure.

$$CH{\equiv}CCH_2OH \xrightarrow[78\%]{CrO_3\ (H_2SO_4)} CH{\equiv}CCO_2H$$

Propargyl alcohol   Propiolic acid

$$\Big\uparrow HCl$$

$$CH{\equiv}CNa \xrightarrow{CO_2} CH{\equiv}CCO_2Na$$

One procedure for effecting addition of acetylene to cyclohexanone to produce 1-ethynylcylcohexanol involves passing acetylene into mechanically stirred liquid ammonia during gradual addition of sodium (1 mole); the blue color of dissolved sodium is discharged rapidly by the acetylene. Cyclohexanone (1 mole) is added by drops and the mixture is allowed to stand for evaporation of most of the ammonia; the yield of distilled product is 70% (*Org. Syn.*). An alternative procedure employs potassium *t*-butoxide in *t*-butanol as the condensing agent.

Ethynylation has many uses in the steroid series, for example, for the preparation of 17α-ethynylestradiol, of value in therapy as an oral estrogen. The procedure employed by Inhoffen[1] at Schering A. -G. utilizes potassium in large excess,

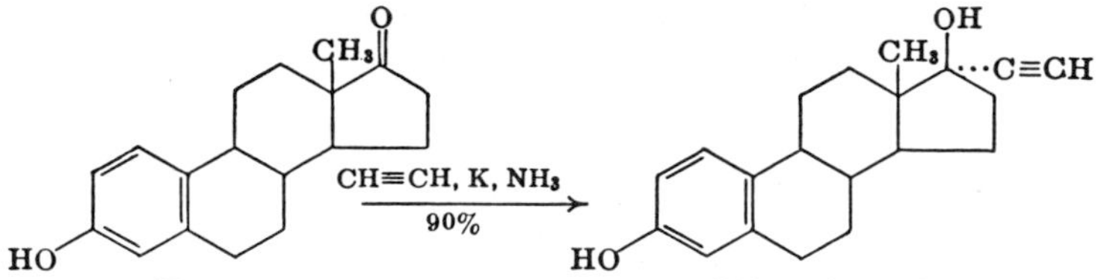

Estrone $CH{\equiv}CH$, K, NH_3 → 90%   17α-Ethynylestradiol

probably to allow for reduction of acetylene to ethylene (3 $CH{\equiv}CH$ + 2 K → 2 $KC{\equiv}CH$ + $CH_2{=}CH_2$). Ammonia (1 l.) is condensed in a flask cooled in acetone–dry ice, potassium (40 g.) is added, and acetylene is passed in until the blue color is completely discharged. A solution of estrone (15 g.) in dioxane (300 ml.) and ether (300 ml.) is run in, the cooling bath is removed, and the mixture is let stand overnight for evaporation of the ammonia. Recovery of the product by ether extraction and one crystallization from methanol–water gave nearly pure product in 90% yield.

Another technique is employed in a process developed by Weizmann[2] for the production of isoprene. Addition of acetylene to acetone is effected by use of powdered potassium hydroxide in a solvent containing O—C—O or O—C—C—O groups. When solid potassium hydroxide is heated with diethylene glycol di-

[1] Hans Herloff Inhoffen, b. 1906 Hannover-Döhren; Ph.D. Göttingen (Windaus); Univ. Göttingen, Braunschweig

[2] Chaim Weizmann, 1874–1952; b. Russia; Ph.D. Berlin, Germany and Freiburg, Switzerland (Bistrzycki); Univ. Manchester; Weizmann Institute of Science. Israel; *J. Chem. Soc.*, 2840 (1953)

methyl ether, $CH_3OCH_2CH_2OCH_2CH_2OCH_3$, the alkali disperses as a highly reactive, finely divided powder which absorbs acetylene with great avidity. Neither sodium nor lithium hydroxide behaves similarly. Acetylene is absorbed with the formation of potassium acetylide and water, and an extra mole of potassium hydroxide is used to bind the water and prevent reversal of the reaction. On

$$HC{\equiv}CH \;+\; 2\,KOH \longrightarrow KC{\equiv}CH \;+\; KOH{-}H_2O$$

$$
\underset{CH_3}{\overset{CH_3}{>}}C{=}O
\xrightarrow{\;KC{\equiv}CH\;}
\underset{CH_3}{\overset{CH_3}{>}}\underset{OK}{C}{-}C{\equiv}CH
\xrightarrow{\;H_2O\;}
\underset{CH_3}{\overset{CH_3}{>}}\underset{OH}{C}{-}C{\equiv}CH
$$

$$
\xrightarrow{\;H_2,\,Pd\;}
\underset{CH_3}{\overset{CH_3}{>}}\underset{OH}{C}{-}CH{=}CH_2
\xrightarrow[-H_2O]{\;Al_2O_3\;}
CH_2{=}\underset{\overset{|}{CH_3}}{C}{-}CH{=}CH_2
$$
$$\text{Isoprene}$$

addition of acetone at $-10°$, a strongly exothermic reaction takes place leading to the potassium derivative of the adduct, which on addition of water is hydrolyzed to 3-methyl-1-butyne-3-ol. Selective hydrogenation and vapor phase dehydration yields isoprene.

6.19   Lewisite (β-Chlorovinyldichloroarsine).—β-Chlorovinyldichloroarsine, or lewisite, is a war gas developed in 1917 by W. Lee Lewis, an American, to meet the demand for a nonpersistent vesicant that would produce immediate casualties and thus be applicable to offensive combat. A method of manufacture was worked out consisting in addition of arsenic trichloride to acetylene in the presence of anhydrous aluminum chloride as catalyst. The

$$
\overset{\ulcorner{-}{-}{-}{-}{-}{-}{-}{-}{-}{-}{-}\urcorner}{CH{\equiv}CH} \;+\; ClAsCl_2 \xrightarrow{\;AlCl_3\;} ClCH{=}CHAsCl_2
$$
$$\text{Lewisite}$$

first lot was ready for shipment overseas only in November, 1918, and after declaration of the Armistice, was destroyed at sea.

Lewisite (b.p. 190°) combines a vesicant action similar to that of mustard gas with the systemic poisoning effect of arsenic, and it is also a lung injurant and a lachrymator. Inhalation of the vapor for ten minutes at a concentration of 0.12 mg. per liter of air is fatal. Like mustard gas, lewisite rapidly penetrates clothing and body tissue. Lewisite is about four times as quick in acting as mustard gas and it is much less persistent. The two halogen atoms attached to arsenic are highly reactive and the substance is hydrolyzed rapidly in moist air to β-chlorovinylarsine oxide. This hydrolysis product is itself a potent vesicant but it is nonvolatile.

$$ClCH{=}CHAsCl_2 \xrightarrow{\;H_2O\;} ClCH{=}CHAsO$$
$$\text{β-Chlorovinylarsine oxide}$$

An antidote to lewisite developed by a British group during World War II is known as BAL (British anti-lewisite). The discovery was based upon the postulate that lewisite is toxic because it combines with sulfhydryl groups (—SH) of enzymes. BAL (2,3-dimercaptopropanol-1) combines with lewisite to form a cyclic, nontoxic derivative. A derivative of BAL in which the sugar glucose is

$$
\begin{array}{ccccc}
\mathrm{CH_2} & & \mathrm{CH_2Br} & & \mathrm{CH_2SH} \\
\| & \xrightarrow{\mathrm{Br_2}} & | & \xrightarrow{\mathrm{2\ NaSH}} & | & \xrightarrow{\mathrm{Cl_2AsCH=CHCl}} \\
\mathrm{CH} & & \mathrm{CHBr} & & \mathrm{CHSH} \\
| & & | & & | \\
\mathrm{CH_2OH} & & \mathrm{CH_2OH} & & \mathrm{CH_2OH} \\
\text{Allyl alcohol} & & & & \text{BAL}
\end{array}
$$

$$
\begin{array}{l}
\mathrm{CH_2\!-\!S} \\
\quad\quad\ \ \diagdown \\
| \qquad\qquad \mathrm{AsCH=CHCl} \\
\mathrm{CH\!-\!S} \\
\quad\quad\ \ \diagup \\
| \\
\mathrm{CH_2OH}
\end{array}
$$

linked to the alcoholic hydroxyl group for increased solubility in water is used as an antidote for poisoning by heavy metals.

6.20   Nature of the Triple Bond. — The reactions and relationships cited provide abundant evidence that the triple bond is less susceptible to attack by electrophiles than the double bond and more reactive to nucleophilic agents. The number of shared electrons is greater, but these electrons do not seem to be as readily available as those of an olefin. The tetranitromethane test affords an apt demonstration of the difference: alkenes are effective electron-donating π-bases and give yellow complexes, but alkynes give no colored π-complexes. Added to a 5% solution in ethyl acetate of the more powerful π-acid tetracyanoethylene, diphenylacetylene gives a cherry red complex and *trans*-stilbene gives an intense purple color. The orbital theory accounts for the difference as follows. The four atoms of acetylene are bonded together in a straight line by sp hybrid orbitals forming σ bonds. Each carbon atom still has two p orbitals perpendicular to one another, each containing one electron, and overlapping of the four p orbitals (a) gives rise to two π-molecular orbitals which over-

(a)   (b)

lap and have cylindrical symmetry, as suggested in the drawing (b). An increased proportion of the s component contained in the sp hybrid orbital of the triple bond, as compared with the sp^2 hybrid of ethylenic carbon contributes to tighter binding and lesser availability of electrons in acetylene; the electrons are concentrated at the center of the molecule to a greater extent in acetylene than in ethylene. Physical evidence of the difference is that the C≡C bond is significantly

$$
\begin{array}{ll}
1.33\ \text{Å} \diagdown\ \ \mathrm{H} & 1.20\ \text{Å} \diagdown \\
\qquad\qquad | & \\
\mathrm{H_2C{=}C\!-\!H} & \mathrm{HC{\equiv}C\!-\!H} \\
\qquad\quad \diagup & \qquad\quad \diagdown \\
\qquad 1.09\ \text{Å} & \qquad 1.06\ \text{Å}
\end{array}
$$

shorter than the C=C bond. Note that the C—H bond is also shorter in acetylene than in ethylene. The sp hybrid forming the C—H bond of acetylene has a greater proportion of the s component than the sp^2 hybrid orbital of ethylenic C—H, a difference which is probably responsible for the greater acidity of a hydrogen atom on triply bound carbon. The acidic hydrogen of hydrogen cyanide is joined by a similarly constructed sp hybrid.

SPECIALIZED TYPES

6.21   Natural Acetylenic Hydrocarbons. — Prior to 1950 only a very limited number of acetylenic compounds had been found to occur in nature. Investigations by Sörensen[1] in Norway, Bohlmann[2] in Germany, and Jones and Whiting in England then revealed that acetylenic acids, alcohols, ketones, and hydrocarbons occur widely, if in small amounts, in higher fungi (Basidiomycetes) and higher plants (Compositae and Umbelliferae). Hydrocarbon types encountered are illustrated by the formulas established for a series of C_{13}-hydrocarbons isolated by Sörensen from Compositae:

$$CH_3CH\!=\!CHC\!\equiv\!CC\!\equiv\!CCH\!=\!CHCH\!=\!CHCH\!=\!CH_2 \text{ (}trans,\ trans,\ trans\text{)}$$
$$CH_3CH\!=\!CHC\!\equiv\!CC\!\equiv\!CC\!\equiv\!CCH\!=\!CHCH\!=\!CH_2 \text{ (}trans,\ trans\text{)}$$
$$CH_3CH\!=\!CHC\!\equiv\!CC\!\equiv\!CC\!\equiv\!CC\!\equiv\!CCH\!=\!CH_2 \text{ (}cis \text{ and } trans\text{)}$$
$$CH_3C\!\equiv\!CC\!\equiv\!CC\!\equiv\!CC\!\equiv\!CCH\!=\!CH_2$$
$$C_6H_5C\!\equiv\!CC\!\equiv\!CCH\!=\!CHCH_3 \text{ (}cis \text{ and } trans\text{)}$$
$$C_6H_5C\!\equiv\!CC\!\equiv\!CC\!\equiv\!CCH_3$$

These compounds are all very unstable and occur in only small amounts, but each was characterized completely and some of the structures were confirmed by synthesis. All known natural acetylenic hydrocarbons are polyacetylenes containing 2–5 conjugated triple bonds, and these are often conjugated with ethylenic linkages. This structural feature gives rise to highly characteristic ultraviolet absorption spectra, which makes detection of even minute quantities easy. Polyacetylenes show very sharp and intense absorption bands in the ultraviolet, and the number of bands depends upon the number of conjugated units. The spacing between the maxima is somewhat greater (about 2,000 cm^{-1}) than for comparable polyenes (1,400 cm^{-1}). An infrared stretching band at 3330 cm^{-1} permits detection of the HC≡C— group, and further infrared bands are useful for detection and assignment of configuration of double bonds. Often spectrographic analysis, coupled with hydrogenation to the parent hydrocarbon, suffices for complete elucidation of structure. Oxidative coupling provides a useful route of synthesis.

6.22   Acetylene–Allene Rearrangement. — Working in the St. Petersburg laboratory of the late Professor Butleroff[3] in 1888, Favorsky[4] sought to prepare ethylacetylene, according to M. Kutscheroff, by converting methyl ethyl ketone to the dichloride and heating this with ethanolic potassium hydroxide at 170°. The product, however, gave no copper or silver derivative and it be-

---

[1] Nils Andreas Sörensen, b. 1909 Oslo; Dr. Techn. Norway Inst. Techn. (C. N. Rüber); Norway Inst. Techn., Trondheim

[2] Ferdinand Bohlmann, b. 1921 Oldenburg, Germany; Ph.D. Göttingen (K. Dimroth); Univ. Braunschweig

[3] Alexander M. Butleroff, 1828–86; b. Tschistopol, Gouv. Kasan, Russia; St. Petersburg

[4] Alexei J. Favorsky, 1860–1945; Ph.D. St. Petersburg; Leningrad

haved like dimethylacetylene when a sample was shaken in a sealed tube with a mixture of one part of water and 5 parts of sulfuric acid. A strongly exothermic reaction set in with separation of crystals of hexamethylbenzene, m.p. 164°.

$$
\text{I.}\quad
\underset{\substack{|\\ \mathrm{CH_2}\\|\\ \mathrm{CH_3}}}{\overset{\substack{\mathrm{CH_3}\\|}}{\mathrm{C{=}O}}}
\xrightarrow{\mathrm{PCl_5}}
\underset{\substack{|\\ \mathrm{CH_2}\\|\\ \mathrm{CH_3}}}{\overset{\substack{\mathrm{CH_3}\\|}}{\mathrm{CCl_2}}}
\xrightarrow[130°]{\mathrm{EtOH,}\ \mathrm{KOH}}
\underset{\substack{|\\ \mathrm{CH_2}\\|\\ \mathrm{CH_3}}}{\overset{\substack{\mathrm{CH}\\ \|\|\\ \mathrm{C}}}{}}
\xrightarrow[170°]{\mathrm{EtOH,}\ \mathrm{KOH}}
\underset{\substack{|\\ \mathrm{C}\\|\\ \mathrm{CH_3}}}{\overset{\substack{\mathrm{CH_3}\\|}}{\mathrm{C}}}\ \|\|\|
$$

Repetition of the dehydrochlorination showed that the normal product is indeed ethylacetylene but that for isolation of this substance the temperature of the alkaline mixture must not exceed 130°. Favorsky then showed that authentic ethylacetylene (b.p. 17°) forms metal derivatives, gives no hexamethylbenzene in the sulfuric acid test, and that the 1-alkyne is isomerized smoothly to the 2-alkyne by ethanolic potassium hydroxide at 170°. He thought that the rearrangement might involve intermediate formation of the allene and so investigated the behavior of isopropylacetylene (2), where production of a 2-alkyne is impossible. Rearrangement occurred and the product was the expected allene,

$$
2.\quad
\underset{\mathrm{CH_3}}{\overset{|}{\mathrm{CH_3CH}}}{-}\mathrm{C{\equiv}CH}
\xrightarrow[170°]{\mathrm{KOH\text{-}EtOH}}
\underset{\mathrm{CH_3}}{\overset{|}{\mathrm{CH_3C}}}{=}\mathrm{C{=}CH_2}
$$

$$
\mathrm{OH^-}\downarrow -\mathrm{H_2O} \qquad\qquad\qquad \mathrm{H_2O}\uparrow -\mathrm{OH^-}
$$

$$
\underset{\mathrm{CH_3}}{\overset{|}{\mathrm{CH_3\bar{C}}}}{-}\mathrm{C{\equiv}CH}
\quad\longleftrightarrow\quad
\underset{\mathrm{CH_3}}{\overset{|}{\mathrm{CH_3C}}}{=}\mathrm{C{=}\bar{C}H}
$$

(a) \qquad\qquad\qquad\qquad\qquad (b)

3-methyl-$\Delta^{1,2}$-butadiene. Favorsky also showed that *t*-butylacetylene is unchanged under comparable conditions, and the observation weakened his postulate that the initial step in the rearrangement involves addition of potassium ethoxide. Jacobs[1] later showed that the rearrangement can be effected with powdered potassium hydroxide at 170° in the absence of ethanol and suggested that the reaction is initiated by abstraction of a proton from an activated position to give an acetylenic carbanion (2a) in resonance with an allenic carbanion (2b), which abstracts a proton from water with formation of the allene and regeneration of the catalytic hydroxide ion. The process is described as a base-catalyzed prototropic rearrangement. A series of similar steps accounts for the alkoxide-catalyzed rearrangement of ethylacetylene to dimethylacetylene, as shown in the formulas:

$$
\mathrm{CH_3CH_2C{\equiv}CH}\xrightarrow[-\mathrm{EtOH}]{\mathrm{EtO^-}}\mathrm{CH_3\bar{C}H{-}C{\equiv}CH}\leftrightarrow\mathrm{CH_3CH{=}C{=}\bar{C}H}\xrightarrow[-\mathrm{EtO^-}]{\mathrm{EtOH}}\mathrm{CH_3CH{=}C{=}CH_2}
$$

$$
\xrightarrow[-\mathrm{EtOH}]{\mathrm{EtO^-}}\mathrm{CH_3\bar{C}{=}C{=}CH_2}\leftrightarrow\mathrm{CH_3C{\equiv}C{-}\bar{C}H_2}\xrightarrow[-\mathrm{EtO^-}]{\mathrm{EtOH}}\mathrm{CH_3C{\equiv}CCH_3}
$$

---

[1] Thomas L. Jacobs, b. 1908 Forest City, Iowa; Ph.D. Cornell (J. R. Johnson); Harvard; Univ. Calif. Los Angeles

For clarification of the first experiment by Favorsky, Jacobs (1951) made a careful study of 1-pentyne (I), 1,2-pentadiene (II), and 2-pentyne (III). Each of the three isomers when heated in 3.7 N ethanolic potassium hydroxide in a

$$CH_3CH_2CH_2C{\equiv}CH \;\rightleftharpoons\; CH_3CH_2CH{=}C{=}CH_2 \;\rightleftharpoons\; CH_3CH_2C{\equiv}CCH_3$$

Pentyne (I)	1,2-Pentadiene (II)	2-Pentyne (III)
b.p. 39°, λ 4.72 μ	b.p. 46°, λ 5.62 μ	b.p. 56°, λ 4.93 μ (small)
1.3%	3.5%	95.2%

sealed tube at 175° for about 3 hrs. gave the same equilibrium mixture, which was analyzed by a combination of infrared spectroscopy and analytical distillation with the results shown under the formulas. Two other possible isomers were shown not to be present: 1,3-pentadiene (conjugated) and 2,3-pentadiene (an allene). That the 2-alkyne predominates in the equilibrium mixture and hence surpasses the other isomers in thermodynamic stability may be because it is stabilized by hyperconjugation involving five hydrogens. Thermochemical data show that in the series $CH{\equiv}CH$, $CH_3C{\equiv}CH$, $CH_3C{\equiv}CCH_3$ each methyl group increases the stability by about 5 kcal. Conversion of 2-pentyne to the less stable 1-pentyne can be accomplished by heating the hydrocarbon with sodamide, for irreversible removal of the 1-alkyne as its sodio derivative displaces the equilibrium. Such isomerization can be accomplished even when the triple bond is more deeply embedded in the carbon chain, as in (3).

3. $CH_3CH_2CH_2CH_2CH_2C{\equiv}CCH_2CH_2CH_2CH_3 \xrightarrow{\text{NaNH}_2;\ \text{H}_2\text{O}}$

$$CH_3CH_2CH_2CH_2CH_2CH_2CH_2CH_2CH_2C{\equiv}CH$$

4. $(C_6H_5)_2CHC{\equiv}CC_6H_5 \xrightarrow[83\%]{\text{Basic Al}_2\text{O}_3} (C_6H_5)_2C{=}C{=}CHC_6H_5$

5. $C_2H_5OCH_2C{\equiv}CH \xrightarrow[89\%]{\text{Solid KOH}} C_2H_5OCH{=}C{=}CH_2$

6. $ClCH_2C{\equiv}CH \xrightarrow{\text{Solid NaOH}} ClCH{=}C{=}CH_2$

The acetylene → allene rearrangement formulated in (4) is promoted by conjugation of the allenic system with the terminal phenyl groups and the reaction proceeds in high yield on mere contact with basic alumina at room temperature. In reactions (5) and (6) the allenic system in the product is in conjugation with an atom carrying unshared electrons.

A rearrangement of a second type is illustrated by the conversion of propargyl bromide into bromoallene (7) under catalysis by a cuprous salt (Jacobs, 1953).

7. $CH{\equiv}C{-}CH_2Br \xrightarrow[-Br^-]{\text{Cu}_2\text{Br}_2,\ 70°} CH{\equiv}C\overset{+}{C}H_2 \leftrightarrow \overset{+}{C}H{=}C{=}CH_2 \xrightarrow{Br^-} BrCH{=}C{=}CH_2$

8. $CH_3{-}\underset{\underset{Cl}{|}}{\overset{\overset{CH_3}{|}}{C}}{-}C{\equiv}CH \xrightarrow{\text{Cu}_2\text{Cl}_2,\ \text{HCl},\ \text{NH}_4\text{Cl}} CH_3{-}\underset{}{\overset{\overset{CH_3}{|}}{C}}{=}C{=}CHCl$

9. $CH_3{-}\underset{\underset{Cl}{|}}{\overset{\overset{CH_3}{|}}{C}}{-}C{\equiv}CH \xrightarrow{\text{Zn}{-}\text{Cu},\ \text{C}_2\text{H}_5\text{OH}} CH_3{-}\underset{}{\overset{\overset{CH_3}{|}}{C}}{=}C{=}CH_2$

Since an anion dissociates and returns to a new site, the reaction is described as an anionotropic rearrangement.   Other examples are formulated in (8) and (9).

The isomerization of β,γ-acetylenic acids such as Δ^3-butynoic acid I was investigated by the group of Jones and Whiting (1954) with interesting results. The substance is rearranged (as anion) to allenecarboxylic acid in 92% yield on

$$CH{\equiv}CCH_2CO_2H \xrightarrow{\ K_2CO_3\ } CH_2{=}C{=}CHCO_2H \rightleftharpoons CH_3C{\equiv}CCO_2H$$

$$\underset{\text{I}}{} \qquad\qquad \underset{\text{II}}{} \qquad\qquad \underset{\text{III}}{}$$

K₂CO₃ (as ester) │   │ NaOC₂H₅ (as ester)

$$\longrightarrow CH_3C{=}CHCO_2CH_3 \longleftarrow$$
$$\underset{\text{IV}}{\overset{|}{O}C_2H_5}$$

standing in potassium carbonate solution at 40° for three hours.   At a temperature of 90° the allene II is isomerized to tetrolic acid (III) in 60% yield.   That the allenic system is more susceptible than the acetylenic system to nucleophilic attack is shown by the fact that the ester of II adds ethanol to give IV under

$$CH_2{=}C{=}CHCH_2C{\begin{smallmatrix}\diagup O\\ \diagdown O^-\end{smallmatrix}} \xrightarrow[-H_2O]{OH^-} CH_2{=}C{=}CHCH{=}C{\begin{smallmatrix}\diagup O^-\\ \diagdown O^-\end{smallmatrix}} \xrightarrow[-OH^-]{H_2O}$$

(1)   (2)

$$CH_2{=}CH{-}CH{=}CHC{\begin{smallmatrix}\diagup O\\ \diagdown O^-\end{smallmatrix}}$$

(3)

catalysis by potassium carbonate; formation of the same compound from the ester of the α,β-acetylenic acid III is accomplished only with a more basic catalyst. Further evidence is that the allenic acid II on reaction with a limited amount of lithium aluminum hydride is reduced to vinylacetic acid, $CH_2{=}CHCH_2CO_2H$, whereas tetrolic acid (III) is reduced to the acetylenic alcohol $CH_3C{\equiv}CCH_2OH$.

The examples cited in illustration of the rearrangement of allenes to acetylenes and of the reverse rearrangements all involve three-carbon systems in which formation of a conjugated diene is not possible.   However, the work of Jacobs cited above shows that the allene $CH_3CH_2CH{=}C{=}CH_2$ rearranges to acetylenic products and not to a diene.   A carboxylate group adjacent to an allenic system, as in the anion (1), promotes allene $\rightarrow$ diene isomerization by providing a center $(-CO_2^-)$ suitable for acceptance of electrons; thus (1) affords the conjugated dienic anion (3) in 80% yield (Whiting).

S. R. Landon and R. Taylor-Smith (1959) effected the stereospecific synthesis of optically active allenes by a scheme involving resolution of the alcohol (1) by conversion to the (+)-hydrogen phthalate (3), crystallization of the brucine salts, and cleavage with lithium aluminum hydride.   The acetylenic alcohols had

$$\underset{\substack{\text{CH}_3\\|\\(\text{CH}_3)_3\text{C}-\text{C}-\text{C}\equiv\text{CH}\\|\\\text{OH}\\(1)\ dl}}{} \xrightarrow{\text{2 EtMgBr}} \underset{\substack{\text{CH}_3\\|\\(\text{CH}_3)_3\text{C}-\text{C}-\text{C}\equiv\text{CMgBr}\\|\\\text{CMgBr}\\(2)}}{} \xrightarrow[\substack{\text{(Py)}}]{\substack{\text{Phthalic}\\\text{anhydride}}}$$

$$\underset{\substack{\text{CH}_3\\|\\(\text{CH}_3)_3\text{C}-\text{C}-\text{C}\equiv\text{C}-\text{OCOC}_6\text{H}_4\text{CO}_2\text{HCOOH-}o\\|\\\text{OH}\\(3)}}{} \xrightarrow[\substack{\text{2. LiAlH}_4}]{\substack{\text{1. Resolution}}} \underset{\substack{\text{CH}_3\\|\\(\text{CH}_3)_3\text{C}-\text{C}-\text{C}\equiv\text{CH}\\|\\\text{OH}\\(4)}}{}$$

$$\xrightarrow{\text{SOCl}_2} \left[\underset{\substack{\text{CH}_3\\|\\(\text{CH}_3)_3\text{C}-\text{C}-\text{C}\equiv\text{CH}\\|\\\text{OSOCl}\\(5)}}{}\right] \xrightarrow[-\text{SO}_2]{\text{Py}} \underset{\substack{\text{CH}_3\\|\\(\text{CH}_3)_3\text{C}-\text{C}=\text{C}=\text{CHCl}\\(6)}}{}$$

specific rotations of $+1.6°$ and $-1.3°$; rearrangement of the former isomer afforded the allene (6) of $\alpha_D +39°$.

6.23   Cumulenes. — A cumulene is a substance having several adjacent double bonds. The first one known, 2,5-dimethylhexatriene-2,3,4 (4) was prepared by Wl. Krestinsky at Leningrad in 1926 by the action of zinc

$$2(\text{CH}_3)_2\text{C}=\text{O} + \text{BrMgC}\equiv\text{CMgBr} \rightarrow \underset{\substack{\quad\ |\quad\ |\\\quad\ \text{OH}\ \ \text{OH}\\(1)\ \text{M.p. }95°}}{(\text{CH}_3)_2\text{C C}\equiv\text{C C}(\text{CH}_3)_2} \xrightarrow{\text{2HBr}}$$

$$\left[\underset{\substack{\ |\quad\ |\\\ \text{Br}\quad\text{Br}\\(2)}}{(\text{CH}_3)_2\text{C C}\equiv\text{C C}(\text{CH}_3)_2}\right] \rightarrow \underset{\substack{(3)\ \text{M.p. }39°}}{(\text{CH}_3)_2\text{C}=\text{CBrCBr}=\text{C}(\text{CH}_3)_2} \xrightarrow{\text{Zn}}$$

$$\underset{\substack{(4)}}{(\text{CH}_3)_2\text{C}=\text{C}=\text{C}=\text{C}(\text{CH}_3)_2}$$

dust in ethanol on the *vic*-dibromide (3). This dibromide had been obtained in nearly quantitative yield by Dupont[1] (1911) by the action of hydrobromic acid at $0°$ on the acetylenic glycol (1) but had been assumed to be the ditertiary dibromide (2). Krestinsky, however, noticed that the bromine atoms are very unreactive and that the substance gives a positive test with tetranitromethane and hence behaves like the diene (3) rather than the acetylene (2). He proved the structure (3) by oxidation to acetone and oxalic acid and by debromination to the cumulene (4). On steam distillation of the reaction mixture the hydrocarbon (4) was obtained as feathery needles of camphorlike odor, m.p. $39°$; on brief exposure to air the substance is transformed into a white amorphous product. The simplest cumulene, butatriene, was not known until 1954, when it was prepared by reaction of 1,4-dibromobutyne-2 with zinc dust in diethylene glycol

[1] Georges Dupont, 1884–1958; b. La Réole; D.Sc. Bordeaux, Paris (Lespieau); Univ. Bordeaux, Paris (École Normal Supérieure)

(Schubert[1]).   The most striking property is the tendency to polymerize, even at
0°.

$$\text{BrCH}_2\text{C}{\equiv}\text{C CH}_2\text{Br} \xrightarrow[85\%]{\text{Zn}} \text{CH}_2{=}\text{C}{=}\text{C}{=}\text{CH}_2$$
Butatriene

R. Kuhn[2] (1938–51) synthesized a series of tetraphenylcumulenes and found
that the simplest one, tetraphenylbutatriene, is yellow, the pentaene is red, and
the heptaene is violet.   The tetraphenylcumulenes are hydrogenated in the
presence of Lindlar catalyst to the corresponding *cis*-polyenes in high yield (Kuhn,
1960).

$(\text{C}_6\text{H}_5)_2\text{C}{=}\text{C}{=}\text{C}{=}\text{C}{=}\text{C}{=}\text{C}(\text{C}_6\text{H}_5)_2$ $(\text{C}_6\text{H}_5)_2\text{C}{=}\text{C}{=}\text{C}{=}\text{C}{=}\text{C}{=}\text{C}{=}\text{C}(\text{C}_6\text{H}_5)_2$

Tetraphenylhexapentaene (red)   Tetraphenyloctaheptaene (violet)

Bohlmann (1954) synthesized a series better adapted to spectroscopic analysis
in which all positions α to the unsaturated system are blocked by methyl groups,

so that isomerization to acetylenes or conjugated dienes is not possible.   The
products are all solids, of m.p. above 100°.   Selective light absorption occurs at
much lower wave length than in resonance-stabilized conjugated polyenes.
Whereas butadiene has an absorption maximum at 220 mμ and the conjugated
triene system absorbs selectively at 265 mμ, the aliphatic cumulene system (a)

(a)   (b)   (c)

shows only a subsidiary maximum, (b) absorbs at 238 mμ, and (c) at 284 mμ.
The hydrocarbons were all synthesized from 2,2,6,6-tetramethylcyclohexanone
(V), prepared by methylating 2-methylcyclohexanone three times by alternate
treatment with sodamide, to form the sodio enolate, and methyl iodide.   The
triene (VII) was obtained by condensation of two moles of V with acetylenedimagnesium bromide to give the diol VI, which on reaction with phosphorus
diiodide gave the cumulene VII.   Kuhn interpreted the synthesis of diphenyl-
cumulenes by this reaction as involving replacement of the two alcoholic hydroxyls
by iodine and spontaneous elimination of iodine.   The unsaturated system of VII
is so highly shielded by the eight methyl groups that it does not add bromine.
The next member of the series, having the system XI, was obtained by the reactions formulated.   Reaction of the diol VIII with phosphorus diiodide was not

[1] (Wolfgang) (Man)fred Schubert, b. 1920 Hannover, Germany; Ph.D. Minnesota (L. I.
Smith); Washington State Univ.

[2] Richard Kuhn, b. 1900 Vienna; Ph.D. Munich (Willstätter); Zurich; Heidelberg; Max
Planck Inst. Med. Res.; Nobel Prize 1938

satisfactory, but on reaction with phosphorus tribromide the initial product **IX** underwent double propargyl rearrangement to give **X**.   The cumulene **XI** adds only one mole of bromine and the product is **X**.

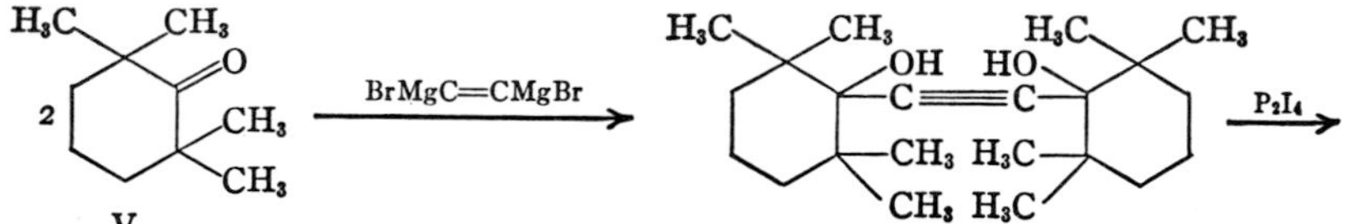

V

BrMgC≡CMgBr →

VI

P₂I₄ →

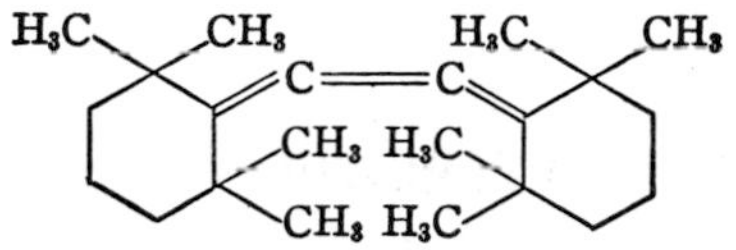

VII

$$2 \underset{}{>}C=O \ + \ BrMgC\equiv C-C\equiv C-MgBr \ \longrightarrow \ \overset{OH}{\underset{}{>}}C-C\equiv C-C\equiv C-\overset{OH}{\underset{}{C}}< \ \xrightarrow{PBr_3}$$

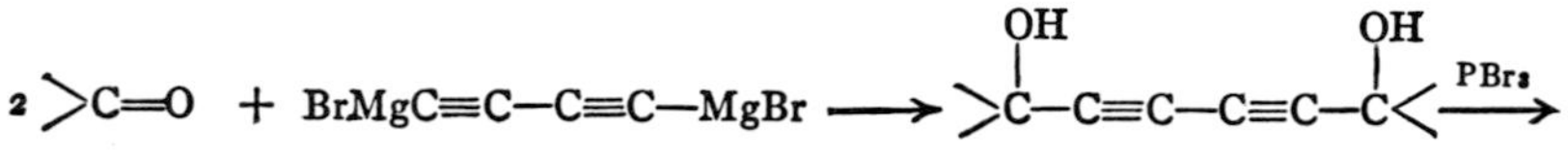

VIII

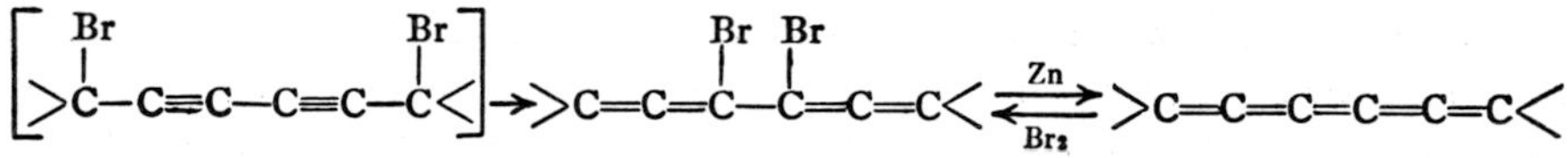

IX   X   XI

PROBLEMS

1. Suggest a possible mechanism for the dehydrohalogenation of $CH_3CHClCH=CH(C\equiv C)_2CH=CHCHClCH_3$ (equation 7, Section 6.6).
2. Show how $ClCH_2C\equiv CCH_2Cl$ can be used for the synthesis of:
   (a) $CH_3C\equiv CC\equiv CH$ (c) $CH_3C\equiv CC\equiv CC\equiv CC\equiv CCH_3$
   (b) $CH_3C\equiv CC\equiv CCH_3$
3. On the assumption of an analogy to the acetylene rearrangement discovered by Favorsky, account for the following isomerization brought about by hot potassium hydroxide solution.

$$CH_2=CHCH_2CH_2CH_2CH_2CO_2H \rightarrow CH_3CH_2CH_2CH_2CH=CHCOOH$$

4. How could phenylacetylene be prepared from acetophenone, $C_6H_5COCH_3$?
5. Suggest a reaction sequence by means of which fumaric acid could be transformed into its geometrical isomer, maleic acid.
6. Write an electronic formulation that accounts for the diazine synthesis of acetylenes.
7. The acid $C_6H_5CH_2CH_2C\equiv CCO_2H$ is isomerized by alkali; what is the product?
8. The reaction of ethoxyacetylene with a carboxylic acid in an inert solvent provides an efficient method for the preparation of an anhydride.   Formulate the reaction.
9. Formulate the following synthesis. (a) Sodium acetylide is prepared by a titration technique which avoids the presence of excess acetylene: acetylene is passed into liquid ammonia and sodium is added in small portions at such a rate that no blue color develops for any length of time. (b) One equivalent of *n*-propyl iodide is added, followed by (c) one equivalent of sodamide, and then by (d) one equivalent of 1-chloro-4-bromobutane.

Chapter 7

PETROLEUM

7.1   **Introduction.** — The theory that petroleum results from the decomposition of organic matter, probably of marine origin, is supported by observation of small but significant optical activity in at least some petroleum fractions.   The dark brown or greenish viscous oil occurs, along with natural gas, in the interstices of granular rocks (limestones, sandstones) in the upper strata of the earth entrapped by overlying nonporous rock (L. *petra*, rock + *oleum*, oil). When a well is drilled through the cap, oil for a time is forced to the surface until the pressure subsides and then is removed by pump.   Natural gas flowing from a well consists largely of methane and gaseous homologs but contains dissolved C_5–C_7 hydrocarbons which are normally liquid.   The raw gas is processed for recovery of this material, known as **natural gasoline,** either by compression sufficient to liquefy the less volatile constituents or by passage of the gas through a scrubber from which the natural gasoline can be recovered by distillation.   Natural gasoline accounts for about 10% of the total straight-run gasoline; it once served largely as a blend to increase the vapor pressure of refinery gasoline, but natural gasoline is now valued as starting material for petrochemical production. The residual gas is either separated into its components or carried by pipeline for use as domestic or industrial fuel.

Petroleum is refined near the oil field if labor and transportation are available, or is shipped by tanker or pipeline to suitably located refineries.   Refining involves separation into fractions of different boiling point ranges by distillation and reprocessing of specific fractions.   The principal fractions are: petroleum ether (b.p. 20–60°, pentanes, hexanes), ligroin or light naphtha (b.p. 60–120°, hexanes, heptanes), gasoline (b.p. 40–205°), kerosene (b.p. 175–325°), gas oil (b.p. above 275°).   Finally, vacuum distillation affords lubricating oil and leaves a residue that is either asphalt or residual fuel oil, depending upon the nature of the petroleum. The United States production of petroleum in millions of barrels per year rose from 0.44 in 1920 to nearly 3.5 in 1960.

CONSTITUENTS

7.2   **Hydrocarbons.** — Natural gas, freed of natural gasoline by com-
           pressors or oil scrubbers, contains methane as the chief hydrocarbon
constituent, together with decreasing amounts of ethane, propane, butane, and isobutane; varying amounts of carbon dioxide, nitrogen, or sometimes helium, are also present. Since the lower paraffins differ considerably in boiling point from one another and from nitrogen and helium, the components of a given natural gas can be separated efficiently by liquefaction and fractional distillation under pressure at low temperature. Pure products obtained in this way and their boiling points are: methane ($-162°$), ethane ($-89°$), propane ($-42°$), and helium ($-269°$). Compressed propane from this source is available in cylinders for use in heating, soldering, and as a motor fuel. Methane and ethane are converted by cracking into acetylene and ethylene.

Natural gasoline contains paraffins ranging from C_3 to C_8 in the following approximate proportion: C_3–C_4, 20%; C_5, 30%; C_6, 24%; C_7, 20%; C_8, 4%; residue, 2%. One useful fraction, called the C_4-cut, is easily separated from propane and from C_5-alkanes and consists of n-butane and isobutane. The C_5-cut contains n-pentane and isopentane in about equal amounts and a negligible

$$CH_3CH_2CH_2CH_3 \qquad\qquad \overset{CH_3}{\underset{CH_3}{\diagdown}}CHCH_3$$

Butane, b.p. $-0.5°$ Isobutane, b.p. $-12°$

$$\underbrace{\qquad\qquad\qquad\qquad\qquad\qquad\qquad\qquad}_{C_4\text{-cut}}$$

$$CH_3CH_2CH_2CH_2CH_3 \qquad \overset{CH_3}{\underset{CH_3}{\diagdown}}CHCH_2CH_3 \qquad CH_3-\overset{CH_3}{\underset{CH_3}{\overset{|}{\underset{|}{C}}}}-CH_3 \text{ (minor component)}$$

n-Pentane, b.p. 36°   Isopentane, b.p. 28°   Neopentane, b.p. 9.5°

$$\underbrace{\qquad\qquad\qquad\qquad\qquad\qquad\qquad\qquad}_{C_5\text{-cut}}$$

amount of neopentane; this fraction is separated easily, since the least volatile C_4-hydrocarbon, n-butane, boils at $-0.5°$, and the most volatile C_5-hydrocarbon, trimethylethylmethane, boils at 49.7°.

Efficient methods now available for the analysis of hydrocarbon mixtures employ gas chromatography, mass spectrometry, and infrared spectroscopy. In 1927, before these techniques had become available, Rossini[1] et al. of the National Bureau of Standards initiated an extensive investigation of a Midcontinent petroleum, largely by precision distillation, and succeeded in isolating and identifying 175 pure hydrocarbons. n-Alkanes accounted for a total of 29% of the

---

[1] Frederick D. Rossini, b. 1912 Buffalo, Iowa; Ph.D. California; Bureau of Standards; Carnegie Inst. Techn.; Univ. Notre Dame

gasoline fraction, and branched alkanes accounted for 15%. All the *n*-alkanes through tritriacontane ($C_{33}H_{68}$) were isolated. Branched chain alkanes isolated (37) included four C_6-isomers, eight C_7-isomers, and seventeen C_8-alkanes.

In addition to the open-type hydrocarbons, petroleum contains varying amounts of cycloparaffins known in petroleum technology as **naphthenes**. Thirty-eight of these have been isolated from the gasoline fraction discussed above; they are alkyl derivatives of cyclopentane and cyclohexane, both of which are also present. Typical naphthenes are shown in the formulas:

$$\begin{array}{cc}
\begin{array}{c} C(CH_3)_2 \\ H_2C \quad\quad CH_2 \\ | \quad\quad\quad | \\ H_2C \text{——} CH_2 \end{array} &
\begin{array}{c} CHCH_3 \\ H_2C \quad\quad CH_2 \\ | \quad\quad\quad | \\ H_2C \text{——} CHCH_3 \end{array}
\end{array}$$

1,1-Dimethylcyclopentane   1,3-Dimethylcyclopentane
(b. p. 87.5°)   (b. p. 90.9°)

$$\begin{array}{cc}
\begin{array}{c} CHCH_2CH_3 \\ H_2C \quad\quad CH_2 \\ | \quad\quad\quad | \\ H_2C \quad\quad CH_2 \\ CH_2 \end{array} &
\begin{array}{c} CHCH_3 \\ H_2C \quad\quad CHCH_3 \\ | \quad\quad\quad | \\ H_2C \quad\quad CH_2 \\ CHCH_3 \end{array}
\end{array}$$

Ethylcyclohexane   1,2,4-Trimethylcyclohexane
(b. p. 131.8°)   (b. p. 141.2°)

Most petroleums also contain aromatic hydrocarbons. The total aromatic content of Borneo crudes is estimated at 39%, and in World War I this petroleum was an important source of toluene, a strategic material for the preparation of the high explosive trinitrotoluene (TNT). Nineteen aromatics were isolated by the Bureau of Standards group from the gasoline fraction. Typical ones are formulated:

Benzene   Toluene   Cumene   Pseudocumene
(b. p. 80.1°)   (b. p. 110.6°)   (isopropylbenzene,   (b. p. 169.2°)
b. p. 152.4°)

The relative proportion of the three types of hydrocarbons varies in different crude gasolines, even from the same general locality; the content of naphthenes and aromatics may vary from a few percent to as much as 40%. The aniline point, defined as the temperature at which a given gasoline is miscible with an equal volume of aniline, has been used as an indication of the approximate hydrocarbon composition. Since aniline, $C_6H_5NH_2$, is a derivative of benzene, aromatic hydrocarbons dissolve even at temperatures as low as −30°. Naphthenes have higher aniline points (35–55°), and paraffins, which are most dissimilar to aniline, the highest (70–76°). The specific gravities have been used also as a similar index of composition; aromatic hydrocarbons have the highest values (benzene = 0.89), straight-chain paraffins the lowest (*n*-hexane = 0.66), and cyclic hydrocarbons intermediate values (cyclohexane = o.78). One method of analysis takes advantage of the fact that aromatics can be separated fairly readily from paraffins and naphthenes by adsorption. In another method the aromatic content is determined from the percent absorbed by sulfuric acid:

$$C_6H_6 + H_2SO_4 \xrightarrow{P_2O_5} C_6H_5SO_3H + H_2O$$

and the amounts of paraffins and naphthenes in the residue are determined from the density and refractive index.

Eleven hydrocarbons isolated from the kerosene fraction of the above Mid-continent crude include one paraffin, n-dodecane (b.p. 216.3°), three alkyl derivatives of benzene, naphthalene, and two alkyl derivatives, α- and β-methylnaph-

Naphthalene   Tetralin

thalene, which had been isolated previously as the less soluble complexes that they form with picric acid, $HOC_6H_2(NO_2)_3$. The additional four substances contain a benzene ring fused to a cycloparaffin ring, such as tetralin (1,2,3,4-tetrahydro-naphthalene, b.p. 207.6°) and two alkyl derivatives, 1- and 2-methyl-5,6,7,8-tetrahydronaphthalene (b.p. 234°, 229°).

7.3   Naphthenic Acid. — Extraction of petroleum with alkali and acidification of the alkaline solution gives a black viscous tar known as naphthenic acid, since the constituents are mainly cycloparaffin acids derived from naphthene components. Investigations by Markownikoff (1899) and by von Braun[1] (1931–33) showed that only minor amounts of paraffinic acids are present [e.g., $(CH_3)_2CHCH_2CH_2CH_2CO_2H$ and n-$C_{15}H_{31}CO_2H$], and that the lowest boiling fraction contains C_8–C_{12} acids of the general formula I, in which n, the number of methylene groups, is 1 to 5. Acids whose analyses indicate the presence of two and three rings were also encountered. The further naphthenic acids II–IV were isolated by Nenitzescu[2] (1938); acids V–VII, two of which are cyclohexane derivatives, were isolated and characterized by a group at the University of Texas. Analysis of fractions from the high-boiling naphthenic acids of lubricating oils indicate that they are monobasic C_{14}–C_{19} acids with an average of 2.6 rings.

I (R=H or alkyl)

Naphthenic acids occur in larger amounts (3%) in Russian, Roumanian, and Polish oils than in American oils (o.1–o.3%), but since extraction of petroleum with alkali is a usual part of the refining operations and since the volume of U. S.

[1] Julius von Braun, 1875–1939; b. Warsaw; Ph.D. Göttingen (Wallach); Univ. Frankfurt, Germany

[2] Costin D. Nenitzescu, b. 1902 Bucharest, Roumania; Dr. Ing. Techn. Hochschule Munich (Hans Fischer); Polytechnical Institute, Bucharest

production is enormous, naphthenic acid is available for technical uses in large quantity. Most uses require conversion into a water-insoluble metallic salt, or soap, of aluminum or of a heavy metal, either by precipitation from an alkaline solution or, in the case of aluminum, by fusion with an aqueous aluminum hy-

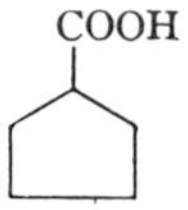

COOH	CH₂COOH	CH₂COOH
Cyclopentane-carboxylic acid	Cyclopentyl-acetic acid	3-Methylcyclopentyl-acetic acid
II	III	IV

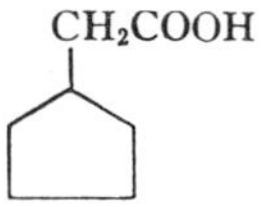

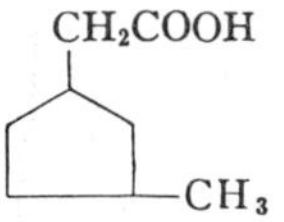

droxide gel. These soaps are amorphous solids or tough gums; in contrast to sodium soaps of paraffinic acids, they are soluble in hydrocarbon solvents.

A certain amount of naphthenic acid goes into the manufacture of the lead, cobalt, and manganese soaps for use as driers (oxidation catalysts) in paint and varnish formulations. Copper naphthenate is used for mildew-proofing sandbags, rope for use at sea, and other wood, cotton, jute, and hemp products. The fungicidal action is associated with the copper present, but copper naphthenate is

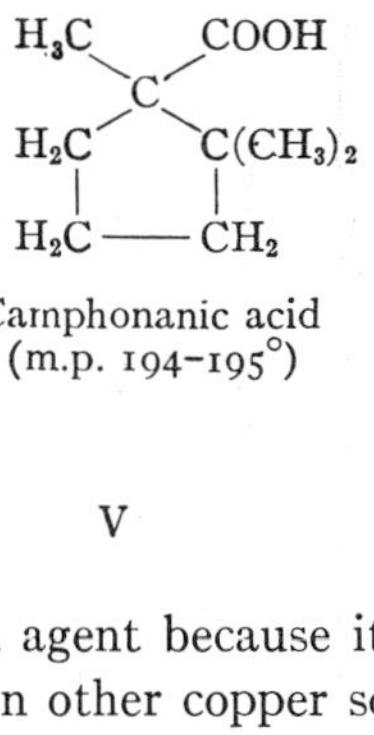

Camphonanic acid (m.p. 194–195°)	4-Methylcyclohexane-carboxylic acid (m.p. 110–111°)	2,2,6-Trimethylcyclo-hexanecarboxylic acid (m.p. 83°)
V	VI	VII

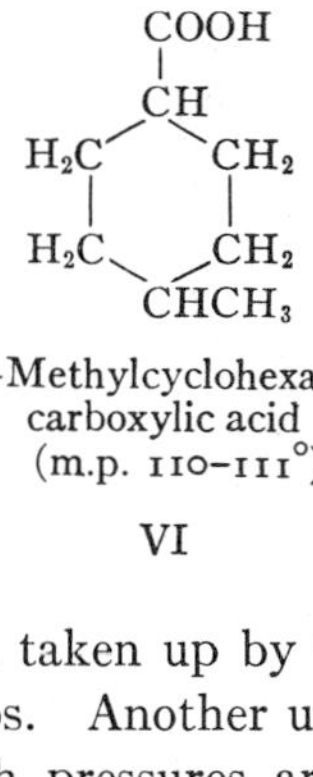

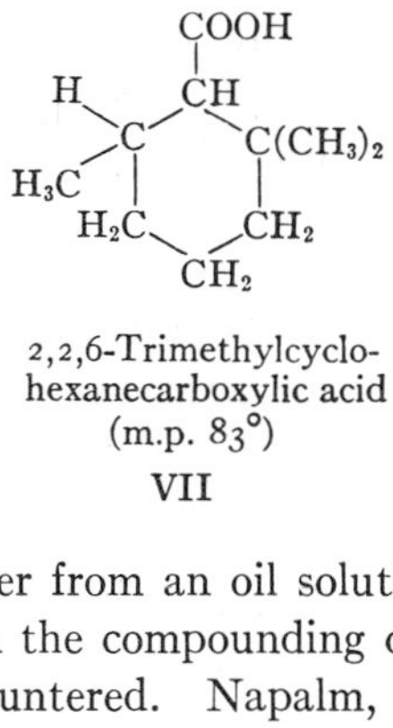

a preferred agent because it is taken up by the fiber from an oil solution more readily than other copper soaps. Another use is in the compounding of special lubricants required where high pressures are encountered. Napalm, a coprecipitated aluminum soap from naphthenic acid and the fatty acids of coconut oil developed in 1942 (L. F. Fieser, G. C. Harris, E. B. Hershberg, M. Morgana, F. C. Novello, and S. T. Putnam), was used in the war for preparation of gasoline gels for incendiary bombs and flame throwers. The granular powder solvates rapidly and brief aging gives a tough, sticky gel which retains the same consistency at temperatures from −40° to over 100°.

7.4   Sulfur and Nitrogen Compounds. — Petroleums contain sulfur compounds in amounts up to about one percent. These are objectionable because of a disagreeable odor (mercaptans) and because even the combined sulfur in gasoline is oxidized during combustion to sulfur dioxide, which is corrosive in the presence of moisture (sulfurous acid). Specifications for government purchases allow 0.10% as the maximum sulfur content of gasoline. A certain number of the sulfur compounds have been identified and they are of the three types corresponding to the paraffins, naphthenes, and aromatics of the hydrocarbon constituents.

$$(CH_3)_2CHCH_2SH$$

Isobutyl mercaptan

$$CH_3SC_2H_5$$

Methyl ethyl sulfide

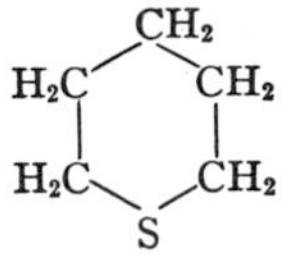

Pentamethylene sulfide 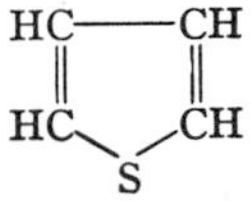   Thiophene

The nitrogen content of most petroleums is very low, for instance, 0.008% for Pennsylvanian oils. Some of the nitrogen compounds are basic and can be extracted with sulfur dioxide or mineral acids. The only nitrogen bases of known structure are quinoline derivatives, formulas VIII–X (J. R. Bailey).

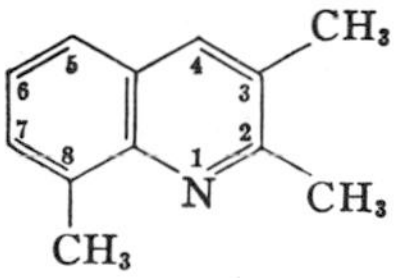

2,3,8-Trimethyl-
quinoline

VIII

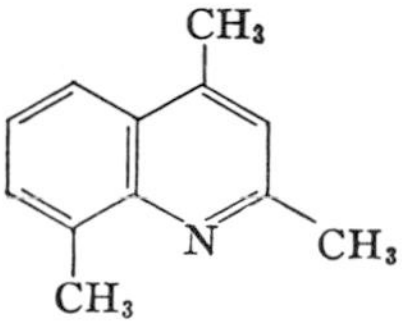

2,4,8-Trimethyl-
quinoline

IX

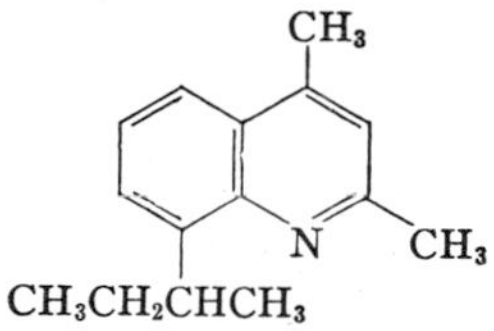

2,4-Dimethyl-8-
sec-butylquinoline

X

MOTOR FUELS

7.5   **Fuel Knock and Octane Rating.** — The knock (or ping) heard when an automobile engine under stress is accelerated too rapidly is a warning that conditions for efficient performance of the engine with the particular gasoline used have been exceeded. In the down-stroke of the piston a mixture of air and gasoline vapor and droplets is drawn from the carburetor into the cylinder, and on the up-stroke the mixture is compressed; the ratio of the initial volume to the final volume is the compression ratio. At the end of the up-stroke a spark from the ignition system ignites the compressed air-gasoline mixture in the immediate vicinity of the spark plug and, in normal operation, the gases expand and a flame-front travels at a regular and orderly rate through the remainder of the fuel mixture to give a power thrust transmitted by the piston to the crankshaft. If the stress is excessive, however, the major portion of the fuel mixture burns in an orderly fashion but in doing so compresses the end gas, that is, the gas furthest from the point of ignition, and produces in it a preflame reaction which lowers its ignition temperature. In consequence, the end gas burns in an explosive and disorderly fashion ahead of the flame front and so produces the sound of knocking. Knocking increases with increasing compression ratio, and since an engine develops more power and requires less fuel with increasing compression ratio, the development of efficient high-compression engines was dependent upon the knocking tendencies of available gasolines.

With recognition that gasolines vary greatly in this property, standards were introduced for rating fuels (1927). Isooctane (2,2,4-trimethylpentane), which detonates only at high compression and which was superior to any gasoline known at the time, was assigned the octane rating of 100, and n-heptane, which is particularly prone to knocking, was given the octane number of 0. The octane number of a given fuel is the percent of isooctane in a blend with n-heptane that has the same knocking characteristics of the fuel under examination in a standard one-cylinder engine operated under specific conditions. Determination of the octane ratings of a large number of synthetic hydrocarbons has shown that in the alkane series octane number decreases as the carbon chain is lengthened and increases with branching of the chain. Alkenes have higher ratings than the corresponding alkanes, and the octane number increases as the double bond is shifted to the center of the molecule. Cycloparaffins are less prone to knock than normal paraffins, and aromatic hydrocarbons have exceptionally high octane numbers.

The straight-run gasolines provided by distillation of petroleum consist mainly of alkanes, and as a result the octane rating varies from as high as 80 to as low as 28 (Michigan). However, technological improvements have so increased octane ratings that engines of the nineteen twenties with a compression ratio of some 4:1 have given place to models of superior efficiency of ratios of 9–10 to 1.

7.6   Antiknock Compound. — The steady improvement in antiknock characteristics of gasoline is due in part to new technological processes, but the first major advance was the discovery that knocking can be suppressed by addition of certain chemicals, the most important of which is tetraethyllead (TEL), developed by T. Midgley and T. A. Boyd (1922). After the initial observation that iodine, aniline, and selenium oxychloride are somewhat effective in decreasing knock, study of innumerable substances led to the organometallic compound, which still retains its supremacy. Most American gasolines contain tetraethyllead; gasolines leaded to the point of an octane rating of about 93 are known to the trade as Ethyl or premium gasoline. An early synthesis utilized the Grignard reaction:

$$4 \ C_2H_5MgBr + 2 \ PbCl_2 \rightarrow Pb(C_2H_5)_4 + 4 \ MgClBr + Pb$$

The commercial process now consists in interaction of a sodium–lead alloy with ethyl chloride at moderate temperatures and pressures:

$$4 \ PbNa + 4 \ C_2H_5Cl \rightarrow Pb(C_2H_5)_4 + 4 \ NaCl + 3 \ Pb$$

The lead derivative is separated by steam distillation, and the lead sludge is smelted into pig lead.

Ethyl fluid contains not only tetraethyllead (63%), but also ethylene dibromide (26%), ethylene dichloride (9%), and a dye (2%). Ethylene dibromide is an essential constituent since it reacts with the lead oxide produced during combustion to form volatile lead bromide, which is swept from the cylinders in the exhaust gases. The manufacture of large amounts of ethylene dibromide presented a problem, since bromine was not available in sufficient quantity. The dificulty was solved by extraction of bromine from sea water, 7.5 tons of which contain one pound of bromine. An early process, operated on board the S.S. "Ethyl," extracted bromine by adding aniline to chlorinated sea water, and recovering bromine from the filtered precipitate of 2,4,6-tribromoaniline. In the modern process, bromine is liberated from natural bromine-containing brines by oxidation

$$3 \text{ Na}_2\text{CO}_3 + 3 \text{ Br}_2 \rightarrow 5 \text{ NaBr} + \text{NaBrO}_3 + 3 \text{ CO}_2$$

with chlorine, entrained in a current of air, and absorbed in sodium carbonate solution, from which it can be recovered easily. The efficiency is 95%.

The amount of tetraethyllead in motor gasoline ranges from 0.75 to 3 ml. per gal., the legal maximum; aviation gasolines are more heavily leaded. The susceptibility of various gasolines depends upon the initial octane number and the hydrocarbon composition. The response is greater for low-octane gasolines, and hence tetraethyllead decreases in effectiveness with increasing concentration. Development of modern high compression engines operating on highly aromatic, high octane gasolines is leading to increased use of tetramethyllead, which is more stable than the ethyl derivative at the high temperatures generated and which gives superior antiknock response under severe engine conditions.

7.7   Diesel and Jet Fuels. — In Diesel engines the air alone is compressed, with the result that the temperature is increased to 290–340°. The fuel is injected almost at the end of the compression stroke and is spontaneously ignited. Diesel fuel need not be volatile, and generally consists of the fraction boiling between kerosene and the heavier lubricating oils. Owing to differences in engine construction, high octane fuels are much less efficient than low ones. The ignition quality is expressed in terms of the cetane number, which refers to a mixture of cetane (*n*-hexadecane, value = 100) and α-methylnaphthalene (value = 0); most automotive Diesel engines require a fuel of cetane number greater than 45; that is, the desirability of hydrocarbons is exactly reversed for the Diesel as compared with the ordinary engine.

Jet fuel is made from kerosene taken from selected crudes and processed for improvement of thermal stability. Aromatics are objectionable because they burn with a smoky flame and lead to fuel loss. *n*-Alkanes burn well but their higher melting points may lead to inferior flow properties at low temperatures.

7.8   Gasoline Manufacture. — The advent of the automobile created a demand for an increase in the amount of gasoline obtainable from crude oil beyond that afforded by simple refinery distillation. The process of thermal cracking, or heating under pressure, met this first objective, for pyrolysis transforms the large molecules of the kerosene fraction into mixtures of smaller hydrocarbons having the desired volatility. Thus thermal cracking more than doubled the yield of motor gasoline obtainable from crude oil. Furthermore, gasolines produced by thermal cracking were found to be superior in quality to most virgin gasolines. Recognition that the difference is due to an increased content of olefins, which have superior antiknock properties, led to development of the process of thermal reforming, in which a straight-run gasoline is heated under pressure to effect transformations that improve the quality of the material as motor fuel. Thermal cracking and thermal reforming both lead to production of considerable amounts of gaseous hydrocarbons, including ethylene and other simple olefins. The availability of these products prompted the search for methods for their utilization. One outlet was found in processes for conversion of the gaseous products, by polymerization and other means, into gasoline; another was in employing olefinic fractions as starting materials for the synthesis of petrochemicals.

The thermal processes, however, had limitations. Study of the knocking characteristics of pure hydrocarbons had indicated that high quality gasoline should consist predominantly of highly branched paraffins, branched and internally unsaturated olefins and cyclic olefins, and aromatics. Thermal cracking does not increase branching, it does not lead to cyclization, and the olefins produced are largely of the undesirable α-olefin type. The search for improvement led to the vastly superior methods of catalytic cracking and catalytic reforming, which increase branching, produce internal olefins, and effect cyclization and aromatization. The catalytic methods thus ideally meet the requirement for improvement in quality and, in gasoline manufacture, have completely supplanted the thermal methods. The difference is one of reaction types. Thermal cracking involves free radical chain reactions (Rice,[1] 1931); catalytic cracking employs an acidic catalyst and proceeds by ionic reactions. Mechanisms worked out by petroleum technologists are summarized in the sections that follow.

7.9   Thermal cracking. — The initiating reaction in thermal cracking, illustrated for simplicity for an n-alkane, is homolysis of a carbon–carbon bond to produce two radicals (1). A radical $R\dot{C}H_2$ can then attack an alkane, as in (2), to produce a smaller alkane, RCH_3, and a new radical in which

$$1. \quad R\overset{H}{\underset{H}{C}}:\overset{H}{\underset{H}{C}}R' \longrightarrow R\overset{H}{\underset{H}{C}}\cdot \;+\; \cdot\overset{H}{\underset{H}{C}}R'$$

$$2. \quad R\dot{C}H_2 \;+\; RCH_2CH_2CH_2CH_2CH_2CH_3 \longrightarrow RCH_3 \;+$$

$$RCH_2CH_2CH_2CH_2\dot{C}HCH_2CH_3$$

$$3. \quad RCH_2CH_2CH_2 | CH_2\dot{C}HCH_2CH_3 \longrightarrow RCH_2CH_2\dot{C}H_2 \;+\; CH_2{=}CHCH_2CH_3$$

$$4. \quad RCH_2 | CH_2\dot{C}H_2 \longrightarrow R\dot{C}H_2 \;+\; CH_2{=}CH_2$$

5.

$$\cdot\dot{C}H_2 \underset{RCH_2CH_2}{\overset{CH_2}{\diagdown}}\underset{CH_2}{\overset{CH_2}{\diagup}} \longrightarrow CH_3 \underset{RCH_2\dot{C}H}{\overset{CH_2}{\diagdown}}\underset{CH_2}{\overset{CH_2}{\diagup}}$$

$$6. \quad RCH_2CH_2\dot{C}H_2 \;+\; \dot{C}H_3 \longrightarrow RCH_2CH_2CH_2CH_3$$

the odd electron is located on an internal carbon atom, since a secondary radical is more stable than a primary one (5.18). The new radical then suffers β-fission

---

[1] Francis O. Rice, b. 1890 Liverpool, England; D.Sc. Liverpool; Johns Hopkins Univ.; Catholic Univ.

(3) to give an α-olefin and a smaller primary radical, which in turn undergoes β-fission to give ethylene (4). Repetition of the process of β-fission accounts for the large amount of ethylene produced in thermal cracking. Free radicals do not undergo isomerization involving either migration of alkyl groups or shift of the odd electron from one carbon atom to the next in the chain. However, since a primary radical is less stable than one that is secondary or tertiary, a long-chain primary radical can coil back on itself as in (5) and transfer the unshared electron to a secondary or tertiary position five or six carbon atoms back along the chain. This reaction is important because it results in production of less ethylene and more gasoline components. The terminating step of recombination of radicals (6) is very fast, but under cracking conditions the radicals are so diluted with hydrocarbons that collision with hydrocarbons is much more frequent than collision with another radical.

7.10   Catalytic Cracking. — The feed to a catalytic cracking unit is ordinarily a gas oil of boiling range of about 250–500°. Vaporized or partly vaporized feed comes in contact with the catalyst under slight pressure at a temperature of 450–550°. The catalysts are solid acids. One type is a natural clay which has been leached with acid to remove alkaline materials and to increase porosity. The most widely used cracking catalyst is a synthetic silica (87%)–alumina (13%) composite similar to the acid-washed clay; it has a surface area of about 500 m.²/g., a pore volume of 0.55 ml./g., and an acidity of 0.25 meq./g. The catalyst in use rapidly becomes deactivated by coke deposits and the activity is restored by frequently burning off the deposits with air.

Catalytic cracking is an ionic process involving carbonium ions, which arise in various ways. One is by donation of a proton by the catalyst to an olefin (1). A proton may be returned to the catalyst or transferred to another olefin, which in turn becomes a carbonium ion, but the position of departure may be different

1. $RCH_2CH{=}CH_2 \underset{}{\overset{H^+}{\rightleftarrows}} RCH_2\overset{+}{C}HCH_3 \underset{}{\overset{-H^+}{\rightleftarrows}} RCH{=}CHCH_3$

2. $(CH_3)_3C{:}H \rightleftarrows (CH_3)_3C^+ + {:}H^-$

3. $(CH_3)_3C{:}H + RCH_2\overset{+}{C}HCH_3 \rightleftarrows (CH_3)_3C^+ + RCH_2CH_2CH_3$

from that of arrival. The result is a shift of the double bond along the chain, with conversion of α-olefins into more valuable internally unsaturated olefins. Other reactions producing carbonium ions are: (2) abstraction of a hydride ion from a paraffin by an electron-deficient zone on the catalyst surface, and (3) withdrawal of hydride ion by another carbonium ion.

Reactions of carbonium ions involved in catalytic cracking are summarized as follows. A hydride shift (4) moves the charge from one carbon to the next. Since the energy level decreases as the charge moves toward the center of the chain and maximum stability is reached when the charge is located two to four carbons from the end of the chain, the process favors formation of internally unsaturated olefins. Equation (5) shows a methide shift followed by shift of a hydride ion to give a tertiary ion; the result is an increase in branching.

Reaction (6), a true cracking process, consists in fission of the carbon chain of a carbonium ion at each position β to the positive charge. The chain usually

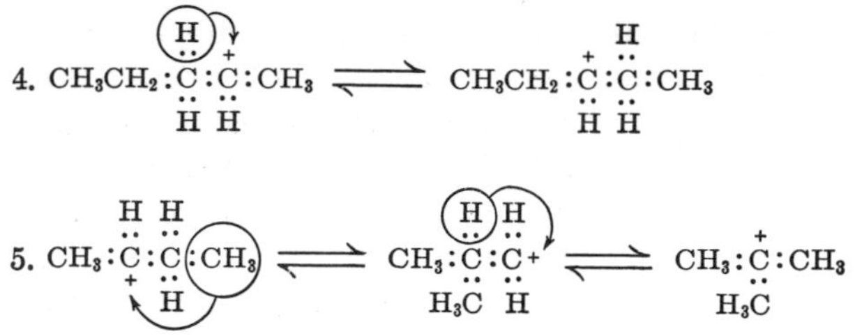

4. $CH_3CH_2:\overset{\overset{(H)}{\cdot\cdot}}{\underset{H}{C}}:\overset{+}{\underset{H}{C}}:CH_3$ $\rightleftharpoons$ $CH_3CH_2:\overset{+}{\underset{H}{C}}:\overset{\overset{H}{\cdot\cdot}}{\underset{H}{C}}:CH_3$

5. $CH_3:\overset{\overset{H}{\cdot\cdot}}{\underset{\overset{+}{H}}{C}}:\overset{\overset{H}{\cdot\cdot}}{C}:(CH_3)$ $\rightleftharpoons$ $CH_3:\overset{\overset{(H)H}{\cdot\cdot}}{\underset{H_3C\ \ H}{C}}:\overset{+}{C}$ $\rightleftharpoons$ $CH_3:\overset{+}{\underset{H_3C}{C}}:CH_3$

breaks at a point such that the smallest fragment contains at least three carbon atoms. The reaction products are smaller carbonium ions and olefins. Unlike β-fission of a free radical, β-fission of an ion does not continue stepwise along the

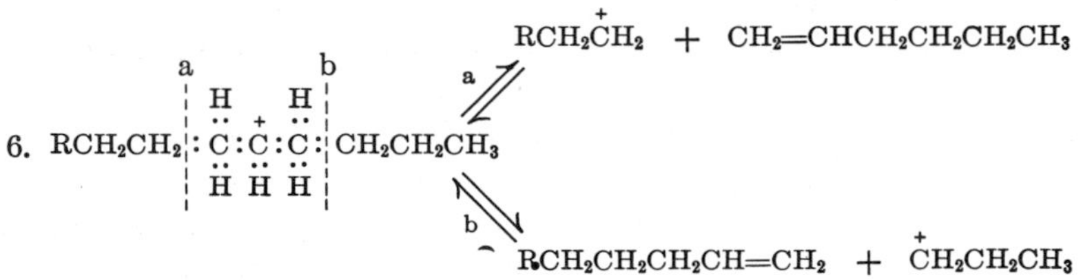

6. $RCH_2CH_2\overset{a}{\vdots}\overset{\overset{H}{\cdot\cdot}}{\underset{H}{C}}:\overset{+}{\underset{H}{C}}:\overset{\overset{H}{\cdot\cdot}}{\underset{H}{C}}\overset{b}{\vdots}CH_2CH_2CH_3$

$\overset{a}{\nearrow}$ $R\overset{+}{C}H_2\overset{+}{C}H_2 \ + \ CH_2{=}CHCH_2CH_2CH_2CH_3$

$\overset{b}{\searrow}$ $RCH_2CH_2CH_2CH{=}CH_2 \ + \ \overset{+}{C}H_2CH_2CH_3$

chain with production of ethylene, probably because the new carbonium ion produced by β-fission is primary and rearranges before further fission can occur.

Cyclization probably involves self-alkylation of an olefinic carbonium ion (7) in a reaction which is essentially a reverse β-fission. Catalytic cracking also pro-

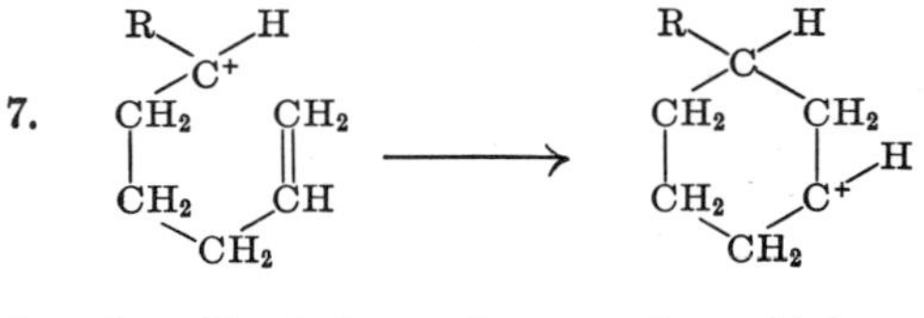

7.

duces large quantities of cyclic olefins and aromatics, which may arise in a series of steps starting with transfer of a proton from a cyclic carbonium ion to an olefin (8a). The cyclic olefin then transfers a hydride ion to the new carbonium ion

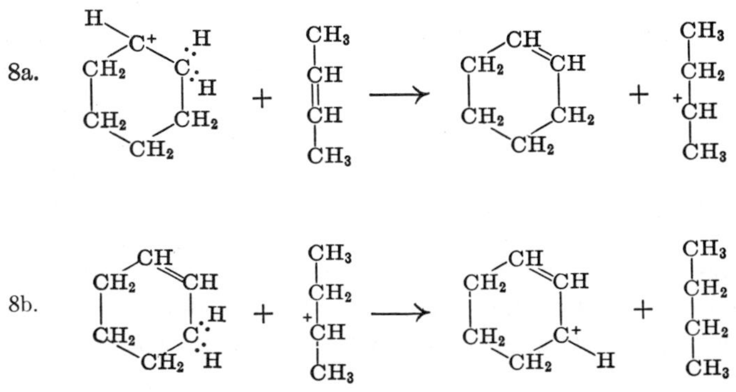

8a.

8b.

(8b) to produce a cyclic olefinic carbonium ion and a paraffin, and repetition of the process eventually affords an aromatic hydrocarbon.

The mechanisms cited show why the catalytic product is rich in branched chain products, in olefins of the most desirable type, and in high quality cyclic olefins and aromatics. Another advantage of catalytic over thermal cracking lies in a more favorable distribution in the boiling range of the fragments. Thus on thermal cracking of cetane the characteristic fragment size is C_2, and ethylene predominates; catalytic cracking gives a maximum at C_4 and the product is a mixture of butanes and butenes. Catalytic cracking of gas oil affords valuable light gasoline components in the C_5 and C_6 range in high yield. In addition to the gasoline fractions produced directly, unsaturated C_3- and C_4-cuts and iso-butane from catalytic cracking are converted into additional high quality gasoline by the processes of polymerization and alkylation.

7.11 **Polymer Gasoline.** — The unsaturated gaseous hydrocarbons pro-duced in cracking are valuable starting materials for the production of high-octane motor fuels. The first large-scale use involved polymerization of a cracked fraction rich in gaseous olefins to a liquid product known as polymer gasoline, of octane number about 90. The process of polymerization, usually induced by phosphoric or sulfuric acid (Ipatieff, 1935), is chiefly one of dimeriza-

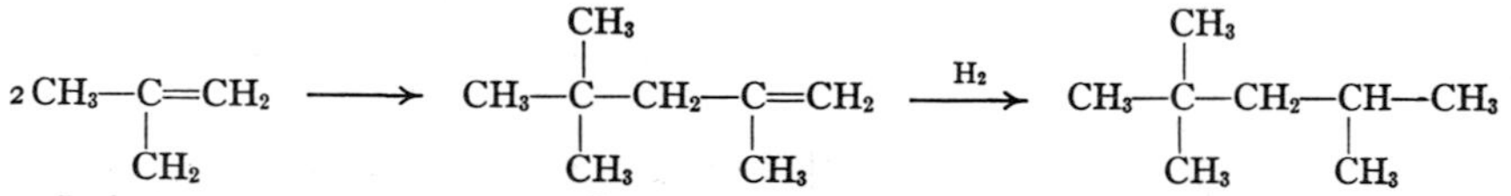

$$2\ CH_3-\underset{\underset{CH_2}{|}}{C}=CH_2 \longrightarrow CH_3-\underset{\underset{CH_3}{|}}{\overset{\overset{CH_3}{|}}{C}}-CH_2-\underset{\underset{CH_3}{|}}{C}=CH_2 \xrightarrow{H_2} CH_3-\underset{\underset{CH_3}{|}}{\overset{\overset{CH_3}{|}}{C}}-CH_2-\underset{\underset{CH_3}{|}}{CH}-CH_3$$

Isobutene   Isooctene   Isooctane
                                       (diisobutylene)

tion. Thus isobutene yields the dimer isooctene, which consists mainly of 2,4,4-trimethylpentene-1 but contains about 20% of 2,4,4-trimethylpentene-2. Both isomers on hydrogenation yield isooctane, which in a pure form ·has an octane number of 100. The acid-catalized polymerization can be interpreted by the following reaction mechanism. A proton first attacks the terminal carbon of the double bond in (a) to give t-butylcarbonium ion (b), rather than the alternate ion (b′), because in (b) the charged carbon is partially stabilized by three electron-releasing methyl groups whereas in (b′) only one stabilizing group is available. The t-butylcarbonium ion (b) then attacks a second molecule of isobutene to give the dimeric ion (c) in which three alkyl groups stabilize the charged center. In the completing step, which balances the initiating step of attack by a proton, a terminal hydrogen is eliminated with the charge as a proton, with consequent appearance of a double bond and formation of 2,4,4-trimethylpentene-1. About 20% of the product is the bond-isomer 2,4,4-trimethylpentene-2, resulting from elimination of hydrogen from (c) at position 3, rather than at position 1.

In practice isobutene is available as a component of the C_4-cut of cracked gaso-line, which also contains butenes (-1 and -2) and butanes (n- and i-). Isobutene, however, has greater affinity for sulfuric acid than the butenes, and when the fraction is passed into 65% sulfuric acid at 20–35°, isobutene is selectively ab-sorbed. The acid solution is then heated at 100° for about a minute, after which polymerization is complete. The product as such is too high-boiling for aviation fuel and is blended with more volatile hydrocarbons. A typical 100-octane aviation gasoline contains about 40% isooctane, 25% isopentane, 35% depen-

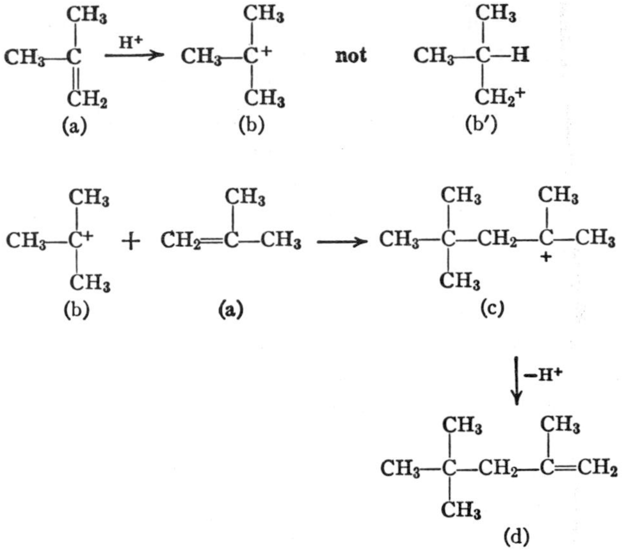

$$
\begin{array}{ccccc}
& \underset{|}{CH_3} & & \underset{|}{CH_3} & & \underset{|}{CH_3} \\
CH_3-\underset{\parallel}{C} & \xrightarrow{H^+} & CH_3-\underset{|}{C^+} & \quad not \quad & CH_3-\underset{|}{C}-H \\
CH_2 & & CH_3 & & CH_2{}^+ \\
(a) & & (b) & & (b')
\end{array}
$$

$$
\begin{array}{ccc}
\underset{|}{CH_3} & & \underset{|}{CH_3} \\
CH_3-\underset{|}{C^+} \ + \ CH_2{=}\underset{}{C}-CH_3 & \longrightarrow & CH_3-\underset{|}{C}-CH_2-\underset{+}{C}-CH_3 \\
CH_3 & & CH_3 \\
(b) & (a) & (c)
\end{array}
$$

$$\downarrow -H^+$$

$$
\begin{array}{c}
\underset{|}{CH_3} \qquad \underset{|}{CH_3} \\
CH_3-\underset{|}{C}-CH_2-\underset{}{C}{=}CH_2 \\
CH_3 \\
(d)
\end{array}
$$

Isooctene (2,4,4-trimethylpentene-1)

tanized base stock, and 4 ml. per gal. of tetraethyllead. Cumene is an excellent blending fuel in high-octane gasoline.

The polymerization reaction is applied extensively to propylene or to propylene-butylene mixtures, for the product then has the volatility required in a gasoline. The chief product from propylene alone is 2,3-dimethylbutene-2, probably formed in a sequence involving a cyclic intermediate.

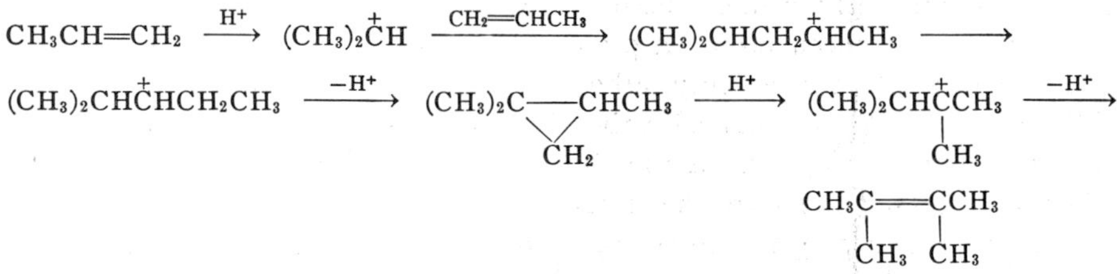

$$CH_3CH{=}CH_2 \xrightarrow{H^+} (CH_3)_2\overset{+}{C}H \xrightarrow{CH_2{=}CHCH_3} (CH_3)_2CHCH_2\overset{+}{C}HCH_3 \longrightarrow$$

$$(CH_3)_2CH\overset{+}{C}HCH_2CH_3 \xrightarrow{-H^+} (CH_3)_2C\underset{\underset{CH_2}{|}}{\overline{\quad\quad}}CHCH_3 \xrightarrow{H^+} (CH_3)_2CH\overset{+}{C}CH_3 \xrightarrow{-H^+}$$

$$CH_3C\underset{\underset{CH_3 \ CH_3}{|\quad\ |}}{\overline{=\!=\!=}}CCH_3$$

7.12   Alkylation. — A second reaction of considerable technological importance is the alkylation of an alkane with an olefin. The alkylation of isobutane with isobutene gives isooctane, and hence this important hydrocarbon

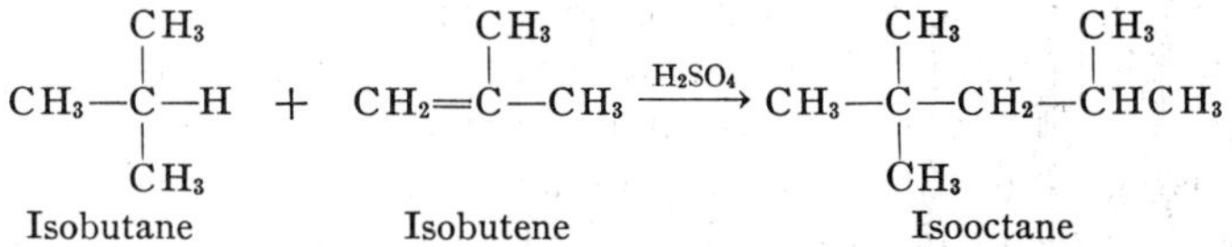

$$
\begin{array}{ccc}
\underset{|}{CH_3} & \underset{|}{CH_3} & \underset{|}{CH_3} \quad \underset{|}{CH_3} \\
CH_3-\underset{|}{C}-H \ + \ CH_2{=}\underset{}{C}-CH_3 & \xrightarrow{H_2SO_4} & CH_3-\underset{|}{C}-CH_2-\overset{}{C}HCH_3 \\
CH_3 & & CH_3 \\
\text{Isobutane} & \text{Isobutene} & \text{Isooctane}
\end{array}
$$

is obtained in one step by partial cracking of the isobutane in the C$_4$-cut to produce a mixture of the two components, which is then treated with sulfuric acid. The reaction is very similar to the dimerization, and it likewise involves in the first step protonation of isobutene to form trimethylcarbonium ion (b) and, in the second step, addition of ion (b) to isobutene to form ion (c), identical with that

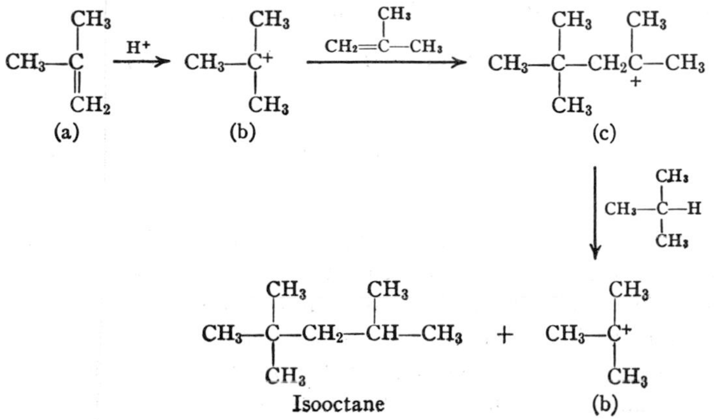

above. However, if isobutane is present when ion (c) is formed, it gives up hydrogen to ion (c) and acquires the charge and thus produces a trimethylcarbonium ion (b), and the intermediate is thereby regenerated.

Alkylation is done at temperatures not above 40° and at a pressure sufficiently high to maintain the reactants in the liquid phase. The catalyst employed is sulfuric acid or anhydrous hydrofluoric acid. Application to gasoline manufacture is largely limited to alkylation of isobutane with either isobutene or butene-2. A reaction of theoretical interest if of no technical importance is the thermal alkyla-

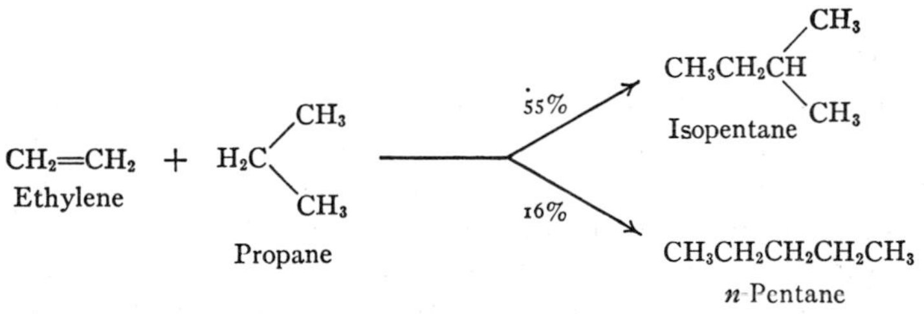

tion of propane with ethylene to give the products shown; the course of the reaction demonstrates that the hydrogen atoms of a methylene group are more reactive than those of a methyl group. Alkylation of isobutane with propylene leads to

$$(CH_3)_3CH \ + \ CH_2{=}CHCH_3 \ \longrightarrow \ \begin{cases} (CH_3)_3CCH_2CH_2CH_3 \ (2,2\text{-Dimethylpentane}) \\ (CH_3)_2CHCH_2CH_2CH_2CH_3 \ (2\text{-Methylhexane}) \\ (CH_3)_3CCH(CH_3)_2 \ (2,2,3\text{-Trimethylbutane}) \end{cases}$$

three products: 2,2-dimethylpentane (60–80%), 2-methylhexane (10–30%), and 2,2,3-trimethylbutane or triptane (7–11%). The last hydrocarbon has a particularly high octane rating.

7.13   **Isomerization.** — This process is employed for conversion of n-pentane and n-hexane into the more desirable branched chain isomers. A catalyst of one type consisting of nickel or platinum deposited on an acidic silica–

alumina carrier is active at a temperature of about 300°. Pressures of 200–400 p.s.i. are employed and hydrogen gas is mixed with the feed to be isomerized. Aluminum chloride catalyzes isomerizations at temperatures around 100°. The catalyst is assumed to abstract a hydride ion from *n*-pentane to produce a second-

$$CH_3CH_2CH_2CH_2CH_3 \xrightarrow[-H^-]{AlCl_3} CH_3CH_2\overset{+}{C}HCH_2CH_3 \xrightarrow{-H^+} CH_3CH\!\!-\!\!CHCH_3 \xrightarrow{H^+}$$
$$\underset{CH_2}{\diagdown\!\diagup}$$

$$CH_3\overset{+}{C}H\!\!-\!\!CHCH_3 \xrightarrow{H^-} CH_3CH_2CHCH_3$$
$$\underset{CH_3}{|} \qquad\qquad \underset{CH_3}{|}$$

ary carbonium ion, which rearranges through a cyclopropane intermediate; recapture of hydride ion completes the sequence leading to isopentane. Isomerization of *n*-hexane is similar but leads to a number of isomers.

7.14   Catalytic Reforming. — The quality of a virgin gasoline fraction from crude oil often can be improved enormously by catalytic reforming, which converts naphthenes and some of the paraffins into aromatic hydrocarbons. One catalyst consists of 10% of molybdic acid deposited on alumina; another is an alumina carrier containing a small amount of platinum. The reaction is carried out by mixing the feed with hydrogen gas in the presence of the catalyst at a temperature of about 500° and a pressure of 200–600 p.s.i. Methylcyclopentane is isomerized to cyclohexane in a reversible reaction, but the equilibrium is upset by dehydrogenation to benzene. Although hydrogen is evolved, an adequate initial concentration of added hydrogen is required for activation of the catalyst. Paraffins present in the feed enter in two reactions. *n*-Heptane, for example, is converted in part into toluene and in part into *n*-pentane and ethane (hydrocracking).

7.15   Motor Gasoline. — The manufacturing processes described afford a number of high quality gasoline components but not a finished product. It is necessary to blend components in proper proportion to give a gasoline of full boiling range. A little butane may be added to adjust the vapor pressure, a light lubricating oil to provide upper cylinder lubrication, and tetraethyllead or tetramethyllead to adjust the octane number; ethylene dibromide and ethylene dichloride present in the antiknock fluid function as scavengers for removal of lead. Other gasoline-soluble additives employed to correct specific difficulties are as follows. Tricresyl phosphate (*omp* mixture) and related phosphates marketed under the trade name TCP are combustion-deposit modifiers used to prevent fouling of spark plugs. The average content of gasolines is equivalent to about 20 parts of phosphorus per million; the U. S. market for 1960 was about 2.5 million pounds of phosphorus. Antirust agents are of several types, exemplified by ammonium polyalkylbenzenesulfonates and unsaturated organic acids. Gum formation results from oxidation-induced polymerization, which is markedly catalyzed by traces of metals, particularly iron and copper, and hence gasolines are protected by addition of an antioxidant (*e.g.*, 2,6-di-*t*-butyl-4-methylphenol, N-butyl-*p*-aminophenol) and of a metal deactivator such as those formulated. The concentration, per 1000 barrels of gasoline, is about 5 lbs. of antioxidant and

1 lb. of deactivator. Additives that inhibit accumulation of troublesome deposits in the carburetor and intake manifold ("cleanliness agents"), exemplified by petroleum neutral oil and by silicone oil, remain liquid in the intake system and

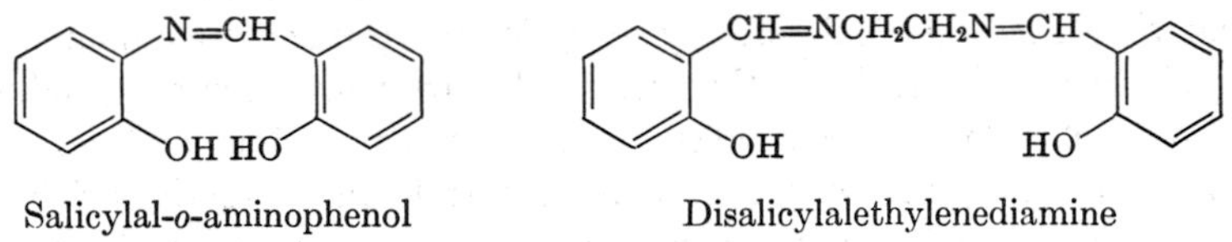

Salicylal-*o*-aminophenol   Disalicylalethylenediamine

Metal deactivators

keep contaminants in solution or suspension so that they are washed through. During the period when an engine is warming up, vaporization of gasoline in the carburetor venturi may cause the parts to become cold enough to form ice from incoming moist air. Anti-icing agents to prevent stalls during warmup are of two types. Isopropyl alcohol and 2-methylpentane-2,4-diol dissolve in the water and lower its freezing point; agents such as amine phosphates function as surfactants. Leaded gasolines contain a dye to give warning of toxicity in case of spillage. Dyes are used also to identify specific gasoline brands and avoid inadvertent mixing in the handling of gasolines in bulk plants. Typical dyes used are: *p*-dimethylaminoazobenzene (yellow), 1-benzeneazo-2-naphthol (orange), 1,4-dialkylaminoanthraquinone (blue).

SPECIALTIES

7.16   **Petrochemicals.** — Organic chemicals derived from petroleum by a combination of distillation, cracking, and isomerization techniques, and often by further chemical processing, are known as petrochemicals. Since such chemicals are available on a huge scale and at low cost, they have acquired enormous importance as starting materials for synthesis and as intermediates for the production of solvents, plastics, rubbers, detergents. Until comparatively recently, benzene, toluene, and the xylenes were available only from coal tar, the amount of which, being governed by steel production capacity, was necessarily limited. During World War II toluene became a strategic chemical required for production of the explosive trinitrotoluene (TNT) in amounts well in excess of that available by coal carbonization. A process for aromatization of petroleum

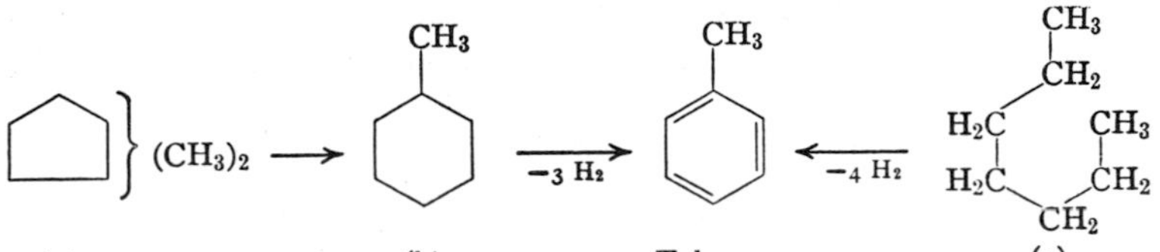

fractions rich in methylcyclohexane made the hydrocarbon available in adequate supply. Toluene is now made not only from methylcyclohexane alone (b, molybdenum catalyst) but also from a dimethylcyclopentane fraction (a, by isomerization and dehydrogenation) and, to a more limited extent, from *n*-heptane (c). The platinum catalyst used is modified by incorporation of acidic components to effect isomerization prior to dehydrogenation. At one time benzene was blended with gasoline for improvement of octane rating. The demand for benzene as a raw material in the chemical industry then rose sharply and the amount available from coal tar was far short of that required, particularly for the production of styrene, phenol, nylon, aniline, and synthetic detergents. Vast additional supplies of benzene are now made by synthesis from petroleum. Fractions rich in cyclo-hexane are aromatized and methylcyclopentane concentrates are isomerized and then aromatized. Since the production of one specific petrochemical is coupled to the manufacture of an array of others, as well as to motor fuel production, by-product hydrogen, hydrocarbon gases, and residues from purification are utilized as such, incorporated into processes for motor fuel production, or burned for energy.

Production of the three xylenes scored another triumph of petroleum tech-nology. Limited amounts of the isomer mixture were available from coal tar, but the components have boiling points too close together to be separable by frac-

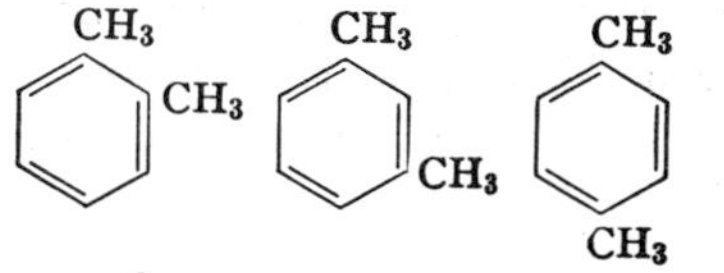

	ortho	*meta*	*para*
B. p.	144°	139°	138°
M. p.	−25°	−48°	13°

tionation in the stills used for processing coal tar products. Aromatization of the C$_8$-cut of petroleum affords a xylene mixture on a scale far surpassing the pro-duction from coal tar. Since the individual hydrocarbons offered a much better potential use than the mixture, petroleum technologists worked on and developed a method for large-scale, low-cost production of substantially pure *o*-, *m*-, and *p*-xylene. The first step utilizes the extraordinarily efficient technique of frac-tional distillation that is one of the key factors in the success of the modern petroleum industry. Although the boiling point of *o*-xylene is only 5° higher than that of the *m*-isomer, *o*-xylene is produced in quantity by fractional distilla-tion of the mixture. The *meta*- and *para*-isomers, of b.p. 139° and 138°, are not separable by known distillation techniques. However, the two isomers differ in melting point by no less than 61°; the more symmetrical *p*-isomer freezes at

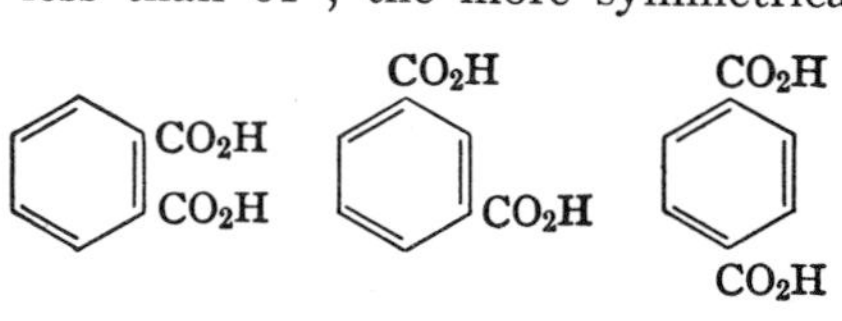

13°, whereas *m*-xylene solidifies only at −48°. Thus the mixture remaining after removal of *o*-xylene by fractionation is separated by freezing out the *p*-isomer. By efficient processes of oxidation, the three xylenes afford the corresponding

benzenedicarboxylic acids: phthalic, isophthalic, and terephthalic acid, which are petrochemicals of increasing importance in chemical technology.

Cumene, made by alkylation of benzene with propylene over a supported phosphoric acid catalyst, is a valuable high-octane blending stock and serves also as

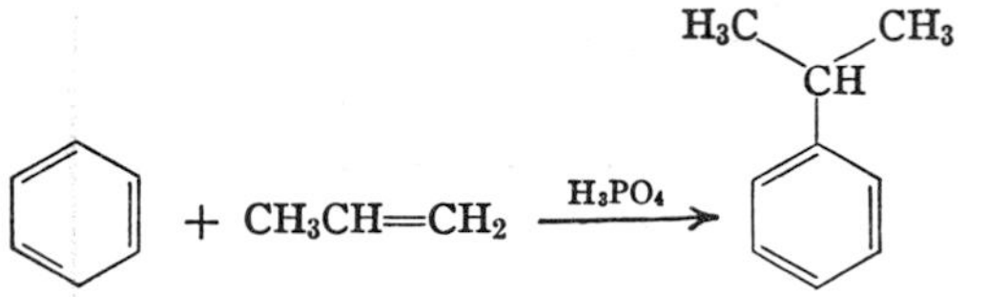

$$\text{benzene} + CH_3CH=CH_2 \xrightarrow{H_3PO_4} \text{Cumene}$$

Cumene (b. p. 152°)

starting material for the production of phenol and acetone (4.16). Ethylbenzene is made by alkylation of benzene with ethylene and converted by dehydrogenative cracking into the useful polymerization monomer styrene: $C_6H_5CH_2CH_3 \rightarrow C_6H_5CH=CH_2 + H_2$.

Aliphatic petrochemicals already mentioned include the chloropentanes obtained by thermal chlorination of the C_5-cut (4.11), ethanol from the hydration of ethylene (5.21) and ether as a by-product of the process, and the corresponding alcohols from propene and from butene-1 and butene-2. Ethylene oxide, a key chemical produced on a huge scale, is made by catalytic air oxidation of ethylene.

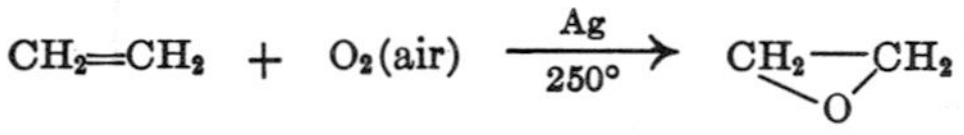

$$CH_2=CH_2 + O_2(\text{air}) \xrightarrow[250°]{Ag} CH_2-CH_2\ (O)$$

Ethylene oxide (b.p. 10.5°)

Ethylene can be produced by thermal cracking of a variety of feeds or from ethane by catalytic dehydrogenation. Olefins are dehydrogenated to conjugated dienes and not to acetylenes. Butadiene, a chemical of key importance, is made by

$$CH_3CH_2CH=CH_2 \xrightarrow{-2H} CH_2=\overset{3}{C}H\overset{1}{C}H=CH_2 \xleftarrow{-2H} CH_3CH=CHCH_3$$
Butene-1   Butadiene   Butene-2

dehydrogenation of a mixture of butene-1 and butene-2. Production of ethylene glycol, glycerol, and other chemicals now derived from petroleum will be described later.

7.17   **Bergius Process.** — The production of fuels by destructive hydrogenation of coal was developed in Germany during World War I by Bergius,[1] and was operated for a time on a large scale. Coal probably is an elaborate network of carbon rings, which are cleaved during the process into fragments that are hydrogenated to open-chain and cyclic hydrocarbons. One ton of gasoline is obtained from 1.5–2 tons of coal. In the early process powdered coal was mixed with heavy tar and 5% of iron oxide, originally added for the purpose of fixing sulfur present in coal but actually a catalyst, and the pasty mass was heated with

[1] Friederich Bergius, 1884–1949; b. Goldschmieden bei Breslau; Ph.D. Leipzig (Hantzsch); Univ. Hannover, Essen, Heidelberg; Nobel Prize 1931

hydrogen at 450–490° at a pressure of 3000 lbs. per sq. in. With more active catalysts (tin, lead, etc.), the reaction is carried out in liquid phase and finally in vapor phase. The product is separated by distillation into gasoline (b.p. to 200°), gas oil (b.p. 200–300°), and a residue that is recycled with fresh coal. A typical gasoline fraction contains 74% paraffins, 22% aromatics, and 4% olefins. Octane numbers of 75–80 are reported.

7.18   Fischer-Tropsch Process. — Synthetic motor fuel was made in Germany in large amounts by hydrogenation of water gas, which is a mixture of carbon monoxide and hydrogen formed by treating coke with steam at high temperatures:

$$C + H_2O \rightarrow CO + H_2$$

The pioneering experiments of Sabatier demonstrated that carbon monoxide can be hydrogenated at high temperatures to methane in the presence of nickel or iron catalysts:

$$CO + 3H_2 \rightarrow CH_4 + H_2O$$

F. Fischer[1] and Tropsch[2] (1933) showed that the hydrogenation can be modified further by certain catalysts for production of a complex mixture of aliphatic

$$nCO + 2nH_2 \rightarrow C_nH_{2n} + nH_2O$$
$$nCO + (2n + 1)H_2 \rightarrow C_nH_{2n+2} + nH_2O$$

products. Hydrogen is added to water gas so that the approximate ratio to carbon monoxide is 2:1; the mixture is treated with an iron oxide catalyst to remove sulfur and finally passed over a cobalt catalyst at 200°. The reaction is believed to involve formation of cobalt carbide (Co_2C) and cleavage of the carbide by hydrogen to cobalt and methylene radicals, which polymerize to give straight-chain alkanes and alkenes. One cubic meter of gas yields 130–140 g. of a hydrocarbon fraction (theory = 209 g.), more than half of which boils in the gasoline range. Because of the preponderance of straight-chain hydrocarbons, the octane rating is only 40, so reforming and leading are required. The higher-boiling fraction has a cetane rating of 85 and is eminently suited for Diesel engines. The Fischer-Tropsch hydrocarbon fraction is accompanied by a smaller but appreciable fraction rich in oxygenated compounds, particularly straight-chain alcohols, aldehydes, and ketones.

7.19   Lubricating Oil. — Although no single compound has been isolated from lubricating oil, it is possible from the chemical and physical properties of the various fractions to draw the following conclusions concerning the composition of the very complex mixture in the oil: approximately 18–26% is composed of straight-chain and possibly branched-chain paraffins; 43–51% of alkylated naphthenes containing 1, 2, or 3 rings; 23% of alkylated naphthene–

[1] Franz Fischer, 1877–1947; b. Freiburg; Ph.D. Giessen (Elbs); Berlin; Mulheim/Ruhr; Kaiser-Wilhelm Inst. Coal Research

[2] Hans Tropsch, 1889–1935; b. Plan (Bohemia); Ph.D. Prague; Coal Research Inst., Prague; Univ. Chicago; *Ber.*, **68A**, 169 (1935)

aromatic hydrocarbons containing 2, 3, or 4 rings; and 8% of "asphaltic" substances, which are considered to be largely aromatic.

Lubricating oils are refined to improve the viscosity and viscosity index, which is a measure of the change of viscosity with temperature. Since lubricating oils are submitted to a wide variety of temperatures, a high viscosity index is desirable. Another important characteristic is the solidifying tendency, measured by the pour-point test or cold test. Substances that crystallize from the oil on chilling are known as petroleum waxes and their removal decreases the pour-point temperature but lowers the viscosity index. The presence of wax is not necessarily harmful in engines operated at temperatures at which the wax remains in solution, but at low temperatures crystallization prevents normal circulation of oil. Originally dewaxing was accomplished by allowing the crude oil to settle during the winter months, and the wax-free layer was poured off or sometimes filtered. In more recent processes solvents are used to increase the rate of filtration and also to permit better separation. Unfortunately no solvents are known that differentiate completely between the waxes and the oil at temperatures above the melting point of the wax, but many solvents are available that completely dissolve the oil at temperatures at which the waxes are crystalline. The usual solvents are liquid propane, benzene–acetone, and chlorinated hydrocarbons such as trichloroethylene and ethylene dichloride. Separation of straight-chain paraffins as urea inclusion complexes offers another possibility for dewaxing. Vaseline is a mixture of paraffin waxes and added oils, but usually waxes for commercial uses (candles, etc.) are freed from residual traces of oil by sweating (gradual application of heat) or by solvents and subsequent pressing.

Greases are solid or semisolid gels prepared by the addition to mineral oils of hydrocarbon-soluble metal soaps or salts of higher fatty acids, for example, calcium stearate, lithium stearate, aluminum naphthenate. The soap content may vary from less than one to as much as thirty percent. Calcium soaps of the rosin acids are used as the gelator in the lubricants known as sett greases. In addition greases contain a certain amount of water as a stabilizer.

Chapter 8

ALCOHOLS

8.1   **Common Alcohols.** — Table 8.1 lists a number of alcohols of low or moderate cost which are available as starting materials for synthesis. As noted earlier (1.13), hydrogen bonding leads to association in the liquid state and hence boiling points are relatively high. Tertiary alcohols have boiling points significantly below those of the primary and secondary isomers. Paraffinic alcohols have somewhat higher densities than the corresponding paraffins but are still lighter than water. In a lower alcohol the hydroxyl group forms a considerable part of the total molecule and hence makes for solubility in water; higher paraffinic alcohols are more like paraffins and dissolve more readily in hydrocarbon solvents than in water. Methyl, ethyl, and n-propyl alcohol are miscible with water in all proportions; the next higher homologs have the following solubilities in water at 20°, expressed in grams dissolved by 100 g. of water; n-butyl alcohol, 8.3 g.; n-amyl alcohol, 2.6 g.; n-hexyl alcohol, 1 g. That structure plays a role in determining solubility is evident from the fact that t-butyl alcohol is miscible with water. Most of the alcohols of low molecular weight are liquids at room temperature; that t-butyl alcohol and cyclohexanol are low-melting solids may be because each substance has a certain symmetry of structure. Normal paraffinic alcohols in the even-carbon series are solids from C_{12} on.

Since an alcohol is already in a partly oxidized condition, the heat release on combustion is lower than that of a corresponding alkane. The heat of combustion of ethanol (b.p. 78°) is 328 kcal./mole, or 5.62 kcal./ml.; values for alkanes in the same boiling range are: n-hexane (b.p. 69°), 7.58 kcal./ml.; n-heptane (b.p. 98°), 7.85 kcal./ml.

Table 8.2 lists commercially available alcohols having two or more hydroxyl groups. In ethylene glycol (CH_2OHCH_2OH) and glycerol ($CH_2OHCHOHCH_2OH$) each carbon carries one hydroxyl group; the same is true of erythritol

264

TABLE 8.1. MONOHYDRIC ALCOHOLS

NAME	FORMULA	M.P. °C.	B.P. °C.	SP. GR.
Methyl alcohol	CH_3OH	−97	64.7	0.792
Ethyl alcohol	CH_3CH_2OH	−114	78.3	.789
n-Propyl alcohol	$n\text{-}C_3H_7OH$	−126	97.2	.804
Isopropyl alcohol	$i\text{-}C_3H_7OH$	−88.5	82.3	.786
Allyl alcohol	$CH_2{=}CHCH_2OH$	−129	97.0	.855
Crotyl alcohol	$CH_3CH{=}CHCH_2OH$		118	.873
n-Butyl alcohol	$n\text{-}C_4H_9OH$	−90	117.7	.810
Isobutyl alcohol	$(CH_3)_2CHCH_2OH$	−108	107.9	.802
sec-Butyl alcohol	$CH_3CH_2CH(OH)CH_3$		99.5	.808
t-Butyl alcohol	$(CH_3)_3COH$	25	82.5	.789
n-Amyl alcohol	$n\text{-}C_5H_{11}OH$	−78.5	138.0	.817
Isoamyl alcohol	$(CH_3)_2CHCH_2CH_2OH$	−117	131.5	.812
t-Amyl alcohol	$CH_3CH_2C(OH)(CH_3)_2$	−12	101.8	.809
Neopentyl alcohol	$(CH_3)_3CCH_2OH$	50	113	
Cyclopentanol	C_5H_9OH	−19	141	.950
n-Hexyl alcohol	$n\text{-}C_6H_{13}OH$	−52	155.8	.820
Cyclohexanol	$C_6H_{11}OH$	24	161.5	.962
n-Octyl alcohol	$n\text{-}C_8H_{17}OH$	−16	194.0	.827
Capryl alcohol (octanol-2)	$n\text{-}C_6H_{13}CH(OH)CH_3$	−39	179.0	.819
n-Decyl alcohol	$n\text{-}C_{10}H_{21}OH$	6	232.9	.829
Lauryl alcohol	$n\text{-}C_{12}H_{25}OH$	24	259	.831
Myristyl alcohol	$n\text{-}C_{14}H_{29}OH$	38	167/15 mm.	.824
Cetyl alcohol	$n\text{-}C_{16}H_{33}OH$	49	189/15 mm.	.798
Stearyl alcohol	$n\text{-}C_{18}H_{37}OH$	58.5	210.5/15 mm.	.812
Benzyl alcohol	$C_6H_5CH_2OH$	−15.3	205.4	1.046
Benzhydrol	$(C_6H_5)_2CHOH$	69		
Cinnamyl alcohol	$C_6H_5CH{=}CHCH_2OH$	33	257	1.040
Triphenylcarbinol	$(C_6H_5)_3COH$	164		

TABLE 8.2. POLYHYDRIC ALCOHOLS

NAME	FORMULA	M.P. °C	B.P. °C	SP. GR.
Ethylene glycol	$HOCH_2CH_2OH$	−12	198	1.12
1,2-Propanediol (dl)	$CH_3CHOHCH_2OH$		188	
1,3-Propanediol (trimethylene glycol)	$HO(CH_2)_3OH$		212	1.06
1,3-Butanediol (dl)	$CH_2OHCH_2CHOHCH_3$		207	
1,4-Butanediol	$HO(CH_2)_4OH$	16	230	1.02
2,3-Butanediol (mixt.)	$CH_3CHOHCHOHCH_3$		183	
1,5-Pentanediol	$HO(CH_2)_5OH$		240	0.99
1,6-Hexanediol	$HO(CH_2)_6OH$	42	250	
1,10-Decanediol	$HO(CH_2)_{10}OH$	74	192/20 mm.	
Pinacol	$(CH_3)_2C(OH)C(OH)(CH_3)_2$	41	174.4	
Glycerol	$CH_2OHCHOHCH_2OH$	18	290	1.26
1,2,4-Butanetriol (dl)	$CH_2OHCHOHCH_2CH_2OH$		151/1 mm.	
1,2,6-Hexanetriol (dl)	$CH_2OHCHOH(CH_2)_3CH_2OH$		160/1 mm.	

($CH_2OHCHOHCHOHCH_2OH$, m.p. 120°). That the *gem*-diol group ordinarily is not stable but loses water to form a carbonyl compound was recognized in 1864 by Erlenmeyer, Sen.,[1] designer of the indispensable Erlenmeyer flask. A

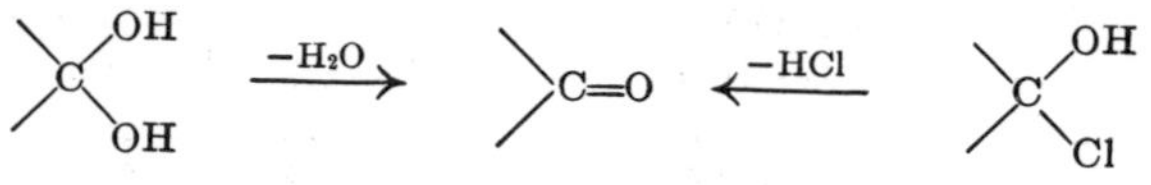

gem-Diol   *gem*-Chlorohydrin

likewise unstable structure is one with a hydroxyl group and a halogen atom on the same carbon.

8.2   From Natural Sources. — Cetyl alcohol, $n\text{-}C_{16}H_{33}OH$, is obtained on hydrolysis of spermaceti, a waxy solid which separates from sperm whale oil and consists largely of the ester cetyl palmitate, $n\text{-}C_{15}H_{31}COOC_{16}H_{33}$. The normal C_{12}-, C_{14}-, C_{16}-, and C_{18}-alcohols can all be prepared from acid constituents of fats. Thus saponification of the glycerides comprising coconut oil affords, as the chief acidic component (48%), lauric acid, which on esterification and reduction of the ester yields lauryl alcohol.

$$n\text{-}C_{11}H_{23}CO_2H \xrightarrow[\text{(H}^+)]{CH_3OH} n\text{-}C_{11}H_{23}CO_2CH_3 \xrightarrow{Na,\ C_2H_5OH}$$

Lauric acid

$$n\text{-}C_{11}H_{23}CH_2OH \ + \ HOCH_3$$
Lauryl alcohol

The eight amyl alcohols ($C_5H_{11}OH$) are so named because two of them were discovered as by-products of the fermentation of crude potato starch to ethyl alcohol (L. *amylum*, starch, fine meal). The isomers were isolated from fusel oil, a higher-boiling contaminant liquid which is formed on fermentation but which is derived not from starch but from accompanying proteins. Proteins are polymer-like substances of high molecular weight made up of chains of amino acid units linked together. During the fermentation of starch, the protein is hydrolyzed to amino acids; two of the units, leucine and isoleucine, are transformed enzymically into amyl alcohols. Leucine has an asymmetric carbon atom and the natural acid

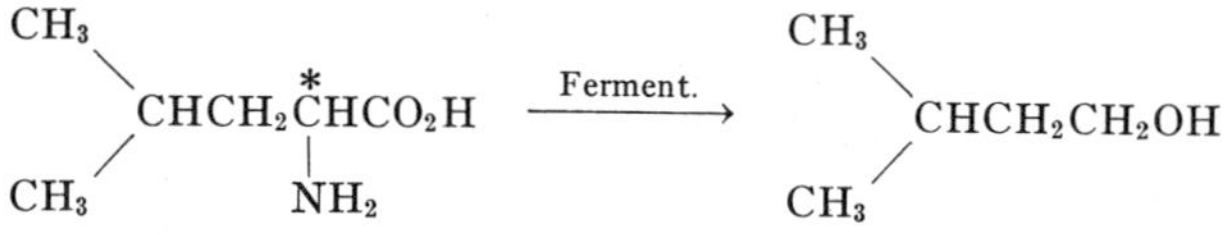

Leucine   Isoamyl alcohol

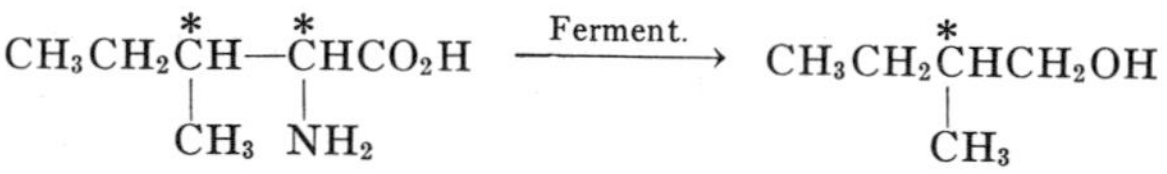

Isoleucine   *act*-Amyl alcohol

is optically active, but asymmetry is lost on fermentation. The product has an isopropyl group, like isopropyl and isobutyl alcohol, and so is described as isoamyl

[1] Emil Erlenmeyer, Sen., 1825–1909; b. Wehen/Wiesbaden, Germany; Ph.D. Giessen; Univ. Heidelberg; Techn. Hochsch. Munich; *Ber.*, **43,** 3645 (1910)

alcohol. Isoleucine has two centers of asymmetry, one of which is retained in the product of fermentation; since this constituent of fusel oil is optically active it is named active amyl alcohol. The fermentative degradation probably involves a series of coupled, enzyme-controlled steps: dehydrogenation, hydrolysis, decar-

$$\underset{\substack{|\\ NH_2}}{RCHCOOH} \xrightarrow{-2H} \underset{\substack{\|\\ NH}}{RCCOOH} \xrightarrow[-NH_3]{H_2O} \underset{\substack{\|\\ O}}{RCCOOH} \xrightarrow{-CO_2}$$

$$\underset{\substack{\|\\ O}}{RCH} \xrightarrow{2H} RCH_2OH$$

boxylation, and reduction.

8.3   **From Castor Oil.** Castor oil, from the seeds of the castor oil plant, contains as the chief component (88%) the glyceride of ricinoleic acid, a monounsaturated *cis* acid having a hydroxyl group β to the double bond; it is 12-hydroxyoleic acid. Four useful products are obtainable from castor oil: (a) capryl alcohol and sebacic acid by fusion with alkali, and (b) *n*-heptaldehyde and Δ^{10}-undecylenic acid by pyrolysis. The alkali fusion process was once operated

$$\underset{\substack{|\\ HO_2C(CH_2)_7CH}}{\overset{\substack{OH\\|}}{CH_3(CH_2)_5CHCH_2CH}} \rightarrow$$
Ricinoleic acid

(a) $\underset{\substack{|\\}}{\overset{\substack{OH\\|}}{CH_3(CH_2)_5CHCH_3}}$ + $HO_2C(CH_2)_8CO_2H$
       Capryl alcohol   Sebacic acid

(b) $CH_3(CH_2)_5CHO$ + $CH_2{=}CH(CH_2)_8CO_2H$
       n-Heptaldehyde Δ^{10}-Undecylenic acid

for production of capryl alcohol for use as an antifoam agent, and in an *Organic Syntheses* procedure reporting a 40–42% yield of the alcohol the dibasic acid is discarded. Sebacic acid is now the more valuable product. After fusion with 70% sodium hydroxide with a lead salt as catalyst, the capryl alcohol is distilled (with some water) and water is added to the cooling mass to the point where disodium sebacate separates from the alkaline liquor. After acidification, sebacic acid is crystallized from water.

From a study of the alkali fusion of sodium ricinoleate at different temperatures and from investigation of model compounds, G. H. Hargreaves (1947) concluded that the initial step is isomerization of the β,γ-unsaturated alcohol (1, homoallylic) to the α,β-unsaturated alcohol (2, allylic). Migration of the double bond through an intermediate carbanion gives a product stabilized by conjugation of the double bond with a lone pair of electrons on oxygen. The next step is fission of the double bond to fragments (3) and (4), each of which has a bivalent carbon atom (carbenes); the first rearranges to the ketone (5) and the second adds water to form the primary alcohol (6). When the temperature is controlled to 200° the volatile product is indeed largely methyl *n*-hexyl ketone (5). At a higher temperature a disproportionation occurs with transfer of hydrogen from the primary alcohol to the ketone to produce the secondary alcohol (7) and the aldehyde-acid salt (8), and the latter reacts with alkali to form disodium sebacate and hydrogen. α,β-Unsaturated acids also undergo alkali cleavage of the conjugated olefinic linkage,

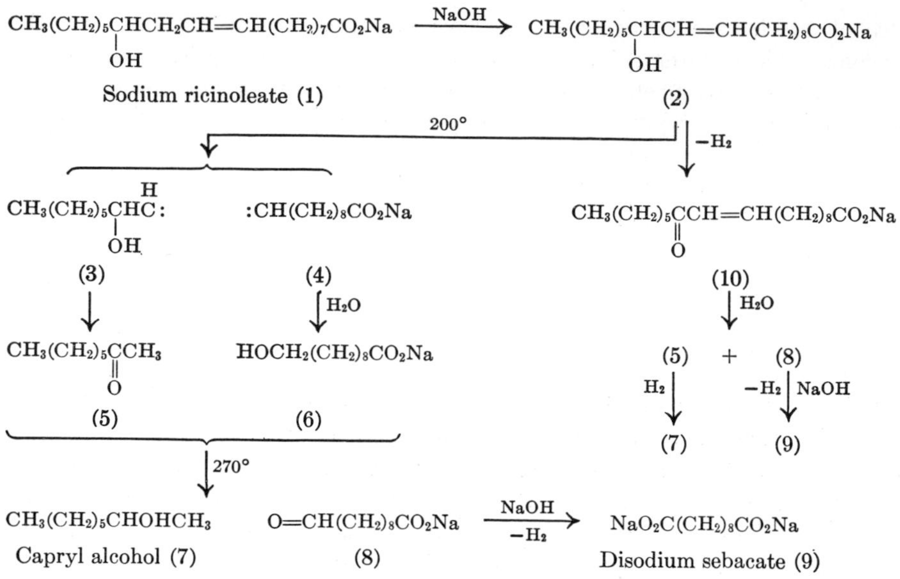

$$CH_3(CH_2)_5CHCH_2CH=CH(CH_2)_7CO_2Na \xrightarrow{NaOH} CH_3(CH_2)_5CHCH=CH(CH_2)_8CO_2Na$$

$$\underset{\underset{OH}{|}}{}$$ $$\underset{\underset{OH}{|}}{}$$

Sodium ricinoleate (1)   (2)

200° $-H_2$

$$CH_3(CH_2)_5CHC:$$ $$:CH(CH_2)_8CO_2Na$$ $$CH_3(CH_2)_5CCH=CH(CH_2)_8CO_2Na$$
$$\underset{\underset{OH}{|}}{}$$ $$\underset{\overset{||}{O}}{}$$

(3)   (4)   (10)

$$\downarrow$$ $\downarrow H_2O$ $\downarrow H_2O$

$$CH_3(CH_2)_5CCH_3$$ $$HOCH_2(CH_2)_8CO_2Na$$ (5) + (8)
$$\underset{\overset{||}{O}}{}$$

(5)   (6) $H_2\downarrow$ $-H_2\downarrow NaOH$

$\downarrow 270°$ (7)   (9)

$$CH_3(CH_2)_5CHOHCH_3 \qquad O=CH(CH_2)_8CO_2Na \xrightarrow[-H_2]{NaOH} NaO_2C(CH_2)_8CO_2Na$$

Capryl alcohol (7)   (8)   Disodium sebacate (9)

and Hargreaves demonstrated the reaction with preformed allylic alcohols. A perhaps more plausible alternative mechanism involves dehydrogenation of (2) to (10), hydration, and cleavage (reverse aldolization).

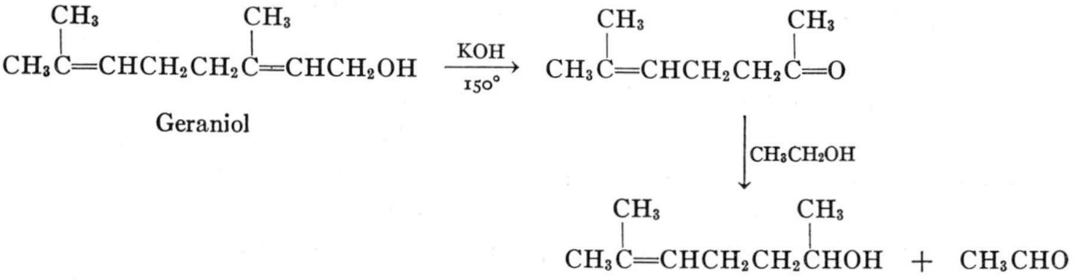

$$\underset{}{CH_3} \qquad \underset{}{CH_3} \qquad\qquad CH_3 \qquad CH_3$$
$$CH_3C=CHCH_2CH_2C=CHCH_2OH \xrightarrow[150°]{KOH} CH_3C=CHCH_2CH_2C=O$$

Geraniol

$$\downarrow CH_3CH_2OH$$

$$\underset{}{CH_3} \qquad\qquad \underset{}{CH_3}$$
$$CH_3C=CHCH_2CH_2CHOH \;+\; CH_3CHO$$

Pyrolysis of castor oil or of methyl ricinoleate affords Δ^{10}-undecylenic acid, a compound of unusual structure available by no other simple route. The other

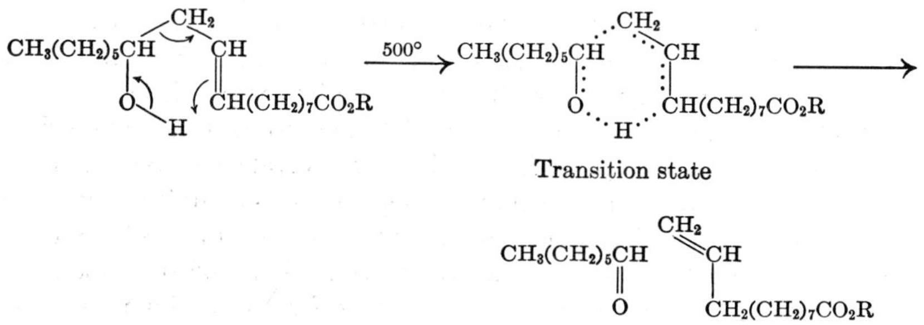

$$CH_3(CH_2)_5CH \overset{CH_2}{\diagup}\underset{}{CH} \xrightarrow{500°} CH_3(CH_2)_5CH \overset{\cdot\cdot CH_2}{\diagup}\underset{}{CH}$$

Transition state

$$CH_2$$
$$CH_3(CH_2)_5CH \qquad CH$$
$$\underset{\overset{||}{O}}{} \qquad CH_2(CH_2)_7CO_2R$$

product, n-heptaldehyde, on reduction with iron powder in aqueous acetic acid affords n-heptyl alcohol in 75–81 % yield. A plausible mechanism involves formation of a cyclic transition state (Arnold,[1] 1959; W. J. Gensler, 1961). Arnold has shown that the cleavage is general for β-hydroxyolefins and has demonstrated its use in the novel method for extending carbon chains formulated (1960).

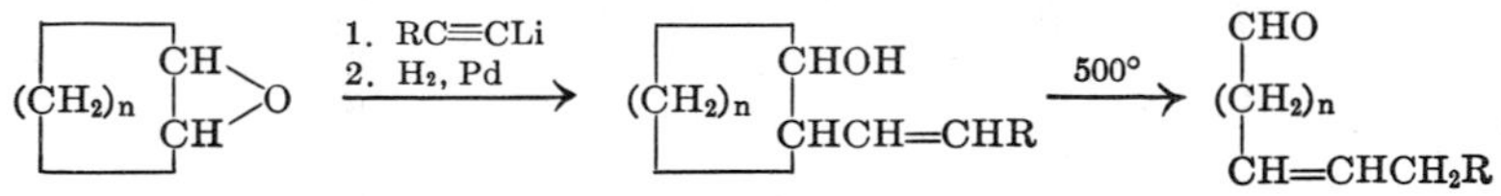

8.4   **Allyl Alcohol.** — Glycerol from fats was once the main source of allyl alcohol. An *Organic Syntheses* procedure based upon an early observation of B. Tollens[2] calls for heating glycerol with three successive portions of formic acid to a temperature of 260° (1½ days) and recovery of allyl alcohol from the distillate (46% yield). Glycerol monoformate is formed and suffers pyrolysis to the unsaturated alcohol, carbon dioxide and water, probably through a cyclic transition state:

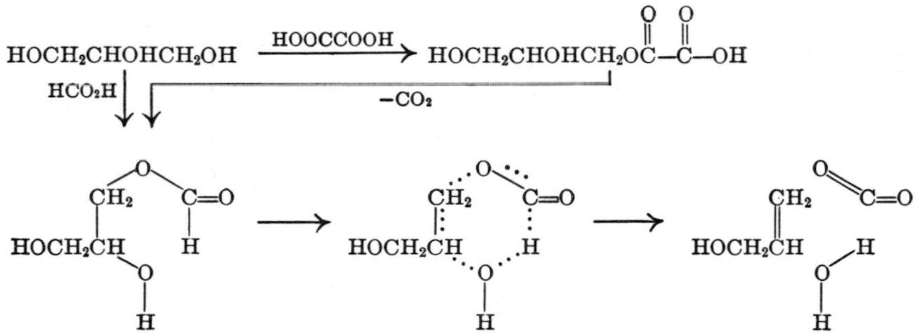

Oxalic acid can also be used to produce the intermediate formate but there is more foaming and the reaction is not so smooth as in the formic acid method.

SYNTHETIC PREPARATION

8.5   **Hydration and Hydrolysis.** — The hydration of alkenes to alcohols has been described (5.21) and mention has been made of the conversion of alkyl halides to alcohols by reaction with silver hydroxide (1.9), as obtained with a suspension of silver oxide in moist ether (alcoholic alkali effects elimination of

$$RCH_2CH_2I + AgOH \rightarrow RCH_2CH_2OH + AgI$$

hydrogen halide). The method has limited application because alcohols usually are more accessible than the corresponding halides.

$$(CH_3)_3CCH_2C(CH_3)=CH_2 \xrightarrow{H_2O_2\ (H^+)} (CH_3)_3CCH_2C(CH_3)_2O_2H \xrightarrow[34-40\%]{H^+}$$

Diisobutylene

$$(CH_3)_3CCH_2OH + CH_3COCH_3$$

A related reaction is illustrated by a procedure for the preparation of neopentyl alcohol (*Org. Syn.*, 1960). Hydrogen peroxide adds to commercial diisobutylene

[1] Richard T. Arnold, b. 1913 Indianapolis; Ph.D. Illinois (Fuson); Minnesota; Alfred P. Sloan Foundation; Mead Johnson and Co.

[2] Bernhard Tollens, 1841–1918, b. Hamburg; Ph.D. Göttingen; Univ. Göttingen

in a solution containing 12.5% of H_2O_2 and 40% H_2SO_4 at 25° to give the hydro-peroxide, which is rearranged by 70% sulfuric acid (25°) to neopentyl alcohol and acetone.

8.6   **Grignard Synthesis.** — Addition of a Grignard reagent to the carbonyl group of a second component and hydrolysis of the addition product provides an efficient method for the synthesis of alcohols of all types. Usually

$$\begin{array}{c} \diagdown \\ \diagup \end{array} C{=}O \ + \ RMgX \ \rightarrow \ \begin{array}{c} \diagdown \\ \diagup \end{array} \underset{R}{\overset{|}{C}}{-}OMgX \ \xrightarrow{HOH} \ \begin{array}{c} \diagdown \\ \diagup \end{array} \underset{R}{\overset{|}{C}}{-}OH \ + \ HOMgX$$

yields are high and the products are pure and of unambiguous structure. The key reaction can be regarded as a nucleophilic addition initiating in attack of the positively polarized carbon of the carbonyl function by a potential or actual car-banion, with acceptance of the charge by oxygen. In the ordinary case a Grig-

$$\overset{\delta^+\ \delta^-}{R_2C{=}O} \ + \ R^-Mg^+Br \ \longrightarrow \ \underset{R}{\overset{|}{R_2C}}{-}O^- \ \xrightarrow{Mg^+Br} \ \underset{R}{\overset{|}{R_2C}}{-}OMgBr$$

nard reagent is prepared in ether solution and a solution of the carbonyl component in ether or tetrahydrofurane is run in at a rate such that refluxing is kept under control. The MgX-derivative of the alcohol often separates as the reaction pro-ceeds. The reaction mixture usually is decomposed by addition of ice and hydro-chloric acid, the latter to keep basic magnesium salts in solution in the aqueous phase; the layers are separated and the product isolated by evaporation of the washed and dried ethereal extract. Another procedure is to add a specific amount of saturated ammonium chloride solution to the stirred reaction mixture; magnesium salts are precipitated and the supernatant liquid is a solution of the reaction product in substantially dry ether.

Alcohols of all three types can be synthesized by the Grignard method. One route to primary alcohols utilizes formaldehyde as the carbonyl component, as in the synthesis of cyclohexylcarbinol (1). Gaseous formaldehyde is generated by

$$\text{1.} \quad \underset{CH_2CH_2}{\overset{CH_2CH_2}{CH_2}} \hspace{-1.2em}\diagup\diagdown\hspace{-1.2em} CHMgCl \ \xrightarrow{CH_2{=}O} \ C_6H_{11}CH_2OMgCl \ \xrightarrow[64\text{-}69\%]{H_2O}$$

$$\underset{CH_2CH_2}{\overset{CH_2CH_2}{CH_2}} \hspace{-1.2em}\diagup\diagdown\hspace{-1.2em} CHCH_2OH$$

Cyclohexylcarbinol

pyrolysis of the solid polymer paraformaldehyde and carried by a slow current of nitrogen into an ethereal solution of cyclohexylmagnesium chloride. Ethylene oxide reacts similarly and gives primary alcohols in which the chain is lengthened by two carbon atoms, as illustrated by the synthesis of *n*-hexyl alcohol (2). A solution of *n*-butylmagnesium bromide is prepared and cooled below 10° in a salt-ice bath and ethylene oxide (b.p. 10.5°) is run in slowly from a weighed cylinder

2. n-C$_4$H$_9$MgBr $+$ CH$_2$—CH$_2$ $\longrightarrow$ n-C$_4$H$_9$CH$_2$CH$_2$OMgBr

$\qquad\qquad\qquad\qquad\qquad\qquad\qquad\qquad \xrightarrow[\text{60-62\%}]{\text{H}_2\text{O}} n$-C$_4H_9CH_2CH_2$OH

as a gas through a tube ending about 2 cm. above the surface of the liquid so that the gas condenses in the reaction mixture. Trimethylene oxide (b.p. 48°), available in moderate yield by the reactions formulated, reacts in an analogous manner and affords the means of introducing a three-carbon chain with a terminal primary alcohol group.

$$
\begin{array}{ccccccc}
\text{CH}_2\text{CH}_2\text{OH} & & \text{CH}_2\text{CH}_2\text{Cl} & & \text{CH}_2\text{CH}_2\text{Cl} & & \text{CH}_2\text{—CH}_2 \\
| & \xrightarrow{\text{HCl}} & | & \xrightarrow{\text{CH}_3\text{CO}_2\text{H}} & | & \xrightarrow{\text{KOH}} & | \quad | \\
\text{CH}_2\text{OH} & & \text{CH}_2\text{OH} & & \text{CH}_2\text{OCOCH}_3 & & \text{CH}_2\text{—O}
\end{array}
$$

Trimethylene oxide

The product of reaction of a Grignard reagent with an aldehyde (other than formaldehyde) is of necessity a secondary alcohol. The reaction sequence (3) illustrates the synthesis of a secondary alcohol as an intermediate to a diene; sequence (4) requires preparation of ethynlmagnesium bromide by the special tech-

3. CH$_3$CH=CHCH=O $\xrightarrow[\text{81-86\%}]{\begin{array}{l}\text{1. CH}_3\text{MgCl}\\ \text{2. H}_2\text{O}\end{array}}$ CH$_3$CH=CHCH—CH$_3$ $\xrightarrow[\text{80\%}]{\text{Al}_2\text{O}_3 \text{ at } 450°}$
$\qquad\qquad\qquad\qquad\qquad\qquad\qquad\qquad\qquad\qquad |$
$\qquad\qquad\qquad\qquad\qquad\qquad\qquad\qquad\qquad\;\text{OH}$

$\qquad\qquad\qquad\qquad\qquad\qquad\qquad\qquad\qquad\qquad\qquad$ CH$_3$CH=CHCH=CH$_2$
$\qquad\qquad\qquad\qquad\qquad\qquad\qquad\qquad\qquad\qquad\qquad$ Piperylene (b.p. 44°)

4. HC≡CH $+$ C$_2$H$_5$MgBr $\xrightarrow{\begin{array}{c}\text{Tetrahy-}\\ \text{drofurane}\end{array}}$ BrMgC≡CH $+$ C$_2$H$_6$

C$_6$H$_5$CH=CHCH=O $+$ BrMgC≡CH $\xrightarrow[\text{55-65\%}]{\begin{array}{l}\text{1. Addition}\\ \text{2. NH}_4\text{Cl-H}_2\text{O}\end{array}}$ C$_6$H$_5$CH=CHCHC≡CH
$\qquad\qquad\qquad\qquad\qquad\qquad\qquad\qquad\qquad\qquad\qquad\qquad\qquad\qquad\quad |$
$\qquad\qquad\qquad\qquad\qquad\qquad\qquad\qquad\qquad\qquad\qquad\qquad\qquad\qquad\;\text{OH}$

$\qquad\qquad\qquad\qquad\qquad\qquad\qquad\qquad\qquad\qquad\qquad\qquad$ 1-Phenyl-1-pentene-
$\qquad\qquad\qquad\qquad\qquad\qquad\qquad\qquad\qquad\qquad\qquad\qquad$ 4-yne-3-ol (m. p. 68°)

nique described (6.6). A ketone reacts to give a tertiary alcohol. Selection of an unsymmetrical ketone and an appropriate Grignard reagent permits synthesis of a tertiary alcohol having three different hydrocarbon groups (5). In example

$\qquad\;\;$ CH$_3$ $\qquad\qquad\qquad\qquad\qquad\qquad\qquad$ CH$_3$
$\qquad\;\;\;|$ $\qquad\qquad$ C$_2$H$_5$MgBr; H$_2$O $\qquad\qquad\quad|$
5. C$_6$H$_5$C=O $\xrightarrow{\qquad\qquad\qquad}$ C$_6$H$_5$—C—OH
$\qquad\qquad\qquad\qquad\qquad\qquad\qquad\qquad\qquad\qquad\quad|$
$\qquad\qquad\qquad\qquad\qquad\qquad\qquad\qquad\qquad\qquad\;$ C$_2$H$_5$

$\quad$ Acetophenone $\qquad\qquad\qquad\qquad$ Methylethylphenylcarbinol

6. (C$_6$H$_5$)$_2$C=O $\xrightarrow[\text{91\%}]{\text{C}_6\text{H}_5\text{MgBr; H}_2\text{O}}$ (C$_6$H$_5$)$_3$COH

$\quad$ Benzophenone $\qquad\qquad\qquad$ Triphenylcarbinol

7. $(C_6H_5)_2C=O$ $\xrightarrow{C_6H_5CH_2MgCl;\ H_2O}$ $(C_6H_5)_2\underset{\underset{OH}{|}}{C}-CH_2C_6H_5$ $\xrightarrow[54-59\%]{20\%\ H_2SO_4}$

$(C_6H_5)_2C=CHC_6H_5$

Triphenylethylene (m.p. 69°)

(6) the ketone contains two phenyl groups and phenylmagnesium bromide introduces a third such group to give a symmetrical product. Example (7) illustrates the synthesis of a tertiary alcohol required as an intermediate to a substituted ethylene.

Tertiary alcohols can also be made by reaction of an ester with two equivalents of Grignard reagent, for example, the reaction of ethyl benzoate with excess phenylmagnesium bromide to give, after hydrolysis of the MgBr-derivative, triphenylcarbinol (8). The initially formed anion (a) does not combine with Mg⁺Br

8. $C_6H_5\overset{\overset{O}{\|}}{C}-OC_2H_5$ $\xrightarrow{C_6H_5^-}$ $C_6H_5-\underset{\underset{C_6H_5}{|}}{\overset{\overset{O^-}{|}}{C}}-OC_2H_5$ $\xrightarrow[-C_2H_5OMgBr]{Mg^+Br}$ $C_6H_5\underset{\underset{C_6H_5}{|}}{\overset{\overset{O}{\|}}{C}}$ $\xrightarrow{C_6H_5MgBr}$

(a)   (b)

$C_6H_5\underset{\underset{C_6H_5}{|}}{\overset{\overset{OMgBr}{|}}{C}}-C_6H_5$ $\xrightarrow[91\%\ overall]{H_2O}$ $C_6H_5-\underset{\underset{C_6H_5}{|}}{\overset{\overset{OH}{|}}{C}}-C_6H_5$

(c)   Triphenylcarbinol

to form an alcoholate, for this would be an unstable *gem*-diol derivative, but affords the ketone (b). The ketone then reacts with a second equivalent of Grignard reagent to give, after hydrolysis, the tertiary alcohol. The alternative routes (6) and (8) are equally satisfactory. Although the initial product of the addition of a Grignard reagent to an ester is a ketone, the reaction of an ester with one equivalent of Grignard reagent is not a practical method of ketone synthesis. The difficulty is that a ketone is so much more reactive than an ester that the ketone initially formed consumes reagent before the starting material has been fully utilized. The decreased reactivity of esters is attributable to a resonance effect which decreases the double-bond character of the carbonyl group:

$R-\underset{\underset{OCH_3}{|}}{C}=O$ $\longleftrightarrow$ $R-\underset{\underset{+OCH_3}{\|}}{C}-O^-$

Use of ethyl formate as the carbonyl component provides an alternate route to secondary alcohols; thus ethyl formate, like other esters, reacts with two moles of Grignard reagent (9). The intermediate in this case is an aldehyde. Esters thus

9. $H-\underset{\underset{OC_2H_5}{|}}{C}=O$ $\xrightarrow{n\text{-}C_4H_9^-}$ $H-\underset{\underset{C_4H_9\text{-}n}{|}}{\overset{\overset{OC_2H_5}{|}}{C}}-O^-$ $\xrightarrow[-C_2H_5OMgBr]{Mg^+Br}$ $H-\underset{\underset{C_4H_9\text{-}n}{|}}{C}=O$ $\xrightarrow{n\text{-}C_4H_9MgBr}$

$$\begin{array}{c} C_4H_9\text{-}n \\ | \\ H\text{—}C\text{—}OMgBr \\ | \\ C_4H_9\text{-}n \end{array} \xrightarrow[83\text{–}85\%]{H_2O} (CH_3CH_2CH_2CH_2)_2CHOH$$

Di-n-butylcarbinol
(b.p. 97°/20 mm.)

serve for the synthesis of secondary and tertiary alcohols in which two of the hydrocarbon groups are the same. In example (10) the alcohol is prepared as an intermediate to an alkene. The Grignard synthesis of a diacetylenic diol (tertiary)

10. $2\ C_6H_5MgBr\ +\ CH_3CO_2C_2H_5 \xrightarrow[\text{2. } H_2O]{\text{1. Addition}} (C_6H_5)_2CCH_3$
$$\underset{OH}{}$$

$$\xrightarrow[67\text{–}70\%]{20\% H_2SO_4} (C_6H_5)_2C\text{=}CH_2$$

1,1-Diphenylethylene
(b.p. 113°/2 mm.)

is illustrated below (**XVI**)

Although Grignard reagents are the most generally useful organometallic compounds, some of the above synthetic reactions can be effected with compounds of other types. Sondheimer[1] employed addition of a sodioacetylene derivative to ethylene oxide as one step in the synthesis of an ethylenic alcohol for comparison with an odoriferous constituent of violet leaf (11).

11. $C_2H_5I \xrightarrow[NH_3]{NaC\equiv CH} C_2H_5C\equiv CH \xrightarrow[NH_3]{NaNH_2} C_2H_5C\equiv CNa$

$$\xrightarrow[(H_2O)]{\begin{array}{c} CH_2\text{—}CH_2 \\ \diagdown\ \diagup \\ O \end{array}} C_2H_5C\equiv CCH_2CH_2OH \xrightarrow{H_2\text{-}Pd} \underset{}{\overset{H\ \ H}{C_2H_5C\text{=}CCH_2CH_2OH}}$$

cis-Δ^3-Hexene-1-ol

Alkyl and aryl derivatives of lithium, RLi and ArLi, enter into the usual Grignard reactions and are prepared by treating a halide with lithium metal in dry ether by essentially the same technique as employed in preparing a Grignard reagent (K. Ziegler, 1930). For example, phenyllithium is obtained from bromobenzene in about 75% yield and reacts quantitatively with benzophenone (12).

12. $C_6H_5Br\ +\ 2\ Li \rightarrow C_6H_5Li\ +\ LiBr$
$(C_6H_5)_2C\text{=}O\ +\ C_6H_5Li \rightarrow (C_6H_5)_3COLi \xrightarrow{H_2O} (C_6H_5)_3COH$

Chlorobenzene also reacts with lithium, whereas it is not reactive enough to form a Grignard reagent. Organolithium compounds are more expensive than Grignard reagents and for most purposes offer no advantages. However, they are more reactive and hence useful in cases where a Grignard reagent adds slowly or not at all. For example, addition of lithium acetylide to a triply unsaturated aldehyde (13) gives the desired ethynylcarbinol in 72% yield, whereas with sodium acetylide

[1] Franz Sondheimer, b. 1926, Stuttgart; Ph.D. Univ. London (Heilbron); Syntex S.A., Weizmann Inst.

13. $CH_3(CH=CH)_3CHO$ $\xrightarrow[\text{NH}_3 \ (72\%)]{\text{LiC}\equiv\text{CH; NH}_4\text{Cl}}$ $CH_3(CH=CH)_3CH(OH)C\equiv CH$

$\Delta^{2,4,6}$-Octatrienal   Deca-4,6,8-triene-1-yne-3-ol(m.p. 73°)

the yield is only about 20%. Lithium is added to liquid ammonia in a Dewar flask to form lithamide; acetylene is passed in to produce lithium acetylide; an ethereal solution of $\Delta^{2,4,6}$-octatrienal is added slowly with gentle passage of acetylene; and the acetylene stream is then replaced by nitrogen. Ammonium chloride is added to decompose the lithium alkoxide, the mixture is poured into a beaker, and the ammonia is allowed to evaporate through cellophane, which protects the sensitive product from air oxidation. The alcohol, collected by ether extraction, crystallizes from petroleum ether in long, colorless needles.

A novel Grignard synthesis reported by D. Seyferth[1] and M. A. Weiner (1959) utilizes the previously unknown **allyllithium** (14). The preparation of allylmag-

14. $(C_6H_5)_3SnCl$ $+$ $CH_2=CHCH_2Cl$ $+$ Mg $\xrightarrow[75-80\%]{}$ $(C_6H_5)_3SnCH_2CH=CH_2$

Triphenyltin   Allyltriphenyltin
chloride   (m.p. 74°)

$(C_6H_5)_3SnCH_2CH=CH_2$ $+$ C_6H_5Li $\rightarrow$ $(C_6H_5)_4Sn$ $+$ $CH_2=CHCH_2Li$

$$CH_2=CHCH_2Li \ + \ CH_3\overset{O}{\overset{\|}{C}}CH_2CH(CH_3)_2 \ \xrightarrow[70-75\%]{(H_2O)} \ CH_2=CHCH_2\underset{\underset{CH_3}{|}}{\overset{\overset{OH}{|}}{C}}CH_2CH(CH_3)_2$$

nesium chloride and its reaction with triphenyltin chloride are combined in one operation (ether, tetrahydrofurane, and benzene) and the resulting allyltriphenyltin is then treated under nitrogen with phenyllithium in ether. The resulting suspension of tetraphenyltin in a solution of allyllithium is then employed for reaction with 4-methyl-2-pentanone for synthesis of 4,6-dimethyl-Δ^1-heptene-4-ol.

Grignard reactions proved useful in elucidation of the structure of **cosmene**, a volatile, light-sensitive hydrocarbon isolated from various Norwegian Compositae by Jörgine S. Sörensen and Nils A. Sörensen (1954) by steam distillation of the plant in a slow stream of pure nitrogen with exclusion of light; crystallization from petroleum ether was effected at −70° (m.p. −1°). The substance is altered so rapidly on contact with air that analyses were not reliable. The Norwegian investigators noticed that the substance has a four-banded ultraviolet spectrum very similar to that reported for octatetraene-1,3,5,7:

	λ max, mμ			
Cosmene	272	278	296	309.7
$CH_2=CH(CH=CH)_2CH=CH_2$	268	283	290.5	304

Woods[2] had found a route to this hydrocarbon in exploring the chemistry of dihydropyrane (II), available by pyrolytic dehydration of tetrahydrofurfuryl alcohol

[1] Dietmar Seyferth, b. 1929 Chemnitz, Germany; Ph.D. Harvard (Rochow); Mass. Inst. Techn.

[2] G. Forrest Woods, b. 1913 Chicago; Ph.D. Harvard (Kohler, Bartlett); Univ. Maryland

I $\xrightarrow{\text{Al}_2\text{O}_3,\ 300°}$ II $\xrightarrow{\text{Br}_2}$ III $\xrightarrow{\text{NH}_3,\ \text{C}_2\text{H}_5\text{OH}}$

I (with CH$_2$OH) → II → III (with Br, Br)

IV $\xrightarrow{\text{NaOC}_2\text{H}_5}$ V $\xrightarrow{\text{H}_3\text{PO}_4}$ VI $\xrightarrow{-\text{H}_2\text{O}}$

IV (Br, OC$_2$H$_5$) → V (OC$_2$H$_5$) → VI $\begin{bmatrix} \text{CH}_2 & \overset{\text{CH}}{} & \text{CH} \\ \text{HOCH}_2 & & \text{CHO} \end{bmatrix}$

VII
$$\overset{\text{CH}}{\underset{\begin{smallmatrix}\text{CH}_2 & \text{CHO}\end{smallmatrix}}{\overset{\text{CH}\ \ \ \text{CH}}{}}}$$
$\xrightarrow{\text{CH}_2=\text{CHCH}_2\text{MgBr}}$

VIII
$$\text{CH}_2=\text{CHCH}=\text{CHCHCH}_2\text{CH}=\text{CH}_2$$
$$\underset{\text{OH}}{|}$$
$\xrightarrow{\text{Al}_2\text{O}_3}$

IX
$$\text{CH}_2=\text{CHCH}=\text{CHCH}=\text{CHCH}=\text{CH}_2$$

(Paul,[1] 1933). In the dibromide III the bromine adjacent to the electron-rich oxygen is labile and easily replaced by an ethoxyl group to give IV. The latter on dehydrohalogenation affords V, which on hydrolysis with phosphoric acid gives a transient product VI, and this loses water and affords $\Delta^{2,4}$-pentadienal (VII). Reaction with allylmagnesium bromide to form VIII and dehydration gave the tetraene IX, m.p. 50°. Sörensen and Sörensen noticed that the spectrum of cosmene matches that of the tetraene IX except for a general bathochromic displacement of about 5 mμ, which could be due to the presence in cosmene of two terminal methyl groups. Since the infrared spectrum shows a strong band at 1372 cm^{-1} characteristic of a methyl group, which is lacking in the spectrum of IX, and shows no ethyl band at 770 cm^{-1}, they suggested the isoprenoid structure X. Whiting promptly established this structure as correct by synthesis. The starting material, 3-methylpentene-1-yne-4-ol-3 (XIII) was prepared according to Oroshnik[2] by reaction of vinyl methyl ketone (XI) with a suspension of lithium acetylide in liquid ammonia and hydrolysis of the lithium alcoholate XII. Whiting converted the carbinol XIII to the dimagnesio halide derivative XIV by reaction with ethyl Grignard reagent, displaced the ether by benzene, and cooled the mixture during addition of α-methacraldehyde (XV). The last step is an application of the newly found reaction of propargylic alcohols with lithium aluminum hydride (6.16); the product, 2,6-dimethyloctatetraene-1,3,5,7 (X), proved to be identical with cosmene.

[1] Raymond-Etienne Paul, b. 1907 Angers, France; Ph.D. Paris (Blanchard, Lespieaux); Univ. Angers; Rhône-Poulenc

[2] William Oroshnik, b. 1914 New York; Ph.D. Polytech. Inst. Brooklyn (Spoerri); Ortho Pharmaceut. Corp.

$$\text{HC} \equiv \text{CLi} + \underset{\overset{\displaystyle \text{O}}{\displaystyle |}}{\overset{\displaystyle \text{CH}_3}{\underset{|}{\text{C}}}}\text{CH}=\text{CH}_2 \xrightarrow{\text{liq. NH}_3} \text{HC} \equiv \text{C} - \underset{\text{OLi}}{\overset{\text{CH}_3}{\text{C}}} - \text{CH}=\text{CH}_2 \xrightarrow{\text{H}_2\text{O, H}^+} \text{HC} \equiv \text{C} - \underset{\text{OH}}{\overset{\text{CH}_3}{\text{C}}} - \text{CH}=\text{CH}_2$$

XI   XII   XIII

$$\xrightarrow{2\ \text{C}_2\text{H}_5\text{MgBr}} \text{BrMgC} \equiv \text{C} - \underset{\text{OMgBr}}{\overset{\text{CH}_3}{\text{C}}} - \text{CH}=\text{CH}_2 \xrightarrow{\text{CH}_2=\overset{\text{CH}_3}{\text{C}}\text{CHO (XV)}}$$

XIV

$$\underset{\text{OH}}{\overset{\text{CH}_3}{\text{CH}_2=\text{C}}} - \text{CH} - \text{C} \equiv \text{C} - \underset{\text{OH}}{\overset{\text{CH}_3}{\text{C}}} - \text{CH}=\text{CH}_2 \xrightarrow{\text{LiAlH}_4} \text{CH}_2=\overset{\text{CH}_3}{\text{CCH}}=\text{CHCH}=\overset{\text{CH}_3}{\text{C}} - \text{CH}=\text{CH}_2$$

XVI   X

8.7   **Oxygenation of Grignard Reagents.** — Ethereal solutions of aliphatic Grignard reagents absorb molecular oxygen with great avidity, and hydrolysis of the oxygenated products affords alcohols in yields of 60–90%:

$$2\ \text{RMgX} + \text{O}_2 \rightarrow 2\ \text{ROMgX} \xrightarrow{\text{H}_2\text{O}} 2\ \text{ROH}$$

Yields of phenols from arylmagnesium halides are lower (10–22%) and many by-products are formed. The oxidation is sometimes attended with spectacular chemiluminescence, as demonstrated by pouring a solution of p-chlorophenylmagnesium bromide from one flask to another in the dark. Since rapid uptake of oxygen is very general, Grignard reagents are advisedly protected during preparation and use by an atmosphere of pure, dry nitrogen. Although oxygenation of alkylmagnesium halides at ordinary temperature finds little preparative use, Walling[1] (1955) discovered that alkyl hydroperoxides can be prepared in good yield by slow addition of Grignard reagents to ether that is cooled to about −70° and kept saturated with oxygen. The yield of t-butyl hydroperoxide (1), determined by titration, is 86%. Reverse addition is necessary, for otherwise t-butyl-

1. $(\text{CH}_3)_3\text{CMgCl} + \text{O}_2 \rightarrow (\text{CH}_3)_3\text{COOMgCl} \xrightarrow[\text{HCl}]{\text{H}_2\text{O}} (\text{CH}_3)_3\text{COOH}$

2. $(\text{CH}_3)_3\text{COOMgCl} + (\text{CH}_3)_3\text{CMgCl} \rightarrow 2\ (\text{CH}_3)_3\text{COMgCl}$

OOMgCl is reduced by the Grignard reagent as in (2) and the final product is the alcohol. Benzyl hydroperoxide, unavailable by autoxidation of toluene, was obtained from benzylmagnesium chloride in 30% yield and found to undergo usual base-catalyzed conversion to the carbonyl compound (4.16), in this case benzaldehyde. Best results were obtained with tertiary chlorides, but cyclo-

$$\text{C}_6\text{H}_5\text{CH}_2\text{OOH} \xrightarrow{\text{OH}^-} \text{C}_6\text{H}_5\text{CH}=\text{O} + \text{H}_2\text{O}$$
Benzyl hydroperoxide
b.p. 56°/1 mm.

---

[1] Cheves Walling, b. 1916 Evanston, Ill.; Ph.D. Chicago (Kharasch); Columbia Univ.

hexyl-MgCl and *n*-butyl-MgCl gave the corresponding hydroperoxides in yields of 66 and 57%. Yields from *n*-butyllithium and from di-*n*-butylzinc were 36 and 48%. Bromides gave poorer results than chlorides, probably because of oxidation of bromide ion to bromine. Acetylenic Grignard reagents proved to be relatively stable to oxygen.

8.8 Reduction of Aldehydes and Ketones. — On addition of hydrogen to the carbonyl group, an aldehyde affords a primary alcohol and a ketone gives a secondary alcohol. Reduction can be effected by catalytic hydrogenation

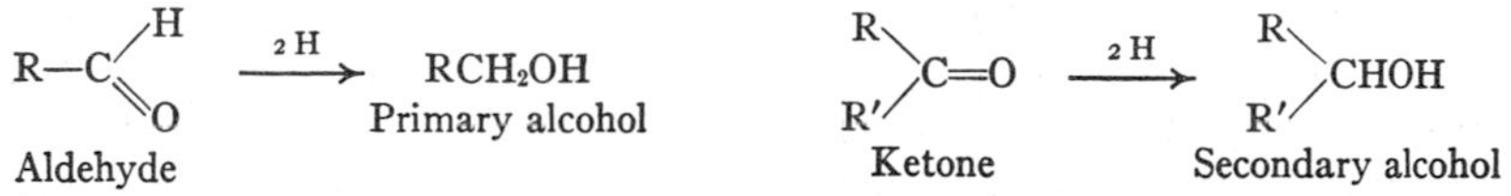

$$R-C{\overset{H}{\underset{O}{}}} \xrightarrow{2H} RCH_2OH \qquad {R \atop R'}C=O \xrightarrow{2H} {R \atop R'}CHOH$$

Aldehyde   Primary alcohol   Ketone   Secondary alcohol

but chemical methods where available are preferred because of greater simplicity. Before metal hydrides became available (see below), however, such procedures as were available were applicable to specific cases and lacked generality. One example is the reduction of *n*-heptaldehyde with iron and acetic acid (8.3), another is the reduction of benzophenone with zinc dust and alcoholic alkali. One limitation

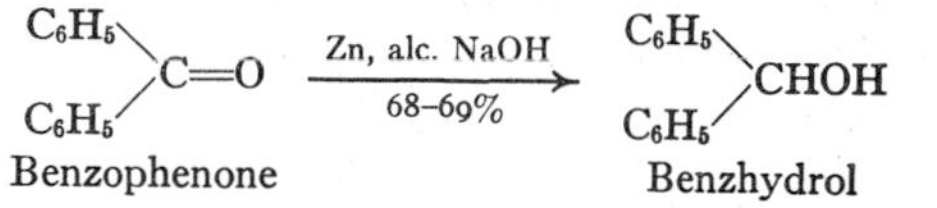

$$\underset{C_6H_5}{\overset{C_6H_5}{}}C=O \xrightarrow[68-69\%]{Zn,\ alc.\ NaOH} \underset{C_6H_5}{\overset{C_6H_5}{}}CHOH$$

Benzophenone   Benzhydrol

to the use of heavy metal combinations is that ketones often afford considerable amounts of bimolecular reduction products (12.34). Another is that the less reactive carbonyl group of an ester is not attacked.

8.9 Reduction of Esters. — The Bouveault[1]-Blanc[2] method of reduction consists in refluxing an ester with sodium and an alcohol; the products are a primary alcohol having the carbon content of the acid residue and an alcohol

$$RCOOCH_3 + 4H \rightarrow RCH_2OH + HOCH_3$$

derived from the alcoholic component. Free acids are resistant to attack by this method. Anhydrous ethanol is commonly used to furnish hydrogen, but a butyl or an amyl alcohol can be employed to provide a higher reflux temperature and more solvent power. Practical examples are as follows:

1. 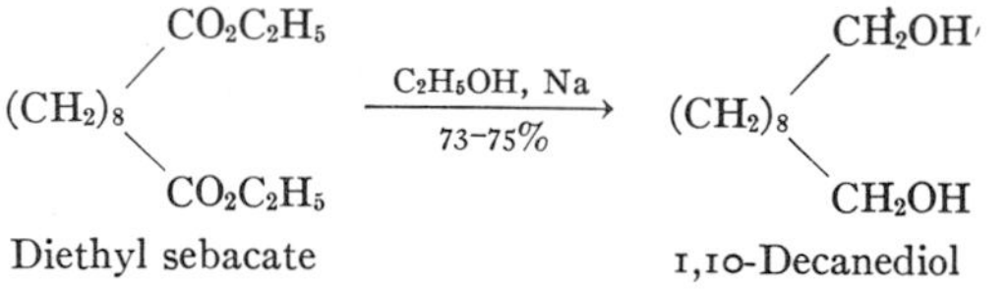 $(CH_2)_8{\overset{CO_2C_2H_5}{\underset{CO_2C_2H_5}{}}} \xrightarrow[73-75\%]{C_2H_5OH,\ Na} (CH_2)_8{\overset{CH_2OH}{\underset{CH_2OH}{}}}$

Diethyl sebacate   1,10-Decanediol

2. $CH_3(CH_2)_7CH=CH(CH_2)_8CO_2C_4H_9 \xrightarrow[82-84\%]{C_4H_9OH,\ Na} CH_3(CH_2)_7CH=CH(CH_2)_7CH_2OH$

Butyl oleate   Oleyl alcohol (b.p. 195°/8 mm.)

---

[1] Louis Bouveault, 1864–1909; b. Nevers, France; Ph.D. Paris (Hanriot); Lyon, Lille, Nancy, Paris; *Ber.*, **42**, 3561 (1909)

[2] Gustave Blanc, 1872–1927; b. Paris; Ph.D. Paris (Friedel); Laboratoire de la Séction technique de l'intendance militaire aux Invalides (Paris); Firme Lautier (Grasse)

High-pressure hydrogenation over Adkins copper chromite catalyst provides a second experimental method, for example:

$$(CH_2)_4 \Big\langle \begin{array}{l} CO_2C_2H_5 \\ CO_2C_2H_5 \end{array} \xrightarrow[85-90\%]{H_2,\ CuCr_2O_4\ (255°,\ 10-15\ atm.)} (CH_2)_4 \Big\langle \begin{array}{l} CH_2OH \\ CH_2OH \end{array}$$

Diethyl adipate   1,4-Hexanediol

Lauryl alcohol, n-$C_{12}H_{25}OH$, and the C_{14}, C_{16}, and C_{18} homologs are produced technically by hydrogenation of the methyl esters of lauric, myristic, palmitic, and stearic acid derived from fats. The Bouveault-Blanc and hydrogenation methods are both generally applicable and both probably involve addition of hydrogen to the carbonyl group with formation of an intermediate aldehyde. Preformed

$$RC\!\!\underset{}{\overset{OCH_3}{=}}\!\!O \xrightarrow{C_2H_5OH;\ Na} RC\!\!\underset{H}{\overset{OCH_3}{\vert}}\!\!-ONa \xrightarrow{-CH_3ONa} RC\!\!\underset{H}{\overset{}{=}}\!\!O \xrightarrow{2H} RCH_2OH$$

aldehydes and ketones are reduced by the sodium-alcohol method.

8.10   Metal Hydride Reduction. — Lithium aluminum hydride was discovered in 1947 by A. E. Finholt, A. C. Bond, Jr., and H. I Schlesinger.[1] The reagent is made by gradual addition of anhydrous aluminum chloride to a stirred slurry of lithium hydride in ether. Lithium chloride pre-

$$4\ LiH + AlCl_3 \rightarrow LiAlH_4 + 3\ LiCl$$

cipitates during the addition, and this, together with excess lithium hydride, is separated by filtration under nitrogen pressure. The solid reagent is available commercially and, if protected from moist air and carbon dioxide, is stable indefinitely at room temperature. At the same time that the discovery was announced, R. F. Nystrom and W. G. Brown reported numerous examples of high-yield reduction of organic compounds with the new reagent. It is usually employed in solution or suspension in anhydrous ether (100 g. dissolves 25–30 g. at 25°); tetrahydrofurane is favored as a higher boiling ether (100 g. dissolves 13 g. at 25°). The metal hydride reacts with water and alcohols with liberation of hydrogen; indeed all hydrogen atoms attached to nitrogen, oxygen, or sulfur are active hydrogens with respect to lithium aluminum hydride and will react with liberation of 1 mole of hydrogen and consumption of 0.25 mole of hydride per active hydrogen.

Lithium aluminum hydride appears to exist in ethereal solution as ionic aggregates of solvated lithium ions and aluminohydride ions, or $Li^+[AlH_4]^-$. Reaction

$$R_2C\!=\!O \xrightarrow{(Li^+)AlH_4^-} \left\{ R_2C\!\!\underset{AlH_3}{\overset{H}{\vert}}\!\!-O^-(Li^+) \right\} \rightarrow R_2CHOAl^-H_3\,(Li^+) \xrightarrow{3R_2C=O}$$

$$(R_2CHO)_4Al^-(Li^+) \xrightarrow{4H_2O} 4R_2CHOH + Al(OH)_3 + LiOH$$

[1] Hermann I. Schlesinger, 1882–1960; b. Minneapolis; Ph.D. Chicago; Univ. Chicago

with a ketone then involves transfer of hydride ion in a bimolecular nucleophilic displacement to produce an alkoxide anion which immediately coordinates with the neutral aluminum hydride to form a new ion. Successive reaction with three more moles of ketone exhausts the reagent, and decomposition of the alcoholate liberates the alcoholic reduction product. Because of its low molecular weight (37.95) and because one mole reduces four moles of an aldehyde or ketone, lithium aluminum hydride has a favorable ratio of reducing capacity to mass. If excess reagent is used, as is often the case (2- to 4-fold excess), destruction of active hydride with water is troublesome because of the large volume of hydrogen evolved. Ethyl acetate is more satisfactory because it is reduced to two moles of ethanol, which should not interfere with isolation of the product. Reduction of an ester doubtless involves intermediate formation of the aldehyde, as in the reductions described in the preceding section.

Typical reductions are as follows:

$$CH_3(CH_2)_5CHO \xrightarrow[86\%]{\text{0.25 LiAlH}_4} CH_3(CH_2)_5CH_2OH$$

$$CH_3CH_2COCH_3 \xrightarrow[80\%]{\text{0.25 LiAlH}_4} CH_3CH_2CH(OH)CH_3$$

$$CH_3CH{=}CHCHO \xrightarrow[70\%]{\text{0.25 LiAlH}_4} CH_3CH{=}CHCH_2OH$$

Crotonaldehyde   Crotyl alcohol

$$C_6H_5COOC_2H_5 \xrightarrow[90\%]{\text{0.5 LiAlH}_4} C_6H_5CH_2OH$$

Ethyl benzoate   Benzyl alcohol

Use of the reagent for reductive fission of a *vic*-oxide (epoxy derivative) has been illustrated (5.17). Note that if the compound being reduced contains an acetoxyl group, this group is cleaved in the course of the reaction; indeed lithium aluminum hydride is useful for deacetylation of acetates of alcohols sensitive to acids or bases:

$$\overset{\displaystyle O}{\underset{\displaystyle \parallel}{RO C CH_3}} \xrightarrow{\text{0.5 LiAlH}_4;\ H_2O} ROH\ +\ HOCH_2CH_3$$

Lithium aluminum hydride is capable of reducing free carboxylic acids, which are resistant to most other methods, and acids of simple types often afford primary alcohols in high yield. Although the tertiary carboxyl group of trimethylacetic

$$(CH_3)_3CCOOH \xrightarrow[92\%]{\text{0.75 LiAlH}_4} {}'(CH_3)_3CCH_2OH$$

Trimethylacetic acid   Neopentyl alcohol

$$HOOC(CH_2)_8COOH \xrightarrow[97\%]{\text{1.5 LiAlH}_4} HOCH_2(CH_2)_8CH_2OH$$

Sebacic acid   Decanediol-1,10

acid (pivalic acid) is somewhat hindered, the acid is reduced readily to neopentyl alcohol. Podocarpic acid (from Javanese and New Zealand resins) has an axial tertiary β-carboxyl group which is close to an axial β-methyl group and hence strongly hindered. Furthermore, the active hydrogens of the carboxyl and phenolic hydroxyl groups consume reagent and give rise to metal oxide groups which

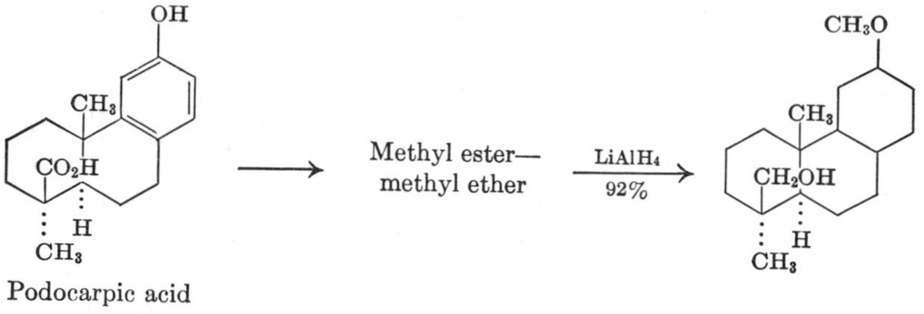

Podocarpic acid → Methyl ester— methyl ether $\xrightarrow[92\%]{\text{LiAlH}_4}$

decrease the solubility. Thus reduction of the free acid over a four-day period afforded podocarpinol in only 56% yield; reduction of the methyl ester methyl ether to podocarpinol methyl ether proceeded much more satisfactorily.

Another complex hydride, sodium borohydride ($NaBH_4$), is insoluble in ether but soluble in water without decomposition. It can be used for effecting reduction in water or methanol of aldehydes and ketones (not acids):

$$CH_3COCH_2CH_2COCH_3 \xrightarrow[86\%]{0.5\,NaBH_4} CH_3CH(OH)CH_2CH_2CH(OH)CH_3$$

Acetonylacetone   Hexanediol-2,5

$$CH_3CH{=}CHCHO \xrightarrow[85\%]{0.25\,NaBH_4} CH_3CH{=}CHCH_2OH$$

Potassium borohydride (mol. wt. 53.95) is less expensive than sodium borohydride (mol. wt. 37.85) but has a somewhat lower ratio of reducing capacity to mass.

Lithium borohydride ($LiBH_4$) is soluble in ether and decomposed by water; solutions in ether (0.5 M) or in tetrahydrofurane (3.5 M) can be employed. The reagent is milder than lithium aluminum hydride and particularly suited to selective reduction of the more reactive of two groups. Aldehydes and ketones are reduced rapidly at 0°; esters are reduced when the solution is refluxed for several hours, and acids are even more resistant:

$$n\text{-}C_{15}H_{31}COOC_4H_9\text{-}n \xrightarrow[95\%]{0.5\,LiBH_4} n\text{-}C_{15}H_{31}CH_2OH$$

n-Butyl palmitate n-Hexadecanol

$$C_6H_5COCH_2CH_2COOH \xrightarrow[78\%]{0.25\,LiBH_4} C_6H_5CH(OH)CH_2CH_2COOH$$

β-Benzoylpropionic acid   (as the lactone)

$$m\text{-}NO_2C_6H_4COCH_3 \xrightarrow[93\%]{0.25\,LiBH_4} m\text{-}NO_2C_6H_4CH(OH)CH_3$$

m-Nitroacetophenone α-(m-Nitrophenyl)-ethanol

INDUSTRIAL PREPARATION

8.11   **Methanol.** — Until 1923 methanol was prepared by destructive distillation of wood, which consists of the carbohydrate cellulose, $(C_6H_{10}O_5)_n$, together with some 20–30% of lignin, a polymeric substance containing aromatic rings bearing methoxyl groups ($—OCH_3$). Methanol derived from wood arises from the lignin component. When wood is heated without access of air to temperatures above 250°, it decomposes into charcoal and a volatile fraction that partly condenses on cooling to a liquor, pyroligneous acid. A dark heavy oil separates from the condensate, and the supernatant aqueous layer contains methanol, acetic acid, traces of acetone and allyl alcohol, and contaminants with a disagreeable odor. Acetic acid can be neutralized with calcium hydroxide, and methanol separated by distillation. At the present time methanol is made largely synthetically in nearly quantitative yield by hydrogenation of carbon monoxide:

$$2\ H_2 + CO \rightleftharpoons CH_3OH$$

Formation of methanol is accompanied by a decrease in volume, and hence pressures of 3000 lbs./sq. in. are commonly employed to promote the conversion. The usual temperature range is 350–400°. The hydrogenation is catalyzed by chromic oxide in combination with zinc oxide.

8.12   **Ethanol.** — Production of ethyl alcohol by fermentation of sugars under the influence of yeast has been known since antiquity. Yeast contains biological catalysts, enzymes, which promote a lengthy sequence of reactions that effect, in about 95% yield, the following overall reaction: $C_6H_{12}O_6 \rightarrow$ $2\ C_2H_5OH + 2\ CO_2$. Elucidation of all the steps was a major triumph of biochemistry. Ethanol is also manufactured from ethylene, available from coke-oven gas and by cracking of petroleum fractions, by absorption in sulfuric acid and hydrolysis of the ethylsulfuric acid formed.

Ordinary commercial alcohol is a constant-boiling mixture of alcohol (95.57% by weight) and water (4.43%), and since this mixture boils at 78.2°, a temperature slightly lower than the boiling point of absolute ethyl alcohol, 78.3°, separation cannot be effected by ordinary distillation. Absolute alcohol can be prepared by chemical methods, for example with use of quicklime, which combines with water but not with alcohol, but it is prepared commercially by azeotropic distillation. When a mixture of 95% alcohol and benzene is distilled, the initial fraction consists of benzene—alcohol—water (64.8°), followed by alcohol—benzene (68.2°), and the final fraction consists of absolute alcohol.

8.13   **Isopropyl Alcohol.** — Isopropyl alcohol is made by hydrogenation of acetone and by hydration of propylene (petroleum); diisopropyl alco-

$$\underset{\text{Acetone}}{CH_3COCH_3} \xrightarrow{\ H_2\ (Ni)\ } \underset{\text{Isopropyl alcohol}}{CH_3CHOHCH_3}$$

hol, a by-product, is valued because it has an octane rating of 98.

8.14   **Butyl Alcohols.** — *n*-Butyl alcohol is made along with acetone by bacterial fermentation of carbohydrates. The process (utilizing *Clostridium acetobutylicum* Weizmann) was developed by Weizmann in 1911 to provide acetone, required by the British for compounding the propellant Cordite; after the war, its major function was to supply *n*-butyl alcohol, required for quick-drying automobile lacquers. *sec*-Butyl alcohol, or butanol-2, is made from the mixture

$$\left.\begin{array}{c} \underset{\text{Butene-2}}{CH_3CH{=}CHCH_3} \\[1em] \underset{\text{Butene-1}}{CH_3CH_2CH{=}CH_2} \end{array}\right\} \xrightarrow[\text{80\%}]{H_2SO_4,\ H_2O} \underset{\text{Butanol-2}}{CH_3CH_2CHOHCH_3}$$

of butene-1 and -2 present to the extent of 30–32% in the C_4-cut of gas obtained on vapor-phase cracking. Isobutene is selectively absorbed in 65% sulfuric acid at 5–10°, and butadiene is removed by treatment with cuprous chloride—ammonium chloride. The butenes are then extracted from butane and isobutane by absorption in concentrated sulfuric acid, and the alcohol is obtained on hydrolysis of the acid solution.

8.15   Amyl Alcohols. — The mixture of chloropentanes prepared by thermal chlorination of the C_5-cut of natural gasoline (4.11) is utilized in part for conversion to a mixture of amyl alcohols. Hydrolysis is effected with hot aqueous sodium hydroxide in the presence of sodium stearate soap to emulsify the water-immiscible layer. The alcohol mixture consists largely of five isomers, and the boiling points are such that separation of a primary and a secondary fraction is possible:

$$\text{Primary} \begin{cases} CH_3CH_2CH_2CH_2CH_2OH \ (138.0°) \\ CH_3CH_2CH(CH_3)CH_2OH \ (128°) \\ (CH_3)_2CHCH_2CH_2OH \ (131.5°) \end{cases} \quad \text{Secondary} \begin{cases} CH_3CH_2CH_2CHOHCH_3 \ (119.5°) \\ (CH_3CH_2)_2CHOH \ (115.6°) \end{cases}$$

Both the total mixture and the segregated cuts are used as solvents and plasticizers, particularly for production of the important lacquer solvent amyl acetate.

Commercial *sec*-amyl alcohol is a mixture made by the sulfuric acid method from pentene-1 and pentene-2, present to an extent of about 30% in the pentane-pentene fraction from cracked gasoline. Pentene-1 forms pentanol-2; pentene-2, a mixture of pentanol-2 (65%) and pentanol-3 (35%). The technical product contains about 80% of pentanol-2 and 20% of pentanol-3.

8.16   Ethylene Glycol. — An early process involved either hydrolysis of ethylene chlorohydrin with soda or conversion of the chlorohydrin into ethylene oxide, which is hydrolyzed rapidly by dilute acid. Ethylene oxide is

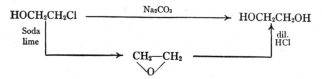

now made by direct catalytic combination of ethylene with oxygen (p. 261). A less direct but efficient route involves the following steps:

$$CH_2{=}O + CO + H_2O \xrightarrow[\text{700 Atm.}]{200°} CH_2OHCO_2H \xrightarrow{ROH}$$
$$CH_2OHCO_2R \xrightarrow{Cr, H_2} CH_2OHCH_2OH + ROH$$

Ethylene glycol is used extensively as an antifreeze agent. Long-lived coolant formulations made from about equal parts of ethylene glycol and deionized water and containing rust inhibitors give freeze protection down to −40° (−40° C. = −40° F.) and boil at about 116°.

Monoalkyl ethers useful as solvents in varnishes and lacquers are obtained by alcoholysis of ethylene oxide. Dioxane is made by acid-catalyzed polymerization of the oxide. Dioxane is a powerful solvent for many organic substances and is

TABLE 8.3. ETHYLENE GLYCOL DERIVATIVES

NAME	FORMULA	SP. GR.	B.P. °C.	G./100 G. H_2O 20°
Ethylene glycol				
Diol	$HOCH_2CH_2OH$	1.12	197	∞
Monomethyl ether	$CH_3OCH_2CH_2OH$	0.97	125	∞
Monoethyl ether	$C_2H_5OCH_2CH_2OH$	0.93	136	∞
Mono-n-butyl ether	$CH_3CH_2CH_2CH_2OCH_2CH_2OH$	0.90	171	5
Dimethyl ether	$CH_3OCH_2CH_2OCH_3$		83	∞
Diethylene glycol				
Diol	$HOCH_2CH_2OCH_2CH_2OH$	1.12	245	∞
Monomethyl ether	$CH_3OCH_2CH_2OCH_2CH_2OH$	1.02	194	∞
Monoethyl ether	$C_2H_5OCH_2CH_2OCH_2CH_2OH$	1.03	195	∞
Monobutyl ether	$n\text{-}C_4H_9OCH_2CH_2OCH_2CH_2OH$	0.95	231	∞
Dimethyl ether	$CH_3OCH_2CH_2OCH_2CH_2OCH_3$	0.95	161	∞
Triethylene glycol				
Diol	$HOCH_2CH_2OCH_2CH_2OCH_2CH_2OH$	1.12	287	∞
Monomethyl ether	$CH_3OCH_2CH_2OCH_2CH_2OCH_2CH_2OH$	1.05	249	∞
Monoethyl ether	$C_2H_5OCH_2CH_2OCH_2CH_2OCH_2CH_2OH$	1.02	256	∞
Dimethyl ether	$CH_3OCH_2CH_2OCH_2CH_2OCH_2CH_2OCH_3$		222	∞

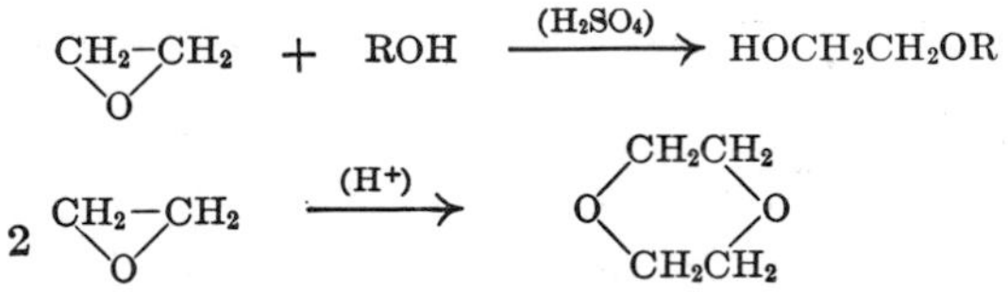

also miscible with water, a property shared by several of the ether derivatives of Table 8.3. Di- and triethylene glycol are water-miscible hydroxylic solvents of high solvent power and are useful solvents for reactions requiring high temperatures; they dissolve potassium hydroxide and are stable to this reagent. The dimethyl ethers are useful as special, nonhydroxylic, water miscible solvents.

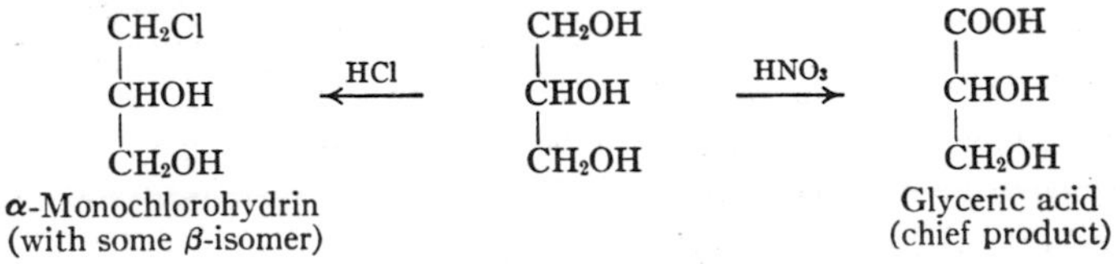

8.17   Glycerol. — Glycerol (Gr. *glykys*, sweet), a viscous, hygroscopic liquid with a sweet taste, was discovered by Scheele in 1779 as a product of hydrolysis of olive oil. The pure substance, b.p. 290°, has a marked tendency to supercool, but it slowly crystallizes and has a melting point of 18°. Glycerol contains both primary and secondary alcoholic groups, and in the reactions with dry hydrogen chloride and with nitric acid, the former type is the more reactive.

Glycerol is a by-product of the manufacture of soap in amounts sufficient except in time of war, when it is required for production of nitroglycerin. During World War I additional quantities were made by fermentation. In 1938 Shell Chemical announced production of synthetic glycerol from petroleum. Propylene on thermal chlorination suffers substitution in the activated methyl group to give

$$
\begin{array}{ccccc}
CH_3 & & CH_2Cl & & CH_2OH \\
| & \xrightarrow[80\%]{Cl_2(400°)} & | & \xrightarrow{(OH^-)} & | & \xrightarrow{HOCl} \\
CH & & CH & & CH \\
|| & & || & & || \\
CH_2 & & CH_2 & & CH_2 \\
\text{Propylene} & & \text{Allyl chloride} & & \text{Allyl alcohol}
\end{array}
$$

$$
\begin{array}{ccccc}
CH_2OH & & CH_2OH & & CH_2OH \\
| & \xrightarrow{\text{Soda lime}} & | & \xrightarrow{H_2O} & | \\
CHOH & & CH & & CHOH \\
| & & \diagdown O & & | \\
CH_2Cl & & CH_2 \diagup & & CH_2OH \\
 & & \text{Glycidol} & & \text{Glycerol}
\end{array}
$$

allyl chloride, which is hydrolyzed to allyl alcohol. At temperatures below 200° the addition reaction predominates, and even at high temperatures some 1,2-dichloropropane is formed; another by-product is 1,3-dichloropropene. Hypochlorite addition and cyclization with base gives glycidol (2,3-epoxypropanol-1), which affords glycerol on hydrolysis. Another useful product, which for an obscure reason bears the name epichlorohydrin, is made from allyl chloride by hypochlorite addition and cyclization. In a second process catalytic air oxidation of

$$
\begin{array}{ccccc}
CH_2Cl & & CH_2Cl & & CH_2Cl \\
| & \xrightarrow{HOCl} & | & \xrightarrow{NaOH} & | \\
CH & & CHOH & & CH \\
|| & & | & & \diagdown O \\
CH_2 & & CH_2Cl & & CH_2 \diagup
\end{array}
$$

Epichlorohydrin (b. p. 118°)

propylene affords acrolein, which is hydroxylated with hydrogen peroxide to an

$$
\begin{array}{ccccccc}
CH_3 & & & CH=O & & CH=O & & CH_2OH \\
| & + O_2 & \xrightarrow{\substack{Cu_2O \\ 370°}} & | & \xrightarrow{H_2O_2} & | & \xrightarrow{H_2,\ Ni} & | \\
CH & & & CH & & CHOH & & CHOH \\
|| & & & || & & | & & | \\
CH_2 & & & CH_2 & & CH_2OH & & CH_2OH \\
 & & & \text{Acrolein} & & \textit{dl-}\text{Glyceraldhyde}
\end{array}
$$

aldehyde reducible to glycerol.

8.18   **Propane-1,3-diol** is a product of bacterial fermentation of glycerol.
In the course of the large-scale production of glycerol from fats in World War I, some batches were found to contain sufficient quantities of this propanediol to lower the specific gravity below the tolerance value for material required for nitroglycerin manufacture. By deliberate fermentation glycerol can be converted into the glycol in 45% yield.

REACTIONS

The dehydration of alcohols has been discussed in a previous chapter (5); displacement reactions are treated in a future one (10).

8.19   With Metals. — When metallic sodium is added continuously in small pieces to excess methanol, the metal rapidly dissolves, hydrogen is evolved, and there is a considerable heat effect, although not sufficient to cause ignition of hydrogen as in the parallel reaction with water. The resulting solution contains sodium methoxide, CH_3ONa (also called sodium methylate). The substance can be obtained as a dry white solid by preparing a suspension of powdered

$$CH_3OH + Na \longrightarrow CH_3ONa + \tfrac{1}{2}H_2$$
$$\text{Sodium methoxide}$$

sodium in absolute ether and adding in portions one equivalent of methanol. Sodium and potassium alkoxides are stable in anhydrous methanol or ethanol but are hydrolyzed by water in an equilibrium reaction, for example:

$$C_2H_5OK + H_2O \rightleftharpoons C_2H_5OH + KOH$$

A solution of potassium hydroxide in ethyl alcohol, alcoholic potassium hydroxide, is an equilibrium mixture containing potassium ethoxide. Alkali metal alkoxides are useful as basic reagents for effecting eliminations and as condensation catalysts. Thus dehydrohalogenation of an alkyl halide involves attack by the alkoxide ion as electron donating nucleophile. An alkoxide ion is a more powerful nucleophile than the hydroxide ion because the inductive drift of electrons away from the alkyl group increases the electron density on oxygen: $CH_3{\rightarrow}O^-$. Since an inductive effect is still greater in the *t*-butoxide ion, potassium *t*-butoxide is a particularly effective condensing agent. A solution is prepared by refluxing potassium with *t*-butanol in a nitrogen atmosphere.

Aluminum isopropoxide, $Al[OCH(CH_3)_2]_3$, m.p. 118°, and aluminum *t*-butoxide have specific synthetic uses and are prepared by heating the anhydrous alcohol with amalgamated aluminum foil and a trace of carbon tetrachloride as catalyst; when hydrogen evolution ceases the molten alkoxide is distilled at reduced pressure.

8.20   Wagner-Meerwein Rearrangement. — In 1901 N. Zelinsky and J. Zelikow heated methyl-*t*-butylcarbinol (I, pinacolyl alcohol) with expectation of producing *t*-butylethylene (II), but found the product to be tetramethylethylene (III), a product of rearrangement of the carbon skeleton. Later

workers found that the normal alkene II is the chief product of dehydration of the alcohol over neutral alumina; passage of the alcohol over alumina with a stream of ammonia affords II in 72 % yield (H. Pines, 1960). The rearrangement reaction is thus associated with the use of an acid catalyst. This and many other acid-catalyzed rearrangements were eventually clarified through investigations by Wagner[1] in the field of terpenes and by Meerwein[2] in a broader field. Studies by Whitmore[3] (1930–40) are largely responsible for the following interpretation. The oxygen atom of the alcohol, functioning as a Lewis base, accepts a hydrogen

$$
\begin{array}{ccc}
\underset{\substack{| \\ \mathrm{CH_3} \\ \mathbf{I}}}{\overset{\substack{\mathrm{CH_3\ OH} \\ | \quad |}}{\mathrm{CH_3-C-C-CH_3}}} \ \ \xrightarrow{\ \mathrm{H^+}\ } \ \
\underset{\substack{| \\ \mathrm{CH_3\ H} \\ (a)}}{\overset{\substack{\mathrm{H} \\ \mathrm{CH_3\ {}^+OH} \\ | \quad |}}{\mathrm{CH_3-C-C-CH_3}}} \ \ \xrightarrow{\ -\mathrm{H_2O}\ } \ \
\underset{\substack{| \\ \mathrm{CH_3\ H} \\ (b)}}{\overset{\substack{[\mathrm{CH_3}] \\ + \\ |}}{\mathrm{CH_3-C-C-CH_3}}}
\end{array}
$$

$$
\xrightarrow{\text{(rearrangement)}} \ \
\underset{\substack{| \\ \mathrm{CH_3\ H} \\ (c)}}{\overset{\substack{\mathrm{CH_3} \\ + \quad | }}{\mathrm{CH_3-C-C-CH_3}}} \ \ \xrightarrow{\ -\mathrm{H^+}\ } \ \
\underset{\substack{| \\ \mathrm{CH_3} \\ \mathbf{III}}}{\overset{\substack{\mathrm{CH_3} \\ | }}{\mathrm{CH_3-C=C-CH_3}}}
$$

ion to form the oxonium ion (a), which loses water to give the carbonium ion (b). This ion is not so stable as the carbonium ion (c), for the charged carbon atom. of (b) carries only two alkyl groups (methyl and t-butyl), whereas that of (c) carries three (two methyls and an isopropyl); alkyl groups, being electron-releasing, partially balance the positive charge and hence increase stability. The difference in stability of the two carbonium ions provides a driving force for rearrangement of (b) to (c) by migration of a methyl group. Ion (c) then loses a proton (hydrogen atom from one carbon and the positive charge from the other), and the product is tetramethylethylene (III). The electronic formulation of the

$$
\begin{array}{ccc}
\underset{\substack{\mathbf{\cdot\cdot} \\ \mathrm{CH_3\ H} \\ \mathbf{I}}}{\overset{\substack{\mathrm{H} \\ \mathbf{\cdot\cdot} \\ \mathrm{CH_3\ \overset{\cdot\cdot}{:}O\overset{\cdot\cdot}{:}}}}{\mathrm{CH_3:C\ :\ C:CH_3}}} \ \xrightarrow{\mathrm{H^+}}\
\underset{\substack{\mathbf{\cdot\cdot} \\ \mathrm{CH_3\ H} \\ (a)}}{\overset{\substack{\mathrm{H}_+ \\ \mathrm{CH_3\ :O:\ H}}}{\mathrm{CH_3:C\ :\ C:CH_3}}} \ \xrightarrow{-\mathrm{H_2O}}\
\underset{\substack{\mathrm{CH_3\ H\ \cdot} \\ (b)}}{\overset{\substack{[\mathrm{CH_3}] \\ + }}{\mathrm{CH_3:C\ :\ C:CH_3}}}
\end{array}
$$

$$
\longrightarrow \
\underset{\substack{\mathrm{CH_3\ H} \\ (c)}}{\overset{\substack{\mathrm{CH_3} \\ + \\ }}{\mathrm{CH_3:C\ :\ C\ :\ CH_3}}} \ \xrightarrow{-\mathrm{H^+}}\
\underset{\substack{\mathrm{CH_3} \\ \mathbf{III}}}{\overset{\substack{\mathrm{CH_3} \\ }}{\mathrm{CH_3:C::C\ :\ CH_3}}}
$$

reaction shows that in both intermediate ions the carbon atom carrying the charge is electron deficient and reactive. The methyl group in migrating carries with it the pair of shared electrons.

Neopentyl alcohol has a structure such that normal dehydration is not possible.

[1] G. Wagner, 1849–1903; b. Kazan, Russia; Ph.D. Kazan (Butleroff, Markownikoff); St. Petersburg Univ.

[2] Hans Meerwein, b. 1879 Hamburg, Germany; Ph.D. Bonn (Schroeter); Univ. Marburg

[3] Frank C. Whitmore, 1887–1947; b. North Attleboro, Mass.; Ph.D. Harvard (E. L. Jackson); Penn. State Univ.; *J. Chem. Soc.*, 1090 (1948)

$$CH_3-\underset{\underset{CH_3}{|}}{\overset{\overset{CH_3}{|}}{C}}-CH_2OH \xrightarrow[-H_2O]{H^+} CH_3-\underset{\underset{CH_3}{|}}{\overset{\overset{CH_3}{|}}{C}}-\overset{+}{C}H_2 \rightarrow CH_3-\underset{\underset{CH_3}{|}}{\overset{\overset{CH_3}{|}}{\overset{+}{C}}}-CH_2CH_3 \xrightarrow{-H^+}$$

Neopentyl alcohol

$$(CH_3)_2C{=}CHCH_3$$

When the substance is heated with sulfuric acid, water is eliminated with rearrangement to trimethylethylene. The reaction involves rearrangement of a primary ion to a more stable tertiary ion.

8.21   Pinacol Rearrangement. — Experimenting at Göttingen in 1860 with pinacol, a diol readily available from acetone (12.34), Fittig found that the substance when refluxed briefly with 30% sulfuric acid is dehydrated to a new compound, to which he assigned the name pinacolone. The structure was estab-

$$\begin{array}{c}(CH_3)_2\overset{|}{C}OH \\ (CH_3)_2\overset{|}{C}OH\end{array} \xrightarrow{H_2SO_4} \begin{array}{c}CH_3C{=}O \\ (CH_3)_3\overset{|}{C}\end{array} \qquad \begin{array}{c}CH_2OH \\ \overset{|}{C}H_2OH\end{array} \xrightarrow{-H_2O} \left[\begin{array}{c}CH-OH \\ \overset{|}{C}H_2\end{array}\right] \rightarrow \begin{array}{c}CH{=}O \\ \overset{|}{C}H_3\end{array}$$

Pinacol   Pinacolone   Ethylene glycol

lished at St. Petersburg in 1873 by Butleroff, who seemed satisfied with a suggested analogy to the conversion of ethylene glycol to acetaldehyde. Actually the latter reaction involves merely dehydration to acetaldehyde enol, whereas the formation of pinacolone involves migration of a methyl group under acid catalysis. Normal dehydration of pinacol over alumina to give 2,3-dimethylbutadiene in high yield has already been cited (5.2). The acid-catalyzed dehydration involving methyl migration is analogous to a Wagner-Meerwein rearrangement and is interpreted by a similar mechanism. The steps of acceptance of a hydrogen ion

$$CH_3-\underset{\underset{OH}{|}}{\overset{\overset{CH_3}{|}}{C}}-\underset{\underset{OH}{|}}{\overset{\overset{CH_3}{|}}{C}}-CH_3 \xrightarrow{H^+} CH_3-\underset{\underset{\underset{H}{+OH}}{|}}{\overset{\overset{CH_3}{|}}{C}}-\underset{\underset{OH}{|}}{\overset{\overset{CH_3}{|}}{C}}-CH_3 \xrightarrow{-H_2O} CH_3-\underset{\underset{\overset{+}{OH}}{|}}{\overset{\overset{CH_3}{|}}{C}}-\underset{OH}{\overset{\overset{[CH_3]}{}}{C}}-CH_3$$

I   (a)   (b)

$$\rightarrow CH_3-\underset{\underset{CH_3}{|}}{\overset{\overset{CH_3}{|}}{\overset{+}{C}}}-\underset{OH}{\overset{|}{C}}-CH_3 \rightarrow CH_3-\underset{\underset{\overset{+}{OH}}{|}}{\overset{\overset{CH_3}{|}}{C}}-\overset{\overset{CH_3}{||}}{C}-CH_3 \xrightarrow{-H^+} CH_3-\underset{\underset{CH_3}{|}}{\overset{\overset{CH_3}{|}}{C}}-\overset{\overset{CH_3}{||}}{\underset{O}{C}}-CH_3$$

(c)   (d)   III

by oxygen (a) and loss of water to form the carbonium ion (b) are the same as before. In the present case, however, methyl migration with rearrangement of carbonium ion (b) to carbonium ion (c) is occasioned not by a difference in the inductive effects of groups in these ions but because carbonium ion (c) is at once stabilized by a shift of the charge from carbon to oxygen to produce the tremendously more stable oxonium ion (d). Ion (d) then loses a hydrogen ion to form pinacolone, III.

The electronic formulations of the transient ions help explain the process. The charged carbon atom of (c), as of (b), carries only six electrons and is hence very

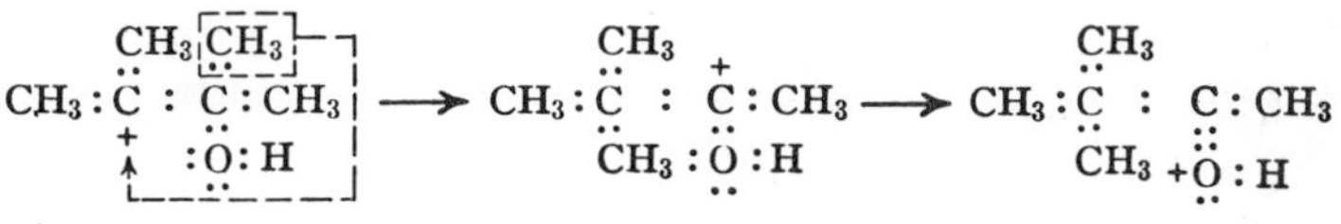

$$CH_3\underset{\underset{\overset{\uparrow}{\overset{+}{}}\,:\overset{..}{O}:H}{\overset{..}{C}}}{:}\,:\,\underset{CH_3}{\overset{\overset{\lceil CH_3\rceil}{}}{\overset{..}{C}}}:CH_3 \longrightarrow CH_3\underset{\underset{CH_3:\overset{..}{O}:H}{\overset{..}{C}}}{:}\,:\,\underset{}{\overset{+}{C}}:CH_3 \longrightarrow CH_3\underset{\underset{CH_3+\overset{..}{O}:H}{\overset{..}{C}}}{:}\,:\,\underset{}{\overset{..}{C}}:CH_3$$

$$\qquad\qquad (b)\qquad\qquad\qquad\qquad (c)\qquad\qquad\qquad\qquad (d)$$

unstable, but the charged oxygen in (d) has the full complement of eight electrons, as does the carbon to which it is attached. The driving force for the rearrangement thus comes from the tendency of electron-deficient intermediates to form a stable oxonium ion. Benzopinacol when heated in acetic acid with a trace of iodine rearranges in 95% yield to benzopinacolone.

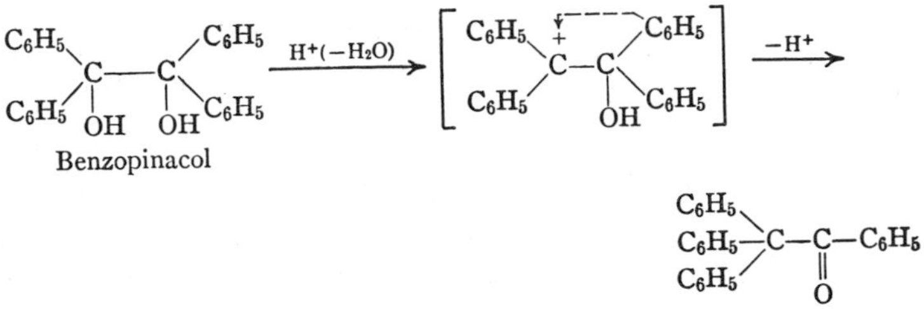

Benzopinacol

Benzopinacolone

In a pinacol of the type ArAr'C(OH)C(OH)ArAr', either group, Ar or Ar', can migrate. Bachmann[1] (1934) and others investigated the tendency of various groups to migrate and established the following values for migratory aptitude with reference to phenyl, assigned the value 1:

$C_6H_4OCH_3$-p	$C_6H_4CH_3$-p	C_6H_4-C_6H_5-p	$C_6H_4Cl(Br)$-p	$C_6H_4Cl(Br)$-m
500	16	12	0.7	0

8.22   Hydroperoxide Rearrangement. — The decomposition of cumene hydroperoxide (4.16) has been studied in homogeneous solution in 50% acetic acid with p-toluenesulfonic acid (p-CH$_3$C$_6$H$_4$SO$_3$H) as catalyst and found to give phenol and acetone in yields of 90 and 80%, respectively (F. H. Seubold, Jr., and W. E. Vaughan, 1953). The reaction is second order, the rate being dependent on the concentrations of hydroperoxide and of hydronium ion. The mechanism suggested involves formation of an intermediate having an electron deficient oxygen atom and its rearrangement to a carbonium ion.

W. Treibs (1961) investigated the autoxidation of partially hydrogenated poly-

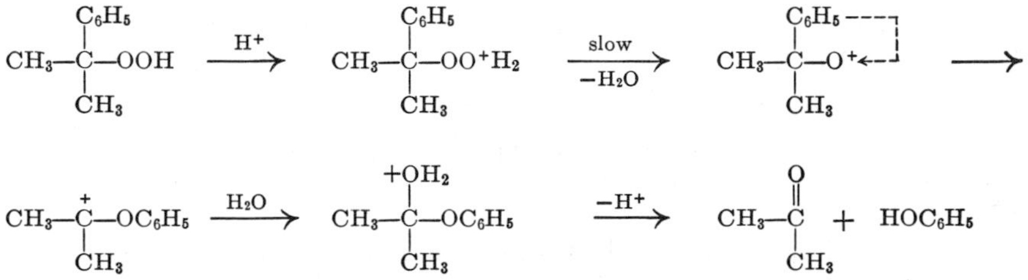

[1] Werner E. Bachmann, 1901–51; b. Detroit; Ph.D. Michigan (Gomberg); Univ. Michigan

cyclic hydrocarbons in methanol containing a trace of sulfuric acid under UV irradiation and isolated in good yield ketals of the type $ArRC(OCH_3)OR$ resulting from reaction of methanol with the intermediate carbonium ion.

8.23   Acylation. — The most generally prepared acyl derivatives of alcohols are the acetyl and benzoyl derivatives, that is, acetates and benzoates. A primary or secondary alcohol is acetylated conveniently by reaction with acetic anhydride in the presence of a catalyst, either overnight at 25° or at the steam

$$RCH_2OH \; + \; \begin{matrix} CH_3C{\diagdown}^O \\ \quad \quad \; \diagdown O \\ CH_3C{\diagdown}_O \end{matrix} \quad \xrightarrow{\text{Catalyst}} \quad \overset{O}{\overset{\|}{RCH_2OCCH_3}} \; + \; CH_3CO_2H$$

bath temperature for 10–15 min. Catalysts include bases, Lewis acids, and mineral acids. Sodium acetate is a weak basic catalyst and pyridine is a more effective one. Gaseous boron fluoride, an electron-seeking Lewis acid, combines

$$\begin{matrix} C_2H_5\!:\!\overset{..}{\underset{..}{O}}\!: & + & \overset{F}{\underset{F}{\overset{..}{B}\!:\!F}} & \longrightarrow & C_2H_5\!:\!\overset{..+}{\underset{..}{O}}\!:\!\overset{..-}{B}\!:\!F \\ \overset{}{C_2H_5} & & & & \underset{}{H_5C_2 \; F} \end{matrix}$$

Lewis base   Lewis acid   Boron fluoride etherate
                                                            (b.p. 126°)

with diethyl ether to form a liquid etherate, which is a convenient acetylation catalyst. Still more effective are strong acids: concentrated sulfuric acid, hydrogen chloride, and p-toluenesulfonic acid. Thus the common acetylation catalysts, listed in the order of increasing effectiveness, are:

$$NaOAc \; < \; Pyridine \; < \; BF_3 \; < \; HCl, \; H_2SO_4, \; CH_3C_6H_4SO_3H\text{-}p$$

A favored procedure, particularly for alcohols of low solubility in common solvents, consists in dissolving the alcohol in pyridine, a powerful solvent, and adding an equal volume of acetic anhydride. This pyridine-Ac_2O method is applicable to almost all primary and secondary alcohols, and fails only in rare instances of excessive steric hindrance. The hydroxyl group of any tertiary alcohol is to some

$$\begin{matrix} CH_3 \\ | \\ CH_3\!-\!\overset{}{\underset{|}{C}}\!-\!OH \\ CH_3 \end{matrix} \qquad \begin{matrix} CH_3 \\ | \\ CH_3CH_2\overset{}{\underset{|}{C}}CH_2CH_3 \\ OH \end{matrix} \qquad \begin{matrix} H_3C{\diagdown}\quad{\diagup}OH \\ \bigcirc \end{matrix}$$

Not acetylated by Ac_2O-Py

extent hindered, and tertiary alcohols such as the three formulated remain unchanged on treatment with acetic anhydride in pyridine. A tertiary alcohol that is sufficiently resistant to acid-catalyzed dehydration can often be acetylated by use of a more potent catalyst, an acid. The favored reagent is p-toluenesulfonic acid, a crystalline solid which is a strong acid but somewhat less destructive than concentrated sulfuric acid.

Cortisol, a steroid hormone of the adrenal gland now manufactured synthetically for use in therapy, is an interesting example of a triol with only one acylable

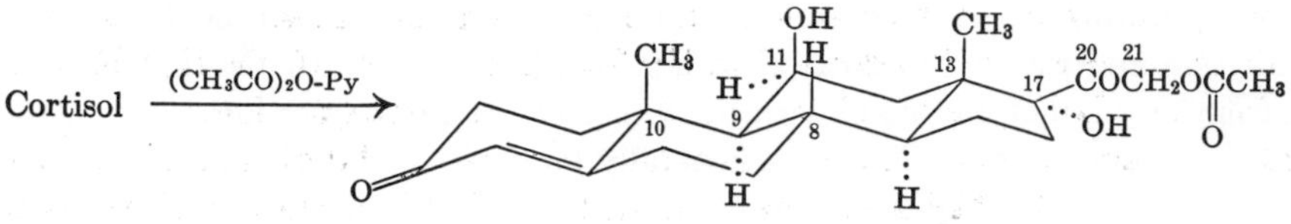

Cortisol $\xrightarrow{(CH_3CO)_2O\text{-}Py}$

Cortisol 21-acetate

hydroxyl group. The side chain at C_{17} is the ketol group $COCH_2OH$, and this hydroxyl is primary and readily acetylated in pyridine. The 17α-hydroxyl group is tertiary and remains unaltered, as does the 11β-hydroxyl group, even though it is secondary. This β-hydroxyl group is strongly hindered by 1:3 repulsions by the two β-methyl groups at C_{10} and C_{13} and the 8β-hydrogen. Thus acetylation of cortisol in pyridine affords the 21-acetate in high yield. The more potent acid-catalyzed acetylation is inapplicable in this case because the 11β-hydroxyl bears the *trans* diaxial relationship to the tertiary 9α-hydrogen and is easily eliminated under the influence of an acid to produce the $\Delta^{9,11}$-olefinic derivative. In related steroids lacking the 11β-hydroxyl group, a tertiary 17α-hydroxyl group can be acetylated with use of *p*-toluenesulfonic acid.

Phenol formally resembles a tertiary alcohol in that the hydroxylated carbon is trisubstituted, but it is free from hindrance and easily acetylated. Phenols are

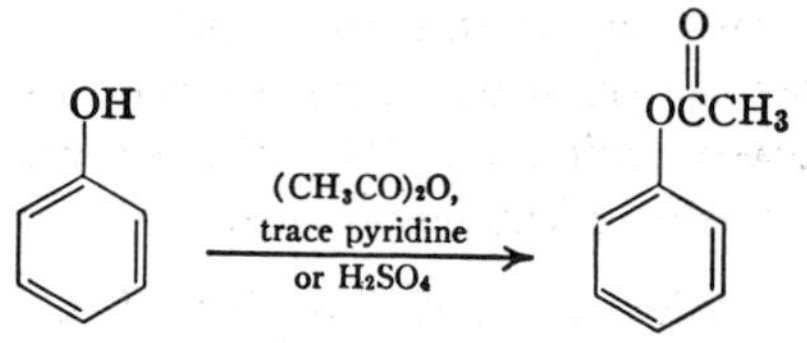

sufficiently acidic to dissolve in sodium hydroxide solution, and a convenient procedure for benzoylation, the Schotten[1]-Baumann method, is to shake a weakly alkaline solution of the phenol with benzoyl chloride.

$$C_6H_5O^-Na^+ \quad + \quad C_6H_5COCl \quad + NaOH \rightarrow \ C_6H_5OCOC_6H_5 \ + NaCl$$

Sodium phenolate   Benzoyl chloride   Phenyl benzoate
(m.p. 71°)

Acetates and benzoates of alcohols and phenols are esters, and they can be hydrolyzed with alkali to sodium acetate or benzoate and the alcoholic component. A convenient method of deacetylation is by alcoholysis catalyzed by alkoxide ion:

$$ROCOCH_3 + C_2H_5OH \xrightarrow{\ ^-OC_2H_5\ } ROH + CH_3CO_2C_2H_5$$

Thus acyl derivatives are often prepared for temporary protection during oxidation of some other group in the molecule, after which the acyl group is removed by saponification. Acetates have lower boiling points than the hydrogen-bonded hydroxy compounds and they are much less strongly adsorbed on a chromatographic column of alumina. Hence an alcoholic or phenolic reaction product is

---

[1] Carl Schotten, 1853–1910; b. Marburg, Germany; Ph.D. Berlin (Hofmann); Univ. Berlin; *Ber.*, **43**, 3703 (1910)

often converted into the acetate for better purification by distillation or chromatography.   An acetate or benzoate may also offer advantages in crystallization.
A hindered acetate may require more severe conditions for hydrolysis than an
unhindered one; the alternative procedure for deacetylation with lithium aluminum hydride (8.10) is often useful.

8.24   Selective Acylation and Hydrolysis. — When a cyclohexane ring is
              locked rigidly to other rings, a substituent hydroxyl group has either
the equatorial or the axial orientation.   Among saturated steroid alcohols, there
is no exception to the rule that an equatorial hydroxyl group is acylated more
readily than an axial group at the same position; the same relationship applies
to the hydrolysis of acetoxyl groups.   Thus the rates of hydrolysis indicated under
the formulas of the benzoates of cholestane-3β-ol (1) and the 3α-epimer (2) show

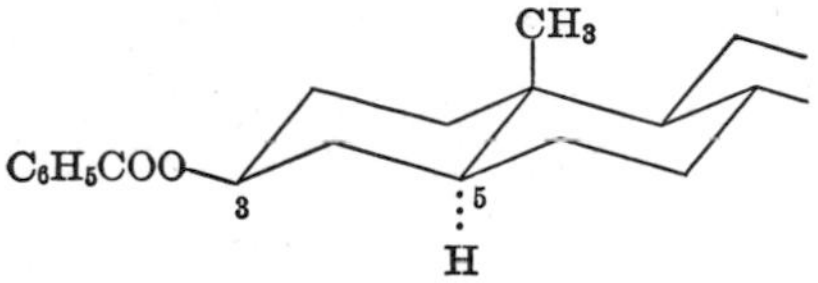

$$k^{69°} = 14.8 \qquad\qquad k^{69°} = 6.2$$
$$(1) \qquad\qquad\qquad (2)$$

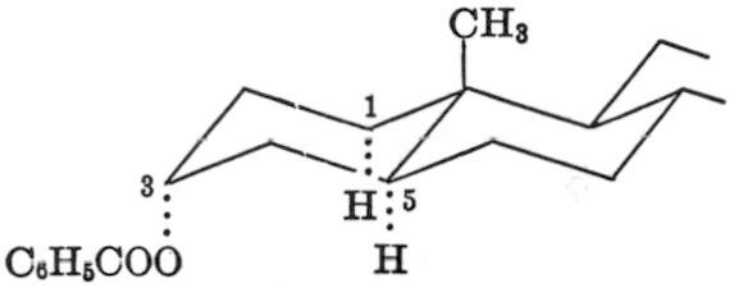

that the equatorial isomer (1) is saponified at over twice the rate of the axial
isomer (2).   The equatorial group is in a more available location, and the axial
group of (2) is hindered by 1:3 interactions with the axial 1α- and 5α-hydrogens.
In 3β,6β-diacetoxycholestane (3) one functional group is equatorial and the other

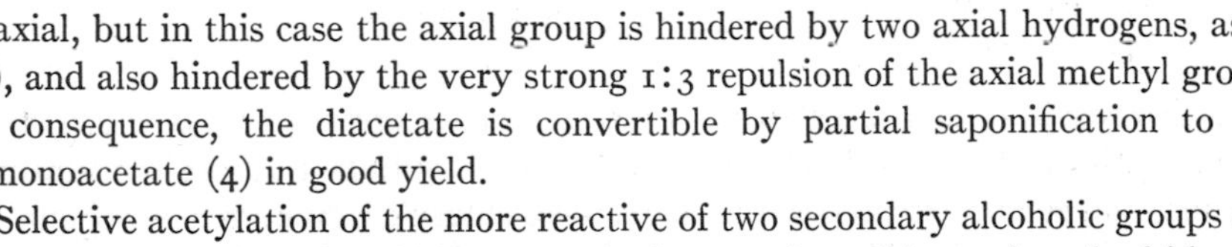

$$(3) \qquad\qquad\qquad\qquad (4)$$

is axial, but in this case the axial group is hindered by two axial hydrogens, as in
(2), and also hindered by the very strong 1:3 repulsion of the axial methyl group;
in consequence, the diacetate is convertible by partial saponification to the
6-monoacetate (4) in good yield.

   Selective acetylation of the more reactive of two secondary alcoholic groups can
sometimes be accomplished, for example, by reaction with acetic anhydride and
pyridine in benzene solution at 25° for a controlled period of time.   Better results
are obtainable with a specific acylating agent, ethyl chloroformate, or cathyl
chloride.   This substance is at the same time an ester and an acid chloride, and it

$$\text{ROH} \ + \ \underset{\substack{\text{Ethyl chloroformate}\\ \text{(b.p. 94°, sp. gr. 1.135)}}}{\text{Cl}-\overset{\overset{\text{O}}{\|}}{\text{C}}-\text{OC}_2\text{H}_5} \ + \ \text{Py} \ \rightarrow \ \underset{\substack{\text{Cathylate}\\ \text{(carbethoxyl derivative)}}}{\text{RO}\overset{\overset{\text{O}}{\|}}{\text{C}}\text{OC}_2\text{H}_5} \ + \ \text{Py·HCl}$$

reacts with an alcohol in pyridine solution, or in dioxane containing one equivalent of pyridine, to give the cathyl derivative (abbreviation of carbethoxyl). A cathylate on saponification affords the alcohol, carbon dioxide, and ethanol. Among all saturated alcohols tested, cathyl chloride reacted with equatorial hydroxyl groups but not with those that are axial (Fieser, 1952). Thus, treated

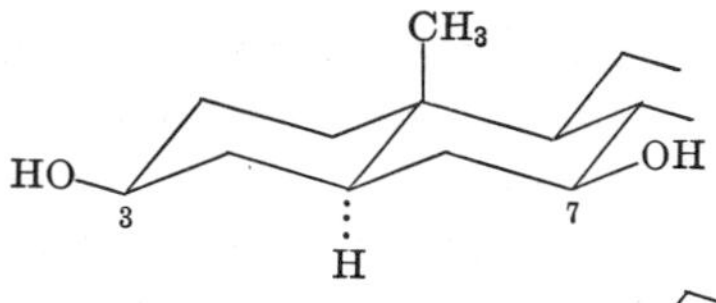

with excess cathyl chloride in pyridine, $3\beta,7\beta$-dihydroxycholestane (5) gives the 3,7-dicathylate whereas the $3\beta,7\alpha$-diol (6) gives the 3-monocathylate; the $3\beta,5\alpha,6\beta$-triol (7) affords the 3-monocathylate in 97% yield. An allylic alcohol has enhanced reactivity due to the adjacent double bond and is capable of forming a cathylate even though the orientation is axial.

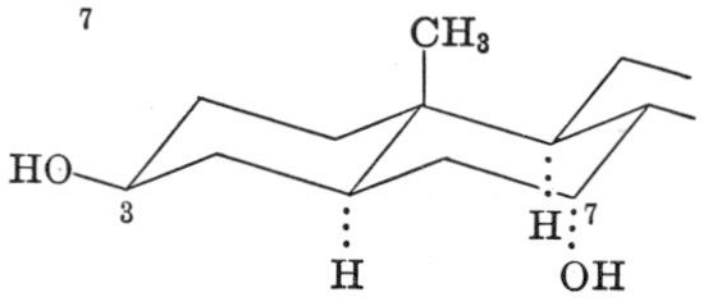

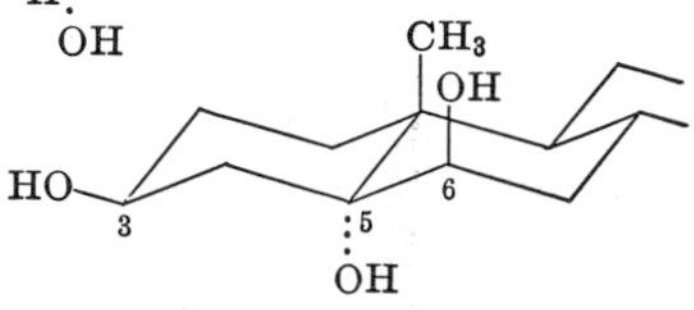

8.25   Tosylates and Mesylates. — The p-toluenesulfonyl and methane-sulfonyl groups usually are identified by the abbreviations tosyl and mesyl, and the corresponding ester derivatives of primary and secondary alcohols

$$p\text{-}CH_3C_6H_4SO_2Cl \;+\; HOR \;+\; Py \;\rightarrow\; p\text{-}CH_3C_6H_4SO_2OR \;+\; Py\cdot HCl$$

Tosyl chloride (TsCl)   Tosylate (TsOR)
m.p. 69°

$$CH_3SO_2Cl \;+\; HOR \;+\; Py \;\rightarrow\; CH_3SO_2OR \;+\; Py\cdot HCl$$

Mesyl chloride (MsCl)   Mesylate (MsOR)
b.p. 50°/8 mm.

are called tosylates and mesylates. These esters are prepared by reaction of the alcohol with tosyl or mesyl chloride in anhydrous pyridine at room temperature. In micro and semimicro preparative work tosyl chloride is preferred over benzenesulfonyl chloride, a liquid, because it can be purified by crystallization. Purity of both reagent and solvent is necessary because of the high reactivity of the esters, particularly tosylates. Because of the greater steric requirement for the larger group, tosyl chloride is the reagent of choice for selective acylation of polyfunctional alcohols; it is slightly less reactive than mesyl chloride. Where other considerations are equal, mesylates are often preferred because of better crystallization properties.

Tosylates and mesylates are considerably different from acetates and benzoates because they are derived from much more strongly acidic acids. The sulfone

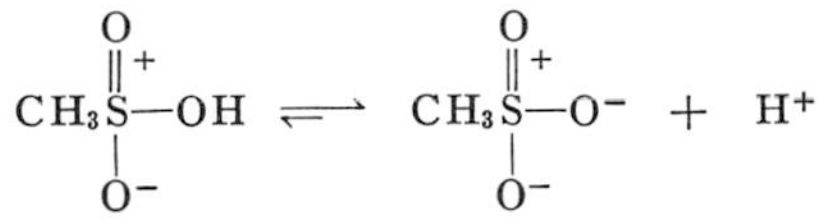

$$CH_3 \overset{\overset{O}{\|^+}}{\underset{\underset{O^-}{|}}{S}} {-}OH \rightleftharpoons CH_3 \overset{\overset{O}{\|^+}}{\underset{\underset{O^-}{|}}{S}} {-}O^- + H^+$$

Methanesulfonic acid   (MsO⁻)

group, —SO₂—, is powerfully electron attracting and exerts an inductive drift of electrons facilitating separation of the hydroxylic hydrogen as a proton. Because of the ready formation of the anions MsO⁻ and TsO⁻, mesylates and tosylates are described as efficient leaving groups. The sulfonic acid esters resemble alkyl halides and enter into similar reactions of displacement, elimination, and hydrolysis.

Typical displacements occur on reaction with sodium iodide, potassium cyanide, potassium thiocyanate, sodium hydrogen sulfide, sodium sulfide, sodium sulfide and sulfur, and potassium thiolacetate. The product of the last reaction is de-

$$RCH_2OSO_2C_6H_4CH_3\text{-}p +$$
$$(RCH_2OSO_2CH_3)$$
$$\begin{cases} NaI & \rightarrow RCH_2I \\ KCN & \rightarrow RCH_2CN \\ KSCN & \rightarrow RCH_2SCN \\ NaHS & \rightarrow RCH_2SH \\ Na_2S & \rightarrow (RCH_2)_2S \downarrow \\ Na_2S + S \rightarrow RCH_2SSCH_2R \\ CH_3COSK \rightarrow RCH_2SCOCH_3 \xrightarrow{NH_3} RCH_2SH + CH_3CONH \end{cases}$$

acetylated by reaction with alcoholic ammonia, which produces the mercaptan (or thiol) and acetamide. All these reactions involve cleavage of the bond between oxygen and the alkyl group; in the reaction of an ester with ammonia the

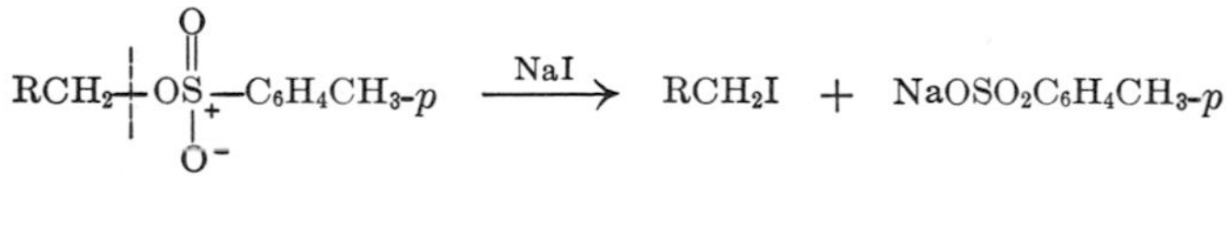

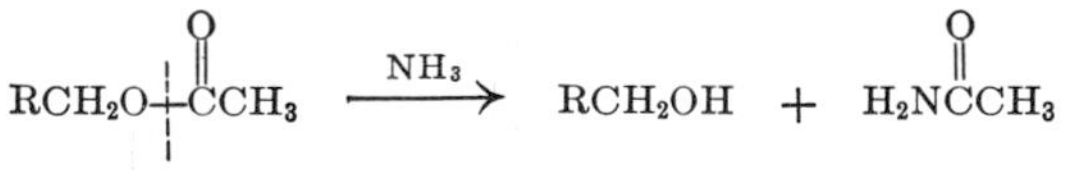

$$RCH_2{-}O\overset{\overset{O}{\|}}{\underset{\underset{O^-}{|^+}}{S}}{-}C_6H_4CH_3\text{-}p \xrightarrow{NaI} RCH_2I + NaOSO_2C_6H_4CH_3\text{-}p$$

$$RCH_2O{-}\overset{\overset{O}{\|}}{C}CH_3 \xrightarrow{NH_3} RCH_2OH + H_2N\overset{\overset{O}{\|}}{C}CH_3$$

bond cleaved is that between oxygen and the acyl group. Acetates do not enter into any of the displacements listed. Neopentyl tosylate, $(CH_3)_3CCH_2OTs$, undergoes smooth displacements without rearrangement on reaction with a number of reagents [NaI, NaSH, $C_6H_5CH_2SNa$, $(NH_2)_2C{=}S$]; with sodium methoxide, however, attack occurs at sulfur and the ultimate product is neopentyl alcohol (Bordwell,[1] 1951).

Reduction of a tosylate affords an efficient method for reductive elimination of the hydroxyl group of a primary alcohol or secondary alcohol. Sodium amalgam

$$R_2CHOH \rightarrow R_2CHOTs \xrightarrow{Na(Hg)\ or\ LiAlH_4} R_2CH_2 + TsOH$$

is the classical reducing agent; lithium aluminum hydride usually gives good

[1] Frederick G. Bordwell, b. 1916 Marmarth, N. Dakota; Ph.D. Minnesota (Suter); Northwestern Univ.

results except in the case of hindered alcohols. These reagents are not applicable to the reduction of an α-ketol tosylate with preservation of the intact carbonyl

$$RCOCH_2OTs \xrightarrow{NaI-AcOH} RCOCH_3 + TsOH$$

group, but in this case sodium iodide in acetic acid has been used with success (H. J. Ringold, 1958). An indirect method is particularly useful for effecting the transformation $—CO_2R \rightarrow —CH_3$. The primary alcohol resulting on reduction

$$RCO_2CH_3 \xrightarrow{LiAlH_4} RCH_2OH \xrightarrow{TsCl} RCH_2OTs \xrightarrow{C_2H_5SH} RCH_2SC_2H_5 \xrightarrow{Ni} RCH_3 + C_2H_6$$

is converted via the tosylate to the ethyl thioether, which is desulfurized with Raney nickel, that is, with nickel catalyst saturated with hydrogen. Probably hydrogen sulfide is formed and is adsorbed on the catalyst. The benzyl thioether is often the intermediate of choice.

Introduction of a double bond by dehydrotosylation often proceeds more readily than direct dehydration. With an alcohol of the type $R_2CH—CH(OTs)—$, the elimination can be effected with sodium acetate in acetic acid. If the hydrogen to be eliminated is secondary, $RCH_2—CH(OTs)—$, refluxing with an organic base such as lutidine or collidine may be required. However, some secondary tosylates of the same type have been converted to olefins by chromatography on slightly alkaline alumina. In another procedure the tosylate is heated to around 100° in dimethylformamide, $HCON(CH_3)_2$, or dimethyl sulfoxide, $(CH_3)_2S^+—O^-$ (H. R. Nace, 1958).

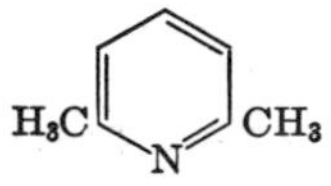

2, 6-Lutidine
b. p. 144°

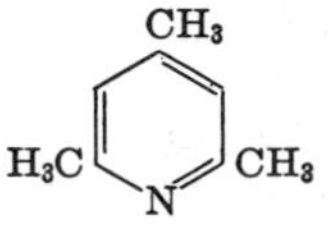

2, 4, 6-Collidine
b. p. 171°

(+)-*sec*-Butyl alcohol (1) is an optically active secondary alcohol in which the carbinol carbon atom is asymmetric. Conversion to the tosylate (2) involves cleavage of the O—H bond and proceeds with retention of configuration, but dis-

$$\begin{array}{c} C_2H_5 \\ | \\ HO—C—H \\ | \\ CH_3 \\ (1)\ +14° \end{array} + ClSO_2C_6H_4CH_3\text{-}p \xrightarrow{Py} \begin{array}{c} C_2H_5 \\ | \\ TsO—C—H \\ | \\ CH_3 \\ (2)\ +11° \end{array} \xrightarrow{C_6H_5CO_2Na} \begin{array}{c} C_2H_5 \\ | \\ H—C—OCOC_6H_5 \\ | \\ CH_3 \\ (3)\ -38° \end{array}$$

placement of the tosylate group by a benzoate group involves breaking of the bond extending to the asymmetric center and proceeds with Walden inversion. The product (3) is the (−)-benzoate, the enantiomer of the product of benzoylation of the alcohol, which has a specific rotation of +39°. All displacements of tosylates of the type (2) proceed with inversion. The reaction is useful for effecting epimerization of alcohols.   The tosylate is either converted to the epimeric acetate or benzoate, which is then saponified, or else hydrolyzed directly, but in either case dehydrotosylation usually occurs to some extent and affords the olefin as a by-product.   Tosylates and mesylates have been converted into the epimeric alcohols in good yield by stirring a solution in benzene–ligroin with alumina for 2–4 days and then eluting the product (Chang,[1] 1958).   Still better results are obtained by heating the sulfonate ester in dimethylformamide at 78° to produce the formate of the inverted alcohol, which is then saponified; as noted above, elimination occurs if the temperature is raised to 100°.

If it is necessary to convert a tosylate into the original alcohol, that is, to avoid cleavage of the R—O bond with attendant inversion, this can be accomplished by reduction with Raney nickel or with sodium in liquid ammonia; the products are the alcohol, toluene, and sulfur in an unidentified form (D. B. Denney, 1956).

$$\text{RO—SO}_2\text{C}_6\text{H}_4\text{CH}_3\text{-}p \xrightarrow{\text{Na, NH}_3} \text{ROH} + \text{C}_6\text{H}_5\text{CH}_3$$

An epoxide sometimes is obtained most conveniently by treatment of a *trans vic*-diol monotosylate or monomesylate with base; the elimination of TsOH is the equivalent of the elimination of HBr from a bromohydrin.   The following example illustrates the transformation of an α-oxide (1) of the cholestane series into the β-oxide (4).   Reaction of Δ²-cholestene with perbenzoic acid gives a product

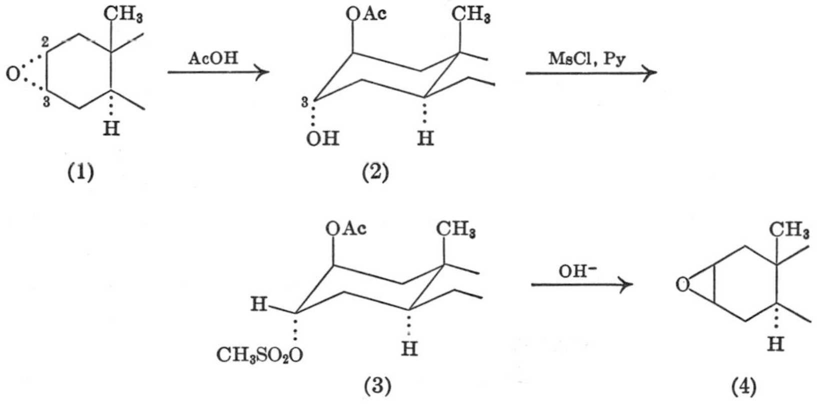

recognized as the α-oxide (rear attack) by identification of the product of hydrogenation or reduction (LiAlH₄) as cholestane-3α-ol (axial).   Acetolysis of the oxide also involves cleavage of the C₂-bond, with inversion at C₂ and formation of the *trans*-diaxial 2-monoacetate (2).   Conversion to the 2-acetate-3-mesylate (3) and reaction with base affords the 2β,3β-oxide (4).   A diol monomesylate or monotosylate, where available, is as satisfactory for the reaction as an acetate-mesylate or acetate-tosylate.

[1] Frederic C. Chang, b. 1905 San Francisco; Ph.D. Harvard (Fieser); Lingnan Univ. (China); Univ. Tennessee, Memphis

TABLE 8.4. ESTERS OF INORGANIC ACIDS

NAME	FORMULA	B.P. °C	SP. GR.
Dimethyl sulfate	$(CH_3O)_2SO_2$	188.5	1.35
Diethyl sulfate	$(C_2H_5O)_2SO_2$	210	1.17
Di-n-butyl sulfate	$(n\text{-}C_4H_9O)_2SO_2$	256	0.97
n-Butyl p-toluenesulfonate	$p\text{-}CH_3C_6H_4SO_2OC_4H_9\text{-}n$	175/10 mm.	1.12
Di-n-butyl sulfite	$(n\text{-}C_4H_9O)_2SO$	109/15 mm.	1.00
Methyl nitrate	CH_3ONO_2	65	1.20
Ethyl nitrate	$C_2H_5ONO_2$	87.5	1.10
Methyl nitrite	CH_3ONO	−12	0.99
Ethyl nitrite	C_2H_5ONO	17	0.90
n-Butyl nitrite	$n\text{-}C_4H_9ONO$	78 dec.	0.91
Tri-n-butyl phosphate	$(n\text{-}C_4H_9O)_3PO$	289 dec.	0.98
t-Butyl hypochlorite	$(CH_3)_3COCl$	78	0.91
Triphenyl phosphite (m.p. 50°)	$(C_6H_5O)_3P$	210/1 mm.	1.21

8.26   Esters of Inorganic Acids. — Methyl and ethylsulfuric acid are formed on cautious addition of sulfuric acid to the alcohol with ice cooling, and on distillation at reduced pressure they afford dimethyl and diethyl sulfate (5.3).   The method fails with higher alcohols because of extensive olefin formation.   For preparation of di-n-butyl sulfate, n-butyl alcohol is first converted into

$$2\ n\text{-}C_4H_9OH\ +\ SOCl_2\ \xrightarrow[77\text{-}84\%]{}\ (n\text{-}C_4H_9O)_2SO\ +\ HCl$$

$$2\ (n\text{-}C_4H_9O)_2SO\ +\ SO_2Cl_2\ \xrightarrow[74\text{-}83\%]{}\ (n\text{-}C_4H_9O)_2SO_2\ +\ 2\ n\text{-}C_4H_9Cl\ +\ SO_2$$

the dialkyl sulfite by heating it with thionyl chloride.   The product is distilled at 14 mm. pressure and treated with one half equivalent of sulfuryl chloride with cooling; the temperature is raised for distillation of n-butyl chloride and removal of sulfur dioxide, and the di-n-butyl sulfate is washed neutral with soda solution, dried and distilled.   The sulfite also can be oxidized to the sulfate with permanganate in acetic acid. n-Butyl p-toluenesulfonate is obtained in 50–54% yield by slow addition of 5 N sodium hydroxide solution to a mixture of the alcohol with p-toluenesulfonyl chloride.   The sulfonate ester and the dialkyl sulfates are useful alkylating agents, for example, for reaction with a Grignard reagent (4.7).

Dodecyl-, tetradecyl-, hexadecyl-, and octadecylsulfuric acids are obtained in a pure state by dropwise addition of chlorosulfonic acid to a solution of the alcohol in chloroform at 5° (*Org. Syn.*, 1961).   The alkylsulfuric acid that crystallizes is collected at 0° on a Büchner funnel supplied with a polyethylene filter cloth, a disc of plastic sheeting, and a rubber dam (yield 61–68%).

Methyl nitrate is prepared by cautious addition of an ice-cold mixture of concentrated nitric acid and concentrated sulfuric acid to an iced solution of methylsulfuric acid.   The ester separates as an oily layer and is washed and used promptly without distillation, which requires special precautions; yield 66–80%. The procedure for preparation of ethyl nitrites is illustrated as follows.   A mixture of n-butyl alcohol, water, and concentrated sulfuric acid is cooled to 0° and added to a stirred aqueous solution of sodium nitrite at $0°$; the ester separates in an upper layer and is washed, dried, and distilled at 43 mm.; yield 79-83%.

Tri-n-butyl phosphate is made by slow addition of phosphorus oxychloride to a stirred solution of the alcohol and pyridine in benzene at a temperature kept below

$$n\text{-}C_4H_9OH + POCl_3 + 3\ C_5H_5N \rightarrow PO(OC_4H_9\text{-}n)_3 + 3\ C_5H_5NHCl$$

$10°$; water is added and the benzene layer is washed, dried, and fractionated.

t-Butyl hypochlorite is useful for chlorination of ketones and for oxidation of alcohols in the presence of pyridine in carbon tetrachloride or ether: cyclohexanol $\rightarrow$ cyclohexanone. It is made by passing chlorine into an alkaline solution of the alcohol.

Triphenyl phosphite, prepared from three moles of phenol and one of phosphorus trichloride, reacts with an alcohol and hydrogen chloride to form the alkyl chloride; other hydrogen halides react in the same way (H. N. Rydon, 1953).

$$(C_6H_5O)_2POC_6H_5 + ROH + HCl \rightarrow RCl + (C_6H_5O)_2POH + HOC_6H_5$$

8.27   Nitroglycerin. — The powerful explosive commonly known as nitroglycerin is more accurately defined as the trinitrate ester of glycerol, or glycerol trinitrate. It is made by cautious addition of anhydrous glycerol to a stirred mixture of concentrated nitric acid and fuming sulfuric acid at a temperature maintained at $10\text{-}20°$ by efficient cooling (exothermic reaction). The nitration is conducted in lead vessels with cooling coils, and agitation is accomplished

$$\begin{array}{l} CH_2OH \\ | \\ CHOH \\ | \\ CH_2OH \\ \text{Glycerol} \end{array} + 3\,HONO_2 \xrightarrow[94\%]{H_2SO_4} \begin{array}{l} CH_2ONO_2 \\ | \\ CHONO_2 \\ | \\ CH_2ONO_2 \\ \text{Nitroglycerin} \end{array}$$

with compressed air. The sulfuric acid absorbs the water liberated and promotes formation of the fully esterified product.

Nitroglycerin is a colorless oily liquid (sp. gr. 1.6) with a sweet burning taste. It is very slightly soluble in water but readily soluble in alcohol or ether. It supercools to a marked degree but crystallizes in two forms, one labile (m.p. $2.9°$) and the other stable (m.p. $13.2°$). The substance has some use for treatment of angina pectoris, usually in the form of a dilute alcoholic solution (which can be handled safely if care is taken to prevent evaporation of solvent).

The most significant property of the nitrate ester is violent detonation on slight shock. More than enough oxygen is present to convert the carbon and hydrogen into the corresponding oxides, with liberation of elemental nitrogen:

$$C_3H_5(ONO_2)_3 \longrightarrow \tfrac{3}{2}N_2 + 3CO_2 + \tfrac{5}{2}H_2O + \tfrac{1}{4}O_2$$

The sudden liberation of this large volume of gas in a space initially occupied by the liquid substance gives an explosion wave of enormous pressure. Nitroglycerin was first prepared in 1846, and some years later Alfred Nobel in Sweden undertook its manufacture. The great sensitivity introduced considerable hazard, and the expedient of transporting the product in the frozen condition, in which state nitroglycerin is somewhat less sensitive to shock than in the liquid form, reduced but did not eliminate accidents. The experience, however, provided a clue that materialized in Nobel's discovery in 1866 of the practical explosive dynamite. Kieselguhr, a diatomaceous earth, will absorb up to three times its weight of nitroglycerin and still remain dry; the absorbed nitroglycerin in this solid form retains explosive properties but shows greatly diminished sensitivity. Commercial dynamites often contain sodium or ammonium nitrate to aid in burning an organic absorbent. Dynamite usually is molded as sticks encased in paraffined paper wrappers. It is sufficiently insensitive to shock to be handled and shipped with comparative safety, and it is exploded with use of a percussion cap containing a detonator, mercury fulminate or lead azide.

$$\overset{-}{C}\!\!\equiv\!\!\overset{+}{N}\!\!-\!\!O\!\!-\!\!Hg\!\!-\!\!O\!\!-\!\!\overset{+}{N}\!\!\equiv\!\!\overset{-}{C} \qquad \overset{-}{N}\!\!=\!\!\overset{+}{N}\!\!=\!\!\overset{-}{N}\!\!-\!\!Pb\!\!-\!\!N\!\!=\!\!\overset{+}{N}\!\!=\!\!\overset{-}{N}$$
$$\text{Mercury fulminate} \qquad\qquad \text{Lead azide}$$

In 1875 Nobel made the further discovery that guncotton can be gelatinized with nitroglycerin to give a jelly of satisfactory stability and powerful explosive properties. Guncotton has much the same appearance as ordinary cotton and consists largely of cellulose trinitrate (nitrocellulose), a polymeric substance of the formula $[C_6H_7O_2(ONO_2)_3]_n$; the substance is a nitric acid ester structurally similar to nitroglycerin, $C_3H_5(ONO_2)_3$, and this similarity may account for the solubility of the solid of high molecular weight in the liquid ester. Nobel's first formulation, called Blasting Gelatin, contained 92% of nitroglycerin and 8% of guncotton; it is one of the most powerful and brisant (shattering) explosives known and is employed for blasting rocks. By greatly reducing the proportion of nitroglycerin to guncotton formulations are obtainable of slow-burning characteristics suitable for use as propellants in shells. A rifled arm requires a particularly slow-burning powder to impart a substantial push to the projectile without building up an excessive pressure in the almost gas-tight space confined by a lead bullet or shell fitting snugly into the spiral grooves of the barrel. Cordite, a superior smokeless powder introduced as the British Service propellant in 1889, has the composition: nitroglycerin, 30%; guncotton, 65%; mineral jelly (crude vaseline), 5%. With this high proportion of guncotton, gelatinization cannot be accomplished by nitroglycerin alone, and acetone is employed as a mutual solvent adapted to the production of a homogeneous gel. A paste of the ingredients, moistened with the solvent, is incorporated in a kneading machine into a stiff dough that is then extruded through a die in the form of cords (hence Cordite) of various sizes, usually having carefully spaced perforations to provide for even burning from within as well as from without. The cords are cut into lengths and dried thoroughly to evaporate the acetone, the bulk of which is recovered.

8.28   Pentaerythritol Tetranitrate (PETN) is a related high explosive prepared by esterification of the alcohol with mixed acid. The substance has considerable brisance, but is more sensitive to shock than other common high explosives, such as TNT, and usually is detonated by impact of a rifle bullet.

$$\underset{\underset{\underset{\text{Pentaerythritol (m.p. 260°)}}{}}{\overset{\overset{\text{CH}_2\text{OH}}{|}}{\underset{|}{\text{HOCH}_2-\text{C}-\text{CH}_2\text{OH}}}}}{} \quad \xrightarrow{\text{HNO}_3,\ \text{H}_2\text{SO}_4} \quad \underset{\underset{\text{PETN (m.p. 138–140°)}}{}}{\overset{\overset{\text{CH}_2\text{ONO}_2}{|}}{\underset{\overset{|}{\text{CH}_2\text{ONO}_2}}{\text{O}_2\text{NOCH}_2-\text{C}-\text{CH}_2\text{ONO}_2}}}}$$

The substance is used chiefly in manufacture of detonating fuse (Primacord), a waterproof textile filled with powdered PETN.

8.29   Oxidation. — Ethanol and higher primary alcohols are oxidized (or dehydrogenated) to aldehydes (alcohol dehydrogenated), and alde-

1. $\text{RCH}_2\text{OH} \xrightarrow{\text{[O]}} \text{RCH}{=}\text{O} \xrightarrow{\text{[O]}} \text{RCO}_2\text{H}$

2. $\text{CH}_3\text{OH} \xrightarrow{\text{[O]}} \text{HCH}{=}\text{O} \xrightarrow{\text{[O]}} \overset{\overset{\text{OH}}{|}}{\text{HC}}{=}\text{O} \xrightarrow{\text{[O]}} \overset{\overset{\text{OH}}{|}}{\text{HO}{-}\text{C}}{=}\text{O} \rightarrow \text{H}_2\text{O} + \text{CO}_2$

3. $\text{R}_2\text{CHOH} \xrightarrow{\text{[O]}} \text{R}_2\text{C}{=}\text{O}$

hydes can be oxidized further to carboxylic acids (1). Methanol similarly yields formaldehyde and then formic acid, but since this acid is at the same time an aldehyde it is oxidized further to carbon dioxide and water. Secondary alcohols on oxidation afford ketones (3), for example, cyclohexanol gives cyclohexanone and, although ketones of this type can be oxidized further, procedures are available for carrying the oxidation to the ketone stage and no further. Aldehydes are more sensitive to further oxidation than ketones but often can be isolated in fair to good yield as primary oxidation products.

Tertiary alcohols are resistant to oxidation in neutral or alkaline solution and can be distinguished from primary and secondary alcohols by a test with dilute alkaline permanganate. If the alcohol is very sensitive to acid-catalyzed dehydration it may suffer oxidation in an acidic medium via the olefin, as in (4). In the

4. $\overset{\overset{\text{OH}}{|}}{\underset{\underset{\text{CH}_3}{|}}{\text{CH}_3-\text{C}-\text{CH}_3}} \xrightarrow{\text{H}^+} \underset{\underset{\text{CH}_3}{|}}{\text{CH}_3-\text{C}{=}\text{CH}_2} \xrightarrow{\text{[O]}} \underset{\underset{\text{CH}_3}{|}}{\text{CH}_3-\text{C}{=}\text{O}} + \text{CO}_2$

more usual case a tertiary alcoholic group withstands oxidation of a primary or secondary group in the same molecule, even under acidic conditions. Thus $3\beta,5\alpha,6\beta$-trihydroxycholestane (7, section 8.24) can be oxidized smoothly to the 3,6-diketo-5α-hydroxy derivative with chromic acid or sodium dichromate in aqueous acetic acid.

In the classical procedure for oxidation with chromic acid a solution of the organic substance in x parts of acetic acid is treated with a solution of chromic anhydride in $x/10$ parts of water. However, the water present slows down the reaction and a suspension of chromic anhydride in anhydrous acetic acid is a much more powerful reagent (see data of Table 8.5). Oxidation of tertiary alcohols by the anhydrous procedure is the basis for a practical synthesis of keto acids (J. Szmuszkovicz, 1948). Thus the phenylcarbinol from cyclohexanone affords δ-benzoylvaleric acid in high yield (5); that the reaction does not involve initial de-

5. $O=$⟨cyclohexanone⟩ $\xrightarrow{C_6H_5MgBr}$ C_6H_5-⟨1-phenylcyclohexanol, HO⟩ $\xrightarrow[81\%]{\substack{CrO_3 \\ AcOH}}$ $C_6H_5-CO\begin{smallmatrix}CH_2-CH_2\\ \\ HO_2C----CH_2\end{smallmatrix}CH_2$

δ-Benzoylvaleric acid
m. p. 78°

6. $CH_3(CH_2)_{13}-$⟨cyclohexanol, HO⟩ $\xrightarrow[80\%]{\substack{CrO_3 \\ AcOH}}$ $CH_3(CH_2)_{13}\overset{\overset{\displaystyle O}{\|}}{C}(CH_2)_5CO_2H$

ε-Ketoarachidic acid
m. p. 89°

hydration is evident from the fact that oxidation of 1-phenylcyclohexene by the same procedure affords the keto acid in only 39% yield. That a phenyl group is not necessary is shown by example (6). Carbinols from cyclopentanone and from cyclooctanone are oxidized in the same way. The first step is formation of the chromate ester, $(RO)_2CrO_2$, and the fission reaction may be related to oxidative rearrangements (7) observed as side reactions (1–4%) in the oxidation of secondary alcohols and interpreted as involving formation and rearrangement of an inter-

7. $R\overset{\overset{\displaystyle OCrO_2(OH)}{|}}{C}HR'$ $\xrightarrow{-CrO_2,\ OH^-}$ $R\overset{\overset{\displaystyle O^+}{|}}{C}HR'$ $\longrightarrow$ $R^+ + R'CHO$
$\overset{\ \ \ \ \ \ \ \ \downarrow OH^-}{\longrightarrow}$ ROH

8. $R\overset{\overset{\displaystyle CH_2-CH_2CH_2}{|}}{\underset{\underset{\displaystyle OCrO_2(OH)}{|}}{C}}-CH_2CH_2$ $\xrightarrow{-CrO_2,\ OH^-}$ $R\overset{\overset{\displaystyle CH_2-CH_2CH_2}{|}}{\underset{\underset{\displaystyle O^+}{|}}{C}}-CH_2CH_2$ $\longrightarrow$ $R\overset{\overset{\displaystyle CH_2-CH_2CH_2}{|}}{\underset{\underset{\displaystyle O}{\|}}{C}}\overset{\overset{\displaystyle +}{}}{CH_2CH_2}$

$\Big\downarrow CrO_3,\ OH^-$

$R\overset{\overset{\displaystyle CH_2-CH_2CH_2}{|}}{\underset{\underset{\displaystyle O}{\|}}{C}}\ HO_2CCH_2$

mediate with an electron deficient oxygen (Mosher,[1] 1949; Fieser, 1960). A similar mechanism (8) accounts for the reaction in question and is closely analogous to that postulated for the hydroperoxide rearrangement (8.22).

Mandelic acid (9) is an α-hydroxy acid in which the alcoholic function is secondary, and by controlled oxidation with permanganate in alkaline solution it can be

9. $C_6H_5\overset{\overset{\displaystyle OH}{|}}{C}HCO_2H$ $\xrightarrow{KMnO_4-NaOH;\ H^+}$ $C_6H_5\overset{\overset{\displaystyle O}{\|}}{C}CO_2H$ $\xrightarrow[-CO_2]{KMnO_4-H_2SO_4}$

Mandelic acid   Phenylglyoxylic acid
                                        m.p. 66°

$C_6H_5CHO \xrightarrow{[O]} C_6H_5CO_2H$

[1] William A. Mosher, ᵇ 1912 Salem, Oregon; Ph.D. Penn. State Univ. (Whitmore); Univ. Delaware

$$\text{10. } (C_6H_5)_2C \overset{\displaystyle OH}{\underset{\displaystyle CO_2H}{\Big\langle}} \xrightarrow{\;CrO_3\;} (C_6H_5)_2C{=}O \; + \; CO_2$$

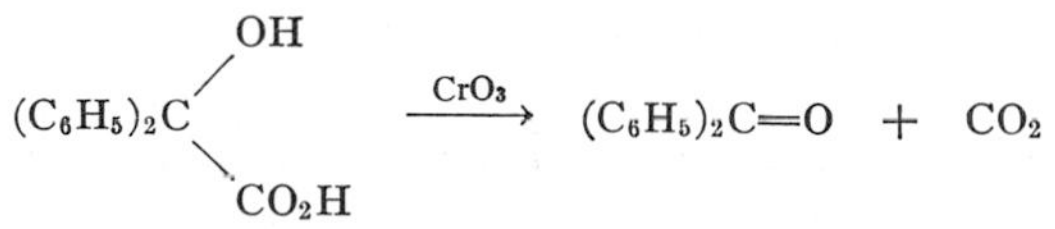

Benzilic acid (m.p. 150°)   Benzophenone

converted in good yield into phenylglyoxylic acid (benzoylformic acid). When this α-keto acid is formed by permanganate oxidation in an acidic solution it is converted rapidly into benzaldehyde, which is then oxidized to benzoic acid. The alcoholic group of benzilic acid (10) is tertiary, but this α-hydroxy acid is oxidized readily by chromic acid to benzophenone and carbon dioxide.

8.30   Steric Acceleration of Oxidation. — The determination of the rates of saponification of the benzoates of cholestane-3β-ol and cholestane-3α-ol (8.24) was done by G. Vavon and Boleslawa Jakubovicz in 1933 for comparison with the rates of chromic acid oxidation of the epimeric secondary alcohols. Their results are recorded in Table 8.5. Since relative rates of saponification

TABLE 8.5. SAPONIFICATION VS. OXIDATION

		CHOLESTANE-3β-OL	CHOLESTANE-3α-OL
Rates of saponification at 69°	Benzoates	14.8	6.2
	Isovalerates	7.2	4.2
Time (min.) for 5% oxidation at 25°	90% AcOH	500	70
	95% AcOH	150	10

afford a measure of relative rates of acylation, the data show that rates of oxidation of the secondary alcohols do not follow the order of rates of acylation. No explanation of the difference was at the time evident. In 1949 Westheimer[1] investigated the kinetics of chromic acid oxidation of 2-deuteropropanol-2, $(CH_3)_2CDOH$, and found that the rate controlling step is removal of the hydrogen (or deuterium) on the hydroxylated carbon atom. When, a year later, Barton advanced the now

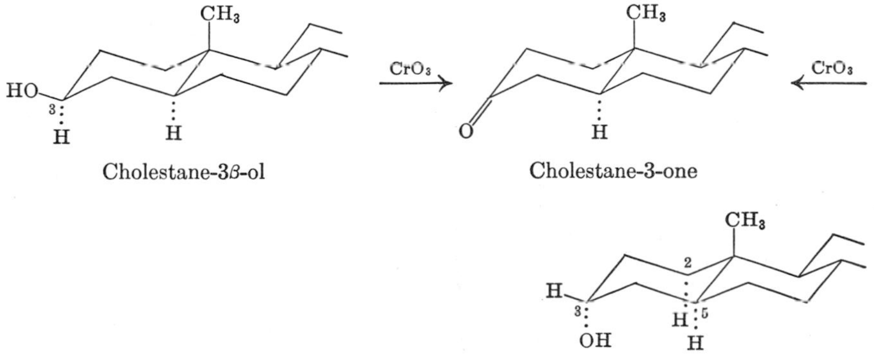

Cholestane-3β-ol   Cholestane-3-one

Cholestane-3α-ol

---

[1] Frank H. Westheimer, b. 1912 Baltimore; Ph.D. Harvard (Conant); Univ. Chicago; Harvard Univ.

well grounded theory that equatorial alcohols are generally more reactive in acylation than alcohols of axial orientation, he suggested that cholestane-3α-ol is oxidized more rapidly than the 3β-ol because the 3β-hydrogen which is attacked is equatorial in the 3α-ol and hence more accessible than an axial 3α-hydrogen. A probably more important factor determining reaction rates in oxidations with chromic acid or other reagent was defined by Eschenmoser[1] (1955), who noticed that transformation of the tetrahedral carbon of an alcoholic group to a trigonal carbon often removes repulsive interactions giving rise to steric strain or instability. Thus cholestane-3α-ol is destabilized by two 1:3 OH:H interactions which disappear on oxidation to the ketone. Relief of steric strain provides a driving force for oxidation of the 3α-ol, whereas the 3β-ol is free from comparable strain (1:3 H:H interactions are negligible). Rate constants for oxidation of axial alcohols with chromic acid in 90.9% acetic acid follow the order expected from esti-

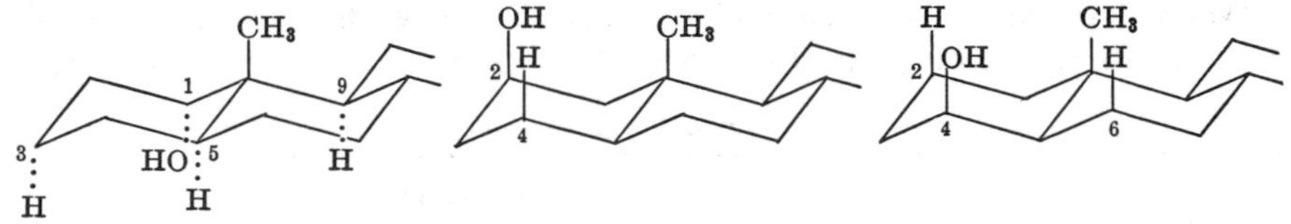

1α-ol	2β-ol	4β-ol
13.0	20.0	35.0

$$k^{25°}$$

mated steric strain. In cholestane-1α-ol there is one more OH:H interaction than in cholestane-3α-ol, for which the rate constant is 3.0. The 2β-ol is destabilized by a strong CH₃:OH interaction and by one weaker OH:H repulsion; the 4β-ol is strained still further by one CH₃:OH and two OH:H interactions.

Steric effects produce such differences in reactivity that selective oxidation of one of two secondary alcoholic groups is often realizable. Thus cholestane-3β,5α,6β-triol on controlled oxidation with chromic acid affords the 6-ketone in

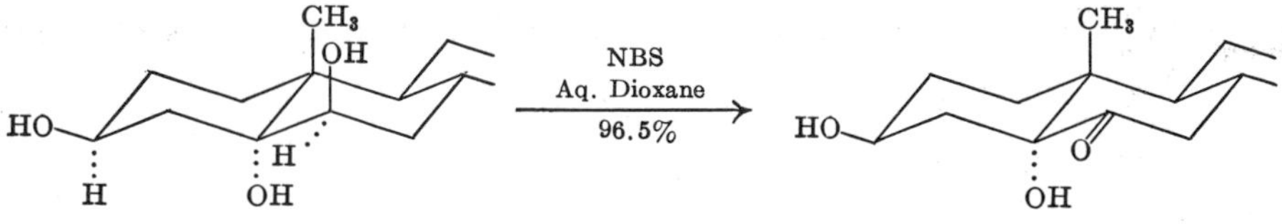

3β, 5α, 6β-Triol   NBS
                    Aq. Dioxane
                       96.5%   →   3β, 5α-Diol-6-one

65% yield. N-Bromosuccinimide in aqueous dioxane is a more selective reagent, for oxidation of the triol with either one or two oxygen equivalents affords the diolone in nearly quantitative yield.

8.31   Oxidation of Allylic Alcohols. — Allylic alcohols, for example, cinnamyl and allyl alcohol, can be oxidized to the corresponding aldehydes by stirring a solution in an organic solvent with suitably prepared manganese

$$C_6H_5CH=CHCH_2OH \xrightarrow[76\%]{MnO_2} C_6H_5CH=CHCH=O$$

[1] Albert Eschenmoser, b. 1925, Erstfeld (Switzerland); Ph.D. ETH, Zurich (Schinz, Ruzicka); ETH, Zurich.

dioxide. The reactions proceed rapidly and yields usually are high. Active oxidant is prepared by slow addition of aqueous potassium permanganate into a stirred solution of manganese sulfate at 90° (O. Mancera, 1953) or by addition of solutions of manganese sulfate and sodium hydroxide to a permanganate solution (J. Attenburrow, 1952); the precipitated oxide is washed and dried for a limited period at 100–130°. Natural pyrolusite ores and other commercial oxides show little activity. Only a part of the oxygen is available, and the amount of oxide used usually is five to fifteen parts per part of alcohol oxidized. The activity of a preparation seems to be dependent upon the degree of hydration. Oxidation probably occurs while the alcohol is adsorbed on the surface of the oxide. Solvents employed include petroleum ether, acetone, chloroform, and carbon tetrachloride. Some batches of oxide are described as active enough to ignite petroleum ether.

Both primary and secondary allylic alcohols can be oxidized smoothly by manganese dioxide, and these alcohols are so much more reactive than saturated alcohols that selective oxidation of polyfunctional compounds can be realized in high yield. The course of such an oxidation can be judged from the intensity of ultraviolet absorption due to the new chromophore formed. The triple bond evidently has an activating effect comparable to that of the double bond, for several propargylic alcohols have been found to undergo ready oxidation. 3-Octyne-2-ol (1 g.), for example, was stirred for 30 min. with a suspension of manganese dioxide (10 g.) in petroleum ether (50 ml.), and evaporation of the filtered

$$CH_3CH_2CH_2CH_2C{\equiv}CCHCH_3 \xrightarrow{\text{MnO}_2} CH_3CH_2CH_2CH_2C{\equiv}CCCH_3$$
$$\underset{OH}{|} \qquad\qquad \underset{O}{\|}$$

solution afforded the ketone, isolated as a derivative in quantitative yield. 1-Hexyne-3-ol, which has acetylenic hydrogen, was recovered unchanged after similar treatment. Oxidation of an allylic secondary alcoholic group without attack of a saturated secondary alcoholic function can be accomplished also with aluminum isopropoxide and acetone at 20° (K. Heusler, 1961).

Some α,β-unsaturated ketones of the type (a) are dehydrogenated to the

$$O{=}C(R)CH{=}C(R)CH_2CH_2{-} \xrightarrow[\text{CHCl}_3]{\text{MnO}_2} O{=}C(R)CH{=}C(R)CH{=}CH{-}$$
$$\text{(a)} \qquad\qquad \text{(b)}$$

dienones (b) by manganese dioxide prepared without the use of alkali (Mancera) but not with that precipitated from an alkaline solution.

ETHERS

8.32 **Properties.** — Constants for a number of ethers of types ROR and ROR′ are recorded in Table 8.6. Being unassociated in the liquid state, methyl ethers have boiling points considerably below those of the parent, hydrogen-bonded alcohols. For example, *n*-butyl alcohol boils at 117.7° and its methyl ether at 70.3°.

Ethers are indifferent to dilute acids, strong bases, and Grignard reagents. Since the methoxyl group withstands oxidation, an alcohol can be alkylated for protec-

TABLE 8.6. ETHERS

NAME	FORMULA	M.P., °C.	B.P., °C.	SP. GR. (LIQ.)
Dimethyl ether	CH_3OCH_3	− 140	− 24.9	0.661
Methyl ethyl ether	$CH_3OCH_2CH_3$		7.9	.697
Diethyl ether	$CH_3CH_2OCH_2CH_3$	$\begin{cases} -116\ (\alpha) \\ -123.5\ (\beta) \end{cases}$	34.6	.714
Di-n-propyl ether	$(CH_3CH_2CH_2)_2O$	− 122	90.5	.736
Diisopropyl ether	$(CH_3)_2CHOCH(CH_3)_2$		68	.735
Methyl n-butyl ether	$CH_3OCH_2CH_2CH_2CH_3$	− 116	70.3	.744
Ethyl n-butyl ether	$CH_3CH_2OCH_2CH_2CH_2CH_3$		92	.752
Di-n-butyl ether	$(CH_3CH_2CH_2CH_2)_2O$		141	.769
Di-n-amyl ether	$(n\text{-}C_5H_{11})_2O$	− 69	187.5	.774
Diisoamyl ether	$[(CH_3)_2CHCH_2CH_2]_2O$		172.2	.777
Di-n-hexyl ether	$(n\text{-}C_6H_{13})_2O$		208.8	
s-Di-(chloromethyl) ether	$ClCH_2OCH_2Cl$		106	1.315
α,β-Dichloroethyl ethyl ether	$CH_3CH_2OCHClCH_2Cl$		145	1.174
Di-(β-chloroethyl) ether	$CH_2ClCH_2OCH_2CH_2Cl$		178	1.213
Ethylene glycol dimethyl ether	$CH_3OCH_2CH_2OCH_3$		83	.863
Divinyl ether	$CH_2{=}CHOCH{=}CH_2$		35	
Diallyl ether	$(CH_2{=}CHCH_2)_2O$		94	.826
Tetrahydrofurane	$\begin{array}{c} CH_2CH_2 \\ \diagup\quad\diagdown \\ \qquad O \\ \diagdown\quad\diagup \\ CH_2CH_2 \end{array}$	− 108	65.4	.888
Diphenyl ether	$C_6H_5OC_6H_5$	26.9	259	1.072
Anisole	$C_6H_5OCH_3$	− 37.3	154	.994

tion during oxidation of another functional group in the molecule. Because ethers are Lewis bases capable of forming oxonium salts, they dissolve in concentrated sulfuric acid and are thus easily distinguishable from alkanes and alkyl halides. That ethers are more reactive than paraffinic hydrocarbons is indicated by the fact that diethyl ether can be chlorinated readily at ordinary temperatures without illumination; the product, α,β-dichloroethyl ethyl ether, $CH_3CH_2OCHCl\text{-}CH_2Cl$, is obtained in about 24% yield.

8.33   Diethyl ether, known simply as ether, is used extensively as a solvent and as an anesthetic. The combination of two hydrocarbon residues linked through an inert oxygen atom confers marked solvent power for organic compounds of most types other than those of a highly hydroxylic character. Ether is an excellent extraction medium because it is a good solvent for organic compounds and dissolves but few inorganic substances, because it is not miscible with water and separates as a discrete upper layer, and because its high volatility (b.p. 34.6°) permits rapid removal from an extract by distillation at a temperature so low as to avoid damage to sensitive substances. Ether falls short of being an ideal extraction solvent because it is not completely insoluble in water; at room temperature ether dissolves 1–1.5% of water and water dissolves 7.5% of ether; hence considerable solvent is lost in extraction operations. The volatile solvent is also highly flammable, and ether vapor, being about two and one half times as heavy as air, tends to settle on bench surfaces and catch fire. Another property calling for caution in handling ether is that on standing for some time in contact with air the substance is partly oxidized to a nonvolatile peroxide, which is left as a residue on evaporation of the solvent and which may explode violently in a distillation carried to dryness with consequent overheating. Ether peroxide is a mixture of which the following constituents have been identified:

$$CH_3CHO \cdot OCHCH_3$$
$$\underset{OH}{|} \quad \underset{OH}{|}$$
Dihydroxyethyl peroxide

$$\left(CH_3CH\underset{O}{\overset{O}{<}} \underset{|}{} \right)_n$$
Ethylidene peroxide polymer

Ether for anesthesia and for most solvent purposes contains a little alcohol and a trace of water, and material of this composition is protected effectively by use as container of a tinplate can surfaced on the inside with a thin layer of electroplated copper or with a layer of copper-tin oxide. Absolute ether requires use of a treated container as well as addition of a preservative, for example, 0.05 part per million of sodium diethyldithiocarbamate, $(C_2H_5)_2NC(=S)S^-Na^+$.

8.34   Ether as an Anesthetic. — Ether was first used in surgical anesthesia by Long in Georgia in 1842, but the results were not published and did not influence medical practice. The safe abolition of pain by inhalation of ether for a period long enough for a surgical operation was rediscovered by the Boston dentist Morton, and introduction of ether anesthesia into surgical practice resulted from a successful demonstration by Morton at the Massachusetts General Hospital in 1846. The term anesthesia (insensibility) was suggested to Morton by Oliver Wendell Holmes. Inhalation of ether vapor produces unconsciousness by depressing activity of the central nervous system. The effect appears to be associated with affinity of ether for cell surfaces, possibly with alteration in the permeability of cells.

Anesthesia with ethylene was employed successfully in clinical surgery in 1923 (Luckhardt and Lewis), but although the hydrocarbon produces a rapid and pleasant induction of unconsciousness, with prompt recovery, the explosiveness of certain mixtures of ethylene and air imposes difficulties, and the method has been little used. Divinyl ether was suggested as an anesthetic by Leake and Chen (1930) and made available in a satisfactory form by Ruigh and Major[1] by synthesis from ethylene chlorohydrin via di-(β-chloroethyl)ether, a nonvesicant analog of mustard gas. The commercial preparation Vinethene contains 3.5% of

$$2 HOCH_2CH_2Cl \xrightarrow[75\%]{H_2SO_4} \underset{\text{Di-}(\beta\text{-chloroethyl)}}{O(CH_2CH_2Cl)_2} \xrightarrow[25\%]{\text{Fused KOH, 200-240°, stream of NH}_3} \underset{\text{Divinyl ether}}{O(CH=CH_2)_2}$$

absolute alcohol to retard evaporation leading to frosting of the anesthetic mask and 0.01% of phenyl-α-naphthylamine as antioxidant. Divinyl ether is about seven times as potent as ether and is characterized by greater rapidity of action, and its use is attended with the danger of rapidly reaching too deep a plane of

[1] Randolph T. Major, b. 1901 Columbus, Ohio; Ph.D. Princeton (L. W. Jones); Merck and Co.; Univ. Virginia

anesthesia. Cyclopropane, first used clinically at the University of Wisconsin General Hospital in 1934, is the most potent anesthetic gas, and in very low concentrations can produce insensibility to pain without unconsciousness. However, the hydrocarbon is expensive, and mixtures with air over the entire anesthetic range are explosive and flammable; an experienced anesthetist with access to special equipment is required. Nitrous oxide was suggested for use in surgical operations by Sir Humphry Davy in 1799, but was investigated for this purpose only subsequent to the American discovery of the similar use of ether. The oxide has found some use in dentistry but not in general surgery, for even undiluted nitrous oxide has only a weak depressant action on the central nervous system, and in an operation lasting more than a minute or two oxygen must be given to prevent anoxemia (insufficient aeration of the blood); this dilution of the anesthetic reduces potency to a low level. Chloroform, formerly employed to some extent as an anesthetic, possesses significant liver toxicity and is now little used except in the tropics, where the low boiling point of ether presents difficulties. Ether thus continues to be the safest and the most widely used general anesthetic.

8.35   Preparation of Ethers. — Diethyl ether is manufactured by the sulfuric acid process and as a by-product of the production of synthetic ethanol from ethylene. Symmetrical ethers are made satisfactorily from primary alcohols (methyl, n-propyl, isoamyl) by the sulfuric acid method; secondary and tertiary alcohols are dehydrated too readily for efficient ether formation. Diisopropyl ether is a by-product of the production of isopropyl alcohol from propylene. Mixed ethers are available by the Williamson synthesis (4.6), for example:

$$\underset{\text{Sodium } n\text{-propoxide}}{CH_3CH_2CH_2ONa} + CH_3CH_2I \xrightarrow{70\%} \underset{\text{Ethyl } n\text{-propyl ether}}{CH_3CH_2CH_2OCH_2CH_3}$$

$$CH_3CH_2ONa + BrCH_2CH_2CH_2CH_3 \xrightarrow{110°} \underset{\text{Ethyl } n\text{-butyl ether}}{CH_3CH_2OCH_2CH_2CH_2CH_3}$$

A variation in the synthesis which utilizes a dialkyl sulfate in place of an alkyl halide is useful for preparation of ethers of phenols. Phenols are acidic enough to dissolve in aqueous alkali, and when dimethyl sulfate is stirred into an alkaline

Anisole

solution of phenol the oily sulfate slowly dissolves and the oily ether separates. The first methyl group of the sulfate reacts more rapidly than the second, but the second can be utilized if desired; when one half mole of dimethyl sulfate is employed the mixture is refluxed for 15 hrs. and the yield is 72–75%.

Diazomethane, CH_2N_2 (11.18), has long been used for methylation of carboxylic acids, for these substances themselves provide the necessary acidic catalysis. Hydrochloric acid is unsatisfactory for promotion of the reaction of an alcohol with the reagent because it is itself methylated by diazomethane. However, fluoroboric acid and boron fluoride etherate are satisfactory catalysts and at a concentration of about 0.7 mole percent promote rapid reaction of primary or unhindered secondary alcohols with diazomethane to give the methyl ethers in

$$C_6H_{11}OH \quad + \quad \bar{C}H_2\!-\!\overset{+}{N}\!\equiv\!N \quad \xrightarrow[92\%]{HBF_4} \quad C_6H_5OCH_3 \quad + \quad N_2$$

Cyclohexanol

high yield (M. C. Caserio, 1958; E. Müller, 1958). M. Neeman (1961) employed the reaction to establish the structure of estriol D-glucosiduronic acid (1), which is excreted in human pregnancy urine as the sodium salt. Since the UV spectrum

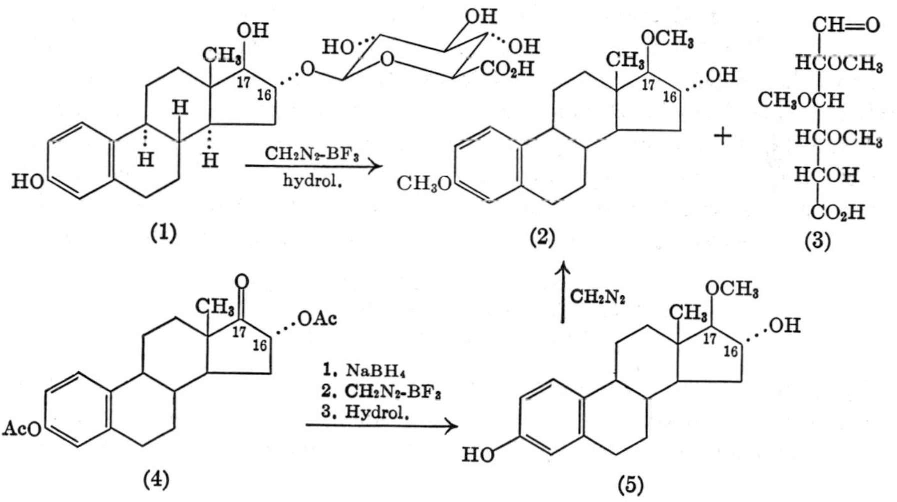

shifts on addition of alkali, the sugar acid is not linked to the hormone at the phenolic hydroxyl group and must be at C_{16} or C_{17}. BF_3-catalyzed methylation of (1) gave the pentamethyl ether methyl ester, and acid hydrolysis removed the methylated sugar acid (3) and gave the dimethyl ether (2), as established by synthesis from (4). Reduction of the carbonyl group, acid-catalyzed methylation, and hydrolysis gave the triol 17-monomethyl ether (5). The phenolic hydroxyl group of this ether is sufficiently acidic to react with diazomethane without catalysis, and the product was (2).

t-Butyl ethers of alcohols and phenols are available by a novel Grignard reaction. Thus phenylmagnesium bromide reacts with *t*-butyl perbenzoate, a stable and commercially available reagent, to give phenyl *t*-butyl ether and benzoic acid (Sven-Olov Lawesson, 1959). The reaction is formulated thus:

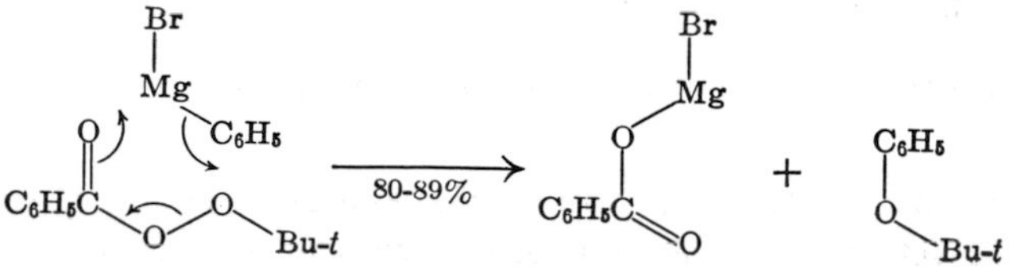

Vinyl methyl ether and vinyl ethyl ether (b.p. $35.5°$) are made commercially by catalytic addition of methanol or ethanol to acetylene. These ethers and propenyl ethyl ether (b.p. $69°$) are useful in synthesis. Thus methylal (from $CH_3CHO + 2\ HOCH_3$) adds to vinyl methyl ether to give a β-methoxy acetal; on

$$CH_3CH(OCH_3)_2\ +\ CH_2{=}CHOCH_3\ \xrightarrow{BF_3}\ CH_3\underset{\underset{OCH_3}{|}}{C}HCH_2CH(OCH_3)_2\ \xrightarrow{H^+}$$

$$CH_3CH{=}CHCH{=}O$$

liberation of the aldehyde group, the β-methoxy group is eliminated and the product is crotonaldehyde.

8.36 Ether Cleavage. — An ether having two different primary groups, ROR′, is cleaved by hydriodic acid at a suitably elevated temperature to two alkyl halides, RI and R′I. For investigation of the direction of cleavage, Michael (1906) employed more moderate conditions such that the products are RI and R′OH. Methyl n-alkyl ethers are cleaved predominantly to give methyl iodide, and methyl sec-alkyl ethers give methyl iodide only; but methyl t-alkyl ethers are cleaved to methyl alcohol and the t-alkyl iodide. Tertiary ethers, moreover, are cleaved more readily than ethers containing primary or secondary

$$RCH_2OCH_3 + HI \rightarrow RCH_2OH + CH_3I$$
$$R_2CHOCH_3 + HI \rightarrow R_2CHOH + CH_3I$$
$$R_3COCH_3 + HI \rightarrow R_3CI + CH_3OH$$

alkyl groups. The results are interpretable on the basis of reaction mechanisms which can be outlined as follows. Methyl t-butyl ether (1) is protonated to give an oxonium ion which decomposes to methanol and a tertiary carbonium ion

$$1.\quad (CH_3)_3COCH_3\ \xrightarrow{H^+}\ (CH_3)_3\underset{H}{\overset{+}{C}}OCH_3\ \longrightarrow\ (CH_3)_3\overset{+}{C}\ +\ HOCH_3$$

$$(CH_3)_3\overset{+}{C}\ +\ I^-\ \longrightarrow\ (CH_3)_3CI$$

stabilized by the inductive effect of three alkyl groups, and this then combines with iodide ion to give t-butyl iodide. A primary or secondary carbonium ion lacks comparable stability, and evidence that such an ion is not formed is afforded by the behavior of optically active methyl ethers in which the carbon atom carrying the methoxyl group is asymmetric. Thus optically active $CH_3CH_2CH(CH_3)$-OCH_3 affords optically active $CH_3CH_2CH(CH_3)OH$. Since a carbonium ion is planar and permits equal opportunity for formation of the $(+)$ or $(-)$ product, a reaction involving such an intermediate would be attended with racemization. Cleavage of a methyl n- or sec-alkyl ether is thus interpreted as following the alternative course (2).

$$2.\quad R_2CHOCH_3\ \xrightarrow{H^+}\ R_2\underset{H}{\overset{+}{C}}HOCH_3\ \xrightarrow{I^-}\ R_2CHOH\ +\ CH_3I$$

Cleavage of an aliphatic ether to two moles of alkyl halide involves reaction (2) followed by reaction of the alcohol formed with more hydrogen iodide. Since phenols do not react similarly with HI, phenol methyl ethers are cleaved to methyl iodide and the phenol. Demethylation of such an ether is done more usually by refluxing the compound with hydrobromic and acetic acid. Other effective methods are: refluxing with anhydrous aluminum chloride in carbon disulfide or nitrobenzene solution and decomposing the product with water (3); heating for

3. $C_6H_5OCH_3 + AlCl_3 \rightarrow C_6H_5OAlCl_2 + CH_3Cl$
$C_6H_5OAlCl_2 + 3 H_2O \rightarrow C_6H_5OH + Al(OH)_3 + 2 HCl$

5–6 hrs. at 200° with pyridine hydrochloride, m.p. 144°, b.p. 218°. Cleavage of ethers can be effected also by adding boron bromide (b.p. 90.6°) to the ice-cold ether (3 equiv.), refluxing the mixture, and removing the alkyl bromide by distil-

$$3 ROR + BBr_3 \longrightarrow (RO)_3B + 3 RBr$$
$$(RO)_3B + 3 H_2O \quad \rangle \quad 3 ROH + H_3BO_3$$

lation; the orthoboric ester is then hydrolyzed with 10% alkali (F. L. Benton, 1942). Alkyl phenyl ethers yield the phenol and the alkyl bromide.

8.37   Zeisel Methoxyl Determination. — Colchicine, an alkaloid of the formula $C_{20}H_{25}O_6N$, has three methoxyl groups on an aromatic ring and also an enol methyl ether group. Such a group is hydrolyzed easily by dilute

$$-\overset{|}{C}=\overset{|}{C}-OCH_3 \quad \xrightarrow{HCl} \quad HOCH_3 + -\overset{|}{C}=\overset{|}{C}-OH$$

Colchicine   Colchiceine

mineral acid without disturbance of the phenolic methoxyl groups. Thus colchicine affords methyl alcohol and colchiceine. This relationship was established in an analytical study by S. Zeisel in Austria in 1886. A 32.9-g. sample of colchicine yielded 28.9 g. (91%) of colchiceine and about 1.5 g. of a liquid corresponding approximately in boiling point (63–67°) to methyl alcohol. To increase the accuracy of both the identification and the weight, Zeisel converted the sample to methyl iodide (6.6 g.). The experience led Zeisel to develop a general method for quantitative determination of methoxyl (or ethoxyl) content. A weighed sample is heated with excess hydriodic acid, the methyl iodide formed (b.p. 42.3°) is distilled into an alcoholic solution of silver nitrate, and the precipitated silver iodide is weighed. Titrimetric methods of determination are used in microanalysis. The other cleavage product must be relatively nonvolatile. An example is the alkaloid papaverine, which was found by Zeisel determination to contain four methoxyl groups.

$$C_{16}H_9N(OCH_3)_4 \quad \xrightarrow{HI} \quad C_{16}H_9N(OH)_4 + 4 CH_3I$$

Papaverine   Nonvolatile residue   Distillate

8.38   Protective Ether Groups. — Since methyl ether derivatives of phenols can be demethylated with relative ease and in good yield, they are satisfactory for providing temporary protection during operations incompatible with the presence of a free phenolic function, for example, a Grignard reaction. In the case of aliphatic alcohols, methyl ether derivatives usually are not suitable as protective groups because the more drastic conditions required for cleavage lead to secondary changes. However, ethers of special types which can be split under mild conditions are available.

Ethers of one type, tetrahydropyranyl ethers, are made by reaction of an alcohol with dihydropyrane under acid catalysis (R. Paul, 1934; G. F. Woods, 1947). A proton attacks dihydropyrane in the direction formulated because the resulting

Dihydropyrane   Tetrahydropyranyl
b. p. 85°   ether

charge at C_2 is stabilized by the adjacent electron-rich oxygen. Tetrahydropyranyl ethers are stable to base, to Grignard reagents, and to oxidation, and the original alcohol can be recovered by gentle hydrolysis with dilute mineral acid. Under catalysis by hydrogen chloride or comparable acid at room temperature, dihydropyrane reacts also with phenols and mercaptans (W. E. Parham, 1954) and with carboxylic acids (R. E. Bowman, 1952).

Freudenberg[1] (1928) introduced use of benzyl ethers as protective derivatives which are stable to dilute acids or bases but which can be cleaved either by catalytic hydrogenation or by chemical reduction (sodium-alcohol). They usually

$$ROCH_2C_6H_5 \xrightarrow{\text{2H}} ROH + CH_3C_6H_5$$

are prepared by interaction of the alcohol with benzyl chloride in the presence of powdered potassium or sodium hydroxide, since yields are generally poor if an aqueous solution is used. A mixture of benzene and dry dioxane is generally suitable as solvent, or else benzyl chloride itself serves as solvent. Alternatively, the alcohol is converted into the sodium alkoxide and this is allowed to react with benzyl chloride in an inert solvent. Reductive fission of a benzyl ether is attributable to activation of the O—C bond by the phenyl group. The effect is accentuated in a triphenylmethyl, or trityl, ether, and these are also cleaved by hydrogenolysis. But, like the tertiary ethers discussed above, trityl ethers are also cleaved by acids, even by dilute acetic acid at room temperature. Primary

$$ROC(C_6H_5)_3 + H_2O \xrightarrow{\text{CH}_3\text{CO}_2\text{H}} ROH + HOC(C_6H_5)_3$$
Trityl ether

alcohols usually are convertible into trityl ethers by reaction with trityl chloride in pyridine at room temperature; several days may be required, but yields are satisfactory. Secondary alcohols do not react appreciably with trityl chloride unless the temperature is raised, and the difference in reactivity is so pronounced that there is no difficulty in selective tritylation of a primary alcoholic group in the presence of secondary groups.

Differences in the conditions for formation and cleavage of benzyl and trityl ethers formed the basis for a synthesis of the coenzyme uridine-diphosphate-

[1] Karl Freudenberg, b. 1886 Weinheim/Baden; Ph.D. Berlin (E. Fischer); Univ. Heidelberg

glucose (UDPG) by Todd[1] (1956). One component, uridine (1), has three acylable groups, one primary (C_5) and two secondary (C_2, C_3); the enolic group in the heterocyclic ring is inert. The synthesis required introduction of a phosphate

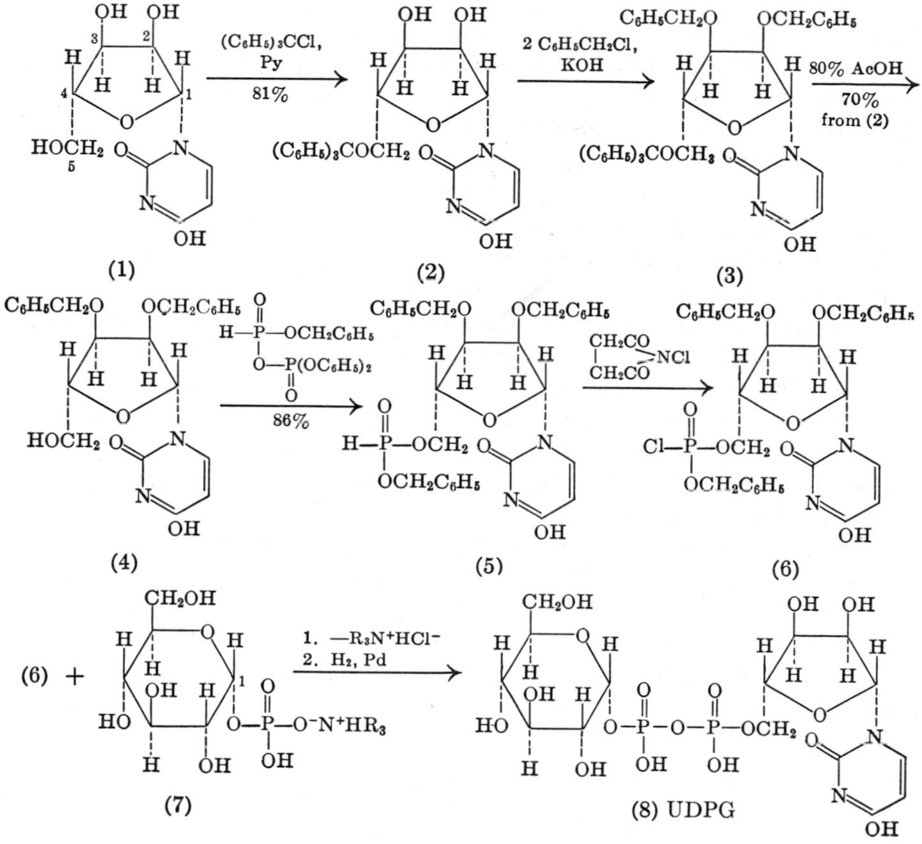

group at the more reactive primary alcoholic function, which was achieved as follows. The primary group was protected by selective tritylation (2), the secondary groups were benzylated (3), and the primary alcoholic group was liberated by acid hydrolysis (4). Reaction of (4) with O-benzyl phosphorus O,O-diphenylphosphoric anhydride in the presence of 2,6-lutidine as catalyst proceeded with elimination of $(C_6H_5O)_2P(=O)OH$ to give the phosphite derivative (5). Reaction of the phosphite (5) with N-chlorosuccinimide to replace hydrogen by chlorine completed the synthesis of the component (6), a phosphorochloridate. The second component was the amine salt (7), α-D-glucose 1-(tri-n-octylamine hydrogen phosphate); this was condensed with the uridine derivative (6) with elimination of the amine hydrochloride, and the product was hydrogenated. A mild platinum catalyst served for removal of the benzyl group of the pyrophosphate linkage, and hydrogenation with palladium black removed the other two benzyl groups.

[1] Sir Alexander Todd, b. 1907 Glasgow; Ph.D. Oxford (Robinson); Cambridge Univ.

Purification through the calcium salt gave a product having the full enzymic activity of UDPG.

SULFUR ANALOGS

8.39   **Mercaptans.** — Sulfur is in the same group as oxygen in the periodic table and forms similar compounds. The sulfur analogs of alcohols, RSH, are known both as mercaptans and as alkane thiols. The —SH group is called the mercapto-, thiol-, or sulfhydryl group. The boiling points are much lower than those of the corresponding alcohols, for example: CH_3SH, 6°; CH_3-CH_2SH, 36°; $CH_3CH_2CH_2SH$, 68°; $CH_3(CH_2)_3SH$, 98°. The boiling point of the last compound, n-butyl mercaptan, is that characteristic of a normal alkane of molecular weight 100, and the molecular weight of the mercaptan is almost the same (90). Mercaptans are thus only slightly associated because, since sulfur is much less negative than oxygen, they are unable to form hydrogen bonds. Inability to form hydrogen bonds with water accounts for the fact that mercaptans are much less soluble in water than alcohols. A distinguishing feature of volatile mercaptans is their disagreeable odor. Mercaptans, unlike alcohols, are acidic and form water-soluble salts with alkalis and insoluble salts with heavy metals (mercury, lead, zinc). The name is derived from this property (*L. mercurium captans*, seizing mercury).

Primary mercaptans can be prepared by reaction of an alkyl halide with sodium or potassium hydrosulfide: $RX + Na(K)SH \rightarrow RSH + Na(K)X$. The yields are satisfactory, however, only if the alkyl group is primary. A method that generally gives high yields involves reaction of either an alkyl halide or a dialkyl sulfate with thiourea (a) to form the S-alkylthiuronium salt (b), which is hydrolyzed by alkali to the mercaptan (c) and cyanamide (d). Another convenient

$$n\text{-}C_{12}H_{25}Br \ + \ S{=}C(NH_2)_2 \ \longrightarrow \ n\text{-}C_{12}H_{25}SC\overset{+}{\underset{NH_2}{\overset{NH_2Br^-}{\diagup}}} \ \xrightarrow[\text{80\% overall}]{NaOH}$$

(a)   (b)

$$n\text{-}C_{12}H_{25}SH \ + \ NaBr \ + \ H_2NC{\equiv}N \ + \ H_2O$$

(c)   (d)

method is reaction of an alkyl halide with potassium thiolacetate to give an acetyl mercaptan, which is hydrolyzed: $RX + CH_3COSK \rightarrow RSCOCH_3 \rightarrow RSH$.

The most characteristic chemical property of mercaptans is that they are reducing agents; they are readily oxidized by hydrogen peroxide or sodium hypohalite to disulfides, from which they can be regenerated by reduction (zinc dust

$$2\,RSH + H_2O_2 \rightarrow RSSR + H_2O$$

and acid). Nitric acid oxidizes either a mercaptan or the corresponding disulfide to the alkylsulfonic acid, RSO_2OH.

8.40   **Sulfides.** — These analogs of ethers can be prepared by a method (1) analogous to the Williamson synthesis. A symmetrical disulfide is obtained most readily by the action of sodium sulfide on an alkyl halide (2).

1. $C_2H_5Br + NaSCH_3 \rightarrow CH_3CH_2SCH_3$

         Methyl ethyl sulfide, b.p. 67°

2. $2\ C_2H_5Br + Na_2S \rightarrow CH_3CH_2SCH_2CH_3$

         Diethyl sulfide, b.p. 92°

Sulfides combine with alkyl halides to form crystalline sulfonium salts (a), comparable to oxonium salts, and they react with chlorine, bromine, or iodine to form dihalides that are similarly constituted. On oxidation (HNO_3, H_2O_2, etc.),

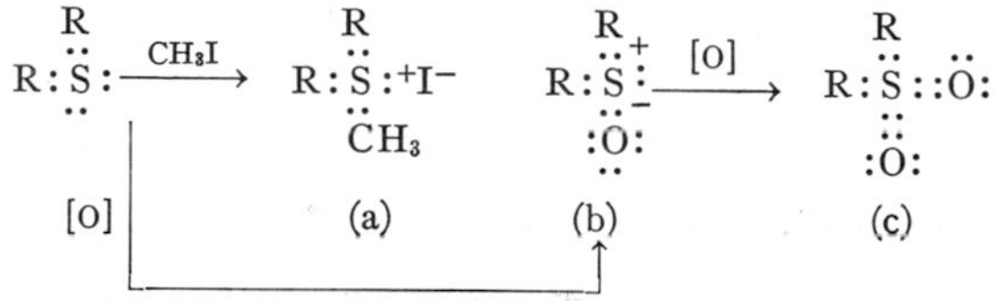

$$R:\overset{\cdot\cdot}{\underset{\cdot\cdot}{S}}: \xrightarrow{\ CH_3I\ } R:\overset{\overset{R}{\cdot\cdot}}{\underset{CH_3}{S}}:{}^{+}I^{-} \qquad R:\overset{\overset{R}{\cdot\cdot}}{\underset{:\overset{\cdot\cdot}{O}:}{S}}:{}^{+}\xrightarrow{\ [O]\ } R:\overset{\overset{R}{\cdot\cdot}}{\underset{:\overset{\cdot\cdot}{O}:}{S}}::\overset{\cdot\cdot}{O}:$$

    [O]   (a)   (b)   (c)

one oxygen equivalent of reagent converts a sulfide into a sulfoxide (b) and a second produces the sulfone (c). The present evidence is that a sulfoxide has a semipolar double bond and a sulfone two covalent bonds; the sulfur atom thus is able to accommodate more than eight electrons in its valance shell.

PROBLEMS

1. Predict the chief products of the following reactions:
   (a) Methyldiethylcarbinol on dehydration
   (b) $(CH_3)_2CHCHBrCH_2CH(CH_3)_2$ + alcoholic KOH
   (c) $(CH_3)_2COHCH_2CH_2CH_2OH$ on partial dehydration (elimination of one molecule of H_2O)
   (d) $CH_3CH_2CH_2COH(CH_3)_2$ + $K_2Cr_2O_7$ in a hot solution of dilute sulfuric acid
   (e) Cyclohexene, heated in acetic acid with hydrogen peroxide, followed by the addition of lead tetraacetate
   (f) Ethylene oxide + n-amyl alcohol, in the presence of dry hydrogen chloride
   (g) Ethylene oxide + ammonia
2. Indicate Grignard syntheses of the following substances from n-propylmagnesium bromide and any second component desired:
   (a) 2-Methylpentanol-2   (d) n-Amyl alcohol
   (b) 4-Methylheptanol-4   (e) Methylethyl-n-propylcarbinol
   (c) n-Butyl alcohol
3. Devise syntheses of the following compounds, starting with any alcohols having not more than three carbon atoms and any desired components readily obtainable from these alcohols (the list of available starting materials thus includes C_3-compounds of the types RX, RMgX, RCHO, RCOR, RCO_2H; also ethylene oxide, allyl alcohol):
   (a) $(CH_3)_2CHCH_2OH$ (f) 4-Methylpentene-1
   (b) $(CH_3)_2C(OH)CH_2CH_3$ (g) 2,3-Dimethylbutene-2
   (c) $(CH_3CH_2)_3COH$ (h) Isobutane
   (d) $CH_3CH_2CH_2CH_2CH_2OH$ (i) 2-Methylpentane
   (e) 2-Methylbutene-2   (j) 2,3,4-Trimethylpentane
4. Give syntheses of the following compounds from the starting materials of (3):
   (a) 4-Ethylheptane
   (b) 4-Methylpentadiene-1,3
   (c) Neopentyl alcohol, $(CH_3)_3CCH_2OH$

5. Devise syntheses of the following compounds starting with alcohols and derived substances having no more than four carbons:
   (a) 2,4-Dimethylpentene-2   (c) 2-Methylhexane
   (b) 3-Methylhexanol-3   (d) 2,2-Dimethylpentane

6. A hydrocarbon C_5H_{10} yields 2-methylbutane on catalytic hydrogenation and adds HBr to form a compound that on reaction with silver hydroxide affords an alcohol. The latter on oxidation gives a ketone. What is the structure of the hydrocarbon?

7. An alcohol $C_5H_{11}OH$ gives a ketone on oxidation, and when it is dehydrated and the resulting alkene is oxidized, a mixture of a ketone and an acid results. What is the structure of the alcohol?

8. Plan a synthesis of octadiene-2,6, starting with cyclohexene.

9. How could you distinguish experimentally between the following isomers?

$$\underset{HOCH_2CHCH_2CH_2CHCH_2OH}{\overset{CH_3 \qquad\quad CH_3}{\mid \qquad\qquad\quad \mid}} \qquad and \qquad \underset{HOCH_2CH_2CH-CHCH_2CH_2OH}{\overset{CH_3 \ \ CH_3}{\mid \quad\ \ \mid}}$$

10. Starting with a natural product that has been formulated, plan a synthesis of:

$$CH_3(CH_2)_5CH(OH)CH_2CHOHCHOH(CH_2)_7CH_2OH$$

11. Predict the relative rates of oxidation of the following axial cholestanols: 1α, 2β, 3α, 4β, 6β, 7α, 11β.

Chapter 9

DISPLACEMENT REACTIONS

Typical displacements are the hydrolysis of an alkyl halide to an alcohol and the transformation of an alcohol to an alkyl halide or to an ether. Such reactions are described also as replacements and as substitutions; the latter term, however, usually is restricted to description of a replacement of hydrogen by another atom or group, as in the nitration of benzene, $C_6H_6 \rightarrow C_6H_5NO_2$, an aromatic substitution.

9.1 **Kinetics.** — A kinetic study of a reaction involves determination of the reaction rate in homogeneous solution and investigation of the effect on the rate of variations in the concentrations of the reactants and of changes in solvent and in temperature. According to the law of mass action, the rate at which a reaction proceeds is directly proportional to the concentrations of the species participating in the reaction. Most organic reactions, however, proceed through more than one step, and the kinetics apply only to the slowest one, the rate determining step. Most reactions are found to correspond to one of three rate expressions. A first order reaction is one in which the rate depends upon the concentration of only one species (A): Rate $= k_1\,[A]$. In a second order reaction the rate depends upon the concentrations of two reactants or upon the square of the concentration of one: Rate $= k_2[A]\,[B]$ or $k_2[A]^2$. The rate of a third order reaction is dependent upon either the concentrations of three reactants or the concentration of one reactant and the square of the concentration of another: Rate $= k_3[A]\,[B]\,[C]$ or $k_3[A]\,[B]^2$. In the latter case the reaction can be described as first order with respect to A and second order with respect to B.

The rate of hydrolysis of α-bromophenylacetic acid to mandelic acid is found to be proportional to the concentration of the acid and inversely proportional to the hydrogen ion concentration. The observed kinetics can be explained on the assumption of an initial rapid dissociation of the acid preceding the rate determining step:

$$C_6H_5CHBrCO_2H \underset{fast}{\rightleftharpoons} C_6H_5CHBrCO_2^- + H^+$$

$$C_6H_5CHBrCO_2^- + H_2O \xrightarrow{slow} C_6H_5CHOHCO_2^- + HBr$$

Water is present in such large excess that the concentration does not change perceptibly and hence does not appear in the kinetic expression: Rate = $k\,[C_6H_5CHBrCO_2^-] = k\,[C_6H_5CHBrCO_2H]/[H^+]$. On the other hand, a reagent involved in a fast step after the rate determining step does not appear in the equation. Thus Lapworth found (1904) that halogenation of acetone in dilute aqueous alkali is a second order reaction, the rate being proportional to the concentrations of acetone and hydroxide ion but independent of the concentration of halogen. The observation suggests that the rate determining step is formation of the hybrid enolate anion, which then reacts rapidly with halogen:

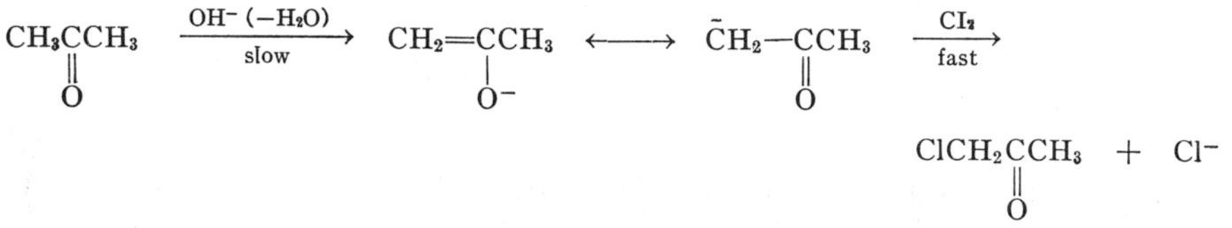

The finding that a reaction is third order does not necessarily mean that it is in fact termolecular, that is, that it involves simultaneous collision of three reactants. Thus the reaction of ethylene oxide with hydrogen bromide to form ethylene bromohydrin follows the third order rate law: Rate = $k_3[\text{Oxide}]\,[H^+]\,[Br^-]$, but probably the rate determining step is nucleophilic attack by Br^- on the conjugate acid of the oxide:

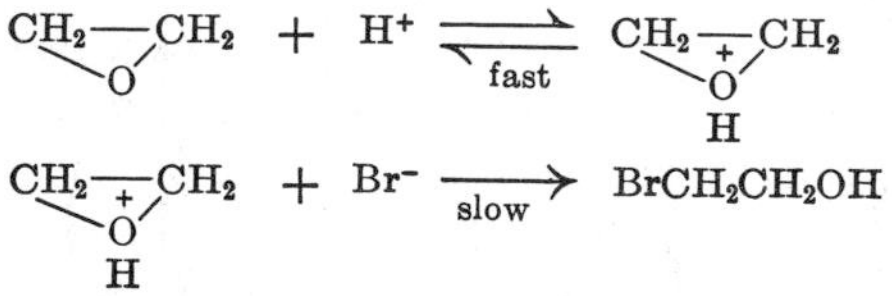

9.2　　　**S_N1 and S_N2 Mechanisms.** — The first detailed kinetic studies of substitution reactions at a saturated carbon atom were described by Ingold and Hughes[1] in a series of more than thirty papers (1933–46). Either electrophilic or nucleophilic reagents can effect displacements, but the following discussion is limited to the nucleophilic type, exemplified by hydrolysis of alkyl

$$HO^- + R{:}Br \longrightarrow HOR + Br^-$$

$$R_3N{:} + R{:}Br \longrightarrow R_3\overset{+}{N}R + Br^-$$

halides and by formation of alkylammonium salts from tertiary amines and alkyl halides. In a study of rates of hydrolysis in 80 % aqueous ethanol at 55° of methyl bromide and of halides derived from it by α-substitution of methyl groups (Table

[1] Edward David Hughes, b. 1906 Caernarvonshire, North Wales; Ph.D. Wales (Watson); D.Sc. London (Ingold); University College, London

TABLE 9.1. RATE OF HYDROLYSIS OF ALKYL BROMIDES
(80% ETHANOL AT 55°)

ALKYL BROMIDE	FIRST-ORDER REACTION CONSTANT sec.$^{-1}$ $k_1 \times 10^5$	SECOND-ORDER REACTION CONSTANT sec.$^{-1}$/(g. mol./l.) $k_2 \times 10^5$
CH_3Br	0.349	2140
CH_3CH_2Br	0.139	171
$(CH_3)_2CHBr$	0.237	4.75
$(CH_3)_3CBr$	1010	—

9.1), Ingold and Hughes observed that hydrolysis of methyl bromide is predominantly a second-order reaction, dependent upon the concentration of halide and of hydroxide ion; a concurrent reaction of first-order kinetics occurs to only a minor extent ($k_1 = 0.349 \times 10^{-5}$). The rate decreases with the α-substitution of one and two methyl groups and passes through a minimum in the case of isopropyl bromide, where both first- and second-order kinetics obtain, though the latter still predominates. The rate rises sharply with introduction of a third methyl group (t-butyl bromide) and is independent of hydroxide ion, the kinetics being of first order.

Two distinct reactions are involved, one unimolecular and the other bimolecular, and they are regarded as proceeding by two distinctly different mechanisms identified by the designations S_N1 and S_N2 (substitution, nucleophilic, first or second order). Since the rate of hydrolysis of methyl, ethyl, or isopropyl bromide is determined by the concentrations of alkyl halide and hydroxide ion, the key step must involve collisions between these species. The S_N2 reaction of methyl bromide is thus envisioned as a one-step process involving approach of a hydroxide ion from the back side to form a transition state in which the negative charge is distributed evenly between the entering and leaving groups. Attack by hydroxide ion and expulsion of bromide ion are synchronous processes. The unimolecular

S_N2 Mechanism:

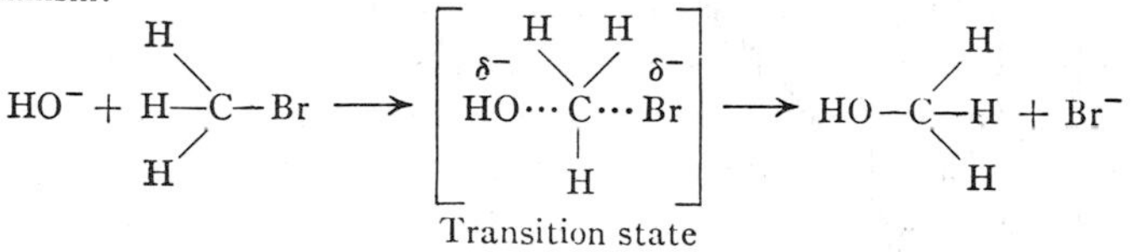

Transition state

reaction (S_N1) is considered to involve a two-step process in which the rate determining step is ionization of the halide to form a carbonium ion, which combines rapidly with an anionoid reagent. S_N1 reactions of significant reaction rate

S_N1 Mechanism:

$$(CH_3)_3C-Br \longrightarrow (CH_3)_3C^+ + Br^- \text{ (relatively slow)}$$
$$(CH_3)_3C^+ + OH^- \longrightarrow (CH_3)_3COH \text{ (fast)}$$

occur only when some special feature of structure, for example that in a tertiary alkyl halide, contributes to the surmounting of the energy barrier required for initial ionization.

Table 9.1 shows that methyl, ethyl, and isopropyl bromide undergo hydrolysis to all but a negligible extent bimolecularly, and that the reactivity, as measured by the second-order rate constants, decreases markedly in the order of listing.

$$CH_3 \rightarrow CH_2Br \qquad \begin{array}{c} CH_3 \\ \diagdown \\ CH_3 \diagup \end{array}\!\!CHBr$$

The progressive decrease in reactivity of ethyl and isopropyl bromide is attributable to the electron-releasing effect of the one and two methyl groups, respectively, joined to the carbon atom undergoing substitution, which should inhibit approach of the hydroxide ion. In tertiary butyl bromide the combined inductive effect of three methyl groups completely suppresses the bimolecular reaction and hydrolysis proceeds unimolecularly; that is, the reaction rate is dependent only on the concentration of alkyl bromide and is not increased by an increase in concentration of hydroxide ion. The transition state can be pictured as involving a weakened C—Br bond and partial charge separation.

$$\underset{\underset{CH_3}{|}}{\overset{\overset{CH_3}{|}}{CH_3{-}C{-}Br}} \longrightarrow \underset{\underset{CH_3}{|}}{\overset{\overset{CH_3}{|}}{CH_3{-}\overset{\delta^+\ \ \delta^-}{C\cdots Br}}} \overset{-Br^-}{\longrightarrow} \underset{\underset{CH_3}{|}}{\overset{\overset{CH_3}{|}}{CH_3{-}C^+}} \overset{OH^-}{\longrightarrow} \underset{\underset{CH_3}{|}}{\overset{\overset{CH_3}{|}}{CH_3{-}COH}}$$

Transition state

The polarity of the group that is being replaced may influence unimolecular substitution more than bimolecular substitution. Displacement of the strongly electron-attracting sulfonium group by bromine is a first-order reaction, in contrast with the bimolecular displacement of chlorine by bromine at a similar carbon atom.

$$(S_{N}1) \quad C_2H_5\overset{+}{S}(C_2H_5)_2 + Br^- \longrightarrow C_2H_5Br + S(C_2H_5)_2$$
$$(S_{N}2) \quad C_2H_5Cl + Br^- \longrightarrow C_2H_5Br + Cl^-$$

9.3   Solvent Effects. — The polarity, or ionizing power, of solvents is correlated with the dielectric constants (32.3) and follows the order: $H_2O \gg C_2H_5OH > CH_3COCH_3 \gg C_6H_6$. Thus water is highly polar; benzene is nonpolar. Since electrostatic attraction between a polar solvent and an ion stabilizes the system by dispersal of the charge over a larger area, polar solvents would be expected to favor $S_{N}1$ reaction, where the transition state is more polar than the initial state. Indeed marked solvent effects have been noted. Thus the rate of hydrolysis of tertiary alkyl halides is greatly enhanced by addition of water. On the other hand, the rate of unimolecular decomposition of t-butyldimethylsulfonium hydroxide is somewhat decreased by addition of water. In this case an ionic substance is converted into neutral products, and dispersal of the

$$(CH_3)_3C\overset{+}{S}(CH_3)_2OH^- \overset{S_{N}1}{\longrightarrow} (CH_3)_3COH + S(CH_3)_2$$

charges in the transition state opposes reaction. A similar situation obtains in the usual $S_{N}2$ reaction of the type $Y^- + RX \rightarrow RY + X^-$; there is no overall change of charge, but in the transition state the charges are dispersed. However, $S_{N}2$ reactions of the type $NH_3 + RCl \rightarrow RN^+H_3Cl^-$, in which an ionic compound is formed from neutral reactants, are favored by polar solvents.

9.4   **Nature of Entering and Leaving Groups.** — The nature of the attacking nucleophile obviously does not influence S_N1 reactions but may influence reactions proceeding by the S_N2 mechanism. In a systematic study of the reaction of trimethylsulfonium salts with various nucleophilic reagents, Ingold and Hughes found that the rates are highly dependent on the nature of the Y^- group. Reactions with hydroxide ion and with phenoxide ion, both of the S_N2

$$Y^- + (CH_3)_3S^+ \rightarrow Y-CH_3 + (CH_3)_2S$$

type, differ in rate by a factor of about 70, the former being the more reactive. The weaker nucleophiles CO_3^-, Br^-, and Cl^- react much more slowly and by the unimolecular mechanism. Nucleophilicity roughly parallels basicity. The order of nucleophilicity in three series is as follows:

$$OH^- > C_6H_5O^- > CO_3^- > CH_3CO_2^- > C_6H_5SO_3^- > H_2O$$
$$NH_2^- > NH_3 > C_6H_5NH_2$$
$$I^- > Br^- > Cl^- > F^-$$

On the other hand, the nature of the leaving group would be expected to affect both S_N1 and S_N2 reactions, and the most effective leaving groups should be those bound to carbon by relatively weak bonds. As already noted (8.25), tosylate and mesylate groups are displaced with particular ease. The approximate order of ease of displacement is:

$$p\text{-}CH_3C_6H_4SO_2O(CH_3SO_2O)^- > I^- > Br^- > Cl^- > F^- > AcO^- > R_3N^+$$

Hydroxyl and alkoxyl groups generally can be displaced only in a strongly acidic medium such that they exist as $^+OH_2$ and ^+OHR; displacement involves loss of H_2O or HOR. The halogens present an anomalous situation in that the order of effectiveness is the same both as attacking and as leaving groups.

9.5   **Steric Effects.** — Intuitive reasoning suggests that unimolecular substitutions should be relatively insensitive to steric hindrance. Since formation of the transition state involves stretching of a bond, this process should decrease any crowding in the original molecule and if anything accelerate the reaction. This effect has been noted in the solvolysis of t-alkyl chlorides with highly branched groups, for the reaction rates are abnormally high (Bartlett, 1955).

Bimolecular substitutions, on the other hand, proceed through a crowded transition state and hence would be expected to show substantial steric retardation. The effect of β-methyl substitution on the bimolecular alkaline hydrolysis of alkyl halides is shown in Table 9.2 (second column). The rate relationships for the first three members accord with expectations from the electron-releasing effect of a β-methyl group, which should decrease the S_N2 reaction rate but less than an α-methyl substituent does. The last member of the series of primary halides, neopentyl bromide, is singularly inert to alkali, and the effect is much greater than expected from the additional substitution of a methyl group. In aqueous alcoholic solution (third column), however, neopentyl bromide undergoes ready unimolecular hydrolysis and is only slightly less reactive than ethyl and n-propyl bromide. In the tertiary series substitution of β-methyl groups actually increases the first-order reaction constant (last column).

TABLE 9.2.   RATE OF ALKALINE HYDROLYSIS OF ALKYL HALIDES

HALIDE (PRIMARY)	SECOND ORDER,[a] $k_2 \times 10^3$	FIRST ORDER,[b] RELATIVE CONSTANT	HALIDE (TERTIARY)	FIRST ORDER,[c] $k_1 \times 10^5$
CH_3CH_2Br	1.97	1	$(CH_3)_3CCl$	0.854
$CH_3CH_2CH_2Br$	0.547	0.69	$CH_3CH_2\!\!\diagdown\!\!CCl$ $(CH_3)_2\!\!\diagup$	1.50
$(CH_3)_2CHCH_2Br$	0.058		$(CH_3CH_2)_2\!\!\diagdown\!\!CCl$	11.7
$(CH_3)_3CCH_2Br$	No reaction [d]	0.57	$(CH_3)_3C\!\!\diagup$	

[a] Reaction with sodium ethoxide in absolute ethanol (55°).
[b] Reaction in aqueous alcohol (no alkali).
[c] Reaction in 80% aqueous ethanol at 25°.
[d] A slow reaction occurs at 95° ($k_2 \times 10^7 = 5.0$).

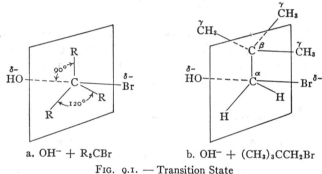

a. $OH^- + R_3CBr$ b. $OH^- + (CH_3)_3CCH_2Br$

FIG. 9.1. — Transition State

The only reasonable explanation of the lack of reactivity of neopentyl halides (first observed by Whitmore, 1933) in bimolecular but not in unimolecular reactions is that a steric factor prevents necessary attack by the nucleophilic reagent. The bimolecular reaction involves formation of a transition complex, the most stable state of which is known from quantum mechanical considerations to have the configuration shown in Fig. 9.1.   In the most stable state of the complex from a trialkylmethyl bromide the attacking group (OH^-), the carbon atom at which substitution takes place, and the displaced group (Br^-) are in linear orientation; and the covalently attached alkyl groups lie in a plane perpendicular to the line of OH^- and Br^-.   If the β-carbon atom of one of the alkyl groups carries a single γ-methyl substituent, this can exert practically no steric effect because of free rotation about the single bond.   In the case of neopentyl bromide, however, the presence of three γ-methyl groups does not allow the stable linear arrangement of the $HO\cdots C\cdots Br$ grouping.

9.6   **Steric Course.** — The steric course of a displacement at an asymmetric carbon atom may be determined by the mechanism of the reaction.   An S_N2 hydrolysis of a bromide (Fig. 9.2) involves backside attack by the nucleophile to produce a transition state in which the three groups covalently bonded to carbon lie in a plane; expulsion of bromide ion of necessity gives an

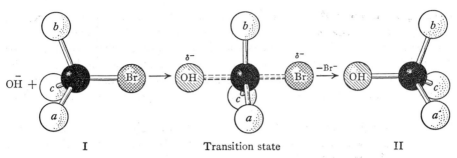

I   Transition state   II

FIG. 9.2. — S_N2 Mechanism

TABLE 9.3. RELATION OF MECHANISM OF SUBSTITUTION TO OPTICAL EFFECTS

HALIDE	REAGENT	MECHANISM	EFFECT ON CONFIGURATION [a]
n-C$_6$H$_{13}$CHBr | CH$_3$	HO$^-$ H$_2$O	S_N2 S_NI	I (96%) I (66%) + Ra
C$_6$H$_5$CHCl | CH$_3$	H$_2$O CH$_3$O$^-$ CH$_3$OH	S_NI S_N2 S_NI	Ra + I (2–17%) I Ra + I (low)
CH$_3$CHBr | CO$_2$H	H$_2$O	S_N2	I (100%)
CH$_3$CHBr | CO$_2$CH$_3$	CH$_3$O$^-$	S_N2	I (100%)
CH$_3$CHBr | CO$_2^-$	HO$^-$ H$_2$O CH$_3$OH	S_N2 S_NI S_NI	I (80–100%) Re (80–100%) Re (90–100%)
CH$_3$CHOH | CH$_3$CHBr	HBr	S_NI	Re (80–90%)

[a] I = Inversion; Ra = Racemization; Re = Retention

alcohol of configuration opposite to that of the starting material. The process is like the turning of an umbrella inside out in the wind. An explanation is thus at hand for the initially baffling phenomena of Walden inversion (3.17, 5.12).

The kinetic evidence of Table 9.1 shows that the hydrolysis of t-butyl bromide follows the S_NI course involving the intermediate carbonium ion, (CH$_3$)$_3$C$^+$. This ion is probably planar, since it is identical in electronic structure with (CH$_3$)$_3$B, which is known from physical measurements to be planar. If an optically active t-alkyl halide forms a planar carbonium ion, there is equal chance for return of the groups to the original or to the opposite configuration, and hence hydrolysis should be attended with racemization. However, the structure may be such as to inhibit formation of a fully planar carbonium ion, or such an ion may be too short-lived for destruction of asymmetry.

Racemization, retention, and inversion of configuration have all been observed experimentally and the results correlated with the mode of substitution. The results generally accord well with expectations. Among the examples listed in Table 9.3, all the S_N2 reactions result in complete or nearly complete inversion; the S_N1 reactions of the first two compounds listed proceed with racemization or incomplete inversion. In the case of α-bromopropionic acid (or its ester) the inductive effect of the electron-attracting carboxyl group completely inhibits the S_N1 mechanism and facilitates S_N2 substitution, which proceeds with quantitative inversion.

9.7 **Neighboring Group Effect.** — Alkaline hydrolysis (HO⁻) of α-bromopropionate ion (Table 9.3) also follows the S_N2 course with inversion, but both hydrolysis and alcoholysis of this ion (1) effected under nonalkaline conditions (H_2O or CH_3OH) apparently proceed by the S_N1 mechanism with practically complete retention of configuration. Hughes and Ingold (1937) postulated that the carboxylate substituent forms a weak electrostatic bond with the carbon atom undergoing substitution and thus maintains the original configuration in the transition state. Winstein made the alternative suggestion that the transition state results from backside attack by the carboxylate group with inversion, and

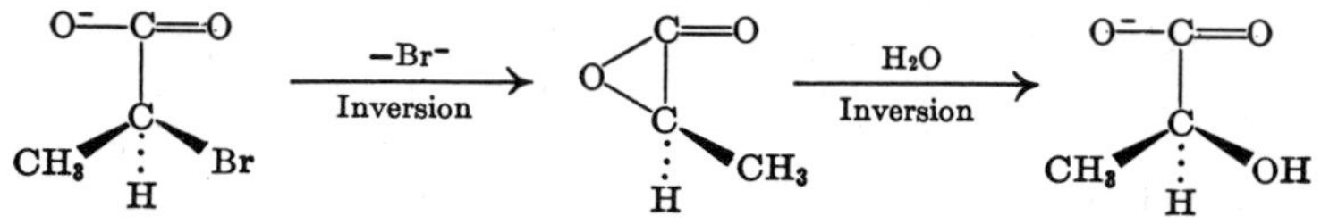

synchronous loss of bromide ion to form the α-lactone (2). The oxide ring is then cleaved rapidly in the normal fashion with a second inversion which restores the original configuration (3). The overall reaction thus involves two normal S_N2 displacements, the first of which is internal. The reaction is regarded as one of a number involving a neighboring group effect, that is, an effect of a group situated β to the center of substitution and controlling the steric course of a reaction (a participant group).

Retention of configuration has been observed when the adjacent carbon bears an atom with an unshared pair of electrons available for displacement or coordination, as in the last example of Table 9.3. The reaction in this case involves S_N1 replacement of the hydroxyl group of an alcohol by bromine at an asymmetric center vicinal to a carbon atom bearing a bromo substituent. Expulsion of the hydroxyl group proceeds by addition of a proton to oxygen and loss of

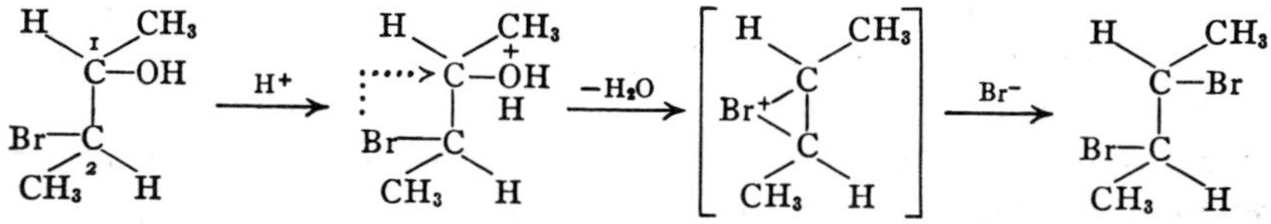

Oxonium ion

water from the oxonium ion. Retention of configuration is attributed to an intramolecular nucleophilic attack resulting in formation of an intermediate bromonium ion. According to this mechanism inversion at C_1 occurs in formation of the three-membered ring and again in its fission, with the net result that absolute configuration is retained.

Participation of a neighboring acetoxyl group is illustrated by the behavior of *trans*-cyclohexane-1,2-diol 1-acetate-2-tosylate (6). Winstein (1942) found that when (6) is refluxed with potassium acetate in dry acetic acid the product is the diacetate of *trans*-cyclohexane-1,2-diol (8), but that if the acetic acid contains enough water to lower the melting point by $1.1°$ the product is chiefly the monoacetate of *cis*-cyclohexane-1,2-diol (11). The interpretation is as follows. In each case the initial step is expulsion of a tosylate ion with inversion at C_2 and formation of the cyclic intermediate (7a). In an anhydrous medium this intermediate, or the resonance structure (7b), is attacked by acetate ion with inversion

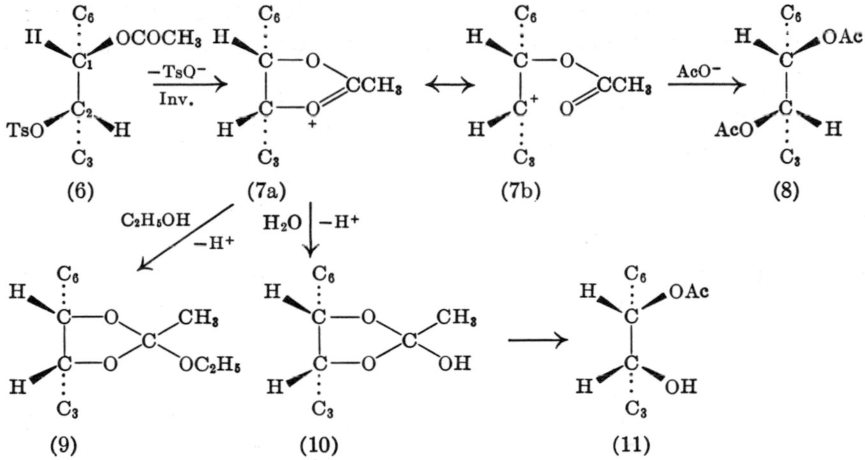

(6)   (7a)   (7b)   (8)

(9)   (10)   (11)

at C_2 and formation of a diacetate (8) of the original *trans* configuration. If enough water is present it reacts with intermediate (7a) to give the orthomonoacetate (10), which isomerizes to the *cis*-diol monoacetate (11). Thus the water-controlled reaction involves one inversion and the seemingly more normal anhydrous reaction involves two. Supporting evidence is that when ethanol was used as solvent the ethyl orthoacetate (9) was isolated.

The same mechanism applies to the reaction of *meso*-stilbene dibromide with silver acetate in acetic acid containing a little water. The product is a mixture of diols, diacetates, and the *dl*-diol monoacetate, which can be isolated easily by chromatography. *dl*-Hydrobenzoin is one of the few known racemates that is

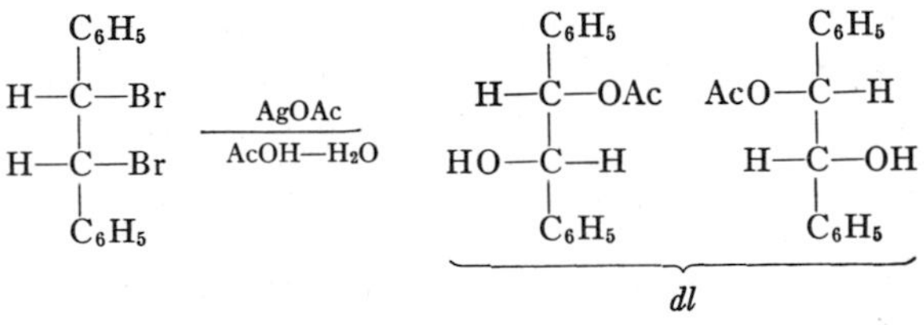

resolvable by simple crystallization; the reaction cited is the best known method of preparation.

Investigations, particularly of Cram and of Roberts,[1] have led to the surprising conclusion that phenyl can function as a neighboring group. Cram (1949) prepared the four optically pure forms of 3-phenyl-2-butanol tosylate, $C_6H_5CH(CH_3)$-$CH(CH_3)OTs$, and heated each of them at 70° for 30 hrs. in acetic acid containing 1% of acetic anhydride and one equivalent of potassium acetate. Acetolysis of each *erythro* tosylate, one of which is shown in formula (1), proceeds with complete retention of configuration, whereas each *threo* tosylate afforded the DL-acetate. If the group order is phenyl → methyl → hydrogen, tosylate → methyl → hydrogen, or acetate → methyl → hydrogen, formula (1) represents an upper counterclockwise carbon (cc) joined to a lower clockwise one (c′); in the product of acetolysis (3) the upper and lower carbon atoms are also counterclockwise and clockwise. The experimental results are interpreted on the postulate of the formation of intermediate bridged ions, the aronium ions (2) and (5); each formula shows

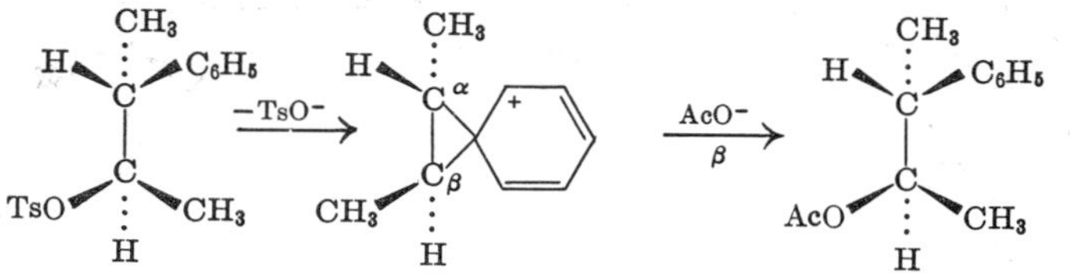

(1) *Erythro* (D or L)   (2)   (3) *Erythro* (D or L)

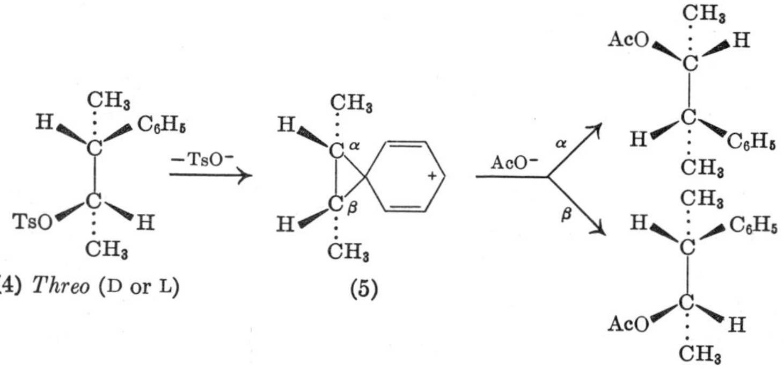

(4) *Threo* (D or L)   (5)

(6) DL-*Threo*

one of several contributors to a hybrid resonant ion.[2] Elimination of the tosylate group from an *erythro* tosylate (1) proceeds with inversion of the lower center of asymmetry and formation of the intermediate cation (2) having a cyclopropane ring (the two rings actually are in planes at right angles to each other and the common carbon atom is tetrahedral). Attack of this intermediate by acetate anion with opening of the bond to the lower carbon (β) gives the optically active

[1] John D. Roberts, b. 1918 Los Angeles; Ph.D. Univ. Calif. Los Angeles (W. G. Young); Mass. Inst. Techn.; Calif. Inst. Techn.

[2] The species was originally described as a phenonium ion but is of the same type as intermediates involved in electrophilic aromatic substitution (Chapter 17) and initially called benzenonium ions. We have used the term aronium ion for description of both types.

erythro acetate (3); if the attack is at α, the product, when turned upside down, is seen to be identical with (3).   Formula (4) represents one of the optically active *threo* tosylates; the upper and lower carbons are, respectively, cc and c'c'.   Attack by acetate ion at the α-carbon gives the cc' acetate, and attack at the β-carbon puts the phenyl group in the alternative position and gives the (cc)'—cc acetate; hence the product is the DL-*threo* acetate (6).

Treatment of 2-amino-3-phenylbutane (7) with nitrous acid in a mixture of aqueous hydrochloric acid and acetic acid at 0° effects conversion to the alcohol (10) in 73% yield.   W. A. Bonner (1958) labeled the 1-methyl group with isotopic

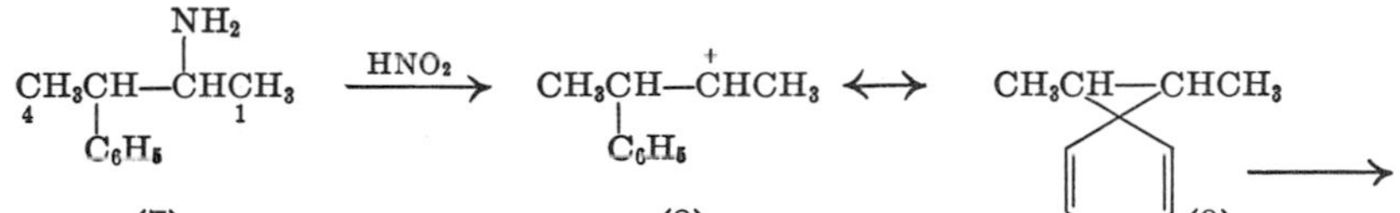

(7)   (8)   (9)

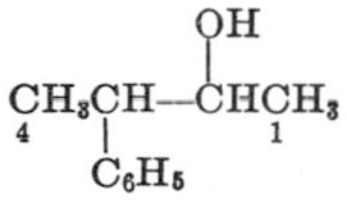

(10)

carbon (C^{14}) and found that radioactivity appears equally in the two methyl groups of the product.   Formation of the intermediate aronium ion (9) accounts for the observation.

Further examples of aryl participation are the conversion of *trans*-4-(4'-hydroxycyclohexyl)-phenol tosylate I into the spiroketone IV (A. S. Dreiding,[1]

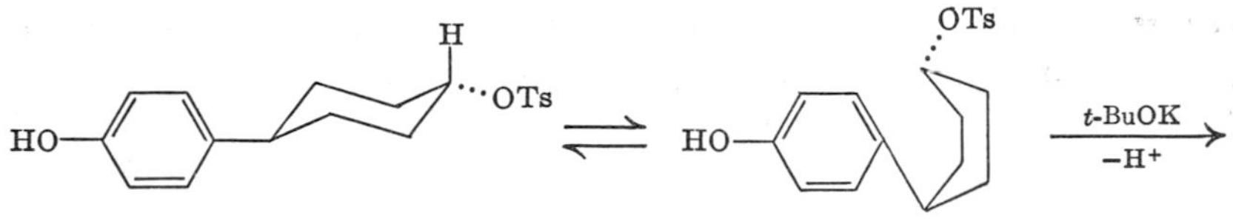

I   II

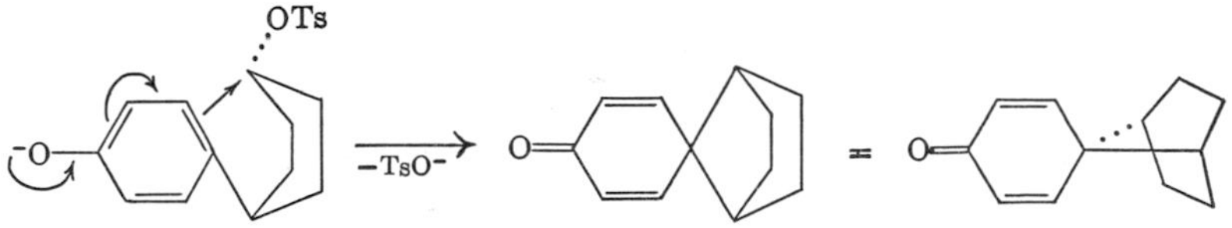

III   IV

1958), and the remarkable base-initiated rearrangement of the norbornyl derivative (1), prepared from the cyclopentadiene-*p*-benzoquinone adduct (J. Meinwald,[2] 1958).   Whereas norbornene epoxide is exceedingly resistant to nucleophilic at-

[1] André S. Dreiding, b. 1919 Zurich, Switzerland; Ph.D. Michigan (Bachmann); Wayne State Univ.; Univ. Zurich

[2] Jerrold Meinwald, b. 1927 New York; Ph.D. Harvard (Woodward); Cornell Univ.

tack, the fused hydroquinone ring plays a special role, for mere saponification of (1) with 2 N sodium hydroxide was attended with rearrangement.

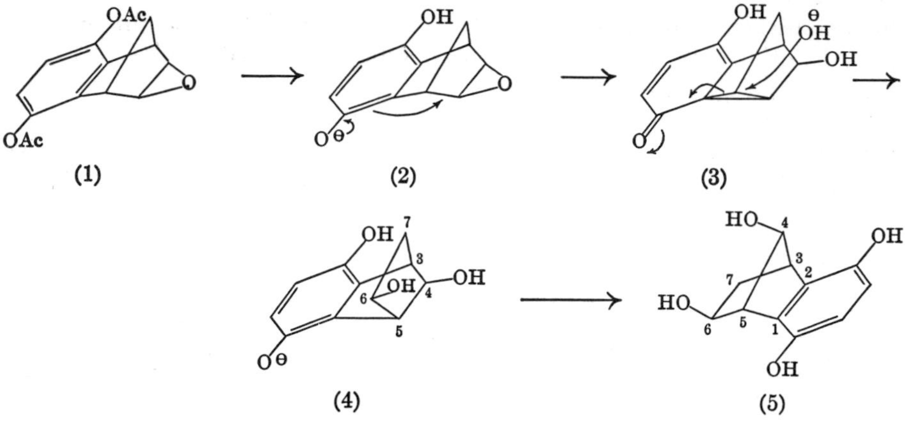

(1)   (2)   (3)

(4)   (5)

(counterclockwise rotation)

9.8   **Displacement of Hydroxyl by Chlorine.** — When thionyl chloride is used to displace the hydroxyl group of an alcohol by chlorine the reaction usually proceeds with retention of configuration, whereas reaction with a phosphorus halide usually results in inversion. Hughes and Ingold (1937) suggested that in either case the first step consists in formation of an ester, for example, the chlorosulfite: ROH + ClSOCl → ROSOCl. They picture this ester as nonlinear and of such a structure to permit operation of mechanism (a), defined as internal substitution (S_Ni), in which an electron pair from the chlorine atom is received at the carbon center simultaneously with release of the electron pair to oxygen; in this way chlorine occupies the place vacated by oxygen and configuration is retained. Alternatively, the ester group can be displaced by chloride ion

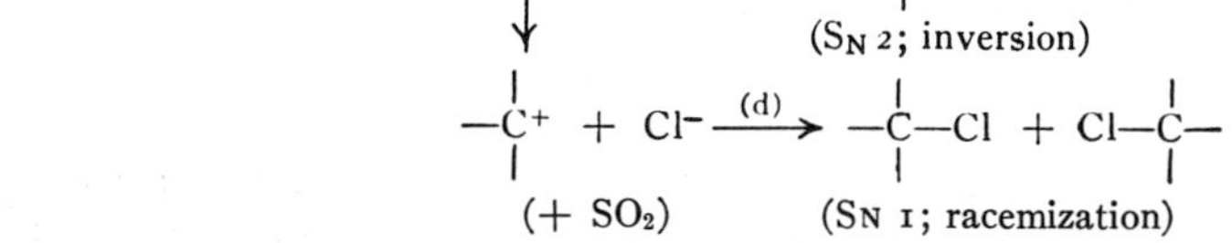

(b) in an S_N2 reaction (inversion), or ionization (c) can lead to an S_N1 displacement (d, racemization). The esters derived from the phosphorus halides, for example R_3C—O—PCl_2, undergo the ionic reactions (b) and (c) with particular facility, and inversion or racemization is commonly observed.

The formation of chlorosulfites as intermediates is well established, but E. S. Lewis (1952–53) found that the steric course of the conversion to a chloride depends upon the solvent.   Almost complete retention of activity is observed when dioxane is the solvent; almost complete inversion is found when the solvent is pyridine.   The rates are practically the same in either case.   The marked dependency on the polarity of the solvent suggests that ionic intermediates are involved.   The reaction in dioxane is regarded as proceeding through a solvated ion pair (Cram); the nucleophilic anion then captures the carbonium ion before it loses its asymmetry:

$$-\overset{|}{\underset{|}{C}}-OSOCl \longrightarrow -\overset{|}{\underset{|}{C}}^{+}\overset{\frown}{OSOCl^-} \longrightarrow -\overset{|}{\underset{|}{C}}^+Cl^- \longrightarrow -\overset{|}{\underset{|}{C}}-Cl$$

Solvated

When pyridine is the solvent the hydrogen chloride produced in the formation of the chlorosulfite is neutralized to afford chloride ion, which reacts with the chloro-sulfite by the S_N2 mechanism with inversion of configuration:

$$Cl^- + -\overset{H}{\underset{H}{\overset{|}{\underset{|}{C}}}}-OSOCl \longrightarrow Cl-\overset{H}{\underset{H}{\overset{|}{\underset{|}{C}}}}- + SO_2 + Cl^-$$

9.9   Rearrangements. — Rearrangements frequently occur during substitution reactions.   Whereas the reaction of neopentyl bromide with ethoxide ion results in formation of the normal product, neopentyl ethyl ether (b, second-order kinetics), reaction with aqueous ethanol leads to formation of

$$\underset{(a)}{\overset{CH_3}{\underset{CH_3}{CH_3-\overset{|}{\underset{|}{C}}-CH_2Br}}} + NaOC_2H_5 \xrightarrow{S_N2} \underset{(b)}{\overset{CH_3}{\underset{CH_3}{CH_3-\overset{|}{\underset{|}{C}}-CH_2OC_2H_5}}}$$

$$-Br \downarrow S_N1$$

$$\underset{(c)}{\overset{[CH_3]}{\underset{CH_3}{CH_3-\overset{|}{\underset{|}{C}}{-}CH_2}}} \longrightarrow \underset{(d)}{\overset{+}{\underset{CH_3}{CH_3-\overset{|}{\underset{|}{C}}-CH_2CH_3}}} \xrightarrow{C_2H_5OH} \underset{(e)}{\overset{OC_2H_5}{\underset{CH_3}{CH_3-\overset{|}{\underset{|}{C}}-CH_2CH_3}}} + H^+$$

t-amyl ethyl ether (e) and must involve rearrangement.   The kinetics are first order.   The first step is considered to be formation of the carbonium ion (c), followed by migration of one of the adjacent methyl groups with its pair of electrons, with transference of the charge from the α- to the β-position (d).   The neopentyl-t-amyl rearrangement is analogous to the Wagner-Meerwein rearrangement.

Rearrangements are particularly common in allylic systems, such as those shown in the formulation below.   The bimolecular reactions of the methylallyl chlorides (a) and (b) with ethoxide ion afford the normal reaction products (c) and (d), respectively.   The unimolecular reactions of the chlorides with ethanol proceed with rearrangement, for each chloride gives a mixture of the two ethers (c) and (d), and the composition of the mixture is the same regardless of the initial halide.

An S_N1 reaction involving intramolecular rearrangement is denoted by the symbol S_N1'. The observations support the postulated ionization in unimolecular substitutions, since the hybrid carbonium ion from one methallyl chloride is identical with that from the other.

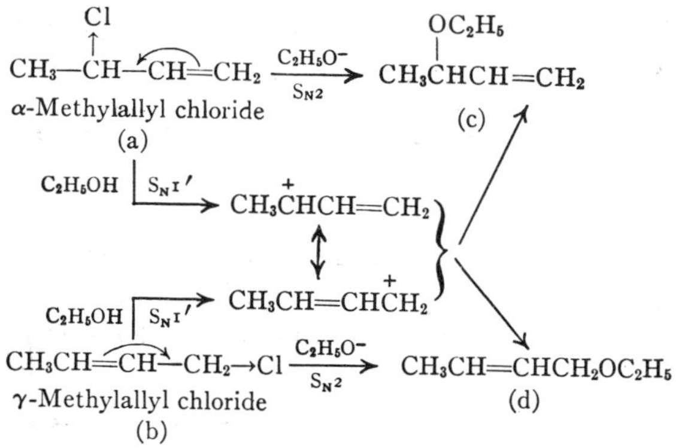

$$
\begin{array}{c}
\overset{Cl}{\underset{|}{CH_3-CH}}\overset{\frown}{-CH}=CH_2 \xrightarrow[S_N2]{C_2H_5O^-} \overset{OC_2H_5}{\underset{|}{CH_3CHCH}}=CH_2 \\
\text{α-Methylallyl chloride} \qquad\qquad\qquad (c) \\
\text{(a)}
\end{array}
$$

$$
C_2H_5OH \Big| S_N1' \xrightarrow{\quad} CH_3\overset{+}{C}HCH=CH_2
$$

$$
CH_3\overset{+}{C}HCH=CH_2 \updownarrow CH_3CH=CH\overset{+}{C}H_2
$$

$$
C_2H_5OH \Big[S_N1' \xrightarrow{\quad} CH_3CH=CH\overset{+}{C}H_2
$$

$$
\begin{array}{c}
CH_3CH=\overset{\frown}{CH}-CH_2{\rightarrow}Cl \xrightarrow[S_N2]{C_2H_5O^-} CH_3CH=CHCH_2OC_2H_5 \\
\text{γ-Methylallyl chloride} \qquad\qquad\qquad (d) \\
\text{(b)}
\end{array}
$$

A bimolecular reaction involving allylic rearrangement, an S_N2' reaction, was first demonstrated by Young (1949) in the reaction of α-ethylallyl chloride (e) with sodiomalonic ester (f). The reaction follows second-order kinetics and gives two products. The major product (g) arises by a normal S_N2 reaction, but the minor product (h), formed to the extent of 23%, is formed by an S_N2' reaction.

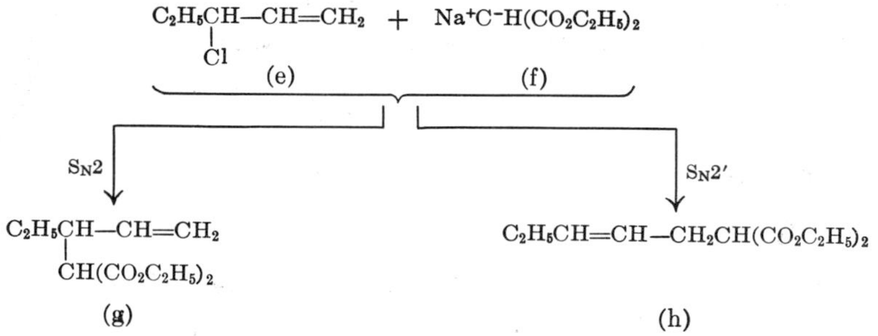

$$
\underset{\overset{|}{Cl}}{C_2H_5CH}-CH=CH_2 \; + \; Na^+C^-H(CO_2C_2H_5)_2
$$

$$
\underbrace{\qquad\qquad}_{(e)} \qquad \underbrace{\qquad\qquad}_{(f)}
$$

$$
S_N2 \downarrow \qquad\qquad\qquad\qquad\qquad S_N2' \downarrow
$$

$$
\underset{\overset{|}{CH(CO_2C_2H_5)_2}}{C_2H_5CH}-CH=CH_2 \qquad\qquad C_2H_5CH=CH-CH_2CH(CO_2C_2H_5)_2
$$

$$
\text{(g)} \qquad\qquad\qquad\qquad\qquad\qquad \text{(h)}
$$

No abnormal products were detected on reaction of sodiomalonic ester with primary allylic halides. Stork[1] (1953) investigated the stereochemistry of an S_N2'

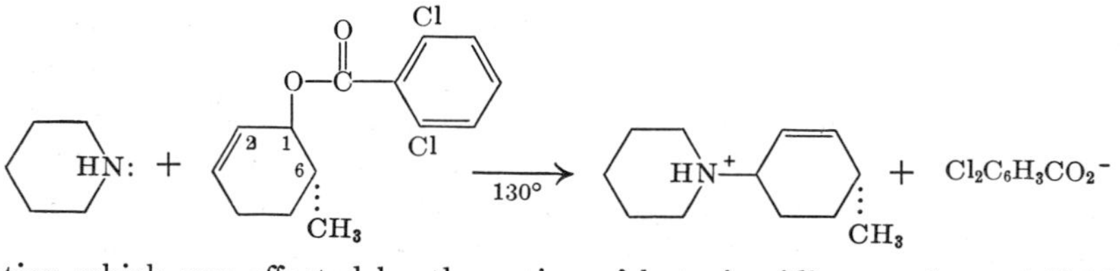

reaction which was effected by the action of hot piperidine on the 2,6-dichlorobenzoate of 6α-methyl-Δ^2-cyclohexene-1β-ol (attempts to prepare the tosylate were

[1] Gilbert Stork, b. 1921 Brussels, Belgium; Ph.D. Wisconsin (McElvain); Harvard Univ.; Columbia Univ.

unsuccessful).   Elimination of the aryloxy group in a reaction of bimolecular kinetics afforded 6α-methyl-1β-piperidino-Δ^2-cyclohexene.   Demonstration that the two groups are in the *trans* orientation established that the entering and leaving groups have the *cis* relationship, in accordance with the postulate of Young and Winstein that in the transition state the allylic system is in the form of a

$$R_3N + \overset{\displaystyle CH}{\underset{\displaystyle CH-}{\Big|}} \overset{\displaystyle OCOAr}{\underset{\displaystyle CH-}{\Big|}} \longrightarrow \underset{\text{Transition state}}{\overset{\overset{\delta+}{R_3N}\qquad\overset{\delta-}{OCOAr}}{\underset{\displaystyle -CH\cdots\cdots CH-}{\vdots\quad CH\quad\vdots}}} \xrightarrow{-ArCO_2^-} \overset{\displaystyle \overset{+}{R_3N}\qquad CH}{\underset{\displaystyle CH\qquad CH-}{\diagdown\diagup}}$$

triangle with the entering group adjacent to the leaving group.   If the usually easier S$_N$2 mechanism is sterically hindered, the S$_N$2' mechanism may predominate.   Thus 1-*t*-butylallyl chloride reacts with ethoxide ion to give exclusively the ether formed by attack at the less hindered 3-position (Hughes, 1958).

$$\overset{3}{CH_2}=\overset{2}{CH}-\underset{\underset{\displaystyle Cl}{\displaystyle |}}{\overset{1}{CH}}C(CH_3)_3 \xrightarrow{-OC_2H_5} CH_2-CH=CHC(CH_3)_3$$
$$\underset{\displaystyle OC_2H_5}{\big|}$$

A rearrangement of homoallylic alcohols has been studied particularly as applied to cholesterol.   The tosylate, shown in partial formula I, when refluxed in aqueous acetone containing potassium acetate affords the acetate III of an alcohol named

| I | IIa | IIb | III |

i-cholesterol before the structure had been established by Wallis[1] (1937); the systematic name is 3,5-cyclocholestane-6β-ol.   Reverse rearrangement to cholesteryl acetate is effected by refluxing with zinc acetate in acetic acid.   Both the forward and the reverse rearrangements are stereospecific; the 3β-tosylate affords only the 6β-acetate and the epimeric 3α-tosylate does not rearrange.   The rate-controlling step is unimolecular and hence probably consists in ionization to a hybrid ion stabilized by distribution of the charge between C$_3$ and C$_6$.

9.10   Electrophilic Substitution. — Most electrophilic substitutions selected for study involve use of organometallic compounds as substrates, since metals form cations readily and hence can serve as entering and leaving electrophiles.   Ingold and Hughes inferred intuitively (1935) that S$_E$1, S$_E$2, and S$_E$i substitutions should all be possible and investigated an S$_E$2 reaction by the following technique (1959).   Optically active *sec*-butylmercuric bromide (1) was prepared by resolution of the cation by crystallization of the (+)-tartrate and the (−)-mandelate and reconversion to the bromide.   The (−)-bromide (1) was then converted by reaction with racemic *sec*-butylmagnesium bromide (2) into di-*sec*-

---

[1] Everett S. Wallis, b. 1899 Waitsfield, Vt.; Ph.D. Princeton (L. W. Jones); Princeton Univ.

butylmercury (3) labeled by optical activity in one of the two alkyl groups. The reaction of this dialkylmercury with mercuric bromide was then examined and found to follow second-order kinetics as expected. Attack of either alkyl group is equally likely. If the configuration is completely retained, the product should

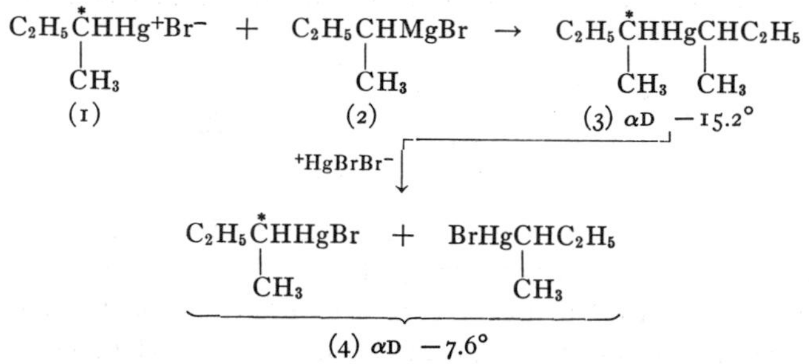

$$C_2H_5\overset{*}{C}HHg^+Br^- \;+\; C_2H_5CHMgBr \;\rightarrow\; C_2H_5\overset{*}{C}HHgCHC_2H_5$$
$$\underset{CH_3}{|} \qquad\qquad \underset{CH_3}{|} \qquad\qquad \underset{CH_3}{|}\;\underset{CH_3}{|}$$
$$(1) \qquad\qquad\qquad (2) \qquad\qquad\qquad (3)\; \alpha_D\; -15.2°$$

$$+HgBrBr^-$$

$$C_2H_5\overset{*}{C}HHgBr \;+\; BrHgCHC_2H_5$$
$$\underset{CH_3}{|} \qquad\qquad\qquad \underset{CH_3}{|}$$

(4) α_D $-7.6°$

have half the optical activity of the starting material; if the asymmetric center is racemized, the activity should be one fourth that of (3); complete inversion would give an optically inactive product. Actually the first possibility was shown to be correct and therefore configuration is retained in the S_E2 reaction.

Winstein (1955) had drawn the same conclusion from a study of the reaction of radioactive mercuric chloride with the mixed mercurial (5). The group containing phenyl is related to a neopentyl group and is called the neophyl group; it was selected for the case at hand to balance possible sluggishness of electrophilic sub-

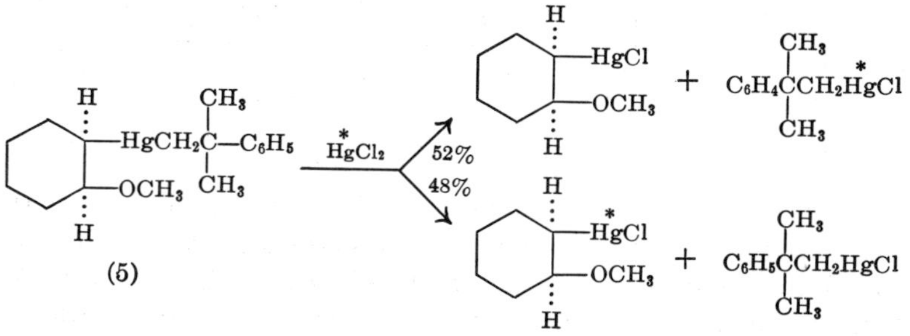

(5)   52%   48%

stitution on the cyclohexane ring. Cleavage of cis-2-methoxycyclohexylneophyl-mercury (5) with mercuric chloride labeled with Hg[203] effected cleavage of the two C—Hg bonds to about the same extent and the radioactivity of the products corresponded to that expected for complete retention of configuration. Retention of configuration in S_E2 reactions shows that the transition state does not resemble that of S_N2 reactions and is consistent with the view that the two electrons of the original carbon–metal bond remain more or less in the original orbital. The properties of carbanions are also consistent with a tetrahedral structure. Thus whereas it is extremely difficult to form a cationic center at a bridgehead position, a carbanion center is readily produced at such a position (Winstein, 1956).

9.11 S_N1 **Reactions of Norbornane Derivatives.** — The parent hydrocarbon norbornane is sometimes represented without stereochemical implication as in (a) or (b); the systematic name includes numbers, listed in descending order, giving the number of atoms in the three bridges: $2(C_2\text{-}C_3)$, 2 $(C_5\text{-}C_6)$, 1 (C_7). The hydrocarbon actually contains a cyclohexane ring locked in a boat conformation by the bridging methylene group at C_7, as shown in (c) and (d). Where both

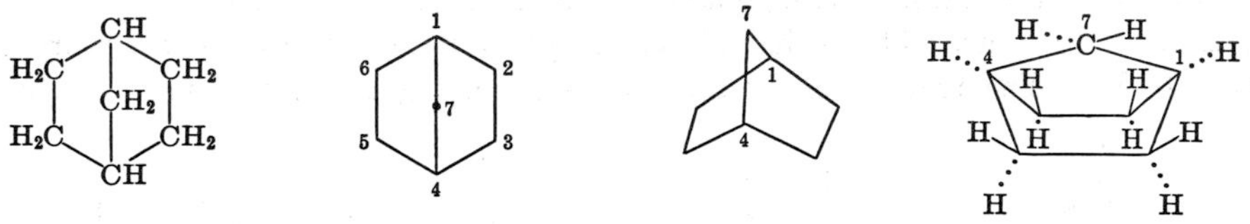

(a)   (b)   (c)   (d)

Norbornane (bicyclo-[2,2,1]-heptane)

chair and boat forms are possible, the chair form is the more stable, but the energy difference is small and no significant strain is associated with the norbornane structure or with that of the terpenoid alcohol borneol or its parent hydrocarbon bornane, which is the $1,7,7$-trimethyl derivative of the hydrocarbon under discussion. A nor derivative is one having one less carbon atom than a structurally related substance; a homo derivative has one carbon atom more. The unmethylated hydrocarbon in precise terminology would be called trisnorbornane, but for simplicity it is called norbornane.

Alder (1940) found that at a suitably elevated temperature cyclopentadiene adds to vinyl acetate to give an unsaturated acetate convertible into a saturated alcohol

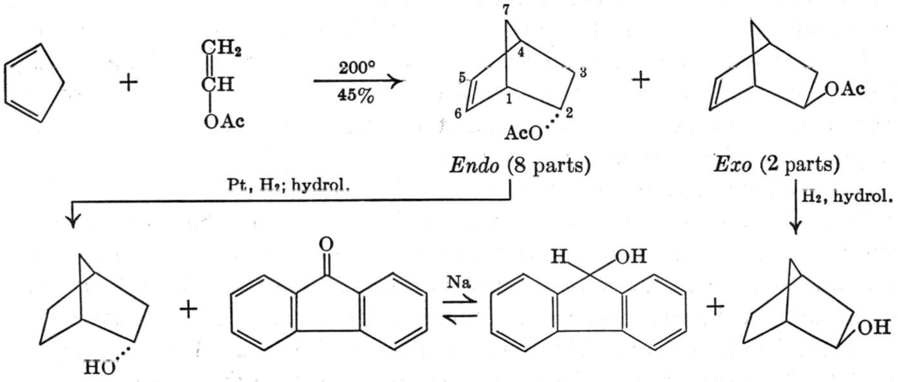

Endo (8 parts)   *Exo* (2 parts)

Endo-2-norborneol   Fluorenone   Fluorenol   *Exo*-2-norborneol

designated *endo*-2-norborneol because the hydroxyl group is inclined in toward the cyclohexane ring. Later workers found that the addition is not fully stereospecific but that the main product is accompanied by some of the *exo* isomer. A better route to the less accessible alcohol (Roberts, 1954) consists in equilibration of the *endo* alcohol with sodium in refluxing toluene containing a trace of fluorenone, which effects epimerization to *exo*-2-norborneol to the extent of about 75%. Doering,[1] reasoning that such an epimerization may involve formation and reduction of the ketone, had found that equilibration is markedly catalyzed by a trace

[1] William von E. Doering, b. 1917 Fort Worth, Texas; Ph.D. Harvard (Linstead); Columbia Univ.; Yale Univ.

of a ketone-alcohol pair capable of rapidly reaching oxidation-reduction equilibrium, such as the fluorenone-fluorenol system. Winstein (1949) found that the epimeric norbornyl tosylates differ markedly in rate of solvolysis. *Endo*-norbornyl tosylate (I), on treatment with potassium acetate in acetic acid, undergoes solvolysis at a rate comparable to that of cyclohexyl tosylate and gives *exo*-norbornyl acetate IV. The reaction is interpreted as involving a rearrangement of the

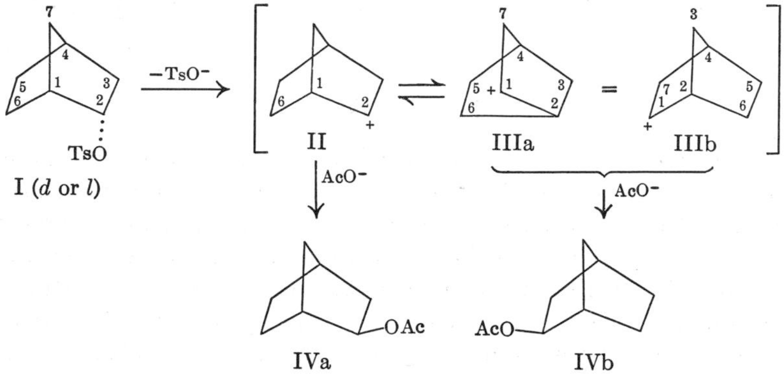

Wagner-Meerwein type: ionization of the tosylate I gives the carbonium ion II, which can rearrange to IIIa, with the charge at C_1 rather than at C_2. The formula can be written equally well as in IIIb, which is the mirror image of II. Attack by acetate ion on II gives IVa, and attack on IIIa or IIIb gives the enantiomer IVb. Acetolysis of optically active tosylate thus should give *dl*-acetate, and indeed almost complete racemization of $(+)$- and $(-)$-*endo*-norbornyl tosylate was observed (at most 7–8% retention of activity), and racemization was found to proceed at the same rate as solvolysis.

Exo-norbonyl tosylate (V) undergoes acetolysis at a rate 500 times that of the *endo*-epimer and the product is again *exo*-norbornyl acetate. Solvolysis of either optically active *exo*-tosylate results in complete racemization (in this case racemization is faster than solvolysis). Winstein reasoned that the enhanced reactivity is indicative of the intermediate formation of an ion significantly more stable than the carbonium ions II and III formulated above and postulated the intermediate ion VI. The orientation of the tosylate group of V is such that separation of the

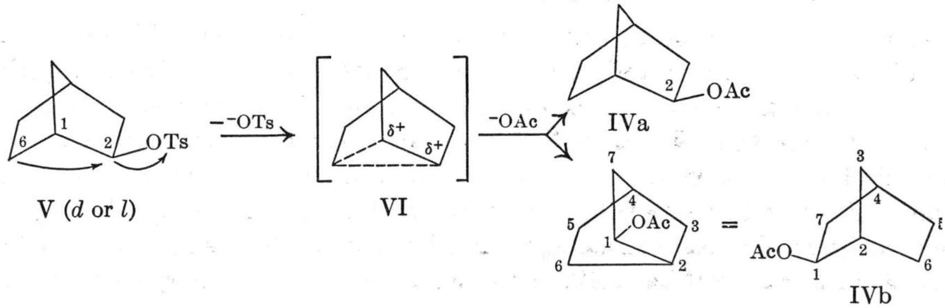

tosylate ion from C_2 invites interaction of C_6 with C_2, with the result that C_6 is partially bonded to C_2 as well as to C_1 and the charge is distributed between C_1

and C_2.   The splitting of the original C_1—C_6 single bond to bind simultaneously the partially charged centers C_1 and C_2 is assumed to enhance the stability of the ion and hence the rate of its formation.   The split-bond ionic intermediate, or bridged ion, accounts for complete racemization of an optically active tosylate, since the probability of attack by acetate ion at C_1 and at C_2 is equal. (See p. 337.)

To test the validity of the postulated bridged ion VI, Roberts synthesized labeled material starting with Diels-Alder addition of cyclopentadiene and vinyl acetate-1,2-C^{14} (obtained via acetylene-1,2-C^{14} generated from barium carbide-C_2^{14}).   The distribution of C^{14} in the *exo*-norborneol resulting from acetolysis of *exo*-norbornyl *p*-bromotosylate and hydrolysis was determined by degradations as shown in the formulas.   If ion VI were the only carbonium ion intermediate, the

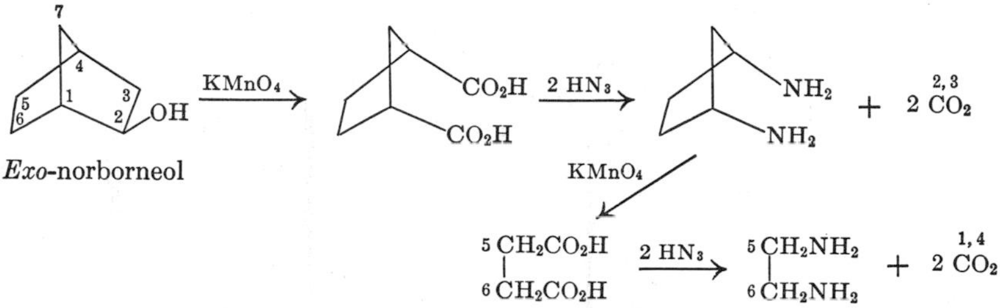

exo-norborneol should contain equal radioactivity at C_1, C_2, C_3, and C_7.   The actual distribution found was: C_1 and C_4, 23 % (C_4 probably zero); C_2 and C_3, 40 %; C_5 and C_6, 15 %; C_7, 23 %.   Thus a greater shuffling of radioactivity is observed than would be expected on the basis of ion VI postulated by Winstein.   Roberts

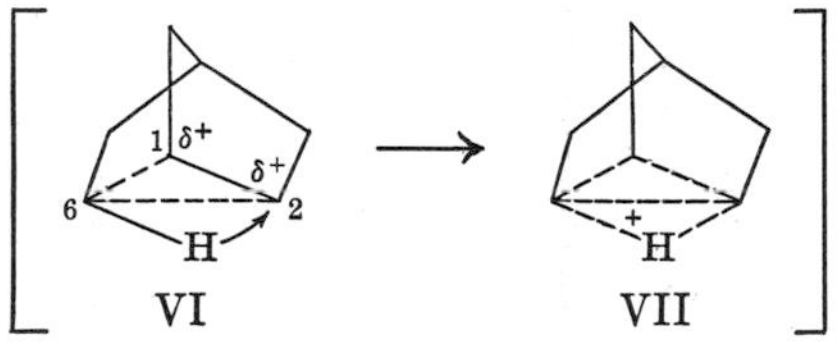

suggests participation of the further intermediate ion VII, arising from a hydride shift from C_6 toward both C_1 and C_2.   Such an ion would have a three-fold symmetry axis and should react with acetate ion with equal probability at the C_1, C_2, and C_6 positions.   Since the C^{14} distribution is intermediate between the values expected for intermediates VI and VII, it is possible that both ions are involved.

A route to a 7-norborneol developed by R. B. Woodward, R. E. Vanelli, and C. J. Norton (1956) involves initial pyrolysis of dicyclopentadienyl 3-acetate (2); reverse Diels-Alder reaction affords a mixture of the products (3)–(6); (4), the normal acetoxy component, is in part isomerized to (5) and (6).   The mixture was heated with ethylene to effect Diels-Alder addition of each component, and the norbornene (7) was easily removed from the resulting mixture by distillation. Hydrolysis of the residual mixture of acetates converted the enol acetate (10) into a ketone (13) removable as the Girard derivative (12.37).   This left a mixture of two unsaturated alcohols, which were separated by chromatography and identified by characterization as secondary (11) and tertiary (12), respectively.   Later work discussed below established that the sole 7-norbornenol isolated has the *anti* configuration shown in (11), with the hydroxyl group on the side opposite that carrying the double bond, rather than the *syn* configuration. Since the same isomer results from reduction of the corresponding ketone (LiAlH₄ or Na), it is

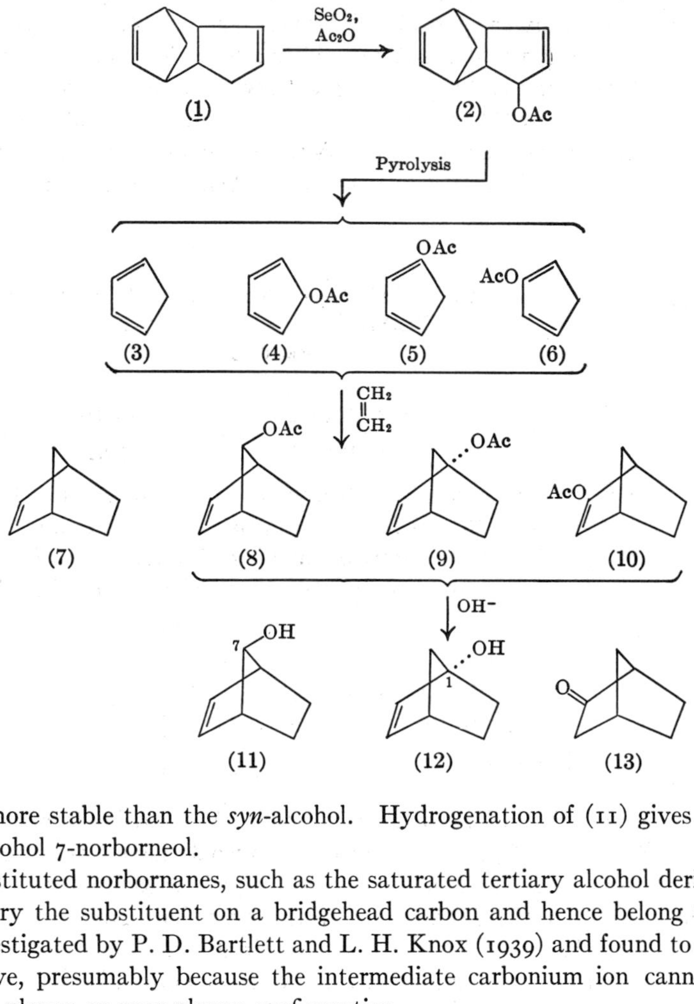

(1) $\xrightarrow{\text{SeO}_2,\ \text{Ac}_2\text{O}}$ (2) OAc

Pyrolysis

(3)   (4) OAc   OAc (5)   AcO (6)

$\downarrow$ CH₂=CH₂

(7)   OAc (8)   (9) OAc   AcO (10)

$\downarrow$ OH⁻

(11) 7 OH   (12) 1 OH   (13) O

clearly more stable than the *syn*-alcohol. Hydrogenation of (11) gives the saturated alcohol 7-norborneol.

1-Substituted norbornanes, such as the saturated tertiary alcohol derived from (12), carry the substituent on a bridgehead carbon and hence belong to a type first investigated by P. D. Bartlett and L. H. Knox (1939) and found to be highly unreactive, presumably because the intermediate carbonium ion cannot flatten out to a planar or near-planar configuration.

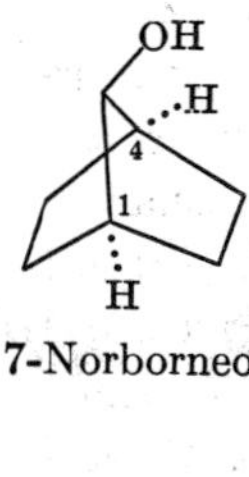

OH H 4 1 H
7-Norborneol

Surprisingly, 7-norborneol, for which only one steric form is possible, is almost as unreactive; the rate of solvolysis of its tosylate, relative to that of the tosylate of cyclohexanol taken as unity, is 10^{-7}. One explanation advanced for the difficulty of formation of a cationic center at C₇ is that the ring system prevents the stabilization by hyperconjugation that is usually possible:

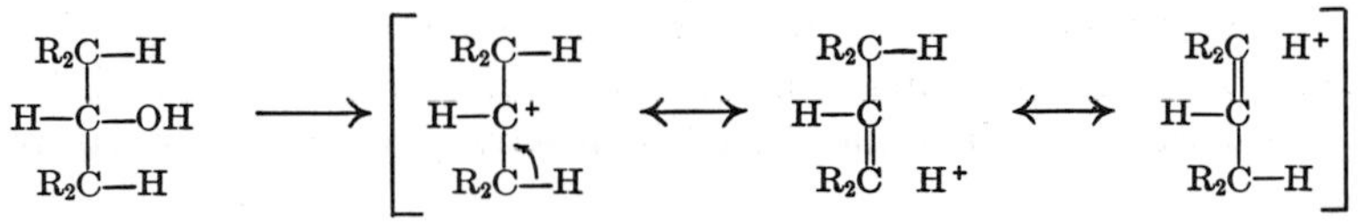

$$
\begin{array}{c}
\text{R}_2\text{C--H} \\
\text{H--C--OH} \\
\text{R}_2\text{C--H}
\end{array}
\longrightarrow
\left[
\begin{array}{c}
\text{R}_2\text{C--H} \\
\text{H--C}^+ \\
\text{R}_2\text{C--H}
\end{array}
\leftrightarrow
\begin{array}{c}
\text{R}_2\text{C--H} \\
\text{H--C} \\
\text{R}_2\text{C} \ \text{H}^+
\end{array}
\leftrightarrow
\begin{array}{c}
\text{R}_2\text{C} \ \ \text{H}^+ \\
\text{H--C} \\
\text{R}_2\text{C--H}
\end{array}
\right]
$$

Comparable resonance structures for the 7-bornyl cation would have a double bond extending to a bridgehead (1,7-; 4,7-) and would thus violate a rule formulated by Bredt.[1]

In contrast to the saturated 7-derivative, the unsaturated *anti*-7-norbornenyl tosylate is extraordinarily reactive; the rate of solvolysis relative to that of cyclohexyl tosylate is 10^4, or 10^{11} times that of the saturated analog. Winstein and Woodward (1956) suggested that the unusual reactivity, which evidently is the

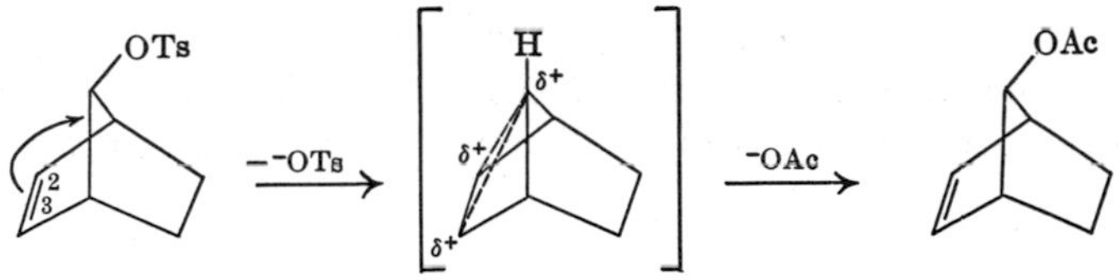

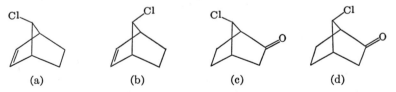

anti-7-Norbornenyl   Bridged cation   *anti*-Acetate
    tosylate

result of a neighboring olefinic group effect, is due to stabilization in the bridged cation formulated, in which C_7 is partially bonded to C_2 and C_3 and the charge is spread over three centers. The formation of this bridged ion requires the *anti* configuration in the tosylate and predicts stereospecific reaction with solvent at C_7 to generate the *anti* acetate. That complete retention of configuration was observed on acetolysis of optically active tosylate strengthened the interpretation of the enhanced reactivity and the mechanistic deduction of the *anti* configuration.

Synthesis of both *syn*- (a) and *anti*- (b) 7-chloronorbornene was accomplished

(a)	(b)	(c)	(d)

by Roberts (1954) by a principle to be illustrated below. The unsaturated chloride (a) was correlated by unambiguous chemical transformations with the saturated chloroketone (c), and (b) was similarly correlated with the chloroketone (d). One chloroketone was assigned the *syn* configuration (d) because it was found to have a larger dipole moment (3.39) than the epimer (2.21); in (d) the chlorine atom is oriented in the same direction as the carbonyl group and hence the two dipoles reinforce one another. Corresponding configurations could then be assigned to the correlated unsaturated chlorides, (a) and (b). Kinetic studies

[1] Julius Bredt. 1855–1937; b. Berlin; Ph.D. Strasbourg (Fittig); Univ. Aachen

(1956) of the saturated and unsaturated 7-chloro derivatives revealed interesting relationships. Reaction rates relative to that of cyclopentyl chloride are shown under the formulas. That the spread in reactivity between the saturated and

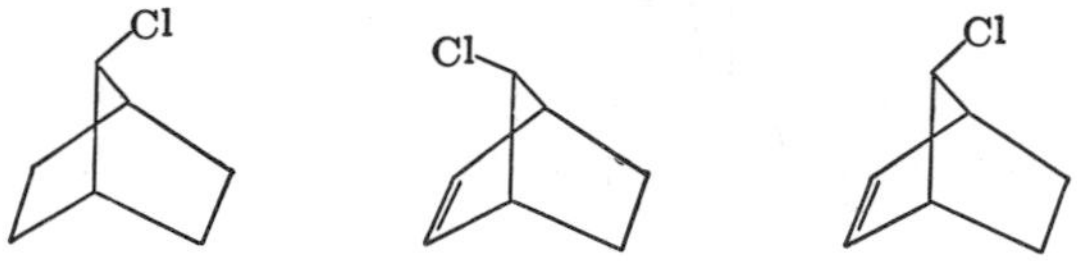

>0.005   >0.01   7

the *anti* unsaturated chlorides is consistent with the spread observed for the corresponding alcohols strengthened the mechanistic deduction of the *anti* configuration of the norbornenol of Woodward and Norton.

A route to *syn*-7-norborneol (VII) developed by Winstein (1957) starts with epoxidation of norbornene (I) and cleavage of the oxide II with hydrogen bromide, which is considered to involve formation of the bridged cation III and backside

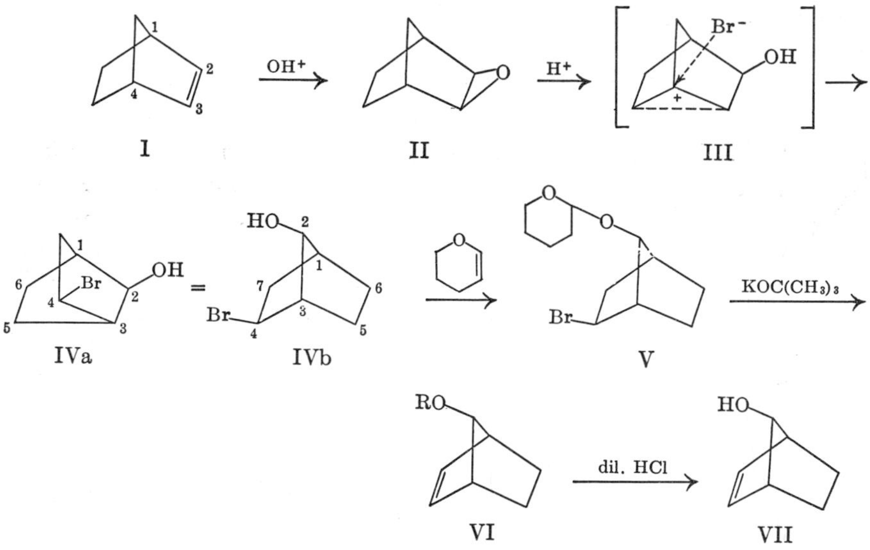

I   II   III

IVa   IVb   V

VI   VII

attack by bromide ion at C_4 with production of the bromohydrin IVa. When the formula is arranged as in IVb, the substance is seen to be a 7-norborneol with the hydroxyl *syn* to the second functional group. Protection of the hydroxyl group as the dihydropyrane derivative V and dehydrobromination gave the *syn*-alcohol VII.

The tosylate of VII, VIII, undergoes solvolysis at a rate of 10^4, as compared to 1 for 7-norbornyl tosylate and to 10^{11} for *anti*-7-norbornenyl tosylate. The reaction product does not possess the norbornane skeleton, but contains a five-membered ring fused to a four-membered ring. The structure IX was established by synthesis of the product from the hydrocarbon XI, which resulted from addition of cyclopentadiene to ketene and Wolf-Kishner reduction of the resulting bicyclic ketone.   Solvolysis of **VIII** thus proceeds with a rearrangement involving participation of the neighboring C$_6$-methylene group.   The C$_1$—C$_6$ linkage is ruptured,

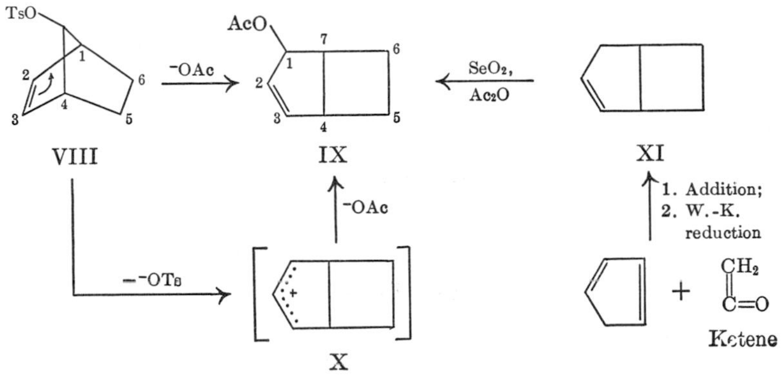

with appearance of the acetoxy group at C$_1$, and C$_6$ becomes bonded to C$_7$.   Winstein postulates an intermediate allylic cation, **X**, and considers that the resonance stabilization of this ion more than compensates for the increased ring strain in the bicyclic system formed.   Introduction into the unsaturated tosylate **VIII** of a second double bond at the 5,6-position enhances the reactivity still more: k = 10^{14} (Winstein, 1960).   P. R. Story and M. Saunders (1960) obtained a norbornadienyl carbanion salt by slow addition at −80° of a soution of 7-norbornadienyl chloride in liquid sulfur dioxide to a similar solution of silver tetrafluoroborate.   The filtered solution of 7-norbornadienyl fluoroborate was sufficiently stable at − 10° for an examination of the n.m.r. spectrum, which afforded evidence of the bridged ion structure.   A new route to 7-norbornadienol involves reaction of norbornadiene with *t*-butyl perbenzoate in benzene in the presence of Cu$_2$Br$_2$ to give 7-*t*-butoxynorbornadiene (25% yield); this on cleavage with perchloric acid in acetic acid gives the 7-acetoxy derivative which is cleaved by methylmagnesium iodide to 7-norbornadienol (P. R. Story, Bell Telephone Lab., 1961).

Note to page 333.—For description of the enhanced reactivity associated with an intermediate bearing a split ionic charge, Winstein uses the term anchimeric acceleration (Gr. *anchi-* + *meros*, adjacent parts).

Chapter 10

HALIDES

10.1   **Properties.** — In the series of alkyl halides (Table 10.1), bromides boil at temperatures distinctly higher than the corresponding chlorides, and iodides are higher boiling than bromides.   There is also a rise in boiling point in each series of homologs; thus an increase in molecular weight due to either a heavier halogen atom or a larger alkyl group results in an increase in boiling point.   The chlorides are much less volatile than the alkanes from which they are derived but do not differ greatly from alkanes of comparable molecular weight. Bromides and iodides are considerably more volatile than comparable alkanes, as is evident from data for C_2H_5Br and n-C_3H_7I: b.p. 38.4° and 102°; mol. wt. 108.98 and 169.99.   Iodides boil at about the same temperatures as alcohols of corresponding structure.   Among the initial members of the series, methyl chloride, ethyl chloride, and methyl bromide are gases at laboratory temperature; liquefied methyl chloride is obtainable commercially in steel cylinders and the other two in sealed glass ampules, which are chilled prior to being opened or resealed.   When a small quantity of a methyl or an ethyl halide is required, convenience in measuring may dictate selection of methyl iodide or ethyl bromide, but the chlorides are cheaper and usually preferable for large-scale operations. The boiling point of ethyl chloride is such that a fine stream of the liquid sprayed on the skin freezes tissues in a localized area by abstraction of heat required for evaporation.   Because of the resulting insensitization to pain, ethyl chloride has found some use as a local anesthetic for minor operations of short duration (*e.g.*, incision of boils).

Alkyl halides are practically insoluble in water and separate from water in layers.   Chlorides are slightly lighter than water, and bromides and particularly iodides are much heavier.   Like alkanes, halogen compounds are insoluble in and inert to cold concentrated sulfuric acid, and extraction with this reagent removes contaminants such as alkenes, alcohols and ethers.

TABLE 10.1. ALKYL HALIDES

NAME	FORMULA	M.P., °C.	B.P., °C.	SP. GR. (LIQ.)
Methyl chloride	CH_3Cl	-97	-23.7	0.920
Methyl bromide	CH_3Br	-93	4.6	1.732
Methyl iodide	CH_3I	-64	42.3	2.279
Ethyl chloride	C_2H_5Cl	-139	13.1	0.910
Ethyl bromide	C_2H_5Br	-119	38.4	1.430
Ethyl iodide	C_2H_5I	-111	72.3	1.933
n-Propyl chloride	$CH_3CH_2CH_2Cl$	-123	46.4	0.890
n-Propyl bromide	$CH_3CH_2CH_2Br$	-110	71	1.353
n-Propyl iodide	$CH_3CH_2CH_2I$	-101	102	1.747
Isopropyl chloride	$(CH_3)_2CHCl$	-117	36.5	0.860
Isopropyl bromide	$(CH_3)_2CHBr$	-89	59.5	1.310
Isopropyl iodide	$(CH_3)_2CHI$	-91	89.4	1.703
n-Butyl chloride	$CH_3(CH_2)_3Cl$	-123	78.1	0.884
n-Butyl bromide	$CH_3(CH_2)_3Br$	-112	101.6	1.275
Isobutyl chloride	$(CH_3)_2CHCH_2Cl$	-131	68.9	0.866
Isobutyl bromide	$(CH_3)_2CHCH_2Br$	-120	91.3	1.250
sec-Butyl chloride	$CH_3CH_2CHClCH_3$		68	0.871
sec-Butyl bromide	$CH_3CH_2CHBrCH_3$		91.3	1.251
t-Butyl chloride	$(CH_3)_3CCl$	-28.5	51.0	0.851
t-Butyl bromide	$(CH_3)_3CBr$	-20	73.3	1.222
n-Amyl bromide	$CH_3(CH_2)_4Br$	-95	129.7	1.223
Isoamyl bromide	$(CH_3)_2CHCH_2CH_2Br$	-112	120.7	1.215
t-Amyl bromide	$(CH_3)_2CBrCH_2CH_3$		109.2	1.190
n-Hexyl bromide	$CH_3(CH_2)_5Br$		156	1.173
n-Octadecyl bromide	$CH_3(CH_2)_{17}Br$	34	170 at 0.5 mm.	
Vinyl chloride	$CH_2{=}CHCl$	-160	-14	
Vinyl bromide	$CH_2{=}CHBr$	-138	15.8	1.517
Allyl chloride	$CH_2{=}CHCH_2Cl$	-136	45.7	0.938
Allyl bromide	$CH_2{=}CHCH_2Br$	-119	70.0	
Allyl iodide	$CH_2{=}CHCH_2I$	-99	102.0	1.848

10.2   Preparation. — As mentioned earlier (4.5), the HX-method for conversion of an alcohol to the alkyl halide is generally satisfactory for the preparation of bromides and iodides but, with the exceptions noted below, is not satisfactory for the preparation of chlorides. However, chlorides can be obtained in high yield by reaction of the alcohol with hydrochloric acid containing zinc chloride as catalyst. Chlorides are obtainable also with phosphorus trichloride or pentachloride or with thionyl chloride and pyridine (11.23). Bro-

$$3\ ROH + PCl_3 \rightarrow 3\ RCl + P(OH)_3$$
$$ROH + PCl_5 \rightarrow RCl + HCl + POCl_3$$

mides can be prepared with use of either preformed phosphorus tribromide or with a mixture of red and yellow phosphorus with bromine. Alkyl iodides are obtainable by generation of phosphorus triiodide by addition of iodine to a suspension of red phosphorus in the alcohol. A procedure by which methyl iodide is obtainable in 90–94% yield consists in reaction of dimethyl sulfate with aqueous potassium iodide in the presence of calcium carbonate. Rydon's triphenylphosphite method has been described (8.26).

Vinyl chloride, a key monomer for the manufacture of plastics, is produced as a petrochemical from ethylene by thermal dehydrohalogenation of ethylene dichloride. Vinyl bromide is formed in good yield by reaction of ethylene dibromide with base. Ethyl chloride is made commercially by chlorination of ethane in

$$CH_2=CH_2 \xrightarrow{Cl_2} ClCH_2CH_2Cl \xrightarrow{Heat} CH_2=CHCl$$

$$BrCH_2CH_2Br \xrightarrow{alc.\ KOH} CH_2=CHBr$$

the vapor phase at 400°. The hydrogen chloride formed is used for hydrochlorination of ethylene.

t-Butyl chloride can be prepared by merely shaking the alcohol with concentrated hydrochloric acid for a few minutes in a separatory funnel at room temperature. Allyl alcohol reacts readily at a higher temperature; the water present

$$\underset{\textit{t-Butyl alcohol}}{(CH_3)_3COH} \xrightarrow[94\%]{concd.\ HCl,\ 25°} \underset{\textit{t-Butyl chloride}}{(CH_3)_3CCl}$$

$$\underset{\text{Allyl alcohol}}{CH_2=CHCH_2OH} \xrightarrow{concd.\ HCl,\ 100°} \underset{\text{Allyl chloride}}{CH_2=CHCH_2Cl}$$

inhibits addition to the double bond. The reactions follow the S_N1 mechanism. *t*-Butyl alcohol reacts with special ease because of the ready formation of a carbonium ion stabilized by the inductive effect of three methyl groups; allyl alcohol forms an ion stabilized by resonance:

$$CH_2=CHCH_2OH \xrightarrow{H^+} CH_2=CH-\overset{+}{C}H_2 \leftrightarrow \overset{+}{C}H_2-CH=CH_2$$

$$\xrightarrow{Cl^-} CH_2=CHCH_2Cl$$

Hunsdiecker[1] and Hunsdiecker[2] discovered that treatment of the dry silver salt of a carboxylic acid in refluxing carbon tetrachloride effects conversion to the corresponding bromide with liberation of carbon dioxide. Examples of the **Hunsdiecker reaction** are: conversion of silver laurate to undecyl bromide (1), of

1. $$n\text{-}C_{11}H_{23}CO_2Ag \xrightarrow[67\%]{Br_2,\ CCl_4} n\text{-}C_{11}H_{23}Br + CO_2 + AgBr$$

2. $$AgO_2C(CH_2)_8CO_2Ag \xrightarrow[62\text{-}81\%]{2\ Br_2,\ CCl_4} Br(CH_2)_8Br + 2\ CO_2 + 2\ AgBr$$

3. $$CH_3O_2C(CH_2)_6CO_2Ag \xrightarrow[70\%]{Br_2,\ CCl_4} CH_3O_2C(CH_2)_6Br + CO_2 + AgBr$$

silver sebacate into octamethylene dibromide (2), and of the silver salt of suberic acid half methyl ester into methyl 7-bromoheptanoate (3). The third reaction is particularly useful because ω-bromo esters are not readily available by other methods.

The initial reaction product is the acyl hypobromite, which is easily isolated,

[1] Heinz Hunsdiecker, b. 1904 Cologne; Ph.D. Cologne (Wintgen); Privatlaborat. Cologne-Braunsfeld; Manager Dr. Vogt and Co., Cologne

[2] Cläre Hunsdiecker, b. 1903 Kiel; Ph.D. Cologne (Wintgen); Privatlaborat. Cologne-Braunsfeld

and several pieces of evidence indicate that its subsequent decomposition is a free radical reaction. Termination steps are combination of R· with another R·

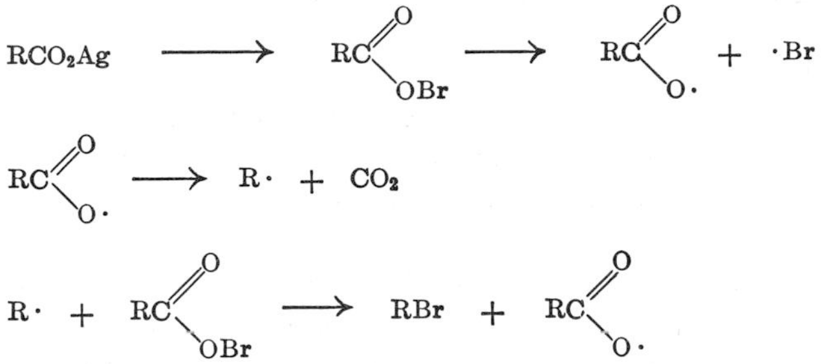

$$RCO_2Ag \longrightarrow RC\underset{OBr}{\overset{O}{<}} \longrightarrow RC\underset{O\cdot}{\overset{O}{<}} + \cdot Br$$

$$RC\underset{O\cdot}{\overset{O}{<}} \longrightarrow R\cdot + CO_2$$

$$R\cdot + RC\underset{OBr}{\overset{O}{<}} \longrightarrow RBr + RC\underset{O\cdot}{\overset{O}{<}}$$

or with $RCO_2\cdot$. This mechanism is consistent with the finding that optically active $CH_3CH_2CH(CH_3)CO_2Ag$ gives racemic $CH_3CH_2CHBrCH_3$ and with the observation that the silver salts of *cis-* and *trans*-4-*t*-butylcyclohexanecarboxylic acid give identical mixtures containing about 65% of the *trans* bromide (Eliel,[1] 1959). See note added in proof on page 357.

J. W. Wilt found (1958) that β,β,β-triphenylpropionic acid silver salt does not undergo the normal Hunsdiecker reaction but yields phenyl β,β-diphenyl-acrylate (3), probably via the acyl radical (1) and the aronium radical (2).

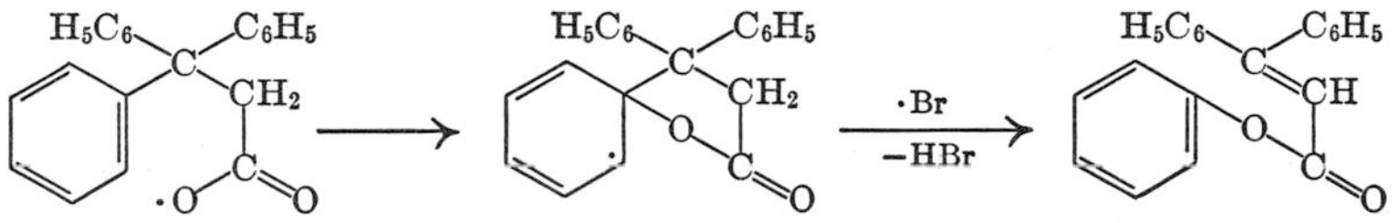

(1)   (2)   (3)

10.3   Reactivity. — The following generalizations roughly define the reactivity of saturated alkyl halides. (1) Primary and secondary bromides react by the S_N2 mechanism with marked decrease in rate in the following order (9.2):

$$CH_3Br > CH_3CH_2Br > (CH_3)_2CHBr$$

Normal bromides higher than ethyl react at essentially the same rate as ethyl bromide. (2) Tertiary alkyl bromides enter into S_N1 displacements and react more rapidly than methyl bromide. (3) Reactivity decreases markedly in the order RI > RBr > RCl. (4) Halides of the allyl and benzyl types are highly reactive. (5) Vinyl-type halides (CH_2=CHBr) are very inert.

The last two points require elaboration. That allyl chloride in a typical displacement reacts 79 times as fast as *n*-propyl chloride is attributable to resonance stabilization of the carbonium ion formed by the S_N1 mechanism. Benzyl halides are of comparable activity; here the aromatic ring participates in resonance and the charge is distributed between the side chain and the *ortho* and *para* positions in the ring. The special reactivity disappears if the double bond or phenyl group is moved out of conjugation with the halogen atom; CH_2=CHCH$_2$CH$_2$Cl is no

[1] Ernest L. Eliel, b. 1921 Cologne, Germany; Ph.D. Illinois (Snyder); Univ. Notre Dame

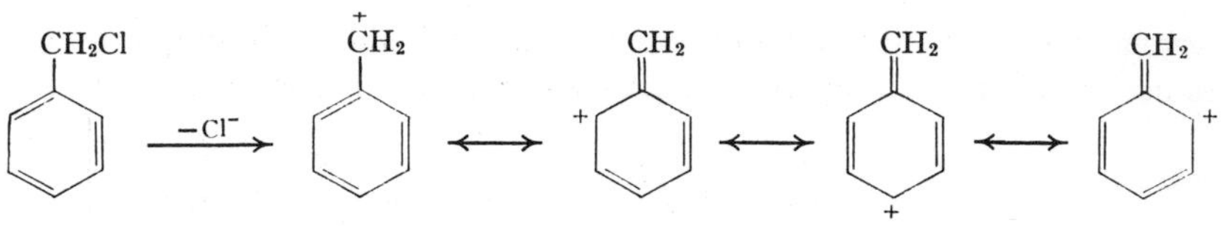

more reactive than n-butyl chloride. In chloromethyl methyl ether, CH_3OCH_2Cl, the unshared electrons on oxygen are conjugated with the chlorine atom and the substance is 918 times as reactive to potassium iodide in acetone as n-butyl chloride.

The enhanced reactivity of allyl halides is utilized in the **Grignard coupling reaction**, in which an alkyl or aryl Grignard reagent combines with an allyl-type halide to produce an α-olefin. Coupling is sometimes observed as a minor side

$$CH_3CH_2CH_2CH_2MgBr + \overset{1}{Br}\overset{2}{C}H_2\overset{3}{C}H{=}\overset{4}{C}H_2 \xrightarrow{\text{(in ether)}}$$

Allyl bromide

$$CH_3CH_2CH_2CH_2CH_2CH{=}CH_2 + MgBr_2$$

Heptene-1

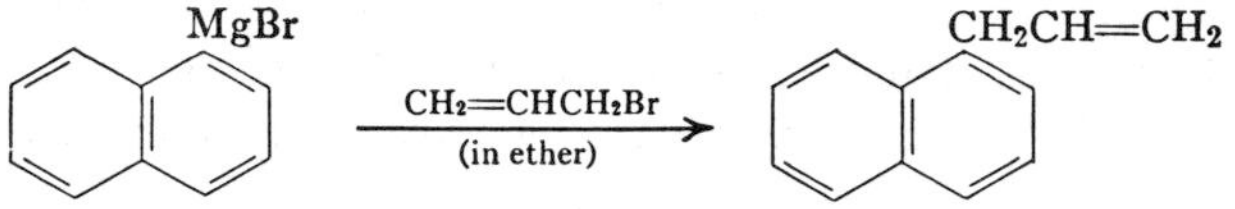

α-Naphthylmagnesium bromide

α-Allylnaphthalene

reaction in the preparation of Grignard reagents, but as applied to allylic halides it has practical use in synthesis.

Table 10.2 shows that propargyl bromide surpasses allyl bromide in reactivity. The reaction of propargyl bromide with iodide ion is a prototropic displacement

$$CH{\equiv}C{-}CH_2Br \xrightarrow{-Br^-} CH{\equiv}C{-}\overset{+}{C}H_2 \leftrightarrow \overset{+}{C}H{=}C{=}CH_2 \xrightarrow{I^-} ICH{=}C{=}CH_2$$

affording iodoallene. The data for vinyl bromide, bromoallene, and β-methylvinyl bromide show that a halogen atom on an unsaturated carbon is very unreactive. A resonance effect accounts for the phenomenon. Vinyl bromide is a hybrid of structure (a) and the polarized structure (b); the corresponding electronic formulations are (c) and (d). That the C—Br bond does indeed have

$$\underset{(a)}{CH_2{=}CH{-}Br} \longleftrightarrow \underset{(b)}{\overset{-}{C}H_2{-}CH{=}\overset{+}{Br}}$$

$$\underset{(c)}{H{:}\underset{H}{\ddot{C}}{::}\underset{H}{\ddot{C}}{:}\ddot{\underset{..}{Br}}{:}} \longleftrightarrow \underset{(d)}{H{:}\overset{-}{\underset{H}{\ddot{C}}}{:}\underset{H}{\ddot{C}}{::}\overset{+}{\underset{..}{Br}}{:}}$$

some double-bond character is shown by the fact that the bond is shorter (1.86 Å) than the normal C—Br bond (1.91 Å). The hybrid bond evidently is more stable than a normal covalent bond. The carbon—halogen bond distance in

TABLE 10.2.   REACTION WITH NaI IN ACETONE (25°)

HALIDE	FORMULA	K(MOLE⁻¹, HR.⁻¹)
Propargyl bromide	$CH{\equiv}CCH_2Br$	612
Allyl bromide	$CH_2{=}CHCH_2Br$	438
Vinyl bromide	$CH_2{=}CHBr$	0.014
Bromoallene	$CH_2{=}C{=}CHBr$	0.0122
β-Methylvinyl bromide	$CH_3CH{=}CHBr$	0.0005

methyl chloride is 1.77 Å, and the distances for vinyl chloride (1.69 Å) and chloro-benzene (1.70 Å) show evidence of shortening due to resonance.

The following synthesis of 3-cyclohexylpropyne-1 illustrates the coupling of a Grignard reagent with an allyl-type halide and the relative reactivity of halogen atoms adjacent to and attached to an ethylenic carbon atom:

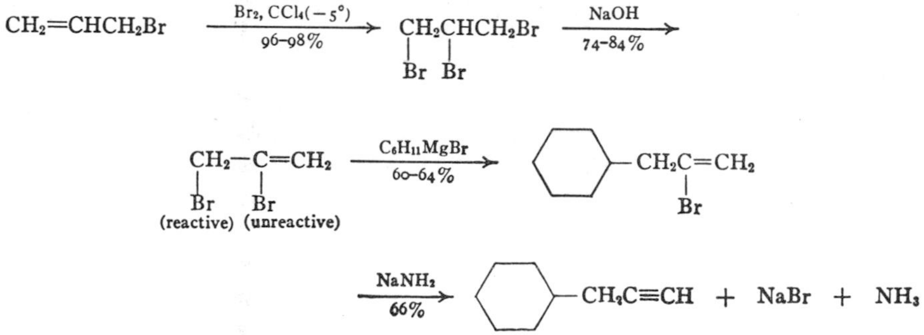

$$CH_2{=}CHCH_2Br \xrightarrow[\text{96-98\%}]{Br_2, CCl_4(-5°)} \underset{\underset{Br\ Br}{|\ \ |}}{CH_2CHCH_2Br} \xrightarrow[\text{74-84\%}]{NaOH}$$

$$\underset{\underset{\substack{Br\ \ \ Br \\ \text{(reactive) (unreactive)}}}{|\ \ \ |}}{CH_2{-}C{=}CH_2} \xrightarrow[\text{60-64\%}]{C_6H_{11}MgBr} \text{⬡}{-}\underset{\underset{Br}{|}}{CH_2C{=}CH_2}$$

$$\xrightarrow[\text{66\%}]{NaNH_2} \text{⬡}{-}CH_2C{\equiv}CH\ +\ NaBr\ +\ NH_3$$

3-Cyclohexylpropyne-1

Early attempts to form Grignard reagents from vinyl halides, even the iodide, by the usual procedure were unsuccessful, but H. Normant (1957) found that vinyl chloride and vinyl bromide readily form vinylmagnesium halides in tetra-hydrofurane or in a diether of di- or triethylene glycol. These solvents form particularly stable complexes with RMgX.

10.4   Other Organometallic Compounds. — With the idea of abstracting iodine from ethyl iodide and producing the free ethyl radical, Frank-land (1849) heated the iodide with zinc in a sealed tube at 150–160°. The product was a liquid which took fire in contact with air and which reacted vigorously with water to produce a gas. The gas proved to be ethane, not ethyl, and the liquid was diethylzinc, formed in reaction sequence 1–2. The modern procedure utilizes a zinc–copper couple and is run at the boiling point of an equimolecular mixture of

1. $C_2H_5I\ +\ Zn\ \rightarrow\ C_2H_5ZnI$
2. $2\ C_2H_5ZnI\ \rightarrow\ (C_2H_5)_2Zn\ +\ ZnI_2$

ethyl iodide and ethyl bromide. Ethyl bromide alone does not react with zinc, but use of a mixture reduces the cost and moderates the reaction. The product is distilled in an atmosphere of carbon dioxide (yield, 81–84%). Both dimethyl-zinc (b.p. 46°) and diethylzinc (b.p. 118°) ignite in the air. The dialkylzincs react like Grignard reagents and prior to Grignard's discovery of the more easily manipulated reagents were employed in synthesis. Both dialkylzincs and alkylzinc chlorides, prepared from Grignard reagents as in (3), are less reactive than Grignard reagents and have found some use in the synthesis of ketones (4) since

3. $\quad\quad C_2H_5MgBr + ZnCl_2 \rightarrow C_2H_5ZnCl + MgBrCl$
4. $\quad\quad (C_2H_5)_2Zn + RCOCl \rightarrow RCOC_2H_5 + C_2H_5ZnCl$
5. $\quad\quad (CH_3)_3CCl + (CH_3)_2Zn \rightarrow (CH_3)_4C + CH_3ZnCl$

they react only very slowly with the ketonic product. The corresponding cadmium derivatives, however, serve the same purpose more effectively (12.8). Another use is illustrated by the synthesis of neopentane (5) from t-butyl chloride and diethylzinc.

Diethylmercury (b.p. 190°), prepared as in (6), is much less reactive than

6. $\quad\quad 2\ C_2H_5I + Na_2Hg \longrightarrow (C_2H_5)_2Hg + 2\ NaI$
7. $\quad\quad (C_2H_5)_2Hg + Zn \longrightarrow (C_2H_5)_2Zn + Hg$

diethylzinc; it is not decomposed by water but is split by mineral acids. Frankland found (1864) that zinc reacts with diethylmercury to form diethylzinc (7).

10.5 **Methylene Halides (Dihalides).** — Methylene chloride, CH_2Cl_2, has high solvent power for organic compounds, is insoluble in water and heavier than water, has a low boiling point (40.8°), and is nonflammable; these properties make the substance useful as an extraction solvent. Methylene chlo-

TABLE 10.3. POLYHALOGEN COMPOUNDS

Name	Formula	M.P., °C.	B.P., °C.	Sp. Gr.
Methylene chloride	CH_2Cl_2	-96	40.8	1.336
Methylene bromide	CH_2Br_2	-53	98.2	2.46
Methylene iodide	CH_2I_2	5	180 dec.	3.322
Chloroform	$CHCl_3$	-63.5	61.2	1.489
Bromoform	$CHBr_3$	7.8	149.6	2.865
Iodoform	CHI_3	119	....	4.1
Carbon tetrafluoride	CF_4	....	-128	....
Carbon tetrachloride	CCl_4	-23	76.8	1.575
Carbon tetrabromide	CBr_4	92.5	189.5	3.42
Dichlorodifluoromethane	CCl_2F_2	-155	-29.8	1.4
Ethylene dichloride (ethylene chloride)	$ClCH_2CH_2Cl$	-35.5	83.8	1.238
Ethylene dibromide	$BrCH_2CH_2Br$	10	131.7	2.182
Ethylidene chloride	CH_3CHCl_2	-97	57.3	1.174
Ethylidene bromide	CH_3CHBr_2	....	110	2.056
s-Tetrachloroethane (acetylene tetrachloride)	$CHCl_2CHCl_2$	-43	146.3	1.600
Hexachloroethane	CCl_3CCl_3	189	185	2.091
s-Dichloroethylene [1] (acetylene dichloride)	$ClCH=CHCl$	-50	48.4	1.259
Trichloroethylene	$CHCl=CCl_2$	-86	87	1.477
Trimethylene bromide	$Br(CH_2)_3Br$	-36	167	1.979
Tetramethylene bromide	$Br(CH_2)_4Br$	-21	198 dec.	1.79
Pentamethylene bromide	$Br(CH_2)_5Br$	-40	221	1.706
Hexamethylene bromide	$Br(CH_2)_6Br$	....	240 dec.	1.599

[1] *trans* form; *cis* form: m.p. $-80.5°$, b.p. 60.3°, sp. gr. 1.265.

ride is also an excellent solvent for crystallization, either alone or as a member of a solvent pair. For example, a methylene chloride solution of a substance to be purified can be clarified with decolorizing carbon, filtered, diluted with methanol, and evaporated to the point of saturation and let stand for crystallization. Methylene chloride is prepared technically as one of the products of chlorination of methane. Methylene bromide and methylene iodide are prepared most readily by reduction of the corresponding trihalomethane derivatives with sodium arsenite in alkaline solution:

$$\underset{\substack{\text{Iodoform}\\\text{(bromoform)}}}{CHI_3(CHBr_3)} + Na_3AsO_3 + NaOH \xrightarrow{88-97\%} \underset{\substack{\text{Methylene iodide}\\\text{(bromide)}}}{CH_2I_2(CH_2Br_2)} + NaI(Br) + Na_3AsO_4$$

Methylene halides yield formaldehyde on hydrolysis and are sometimes employed as a potential source of this reagent:

$$CH_2X_2 \xrightarrow{H_2O} \left[CH_2 \begin{array}{c} OH \\ OH \end{array} \right] \longrightarrow CH_2{=}O$$

10.6   Haloforms. — Chloroform is so named because it yields formic acid on hydrolysis. It is a sweet-smelling heavier than water liquid of high solvent power and it is the standard solvent for determination of optical rotation. The liquid is not flammable but the vapor can burn. On exposure to air and sunlight, chloroform suffers slow oxidation to the highly toxic phosgene, possibly by formation and decomposition of the hydroperoxide:

$$Cl_3CH \xrightarrow{O_2} \left[\begin{array}{c} Cl \\ | \\ Cl{-}\underset{|}{\overset{|}{C}}OOH \\ Cl \end{array} \right] \xrightarrow{-HOCl} \underset{\substack{| \\ Cl \\ \text{Phosgene}}}{Cl{-}C{=}O}$$

Commercial preparations are stored in brown bottles and contain 0.75% ethanol to destroy any trace of phosgene which may arise. Steroids of the partial structure I, in which the 6β-acetoxyl group is axial, can be epimerized to the equatorial 6α-acetates II by the action at 0° of dry hydrogen chloride in commercial chloroform containing ethanol, but not in pure chloroform. Chloroform is made

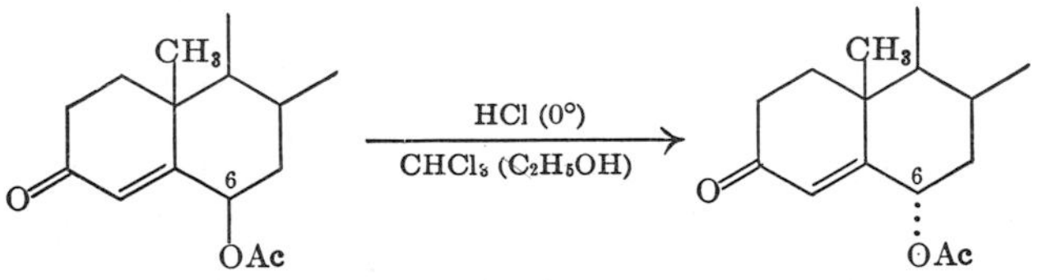

$$\xrightarrow[\text{CHCl}_3\ (\text{C}_2\text{H}_5\text{OH})]{\text{HCl (0°)}}$$

           I   II

both by the haloform reaction described below and by reduction of carbon tetrachloride with iron and water:

$$CCl_4 + 2\ H\ (Fe,\ H_2O) \rightarrow CHCl_3 + HCl$$

Bromoform, being a liquid of unusually high specific gravity (2.865), is used as a component in flotation methods of mineral analysis. **Iodoform** is a crystalline yellow solid of characteristic melting point and odor. This substance and carbon tetraiodide, which is red, are the only organic compounds which are colored but not unsaturated; the iodine present accounts for 97–98% of the molecule. Iodoform was once used as a topical antiseptic, but it is not very effective.

10.7 Haloform Reaction. — One example of this general method for producing haloforms is the reaction of acetone with a solution of sodium hypochlorite or bleaching powder. One methyl group is fully substituted to

$$CH_3\overset{O}{\overset{\|}{C}}CH_3 \xrightarrow{\text{3 NaOCl}} CH_3\overset{O}{\overset{\|}{C}}CCl_3 \xrightarrow{\text{NaOH}} CH_3COONa + HCCl_3$$

give 1,1,1-trichloroacetone, which undergoes cleavage in the alkaline medium to sodium acetate and chloroform. Chloroform, bromoform, and iodoform are obtainable by this reaction in high yield. Since the haloform reaction is generally applicable to methyl ketones, it is useful for the preparation of acids, for example, for the preparation of trimethylacetic acid from pinacolone; in this case the first step is conducted at room temperature and then the mixture is heated to bring

$$(CH_3)_3CCOCH_3 \xrightarrow[71-74\%]{\text{NaOBr}} (CH_3)_3CCO_2H$$

the alkaline fission to completion and to eliminate bromoform (and a small amount of carbon tetrabromide formed from it). Methyl ketones of the aromatic series are readily available by the general Friedel-Crafts reaction and afford a convenient route to aryl acids, as illustrated for one derived from toluene; an ordinary oxidizing agent would attack the methyl group as well. That olefinic linkages

$$C_6H_5CH_3 \xrightarrow[\text{AlCl}_3]{\text{CH}_3\text{COCl}} CH_3COC_6H_4CH_3\text{-}p \xrightarrow{\text{NaOCl}} HO_2CC_6H_4CH_3\text{-}p$$

are not affected is shown by hypohalite oxidation of β-ionone to a crystalline acid (the yield reported is after four crystallizations).

β-Ionone → M. p. 107°

CH₃OH-aq. KOCl, 12 hrs. at 25°, 49.5%

The first step in the haloform reaction has been discussed (9.1) and formulated as involving electrophilic attack of the enolate anion (1). Since the second and third chlorines attack the same position as the first, enolization must favor the

$$(1)\quad CH_3\overset{O}{\overset{\|}{C}}CH_3 \xrightarrow[-H_2O]{OH^-} CH_3\overset{O^-}{\overset{|}{C}}=CH_2 \longleftrightarrow CH_3\overset{O}{\overset{\|}{C}}-\overset{-}{C}H_2 \xrightarrow[-Cl^-]{Cl_2} CH_3\overset{O}{\overset{\|}{C}}-CH_2Cl$$

$$(2)\quad CH_3\overset{O}{\overset{\|}{C}}CH_2Cl \xrightarrow[-H_2O]{OH^-} CH_3\overset{O^-}{\overset{|}{C}}=CHCl \longleftrightarrow CH_3\overset{O}{\overset{\|}{C}}-\overset{-}{C}HCl \xrightarrow[-Cl^-]{Cl_2} CH_3\overset{O}{\overset{\|}{C}}-CHCl_2$$

chlorinated over the unchlorinated carbon, as in (2): the electron-attracting chlorine promotes separation of a proton from the carbon to which it is linked. The alkaline fission of the trihaloketone may involve the transition state formulated:

$$
HO^- \ + \ \underset{R}{\overset{O}{\underset{|}{\overset{\|}{C}}}}{-}CCl_3 \longrightarrow HO\cdots\overset{O}{\overset{\|}{\underset{R}{\underset{|}{C}}}}\overset{\delta^-}{\cdots}\overset{\delta^-}{CCl_3} \longrightarrow HO{-}\underset{R}{\overset{O}{\overset{\|}{C}}} \ + \ \bar{C}Cl_3
$$

$$\downarrow H_2O$$

$$HCCl_3 \ + \ OH^-$$

Here the electron drift toward the three halogens favors acceptance of a negative charge by carbon.

10.8   Iodoform Test. — Since iodoform can be detected from its yellow color and characteristic odor and identified by mixed melting point determination, the reaction of an alcohol with a solution of iodine in alkali affords a useful test for diagnosis of alcohol type. Ethanol gives a positive iodoform test because it is initially oxidized by hypoiodite to acetaldehyde, which affords

$$CH_3CH_2OH \xrightarrow{NaOI} CH_3CH{=}O \xrightarrow{3\ NaOI} CI_3CH{=}O \xrightarrow{NaOH} CHI_3 + HCO_2Na$$
$$RCHOHCH_3 \xrightarrow{NaOI} RCOCH_3 \xrightarrow{3NaOI} RCOCI_3 \xrightarrow{NaOH} RCO_2Na + CHI_3$$

the triiodo derivative and then iodoform and sodium formate. No other primary alcohol affords iodoform; the test can be used to distinguish ethanol from methanol. Secondary alcohols that on oxidation afford methyl ketones give a positive response. Thus the iodoform test is specific for methyl ketones, ethanol, and secondary alcohols oxidizable to methyl ketones. Pinacolone is an exception to the rule; this hindered ketone affords bromoform satisfactorily, as noted, but the reaction with hypoiodite stops at the stage of the diiodo compound $(CH_3)_3CCO$-CHI_2.

10.9   Carbon tetrachloride is manufactured by chlorination of carbon disulfide, obtained by heating sulfur with coke in an electric furnace. Antimony pentachloride, aluminum chloride, or ferric chloride is employed as a catalyst, or halogen carrier:

$$CS_2 \ + \ 3\,Cl_2 \xrightarrow{SbCl_5} CCl_4 \ + \ S_2Cl_2$$
$$\text{Sulfur}$$
$$\text{monochloride}$$

Having no hydrogen atoms, carbon tetrachloride is one of the rare instances of a noncombustible organic compound, and it is used in fire extinguishers. It has a low boiling point ($76.8°$) and volatilizes readily when sprayed on a fire, and the heavy vapor settles over the flame and smothers it by excluding oxygen; some phosgene is formed, and hence adequate ventilation is essential. The substance is used in the laboratory as a heavier than water extraction solvent. It is a powerful solvent for greases and is preferred for use in commercial dry cleaning and as a household cleaning fluid because of the freedom from fire hazard.

10.10   Ethane Derivatives. — **Ethylene dichloride,** $ClCH_2CH_2Cl$, is made by addition of chlorine to ethylene, and **s-tetrachloroethane,** $Cl_2CHCHCl_2$, is produced by addition of two moles of chlorine to acetylene. The dichloro compound is an excellent extraction solvent of moderate boiling point (83.8°), and the tetrachloro derivative is a powerful, higher-boiling (146.3°) solvent. **Ethylidene chloride,** CH_3CHCl_2, is less used; it can be prepared by the action of phosphorus pentachloride on acetaldehyde and by addition of hydrogen chloride to vinyl chloride. **Hexachloroethane** can be prepared by the action of amalgamated aluminum on carbon tetrachloride, but is produced industrially as a by-product in the reaction of acetylene with chlorine or by chlorination of s-tetrachloroethane in the presence of aluminum chloride. It is a crystalline solid of camphorlike odor having a marked tendency to sublime. The melting point, determined by heating the substance in a sealed capillary tube, is practically the same as the boiling point. Hexachloroethane is a component of a mixture used in smoke candles and smoke pots, consisting of zinc dust (36%), hexachloroethane (44%), ammonium perchlorate (10%), and ammonium chloride (10%). When started with a suitable igniter, the reaction between zinc dust and the organic halide proceeds with liberation of sufficient heat (temperature of 1200°)

$$3 \ Zn + C_2Cl_6 \rightarrow 3 \ ZnCl_2 + 2 \ C$$

to volatilize the zinc chloride formed and produces a dense smoke having nearly half the obscuring power of the smoke from the burning of white phosphorus.

10.11 **Ethylene Derivatives.** — Three chlorinated derivatives of value as nonflammable and noncorrosive solvents for fats, oils, and resins are made from the product of addition of two moles of chlorine to acetylene. Dechlorination with zinc dust gives **s-dichloroethylene**, and dehydrochlorination

$$CH{\equiv}CH \xrightarrow{\ Cl_2\ } CHCl_2CHCl_2 \xrightarrow{\ Zn\ } CHCl{=}CHCl$$

$$\downarrow Ca(OH)_2$$

$$CHCl{=}CCl_2 \xrightarrow{\ Cl_2\ } CHCl_2CCl_3 \xrightarrow{\ Ca(OH)_2\ } CCl_2{=}CCl_2$$

with lime gives **trichloroethylene.** Further addition of chlorine and dehydrohalogenation affords **perchloroethylene,** m.p. −22.4°, b.p. 121°. Perchloroethylene is manufactured in the U.S.A. on a scale of over 200 million lbs. per year for use in the dry cleaning industry. It is preferred to the cheaper petroleum solvents (*e.g.* Stoddard Solvent, average b.p. about 200°) because it is nonflammable and a better solvent and because recovery is more efficient.

10.12 **Polymethylene Dihalides.** — Halides containing two functional groups, $X{-}(CH_2)_n{-}X$, are useful in synthesis because of the opportunity for conducting simultaneous operations at the ends of the carbon chain. The dibromides of the series are obtainable in yields of 75–90% by the action of dry hydrogen bromide at 135° on the corresponding glycols, where these starting materials are available. Trimethylene glycol is available as a fermentation product, and tetramethylene and hexamethylene glycol can be produced satisfactorily from the corresponding dibasic acids (8.9); hence the derived bromides $Br(CH_2)_3Br$, $Br(CH_2)_4Br$, $Br(CH_2)_6Br$ are useful synthetic starting materials.

Pentamethylene dibromide can be produced efficiently by a process utilizing a fairly readily accessible intermediate (von Braun reaction):

$$\underset{\substack{\text{Benzoylpiperidine}}}{\begin{array}{c}\text{CH}_2\\\text{H}_2\text{C}\diagup \quad \diagdown\text{CH}_2\\| \qquad |\\\text{H}_2\text{C} \diagdown \quad \diagup \text{CH}_2\\\text{N}\\|\\\text{C}_6\text{H}_5\text{C}=\text{O}\end{array}} \xrightarrow[\substack{65\text{-}72\%}]{\text{PBr}_5} \underset{\substack{\text{Pentamethylene dibromide}}}{\text{BrCH}_2\text{CH}_2\text{CH}_2\text{CH}_2\text{CH}_2\text{Br}} + \text{C}_6\text{H}_5\text{CN} + \text{POBr}_3$$

Pentamethylene dibromide can be obtained also by an efficient four-step process starting with the abundantly available furfural (12.15).

One use of polymethylene dihalides in syntheses involves temporarily protecting one of the two functional groups by conversion into an ether group so that the other can be utilized selectively. The half-ether can be obtained by interaction of a sodium alkoxide with an excess of the halide. The monohalide can be used

$$\underset{\substack{\text{Sodium phenoxide}}}{\text{C}_6\text{H}_5\text{ONa}} + \text{BrCH}_2\text{CH}_2\text{CH}_2\text{Br} \xrightarrow[84\text{-}85\%]{} \underset{\substack{\gamma\text{-Phenoxypropyl bromide}}}{\text{C}_6\text{H}_5\text{OCH}_2\text{CH}_2\text{CH}_2\text{Br}}$$

in Grignard or other syntheses and the ether group subsequently cleaved with hydrogen bromide to the bromo derivative.

10.13   Free Radicals. — An authentic free radical was prepared for the first time by Gomberg[1] at the University of Michigan in 1900. Gomberg had synthesized tetraphenylmethane (m.p. 285°) and was interested to observe that the tetranitro derivative of this hydrocarbon, which has no hydrogen on the methane carbon atom, gave no color reaction with alcoholic potassium hydroxide and thereby contrasted with trinitrotriphenylmethane, $(p\text{-NO}_2\text{C}_6\text{H}_4)_3\text{CH}$. In order to determine whether the difference was general, Gomberg sought to synthesize the completely phenylated ethane, hexaphenylethane, by the following coupling reaction:

$$\underset{\substack{\text{Triphenylchloro-}\\\text{methane (m.p. }113°)}}{2\,(\text{C}_6\text{H}_5)_3\text{CCl}} + 2\,\text{Ag} \longrightarrow \underset{\substack{\text{Hexaphenylethane}}}{(\text{C}_6\text{H}_5)_3\text{C}\!-\!\text{C}(\text{C}_6\text{H}_5)_3} + 2\,\text{AgCl}$$

The product was a high-melting, sparingly soluble, white solid resembling tetraphenylmethane in physical properties and in its inert character. Analysis, however, showed that it was no hydrocarbon but an oxygen-containing compound $(\text{C}_{38}\text{H}_{30}\text{O}_2)$. The experiment was then repeated with exclusion of air by shaking a solution of triphenylchloromethane in benzene with finely divided silver or zinc in an atmosphere of carbon dioxide. A yellow solution resulted which, on evaporation in the absence of air, deposited colorless crystals of a hydrocarbon having the composition expected for hexaphenylethane but exhibiting remarkable reac-

---

[1] Moses Gomberg, 1866–1947; b. Elisabetgrad, Russia; Ph.D. Michigan (Prescott); Univ. Michigan; *J. Am. Chem. Soc.*, **69**, 2921 (1947)

tivity. Solutions in benzene or carbon disulfide absorbed oxygen with avidity, with separation of the white oxygen compound, and in the absence of oxygen they absorbed chlorine, bromine, and iodine. When the colorless hydrocarbon was first dissolved in a solvent, the solution was momentarily colorless, but within a few seconds became tinged with yellow, and the color soon deepened to a point of maximum intensity. The change was reversible, for by evaporation of the solution, the colorless hydrocarbon could be recovered. Gomberg interpreted the results as follows: "The experimental evidence . . . forces me to the conclusion that we have to deal here with a free radical triphenylmethyl $(C_6H_5)_3C$—. The action of zinc results, as it seems to me, in a mere abstraction of the halogen:

$$2\,(C_6H_5)_3C—Cl \;+\; Zn \;\longrightarrow\; 2\,(C_6H_5)_3C— \;+\; ZnCl_2$$

Now, as a result of the removal of the halogen atom from triphenylchloromethane, the fourth valence of the methane is bound either to take up the complicated group $(C_6H_5)_3C$— or remain as such, with carbon as trivalent. Apparently the latter is what happens."

Molecular weight determinations established that the colorless solid is hexaphenylethane and that in solution it undergoes dissociation to colored triphenylmethyl radicals to a point of equilibrium. The free radical combines with halo-

Hexaphenylethane   Triphenylmethyl
(colorless, m.p. 147° dec.)   (yellow)

gens to produce triphenylmethyl halides, and with molecular oxygen to form the colorless peroxide, $(C_6H_5)_3C—O:O—C(C_6H_5)_3$ m.p. 186°, with disturbance of the equilibrium and eventual dissociation of the whole of the hexaphenylethane. Many other hexaarylethanes and related compounds subsequently have been examined, and the degree of dissociation determined from the molecular weights observed at the boiling points and freezing points of various solvents. The point of equilibrium between the ethane and the radical at any temperature can be determined by measurement of either the molecular extinction coefficients of the colored solutions or of the paramagnetic susceptibilities of solutions containing the paramagnetic free radical (attracted by a magnet) and the diamagnetic ethane (not attracted). The extent of dissociation is dependent on the specific compound, concentration, solvent, and temperature. Values found for dissociation of hexaphenylethane in benzene at 20° are: 3.6% in a 4% solution, 9.6% in a 0.5% solution, 25.8% in a 0.055% solution. The dissociation constant for this substance is slightly less in acetone (1.7×10^{-4}) or in dioxane (2.5×10^{-4})

than in benzene (4.1×10^{-4}), but considerably greater in carbon disulfide (19.2×10^{-4}). An increase in temperature favors dissociation; for example, a 0.07% solution in benzene contains 18% of the free radical at 13° and 42% at 43°. Some of the more striking variations in the extent of dissociation with changes in the nature of the aryl groups are illustrated in the formulas, which include the percent of the radical present at equilibrium in benzene at 5° in approximately 0.08 molar solution; such a solution contains about 3% of triphenylmethyl. In general, the order of effectiveness of aryl groups in promoting

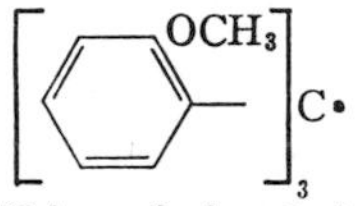

Tri-*o*-anisylmethyl
95–100% (orange)

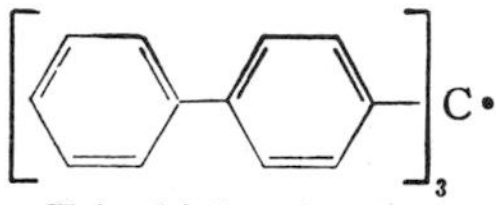

Tri-*p*-biphenylmethyl
74% (deep violet)

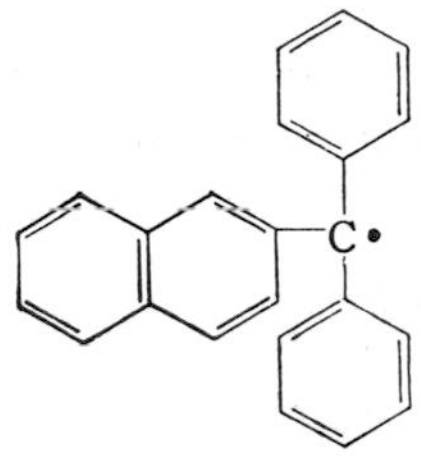

Diphenyl-β-naphthylmethyl
7–9% (wine red)

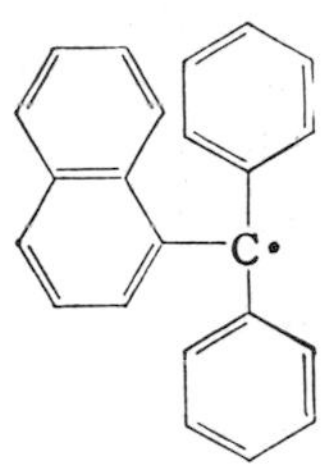

Diphenyl-α-naphthylmethyl
28–31% (deep red-brown)

dissociation is: α-naphthyl > *o*-anisyl > *p*-anisyl > *p*-biphenyl > β-naphthyl > *p*-alkylphenyl > phenyl > *p*-chlorophenyl.

An empirical correlation of the dissociation of hexaphenylethane with other phenomena, such as the susceptibility of triphenylmethane to oxidation, is that the bond connecting the two ethane carbon atoms is subject to the activating influence of all six unsaturated phenyl groups, and indeed thermochemical studies have shown that this bond is weaker than that in ethane by about 30 kcal. (H. E. Bent, 1936). Steric hindrance between the two clusters of benzene rings may contribute to weakening the linkage. However, the dissociation to radicals is determined less by weakening of the ethane linkage than by stabilization of the free radical through resonance. The triphenylmethyl radical contains an unpaired electron, and the paramagnetic property of the substance is due to the presence of an odd electron that is not compensated magnetically. Pauling

$$(C_6H_5)_3C:C(C_6H_5)_3 \rightleftharpoons 2(C_6H_5)_3C\cdot$$

(1933) and Hückel[1] (1933) developed by quantum-mechanical calculations a concept, stated qualitatively by Ingold (1929), that the odd electron is distributed between the methane carbon atom and all *ortho* and *para* positions in the three phenyl groups, as shown in the formulas for one of the rings. In all, there are

[1] Erich Hückel, b. 1896 Charlottenburg, Germany; Ph.D. Göttingen (Debye); Univ. Stuttgart, Marburg

ten structures that can contribute to the resonance state, and resonance results in marked stabilization of the radical.

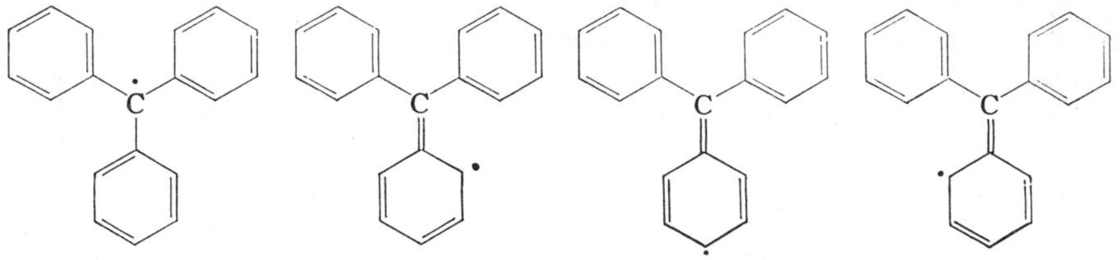

The triphenylmethyl group can form both positive and negative ions. Colorless solutions of triphenylcarbinol in alcohol or acetic acid become intensely colored on addition of mineral acids owing to formation of ionized halochromic salts:

$$(C_6H_5)_3COH + HX \longrightarrow [(C_6H_5)_3C]^+ + X^- + H_2O$$

On the other hand, addition of finely powdered sodium to a solution of the triphenylmethyl radical in ether—benzene or in liquid ammonia produces intensely red solutions of the ionic but nevertheless ether-soluble triphenylmethylsodium:

$$(C_6H_5)_3C + Na \longrightarrow [(C_6H_5)_3C]^- + Na^+$$

The relationship of the two ions to the radical is shown in the following electronic formulas:

$$\left[\begin{matrix} & C_6H_5 \\ C_6H_5 : & \ddot{\underset{\cdot\cdot}{C}} \\ & C_6H_5 \end{matrix}\right]^+ \qquad \begin{matrix} & C_6H_5 \\ C_6H_5 : & \ddot{\underset{\cdot\cdot}{C}}\cdot \\ & C_6H_5 \end{matrix} \qquad \left[\begin{matrix} & C_6H_5 \\ C_6H_5 : & \ddot{\underset{\cdot\cdot}{C}}: \\ & C_6H_5 \end{matrix}\right]^-$$

Triphenylmethyl carbonium ion — Triphenylmethyl radical — Triphenylmethyl carbanion

The three benzene rings of the triphenylmethyl radical do not lie in a plane but are out of plane by an angle of about 20° (G. Briegleb, 1943), and resonance stabilization is not so effective as would be expected for a fully planar structure. O. Neunhoeffer (1958) prepared the radical II (5,9-dioxa-9,14-dihydrocoeranthryl), which is considered to have a planar structure, and found, indeed, that it

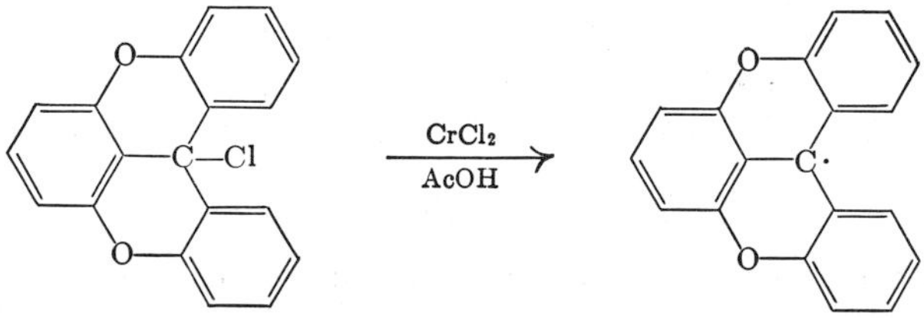

I II

has no tendency to dimerize. This stable radical is very reactive, and air must be excluded scrupulously during preparation by reduction of the chloride and collection of the red crystals (m.p. 161°). Resonance stabilization is attributable not only to the planar structure but to the opportunity for increased resonance involving oxonium structures.

Use of triphenylchloromethane (trityl chloride) for selective alkylation of primary alcohols (8.38) is based upon the high reactivity of this chloride associated with the tertiary structure and activation by three phenyl groups. Manifestations of reactivity in the corresponding alcohol are as follows. Triphenylcarbinol on brief heating in acetic acid with hydrobromic acid affords trityl bromide (m.p. 152°); with hydriodic acid, the product is triphenylmethane (m.p. 94°). Refluxed in methanol containing hydrobromic acid, triphenylcarbinol is converted into its methyl ether (m.p. 97°). When the solid carbinol is fused with malonic acid at about 150°, water is eliminated and the substituted malonic acid loses carbon

$$(C_6H_5)_3COH \ + \ CH_2(CO_2H)_2 \ \xrightarrow{-H_2O} \ \left[(C_6H_5)_3CCH(CO_2H)_2\right] \xrightarrow{-CO_2}$$

$$(C_6H_5)_3CCH_2CO_2H$$
Triphenylmethylacetic acid
(m.p. 176°)

dioxide and forms triphenylmethylacetic acid. The reduction of triphenylcarbinol to triphenylmethyl theoretically requires 0.5 mole of stannous chloride: $2\ (C_6H_5)_3COH \ + \ SnCl_2 \ + \ 2\ HCl \ \rightarrow \ 2\ (C_6H_5)_3C\cdot \ +$ $SnCl_4 \ + \ 2\ H_2O$, but for efficient reduction it is necessary to use a five-fold excess of reagent, probably in order to maintain a satisfactory reduction potential. Conducted in acetic acid on the steam bath, the reaction is complete in 1 hr. and affords not triphenylmethyl but the product of condensation of one radical into the *p*-position of another: *p*-benzhydryltetraphenylmethane (m.p. 230°, corr.). Although the structure of this sparingly soluble hydrocarbon of the formula $C_{38}H_{30}$ was established by Chichibabin,[1] the substance should not be confused with a hydrocarbon $C_{30}H_{28}$ first described by the Russian investigator and known as the Chichibabin hydrocarbon. The later substance, made by dechlorination of (1) has two quinonoid rings; solutions are deep red violet and

p-Benzhydryl-
tetraphenylmethane

the crystals are dark violet and have a metallic luster. The diradical form (3) was formerly regarded as nonexistent because magnetic susceptibility measurements failed to detect paramagnetism in the Chichibabin hydrocarbon. However, the spin of an unpaired electron produces an electron-spin resonance (ESR) which gives rise to a spectrum by means of which odd electrons are detectable at extremely low concentration, and ESR absorption of the hydrocarbon indicates that about 4% is present as the diradical (E. Müller, 1935; W. R. Vaughan,[2] 1957).

[1] Alexei E. Chichibabin, 1871–1945; b. Gouv. Poltowa, Russia; Ph.D. St. Petersburg; Moscow; Paris; *J. Chem. Soc.*, 760 (1946)

[2] Wyman R. Vaughan, b. 1916 Minneapolis, Minn.; Ph.D. Harvard (Fieser); Univ. Michigan

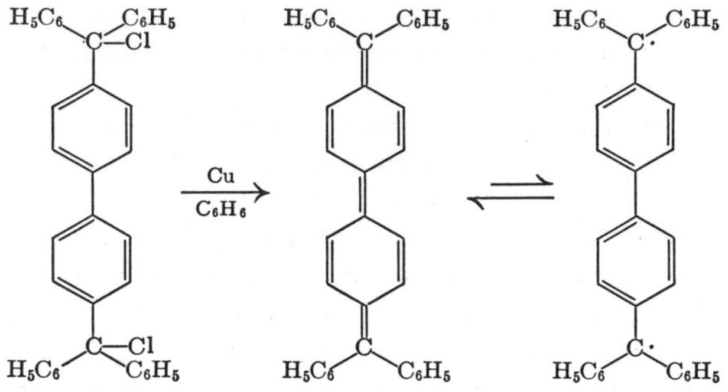

(1)   (2)   (3)

Chichibabin hydrocarbon

10.14   Fluoro Compounds. — Fluorinated hydrocarbons are not readily obtainable by interaction of an alcohol with concentrated or even anhydrous hydrogen fluoride, since the position of equilibrium favors hydrolysis, and the reaction cannot be promoted satisfactorily by use of sulfuric acid, which causes formation of alkenes from fluorides. One route to fluorides is addition of hydrogen fluoride to a double bond, (1) and (2), even though the reverse reaction is prone to occur. A second method consists in metathesis of an organic halide with an inorganic fluoride, usually mercuric fluoride or antimony trifluoride, (3) and (4).

1. $$CH_2{=}CH_2 + HF \xrightarrow[81\%]{90°} CH_3CH_2F$$

M.p. − 143°, b.p. − 38°

2. $$CH_3CH{=}CH_2 + HF \xrightarrow[61\%]{0°} CH_3CHFCH_3$$

M.p. − 133°, b.p. − 10°

3. $$2\,CH_3CH_2Br + HgF_2 \xrightarrow[(quant.)]{0°} 2\,CH_3CH_2F + HgBr_2$$

4. $$2\,CHBrF_2 + HgF_2 \xrightarrow[80\%]{50°} 2\,CHF_3 + HgBr_2$$

B.p. − 14.5°   M.p. − 163°, b.p. 82°

Although monofluorides are markedly unstable, polyfluorides in which more than one fluorine atom is situated on the same carbon atom are chemically inert; for example, as-difluoroethylene, $CH_2{=}CF_2$, is stable to air oxidation, in contrast with the corresponding dichloro compound, which under the same conditions is rapidly attacked. The stabilizing effect of fluorine atoms extends to other halogen atoms situated on the same or on an adjacent carbon atom, for dichlorodifluoromethane, CCl_2F_2, is completely impervious to hydrolysis and to molten sodium. One explanation of the inertness of polyfluorides (Brockway, 1937) is based upon the observation that the normal carbon–fluorine bond distance of 1.42 Å in monofluorides is decreased to 1.35 Å in polyfluorides and that the carbon–chlorine bond distance in mixed chloropolyfluorides is also shortened by 0.03–0.07 Å; no comparable shortening of bond length is observed with polychlorides.

Useful products are often obtainable by addition of a nucleophile (RO−, RNH−,

CN⁻) to a polyfluoroolefin. An example is the conversion of chlorotrifluoro-ethylene to 3-chloro-2,2,3-trifluoropropionic acid (D. C. England and L. R. Melby, du Pont Co., 1960). A hydrogenation bottle containing acetonitrile and

$$CFCl=CF_2 + NaCN + H_2O \rightarrow ClCHFCF_2CO_2Na + NH_3$$
$$H^+ \Big\downarrow$$
$$\longrightarrow ClCHFCF_2CO_2H$$

aqueous sodium cyanide is pressurized with chlorotrifluoroethylene (40 lbs.) and shaken with cooling to 75–80°; the yield of acid is 76–79%.

Dichlorodifluoromethane has ideal properties for use as a refrigerant liquid for domestic refrigerators and for air-conditioning units and has been employed widely for this purpose since its introduction (Midgley and Henne,[1] 1930). It is used also as a propellant for aerosol sprays. It is nonflammable, nontoxic, non-corrosive, nearly odorless, and stable up to 550°. The boiling point (−29.8°), indicative of the desired degree of volatility, is not far from that of the earlier, flammable refrigerant methyl chloride (b.p. −23.7°). Preparation is accomplished by replacement of two chlorine atoms of carbon tetrachloride by fluorine by the action of antimony trifluoride containing antimony pentahalide as catalyst. The industrial process utilizes liquid hydrogen fluoride as a cheap source of the fluorine substituents and involves continuous regeneration of a small initial batch of antimony trifluoride containing pentahalide:

$$3\,CCl_4 + 2\,SbF_3 \xrightarrow{(SbCl_5)} 3\,CCl_2F_2 + 2\,SbCl_3$$
$$6\,HF + 2\,SbCl_3 \longrightarrow 2\,SbF_3 + 6\,HCl$$

The dichlorodifluoro compound and hydrogen chloride (b.p. −85°, insoluble in liquid HF) liberated are taken off through a column that easily separates and returns to the mixture the partially fluorinated substance CCl_3F (b.p. 25°). The mixed halides $CClF_2CClF_2$, b.p. 3.8°, and $CHClF_2$, b.p. −40°, are used in household refrigerators and in deepfreeze units, respectively.

A second development of considerable technical importance was the discovery (du Pont, 1941) of the polymerization of tetrafluoroethylene to polytetrafluoro-ethylene, a plastic of remarkable thermal stability and resistance to chemicals.

$$nCF_2=CF_2 \rightarrow \cdots(CF_2-CF_2)n\cdots$$

Moissan,[2] discoverer of elemental fluorine (1886), found that fluorine reacts explosively with hydrocarbons and that finely divided carbon burns in the gas to form a small amount of liquid thought to be CF_4. Owing to difficulties encountered in the preparation of fluorine and in conducting reactions with the extraordinarily reactive reagent, further progress was so slow that it was only in 1926 that P. Lebeau and A. Damiens isolated pure CF_4 as one of the reaction products and showed that the combustion of carbon in fluorine gives a mixture of CF_4,

[1] Albert L. Henne, b. 1901 Brussels, Belg.; Ph.D. Brussels; Ohio State Univ.
[2] Henri Moissan, 1852–1907; Paris; Nobel Prize, 1906

C_2F_6, and probably C_3F_8.   In 1937 Joseph H. Simons[1] and L. P. Block discovered, through a fortunate accident, that a small amount of a mercury compound added to the carbon functions catalytically and makes it possible to conduct the reaction without explosion at a moderate temperature.   Separation of the reaction mixture afforded 54% of CF_4, b.p. $-128°$, 27% of other gaseous fluorocarbons in the range C_2F_6 to C_4F_{10}, and 18% of a fraction liquid at room temperature and containing, for example, cyclo-C_5F_{10} (b.p. 22.5°), cyclo-C_6F_{12}, and cyclo-C_7F_{14}.   Impressed with the stability and inertness of the new compounds, Simons thought that a liquid fluorocarbon might be resistant to the chemical attack by uranium hexafluoride and hence useful as sealant and coolant in direct contact with this material, and in 1940 he sent a 2-ml. sample, nearly the entire supply on hand, to H. C. Urey[2] and A. V. Grosse,[3] who were working at Columbia on the separation of isotopes by diffusion of uranium hexafluoride.   The trial was successful and the discovery created a demand for large quantities of fluorocarbons and set in motion intensive studies in the United States and Great Britain.   Because of the secrecy at the time surrounding all phases of atomic energy research, fluorocarbons acquired the code name "Joe's stuff," from the given name of J. H. Simons.

The first attempt to fluorinate a simple hydrocarbon was made in 1905 by Moissan and Chavanne, who tried to bring about a reaction of solid methane with liquid fluorine at $-187°$; in spite of the low temperature and the skill of the investigators, the result was a disastrous explosion.   K. Fredenhagen and G. Cadenbach (1934) found that introduction of fluorine to a hydrocarbon vapor through the meshes of a roll of copper wire screen moderates the reaction considerably, and wartime researches of Bigelow,[4] Cady,[5] Grosse and others led to development of practical vapor phase processes.   Coating the copper catalyst with fluorides of silver, gold, or cobalt enhances the activity (temperature: 200°). In one process hydrocarbon vapor and fluorine, each diluted with nitrogen, are introduced into opposite sides of a reactor packed with copper turnings coated with silver difluoride (200–350°) and allowed to mix gradually.   A slight excess of fluorine is used and the products, collected in a series of cold traps, are fluorocarbons and hydrogen fluoride.   A method developed at Johns Hopkins by Fowler[6] and co-workers in which hydrocarbons are fluorinated to saturated fluorocarbons by cobalt trifluoride was used on a small industrial scale during the war to produce fluorocarbon lubricants which, however, have been disappointing.   In 1941 Simons' group at Pennsylvania State University developed a process for

[1] Joseph H. Simons, b. 1897, Chicago; Ph.D. California; Puerto Rico; Northwestern; Penn. State Coll.; Univ. Florida

[2] Harold C. Urey, b. 1893 Walkertown, Ind.; Ph.D. California; Columbia Univ.; Univ. Chicago, California, LaJolla; Nobel Prize, 1934

[3] Aristid V. Grosse, b. 1905 Riga, Russia; D. Ing. Tech. Hochsch. Berlin; Res. Inst., Temple Univ.

[4] Lucius A. Bigelow, b. 1892 Boston; Ph.D. Yale; Brown; Duke Univ.

[5] George H. Cady, b. 1906 Lawrence, Kans.; Ph.D. Calif., Berkeley; Washington State Univ.

[6] Robert Dudley Fowler, b. 1905 San Francisco, Calif.; Ph.D. Michigan; Johns Hopkins Univ.; Los Alamos Sci. Lab.

producing fluorocarbons by passing an electric current through a solution of an organic compound in liquid hydrogen fluoride (a powerful solvent). A copper or iron cell is operated at a potential (5–6 v.) below that at which fluorine is generated; separation of anode and cathode compartments is not necessary, since fluorocarbons do not react with the hydrogen produced simultaneously. A variety of compounds (alcohols, carboxylic acids, ethers, amines) can be used as well as hydrocarbons.

Significant industrial uses for the still expensive fluorocarbons are developing, and the compounds have attracted considerable attention because of their unusual properties. That fluorocarbons are much more volatile than hydrocarbons of the same molecular weight is illustrated by the following comparison: CF_4, mol. wt. 88, b.p. $-128°$; $n\text{-}C_6H_{14}$, mol. wt. 86, b.p. 69°. Saturated fluorocarbons have boiling points close to those of the corresponding alkanes, as shown by the following comparison: $n\text{-}C_4F_{10}$, b.p. $-1.7°$; $n\text{-}C_4H_{10}$, b.p. $-0.5°$. Liquid fluorocarbons are poor solvents for most organic compounds, but they dissolve other substances of similarly low internal pressures, for example, SF_6 and WF_6. Fluorocarbons are much more stable and inert than hydrocarbons; in many ways they resemble the rare gases.

PROBLEMS

1. Suggest methods suitable for the preparation of each of the following halides from the corresponding alcohol:
   (a) $n\text{-}C_{18}H_{37}Cl$
   (b) $CH_3CH_2CCl(CH_3)_2$
   (c) $CH_3CH_2CH_2CHBrCH_3$
   (d) $n\text{-}C_6H_{13}I$
2. Arrange the following compounds in the expected order of decreasing activity:
   (a) $CH_3CHBrCH_2CH_2CH_3$
   (b) $(CH_3)_2CHCH_2CH_2Br$
   (c) $(CH_3)_2C\!=\!CBrCH_2CH_3$
   (d) $(CH_3)_2C\!=\!CHCH_2Br$
3. Which of the following substances would be expected to give a positive iodoform test?
   (a) $CH_3CH_2CH_2CH(CH_3)CH_2OH$
   (b) $CH_3CH_2CH_2CHOHCH_3$
   (c) $CH_3CH(CH_3)CHOHCH_2CH_3$
   (d) CH_2OHCH_2OH
   (e) $CH_3COCH_2CH_2CH_2COOH$
   (f) CH_3COOH
   (g) $C_6H_5CHOHCH_3$
   (h) $(CH_3)_3COH$
4. Starting with allyl bromide and any other components desired, suggest syntheses for:
   (a) 4-Methylpentene-1
   (b) 1,2,3-Tribromopropane
   (c) 1,2-Dibromopropane
   (d) 2,3-Dibromopropene-1
5. Glycerol on treatment with concd. sulfuric acid yields the substance C_3H_4O. Predict the structure of the product.
6. Write electronic formulas for allyl bromide and its resonance-hybrid ion. Calculate the formal charges. Does each carbon atom have an octet of electrons?
7. (a) Test the electronic formulas for vinyl bromide and for the structure contributing to resonance by calculation of formal charges. (b) How could you deduce, without such calculation, that the terminal carbon atom carries a negative charge? (c) Why does not the structure $\overset{+}{C}H_2\text{—}CH\!=\!Br^-$ contribute to the resonance?
8. A substance is known isomeric with the Chichibabin hydrocarbon but having the two diphenylmethyl groups *meta* to the diphenyl linkage, rather than *para*. In what form would you expect it to exist?

Note to page 340.—In a modification of the Hunsdiecker reaction, stearic acid is treated in carbon tetrachloride with bromine and red mercuric oxide; 93% yield of RBr (S. J. Cristol, 1961).

Chapter 11

CARBOXYLIC ACIDS

11.1 **Acidic Character.** — In Chapter 2 the acidic character of the carboxylic acids was attributed to activation by a 3,4-double bond of the hydroxylic hydrogen at position 1 and separation of this hydrogen as a proton under

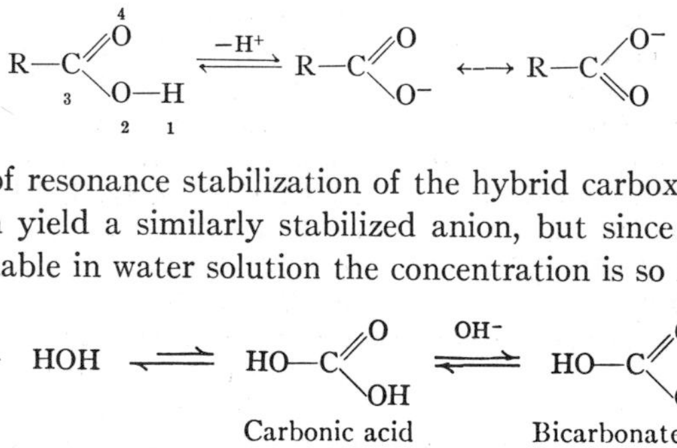

$$
R-C\overset{\overset{4}{\nearrow}O}{\underset{\underset{2}{\searrow}O-H}{}} \; \underset{}{\overset{-H^+}{\rightleftharpoons}} \; R-C\overset{\nearrow O}{\underset{\searrow O^-}{}} \; \longleftrightarrow \; R-C\overset{\nearrow O^-}{\underset{\searrow O}{}}
$$

the driving force of resonance stabilization of the hybrid carboxylate ion formed. Carbonic acid can yield a similarly stabilized anion, but since this acid, unlike acetic acid, is unstable in water solution the concentration is so low that the sub-

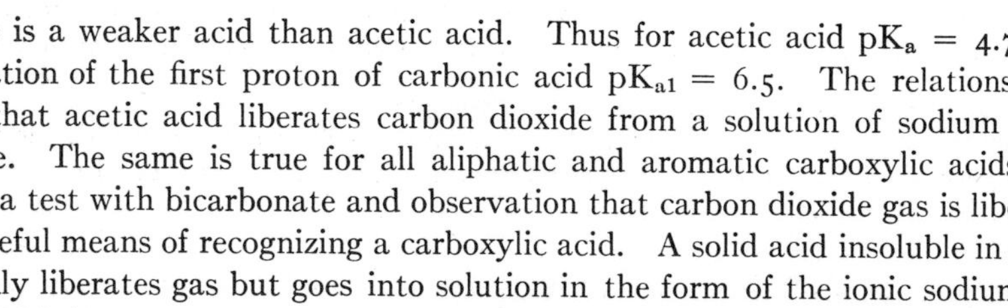

$$
O{=}C{=}O \; + \; HOH \; \rightleftharpoons \; HO-C\overset{\nearrow O}{\underset{\searrow OH}{}} \; \overset{OH^-}{\rightleftharpoons} \; HO-C\overset{\nearrow O}{\underset{\searrow O^-}{}} \; \longleftrightarrow
$$

$$
\text{Carbonic acid} \qquad\qquad \text{Bicarbonate ion}
$$

$$
HO-C\overset{\nearrow O^-}{\underset{\searrow O}{}} \; + \; H_2O
$$

stance is a weaker acid than acetic acid. Thus for acetic acid $pK_a = 4.76$; for separation of the first proton of carbonic acid $pK_{a1} = 6.5$. The relationship is such that acetic acid liberates carbon dioxide from a solution of sodium bicarbonate. The same is true for all aliphatic and aromatic carboxylic acids, and hence a test with bicarbonate and observation that carbon dioxide gas is liberated is a useful means of recognizing a carboxylic acid. A solid acid insoluble in water not only liberates gas but goes into solution in the form of the ionic sodium salt, $RCOO^-Na^+$.

358

Nitrous, nitric, sulfurous, and sulfuric acids all have a hydroxylic hydrogen atom activated by a 3,4-double bond, and hence are analogous to acetic acid. The

$$\overset{1\ 2}{HO}\!-\!\overset{3}{N}\!=\!\overset{4}{O} \;\rightleftharpoons\; H^+ + {}^-O\!-\!N\!=\!O \;\longleftrightarrow\; O\!=\!N\!-\!O^-$$

Nitrous acid

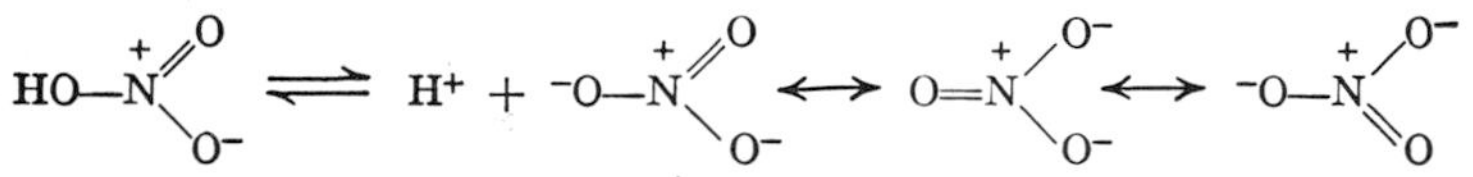

Nitric acid

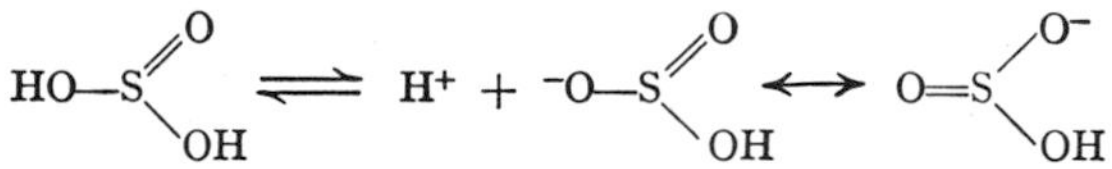

Sulfurous acid

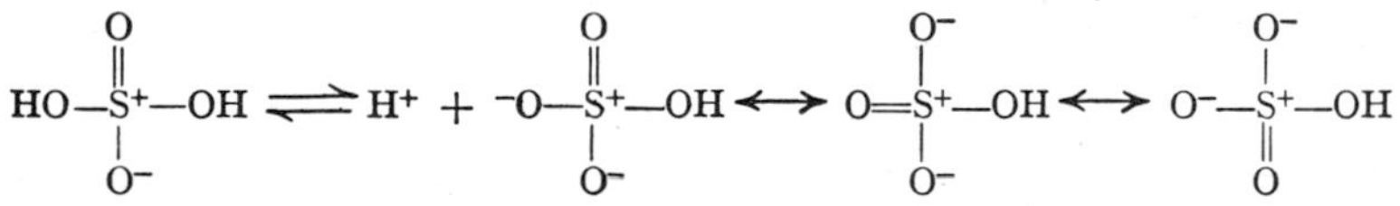

Sulfuric acid

higher-valence acids (nitric, sulfuric) are more unsaturated than the lower-valence analogs and they are more strongly acidic. Phenol has a hydroxylic hydrogen atom activated by the unsaturated phenyl group. This type of unsaturation does not produce as much activation as the potent carbonyl group of the carboxylic acids and hence phenol is only weakly acidic, $pK_a = 10.0$. Thus

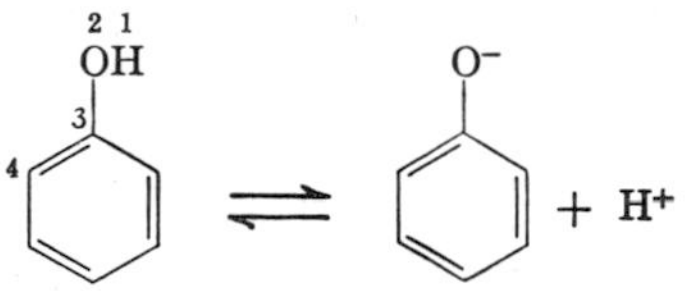

Phenol (m. p. 43°)   Phenoxide ion
$pK_a = 10.0$

a phenol that is insoluble in water dissolves in sodium hydroxide solution as does a carboxylic acid, but its phenolic character can be recognized from the fact that it does not dissolve in sodium bicarbonate solution. Since phenol is a weaker acid than carbonic acid, addition of carbon dioxide (*e.g.* as dry ice) to an aqueous solution of sodium phenoxide causes precipitation of free phenol.

11.2   Properties. — The acids of Table 11.1 are listed by their common names. In the Geneva system the carbon of the carboxyl group is taken as the first carbon of the longest carbon chain in the molecule. Thus *n*-heptylic acid is heptanoic acid, pelargonic acid (C$_9$) is nonanoic acid. The acid CH_2=$CH(CH_2)_8CO_2H$ is usually called Δ^{10}-undecylenic acid, but the Geneva name is Δ^{10}-undecylenoic acid.

Boiling points are even higher than those of alcohols of comparable molecular weight, as is evident from the following comparison:

$CH_3CH_2CH_2CH_2CO_2H$	Mol. wt. 102.13	B.p. 187°
$CH_3CH_2CH_2CH_2CH_2CH_2OH$	Mol. wt. 102.17	B.p. 155.8°

TABLE 11.1. CARBOXYLIC ACIDS

ACID	FORMULA	M.P., °C.	B.P., °C.	SP. GR.	pK$_a$$^{25°}$
Formic	HCOOH	8.4	100.5	1.220	3.77
Acetic	CH$_3$COOH	16.6	118	1.049	4.76
Propionic	CH$_3$CH$_2$COOH	− 22	141	0.992	4.88
n-Butyric	CH$_3$CH$_2$CH$_2$COOH	− 4.7	162.5	.959	4.82
Isobutyric	(CH$_3$)$_2$CHCOOH	− 47	154.4	.949	4.85
n-Valeric	CH$_3$(CH$_2$)$_3$COOH	− 34.5	187	.939	4.81
Trimethylacetic	(CH$_3$)$_3$CCOOH	35.5	163.8	.905	5.02
Caproic	CH$_3$(CH$_2$)$_4$COOH	− 1.5	205	.929	4.85
n-Heptylic	CH$_3$(CH$_2$)$_5$COOH	− 11	223.5	.922	4.89
Caprylic	CH$_3$(CH$_2$)$_6$COOH	16	237	.910	4.85
Pelargonic	CH$_3$(CH$_2$)$_7$COOH	12.5	254	.907	4.96
Fluoroacetic	CH$_2$FCOOH	33	165	.....	2.66
Chloroacetic	CH$_2$ClCOOH	63	189.5	1.37	2.81
Bromoacetic	CH$_2$BrCOOH	50	208	1.934	2.87
Iodoacetic	CH$_2$ICOOH	82	......	.....	3.13
Dichloroacetic	CHCl$_2$COOH	10	193.5	1.563	1.29
Trichloroacetic	CCl$_3$COOH	58	196	1.617	0.08*
α-Chloropropionic	CH$_3$CHClCOOH	......	186	1.306	2.8
β-Chloropropionic	CH$_2$ClCH$_2$COOH	39	204	.....	4.1
Glycolic	HOCH$_2$COOH	79	......	.....	3.83
Lactic	CH$_3$CHOHCOOH	18	122$^{15mm.}$	1.249	3.87
Methoxyacetic	CH$_3$OCH$_2$COOH	.....	204	1.777	3.48
Thioglycolic	HSCH$_2$COOH	− 16.5	123$^{29mm.}$	1.325	3.55
Cyanoacetic	N≡CCH$_2$COOH	66	dec.	.....	2.44
Glyoxylic	O=CHCOOH	......	......	.....	3.3
Malonic	HOOCCH$_2$COOH	135	......	1.631	2.80
Acrylic	CH$_2$=CHCOOH	13	141	.....	4.26
Vinylacetic	CH$_2$=CHCH$_2$COOH	− 39	163	1.013	4.35
Phenylacetic	C$_6$H$_5$CH$_2$COOH	78	265	.....	4.31

* A 0.03 M solution is 89.5% ionized; comparable solutions of acetic acid and the mono- and dichloro derivatives are ionized to the extent of 2.4%, 22.5%, and 70%.

The difference is attributable to more effective hydrogen bonding. Cryoscopic determinations in hydrocarbon solvents and X-ray crystallographic measurements both indicate that carboxylic acids exist largely in a dimeric form, formulated as shown. The boiling point of formic acid (100.5°) is about that characteristic of unassociated substances of molecular weight comparable to that of formic acid dimer (92).

Solubility relationships of carboxylic acids conform to the usual rule for hydroxylic compounds. Formic, acetic, propionic, and n-butyric acid are miscible with water in all proportions, the next few members of the series are partially soluble, and the C$_9$-acids and higher homologs are practically insoluble in water.

Examination of the melting points of the homologous straight-chain acids reveals an alternation; each even-carbon acid melts higher than its two immediate odd-carbon neighbors.

The lower acids are sufficiently soluble in water to produce an appreciable concentration of hydrogen ion and give a sour taste. The three lower acids have sharp, acrid odors; acids from butyric through caprylic have rank, disagreeable odors. Butter (L. *butyrum*) is a mixture of glycerides containing fourteen fatty acids, including butyric (3%), caproic (1.4%), and caprylic (1.5%) acids, and the rancidity of butter is due to liberation of these volatile acids. Caproic acid has been isolated from butter made from goats' milk (L. *caper*, goat), from coconut oil, and from Limberger cheese. The higher acids are nonvolatile and odorless.

11.3   **Acidic Strength.** — The pK_a values of a number of carboxylic acids listed in Table 11.1 show that in the series of normal acids from acetic (C_2) to pelargonic (C_9) the values all fall in the range pK_a 4.8–5, and that the effect of branching the chain is minor. Formic acid, the first member of the series, is exceptional and is distinctly more strongly acidic (pK_a 3.77) than any of the homologs (RCOOH) having an alkyl group rather than hydrogen attached to the carboxyl group. Values for the second and third series of acids listed in the table show that substitution of halogen, hydroxyl, and other groups often produces a profound increase in acidic strength.

A rational explanation of the effect of substituents on the ionization of acids was advanced by G. N. Lewis (1923). In a symmetrical molecule such as CH_3:CH_3 or Cl:Cl, the pair of electrons constituting the covalent bond is shared equally by the two atomic centers. In an unsymmetrical molecule, however, one center may have a greater attraction for electrons than the other, and hence the electron pair will be displaced toward that center. Such a displacement or inductive effect can be represented by an arrow pointing in the direction of the drift of electrons, B→A. If, in an acid A—COOH, the group A attracts electrons, the inductive displacement of the electron pair between C and A in the direction of A will cause secondary displacements of electrons of the C:O and O:H bonds and hence facilitate separation of the hydroxylic hydrogen as a proton:

$$A{\leftarrow}\overset{\displaystyle O}{\overset{\|}{C}}{:}\overset{..}{\underset{..}{O}}{:}H \rightleftharpoons A{-}\overset{\displaystyle O}{\overset{\|}{C}}{:}\overset{..}{\underset{..}{O}}{:}^- + H^+$$

A group B that repels electrons will produce a displacement in the opposite direction and decrease the extent of ionization:

$$B{\rightarrow}\overset{\displaystyle O}{\overset{\|}{C}}{:}\overset{..}{\underset{..}{O}}{:}H \rightleftharpoons B{-}\overset{\displaystyle O}{\overset{\|}{C}}{:}\overset{..}{\underset{..}{O}}{:}^- + H^+$$

The fact that acetic acid is a weaker acid than formic acid means that the methyl group has less attraction for electrons than a hydrogen atom, or is relatively electron-repelling. The higher normal homologs are so close to acetic acid in pK_a values that any difference in electron release between methyl, ethyl, and higher *n*-alkyl groups must be so slight as to be obscured in the transmissal of the inductive effect through two covalent links.

Substitution of one of the α-hydrogen atoms of acetic acid by chlorine greatly increases the acidic strength: $CH_2ClCOOH$, pK_a 2.81. Chlorine, therefore, is strongly electron-attracting and produces displacements of the type Cl←C(=O)← O←H. Bromine is less effective than chlorine, and iodine is less effective than bromine; the order of electron attraction, as measured by the inductive effect, corresponds with the order of decreasing electronegativity. That the inductive effect of a substituent decreases rapidly with increasing distance from the hydroxylic hydrogen is shown by comparison of α- and β-chloropropionic acid. The α-chloro acid is much more acidic than the parent acid, whereas the β-chloro isomer is only a little more acidic. Substitution in acetic acid of one, two, and

$$CH_3CH_2COOH \qquad\qquad \underset{\underset{Cl}{|}}{CH_3CHCOOH} \qquad\qquad \underset{\underset{Cl}{|}}{CH_2CH_2COOH}$$

Propionic acid α-Chloropropionic acid β-Chloropropionic acid
pK$_a$ 4.88   pK$_a$ 2.8   pK$_a$ 4.1

three α-chlorine atoms produces progressive shifts to greater acidic strength, and trichloroacetic acid almost reaches the acidic strength of mineral acids.

The pK$_a$ values of the acids listed in the third series of Table 11.1 indicate that the following groups, like halogen, are electron-attracting: hydroxyl, methoxyl, sulfhydryl (—SH), cyano (—C≡N), aldehydo (—CH═O), carboxyl, vinyl (—CH═CH$_2$), phenyl (—C$_6$H$_5$); the last five groups are unsaturated. The order of inductive effect of substituent groups, deduced partly from the effect on the strength of acids and bases, is as follows:

Cl > Br > I > OCH$_3$ > OH > C$_6$H$_5$ > CH═CH$_2$ > H < CH$_3$ < CH$_2$CH$_3$ < CH(CH$_3$)$_2$ < C(CH$_3$)$_3$

————————————————————→   ←————————————————————

Decreasing electron attraction   Decreasing electron release
(+ I groups)   (− I groups)

The pK$_a$ values of propionic, acrylic, and benzoic acid show that the inductive effects of the vinyl and phenyl groups are about the same. Striking inductive

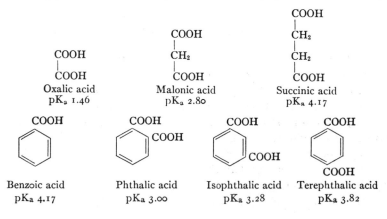

CH$_3$CH$_2$COOH   CH$_2$═CHCOOH
Propionic acid   Acrylic acid   COOH
pK$_a$ 4.88   pK$_a$ 4.26   Benzoic acid
                                               pK$_a$ 4.17

effects are observable in both aliphatic and aromatic dibasic acids. The carboxyl group is strongly electron-attracting, and one carboxyl joined to another (oxalic)

COOH   COOH   COOH
| | CH$_2$
COOH   CH$_2$ |
Oxalic acid | CH$_2$
pK$_a$ 1.46   COOH |
                Malonic acid   COOH
                pK$_a$ 2.80   Succinic acid
                                       pK$_a$ 4.17

Benzoic acid   Phthalic acid   Isophthalic acid   Terephthalic acid
pK$_a$ 4.17   pK$_a$ 3.00   pK$_a$ 3.28   pK$_a$ 3.82

greatly increases the acidic strength. The effect is still strong if the two carboxyls are separated by one methylene group (malonic), but nearly disappears if
there are two intervening carbon atoms. The effect of one carboxyl on another is
transmitted more efficiently along carbon atoms of the resonant benzene ring.
The case of maleic and fumaric acids is interesting. The carboxyl groups are closer

$$H-C-CO_2H$$
$$\parallel$$
$$H-C-CO_2H$$
pK_{a1} 1.9, pK_{a2} 6.5

$$H-C-CO_2H$$
$$\parallel$$
$$HO_2C-C-H$$
pK_{a1} 3.0, pK_{a2} 4.5

together in the *cis* than in the *trans* acid, and maleic acid is the stronger acid.
However, once the *cis* acid has lost a first proton, the negative charge close to the
second ionizable group opposes separation of the second proton. Thus the *trans*
acid has the lower pK_{a2} value, and the spread between pK_{a1} and pK_{a2} is less than
in the *cis* acid.

11.4   **Occurrence and Special Sources.** — **Formic acid,** a vesicatory liquid of
pungent odor, was so named because it is a constituent of certain ants
(L. *formica*, ant). It occurs also in several plants, including the nettle, and the
irritating effect resulting from contact with the plant is due in part to injection
of the acid under the skin. On macerating ants or nettles with water and distilling, a dilute aqueous solution of formic acid passes into the distillate. The
method of manufacture involves combination of carbon monoxide with pulverized

$$NaOH + CO \xrightarrow[\text{100 lbs./sq. in.}]{120-150°} H-C\underset{ONa}{\overset{O}{\diagup}}$$

Sodium formate

sodium hydroxide at moderate temperatures and pressures; the resulting sodium
formate when treated with sulfuric acid yields free formic acid.

Formic acid combines the structural features of a carboxylic acid and an
aldehyde and hence has reducing properties. It reduces ammoniacal silver hydroxide to metallic silver, and triphenylcarbinol to triphenylmethane. Like
formaldehyde, it has strong bactericidal activity and is used for disinfection of
wine casks. A technical water-containing grade is used in the textile and rubber
industries as a cheap acidifying agent in place of acetic or sulfuric acid. Acid
of high concentration has a pungent odor and is dangerously caustic to the skin.
Heated to about 160° in a closed system, formic acid is decomposed to carbon
dioxide and hydrogen; the reaction can be brought about at room temperature
under the influence of palladium catalyst.

Since the boiling point (100.5°) is close to that of water, a concentration beyond
about 75% cannot be achieved by distillation. Addition of concentrated sulfuric
acid to dry sodium formate converts part of the anhydrous acid liberated into
carbon monoxide (see decarbonylation, 11.9). The technical method of producing 85-90% formic acid with minimum loss by decomposition consists in
adding concentrated sulfuric acid to a slurry of powdered sodium formate in a
sufficient quantity of preformed 85-90% acid to moderate the reaction and promote rapid conversion of all the sulfuric acid into sodium sulfate. Anhydrous acid

can be prepared in the laboratory by the action of dry hydrogen sulfide on lead formate at 100°.

Acetic acid is the sour principle of vinegar resulting from air oxidation of ethanol present in wine or hard cider under the influence of specific bacteria (*e.g.*, in mother of vinegar), which provide enzymes that promote oxidation. If not deliberately added, microorganisms from the atmosphere find access to exposed solutions. The fortified wines port and sherry do not turn sour on standing in opened bottles because the delicate enzyme is inactivated by ethanol in any but very dilute solutions. Dilute solutions of pure ethanol in water fail to undergo microbiological oxidation because the microorganism requires for normal growth nitrogenous substances and mineral salts such as are present in beers and wines. It has never been practicable to produce concentrated or pure acetic acid from crude vinegars. Formerly the chief source was pyroligneous acid, the dilute aqueous solution of methanol and acetic acid resulting from destructive distillation of woods, for this yielded the two products methanol and calcium acetate, and distillation of the dry salt with sulfuric acid afforded substantially pure acetic acid. Pure acetic acid, m.p. 16.6°, is called glacial because it freezes at temperatures frequently encountered in the laboratory, and the melting point is depressed to such an extent by small amounts of water that samples observed to remain liquid on cooling are readily recognized as impure. Modern processes of manufacture involve air oxidation of ethanol over a metal catalyst and hydration of acetylene and oxidation of the resulting acetaldehyde.

PREPARATION

11.5   **Oxidation Reactions.** — Acids can be obtained by oxidation of primary alcohols or aldehydes. Thus *n*-heptaldehyde, obtainable from castor oil, provides a source of *n*-heptylic acid, and β-chloropropionic acid can be prepared by a synthesis utilizing oxidation of a primary alcohol:

1. $n\text{-}C_6H_{13}CHO \xrightarrow[\text{76-78\%}]{\text{KMnO}_4,\ \text{H}_2\text{SO}_4\ (20°)} n\text{-}C_6H_{13}COOH$
       n-Heptaldehyde   *n*-Heptylic acid

2. $HOCH_2CH_2CH_2OH \xrightarrow[\text{50-60\%}]{\text{dry HCl}} ClCH_2CH_2CH_2OH \xrightarrow[\text{78-79\%}]{\text{HNO}_3\ (25-30°)} ClCH_2CH_2COOH$
       Trimethylene glycol   Trimethylene β-Chloropropionic
                                               chlorohydrin   acid

Oxidation of ethylenic compounds having the grouping RCH= also affords carboxylic acids, and the method has applications to unsaturated substances derived from fats. Acids are also obtainable by hypohalite oxidation of methyl ketones or of alcohols of the type RCHOHCH$_3$.

Although acids higher than acetic usually are obtainable in reasonably good yield by chromic acid oxidation of olefinic materials, they are not fully resistant to the oxidizing agent; thus stearic acid can be oxidized to a mixture of lower acids. Acetic acid, however, is completely unattacked and is frequently used as solvent for chromic acid oxidation of alcohols and alkenes. Furthermore acetic acid is almost invariably produced on drastic oxidative degradation of both saturated and unsaturated compounds containing methyl groups attached to carbon, and the reaction is used in the **Kuhn-Roth determination** of the number of C-methyl groups present (1933). Oxidation is accomplished by chromic acid in sulfuric acid solution, excess reagent is reduced with hydrazine, the mixture is neutralized with alkali, phosphoric acid is added, and the acetic acid is distilled and determined by titration with standard alkali. Natural products containing the grouping —$CH_2C(CH_3)$=$CHCH_2$— give one equivalent of acetic acid for every such unit present. Kuhn-Roth analysis of $CH_3(CH_2)_{16}CO_2H$ indicates one methyl group (terminal), whereas two C-methyl groups are found for $CH_3(CH_2)_7CH(CH_3)$-$(CH_2)_8CO_2H$. A *gem*-dimethyl group, —$C(CH_3)_2$—, gives rise to but one equivalent of acetic acid.

11.6   Grignard and Nitrile Syntheses. — Replacement of the halogen atom of an alkyl halide by a carboxyl group can be accomplished by two methods. One is addition of a Grignard reagent to the carbonyl group of carbon dioxide and hydrolysis of the magnesiohalide derivative:

$$(CH_3)_3CCl \xrightarrow{\text{Mg, ether}} (CH_3)_3\text{\text{C}MgCl} + C\!\!\begin{array}{c}O\\O\end{array} \longrightarrow$$

$$(CH_3)_3CC\!\!\begin{array}{c}O\\OMgCl\end{array} \xrightarrow[\text{69-70\% overall}]{H_2O} \underset{\text{Trimethylacetic acid}}{(CH_3)_3CCOOH}$$

The carbonation of an alkylmagnesium halide can be accomplished by bubbling carbon dioxide into a solution of the Grignard reagent or by pouring the solution on dry ice.

The second synthesis consists in preparation and hydrolysis of a substance of the type $RC\equiv N$, known both as an alkyl cyanide and as a nitrile. This is obtained by interaction of an alkyl halide with sodium or potassium cyanide in aqueous-alcoholic solution, and complete hydrolysis is accomplished under catalysis with either an acid or a base:

$$RX + KCN \longrightarrow \underset{\substack{\text{Alkyl cyanide}\\\text{(nitrile)}}}{RC\equiv N} + KX$$

$$RC\equiv N + 2H_2O \xrightarrow{H^+ \text{ or } OH^-} RCOOH + NH_3$$

If hydrochloric acid is employed for hydrolysis, the ammonia is bound as ammonium chloride, whereas on alkaline hydrolysis ammonia is liberated and the carboxylic acid is obtained by acidification of the reaction mixture containing the alkali salt. Typical applications to synthesis are:

1. $Br(CH_2)_3Br \xrightarrow[\text{77-86\%}]{2NaCN} NC(CH_2)_3CN \xrightarrow[\text{83-85\%}]{HCl} \underset{\text{Glutaric acid}}{HOOC(CH_2)_3COOH}$

2. $\underset{\substack{\text{Ethylene}\\\text{chlorohydrin}}}{HOCH_2CH_2Cl} \xrightarrow[\text{79-80\%}]{NaCN} \underset{\text{Ethylene cyanohydrin}}{HOCH_2CH_2CN} \xrightarrow[\text{75-80\%}]{NaOH} \underset{\beta\text{-Hydroxypropionic acid}}{HOCH_2CH_2COOH}$

The intermediate alkyl cyanides are called nitriles when it is desired to emphasize the structural relation to the acids which they yield on hydrolysis; thus methyl cyanide, CH_3CN, is the nitrile of acetic acid, or acetonitrile; ethyl cyanide, CH_3CH_2CN, is propionitrile.

Cyanides are stable substances boiling at temperatures some 60–80° higher than the chlorides from which they can be prepared, for example capronitrile, or n-amyl cyanide (n-$C_5H_{11}CN$): b.p. 162–163°, sp. gr. 0.809, mol. wt. 97.16. The triple bond between carbon and nitrogen can enter into various additions. Hydrolysis can be conducted in two steps, the first of which affords an amide. Nu-

$$R—C≡N \xrightarrow{OH^-} \left[\begin{array}{c} R—C=N^- \\ | \\ OH \end{array} \xrightarrow{H^+} \begin{array}{c} R—C=NH \\ | \\ OH^- \end{array} \right] \longrightarrow \begin{array}{c} R—C—NH_2 \\ || \\ O \end{array}$$

Amide

cleophilic attack of the triple bond and rearrangement of an activated hydrogen atom of the intermediate find analogy in the hydration of acetylene. Amides can be prepared as products of mild hydrolysis and can be hydrolyzed to acids under more drastic conditions.

Of the two methods available for conversion of alkyl halides into acids, the Grignard synthesis is the more generally applicable. The alternate cyanide procedure usually gives good results as applied to primary halides, but the reagent is so strongly basic that with secondary and tertiary halides some alkene formation is inevitable. Thus t-butyl bromide is converted by sodium cyanide largely into isobutylene.

The Grignard reaction is also applicable to the synthesis of an acid in the form of the ethyl ester, for example, by the reaction of α-naphthylmagnesium bromide with diethyl carbonate. The reaction of α-bromonaphthalene with magnesium

$$\alpha\text{-}C_{10}H_7MgBr + O=C(OC_2H_5)_2 \xrightarrow[68\text{-}73\%]{} \alpha\text{-}C_{10}H_7\overset{\overset{O}{||}}{C}OC_2H_5 + C_2H_5OMgBr$$

is conducted in ether, and benzene is added to the warm solution to dissolve the deposit of oily organometallic derivative before it solidifies; the solution is then added gradually from a separatory funnel to a stirred solution of diethyl carbonate in ether.

PROPERTIES AND REACTIONS

Accounts have been given of the Kolbe electrolysis of acid salts (4.4) and of decarboxylation (4.9, 6.4).

11.7   **Metal Salts.** — The series of acids includes water-soluble liquids (CH_3CO_2H, $C_2H_5CO_2H$), water-insoluble liquids (n-$C_5H_{11}CO_2H$), solids readily soluble in hot water (benzoic), and solids sparingly soluble in water (α-naphthoic acid). Acids of all these types are soluble in ether. The corresponding sodium and potassium salts, being ionic, are all soluble in water and insoluble in ether. Sodium salts of higher fatty acids have sufficient water solubility to function as surface-active soaps. Aluminum, copper, lead, cobalt, and manganese salts of the higher acids are water-insoluble, oil-soluble, nondetergent soaps (7.3). Melting points, where known, are high: HCO_2Na, 253°; NaOAc, 324°; KOAc, 292°; $Pb(OAc)_2$, 280°; $Zn(OAc)_2$, 242°. Lead tetraacetate is prepared by gradual addition of red lead to a stirred mixture of acetic acid and acetic anhydride at 55–80°; the crude acetate separates on cooling and is recrystallized from acetic acid.

11.8   **Halogenation.** — Acetic acid can be chlorinated in the presence of a trace of iodine, red phosphorus, or with exposure to sunlight, and yields in succession chloroacetic acid, di-, and trichloroacetic acid. In contrast with the photochemical chlorination of methane, halogen substitution can be conducted in

$$CH_3COOH \xrightarrow{Cl_2(I_2)} CH_2ClCOOH \xrightarrow{\text{Higher temp.}} CHCl_2COOH \xrightarrow{\text{Higher temp.}} CCl_3COOH$$

discrete stages, and either the mono- or the dichloro compound can be prepared in good yield and in satisfactory purity by merely introducing chlorine slowly until the proper increase in weight is observed. Fortunately no separation of mixtures is required, for the three chlorinated acids all boil at nearly the same temperature (Table 11.1). Trichloroacetic acid is obtained most conveniently by oxidation of chloral, CCl_3CHO (12.15), with concentrated nitric acid. The iodine catalyst is described as a halogen carrier, and probably iodine trichloride is the effective chlorinating agent:

$$I_2 + 3\,Cl_2 \longrightarrow 2\,ICl_3$$
$$ICl_3 + 2\,CH_3COOH \longrightarrow ICl + 2\,CH_2ClCOOH$$
$$ICl + Cl_2 \longrightarrow ICl_3$$

Bromination of acids also can be effected readily, for example with use of a small amount of phosphorus trichloride as catalyst:

$$\underset{\alpha}{CH_3CH_2CH_2CH_2CH_2CO_2H} \xrightarrow[83-89\%]{Br_2(PCl_3),\ 65-70°} \underset{\overset{|}{Br}}{CH_3CH_2CH_2CH_2CHCO_2H}$$

Caproic acid   α-Bromocaproic acid

Only activated α-hydrogen atoms are replaceable by halogen. Thus caproic acid yields first the α-bromo acid and then α,α-dibromocaproic acid and the reaction then stops. Trimethylacetic acid has no α-hydrogen and is resistant to halogenation. Thus bromination of an acid of unknown structure and determination of the degree of substitution reveals the number of α-hydrogen atoms present.

The facts suggest that α-halogenation involves the enol form in equilibrium with the acid in low concentration. In the Hell-Volhard-Zelinsky[1] procedure

$$R_2CH\overset{O}{\underset{OH}{C}} \rightleftharpoons R_2C{=}\underset{OH}{\overset{OH}{C}} \xrightarrow{Br^+} R_2\underset{Br}{\overset{+}{C}}{-}\underset{OH}{\overset{OH}{C}} \xrightarrow{Br^-} R_2\underset{Br}{C}{-}\underset{OH}{\overset{O}{C}} + HBr$$

(1881–87) an acid is treated with sufficient bromine and red phosphorus to form the acid bromide and then convert it into the α-bromoacid bromide, which is

---

[1] Nikolai D. Zelinsky, 1861–1953; b. Tiraspol, Russia; Ph.D. Odessa; Moscow Univ.

hydrolyzed by water to the α-bromo acid. The method is particularly efficient because an acid bromide is more prone to enolize than the free acid.

$$RCH_2CO_2H \xrightarrow{\text{P-Br}_2} RCH_2COBr \xrightarrow{\text{P-Br}_2} RCHBrCOBr \xrightarrow{H_2O} RCHBrCO_2H$$

α-Iodo acids cannot be prepared by direct halogenation but can be obtained by metathesis from the bromo compounds:

$$RCHBrCOOH + KI \rightarrow RCHICOOH + KBr$$

11.9   **Decarbonylation.** — When warmed with concentrated sulfuric acid, formic acid is decomposed with liberation of carbon monoxide: $HCOOH \rightarrow CO + H_2O$. Thus carbon monoxide can be generated in the laboratory by dropping 85–90% formic acid into concentrated sulfuric acid at 60–70°. Studies with isotopically labeled formic acid and related acids (G. A. Ropp, 1960) indicate that the reaction proceeds essentially as suggested by Hammett[1] in 1940. Protonation of the acid occurs chiefly on the carbonyl oxygen (1a), but the less abundant form (b) is better suited for bond-breaking in the rate-controlling step

1.

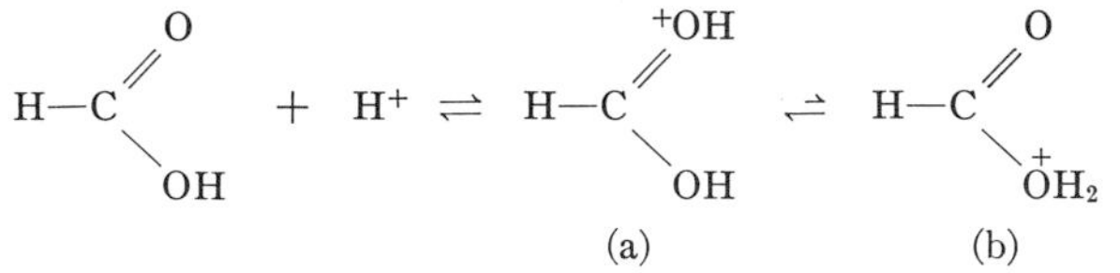

(a)   (b)

2

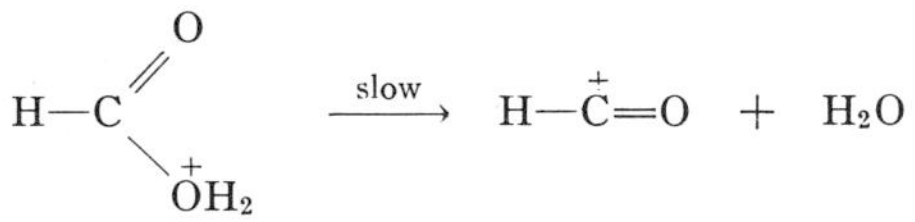

3. $H-\overset{+}{C}{=}O \rightarrow CO + H^+$

(2) with elimination of water and formation of a carbonium ion, which decomposes (3) to carbon monoxide and a proton. Benzoylformic acid (4) undergoes decarbonylation to benzoic acid by the same mechanism; in this case the cation pro-

4. $C_6H_5COCO_2H \xrightarrow[\text{96\% H}_2\text{SO}_4]{} C_6H_5CO_2H + CO$

5. $C_6H_5\underset{\underset{OH}{|}}{C}HCO_2H \xrightarrow[130°]{\text{dil. H}_2\text{SO}_4} C_6H_5CHO + HCO_2H$

6. $(C_6H_5)_3CCO_2H \xrightarrow{\text{concd. H}_2\text{SO}_4} (C_6H_5)_3COH + CO$

duced in step (3) is the carbonium ion $C_6H_5C^+{=}O$. The behavior of α-hydroxy acids is exemplified by mandelic acid (5), which affords carbon monoxide when heated with concentrated sulfuric acid; reaction with dilute acid at 130° shows, however, that the initial fission affords benzaldehyde and formic acid (compare lactic acid, 3.4). Triphenylacetic acid (6) reacts by the steps outlined above; here the intermediate in step (3) is the tertiary trityl ion. Acid-catalyzed decarbonylation distinguishes tertiary acids from primary and secondary types and hence is a

[1] Louis P. Hammett, b. 1894 Wilmington, Del.; Ph.D. Columbia (Beans); Columbia Univ.

useful diagnostic test.   Acids such as acetic and isobutyric are stable to sulfuric acid because the carbonium ions required as intermediates are not so stable as a tertiary ion or a proton.

Tracer studies show that in all the reactions cited the carbon monoxide is derived from the carboxyl group.   Esters of the α-keto acids lose carbon monoxide when heated to temperatures of 100–175°, and experiments with labeled ethyl pyruvate (7, Calvin,[1] 1947) and with isotopic dimethyl phenyloxalacetate (8, H.

7. $CH_3C^{14}OCO_2C_2H_5 \xrightarrow{130°} CH_3C^{14}OOC_2H_5 + CO$

8. $CH_3OOCCH(C_6H_5)COC^{14}O_2CH_3 \xrightarrow{175°} CH_3OOCCH(C_6H_5)CO_2CH_3 + C^{14}O$

9. $C_6H_5COCOC_6H_5 \xrightarrow[200°]{UV} C_6H_5COC_6H_5 + CO$

Schmid,[2] 1959) have shown that the carbon monoxide comes from the carboxylate group and not the keto group.   The α-diketone benzil (9) affords benzophenone and carbon monoxide when heated under ultraviolet irradiation or when the vapor is passed over hot lead oxide.   The decomposition of the α-keto esters and α-diketones is perhaps due to the presence of adjacent positively polarized carbon centers.

The course of protonation of the carboxyl group calls for comment.   Formulation (1), above, indicates protonation of the carbonyl oxygen atom rather than the hydroxylic oxygen.   This mode of combination appeared the more probable both because the doubly bound oxygen in the carbonyl group is negatively polarized and because protonation at this point permits resonance stabilization whereas protonation of the hydroxylic oxygen does not.   Stewart[3] (1960) found a close correlation between the basicities of a series of substituted benzoic acids and the corresponding acetophenones which supports carbonyl protonation.

11.10   **Inertness to Addition.** — Early chemists were puzzled by the fact that carboxylic acids and carboyxlate ions do not enter into addition reactions characteristic of carbonyl compounds, whereas esters do.   Thus Grignard reagents react readily with esters, but reaction with an acid is limited to formation of the magnesium halide salt, $RCOO^-Mg^+Br$, which on decomposition with water affords the unchanged acid.   Hantzsch observed that acids and their salts lack the power to absorb ultraviolet light characteristic of esters.   Since absorption of light is indicative of unsaturation, Hantzsch regarded esters as true carbonyl compounds, and acids and salts as substances in which the hydrogen or metal atom is linked equally to both oxygen atoms, with obliteration of carbonyl characteristics (a).   The Hantzsch postulate can now be interpreted as a rough equivalent of the concept of a resonant hybrid ion (b), in which neither C—O bond has true carbonyl character.   The lack of reactivity of acids to Grignard reagents is thus attributable to resonance in the anion of the initially formed $RCOO^-Mg^+Br$.   Lithium alumi-

[1] Melvin Calvin, b. 1911 St. Paul; Ph.D. Minnesota (Glockler); Univ. Calif., Berkeley

[2] Hans Schmid, b. 1917 Austria; Ph.D. Vienna (Späth, Karrer); Univ. Zurich

[3] Ross Stewart, b. 1924 Vancouver, Canada; Ph.D. Washington State Univ. (Wiberg); Royal Roads College; Univ. British Columbia

num hydride has such enhanced additive power that it adds to the initially formed $RCOO^-AlH_3Li^+$ and reduces the acid to RCH_2OH. Diborane (B_2H_6) is more effective than lithium aluminum hydride for the reduction of carboxylic acids

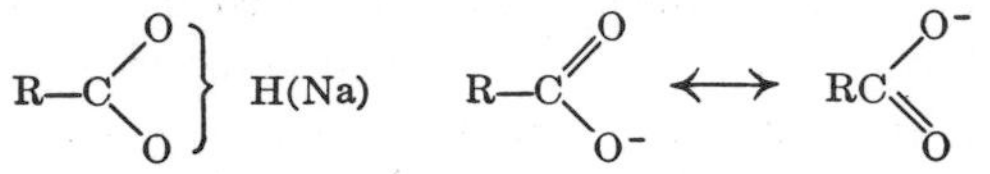

(a)   (b)

(H. C. Brown, 1960); esters are also reduced by this reagent, but more slowly. That an unionized acid lacks carbonyl character is attributable to hydrogen bonding in the dimer. Esters behave more like true carbonyl compounds.

ESTERS

11.11   **Properties.** — Esters are one of three common types of derivatives of carboxylic acids. They are readily obtainable by acid-catalyzed esterification or by one of the alternate methods described below, and they can be reconverted efficiently into the acids by alkaline hydrolysis. Because of the ready interconversion and because esters possess certain advantageous physical characteristics, it is frequently expedient to esterify an acid or acid mixture in order to effect purification, separation, or characterization. Methyl and ethyl esters are unassociated liquids and distil at temperatures lower than the corresponding associated acids, even though the molecular weights are higher. The comparative data of Table 11.2 show that methyl esters boil an average of 62° below the acids; the ethyl esters boil some 42° below the acids. Both methyl and ethyl formate boil at temperatures lower than the component acid and alcohols. The more volatile esters are also more stable to heat than the free acids and can be distilled satisfactorily in cases where the acid undergoes decomposition. Esters of solid acids melt at lower temperatures than the acids and often more sharply and without decomposition; they are more soluble in organic solvents and crystallize more satisfactorily. A methyl ester invariably has a higher melting point than the corresponding ethyl ester.

Volatile esters are liquids of characteristic fruity odors. The disagreeable-smelling acids butyric and valeric are converted by esterification into pleasantly fragrant derivatives. Esters, usually in the form of mixtures, are responsible for the flavor and fragrance of many fruits and flowers, and artificial flavoring essences are mixtures of synthetic esters empirically compounded to reproduce the flavor

TABLE 11.2. BOILING POINTS OF ACIDS AND ESTERS, °C.

	ACID	METHYL ESTER	DIFFERENCE
Formic	100.5	32	68.5
Acetic	118	57	61
Propionic	141	79.7	61.3
n-Butyric	162.5	102.3	60.2
n-Valeric	187	127.3	59.7

TABLE 11.3 ESTERS (ALL LIQUIDS)

NAME	FORMULA	B.P., °C.	SP. GR.
Methyl formate	HCO_2CH_3	32	0.974
Ethyl formate	$HCO_2C_2H_5$	54	.906
Methyl acetate	$CH_3CO_2CH_3$	57	.924
Ethyl acetate	$CH_3CO_2C_2H_5$	77.1	.901
n-Propyl acetate	$CH_3CO_2C_3H_7(n)$	101.7	.886
n-Butyl acetate	$CH_3CO_2C_4H_9(n)$	126.5	.882
n-Amyl acetate	$CH_3CO_2C_5H_{11}(n)$	147.6	.879
Isobutyl acetate	$CH_3CO_2C_4H_9(i)$	118	.871
t-Butyl acetate	$CH_3CO_2C(CH_3)_3$	97	.896
Isoamyl acetate	$CH_3CO_2C_5H_{11}(i)$	142	.876
n-Octyl acetate	$CH_3CO_2C_8H_{17}(n)$	210	.885
Methyl propionate	$C_2H_5CO_2CH_3$	79.7	.915
Ethyl propionate	$C_2H_5CO_2C_2H_5$	99.1	.891
Methyl n-butyrate	$n\text{-}C_3H_7CO_2CH_3$	102.3	.898
Ethyl n-butyrate	$n\text{-}C_3H_7CO_2C_2H_5$	121	.879
Isoamyl n-butyrate	$n\text{-}C_3H_7CO_2C_5H_{11}(i)$	178.6	.866
Methyl n-valerate	$n\text{-}C_4H_9CO_2CH_3$	127.3	.910
Ethyl n-valerate	$n\text{-}C_4H_9CO_2C_2H_5$	145.5	.877
Methyl isovalerate	$i\text{-}C_4H_9CO_2CH_3$	117	.881
Isoamyl isovalerate	$i\text{-}C_4H_9CO_2C_5H_{11}(i)$	194	.858
Ethyl n-heptylate	$n\text{-}C_6H_{13}CO_2C_2H_5$	187	.872
Ethyl pelargonate	$n\text{-}C_8H_{17}CO_2C_2H_5$	228	.866

and aroma of natural fruits and extracts (apple, raspberry, cherry, rum, etc.). The ester mixtures are usually prepared in an alcoholic solution containing glycerol, chloroform, or acetaldehyde as fixatives to retain the fragrant principles, and organic acids are added to simulate the tartness of fruits. The esters most extensively employed are ethyl formate, ethyl and isoamyl acetate, ethyl and isoamyl n-butyrate, ethyl and isoamyl n-valerate, and ethyl heptylate. One formulation for artificial raspberry flavor utilizes nine esters, two organic acids, acetaldehyde, glycerol, and alcohol.

The esters listed in Table 11.3 are all slightly lighter than water, and all but those of low molecular weight are practically insoluble. At room temperature, 100 g. of water dissolves 30 g. of methyl formate, 33 g. of methyl acetate, 8.5 g. of ethyl acetate, or 6.5 g. of methyl propionate.

11.12   Fischer Esterification. — The esterification procedure introduced by E. Fischer and A. Speier (1895) consists in refluxing the acid with excess methanol or ethanol in the presence of about 3% of hydrogen chloride. The catalysts now generally preferred are sulfuric acid or boron fluoride etherate (Lewis acid); use of the milder catalyst ethanesulfonic acid makes possible the esterification of sensitive acids, e.g. pyruvic acid, CH_3COCO_2H. The reaction reaches a point of equilibrium, but in a small-scale experiment a conversion of 60–80% can be achieved by use of a large excess of the alcohol. On a larger scale, where economy of alcohol and high yield are important, various expedients have been employed for removal of the water formed. One is by fractional distillation in an elaborate apparatus (*Org. Syn.*); another involves addition of chloroform and refluxing under a Soxhlet condenser containing anhydrous magnesium sulfate (B. R. Baker, 1943). Use of ethylene dichloride as the additive eliminates the necessity for continuous drying. This solvent retains the ester; water, methanol, and sulfuric acid separate in an upper layer (R. O. Clinton, 1948). Dimethyl oxalate (m.p. 53°) can be prepared in 68–76% yield by slowly adding concentrated sulfuric acid (35 ml.) to a stirred mixture of anhydrous oxalic acid (1 mole) and methanol (2.5 moles) and letting the mixture stand at 15° for 24 hrs. (*Org. Syn.*); the large amount of sulfuric acid serves for catalysis and dehydration. A simple means of eliminating water is to use an excess of acetone dimethylacetal, which reacts with the water formed to produce two moles of methanol and one of acetone (N. B. Lorette, 1959). Thus a mixture of adipic acid (4 moles), methanol (5 moles), and

$$HO_2C(CH_2)_4CO_2H \ + \ 2 \ CH_3OH \ \underset{}{\overset{p\text{-}CH_3C_6H_4SO_3H}{\rightleftharpoons}} \ CH_3O_2C(CH_2)_4CO_2CH_3 \ + \ H_2O$$

Adipic acid — Dimethyl adipate

$$(CH_3)_2C(OCH_3)_2 \ + \ H_2O \ \rightarrow \ (CH_3)_2CO \ + \ 2 \ HOCH_3$$

Acetone dimethylacetal
(see 12.40)

p-toluenesulfonic acid (5 g.) is stirred at 40–60° and acetone dimethylacetal (8 moles) is added in portions; after 4 hrs. the conversion is 99% complete. Advantages of the method are that a high reaction rate is maintained throughout and that acid hydrates, for example $(CO_2H)_2 \cdot 2 \ H_2O$, can be esterified (methanol as such is not required).

11.13 **Mechanism of Esterification.** — Esterification of acids and acid hydrolysis of esters can be considered together, since acid-catalyzed esterification is reversible and esterification proceeds by reversal of the steps leading to hydrolysis. The hydrolytic reaction is often selected for mechanistic studies. Although hydrolysis is usually conducted under basic catalysis, reversal

$$1. \quad R-\overset{O}{\underset{}{\overset{\|}{C}}}-OH \ + \ H^+ \ \underset{slow}{\overset{fast}{\rightleftharpoons}} \ R-\overset{\overset{+}{O}H}{\underset{}{\overset{\|}{C}}}-OH$$

$$2. \quad R-\overset{\overset{+}{O}H}{\underset{}{\overset{\|}{C}}}-OH \ + \ HOCH_3 \ \underset{fast}{\overset{slow}{\rightleftharpoons}} \ R-\overset{OH}{\underset{\underset{H}{+OCH_3}}{\overset{|}{\underset{}{C}}}}-OH$$

$$3. \quad R-\overset{OH}{\underset{\underset{H}{+OCH_3}}{\overset{|}{\underset{}{C}}}}-OH \ \underset{slow}{\overset{fast}{\rightleftharpoons}} \ R-\overset{O}{\underset{H}{\overset{\|}{C}}}-\overset{+}{O}CH_3 \ + \ H_2O$$

$$4. \quad R-\overset{O}{\underset{H}{\overset{\|}{C}}}-\overset{+}{O}CH_3 \ \rightleftharpoons \ R-\overset{O}{\underset{}{\overset{\|}{C}}}-OCH_3 \ + \ H^+$$

of this reaction is precluded by the stability of the hybrid carboxylate ion. Esterification is a complicated phenomenon, and kinetic studies have disclosed several different paths. We shall consider only mechanisms which appear to apply to the vast majority of cases. In a fast step (1) a proton (or Lewis acid) attacks the negatively polarized carbonyl oxygen to produce an oxonium ion which then reacts more slowly with methanol (2). Expulsion of water (3) and then of a proton (4) affords the ester. In esterification the rate-controlling step is bimolecular attack of methanol on the protonated acid (2); in hydrolysis the slow step is attack of water on the protonated ester (3). The process is known as the $A_{ac}2$ mechanism, A standing for acid-catalyzed, 2 having the usual meaning of molecularity, and ac referring to acyl cleavage, that is, severance of the C—O bond of the acid or the C—OCH_3 bond of an ester. Alkyl cleavage (al) refers to cleavage of the O—CH_3 bond of an ester. The mechanism is supported by isotopic studies of oxygen exchange. M. L.'Bender[1] (1958) studied the hydrolysis of labeled esters of the type $RCO^{18}OR'$ in ordinary water and of unlabeled esters in H_2O^{18} and found in each case that oxygen is exchanged at a rate approximately equal to that of hydrolysis, which shows that the reaction proceeds through an intermediate having two equivalent hydroxyl groups.

Esters of tertiary alcohols undergo acid-catalyzed hydrolysis by a different mechanism. Thus acid hydrolysis of t-butyl acetate with H_2O^{18} yields labeled

$$5. \ (CH_3)_3C \mid OCOCH_3 \ + \ HO^{18} \mid H \ \xrightarrow{H^+} \ (CH_3)_3CO^{18}H \ + \ CH_3CO_2H$$

t-butyl alcohol, showing that the process is one of alkyl cleavage. The reaction is unimolecular, and the mechanism attributed to this $A_{al}1$ reaction is shown in formulations 6–9. The reactions are reversible, but in practice esters of tertiary

$$6. \ CH_3\overset{O}{\overset{\|}{C}}-OC(CH_3)_3 \ + \ H^+ \ \underset{fast}{\overset{fast}{\rightleftarrows}} \ CH_3\overset{+OH}{\overset{\|}{C}}-OC(CH_3)_3$$

$$7. \ CH_3\overset{+OH}{\overset{\|}{C}}-OC(CH_3)_3 \ \rightleftarrows \ CH_3\overset{O}{\overset{\|}{C}}-\overset{+}{\underset{H}{O}}-C(CH_3)_3 \ \underset{fast}{\overset{slow}{\rightleftarrows}} \ CH_3COOH \ + \ \overset{+}{C}(CH_3)_3$$

$$8. \ (CH_3)_3\overset{+}{C} \ + \ H_2O \ \underset{slow}{\overset{fast}{\rightleftarrows}} \ (CH_3)_3C-\overset{|}{\underset{H}{O}}H$$

$$9. \ (CH_3)_3C-\overset{+}{\underset{H}{O}}H \ \underset{fast}{\overset{fast}{\rightleftarrows}} \ (CH_3)_3COH \ + \ H^+$$

alcohols are prepared by other methods (see below).

The course of the base-catalyzed hydrolysis of n-amyl acetate (10) shows that acyl cleavage is involved. The reaction follows second order kinetics and is de-

$$10. \ CH_3\overset{O}{\overset{\|}{C}}\!\mid\!OC_5H_{11}\text{-}n \ + \ O^{18}H^- \ \longrightarrow \ CH_3\overset{O}{\overset{\|}{C}}-O^{18}H \ + \ n\text{-}C_5H_{11}O^-$$

[1] Myron L. Bender, b. 1924 St. Louis, Mo.; Ph.D. Purdue (Hass); Illinois Inst. Techn.; Northwestern Univ.

scribed as a $B_{ac}2$ process (B = base-catalyzed). In the mechanism assigned to the hydrolysis of a methyl ester (11–13) the slow step (11) resembles an S_N2 replace-

$$11. \quad HO^- \; + \; \underset{R}{\overset{O}{\underset{|}{\overset{||}{C}}}}-OCH_3 \; \underset{fast}{\overset{slow}{\rightleftharpoons}} \; HO-\underset{R}{\overset{O^-}{\underset{|}{\overset{|}{C}}}}-OCH_3$$

$$12. \quad HO-\underset{R}{\overset{O^-}{\underset{|}{\overset{|}{C}}}}-OCH_3 \; \underset{slow}{\overset{fast}{\rightleftharpoons}} \; HO-\underset{R}{\overset{O}{\underset{|}{\overset{||}{C}}}} \; + \; {}^-OCH_3$$

$$13. \quad HO-\underset{R}{\overset{O}{\underset{|}{\overset{||}{C}}}} \; + \; {}^-OCH_3 \; \xrightarrow{fast} \; R-C\overset{O}{\underset{O^-}{\diagup}} \; + \; HOCH_3$$

ment. The first two steps undoubtedly are reversible, but the transfer of a proton ion (13) is irreversible for the reason stated.

11.14   **Esters of Tertiary Alcohols.** — *Organic Syntheses* describes four methods for the preparation of *t*-butyl acetate (b.p. 97°). In one a mixture of *t*-butyl alcohol, acetic anhydride, and a trace of zinc chloride is gradually brought to the reflux temperature, refluxed for 2 hours, and distilled; the ester layer is washed, dried, and distilled; yield 53–60%. In the second method acetyl chloride is added gradually to a refluxing mixture of *t*-butyl alcohol and N,N-dimethylaniline in ether; yield 63–68%. The third method consists in addition of acetyl chloride in ether to an ethereal solution of *t*-butyl alcohol in which one equivalent of powdered magnesium is suspended; yield 45–55%. In the fourth method isobutylene is condensed into a tube cooled in dry ice and the liquid poured into a

$$CH_3COOH \; + \; (CH_3)_2C{=}CH_2 \; \xrightarrow{H_2SO_4} \; CH_3COOC(CH_3)_3$$

pressure bottle containing acetic acid, ether, and a catalytic amount of concentrated sulfuric acid. The bottle is closed with a wired-on rubber stopper and let stand for about 6 hrs.; yield 50%. In the preparation of di-*t*-butyl malonate by this method the bottle is shaken mechanically until the solid acid has dissolved (yield 58–60%). The acid-catalyzed reaction of succinic acid with isobutylene is conducted advantageously with dioxane as solvent in place of ether (yield 52%).

11.15   **Symmetrical esters,** for example, *n*-butyl butyrate and *n*-heptyl *n*-heptanoate, can be prepared in yields of 60–70% by gradual addition at 10° of a solution of dichromate in 44% sulfuric acid to a mixture of the appropriate alcohol and acetic acid (to prevent acetal formation). The hemiacetal is postulated as the intermediate (J. Cymerman Craig, 1954–60).

$$RCH_2OH \; \xrightarrow{[O]} \; RCH{=}O \; \xrightarrow{RCH_2OH} \; \underset{Hemiacetal}{RCH\overset{OH}{\underset{|}{\overset{|}{O}}}OCH_2R} \; \xrightarrow{[O]} \; R\overset{O}{\overset{||}{C}}OCH_2R$$

11.16   **Rates of Esterification.** — Variation in the size and structure of the alkyl groups of saturated aliphatic acids can lead to wide differences in rates of Fischer esterification, and, since the same changes have little effect on ionization constants, steric factors rather than polar factors must be involved. Thus trimethylacetic acid (pK$_a$ 5.02) is nearly as strongly acidic as acetic acid (pK$_a$ 4.76), but the data of Table 11.4 show that the rate of esterification is only 0.037, relative to the rate for acetic acid taken as unity. The three α-methyl

$$\underset{6\ 5\ 4\quad 3\ 2\ 1}{}$$

$$\begin{array}{cccc}
\underset{\displaystyle \underset{\text{OH}}{|}}{(CH_3)_3CC{=}O} &
\underset{\displaystyle \underset{\text{OH}}{|}}{\overset{6\ 5\ 4\quad 3\ 2\ 1}{(H_3CCH_2)_3CC{=}O}} &
\underset{\displaystyle \underset{\text{OH}}{|}}{CH_3CH_2C{=}O} &
\underset{\displaystyle \underset{\text{OH}}{|}}{\overset{6\ 5\ 4\quad 3\ \ 2\ 1}{H_3CCH_2CH_2C{=}O}} \\
0.037 & 0.0016 & 0.84 & 0.50
\end{array}$$

Relative rates (Table 11.4)

groups thus exert considerable steric hindrance.   Newman (1950) noted that substituents on the β-carbon atom are somewhat more effective in retarding esterification than α-substituents.   Thus the rate of esterification of triethylacetic acid is only $\frac{1}{23}$ that for trimethylacetic acid; n-butyric acid differs more from propionic acid than the latter differs from acetic acid (rate = 1).   On the basis of these and

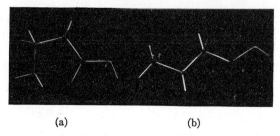

(a)   (b)

other comparisons, Newman formulated an empirical rule of six.   Atoms in the chain are numbered as shown in the formulas, and the rule states that the steric effect increases with increase in the number of atoms in the six-position, the six-

TABLE 11.4.   RELATIVE RATES OF ESTERIFICATION (40°) WITH METHANOL
0.005 M in HCl

ACID	ATOMS IN POSITION 6		RELATIVE RATE
	H	C	
CH_3CO_2H	0	0	1
$CH_3CH_2CO_2H$	0	0	0.84
$CH_3CH_2CH_2CO_2H$	3	0	0.50
$(CH_3)_2CHCO_2H$	0	0	0.33
$(CH_3)_3CCO_2H$	0	0	0.037
$(CH_3)_2CHCH_2CO_2H$	6	0	0.12
$(CH_3)_3CCH_2CO_2H$	9	0	0.23
$(CH_3)_2CHCH_2CH_2CO_2H$	1	2	0.10
$(CH_3)_3CCH_2CH_2CO_2H$	0	3	0.46
$(CH_3)_3CCH(CH_3)CO_2H$	9	0	0.00062
$(CH_3)_3CC(CH_3)_2CO_2H$	9	0	0.00013
$(CH_3CH_2)_3CCO_2H$	9	0	0.00016

number.   The six-number of triethylacetic acid is 9, that of n-butyric acid is 3. A carbon atom in the six-position has a somewhat greater effect than a hydrogen atom.   The rationale of the rule of six is evident from the photographs of two models of n-butyric acid.   The extended structure (b) may represent maximum stability, but the acid can also exist to some extent in the coiled form (a), in which the hydrogens in the six-position shield the carbonyl group.   Analogous coiling back of free radical chains has been noted (7.9).   The data of Table 11.4 provide a number of comparisons of interest for evaluation of the rule of six.

11.17   **Silver Salt Method.** — In those instances where direct acid-catalyzed esterification is slow or inefficient, satisfactory results can be obtained by treatment of the dry silver salt of the acid with an alkyl halide:

$$RCOO\underline{Ag \; + \; X}R' \longrightarrow RCOOR' + AgX$$

The reaction, analogous to the Williamson synthesis of ethers, apparently proceeds through simple metathesis involving fission of the O—Ag bond, for it is not materially impeded by the presence of branching alkyl groups.   The silver salt often can be precipitated by dissolving the acid in dilute aqueous ammonia, boiling off the excess, and adding silver nitrate solution.   The method has the objection of being lengthy and expensive.

11.18   **Esterification with Diazomethane.** — Discovery of diazomethane (von Pechmann,[1] 1894) provided organic chemists with a highly reactive reagent which has found several synthetic uses, one of which is for the methylation of acids, phenols, and enols (also alcohols, 8.35).   The reagent is a

$$RCOOH \quad + \quad CH_2N_2 \longrightarrow RCOOCH_3 \quad + \quad N_2$$

$$\text{Diazomethane} \qquad\qquad \text{Methyl ester}$$

toxic yellow gas (m.p. $-145°$, b.p. $-23°$) which may explode when heated to $100°$ or on contact with a rough glass surface; the undiluted liquid may explode violently.   However, a solution of the gas in ether can be prepared without hazard prior to use and can be stored at $0°$ for a day or so with little loss.   On addition of the yellow ethereal solution in portions to the acid, or to a solution or suspension of the acid in ether, nitrogen is evolved at once and the yellow color is discharged; when the yellow color persists, the solution is warmed on the steam bath to expel excess reagent and leave a colorless ethereal solution of the ester.

Diazomethane is a resonance hybrid (1); resonance in these unsaturated structures accounts for the color.   The reaction with a carboxylic acid may be repre-

1. $CH_2{=}\overset{+}{N}{=}\overset{-}{N} \longleftrightarrow \overset{-}{C}H_2\overset{+}{N}{\equiv}N$

2. $H^+ \; + \; \overset{-}{C}H_2\overset{+}{N}{\equiv}N \; + \; \overset{-}{O}{-}\overset{\overset{O}{\|}}{C}{-}R \longrightarrow$

$$\overset{\delta^+ \;\; \delta^-}{H{\cdots}CH_2}\overset{\delta^+}{\cdots}\overset{\delta^-}{N{\equiv}N}{\cdots}O{-}\overset{\overset{O}{\|}}{C}{-}R \longrightarrow CH_3O{-}\overset{\overset{O}{\|}}{C}{-}R \; + \; N_2$$

sented as in (2).   Hydrochloric acid reacts to give methyl chloride.

[1] Hans Frh. von Pechmann, 1850–1902; b. Nuremberg; Ph.D. Greiswald; Univ. Munich; Tübingen

von Pechmann obtained diazomethane by the action of alcoholic potassium hydroxide on an ethereal solution of the liquid nitrosomethylurethane, an active skin irritant (3). A related method (Arndt,[1] 1930) involves shaking solid nitroso-

3. $\underset{\underset{NO}{|}}{CH_3NCO_2C_2H_5} \xrightarrow{C_2H_5O^-} \underset{\underset{NO}{|}}{CH_3NCO_2H} \xrightarrow{-CO_2, -H_2O} CH_2{=}\overset{+}{N}{=}\overset{-}{N}$

Nitrosomethyl-
urethane

$\Big\uparrow$ aq. KOH, ether

4. $CH_3NH_3Cl \xrightarrow[-NH_4Cl]{H_2NCONH_2} CH_3NHCONH_2 \rightarrow \underset{\underset{NO}{|}}{CH_3NCONH_2} \Big\rfloor$

Nitrosomethylurea

5. $CHCl_3 + H_2NNH_2 \xrightarrow{KOH} [C{=}NNH_2] \rightarrow CH_2{=}\overset{+}{N}{=}\overset{-}{N}$

methylurea with aqueous potassium hydroxide and ether at 5° (4). Staudinger[2] (1912) prepared the reagent by adding chloroform to a mixture of anhydrous hydrazine and a hot solution of potassium hydroxide in absolute alcohol (5); yield about 20%. Methods later favored because they involve stable intermediates available commercially employ the precursor (a) of A. F. McKay (1948) and the comparable precursor (b) of Th. J. de Boer and H. J. Backer (1954).

$$CH_3NH_3^+Cl^- + \underset{Nitroguanidine}{H_2N\overset{\overset{NH}{\|}}{C}NHNO_2} \xrightarrow[84\%]{KOH} CH_3NH\overset{\overset{NH}{\|}}{C}NHNO_2 \xrightarrow[90\%]{HNO_2}$$

$$\underset{\underset{NO}{|}}{CH_3N}\overset{\overset{NH}{\|}}{C}NHNO_2 \xrightarrow{KOH} CH_2{=}\overset{+}{N}{=}\overset{-}{N} \leftarrow \underset{\underset{NO}{|}}{CH_3NSO_2C_6H_4CH_3\text{-}p}$$

(a) N-Methyl-N-nitroso-
    N'-nitroguanidine

(b) p-Tolylsulfonyl-
    methylnitrosamide

The latest precursor reagent (c) is available in a mixture with 30% white mineral oil as stabilizer from the du Pont Explosives Department, Gibbstown, N. J. under the trade name EXR-101. An *Organic Syntheses* procedure (J. A. Moore, 1961)

$$\underset{\underset{O}{\|}}{\overset{\overset{NO}{|}}{CH_3N}C}\langle\bigcirc\rangle\underset{\underset{O}{\|}}{\overset{\overset{NO}{|}}{C}NCH_3} \xrightarrow[76\text{-}86\%]{2\,NaOH} 2\,CH_2N_2 + NaO_2C\langle\bigcirc\rangle CO_2Na$$

(c) Bis-(N-methyl-N-nitroso)-
    terephthalamide

describes the preparation of 0.8 mole of diazomethane in one batch by distillation with ether from a mixture of diethylene glycol monomethyl ether and 30% aqueous sodium hydroxide after chilling to 0° and adding the reagent. This nitrosoamide

---

[1] Fritz Arndt, b. 1885 Hamburg; Ph.D. Freiburg (Howitz); Univ. Breslau; Istanbul; Hamburg
[2] Hermann Staudinger, b. 1881 Worms; Ph.D. Halle (Vorländer); Univ. Strasbourg, Karlsruhe, ETH Zurich, Freiburg; Nobel Prize 1953

has the advantage of availability, low cost, indefinite stability at room temperature, and suitability for large-scale preparations.

Ethyl diazoacetate, a yellow oil, is made by reaction of sodium nitrite with

$$CH_2CO_2C_2H_5 \xrightarrow{\text{NaNO}_2} \overset{-}{N}=\overset{+}{N}=CHCO_2C_2H_5$$
$$\underset{NH_2 \cdot HCl}{|}$$

glycine ethyl ester hydrochloride at 0–2°. Ether extraction gives a product suitable for use without distillation.

11.19   Ester Interchange (Transesterification). — When the methyl ester of an acid is refluxed with excess ethyl alcohol containing a few percent of hydrogen chloride or sulfuric acid, it is converted to a large extent into the ethyl ester. An equilibrium is set up, and the extent of conversion is dependent upon the relative amounts of methyl and ethyl alcohol present in either the free or combined form:

$$\underset{\text{(excess)}}{RCOOCH_3 \ + \ C_2H_5OH} \ \underset{}{\overset{H^+}{\rightleftharpoons}} \ RCOOC_2H_5 \ + \ CH_3OH$$

An ethyl ester can be transformed similarly into the methyl derivative by ester interchange. Rapid interchange of alkyl groups also can be brought about with a catalytic amount of sodium alkoxide. Sodium borohydride also catalyzes transesterification; thus thoughtless choice of ethanol as solvent for the borohydride reduction of a keto methyl ester led to confusion because the alcoholic reduction product proved to be the ethyl ester. A technical application of ester interchange is the production of lauryl alcohol from the glyceride trilaurin with recovery of glycerol. Refluxing the glyceride with methanol and sulfuric acid affords the methyl ester, which separates as an oil on addition of water; the glycerol is recovered from the aqueous solution:

$$
\begin{array}{llll}
C_{11}H_{23}COOCH_2 & & & CH_2OH \\
| & & & | \\
C_{11}H_{23}COOCH & + \ 3\,CH_3OH & \xrightarrow{H_2SO_4} & 3\,C_{11}H_{23}COOCH_3 \ + \ CHOH \\
| & & \text{Methyl laurate} & | \\
C_{11}H_{23}COOCH_2 & & \text{(m.p. 5°)} & CH_2OH \\
\text{Trilaurin} & & & \text{Glycerol} \\
\text{(m.p. 46°)} & & &
\end{array}
$$

Methyl laurate is then reduced by catalytic hydrogenation to lauryl alcohol; direct hydrogenation of the glyceride is attended with the destruction of glycerol.

11.20   Esters of Carbonic and Formic Acids. — Ortho acids, known only in the form of esters, contain the maximum number of hydroxyl groups: orthocarbonic acid, $C(OH)_4$; orthoformic acid, $HC(OH)_3$. Ethyl orthocarbonate is made by the action of sodium ethoxide on trichloronitromethane, a substance which was named chloropicrin by its discoverer J. Stenhouse (Glasgow, 1848), who obtained it in good yield by the action of sodium hypochlorite on picric acid (sample prepared from indigo). Chloropicrin is a powerful lachrymator. Ethyl orthoformate is prepared by a method discovered by Williamson, reaction of

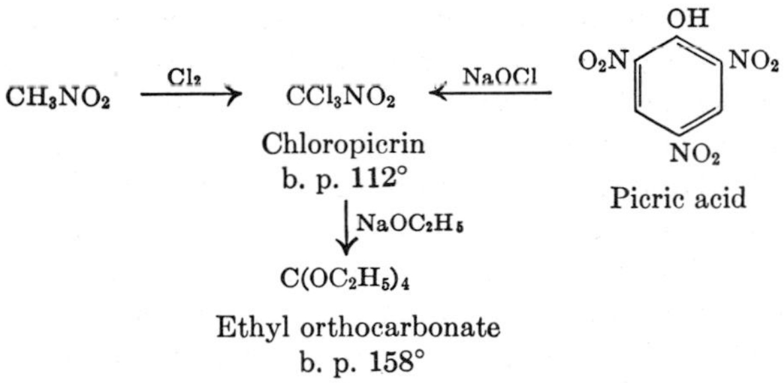

$$CH_3NO_2 \xrightarrow{Cl_2} CCl_3NO_2 \xleftarrow{NaOCl}$$

Chloropicrin
b. p. 112°

Picric acid

$$\downarrow NaOC_2H_5$$

$C(OC_2H_5)_4$

Ethyl orthocarbonate
b. p. 158°

chloroform with sodium ethoxide. Since the reaction is very much faster than the reaction of carbon tetrachloride or of methylene chloride with sodium ethoxide,

$$HCCl_3 + 4\ NaOC_2H_5 \rightarrow HC(OC_2H_5)_3$$
Ethyl orthoformate
(b.p. 146°)

it is not of the ordinary Williamson type and probably involves initial formation of dichlorocarbene (J. Hine,[1] 1950); see note on p. 394:

$$CHCl_3 \xrightarrow{C_2H_5O^-} :CCl_2 \xrightarrow[-2HCl]{3C_2H_5OH} (C_2H_5O)_3CH$$

Ethyl orthoformate is stable to base but it is hydrolyzed easily by dilute acid with initial formation of ethyl formate.

Cevine is a steroid alkaloid of the elaborate structure and stereochemistry shown in formula (1). On acetylation in pyridine solution cevine is converted

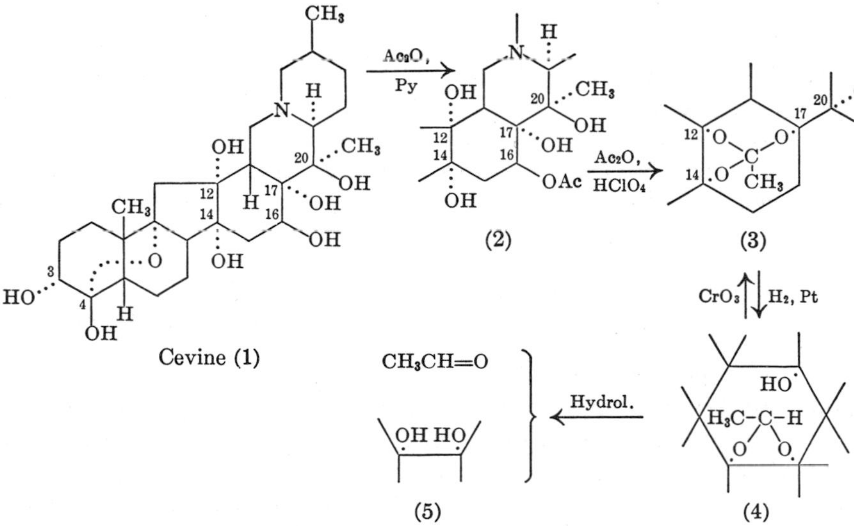

Cevine (1)

(2)

(3)

(5)

(4)

into the 3,4,16-triacetate, for which (2) is a partial formula. The 16-hydroxyl group, being secondary, is acetylated, but the tertiary hydroxyl groups at posi-

---

[1] Jack Hine, b. 1923 Coronado, Calif.; Ph.D. Illinois (R. Adams); Georgia Inst. Techn.

tions 12, 14, 17, and 20 remain untouched. However, three of these groups, namely those at C_{12}, C_{14}, and C_{17} are all α-oriented (dotted line, to the rear) and close to one another, and when cevine triacetate is treated with acetic anhydride and a trace of the powerfully catalytic perchloric acid they react to form the orthoacetate (3). Note that the tertiary 20-hydroxyl group remains unaffected. Evidence of the orthoester structure is that hydrogenation of the derivative cleaves one of the three oxygen bridges (the identity of the bridge cleaved is not known) and affords a dihydro derivative characterized as an acetal (4) by hydrolysis to acetaldehyde. Chromic acid oxidation of the acetal (4) regenerates the orthoacetate.

Two esters useful in synthesis are made from phosgene. Cautious reaction

$$Cl-\overset{\overset{\displaystyle O}{\|}}{C}-Cl \ + \ HOC_2H_5 \ \rightarrow \ Cl-\overset{\overset{\displaystyle O}{\|}}{C}-OC_2H_5 \ + \ HCl$$

Ethyl chloroformate (b.p. 94°)

$$C_2H_5O-\overset{\overset{\displaystyle O}{\|}}{C}-OC_2H_5 \longleftarrow \qquad\qquad \Big| \ NaOC_2H_5$$

Diethyl carbonate (b.p. 127°)

with ethanol gives ethyl chloroformate, which reacts with a solution of sodium ethoxide in ethanol to give diethyl carbonate.

11.21   Ammonolysis. — Esters react with ammonia to form amides. For example, a mixture of ethyl acetate and concentrated ammonia solution is shaken occasionally until the two-phase system becomes homogeneous

$$CH_3COOC_2H_5 + NH_3 \rightarrow CH_3CONH_2 + H_2O$$

Acetamide

(1–2 days) and the acetamide is isolated by distillation. The reaction shows that the C—O bond of an ester is weaker than the C—N bond of an amide; ammonolysis provides a convenient method of deacetylation (8.25). Ammonolysis of an ester usually is carried out with either aqueous or alcoholic ammonia at room temperature; sometimes the mixture is cooled in order to avoid attack of another reactive group in the molecule, for example:

$$ClCH_2COOC_2H_5 \ + \ aq. \ NH_3 \ \xrightarrow[62-87\%]{0-5°} \ ClCH_2CONH_2$$

Ethyl chloroacetate   Chloroacetamide (m.p. 120°)

With the exception of formamide, amides are crystalline solids at room temperature, and they are frequently prepared from liquid acids or esters for purposes of identification by mixed melting-point determinations. The data of Table 11.5, however, show that among the amide derivatives of straight-chain aliphatic acids there is little change in the melting point from the C_5-compound on. The amides boil at temperatures higher than the acids from which they are derived, and the boiling points are less regular than usual and show less increase with increasing molecular weight, a relationship which suggests that in the liquid state amides are associated to varying degrees. Dimethylformamide, $HCON(CH_3)_2$ (b.p. 153°), is a useful solvent.

TABLE 11.5. AMIDES

NAME	FORMULA	M.P., °C.	B.P., °C.	SP. GR.	SOLUBILITY IN WATER
Formamide	$HCONH_2$	2	193	1.139	sol.
Acetamide	CH_3CONH_2	82	222	1.159	sol.
Propionamide	$C_2H_5CONH_2$	80	213	1.042	sol.
n-Butyramide	$n\text{-}C_3H_7CONH_2$	116	216	1.032	sol.
n-Valeramide	$n\text{-}C_4H_9CONH_2$	106		1.023	sol.
n-Caproamide	$n\text{-}C_5H_{11}CONH_2$	101		0.999	sol. hot
Stearamide	$n\text{-}C_{17}H_{35}CONH_2$	109	$251^{12mm.}$		insol.

Other substances derived from ammonia react with esters in an analogous manner; hydrazine, for example, reacts as follows:

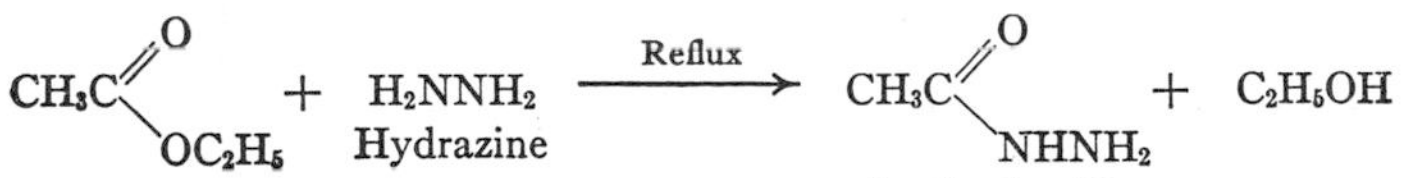

$$CH_3C\underset{OC_2H_5}{\overset{O}{<}} + H_2NNH_2 \xrightarrow{Reflux} CH_3C\underset{NHNH_2}{\overset{O}{<}} + C_2H_5OH$$

Hydrazine

Acethydrazide
(m.p. 67°)

Grignard reactions of esters (8.6) and reduction of esters (8.9) have been described.

ACYL HALIDES

11.22   Properties. — Acyl halides are reactive, low-boiling derivatives in which the hydroxyl group of an acid is replaced by a halogen atom. They bear the same relationship to acids as alkyl halides do to alcohols, and re-

$$R—C\underset{X}{\overset{O}{<}} \qquad\qquad R—C\overset{O}{<}$$

Acyl halide   Acyl radical

placement of hydroxyl by halogen has a similar effect on the boiling point in each case:

$n\text{-}C_3H_7CO\boxed{OH}$, b.p. 162.5° $n\text{-}C_5H_{11}\boxed{OH}$, b.p. 138.0°

$n\text{-}C_3H_7CO\boxed{Cl}$, b.p. 102° $n\text{-}C_5H_{11}\boxed{Cl}$, b.p. 105.7°

(mol. wt. 106.55)   (mol. wt. 106.60)

The acyl chloride and alkyl chloride selected for illustration have practically the same molecular weights, and the boiling points are very close to each other and to that of n-heptane. Properties of other acyl halides are recorded in Table 11.6. The initial member, the chloride of formic acid, is stable only at −190°, but in some reactions a mixture of carbon monoxide and hydrogen chloride functions as though the substance is produced in a transient phase:

$$\underset{Cl}{\overset{H}{|}} + C{=}O \rightleftharpoons \underset{Cl}{\overset{H}{\diagdown}}C{=}O$$

TABLE 11.6. ACYL HALIDES[1]

NAME	FORMULA	B.P., °C.	SP. GR.
Acetyl fluoride	CH_3COF	20.5	0.993
Acetyl chloride	CH_3COCl	52	1.104
Acetyl bromide	CH_3COBr	76.7	1.52
Acetyl iodide	CH_3COI	108	1.98
Chloroacetyl chloride	$CH_2ClCOCl$	105	1.495
Bromoacetyl bromide	$CH_2BrCOBr$	150	2.317
Propionyl chloride	CH_3CH_2COCl	80	1.065
n-Butyryl chloride	$CH_3CH_2CH_2COCl$	102	1.028
Isobutyryl chloride	$(CH_3)_2CHCOCl$	92	1.017
n-Valeryl chloride	$CH_3CH_2CH_2CH_2COCl$	128	1.016
Isovaleryl chloride	$(CH_3)_2CHCH_2COCl$	113	
n-Caproyl chloride	$n\text{-}C_5H_{11}COCl$	153	
Capryl chloride	$CH_3(CH_2)_6COCl$	196	0.975
Stearoyl chloride	$CH_3(CH_2)_{16}COCl$	$215^{15\,mm.}$	
Benzoyl chloride	C_6H_5COCl	197.2	1.212

[1] All liquids except stearoyl chloride, m.p. 23°.

11.23   **Preparation.** — Replacement of the hydroxyl group of acids by chlorine can be accomplished with phosphorus trichloride, phosphorus penta-chloride, thionyl chloride. The type reactions are:

$$3RCOOH + PCl_3 \longrightarrow 3RCOCl + H_3PO_3$$
$$RCOOH + PCl_5 \longrightarrow RCOCl + POCl_3 + HCl$$
$$RCOOH + SOCl_2 \longrightarrow RCOCl + SO_2 + HCl$$

Some considerations guiding the choice of reagent are indicated by the following combinations found satisfactory for preparative purposes:

1. $CH_3COOH \xrightarrow[70\%]{PCl_3} CH_3COCl$ (b.p. 52°) $+ H_3PO_3$ (dec. 200°)
       Acetic acid   Acetyl chloride

2. $C_6H_5COOH \xrightarrow[90\%]{PCl_5} C_6H_5COCl$ (b.p. 197.2°) $+ POCl_3$ (b.p. 107.2°)
       Benzoic acid   Benzoyl chloride

3. $n\text{-}C_3H_7COOH \xrightarrow[85\%]{SOCl_2 \text{ (b.p. 77°)}} n\text{-}C_3H_7COCl$ (b.p. 102°) $+ SO_2 + HCl$
       n-Butyric acid   n-Butyryl chloride

Acid chlorides are so sensitive to hydrolysis, particularly when liquid, that it is impracticable to separate the reaction products from accompanying inorganic materials by extraction of the latter with water, and the only method of purification available is distillation. Phosphorus trichloride is a satisfactory reagent in example (1) because the low-boiling acetyl chloride can be distilled from the non-volatile residue of phosphorous acid. If phosphorus trichloride were used in the case of benzoic acid, however, benzoyl chloride could not be distilled from the reaction mixture because it boils at about the temperature at which phosphorous acid begins to decompose; phosphorus pentachloride is better in this case because the inorganic product is phosphorus oxychloride, which is more volatile than the organic product and can be removed by distillation prior to distillation of the benzoyl chloride (2). Phosphorus pentachloride would be a poor choice for the preparation of *n*-butyryl chloride because the boiling point of this substance is close to that of phosphorus oxychloride; thionyl chloride gives satisfactory results (3). It may be necessary to employ excess thionyl chloride, and hence the boiling point of the product must be sufficiently above or below that of thionyl chloride to permit separation. For some purposes the crude materials can be used without purification. Thus benzoic acid can be warmed with phosphorus trichloride, the mixture cooled, and the upper layer of the acid chloride decanted from a lower layer of phosphorous acid and employed directly.

The thionyl chloride method of preparing acid chlorides fails with some carboxylic acids (*e.g.* p-$NO_2C_6H_4CO_2H$) and with all sulfonic acids (*e.g.* $C_6H_5SO_3H$). Pyridine catalyzes the reaction with carboxylic acids but not that with sulfonic acids. Dimethylformamide, however, has been found to catalyze both reactions, either when used as the solvent or when employed in catalytic amount in an inert solvent (H. H. Bosshard, 1959). A reactive, highly hygroscopic amide chloride (m.p. about 140°) which may be an intermediate was isolated from a mixture of one equivalent each of thionyl chloride and dimethylformamide, and also by reaction of the amide with phosgene, oxalyl chloride, or phosphorus pentachloride.

$$(CH_3)_2N\overset{O}{\overset{\|}{C}}-H \xrightarrow[-SO_2]{SOCl_2} (CH_3)_2\overset{+}{N}=C\overset{Cl}{\underset{Cl^-\ H}{\diagdown}} \longleftrightarrow (CH_3)_2\overset{+}{N}C\overset{Cl}{\underset{Cl^-\ H}{\diagdown}}$$

Dimethylformamide chloride

This substance converts acids to their acid chlorides with regeneration of dimethyl formamide. In one example, 0.3 mole of p-nitrobenzoic acid was heated briefly at 90–95° with 0.315 mole of thionyl chloride and 0.03 mole of dimethylformamide in 160 ml. of chlorobenzene; yield of acid chloride: 87.7%. In another, a suspension of sodium β-naphthalenesulfonate in dimethylformamide was treated with thionyl chloride at 10–15°; after 5 min. sodium chloride had separated and addition of ice and water precipitated β-naphthalenesulfochloride (m.p. 76°) in quantitative yield.

Oxalyl chloride (b.p. 62°) is sometimes the preferred reagent for the preparation of acid chlorides (R. Adams, 1920), for example, of the half-esters of phthalic, succinic, and glutaric acids. A very sensitive acid can be converted into the dry sodium salt and suspended in benzene (trace of pyridine) and treated with oxalyl chloride at ice-bath temperature.

Acyl fluorides that are stable substances whereas the corresponding chlorides are nonexistent or unstable are as follows:

Formyl fluoride, HCOF, b.p. $-29°$
Perchloryl fluoride, $FClO_3$, b.p. $-48°$
Acetoacetyl fluoride, CH_3COCH_2COF, b.p. 133°

Perchloryl fluoride, the fluoride of perchloric acid, is a commercially available fluorinating agent. Diketene reacts with liquid hydrogen fluoride at a subzero temperature to give acetoacetyl fluoride and some dehydroacetic acid (G. Olah,

$$CH_2=\overset{|}{C}-\overset{|}{C}H_2 \xrightarrow[65\%]{HF} CH_3COCH_2COF$$
$$\quad\ O-C=O$$

1960). The proton resonance spectrum indicates an enol content of 7.4%. Acetoacetyl fluoride reacts with primary and secondary alcohols to form the acetoacetonides; in an ethereal solution containing an acid-binding agent (trimethylamine) it reacts smoothly with primary and secondary alcohols to give the corresponding esters.

11.24   Replacement Reactions. — Acetyl chloride fumes in moist air as the result of liberation of hydrogen chloride. The higher acid chlorides are somewhat more resistant to the action of water because they are less soluble in water. Alcohols and ammonia act upon acid chlorides in the same way. In

Hydrolysis	$RCOCl + HOH \rightarrow RCOOH + HCl$
Alcoholysis	$RCOCl + HOR' \rightarrow RCOOR' + HCl$
Ammonolysis	$RCOCl + HNH_2 \rightarrow RCONH_2 + HCl$

these reactions resulting in replacement of halogen by a hydroxyl, alkoxyl, or amino group, acid chlorides are more reactive than alkyl chlorides or even than alkyl iodides. This reactivity seems surprising when it is considered that the chlorine atom is linked to an unsaturated carbonyl group, for unsaturated halides of the type of vinyl chloride, $CH_2\!=\!CHCl$, are notably unreactive. An explanation is based on the fact that the carbonyl group is endowed with specific additive power not shared by an ethylenic double bond. Probably all three of the apparent replacements proceed by an addition, with formation of an unstable intermediate from which hydrogen chloride is eliminated with the same ease that water separates from an unstable *gem*-diol, for example:

$$\underset{\overset{|}{R\!-\!C\!=\!O}}{\overset{Cl}{}} + HOCH_3 \rightleftharpoons \left[\underset{\overset{|}{OCH_3}}{\overset{Cl}{\underset{|}{R\!-\!C\!-\!O\,H}}} \right] \longrightarrow \underset{\overset{|}{OCH_3}}{\overset{}{R\!-\!C\!=\!O}} + HCl$$

The halogen atom is apparently susceptible to replacement not because it is actually labile but as a consequence of its being linked to a functional group capable of entering into additions; even if the addition reaction is an equilibrium proceeding to only a slight extent, the irreversible decomposition of the addition product can displace the equilibrium and lead to complete conversion.

11.25   Grignard Reaction. — In the reaction with a Grignard reagent an acid chloride, like an ester, yields first a ketone and then, with more reagent, a tertiary alcohol:

$$RCOCl \xrightarrow{R'MgX} RCOR' \xrightarrow{R'MgX,\ H_2O} \underset{R'}{\overset{R}{\underset{}{\rangle}}}\!COH$$

The initial step proceeds more rapidly than the corresponding reaction of an ester, and there is more differentiation between the first and second steps. Consequently ketones can be prepared in reasonable yield by using just one equivalent of Grignard reagent and adding it by portions to a solution of the acid chloride (inverse Grignard reaction), in order to avoid exposure of the ketone formed to the action of the reagent. Investigations of other organometallic compounds have established the cadmium derivatives as preferred reagents for conversion of acid chlorides into ketones (Gilman,[1] 1936). Addition to an ethereal solution of phenylmagnesium bromide of one equivalent of anhydrous cadmium chloride affords a solution of phenylcadmium chloride, which reacts with acetyl chloride to give acetophenone in high yield. Reaction of two moles of Grignard reagent

$$C_6H_5MgBr \xrightarrow[-MgBrCl]{CdCl_2} C_6H_5CdCl \xrightarrow[83\%]{CH_3COCl} C_6H_5COCH_3 + CdCl_2$$

$$2\ C_6H_5MgBr \xrightarrow{CdCl_2} (C_6H_5)_2Cd + MgBr_2 + MgCl_2$$

$$85\% \Big\downarrow CH_3COCl$$

$$2\ C_6H_5COCH_3 + CdCl_2$$

with one mole of cadmium chloride gives diphenylcadmium, which reacts equally well with the same acid chloride. The second method was selected for the synthesis of methyl 4-keto-7-methyloctanoate; the required half ester-half acid

$$[(CH_3)_2CHCH_2CH_2]_2Cd + 2\ ClCOCH_2CH_2CO_2CH_3 \xrightarrow{73\text{-}75\%}$$

β-Carbomethoxy-
propionyl chloride

$$2\ (CH_3)_2CHCH_2CH_2COCH_2CH_2CO_2CH_3 + CdCl_2$$

Methyl 4-keto-7-methyloctanoate

chloride is made by the action of thionyl chloride on methyl hydrogen succinate (11.31).

Formation of a ketone in the reaction of an acyl halide with an organometallic halide can be interpreted as the result of either direct replacement or initial addition to the carbonyl group and subsequent elimination of a metal dihalide, as follows:

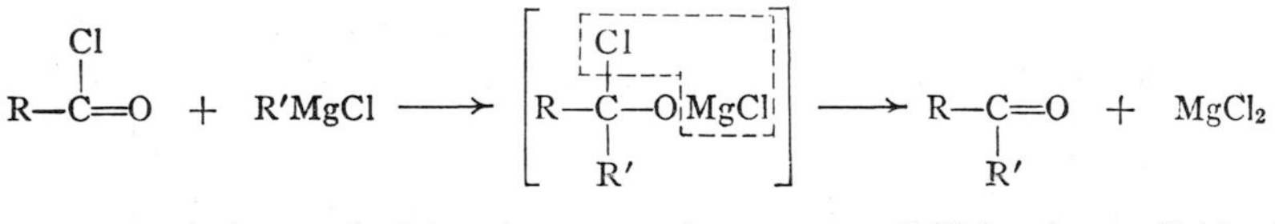

$$\begin{array}{c}Cl \\ | \\ R-C=O \end{array} + R'MgCl \longrightarrow \left[\begin{array}{c} Cl \\ | \\ R-C-OMgCl \\ | \\ R' \end{array}\right] \longrightarrow \begin{array}{c} R-C=O \\ | \\ R' \end{array} + MgCl_2$$

Evidence permitting a decision between the two possibilities is available from a study of the reactivity of a series of acid fluorides, chlorides, and bromides to a given Grignard reagent as evaluated in competitive experiments (J. R. Johnson[2]). The order of reactivity is found to be RCOF > RCOCl > RCOBr, which is just the reverse of the order of lability of the carbon–halogen bonds in alkyl halides as determined in replacement reactions: C—Br > C—Cl > C—F. That the acid fluoride is the most, rather than the least, reactive member of the series indicates that the reaction can hardly involve direct severance of the carbon–halogen linkage and suggests an initial addition to the carbonyl group. The halogen atom then influences the speed of the reaction merely to the extent that it modifies the

---

[1] Henry Gilman, b. 1893 Boston; Ph.D. Harvard (Kohler); Iowa State College
[2] John R. Johnson, b. 1900 Chicago; Ph.D. Illinois (Adams); Cornell Univ.

TABLE 11.7. ATOMIC DIMENSIONS

BOND	DISTANCE BETWEEN ATOMIC CENTERS, Å	RADIUS OF THE HALOGEN ATOM, Å
C—C	1.54	....
C—F	1.41	0.64
C—Cl	1.76	.99
C—Br	1.91	1.14
C—I	2.10	1.33

additive power of the carbonyl group, and this effect may be partly a function of its size, a large atom tending to block free access of the Grignard reagent to the unsaturated center. The space factor can be evaluated from the interatomic distances given in Table 11.7; the differences between the halogens are very marked. The relationship between an acid fluoride and an acid bromide is indicated schematically as follows:

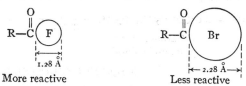

More reactive　　　　　　　　Less reactive

A second factor is the relative electronegativity of the halogens, for the addition reaction requires partial polarization of the carbonyl group in the sense $>\overset{+}{C}\!-\!\overset{-}{O}$. Since fluorine is the most electronegative, or electron-accepting, of the halogens, the fluorine atom would cause a drift of electrons away from the carbon atom and hence increase the fractional positive charge to an extent greater than is realized in an acid chloride or bromide.

11.26　　Arndt-Eistert Reaction. — The first step in the Arndt-Eistert reaction is condensation of an acid chloride with diazomethane to form a diazoketone. The condensation had been investigated in England in 1915, but the

$$R-\overset{O}{\overset{\|}{C}}\!-\!\overline{[Cl + H]}\!-\!CH\!=\!\overset{+}{N}\!=\!\overset{-}{N} \longrightarrow R-\overset{O}{\overset{\|}{C}}\!-\!CH\!=\!\overset{+}{N}\!=\!\overset{-}{N} + HCl$$
Diazoketone

$$R-\overset{O}{\overset{\|}{C}}\!-\!CH\!=\!\overset{+}{N}\!=\!\overset{-}{N} + HCl \longrightarrow R-\overset{O}{\overset{\|}{C}}\!-\!CH_2Cl + N_2$$

product isolated was not the diazoketone but the chloroketone formed from it by reaction with the hydrogen chloride liberated in the first step. Arndt and Eistert in Germany in 1927 recognized this difficulty, noted that the earlier workers had used only one mole of diazomethane and had added it to the acid chloride, and found that by suitable increase in the amount of reagent and by adding the acid chloride slowly to the diazomethane, rather than the reverse, so that the hydrogen chloride formed would be destroyed by reaction with the reagent, diazoketones can be prepared without difficulty in high yield.

In the completing step of the Arndt-Eistert reaction the diazoketone is heated with water in the presence of colloidal silver as catalyst. The reaction would appear to involve a rearrangement, for the R group initially joined to the carbonyl

$$R-\overset{O}{\overset{\|}{C}}-CH{=}N^{+}{=}N^{-} \ + \ H_2O \ \xrightarrow{\ Ag\ } \ R-CH_2C\overset{O}{\underset{OH}{\diagup}}$$

group is joined in the product to a methylene group. Indeed rearrangement has been proved to occur by an experiment with an isotopically labeled diazoketone:

$$C_6H_5\overset{O}{\overset{\|}{C^{13}}}-CH{=}N^{+}{=}N^{-} \ \xrightarrow{\ H_2O(Ag)\ } \ C_6H_5CH_2C^{13}\overset{O}{\underset{OH}{\diagup}}$$

A further clue to the mechanism of the reaction is that diazoketones when decomposed in the absence of water yield ketenes of the formula $RCH{=}C{=}O$. Ketene itself adds water to form acetic acid. The carboxylic acid formed when a diazoketone is decomposed in the presence of water evidently arises by addition of

$$RCH{=}C{=}O \ + \ HOH \ \rightleftharpoons \ RCH{=}C\overset{OH}{\underset{OH}{\diagup}} \ \longrightarrow \ RCH_2C\overset{O}{\underset{OH}{\diagup}}$$

water to the intermediate ketene. With the further knowledge that the carbony group of the diazoketone becomes part of the carboxyl group of the acid, the reaction can be inferred to take the following course. Loss of nitrogen from the

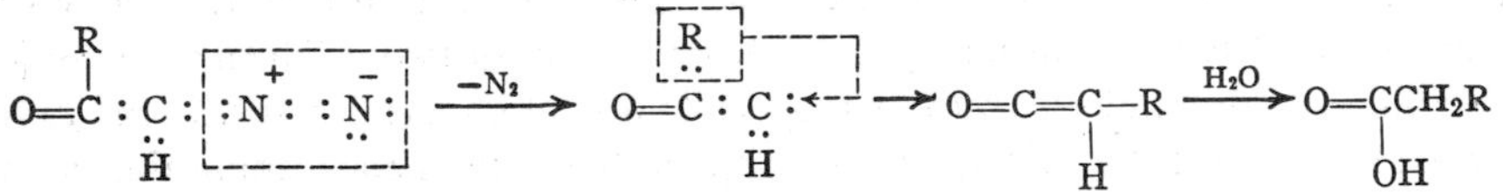

(a)   (b)   (c)   (d)

diazoketone (a) produces the intermediate (b) having an electron-deficient carbon. The alkyl group therefore migrates with the pair of shared electrons to fill the open sextet and give the ketene (c), which adds water to form the acid (d).

The Arndt-Eistert reaction is useful in synthesis because it provides a means of lengthening an acid chain: $RCOOH \rightarrow RCH_2COOH$. The decomposition of the diazoketone can be effected with silver oxide catalyst in the presence

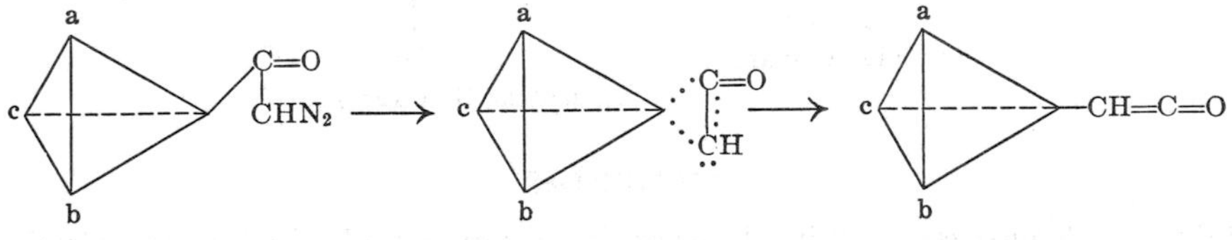

of methanol, in which case the product is the methyl ester. In an improved procedure (Wilds,[1] 1948) a higher boiling alcohol is used (benzyl alcohol, octanol-2) and the reaction conducted at 160–180°; a catalyst is not essential, but addition of collidine improves the yield. Experiments with acids in which the migrating

[1] Alfred L. Wilds, b. 1915 Kansas City; Ph.D. Michigan (Bachmann); Univ. Wisconsin

group is asymmetric have established that the group migrates with retention of configurations (Wallis, 1933; Wiberg,[1] 1956), perhaps because a cyclic transition state is involved.

11.27 Phosgene (COCl₂). — Phosgene was discovered by J. Davy (1812) as a product of the combination of carbon monoxide and chlorine under the influence of light (Gr. *phos*, light; L. *genere*, to be born), and it is now manufactured from these reagents with activated charcoal as catalyst. The substance

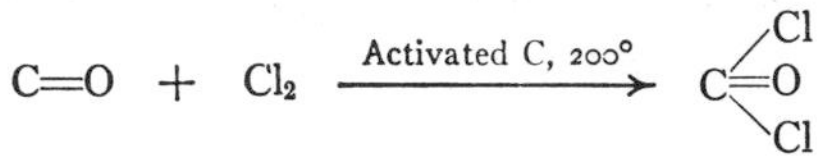

$$C{=}O \ + \ Cl_2 \ \xrightarrow{\text{Activated C, 200°}} \ C{\underset{Cl}{\overset{Cl}{\lessgtr}}}O$$

Phosgene
(b.p. 8.3°)

is a highly toxic gas having an odor resembling that of newmown hay; it is available in the liquefied form in steel cylinders.

Phosgene is the diacid chloride of the unstable carbonic acid and is sometimes called carbonyl chloride. It enters into typical reactions of hydrolysis to carbonic acid and ammonolysis to urea:

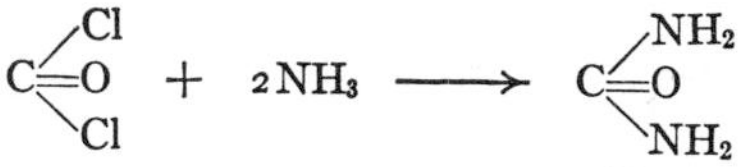

$$C{\underset{Cl}{\overset{Cl}{\lessgtr}}}O \ + \ 2NH_3 \ \longrightarrow \ C{\underset{NH_2}{\overset{NH_2}{\lessgtr}}}O$$

Urea

Phosgene was introduced as a war gas by the Germans in 1915 and was responsible for about 80% of the gas casualties in World War I. It is a lung injurant similar to chlorine but about ten times as toxic; it is also more insidious in action, since it gives no warning symptoms for an hour or two. The irritant action is attributed to hydrolysis in the tissues to hydrochloric acid, which is the agent directly toxic to cells. Phosgene is nonpersistent and hence applicable as an attacking agent. It is ineffective in wet weather as the result of ready hydrolysis, and it is stopped effectively by modern gas masks. The substance diphosgene is convertible into phosgene and has also been used as a war gas. It is trichloromethyl chloroformate, ClCOOCCl₃, and is made by chlorination of methyl chloroformate, derived from phosgene and methanol:

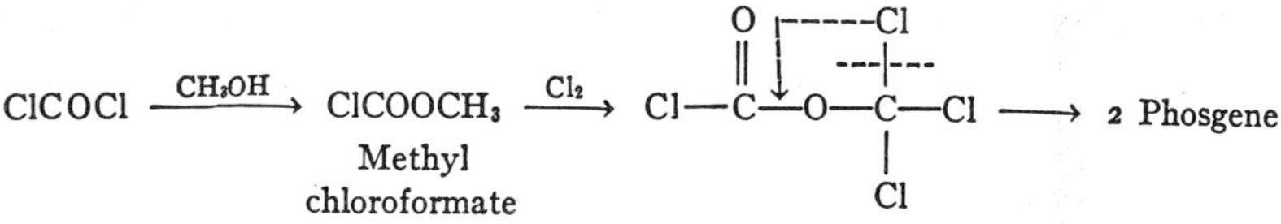

$$ClCOCl \ \xrightarrow{CH_3OH} \ ClCOOCH_3 \ \xrightarrow{Cl_2} \ Cl{-}C{-}O{-}C{-}Cl \ \longrightarrow \ 2 \ \text{Phosgene}$$

Methyl
chloroformate

Diphosgene (b.p. 127°)

ANHYDRIDES

11.28 Properties. — With the exception of formic acid, which on dehydration yields carbon monoxide, the carboxylic acids form anhydrides in which water is eliminated between two molecules of the acid. Anhydrides of normal acids up to C₁₂ are liquids (Table 11.8); acetic anhydride is a mobile liquid

[1] Kenneth B. Wiberg, b. 1927 Brooklyn, N. Y.; Ph.D. Columbia (Doering); Univ. Washington; Yale Univ.

TABLE 11.8. ANHYDRIDES

NAME	FORMULA	M.P., °C.	B.P., °C.	SP. GR.
Acetic anhydride	$(CH_3CO)_2O$	−73	139.6	1.082
Propionic anhydride	$(C_2H_5CO)_2O$	−45	168	1.012
n-Butyric anhydride	$(n\text{-}C_3H_7CO)_2O$	−75	198	0.969
n-Valeric anhydride	$(n\text{-}C_4H_9CO)_2O$		$218^{754mm.}$	.929
Stearic anhydride	$(n\text{-}C_{17}H_{35}CO)_2O$	72		
Succinic anhydride	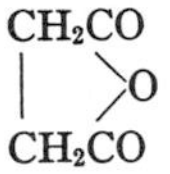 $\begin{matrix} CH_2CO \\ \mid \quad\quad >O \\ CH_2CO \end{matrix}$	119.6	261	1.104
Benzoic anhydride	$(C_6H_5CO)_2O$	42	360	1.199
Phthalic anhydride	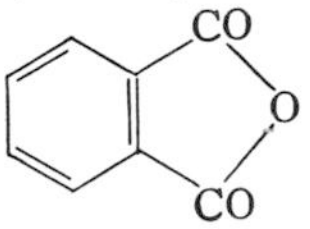	132	284.5	1.527

with a pungent irritating odor. Anhydrides have nearly twice the molecular weights of the acids from which they are derived, and they boil at somewhat higher temperatures. Acetic anhydride (b.p. 139.6°, mol. wt. 102.09) boils at a higher temperature than esters, halogen compounds, and hydrocarbons of comparable molecular weight.

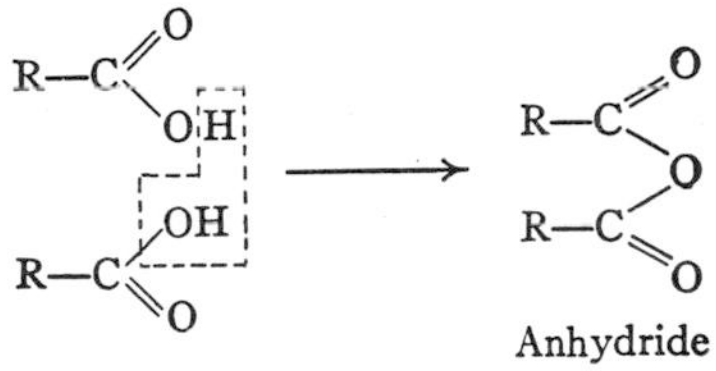

Anhydride

11.29   Preparation. — A laboratory method of preparing acetic anhydride is the reaction of acetyl chloride with anhydrous sodium acetate (compare the Williamson synthesis of an ether). Several variations of this method

$$CH_3COO\,Na \atop + \atop CH_3CO\,Cl \quad \longrightarrow \quad {CH_3CO \atop CH_3CO} >O \; + \; NaCl$$

have been used; for example, when phosphorus oxychloride acts upon excess sodium acetate, acetyl chloride is formed, and this then reacts with more sodium acetate as above, the net result being:

$$4\,CH_3COONa \; + \; POCl_3 \quad \longrightarrow \quad 2\,(CH_3CO)_2O \; + \; NaPO_3 \; + \; 3\,NaCl$$

Sulfur chloride is employed as the active halide in another procedure.

A modern industrial process for making acetic anhydride utilizes the highly unsaturated and reactive ketene, prepared by cracking acetone:

$$CH_3COCH_3 \xrightarrow{700\text{-}750°} CH_2{=}C{=}O \; + \; CH_4$$

Ketene
(b.p. −56°)

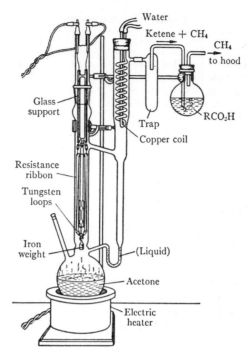

Water
Ketene + CH₄
CH₄ to hood
Glass support
Trap
Copper coil
RCO₂H
Resistance ribbon
Tungsten loops
Iron weight
(Liquid)
Acetone
Electric heater

FIG. 11.1 — Ketene Generator

The reaction undoubtedly involves radicals and probably follows the path of thermal cracking of hydrocarbons (7.9) as suggested in the formulation. Cleavage

$$CH_3COCH_3 \rightarrow \dot{C}H_3 + CH_3\dot{C}O$$
$$CH_3\dot{C}O \rightarrow \dot{C}H_3 + CO$$
$$\dot{C}H_3 + CH_3COCH_3 \rightarrow CH_4 + \dot{C}H_2COCH_3$$
$$\dot{C}H_2COCH_3 \rightarrow CH{=}C{=}O + \dot{C}H_3$$

of a carbon–carbon bond gives methyl and acetyl radicals, and the acetyl radical can break down to carbon monoxide and another methyl radical. A methyl radical abstracts hydrogen from acetone to form methane and $\cdot CH_2COCH_3$, which then suffers β-fission to ketene and a methyl radical. Combination of two methyl radicals terminates the chain. A laboratory ketene generator is shown in Fig. 11.1. Refluxing acetone comes in contact with a glowing grid of resistance wire and undergoes cracking; unchanged acetone is condensed and returned to the boiling flask, and the ketene evolved in the gas stream along with methane is absorbed directly by a liquid reagent or in a solution.

Ketene combines with most reagents containing either hydroxyl or amino groups; it reacts readily with acetic acid to give acetic anhydride, probably by addition to the carbonyl group and migration of the enolic hydrogen atom:

$$CH_3COOH + CH_2{=}C{=}O \longrightarrow \begin{bmatrix} CH_2{=}C{-}OH \\ \quad\quad\quad O \\ CH_3C{=}O \end{bmatrix} \longrightarrow \begin{matrix} CH_3C{=}O \\ \quad\quad O \\ CH_3C{=}O \end{matrix}$$

Mixed anhydrides of the type $CH_3CO \cdot O \cdot COR$ can be prepared by addition of a higher acid, $RCOOH$, to ketene and distillation at a greatly reduced pressure, but unless the temperature is kept low the mixed anhydride rearranges and the more volatile acetic anhydride distills first.   By deliberate maintenance of a temperature favoring rearrangement, ketene can be employed for conversion of higher acids into their anhydrides, for example:

$$2\,CH_3(CH_2)_4CO_2H \; + \; CH_2{=}C{=}O \xrightarrow[80-87\%]{} [CH_3(CH_2)_4CO]_2O \; + \; CH_3CO_2H$$

Caproic anhydride
(b.p. 243°)

Higher anhydrides that are crystalline solids are prepared by heating the acid with either acetic anhydride or acetyl chloride; in either case acetic acid is formed and serves as a solvent from which the higher anhydride crystallizes on cooling. Example 2 illustrates the conversion of a dibasic acid into a cyclic anhydride.

1.

$$C_6H_5COOH \xrightarrow[72-74\%]{(CH_3CO)_2O \,+\, H_3PO_4 \text{ (trace)}} (C_6H_5CO)_2O$$

Benzoic acid   Benzoic anhydride

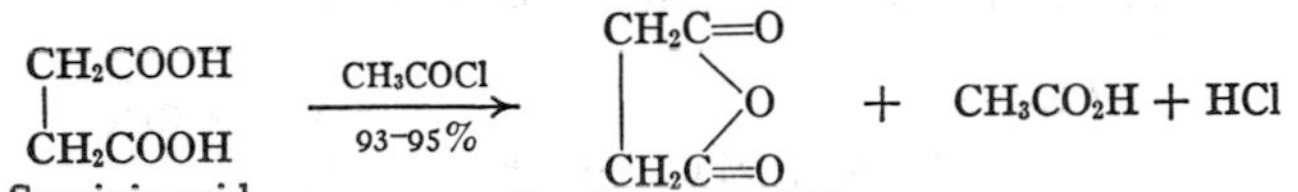

2.

A method for conversion of an acid into its anhydride under very mild conditions consists in reaction with one half equivalent of methoxyacetylene (J. F. Arens, 1950).   Wasserman[1] (1960) found that the reaction of benzoic acid with one

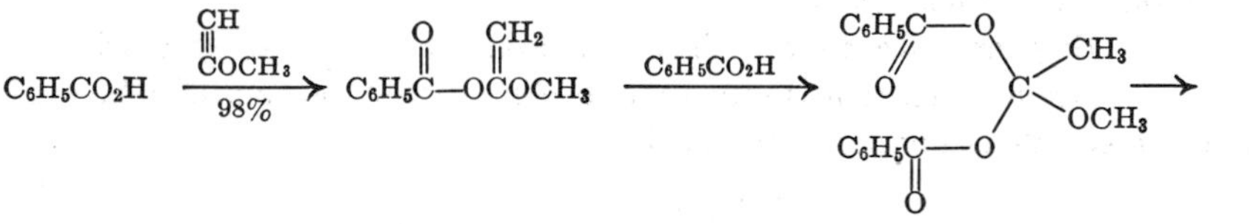

(1)   (2)

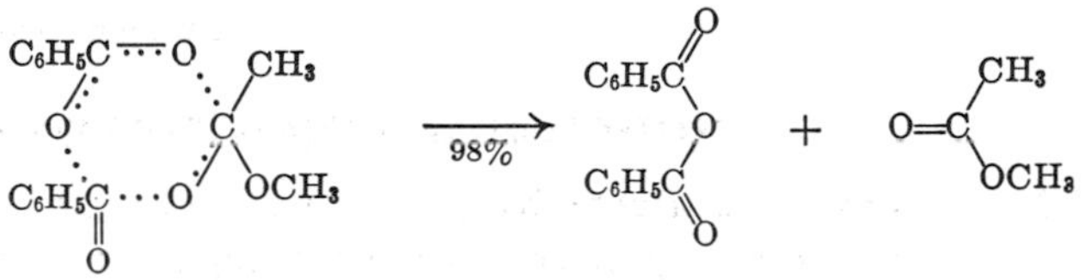

(3)   (4) M. p. 45°

equivalent of methoxyacetylene can be controlled to permit isolation of 1-methoxy-vinylbenzoate (1) by operating at a low temperature with addition of a trace of mercuric benzoate to selectively catalyze addition to the triple bond.   E. R. H. Jones (1954) postulated that the unstable orthoester (2) decomposes intramolecularly through the cyclic transition state (3) to the anhydride and methyl acetone, and Wasserman established that this indeed is the path: reaction of the monoadduct (1) with benzoic acid-O^{18} resulted in equal distribution of isotope between the anhydride and the ester.

[1] Harry H. Wasserman, b. 1920 Boston, Mass.; Ph.D. Harvard (Woodward); Yale Univ.

11.30   Hydrolysis and Ammonolysis. — Anhydrides are not so sensitive to water as acyl halides, but are more easily hydrolyzed than esters. Thus acetic anhydride can be hydrolyzed in a few minutes by boiling water. The anhydride dissolves in cold water to the extent of about 12 g. per 100 g., and if the solution is kept at room temperature, the substance undergoes complete hydrolysis only after an hour or two, whereas acetyl chloride is hydrolyzed at once.

$$\begin{array}{c} CH_2CO \\ | \quad\quad >O \; + \; HNH_2 \; \longrightarrow \\ CH_2CO \end{array} \quad\quad \begin{array}{l} CH_2CONH_2 \\ | \\ CH_2COOH \end{array}$$

Succinamic acid
(m.p. 157°)

The reaction with ammonia parallels that with water and is used for preparation of the monoamides of dibasic acids.

11.31   Alcoholysis; Acetylation of Alcohols. — Anhydrides react with alcohol as with water and ammonia; succinic anhydride, for example, affords the monoester of the corresponding dibasic acid:

$$\begin{array}{c} CH_2CO \\ | \quad\quad >O \; + \; HOCH_3 \; \longrightarrow \\ CH_2CO \end{array} \quad\quad \begin{array}{l} CH_2COOCH_3 \\ | \\ CH_2COOH \end{array}$$

Methyl hydrogen succinate
(m.p. 58°)

The most important application of the general reaction is acetylation of primary and secondary alcohols (8.23).

11.32   Grignard Reaction. — The reaction of a cyclic anhydride with Grignard reagent is sometimes useful for the synthesis of γ-keto acids, for example, β-benzoylpropionic acid:

$$C_6H_5MgBr \; + \; \begin{array}{c} CH_2CO \\ | \quad\quad >O \\ CH_2CO \end{array} \; \rightarrow \; C_6H_5COCH_2CH_2CO_2H$$

β-Benzoylpropionic acid

PROTECTION AND CHARACTERIZATION

11.33   Protective Derivatives. — During synthetic sequences, it is often necessary to protect a carboxyl group as an ester while operations are performed on another part of the molecule, and the ester chosen must be one from which the acid can be recovered without difficulty. Methyl and ethyl esters are satisfactory except in the case of a base-sensitive acid which will not withstand the fairly drastic conditions of alkaline hydrolysis. Benzyl esters are sometimes used to advantage since they can be cleaved by hydrogenation: $RCO_2CH_2C_6H_5 +$ $2 H \rightarrow RCO_2H + CH_3C_6H_5$. They are also subject to acid cleavage under mild conditions.

Tetrahydropyranyl esters, useful as protective derivatives, are made by acid-catalyzed reaction of the acid with 2,3-dihydropyrane at 20–30° (compare 8.38). They are cleaved by p-toluenesulfonic acid monohydrate in refluxing acetic acid.

The occasion may arise for providing temporary protection to the free carboxyl group of a diacid monomethyl ester. The substance can be transformed into the methyl tetrahydropyranyl ester, the operation performed, and the tetrahydropyranyl group removed by hydrolysis as above without disturbance of the methyl ester group.

t-Butyl esters offer the advantage that they are labile and can be split by various methods to the acid and isobutylene:

$$
\begin{array}{ccc}
\quad\ CH_3 & & CH_2 \\
\quad\ | & & \| \\
RCOOC-CH_3 & \rightarrow\ RCOOH\ +\ & C-CH_3 \\
\quad\ | & & | \\
\quad\ CH_3 & & CH_3
\end{array}
$$

Anhydrous *p*-toluenesulfonic acid in glacial acetic acid containing a trace of acetic anhydride effects smooth cleavage and the course of the reaction can be followed by means of a constant-pressure eudiometer. *t*-Butyl esters are also cleaved by concentrated sulfuric acid or by treatment at room temperature with gaseous hydrogen chloride in dioxane. In case the presence of a strong acid is objectionable, cleavage can be effected by pyrolysis (30 min. at 210°).

11.34 **Characterization of 1,4- and 1,5-Diacids.** — Diacids of the succinic and glutaric type produced on oxidation of natural products are often difficult to isolate or purify, either because of unfavorable solubility relationships or because a small amount of contaminant prevents crystallization, even though the pure acid is high melting. A useful expedient is to convert the crude acid to the anhydride (acetic anhydride or acetyl chloride), form the anilic acid by reaction in chloroform with *p*-aminoazobenzene, and cyclize the product with acetyl chloride (H. B. Henbest, 1955). Chromatographed on alumina, the anils form deep yellow bands and are easily separated; their light-absorption properties (UV and IR) facilitate identification.

PROBLEMS

1. Compare the acidity constants (pK_a) of acids of type $A-CH_2CO_2H$, where A = CH_3, OH, I, and Cl. What are the relative positions in the periodic table of the key elements in the group A?
2. Predict the relative order of the acidity constants for the separation of a second proton from phthalic and isophthalic acid.
3. Write formulas for (*a*) 3,6-dimethyl-Δ^2-heptenoic acid; (*b*) decane-1,10-dioic acid.
4. Which synthesis, Grignard or nitrile, would you pick for effecting the following transformations:
   (*a*) $CH_3CH_2CHBrCH(CH_3)_2 \rightarrow$ Ethylisopropylacetic acid
   (*b*) $CH_3CHOHCH_2CH_2Cl \rightarrow \gamma$-Hydroxyvaleric acid
5. Devise a synthesis of succinic acid, $HO_2CCH_2CH_2CO_2H$, from ethanol.
6. How could $(CH_3)_2CHCH_2COCH_3$ be converted into isovaleric acid?
7. Outline a procedure for the isolation of *n*-butyric acid from a mixture of the substance with *n*-amyl alcohol, *n*-amyl chloride, and ethyl *n*-valerate.
8. What method of experimentation would distinguish between the following isomeric acids?
   (*a*) $CH_3CH_2CH(CH_3)CO_2H$ (*c*) $(CH_3)_3CCO_2H$
   (*b*) $(CH_3)_2CHCH_2CO_2H$

9. Suggest methods for the preparation of the methyl esters of each of the following acids. If a catalyst is to be used, suggest a specific one.

(a) $(CH_3)_3CCH_2CO_2H$

(b) $CH_3CH_2C(CH_3)_2CO_2H$

(c) $CH_3CH{=}CHCO_2H$

(d) $n\text{-}C_{11}H_{23}COOH$, starting with $n\text{-}C_{11}H_{23}COOCH_2CH_2CH_3$

10. Write an electronic formulation showing the mechanism of the esterification of acetic acid with methanol, with boron fluoride as catalyst.

11. Indicate a synthesis of $(CH_3)_2CHCOCH_3$ from isobutyric acid.

12. Rates of esterification with methanol (as in Table 11.4) have been determined for the following acids. Predict the order of decreasing reactivity:

(a) $[(CH_3)_2CH]_2CHCO_2H$

(b) $(CH_3)_2CHCH(C_2H_5)CO_2H$

(c) $(CH_3CH_2)_2CHCO_2H$

(d) $(CH_3)_3CC(CH_3)_2CO_2H$

(e) $(CH_3)_3CCH_2C(CH_3)_2CO_2H$

13. How could bromoacetyl chloride be prepared from acetic acid?

14. What products would you expect to result from the interaction of ketene with water and with ethanol?

15. By what sequence of reactions could succinic acid be transformed into $CH_3OCOCH_2CH_2COCl$?

16. A substance of the formula $C_4H_{10}O_4$ yields on acetylation with acetic anhydride a derivative of the formula $C_{12}H_{18}O_8$. How many hydroxyl groups are present in the substance? What is the probable structure?

17. Devise a synthesis of $2,5$-dimethylhexadiene-$2,4$ starting with succinic acid.

18. Compare the reactivities of acid chlorides, anhydrides, esters, and ethers.

19. Indicate two reaction sequences by which n-heptylic acid can be prepared from castor oil (see pp. 267–269).

Note to p. 379.—Dichlorofluoromethane reacts with potassium isopropoxide in isopropyl alcohol to give triisopropyl orthoformate as the only organic product detected (71% yield) whereas chloroform and bromoform give, in addition, propylene, diisopropyl ether, acetone, carbon monoxide, a methylene halide, and sometimes dark-colored resinous products (J. Hine, 1960).

Chapter 12

ALDEHYDES AND KETONES

12.1   **Properties.** — The boiling points of aldehydes and of ketones are
        slightly higher than those of paraffins of comparable molecular weight,
probably because of association due to polarization of the carbonyl group.   Properties of common aldehydes and ketones are recorded in Tables 12.1 and 12.2.   In

Compound	Mol. Wt.	B.P., °C.
$CH_3CH_2CH_2CH_2CH_2CHO$	100.16	129
$CH_3COCH_2CH_2CH_2CH_3$	100.16	127.2
$CH_3CH_2COCH_2CH_2CH_3$	100.16	124
$CH_3CH_2CH_2CH_2CH_2CH_2CH_3$	100.20	98.4

each series the first few members are soluble in water and those from C_5 on are
sparingly soluble or insoluble.

12.2   **Paraldehyde.** — Acetaldehyde, a volatile liquid having a pungent
        smell, rapidly polymerizes under acid catalysis to the less volatile
and unreactive trimer, **paraldehyde**.   At equilibrium, conversion is about 95%

$$3\ CH_3CHO \xrightleftharpoons{H_2SO_4} (CH_3CHO)_3$$

Acetaldehyde   Paraldehyde
(b.p. 20.8°)   (b.p. 124°)

complete.   Since paraldehyde is not oxidizable and shows no carbonyl reactions,
it is formulated as a six-membered heterocycle.   Addition of a trace of sulfuric

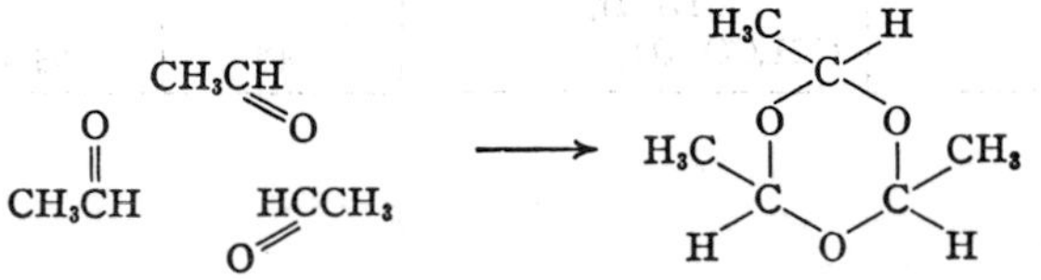

395

TABLE 12.1. ALDEHYDES

NAME	FORMULA	M.P., °C.	B.P., °C.	SP. GR.
Formaldehyde	CH_2O	−92	−21	0.815
Acetaldehyde	CH_3CHO	−123	20.8	.781
Chloral	CCl_3CHO	−57.5	97.8	1.512
Glyoxal	$O{=}HC \cdot CH{=}O$	15	50.4	1.14
Propionaldehyde	CH_3CH_2CHO	−81	48.8	0.807
n-Butyraldehyde	$CH_3CH_2CH_2CHO$	−97	74.7	.817
Isobutyraldehyde	$(CH_3)_2CHCHO$	−66	61	.794
n-Valeraldehyde	$CH_3CH_2CH_2CH_2CHO$	−92	103.7	.819
Isovaleraldehyde	$(CH_3)_2CHCH_2CHO$	−51	92.5	.803
n-Caproaldehyde	$CH_3(CH_2)_4CHO$		129	.834
n-Heptaldehyde (enanthol)	$CH_3(CH_2)_5CHO$	−45	155	.850
Stearaldehyde	$CH_3(CH_2)_{16}CHO$	38		
Acrolein	$CH_2{=}CHCHO$	−88	52.5	.841
Crotonaldehyde	$CH_3CH{=}CHCHO$	−76.5	104	.859
Benzaldehyde	C_6H_5CHO	−56	179	1.046
Furfural	$\begin{array}{c}CH{-}CH\\ \| \quad \|\\ CH \quad CCHO\\ \diagdown O \diagup\end{array}$	−31	162	1.156

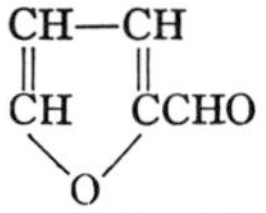

TABLE 12.2. KETONES

NAME	FORMULA	M.P., °C.	B.P., °C.	SP. GR.
Acetone	CH_3COCH_3	−95	56.1	0.7915
Methyl ethyl ketone	$CH_3COCH_2CH_3$	−86	79.6	.805
Methyl n-propyl ketone	$CH_3CH_2CH_2COCH_3$	−77.8	102.1	.812
Diethyl ketone	$CH_3CH_2COCH_2CH_3$	−42.0	101.7	.814
Hexanone-2	$CH_3CH_2CH_2CH_2COCH_3$	−56.9	127.2	.830
Hexanone-3	$CH_3CH_2CH_2COCH_2CH_3$		124	.818
Methyl t-butyl ketone (pinacolone)	$CH_3COC(CH_3)_3$	−52.5	106.3	.811
Di-n-propyl ketone	$(CH_3CH_2CH_2)_2CO$	−34	144.2	.821
Diisopropyl ketone	$[(CH_3)_2CH]_2CO$		125	.806
Diisobutyl ketone	$[(CH_3)_2CHCH_2]_2CO$		166	.833
Di-n-amyl ketone	$(n\text{-}C_5H_{11})_2CO$	14.6	228	.826
Stearone	$(n\text{-}C_{17}H_{35})_2CO$	88.5	$345^{12mm.}$	.793
Chloroacetone	CH_3COCH_2Cl	−44.5	119	1.162
s-Dichloroacetone	$ClCH_2COCH_2Cl$	45	173.4	1.383
Diacetyl	$CH_3COCOCH_3$		89	0.975
Acetylacetone	$CH_3COCH_2COCH_3$	−23.2	137	.976
Mesityl oxide	$(CH_3)_2C{=}CHCOCH_3$	−59.0	131	.863
Phorone	$[(CH_3)_2C{=}CH]_2CO$	28	198.2	.885
Cyclohexanone	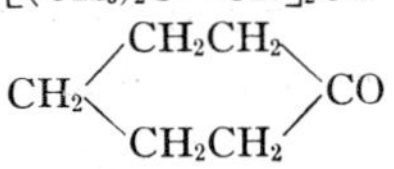 $CH_2\big\langle\begin{smallmatrix}CH_2CH_2\\ \\ CH_2CH_2\end{smallmatrix}\big\rangle CO$		156.7	.949
Benzophenone	$C_6H_5COC_6H_5$	48	305.4	1.083

acid to acetaldehyde initiates exothermal polymerization which soon reaches equilibrium; washing with water removes the small amount of monomer present and the acid catalyst, and the residual paraldehyde is dried and distilled. Depolymerization is accomplished by addition of a trace of sulfuric acid and slow distillation to remove the monomer and displace the equilibrium. Paraldehyde is thus a convenient form in which to store potential acetaldehyde

12.3   **Polymers of Formaldehyde.** — Distillation of formaldehyde from a 60% solution containing 2% sulfuric acid and extraction with chloro-orm affords the trimer trioxane. The carbonyl group of formaldehyde is less

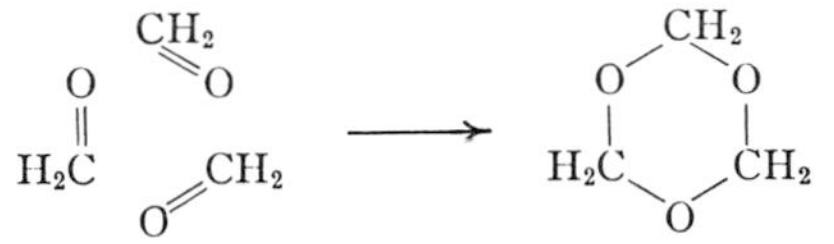

$$\underset{\begin{array}{c}\text{Trioxane}\\\text{(m.p. 62°, b.p. 115°)}\end{array}}{}$$

Trioxane
(m.p. 62°, b.p. 115°)

hindered and hence more reactive than that of higher aldehydes, and the equilibrium in water solution is particularly favorable to the *gem*-diol, or hydrate.

$$CH_2{=}O \;+\; HOH \;\rightleftharpoons\; CH_2\hspace{-2pt}\begin{array}{c}OH\\OH\end{array}$$

Formaldehyde hydrate

Evaporation of the aqueous solution gives a mixture of chain polymers of varying chain length, evidently arising from elimination of water between successive molecules of formaldehyde hydrate. The usual polymer mixture known as para-

$$HOCH_2OH \;+\; nHOCH_2OH \;+\; HOCH_2OH \;\longrightarrow\; HOCH_2(OCH_2)_nOCH_2OH$$

Paraformaldehyde

formaldehyde is an amorphous solid of high molecular weight that is insoluble in water. Depolymerization occurs at a temperature of 180–200°, and hence paraformaldehyde is a convenient source of anhydrous, gaseous formaldehyde.

PREPARATION

12.4   **Oxidation of Alcohols.** — A primary alcohol on oxidation yields initially an aldehyde, but since the aldehyde is easily oxidized further to the acid, yields are apt to be low. In the case of the lower aldehydes advantage can be taken of the fact that the oxidation product is more volatile than the hydrogen-bonded alcohol. Thus ethanol (b.p. 78.3°) affords acetaldehyde (b.p. 20.8°) in fair yield on oxidation with a solution of potassium dichromate in dilute

$$\underset{\text{b.p. 97.2°}}{CH_3CH_2CH_2OH} \xrightarrow[\text{45-40\%}]{K_2Cr_2O_7,\text{ dil. }H_2SO_4} \underset{\text{b.p. 48.5°}}{CH_3CH_2CHO}$$

sulfuric acid kept at 50°; the aldehyde distills as formed and the alcohol is retained. The oxidation of *n*-propyl alcohol is carried out by gradual addition of the oxidizing mixture to the alcohol in a flask fitted with a condenser with water circulating at 60° to return the alcohol and connected at the top with a second, cooled condenser set for downward distillation of the aldehyde.

Ketones can be oxidized by alkaline permanganate or by nitric acid under drastic conditions, but procedures are available for oxidation of secondary alcohols under conditions such that the ketones are not attacked further. For example menthol, the chief constituent of oil of peppermint, can be oxidized by gradual addition of potassium dichromate in dilute sulfuric acid and the corresponding ketone extracted from the cooled reaction mixture with ether. Cyclohexanol

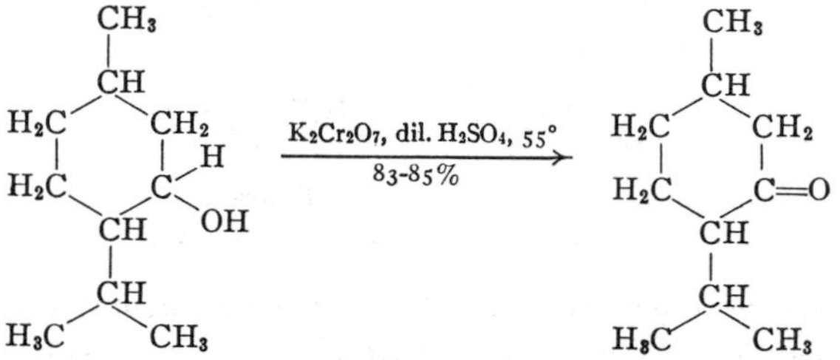

$$\text{l-Menthol} \xrightarrow[83-85\%]{K_2Cr_2O_7,\ dil.\ H_2SO_4,\ 55°} \text{l-Menthone}$$

l-Menthol
(m.p. 42.5°)

l-Menthone
(b.p. 207°)

can be oxidized to cyclohexanone in 85% yield with a solution of sodium dichromate dihydrate in acetic acid at 60°. A new method employs chromic anhydride in dimethylformamide with sulfuric acid as catalyst (G. Snatzke, 1961).

12.5   Dehydrogenation. — An alternative experimental procedure for conversion of an alcohol into an aldehyde or a ketone is passage of the vaporized substance over metallic copper in the temperature range 200–300°. Hydrogen is eliminated as such. The reaction can be conducted in an assembly

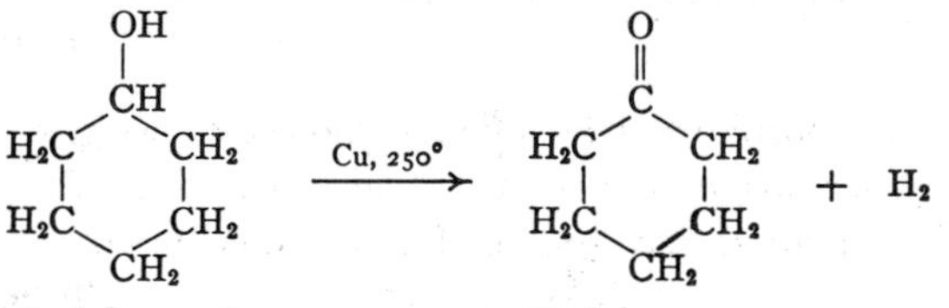

$$\text{Cyclohexanol} \xrightarrow{Cu,\ 250°} \text{Cyclohexanone} + H_2$$

Cyclohexanol

Cyclohexanone

similar to the ketene generator (Fig. 11.1) except that the vapor space is provided with a heated copper grid or with a heated tube charged with reduced copper chromite, a particularly efficient catalyst. Excellent yields are obtainable, and the method is well adapted to the technical production of volatile aldehydes and ketones (formaldehyde, acetaldehyde, acetone, cyclohexanone). Formaldehyde is made by passing methanol vapor and air over heated silver or copper catalyst. The reaction probably consists in dehydrogenation followed by combustion of the

$$CH_3OH + \tfrac{1}{2}O_2 \xrightarrow{Ag,\ 250°} CH_2O + H_2O$$

hydrogen produced, and enough heat is liberated to maintain the required temperature. The oxidation is controlled to a point short of complete conversion, and the gaseous mixture is absorbed in water and marketed under the name formalin, a 40% solution of formaldehyde containing some methanol. Formalin is employed as a convenient source of formaldehyde for manufacture of synthetic resins, preserving anatomical specimens, hardening photographic film, etc.

12.6   **Tosylate Method.** — Kornblum found (1959) that primary saturated alcohols are converted into aldehydes in 60–85% yield by oxidation of the tosylates with dimethyl sulfoxide in the presence of sodium bicarbonate at 150° (3 min.). Benzylic tosylates are oxidized smoothly at 100°. The required esters can be prepared from the halides; for example, by reaction of n-octyl iodide dissolved in acetonitrile with silver tosylate. Dimethyl sulfoxide catalyzed by boron fluoride oxidizes cyclohexene oxide to 2-hydroxycyclohexanone (T. Cohen, 1961).

12.7   **Oppenauer Oxidation.** — The method introduced by R. V. Oppenauer in 1937 consists in refluxing a secondary alcohol in acetone and benzene or toluene with aluminum t-butoxide; the net result is dehydrogenation of the alcohol with transference of the two hydrogen atoms to acetone as acceptor. The reaction involves exchange of metal between the secondary alcohol and aluminum

$$
\begin{array}{c}
R \\
\diagdown \\
CHOH \\
\diagup \\
R'
\end{array}
+ (CH_3)_2C{=}O \underset{\text{(excess)}}{\overset{Al[OC(CH_3)_3]_3}{\rightleftharpoons}}
\begin{array}{c}
R \\
\diagdown \\
C{=}O \\
\diagup \\
R'
\end{array}
+ (CH_3)_2CHOH
$$

t-butoxide; aluminum isopropoxide serves equally well. Use of a large excess of acetone displaces the equilibrium in the desired direction. Since the initial step is attack by the alkoxide on the hydroxylic hydrogen, Oppenauer oxidation differs in steric requirement from chromic acid oxidation (8.30). Hindered alcoholic groups react less readily than unhindered ones, and in a cyclohexane derivative of rigid structure an axial hydroxyl group is attacked less readily than an equatorial group. The order of reactivity is thus the reverse of that in chromic acid oxidation. The mechanism of the reaction is discussed in section 12.35.

Since Oppenauer oxidation is specific to the alcoholic group, and leaves double bonds unattacked, it finds many uses for oxidation of unsaturated alcohols, **for** example:

$$
\underset{\substack{| \\ OH}}{CH_3CHCH}{=}CHCH{=}\underset{\substack{| \\ CH_3}}{CCH}{=}CH_2 \xrightarrow[\substack{\text{Acetone-benzene} \\ 80\%}]{(t\text{-BuO})_3Al} \underset{\substack{\| \\ O}}{CH_3CCH}{=}CHCH{=}\underset{\substack{| \\ CH_3}}{CCH}{=}CH_2
$$

6-Methyl-$\Delta^{3,5,7}$-octatriene-2-ol   6-Methyl-$\Delta^{3,5,7}$-octatriene-2-one

Like allylic alcohols, homoallylic alcohols yield α,β-unsaturated ketones, since the initially formed β,γ-unsaturated ketone is isomerized readily by alkoxide ion

$$
\left.
\begin{array}{c}
\underset{\substack{| \\ OH}}{RCH_2CH}{=}CHCHR' \\[8pt]
\underset{\substack{| \\ OH}}{RCH}{=}CHCH_2CHR'
\end{array}
\right\} \xrightarrow[\text{Acetone}]{(t\text{-BuO})_3Al} \underset{\substack{\| \\ O}}{RCH_2CH}{=}CHCR'
$$

to the conjugated ketone. The reaction finds numerous applications for oxidation of cholesterol and other homoallylic Δ^5-stenols. A particularly interesting application by the Syntex group (H. J. Ringold, 1956) is based upon their discovery that a formate, unlike an acetate or a benzoate, is easily oxidized and gives the same product as the free alcohol.   Initial oxidation of the formyl group gives a product

$$R_2CHOCH \xrightarrow{[O]} R_2CHOCO^-H^+ \xrightarrow{-CO_2} R_2CHOH \xrightarrow[\text{(CH}_3)_2C=O]{\text{Al(OR)}_3} R_2C=O$$

with a carboxyl group on oxygen, and this electron-attracting atom promotes spontaneous elimination of carbon dioxide from the anion.   Use was made of this finding in development of a neat process for production of testosterone acetate, a derivative of the androgenic hormone of value in therapy, from Δ^5-androstene-3β-ol-17-one.   The conversion required reduction at C_{17}, oxidation at C_3, and selective acylation at C_{17}.   The starting material was formylated by heating it

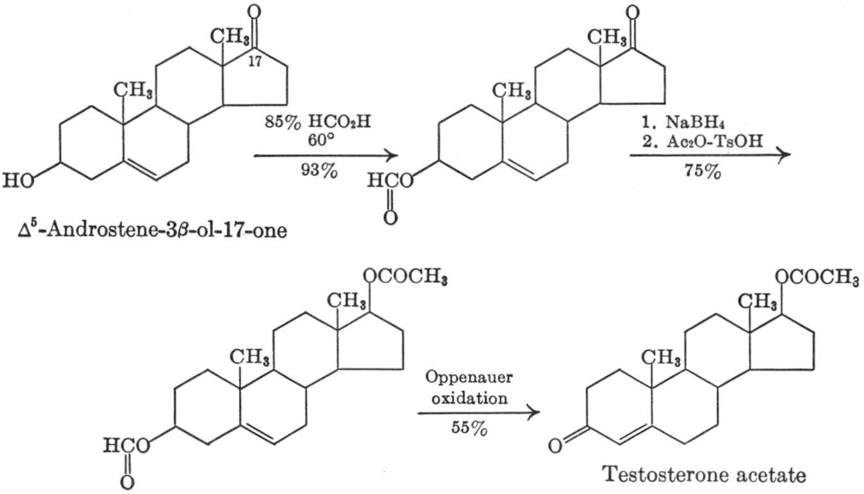

Δ^5-Androstene-3β-ol-17-one

Testosterone acetate

with 85% formic acid at 60° for 1 hr., and the formate was reduced with sodium borohydride in tetrahydrofurane; the reaction proceeded exclusively by rear attack to give the 17β-ol.   Acetylation gave the unsaturated 3-formate-17-acetate, which was refluxed with aluminum isopropoxide and cyclohexanone in a suitable solvent: xylene (b.p. 140°) in Mexico City (570 mm.); toluene (b.p. 111°) at sea level.   Use of cyclohexanone raises the reaction temperature and hence decreases the time required, and excess hydrogen acceptor is easily removed by steam distillation.

The Oppenauer reaction has limited use for oxidation of primary alcohols, for some expedient is required to prevent condensation of the aldehyde with the hydrogen acceptor.

12.8   Grignard Synthesis. — Ketones can be prepared efficiently according to Gilman by the reaction of an acid chloride with an alkyl or aryl cadmium derivative (11.25).   Another method is by reaction of an alkyllithium

$$R\overset{O}{\overset{\|}{C}}-OH \xrightarrow[-CH_4]{CH_3Li} R\overset{O}{\overset{\|}{C}}-OLi \xrightarrow{CH_3Li} R\underset{CH_3}{\overset{OLi}{\overset{|}{\underset{|}{C}}}}-OLi \xrightarrow{H_2O} R\underset{CH_3}{\overset{|}{C}}=O + 2LiOH$$

with a carboxylic acid; unlike an MgBr salt, the lithium salt initially formed has a reactive carbonyl group. In 1934, before these methods were available, A. M. Seligman required a diaryl ketone for the synthesis of a certain hydrocarbon (methylcholanthrene) and obtained it in 40% yield by reaction of a Grignard reagent, ArMgBr, with α-naphthoyl chloride (a). Later, the yield was more than

(a) $ArMgBr \ + \ \alpha\text{-}C_{10}H_7COCl \ \xrightarrow[40\%]{} \ ArCOC_{10}H_7\text{-}\alpha \ + \ MgBrCl$

(b) $ArC{\equiv}N \ \xrightarrow{\alpha\text{-}C_{10}H_6MgBr} \ Ar\overset{\overset{\displaystyle NMgBr}{\|}}{C}C_{10}H_7\text{-}\alpha \ \xrightarrow{H_2O}$

$Ar\overset{\overset{\displaystyle NH}{\|}}{C}C_{10}H_7\text{-}\alpha \ \xrightarrow[87\%\ overall]{HCl} \ Ar\overset{\overset{\displaystyle O}{\|}}{C}C_{10}H_7\text{-}\alpha$

doubled by reaction of the nitrile, ArCN, with α-naphthylmagnesium bromide (b). Decomposition of the reaction product with dilute hydrochloric acid afforded the ketimine in the form of a crystalline yellow hydrochloride, which was hydrolyzed to the ketone by refluxing it with a mixture of aqueous hydrochloric acid, acetic acid, and toluene.

Aldehydes are available by the reaction of a Grignard reagent with ethyl orthoformate, which displaces one of the three alkoxy groups to give the diethyl acetal,

$n\text{-}C_5H_{11}MgBr \ \xrightarrow{HC(OC_2H_5)_3} \ n\text{-}C_5H_{11}CH(OC_2H_5)_2 \ \xrightarrow[45\text{-}50\%]{dil.\ H_2SO_4} \ n\text{-}C_5H_{11}CH{=}O$

n-Hexaldehyde

which is then hydrolyzed to the aldehyde with dilute acid.

12.9   Unsaturated Aldehydes. — Acetylenic aldehydes are available by a synthesis also involving a diethyl acetal intermediate (B. W. Howk,[1] 1958). For example, a mixture of phenylacetylene, ethyl orthoformate, and a

$C_6H_5C{\equiv}CH \ + \ HC(OC_2H_5)_3 \ \xrightarrow[72\text{-}78\%]{ZnI_2} \ C_6H_5C{\equiv}CCH(OC_2H_5)_2 \ + \ C_2H_5OH$

$\Big\downarrow dil.\ HCl$

$C_6H_5C{\equiv}CCH{=}O$

Phenylpropargyl aldehyde

catalytic amount of zinc iodide is heated gradually to 200° until ethanol is completely eliminated. The resulting diethyl acetal is hydrolyzed to the aldehyde in high yield. The synthesis is like the ethoxyacetylene synthesis of α,β-unsaturated aldehydes (6.9). A related synthesis of substances of this type involves conversion of an aldehyde into the diethyl acetal and addition of this to the double bond of ethyl vinyl ether to give a β-ethoxy acetal, which is then hydrolyzed with acid (for examples, see 13.20).

$R\overset{\overset{\displaystyle OC_2H_5}{|}}{C}HOC_2H_5 \ + \ CH_2{=}\overset{\overset{\displaystyle OC_2H_5}{|}}{C}H \ \rightarrow \ R\overset{\overset{\displaystyle OC_2H_5}{|}}{C}H{-}CH_2CH(OC_2H_5)_2 \ \xrightarrow{H^+} \ RCH{=}CHCHO$

12.10   From Acids. (*a*) **Pyrolysis of Metal Salts.** — When calcium acetate is heated strongly it undergoes decomposition to acetone and calcium carbonate. The reaction is like the thermal decomposition of sodium acetate in

[1] Benjamin W. Howk, b. 1907 Momence, Ill.; Ph.D. Wisconsin (McElvain); du Pont Co.

$$\begin{array}{c} CH_3CO|O \\ \\ CH_3|COO \end{array}\!\!\Big\rangle Ca \xrightarrow{\text{Heat}} \begin{array}{c} CH_3 \\ \\ CH_3 \end{array}\!\!\Big\rangle C=O \;+\; CaCO_3$$

the presence of sodium hydroxide to give the more stable carbonate and methane. The pyrolysis illustrated once constituted the chief method of manufacturing acetone; the required calcium acetate, known as gray acetate of lime, was obtained from pyroligneous acid. The reaction has general application for synthesis of symmetrical ketones. In some instances improved results have been obtained

$$(RCOO)_2Ca \xrightarrow{\text{Heat}} R_2CO \;+\; CaCO_3$$

with the barium, manganese, or thorium salts. Instead of preparing the salt as a dry solid prior to pyrolysis, the acid can be distilled through a heated tube packed with the metal oxide. Thus manganous oxide impregnated on pumice is employed in a catalytic process for conversion of acetic acid into acetone; the

$$2\,CH_3COOH \xrightarrow{MnO,300^\circ} (CH_3)_2CO \;+\; H_2O \;+\; CO_2$$

vaporized acid passing through the catalyst tube forms manganous carbonate, which breaks down to the oxide and carbon dioxide.

If a mixture of the calcium salts of two different acids is pyrolyzed, three reaction products are possible because each salt can decompose independently or interact with the other one. Such a reaction inevitably gives mixtures and is practicable

$$\begin{array}{c} (RCO|O)_2Ca \\ \\ (R'|COO)_2Ca \end{array} \longrightarrow \begin{array}{c} R \\ \\ R' \end{array}\!\!\Big\rangle C=O \;+\; \begin{array}{c} R \\ \\ R \end{array}\!\!\Big\rangle C=O \;+\; \begin{array}{c} R' \\ \\ R' \end{array}\!\!\Big\rangle C=O$$

n the preparation of unsymmetrical ketones only when an easy method of separation is at hand. For example, methyl benzyl ketone can be obtained by dropping a mixture of phenylacetic acid and two equivalents of acetic acid through a heated tube of thorium oxide catalyst deposited on pumice. The cheaper reagent, acetic

$$\underset{\text{Phenylacetic acid}}{C_6H_5CH_2COOH} \;+\; CH_3COOH \xrightarrow[55-65\%]{ThO_2,\,430-450^\circ} \underset{\text{Methyl benzyl ketone}}{C_6H_5CH_2COCH_3}$$

acid, is taken in excess in order to allow for formation of acetone as an easily eliminated by-product. The other by-product is dibenzyl ketone, $C_6H_5CH_2$-$COCH_2C_6H_5$, which has a much higher molecular weight than the desired product and is distinctly less volatile (b.p. about 200° at 21 mm.; methyl benzyl ketone, b.p. 110–115° at 21 mm.). Similarly, aldehydes can be synthesized by pyrolysis of a mixture of excess calcium formate with the salt of a higher homolog. A

$$\begin{array}{c} (RCO|O)_2Ca \\ \\ (H|COO)_2Ca \end{array} \longrightarrow \begin{array}{c} R \\ \\ H \end{array}\!\!\Big\rangle C=O \;+\; \begin{array}{c} R \\ \\ R \end{array}\!\!\Big\rangle C=O \;+\; \begin{array}{c} H \\ \\ H \end{array}\!\!\Big\rangle C=O$$

ketone is formed as a by-product, but aldehydes and ketones differ sufficiently in properties to allow fairly sharp separation.

An application of the pyrolytic method is used in the preparation of cyclic ketones from dibasic acids; for example, a mixture of adipic acid with about 5% of barium hydroxide is heated until distillation of the reaction product is complete.

$$CH_2CH_2CO{\cdot}OH \qquad \xrightarrow[\text{75–80\%}]{\text{Ba(OH)}_2,\ 285\text{–}295°} \qquad CH_2\text{—}CH_2$$

$$CH_2CH_2{\cdot}COOH \qquad\qquad CH_2\text{—}CH_2 \diagdown C{=}O$$

Adipic acid   Cyclopentanone
                              (b.p. 130.6°)

The reaction proceeds best in the production of five- and six-membered ring compounds (for application to larger rings, see 15.28).

12.11   (*b*) **Rosenmund**[1] **Reaction.** — A useful method of transforming an acid into an aldehyde is by catalytic hydrogenation of the acid chloride. The success of the method depends upon differentiation between the speed of

$$R\text{—}C\diagup^{O}\diagdown_{Cl} \ +\ H_2\ \xrightarrow{\text{Catalyst}}\ R\text{—}C\diagup^{O}\diagdown_{H}\ +\ HCl$$

replacement of halogen by hydrogen and that of hydrogenation of the resulting aldehyde. The technique introduced by Rosenmund consists in adding a small amount of a sulfur-quinoline poison, which does not seriously inhibit the desired reduction of the highly reactive acid chloride but effectively stops hydrogenation of the aldehyde. A stream of hydrogen is passed through a boiling solution of the

$$\text{(β-Naphthoyl chloride)}\ \xrightarrow[\text{74–81\%}]{\text{H}_2,\ \text{Pd—BaSO}_4,\ \text{poison}}\ \text{(β-Naphthaldehyde)}\ +\ HCl$$

β-Naphthoyl chloride   β-Naphthaldehyde

acid chloride in a hydrocarbon solvent and the exit gas is passed into standard alkali; the course of the reaction is followed from the amount of hydrogen chloride absorbed. A hindered acid chloride may require no poisoning of the catalyst.

12.12   (*c*) **Grundmann Synthesis.** — As an alternative to the Rosenmund reaction, Ch. Grundmann (1936) developed the following route:

$$RCOCl\ \xrightarrow[-\text{CH}_3\text{Cl}]{2\ \text{CH}_2\text{N}_2}\ RCOCHN_2\ \xrightarrow{\text{HOAc}}\ RCOCH_2OAc\ \xrightarrow{\text{Hydrol.}}$$

$$RCOCH_2OH\ \xrightarrow{\text{LiAlH}_4}\ RCHOHCH_2OH\ \xrightarrow{\text{HIO}_4}\ RCH{=}O$$

The acid chloride is converted into the diazoketone, which reacts with acetic acid to give a ketol acetate. Hydrolysis and reduction gives a glycol, which on cleavage with either periodic acid or lead tetraacetate affords the aldehyde. Although several steps are involved, overall yields of saturated and unsaturated aliphatic aldehydes and of aromatic aldehydes are in the range 40–60%.

---

[1] Karl W. Rosenmund, b. 1884 Berlin; Ph.D. Berlin (Diels); Univ. Kiel

12.13   **From Alkenes.** — The methods of hydroxylation and glycol cleavage (5.27) and of ozonization (5.31) have been discussed.

12.14   **Hydroformylation of Alkenes.** — In this process, developed in Germany (1943) and investigated in this country by Adkins (1948–49), aldehydes are prepared by reaction of an alkene with carbon monoxide and hydrogen in the presence of a catalyst such as dicobalt octacarbonyl, $[Co(CO)_4]_2$:

$$RCH{=}CH_2 + CO + H_2 \xrightarrow[\text{1000–6000 lbs./sq. in.}]{[Co(CO)_4]_2,\ 125°,} \begin{cases} RCH_2CH_2CHO \ \text{(a)} \\ RCHCH_3 \\ | \quad\quad \text{(b)} \\ CHO \end{cases}$$

A mixture of the two possible aldehydes often results, but the primary aldehyde (a) generally predominates.

Examples:

1. $CH_3(CH_2)_3CH{=}CH_2 \xrightarrow{CO,\ H_2} CH_3(CH_2)_5CHO + CH_3(CH_2)_3\overset{\displaystyle CHO}{\underset{}{C}}HCH_3$

       Hexene-1   32%   32%

2. $CH_3COOCH_2CH{=}CH_2 \xrightarrow[69\%]{CO,\ H_2} CH_3COOCH_2CH_2CH_2CHO$

       Allyl acetate   γ-Acetoxybutyraldehyde

3.

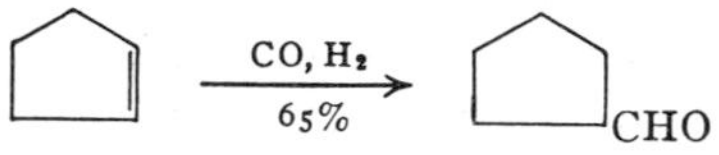

       Cyclopentene   Formylcyclopentane

4. $C_2H_5OCOCH{=}CHCOOC_2H_5 \xrightarrow[51\%]{CO,\ H_2} C_2H_5OCO\overset{\displaystyle CHO}{\underset{}{C}}HCH_2COOC_2H_5$

       Diethyl fumarate   Diethyl α-formylsuccinate

The process is similar to the oxo process for production of alcohols, in which the addition of one mole of carbon monoxide and two moles of hydrogen to an olefin is effected with a Fischer-Tropsch catalyst. A convenient route to normal paraffinic hydrocarbons involves reversal of the oxo process:

$$n\text{-}C_{15}H_{31}CH_2CH_2CH_2OH \xrightarrow[240\ atm.]{Ni,} [C_{15}H_{31}CH_2CH_2CHO \xrightarrow{-CO}$$

Stearyl alcohol

$$C_{15}H_{31}CH{=}CH_2] \xrightarrow{H_2} n\text{-}C_{17}H_{36}$$

n-Heptadecane
(yield 95%)

12.15   **Special Methods.** — Production of **acetaldehyde** by catalyzed hydration of acetylene has been mentioned (6.13); the preparation of **acetone** by bacterial fermentation of sugars is described (8.14). **Chloral** is made by the action of chlorine on ethanol; the alcoholic group is oxidized by the halogen

$$CH_3CH_2OH + 4\,Cl_2 \longrightarrow CCl_3CHO + 5\,HCl$$

Chloral

during the reaction.   Chloral is an intermediate in the reaction of ethanol with sodium hypochlorite, and the material prepared under nonalkaline conditions is cleaved by alkali to chloroform and sodium formate.

The α,β-unsaturated aldehyde **acrolein** is obtained by dehydration of glycerol with acidic reagents.   The reaction apparently involves preferential elimination of the secondary, rather than a primary, hydroxyl group, a hydrogen shift in the resulting enol, and elimination of water between an activated α-hydrogen atom and a hydroxyl group in the β-position.   A commercial process for production of acrolein involves air oxidation of propylene over copper oxide catalyst.   Acrolein

$$
\underset{\underset{\text{OH OH OH}}{|\;\;\;|\;\;\;|}}{\text{CH}_2\text{CH}-\text{CH}_2} \xrightarrow{\text{KHSO}_4,\ 215-230°} \left[\underset{\underset{\text{OH}\;\;\;\;\;\;\text{OH}}{|\;\;\;\;\;\;\;\;|}}{\text{CH}_2\text{CH}=\text{CH}} \longrightarrow \overset{\beta\;\;\;\alpha}{\underset{\underset{\text{OH H}}{|----|}}{\text{CH}_2\text{CHC}}}\diagdown\text{H} \atop \diagup\!\!\searrow\text{O} \right]
$$

$$
\xrightarrow[\text{33-48\% (overall)}]{} \quad \underset{\text{Acrolein}}{\text{CH}_2=\text{CHCHO}}
$$

is a highly reactive, volatile liquid with a sharp irritating odor and a marked tendency to polymerize.

Acrolein diethyl acetal is the starting material for the preparation of *dl*-glyceraldehyde; this base-stable protective derivative is made by acid-catalyzed reaction of acrolein with ethanol.   The acetal is hydroxylated by controlled permanganate

$$
\underset{\underset{\text{CH}_2}{\|}}{\overset{\text{CH(OC}_2\text{H}_5)_2}{\underset{|}{\text{CH}}}} \xrightarrow[67\%]{\text{aq. KMnO}_4,\ 5°} \underset{\underset{\text{CH}_2\text{OH}}{|}}{\overset{\text{CH(OC}_2\text{H}_5)_2}{\underset{|}{\text{CHOH}}}} \xrightarrow[80\%]{\underset{20°,\ 1\ \text{wk.}}{0.1\ \text{N H}_2\text{SO}_4}} \underset{\underset{\text{CH}_2\text{OH}}{|}}{\overset{\text{CH}=\text{O}}{\underset{|}{\text{CHOH}}}}
$$

$$
\textit{dl}\text{-Glyceraldehyde}
$$
$$
\text{m.p. 139°}
$$

oxidation and the protective group is removed by hydrolysis with dilute acid; the reaction is slow but affords a crystalline product which can be described as a C_3-sugar aldehyde, or aldotriose.

Furfural is easily prepared from carbohydrates present in corncobs (pentosans). The immediate precursor is a mixture of pentoses, and the reaction in-

$$
\underset{\underset{\underset{\text{OH}\;\;\;\;\text{OH}}{|\;\;\;\;\;\;\;\;|}}{\text{CH}_2\;\;\text{CHCHO}}}{\overset{\text{HOCH}-\text{CHOH}}{|\;\;\;\;\;\;\;\;\;|}} \xrightarrow[\text{Distillation}]{10\%\ \text{H}_2\text{SO}_4,\ \text{NaCl}} \underset{\text{Furfural}}{\boxed{}\!\!\diagdown_{\text{O}}\diagup\text{CHO}}
$$

$$
\text{Pentose}
$$

volves elimination of three moles of water with formation of two double bonds and closing of an oxide bridge.   A mixture of 1.5 kg. of ground dry corncobs with dilute sulfuric acid and salt is heated in an apparatus provided with a separator for collection of the heavier-than-water aldehyde and return of the bulk of the water to the boiling flask; yield about 200 g. of furfural.

2,5-Dimethoxy-2,5-dihydrofurane (2), the cyclic acetal of malealdehyde (3), is used to generate this substance *in situ* and can be hydrogenated (Raney Ni, 25°)

to the cyclic acetal of succindialdehyde (J. Fakstorp, 1950). The dihydrofurane (2) is made by reaction of furane with bromine and methanol at −25°, followed

(1) (2) (3)

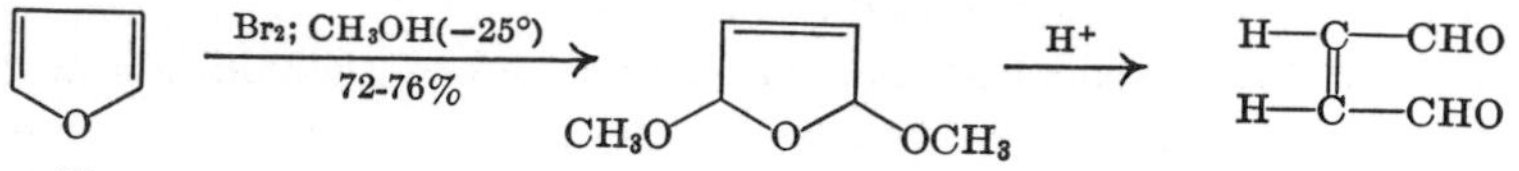

by neutralization of the mixture with ammonia; the ammonium bromide formed salts out the product (N. Clauson-Kaas, 1952; D. M. Burness, 1960). The reaction probably involves 1,4-addition of bromine and solvolysis of the allylic dibromide.

12.16 Ketenes. — Ketene itself, useful as an acetylating agent and in synthesis, is made by the pyrolysis of acetone (11.29). One general method for the preparation of substituted ketenes is by dehydrohalogenation of an acid chloride with triethylamine (preferred), quinoline, or granulated zinc.

Diphenylacetyl chloride — Diphenylketene b.p. 120°/35 mm.

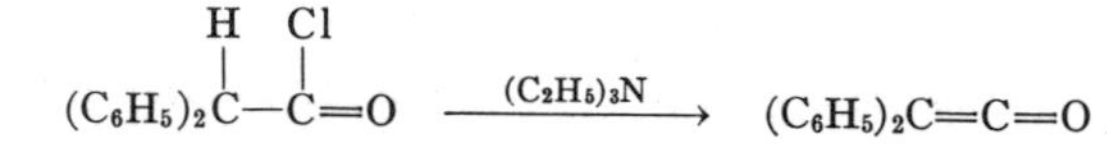

Staudinger (1905) developed these routes to diphenylketene but later preferred the method of Schroeter[1] (1909), starting with benzil. On dropwise addition of 85% hydrazine hydrate to a solution of the α-diketone in hot ethanol the monohydrazone separates in nearly quantitative yield (preparation of the bishydrazone requires refluxing for 60 hrs. in *n*-propyl alcohol). The hydrazone is oxidized with

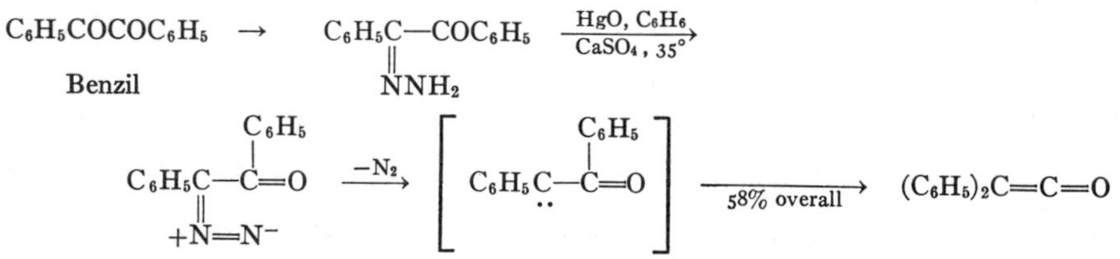

yellow mercuric oxide and the resulting benzoylphenyldiazomethane is dropped into a flask heated at 110°; expulsion of nitrogen gives a product with an electron-deficient carbon atom (a carbene) which rearranges to diphenylketene.

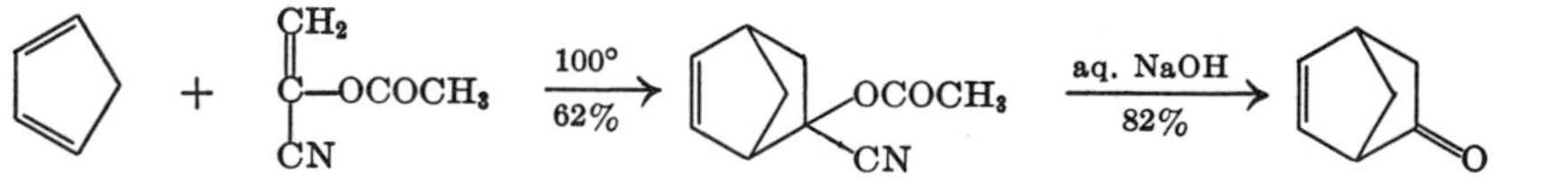

α-Acetoxyacrylonitrile — Dehydronorcamphor (m. p. 23°)

α-Acetoxyacrylonitrile, made by reaction of ketene with hydrogen cyanide, is a superior dienophile with which to introduce the elements of ketene in a Diels-

[1] Georg Schroeter, 1869–1943; b. Passenheim (East Prussia); Ph.D. Bonn (Anschütz); Tierärztl. Hochschule Berlin

Alder reaction (Bartlett, 1956). The carbonyl group is regenerated by alkaline hydrolysis.

KETO-ENOL TAUTOMERISM

12.17   **Ethyl Acetoacetate.** — The classical example of a tautomeric system is that comprising the keto and enol forms of ethyl acetoacetate, $CH_3COCH_2CO_2C_2H_5$ (commonly called acetoacetic ester). The methylene group of this β-keto ester is so activated by both the carbonyl and the carboxylate group that the enolic form is considerably more stable than that of an ordinary ketone. The liquid ester, or a solution of the ester in a neutral solvent, is a mobile equi-

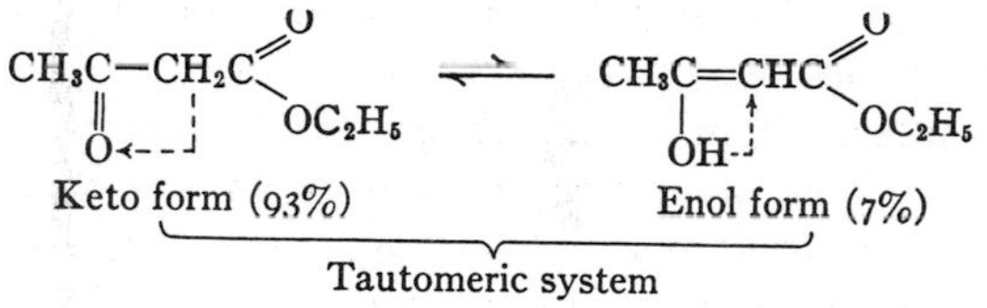

librium of the two forms. An activated hydrogen of the keto form migrates from carbon by an α,γ-shift to give the enol; the activated hydroxylic hydrogen of the enol migrates by an α,γ-shift in the reverse direction.

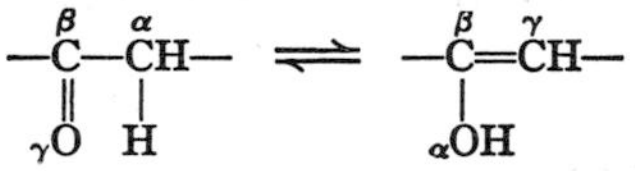

That ethyl acetoacetate has a dual nature was first recognized from its behavior in test reactions. It responds to tests with the usual carbonyl reagents, but it also responds to tests that are negative with ordinary ketones. Thus the ester gives a red color when treated with alcoholic ferric chloride; the formation of colored ferric chloride complexes is characteristic of many, if not all, phenols. Like phenols, the ester is weakly acidic and forms metal salts. Shaking an ethereal solution of ethyl acetoacetate with aqueous copper acetate gives a precipitate of the copper salt, $Cu(C_6H_9O_3)_2$, which crystallizes from benzene in green needles, m.p. 193°. When a solution of the ester in benzene is treated with one equivalent of sodium and warmed, hydrogen is evolved with the formation of a precipitate of the sodio derivative. A solution of the sodio derivative can be prepared by adding the ester to an equivalent amount of a solution prepared by dissolving sodium in absolute ethanol: $C_6H_{10}O_3 + C_2H_5ONa \rightarrow Na(C_6H_9O_3) + C_2H_5OH$.

Knorr[1] thought the isolation of the pure keto and enol forms might be accomplished by operating at a low temperature and found indeed that at $-78°$, the temperature of an ether–dry ice mixture, the equilibrium between the tautomers is practically frozen; the position of the equilibrium is essentially free from a temperature effect. Knorr cooled a solution of ethyl acetoacetate in alcohol, ether, or hexane to $-78°$ in an apparatus permitting collection and washing of crystals at $-78°$ in a moisture-free atmosphere. The product that crystallized

[1] Ludwig Knorr, 1859–1921; b. Munich; Ph.D. Erlangen; Univ. Würzburg, Jena

proved to be the keto form, and on washing the crystals with dimethyl ether (b.p. $-24°$) to remove enol retained in the mother liquor he isolated the pure keto form, m.p. $-39°$.   The substance is stable at $-78°$ but reverts to the equilibrium mixture at room temperature.   Treated with ferric chloride solution at $-78°$, the equilibrium mixture gave a red color at once and the solution of the pure keto form remained colorless for over an hour.   Since the sodio derivative must be de-

$$CH_3C{=}CHCO_2C_2H_5 \xrightarrow{\text{HCl}} CH_3C{=}CHCO_2C_2H_5$$
$$\underset{O^-Na^+}{\big|} \qquad\qquad \underset{OH}{\big|}$$

rived from the enol form, Knorr suspended the solid sodio derivative in dimethyl ether at $-78°$ and passed in dry hydrogen chloride in amount a little short of that required for complete neutralization (to avoid acid-catalyzed isomerization). The solution was filtered from sodium chloride and evaporated in high vacuum at $-78°$, and the residual oil (which crystallized only at a lower temperature) was the pure enol.   Tested at $-78°$, this form gives an immediate ferric chloride color reaction.   Interconversion of the two forms is markedly catalyzed by both acids and bases.   K. H. Meyer[1] (1911) isolated enol ethyl acetoacetate by very slow distillation of the equilibrium mixture in a quartz apparatus (b.p. 180°); quartz is required because glass has a sufficiently alkaline reaction to catalyze equilibration.   The unusual volatility of the enol is attributed to intramolecular

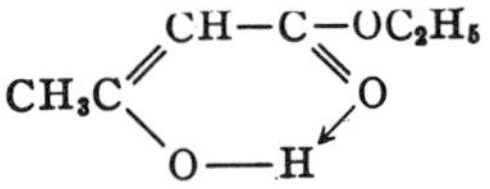

Enol-acetoacetic ester 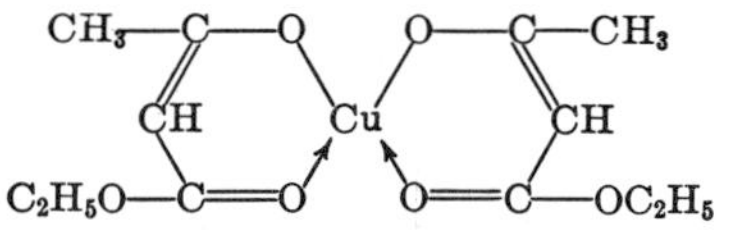   Copper salt

hydrogen bonding to form what is described as a chelate ring (Gr. *chēlē*, claw), with consequent decrease in association due to intermolecular hydrogen bonding. The copper derivative is also chelated.

$$CH_3C{=}CHCO_2C_2H_5 \xrightarrow{\text{Br}_2} CH_3COCHBrCO_2C_2H_5 \; + \; HBr$$
$$\underset{OH}{\big|}$$ 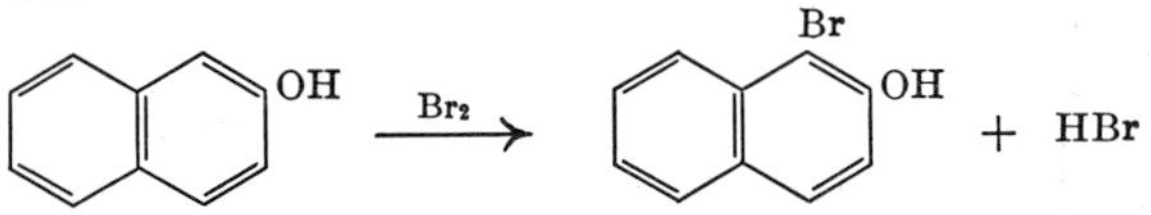

$$CH_3COCHBrCO_2C_2H_5 \; + \; HI \longrightarrow CH_3COCH_2CO_2C_2H_5 \; + \; HBr \; + \; \tfrac{1}{2}I_2$$

From comparison of the refractive index (n_D^{10}) of the equilibrium mixture (1.4232) with values for the keto form (1.4225) and the enol form (1.4480), Knorr concluded that the equilibrium mixture contains only a few per cent of the enol.   Meyer developed a method of analysis based upon the fact that the enolic form alone

[1] Kurt Hans Meyer, 1883–1952; b. Dorpat, Germany; Ph.D. Leipzig; BASF Ludwigshaven, Univ. Geneva; *Angew. Chem.*, **64,** 521 (1952)

TABLE 12.3. ENOL CONTENT
(liquid state,[a] aqueous solution[b])

		% Enol
Diethyl malonate[a]	$C_2H_5O_2CCH_2CO_2C_2H_5$	0.0
Acetone[a]	CH_3COCH_3	0.00025
Ethyl C-methylacetoacetate[a]	$CH_3COCH(CH_3)CO_2C_2H_5$	4
Ethyl acetoacetate[a]	$CH_3COCH_2CO_2C_2H_5$	7.5
Acetylacetone[a]	$CH_3COCH_2COCH_3$	80
Benzoylacetone[a]	$C_6H_5COCH_2COCH_3$	99
Cyclopentanone[a]	$CH_2CH_2CH_2CH_2CO$	0.0048
Cyclohexanone[a]	$CH_2CH_2CH_2CH_2CH_2CO$	0.020
Diacetyl[a]	$CH_3COCOCH_3$	0.0056
Cyclopentane-1,2-dione[b]	$CH_2CH_2CH_2COCO$	100
Cyclohexane-1,2-dione[b]	$CH_2CH_2CH_2CH_2COCO$	40

reacts rapidly with bromine at 0°. A solution of the ester is treated at 0° with somewhat more than the required amount of bromine and a solution of β-naphthol is added rapidly to remove excess reagent. On acidification and addition of sodium iodide, the α-bromoketone is reduced by hydrogen iodide; titration of the iodine formed with thiosulfate solution gives a measure of extent of reaction and hence of the enol content. Meyer's method indicated that ethyl acetoacetate at equilibrium contains 7.5% of the enolic form. A modified flow method (G. Schwarzenbach, Univ. Zurich, 1947) is capable of detecting very minute amounts of enol (Table 12.3). Solutions of the ketone and of an acidified bromide-bromate solution are flowed into a mixing chamber and past a platinum electrode; the flows are adjusted until the potential rises sharply, corresponding to the endpoint in a titration of the enol with bromine. Nuclear magnetic resonance spectroscopy affords a useful means of structural and kinetic analysis of tautomeric systems.

The position of the equilibrium varies somewhat with solvent and with concentration: the enol content is favored by a solvent of low polarity (carbon disulfide, hexane) and by dilution. Structural features are more important. Acetone is essentially ketonic, β-keto esters are more enolic than simple ketones, and the high enol content of the 1,3-diketones acetylacetone and benzoylacetone shows that activation by two carbonyl groups is much more effective than activation by the combination of a keto and an ester group; note that a phenyl group conjugated with the double bond of the enol favors enolization. The two ester groups of diethyl malonate are not sufficient to produce a measurable amount of enol; this ester, however, reacts with sodium to form a sodio derivative. Enolization is favored in cyclic ketones: the enol content of cyclohexanone is one hundred times that of acetone. The aliphatic α-diketone diacetyl is predominantly ketonic, whereas the cyclic C_5- and C_6-1,2-diones are largely enolic. The order of relative enol stability in the cyclic diketones is the reverse of that in the cyclic ketones.   The acidity constants (pK$_a$) of the enolic forms of cyclopentane-1,2-dione (pK$_a$ 9.14) and cyclohexane-1,2-dione (pK$_a$ 10.30) show that these substances are weak acids comparable to phenols.   By contrast, the enolic forms of 1,3-diketones are comparable in acidic strength to carboxylic acids, probably because they offer comparable opportunity for resonance stabilization:

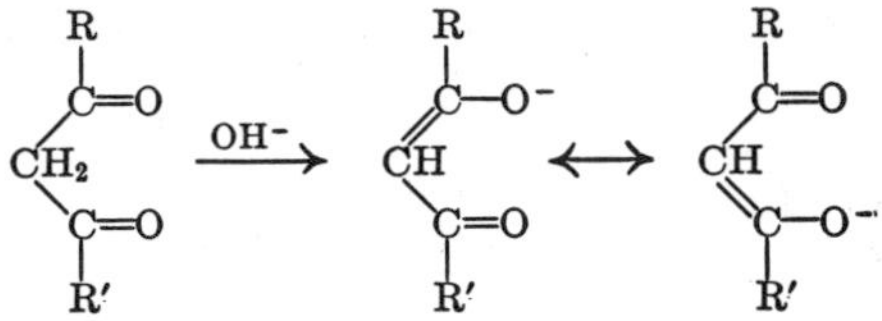

A likely interpretation of basic catalysis of enolization is that the base abstracts a proton from the ketone to give a carbanion, which is one resonance form of the

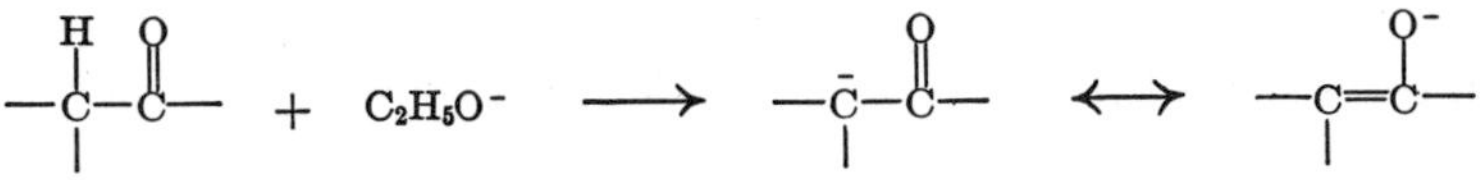

enolate anion.   The kinetic evidence regarding acid catalysis is complicated One possibility, illustrated for acetic acid, is a concerted attack, as in (a).   Alterna

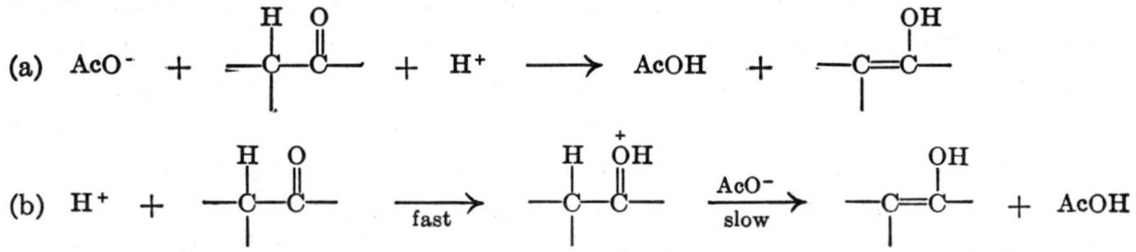

(a)   AcO$^-$ + + H$^+$ $\longrightarrow$ AcOH +

(b)   H$^+$ + $\xrightarrow{\text{fast}}$ $\xrightarrow[\text{slow}]{\text{AcO}^-}$ + AcOH

tively, a two-step mechanism (b) is possible.

12.18   Enol acetates. — Vinyl acetate (CH_2=CHOCOCH$_3$), the enol acetate of acetaldehyde, is made by acid catalyzed addition of acetic acid to acetylene (6.13).   The enol acetate of acetone, isopropenyl acetate, is made commercially by sulfuric acid catalyzed reaction of ketene with acetone (H. J. Hagemeyer, 1949).   Conversion of higher ketones into their enol acetates was formerly

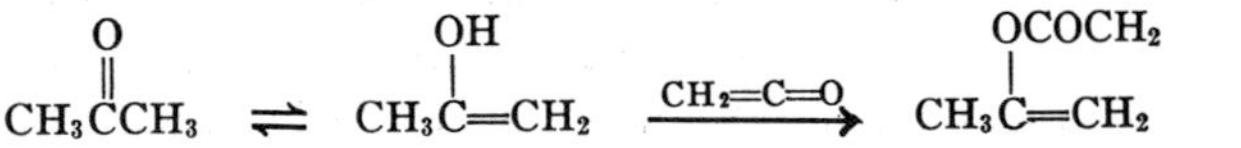

Isopropenyl acetate
b.p. 96°/750 mm.

done by reaction with acetic anhydride and acetyl chloride.   The method now preferred consists in acetate exchange with isopropenyl acetate in the presence of *p*-toluenesulfonic acid.   Enol acetates are very sensitive to hydrolysis by dilute acids.   When a ketone is of such a structure that enolization in two directions is possible, conversion to the enol acetate and ozonization establishes the major direction of enolization.

Enol ethers are discussed in section 12.46.

α-HALOKETONES

12.19   Bromination of Ketones. — Ketones having at least one α-hydrogen atom readily afford α-bromoketones on reaction with bromine in acetic acid containing a trace of hydrobromic acid. Crystalline pyridinium bromide perbromide, $C_5H_5N^+HBr_3^-$, is a convenient brominating reagent (in acetic acid) and has higher stereospecificity than bromine itself. Bromination can be effected also by refluxing the ketone with N-bromosuccinimide in carbon tetrachloride for 1-2 min. in strong light or for 30 min. in the dark. α-Bromination of a ketone,

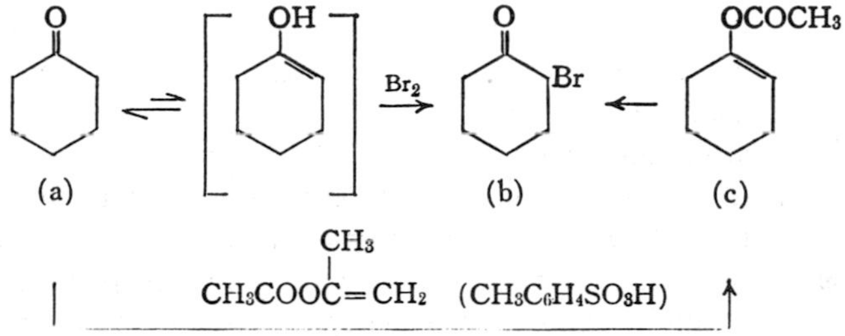

(a)   (b)   (c)

$$CH_3COOC(CH_3)=CH_2 \quad (CH_3C_6H_4SO_3H)$$

for example cyclohexanone (a), is known to proceed through the enol, since the same product is formed much more rapidly from the enol acetate (c). The reaction is catalyzed by base, as is the haloform reaction (10.6), and also by acid, and in each case the reaction rate is dependent upon the concentration of the ketone and of the acid or base but is independent of the concentration of halogen. In acid-catalyzed bromination protonation of the carbonyl oxygen facilitates separation of the α-hydrogen as a proton to form the enol, which is then brominated.

The direction of bromination of steroid 3-ketones is dependent upon the configuration at C_5. Cholestane-3-one, of 5α-configuration, is brominated at C_2 (1), whereas the 5β-isomer coprostanone is brominated at C_4 (4). The method by

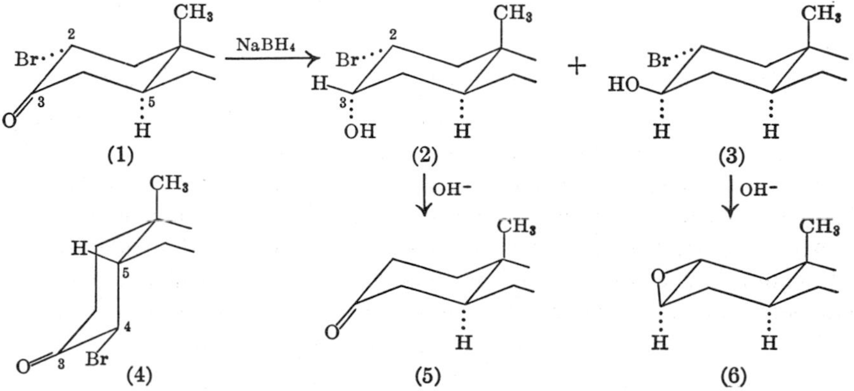

(1)   (2)   (3)

(4)   (5)   (6)

which the stereochemistry of these bromoketones was established is as follows. Sodium borohydride reduction of the 2-bromocholestanone (1) gave a mixture of bromohydrins, (2) and (3); these were separated by chromatography and each was hydrogenated (Pd) in alcoholic alkali to replace bromine by hydrogen. One isomer (2) gave the known cholestane-3α-ol and the other (3) the 3β-ol, and hence the configurations at C_3 are as shown. When refluxed with alcoholic alkali, one bromohydrin (2) gave a ketone and the other (3) gave an oxide. Formation of a ketone from (2) must result from *trans* elimination of HBr to give the enolic form of the ketone and, since the 3-H eliminated is β, the 2-Br must be α, as in (2). Formation of an oxide means that the 3α-H is *cis* to the bromine and hence not eliminated, but that hydroxyl and bromine are *trans*, as in (3). Similar evidence established the configuration of (4).

The products of bromination of both cholestanone and coprostanone are equatorial bromides. However, there is reason to believe that these are not the products initially formed but merely the thermodynamically more stable isomers. Thus axial 2β-bromocholestane-3-one ($α_D$ + 110°) has been prepared by an indirect method and found to be isomerized to the equatorial 2α-bromo derivative (+42°) on brief contact with alumina in benzene solution. Some ketosteroids on bromination afford a labile bromo derivative which can be isomerized to a stable epimer, and in all cases known the labile epimer is axial and the stable one equatorial. The simplest explanation for the preferential formation of the axial bromoketone is that the reaction involves formation and cleavage of a cyclic bromonium ion. The mechanism may be illustrated for the case of 7-keto-

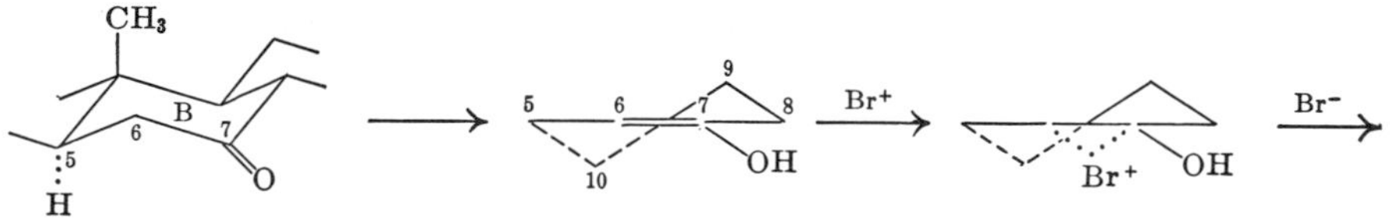

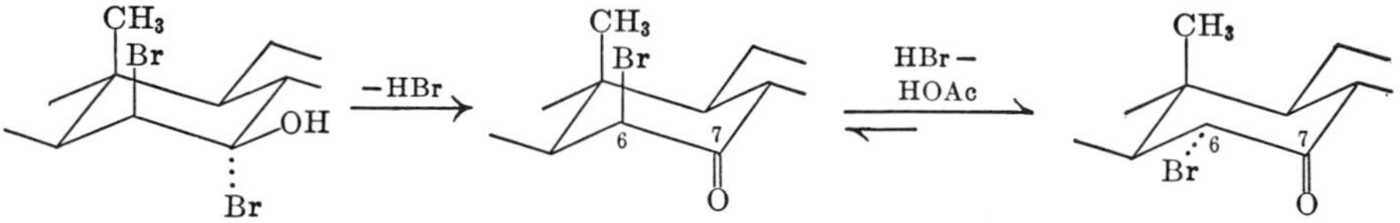

cholestanyl acetate (1), which forms the 6,7-enol. The double bond of the enol forces ring B to assume the half-chair conformation (2), in which the double bond and the two adjoining carbons lie in a plane. α-Attack by Br^+ gives the bromonium ion (3), and completion of the steps gives as the chief product of bromination the axial 6β-bromide (5), which is easily isomerized to the 6α-bromide (6).

A route to halomethyl ketones involves the reaction of a diazoketone with a hydrogen halide (a). The diazoketone need not be isolated, for slow addition of

(a) $RCOCHN_2 + HCl \rightarrow RCOCH_2Cl + N_2$
(b) $RCOCl + CH_2N_2 \rightarrow RCOCH_2Cl + N_2$

one equivalent of diazomethane to the acid chloride (b) permits the hydrogen chloride initially produced to attack the diazoketone as it is formed.

An operation required in the synthesis of adrenocortical hormones is the conversion of a 20-ketone (7) into the 21-acetoxy derivative (9). Initial bromination

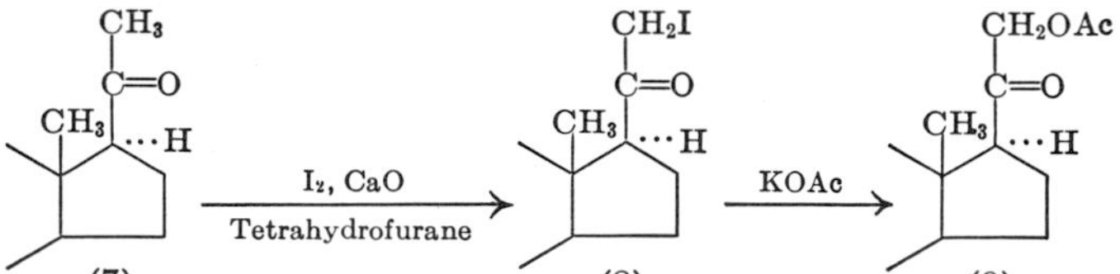

at C_{21} suffers from the difficulty that the 20-ketone is brominated at both C_{17} and C_{21} and also that a double bond elsewhere in the molecule is attacked by bromine. Iodination with excess iodine in the presence of calcium oxide affords the 21-iodo compound in good yield (H. J. Ringold, 1958). In the case of the unsaturated

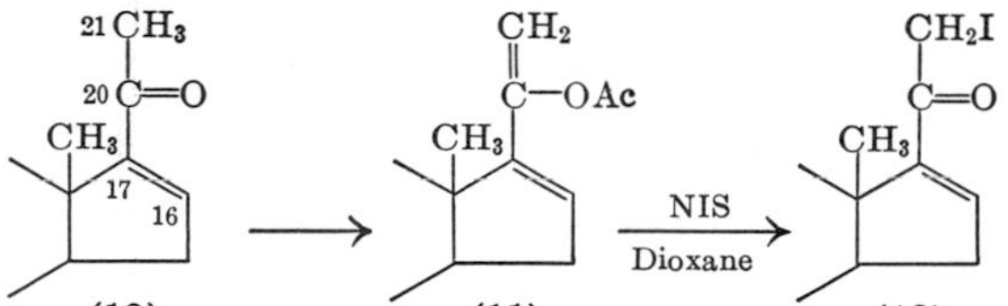

20-ketone (10), the problem was solved by reaction with isopropenyl acetate to form the enol acetate (11), which reacts with N-iodosuccinimide to give the iodo derivative (12) without attack of double bonds at the 5,6- and 16,17-positions (C. Djerassi, 1954).

12.20 α,β-Unsaturated Ketones.

— α-Haloketones are often prepared as intermediates to the α,β-unsaturated ketones derived from them by dehydrohalogenation. The preparation of 2-methyl-2-cyclohexenone illustrates the reaction sequence (E. W. Warnhoff, 1953). Direct chlorination of 2-methyl-

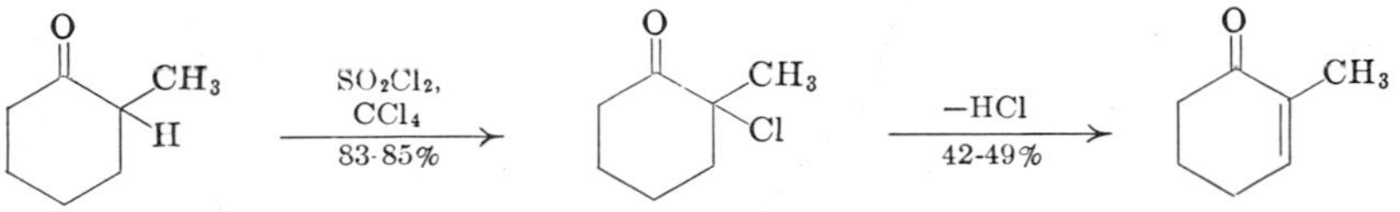

2-Methyl-2-cyclohexenone

cyclohexanone gives a mixture of the 2- and 6-chloro compounds, but chlorination with sulfuryl chloride in carbon tetrachloride affords the 2-chloro isomer in high yield. Elimination of hydrogen chloride was effected by two methods. In one, the crude product of chlorination was heated briefly with collidine at 150°. The second method was that of R. P. Holysz (1953): the crude chloroketone was stirred at 100° with lithium chloride in dimethylformamide in a nitrogen atmosphere. After a mildly exothermic reaction, the mixture was cooled, diluted with ether and 2.5% sulfuric acid, and stirred to hydrolyze the dimethylformamide.

If the halogen is *cis* to the hydrogen eliminated, base-catalyzed elimination by ordinary techniques proceeds poorly. The terminal step in the first practical synthesis of cortisone involved *cis* elimination from a 4β-bromo-3-ketone of the

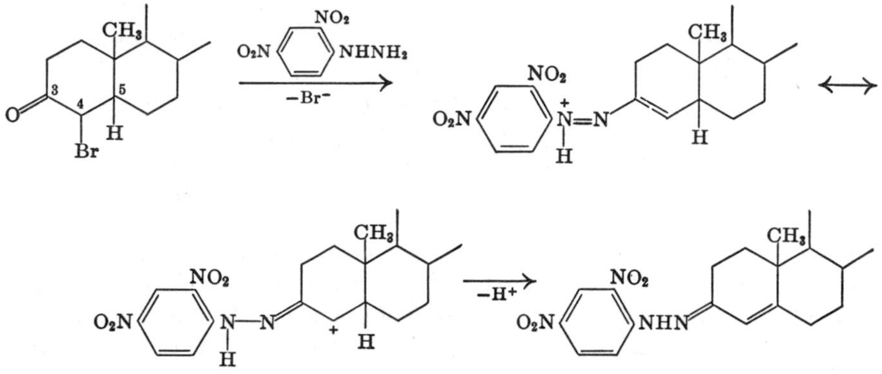

5β-series and the best yield obtainable by dehydrohalogenation with pyridine, lutidine, and other bases was 25%. However, V. C. Mattox and E. C. Kendall[1] discovered (1942) that the bromoketone reacts with 2,4-dinitrophenylhydrazine with elimination of bromine and formation of the red 2,4-dinitrophenylhydrazone of the desired unsaturated ketone in 78% yield (the derivatives of saturated ketones are yellow). Since the elimination follows a nonstereospecific pathway, the *cis* orientation is not disadvantageous. The α,β-unsaturated ketone is obtained in 80% yield by cleavage with hydrogen bromide in a mixed solvent with use of pyruvic acid as acceptor.

1-Acetylcyclohexene (4) is readily available by addition of acetylene to cyclohexanone and treatment of the resulting 1-ethynylcyclohexanol (1) with formic acid. The yield of the α,β-unsaturated ketone of 60–70% is raised to

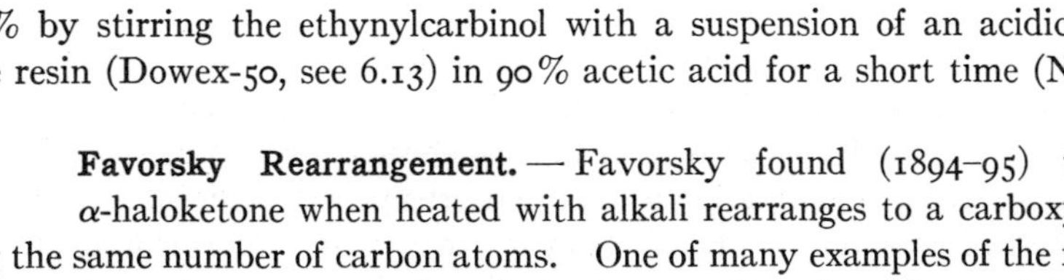

(1)　　　　　　(2)　　　　　　(3)　　　　　　(4)

84–87% by stirring the ethynylcarbinol with a suspension of an acidic ion-exchange resin (Dowex-50, see 6.13) in 90% acetic acid for a short time (Newman, 1953).

12.21　　Favorsky Rearrangement. — Favorsky found (1894–95) that an α-haloketone when heated with alkali rearranges to a carboxylic acid having the same number of carbon atoms. One of many examples of the reaction, first demonstrated by Wallach (1903), is the reaction of α-chlorocyclohexanone

[1] Edward C. Kendall, b. 1886 South Norwalk, Conn.; Ph.D. Columbia (H. C. Sherman); Mayo Foundation; Nobel Prize, 1950

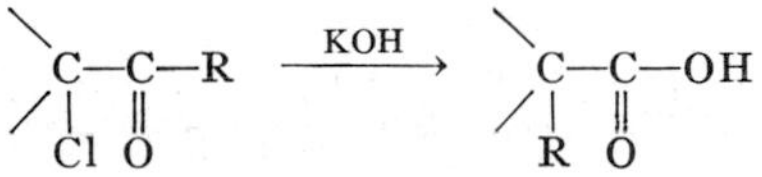

$$\underset{\underset{\text{Cl}}{|}}{\overset{\diagdown}{\underset{\diagup}{\text{C}}}} - \underset{\underset{\text{O}}{\|}}{\text{C}} - \text{R} \quad \xrightarrow{\text{KOH}} \quad \underset{\underset{\text{R}}{|}}{\overset{\diagdown}{\underset{\diagup}{\text{C}}}} - \underset{\underset{\text{O}}{\|}}{\text{C}} - \text{OH}$$

with alkali to give cyclopentanecarboxylic acid; reaction with sodium ethoxide gives the corresponding ester (yield 56–61%). This particular rearrangement was later studied by R. B. Loftfield[1] (1951) using α-chlorocyclohexanone-1,2-C^{14} with a view to distinguishing between several mechanisms that had been suggested. The radioactive ketone was rearranged with sodium isoamyl oxide in

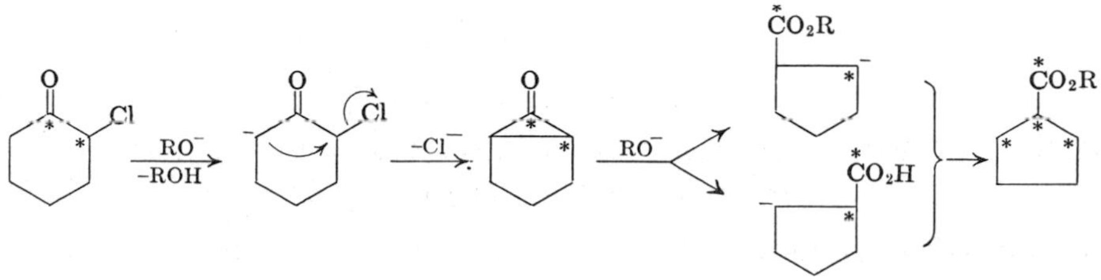

isoamyl alcohol and the isoamyl ester produced was degraded in order to locate the radioactive centers. Half of the radioactivity was found in the carboxyl carbon atom, one quarter was at the α-carbon atom, and the other quarter was distributed between the two β-carbon atoms. The reaction thus proceeds through a symmetrical intermediate, which Loftfield suggests is a cyclopropanone. A cyclopropanone has never been prepared, but such a structure would not be expected to survive the conditions of the Favorsky reaction. N. L. Wendler[2] (1958) studied a Favorsky rearrangement which affords two epimeric products and concluded that epimeric cyclopropanones are the key intermediates. Rearrangements have been observed with compounds in which a cyclopropanone ring is not possible, for example, α-chlorocyclohexyl phenyl ketone, which affords a rearranged acid when refluxed in toluene with powdered sodium hydroxide (C. L. Stevens, 1952). In this case a bridged aronium ion may be the intermediate (compare 9.7).

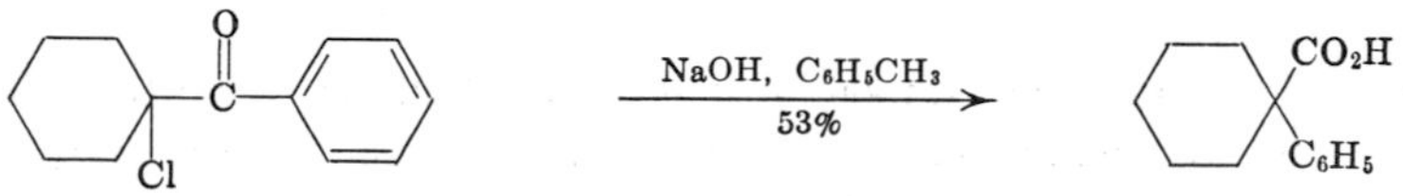

Investigations of Wagner[3] and Moore[4] (1949–50) have established that α,α'-dibromoketones are rearranged by alkoxide to α,β-unsaturated esters (1), and that α,β-dibromoketones afford mainly the β,γ-unsaturated esters (2).

[1] Robert B. Loftfield, b. 1919 Detroit; Ph.D. Harvard (Woodward); Mass. Gen. Hospital

[2] Norman L. Wendler, b. 1915 Stockton, Calif.; Ph.D. Michigan (W. E. Bachmann); Merck Sharp and Dohme Co.

[3] Romeo B. Wagner, b. 1917 Hopewell, Va.; Ph.D. Penn. State (Whitmore); Penn. State Univ.; Hercules Powder Co.

[4] James A. Moore, b. 1922 Johnstown, Pa.; Ph.D. Penn. State (Wagner); Univ. Delaware

1. $(CH_3)_2\overset{\overset{\displaystyle O}{\|}}{C}CCH_2Br$ $\xrightarrow[58\%]{NaOCH_3-Ether}$ $(CH_3)_2C{=}CHCO_2CH_3$

        $|$
        Br

       1,3-Dibromo-3-   Methyl β,β-dimethyl-
        methylbutanone   acrylate

2. $\overset{\displaystyle CH_3}{\underset{\displaystyle Br\ Br}{CH_3CHCCOCH_3}}$ $\xrightarrow{NaOCH_3-Ether}$ $\begin{cases} \overset{\displaystyle CH_3}{\underset{\displaystyle H}{CH_3C{=}CCH_2CO_2CH_3}}\ (55\%) \\ \\ CH_3COC(CH_3){=}CHCH_3\ (15\%) \end{cases}$

ADDITION REACTIONS

12.22   Aldol Condensation. — In the presence of a trace of alkali acetaldehyde undergoes self-addition to yield aldol, which easily loses a

$$CH_3CH{=}O\ +\ CH_3CH{=}O \xrightarrow{OH^-} CH_3\underset{\underset{\displaystyle OH}{|}}{C}HCH_2CHO \xrightarrow[-H_2O]{} CH_3CH{=}CHCHO$$

                                       Aldol   Crotonaldehyde

molecule of water to give crotonaldehyde. Since the overall reaction involves an elimination and hence is a "condensation," even the initial aldolization is known as an aldol condensation. This reaction, and a number of related ones involving esters as well as aldehydes and ketones, are described in Chapter 13.

12.23   Sodium Bisulfite. — A reaction characteristic of aldehydes and of some ketones is addition of sodium bisulfite, employed in a saturated (40%) aqueous solution. Equilibrium is reached, but the carbonyl component can be converted almost entirely into the addition product by use of excess bisulfite. The addition product is a crystalline salt and has the usual charac-

$$RC\overset{\displaystyle H}{\underset{\displaystyle O}{\diagdown}}\ +\ \underset{\text{(large excess)}}{NaHSO_3} \rightleftharpoons RC\overset{\displaystyle H}{\underset{\displaystyle SO_3Na}{\diagup\ OH}}$$

                                        Bisulfite-addition
                                        compound

teristics of an ionic metal compound; it is very soluble in water but subject to salting out by the common-ion effect, and it is insoluble in ether, infusible, and nonvolatile. Since the reaction is reversible, the aldehyde can be regenerated by adding to an aqueous solution of the product an amount of sodium carbonate or hydrochloric acid sufficient either to neutralize or to destroy the free sodium

$$RC\overset{\displaystyle H}{\underset{\displaystyle SO_3Na}{\diagup\ OH}} \rightleftharpoons RCHO\ +\ NaHSO_3 \begin{matrix} \xrightarrow{\frac{1}{2}Na_2CO_3} Na_2SO_3\ +\ \frac{1}{2}CO_2\ +\ \frac{1}{2}H_2O \\ \\ \xrightarrow{HCl} NaCl\ +\ SO_2\ +\ H_2O \end{matrix}$$

bisulfite present in equilibrium. Because of their specific physical properties and ease of formation and decomposition, bisulfite-addition products are useful for separation and purification of carbonyl compounds. To separate an aldehyde from an alcohol, for example, the mixture is shaken with excess saturated sodium bisulfite solution to form and to salt out the addition product; this is collected as a white solid and washed with bisulfite solution, ethanol, and then ether, to eliminate all traces of the original alcohol; the dried solid is dissolved in water and treated with sodium carbonate or hydrochloric acid; the liberated aldehyde is precipitated or obtained by distillation or by extraction with ether. Similar separations can be made from hydrocarbons, ethers, alkyl halides, carboxylic acids, and esters, since the carbonyl group of an ester is not sufficiently reactive to combine with sodium bisulfite. An aldehydic component that is insoluble in water often can be converted into an addition product by being dissolved in alcohol prior to treatment with aqueous bisulfite solution.

The relative additive power of carbonyl compounds is shown by figures for the amount of addition product formed in one hour with just one equivalent of sodium bisulfite. That acetone adds to a lesser extent than acetaldehyde can be at-

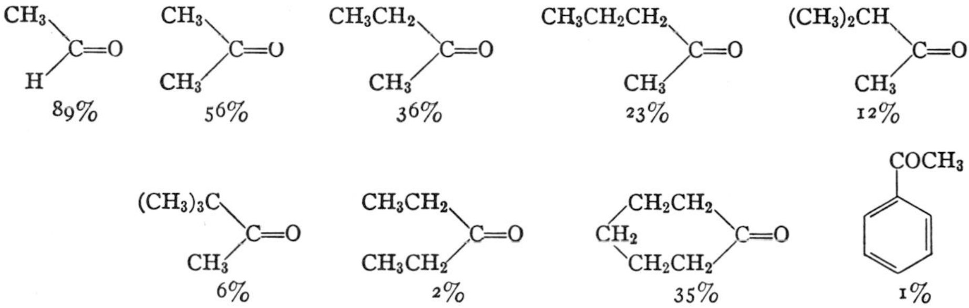

tributed to the greater steric hindrance of two methyl groups, as compared to one methyl group and one hydrogen atom. The larger the two groups attached to carbon, the greater is the impediment to approach of the reagent. In the series of ketones having one methyl group, the extent of blocking increases as the second group is enlarged from methyl to ethyl to n-propyl. The branched groups isopropyl and t-butyl exert considerable hindrance to the addition. The reaction is practically stopped if both groups are larger than methyl, as shown by the behavior of diethyl ketone. Cyclohexanone can be regarded as derived from diethyl ketone by insertion of a methylene group to bridge the two C$_2$-units. The bridge seems to restrict these C$_2$-units and so to decrease the hindrance which they exert, for cyclohexanone reacts with bisulfite to a considerably greater extent than the noncyclic ketone. The very limited reaction of acetophenone is probably attributable to resonance involving the benzene ring; contribution of

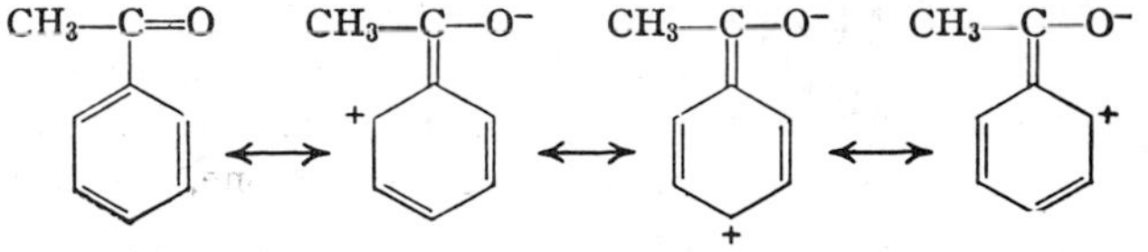

Acetophenone

the resonance structures formulated decreases the double-bond character of the carbonyl group.

In qualitative organic analysis the bisulfite test is preferred to the silver mirror test for distinguishing between aldehydes and ketones, since methyl ketones are easily recognized by the iodoform test.   That esters do not form bisulfite-addition

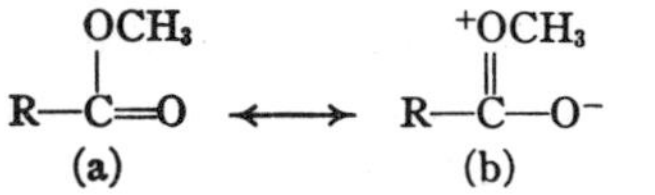

$$R—\underset{\underset{\text{(a)}}{|}}{\overset{\overset{OCH_3}{|}}{C}}{=}O \longleftrightarrow R—\underset{\underset{\text{(b)}}{|}}{\overset{\overset{+OCH_3}{||}}{C}}—O^-$$

products is attributable to partial charge separation (b) with decrease in double-bond character.

12.24   **Hydrogen Cyanide.** — Hydrogen cyanide adds to carbonyl compounds by nucleophilic attack of the positively polarized carbon atom; the reaction product is a cyanohydrin.   Anhydrous liquid hydrogen cyanide

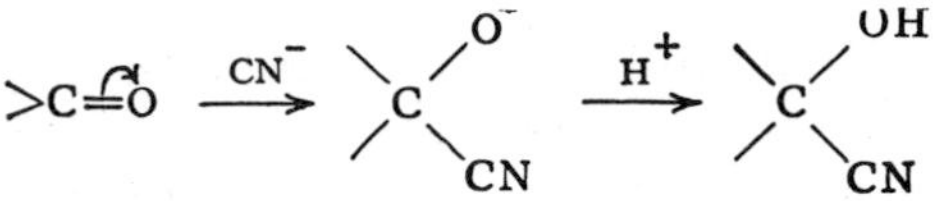

$$>C{=}O \xrightarrow{CN^-} \underset{CN}{\overset{O^-}{>C<}} \xrightarrow{H^+} \underset{CN}{\overset{OH}{>C<}}$$

reacts satisfactorily, particularly under basic catalysis, but the reagent is volatile and so toxic that it is advantageously generated in the course of the reaction. One procedure is to mix the carbonyl compound with an aqueous solution of sodium or potassium cyanide and add a mineral acid.   Another is to convert the

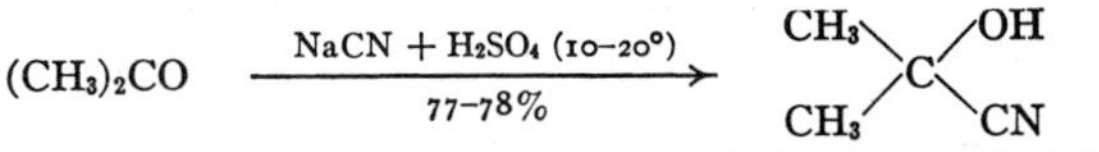

$$(CH_3)_2CO \xrightarrow[77-78\%]{NaCN + H_2SO_4 \text{ (10-20°)}} \underset{CH_3}{\overset{CH_3}{>}}C\underset{CN}{\overset{OH}{<}}$$

Acetone cyanohydrin
(b.p. 82° at 23 mm.)

carbonyl compound into its bisulfite-addition product, which is then treated with an equivalent amount of sodium cyanide, as in the synthesis of mandelic acid. Sodium cyanide acts as a base and neutralizes the sodium bisulfite in equilibrium

$$C_6H_5CHO \xrightarrow{NaHSO_3} C_6H_5CH(OH)SO_3Na \xrightarrow{NaCN}$$

Benzaldehyde

$$C_6H_5CH(OH)CN \xrightarrow[67\% \text{ (overall)}]{\text{Hydrolysis (HCl)}} C_6H_5CH(OH)COOH$$

Mandelonitrile
(m.p. −10°)

Mandelic acid
(m.p. 118°)

with the bisulfite compound with formation of sodium sulfite; the simultaneously liberated aldehyde and hydrogen cyanide then combine to give the cyanohydrin.

The method of exchange with a hydrogen cyanide donor, transcyanohydrination, has been applied with success in the steroid series (A. Ercoli,[1] 1953).   In a procedure for the preparation of the hormone testosterone, the cyanohydrin was

[1] Alberto Ercoli, b. 1905 Codogno (Milan), Italy; Ph.D. Pavia; Vismara Terapeutici, Vister Co., Casatenovo

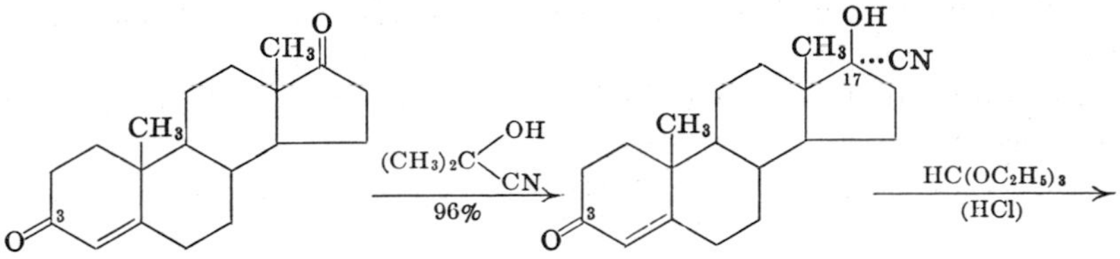

Δ⁴ –Androstene-3,17–dione   (1)

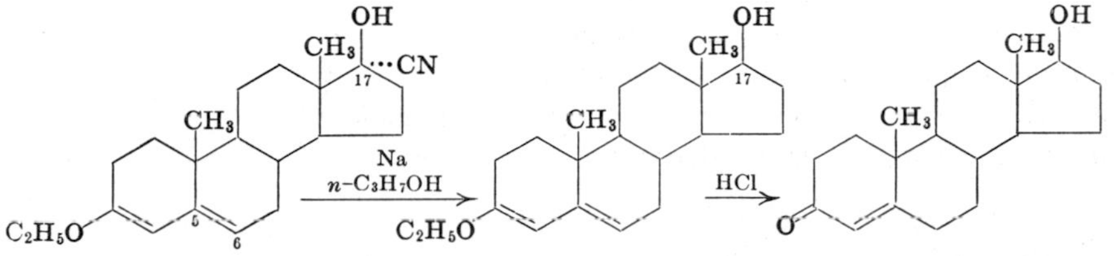

(2)   (3)   Testosterone

employed as a protective derivative to permit operation on one of the two keto groups of Δ^4-androstene-3,17-dione. A 20-g. portion of the dione was dissolved by gentle heating in acetone cyanohydrin, prepared as described above, and the solution on cooling deposited the crystalline 17-cyanohydrin (1). The formation of this product in high yield in the presence of a large excess of reagent shows that in this particular addition the saturated 17-keto group is considerably more reactive than the α,β-unsaturated 3-keto group. The derivative (1) was then transformed into the enol ethyl ether (2) by reaction with ethyl orthoformate in dry benzene and absolute ethanol containing a trace of hydrogen chloride at 65°; soon the solid dissolved and the product (2) began to crystallize. The next step, reduction with sodium and n-propyl alcohol, effected two changes: elimination of hydrogen cyanide by the basic reagent, and reduction of the 17-carbonyl group liberated (rear attack). The product (3) is the enol ethyl ether of testosterone, and it was hydrolyzed to testosterone by acidification of the reaction mixture. When the reactions were carried out without isolation of intermediates, the yield of testosterone was 92%. An earlier method (A. Serini, 1938) was based upon the fact that on reaction of Δ^4-androstene-3,17-dione with ethyl orthoformate the 3-keto group reacts preferentially and the 3-enol ethyl ether is the chief product. This substance was then reduced at C_{17} and hydrolyzed to testosterone. However, if the theoretical amount of ethyl orthoformate is used, conversion is incomplete; if an excess is employed, the 17-keto group reacts as well. That the order of reactivity of the 3- and 17-keto groups to ethyl orthoformate is the reverse of that in cyanohydrin formation may be because one enol ether has a conjugated diene system and the other an isolated double bond.

The example just cited illustrates reversal of hydrogen cyanide addition in the reaction of (2) with sodium alkoxide. The cyanohydrin (1) affords the corresponding 17-ketone on treatment with pyridine in ethanol. A method for reversal of HCN-addition favored by sugar chemists consists in treatment of a cyanohydrin with moist silver oxide.

1,4-Addition of hydrogen cyanide is illustrated by the reaction of benzalacetophenone:

$$C_6H_5CH=CHCOC_6H_5 \xrightarrow[93-96\%]{C_2H_5OH,\ CH_3CO_2H,\ aq.\ KCN} C_6H_5CH(CN)CH_2COC_6H_5$$

Benzalacetophenone   α-Phenyl-β-benzoyl-
                                                       propionitrile

12.25   Grignard Reaction. — Steric hindrance in either the reagent or the carbonyl component sometimes limits Grignard addition to an aldehyde or ketone. Diisopropyl ketone adds methylmagnesium iodide normally but with isopropylmagnesium bromide the addition reaction is repressed, and the ketone instead suffers reduction at the expense of the organometallic reagent with formation of the magnesiohalide derivative of diisopropylcarbinol and propylene:

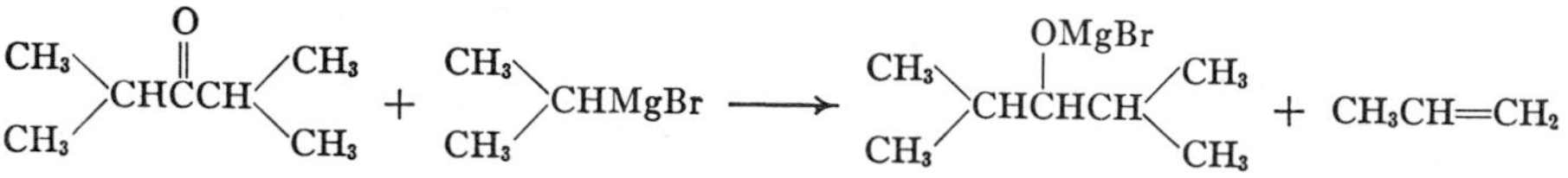

Di-*t*-butyl ketone adds methylmagnesium iodide but not phenylmagnesium bromide, and it is merely reduced to the carbinol by *t*-butylmagnesium chloride.

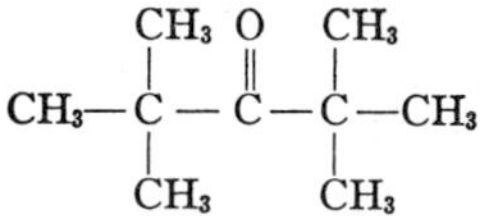

Di-*t*-butyl ketone 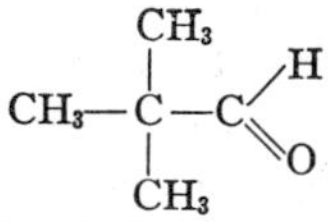   Trimethylacetaldehyde

This tertiary Grignard reagent also reduces rather than adds to trimethylacetaldehyde.

The reducing action of reagents with branched alkyl groups is accounted for by a mechanism advanced by Whitmore (1943). The reaction is pictured as

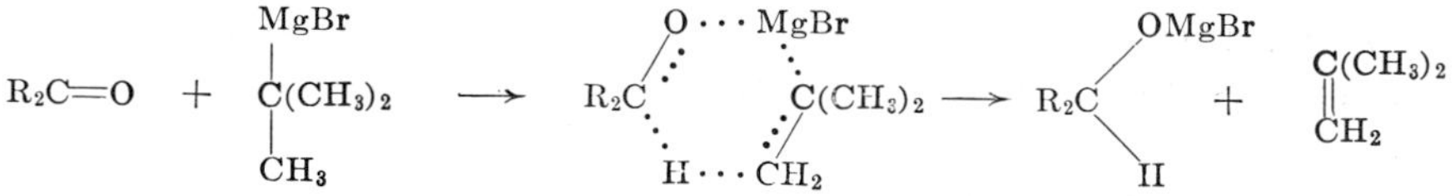

involving a cyclic transition state which undergoes internal rearrangement with transfer of a hydride ion (H:) from the Grignard reagent to the relatively positive carbon atom of the carbonyl group. The mechanism is supported by demonstration of partial asymmetric reduction of methyl *t*-butyl ketone by the Grignard reagent from (+)-2-methylbutyl chloride (Mosher,[1] 1950). The postulated

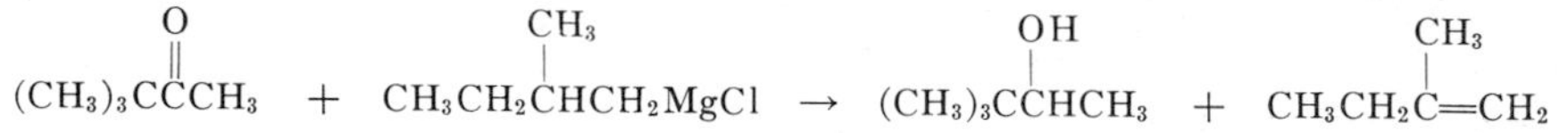

transition state allows for stereospecific reduction of the ketone simultaneously with destruction of asymmetry of the Grignard reagent.

[1] Harry S. Mosher, b. 1915 Salem, Oregon; Ph.D. Penn. State (Whitmore); Stanford Univ.

Even though the carbonyl component may contain hydroxyl or carboxyl groups that rapidly destroy the Grignard reagent, just as water does, a satisfactory addition sometimes can be accomplished by using sufficient excess reagent to allow for destruction of an amount equivalent to the hydroxyl groups present. For example, such substances as

$$RCO(CH_2)_nCH_2OH \qquad\qquad HOOC(CH_2)_nCHO$$

react with a first mole of methylmagnesium iodide with liberation of methane, and then add a second mole to form the derivatives:

$$\begin{array}{c} OMgI \\ | \\ RC(CH_2)_nCH_2OMgI \\ | \\ CH_3 \end{array} \qquad\qquad \begin{array}{c} \\ IMgOOC(CH_2)_nCHOMgI \\ | \\ CH_3 \end{array}$$

12.26   Zerewitinoff Determination. — Liberation of methane by compounds with hydroxyl or other active-hydrogen groups is the basis of a useful analytical method introduced by Zerewitinoff (1912) and elaborated by others, particularly Kohler[1] (1930). In the original method a weighed sample is treated with excess methyl Grignard reagent and the volume of evolved methane measured; the number of equivalents of gas liberated indicates the number of hydroxyl groups. The procedure can be modified to include determination of the amount of reagent that adds to the molecule by using a measured amount of Grignard solution of known content, measuring the methane evolved on reaction with the test sample, and then adding water and measuring the methane evolved from the remaining reagent not utilized for addition. A microapparatus (Kohler: Grignard machine) including technical improvements introduced by W. M. Lauer is illustrated in Fig. 12.1. A measured volume of Grignard solution, withdrawn from a reservoir with a hypodermic syringe and introduced into the apparatus without exposure to moist air, is mixed with a weighed sample of the substance to be analyzed, and the mixture is agitated by oscillation of a glass-covered steel ball.

12.27   1,4-Addition. — Replacement of one of the phenyl groups of triphenylcarbinol greatly decreases the reactivity, for example, the ability to form halochromic salts with strong acids. In 1903 Kohler, then at Bryn Mawr, was interested in examining diphenylstyrylcarbinol, $C_6H_5CH=CHCOH(C_6H_5)_2$, for comparison of the phenylvinyl group with the phenyl group. From all information at the time available, the substance should be obtainable by the reaction of phenylmagnesium bromide with benzalacetophenone, $C_6H_5CH=CHCOC_6H_5$. To his surprise, Kohler found that gradual addition of this ketone to one equivalent of phenylmagnesium bromide gave a dimeric product and not the carbinol sought. He had observed, however, that when approximately half of the ketone had been added the solution acquired a pale yellow color, and when he stopped the reaction at this point he obtained the monomeric addition

[1] Elmer Peter Kohler, 1865–1938; b. Egypt, Penna.; Ph.D. Johns Hopkins (Remsen); Bryn Mawr College, Harvard Univ.

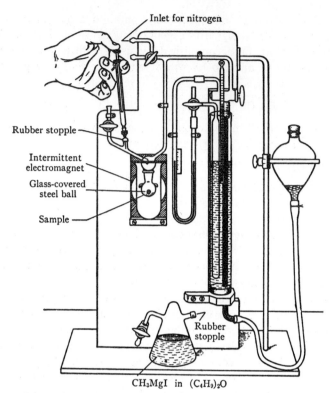

Inlet for nitrogen

Rubber stopple

Intermittent
electromagnet

Glass-covered
steel ball

Sample

Rubber
stopple

CH₃MgI in (C₄H₉)₂O

Fɪɢ. 12.1. — Grignard Machine for the Determination of Active Hydrogen Atoms and
Carbonyl Groups

product in fair yield.   By use of two equivalents of Grignard reagent he raised
the yield to 9ɔ%.

Kohler reported a number of properties consistent with formulation of the
reaction product as diphenylstyrylcarbinol, but he also called attention to certain
abnormalities: the substance did not behave like an alcohol; reaction with phosphorus pentachloride gave a monochloro derivative which was notably unreactive;
the "dibromide" lost hydrogen bromide and was too unstable to be isolated.   A
year later, Kohler wrote "Since publication of the paper I have found that all
these peculiarities are explained by the fact that the substance is not an alcohol at
all, but an isomeric ketone represented by the formula $(C_6H_5)_2CHCH_2COC_6H_5$."
This ketone, β,β-diphenylpropiophenone, could arise either by addition to the
carbon–carbon double bond or by 1,4-addition to the conjugated system.   Kohler
preferred the latter explanation but did not commit himself until he had proved
the point experimentally (19ɔ6).   He knew that an enolic system is stabilized by
substituent phenyl groups (due to increased conjugation), and found that addition of phenylmagnesium bromide to benzaldesoxybenzoin (1) gave a magnesium
halide derivative (2), which on hydrolysis gave an enol (3) stable enough for
isolation, characterization, and determination of the rate of its isomerization to

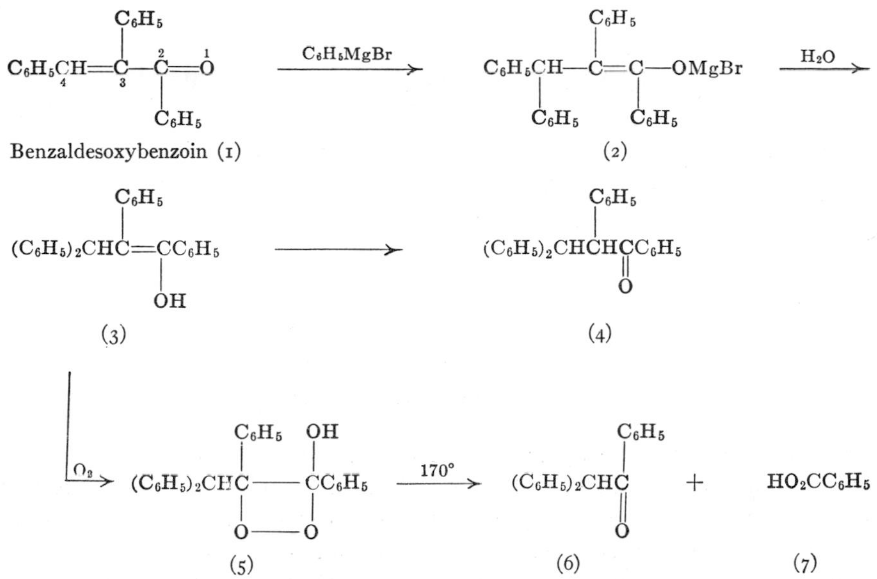

$$
\underset{\text{Benzaldesoxybenzoin (1)}}{\overset{\overset{\displaystyle C_6H_5}{|}}{C_6H_5\overset{4}{C}H=\overset{3}{\underset{\underset{\displaystyle C_6H_5}{|}}{C}}-\overset{2}{\overset{1}{C}}=O}} \xrightarrow{C_6H_5MgBr} \underset{(2)}{\overset{\overset{\displaystyle C_6H_5}{|}}{C_6H_5CH-\underset{\underset{\displaystyle C_6H_5}{|}}{C}=\underset{\underset{\displaystyle C_6H_5}{|}}{C}-OMgBr}} \xrightarrow{H_2O}
$$

$$
\underset{(3)}{\overset{\overset{\displaystyle C_6H_5}{|}}{(C_6H_5)_2CH\underset{\underset{\displaystyle OH}{|}}{C}=CC_6H_5}} \longrightarrow \underset{(4)}{\overset{\overset{\displaystyle C_6H_5}{|}}{(C_6H_5)_2CHCH\underset{\underset{\displaystyle O}{\|}}{C}C_6H_5}}
$$

$$
\xrightarrow{O_2} \underset{(5)}{\overset{\overset{\displaystyle C_6H_5}{|}\ \ \overset{\displaystyle OH}{|}}{(C_6H_5)_2CHC\underset{O-O}{\underset{|\ \ \ |}{}}CC_6H_5}} \xrightarrow{170°} \underset{(6)}{\overset{\overset{\displaystyle C_6H_5}{|}}{(C_6H_5)_2CH\underset{\underset{\displaystyle O}{\|}}{C}}} + \underset{(7)}{HO_2CC_6H_5}
$$

the ketone (4) in ether at 0° (about 20% in 24 hrs.). When air was drawn through an ethereal solution of the crystalline enol at 0° for several hours the substance afforded the peroxide (5). The peroxide does not liberate iodine from potassium iodide, but liberates methane in the Zerewitinoff test and on decomposition at 170° affords the ketone (6) and benzoic acid. The ketonic product of isomerization, (4), is stable to oxygen. Therefore the Grignard reaction is a 1,4-addition.

Almost all Grignard reactions of α,β-unsaturated aldehydes are 1,2-additions. Structural features influencing the direction of addition to α,β-unsaturated ketones are evident from Table 12.4 (Kohler, 1907). Groups that shield the carbonyl group suppress 1,2-addition, and β-substituents suppress 1,4-addition. The ethyl Grignard reagent usually gives a higher proportion of the 1,4-product than phenylmagnesium bromide. In the case of benzalacetophenone, phenylmagnesium bromide gives 94% 1,4-addition whereas the more reactive phenyllithium gives 13% of 1,4-product and 69% of 1,2-product. Kharasch (1941) discovered,

TABLE 12.4. PERCENT 1,4-ADDITION (THE REMAINDER IS 1,2-ADDITION)

	C_6H_5MgBr	C_2H_5MgBr
$C_6H_5CH=CHCOCH_3$	12	60
$C_6H_5CH=CHCOCH_2CH_3$	40	71
$C_6H_5CH-CHCOCH(CH_3)_2$	88	100
$C_6H_5CH=CHCOC(CH_3)_3$	100	100
$C_6H_5CH=CHCOC_6H_5$	94	99
$(C_6H_5)_2C=CHCOC_6H_5$	0	18
$C_6H_5CH=C(C_6H_5)COC_6H_5$	100	100
$C_6H_5C(CH_3)=CHCOC_6H_5$	44	41

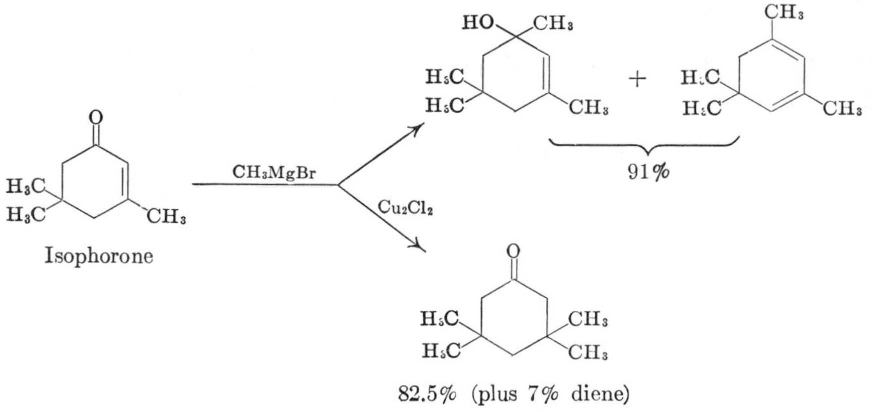

Isophorone

91%

82.5% (plus 7% diene)

surprisingly, that methylmagnesium bromide reacts with isophorone to give exclusively products of 1,2-addition (either direct or inverse procedure), but that when the ketone is added to a solution of methylmagnesium bromide containing one mole percent of cuprous chloride addition is almost exclusively 1,4.

12.28   The Reformatsky[1] reaction (1887) depends on interaction between a carbonyl compound, an α-halo ester, and activated zinc in the presence of anhydrous ether or ether-benzene, followed by hydrolysis. The halogen component, for example ethyl bromoacetate, combines with zinc to form an organozinc bromide that adds to the carbonyl group of the second component to give a complex readily hydrolyzed to a carbinol. The reaction is conducted by

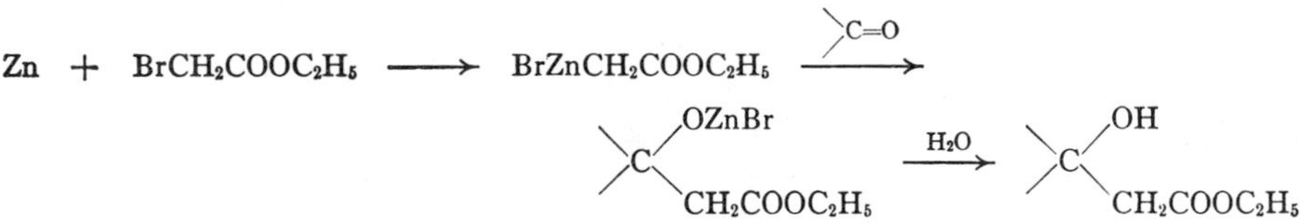

the usual Grignard technique except that the carbonyl component is added at the start. Magnesium has been used in a few reactions in place of zinc but with poor results, for the more reactive organometallic reagent tends to attack the ester group; with zinc this side reaction is not appreciable, and the reactivity is

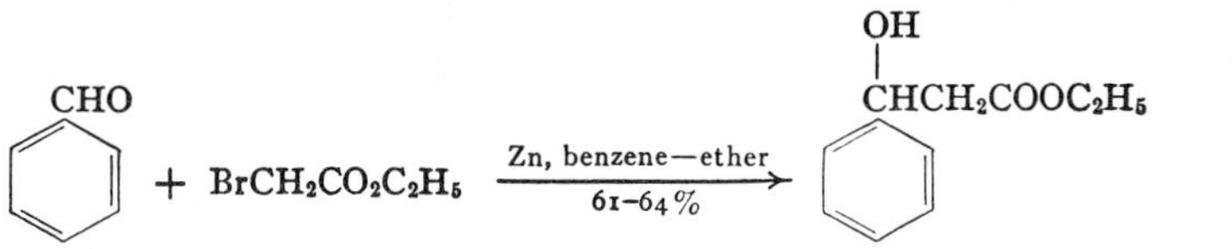

Ethyl β-phenyl-β-hydroxy-
propionate (b.p. 130°/6 mm.)

sufficient for addition to the carbonyl group of aldehydes and ketones of both the aliphatic and aromatic series. The product of the reaction is a β-hydroxy

[1] Sergius Reformatsky, 1860–1934; b. Russia; Kiev; *Ber.*, **68A**, 61 (1935)

ester and can be dehydrated to the α,β-unsaturated ester; thus the product from benzaldehyde and ethyl bromoacetate yields ethyl cinnamate. α-Bromo esters of the types $RCHBrCO_2C_2H_5$ and $RR'CBrCO_2C_2H_5$ react satisfactorily, but β- and γ-bromo derivatives of saturated esters do not have adequate reactivity. Methyl γ-bromocrotonate ($BrCH_2CH{=}CHCO_2CH_3$), however, has a reactive, allylic bromine atom and enters into the Reformatsky reaction.

OXIDATION-REDUCTION

12.29 **Test for Aldehydes.** — Aldehydes are subject to ready oxidation, whereas ketones are not, and the two types can be distinguished by qualitative tests with oxidizing agents specific for aldehydes. One reagent is a solution of silver nitrate in excess ammonium hydroxide, containing the complex

$$RCHO + 2\,Ag(NH_3)_2OH \longrightarrow RCOONH_4 + 2\,Ag + 3\,NH_3 + H_2O$$

ion $Ag(NH_3)_2{}^+$. The aldehyde is oxidized to the acid, which forms the ammonium salt, and the complex metal ion is reduced to metallic silver, which is deposited on the walls of a test tube as an adherent mirror. A second test reagent, Fehling solution, is made by mixing a solution of copper sulfate with an alkaline solution of a salt of tartaric acid; this combination results in a deep blue solution containing a complex cupric ion, and on interaction with an aldehyde the copper is reduced to the univalent stage, and a red precipitate of cuprous oxide is indicative of a reaction. Thus aldehydes give a positive silver-mirror test and

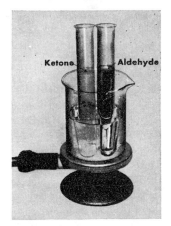

Ketone   Aldehyde

$$RCHO + 2\,Cu^{++} + NaOH + H_2O \longrightarrow RCOONa + Cu_2O + 4\,H^+$$
(Fehling
solution)

reduce Fehling solution, whereas ketones do not. These reagents do not attack alcohols or ethylenic compounds, but they oxidize α-ketols as well as aldehydes (activation by the carbonyl group).

$$\begin{array}{ccc} -C{=}O & & -C{=}O \\ | & \xrightarrow{[O]} & | \\ -CHOH & & -C{=}O \\ \alpha\text{-Ketol} & & \alpha\text{-Diketone} \end{array}$$

12.30 **Oxidative Fission.** — Although ketones are resistant to oxidation by hexavalent chromium in an acidic medium, those of the type RCH_2COCH_2R' can be oxidized with alkaline permanganate or hot nitric acid. Since the chain can be ruptured on both sides of the carbonyl group and four

$$RCH_2|CO|CH_2R' \xrightarrow{HNO_3} RCO_2H + RCH_2CO_2H + R'CO_2H + R'CH_2CO_2H$$

acidic fragments formed, such reactions are seldom of value. However, in a cyclic ketone, for example cyclohexanone, oxidative fission gives a dibasic acid;

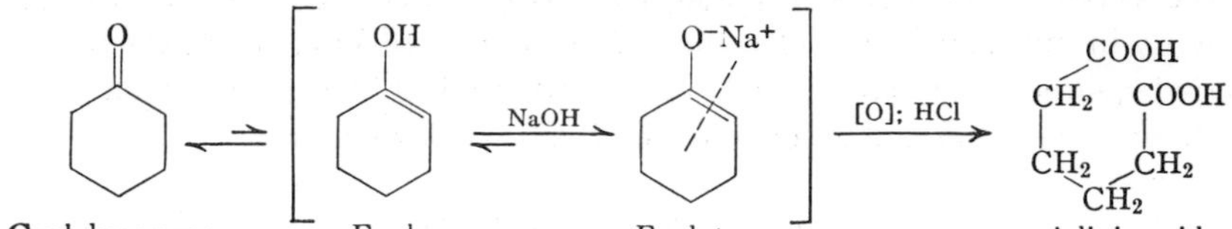

Cyclohexanone   Enol   Enolate   Adipic acid

since the starting material is symmetrical, the same acid results from cleavage of either connecting link. No reaction occurs when cyclohexanone is shaken with aqueous permanganate at room temperature, but addition of a little sodium hydroxide causes a prompt temperature rise with separation of manganese dioxide, and adipic acid can be obtained in good yield. Alkali promotes enolization because the enol is acidic; oxidation involves attack of the double bond of the enolate. Adipic acid can be prepared by oxidation of either cyclohexanone or cyclohexanol with 50% nitric acid at 85–90°; the yield from the alcohol is 53–55%. A higher yield is reported for oxidation of cyclopentanone to glutaric acid with vanadium pentoxide as catalyst.

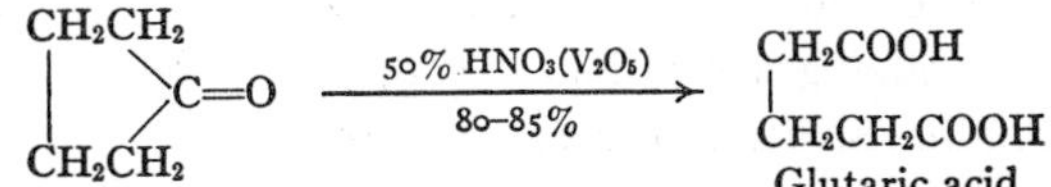

Cyclopentanone   Glutaric acid

Bromination experiments cited above show that cholestanone and coprostanone form the 2,3- and 3,4-enol, respectively. Thus on oxidative fission cholestanone is cleaved chiefly to the 2,3-seco-dioic acid and coprostanone to the 3,4-seco-dioic acid (L. *secare*, to cut).

12.31   Selenium Dioxide Oxidation (Riley Reaction). — H. L. Riley (1932) introduced a new oxidizing agent which is commonly known as selenium dioxide. Oxidations are usually conducted in alcohol, acetic acid, acetic acid–benzene, and the oxide is dissolved in a small volume of hot water. The actual reagent is thus selenious acid, $(HO)_2Se{=}O$, and it is a convenience to use the preformed reagent. Riley found that the reagent effects the oxidation of —CH_2CO— to —$COCO$—, the Riley reaction; selenious acid also effects allylic hydroxylations and dehydrogenations. A typical Riley reaction is the

$$C_6H_5COCH_3 + H_2SeO_3 \xrightarrow[69-72\%]{} C_6H_5COCHO + Se + H_2O$$
Acetophenone   Phenylglyoxal

oxidation of acetophenone in dioxane–acetic acid to phenylglyoxal; phenylacetaldehyde can be used in place of acetophenone. Another is the oxidation of diethyl malonate to diethyl oxomalonate, although *Organic Syntheses* gives

$$CH_2(CO_2C_2H_5)_2 \xrightarrow[74-76\%]{N_2O_3} CO(CO_2C_2H_5)_2$$
Diethyl malonate   Diethyl oxomalonate

preference to nitric anhydride as oxidant; the product distills as a golden yellow liquid, b.p. 104°/15 mm.

Study of the oxidation of desoxybenzoin to benzil by selenious acid in 70% acetic acid at 89° (Corey,[1] 1960) showed that the reaction rate is proportional to

$$C_6H_5CH_2COC_6H_5 \xrightarrow[90\%]{H_2SeO_3} C_6H_5COCOC_6H_5$$
Desoxybenzoin   Benzil

the concentrations of the ketone, of H_2SeO_3, and of H^+. Since the rate is dependent upon the concentration of the oxidizing agent, the reaction does not involve enolization as the slow step. Replacement of the methylene hydrogens by deuterium depresses the rate several fold and hence the rate-determining step must involve C—H bond breaking. The effect of substituent groups in one or the other phenyl group suggests that an enol ester, if not the enol itself, is involved. Thus electron-withdrawing groups *para* to the methylene group facilitate enolization and also accelerate oxidation; the opposite is true for substituents in the benzoyl group. Cholestanone forms the 2,3-enol and is oxidized by selenious acid to cholestane-2,3-dione. Corey considers that the reaction involves the protonated electrophile $(HO)_3Se^+$ [selenious acid, $(HO)_2Se$

$$C_6H_5COCH_2C_6H_5 \quad + \quad (HO)_3Se^+ \quad \xrightarrow{k_1} \quad \overset{\overset{O}{\|}}{\underset{|}{OSeOH}} C_6H_5C{=}CHC_6H_5 \quad + \quad H_3O^+$$

(1)

$$\overset{\overset{O}{\|}}{\underset{|}{OSeOH}} C_6H_5C{=}CHC_6H_5 \quad \xrightarrow{k_2} \quad C_6H_5\overset{O}{\underset{}{C}}{-}\overset{OSeOH}{\underset{}{C}}HC_6H_5 \quad \xrightarrow[-Se, H_2O]{fast} \quad C_6H_5\overset{O}{\underset{}{C}}{-}\overset{O}{\underset{}{C}}C_6H_5$$

(1)   (2)   (3)

=O, + H^+], which attacks the carbonyl oxygen with synchronous departure of an α-hydrogen atom, a molecule of water, and the ionic charge as a hydronium ion. The Se-IV selenite ester formed (1) rearranges to the Se-II ester (2), which decomposes to the diketone (3), selenium, and water. Results of a study of the selenious acid oxidation of 1,2-dibenzoylethane to dibenzoylethylene (J. P. Schaefer, 1960) are interpreted similarly.

12.32   Peracid Oxidation (Baeyer-Villiger Reaction). — A. Baeyer and V. Villiger (1899–1900) found that cyclic ketones, such as camphor, are oxidized to cyclic lactones by permonosulfuric acid, $HOOSO_3H$ (= H_2SO_5, Caro's acid). Oxidizing agents preferred by modern workers are perbenzoic, monoperphthalic, peracetic, and trifluoroperacetic acid. The reaction, RCOR′ → RCOOR′, is generally applicable to aliphatic, cyclic, and aromatic ketones. α-Diketones are converted into acid anhydrides: RCOCOR′ → RCOOCOR′

[1] Elias J. Corey, b. 1928 Methuen, Mass.; Ph.D. Mass. Inst. Techn.; Univ. Illinois; Harvard Univ.

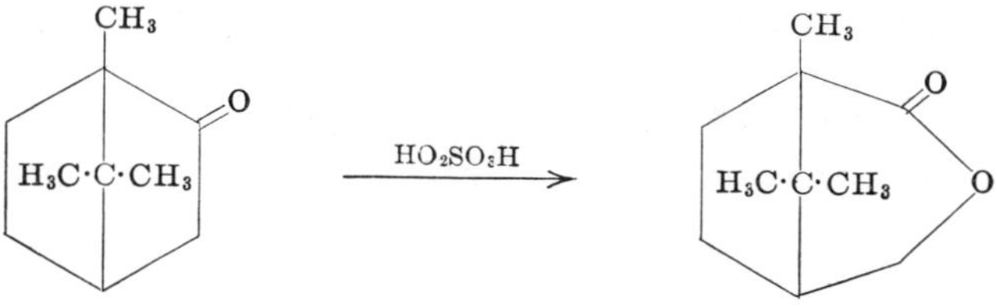

Camphor ε-Lactone

(Karrer,[1] 1946); α,β-unsaturated ketones yield enol esters: RCH═CHCOR′ → RCH═CHOCOR′ (Böeseken, 1931–36). Criegee (1948) postulated the following sequence, as illustrated for the perbenzoic acid oxidation of methyl cyclohexyl

$$CH_3{-}\overset{O}{\overset{\|}{C}}{-}C_6H_{11} \xrightarrow{C_6H_5CO_3H} CH_3{-}\underset{OOCOC_6H_5}{\underset{|}{\overset{OH}{\overset{|}{C}}}}{-}C_6H_{11} \xrightarrow{-C_6H_5COO^-} CH_3{-}\underset{O^+}{\underset{|}{\overset{OH}{\overset{|}{C}}}}{-}C_6H_{11} \rightarrow$$

Methyl
cyclohexyl ketone

$$CH_3{-}\underset{OC_6H_{11}}{\underset{|}{\overset{OH}{\overset{|}{C}}}}{}^+ \xrightarrow[67\%]{-H^+} CH_3\underset{OC_6H_{11}}{\underset{|}{\overset{O}{\overset{\|}{C}}}}$$

Cyclohexyl
acetate

ketone: addition to the carbonyl group, expulsion of benzoate anion to give an intermediate with an electron-deficient oxygen atom, migration of one of the two groups to give a carbonium ion, and loss of a proton with formation of the ester. In the case cited the migrating group is secondary and that retained is primary. The mechanism is in accord with the later finding of Doering (1953) that in the peracid oxidation of benzophenone-O^{18} the activity is retained completely in the carbonyl oxygen:

$$C_6H_5\overset{O^{18}}{\overset{\|}{C}}C_6H_5 \xrightarrow{C_6H_5CO_3H} C_6H_5O\overset{O^{18}}{\overset{\|}{C}}C_6H_5 \xrightarrow{LiAlH_4} C_6H_5OH + C_6H_5CH_2O^{18}H$$

The result rules out any alternative mechanism in which two oxygen atoms become equivalent.

The reaction thus bears some analogy to the pinacol and Beckmann (12.39) rearrangements, and the order of migratory aptitude corresponds to those in these rearrangements. The order of migratory aptitude in the alkyl series is tertiary > secondary > primary (S. L. Friess,[2] 1950); in the aryl series the order is p-$CH_3OC_6H_4$— > p-$CH_3C_6H_4$— > C_6H_5— > p-ClC_6H_4— > p-$O_2NC_6H_4$— > p-$H_2NC_6H_4$— > (Doering, 1950). That the migrating group is thus the one with greater capacity for electron release supports the hypothesis of an electron-

[1] Paul Karrer, b. 1889 Moscow; Ph.D. Zurich (Werner); Univ. Zurich; Nobel Prize 1937

[2] S. L. Friess, b. 1922 Detroit; Ph.D. Univ. Calif. Los Angeles (Geissman); U. S. Naval Med. Res. Inst., Bethesda, Md.

deficient intermediate. The fact that the reaction is catalyzed by acids is a further indication that one step involves addition to the carbonyl group. Moreover the migrating group retains its configuration (R. B. Turner, 1950; K. Mislow, 1953). Thus *cis-* and *trans*-1-acetyl-2-methylcyclohexane give, respectively,

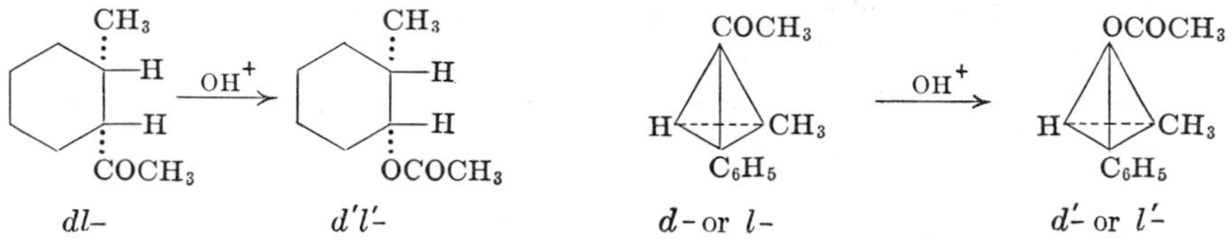

cis- and *trans*-2-methylcyclohexanyl acetate, and optically active 3-phenyl-2-butanone affords optically active phenylmethylcarbinol acetate. The results support the idea that the reaction is an internal substitution (S_Ni, see 9.8). Retention of configuration is characteristic of rearrangements of the Wagner-Meerwein and related types.

The direction of cleavage of alkyl aryl ketones is variable, although acetophenone and propiophenone afford phenyl acetate and phenyl propionate in yield of 63 and 73%, and α-tetralone is cleaved chiefly between the keto group and the benzenoid ring. That the phenyl group migrates in preference to the electron-releasing alkyl groups suggests involvement of an aronium ion intermediate (9.7):

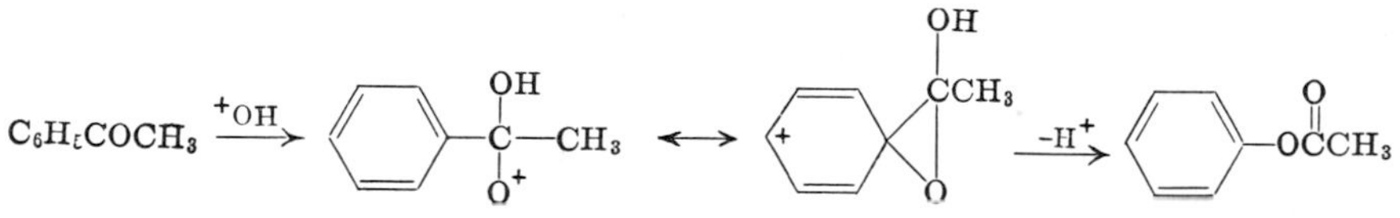

12.33   **Air Oxidation.** — E. J. Bailey and J. Elks (1960) report that steroid ketones of the partial structure (1) react with molecular oxygen

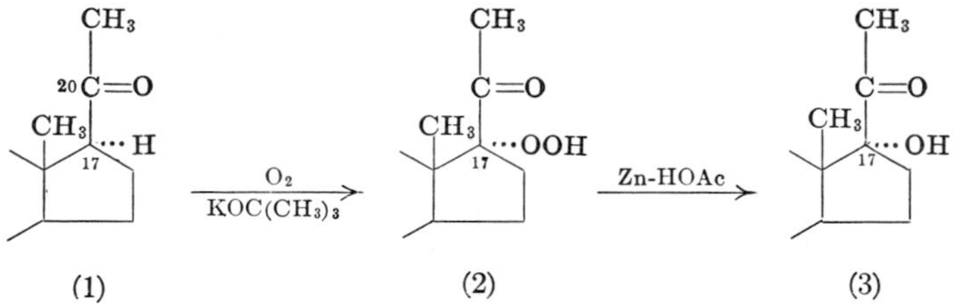

in *t*-butyl alcohol in the presence of potassium *t*-butoxide to form 17α hydroperoxides (2) reducible with zinc and acetic acid to the 17α-hydroxy derivatives (3). Overall yields in this novel method for effecting 17α-hydroxylation of 20-ketones are in the order of 23–57%.

12.34   **Bimolecular Reduction.** — Normal reduction of aldehydes and ketones can be effected smoothly with a borohydride, by catalytic hydrogenation (Pt, Raney nickel), or by the sodium–alcohol method. Other metal combinations (iron powder and acetic acid; zinc dust and alcoholic alkali) are sometimes satisfactory for reduction of aldehydes; ketones, however, undergo both normal and bimolecular reduction, and the latter reaction has synthetic applications. Thus the standard laboratory method for the preparation of pinacol is by reduction of dry acetone with amalgamated magnesium in benzene, followed by hydrolysis of the solid magnesium derivative formed. The reaction probably involves attachment of magnesium to the oxygen atoms of two molecules of acetone to form a transient diradical and then magnesium pinacolate, which is

$$2(CH_3)_2CO \xrightarrow{Mg} \begin{array}{c} (CH_3)_2C-O \\ \vdots \\ (CH_3)_2C-O \end{array}\!\!\!\!Mg \longrightarrow \begin{array}{c} (CH_3)_2C-O \\ | \\ (CH_3)_2C-O \end{array}\!\!\!\!Mg \xrightarrow[43\text{-}50\%]{H_2O} \begin{array}{c} (CH_3)_2COH \\ | \\ (CH_3)_2COH \end{array}$$

Pinacol

subsequently hydrolyzed to pinacol. Anhydrous pinacol is a liquid, b.p. 174.4°; it forms a crystalline hydrate containing six molecules of water. Pinacol hydrate, $C_6H_{12}(OH)_2 \cdot 6H_2O$ (named from *pinako-*, Gr., tabletlike, referring to the crystalline form of the hydrate), melts at 45°. The aluminum amalgam reduction of acetone yields isopropyl alcohol along with pinacol, but on addition of an appropriate amount of water to a benzene solution of the mixture pinacol hydrate separates in crystalline form. Aliphatic aldehydes are more reactive than ketones and are reduced unimolecularly. A phenyl group depresses the additive power of the carbonyl group (see 12.23), and benzaldehyde on reaction with aluminum amalgam or sodium amalgam is reduced bimolecularly to *meso*-hydrobenzoin and a trace of *dl*-hydrobenzoin: $C_6H_5CH(OH)CH(OH)C_6H_5$.

12.35   Meerwein-Ponndorf Reduction. — Introduced (1925–26) prior to Oppenauer oxidation (12.7), this method of reduction is the reverse of dehydrogenation of an alcohol with excess acetone. A carbonyl compound is heated with aluminum isopropoxide (or aluminum *t*-butoxide) in benzene or toluene solution and the acetone is distilled from the resulting equilibrium.

$$\begin{array}{c} R \\ \diagdown \\ R' \end{array}\!\!\!C=O \ + \ Al[OCH(CH_3)_2]_3 \ \rightleftharpoons \ \left[\begin{array}{c} R \\ \diagdown \\ R' \end{array}\!\!\!CHO\right]_3\!Al \ + \ O=C(CH_3)_2$$

Aluminum isopropoxide

(R′ = alkyl or H)

dil. H_2SO_4 ↓

$$\begin{array}{c} R \\ \diagdown \\ R' \end{array}\!\!\!CHOH$$

The reaction is specific to the carbonyl group, and can be employed for reduction of unsaturated aldehydes and ketones, for example:

$$CH_3CH=CHCHO \xrightarrow[85\text{-}90\%]{Al(OC_3H_7)_3} CH_3CH=CHCH_2OH$$

Crotonaldehyde   Crotyl alcohol

The reaction has been carried out also by treating a mixture of ketone and hydrogen donor with potassium *t*-butoxide.

The Meerwein-Ponndorf and Oppenauer reactions are regarded as proceeding through a cyclic transition state similar to that postulated for reduction by a Grignard reagent (12.25). The postulated direct carbon to carbon transfer of

$$R_2C=O \quad + \quad Al[OCH(CH_3)_2]_3 \quad \rightleftharpoons \quad \begin{array}{c} O\cdots Al[OCH(CH_3)_2]_2 \\ R_2C \\ H\cdots C \\ H_3C \quad CH_3 \end{array} \quad \rightleftharpoons$$

$$\begin{array}{c} O{-}Al[OCH(CH_3)_2]_2 \\ R_2C \\ H \end{array} \quad + \quad \begin{array}{c} O \\ \parallel \\ C \\ H_3C \quad CH_3 \end{array}$$

hydrogen with its electrons is supported by the observation that when the reaction is carried out in the presence of deuterium oxide no deuterium is incorporated.

12.36　　Cannizzaro Reaction of Aldehydes. — Another reaction, characteristic of aldehydes having no α-hydrogen atoms and applicable chiefly in the aromatic series, is oxidation of one molecule of the aldehyde at the expense of another, which suffers reduction. The reaction, which bears the name of the discoverer, Cannizzaro[1] (1853), is brought about by the action of a concentrated solution of sodium or potassium hydroxide on an aldehyde of the type indicated, for example benzaldehyde:

$$2\,C_6H_5C{\overset{H}{\underset{O}{\big\langle}}} \quad + \quad KOH \quad \xrightarrow{60\% \text{ KOH}} \quad C_6H_5C{\overset{OK}{\underset{O}{\big\langle}}} \quad + \quad C_6H_5CH_2OH$$

Potassium benzoate　　　　　Benzyl alcohol

The oxidation product, benzoic acid, can be isolated in 85–95% yield, and the reduction product, benzyl alcohol, in 80% yield. This type of compensated oxidation-reduction process is called disproportionation.

The first step in the Cannizzaro reaction is formation of a complex containing one mole of metal hydroxide and two moles of the aldehyde, and indeed such complexes have been isolated (see E. Pfeil, 1951). The hydroxide ion of the com-

$$\begin{array}{ccc} C_6H_5{-}C{\overset{H}{\underset{O}{\big|}}}\overset{H}{\underset{O}{\big|}}C{-}C_6H_5 & \longrightarrow & C_6H_5{-}C{\overset{OH}{\underset{O}{\big|}}}\overset{H}{\underset{O}{\big|}}C{-}C_6H_5 & \longrightarrow & C_6H_5{-}C{\overset{OH}{\underset{O}{\big|}}} \quad + \quad H{-}C{\overset{H}{\underset{O^-Na^+}{\big|}}}{-}C_6H_5 \\ \overset{-}{O}H \cdots Na^+ & & O^-{\cdots}Na^+ & & O \end{array}$$

plex attacks one of the carbonyl groups, and the resulting increased electron density at the carbon center promotes transfer of a hydride ion (H^-) to the other

---

[1] Stanislao Cannizzaro, 1826–1910; b. Palermo, Italy; stud. Pisa (Piria); Univ. Genoa, Palermo, Rome; *J. Chem. Soc.*, **111**, 1677 (1912)

carbonyl group with synchronous electron displacements to give the acid and the alcohol anion.

Application of the Cannizzaro reaction in the aliphatic series is limited, for substances having an α-hydrogen atom enter more readily into aldol condensation.

DERIVATIVES

12.37   Condensation with Amines. — Among reagents for the carbonyl group are various amine derivatives of ammonia. One, hydroxylamine, represents a combination of the structures of water and of ammonia; another, hydrazine, is structurally comparable to hydrogen peroxide, to which it bears the same relation as ammonia does to water. These amine reagents condense with

$$\left.\begin{array}{l} \text{H·OH} \\ \text{H·NH}_2 \end{array}\right\} \text{HO·NH}_2, \text{Hydroxylamine}$$

$$\text{HO·OH} \} \text{H}_2\text{N·NH}_2, \text{Hydrazine}$$

aldehydes and ketones with the net result that water is eliminated between the two molecules and an unsaturated nitrogen-containing derivative is formed.

$$\text{>C=O + H}_2\text{N}- \longrightarrow \text{>C=N}-$$

The products of condensation with hydroxylamine are called oximes, and can be designated as aldoximes or ketoximes, according to the nature of the carbonyl component. The condensations proceed readily on warming the components in

$$\text{CH}_3\text{CH=O + H}_2\text{NOH} \longrightarrow \underset{\substack{\text{Acetaldoxime} \\ \text{(m.p. 47°)}}}{\text{CH}_3\text{CH=NOH}}$$

$$\begin{array}{c} \text{CH}_3 \\ \diagdown \\ \diagup \\ \text{CH}_3 \end{array}\text{C=O + H}_2\text{NOH} \longrightarrow \underset{\substack{\text{Acetoxime} \\ \text{(m.p. 60°)}}}{\begin{array}{c} \text{CH}_3 \\ \diagdown \\ \diagup \\ \text{CH}_3 \end{array}\text{C=NOH}}$$

aqueous or alcoholic solution, and the examples indicate that oximes are crystalline solids even though the carbonyl compounds from which they are derived are volatile liquids. Oximes are thus solid derivatives of service for identification.

An interesting use of an aldoxime is for preparation of an acid from an aldehyde

$$\underset{\substack{| \\ \text{CH}_3}}{\text{CH}_3}\underset{\substack{| \\ \text{CH}_3}}{\text{CH}_3} \\ \text{CH}_3\text{CH(CH}_2)_3\text{CHCH=CHCH=O} \xrightarrow{\text{H}_2\text{NOH}}$$

$$\underset{\substack{| \\ \text{CH}_3}}{\text{CH}_3}\underset{\substack{| \\ \text{CH}_3}}{\text{CH}_3} \\ \text{CH}_3\text{CH(CH}_2)_3\text{CHCH=CHCH=NOH} \xrightarrow[-\text{NH}_3]{\text{KOH; acidification}}$$

$$\underset{\substack{| \\ \text{CH}_3}}{\text{CH}_3}\underset{\substack{| \\ \text{CH}_3}}{\text{CH}_3} \\ \text{CH}_3\text{CH(CH}_2)_3\text{CHCH=CHCO}_2\text{H}$$

resistant to oxidation by usual methods (*e.g.* Ag_2O), for example the α,β-unsaturated aldehyde formulated. This reaction, discovered in 1891 by the Italian C. U. Zanetti, probably is analogous to the disproportionation discovered in Italy by Cannizzaro: cleavage to the components, reaction with KOH to produce

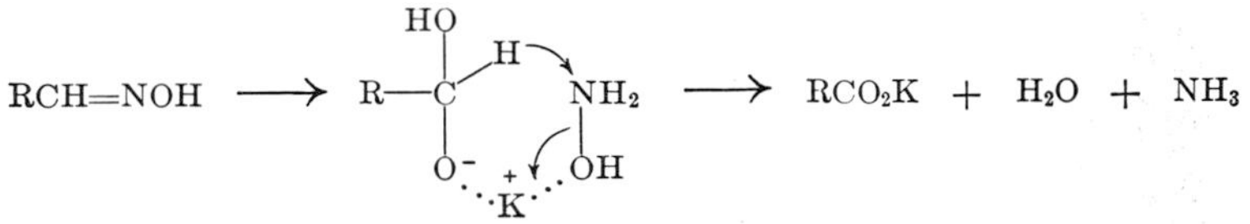

$$RCH=NOH \longrightarrow R-\overset{\overset{\textstyle HO}{|}}{\underset{\underset{\textstyle \overset{+}{K}}{O^-}}{C}}\overset{H}{\diagdown}NH_2 \longrightarrow RCO_2K + H_2O + NH_3$$

a cyclic complex, and hydride transfer.

Hydrazine reacts with a carbonyl compound to form a hydrazone, but this derivative possesses a free amino group and can condense with another molecule of the carbonyl component to form an azine. Derivatives of hydrazine in which

$$\underset{\text{Aldehyde}}{RCH=O} + \underset{\text{Hydrazine}}{H_2NNH_2} \longrightarrow \underset{\text{Hydrazone}}{RCH=NNH_2} \overset{RCHO}{\longrightarrow} \underset{\text{Azine}}{RCH=NN=CHR}$$

this double condensation is obviated by the presence of a substituent group have more practical value than hydrazine itself. One is phenylhydrazine, which yields phenylhydrazone derivatives. The phenylhydrazone of acetaldehyde is also a

$$\underset{\substack{\text{Benzaldehyde}\\(\text{liquid})}}{C_6H_5CHO} \overset{H_2NNHC_6H_5}{\longrightarrow} \underset{\substack{\text{Benzaldehyde phenylhydrazone}\\(\text{m.p. } 156°)}}{C_6H_5CH=NNHC_6H_5}$$

crystalline solid, m.p. 99°. Replacement of the oxygen atom of a carbonyl group by the residue $=NNHC_6H_5$ is attended with decided increase in molecular weight and consequent decrease in solubility, and hence an aldehyde or a ketone often can be precipitated from a dilute solution as the phenylhydrazone and identified by the melting point of this derivative. Derivatives of still higher melting point and decreased solubility are obtained with 2,4-dinitrophenylhydrazine (m.p. 197°). The carbonyl component is added to a solution of 1 g. of the red reagent

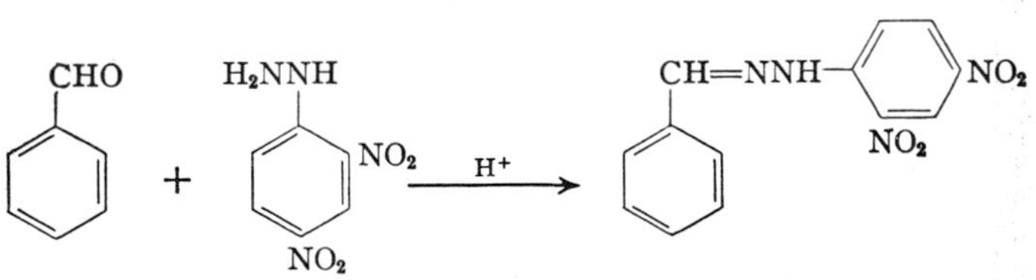

in 30 ml. of diethylene glycol dimethyl ether, followed by a drop of hydrochloric acid, which causes prompt separation of the derivative (H. J. Shine,[1] 1959); the derivative formulated melts at 237°. When the reaction is catalyzed by acetic acid (5 drops), the derivative first begins to appear in about 15 minutes. The

[1] Henry J. Shine, b. 1923 London, England; Ph.D. London; U. S. Rubber Co.; Texas Tech. College

2,4-dinitrophenylhydrazones of saturated aldehydes and ketones are yellow, and those of α,β-unsaturated carbonyl compounds are orange or red. In structure

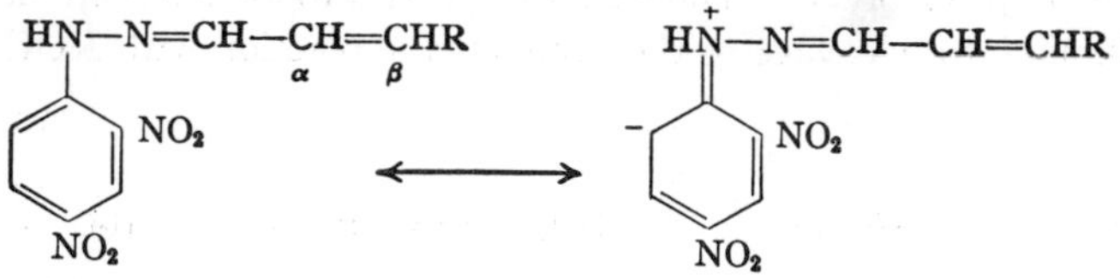

HN—N=CH—CH=CHR $\quad\quad$ HṄ—N=CH—CH=CHR

(a) $\quad\quad\quad\quad\quad$ (b)

(a) the chromophoric dinitrophenyl group is not conjugated with the —N=CH— bond and hence not influenced by the additional α,β-double bond; full conjugation is achieved, however, in resonance structures such as (b). Another reagent is

$$CH_3CHO \;+\; H_2NNHCONH_2 \longrightarrow CH_3CH=NNHCONH_2$$

$\quad\quad\quad\quad\quad\quad$ Semicarbazide $\quad\quad\quad\quad$ Acetaldehyde semicarbazone
$\quad\quad\quad\quad\quad\quad\quad\quad\quad\quad\quad\quad\quad\quad\quad\quad$ (m.p. 162°)

semicarbazide, $H_2NNHCONH_2$; this generally gives derivatives that melt at higher temperatures than oximes or phenylhydrazones. Because of their sparing solubility and because they can be hydrolyzed readily, semicarbazones are often useful for isolation of a ketone from a complex reaction mixture. Exchange with pyruvic acid, CH_3COCO_2H, affords an efficient method of cleavage. The reaction is conducted in acetic acid containing sodium acetate to the end that on eventual addition of water the exchange semicarbazone is retained in solution as the salt: $CH_3C(=NNHCONH_2)CO_2Na$. Another scheme of separation involves conversion of a ketone into a water-soluble derivative with use of Girard's reagent, trimethylaminoacetohydrazide chloride, readily prepared from trimethylamine, ethyl chloroacetate, and hydrazine. The reagent combines with ketonic sub-

$$(CH_3)_3N \;+\; ClCH_2COOC_2H_5 \;+\; H_2NNH_2 \;\xrightarrow[83-89\%]{C_2H_5OH,\ HCl,\ o-6o°}\; [(CH_3)_3\overset{+}{N}CH_2CONHNH_2]Cl^-$$

$\quad\quad\quad\quad\quad\quad\quad\quad\quad\quad\quad\quad\quad\quad\quad\quad\quad\quad\quad\quad\quad\quad\quad\quad\quad\quad$ Girard's reagent

stances to form hydrazone derivatives having a polar group that renders the substances soluble in water; after separation from nonketonic materials, the ketones are easily regenerated by hydrolysis of the Girard derivatives with mineral acid:

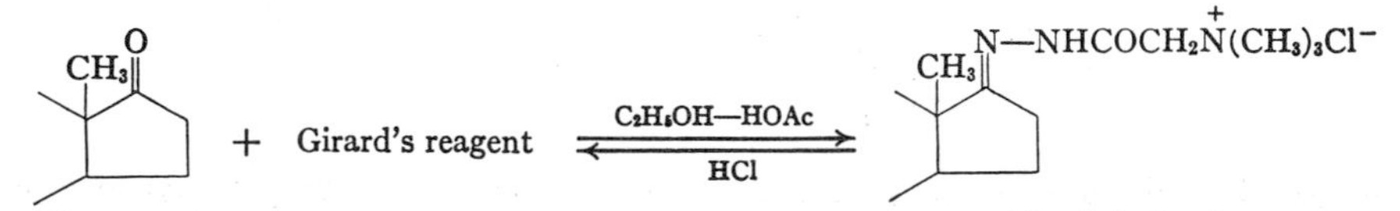

17-Ketosteroid $\quad$ + Girard's reagent $\;\xrightarrow[HCl]{C_2H_5OH—HOAc}\;$ Girard derivative

The reagent was introduced by A. Girard (1934) for the express purpose of facilitating isolation of the hormone estrone, a 17-ketosteroid, from urinary extracts.

The mechanism of the amine condensations appears to vary with the reagent. The reaction with hydroxylamine is base-catalyzed and appears to proceed by an addition-elimination mechanism initiated by abstraction of a proton from the

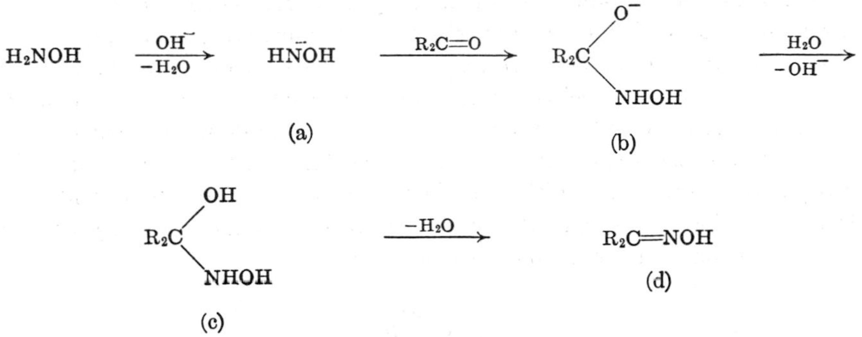

$$H_2NOH \xrightarrow[-H_2O]{OH^-} H\overset{..}{N}OH \xrightarrow{R_2C=O} R_2C\overset{\displaystyle O^-}{\underset{NHOH}{\diagdown}} \xrightarrow[-OH^-]{H_2O}$$

(a)　　　　　　　　　　(b)

$$R_2C\overset{\displaystyle OH}{\underset{NHOH}{\diagdown}} \xrightarrow{-H_2O} R_2C=NOH$$

(c)　　　　　　　　　　(d)

reagent (e.g., hydroxylamine) by hydroxide ion, and addition of the anion (a) to the carbonyl group, with eventual formation of (c) and dehydration to (d). On the other hand, the condensation with semicarbazide is catalyzed by acids but not by bases and is formulated as follows:

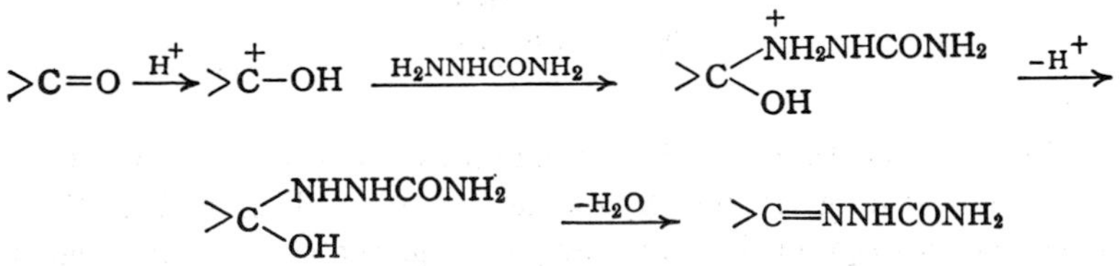

$$>C=O \xrightarrow{H^+} >\overset{+}{C}-OH \xrightarrow{H_2NNHCONH_2} >C\overset{\displaystyle \overset{+}{N}H_2NHCONH_2}{\underset{OH}{\diagdown}} \xrightarrow{-H^+}$$

$$>C\overset{\displaystyle NHNHCONH_2}{\underset{OH}{\diagdown}} \xrightarrow{-H_2O} >C=NNHCONH_2$$

As noted above, the reaction with 2,4-dinitrophenylhydrazine (and other hydrazines) requires acid catalysis. In the reaction of a number of aldehydes and ketones with semicarbazide or hydroxylamine in neutral or basic solution the addition compound, a carbinolamine (c), is formed rapidly and dehydration is the rate-controlling step. However, in strongly acidic solution the formation of the carbinolamine appears to be the slow step (W. P. Jenks, 1959).

Dianilinoethane is a useful reagent for characterization of aldehydes and for distinguishing an aldehyde from a ketone (H.-W. Wanzlick, Berlin, 1953). When a

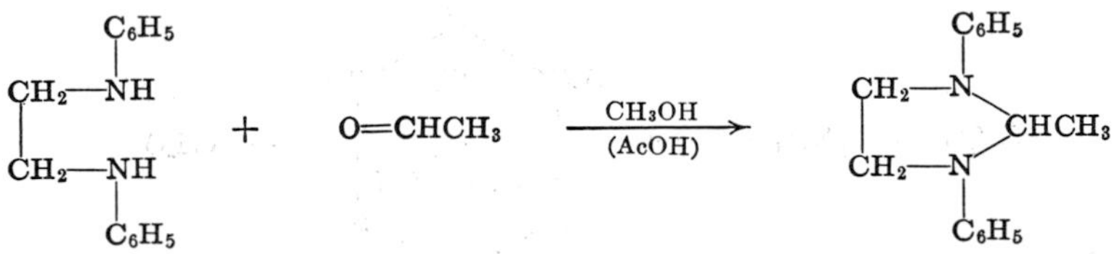

$$\begin{array}{c} C_6H_5 \\ | \\ CH_2-NH \\ | \\ CH_2-NH \\ | \\ C_6H_5 \end{array} \quad + \quad O=CHCH_3 \quad \xrightarrow[(AcOH)]{CH_3OH} \quad \begin{array}{c} C_6H_5 \\ | \\ CH_2-N \\ | \qquad \diagdown \\ CH_2-N \quad CHCH_3 \\ | \\ C_6H_5 \end{array}$$

Dianilino-　　　　　　　　　　　　　　2-Methyl-1,3-diphenyl-
ethane (m. p. 67°)　　　　　　　　　　imidazolidine (m. p. 102°)

solution of the reagent and the aldehyde in methanol is treated with a catalytic amount of acetic acid, the derivative separates in 1–2 min. Even the formalde-

hyde derivative is a solid (m.p. 126°). For recovery of the aldehyde, the derivative is shaken with 10% hydrochloric acid and the aldehyde extracted with ether.
Ketones do not react. Derivatives of still higher melting point are obtained
from *dl*-1,2-dianilino-1,2-diphenylethane (R. Jaunin, Lausanne, 1961).

A solution of acetaldehyde in ether absorbs dry ammonia gas and gives a crystalline, white precipitate, aldehyde ammonia, which presumably is the addition
product, for it yields acetaldehyde when neutralized with dilute mineral acid in the
cold, but it is unstable and is not obtainable in pure condition. The trichloro derivative, chloral, has greater additive power and forms with ammonia and with
hydroxylamine authentic addition products sufficiently stable to permit their
isolation and characterization; the product from hydroxylamine slowly changes
into the oxime on standing at room temperature:

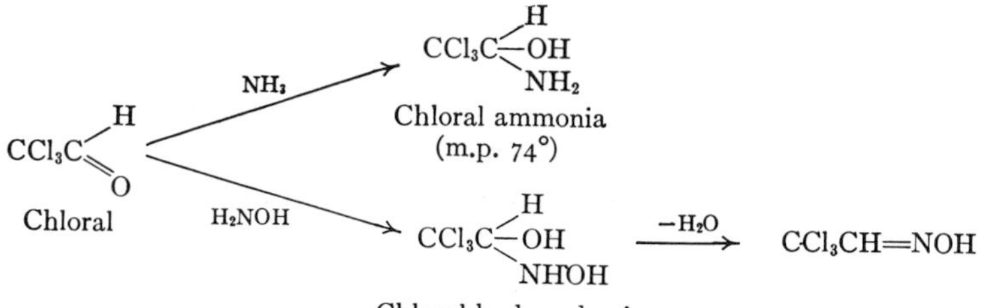

The amine reagents also react with esters; for example, ammonia reacts to form
amides and hydrazine gives acid hydrazides (11.21). The condensations with
esters, however, proceed much more slowly or require a considerably higher temperature. Thus in the preparation of acethydrazide from ethyl acetate and hydrazine hydrate, the mixture is refluxed for two days. The more reactive aldehydes and ketones combine with hydrazine or phenylhydrazine rapidly at room
temperature.

Formaldehyde, which is particularly reactive, condenses with ammonia to give a
crystalline solid of the formula $C_6H_{12}N_4$, or $(CH_2)_6N_4$, hexamethylenetetramine.
The substance, which can be prepared merely by allowing a mixture of formalin
and concentrated ammonia solution to evaporate, has a polycyclic structure made

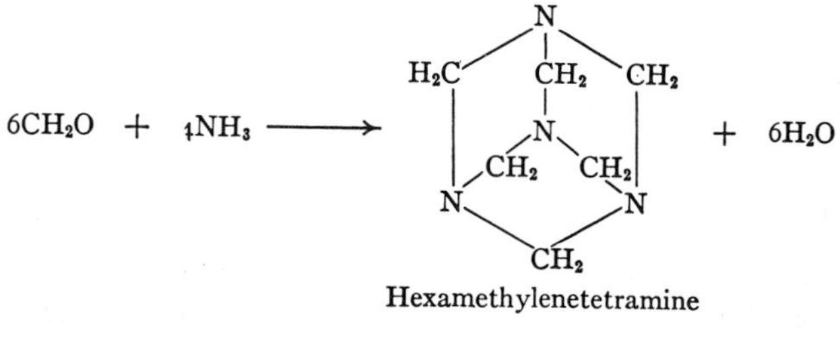

$$6CH_2O \;+\; 4NH_3 \longrightarrow \qquad\qquad +\; 6H_2O$$

Hexamethylenetetramine

up of methylene groups bridged by nitrogen atoms. The model shows that the
four six-membered rings present all have the chair conformation. The three

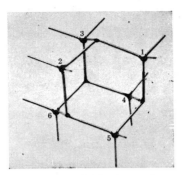

bridges extending from the central nitrogen atom are linked axially to the horizontal ring.   The product presumably arises as the result of a series of additions of ammonia or of ammonia-addition products to the carbonyl group of successive formaldehyde molecules.   Hexamethylenetetramine (urotropin, renders urine

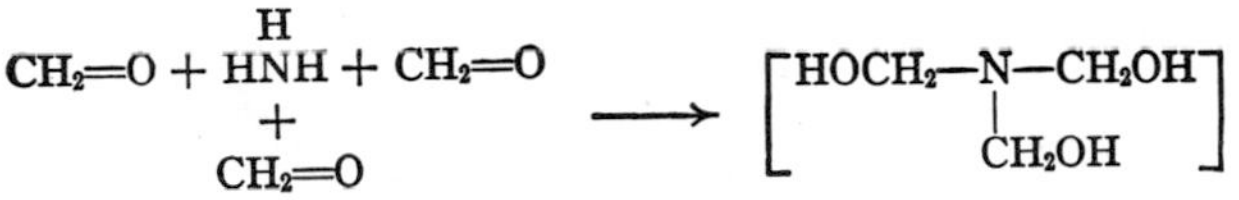

$$CH_2{=}O + \underset{\underset{CH_2{=}O}{+}}{\overset{H}{HNH}} + CH_2{=}O \longrightarrow \left[\underset{CH_2OH}{HOCH_2{-}N{-}CH_2OH} \right]$$

basic) is employed in medicine as a urinary antiseptic, and is effective because it slowly releases formaldehyde by reversal of the reactions leading to its formation. Another use is for preparation of a powerful high explosive known as cyclonite. This is made by treating hexamethylenetetramine with fuming nitric acid, when the inner bridge system is destroyed by oxidation and the peripheral nitrogen atoms are nitrated.   Since the ballistic strength is 150.2 relative to that of TNT taken

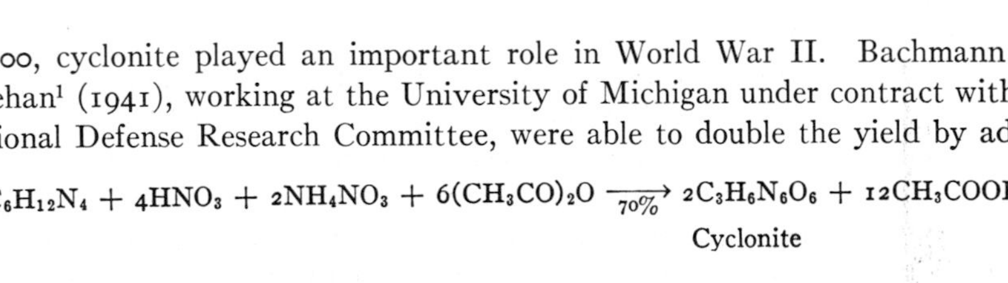

$$\xrightarrow{3HNO_3}\ + \ 3HCHO \ + \ NH_3$$

Cyclonite (m.p. 203°)

as 100, cyclonite played an important role in World War II.   Bachmann and Sheehan[1] (1941), working at the University of Michigan under contract with the National Defense Research Committee, were able to double the yield by adding

$$C_6H_{12}N_4 + 4HNO_3 + 2NH_4NO_3 + 6(CH_3CO)_2O \xrightarrow[70\%]{} 2C_3H_6N_6O_6 + 12CH_3COOH$$

Cyclonite

ammonium nitrate and acetic anhydride to the reaction mixture; one mole of hexamethylenetetramine then yields two moles of cyclonite rather than one.

[1] John C. Sheehan, b. 1915 Battle Creek, Mich.; Ph.D. Michigan (Bachmann); Mass. Inst. Techn.

12.38   **Wolff-Kishner Reduction.** — This method was discovered indepen-
.dently in Germany (Wolff,[1] 1912) and in Russia (Kishner,[2] 1911).   A
ketone (or aldehyde) is converted into the hydrazone, and this derivative is heated
in a sealed tube or an autoclave with sodium ethoxide in absolute ethanol.   After
preliminary technical improvements (M. D. Soffer; F. C. Whitmore, 1945), Huang-

$$\text{>C=O} \xrightarrow{\text{H}_2\text{NNH}_2} \text{>C=NNH}_2 \xrightarrow{\text{NaOC}_2\text{H}_5,\ 200°} \text{>CH}_2 + \text{N}_2$$

Minlon (1946) introduced a modified procedure by which the reduction is conducted on a large scale at atmospheric pressure with efficiency and economy.   The
ketone is refluxed in a high-boiling water-miscible solvent (usually di- or triethylene glycol) with aqueous hydrazine and sodium hydroxide to form the hydrazone;
water is then allowed to distil from the mixture till the temperature rises to a point
favorable for decomposition of the hydrazone (200°); and the mixture is refluxed
for three or four hours to complete the reduction.

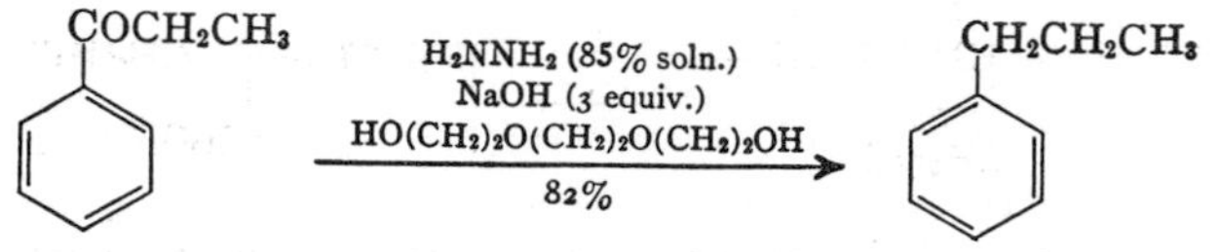

Propiophenone   n-Propylbenzene

12.39   **Stereoisomerism and Beckmann Rearrangement of Oximes.** —
Oximes of aliphatic and aromatic aldehydes are known in *cis* and
trans forms (also called *syn* and *anti*).   Thus the product of the reaction of benzaldehyde with hydroxylamine in the presence of excess sodium hydroxide is the low-
melting *cis* form, which is stable to alkali but rapidly rearranged by acids to the
higher-melting *trans* form.   The isomerization, which is comparable to the acid-

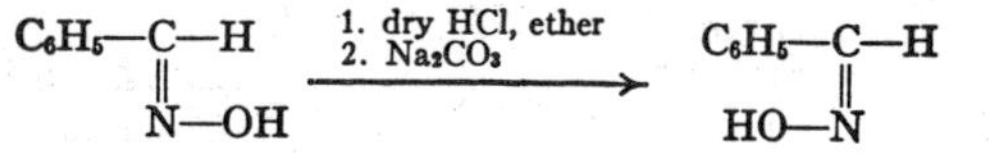

cis-Benzaldoxime   *trans*-Benzaldoxime
(m.p. 35°)   (m.p. 130°)

catalyzed conversion of maleic into fumaric acid, is accomplished by passing dry
hydrogen chloride into an ethereal solution of the *cis* form; a crystalline precipitate
separates consisting of the hydrochloride of the *trans* isomer, from which the free
oxime is obtained on neutralization with soda solution.   The reverse change occurs
on irradiation of the benzene solution (compare fumaric → maleic acid).   The
trans oxime undergoes dehydration to benzonitrile, for example under the influence
of hot acetic anhydride, more readily than the *cis* form; the ready elimination of
water between hydrogen and hydroxyl on opposite sides of the molecule corre-

[1] Ludwig Wolff, 1857–1919; b. Neustadt/Hardt; Ph.D. Strasbourg (Fittig); Univ. Jena; *Ber.*,
62A, 145 (1929)
[2] N. M. Kishner, 1867–1935; b. Moscow; Ph.D. Moscow (Markownikoff); Univ. Tomsk, Moscow

sponds to the normally occurring *trans* elimination observed in dehydration of alcohols.

Oximes of certain ketones also have been isolated in two geometrical forms, and in this series the configuration determines the course of a characteristic rearrangement discovered by Beckmann[1] (1886). The **Beckmann rearrangement,** for example of benzophenone oxime, is brought about by treatment of the oxime with phosphorus pentachloride in ether solution and results in conversion into benzanilide by exchange of place between the hydroxyl group and a phenyl group on the opposite side of the molecule, and ketonization of the enolic intermediate. Evi-

$$C_6H_5\text{—}\overset{\text{⌐-----⌐}}{\underset{\parallel}{C}}\text{—}C_6H_5 \quad \xrightarrow{\text{PCl}_5,\ \text{ether}} \quad C_6H_5\text{—}\underset{\parallel}{C}\text{—OH} \quad \longrightarrow \quad C_6H_5C{=}O$$

$$\text{HO—N} \qquad\qquad\qquad C_6H_5\text{—N} \qquad\qquad\qquad NHC_6H_5$$

Benzophenone oxime （m.p. 144）　　　　　　　　　　　　　　　　　　　　　　　　　　Benzanilide

dence for a *trans* exchange of groups is derived from experiments with unsymmetrical diaryl ketoximes that have been isolated in two geometrical forms of established configuration; for example the isomeric oximes of *p*-methoxybenzophenone:

$$C_6H_5\text{—}\underset{\parallel}{C}\text{—}C_6H_4OCH_3 \quad \xrightarrow{\text{PCl}_5,\ \text{ether},\ -10°} \quad O{=}CC_6H_4OCH_3$$

$$N\text{—OH} \qquad\qquad\qquad\qquad\qquad NHC_6H_5$$

（m.p. 147°）　　　　　　　　　　　　　Anisanilide (m.p. 171°)

Ultraviolet light $\Big\updownarrow$

$$C_6H_5\text{—}\underset{\parallel}{C}\text{—}C_6H_4OCH_3 \quad \xrightarrow{\text{PCl}_5,\ \text{ether}} \quad C_6H_5C{=}O$$

$$HO\text{—N} \qquad\qquad\qquad\qquad\qquad NHC_6H_4OCH_3$$

（m.p. 117°）　　　　　　　　　　　Benz-*p*-anisidide （m.p. 156°）

In each case the group that migrates from carbon to nitrogen is the one *trans* to the hydroxyl group.

The reaction has useful application to oximes of ketones of the type ArCOR readily obtainable by the Friedel-Crafts reaction; for example, acetyl chloride reacts with benzene in the presence of aluminum chloride to give acetophenone. Acetophenone affords only one oxime, which is converted on Beckmann rearrange-

$$C_6H_5\text{—}\underset{\parallel}{C}\text{—}CH_3 \quad \longrightarrow \quad \left[HO\text{—}\underset{\parallel}{C}\text{—}CH_3\right] \quad \longrightarrow \quad O{=}CCH_3$$

$$N\text{—OH} \qquad\qquad\qquad NC_6H_5 \qquad\qquad\qquad NHC_6H_5$$

Acetophenone oxime （m.p. 59°）　　　　　　　　　　　　　　　　　　　　　Acetanilide

ment with sulfuric acid at 100° into acetanilide. The oxime formed is that in which the phenyl group is *trans* to the hydroxyl group, and hence it is the phenyl

---

[1] Ernst Beckmann, 1853–1923; b. Solingen, Germany; Ph.D. Leipzig (Kolbe); Univ. Giessen, Erlangen, Leipzig, KWI Berlin; *Ber.*, **61A**, 87 (1928)

group which migrates.   The behavior is typical of aryl methyl ketoximes, and hence these substances always afford aryl derivatives of aromatic, rather than of aliphatic amines.

Other reagents which promote rearrangement are hydrogen chloride in acetic acid, benzenesulfonyl chloride in pyridine, aluminum chloride in benzene.   Newer Beckmann reagents (C. R. Hauser,[1] 1955) are boron fluoride and polyphosphoric acid; these catalysts sometimes lead to abnormal rearrangements (S. Wawzonek, 1959).   Tosylate esters of ketoximes have been found to undergo a related rearrangement, and this observation suggests that an ester or the equivalent is an intermediate in the ordinary Beckmann rearrangement and provides an efficient leaving group.   A mechanism suggested by Huisgen[2] postulates intermediate formation

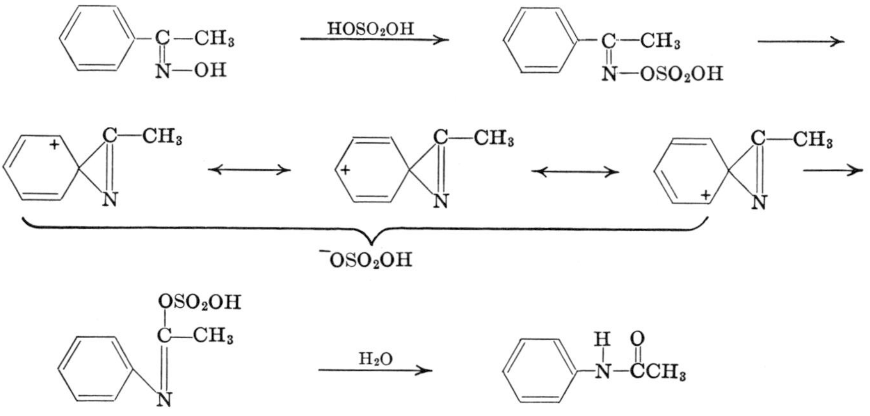

of an ethyleneimine; that from acetophenone oxime is formulated as a hybrid of three resonance structures.   An intermediate ethyleneimine of the type postulated was isolated by P. W. Neber (1932) and the structure was later confirmed by Cram (1953).   The substance II is formed on rearrangement of the tosylate of 2,4-dini-

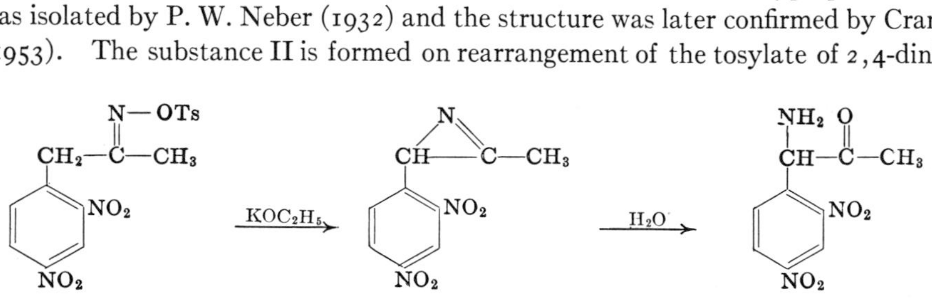

| I | II | III |

trophenylacetone oxime (I) with potassium ethoxide or pyridine.   The Huisgen mechanism is thus applicable to purely aliphatic oximes as well as to those of the aryl alkyl type.

One use for the Beckmann rearrangement is in elucidation of the structure of a ketone; rearrangement of the oxime and hydrolysis of the amide affords an acid

[1] Charles R. Hauser, b. 1900 San Jose, Calif.; Ph.D. Iowa (Coleman); Duke Univ.
[2] Rolf Huisgen, b. 1920 Gerolstein, Germany; Ph.D. Univ. Munich; Univ. Munich

and an amine component from which the original structure may be deducible. Preparative use in the aliphatic series is illustrated by the synthesis of ε-aminocaproic acid from cyclohexanone oxime. Rearrangement of the oxime is carried

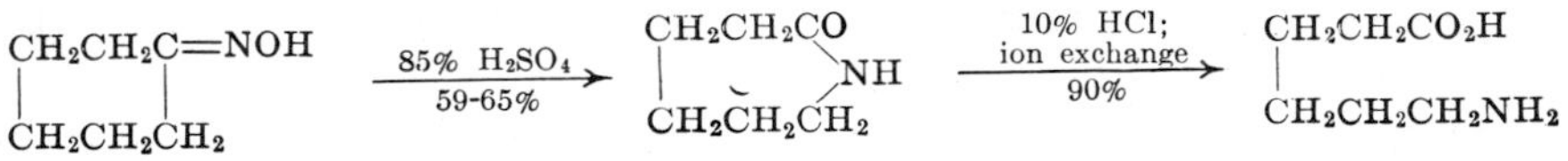

$$CH_2CH_2C{=}NOH \quad \xrightarrow[59-65\%]{85\%\ H_2SO_4} \quad CH_2CH_2CO{>}NH \quad \xrightarrow[90\%]{\substack{10\%\ HCl;\\ ion\ exchange}} \quad CH_2CH_2CO_2H$$

| Cyclohexanone oxime | Lactam | ε-Aminocaproic acid (m.p. 203°) |

out in an open beaker in 10-g. portions because of the violence of the reaction induced by brief heating. Hydrolysis is effected by boiling the lactam with hydrochloric acid until a clear solution results (1 hr.). Evaporation to dryness gives the hydrochloride of the amino acid, and this is converted into the amino acid by passing a solution of the salt through a column containing Amberlite IR-413 resin (see 14.25). Another preparative use for ε-caprolactam (1) is for conversion via the Schiff base (5) into 1,11-diaminoundecanone-6 dihydrochloride (6, G. Nawrath, 1960).

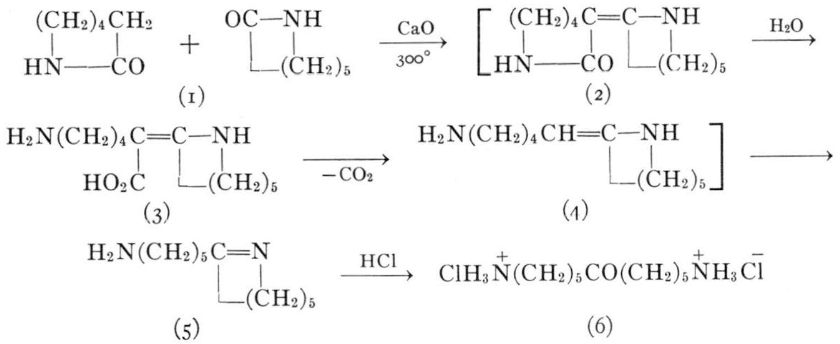

(reaction scheme with structures 1, 2, 3, 4, 5, 6)

$$(6) \quad ClH_3\overset{+}{N}(CH_2)_5CO(CH_2)_5\overset{+}{N}H_3\overset{-}{C}l$$

12.40   Acetals and Ketals.

— Under the catalytic influence of dry hydrogen chloride a typical aldehyde adds a molecule of ethyl alcohol to form a moderately stable hemiacetal, which combines with a second molecule of the alcohol and yields a stable acetal. Acetals are *gem*-diethers but, unlike the correspond-

$$CH_3CH{=}O + HOC_2H_5 \xrightarrow{HCl} CH_3CH{<}^{OH}_{OC_2H_5} \xrightarrow{HOC_2H_5(H^+)} CH_3CH{<}^{OC_2H_5}_{OC_2H_5}$$

| | Hemiacetal | Acetal (b.p. 104°) |

$$CH_2{=}O + 2HOCH_3 \xrightarrow{H^+} CH_2(OCH_3)_2$$
Methylal (b.p. 42°)

$$CH_2{=}O + 2HOC_2H_5 \xrightarrow{H^+} CH_2(OC_2H_5)_2$$
Ethylal (b.p. 88°)

ing unstable *gem*-diols, can be obtained as pure, distillable liquids. Acetal formation is reversible, and acetals are hydrolyzed easily with water and a mineral acid catalyst. Acetals are considerably more stable to alkalis than to acids, and they are so much more stable than free aldehydes to basic reagents and oxidizing agents that aldehydic compounds are often converted into the acetals to protect the aldehydic function during synthetic operations involving other groups of the molecule.   Acetals usually are prepared by passing about one percent of hydrogen chloride gas into a solution of the aldehyde in methanol or ethanol.   The order of reactivity for the alcoholic component is: primary $>$ secondary $>$ tertiary, in the ratio of about $80:45:20$.

Ketones are less reactive and are not convertible into ketals satisfactorily by acid-catalyzed reaction with methanol or ethanol.   L. Claisen (Aachen, 1896) found a satisfactory method in reaction of the ketone with ethyl orthoformate, which is converted into ethyl formate.   Later (Kiel, 1898) Claisen simplified the

$$(CH_3)_2C{=}O + HC(OC_2H_5)_3 \rightarrow \quad (CH_3)_2C(OC_2H_5)_2 \; + \; HCO_2C_2H_5$$

b.p. 146°   Acetone diethyl acetal   b.p. 54°

(b.p. 114°)

process by generation of ethyl orthoformate *in situ*.   A. Pinnen (1892) had found that hydrogen cyanide, ethanol, and hydrogen chloride combine smoothly to yield formimidoethyl ether hydrochloride (1), which reacts with ethanol to yield ethyl orthoformate and ammonium chloride (2).   For ketalization of acetophenone (3),

1. $HC{\equiv}N \; + \; C_2H_5OH \; + \; HCl \longrightarrow HC\begin{smallmatrix}\nearrow N^+H_2Cl^- \\ \searrow OC_2H_5\end{smallmatrix}$

Formimidoethyl ether hydrochloride

2. $HC\begin{smallmatrix}\nearrow N^+H_2Cl^- \\ \searrow OC_2H_5\end{smallmatrix} \; + \; C_2H_5OH \longrightarrow CH(OC_2H_5)_3 \; + \; NH_4Cl$

3. $C_6H_5COCH_3 + HC\begin{smallmatrix}\nearrow N^+H_2Cl^- \\ \searrow OC_2H_5\end{smallmatrix} \; + \; 2\,C_2H_5OH \xrightarrow{92\%} C\begin{smallmatrix}\nearrow C_6H_5 \;\; \searrow OC_2H_5 \\ \searrow CH_3 \;\; \nearrow OC_2H_5\end{smallmatrix}$

$+ \; NH_4Cl \; + \; HCO_2C_2H_5$

for example, a solution of the ketone in excess ethanol (about 5 moles) is cooled during gradual addition of formimidoethyl ether hydrochloride and the mixture let stand at 0° for 4–6 days.

12.41   Ethyleneketals and Ethylenethioketals. — Since ethylene glycol has a high boiling point (197.5°), the equilibrium in its reaction with a ketone in the presence of an acid catalyst can be displaced by refluxing the mixture under a take-off condenser for removal of the water formed.   The product is known both

$$\begin{smallmatrix}R\searrow \\ R'\nearrow\end{smallmatrix}C{=}O \; + \; \begin{smallmatrix}HOCH_2 \\ | \\ HOCH_2\end{smallmatrix} \xrightarrow{H^+} \begin{smallmatrix}R\searrow \\ R'\nearrow\end{smallmatrix}C\begin{smallmatrix}\nearrow O-CH_2 \\ | \\ \searrow O-CH_2\end{smallmatrix} \; + \; H_2O$$

Ethyleneketal

as an ethyleneketal and as a dioxolane.   *p*-Toluenesulfonic acid is the favored catalyst for both the direct reaction and exchange dioxolonation with butanone dioxolane (H. J. Dauben, 1954). Ketalization is useful for protection of a keto group during operation on other functions present under nonacidic conditions, for the keto group is easily regenerated by hydrolysis with dilute mineral acid.

Ketones react with mercaptans much more readily than with alcohols to form thioketals, $(RS)_2CR_2$. Ethanedithiol, analogous to ethylene glycol, is a favored reagent and gives cyclic ethylenethioketals which, like thioketals, can be desulfurized by reaction with Raney nickel (with adsorbed hydrogen), with the result that

$$\underset{R'}{\overset{R}{\diagdown}}C{=}O \xrightarrow[\text{BF}_3\cdot\text{HOAc}]{\text{HSCH}_2\text{CH}_2\text{SH}} \underset{R'}{\overset{R}{\diagdown}}C\underset{S-CH_2}{\overset{S-CH_2}{\diagup}}\ \xrightarrow{\text{Ni, H}_2}\ \underset{R'}{\overset{R}{\diagdown}}CH_2$$

Ethylenethioketal

the original carbonyl oxygen is replaced by two atoms of hydrogen (Bougault, 1938; Mozingo, 1943; Wolfrom,[1] 1944). The condensation with ethanedithiol proceeds rapidly and in high yield at room temperature in the presence of boron fluoride etherate, alone or in acetic acid solution. Thioketals are hydrolyzed with too great difficulty to be useful as protective derivatives. Ethylenesemithioketals, made in the same way with β-mercaptoethanol, $HSCH_2CH_2OH$, are reconverted to the ketones by Raney nickel.

12.42   Stable Hydrates. — Ordinary aldehydes do not form stable addition products with water, although small amounts of the unstable *gem*-diols may exist in equilibrium with the aldehyde, just as carbonic acid is present in aqueous solutions of carbon dioxide. The tendency of formaldehyde to form chain polymers in aqueous solution indicates that the equilibrium is more favorable to formation of a hydrate than in the case of acetaldehyde and the higher homologs. A few aldehydes of specialized types surpass formaldehyde in additive power and form stable hydrates. One is chloral, a liquid substance which combines exothermally with water to form a stable crystalline hydrate. The reactivity of the

$$CCl_3C\underset{\diagdown O}{\overset{\diagup H}{}} + HOH \longrightarrow CCl_3C\underset{\diagdown OH}{\overset{\diagup H}{\diagup}OH}$$

Chloral   Chloral hydrate
(m.p. 51.7°)

carbonyl group of chloral is further shown by formation of products of addition with ammonia and with hydroxylamine, cited above. The modifying influence of the α-chloro atoms on the additive power of the carbonyl group finds a parallel in the effect of similar substitution on the acidic strength of acetic acid. In the present instance the effect is ascribable to the electron-attracting character of the three chlorine atoms; withdrawal of electrons from the carbon atom of the carbonyl group renders this center relatively positive and hence vulnerable to attack by hydroxide ion. Other examples of the formation of stable, isolable hydrates are as follows:

[1] Melville L. Wolfrom, b. 1900 Bellevue, Ohio; Ph.D. Northwestern (W. L. Lewis); Ohio State Univ.

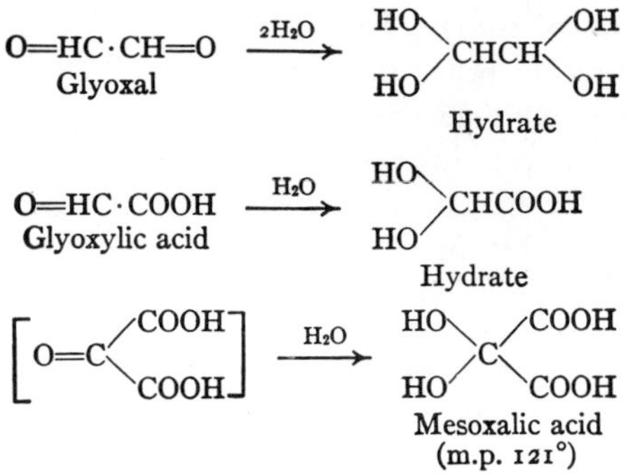

$$O{=}HC{\cdot}CH{=}O \xrightarrow{2H_2O} \begin{array}{c} HO \\ HO \end{array}{>}CHCH{<}\begin{array}{c} OH \\ OH \end{array}$$

Glyoxal   Hydrate

$$O{=}HC{\cdot}COOH \xrightarrow{H_2O} \begin{array}{c} HO \\ HO \end{array}{>}CHCOOH$$

Glyoxylic acid   Hydrate

$$\left[O{=}C{<}\begin{array}{c} COOH \\ COOH \end{array} \right] \xrightarrow{H_2O} \begin{array}{c} HO \\ HO \end{array}{>}C{<}\begin{array}{c} COOH \\ COOH \end{array}$$

Mesoxalic acid
(m.p. 121°)

Diacetyl derivatives of *gem*-diols are stable substances most conveniently obtainable by reaction of a carbonyl compound with acetic anhydride in the presence

$$C_6H_5CH{=}CHCHO \xrightarrow[71\%]{Ac_2O\ (CuSO_4\cdot5H_2O)} C_6H_5CH{=}CHCH(OCOCH_3)_2$$

Cinnamaldehyde, m.p. −7.5°   Cinnamal diacetate, m.p. 86°

of a catalyst: H_2SO_4, PCl_3, $SnCl_2\cdot2H_2O$, $CuSO_4\cdot5H_2O$ (Knoevenagel, 1913).

gem-Dithiols, $R_2C(SH)_2$, considerably more stable than *gem*-diols, are formed, along with polysulfide, when an aldehyde or ketone is heated with hydrogen sulfide at pressures of 35–8500 atmospheres (T. L. Cairns, 1952). A 5-g. sample of 1,1-propanedithiol, $CH_3CH_2CH(SH)_2$, can be distilled at atmospheric pressure (b.p. 142°) without appreciable decomposition. *gem*-Dithiols initially form salts with alkali but are decomposed by the reagent. They are stable to acids, and indeed the condensation with hydrogen sulfide is markedly catalyzed by hydrogen chloride. Thus when hydrogen sulfide and hydrogen chloride are passed into a chilled alcoholic solution of dibenzyl ketone, the dithiol separates as a crystalline solid (Campaigne,[1] Carmack,[2] 1959).

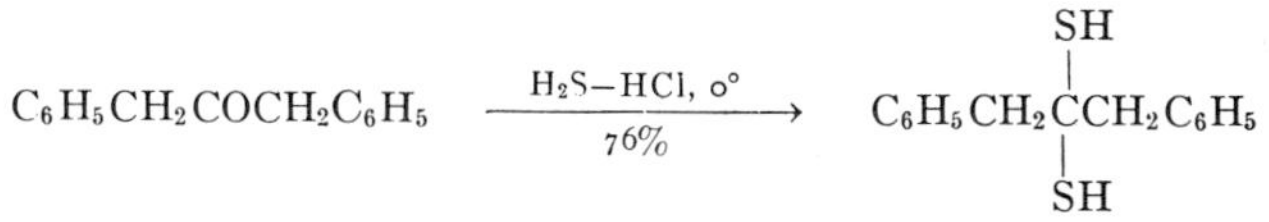

$$C_6H_5CH_2COCH_2C_6H_5 \xrightarrow[76\%]{H_2S{-}HCl,\ 0°} \begin{array}{c} SH \\ | \\ C_6H_5CH_2CCH_2C_6H_5 \\ | \\ SH \end{array}$$

2,2-Dimercapto-1,3-
diphenylpropane, m.p. 83°

ALKYLATION

12.43   Alkylation of Simple Ketones. — Nef (1900) found that simple ketones can be alkylated by reaction with methyl iodide and powdered potassium hydroxide in a sealed tube at 100°. All available α-hydrogen atoms are replaceable: acetone alkylated with one mole of methyl iodide gave a mixture of mono-, di-, tri-, tetra-, and pentamethyl derivatives. Thus the reaction is useful only for preparation of peralkyl derivatives, for example, *t*-butyl phenyl ketone.

[1] Ernest E. Campaigne, b. 1914 Chicago; Ph.D. Northwestern (Fosdick); Indiana Univ.
[2] Marvin Carmack, b. 1913 Dana, Ind.; Ph.D. Michigan (W. E. Bachmann); Univ. Pennsylvania; Indiana Univ.

By alkylating acetophenone three times, Nef obtained the trimethyl derivative in moderate yield. A strong base is required to abstract a proton and produce a carbanion, which then reacts with the alkylating reagent (S_N2). Claisen (1905)

$$C_6H_5COCH_3 \xrightarrow[57\%]{KOH,\ CH_3I\ (excess),\ 100°} C_6H_5COC(CH_3)_3$$

and A. Haller and Ed. Bauer (France, 1900) found that use of sodamide as base permits alkylation in refluxing benzene. The sodium enolate is formed and on addition of methyl iodide, sodium iodide soon separates. Use of this procedure for the preparation of 2,2,6,6-tetramethylcyclohexanone has been described (6.23). Limited use has been made of exhaustive methylation as a route to tertiary acids. Thus Nef found that t-butyl phenyl ketone is cleaved slowly by potassium hydroxide at 160° to benzene and trimethylacetic acid. Haller and Bauer found

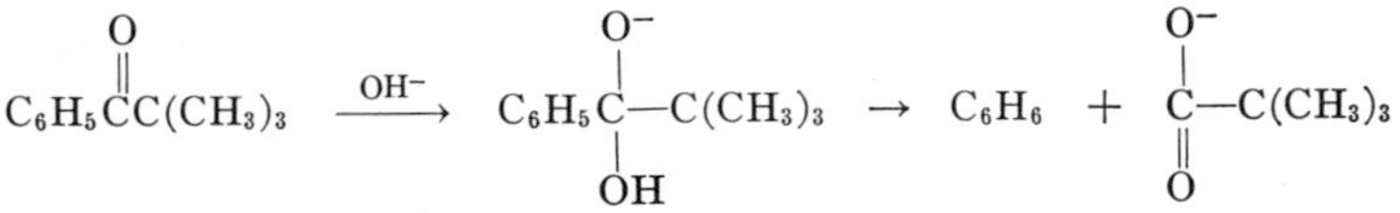

$$C_6H_5\overset{O}{\overset{\|}{C}}C(CH_3)_3 \xrightarrow{OH^-} C_6H_5\overset{O^-}{\underset{OH}{\overset{\|}{C}}}{-}C(CH_3)_3 \rightarrow C_6H_6 + \overset{O^-}{\underset{O}{\overset{\|}{C}}}{-}C(CH_3)_3$$

that this reaction, like alkylation, proceeds better with sodamide as the base; the product is then the acid amide: $RR_2'CCOR'' \rightarrow RR_2'CCONH_2 + R''H$. The reaction is limited to ketones with no α-hydrogens (nonenolizable), for example, $C_6H_5COC_6H_5 \rightarrow C_6H_5CONH_2 + C_6H_6$. In a mixed ketone, the group of greater electron attraction is split off as a hydrocarbon (e.g. phenyl rather than t-butyl). Unless the difference is considerable, a mixture results.

Alkylation has been useful as applied to cyclic ketones, particularly for the introduction of angular methyl groups in the synthesis of steroids or model compounds. R. Robinson (1917) found potassium t-butoxide an effective strong base for production of the required enolate anion, and this is the usual procedure. The

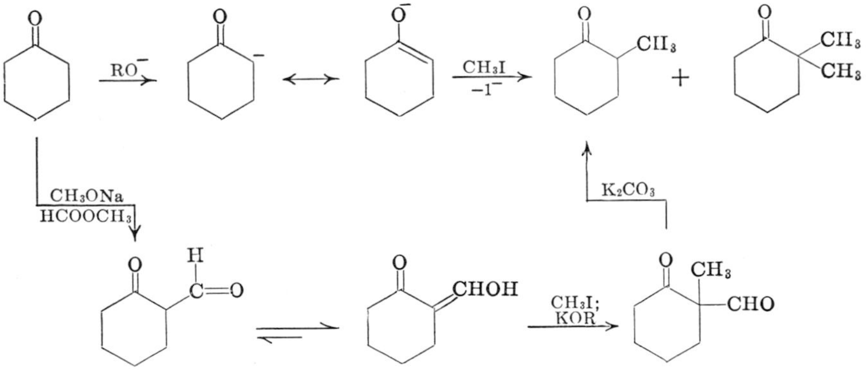

alkylation of cyclohexanone is complicated by the production of both the 2-methyl and the 2,2-dimethyl derivative (and unchanged starting material); in this case the tertiary α-hydrogen is more vulnerable than a secondary α-hydrogen. A method for producing only the monomethyl derivative (H. K. Sen and K. Mondal, 1928) involves acylation with methyl formate and sodium methoxide and methylation of the 2-formyl (or 2-hydroxymethylene) derivative. The product is a 1-one-3-al, and, like 1,3-diketones, it is easily cleaved by potassium carbonate with removal of the formyl group. The preparation of methylcyclohexanone is cited merely to illustrate the method; the ketone is available by oxidation of commercially available 2-methylcyclohexanol (hydrogenation of o-cresol). 2,6-Dimethylcyclohexanone has been prepared by formylation of 2-methylcyclohexanone in the 6-position, methylation at the 6-position, and removal of the formyl group; starting material is removed as the bisulfite compound.

From the behavior of 2-methylcyclohexanone, methylation of α-decalone would be expected to favor attack of the tertiary 9-hydrogen atom at the bridgehead, but direct alkylation yields the 2-methyl derivative as the chief product. Various indirect methods for alkylation at C_9 depend on blocking the 2-methylene group. In one (W. S. Johnson, 1947) the ketone I is condensed with ethyl formate and the hydroxymethylene derivative II is converted into the O-isopropyl derivative III

α-Decalone (I)   II   III

IV   V   VI

$trans/cis = 3/1$

by alkylation with isopropyl iodide. The hydroxymethylene derivative II, like the enol of a 1,3-diketone, forms a hybrid enolate in which the negative charge is distributed between oxygen and carbon, and in such a system the occurrence of C- or O-alkylation depends upon the structure, the alkylating agent, and the conditions; alkylation in acetone in the presence of sodium carbonate favors O-alkylation (method of Claisen). In the case at hand, II gives the C-alkyl derivative with methyl iodide but the O-alkyl derivative with isopropyl iodide. The ether III can give only the desired product of angular methylation, IV. The blocking group is then removed by acid hydrolysis of the enol ether and alkaline cleavage of V. This synthesis afforded chiefly the *trans* form of 9-methyl-1-decalone (VI), investigated as a model compound. Applied in the steroid series, however, the method gave only the undesired *cis* form.

12.44   Acetoacetic Ester Synthesis. — The acetoacetic ester synthesis of ketones is based upon the fact that this readily available (13.9) β-keto ester affords C-alkyl derivatives in good yield and that the β-keto acids produced

$$CH_3COCH_2CO_2C_2H_5 \xrightarrow[RX]{NaOC_2H_5} CH_3COCHRCO_2C_2H_5 \xrightarrow{OH^-}$$

$$CH_3COCHRCO_2H \xrightarrow{-CO_2} CH_3COCH_2R$$

on saponification are easily decarboxylated (100°). The latter reaction calls for some comment. Since the rate of decomposition of a β-keto acid is independent of the solvent, the reaction can hardly follow the anionic mechanism applicable to ordinary carboxylic acids (4.9). Moreover, the immediate product is the enolic form of the ketone. A concerted mechanism involving a cyclic transition state (Westheimer, 1941) provides a reasonable interpretation of the facts. The double

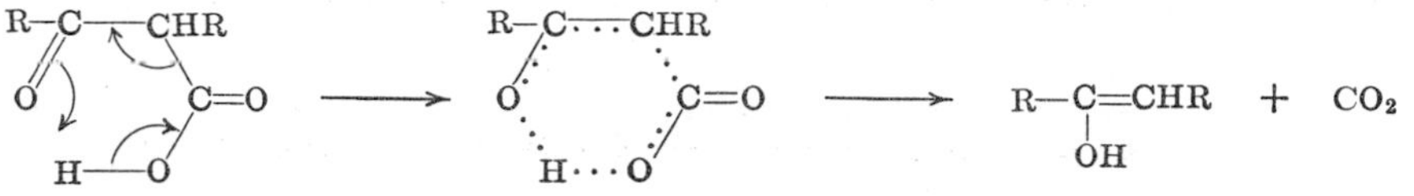

bond of a β,γ-unsaturated acid promotes decarboxylation, although the effect is less than that of a β-keto group, and the reaction is attended with a shift of the double bond. Arnold (1950) has pointed out that a similar cyclic transition state accounts for the facts of the case. Arnold noted also that decarboxylation of an

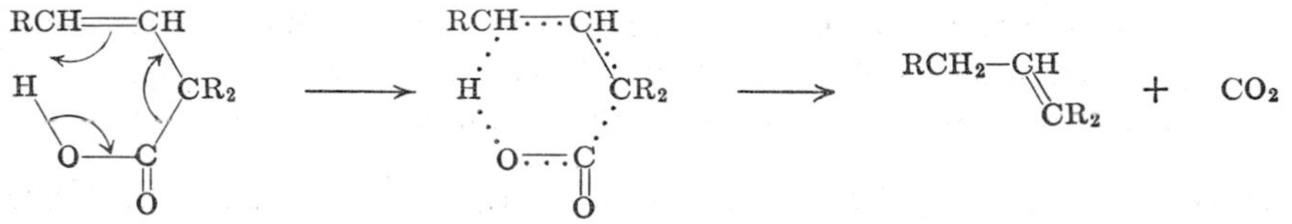

α,β-unsaturated acid probably proceeds by isomerization to the β,γ-unsaturated isomer and restoration of the double bond to the original position by the mechanism cited. Indeed the acid $(CH_3)_3CCH=CHCO_2H$, which is incapable of such isomerization, is stable at high temperatures.

When ethyl acetoacetate is introduced into a solution of one equivalent of sodium in absolute ethanol it is converted into the sodio derivative. Reaction with an

$$CH_3COCH_2CO_2C_2H_5 \xrightarrow[C_2H_5OH]{NaOC_2H_5} Na^+[CH_3COC^-HCO_2C_2H_5] \xrightarrow{RI}$$

$$CH_3COCHRCO_2C_2H_5 \xrightarrow{Saponif\,;\,-CO_2} CH_3COCH_2R$$

$$\downarrow NaOC_2H_5;\ RI$$

$$CH_3COCR_2CO_2C_2H_5 \xrightarrow{Saponif.;\,-CO_2} CH_3COCHR_2$$

alkyl halide affords the monoalkyl derivative, which on saponification and decarboxylation yields a monosubstituted acetone. The monoalkyl ester also can be alkylated further for production of a disubstituted acetone. Hydrolysis for ultimate production of a ketone is done with dilute alkali and is called **ketonic hy-**

$$\text{Na}^+ [\text{CH}_3\text{COCHCOOC}_2\text{H}_5]^- + \text{CH}_3(\text{CH}_2)_2\text{CH}_2\text{Br} \xrightarrow[69-72\%]{} \begin{array}{c} \text{CH}_3\text{COCHCOOC}_2\text{H}_5 \\ | \\ \text{CH}_2(\text{CH}_2)_2\text{CH}_3 \end{array} \xrightarrow{5\% \text{ NaOH}}$$

Sodioacetoacetic ester

Ethyl *n*-butylacetoacetate
(b.p. 114°/16 mm.)

$$\left[\begin{array}{c} \text{CH}_3\text{COCHCOOH} \\ | \\ \text{CH}_2(\text{CH}_2)_2\text{CH}_3 \end{array} \right] \xrightarrow[52-61\%, \text{ overall from acetoacetic ester}]{\text{dil. H}_2\text{SO}_4} \text{CH}_3\text{CO(CH}_2)_4\text{CH}_3 + \text{CO}_2$$

Methyl *n*-amyl ketone
(b.p. 150°)

drolysis. An example is the synthesis of methyl *n*-amyl ketone. Concentrated alkali cleaves β-keto esters at the position adjacent to the carbonyl group, and since the two products are acids the process is called **acid hydrolysis**. By alkyla-

$$\underset{\text{R}}{\underset{|}{\overset{\text{O}}{\overset{\|}{\text{CH}_3\text{C}}}}\text{CHCOOC}_2\text{H}_5} \xrightarrow{\text{OH}^-(-\text{C}_2\text{H}_5\text{OH})} \overset{\text{OH}}{\overset{|}{\text{CH}_3\text{C}}}=\text{O} + \text{RCH}_2\text{COOH}$$

tion of acetoacetic ester and cleavage in this second way, acids of the types $\text{RCH}_2\text{CO}_2\text{H}$ and $\text{RR}'\text{CHCO}_2\text{H}$ can be synthesized. However the malonic ester synthesis described below accomplishes the same end and is more widely used.

A novel modification of the acetoacetic ester synthesis provides a route to acyloins, or α-hydroxyketones (S.-O. Lawesson, 1960). *t*-Butyl acetoacetate, easily prepared in high yield from *t*-butyl alcohol and diketene, is alkylated and the benzoyloxy group is introduced into the α-position by reaction of the sodio

$$\begin{array}{c} \text{CH}_2\!=\!\text{C}\!-\!\text{O} \\ | \quad\quad | \\ \text{CH}_2\!-\!\text{C}\!=\!\text{O} \end{array} \xrightarrow[85-95\%]{\text{HOC(CH}_3)_3,\ \text{C}_2\text{H}_5\text{ONa}} \begin{array}{c} \text{CH}_2\!=\!\text{C}\!-\!\text{OH} \\ | \\ \text{CH}_2\text{COOC(CH}_3)_3 \end{array} \xrightarrow[67\%]{n\text{-C}_5\text{H}_{11}\text{Br},\ \text{C}_2\text{H}_5\text{ONa}}$$

Diketene

$$\underset{\text{CH}_3\overset{\text{O}}{\overset{\|}{\text{C}}}-\overset{\text{C}_5\text{H}_{11}\text{-}n}{\overset{|}{\text{CH}}}\text{CO}_2\text{C(CH}_3)_3}{} \xrightarrow{\text{NaH, C}_6\text{H}_6} \text{Sodio derivative} \xrightarrow[83\%]{(\text{C}_6\text{H}_5\text{COO})_2\ (0°)]}$$

$$\begin{array}{c} \text{O} \quad \text{C}_5\text{H}_{11}\text{-}n \\ \| \quad\quad | \\ \text{CH}_3\text{C}\!-\!\text{CCO}_2\text{C(CH}_3)_3 \\ | \\ \text{OCOC}_6\text{H}_5 \end{array} \xrightarrow[51\%]{\text{TsOH; OH}^-} \begin{array}{c} \text{O} \\ \| \\ \text{CH}_3\text{CCHC}_5\text{H}_{11}\text{-}n \\ | \\ \text{OH} \end{array} + (\text{CH}_3)_2\text{C}\!=\!\text{CH}_2 + \text{CO}_2$$

Octane-2-one-3-ol

derivative with dibenzoyl peroxide in benzene. Elimination of the *t*-butyl group and decarboxylation is accomplished by heating the ester at 160° with a catalytic amount of *p*-toluenesulfonic acid; saponification under mild conditions then gives the (base-sensitive) acyloin.

12.45   Malonic Ester Synthesis. — Diethyl malonate, commonly called malonic ester, is made by the action of ethanol and a mineral acid on sodium cyanoacetate. The carboxyl group is liberated and esterified, and addition of ethanol to the nitrile group gives the imino ester, which is hydrolyzed on addition of water.

$$\underset{\overset{|}{\text{CN}}}{\text{CH}_2\text{CO}_2\text{Na}} \xrightarrow{\text{C}_2\text{H}_5\text{OH, H}^+} \underset{\overset{|}{\text{C}\equiv\text{N}}}{\text{CH}_2\text{CO}_2\text{C}_2\text{H}_5} \xrightarrow{\text{C}_2\text{H}_5\text{OH. H}^+}$$

$$\underset{\underset{\text{Imino ester}}{\text{HN}=\text{C}-\text{OC}_2\text{H}_5}}{\text{CH}_2\text{CO}_2\text{C}_2\text{H}_5} \xrightarrow{\text{H}_2\text{O}} \underset{\underset{\text{Diethyl malonate}}{\text{CO}_2\text{C}_2\text{H}_5}}{\text{CH}_2\text{CO}_2\text{C}_2\text{H}_5}$$

Unlike β-keto esters and β-diketones, malonic ester does not form an enolate that is isolable or present in any but trace amounts at equilibrium. It does, however, react with sodium like these substances to form an enolate ion, stabilized by resonance. The enolate, represented for convenience as $\overset{+}{\text{Na}}\overset{-}{\text{C}}\text{H}(\text{CO}_2\text{C}_2\text{H}_5)_2$, can

be alkylated to $\text{RCH}(\text{CO}_2\text{C}_2\text{H}_5)_2$, and when this is hydrolyzed the substituted malonic acid readily loses carbon dioxide and affords a substituted monocarboxylic

$$\text{RCH}\underset{\text{COOC}_2\text{H}_5}{\overset{\text{COOC}_2\text{H}_5}{<}} \xrightarrow{\text{Hydrol.}} \text{RCH}\underset{\text{COOH}}{\overset{\text{COOH}}{<}} \xrightarrow{\text{Heat}} \text{RCH}_2\text{COOH} \;+\; \text{CO}_2$$

acid. An example is the synthesis of caproic acid starting with n-butyl bromide. Metallic sodium is dissolved in ethanol to give a solution of sodium ethoxide, and malonic ester is slowly introduced followed by an equivalent amount of n-butyl

$$\text{CH}_3(\text{CH}_2)_2\text{CH}_2\text{Br} \;+\; \text{CH}_2(\text{COOC}_2\text{H}_5)_2 \;+\; \text{NaOC}_2\text{H}_5 \xrightarrow[80\text{-}90\%]{}$$

$$\underset{\underset{\text{Diethyl }n\text{-butylmalonate (b.p. 235–240°)}}{}}{\text{CH}_3(\text{CH}_2)_2\text{CH}_2\text{CH}\underset{\text{COOC}_2\text{H}_5}{\overset{\text{COOC}_2\text{H}_5}{<}}} \xrightarrow{50\% \text{ KOH, reflux}}$$

$$\underset{\substack{n\text{-Butylmalonic acid}\\ \text{(m.p. 101.5°)}}}{\text{CH}_3(\text{CH}_2)_2\text{CH}_2\text{CH}\underset{\text{COOH}}{\overset{\text{COOH}}{<}}} \text{(as salt)} \xrightarrow[75\%,\text{ from butylmalonate}]{\text{dil. H}_2\text{SO}_4,\text{ reflux}} \underset{\text{Caproic acid}}{\text{CH}_3\text{CH}_2\text{CH}_2\text{CH}_2\text{CH}_2\text{COOH}}$$

bromide. The substituted malonic ester is separated by removing the bulk of the alcohol and adding water, and it is hydrolyzed with boiling potassium hydroxide solution. The resulting n-butylmalonic acid can be isolated as a solid and the decarboxylation conducted by heating the molten material at 150°. A simpler method is to render the aqueous solution strongly acidic with sulfuric acid and reflux the mixture; the mineral acid catalyzes loss of carbon dioxide at a temperature not much above 100°.

A monosubstituted malonic ester still has a hydrogen atom replaceable by sodium and therefore available for a second alkylation. An example is the synthesis of diethylacetic acid. Malonic ester is either converted into the mono- and then the diethyl derivative or treated with two equivalents each of sodium ethoxide and ethyl iodide and so diethylated directly. The disubstituted malonic ester is hindered and hence more resistant to alkaline hydrolysis than a monosubstituted ester.

$$CH_2(CO_2C_2H_5)_2 \longrightarrow C_2H_5CH(CO_2C_2H_5)_2 \longrightarrow (C_2H_5)_2C(CO_2C_2H_5)_2 \longrightarrow$$

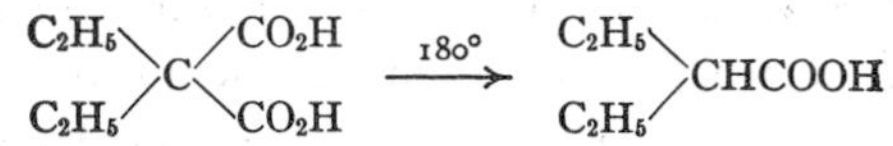

$$\underset{\substack{\text{Diethylmalonic acid}\\ \text{(m.p. 121°)}}}{\overset{C_2H_5}{\underset{C_2H_5}{>}}C\overset{CO_2H}{\underset{CO_2H}{<}}} \quad \overset{180°}{\longrightarrow} \quad \underset{\substack{\text{Diethylacetic acid}\\ \text{(b.p. 190°)}}}{\overset{C_2H_5}{\underset{C_2H_5}{>}}CHCOOH}$$

12.46   β-Diketones. — Data tabulated in section 12.17 show that cyclopentanone and cyclohexanone are more enolic than open-chain analogs and that acetylacetone is 80% enolic. Hence related cyclic 1,3-diones would be expected to be very largely enolic, and spectrographic evidence shows that in the case of cyclohexane-1,3-dione (dihydroresorcinol) and dimedone (5,5-dimethyl-cyclohexane-1,3-dione) the ketonic form is practically nonexistent (E. G. Meek, 1953). Thus the ultraviolet absorption bands of the two compounds in ethanol

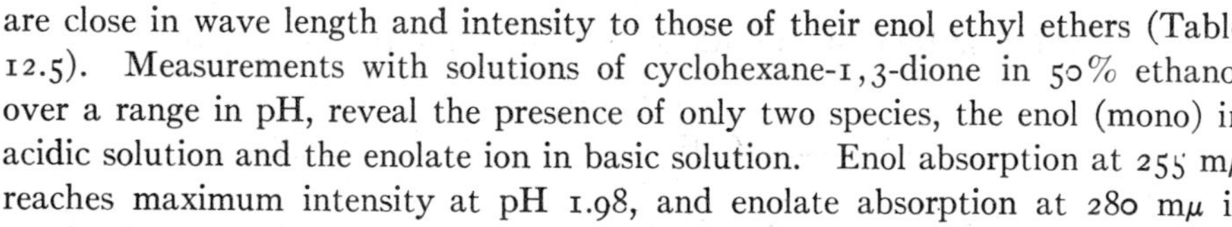

Cyclohexane-1,3-dione   Enol ethyl ether   Dimedone

are close in wave length and intensity to those of their enol ethyl ethers (Table 12.5). Measurements with solutions of cyclohexane-1,3-dione in 50% ethanol over a range in pH, reveal the presence of only two species, the enol (mono) in acidic solution and the enolate ion in basic solution. Enol absorption at 255 mμ reaches maximum intensity at pH 1.98, and enolate absorption at 280 mμ is maximal at pH 7.99.

Cyclohexane-1,3-dione is obtained easily by hydrogenation of resorcinol with

TABLE 12.5.   CYCLIC β-DIKETONES

	$\lambda^{\text{EtOH}}(m\mu)$	ϵ	pK_a	$\lambda^{\text{Chf}}(\mu)$
Cyclohexane-1,3-dione	253	22,300	5.89	
Enol ethyl ether	249	18,700		
Dimedone	255	17,800	6.05	6.03, 6.15
Enol ethyl ether	250	19,200		

Raney nickel in aqueous alkali; the preparation of dimedone is described later (13.10). The enol ethyl ethers are prepared in about 75% yield either by heating the dione with p-toluenesulfonic acid in ethanol–benzene, with azeotropic distillation of water, or from the dione, ethyl orthoformate, and sulfuric acid as catalyst. The enol ethers are hydrolyzed by moisture of the air unless especially protected. C-Alkylation, for example preparation of 2-methylcyclohexane-1,3-dione, is effected with methyl iodide and sodium methoxide in methanol (58% yield). A similar alkylation may account for the formation of tetraacetylethane by the action

$$2\ CH_3COCH_2COCH_2 \xrightarrow[59\text{–}67\%]{2\ NaOH} 2\ [CH_3COC^-HCOCH_3]\ Na^+ \xrightarrow[41\text{–}59\%]{I_2}$$

$$CH_3COCHCOCH_3$$
$$|$$
$$CH_3COCHCOCH_3$$

Tetraacetylethane
m.p. 193°

of iodine on sodium acetylacetonate, which is obtained as a crystalline solid on addition of acetylacetone to an aqueous–methanolic solution of sodium hydroxide; the vacuum-dried salt can be stored indefinitely.

A general method of obtaining α,β-unsaturated ketones from the enol ethers of β-dicarbonyl compounds is illustrated by a procedure for the preparation of Δ^2-cyclohexenone (R. Pappo, 1953; H. O. House, 1960). Cyclohexane-1,3-dione enol ethyl ether is reduced with lithium aluminum hydride and the product shaken

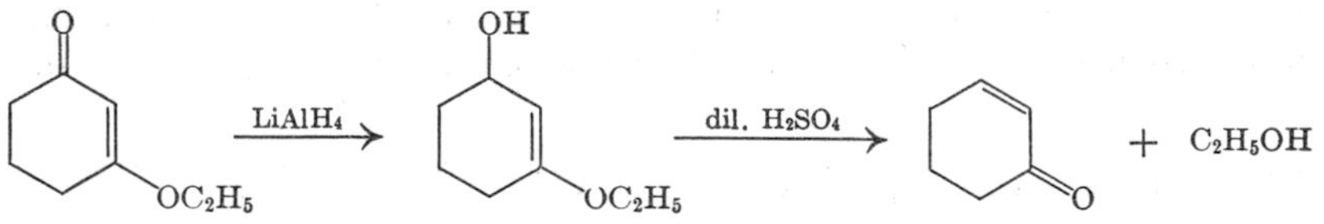

with ether and dilute sulfuric acid, which hydrolyzes the enol ether to the β-hydroxyketone and dehydrates the latter to the conjugated ketone.

β-Diketones are characterized by their tendency to undergo basic cleavage. The reaction of acetylacetone probably follows the course indicated.

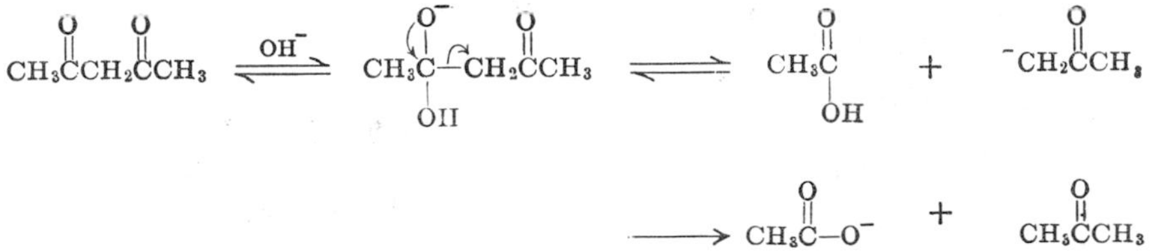

RING ENLARGEMENT AND CONTRACTION

12.47　　Diazomethane Method. — Diazomethane reacts readily with simple aldehydes and ketones in a polar solvent (water or alcohol) with liberation of nitrogen and formation of a mixture of products (Arndt, 1928). An aldehyde gives chiefly a methyl ketone and an epoxide; a ketone gives homologous

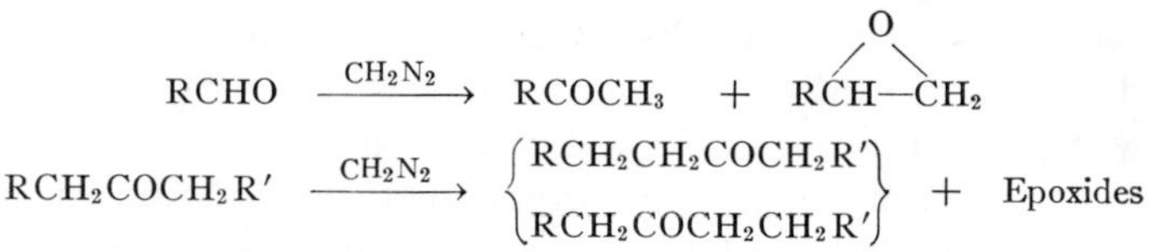

$$RCHO \xrightarrow{CH_2N_2} RCOCH_3 + \underset{\substack{\diagup \diagdown \\ RCH-CH_2}}{\overset{O}{}}$$

$$RCH_2COCH_2R' \xrightarrow{CH_2N_2} \left\{ \begin{array}{l} RCH_2CH_2COCH_2R' \\ RCH_2COCH_2CH_2R' \end{array} \right\} + \text{ Epoxides}$$

ketones with inserted methylene groups and epoxides. Mosettig[1] and Burger[2] (1930) investigated the reaction of cyclohexanone with diazomethane as a possible route to the epoxide IV, but found that this substance is formed in only small

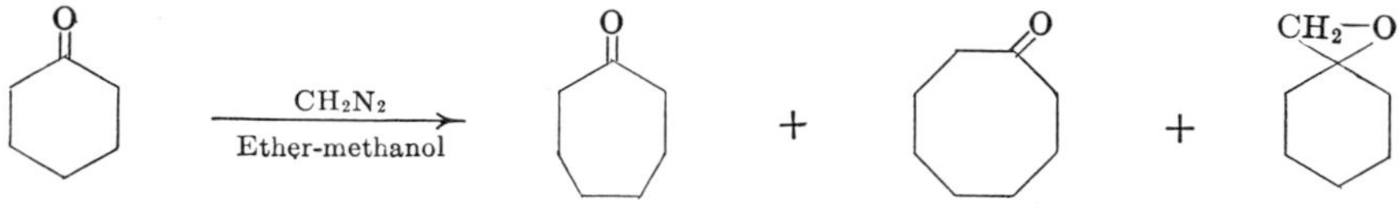

$$I \qquad\qquad II\ (33\text{-}36\%) \qquad\qquad III \qquad\qquad IV$$

amount and that the main reaction is ring enlargement to cycloheptanone; a further reaction of the same type affords cyclooctanone. Mosettig and Burger let a solution of cyclohexanone (24 g.) and 13.6 g. of diazomethane in dry ether (900 ml.) stand at 0° but observed no reaction. Addition of methanol (200 ml.) initiated rapid evolution of nitrogen at 0°; when the reaction subsided the solution was let stand at room temperature until it became colorless (3 days). The solution was filtered free of a slight flocculent precipitate (polymethylenes) and evaporated. Fractional distillation afforded 4% of the epoxide IV; the higher-boiling ketonic material was treated with aqueous sodium bisulfite and the solid cycloheptanone addition product was collected, washed with ether, and decomposed with sodium

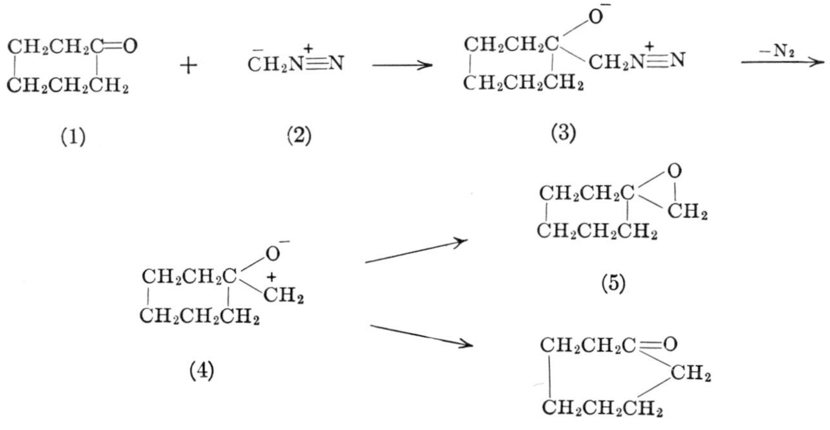

carbonate. The cyclooctanone formed as a by-product was thus eliminated, since it does not form a bisulfite product. Cycloheptanone was obtained in 52% yield.

[1] Erich Mosettig, b. 1898 Vienna; Ph.D. Vienna (Späth); Univ. Virginia; National Institutes of Health

[2] Alfred Burger, b. 1905 Vienna; Ph.D. Vienna (Späth); Univ. Virginia

Kohler and co-workers (1939) conducted the reaction on a 500-ml. scale by drop-wise addition of nitrosomethylurethane to a stirred solution of cyclohexanone in methanol containing a small amount of suspended sodium carbonate (20–25°); fractional distillation afforded the epoxide in 15 % yield and cycloheptanone in 63 % yield.

Arndt's studies indicated that the reaction probably involves addition of diazomethane to the carbonyl group prior to elimination of nitrogen. The fact that the reaction is catalyzed by polar solvents suggests that the ionic species (4) is involved, and a plausible precursor is the addition product (3). The ionic centers of (4) can then interact to form the epoxide (5), or a 1,2-shift can afford the ring-enlarged ketone (6). In the case of the intermediate ion (8) from an aliphatic aldehyde, hydrogen enters into a 1,2-shift in preference to the alkyl group.

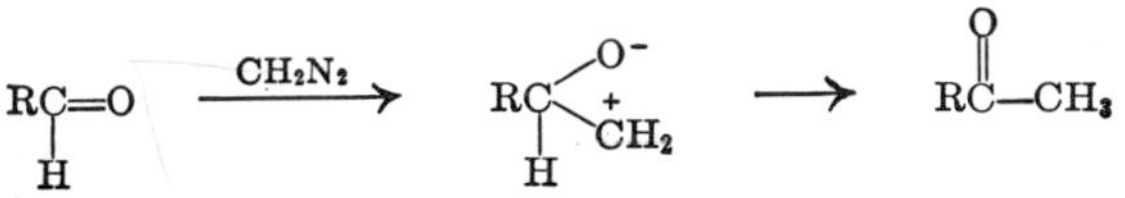

House[1] (1960) found that use of boron fluoride as a catalyst markedly accelerates formation of a ketone and so suppresses epoxide formation and from the ratios of the two possible ketonic products derived from ketones of the type RCOR' established the following order of migratory aptitudes: $C_6H_5 > CH_3 > (CH_3)_2CH$.

12.48   Ring Contraction. — A general method for the conversion of cyclo-hexenones to corresponding cyclopentanones is illustrated by the synthesis of 2,4,4-trimethylcyclopentanone from isophorone (H. O. House, 1957). The oxide (2) is prepared by dropwise addition of aqueous sodium hydroxide to a solution of isophorone and 30 % hydrogen peroxide in methanol at 15–20° and

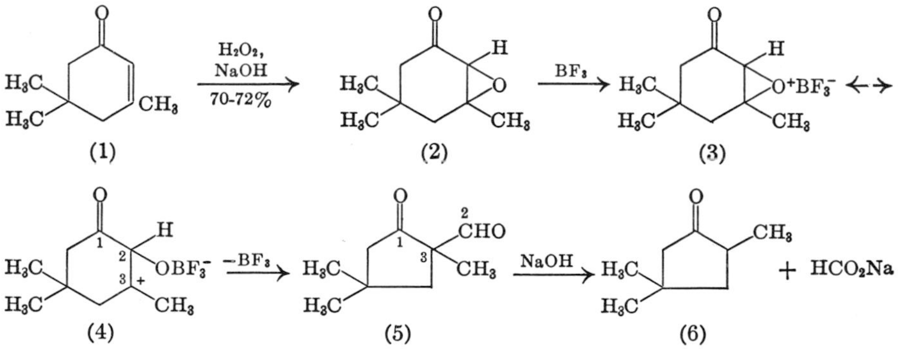

treated in benzene solution with boron fluoride etherate at room temperature (30 min.). The ionic intermediate (4) is more stable than the alternative one with the charge at C_2 because the latter incorporates two adjacent atoms bearing at least a partial positive charge. Rearrangement of (4) involves acyl migration of C_1 to C_3 to give the α-formyl ketone (5), a 1,3-dione which is rapidly cleaved by

[1] Herbert O. House, b. 1929 Willoughby, Ohio; Ph.D. Illinois (Fuson); Mass. Inst. Techn.

shaking a benzene–ether solution with aqueous alkali. The overall yield of the trimethylcyclopentanone (6) from the oxide (2) is 56–63%.

12.49   Tiffeneau[1] Rearrangement (1937). — A procedure for the preparation of cycloheptanone by the Tiffeneau rearrangement reported by H. J. Dauben (1951) is as follows. Aldol condensation of nitromethane with cyclohexanone is conducted efficiently with one equivalent of sodium ethoxide in absolute ethanol. The resulting sodio derivative II is collected and stirred with dilute acetic acid for conversion to 1-(nitromethyl)-cyclohexanol (III), which is reduced to the amino alcohol IV by shaking an acetic acid solution with W-4 Raney

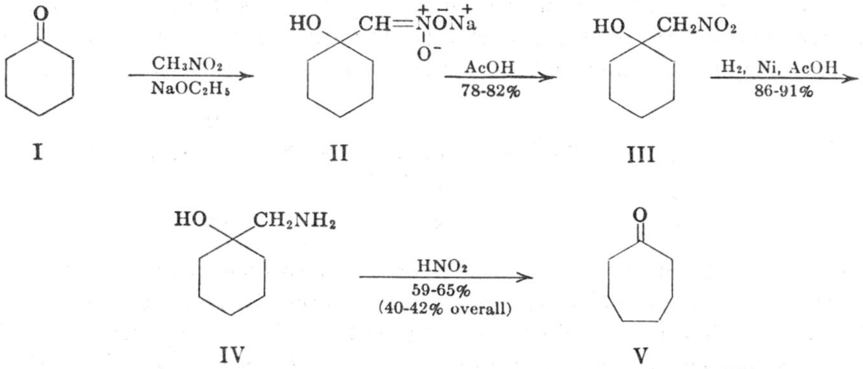

nickel and hydrogen at 35°. The filtered solution is diluted with ice water and treated with aqueous sodium nitrite solution to effect rearrangement to cycloheptanone (V). The last step involves initial formation of the diazonium salt VI;

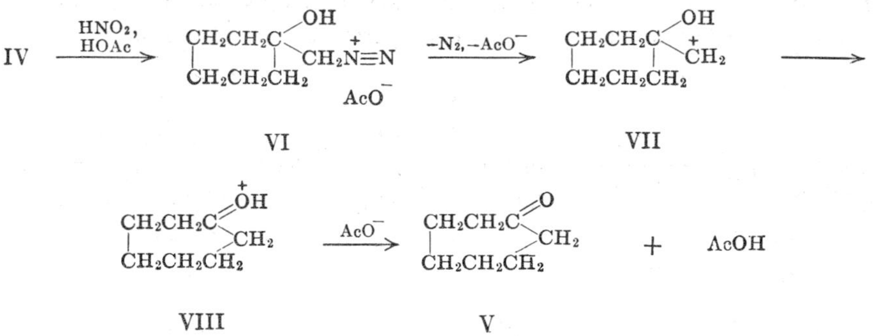

aromatic diazonium salts are stable enough to be isolated, since the unsaturated group is conjugated with an aromatic ring, but the aliphatic salt VI loses nitrogen spontaneously to form the carbonium ion VII, which undergoes a 1,2-shift of carbon to give VIII, the conjugate acid of cycloheptanone. The intermediate VI is similar to the dipolar ion postulated in ring enlargement with diazomethane.

PROBLEMS

1. Suggest a method for effecting the conversion of $C_6H_5CH_2CH_2Cl$ into $C_6H_5CH_2CHO$.
2. Suggest an appropriate method for preparation of the following compounds from the starting materials indicated:

---

[1] Marc Tiffeneau, 1873–1945; b. France; Univ. Paris (Sorbonne); *J. Chem. Soc.*, 1668 (1949)

(a) Methyl ethyl ketone from sec-butyl alcohol

(b) Methyl n-hexyl ketone from capryl alcohol, $CH_3(CH_2)_5CH(OH)CH_3$

(c) Methyl allyl ketone, starting with acetaldehyde and allyl bromide

(d) Sebacic acid-half aldehyde, $O=CH(CH_2)_8COOH$, from undecylenic acid, $CH_2=CH(CH_2)_8COOH$

(e) n-Valeraldehyde from n-valeric acid

3. Indicate the steps required for transformation of cyclohexanone into cyclopentanone. How could the reverse transformation be accomplished?

4. Summarize the quantitative and qualitative differences in reactions of aldehydes and ketones.

5. Cite specific comparisons that establish the order of reactivity of the carbonyl groups in the following compounds: acetone, diethyl ketone, acetaldehyde, chloral, diisopropyl ketone.

6. How could cinnamaldehyde, $C_6H_5CH=CHCHO$, be converted into cinnamyl alcohol, $C_6H_5CHCH=CH_2OH$?

7. What products would you expect to obtain from cholestane-$2\beta,3\beta$-oxide on (a) acetolysis; (b) reduction with $LiAlH_4$?

8. Predict the result of the action of a concentrated solution of alkali on trimethylacetaldehyde.

9. Suggest a synthesis of β-hydroxyisovaleric acid, $(CH_3)_2C(OH)CH_2COOH$, starting with acetone.

10. Suggest a procedure by which the aldehydic group of the compound $CH_3COCH_2CH_2CHO$ could be protected and the substance converted into the aldehyde-acid $HOOCCH_2CH_2CHO$.

11. Suggest a method for the synthesis from cyclohexanone of $C_6H_{11}=CHCO_2C_2H_5$.

12. Cite specific examples establishing the relative reactivity of the carbonyl group of ketones and esters.

13. A substance $C_5H_{12}O$ yields an oxidation product $C_5H_{10}O$ that reacts with phenylhydrazine and gives a positive iodoform test. The original substance also can be dehydrated with sulfuric acid to a hydrocarbon C_5H_{10}, and this on oxidation yields acetone. What is the structure of the substance?

14. A substance $C_5H_8O_2$ forms a dioxime, gives a positive iodoform test and a positive bisulfite test, and can be converted into n-pentane. What is its structure?

15. Predict the result of the following reactions:

(a) Ethylene oxide + HCN

(b) $CH_3COC(CH_3)_3 + C_6H_5CO_3H$

16. Starting with three-carbon components, devise syntheses for:

(a) Diethyl ketone   (c) $(CH_3)_2C=CHCH=CH_2$

(b) Hexanone-3

17. A hydrocarbon C_7H_{12} yields cyclopentanecarboxylic acid on chromic acid oxidation. On reaction with concentrated sulfuric acid followed by hydrolysis it yields an alcohol, $C_7H_{14}O$, that gives a positive iodoform test. What is the structure of the hydrocarbon?

18. A compound $C_7H_{14}O_2$ (I) reacts with acetic anhydride to give $C_7H_{13}O(OCOCH_3)$ (II); it does not react with phenylhydrazine. When treated with $Pb(OAc)_4$, I gives $C_7H_{12}O_2$ (III), which reacts with H_2NOH to give $C_7H_{12}(=NOH)_2$, reduces Fehling solution, and on treatment with NaOI consumes 4 moles of the reagent to give iodoform and $HOOC(CH_2)_4COOH$. Give a brief interpretation of the significance of each of the observations recorded and deduce the structure of I.

19. Suggest a method for reduction of $CH_3COCH_2CO_2C_2H_5$ to $CH_3CH_2CH_2CO_2C_2H_5$.

20. Phenylglyoxal, C_6H_5COCHO, under the influence of base, undergoes a Cannizzaro-like intramolecular reaction to form a substance $C_8H_8O_3$. What is the structure?

21. Formulate syntheses for the following compounds from malonic ester and any halogen compound desired:

(a) $(CH_3)_2CHCH_2CO_2H$ (c) $HOOCCH_2CH_2CH_2CH_2CH_2CH_2CO_2H$

(b) $CH_3CH_2CH(CH_3)CO_2H$

22. Predict the relative enol content of the C-methyl and C-acetyl derivatives of acetoacetic ester:

$$CH_3COCH(CH_3)CO_2C_2H_5 \quad \text{and} \quad CH_3COCH(COCH_3)CO_2C_2H_5$$

Chapter 13

CONDENSATIONS

13.1   **Introduction.** — Description of a reaction as a condensation implies that elimination of a molecule of water or alcohol between two react-ants is involved, rather than simple addition.   The distinction, however, is not clearly defined, for some reactions can be stopped at the stage of an addition or else carried a step further, as desired.   In this chapter we have assembled a group of reactions which are not all condensations in the strict sense but which have a general mechanistic pattern and in which the acceptor component is an aldehyde, a ketone, or an ester.   Some of the reactions are interrelated in origin, and we shall discuss them roughly in chronological order.

13.2   **Aldol Condensation.** — When acetaldehyde is treated with a small quantity of sodium hydroxide, two molecules combine in an equilib-rium process and afford aldol, or β-hydroxy-n-butyraldehyde.   The reaction

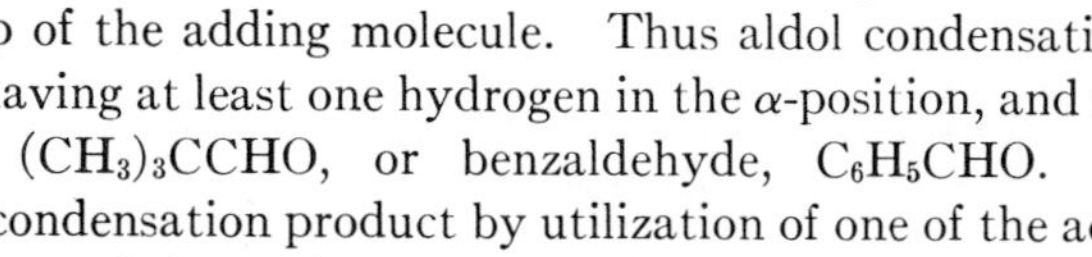

$$\overset{\text{H}}{\underset{}{\text{CH}_3\text{C}}}\!\!=\!\!\text{O} + \text{H}\cdot\overset{\alpha}{\text{CH}_2\text{CHO}} \xrightarrow{\text{OH}^-} \text{CH}_3\text{CHCH}_2\text{CHO}$$
$$\underset{\text{OH}}{|}$$

Aldol (b.p. 83°/20 mm.)

involves addition of one molecule of acetaldehyde to the carbonyl group of another molecule, and is dependent upon an activated hydrogen in the α-position to the carbonyl group of the adding molecule.   Thus aldol condensation is shown only by aldehydes having at least one hydrogen in the α-position, and not by trimethyl-acetaldehyde, $(\text{CH}_3)_3\text{CCHO}$, or benzaldehyde, $\text{C}_6\text{H}_5\text{CHO}$.   Propionaldehyde gives an aldol condensation product by utilization of one of the activated α-hydro-gens, and not one of the hydrogens in the β-position:

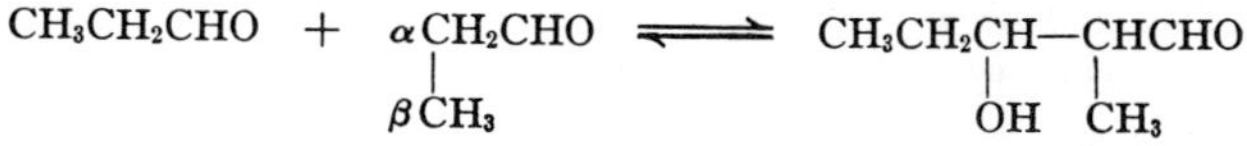

$$\text{CH}_3\text{CH}_2\text{CHO} + \underset{\beta\,\text{CH}_3}{\overset{\alpha\,\text{CH}_2\text{CHO}}{|}} \rightleftharpoons \text{CH}_3\text{CH}_2\text{CH}\!-\!\underset{\text{OH}\ \ \text{CH}_3}{\text{CHCHO}}$$

456

Base-catalyzed aldolization, like cyanohydrin formation, involves nucleophilic addition. In an initial, slow step (a) the basic catalyst abstracts a proton from the aldehyde to give the anion required for the more rapid step of addition (b); the terminal step (c) regenerates the catalytic anion.

(a)　　$OH^- + HCH_2CHO \rightleftharpoons H_2O + \overset{-}{C}H_2CHO$

(b)　　$CH_3CH{=}O + \overset{-}{C}H_2CHO \rightleftharpoons CH_3\underset{\underset{O^-}{|}}{C}HCH_2CHO$

(c)　　$CH_3\underset{\underset{O^-}{|}}{C}HCH_2CHO + H_2O \rightleftharpoons CH_3\underset{\underset{OH}{|}}{C}HCH_2CHO + OH^-$

Aldol is subject to ready dehydration because of the presence of a β-hydroxy group adjacent to an activated α-hydrogen atom. Conditions are thus particularly favorable for elimination of water, and aldol is converted into crotonaldehyde either by heating the isolated product alone or with a trace of mineral acid or by merely warming the aqueous solution of the equilibrium mixture resulting from aldolization. If acetaldehyde is warmed with strong alkali, it is converted into

$$\overset{\beta\quad\ \alpha}{CH_3CH{-}CHCHO} \xrightarrow{\ -H_2O\ } \overset{\quad\beta\quad\ \alpha}{CH_3CH{=}CHCHO}$$
$$\underset{\text{Aldol}}{\underset{OH\ \ H}{}} \qquad\qquad \text{Crotonaldehyde}$$

a resinous product resulting from repeated aldol condensations among aldol, crotonaldehyde, and acetaldehyde.

A reaction sequence of use in the industry consists in aldol condensation, dehydration, and hydrogenation. 2-Ethyl-1-hexanol is made by this process (a) and used for oxidation to 2-ethylhexanoic acid. A mixture of C_2- and C_4-aldehydes

(a)　　$2CH_3CH_2CH_2CHO \xrightarrow{\ -H_2O;\ H_2\ } CH_3CH_2CH_2CH_2\underset{\underset{CH_2CH_3}{|}}{C}HCH_2OH$

(b)　　$CH_3CHO + CH_3CH_2CH_2CHO \xrightarrow{\ -H_2O;\ H_2\ } \begin{cases} CH_3CH_2CH_2CH_2CH_2CH_2OH \\ (CH_3CH_2)_2CHCH_2OH \end{cases}$

(b) affords a mixture of two C_6-primary alcohols of use for manufacture of lacquer solvents.

The carbonyl group of acetone has less additive power than that of acetaldehyde, although comparably activated α-hydrogen atoms are present. Aldol condensation occurs under basic catalysis, but the position of equilibrium is very unfavor-

$$\underset{\substack{CH_3 \\ \text{Acetone (b.p. 56.1°)}}}{\overset{CH_3}{>}}C{=}O + H\cdot CH_2COCH_3 \underset{\xleftarrow{\hspace{1cm}}}{\overset{Ba(OH)_2}{\xrightarrow{\hspace{1cm}}}} \underset{\substack{CH_3 \\ \text{Diacetone alcohol (b.p. 166°)}}}{\overset{CH_3}{>}}\underset{\underset{OH}{|}}{C}{-}CH_2COCH_3$$

able to formation of the condensation product, diacetone alcohol. Even so, a special technique of conducting the reaction makes possible efficient preparation of the condensation product. Solid barium hydroxide is used as catalyst and promotes reaction on contact with acetone without dissolving in it. The catalyst is placed in a filter-paper thimble in an extraction apparatus (Soxhlet) in which acetone is distilled into a vertical condenser, the condensate trickles over the solid catalyst and the liquid then filters by gravity through the thimble and is returned to the boiling flask. The acetone flowing over the barium hydroxide is converted into diacetone alcohol in small amounts approaching the equilibrium concentration, but once the resulting solution has passed through the filter and is out of contact with catalyst the dimeric condensation product does not revert to acetone but accumulates in the boiling flask as the more volatile acetone is continually removed by distillation and recycled. By operation of such a unit for about four days, 1 5 liters of acetone can be converted into diacetone alcohol in 71 % yield.

Diacetone alcohol can be dehydrated by adding a small amount of iodine as catalyst and slowly distilling the somewhat more volatile reaction product. The resulting substance, a colorless liquid having a peppermint-like odor and a burning taste, was assigned the name mesityl oxide at an early date because of an errone-

$$
\begin{array}{ccc}
CH_3 & & CH_3 \\
\diagdown C-CH_2COCH_3 & \xrightarrow{I_2} & \diagdown C=CHCOCH_3 \\
CH_3 \diagup \; | & & CH_3 \diagup \\
\quad OH & & \\
\text{Diacetone alcohol (b.p. 166}^\circ) & & \text{Mesityl oxide (b.p. 131}^\circ)
\end{array}
$$

ous conception of its chemical nature. By the action of sodium hypochlorite it can be converted in good yield into β,β-dimethylacrylic acid, $(CH_3)_2C=CHCOOH$ (m.p. 70°, b.p. 195°). Mesityl oxide is also obtainable directly from acetone by the action of dry hydrogen chloride, but the yields are low, and the substance is accompanied by a product of further condensation with another molecule of

$$
\begin{array}{ccc}
CH_3 & & CH_3 \\
\diagdown C=\lceil O \; + \; H_2 \rceil CHCOCH_3 \xrightarrow{HCl} & & \diagdown C=CHCOCH_3 \xrightarrow{(CH_3)_2CO} \\
CH_3 \diagup & & CH_3 \diagup \\
& & \text{Mesityl oxide}
\end{array}
$$

$$
\begin{array}{cc}
CH_3 & CH_3 \\
\diagdown C=CHCOCH=C \diagup \\
CH_3 & CH_3 \\
\text{Phorone}
\end{array}
$$

acetone, phorone. These reactions doubtless proceed through aldol-type products, which are dehydrated under the influence of the acidic condensing agent. Phorone, so named because of a chance correspondence of the empirical formula with that of a camphor derivative (camphor + acetone), is a yellow crystalline solid having a geranium odor. Isophorone (12.27) has been obtained from acetone under various conditions of acidic and basic catalysis. Mesityl oxide, phorone, and isophorone are all produced commercially.

Reverse aldolization is sometimes useful in structure elucidation. Thus a ketol having an α-methylol group can be recognized because it liberates formaldehyde on treatment with base:

$$RCOCR_2CH_2OH \xrightarrow{OH^-} R\overset{\overset{\displaystyle O}{\|}}{C}CHR_2 \;+\; CH_2{=}O$$

The formaldehyde produced is conveniently isolated and identified by reaction in aqueous solution with dimedone, a $1,3$-diketone which exists almost entirely in

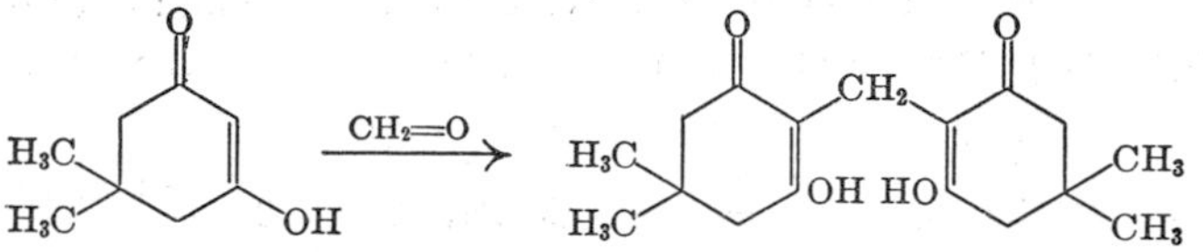

Dimedone, m. p. 148°   Methylene-bisdimedone, m. p. 188°

the enolic form (12.17). No catalyst is required, and the gaseous aldehyde affords a crystalline solid with a ten-fold increase in mass. If the formaldehyde liberated in a cleavage can react with some other functional group in the molecule, it can be trapped by conducting the reverse aldolization in the presence of dimedone.

CONDENSATIONS OF FORMALDEHYDE

13.3   **Aldol Condensations.** — Formaldehyde has no α-hydrogen for donation and the carbonyl group surpasses that of other aldehydes in additive ability. Aldol addition to formaldehyde of another aldehyde is thus of preparative value. One process for the production of acrolein involves condensation of equivalent amounts of acetaldehyde and formaldehyde (yield 75%). If

$$O{=}CH_2 \;+\; HCH_2CHO \longrightarrow [HOH_2CCH_2CHO] \xrightarrow{-H_2O} \underset{\text{Acrolein}}{H_2C{=}CHCHO}$$

enough formaldehyde is present, all three α-hydrogens of acetaldehyde are utilized. Thus pentaerythritol, required for the production of the explosive PETN and of surface-active agents, is made by the reaction of acetaldehyde with about five equivalents of formaldehyde in an aqueous solution of calcium hydroxide. After

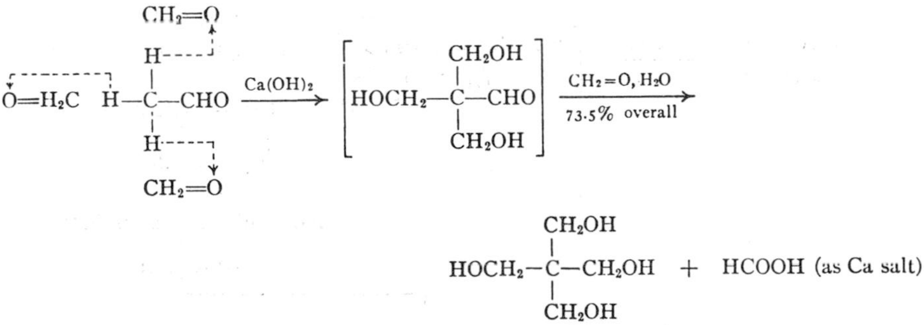

$$\underset{\text{Pentaerythritol (m.p. 260°)}}{HOCH_2{-}\overset{\overset{\displaystyle CH_2OH}{|}}{\underset{\underset{\displaystyle CH_2OH}{|}}{C}}{-}CH_2OH \;+\; HCOOH \text{ (as Ca salt)}}$$

addition, the next step is a crossed Cannizzaro reaction, or disproportionation, between the trihydroxyaldehyde and formaldehyde resulting in reduction of the former to pentaerythritol and oxidation of the latter to formic acid.

Aldol addition of isobutyraldehyde to formaldehyde is the first step in a process for the production of an intermediate in the synthesis of pantothenic acid (Merck, 1940). Addition of hydrogen cyanide and hydrolysis gives the hydroxy acid II, which cyclizes to the γ-lactone III. The dl-lactone is resolved by dissolving it in one equivalent of alkali, when the sodium salt of the acid II is formed, and adding one-half equivalent of quinine hydrochloride (Pope procedure); the quinine salt of one enantiomer crystallizes selectively (86% yield) and affords the desired levorotatory form of the lactone III (m.p. 91°, yield 71%). The other enantiomer,

$$O=CH_2 \ + \ H-\overset{\overset{\displaystyle CH_3}{|}}{\underset{\underset{\displaystyle CH_3}{|}}{C}}-CHO \ \xrightarrow{K_2CO_3,\ 20°} \ HOCH_2-\overset{\overset{\displaystyle CH_3}{|}}{\underset{\underset{\displaystyle CH_3}{|}}{C}}-CHO \ \xrightarrow{aq.KCN\ and\ CaCl_2}$$

Isobutyraldehyde α,α-Dimethyl-β-hydroxy-propionaldehyde, I (m.p. 96–97°)

$$\left[\ HOCH_2-\overset{\overset{\displaystyle CH_3}{|}}{\underset{\underset{\displaystyle CH_3}{|}}{C}}-\overset{}{\underset{\underset{\displaystyle OH}{|}}{C}}HCN \ \longrightarrow \right.$$

$$\left[H OCH_2-\overset{\overset{\displaystyle CH_3}{|}}{\underset{\underset{\displaystyle CH_3}{|}}{C}}-\overset{}{\underset{\underset{\displaystyle OH}{|}}{C}}H-CO OH \right] \ \xrightarrow[77-81\%\ from\ I]{} \ CH_2-\overset{\overset{\displaystyle CH_3}{|}}{\underset{\underset{\displaystyle CH_3}{|}}{C}}-\overset{}{\underset{\underset{\displaystyle OH}{|}}{C}}H-CO$$

II dl-α-Hydroxy-β,β-dimethyl-butyrolactone, III (m.p. about 80°)

which is valueless for the synthesis of pantothenic acid, is then racemized by heating an aqueous solution of its sodium salt at 150° for eighteen hours, and the resulting dl-product is added to the next batch of synthetic material submitted to resolution; in this manner the entire lot, rather than half, of the intermediate can be utilized.

$$\overset{\displaystyle CH(CO_2H)_2}{\underset{\displaystyle CH_2CO_2H}{|}} \ \xrightarrow{CH_2=O} \ \left[\overset{\displaystyle HOCH_2C(CO_2H)_2}{\underset{\displaystyle CH_2CO_2H}{|}} \right]$$

$$\xrightarrow[-H_2O]{-CO_2} \ \overset{\displaystyle CH_2=CCO_2H}{\underset{\displaystyle CH_2CO_2H}{|}} \ Itaconic\ acid\ (m.\ p.\ 161°)$$

Paraconic acid (m. p. 57°)

−H₂O | Distil

$$\overset{\overset{\displaystyle OH}{|}}{HO_2C-CH_2-\underset{\underset{\displaystyle CH_2CO_2H}{|}}{C}-CO_2H} \ \xrightarrow[37-47\%]{Dist.} \ H_2C=C \begin{matrix} & C=O \\ | & \ \ | \ \ O \\ CH_2- & C=O \end{matrix} \ \xrightarrow[62-66\%]{Heat} \ CH_3-C \begin{matrix} & C=O \\ | & \ \ | \ \ O \\ CH- & C=O \end{matrix}$$

Citric acid Itaconic anhydride (m. p. 68°) Citraconic anhydride (m. p. 8°)

Michael (1933) synthesized paraconic acid by allowing a mixture of paraformaldehyde and carboxysuccinic acid in acetic acid–acetic anhydride to stand at room temperature for two weeks and then heating it on the steam bath. The minor product (16%), itaconic acid, crystallized readily; paraconic acid (80%) crystallized slowly. The initial addition involves the more reactive α-hydrogen of the malonic acid group (condensation occurs readily with acetaldehyde as well). Paraconic acid on distillation loses water and affords itaconic anhydride, a substance discovered by Baup (France, 1836) as a product of the destructive distillation of citric acid. The yields shown for this reaction and for the thermal isomerization to citraconic anhydride are those of *Organic Syntheses*. Condensation of malonic ester with two moles of aqueous formaldehyde in the presence of potassium bicarbonate as catalyst affords diethyl bis-(hydroxymethyl)-malonate (*Org. Syn.*, 1960).

$$2\ CH_2{=}O + CH_2(CO_2C_2H_5)_2 \xrightarrow[72-75\%]{KHCO_3} (HOCH_2)_2C(CO_2C_2H_5)_2$$
$$\text{(m.p. } 52°)$$

The base-catalyzed condensation of nitromethane (Louis Henry, 1895) with one, two, or three molecules of formaldehyde is a variation of the aldol condensa-

$$CH_3NO_2 \xrightarrow{CH_2O} HOCH_2CH_2NO_2 \xrightarrow{CH_2O} (HOCH_2)_2CHNO_2 \xrightarrow{CH_2O} (HOCH_2)_3CNO_2$$

tion reaction. Unusually rapid condensation is achieved by interaction of the sodium salt of the aci-nitroparaffin with the bisulfite compound of the aldehyde

$$RCHOHSO_3Na + CH_2{=}NONa \longrightarrow RCHOHCH_2NO_2 + Na_2SO_3$$

(J. Kamlet, 1939).

In an interesting application of the Henry reaction described by Urbański[1] (1959) nitroethane is first condensed with two moles of formaldehyde (NaHCO₃) to give the diol (1), which shows no nitro group absorption at 270 mμ and therefore appears to be hydrogen bonded, as in (1a). Treatment with base effects reverse aldolization to (2) with liberation of one mole of formaldehyde. The nitrodiol

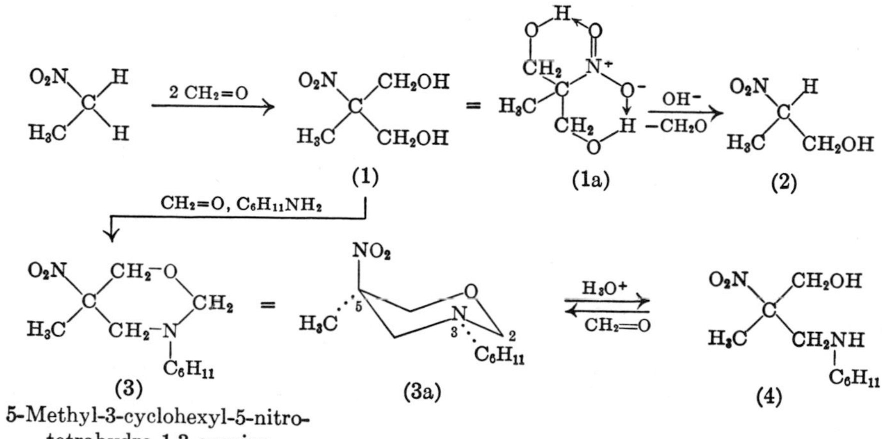

(1)   (1a)   (2)

(3)   (3a)   (4)

5-Methyl-3-cyclohexyl-5-nitro-
   tetrahydro-1,3-oxazine

[1] T. Urbański, b. 1901; Ph.D. Warsaw Inst. Techn.; Warsaw Inst. Tech., Poland

(1) on reaction with formaldehyde and cyclohexylamine affords the six-membered heterocycle (3). Dipole moment data indicate that this substance has the conformation (3a), in which the methyl and cyclohexyl groups are equatorial and the nitro group is axial. The 4-methylene group of the 1,3-oxazine (3) is labile and easily eliminated on acid hydrolysis, with conversion to the amino alcohol (4). Variation in the nitroparaffin and amine component affords a series of 1,3-oxazines, some of which have shown promise in cancer chemotherapy.

13.4   Prins Reaction. — Formaldehyde (also other aldehydes) condenses with olefins in the presence of an acid catalyst to give a mixture of a 1,3-glycol and a 1,3-dioxane (H. J. Prins, 1919). Ethylene itself reacts only under

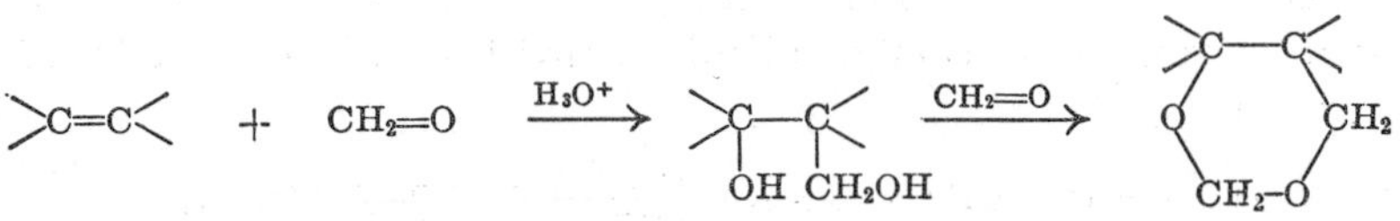

drastic conditions; olefins of the types $R_2C=CH_2$ and $RCH=CH_2$ give mainly 1,3-dioxanes; olefins of the type $RCH=CHR'$ afford 1,3-glycols, but usually in low yield.

Blomquist (1957) found that addition of cyclohexene to a slurry of paraformaldehyde in acetic acid–sulfuric acid at 50–70° affords, as the major products, *trans*-2-hydroxymethyl-1-cyclohexanol diacetate (5, yield 26%) and the *trans*-1,3-dioxane (8, yield 10%); two minor products were also characterized. The mechanism generally accepted for the acid-catalyzed reaction is protonation of

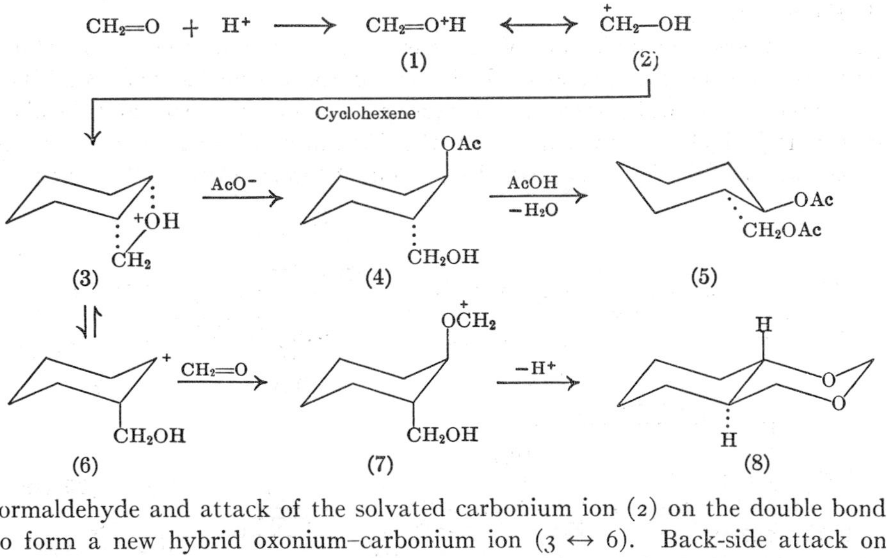

formaldehyde and attack of the solvated carbonium ion (2) on the double bond to form a new hybrid oxonium–carbonium ion (3 ↔ 6). Back-side attack on (3) by acetate ion gives the diaxial intermediate (4), and the final product is the *trans*-diequatorial diacetate (5). The *trans*-1,3-dioxane (8) may arise through the sequence shown.

In another study of the Prins reaction, a mixture of 2-methyl-2-butene, trioxymethylene, and stannic chloride in chloroform was stirred at room temperature for 18 hrs. (N. C. Yang,[1] 1959). The products isolated were the β,γ-unsaturated alcohol (3, 28%) and its formate (20%). The mechanism suggested for the

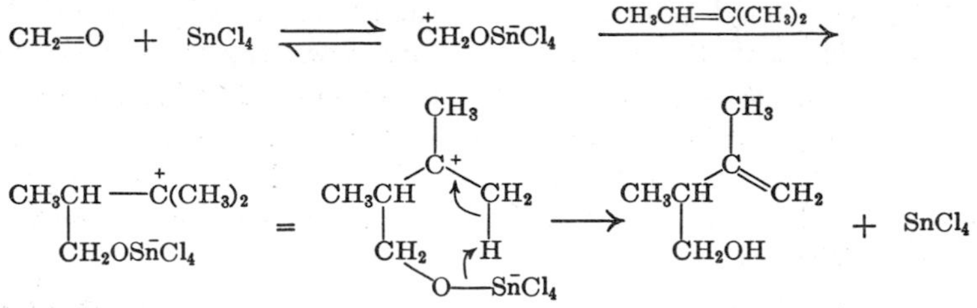

$$CH_2{=}O \;+\; SnCl_4 \;\rightleftharpoons\; \overset{+}{C}H_2OS\bar{n}Cl_4 \xrightarrow{\;CH_3CH{=}C(CH_3)_2\;}$$

$$
\underset{(1)}{\underset{\underset{CH_2OS\bar{n}Cl_4}{|}}{CH_3\overset{+}{C}H-\overset{+}{C}(CH_3)_2}}
\;=\;
\underset{(2)}{[\text{quasi-cyclic intermediate}]}
\;\longrightarrow\;
\underset{(3)}{[\text{unsat. alcohol}]}
\;+\; SnCl_4
$$

stannic chloride-catalyzed reaction postulates combination of formaldehyde with the Lewis acid (expanded electron shell) to form a polarized complex which adds to the olefin in the Markownikoff sense to form a quasi-cyclic intermediate (2). Collapse of the intermediate with electronic rearrangement affords the unsaturated alcohol with regeneration of the catalyst.

The cleavage of 1,3-ditertiary glycols by sulfuric acid in ethanol (H. E. Zimmerman and J. English, Jr.,[2] 1954) can be regarded as a reversal of the Prins reaction. Both stereoisomeric forms of 1,1,3-triphenyl-2-methylpropane-1,3-diol are

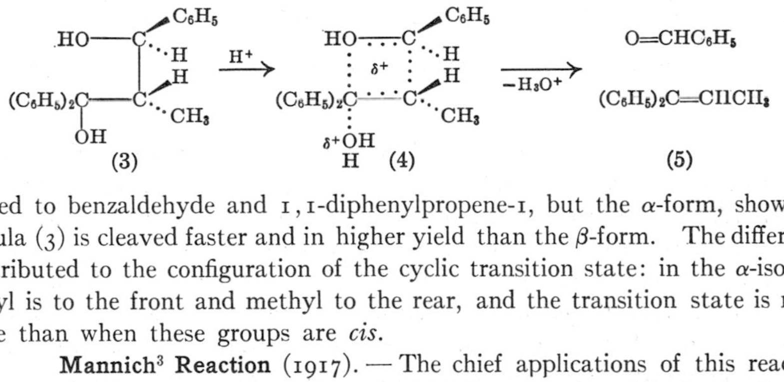

cleaved to benzaldehyde and 1,1-diphenylpropene-1, but the α-form, shown in formula (3) is cleaved faster and in higher yield than the β-form. The difference is attributed to the configuration of the cyclic transition state: in the α-isomer, phenyl is to the front and methyl to the rear, and the transition state is more stable than when these groups are *cis*.

13.5   **Mannich[3] Reaction** (1917). — The chief applications of this reaction involve condensation of formaldehyde and a secondary amine hydrochloride with a ketone having an active hydrogen atom. Acetophenone, for example, is refluxed in 80% ethanol with dimethylamine hydrochloride, para-formaldehyde, and a trace of hydrochloric acid; when the solution is filtered and

$$C_6H_5COCH_3 \;+\; CH_2{=}O \;+\; (CH_3)_2\overset{+}{N}H_2\bar{C}l \xrightarrow[63\%]{}$$

$$C_6H_5COCH_2CH_2\overset{+}{N}H(CH_3)_2\bar{C}l \xrightarrow{\;Heat\;} C_6H_5COCH{=}CH_2 \;+\; (CH_3)_2\overset{+}{N}H_2\bar{C}l$$

Dimethylaminopropiophenone   Phenyl vinyl
hydrochloride (m.p. 156°)   ketone

---

[1] Nien-Chu Yang, b. 1928 Shanghai, China; Ph.D. Chicago (Kharasch); Univ. Chicago

[2] James English, Jr., b. 1912 New Haven, Conn.; Ph.D. Yale (DonLeavy); Yale Univ.

[3] Carl Mannich, 1877–1947; b. Breslau, Germany; Ph.D. Basel (Thoms); Univ. Berlin; *Ber.*, **88**, 1 (1955)

allowed to cool, the Mannich base crystallizes as the hydrochloride. The free base, an oil, can be distilled at $111°/14$ mm., but the salt is labile to heat and easily eliminates dimethylamine hydrochloride. Thus steam distillation of the salt affords phenyl vinyl ketone in nearly quantitative yield. Since Mannich salts are solids of indefinite shelf life, they are often employed in synthesis in place of the liquid, reactive α,β-unsaturated ketones. The Mannich salt from acetophenone and piperidine hydrochloride is obtained by the same procedure in 90% yield; the product from cyclohexanone, formaldehyde, and dimethylamine hydrochloride is obtained in 85% yield. Phenylacetylene forms the Mannich base $C_6H_5C{\equiv}CCH_2N(CH_3)_2$.

13.6   **Perkin Reaction** (1867). — The first aldehyde reaction associated with the name of a specific investigator is that discovered by Cannizzaro in 1853 (12.36). The next was one devised by Perkin[1] (1868) for the synthetic preparation of coumarin. Coumarin is a crystalline solid of fragrance resembling that of new-mown hay and is used in the perfume industry. Treatment of the substance with alkali was known to give coumarinic acid under mild

Coumarin   Coumarinic acid   Salicylaldehyde
M. p. 67°, b. p. 291°

conditions and salicylaldehyde at a higher temperature. Coumarinic acid (*cis*) is isolated as the potassium salt; the free acid liberated on acidification (even with carbon dioxide) cyclizes to coumarin. (The *trans* acid, coumaric acid, m.p. 208°, is incapable of lactonization.) Since coumarin differs from salicylaldehyde by two carbon atoms, and since acetic acid is eliminated in the fusion, Perkin thought that coumarin might be obtainable by reaction of salicylaldehyde with acetic anhydride, but initial attempts were unsuccessful. He then prepared the yellow sodium salt of salicylaldehyde and heated it with acetic anhydride in the hope of first replacing sodium by acetyl; the salt rapidly lost its color and then dissolved and the reaction product was coumarin. Perkin succeeded in preparing the postulated intermediate acetylsalicylaldehyde by treating an ethereal solution of the sodium salt with acetic anhydride, but was surprised to find that the substance when heated with acetic anhydride yielded a product other than coumarin $[AcOC_6H_4CH(OAc)_2]$. Coumarin was formed, however, when the acetate was heated with acetic anhydride and sodium acetate. Thinking it unlikely that the sodium of sodium acetate could have replaced the phenolic hydrogen of salicylaldehyde, Perkin (1877) was led to try the action of acetic anhydride and sodium acetate on benzaldehyde. The product was cinnamic

[1] Sir William Henry Perkin, 1838–1907; b. London; Sudbury/London; *J. Chem. Soc.*, **93**, 2214 (1908)

acid; a modern procedure for conducting this, the simplest example of a Perkin

$$C_6H_5CHO + (CH_3CO)_2O \xrightarrow[60-54\%]{CH_3CO_2K, 180°, 8 \text{ hrs.}} C_6H_5CH=CHCO_2H$$

Cinnamic acid

reaction, is shown in the formulation.

Perkin thought that the key reaction is between the aldehyde and the anhydride and regarded sodium acetate as a catalyst. Fittig (1868) deduced the correct structure of coumarin, but was led from reactions of benzaldehyde with mixtures of $(RCO)_2O$ and $R'CO_2Na$ to the view that the salt is the reacting species. Michael (1901) contested Fittig's position and showed that the mixtures of Fittig reach rapid equilibrium at 100° and hence that the identity of the reacting component cannot be inferred from the structures of the starting materials. The debate continued for some years before the position of Perkin and Michael was generally accepted as correct. The simplest evidence is the demonstration by P. Kalnin (1928) that benzaldehyde reacts readily with acetic anhydride in the presence of potassium carbonate or trimethylamine but does not react with sodium acetate in the presence of these catalysts. The Perkin reaction, in fact, is a form of aldol condensation.

As in an aldol condensation, a carbanion derived by abstraction of an α-hydrogen of the anhydride adds to the carbonyl group of the aldehyde. In a reaction involving the anhydride of one acid and the salt of another, both anhydrides are available through equilibration and the one with the more reactive methylene group is the one that participates. Thus condensation of benzaldehyde with potassium phenylacetate and acetic anhydride gives the product of reaction with the component originally introduced as a salt; the effective reactant must be the mixed anhydride. An improved procedure utilizes triethylamine as the base;

$$C_6H_5CHO \xrightarrow[(C_2H_5)_3N, \text{ refl. } 0.5 \text{ hr.}]{C_6H_5CH_2CO_2H, (CH_3CO)_2O} \begin{array}{c} C_6H_5-C-CO_2H \\ \| \\ C_6H_5-C-H \end{array} + \begin{array}{c} C_6H_5-C-CO_2H \\ \| \\ H-C-C_6H_5 \end{array}$$

cis   trans
71%; pKa 6.1   7%; pKa 4.8

acidification of an alkaline solution of the reaction mixture with acetic acid precipitates the *cis* acid, and addition of hydrochloric acid to the filtrate precipitates the *trans* acid.

Perkin applied the reaction to the preparation of the doubly unsaturated cinnamalacetic acid (1). Another variation was utilized by Kuhn (1928) for

1. $C_6H_5CH=CHCHO + (CH_3CO)_2O \xrightarrow[25\%]{NaOAc, 167°} C_6H_5CH=CHCH=CHCOOH$

    Cinnamaldehyde   Cinnamalacetic acid
                                                          (m.p. 166°)

synthesis of diphenylpolyenes, as illustrated in examples 2 and 3. Lead oxide functions as the basic catalyst and also promotes decarboxylation of the intermediate unsaturated acids.

Although aliphatic aldehydes give very low yields in the standard Perkin reaction, Fittig (1885) found that *n*-heptaldehyde, for example, reacts with acetic

2. $C_6H_5CH=CHCH\underbrace{O}_{}$ + $\underbrace{C}H_2 C_6H_5$ $\quad\xrightarrow{PbO,\ (CH_3CO)_2O}\quad$ $\left[\begin{array}{c}C_6H_5CH=CHCH=CC_6H_5\\ \underbrace{COOH}\end{array}\right]$

COOH

$\xrightarrow[23-25\%]{Heat}$ $C_6H_5CH=CHCH=CHC_6H_5$
1,4-Diphenylbutadiene
(*trans-trans* form, m.p. 153°)

3. $2\,C_6H_5CH=CHCHO$ + $HOOCCH_2CH_2COOH$ $\xrightarrow[16\%]{PbO,\ (CH_3CO)_2O,\ reflux}$

$C_6H_5CH=CHCH=CHCH=CHCH=CHC_6H_5$
1,8-Diphenyloctatetraene
(yellow, m.p. 232°)

anhydride and sodium succinate more smoothly, and at a lower temperature (120°) than it reacts with acetic anhydride and sodium acetate (170°). Although few yields are recorded, satisfactory results apparently were obtained with a number of aliphatic aldehydes   In the light of the above discussion, we formulate the reaction as involving succinic anhydride, with sodium acetate functioning as basic catalyst.   Presumably the aldol-like product (3) isomerizes to γ-*n*-hexyl-

$n\text{-}C_6H_{13}CH=O$ + $\begin{array}{c}CH_2CO\\ \\ CH_2CO\end{array}\!\!>\!O$ $\xrightarrow[120°,\ 20\ hrs.]{NaOAc}$ $\left[\begin{array}{c}n\text{-}C_6H_{13}CHCH\!\!-\!\!-\!\!CO\\ \\ OH\\ CH_2O\\ CO\end{array}\right]\longrightarrow$

(1)$$(2)$$(3)

$\begin{array}{c}n\text{-}C_6H_{13}CH\!\!-\!\!-\!\!CHCO_2H\\ \\ OCH_2\\ CO\end{array}$ $\xrightarrow[-CO_2]{300°}$ $n\text{-}C_6H_{13}CH=CHCH_2CO_2H$ + $\begin{array}{c}n\text{-}C_6H_{13}CH\!\!-\!\!-\!\!CH_2\\ \\ OCH_2\\ CO\end{array}$

γ-*n*-Hexylparaconic acid (4)$$(5)$$(6)

paraconic acid (4) by attack of the hydroxyl group on the anhydride linkage. Heated to 300°, the paraconic acid loses carbon dioxide with formation of the β,γ-unsaturated Δ³-decenoic acid (5), together with a small amount of lactone (6) resulting from the acid by intramolecular addition.   The formation of the nonconjugated acid (5) is accounted for on the assumption of an electron shift in

(4) $\xrightarrow{-H^+}$ $\begin{array}{c}RCH\!\!-\!\!-\!\!CHC\!\!\nearrow\!\!^O\\ \\ OCH_2\\ C\\ O\end{array}$ $\xrightarrow{-CO_2}$ $\begin{array}{c}RCH=CH\\ \\ {}^-OCH_2\\ C\\ O\end{array}$

the anion from (4).   Surprisingly, Fittig's modified method as applied to benzaldehyde afforded β-phenylparaconic acid in only 2% yield.   Note that the Kuhn synthesis (3, above) is an adaptation of the Fittig reaction.

The yields in most of the Perkin reactions cited are for the most part moderate or low.   The high temperature required and the basic catalyst both contribute to tar formation and side reactions.   Chemists of the day thus were stimulated by the shortcomings of the reaction, as well as by its remarkable versatility, to seek other methods for effecting the same or similar transformations.

13.7   Claisen-Schmidt Condensation (1881). — This useful reaction consists in basic condensation of an aromatic aldehyde, or other aldehyde having no α-hydrogen atom, with an aliphatic aldehyde or ketone.   For example, cinnamaldehyde can be prepared by shaking a mixture of benzaldehyde and acetaldehyde with about ten parts of dilute alkali and letting the mixture stand for 8–10 days.   Under these conditions two aldols are formed in equilibrium reactions, but the one in which the β-hydroxyl group is activated by the phenyl group

$$
C_6H_5CHO \ + \ CH_3CHO\,[NaOH] \underset{\displaystyle \left[\begin{array}{c} C_6H_5CHCH_2CHO \\ | \\ OH \end{array}\right] \xrightarrow{-H_2O} \underset{\substack{Cinnamaldehyde \\ (b.p.\ 127^\circ/15\ mm.)}}{C_6H_5CH{=}CHCHO}}{\overset{\displaystyle \overset{CH_3CHO}{\underset{\textstyle \substack{CH_3CHCH_2CHO \\ | \\ OH}}{}}}{\rightleftarrows}}
$$

loses water irreversibly to give cinnamaldehyde (*trans*, m.p. − 7.5°).   The yield in this example is not recorded and presumably is low.   The same is true of the first recorded example of a reaction of this type.   In 1880 J. Gustav Schmidt, in Victor Meyer's laboratory at Zurich, condensed furfural with acetaldehyde in the presence of dilute alkali at about 60° and obtained furfuralacetaldehyde, m.p. 51°.   The product was identified by oxidation with silver oxide in water at 100° to furfuralacetic acid, identical with a comparison sample secured from Baeyer.   H. Röhman (1898) described an improved procedure but likewise recorded no yield.

Claisen,[1] at Bonn in 1881, thought it might be possible to effect a Perkin-like condensation of the type $CH_3CHO \ + \ CH_3CO_2C_2H_5 \rightarrow CH_3CH{=}CHCO_2C_2H_5$ under the influence of dry hydrogen chloride, but all attempts led only to croton-aldehyde and resins.   However, when he passed hydrogen chloride into an ice-cold mixture of acetaldehyde and ethyl acetoacetate until the mixture had gained approximately half its weight he obtained a product of the expected composition in high yield.   His evidence of structure is novel.   If, as seemed likely, the reac-

$$
\underset{}{CH_3CH{=}O} \ + \ \overset{\textstyle COCH_3}{\underset{\textstyle |}{CH_2CO_2C_2H_5}} \xrightarrow[98\%]{HCl,\ 0^\circ} \underset{\substack{Ethyl\ ethylideneacetoacetate \\ (b.p.\ 210\text{-}212^\circ)}}{\overset{\textstyle COCH_3}{\underset{\textstyle |}{CH_3CH{=}CCO_2C_2H_5}}}
$$

tion involves the carbonyl group of the aldehyde and the methylene group of the β-keto ester, then benzaldehyde should react in the same way as acetaldehyde and acetoacetic ester should be replaceable by malonic ester.   Both reactions proceeded in the manner expected.

These results suggested trial of the acid-catalyzed condensation of benzaldehyde with acetone.   The first reaction was done with equivalent amounts of reactants,

$$
2\,C_6H_5CHO \ + \ CH_3COCH_3 \xrightarrow{HCl\ (0^\circ)} \underset{\text{Dibenzalacetone (m.p. 112°)}}{C_6H_5CH{=}CHCOCH{=}CHC_6H_5}
$$

[1] Ludwig Claisen, 1851–1930; b. Cologne; Ph.D. Bonn (Kekulé); Univ. Bonn; Owens College (Manchester); Univ. Munich, Aachen, Kiel, Berlin; Godlesberg (private laboratory); Ber., **69A,** 97 (1936)

saturated with hydrogen chloride, but the product, unexpectedly, proved to be dibenzalacetone. The diketone is characterized by the formation of intensely colored halochromic salts with mineral acids; thus in the preparation of the compound the reaction mixture acquires a "prachtvolle Rothfärbung."

These results were published in February, 1881. In June of the same year Schmidt, in extension of the work cited, described the reaction of benzaldehyde with acetone in dilute aqueous sodium hydroxide at about 60°. The crystalline product (m.p. 110°) appeared anomalous, for two analyses indicated a carbon content (85.65; 86.17%) corresponding approximately to the condensation of 5 moles of benzaldehyde with 2 moles of acetone with loss of 3 moles of water. In a paper of November, Claisen described a reinvestigation of the alkaline condensation. Schmidt's compound corresponded so closely in melting point, solubility, and color reactions to his compound that Claisen thought that the only point of question was whether his formula or Schmidt's was correct. He ran the reaction exactly as described by Schmidt and obtained the crystalline product reported. Analysis indicated the composition of dibenzalacetone (Found: C, 87.29%; H, 5.96%. Calcd.: C, 87.18%; H, 5.98%), and the samples indeed were identical. But Claisen found that this is a minor reaction product and that the major product is benzalacetone. When the reaction mixture, without being warmed, was let stand 2–3 days at room temperature, pure benzalacetone was obtained in high yield (1). Alkaline condensation thus affords an excellent method for selective

1. C_6H_5CHO + CH_3COCH_3 $\xrightarrow[\text{65–78\%}]{\text{10\% aq. NaOH, 25–31°}}$ $C_6H_5CH{=}CHCOCH_3$
                  (excess)   Benzalacetone
                                                     (yellow, m.p. 42°, b.p. 262°)

2. C_6H_5CHO + $CH_3COC_6H_5$ $\xrightarrow[\text{85\%}]{\text{aq.-alc. NaOH, 15–30°}}$ $C_6H_5CH{=}CHCOC_6H_5$
                                                            Benzalacetophenone
                                                     (yellow, m.p. 62°)

reaction with one of two available groups. The yield is nearly as high as in the condensation of benzaldehyde with acetophenone (2). One technical route to cinnamic acid is oxidation of benzalacetone with sodium hypochlorite.

Kuhn (1929) explored two routes to cinnamalacetaldehyde (5-phenylpentadienal), required in his synthesis of diphenylpolyenes; condensation of benzalde-

C_6H_5CHO + $CH_3CH{=}CHCHO$ $\xrightarrow[\text{10\%}]{\text{NaOH, C}_2\text{H}_5\text{OH}}$

$C_6H_5CH{=}CHCH{=}CHCHO$
Cinnamalacetaldehyde
(yel. liq.)

$C_6H_5CH{=}CHCHO$ + CH_3CHO $\xrightarrow[\text{15\%}]{\text{NaOH, CH}_3\text{OH}}$

hyde with crotonaldehyde, and condensation of cinnamaldehyde with acetaldehyde. These sodium alkoxide-catalyzed condensations involving aliphatic aldehydes both afford the doubly unsaturated aldehyde in only very low yield. Piperidine acetate is a better catalyst for the condensation. With cinnamaldehyde as the aldehydic component, the synthesis of higher phenylpolyenals can be accomplished by single and multiple condensation with crotonaldehyde; simplified procedures described by J. Schmitt (1941) are summarized as follows:

Piperidine acetate,
1. $C_6H_5CH=CHCHO$ + $CH_3CH=CHCHO$ $\xrightarrow{70\% \text{ alcohol}}$
   Cinnamaldehyde   Crotonaldehyde

$C_6H_5CH=CHCH=CHCH=CHCHO$ +
7-Phenylheptatrienal
(50%; orange-yellow, m.p. 116°)

$C_6H_5CH=CHCH=CHCH=CHCH=CHCHO$
11-Phenylundecapentaenal
(20%; orange, m.p. 183°)

Piperidine acetate,
benzene
2. $C_6H_5(CH=CH)_5CHO$ + $CH_3CH=CHCHO$ $\xrightarrow[80\%]{}$ $C_6H_5(CH=CH)_7CHO$
                                                                     15-Phenylpentadecahepta-
                                                                     enal (deep red, m.p. 232°)

13.8   Claisen Reaction (1890). — After a brief period at Manchester
(1882–85), Claisen found a place in Baeyer's laboratory at Munich
(1886–91), along with Bamberger, Curtius, Königs, von Pechmann, and Perkin,
Jr. In continuation of the earlier studies, he found (1887) in sodium ethoxide a
superior condensing agent permitting operation in an organic solvent and hence
obviating the large volumes of the original Claisen-Schmidt procedure. For
example, when a mixture of benzaldehyde (10.5 g.) and acetophenone (12 g.)
was treated with 20% sodium ethoxide solution (3 ml.) and let stand for a few
days at winter temperature, benzalacetophenone was obtained in 90% yield.
With this reagent Claisen was able to condense benzaldehyde with ethyl acetate
to give ethyl cinnamate in about 40% yield, but he then found that the reaction
proceeds even better under the influence of metallic sodium and a trace of alcohol

$$C_6H_5CHO + CH_3COOC_2H_5 \xrightarrow[68-74\%]{Na, \, 0-5°} C_6H_5CH=CHCOOC_2H_5$$
                                                         Ethyl cinnamate

at a low temperature, as illustrated for benzaldehyde. The Claisen reaction, condensation of an aromatic aldehyde with an ester, is a useful, high-yield route to
α,β-unsaturated esters rivalling the Perkin route to the corresponding acids.

A novel Claisen condensation has been observed with methyl trityl ketone (**1**),
prepared from benzil ($C_6H_5COCOC_6H_5$) by successive treatment with phenyl
and methyl Grignard reagents, followed by dehydration of the resulting tri-

$$(C_6H_5)_3CCCH_3 \xrightarrow[-(C_6H_5)_3CH]{(C_6H_5)_3C^-} (C_6H_5)_3CCCH_2^- \xrightarrow{(C_6H_5)_3CCCH_3}$$
      (1)   (2)

$$(C_6H_5)_3CCCH_2CCH_3 \rightarrow (C_6H_5)_3CCCH_2CCH_3 + (C_6H_5)_3C^-$$
              $\overset{|}{C(C_6H_5)_3}$
         (3)   (4)

phenylpropanediol (H. D. Zook,[1] 1958). The carbanion (**2**) produced by reaction
of (**1**) with trityl carbanion adds to a second mole of (**1**) to give the enolate anion

[1] Harry D. Zook, b. 1916 Milroy, Pa.; Ph.D. Penn. State Univ. (Whitmore); Penn. State Univ.

(3), which dissociates to the β-diketone (4) and trityl carbanion. Cleavage of (3), in preference to formation of the hydroxy ketone as in an aldol condensation, is attributable to the special stability of the trityl carbanion.

13.9   Ester Condensation (1887). — In 1863 the German chemist A. Geuther attempted to alkylate ethyl acetate with methyl iodide and accidentally discovered ethyl acetoacetate and the acetoacetic ester alkylation reaction (12.44). The reaction involves elimination of the ethoxyl group of one molecule of ester and an α-hydrogen atom of another molecule, with formation of the so-

$$CH_3COOC_2H_5 \;+\; HCH_2CO_2C_2H_5 \xrightarrow{\text{NaOC}_2\text{H}_5} [CH_3CO\bar{C}HCO_2C_2H_5]Na^+$$

$$\xrightarrow[\text{75-76\%}]{\text{HOAc}} CH_3COCH_2CO_2C_2H_5$$

Ethyl acetoacetate

dium enolate. In a modern procedure sodium (1 equiv.) is dissolved in portions in absolute ethanol, ethyl acetate (2 equiv.) is added, and the solution is refluxed for 8 hrs. The resulting solution of enolate is acidified with 33% acetic acid and the product extracted with ether.

E. Frankland and B. F. Duppa (1866) made a few experiments and suggested that the reaction involves an elimination in the sense: $CH_3CO—OC_2H_5 +$ $H—CHNaCO_2C_2H_5$, but the first substantial investigations of the ester condensation reaction were begun in 1887 by Claisen at Munich and by Wislicenus at Würzburg. Claisen discounted the suggestion of Frankland and Duppa and thought that the first step might be addition of sodium ethoxide to the carbonyl group of ethyl acetate. Indeed, a suspension of alcohol-free sodium ethoxide in ethyl benzoate when heated on the steam bath soon set to a solid mass, and after adding ethyl acetate, refluxing the mixture, and acidification, Claisen isolated pure ethyl benzoylacetoacetate. The modern interpretation of the reactions, represented in the following formulation (1) without showing all possible resonance structures, is essentially that suggested by Claisen. Higher esters undergo self-

1. $CH_3CO_2C_2H_5 \xrightarrow{\text{C}_2\text{H}_5\text{O}^-} \bar{C}H_2CO_2C_2H_5 \xrightarrow{\text{C}_6\text{H}_5\text{CO}_2\text{C}_2\text{H}_5}$

$$C_6H_5\overset{\overset{\displaystyle O^-}{|}}{\underset{\underset{\displaystyle OC_2H_5}{|}}{C}}CH_2CO_2C_2H_5 \xrightarrow{-\text{C}_2\text{H}_5\text{OH}} C_6H_5\overset{\overset{\displaystyle O^-}{|}}{C}=CHCO_2C_2H_5 \xrightarrow{\text{H}^+}$$

$$C_6H_5COCH_2CO_2C_2H_5$$

Ethyl benzoylacetate

condensation less readily than ethyl acetate, but a compensating expedient is to remove the alcohol formed by periodic distillation (McElvain,[1] 1937).

The initial reactions formulated are reversible, but formation of the resonance-stabilized sodioenolate favors completion of the condensation. Ethyl isobutyrate, having but one α-hydrogen, cannot form a comparable enolate and it fails to undergo self-condensation under the influence of sodium ethoxide. However,

---

[1] Samuel M. McElvain, b. 1897 Duquoin, Ill.; Ph.D. Illinois (Adams); Univ. Wisconsin

Hauser found (1937) that the reaction can be effected by using the very strong base triphenylmethylsodium, trityl sodium (2).

2. $(CH_3)_2CHCO_2C_2H_5 \xrightarrow{(C_6H_5)_3\bar{C}Na^+} (CH_3)_2\bar{C}CO_2C_2H_5(Na^+) + (C_6H_5)_3CH$

$(CH_3)_2\bar{C}CO_2C_2H_5(Na^+) + (CH_3)_2CHCO_2C_2H_5 \longrightarrow$

$(CH_3)_2CHCOC(CH_3)_2CO_2C_2H_5 + C_2H_5OH$

Mixed condensation of two esters having active hydrogens can lead to four products and is seldom satisfactory. Wislicenus noted, however, that diethyl oxalate has no α-hydrogen, and found (1887) that it condenses readily with ethyl acetate to form diethyl oxaloacetate, $CH_2(CO_2C_2H_5)COCO_2C_2H_5$. An example for illustration is the condensation of diethyl oxalate with ethyl propionate (3). Wislicenus (1894) found that oxalyl esters undergo smooth decarbonylation

3. 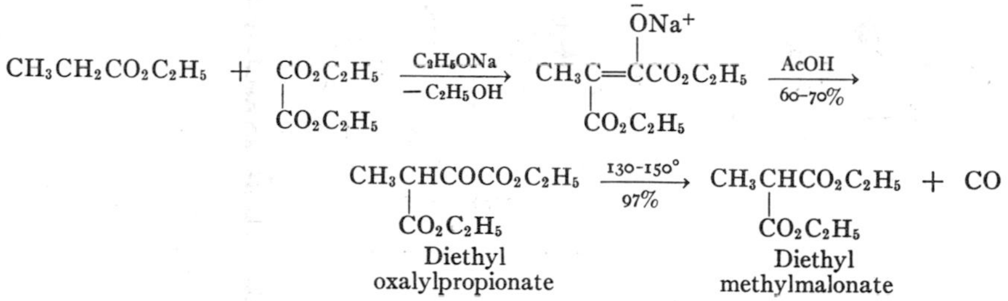 $CH_3CH_2CO_2C_2H_5 + \underset{CO_2C_2H_5}{\overset{CO_2C_2H_5}{|}} \xrightarrow[-C_2H_5OH]{C_2H_5ONa} \underset{CO_2C_2H_5}{\overset{\overset{\bar{O}Na^+}{|}}{CH_3C=CCO_2C_2H_5}} \xrightarrow[60-70\%]{AcOH}$

$\underset{\underset{\text{Diethyl}}{CO_2C_2H_5}}{\overset{CH_3CHCOCO_2C_2H_5}{|}} \xrightarrow[97\%]{130-150°} \underset{\underset{\text{Diethyl}}{CO_2C_2H_5}}{\overset{CH_3CHCO_2C_2H_5}{|}} + CO$

oxalylpropionate   methylmalonate

at moderate temperatures (compare 11.9), and hence these readily available esters provide a convenient route to monosubstituted malonic esters. Thus the oxalyl ester of the example cited affords methylmalonic ester in high yield. Preparation of pure monoalkyl derivatives by alkylation of malonic ester presents the difficulty of separation from unalkylated and dialkylated ester. Phenylmalonic ester, available only recently by direct substitution (25.17) can be obtained easily through the oxalyl ester (H. Schmid, 1959).

Condensation of diethyl oxalate with diethyl succinate, a 1,4-diester (4), provides another synthetic variation (Wislicenus, 1895). Acid hydrolysis of the

4. 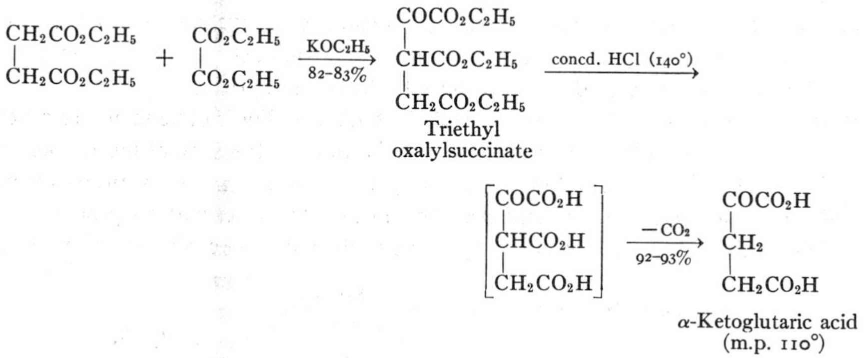 $\underset{CH_2CO_2C_2H_5}{\overset{CH_2CO_2C_2H_5}{|}} + \underset{CO_2C_2H_5}{\overset{CO_2C_2H_5}{|}} \xrightarrow[82-83\%]{KOC_2H_5} \underset{\underset{CH_2CO_2C_2H_5}{CH_2CO_2C_2H_5}}{\overset{\overset{COCO_2C_2H_5}{|}}{CHCO_2C_2H_5}} \xrightarrow{\text{concd. HCl (140°)}}$

Triethyl
oxalylsuccinate

$\begin{bmatrix} COCO_2H \\ | \\ CHCO_2H \\ | \\ CH_2CO_2H \end{bmatrix} \xrightarrow[92-93\%]{-CO_2} \underset{\underset{CH_2CO_2H}{CH_2}}{\overset{\overset{COCO_2H}{|}}{CH_2}}$

α-Ketoglutaric acid
(m.p. 110°)

condensation product gives a triacid in which the central carboxyl group is β to a keto group and β to a carboxyl group, and the substance loses carbon dioxide during hydrolysis and affords α-ketoglutaric acid.

Ninhydrin, a reagent useful in paper chromatography, can be prepared by a reaction sequence starting with a double ester condensation of dimethyl phthalate with ethyl acetate under the influence of sodium to give the yellow enolate II (Wislicenus, 1888). Ester interchange occurs during the process and the salt is largely the methyl ester. When the enolate is heated with dilute hydrochloric

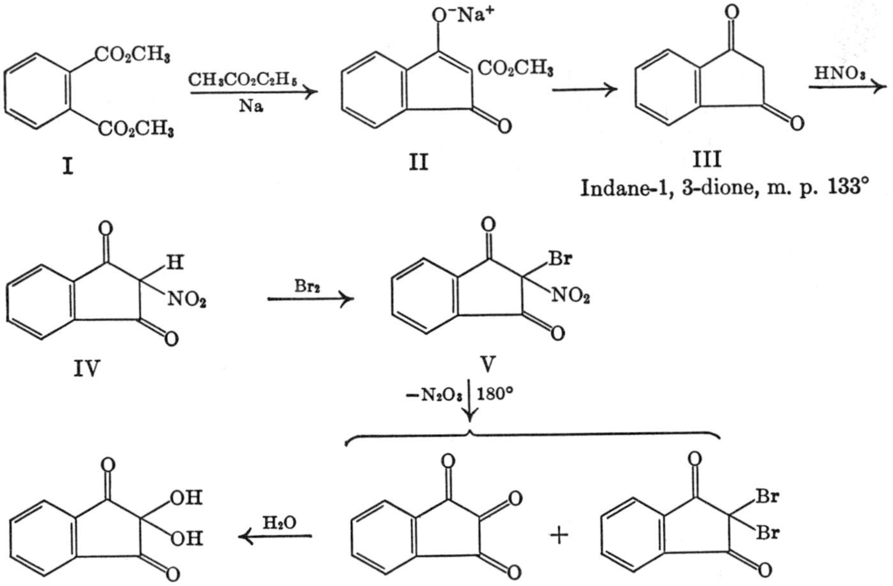

Indane-1, 3-dione, m. p. 133°

VI
Ninhydrin, dec. 125°

VII
Red, m. p. 180°

acid, the β-keto acid initially formed loses carbon dioxide and gives indane-1,3-dione (III). This substance is nitrated and then brominated, and the bromonitro diketone V is heated for a few minutes in o-dichlorobenzene at 180°, when it undergoes decomposition to give equal parts of the trione VII and the dibromoketone VIII. The solution on cooling deposits large red needles of the trione, and VIII is retained in the mother liquor. Red indane-1,2,3-trione on crystallization from water affords the colorless hydrate, ninhydrin.

13.10   Condensation of Esters with Ketones. — The condensation of an ester with a ketone usually is successful only in the case of methyl ketones, and even here yields are low. Thus *Organic Syntheses* reports preparation of acetylacetone by the ester condensation (1) and by an acylation procedure due to Meerwein (2); the latter is clearly to be preferred. The condensation of ethyl

1. $CH_3CO_2C_2H_5 + CH_3COCH_3 \xrightarrow[38-45\%]{NaOC_2H_5;\ H_2SO_4}$

$CH_3COCH_2COCH_3$

2. $(CH_3CO)_2O + CH_3COCH_3 \xrightarrow[80-85°]{BF_3}$ Acetylacetone

formate with acetone, first investigated by Claisen (1888), is of interest even though the yield is low. Ester condensation in ether–ethanol gives acetylacetalde-

$$HCOOC_2H_5 \; + \; CH_3COCH_3 \xrightarrow{\quad NaOC_2H_5;\; AcOH \quad} O=\overset{\overset{\displaystyle H}{|}}{C}CH_2COCH_3$$

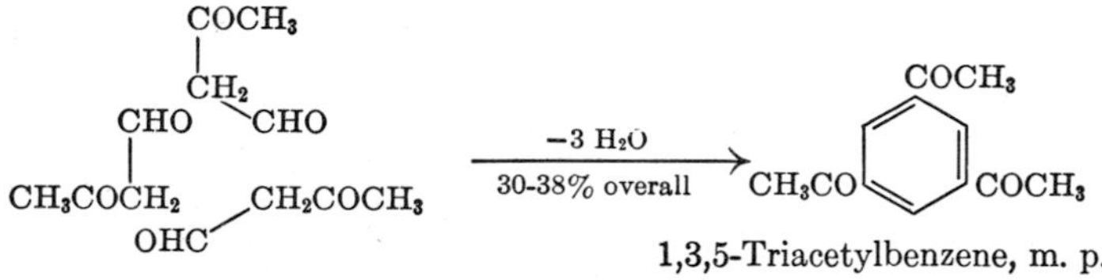

1,3,5-Triacetylbenzene, m. p. 163°

hyde enolate, which is extracted with water. The solution is made acid with acetic acid and warmed at 50° to effect trimerization, and on cooling 1,3,5-triacetylbenzene separates in shiny white needles.

Dimedone, 5,5-dimethylcyclohexane-1,3-dione, is made efficiently by base-catalyzed condensation of malonic ester with mesityl oxide (Vorländer,[1] 1897). Probably a first step of Michael addition (13.14) to the unsaturated ketone is followed by an ester condensation closing the ring. The resulting enolate is

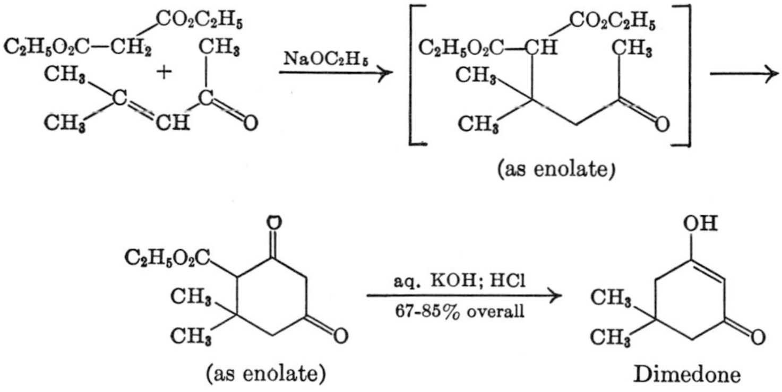

heated with aqueous potassium hydroxide to hydrolyze the ester group, and on acidification the β-keto acid loses carbon dioxide and affords dimedone.

13.11   **Acylation of Acetoacetic Ester.** — Claisen (Aachen, 1896) developed an efficient method for the C-benzoylation of acetoacetic ester and for conversion of the product to ethyl benzoylacetate. The *Organic Syntheses* adapta-

$$CH_3COCH_2CO_2C_2H_5 \xrightarrow[-1/2\,H_2]{Na,\; C_6H_6} [CH_3CO\bar{C}HCO_2C_2H_5]Na^+ \xrightarrow[63-75\%]{C_6H_5COCl}$$

$$\underset{\text{Ethyl benzoylacetoacetate}}{\overset{\overset{\displaystyle COC_6H_5}{|}}{CH_3COCHCO_2C_2H_5}} \xrightarrow[77-78\%]{NH_3,\; H_2O,\; NH_4Cl,\; 42°} \underset{\text{Ethyl benzoylacetate}}{C_6H_5COCH_2CO_2C_2H_5} \; + \; CH_3CONH_2$$

---

[1] Daniel Vorländer, 1867–1941; b. Eupen (Aachen); Ph.D. Halle (Tiemann); Univ. Halle; *Ber.*, **76A,** 41 (1943)

tion of the reaction sequence is shown in the formulation. The sodium enolate of the β-keto ester is prepared by refluxing with sodium in benzene (24 hrs.) and the salt is then refluxed with benzoyl chloride (8 hrs.). The ethyl benzoylaceto-acetate is collected and cleaved to ethyl benzoylacetate and acetamide by reaction, in 10-g. portions, with aqueous ammonia–ammonium chloride.

13.12   Stobbe Reaction. — Hans Stobbe (Leipzig, 1893) thought it of interest to see if condensation of ethyl acetate with diethyl succinate would result in double ester condensation (Claisen) or cyclization to a diketo ester (Wislicenus). He added a mixture of acetone and diethyl succinate to a suspension of alcohol-free sodium ethoxide (2 equivalents) in absolute ether, let the mixture stand for several days, and on working up the product (after saponification) was surprised to find it to be teraconic acid, $(CH_3)_2C{=}C(CO_2H)CH_2CO_2H$

$$(CH_3)_2C{=}O \;+\; \overset{\displaystyle CO_2C_2H_5}{\overset{|}{CH_2CH_2CO_2C_2H_5}} \;+\; KOC(CH_3)_3 \;\xrightarrow[\;92\%\;]{\text{Refl. o.5 hr. in } t\text{-BuOH}}$$

$$\overset{\displaystyle CO_2C_2H_5}{\overset{|}{(CH_3)_2C{=}CCH_2CO_2K}} \;+\; C_2H_5OH \;+\; (CH_3)_3COH$$

(m.p. 161°). Stobbe's yield was only 53%, but the same reaction conducted by modern techniques affords teraconic acid (isolated as diester) in high yield. As the equation shows, the reaction requires only one equivalent of alkoxide and affords the salt of the diacid half ester. The reaction is now known to be widely applicable to aldehydes and ketones, aliphatic and aromatic, saturated and α,β-unsaturated, and to diketones, keto esters, and cyano ketones. W. S. Johnson (1945) found many synthetic uses for the Stobbe reaction. For example, γ-2-naphthylvaleric acid can be prepared from 2-acetonaphthalene by Stobbe condensation, decarboxylation (with lactonization), and hydrogenation in alkaline solution:

$$\overset{\displaystyle CH_3}{\overset{|}{C_{10}H_7C{=}O}} \;+\; \overset{\displaystyle CH_2CO_2C_2H_5}{\overset{|}{CH_2CO_2C_2H_5}} \;\xrightarrow{KOC(CH_3)_3}\; \overset{\displaystyle CH_3}{\underset{\displaystyle CO_2C_2H_5}{\overset{|}{\underset{|}{C_{10}H_7C{=}CCH_2CO_2H}}}} \;\xrightarrow{HCl-HOAc}$$

$$\overset{\displaystyle CH_3}{\overset{|}{C_{10}H_7CCH_2CH_2CO}} \;\xrightarrow[\substack{74\%\\ \text{overall}}]{\substack{H_2,\ Cu-Cr,\\ NaOH}}\; \overset{\displaystyle CH_3}{\overset{|}{C_{10}H_7CHCH_2CH_2CO_2H}}$$
$$\underset{\displaystyle O}{\rule{1.6cm}{0.4pt}} \qquad\qquad \gamma\text{-2-Naphthylvaleric acid}$$

Sodium methoxide is too weak a condensing agent; sodium ethoxide is stronger but gives rise to oxidation-reduction complications. Potassium t-butoxide does not have this disadvantage and is considerably more powerful than sodium ethoxide and affords better products in higher yield and shorter time. Some reduction occurs when the t-butoxide is used in combination with diethyl succinate. This difficulty is obviated by use of dimethyl succinate, but a shortcoming of the dimethyl ester is its susceptibility to self-condensation to dimethyl cyclohexane-1,4-dione-2,5-dicarboxylate. Use of di-t-butyl succinate largely obviates these difficulties; reduction is impossible and self-condensation is negligible. However, the Stobbe condensation itself is retarded by use of this hindered ester, and longer reaction periods are required. Use of this ester in combination with sodium hydride as condensing agent offer promise (solvent: benzene). The reagent is easy to use, powerful, and permits following the progress of the reaction by measuring the hydrogen evolved: two moles of gas for each half ester salt formed.

Although the carbonyl component can be varied over a wide range, the Stobbe reaction is specific to esters of succinic acid, just as the Fittig reaction is specific to succinic anhydride. Benzophenone condenses with diethyl succinate to give $(C_6H_5)_2C=C(CO_2C_2H_5)CH_2CO_2H$ in 90% yield, but under the same conditions it fails to react with ethyl or t-butyl acetate. The methylene group of diethyl malonate, $CH_2(CO_2C_2H_5)_2$, is more reactive to most reagents than that of a succinic ester, but diethyl malonate fails to condense with benzophenone. These facts, as well as the analogy to the Fittig reaction, support Stobbe's postulate that a paraconic ester is an essential intermediate; by stopping the reaction after a brief reaction period, Stobbe was able to isolate paraconic esters, which indeed are cleaved by alkoxide to unsaturated half-esters. The sequence of events appears to start with the aldol-like abstraction of an α-hydrogen from the diester to

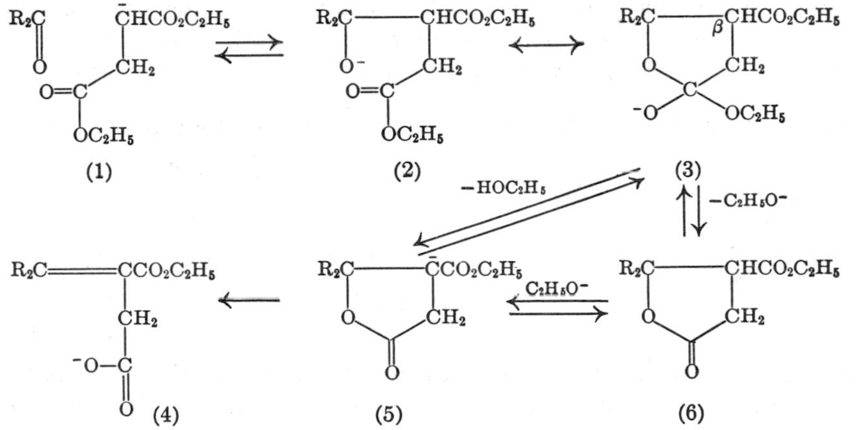

form the carbanion (1), which attacks the carbonyl component in the usual way to give the hybrid anion (2) ↔ (3). The intermediate (3) can expel ethoxide ion to give the paraconic acid derivative (6), or it can expel ethanol to give the carbanion (5). These reversible steps are followed by the irreversible conversion of carbanion (5) into the unsaturated half-ester anion (4).

13.13   **Dieckmann[1] Reaction** (1894). — At Baeyer's suggestion Dieckmann at Munich investigated the ester condensation of diesters capable of cyclizing to five- and six-membered β-keto esters. He found that diethyl adipate and the next higher homolog do indeed afford cyclic esters in good yield. The cyclic β-keto ester shown in the example has an α-hydrogen replaceable by alkyl through the sodio enolate. Dieckmann condensation can be effected with sodium, sodium ethoxide, sodium hydride, or potassium t-butoxide (in xylene, see 15.28).

[1] Walter Dieckmann, 1869–1925; b. Hamburg, Germany; Ph.D. Munich (Bamberger); Univ. Munich

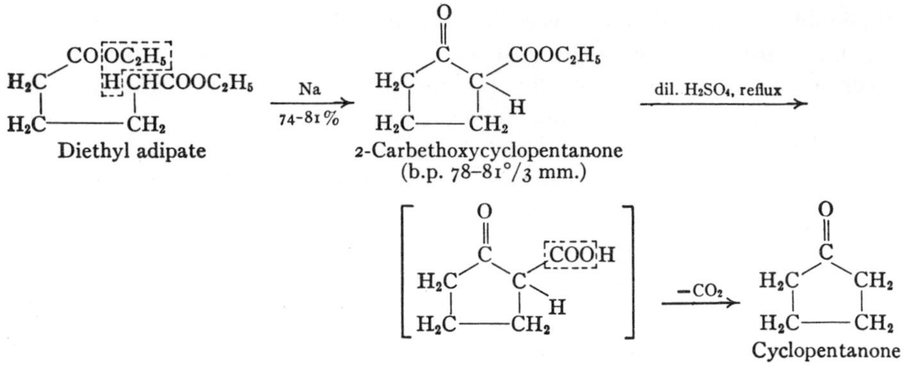

Diethyl adipate → (Na, 74–81%) → 2-Carbethoxycyclopentanone (b.p. 78–81°/3 mm.) → (dil. H₂SO₄, reflux) → [intermediate] → (−CO₂) → Cyclopentanone

13.14   Michael Reaction. — In 1887, when activity in Germany on the development of new synthetic methods was at a peak, German-trained Arthur Michael at Tufts University wrote "I shall describe in this paper a synthetical method of building up carbon derivatives by the direct union of carbon and sodium to unsaturated carbons." In the first of several examples of the new reaction, Michael added diethyl malonate to a solution of one equivalent of sodium ethoxide in ethanol, when sodiomalonic ester soon separated, and then added one equivalent of ethyl cinnamate. The precipitate gradually dissolved, and on

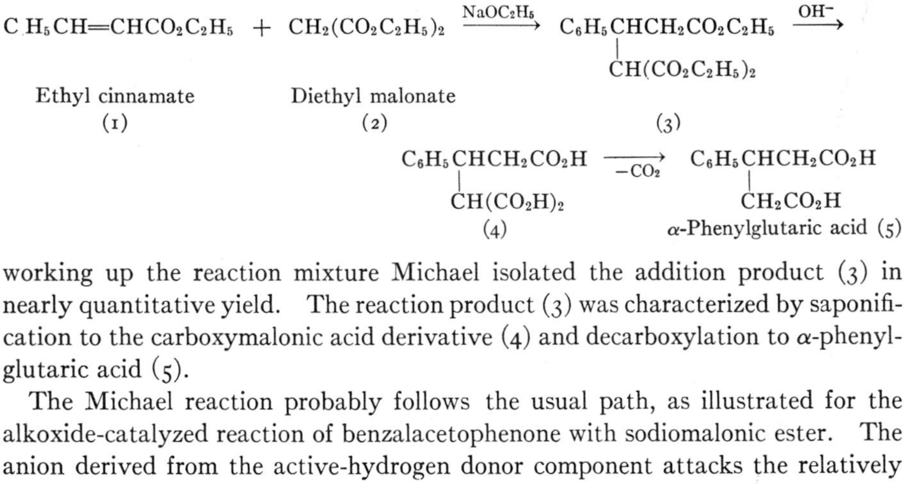

$$C_6H_5CH{=}CHCO_2C_2H_5 \; + \; CH_2(CO_2C_2H_5)_2 \xrightarrow{\text{NaOC}_2\text{H}_5} \underset{\underset{\text{(3)}}{CH(CO_2C_2H_5)_2}}{C_6H_5CHCH_2CO_2C_2H_5} \xrightarrow{\text{OH}^-}$$

Ethyl cinnamate   Diethyl malonate
(1)   (2)

$$\underset{\underset{\text{(4)}}{CH(CO_2H)_2}}{C_6H_5CHCH_2CO_2H} \xrightarrow[-CO_2]{} \underset{\text{CH}_2\text{CO}_2\text{H}}{C_6H_5CHCH_2CO_2H}$$

α-Phenylglutaric acid (5)

working up the reaction mixture Michael isolated the addition product (3) in nearly quantitative yield. The reaction product (3) was characterized by saponification to the carboxymalonic acid derivative (4) and decarboxylation to α-phenylglutaric acid (5).

The Michael reaction probably follows the usual path, as illustrated for the alkoxide-catalyzed reaction of benzalacetophenone with sodiomalonic ester. The anion derived from the active-hydrogen donor component attacks the relatively

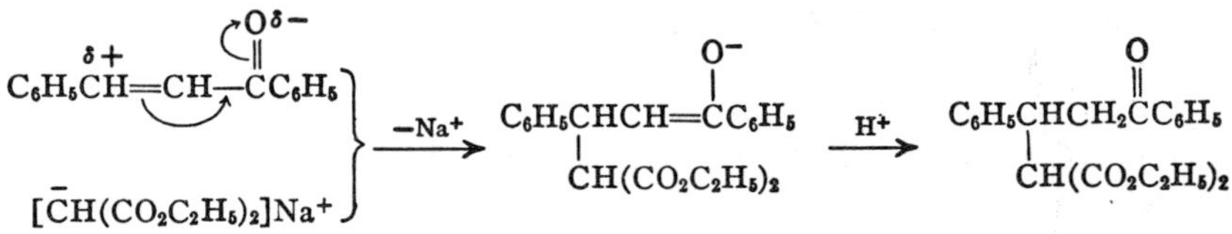

positive carbon atom of the acceptor system to produce an enolate anion, which abstracts a proton from ethanol to give the product and regenerate ethoxide ion. Presumably the rate-determining step is that in which a new carbon–carbon bond is established. Alkyl and, particularly, aryl groups in the α- or β-position of the acceptor inhibit the reaction.

The Michael reaction is widely applicable. Donor components include active-hydrogen esters, ketones, nitriles, and nitro compounds. The acceptor component can be an α,β-unsaturated ester, aldehyde, or ketone. A few hydrocarbons react, for example, dimethyltetraacetylene (Bohlmann, 1957):

$$CH_3(C{\equiv}C)_3C{\equiv}CCH_3 \xrightarrow{CH_2(CO_2C_2H_5)_2} CH_3(C{\equiv}C)_3CH{=}CCH_3$$
$$\underset{CH(CO_2C_2H_5)_2}{|}$$

In compounds containing two double bonds conjugated with a carbonyl group, 1,6-addition generally predominates over 1,4-addition. Thus methyl sorbate adds malonic ester to give chiefly the 1,6-product.

$$\underset{\text{Methyl sorbate}}{CH_3CH{=}CHCH{=}CHCO_2CH_3} \xrightarrow{CH_2(CO_2C_2H_5)_2}$$

$$\begin{cases} CH_3CHCH{=}CHCH_2CO_2CH_3 \ (72\%) \\ \quad\underset{CH(CO_2C_2H_5)_2}{|} \\ CH_3CH{=}CHCHCH_2CO_2CH_3 \ (8\%) \\ \qquad\qquad\underset{CH(CO_2C_2H_5)_2}{|} \end{cases}$$

A method introduced by R. Robinson (1937) of great value for the synthesis of carbocyclic systems combines the Michael reaction with aldolization. Methyl

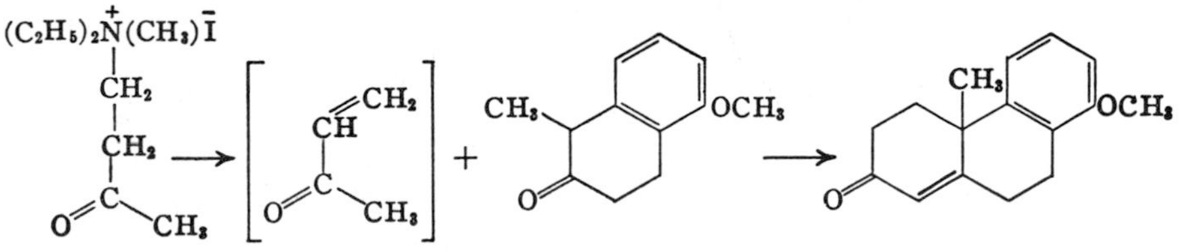

$(C_2H_5)_2\overset{+}{N}(CH_3)\bar{I}$

I   II   III   IV

vinyl ketone (II) is generated *in situ* from the Mannich base methiodide I (prepared from acetone, diethylamine hydrochloride, and formaldehyde, followed by reaction with methyl iodide). A solution of the methiodide, which need not be isolated, is condensed with the active-hydrogen component in the presence of a base ($NaOC_2H_5$, $NaNH_2$, t-BuOK). Michael addition is followed by aldolization and dehydration.

Michael addition can be reversed by pyrolysis. Cornforth[1] (1957) employed two reverse Michael reactions in degrading cholesterol prepared by biosynthesis from $C^{14}H_3CO_2H$ and from $CH_3C^{14}O_2H$ with the objective of determining the extent of isotope incorporation in each of the twenty-seven carbon atoms. In one,

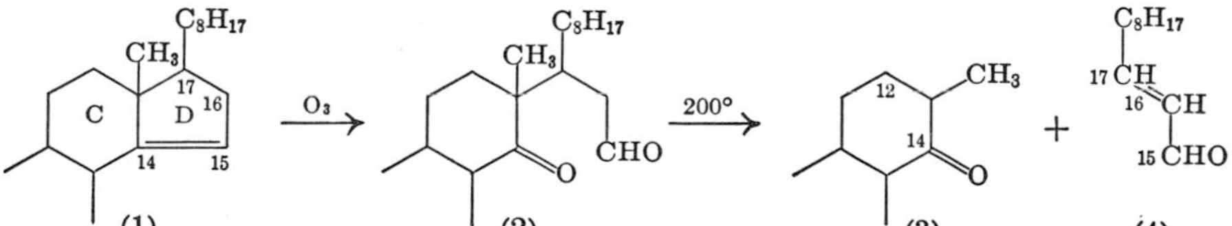

(1)   (2)   (3)   (4)

[1] John Warcup Cornforth, b. 1917 Australia; Ph.D. Oxford (Robinson); Nat. Inst. Med. Res.

cholesteryl acetate was transformed into the isomer (1) having the double bond at the 14,15-position in ring D. Ozonization gave the ketoaldehyde (2), which on pyrolysis in cyclohexane at 200° gave the ketone (3) and the unsaturated aldehyde (4). Further degradation of the fragments revealed the origins, methyl or carboxyl, of carbon atoms 12, 14, 15, 16, and 17.

13.15   Cyanoethylation. — A Michael reaction of a specialized type involves addition of an active-hydrogen compound to acrylonitrile in the presence of a basic catalyst. Primary and secondary amines function as their own catalysts; for example, a mixture of diethylamine and acrylonitrile is heated briefly

$$(C_2H_5)_2NH \ + \ \overset{\delta+}{CH_2}\!\!=\!\!CH\!-\!\overset{\delta-}{C}\!\!\equiv\!\!N \xrightarrow[97\%]{} (C_2H_5)_2NCH_2CH_2CN$$

and let stand; the yield of β-diethylaminopropionitrile is nearly quantitative. Some of the many compound types which can be cyanoethylated are: alcohols, mercaptans, aldehydes, ketones, malonic ester, nitromethane, bromoform. Amines generally react more readily than compounds of other types. A metal alkoxide can be used as catalyst for condensation of neutral components, but trimethylbenzylammonium hydroxide (Triton B) is favored because of its solubility in organic solvents. Cyanoethylation usually can be continued until all available active hydrogens are used up.

13.16   Knoevenagel[1] Reaction (1898). — Aldehydes, both aliphatic and aromatic, condense readily with malonic acid and other compounds having a methylene group activated by carbonyl, nitrile, or nitro groups under basic catalysis. In the condensation with malonic acid the initially formed unsaturated malonic acid undergoes decarboxylation during the condensation. Knoeve-

$$ArCHO + CH_2(CO_2H)_2 \xrightarrow{\text{Base}} [ArCH\!\!=\!\!C(CO_2H)_2] \xrightarrow{-CO_2} ArCH\!\!=\!\!CHCO_2H$$

nagel used ammonia or a primary or secondary amine to effect condensation, but pyridine, or pyridine with a trace of piperidine, is more satisfactory. With the latter combination piperonal, $C_7H_5O_2CHO$, is converted in 85–90% yield to β-piperonylacrylic acid, $C_7H_5O_2CH\!\!=\!\!CHCO_2H$; crotonaldehyde similarly affords sorbic acid (m.p. 134°), $CH_3CH\!\!=\!\!CHCH\!\!=\!\!CHCO_2H$ (30% yield). If such condensation is carried out in acetic acid solution rather than in the presence of a base the unsaturated malonic acid sometimes can be isolated.

Variations in the general reaction are illustrated by procedures for the preparation of a nitrile and of a nitro compound.

$$C_6H_5CHO \ + \ C_6H_5CH_2CN \xrightarrow[83-91\%]{C_2H_5ONa,\ C_2H_5OH} C_6H_5CH\!\!=\!\!C(CN)C_6H_5$$

$$\alpha\text{-Phenylcinnamonitrile}$$

$$C_6H_5CHO \ + \ CH_3NO_2 \xrightarrow[80-83\%]{\substack{\text{1. Aq. NaOH, 15°} \\ \text{2. HCl}}} C_6H_5CH\!\!=\!\!CHNO_2$$

$$\beta\text{-Nitrostyrene}$$

---

[1] Emil Knoevenagel, 1865–1921; b. Linden/Hannover, Germany; Ph.D. Göttingen; Univ. Heidelberg

13.17   The Darzens[1] condensation (1904) is exemplified by the addition of ethyl chloroacetate to the carbonyl group of acetophenone under catalysis by a strong base (potassium *t*-butoxide is particularly effective, as it is in the Stobbe condensation). The initial chlorohydrin (1) cyclizes irreversibly to

$$C_6H_5\overset{\overset{\text{CH}_3}{|}}{C}=O \ + \ ClCH_2CO_2C_2H_5 \ \underset{\rightleftarrows}{\overset{NaNH_2}{\longrightarrow}} \ C_6H_5\overset{\overset{\text{CH}_3}{|}}{\underset{\underset{\text{OH}}{|}}{C}}-\overset{\overset{}{}}{\underset{\underset{\text{Cl}}{|}}{C}}HCH_2CO_2C_2H_5 \ \xrightarrow{63\%}$$

(1)

$$C_6H_5\overset{\overset{\text{CH}_3}{|}}{C}-CHCO_2C_2H_5 \ \xrightarrow{NaOR;\ H^+} \ \ \ \ \xrightarrow{-CO_2,\ -H^+}$$
(2)   (3)

$$C_6H_5\overset{\overset{\text{CH}_3}{|}}{\underset{\underset{\text{OH}}{|}}{C}}=CH \ \longrightarrow \ C_6H_5\overset{\overset{\text{CH}_3}{|}}{C}HC\overset{H}{\underset{O}{}}$$

(4)   (5)

the α,β-epoxy ester (2), described as a glycidic ester (ethyl β-methyl-β-phenyl-glycidate). The ester group is saponified and the glycidic acid (3) warmed with dilute mineral acid to effect oxide cleavage and decarboxylation to the aldehyde (5).

Epoxidation of α,β-unsaturated esters by usual techniques is seldom successful, but glycidic esters have been prepared with peroxytrifluoroacetic acid in the presence of disodium hydrogen phosphate buffer (W. D. Emmons, 1955) and with pure peracetic acid (5.17) in ethyl acetate or acetone (D. L. MacPeek, 1959).

13.18   Isonitroso (or Oximido) Derivatives. — Victor Meyer (Zurich, 1883) dissolved ethyl acetoacetate in one equivalent of very dilute potassium hydroxide in the cold, added one equivalent of potassium nitrite, and then acidified the solution with sulfuric acid with cooling. After a brief reaction period, he made the solution alkaline again, removed unchanged acetoacetic ester (weakly acidic) by ether extraction, acidified the aqueous layer and by ether extraction isolated the acid reaction product, ethyl isonitrosoacetoacetate (an oxime). The

$$CH_3COCH_2CO_2C_2H_5 \ \xrightarrow{HNO_2} \ CH_3\overset{\overset{O}{||}}{C}-\overset{\overset{NOH}{||}}{C}CO_2C_2H_5$$

Ethyl isonitrosoacetoacetate,
m.p. 54°

$\downarrow$ Saponif.

$$CH_3COCH_3 \ \xrightarrow[HCl]{(CH_3)_2CHCH_2ONO} \ CH_3COCH=NOH \ \xrightarrow{H^+} \ CH_3COCHO$$

Isonitrosoacetone   Methylglyoxal
(m.p. 69°)

[1] Georges Darzens, 1886–1954; b. Moscow (French parentage); M.D. École Polytechnique, Paris; École Polytechnique; *Bull. Soc. Chim.*, 169 (1955).

product, a colorless oil, had the correct analysis but several batches failed to crystallize, even at $-25°$. Then a sample prepared several months earlier was observed to contain crystals, and when a seed crystal was rubbed into a fresh batch of liquid the entire product could be obtained crystalline in 1–2 days. Indeed the compound forms unusually well-formed, centimeter-thick prisms. For further exploration of an easily prepared new class of compounds which "durch Krystallizationsfähigkeit ausgezeichnet sind," Meyer assigned the problem to a student.

The colorless isonitroso compound forms a yellow solution in alkali, and when the solution is warmed and then acidified, carbon dioxide is lost and the product is isonitrosoacetone, a colorless solid soluble in alkali (yellow color). A few years later Claisen (Munich, 1887) found that the latter substance is obtained more easily by warming a mixture of acetone, isoamyl nitrite, and hydrochloric acid. The reaction is fairly general and provides a route to α-aminoketones (zinc–acetic acid). Another use is illustrated by the acid hydrolysis of isonitrosoacetone to methylglyoxal, a mobile yellow liquid which when heated partly boils at $72°$ and partly polymerizes.

Nitrite condensation is illustrated further by the preparation of isonitrosopropiophenone (1-phenylpropane-1,2-dione-2-oxime). Methyl nitrite is generated

$$C_6H_5COCH_2CH_3 \xrightarrow[65-68\%]{CH_3ONO,\ HCl} C_6H_5CO\overset{\overset{\displaystyle NOH}{\|}}{C}CH_3$$

Propiophenone   Isonitrosopropiophenone
(m.p. 113°)

$$\downarrow\ 10\%\ H_2SO_4\ \big|\ 66-70\%$$

$$C_6H_5COCOCH_3$$

1-Phenylpropane-1,2-dione
(b.p. 115°, 20 mm.)

by dropping dilute sulfuric acid into a mixture of sodium nitrite, methanol, and water, and the gaseous ester is passed into a stirred solution of propiophenone in ether while hydrogen chloride is being passed in through a second addition tube. After several hours, the ethereal solution is extracted with alkali as long as the extracts are yellow; acidification gives a solid product which forms snow-white crystals from toluene. Steam distillation of a mixture of this isonitroso compound with 10% sulfuric acid affords 1-phenylpropane-1,2-dione (acetylbenzoyl), a yellow liquid.

A. Treibs[1] and D. Dinelli (1935) made several attempts to convert cyclohexanone into the monoisonitroso derivative but obtained only the di derivative. Application of the Victor Meyer route solved the problem: a solution of 4 g. of cyclohexanone-2-carboxylic acid in 4 ml. of acetic acid and 6 ml. of water (or in 10 ml. of acetic acid) was cooled at 5–10° during dropwise addition of aqueous sodium nitrite; each drop caused evolution of carbon dioxide. The next intermediate required, 2-aminocyclohexanone, when produced by reduction with zinc dust and

---

[1] Alfred Treibs, b. 1899 Oberstein, Rheinland; Dr. Ing. Techn. Hochschule Munich (Hans Fischer); Techn. Hochschule Munich

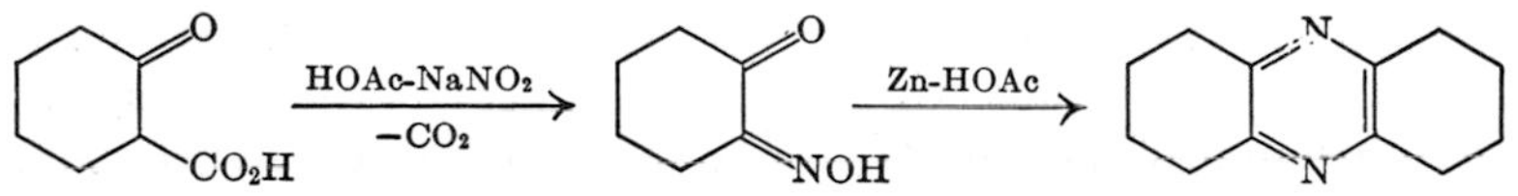

Octahydrophenazine (m. p. 108°)

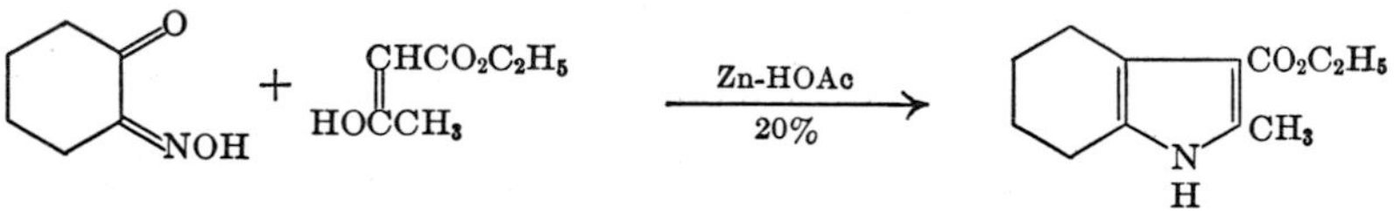

2-Methyl-3-carbethoxy-
tetrahydroindole, m. p. 134°

acetic acid condenses to octahydrophenazine. However, the amine was required for condensation with ethyl acetoacetate, and when the reduction was conducted in the presence of this reagent the desired indole synthesis was realized.

13.19   Fulvenes. — Thiele[1] (Munich, 1900), curious to know if the activating effect of the two double bonds of the system $C{=}CCH_2C{=}C$ would be comparable to the effect of a single carbonyl group, decided to investigate cyclopentadiene (1), which was already known to be acidic enough to form a sodio

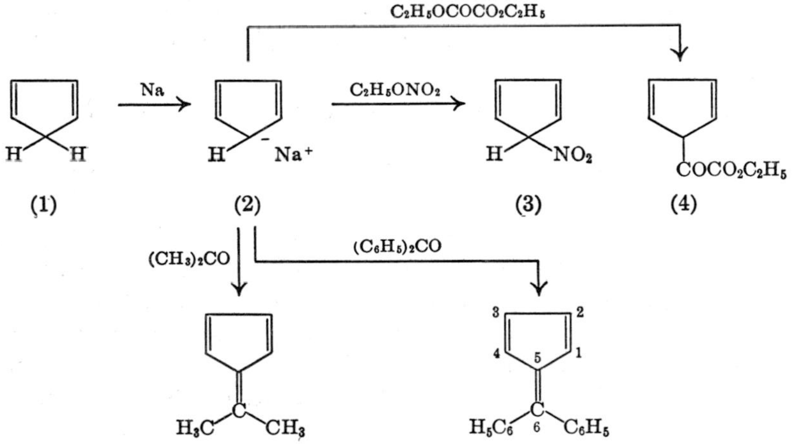

derivative (2). He found that the hydrocarbon indeed enters into some reactions characteristic of ketones: the sodio derivative reacts with ethyl nitrite to form an oximido (isonitroso) derivative, isolated as a dimer; it reacts with ethyl nitrate to form a salt of the nitro derivative (3); condensation with diethyl oxalate gives the oxalyl ester (4). Thiele also observed that in the presence of sodium ethoxide cyclopentadiene condenses with acetone to form the orange hydrocarbon (5) and with benzophenone to give the hydrocarbon (6), which crystallizes in deep red prisms. Since the parent hydrocarbon is yellow (see below), Thiele named it fulvene (L. *fulvus*, yellow); the numbering system now employed is shown in

[1] Johannes Thiele, 1848–1937; b. Ratibon, Germany; Ph.D. Halle; Univ. Munich, Strasbourg; *Ber.*, **60A**, 75 (1927)

formula (6) for 6,6-diphenylfulvene. Cyclopentadiene has a weak absorption maximum at 238.5 mμ; fulvenes are characterized by a strong band at about 270 mμ and a somewhat weaker band at 365 mμ, corresponding to the visible color. Fulvenes are highly reactive, easily polymerized, subject to autoxidation, and in general very susceptible to attack by free radicals (J. L. Kice and W. E. Parham[1]). They can function in the Diels-Alder reaction both as the diene and as the dienophile.

On reaction of cyclopentadiene with formaldehyde, Thiele obtained a yellow oil which rapidly polymerized. Fulvene prepared by his method was later found stable enough in dilute solution for spectrographic characterization, and this technique served for identification of fulvene formed in minute amount on irradiation of benzene (J. M. Blair, 1957). The yellow solution containing 0.1 g. of fulvene/l. codistilled with benzene through a 10-plate column, but the concentration could be increased five-fold by fractional freezing.

Although Thiele's discovery of a reaction of ketones with a reagent that replaces the carbonyl oxygen by the $=CR_2$ group has led to no practical synthetic uses, it is an interesting precursor of the very useful reaction described in the next section.

13.20   Wittig[2] Reaction. — G. Wittig (1954) discovered a widely applicable method for the replacement of the carbonyl oxygen atom by a methylene group, for example:

$$(C_6H_5)_2C=O \quad + \quad (C_6H_5)_3P=CH_2 \quad \xrightarrow{84\%} \quad (C_6H_5)_2C=CH_2 \quad + \quad (C_6H_5)_3PO$$

| Benzophenone | Triphenylphos-phinemethylene | 1,1-Diphenyl-ethylene | Triphenyl-phosphine oxide |

Triphenylphosphinemethylene, the simplest member of the series, is a crystalline yellow solid (m.p. 79°), but since it is unstable to air and moisture it is generated in solution in the presence of the carbonyl component by the following method. A mixture of triphenylphosphine (Metal and Thermite Corp.) and methyl bromide on standing for a few days deposits crystals of methyltriphenylphosphonium bromide (m.p. 229°). When this salt is dehydrohalogenated by treatment with a

$$(C_6H_5)_3P: \quad + \quad CH_3Br \rightarrow \quad (C_6H_5)_3\overset{+}{P}CH_3(\overset{-}{Br}) \quad \xrightarrow{C_6H_5Li}$$

| Triphenylphosphine | | Methyltriphenylphosphonium bromide |

$$(C_6H_5)_3P=CH_2 \quad \leftrightarrow \quad (C_6H_5)_3P^+-\overset{-}{C}H_2$$

(a) methylene   (b) ylide

base, usually phenyllithium in dry ether under nitrogen, the product is a resonance hybrid of the triphenylphosphinemethylene (a) and the ylide (b). The formation of this highly reactive reagent is attributable to the ability of phosphorus to accommodate an expanded outer shell of ten electrons. When the ethereal solution

[1] William E. Parham, b. 1922 Denison, Texas; Ph.D. Illinois (Fuson); Univ. Minnesota

[2] Georg Wittig, b. 1897 Berlin; Ph.D. Marburg (von Auwers); Univ. Freiburg, Tübingen, Heidelberg

of the reagent, prepared as described, is treated with benzophenone and let stand for several hours at room temperature, the adduct of triphenylphosphine oxide and lithium bromide separates and unsaturated hydrocarbon can be isolated from the filtered solution. The mechanism suggested by Wittig (1950) involves a four-membered cyclic transition state:

$$(C_6H_5)_3P{=}CH_2 \qquad (C_6H_5)_3P\overset{\cdots}{\cdots}CH_2 \qquad (C_6H_5)_3P \qquad CH_2$$
$$\xrightarrow{\hspace{1cm}} \qquad\quad \vdots \qquad \vdots \qquad \xrightarrow{\hspace{1cm}} \qquad \| \;\; + \;\; \|$$
$$O{=}C(C_6H_5)_2 \qquad\quad O\overset{\cdots}{\cdots}C(C_6H_5)_2 \qquad\qquad O \qquad C(C_6H_5)_2$$

Other examples of reactions with the methylene ylide are as follows:

$$\begin{array}{l} C_6H_5COCH_3 \\ (CH_2)_5C{=}O \\ C_6H_5CH{=}O \end{array} \bigg\} \xrightarrow{(C_6H_5)_3P{=}CH_2} \begin{cases} (74\%)\; C_6H_5\overset{CH_3}{\underset{|}{C}}{=}CH_2 \;(\alpha\text{-Methylstyrene}) \\ (48\%)\; (CH_2)_5C{=}CH_2 \;(\text{Methylenecyclohexane}) \\ (67\%)\; C_6H_5CH{=}CH_2 \;(\text{Styrene}) \end{cases}$$

1-Phenylbutadiene (*cis-trans* mixture) has been prepared by the condensation

$$C_6H_5CH{=}CHCHO \;+\; (C_6H_5)_3P{=}CH_2 \qquad\qquad C_6H_5CHO \;+\; (C_6H_5)_3P{=}CHCH{=}CH_2$$
$$\underset{69\%}{\longrightarrow}\; C_6H_5CH{=}CHCH{=}CH_2 \;\underset{58\%}{\longleftarrow}$$

of cinnamaldehyde with the methylene ylide and from benzaldehyde and the vinylmethylene ylide obtained by use of allyl bromide instead of methyl bromide in the first step. *trans,trans*-1,4-Diphenylbutadiene is obtainable from the phosphonium salt of cinnamyl chloride and benzaldehyde in twice the yield of the modified Perkin reaction cited (13.6). The initially formed dipolar ion evidently is stabilized by resonance, for when generated in alcohol in the absence of an

$$C_6H_5CH{=}CHCH_2\overset{Cl^-}{P^+}(C_6H_5)_3 \xrightarrow[-HCl]{LiOC_2H_5}$$

$$\begin{bmatrix} C_6H_5CH{=}CHC^-HP^+(C_6H_5)_3 \\ \updownarrow \\ C_6H_5C^-HCH{=}CHP^+(C_6H_5)_3 \end{bmatrix} \xrightarrow[55\text{-}62\% \text{ overall}]{C_6H_5CHO} C_6H_5CH{=}CHCH{=}CHC_6H_5$$

aldehyde it gives rise to a brilliant red-orange color which persists for a considerable period. T. W. Campbell[1] and co-workers, responsible for the procedure described, found it to afford the best available route to *p*-quinquephenyl. *p*-Xylylene dichloride (Hooker Electrochemical Co.) is converted to the bis-phosphonium salt, which on reaction with cinnamaldehyde affords 1,4-bis-(4-phenylbutadienyl)-benzene. The adduct prepared from this hydrocarbon and diethyl acetylenedicarboxylate in refluxing *o*-dichlorobenzene on saponification gives a brilliant yellow solution of the potassium tetracarboxylate. Addition of potassium ferricyanide

[1] Tod W. Campbell, b. Seattle, Wash.; Ph.D. Univ. Calif. Los Angeles (W. G. Young); du Pont Co.

$(C_6H_5)_3P^+CH_2C_6H_4CH_2P^+(C_6H_5)_3[2Cl^-]$ $\xrightarrow[\text{69-75\%}]{2\ C_6H_5CH=CHCHO\ (LiOC_2H_5)}$

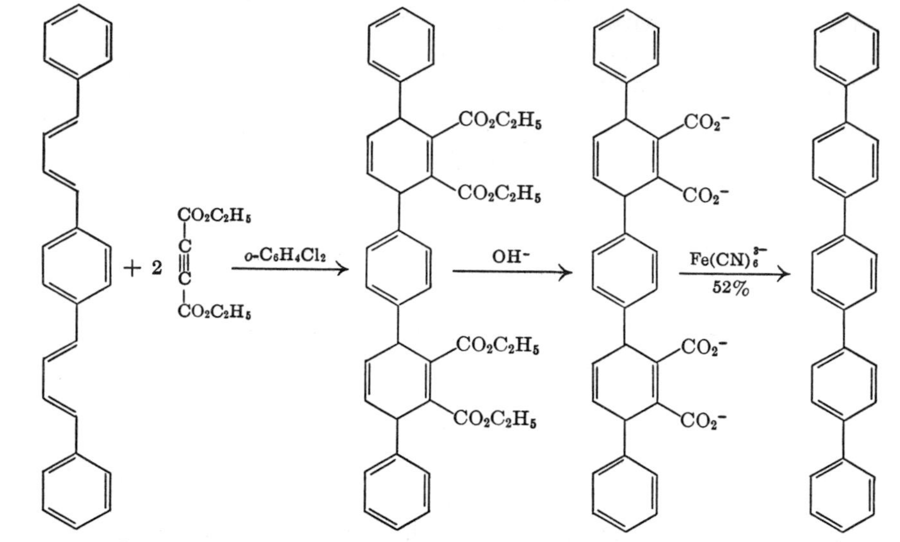

m.p. 287°　　　　　　　　　　　　　　　　　　　　　　　　m.p. 390°

to a weakly alkaline (Na_2CO_3) solution of the salt at room temperature effects decarboxylation and aromatization to give quinquephenyl in 52% yield.

The ylide form (b) of methyltriphenylphosphonium bromide is a betaine, the cation of which contains a central phosphorus atom surrounded by complexing phenyl groups as ligands. Replacement of the phenyl groups by *p*-tolyl- or *p*-methoxyphenyl groups favors formation of the ylide but inhibits its reaction with carbonyl compounds (Wittig, 1961).

The Wittig reaction has been particularly valuable in the synthesis of isoprenoid polyenes related to vitamin A. For example, the reaction was used by Isler[1] and six co-workers in an efficient synthesis of lycopene, the red pigment of the tomato. The first step was reaction of methacrolein with acetylenedimagnesium bromide to form the diol (1), which underwent double allylic rearrangement in ethanol containing a little acid (55°) to the diprimary diol (2), and this was oxidized to the C_{10}-dialdehyde (3). The chain was then lengthened at each end by a process represented in the chart for one terminal group. Reaction with ethyl orthoformate in ethanol (TsOH) gave the diethyl acetal (4), which was condensed with ethyl vinyl ether in ethyl acetate in the presence of zinc chloride and boron fluoride to give the ether–acetal derivative (5). Acid hydrolysis of (5) liberated the aldehyde function and eliminated the β-acetoxy group, giving (6). Conversion to the diethyl acetal (7) and condensation with ethyl propenyl ether extended the chain by three carbons (at each end) and gave (8), and this on hydrolysis gave the C_{20}-dialdehyde shown in the complete formula (9). Selective hydrogenation of the triple bond (Lindlar Pd–Pb catalyst) then afforded crocetin dialdehyde (10,

[1] Otto Isler, b. 1910 Schaffhausen; D.Sc. ETH Zurich (Ruzicka); Hoffmann-La Roche, Basel

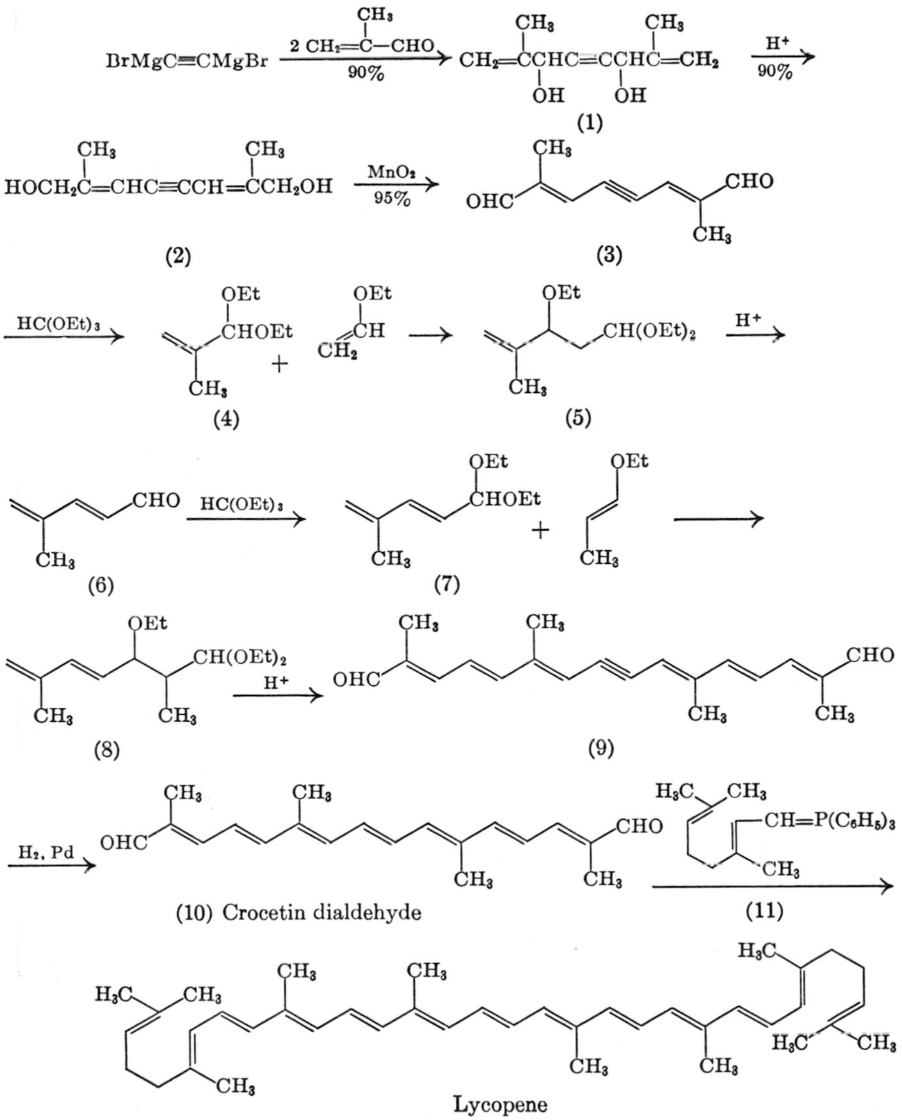

The structures and reaction schemes (1) through (11) and Lycopene are shown.

(1)

(2) → (3)

(4) + → (5)

(6) → (7) +

(8) → (9)

(10) Crocetin dialdehyde

(11)

Lycopene

violet-red plates, m.p. 191°), one component for the Wittig reaction. The other component was the ylide (11), prepared from readily available geranyl bromide. The reaction product crystallized in red needles, m.p. 173°, and proved to be identical with lycopene isolated from tomato juice. The yields throughout were high; for example, 20 g. of crocetin dialdehyde yielded 25 g. of pure lycopene.

Inhoffen's group (1960) employed Wittig reactions at two stages of a total synthesis of vitamin D_3. Attachment of a side chain to the bicyclic ketone (1) was accomplished by an interesting variation of the Grignard synthesis. Reaction with crotylmagnesium bromide proceeds through a cyclic transition state (2) to

give the carbinol (3).   Cleavage of the double bond [OsO$_4$; Pb(OAc)$_4$] and dehydration gave two 17,20-unsaturated aldehydes, one of which on hydrogenation (rear
attack) gave the aldehyde (4) of appropriate stereochemistry at C$_{17}$ and C$_{20}$.

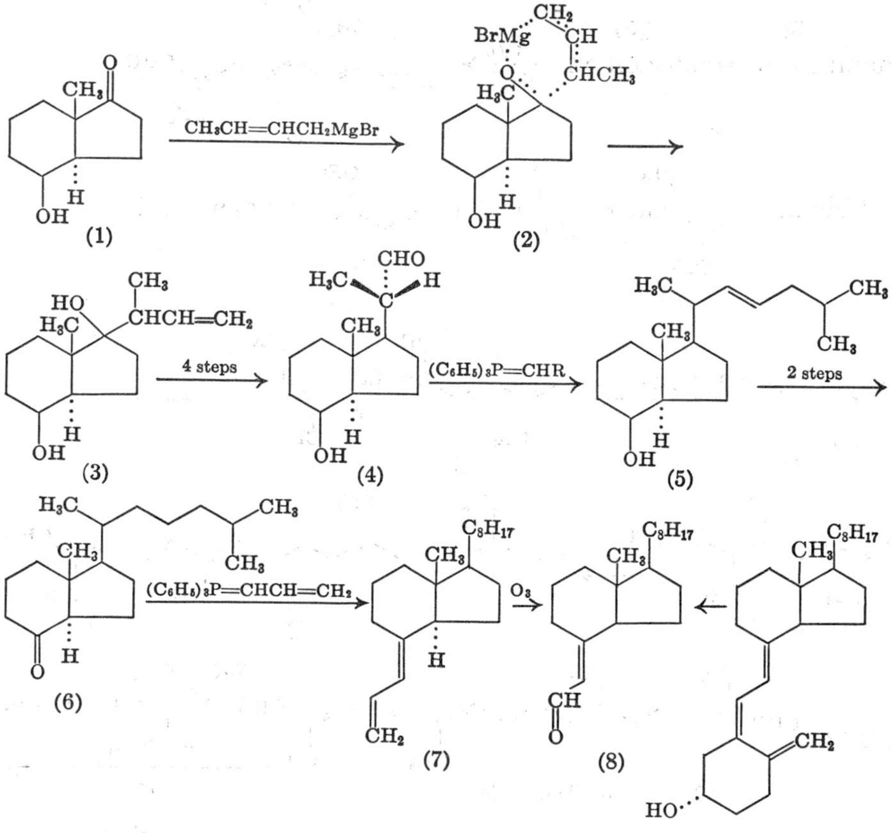

Condensation of (4) with the Wittig reagent prepared from isoamyl bromide gave
the unsaturated alcohol (5), and hydrogenation of the double bond and oxidation
gave the ketone (6), in which the side chain corresponds in structure and stereochemistry to that of cholesterol and vitamin D$_3$.   Condensation of (6) with the
Wittig reagent from allyl bromide afforded almost exclusively the desired *trans*
diene (7), and this on selective ozonization gave the α,β-unsaturated aldehyde
(8), a product of degradation of vitamin D$_3$ which already had been reconverted
into D$_3$ by partial synthesis.

PROBLEM

(The experimentally determined facts leading to elucidation of the structure of chloramphenicol are presented and left for the reader to interpret, step by step.   An analysis
of the data is given in the back of the book.)

The isolation of the valuable antibiotic streptomycin from several strains of *Streptomyces*
(S. Waksman, 1942–44) prompted widespread investigations of other strains.   A strain named

S. venezuelae, because it was isolated from a sample of soil obtained from Venezuela, was found to yield another antibiotic, investigated particularly by Parke, Davis and Co. (Q. R. Bartz, J. Controulis, *et al.*, 1949).

Physical constants and analytical data for chloramphenicol are as follows: colorless needles, m.p. 150°, $\alpha_D + 19°$ (ethanol), $-25.5°$ (ethyl acetate); empirical formula, $C_{11}H_{12}O_5N_2Cl_2$ (both chlorines inert to silver ion); mol. wt. (Rast), 310; inert to carbonyl reagents and to dilute bromine solution; neutral. The substance has an ultraviolet maximum at 278 mμ similar to that of benzene. Chloramphenicol forms a diacetate from which it is regenerated under hydrolytic conditions so mild as to indicate that both acetyl groups are linked to oxygen rather than nitrogen.

Further evidence is that on catalytic hydrogenation of the antibiotic three moles of hydrogen are absorbed rapidly without marked alteration of the spectrum. Reduction with tin and hydrochloric acid followed by reaction with nitrous acid gave a diazonium salt.

Chloramphenicol had been observed to suffer decrease in biological activity in contact with alkali, and hence alkaline hydrolysis was tried and found to give an easily distillable, strongly acidic fragment of the formula $C_2H_2O_2Cl_2$ and a crystalline, optically active base, $C_9H_{12}O_4N_2$, which forms a triacetate. The results of the degradation permit a further significant inference. Although chloramphenicol itself is stable to periodic acid under conditions ordinarily employed for determination of vicinal hydroxyl groups, the base $C_9H_{12}O_4N_2$ readily consumed two oxygen equivalents of the reagent and the following four products were identified: ammonia, formaldehyde, formic acid, and an aldehyde of the formula $C_7H_5O_3N$. The aldehyde was identified readily by the Parke, Davis group, but for the purpose of the present problem it will be described as a substance convertible into *p*-toluidine, $CH_3C_6H_4NH_2\text{-}p$.

At this point, the Parke, Davis group regarded the evidence for the structure of the antibiotic as conclusive, took stock of the number of possible stereoisomers, and considered possibilities for synthesis. The reader should do likewise. Synthetic methods will, of course, lead to one or more *dl*-mixtures which have to be resolved, and if two racemates are possible one can more or less expect to obtain a mixture of both but has no way of predicting whether the desired or undesired racemate will predominate.

The Parke, Davis group, reported a synthesis of chloramphenicol in 1949. From a broad outline of the chemical reactions involved, the reader may be able to fill in the details; the stereochemistry is summarized in the analysis at the end of the book. The synthesis started with a sodium methoxide-induced aldol-type condensation of benzaldehyde with β-nitroethanol, $HOCH_2CH_2NO_2$,* to give an addition product which on catalytic hydrogenation absorbed 3 moles of hydrogen and gave an amino diol. This afforded a triacetate, actually a mixture of two diastereomeric triacetates. Nitration and deacetylation gave a mixture of two diastereomeric nitrophenylaminodiols, which were separated. A levorotatory base from one of the racemates on reaction with methyl dichloroacetate gave a product identical with natural chloramphenicol.

Chloramphenicol is a broad-spectrum antibiotic; it is currently the drug of choice for treatment of typhoid fever and rickettsial infections.

---

* Prepared (a) from ethylene chlorohydrin and silver nitrate or (b) as follows: $O{=}CH_2 + CH_3NO_2 \rightarrow HOCH_2CH_2NO_2$.

Chapter 14

AMINES

14.1   **Steric Character.** — Since the nitrogen atom has five electrons in the outer shell, it would be expected to complete an octet by forming three electron-pair bonds with three unpaired $2p$ electrons. Ammonia, then, would be pyramidal, with N—H bond angles of 90° (nitrogen at one corner of a tetrahedron and hydrogen at the other three corners). However, hydrogen interactions and a partial ionic character of the N—H bond due to a difference in electronegativity distort this arrangement so that the actual bond angle is 109°, almost identical with the tetrahedral angle (109°28′). Evidently some hybridization of $2s$ and $2p$ orbitals takes place, with three of the four resulting sp^2 orbitals being used to bind hydrogen atoms and the unshared pair of electrons occupying the remaining tetrahedral position. The Dreiding nitrogen model resembles a carbon model with one bond removed and with the N—H bonds scaled to the bond distance of 1.01 Å. Compounds of the type Nabc should be capable of existing in enantiomeric forms, but attempted resolutions of noncyclic amines have all failed. Thus the wide bond angle and the absence of a fourth group appear to permit trivalent nitrogen to undergo Walden inversion with great ease. This fact was only recognized by

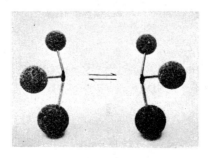

Meisenheimer[1] in 1924 after numerous investigators had sought in vain to effect resolutions. Julius Tröger (1887) condensed p-toluidine with methylal in concentrated hydrochloric acid and obtained a substance (m.p. 134°) now called Tröger's base. Structures suggested by Tröger and by later workers proved to be incorrect, but Spielman[2] (1935) deduced the structure formulated and established

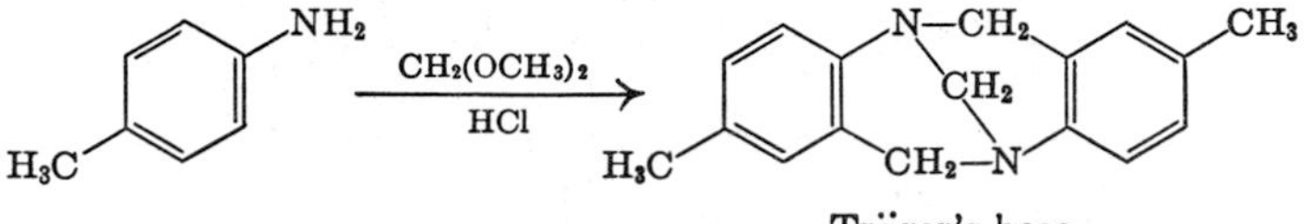

Tröger's base

it by synthesis. V. Prelog and P. Wieland (1944) thought that the caged ring system should inhibit Walden inversion and undertook resolution of Tröger's base. Attempted resolution with optically active acids was only partially successful, for the diamine is a relatively weak base and it is also rapidly racemized in acid solution. Chromatographic resolution proved successful. When the base was adsorbed on specially ground (+)-lactose hydrate and the column eluted with petroleum ether, initial fractions were dextrorotatory, intermediate fractions inactive, and terminal fractions levorotatory. The enantiomers melt at 128°; α_D

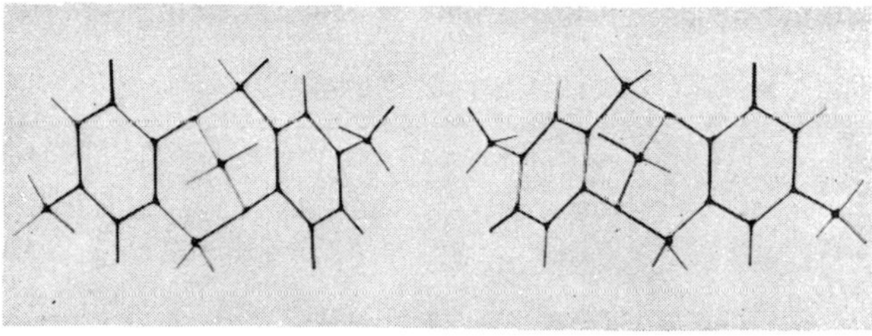

±7°. Dissolved in 0.1 N HCl in absolute ethanol, they undergo rapid racemization.

A derivative of ammonium chloride having four different groups covalently bonded to nitrogen should be resolvable into optically active forms, and Pope in 1899 effected the first of a number of such resolutions. The d- and l-forms of methylallylbenzylphenylammonium iodide were obtained by crystallization of the

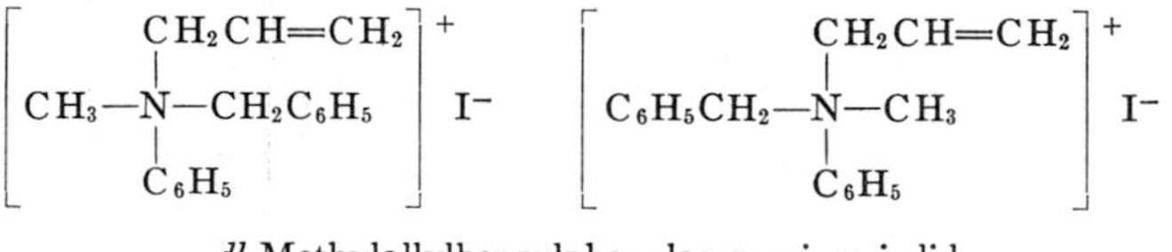

dl-Methylallylbenzylphenylammonium iodide

d-α-bromo-π-camphorsulfonates and decomposition of the two salts with potassium iodide.

[1] Jacob Meisenheimer, 1876–1934; b. Greisheim; Ph.D. Munich; Univ. Berlin, Greifswald, Tübingen; *Ber.*, **68A**, 32 (1935)

[2] Marvin A. Spielman, b. 1906 Dotson, Minn.; Ph.D. Minnesota (Lauer); Abbott Laboratories

The heterocyclic secondary amine piperidine has a ring similar in shape to that of cyclohexane. Since conformation (b) is destabilized by two more diaxial hydrogen interactions than (a), (a) might be expected to be the more stable form, but some evidence suggests that a lone pair on nitrogen may occupy more space than a hydrogen atom.

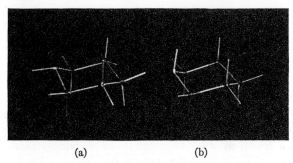

(a)   (b)

14.2   Physical Properties. — Methylamine is a gas under ordinary conditions (Table 14.1) and has a boiling point somewhat higher than that of ammonia (b.p. $-33.3°$). The odor of the also volatile ethylamine is so similar to that of ammonia that when Wurtz, the discoverer (1849), first had the material in hand he did not recognize it as a new substance until, in the course of experi-

TABLE 14.1.   AMINES

NAME	FORMULA	M.P., °C.	B.P., °C.	SP. GR.
Methylamine	CH_3NH_2	-92.5	-6.5	0.699
Dimethylamine	$(CH_3)_2NH$	-96.0	7.4	.680
Trimethylamine	$(CH_3)_3N$	-124.0	3.5	.662
Ethylamine	$CH_3CH_2NH_2$	-80.6	16.6	.689
Diethylamine	$(CH_3CH_2)_2NH$	-38.9	56.0	.711
Triethylamine	$(CH_3CH_2)_3N$	-114.8	89.5	.728
n-Propylamine	$CH_3CH_2CH_2NH_2$	-83.0	48.7	.719
Di-n-propylamine	$(CH_3CH_2CH_2)_2NH$	-39.6	110.7	.738
Tri-n-propylamine	$(CH_3CH_2CH_2)_3N$	-93.5	156	.757
n-Butylamine	$CH_3CH_2CH_2CH_2NH_2$	-50.5	76	.740
n-Amylamine	$CH_3CH_2CH_2CH_2CH_2NH_2$	-55.0	104	.766
n-Hexylamine	$CH_3(CH_2)_5NH_2$	-19	$130^{742mm.}$	
Laurylamine	$CH_3(CH_2)_{11}NH_2$	28	$135^{15mm.}$	
Ethylenediamine	$H_2NCH_2CH_2NH_2$	8.5	117	.892
Trimethylenediamine	$H_2NCH_2CH_2CH_2NH_2$		135.5	.884
Tetramethylenediamine	$H_2NCH_2CH_2CH_2CH_2NH_2$	27	158	
Pentamethylenediamine	$H_2NCH_2CH_2CH_2CH_2CH_2NH_2$	9	178	.855
Hexamethylenediamine	$H_2N(CH_2)_6NH_2$	39	196	
Ethanolamine	$HOCH_2CH_2NH_2$		171	1.022
Diethanolamine	$(HOCH_2CH_2)_2NH$	28	270	1.097
Triethanolamine	$(HOCH_2CH_2)_3N$	21	$279^{150mm.}$	1.124
Allylamine	$CH_2{=}CHCH_2NH_2$		53.2	0.761
Aniline	$C_6H_5NH_2$	-6	184	1.022

mentation, the alkaline gas by chance came near a flame and took fire. In general, amines that are either gases or fairly volatile liquids of moderate molecular weight have a pronounced odor similar to that of ammonia but less pungent and more fishlike. Dimethylamine and trimethylamine are constituents of herring brine. The lower amines are very soluble in water; among compounds having normal alkyl groups the limiting members in the three series showing significant solubility are: *n*-amylamine, di-*n*-propylamine, and triethylamine.

Comparative data of isomeric compounds of molecular weight 101.19 show that straight-chain amines boil at temperatures only slightly above those characteristic of unassociated liquids of this molecular weight (b.p. about 100°) and that branching of

COMPOUND (MOL. WT. 101.19)	B.P.
$CH_3CH_2CH_2CH_2CH_2CH_2NH_2$	130°/742mm.
$CH_3CH_2CH_2NHCH_2CH_2CH_3$	110.7°
$CH_3{>}CHNHCH{<}^{CH_3}_{CH_3}$ (CH₃ top)	84°
$CH_3CH_2{>}N{-}CH_2CH_3$ with CH_3CH_2 below	89.5°

the chain is attended by enhanced volatility. Diethanolamine (mol. wt. 105.14) has a much higher boiling point (270°), indicative of association attributable to the hydroxyl groups. Pentamethylenediamine (mol. wt. 102.18) has a boiling point (178°) considerably above the normal value for unassociated liquids, and this property is in line with the fact that even monoamines show some tendency to exist in an associated condition. The association is attributable to hydrogen bonding; since nitrogen is less electronegative than oxygen, hydrogen bonding in primary and secondary amines is less pronounced than that in alcohols.

14.3   Definition of Acids and Bases. — The Ostwald-Arrhenius definition of acids and bases (1880–90) as substances that give rise to hydrogen or hydroxide ions in aqueous solution has limitations as applied to the behavior of organic compounds in nonaqueous solvents. Thus a solution of sodium hydroxide in ethanol contains ethoxide anion not hydroxide ion. A further difficulty is that free hydrogen ions are not present in any solvent; in water the "hydrogen ion" is H_3O^+, in ethanol it is $C_2H_5O^+H_2$, and in ammonia it is NH_4^+. A particular ambiguity exists in the definition of bases, since some, *e.g.* amines, produce the hydroxide ion in aqueous solution indirectly:

$$R_3N + H_2O \rightleftharpoons R_3N^+H + OH^-$$

A more general definition was proposed by J. N. Brønsted (1923). A Brønsted acid is a substance that loses a proton and a Brønsted base one that accepts a proton: A (acid) $\rightleftharpoons$ B (base) + H^+. Salts are not related directly to acids or bases, but rather B is the conjugate base of acid A and A is the conjugate acid of base B. An acid or base can function as such only in the presence of another base or acid; hence acid-base equilibrium reduce to the generalized form 1, Table 14.2. Typical examples are formulated. The Brønsted definition of an acid includes substances defined as acids in the classical dissociation theory (HCl, CH_3CO_2H), but it includes in addition the ions N^+H_4 and $CH_3N^+H_3$. It also includes nitromethane ($CH_3NO_2 \rightarrow {}^-CH_2NO_2 + H^+$), originally called a pseudo acid. The change in definition of bases is more profound. Ammonia and amines are

TABLE 14.2. BRØNSTED ACIDS (A) AND BASES (B)

1	A_1	+	B_2	⇌	A_2	+	B_1
2	CH_3COOH	+	H_2O	⇌	H_3O^+	+	CH_3COO^-
3	H_2O	+	CH_3COO^-	⇌	CH_3COOH	+	OH^-
4	CH_3COOH	+	NH_3	⇌	NH_4^+	+	CH_3COO^-
5	NH_4^+	+	H_2O	⇌	H_3O^+	+	NH_3
6	RN^+H_3	+	H_2O	⇌	H_3O^+	+	RNH_2

Brønsted bases because of their ability to combine with protons (5, 6); an ether is a base in a strongly acidic medium.

The Lewis concept (1923) of an acid as an electron acceptor and a base as an electron donor (1.11) is more generally useful in the organic field than the Brønsted concept. A Lewis base and a Brønsted base are essentially the same, since a molecule that adds a proton does so because it has an unshared pair of electrons: $H^+ + (CH_3)_3N: \rightarrow (CH_3)_3N^+:H$. However, a Lewis acid can be considerably different from a Brønsted acid. Thus hydrogen chloride and acetic acid are not themselves acids; the acid is the proton which the substances can give up. Typical Lewis acids are not acids in the Brønsted sense but compounds with an atom that can expand its outer valence shell. Examples already cited are boron fluoride and methylmagnesium bromide, which combine with one and two molecules of the Lewis base diethyl ether. Another is trimethylboron, which combines with the

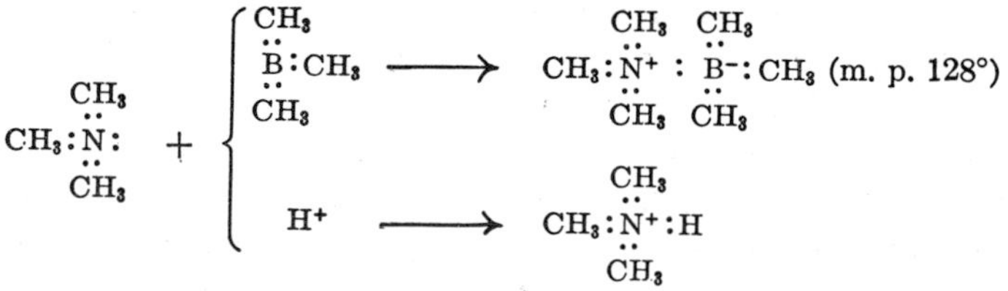

Lewis base trimethylamine just as a proton does.

14.4 **Basic Strength.** — The alkaline reaction noted on dissolving an amine in water is due to withdrawal of hydrogen ion by combination with the base, and the overall result can be represented thus:

$$R_3N: + \overset{+}{H}OH^- \rightleftharpoons R_3\overset{+}{N}:H + OH^-$$

The amine may be present partly as the unstable hydrate, R_3NHOH. The basic dissociation constant of an amine (k_b) is expressed as the product of the concentrations of the ammonium and hydroxide ions divided by the total concentration of unionized material, $[CH_3NH_2]$, for example:

$$k_b = \frac{[CH_3NH_3^+][OH^-]}{[CH_3NH_2]}$$

Basic strength is conveniently expressed as the negative logarithm of the basic dissociation constant; thus $pK_b = - \log k_b$. A strong base has a low pK_b value,

TABLES 14.3.　BASIC DISSOCIATION, $pK_b^{25°}$

NH₃, 4.75	
CH_3NH_2, 3.37	$CH_3CH_2NH_2$, 3.27
$(CH_3)_2NH$, 3.22	$(CH_3CH_2)_2NH$, 2.89
$(CH_3)_3N$, 4.20	$(CH_3CH_2)_3N$, 3.36
$C_6H_5NH_2$ (Aniline), 9.30	

a weak one has a value approaching the limit $pK_b = 14$.　The typical aliphatic amines listed in Table 14.3 are all more strongly basic than ammonia; aromatic amines, typified by aniline, are much weaker bases.　That methylamine and ethylamine are stronger bases than ammonia by 1.4–1.5 pK_b units is attributable to the electron release of the methyl or ethyl group, which increases the electron density on nitrogen and hence increases its affinity for a proton.　That the effect of a second group is much less than that of the first is consistent with the effect of one and two chlorine atoms on the ionization of acetic acid, but the marked and uneven decrease in basic strength in the tertiary series is difficult to understand.　H. C. Brown (1944) has suggested an interpretation based on the assumption of strains (B- and F-strain) in the ammonia molecule that influence attack by the proton.

14.5　　Salts. — Salts with minerals acids are analogous to ammonium salts, and are formed both in aqueous solution and under anhydrous conditions, for example by passing hydrogen chloride gas into an ethereal solution of the amine, in which case the amine salt separates quantitatively as a white solid. Conventional methods of formulating and naming amine salts are illustrated for the salt of methylamine and hydrochloric acid:

$CH_3N^+H_3Cl^-$　　　　　　　　$CH_3NH_2 \cdot HCl$
Methylammonium　　　　　　　Methylamine
chloride　　　　　　　　　　　hydrochloride

Salt formation involves an increase in the valence of nitrogen from three to five, and the fifth linkage is polar; the reaction is represented as follows:

$$\begin{array}{ccc} CH_3 & & CH_3 \\ CH_3:\ddot{N}: & + \quad H^+:\ddot{Br}:^- \longrightarrow & CH_3:\ddot{N}:H^+:\ddot{Br}:^- \\ CH_3 & & CH_3 \end{array}$$

Trimethylamine　　　　　　　　Trimethylammonium
　　　　　　　　　　　　　　　bromide (trimethyl-
　　　　　　　　　　　　　　　amine hydrobromide)

The hydrogen ion accepts the unshared pair of electrons of the nitrogen atom with formation of a covalent bond, and the nitrogen-containing group thereby acquires a positive charge.　Amine salts, owing to their ionic character, contrast with amines in physical properties.　They are all odorless, nonvolatile solids, even though the amines from which they are derived are odoriferous gases or liquids, and they are insoluble in ether or in hydrocarbon solvents, which dissolve the typically organic amines.　With the exception of substances of very high molecular weight, the salts are readily soluble in water and exist in the solution in ionized

TABLE 14.4. AMINE SALTS

FORMULA	M.P.	FORMULA	M.P.
$CH_3NH_2 \cdot HCl$	226°	$(C_2H_5)_2NH \cdot HCl$	217°
$C_2H_5NH_2 \cdot HCl$	109°	$(C_2H_5)_3N \cdot HCl$	254°
$C_2H_5NH_2 \cdot HBr$	159.5°	$C_6H_5NH_2 \cdot HCl$	198°
$C_2H_5NH_2 \cdot HI$	188.5°	$C_6H_5NH_2 \cdot HBr$	286°

condition. The solubility in water is decreased by addition of excess of the appropriate mineral acid, and use is made of the common-ion effect in crystallization of amine salts. Ability to form salts is a property distinctive of amines and can be recognized easily by simple qualitative tests. An amine of low molecular weight may be substantially as soluble in water as it is in dilute hydrochloric acid, but if so it will be in the range of the odoriferous amines, and the fact of salt formation will be evident from obliteration of the odor on addition of excess acid. Odorless amines invariably are at most only partially soluble in water, and salt formation is apparent from the fact that they can be brought into solution by addition of a mineral acid. Similarly, an amine salt can be recognized by addition of sodium hydroxide to the aqueous solution. The alkali is a much stronger base than the amine, and liberation of the amine is evident either from the odor or from separation of an oil or solid. For recovery of an amine from a salt, the material set free by addition of alkali is collected by suction filtration of a solid or by extraction with ether or steam distillation of a volatile amine.

Amine salts of the halogen acids often possess characteristic melting points, or points of decomposition, as shown in Table 14.4. Amine hydrochlorides, although insoluble in ether, ligroin, or benzene, often are somewhat soluble in methanol or ethanol and can be separated from a mixture containing ammonium chloride by extraction with a lower alcohol. The sulfates usually are less fusible and less soluble in water. Acetic acid forms salts of slight stability, but strongly acidic organic acids (e.g., picric acid, oxalic acid) give stable salts which, being of more organic character than mineral acid salts, tend to be less soluble in water and more readily fusible and which are therefore useful for identification. Volatile amines are conveniently prepared for analysis in the form of their sparingly soluble salts with chloroplatinic acid, for example $(RNH_3)_2PtCl_6$.

14.6   **Quaternary Ammonium Compounds.** — Tertiary amines when heated with alkyl halides combine to form compounds similar to ammonium salts but having four alkyl groups attached to nitrogen and hence called quaternary ammonium salts. These salts are solid ionic substances readily soluble in water

$$(CH_3)_3N \xrightarrow{CH_3I} (CH_3)_4\overset{+}{N}I^-$$

Tetramethylammonium
iodide

and insoluble in ether and comparable to hydrochlorides and hydrobromides of the same tertiary amines. They are also difficultly fusible substances that when strongly heated decompose into a tertiary amine and an alkyl halide. The tetraalkylammonium salts contrast with amine hydrohalides and simple ammonium salts in behavior toward alkalis, for no free amine is liberated and instead there results an equilibrium mixture containing a stable quaternary ammonium hydroxide, for example:

$$(CH_3)_4\overset{+}{N}I^- \quad + \quad KOH \quad \rightleftharpoons \quad (CH_3)_4\overset{+}{N}OH^- \quad + \quad KI$$

Tetramethylammonium
hydroxide

The tetraalkyl derivative cannot decompose by loss of water in the manner characteristic of ammonium hydroxide and amine hydrates and therefore affords a high concentration of hydroxide ion. The substance is a strong base comparable to sodium or potassium hydroxide, which explains why the equilibrium constant in the above reaction is close to unity. The preparation of a quaternary ammonium base is accomplished by treatment of the halide in aqueous solution with silver hydroxide, for silver halide precipitates and the equilibrium is displaced. The filtered aqueous solution can be evaporated without decomposition of the

$$(CH_3)_4\overset{+}{N}I^- \quad + \quad AgOH \quad \longrightarrow \quad (CH_3)_4\overset{+}{N}OH^- \quad + \quad AgI$$

organic base, which can be obtained as a crystalline solid, usually as a deliquescent hydrate. Concentrated solutions of quaternary ammonium hydroxides have a caustic, corrosive action similar to alkalis and cannot be stored in glass vessels without contamination due to attack of the container. Use of benzyltrimethylammonium hydroxide as a basic catalyst has been mentioned (13.15).

PREPARATION

14.7 **Amination of Alkyl Halides.** — Hofmann discovered (London, 1849; see biog., 4.4) that alkyl groups can be introduced directly into ammonia by interaction with an alkyl halide and subsequent treatment with alkali. The reaction is general, but it has the disadvantage that higher substitution is

$$1. \quad CH_3CH_2Br \; + \; NH_3 \; \longrightarrow \; CH_3CH_2N^+H_3Br^- \; \xrightarrow{\;NaOH\;} \; CH_3CH_2NH_2$$

inevitable. Thus in the reaction of ethyl bromide with ammonia the ethylammonium bromide as it is formed enters into equilibrium with ammonia still present with liberation of ethylamine (2). The primary amine then competes with ammonia for the alkyl halide and yields some of the secondary amine salt (3). However, a simple expedient for suppression of the unwanted secondary amine is

$$2. \quad CH_3CH_2N^+H_3Br^- \; + \; NH_3 \; \rightleftharpoons \; CH_3CH_2NH_2 \; + \; NH_4^+Br^-$$

$$3. \quad CH_3CH_2NH_2 \; + \; CH_3CH_2Br \; \longrightarrow \; (CH_3CH_2)_2N^+H_2Br^-$$

to use so large an excess of ammonia that the competitive reaction (3) has little chance of occurring. An example is the amination of α-bromopropionic acid (4).

$$4. \quad \underset{\underset{Br}{|}}{CH_3CHCO_2H} \; \xrightarrow[65-70\%]{NH_3 \;(70 \text{ equivalents})} \; \underset{\underset{NH_2}{|}}{CH_3CHCO_2H}$$

Alanine

Secondary amines can be made by alkylation of primary amines and tertiary amines by repetition of the process (5). These reactions are not easily controlled

5.

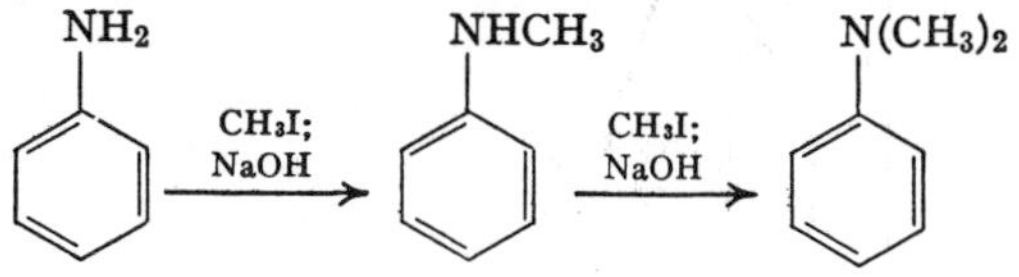

NH_2 $\xrightarrow[\text{NaOH}]{\text{CH}_3\text{I};}$ $NHCH_3$ $\xrightarrow[\text{NaOH}]{\text{CH}_3\text{I};}$ $N(CH_3)_2$

N-Methylaniline   N,N-Dimethylaniline

to just the desired stage of alkylation, and the reaction products require extensive purification. For amination of chloroacetal (6), a hydrogenation bomb is cooled in dry ice–acetone and charged with the halide, methanol, and liquid ammonia

6. $ClCH_2CH(OC_2H_5)_2$ $\xrightarrow[71\text{-}74\%]{\substack{\text{NH}_3 \text{ (18 equiv.)} \\ \text{CH}_3\text{OH, 140}^\circ}}$ $H_2NCH_2CH(OC_2H_5)_2$

      Chloroacetal   Aminoacetal

and the mixture is shaken at 140°. Distillation of the product leaves a residue of diacetalylamine.

14.8　　　**Reductive Amination** (R. Leuckart, 1885). — In the Leuckart reaction an aldehyde or ketone is heated with formic acid and ammonia, a primary amine, or a secondary amine. Use of formaldehyde as the carbonyl component affords a method of methylation. Thus benzylamine, refluxed with form-

$C_6H_5CH_2NH_2$ $\xrightarrow[80\%]{\text{CH}_2\text{O, HCO}_2\text{H}}$ $C_6H_5CH_2N(CH_3)_2$ + CO_2 + H_2O

Benzylamine   N,N-Dimethyl-
                              benzylamine

aldehyde (2.2 equiv.) and formic acid (5 equiv.) until evolution of carbon dioxide ceases, affords the N,N-dimethyl derivative in good yield. Methylamine hydrochloride can be prepared by heating a mixture of formalin and ammonium chloride. The yield reported is for hydrochloride recrystallized from absolute ethanol and is

$2\ CH_2O$ + NH_4Cl $\xrightarrow[45\text{-}51\%]{104^\circ}$ $CH_3N^+H_3Cl^-$ + HCO_2H

based upon ammonium chloride consumed. Here, formaldehyde serves both as carbonyl component and as reducing agent and is oxidized to formic acid. In the preparation of trimethylamine hydrochloride, paraformaldehyde is employed

$3\ (CH_2O)_3$ + $2\ NH_4Cl$ $\xrightarrow[80\%]{160^\circ}$ $2\ (CH_3)_3N^+HCl^-$ + $3\ CO_2$ + $3\ H_2O$

rather than the aqueous solution to permit a higher reaction temperature, and the ratio of reagents is that corresponding to complete utilization of formaldehyde. At the end of the reaction, alkali is added and the free amine distilled into hydrochloric acid. The salt that crystallizes after evaporation is soluble in chloroform and therefore completely free from ammonium chloride and methylamine hydrochloride; a negative Hinsberg test (14.17) shows the absence of secondary amine hydrochloride.

The transformation of a ketone into a primary amine ($R_2CO \rightarrow R_2CHNH_2$) is illustrated for the case of benzophenone. A mixture of the ketone with five

$$C_6H_5COC_6H_5 \xrightarrow[\text{Refl. 9 hrs.}]{NH_3,\ HCO_2H,\ 160°} \underset{\overset{|}{NHCHO}}{C_6H_5CHC_6H_5} \xrightarrow[80\%]{HCl} \underset{\overset{|}{NH_2}}{C_6H_5CHC_6H_5}$$

Benzhydrylamine

equivalents each of 28% ammonia and 90% formic acid is heated to distil water until the temperature reaches 160° and is then refluxed for 9 hrs. Hydrochloric acid is added and the mixture refluxed for 8 hrs. to hydrolyze the formyl derivative formed. Formamide or a derivative is often employed to supply the amine component. Thus cholestane-3-one on being heated at 165° with formic acid and dimethylformamide gave 3β-dimethylaminocholestane (m.p. 105°) in 53% yield; chromatography of the mother liquor afforded the 3α-epimer in 5% yield (R. R. Sauers, 1958). The main product is thus that resulting from attack from the rear.

The Leuckart reaction with ammonia or with a primary amine is considered to involve addition to the carbonyl group and formation of an unsaturated derivative

$$R_2C{=}O \xrightarrow{RNH_2} \underset{\overset{|}{OH}}{R_2C{-}NHR} \xrightarrow{-H_2O} R_2C{=}NR$$

Schiff base

$$R_2C{=}NR + HCO_2H \rightarrow R_2\overset{+}{C}{-}NHR + HCO_2{}^- $$
$$\hookrightarrow R_2CHNHR + CO_2$$

known as a Schiff base. This intermediate is then reduced by formic acid by successive transfer of a proton and then a hydride ion. In the case of a secondary amine a slight variation in mechanism is applicable.

$$R_2C{=}O \xrightarrow{R_2NH} \underset{\overset{|}{OH}}{R_2C{-}NR_2} \xrightarrow[-H_2O]{HCO_2H} R_2\overset{+}{C}{-}NR_2 + HCO_2{}^-$$
$$\hookrightarrow R_2CHNR_2$$

14.9   Enamines. — Little was known of the behavior of aliphatic aldehydes other than formaldehyde in the Leuckart reaction until 1950, when P. L. DeBenneville and J. H. Macartney (Rohm and Haas Co.) investigated the condensation of secondary amines with a number of aldehydes and noted that aldehydes with an α-hydrogen atom react more readily than ketones and aromatic aldehydes. The observation suggested that the reaction, for example of n-nonaldehyde (1) with dimethylamine, involves intermediate formation of an enamine (3). Mannich (1936) had found that in the presence of solid potassium carbonate at 5° an aldehyde combines with two molecules of dimethylamine to form a bis-

dimethylamino derivative of type (2) and that this on distillation loses one mole
of amine and yields an enamine (3).   The Rohm and Haas investigators prepared

$$n\text{-}C_8H_{17}CHO \xrightarrow{\text{2 HN(CH}_3)_2} n\text{-}C_7H_{15}CH_2CH\begin{smallmatrix}N(CH_3)_2\\ \\ N(CH_3)_2\end{smallmatrix} \xrightarrow{-\text{HN(CH}_3)_2}$$

(1)   (2)

$$n\text{-}C_7H_{15}CH=CHN(CH_3)_2 \xrightarrow[\text{84\% overall}]{\text{HCO}_2\text{H}} n\text{-}C_8H_{17}CH_2N(CH_3)_2$$

(3) Enamine   (4)

a number of enamines and found that they are indeed reduced in good yield by
formic acid (4).

   Although the Mannich procedure had been applied to ketones only in limited
instances, investigations at the Upjohn laboratory initiated by M. E. Herr and
F. W. Heyl[1] (1952) led to a highly efficient route to enamine derivatives of steroid
aldehydes and ketones: the substance is refluxed with a secondary amine and a
trace of *p*-toluenesulfonic acid in benzene under a trap for removal of water.
Yields are very high.   The favored bases are piperidine and pyrrolidine, although
the Rohm and Haas work would suggest that morpholine is equally satisfactory.

Piperidine   Pyrrolidine   Morpholine
B. p. 106°   B. p. 87°   B. p. 206°

One synthetic use for enamines is illustrated by the conversion of the aldehyde (1)
into the norketone (3); enamine formation (2) establishes a double bond at C_{20} and

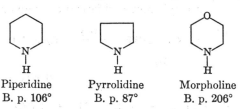

(1)   (2)   (3)

oxidation produces the 20-ketone (3).   Conversion to an enamine as a protective
derivative has applications based on the high selectivity of the reaction and the
fact that enamines can be hydrolyzed efficiently with dilute acid.   Thus the
aldehyde shown in partial formula (1) also has an α,β-unsaturated keto group in
ring A which remained unattacked (the reaction is stopped when one equivalent
of water has been collected).   However the unsaturated 3-keto group reacts in
perference to a keto group at C_{17}, as illustrated by a synthesis of testosterone

[1] F. W. Heyl, b. 1885 New Haven, Conn.; Ph.D. Yale; Univ. Wyoming; Upjohn Co.

rivalling that of Ercoli (12.24). Enamines are also useful as intermediates for α-alkylation or acylation of aldehydes and ketones (Stork, 1954, 1956).

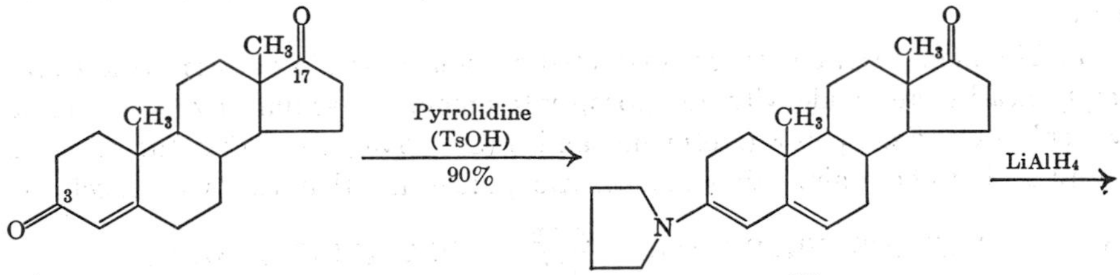

Δ⁴-Androstene-3, 17-dione   (2)

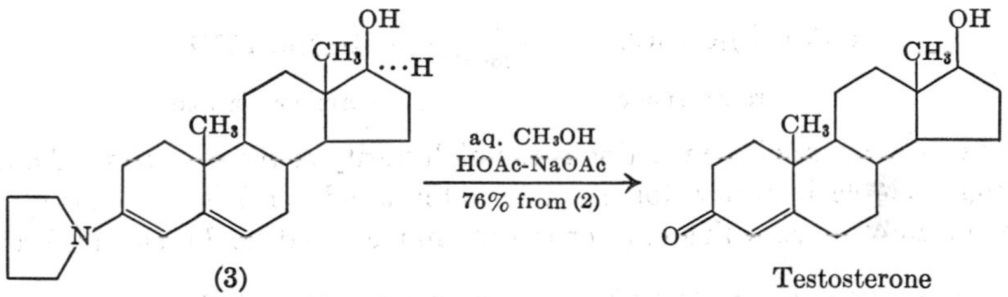

(3)   Testosterone

14.10   Hofmann Reaction. — The difficulty in preparing pure primary amines by the amination reaction discovered by Hofmann in London in 1849 is completely eliminated in a method which Hofmann discovered in Berlin in 1882. A year earlier he had made the puzzling observation that slow addition of 10% potassium hydroxide to a solution of acetamide in 0.5 mol. equiv. of bromine affords N-methyl-N′-acetylurea (1). Realizing that several steps are involved, he

1. $2 \, CH_3CONH_2 + Br_2 \xrightarrow{KOH} CH_3NHCONHCOCH_3$ (m.p. 180°)

2. $CH_3CONH_2 + Br_2 \xrightarrow{KOH} CH_3CONHBr$ (m.p. 108°)

3. $CH_3CONHBr + CH_3CONH_2 \xrightarrow{KOH} CH_3NHCONHCOCH_3$

4. $CH_3CONHBr + KOH \rightarrow CH_3NH_2 + KBr + CO_2$

5. $2 \, CH_3CONHBr + Ag_2CO_3 \rightarrow CH_3N{=}C{=}O + AgBr + CO_2 + H_2O$

6. $CH_3N{=}C{=}O + H_2O \rightarrow [CH_3NHCO_2H] \rightarrow CH_3NH_2 + CO_2$

7. $CH_3N{=}C{=}O + H_2NCOCH_3 \rightarrow CH_3NHCONHCOCH_3$

proceeded to trace the course of events. Repetition of the process with an equimolecular mixture of amide and bromine gave the initial product, N-bromoacetamide (2). As expected, this substance combined with acetamide in the presence of alkali as in (3) to give the product of reaction (1). The most interesting finding was that a solution of N-bromoacetamide in cold alkali when warmed to about 60° gave off a gas, which Hofmann recognized as methylamine from its odor, alkalinity, and combustibility (4). Distillation from a mixture of reactants into hydrochloric acid afforded methylamine hydrochloride in 80-90% yield. Study of the reaction in an open vessel was rewarding, for, at an intermediate stage which was only transient, Hofmann noticed the unmistakable, pungent odor of methylisocyanate. He confirmed his identification of this intermediate by gentle heating of a mixture of N-bromoacetamide and silver carbonate (diluted with sand to moderate the reaction) and isolated methylisocyanate (5). This ketenelike substance was known to add water to form methylamine and carbon dioxide (6), and a similar addition of acetamide (7) accounts for reactions (1) and (3).

The Hofmann reaction can be conducted without isolation of intermediates by simply heating an amide with an appropriate amount of sodium hypobromite or hypochlorite. Examples 8 (Hofmann) and 9 (*Org. Syn.*) show that the reaction is applicable to both aliphatic and aromatic amides and that yields are excellent.

8.
$$CH_3CH_2CH_2CH_2CH_2CONH_2 \xrightarrow[88\%]{NaOBr} CH_3CH_2CH_2CH_2CH_2NH_2$$

Caproamide   *n*-Amylamine

9.
$$3,4(CH_3O)_2C_6H_3CONH_2 \xrightarrow[80-82\%]{NaOCl} (CH_3O)_2C_6H_3NH_2$$

Veratric amide   4-Aminoveratrole

A particular feature of the reaction is the high purity of the products. An amide sparingly soluble in water, for example palmitamide (10), can be dissolved in methanol and treated with a solution of sodium methoxide and then with bromine.

10.
$$n\text{-}C_{15}H_{31}CONH_2 \xrightarrow[84-94\%]{CH_3ONa, Br_2} n\text{-}C_{15}H_{31}NHCO_2CH_3 \xrightarrow{CaO} n\text{-}C_{15}H_{31}NH_2$$

Palmitamide   Methyl *n*-pentadecyl-carbamate   Pentadecyl-amine

The product is a urethane resulting from addition of methanol to the intermediate isocyanate, and on saponification it affords pentadecylamine in nearly quantitative yield.

Hofmann's paper of 1882 described all intermediates that have ever been isolated and clarified all steps in the reaction except the rearrangement evidently involved in the conversion of N-bromoacetamide to methylisocyanate (5). In modern theory the reaction conforms to the general pattern of rearrangements. Thus elimination of hydrogen bromide from the bromoamide gives an intermediate

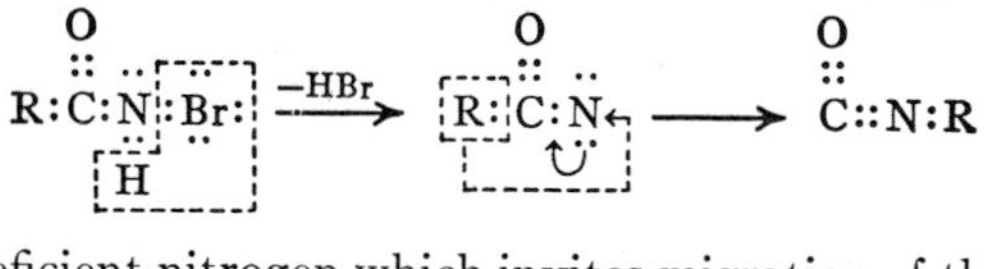

$$\overset{O}{\underset{H}{R:C:N:Br:}} \xrightarrow{-HBr} \overset{O}{R:C:N} \longrightarrow \overset{O}{C::N:R}$$

with an electron-deficient nitrogen which invites migration of the alkyl group with its pair of electrons from carbon to nitrogen. The formation of an isocyanate is analogous to the formation of a ketene in the Arndt-Eistert reaction (11.26). Isocyanates are usually prepared by condensation of an amine with phosgene (11), and they are hydrolyzed readily (12) by alkali to carbamic acids, which spontaneously lose carbon dioxide to give amines. These are the reactions employed by

11. $RNH_2 + ClCOCl \rightarrow RNHCOCl \rightarrow RN{=}C{=}O + HCl$

12. $RN{=}C{=}O \xrightarrow{HOH} RN{=}C \overset{OH}{\underset{OH}{\diagup}} \rightarrow RNHCO_2H \rightarrow RNH_2 + CO_2$

Carbamic acid

Wurtz in the first preparation of an alkylamine.

Working on products of the degradation of camphor in the period 1894–1914, Noyes[1] established a number of interrelationships which were recognized later (S. Archer, 1940) as defining the stereochemistry of the Hofmann reaction. For example, one form of camphoric acid is *cis* (I), since it forms an anhydride. One

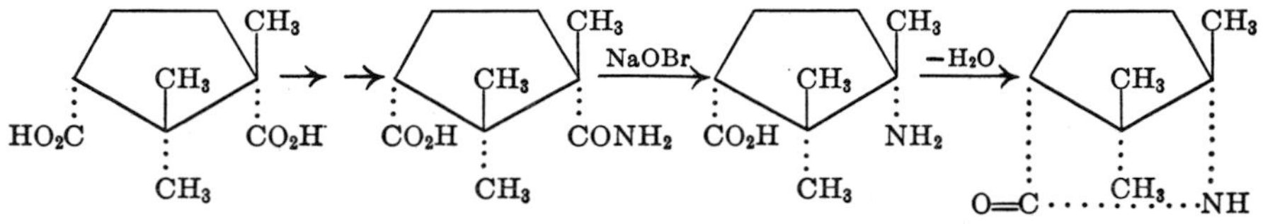

cis-Camphoric acid (I)   II   III   IV

of two monoamides (II) obtainable from it was available in *d*- and *l*-forms, and each on reaction with hypobromite gave an optically pure amine, III, in which the amino group was recognized as *cis* to the carboxyl group by formation of the lactam IV, from which III was recovered on hydrolysis. The migratory group thus retains its configuration in the rearrangement. Wallis (1933) studied the Hofmann rearrangement of an amide (V) in which optical activity is due to restriction of rotation about the pivotal bond between the substituted phenyl group and the α-naphthyl group. If the migratory phenyl group could become free during the

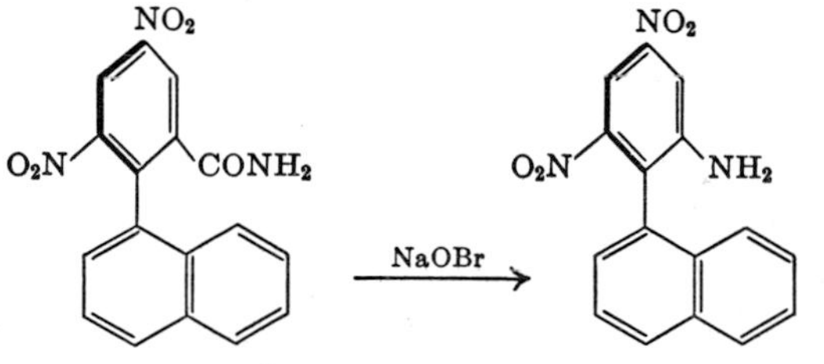

V (αD + 37°)   VI (αD + 398°)

rearrangement, the restriction would be removed and at least some racemization would occur. The amine produced, however, proved to be optically pure. Hence the reaction must proceed through a transition state in which the migratory group is partially bonded to both the migration origin and the migration terminus:

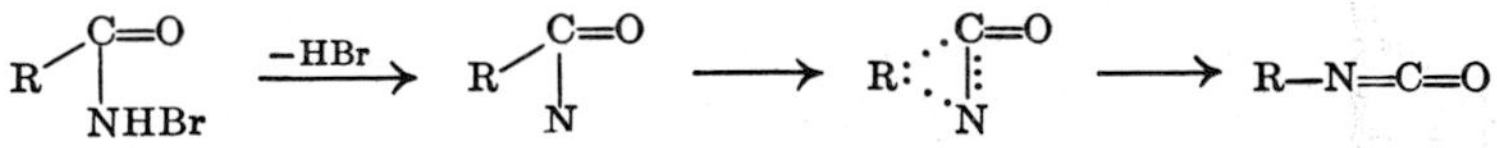

14.11   **Curtius Reaction.** — Curtius (Kiel, 1894) discovered an alternative route to primary amines that utilizes an acyl azide prepared either from an acid chloride and sodium azide ($RCOCl + NaN_3$) or by the action of nitrous acid on an acyl hydrazide (from an ester and hydrazine, 11.21). When heated in a solvent, the acyl azide loses nitrogen with rearrangement to an isocyanate, as in the Hofmann reaction. Loss of nitrogen gives an electronically

---

[1] William Albert Noyes, 1857–1941; b. Independence, Iowa; Ph.D. Johns Hopkins (Remsen); Minnesota; Tennessee; Rose Polytechnic Inst.; National Bureau of Standards; Univ. Illinois

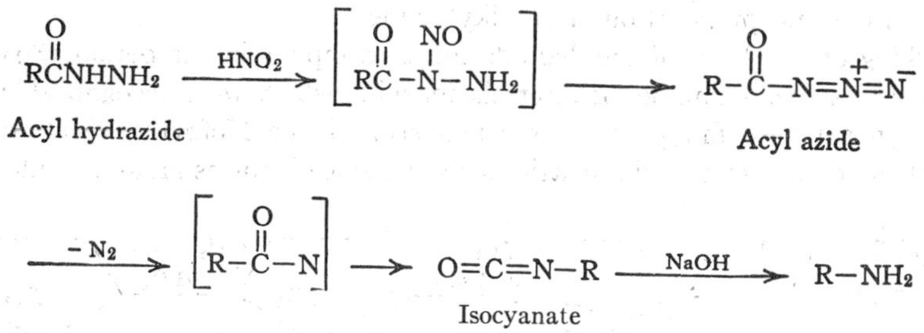

$$RCNHNH_2 \xrightarrow{HNO_2} \left[RC-N-NH_2 \right] \longrightarrow R-C-N=N=N^-$$

Acyl hydrazide   Acyl azide

$$\xrightarrow{-N_2} \left[R-C-N \right] \longrightarrow O=C=N-R \xrightarrow{NaOH} R-NH_2$$

Isocyanate

deficient nitrogen atom which acquires stability by alkyl migration. In one of

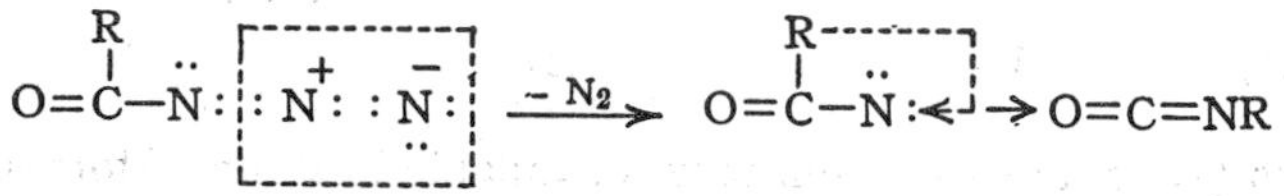

$$O=C-N \left[N : N \right] \xrightarrow{-N_2} O=C-N \rightarrow O=C=NR$$

several procedures the azide is decomposed in refluxing absolute ethanol to produce a urethane, which is then hydrolyzed; for example, as in the preparation of benzylamine from ethyl phenylacetate (overall yield about 80%). The ester is refluxed with hydrazine in absolute ethanol (6 hrs.); a solution of the hydrazide

$$C_6H_5CH_2CO_2C_2H_5 \xrightarrow[C_2H_5OH]{H_2NNH_2} C_6H_5CH_2CONHNH_2 \xrightarrow[Ether]{HCl, NaNO_2, 0°}$$

Ethyl phenylacetate   Phenylacethydrazide

$$C_6H_5CH_2CON_3 \xrightarrow[Refl.]{C_2H_5OH} C_6H_5CH_2NHCOC_2H_5 \xrightarrow[AcOH]{HCl} C_6H_5CH_2N^+H_3Cl^-$$

Ethyl N-benzyl-   Benzylamine
urethane   hydrochloride

is treated at 0° with sodium nitrite in the presence of ether; an ethereal extract of the azide is dried, absolute ethanol is added, and the solution heated on the steam bath to expel the ether and complete the decomposition. The urethane, a low-melting solid, is refluxed with hydrochloric acid and acetic acid until the oily layer disappears (12–36 hrs.) and the amine hydrochloride is obtained by evaporation to dryness and crystallization from absolute ethanol.

14.12   Schmidt Reaction. — A method for the direct conversion of a carboxylic acid into an amine in one step is due to Karl Friedrich Schmidt[1] (Åbo, Finland, 1923). On reaction with hydrazoic acid in benzene in the presence of sulfuric acid, a carboxylic acid is converted not to the acyl azide (a) but to the conjugate acid (b), which loses nitrogen more easily than the azide itself, with re-

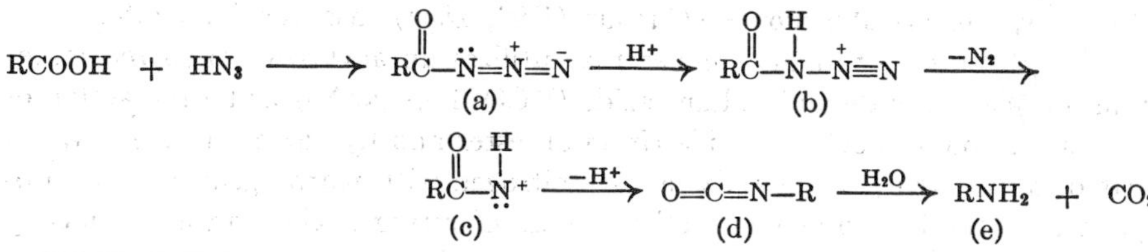

$$RCOOH + HN_3 \longrightarrow \underset{(a)}{RC-N=N=N} \xrightarrow{H^+} \underset{(b)}{RC-N-N\equiv N} \xrightarrow{-N_2}$$

$$\underset{(c)}{RC-N^+} \xrightarrow{-H^+} \underset{(d)}{O=C=N-R} \xrightarrow{H_2O} \underset{(e)}{RNH_2 + CO_2}$$

[1] Karl Friedrich Schmidt, b. 1887 Heidelberg; Ph.D. Heidelberg; Åbo, Finland; Knoll Co., Mannheim

arrangement to the isocyanate (d). The one-step procedure is convenient and yields are high. For example, a solution of stearic acid (15 g.) in benzene (500 ml.) is treated with concentrated sulfuric acid (30 ml.) and the mixture is stirred

$$CH_3(CH_2)_{16}CO_2H \xrightarrow[96\%]{HN_3,\ H^+;\ H_2O} CH_3(CH_2)_{16}NH_2 + CO_2 + N_2$$

Stearic acid　　　　　　　　　　　　　Heptadecylamine

at 40° during addition of a 5% solution of hydrazoic acid in benzene. After the reaction has ceased, the acid layer is poured into water to precipitate heptadecyl-amine sulfate, which is collected and crystallized from ethanol. The solution of hydrazoic acid is made by dropping sulfuric acid into a stirred mixture of sodium azide, water, and benzene at 0–10° and drying the benzene layer.

14.13　　　Gabriel Synthesis. — Working in Hofmann's laboratory, S. Gabriel (1887) introduced a useful method of preparing pure primary amines consisting in alkylation of a derivative of ammonia in which two of the positions

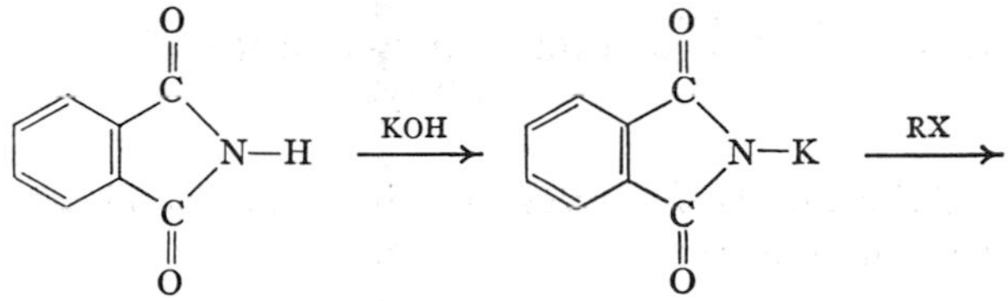

Phthalimide　　　　　　　Potassium phthalimide
(pK$_a$ 8.30)

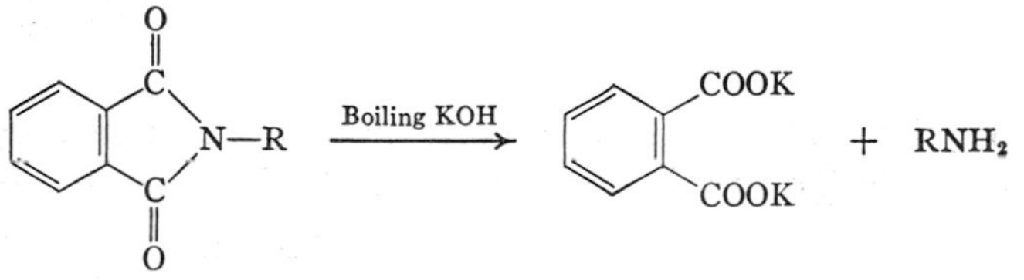

are temporarily occupied by blocking groups to prevent introduction of more than a single alkyl substituent. The cyclic substance phthalimide, employed as the ammonia derivative, possesses a hydrogen atom doubly activated by the carbonyl groups and hence acidic and capable of forming metal salts, which react with alkyl halides. The alkylated phthalimide is then hydrolyzed with alkali and the liberated amine is removed from the alkaline mixture by steam distillation.

An example for illustration is the synthesis of γ-aminobutyric acid by the following reaction sequence. Treatment of trimethylene glycol with hydrogen chloride

$$HOCH_2CH_2CH_2OH \xrightarrow[50-60\%]{HCl,\ 160°} ClCH_2CH_2HC_2OH \xrightarrow{PBr_3}$$

$$ClCH_2CH_2CH_2Br \xrightarrow[60-70\%]{KCN\ Alcohol-water} ClCH_2CH_2CH_2CN \xrightarrow[160°]{C_6H_4(CO)_2NK}$$

$$C_6H_4(CO)_2NCH_2CH_2CH_2CN \xrightarrow[47-62\%]{H_2SO_4-H_2O} H_2NCH_2CH_2CH_2CO_2H$$

γ-Aminobutyric acid

at 160° gives a mixture from which trimethylene chlorohydrin can be isolated in modest yield by fractionation. The hydroxyl group is replaced by bromine and then bromine is replaced by a cyanide group. γ-Chlorobutyronitrile is then heated with powdered potassium phthalimide and the cooled mixture extracted with water. The residual phthalimide derivative is refluxed with strong sulfuric acid to effect hydrolysis and the solution let stand for separation of phthalic acid, which is removed. Sulfuric acid is removed with excess barium carbonate, which does not react with the dipolar amino acid, $H_3N^+(CH_2)_3CO_2^-$. The filtered solution is evaporated and the amino acid precipitated with absolute ethanol.

14.14   Reduction of Unsaturated Nitrogen Compounds. — The preparation of amines by the reduction of **nitro compounds** is particularly useful in the aromatic series, for the required intermediates are obtained easily by nitration: $C_6H_6 + HNO_3 \rightarrow C_6H_5NO_2 \rightarrow C_6H_5NH_2$. Reduction of **nitriles** with sodium and alcohol is only moderately satisfactory. Hydrogenation of nitriles proceeds

$$CH_3CH_2CH_2CH_2CH_2C\equiv N \xrightarrow[70\%]{Na,\ C_2H_5OH} CH_3CH_2CH_2CH_2CH_2CH_2NH_2$$
Capronitrile n-Hexylamine

readily in the presence of nickel catalysts but yields, surprisingly, a considerable amount of the secondary amine, for example:

$$C_6H_5CH_2CN \xrightarrow{H_2,\ Raney\ Ni,\ 140°} \begin{cases} C_6H_5CH_2CH_2NH_2\ (71\%) \\ \beta\text{-Phenylethylamine} \\ (C_6H_5CH_2CH_2)_2NH\ (20\%) \\ Di\text{-}\beta\text{-phenylethylamine} \end{cases}$$
Benzyl cyanide

The by-product is regarded as resulting from addition of some of the primary amine to the initially produced imine ($RCH=NH$), followed by hydrogenolysis.

$$RCH_2NH_2 + RCH=NH \longrightarrow \begin{array}{c} RCH-NH_2 \\ \diagdown \\ \diagup NH \\ RCH_2 \end{array} \xrightarrow{2H} \begin{array}{c} RCH_2 \\ \diagdown \\ \diagup NH + NH_3 \\ RCH_2 \end{array}$$

Formation of the secondary amine is suppressed by conducting the hydrogenation in either liquid ammonia or a solution of dry ammonia in methanol; under these conditions β-phenylethylamine is obtained in yields of 85–90%.

Reduction of nitriles by lithium aluminum hydride proceeds smoothly and secondary amines are not formed. The yields in the reduction of aliphatic mononitriles are high (lauronitrile, 90%); reduction of dinitriles proceeds with some

$$2\ RC\equiv N + LiAlH_4 \longrightarrow (RCH_2N)_2LiAl \xrightarrow{H_2O} 2\ RCH_2NH_2$$

Examples:

$$C_6H_5C\equiv N \xrightarrow[72\%]{LiAlH_4} C_6H_5CH_2NH_2$$
Benzonitrile   Benzylamine

$$N\equiv C(CH_2)_8C\equiv N \xrightarrow[40\%]{LiAlH_4} H_2NCH_2(CH_2)_8CH_2NH_2$$
Sebaconitrile   1,10-Diaminodecane

difficulty. Nitriles are also reduced by diborane. Phenylacetonitrile, for example, gives 2-phenylethylamine in 88% yield (H. C. Brown, 1960). Amides of the types $RCONH_2$, $RCONHR'$ and $RCONR'R''$ are reduced by lithium aluminum hydride to primary, secondary and tertiary amines, respectively. The

Examples:

$$C_6H_5N\begin{array}{c}H\\\\COCH_3\end{array} \xrightarrow[60\%]{\text{LiAlH}_4} C_6H_5N\begin{array}{c}H\\\\CH_2CH_3\end{array}$$

Acetanilide   N-Ethylaniline

$$C_6H_5N\begin{array}{c}CH_3\\\\COCH_3\end{array} \xrightarrow[91\%]{\text{LiAlH}_4} C_6H_5N\begin{array}{c}CH_3\\\\CH_2CH_3\end{array}$$

N-Methylacetanilide   N,N-Methylethylaniline

reduction of an amide of type $RCONH_2$ apparently proceeds through initial dehydration to the nitrile (Newman, 1960). Amides are rather unreactive substances and are not reducible by other chemical methods. Hydrogenation can be accomplished at high temperatures and pressures, but mixtures usually result; for example:

$$CH_3(CH_2)_9CH_2CONH_2 \xrightarrow[250°, 300 \text{ atm.}]{H_2, \text{ Cu—Cr, dioxane,}} CH_3(CH_2)_9CH_2CH_2NH_2$$

Lauramide   Laurylamine
                                              (with 49% of the
                                              secondary amine)

Oximes are also reducible to primary amines, presumably by addition of hydrogen to the double bond and replacement of the hydroxyl group by hydrogen:

$$RCH{=}NOH \xrightarrow{2H} \left[RCH_2N\begin{array}{c}H\\\\OH\end{array} \right] \xrightarrow{2H} RCH_2NH_2 + H_2O$$

Such reductions are often accomplished successfully with sodium and alcohol or with sodium amalgam and dilute acetic acid, as in the example:

$$CH_3(CH_2)_5CH{=}NOH \xrightarrow[60-73\%]{Na, C_2H_5OH} CH_3(CH_2)_5CH_2NH_2$$

n-Heptaldoxime   n-Heptylamine

On hydrogenation of the same oxime over a nickel catalyst supported on kieselguhr, n-heptylamine is obtained in 61% yield, accompanied by 20% of di-n-heptylamine; a further example of the method is as follows:

$$\begin{array}{c}CH_2{-}CH_2\\| \qquad \rangle C{=}NOH\\CH_2{-}CH_2\end{array} \xrightarrow[80\%]{H_2, \text{ Ni (kieselguhr), } 90°} \begin{array}{c}CH_2{-}CH_2\\| \qquad \rangle CHNH_2\\CH_2{-}CH_2\end{array}$$

Cyclopentanone oxime   Cyclopentylamine
                                              (with 10% of the
                                              secondary amine)

Some secondary amine invariably is formed in the hydrogenation and may result from initial condensation of the primary amine with the starting material.

Nitroalkanes are reducible with lithium aluminum hydride to amines; for example, 2-nitrobutane gives sec-butylamine in 85% yield (see also 12.49).

Schiff bases, for example benzylidenaniline from benzaldehyde and aniline, are reduced rapidly and efficiently by dimethylamine borane in acetic acid solution or suspension (J. H. Billman,[1] 1961). Unlike other borohydrides, dimethylamine

$$3\,C_6H_5CH{=}NC_6H_5 \;+\; (CH_3)_2N^+HB^-H_3 \;+\; 3\,CH_3CO_2H \xrightarrow{84\%} 3\,C_6H_5CH_2NHC_6H_5 \;+\; (CH_3)_2NH \;+\; (CH_3CO_2)_3B$$

borane can be used in boiling acetic acid with little loss of active hydrogen (25% excess reagent is recommended). Borane appears to be the effective reagent and to be liberated from the complex as it is utilized. Yields are high and the following groups are not affected: NO_2, Cl, OH, OCH_3, CO_2H, $CO_2C_2H_5$, SO_2NH_2.

14.15 **Ethanolamines** are produced technically from ammonia and ethylene oxide.

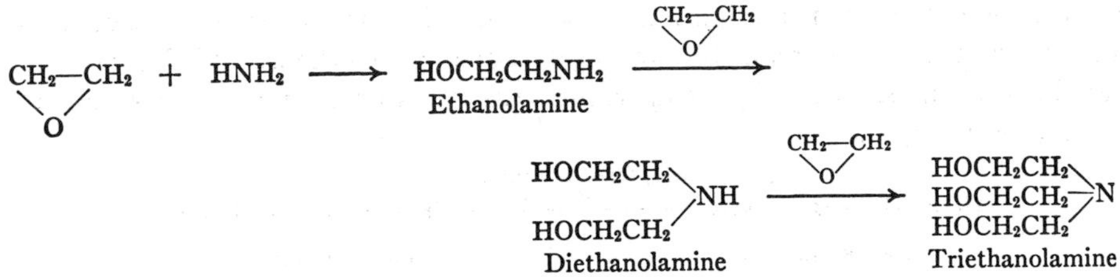

REACTIONS

14.16 **Acylation.** — Primary and secondary amines can be acetylated efficiently with acetic anhydride at room temperature. A primary amine can be converted into a diacetyl derivative, but only under special conditions.

$$\underset{\text{Primary amine}}{(CH_3)_2CHCH_2NH_2} \xrightarrow{(CH_3CO)_2O} \underset{\substack{\text{Acetylisobutylamine}\\ \text{(m.p. 107°)}}}{(CH_3)_2CHCH_2NHCOCH_3} \;+\; CH_3CO_2H$$

$$\underset{\text{Secondary amine}}{[(CH_3)_2CH]_2NH} \xrightarrow{CH_3COCl} \underset{\substack{\text{Acetyldiisopropylamine}\\ \text{(liq., b.p. 222–225°)}}}{[(CH_3)_2CH]_2NCOCH_3} \;+\; HCl$$

Aniline can be converted into acetanilide, $C_6H_5NHCOCH_3$, by refluxing a solution in acetic acid for about 4 hrs. Formyl derivatives of amines are obtainable by reaction with formic acid under milder conditions. Acetylation of an amine can be accomplished also with acetic anhydride in aqueous solution; the amine evidently is very much more reactive than water, since the relative concentrations would favor hydrolysis. The easily formed amide linkage of an acylamine is considerably more resistant to hydrolysis than an ester linkage, and hence an N-acetyl derivative of an acid ester is easily convertible by partial hydrolysis into

[1] John Henry Billman, b. 1912 Brooklyn, N. Y.; Ph.D. Princeton (Audrieth); Indiana Univ.

the N-acetylamino acid. The N,N-diacetate of a water-soluble primary amine can be obtained by reaction with acetic anhydride in alkaline solution.

Acetyl derivatives of liquid amines are often crystalline solids useful for identification. Acetylamines, like other amides, are neutral. Since a tertiary amine is not acylable, a crude tertiary amine contaminated with primary or secondary amines can be purified by addition of sufficient acetic anhydride to react with such substances and extraction of an ethereal solution of the mixture with hydrochloric acid. Alternatively, a little acetic anhydride is added and the tertiary amine separated by distillation from the less volatile acetyl derivatives.

Trichloroacetyl derivatives of both aliphatic and aromatic amines are obtainable in 80–90% yield by reaction with hexachloroacetone (Allied Chem. Corp.) in hexane (*Org. Syn.*, 1961).

$$(CH_3)_2NH \xrightarrow{-H^+} (CH_3)_2\bar{N} \xrightarrow{CCl_3COCCl_3}$$

$$(CH_3)_2N-\overset{\overset{\displaystyle CCl_3}{|}}{\underset{\underset{\displaystyle CCl_3}{|}}{C}}-O^- \xrightarrow{H^+} (CH_3)_2N-\overset{\overset{\displaystyle CCl_3}{|}}{C}=O \ + \ CHCl_3$$

14.17   **Sulfonamides.** — In extension of Baumann's work on benzoylation in an alkaline medium (8.23), his student O. Hinsberg (1890) found in benzenesulfonyl chloride a useful reagent for distinguishing between amine types. In the **Hinsberg test** a primary amine when shaken with the liquid reagent in dilute alkali gives a benzenesulfonamide which is soluble in alkali; a secondary amine gives a Hinsberg derivative, but this has no replaceable hydrogen and is insoluble in alkali; a tertiary amine fails to react. The acidity of the primary

$$C_6H_5SO_2Cl \ + \ H_2NR \xrightarrow{-HCl} C_6H_5SO_2NR \xrightarrow{NaOH} C_6H_5SO_2\bar{N}R$$
$$\underset{\substack{\text{Primary} \\ \text{amine}}}{} \qquad\qquad \underset{\substack{H \\ \text{(soluble} \\ \text{in alkali)}}}{} \qquad\qquad \underset{Na^+}{}$$

$$C_6H_5SO_2Cl \ + \ HNR_2 \xrightarrow{-HCl} C_6H_5SO_2NR_2$$
$$\underset{\substack{\text{Secondary} \\ \text{amine}}}{} \qquad\qquad \underset{\substack{\text{(insoluble} \\ \text{in alkali)}}}{}$$

amine derivative is attributable to the presence of the sulfone group. Like other acyl derivatives, benzenesulfonamides of both types can be hydrolyzed, with regeneration of the amines. The benzenesulfonamide from a primary amine can be alkylated and the product hydrolyzed, and in this way the original amine can be converted into a pure N-alkyl derivative:

$$RNH_2 \xrightarrow{C_6H_5SO_2Cl, \ NaOH} R\bar{N}SO_2C_6H_5 \xrightarrow{(CH_3)_2SO_4} RNSO_2C_6H_5 \xrightarrow{Hydrol.} RNH$$
$$\underset{Na^+}{} \qquad\qquad \underset{CH_3}{} \qquad\qquad \underset{CH_3}{}$$

Sulfonamides of primary amines can be used to effect reductive deamination (Nickon,[1] 1960). The methanesulfonamide (or an arylsulfonamide) is treated

$$C_6H_5CH_2NHSO_2CH_3 \xrightarrow[-H_2SO_4]{H_3N^+OSO_3^-, \ OH^-} C_6H_5CH_2NSO_2CH_3 \xrightarrow{-CH_3SO_2H}$$
$$\underset{NH_2}{|}$$

$$C_6H_5CH_2N=NH \xrightarrow{-N_2} C_6H_5CH_3$$

in aqueous alcoholic alkali with 15–25 equivalents of the alkali-unstable reagent hydroxylamine-O-sulfonic acid (a solid). The formulation shows the pathway postulated.

14.18   **Reaction with Nitrous Acid.** — It was noted in section 12.47 that a diazonium salt derived from a primary aliphatic amine decomposes

$$RCH_2N^+H_3Cl^- \xrightarrow{HNO_2} \underset{\text{Diazonium salt}}{[RCH_2N^+\equiv N]Cl^-} \xrightarrow{-N_2} RC^+H_2 + N_2 + Cl^-$$

spontaneously to nitrogen and a carbonium ion. Such an ion can then react with water to form an alcohol, but usually rearrangement occurs and the alcohol is not that structurally related to the amine. Thus on treatment with nitrous acid at pH 3 *n*-propylamine gives isopropyl alcohol, propylene, and a trace of *n*-propyl alcohol; methylamine gives no methanol. Neopentylamine gives rise to *t*-amyl alcohol as the only alcoholic product. The rearrangement is of the Wagner-

$$\underset{(CH_3)_2\overset{\displaystyle CH_3}{\underset{|}{C}}CH_2NH_2}{} \xrightarrow{HNO_2} \underset{(CH_3)_2\overset{\displaystyle CH_3}{\underset{|}{C}}\overset{+}{-}\overset{\cdot}{C}H_2}{} \xrightarrow{OH^-} \underset{(CH_3)_2\overset{\displaystyle OH}{\underset{|}{C}}-CH_2CH_3}{}$$

Meerwein type but is generally named after N. J. Demjanov, who used the reaction for expanding and contracting alicyclic ring systems: cyclobutylamine → cyclopropylcarbinol; cyclobutylmethylamine → cyclopentanol. The reaction provides a most satisfactory procedure for generation of carbonium ions under irreversible and mild conditions. Since liberation of nitrogen is quantitative, the reaction is also of use for determination of the amount of primary amino nitrogen present in a given substance or mixture.

Secondary amines on reaction with nitrous acid yield N-nitrosoamines, which

$$\underset{R'}{\overset{R}{>}}N-H + HON=O \longrightarrow \underset{R'}{\overset{R}{>}}N-N=O + H_2O$$

Secondary amine   Nitrosoamine

are neutral yellow oils or solids sparingly soluble in water. They can be hydrolyzed to the components and on reduction they afford substituted hydrazines.

$$\underset{CH_3}{\overset{CH_3}{>}}N\cdot NO \qquad\qquad \underset{(CH_3)_2CH}{\overset{(CH_3)_2CH}{>}}N\cdot NO$$

N-Nitrosodimethylamine   N-Nitrosodiisopropylamine
(yellow oil, b.p. 153°)   (volatile yellow solid, m.p. 46°)

Tertiary aliphatic amines are indifferent to nitrous acid.

[1] Alex Nickon, b. 1927 Cholojow, Poland; Ph.D. Harvard (Fieser); Johns Hopkins Univ.

14.19   **Hofmann Degradation,** 1881. — Piperine, an alkaloid isolated from black pepper (*Piper nigrum*) by Pelletier[1] (1821), is an amide, and the acidic and basic components which it yields on hydrolysis with alcoholic alkali were named piperic acid and piperidine. Auguste Cahours (1857) characterized the new base as a secondary amine of the formula $C_5H_{10}N$ but did not deduce the structure. The problem attracted the attention of Hofmann, but a first attempt to cleave the molecule to smaller fragments by the action of hydrogen chloride at a high temperature failed. A second approach was based upon observations reported 30 years earlier when Hofmann had discovered the quaternary ammonium hydroxides. He had found these substances to undergo smooth thermal decomposition. Whereas tetramethylammonium hydroxide yields trimethylamine and methanol, the decomposition of tetraethylammonium hydroxide

$$[(CH_3)_4N]^+OH^- \xrightarrow{130-135°} (CH_3)_3N + CH_3OH$$

Tetramethylammonium
hydroxide (pentahydrate, m.p. 63°)

occurs at a lower temperature and the products are triethylamine, ethylene, and water. Higher alkyl groups all behave like the ethyl group and give rise to

$$[(CH_3CH_2)_4N]^+OH^- \xrightarrow{100°} (CH_3CH_2)_3N + CH_2{=}CH_2 + H_2O$$

(tetrahydrate, m.p. 50°)

alkenes. Hofmann then established that in compounds of mixed types containing one methyl group, this group, which alone can afford no alkene, is always retained by the nitrogen, for example:

$$[CH_3(C_2H_5)_2C_5H_{11}]N^+OH^- \rightarrow [CH_3(C_2H_5)C_5H_{11}]N + CH_2{=}CH_2$$
$$[CH_3(C_2H_5)(n\text{-}C_5H_{11})C_6H_5]N^+OH^- \rightarrow [CH_3(n\text{-}C_5H_{11})C_6H_5]N + CH_2{=}CH_2$$

For investigation of the structure of piperidine (1), Hofmann exhaustively methylated the base, converted the iodide into the methohydroxide (2), and pyrolyzed this substance in the expectation of obtaining an unsaturated hydrocarbon. The product, however, was an amine, eventually recognized as having structure

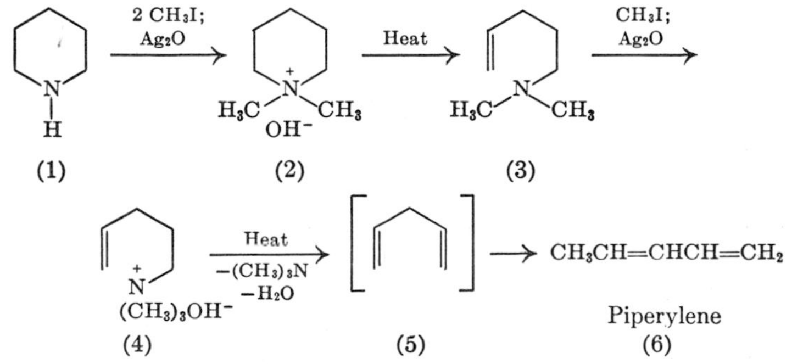

[1] P. Joseph Pelletier, 1788–1842; b. Paris; Paris

(3); the base absorbed carbon dioxide from the air too rapidly for reliable analysis but gave a crystalline yellow complex salt, $C_7H_{15}N^+AuCl_4^-$. Exhaustive methylation of this base, conversion to the methohydroxide (6), and pyrolysis afforded trimethylamine and a new hydrocarbon, C_5H_8, to which Hofmann assigned the name piperylene. The hydrocarbon was characterized as doubly unsaturated by conversion to a crystalline tetrabromide, m.p. 114.5°. It was assumed to be divinylmethane (5) until Thiele (1901) tried to condense it with benzaldehyde and with diethyl oxalate under the conditions which he had used in the case of cyclopentadiene (13.19). Finding the hydrocarbon inert to these reagents, he oxidized a sample ($KMnO_4$, 0°) and showed by isolation of acetic acid and formic acid, and no malonic acid, that the substance is 1,3-pentadiene (6); the initial product (5) is isomerized in the alkaline medium to the conjugated diene. Thiele's assumption that a hydrocarbon of structure (5) would behave like cyclopentadiene turned out to be incorrect. Indeed he himself showed that cycloheptadiene-1,5 does not form fulvenes and related products.

The conversion of piperidine to piperylene by two Hofmann degradations settled a problem which might have been solved by correlation of the secondary amine with pyridine. Pyridine had been obtained by oxidation of piperidine, but the yield was very low. Reduction of pyridine to piperidine was later accomplished with sodium and alcohol, but the reaction proceeded so poorly that unchanged pyridine had to be eliminated by formation of the N-nitroso derivative, oxidation with permanganate in acetone, and hydrolysis of the nitroso derivative (HCl in toluene). Piperidine poisons platinum catalysts, but piperidine hydrochloride can be hydrogenated efficiently in absolute ethanol (R. Adams, 1928).

Where *cis* and *trans* forms of the olefin are possible, the pyrolytic reaction normally proceeds by *trans* elimination (see p. 586 for example).

An adaptation of the Hofmann reaction has been employed for the construction of interesting ring systems (H. E. Winberg, du Pont Co., 1960). Pyrolysis of the quaternary base (1) effected 1,6-Hofmann elimination to the triene (2), isolated

$$H_3C \quad O \quad CH_2N^+(CH_3)_2OH^- \qquad H_2C \quad O \quad CH_2$$

(1)   (2)   (3)

by quenching at −78°. When warmed in the presence of hydroquinone to inhibit polymerization, the substance dimerized to give (3) in high yield. Because of the relationship to hydrocarbon analogs (18.19), (3) is described as a heterocyclophane. It was degraded to cyclododecane by hydrogenolysis, acetylation, pyrolysis, and hydrogenation. The sulfur analog of (2) was not isolated, and the analog of (3) was obtained in only 19% yield.

14.20   Mechanism of the Hofmann Elimination. — Hofmann's experiments with ammonium hydroxides of mixed types led him to formulate the empirical rule that the group participating preferentially in the β-elimination is

$$(CH_3)_3\overset{+}{N}\!-\!\overset{|}{\underset{\beta}{C}}\!-\!\overset{|}{\underset{|}{C}}H\!-\!\longrightarrow\ (CH_3)_3N\ +\ \overset{|}{C}\!=\!\overset{|}{C}\ +\ H_2O$$
$$OH^-$$

the one capable of forming an olefin carrying the smallest number of alkyl groups. Thus in the second example cited above, an ethyl group is eliminated in preference to an n-amyl group. A theoretical interpretation of the rule emerged from kinetic studies by the Ingold school (1927–48) of β-eliminations of quaternary ammonium hydroxides and the related sulfonium hydroxides. These eliminations exhibit second-order kinetics (E_2 reaction) and are formulated by Ingold as shown in (1) for the basic decomposition of ethyldimethylsulfonium ion. That dimethylethyl-

1. $CH_3CH_2\overset{+}{S}(CH_3)_2 \xrightarrow[(E_2)]{OH^-} [HO\cdots H\cdots CH_2\!:\!:\!:\!CH_2\cdots S(CH_3)_2]$
   　　　　　　　　　　　　　　　　Transition state

   $$\longrightarrow H_2O + CH_2\!=\!CH_2 + S(CH_3)_2$$

n-propylammonium hydroxide (2) yields ethylene rather than propylene is interpreted as follows. The positively charged nitrogen atom produces an inductive

2. $$CH_3\!\rightarrow\!\underset{\beta'}{C}H_2\underset{\alpha'}{C}H_2\overset{+}{N}\!-\!\underset{\alpha}{C}H_2\!\overset{\overset{H}{|}}{\underset{\beta}{C}}H_2 \xrightarrow[E_2]{OH^-} CH_2\!=\!CH_2$$
   　　　　　　　　$\overset{}{CH_3}\ \overset{}{CH_3}$

drift of electrons from the surrounding carbon atoms sufficient to loosen and promote elimination of a β-proton. The β'-methyl substituent in the n-propyl group is electron-releasing and hence opposes the effect of the nitrogen pole, with the result that this group remains joined to nitrogen and the ethyl group suffers fission. A β'-substituent that is electron-attracting, for example halogen, augments the effect of the nitrogen pole and promotes preferential elimination, as illustrated in (3). The reaction proceeds in the same direction when the β'-sub-

3. $$Cl\!\leftarrow\!\overset{\overset{H}{|}}{C}H\!-\!CH_2\!-\!\overset{+}{S}\!-\!CH_2CH_3 \xrightarrow[(E_2)]{OH^-} ClCH\!=\!CH_2$$
   　　　　　　　　　　　　CH_3

stituent is phenyl rather than chlorine.

The relative ease with which various alkyl groups form olefins, as determined by kinetic studies of the decomposition of ions of the types $RS^+(CH_3)_2$ and $RN^+(CH_3)_3$, is shown in (4). The results substantiate predictions; thus the isobutyl group, which carries two β-alkyl substituents, is eliminated with particular difficulty.

4. 　ethyl > n-propyl > n-butyl　>　n-amyl　>　isoamyl > isobutyl

$$\underset{\beta}{C\!-\!C}\quad \underset{\beta}{C\!\rightarrow\!C\!-\!C}\quad \underset{\beta}{C\!-\!C\!\rightarrow\!C\!-\!C}\quad \underset{\beta}{C\!-\!C\!-\!C\!\rightarrow\!C\!-\!C}\quad \overset{C}{\underset{C}{\diagdown}}\!\!\underset{\beta}{C\!\rightarrow\!C\!-\!C}\quad \overset{C}{\underset{C}{\diagup}}\!\!\underset{\beta}{C\!-\!C}$$

Onium ions of special structural types are capable under suitable conditions of undergoing decomposition by a reaction that follows first-order kinetics (E_1). Unimolecular elimination, like unimolecular substitution, is considered to involve two stages (5): formation of a carbonium ion, followed by rapid loss of a proton. Unimolecular eliminations have been observed only when one of the alkyl groups is secondary or tertiary, as in the example cited (5, dimethyl-t-butylsulfonium

$$5. \quad CH_3 \rightarrow \overset{\overset{CH_3}{\downarrow}}{\underset{\overset{\uparrow}{CH_3}}{C}} \overset{+}{S}(CH_3)_2 \xrightarrow[\text{(slow)}]{E_1} CH_3 - \overset{+}{\underset{\underset{CH_3}{|}}{C}} - CH_3 + S(CH_3)_2$$

$$H_2C \overset{\overset{--H--}{\overset{\overset{\cdot}{|}}{\cdot}}}{\overset{+}{C}} - CH_3 \xrightarrow[\text{(fast)}]{} H^+ + H_2C = \overset{\underset{CH_3}{|}}{C} - CH_3$$

iodide), for the combined inductive effect of two or three alkyl substituents is required to surmount the energy barrier involved in production of the carbonium ion. In unimolecular elimination the Hofmann rule no longer applies, and the olefin formed preferentially carries the largest number of alkyl substituents. The contrasting results are seen in the decomposition of dimethyl-t-amylsulfonium iodide (6), which proceeds largely unimolecularly in 98% ethanol and largely bimolecularly in 80% aqueous ethanol. The E_1 reaction yields the trialkylalkene (a) and the E_2 reaction, in accordance with the Hofmann rule, yields the dialkylalkene (b).

$$6. \quad CH_3CH_2\overset{\overset{CH_3}{|}}{\underset{\overset{|}{CH_3}}{\overset{+}{C}}}-\overset{+}{S}(CH_3)_2$$

$$\xrightarrow[E_1]{98\% \text{ EtOH}} CH_3CH = \overset{\overset{CH_3}{|}}{\underset{\overset{|}{CH_3}}{C}} \quad \begin{matrix} 85\% \\ (+15\% \text{ b}) \end{matrix} \quad (a)$$

$$\xrightarrow[E_2]{80\% \text{ EtOH}} CH_3CH_2\overset{\overset{CH_3}{|}}{\underset{\overset{\|}{CH_2}}{C}} \quad \begin{matrix} 86\% \\ (+14\% \text{ a}) \end{matrix} \quad (b)$$

G. Wittig (1956–60) investigated the decomposition of quaternary ammonium salts with the very strongly basic phenyllithium or butyllithium and found that in at least some cases the reaction does not proceed by pure β-elimination but by a process described as an α',β-elimination. Experiments with tritium-containing trimethylethylammonium hydroxide showed that the base first abstracts a proton from a methyl group (α'); β-elimination then occurs through a quasi-cyclic

$$(CH_3)_2\overset{+}{N}\overset{\underset{\overset{|}{CH_3}}{\overset{|}{CH_2}}}{\underset{\underset{\beta}{\overset{\alpha'}{}}}{}} \xrightarrow[-C_6H_6]{C_6H_5^-} (CH_3)_2\overset{+}{N}\cdots CH_2 \quad \longrightarrow \quad (CH_3)_2N: + \; CH_2$$

transition state, with reformation of the methyl group. V. Franzen (1960) found that organoalkali compounds react much more rapidly with trialkylsulfonium salts than with the quaternary ammonium salts and that the reactions proceed almost exclusively by α',β-elimination. Thus the reaction of $(CH_3CD_2)_3S^+Br^-$ with triphenylmethylsodium gives a hydrocarbon containing 75% of $(C_6H_5)_3CD$. Since the five atoms involved in the α',β-elimination are planar in the transition state, the steric course of an elimination may depend upon conformational stability. Thus n-heptyl-(4)-dimethylsulfonium bromide on reaction with tritylsodium gives *trans*-heptene-3.

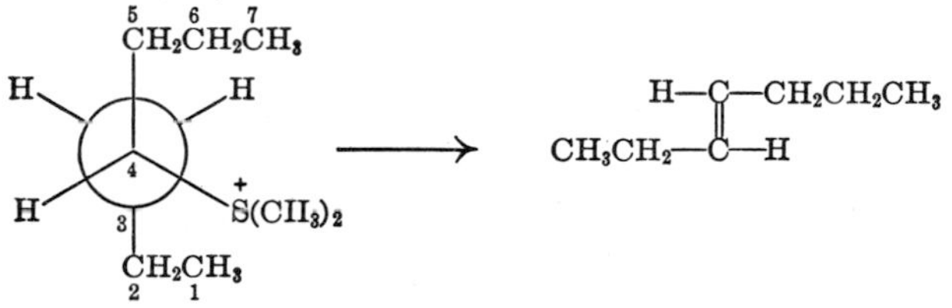

14.21   Oxidation.

— Amine salts are stable to oxidation, but not the free bases. Thus a *vic*-aminoalcohol is cleaved by periodic acid or lead tetraacetate (1) just as a *vic*-glycol is cleaved. Primary amines (both aliphatic

$$1. \quad \underset{\overset{|}{OH} \;\; \overset{|}{NH_2}}{RCH-CHR'} \xrightarrow{HIO_4} RCH=O + O=CHR' + NH_3$$

$$2. \quad n\text{-}C_3H_7CH_2NH_2 \xrightarrow{H_2O_2 \;(Na_2WO_2)} n\text{-}C_3H_7CH_2NHOH \xrightarrow[57\%]{} n\text{-}C_3H_7CH=NOH$$

and aromatic) on oxidation with hydrogen peroxide in the presence of a catalytic amount of sodium tungstate are converted to the aldoximes through intermediate hydroxylamines (2; Kurt Kahr, 1960).

The oxidation of tertiary amines is particularly interesting. Trimethylamine on reaction with aqueous hydrogen peroxide yields trimethylamine oxide hydrate (1), which when warmed in vacuum slowly yields anhydrous trimethylamine

$$(CH_3)_3N \xrightarrow{HOOH} [(CH_3)_3\overset{+}{N}OH]OH^- \xleftarrow{Ag_2O} [(CH_3)_3\overset{+}{N}OH]I^- \xleftarrow{CH_3I} (CH_3)_2NOH$$

$$\text{(1) m. p. 98°} \qquad\qquad \text{(2)} \qquad\qquad \text{(3)}$$

$$\downarrow$$

$$(CH_3)_3\overset{+}{N}-\overset{-}{O} \quad = \quad (CH_3)_3N\rightarrow O \quad = \quad CH_3\cdot\overset{..CH_3}{\underset{..CH_3}{N^+}}:\overset{..}{\underset{..}{O}}^-:$$

$$\text{(4) m. p. 208°} \qquad\qquad \text{(5)} \qquad\qquad \text{(6)}$$

oxide. A second route to the hydrate is from N,N-dimethylhydroxylamine (3). The oxide has a semipolar bond, represented as in (4) or as in (5), or in the electronic formulation (6). The saltlike character of the oxide is evident from its high melting point and because it is soluble in water and insoluble in ether. The hydrate is in fact a quaternary ammonium hydroxide. Meisenheimer (1913) proved that the two hydroxyl groups are bound in different ways by synthesis and thermal decomposition of isomers I and II. Meisenheimer (1908) also demon-

$$\left[\begin{array}{c} CH_3 \\ CH_3 \end{array} \!\! \diagdown \!\! N \!\! \diagup \!\! \begin{array}{c} CH_3 \\ OCH_3 \end{array} \right]^+ OH^- \longrightarrow (CH_3)_3N + CH_2O + H_2O$$

I

$$\left[\begin{array}{c} CH_3 \\ CH_3 \end{array} \!\! \diagdown \!\! N \!\! \diagup \!\! \begin{array}{c} CH_3 \\ OH \end{array} \right]^+ OCH_3^- \longrightarrow (CH_3)_3NO + CH_3OH$$

II

strated that suitably substituted amine oxides can be obtained in $(+)$ and $(-)$ forms.

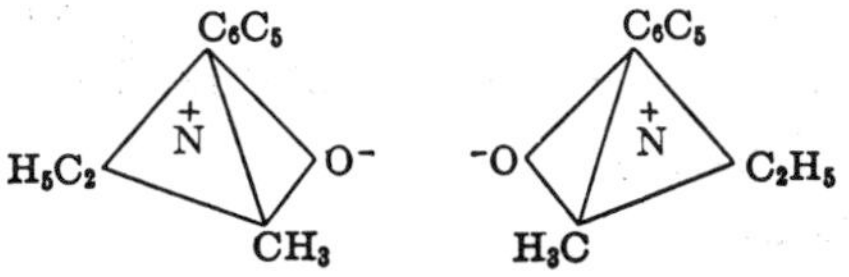

Cope and co-workers, who discovered a reaction to be discussed presently, employed a preparative procedure here illustrated for the case of N,N-dimethyl-(α-phenylethyl)-amine oxide. The tertiary amine is stirred with 150% excess

$$C_6H_5\underset{\underset{CH_3}{|}}{CH}N(CH_3)_2 \xrightarrow[98\%]{35\% \ H_2O_2} C_6H_5\underset{\underset{CH_3}{|}}{CH}\overset{\overset{O^-}{|}}{N^+}(CH_3)_2$$

35% hydrogen peroxide for 11 hrs. at room temperature (methanol is added if the amine is sparingly soluble). Platinum catalyst is added to decompose the hydrogen peroxide, and the solution is stirred for 5 hrs.; tests for hydrogen peroxide (lead sulfide paper) and for amine (phenolphthalein spot test) are then negative. An aliquot portion of the aqueous solution is converted for analysis into the picrate, m.p. 156°; the remainder is evaporated to a sirup.

Cope found (1949) that the oxide just discussed decomposes on moderate heating to styrene and N,N-dimethylhydroxylamine. The **Cope reaction** bears a

$$C_6H_5\underset{\underset{CH_3}{|}}{CH}\overset{\overset{O^-}{|}}{N^+}(CH_3)_2 \xrightarrow[98\%]{70-115°} C_6H_5CH{=}CH_2 + (CH_3)_2NOH$$

formal analogy to the Hofmann decomposition, for each reaction requires a hydrogen atom β to a positively charged nitrogen. However, the reaction proceeds by *cis* elimination (Cope, 1953; Cram, 1954) and the more highly substituted olefin is formed to a slightly greater extent than the less substituted olefin. Cope considers that the reaction involves a cyclic transition state; it is thus analogous

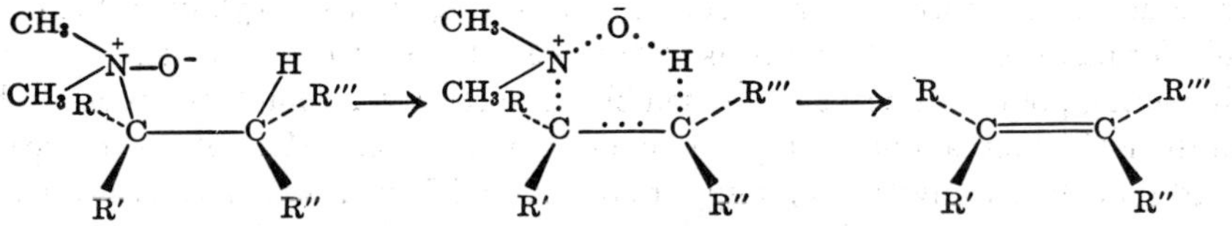

to the Tschugaeff reaction (5.7) and the ester pyrolysis. (5.20).

The reaction is useful for the preparation of alicyclic olefins, for example, pyrolysis of N,N-dimethylcyclooctylamine oxide affords *cis*-cyclooctene in yield of 90%. Decomposition of N,N,N-trimethylcyclooctylammonium hydroxide gave both *trans*-cyclooctene (54%) and *cis*-cyclooctene (36%).

The Cope group prepared 1-methylcyclohexylamine (6), and the 5- and 7-ring analogs, by the **Ritter[1] reaction** (1948–50), which involves addition of sulfuric acid

$$\begin{array}{c}CH_2CH_2C{=}O\\|\qquad\quad\ |\\CH_2CH_2CH_2\\(1)\end{array}\xrightarrow[\substack{60\%}]{\substack{1.\ CH_3MgI\\2.\ TsOH}}\begin{array}{c}CH_2CH{=}CCH_3\\|\qquad\qquad\ |\\CH_2CH_2{-}CH_2\\(2)\end{array}\xrightarrow{H_2SO_4}\begin{array}{c}OSO_3H\\|\\CH_2CH_2CCH_3\\|\qquad\qquad\ |\\CH_2CH_2CH_2\\(3)\end{array}\xrightarrow{HCN}$$

$$\begin{array}{c}N{=}CHOSO_2OH\\|\\CH_2CH_2CCH_3\\|\qquad\qquad\ |\\CH_2CH_2CH_2\\(4)\end{array}\xrightarrow{H_2O}\begin{array}{c}HNCH{=}O\\|\\CH_2CH_2CCH_3\\|\qquad\qquad\ |\\CH_2CH_2CH_2\\(5)\end{array}\xrightarrow{OH^-}\begin{array}{c}NH_2\\|\\CH_2CH_2CCH_3\\|\qquad\qquad\ |\\CH_2CH_2CH_2\\(6)\end{array}$$

to a mixture of the olefin (2), or the corresponding *t*-alcohol, with sodium cyanide in acetic acid. Addition of (3) to hydrogen cyanide gives the ester (4), which is hydrolyzed to the N-alkylformamide (5); saponification then affords the *t*-carbinamine (6). The six-ring olefin produced from both the amine oxide (7) and the

$$(6)\quad\rightarrow\quad\begin{cases}\begin{array}{c}(CH_3)_2N^+{-}O^-\\|\\CH_2CH_2CCH_3\\|\qquad\qquad\ |\\CH_2CH_2CH_2\\(7)\end{array}\quad{-}(CH_3)_2NOH\\[2em]\begin{array}{c}(CH_3)_3N^+OH\\|\\CH_2CH_2CCH_3\\|\qquad\qquad\ |\\CH_2CH_2CH_2\\(8)\end{array}\quad{-}(CH_3)_3N,\ H_2O\end{cases}\rightarrow\begin{array}{c}CH_2CH_2C{=}CH_2\\|\qquad\qquad\ |\\CH_2CH_2CH_2\\(9)\end{array}$$

methohydroxide (8) was the exocyclic isomer (9), shown by gas chromatography to contain only trace amounts (1–3%) of endocyclic material. The corresponding derivatives of cyclopentane and cycloheptane behaved the same in the Hofmann elimination, giving exo olefins, but in the Cope reaction gave chiefly endo olefins. The deviating behavior of the six-ring amine oxide is attributed to the stability of the chair conformation; the bulky amine oxide group assumes the equatorial orientation in which the only planar cyclic transition state involves a β-hydrogen of the methyl group.

N,N-Dimethylcyclohexylmethylamine (10) is obtained efficiently from cyclohexanecarboxylic acid by the steps formulated (*Org. Syn.*, 1959). The Cope reac-

[1] John J. Ritter, b. 1895 New York; Ph.D. Columbia (Bogert); Washington Square College, New York University

tion (11) affords methylenecyclohexane in 79–88% yield and N,N-dimethyl-hydroxylamine in 78–90% yield; the hydrocarbon prepared in this way contains less than 0.01% of 1-methylcyclohexene. The five- and seven-ring analogs of

$$C_6H_{11}CO_2H \xrightarrow{SOCl_2} C_6H_{11}COCl \xrightarrow[85-89\%]{} C_6H_{11}CON(CH_3)_2 \xrightarrow[88\%]{LiAlH_4}$$

$$C_6H_{11}CH_2N(CH_3)_2 \rightarrow \left\{ \begin{array}{c} N^+\!\!-\!O^- \\ | \\ C_6H_{11}CH_2N(CH_3)_2 \\ (11) \\[2mm] C_6H_5CH_2N^+(CH_3)_3\,OH^- \\ (12) \end{array} \right\} \rightarrow C_6H_{10}\!=\!CH_2$$

       (10)   (9)

(11) likewise give exclusively the exo olefins. The methohydroxide (12) and its analogs give the exo olefins as the chief products, but considerable amounts of endo olefins are often present.

14.22 Hofmann-Löffler Reaction.

— Coniine, a dextrorotatory alkaloid which occurs with four companions in the hemlock herb, was isolated in 1831 but it was not until 1885 that Hofmann established the structure. In

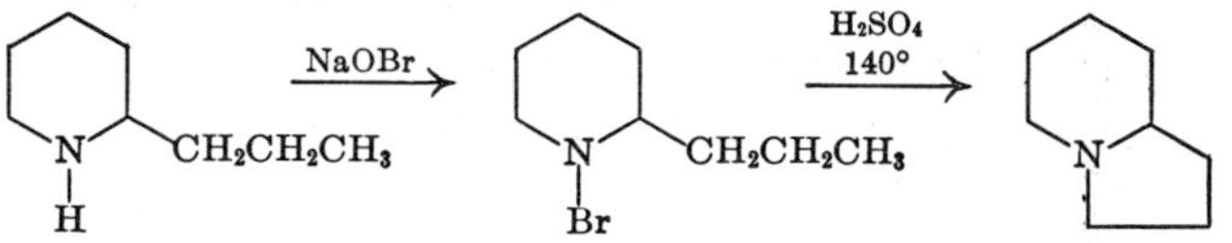

Coniine   δ-Coneceine

the course of the work Hofmann (1883) heated N-bromoconiine with sulfuric acid and obtained a new base, δ-coneceine, the structure of which was deduced by E. Lellmann (1900). The remarkable ring closure went neglected for a time, but investigations by K. Löffler (1909–10) and particularly by Coleman[1] (1938–41) showed the reaction to afford a general route to pyrrolidines. For example, di-*n*-

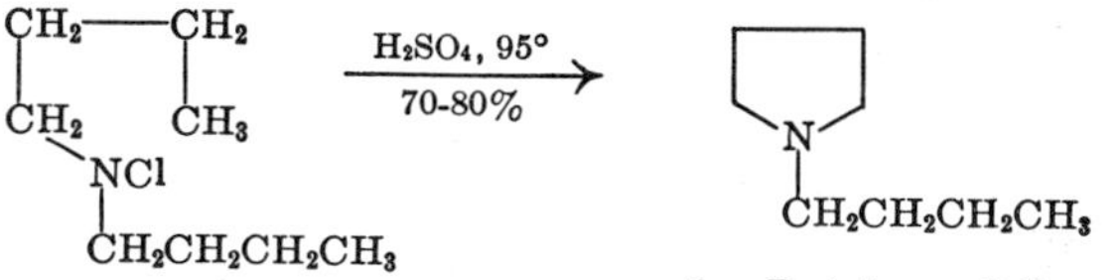

1-*n*-Butylpyrrolidine

butylamine is converted to the N-chloro derivative (NaOCl), this is heated with sulfuric acid, the crude amine is treated with a little benzenesulfonyl chloride and alkali, and the pyrrolidine is separated by steam distillation from the Hinsberg derivative of di-*n*-butylamine.

More recently Wawzonek[2] (1951–52) found that higher yields are obtained

[1] George H. Coleman, b. 1891 Evansville, Wis.; Ph.D. Illinois (Noyes); Iowa; Wayne State Univ.

[2] Stanley Wawzonek, b. 1914 Valley Falls, R. I.; Ph.D. Minnesota (Koelsch); State Univ. Iowa

by irradiation of a solution in 85% sulfuric acid with ultraviolet light at room temperature, a fact which clearly pointed to a free radical reaction. Wawzonek suggested that the first step is formation of the chloroammonium ion (1), which on homolysis affords a chlorine radical and the amininium radical (2). This

$$\underset{\overset{|}{\underset{Cl}{C_4H_9N^+CH_2CH_2CH_2CH_3}}}{\overset{\overset{H}{|}}{}} \quad \xrightarrow[-Cl\cdot]{h\nu} \quad \underset{(2)}{\overset{\overset{H}{|}}{C_4H_9N^+CH_2CH_2CH_2CH_3}} \quad \longrightarrow$$

(1)

$$\underset{\overset{|}{H}}{\overset{\overset{H}{|}}{C_4H_9N^+CH_2CH_2CH_2\overset{\cdot}{C}H_2}} \xrightarrow{Cl\cdot} \underset{\overset{|}{H}}{\overset{\overset{H}{|}}{C_4H_9N^+CH_2CH_2CH_2CH_2Cl}} \xrightarrow{OH^-} \underset{\overset{|}{C_4H_9}}{\overset{}{\boxed{}N}}$$

(3)   (4)   C₄H₉

radical then abstracts hydrogen from the δ-position in the chain to form a new carbon radical (3), and reaction with a chlorine radical gives the δ-chloro derivative (4). Terminal treatment with alkali then induces ring closure to the pyrrolidine. Indeed Wawzonek (1960) isolated intermediate (4) as the hydrochloride after partial neutralization of the acid solution with sodium bicarbonate and removal of the sulfate with barium chloride. A similar intermediate in the steroid series was isolated by Corey (1958).

Barton *et al.* (1960) effected novel transformations in the steroid series by a related rearrangement. An alcohol (1) in which the hydroxyl group is strategically

$$\underset{(1)}{\overset{\overset{OH}{|}\quad\overset{CH_3}{|}}{RCHCH_2\overset{}{C}R'R''}} \xrightarrow[Py]{ClNO} \underset{(2)}{\overset{\overset{ON=O}{|}\quad\overset{CH_3}{|}}{RCHCH_2\overset{}{C}HR'R''}} \xrightarrow[Benzene]{h\nu} \underset{(3)}{\overset{\overset{OH}{|}\quad\overset{CH=NOH}{|}}{RCHCH_2\overset{}{C}R'R''}}$$

$$\xrightarrow{aq.\ NaNO_2-AcOH} \underset{(4)}{\overset{\overset{O\text{---}CHOH}{|\qquad\quad|}}{RCHCH_2\overset{}{C}R'R''}}$$

located with respect to an angular methyl group is converted into the nitrite ester (2) by reaction with nitrosyl chloride in pyridine. Irradiation of the nitrite ester effects rearrangement to the γ-hydroxy aldoxime (3). Hydrolysis, effected with nitrous acid, affords the hydroxyaldehyde, which cyclizes to the hemiacetal (4). Yields in the irradiation step are only 20–30%, but functionalization of a saturated group at a distance in any yield is remarkable.

A related free radical reaction is the formation of the cyclobutanol derivative

$$\underset{\text{2-Nonanone}}{\overset{\overset{O}{\|}\quad\overset{H}{|}}{\underset{\overset{|}{CH_2-CH_2}}{CH_3C\qquad CHC_4H_9}}} \xrightarrow{h\nu} \underset{(5)\ 10\%}{\overset{\overset{OH}{|}}{\underset{\overset{|}{CH_2CH_2}}{CH_3C\text{---}CHC_4H_9}}} + \underset{60\%}{\overset{\overset{O}{\|}}{\underset{\overset{|}{CH_3}}{CH_3C}}} + \underset{60\%}{\overset{}{\underset{\overset{\|}{CH_2}}{CHC_4H_9}}}$$

(5) on irradiation of 2-nonanone (Yang, 1958). The reaction is general for ketones having a γ-hydrogen, but yields are in the range 10–20%.

14.23   Nitrogen Mustards. — Tertiary amines of the general formula $RN(CH_2CH_2Cl)_2$ have vesicant properties similar to those of mustard gas, $S(CH_2CH_2Cl)_2$; hence they were investigated intensively during World War II as possible chemical warfare agents. They can be prepared by reaction of

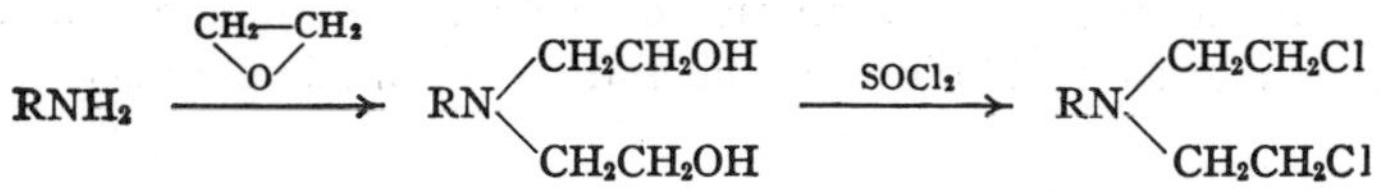

$$RNH_2 \xrightarrow{\overset{CH_2-CH_2}{\diagdown O \diagup}} RN\diagup^{CH_2CH_2OH}_{\diagdown CH_2CH_2OH} \xrightarrow{SOCl_2} RN\diagup^{CH_2CH_2Cl}_{\diagdown CH_2CH_2Cl}$$

ethylene oxide with the appropriate amine followed by reaction with thionyl chloride in boiling benzene. Toxicity of the nitrogen mustards is believed to be due to reaction with tissue proteins, built up of amino acids of the formula $RCH(NH_2)COOH$, according to the general scheme:

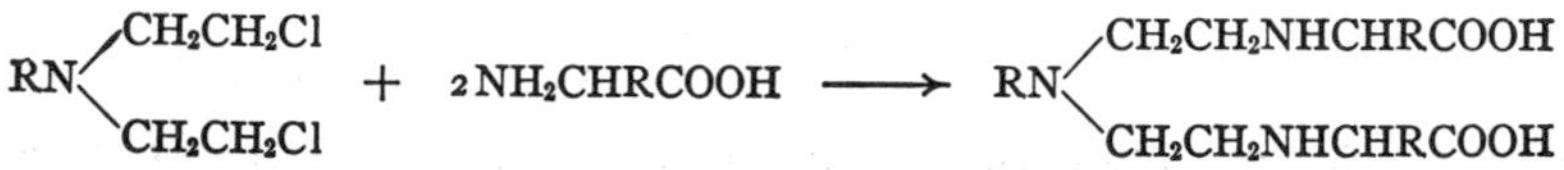

$$RN\diagup^{CH_2CH_2Cl}_{\diagdown CH_2CH_2Cl} + 2NH_2CHRCOOH \longrightarrow RN\diagup^{CH_2CH_2NHCHRCOOH}_{\diagdown CH_2CH_2NHCHRCOOH}$$

Nitrogen mustards are all somewhat unstable and eventually are transformed even at room temperature into cyclic piperazinium dimers:

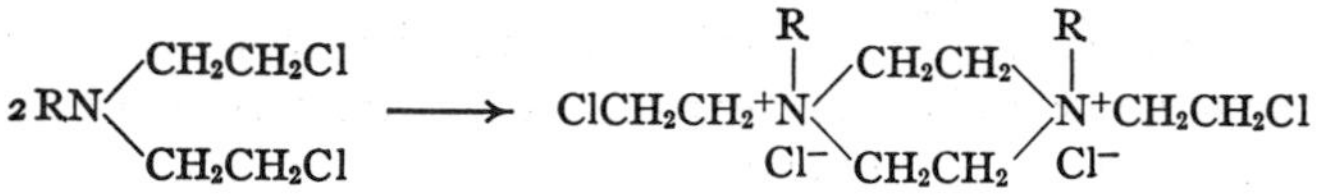

$$2RN\diagup^{CH_2CH_2Cl}_{\diagdown CH_2CH_2Cl} \longrightarrow ClCH_2CH_2^+\overset{\overset{R}{|}}{N}\diagup^{CH_2CH_2}_{\diagdown CH_2CH_2}\overset{\overset{R}{|}}{N}{}^+CH_2CH_2Cl$$
$$Cl^- \qquad Cl^-$$

Nitrogen mustards have been investigated clinically (1946–47) for chemotherapy of cancer, particularly in treatment of lymphatic diseases. However, they do not distinguish between normal and neoplastic tissue, and the regressions of tumor observed are only temporary.

AMIDES

14.24   Properties. — Constants of representative amides of the type $RCONH_2$ are given in Table 11.15 (section 11.21), and a few are repeated below. All the simple amides are solids at room temperature except formamide (m.p. 2°) and N,N-dimethylformamide, $HCON(CH_3)_2$ (m.p. 2.6°,

CH_3CONH_2	$CH_3CH_2CONH_2$	$CH_3(CH_2)_{16}CONH_2$	$C_6H_5CONH_2$
Acetamide	Propionamide	Stearamide	Benzamide
(m.p. 82.0°, b.p. 222°)	(m.p. 80°, b.p. 213°)	(m.p. 109°)	(m.p. 130°)

b.p. 193°). The latter substance is useful both as a reagent and as a solvent. Liquid acids are often converted into their solid amides for identification and char-

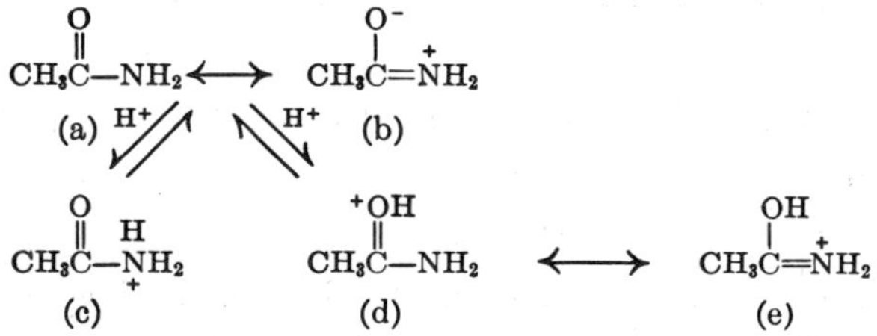

$$\overset{O}{\overset{\|}{CH_3C}}-NH_2 \longleftrightarrow \overset{O^-}{\overset{|}{CH_3C}}=\overset{+}{N}H_2$$
$$(a) \qquad \qquad (b)$$
$$H^+ \qquad \qquad H^+$$

$$\overset{O}{\overset{\|}{CH_3C}}-\overset{H}{\underset{+}{N}}H_2 \qquad \overset{+OH}{\overset{\|}{CH_3C}}-NH_2 \longleftrightarrow \overset{OH}{\overset{|}{CH_3C}}=\overset{+}{N}H_2$$
$$(c) \qquad \qquad (d) \qquad \qquad (e)$$

acterization. Boiling points are usually high: *n*-butyramide, of molecular weight 87.12, boils at 216°.

Amides of types CH_3CONH_2 and $CH_3CONHCH_3$ are neutral in the classical sense but basic enough to accept a proton from a strong acid. Is it nitrogen or oxygen which is protonated? Acetamide is a hybrid of (a) and (b) and protonation of nitrogen (c) would eliminate resonance stabilization whereas protonation of oxygen (d, e) would not, and hence the oxygen-protonated system should be the more stable. Potentiometric titrations of a series of amides with perchloric acid in acetic acid (Huisgen, 1957) and nuclear magnetic resonance data in 96–100% sulfuric acid (C. Niemann,[1] 1958) indicate O-protonation. However, a minute equilibrium concentration of the N-protonated species (c) probably accounts for the decarbonylation of formamide by hydrochloric acid and for the acid hydrolysis of amides (14.26).

$$\underset{\text{HC—NH}_2}{\overset{\overset{\text{O}}{\|}}{}} \xrightarrow{\text{H}^+} \underset{\text{HC—}\overset{+}{\text{N}}\text{H}_3}{\overset{\overset{\text{O}}{\|}}{}} \rightarrow CO + NH_4{}^|$$

14.25 Preparation. — Acids can be converted into amides by the action of ammonia on their ester, acid chloride, or anhydride derivatives, as already noted; the route through the halide is usually the most convenient. A useful technical method consists in pyrolysis of the ammonium salt of the acid.

$$\underset{\text{[from CH}_3\text{COOH + (NH}_4\text{)}_2\text{CO}_3]}{CH_3COONH_4} \xrightarrow[87-90\%]{\text{Slow distillation}} CH_3CONH_2 + H_2O$$

Amides also result from partial hydrolysis of nitriles (11.6). One improvement in the procedure for conversion of nitriles into amides consists in use of alkaline hydrogen peroxide at 45–55°. Another is use as catalyst of an ion-exchange basic resin, for example, the commercial product Amberlite IR-400, a water-insoluble polymer containing quaternary ammonium chloride groups. The resin is stirred with dilute alkali and the resulting resin base is washed free of sodium chloride and of excess alkali and added to a solution of the nitrile. Brief boiling (1 hr.) of

Nicotinonitrile   Nicotinamide

the suspension effects hydrolysis to the amide stage and no further, and the filtered solution of the amide is free from inorganic salts.

14.26 Hydrolysis. — Hydrolysis of amides to acids proceeds smoothly but requires somewhat drastic conditions, for these substances are much less reactive than esters. Prolonged refluxing with a mixture of acetic and hydrochloric acid or with alcoholic alkali (in a copper flask) may be required, but the material is not damaged in the process, and the acid is usually obtainable in good yield. The primary amino group present is attacked by nitrous acid in the manner characteristic of primary amines, and this reaction has afforded a satisfactory method of hydrolysis in some instances:

[1] Carl Niemann, b. 1908 St. Louis, Mo.; Ph.D. Wisconsin (Link); Calif. Inst. Techn.

$$R-C\overset{O}{\underset{NH_2}{\diagdown}} + HNO_2 \longrightarrow R-C\overset{O}{\underset{OH}{\diagdown}} + N_2 + H_2O$$

In both acid- and base-catalyzed hydrolytic reactions the rate is proportional to the concentration of the amide and of the acid or base. In the case of basic hydrolysis, oxygen exchange between amide and water has been observed, and this exchange is interpreted, as in the basic hydrolysis of an ester, in terms of a symmetrical intermediate:

$$RCO^{18}NH_2 + H_2O \underset{\longleftarrow}{\overset{slow}{\longrightarrow}} \underset{OH}{\overset{OH}{RC-NH_2}} \underset{\longleftarrow}{\overset{fast}{\longrightarrow}} \underset{OH}{\overset{O^-}{RC-NH_2}} \underset{\longleftarrow}{\overset{fast}{\longrightarrow}} \underset{OH}{\overset{O}{RC}} + \bar{N}H_2$$

$$\bar{N}H_2 + RCO_2H \overset{fast}{\longrightarrow} RCO_2^- + NH_3$$

No exchange occurs during acid-catalyzed hydrolysis, and the probable mechanism is as follows:

$$\underset{CH_3}{\overset{O}{C-NH_2}} \overset{H^+}{\longrightarrow} \underset{CH_3}{\overset{O}{CN^+H_3}} \overset{H_2O}{\longrightarrow} \underset{CH_3}{\overset{O^-}{H_2O^+-C-N^+H_3}} \rightarrow \underset{CH_3}{\overset{O}{HO-C}} + \overset{+}{N}H_4$$

The hydrolysis of amides is catalyzed not only by mineral acids but also by acetic and other carboxylic acids. Bender (1958) investigated the interesting case of phthalamic acid in which a carboxyl group is adjacent to an amide group. At pH 3 the hydrolysis of phthalamic acid is 10^5 faster than the hydrolysis of benzamide.

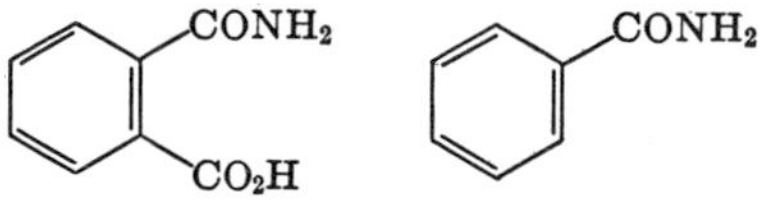

Phthalamic acid   Benzamide

14.27   **Dehydration to Nitriles.** — The formation of an amide by partial hydrolysis of a nitrile can be reversed and an amide dehydrated to a nitrile. One procedure is illustrated by the conversion of isobutyramide into isobutyronitrile. A mixture of the solid amide and phosphorus pentoxide is

$$(CH_3)_2CHCONH_2 \xrightarrow[\text{69-86\%}]{P_2O_5\,,\ 200-220°,\ 9\ hrs.} (CH_3)_2CHCN$$

Isobutyramide   Isobutyronitrile

heated until distillation of the nitrile ceases. Dehydration of cyanoacetamide is accomplished by refluxing a solution of the amide in ethylene dichloride with phosphorus oxychloride in the presence of solid sodium chloride. In the case of

$$NCCH_2CONH_2 \xrightarrow[\text{57-66\%}]{POCl_3,\ ClCH_2CH_2Cl,\ NaCl,\ refl.\ 8\ hrs.} CH_2(CN)_2$$

Cyanoacetamide   Malononitrile

amides containing hydroxyl groups (sugar series), the preferred dehydrating agent is acetic anhydride; the product is then an acetoxy nitrile.

14.28   **Degradation of a Lactam (Cyclic Amide).** — One phase of the work of Cornforth and Popjak on the isotope pattern of cholesterol produced by biosynthesis from labeled acetate (13.14) involved degradation of Δ^5-cholestene (1) to the diketo acid (4), the carboxyl group of which contains C_6. When (4) derived by biosynthesis from $CH_3C^{14}O_2H$ was heated to 200°, the carbon dioxide carried the label; when material derived from $C^{14}H_3CO_2H$ was employed, the carbon dioxide was nonisotopic; therefore C_6 is carboxyl-derived. The keto aldehyde (5) was then pyrolyzed with potassium carbonate at 450° to effect reverse

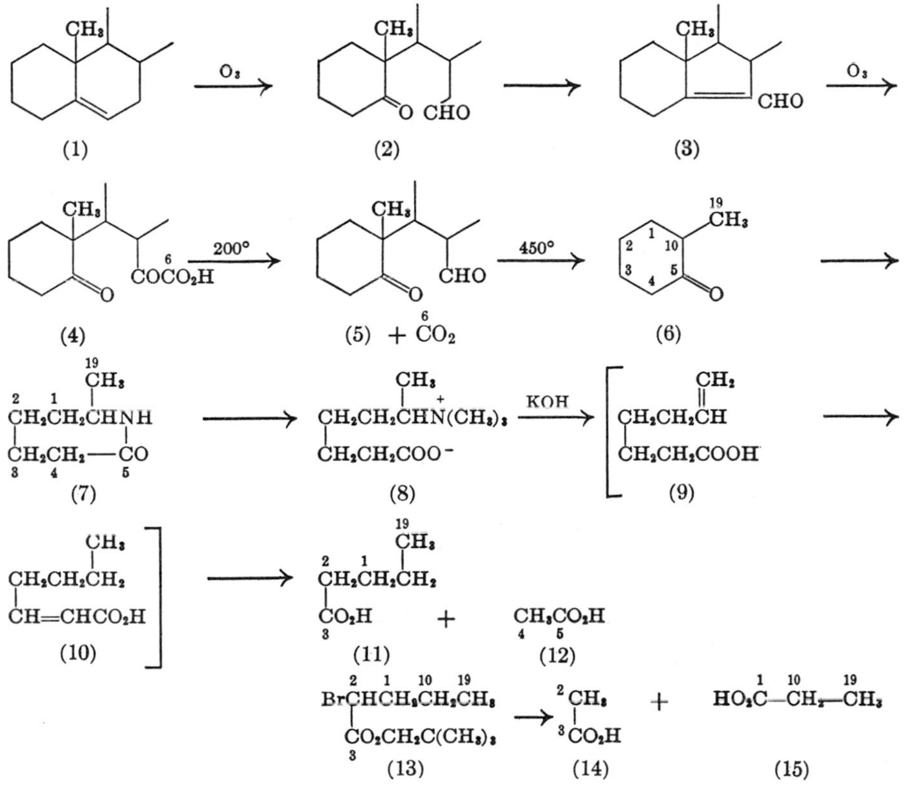

Michael reaction and split off the entire ring A in the form of 2-methylcyclohexanone. "The next task was to break down this ketone into the seven constituent carbon atoms." The ketone was converted by the Schmidt reaction (HN_3) into the lactam (7), which in turn was converted by hydrolysis and methylation into the betaine (8). When this betaine was heated with potassium hydroxide to 350°, trimethylamine was split off smoothly but the product was not the acid (9) with a terminal double bond, but a mixture of *n*-valeric acid and acetic acid. The transformation is similar to one discovered in 1840 by F. Varrentrapp, when he fused oleic acid with potassium hydroxide and obtained palmitic acid. Cornforth and Popjak found that a nonconjugated acid is isomerized by alkali fusion at about 150° to the α,β-unsaturated acid and that this is cleaved on raising the temperature to 350°. The bond migration along the chain can occur, as in an analogous case (p. 238), by nucleophilic attack with abstraction of an allylic proton to form a carbanion (b), which through resonance (c) and recapture of a proton

$$RCH{=}CH_2CH_2CO_2K \xrightarrow[-H_2O]{OH^-} RCH{=}CH\overset{-}{C}HCH_2CO_2K \longleftrightarrow$$

$$\text{(a)} \hspace{5cm} \text{(b)}$$

$$\overset{-}{R}CHCH{=}CHCH_2CO_2K \xrightarrow[-OH^-]{H_2O} RCH_2CH{=}CHCH_2CO_2K \xrightarrow[H_2O]{OH^-}$$

$$\text{(c)} \hspace{5cm} \text{(d)}$$

$$RCH_2CH{=}CH\overset{-}{C}HCO_2K \longleftrightarrow RCH_2\overset{-}{C}HCH{=}CHCO_2K \xrightarrow[-OH^-]{H_2O}$$

$$\text{(e)} \hspace{5cm} \text{(f)}$$

$$RCH_2CH_2CH{=}CHCO_2K \xrightarrow{H_2O} RCH_2CH_2CHCH_2CO_2K \longrightarrow$$
$$\hspace{8cm} |$$
$$\hspace{8cm} OH$$

$$\text{(g)} \hspace{5cm} \text{(h)}$$

$$RCH_2CH_2CH{=}O \; + \; CH_3CO_2K$$

$$\text{(i)} \hspace{3cm} \text{(j)}$$

$$\Big\downarrow \text{ KOH}$$

$$RCH_2CH_2CO_2K \; + \; H_2$$

$$\text{(k)}$$

affords the isomeric salt (d). Repetition of the process gives the conjugated salt (g); resonance stabilization in this salt forces a double bond to migrate from an initially remote position. Cleavage of (g) to two acid salts is interpreted as involving 1,4-addition of water (h), reverse aldolization to (i) and (j), and disproportionation of the aldehyde with potassium hydroxide to the acid salt (k) and hydrogen (compare 8.3).

The acetic acid (12) derived from the degradation was converted to the silver salt, which was analyzed for C^{14} ($C_4 + C_5$) and then decarboxylated with bromine (Hunsdiecker reaction) to give carbon dioxide coming from C_5 alone. The *n*-valeric acid (11) was converted through the α-bromo acid to the neopentyl ester (13), which on dehydrohalogenation with dimethylaniline and fusion with alkali gave acetic acid and propionic acid.

14.29   Imides. — The dibasic succinic acid can be converted by usual methods into a neutral diamido derivative, succinamide. This substance when strongly heated could conceivably suffer dehydration to a nitrile, but instead it loses ammonia and yields a cyclic diacyl-substituted ammonia derivative, succinimide. Succinimide is a weak acid (pK_a 10.52) capable of forming salts with alkalis. Phthalimide (14.13), a substance of similar structure, is even more strongly acidic. Two acyl substituents more than compensate for the basic character inherent in the trivalent nitrogen atom; the imido hydrogen atom is activated by both carbonyl groups, and separates as a proton. Imides are hydrolyzed more readily than the usual amides. Thus succinimide is convertible in good yield to the monoamido compound succinamic acid, $HOOCCH_2CH_2CONH_2$, m.p. 157°. This half-amide probably is an intermediate in the reaction

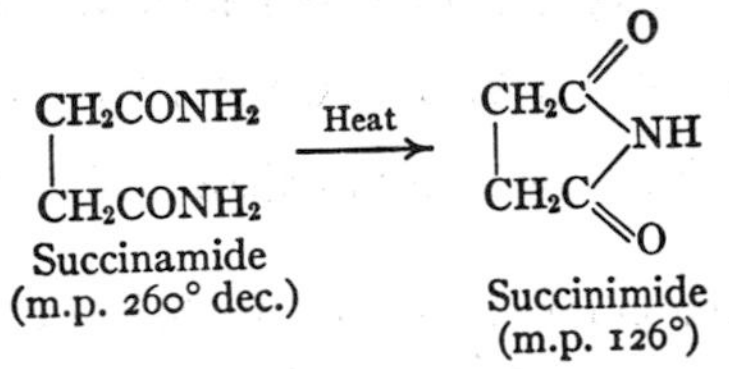

CH₂CONH₂ / CH₂CONH₂   Succinamide (m.p. 260° dec.) → Heat →   Succinimide (m.p. 126°)

of succinimide with sodium or potassium hypobromite, which is a useful application of the Hofmann reaction to the preparation of an amino acid:

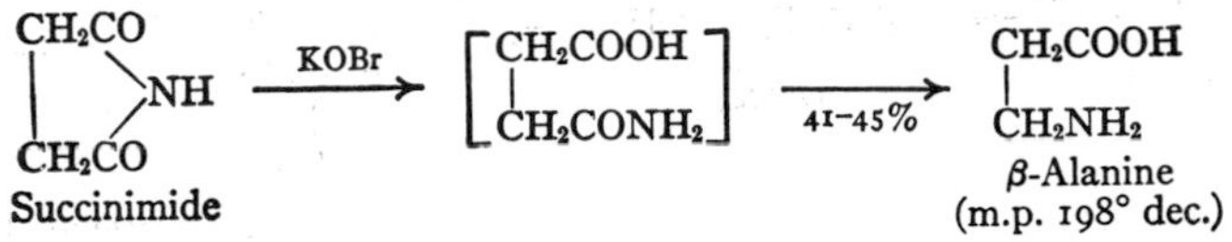

Succinimide → KOBr → [CH₂COOH / CH₂CONH₂] → 41–45% → CH₂COOH / CH₂NH₂   β-Alanine (m.p. 198° dec.)

By adding bromine to an ice-cold solution of succinimide in alkali and quickly collecting the material that precipitates, N-bromosuccinimide of about 97% purity can be prepared in high yield. The bromine atom in this bromoimide is

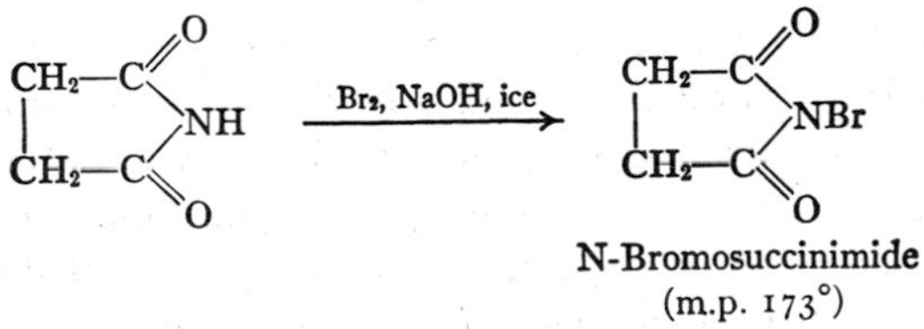

→ Br₂, NaOH, ice → N-Bromosuccinimide (m.p. 173°)

described as a positive halogen, since on hydrolysis it combines with the negative hydroxide ion to form hypobromous acid; an alkyl bromide affords hydrobromic acid.

Maleinimide (m.p. 93°), the dehydro derivative of succinimide, is obtainable in good yield via the adduct of cyclopentadiene with maleic anhydride (P. O. Tawney, U. S. Rubber Co., 1961). It undergoes base-catalyzed polymerization but reacts smoothly with formaldehyde to give N-methylolmaleinimide.

14.30   **Urea** is made in the industry by heating carbon dioxide with ammonia under pressure (1) and by partial hydrolysis of cyanamide (2). At

1. 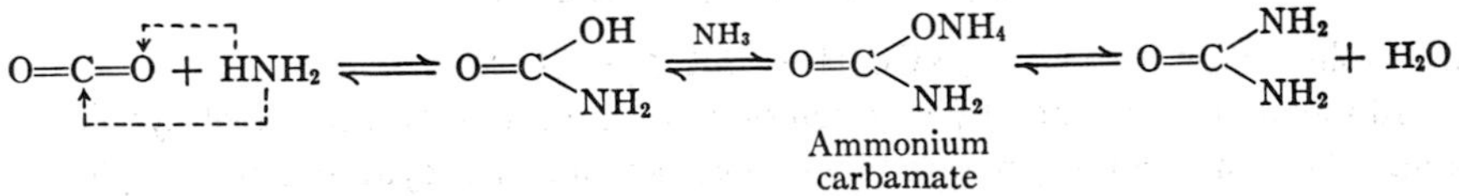 O=C=O + HNH₂ ⇌ O=C(OH)(NH₂) ⇌ O=C(ONH₄)(NH₂) ⇌ O=C(NH₂)(NH₂) + H₂O   Ammonium carbamate

2. 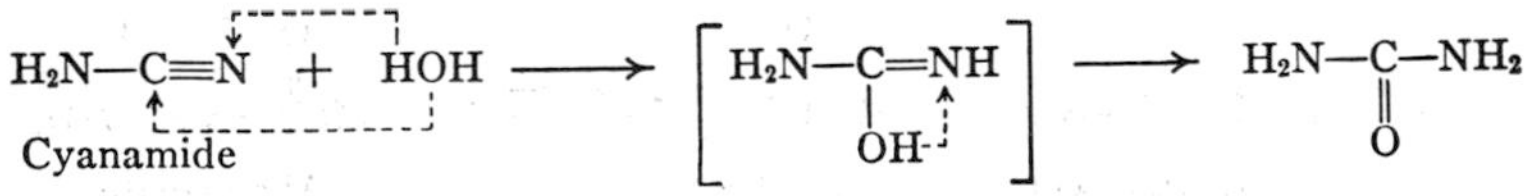   H₂N—C≡N + HOH → [H₂N—C=NH / OH⁻] → H₂N—C(=O)—NH₂   Cyanamide

room temperature 1 g. of urea dissolves in 1 ml. of water, 10 ml. of 85% ethanol, or 20 ml. of absolute ethanol; it is practically insoluble in ether or chloroform. A

10% aqueous solution shows a pH of 7.2, but since urea has two basic groups and only one acidic group it is basic enough to form a stable salt with 71% nitric acid, urea nitrate, $H_2NCON^+H_3NO_3^-$. It forms a crystalline $1:1$ complex with hydrogen peroxide. Like primary amines, urea reacts with nitrous acid with libera-

$$H_2NCONH_2 + 2\ HNO_2 \rightarrow CO_2 + 2\ N_2 + 3\ H_2O$$

tion of nitrogen. Thus urea can be added to nitric acid to destroy nitrous acid and oxides of nitrogen present.

Heated above its melting point, urea is converted into biuret, cyanuric acid (a solid trimer), and ammonia. A minute amount of biuret is detectable from a

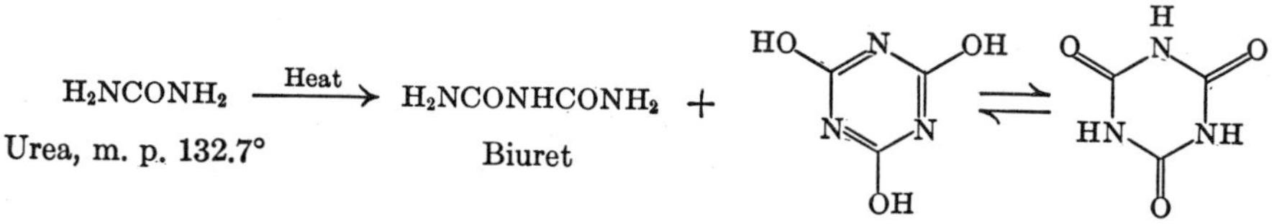

$$\underset{\text{Urea, m. p. } 132.7°}{H_2NCONH_2} \xrightarrow{\text{Heat}} \underset{\text{Biuret}}{H_2NCONHCONH_2} +$$

Cyanuric acid
pK$_{a1}$ 7.2; pK$_{a2}$ 11.1

reddish violet color formed on reaction with aqueous copper sulfate and alkali: all reagent grade urea gives a biuret test.

The normal individual excretes in the urine 28–30 g. of urea per day; it is a product of metabolism of proteins. Isolation of the nitrate from urine, once a favored experiment for students, is accomplished by evaporation on the steam bath (hood) to a sirup, extraction with alcohol, evaporation, and treatment with nitric acid (yield 8–11 g.). Urease, a crystalline enzyme present in Jack beans to the extent 0.12%, catalyzes hydrolysis of urea to ammonia and carbon dioxide. Urea is used in the production of plastics, in animal feeds, and as a fertilizer (high content of easily available nitrogen).

14.31   Urethanes and Allophanates. — Urethane, or ethyl carbamate, is made by heating urea with ethanol under pressure or by reaction of urea nitrate with sodium nitrite and alcohol. Hydrolysis of urethane gives

$$H_2NCONH_2 + HOC_2H_5 \xrightarrow{-NH_3} H_2NCOOC_2H_5$$

Urethane, m.p. 50°, b.p. 183°

$$H_2NCON^+H_3NO_3^- + NaNO_2 + HOC_2H_5\uparrow$$

unstable carbamic acid ($H_2NCO_2H \rightarrow NH_3 + CO_2$).

Allophanates are made by reaction of an alcohol with two moles of cyanic acid, a gas. Cyanic acid is generated by depolymerization of cyanuric acid at 360–400°

$$\underset{}{ROH} + \underset{\text{Cyanic acid}}{O=C=NH} \rightarrow \underset{\text{A urethane}}{RO\overset{O}{\overset{\|}{C}}NH_2} \xrightarrow{O=C=NH} \underset{\text{Allophanate}}{RO\overset{O}{\overset{\|}{C}}-\overset{H}{\underset{}{N}}-\overset{O}{\overset{\|}{C}}NH_2}$$

in a slow stream of carbon dioxide and the gas is absorbed directly in a liquid alcohol or in ether; in the latter case a 30% ethereal solution is added to a solution of the alcohol in benzene (F. Zobrist, 1952). If insufficient reagent is used the chief product is the urethane; excess reagent polymerizes to products insoluble in benzene. Allophanates usually are high-melting, well crystalline derivatives suitable for characterization and isolation. Since the reaction involves addition to a ketenelike, neutral substance, acid-sensitive alcohols and tertiary alcohols are convertible into allophanates. Warming the allophanate with methanolic alkali regenerates the alcohol.

α-Naphthylisocyanate is useful as a reagent for characterizing phenols. A mixture of the components is treated with a drop of pyridine or trimethylamine

$$\alpha\text{-}C_{10}H_7N\text{=}C\text{=}O \quad + \quad C_6H_5OH \quad \rightarrow \quad \alpha\text{-}C_{10}H_7NHCO_2C_6H_5$$

　　α-Naphthylisocyanate　　　　　　　　　　　Phenyl α-naphthylurethane

and warmed gently.

Urethane itself has mild hypnotic properties. The bisurethane or biscarbamate of 2-methyl-2-n-propylpropane-1,3-diol is widely used as a tranquilizer (Miltown

$$\underset{\text{Meprobamate}}{H_2N\overset{O}{\overset{\|}{C}}OCH_2\underset{\underset{CH_2CH_2CH_3}{|}}{\overset{\overset{CH_3}{|}}{C}}CH_2O\overset{O}{\overset{\|}{C}}NH_2}$$

is one of twenty-two trade names).

14.32　　Uric Acid. — Uric acid, a white crystalline solid very sparingly soluble in water and decomposing above 400° without melting, was discovered by Scheele in 1776 as a constituent of human urinary calculi (pebbles). It was later found to be the chief end product of nitrogenous metabolism in snakes and birds. Thus uric acid constitutes 90% of the excrement of the boa constrictor and is a major component of guano deposits. It occurs normally in human urine in only very small amounts, but excessive amounts are present in the urine of patients suffering from gout, a disease which is thus recognizable from the results of urine analysis.

Wöhler (1829) extended Scheele's study of the pyrolysis of uric acid and identified one of the products as urea, and Liebig (1834) established the empirical formula of uric acid: $C_5H_4O_3N_4$. These two chemists then undertook a joint investigation which resulted in the publication, in 1838, of a paper reporting characterization of no less than twelve new compounds obtained by various degradations of uric acid. Each was analyzed accurately and fully characterized, but interpretation of the results was not possible. Then Adolf von Baeyer undertook research on the problem (Berlin, 1863–64) and finally clarified empirical correlations between many known degradation products and some new ones, particularly a key compound in the series which he discovered and named barbituric acid in honor of a friend, Barbara. Although the work was published a few years after Kekulé's structural theory, Baeyer interpreted the extensive results only in empirical formulations. Strecker (1868) reported that uric acid is hydrolyzed by treatment with hydrochloric acid at 160° and affords ammonia, carbon dioxide, and glycine, $H_2NCH_2CO_2H$. The observation established the presence in uric acid of an N—C—C grouping, as well as the N—C—N grouping evident from degradation to urea. A synthesis of barbituric acid by E. Grimaux (1879) advanced the problem. Then Emil Fischer, in work completed in 1899 established a structure suggested in 1875 by Medicus and clarified the host of interrelated degradation products characterized by the earlier investigators.

The structure finally established is represented in the classical literature by formula (a), in which one ureide grouping occupies the 1,2,3-position in a six-

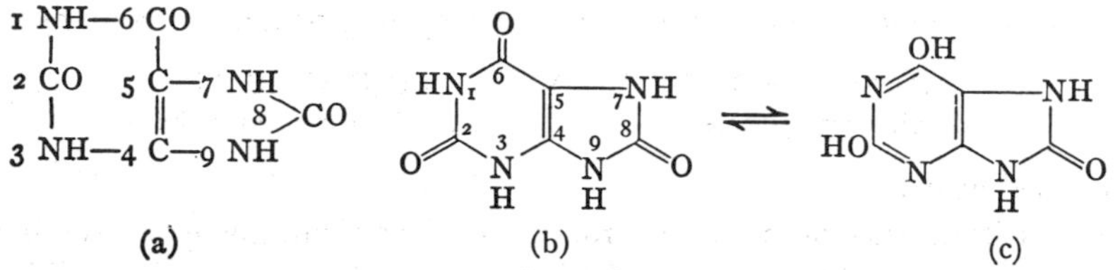

(a)   (b)   (c)

Uric acid

(pKa 5.7; solubility in water at 18°, 1:39,480)

membered ring and a second the 7,8,9-position in a five-membered ring. The equivalent triketo formula (b) provides a convenient expression of the possibility, considered by Fischer, of tautomerism to the dienolic (phenolic) form (c). Formula (b) agrees better with spectrographic data, and it affords a better insight into the degradations. The major degradations involve opening of one or the other of the two rings. Oxidation with nitric acid cleaves the smaller ring with formation of urea and alloxan. Scheele had observed the formation of alloxan,

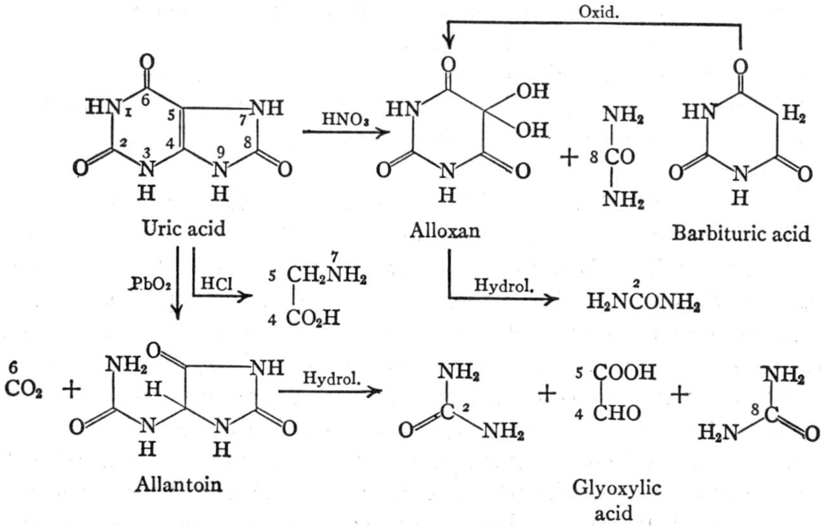

later characterized by Liebig and Wöhler, and had devised a useful test for uric acid based upon specific color reactions characteristic of alloxan. Alloxan is a stable hydrate of a 1,2,3-triketone. Fischer converted alloxan into a derivative of barbituric acid in a series of steps, but the correlation of the two substances is established most simply by the fact that barbituric acid yields alloxan on oxidation. Proof of the structure of barbituric acid by synthesis from urea thus established the structure of one ring of uric acid. The nature of the second ring follows from another degradation in which the six-membered ring is cleaved. Liebig and Wöhler found that uric acid on mild oxidation loses carbon dioxide and affords a product named allantoin because it is identical with a substance isolated from the allantoic liquid of cows. (The two urea residues are now equivalent.) In the classical investigations allantoin was degraded further in a variety of ways, but the simplest reaction revealing the structure is hydrolysis to two moles of urea and one of glyoxylic acid.

A half century after Fischer's experiments had brought the classical investigations of structure to a successful conclusion, some of the degradative reactions on which the structure is based were put to new use for mapping out the pathway of biosynthesis of uric acid. The degradations formulated above involve conversion into the small fragments urea, glycine, carbon dioxide, and glyoxylic acid, and hence these substances would appear to be possible precursors, in the sense of supplying some parts of the uric acid molecule. That a suspected substance is in fact a biogenetic precursor can be determined by preparation of an isotopically labeled form and administration to an animal; in the present case, pigeons and man were used. Biosynthetic uric acid is then isolated from the urine and put through degradations revealing the positions of any labeled atoms incorporated. When isotopically labeled carbonate was administered and the biosynthetic uric acid was oxidized to allantoin, the carbon dioxide formed contained the isotope, and hence this is indeed the precursor of C_6. In contrast, isotopic formic acid gives material which on oxidation with lead dioxide affords nonisotopic carbon dioxide. However, nitric acid oxidation of the same uric acid reveals that the labeled carbon of formic acid enters the molecule at other sites. Both the urea formed in the oxidation and that resulting from hydrolysis of alloxan, when treated with the enzyme urease to effect conversion to carbon dioxide and ammonia, gave isotopic carbon dioxide, which shows that formic acid supplies C_2 and C_8. Experiments with donors of labeled ammonia established that this precursor supplies N_1, N_3 and N_9, but not N_7. Acid hydrolysis of uric acid derived from N^{15}-labeled glycine gave glycine bearing isotopic nitrogen, and hence N_7 is supplied by the amino group of glycine. That C_4 and C_5 are supplied, respectively, by the carboxyl and methylene groups of glycine was established in parallel experiments with glycine labeled in each of these positions. The resulting uric acid was oxidized to allantoin, which was hydrolyzed to glyoxylic acid, isolated as the semicarbazone, $HO_2CCH=NNHCONH_2$. On permanganate oxidation of this derivative, carbon dioxide derived from the carboxyl group of glyoxylic acid appears rapidly (7 min.) and that from the aldehydic group is formed slowly (several hrs.), and hence the two positions are distinguishable. The results established that the carboxyl group of glycine is the precursor of C_4 and that the methylene group supplies C_5. Hence all the atoms in the bicyclic ring system are accounted for. The enzymic synthesis of uric acid from the precursors indicated has been realized.

The classical uric acid work also resulted in a practical application to medicine. The first synthesis of barbituric acid was accomplished by condensing urea with malonic acid under the influence of phosphorus trichloride, but the procedure is improved by use of diethyl malonate in place of the acid and sodium ethoxide as the condensing agent; note the resemblance to an ester condensation (13.9). In 1903 E. Fischer and J. von Mering applied this procedure to the synthesis of a number of derivatives of barbituric acid, some of which were found valuable as soporifics. 5,5-Diethylbarbituric acid has been widely used under the name

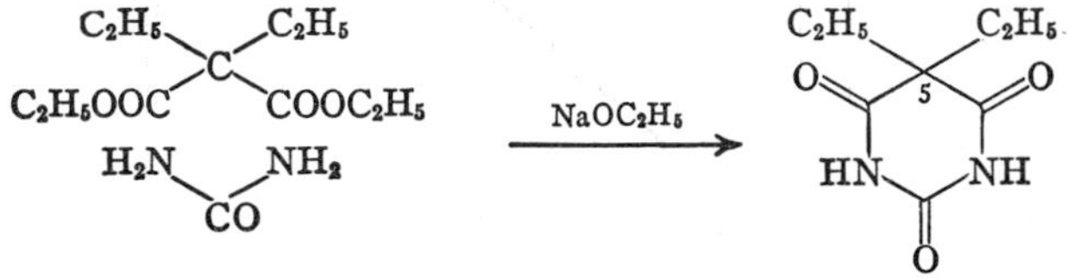

Diethylbarbituric acid
(veronal, m. p. 191°, pKa 7.4)

veronal or barbital to induce sleep and to some extent as a sedative and in anesthesia.

It is curious that the alkaloids caffeine, theophylline, and theobromine bear a certain structural analogy to the barbiturates but have physiological activity of directly opposite type: they are stimulants. The coffee bean contains caffeine

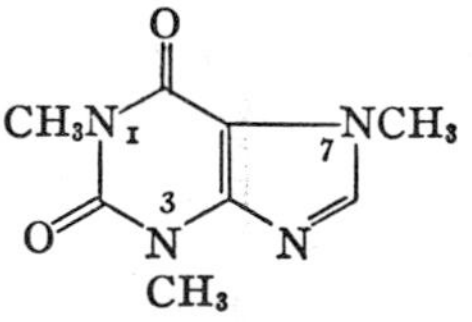

Caffeine

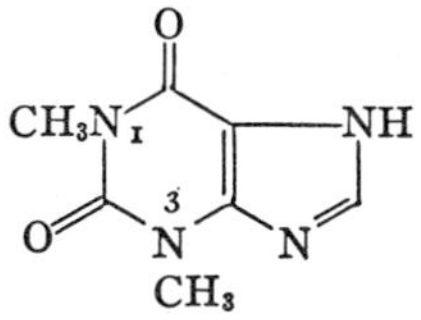

Theophylline

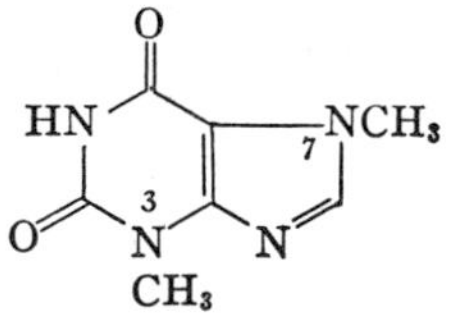

Theobromine

(1.5%); tea leaves contain caffeine (5%) and theophylline (trace); cocoa beans (*Theobroma cacao*) contain theobromine (1.8%).

In the present systematic nomenclature, substances having the skeletal structure of uric acid are defined as purines, from the name assigned by E. Fischer to the parent compound (L. *purum uricum*). The six-membered ring of alloxan and

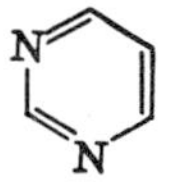

Pyrimidine, or
1,3-diazine
(m.p. 22°, b.p. 124°)

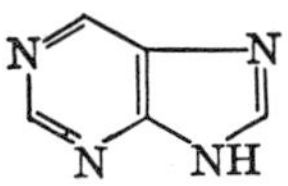

Purine
(m.p. 216°)

barbituric acid is known both as a pyrimidine and as a 1,3-diazine ring.

14.33   **Natural Isobutylamides.** — Affinin, an insecticidal isobutylamide, was isolated by F. Acree, Jr., M. Jacobson, and H. L. Haller[1] (1945)

[1] H. L. Haller, b. 1894 Cincinnati, Ohio; Ph.D. Columbia (Ambler); Insecticide Div., U. S. Dept. Agr.

as a pale yellow, viscous oil from roots of *Heliopsis longipes*, a plant native to the environs of Mexico City and used in the preparation of native insecticides.   Iso-

$$CH_3CH\overset{8}{=}CHCH\overset{6}{=}CHCH_2CH_2CH\overset{t}{\underset{=}{}}\overset{2}{C}HC\overset{1}{O}NHCH_2CH(CH_3)_2$$

Affinin (m.p. 23°)

butylamine was identified as the basic product of saponification.   Hydrogenation of affinin yields a hexahydro derivative which on hydrolysis affords isobutylamine and capric acid $CH_3(CH_2)_8CO_2H$.   The three double bonds were located at the positions shown in the formula by permanganate oxidation to acetic acid, oxalic acid, succinic acid, and N-isobutyloxamic acid, $(CH_3)_2CHCH_2NHCOCO_2H$.   The presence of a diene system isolated from a C=C—C=O system accounts for a spectrum with one intense absorption band, λ 228.5 mμ (ϵ 33,700).   The double bond at either the C_6- or the C_8-position in affinin is *cis*, for the substance is isomerized by ultraviolet light or by selenium to all-*trans*-affinin, λ 228.5 mμ (ϵ 37,100). This isomer, which is nontoxic to insects, has been prepared by total synthesis (M. Jacobson, 1955).

The structure of neoherculin, isolated from several plants, was elucidated by L. Crombie[1] (Imperial College, 1957).   Like affinin, neoherculin is highly unstable and

$$CH_3CH\overset{t}{\underset{=}{}}CHCH\overset{t}{\underset{=}{}}CHCH\overset{c}{\underset{=}{}}CHCH_2CH_2CH\overset{t}{\underset{=}{}}CHCONHCH_2CH(CH_3)_2$$

Neoherculin (m.p. 69°)

is isomerized to the all-*trans* form by iodine.   Anacyclin is a diene diyne iso-

$$CH_3CH_2CH_2C\equiv CC\equiv CCH_2CH_2CH\overset{t}{\underset{=}{}}CH—CH\overset{t}{\underset{=}{}}CHCONHCH_2CH(CH_3)_2$$

Anacyclin (m.p. 121°)

butylamide with a C_{14}- rather than a C_{12}-acyl chain (Crombie, 1957).   It is not insecticidal but becomes so on selective hydrogenation of the two acetylenic bonds. Other members of the group have similar structures.   All have a *trans* double bond conjugated with the amide linkage.   One or more *cis* double bonds in the interior of the chain are apparently necessary for high insecticidal activity.

PROBLEMS

1. Examine the model of hexamethylenetetramine (p. 437).   (a) Would replacement of one hydrogen give a resolvable compound?   (b) Would a substance with a methyl and an ethyl group at C_1 and the same two groups at C_6 be capable of resolution?

2. Arrange the following compounds in order with respect to their acidic or basic properties: methylamine, acetamide, phthalimide, tetramethylammonium hydroxide, urea, acetylmethylamine, succinimide, β-alanine ($H_2NCH_2CH_2COOH$).

3. Suggest convenient chemical methods for isolating in a pure form the chief component of each of the following mixtures:
   (*a*) Triethylamine, containing traces of ethylamine and diethylamine
   (*b*) Diethylamine, contaminated with ethylamine and triethylamine
   (*c*) Ethylamine, containing di- and triethylamine

4. How could *n*-propylamine and *n*-amylamine be prepared from *n*-butyl alcohol?

---

[1] Leslie Crombie, b. 1923 York, England; Ph.D., D.Sc. London (Harper, Linstead); Imperial College and King's College, Univ. London

5. Suggest a method other than one proceeding through the halogen derivative for the preparation of *sec*-butylamine from *sec*-butyl alcohol.

6. If *n*-butyl bromide is to be converted into *n*-butylamine, what would be the advantage of using the Gabriel synthesis rather than direct ammonolysis? Comment on the practicability of converting the alcohol into the aldehyde, preparing the oxime, and reduction.

7. Indicate the steps involved in the transformation of a nitrile into an acid and of an acid into a nitrile. Would you expect an aldoxime to be convertible directly to a nitrile?

8. Formulate the Hofmann degradation as applied to cyclohexylamine.

9. Is there any similarity in electronic state between trimethylboron and the trimethylcarbonium ion?

10. What structures can contribute to the resonant hybrid anion from succinimide?

11. With the aid of electronic formulas, explain more fully the statement in section 14.29 that the bromine atom in N-bromosuccinimide is relatively positive since the substance on hydrolysis affords HOBr, whereas RBr yields HBr.

12. The thermal decomposition of quaternary ammonium hydroxides with the formation of alkenes is an example of the rather general phenomenon that high or moderately high temperatures favor the formation of unsaturated compounds. A number of other examples have been cited in earlier chapters; how many can you cite?

13. Mescal, a preparation from the tops of the small cactus *Lophophora williamsii*, is used as a stimulant and antispasmodic, especially among Mexican Indians, who also employ it as a mild intoxicant in various ceremonials. The active principle, mescaline, was isolated in 1896 by A. Heffter (Leipzig) from material supplied by Parke, Davis and Co. Mescaline (A), $C_{11}H_{17}O_3N$, melts at 36°, is optically inactive, sparingly soluble in water or in sodium hydroxide solution, but soluble in dilute hydrochloric acid. Zerewitinoff determination shows the presence of one active hydrogen, and reaction with acetic anhydride in pyridine gives a neutral derivative (B), $C_{13}H_{19}O_4N$. When A is shaken with benzenesulfonyl chloride and aqueous alkali the substance gradually dissolves, and acidification of the solution gives a crystalline precipitate (C), $C_{17}H_{21}O_5NS$. Mescaline on reaction with excess methyl iodide, followed by treatment of the product with moist silver oxide, gives a product D, $C_{14}H_{25}O_4N$, which when heated decomposes to trimethylamine and a neutral compound E, $C_{11}H_{14}O_3$. Ozonization of E gives formaldehyde and an aromatic aldehyde, F, $C_{10}H_{12}O_4$, characterized by Zeisel determination as having three methoxyl groups. The trihydroxy compound resulting on demethylation has an infrared absorption band characteristic of an unchelated aldehydic group. Deduce the structure of mescaline and suggest a synthesis from the aldehyde F.

Chapter 15

RING FORMATION AND STABILITY

15.1   **Cycloalkanes.** — Cycloalkanes boil 10–20° higher than corresponding
n-alkanes and densities are about 20% greater.   The heat of combustion of cyclohexane (939 kcal./mole, 11.16 kcal./g.) is slightly lower than that
of *n*-hexane on a weight basis, but the value of 8.68 kcal./ml. is considerably higher
than the value (7.58 kcal./ml.) for *n*-hexane.

TABLE 15.1.   CYCLOALKANES

	M.P., °C.	B.P., °C.	SP. GR. (LIQ.)
Cyclopropane	−127	−32.9	0.688
Cyclobutane	−80	11	.7038
Cyclopentane	−94	49.5	.7460
Cyclohexane	6.4	80.8	.7781
Cycloheptane	−13	117	.8100
Cyclooctane	14	147	.8304

15.2   **Cyclopropane Series.** — Cyclopropane was prepared for the first time
by O. Freund (1881) by the action of sodium on trimethylene dibromide (1).   The yield in the Freund reaction is raised to about 70% by use of
zinc dust in alcohol (G. Gustavson, 1887).   A technical process (H. B. Hass,
1936) involves reaction of trimethylene dichloride with zinc dust in aqueous
alcohol containing sodium iodide and sodium carbonate.   The first synthetic
routes to cyclopropane derivatives having functional groups were developed by
Perkin, Jr. at Munich in 1885–86.   One (2) involves condensation of ethylene
dibromide with sodiomalonic ester and affords diethyl cyclopropane-1,1-dicar-
boxylate.   Perkin saponified the ester and by mild pyrolytic decarboxylation of

531

the malonic acid obtained cyclopropanecarboxylic acid (m.p. 19°, pK$_a$ 4.8). Perkin's second method (3) involves the reverse process: preparation of a disodiomalonic ester derivative and ring closure by reaction with bromine (or iodine). Reaction (4) illustrates one of several routes to cyclopropanes involving intramolecular dehydrohalogenation of a compound with a reactive α-hydrogen atom. Example (5) illustrates a reaction discovered by E. Buchner (1890). Diazomethane adds to α,β-unsaturated carbonyl compounds to form pyrazolines, which on heating lose nitrogen and afford cyclopropane derivatives. According to a

1. $\text{CH}_2\text{CH}_2\text{Br}$ / CH_2Br $\xrightarrow{\text{Zn}}$ $\text{CH}_2\!\!>\!\!\text{CH}_2$ / CH_2

2. CH_2Br / CH_2Br $\xrightarrow{\text{NaCH(CO}_2\text{C}_2\text{H}_5)_2}$ $\text{CH}_2\text{CH(CO}_2\text{C}_2\text{H}_5)_2$ / CH_2Br $\xrightarrow{\text{NaCH(CO}_2\text{C}_2\text{H}_5)_2}$

$\text{CH}_2\text{CNa(CO}_2\text{C}_2\text{H}_5)_2$ / CH_2Br $\longrightarrow$ $\text{CH}_2\!\!>\!\!\text{C(CO}_2\text{C}_2\text{H}_5)_2$ / CH_2

3. $\text{CH}_2\!\!<^{\text{CNa(CO}_2\text{C}_2\text{H}_5)_2}_{\text{CNa(CO}_2\text{C}_2\text{H}_5)_2}$ $\xrightarrow{\text{Br}_2}$ $\text{CH}_2\!\!<^{\text{C(CO}_2\text{C}_2\text{H}_5)_2}_{\text{C(CO}_2\text{C}_2\text{H}_5)_2}$

4. $\text{CH}_2\text{CH}_2\text{COCH}_3$ / CH_2Br $\xrightarrow{\text{KOH}}$ $\text{CH}_2\!\!>\!\!\text{CHCOCH}_3$ / CH_2

5. $^-\text{CH}_2$ / $^+\text{N}\!\equiv\!\text{N}$ $+$ $\text{CHCO}_2\text{C}_2\text{H}_5$ / $\text{CHCO}_2\text{C}_2\text{H}_5$ $\longrightarrow$ $\text{N}\!\!<^{\text{CH}_2\!-\!\text{CHCO}_2\text{C}_2\text{H}_5}_{\text{N}\!-\!\text{CHCO}_2\text{C}_2\text{H}_5}$ $\xrightarrow{-\text{N}_2}$ $\text{CH}_2\!\!<^{\text{CHCO}_2\text{C}_2\text{H}_5}_{\text{CHCO}_2\text{C}_2\text{H}_5}$

(pyrazoline)

preliminary report (K. L. Rinehart, Jr., 1960) light-induced decomposition of the pyrazoline is free from side reactions and proceeds stereospecifically.

A synthesis of cyclopropene reported by N. J. Demjanov (1923) and confirmed by Schlatter[1] (1941) involves exhaustive methylation of cyclopropylamine and

$\text{CH}_2\text{CH}_2\text{CN}$ / CH_2Cl $\xrightarrow{\text{NaNH}_2}$ $\text{CH}_2\!\!>\!\!\text{CHCN}$ / CH_2 $\xrightarrow{\text{C}_2\text{H}_5\text{OH}-\text{HCl}}$ $\text{CH}_2\!\!>\!\!\text{CHC}\!\!<^{\text{OC}_2\text{H}_5}_{\text{NH}\cdot\text{HCl}}$ / CH_2 $\xrightarrow{\text{Heat}}$

$\text{CH}_2\!\!>\!\!\text{CHCONH}_2$ / CH_2 $\xrightarrow[\text{NaOCH}_3]{\text{Br}_2,}$ $\text{CH}_2\!\!>\!\!\text{CHNHCO}_2\text{CH}_3$ / CH_2 $\xrightarrow{\text{H}_2\text{O}_2}$ $\text{CH}_2\!\!>\!\!\text{CHNH}_2$ / CH_2 $\xrightarrow{\text{CH}_3\text{I}}$

$\text{CH}_2\!\!>\!\!\text{CHN(CH}_3)_3\text{I}^-$ / CH_2 $\xrightarrow{\text{Ag}_2\text{O}}$ $\text{CH}_2\!\!>\!\!\text{CHN(CH}_3)_3\text{OH}^-$ / CH_2 $\xrightarrow{325°}$ $\text{CH}_2\!\!>\!\!\text{CH}$ / CH

Cyclopropene

Hofmann elimination of the methohydroxide. Cyclopropene is stable as a solid at liquid nitrogen temperature and several reactions and properties have been investigated (K. B. Wiberg, 1960–61). The hydrocarbon (b.p. −36°) polymerizes

[1] Maurice J. Schlatter, b. 1916 Chicago; Ph.D. Calif. Inst. Techn. (Lucas, Buchman); Hyland Laboratories; Calif. Research Corp.

slowly in a dry ice–acetone bath.   Passed with helium over glass helices at 425°, it rearranges to methylacetylene; the enthalpy of isomerization is less than -3.4 kcal./mole, as compared to -7.9 kcal./mole for the cyclopropane–propylene rearrangement (J. W. Knowlton and F. D. Rossini, 1949).   The extra strain energy of cyclopropene as compared to cyclopropane is at least 8 kcal./mole and possibly considerably greater.   The strain of the unsaturated hydrocarbon accounts for the ready formation and unusual stability of the dibromide and diiodide; the diiodide does not react with iodide ion or with zinc dust.   The dibromide is characterized by the proton nuclear resonance absorption to be *cis*-oriented.   It is the only

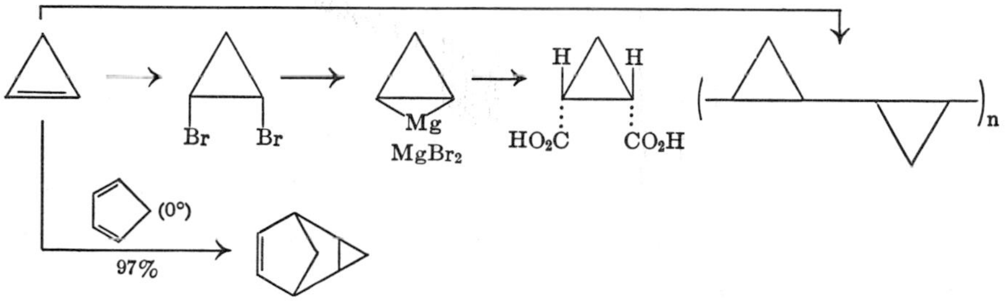

simple *vic*-dibromide that forms a di Grignard reagent, formulated as a complex $R_2Mg \cdot MgBr_2$.   Carbonation of the reagent affords *cis*-cyclopropane-1,2-dicarboxylic acid.   The strained hydrocarbon is a highly reactive dienophile; thus the gas was largely absorbed when passed with nitrogen into a solution of cyclopentadiene in methylene chloride at 0°.   The adduct probably has the *endo* configuration; the *exo* isomer had been prepared by the carbene reaction of Simmons and Smith (15.4).   The yield of adduct with the less reactive butadiene was only 37%.   J. G. Traynham[1] (1956) determined equilibrium constants for formation of π-complexes between aqueous silver ion and cyclic olefins and found that strain in the olefin facilitates complex formation.   Thus values for K_{eq}, l./mole are: cyclopentene, 0.11; cyclohexene, 0.019; cycloheptene, 0.22; bicycloheptene, 0.27; bicyclooctene, 0.098.   For cyclopropene, the formation constant is of the order of 10^7.

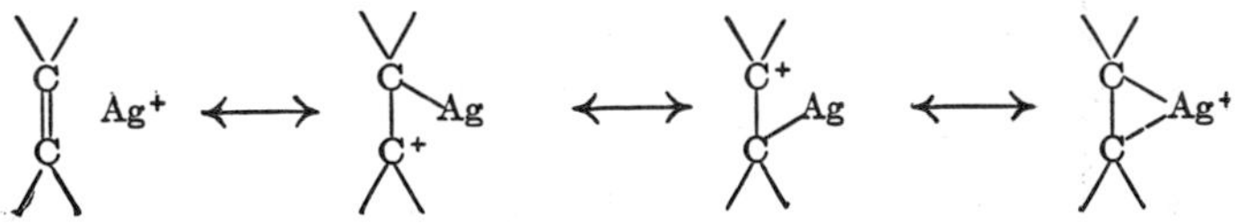

Many attempts to prepare cyclopropanol resulted only in the formation of allyl alcohol.   However, D. L. Cottle (1943) found that the alcohol can be obtained in reasonable yield by the reaction of epichlorohydrin with ethylmagnesium bromide.

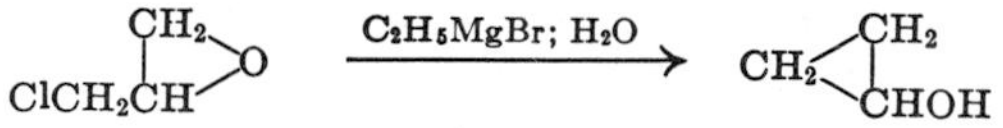

---

[1] James G. Traynham, b. 1925 Broxton, Ga.; Ph.D. Northwestern (Letsinger); Louisiana State Univ.

Cyclopropanol rearranges to propionaldehyde on distillation but was characterized as the phenylurethane (m.p. 102°) and the 3,5-dinitrobenzoate (m.p. 109°). Cyclopropanone is probably formed in the reaction of diazomethane with excess ketene in absolute ether, but the only products isolated are polymeric substances.

$$\bar{C}H_2N\overset{+}{\equiv}N \ + \ CH_2=C=O \ \xrightarrow{-N_2} \ \left[\begin{array}{c} CH_2 \\ | \quad \diagdown \\ | \quad \diagup C=O \\ CH_2 \end{array} \right]$$

The reactions of cyclopropane characterize the hydrocarbon as somewhat less reactive than ethylene. Catalytic hydrogenation to *n*-propane proceeds rather

$$\begin{array}{c} CH_2{-}CH_2 \\ \diagdown \ \diagup \\ CH_2 \end{array} \quad \xrightarrow{H_2, \ Ni \ (120°)} \quad CH_3CH_2CH_3$$

readily, and the ring is opened also by reaction with bromine, hydrogen bromide, or sulfuric acid. Addition of hydrogen bromide to substituted cyclopropanes follows the Markownikoff rule: the ring is opened between the carbons carrying the smallest and the largest number of alkyl groups and the halogen appears at the latter position, as in the examples. Kohler (1917) neatly proved the existence

$$\begin{array}{c} CH_3CH_2CH{\vdots}{-}CH_2 \\ \diagdown \ \diagup \\ CH_2 \end{array} \quad \xrightarrow{HBr} \quad \begin{array}{c} CH_3CH_2CHCH_2CH_3 \\ | \\ Br \end{array}$$

$$\begin{array}{c} CH_3 \diagdown \\ \qquad C{-}CHCH_3 \\ CH_3 \diagup \ \cdot\times\diagup \\ \qquad CH_2 \end{array} \quad \xrightarrow{HBr} \quad \begin{array}{c} CH_3 \diagdown \qquad \diagup CH_3 \\ \qquad C{-}CH \\ CH_3 \diagup \ | \ \diagdown CH_3 \\ \qquad Br \end{array}$$

of a three-membered ring by cleaving a substituted cyclopropane at each of the three sides of the triangle. Since the reactions all proceed by 1,4-addition, they show that a cyclopropane ring and an adjacent carbonyl group form a conjugated

$$\begin{array}{c} \qquad\qquad CHCOC_6H_5 \\ C_6H_5CH \diagup \ | \\ \qquad\qquad C(CO_2C_2H_5)_2 \end{array}$$

$$\text{HBr} \diagup \qquad \big\downarrow \text{Zn, AcOH} \qquad \diagdown \text{Mg(OCH}_3)_2$$

$$\begin{array}{c} Br \\ | \\ C_6H_5CH \ | \begin{array}{c} CH_2COC_6H_5 \\ C(CO_2C_2H_5)_2 \end{array} \end{array} \qquad C_6H_5CH \diagup \begin{array}{c} CH_2COC_6H_5 \\ CH(CO_2C_2H_5)_2 \end{array} \qquad C_6H_5CH \diagup \begin{array}{c} CCOC_6H_5 \\ CH(CO_2C_2H_5)_2 \end{array}$$

system. Ultraviolet spectroscopy confirms this finding, since substances having a cyclopropylethylene group absorb at a wave length of 210 mμ, not far from the value for butadiene (220 mμ). Pseudoconjugate properties of the three membered ring, demonstrated also by dipole moments and other physical data, indicate that the C—C bond electrons are more weakly bound than the usual σ electrons and tend to exhibit characteristics associated with mobile π electrons. This concept accounts for the direction of addition of hydrogen bromide (intermediate π-complex, as with an olefin) and for the fact that cyclopropane forms a yellow π-complex with tetranitromethane.

Cyclopropyl sulfones are available by a simple elimination reaction effected with sodamide in a special solvent, ethylene glycol dimethyl ether (L. Lindy and W. E.

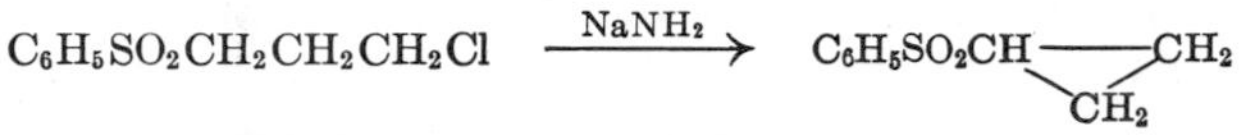

$$C_6H_5SO_2CH_2CH_2CH_2Cl \xrightarrow{\text{NaNH}_2} C_6H_5SO_2CH\overset{\displaystyle\diagdown}{\underset{\displaystyle CH_2}{\diagup}}CH_2$$

Truce,[1] 1960). Phenyl cyclopropyl sulfone on reaction with Raney nickel in refluxing ethanol yields cyclopropane. Unlike the behavior of the corresponding cyclopropyl ketones, the cyclopropane ring in the sulfones is not opened by HX-reagents.

In contrast with ethylene, cyclopropane is not attacked by aqueous permanganate solution or by ozone. The difference is illustrated by the permanganate oxidation of the unsaturated cyclopropane derivative shown in the formulation. Indeed compounds containing the cyclopropane ring can be distinguished from ethylenic substances by a qualitative test with permanganate, and the reagent is also useful

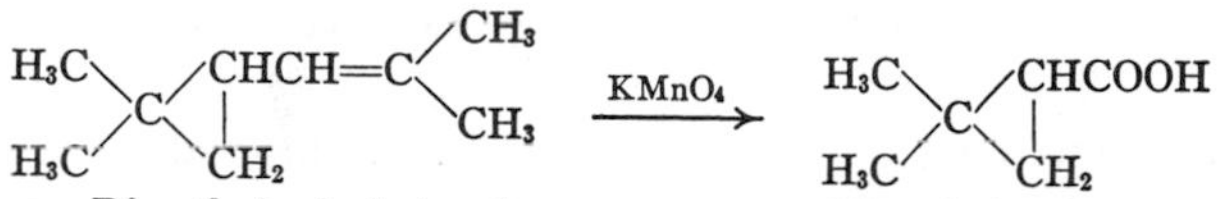

$$\overset{H_3C}{\underset{H_3C}{\diagdown}}C\overset{CHCH=C\diagdown CH_3}{\underset{CH_2}{\diagup}}\xrightarrow{\text{KMnO}_4}\overset{H_3C}{\underset{H_3C}{\diagdown}}C\overset{CHCOOH}{\underset{CH_2}{\diagup}}$$

| 1,1-Dimethyl-2-isobutenyl- | 1,1-Dimethylcyclopropane- |
| cyclopropane | 2-carboxylic acid |

for removing traces of propylene from cyclopropane. The three-membered ring also resists attack by ozone.

15.3   The Feist Acid. — Geuther, discoverer of ethyl acetoacetate (1863), encountered a dimeric product derived from it known as dehydroacetic acid. The crystalline, highly reactive substance can be prepared by heating acetoacetic ester with a trace of sodium bicarbonate at 200° and removal of ethanol with a trap (F. Arndt, 1924). The base-catalyzed reaction (1) is formulated as proceeding through an initial ester condensation in order to distinguish it from the acid-catalyzed condensation (2) to isodehydroacetic acid, which may

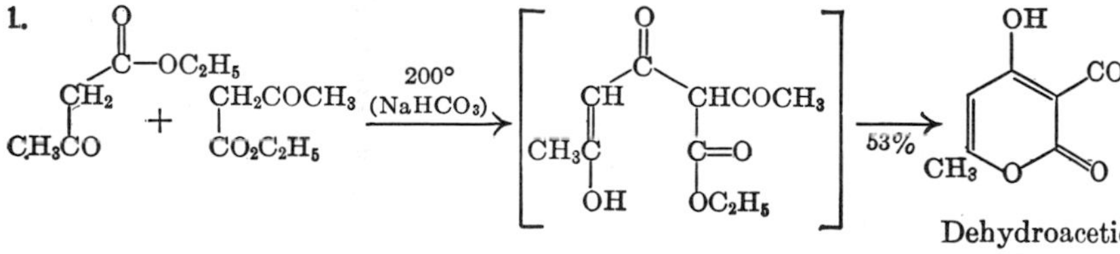

1.

Dehydroacetic acid
M. p. 109°

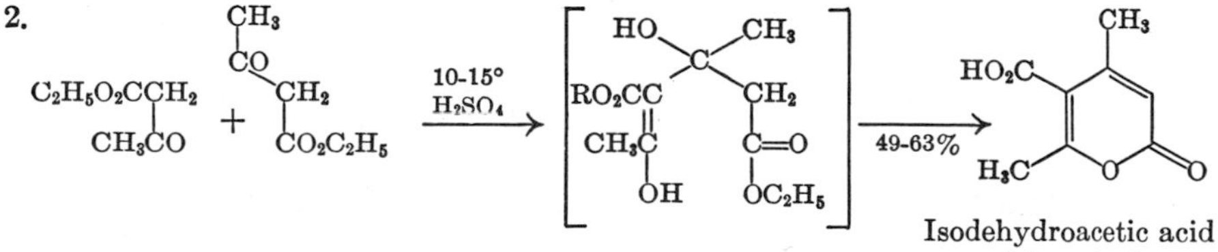

2.

Isodehydroacetic acid
M. p. 155°

---

[1] William E. Truce, b. 1917 Chicago; Ph.D. Northwestern (Suter); Purdue Univ.

proceed through an initial aldolization. The reaction product is isolated in part as the free acid and in part as the ester; the systematic name of the iso acid is 4,6-dimethyl-2-pyrone-5-carboxylic acid. This condensation was described first by Hantzsch (1883).

In investigating the action of alcoholic potassium hydroxide on 3-bromo-5-carbethoxy-4,6-dimethyl-2-pyrone (I), a derivative of isodehydroacetic acid, F. Feist (Zurich, 1893) encountered a remarkable product, $C_6H_6O_4$, later known as the Feist acid. The Feist acid, m.p. 200°, is dibasic, and hence only the residual unit C_4H_4 needed to be identified. Resolution to enantiomers, $\alpha_D + 116°$ and $-128°$, provided one clue. The problem attracted several investigators, par-

ticularly Ingold and Thorpe[1] (1922–25), who concluded that the substance is 1-methylcyclopropene-2,3-dicarboxylic acid (II). Thirty years after discovering the acid, Feist (Kiel, 1924) reinvestigated the substance and concluded that formula II is correct. However, Ettlinger[2] later (1952) found from Kuhn-Roth determination (11.5) that the Feist acid contains no C-methyl group and presented chemical evidence that the substance in fact is 1-methylenecyclopropane-*trans*-2,3-dicarboxylic acid (III).

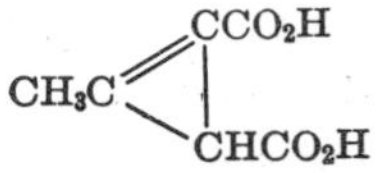

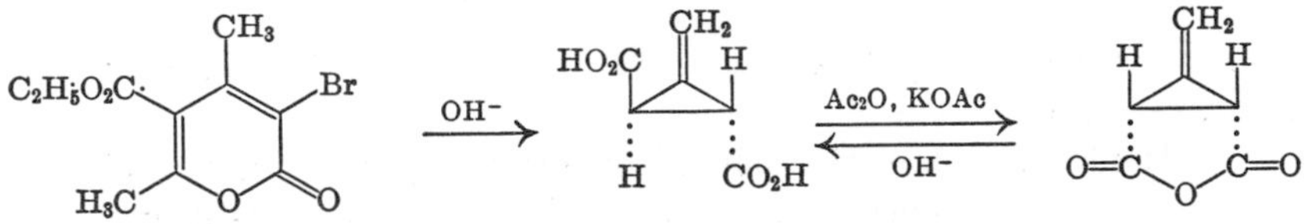

I   III (d- or l-)   IV

15.4   **Carbenes.** — The entity :CH_2, a methylene group with a lone electron pair, is known as carbene (the name methylene is also used). Irradiation of ketene with light of wave length 300–370 mμ causes decomposition with eventual formation of ethylene and carbon monoxide as the major products in the approximate ratio 1:2 (R. G. W. Norrish, 1933). Detailed investigations by G. B. Kistiakowsky (1933–61) of flash photochemical decomposition of ketene in the gas phase revealed that the primary products are carbene and carbon monoxide (1). The ethylene formed does not arise from the coupling of two

1. $CH_2{=}C{=}O \longrightarrow$:CH_2 + CO

2. :CH_2 + $CH_2{=}C{=}O \longrightarrow CH_2{=}CH_2$ + CO

molecules of carbene but by a complex series of reactions which can be approximated by the step (2). One characteristic and unusual reaction of this highly labile species is attack of a C—H bond with formation of C—CH_3, an insertion

$$CH_3CH_2CH_3 + :CH_2 \longrightarrow CH_3CH_2CH_2CH_3 + CH_3\overset{\displaystyle CH_3}{\underset{\displaystyle |}{C}}HCH_3$$

[1] Jocelyn Field Thorpe, 1872–1940; b. Clapham, England; Ph.D. Heidelberg (von Auwers); Manchester Univ.; Imperial College, London

[2] Martin G. Ettlinger, b. 1925 Austin, Texas; Ph.D. Harvard (Fieser); Rice Univ.

reaction. Thus carbene generated from ketene reacts with propane to give *n*-butane and isobutane in the ratio 7:4 (gas phase). If the attack were entirely random the ratio would be 6:2. Consequently carbene, like a chlorine radical in photochemical chlorination (4.11), reacts more readily with secondary hydrogen bonds than with primary bonds. Meerwein found (1942) that carbene generated in the presence of diethyl ether by irradiation or pyrolysis of diazomethane reacts by insertion in two ways:

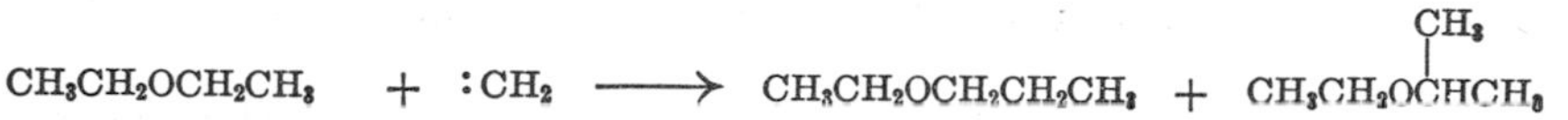

$$\overset{H}{\underset{\cdot\cdot}{H:\overset{+}{C}::\overset{-}{N}::\overset{-}{N}:}} \longrightarrow \overset{H}{\underset{\cdot\cdot}{H:\overset{\cdot\cdot}{C}:}} + N_2$$

$$CH_3CH_2OCH_2CH_3 + :CH_2 \longrightarrow CH_3CH_2OCH_2CH_2CH_3 + CH_3CH_2O\overset{CH_3}{\overset{|}{C}HCH_3}$$

A further unusual reaction of carbenes is addition to a double bond to give a cyclopropane derivative (Doering, 1954; Skell,[1] 1956). Dichlorocarbene, generated in the presence of an olefin by the action of potassium *t*-butoxide on chloroform, reacts with the olefin to form a 1,1-dichlorocyclopropane. The carbene is considered to arise by the steps formulated. Yields are improved by generating dichlorocarbene from ethyl trichloroacetate and potassium *t*-butoxide (W. E. Parham, 1959). Skell (1956) established that the reaction is stereospecific. Thus

$$HCCl_3 + t\text{-}BuO^- \rightleftharpoons C^-Cl_3 + t\text{-}BuOH$$

$$C^-Cl_3 \longrightarrow :CCl_2 + Cl^-$$

dibromocarbene reacts with *cis*-2-butene to give *cis*-1,1-dibromo-2,3-dimethylcyclopropane and the *trans* isomer gives the corresponding *trans* cyclopropane.

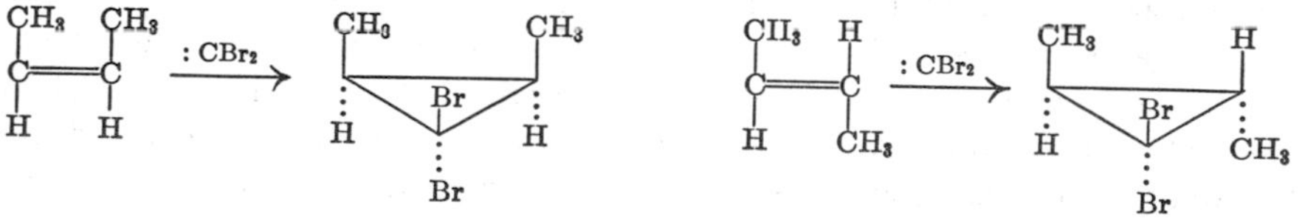

H. D. Hartzler[2] (1959) found that treatment of 3-chloro-3-methylbutyne-1 with potassium *t*-butoxide in styrene produces an allenylcarbene which reacts with the olefin to give 1-(2-methylpropenylidene)-2-phenylcyclopropane. He showed also

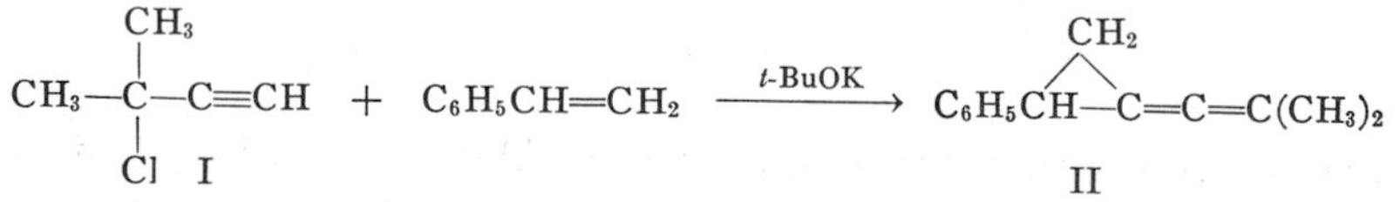

$$\underset{\overset{|}{Cl}\ I}{CH_3-\overset{\overset{CH_3}{|}}{C}-C\equiv CH} + C_6H_5CH=CH_2 \xrightarrow{t\text{-}BuOK} \underset{II}{\overset{CH_2}{C_6H_5CH-\overset{\triangle}{C}=C=C(CH_3)_2}}$$

that reactions of the allenylcarbene with the 2-butenes are stereospecific *cis* additions.

Skell (1956) and Doering (1958) found that the rates of addition of dibromocarbene and of dichlorocarbene parallel the rates of bromination and of epoxidation

[1] Philip S. Skell, b. 1918 New York; Ph.D. Duke (Hauser); Pennsylvania State Univ.
[2] Harris D. Hartzler, b. 1932; Ph.D. Chicago (Urry); du Pont Co.

of the same alkenes; the relative rates were determined by competition of pairs of olefins for a given carbene. Thus tetramethylethylene reacts more rapidly than trimethylethylene, which reacts more rapidly than isobutylene. The correlation of rates and the stereospecificity both suggest that carbene addition involves a similar cyclic transition state. It would appear that a carbene is not a diradical, that is, it does not contain two unpaired electrons. The structure is probably

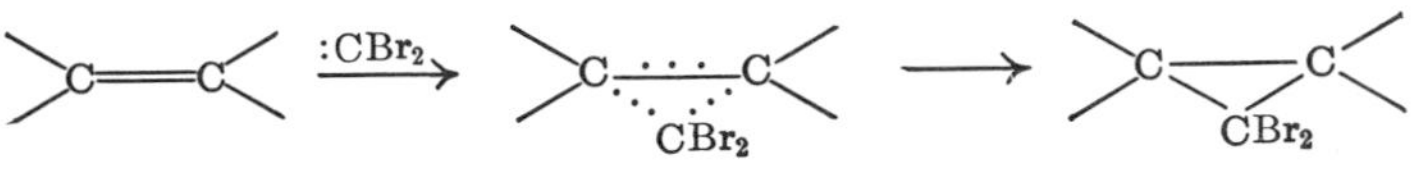

planar, like a carbonium ion, with two electrons in one orbital and with one vacant orbital.

Another method for generation of a halocarbene is by reaction of a polyhalide with an alkyllithium (G. L. Closs[1] and L. E. Closs,[2] 1960; W. T. Müller, Jr., 1960). For example, treatment of bromotrichloromethane with n-butyllithium in ether at $-60°$ in the presence of cyclohexene gives 7,7-dichloronorcarane (1). Use of

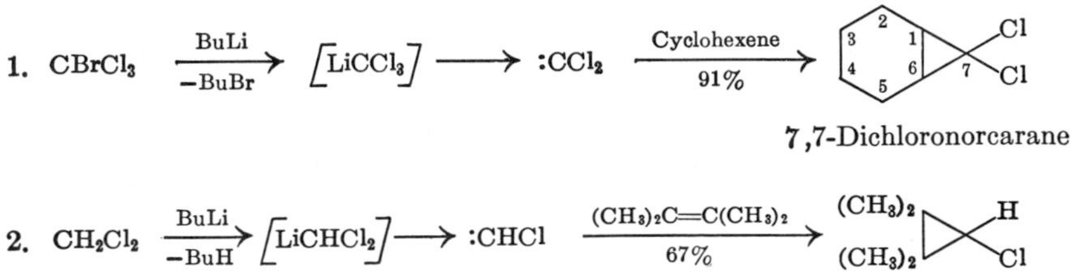

methylene chloride (2) leads to generation of chlorocarbene and provides a synthesis of monochlorocyclopropanes. *trans*-Butene-2 gives exclusively the product of *cis* addition (yield 40%). As with dichlorocarbene, yields increase with increasing nucleophilicity of the olefin. The possible intermediates $LiCCl_3$ and $LiCHCl_2$ could not be detected by hydrolysis or by carbonation at $-70°$. Analogy with a mechanism cited below (Simmons and Smith) suggests the following cyclic transition state (in reaction 1):

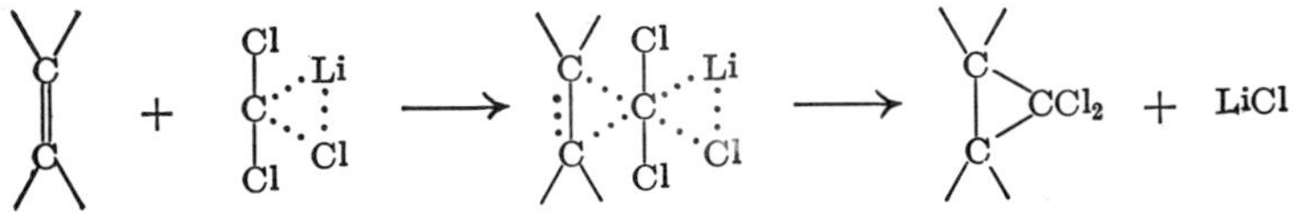

The production of phenylcarbene from benzyl chloride and n-butyllithium has been demonstrated by a trapping experiment. When chlorocarbene is generated from an alkyllithium (1) in the absence of another nucleophilic substrate, it reacts with the organolithium compound to form olefins and cyclopropanes (Closs, 1960). Thus n-amyllithium on reaction with methylene chloride (3) gives 1-hexene (95%) and n-propylcyclopropane (5%). The mechanism suggested postulates addition

[1] Gerhard L. Closs, b. 1928 Wuppertal, Germany; Ph.D. Tübingen (Wittig); Univ. Chicago
[2] Liselotte E. Closs, b. 1927 Berlin; Ph.D. Tübingen (Wittig).

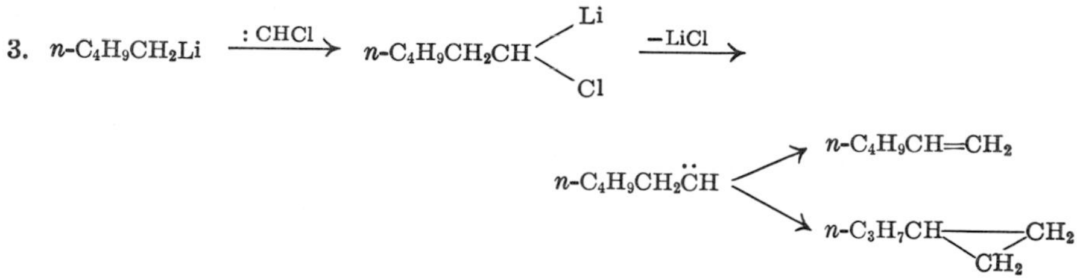

3. $n\text{-}C_4H_9CH_2Li$ $\xrightarrow{\;:\,CHCl\;}$ $n\text{-}C_4H_9CH_2CH \overset{Li}{\underset{Cl}{\diagdown\diagup}}$ $\xrightarrow{\;-LiCl\;}$

$$n\text{-}C_4H_9CH_2\ddot{C}H \diagdown \begin{array}{l} \nearrow\; n\text{-}C_4H_9CH{=}CH_2 \\[6pt] \searrow\; n\text{-}C_3H_7CH\!\!\!-\!\!\!-\!\!\!CH_2 \\ \qquad\qquad CH_2 \end{array}$$

of RLi to chlorocarbene, elimination of lithium chloride to form an alkylcarbene, which rearranges to stable products by hydrogen or alkyl migration or by intramolecular insertion. Another novel reaction leading to an olefin utilizes the even more strongly electrophilic difluorocarbene (V. Franzen,[1] 1960). Generated from CF_2Br_2 and n-butyllithium in the presence of an alkane, difluorocarbene reacts in the manner formulated in (4). This carbene also reacts with olefins to give 1,1-

4. RCH_2Li $\xrightarrow[-LiF]{\;:\,CF_2\;}$ $RCH_2\ddot{C}F$ $\xrightarrow[-LiF]{\;RLi\;}$ $RCH_2\ddot{C}R \longrightarrow RCH{=}CHR$

difluorocyclopropanes. Carbene is formed on reaction of methyl chloride with phenylsodium (L. Friedman, 1960), and phenoxycarbene can be generated from $C_6H_5OCH_2Cl$ and butyllithium (U. Schollkopf, 1961).

The synthetic potentiality of the dihalocarbene–olefin addition is illustrated by a procedure developed by K. Hofmann (1959) for the preparation of *cis*-cyclopropane-1,2-diacetic acid (4), required for the synthesis of dihydrosterculic acid (15.8). Bromoform was added slowly to a suspension of powdered potassium

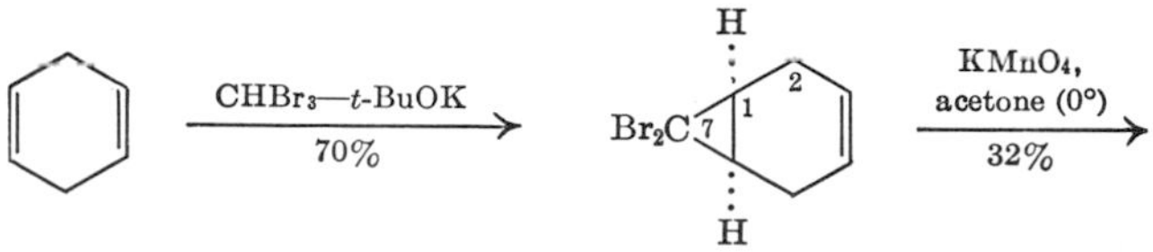

(1)   (2) M. p. 37°, λ 9.5 μ

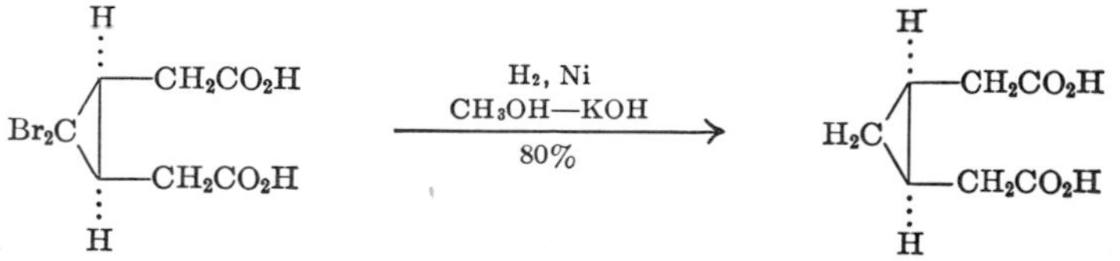

(3) M. p. 181°, λ 9.2, 9.9 μ   (4) M. p. 133°, λ 9.7 μ

t butoxide in a solution of 1,4-cyclohexadiene in *n*-pentane at 0–5°, and the resulting 7,7-dibromo-3-norcarene (2) was oxidized to the diacid (3) with permanganate in acetone; pimelic acid, $HO_2C(CH_2)_5CO_2H$, was isolated as a by-product (10%).

[1] Volker Franzen, b. 1924 Hamburg; Ph.D. Heidelberg; Max-Planck Inst. Med. Res., Heidelberg

The best method found for removal of halogen was by Raney nickel hydrogenation in a basic medium. The infrared bands indicated under the formulas are just those attributable to the cyclopropane ring.

Carbene itself adds to the double bond of cyclohexene to some extent, but addition here competes with several insertion reactions (Doering, 1956). Although the reaction of carbene itself with olefins is unsatisfactory as a route to

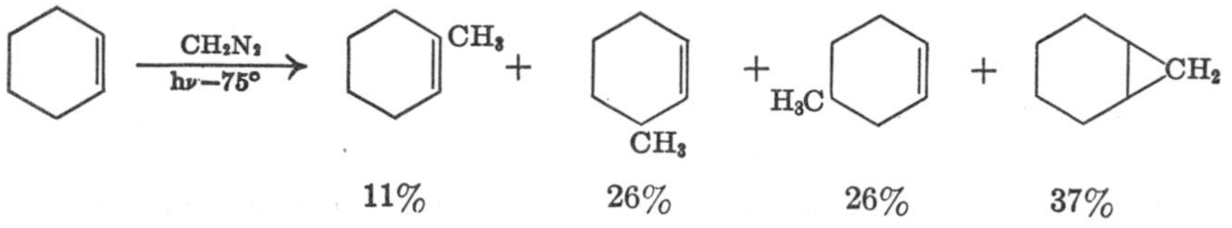

11%　　　　　26%　　　　　26%　　　　　37%

halogen-free cyclopropanes, a reaction developed by H. E. Simmons[1] and R. D. Smith[2] (du Pont, 1959) makes the addition products available in reasonable yield. The active reagent is iodomethylzinc iodide, generated by reaction of methylene iodide in ether with an active zinc–copper couple prepared from acid-washed zinc dust and copper sulfate solution and washed with water, absolute ethanol, and

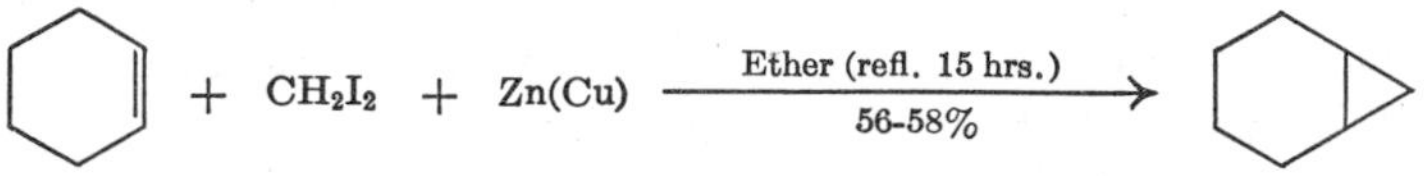

Norcarane

absolute ether. A suspension of the couple in anhydrous ether is treated with a crystal of iodine followed by the olefin and methylene iodide. After a suitable reflux period, the ethereal solution is decanted from finely divided copper, washed with saturated ammonium chloride, dried and evaporated. Yields reported for some thirty examples are mostly in the range 30–60%. The reaction is applicable to vinyl acetate (yield 30%), dihydropyrane (65%), styrene (32%), 1-(o-, m-, and p-methoxy)-phenylpropene (60–70%). The reaction of excess reagent with D-limonene to give a monoadduct offers evidence of a considerable steric require-

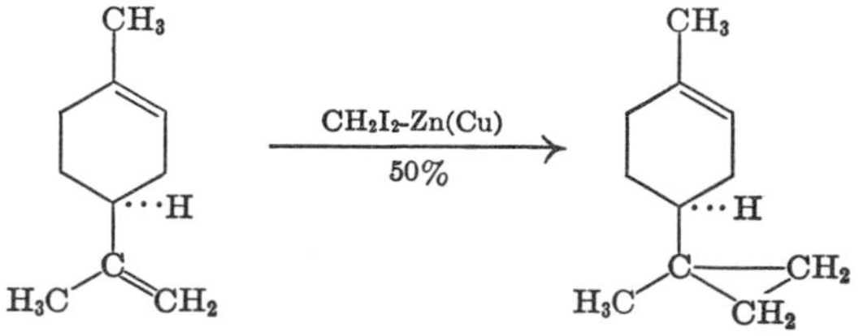

D-Limonene (+ 106°)　　　　　+ 51°

ment of the reagent. The high optical rotation of the product suggests that little or no racemization occurs, even though the asymmetric carbon atom is adjacent

[1] Howard E. Simmons, b. 1929 Norfolk, Va.; Ph.D. Mass. Inst. Techn. (J. D. Roberts, A. C. Cope); du Pont Co.

[2] Ronald D. Smith, b. 1930 Oakland, Calif.; Ph.D. Mass. Inst. Techn. (Cope); du Pont Co.

to the double bond undergoing reaction. Cyclopropane formation is a stereo-specific *cis* addition: *cis*- and *trans*-hexene-3 gave pure *cis*- and *trans*-1,2-diethyl-cyclopropane, respectively (b.p. 93.5° and 86.5°). The du Pont workers regard iodomethylzinc iodide as a relatively strongly bonded complex of carbene and zinc iodide (a) in which the carbon atom is electrophilic. The three-center transi-

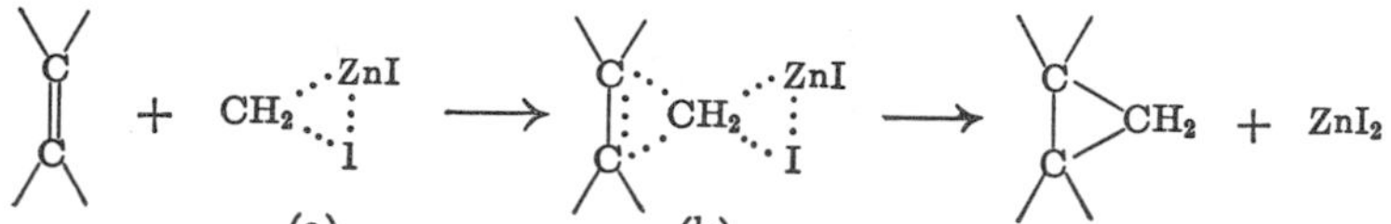

tion state (b) accounts for the large steric requirement and for *cis* addition.

The nucleophilic character of triphenylphosphine and the electrophilic character of carbenes suggested that the two reagents should combine to form ylides of a new type of use in expansion of the Wittig reaction (A. J. Speziale,[1] 1960; D. Seyferth, 1960). Thus triphenylphosphine on treatment in pentane with chloro-form and potassium *t*-butoxide at 0° gives yellow triphenylphosphinedichloro-methylene, which reacts with benzophenone to yield 1,1-diphenyl-2,2-dichloro-

1. $(C_6H_5)_3P \xrightarrow{:CCl_2} (C_6H_5)_3P=CCl_2 \xrightarrow[46\%]{(C_6H_5)_2CO} (C_6H_5)_2C=CCl_2$

2. $(C_6H_5)_3P + n\text{-BuLi} + CH_2Cl_2 \longrightarrow (C_6H_5)_3P=CHCl \xrightarrow[46\%]{C_6H_5COCH_3}$

$$C_6H_5C(CH_3)=CHCl$$

cis and *trans*

ethylene (1). Generation of chlorocarbene from *n*-butyllithium and methylene chloride in the presence of triphenylphosphine (2) gives triphenylphosphinechloro-methylene, which reacts with acetophenone to give a mixture of *cis*- and *trans*-1-chloro-2-phenyl-1-propene.

A trapping experiment with cyclohexene as acceptor has demonstrated formation of carbene in the reaction (3) of tetramethylammonium bromide with phenyl-lithium–phenylsodium (1:10); isolation of norcarane in 5–18% yields shows that

3. $(CH_3)_4N^+Br^- \xrightarrow{C_6H_5Na(Li)} (CH_3)_3\overset{+}{N}-\overset{-}{C}H_2 \longrightarrow (CH_3)_3N + :CH_2$

the intermediate trimethylammoniummethylide decomposes to trimethylamine and carbene (V. Franzen and G. Wittig, 1960). A similar experiment demon-strated the formation of dichlorocarbene in high yield on decomposition of sodium trichloroacetate in refluxing 1,2-dimethoxyethane (W. M. Wagner, 1959); the carbanion (4.9) may be involved: $^-CCl_3 \rightarrow :CCl_2 + Cl^-$.

Spirocyclopentane (3) was discovered by G. Gustavson (1896) as a product of the action of zinc dust on pentaerythritol tetrabromide (1) in aqueous ethanol. Later workers, chiefly N. D. Zelinsky (1912) and I. N. Shokhor (1954), investi-

[1] A. John Speziale, b. 1916 Rocky Hill, Conn.; Ph.D. Illinois (Fuson); Monsanto Chem. Co.

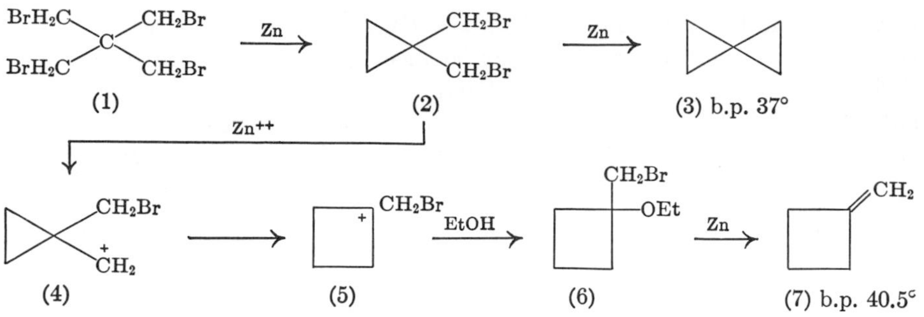

(1)   (2)   (3) b.p. 37°

(4)   (5)   (6)   (7) b.p. 40.5°

gated the reaction extensively without finding a way to inhibit extensive production of methylenecyclobutane (7), a by-product probably arising by electrophilically induced rearrangement of the intermediate dibromide (2) via the intermediates (4–6).   D. E. Applequist[1] (1958) devised a simple expedient which confirms the mechanism of the rearrangement and raises the yield of spirocyclopentane (94 % pure) to 81 %: addition of tetrasodium ethylenediaminetetraacetate to sequester zinc ion.   Preparation of derivatives presents difficulties; thus free-radical chlorination of the hydrocarbon gives chlorospiropentane and three other major products (D. E. A., 1960).   Chlorospiropentane is not attacked appreciably on prolonged refluxing with aqueous silver nitrate.   It was converted into spiropentylamine by reaction of the Grignard reagent with ethyl chloroformate and Curtius degradation (D. E. A., 1960).   The amine is converted by nitrous acid into a mixture of 2- and 3-methylenecyclobutanols (yields 7 % and 32 %); the mechanism is under study.   For a new route to spiropentanes, see p. 604.

A new synthetic route utilizes the reaction of a cyclopropylindenecarbene with an olefin (W. M. Jones,[2] 1960).   The starting material, 2,2-diphenylcyclopropanecarboxylic acid (1) was prepared according to H. M. Walborsky[3] (1955) by reaction of diphenyldiazomethane with methyl acrylate and converted via the acid

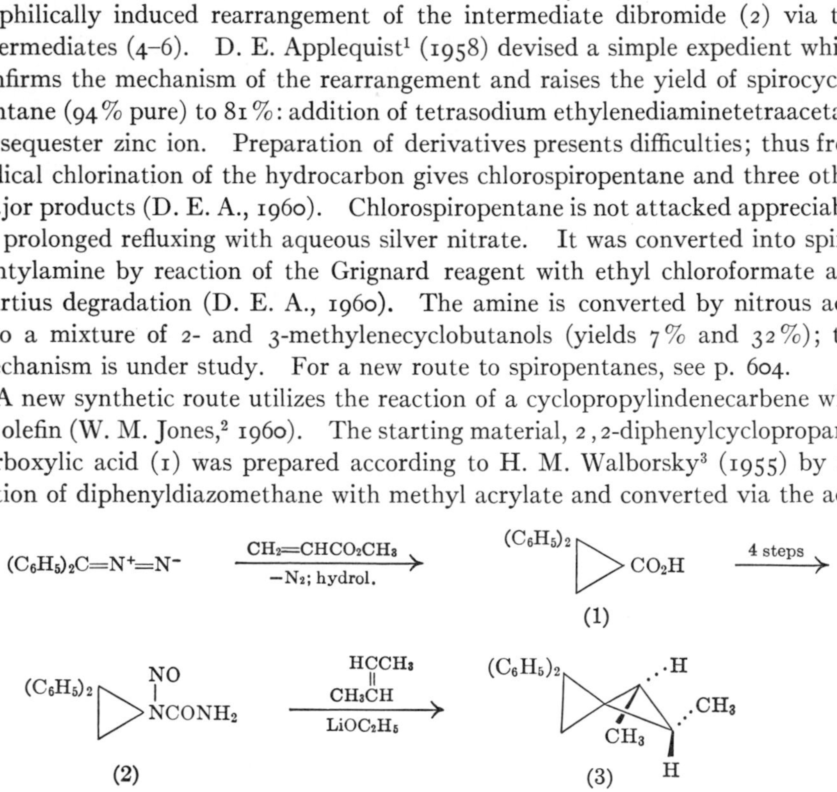

(1)

(2)   (3)

chloride, acid azide, isocyanate, and urea into the unusually stable nitrosourea (2). The cyclopropylindenecarbene was then generated in the presence of *cis*- and

[1] Douglas E. Applequist, b. 1930 Salt Lake City, Utah; Ph.D. Calif. Inst. Techn. (Roberts); Univ. Illinois

[2] William M. Jones, b. 1930 Campbellsville, Ky.; Ph.D. Southern Calif. (Berson); Univ. Florida

[3] Harry M. Walborsky, b. 1923 Lodz, Poland; Ph.D. Ohio State (Newman); Florida State Univ.

trans-2-butene by treatment of (2) with lithium ethoxide.   Crystalline products (m.p. 32°, 52°) were isolated and characterized as sterically pure diphenyldimethyl-spirocyclopentanes.

A cyclopropene synthesis by G. L. Closs and L. E. Closs (1961) is illustrated by the reaction of 1,2-dimethylpropenyllithium (1) with methylene chloride in tetrahydrofurane at $-35°$ to give, after hydrolysis, 1,3,3-trimethylcyclopropene

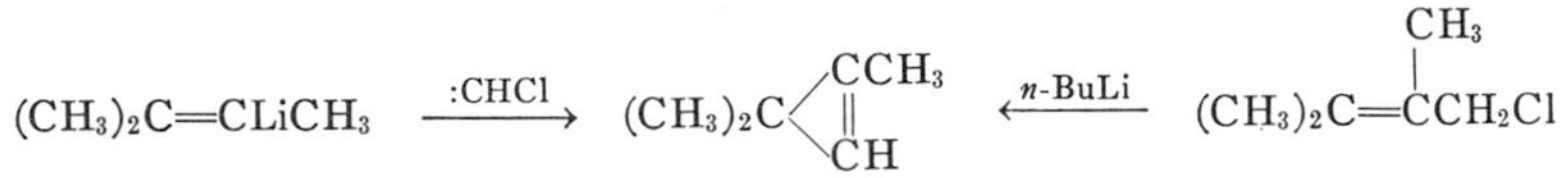

$$(CH_3)_2C{=}CLiCH_3 \xrightarrow{:CHCl} (CH_3)_2C{\Big\langle}^{CCH_3}_{CH} \xleftarrow{n\text{-BuLi}} (CH_3)_2C{=}\overset{CH_3}{\overset{|}{C}}CH_2Cl$$

(1)   (2)   (3)

(2).   The same product results also from 1-chloro-2,3-dimethyl-2-butene (3), but yields are low.   However decomposition of the tosylhydrazone $(CH_3)_2C{=}$ $C(CH_3)CH{=}NNHTs$ with base (150°) affords (2) in 72% yield.   A novel route to highly strained systems described by W. R. Moore[1] (1961) involves reaction of 7,7-

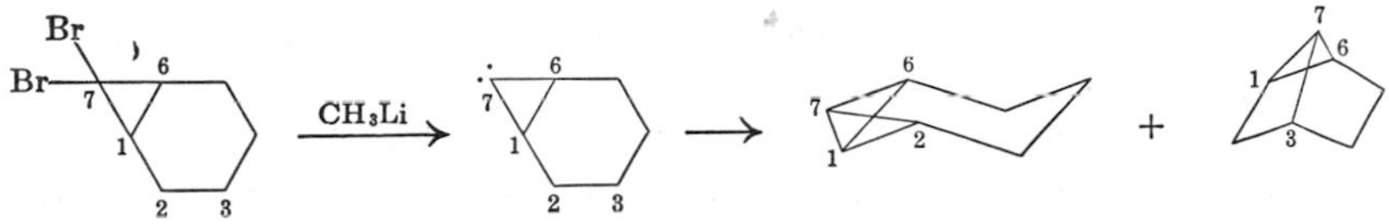

I   II   III   IV

dibromonorcarane (I) with methyllithium to produce the cyclopropylidene carbene II.   This intermediate undergoes intramolecular condensation, or self-insertion.   The major product is the hydrocarbon III, resulting from attack by C_7 at C_2; one of two minor products (IV) is formed by attack by C_7 at C_3.   The names are: III, tricyclo[4.1.0.0^{2,7}] heptane; IV, tricyclo[4.1.0.0^{3,7}]heptane.

Preliminary reports of the isolation of carbenes await confirmation.   Wanzlick[2] (1960) found that the product of reaction of dianilinoethane (12.37) with chloral when heated in an inert solvent loses chloroform and gives a colorless crystalline solid regarded as a carbene because it reacts with oxygen of the air to form 1,3

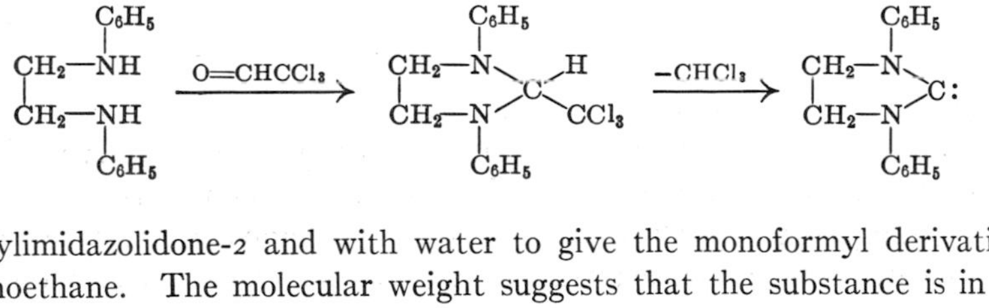

diphenylimidazolidone-2 and with water to give the monoformyl derivative of dianilinoethane.   The molecular weight suggests that the substance is in equilibrium with its dimer.

15.5   Cyclobutane Series. — The first known member of the series, diethyl cyclobutane-1,1-dicarboxylate (1), was obtained by Perkin, Jr. by his malonic ester synthesis (1887).   Saponification and pyrolysis of the malonic

---

[1] William R. Moore, b. 1928 Minneapolis; Ph.D. Minnesota (Arnold, Fenton); Mass. Inst. Techn.

[2] Hans-Werner Wanzlick, b. 1917 Berlin; Techn. Univ. Berlin

$$
\begin{array}{cc}
\underset{\text{CH}_2\text{—CH}_2\text{Br}}{\overset{\text{CH}_2\text{Br}}{|}} & \xrightarrow{\text{NaCH(CO}_2\text{C}_2\text{H}_5)_2} \quad \boxed{}^{(\text{CO}_2\text{C}_2\text{H}_5)_2} \xrightarrow{\text{OH}^-} \boxed{}^{(\text{CO}_2\text{H})_2} \xrightarrow{\text{Heat}} \\
 & \quad\quad\quad (1) \quad\quad\quad\quad\quad (2)
\end{array}
$$

$$
\boxed{}^{\text{CO}_2\text{H}} \longrightarrow \boxed{}^{\text{CONH}_2} \longrightarrow \boxed{}^{\text{NH}_2} \xrightarrow{\text{CH}_3\text{I}} \boxed{}^{\text{N}^+(\text{CH}_3)_3\text{I}^-}
$$

$$
(3) \quad\quad\quad\quad (4) \quad\quad\quad\quad\quad (5) \quad\quad\quad\quad\quad (6)
$$

$$
\xrightarrow{\text{Ag}_2\text{O}} \boxed{}^{\text{N}^+(\text{CH}_3)_3\text{OH}^-} \xrightarrow{\text{Heat}} \boxed{} \xrightarrow{\text{H}_2,\ \text{Pt}} \boxed{}
$$

$$
(7) \quad\quad\quad\quad\quad (8) \quad\quad\quad\quad (9)
$$

acid afforded cyclobutanecarboxylic acid (3), but Perkin's attempts to obtain the parent cycloalkane by pyrolysis of the calcium salt led only to the production of ethylene. The synthesis of cyclobutane was first achieved by Willstätter[1] (1907) by the following lengthy and low-yield process. Perkin's carboxylic acid was converted via the acid chloride and amide (4) to the amine (5), which was converted by exhaustive methylation (6) and Hofmann elimination of the methohydroxide (7) to cyclobutene (8). Careful hydrogenation then afforded cyclobutane (9), along with butadiene.

On undertaking to prepare a batch of cyclobutane for physiochemical investigation by his associates at Berkeley, Cason (1949) first tried the Freund synthesis, but found that the reaction of tetramethylene dibromide with sodium in boiling toluene afforded a mixture of about 7 % each of cyclobutane and n-butane, which differ in boiling point by only 12°. He then found a practicable process starting with a Hunsdiecker reaction (10.2) of silver cyclobutanecarboxylate (10), added

$$
\boxed{}^{\text{CO}_2\text{Ag}} \xrightarrow[\ -25°\ ]{\overset{\text{Br}_2\text{—CCl}_4}{\underset{53\%}{}}} \boxed{}^{\text{Br}} \xrightarrow{\text{Mg, Bu}_2\text{O}} \boxed{}^{\text{MgBr}} \xrightarrow[\ 83\%\ ]{\text{BuOH}} \boxed{}
$$

$$
(10) \quad\quad\quad\quad (11) \quad\quad\quad\quad (12) \quad\quad\quad\quad (13)
$$

to a solution of bromine in carbon tetrachloride at −25°. The resulting cyclobutylbromide (11) was converted to the Grignard reagent in di-n-butyl ether, and addition of butanol liberated the cycloalkane in easily isolable form.

Cyclobutane is considerably less reactive than cyclopropane. It is not only inert to permanganate and ozone, but stable to bromine and hydrogen iodide at ordinary

$$
\underset{\text{CH}_2\text{—CH}_2}{\overset{\text{CH}_2\text{—CH}_2}{|\quad\quad|}} \xrightarrow{\text{H}_2,\ \text{Ni (200°)}} \text{CH}_3\text{CH}_2\text{CH}_2\text{CH}_3
$$

temperature. The ring can be opened by hydrogenation, but at a higher temperature than suffices for hydrogenation of cyclopropane. Cyclopentane and

[1] Richard Willstätter, 1872–1942; Ph.D. Munich (Einhorn); Univ. Zurich, Berlin, Munich; Nobel Price 1930; *J. Chem. Soc.*, 999 (1953)

cyclohexane are fully resistant to hydrogenation and are as inert as the normal alkanes.

15.6   Demjanov Rearrangement. — In investigating the reaction of primary amines with nitrous acid (14.18), Demjanov noted that cyclopropanemethylamine and cyclobutylamine both react with nitrous acid to give a

$$\triangle\text{—CH}_2\text{NH}_2 \xrightarrow{\text{HNO}_2} \triangle\text{—CH}_2\text{OH} \quad + \quad \square\text{—OH} \xleftarrow{\text{HNO}_2} \square\text{—NH}_2$$

48%   47%

mixture of cyclopropylcarbinol and cyclobutanol. The reaction, now known to involve carbonium ion intermediates, was investigated with isotopic labels by Roberts (1959), who found that each amine gives essentially the same mixture. The interpretation is that the two systems give rise to the same carbonium ion, a bridged bicyclobutonium ion. This can exist in two isomeric forms of equal energy.

$$\begin{array}{c}\text{CH}_2\cdots\text{CH}_2 \\ \vdots\; + \vdots \\ \text{CH}\text{—CH}_2\end{array} \rightleftharpoons \begin{array}{c}\text{CH}_2\text{—CH}_2 \\ \vdots\; + \vdots \\ \text{CH}\cdots\text{CH}_2\end{array}$$

15.7   The C₂ + C₂ Route. — Dimerization of simple olefins is not feasible— for only the reverse reaction is known. Fluorinated olefins, however, undergo this reaction readily. For example, dimerization of 1,1-dichloro-2,2,

$$CF_2\!\!=\!\!CCl_2 \xrightarrow[80\text{-}85\%]{200°} \begin{array}{c}CF_2\text{—}CCl_2 \\ | \qquad | \\ CF_2\text{—}CCl_2\end{array}$$

difluoroethylene to 1,1,2,2-tetrachloro-3,3,4,4-tetrafluorocyclobutane is effected by heating the substance in a pressure bomb in the presence of hydroquinone or other polymerization inhibitor (D. D. Coffman, du Pont Co., 1949). Roberts (1953–) extended the reaction by cycloaddition of phenylacetylene with fluorinated olefins and devised means for subsequent removal of the halogen atoms. Thus reaction of phenylacetylene with 1,1-dichloro-2,2-difluoroethylene affords the cyclobutene (1). Treatment of (1) with sulfuric acid hydrolyzes the fluorine atoms and gives the 2,2-dichloroenone (2), and this in the presence of triethylamine undergoes an allylic type rearrangement to the isomeric 2,4-dichloroenone (3). The observation that this substance is incapable of enolization is an indica-

$$\begin{array}{c}CH \\ C_6H_5C\end{array} + \begin{array}{c}CF_2 \\ CCl_2\end{array} \xrightarrow[85\%]{100°} \underset{C_6H_5}{\square}\overset{F_2}{\underset{Cl_2}{}} \xrightarrow{H_2SO_4} \underset{C_6H_5}{\square}\overset{O}{\underset{Cl_2}{}} \xrightarrow{R_3N} \underset{C_6H_5}{\square}\overset{Cl}{\underset{Cl}{\overset{O}{}}}\text{—H}$$

(1)   (2)   (3)

tion of the instability of the cyclobutadiene system. The adduct of chlorotrifluoroethylene and phenylacetylene of structure (4) on hydrolysis with sulfuric acid yields phenylcyclobutenedione (5). This substance is yellow and has a formal resemblance to an *ortho*-quinone, but it does not behave like a quinone; it is not

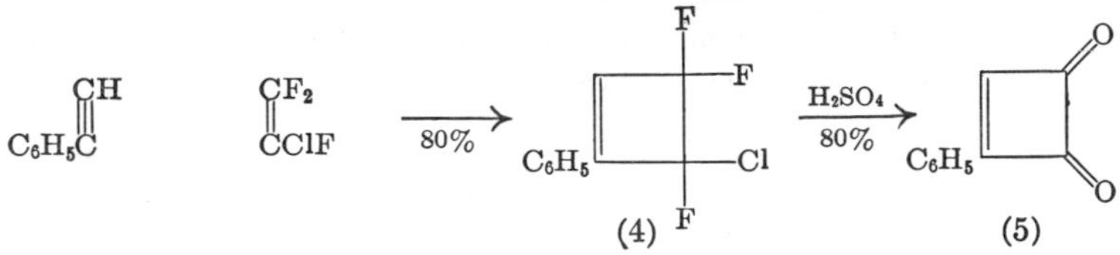

reduced to cyclobutadienediol and the product of condensation with *o*-phenylene-diamine no longer contains the cyclobutene ring. Blomquist (1961) prepared diphenylcyclobutenedione (8, yellow, m.p. 97°) via (6) and (7) and found that on standing in ethanol at room temperature the substance is transformed into diethyl α,α'-diphenylsuccinate (10, *dl*- and *meso*), probably through isomerization to

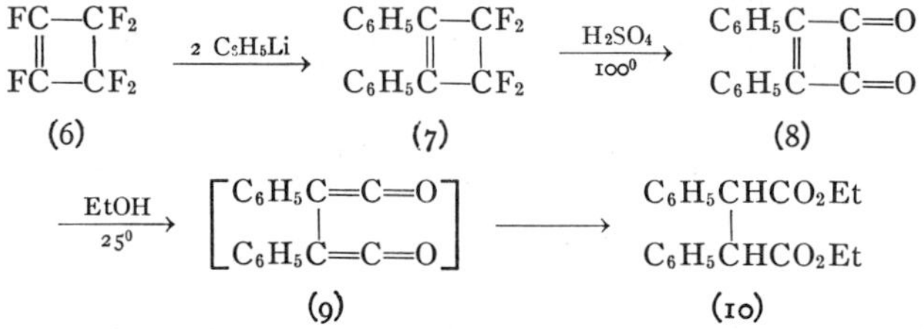

bis-phenylketene (9).

Dimerization of ketenes affords another route to 1,3-cyclobutanediones. Thus tetramethyl-1,3-cyclobutanedione (1) is obtained in modest yield on dehydrohalogenation of α-bromoisobutyryl bromide with triethylamine in benzene. The substance is cleaved by sodium ethoxide to ethyl 2,2,4-trimethyl-3-oxovalerate.

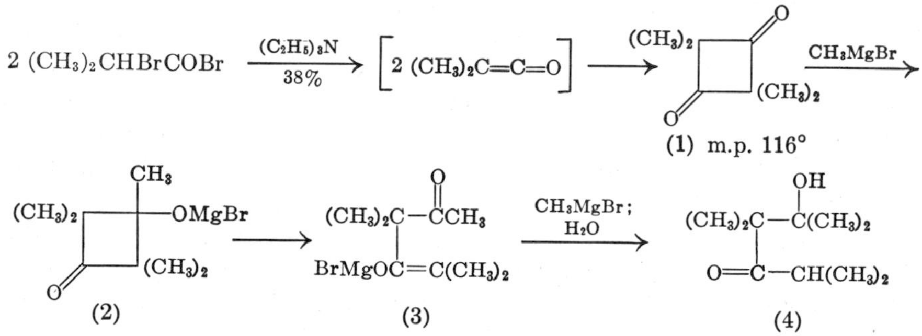

It is also cleaved by Grignard reagents (J. L. E. Erickson, 1946). The initial product of addition of methylmagnesium bromide, (2), undergoes reverse aldolization to the ketone (3), which reacts with further reagent with eventual formation of the keto alcohol (4). Tetramethyl-1,3-cyclobutanedione and the diol mixture derived from it are available in semicommercial quantities (Eastman Chemical Products). Hydrogenation of the dione with usual catalysts is unsatisfactory but

proceeds well in methanol in the presence of ruthenium on alumina powder and
gives, in 98% yield, a mixture of nearly equal parts of *cis*-2,2,4,4-tetramethyl-
cyclobutane-1,3-diol (m.p. 148°) and the
trans-diol (m.p. 163°). The diformate ester of the mixture is separable into solid
and liquid fractions which afford, respectively, the *trans*-diol (24%) and the
cis-diol (7%). The stereochemistry of
the *cis*-diol is shown in a photograph of a
model constructed from parts designed by
Petersen[1] and distributed by the Central
Scientific Co.; carbon atoms of neoprene
make possible the construction of highly
strained ring systems.

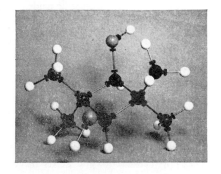

   2,3-Dimethyl-1,4-benzoquinone (I) on brief exposure to sunlight is converted
into a weakly yellow dimer shown to be the cyclobutane derivative II (W. Flaig,
1960). Further irradiation closes another four-membered ring by establishment
of 6,2'- and 5,3'-bridges to give the three-dimensional structure III. Pyrolysis
of this colorless dimer gives 2,5-dimethyl-1,4-benzoquinone (IV), evidently re-

sulting from cleavage along the horizontal axis, rather than the vertical axis of
formation.

15.8   Occurrence of Small-Ring Compounds in Nature. — A few natural
        products contain a small ring fused to or inserted into a six-membered
ring, but these played no part in the development of ideas about the stability and
reactivity associated with rings of three and four carbon atoms. Compounds with
isolated small rings are even rarer. The first ones known were a series of stereoisomeric truxillic and truxinic acids isolated by Liebermann (1889) from coca leaves
(coca from a place named Truxillo was found to be a particularly rich source).

[1] Quentin R. Petersen, b. 1924 Bridgeport, Conn.; Ph.D. Northwestern (R. H. Baker); Wes-
leyan Univ.; Wabash College

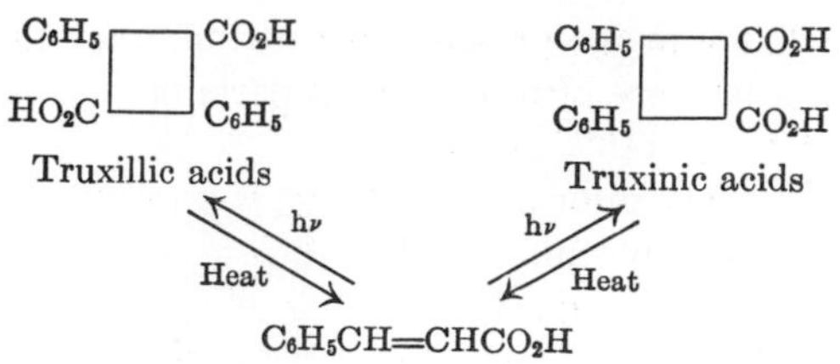

C_6H_5 ⎡‾‾‾⎤ CO_2H C_6H_5 ⎡‾‾‾⎤ CO_2H

HO_2C ⎣___⎦ C_6H_5 C_6H_5 ⎣___⎦ CO_2H

Truxillic acids   Truxinic acids

$h\nu$ / Heat $h\nu$ / Heat

$C_6H_5CH=CHCO_2H$

Liebermann determined the molecular weights of these diacids, found that on pyrolytic distillation they afford cinnamic acid, and inferred the structures. Subsequent work established that cinnamic acid can be converted by irradiation into mixtures of truxillic and truxinic acids. Five optically inactive truxillic acids are theoretically possible, and they are all known. The four possible cyclobutane-1,2,3,4-tetracarboxylic acids have been produced by synthesis (G. W. Griffin, 1960).

No further small ring compounds were reported until 1924, when Staudinger and Ruzicka[1] isolated from pyrethrum flower heads two highly insecticidal components, pyrethrin I and pyrethrin II. The substances were characterized as esters of the structures shown. Each on hydrolysis gives an acid derived from cyclopropane

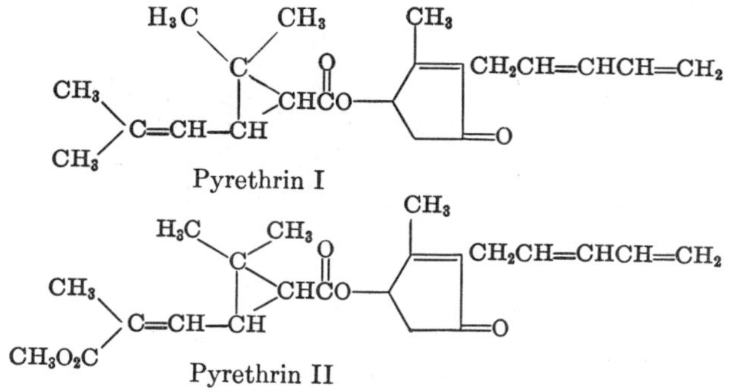

Pyrethrin I

Pyrethrin II

and a keto alcoholic derivative of cyclopentene.

Since the usual acids from fats contain an even number of carbon atoms, isolation of two C_{19}-acids was a surprise. Nunn[2] gave the name sterculic acid to the main constituent of the kernel oil (saponified) of *Sterculia foelida,* a tropical tree. Extraction of the kernels with 2-methylpentane gives the glyceride as a yellow oil; the free acid undergoes rapid thermal polymerization. Earlier workers had been unable to isolate pure material but had inferred from hydrogenation experiments that the crude product contains 72% of a conjugated diene. Nunn isolated the acid as the more stable urea inclusion complex; addition of controlled amounts of powdered urea to the methanolic filtrates from successive batches afforded an efficient means of fractionation. The acid was identified as having a cyclopropene

[1] Leopold Ruzicka, b. 1887 Vukova, Yugoslavia; Ph.D. Karlsruhe (Staudinger); Utrecht; Zurich ETH; Nobel Prize 1939

[2] John R. Nunn, b. 1919 Cape Town, South Africa; Ph.D. Cape Town; Council for Sci. and Ind. Research, Pretoria

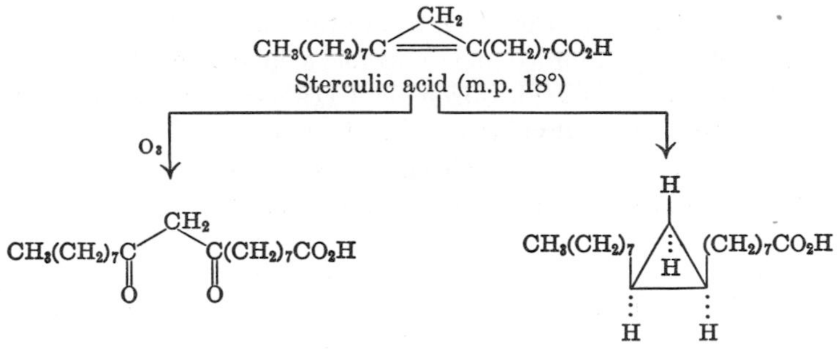

$$CH_3(CH_2)_7C \overset{CH_2}{=\!\!=\!\!=} C(CH_2)_7CO_2H$$

Sterculic acid (m.p. 18°)

O_3

$$CH_3(CH_2)_7\underset{O}{C} \overset{CH_2}{} \underset{O}{C}(CH_2)_7CO_2H$$

$$CH_3(CH_2)_7 \overset{H}{\underset{H}{\triangle}} (CH_2)_7CO_2H$$

9,11-Diketononadecanoic acid
M.p. 58°

Dihydrosterculic acid
M.p. 39°, λ 9.8 μ

group at the middle of the chain by ozonization to a product recognized as a 1,3-diketone (UV spectrum in ethanol and in ethanolic NaOH) and established to be 9,11-diketononadecanoic acid by oxidation to pelargonic and azelaic acids. Hydrogenation of sterculic acid in ethanol in the presence of palladium on calcium carbonate gave dihydrosterculic acid (stable to $KMnO_4$); in acetic acid in the presence of the Adams platinum catalyst, the dihydro acid absorbed one more mole of hydrogen. Hofmann[1] (1959) proved the *cis* configuration by an unequivocal synthesis from *cis*-cyclopropane-1,2-diacetic acid (15.4). Simmons and Smith (1959) obtained dihydrosterculic acid in 51% yield by synthesis from methyl oleate, methylene iodide, and zinc–copper couple. N. T. Castellucci and C. E. Griffin (1960) synthesized sterculic acid from stearolic acid by the Simmons-Smith method.

The second C_{19}-acid, lactobacillic acid, was isolated by Hofmann (1950) from *Lactobacillus arabinosus* and *L. casei*. The composition of the acid, its stability to oxidation but lability to hydrogenation, and the presence of a band at 9.8 μ in the infrared absorption spectrum pointed to the presence of a cyclopropane ring somewhere in the chain. In a later investigation (1954) the methylene bridge was shown to be between C_{11} and C_{12} by the following micromethod. Reaction with hydrogen bromide in acetic acid at 100° opened the cyclopropane ring in the Markownikoff sense to give the two bromo acids (a) and (b). Boiling collidine

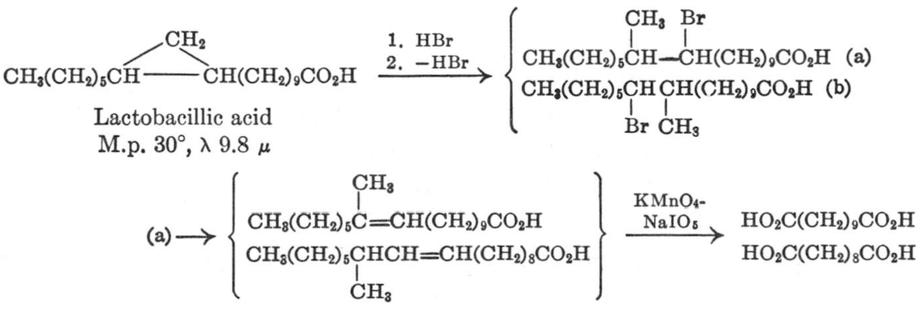

$$CH_3(CH_2)_5CH \overset{CH_2}{-\!\!\!-\!\!\!-} CH(CH_2)_9CO_2H$$

Lactobacillic acid
M.p. 30°, λ 9.8 μ

1. HBr
2. −HBr

$$CH_3(CH_2)_5\overset{CH_3}{\underset{}{C}}H\!-\!\overset{Br}{\underset{}{C}}H(CH_2)_9CO_2H \quad (a)$$
$$CH_3(CH_2)_5\overset{}{\underset{Br}{C}}H\overset{}{\underset{CH_3}{C}}H(CH_2)_9CO_2H \quad (b)$$

(a) →

$$CH_3(CH_2)_5\overset{CH_3}{\underset{}{C}}\!=\!CH(CH_2)_9CO_2H$$
$$CH_3(CH_2)_5CHCH\!=\!CH(CH_2)_8CO_2H$$
$$\underset{CH_3}{|}$$

KMnO₄-
NaIO₅

$HO_2C(CH_2)_9CO_2H$
$HO_2C(CH_2)_8CO_2H$

---

[1] Klaus H. Hofmann, b. 1911 Karlsruhe, Germany; Ph.D. ETH Zurich (Ruzicka); Univ. Pittsburgh School of Medicine

evidently eliminated hydrogen bromide from bromide (a) in both directions, for Lémieux oxidation (5.30) afforded undecanedioic acid and sebacic acid, separated by chromatography on silicic acid. Bromide (b) cannot give rise to either of these diacids but can yield the methyl keto acid $CH_3CO(CH_2)_9CO_2H$; bromide (a) can yield the methyl ketone $CH_3(CH_2)_5COCH_3$. Indeed both the acidic and neutral fractions on reaction with hypoiodite yielded iodoform, derived from the methylene bridge.

At a time when the position of the methylene bridge in the C_{18}-chain was not known, E. M. Kosower[1] (1951) suggested what proved to be the correct structure on biogenetic grounds. Ricinoleic acid, the suggested precursor, is a homoallylic alcohol and a phosphate ester might undergo the i-cholesterol rearrangement (9.9) with closure of a three-membered ring. Addition of another carbon at the car-

$$CH_3(CH_2)_5\overset{|}{\underset{OH}{C}}H \quad \overset{CH_2}{\diagup} \quad CH=CH(CH_2)_7CO_2H \quad \xrightarrow[(+C_1)]{?} \quad CH_3(CH_2)_5\overset{CH_2}{\overset{\diagup}{C}}H\text{——}CH(CH_2)_9CO_2H$$

Ricinoleic acid   Lactobacillic acid

boxyl end of the chain might occur through phosphorylation, reaction with acetate to form the 2-keto acid, and decarbonylation. Kosower noted that a C_{19}-acid with a cyclopropane ring is really analogous to a C_{18}-acid with a double bond.

15.9 **Baeyer Strain Theory.** — In his Pedler lecture of 1929, Perkin, Jr.[2] looked back to the time when organic compounds were regarded as of just two classes, open chain and aromatic. "It was thought to be so out of the question that intermediate carbon rings containing 3, 4, or 5 atoms could be capable of existence that no one seems to have given them serious attention or to have attempted to construct them. Thus we find Victor Meyer in 1876 writing an interesting *Annalen* paper . . . from which it is clear . . . that he was firmly per-suaded that there is no evidence to warrant the supposition that other rings smaller than six are ever likely to be obtained." Shortly after going to Germany in 1880, Perkin translated this paper for practice in German and was "much impressed with the interesting way the subject was presented." After studying for two years under Wislicenus, he went to Munich to continue research under Baeyer. On one of Meyer's visits to the Munich laboratory, Perkin ventured to ask him if he was still of the same opinion and was invited to spend the evening at the Hofbräuhaus. When Perkin expressed his intention of trying to prepare rings of 3, 4, or 5 carbon atoms, Meyer was impressed with Perkin's enthusiasm but ad-vised him to work on something more promising. Meyer's main arguments were that synthetic experiments had frequently yielded derivatives of benzene, but not rings smaller than six, and that no small-ring compounds had been isolated from natural sources. Consulted the next day, Baeyer said that all experience was

[1] Edward M. Kosower, b. 1929 Brooklyn, N. Y.; Ph.D. Univ. Calif., Los Angeles (Winstein); Univ. Wisconsin; State Univ. of New York College on Long Island

[2] William Henry Perkin, Jr., 1860–1929; b. Sudbury/London; Ph.D. Würzburg (Wislicenus); Univ. Munich, Edinburgh, Manchester, Oxford; *Nature*, **124**, 263 (1929); Pedler Lecture: "Early History of the Synthesis of Closed Carbon Rings," *J. Chem. Soc.*, 1347 (1929)

against the assumption that small rings could exist. Later, however, he made encouraging remarks when Perkin said that he was about to start work on the problem. Emil Fischer, on a visit to Munich, expressed the view that even if small-ring compounds could be produced they probably would exhibit so little stability that it would be very difficult to demonstrate their existence sufficiently to convince the chemical world.

The problem assigned to Perkin by Baeyer, investigation of ethyl benzoylacetate, proved tedious and disappointing, mainly because the method of fractional distillation under low pressure had not then been developed (the Claisen flask was described in 1893). In possession of a batch of trimethylene dibromide prepared for another purpose, Perkin tried condensation of this substance with sodio acetoacetic ester and obtained an ester of the composition required for the cyclobutane derivative (1), and this on hydrolysis gave a beautifully crystalline acid (which,

$$
\begin{array}{ccc}
CH_2\!\!<\!\!\begin{array}{l}CH_2Br\\CH_2Br\end{array} \;+\; \begin{array}{l}CO_2C_2H_5\\CH_2\\COCH_3\end{array} & \xrightarrow{\;\;\not{\;\;}\;\;} & CH_2\!\!<\!\!\begin{array}{l}CH_2\\CH_2\end{array}\!\!>\!\!C\!\!<\!\!\begin{array}{l}CO_2C_2H_5\\COCH_3\end{array}\\
 & & (1)
\end{array}
$$

$$
\begin{array}{ccc}
\begin{array}{l}CH_2\!-\!CCO_2C_2H_5\\CH_2\quad CCH_3\\CH_2Br\;\;OH\end{array} & \longrightarrow & \begin{array}{l}CH_2\!-\!CCO_2C_2H_5\\CH_2\quad CCH_3\\CH_2\!-\!O\end{array}\\
(2) & & (3)
\end{array}
$$

however, did not lose carbon dioxide readily). Baeyer thought the observation so important that he decided to communicate the result to the Bavarian Academy the same day and not wait for the next number of the *Berichte*. "Victor Meyer not only wrote me a charming letter but when he visited Baeyer shortly afterwards he told him how greatly interested he was in the results." Three years later, Perkin found, quite accidentally, that his interpretation had been incorrect and that the reaction product is not the cyclobutane derivative (1) but the cyclic enol ether (3). However, he had launched a program in which a few failures were more than offset by successes. In 1883 he synthesized diethyl cyclobutane-1,1-dicarboxylate from trimethylene dibromide and malonic ester (15.5) and from it obtained cyclobutanecarboxylic acid. In the same year Perkin synthesized diethyl cyclopropane-1,1-dicarboxylate from ethylene dibromide and malonic ester (15.2). Fittig in an extensive investigation of lactones prepared the same compound independently and thought it should be formulated differently, but Perkin's interpretation proved to be correct. The next obvious goal was to produce a 5-ring ester by condensation of tetramethylene dibromide with malonic ester. But the required dibromide was unknown; the experiment was performed, but only after a lapse of ten years, when tetramethylene dibromide became available through a fortuitous circumstance. With the collaboration of E. Haworth at Owens College, Manchester, Perkin (1894) had prepared pentamethylene dibromide by the sequence (1) for use in the synthesis of hexamethylenedicarboxylic acid. The product proved to be a mixture and on fractionation afforded, along with pentamethylene

1. $Br(CH_2)_3Br \rightarrow NC(CH_2)_3CN \rightarrow H_2N(CH_2)_5NH_2 \rightarrow HO(CH_2)_5OH \rightarrow Br(CH_2)_5Br$
         $\downarrow$ KCN

2. $HO(CH_2)_3Br \rightarrow HO(CH_2)_3CN \rightarrow HO(CH_2)_4NH_2 \rightarrow HO(CH_2)_4Br \rightarrow Br(CH_3)_4Br$

dibromide, the long sought tetramethylene dibromide. The strongly alkaline potassium cyanide in common use in those days had effected partial hydrolysis, leading to sequence (2). Digestion of the new dibromide with sodiomalonic ester gave diethyl cyclopentane-1,1-dicarboxylate in nearly quantitative yield, and this on hydrolysis and decarboxylation gave cyclopentanecarboxylic acid, a substance characterized by great stability.

However, shortly after becoming Privatdozent at Munich (1889), Perkin sought another route to five-carbon rings. He had noticed that in the condensation of ethylene dibromide with sodiomalonic ester the cyclopropanedicarboxylic ester produced is accompanied by a small amount of the higher boiling tetraester formed by condensation of the dibromide with two equivalents of malonic ester. By adjusting the proportions of trimethylene dibromide and sodium salt and conducting the reaction at room temperature, Perkin obtained the tetraester in good

yield and found that treatment of the disodio derivative with bromine affords the cyclopentane tetraester in almost quantitative yield. This was the first synthesis of the carbon five-ring. That the cyclopentane-1,2-dicarboxylic acid derived from the easily formed tetraester "should prove to be a substance of such marked, it might even be said unusual, stability excited a great deal of interest at the time."

This work was published in 1885, four months after appearance of the classical paper describing the Baeyer strain theory. The information available to Baeyer was extremely limited. Perkin had shown that three- and four-membered rings are easily formed, and he had observed that the three-ring compounds are less reactive than olefinic derivatives but more reactive than four-ring compounds. Thus cyclopropane-1,2-dicarboxylic acid does not add bromine but is cleaved easily by hydrogen bromide to γ-bromoethylmalonic acid, $BrCH_2CH_2CH(CO_2H)_2$. Cyclobutanecarboxylic acid is inert to both bromine and hydrogen bromide. Cyclopentane and cyclohexane derivatives were not known, and Baeyer's ideas about the character of six-membered rings were based on the properties of benzene. His theory was thus largely a prediction, and indeed Baeyer expressly stated that his views were presented in order that they could receive the widest possible evaluation.

Baeyer postulated that any deviation from the normal tetrahedral angle of 109°28' would result in internal strain. The linking together of two carbon atoms by a double bond must then be attended with distortion of the normal valence

TABLE 15.2. HEATS OF COMBUSTION AND VALENCE ANGLES

HYDROCARBON	ETHYLENE	CYCLO-PROPANE	CYCLO-BUTANE	CYCLO-PENTANE	CYCLO-HEXANE	CYCLO-HEPTANE
Molecular heat of combustion (kg.-cal.)	340	505.5	662.5	797	939	1103
kcal. per >CH$_2$	170	168.5	165.5	158.7	157.5	158.3
Deviation from normal angle	$+54°$ 44'	$+24°$ 44'	$+9°$ 44'	$+0°$ 44'	$(-5°$ 16')	$(-9°$ 33')

angle for each carbon atom of ½ (109°28') or $+54°44'$. In cyclopropane the deviation is ½ (109°28'–60°) = $+24°44'$; other calculations are: C$_4$, ½ (109°28'–90°) = $+9°44'$; C$_5$, ½ (109°28'–108°) = $+0.44'$. In the case of cyclohexane, Baeyer assumed a planar structure with expansion of the normal angle amounting to a deviation of $-5°16'$ per carbon atom. The assumption of a planar ring of course was not justified and this part of the theory is now meaningless. Inclusion of the calculation for an as yet unknown hydrocarbon was unfortunate, for it probably discouraged Perkin and others from seeking routes to rings larger than six. As applied to the smaller rings, the strain theory accounted well for the few facts known at the time and promptly received added support from Perkin's synthesis of the di- and tetraacids of the cyclopentane series. It accounts also for the relative reactivities evident from later work (15.2, 15.5) and with the energy relationships evident from heats of combustion (Table 15.2). The energy content per methylene group falls off in the order of decreasing angle strain.

15.10   **Strain-Free Rings.** — In 1890 H. Sachse suggested that the carbon atoms of cyclohexane do not lie in a plane but rather form a puckered, strain-free ring which can assume either of two forms, now identified as the boat and chair forms. Perhaps because the paper was poorly written and the postu-

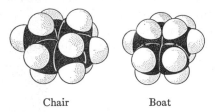

Chair   Boat

lated forms illustrated with obscure diagrams, the suggestion received no attention until 1918, when E. Mohr[1] in a scholarly paper illustrated with well-executed drawings of models presented a strong case for nonplanar strain-free rings in both simple compounds and in complex polycyclic systems. Although Mohr had no new experimental evidence of his own, he could point to existing evidence not previously recognized. Baeyer had concluded his paper with the comment that

[1] Ernst Mohr, 1873–1926; b. Dresden; Ph.D. Kiel (Curtius); Univ. Heidelberg; *Ber.*, **59A.** 39 (1926)

probably the most stable arrangement of carbon atoms is that in black coal. Mohr observed that the statement needed correction only in replacing "black coal" by "diamond," for, from analysis of the X-ray data of W. H. and W. L. Bragg, he was able to show that the crystal lattice of the diamond is made up of rings of carbon atoms in the chair conformation, as shown in the model.   Mohr

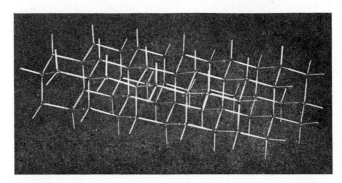

thought that the two forms of cyclohexane should be too easily interconvertible for isolation, but predicted the existence of two forms of decalin, *cis* and *trans*.

The first supporting evidence was adduced by Böeseken[1] (1921–23), who differentiated between *cis*- and *trans*-cyclohexane-1,2-diol by two methods.   One was by noting the effect on the electrical conductivity of a solution of boric acid.   The *cis*-diol increases the conductivity because it forms an ionic complex with the

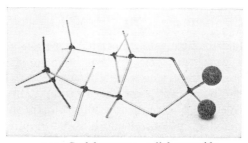

inorganic acid; the *trans*-diol has little effect.   The second method was acetonide formation: the *cis*-C_6-diol forms an acetonide and the *trans*-isomer does not.   However, *trans*-cycloheptane-1,2-diol (m.p. 63°), as well as the *cis*-isomer (m.p. 46°), forms an acetonide and a boric acid complex.   That these cyclic structures can be accommodated in a puckered ring without strain is evident from the photograph of the *trans*-diol acetonide.

trans-Cycloheptane-1,2-diol acetonide

[1] Jacob Böeseken, 1868–1948; b. Rotterdam; Ph.D. Basel; Techn. Univ. Delft, Netherlands

The next piece of evidence was isolation by W. Hückel[1] (1925) of *cis*- and *trans*-decalin (Mohr's only error had been in representing *cis*-decalin in a boat-boat conformation).   Hydrogenation of naphthalene with platinum catalyst in acetic acid gives mainly *cis*-decalin, and hydrogenation in the gas phase by the Sabatier-

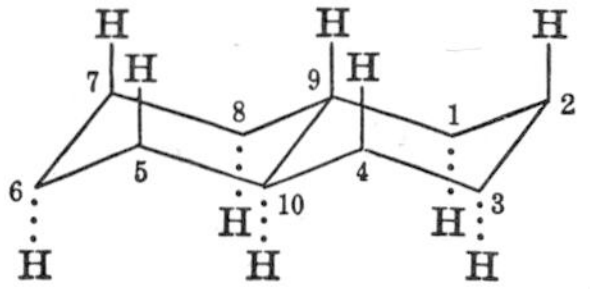

trans-Decalin 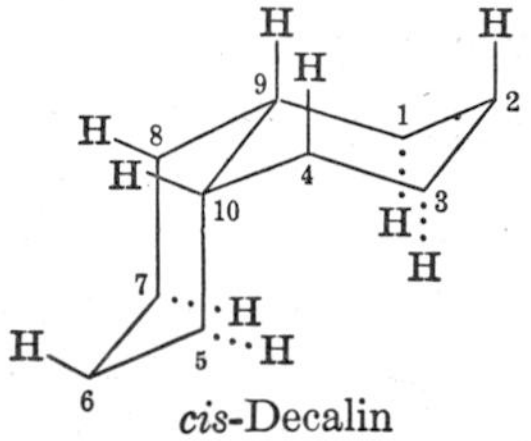   *cis*-Decalin

Senderens method gives chiefly *trans*-decalin. The isomers are separable by fractional distillation and can be identified from the values for the density and refractive index.   Zelinsky (Moscow, 1932) found that *cis*-decalin can be isomerized to the *trans* hydrocarbon by stirring it with aluminum chloride at room temperature for 22 hrs.   The same order of relative thermodynamic stability is indicated

TABLE 15.3.   DECALINS

	trans	*cis*
Melting point	$-31.3°$	$-43.3°$
Boiling point	$185.4°$	$194.6°$
Density, d_4^{20}	0.871	0.898
Refractive index, n_D^{20}	1.4713	1.482
Heat of combustion, kcal./mole	1500.3	1502.4

TABLE 15.4.   DECALONES

	M.P., °C.	n_D^{20}
cis-α-Decalone	2°	1.4963
trans α Decalone	33°	1.4837
cis-β-Decalone	$-14°$	1.4918
trans-β-Decalone	6°	1.4809

by the higher heat of combustion of the *cis*-isomer (Table 15.3).   *trans*-Decalin is mildly destabilized by 1,2- and 1,3-H:H interactions; *cis*-decalin is destabilized also by three transannular interactions (1α,5α at 2.0 Å; 1α,7α at 2.0 Å; 3α,5α at 2.0 Å).

Hückel characterized all eight optically active decalols (α- and β-, *cis* and *trans*) and all of the eight amines.   The decalones are of particular interest (Table 15.4). *cis*-α-Decalone is less stable than the *trans* isomer but is easily obtained by convert-

[1] Walter Hückel, b. 1895 Charlottenburg; Ph.D. Göttingen (Windaus); Univ. Freiburg, Greifswald, Breslau, Tübingen

ing the equilibrium mixture into the bisulfite addition compound and decomposing this with sodium carbonate. The *cis* isomer can be distilled at reduced pressure, but it is isomerized to *trans-α*-decalone by the action of alcoholic potassium hydroxide or by distillation at 760 mm.; the equilibrium mixture obtained on distillation is estimated to contain about 95% of the *trans* isomer. That isomerization proceeds through the enol is evident from the fact that *cis*- and *trans-β*-decalone are both stable to alkali and to heat.

15.11   **Muscone and Civetone.** — Baeyer's inference that multimembered ring compounds would be too unstable to exist was disproved finally in work of Ruzicka at Zurich (1926) on the active principles of the rare perfume bases musk and civet. Dried musk is a dark-colored powdery substance of powerful odor obtained from an egg-sized gland situated near the abdomen of the male musk deer, a small wild animal found in mountainous regions of central Asia, particularly the Himalayas; the apparent function of musk is to attract the female animal. From about 60,000 deer killed per year, there results an average of 2000 kg. of the valuable musk, the active principle of which, muscone (H. Wahlbaum, 1906), is present to the extent of about 1%. Civet, valued at about one third the price of musk, occurs similarly in the African civet cat (male and female), and the active fragrant principle, which occurs along with the evil-smelling skatole, is civetone. Muscone (liq.), the principle of musk, is an optically active saturated ketone and civetone (m.p. 31°) is an inactive, unsaturated ketone. Civetone on hydrogenation absorbed an amount of gas indicative of the presence of one double bond and gave a saturated ketone (2) which on oxidation yielded a dibasic acid (3) of the same carbon content, which shows that the carbonyl group is present in a ring. Reduction of the carbonyl group of civetone to a methylene group

$$C_{17}H_{30}O \xrightarrow{2H} C_{17}H_{32}O \xrightarrow{CrO_3} C_{15}H_{30}\begin{array}{l} CO_2H \\ \\ CO_2H \end{array}$$

$$\text{Civetone (1)} \qquad\qquad (2) \qquad\qquad\qquad (3)$$

$$\Big\downarrow \text{Reduction} \qquad C_{17}H_{32} \xrightarrow{\hspace{3cm}} \uparrow$$

$$(4)$$

(4) and oxidation gave an identical acid (3), and hence the carbonyl group and the double bond of the natural product must be in the same ring. Oxidation of civetone itself gave the acids $HO_2C(CH_2)_3CO_2H$, $HO_2C(CH_2)_6CO_2H$, and $HO_2C(CH_2)_7CO_2H$, the last of which shows that the ring must include at least

$$\begin{array}{ccccc}
 & & CH_2(CH_2)_7 & & \\
 & & | \qquad\qquad C=O & & \\
 & \nearrow & CH_2(CH_2)_7 & \searrow & \\
CH(CH_2)_7 & & (2) & & (CH_2)_{15}\begin{array}{l}CO_2H \\ CO_2H\end{array} \\
\| \qquad\qquad C=O & & & \nearrow & \\
CH(CH_2)_7 & \searrow & CH(CH_2)_7 & & II \\
\text{I} & & \| \qquad\qquad CH_2 & & \\
 & & CH(CH_2)_7 & & \\
 & & (4) & &
\end{array}$$

seven methylene groups.   Formula I meets this requirement and also accounts for the production from (2) and (4) of a common oxidation product, shown by synthesis to have the structure II.   Structure I for civetone was finally proved by controlled permanganate oxidation to a keto dibasic acid, the structure of which was established by synthesis:

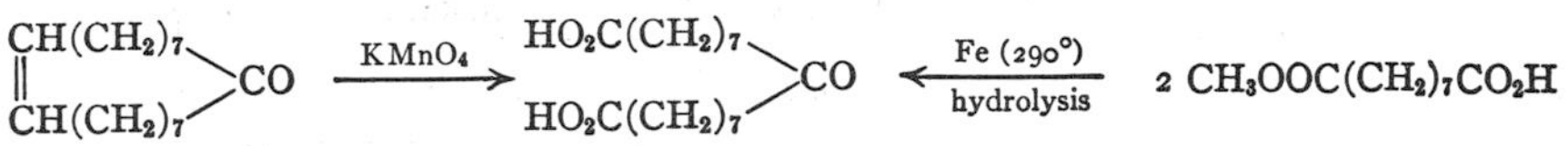

$$
\begin{array}{c} CH(CH_2)_7 \\ \| \\ CH(CH_2)_7 \end{array}\!\!\!\!>CO \quad \xrightarrow{KMnO_4} \quad \begin{array}{c} HO_2C(CH_2)_7 \\ \\ HO_2C(CH_2)_7 \end{array}\!\!\!\!>CO \quad \xleftarrow[hydrolysis]{Fe\ (290°)} \quad 2\ CH_3OOC(CH_2)_7CO_2H
$$

Civetone and muscone occur in secretions rich in fat, and it may be significant that civetone is structurally related to one common fat component, oleic acid, and that muscone has at least the carbon skeleton of another, palmitic acid.

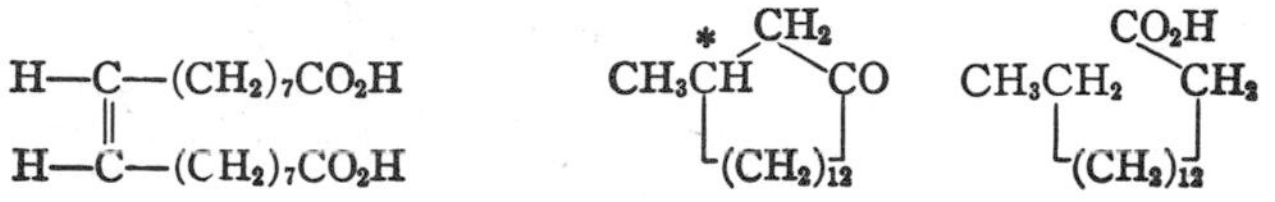

$$
\begin{array}{c} H\!-\!C\!-\!(CH_2)_7CO_2H \\ \| \\ H\!-\!C\!-\!(CH_2)_7CO_2H \end{array} \qquad\qquad \begin{array}{c} ^*CH_2 \\ CH_3CH \quad CO \\ \lfloor(CH_2)_{12}\rfloor \end{array} \qquad \begin{array}{c} CO_2H \\ CH_3CH_2 \quad CH_2 \\ \lfloor(CH_2)_{12}\rfloor \end{array}
$$

Oleic acid   Muscone   Palmitic acid

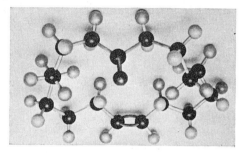

Civetone

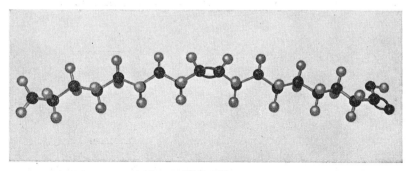

Oleic acid

M. Stoll[1] (1948) found that the relationship of civetone to oleic acid extends to the stereochemistry.   The carbonyl group of civetone was protected by ketal

[1] Max Stoll, b. 1899 Zurich; Ph.D. and D.Sc. Zurich ETH (Ruzicka); Firmenich and Co., Geneva

formation, bromine was added to the double bond, and the dibromide was dehydrohalogenated (KOH, amyl alcohol) to the acetylene. Selective hydrogenation under conditions suitable for production of a *cis*-ethylene and hydrolytic elimination of the ketal group gave material identical with natural civetone.

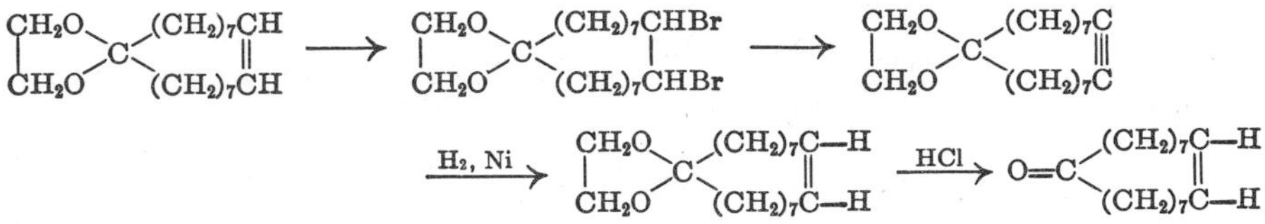

$$\begin{array}{c}CH_2O\\ \\ CH_2O\end{array}\hspace{-0.3em}\Big\rangle C\hspace{-0.3em}\Big\langle\hspace{-0.3em}\begin{array}{c}(CH_2)_7CH\\ \parallel\\ (CH_2)_7CH\end{array} \longrightarrow \begin{array}{c}CH_2O\\ \\ CH_2O\end{array}\hspace{-0.3em}\Big\rangle C\hspace{-0.3em}\Big\langle\hspace{-0.3em}\begin{array}{c}(CH_2)_7CHBr\\ \mid\\ (CH_2)_7CHBr\end{array} \longrightarrow \begin{array}{c}CH_2O\\ \\ CH_2O\end{array}\hspace{-0.3em}\Big\rangle C\hspace{-0.3em}\Big\langle\hspace{-0.3em}\begin{array}{c}(CH_2)_7C\\ \parallel\\ (CH_2)_7C\end{array}$$

$$\xrightarrow{H_2,\ Ni} \begin{array}{c}CH_2O\\ \\ CH_2O\end{array}\hspace{-0.3em}\Big\rangle C\hspace{-0.3em}\Big\langle\hspace{-0.3em}\begin{array}{c}(CH_2)_7C\!-\!H\\ \parallel\\ (CH_2)_7C\!-\!H\end{array} \xrightarrow{HCl} O\!=\!C\hspace{-0.3em}\Big\langle\hspace{-0.3em}\begin{array}{c}(CH_2)_7C\!-\!H\\ \parallel\\ (CH_2)_7C\!-\!H\end{array}$$

Stoll synthesized the *trans* isomer as well. The large-ring compounds have no unusual chemical properties and are evidently free from strain.

Investigations of large-ring natural compounds not only enriched the science but also pointed the way to synthetic substances of a new type of value to the perfume industry. Synthetic cyclopentadecanone (Exaltone) not only matches closely the fragrance of muscone but enhances the harmony of odors of a mixture of ingredients. Two natural substances of plant origin employed in perfumes and having musklike odors have been characterized as large-ring lactones of the following structures (M. Kerschbaum, 1927):

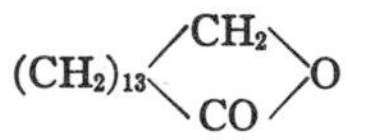

$$(CH_2)_{13}\hspace{-0.3em}\Big\langle\hspace{-0.3em}\begin{array}{c}CH_2\\ \\ CO\end{array}\hspace{-0.3em}\Big\rangle O \hspace{3em} \begin{array}{c}CH(CH_2)_7CH_2\\ \parallel\\ CH(CH_2)_5\cdot CO\end{array}\hspace{-0.3em}\Big\rangle O$$

Lactone of 15-hydroxypentadecylic acid,   Ambrettolide
m.p. 31° (principle of angelica oil)   (musk ambrette)

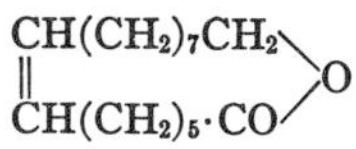

15.12   Conformation of Cyclohexane. — One method of estimating the relative stability of alternative conformations of a given compound is with reference to interactions of the three types, staggered, skew, and eclipsed,

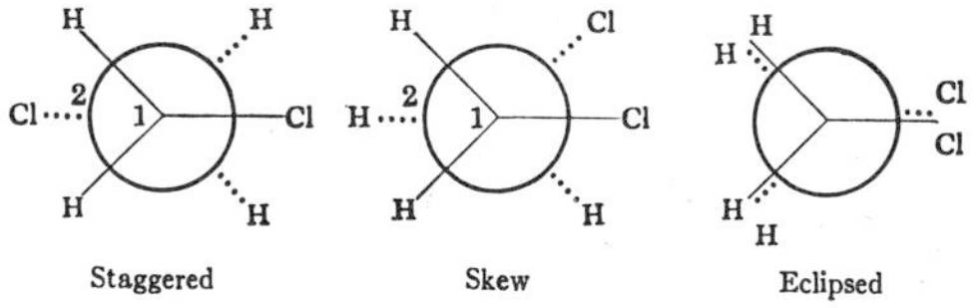

Staggered   Skew   Eclipsed

as illustrated for 1,2-dichloroethane; the interactions are listed in order of increasing strain energy. The models below show that in the chair form of cyclohexane all the H:H repulsions are skew, whereas in the boat form the hydrogens along the sides of the boat are eclipsed; therefore the boat form must be less stable than the chair form. This method of estimation is purely qualitative and it is not well adapted to consideration of the higher cycloalkanes or to a modified boat-cyclohexane discussed below.

We prefer analysis based upon separation distances. With the conventional chair and boat forms, these distances can be calculated by vector analysis; in other cases they can be measured on a model with a ruler (SASM models are particularly convenient for the purpose). The diagram gives calculated inter-nuclear distances for the chair form of cyclohexane and for methylcyclohexane, oriented as in a steroid. Severity of repulsion increases exponentially with decreasing separation distances, and E. A. Mason and M. M. Kreevoy (1955) developed an equation defining the relationship between internuclear distance and potential energy. This equation includes a constant (K) of uncertain magnitude; since the upper and lower limits appear to be 1.0 and 0.5, we used the value K = 0.75 for calculations reported in *Steroids* (1959) and reproduced with some refinements, in Table 15.5.

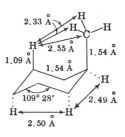

TABLE 15.5. ENERGY OF H:H INTERACTIONS

DISTANCE, Å	KCAL./MOLE	DISTANCE, Å	KCAL./MOLE
1.80	9.10	2.40	1.43
1.84 (bow-stern)	8.25	2.49 (skew)	1.07
1.90	6.80	2.50 (1:3)	1.04
2.00	5.00	2.60	0.89
2.10	3.60	2.70	0.57
2.20	2.70	2.80	0.32
2.27 (eclipsed)	2.14	2.90	0.13
2.30	1.90	3.00	0.0

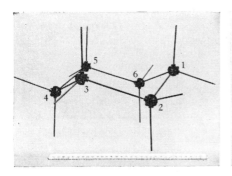
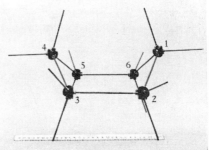

In chair-cyclohexane the 1β-H is 2.49 Å distant from the 2β-H, the 1α-H is 2.49 Å distant from both the 2α-H and the 2β-H, and the diaxial 1β,2α-pair are too distant (3.0 Å) for interaction. There are in all twelve skew interactions at a distance of 2.49 Å, equivalent to 1.07 kcal., and six 1:3 interactions at 2.50 Å (1.04 kcal.). Hence the strain energy is (12 × 1.07) + (6 × 1.04) = 19.1 kcal. The regular boat form of cyclohexane includes five types of hydrogen pairs. One is a 1β,4β bow-stern interaction at close distance (1.84 Å) and consequent high strain energy (8.25 kcal.). As summarized in Table 15.6, there are four eclipsed hydrogen pairs and twelve skew interactions which contribute to in-

TABLE 15.6. BOAT-CYCLOHEXANE

H:H INTERACTION		REGULAR		HALF-BOAT	
Type[a]	Positions	Å	Kcal.	Å	Kcal.
Bow-stern	$1\beta,4\beta$ $1\beta,4\beta; 2\alpha,5\alpha$	1.84	8.25	2.45	2 × 1.22
Eclipsed	$2\alpha,3\alpha; 2\beta,3\beta; 5\alpha,6\alpha; 5\beta,6\beta$	2.27	4 × 2.14	2.33	4 × 1.74
Skew	$1\alpha,2\beta; 1\alpha,2\alpha; 1\beta,2\beta; 3\alpha,4\alpha;$ $3\beta,4\alpha; 3\beta,4\beta; 4\alpha,5\alpha; 4\alpha,5\beta;$ $4\beta,5\beta; 6\beta,1\alpha; 6\beta,1\alpha; 6\beta,1\beta$	2.49	12 × 1.07	2.44	12 × 1.26
Diaxial	$1\beta,2\alpha; 3\alpha,4\beta; 4\beta,5\alpha; 6\alpha,1\beta$	3.0	0	3.0	0
Trans	$2\alpha,3\beta; 2\beta,3\alpha; 5\alpha,6\beta; 5\beta,6\alpha$	3.0	0	2.80	4 × 0.32
Total			29.6		25.8

[a] In the half-boat form: quasi-

stability. The total strain energy of this regular boat form is thus 29.6 kcal. If a model of the boat form is grasped at C_1 and C_4 and these carbon atoms are moved apart, as for relief of the bow-stern interaction, a new boat is formed with a bow-stern interaction between the $2\alpha,5\alpha$ pair. An intermediate form, the half-boat conformation, can be constructed by making the potential $1\beta,4\beta$ and $2\alpha,5\alpha$ bow-stern equidistant, whereby a single interaction contributing 8.25 kcal. is replaced by two totalling 2.44 kcal. The figures given in Table 15.6 show that the now quasi-eclipsed interactions are also less severe. The quasi-skew interactions lose their original identity and individual interactions vary in distance

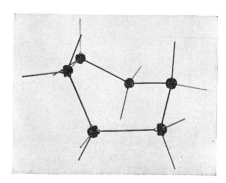

Half-boat Form

from 2.2 to 2.6 Å (the values tabulated are all averages; the energy values were read from a graph of the data of Table 15.5). The net effect of the change to quasi-skew interactions is a stabilization. Two of the *trans* interactions also become appreciable (2.6 Å) and the others remain negligible (3.0 Å). The totals show that the half-boat form is more stable than the regular form by 3.8 kcal.; hence the energy difference between the boat and chair forms is taken to be $(25.8 - 19.1) = 6.7$ kcal.

Other theoretical estimates of the energy difference between the chair and boat forms vary from 1.3 kcal. (Barton, 1948) to 10.6 kcal. (Turner, 1956). Experimental evidence presented by W. S. Johnson (1961) involved synthesis of the isomeric lactones (3) and (6) starting with condensation of *trans*-2-octalin oxide

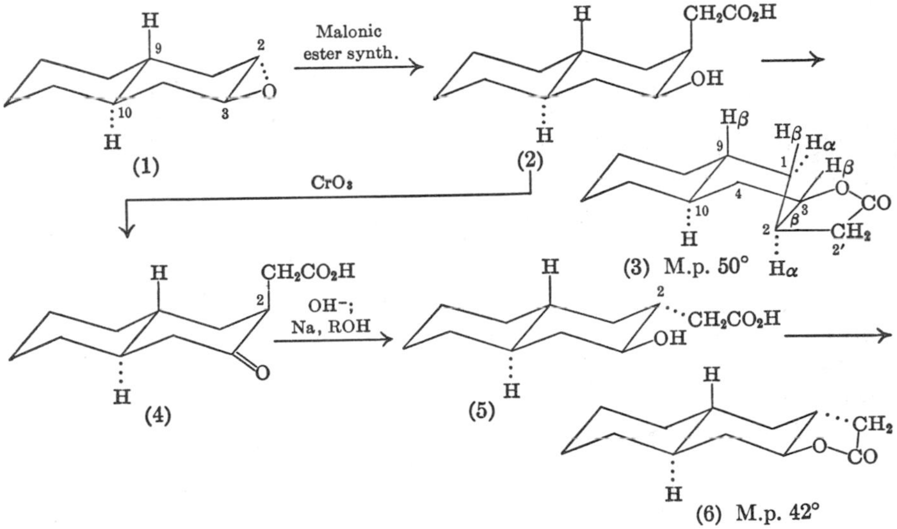

(1) with sodiomalonic ester, saponification, and decarboxylation. Lactonization of (2), which forces ring B into a boat conformation (3), required drastic conditions, *i.e.* treatment with dicyclohexylcarbodiimide ($C_6H_{11}N{=}C{=}NC_6H_{11}$) or prolonged refluxing with *p*-toluenesulfonic acid in xylene. Oxidation of (2) gave the keto acid (4) which was epimerized by base at C_2; reduction with sodium and isopropyl alcohol then gave the diequatorial hydroxy acid (5), which readily afforded the lactone (6). Thermochemical determinations on carefully purified samples of the lactones indicated that ΔS for the chair-boat form (3) is higher by 5.3 kcal./mole than that for the chair form (6). A model of the chair-boat lactone shows that ring B is a somewhat distorted regular boat. Measurement of the non-cancelling interactions in the two lactones (Table 15.7) indicates an energy difference of 4.7 kcal., not far from the experimental value of 5.3 kcal.

15.13   Auwers-Skita Rule. — K. von Auwers (Marburg, 1925) and A. Skita (Freiburg, 1925) noted a relationship between physical properties which they expressed as a rule for predicting the direction of hydrogenation in acidic and basic media. Rephrased in terms of conformational stability (rather than *cis-trans* relationship) and without reference to mode of formation, the Auwers-Skita rule states that with a pair of cyclic *cis-trans* isomers the one of lower

TABLE 15.7. ENERGY OF NONCANCELLING INTERACTIONS

CHAIR-CHAIR LACTONE (3)		CHAIR-BOAT LACTONE (6)	
Interaction	Å	Interaction	Å
$9\beta,1\beta$	2.34	$9\beta,3\beta$ (bow-stern)	2.12
$1\beta,2\beta$	2.33	$9\beta,1\beta$	2.30
$2\beta,2'\beta$	2.34	$1\alpha,2\alpha$	2.36
$1\alpha,2'\alpha$	2.40	$1\beta,2'\beta$ (1:3)	2.20
$2\beta,3\beta$	2.32	$2\alpha,2'\alpha$	2.28
$3\beta,4\alpha$	2.66	$3\beta,4\beta$	2.32
$4\alpha,10\alpha$	2.31	$4\alpha,10\alpha$	2.33
	Av. 2.39		Av. 2.27
$7 \times 1.47 = 10.3$ kcal.		$7 \times 2.14 = 15.0$ kcal.	

TABLE 15.8. DIMETHYLCYCLOHEXANES

	B.P., °C.	REFR. INDEX n_D^{25}	DENSITY d_4^{25}	CONFIGURA- TION	RELATIVE STABILITY	
					Pre- dicted	Found
1,2-*cis*	129.7°	1.4336	0.7922	ea		
1,2-*trans*	123.4°	1.4247	0.7720	ee	*	*
1,3-*cis*	120.1°	1.4206	0.7620	ee	*	*
1,3-*trans*	124.5°	1.4284	0.7806	ea		
1,4-*cis*	124.3°	1.4273	0.7787	ea		
1,4-*trans*	119.4°	1.4185	0.7584	ee	*	*

refractive index, lower density (and often lower boiling point) is the one of greater conformational stability (R. B. Kelley, 1957). Data for the dimethylcyclohexanes (Table 15.8) show that the more stable diequatorial isomer in each case has the lower constants.

Cyclohexanol exists chiefly in the more stable form with the hydroxyl group equatorially oriented. For study of reactions involving axial hydroxyl groups, Winstein, Eliel, and others have used the device of introducing a bulky alkyl group which assumes an equatorial position and makes possible isolation of conformationally pure *cis* and *trans* isomers, such as those formulated. Diequatorial *cis*-3-*t*-butylcyclohexanol (1) is lower in refractivity than the less stable isomer (2) and diequatorial *trans*-4-isopropylcyclohexanol (4) is lower in both refractivity and density than isomer (3). Notice that the boiling point relationship in the latter case is not a reliable guide. The rates of ester hydrolysis, tosylate solvolysis, and oxidation of (3) and (4) and of the two 3-*t*-butyl-1-cyclohexanols bear the expected relationships (Winstein, 1955). The relative tendency to maintain the equatorial orientation decreases in the order: *t*-butyl $\gg$ isopropyl $>$ *n*-butyl $>$ *n*-propyl $>$ ethyl $>$ methyl $>$ OTs $>$ OCOCH$_3$ $>$ OH.

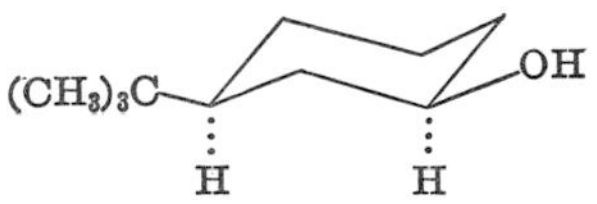

$(CH_3)_3C$—⋯OH

(1) *cis*
M.p. 41°
n_D^{25} 1.4660

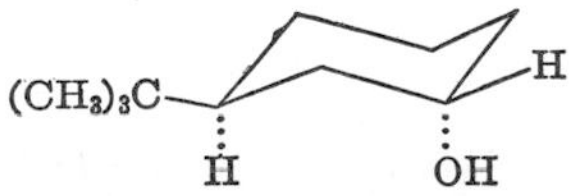

$(CH_3)_3C$—⋯H   ÖH

(2) *trans*
M.p. 49°
n_D^{25} 1.4684

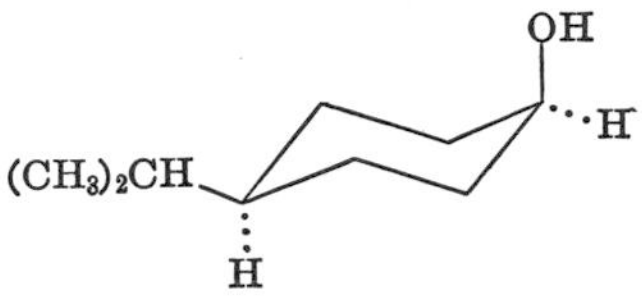

OH ⋯H
$(CH_3)_2CH$—

(3) *cis*
B.p. 74.5°/2.2 mm.
n_D^{20} 1.4671
d^{20} 0.9212

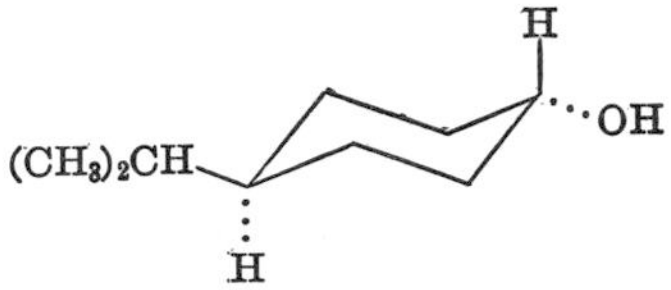

H ⋯OH
$(CH_3)_2CH$—

(4) *trans*
B.p. 81°/2.2 mm.
n_D^{20} 1.4658
d^{20} 0.9158

15.14   **Conformation of Cyclohexene.** — A double bond (or an oxide ring) in a six-membered ring causes the ring to assume the half-chair conformation shown in a model (a) and in the perspective formula (b). The four

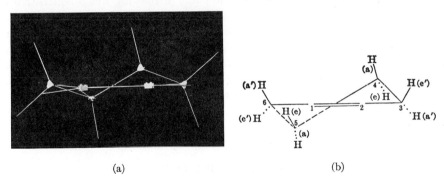

(a)   (b)

carbon atoms associated with the olefinic system C_6—C_1—C_2—C_3 lie in a plane and C_4 is above this plane and C_5 is below it. The bonds extending to hydrogen at C_4 and C_5 are normal axial or equatorial bonds (a, e), but those at C_3 and C_6 differ and are described as quasi-axial (a') or quasi-equatorial (e'). The separation distance for hydrogen pairs $3\alpha,4\alpha$; $3\beta,4\beta$; $5\alpha,6\alpha$; $5\beta,6\beta$ is only 2.4 Å; hence half-chair cyclohexene is slightly less stable than chair cyclohexane. A half-boat cyclohexene is possible in which C_4 and C_5 are both above the plane, but this form is less stable than the one formulated.

15.15   **Conformation of Cyclopentane.** — J. E. Kilpatrick, K. S. Pitzer,[1] and R. Spitzer (1947) suggested that cyclopentane exists in the puckered conformation shown in the model; this is known as the C_s or envelope form. A planar molecule would be destabilized by ten eclipsed interactions (2.27 Å) contributing a strain of 21.4 kcal. In the puckered form four such interactions (C_1—C_2; C_1—C_5) are replaced by quasi-eclipsed interactions at a separation dis-

[1] Kenneth S. Pitzer, b. 1914 Pomona, Calif.; Ph.D. Calif., Berkeley; Univ. Calif., Berkeley

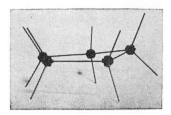

tance of 2.31 Å and the calculated strain is 20.2 kcal. Note that the strain per methylene group in cyclopentane is 4.0 kcal. and that the heat of combustion per methylene group is 158.7 kcal.; for cyclohexane, the values are 3.2 and 157.4 kcal. Puckering lowers the bond angle below that demanded in a planar structure, and hence in the five-membered ring the angles are slightly less than 108°; there is no angle strain.

The Pitzer group suggested that the puckering rotates around the ring (pseudo-rotation). X-ray analysis of cyclopentane derivatives agrees with this configuration for the crystalline state (F. V. Brutscher, Jr., 1959). In this form carbon atoms 1, 2, and 5 have axial and equatorial bonds, but the bonds at C_3 and C_4, called bisectional, form an angle with the plane of the ring which is half that of the tetrahedral angle. Another conformation suggested for cyclopentane (Hassel, 1949) is similar to the half-chair conformation for cyclohexene: three adjacent carbon atoms lie in a plane and the two remaining ones lie 0.4 Å above and below this plane. In this form one carbon atom has bisectional bonds, two have axial and equatorial bonds, and the remaining two have quasi-axial and quasi-equatorial bonds. According to Pitzer (1959) these two forms differ very slightly in energy. No one form describes cyclopentane, but a substituent may well stabilize one form. However, in contrast to the situation in cyclohexane, there is little difference between an equatorial and an axial methyl group (about 0.5 kcal./mole).

CYCLIC ANHYDRIDES, LACTONES

15.16 **ω,ω-Dicarboxylic Acids.** — The normal diacids of Table 15.9 are all crystalline solids of much higher melting point than monoacids of comparable molecular weight. Melting points fall off somewhat as the paraffinic part of the molecule becomes larger, and an alternation is apparent in both melting point and solubility.

15.17 **Oxalic Acid.** — The acid occurs as potassium hydrogen oxalate in the cell sap of many plants, such as *Oxalis* and *Rumex*. An early method of production involved fusion of sawdust with alkali at about 240°; the acid is derived from —CHOHCHOH— units of cellulose. A modern process consists in heating sodium formate with sodium hydroxide, which affords sodium oxalate. The acid crystallizes as the dihydrate, m.p. 101°; azeotropic distillation

$$2HCO_2Na \xrightarrow{\text{NaOH, } 360°} (CO_2Na)_2 + H_2$$

of the water with carbon tetrachloride gives anhydrous material. Unlike other members of the series, oxalic acid is oxidized quantitatively by permanganate and is used in volumetric analysis for standardization. Heat decomposes the acid in

TABLE 15.9. ω,ω-DICARBOXYLIC ACIDS

ACID	FORMULA	M.P.,°C.	SOLUBILITY, G./100G. H$_2$O	ACIDIC DISSOCIATION	
				pK$_{a_1}$	pK$_{a_2}$
Oxalic	HOOC·COOH	189	10.2$^{20°}$	1.46	4.40
Malonic	HOOCCH$_2$COOH	135	138$^{16°}$	2.80	5.85
Succinic	HOOCCH$_2$CH$_2$COOH	185	6.8$^{20°}$	4.17	5.64
Glutaric	HOOCCH$_2$CH$_2$CH$_2$COOH	97.5	63.9$^{20°}$	4.33	5.57
Adipic	HOOC(CH$_2$)$_4$COOH	151	1.4$^{15°}$	4.43	5.52
Pimelic	HOOC(CH$_2$)$_5$COOH	105	2.5$^{14°}$	4.47	5.52
Suberic	HOOC(CH$_2$)$_6$COOH	142	0.14$^{16°}$	4.52	5.52
Azelaic	HOOC(CH$_2$)$_7$COOH	106	.2$^{15°}$	4.54	5.52
Sebacic	HOOC(CH$_2$)$_8$COOH	134	.1$^{17°}$	4.55	5.52
Undecanedioic	HOOC(CH$_2$)$_9$COOH	111			
Dodecanedioic	HOOC(CH$_2$)$_{10}$COOH	128			
Brassylic	HOOC(CH$_2$)$_{11}$COOH	113			
Thapsic	HOOC(CH$_2$)$_{14}$COOH	125			

part to carbon monoxide, carbon dioxide, and water, and in part to formic acid and carbon dioxide. Sulfuric acid promotes decomposition at a lower temperature; probably the acid is first decarboxylated to formic acid which is then dehydrated to yield carbon monoxide.

15.18   Malonic acid was discovered (1858) as an oxidation product of malic acid (*L. malum*, apple) and was named accordingly. It is usually prepared from chloroacetic acid by the cyanide synthesis; the sodium or potassium

$$\text{HOOCCH}_2\text{CHOHCOOH} \xrightarrow{[O]} \text{HOOCCH}_2\text{COCOOH} \xrightarrow{[O]} \text{HOOCCH}_2\text{COOH} + \text{CO}_2$$

Malic acid   Oxalacetic acid   Malonic acid
(two forms, m.p. 152°
and 184°)

salt is treated with potassium cyanide, and the resulting nitrile hydrolyzed to the dibasic acid.

$$\begin{array}{ccc}
\text{CH}_2\text{COONa} & \xrightarrow{\text{KCN}} & \text{CH}_2\text{COONa} & \xrightarrow{\text{Hydrol.}} & \text{CH}_2\text{COOH} \\
| & & | & & | \\
\text{Cl} & & \text{CN} & & \text{COOH}
\end{array}$$

Sodium chloroacetate   Sodium cyanoacetate

The acid begins to decompose to acetic acid and carbon dioxide at about 130°. By heating malonic acid with phosphorus pentoxide, Diels (1908) effected dehydration to carbon suboxide. This reactive substance adds water to reform the

$$\begin{array}{c}
\text{OH} \quad\quad \text{OH} \\
| \quad\quad\quad | \\
\text{O}=\text{C}-\text{CH}_2-\text{C}=\text{O} \xrightarrow{\text{P}_2\text{O}_5} \text{O}=\text{C}=\text{C}=\text{C}=\text{O}
\end{array}$$

Carbon suboxide
(m.p. $-108°$, b.p. 7°)

acid and ethanol to give diethyl malonate. It adds deuterium oxide to give completely deuterated malonic acid, which on heating gives completely deuterated acetic acid (C. L. Wilson, 1935).

$$O{=}C{=}C{=}C{=}O \xrightarrow{2D_2O} DO_2CCD_2CO_2D \rightarrow CD_3CO_2D + CO_2$$
(m.p. 128–130°)   (m.p. 15.75°)

15.19   Succinic acid occurs widely in nature; it was first mentioned by Agricola in 1550 as a product of distillation of the fossil resin amber (L. *succinum*, amber), in which it is present in combined form. The substance

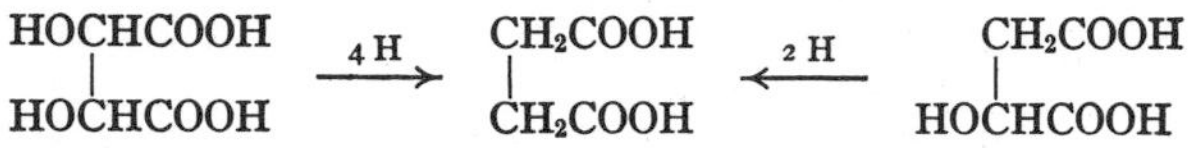

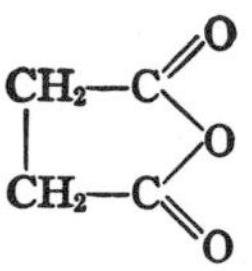

$$\begin{array}{ccc} HOCHCOOH & & CH_2COOH & & CH_2COOH \\ | & \xrightarrow{4H} & | & \xleftarrow{2H} & | \\ HOCHCOOH & & CH_2COOH & & HOCHCOOH \end{array}$$

can be prepared by bacterial fermentation (reductive) of either tartaric or malic acid. Another method of technical application is hydrogenation of maleic acid.

Succinic anhydride (m.p. 120°)

The property most characteristic of succinic acid and substituted succinic acids has been mentioned repeatedly: ready dehydration to cyclic anhydrides containing a five-membered ring.

15.20   Glutaric acid, so named because of relationships to glutamic acid, $HO_2CCH(NH_2)CH_2CH_2CO_2H$, and tartaric acid, is less available than the lower homologs, but can be prepared by nitric acid oxidation of cyclopentanone or synthesized from trimethylene glycol. Like succinic acid, glutaric acid readily forms a cyclic anhydride; in this case the heterocyclic ring is six-membered. Parallel experiments in which succinic and glutaric acids were treated in tetrahydrofurane with 1.1 mole of acetic anhydride at 25° for limited periods of time and the cyclic anhydrides converted for isolation into the *p*-toluidinic acids have shown that glutaric anhydride is formed more rapidly than succinic anhydride (Vivian Viegas and L. F. Fieser, unpublished).

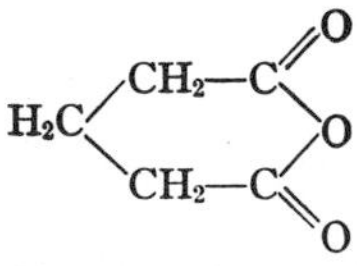

Glutaric anhydride (m.p. 57°)

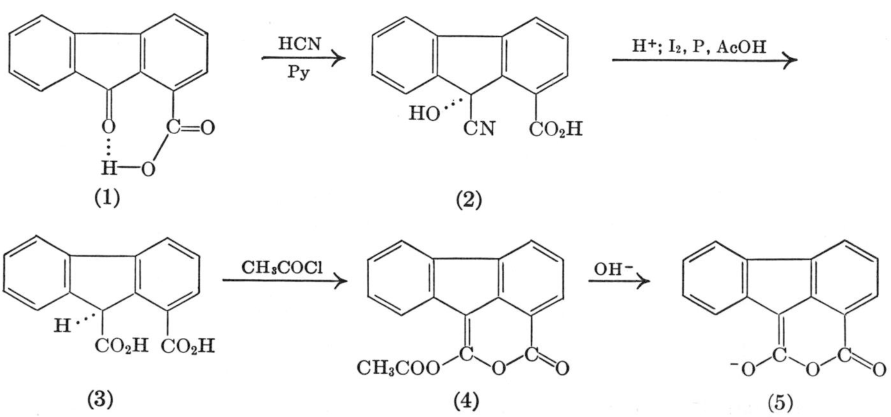

Fluorene-1,9-dicarboxylic acid (3) does not form an anhydride, which would be nonplanar and strained, but is converted by acetyl chloride into the ketene acylal (4) which is planar (R. Kuhn, 1961). A solution of (4) in alcohol is yellow; addition of base gives a deep orange color attributed to the anion (5, unstable). Since fluorenone itself does not add hydrogen cyanide, the ready reaction of the 1-carboxylic acid (1) is attributed to enhanced polarization of the carbonyl group as the result of hydrogen bonding.

15.21   Adipic acid, originally obtained by oxidation of various fats (L. *adipis*, of fat), is now produced in large quantities for the manufacture of nylon by oxidation of cyclohexanol. Adipic acid is converted by treatment with acetic anhydride at reflux temperature into a microcrystalline polymeric anhydride melting after recrystallization in the range 70–85°. Properties and reactions of the substance indicate that it is a mixture of chain polymers of varying chain length:

$$\text{HOOCCH}_2\text{CH}_2\text{CH}_2\text{CH}_2\text{CO}\overline{|\text{OH}|} + n\overline{|\text{H}|}\text{OOCCH}_2\text{CH}_2\text{CH}_2\text{CH}_2\text{COOH} \xrightarrow{-n\text{H}_2\text{O}}$$

$$\text{HOOCCH}_2\text{CH}_2\text{CH}_2\text{CH}_2\overset{\overset{\text{O}}{\|}}{\text{C}}-\text{O}-\left[\overset{\overset{\text{O}}{\|}}{\text{C}}\text{CH}_2\text{CH}_2\text{CH}_2\text{CH}_2\overset{\overset{\text{O}}{\|}}{\text{C}}-\text{O}\right]_n\text{H}$$

Instead of intramolecular cyclization to a 7-ring structure, the predominating reaction is intermolecular condensation, and the contrast in behavior to that of succinic and glutaric acids is attributable to a difference in relative opportunities for the two reactions. One carboxyl group separated from the other by a chain of four methylene groups has many opportunities to combine with functional groups of other molecules and relatively few chances of colliding and interacting with the group attached to the same chain, for the chain can assume many positions, and only a few of these bring the functional groups into proximity. Thus the longer the chain the less chance there is for intramolecular cyclization and the greater the tendency to form polymers. Pimelic acid and suberic acid similarly yield chain polymers on treatment with dehydrating agents.

Although the monomeric form of adipic anhydride is not available by any known process of direct dehydration, J. W. Hill[1] (1930) found that when the polymer is heated in high vacuum a distillate slowly accumulates consisting of the pure cyclic anhydride. Evidently the polymerization is reversible and the volatile monomer distils from the equilibrium mixture, with eventual reversion of the bulk of the nonvolatile polymer. Monomeric adipic anhydride is stable but re-

$$\underset{\text{Polymer}}{\text{HOOC(CH}_2)_4\text{COO[CO(CH}_2)_4\text{COO]}_n\text{H}} \xrightarrow[\text{0.1 mm.}]{98-100°} \quad \underset{\substack{\text{Monomeric adipic}\\ \text{anhydride}\\ \text{(m.p. 20°)}}}{\begin{matrix}\text{CH}_2\text{CH}_2\text{CO}\\ |\qquad\quad\searrow\\ \qquad\qquad\text{O}\\ |\qquad\quad\nearrow\\ \text{CH}_2\text{CH}_2\text{CO}\end{matrix}}$$

active, and it is repolymerized by the catalytic action of a trace of water. The principle of converting a polymeric substance into a cyclic monomer by heating

---

[1] Julian W. Hill, b. 1904 St. Louis, Mo.; Ph.D. Mass. Inst. Techn. (T. L. Davis); du Pont Co.

in high vacuum to a temperature approaching the decomposition point, in the presence of a catalyst where required, has been applied extensively to the preparation of large-ring compounds of several types by Carothers[1] and Hill (1930–33).

15.22   Higher Acids. — **Pimelic acid,** also isolated as a product of oxidation of fats (Gr. *pimelē*, fat), can be prepared from salicylic acid (1) by a novel reaction involving fission of the aromatic ring. A 1,4-addition across the ring (2) is followed by ketonization (3), cleavage of the β-keto acid (4), migration of the double bond to a position of conjugation (14.28), and reduction. In a

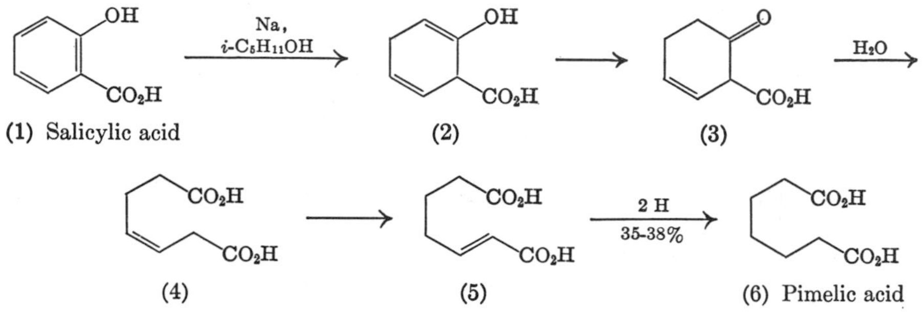

(1) Salicylic acid   (2)   (3)

(4)   (5)   (6) Pimelic acid

process developed in Germany (1949) salicylic acid is hydrogenated (as ester, I) to *cis*-hexahydrosalicylic acid (II), and when this is heated at 310° in an autoclave with strong alkali a mole of hydrogen is evolved and pimelic acid (V) is formed in high yield. The expected reaction was dehydrogenation of the secondary alcoholic group of II and cleavage of the β-keto acid, cyclohexanone-2-carboxylic acid; however, treatment with alkali at a lower temperature afforded Δ^1-cyclo-

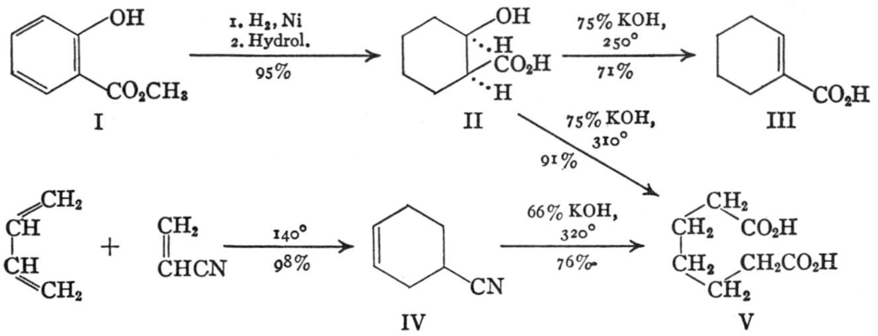

I   II   III

IV   V

hexene-1-carboxylic acid, III (*trans* elimination), which thus may be the intermediate in the high-temperature process. The observation suggested a further efficient synthesis consisting in Diels-Alder condensation of butadiene with acrylonitrile to the nitrile (IV) of Δ^3-cyclohexene-1-carboxylic acid and alkaline hydrolysis and cleavage; the double bond of IV migrates to a position of conjugation with the carboxyl group; cleavage can then occur by the mechanism suggested in section 14.28. Other syntheses are described on p. 604.

[1] Wallace H. Carothers, 1896–1937; b. Burlington, Iowa; Ph.D. Illinois (Adams); du Pont Co.; *J. Chem. Soc.*, 100 (1940)

Suberic acid (L. *suber*, cork) is one product of the oxidation of cork; it is not readily accessible. **Azelaic acid** also is a rather expensive chemical; the name apparently is derived from the fact that the substance is one of the products of oxidation of oleic acid with nitric acid (az, from *azote*, nitrogen, + Gr. *elaion*, olive oil):

$$CH_3(CH_2)_7CH{=}CH(CH_2)_7COOH \xrightarrow{HNO_3} HOOC(CH_2)_7COOH$$

　　　　　　Oleic acid　　　　　　　　　　　　　Azelaic acid

For the preparation of sebacic acid from castor oil, see 8.3.

Traumatic acid, a plant constituent which induces division and extension of certain plant cells, is *trans*-1-decene-1, 10-dicarboxylic acid (Haagen-Smit,[1] 1939). Actually linoleic, linolenic, and lauric acid are considerably more active than traumatic acid.

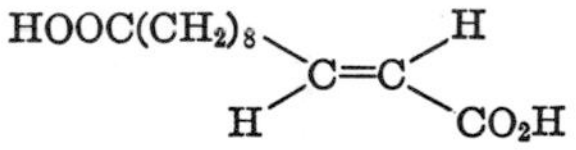

A novel method for the synthesis of symmetrical compounds such as $HO(CH_3)_2CCH_2$-$CH_2C(CH_3)_2OH$ involves dimerization effected by hydroxyl radicals (D. D. Coffman[2] and E. L. Jenner,[3] 1960). A solution of *t*-butyl alcohol in dilute sulfuric acid is placed in a flask having creased sides and a conical indentation in the bottom and equipped with a high-speed stirrer. Solutions of hydrogen peroxide and ferrous sulfate are run in equivalently at 20°. A hydroxyl radical removes a hydrogen

Traumatic acid (m.p. 166°)

$$Fe^{2+} + H_2O_2 \xrightarrow{H_2SO_4} Fe^{3+} + OH^- + \cdot OH$$

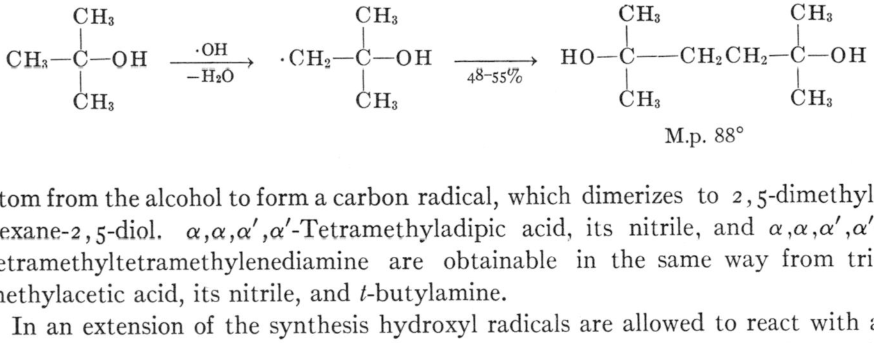

atom from the alcohol to form a carbon radical, which dimerizes to 2,5-dimethylhexane-2,5-diol. $\alpha,\alpha,\alpha',\alpha'$-Tetramethyladipic acid, its nitrile, and $\alpha,\alpha,\alpha',\alpha'$-tetramethyltetramethylenediamine are obtainable in the same way from trimethylacetic acid, its nitrile, and *t*-butylamine.

In an extension of the synthesis hydroxyl radicals are allowed to react with a saturated aliphatic compound in the presence of a 1,3-diene; the result is an additive dimerization. Thus the carbon radical from *t*-butyl alcohol adds rapidly to butadiene to form a resonance-stabilized radical of greatly reduced reactivity, which, since it does not abstract hydrogen and adds another molecule of butadiene only reluctantly, dimerizes, in this case almost exclusively by 1,4-addition, since the product on hydrogenation afforded 2,13-dimethyltetradecane-2,13-diol.

[1] A. J. Haagen-Smit, b. 1900 Utrecht, Holland; Ph.D. Utrecht; Calif. Inst. Techn.

[2] Donald D. Coffman, b. 1905 Sidney, Ohio; Ph.D. Illinois (Marvel); du Pont Co.

[3] Edward L. Jenner, b. 1918 Pontiac, Mich.; Ph.D. Michigan (Blicke); du Pont Co.

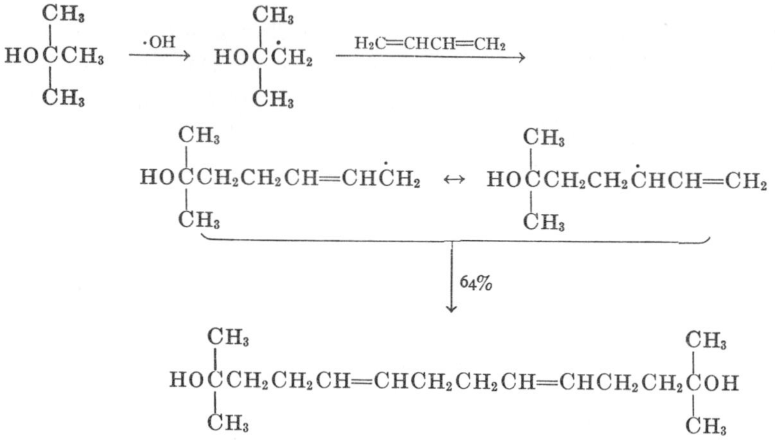

$$\underset{\underset{CH_3}{|}}{\overset{\overset{CH_3}{|}}{HOC}}CH_3 \xrightarrow{\cdot OH} \underset{\underset{CH_3}{|}}{\overset{\overset{CH_3}{|}}{HOC}}\dot{C}H_2 \xrightarrow{H_2C=CHCH=CH_2}$$

$$\underset{\underset{CH_3}{|}}{\overset{\overset{CH_3}{|}}{HOC}}CH_2CH_2CH=CH\dot{C}H_2 \leftrightarrow \underset{\underset{CH_3}{|}}{\overset{\overset{CH_3}{|}}{HOC}}CH_2CH_2\dot{C}HCH=CH_2$$

$$\Big\downarrow \text{64\%}$$

$$\underset{\underset{CH_3}{|}}{\overset{\overset{CH_3}{|}}{HOC}}CH_2CH_2CH=CHCH_2CH_2CH=CHCH_2CH_2\underset{\underset{CH_3}{|}}{\overset{\overset{CH_3}{|}}{C}}OH$$

The additive dimer from *t*-butyl alcohol and maleic anhydride corresponded approximately in composition to the dilactonic diacid formulated. *t*-Butyl al-

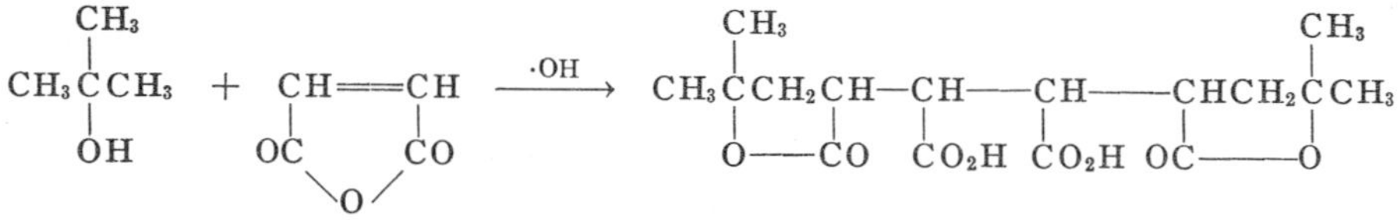

$$\underset{\underset{OH}{|}}{\overset{\overset{CH_3}{|}}{CH_3C}}CH_3 + \overset{CH=\!=\!CH}{\underset{OC\diagdown_{O}\diagup CO}{}} \xrightarrow{\cdot OH} \underset{\underset{O---CO}{|}}{\overset{\overset{CH_3}{|}}{CH_3C}}CH_2CH\!-\!\underset{\underset{CO_2H}{|}}{CH}\!-\!-\!\underset{\underset{CO_2H}{|}}{CH}\!-\!-\!\underset{\underset{OC-----O}{|}}{CHCH_2}\overset{\overset{CH_3}{|}}{\underset{\underset{CH_3}{|}}{C}}CH_3$$

cohol is a preferred substrate for synthesis merely because all nine hydrogens are identical. Other aliphatic compounds, for example, *n*-butyl alcohol, propionic acid, glutaric acid, and cyclopentanone react readily, but, since attack by the extremely reactive hydroxyl radical is relatively nonselective, isomer mixtures result. Usually products arising from both 1,2- and 1,4-incorporation of diene are formed.

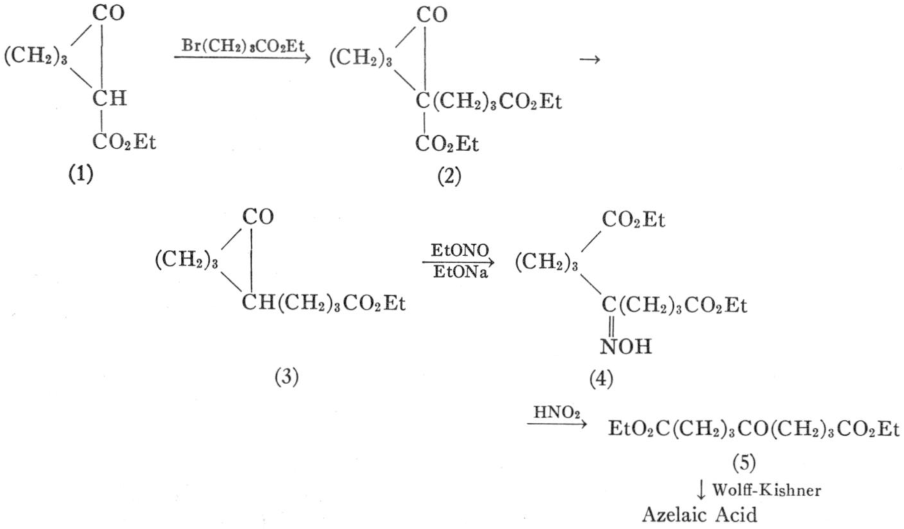

$$\underset{(1)}{(CH_2)_3\overset{\diagup CO}{\underset{\diagdown CH}{|}}\underset{CO_2Et}{|}} \xrightarrow{Br(CH_2)_3CO_2Et} \underset{(2)}{(CH_2)_3\overset{\diagup CO}{\underset{\diagdown C(CH_2)_3CO_2Et}{|}}\underset{CO_2Et}{|}} \rightarrow$$

$$\underset{(3)}{(CH_2)_3\overset{\diagup CO}{\underset{\diagdown CH(CH_2)_3CO_2Et}{|}}} \xrightarrow[EtONa]{EtONO} \underset{(4)}{(CH_2)_3\overset{\diagup CO_2Et}{\underset{\diagdown C(CH_2)_3CO_2Et}{\underset{\underset{NOH}{\|}}{|}}}}$$

$$\xrightarrow{HNO_2} EtO_2C(CH_2)_3CO(CH_2)_3CO_2Et$$

$$(5)$$

$$\Big\downarrow \text{Wolff-Kishner}$$

Azelaic Acid

A generally applicable route to diacids introduced by Huisgen (1961) is illustrated for the synthesis of azelaic acid from 2-carbethoxycyclopentanone (1) and ethyl γ-bromobutyrate. The product of alkylation (2) on hydrolysis, decarboxylation, and reesterification gave (3). Ring cleavage with ethyl nitrite and sodium ethoxide in ethanol at 0° gave the oximino derivative (4), which was split by HNO_2–HNO_3 to the keto diester (5). Wolff-Kishner reduction completed the synthesis.

15.23   Half Esters of Diacids. — Monoesters of succinic and glutaric acids are obtained easily by refluxing the anhydrides with methanol or ethanol without catalyst. A substituted diacid in which one carboxyl group is more hindered than the other, for example phenylsuccinic acid (1), can be converted into the β-monoester (2) by partial Fischer esterification or (in better

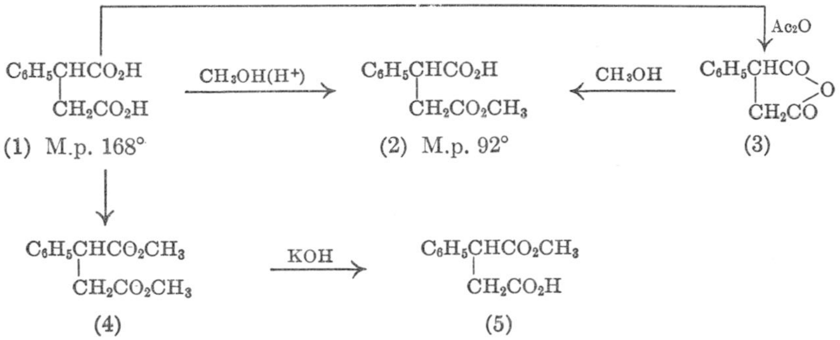

yield) by methanolysis of the anhydride (3). The isomeric α-monoester (5) is formed on selective saponification of the diester (4).

One route to half esters of higher straight-chain dibasic acids and of malonic acid is by half-saponification of the diester. Thus gradual addition of a solution of potassium hydroxide (1 equiv.) in absolute ethanol to a stirred solution of diethyl malonate in the same solvent at room temperature causes separation of potassium ethyl malonate; acidification of an aqueous solution of the salt at 5° and extraction with ether affords ethyl hydrogen malonate in 75–82% yield. Half-saponification of dimethyl undecanedioate, $CH_3O_2C(CH_2)_9CO_2CH_3$ is done with a 0.9 N solution of barium hydroxide in anhydrous methanol at room temperature; the barium salt separates and is converted into the free acid by acidification and ether extraction (yield 60–64%). The method is not suitable for the preparation of ethyl esters because barium hydroxide is not sufficiently soluble in ethanol. It is not satisfactory for azelaic acid, $HO_2C(CH_2)_7CO_2H$, or lower acids because the barium salts are too soluble in methanol. An alternative method which is applicable in this range consists essentially in equilibrating a mixture of equivalent amounts of diacid and diester in the presence of hydrochloric acid; yields of ethyl hydrogen sebacate, $C_2H_5O_2C(CH_2)_8CO_2H$, and ethyl hydrogen adipate, $C_2H_5O_2C(CH_2)_4CO_2H$, are 60–65 and 71–75%.

15.24   Blanc Rule (1907). — Pyrolysis of the barium salt of adipic acid affords cyclopentanone in 80% yield, and cyclohexanone is produced in high yield from pimelic acid by the same method. Five- and six-membered cyclic ketones are produced so readily that acids of the adipic and pimelic types often can be converted into the ketones by simply heating the dibasic acid with acetic anhydride and distilling the excess reagent and the product, if it is volatile,

$$
\begin{array}{c}
\text{CH}_2\text{CH}_2\text{CO}\,\vert\text{OH}\vert \\
\vert \qquad\qquad \\
\text{CH}_2\text{CH}_2\vert\text{COOH}\vert
\end{array}
\quad\xrightarrow[\;]{(\text{CH}_3\text{CO})_2\text{O, distil}}\quad
\begin{array}{c}
\text{CH}_2\text{—CH}_2 \\
\vert \qquad\quad \rangle\text{CO} \\
\text{CH}_2\text{—CH}_2
\end{array}
\;+\; \text{CO}_2 \;+\; \text{H}_2\text{O}
$$

Adipic acid   Cyclopentanone

at atmospheric pressure.   Probably the acid is converted first into the polymeric anhydride, which then suffers pyrolysis rather than the depolymerization to the monomer observed when distillation is conducted in vacuum at a lower temperature, for pyrolysis of such polymers at atmospheric pressure affords ketones. Blanc observed that acids of the glutaric type, when submitted to the same process of distillation with acetic anhydride, are converted into anhydrides and not into cyclobutanone derivatives, and proposed this reaction as a diagnostic test for distinguishing between dibasic acids having a chain of five carbon atoms

$$
\text{H}_2\text{C}\!\!\begin{array}{c}\nearrow\text{CH}_2\text{COOH} \\[2pt] \searrow\text{CH}_2\text{COOH}\end{array}
\quad\xrightarrow[\text{Distil}]{(\text{CH}_3\text{CO})_2\text{O}}\quad
\text{H}_2\text{C}\!\!\begin{array}{c}\nearrow\text{CH}_2\text{CO} \\[2pt] \qquad\quad \searrow\text{O} \\[2pt] \searrow\text{CH}_2\text{CO}\end{array}
$$

Glutaric acid   Anhydride

$(\text{HOOC}\cdot\text{C}\cdot\text{C}\cdot\text{C}\cdot\text{COOH})$ and those having six or more carbon atoms in the chains (Blanc rule).   Although the generalization accurately describes the behavior of the majority of acids, exceptions have been encountered in the case of certain highly substituted compounds of the adipic acid type that yield anhydrides rather than ketones.

15.25   Lactones. — Carboxylic acids containing alcoholic hydroxyl groups respond differently to the action of heat or of dehydrating agents depending upon the relative positions of the two functional groups.   The α-hydroxy acid HOCH_2COOH, glycolic acid, contains both types of groups required for esterification, and opportunity therefore exists either for formation of an internal ester linkage or for production of a polyester under the influence of an acidic esterification catalyst or of heat.   Actually the substance is convertible into either a polyester formed by condensation polymerization or a cyclic ester formed by esterification occurring between two molecules of the acid.   The cyclic

$$
\begin{array}{c}
\vert\text{H}\vert\text{O}-\text{CH}_2-\text{CO}\vert\text{OH}\vert \\
+ \\
\vert\text{HO}\vert\text{OC}-\text{CH}_2-\text{O}\vert\text{H}\vert
\end{array}
$$

Glycolic acid

$(\text{C}_2\text{H}_2\text{O}_2)_n$
Polyglycolide
(m. p. 223°)

Heat $\Big\Updownarrow$ Vacuum distillation

$$
\begin{array}{c}
\text{O}-\text{CH}_2-\text{C}\!\!=\!\!\text{O} \\
\vert \qquad\qquad\quad \vert \\
\text{O}\!\!=\!\!\text{C}-\text{CH}_2-\text{O}
\end{array}
$$

Glycolide (m. p. 86°)

anhydro compound glycolide has a heterocyclic ring of six atoms, which is evidently more easily formed or more stable than the three-membered ring that would result from a monomeric cyclization.   Lactic acid yields an analogous ring compound, lactide:

$$\overline{CH_3CHCO \cdot OCH(CH_3)CO \cdot O}$$
dl-Lactide (m.p. 125°)

The behavior is characteristic of α-hydroxy acids in general.

β-Hydroxy acids on similar treatment undergo dehydration to α,β-unsaturated acids.   Combination of an activated hydrogen atom in the α-position and a

$$\overset{\beta}{R}\overset{\alpha}{C}HCH_2COOH \xrightarrow{-H_2O} RCH{=}CHCOOH$$
$$\underset{OH}{|}$$

hydroxyl group at the adjacent β-position affords so favorable an opportunity for elimination of water with establishment of a double bond that this reaction takes precedence over either polymerization or formation of a four-ring structure by monomeric cyclization or of an eight-ring structure by dimeric cyclization.

Although β-lactones are not formed on dehydration of β-hydroxy acids, they arise in certain condensation reactions of ketene.   One is condensation of ketene with formaldehyde in the presence of zinc or aluminum chloride.   The reaction

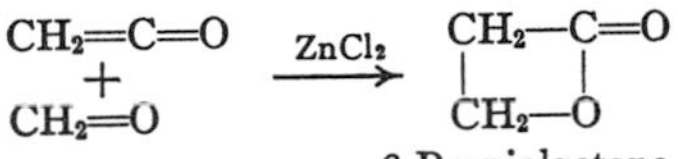

$$\begin{array}{c} CH_2{=}C{=}O \\ + \\ CH_2{=}O \end{array} \xrightarrow{ZnCl_2} \begin{array}{c} CH_2{-}C{=}O \\ | \quad | \\ CH_2{-}O \end{array}$$
β-Propiolactone
(m.p. −33.4°, b.p. 51°/10 mm.)

which can be conducted on a technical scale, affords β-propiolactone, a highly reactive substance of promise for many syntheses (T. L. Gresham, J. E. Jansen, 1948).   The lactone can be polymerized by acid catalysis to a solid polyester-acid (molecular weight about 1000); this affords ethyl hydracrylate on alcoholysis

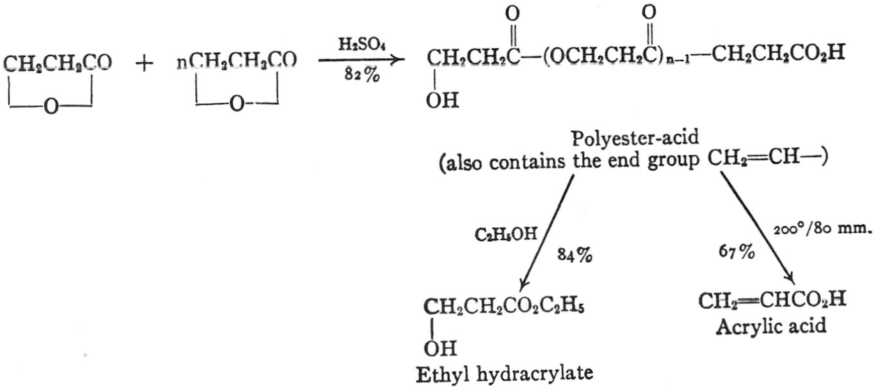

$$\underset{\underset{O}{|\_\_\_|}}{CH_2CH_2CO} + \underset{\underset{O}{|\_\_\_|}}{nCH_2CH_2CO} \xrightarrow[82\%]{H_2SO_4} \underset{OH}{\overset{\overset{O}{\|}}{CH_2CH_2C}}{-}(OCH_2CH_2\overset{\overset{O}{\|}}{C})_{n-1}{-}CH_2CH_2CO_2H$$

Polyester-acid
(also contains the end group $CH_2{=}CH{-}$)

$$C_2H_5OH \diagdown 84\% \qquad\qquad 67\% \diagup 200°/80\ mm.$$

$$\underset{OH}{\overset{|}{CH_2CH_2CO_2C_2H_5}} \qquad\qquad \underset{Acrylic\ acid}{CH_2{=}CHCO_2H}$$
Ethyl hydracrylate

and acrylic acid on pyrolysis.   β-Propiolactone reacts with aqueous sodium chloride, sodium hydrogen sulfide, and ammonia in acetonitrile solution to give β-substituted propionic acids in high yield. Curiously, the base-catalyzed reaction with methanol opens the lactone ring to form the ester, whereas the product of reaction with methanol without catalyst and the primary product of the acid-

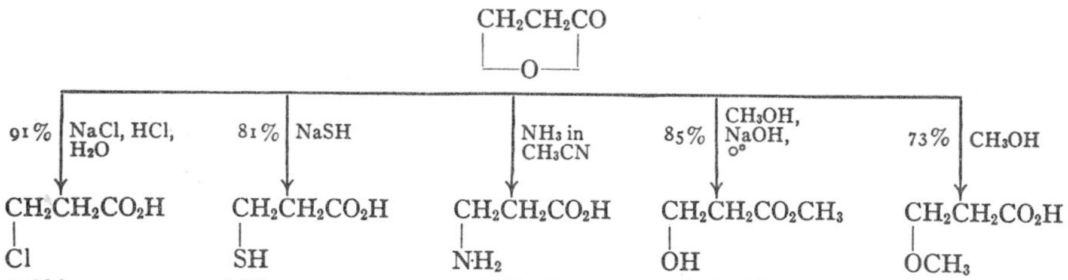

$$CH_2CH_2CO$$
$$\underset{O}{\rule{1.2cm}{0.4pt}}$$

91% NaCl, HCl, H_2O	81% NaSH	NH_3 in CH_3CN	85% CH_3OH, NaOH, 0°	73% CH_3OH
$CH_2CH_2CO_2H$ $\mid$ Cl	$CH_2CH_2CO_2H$ $\mid$ SH	$CH_2CH_2CO_2H$ $\mid$ NH_2	$CH_2CH_2CO_2CH_3$ $\mid$ OH	$CH_2CH_2CO_2H$ $\mid$ OCH_3
β-Chloropro-pionic acid	β-Mercaptopro-pionic acid	β-Alanine	Methyl hydra-crylate	β-Methoxypro-pionic acid

catalyzed reaction is the ether acid, formed by cleavage of the ether rather than of the ester linkage of the lactone.

β-Lactones are key intermediates in a generally applicable method for the synthesis of acids of the type exemplified by α-methyltropic acid (3) (E. Testa, Milan, 1961). An α-alkyl or α-aryl β-amino acid (1) on diazotization in aqueous

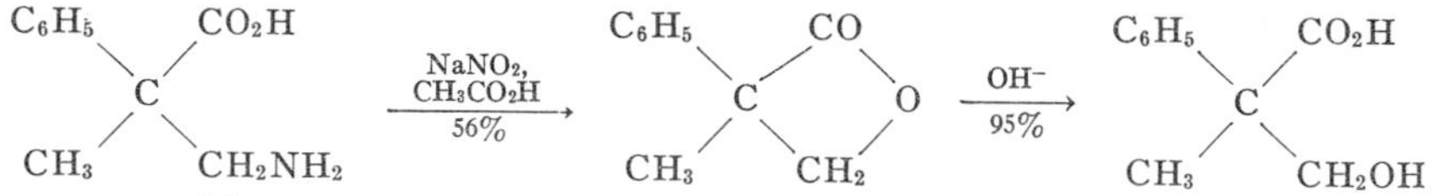

$$
\begin{array}{ccc}
\underset{CH_3}{\overset{C_6H_5}{>}}C\underset{CH_2NH_2}{\overset{CO_2H}{<}} & \xrightarrow[56\%]{NaNO_2,\ CH_3CO_2H} & \underset{CH_3}{\overset{C_6H_5}{>}}C\underset{CH_2}{\overset{CO}{<}}O & \xrightarrow[95\%]{OH^-} & \underset{CH_3}{\overset{C_6H_5}{>}}C\underset{CH_2OH}{\overset{CO_2H}{<}}
\end{array}
$$

(1)   (2) liq.   (3) m.p. 88°

acetic acid at 0° affords a β-lactone (2), which yields the β-hydroxy acid on saponification.

γ-Hydroxy acids present the possibility for formation of lactones having a favored five-membered ring, and this reaction proceeds with great readiness and predominates over other processes, for example:

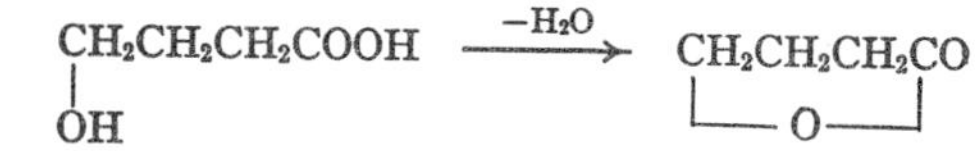

$$
\underset{\substack{\mid \\ OH}}{CH_2CH_2CH_2COOH} \xrightarrow{-H_2O} \underset{O}{CH_2CH_2CH_2CO\rule{1cm}{0.4pt}}
$$

γ-Hydroxybutyric acid   γ-Butyrolactone (b.p. 206°)

Cyclic esters derived from γ-hydroxy acids are γ-lactones. The five-membered ring system is formed with such ease that γ-hydroxy acids are often difficult to isolate in the free state and tend to revert to the γ-lactones on acidification of an alkaline solution of the hydroxy acid unless the temperature is kept low and excess mineral acid is avoided. γ-Lactones are stable, neutral substances, but the lactone ring usually can be opened by the action of warm alkali. Substances of this type are often formed by isomerization of unsaturated acids by heat or by treatment with hydrobromic or sulfuric acid. In the example shown a δ-lactone

$$\overset{\delta}{CH_2}=\overset{\gamma}{CH}\overset{\beta}{CH_2}\overset{\alpha}{CH_2}COOH \xrightarrow{\text{dil. } H_2SO_4} CH_3CHCH_2CH_2CO$$

Allylacetic acid
(b.p. 188°)

γ-Valerolactone
(b.p. 207°)

would also be possible but is not formed. The marked preference for formation of the five-membered γ-lactone ring is further illustrated by the behavior of acids of the sugar series that have hydroxyl groups in the α-, β-, γ-, δ-, and ϵ-positions; these regularly form γ-lactones:

$$\overset{\epsilon}{CH_2}-\overset{\delta}{CH}-\overset{\gamma}{CH}-\overset{\beta}{CH}-\overset{\alpha}{CH}-CO\text{OH} \xrightarrow{-H_2O} CH_2-CH-\overset{\gamma}{CH}-CH-CH-CO$$

$$\underset{OH}{\ \ }\ \underset{OH}{\ \ }\ \underset{OH}{\ \ }\ \underset{OH}{\ \ }\ \underset{OH}{\ \ } \qquad \underset{OH}{\ \ }\ \underset{OH}{\ \ }\qquad \underset{OH}{\ \ }\ \underset{OH}{\ \ }$$

δ-Hydroxy acids sometimes can be converted into the corresponding δ-lactones when no other course of reaction is open. Production of lactones by Baeyer-Villiger oxidation of cyclic ketones (12.32), as illustrated for oxidation of β-hy-

drindone to the lactone of o-(hydroxymethyl)-phenylacetic acid, provides a route to large-ring lactones. Lactones are also obtainable by reduction of anhydrides, for example, succinic anhydride yields γ-butyrolactone. This lactone

γ-Butyrolactone

has been obtained in quantitative yield by oxidation of tetrahydrofurane with ruthenium tetroxide in carbon tetrachloride at 0° (L. M. Berkowitz, 1958). The reagent, which is less volatile, less toxic, less expensive, and more powerful than osmium tetroxide, oxidizes ethers to esters, but is without effect on esters and lactones. Double bonds are cleaved, rather than hydroxylated. Thus cyclohexene is converted into adipaldehyde, and 1-octene affords heptaldehyde (and presumably formaldehyde). Benzyl alcohol affords benzaldehyde, but aliphatic primary alcohols yield the corresponding acids.

Lactones are cyclic esters and enter into usual ester reactions. γ-Lactones are recognizable from a characteristic infrared carbonyl absorption band at 5.62–5.63 μ (1781–1777 cm^{-1}), since with open-chain esters the band appears in the range 5.74–5.82 μ (1742–1717 cm^{-1}); δ-lactones are similar, 5.73–5.74 μ (1744–1742 cm^{-1}).

15.26   **Nepetalactone.** — An investigation of the active principle of catnip responsible for the attractiveness of the plant to certain species of the cat family was commenced in the department of pharmaceutical chemistry at

Wisconsin and continued by a group in the chemistry department headed by
S. M. McElvain (1941–42). Steam distillation of the plant (*Nepeta cataria*) gives
about 0.3% of a volatile, odoriferous oil, about 80% of which dissolves in alkali.
Careful acidification gives crystalline, odorless nepetalic acid, a tautomeric mixture of the enol IIa, the lactol (IIb: IR bands at 3.04 and 5.85 μ), and the aldehyde (IIc: Tollens test). The enol IIa accounts for ready cyclization with acid
to the volatile, physiologically active nepetalactone (I, liq., αD −13°). Oxidation

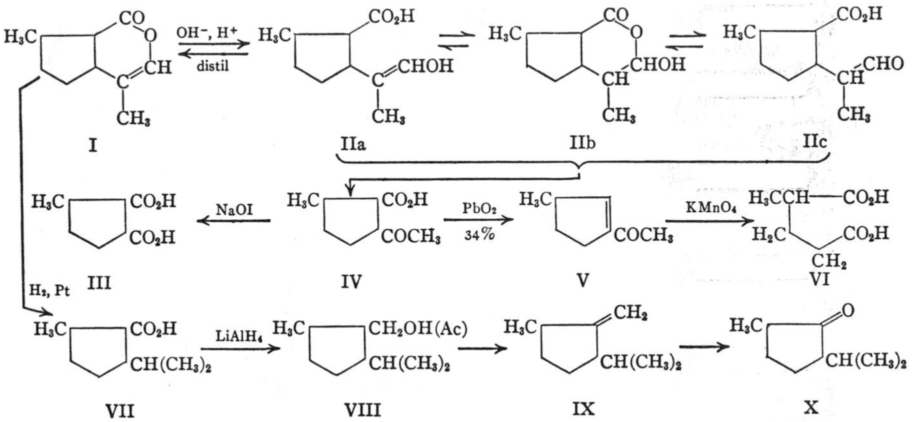

of nepetalic acid (probably as IIa) with alkaline hydrogen peroxide gives formic
acid and nepetonic acid (IV), recognized as a methyl ketone by hypoiodite oxidation
to the dibasic acid III, which on Kuhn-Roth determination was found to contain
one C-methyl group. McElvain concluded that nepetalactone contains a cyclopentane ring with a methyl group at the position shown in I or at one of the other
two possible positions.

The alkali-insoluble fraction of the steam-volatile oil from catnip proved to be
a mixture of nepetalactone, nepetalic anhydride, and the known caryophyllene,
a hydrocarbon constituent of oil of cloves which has an odor midway between
that of cloves and that of turpentine. Tests for physiological activity were
carried out at the Madison zoo with ten African lions, including lions of both
sexes, three cubs, and a partially blind female 25–30 years old. All but the cubs
responded to nepetalactone as they had to the fresh plant, regularly given to them
in the summer. They showed no interest in caryophyllene or in nepetalic acid or
other odorless members of the series. The playful reaction of the adult lions to
nepetalactone, the evident active principle, was similar to that of an ordinary
house cat. Caryophyllene is a C_{15}-compound in which the carbon skeleton con-

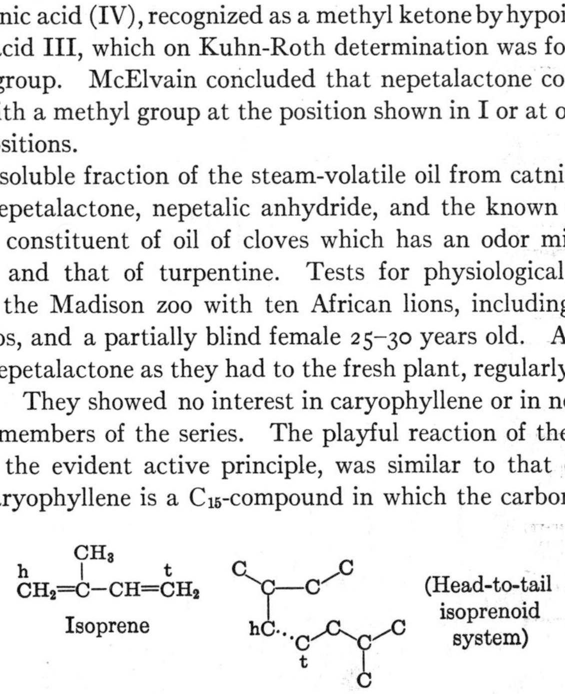

tains three isoprene units linked head-to-tail. Meinwald (1954) noted that of the three structures indicated by the Wisconsin work as possible, only one (I) can be constructed from two head-to-tail linked isoprene units, and he established this structure as correct by the following degradation: hydrogenation to VII (hydrogenolysis of the allylic C—O bond), reduction to the alcohol VIII, pyrolysis of the acetate, and ozonization to formaldehyde and the known 2-methyl-5-isopropylcyclopentanone, X.

McElvain later (1955) effected another degradation which helped in elucidation of the stereochemistry. Doering (1952) had found that 1,2-diacids of type (1) are oxidized by lead dioxide to 1,2-olefins (2); C. A. Grob (1958) found that

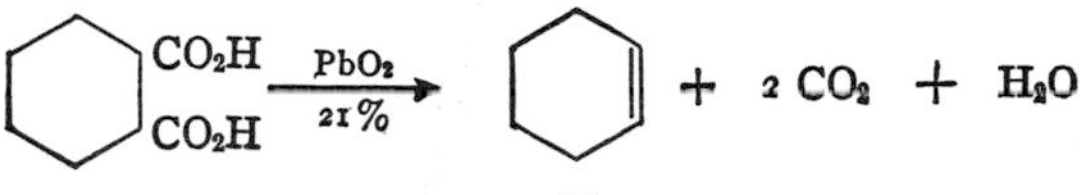

yields are improved by use of lead tetraacetate and pyridine in benzene or acetonitrile. Nepetonic acid is similarly oxidized, possibly through the transition state formulated, to the acetoolefin V, an α,β-unsaturated ketone, λ 237 mμ;

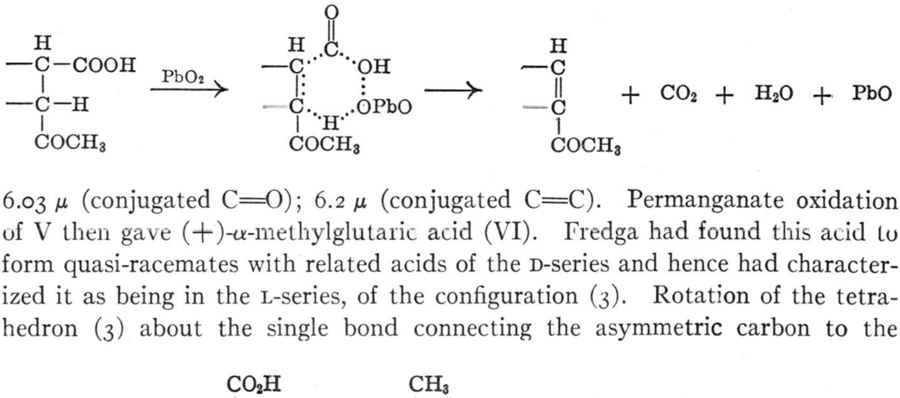

6.03 μ (conjugated C=O); 6.2 μ (conjugated C=C). Permanganate oxidation of V then gave (+)-α-methylglutaric acid (VI). Fredga had found this acid to form quasi-racemates with related acids of the D-series and hence had characterized it as being in the L-series, of the configuration (3). Rotation of the tetrahedron (3) about the single bond connecting the asymmetric carbon to the

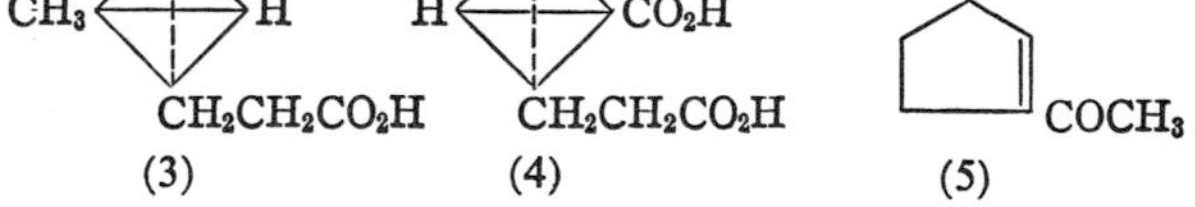

—CH$_2$CH$_2$CO$_2$H group gives (4), and the corresponding configuration thus established for the unsaturated ketone V is (5). In nepetalactone, then, the ring methyl group extends to the rear and hydrogen is to the front.

Nepetic acid, III (m.p. 118°, αD −35°), had been converted into a stereoisomer (αD +69°), but characterization of these acids left some uncertainty about the orientation of the carboxyl groups. Consequently the synthesis of the four possible dl-3-methylcyclopentane-1,2-dicarboxylic acids was undertaken (1958). The acid (11) corresponding in configuration to nepetalactone was obtained from 5-methyl-

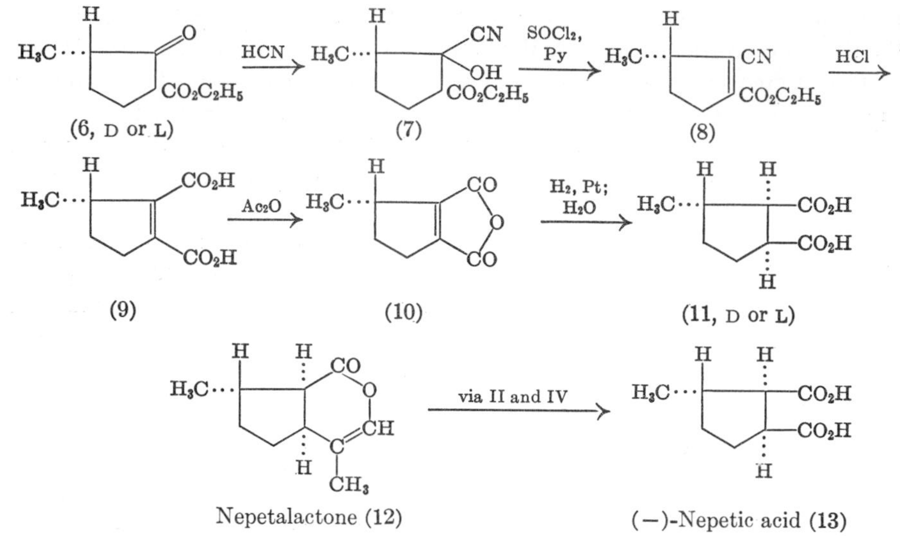

(6, D or L)   (7)   (8)

(9)   (10)   (11, D or L)

Nepetalactone (12)   (−)-Nepetic acid (13)

2-carbethoxycyclopentanone (6, Dieckmann) via the intermediates 7–10. Hydrogenation of the unsaturated anhydride (10) gave both possible products of *cis* addition, and the minor product (11), a DL-acid, m.p. 118°, corresponded in infrared spectrum with (−)-nepetic acid (13). Therefore nepetalactone has the configuration shown in formula (12).

15.27   Conformation of Heterocyclic Rings. — The accompanying chart summarizes bond lengths and interbond angles for compounds of oxygen, carbon and nitrogen. Note that the interbond angle of oxygen increases

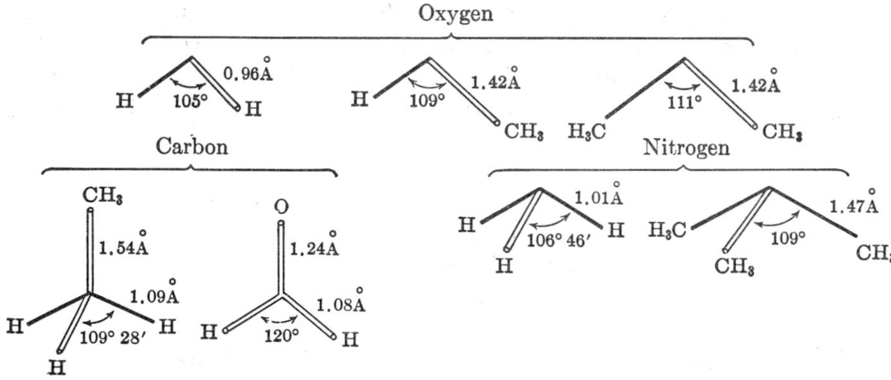

in the series HOH, HOCH$_3$, CH$_3$OCH$_3$ and that the same is true for nitrogen in the series NH$_3$, N(CH$_3$)$_3$. The order is the reverse of that expected if repulsions between nonbonded atoms were the controlling effect in operation. An interpretation suggested by H. A. Bent (1960) is that, since methyl is less electronegative than hydrogen, replacement of H in HOH by methyl causes the oxygen atom to rehybridize slightly so as to shift some of its *s*-character from the O—H bond to the O—CH$_3$ bond, with attendant lengthening of the O—H bond. This concept provides a mechanism for operation of the inductive effect.

That a nonbonded interaction between A and B in the system A—X—B is inherently different from one in the systems A—C—C—B (ethane) and A—C—C—C—B (1:3 interaction in cyclohexane) is a point of importance. The closest approach of two hydrogens in cyclohexane (chair) is 2.5 Å, whereas in methane the separation distance is only 1.7 Å. From what is known of the correlation of potential energy with internuclear distance (15.12) it is evident that, if nonbonded repulsions in methane were like those in cyclohexane, methane would be extremely unstable and carbon tetrachloride would be incapable of existence.

Since the interbond angles of the hetero atoms in dimethyl ether and in trimethylamine are almost identical with the tetrahedral angle, ring compounds of oxygen and nitrogen usually have the conformations of the corresponding carbocyclic substances. Thus the five-membered rings of tetrahydrofurane and pyrrolidine are nearly planar and the six-membered rings of tetrahydropyrane (1) and of piperidine have the chair conformation. Note that the oxide (1) is destabilized

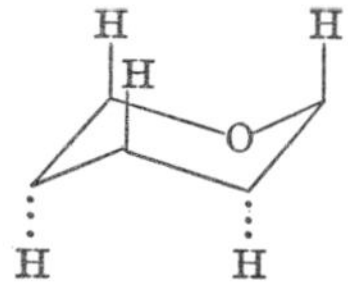

(1) 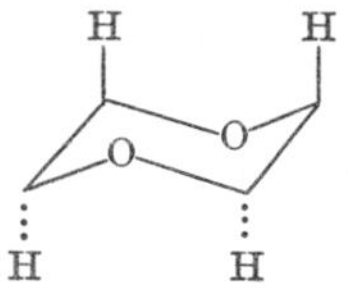   (2) 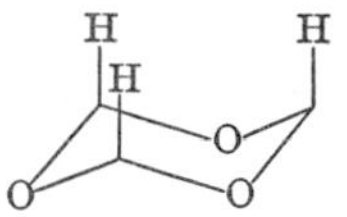   (3) 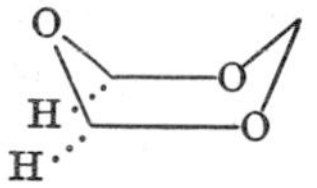   (4)

by only four H:H interactions, as compared to six in cyclohexane and that in 1,4-dioxane the number is reduced to two. Trioxane, with three axial β-hydrogens in the chair form (3) may be more stable in the boat form (4).

In diphenyl ether the lone pair electrons on oxygen can be partially delocalized

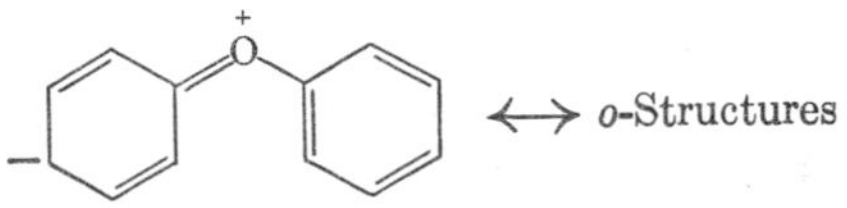

⟷ o-Structures

into the ring; hence the O—C bond acquires some double bond character and the bond angle is expanded to 124° (R. J. Gillespie,[1] 1960).

LARGE AND MEDIUM SIZE RINGS

15.28   Cyclic Ketones. — When the work of the Ruzicka group on muscone and civetone reached a point where synthesis was in order, the method explored was pyrolysis of salts of dibasic acids, since adipic and pimelic acids are convertible by this method into cyclopentanone and cyclohexanone in about 80% yield. The results obtained on pyrolysis of a series of acids mixed with barium, calcium, thorium, or cesium oxide were surprising. The yield of the C$_7$-ketone was moderate and that of the C$_8$-ketone fair (20%), but ketones in the range C$_9$–C$_{12}$ were obtained under optimum conditions in yields of no more than

[1] Ronald J. Gillespie, b. 1924 London, England; Ph.D. London (Ingold); McMaster Univ., Canada

0.5%. From C_{13} on, however, the yields improve and reach a secondary maximum of about 5% for the C_{18}-ketone, and then level off at about 2%. That cyclopentadecanone, valued as a synthetic perfume base, is obtained from a costly diacid in less than 5% yield stimulated efforts to develop a better synthesis. Ziegler (1933) applied to the problem a principle that had appeared in the literature (P. Ruggli,[1] 1912) but had received little attention. The chief obstacle to formation of large-ring compounds is interference from the competing reaction of polymerization. Under ordinary conditions of experimentation a functional group B collides many more times with the group A of surrounding molecules than with that present in the same molecule, and hence polymerization predominates. Any variation in the conditions of the reaction that will suppress

A /\/\/\/\/\/\/\/\ B A /\/\/\/\/\/\/\/\ B

Cyclic monomer   Polymer

polymerization must increase opportunity for intramolecular cyclization, and a means of achieving this objective consists merely in conducting the reaction at high dilution. If each molecule is surrounded largely by solvent molecules and is relatively remote from others of its kind, opportunity for intermolecular collisions is diminished and cyclization given a chance to proceed, even if slowly. As with any other monomolecular reaction, the rate of cyclization is independent of the concentration, and the reaction is just as rapid in a very dilute solution as in a concentrated one, whereas the velocity of polymerization, which is bimolecular in the initial phase, can be decreased enormously by operating at high dilution.

For utilization of the dilution principle in the preparation of large-ring ketones it was necessary to employ a cyclization reaction capable of being conducted in a homogeneous liquid phase with all the reactants in solution, and Ziegler worked out a suitable adaptation of the Dieckmann reaction meeting this requirement. A dinitrile was used in place of a diester, and a condensing agent to replace sodium or sodium ethoxide was found in ether-soluble lithium ethylanilide, $LiN(C_2H_5)$-C_6H_5. The full sequence of reactions is formulated:

$$(CH_2)_n \begin{cases} -CH_2C{\equiv}N \\ \\ -CH_2C{\equiv}N \end{cases} + Li-N{<}^{C_2H_5}_{C_6H_5} \longrightarrow (CH_2)_n \begin{cases} -CH_2C{\equiv}N \\ \\ -CHC{\equiv}N \\ \quad| \\ \quad Li \end{cases} \longrightarrow$$

Dinitrile $[+H-N(C_2H_5)C_6H_5]$

$$(CH_2)_n \begin{cases} -CH_2C{=}NLi \\ \\ -CHC{\equiv}N \end{cases} \xrightarrow{Hydrol.} (CH_2)_n \begin{cases} -CH_2C{=}O \\ \\ -CH{:}COO{:}H \end{cases} \xrightarrow{-CO_2} (CH_2)_n \begin{cases} -CH_2CO \\ \\ -CH_2 \end{cases}$$

Li derivative of ketimino β-Keto acid   Ketone
nitrile

---

[1] Paul Ruggli, 1884–1945; b. Montevideo (German parentage); Ph.D. Leipzig (Hantzsch); Univ. Basel; *Helv. Chim. Acta*, **29**, 796 (1946)

The dinitrile is converted into a lithium derivative, which undergoes cyclization, pictured in the formulas as addition of the C-lithium to the second nitrile group. Water liberates the imino nitrile, converted by hydrolysis and decarboxylation into the cyclic ketone. High dilution at the critical stage of cyclization is accomplished without use of a large volume of solvent by adding a solution of the dinitrile in ether at a very slow rate to a vigorously stirred refluxing solution of the condensing agent in ether. Remarkably high yields were obtained. Thus the yields of cycloheptanone and cyclooctanone were 95% and 88%, respectively, and cyclopentadecanone (Exaltone) and cycloheptadecanone (dihydrocivetone) were obtained in yields of 60% and 70%. Although all the ketones in the series C_{14} to C_{25} as well as the C_5–C_8 ketones could be obtained in yields of 60% and higher, in the series from C_9 to C_{13} the yields dropped to a practically negligible point with the C_9–C_{11} ketones and to 8% and 15% with the next two members. A yield minimum thus exists in this refined method of cyclization, as in the pyrolytic process.

An alternative cyclization process utilizing an intramolecular acetoacetic ester alkylation was applied by Hunsdiecker (1943) to the synthesis of civetone. The starting material was aleuritic acid, a C_{16}-acid available from shellac. The substance contains a terminal primary alcohol group, and two vicinal hydroxyl groups near the middle of the chain provide a means of introducing the necessary double bond. The ω-bromo unsaturated acid is prepared as shown and condensed as the acid chloride with acetoacetic ester; the product of acid hydrolysis contains an activated methylene group adjacent to one end of the chain, and intramolecular condensation is carried out in very dilute solution. The resulting β-keto ester on hydrolysis and decarboxylation yields civetone.

$$HOCH_2(CH_2)_5CHOHCHOH(CH_2)_7COOH \xrightarrow[96\%]{HBr} Br(CH_2)_6CHBrCHBr(CH_2)_7COOH \xrightarrow[61\%]{Zn}$$

Aleuritic acid

$$Br(CH_2)_6CH{=}CH(CH_2)_7COOH \xrightarrow{\substack{1.\ SOCl_2 \\ 2.\ CH_3COCH_2COOC_2H_5}}$$

Δ^9-16-Bromohexadecenoic acid

$$\left[Br(CH_2)_6CH{=}CH(CH_2)_7CO\underset{\diagdown COOC_2H_5}{\overset{\diagup COCH_3}{C}H} \right] \xrightarrow[60\text{–}70\%]{Na,CH_3OH}$$

$$Br(CH_2)_6CH{=}CH(CH_2)_7COCH_2COOCH_3 \xrightarrow[86\%]{\substack{1.\ NaI \\ 2.\ K_2CO_3}}$$

$$\underset{\overset{\|}{CH(CH_2)_6CHCOOCH_3}}{CH(CH_2)_7CO} \xrightarrow[80\%]{KOH} \underset{CH(CH_2)_7}{\overset{CH(CH_2)_7}{\Big\rangle}}C{=}O$$

Civetone

Still another method utilizes intramolecular condensation of a bifunctional ketene (Blomquist, 1948). Ketene itself readily dimerizes when liquid condensed in a dry ice–acetone bath is allowed to come to room temperature. Diketene is an unsaturated lactone reducible to β-butyrolactone, and it is hydrolyzed by water to acetoacetic acid. When the acid chloride of a higher dibasic acid is treated with triethylamine in ether solution, the bifunctional ketene resulting on dehydro-

$$
\begin{array}{c}
\underset{+}{\mathrm{CH_2{=}C{=}O}} \\
\mathrm{CH_2{=}C{=}O}
\end{array}
\longrightarrow
\begin{array}{c}
\mathrm{CH_2{=}C{-}\!-\!O} \\
\mathrm{CH_2{-}\!-\!C{=}O}
\end{array}
\xrightarrow{\ \mathrm{H_2O}\ }
\left[
\begin{array}{c}
\mathrm{CH_2{=}C{-}OH} \\
\mathrm{CH_2CO_2H}
\end{array}
\right]
\longrightarrow
$$

Diketene
(b.p. 68°/92 mm.)

$$
\begin{array}{c}
\mathrm{CH_2C{=}O} \\
\mathrm{CH_2CO_2H}
\end{array}
$$

halogenation undergoes similar intramolecular condensation to a product that on hydrolysis and decarboxylation gives a cyclic ketone. Civetone and *dl*-muscone

$$
\begin{array}{c}
\mathrm{CH_2COCl} \\
\mathrm{(CH_2)_{12}CH_2COCl}
\end{array}
\xrightarrow[\mathrm{ether}]{\mathrm{(C_2H_5)_3N,}}
\left[
\begin{array}{c}
\mathrm{CH{=}C{=}O} \\
\mathrm{(CH_2)_{12}CH{=}C{=}O}
\end{array}
\right]
\longrightarrow
\left[
\begin{array}{c}
\mathrm{CH{=}C{-}\!-\!O} \\
\mathrm{(CH_2)_{12}CH{-}\!-\!C{=}O}
\end{array}
\right]
\xrightarrow{\mathrm{KOH}}
$$

Thapsic acid chloride

$$
\left[
\begin{array}{c}
\mathrm{CH_2{-}\!-\!C{=}O} \\
\mathrm{(CH_2)_{12}CHCOOH}
\end{array}
\right]
\xrightarrow[\mathrm{14\text{-}20\%}]{\mathrm{(-CO_2)}}
\begin{array}{c}
\mathrm{CH_2{-}\!-\!C{=}O} \\
\mathrm{(CH_2)_{12}CH_2}
\end{array}
$$

Exaltone

were prepared by this synthesis. The yields are lower than in the Ziegler or Hunsdiecker processes, owing to considerable linear polymerization, but the starting materials are more readily available.

The curious yield minimum stimulated interest in investigation of compounds of medium size rings, but the most interesting ones were too difficultly accessible for study until 1947, when a vastly improved method of cyclization was developed independently by M. Stoll and by Prelog. The key step is an acyloin condensation, in which a solution of the diester of an α,ω-dicarboxylic acid in hot xylene is stirred vigorously with molten sodium. The first step is analogous to the reduction of a ketone to a pinacol, and the next reduction is a 1,4-addition of sodium. The enediol liberated on acidification ketonizes to the acyloin, which can be reduced to the ketone with zinc and hydrochloric acid or by dehydration and hydrogenation of the α,β-unsaturated ketone. The acyloin condensation is conducted under nitrogen, since the enediol is very sensitive to air oxidation, but

$$
\underset{(CH_2)_n}{\left[
\begin{array}{c}
\mathrm{-COOCH_3} \\
\mathrm{-COOCH_3}
\end{array}
\right.}
\xrightarrow{\ 4\,\mathrm{Na}\ }
\underset{(CH_2)_n}{\left[
\begin{array}{c}
\mathrm{-C{-}ONa} \\
\mathrm{-C{-}ONa}
\end{array}
\right.}
\ +\ 2\,\mathrm{CH_3ONa}
$$

$$
\downarrow \mathrm{H_2O}
$$

$$
\left[
\underset{(CH_2)_n}{
\begin{array}{c}
\mathrm{-C{-}OH} \\
\mathrm{-C{-}OH}
\end{array}}
\right]
\longrightarrow
\underset{(CH_2)_n}{
\begin{array}{c}
\mathrm{-C{=}O} \\
\mathrm{-CHOH}
\end{array}}
$$

Acyloin

high dilution is not required and the yields are spectacular (C_{21}-acyloin, 96%). Even in the region of low yield (C_9–C_{12}), yields of 40% are realized.

Whether a given α,ω-diester undergoes acyloin or Dieckmann condensation appears to depend chiefly on the nature and proportion of the condensing agent. The acyloin reaction requires four equivalents of an alkali metal, whereas Dieckmann condensations have been effected with one equivalent of either sodium or an alkoxide. Thus diethyl adipate reacts with one equivalent of sodium to give the Dieckmann keto ester in 78% yield, and diethyl adipate has been converted into the acyloin in 55% yield by reaction in toluene with 4 g. atoms of sodium in a nitrogen atmosphere and a stirring speed of 2500 r.p.m. (Sheehan, 1950). The Dieckmann reaction is reversible and acyloin formation is not. Dieckmann cyclization of α,ω-diesters with potassium t-butoxide in xylene at high dilution under nitrogen affords C_{14}–C_{16}-monoketones in 24–48% yield, and diametric C_{18}-, C_{20}-, C_{22}-, and C_{24}-diketones in somewhat lower yield (N. J. Leonard,[1] 1959). The method fails, however, as applied to the synthesis of ring compounds in the interesting range C_8–C_{12}.

Wasserman[2] reported (1960) an interesting reaction yielding a small but demonstrable amount of a product with interlocking rings. First, the labeled C_{34}-cycloalkane III was prepared by reduction of the acyloin II in the presence of

$$
\underset{\text{I}}{(CH_2)_{32}\!\!\begin{array}{l}-CO_2C_2H_5\\-CO_2C_2H_5\end{array}} \xrightarrow[\text{Na, Xylene}]{140^\circ} \underset{\text{II}}{(CH_2)_{32}\!\!\begin{array}{l}C=O\\CHOH\end{array}} \xrightarrow[\text{HCl, DCl}]{Zn(Hg)} \underset{\text{III}}{(CH_2)_{32}\!\!\begin{array}{l}CD_2\\CD_2\end{array}}
$$

$$
\underset{\text{IV}}{(CH_2)_{32}\!\!\begin{array}{l}C\!\!=\!\!O\\CHOH\end{array}\!\!\begin{array}{l}(CH_2)_{32}\\CD_2\\CD_2\end{array}} \xrightarrow{H_2O_2,\ OH^-} \underset{\text{V}}{HO_2C(CH_2)_{32}CO_2H} + \text{III}
$$

heavy water; the product contained 3–4 atoms of deuterium per mole. Acyloin condensation of the diester I in the presence of the macrocyclic hydrocarbon III and removal of unchanged III by chromatography gave an acyloin fraction (67% yield) shown by rechromatography not to be contaminated with the hydrocarbon. This acyloin fraction showed infrared bands at 2105, 2160, and 2200 cm^{-1} (C—D stretch) characteristic of the labeled hydrocarbon, and oxidation to the diacid V gave neutral material shown to contain III by the infrared spectrum and the chromatographic behavior. The evidence thus points to the presence in the acyloin fraction of the catenane IV (L. *catena*, chain); cleavage of the acyloin ring results in unthreading to give III.

15.29 Compounds with Bridged Benzene Rings. — Macrocyclic compounds of another type have been synthesized, for example, by reaction of hydroquinone with a polymethylene dihalide and cyclization of the half-ether with sodium ethoxide at high dilution (Lüttringhaus,[3] 1937). The products are

[1] Nelson J. Leonard, b. 1916 Newark, N. J.; Ph.D. Columbia (Elderfield); Univ. Illinois

[2] Edel Wasserman, b. 1932 New York; Ph.D. Harvard (Moffitt); Bell Telephone Laboratories

[3] Arthur Lüttringhaus, b. 1906 Cologne-Mülheim; Ph.D. Göttingen (Windaus, Ziegler); Univ. Berlin, Greifswald, Halle, Freiburg Br.

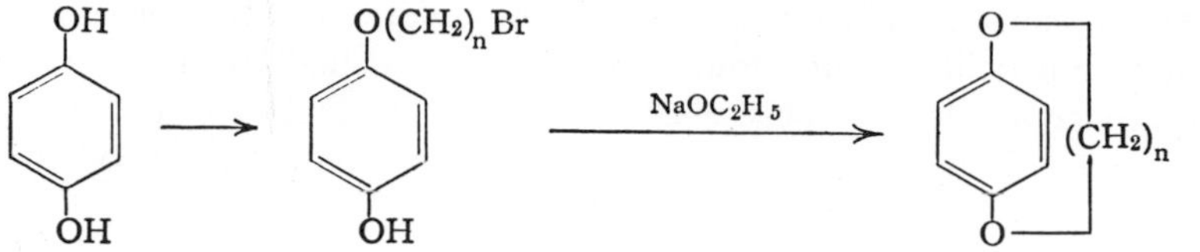

OH $O(CH_2)_n Br$

$\xrightarrow{\hspace{1cm}}$ $\xrightarrow{NaOC_2H_5}$ $(CH_2)_n$

OH   OH

Hydroquinone   Ansa-compound

called ansa compounds (L. *ansa*, a handle). In the case illustrated ring closure succeeds only if the chain contains eight or more methylene groups. Optical isomerism is possible if the benzene ring is unsymmetrically substituted and if the *ansa* ring is small enough to restrict rotation of the benzene ring about the $1,4$-axis. Thus in the series of *o*-carboxylic acid derivatives resolution has been accomplished when $n = 8$ but not when $n = 10$.

Treatment of an ω-phenyl fatty acid chloride with aluminum chloride or bromide in carbon disulfide can effect intramolecular Friedel-Crafts cyclization to either an *o*-phenylenalkanone (I) or a *p*-phenylenalkanone (III); both types are known also

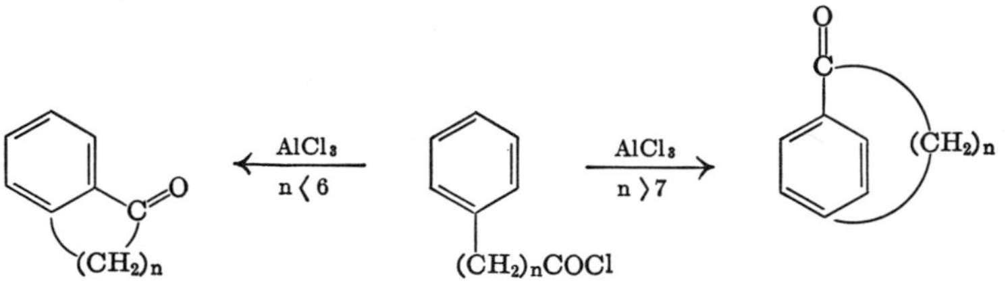

$\xleftarrow[n\langle 6]{AlCl_3}$ $\xrightarrow[n\rangle 7]{AlCl_3}$ $(CH_2)_n$

$(CH_2)_n$ $(CH_2)_nCOCl$

I   II   III

as "benzocyclenones." Huisgen (1956) found that when the side chain contains five or less methylene groups, *ortho* products (I) are formed in high yield (Table 15.10); these ketones have rings of 5–8 carbon atoms. The C_9- and C_{10}-*o*-ketones could be obtained in traces only, even with use of the high-dilution technique. From $n = 8$ on, *p*-ketones were obtained in progressively increasing yield. From the model of the *p*-ketone with an octamethylene bridge, it is evident that this contains the smallest strain-free ring. Notice that the carbonyl group (to the left) is perpendicular to the plane of the benzene ring and hence that resonance and light absorption should be at a minimum. Huisgen compared the

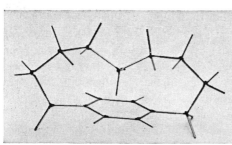

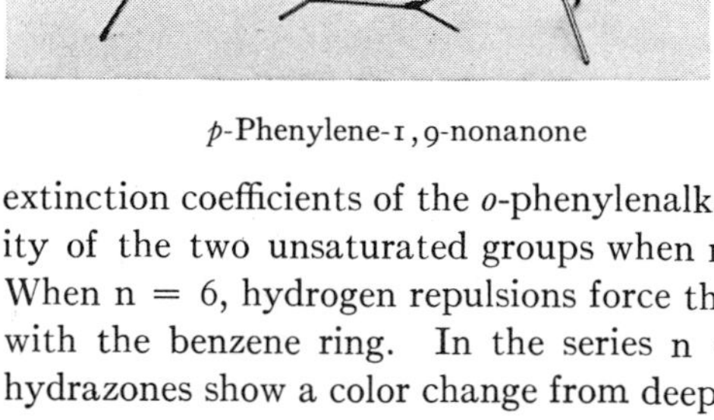

p-Phenylene-$1,9$-nonanone

extinction coefficients of the *o*-phenylenalkanones and found evidence of coplanarity of the two unsaturated groups when $n = 2$ or 3 (indanone-1, α-tetralone). When $n = 6$, hydrogen repulsions force the carbonyl group to an angle of 50–$60°$ with the benzene ring. In the series $n = 3$ to $n = 5$ the $2,4$-dinitrophenylhydrazones show a color change from deep red to yellow.

TABLE 15.10. PREPARATION OF PHENYLENALKANONES

n	2	3	4	5	6	7	8	9	10	11	12	13	15
Orientation	o	o	o	o	—	—	p	p	p	p	p	p	p
AlCl₃; % yield	95	91	88	77	o	o	1	22	28	36	36	35	
AlBr₃; % yield				84	2	1	5					56	75

Two *meta*-ring derivatives of *p*-nitrophenol show interesting differences in properties. Compound (1), with a bridge of six methylene groups, has phenolic properties, but (2), with a five-carbon bridge, behaves as a nonaromatic ketone.

(1)   (2)

15.30   Physical Properties. — The properties of medium-size ring compounds are indeed abnormal. Whereas in the series of homologous *n*-alkanes density increases steadily with increasing molecular weight and molecular refraction decreases, in the cycloalkanes from C_6 on density increases more rapidly and passes through a maximum and then falls off to the level of the higher *n*-alkanes, and the molecular refraction curve exhibits a minimum inflection. R. W. Fawcett and J. O. Harris (King's Coll., Univ. Durham, 1954) completed a series of conjugated cyclo-1,3-dienes, prepared for the most part by allylic bromination of the enes (NBS) and dehydrohalogenation (quinoline), and found that ultraviolet light absorption varies markedly with ring size, as can be seen from figures given for the

Ring	C_5	C_6	C_7	C_8	C_9	C_{10}	C_{11}	C_{12}
λ_{max}, mμ	265	256	248	228	219.5	224	227.5	230

positions of the absorption bands. In this series, λ_{max} decreases to a minimum in the C_9-diene and then rises to a level comparable with that characteristic of openchain dienes of the type $RCH{=}CHCH{=}CHR$ (227 mμ).

Precision combustion measurements (Table 15.11) demonstrate that the heat of combustion per methylene group increases in order from C_6 to C_9 and then falls to the level of C_6. On the assumption that the high energy content of the medium size rings is due entirely to hydrogen : hydrogen repulsions, we have calculated strain energies per methylene group (last line table) as follows. A model is arranged so that transannular interactions on the α- and β-sides are matched and at maximal separation distances, which are measured. Distances are measured also for all transannular, 1:2, and 1:3 interactions, and all interactions measuring 2.90 Å or under are averaged. The equivalent energy value (Table 15.5) then serves for calculation of the interaction energy per mole and per methylene group. Since the values found follow reasonably well the order of the heats of combustion,

TABLE 15.11. CYCLOALKANES; ENERGY RELATIONSHIPS
Heat of combusion ($-\Delta H$) and Estimated Strain Energy per CH_2

	C_5	C_6	C_7	C_8	C_9	C_{10}	C_{15}	C_{17}
$-\Delta H$ kcal.	158.7	157.5	158.3	158.7	158.9	158.6	157.1	157.0
H-Interactions	10	18	28	38	38	46		
Distance, Å (av.)	2.29	2.49₃	2.47	2.51	2.47	2.47		
Kcal. (av.)	2.02	1.06	1.14	1.00	1.14	1.14		
Strain, kcal./CH_2	4.0	3.2	4.6	4.7	4.8	5.2	3.2	3.2

hydrogen:hydrogen interaction is probably the chief factor contributing to instability.

15.31   **Cycloalkenes.** — Ring size influences in an interesting way the stability and reactivity of *cis* and *trans* double bonds incorporated into a carbon ring. Cyclohexene and cycloheptene are known only in the *cis* forms, but *cis* and *trans* pairs from C_8 to C_{12} have been fully characterized. K. Ziegler (1950) was the first to demonstrate that such isomers can exist. M. Godchot (1927), E. P. Kohler (1939), and others had investigated the acid-catalyzed dehydration of cyclooctanol and obtained a cyclooctene of refractive index 1.4693. R. Willstätter and E. Waser (1910), however, had reported n_D^{20} 1.4739 for material obtained by pyrolysis of cyclooctyltrimethylammonium hydroxide. Ziegler confirmed both observations, found that the product of the Hofmann degradation is labile and easily isomerized by acids to the hydrocarbon of lower refractive index, and showed that the stable and labile isomers are, respectively, *cis*- and *trans*-cyclooctene. Both eliminations give initially the labile *trans* olefin, but this is isomerized under the conditions of the acidic dehydration. *cis*-Cyclooctene is formed as the primary product of partial hydrogenation of cyclooctatetraene-1,3,5,7 and of reduction of cyclooctadiene-1,3 with lithium and methylaniline (conjugated dienes are reducible, an isolated double bond is not affected). Procedures used by Cope for the preparation of highly purified samples of isomeric cycloalkenes are described in section 6.15.

Manipulation of a model of *cis*-cyclooctene shows it to be very flexible, like boat-cyclohexane, and easily flipped from the chair-form (a) to the boat-form (b).

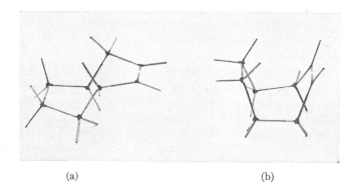

    (a)   (b)

Each of these regular forms is destabilized by several severe interactions, and the substance probably assumes an intermediate, irregular form. The model of *trans*-cyclooctene (c) is very rigid and can be constructed only with slight bond bending. Rigidity and severe bending of bonds is so evident in cyclooctyne (d) that the

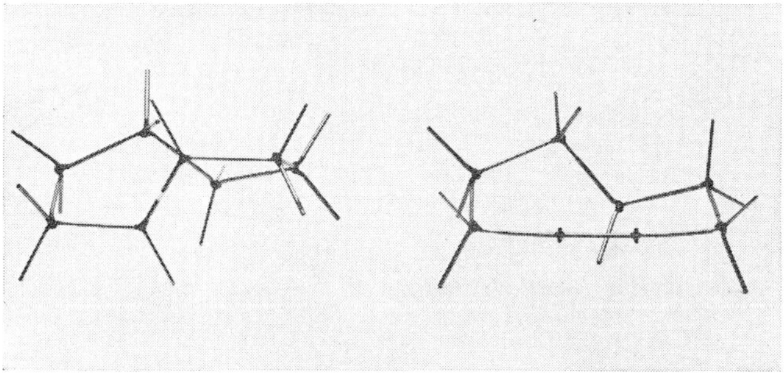

(c)   (d)

existence of this substance seems miraculous (for preparation by the Curtius reaction, see p. 219). Calculation of hydrogen:hydrogen interaction energies for the cycloalkenes lacks significance, for certain transannular carbon atoms become so close that carbon:carbon repulsions probably contribute to instability; in an open-chain olefin with the system —CH_2CH=$CHCH_2$— interaction between the methylene groups in the *cis* form destabilizes this form by a factor of about 1 kcal. (for *cis*-di-*t*-butylethylene the value is 35.5 kcal.).

Heats of hydrogenation determined by Turner (Table 15.12) demonstrate the severe strain that accompanies incorporation of a *trans* double bond in the eight-membered ring. The difference of 9.3 kcal. is the largest yet observed for any *cis-trans* pair. The data for the C_9 and C_{10} series show the *cis* isomers also to be the more stable (Δ = 2.9 and 3.3 kcal./mole). In a very large ring nonbonded interactions beyond those in an open-chain olefin disappear and the usual order of stability, *trans* > *cis*, is restored. Cope's equilibration studies (Table 15.12) demonstrate that the turn-over point is at C_{11}. That the *cis* C_9 and C_{10} ring olefins have greater thermodynamic stability than the *trans* isomers is in agreement with the thermochemical data. That the decrease in enthalpy in the isomerization of *trans*- to *cis*-cyclodecene (ΔH = −3.6 kcal./mole) is greater than that for the isomerization of *trans*- to *cis*-cyclononene (−2.9 kcal.) is surprising, particularly in view of the corresponding entropy changes.

Ring size also affects reaction rates. Ziegler found the reaction with phenyl-azide in ether useful for characterization of the liquid cycloalkenes; thus *cis*- and

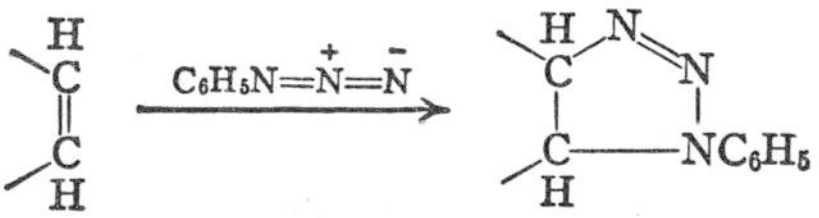

trans-cyclooctene form crystalline adducts melting at 87° and 111°, respectively. Approximate rates of reaction of *trans*-cycloalkenes with phenylazide (Ziegler, 1954) correspond to the following ratios: C_8, 20,000; C_9, 2,000; C_{10}, 10; C_{11}, 1. Cyclooctanone forms no bisulfite addition product (12.47) and cyclodecanone does not add hydrogen cyanide. In the Stuart model (a) of cyclooctanone the

TABLE 15.12. CYCLOALKENES; ENERGY RELATIONSHIPS

	HEAT OF HYDRO-GENATION (CH₃CO₂H, 25°) kcal./mole[a]	trans→cis ISOMERIZATION IN ACETIC ACID AT 100.4°[b]			
		Free energy kcal./mole	Enthalpy kcal./mole	Entropy kcal./mole	Equilibrium, cis/trans
C_6-*cis*	27.10				
C_7-*cis*	25.85				
C_8-*cis*	22.98				
C_8-*trans*	32.24				
C_9-*cis*	23.62	−4.04	−2.9	3.0	232
C_9-*trans*	26.49				
C_{10}-*cis*	20.67	−1.86	−3.6	−4.7	12.2
C_{10}-*trans*	24.01				
C_{11}-*cis*		0.67	0.12	−1.5	0.406
C_{11}-*trans*					
C_{12}-*cis*		0.49	−0.41	−2.4	0.517
C_{12}-*trans*					

[a] R. B. Turner and W. R. Meador (1957).　[b] A. C. Cope, P. T. Moore, and W. R. Moore (1960).

(a)　　　　　　　　(b)　　　　　　　　(c)

carbonyl group does not appear to be more hindered than that of cyclohexanone (c), but repulsive interactions may force the molecule to assume more hindered conformations, for example (b).

15.32　　Transannular Reactions.—Abnormalities in certain reactions of C_8–C_{11} cyclic compounds were observed in 1952 by Cope and by Prelog. Cope, investigating the preparation of the *cis*- and *trans*-cyclooctane-1,2-diols, obtained the former, as expected, by oxidation of *cis*-cyclooctene with osmium tetroxide in combination with hydrogen peroxide or sodium chlorate. The reaction of *cis*-cyclooctene with performic acid, the standard reagent for preparation of *trans* diols (through formation and diaxial opening of the oxide), gave a mixture of approximately equal parts of two diols. One, shown to be *trans*-cyclooctane-$1,2$-diol by quantitative reaction with periodic acid at room temperature (titration) and by oxidation with permanganate to suberic acid, was isolated by treatment of the mixture with acetone and anhydrous copper sulfate and distillation of the *trans*-diol acetonide from the less volatile residual diol. The latter, which crystallizes from ethyl acetate in needles, m.p. 86°, was also obtained along with the *trans*-$1,2$-diol by the action of formic acid on the preformed oxide I, followed by saponification of the initially formed formate. The abnormal diol forms a diacetate and on Oppenauer oxidation yields a diketone, and therefore it is a disecondary alcohol. Failure to react with periodic acid and with acetone showed that it is not a *vic*-glycol. Oxidation with permanganate and identification of the products as oxalic and adipic acid established the presence of the chains CCCCCC and CC, consistent with formula III. That the carbon skeleton is still intact was shown by pyrolysis

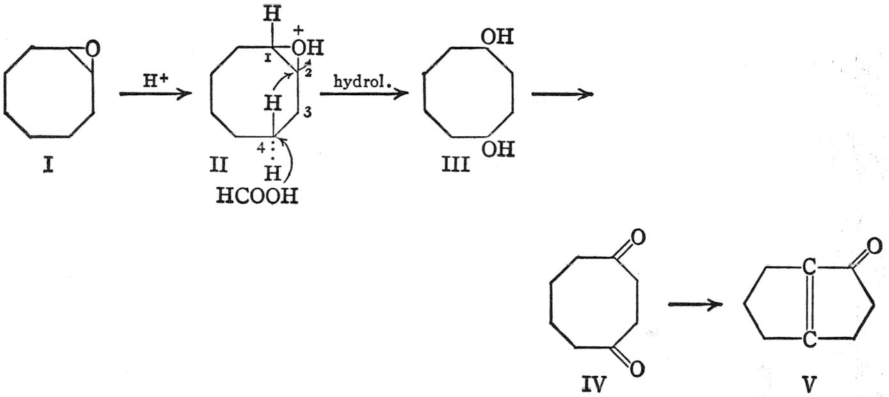

to a mixture of dienes, which on hydrogenation afforded cyclooctane. That the abnormal product is actually cyclooctane-$1,4$-diol (III) was proved by treatment of the diketone IV with sulfuric acid, which induced intramolecular aldolization to give the known bicyclo ketone V (liquid), isolated by steam distillation and characterized as the semicarbazone (m.p. 238°).

The explanation of the abnormal reaction advanced by Cope is that a hydrogen atom at C_4, which in the eight-membered ring is sterically adjacent to the $1,2$-oxide ring, participates in the displacement reaction resulting in ring fission. The reaction can be interpreted as a hydride ion shift from C_4 to C_2 in the protonated oxide (II) with synchronous attack by the solvent at the resulting C_4-carbonium ion. This proximity, or transannular, effect is evidently due to the special conformation of the medium size ring. Later work of the Cope group (1960) established that solvolysis of the oxide I with formic acid affords the following abnormal products in addition to *cis*-$1,4$-cyclooctandiol III: 3-cyclooctene-1-ol (VI) and 4-cyclo-octene-1-ol (VII). Study of the reaction with deuterium labeling on C_5 and C_6 of the oxide established that III is formed to the extent of 61% by a $1,5$-hydride shift and 39% by a 1,3-hydride shift, whereas VI results from 1,5-hydride (94%) and 1,3-hydride (6%) shifts.

Whereas *cis*-cycloheptene and *cis*- and *trans*-cyclododecene react normally on performic acid oxidation, the C_9, C_{10}, and C_{11} cycloalkenes give chiefly abnormal products. Thus *trans*-cyclodecene (I) gave a complicated mixture from which five products were separated by chromatography. Three were identified as cyclo-

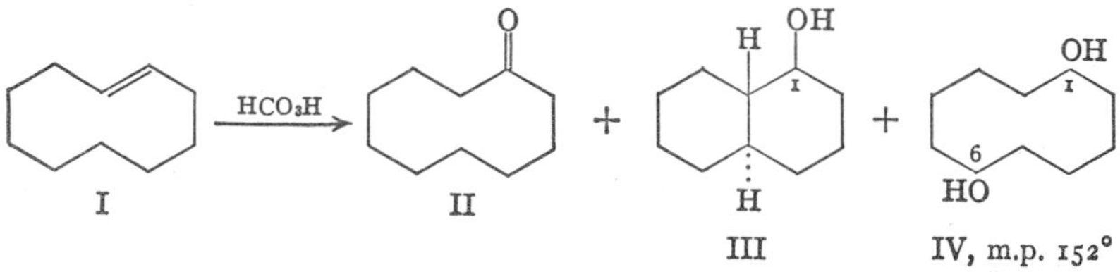

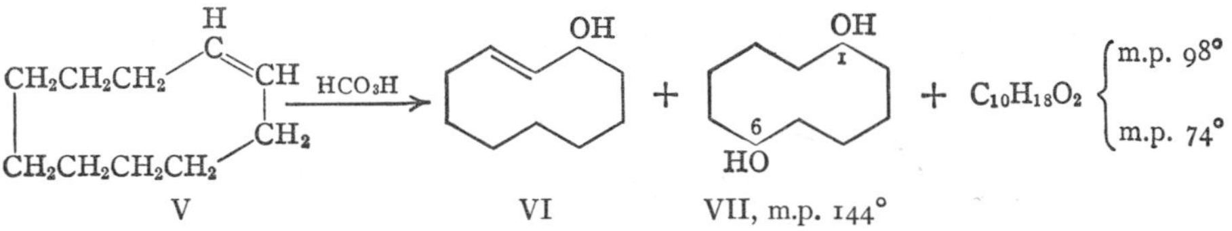

decanone (II), a *trans*-α-decalol (III), and cyclodecane-1,6-diol (IV); the latter product evidently arises through a transannular displacement similar to that discussed above. The other two products, m.p. 98° and 63°, have the composition of bicyclic diols, $C_{10}H_{18}O_2$. *cis*-Cyclodecene (V) on oxidation gave the allylic alcohol VI, a 1,6-diol (VII) stereoisomeric with IV, and two isomers of the formula $C_{10}H_{18}O_2$, one (m.p. 98°) identical with that in the other series. A proximity effect is operative also in peracid oxidation of cyclononene, for two stereoisomeric 1,5-diols were isolated.

Comparison of the rates of reaction of the cyclononenes and cyclooctenes with peracids established that the *trans* double bond is more reactive than the *cis* and therefore more strained. This observation was useful in elucidation of the configuration of caryophyllene, a hydrocarbon constituent of oil of cloves. Early work (1834–88) established the formula $C_{15}H_{24}$ and the presence of two double bonds, and therefore of two rings. Oxidative degradations in several laboratories eventually established the presence of a four-membered ring fused to a nine-membered ring in a carbon skeleton made up of three isoprene units linked head-to-tail. The larger ring contains one exocyclic double bond (=CH₂) and one endocyclic

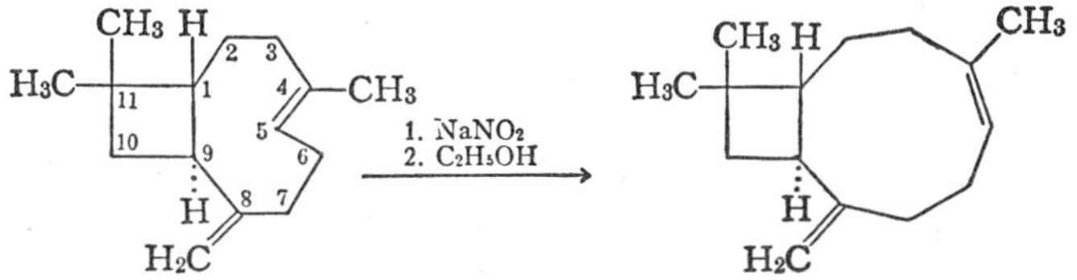

Caryophyllene   Isocaryophyllene

double bond, the configuration of which remained to be elucidated. Caryophyllene very readily undergoes isomerization and cyclization and thus appears strained. It reacts with nitrous acid to form a beautiful blue addition compound, which is decomposed by the action of ethanol with regeneration of a hydrocarbon which, however, is the isomeric substance isocaryophyllene. Barton (1953) found

$$RR'C{=}CHR'' \xrightarrow[C_2H_5OH]{HNO_2} RR'C{-}{-}CHR''$$

$$\begin{array}{cc} | & | \\ NO_2 & NO \end{array}$$

Nitrosite

that caryophyllene reacts more rapidly than isocaryophyllene with peracids and deduced the *trans* configuration for the former and the *cis* for the latter.

An abnormal reaction of a different type was observed by Blomquist (1955) on pyrolysis of cyclononyl acetate. Cyclononene was a minor product (25%), and the main product (70%) is the open-chain diene, 1,8-nonadiene. Blomquist

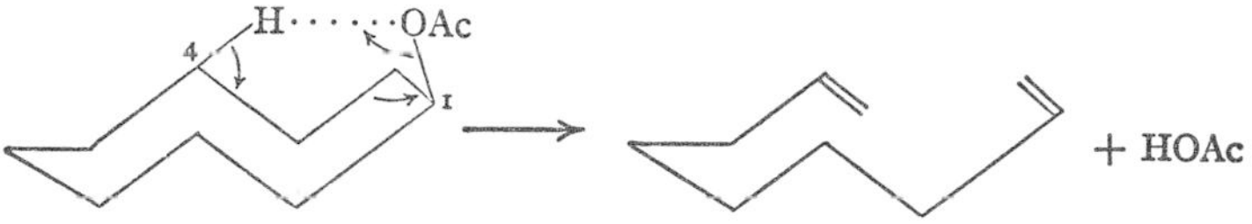

interprets the formation of the diene as a transannular 1,4-elimination of acetic acid involving an intermediate six-membered ring transition state.

R. Robinson postulated a transannular interaction to account for the fact that certain salts of the alkaloid cryptopine (1) do not show infrared absorption characteristic of the carbonyl group. He suggested that these salts are neutralized in-

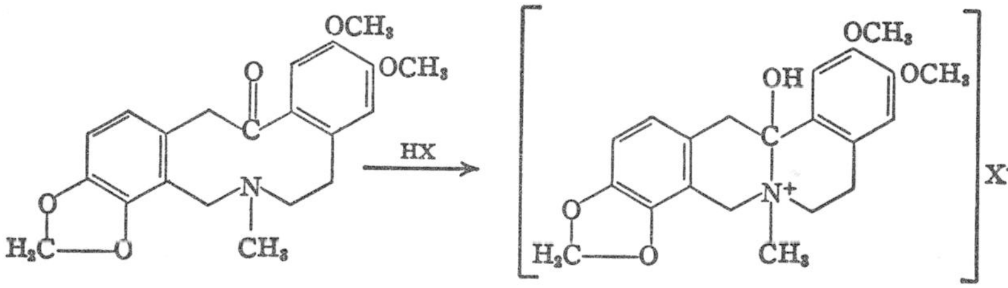

(1)   (2)

ternally and have the structure (2). This proximity effect has been investigated extensively with simpler related bases by Leonard (1954–55). Internal bonding is appreciable only in C_9 and C_{10} rings and disappears from C_{11} on; it decreases with increasing size of the N-alkyl group, and is dependent upon the relative positions of the tertiary nitrogen and the carbonyl group.

Cope (1955) encountered a proximity effect of a further type in investigating the reduction of cyclodecane-1-ol-6-one oxime (I). The amino alcohol was produced

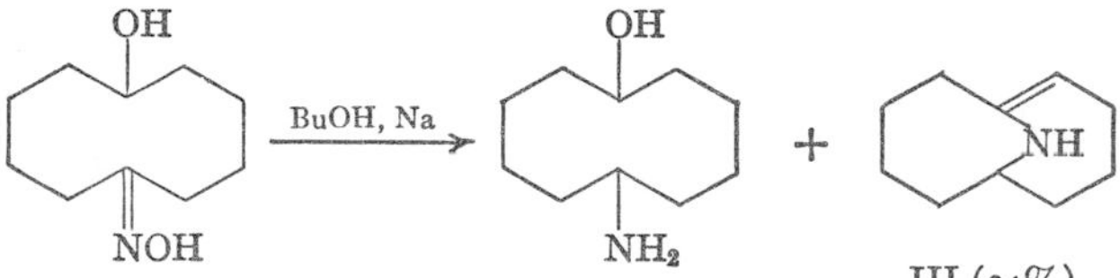

1   II (72%)   III (24%)

in both *cis* and *trans* forms, but was not the exclusive product of either hydrogenation or chemical reduction (sodium–butanol). In the latter case the amine III was obtained in appreciable amounts. Hydrogenation of III established the presence of one double bond and its position was deduced from the appearance in the ultraviolet spectrum of an absorption band at 226 mμ characteristic of a vinylamine (confirmed by infrared absorption). Formation of an alkali-insoluble benzenesulfonamide confirmed the secondary amine character, and Hofmann degradation established the cyclic structure. Formation of III is considered due to the spatial proximity of the two functional groups in I. Transannular participation of the double bond in carbonium ion reactions of the ester IV (p-nitrobenzoate of $trans$-Δ^5-cyclodecene-1-ol) is manifest in greatly enhanced reactivity and in the formation of bicyclic products (Goering,[1] 1960). Solvolysis in 90% acetone

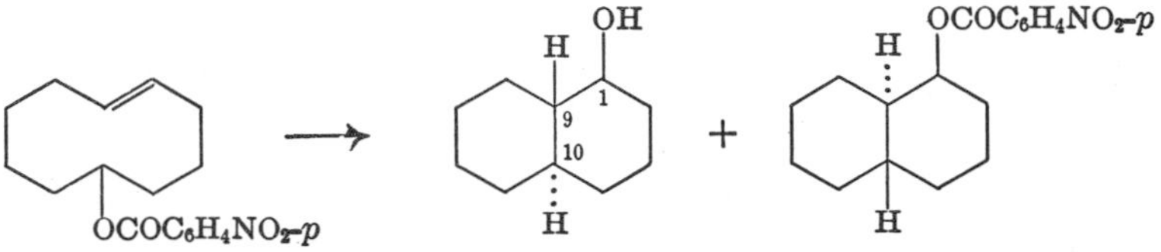

IV   V   VI

at 120° gives mainly $trans$-decalol-1β, of stereochemistry established by Dauben (1954), accompanied by the product of intramolecular rearrangement, VI.

15.33   Lactones and Lactams. — Huisgen (1951–56) noted that in an ordinary ester resonance with a limiting dipolar ion structure imparts partial double-bond character to the C—O bond, which flattens the carboxylate group and makes possible the existence of cis and $trans$ forms. The $trans$ form, since it

cis $trans$

has the lower electrical moment, must be the preferred configuration; hence noncyclic esters are all $trans$ compounds. The five-membered ring of γ-butyrolactone

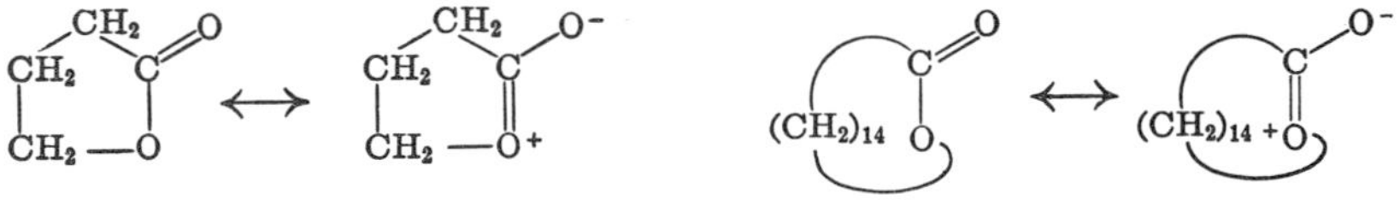

γ-Butyrolactone   Exaltolide
cis $trans$

forces the substance to assume the energy-rich cis configuration, and in consequence the rate of saponification is 10^4 higher than that for open-chain esters. Higher lactones, for example exaltolide, can assume the more stable $trans$ configuration.

[1] Harlan L. Goering, b. 1921 McPherran, Kans.; Ph.D. Colorado (Cristol); Univ. Wisconsin
[2] William G. Dauben, b. 1919 Columbus, Ohio; Ph.D. Harvard (Linstead); Univ. Calif., Berkeley

The C—N bond of an amide also has partial double-bond character and gives rise to *cis* and *trans* structures recognizable by measurement of the dielectric constant in benzene solution over a range of concentration. A *cis*-lactam, like an open-chain amide, forms a hydrogen-bonded dimer in which the two electrical moments (arrows) are balanced; increasing the concentration increases association

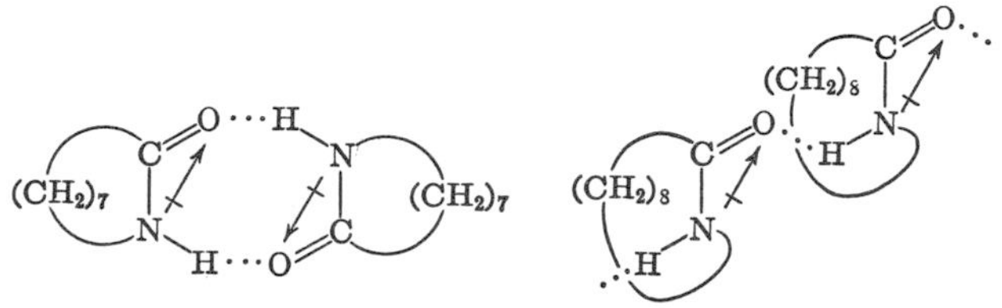

cis-Lactam   *trans*-Lactam

and hence is attended with a sharp decrease in dielectric constant. A *trans*-lactam, however, can form only a chain aggregate in which the electrical moments are additive, and hence the dielectric constant in benzene solution increases with increasing concentration. The C_9 and lower lactams were found to be *cis*; those having rings of 10–19 members are *trans*.

When dissolved in an organic solvent, a nitrosolactam undergoes spontaneous decomposition with liberation of nitrogen, and investigations of Huisgen (1949–51) and of DeTar[1] (1951) have shown that the rate-controlling step is acyl migration through a cyclic transition state to a diazoester which, in a more rapid reaction

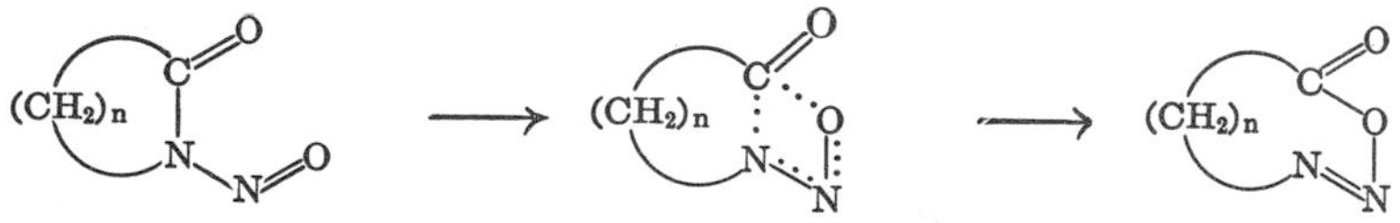

Nitrosolactam   Diazoester

decomposes to nitrogen and a polyester. Reaction rates (Table 15.13; Huisgen) increase as the *cis* ring reaches medium size (n = 7; 9-membered ring), and then fall off (n = 8, 9) to the level characteristic of open-chain analogs (*trans*).

TABLE 15.13. RATE ISOMERIZATION OF NITROSOLACTAMS

n	$k_{40°}10^7$ sec^{-1}	n	$k_{40°}10^7$ sec^{-1}
3	0.0003	7	57,500
4	0.65	8	443
5	1,540	9	157
6	24,200		

15.34   Oxide Ring Size and Stability. — The behavior of sugar acids shows that where a choice is open a five-membered γ-lactone ring is formed in preference to a six-membered ring. On the other hand, D-glucose reacts with

[1] DeLos F. DeTar, b. 1920 Kansas City; Ph.D. Pennsylvania (Carmack); Univ. South Carolina

methanol under acid catalysis to form the cyclic derivative β-methyl D-glucoside, in which the ring is six-membered rather than five-membered. Other sugars react in the same way to form ether derivatives described as pyranosides (6-ring), in

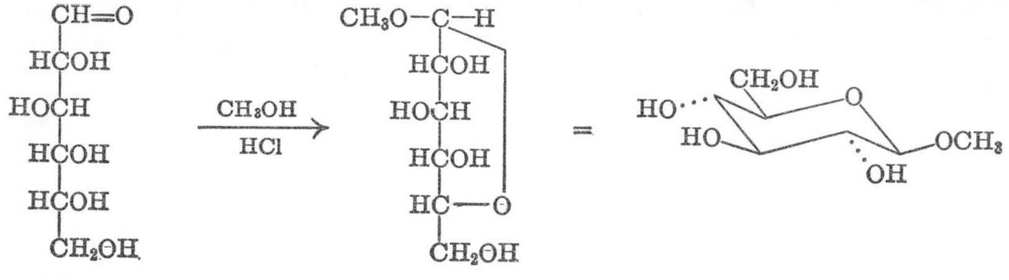

D-Glucose   β-Methyl-D-glucoside

contradistinction to the less stable five-membered furanosides, some of which occur in nature. Many alcohols and phenols occur in nature as derivatives of cyclized glucose and are called glucosides; the generic name is glycoside.

Why do sugar acids preferentially form five-membered lactone rings whereas sugars form six-membered oxides? Since six-membered carbocyclic rings are more stable than five-membered ones, the anomaly appears to lie with the lactones. A possible explanation is as follows. The nearly planar ring of a γ-lactone permits resonance stabilization (1), whereas a δ-lactone must assume either the chair con-

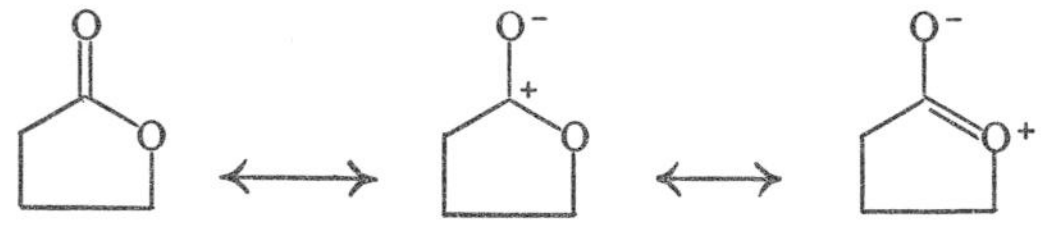

formation (2), in which the —O—C=O system is nonplanar and not comparably stabilized, or the boat form (3), which permits resonance but which is destabilized

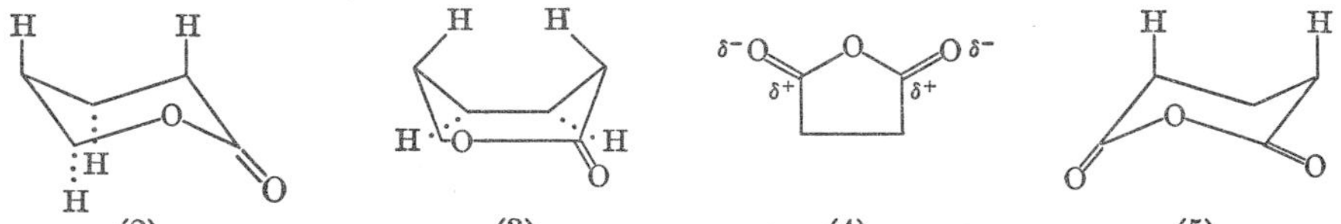

(2)   (3)   (4)   (5)

by two severe H:H interactions. In a cyclic anhydride of any size, the ring oxygen is restricted from acceptance of a positive charge by the adjacent polarized carbonyl group. The observed greater rate of cyclization of glutaric over succinic acid (15.20) is attributable to a difference in steric strain: two H:H interactions in (4) at a distance of 2.3 Å, over one in (5) at a distance of 2.5 Å.

RING FORMATION IN HORMONE SYNTHESIS

15.35   **Cortisone.** — Of no less than 43 steroids isolated from adrenal cortical glands, the most important are the hormones cortisone, an 11-ketone, and cortisol, the corresponding 11β-alcohol. These substances were isolated in the period 1936–43 by the research groups of T. Reichstein,[1] E. C. Kendall, and O.

---

[1] Tadeus Reichstein, b. 1897 Wloclawek, Poland; Ph.D. ETH Zurich (Staudinger); ETH Zurich; Univ. Basel; Nobel Prize 1950

Wintersteiner.[1] The amounts obtainable were extremely small: 85–200 mg. of cortisone and 34–37 mg. of cortisol from 1000 lbs. of beef adrenal glands. Micro-techniques of degradation and characterization led to elucidation of structure and stereochemistry. Preliminary bioassays with the tiny supplies available indicated physiological activities of various types without revealing any promising applica-tion of the hormones in therapy. In 1942 a group of cooperating American labora-tories under sponsorship of the National Research Council initiated research with the objective of finding a method for the synthesis of enough cortisone for adequate exploration of its possible application to medicine. Eventually a route was found. Desoxycholic acid from ox bile was converted, via a novel $3\alpha,9\alpha$-oxide discovered by Kendall, in a total of 32 steps into a product identical with natural cortisone. The process requires transposition of the oxygen function from C_{12} to C_{11}, degrada-

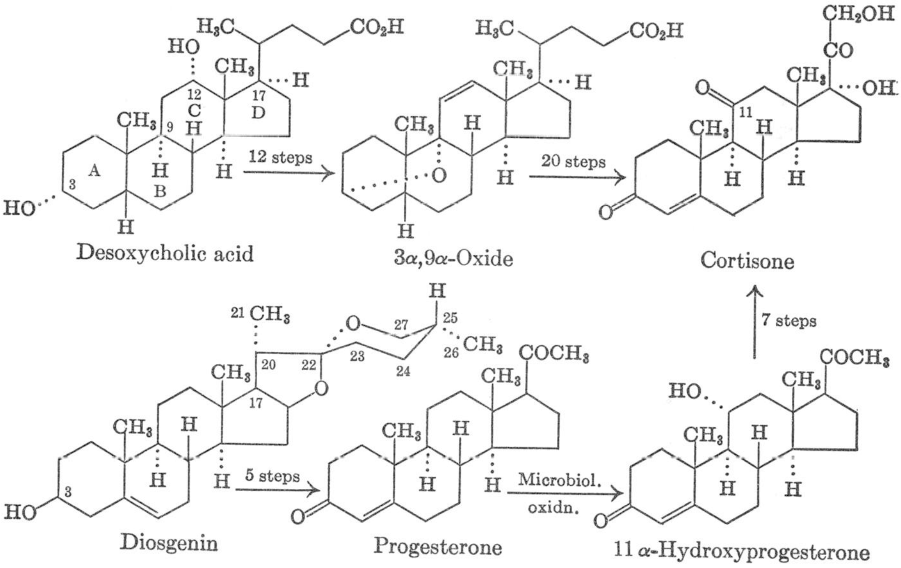

Desoxycholic acid $3\alpha,9\alpha$-Oxide   Cortisone

Diosgenin   Progesterone   11 α-Hydroxyprogesterone

tion of the side chain, introduction of a 17α-hydroxyl group, and construction of the α,β-unsaturated keto function in ring A. Some of the steps in the American process were improved by modifications introduced by Reichstein's group and by workers at the firm Ciba in Basel. In 1946 a small development team at Merck and Co. undertook the laboratory production of cortisone. Over a three year period they processed a total of 1,270 lbs. of desoxycholic acid. The work was constantly spurred by the enthusiasm and experimentation of Kendall at the Mayo Clinic, who had been the first to isolate cortisone. Thanks to a number of im-provements, the total cortisone acetate produced was 938 g., about ten times the amount originally expected.

Early clinicians had noticed that women suffering from rheumatoid arthritis are frequently relieved of symptoms during pregnancy. Rheumatologist Philip S.

[1] Oskar Wintersteiner, b. 1898 Bruck, Austria; Ph.D. Graz (Pregl); College Phys. and Surg., Columbia Univ.; Squibb Inst. Med. Res.

Hench of the Mayo Clinic noted in 1929 that rheumatic patients sometimes also are relieved by an attack of jaundice. Since the steroid hormone progesterone was known to exert a favorable control over pregnancy but to be without influence on arthritis, Hench speculated that during pregnancy and jaundice some other steroid hormone capable of controlling arthritis is released into the blood stream. Cortisone was an obvious choice for trial. The first material for clinical use reached the Mayo Clinic in May 1948. In April 1949 Hench and Kendall announced dramatic success in the control of rheumatoid arthritis with cortisone.

Even before the public announcement, Merck undertook the unprecedented task of adapting to large-scale production a multistep process utilizing expensive reagents (OsO_4, NBS, O_3, C_6H_5MgBr, 2,4-dinitrophenylhydrazine, and semicarbazide), reactions requiring critical control, and a sensitive final product. Nevertheless, cortisone was offered to physicians in limited amounts late in 1949 at $200/g. Steady improvements in the process reduced the price to $10/g. in 1951.

In 1952 the Upjohn Co. announced a surprising new route to the cortical hormones. Having set out with the deliberate objective of finding a soil microorganism capable of hydroxylating a steroid at position 11, a group headed by D. H. Peterson found that a culture of *Rhizopus arrhizus* isolated from Kalamazoo air on exposure of an agar plate on a window sill converts progesterone to 11α-hydroxyprogesterone in 50% yield. With other microorganisms yields up to 90% have been achieved. In a subsequent surge of investigation in several laboratories, hydroxylation at a total of 17 positions has been realized. 11α-Hydroxyprogesterone is convertible into cortisone in seven synthetic steps. Furthermore, the pregnancy hormone progesterone had become available from diosgenin. This steroid sapogenin had been isolated by T. Tsukamoto in 1936 from a Japanese *Dioscorea*, and in 1940 Russell E. Marker, then at Pennsylvania State College, applied to material of Japanese origin a general method for side-chain degradation and obtained progesterone in overall yield later raised to over 60%. Marker then launched a series of botanical collection trips in Southern United States and Mexico, discovered twelve new sapogenins, and found a Mexican *Dioscorea* known as *cabeza de negro* to be very rich in diosgenin. Marker then transferred to Mexico City (1944), joined with others to establish the firm Syntex, and within a year Syntex was offering progesterone at a price of $80/g. Marker shortly broke off his connection with the firm, but Syntex flourished and eventually became a powerful factor in the pharmaceutical field. The toxic saponin of a *Dioscorea* used by Mexican Indians as a fish poison was identified as a diosgenin glycoside (1949) and found to yield 3–10 times as much diosgenin as *cabeza de negro*. A richer source, coupled with process improvements, had cut the price of progesterone as a sex hormone to $1.75/g. When Upjohn sought a manufacturer capable of supplying the hormone in the ton quantities required for production of cortisone, Syntex accepted the challenge and was able to offer progesterone as an intermediate at $0.48/g. (later about $0.19/g.). The lengthy bile acid process evidently had been perfected to so high a degree that it was not dislodged by the Upjohn process; indeed it has been operated not only by Merck but also by Schering-New Jersey and by Roussel-Uclaf in Paris. The lively competition, however, reduced the price of cortisone to about \$3.50/g.　Ten years after the initial production of cortisone, U. S. production of corticoid drugs reached a sales volume of about \$100 million per year.

These partial syntheses utilize starting materials having the preformed tetra-cyclic steroid structure and the correct stereochemistry at all the asymmetric centers.　A total synthesis, however, requires the forming of some or all of the rings, control of the steric course of each reaction used, and a resolution, preferably at an early stage in the process.　Several ingenious methods of building on rings were employed in three syntheses of cortisone.　The first was reported by R. B. Woodward[1] and co-workers in 1951.　In the first step addition of butadiene to 4-methoxy-2,5-toluquinone (1) gave the *cis* adduct (2), which could be isomerized through the enolate to the *trans* isomer (3).　Reduction with lithium aluminum

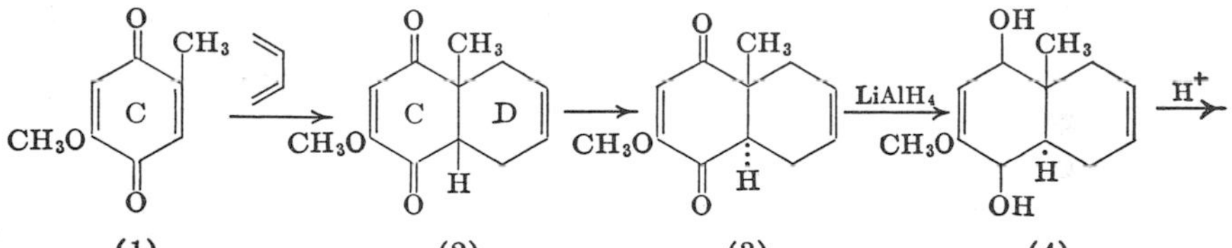

(1)　　　　(2)　　　　(3)　　　　(4)

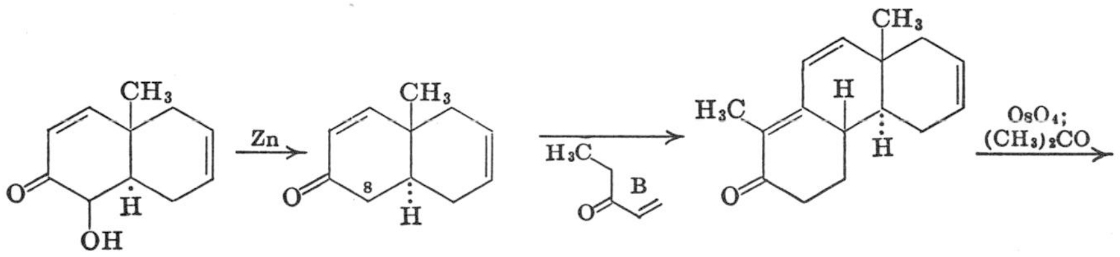

(5)　　　　(6)　　　　(7)

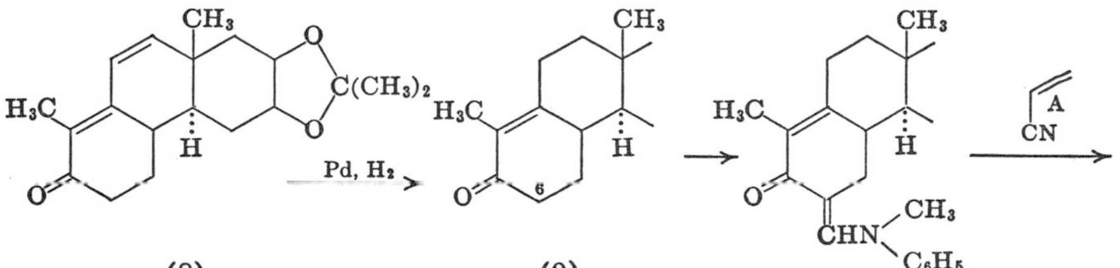

(8)　　　　(9)　　　　(10)

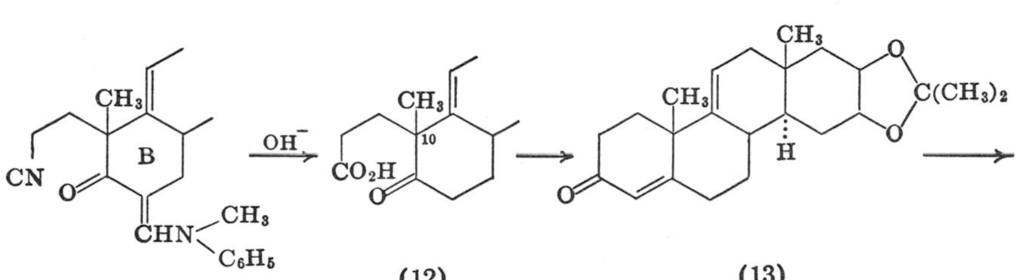

(11)　　(12)　　　　(13)

[1] Robert B. Woodward, b. 1917 Boston: Ph.D. Mass. Inst. Techn.; Harvard Univ.

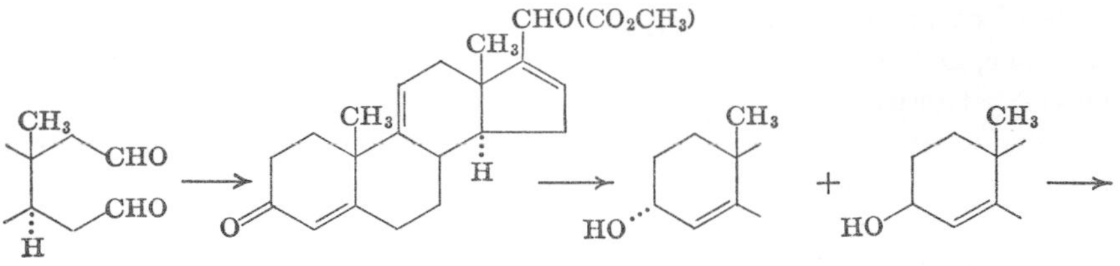

(14)   (15) dl   (16)   (17) d

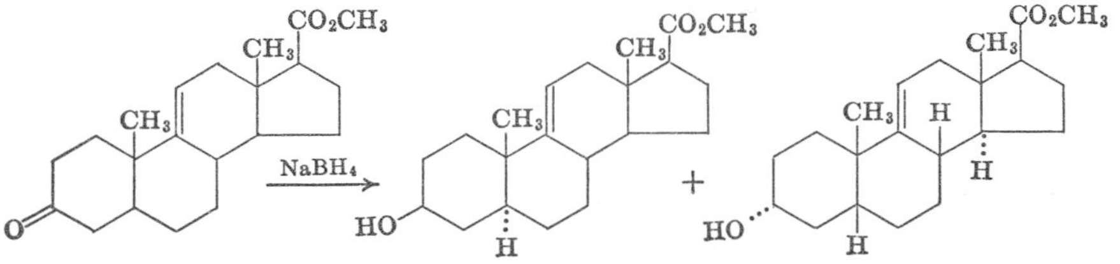

(18) 5α and 5β   (19)   (20)

hydride gave the glycol enol methyl ether (4), and the β-hydroxyketone liberated on acid hydrolysis lost water and gave the ketol (5). Reduction of the ketol acetate with zinc in boiling xylene or acetic anhydride eliminated the α-acetoxyl group to give the bicyclic ketone (6). Ring B was then added by a procedure developed by C. H. Shunk and A. L. Wilds: formylation at C_8 (sterol numbering), addition to ethyl vinyl ketone, and treatment with potassium hydroxide in dioxane to close the ring, with elimination of the formyl group and formation in good yield of a single tricyclic ketone (7), of the correct stereochemistry. The double bond in potential ring D was then protected by hydroxylation with osmium tetroxide and conversion of the more abundant of two cis glycols formed to the acetonide (8) and the γ,δ-double bond was reduced by selective hydrogenation (9). Position 6 was then blocked with a methylanilinomethylene group, and the product (10) was condensed with acrylonitrile in the presence of Triton B to form the nitrile (11). Alkaline hydrolysis of the nitrile group also removed the blocking group and gave the keto acid (12) and its C_{10}-epimer. The keto acid (12) was then converted into the $Δ^4$-3-ketone (13) by conversion to the enol lactone, reaction with methylmagnesium iodide, and cyclization (method of R. B. Turner). Ring D was then contracted by acid hydrolysis of the acetonide (13) to the cis glycol, periodic oxidation to the dialdehyde (14), and cyclization under catalysis by piperidine acetate to the unsaturated aldehyde (15), converted by oxidation and esterification into the corresponding etio ester. Resolution of this dl-ester was accomplished by a method developed by Windaus[1] and based upon his discovery (1909) that 3β-hydroxy steroids usually are precipitated from 90% ethanol by the steroid saponin digitonin, whereas the 3α-epimers are not. Borohydride reduction of the unsaturated keto ester gave a mixture of 3α- and 3β-hydroxy esters from which digitonin precipitated selectively the dextrorotatory form of the 3β-alcohol (17), and after

[1] Adolf Windaus, 1876–1959; b. Berlin; Ph.D. Freiburg (Kiliani); Univ. Freiburg, Innsbruck, Göttingen

two repetitions the substance was obtained in pure form.   After reoxidation of the optically active product at C_3, hydrogenation saturated the 4,5- and 16,17-double bonds and gave a mixture of the 5α- and 5β-Δ$^{9(11)}$-keto esters (18).   Borohydride reduction then gave a mixture of the two equatorial alcohols, the 5α-3β-ol (19) and the 5β-3α-ol (20).   The mixture was easily separated by precipitation of (19) with digitonin, and acetylation of the nonprecipitated isomer afforded the known methyl 3α-acetoxy-Δ$^{9(11)}$-etienate.   Since this ester had been converted to cortisone in a series of steps described in the literature, the work cited completed a synthesis of cortisone.   This formal total synthesis was extended to a total synthesis of the hormone by the Monsanto group of L. B. Barkley *et al.* (1954).

A total synthesis of cortisone reported in 1952 by a Merck group headed by L. H. Sarett[1] is noteworthy for the high degree of stereospecificity in each step. The *cis* adduct (1) from benzoquinone and 3-ethoxypentadiene-1,3 carries an oxygen atom at future position 11 and a future methyl group at C_{10}.   Selective hydrogenation (Ni) saturated the double bond flanked by two keto groups, and lithium aluminum hydride reduction gave a single diol (2).   After acid hydrolysis to produce the ketone (3), ring A was added by condensation with methyl vinyl ketone in the presence of Triton B; attack from the less hindered rear side leads to the β-orientation of the angular methyl group in the product (4).   The unsaturated ketone system was then converted into the 3-ethyleneketal and the protective group was kept in place until the terminal step of the synthesis.   Oppenauer oxidation of this derivative selectively attacked the less hindered 14-hydroxyl group and effected isomerization at C_8 to give the more stable *trans* ring fusion. Methylation (CH_3I, *t*-BuOK) at C_{13} gave a single stereoisomer, regarded as the equatorial 13α-methyl derivative (5).

A novel scheme for introduction of a carbon chain to provide C_{17}, C_{20}, and C_{21} involved alkylation of (5) at C_{13} with methallyl iodide (*t*-BuOK) to produce (6), the stable form of which is that with the smaller of two groups at C_{13} axial (β) to the axial (β) hydroxyl at C_{11}.   Since the 11β-hydroxyl group would be eliminated in a later step (8–9), it was oxidized at this point prior to addition of ethoxyacetyl-

(1)   (2)

(3)   (4)   (5)

[1] Lewis H. Sarett, b. 1917 Champaign, Ill.; Ph.D. Princeton (Wallis); Merck, Sharp and Dohme Co.

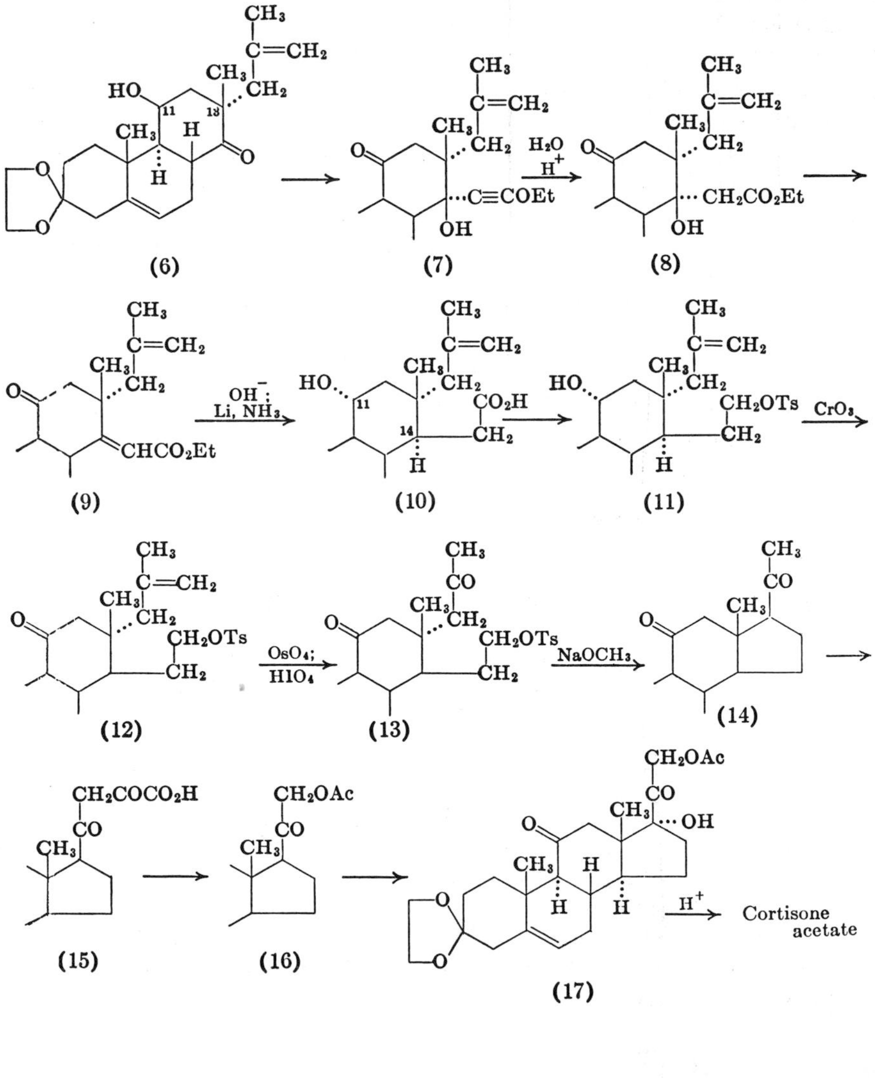

enemagnesium bromide to the 14-keto group to produce the ethoxyethynyl-carbinol (7). Acid-catalyzed rearrangement of this substance, conducted under very mild conditions in order to preserve the protective group in ring A, gave the unsaturated ester (9). Reduction of the free acid with lithium in ammonia saturated the $\Delta^{\alpha, \beta}$-double bond and also afforded the 11α-ol (equatorial), to give (10), of correct configuration at C_{14} (if the 11-hydroxyl is β the course of reduction is reversed). Ring closure was then effected by reduction of the ester of (10) with lithium aluminum hydride, selective tosylation of the primary alcoholic function (11), oxidation (CrO₃–Py) to the 11-ketone (12), conversion of the methylene group to carbonyl (13) by successive treatment with osmium tetroxide and periodic acid, and finally treatment with one mole of sodium methoxide to produce the 3-ketal of dl-11-ketoprogesterone (14). The infrared spectrum was identical with that of the corresponding derivative of natural progesterone. The method selected for introduction of the 21-acetoxyl group involved condensation with diethyl oxalate, iodination, saponification, and reaction with potassium acetate:

$$RCOCH_3 \rightarrow RCOCH_2COCO_2Et \rightarrow RCOCHICOCO_2Et \rightarrow RCOCH_2I \rightarrow RCOCH_2OAc$$

This proved convenient because the free oxalyl derivative (15) could be resolved by crystallization of the strychnine salts. The *d*-acid was then treated with iodine and then potassium acetate to produce the ketol acetate (16). The 20-cyanohydrin was formed by reaction with hydrogen cyanide and triethylamine in ethylene dichloride–ether solution and dehydrated to the 20-cyano-17,20-ene. Selective hydroxylation was achieved by permanganate oxidation in acetone to produce cortisone 3-ketal acetate (17). Acid hydrolysis then afforded cortisone acetate.

Neither of the two total syntheses described proved suitable for commercial production. The practical value of a synthesis announced in 1960 is yet to be determined. This synthesis was achieved by the group of Léon Velluz of the firm Roussel-Uclaf in Paris. It has the novelty of providing routes not only to cortisone but to estrogenic female sex hormones and to a group of steroids which lack the angular methyl group at C_{10} containing carbon atom 19 and which are called 19-norsteroids. Norprogesterone has eight times the potency of natural progesterone; products derived from nortestosterone are useful as anabolic agents. These products are all derived from a common intermediate, the tricyclic nor-compound (10). The synthesis of (10) was accomplished largely by a combination of methods introduced by W. E. Bachmann, W. S. Johnson, D. K. Banerjee, and, particularly, by G. Stork (construction of ring A, 1956). 6-Methoxy-1-tetralone (1) is converted in succession into the formyl derivative (CHCH=O), its oxime (CHCH=NOH), and the corresponding nitrile derived by dehydration (CHC≡N), which is then methylated to the ketonitrile (2). Stobbe condensation with diethyl succinate affords the tricyclic ester (3) in overall yield from (1) of 50%. This substance has only one center of asymmetry (C_{13}) and, since the ring system containing nine trigonal carbon atoms is essentially planar, the β-an-

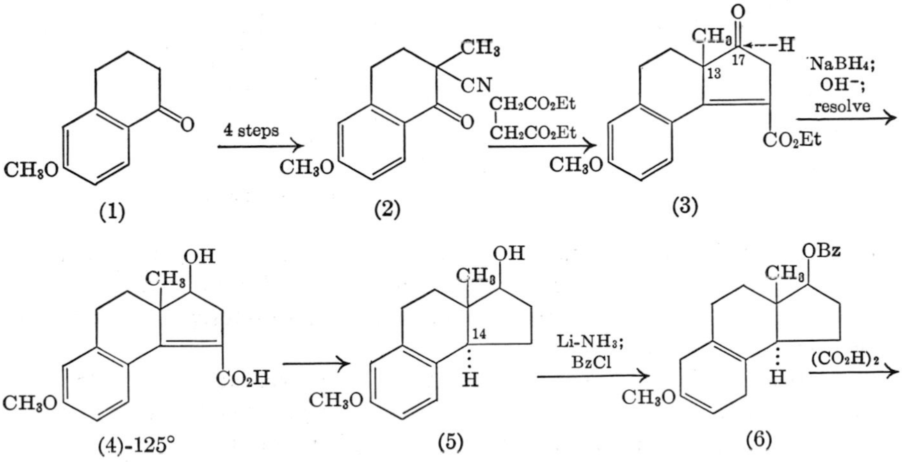

(1)   (2)   (3)

(4)-125°   (5)   (6)

gular methyl group projecting in front of this plane controls borohydride reduction to rear attack. After saponification, the unsaturated acid is resolved with optically active chloramphenicol base, and the levorotatory isomer (4) is decarboxylated (ethanolic HCl) and the product is hydrogenated stereospecifically to (5, 14α-H). Birch reduction of the aromatic ring and benzoylation then affords the dienol methyl ether (6). On hydrolysis of (6) with 10% methanolic hydrogen chloride the double bond moves into conjugation with the carbonyl group, but on hydrolysis with 3% oxalic acid in 90% ethanol the product is the nonconjugated ketone (7). This ketone is alkylated at the reactive 10-position by reaction with 1,3-dichlorobutene-2 to form the nonconjugated ketone (8), which is isomerized easily under acid catalysis to the conjugated ketone (9), in which the hydrogen atom at C$_8$ assumes the desired β-orientation. Hydrolysis of the vinyl chloride group of (9) then leads to the tricyclic nor-compound (10). Hydrogenation proceeds by rear attack to give the product (11), in which the hydrogen atom at C$_{10}$

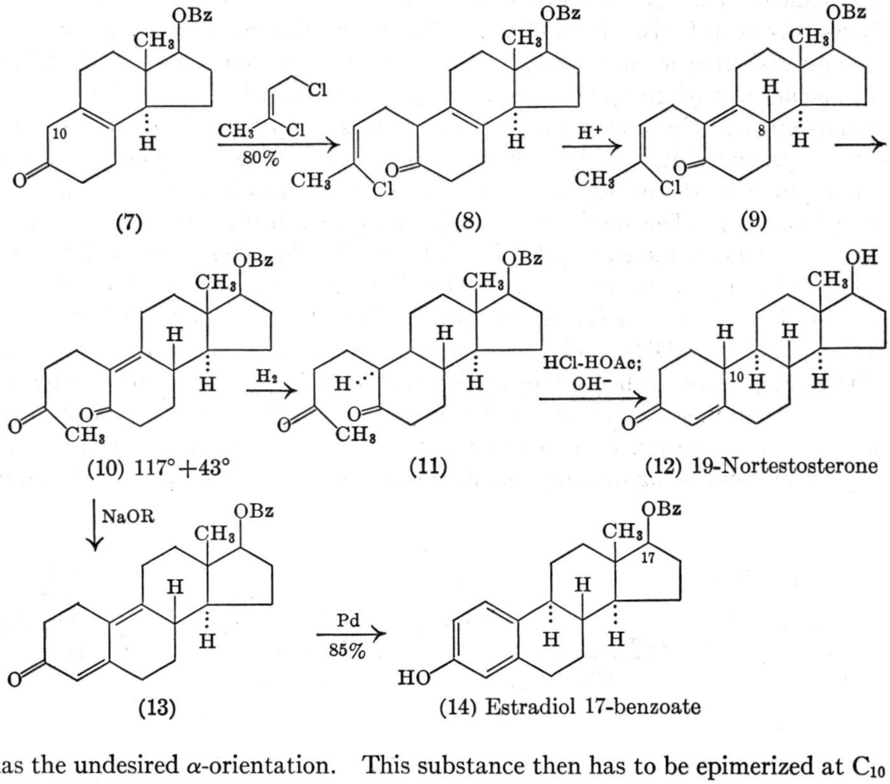

(7)   (8)   (9)

(10) 117°+43°   (11)   (12) 19-Nortestosterone

(13)   (14) Estradiol 17-benzoate

has the undesired α-orientation. This substance then has to be epimerized at C$_{10}$ and cyclized by aldolization. In a mixture of acetic and hydrochloric acid epimerization at C$_{10}$ precedes cyclization and the product is exclusively 19-nortestosterone benzoate (yield 95%).

Aromatization of ring A is accomplished easily by cyclization of the tricyclic nor-compound (10) with the sodio derivative of t-amyl alcohol to (13) and isomerization with palladium catalyst to estradiol 17-benzoate (14).

For production of cortisone, the future 3-keto group of the tricyclic nor-compound is first protected by conversion to the dioxolane (15). Methylation at C_{10} is attended by migration of the double bond to the 9,11-position to give (16). Acidic hydrolysis eliminates the protective group at C_3, treatment with alkali closes ring A by aldolization and removes the benzoate group, and oxidation at C_{17} affords the doubly unsaturated diketone (17). Addition of hypobromous acid to the 9,11-double bond (18), oxidation at C_{11}, and reductive removal of the 9α-

(15) (16) (17)

(18) (19) Adrenosterone (20)

(21, 22) (23) Cortisone acetate

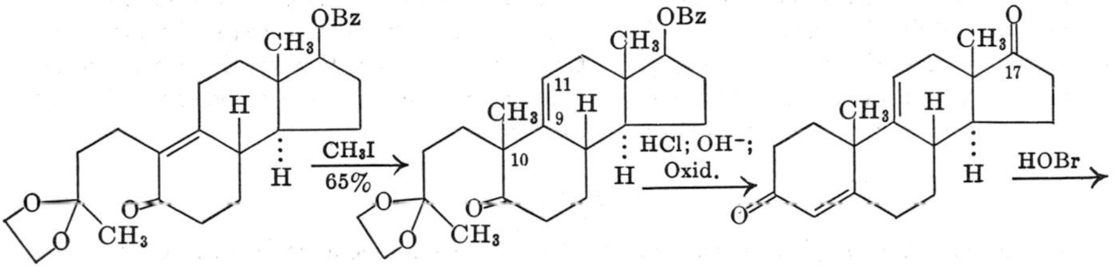

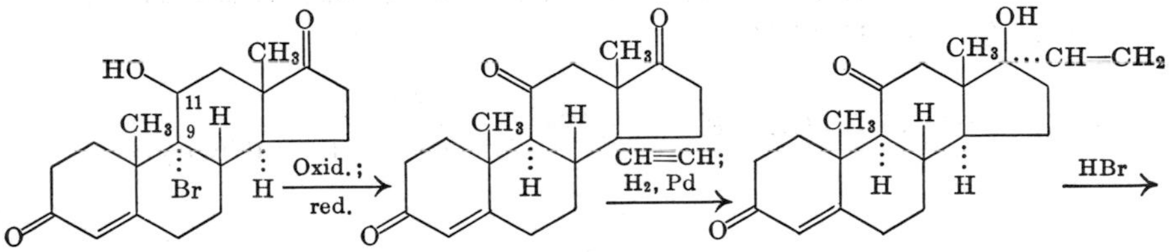

bromine atom leads to adrenosterone (19), which is convertible into cortisone acetate (23) by known methods: ethynylation at C_{17}, partial reduction to the vinyl carbinol (20), reaction with hydrogen bromide with allylic rearrangement to the primary bromide (21), conversion to the corresponding *trans* acetate (22), and oxidative hydroxylation.

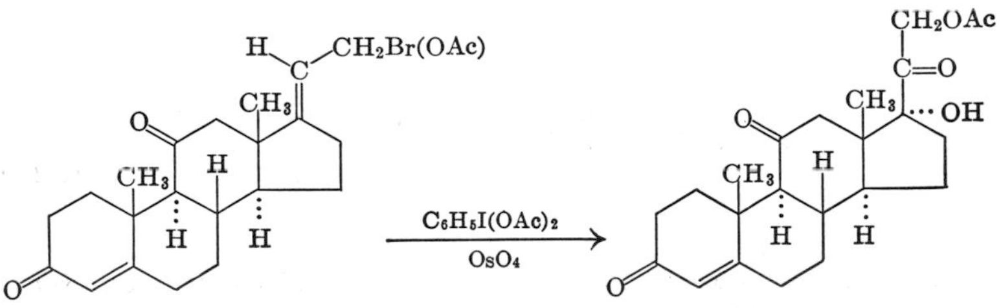

PROBLEMS

1. Cite experimental tests that would distinguish between the following isomers of the formula C_5H_{10}: pentene-2, 1,2-dimethylcyclopropane, and cyclopentane.
2. Explain why optically active muscone yields an optically inactive hydrocarbon on reduction of the carbonyl group to a methylene group.
3. Formulate a synthesis of *cis*-cyclohexane-1,2-dicarboxylic acid.
4. Summarize reactions cited in earlier chapters in which a carbene is postulated as an intermediate.

5. Formulate the five stereoisomeric truxillic acids. Which one lacks a plane of symmetry but is superposable on its mirror image?

6. Glutaric acid can be prepared in 48% overall yield by a series of reactions starting with the condensation of formaldehyde with diethyl malonate in the presence of diethylamine to $CH_2[CH(COOC_2H_5)_2]_2$. Formulate the process.

7. (a) Explain the formation of malonic acid by the action of water on carbon suboxide. (b) What product would you expect to result from treatment of carbon suboxide with ammonia?

8. From the separation distances shown in the chart of section 15.12 and the energy equivalents of Table 15.5, calculate the difference in H:H repulsive strain in *cis*- and *trans*-decalin. Compare your result with the difference of 2.1 kcal./mole calculated from heats of combustion.

9. From inspection of a model make a qualitative estimate of the effect on the relative stability of *cis*- and *trans*-decalin of replacement of the 9β-hydrogen by a methyl group. Would the energy difference be greater or smaller than before?

Notes

To page 542.—On applying the Simmons-Smith synthesis to the allene I, E. F. Ullman (1961) isolated II as the initial product and then the spiropentane III. Pyrolysis of II at 250° gave IV. The structure followed from analogy to that assigned (Ullman, 1959–60) to a long known product of rearrangement of the Feist ester.

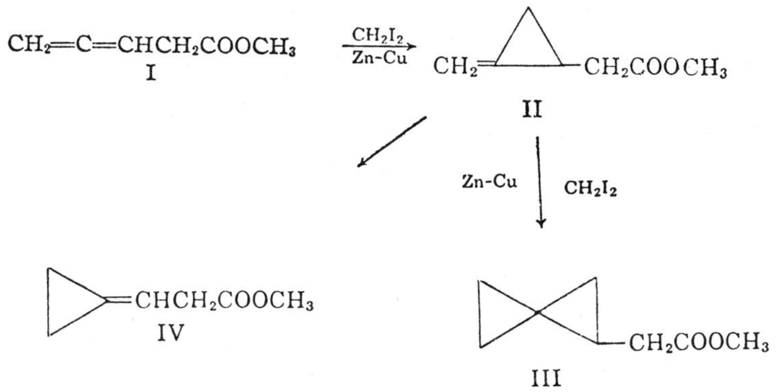

$$CH_2=C=CHCH_2COOCH_3 \qquad \xrightarrow[\text{Zn-Cu}]{CH_2I_2}$$
$$\text{I}$$

II

Zn-Cu | CH_2I_2

IV

III

To page 568.—A new route to diacids described by S. Hünig (1959, *Org. Syn.*, 1961) involves condensation of cyclohexanone with morpholine and acylation of the enamine with sebacic acid dichloride. Acid hydrolysis to remove the enamine group, ring fission, and reduction with hydrazine and alkali in triethanolamine affords ω,ω-docosanedicarboxylic acid. Use of triethanolamine in the Huang-Minlon procedure was introduced by P. D. Gardner (1956) in a neat synthesis of pimelic acid from furfural via furylacrylic acid and γ-ketopimelic acid.

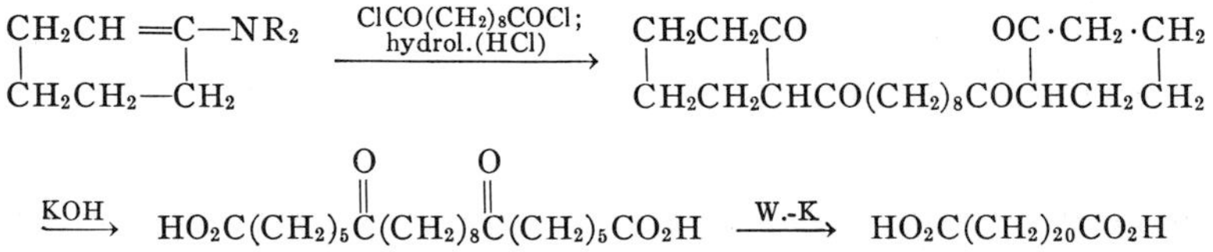

$$\xrightarrow{KOH} \quad HO_2C(CH_2)_5\overset{O}{\overset{\|}{C}}(CH_2)_8\overset{O}{\overset{\|}{C}}(CH_2)_5CO_2H \quad \xrightarrow{W.-K.} \quad HO_2C(CH_2)_{20}CO_2H$$

Chapter 16

HISTORY OF THE BENZENE PROBLEM

16.1   **Discovery of Benzene.** — The earliest known derivatives of benzene
were fragrant substances derived from balsams, resins, and essential
oils.   Because of their aroma and because they seemed differentiated from aliphatic compounds by a low hydrogen content and an apparently saturated
character, they became known as aromatic compounds.   The group included
benzoic acid ($C_7H_6O_2$) and benzyl alcohol (C_7H_8O), from gum benzoin; benzaldehyde (C_7H_6O) from oil of bitter almonds, oxidizable to benzoic acid; toluene
(C_7H_8) from tolu balsam, similarly correlated with benzoic acid; salicylic acid
($C_7H_6O_3$), from many plants and fruits and correlated with phenol (C_6H_5OH).
Kekulé was the first to recognize that these compounds all contain a C_6-unit
which is retained through usual chemical transformations and degradations.
The parent hydrocarbon benzene was discovered in 1825 by Michael Faraday,
who isolated the substance from an oily condensate deposited from compressed
illuminating gas.   He established that it is composed of equal numbers of carbon
and hydrogen atoms and named it carbureted hydrogen.   Mitscherlich (1834)
found that benzoic acid can be converted by dry distillation with lime into an
identical hydrocarbon, which he further characterized by vapor density measurements as having the formula C_6H_6.   As a convenient name indicating the relationship to derivatives designated as benzoic, benzoyl, and benzyl because they
had been obtained from gum benzoin, Mitscherlich coined the German word
benzin, but Liebig, influential editor of the leading chemical journal of the day,
criticized the name as implying a relationship to strychnine and quinine and
recommended a change to benzol, based on oleum, or the German _öl_, oil.   Laurent[1]
(1837) proposed the alternate name pheno from the Greek "I bear light," in
recognition of the discovery of the hydrocarbon in illuminating gas, and this

[1] Auguste Laurent, 1807–53; b. Langres, France; Bordeaux, Paris

gained usage in the form of the name phenyl for the C_6H_5 group though not for the hydrocarbon itself. The name benzol soon became established in the German literature, but in England and France the ending eventually was changed to -ene to avoid confusion with the systematic designation of alcohols. The German literature still employs the names benzol, toluol, xylol, whereas benzene, toluene, and xylene are employed in English and French literature.

Hofmann's first research in Germany (Giessen, 1843) was on aniline, a substance so named by Fritsche, who obtained it as a product of the fusion of indigo with potassium hydroxide. Three other names had been given to preparations made by mere heating of indigo (Unverdorben), from coal tar oil by nitration and reduction (Runge), and from Mitscherlich's benzene from benzoic acid, via nitrobenzene (Zinin). Hofmann showed that these preparations were all the same compound and elected to use Fritsche's name aniline. At that time organic chemistry was little known in England and English students migrated to the laboratory of Liebig at Giessen or to that of Wöhler at Göttingen. However, a tour of England by the illustrious Baron von Liebig so stimulated interest in the science that, at the suggestion of German-born Prince Consort Albert and on recommendation of Liebig, Hofmann (age 27) was called to London in 1845 to establish research and teaching at the Royal College of Chemistry. With a steadily increasing group of students, Hofmann extended in several directions his earlier investigations of aniline, practically all of which was procured by the laborious and costly process of distilling indigo with potash. Having shown that benzene must exist in coal tar by the preparation of aniline from this source, Hofmann (1845) encouraged his pupil Charles Mansfield in a successful attempt to isolate benzene from coal tar. Having available for fractional distillation only crudely fashioned glass retorts with the thermometer in the liquid, Mansfield isolated substantially pure benzene, toluene, and pseudocumene (1,2,4-trimethylbenzene).

16.2   Perkin's Mauve. — Coal tar, available as a by-product of the manufacture of coal gas, was subsequently recognized as an abundant source of naphthalene, anthracene, and a shower of other aromatics, and development of the coal tar industry gained momentum from a discovery by another of Hofmann's students, William Henry Perkin. Perkin worked on a succession of problems assigned to him by Hofmann, but in evenings and on holidays he worked on projects of his own at home in an improvised laboratory. A paper by Hofmann suggesting the possibility of the artificial formation of the alkaloid quinine stimulated Perkin to devise the plan of effecting this synthesis by oxidation of allyltoluidine:

$$2\ C_{10}H_{13}N + 3\ O \xrightarrow{\ ?\ } C_{20}H_{21}O_2N_2 + H_2O$$
$$\text{Allyltoluidine} \qquad\qquad \text{Quinine}$$

The reaction was unpromising, for the product was a dirty reddish-brown precipitate, but Perkin decided to study oxidation of the simpler base aniline (impure). He explored the reaction during the Easter vacation, obtained a black product, and on extraction of this with methanol isolated a small amount of a brightly colored pigment having the properties of a dye. Further work during the summer led to application for a patent for the first synthetic dye, later known as mauve, mauveine, or aniline purple. The discoverer, age 18, against the advice of Hofmann, resigned his assistantship, formed a company with his father and brother, set up a factory, and was soon manufacturing mauve. The new dye, the first rival of natural indigo and alizarin, acquired great popularity and once brought as high a price as platinum. Rival firms sprang up in England and engaged English chemists trained by Hofmann as well as competent German chemists (Caro, Martius, Griess) attracted to the exciting and expanding new field. Hofmann supported the new industry and played a leading part in the scientific study of the new products. Plants were set up for the refining of coal tar and for production of sulfuric acid and alkalis. At the firm of Roberts and Dale in Manchester, Caro discovered a new process for making mauve and, with Martius, introduced the new dyes Manchester Brown and Martius Yellow. Other dyes that appeared at the time included Crysaniline, Rosolic Acid, Spirit Blue, Paeonin, Regina Violet, Methylrosaniline, Aniline Green, Aniline Black, and Diphenylamine Blue.

16.3   **Kekulé Formula** (1865). — The new dyes had been discovered empirically, without knowledge of the structures of natural dyes or of the coal tar products from which the synthetic ones were made, chiefly benzene, toluene, naphthalene, and their amino derivatives. About ten years after Perkin's discovery of mauve, progress of the new industry began to slacken; discoveries based largely upon chance or accident could not continue indefinitely.

A pressing practical need thus lent added importance to the challenging problem of deducing the structure of benzene. The problem was perplexing because the formula C_6H_6 indicated the same degree of unsaturation as in acetylene, C_2H_2, and yet benzene does not display the reactivity characteristic of unsaturated aliphatic compounds. Whereas alkenes are oxidized rapidly by cold alkaline permanganate, add bromine or sulfuric acid at $0°$, and are oxidized by nitric acid, benzene does not react appreciably with these reagents under comparable conditions. Benzene does react when heated with bromine and a catalyst, and it

$$C_6H_6 \;+\; Br_2 \;\xrightarrow{\text{FeBr}_3 \text{ catalyst, heat}}\; \underset{\text{Bromobenzene}}{C_6H_5Br} \;+\; HBr$$

$$C_6H_6 \;+\; H_2SO_4 \;\xrightarrow{\text{Heat}}\; \underset{\substack{\text{Benzenesulfonic} \\ \text{acid}}}{C_6H_5SO_3H} \;+\; H_2O$$

$$C_6H_6 \;+\; HNO_3 \;\xrightarrow{\text{Heat}}\; \underset{\text{Nitrobenzene}}{C_6H_5NO_2} \;+\; H_2O$$

reacts with sulfuric acid and with nitric acid on heating, but the products do not result from additions but from substitutions. Since the behavior is different from that of known unsaturated hydrocarbons, the structure was not deducible from analogy.

Kekulé, on realizing that the C_6-unit of benzene recurs in all aromatic compounds, saw another approach to the problem in determination of the number of substitution products.   The fact that propane affords two mono-, four di-, and five trichloro derivatives can be cited as evidence in support of the accepted structure.   From an evaluation of the still fragmentary and partly erroneous data on hand, Kekulé concluded that benzene must have a structure allowing for only a single product of monosubstitution and for three disubstitution products, and saw that these relationships can be accounted for only by a cyclic formula.   A ring of six carbon atoms, each carrying a hydrogen atom, would explain the equivalence of all six possible positions for monosubstitution and account for the existence of three di derivatives.   The possibilities for di- and trisubstitution are shown with outline formulas.   As new compounds were prepared and charac-

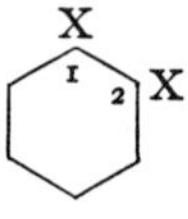

ortho
1,2

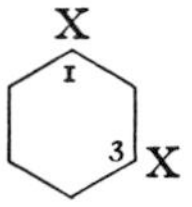

meta
1,3

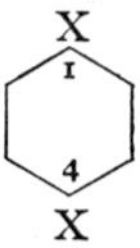

para
1,4

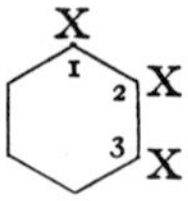

Vicinal (*vic-*)
1,2,3

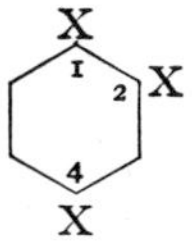

Asymmetrical (*as-*)
1,2,4

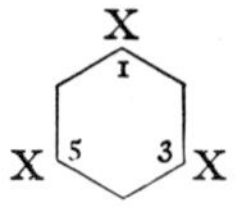

Symmetrical (*s-*)
1,3,5

terized and old ones reinvestigated, abundant evidence soon accumulated that left no doubt of the correctness of this part of Kekulé's theory, for the number of isomers in different series invariably corresponded with the predicted number.

Confirmation of another nature came from correlation of benzene derivatives with compounds of the cyclohexane series.   Baeyer, in a classical investigation of

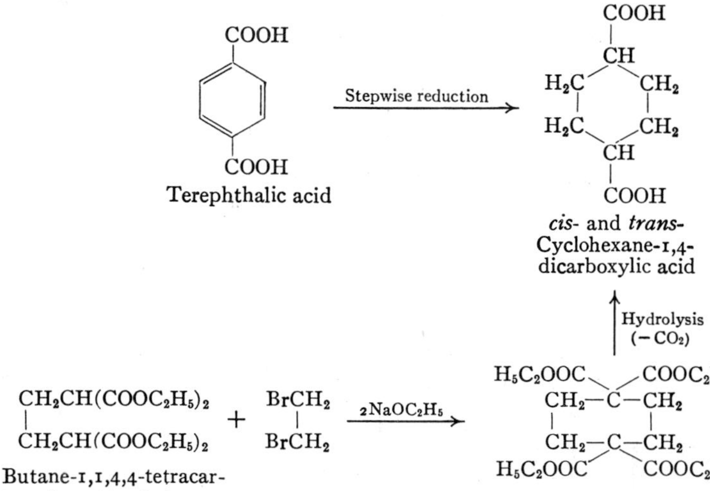

Terephthalic acid

cis- and *trans-*
Cyclohexane-1,4-
dicarboxylic acid

Butane-1,1,4,4-tetracar-
boxylic acid ethyl ester

the reduction of benzenedicarboxylic acids (1887–92), isolated hexahydro derivatives that could be identified by synthesis. The *para* isomer, for example, afforded both the *cis* and *trans* forms of the reduced acid, and these were synthesized by Perkin, Jr. (1892) by an adaptation of the malonic ester synthesis, as formulated. Cyclohexane itself was later obtained by hydrogenation of benzene (Sabatier and Senderens, 1901). Independent evidence came from the field of physics. The interesting substance mellitic acid of the formula $C_6(COOH)_6$, occurring in a mineral found in brown coal, can be converted into and obtained from known derivatives of benzene, and it also can be produced by oxidation of graphite or amorphous carbon with nitric acid. X-ray crystallographic analysis (Debye and Scherrer, 1917) established that graphite is made up of a series of interconnected honeycombs of six-membered carbon rings (in graphite the rings appear to be planar, whereas the diamond molecule contains puckered rings (15.10). Since graphite is correlated with benzene, benzene must have a six-membered ring structure. Later direct X-ray analysis of hexamethylbenzene (Bragg, Lonsdale, 1922–29) not only confirmed the presence of a ring but established the interatomic distances in the molecule.

16.4   Orientation of Substituents. — The early work of testing the postulated ring structure by chemical methods included development of proof of the symmetry of benzene through establishment of the equivalence of the six positions. For example, Ladenburg[1] (1876) succeeded in interconverting benzoic acid (C_6H_5COOH) and phenol (C_6H_5OH), and in transforming all three hydroxybenzoic acids into benzoic acid on the one hand and into phenol on the other; since all samples of each substance were identical in every case, four positions in the molecule are equivalent.

Some early inferences regarding the structures were speculative but nevertheless correct. Thus mesitylene, a trimethyl derivative of benzene resulting from condensation of three molecules of acetone under the influence of concentrated sulfuric acid, was regarded by Baeyer as the symmetrical, or $1,3,5$-derivative because of the manner of its formation, and Ladenburg (1874) proved this structure by demonstrating, through interconversions of nitro and amino derivatives of the hydrocarbon, that any two of the positions not occupied by methyl groups are equivalent; this relationship is consistent with the $1,3,5$-structure but not with the $1,2,3$- or $1,2,4$-formulation. In mesitylene each of the three methyl groups occupies a position *meta* to the other two groups, and since the hydrocarbon can be degraded to one of the xylenes that is convertible by oxidation into isophthalic acid, the xylene and the acid must have the *meta*, or $1,3$-structure. Victor Meyer (1870) correlated one of the hydroxybenzoic acids with isophthalic acid and so characterized it as a *meta* derivative. Since phthalic acid is the only benzenedicarboxylic acid which forms a cyclic anhydride, it was inferred to have the *ortho* structure. Salicylic acid was also classified as an *ortho* compound because of the formation of cyclic de-

CH₃

H₃C   CH₃
Mesitylene

[1] Albert Ladenburg, 1842–1911; b. Mannheim, Germany; Ph.D. Heidelberg; Univ. Kiel

rivatives. Through a rather elaborate series of transformations, Ladenburg was able to characterize as *para* isomers certain key compounds of the dimethyl, dicarboxy, and hydroxycarboxy series, and these served as points of reference for elucidation of the structures of other compounds.

COOH / COOH
Phthalic acid   Salicylic acid

Other early inferences were less secure, and in some instances proved to be erroneous. In 1874 Körner[2] pointed out that any method of orientation involving a sequence of transformations must be subject to some uncertainty because it is based on the assumption that the reactions proceed normally, with one group directly replacing another. He proposed and experimentally exploited a new principle that is free from any such uncertainty. Körner's absolute method consists in establishment of the number of isomeric substitution products of a given kind derivable from a substance under investigation. The three xylenes, for example, offer different opportunities for monosubstitution. The *ortho* isomer can give rise to two derivatives containing the group A, for this can be placed at either the 3- or 4-position as shown in the outline formulas I and II. If A is introduced at position 5, the structure is identical with II, and substitution at position 6 is equivalent to that at 3; the formula stands for a symmetrical ring, and the identity of the pairs of structures can be seen by rotating or inverting

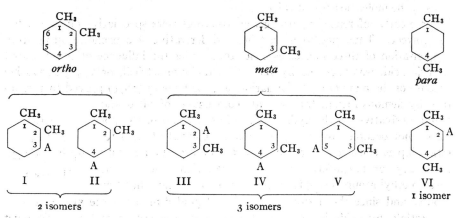

one ring. The rule for numbering is the obvious one of starting with a substituted position and counting in a direction that gives the simplest set of numbers, and hence if a bromine atom were located at either position 3 or 6, as formula I is written, the substance would be named 1,2-dimethyl-3-bromobenzene. The structure of the *meta* compound permits three different orientations of the A-sub-

[2] Wilhelm Körner, 1839–1925; b. Kassel, Germany; Univ. Giessen, Milan; *J. Chem. Soc.*, **127**, 2975 (1925)

stituted derivative, III–V, whereas in the *para* isomer, all available nuclear positions are identical, and only one monosubstitution product (VI) is possible. Thus the *ortho*, *meta*, and *para* compounds can be differentiated by establishing which one leads to two mononitro, monobromo, or other derivatives, which gives three isomers, and which but one.

Application of the principle is not easy, for the derivatives are not all obtainable by direct substitution, and even when the direct method can be employed, mixtures often result and care is required to secure pure substances. In experiments characterized by scrupulous attention to purity of the products, Körner established the structures of the dibromobenzenes by determining the number of mononitro derivatives and of the tribromobenzenes derivable from each isomer; this research also fixed the structures of the tribromo compounds. Griess (1874) characterized the isomeric diaminobenzenes (phenylenediamines) by eliminating the carboxyl group from each member of the series of six diaminobenzoic acids by distillation with lime. Two of these gave the same diamine, m.p. 103°, three gave an isomer, m.p. 63°, and the sixth afforded a third diamine, m.p. 140°.

16.5　　Bond Structure of Benzene. — If benzene consists of a symmetrical ring of six equivalent CH groups, the question of the disposition of the fourth valence of each carbon atom remains. Kekulé suggested that these valences are utilized in formation of three double bonds and that benzene is cyclohexatriene. Although the hydrocarbon does not exhibit the reactivity characteristic of open-chain dienes and trienes and reacts, if at all, chiefly by substitution rather than addition, instances of addition do exist and seem to indicate the presence of three double bonds. Thus though benzene is resistant to catalytic hydrogenation as compared with olefins, it does absorb three moles of hydrogen under the influence of nickel catalyst at high temperatures or of an active platinum catalyst in an acidic medium at room temperature, and affords cyclohexane. The characteristic action of bromine on benzene is substitution of hydrogen by bromine, catalyzed by a trace of an iron salt, but when the catalyst is excluded and the pure reagents are brought together in sunlight and in the absence of oxygen the hydrocarbon forms a hexabromide. Chlorine also adds under these

α-Benzene hexabromide
(m.p. 212°)

special conditions and gives a hexachloride (α-form, m.p. 157°). Ozone, a reagent that affords one of the most reliable means of probing for double bonds, also adds to benzene. The reaction proceeds with difficulty, but a triozonide has been isolated and characterized by decomposition to three molecules of glyoxal (Harries, 1904), as shown.

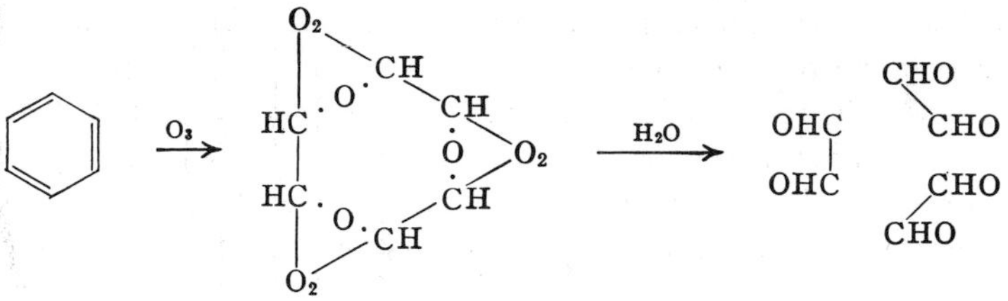

Triozonide   Glyoxal

   Although these additions tend to indicate the presence of three double bonds, Ladenburg noted (1879) that the Kekulé cyclohexatriene formula predicts the existence of more disubstitution products than actually exist. The theory would allow the existence of an *ortho* derivative in two forms, VIIa and VIIb, and of an unsymmetrically substituted *meta* derivative in the forms VIIIa and VIIIb, differing in the location of the double bonds with respect to the substituted posi-

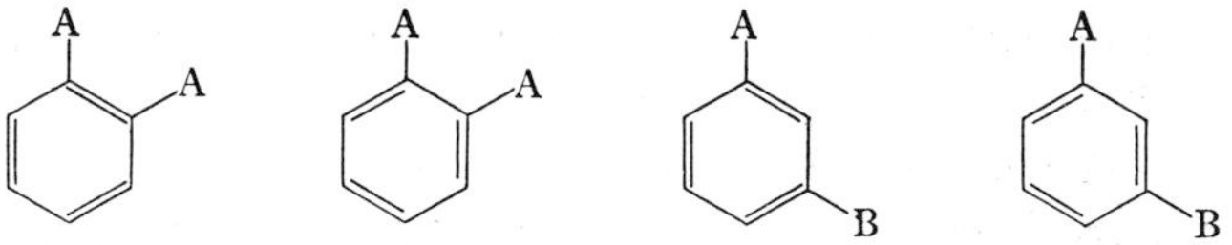

VIIa   VIIb   VIIIa   VIIIb

tions whereas no such isomerism has been observed. Victor Meyer had suggested (1870) that the difference between such possible isomers may be too subtle to be detected; Kekulé pointed out that the double bonds may be in a state of constant oscillation between the two possible structures. After the lapse of many years, the latter view received striking support in the work of A. A. Levine and A. G. Cole (1932) on the ozonization of *o*-xylene. The hydrocarbon affords the following three fragments: glyoxal ($OHC \cdot CHO$ = A), diacetyl ($CH_3CO-COCH_3$ = B), and methylglyoxal (CH_3COCHO = C). The fragments A and

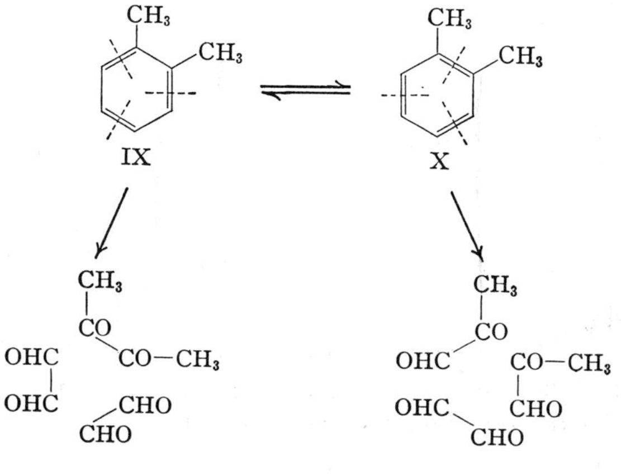

B can come from one Kekulé structure (IX) in the ratio of two to one, and A and C from the other structure (X), but neither structure alone can give rise to all three substances; therefore *o*-xylene must exist in both forms. In a quantitative reinvestigation of the reaction Wibaut[1] observed (1941) that the three dicarbonyl compounds are produced in the relative amounts calculated for a mixture of equal parts of the two Kekulé forms. Ozonization of 1,2,4-trimethylbenzene also indicated a 50:50 ratio between the two structures. The hydrocarbons can hardly consist of equilibrium mixtures, for some preferential stability would be manifested in a predominance of one form.

The possibility was also considered that benzene has a symmetrical structure containing some unique linkage different from a double bond but responsive to some double-bond reagents. The marked difference in reactivity seemed to many of Kekulé's contemporaries to indicate that a unique linkage must be present, and the relatively inert character of benzene was an objection to the cyclohexatriene formula that could not be answered as plausibly as Ladenburg's criticism. One of the alternative benzene formulas devised in an attempt to avoid this objection is Ladenburg's prismatic formula (1869), which is symmetrical but contains no double bonds. Formulas utilizing diagonal, or *para* bonds were suggested by Claus (1867) and by Dewar (1867). Another concept, advanced in 1887 by Armstrong[2] in England and by Baeyer in Germany, was that of a centric formula in which the fourth valence of each carbon is directed

Ladenburg

Claus

Dewar

Armstrong-
Baeyer

Thiele

toward the center. Thiele (1899) introduced a useful concept based on the observation that conjugated systems of double and single bonds function as a unit and are more stable than unconjugated systems of the same degree of unsaturation. He considered each carbon atom of a double bond to possess a certain partial valence, represented by a dotted line, and postulated that in a diene the partial valences on the pair of central carbon atoms neutralize each other with resulting accumulation of residual energy at the ends of the conjugated system. The

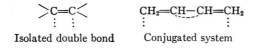

| Isolated double bond | Conjugated system |

Kekulé formula, Thiele noted, represents a closed conjugated system without terminal positions, which permits neutralization of all six partial valences in pairs to form three inactive double bonds alternating with the original deactivated double bonds, or a system of six nearly equivalent inert linkages.

---

[1] Johan Pieter Wibaut, b. 1886 Middleburg, Netherlands; D.Sc. Amsterdam; Amsterdam
[2] Henry E. Armstrong, 1848–1937; b. England; Ph.D. Leipzig (Kolbe); South Kensington

Baeyer's researches on the hydrophthalic acids refuted the Ladenburg formula, for the positions in the prism, numbered in accordance with the requirements for o (1,2)-, m (1,3)-, and p (1,4)-substitution in accordance with the Körner principle do not correspond to the location of substituents in the cyclohexane derivatives resulting on reduction. X-ray analyses of crystalline hexaalkyl derivatives of benzene prove that the six carbon atoms of the ring all lie in a plane and that attached alkyl groups radiate from the ring in this plane, and thus exclude the Ladenburg formula. Interatomic distances determined by the X-ray method also are incompatible with a *para* bond formula, for the distances are such that a linkage extending between *para* carbon atoms would have a length (2.80 Å) considerably greater than in any known compound. Thus the distance between carbon centers in saturated paraffinic hydrocarbons is 1.54 Å, and the normal distance for the olefinic C=C bond is 1.33 Å. Since a bond of abnormal length would correspond to a weak attachment and a consequently reactive system, a formulation utilizing such a linkage is inconsistent with the properties of benzene.

16.6   **Cyclooctatetraene.** — In 1905 Willstätter carried out a degradation of the alkaloid pseudopelletierine which characterized the substance as having an eight-carbon ketonic ring containing a methylamino bridge. The substance was thus a possible starting point for the synthesis of cyclooctatetraene, which has the same closed system of alternating single

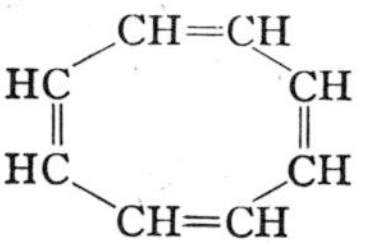

CH=CH
HC   CH
HC   CH
CH=CH
Cyclooctatetraene

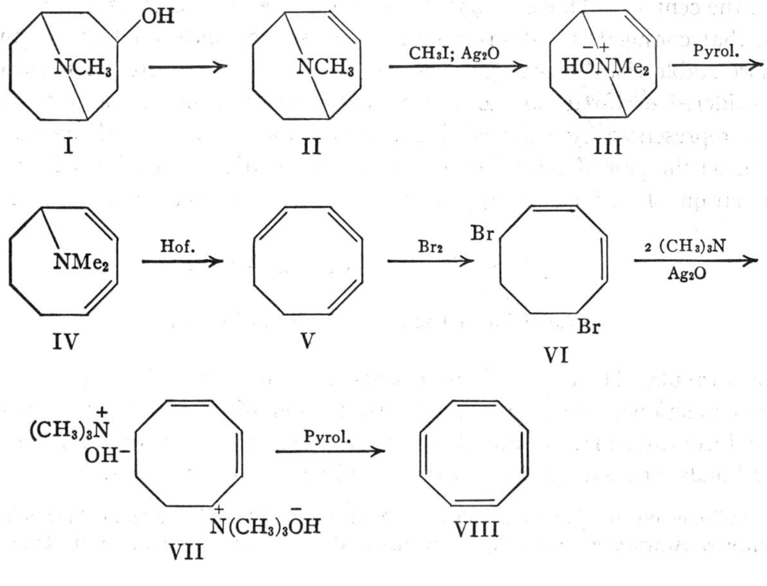

and double bonds as benzene. Since knowledge of the properties of the hydrocarbon might cast some light on the structure of benzene Willstätter with E. Waser (1911) and M. Heidelberger (1913) undertook the synthesis. The alkaloid, which was costly and could be purchased in only small amounts, was reduced to the alcohol I; this was dehydrated to II, which was exhaustively methylated and converted into the methohydroxide III. Distillation in vacuum gave the dienic base IV, which was put through a second Hofmann degradation to give cyclooctatriene (V). Reaction with bromine proceeded by 1,6-addition and afforded the dibromide VI, which on reaction with two equivalents of trimethylamine, followed by treatment of the quaternary bromide with silver oxide, gave the methohydroxide VII. Finally, distillation in vacuum gave, in very low yield, a light yellow liquid characterized as cyclooctatetraene (VIII) by hydrogenation to cyclooctane (absorption of 4 moles of hydrogen). The substance proved to be wholly unlike benzene and comparable in reactivity to open-chain polyenes: it is hydrogenated with ease and is oxidized by permanganate; it adds bromine and on reaction with nitric acid it is resinified and not nitrated.

In later years (1939–45) indirect evidence of three kinds was interpreted as indicating that the Willstätter product may not have been 1,3,5,7-cyclooctatetraene. However, Cope (1948) repeated and verified the synthesis, starting with synthetically prepared pseudopelletierine; the yield in the last step was 6.5–8.6%. In the meantime Reppe at the I. G. Farbenindustrie found that by operating at a suitable high pressure (in tetrahydrofurane in the presence of a nickel catalyst) acetylene can be polymerized to cyclooctatetraene. The method is suitable for large-scale production. A third method of preparation (Cope, 1948) utilizes as the initial step the dimerization of chloroprene to an octadiene.

$$\begin{array}{ccc}
ClC-CH=CH_2 & & ClC=CH-CH_2 \\
\| & & | \quad\quad | \\
CH_2 & \longrightarrow & H_2C \quad\quad CH_2 \\
\quad\quad CH_2 & & | \quad\quad | \\
\quad\quad \| & & H_2C-CH=CCl \\
H_2C=CH-CCl & & \\
Chloroprene & &
\end{array}$$

Samples prepared by both processes are identical with Willstätter's material, and hence his observation of the high reactivity of cyclooctatetraene is confirmed. Constants for cyclooctatetraene are as follows: m.p. $-7°$, b.p. $42°/17$ mm., d_4^{24} 0.9206, n_D^{25} 1.5290.

Cyclooctatetraene is particularly likely to undergo reactions leading to aromatic compounds, two examples of which are shown in the formulas. All four

$$\begin{array}{ccc}
\text{CH}_2\text{CHO} & \xleftarrow{\substack{\text{H}_2\text{O} \\ (\text{HgSO}_4)}} \quad \xrightarrow{\text{NaOCl}} & \text{CHO} \\
& & \text{CHO}
\end{array}$$

Phenylacetaldehyde   Terephthalaldehyde

bonds are reducible by hydrogen (cyclooctane, m.p. 13°); in a neutral medium the reaction proceeds very slowly after addition of three moles of hydrogen. Thus cyclooctene, b.p. 142°, can be prepared in about 90% yield by hydrogenation with palladium catalyst in methanol. Oxidation of cyclooctene with chromic acid leads to suberic acid (64% yield). Even with excess perbenzoic acid, cyclooctatetraene forms only a monoepoxide, which on hydrogenation affords cyclooctanol.

The fact that cyclooctatetraene lacks aromatic character seemed to Willstätter to rule out the formulas for benzene proposed by Kekulé and by Thiele and to support the Armstrong-Baeyer centric formula; for full stabilization the peripheral carbon atoms must be close to the mid-point of the ring.

16.7   **Resonance Stabilization.** — The distance between adjacent carbon centers in the benzene ring, as determined by the X-ray method and confirmed by electron-diffraction studies, is 1.40 Å, a value intermediate between the paraffinic C—C (1.54 Å) and C=C (1.33 Å) distances, whereas the $C_{aliphatic}$— $C_{aromatic}$ bond between an alkyl substituent and a nuclear carbon atom corresponds in length (1.54 Å) to a paraffinic C—C bond. Furthermore all six connecting bonds in the ring are identical. The equivalence of the six bonds could be regarded as consistent with the Armstrong-Baeyer or the Thiele formula or with

$$
\begin{array}{ccc}
& \text{H} & \\
& \text{C} & \\
\text{HC} & & \text{CH} \\
\text{HC} & & \text{CH} \\
& \text{C} & \\
& \text{H} &
\end{array}
\quad\longleftrightarrow\quad
\begin{array}{ccc}
& \text{H} & \\
& \text{C} & \\
\text{HC} & & \text{CH} \\
\text{HC} & & \text{CH} \\
& \text{C} & \\
& \text{H} &
\end{array}
$$

the idea of two oscillating Kekulé structures. The electronic theory of valence, however, provided a clear decision between these alternatives. The well-established concept of the covalent bond as a pair of shared electrons describes in exact terms the nature of the single and double bonds pictured in the Kekulé formula, but does not provide any modern counterpart for neutralized or centrally directed bonds or for partial valences. Thus neither the Armstrong-Baeyer formula nor the Thiele formula has any physical reality. The Kekulé formulation can be translated directly into an electronic equivalent in which the carbon atoms are joined alternately by one and by two pairs of shared electrons, and inspection of the two forms, which Kekulé described as being in a state of dynamic oscillation, shows that the phenomenon is that of resonance. The two forms are equivalent, and their interconversion requires only redistribution of electrons in the planar system, without movement of atomic centers. Results of the ozonization experiments cited above accord with the concept of two resonant Kekulé forms contributing in equal extent to the structure. Since each bond has the same hybrid character and is intermediate between a single and a double bond, the six bonds in the benzene ring have the same length. That there is a shortening of the bond distance to 1.40 Å, as compared with the average value 1.44 Å for three double and three single bonds, finds a parallel in noncyclic resonant systems.

Resonance also provides a concrete expression of Thiele's idea that a closed conjugated system would possess special stability. A measure of the energy content of benzene as compared with nonbenzenoid hydroderivatives of benzene is available from determination of the heats of hydrogenation (Kistiakowsky,

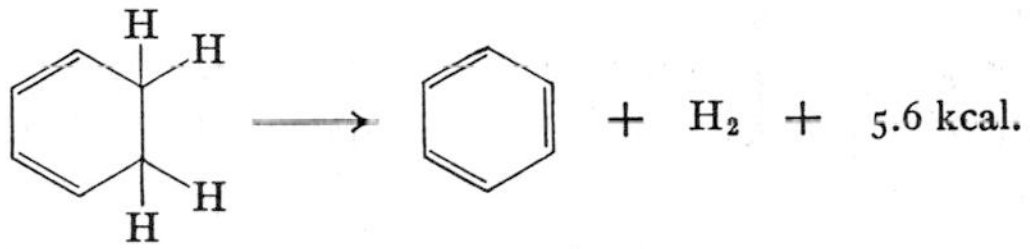

$$\text{(structure)} \longrightarrow \text{(structure)} + H_2 + 5.6 \text{ kcal.}$$

1936). Whereas establishment of a double bond by removal of two hydrogen atoms is ordinarily an endothermic reaction requiring an energy input of some 28–30 kcal./mole, the conversion of 1,2-dihydrobenzene (cyclohexadiene-1,3) into benzene and hydrogen is weakly exothermic and tends to proceed spontaneously, with liberation of energy. The thermodynamic stability, or low energy content, of benzene and the consequent low order of reactivity are distinguishing attributes of aromaticity. Calculations from thermochemical data indicate that benzene is more stable than hypothetical nonresonant cyclohexatriene by 36 kcal./mole in consequence of resonance energy (Pauling, 1933).

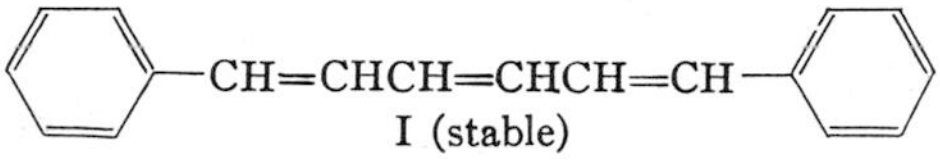

$$\text{(ring)}-CH{=}CHCH{=}CHCH{=}CH-\text{(ring)}$$
$$\text{I (stable)}$$

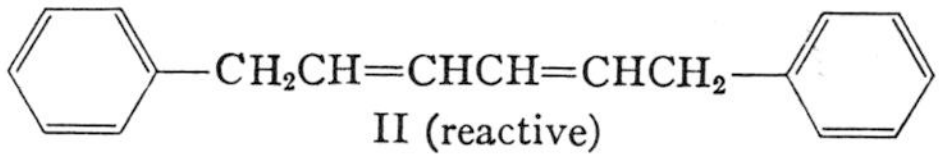

$$\text{(ring)}-CH_2CH{=}CHCH{=}CHCH_2-\text{(ring)}$$
$$\text{II (reactive)}$$

1,6-Diphenylhexatriene-1,3,5 (I) contains an open-chain conjugated system that approaches the inert triene system of the benzene ring in stability, for the substance is unusually resistant to oxidation by alkaline permanganate and does not add hydrogen bromide (Kuhn, 1928). Here the open-chain system is conjugated at the ends of the chain with benzene rings that contribute to the resonance of the system as a whole. The hydrocarbon undergoes 1,6-reduction to the dihydride II, in which the terminal rings are no longer conjugated with the chain, and which does not possess similar stability but resembles the usual, reactive polyenes.

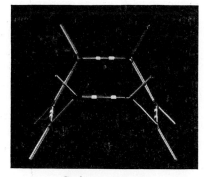

Cyclooctatetraene

Cyclooctatetraene lacks aromatic character because the ring is not planar but puckered and hence incapable of resonance stabilization. X-ray data, electron diffraction measurements, and diamagnetic susceptibility data indicate the presence of alternating single and double bonds of lengths 1.46 Å and 1.33 Å, respectively, arranged in the three-dimensional structure shown in the model. This structure is completely rigid.

16.8   Orbital Theory.— The interpretation of the properties of benzene
afforded by the orbital theory is as follows.   Each carbon atom can
provide three bonds lying in a plane by sp^2, or trigonal, hybridization (5.9, Fig.
5.2), which prepares the atoms for formation of σ bonds of maximal strength if
the valence angle of 120° is preserved.   This condition is uniquely fulfilled in a
six-carbon ring, and hence benzene has a strongly σ-bonded, coplanar ring (Fig.
16.1 a).   The conditions are also ideal for multiple overlapping of p orbitals as

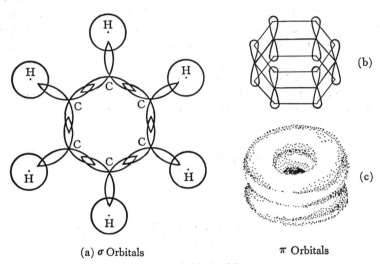

(a) σ Orbitals π Orbitals

FIG. 16.1. — Orbitals of Benzene

shown schematically in the loop-diagram of Fig. 16.1 b.   Because the system is
cyclic, each p orbital overlaps an orbital on either side of it, with particularly
extensive delocalization and consequently high resonance energy.   The cloud
charge of the π orbital takes on the shape of a pair of doughnuts (Fig. 16.1 c),
and all six bonds of benzene are identical and of a unique character.   The orbital
shown accommodates only two electrons (Pauli exclusion principle); the other
four are assumed to occupy two additional π orbitals that encompass all six
nuclei, each with a nodal plane perpendicular to the plane of the ring in addition
to the primary node coplanar with the ring.   The orbital theory provides a
simple explanation of the fact that cyclooctatetraene lacks aromaticity: overlapping of atomic orbitals requires coplanarity of the atoms concerned.

PROBLEMS

1. Suggest a synthesis of cyclohexane-1,3-dicarboxylic acid similar to that of the 1,4-isomer by
   Perkin (16.3).   How can the tetracarboxylic acid esters required for these two syntheses be
   obtained?
2. Could Körner's absolute method of determining structures be applied to the three isomeric
   trimethylbenzenes?
3. Explain why the Körner principle requires numbering the positions in the Ladenburg formula
   in the manner indicated in section 16.5.

4. Write formulas for the six diaminobenzoic acids, and explain the significance of the results obtained by Griess on decarboxylation of these substances.
5. What type of isomerism would be expected in benzene hexabromide?
6. Calculate the molecular ratio of the reaction products expected to result from ozonization of 1,2,4-trimethylbenzene on the theory of a resonance system of the two possible Kekulé forms.

Chapter 17

AROMATIC SUBSTITUTIONS

17.1   **Mechanism of Electrophilic Substitutions.** — Most functional derivatives of aromatic hydrocarbons are obtainable via one of five generally
applicable substitutions. One, chlorination or bromination (1), requires an

1.   Bromination: $C_6H_6 + Br_2 \xrightarrow{FeBr_3} C_6H_5Br + HBr$
2.   Friedel-Crafts alkylation: $C_6H_6 + CH_3Cl \xrightarrow{AlCl_3} C_6H_5CH_3 + HCl$
3.   Friedel-Crafts acylation: $C_6H_6 + CH_3COCl \xrightarrow{AlCl_3} C_6H_5COCH_3 + HCl$
4.   Nitration: $C_6H_6 + HONO_2 \longrightarrow C_6H_5NO_2 + H_2O$
5.   Sulfonation: $C_6H_6 + HOSO_3H \longrightarrow C_6H_5SO_3H + H_2O$

ionic catalyst ($FeBr_3$, $AlCl_3$, $SbCl_5$, I_2) and differs from the halogenation of an
olefin in the requirement of a catalyst and in involving substitution rather than
addition. The Friedel-Crafts reactions of alkylation (2) and acylation (3) require
similar catalysts ($AlCl_3$, BF_3, HF, H_2SO_4). In all three reactions the catalyst
combines with the reagent to form a cationoid electrophile, which is the attacking
species:

$$Br_2 + FeBr_3 \rightarrow Br^+[FeBr_4]^-$$
$$CH_3Cl + AlCl_3 \rightarrow C^+H_3[AlCl_4]^-$$
$$CH_3COCl + AlCl_3 \rightarrow CH_3C^+{=}O[AlCl_4]^-$$

Nitration involves attack by the nitronium ion, NO_2^+ (Ingold and Hughes).
The reaction is often carried out in a mixture of nitric and sulfuric acid (mixed
acid) and the presence of the nitronium ion in the solution is established by the
extent of the depression of the freezing point of sulfuric acid by added nitric acid.
The depression is exactly four times that of an ideal solute, which means that four
ions are produced quantitatively, corresponding to the reaction:

$$HNO_3 + 2H_2SO_4 \rightarrow NO_2^+ + H_3O^+ + 2HSO_4^-$$

Nitration in acetic acid solution involves two steps, the slower of which is formation of the nitronium ion.

Nitration also can be effected with various stable nitronium salts, such as nitronium tetrafluoroborate, conveniently prepared (1) by adding anhydrous hydrogen

$$HNO_3 + HNO_3 \rightleftharpoons H_2NO_3^+ + NO_3^-; \quad H_2NO_3^+ \xrightarrow{\text{slow}} NO_2^+ + H_2O$$

fluoride to a solution of dinitrogen pentoxide in nitromethane at $-20°$ and saturating the solution with boron fluoride (G. Olah, 1956–61). Nitration of benzene,

1. $N_2O_5 + 2HF + 2BF_3 \xrightarrow[94\%]{-20°} 2NO_2^+BF_4^- + H_2O$

    Nitronium tetra-
    fluoroborate

2. $ArH + NO_2^+BF_4^- \rightarrow ArNO_2 + HF + BF_3$
3. $ArH + NO_2Cl + AgBF_4 \rightarrow ArNO_2 + AgCl + HF + BF_3$
    Nitryl
    chloride

toluene, or chlorobenzene is effected by adding the aromatic compound in portions to the reagent with ice cooling. Less reactive compounds (*e.g.* nitrobenzene) may require a temperature of 20–130°, more reactive ones (naphthalene, thiophene) are nitrated in 5–10% solution in ether. Yields based on mononitration are in the range 65–90%. Alternatively, the aromatic compound can be nitrated with a mixture of nitryl chloride and anhydrous silver tetrafluoroborate (3).

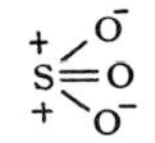

Studies of sulfonation are less extensive but indicate that the active species probably is sulfur trioxide, in which the sulfur atom is strongly electrophilic. The reactions thus are all electrophilic substitutions and are generally carried out in a medium of high dielectric constant which promotes ionization.

Kinetic studies of bromination and nitration have shown that the rate-determining step is bimolecular, the rate being dependent upon the concentrations of the reagent and of the aromatic compound (S_E2 reactions). Indirect evidence that increase in the polarity of the solvent does not increase the rate of substitution shows that ionic charges are neither created nor destroyed in the rate-determining step. The following mechanism for the case of bromination is consistent with this requirement and with further evidence to be cited. A bromonium ion derived from $Br^+[FeBr_4]^-$ combines with benzene to form an ion in which the positive charge is distributed among three carbon atoms (1–3); in a faster step

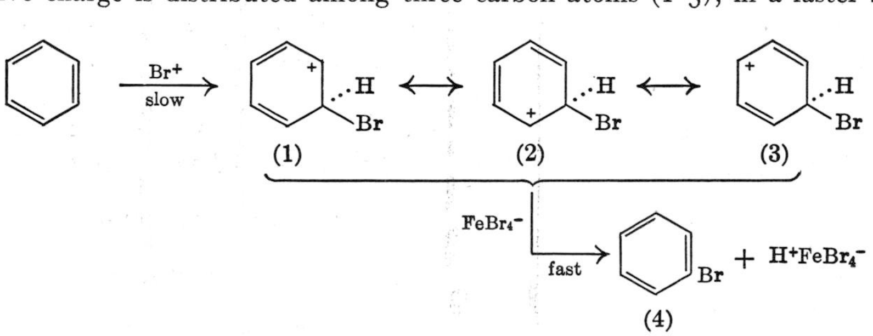

the proton at the site of attack is captured by $[FeBr_4]^-$ or other base to give bromobenzene. Note that the intermediate hybrid ion is formulated with hydrogen to the rear and bromine to the front. Thus Br^+ attacks from the front (or rear) of the plane of the aromatic ring and the carbon atom undergoing substitution becomes tetrahedral. The conversion of a carbon atom having the planar, aromatic bonds to one having four tetrahedrally arranged aliphatic bonds is a transition from sp^2 to sp^3 hybridized electron orbitals. The hybrid cation (1–3) is described as an aronium ion (9.7); the complex resulting from combination of this aronium ion with an anion is called a σ-complex, since the entering substituent and the hydrogen atom are linked to carbon by σ-bonds. Zollinger[1] in a review (1956) emphasized the point that this σ-complex is an intermediate and not a transition state.

Nitration and sulfonation follow the same pattern. Friedel-Crafts reactions involve attack by an electrophile such as $^+CH_3$ or $CH_3C^+{=}O$; the proton-

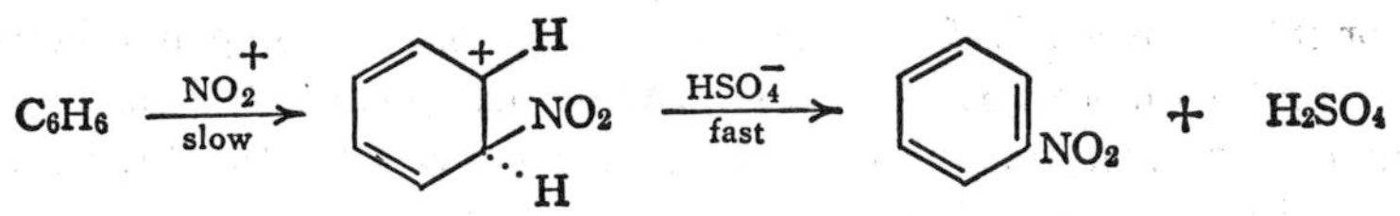

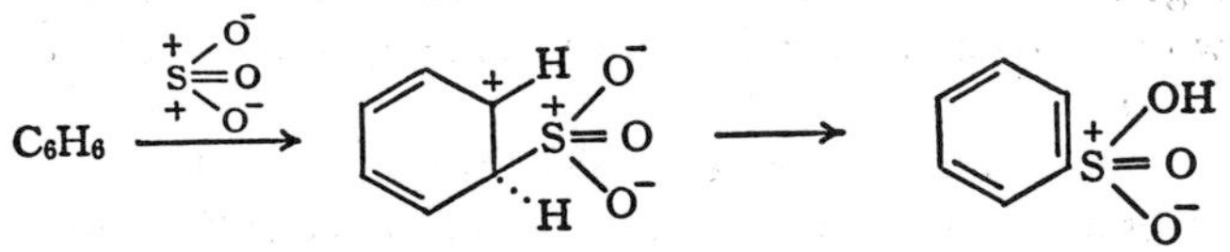

accepting base is an ion such as $AlCl_4^-$ or $FeBr_4^-$.

Evidence that loss of the proton is not the rate-determining step was adduced by Melander[2] (1950–57) by showing that in general aromatic substitutions are not subject to isotope effects. Since the vibrational energy of a bond from carbon to ordinary hydrogen, which is called protium when a distinction is desirable, or to deuterium (at. wt. 2) or to tritium (at. wt. 3) is inversely proportional to the atomic weight, calculation shows that, if the rate-controlling step of substitution were cleavage of the C—H bond, replacement of protium by deuterium should cause the reaction to proceed 5–8 times more slowly, and replacement by tritium should cause it to proceed 20–30 times more slowly. Melander found that hydrocarbons containing tritium are nitrated and brominated at the same rate as the corresponding ordinary protium compounds; Lauer[3] and Noland[4] (1953) made the same observation concerning the nitration of deuterobenzene.

17.2   Aronium Salts (σ-Complexes). — The ionic product of combination of benzene with Br^+, represented in formulas (1)–(3) above as a hybrid of three contributing structures, can be represented also as in formula (5)

---

[1] Heinrich Zollinger, b. 1919 Aaruf, Switzerland; D.Sc. ETH Zurich (Fierz-David); Univ. Basel; ETH Zurich

[2] Lars Melander, b. 1919 Stockholm, Sweden; Ph.D. Univ. Stockholm; Nobel Institute of Physics and Univ. Stockholm

[3] Walter M. Lauer, b. 1895 Thomasville, Pa.; Ph.D. Minnesota (W. H. Hunter); Univ. Minnesota

[4] Wayland E. Noland, b. 1926 Madison, Wis.; Ph.D. Harvard (Bartlett); Univ. Minnesota

for a complex of the ion with Br^-. This dipolar intermediate no longer has the stability of an aromatic ring but is
stabilized by resonance and should be capable of existence.
Indeed an analogous compound (7) was isolated by Pfeiffer[1]
and Winzinger (1928) on bromination of 1,1-(di-p-dimeth-
ylaminophenyl)ethylene (6). The double bond in this sub-
stance has aromatic character since the ultimate product is not the dibromide but
the substitution product (8). The intermediate (7), analogous to (5), is deep

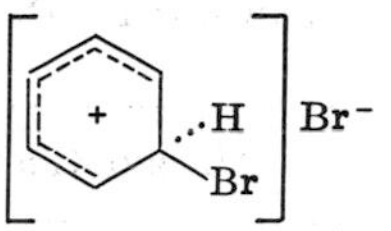

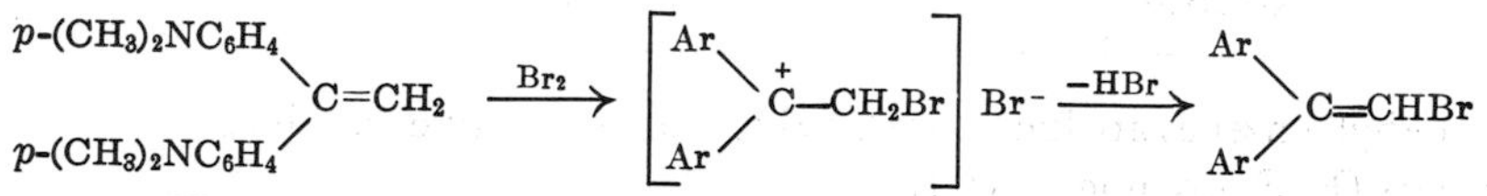

blue; the corresponding compound with methoxyl groups in place of the dimethylamino groups gives a transient red violet coloration on exposure to bromine vapor but the intermediate has not been isolated.

An even closer analogy is afforded by the discovery by D. A. McCaulay[2] and
A. P. Lien (1951–59) of σ-complexes (10) of polyalkylbenzenes with hydrogen
fluoride and boron fluoride. Since the reaction involves combination of an

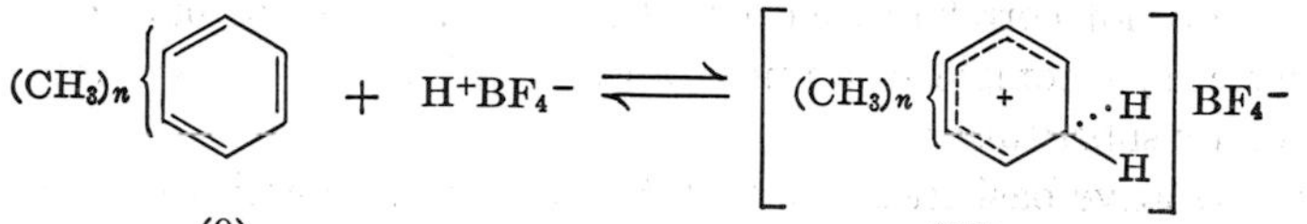

aromatic hydrocarbon with a proton, the extent of reaction provides a direct
measure of the basicity of the hydrocarbon. Benzene is too weak an electron
donor to function as an effective σ-base, but the xylenes and the more highly
alkylated benzenes when distributed between n-heptane and liquid hydrogen
fluoride in the presence of a suitable amount of boron fluoride form complexes
which appear in the hydrogen fluoride layer. Since the stability of the σ-complex
varies with the nature, number, and orientation of the alkyl groups, fractional
extraction of mixtures is possible. When the three xylenes are allowed to compete
for a limited amount of boron fluoride in the presence of excess hydrogen fluoride,
m-xylene, the strongest base, is extracted first and p-xylene is the last to be extracted.

The separation factors relative to that of p-xylene given in Table 17.1 demonstrate the marked enhancement of basicity attending polymethylation. It is
significant that these separation factors are quantitatively related to the rates of
aromatic electrophilic substitution. The log relative rates of halogenation of

[1] Paul Pfeiffer, 1875–1951; b. Elberfeld; Ph.D. Univ. Zurich (Werner); Univ. Bonn; *Helv. Chim. Acta*, **36**, 2032 (1953)

[2] David A. McCaulay, b. 1913 Chicago; M.S. Chicago (R. W. Johnson); People's Gas and Coke; Manhattan District, Columbia Univ.; Standard Oil Co., Indiana

TABLE 17.1. DISTRIBUTION OF METHYLBENZENES BETWEEN n-HEPTANE AND HF–BF$_3$:
RELATIVE SEPARATION FACTORS

METHYL GROUPS	FACTOR	METHYL GROUPS	FACTOR
CH$_3$	(ca. 0.01)	1,2,3,4-(CH$_3$)$_4$	170
1,4-(CH$_3$)$_2$	1	1,3,5-(CH$_3$)$_3$	2,800
1,2-(CH$_3$)$_2$	2	1,2,3,5-(CH$_3$)$_4$	5,600
1,3-(CH$_3$)$_2$	20	(CH$_3$)$_5$	8,760
1,2,4-(CH$_3$)$_3$	40	(CH$_3$)$_6$	89,000
1,2,4,5-(CH$_3$)$_4$	120		

the methylbenzenes are linearly related to the log relative basicities of the methyl-benzenes (F. E. Condon,[1] 1952):

$$\log \text{(relative rate)} = 1.27 \log \text{(relative basicity)} + \text{a constant}$$

This equation is further evidence for the role of σ-complexes in aromatic halogenation. Since a Hammett-type relation has been demonstrated between the halogenation of toluene and several other toluene substitutions (H. C. Brown, 1953), σ-complexes are quite likely involved in most electrophilic aromatic substitutions.

The basicity of methylbenzenes toward hydrogen chloride is believed to be due to the formation of π-complexes (H. C. Brown, 1952). Since the relative basicities to HCl do not correlate well with the relative rates of halogenation of the methylbenzenes, π-complexes do not appear to play a significant role in electrophilic aromatic substitution.

Since the relative basicities toward HF$\cdot$BF$_3$ correlate with the rates of electrophilic aromatic substitution, then *ortho-para* directing groups should promote basicity. Methyl *meta* to added protium promotes the stability of aronium ion somewhat, and methyl *ortho* or *para* to added protium promotes the stability of aronium ion profoundly. All four positions of *p*-xylene are *ortho* to one methyl and *meta* to another. As shown in I, the profound enhancement of stability produced by an *ortho* methyl group is due to the contribution of a tertiary aronium ion. In *o*-xylene, two positions are *ortho* to one methyl group and *meta* to the other (II), and two positions are *para* to one methyl group and *meta* to the other (III). In *m*-xylene, three positions are either *ortho* to both methyl groups (IV) or *ortho* to one methyl group and *para* to the other (VI). Similar reasoning makes sensible the extreme basicity of 1,3,5-trimethylbenzene.

Whereas McCaulay and Lien had investigated the reaction of aromatic hydrocarbons with boron fluoride and excess hydrogen fluoride, Olah[2] (1958–61) added just 0.5 mole of boron fluoride at $-20°$ to $-80°$ to a stirred two-phase mixture of 0.5 mole each of liquid hydrogen fluoride and toluene, *m*-xylene, mesitylene, or isodurene (1,2,3,5-tetramethylbenzene). In each instance the gas was absorbed to give a brightly colored, homogeneous 1:1:1 complex, which was characterized

[1] Francis E. Condon, b. 1919 Abington, Mass.; Ph.D. Harvard (Bartlett); Phillips Petrol. Co.; City College, N. Y.

[2] George A. Olah, b. 1927 Budapest, Hungary; Ph.D. Budapest, Techn. Univ. (Zemplén); Budapest, Techn. Univ.; Dow Chemical of Canada

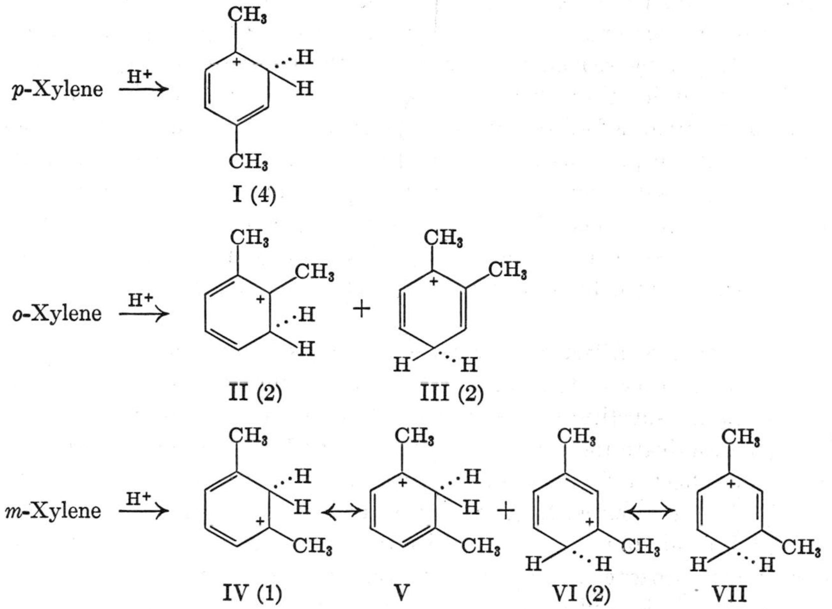

p-Xylene $\xrightarrow{H^+}$

I (4)

o-Xylene $\xrightarrow{H^+}$

II (2)   +   III (2)

m-Xylene $\xrightarrow{H^+}$

IV (1)   V   +   VI (2)   ↔   VII

by determination of freezing and decomposition points and by electrical conductivity. Properties of the mesitylene σ-complex are shown under the formula;

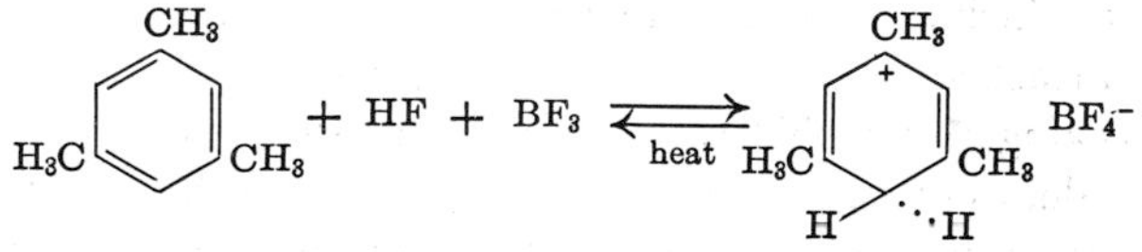

$$+ \ HF + BF_3 \ \underset{heat}{\overset{\longrightarrow}{\rightleftarrows}} \ \ BF_4^-$$

yellow, m.p. −15°

colors and melting points of the complexes of toluene, mesitylene, and isodurene
are: toluene, yellow-green, −65°; m-xylene, yellow, −55°; isodurene, orange,
−10°. The saltlike character is indicated by the specific conductivities and

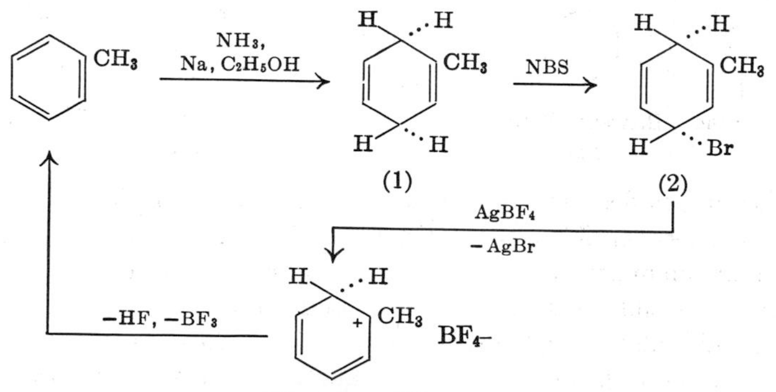

$\xrightarrow{\substack{NH_3, \\ Na, C_2H_5OH}}$ (1) $\xrightarrow{NBS}$ (2)

$\xrightarrow{\substack{AgBF_4 \\ - \ AgBr}}$

−HF, −BF₃

(3) m.p. −64°

insolubility in organic solvents. Synthesis of a complex from toluene provides further proof of structure. 1-Methylcyclohexadiene-1,4 (1), prepared according to Wibaut (1950) by reduction of toluene with sodium and alcohol in liquid ammonia and purified through the tetrabromide (m.p. 171°), on treatment with N-bromosuccinimide afforded the monobromide (2). On addition of silver tetrafluoroborate in portions to the bromide at −60°, the reagent dissolved in the organic layer with immediate precipitation of silver bromide and formation of the complex (3). When the complex is heated, boron fluoride is evolved to leave a two-phase system of toluene (90%) and hydrogen fluoride. Salts of the same type were shown to be formed as intermediates in typical Friedel-Crafts reactions.

17.3   Inductive Effect of Groups. — A substituent already present in the benzene ring often influences markedly the ease with which any of five electrophilic substitution reactions will proceed. Some groups decrease activity, or deactivate the benzene ring for substitution, and other groups have an activating effect and enable substitution to be carried out under conditions milder than those required for substitution of benzene. Thus benzene can be nitrated with a mixture of concentrated nitric and sulfuric acids at 60°, but conversion of nitrobenzene into a dinitrobenzene requires fuming nitric acid and concentrated sulfuric acid at 95°. The nitro group is thus a deactivator. On the other hand, phenol can be nitrated with 20% nitric acid at 25°; the hydroxyl group therefore activates the ring for substitution.

The activating or deactivating influence of a substituent is attributable to an inductive effect, which can operate in either of two directions. A group in which the key atom attached to the ring is positively charged or positively polarized repels the attacking electrophile and so decreases susceptibility to substitution. A group which does not carry a positive charge but which is electron-attracting also has a deactivating inductive effect. Since the nitro group contains a semipolar bond, the nitrogen atom carries a positive charge and renders the group strongly electron-attracting. Thus the nitro group induces a drift of electrons in

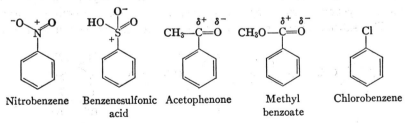

| Nitrobenzene | Benzenesulfonic acid | Acetophenone | Methyl benzoate | Chlorobenzene |

its direction and so decreases the electron density at all positions in the ring and makes them less susceptible to attack by Br^+, NO_2^+, etc. The positive pole of the trimethylammonium group, $-N^+(CH_3)_3$, is the most powerful of the deactivating groups. The sulfonic acid group has a positively charged key atom attached to the ring and is also strongly deactivating. The carbonyl group of ketones and esters has a partially polarized carbon atom and exerts a deactivating inductive effect, which, however, is not so strong as that of the nitro group.

The direction and magnitude of the inductive effects of different groups can be inferred from dipole moment data. Benzene has no dipole moment and neither has p-xylene, but a small dipole moment is observed for toluene (0.41) and a large one for nitrobenzene (3.97). The experimental observations do not indicate whether the methyl group displaces the electric center in the same sense as the nitro group or in the opposite sense, but a decision can be reached from the observation that p-nitrotoluene has a dipole moment of 4.40, which corresponds closely to the sum of the values noted and not to the difference; hence the substituents attached to opposite positions in the ring cooperate in producing a drift of electrons in the same direction. If the nitro group at one terminal position attracts electrons, then the methyl group at the other extremity must repel elec-

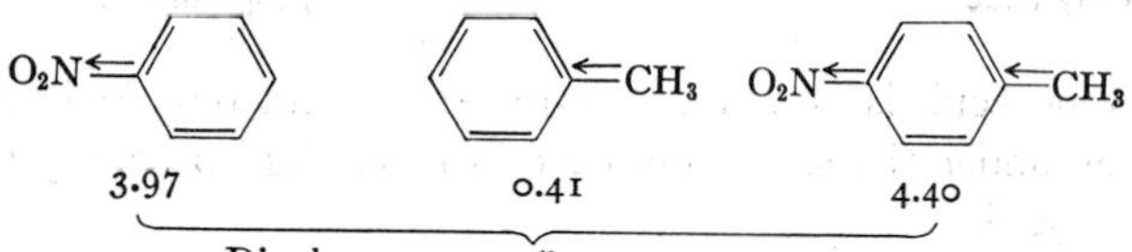

Dipole moments (benzene solution)

trons. By this method of comparison the direction of the inductive effect of a given group is established, and the magnitude is revealed by the dipole moment of the monosubstituted benzene derivative, as recorded in Table 17.2. Strongly ionized groups fall outside the scope of the experimental method, but the other groups can be classified as electron-attracting, if they operate in the same sense as the nitro group, and electron-releasing, if they operate in the opposite sense.

TABLE 17.2. DIPOLE MOMENTS OF BENZENE DERIVATIVES
(IN BENZENE SOLUTION AT 22–25°)

ELECTRON-ATTRACTING		ELECTRON-RELEASING	
Substituent	Dipole moment	Substituent	Dipole moment
—NO_2	3.97	—$N(CH_3)_2$	1.58
—CN	3.90	—NH_2	1.52
—$COCH_3$	2.93	—OH	1.61
—CHO	2.75	—$OCOCH_3$	1.52
—$COOC_2H_5$	1.91	—OCH_3	1.16
—Cl	1.56	—CH_3	0.41
—Br	1.53		
—I	1.30		
—COOH	1.0		

The nitro and nitrile groups are powerful deactivators, carbonyl-containing groups come next, and halogen and carbonyl are weakly electron-attracting. In nitration, sulfonation, and halogenation a single deactivating group merely necessitates use of conditions more forcing than if the substituent were not present. In the case of Friedel-Crafts reactions, however, a single potently electron-attracting group completely inhibits reaction. Thus nitrobenzene can neither be alkylated with an alkyl chloride in the presence of aluminum chloride nor acylated with acetyl chloride or acetic anhydride in combination with the same catalyst. Similarly indifferent to Friedel-Crafts reactions are aromatic nitriles, ketones, aldehydes, esters, and acids.   The weakly deactivating chlorine atom does not stop the Friedel-Crafts reaction but it does lead to lower yields.   Thus chlorobenzene can be acylated with succinic anhydride, but the product, $\beta(p\text{-chloro-}$

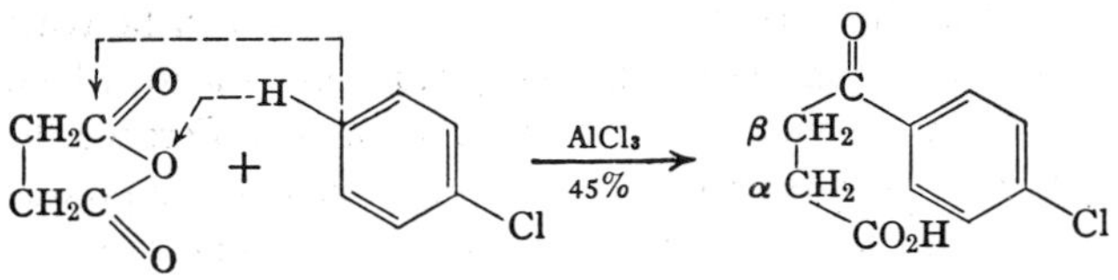

Succinic $\beta(p\text{-Chlorobenzoyl})$-
anhydride   propionic acid

benzoyl)propionic acid, is obtained in only 45% yield (checked in two laboratories), whereas under the same conditions the yield of β-benzoylpropionic acid from benzene is 90%.

An electron-releasing group displaces electrons in such a way as to increase the electron density at the available centers and so activates these sites for electrophilic attack.   Aromatic inductive effects cannot be evaluated from the inductive

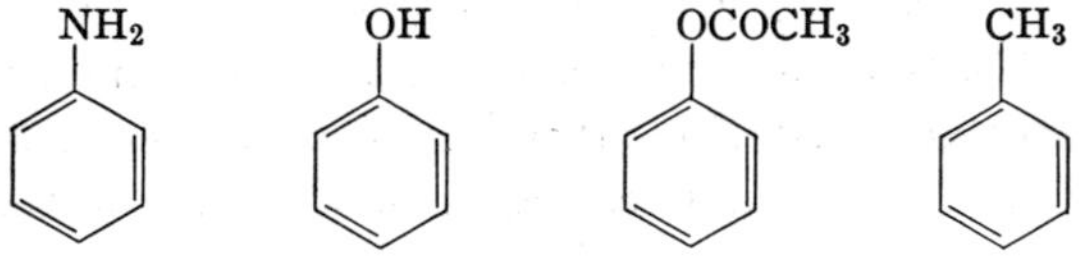

Aniline   Phenol   Phenylacetate   Toluene

effects of the groups in aliphatic systems because of the modifying influence of resonance, as described below, but can be inferred from the dipole moments of Table 17.2, since the dipole moment reveals the character of a group as it functions when linked to the resonant aromatic system.   Thus the amino and hydroxy groups, and derived groups, are particularly potent, and methyl is a feeble activator.

17.4   **Directive Effect of Groups.** — Groups of one type direct the entering substituent into the *meta* position.   The nitro group is of this type and nitrobenzene on further nitration yields *m*-dinitrobenzene; on chlorination it yields *m*-nitrochlorobenzene; the product of sulfonation is *m*-nitrobenzenesulfonic

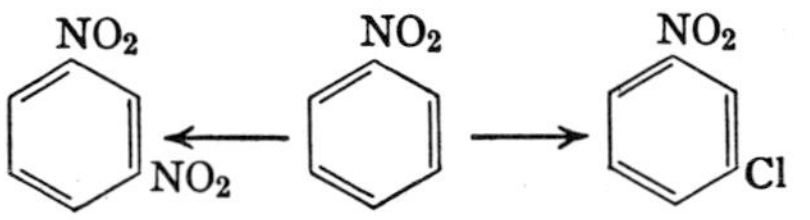

m-Dinitrobenzene   *m*-Nitrochlorobenzene

acid.   Other *meta* directors are listed roughly in the order of decreasing effectiveness.   The strongly ionic trimethylammonium group heads the list, for phenyltrimethylammonium nitrate is substituted with great difficulty and exclusively in the *meta* position.   The ammonium group —N^+H_3 is weakly *meta* directing.

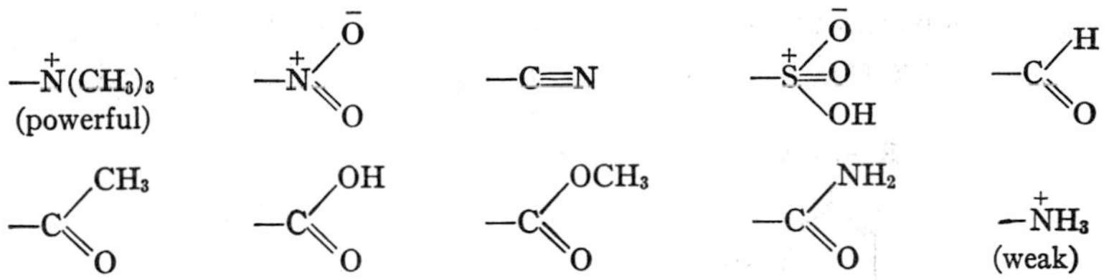

$$-\overset{+}{N}(CH_3)_3 \qquad -\overset{+}{N}\overset{\overset{\bar{O}}{\parallel}}{\diagdown O} \qquad -C\equiv N \qquad -\overset{+}{\underset{\diagdown OH}{S}}\overset{\overset{\bar{O}}{\parallel}}{} \qquad -C\overset{\diagup H}{\diagdown O}$$

(powerful)

$$-C\overset{\diagup CH_3}{\diagdown O} \qquad -C\overset{\diagup OH}{\diagdown O} \qquad -C\overset{\diagup OCH_3}{\diagdown O} \qquad -C\overset{\diagup NH_2}{\diagdown O} \qquad -\overset{+}{N}H_3$$

(weak)

Meta directors

Groups of a second type cause the substituent to enter the *ortho* or *para* position or both. Direction to the *para* position usually is stronger than *ortho* direction, as exemplified by the nitration of acetanilide. All *meta* directing groups are also deactivators, and most *ortho-para* directing groups have an activating inductive

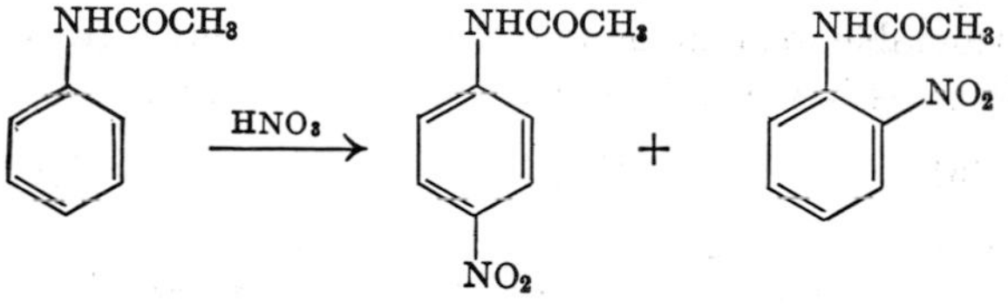

(major product)   (minor product)

effect. Halogen, however, has a deactivating effect but nevertheless directs substitution to *op*-positions. Thus direction of substitution is not determined by the

$$\underbrace{-N(CH_3)_2 \qquad -NH_2 \qquad -OH}_{\text{(very powerful)}} \qquad -OCH_3 \qquad -NHCOCH_3 \qquad -OCOCH_3$$

$$-CH_3 \qquad -Cl, Br, I \qquad -C_6H_5 \qquad -CH_2COOH \qquad -CH=CHCOOH$$

op-Directors

nature of the inductive effect.

The factor determining the direction of substitution appears, in most instances, to be a **resonance effect.** Nitrobenzene is a resonance hybrid involving four structures; since resonance is possible only when a transition from one form to another involves no movement of atoms, the atoms in all the structures lie in a single plane. The effect of resonance in nitrobenzene is to set up positive centers

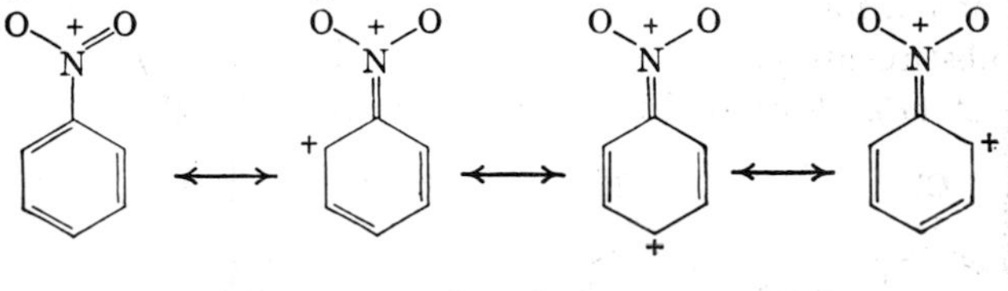

at the *ortho* and *para* positions, and hence to render these sites particularly inaccessible to electrophilic agents; the *meta* carbon atoms are deactivated by induction, along with the rest, but at least offer better points for attack than *ortho-para* positions. Thus nitrobenzene is nitrated with difficulty because of inductive repulsion of NO_2^+ and the orientation is *meta* in consequence of resonance. Similar interpretations can be made of the weaker directive influences of less potently electron-attracting carbonyl functions (a), since initial charge separation (b)

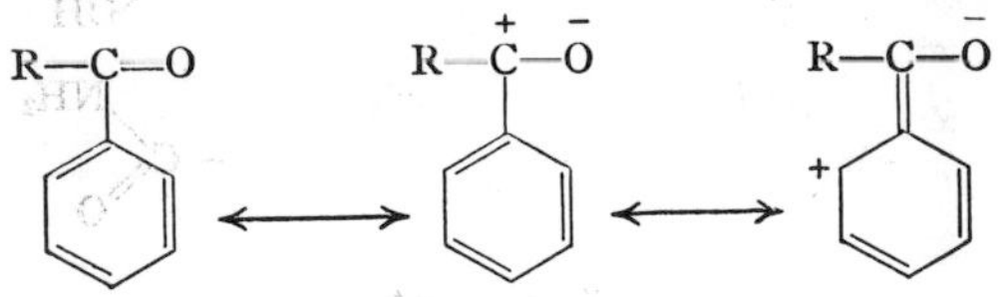

$$R\!-\!\overset{\text{O}}{\underset{}{C}}\!-\!O \qquad R\!-\!\overset{+}{\underset{}{C}}\!-\!\overset{-}{O} \qquad R\!-\!\overset{-}{\underset{}{C}}\!-\!O$$

(a)   (b)   (c)

is promoted by distribution of the positive charge into the ring, as in (c).

Although in aliphatic compounds the hydroxyl group is electron-attracting, the dipole moment data show that hydroxyl attached to a benzene ring is strongly electron-releasing. Thus the high susceptibility of phenol to electrophilic substitution is attributable to an inductive effect. Resonance is possible, since a pair of unshared electrons is available on oxygen to move in and form a double bond

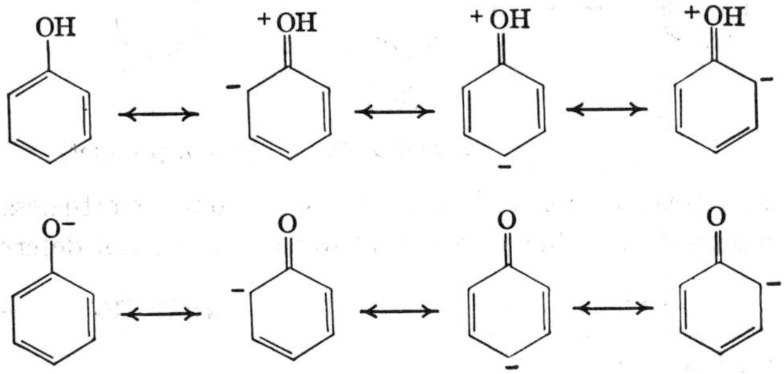

with charge separation. Distribution of the negative charge among three centers increases the electron density at these positions and results in *ortho-para* substitution. Replacement of the phenolic hydrogen by methyl or by acetyl produces some diminution in the inductive activation but does not influence the direction of substitution as determined by resonance. The negative pole of the phenoxide ion has a powerful inductive effect and renders the ring even more susceptible to electrophilic substitution than with nonionized phenol; resonance again controls *ortho-para* orientation. The nonionized amino group, like hydroxyl, has a key atom with unshared electrons and the inductive and resonance effects in amines are like those in phenols.

Halogen substituents present a special case. Resonance establishes electron-rich centers at *ortho-para* positions and determines the course of substitution.

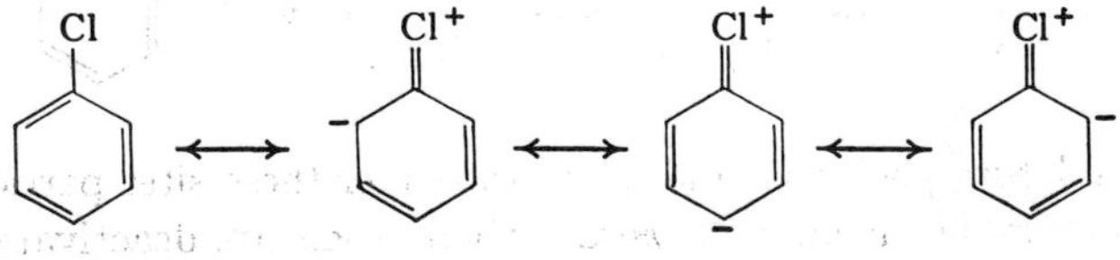

However, unlike other *ortho-para* directing groups, aromatic halogen like aliphatic halogen is electron-attracting and so the inductive effect deactivates the ring; hence chlorobenzene is nitrated less readily than benzene. The partial double-bond character of aromatically bound chlorine is evident from a shortening in bond length: CH_3—Cl, 1.76 Å; C_6H_5—Cl, 1.70 Å.

The trimethylammonium group presents an open problem. This is the most powerfully deactivating group known, and it directs substitution exclusively to the *meta* position. The explanation advanced in the case of nitrobenzene is not applicable because of the requirement that one valence of pentavalent nitrogen retain its polar character. Thus in the ion $C_6H_5N^+(CH_3)_3$ the charge is not free to shift to a position in the ring; the ionic nitrogen has a shell of eight electrons and is incapable of sharing another pair with carbon. One idea is based on consideration of the aronium ions that could lead to *o*-, *m*-, and *p*-nitro derivatives. Of the three possible intermediates, (a), (b), and (c), the first two place a positive

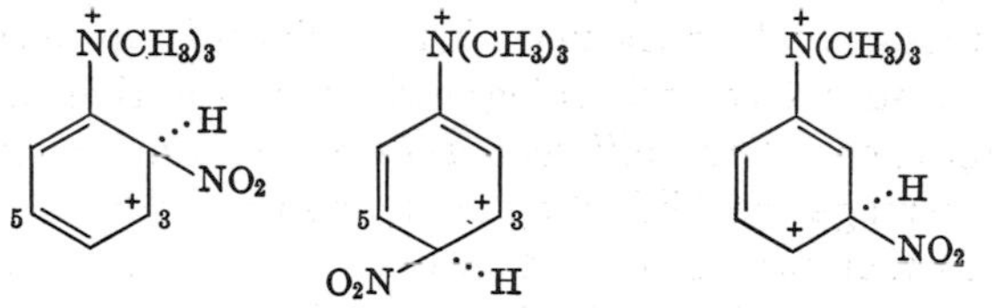

(a)　　　　　　　(b)　　　　　　　(c)

charge at C_1, C_3, and C_5 and this involves adjacent positive charges at C_1. In ion (c), intermediate to the *meta* derivative, the two positive charges are maximally separated.

The methyl group in toluene is weakly electron-releasing and produces an enhancement of reactivity, which however is minor as compared to the effect of a hydroxyl or an amino group. That methyl also directs *ortho-para* presents a problem in interpretation, but a minor one, since the directive effect is feeble. Resonance of the type formulated above is impossible, and the C—C bond distance connecting the group to the nucleus is the same as that of an aliphatic single-carbon link. Hyperconjugation provides a possible explanation. The electrons

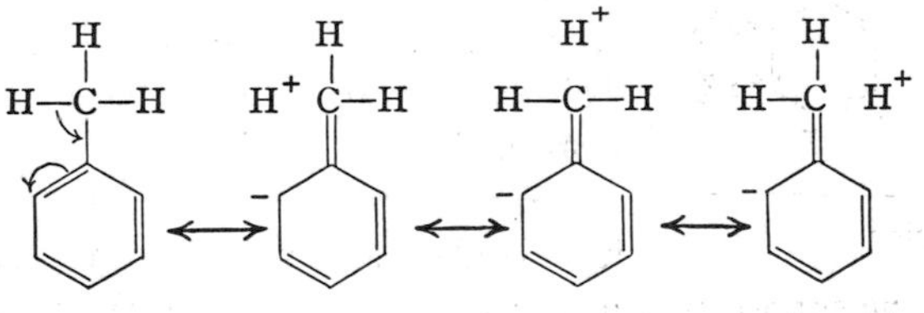

of each of the three C—H bonds in turn are considered to participate in displacements in the same way as unshared electrons of oxygen, nitrogen, or halogen participate, but to a lesser extent. Furthermore, *op* attack by a nucleophile places part of a positive charge at C_1 to produce a tertiary carbonium ion and lower the energy of the system.

The directive effect of the methyl group undergoes a gradual transition to the *meta* type on introduction of halogen into the side chain. Thus whereas toluene gives only 4% of the *meta* isomer on nitration, chloro derivatives give the following percentages of *m*-nitro compounds: $C_6H_5CH_2Cl$, 12%; $C_6H_5CHCl_2$, 34%;

$C_6H_5CCl_3$, 64%. Electron-attracting halogen atoms, in adequate number, produce an electron displacement sufficient to render the carbon atom positive with respect to the ring. The following figures for the percentage of *meta* substitution demonstrate a decreasing transmission of an inductive effect as a nitro group is moved to positions progressively remote from the aromatic ring: $C_6H_5NO_2$, 93%; $C_6H_5CH_2NO_2$, 50%; $C_6H_5CH_2CH_2NO_2$, 13%.

17.5   *Meta* **Substitutions.** — The rules of orientation are useful in predictions of the chief products of substitution reactions, but they indicate the predominant, rather than the exclusive products. Careful quantitative studies have been made by the Netherlands school of Holleman,[1] Wibaut, and others to determine, often by physical methods of analysis, the exact proportion of the isomers present, even in small amounts, in reaction mixtures resulting from various substitutions, usually nitration. The results are conveniently summarized by a formula of a substance undergoing a given substitution with figures representing the proportions of the different isomers found in the total substitution product; the percentages established by analysis should not be confused with the percentage yields that can be secured in practice. Thus in actual preparative work *m*-dinitrobenzene can be obtained in 88% yield by nitration of nitrobenzene,

but analysis of the total nitrated material has shown that the *meta* isomer amounts to 93% of the whole and that the *ortho* and *para* isomers are present to the extent of 6% and 1%, respectively, as indicated in the abbreviated summary. The *ortho* and *para* isomers are produced in such small amounts that they are easily eliminated during crystallization. The trimethylammonium group is even more potent than the nitro group because it affords exclusive *meta* substitution, and carboxyl is weaker than nitro because it allows *ortho-para* substitution to proceed to a considerable extent. Positively charged or highly unsaturated groups direct

an entering group to the *meta* position by deactivating all positions, with particular suppression of attack at the *ortho* and *para* carbon atoms. This is illustrated by results of nitration of *p*-nitrobenzoic acid. The only positions available are *ortho* to either a carboxyl or a nitro group, and it is understandable that the reaction proceeds with difficulty; the suppression of *ortho* substitution is greater for the nitro substituent, and the group introduced takes a place *ortho* to the weaker carboxyl.

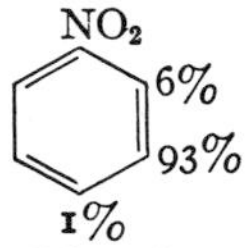

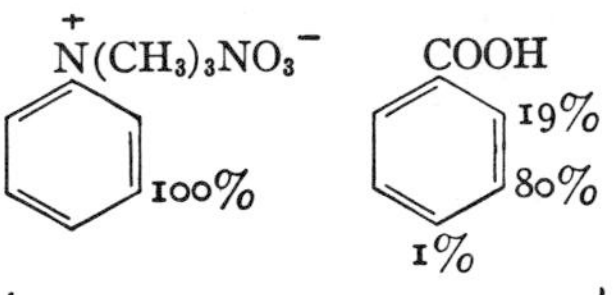

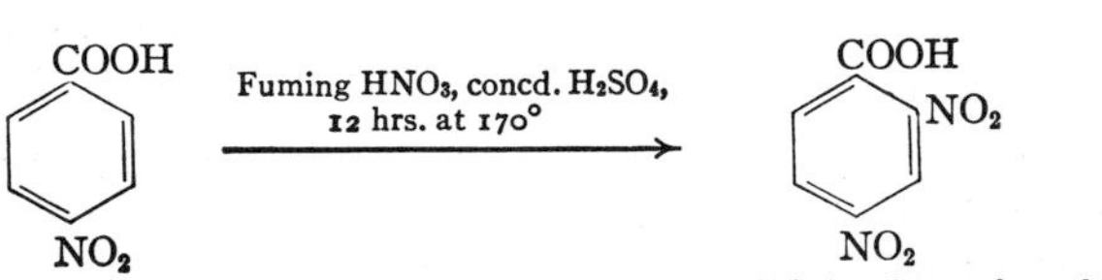

2,4-Dinitrobenzoic acid
(m.p. 182°)

---

[1] Arnold Frederick Holleman, 1859–1953; b. Oisterwyk, Netherlands; Ph.D. Leiden (Franchimont); Univ. Amsterdam

The deactivating influence of *meta* directing groups controls the course of substitution of polynuclear compounds. In 4-nitrodiphenyl, for example, one of the

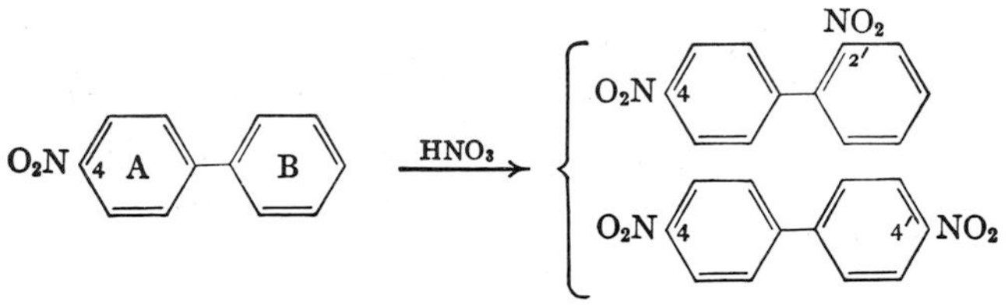

benzene rings (A) is deactivated whereas the other is not, and substitution occurs in the *ortho* (2'-) and *para* (4'-) positions of the unsubstituted ring (B). The same is true of derivatives of diphenylmethane ($C_6H_5CH_2C_6H_5$) and dibenzyl ($C_6H_5CH_2CH_2C_6H_5$), which are attacked preferentially at the *ortho* and *para* positions of the ring containing no nitro or other *meta* directing groups. A nitro

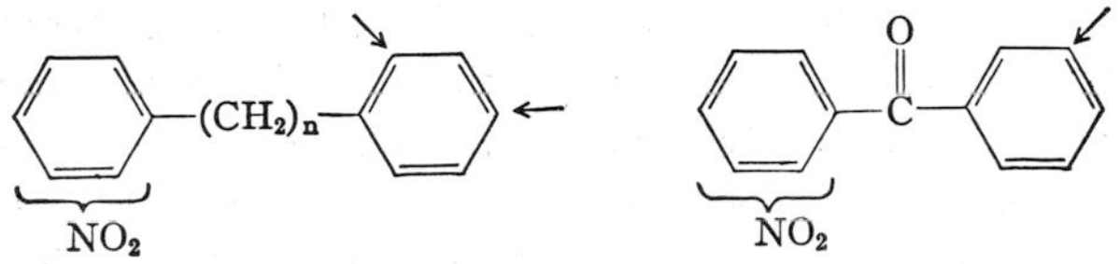

or similar derivative of benzophenone undergoes reaction at the *meta* position of the unsubstituted ring.

17.6   Ortho-Para Substitutions. — The relative effectiveness of the various *ortho-para* directing groups is gauged less accurately from the extent to which *meta* substitution is allowed than by results of competition between two groups in the same molecule, preferably in the *para* position. In *p*-aminophenol substitution occurs preferentially in the position *ortho* to the amino group, which therefore is more powerful in its influence than hydroxyl. If either the

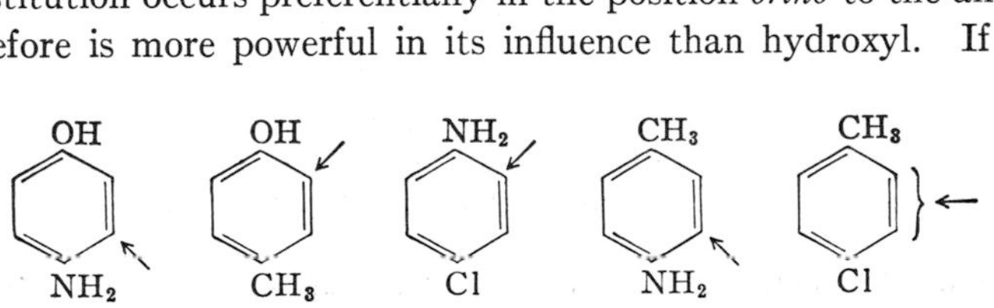

amino or hydroxyl group is pitted against methyl or other alkyl group, or against halogen, substitution is dominated by the —NH₂ or —OH group. The dimethylamino, amino, and hydroxyl groups so far surpass all other groups of the *ortho-para* type that amines and phenols undergo special substitutions not applicable to other aromatic compounds. The other *ortho-para* directing groups included in the list given above are arranged in the approximate order of effectiveness, as judged by competition reactions, but in this category of second-order effectiveness the differences are relatively slight. There is so little difference between methyl and halogen, for example, that the *p*-halotoluenes ordinarily afford mixtures of the two possible monosubstitution products.

Electron-releasing groups transmit an activating influence to both the *ortho* and *para* positions, but the ratio of *ortho* and *para* substitution varies over a rather wide range, as illustrated by the following summary:

NHCOCH₃   OH   Cl   CH₃
5%   40%   30%   59%
                       4%
95%   60%   70%   37%

Nitration

Para substitution generally predominates over substitution in the *ortho* position. Toluene is an exception, but in this case the *ortho-para* ratio is sensitive to conditions and varies from 3:2 to 2:3 according to the nitrating agent; the methyl group is a weakly effective member of the series and permits some *meta* substitution.

17.7   Ortho Effect. — The ratio of isomers produced in nitrations and in halogenations does not vary greatly with the temperature at which the reaction is carried out or with steric factors. In *op*-directed sulfonations and Friedel-Crafts alkylations, but not in nitrations or brominations, substituting groups tend to avoid the *ortho* position, particularly if the directing group is sizeable or if the reaction is done at a high temperature. Since these two reactions are reversible, it is possible that the substituent, SO₃H or R, enters the *ortho* position only to be displaced. However, the Friedel-Crafts acylation is not so readily reversible, but unhindered *para* products are usually formed. Thus the chief products of the two reactions with alkylbenzenes are the *para* derivatives.

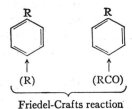

R   R

(R)   (RCO)

Friedel-Crafts reaction

Comparison of the quantitative data for the proportion of isomers formed on nitration and on sulfonation of chlorobenzene and toluene shows that sulfonation is subject to a striking steric effect. The effect of temperature is illustrated by

Cl   Cl   CH₃   CH₃
30%   59%   32%
                       4%   6%
70%   100%   37%   62%
Nitration Sulfonation Nitration Sulfonation

results for the sulfonation of toluene at 0° and 100°. The marked decrease in the *o/p* ratio at the higher temperature shows that increased vibration of groups enhances the *ortho* effect. That hindrance increases also with size of the group is evident from results for the sulfonation of toluene and *t*-butylbenzene.

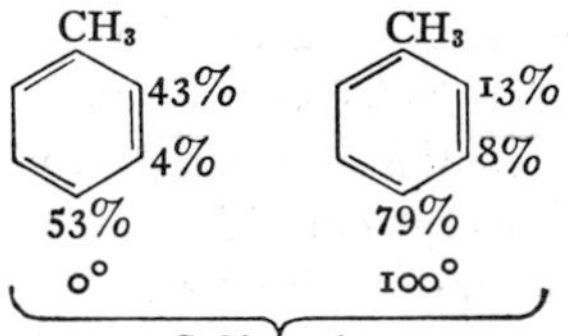

CH₃ 43% 4% 53% 0°   CH₃ 13% 8% 79% 100°

Sulfonation

That even nitration can be influenced by the steric factor is evident from com-

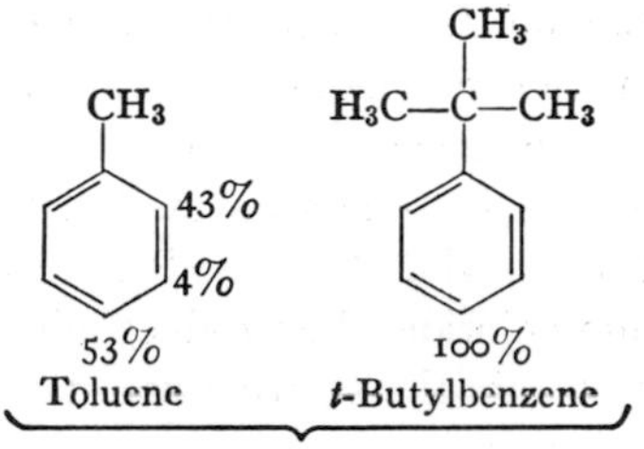

CH₃ 43% 4% 53% Toluene $H_3C-\underset{\underset{CH_3}{|}}{\overset{\overset{CH_3}{|}}{C}}-CH_3$ 100% *t*-Butylbenzene

Sulfonation at 0°

parison of the nitration of toluene and *t*-butylbenzene with mixed acid (H. C. Brown, 1951). Since the *meta* position is not conjugated with C_1 and hence not

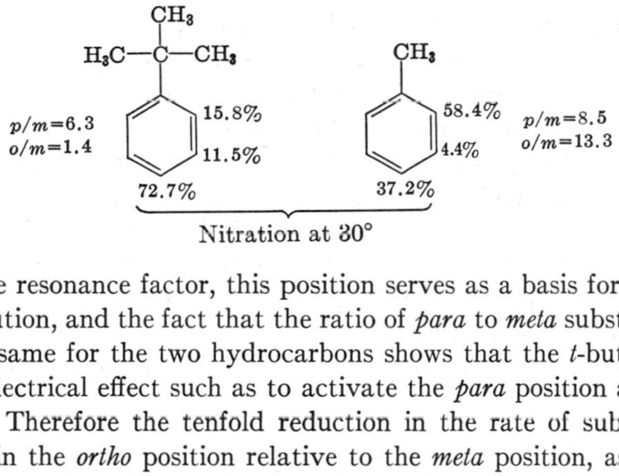

$p/m=6.3$
$o/m=1.4$ $H_3C-\underset{\underset{CH_3}{|}}{\overset{\overset{CH_3}{|}}{C}}-CH_3$ 15.8% 11.5% 72.7%   CH₃ 58.4% 4.4% 37.2% $p/m=8.5$
$o/m=13.3$

Nitration at 30°

affected by the resonance factor, this position serves as a basis for correlation of isomer distribution, and the fact that the ratio of *para* to *meta* substitution is substantially the same for the two hydrocarbons shows that the *t*-butyl group does not exert an electrical effect such as to activate the *para* position at the expense of the *ortho*. Therefore the tenfold reduction in the rate of substitution of *t*-butylbenzene in the *ortho* position relative to the *meta* position, as compared to toluene, can be attributed to the large steric requirement of the *t*-butyl group.

17.8   Mono- and Polysubstitution. — The contrast between the effect of *meta* directing groups in deactivating the benzene ring for substitutions and the substitution-promoting influence of *ortho-para* directors has important consequences. When benzene is nitrated, the reaction comes to a sharp stopping point with introduction of one nitro group, for the resistance to substitution is so increased that a second group can be introduced only under much more drastic conditions. The mononitro derivative is thus obtainable in high yield and without contamination by polynitro compounds. Since the group introduced on sulfonation is of the same type, hydrocarbons can be converted easily into their monosulfonic acids, and forcing conditions are required for introduction of a second group *meta* to the first.   Successive stages of halogenation also are attainable in discrete steps.   In the Friedel-Crafts ketone synthesis, the maximum intensity obtainable is such that the reaction is limited to monosubstitution.   Thus even with considerable excess of acetyl chloride and aluminum chloride, benzene is converted into acetophenone and no further.   The *meta* directing group introduced inhibits further reaction, and this suppression accounts for the generally satisfactory character of the synthesis.   Other *meta* directing groups also have an inhibitory influence, and the Friedel-Crafts acylation and alkylation reactions are inapplicable to such compounds as nitrobenzene, benzaldehyde, or benzonitrile. Friedel-Crafts alkylation is the one instance in which the group introduced facilitates further substitution.   Toluene is distinctly more susceptible than benzene to nitration and sulfonation; also it undergoes methylation more readily than the parent hydrocarbon, and hence when benzene is condensed with methyl chloride in the presence of aluminum chloride, the product initially formed inevitably consumes some of the reagent before the starting material is exhausted, with formation of polysubstitution products.

17.9   Reactions of Polysubstituted Compounds. — When more than one group is present in a substance undergoing substitution, the location and nature of the groups may exert either an antagonistic or a reinforcing influence on the course of the reaction.   In mesitylene each of the three equivalent positions is under the substitution-facilitating influence of one *para*-methyl and two *ortho*-methyl groups, and consequently the hydrocarbon undergoes ready substitution even though the only position attacked is hindered by two adjacent methyl groups.   Among the xylenes, the order of reactivity as indicated by sulfonation and desulfonation reactions employed in the separation (18.12) is: $m > o > p$.   The superior reactivity of m-xylene can be attributed to the reinforcing influence of the strong *para* and moderate *ortho* direction to the 4-position, the site of the sulfonation; both methyl groups exert a moderate activating influence at position 2, but this position is well blocked, particularly to a reaction notably subject to steric hindrance.   Of the

two positions available in o-xylene, one (4) is under the strong *para* influence of a methyl group, and the other (3) is *ortho* activated and moderately hindered; hence sulfonation occurs at the former position.   In p-xylene the only position available corresponds to the less reactive 3-position of o-xylene, and consequently the hydrocarbon is the least readily sulfonated of the three isomers.

p-Nitrophenol contains groups of different types, but these are not antagonistic. The nitro group deactivates position 3 strongly but influences the *meta* position

2 only moderately in an adverse sense, and since the latter position is under the powerful *ortho* influence of the hydroxyl group, it is the exclusive site of mono-

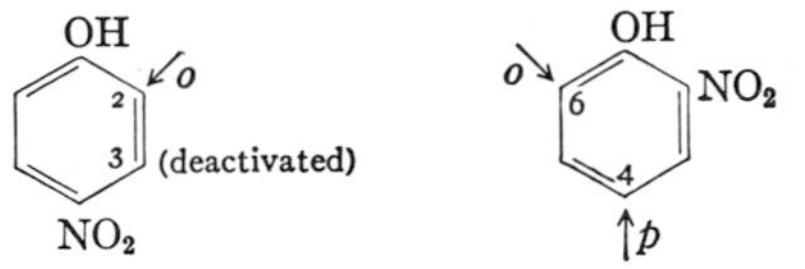

substitution, for example, on nitration or bromination. In *o*-nitrophenol the expected sites of substitution are positions 4 and 6, which are *para* and *ortho*, respectively, to the hydroxyl and *meta* to the nitro group. Since *para* orientation ordinarily is stronger than *ortho*, predominance of attack at position 4 would be anticipated. Actually sulfonation gives the 4-sulfonic acid exclusively; bromination affords the 4-monobromo compound along with the 4,6-dibromo derivative; and nitration gives chiefly 2,4-dinitrophenol, along with a small amount of the isomeric 2,6-dinitrophenol.

17.10 **Homolytic Substitutions.** — Aromatic substitutions effected by free radicals are of more theoretical than preparative interest. Phenyl radicals are generated by thermal decomposition of dibenzoyl peroxide. Methyl radicals are obtainable from diacetyl peroxide, but di-*t*-butyl peroxide is the reagent of choice. In a typical experiment a solution of 13 g. of di-*t*-butyl peroxide in 100 ml. of chlorobenzene is refluxed for 72 hrs., and the *t*-butyl alcohol and

$$(CH_3)_3COOC(CH_3)_3 \rightarrow (CH_3)_3CO\cdot \rightarrow (CH_3)_2C{=}O + \cdot CH_3$$

$$ClC_6H_5 + \cdot CH_3 + (CH_3)_3CO\cdot \rightarrow ClC_6H_4CH_3 + (CH_3)_3COH$$

acetone are removed as formed. Low-boiling products and excess chlorobenzene are removed by fractionation and the residue is analyzed by gas chromatography. Investigations chiefly by Hey[1] and Waters[2] (1959) are summarized in the Tables.

TABLE 17.3. ISOMER DISTRIBUTION IN METHYLATION

COMPOUND	o	m	p	TEMP.	COMPOUND	o	m	p	TEMP.
PhCl	64	25	11	130°	PhNO₂	65.5	6	28.5	143°
PhBr	67.5	23	9.5	145°	PhCN	48	9	43	133°
PhOCH₃	74	15	11	140°	PhCH₃	56.5	26.5	17	110°

Significant features are the high proportion of *ortho* products and the tendency of the *meta/para* ratio to fall below the statistical figure of 2 (Table 17.4). With groups that are *op*-directing in heterolytic electrophilic substitution, the *meta/para* ratio is higher for homolytic methylation than for phenylation, whereas with the

[1] Donald Holroyd Hey, b. 1904 Swansea; D.Sc. Manchester (Lapworth); Imperial College; King's College, Univ. London

[2] William A. Waters, b. 1903 Cardiff, Wales; Ph.D. Cambridge Univ. (McCombie, Scarborough); Univ. Durham; Oxford Univ.

TABLE 17.4. PHENYLATION AND METHYLATION

	PhCH₃	PhCl	PhBr	PhOCH₃	PhNO₂	PhCN
			% Ortho			
Phenylation	71	62	49	67	62.5	60
Temp.	80°	80°	80°		80°	
Methylation	56.5	64	67.5	74	65.5	48
Temp.	110°	130°	145°	140°	143°	133°
			Meta/para Ratio			
Phenylation	1.32	1.71	1.91	1.20	0.36	0.33
Methylation	1.56	2.27	2.42	1.36	0.21	0.21

m-directing nitro and cyano groups the reverse is the case.   Nitrobenzene undergoes nucleophilic substitution (19.7) and the orientation is chiefly *para* (with some *ortho*); hence the methyl radical is more like a nucleophile than the phenyl radical, that is, it has a greater tendency to donate electrons.   These and other data for homolytic aromatic substitutions indicate the following order of increasing electrophilicity: $CH_3 > C_6H_5 > C_6H_5Cl, C_6H_5NO_2$.

Both benzene and maleic anhydride undergo simple chlorine addition by photochemical chain reactions.   When a solution of maleic anhydride in benzene is chlorinated under illumination at 70°, chlorine addition to benzene proceeds to the stage of formation of the resonance-stabilized radical (1) and this is then intercepted by maleic anhydride to form the radical (2).   This radical attacks a

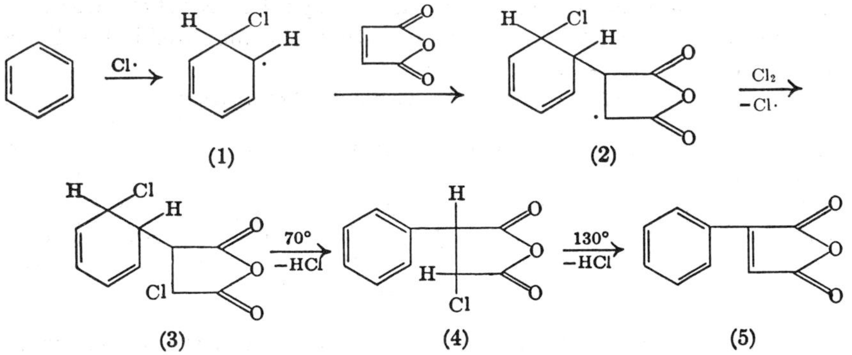

chlorine molecule to regenerate a chlorine radical and produce (3), which in part reverts to the aromatic type (4) and in part adds two moles of chlorine to form a stable by-product (A. J. Kolka,[1] 1956).   Thermal dehydrochlorination of (4) affords phenylmaleic anhydride (5).

[1] Alfred J. Kolka, b. 1914 Irma, Wis.; Ph.D. Notre Dame (Vogt); Allied Chemical and Dye Corp.; Ethyl Corp.; Koppers Co.

PROBLEM

Predict the chief products of the following reactions:

(a) Nitration of resorcinol dimethyl ether (1,3-dimethoxybenzene)

(b) Monobromination of p-CH$_3$CONHC$_6$H$_4$OCOCH$_3$

(c) Sulfonation of p-cymene, p-CH$_3$C$_6$H$_4$CH(CH$_3$)$_2$

(d) Sulfonation of p-methylacetophenone

(e) Nitration of phenol-p-sulfonic acid

(f) Condensation of 1,2,4-trimethylbenzene with acetyl chloride in the presence of aluminum chloride

(g) Nitration of m-dichlorobenzene

(h) Friedel-Crafts condensation of succinic anhydride with desoxybenzoin, C$_6$H$_5$COCH$_2$C$_6$H$_5$

(i) Nitration of diphenylmethane-p-carboxylic acid

(j) Friedel-Crafts methylation of p-chlorodiphenylmethane

(k) Mononitration of 4-methyl-4'-hydroxydiphenyl

(l) Nitration of C$_6$H$_5$CH$_2\overset{+}{\text{N}}$(CH$_3$)$_3$NO$_3^-$

(m) Chlorination of C$_6$H$_5$CCl$_3$ in the presence of FeCl$_3$

Chapter 18

AROMATIC HYDROCARBONS

18.1   **From Coal.** — The heating of bituminous coal at temperatures in the range 1000–1300° in a retort without access of air converts the bulk of the material into coke, a hard porous residuum consisting largely of carbon admixed with ash, and affords a quantity of gas (coal gas) and a mixture of less volatile products separating as a condensate consisting of black viscous coal tar and a water layer containing ammonia. The coking process can be conducted somewhat differently and with utilization of different types of coals according as coal gas or metallurgical coke is the chief objective, which varies with localities and economic conditions. The optimum conditions and type of coal for production of coal gas of high calorific value afford a soft inferior coke, and if conditions are chosen to give a coke hard enough for use in the reduction of iron oxide, the gas is not of the highest quality. It is most economical to manufacture high-grade coke in by-product ovens so constructed as to permit recovery of coal tar, ammonia, and coal gas, and to use a part of the gas as fuel for the ovens and the rest mixed with either natural gas or water gas for distribution through city gas mains. Refined **coke-oven gas,** amounting to some 11,200 cu. ft./ton of coal, consists largely of hydrogen (52% by volume) and methane (32%), with smaller amounts of carbon monoxide (4–9%), carbon dioxide (2%), nitrogen (4–5%), and ethylene and other olefins (3–4%). The average calorific value is 570 B.T.U./cu. ft. In the refining process, the gas passes through tar and ammonia scrubbers and through oil-absorption tanks for recovery of **light oil,** a crude oil amounting to 3.2 gal./ton of coal and containing benzene (60%), toluene (15%), xylenes, and naphthalene. A small additional amount of comparable light oil results from distillation of coal tar, but in the modern process over 90% of the benzene and toluene obtainable from coal is derived from the scrubbing of coke-oven gas. Introduction of the recovery process made available vast amounts of previously unutilized benzene of value as a motor fuel.

640

The yield of **coal tar** is about 3% of the weight of the coal. Initial refining is done by batch distillation; each fraction is further refined by extraction with alkali to separate the weakly acidic aromatic hydroxy compounds (phenols), by extraction of nitrogen bases with dilute mineral acid, and by refractionation. The principal hydrocarbons available commercially from coal tar are listed in Chart I in the order of increasing boiling points; melting points are included for

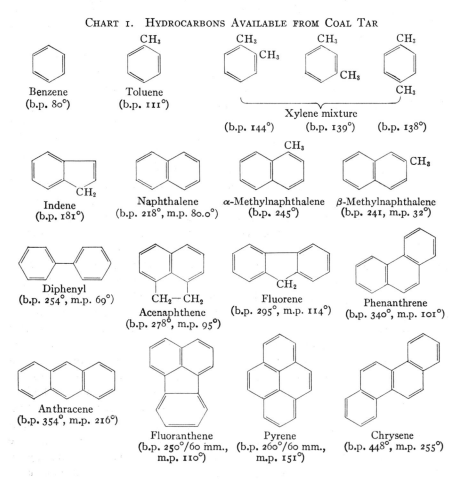

CHART I. HYDROCARBONS AVAILABLE FROM COAL TAR

Benzene
(b.p. 80°)

Toluene
(b.p. 111°)

Xylene mixture
(b.p. 144°)   (b.p. 139°)   (b.p. 138°)

Indene
(b.p. 181°)

Naphthalene
(b.p. 218°, m.p. 80.0°)

α-Methylnaphthalene
(b.p. 245°)

β-Methylnaphthalene
(b.p. 241, m.p. 32°)

Diphenyl
(b.p. 254°, m.p. 69°)

Acenaphthene
(b.p. 278°, m.p. 95°)

Fluorene
(b.p. 295°, m.p. 114°)

Phenanthrene
(b.p. 340°, m.p. 101°)

Anthracene
(b.p. 354°, m.p. 216°)

Fluoranthene
(b.p. 250°/60 mm.,
m.p. 110°)

Pyrene
(b.p. 260°/60 mm.,
m.p. 151°)

Chrysene
(b.p. 448°, m.p. 255°)

substances that are solids at ordinary temperature. In addition to aromatic hydrocarbons, coal tar is a practical source of cyclopentadiene (b.p. 41°), which can be stored as the more stable dimer and regenerated when required by slow distillation. Cyclopentadiene is found in light oil, which also contains small amounts of a number of paraffinic and olefinic hydrocarbons. The benzene and toluene found in light oil can be separated effectively by fractional distillation, but each is accompanied by a small amount of a heterocyclic analog of nearly the same boiling point. Thus coal-tar benzene, unless specially processed, contains a trace of thiophene. This unsaturated substance displays aromatic charac-

HC——CH
HC   CH
\ /
S

Thiophene (b.p. 84°)

teristics, for it undergoes sulfonation and nitration and is more stable and chemically inert than olefins. The resemblance to benzene is so marked that the presence of the substance in coal-tar benzene remained unsuspected till an incident in one of Victor Meyer's lectures provided a clue leading to the discovery of the sulfur compound (1882). Meyer periodically demonstrated a supposedly characteristic color test for benzene, which consists in shaking a sample with concentrated sulfuric acid and a crystal of isatin (Baeyer's indophenine reaction), but on one occasion he applied the test in expectation of proving that benzoic acid on decarboxylation gives benzene. The beautiful blue color failed to appear, since the color reaction is specific for the previously unknown thiophene and not for benzene.

The three xylenes boil at too nearly the same temperature to be separable by the distillation techniques of coal tar refineries, and a xylene mixture is obtained to the extent of about 1% of the weight of dry coal tar (for separation in the petrochemical industry, see 7.16). Naphthalene is the most abundant single constituent (average yield about 11%); it also is accompanied by a sulfur analog, thionaphthene (b.p. 220°). In addition to α- and β-methylnaphthalene and acenaphthene, coal tar affords a considerable fraction containing dimethylnaphthalenes (2,3-, 2,6-, 2,7-, and 1,6-; b.p. 261–262°), which are separable by elaborate processing and have appeared on the market only briefly. Anthracene was valued in the early days of coal-tar technology as the starting material for production of alizarin, the first natural dye that was prepared synthetically (1868), and it gained new importance with discovery of the indanthrone vat dyes (1901), also obtainable from this hydrocarbon. Thus the higher-boiling fractions of the coal-tar distillate have long been worked for anthracene. Some of the other hydrocarbons shown in the chart, though currently available, are rare and expensive. The processing often includes such chemical methods as sulfonation and desulfonation and treatment with alkali or sodium. Thus technical anthracene has a yellowish tinge due to a trace of naphthacene, and gives a positive

Naphthacene
(orange, m.p. 335°)

test for nitrogen, owing to the presence of the heterocyclic analog carbazole (see Chart 2). Naphthacene can be eliminated on a small scale by chromatographic adsorption and on a large scale by selective distillation of the anthracene with ethylene glycol. Pure anthracene (m.p. 216°) exhibits a spectacularly beautiful blue fluorescence in either the crystalline or dissolved state; the fluorescence disappears on fusion of the solid and reappears on solidification of the melt. Although naphthacene does not inhibit the fluorescence of anthracene in solution, as little as 0.1% of this persistent contaminant present in solid solution in anthracene gives rise to a distinctly altered fluorescence spectrum (J. A. Miller and C. A. Baumann, 1943). Naphthacene also persists in repeatedly crystallized samples of chrysene, to which it imparts a beautiful golden color that was the basis for the name (Gr. *chrysos*, gold), though by special techniques completely colorless and fluorescent chrysene can be obtained. Carbazole is comparable in structure to succinimide, and is not extracted by washing with dilute acid; since it is sufficiently acidic to form a sodium salt, it can be eliminated by fusion of technical anthracene with alkali.

The chief nitrogen components produced commercially are listed in Chart 2. These are all basic except indole and carbazole, which are weakly acidic.   The

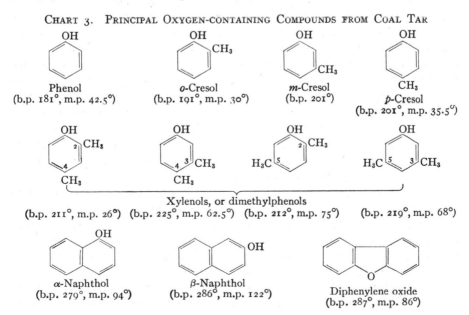

CHART 2. PRINCIPAL NITROGEN COMPOUNDS FROM COAL TAR

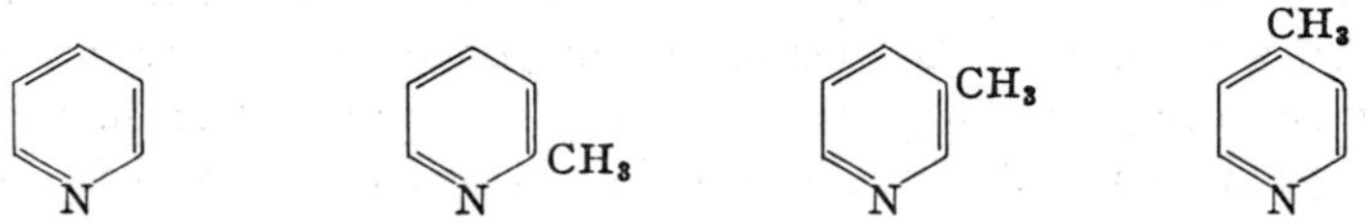

Pyridine
(b.p. 115°)

α-Picoline
(b.p. 129°)

β-Picoline
(b.p. 143°)

γ-Picoline
(b.p. 143°)

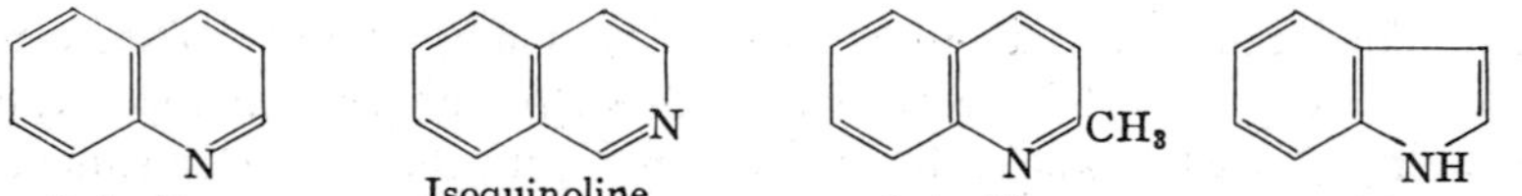

Quinoline
(b.p. 238°)

Isoquinoline
(b.p. 242°, m.p. 25°)

Quinaldine
(b.p. 247°)

Indole
(b.p. 253°, m.p. 52°)

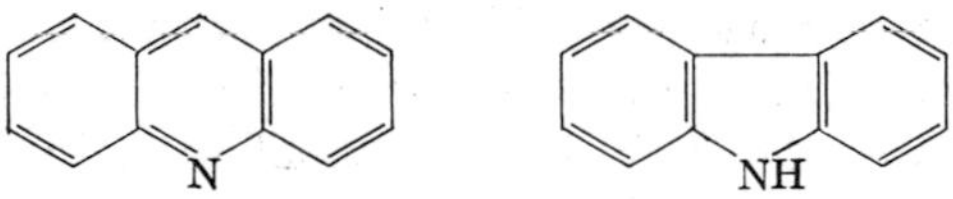

Acridine
(b.p. 345°, m.p. 111°)

Carbazole
(b.p. 354°, m.p. 238°)

oxygen-containing substances produced from coal tar are listed in Chart 3.   The phenolic constituents can be separated from the neutral and basic constituents of

CHART 3. PRINCIPAL OXYGEN-CONTAINING COMPOUNDS FROM COAL TAR

Phenol
(b.p. 181°, m.p. 42.5°)

o-Cresol
(b.p. 191°, m.p. 30°)

m-Cresol
(b.p. 201°)

p-Cresol
(b.p. 201°, m.p. 35.5°)

Xylenols, or dimethylphenols
(b.p. 211°, m.p. 26°) (b.p. 225°, m.p. 62.5°) (b.p. 212°, m.p. 75°)   (b.p. 219°, m.p. 68°)

α-Naphthol
(b.p. 279°, m.p. 94°)

β-Naphthol
(b.p. 286°, m.p. 122°)

Diphenylene oxide
(b.p. 287°, m.p. 86°)

coal-tar distillates by extraction with alkali, and efficient fractionation on a technical scale affords cuts consisting preponderantly of phenol, o-cresol, and a mixture of m- and p-cresol. Isolation of pure components of the cresol and xylenol fractions is accomplished by selective precipitation and by sulfonation.

Some forty compounds have been mentioned here as derived from the coking process, but the total number of identified substances from this source is one hundred twenty-two. Only those substances listed in the charts are normally available for synthetic uses. The benzenoid compounds are not present as such in coal, but arise in the course of pyrolysis. Coal is a product of gradual decomposition of vegetable material containing cellulose, $(C_6H_{10}O_5)_n$, without free access of air, often under the influence of moisture and increased pressure and temperature, and is formed through the successive stages of peat, lignite or brown coal, bituminous or soft coal, and anthracite or hard coal, characterized by increasing carbon content. The bituminous coal ordinarily employed in by-product coking contains about 80–82% carbon, 5–6% hydrogen, 1–2% each of nitrogen and sulfur, 3–5% oxygen, and 5–7% ash. The carbon is combined with the other elements present in the form of large polymeric molecules. The coking process conducted at 1000–1300° must involve cracking of the large molecules, probably followed by an elaborate sequence of reforming steps. The low-temperature carbonization of coal has been investigated on an experimental scale with results indicating that at temperatures of 500–700° the tar is richer in paraffinic and hydroaromatic compounds, which suggests that in the usual process a terminal step consists in thermal dehydrogenation.

18.2   Properties. — The most frequently encountered benzenoid hydrocarbons are included in Table 18.1. Some are obtainable on a practical scale directly from coal tar, but the majority are synthesized from starting materials derived from coal tar. Benzene and its more volatile homologs are characterized by a strong and rather pleasant aromatic odor. The liquids are highly refractive, lighter than water, and very sparingly soluble in water. They possess marked toxicity, and continued breathing of the vapors is dangerous. Benzene vapor is also heavy and highly flammable. Like other members of the series, the hydrocarbon burns with a luminous sooty flame and has a high calorific value. The heat of combustion is 781 kcal./mole, or 8.79 kcal. (34.87 B.T.U.)/ml. The values for toluene (8.79 kcal./ml.) and for the xylenes and ethylbenzene (8.86 kcal./ml.) are similar; the available aromatic hydrocarbons are distinctly more efficient fuels, on a volume basis, than hexane (7.58 kcal./ml.) and are slightly superior to cyclohexane (8.68 kcal./ml.).

In the series of alkylbenzenes, the boiling points show a regular relationship to the molecular weight and are almost independent of the positions of substituents in the ring. Thus the xylenes all boil at nearly the same temperatures, an average of 29° higher than the temperature at which toluene boils, and the tri- and tetramethylbenzenes fall into groups of boiling points about 30° apart. A similar progressive decrease in volatility with increasing molecular weight attends lengthening of the chain of the alkyl substituent. The most noteworthy feature of the melting point data is that substances of symmetrical structure usually melt at

TABLE 18.1. BENZENOID HYDROCARBONS[1]

NAME	FORMULA	M.P., °C.	B.P., °C.
Benzene	C_6H_6	5.4	80.1
Toluene	$C_6H_5CH_3$	−93	110.6
o-Xylene	$1,2\text{-}(CH_3)_2C_6H_4$	−28	144
m-Xylene	$1,3\text{-}(CH_3)_2C_6H_4$	−54	139
p-Xylene	$1,4\text{-}(CH_3)_2C_6H_4$	13	138
Hemimellitene	$1,2,3\text{-}(CH_3)_3C_6H_3$	liq.	176
Pseudocumene	$1,2,4\text{-}(CH_3)_3C_6H_3$	liq.	169
Mesitylene	$1,3,5\text{-}(CH_3)_3C_6H_3$	−57	165
Prehnitene	$1,2,3,4\text{-}(CH_3)_4C_6H_2$	−4	205
Isodurene	$1,2,3,5\text{-}(CH_3)_4C_6H_2$	liq.	196
Durene	$1,2,4,5\text{-}(CH_3)_4C_6H_2$	80	195
Pentamethylbenzene	$C_6H(CH_3)_5$	53	231
Hexamethylbenzene	$C_6(CH_3)_6$	166	265
Ethylbenzene	$C_6H_5CH_2CH_3$	−93	136
n-Propylbenzene	$C_6H_5CH_2CH_2CH_3$	liq.	159.5
Cumene	$C_6H_5CH(CH_3)_2$	liq.	152
n-Butylbenzene	$C_6H_5CH_2CH_2CH_2CH_3$	liq.	180
t-Butylbenzene	$C_6H_5C(CH_3)_3$	liq.	168
p-Cymene	$p\text{-}CH_3C_6H_4CH(CH_3)_2$	−73.5	177
1,3,5-Triethylbenzene	$1,3,5\text{-}(CH_3CH_2)_3C_6H_3$	liq.	215
Hexaethylbenzene	$C_6(CH_2CH_3)_6$	129	305
Styrene	$C_6H_5CH{=}CH_2$	liq.	146
Allylbenzene	$C_6H_5CH_2CH{=}CH_2$	liq.	156
Stilbene (trans)	$C_6H_5CH{=}CHC_6H_5$	124	307
Diphenylmethane	$(C_6H_5)_2CH_2$	27	262
Triphenylmethane	$(C_6H_5)_3CH$	92.5	359
Tetraphenylmethane	$(C_6H_4)_4C$	285	431
Diphenyl	$C_6H_5 \cdot C_6H_5$	70.5	254
p-Terphenyl	$C_6H_5 \cdot C_6H_4 \cdot C_6H_5$	171	
p-Quaterphenyl	$C_6H_5 \cdot C_6H_4 \cdot C_6H_4 \cdot C_6H_5$	320	$428^{18\,mm.}$
1,3,5-Triphenylbenzene	$1,3,5\text{-}(C_6H_5)_3C_6H_3$	174.5	

[1] The hydrocarbons listed that contain only one benzene ring have specific gravities in the range 0.86–.90.

higher temperatures than unsymmetrical isomers. Thus p-xylene freezes at 13°, whereas the *ortho* and *meta* isomers remain liquid at temperatures well below zero. The symmetrical 1,2,4,5-tetramethyl derivative durene melts at 80°, whereas its isomers are liquids; hexamethylbenzene is a high-melting solid (166°).

PREPARATION

18.3   Dehydrogenation of Hydroaromatic Hydrocarbons. — Hydro derivatives of aromatic compounds are called hydroaromatic: cyclohexane, cyclohexanol, 1,2,3,4-tetrahydronaphthalene (tetralin), perhydronaphthalene (decalin). Alicyclic substances containing six-membered rings but having carbon substituents that block conversion to the aromatic state unless they are eliminated (*e.g.* camphor and 1,1-dimethylcyclohexane) are not classified as hydroaromatic. Hydroaromatic compounds can be aromatized by various methods of dehydrogenation. The chief experimental methods, illustrated for a general case, include dehydrogenation with sulfur at a rather low temperature (Vesterberg, 1903), dehydrogenation with the less active and often less destructive selenium at distinctly higher temperatures (Diels, 1927), and catalytic dehydrogenation (Zelinsky, 1911). Dehydrogenation over a 10% palladium charcoal catalyst, prepared by reduction of palladium chloride in an alkaline suspension of activated carbon (Norit) with formaldehyde, often proceeds very smoothly. The reaction can be conducted in the vapor phase by distillation of the hydroaromatic com-

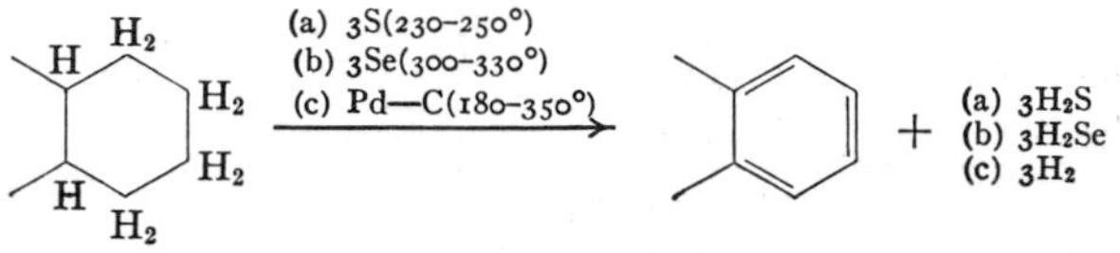

pound through a tube containing the catalyst at temperatures in the range 300–350°, but the liquid-phase method is usually more convenient. If the substance to be dehydrogenated is heated with one tenth part of palladium charcoal to about 310–320°, hydrogen is evolved steadily and the material is soon aromatized. The reaction is promoted by passing carbon dioxide into the solution to entrain and remove the evolved hydrogen from the equilibrium mixture, and also by vigorous boiling, which helps to dislodge the hydrogen from the active surface of the catalyst (Linstead, 1940). Tetralin, b.p. 207°, can be dehydrogenated to naphthalene by heating it with catalyst at the boiling point in a stream of carbon dioxide, and the reaction can be made to proceed at temperatures as low as 185° by addition of a diluent boiling at this temperature.

Although aromatic hydrocarbons are end products of dehydrogenations conducted at temperatures near 500°, further dehydrogenation to a diaryl sometimes can be accomplished at still higher temperatures. Thus diphenyl is manufactured by passing benzene vapor through an iron tube packed with pumice at temperatures in the range 650–800°: $2C_6H_6 \rightarrow C_6H_5 \cdot C_6H_5 + H_2$. In another process the vapor is bubbled through molten lead. Diphenyl is used as a heat-transfer fluid, particularly as a component of Dowtherm A, a eutectic mixture of 73.5% diphenyl ether and 26.5% diphenyl. The mixture (b.p. 260°) is fluid above 12° and can be used at operating temperatures up to about 400° (150 lbs./sq. in.).

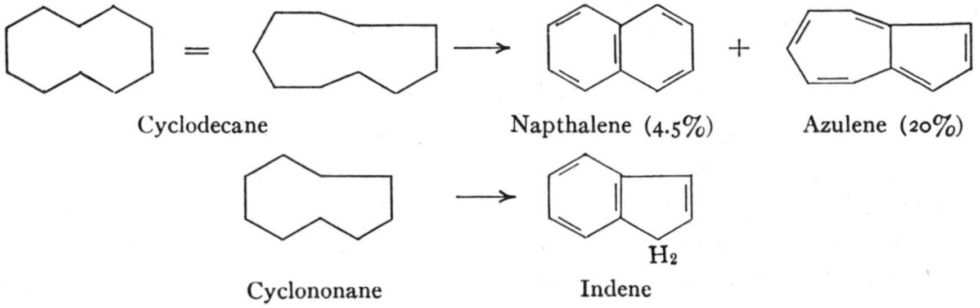

Cyclodecane   Napthalene (4.5%)   Azulene (20%)

Cyclononane   Indene

The catalytic dehydrogenation of macrocyclic hydrocarbons was studied by Plattner.[1]   Heated in the gas phase in the presence of palladium-charcoal, cyclodecane undergoes cyclodehydrogenation to give naphthalene and azulene, a blue, resonance-stabilized isomer of naphthalene.   Cyclononane gives indene as the main aromatic product.   At 440° cyclooctane is converted into p-xylene.

18.4   From Other Alicyclic Compounds. — The production of p-cymene by the action of dehydrating agents on camphor demonstrates the stability and ease of formation of the aromatic system; a rearrangement with

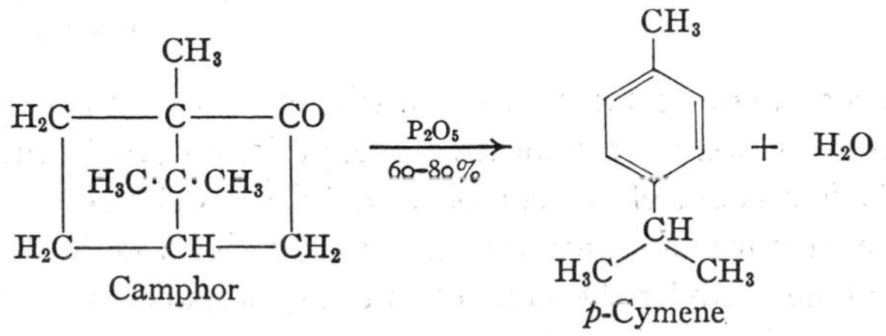

rupture of the bridge linkage carrying the *gem*-dimethyl group is involved, but p-cymene is produced in good yield. p-Cymene can be obtained from several other terpenes (isoprenoids); it occurs along with terpenes in many essential oils (volatile, fragrant oils) and is available from spruce turpentine.

18.5   Condensation and Trimerization Reactions. — Mesitylene can be obtained by adding concentrated sulfuric acid to acetone at 5–10° and letting the mixture come to room temperature.   Mesityl oxide, phorone, and other condensation products are formed and the yield is low.   1,3,5-Triphenyl-

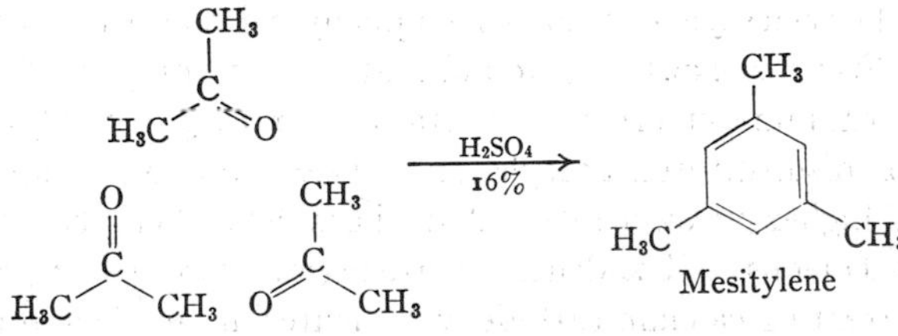

benzene is formed similarly from acetophenone, $C_6H_5COCH_3$.   The reaction has been applied to synthesis of the interesting tetracyclic hydrocarbon dodecahydrotriphenylene from cyclohexanone; the product crystallizes from the reaction mixture in large, sparlike needles.   Several other methods have been tried for effecting this cyclodehydration; the best yield (13%) was obtained by heating cyclohexanone with alumina containing 4.5% of thorium oxide at 280°/57 atm. for 32 hrs. (C. C. Barker, 1958).   Dehydrogenation to triphenylene with palladium charcoal is practically quantitative.

M. Berthelot (1868) found that acetylene passed through a porcelain tube heated to dull redness is converted in part into benzene.   Work of Favorsky cited in section 6.22 shows that in 1888 trimerization of dimethylacetylene to

[1] Placidus Andreas Plattner, b. 1904 Chur, Switzerland; Ph.D. Zurich ETH (Ruzicka, Cherbuliez); Zurich ETH; Hofmann La Roche, Basel

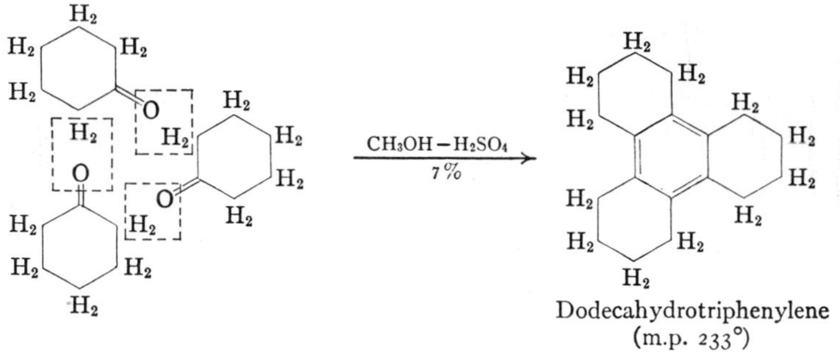
CH₃OH – H₂SO₄
7%
Dodecahydrotriphenylene
(m.p. 233°)

hexamethylbenzene under catalysis by sulfuric acid was a well-established reaction; yields, however, were not recorded. Reppe found (1948) that, in the presence of a catalytic amount of the complex $Ni(CO)_2 \cdot [(C_6H_5)_3P]_2$, acetylene reacts at 60–70° and a pressure of 15 atmospheres to give benzene in 88% yield along with 12% of styrene. Under the same conditions, propargyl alcohol is converted in high yield into a mixture of equal parts of 1,3,5- and 1,2,4-trimethylolbenzene.

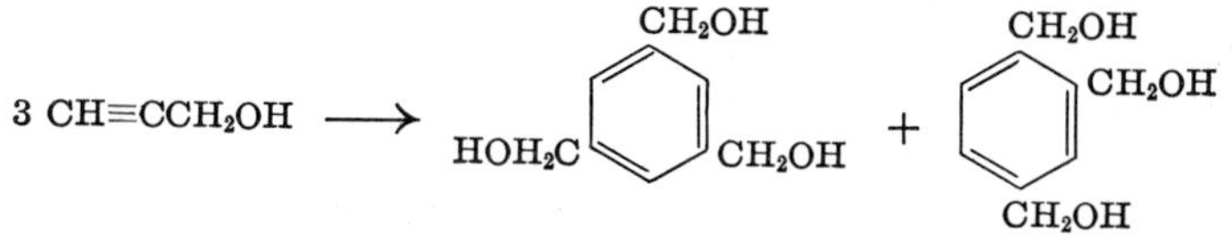
3 CH≡CCH₂OH
CH₂OH
HOH₂C
CH₂OH
+
CH₂OH
CH₂OH
CH₂OH

W. Hübel (1960) found still more effective catalysts in the complexes $Co_2(CO)_8$ and $[Co(CO)_4]_2Hg$. Trimerization of phenylacetylene in refluxing dioxane in the presence of the complex mercury derivative affords 1,2,4-triphenylbenzene in 70% yield; diphenylacetylene affords hexaphenylbenzene (m.p. 427°, uncor.) in 90% yield. B. Franzus[1] *et al.* (1959) found that catalysts prepared from triisobutylaluminum and titanium chloride in the ratios 1/1 to 3/1 catalyze quantitative trimerization of disubstituted acetylenes to hexaalkyl- or hexaphenylbenzenes. Preparations of higher or lower ratios than those defined catalyze polymerization of acetylenes and olefins. Hexadeuterobenzene (m.p. 6.8°, b.p. 79.3°, d_4^{25} 0.9429) is prepared by treating calcium carbide with deuterium oxide and circulating the acetylene-D_2 through a bed of silica-alumina catalyst at room temperature (I. Shapiro, 1957).

The principle of carbon-skeleton synthesis during complex formation offers a new route to the formation of organic compounds which may have practical

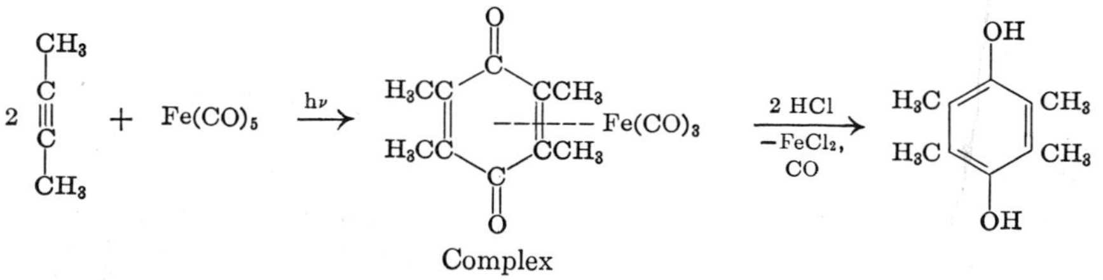
2
+ Fe(CO)₅
hν
Fe(CO)₃
Complex
2 HCl
–FeCl₂,
CO
OH
H₃C
CH₃
H₃C
CH₃
OH

[1] Boris Franzus, b. 1924 Chicago; Ph.D. Colorado (Cristol); Phillips Petrol. Co.

synthetic value (H. W. Sternberg,[1] 1958). Exposure to sunlight of a mixture of dimethylacetylene and $Fe(CO)_5$ causes separation of orange crystals of the composition $Fe(CO)_5(CH_3C{\equiv}CCH_3)_2$. This substance is formulated as a π-complex formed by union of the two alkyne molecules with two carbonyl groups, since on exposure to air the complex affords duroquinone and on treatment with acid it yields durohydroquinone and carbon monoxide quantitatively.

18.6   Wurtz-Type Synthesis. — Examples of the Wurtz-Fittig synthesis of aralkyl hydrocarbons have been cited (4.6). A Wurtz-type reaction is involved in the synthesis of acenaphthene from naphthalic anhydride by reduc-

tion to the diol, conversion to the dibromide, and condensation with phenyl‑lithium in place of sodium (Bergmann[2] and Szmuszkovicz, 1953).

18.7   Friedel-Crafts Alkylation. — In 1877 the French chemist Friedel[3] and his American collaborator Crafts[4] investigated the action of metallic aluminum on alkyl halides, possibly with a view to varying the Wurtz reaction. Little change occurred at first, even on heating, but after an induction period a reaction set in, with evolution of hydrogen chloride, and became particularly brisk whenever a considerable amount of aluminum chloride was formed. The inference that aluminum chloride was the effective catalytic agent was confirmed by experiments on the action of this substance on amyl chloride. A reaction was easily initiated, with evolution of hydrogen chloride and production of amylene and a mixture of other hydrocarbons. Investigation showed that this mixture could hardly consist merely of polymerized amylene and suggested that, under the influence of aluminum chloride, amyl chloride may have condensed with amylene or other hydrocarbon. This inference led to trial condensation with a preformed hydrocarbon, which showed that amyl chloride reacts smoothly with benzene in the presence of aluminum chloride as catalyst to yield amylbenzene. A general synthetic reaction of broad application was thereby discovered, for Friedel and Crafts and later workers found that almost any alkyl chloride or bromide can be condensed catalytically with an aromatic hydrocarbon to produce a hydrocarbon of mixed type, as indicated for the general case as follows:

$$Ar{\cdot}H \ + \ RX \ \longrightarrow \ Ar{\cdot}R \ + \ HX$$

---

[1] Heinz W. Sternberg, b. 1911 Vienna, Austria; Ph.D. Univ. Vienna (Spaeth); U. S. Bureau of Mines

[2] Ernst David Bergmann, b. 1903 Karlsruhe, Germany; Ph.D. Berlin (Schlenk); Hebrew University, Jerusalem, and Scientific Department, Israel Ministry of Defence

[3] Charles Friedel, 1832–99; b. Strasbourg, France; Paris; *Ber.*, **32**, 3721 (1899); *Bull. Soc. Chem.*, [4], **51**, 1493 (1932); *J. Chem. Ed.*, **26**, 3 (1949)

[4] James M. Crafts, 1839–1917; b. Boston; Ph.D. Harvard; Mass. Inst. Techn.

Ordinarily the hydrocarbon must be aromatic and the halogen compound aliphatic. Thus benzene reacts with ethyl chloride or ethyl bromide in the presence of anhydrous aluminum chloride to form ethylbenzene, but the hydrocarbon cannot be synthesized in a comparable manner from ethane and chlorobenzene. Useful applications of the Friedel-Crafts reaction are the syntheses of the di- and triphenyl derivatives of methane:

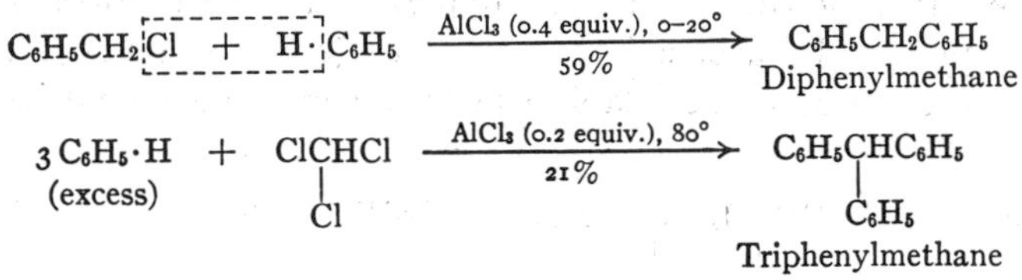

$$C_6H_5CH_2\underline{Cl} + H\cdot\underline{C_6H_5} \xrightarrow[59\%]{\text{AlCl}_3 \text{ (0.4 equiv.), } 0-20°} C_6H_5CH_2C_6H_5$$
Diphenylmethane

$$\underset{\text{(excess)}}{3\,C_6H_5\cdot H} + \underset{\overset{|}{Cl}}{ClCHCl} \xrightarrow[21\%]{\text{AlCl}_3 \text{ (0.2 equiv.), } 80°} C_6H_5\underset{\overset{|}{C_6H_5}}{CHC_6H_5}$$
Triphenylmethane

A severe limitation of Friedel-Crafts alkylation is that the group introduced is electron-releasing and activates the ring for further substitution. Polysubstitution cannot be avoided, and hence yields are low and a given product requires extensive purification.

The reaction provides a practical synthesis of durene, 1,2,4,5-tetramethylbenzene. This symmetrically substituted hydrocarbon has a higher melting point and lower solubility than any of its isomers or than the tri- and pentamethylbenzenes that invariably accompany it in the reaction of benzene with four equivalents of methyl chloride, and hence can be separated from the reaction mixture by freezing and purified by recrystallization. The preparation is modified

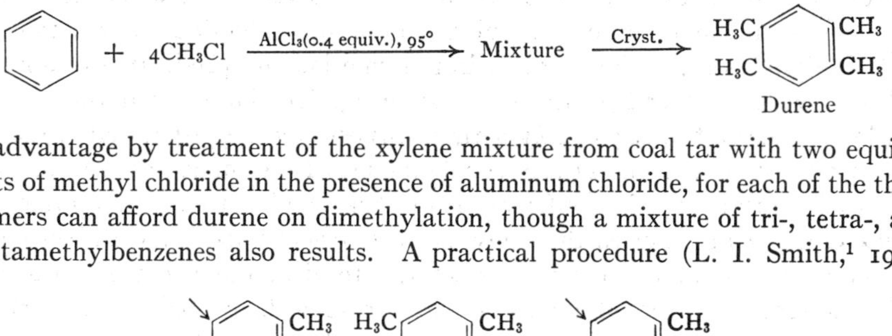

Durene

to advantage by treatment of the xylene mixture from coal tar with two equivalents of methyl chloride in the presence of aluminum chloride, for each of the three isomers can afford durene on dimethylation, though a mixture of tri-, tetra-, and pentamethylbenzenes also results. A practical procedure (L. I. Smith,[1] 1926)

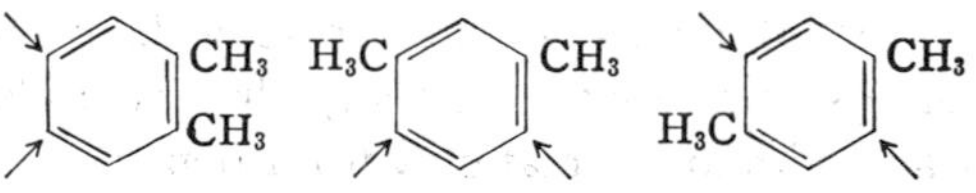

consists in passing methyl chloride (2.3 moles) under slight pressure into technical xylene (1 mole) and aluminum chloride (0.4 mole) at 95°, separating the crude tri-, tetra-, and pentamethylbenzene fractions by distillation, freezing the durene from the middle fraction, and crystallizing it three times from alcohol. The yield of pure durene is 10–11%, but can be raised to 18–25% by submitting the trimethylbenzene fraction to methylation and by heating the liquid portion of the tetramethylbenzene fraction with aluminum chloride. Pure pentamethylbenzene can be isolated from the highest-boiling fraction in 8% yield by redistillation and

[1] Lee Irvin Smith, b. 1891 Indianapolis; Ph.D. Harvard (Kohler); Univ. Minnesota

crystallization.   Hexamethylbenzene is prepared by methylation of pentamethyl-benzene with methyl chloride and aluminum chloride; the yield of the high-melt-ing, easily purified hydrocarbon is 24–30%.

Although aluminum chloride has been the most frequently used catalyst, several other catalysts are available of varying activity below that of aluminum chloride, and hence condensation can be moderated by use of these milder agents.   Suitable anhydrous inorganic halides, listed in the order of decreasing potency, are as follows:

$$AlCl_3 > FeCl_3 > SnCl_4 > BF_3 > ZnCl_2$$

The reagents are all electron-acceptors, or Lewis acids.   In some variations of the general reaction the following catalysts are used:

$$HF > H_2SO_4 \ (96\%) > P_2O_5 > H_3PO_4$$

Hydrogen fluoride, employed as the anhydrous liquid (b.p. 19.4°), is a particularly valuable reagent introduced in 1938–39 (J. H. Simons, W. S. Calcott).   The control that is possible through the choice and amount of catalyst and regulation of the temperature is important in polysubstitutions, for under mild conditions the entering groups tend to become oriented in *ortho* and *para* positions, whereas under forcing conditions *meta* orientation obtains (*ortho* effect).   Thus trisubsti-tution can be directed to afford chiefly either the 1,2,4- or the 1,3,5-derivative. Substitution in the *meta* position is favored by use of a considerable amount (usually 2 equivalents) of aluminum chloride, the most active catalyst, or of a high reaction temperature.   The effect of temperature is seen in the fact that the

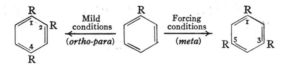

reaction of benzene with three moles of methyl chloride gives chiefly 1,2,4-trimethylbenzene when conducted at 0°, but yields chiefly the 1,3,5-isomer when carried out at 100°.   The proportion of catalyst is even more important.   Durene is formed in a series of *ortho* and *para* substitutions, and the procedure for its preparation cited above calls for use of 0.4 equivalent of aluminum chloride (calculated as $AlCl_3$) at 95°.   If the amount of catalyst is increased to 2 equiva-lents of $AlCl_3$ (or 1 of the actual double molecule Al_2Cl_6), the *meta* derivative mesitylene can be obtained in yields up to 63% in a reaction conducted at 100° (J. F. Norris,[1] 1938–39).   *Meta* ethylation can be realized even at a low temperature by employing sufficient catalyst and allowing an extended period for reaction, as shown in the example.   Aluminum chloride has such a tendency to give *meta* derivatives that milder catalysts are preferred where the alternative course of reaction is desired.   Boron fluoride, introduced in the reaction mixture as a gas,

[1] James F. Norris, 1871–1940; b. Baltimore; Ph.D. Johns Hopkins Univ.; Mass. Inst. Techn.

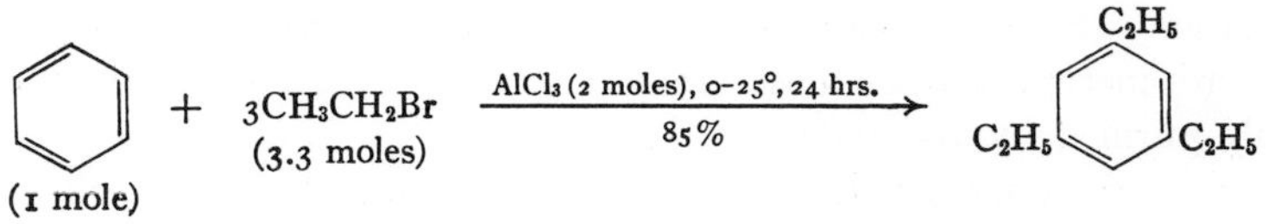

is particularly satisfactory for the preparation of *p*-dialkylbenzenes, for example:

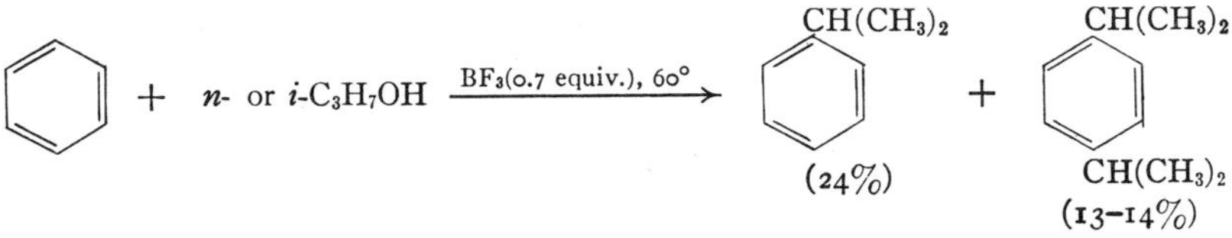

The example illustrates use of an alcohol in place of an alkyl halide as the alkylating agent, and this variation is generally applicable also when aluminum chloride is employed as catalyst.

A likely explanation of the remarkable variation in the course of the reaction with conditions is found in the fact that the Friedel-Crafts reaction is reversible. If an alkylbenzene is treated with aluminum chloride in the absence of an alkylating agent, it is converted in part into a mixture of higher and lower substitution products; alkyl groups evidently are severed from one molecule and transposed to another. Furthermore, 1,2,4-trimethylbenzene rearranges to mesitylene in the presence of aluminum chloride. Therefore production of 1,3,5-derivatives under forcing conditions may be the result of initial *ortho-para* substitution followed by elimination of one group and substitution at a more secure position (C. C. Price, 1941, see next section).

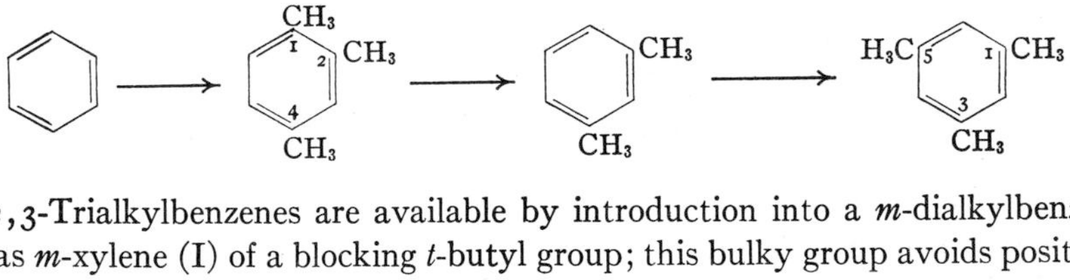

1,2,3-Trialkylbenzenes are available by introduction into a *m*-dialkylbenzene such as *m*-xylene (I) of a blocking *t*-butyl group; this bulky group avoids positions *ortho* to the methyl substituents and gives II in good yield. This derivative

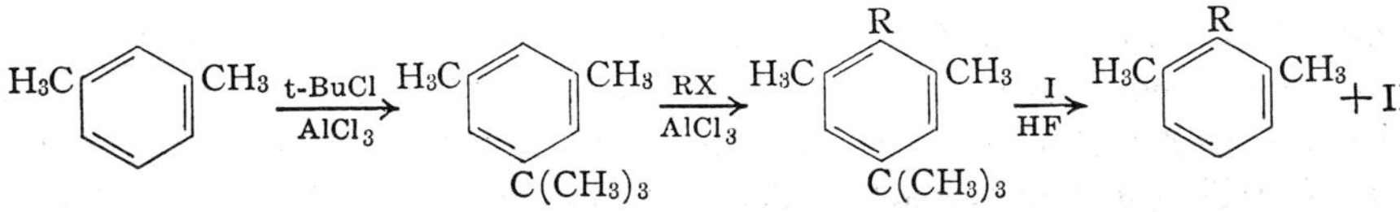

undergoes alkylation in the position *para* to the *t*-butyl group; the blocking group is then removed by transfer to *m*-xylene to regenerate II and yield the 1,2,3-trisubstituted benzene IV (M. J. Schlatter, 1954). A related observation is that under Friedel-Crafts conditions (boiling CS_2) hexaethylbenzene reacts with acetyl chloride to give pentaethylacetophenone in 80% yield (H. Hopff, 1960). Hexamethylbenzene is less reactive and gives mainly tars.

Both olefins and alcohols can be employed in the Friedel-Crafts reaction in place of alkyl halides. Examples of these variations in the general method are shown in reactions 1 to 4. Alkylation of benzene by propylene with production

1. C_6H_6 + $CH_3CH{=}CH_2$ $\xrightarrow[84\%]{HF,\,0^\circ}$ $C_6H_5CH(CH_3)_2$
                                                        Cumene

2.   + $\xrightarrow[62\%]{HF,\,0^\circ}$
        Cyclohexene   Cyclohexylbenzene
                                            (m.p. 8°)

3.   + HO $\xrightarrow{BF_3(0.7\ \text{equiv.}),\,60^\circ}$ $\begin{cases} 56\%\ \text{Cyclohexylbenzene} \\ 27\%\ p\text{-Dicyclohexylbenzene} \end{cases}$
            Cyclohexanol

4.   + $3(CH_3)_2CHOH$ $\xrightarrow[94.5\%]{HF,\,25^\circ}$

                                                    2,4,6-Triisopropylphenol
                                                       (b.p. 125° at 7 mm.)

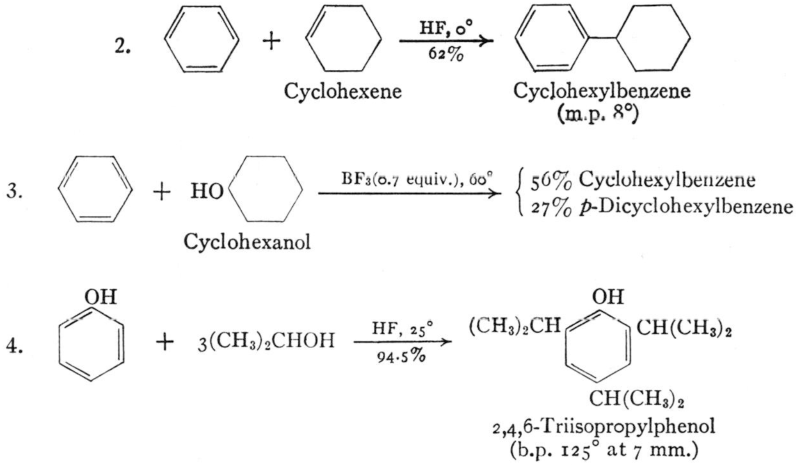

of cumene has been accomplished also with use of ferric chloride, sulfuric acid, or phosphoric acid in place of hydrogen fluoride.

A peculiarity of Friedel-Crafts alkylation is that the hydrocarbon group of the alkyl halide, olefin, or alcohol frequently rearranges in the process. Thus *n*-propyl bromide and isopropyl bromide on reaction with benzene in the presence of aluminum chloride both yield cumene (G. Gustavson, 1878). *n*-Alkyl bro-

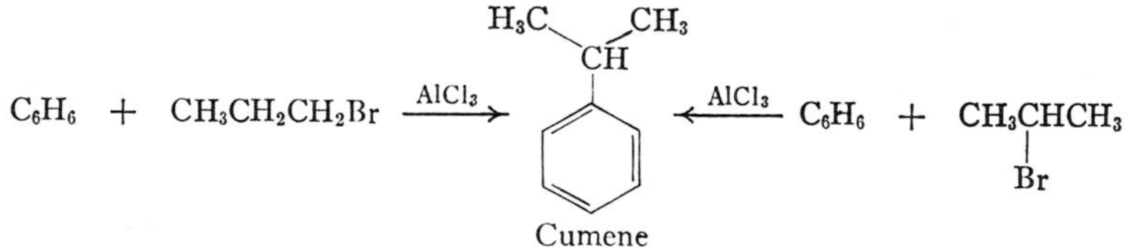

C_6H_6 + $CH_3CH_2CH_2Br$ $\xrightarrow{AlCl_3}$ $\xleftarrow{AlCl_3}$ C_6H_6 + CH_3CHCH_3
                                                                                          |
                                                                                          Br
                                            Cumene

mides usually give rearranged products. Alkylation with an *n*-alkyl chloride or a primary alcohol usually give rearranged products when sulfuric acid is used as catalyst but may yield normal products in the presence of aluminum chloride (Ipatieff, 1940). In the alkylation of benzene with either of the chlorides (1) or (2), the product (3) predominates when the catalyst is aluminum chloride or zirconium chloride, whereas when the reaction is carried out with ferric chloride or with aluminum chloride in nitromethane (4) is the chief product (L. Schmerling,[1] 1954.) Kekulé's observation (1879) that *n*-propyl bromide is isomerized

[1] Louis Schmerling, b. 1912 Milwaukee; Ph.D. Northwestern (Hurd); Universal Oil Products Co.

$$CH_3\overset{\overset{\displaystyle CH_3}{|}}{\underset{\underset{\displaystyle CH_3}{|}}{C}}CH_2CH_2Cl$$

(1)

$$CH_3\overset{\overset{\displaystyle CH_3}{|}}{CH}-\overset{\overset{\displaystyle CH_3}{|}}{\underset{\underset{\displaystyle Cl}{|}}{C}}CH_3$$

(2)

$$CH_3\overset{\overset{\displaystyle CH_3}{|}}{\underset{\underset{\displaystyle CH_3}{|}}{C}}-CHC_6H_5$$

(3)

$$CH_3\overset{\overset{\displaystyle CH_3}{|}}{CH}-\overset{\overset{\displaystyle CH_3}{|}}{\underset{\underset{\displaystyle C_6H_5}{|}}{C}}CH_3$$

(4)

by aluminum chloride to isopropyl bromide later led to the supposition that the reagent catalyzes formation of the primary carbonium ion, which rearranges to the

$$CH_3CH_2CH_2Br \xrightarrow{-Br^-} [CH_3CH_2\overset{+}{C}H_2 \longrightarrow CH_3\overset{+}{C}HCH_3] \xrightarrow{Br^-} CH_3CHBrCH_3$$

more stable secondary ion. The Friedel-Crafts reaction of isobutyl chloride with benzene to give *t*-butylbenzene would then involve isomerization of a primary to a

$$(CH_3)_2CHCH_2Cl \xrightarrow{-Cl^-} [(CH_3)_2CH\overset{+}{C}H_2 \longrightarrow (CH_3)_2\overset{+}{C}CH_3] \xrightarrow{C_6H_6} (CH_3)_3CC_6H_5$$

tertiary carbonium ion. H. C. Brown (1953) found that *n*-propyl bromide combines with aluminum bromide to form the 1:1 complex $CH_3CH_2CH_2{}^+AlBr_4{}^-$ and suggested that a process alternative to ionization of the complex to the carbonium ion and $AlBr_4{}^-$ is an intramolecular rearrangement of the Wagner-Meerwein type

$$CH_3-\overset{\overset{\displaystyle H}{\cdot\cdot}}{\underset{\underset{\displaystyle H}{|}}{C}}-CH_2\!:\overset{\overset{\displaystyle Br}{|}}{\underset{\underset{\displaystyle Br}{\cdot\cdot}}{Br}}\!:\!\overset{+}{Al}\!:\!Br \longrightarrow CH_3-\overset{\overset{\displaystyle H}{|}}{\underset{\underset{\displaystyle :Br:}{\cdot\cdot\ +}}{C}}-CH_3$$

$$Br:\overset{|}{Al}:Br$$
$$\overset{|}{Br}$$

in which a hydrogen atom and the bromine atom shift simultaneously. This mechanism is supported by the observation that in the presence of ferric bromide

1,1-dibromocyclohexane rearranges to *cis*-1,2-dibromocyclohexane (H. L. Goering, 1957). The stereospecificity of the rearrangement indicates that an intermediate carbonium ion can hardly be involved.

18.8   **Catalytic Isomerization.** — Under the influence of a Friedel-Crafts catalyst ($AlCl_3$, $AlBr_3$, $HF \cdot BF_3$) the xylenes can be caused to undergo both disproportionation to toluene and trimethylbenzenes and isomerization, but conditions can be adjusted to inhibit disproportionation and permit quantitative study of isomerization. In one of several investigations (R. H. Allen,[1] 1959)

[1] Robert H. Allen, b. Orange, Mass.; Ph.D. Calif., Berkeley (Rapoport); Dow Chem. Co.

each xylene was equilibrated in toluene solution at 50° with 5 mole % of $AlCl_3$ in the presence of HCl. Analysis by vapor phase chromatography and IR spectroscopy indicated the following equilibrium percentages: *meta*, 62; *para*, 21; *ortho*, 17. The data show that *o*- and *p*-xylene do not interconvert and therefore that the isomerization proceeds by an intramolecular 1,2-shift of the methyl group

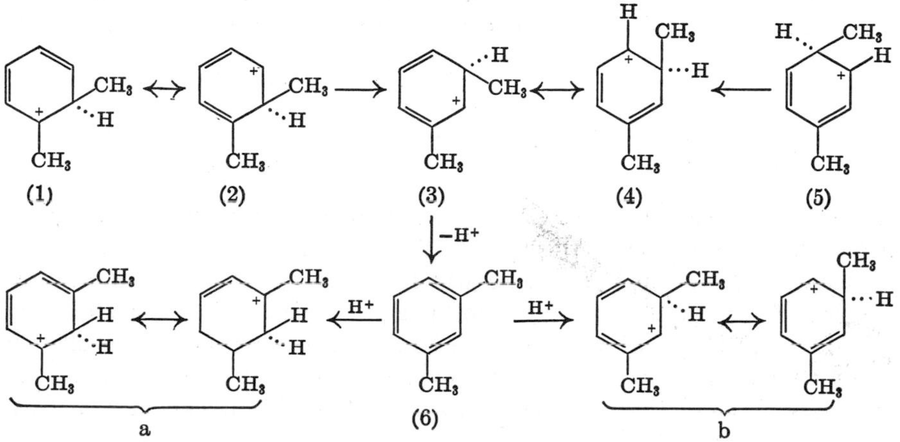

with its pair of electrons. *o*-Xylene on protonation can form the tertiary aronium ion (1), which is in resonance with the less stable secondary ion (2). Ion (2), by a 1,2-methyl shift (3) and expulsion of a proton, yields *m*-xylene (6). A 1,2-shift in the secondary ion (5) from *p*-xylene yields (4), in resonance with (3). The formulas are arranged in such a way as to suggest that the 1,2-shifts involve transition states in which the migrating methyl group is partially bonded to both carbon atoms. Protonation of *m*-xylene at unsubstituted positions (see 17.2) gives tertiary ions of type (a), which are not subject to methyl migration. Protonation at substituted positions give secondary ions of type (b), which can rearrange to *o*- and *p*-xylene.

Study of the isomerization of *o*-, *m*-, and *p*-cymene in toluene shows that the relative distribution at equilibrium is also $m > p > o$ but that the reaction in-

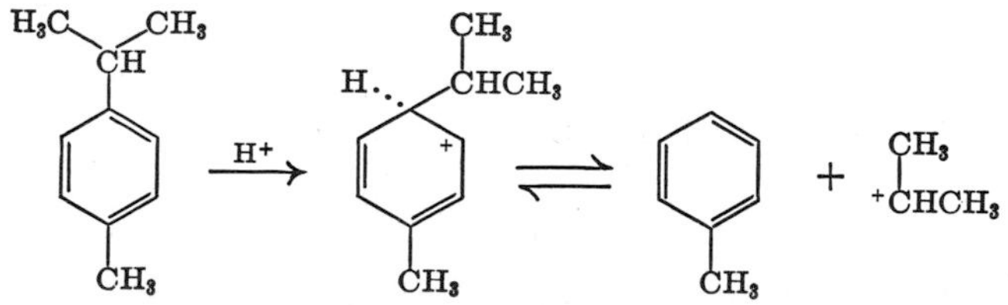

volved is intermolecular. Hence the aronium ion dissociates to the isopropyl ion.

18.9   Friedel-Crafts Acylation. — In the usual case this reaction involves condensation of an acid chloride of either the aliphatic or the aromatic series with an aromatic hydrocarbon in the presence of a molecular equivalent of anhydrous aluminum chloride:

$$\underset{\text{Acyl halide}}{\text{RCO}\overline{\text{Cl}} + \overline{\text{H}}\text{Ar}} \xrightarrow{\text{AlCl}_3} \text{RCOAr} + \text{HCl}$$

$$\underset{\text{Aroyl halide}}{\text{ArCO}\overline{\text{Cl}} + \overline{\text{H}}\text{Ar}'} \xrightarrow{\text{AlCl}_3} \text{ArCOAr}' + \text{HCl}$$

The reaction proceeds readily and affords pure products in high yield, as in the synthesis of the diaryl ketone benzophenone. Excess benzene or carbon disulfide

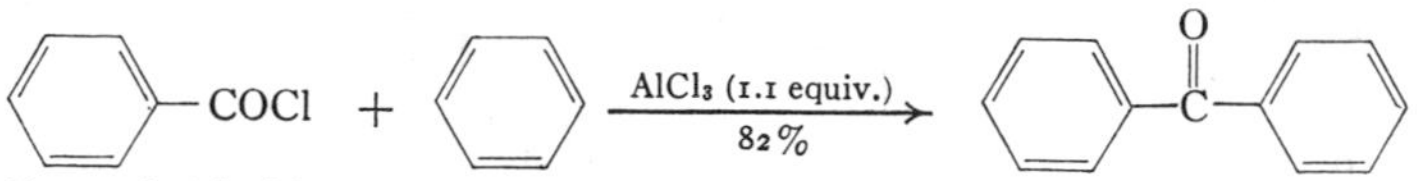

Benzoyl chloride   AlCl₃ (1.1 equiv.) 82%   Benzophenone

can be used as solvent; in either case the reaction proceeds exothermally for a time and can be completed by brief refluxing. The mixture is then cooled and treated cautiously with ice and hydrochloric acid to decompose an aluminum chloride complex and bring aluminum salts into the aqueous phase; the ketonic reaction product is then recovered from the washed and dried organic layer by distillation of the solvent. Acid anhydrides generally enter into the same reactions as acid chlorides and can replace these substances in the Friedel-Crafts reaction, as illustrated for the preparation of acetophenone.

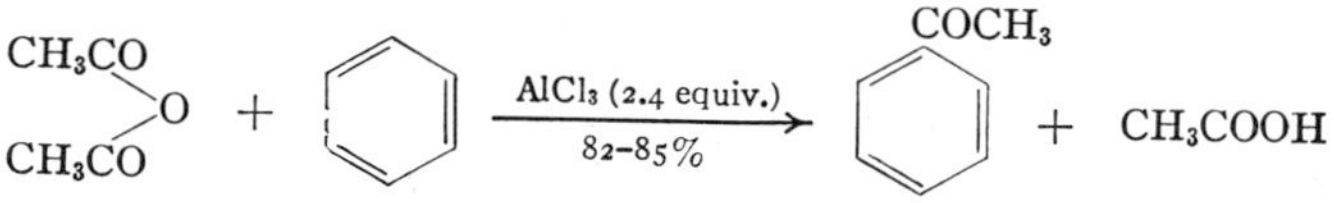

Acetophenone

More aluminum chloride is required in the synthesis of ketones than in the alkylation reaction because this reagent combines with oxygen-containing compounds to form oxonium-salt complexes. Thus when benzoyl chloride and aluminum chloride in equivalent amounts are heated together or refluxed in

(a) $C_6H_5\overset{\text{Cl}}{\underset{}{\text{C}}}=\ddot{\text{O}}: + \text{Al}:\text{Cl} \rightleftharpoons C_6H_5\overset{\text{Cl}}{\underset{}{\text{C}}}=\ddot{\text{O}}:\overset{+}{\text{Al}}:\text{Cl}$

(b) $C_6H_5\overset{\text{Cl}}{\underset{}{\text{C}}}=\ddot{\text{O}}:\overset{+}{\text{Al}}:\text{Cl} \rightleftharpoons C_6H_5\overset{+}{\text{C}}=\text{O} + \text{Cl}:\overset{-}{\text{Al}}:\text{Cl}$

(c) $C_6H_5\overset{+}{\text{C}}=\text{O} + C_6H_6 \longrightarrow C_6H_5\overset{C_6H_5}{\underset{}{\text{C}}}=\text{O} + \text{H}^+$

(d) $(C_6H_5)_2\text{C}=\text{O} + \text{AlCl}_4^- \rightleftharpoons (C_6H_5)_2\text{C}=\text{O}:\overset{+}{\text{Al}}:\text{Cl} + \text{Cl}^-$

(e) $(C_6H_5)_2\overset{+}{\text{C}}=\text{O}:\text{Al}\bar{\text{Cl}}_3 + \text{H}_2\text{O} \longrightarrow (C_6H_5)_2\text{C}=\text{O} + \text{Al(OH)Cl}_2 + \text{HCl}$

carbon disulfide solution, they unite to form a crystalline complex that, like aluminum chloride, is bimolecular in solution (Kohler, 1900). In the formulation (p 656) of the probable mechanism for formation and reaction of the complex, the aluminum salts are written as single molecules, but they actually have twice the molecular weights indicated. In the first step (a) aluminum chloride functions as a Lewis acid and accepts a pair of electrons from the ketonic oxygen atom to form a coordinate covalent complex. This complex dissociates (b) to a certain extent to give the benzoyl cation, which is the effective agent in electrophilic attack of benzene (c), with expulsion of a proton. The reaction product, benzophenone, combines with the ion $AlCl_4^-$ to form a second coordinate covalent complex (d) which, at the end of the reaction, is decomposed by water (e). Complex formation thus binds an equivalent quantity of the metal halide. When an anhydride is the acylating agent, sufficient aluminum chloride must be used to allow for oxonium-salt formation at both carbonyl groups.

A useful application of the synthetic method is the preparation of keto acids by interaction of an aromatic hydrocarbon with one of the readily available cyclic anhydrides, as illustrated in the examples. The γ-keto acids of the aromatic and mixed aliphatic-aromatic types obtainable in this way are important intermediates for further syntheses. If toluene is employed in place of benzene, the orientation of the substituent is almost exclusively in the position *para* to the methyl group (*ortho* effect).

1. Phthalic anhydride (excess) → AlCl₃ (2.6 equiv.) 88% → *o*-Benzoylbenzoic acid (m.p. 128°)

2. Succinic anhydride + (excess) → AlCl₃ (2.2 equiv.) 92–95% → $C_6H_5COCH_2CH_2COOH$ β-Benzoylpropionic acid (m.p. 116°)

The reactions proceed smoothly and stop abruptly with introduction of a single deactivating acyl group, and the primary condensation product is not contaminated with polysubstituted products. This behavior is both an advantage and a limitation, for the reaction usually is inapplicable to benzene derivatives having a *meta*-directing group on the aromatic nucleus, for example: $C_6H_5CH{=}O$, $C_6H_5COOCH_3$, C_6H_5CN, $C_6H_5NO_2$ (under forcing conditions acetophenone reacts with *n*-propyl bromide to give *m*-isopropylacetophenone). Nitrobenzene is so inert to acylation and has such a marked and specific solvent power for aluminum chloride (with which it forms an oxonium-salt complex) that it is frequently employed as solvent for Friedel-Crafts condensations with other aromatic compounds. The rearrangement of the substituting group observed in alkylations does not apply to the ketone synthesis, and the reactions of acyl halides and anhydrides are generally more satisfactory than those of alkyl halides. Although a larger proportion of catalyst is required, the same relationships hold with respect to the applicability and effectiveness of the various catalytic agents. Thus aluminum chloride is the most potent of the common catalysts; stannic chloride and boron fluoride are mild but effective catalysts; and fused zinc chloride is a weakly active agent. These substances are useful where moderation of the reaction is desirable. For example, thiophene is so much more reactive than benzene that it is polymerized to a considerable extent in a reaction mixture containing aluminum chloride, and its acylation is accomplished best by use of the less potent catalyst stannic chloride. Liquid hydrogen fluoride has some

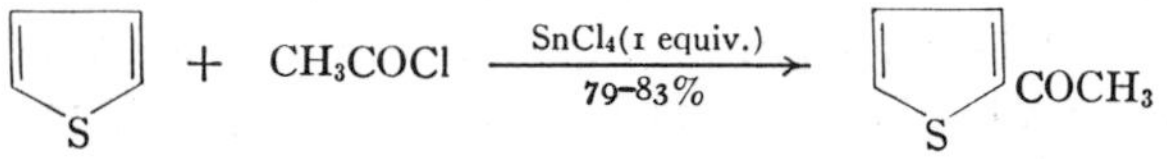

$$\text{(thiophene)} \quad + \quad CH_3COCl \quad \xrightarrow[\text{79-83\%}]{\text{SnCl}_4(\text{1 equiv.})} \quad \text{(methyl 2-thienyl ketone)} COCH_3$$

Thiophene

Methyl 2-thienyl ketone
(b.p. 89–91°/9 mm.)

advantage as catalyst for the ketone synthesis in that the free acid, rather than the acid chloride or anhydride, can be employed as the acylating agent; with polynuclear hydrocarbons, the reagent is also useful in leading to an orientation different from that encountered with the metal halide catalysts.

A useful application of the reaction is the synthesis of cyclic ketones by intramolecular Friedel-Crafts cyclization between an aromatic ring and an acid chloride group in an attached side chain, as illustrated by the preparation of α-tetralone. Five- and six-membered ring ketones are generally obtainable in good yield by

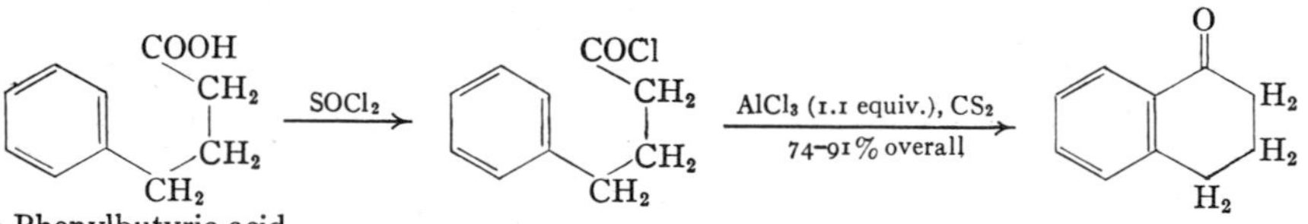

$$\text{γ-Phenylbutyric acid} \xrightarrow{SOCl_2} \quad \xrightarrow[\text{74-91\% overall}]{\text{AlCl}_3 \text{ (1.1 equiv.), CS}_2} \quad \text{α-Tetralone}$$

γ-Phenylbutyric acid

α-Tetralone
(b.p. 105–107°/2 mm.)

this method. An alternative procedure that is often effective consists in treatment of the free acid with liquid hydrogen fluoride. γ-Phenylbutyric acid can

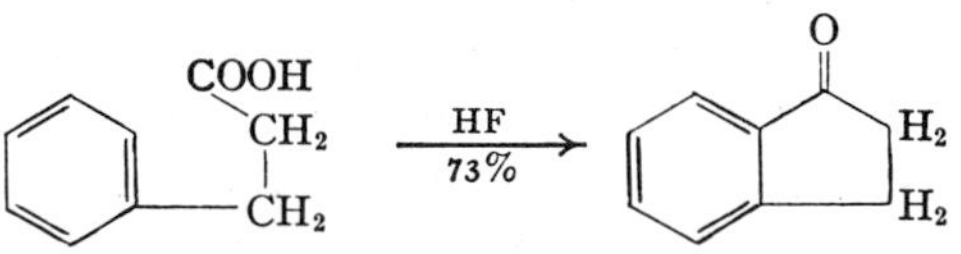

$$\text{Hydrocinnamic acid} \xrightarrow[\text{73\%}]{HF} \quad \text{α-Hydrindone}$$

Hydrocinnamic acid
(m.p. 48.5°)

α-Hydrindone
(m.p. 42°)

be cyclized directly to α-tetralone by this method in 92% yield. Polyphosphoric acid (a mixture of phosphoric acid and phosphorus pentoxide) is often employed for these cyclodehydrations.

Phenyl groups that are deactivated by an acyl group and thereby rendered incapable of undergoing intermolecular acylation may participate in intramolecular acylation if this provides a 5- or 6-membered ring (G. Baddeley,[1] 1956). Thus, whereas 1-indanone and 1-tetralone are not acylable, the acetylated acids (1) can

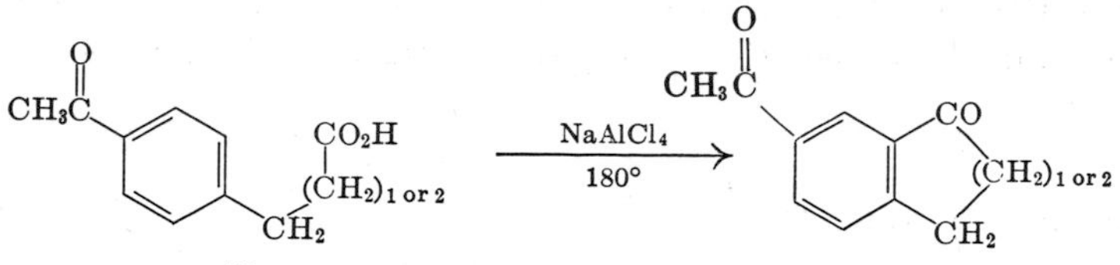

be cyclized smoothly by heating with a melt of sodium chloride and aluminum chloride. Rearrangements are less prone to occur in intramolecular cyclizations than in ordinary Friedel-Crafts reactions. Thus the chlorides (3) and (6) give

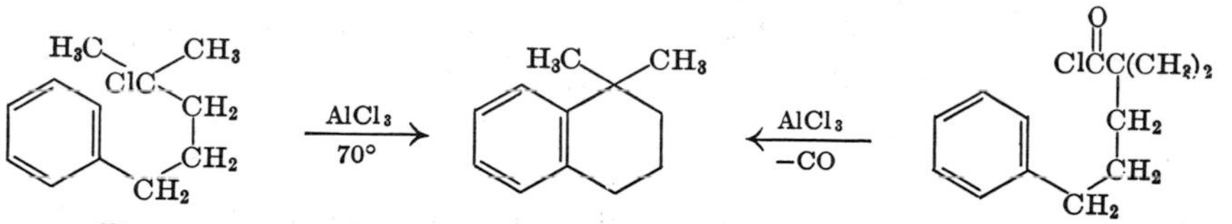

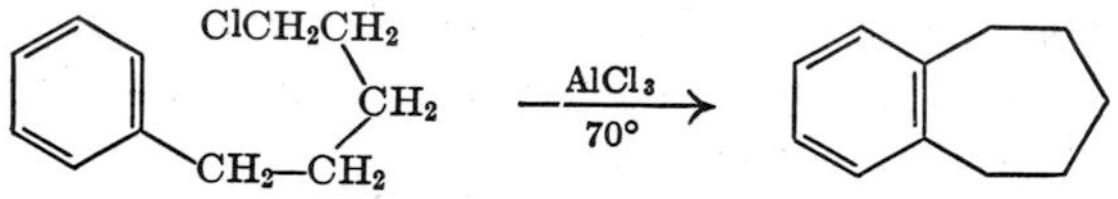

the products of normal cyclization, (4) and (7, benzosuberane). 1,1-Dimethyltetralin (4) is also the product of cyclization of the acid chloride (5); the reaction is attended with decarbonylation (E. Rothstein, 1954).

Symmetrical diaryl ketones are obtainable by an interesting method of trans-decarbonylation (R. C. Fuson,[2] 1959). When duroic acid is heated for an extended period with polyphosphoric acid and a sufficiently reactive hydrocarbon, for example m-xylene, the products are durene and 2,2',4,4'-tetramethyl-

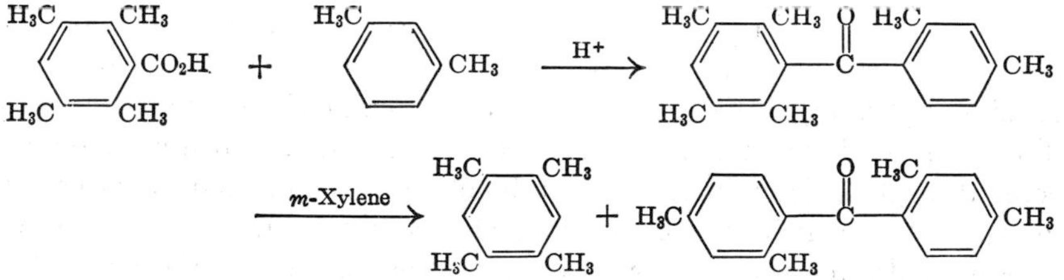

benzophenone. The formation of the mixed ketone as an intermediate was demonstrated by isolation of this product after a shorter reaction period. Some cleavage on the side of the less hindered aryl group was demonstrated by isolation

[1] George Baddeley, b. 1906 Leek, Staffordshire; D.Sc. Manchester (Kenner); Univ. Manchester

[2] R. C. Fuson, b. 1895 Wakefield, Ill.; Ph.D. Minnesota (W. H. Hunter); Univ. Illinois

of 2,4-dimethylbenzoic acid. The reaction is applicable to anisole and diphenyl ether.

A novel Friedel-Crafts cycloalkylation is effected with 2,2,5,5-tetramethyl-3-keto-tetrahydrofurane (III), a reagent obtainable in 80% yield by catalytic

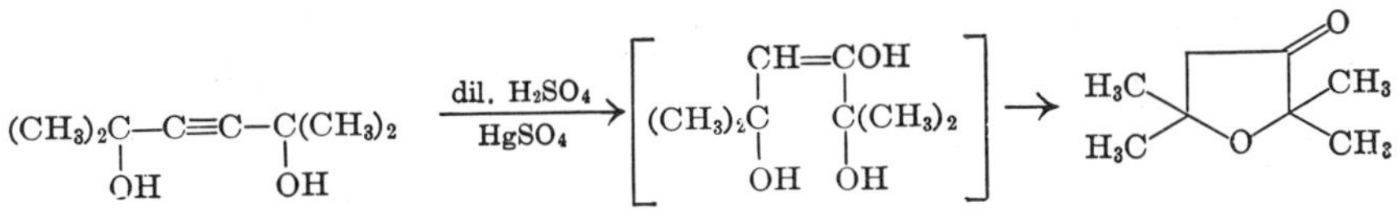

hydration of 2,5-dimethyl-3-hexyne-2,5-diol (Air Reduction Chem. Co.). In the presence of aluminum chloride, this substance reacts with benzene to give the highly hindered ketone IV which, on oxidation with permanganate in the presence of magnesium sulfate as a buffer to prevent alkaline rearrangements, affords *o*-phenylenediisobutyric acid V (H. A. Bruson,[1] 1958).

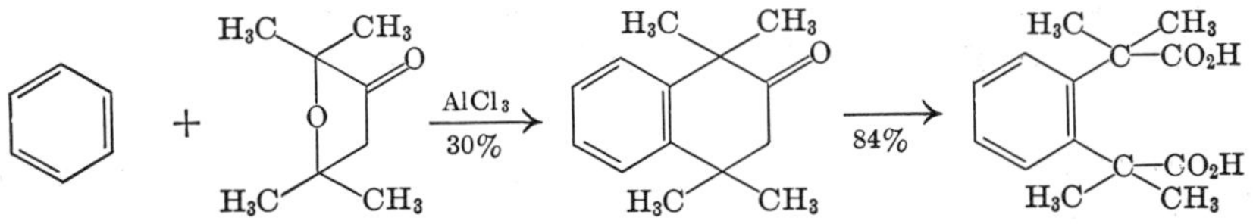

18.10   Reduction of Carbonyl Compounds. — Several efficient methods are available for reduction of carbonyl compounds, including the ketones produced by the Friedel-Crafts synthesis. One, the **Clemmensen**[2] **method of reduction** (1913), consists in refluxing a ketone with amalgamated zinc and hydrochloric acid. Acetophenone, for example, is reduced to ethylbenzene. The

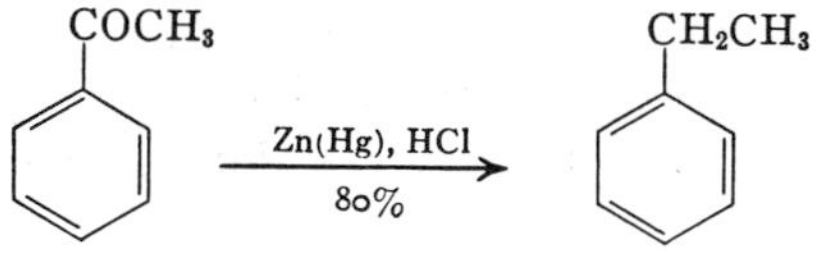

method is applicable to the reduction of most aromatic-aliphatic ketones and to at least some aliphatic and alicyclic ketones. The reaction apparently does not proceed through initial reduction to a carbinol, for carbinols that might be intermediates are stable under the conditions used. With substances sparingly soluble in aqueous hydrochloric acid, improved results sometimes are obtained by addition of a water-miscible organic solvent such as ethanol, acetic acid, or dioxane. Particularly favorable results are obtained by addition of the water-insoluble solvent

[1] Herman A. Bruson, b. 1901 Middletown, Ohio; D.Sc. ETH Zurich (Staudinger); Rohm and Haas Co.; Olin Mathieson Chem. Corp.

[2] E. Ch. Clemmensen, 1876–1941; b. Odense, Denmark; Ph.D. Copenhagen; Clemmensen Chem. Corp., Newark, N. Y.

toluene (E. L. Martin,[1] 1936), stirring the mixture vigorously, and using for amalgamation zinc that has been freshly melted and poured into water (C. S. Sherman, 1948). The ketone is retained largely in the upper toluene layer and is distributed into the aqueous solution of hydrochloric acid in contact with the zinc at so high a dilution that the side reaction of bimolecular reduction is suppressed.

The Clemmensen method of reduction is applicable to the γ-keto acids obtainable by Friedel-Crafts condensations with succinic anhydride (succinoylation) and to the cyclic ketones formed by intramolecular condensation.

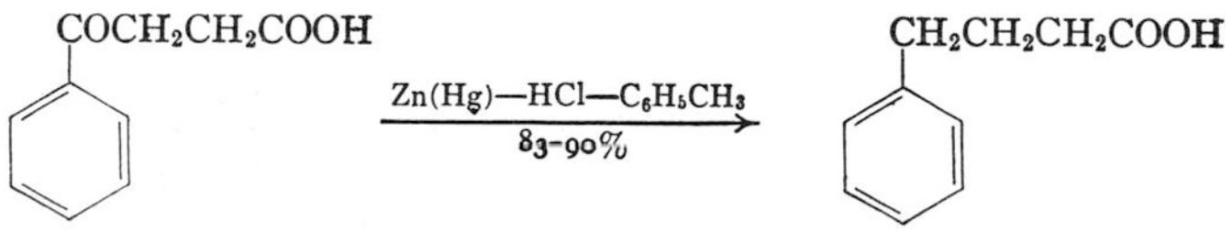

$COCH_2CH_2COOH$

$$\xrightarrow[\text{83-90\%}]{Zn(Hg)-HCl-C_6H_5CH_3}$$

$CH_2CH_2CH_2COOH$

β-Benzoylpropionic acid

γ-Phenylbutyric acid

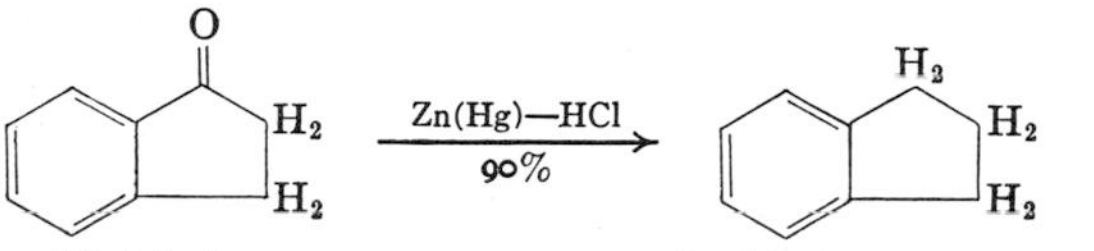

$$\xrightarrow[\text{90\%}]{Zn(Hg)-HCl}$$

α-Hydrindone

Hydrindene or indane
(b.p. 177°)

This and the Wolff-Kishner method of reduction supplement each other; the Clemmensen method is inapplicable to acid-sensitive compounds and the Wolff-Kishner method cannot be used with compounds sensitive to alkali or containing other functional groups that react with hydrazine. A number of substituted benzophenones have been reduced in high yield by adding aluminum chloride to a suspension of lithium aluminum hydride in ether, adding the ketone, and refluxing for 30 min. (J. Blackwell, 1961).

Ketones of the type of acetophenone and α-tetralone can also be reduced to hydrocarbons by **catalytic hydrogenation** (Pd catalyst); β-aroylpropionic acids

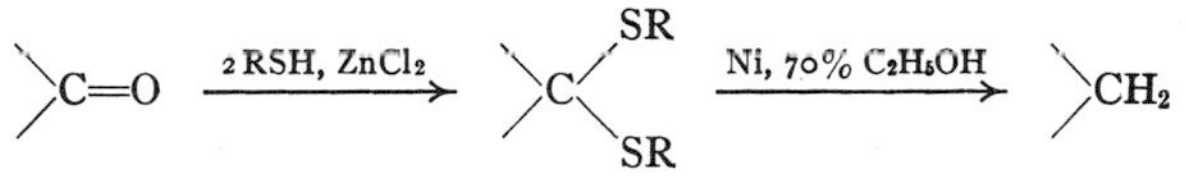

$$\begin{array}{ccccc} \diagup\diagdown C{=}O & \xrightarrow{2\,RSH,\,ZnCl_2} & \diagup\diagdown C\diagup\diagup^{SR}_{SR} & \xrightarrow{Ni,\,70\%\,C_2H_5OH} & \diagup\diagdown CH_2 \end{array}$$

Dialkyl thioacetal

are reduced to γ-arylbutyric acids. A fourth method consists in hydrogenolysis of a dialkyl thioacetal derivative with Raney nickel (12.41).

A new method for the synthesis of prehnitene involves reduction of 3,6-dimethylphthalic anhydride (IV), an intermediate obtainable in good yield by the method of M. Freund (1916). Friedel-Crafts condensation of p-xylene with diethylmalonyl chloride gives the indane-1,3-dione (I), which on alkaline cleavage affords the keto acid II. Oxidation with concentrated nitric acid on the steam bath yields 3,6-dimethylphthalic acid, III, convertible to the anhydride IV by

---

[1] Elmore L. Martin, b. 1909 Pratt, Kansas; Ph.D. Harvard (Fieser); du Pont Co.

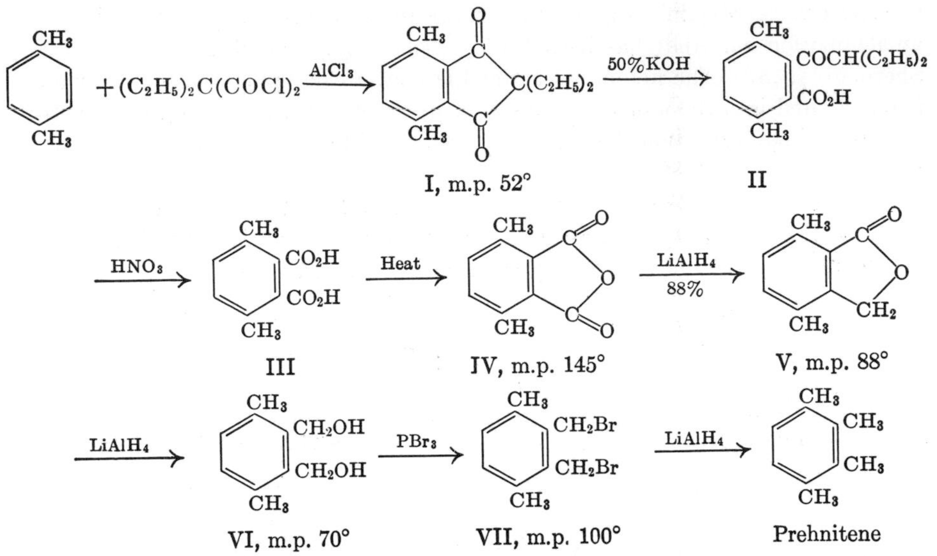

I, m.p. 52° II

III IV, m.p. 145° V, m.p. 88°

VI, m.p. 70° VII, m.p. 100° Prehnitene

pyrolysis. E. Buchta found that lithium aluminum hydride in ether reduces only one of the carbonyl groups (V), whereas both groups of phthalic anhydride are reduced. Evidently hindrance of the two *o*-methyl groups permits formation of a complex with only one of the carbonyl groups. Reduction of the phthalide to VI requires production of only one complex and is accomplished under the same experimental conditions. Completion of the synthesis involves formation and reduction of the dibromide VII, accomplished by refluxing with lithium aluminum hydride in tetrahydrofurane (24 hrs.).

18.11   Synthetic Sequences. — Synthesis and dehydrogenation of hydro-aromatic hydrocarbons provides a route to a variety of aromatic compounds of structure fixed by the synthesis. α-Tetralone, readily obtainable

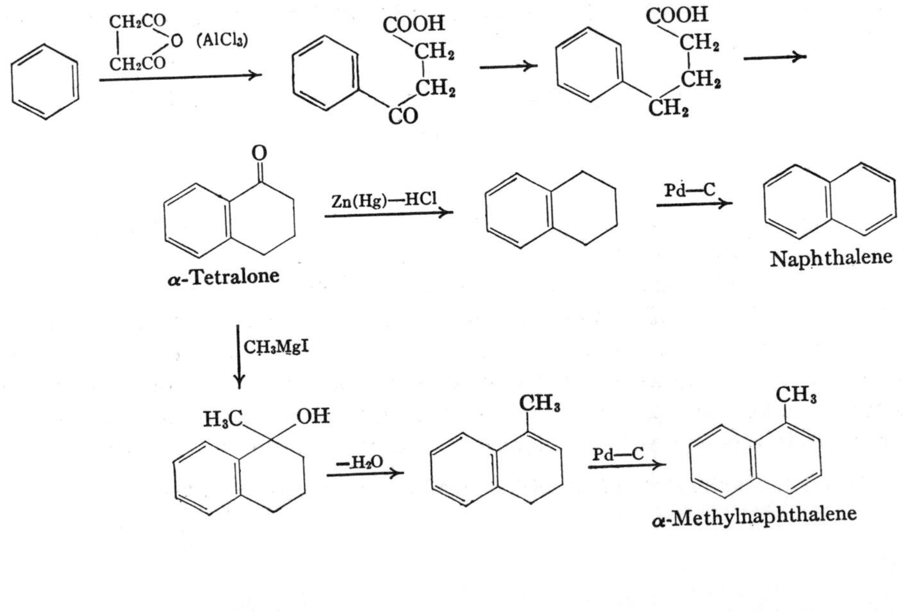

α-Tetralone Naphthalene

α-Methylnaphthalene

by Friedel-Crafts succinoylation of benzene, Clemmensen reduction, and cyclization, can be converted into naphthalene by Clemmensen reduction to tetralin and
dehydrogenation, or it can be condensed with methylmagnesium iodide and the
resulting carbinol dehydrated to a methyldihydronaphthalene which is dehydrogenated to 1-methylnaphthalene. Since toluene is succinoylated in the *p*-position,
application of the same sequences to toluene leads to β-methylnaphthalene and
to 1,7-dimethylnaphthalene. With *p*-xylene as the starting material, the products are 1,4-dimethyl- and 1,4,5-trimethylnaphthalene.

18.12   Grignard Syntheses. — The Grignard reaction can be applied in
numerous ways to synthesis of hydrocarbons of mixed aromatic-
aliphatic type, containing both saturated and unsaturated side chains. One type

1.

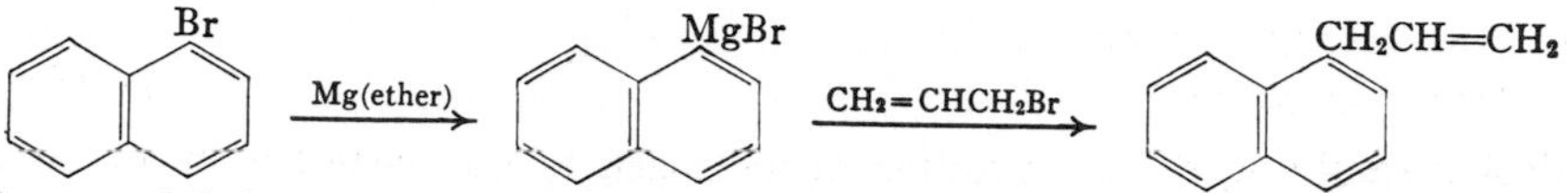

α-Bromonaphthalene   α-Naphthylmagnesium   α-Allylnaphthalene
                                    bromide   (b.p. 266°)

of synthesis, illustrated in examples (1), (2), and (3), utilizes the aryl Grignard
reagents easily prepared by interaction of aromatic bromides or iodides with
magnesium.

2. 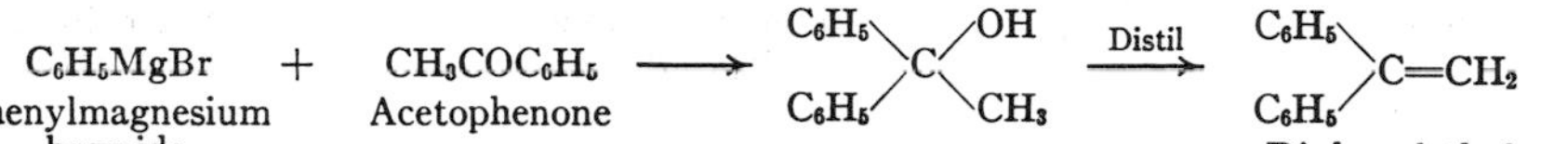 C_6H_5MgBr + $CH_3COC_6H_5$ $\longrightarrow$

Phenylmagnesium   Acetophenone
    bromide

α,α-Diphenylethylene
(b.p. 275°)

A generally useful reaction consists in introduction of a nuclear methyl group
by interaction of an aryl Grignard reagent with dimethyl sulfate. The net result
is equivalent to a Wurtz-Fittig synthesis, but methylation of a Grignard reagent
often proceeds more smoothly and is applicable to more selective synthetic
operations, as illustrated in example (3).

3.

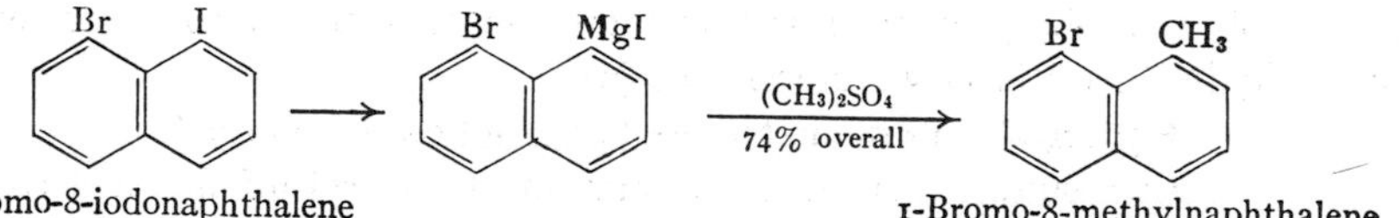

1-Bromo-8-iodonaphthalene   1-Bromo-8-methylnaphthalene
     (m.p. 100°)   (m.p. 78°)

Other elaborations of the Grignard reaction involve addition of an alkylmagnesium halide to a carbonyl component of the aromatic series, as illustrated by the
synthesis of *p*-cymene (4). Saturation of the double bond in the side chain can
be accomplished either by catalytic hydrogenation in the presence of platinum
or by reduction with sodium and absolute ethanol. That this reduction method
is specific for conjugated systems and is not applicable to isolated double bonds
is shown by the behavior of 1-phenylbutadiene, conveniently synthesized by a
further application of the Grignard method (5). Reduction with sodium and

4.

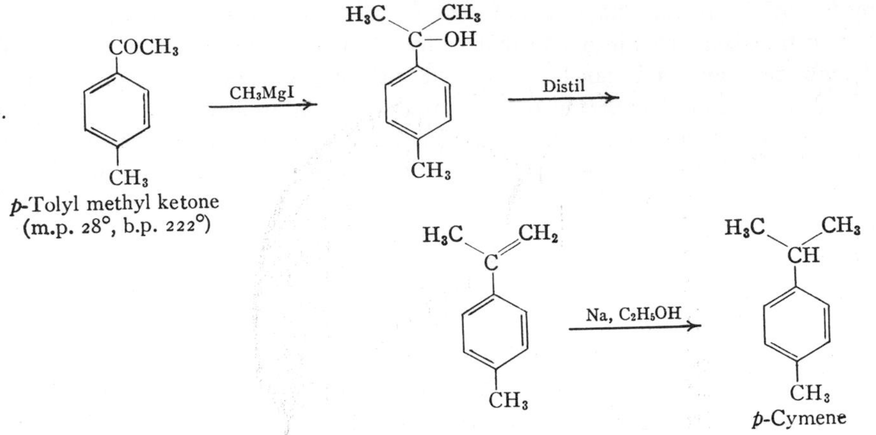

p-Tolyl methyl ketone
(m.p. 28°, b.p. 222°)

alcohol results in the 1,4-addition of hydrogen to the diene system of the side chain and affords 1-phenylbutene-2, which has an isolated double bond not

5. $C_6H_5CH{=}CHCHO$ $\xrightarrow{CH_3MgBr}$ $C_6H_5CH{=}CHCH(OH)CH_3$ $\xrightarrow[70\% \text{ overall}]{30\% \text{ } H_2SO_4}$
　　Cinnamaldehyde

$C_6H_5CH{=}CHCH{=}CH_2$ $\xrightarrow{Na,\ C_2H_5OH}$ $C_6H_5CH_2CH{=}CHCH_3$ $\xrightarrow{alc.\ KOH}$ $C_6H_5CH{=}CHCH_2CH_3$
1-Phenylbutadiene-1,3　　　　　　　　　1-Phenylbutene-2　　　　　　　　1-Phenylbutene-1
(b.p. 86°/11 mm.)　　　　　　　　　　(β-butenylbenzene,　　　　　　　(α-butenylbenzene
　　　　　　　　　　　　　　　　　　　b.p. 176°)　　　　　　　　　　b.p. 188°)

conjugated with the ring and therefore is not attacked by the reagent and can be isolated in good yield. This hydrocarbon can be isomerized by boiling alcoholic potassium hydroxide to the conjugated and more stable 1-phenylbutene-1, which

6. C_6H_5CHO $\xrightarrow{n\text{-}C_3H_7MgI}$ $C_6H_5CH(OH)CH_2CH_2CH_3$ $\xrightarrow{HCl\ in\ ether}$

　　　　　　　　$C_6H_5CHClCH_2CH_2CH_3$ $\xrightarrow{Pyridine,\ 125°}$ $C_6H_5CH{=}CHCH_2CH_3$
　　　　　　　　　　　　　　　　　　　　　　　　　　　　　　1-Phenylbutene-1

is reducible to n-butylbenzene with sodium and alcohol. A Grignard synthesis of the hydrocarbon is shown in example (6).

18.13　　Hydrolysis of Sulfonates. — The reaction of an aromatic hydrocarbon with sulfuric acid with production of an arylsulfonic acid ($ArSO_3H$) is reversible, and under suitable conditions the hydrocarbon can be regenerated from the sulfonic acid or the alkali salt, or sulfonate ($ArSO_3Na$). The hydrolysis, or desulfonation, usually proceeds best in an aqueous solution of dilute sulfuric acid at temperatures of 135–200°, and can be carried out by heating the reagents in a sealed tube or by passing superheated steam into a dilute sulfuric acid solution of the sulfonic acid or sulfonate; the hydrocarbon steam distills from the reaction mixture as it is formed. Desulfonation is valuable in the isolation of pure hydro-

$$ArSO_3H(Na)\ +\ H_2O\ \xrightarrow{dil.\ H_2SO_4\ (heat)}\ ArH\ +\ H_2SO_4(NaHSO_4)$$

carbons from the isomer mixtures derived from coal tar or petroleum (xylenes, dimethylnaphthalenes). The mixture can be sulfonated and the sulfonic acids converted into the solid water-soluble sodium or potassium salts, which are fractionally crystallized; hydrolysis of the isolated sulfonates then affords the liquid or solid hydrocarbons.

The xylene fraction from coal tar contains 50–60% of *m*-xylene and 10–25% each of the *ortho* and *para* isomers, along with some ethylbenzene (Eastman xylene: 15.2% *ortho*, 61% *meta*, 23.8% *para*). Separations have been worked out that utilize in part differences in the ease of sulfonation and desulfonation. *m*-Xylene is the most reactive isomer and slowly dissolves in 80% sulfuric acid at room temperature as the result of conversion into the derivative I; *o*- and *p*-xylene are not attacked on being shaken with 80% acid but undergo sulfonation with 84% acid to give the sulfonic acids II and III, respectively. Other experiments show that *o*-xylene is slightly more reactive than the *para* isomer. Thus

CH₃ structure with SO₃H and CH₃
m-Xylene-4-
sulfonic acid
I

CH₃ structure with CH₃ and SO₃H
o-Xylene-4-
sulfonic acid
II

CH₃ structure with SO₃H and CH₃
p-Xylene-2-
sulfonic acid
III

in one method of separation the mixture is partially sulfonated with concentrated sulfuric acid at 20°; the residue is rich in *p*-xylene, which is sulfonated with oleum. The acid III is crystallized from dilute acid in which it is less soluble than the isomers. The mixture containing I and II on crystallization of the sodium salts affords the *o*-derivative II in the least soluble fraction, whereas the *m*-derivative I concentrates in the more soluble fraction. The purified acids or their salts are hydrolyzed with hydrochloric acid at 190–195°. In another process crude xylene is sulfonated completely, and the mixture of sulfonic acids heated with hydrochloric acid at 122°, when the particularly reactive *m*-xylene derivative I alone is hydrolyzed.

Another use of the reversible sulfonation reaction is for introduction of blocking groups that permit special orientations, as in the example shown:

OH → (H₂SO₄) → OH with SO₃H and SO₃H → (Na salt + Br₂) → OH with Br, SO₃Na, SO₃Na → (dil. H₂SO₄, 200°, 42–44% overall) → OH with Br

18.14   Jacobsen Reaction.

— O. Jacobsen[1] discovered (1886) that the product of sulfonation of a tetra- or pentamethylbenzene rearranges on contact with sulfuric acid with migration of a methyl group. Thus durenesulfonic acid is rearranged chiefly to prehnitenesulfonic acid, which on desulfonation affords the hydrocarbon prehnitene in yield of about 41%. A water-insoluble tar re-

[1] Oskar Jacobsen, 1840–89; b. Ahrensburg Holstein, Germany; Ph.D. Kiel; Univ. Rostock

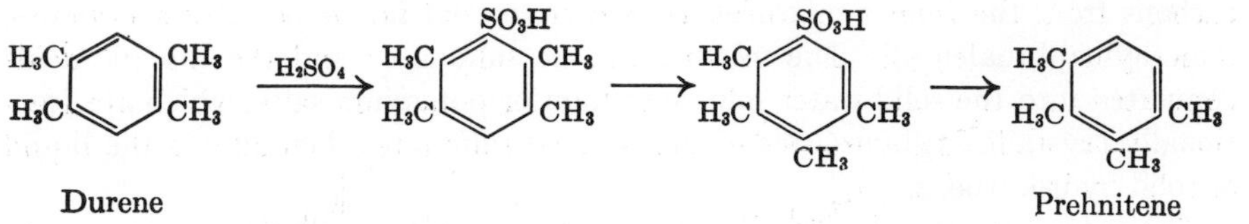

Durene   Prehnitene

moved prior to desulfonation contains hexamethylbenzene, and the acidic fraction contains the sulfonic acids of pentamethylbenzene and 1,2,4-trimethylbenzene as by-products. Investigations of L. I. Smith (1932–40) showed that only *vic*-tetra- or pentaalkyl acids rearrange, that the migrating alkyl group always enters a vicinal position, and that acids other than sulfuric catalyze the rearrangement of sulfonic acids. We suggest that the reaction involves protonation of the sulfonic

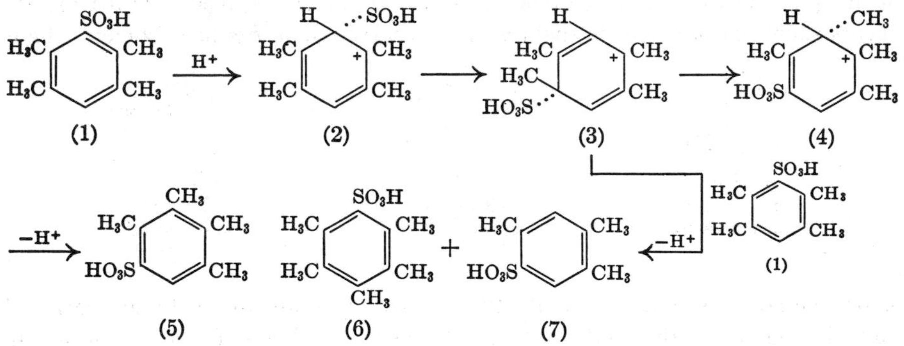

acid (1) to form the aronium ion (2), which undergoes allylic migration of the sulfonic acid group (3) and reverse migration of a methyl group (4), followed by expulsion of a proton to form prehnitenesulfonic acid (5). Hindrance by the two *ortho* alkyl groups in durenesulfonic acid (1) promotes formation of the more stable, nonplanar aronium ions (2–4). The less hindered prehnitenesulfonic acid (5) does not rearrange. The aronium ion (3) can transfer a methyl group to durenesulfonic acid to form pentamethylbenzenesulfonic acid (6) and 1,2,4-trimethylsulfonic acid (7). Reversibility of most of the reactions except the final step leading to prehnitenesulfonic acids accounts for the production of prehnitene from pentamethylbenzene in overall yield of 27%. A high-yield

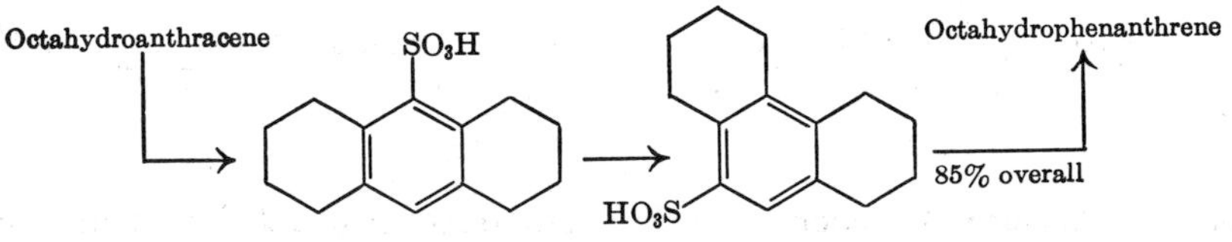

application of the Jacobsen reaction is the isomerization of octahydroanthracene to octahydrophenanthrene (G. Schroeter, 1927).

Sulfonic acids derived from the three trimethylbenzenes are stable to sulfuric acid because they are unhindered or, in the case of mesitylene, because there is no *meta* methyl group available for migration. Polyalkylbenzenes containing amino or methoxyl groups do not undergo Jacobsen rearrangement because of preferential protonation of nitrogen or oxygen functions.   Nitro and carboxyl substituents prevent rearrangement by inductive inhibition of development of a positive charge in the ring.   Rearrangements have been observed with halopoly-alkylbenzenes, but usually complicated mixtures are formed.   One practical application is isomerization of 4,6-dibromo-*m*-xylene to the otherwise inaccessible 2,4-dibromo-*m*-xylene.

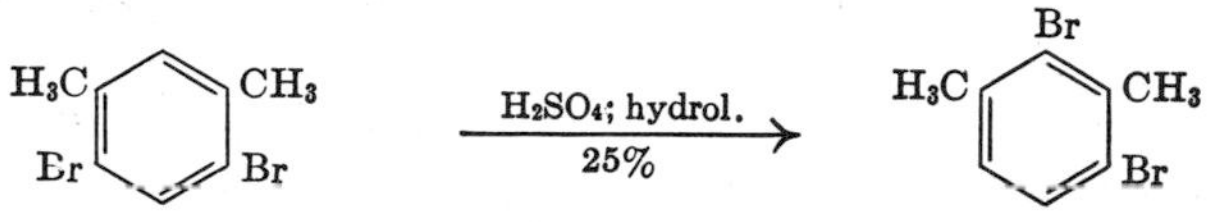

18.15   **Decarboxylation.** — A degradative method sometimes offering a useful route to a hydrocarbon consists in heating the sodium salt of a carboxylic acid with soda lime to effect decarboxylation.   Thiophene-free benzene was first prepared by this method (17.1).   A usually satisfactory procedure consists in heating the acid with copper-powder catalyst in quinoline solution (J. R. Johnson, 1930).   A practical application is the preparation of furane, a heterocyclic oxygen compound exhibiting aromatic characteristics to a moderate degree.   Furfural, available on a technical scale by the processing of oat hulls (cf. 12.15), is converted in part by the Cannizzaro reaction into 2-furoic acid, which is decarboxylated.

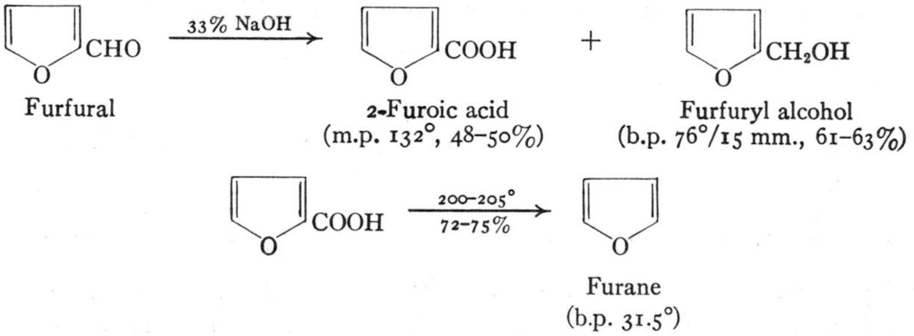

Furfural

2-Furoic acid
(m.p. 132°, 48–50%)

Furfuryl alcohol
(b.p. 76°/15 mm., 61–63%)

Furane
(b.p. 31.5°)

18.16   **Zinc-Dust Distillation of Phenols.** — Phenols are convertible into the parent hydrocarbons by interaction with zinc dust at a red heat; presumably the oxygen is eliminated as zinc oxide.   The reaction is carried out

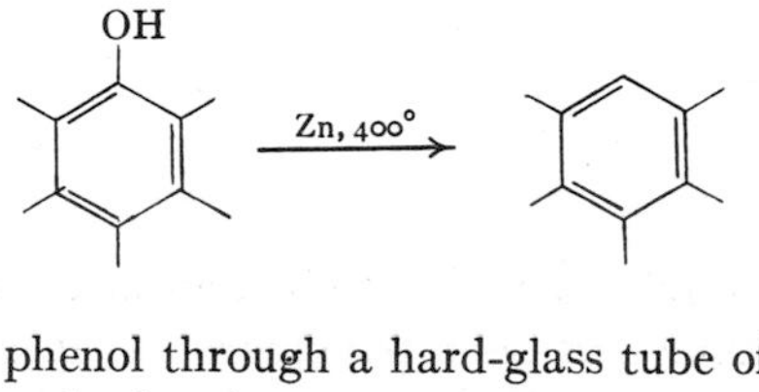

either by distilling the phenol through a hard-glass tube of zinc dust heated to a dull glow in a furnace or by heating a gram or two of the phenol with 25–50 g. of zinc dust in a sealed-off Pyrex distilling flask until the glass begins to soften. The degradative reaction is useful in investigation of substances of unknown structure because it affords a means of establishing the nature of the parent hydrocarbon. Thus the alkaloid morphine was first recognized as a phenanthrene derivative by degradation to phenanthrene, and the method provided the first clue that the natural dye alizarin is a member of the anthracene series. The

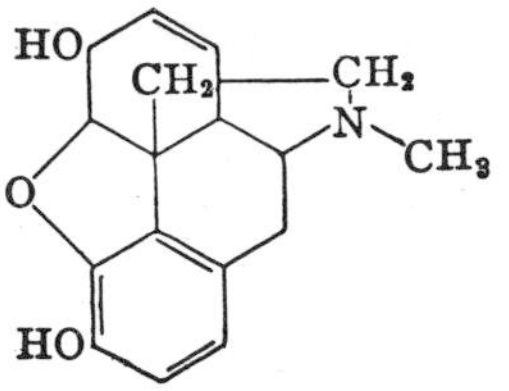

Morphine
(opium)

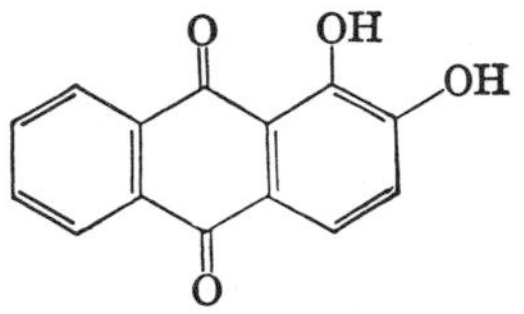

Alizarin

degradation of alizarin involves initial reduction of the central quinone group to the hydroquinone, which has two phenolic hydroxyl groups, and then elimination of the four hydroxyl groups.

18.17 Chemical Reduction of Phenols. — An alternative method for the reduction of phenols to aromatic hydrocarbons is of particular value to the natural product chemist because it is applicable to small quantities (50–200 mg.) and because the conditions are so mild as to preclude rearrangement (S. W. Pelletier,[1] 1958). A solution of the phenol and diethyl hydrogen phosphite in carbon tetrachloride is treated with triethylamine and allowed to stand for 24 hrs. for complete separation of triethylamine hydrochloride (1). The phenol

1. $ArOH + HO-P(OC_2H_5)_2 + CCl_4 + (C_2H_5)_3N \longrightarrow$

$$ArO-\overset{O^-}{\underset{|}{P}}{}^+(OC_2H_5)_2 + CHCl_3 + (C_2H_5)_3N \cdot HCl$$

2. $ArO-\overset{O^-}{\underset{|}{P}}{}^+(OC_2H_5)_2 + 2\ Na + NH_3 \rightarrow ArH + NaNH_2 + NaO\overset{O^-}{\underset{|}{P}}{}^+(OC_2H_5)_2$

diethyl phosphate ester is collected, dissolved in tetrahydrofurane, and reduced with sodium and liquid ammonia (2). Yields of pure polycyclic hydrocarbons from some twelve phenolic derivatives are in the range 18–52% and hence fully adequate for the purpose of identification.

18.18 Oxidation of Alkylbenzenes. — A characteristic reaction of toluene is oxidation to benzoic acid, accomplished by heating with dilute nitric

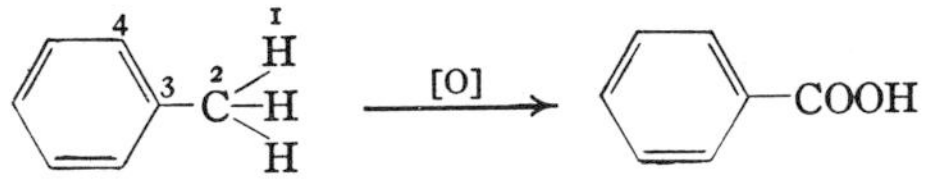

acid in a sealed tube, by refluxing with potassium dichromate and sulfuric acid, or by the action of alkaline potassium permanganate at 95° (nearly quantitative yield). The reaction illustrates both the stability of the benzene ring and the

[1] S. William Pelletier, b. 1924 Kankakee, Ill.; Ph.D. Cornell (J. R. Johnson); Rockefeller Inst. Med. Res.

activating effect of the unsaturated group on the hydrogen atoms of the adjacent methyl group. The lone methane hydrogen atom of triphenylmethane is so

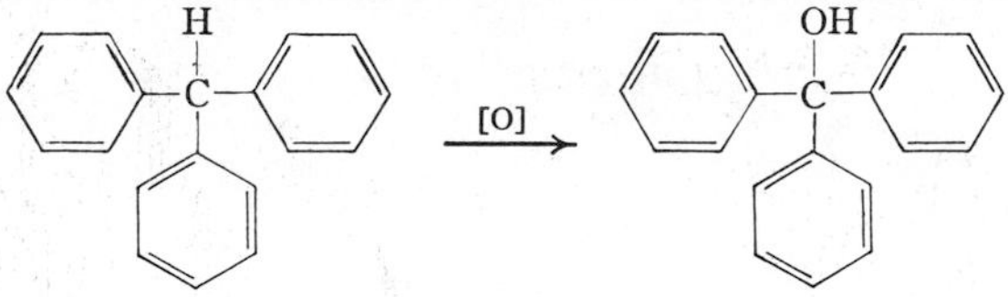

Triphenylmethane   Triphenylcarbinol (m.p. 162°)

labile that oxidation to triphenylcarbinol can be effected by passing air into a solution of the hydrocarbon in carbon disulfide in the presence of a trace of aluminum chloride. The *t*-butyl group, which has no hydrogen in a position to be activated, is stable to oxidation.

18.19   **Paracyclophanes.** — A paracyclophane is a hydrocarbon having two phenyl groups linked through polymethylene bridges at the *para* positions as in (4); since each bridge contains two methylene groups, the hydrocarbon is described as [2.2] paracyclophane. This interesting hydrocarbon was obtained for the first time as a product of pyrolysis of *p*-xylene (C. J. Brown, Imperial Chemical Industries, 1949). The convenient preparative procedure formulated is due to H. E. Winberg and F. S. Fawcett (du Pont Co., 1960).

$$2\ p\text{-}CH_3C_6H_4CH_2Br \xrightarrow{(CH_3)_3N} 2\ p\text{-}CH_3C_6H_4CH_2N^+(CH_3)_3Br^- \xrightarrow{Ag_2O}$$
$$(1) \hspace{8cm} (2)$$

$$2\ p\text{-}CH_3C_6H_4CH_2N^+(CH_3)_3OH^- \xrightarrow[17\text{-}19\%]{} \hspace{4cm} +\ 2(CH_3)_3N\ +\ 2\ H_2O$$
$$(3)$$

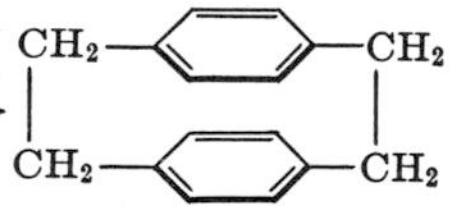

(4) m.p. 287°

Trimethylamine is quaternized with α-bromo-*p*-xylene (m.p. 36°), an aqueous solution of the salt is treated with silver oxide, and a filtered solution of the methohydroxide (3) is heated with toluene under a take-off condenser. When the water has been eliminated, decomposition occurs with formation of solid polyparaxylene and the paracyclophane (4), which is easily isolated by extraction of the dried mixture with toluene. Addition of phenothiazine as a polymerization inhibitor

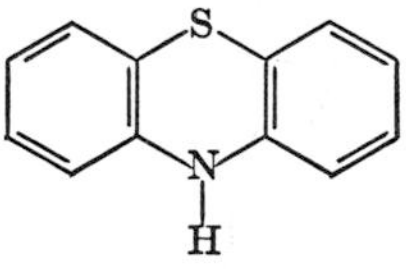

Phenothiazine 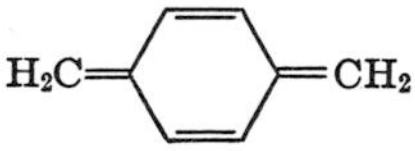   *p*-Xylylene

appears to increase the amount of dimer formed. The reaction involves a 1,6-Hofmann elimination to give *p*-xylylene, which then dimerizes and polymerizes. L. A. Errede (Minnesota Mining and Mfg. Co., 1957–60) developed a technique for preparing a solution of *p*-xylylene by fast-flow pyrolysis of *p*-xylene at low

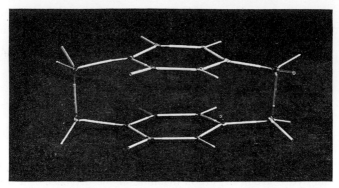

[2.2] Paracyclophane

pressure, followed by instantaneous quenching of the pyrolysate directly into a solvent at −78°. At −78° the solutions have a half life of about 21 hrs. At room temperature *p*-xylylene forms [2.2] paracyclophane and polymer. *p*-Xylylene is diamagnetic but is described as a pseudodiradical because it reacts with iodine to form *p*-xylylene diodide and with oxygen to form poly-*p*-xylylene peroxide, which on decomposition at 125° affords terephthalaldehyde in high yield. Reaction of *p*-xylylene dibromide with phenyllithium in ether affords poly-*p*-xylylene in 74% yield (J. H. Golden, 1961).

The Dreiding model of the [2.2] paracyclophane gives a rough idea of the geometry of the molecule. X-ray diffraction analysis shows that the benzene rings are not flat but that each pair of *p*-carbon atoms is displaced by 0.13 Å, or at an angle of 11°, from the plane of the other four carbons and that these two planes lie 3.09 Å apart. D. J. Cram (1951) prepared (4) and a series of higher homologs by intramolecular Wurtz reactions at high dilution and compared the spectra with those of noncyclic analogs. The first two members, [2.2] and [3.3] paracyclophane, do not show ultraviolet absorption characteristic of ordinary benzene rings because the rings are nonplanar. [4.4] Paracyclophane shows a normal ultraviolet absorption spectrum, but since Friedel-Crafts acylation stops with introduction of a single acetyl group the effect of the deactivating group must be transmitted transannularly to the second ring. In the case of [6.6] paracyclophane, both rings are acylated.

By fast flow pyrolysis of the methohydroxide (1) and quenching at $-78°$, Errede (1961) obtained o-xylylene (2) in good yield. At low temperatures the hydrocarbon dimerizes to the very reactive spiro-di-o-xylylene (4), and at medium temperatures it cyclizes to cyclo-di-o-xylylene.

18.20   Quinonemethane Systems. — Diphenyl has long been recognized as a product of the thermal decomposition of dibenzoyl peroxide in solution, along with carbon dioxide and benzoic acid. Study of the decomposition in benzene at relatively high dilution at the reflux temperature under nitrogen led to the discovery of two additional hydrocarbons (D. F. DeTar, 1958). One was identified as 1,4-dihydrodiphenyl (3, m.p. $-4°$) and

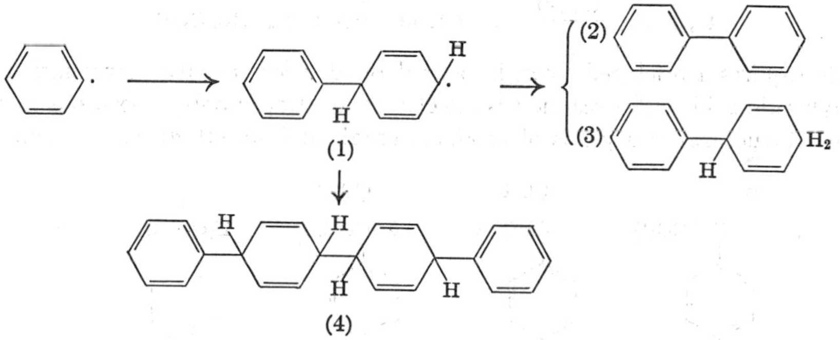

the other as cis, cis-1',4',1'',4''-tetrahydro-p-quaterphenyl (4, m.p. 146°). The key intermediate clearly is the radical (1), which disproportionates to diphenyl (2) and its dihydride (3), and which yields (4) by dimerization. Reaction of diphenyl with sodium in liquid ammonia gives deep red diphenyldisodium, which on quenching with solid ammonium chloride under nitrogen affords 1,4-dihydrodiphenyl (W. Hückel, 1956); Birch reduction (sodium, ethanol, liquid ammonia) of diphenyl attacks both rings.

7,7,8,8-Tetracyanoquinonedimethane (I), synthesized by condensation of cyclohexane-1,4-dione with malonitrile, bromination, and dehydrohalogenation with pyridine, has properties similar to those of tetracyanoethylene (5.11) and is a π-acid of comparable strength (D. S. Acker, R. E. Benson,[1] et al. 1960). The

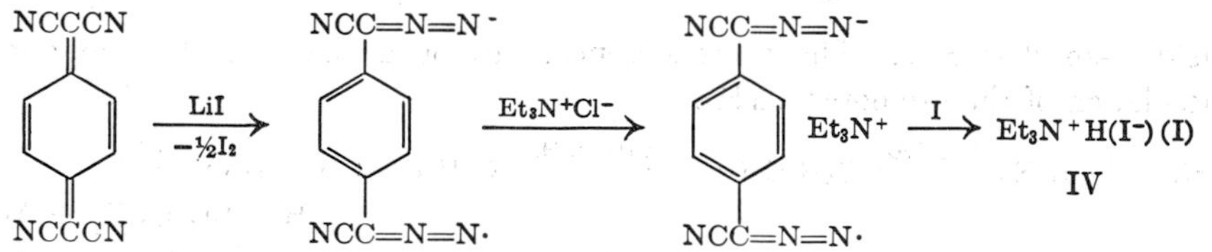

equilibrium constant for π-complex formation with pyrene is 78.4 as compared to 29.5 for the tetracyanoethylene-pyrene complex, probably because the molecule is sufficiently large for effective overlap with the large π-system in pyrene. The substance undergoes one-electron reduction, for example with lithium iodide in acetonitrile, to form a crystalline, saltlike π-complex (II), the anion of which is a

[1] Richard Edward Benson, b. 1920 Racine, Wis.; Ph.D. Nebraska (Hamilton); du Pont Co.

radical (the formula shows one of many resonance structures). Salts of this first type are characterized by high electrical resistivity (10^4–10^{21} ohm cm.). The salt II reacts with aqueous ammonium chloride to form the blue salt III. Addition of neutral I to an acetonitrile solution of the complex III yields purple-black crystals of the anion-radical complex IV, which has a resistivity of only 20 ohm cm. Complexes of this second type have the lowest electrical resistivities yet reported for organic compounds.

18.21   Side-Chain Metalation. — Side-chain metalation of toluene is effected efficiently at 90° by high-speed stirring with a mixture of potassium sand and sodium oxide (A. A. Morton,[1] 1955). The reaction mixture,

$$C_6H_5CH_3 \xrightarrow{\text{K, Na}_2\text{O}} C_6H_5CH_2M \xrightarrow[87\%]{\text{CO}_2} C_6H_5CH_2COOH$$

which acquires a brick red color, is poured on dry ice to effect carbonation to phenylacetic acid. The reaction is selective and attacks only α-positions in the chain. Structures and yields of products obtained from ethylbenzene, cumene,

CH$_2$CO$_2$H	CHCH$_3$ / CO$_2$H	H$_3$CCCH$_3$ / CO$_2$H	H$_3$CCCH$_3$ / H ... CH$_2$CO$_2$H
87%	31%	11%	58%

and *p*-cymene are shown in the formulation. Clearly the methyl group is more vulnerable to attack than the ethyl or isopropyl group.

Side-chain α-ethylation is accomplished with ethylene under pressure in the presence of a catalyst consisting of sodium and anthracene as promotor (H. Pines,[2] 1955). Toluene gives *n*-butylbenzene and 3-phenylpentane; cumene

$$C_6H_5CH_3 \xrightarrow[200°]{\text{CH}_2\!=\!\text{CH}_2} C_6H_5CH_2CH_2CH_3 + C_6H_5CH(CH_2CH_3)_2$$

$$C_6H_5CH(CH_3)_2 \xrightarrow[200°]{\text{CH}_2\!=\!\text{CH}_2} C_6H_5C(CH_3)_2CH_2CH_3$$

yields *t*-amylbenzene. The process appears to be a chain reaction involving metalation of the promoter (ArH).

$$\text{ArH} \xrightarrow{\text{Na}} \text{ArNa} \xrightarrow{C_6H_5CH_3} C_6H_5CH_2Na \xrightarrow{\text{CH}_2\!=\!\text{CH}_2} C_6H_5CH_2CH_2CH_2Na \xrightarrow{\text{ArH}}$$
$$C_6H_5CH_2CH_2CH_3 + \text{ArNa}$$

18.22   Hexaethylbenzene.—Photochemical bromination of hexaethylbenzene in refluxing carbon tetrachloride affords in almost quantitative yield hexa-(α-bromoethyl)benzene (H. Hopff,[3] 1961). Dehydrobromination of

[1] Avery A. Morton, b. 1892 St. Lawrence, So. Dakota; Ph.D. Mass. Inst. Techn. (J. F. Norris); Mass. Inst. Techn.

[2] Herman Pines, b. 1902 Lodz, Poland; Ph.D. Chicago; Northwestern Univ.

[3] Heinrich Hopff, b. 1896 Kaiserlautern, Germany; Ph.D. Munich (R. Willstätter, K. H. Meyer); I. G. Farbenindustrie; Univ. Mainz; ETH Zurich.

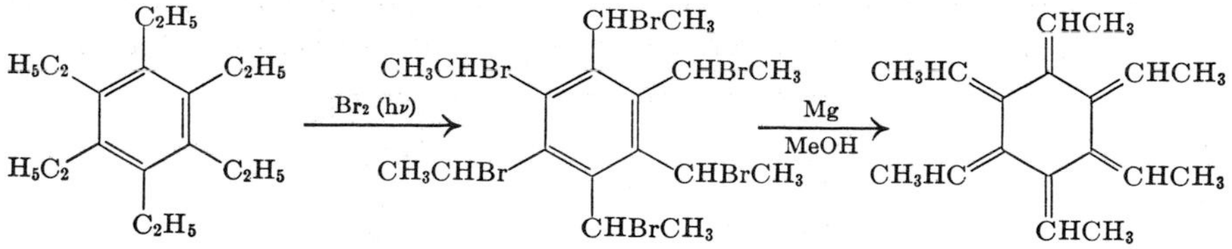

$$
\begin{array}{ccccc}
\text{(1)} & \xrightarrow{\text{Br}_2\,(h\nu)} & \text{(2)} & \xrightarrow[\text{MeOH}]{\text{Mg}} & \text{(3)}
\end{array}
$$

λ 266 mμ, log ε 3.76

this substance with magnesium and methanol gives in 29% yield a hydrocarbon characterized as hexaethylidenecyclohexane (3) by reconversion to (1) and to (2) and from the nuclear magnetic resonance spectrum. The hydrocarbon (m.p. 134°) is colorless but forms an orange π-complex with tetranitromethane.

18.23　　Aromatic Heterocycles.—The resonance energy of pyridine is 43 kcal./mole, significantly higher than that of benzene (36 kcal.). In this heterocycle the possibility for resonance extends beyond the two identical Kekulé structures (a) and (b) to three additional structures (c–e), in which the relatively electron-attracting nitrogen atom acquires an additional pair of electrons from a carbon atom in the α- or γ-position, which thereby becomes positively

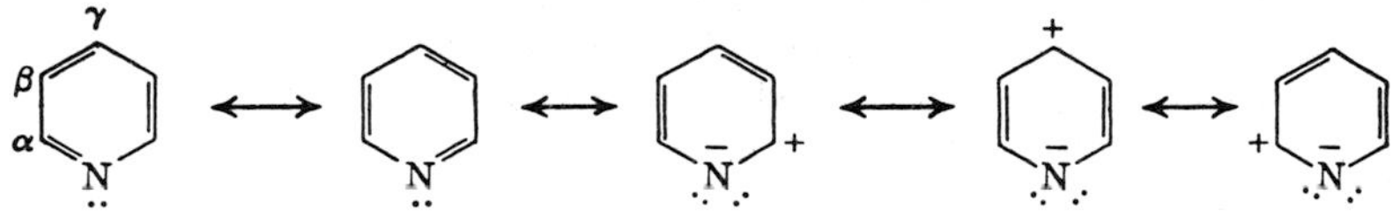

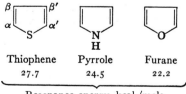

(a)　　　(b)　　　(c)　　　(d)　　　(e)

charged. Thus electrophilic substitution occurs only at the β-position. Actually, such substitution is realizable only under forcing conditions. Bromination can be accomplished only in the vapor phase at a temperature of about 300°, and sulfonation and nitration can be effected only with difficulty. Attempted Friedel-Crafts reactions are invariably negative. Thus pyridine corresponds in aromaticity to nitrobenzene rather than to benzene.

The five-membered heterocycles thiophene, pyrrole, and furane can be seen from their resonance energies to be less aromatic than benzene but nevertheless resonance-stabilized. Stabilization cannot be achieved as in benzene and pyri-

Thiophene	Pyrrole	Furane
27.7	24.5	22.2

Resonance energy, kcal./mole

dine by resonance involving two equivalent Kekulé structures, but the hetero atom is responsible for an evidently weaker resonance effect. In thiophene (a) displacement of a pair of unshared electrons of the sulfur atom to one adjacent carbon atom, with separation of charge, gives structure (b), and displacement to the other α-carbon gives (c). Structures (b) and (c), with centers of high electron density at α-positions, account for the fact that thiophene is substituted in elec-

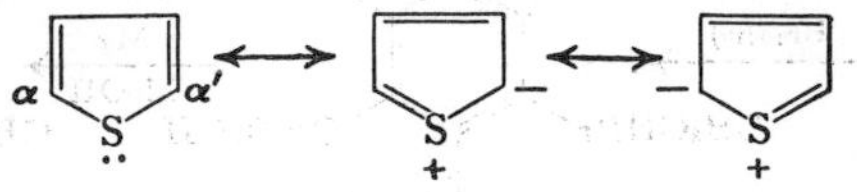

(a)   (b)   (c)

trophilic reactions in the α-position. That such substitutions occur more easily than in the case of benzene is shown by the fact that Friedel-Crafts reaction of acetyl chloride with thiophene can be effected with the mild catalyst zinc chloride; aluminum chloride is liable to cause resinification. Coal-tar benzene can be freed of thiophene by shaking it in the cold with concentrated sulfuric acid; thiophene is sulfonated preferentially and is removed with the acid. Since the hetero atoms of pyrrole and of furane carry unshared electrons, resonance stabilization is achieved in the same way as with thiophene.

PROBLEMS

1. Suggest methods for the Friedel-Crafts synthesis of (a) t-butylbenzene, (b) p-di-t-butylbenzene.
2. How could p-$(CH_3)_3CC_6H_4CO_2H$ be synthesized starting with toluene?
3. Devise a synthesis of p-$(CH_3)_2CHC_6H_4CO_2H$ starting with benzene.
4. What products would you expect to result from the following reactions?
   (a) $C_6H_6 + (CH_3)_2C{=}CH_2 + HF$
   (b) $C_6H_5CH_2CH_3 + (CH_3)_2CHCl + BF_3$
   (c) $C_6H_5CH_2CH_3 + 2CH_3CH_2Cl + AlCl_3$ (2 equivalents, no cooling)
   (d) $C_6H_5CH_3 + CH_3COCl + AlCl_3$ (1 equivalent)
5. Indicate syntheses of n-butylbenzene utilizing any aliphatic components desired and starting with: (a) benzene, (b) bromobenzene, (c) benzaldehyde.
6. Formulate a synthesis of α-phenylnaphthalene starting with benzene and succinic anhydride.
7. What di- and trimethylnaphthalenes would be obtained by syntheses starting with the Friedel-Crafts condensation of methylsuccinic anhydride with toluene?
8. Formulate the following synthesis. Acetophenone is monobrominated (side chain), the product is condensed with the sodio derivative of diethyl malonate, the ester is saponified and heated with dilute acid, and the sequence is completed by Clemmensen reduction and cyclization with liquid hydrogen fluoride. What is the product?
9. How could the synthesis of (8) be varied and extended for the synthesis of:
   (a) 2,7-Dimethylnaphthalene
   (b) 2,3,7-Trimethylnaphthalene
10. Give two ways of preparing α-methylnaphthalene from α-bromonaphthalene.
11. Suggest a synthesis of $C_6H_5(CH_2)_5COOH$, starting with bromobenzene and cyclohexanone.

Chapter 19

NITRO COMPOUNDS

19.1   **Properties.** — Nitration, conducted with nitric acid alone or in combination with acetic acid, acetic anhydride, or sulfuric acid, provides an efficient method for preparation of mono-, di-, and trinitro derivatives of many aromatic hydrocarbons and of hydroxy, halo, and other substitution products.   The polynitro compounds accessible by the direct route have the *meta* orientation, and *ortho* and *para* dinitro compounds, though obtainable by indirect methods, are rare.   Products of nitration find use as solvents, explosives, dyes, perfumes, and analytical reagents, and are important as intermediates for primary amines, into which they are convertible by reduction.

As can be seen from the properties of representative compounds listed in Table 19.1, polynitro derivatives have relatively high melting points, particularly if they are symmetrical (*para*; 1,3,5).   Introduction of the nitro group produces an increase in boiling point out of proportion to the increase in molecular weight, amounting to 120–130° for the nitro derivatives of benzene and toluene.   Nitrobenzene has about the same molecular weight (123.11) as mesitylene (120.19), but the boiling point is higher by 46°.   Electrostatic interaction of the semipolar bonds of contiguous molecules evidently promotes association in the liquid state. Nitro compounds are heavier than water, and unless they contain a solubilizing group, they are practically insoluble in water.   They dissolve in cold concentrated sulfuric acid, usually without permanent change, as the result of formation of oxonium salts.   Technical preparations of nitrobenzene, trinitrobenzene, and trinitrotoluene usually have a yellowish color, but purified substances are colorless.

19.2   **Nitrobenzene.** — Nitrobenzene can be produced on a technical scale in yields up to 98% by nitration of benzene with mixed acid at 50–55°.   It is a colorless hygroscopic liquid, immiscible with water and volatile with steam, d_4^{25} 1.197.   It has a characteristic sweetish almondlike odor.   Nitrobenzene has remarkable solvent power for organic compounds and is employed as a crystallizing solvent for substances that are practically insoluble in more usual solvents, though it has the disadvantage of being difficult to remove from

TABLE 19.1. NITRO COMPOUNDS

NAME	FORMULA	M.P., °C.	B.P., °C.
Nitrobenzene	$C_6H_5NO_2$	5.7	210
o-Dinitrobenzene	$C_6H_4(NO_2)_2(1,2)$	118	$319^{774\,mm.}$
m-Dinitrobenzene	$C_6H_4(NO_2)_2(1,3)$	89.8	$303^{770\,mm.}$
p-Dinitrobenzene	$C_6H_4(NO_2)_2(1,4)$	174	$299^{777\,mm.}$
1,3,5-Trinitrobenzene	$C_6H_3(NO_2)_3(1,3,5)$	122	
o-Nitrotoluene	$CH_3C_6H_4NO_2(1,2)$	$\left\{\begin{array}{l}-9.5\alpha\\-4\beta\end{array}\right\}$	222
m-Nitrotoluene	$CH_3C_6H_4NO_2(1,3)$	16	231
p-Nitrotoluene	$CH_3C_6H_4NO_2(1,4)$	52	238
2,4-Dinitrotoluene	$CH_3C_6H_3(NO_2)_2(1,2,4)$	70	
2,4,6-Trinitrotoluene	$CH_3C_6H_2(NO_2)_3(1,2,4,6)$	80.6	
2,4,6-Trinitro-m-xylene	$(CH_3)_2C_6H(NO_2)_3(1,3,2,4,6)$	182	
Picric acid	$HOC_6H_2(NO_2)_3(1,2,4,6)$	122.5	
2,4,6-Trinitroresorcinol	$(HO)_2C_6H(NO_2)_3(1,3,2,4,6)$	176	
Tetryl	$CH_3(NO_2)NC_6H_2(NO_2)_3(1,2,4,6)$	129	
o-Nitrochlorobenzene	$ClC_6H_4NO_2(1,2)$	32.5	245
m-Nitrochlorobenzene	$ClC_6H_4NO_2(1,3)$	47.9	236
p-Nitrochlorobenzene	$ClC_6H_4NO_2(1,4)$	83	239
2,4-Dinitrochlorobenzene	$ClC_6H_3(NO_2)_2(1,2,4)$	53	
Picryl chloride	$ClC_6H_2(NO_2)_3(1,2,4,6)$	83	
o-Nitrodiphenyl	$C_6H_5 \cdot C_6H_4NO_2(1,2)$	37	320
p-Nitrodiphenyl	$C_6H_5 \cdot C_6H_4NO_2(1,4)$	114	340

the crystals because of its low volatility (b.p. 210°) and of acting as a mild oxidizing agent at temperatures near the boiling point. It also dissolves anhydrous aluminum chloride as the result of complex formation, and is a useful solvent for the Friedel-Crafts reaction.

Nitrobenzene is toxic and is taken into the body both by inhalation of the vapor and by absorption through the skin. It produces chronic intoxication and turns the blood a chocolate brown color owing to either oxidation of hemoglobin to methemoglobin or formation of a complex, Hb–nitrobenzene. The substance is excreted in part as p-aminophenol. The methyl homologs do not share the poisonous quality, apparently because a mechanism is available for their elimina-

Fuming HNO₃ + concd. H₂SO₄, 95°
88% yield

tion from the system. Thus p-nitrotoluene is oxidized in the body to p-nitro-benzoic acid, which presumably is excreted in conjugation with glycine.

Nitration of nitrobenzene under rather drastic conditions affords m-dinitro-benzene; reaction with fuming sulfuric acid gives m-nitrobenzenesulfonic acid with only traces of the *ortho* and *para* isomers; and the chief product of catalyzed chlorination is *m*-nitrochlorobenzene.

19.3   Nitrotoluenes. — The mixtures of *o*- and *p*-nitrotoluene resulting in nearly theoretical yield from nitration of toluene with nitric acid or with mixed acid can be separated on a technical scale by fractional distillation in vacuum, for the isomers differ more than usual in boiling point (16° at 760 mm.). The more volatile fraction containing the *ortho* isomer can be freed from some 4–5% of *p*-nitrotoluene by prolonged heating with alcoholic alkali, when the slightly more reactive *para* compound suffers dehydrogenation to p,p'-dinitrostilbene, $NO_2C_6H_4CH$＝$CHC_6H_4NO_2$. Preferential reduction of the *para* isomer with an arsenate also can be utilized for separation. *m*-Nitrotoluene is obtained in 4% yield as a by-product of nitration.

19.4   *op*-Dinitrobenzenes. — The *ortho* and *para* isomers are obtainable in two steps from the appropriate nitroaniline, which can be oxidized with Caro's acid (H_2SO_5) to the nitroso compound, as in the example. The nitroso derivative is then oxidized with dilute nitric acid or with nitric acid con-

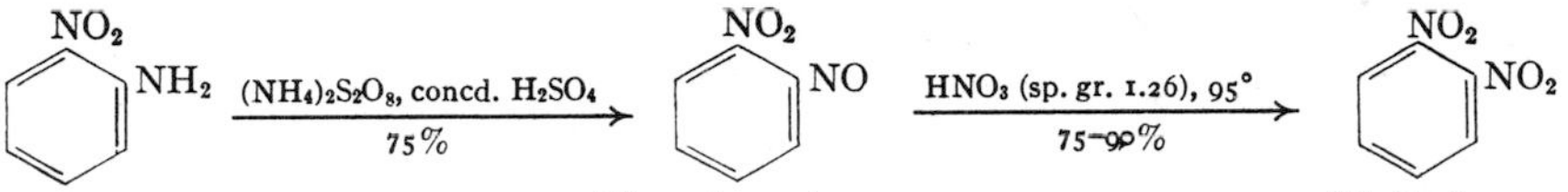

o-Nitroaniline   *o*-Nitronitrosobenzene   *o*-Dinitrobenzene
                         (yellow, m.p. 127°)

taining hydrogen peroxide. A superior one-step process consists in oxidation of the aromatic amine with pertrifluoroacetic acid (5.17) in refluxing methylene chloride (W. D. Emmons, 1954). Oxidation of *o*- and *p*-nitroaniline by this method affords *o*- and *p*-dinitrobenzene in yields of 92 and 86%. Other compounds obtainable with difficulty if at all by other methods but which can be made easily from available amines are: 2,4,6-tribromo- and 2,4,6-trichloronitrobenzene (yields 100 and 98%), 1,2,4-trinitrobenzene (87%).

19.5   Nitrochlorobenzenes. — All three mononitrochlorobenzenes can be obtained from benzene by combination of nitration and halogenation, for the order of the operations determines the final orientation. *m*-Nitrochlorobenzene is obtained by nitration of benzene followed by chlorination, but if the

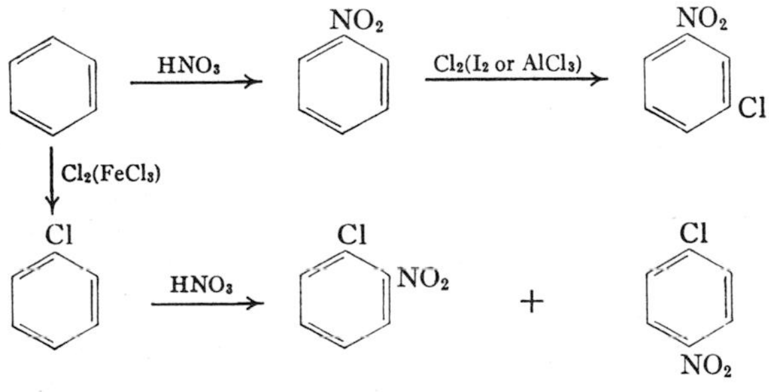

order is reversed and the nitro group is introduced in the second step, a mixture results containing about two parts of the *para* isomer to one of the *ortho*. On a technical scale fairly sharp separation of the isomers resulting from nitration is made by freezing out the bulk of the higher-melting *para* compound, refractionating the liquid portion, and further freezing. Samples free from traces of isomers are best prepared from the corresponding nitroanilines by the Sandmeyer reaction (21.24).

2,4-Dinitrochlorobenzene is reported to be formed in 97% yield by nitration of chlorobenzene in fuming sulfuric acid. Since the halogen atom has a deactivating influence, the reaction proceeds with considerable difficulty beyond the introduction of two substituents, and 2,4,6-trinitrochlorobenzene (picryl chloride) is obtained more readily from the corresponding phenol (19.11).

19.6   Nucleophilic Displacements. — The *ortho* and *para* dinitro derivatives of benzene exhibit a sensitivity to attack by basic reagents not shared by *m*-dinitrobenzene. Thus when *o*-dinitrobenzene is warmed with dilute sodium hydroxide or with a solution of sodium methoxide one nitro group is displaced by a hydroxyl or methoxyl group. Reaction with alcoholic ammonia, or with a primary or secondary amine gives the *o*-aminonitro derivative, and reaction with

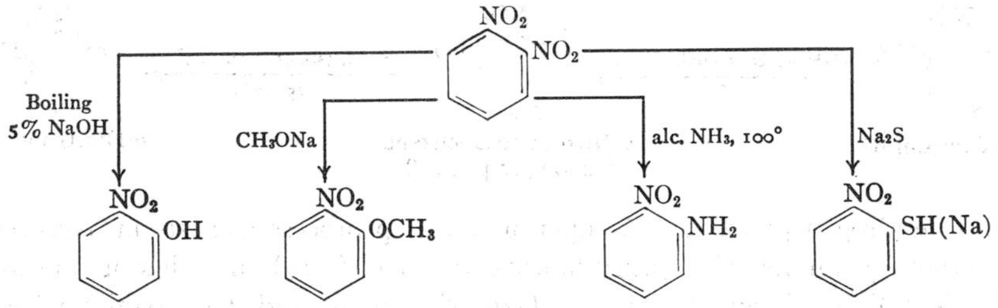

one mole of sodium sulfide affords *o*-nitrothiophenol (as sodium salt). *p*-Dinitrobenzene enters into the same nucleophilic displacements, but the *meta* isomer does not. Thus *m*-dinitrobenzene is stable to alcoholic ammonia even at 250°.

The vulnerability of the *op*-isomers to nucleophilic attack is easily explained. In one of the resonance structures of the *o*-dinitro compound a positive charge on the carbon carrying one nitro group invites attack by the hydroxide anion

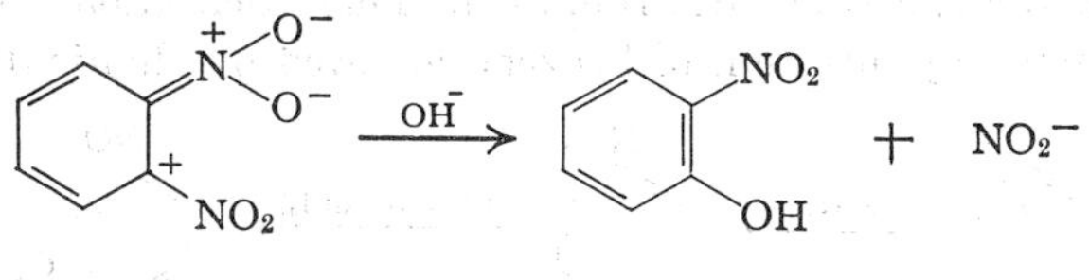

with expulsion of nitrite ion. In *p*-dinitrobenzene a positive charge at the site of one nitro group labilizes this group for nucleophilic displacement. A similar resonance effect is inoperable in the *meta* isomer. Ammonia functions as a nucleophile because of the lone pair of electrons on nitrogen.

The halogen atom in *o*- or *p*-nitrochlorobenzene is similarly labilized and subject to nucleophilic displacement, as shown in the examples. Chlorobenzene and *m*-nitrochlorobenzene show none of these reactions; for example, they are inert to amines even in the temperature range 180–190°. The combined resonance effect of the two *op*-nitro groups in 2,4-dinitrochlorobenzene labilizes the chlorine

$$C_6H_3ClNO_2 \xrightarrow{\text{aq. Na}_2CO_3,\ 130°} \text{C}_6\text{H}_4(\text{OH})(\text{NO}_2)\ \ o\text{-Nitrophenol}$$

$$\xrightarrow{\text{aq. CH}_3\text{OH—KOH}} \text{C}_6\text{H}_4(\text{OCH}_3)(\text{NO}_2)\ \ o\text{-Nitroanisole}$$

$$\xrightarrow{\text{alc. CH}_3\text{NH}_2,\ 160°} \text{C}_6\text{H}_4(\text{NHCH}_3)(\text{NO}_2)\ \ o\text{-Nitro-N-methylaniline}$$

atom to such an extent that nucleophilic displacements occur with great ease. Thus the reaction with hydrazine in triethylene glycol proceeds so readily (and exothermally) that ice cooling of the stirred mixture is required for maintenance

$$\text{(Cl, NO}_2, \text{NO}_2\text{-benzene)} + \text{H}_2\text{NNH}_2\ \text{(64\% solution)} \xrightarrow[\text{HO(CH}_2\text{CH}_2\text{O)}_3\text{H}]{20°} \text{(NHNH}_2, \text{NO}_2, \text{NO}_2\text{-benzene)} + \text{HCl}$$

2,4-Dinitrophenylhydrazine

of a temperature of 20°. Here the special solvent plays a role, for a procedure utilizing ethanol as solvent calls for refluxing the mixture for one hour.

Bunnett[1] (1958) has shown that the reactions of 2,4-dinitrochlorobenzene with several nucleophiles in 60% dioxane at 25° follow second-order kinetics; rate coefficients (1. mole^{-1} sec.$^{-1}$ $\times$ 10^{-3}) are as follows: $C_6H_5NH_2$, 0.08; OH$^-$, 1.10; H_2NNH_2, 3.87; $C_6H_5O^-$, 12.7; piperidine, 74.6. Evidence of several types argue against a one-step S_N2-like mechanism. In the condensation of 1-substituted 2,4-dinitrobenzenes with piperidine in methanol the 1-substituent fluoro, nitro, and p-toluenesulfonoxy groups are displaced very rapidly, whereas chlorine and bromine and four other substituents are displaced more slowly and with little variation in rate among the six. The three halogens clearly do not fall in the order expected for an S_N2 reaction (Br > Cl > F), and the similarity of rates for six groups containing five different elements demonstrates the absence of an element effect and shows that breaking of the C—X bond is not involved in rate-determining transition states of the displacements. The evidence, on the other hand, is consistent with the concept of a two-step mechanism involving the intermediate complex (2), which is similar to the intermediates postulated for electrophilic substitution. Bunnett reasoned that a base, such as acetate ion, should remove hydrogen from the ammonium nitrogen of intermediate (2) to form intermediate (4), from which expulsion of the fluoride ion to form product (3) should be easy and expulsion of the N-methylanilide ion with regeneration of (1) should be difficult. Trial showed that the reaction is very sensitive to base

---

[1] Joseph F. Bunnett, b. 1921 Portland, Oregon; Ph.D. Rochester (Tarbell); Reed College; Univ. North Carolina; Brown Univ.

catalysis: added potassium acetate accelerates displacement of fluorine by 1400%. Furthermore, intermediate salts isolated by Meisenheimer in 1902 are now recog-

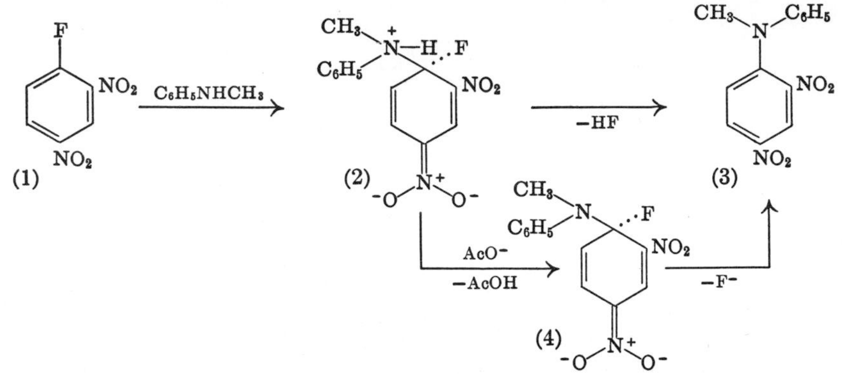

nized as conforming to the type postulated. Thus reaction of either 2,4,6-trinitroanisole (5) with potassium ethoxide or of 2,4,6-trinitrophenetole (7) with potassium methoxide gives a yellow salt (6) which on acidification affords a mixture of the two trinitro ethers, (5) and (7). The fact that alkoxyl is a rela-

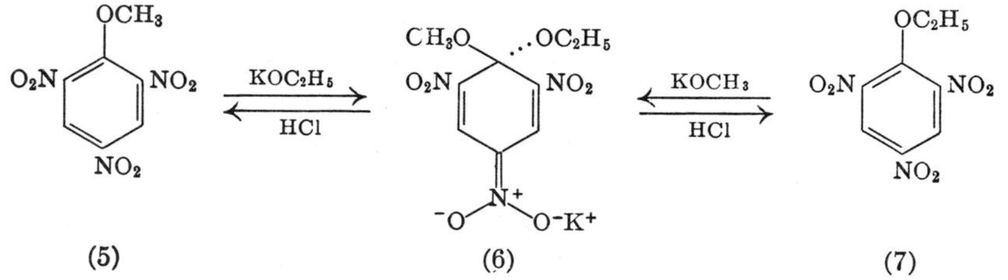

tively inefficient leaving group probably contributes to the stability of the complex salt (6). The infrared spectra of seven Meisenheimer complexes are in accord with the structures assigned (L. K. Dyall, 1960).

19.7   Nucleophilic Substitution. — Attack of an aromatic ring by a nucleophile with displacement of hydrogen has been observed in a few instances. Thus *m*-dinitrobenzene can be partially hydroxylated by oxidation with alkaline potassium ferricyanide. Resonance sets up positive centers in the

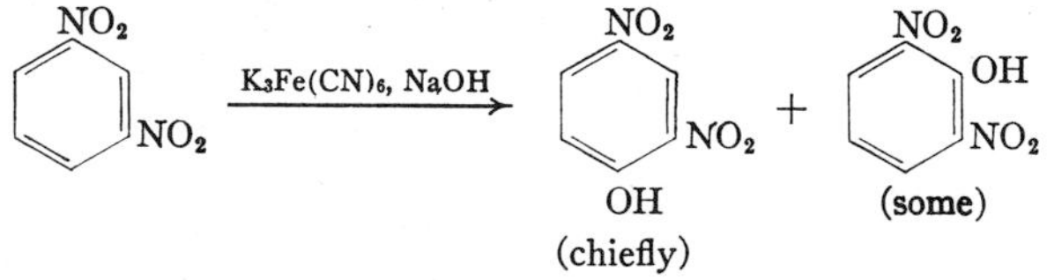

ortho and *para* positions inviting attack by OH⁻ to give *op*-products. Thus the nitro group directs electrophilic substitution at the *meta* position but is *op*-directing in nucleophilic substitution. When warmed with powdered potassium hydroxide, nitrobenzene is converted in part into a mixture of the oxidation products *o*- and *p*-nitrophenol, in which the former predominates, and in part into a product of reduction, azoxybenzene. The reaction proceeds in the absence of

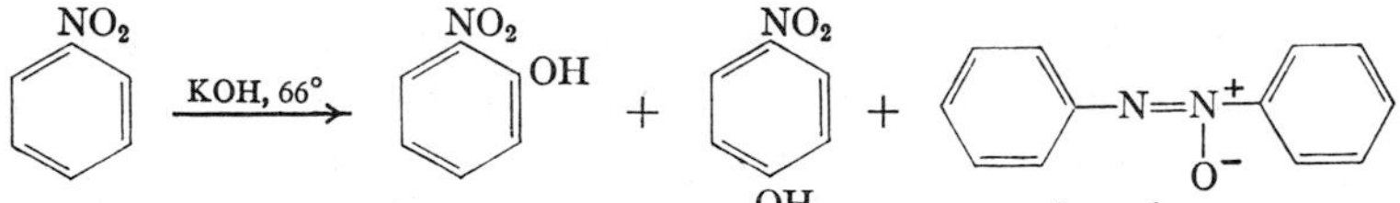

Azoxybenzene

oxygen and is a disproportionation. 1,3,5-Trinitrobenzene undergoes nucleophilic substitution with ease. It is oxidized by alkaline ferricyanide to picric acid and it reacts with hydroxylamine to form picramide.

19.8   Homolytic Methylation. — Since nitro groups enhance the susceptibility of the aromatic ring to attack by methyl radicals (17.10), polynitrobenzenes can be methylated by radicals generated by the decomposition of lead tetraacetate (L. F. Fieser, 1942). Thus 2,4,6-trinitrotoluene affords trinitro-*m*-xylene; this less soluble and higher melting product is easily separated

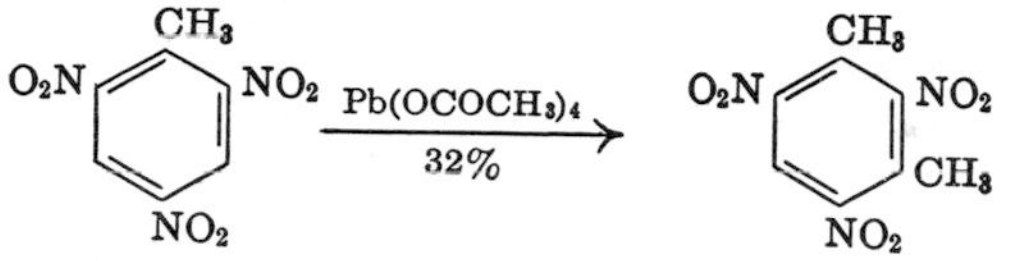

M.p. 80.6°   M.p. 182°

from unchanged starting material. Nitrobenzene is converted in low yield into *o*- and *p*-toluene, but toluene affords benzyl acetate (18%).

19.9   2,4,6-Trinitrotoluene (TNT). — The preparation of this important high explosive is accomplished by nitration of toluene with mixed acid, usually in three steps, with utilization of the spent acid from trinitration for the dinitration, and of the spent acid from dinitration for mononitration. The main end product, the 2,4,6-trinitro derivative (VI), is formed through the intermediates II-V. Monosubstitution gives the *ortho* and *para* isomers in a

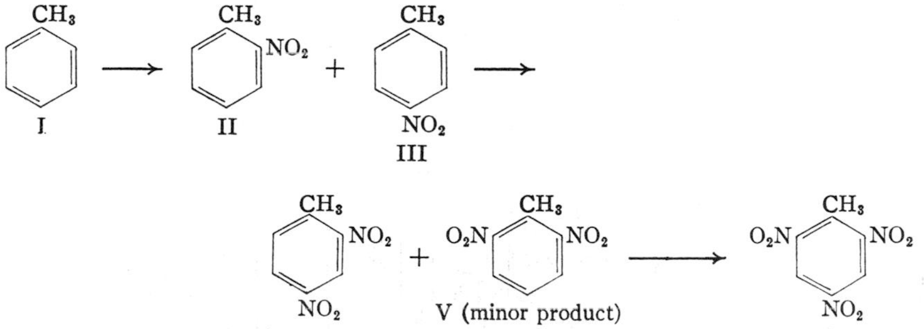

I   II   III

IV (chief product)   V (minor product)   VI

ratio varying somewhat with temperature, and the mixture contains a small amount (4%) of *m*-nitrotoluene. In the next step the *p*-nitro compound III yields exclusively 2,4-dinitrotoluene (IV) by substitution *ortho* to the methyl and *meta* to the nitro group; in the *o*-nitro isomer II, comparable positions are available at 4 and 6 but substitution occurs preponderantly at the point of the stronger *para* direction by the methyl group and gives the same 2,4-isomer; 2,6-dinitrotoluene (V, m.p. 65°) is produced in only minor amounts. Both dinitro compounds are converted on further nitration into the same trinitro derivative VI, or TNT. The crude 2,4,6-trinitrotoluene (α-TNT) is contaminated by small amounts of the isomers VII and VIII (β- and γ-TNT), which arise from nitration of *m*-nitrotoluene. These by-products depress the melting point of the main product (m.p. 80.6°) and impart a greasy character; they are objectionable also because they contain labile *o*- and *p*-nitro groups which render the material subject to hydrolysis with liberation of free nitric acid. The reactive character of the contaminants provides the basis of efficient methods for their

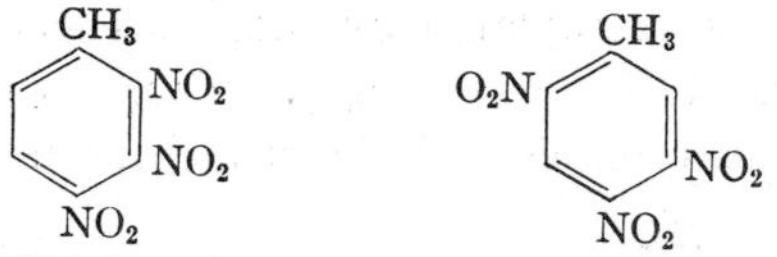

CH$_3$
NO$_2$
NO$_2$
NO$_2$
2,3,4-Trinitrotoluene
(m.p. 112°)
VII

CH$_3$
O$_2$N
NO$_2$
NO$_2$
2,4,5-Trinitrotoluene
(m.p. 104°)
VIII

elimination by nucleophilic displacement. When crude TNT is warmed in a 5% aqueous solution of sodium sulfite, a labile nitro group in VII and VIII is replaced by a sodium sulfonate group to give the water-soluble derivatives IX and X (reddish sulfite extract). A process for utilization of these otherwise wasted by-products consists in conversion into the nitramine XI, a useful explosive

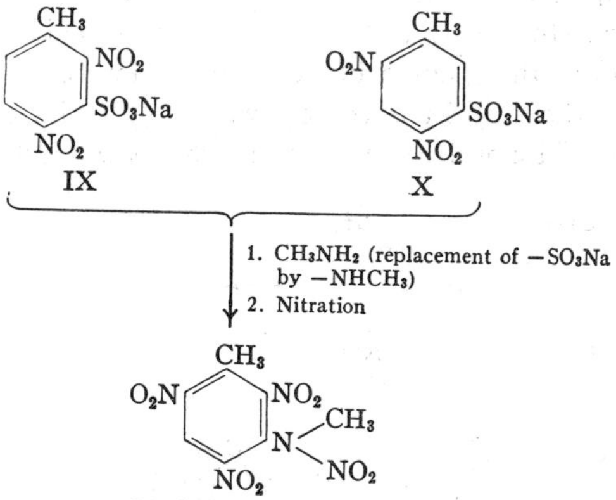

CH$_3$
NO$_2$
SO$_3$Na
NO$_2$
IX

CH$_3$
O$_2$N
SO$_3$Na
NO$_2$
X

1. CH$_3$NH$_2$ (replacement of —SO$_3$Na by —NHCH$_3$)
2. Nitration

CH$_3$
O$_2$N
NO$_2$
CH$_3$
N
NO$_2$
NO$_2$
3-Methyltetryl (m.p. 102°)
XI

The isomeric trinitro compounds also can be eliminated by alkaline hydrolysis to the dinitro-*m*-cresols, which can be converted into explosives by nitration. On a technical scale, overall yields of purified TNT up to 85% are realized.

In addition to the explosive character and ability to form complexes, discussed below, trinitrotoluene is distinguished by the fact that its methyl group possesses reactivity to aldehydic reagents comparable to that of the methyl group of acetaldehyde or of nitromethane. Thus in the presence of the basic catalyst piperidine, the nitro compound reacts with benzaldehyde in a manner analogous

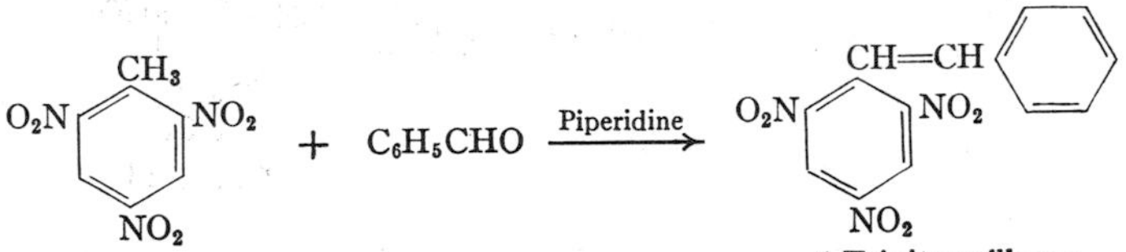

2,4,6-Trinitrostilbene
(yellow, m.p. 158°)

to an aldol condensation. 2,4-Dinitrotoluene condenses similarly under the influence of piperidine or sodium ethoxide at 170°, and affords 2,4-dinitrostilbene, m.p. 140°.

19.10   1,3,5-Trinitrobenzene (TNB). — The marked influence of nitro groups in deactivating the benzene ring is illustrated by the difficulty of preparing trinitrobenzene by direct nitration. One procedure calls for heating 60 g. of m-dinitrobenzene with 1 kg. of fuming sulfuric acid and $\frac{1}{2}$ kg. of fuming nitric acid (sp. gr. 1.52) at 100–110° for five days; the yield is 45%. No practical procedure has been found for preparing trinitrobenzene from benzene, though the substance has greater explosive power than trinitrotoluene. Trinitrotoluene is the commonly used high explosive because it can be prepared readily by direct nitration of the hydrocarbon, thanks to the activating influence of the methyl group in counteracting, to a sufficient extent, the influence of the nitro groups. The methyl group in TNT thus is required for the production, and not for the functioning, of the substance. The usual laboratory preparation of trinitro-

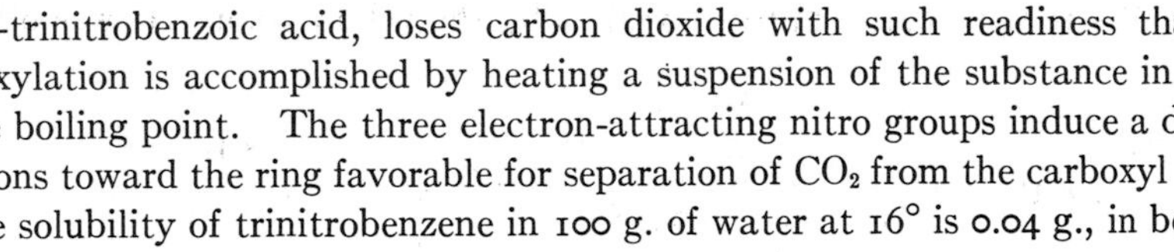

benzene is indirect and consists in degradation of trinitrotoluene by oxidation in concentrated sulfuric acid solution with solid sodium dichromate. The product, 2,4,6-trinitrobenzoic acid, loses carbon dioxide with such readiness that decarboxylation is accomplished by heating a suspension of the substance in water to the boiling point. The three electron-attracting nitro groups induce a drift of electrons toward the ring favorable for separation of CO_2 from the carboxyl anion.

The solubility of trinitrobenzene in 100 g. of water at 16° is 0.04 g., in benzene 6.2 g., and in alcohol 1.9 g.

19.11   Picric Acid. — Picric acid, 2,4,6-trinitrophenol, cannot be prepared satisfactorily by the action of nitric acid because phenol is so sensitive to oxidation that it is mainly destroyed rather than nitrated. A satisfactory procedure consists in first sulfonating phenol to the 2,4-disulfonic acid and then adding nitric acid to the reaction mixture. The unsaturated sulfonic acid groups stabilize the molecule and provide protection against the oxidizing action of nitric acid, and since sulfonation is reversible, the acid groups are smoothly replaced by nitro groups.   The process is simple and a yield of 70% is obtainable.

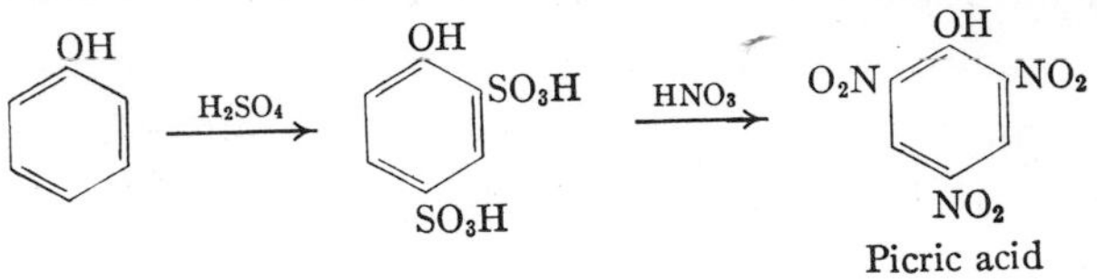

Picric acid

A still more economical method utilizes chlorobenzene as starting material; this can be converted efficiently into the 2,4-dinitro derivative, which is readily hydrolyzed to the dinitrophenol; the latter is then nitrated.   Chlorobenzene is a

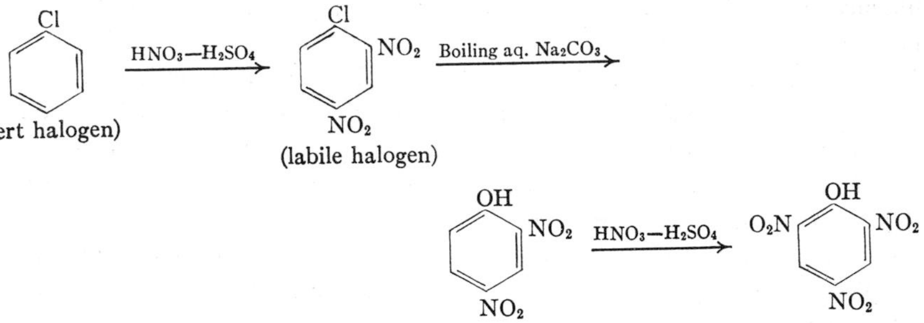

(inert halogen)   (labile halogen)

cheaper starting material than phenol, and in a modern process phenol is made from chlorobenzene in a reaction requiring a high temperature and pressure because of the inert character of the halogen (22.3).   In the picric acid process, replacement of halogen by hydroxyl is accomplished at a stage where it proceeds under mild conditions.

Picric acid is formed by the action of nitric acid on a number of organic substances containing a benzene ring, often as a result of extensive oxidative degradation, displacement of attached groups by nitro substituents, and hydrolysis of a nitrogen substituent with formation of a hydroxyl group.   Thus the substance arises from the action of nitric acid on salicylic acid or on indigo, and was first obtained from the latter source (1771).   Picric acid is characterized by a bitter taste and strongly acidic nature as well as by the yellow color.   It was observed

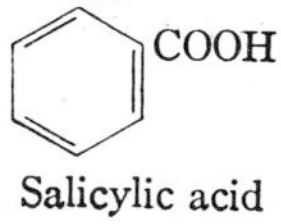

Salicylic acid 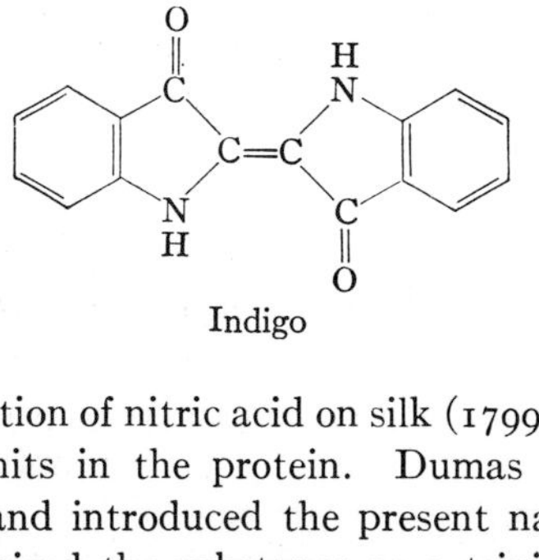   Indigo 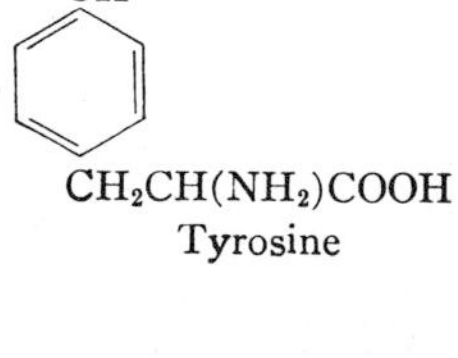   Tyrosine

to be formed by the action of nitric acid on silk (1799), the specific source probably being the tyrosine units in the protein.   Dumas (1836) established the composition by analysis and introduced the present name (Gr. *pikros*, bitter), and Laurent (1841) recognized the substance as a trinitro derivative of phenol and prepared it from the parent compound. Picric acid was found to stain proteins yellow and was introduced as a dye for silk in 1849, the first instance of use of an artificial dye. Application as an explosive was announced in an English patent (Sprengel, 1871). The versatile nitro compound also has bactericidal activity and formerly found use in treatment of burns, and it is employed in the laboratory for characterization of organic bases (amine picrates) and of polynuclear hydro-carbons.

Picric acid crystallizes from water in bright yellow plates, but separates from solutions in ligroin or in strong hydrochloric acid as nearly colorless crystals, which become yellow on the surface in contact with moisture of the air. The solubility in 100 g. of water at 25° is 1.4 g. and at 100°, 7.2 g.; in benzene, at 20° it is 5.3 g. and at the boiling point, 123 g. The substance has a pK_a of 0.80 and approaches mineral acids in acidic strength and ability to corrode metals. Since phenol is but weakly acidic (pK_a 10.01), the nitro groups evidently are responsible for a very marked enhancement in the tendency to ionize. Charac-teristic transformations of the compound are illustrated in the chart. Ready replacement of the phenolic hydroxyl group by halogen is a reaction specific to

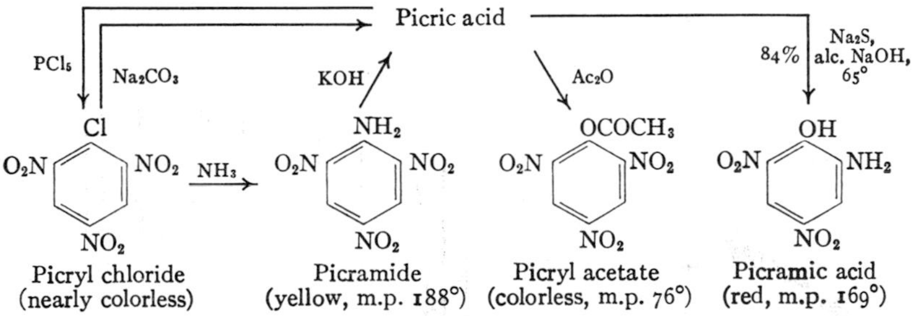

polynitro compounds and is not realizable with ordinary phenols. An improved method of converting picric acid into picryl chloride is the action of p-toluenesul-fonyl chloride ($CH_3C_6H_4SO_2Cl$) in the presence of dimethylaniline in nitrobenzene solution (70% yield); the method is applicable also to 2,4-dinitrophenol (Ull-mann,[1] 1908).

19.12   2,4,6-Trinitroresorcinol (Styphnic Acid). — In analogy with picric acid, this substance is best prepared by sulfonation followed by nitra-tion. It is also obtained from m-nitrophenol, which on nitration yields a tetranitro

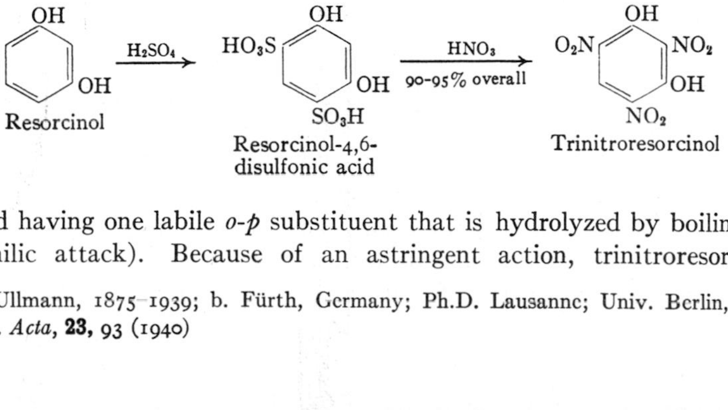

compound having one labile o-p substituent that is hydrolyzed by boiling water (nucleophilic attack). Because of an astringent action, trinitroresorcinol is

---

[1] Fritz Ullmann, 1875–1939; b. Fürth, Germany; Ph.D. Lausanne; Univ. Berlin, Geneva; *Helv. Chim. Acta,* **23,** 93 (1940)

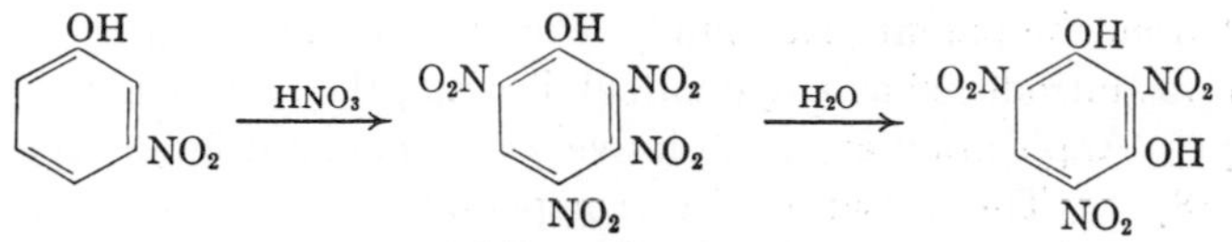

2,3,4,6-Tetranitrophenol

known as styphnic acid (Gr. *styphein*, to contract). Like picric acid, it is yellow, strongly acidic, and forms hydrocarbon complexes.

19.13 Tetryl. — The common name of this useful explosive is an abbreviation of N,2,4,6-tetranitro-N-methylaniline, and the compound can be described also as methyl-2,4,6-trinitrophenylnitramine. One nitro group is affixed to nitrogen by displacement of hydrogen in the methylamino group: $-NHCH_3 + HONO_2 \rightarrow -N(NO_2)CH_3 + H_2O$; this reaction can be reversed by the action of concentrated sulfuric acid, for a nitro group attached to nitrogen is less firmly held than one in the nucleus (tetryl → methylpicramide, m.p. 112°). Tetryl can be obtained from N-methylaniline, but it is prepared more economically from the less expensive N,N-dimethylaniline, which suffers loss of one methyl group by oxidation:

$$-N(CH_3)_2 \longrightarrow -N(CH_3)COOH \longrightarrow -NHCH_3 + CO_2$$

The steps indicated in the accompanying formulation have been established by isolation of the intermediates. The initial reaction is an *ortho-para* substitution of the amine in sulfuric acid solution, that is, under conditions such that ionization might occur with resulting *meta* direction. *Meta* substitution does indeed occur if a large excess of sulfuric acid is employed, but with limited reagent substitution can be controlled to the direction desired. An alternate preparation

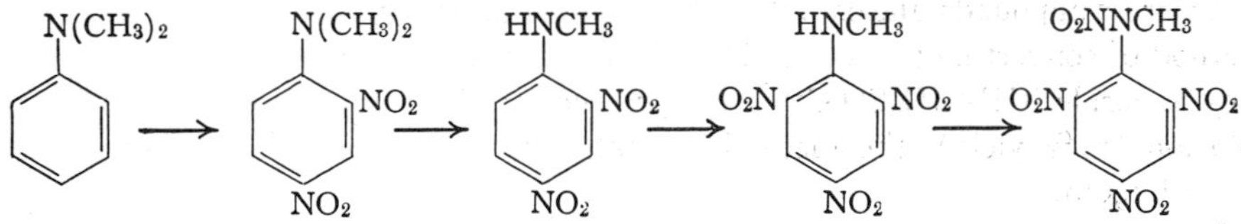

Tetryl

that avoids the loss of nitric acid expended in oxidation of the methyl group consists in condensation of 2,4-dinitrochlorobenzene with methylamine and nitration of the product.

19.14 Explosives. — In the series of compounds with adequate explosive power, the most important factor in determining the specific applications of the substances is the sensitivity to the shock of impact. Although the impact sensitivity, as measured by the height from which a weight must fall for its impact to cause a small sample of the substance to explode, is dependent somewhat on the physical state of the sample and varies with the size, shape, and extent of confinement of the metal cup used as container for the charge, the common explosives falling outside the group of propellants can be arranged in the following order of sensitivity:

Increasing impact sensitivity	Trinitrobenzene Ammonium picrate TNT	} High explosives
	Compressed picric acid Tetryl	} Boosters
	Lead azide Mercury fulminate	} Detonators (See 8.27)

A 5-kg. weight must fall 150 cm. to explode trinitrobenzene, but only 110 cm. to explode TNT, whereas mercury fulminate detonates when struck by a 2-kg. weight falling only 5 cm. The relatively impact-resistant nitro compounds are classified as high explosives; they are not exploded easily by heat or by shock, and in practice are detonated by the shock of a primary explosive. Mercury fulminate is highly sensitive to either impact or heat and is the primary explosive used in small percussion caps and electric squibs to initiate explosion of less sensitive material. Lead azide is a preferred detonator for military uses because it is slightly less sensitive than fulminate and is less subject to accidental or prema-

$$\overset{-}{C}\!\equiv\!\overset{+}{N}\!-\!O\!-\!Hg\!-\!O\!-\!\overset{+}{N}\!\equiv\!\overset{-}{C} \qquad \overset{-}{N}\!=\!\overset{+}{N}\!=\!N\!-\!Pb\!-\!N\!=\!\overset{+}{N}\!=\!\overset{-}{N}$$

Mercury fulminate   Lead azide

ture detonation and because much less material is required to detonate a given charge ($\frac{1}{10}$ to $\frac{1}{5}$ the weight of fulminate). Tetryl occupies an intermediate place in the scale, and is not sensitive enough to serve as a detonator but is too easily exploded to be employed as the main charge in a shell or bomb; the intermediate character renders the substance ideally suited to the function of a booster, as illustrated in an example cited below.

TNT is the most widely used filling for shells and air-borne demolition bombs. It is sufficiently insensitive to withstand the shock entailed in the ejection of a shell from a gun barrel under the pressure developed from ignition of a propellant charge, and can be caused to explode on operation of an impact- or time-fuse mechanism firing a detonator-booster element. It is the only one of the explosive nitro compounds of aromatic or heterocyclic type (cyclonite, 12.37) that melts below 100°, and it is conveniently melted with steam and poured into shells and bombs. Cast TNT is less sensitive than crystalline or pelleted material and is not exploded by a fulminate blasting cap or a lead azide detonator, but satisfactory operation is obtained with either type of detonator in combination with a charge of tetryl representing only a fraction of the charge of TNT; the booster is exploded by the detonator and produces a wave sufficient to set off the TNT. The more sensitive crystalline form of the explosive has been employed in the form of Cordeau detonating fuse, made by casting molten TNT into a 1-inch lead pipe and drawing this down repeatedly, with crushing of the filling, until the tube is about $\frac{3}{8}$ inch in diameter and the explosive is in the form of a fine crystalline powder. Cordeau tubing, which is sensitive enough to be detonated by a fulminate blasting cap, is used to set off multiple charges, but has been largely displaced by PETN-Primacord (8.28).

Picric acid as such was used extensively for a time as a military explosive, but has been abandoned because of the serious disadvantage that the strongly acidic substance corrodes metal surfaces of shells with formation of highly sensitive heavy-metal picrates. The iron (ferric), nickel, and chromium salts of picric acid are more sensitive to impact than tetryl and fall in the range of the detonators; lead picrate is particularly dangerous owing to its sensitivity to heat or shock. Cast picric acid requires a booster of the tetryl type, and it is interesting that the more sensitive compressed picric acid serves this function. Ammonium picrate is less sensitive to shock than the phenol and is free from the disadvantage of tending to form dangerous metal salts. It is at least equal to TNT in power and brisance and is less sensitive than this substance, but can be used satisfactorily with a tetryl booster. Ammonium picrate might be preferred to TNT as a general shell filling if it were not a high-melting solid (m.p. about 270°, dec.) that cannot be loaded by casting. It finds specific use as a charge for armor-piercing shells because it withstands the severe shock of impact better than TNT and is conserved for explosion under detonation after the shell has penetrated. The ammonium salt can be crystallized from water in a bright red metastable form or in a stable yellow one; the two forms do not differ in explosive properties.

Tetryl is employed as a booster for TNT, trinitrobenzene, cyclonite, ammonium picrate, and is the usual component, in combination with lead azide, of reinforced detonators. It is used also to increase the sensitivity of TNT; a mixture of 65% TNT and 35% tetryl melts below the boiling point of water and is fired by an ordinary fulminate blasting cap. For use as a booster, tetryl is compressed into pellets, either alone or mixed with 1–2% of graphite.

19.15   Artificial Nitro Musks. — The polynitro derivatives of certain benzenoid hydrocarbons containing the tertiary butyl group have an odor roughly approximating that of natural musk (Baur, 1891), and they are employed in perfuming cheap soaps. One of these derivatives is prepared from toluene; a t-butyl group is introduced in the meta position by Friedel-Crafts alkylation conducted at high temperature, and the product is then nitrated. The

"Baur musk"
(m.p. 97°)

musklike odor is retained on introduction of an additional methyl group or of an acetyl group.

"Xylene musk" (m.p. 113°)   "Musk ketone" (m.p. 136°)

REDUCTION OF NITRO COMPOUNDS

19.16   Nitrobenzene. — By reduction with a sufficiently powerful reagent (*e.g.*, stannous chloride) nitrobenzene can be converted in high yield into aniline. By use of milder reagents and by control of the acidity or alkalinity of the reaction mixture, it is possible to produce a number of substances of various intermediate stages of reduction, some of which are products of direct reduction, whereas others arise through secondary changes. Particularly comprehensive studies have been made of electrolytic reduction (Haber, 1900), where exact control is possible through adjustment of the imposed potential, current density, and hydrogen-ion concentration, and the results indicate that the sequence of primary reduction steps is as follows:

$$C_6H_5NO_2 \xrightarrow{2\,H} C_6H_5NO \xrightarrow{2\,H} C_6H_5NHOH \xrightarrow{2\,H} C_6H_5NH_2$$

Nitrobenzene   Nitrosobenzene   Phenylhydroxyl-   Aniline
                                                          amine

Nitrosobenzene is reduced to phenylhydroxylamine too readily to be isolable as such, but its formation as the initial product of reduction has been demonstrated by special tests. Both nitrosobenzene and phenylhydroxylamine are reactive, and under the catalytic influence of alkali they condense with elimination of a molecule of water in the manner of an aldol condensation and afford azoxybenzene. Azoxybenzene is made up of two units derived from nitrobenzene molecules

$$C_6H_5N{=}O \quad + \quad HN{-}C_6H_5 \xrightarrow{OH^-(-H_2O)} C_6H_5{-}N{=}\overset{+}{N}{-}C_6H_5$$

Nitrosobenzene | |
                                  OH   O⁻

          Phenylhydroxylamine   Azoxybenzene

linked through the nitrogen atoms, one of which carries an oxygen atom joined by a semipolar bond. This oxygen is readily removed during electrolytic reduction or by treatment with iron powder and water, with formation of azobenzene, which, in turn, can add two hydrogen atoms and form hydrazobenzene. A terminal reaction stage is reached with reductive fission of the N—N bond in

$$C_6H_5{-}N{=}\overset{+}{N}{-}C_6H_5 \xrightarrow{2\,H} C_6H_5N{=}NC_6H_5 \xrightarrow{2\,H} C_6H_5N{-}NC_6H_5$$

          | Azobenzene | |
         O⁻   H   H

  Azoxybenzene   Hydrazobenzene

hydrazobenzene, with formation of two molecules of aniline. Both the intermediate reduction products and the substances indicated as derived from them

$$C_6H_5N{+}NC_6H_5 \xrightarrow{2\,H} C_6H_5NH_2 \quad + \quad H_2NC_6H_5$$

          | | Aniline
         H   H

  Hydrazobenzene

by secondary transformations are thus convertible into aniline. Procedures have been devised for the efficient preparation of all these intermediate compounds by chemical methods, as recorded in the following summary.

Phenylhydroxylamine can be prepared in moderate yield by addition of zinc dust to a mixture of nitrobenzene, ammonium chloride and water.

$$C_6H_5NO_2 \xrightarrow[\text{62–68\%}]{\text{Zn, aq. NH}_4\text{Cl, 65°}} C_6H_5NHOH$$
$$\text{(m.p. 81°)}$$

Nitrosobenzene. — This sensitive primary reduction product of nitrobenzene is best prepared by oxidation of its successor in the reduction process (Bamberger,[1] 1894). Nitrosobenzene forms colorless crystals melting at 67.5–68° to a green liquid, which solidifies again to the colorless form; the substance also

$$C_6H_5NHOH \xrightarrow[\text{77\%}]{\text{K}_2\text{Cr}_2\text{O}_7, \text{ H}_2\text{SO}_4, \text{ 0°}} C_6H_5NO$$

gives green solutions. The colorless solid is bimolecular and dissociates to a green monomer in solution or on melting.

Azoxybenzene. — When nitrobenzene is reduced with a mild reagent in an alkaline medium, opportunity arises for condensation between the first two products of reduction, nitrosobenzene and phenylhydroxylamine.

$$2\,C_6H_5NO_2 \xrightarrow[\text{71–74\%}]{\text{Glucose, NaOH, 100°}} C_6H_5-N=\overset{+}{N}-C_6H_5$$
$$\underset{O^-}{}$$
$$\text{(yellow, m.p. 36°)}$$

Azoxybenzenes substituted in one or both rings are obtainable by condensation of a nitro compound with an amine in the presence of powdered sodium hydroxide and by oxidation of an azobenzene with hydrogen peroxide. The second method

$$o\text{-CH}_3\text{OC}_6\text{H}_4\overset{\overset{O^-}{|}}{\text{N}^+}=O \;+\; \text{H}_2\text{NC}_6\text{H}_4\text{Br-}p \xrightarrow{\text{NaOH (175°)}} o\text{-CH}_3\text{OC}_6\text{H}_4\overset{\overset{O^-}{|}}{\text{N}^+}=\text{NC}_6\text{H}_4\text{Br-}p$$

$$p\text{-BrC}_6\text{H}_4\text{N}=\text{NC}_6\text{H}_5 \xrightarrow{\text{H}_2\text{O}_2} p\text{-BrC}_6\text{H}_4\overset{\overset{O^-}{|}}{\text{N}^+}=\text{NC}_6\text{H}_5 \;+\; p\text{-BrC}_6\text{H}_4\text{N}=\overset{\overset{O^-}{|}}{\text{N}^+}\text{C}_6\text{H}_5$$

usually gives a mixture of both possible products, separable by chromatography.

Azobenzene. — This compound containing two doubly bound nitrogen atoms can be prepared by reduction of nitrobenzene in boiling methanolic sodium hydroxide solution with the calculated amount of zinc dust. The reduction of a

$$C_6H_5NO_2 \xrightarrow[\text{84–86\%}]{\text{Zn, NaOH, CH}_3\text{OH}} C_6H_5N=NC_6H_5$$
$$\text{(orange-red, m.p. 68°)}$$

nitrobenzene to an azobenzene with lithium aluminum hydride in ether is used for the quantitative determination of the nitro group.

---

[1] Eugen Bamberger, 1857–1932; b. Berlin; Ph.D. Berlin (Liebermann); Zurich ETH; *Helv. Chim. Acta*, **16**, 644 (1933)

A general route to substituted azobenzenes involves oxidation of an amine, for example p-aminoacetanilide, with sodium perborate (*Org. Syn.*, 1960). 4,4'-Diaminoazobenzene is useful for the study of colored derivatives such as the diisocyanate.

$$AcNHC_6H_4NH_2\text{-}p \xrightarrow[H_3BO_3]{NaBO_2} p\text{-}AcNHC_6H_4\text{---}N\text{=}N\text{---}C_6H_4NHAc\text{-}p$$

$$\xrightarrow[\text{52-56\% overall}]{HCl\text{---}CH_3OH;\ NaOH} p\text{-}H_2NC_6H_4N\text{=}NC_6H_4NH_2\text{-}p$$
$$\text{(yellow, m.p. 241}° \text{ dec.)}$$

Hydrazobenzene is obtained by reduction of nitrobenzene with zinc dust and alcoholic alkali in the manner just described, but with sufficient zinc to carry the reaction to the desired stage, as indicated by the discharge of the red color; yield 88%. The pure substance forms colorless crystals, m.p. 126°. It is sensitive to air oxidation, and is cleaved to aniline by powerful reducing agents (stannous chloride). Lithium aluminum hydride alone reduces azobenzene only under forcing conditions, but in the presence of 0.01 mole of certain metal halides, reduction to hydrazobenzene is complete in a few minutes (Olah, 1959). Some of the effective catalysts are: $MoCl_5$, $TiCl_4$, $FeCl_3$, Cu_2Cl_2, and $SbCl_5$; aluminum halides are inactive.

19.17   Isomerism of Azobenzene. — Hartley[1] (1937–38) observed that exposure of ordinary azobenzene (m.p. 68°) to light effects isomerization to a substance (m.p. 71°) which is stable in the crystalline state in the dark

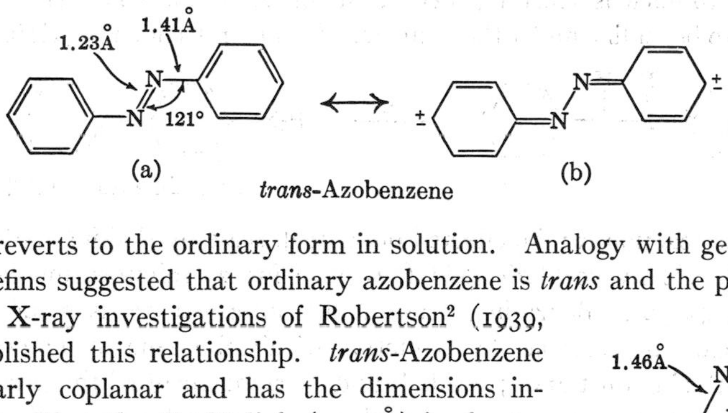

(a)   (b)
trans-Azobenzene

but which reverts to the ordinary form in solution. Analogy with geometrically isomeric olefins suggested that ordinary azobenzene is *trans* and the photoisomer is *cis*, and X-ray investigations of Robertson[2] (1939, 1941) established this relationship. *trans*-Azobenzene is very nearly coplanar and has the dimensions indicated (a). That the C—N link (1.41 Å) is shorter than the normal value (1.47 Å) indicates that excited structures (b) make some contribution. The *cis* isomer, on the other hand, is not coplanar, the benzene rings being rotated about 50° out of the plane containing the two nitrogen atoms. Departure from planarity suppresses resonance stabilization. See note on page 695.

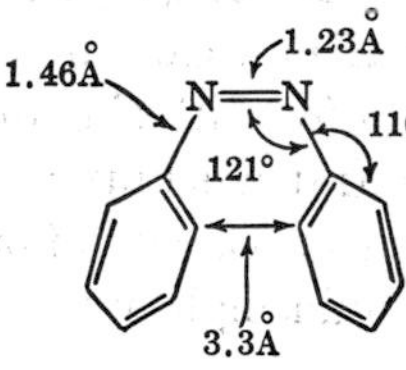

cis-Azobenzene

---

[1] G. Spencer Hartley, b. 1906 Leek, Staffs., England; Ph.D. Cambridge (Donnan); Univ. College, London

[2] J. Monteath Robertson, b. 1900 Auchterarder, Perthshire, Scotland; Ph.D. Glasgow; Univ. Glasgow

19.18   Rearrangement of Phenylhydroxylamine. — Under the influence of an acid catalyst, phenylhydroxylamine rearranges to p-aminophenol. This side-chain-to-nucleus rearrangement can hardly be intramolecular, since the identity of the product depends upon the solvent used. With aqueous sulfuric acid the product is p-aminophenol; rearrangement with sulfuric acid in methanol or in ethanol affords the corresponding methyl or ethyl ether, p-anisidine or p-phenetidine. If hydrochloric acid is used as catalyst, p-chloroaniline is the predominant product (Bamberger, 1921–25). Evidently the rearrangement involves nucleophilic attack. Ingold, finding that the reaction rate is proportional to the acidity, concluded that the conjugate acid of phenylhydroxylamine must be involved and postulated the following steps:

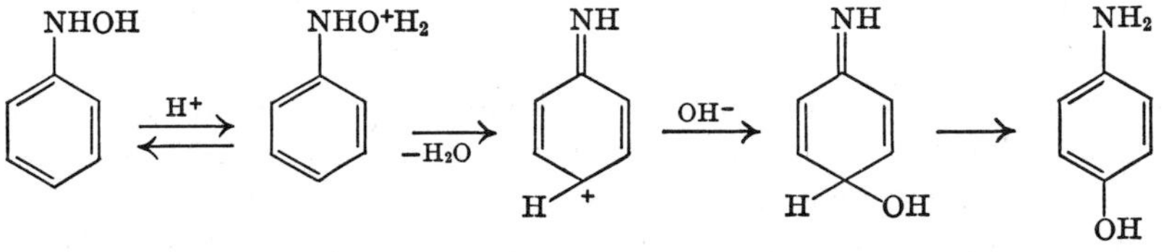

Gattermann[1] (1893) devised a convenient procedure for the preparation of p-aminophenols in which a nitro compound is reduced electrolytically in 80–90% sulfuric acid; the arylhydroxylamine rearranges as formed and the aminophenol is isolated as the sulfate.

19.19   Benzidine and Semidine Rearrangements. — A double side-chain-to-nucleus rearrangement is involved in the conversion of hydrazo-benzene into benzidine under the influence of a mineral acid, a benzidine rearrange-

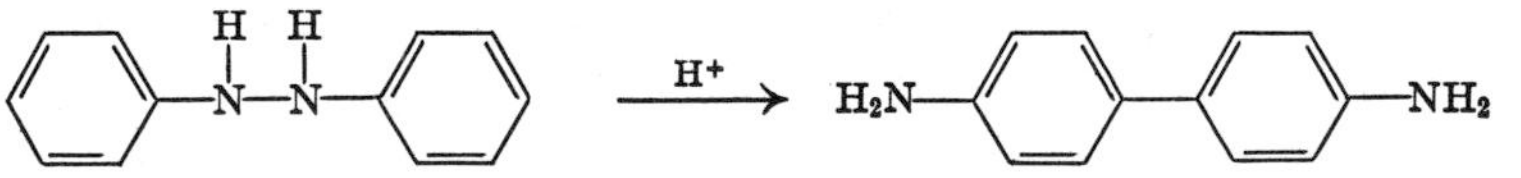

Benzidine (m.p. 127°)

ment. The reaction can be effected on a small scale by shaking hydrazobenzene (5 g.) with 3% hydrochloric acid (125 ml.) for 20 minutes and warming the mixture to 45–50°. Benzidine, a useful dye intermediate, is made industrially in high yield; for example, by reduction of nitrobenzene in o-dichlorobenzene solution with zinc dust and 5% alkali and rearrangement of the product in concentrated sulfuric acid. The hydrazobenzene derived from o-nitrotoluene on rearrangement affords a diamine known as o-tolidine, 3,3'-dimethyl-4,4'-diaminodiphenyl.

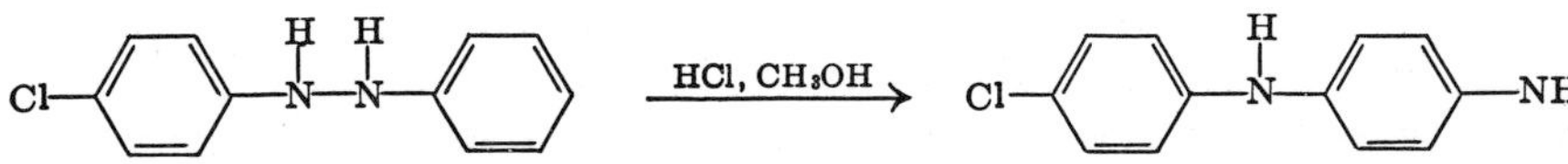

The less smooth semidine rearrangement is applicable to p-monosubstituted hydrazobenzenes. Thus p-chlorohydrazobenzene is rearranged by hydrogen chloride in methanol to 4-amino-4'-chlorodiphenylamine and other products.

---

[1] Ludwig Gattermann, 1860–1920; b. Goslar, Germany; Ph.D. Göttingen (Hübner); Univ. Freiburg; *Ber.*, **54A**, 115 (1921)

When two different hydrazobenzenes are rearranged in the same solution only two benzidines are formed and products of cross-coupling are absent. The result shows that the rearrangement is intramolecular. Hammond[1] found (1950) that the rate of rearrangement is proportional to the concentration of hydrazobenzene and the square of the hydrogen ion concentration and concluded that the first two steps involve protonation of the nitrogen atoms. Repulsion between

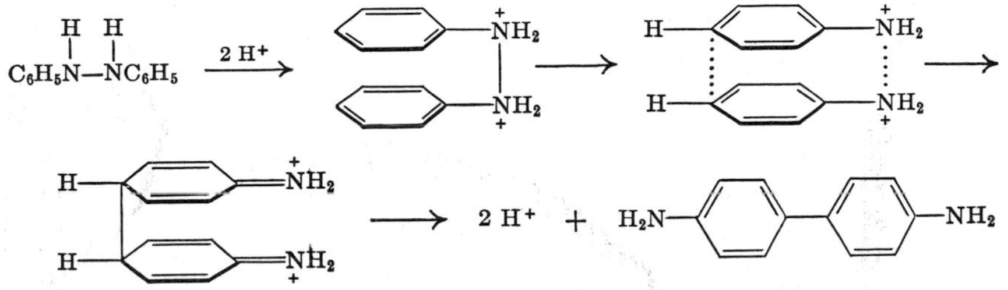

the two positively charged nitrogen atoms weakens the N—N linkage and facilitates formation of a new C—C bond.

19.20   Rearrangement of Azoxy Compounds. — W. M. Cumming (Glasgow, 1925) found that irradiation of a solution of azoxybenzene (yellow) in ethanol with a mercury vapor lamp for 50 hrs. effects partial isomerization to red o-hydroxyazobenzene. Badger[2] (1954) investigated exposure to sunlight

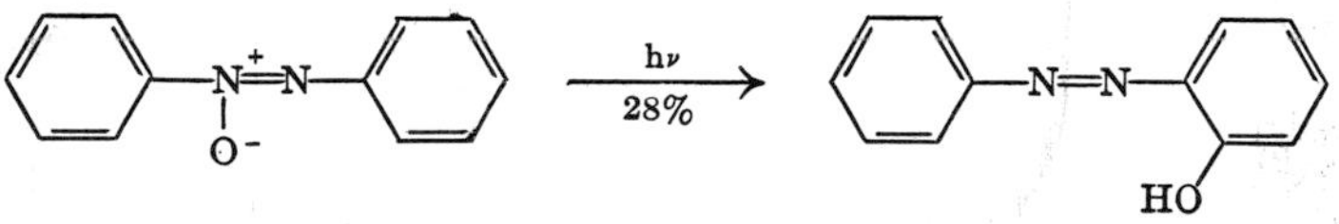

in benzene solutions for one month of a series of unsymmetrically substituted azoxybenzenes and established that oxygen migrates to the nonadjacent aromatic ring; in the example formulated, this is the ring containing bromine. Since the

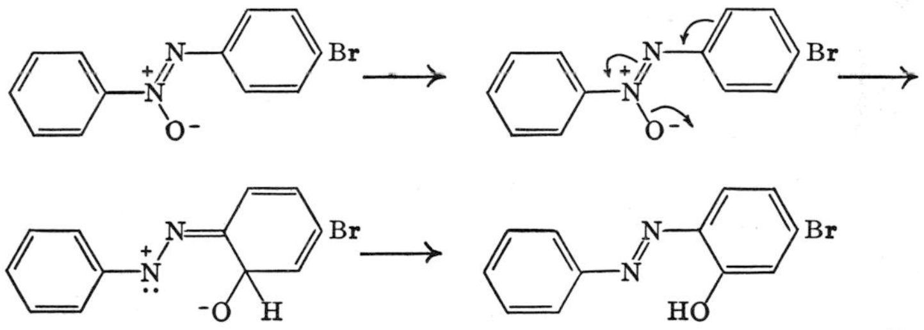

—N═ valency angle is 120°, the oxygen atom is closer to the *ortho* position in the substituted ring than to that in the adjacent ring. An intramolecular mechanism thus accounts for the known facts.

[1] George S. Hammond, b. 1921 Auburn, Maine; Ph.D. Harvard (Bartlett); State Univ. Iowa; Calif. Inst. Techn.
[2] Geoffrey M. Badger, b. 1916 South Australia; Ph.D. Univ. London (J. W. Cook); Univ. Adelaide, South Australia

HYDROCARBON–POLYNITRO COMPOUND COMPLEXES

19.21   When concentrated solutions of picric acid and naphthalene in benzene or alcohol are mixed at room temperature, crystallization soon occurs with separation of a golden yellow substance having a higher melting point (150°) than either component and having a more pronounced yellow color than picric acid. The substance is a π-complex containing equivalent amounts of the hydrocarbon and the polynitro compound, and in solution it dissociates to the components till equilibrium is established. Benzene forms only a very labile complex that reverts to picric acid on brief exposure to air, but the more basic naphthalene, anthracene, phenanthrene, and other higher hydrocarbons form stable complexes. The behavior finds some parallel in chemical reactivities, for the condensed-ring hydrocarbons are all more reactive than benzene; however, a high degree of alkyl substitution also results in increased stability of the picric acid derivatives, as shown by the formation of complexes with penta- and

TABLE 19.2. MELTING POINTS OF COMPLEXES, °C.

HYDROCARBON	NITRO COMPONENT		
	Picric acid	Trinitrobenzene	Trinitrofluorenone
Naphthalene	150 (yellow)	153 (yellow)	154 (yellow)
Acenaphthene	162 (orange)		176 (red)
Anthracene	142 (red)	164 (red)	194 (red)
Phenanthrene	145 (yellow)		197 (yellow)
Methylcholanthrene (light yellow, m.p. 180°)	182.5 (purplish black)	204.5 (dark red)	254 (green)
3,4-Benzpyrene (light yellow, m.p. 179°)	198 (purple-brown)	227 (bright red)	

hexamethylbenzene (m.p. 131° and 170°). The complexes are called picrates, but should not be confused with salts of the acid with amines or inorganic bases. The condensed-ring polynuclear hydrocarbons form similar π-complexes with trinitrobenzene, trinitrotoluene, trinitroresorcinol, 2,4,7-trinitrofluorenone (Orchin, 1946–47), picryl chloride, and picramide; some examples are listed in Table 19.2. The picric acid, trinitrobenzene, and trinitrofluorenone derivatives have considerable value in identification and purification of hydrocarbons and in isolation of hydrocarbons from reaction mixtures because of their superior crystallizing tendency, sparing solubility, and relatively high melting points. The derivatives often have identifying colors, and the phenomenon of color intensification is particularly marked with the two hydrocarbons listed at the end of the table, which are carcinogenic agents of exceptional chemical reactivity. The complexes are easily purified by crystallization, sometimes in the presence of a slight excess of the nitro component to suppress dissociation and decrease solubility. A hydrocarbon can be regenerated from its purified picrate by extraction of the acidic component from a benzene or ether solution with aqueous ammonia. Complexes can be split by passing a benzene solution through a column packed with activated (heat-treated) alumina; the nitro component is adsorbed more strongly than the hydrocarbon and the latter appears first in the filtrate. A hydrocarbon–trinitrobenzene derivative also can be reduced with stannous chloride and hydrochloric acid to convert the nitro compound into an acid-soluble amine incapable of complex formation.

PROBLEMS

1. How can the following compounds be prepared from aniline:
   (a) 2,4,6-Trinitrobromobenzene
   (b) 1,2,4-Trinitrobenzene
2. Which of the three tetrachlorobenzenes should be the most susceptible to nucleophilic displacement?
3. Predict the products of the reactions:
   (a) Mononitration of α-tetralone
   (b) Dinitration of diphenyl ether
   (c) Reaction of 3,4-dichloronitrobenzene with NaOCH₃

Note to p. 691.—The reaction of benzenediazonium fluoroborate with diphenylzinc in dimethylformamide solution gives *trans*-azobenzene in 92% yield (D. Y. Curtin, 1961). Use of diphenylzinc generated by the action of granulated zinc on diphenylmercury in xylene led to the discovery that when 0.03 mole of diphenylzinc in xylene–dimethylformamide was treated with 0.15 mole of diphenylmercury, followed by 0.01 mole of benzenediazonium fluoroborate, 80% of the azobenzene formed was the *cis*-isomer. Diphenylmercury alone is without action on the diazonium salt.

Chapter 20

SULFONIC ACIDS

20.1   **Free Acids and Salts.** — The usual sulfonation procedure requires mere adjustment of the concentration of acid and the temperature in accordance with the reactivity of the aromatic compound and the degree and direction of substitution desired.   Thus for production of p-toluenesulfonic acid the hydrocarbon is shaken with concentrated sulfuric acid at steam-bath temperature; disulfonation of benzene is effected with fuming sulfuric acid at $245°$, which gives the *meta* and *para* isomers in the ratio of $3:1$.   A minor by-product sometimes formed is the diaryl sulfone, $ArSO_2Ar$, but this is insoluble in water and easily eliminated.

Sulfonation also can be effected with the $(1:1)$ complexes of sulfur trioxide with pyridine and with dioxane.   Pyridine–sulfur trioxide (m.p. $175°$) is made by dropping pyridine into a cooled suspension of crushed sulfur trioxide and carbon tetrachloride or by dropping chlorosulfonic acid into a chilled solution of pyridine in carbon tetrachloride.   Dioxane–sulfur trioxide is precipitated on addition of dioxane to a solution of sulfur trioxide in ethylene dichloride.   The dioxane complex is much more reactive than the pyridine complex.   Sulfonation of styrene with dioxane–sulfur trioxide in ethylene dichloride, followed by hydrolysis and neutralization, gives chiefly either $C_6H_5CH(OH)CH_2SO_3Na$ (sodium 2-hydroxy-2-phenylethane-1-sulfonate, below $5°$) or $C_6H_5CH{=}CHSO_3Na$ (sodium β-styrene-sulfonate, formed at the reflux temperature).

A recent finding is that aromatic hydrocarbons and aryl halides are sulfonated rapidly and in high yield in the presence of thionyl chloride at room temperature (J. A. Bradley,[1] 1960).   With moderate excess of the aryl compound and of

$$ArH + H_2SO_4 + SOCl_2 \longrightarrow ArSO_3H + SO_2 + 2\ HCl$$

---

[1] James A. Bradley, b. 1892 Boston; A.M. Harvard (Conant); Newark College of Engineering

thionyl chloride it is possible to use practically all the sulfuric acid. The process is endothermic and temperature drops of as much as 20° have been observed. Alkyl groups and fluorine atoms increase the reaction rate; chlorine and bromine decrease the rate. A nitro group inhibits reaction unless an appropriate activating group is present. The sulfone, usually a minor product, can be made the sole product by use of a large excess of thionyl chloride.

Arylsulfonic acids ($ArSO_3H$) are comparable to sulfuric acid in acidic strength, liberally soluble in water, and very hygroscopic. Free acids, particularly *p*-toluenesulfonic acid and naphthalene-β-sulfonic acid, are useful as catalysts for esterification, dehydration, polymerization, and depolymerization. They are as effective as sulfuric acid and less damaging to reactants, and they are solids. Isolation is accomplished by diluting the sulfonation mixture with a moderate amount of water and adding concentrated hydrochloric acid to decrease the solubility; the sulfonic acid crystallizes on cooling, usually as a hydrate. Benzenesulfonic acid dried over concentrated sulfuric acid melts at 44° and varies in composition: $C_6H_5SO_3H \cdot 1\frac{1}{2}-2\ H_2O$; drying at 100° gives anhydrous material, m.p. 104°. *p*-Toluenesulfonic acid and naphthalene-β-sulfonic acid crystallize as the monohydrates, m.p. 104–106° and 120–122°, respectively.

Usually the free sulfonic acid is not isolated but converted into the sodium salt. The sulfonation mixture is poured into water and the solution is partially neutralized with sodium bicarbonate and heated to boiling. Sufficient sodium chloride is added to produce a saturated solution, which is then let stand for crystallization. With sulfonates of low molecular weight the amount of common salt required for salting out is excessive and the product is liable to be contaminated with salt. A pure product may be obtainable by crystallization from absolute ethanol, in which lower sodium sulfonates are sparingly soluble and sodium chloride is insoluble. A higher sodium sulfonate insoluble in ethanol or methanol can be obtained salt-free by first salting it out repeatedly from aqueous solution with sodium acetate in order to replace sodium chloride as contaminant. The salt is then dried and powdered and the sodium acetate removed by repeated extraction with boiling methanol. Another method of obtaining a sodium salt from a sulfonation reaction mixture containing excess sulfuric acid is to neutralize the diluted mixture with calcium hydroxide or with barium or lead carbonate. The calcium, barium, or lead sulfonate can be extracted with hot water and thus separated from a residue of inorganic sulfate, and the aqueous extract is then treated with sodium carbonate to precipitate an insoluble carbonate and give a solution that on evaporation affords the sodium salt of the sulfonic acid. A lead sulfonate also can be decomposed with hydrogen sulfide to give a solution of the free acid.

Usually sodium and ammonium sulfonates are more soluble in water than other salts; potassium salts are slightly less soluble and often crystallize better, and barium and calcium salts are distinctly less soluble. The metal salts are infusible and completely insoluble in ether. Amine salts, such as those formed with *p*-toluidine, are composed of two organic parts, and they are less soluble in water than the alkali-metal salts and often crystallizable from alcohol or alcohol–water mixtures; also they have characteristic melting points. The *p*-toluidine

$$ArSO_3H + CH_3C_6H_4NH_2 \longrightarrow ArSO_3\overset{-}{N}\overset{+}{H_3}C_6H_4CH_3$$
$$\text{\textit{p}-Toluidine salt}$$

salts thus are useful derivatives for characterization, and they are easily prepared by addition of the amine and hydrochloric acid to a solution of a sodium salt.

$$ArSO_3Na + NH_2C_6H_4CH_3 + HCl \longrightarrow ArSO_3\overset{-}{N}\overset{+}{H_3}C_6H_4CH_3 + NaCl$$

The sulfonate group often is introduced to provide water solubility, particularly in the case of dyes.

20.2   Acid Chlorides. — Arylsulfonic acids, either free or as salts, are convertible into acid chlorides by the methods applicable to preparation of chlorides of carboxylic acids, namely by interaction with phosphorus halides. Alternative procedures for the preparation of benzenesulfonyl chloride are indicated (1, 2). The reaction mixture is cooled and treated with water and ice

1. $3 C_6H_5SO_2ONa + PCl_5 \xrightarrow[75-80\%]{170-180°} 3 C_6H_5SO_2Cl + 2 NaCl + NaPO_3$

2. $2 C_6H_5SO_2ONa + POCl_3 \xrightarrow[74-87\%]{170-180°} 2 C_6H_5SO_2Cl + NaCl + NaPO_3$

and the acid chloride separating as an oil is collected, dried, and distilled. Another method is the action of at least two equivalents of chlorosulfonic acid on benzene (3). If chlorosulfonic acid is not used in considerable excess, a significant amount

3. $C_6H_6 + 2 ClSO_2OH \xrightarrow[75-77\%]{20-25°} C_6H_5SO_2Cl + H_2SO_4 + HCl$
   (3 equiv.)

of diphenyl sulfone is formed as a by-product, and when an aromatic hydrocarbon is treated in carbon tetrachloride solution with just one equivalent of chlorosulfonic acid the reaction product is the free sulfonic acid. Production of the acid chloride with the use of excess reagent probably proceeds through formation of

$$C_6H_6 + ClSO_2OH \rightarrow C_6H_5SO_2OH + HCl$$

the free acid and replacement of hydroxyl by the chlorine of chlorosulfonic acid.

The preparation of arylsulfonyl chlorides with thionyl chloride in dimethylformamide solution has been described (11.23).

Benzenesulfonyl chloride is an easily solidified liquid, m.p. 14.4°, b.p. 251.5°. It can be digested with cold water with little hydrolysis, but reacts readily with alcohols and with ammonia, as described below, and it is useful as a reagent in the Hinsberg test for characterization of amines of different types (14.17). A reagent often preferred because it is a solid is *p*-toluenesulfonyl chloride (tosyl chloride), m.p. 69°.

20.3   Esters. — Ester derivatives of sulfonic acids are sometimes prepared for purposes of identification, but they are lower melting and much less easily prepared than the *p*-toluidine salts. The preparation is accomplished either (1) by heating the solid sodium salt of the acid with dimethyl or diethyl sulfate or (2) by the action of an alcohol or of a sodium alkoxide (in ether) on

1. $ArSO_3Na + (CH_3)_2SO_4 \xrightarrow{150-160°} ArSO_3CH_3 + CH_3NaSO_4$

2. $ArSO_2Cl + HOCH_3 \longrightarrow ArSO_2OCH_3 + HCl$

the acid chloride. The methyl ester of benzenesulfonic acid is a liquid and is slowly hydrolyzed by water at room temperature. Methyl p-toluenesulfonate, $CH_3C_6H_4SO_3CH_3$, melts at 28°.

20.4   Sulfonamides. — The acid chlorides react readily with ammonia or with amines to form sulfonamides. Thus benzenesulfonyl chloride affords benzenesulfonamide when shaken with aqueous ammonia or on interaction with ammonium carbonate. This easily prepared neutral derivative crystallizes

$$C_6H_5SO_2Cl + NH_3 \longrightarrow C_6H_5SO_2NH_2 + HCl$$
Benzenesulfonamide
(m.p. 156°)

well from alcohol, and in general sulfonamides are satisfactory derivatives for characterization of aromatic sulfonic acids.

The product of reaction of equimolecular quantities of p-toluenesulfonyl chloride with o-phenylenediamine is known as T-sulfonamidine and is useful as a highly specific reagent for the quantitative precipitation of cupric ion, with which it forms a green chelate (J. H. Billman, 1960).

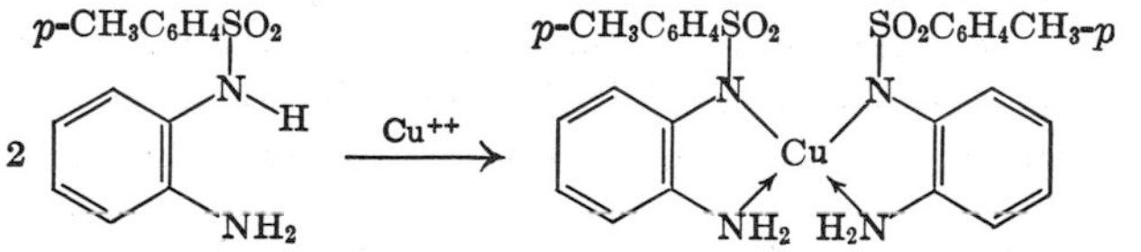

p-Toluenesulfonylhydrazide is obtained in 90% yield by gradual addition to a stirred solution of p-toluenesulfonyl chloride in tetrahydrofurane at 15° of 2 moles of hydrazine hydrate (*Org. Syn.*, 1960). The product of condensation of this reagent with benzyl methyl ketone, a tosylhydrazone, reacts with sodio ethyleneglycolate to give a diazonium compound which decomposes with elimination of nitrogen to form an olefin (W. R. Bamford and T. S. Stevens, 1952). A useful

$$\overset{\overset{\displaystyle CH_3}{|}}{C_6H_5CH_2C}=NNHTs + NaOCH_2CH_2OH \rightarrow \overset{\overset{\displaystyle CH_3}{|}}{C_6H_5CH_2C}=N^+=N^-$$

$$\rightarrow C_6H_5CH=CHCH_3 + N_2$$

application of the reaction is for conversion of an α-diketone into the corresponding α-diazoketone (M. P. Cava,[1] 1958). 1,2-Indanedione, prepared conveniently via the 2-oximido derivative, reacts with tosylhydrazide to form the monotosylhydrazone. Treatment with base effects elimination of the tosyloxy anion with

---

[1] Michael P. Cava, b. 1926 Brooklyn, N. Y.; Ph.D. Michigan (W. E. Bachmann); Ohio State Univ.

formation of 2-diazo-1-indanone in good yield. Quinones are convertible by this method into diazo derivatives. 2,6-Dimethyl-1,4-benzoquinone yields 2,6-di-

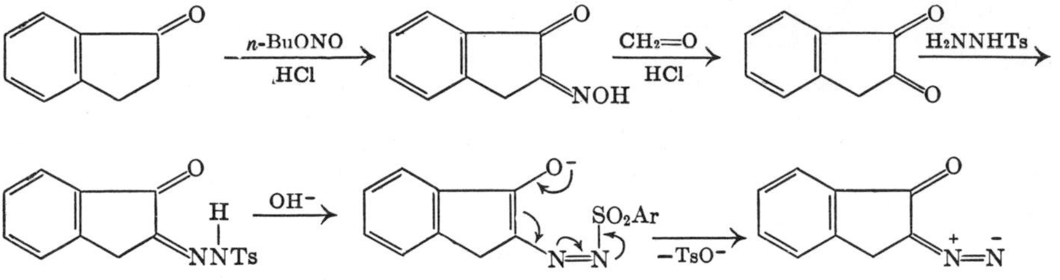

methyl-1,4-benzoquinone-4-diazide and 4,5-dimethyl-1,2-benzoquinone yields 4,5-dimethyl-1,2-benzoquinone-1-diazide (W. Reid, 1961). Another elimination which involves a Wagner-Meerwein type rearrangement with contraction of one ring and enlargement of another is effected by the action of hot alkali on the tosylhydrazone of the steroid 12-ketone hecogenin (N. L. Wendler, 1954).

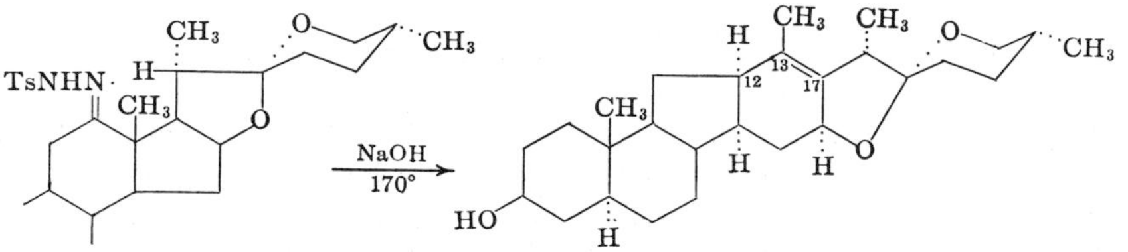

20.5 **Chloroamides.** — The action of sodium hypochlorite on a sulfonamide results in substitution of halogen for an amide hydrogen atom. p-Toluenesulfonamide is converted initially into the N-monochloro derivative, known as chloramine-T. This substance slowly liberates hypochlorous acid on

$$p\text{-CH}_3\text{C}_6\text{H}_4\text{SO}_2\text{NH}_2 \ + \ \text{NaOCl} \ \longrightarrow \ p\text{-CH}_3\text{C}_6\text{H}_4\text{SO}_2\text{NHCl} \ + \ \text{NaOH}$$

contact with water and is an effective antiseptic agent used for treatment of wounds. The active chlorine atom is positive. Chloramine-T is employed for external application in the form of a dilute (0.2%) aqueous solution of the sodium salt, $[p\text{-CH}_3\text{C}_6\text{H}_4\text{SO}_2\text{NCl}]^-\text{Na}^+$. The second amide hydrogen can be replaced by further treatment with hypochlorite to give dichloramine-T, $p\text{-CH}_3\text{C}_6\text{H}_4\text{SO}_2\text{NCl}_2$; this is insoluble in water and is employed as an antiseptic spray in the form of a solution in chlorinated paraffin. A related chloroamide halozone, $p\text{-HOOCC}_6\text{H}_4\text{-SO}_2\text{NCl}_2$, is pelleted with sodium carbonate into tablets suitable for sterilization of drinking water; addition to water produces a solution of the sodium carboxylate.

Chloroamides are the only practical agents for decontamination of mustard gas, $S(\text{CH}_2\text{CH}_2\text{Cl})_2$, which is converted by the active-halogen compounds into the sulfoxide, $O{=}S(\text{CH}_2\text{CH}_2\text{Cl})_2$, and the chlorosulfoxide, $\text{ClCH}_2\text{CHClS}({=}O)\text{-CH}_2\text{CH}_2\text{Cl}$. Haloamides useful as antiseptic and decontaminating agents are derived from the amides of carboxylic as well as sulfonic acids. Thus the substance $2,4\text{-Cl}_2\text{C}_6\text{H}_3\text{N}(\text{Cl})\text{COC}_6\text{H}_5$ is employed for impregnation of clothing to provide protection against mustard gas (British Impregnite).

20.6   Saccharin and Other Sweetening Agents. — Saccharin, o-sulfobenzoic acid imide, was first prepared by Remsen[1] (1879) and found to have extraordinary sweetness of taste. The substance is about 550 times as sweet as cane sugar (sucrose), and the aqueous solution retains a detectable sweet taste at a dilution of 1:100,000. It is employed as a sweetening agent by diabetics incapable of tolerating sugar, and is excreted unchanged in the urine. The technical preparation is essentially that introduced by Remsen, namely oxidation of o-toluenesulfonamide with aqueous permanganate solution at 35°. The o-sulfonamidobenzoic acid initially formed undergoes spontaneous loss of water in a neutral or weakly alkaline solution with closure of the heterocyclic ring. The starting material is obtained from the mixture of *ortho* and *para* acids resulting from sulfonation of toluene; the acids are converted into the acid chlorides by

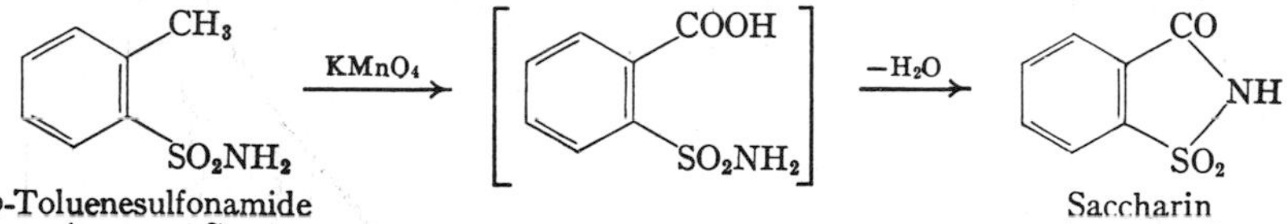

o-Toluenesulfonamide
(m.p. 155°)

Saccharin
(m.p. 229°)

the action of phosphorus pentachloride, the solid p-toluenesulfonyl chloride is largely removed by freezing, and the liquid residue containing the *ortho* compound treated with ammonia. Saccharin is sparingly soluble in cold water, but the doubly activated imino hydrogen atom is acidic, and saccharin forms a water-soluble sodium salt.

5-Nitro-2-n-propoxyaniline (Verkade,[2] 1946) is 4100 times as sweet as sucrose and leaves no bitter aftertaste. The substance initially found use as a sweetener but was later withdrawn because of toxicological considerations. The sugar substitute now most widely used is calcium cyclohexylsulfamate (Sucaryl calcium), prepared by sulfonation of cyclohexylamine with chlorosulfonic acid (3 equivalents) and conversion to the calcium salt. Finding that sodium phenylsulfamate

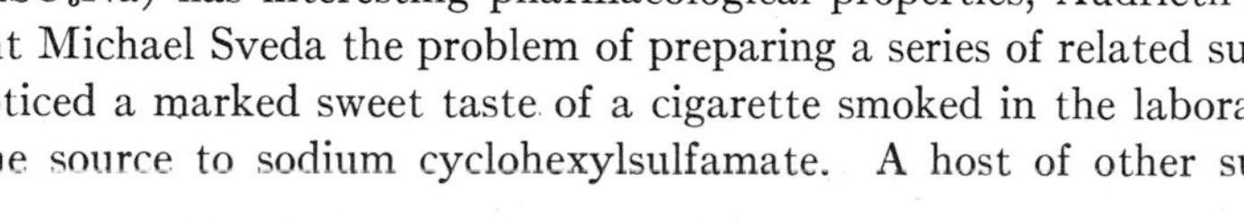

Calcium cyclohexyl-
sulfamate

$(C_6H_5NHSO_3Na)$ has interesting pharmacological properties, Audrieth[3] assigned to student Michael Sveda the problem of preparing a series of related sulfamates. Sveda noticed a marked sweet taste of a cigarette smoked in the laboratory and traced the source to sodium cyclohexylsulfamate. A host of other sulfamates

[1] Ira Remsen, 1846–1927; b. New York; Ph.D. Göttingen; Williams College, Johns Hopkins Univ.; *J. Chem. Soc.*, 3182 (1927)

[2] Peter E. Verkade, b. 1891 Zaandam, Netherlands; Ph.D. Delft (Böeseken); Univ. Rotterdam, Delft

[3] Ludwig F. Audrieth, b. 1901 Vienna, Austria; Ph.D. Cornell; Univ. Illinois

subsequently prepared proved less sweet than the first one discovered.   Calcium cyclohexylsulfamate is approximately 35 times as sweet as sucrose, nontoxic, and free from bitter aftertaste when used in normally required amounts.

20.7   Alkali Fusion of Sulfonates. — An important use of sulfonates is for the preparation of phenols, accomplished by fusion with molten sodium or potassium hydroxide in the temperature range 290–340°.   The sulfonate

$$ArSO_3Na \; + \; NaOH \; \longrightarrow \; ArONa \; + \; NaHSO_3$$
$$ArONa \; + \; HCl \; \xrightarrow{\;\;\;} \; ArOH \; + \; NaCl$$

group is replaced by the —ONa(K) group, and the phenol is obtained by treating the cooled melt with ice and hydrochloric acid.   A typical laboratory procedure is illustrated for the preparation of β-naphthol.   A charge of potassium hydroxide is placed in a nickel, copper, or iron crucible, along with a small amount of water to render the material more easily fusible, and heated over a free flame to a tem-

Sodium naphthalene-
β-sulfonate   β-Naphthol

perature of about 250°.   The melt is stirred with a thermometer enclosed in a protective metal case while the fully dried and powdered sodium naphthalene-β-sulfonate is added.   The solid only partly dissolves and there is no initial reaction, but as the temperature is gradually raised a critical point is reached (300°) at which the mass rapidly changes, with separation of a mobile yellow-brown layer of potassium β-naphtholate floating on an almost clear layer of alkali.   The fusion is soon over, and the cooled melt is added in portions to ice and hydrochloric acid and the precipitated β-naphthol collected.   The cheaper sodium hydroxide is employed where possible in technical operations, but it has less solvent action than potassium hydroxide, gives a less mobile melt, and may prove unsatisfactory. A successful compromise in some instances consists in use of mixtures of the two alkalis, as in the second example, where sodium hydroxide alone gives none of the desired product.   A further variation, used widely in the industry, is to

Sodium p-toluene-
sulfonate   p-Cresol

conduct the fusion in pressure vessels with aqueous solutions of alkali.   Alkali fusion is not applicable to sulfonated compounds containing nitro or halo substituents, which may undergo nucleophilic displacement; the conversion of a sulfonate to a phenol is itself a nucleophilic displacement.

20.8   Conversion to Nitriles. — A reaction that would appear analogous to alkali fusion is conversion of a sulfonate into a nitrile by heating with potassium cyanide or potassium ferricyanide.   The nitrile reaction, however, differs in that the mixture of the dry salts remains unfused even at very high temperatures. The conditions thus are unfavorable for both chemical interaction

$$C_6H_5SO_3K \; + \; KCN \xrightarrow{\text{Pyrolysis}} C_6H_5CN \; + \; K_2SO_3$$
$$\text{Benzonitrile}$$

and heat interchange. Only a small quantity of the mixture can be processed in one charge in a glass flask or retort, or else the material in the interior will not reach the pyrolysis temperature; even so the vessel usually is damaged at the temperature required to obtain the maximum amount of nitrile, which distills from the salt mixture. The yields often are poor and at best seldom exceed 50%.

20.9   **Bromodesulfonation.** — Reversal of the sulfonation reaction represents displacement of the sulfonic acid group by hydrogen. The sulfonic acid group can also be displaced by bromine. Since bromodesulfonation is facili-

$$C_6H_5SO_2O^- + H_2O + Br_2 \longrightarrow C_6H_5Br + HBr + HOSO_2O^-$$

tated by electron-releasing amino, hydroxyl, methoxyl, or alkyl groups *ortho* or *para* to the sulfonic acid group, the reaction is a typical electrophilic substitution. In the case of sodium 2,6-dibromophenol-4-sulfonate, formulated as the anion (1), the reaction has been shown by L. G. Cannell (1957) to proceed through the dienone (2). When dilute aqueous solutions of the dibromophenolsulfonate

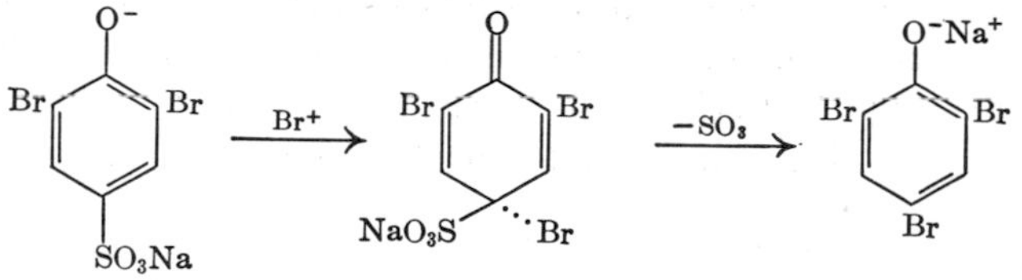

and bromine are mixed at 0° the bromine color disappears immediately and the spectrum is that expected for the enedione (2), λ 278–279 mμ ($\epsilon = 11,400$). Addition to a freshly prepared solution of the intermediate of one equivalent of sodium iodide reverses the conversion of (1) into (2), and the titer falls off with time as (2) is converted into the aromatic product (3).

20.10   **RELATED SULFUR COMPOUNDS**

An arylsulfonate ion offers opportunity for three resonance structures within the substituent group, and is very stable and resistant to reduction. The situation is changed on conversion into the sulfonyl chloride, which is reducible by

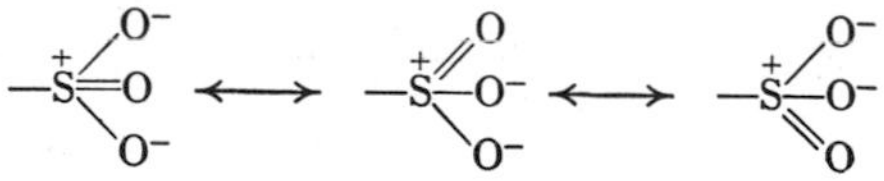

chemical means. The case is analogous to that of the unreactive carboxylic acids and corresponding chlorides, which are convertible to aldehydes by catalytic hydrogenation. The initial reduction product of a sulfonyl chloride is a sulfinic acid, $ArSO_2H$, obtained by reduction with zinc dust and water. Sulfinic acids differ markedly from the more highly oxidized and more stable sulfonic acids.

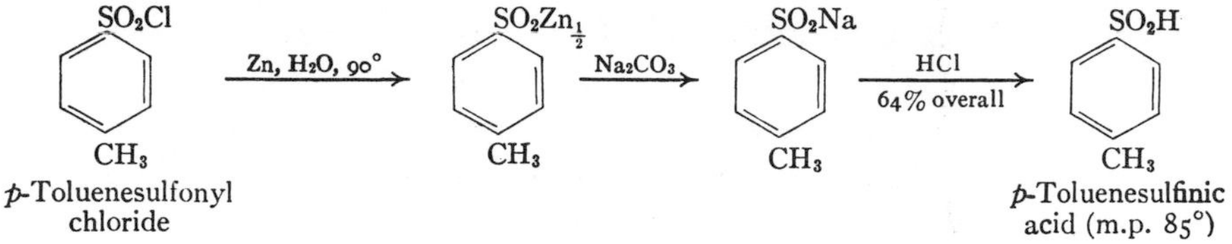

SO$_2$Cl	SO$_2$Zn$_{\frac{1}{2}}$	SO$_2$Na	SO$_2$H
p-Toluenesulfonyl chloride			p-Toluenesulfinic acid (m.p. 85°)

p-Toluenesulfonyl chloride $\xrightarrow{\text{Zn, H}_2\text{O, 90°}}$ $\xrightarrow{\text{Na}_2\text{CO}_3}$ $\xrightarrow[\text{64\% overall}]{\text{HCl}}$ p-Toluenesulfinic acid

Benzenesulfinic acid, m.p. 84°, is subject to air oxidation and can be converted into the sulfonic acid with chlorine water; it decomposes when heated above 100°, and samples cannot be stored for long without deterioration. It is soluble in benzene, ether, or hot water, but unlike the sulfonic acid, is sparingly soluble in cold water. The substance is distinctly less acidic (pK$_a$ 1.80) than benzenesulfonic acid and is liberated from its metal salts by mineral acids, as illustrated in the preparation cited. An alternative method of preparation is by the Grignard

$$C_6H_5MgBr + SO_2 \longrightarrow C_6H_5SO_2MgBr \xrightarrow{H_2O} C_6H_5SO_2H$$

reaction. Arylsulfinic acids are comparable to sodium bisulfite in ability to add to carbonyl and related unsaturated nitrogen compounds (azomethines).

Sulfinic acids are reducible in turn to **thiophenols** or **aryl mercaptans,** which are obtained on reduction of sulfonyl chlorides with the more powerful combination of zinc dust and hydrochloric or sulfuric acid. Thiophenol, a very feebly acidic liquid of repulsive odor, is readily oxidized by air, particularly when dis-

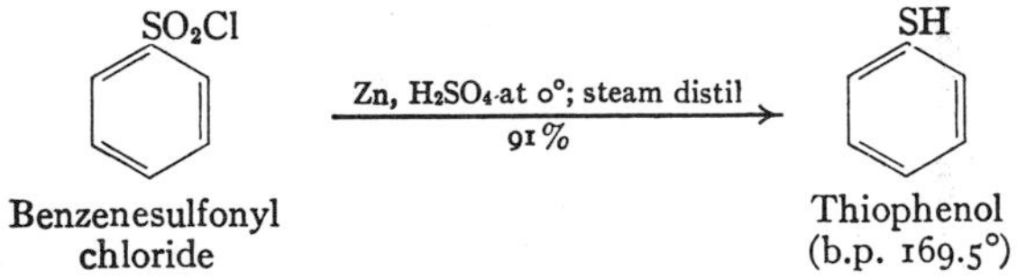

SO$_2$Cl $\xrightarrow[\text{91\%}]{\text{Zn, H}_2\text{SO}_4\cdot\text{at 0°; steam distil}}$ SH

Benzenesulfonyl chloride　　　　　　　　Thiophenol (b.p. 169.5°)

solved in alcoholic ammonia, to diphenyl disulfide, C_6H_5S—SC_6H_5 (m.p. 61°). It is oxidized by nitric acid to benzenesulfonic acid. Thiophenols have about the same physical properties as the corresponding hydroxy compounds: thio-o-cresol, m.p. 15°; thio-p-cresol, m.p. 43°; thio-β-naphthol, m.p. 81°. They also result from interaction of arylmagnesium halides with sulfur.

Benezenesulfonyl chloride enters into Friedel-Crafts condensations in the same manner as benzoyl chloride. The aluminum chloride catalyzed reaction with

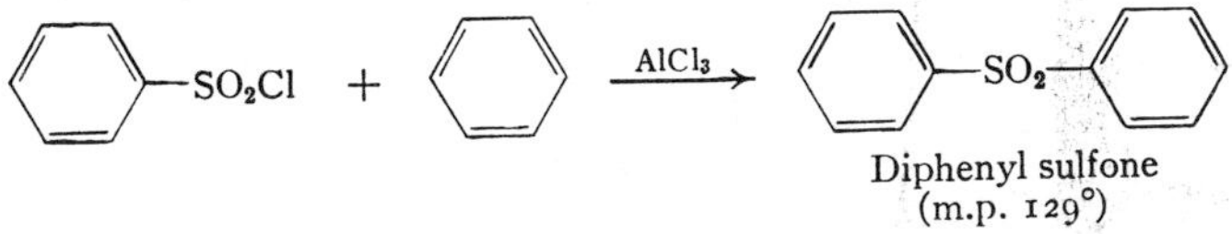

—SO$_2$Cl + $\xrightarrow{\text{AlCl}_3}$ —SO$_2$—　　Diphenyl sulfone (m.p. 129°)

benzene affords **diphenyl sulfone,** encountered as a by-product in the sulfonation of benzene with fuming sulfuric acid. Diphenyl sulfone is stable to oxidation and reduction, and is the end product of the oxidation of **diphenyl sulfide,** which can be prepared by a process akin to a Friedel-Crafts condensation. Diphenyl sulfide

$$2\,C_6H_6 \;+\; S_2Cl_2 \xrightarrow[\substack{81\text{-}83\%}]{\text{AlCl}_3,\ 10\text{--}30^\circ} C_6H_5SC_6H_5 \;+\; S \;+\; 2\,HCl$$

               Sulfur   Diphenyl sulfide
               chloride   (b.p. 296°)

is oxidized to **diphenyl sulfoxide** by one equivalent of hydrogen peroxide in acetic acid solution, and to diphenyl sulfone by more than one equivalent.

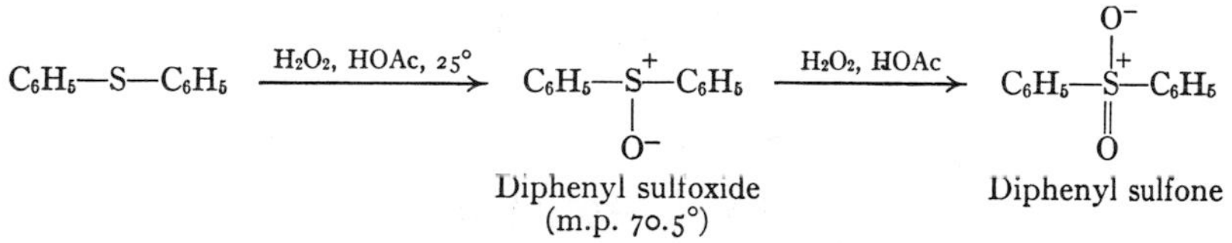

Diphenyl sulfoxide (m.p. 70.5°)   Diphenyl sulfone

    Dimethyl sulfoxide (b.p. 189°), made by air oxidation of dimethyl sulfide in the presence of nitrogen oxides, has remarkable solvent properties (solvent for Orlon; paint and varnish remover). It is miscible with water and highly hygroscopic.

    2,4-Dinitrobenzenesulfenyl chloride (m.p. 95°) is made from 2,4-dinitrochlorobenzene (1) by conversion to the dinitrophenyl disulfide (2) and cleavage with chlorine in ethylene dibromide solution. The reagent enters into a number of

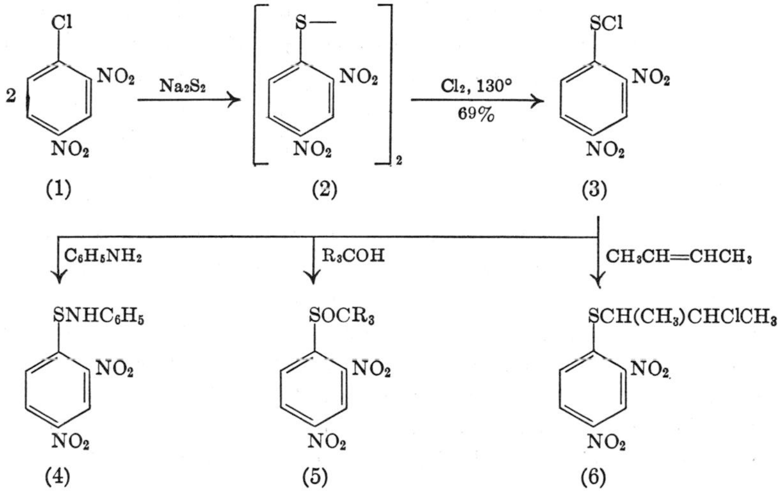

ionic reactions involving attack on sulfur by a nucleophile with displacement of chlorine (Kharasch,[1] 1947–60), for example in the reaction with aniline (4). Alcohols, including tertiary alcohols, react with the reagent, as in (5). The reagent adds stereospecifically (*trans*), for example to the two 2-butenes (6), and to alkynes. The 2,4-dinitrosulfenyl derivatives thus formed are colored solids readily purified by crystallization or chromatography and hence are useful for purposes of identification.

---

[1] Norman Kharasch, b. 1914 Poland; Ph.D. Northwestern (Hurd); Univ. Southern Calif.

Chapter 21

ARYL AMINES

21.1   **Preparation.** — Aniline was first obtained by destructive distillation of
indigo (Unverdorben, 1826) and later was isolated from a coal-tar
distillate (Runge, 1834). Fritzsche (1840) introduced an improved method of
preparation consisting in heating indigo with concentrated alkali, established the
formula, and proposed the subsequently accepted name (Spanish *añil*, Sanskrit
nēlē, indigo); for a time this method was the best route to the then rare chemical.
A base subsequently recognized as aniline was obtained (Zinin, 1842) by reduction
of nitrobenzene; and with development of the coal-tar industry this reaction
eventually became the standard method for the technical production of a key
chemical on a scale mounting to several million pounds per year. Aniline is convertible into various nuclear substitution products or, by alkylation on the nitrogen atom, into N-methyl- and N,N-dimethylaniline.

Primary aromatic amines are obtained almost entirely by combination of nitration and reduction. A number of methods of reduction are available. Small-
scale reductions are often carried out with tin and hydrochloric acid ($C_6H_5NO_2 \rightarrow$
$C_6H_5NH_2$, 80%), or somewhat more cleanly with a solution of stannous chloride
in concentrated hydrochloric acid; the basic product usually is isolated from the

1.

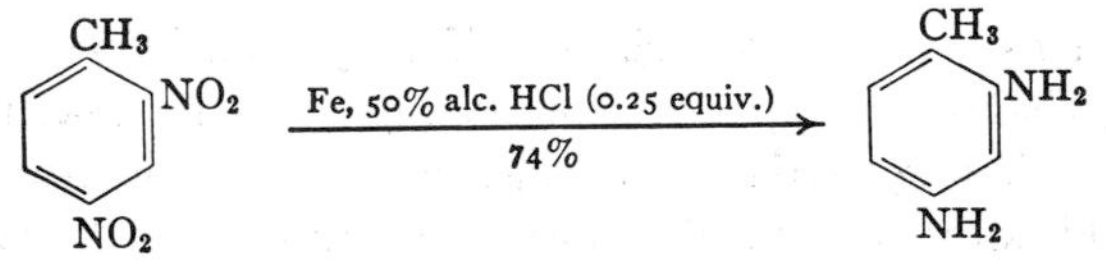

Fe, 50% alc. HCl (0.25 equiv.)

74%

diluted reaction mixture either by addition of enough alkali to neutralize the acid
and dissolve the tin in the form of sodium stannite and sodium stannate or by
precipitation of the metal as sulfide. In technical practice it is more economical
to reduce the nitro compound with iron powder and water, with addition of either

706

hydrochloric or acetic acid as catalyst. Where proper reaction conditions have been worked out, this procedure also serves for laboratory preparations, as in the reduction of 2,4-dinitrotoluene (1). Reduction with zinc dust and alkali is less widely employed but sometimes gives excellent results (2).

2.

$$\text{(structure: benzene ring with NH}_2 \text{ and NO}_2) \xrightarrow[85\%]{\text{Zn, alc. NaOH, reflux}} \text{(benzene ring with NH}_2 \text{ and NH}_2)$$

If the nitro compound contains an acetylamino or acetoxyl group reduction in either an acidic or a basic medium results in hydrolysis of the acetyl groups. In example 3 hydrolysis is not objectionable because the desired product was the

3.

$$\text{CH}_3\text{CONH} \langle \rangle \text{SO}_2 \langle \rangle \text{NO}_2 \xrightarrow[74\text{--}77\%]{\text{Sn, HCl}} \text{H}_2\text{N} \langle \rangle \text{SO}_2 \langle \rangle \text{NH}_2$$

p-Acetylamino-p′-nitrodiphenyl   p,p′-Diaminodiphenyl
sulfone (m.p. 228°)   sulfone (m.p. 178°)

deacetylated diamine. If retention of an acetyl group is required, as in the preparation of the monoacetyl derivative of o-phenylenediamine (4), the most satisfactory method of reduction is catalytic hydrogenatio n in a neutral medium. Ethy

4.

$$\text{(benzene ring, NH}_2\text{, NO}_2) \xrightarrow[93\%]{\substack{(\text{CH}_3\text{CO})_2\text{O in C}_6\text{H}_6,\\ \text{trace H}_2\text{SO}_4}} \text{(benzene ring, NHCOCH}_3\text{, NO}_2) \xrightarrow[90\%]{\text{Pt, H}_2\text{, in alcohol}} \text{(benzene ring, NHCOCH}_3\text{, NH}_2)$$

o-Aminoacetanilide
(m.p. 133°)

p-nitrobenzoate (m.p. 57°) can be reduced by the same method in nearly quantitative yield to ethyl p-aminobenzoate, $p\text{-}H_2NC_6H_4COOC_2H_5$ (m.p. 92°). Another catalytic process is illustrated by hydrogenation of 2-nitro-p-cymene in alcoholic solution over Raney nickel catalyst at 100–200° and 1000–1500 lbs. pressure; the yield of 2-amino-p-cymene (b.p. 242°) is 87–90%. The method of S. Pietra (1955) is illustrated by a procedure for the preparation of 2-aminofluorene: a mixture of 2-nitrofluorene, hydrazine hydrate and palladized charcoal or Raney nickel is stirred under reflux; yield 93–96% (P. M. G. Bavin, *Org. Syn.*, 1960).

Selective reduction of one group in a polynitro compound often can be accomplished with use of the calculated amount of sodium or ammonium sulfide or hydrosulfide. One example is reduction of picric acid to picramic acid (19.11); another is shown in example 5. The reactions can be conducted with a weighed

5.

$$\text{(benzene ring, NO}_2\text{, NO}_2) \xrightarrow[70\text{--}80\%]{\text{H}_2\text{S, alc. NH}_3} \text{(benzene ring, NH}_2\text{, NO}_2)$$

quantity of crystalline sodium sulfide or by dissolving the nitro compound in alcoholic ammonia and passing in hydrogen sulfide to a given gain in weight. The reagent reduces one nitro group before attacking another, but the reaction will proceed beyond this stage unless the amount of reagent is controlled.

The preparation of 2,4,5-triaminonitrobenzene (6) from *m*-dichlorobenzene involves nitration, nucleophilic displacement of the two halogen atoms, and selective reduction, effected by adding to a stirred slurry of the dinitro compound in boiling water a clear orange-red solution of sodium polysulfide prepared from sodium sulfide and sulfur (J. H. Boyer, *Org. Syn.*, 1960). The selective reduction of 2,4-di-

6.

$$Cl\underset{}{\bigcirc}Cl \xrightarrow[70-71\%]{\underset{KNO_3-H_2SO_4}{135°}} \underset{O_2N}{Cl}\underset{}{\bigcirc}\underset{NO_2}{Cl} \xrightarrow[88-95.5\%]{\underset{HOCH_2CH_2OH}{NH_3}}$$

Yellow, m.p. 104°

$$\underset{O_2N}{H_2N}\underset{}{\bigcirc}\underset{NO_2}{NH_2} \xrightarrow[\text{Boiling water}]{Na_2S_2} \underset{O_2N}{H_2N}\underset{}{\bigcirc}\underset{NH_2}{NH_2}$$

Orange   Red, m.p. 207°

nitro-1-naphthol to 2-nitro-4-amino-1-naphthol illustrates another procedure. A solution of stannous chloride dihydrate (15 g.) in ethanol (20 ml.) is stirred into a suspension of the dinitronaphthol (5 g.) in concentrated hydrochloric acid (20 ml.) and ethanol (10 ml.); pale yellow needles of the amine hydrochloride separate in 98% yield.

21.2   Physical Properties; Basic Character. — The more commonly encountered amines of the benzene and diphenyl series are listed in Table 21.1. Among the isomeric toluidines, nitroanilines, and phenylenediamines, the symmetrical *para* isomer invariably has the highest melting point. It is noteworthy that the boiling points of methyl- and of dimethylaniline are practically the same and only slightly higher than that of aniline, and also that in the series of the toluidines, phenylenediamines, and chloroanilines, the *ortho* isomer has a lower boiling point than the *meta* and *para* compounds.

Aniline has only weak basic properties (pK$_b$ 9.4) as compared with methylamine (pK$_b$ 3.4). The diminished basicity of aromatic amines can be attributed empirically to the unsaturated aromatic ring, in analogy with the relationship of acetamide to ammonia. The explanation provided by the resonance theory is that the anilinium ion is incapable of resonance involving the nitrogen, for a reason already stated (17.3), whereas resonance stabilization is possible in the free aniline molecule; there is thus little driving force to promote ionization. The N-methyl derivatives of aniline and the three toluidines all have dissociation constants in the same range as the parent amine, and hence alkyl substitution in either the amino group or the ring has little influence on the basic strength. Introduction of a nitro substituent, however, results in a marked decrease in basicity, particularly prominent in the case of *o*-nitroaniline. The feebly basic character of nitroanilines is evidenced by the fact that the colorless salts formed by these substances with concentrated sulfuric or hydrochloric acid are hydrolyzed on dilution with moderate amounts of water to yellow, water-insoluble bases; the *ortho* isomer is precipitated most readily, the *para* compound separates next, and *m*-nitroaniline separates only on more extensive dilution. Decrease in basicity attending introduction of the nitro group at any position in the ring can be attributed to the inductive effect; the positively polarized nitro group induces a drift of electrons in the sense of withdrawal from the ring and from the amino nitrogen atom, and hence affinity of the nitrogen for protons is decreased. The effect is magnified

TABLE 21.1. AMINES

NAME	FORMULA	M.P., °C.	B.P., °C.	pK_b
Aniline	$C_6H_5NH_2$	-6	184	9.42
Methylaniline	$C_6H_5NHCH_3$	liq.	194	9.20
Dimethylaniline	$C_6H_5N(CH_3)_2$	2	193	9.42
Diethylaniline	$C_6H_5N(C_2H_5)_2$	-39	215	
o-Toluidine	$CH_3C_6H_4NH_2(1,2)$	-15.5	197	9.47
m-Toluidine	$CH_3C_6H_4NH_2(1,3)$	liq.	203	9.30
p-Toluidine	$CH_3C_6H_4NH_2(1,4)$	44	200	8.93
o-Nitroaniline	$H_2NC_6H_4NO_2(1,2)$	71.5		14.28
m-Nitroaniline	$H_2NC_6H_4NO_2(1,3)$	114		11.40
p-Nitroaniline	$H_2NC_6H_4NO_2(1,4)$	146		13.0
2,4-Dinitroaniline	$H_2NC_6H_3(NO_2)_2(1,2,4)$	187		
o-Phenylenediamine	$C_6H_4(NH_2)_2(1,2)$	103	257	9.48
m-Phenylenediamine	$C_6H_4(NH_2)_2(1,3)$	63	284	9.12
p-Phenylenediamine	$C_6H_4(NH_2)_2(1,4)$	140	267	8.0
o-Anisidine	$H_2NC_6H_4OCH_3(1,2)$	5.2	225	9.7
p-Anisidine	$H_2NC_6H_4OCH_3(1,4)$	57	244	8.82
p-Phenetidine	$H_2NC_6H_4OC_2H_5(1,4)$	2	254	8.70
o-Chloroaniline	$H_2NC_6H_4Cl(1,2)$	liq.	2:9	11.38
m-Chloroaniline	$H_2NC_6H_4Cl(1,3)$	liq.	236	10.40
p-Chloroaniline	$H_2NC_6H_4Cl(1,4)$	70	231	10.19
p-Bromoaniline	$H_2NC_6H_4Br(1,4)$	66		10.0
2,4,6-Trichloroaniline	$H_2NC_6H_2Cl_3(1,2,4,6)$	78	262	
2,4,6-Tribromoaniline	$H_2NC_6H_2Br_3(1,2,4,6)$	118	300	
Diphenylamine	$C_6H_5NHC_6H_5$	54	302	
Triphenylamine	$(C_6H_5)_3N$	126	348	
Benzidine	$(4)H_2NC_6H_4-C_6H_4NH_2(4')$	127	$401^{740mm.}$	12.13
o-Tolidine	$[-C_6H_3(CH_3)NH_2]_2(3,3',4,4')$	129		
o-Dianisidine	$[-C_6H_3(OCH_3)NH_2]_2(3,3',4,4')$	131		

in the polynitro compounds 2,4-dinitroaniline and picramide (2,4,6-trinitroaniline); the latter compound forms with concentrated sulfuric acid a salt scarcely more stable than oxonium salts of ethers. The three chloroanilines are distinctly weaker bases than aniline, but show an alternation owing to substitution in the three positions that conforms to the order in the series of nitro compounds but is less profound. Since the chlorine atom is known from dipole moment data to be electron-attracting, a comparable inductive effect evidently is responsible for the relationship. A slight effect in the opposite direction is observed in the *para* methoxyl and ethoxyl derivatives, *p*-anisidine and *p*-phenetidine, which are stronger bases than aniline. As would be anticipated, diphenylamine is feebly basic and salts formed with concentrated acids are readily hydrolyzed.

21.3   **Acid Salts.** — Aniline, as well as the toluidines and other amines of comparable basic strength and molecular weight, dissolves readily in dilute solutions of mineral acids with formation of salts which are so soluble in water that they are not easily precipitated by excess acid.   Hydrochloride salts of this type are isolated most easily by passing dry hydrogen chloride gas into an ethereal solution of the amine, for the salts are insoluble in ether and separate quantitatively.   Salts of higher amines, for example those of the naphthalene series, are less soluble in water and can be crystallized from an aqueous medium, with use of excess acid where required to decrease solubility.   Salts of moderate molecular weight often have sharp melting points and are even distillable; for example: aniline hydrochloride, m.p. 198°, b.p. 245°; methylaniline hydrochloride, m.p. 122°; dimethylaniline hydrochloride, m.p. 85°; m-toluidine hydrochloride, m.p. 228°, b.p. 250°.   The picrate of aniline melts at 181° dec., that of dimethylaniline at 142°.   Dimethylaniline also forms a complex molecular compound with trinitrobenzene, m.p. 108° (dark violet).

21.4   **Inner Salts.** — Sulfanilic acid (p-$H_2NC_6H_4SO_3H$), a typical amine sulfonic acid, has properties indicative of a dipolar ion, or inner salt structure, as shown in the formula.   It is insoluble in ether and soluble in water at room temperature only to the extent of about 1%, and when heated in a capillary tube

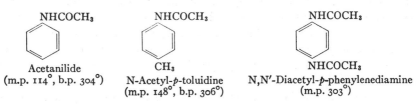

Sulfanilic acid
(sparingly soluble in water)

Sodium sulfanilate
(readily soluble in water)

it begins to decompose at 280°.   Sulfanilic acid dissolves readily when warmed with aqueous sodium carbonate solution with formation of the sodium salt, but it has so little tendency to combine with mineral acids that the original substance crystallizes from the solution in concentrated hydrochloric acid (anhydrous form; the commercial preparation is the monohydrate).   Sulfanilic acid has a logarithmic acidity constant pK = 3.22, attributable to separation of a proton from the —NH_3^+ group.

21.5   **Acetyl Derivatives.** — As in the aliphatic series, acetylation obliterates basic characteristics of aromatic amines.   Acetanilide is neutral and no more soluble in dilute hydrochloric acid than in water.   An acetyl derivative is prepared easily either by the action of acetic anhydride on the anhydrous amine

Acetanilide
(m.p. 114°, b.p. 304°)

N-Acetyl-p-toluidine
(m.p. 148°, b.p. 306°)

N,N′-Diacetyl-p-phenylenediamine
(m.p. 303°)

or by dissolving the amine with an equivalent quantity of hydrochloric acid in water and adding acetic anhydride, followed by enough sodium acetate to react with the hydrochloride salt and liberate the free amine. The acetyl derivatives melt at higher temperatures than the free amines and are useful for characterization. They are also useful because of stability to oxidation, in contrast with free amines, and because of moderation in the substitution-facilitating influence of the amino group.

PREPARATION OF SPECIFIC AMINES

21.6   Aniline. — The standard industrial preparation of aniline involves reduction of nitrobenzene with iron chips and 30% hydrochloric acid. After the reaction is complete the mixture is neutralized with soda, and the aniline removed by distillation with steam saturated with aniline. Since aniline is slightly soluble in water (3 g. in 100 g. H_2O), sodium chloride is added to the distillate to make a 20% solution of sodium chloride, in which aniline is insoluble. After separation of the two layers, aniline is obtained pure by distillation in practically quantitative yield. Reduction with hydrogen or water gas in the presence of a catalyst is also used. In one process aniline is made by treating chlorobenzene with ammonia at 340° and 340 atmospheres.

21.7   Methyl- and Dimethylaniline. — Methylation of aniline by any standard method of alkylation is liable to afford mixtures of the mono- and dimethyl derivatives, along with unchanged starting material, but by control of the conditions one or the other derivative can be obtained as the chief product. A technical process for production of dimethylaniline consists in heating a mixture of aniline, methanol, and concentrated sulfuric acid at 230–235° and a pressure of 25–30 atmospheres (97% yield). Small amounts of aniline and methylaniline present in technical preparations can be eliminated by adding enough acetic anhydride to react with these contaminants and distilling the unattacked tertiary amine from a residue containing the much less volatile acetyl derivatives. Technical methylaniline is produced by heating aniline with methanol and hydrochloric acid at 180° in an autoclave. A generally applicable laboratory method consists in alkylation of the arylsulfonyl, or Hinsberg, derivative of a primary amine in the orm of the sodium salt (Ullmann):

$$C_6H_5NH_2 \xrightarrow{C_6H_5SO_2Cl} \underset{H}{C_6H_5N}-SO_2C_6H_5 \xrightarrow{NaOH}$$

$$\underset{Na}{C_6H_5NSO_2C_6H_5} \xrightarrow{(CH_3)_2SO_4} \underset{CH_3}{C_6H_5NSO_2C_6H_5} \xrightarrow{Hydrol.} \underset{CH_3}{C_6H_5NH}$$

The preparation of N-alkyl derivatives by various processes of reductive amination is described in section 14.8. A variation of the general method of reduction of a mixture of an amine and a carbonyl compound involves generation of the

$$C_6H_5NO_2 + n\text{-}C_4H_9CHO \xrightarrow[84\%]{\text{Raney Ni, } H_2, \text{ NaOAc}} \underset{\text{N-}n\text{-Amylaniline}}{C_6H_5NHC_6H_{11}(n)}$$

amine in the reaction mixture by hydrogenation of a nitro compound in the presence of sodium acetate as condensing agent.

21.8   **C-Alkyl Derivatives.** — The *ortho* and *para* methyl derivatives of
aniline are obtained technically by reduction of the corresponding
nitrotoluenes with iron powder and a catalytic amount of hydrochloric acid.   Prior
to the development of distillation technique for separation of the nitro compounds
by fractionation, the *o-p* mixture was reduced and the toluidines separated through
the oxalate salts.   The oxalate of **o-toluidine** is much more soluble in either water
or ether than that of **p-toluidine**, and separation can be accomplished by preferential precipitation of the *para* isomer by the measured addition of oxalic acid to a
solution of the mixture of amines in ether.   In technical practice **m-toluidine** is
made from *m*-nitrotoluene, available in small yield in production of the *o*- and
p-isomers.

Nitration of coal tar xylene and reduction gives a mixture of five isomers containing 40–60% of **m-xylidine** (2,4-dimethylaniline) and 10–20% of **p-xylidine**
(2,5-dimethylaniline).   On treatment with hydrochloric acid, the isomers crystallize as a mixture of the hydrochlorides.   Separation is accomplished by sulfonation, since *m*-xylidinesulfonic acid is sparingly soluble in water whereas the
p-isomer is readily soluble.   **Mesidine** (2,4,6-trimethylaniline) and **cumidine**
(*p*-isopropylaniline) are obtained by nitration of mesitylene and cumene, followed
by reduction.   **Pseudocumidine** (m.p. 68°) is the name applied to 2,4,5-trimethyl-
aniline.

21.9   **Nitroanilines.** — Nitration of aniline with nitric acid alone is not satisfactory because the amine is sensitive to oxidation and is subject to
considerable destruction as a result of the oxidizing action of the reagent.   The
amine is stabilized against oxidation by dissolving it in sulfuric acid, and nitration
in such a solution proceeds somewhat more smoothly and affords *m*-nitroaniline
as the chief product, though in only moderate yield, for the amine is present largely
as the ionic salt and substitution occurs under the influence of the rather weakly
meta directing ammonium group, $—NH_3^+$.   The reaction has no practical use
since *m*-nitroaniline can be prepared more efficiently by partial reduction
of *m*-dinitrobenzene with ammonium hydrosulfide.

Acetylation of aniline provides stabilization to oxidation and does not lead to a
meta directing ionic group.   Acetanilide on nitration with mixed acid reacts

smoothly with almost exclusive production of *p*-nitroacetanilide (m.p. 215°); a
small amount of *o*-nitroacetanilide (m.p. 94°) is formed but is easily eliminated by
crystallization of the much higher-melting and less soluble *para* isomer.   Acid
hydrolysis of the recrystallized product affords *p*-nitroaniline in good overall
yield.   In a large-scale operation, a certain amount of *o*-nitroaniline can be recovered from the mother liquors of crystallization of the nitration product by

hydrolysis and steam distillation (volatility ascribable to chelation, see 12.17). A more efficient process is that formulated. Sulfonation of acetanilide blocks the

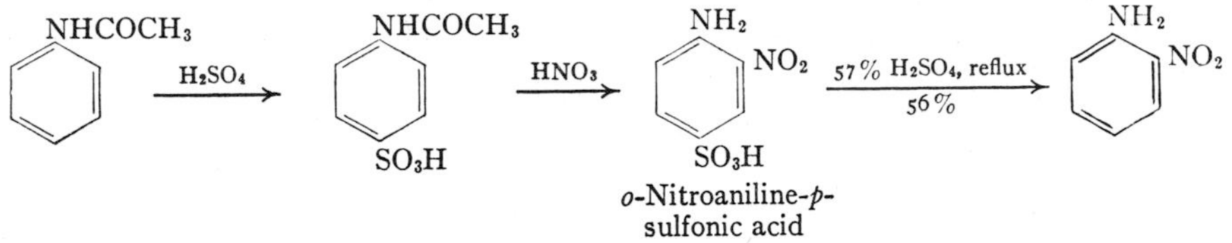

o-Nitroaniline-p-
sulfonic acid

para position, and on reaction with nitric acid in sulfuric acid solution a nitro group is introduced at the 2-position and the acetyl group is eliminated. Hydrolysis of the sulfonic acid substituent then affords o-nitroaniline.

The diminished basicity of nitroanilines has been noted. Another deviation from the behavior of aniline, shown by o- and p-nitroaniline but not by the *meta* isomer, is the ready reaction with alkalis with displacement of the amino group by hydroxyl. This reaction is another manifestation of the sensitivity of nitro com-

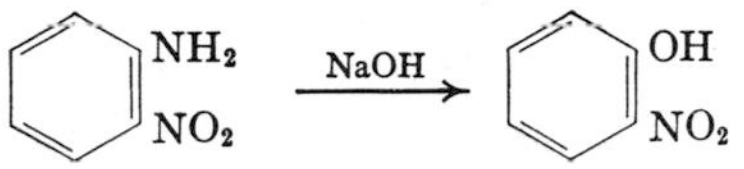

pounds to nucleophilic attack in the *ortho* and *para* positions.

21.10   Phenylenediamines. — The *ortho* and *para* diamino derivatives of benzene are obtainable by reduction of the corresponding nitroanilines; a specific procedure for preparation of o-phenylenediamine is indicated in example 2, section 21.1. *m*-Phenylenediamine is prepared by reduction of the readily available *m*-dinitro compound.

21.11   Halogen Derivatives. — Aniline combines with bromine with such avidity that interaction of the amine with a dilute aqueous solution of bromine affords a precipitate of the sparingly soluble 2,4,6-tribromoaniline.

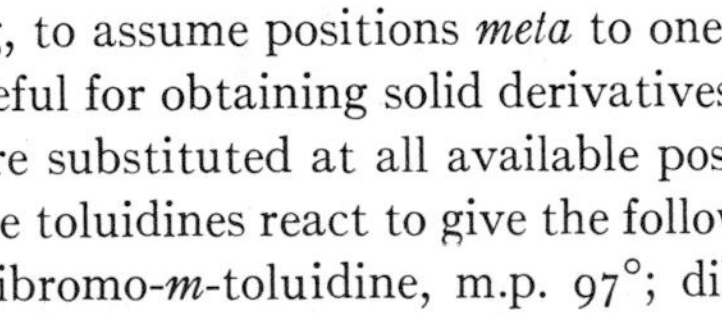

The reaction demonstrates the powerful substitution-facilitating influence of the amino group, for this directing group causes the three bromine atoms, which ordinarily are o-p directing, to assume positions *meta* to one another. Bromination in aqueous solution is useful for obtaining solid derivatives for identification, since most aromatic amines are substituted at all available positions *ortho* and *para* to the amino group; thus the toluidines react to give the following products: dibromo-o-toluidine, m.p. 50°; tribromo-*m*-toluidine, m.p. 97°; dibromo-p-toluidine, m.p. 73°. Bromination of aniline proceeds so rapidly even at high dilution that an early process for extraction of bromine from sea water consisted in the addition of chlorine to liberate bromine from the sodium bromide, followed by aniline to combine with the free halogen and give a filterable precipitate.

The effect of the amino group in promoting halogenation is so powerful that the acetyl derivative is used to control the reaction to the stage of monosubstitution. Acetanilide reacts to give almost exclusively the *p*-bromo derivative, which is hydrolyzed easily to the amine.   *p*-Chloroaniline is obtainable similarly; a small

$$\text{NHCOCH}_3 \xrightarrow[80\%]{\text{Br}_2,\ \text{HOAc}} \text{NHCOCH}_3\ (\text{Br}) \xrightarrow{\text{H}^+\ \text{or}\ \text{OH}^-} \text{NH}_2\ (\text{Br})$$

p-Bromoacetanilide
(m.p. 166°)

p-Bromoaniline

amount of the *ortho* compound is formed, and in technical practice the mixture is separated, after hydrolysis, by steam distillation of the *o*-chloroaniline.   The *meta* isomer is prepared by reduction of *m*-nitrochlorobenzene.

21.12   Sulfanilic Acid and Isomers. — Sulfanilic acid, used extensively as a dye intermediate, is prepared by mixing equal moles of aniline and concentrated sulfuric acid and baking the resulting acid sulfate at 180° until a test portion when neutralized with sodium hydroxide no longer liberates aniline.

$$\text{NH}_3\text{OSO}_3\text{H} \xrightarrow{180-190°} \text{NH}_2\ (\text{SO}_3\text{H}) + \text{H}_2\text{O}$$

Aniline monosulfate

Sulfanilic acid

Sulfanilic acid monohydrate crystallizes on pouring the cooled mixture into water. The reaction involves migration of the sulfonic acid group from the side chain to the ring and dehydration; experiments of Bamberger (1897) established that the initial reaction is loss of water from the sulfate with formation of phenyl-sulfamic acid, a dehydration comparable to the pyrolytic conversion of an ammonium salt into an amide.   When phenylsulfamic acid is heated cautiously, the sulfonic acid group first migrates to the *ortho* position, giving orthanilic acid, which rearranges at 180° to sulfanilic acid.   The progressive migrations to the *ortho* and then the *para* position can be correlated empirically with other phenomena; for

NH₃OSO₃H   αNHSO₃H   NH₂ SO₃H   NH₂

$$\xrightarrow{-\text{H}_2\text{O}}$$

Phenylsulfamic acid

Orthanilic acid

SO₃H
Sulfanilic acid

example, the shift of a hydrogen atom in an enol to give the corresponding keto form, and the reverse process.   Lapworth (1898) described each process as a shift of hydrogen from the α- to the γ-position in a system having a double bond between the β- and γ-atoms in the chain.   Phenylsulfamic acid affords orthanilic acid by an α,γ-shift of the sulfonic acid group to the *ortho* position, with a similar shift of hydrogen in the reverse direction.   Another α,γ-shift brings the acid group into the evidently more stable *para* position, and this interpretation accounts for the absence of the *meta* derivative from the reaction. Several com-

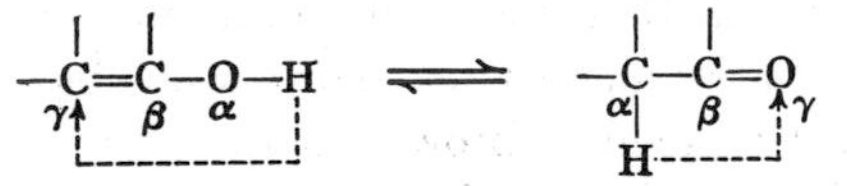

$$-\overset{|}{\underset{\gamma}{C}}=\overset{|}{\underset{\beta}{C}}-\overset{|}{\underset{\alpha}{O}}-H \;\; \rightleftharpoons \;\; -\overset{|}{\underset{\alpha}{C}}-\overset{|}{\underset{\beta}{C}}=\overset{O}{\underset{\gamma}{\;}}$$

Enol form   Keto form

parable rearrangements involve migration of a group from an initial position of attachment to nitrogen or to oxygen into *ortho* or *para* positions in the ring; for example, the acid-catalyzed rearrangement of phenylhydroxylamine to *p*-aminophenol (19.18).

Orthanilic acid is also employed technically and is prepared by the procedure shown.

2,2'-Dinitrodiphenyl disulfide (m.p. 199°)

o-Nitrobenzenesulfonyl chloride (m.p. 69°)   Orthanilic acid (dec. about 325°)

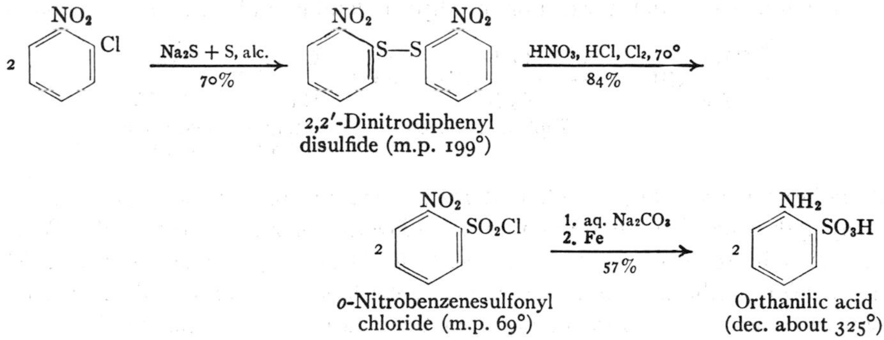

Metanilic acid, used to some extent in production of dyes, is prepared by sulfonating nitrobenzene with fuming sulfuric acid (25% SO_3) at 60–70° and reducing the resulting *m*-nitrobenzenesulfonic acid.

21.13   **Anisidines.** — The *o*- and *p*-methoxy derivatives of aniline are prepared by reduction of the corresponding nitroanisoles (m.p. 9° and 54°), which in turn are obtainable by nitration of anisole, by the action of methyl alcoholic potassium hydroxide on the nitrochlorobenzenes, or by methylation of the nitrophenols (sodium salts) with dimethyl sulfate in boiling toluene.

21.14   **Diphenylamine** is prepared by heating aniline hydrochloride with a small excess of aniline (1.1 equiv.) under slight pressure; the aniline is extracted from the resulting melt with warm dilute hydrochloric acid, and an oily

$$C_6H_5NH_3Cl \;+\; C_6H_5NH_2 \;\xrightarrow[82\%]{210-240°, \, 6 \, atm.}\; C_6H_5NHC_6H_5 \;+\; NH_4Cl$$

layer of the feebly basic diarylamine is collected and distilled.

21.15   **Triphenylamine.** — Introduction of a third phenyl group can be accomplished by dissolving potassium (two moles) in hot aniline and adding bromobenzene to the resulting melt of the potassium derivative, $C_6H_5NK_2$; a more convenient procedure is as follows:

$$2(C_6H_5)_2NH \;+\; 2C_6H_5I \;+\; K_2CO_3 \;\xrightarrow[82-85\%]{Boiling \, C_6H_5NO_2}\; 2(C_6H_5)_3N \;+\; 2KI \;+\; H_2O \;+\; CO_2$$

SPECIAL CHEMICAL PROPERTIES

21.16   **Oxidation.** — Primary and secondary aromatic amines are so sensitive
to oxidation that they often deteriorate in storage owing to attack by
atmospheric oxygen. Pure aniline is a colorless oil, but on exposure to air it
eventually acquires a deep reddish brown color. Pure samples deteriorate less
rapidly than technical preparations, which initially are somewhat colored. The
extent of oxidation, however, is not great, and practically colorless aniline can be
recovered in good yield from very dark material by distillation from a trace of zinc
dust. Solid amines (*e.g.*, *p*-toluidine) are less vulnerable to air oxidation than
liquid amines. An inference regarding the initial phase of oxidation can be made
on the basis of the established course of oxidation of diphenylamine. Wieland
(1911) discovered that diphenylamine on careful oxidation with potassium permanganate in acetone solution is converted into tetraphenylhydrazine, apparently
through formation and association of diphenylamino radicals. Association of

$$2 \begin{array}{c}C_6H_5\\C_6H_5\end{array}\!\!\!>\!NH \xrightarrow{[O]} 2\begin{array}{c}C_6H_5\\C_6H_5\end{array}\!\!\!>\!N\cdot \rightleftharpoons \begin{array}{c}C_6H_5\\C_6H_5\end{array}\!\!\!>\!N\!-\!N\!<\!\!\begin{array}{c}C_6H_5\\C_6H_5\end{array}$$

Diphenylnitrogen   Tetraphenylhydrazine
                                         (m.p. 147° dec.)

the radicals is practically complete at room temperature, for the colorless tetraphenylhydrazine gives solutions that are likewise colorless in the cold. When
a solution in toluene is heated to about 70°, however, it acquires a greenish
brown color attributable to the radical; the color fades on cooling, and the original
hydrazine derivative is recoverable from the solution. The behavior is similar
to that of hexaphenylethane, except that the diphenylamino radical does not
combine with oxygen (or with iodine) and is present in equilibrium with the di-
arylhydrazine in amounts too small to be determined. Evidence of dissociation
to free radicals, apart from the color phenomena, is provided by interaction of the
substance with triphenylmethyl to form the compound $(C_6H_5)_3C\!-\!N(C_6H_5)_2$ and
with sodium to give $(C_6H_5)_2NNa$.

With the use of different oxidizing agents under varying conditions, aniline is
convertible into a host of products, including azobenzene, azoxybenzene, nitrobenzene, quinone, the dye Aniline Black and intermediates, and many products
resulting from secondary processes of condensation. Most of the products appear derivable through an initial abstraction of one amino hydrogen atom with

Unstable radical   Quinone

formation of a transient free radical sensitive to further attack, either at the nitrogen atom or at the *para* position of the nucleus.

21.17   Action of Nitrous Acid on Primary Amines. — The response of aromatic amines of the three classes to nitrous acid parallels only in part the behavior of aliphatic amines. Whereas a primary alkylamine on treatment with nitrous acid in hydrochloric acid solution affords an alcohol and nitrogen, aniline hydrochloride is convertible under controlled conditions (low temperature, excess acid) into a crystalline salt of the formula $C_6H_5N_2^+Cl^-$, benzenediazonium chloride. The product undergoes hydrolytic decomposition when boiled with dilute acid, and hence the overall reaction resembles that in the ali-

$$C_6H_5NH_2Cl \; + \; HONO \; \xrightarrow{\; 0° \;} \; C_6H_5N_2^+Cl^- \; + \; 2\,H_2O$$

$$C_6H_5N_2Cl \; + \; H_2O \; \xrightarrow{\text{dil. } H_2SO_4, \text{ heat}} \; C_6H_5OH \; + \; N_2 \; + \; HCl$$

phatic series. The diversified reactions of aryldiazonium salts are described later.

21.18   N-Nitroso Compounds. — Secondary aromatic amines, like dialkylamines, combine with nitrous acid to form N-nitroso derivatives, or nitrosoamines. The product from methylaniline is known as either N-nitroso-N-

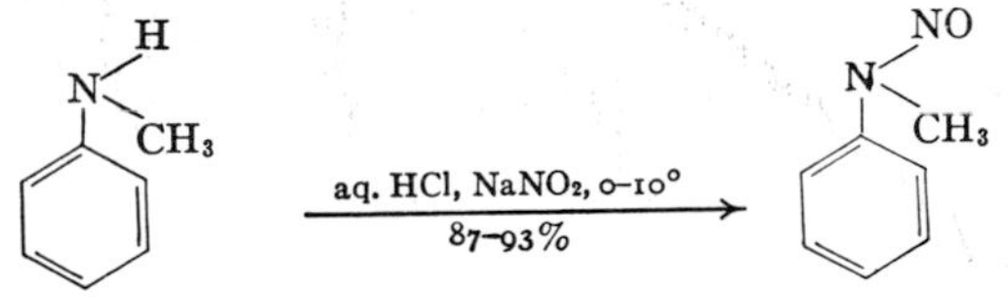

N-Nitroso-N-methylaniline
(yellow, m.p. 15°)

methylaniline or methylphenylnitrosoamine; it is a bright yellow oil that crystallizes on cooling and can be distilled in vacuum but not at atmospheric pressure. The N-nitroso derivative of N-methyl-*p*-toluidine is a yellow solid which melts at 54°; that of diphenylamine melts at 67°. N-Nitrosodiphenylamine undergoes nitration in acetic acid solution to a mixture of the 2- and 4-nitro derivatives. A reaction of preparative value consists in reduction of nitroso compounds to the substituted hydrazines with zinc dust and dilute acetic acid or with sodium amalgam (see example). Reduction with a more powerful reagent such as tin or zinc and a

α-Methylphenylhydrazine
(b.p. 107°/13 mm.)

mineral acid results in fission of the N–N linkage and formation of the amine:

$$C_6H_5N(NO)CH_3 \; \longrightarrow \; C_6H_5NHCH_3 \; + \; NH_3$$

N-Nitroso-N-methylaniline readily undergoes rearrangement under the catalytic influence of hydrochloric acid. When a solution in alcohol is treated with concentrated hydrochloric acid and allowed to stand for a time at room temperature, the substance rearranges to *p*-nitroso-N-methylaniline, which separates as the crystalline hydrochloride (yellow, see next page).

The N-nitroso derivative of phenylhydroxylamine is employed as the colorless ammonium salt, cupferron, in quantitative analysis as a reagent for the precipita-

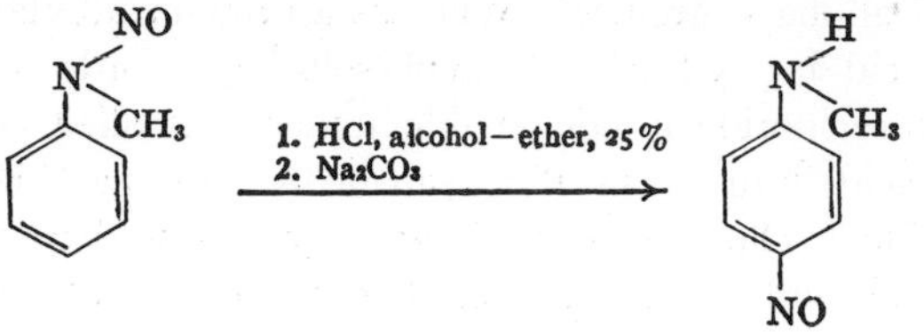

$$
\begin{array}{ccc}
\underset{\text{(blue-green, m.p. 118°)}}{\underset{\textit{p}\text{-Nitroso-N-methylaniline}}{}} & \xrightarrow[\textbf{2. Na}_2\textbf{CO}_3]{\textbf{1. HCl, alcohol—ether, 25\%}} &
\end{array}
$$

p-Nitroso-N-methylaniline
(blue-green, m.p. 118°)

tion of copper and iron. The salt is prepared by passing ammonia gas into an ethereal solution of phenylhydroxylamine and *n*-butyl nitrite. The marked acidic

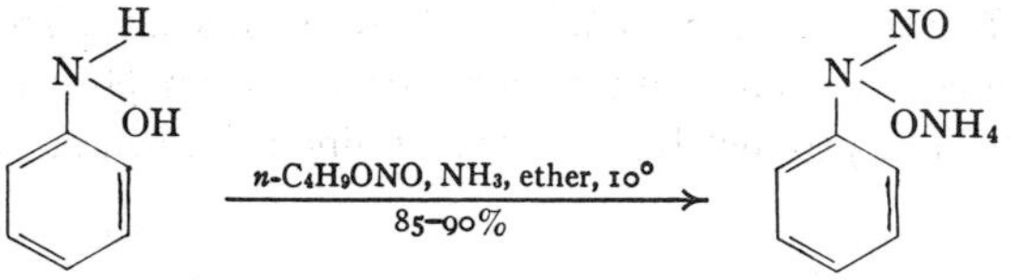

Phenylhydroxylamine $\xrightarrow[85-90\%]{\textit{n}\text{-C}_4\text{H}_9\text{ONO, NH}_3\text{, ether, 10}°}$ Cupferron

character of free N-nitrosophenylhydroxylamine (colorless, m.p. 51°, pK$_a$ 5.3) suggests that the substance exists largely not in the nitroso hydroxy form (*a*) but in the tautomeric amine oxide form (*b*), which has a hydroxyl group joined to an unsaturated nitrogen atom. The sparingly soluble copper and iron salts are formulated as derivatives of the amine oxide form (*b*), which permits formation of

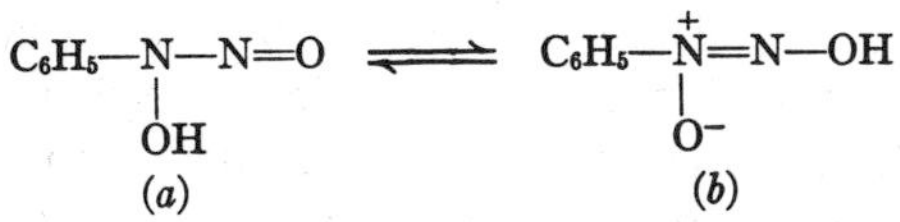

$$
\begin{array}{ccc}
\underset{\overset{|}{\text{OH}}}{\text{C}_6\text{H}_5\text{—N—N}\text{=}\text{O}} & \rightleftharpoons & \underset{\overset{|}{\text{O}^-}}{\text{C}_6\text{H}_5\text{—}\overset{+}{\text{N}}\text{=}\text{N—OH}} \\
(a) & & (b)
\end{array}
$$

stabilizing chelate rings:

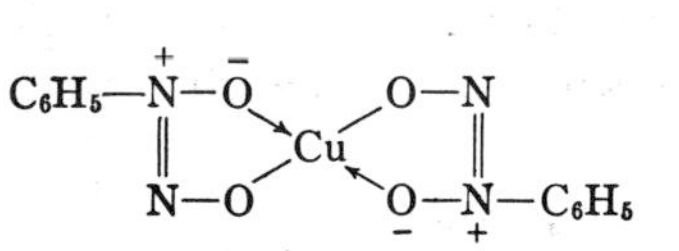

$$
\underset{\text{N—O}}{\overset{+\quad -}{\text{C}_6\text{H}_5\text{—N—O}}} \diagdown \underset{\text{O—N}}{\overset{\text{O—N}}{\text{Cu}}} \text{—C}_6\text{H}_5
$$

21.19   C-Nitroso Compounds. — Whereas tertiary aliphatic amines are inert to nitrous acid, those of the aromatic series undergo nitrosation in the nucleus with formation of C-nitroso compounds. Nitrosation proceeds rapidly

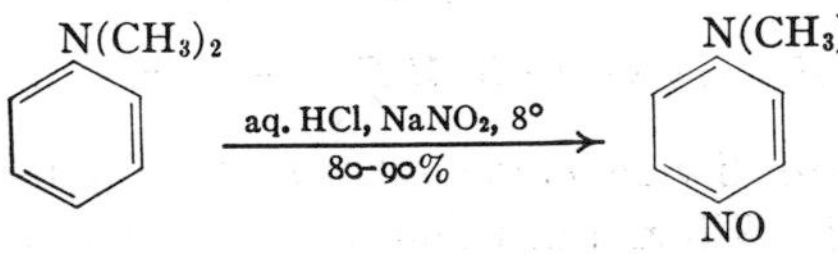

$$
\xrightarrow[80-90\%]{\text{aq. HCl, NaNO}_2\text{, 8}°}
$$

(isolated as the hydrochloride)

p-Nitrosodimethylaniline
(green, m.p. 86°)

at 0°, usually with exclusive substitution in the *para* position, if available, or otherwise in the *ortho* position. Phenols also yield C-nitroso derivatives, in transformations characterized by the low temperature of reaction and by exclusive attack at the *para* position, whereas neither aromatic hydrocarbons nor any derivatives other than the free amines and phenols react with nitrous acid.   C-Nitrosation is applicable only to compounds containing the powerful substitution-facilitating dialkylamino or hydroxyl group.

p-Nitrosodimethylaniline crystallizes in green plates and forms a yellow hydrochloride (dec. 177°).   It is hydrolyzed quantitatively by hot alkali to *p*-nitrosophenol and dimethylamine, and this hydrolysis has found some use in preparation

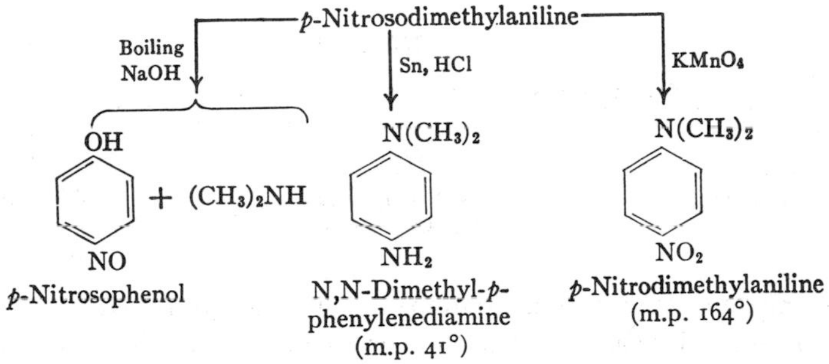

of secondary aliphatic amines.   The reaction probably involves the tautomer *p*-benzoquinone monoxime.   Reduction of the nitroso derivative affords the N,N-dimethyl derivative of *p*-phenylenediamine, and oxidation with permanganate yields the corresponding nitro compound.   *p*-Nitrosodimethylaniline is employed as a dye intermediate.

21.20   Ureides, Isocyanates, Urethanes, and Other Derivatives. — Aniline combines readily with phosgene to form **s-diphenylurea**; the reaction is general for primary and secondary amines.   A preparative method that affords

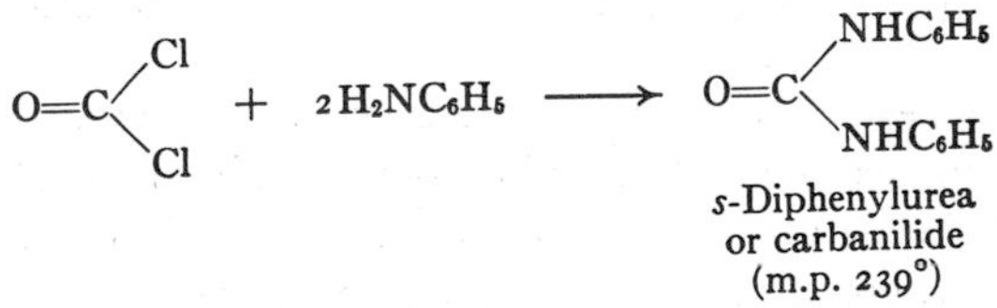

phenylurea along with the N,N'-disubstituted urea consists in boiling an aqueous solution of aniline hydrochloride and urea, when ammonium chloride is eliminated between the reactants; the diphenyl derivative separates from the hot solution and

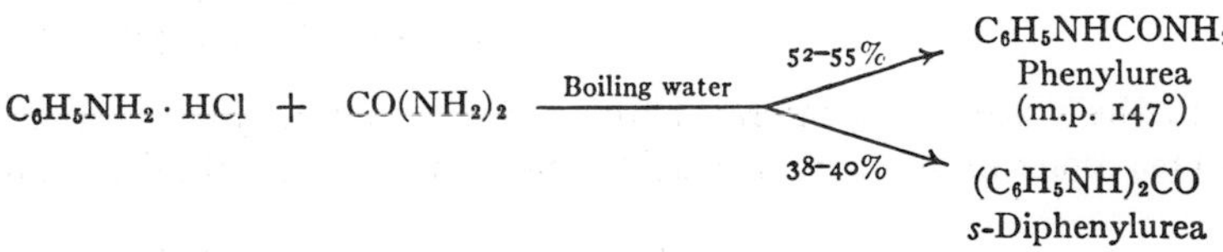

phenylurea is deposited on cooling.   Another route to these ureides starts from **phenyl isocyanate**, $C_6H_5N{=}C{=}O$, an offensive smelling, lachrymatory liquid, b.p. 164°; this reactive compound with twinned double bonds combines with ammonia to yield phenylurea and with aniline to give s-diphenylurea, probably by addition to the carbonyl group and ketonization.   Aryl isocyanates usually are

$$C_6H_5N=C=O \;+\; H_2NC_6H_5 \;\longrightarrow\; \left[\begin{array}{c} C_6H_5N=C-OH \\ | \\ C_6H_5NH \end{array} \right] \;\longrightarrow\; \begin{array}{c} C_6H_5NHC=O \\ | \\ C_6H_5NH \end{array}$$

Phenyl isocyanate   s-Diphenylurea

prepared by condensation of an amine with one equivalent of phosgene and heating or distilling the resulting arylcarbamyl chloride, ArNHCOCl, when hydrogen chloride is readily eliminated (see example).   Ethanol adds to phenyl isocyanate

NH₂ → COCl₂ in C₂H₅OAc → NHCOCl → Mild heat 85–95% overall → N=C=O

NO₂   NO₂   NO₂
p-Nitroaniline   p-Nitrophenyl-   p-Nitrophenyl
                           carbamyl chloride   isocyanate
                                                          (m.p. 57°)

in the same manner as ammonia or aniline to form **phenylurethane**.   This method of preparing solid derivatives of alcohols is useful for identification and has the

$$C_6H_5N=C=O \;+\; HOC_2H_5 \;\longrightarrow\; \left[C_6H_5N=C\!\!\begin{array}{c} {}^{OC_2H_5} \\ {}_{OH} \end{array} \right] \;\longrightarrow\; C_6H_5NHCOOC_2H_5$$

Phenylurethane (ethyl N-phenylcarbamate, m.p. 53°)

advantage of being applicable to tertiary, as well as to primary and secondary, alcohols.   Urethanes also are used for characterization of amines, for they are obtainable by acylation with ethyl chlorocarbonate:

$$C_6H_5NH_2 \;+\; ClCOOC_2H_5 \;\xrightarrow{\text{aq. Na}_2CO_3,\; 0°}\; C_6H_5NHCOOC_2H_5$$

s-Diphenylthiourea, employed as an accelerator for vulcanization of rubber, can be prepared by heating aniline and carbon disulfide in alcohol with powdered potassium hydroxide as catalyst.   The reaction probably proceeds through addition of aniline to carbon disulfide, elimination of hydrogen sulfide, and addition of

$$2\,C_6H_5NH_2 \;+\; CS_2 \;\xrightarrow[78\%]{\text{Boiling alcohol, KOH}}\; \begin{array}{c} C_6H_5NH \\ \diagdown \\ C_6H_5NH \end{array}\!\!C=S \;+\; H_2S$$

s-Diphenylthiourea
(thiocarbanilide, m.p. 153°)

aniline to the unsaturated intermediate, phenyl isothiocyanate.   The terminal addition reaction can be reversed by acids, and this reaction is the standard method

$$C_6H_5NH_2 \;\xrightarrow{CS_2}\; C_6H_5NHC\!\!\begin{array}{c} {}^{S} \\ {}_{SH} \end{array} \;\xrightarrow{-H_2S}\; C_6H_5N=C=S \;\xrightarrow{C_6H_5NH_2}\; (C_6H_5NH)_2CS$$

Phenyldithio-   Phenyl isothio-
carbamic acid   cyanate

of preparing **phenyl isothiocyanate** (b.p. 221°), also called **phenyl mustard oil** because of the mustardlike odor and the relationship to the active component of mustard, allyl isothiocyanate ($CH_2=CHCH_2N=C=S$). Another property of s-diphenylthiourea is ready replacement of sulfur by the imino group ($=NH$) through an unsaturated intermediate that can be isolated in the absence of ammonia:

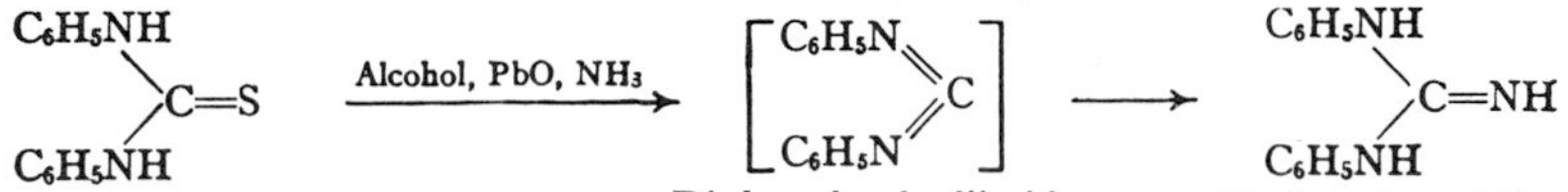

$$
\begin{array}{c}
C_6H_5NH \\
\diagdown \\
C=S \\
\diagup \\
C_6H_5NH
\end{array}
\xrightarrow{\text{Alcohol, PbO, NH}_3}
\left[
\begin{array}{c}
C_6H_5N \\
\diagdown \\
C \\
\diagup \\
C_6H_5N
\end{array}
\right]
\longrightarrow
\begin{array}{c}
C_6H_5NH \\
\diagdown \\
C=NH \\
\diagup \\
C_6H_5NH
\end{array}
$$

Diphenylcarbodiimide Diphenylguanidine
(liq., b.p. 331°) (m.p. 147°)

Until recently the only route to **carbodiimides** such as diphenylcarbodiimide was by oxidation of a thiourea. Thus N,N'-dicyclohexylcarbodiimide (DCC) is made by mercuric oxide oxidation of N,N'-dicyclohexylthiourea. The ketene-like reagent adds water with great avidity and is useful for effecting dehydrations

$$C_6H_{11}NHCSNHC_6H_{11} \xrightarrow{\text{HgO}} C_6H_{11}N=C=NC_6H_{11}$$
$$\text{DCC}$$

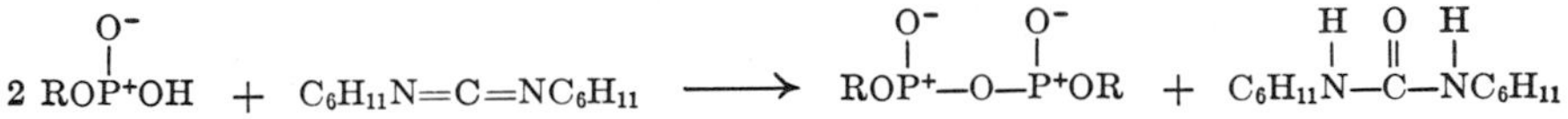

that proceed with difficulty. DCC reacts rapidly and almost quantitatively at 25° in ether solutions with mono and di esters of phosphoric acid to yield the corresponding symmetrical di or tetra esters of pyrophosphoric acid, with immediate precipitation of dicyclohexylurea (H. G. Khorana,[1] 1953).

$$2\ ROP^+OH + C_6H_{11}N=C=NC_6H_{11} \longrightarrow ROP^+{-}O{-}P^+OR + C_6H_{11}N{-}C{-}NC_6H_{11}$$

du Pont chemists (T. W. Campbell, *et al.*, 1961) found a novel route to carbodiimides involving self-condensation of an isocyanate under catalysis by a phospholine oxide, such as 1-ethyl-3-methylphospholine oxide (I). In the presence of this catalyst an aryl isocyanate dimerizes smoothly to a carbodiimide with elimination of carbon dioxide: $2\ Ar{-}N=C=O \rightarrow$ $Ar{-}N=C=N{-}Ar + CO_2$. Kinetic studies indicate that the reaction is reversible, has a low energy of activation, and proceeds in two steps. A suggested sequence of events is shown in the formulation. The reaction conditions are mild enough to permit preparation of highly reactive substances not previously available, such as 4,4'-dinitrodiphenylcarbodiimide. That

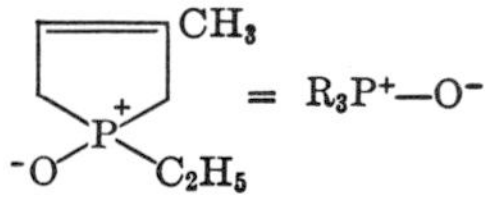

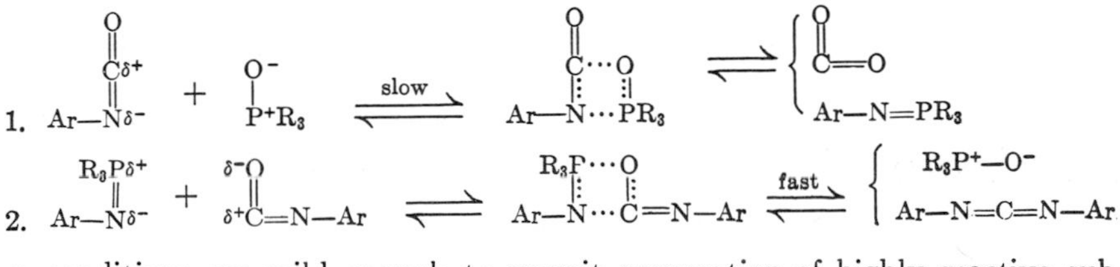

---

[1] H. G. Khorana, b. 1922 Raipur, India; Ph.D. Liverpool; Cambridge Univ.; Univ. British Columbia; Inst. Enzyme Res., Univ. Wisconsin

the formation of the carbodiimide is essentially quantitative is shown by the fact that addition of a trace of the phospholine oxide catalyst to the diisocyanate II produces a polymer (III) shown by infrared analysis to contain only carbodiimide links. The polymer forms tough, nylonlike films and fibers which are remarkably inert to chemical reagents.

II

III

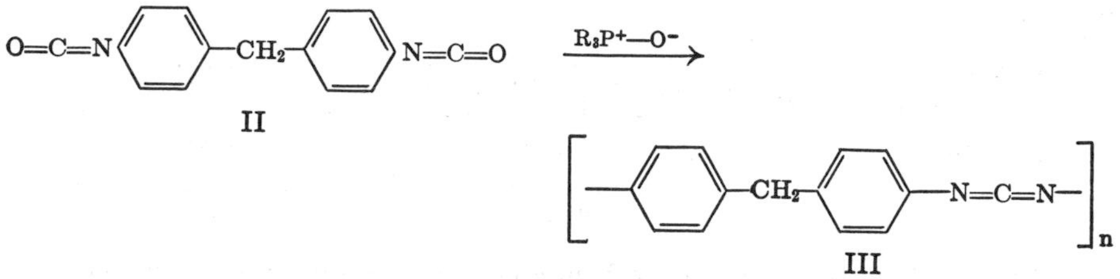

Another type of amine derivative obtainable through the hydrazine is illustrated by **phenyl azide,** $C_6H_5N_3$, a pale yellow, pungent smelling oil that explodes when heated. The usual preparation involves the action of nitrous acid on phenylhydrazine, when the nitroso compound initially formed loses water, with rearrangement to the azide structure. The substance does not have a cyclic structure ex-

$$C_6H_5NHNH_2 \xrightarrow{\text{aq. HCl, NaNO}_2\text{, 0°}} C_6H_5N(NO)\text{—}NH_2 \xrightarrow[65\text{–}68\%]{-H_2O} C_6H_5N_3$$

Phenyl azide (b.p. 50°/5 mm.)

pected from the mode of formation but is a hybrid of resonance forms:

$$C_6H_5N{=}\overset{+}{N}{=}\overset{-}{N} \longleftrightarrow C_6H_5\overset{-}{N}\text{—}\overset{+}{N}{\equiv}N$$

Phenyl isocyanide, $C_6H_5N{=}C$, is formed on heating aniline with chloroform and alcoholic potassium hydroxide (Hofmann, 1867). The isocyanide (or iso-

$$C_6H_5NH_2 + HCCl_3 \xrightarrow{KOH} C_6H_5N{=}C$$

Phenyl isocyanide (b.p. 166°)

nitrile) is toxic, and has a penetrating, characteristic odor resembling that of hydrogen cyanide, and since the substance can be recognized by smell, its formation from a drop of aniline is used as a test (general for primary amines). It is colorless when freshly distilled, but is unstable in the presence of air and becomes discolored on brief exposure and soon resinifies. Phenyl isocyanide is formulated conventionally as containing bivalent carbon, but dipole moment data indicate the presence of one polar link $C_6H_5N^+{\equiv}C^-$; the substance has a marked tendency to enter into reactions by which the carbon atom acquires its normal condition.

$$C_6H_5N{=}C \xrightarrow{\text{S, heat}} C_6H_5N{=}C{=}S$$

Phenyl isothiocyanate

$$C_6H_5N{=}C \xrightarrow{Cl_2} C_6H_5N{=}CCl_2$$

N-(Dichloromethylene)-aniline (b.p. 210°)

$$C_6H_5N{=}C \xrightarrow{\text{Na, }C_5H_{11}OH} C_6H_5NHCH_3$$

N-Methylaniline

Nef suggested in 1897 that an intermediate in the isocyanide reaction is the substance now known as dichlorocarbene (1). This mechanism is supported by

1. $CHCl_3 \xrightarrow{OH^-} :CCl_2 \xrightarrow{C_6H_5NH_2} C_6H_5\overset{H}{\underset{|}{N}}-\overset{H}{\underset{|}{C}}Cl_2 \xrightarrow{-2HCl} C_6H_5N{=}C$

2. $R_2NH \xrightarrow{:CCl_2} R_2\overset{+}{\underset{H}{N}}-\overset{-}{C}Cl_2 \longrightarrow R_2N-CHCl_2 \xrightarrow{H_2O} R_2NCH{=}O$

work of J. Hine (1950) and of M. Saunders[1] (1960), who generated dichlorocarbene ($CHCl_3$ + t-BuOK) at a low temperature in the presence of various secondary amines (2) and isolated the corresponding dialkylformamides in yields up to 31% (piperidine).

DIAZONIUM SALTS

21.21   **Diazotization.** — Diazonium salts of the type $ArN_2^+Cl^-$ were discovered by Griess.[2] The name is based on the presence of two nitrogen atoms (Fr. *azote*, nitrogen) and on analogy to ammonium compounds. Benzenediazonium chloride, $C_6H_5N_2^+Cl^-$, the product of the reaction between aniline hydrochloride and nitrous acid in the presence of excess hydrochloric acid at ice-bath temperature, is an ionic salt very soluble in water and insoluble in ether and other organic solvents, and in aqueous solutions it is completely dissociated. The crystalline solid is very sensitive to shock when fully dried and detonates violently on mild heating. Preparation of the solid can be accomplished by employing the combination of an organic nitrite and an organic acid as the source of nitrous acid, for the diazonium salt is then the only ether-insoluble product and is precipitated from this solvent. The reaction product is sensitive

$$C_6H_5NH_2Cl + n\text{-}C_4H_9ONO + CH_3COOH \xrightarrow{Ether} C_6H_5N_2Cl + CH_3COOC_4H_9$$

and requires careful handling. Fortunately, for nearly all reactions, isolation of the dry solid is not required, for the reactions can be carried out satisfactorily with use of the readily prepared aqueous solutions. Preparation of such a solution, or diazotization of an amine, is conducted as follows. The amine is dissolved in water containing three equivalents of hydrochloric acid, by heating if required, and the solution is cooled well in ice, when the amine hydrochloride usually crystallizes. With control of the temperature to 0–5°, an aqueous solution of sodium nitrite is added in portions until, after allowing a few minutes for reaction, the solution gives a positive test for excess nitrous acid with starch-iodide paper. The amine hydrochloride dissolves in the process to give a clear solution of the much more soluble diazonium salt. One equivalent of hydrochloric acid is bound by the amine and provides the anion of the reaction product, a second reacts with sodium nitrite to liberate nitrous acid, and the third maintains proper acidity required to stabilize the diazonium salt by inhibition of secondary changes. The

[1] Martin Saunders, b. New York; Ph.D. Harvard (Woodward); Yale Univ.

[2] Peter Griess, 1829–88; b. Kirchhosbach, Germany; asst. to Hofmann in London; chemist in an English brewery; *Ber.*, **24** (3), 1007 (1891)

process can be summarized as follows:

$$ArNH_2 \ + \ 3HCl \ + \ NaNO_2 \ \xrightarrow{\text{In water at 0°}} \ ArN_2Cl \ + \ NaCl \ + \ HCl \ + \ 2H_2O$$

The expected mode of formation of a diazonium salt is via the N-nitroso derivative, the final product in the reaction of nitrous acid with a secondary amine,

$$\left[\overset{+}{C_6H_5\underset{H}{N}}\!-\!\underset{H}{H}\right]Cl^- \xrightarrow{\text{HONO}} \left[\overset{+}{C_6H_5\underset{H}{N}}\!-\!N\!=\!\underset{H\text{----}}{O}\right]Cl^- \longrightarrow$$

$$\left[C_6H_5\overset{+}{N}\!=\!N\!-\!OH\atop H\right]Cl^- \xrightarrow{-H_2O} \left[C_6H_5\overset{+}{N}\!\equiv\!N\right]Cl^-$$
$$\text{Benzenediazonium}$$
$$\text{chloride}$$

and this inference has been verified by Hughes and Ingold (1958). These investigators found that the kinetic order is dependent upon the acid concentration. At a high concentration of acid the rate is third order, rate $= k_3[H^+][HNO_2][ArNH_2]$, and the reaction is interpreted as involving the steps 1–3:

1. $H^+ + HNO_2 \ \dashrightarrow \ H_2^+NO_2$ (fast)
2. $H_2^+NO_2 + ArNH_2 \ \longrightarrow \ ArNHNO + H^+ + H_2O$ (slow)
3. $ArNHNO \ \xrightarrow{\text{fast}} \ ArN\!=\!NOH \ \xrightarrow{\text{fast}} \ ArN^+\!\equiv\!N + OH^-$

At low concentration of mineral acid the nitrosating agent is dinitrogen trioxide, formed from nitrous acid in the rate-controlling step 4. Addition of alkali to a

4. $2 HNO_2 \ \rightleftharpoons \ N_2O_3 + H_2O$ (slow)
5. $N_2O_3 + ArNH_2 \ \longrightarrow \ ArNHNO + HNO_2$ (fast)

well-cooled solution of benzenediazonium chloride may result in initial conversion to the quaternary ammonium hydroxide, $[C_6H_5N^+\!\equiv\!N]OH^-$, which isomerizes at once to a weakly acidic substance, benzenediazoic acid, characterized as metal salts, or diazotates. The aryldiazoic acids, referred to also as diazo hydroxides or diazo hydrates, are comparable in structure and degree of acidity to nitrous acid;

$$[C_6H_5\overset{+}{N}\!\equiv\!N] \ + \ OH^- \ \rightleftharpoons \ \underset{\substack{\text{Benzenediazoic}\\ \text{acid}}}{C_6H_5N\!=\!NOH} \ \overset{\text{KOH}}{\rightleftharpoons} \ \underset{\substack{\text{Potassium benzene-}\\ \text{diazotate}}}{C_6H_5N\!=\!NOK}$$

they have not been isolated in crystalline form, for acidification of the alkaline solution, even with acetic acid, results largely in reversal of the equilibrium and reconversion to the diazonium salt. Potassium salts have been isolated as crystallizates from concentrated alkaline solutions and purified by precipitation from alcoholic solution with ether. Two forms have been isolated and characterized

$$\underset{\substack{\textit{cis} \text{ Form}\\ \text{(normal diazotate)}}}{\overset{\displaystyle C_6H_5\!-\!N}{\underset{\displaystyle KO\!-\!N}{\|}}} \ \longrightarrow \ \underset{\substack{\textit{trans} \text{ Form}\\ \text{(isodiazotate)}}}{\overset{\displaystyle C_6H_5\!-\!N}{\underset{\displaystyle N\!-\!OK}{\|}}}$$

by Hantzsch as geometrical isomers. The initially produced form (normal, or cis) of potassium benzenediazotate is labile, and is more reactive and has a higher energy content than the *iso* form (*trans*) to which it changes rather rapidly in either the solid or the dissolved state. A freshly alkalized solution of benzenediazonium chloride thus consists principally of the alkali salt of the *cis* form of benzenediazoic acid; the *trans* form predominates in an aged solution.

Huisgen established that the benzenediazoacetate (*b*) formed from N-nitrosoacetanilide (*a*) by acyl migration has the *trans* configuration in an investigation of the rearrangement of nitrosolactams to cyclic diazo esters (15.33).

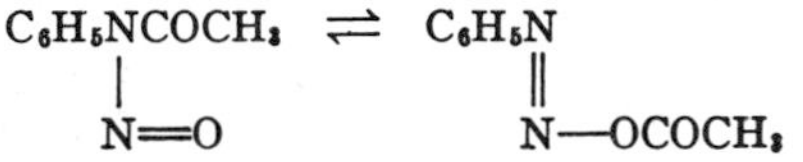

$$C_6H_5NCOCH_3 \rightleftharpoons C_6H_5N$$

$$\begin{array}{cc} | & \| \\ N{=}O & N{-}OCOCH_3 \\ (a) & (b) \end{array}$$

A weakly basic amine, for example 2,4-dinitro-1-naphthylamine, can be diazotized rapidly and completely by the method of Hodgson[1] (1933): addition of a solution of the amine in acetic acid to a cold solution of sodium nitrite in concentrated sulfuric acid. The method is generally applicable. Thus *o*-, *m*-, and *p*-phenylenediamine can be tetrazotized smoothly by this method but not by the ordinary procedure. Treatment of an aqueous solution of *o*-phenylenediamine

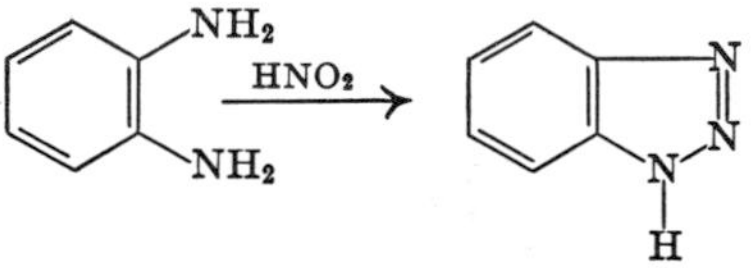

with nitrous acid effects conversion to benzotriazole. The *para* isomer is oxidized readily to quinonediimine.

Most aromatic primary amines can be diazotized in aqueous solution. Usually a clear colorless solution of the diazonium salt results, even though the amine salt used is only sparingly soluble, but in some instances the diazonium salt crystallizes. This is the case with sulfanilic acid because of the formation of an inner salt. The substance is diazotized by bringing it into solution as the sodium salt, adding the requisite amount of sodium nitrite, and pouring the solution on a mixture of ice and hydrochloric acid; nitrous acid and the dipolar sulfanilic acid are liberated together and after a few seconds the dipolar diazonium salt separates. Difficulty in effecting diazotization is experienced with very weakly basic amines, particu-

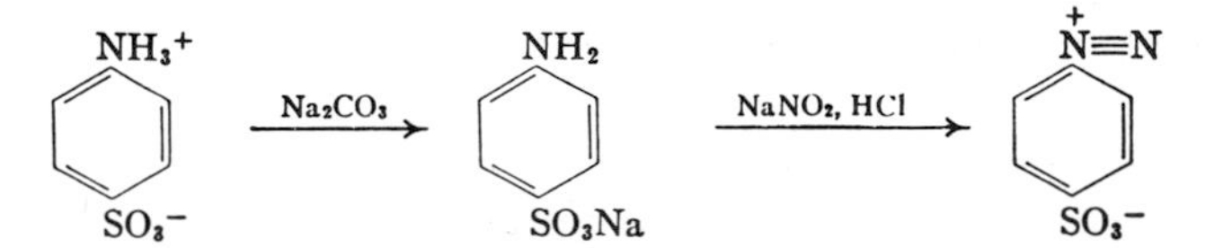

larly polynitro compounds such as picramide, but satisfactory procedures have been developed for conducting such diazotizations in a mixture of concentrated

[1] Herbert Henry Hodgson, b. 1883 Bradford, England; Ph.D. Heidelberg; Huddersfield Techn. College

sulfuric acid and acetic acid or in concentrated sulfuric acid alone. Another limiting factor is that nitrous acid has oxidizing properties and is liable to attack sensitive compounds (o- and p-aminophenols), but oxidation often can be inhibited by a zinc or copper salt.

Phenols and tertiary amines can be converted directly into p- or o-diazonium salt derivatives in aqueous acetone by treatment with a large excess of sodium nitrite and a small excess of hydrochloric acid; the excess nitrite acts as a buffer and maintains a constant pH of 3–4 (J. M. Tedder,[1] 1959). The initial product is the nitroso derivative, and, in the buffered solution, the reactive species in the next step probably is dinitrogen trioxide. The effect of substituents is that

$$C_6H_5OH \xrightarrow{HNO_2} p\text{-}HOC_6H_4N{=}O \xrightarrow{N_2O_3} p\text{-}HOC_6H_4N{-\!\!-\!\!-}N{=}O$$

$$\xrightarrow[-HNO_3]{HNO_2} p\text{-}HOC_6H_4N{=\!\!=}N \longleftrightarrow p\text{-}HOC_6H_4\overset{+}{N}{\equiv}NNO_3^-$$

expected for a normal electrophilic substitution. Thus yields are high except when a deactivating group opposes the directive influence of the hydroxyl group (p-chlorophenol, m-nitrophenol). Since the nitrosonaphthols are stable in the quinoneoxime forms, these substances are obtained in good yield and do not react further to form diazonium salts. p-Cresol affords the diazonium salt in 77% yield, but when cupric ion is present to trap the nitroso intermediate as the chelate no diazonium salt is formed. Mesitylene is convertible into its diazonium salt by reaction with nitrous acid in a solution in concentrated sulfuric acid; the reactive species here appears to be the nitrosonium ion, N^+O. Compounds deactivated by a nitro group, p-nitroanisole for example, react readily in concentrated sulfuric acid in the presence of a trace of mercuric ion, which appears to function by effecting initial mercuration. The intense red brown sulfuric acid solution contains no diazonium salt; this salt is formed when the solution is poured into water. When the solution is poured into sulfamic acid, p-nitrosoanisole is obtained in 88% yield.

21.22   Diazo anhydrides. — Bamberger found (1896) that diazonium salts or salts of normal diazotates are converted in the pH range 5.5–7.5 into water-insoluble, highly explosive, yellow anhydrides, later shown to have the structure ArN=N—O—N=NAr (T. Kauffmann, 1960). The diazo anhydride prepared from p-chloraniline is stable for a month at 0° but explodes at room temperature with quantitative release of one mole of nitrogen and formation of the diazo ether, $p\text{-}ClC_6H_5N{=}N{-}OC_6H_4Cl\text{-}p$, which is a stable substance. If the cis configuration of the normal diazotate is retained, both —N=N— links

[1] J. M. Tedder, b. 1926 London; Ph.D. Birmingham; Univ. Sheffield

must be *cis* (1) and the decomposition is then a *cis* elimination and must involve a cyclic transition state (2, stabilized by resonance with a second identical structure). The diazo anhydride (1) is split by ethanol at room temperature

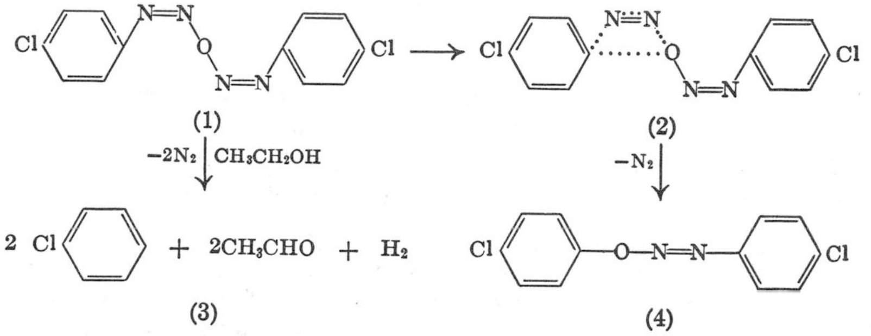

(1)

(2)

$-2N_2$ | CH_3CH_2OH

$-N_2$

$2\ Cl\langle\ \rangle\ +\ 2CH_3CHO\ +\ H_2$

(3)

$Cl\langle\ \rangle{-}O{-}N{=}N{-}\langle\ \rangle Cl$

(4)

to chlorobenzene with liberation of nitrogen and formation of acetaldehyde and water.

21.23   Hydrolysis to Phenols. — When an aqueous solution of a diazonium salt is strongly acidified with sulfuric acid and heated at the boiling point, nitrogen is evolved and the amine derivative is converted into the corresponding phenol. Usually 40–50% sulfuric acid is used in order to attain a reflux

$$[Ar\overset{+}{N}{\equiv}N]Cl^-\ +\ HOH\ \longrightarrow\ ArOH\ +\ N_2\ +\ HCl$$

temperature sufficiently high to promote reasonably rapid hydrolysis, and the strong acid may have a destructive action on the sensitive hydroxy compound. The crude reaction product may be deeply colored owing to contamination with azo compounds almost invariably formed as by-products, but purification can be accomplished by extraction with alkali or by steam distillation, and the pure phenol obtained in moderate yields. Since the diazonium salt need not be isolated, introduction of a hydroxyl group can be accomplished in essentially three steps: nitration, reduction to the amine, and diazotization in aqueous medium followed by hydrolysis in the same solution. The overall process is more elaborate than that of sulfonation and alkali fusion, and ordinarily the yields are not so satisfactory. The chief preparative application of the route through the diazonium derivative is in instances where the alternative method is inapplicable. Thus *m*-nitrophenol cannot be prepared through the sulfonate because of the sensitivity of nitro compounds to alkali, but is obtainable through the diazo reaction. Halogen substituents also are liable to be attacked by alkali at the

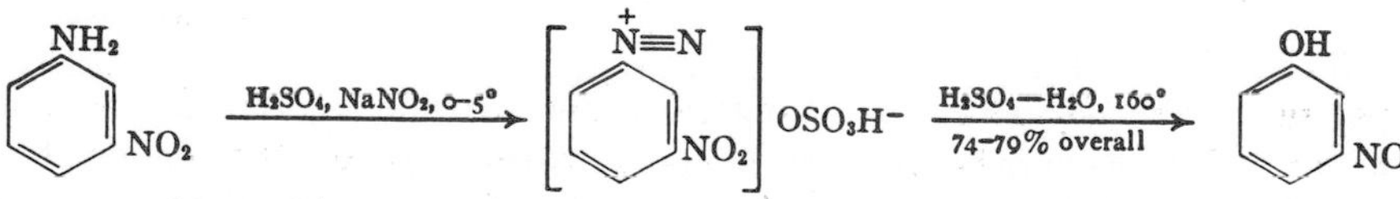

elevated temperatures required for alkali fusion of a sulfonate, but *o*- and *p*-chlorophenol, for example, can be prepared satisfactorily from the corresponding amines by diazotization and hydrolysis.

The decomposition of a diazonium salt in water is unimolecular and is believed to proceed by an S_N1 mechanism involving phenyl cation (E. S. Lewis,[1] 1958).

$$C_6H_5N^+\!\equiv\!N - N_2 \xrightarrow{\text{slow}} C_6H_5^+ + N_2$$

$$C_6H_5^+ + H_2O \xrightarrow{\text{fast}} C_6H_5OH + H^+$$

This cation is very reactive and any nucleophilic reagent present may give rise to a product other than the phenol. In aqueous methanol the products are the phenol and its methyl ether. Chloride ion gives rise to chlorobenzene, and hence hydrochloric acid is less satisfactory than sulfuric acid for effecting hydrolysis of diazonium salts.

21.24   Sandmeyer Reaction. — When an aqueous solution of benzenediazonium chloride is treated with one equivalent of potassium iodide and warmed, the benzenediazonium iodide present in the equilibrium mixture decomposes with evolution of nitrogen and formation of iodobenzene in good yield. Neither chloro- nor bromobenzene can be prepared satisfactorily by this proce-

$$C_6H_5NH_2 \xrightarrow{\text{aq. HCl, NaNO}_2,\,5°} [C_6H_5\overset{+}{N}\!\equiv\!N]Cl^- \xrightarrow[\substack{74-76\% \\ \text{overall}}]{\text{KI, 95°}} C_6H_5I + N_2 + KCl$$

dure, but Sandmeyer[2] (1884) discovered that replacement of the diazonium salt group by halogen is catalyzed markedly by cuprous salts and thereby contributed a practical preparative method capable of wide application and of certain elaborations that can be described as Sandmeyer-type displacements. For the preparation of aryl chlorides by the Sandmeyer procedure, the amine is diazotized in ice-cold solution in hydrochloric acid with sodium nitrite, and a solution of one equivalent of cuprous chloride in hydrochloric acid is added; a brown, sparingly soluble complex separates consisting of a double molecule of the diazonium salt and cuprous chloride, and when the suspension of this substance is warmed, decomposition sets in with evolution of nitrogen, disappearance of the solid, and

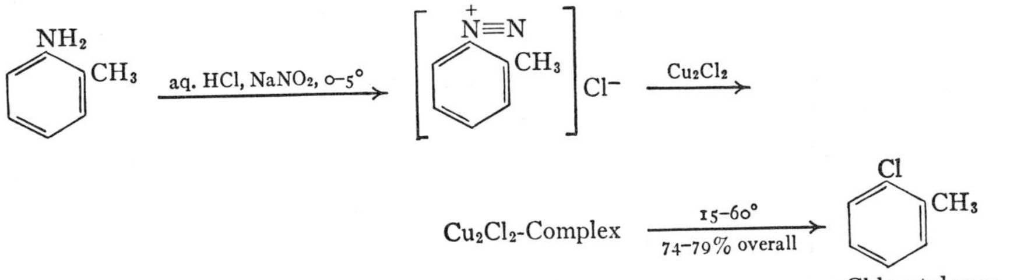

separation of an oily layer containing the organic halide. Although the crude reaction mixture usually is dark colored, separation of the halide from contaminants and inorganic salts can be accomplished by steam distillation. Both

[1] Edward S. Lewis, b. 1920 Berkeley, Calif.; Ph.D. Harvard (Bartlett); Rice Univ.

[2] Traugott Sandmeyer, 1854–1922; b. Wettingen, Switzerland; asst. to V. Meyer and Hantzsch; Geigy Co., Basel

o- and *p-*chlorotoluene can be prepared in good yield; this method is convenient for obtaining *m-*nitrochlorobenzene free from isomers, since pure *m-*nitroaniline is available (yield 68–71%). For preparation of a bromide by the Sandmeyer reaction, the amine is diazotized in sulfuric acid solution and the resulting aryl-diazonium sulfate treated with a solution of cuprous bromide in excess hydrobromic acid; the complex is then decomposed by heating. *p-*Bromotoluene can be prepared from *p-*toluidine in 70–73% yield, and *o-*chlorobromobenzene is obtainable from *o-*chloroaniline with equal success. The reaction can be applied to preparation of nitriles, which result from the action of a solution of cuprous cyanide in excess potassium cyanide on a diazonium salt, as shown in the example (the yield is the same for the conversion of *p-*toluidine into *p-*tolunitrile, m.p.

$$\underset{\text{1. aq. HCl + NaNO}_2,\ 0\text{–}5^\circ}{\overset{\text{2. Cu}_2\text{(CN)}_2 + \text{KCN, }50^\circ}{\xrightarrow{\hspace{1cm}64\text{–}70\%\hspace{1cm}}}}$$

*o-*Tolunitrile
(b.p. 205°)

29°, b.p. 218°). Excellent results are obtained by preparing a solution of the diazonium salt in acetone–sulfuric acid (Hodgson, 21.21) and pouring it into a solution of cuprous chloride in concentrated sulfuric acid. Decomposition occurs at once and the pure halide precipitates in yield of about 80% (*e.g.,* conversion of the phenylenediamines to the dichlorides).

In the examples cited a molecular equivalent of the cuprous salt component is required, apparently because of formation of the intermediate molecular complex. The structure of the complex is not known but the reaction is considered to follow a free-radical mechanism. Gattermann (1890) discovered that freshly precipitated copper powder (zinc dust and copper sulfate solution) can replace the cuprous salt as promoter for the replacement and is effective in catalytic amounts and at temperatures lower than required in the Sandmeyer procedure. Gattermann's procedure is the simpler of the two, but the yields, though high in some instances, never surpass those of the Sandmeyer procedure and are sometimes lower. If a cuprous salt is not available, the copper-catalyzed reaction of Gattermann is

$$p\text{-CH}_3\text{C}_6\text{H}_4\text{NH}_2 \xrightarrow[\text{43–47\%}]{\substack{\text{1. aq. HBr, NaNO}_2,\ 10^\circ \\ \text{2. Cu powder, gentle heat}}} p\text{-CH}_3\text{C}_6\text{H}_4\text{Br}$$

applicable. Thus benzenediazonium sulfate is converted in good yield into benzenesulfinic acid by the action of sulfur dioxide and copper powder, and when treated with potassium cyanate and copper affords phenyl isocyanate, C_6H_5NCO, though in low yield (20%).

A further variation of the Sandmeyer reaction is the preparation of aryl thiocyanates, or rhodanates, ArSCN, from diazonium salts and cuprous thiocyanate. In other instances the replacement reaction can be brought about with a catalyst other than copper or a copper salt, or even proceeds without a catalyst (compare $C_6H_5N_2I \rightarrow C_6H_5I$). Replacement by the sulfhydryl group (—SH), the thioglycolyl residue (—SCH$_2$COOH), and the azide group (—N$_3$) in the absence of a catalyst is brought about by the reagents KSH, HSCH$_2$COOH, and NaN$_3$, respectively.

Several procedures are available for replacement of the diazonium salt group by a nitro group. One involves reaction with sodium nitrite in the presence of precipitated cuprous oxide. Another involves preparation of fluoroboric acid by stirring solid boric acid into 50% hydrofluoric acid in a copper, lead, or silver plated container, dissolving p-nitroaniline in the solution, and dropping in aqueous sodium nitrite. The solid diazonium tetrafluoroborate that separates is washed

$$p\text{-NO}_2\text{C}_6\text{H}_4\text{N}_2{}^+\text{Cl} \xrightarrow{\text{HBF}_4} p\text{-NO}_2\text{C}_6\text{H}_4\text{N}_2{}^+\text{BF}_4{}^- \xrightarrow[\text{67-82\%}]{\text{NaNO}_2 \ (\text{Cu})} p\text{-NO}_2\text{C}_6\text{H}_4\text{NO}_2$$

in turn with water, alcohol, and ether and added slowly to a stirred suspension of copper powder in an aqueous solution of sodium nitrite. Foaming occurs and the p-dinitrobenzene that separates is collected and extracted with benzene (E. B. Starkey, 1937). A diazonium cobaltinitrite is decomposed by a cold solution of

$$(\text{ArN}_2{}^+)_3\text{Co}^{-3}(\text{NO}_2)_6 \xrightarrow{\text{NaNO}_2 \ (\text{Cu}_2\text{O})} 3\text{ArNO}_2$$

sodium nitrite in the presence of cuprous oxide and copper sulfate to give the nitro compound in yield of about 60% (H. H. Hodgson and E. Marsden, 1944). A yield of 90% is reported for the conversion of o-nitrobenzenediazonium chloride into o-dinitrobenzene by treatment with sodium nitrite and sodium bicarbonate.

21.25   Schiemann Reaction. — Aromatic monofluoro compounds cannot be prepared by direct fluorination but are available by a method introduced by G. Schiemann (1927). In the first step an aryldiazonium tetrafluoroborate is prepared by diazotization of an arylamine in aqueous fluoroboric acid (1). The precipitated diazonium fluoroborate is collected, dried, and heated

1. $\text{ArN}^+\text{H}_3\text{BF}_4{}^- + \text{HNO}_2 \longrightarrow \text{ArN}_2{}^+\text{BF}_4{}^- + 2\ \text{H}_2\text{O}$

2. $\text{ArN}_2{}^+\text{BF}_4{}^- \xrightarrow{\text{heat}} \text{ArF} + \text{N}_2 + \text{BF}_3$

intermittently with a free flame, when it decomposes smoothly with evolution of nitrogen and boron fluoride to give the aryl fluoride. Fluorobenzene is obtainable by this procedure in 51–57% yield. In an alternative procedure (U. Wannagat, 1955) the diazonium tetrafluoroborate is prepared from the amine and nitrosonium tetrafluoroborate (4), obtainable by reaction (3).

3. $\text{N}_2\text{O}_3 + 2\ \text{H}^+\text{BF}_4{}^- \longrightarrow 2\ \text{NO}^+\text{BF}_4{}^- + \text{H}_2\text{O}$

4. $\text{ArNH}_2 + \text{NO}^+\text{BF}_4{}^- \longrightarrow \text{ArN}_2{}^+\text{BF}_4{}^- + \text{H}_2\text{O}$

Aryldiazonium tetrachloroborates and tetrabromoborates have been prepared in the following way (G. A. Olah, 1961). A solution of the amine in chloroform is added to a solution of nitrosyl chloride (5, or bromide) in chloroform–petroleum ether at −18° and the white precipitate of aryldiazonium salt is collected (and can be stored under petroleum ether below 0°). Boron chloride is then added to a stirred suspension of the diazonium salt in chloroform–petroleum ether at −18° (6) and the off-white precipitate of aryldiazonium tetrahaloborate is col-

5. $ArNH_2 + NOCl \longrightarrow ArN_2^+Cl^- + H_2O$

6. $ArN_2^+Cl^- + BCl_3 \longrightarrow ArN_2^+BCl_4^-$

lected. These salts when heated often decompose explosively, but the reaction can be controlled by use of an inert diluent (ligroin, b.p. 110–115°) and the corresponding aromatic chlorides or bromides obtained in yields of 80–90%.

21.26   Bart Reaction. — Introduction of the arsonic acid group (AsO_3H) is accomplished by decomposition of a diazonium salt with sodium arsenite in the presence of a copper salt (1; Heinrich Bart, Heidelberg, 1912). Use of sodium carbonate as a buffer improves the yield. Alternatively, a suspension

1. $C_6H_5N_2^+Cl^- + Na_3AsO_3 \xrightarrow{CuSO_4 \ (Na_2CO_3)}$

              $C_6H_5AsO_3Na_2 + NaCl + N_2 \xrightarrow[86\%]{HCl} C_6H_5AsO_3H_2$

                                                              Phenylarsonic
                                                              acid

2. $C_6H_5N_2^+BF_4^- + NaAsO_2 + H_2O \xrightarrow{Cu_2Cl_2} C_6H_5AsO_3H_2 + NaF + N_2 + BF_3$

of an aryldiazonium tetrafluoroborate is added to a solution of sodium metaarsenite in the presence of a catalytic amount of cuprous chloride (Hartung,[1] 1942). *p*-Nitrophenylarsonic acid is obtained by this procedure in 79% yield as compared with 45% by the original method.

21.27   Aryl Coupling. — One method for coupling two aryl rings to establish a diphenyl linkage is known as the **Gomberg reaction** (M. Gomberg and W. E. Bachmann, 1924). In one procedure an amine, for example *p*-bromoaniline, is diazotized, a large excess of liquid aryl component such as benzene or anisole is added, and sodium hydroxide solution is then dropped into the vigorously stirred two-phase system. The *cis*-aryldiazoic acid formed is extracted into the

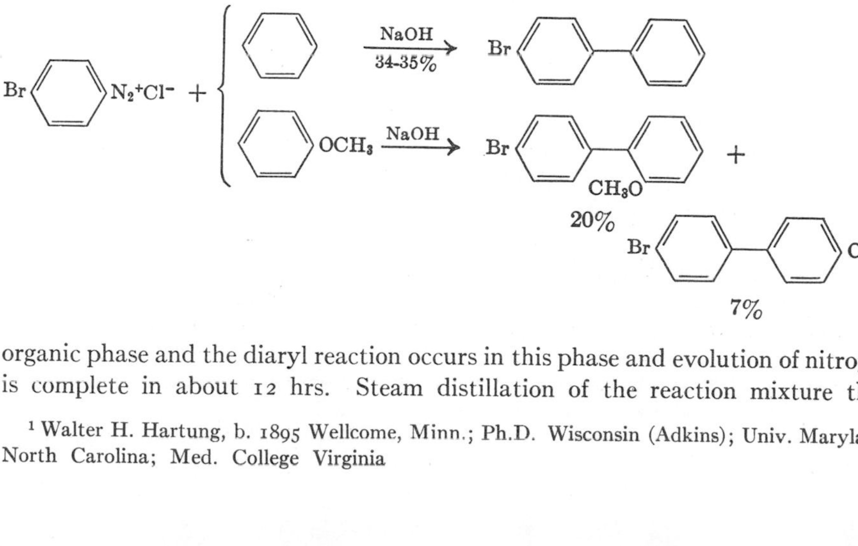

organic phase and the diaryl reaction occurs in this phase and evolution of nitrogen is complete in about 12 hrs. Steam distillation of the reaction mixture then

[1] Walter H. Hartung, b. 1895 Wellcome, Minn.; Ph.D. Wisconsin (Adkins); Univ. Maryland, North Carolina; Med. College Virginia

eliminates the excess aryl component and may effect separation of the diphenyl derivatives. The reaction with benzene affords *p*-bromodiphenyl, that with anisole affords 2-methoxy- and 4-methoxy-4'-bromodiphenyl. Yields are low, but the reaction provides a unique route to unsymmetrical diphenyls. Usual directive effects of groups are not operative, for nitrobenzene, like bromobenzene, is substituted in the *ortho* and *para* positions. The Gomberg reaction is thus analogous to homolytic substitution (17.10) and probably is also a free-radical reaction.

Another method, suggested by brief work of D. Vorländer and F. Meyer (1902) and worked out by Atkinson[1] (1940–), is illustrated by the preparation of diphenic acid from anthranilic acid by slow addition of a solution of the diazonium salt to a

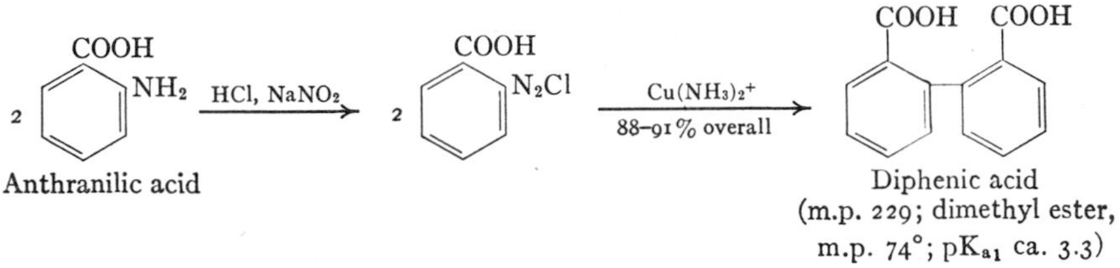

Anthranilic acid

Diphenic acid
(m.p. 229; dimethyl ester,
m.p. 74°; pK_{a_1} ca. 3.3)

solution of cuprous ammonium hydroxide prepared by reduction of copper sulfate in ammonia with hydroxylamine. Reductive coupling by this method is less satisfactory with other amines and by-products isolated are as follows: ArN=NAr, ArOAr, ArNHAr, ArCl, ArOH. With *o*-nitroaniline no diaryl was found and the azo compound was formed in yield of 30%. The yield of 3,3'-dinitrodiphenyl from *m*-nitroaniline was 45%.

A useful application of the aryl displacement reaction is in a general method developed by Pschorr[2] (Berlin, 1896) for the synthesis of phenanthrene derivatives. Perkin condensation of an *o*-nitrobenzaldehyde with sodium phenylacetate (or a derivative) and acetic anhydride gives chiefly the *cis*-α-phenyl-*o*-nitro-

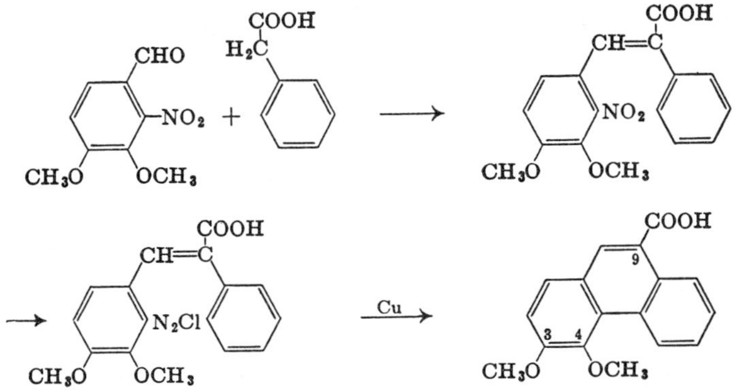

---

[1] Edward R. Atkinson, b. 1912 Boston; Ph.D. Mass. Inst. Techn. (Huntress); Univ. New Hampshire; Dewey and Almy Chem. Co.; Arthur D. Little Co.

[2] Robert Pschorr, 1868–1930; b. Munich; Ph.D. Jena; Univ. Berlin; *Angew. Chem.*, **43**, 245 (1930)

cinnamic acid, which is converted via the amine to the diazonium salt, and under catalysis by copper powder this loses nitrogen and hydrogen chloride with ring closure to the 9-phenanthroic acid. The product formulated in the example on decarboxylation gave 3,4-dimethoxyphenanthrene, identical with a degradation product of morphine.

21.28   **Meerwein Arylation Reaction.** — A reaction introduced by Meerwein in 1939 differs from aryl coupling in that the substance arylated is a nonaromatic unsaturated compound, for example acrylic acid (1), cinnamonitrile (2), or styrene (3). An amine is diazotized in the usual way, the solution is

1. $p\text{-ClC}_6\text{H}_4\text{N}_2\text{Cl} + \text{CH}_2=\text{CHCO}_2\text{H} \xrightarrow{\text{Cu}^{++}} p\text{-ClC}_6\text{H}_4\text{CH}=\text{CHCO}_2\text{H} + \text{N}_2 + \text{HCl}$

2. $p\text{-ClC}_6\text{H}_4\text{N}_2\text{Cl} + \text{C}_6\text{H}_5\text{CH}=\text{CHCN} \xrightarrow[78\%]{\text{Cu}^{++}} \text{C}_6\text{H}_5\text{CH}=\text{CCN}$
                                                            $|$
                                                          $\text{C}_6\text{H}_4\text{Cl-}p$

3. $\text{C}_6\text{H}_5\text{N}_2\text{Cl} + \text{CH}_2=\text{CHC}_6\text{H}_5 \xrightarrow[28\%]{\text{Cu}^{++}} \text{C}_6\text{H}_5\text{CH}=\text{CHC}_6\text{H}_5 + \text{N}_2 + \text{HCl}$

adjusted to pH 3–4 by addition of sodium acetate, the solution is mixed with a solution of the unsaturated compound in water, acetone, or other solvent, and about 0.1 mole of cupric chloride dihydrate is added, which usually initiates liberation of nitrogen. Yields usually are low, but the reaction affords the most convenient route to compounds of specific types, for example 2-hydroxy-3-aryl-1,4-naphthoquinones (4) and 5-arylfurfurals (5). A simple route to arylmaleic anhydrides is by arylation of N-phenylmaleimide followed by saponification and

(4)   (5)

10–20%   Yields   50–90%

6.

recyclization (6). In some cases, for example with the dimethyl esters of maleic and fumaric acids, the reaction affords an addition product (7, two stereoisomers).

7. $\underset{\text{CHCO}_2\text{CH}_3}{\overset{\text{CHCO}_2\text{CH}_3}{\|}}$ $\xrightarrow{p\text{-Cl-C}_6\text{H}_4\text{N}_2\text{Cl}}$ $\underset{\text{ClCHCO}_2\text{CH}_3}{\overset{p\text{-ClC}_6\text{H}_4\text{CHCO}_2\text{CH}_3}{|}}$

In general, reaction is facilitated by electron-attracting groups on the olefinic double bond and by electron-releasing groups in the diazonium salt. Thus benzenediazonium chloride fails to react with acrylic acid as its p-chloro derivative does (1). Dienes react particularly well to give products of 1,4-addition (8), convertible by dehydrohalogenation into aryldienes. A free-radical mechanism is now favored.

8. $p\text{-}NO_2C_6H_4N_2Cl \xrightarrow{\quad CH_2=CHCH=CH_2 \quad}$

$$p\text{-}NO_2C_6H_4CH_2CH=CHCH_2Cl \xrightarrow[\text{57-61\%(overall)}]{\quad KOH \quad} p\text{-}NO_2C_6H_4CH=CHCH=CH_2$$

1-p-Nitrophenylbutadiene-1,3
(m.p. 79°)

21.29   Reduction to Arylhydrazines. — Reduction of a diazonium salt with the calculated amount of stannous chloride at a low temperature, or better with excess sodium sulfite in a warm solution, results in formation of the corresponding arylhydrazine. The reaction probably proceeds through the diazo chloride ($C_6H_5N=NCl$) or diazo sulfonate ($C_6H_5N=NSO_3Na$) present in equilibrium with the diazonium salt. The product can be isolated as either the hydro-

$$[Ar\overset{+}{N}\equiv N]\overset{-}{X} \;\rightleftharpoons\; ArN=N-X \xrightarrow{4\,H} ArNHNH_3X \xrightarrow{NaOH} ArNHNH_2$$

chloride or the free base. An efficient procedure for the preparation of **phenylhydrazine** consists in diazotization of aniline in hydrochloric acid solution, reduction with sodium sulfite, treatment with hydrochloric acid to destroy excess

NH₂   1. HCl + NaNO₂, 0°
      2. Na₂SO₃, 60-70°   NHNH₂
      3. HCl, 100°
      4. NaOH
      ⟶
      80-84%

Phenylhydrazine (m.p. 24°,
b.p. 243°, pK_b 8.80)

sulfite and decompose the sulfamic acid sodium salt ($C_6H_5NHNHSO_3Na$), and liberation of the base with alkali. Phenylhydrazine when freshly distilled is a nearly colorless liquid, but it darkens rather rapidly on exposure to air as the result of oxidation. The hydrochloride, m.p. 243° dec., is more stable. Phenylhydrazine is toxic and must be kept off the skin; it is a valuable reagent for carbonyl compounds.

p-Nitrophenylhydrazine (m.p. 157°) is prepared by reduction of the diazonium salt with sodium sulfite. 2,4-Dinitrophenylhydrazine is prepared by condensation of 2,4-dinitrochlorobenzene with hydrazine (19.6).

21.30   Deamination. — Methods of reduction are available for replacement of the diazonium salt group by hydrogen, and hence for elimination of a primary amino substituent; the reaction is described as a deamination. The first known experimental procedure, discovered by Griess in 1864, consists in treatment of the diazonium salt with ethanol, which serves as a hydrogen donor and becomes oxidized to acetaldehyde. An appreciable amount of water must

$$ArN_2Cl + CH_3CH_2OH \longrightarrow ArH + N_2 + HCl + CH_3CHO$$

be avoided or else hydrolysis will occur, but the isolation of the dry diazonium salt is not always required. The utility of deamination is illustrated by the preparation of s-tribromobenzene, which is not accessible by direct bromination, for it contains o-p directing groups *meta* to one another. The desired orientation is achieved in the bromination of aniline because of the dominating directive influence of the amino group. Thus 2,4,6-tribromoaniline is obtainable from aniline in nearly quantitative yield, and can be converted into s-tribromobenzene by reduction of the diazotized amine with ethanol. The moist precipitate of tribromoaniline is dissolved in ethanol containing some benzene as diluent and

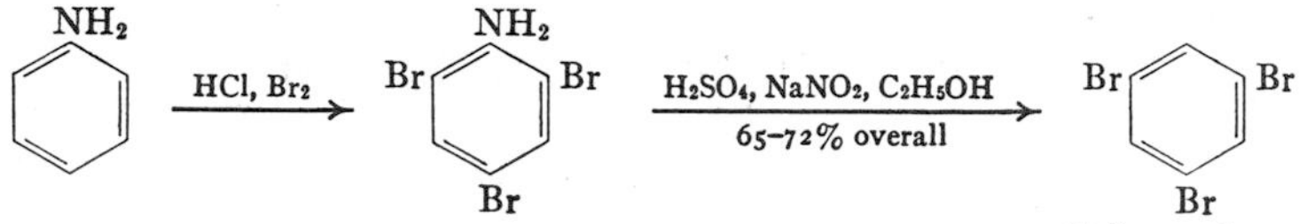

s-Tribromobenzene

treated with concentrated sulfuric acid followed by solid sodium nitrite; the diazonium salt is reduced as formed, with evolution of nitrogen and production of the deaminated product and acetaldehyde.

Deamination with ethanol gives good results with the diazonium salts of several polyhalo- and polynitroamines, but with simpler compounds a considerable amount of material is converted into the corresponding ethyl ether by the side reaction:

$$ArN_2Cl + HOC_2H_5 \rightarrow ArOC_2H_5 + N_2 + HCl$$

A superior and more convenient procedure is reduction of the diazonium salt in aqueous solution with a large excess of hypophosphorous acid, H_3PO_2 (J. Mai, 1902). The reaction proceeds in the cold, and the reagent can be added to the aqueous solution of the diazotized amine. The example cited illustrates the preparation through an amine derivative of a hydrocarbon difficult accessible

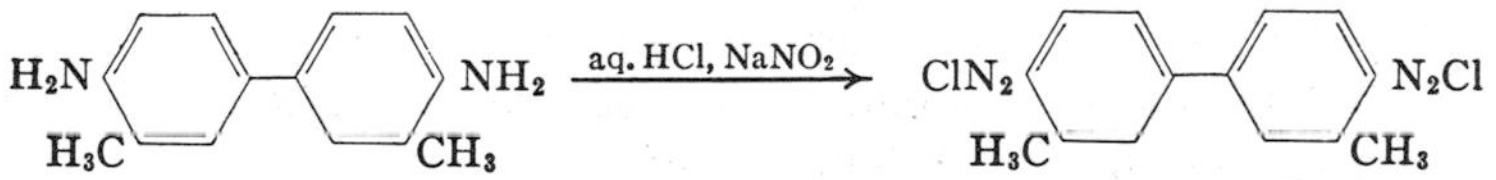

o-Tolidine　　　　　　　　　　Tetrazotized o-tolidine

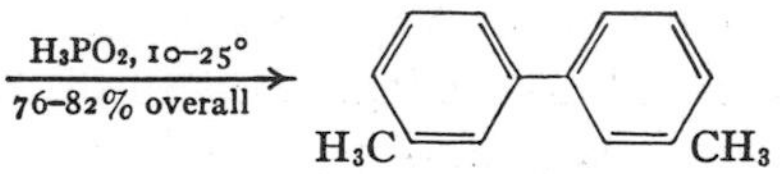

3,3'-Dimethyldiphenyl
(m-ditolyl, b.p. 115°/3 mm.)

by other methods. Diazonium salts can also be reduced in aqueous solution with sodium stannite (Friedländer,[1] 1889) or with alkaline formaldehyde solution (Brewster,[2] 1939). A further example of the value of deamination is the method for preparation of m-toluidine from p-toluidine. The amine is acetylated both to prevent oxidation and to permit ortho orientation, a nitro group is introduced, and after deacetylation the amino substituent is eliminated. The diazonium salt is not isolated but is produced under conditions suitable for the replacement reaction; thus m-nitro-p-toluidine is suspended in alcohol, treated with concen-

---

[1] Paul Friedländer, 1857–1923; b. Königsberg, Germany; asst. to Baeyer in Munich; Univ. Darmstadt; Ber., **57A**, 13 (1924)

[2] Ray Q. Brewster, b. 1892 Guthrie, Okla.; Ph.D. Chicago (Dains); Univ. Kansas

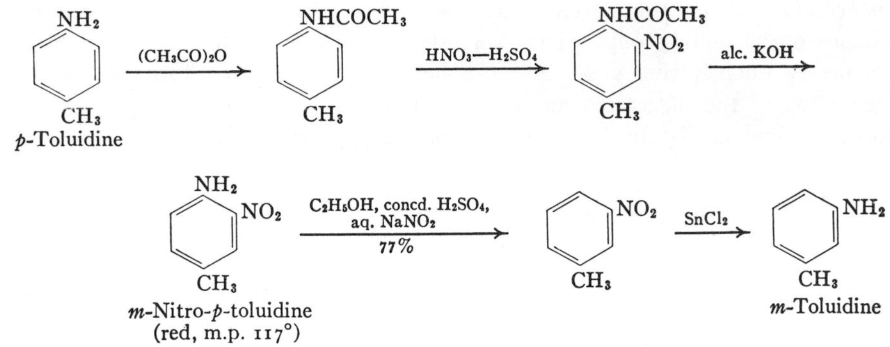

NH₂ → (CH₃CO)₂O → NHCOCH₃ → HNO₃—H₂SO₄ → NHCOCH₃ NO₂ → alc. KOH →

p-Toluidine (CH₃)   CH₃   CH₃

NH₂ NO₂ / CH₃ → C₂H₅OH, concd. H₂SO₄, aq. NaNO₂ / 77% → NO₂ / CH₃ → SnCl₂ → NH₂ / CH₃

m-Nitro-p-toluidine
(red, m.p. 117°)

m-Toluidine

trated sulfuric acid, and, after cooling, a concentrated aqueous solution of sodium nitrite is added in portions. Deamination provides a convenient route for preparation of 2,4,6-tribromobenzoic acid from m-nitrobenzoic acid.

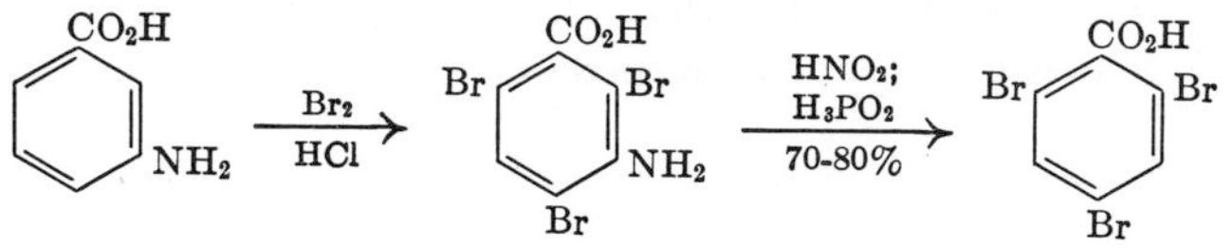

CO₂H / NH₂ → Br₂ HCl → CO₂H Br Br / NH₂ Br → HNO₂; H₃PO₂ 70-80% → CO₂H Br Br / Br

A new method of deamination conducted in a nonaqueous medium utilizes the readily precipitated borofluoride salts (J. B. Hendrickson, 1961). Either solid sodium borohydride is added to a chilled solution or suspension of the diazonium borofluoride or a chilled solution of NaBH₄ in dimethylformamide is added to a chilled solution of the diazonium salt in the same solvent. Yields are in the range 50–75%; NO₂, CO₂H, CO₂R, OR groups are not affected.

21.31   Coupling Reaction. — Diazonium salts react readily with phenols and aromatic amines to form bright-colored azo compounds in which the two aromatic rings are linked through the azo grouping, —N=N—. The smoothly proceeding union of the diazo component with the phenol or amine is described as coupling. Benzenediazonium chloride couples with phenol in alkaline solution very rapidly at ice-bath temperature to form p-hydroxyazobenzene (or p-benzeneazophenol). Since a diazonium salt undergoes change in alkaline

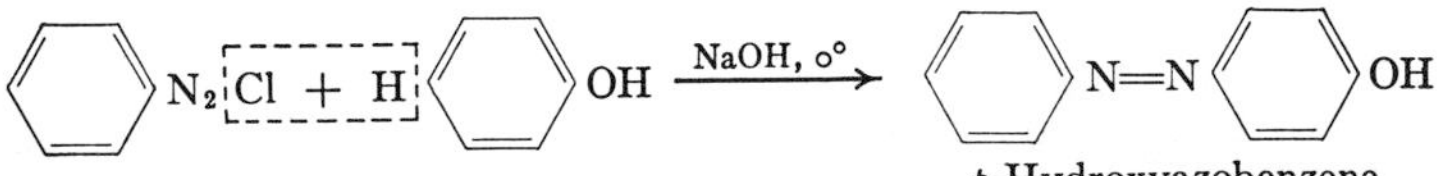

N₂Cl + H OH → NaOH, 0° → N=N OH

p-Hydroxyazobenzene
(orange, m.p. 152°)

solution with eventual formation of the *trans* diazotate, which fails to couple, the proper procedure is to stir the solution of benzenediazonium chloride slowly into a chilled solution of phenol containing sufficient alkali to neutralize the organic and inorganic acids in the resulting mixture and maintain suitable alkalinity. Coupling occurs so rapidly as to preclude destruction of the diazo component. Dimethylaniline couples in an analogous manner in an aqueous medium that is either neutral or weakly acidified with acetic acid, and gives a yellow p-benzeneazo

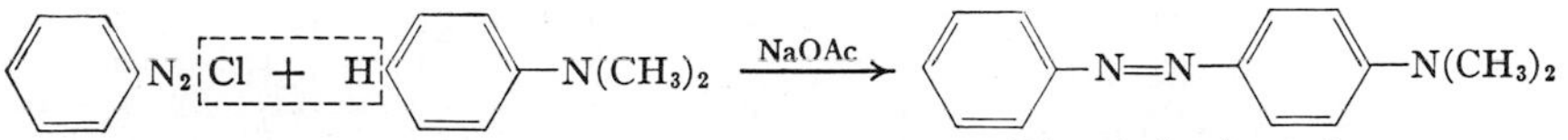

p-Dimethylaminoazobenzene
(yellow, m.p. 117°)

compound. These examples illustrate a reaction that is general to phenols and to tertiary amines having available a free position *ortho* or *para* to the hydroxyl or amino group. Where a choice is open, coupling occurs practically exclusively in the *para* position. The product of coupling of benzenediazonium chloride with phenol contains at most 1% of *o*-hydroxyazobenzene (orange, m.p. 83°); the small amount of *ortho* isomer can be separated from the nonvolatile *para* compound by steam distillation. Although there is a marked preference for *para* substitution, coupling occurs readily enough in the *ortho* position if this alone is available, for example:

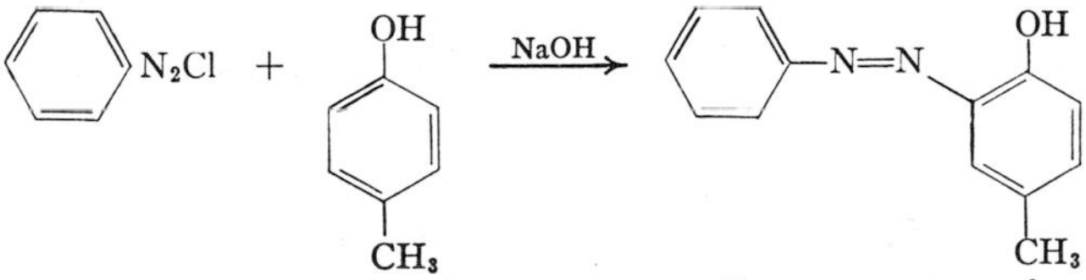

p-Cresol   Benzeneazo-*p*-cresol
(yellow, m.p. 108°)

E. L. Martin discovered (1961) a new class of colored compounds exemplified by the bright red product readily formed by reaction of N,N-dimethylaniline in dimethylformamide with 3-chloro-2-cyanomaleimide. Elimination of hydrogen chloride between the two reactants gives *p*-(2-cyano-3-maleimidyl)-N,N-dimethylaniline.

The coupling reaction is spectacular because of the rapid formation of brightly colored products from colorless components. The reaction is comparable to that of C-nitrosation with nitrous acid (21.19) with respect to exclusive *para* orientation and rapidity of combination in aqueous solution even at 0°. Both reactions are specific to amines and phenols and depend on the powerful directive influence of the hydroxyl and amino group. Studies of the rate of coupling in solutions of varying acidity indicate that one reacting species is always the electrophilic diazonium ion and that the other, in an amine coupling (1), is the nonionized amine, and in a phenol coupling (2), is the phenoxide ion (Bartlett, 1941). In the pH range 2–6 the velocity of an amine coupling increases with decreasing acidity till

1. ArN_2^+ + $C_6H_5N(CH_3)_2$

2. ArN_2^+ + $C_6H_5O^-$

the concentration of free amine reaches a maximum, and in a phenol coupling in the region pH 5–8 the rate of reaction increases with increasing pH because a greater proportion of the reactive phenoxide component becomes available. This interpretation not only accords with the general concept of other aromatic substitutions but extends the evidence. Here the entering group is an actual cation, and that it is attracted to the phenoxide ion more strongly than to the phenol is a consequence of the inductive and resonance effect of the negatively charged oxygen, which results in increased electron density at the *ortho* and *para* positions. A positive charge on the nitrogen atom of an amine would have the opposite effect, and hence it is the free amine that couples.

Just as primary and secondary amines are attacked by nitrous acid in the amino group rather than in the ring, such amines ordinarily react with diazonium salts to give N-substitution products known as diazoamino derivatives. Thus benzenediazonium chloride and aniline combine to form diazoaminobenzene. A convenient procedure consists in dissolving two equivalents of aniline in three

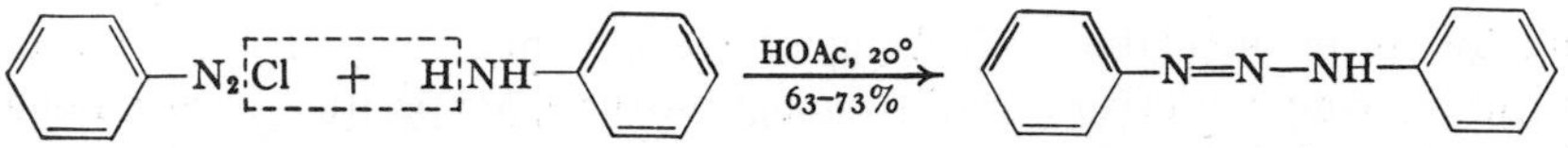

Diazoaminobenzene
(yellow, m.p. 98°)

equivalents of hydrochloric acid and adding one equivalent of sodium nitrite, followed by two equivalents of sodium acetate. The hydrogen in the system —N=N—NH— is activated and apparently labile, for the same product results from condensation of benzenediazonium chloride with *p*-toluidine as from *p*-toluenediazonium chloride with aniline; the probable structure is indicated. Like

$$C_6H_5N_2Cl \ + \ p\text{-}H_2NC_6H_4CH_3 \qquad\qquad C_6H_5NH_2 \ + \ p\text{-}CH_3C_6H_4N_2Cl$$

$$C_6H_5N{=}NNHC_6H_4CH_3(p)$$
4-Methyldiazoamino-
benzene (yellow, m.p. 91°)

N-nitrosoamines, diazoamino compounds rearrange under the influence of acid catalysts with transposition of the arylazo group to the *para* position. Thus diazoaminobenzene rearranges to *p*-aminoazobenzene, the product that would have

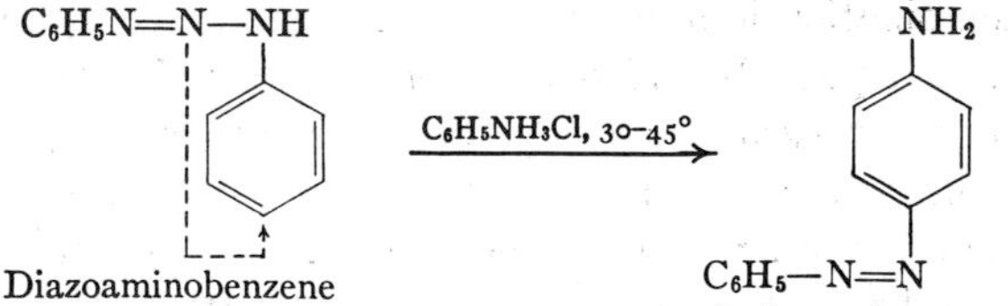

$$C_6H_5N{=}N{-}NH$$
Diazoaminobenzene

$$C_6H_5NH_3Cl, \ 30\text{-}45°$$

NH₂

$$C_6H_5{-}N{=}N$$
p-Aminoazobenzene
(yellow, m.p. 126°)

resulted from direct coupling. Such rearrangements proceed slowly under the influence of mineral acids at room temperature and can be brought about more readily by gentle heating in the presence of the amine hydrochloride, often with use of an excess of the free amine as diluent. Test experiments indicate that the rearrangement actually involves fission of the diazoamino compound under the influence of the acidic catalyst to the diazonium salt and the amine and recombination of the components with ring substitution. Secondary amines, N-methylaniline for example, react similarly, and yield as the initial product the N-substituted aryldiazoamino compound, which can be rearranged to the azo compound. An initial attachment of the diazo residue to nitrogen is the usual but not the invariable mode of reaction of primary and secondary amines. Direct coupling to an aminoazo compound occurs under the following conditions: (1) with a particularly reactive amino component (*m*-phenylenediamine, *m*-toluidine, naphthylamines), (2) with a highly reactive diazo component (*p*-nitrobenzenediazonium chloride), or (3) in aqueous formic acid solution, which is acidic enough to cause the N-azo compound to be unstable but not to inhibit combination of the diazonium salt with the amine.

Very few aromatic compounds other than phenols and amines are capable of diazo coupling. Mesitylene couples, but only with a particularly reactive diazonium salt. An electron-attracting nitro group *ortho* or *para* to the diazonium salt group enhances the electrophilic character of the ion, and a progressive increase in reactivity is noted with the 2,4-dinitro and 2,4,6-trinitro derivatives. Thus mesitylene couples with the powerfully electrophilic 2,4,6-trinitrobenzenedi-

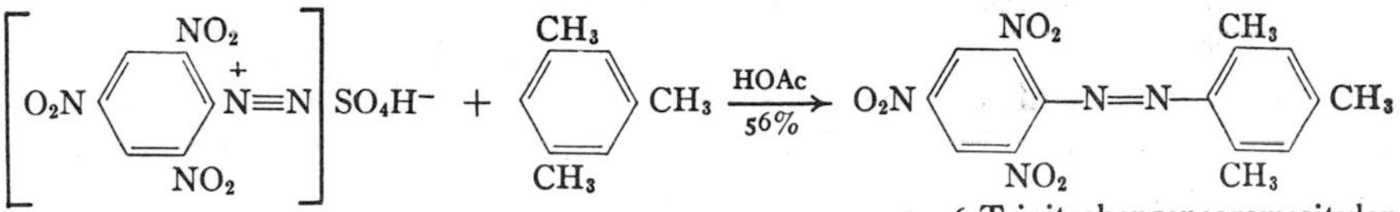

2,4,6-Trinitrobenzeneazomesitylene
(dark red, m p. 189° dec.)

azonium sulfate (diazotized picramide). Halogen atoms in *ortho* and *para* positions have some influence in increasing the coupling potency of the diazo component.

Phenol ethers are distinctly less reactive than free phenols in nitrations and brominations, and they do not couple with benzenediazonium chloride. With suitable activation by nitro substituents in the diazo component, however, coupling can be accomplished in acetic acid solution; for example anisole couples with 2,4-dinitrobenzenediazonium chloride.

The outstanding property of the azo compounds is the color, and a considerable number of the products obtainable by coupling possess other attributes required in dyes. A preparative use is the synthesis of *ortho* and *para* aminophenols and diamines, obtainable by reductive fission of the azo linkage. Thus *p*-hydroxyazobenzene is cleaved by reduction with stannous chloride or sodium hydrosulfite to *p*-aminophenol and aniline. An amino group can be introduced into the *para* position of phenol by coupling with diazotized aniline and reduction of the azo compound. Separation of the two amines resulting on reduction is facilitated by

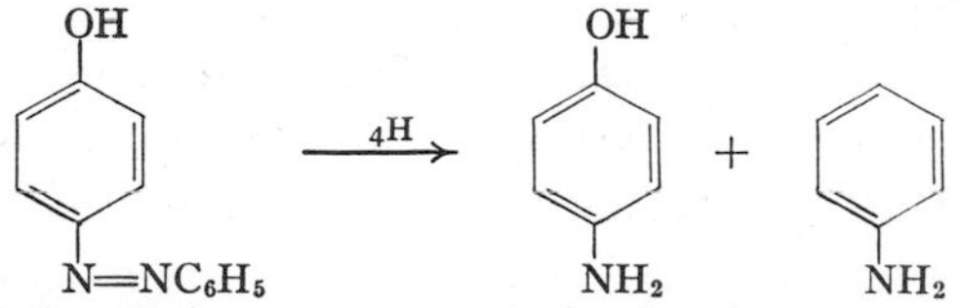

p-Hydroxyazobenzene   *p*-Aminophenol

employing *p*-diazobenzenesulfonic acid, for the sulfanilic acid subsequently formed on reduction is easily removed as the water-soluble sodium salt:

$$p\text{-HOC}_6\text{H}_4\text{N}{=}\text{NC}_6\text{H}_4\text{SO}_3\text{Na} \xrightarrow{\text{Na}_2\text{S}_2\text{O}_4} p\text{-HOC}_6\text{H}_4\text{NH}_2 + \text{H}_2\text{NC}_6\text{H}_4\text{SO}_3\text{Na}$$

An interesting difference is observable in the properties of azo compounds having a hydroxyl group in the positions *ortho* and *para* to the azo linkage. The *para* hydroxy compounds dissolve freely in aqueous alkali, whereas the *ortho* compounds are either insoluble in dilute alkali in the cold or at most moderately soluble in hot alkali. The difference is illustrated in the properties of two isomeric

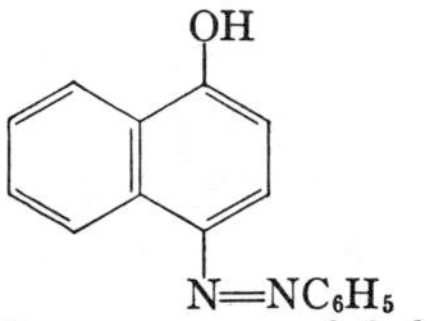

4-Benzeneazo-1-naphthol

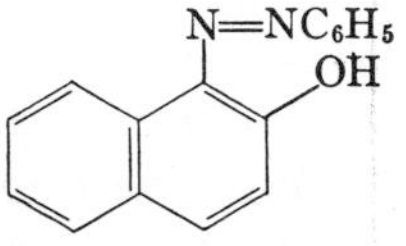

1-Benzeneazo-2-naphthol

hydroxyazo compounds of the naphthalene series; the first is soluble in alkali and the second insoluble. A likely explanation of the striking difference is that the *ortho* compounds exist in a chelated condition, as represented in the formulation. The presence of a chelate ring would account also for the fact, noted above, that *o*-hydroxyazobenzene is volatile with steam, whereas the *para* isomer is not, since hydrogen bonding would moderate the hydroxylic characteristics of the *ortho* compound.

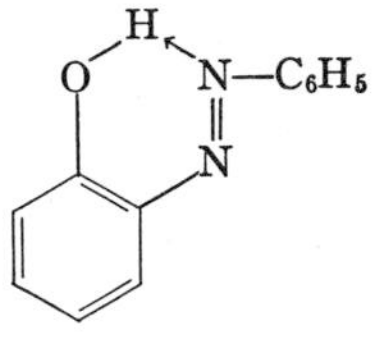

REARRANGEMENTS

21.32   Stevens Rearrangement. — Stevens[1] found (1928) that the quaternary ammonium salt (1), when generated from the bromide in water solution undergoes smooth rearrangement with migration of the benzyl group from

$$\text{C}_6\text{H}_5\text{COCH}_2\overset{+}{\text{N}}(\text{CH}_3)_2\text{OH}^- \underset{\underset{\text{CH}_2\text{C}_6\text{H}_5}{|}}{\xrightarrow{-\text{H}_2\text{O}}} \text{C}_6\text{H}_5\text{COCHN(CH}_3)_2$$

(1)   (2)

nitrogen to carbon. The migrating group also can be of the types: allyl, benzhydryl = $(\text{C}_6\text{H}_5)_2\text{CH}—$, or phenacyl = $\text{C}_6\text{H}_5\text{COCH}_2—$. That the rearrangement is intramolecular was established by rearrangement of two different quaternary ammonium salts and isolation of no crossed products. Unlike the usual rearrangements which proceed through carbonium ions, the Stevens rearrangement must proceed through a carbanion, in the present case an internal salt (4, an ylide or alkylide), and the benzyl group migrates with only a sextet of electrons (Hauser,

[1] Thomas Stevens Stevens, b. 1900 Renfrew, Scotland; Ph.D. Oxford (Perkin, Jr.); Univ. Sheffield

1951). The reaction is of the $S_{N}i$ type and a migrating α-phenylethyl group retains its configuration (Brewster,[1] 1952).

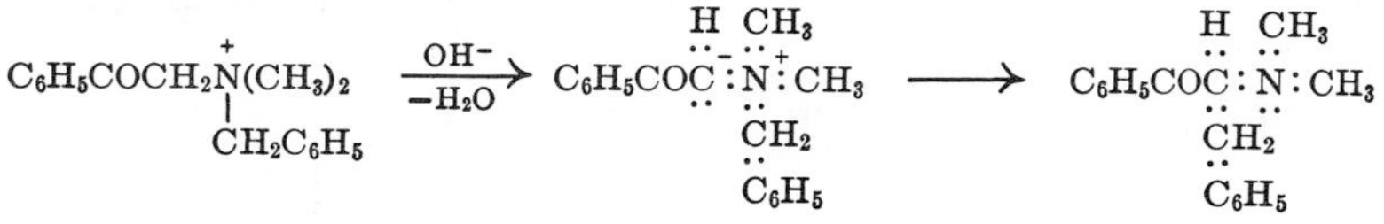

$$C_6H_5COCH_2\overset{+}{N}(CH_3)_2 \quad \xrightarrow[-H_2O]{OH^-} \quad C_6H_5CO\overset{H}{\underset{\underset{C_6H_5}{\overset{|}{CH_2}}}{C}}:\overset{CH_3}{\underset{}{N}}:CH_3 \quad \longrightarrow \quad C_6H_5CO\overset{H}{\underset{\underset{C_6H_5}{\overset{|}{CH_2}}}{C}}:\overset{CH_3}{\underset{}{N}}:CH_3$$

$$\underset{CH_2C_6H_5}{|}$$

$$\text{(3)} \qquad\qquad\qquad \text{(4)} \qquad\qquad\qquad \text{(5)}$$

21.33   Sommelet Rearrangement. — An analogous rearrangement reported by Marcel Sommelet (1937) involves conversion of benzhydryltrimethylammonium hydroxide into o-benzylbenzyldimethylamine. The ylide mechanism formulated was postulated by Wittig (1948) and by Hauser (1951).

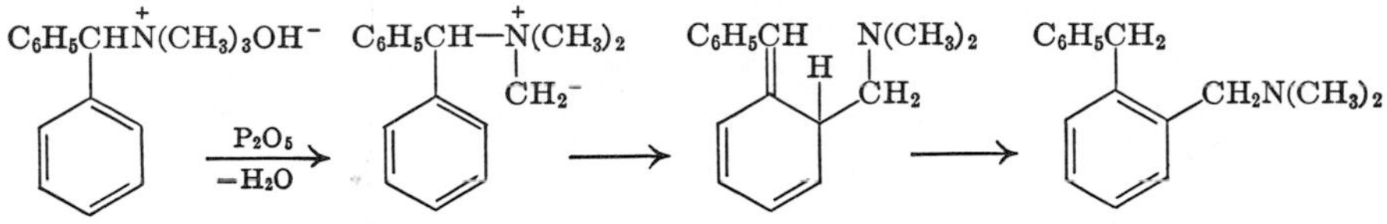

$$C_6H_5\overset{+}{CH}N(CH_3)_3OH^- \quad C_6H_5CH-\overset{+}{N}(CH_3)_2 \quad C_6H_5\overset{H}{\underset{}{CH}}\;N(CH_3)_2 \quad C_6H_5CH_2$$

$$\xrightarrow[-H_2O]{P_2O_5} \qquad \longrightarrow \qquad \longrightarrow \qquad CH_2N(CH_3)_2$$

Benzyltrimethylammonium hydroxide is rearranged by sodamide in liquid ammonia in high yield. Similar treatment of 2,4,6-trimethylbenzyltrimethyl-

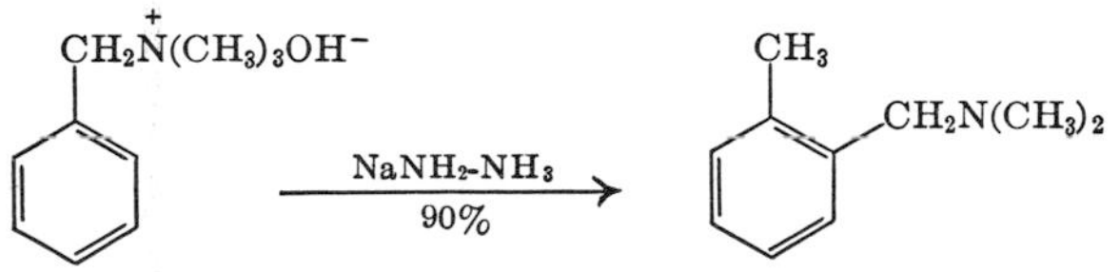

$$CH_2\overset{+}{N}(CH_3)_3OH^-$$

$$\xrightarrow[90\%]{NaNH_2-NH_3}$$

$$CH_3$$
$$CH_2N(CH_3)_2$$

ammonium hydroxide (1) afforded the intermediate alicyclic amine (2), isolated by steam distillation of the alkaline reaction mixture (Hauser, 1956). On treatment with acid the alicyclic amine is converted into isodurene (3); when heated it undergoes rearrangement to the aromatic amine (4).

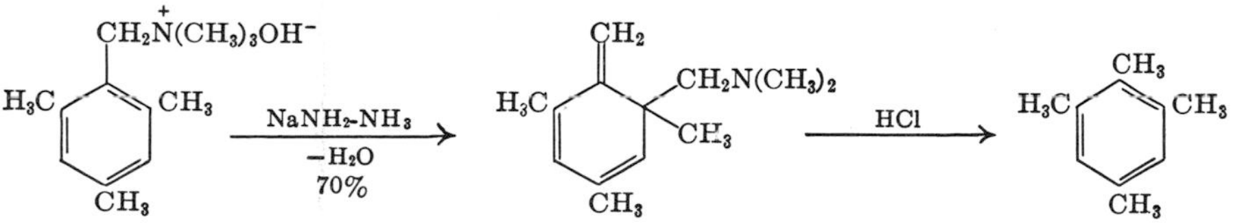

$$CH_2\overset{+}{N}(CH_3)_3OH^-$$

$$H_3C \qquad CH_3 \qquad \xrightarrow[70\%]{NaNH_2-NH_3 \atop -H_2O} \qquad H_3C \qquad \underset{CH_3}{\overset{CH_2}{\Big|}} \qquad \overset{CH_2N(CH_3)_2}{\underset{CH_3}{\Big|}} \qquad \xrightarrow{HCl} \qquad H_3C \qquad \overset{CH_3}{\underset{CH_3}{\Big|}} CH_3$$

$$\underset{CH_3}{|}$$

$$\text{(1)} \qquad\qquad\qquad\qquad \text{(2)} \qquad\qquad\qquad\qquad \text{(3) Isodurene}$$

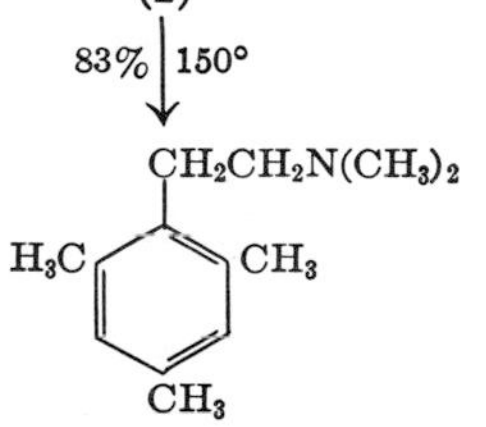

$$83\% \Big| 150°$$

$$CH_2CH_2N(CH_3)_2$$

$$H_3C \qquad CH_3$$

$$\underset{CH_3}{|}$$

$$\text{(4)}$$

James H. Brewster, b. 1922 Ft. Collins, Colo.; Ph.D. Illinois (Snyder); Purdue Univ.

21.34   Wittig Ether → Carbinol Rearrangement. — This reaction is related
to the Stevens rearrangement: benzyl ethers are rearranged to carbinols by means of phenyllithium (Wittig, 1942–47) or of potassium amide (Hauser,
1951).

$$\underset{C_6H_5CH_2O}{\overset{CH_3}{|}} \quad \xrightarrow[-NH_3]{KNH_2} \quad \underset{C_6H_5C\text{-}HO}{\overset{CH_3}{|}} \quad \longrightarrow \quad \underset{C_6H_5CHO^-}{\overset{CH_3}{|}} \quad \xrightarrow{H^+} \quad \underset{C_6H_5CHOH}{\overset{CH_3}{|}}$$

PROBLEMS

1. Write equations for the alternative methods of preparing *o*- and *p*-anisidine mentioned in 21.13.
2. In what respects are amines subject to oxidation? Indicate two methods by which stabilization can be achieved, and explain how each modification influences substitutions.
3. Describe three instances of initial attack by a reagent on the nitrogen atom of an amine, with
   subsequent rearrangement into the ring.
4. How can *p*-bromophenol be prepared from acetanilide?
5. Indicate reactions by which *o*-toluidine can be converted into phthalic acid.
6. Utilizing *p*-toluidine as the starting material, devise methods for the preparation of:
   (*a*) *p*-Bromobenzoic acid   (*d*) 4,4′-Dimethyldiphenyl
   (*b*) *p*-Tolylhydrazine   (*e*) 4-Methyl-2-aminophenol
   (*c*) 3,5-Dibromotoluene   (*f*) N-Methyl-*p*-toluidine
7. How could N-methylaniline be converted into 4-amino-N-methylaniline?
8. Suggest methods for the preparation of the following compounds:
   (*a*) *m*-Chloroaniline   (*b*) *m*-Cresol   (*c*) *m*-Bromochlorobenzene
9. Starting with hydrocarbons available from coal tar or by ready synthesis, suggest methods for
   the preparation of the following compounds:
   (*a*) 2,4,6-Trimethylphenol   (*d*) 2,5-Dimethyl-4-aminophenol
   (*b*) 2-Cyano-1,4-dimethylbenzene   (*e*) 3-Amino-4-methylacetophenone
   (*c*) 4-Chlorobenzene-1,3-dicarboxylic acid

Chapter 22

PHENOLS

22.1   **Properties.** — Phenols usually are crystalline solids, but certain alkylphenols are liquids (*m*-cresol). Phenol itself is a solid at room temperature, but the melting point (43°) is greatly depressed by small amounts of water, and liquid preparations containing 2–10% of water find some use in medicine (cauterization) and in extraction operations. Introduction of the phenolic hydroxyl group produces a marked increase in boiling point and also raises the r   ; point, particularly when in the *para* position to a methyl, halogen, or   substituent, as shown by the data in Table 22.1.

The most   inctive property of phenols is the weakly acidic character, attributable to combination of a hydroxyl group with an unsaturated ring, or to the presence of an enolic grouping: —CH=C(OH)—. Phenol is a weak acid, pK_a 10.0, and it forms salts (phenolates) with sodium hydroxide but not with the carbonate. This behavior is typical and distinguishes phenols from carboxylic acids, which react with bicarbonate. An aromatic substance found to be more soluble in sodium hydroxide solution than in water but showing no increased solubility in the presence of sodium carbonate is likely to be a phenol. Dissociation constants of substituted phenols show little regularity, except in the series of nitro compounds. The three mononitrophenols are more acidic (pK_a 7.2–8) than the parent substance, and the effect is greatly magnified in 2,4-dinitrophenol (pK_a 4.0) and in picric acid, which is nearly as strongly acidic as a mineral acid. Stabilization of the anionic form by nitro groups is the counterpart of suppression of the basic dissociation of the amines, and likewise can be attributed to inductive and resonance effects.

Properties of representative polyhydric phenols are listed in Table 22.2. Among dihydroxy compounds the symmetrical *para* derivative, hydroquinone, has the

TABLE 22.1. MONOHYDRIC PHENOLS

NAME	FORMULA	M.P., °C.	B.P., °C.	$pK_a^{25°}$
Phenol	C_6H_5OH	43	181	10.0
o-Cresol	$CH_3C_6H_4OH(1,2)$	30	191	10.20
m-Cresol	$CH_3C_6H_4OH(1,3)$	11	201	10.01
p-Cresol	$CH_3C_6H_4OH(1,4)$	35.5	201	10.17
o-Chlorophenol	$ClC_6H_4OH(1,2)$	8	176	9.11
m-Chlorophenol	$ClC_6H_4OH(1,3)$	29	214	
p-Chlorophenol	$ClC_6H_4OH(1,4)$	37	217	9.39
p-Bromophenol	$BrC_6H_4OH(1,4)$	64	236	
2,4,6-Trichlorophenol	$HOC_6H_2Cl_3(1,2,4,6)$	69	244	7.59
2,4,6-Tribromophenol	$HOC_6H_2Br_3(1,2,4,6)$	95		
o-Nitrophenol	$HOC_6H_4NO_2(1,2)$	44.5	214	7.21
m-Nitrophenol	$HOC_6H_4NO_2(1,3)$	96		8.0
p-Nitrophenol	$HOC_6H_4NO_2(1,4)$	114		7.16
2,4-Dinitrophenol	$HOC_6H_3(NO_2)_2(1,2,4)$	113		4.0
Guaiacol	$HOC_6H_4OCH_3(1,2)$	32	205	7.0
Anol	$HOC_6H_4CH{=}CHCH_3(1,4)$	93		
Eugenol	$HOC_6H_3(OCH_3)CH_2CH{=}CH_2(1,2,4)$		248	
Isoeugenol	$HOC_6H_3(OCH_3)CH{=}CHCH_3(1,2,4)$	33	267	
Saligenin	$HOC_6H_4CH_2OH(1,2)$	87		
Carvacrol	$HOC_6H_3(CH_3) \cdot CH(CH_3)_2(1,2,5)$	1	237	8.4
Thymol	$HOC_6H_3(CH_3) \cdot CH(CH_3)_2(1,5,2)$	51	233	
o-Hydroxyacetophenone	$HOC_6H_4COCH_3(1,2)$	liq.	97 [10 mm.]	
p-Hydroxyacetophenone	$HOC_6H_4COCH_3(1,4)$	110	148 [3 mm.]	
o-Hydroxydiphenyl	$C_6H_5C_6H_4OH(1,2)$	56	275	
p-Hydroxydiphenyl	$C_6H_5C_6H_4OH(1,4)$	165	308	
o-Cyclohexylphenol	$C_6H_{11}C_6H_4OH(1,2)$	57		
p-Cyclohexylphenol	$C_6H_{11}C_6H_4OH(1,4)$	133		

TABLE 22.2. POLYHYDRIC PHENOLS AND AMINOPHENOLS

NAME	FORMULA	M.P., °C.	B.P., °C.	$pK_a^{20-25°}$	SOLUBILITY, g./100 cc. $H_2O^{20°}$
Catechol	$C_6H_4(OH)_2(1,2)$	105	245	9.4	45
Resorcinol	$C_6H_4(OH)_2(1,3)$	110	281	9.4	123
Hydroquinone	$C_6H_4(OH)_2(1,4)$	170		10.0	8
Pyrogallol	$C_6H_3(OH)_3(1,2,3)$	133	309	7.0	62
Hydroxyhydroquinone	$C_6H_3(OH)_3(1,2,4)$	140			
Phloroglucinol	$C_6H_3(OH)_3(1,3,5)$	219		7.0	1
o-Aminophenol	$HOC_6H_4NH_2(1,2)$	174		9.7	
m-Aminophenol	$HOC_6H_4NH_2(1,3)$	123			
p-Aminophenol	$HOC_6H_4NH_2(1,4)$	186		8.16	

highest melting point, and the symmetrically trisubstituted 1,3,5-compound, phloroglucinol, melts higher than its isomers. Solubility data indicate that multiple hydroxyl groups increase the solubility in water, but that the effect is counteracted by symmetry of structure.

PREPARATION

22.2 General Methods. — Generally applicable methods for preparation of phenols are **alkali fusion of a sulfonate** (20.7) and **hydrolysis of a diazonium salt** (21.23), and these two reactions render phenols available from hydrocarbons through initial sulfonation or nitration. A third method, alkaline **hydrolysis of an aryl halide,** is applied industrially to the preparation of phenol from chlorobenzene at a high temperature and pressure, and is applicable under ordinary conditions to the highly reactive polynitro halogen compounds. A fourth method, effective in special instances, consists in **dehydrogenation of a hydroaromatic ketone** conducted either with a palladium or platinum catalyst or with sulfur or

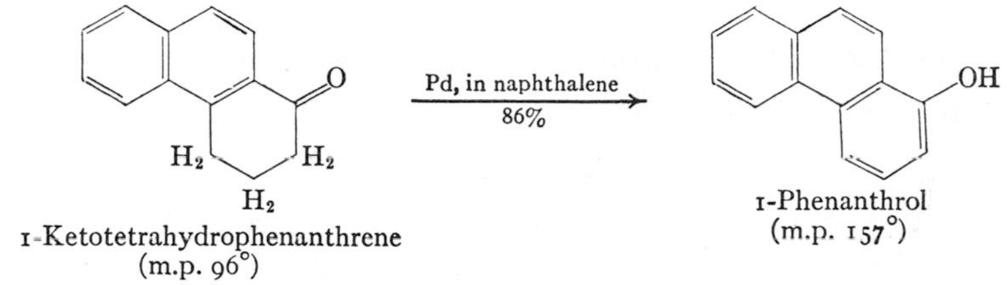
O
H2
H2
H2
1-Ketotetrahydrophenanthrene
(m.p. 96°)
Pd, in naphthalene
86%
OH
1-Phenanthrol
(m.p. 157°)

selenium. The reaction probably proceeds by removal of two hydrogen atoms with formation of an unstable keto form of dihydrobenzenoid structure, which isomerizes to the phenol. Temperature control is essential, for under too drastic

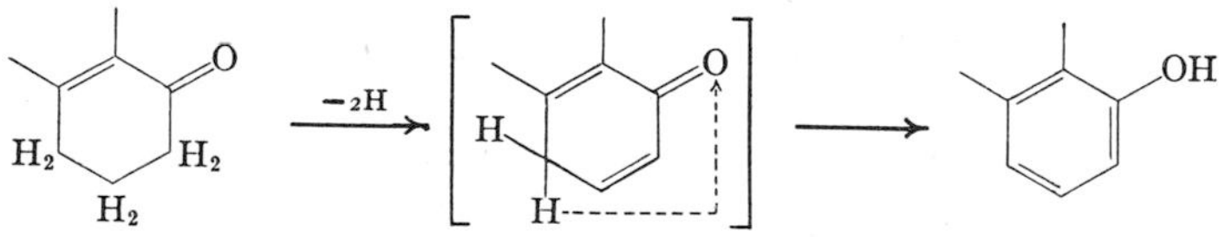
O
H2
H2
H2
−2H
H
H
O
OH

conditions the hydroxyl group is lost. An alternative procedure involving the same intermediate is α-bromination of the ketone and elimination of hydrogen bromide by treatment with a basic reagent as in the following example:

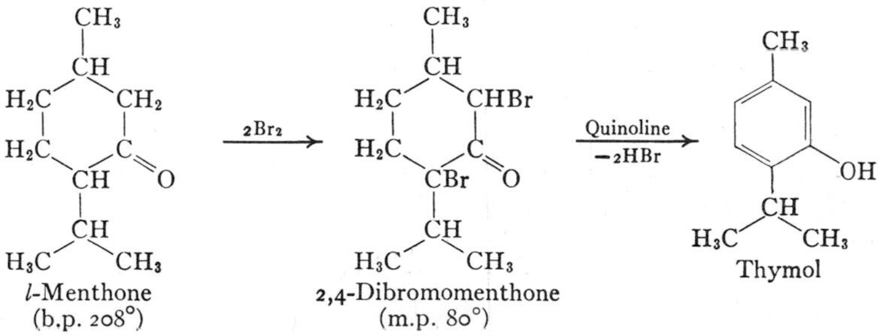
CH3
CH
H2C
CH2
H2C
C
CH
O
CH
H3C
CH3
l-Menthone
(b.p. 208°)
2Br2
CHBr
CBr
2,4-Dibromomenthone
(m.p. 80°)
Quinoline
−2HBr
OH
Thymol

A novel route to phenols is based upon Walling's discovery (8.7) of the reaction ROOMgBr + RMgBr → 2 ROMgBr (Lawesson,[1] 1959). *t*-Butyl hydroperoxide is treated with one equivalent of ethylmagnesium bromide to form the MgBr

[1] Sven-Olav Lawesson, b. 1926 Bräcke, Sweden; Ph.D. Uppsala (Fredga); Univ. Uppsala

$$(CH_3)_3COOH + C_2H_5MgBr \rightarrow (CH_3)_3COOMgBr + C_2H_6$$
$$(CH_3)_3COOMgBr + C_6H_5MgBr \rightarrow (CH_3)_3COMgBr + C_6H_5OMgBr$$

derivative, and one equivalent of phenylmagnesium bromide is then added. Hydrolysis of the reaction mixture affords phenol in 80% yield. Alkyl halides react similarly to give alcohols, and yields of phenols and alcohols are generally high. The reaction is useful for replacement of halogen by hydroxyl where direct hydrolysis is inapplicable or complicated by side reactions of elimination or rearrangement. Another method involves slow addition of phenylmagnesium bromide solution to methyl borate at $-80°$ (Hawthorne,[1] 1957). The resulting mixture of phenyl-

$$C_6H_5MgBr \xrightarrow{(CH_3O)_3B; H_2O (H^+)} \begin{Bmatrix} C_6H_5B(OH)_2 \\ (C_6H_5)_2BOH \end{Bmatrix} \xrightarrow{H_2O_2} C_6H_5OH$$

boronic and diphenylboronic acid is cleaved with hydrogen peroxide in ether to give the phenol (yields 60–78%).

SPECIFIC PREPARATIONS

22.3   **Phenol.** — During World War I the phenol required for production of picric acid was produced from benzene by sulfonation and alkali fusion.   The overall yield was only 60–75%, and a considerable loss was entailed

$$C_6H_6 \xrightarrow{H_2SO_4 + 9.5\% SO_3, 50-70°} C_6H_5SO_3H(Na) \xrightarrow{NaOH, 320-350°} C_6H_5ONa(H)$$

in the sulfonation process, which reaches equilibrium with the accumulation of water from the reaction. In a vapor-phase process introduced in 1923 with resumption of production of synthetic phenol to meet increasing requirements of material for production of phenol-formaldehyde plastics, sulfonation was accomplished at 170–180° with concentrated sulfuric acid.

An innovation, announced by the Dow Chemical Company in 1928, consists in hydrolysis of chlorobenzene by a dilute aqueous solution of alkali at high temperature and pressure. Hydrolysis is conducted as a continuous process by flowing the reactants through a pipe line system capable of maintaining the

$$C_6H_5Cl \xrightarrow[2000-3000 \text{ lbs./sq. in.}]{6-8\% \text{ aq. NaOH, 300°,}} C_6H_5ONa \xrightarrow{HCl} C_6H_5OH$$

required temperature and pressure and of suitable length (about one mile) to provide the period required for reaction (about twenty minutes). An inevitable side reaction results in formation of diphenyl oxide, and accumulation of this

$$C_6H_5ONa + C_6H_5OH \rightleftharpoons C_6H_5OC_6H_5 + NaOH$$
Diphenyl oxide

material, for which no large-scale use has arisen, would detract from the efficiency of the process. A solution of this apparent difficulty followed from the observation that the by-product is formed in a reversible reaction and can be kept from

---

[1] M. F. Hawthorne, b. Ft. Scott, Kans.; Ph.D. Univ. Calif. Los Angeles (Cram); Rohm and Haas Co.

accumulating by simply recirculating the amount necessary to meet the equilibrium requirement.   The tar waste remaining from distillation of the phenol contains 20–25% of a mixture of *o*- and *p*-hydroxydiphenyl, in which the *para* isomer predominates.   These by-products, which find some use, arise either from condensation of chlorobenzene to the chlorodiphenyls and hydrolysis ($2C_6H_5Cl \rightarrow C_6H_5C_6H_4Cl \rightarrow C_6H_5C_6H_4OH$) or by condensation of chlorobenzene with phenol ($C_6H_5Cl + C_6H_5OH \rightarrow C_6H_5C_6H_4OH$).

In the German Raschig process, benzene is converted through chlorobenzene into phenol by a sequence of reactions at atmospheric pressure with utilization of atmospheric oxygen as the only reagent not regenerated.   Benzene is chlorinated by halogen generated by the catalyzed oxidation of hydrogen chloride with oxygen, and on catalytic hydrolysis hydrogen chloride is regenerated (97% recovery):

$$C_6H_6 + HCl + \tfrac{1}{2}O_2 \xrightarrow{\text{Catalyst, 230°}} C_6H_5Cl + H_2O$$

$$C_6H_5Cl + H_2O \xrightarrow{\text{Catalyst, 425°}} C_6H_5OH + HCl$$

A newer process involving alkaline fission of cumene hydroperoxide has been described (4.16).

22.4   **Derivatives of Phenol.** — The ether derivatives, **anisole**, $C_6H_5OCH_3$ (b.p. 154°), and **phenetole**, $C_6H_5OC_2H_5$ (b.p. 172°), are liquids with an aromatic fragrance, obtained conveniently by alkylation of phenol with dimethyl or diethyl sulfate in a weakly alkaline aqueous medium.   This method is usual in preparation of phenol ethers, but in special instances alkylation is accomplished with diazomethane or diazoethane.   A phenol often is converted into its ether to provide protection against oxidation or other undesired side reaction during transformations not involving the oxygen function, for the masking group subsequently can be removed and the hydroxyl group regenerated.   Anisole can be demethylated by refluxing in acetic acid solution with 48% hydrobromic acid or by heating with hydriodic acid at 130°: $C_6H_5OCH_3 + HX \rightarrow C_6H_5OH + CH_3X$.   Aluminum chloride is a further effective dealkylating agent; the ether can be heated with aluminum chloride alone at 120°, or more sensitive ethers are refluxed in benzene or carbon disulfide solution with an amount of the reagent equivalent to the number of alkoxyl groups present.   High yields in the fission

$$C_6H_5OCH_3 \xrightarrow{AlCl_3} \left[\begin{array}{c} C_6H_5 \\ \diagdown \\ \overset{+}{O}\text{—}AlCl_2 \\ \diagup \\ CH_3 \end{array} \right] Cl^- \xrightarrow{\text{Heat}} C_6H_5OAlCl_2 \xrightarrow{H_2O} C_6H_5OH + HOAlCl_2$$
$$(+CH_3Cl)$$

of aromatic ethers have been obtained by heating with pyridine hydrochloride and by the action of sodium in refluxing pyridine (V. Prey, 1942–43).

Phenoxyacetic acid, $C_6H_5OCH_2COOH$, is a solid ether derivative useful for identification; it is prepared by slow addition of aqueous alkali to a melt of phenol and chloroacetic acid.   The product separates as the sodium salt, which is collected and acidified.

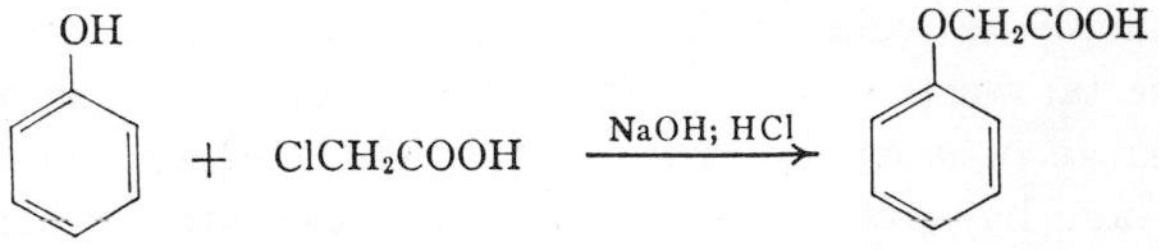

Phenoxyacetic acid
(m.p. 98°, b.p. 285° dec.)

Phenyl acetate, $C_6H_5OCOCH_3$, is a liquid, b.p. 196°; acetyl derivatives in general are prepared by warming the phenol with excess acetic anhydride with addition of either a basic catalyst (fused sodium acetate, pyridine, triethylamine) or an acid catalyst (sulfuric acid, boron fluoride etherate). **Phenyl benzoate,** $C_6H_5COOC_6H_5$ (m.p. 71°), is obtained by shaking a weakly alkaline solution of phenol with benzoyl chloride (Schotten-Baumann reaction, 8.23) or by interaction of the components in cold pyridine solution. The Schotten-Baumann procedure is applicable to the preparation of **phenyl p-toluenesulfonate** (m.p. 95°):

$$C_6H_5OH \ + \ p\text{-}CH_3C_6H_4SO_2Cl \ \longrightarrow \ C_6H_5OSO_2C_6H_4CH_3(p)$$

22.5   Benzyne Intermediates. — The idea that intermediates of a novel type are involved in certain nucleophilic displacements stems from experiments reported by Wittig in 1940. In the reaction of n-butyllithium with n-butyl halides to form octane, the reaction rate falls off sharply in the usual order: $RI > RBr > RCl$. Hence on allowing phenyllithium to react in ether with equivalent amounts of aryl halides to form diphenyl, it was a surprise to find that the extent of reaction after 20 hrs. was: C_6H_5I, 5%; C_6H_5Br, 7%; C_6H_5Cl, 5%; C_6H_5F, 75%. The peculiarly high reactivity of fluorobenzene suggested the possibility that the reaction involves formation of o-fluorophenyllithium (1) and its reaction with phenyllithium to give o-diphenyllithium (2), which on hydrolysis would

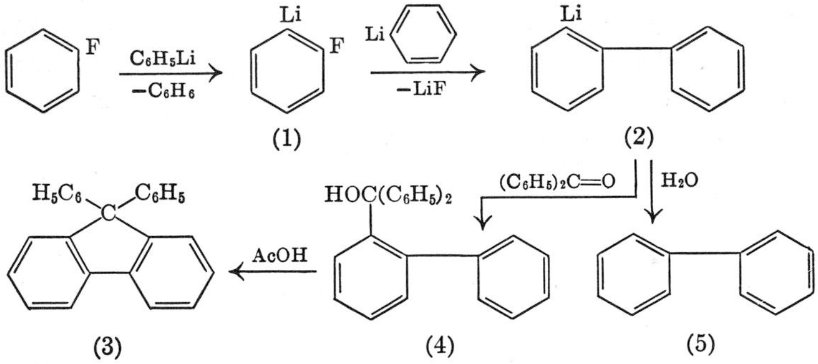

afford diphenyl (5). That the aryllithium (2) is in fact an intermediate was established by treating the reaction mixture with benzophenone instead of water, for the product proved to be o-phenyltriphenylcarbinol (4), converted by hot acetic acid into 9,9-diphenylfluorene (3, m.p. 220°). The unusual reactivity of fluorobenzene would then be attributed to labilization of an *ortho* hydrogen by the strongly electronegative fluorine atom.

However, the initial work included no evidence that *o*-fluorophenyllithium (1) is an intermediate, and in 1942 Wittig considered the alternative possibility that the initial step is dehydrohalogenation to benzyne, a dienyne, and that phenyl-

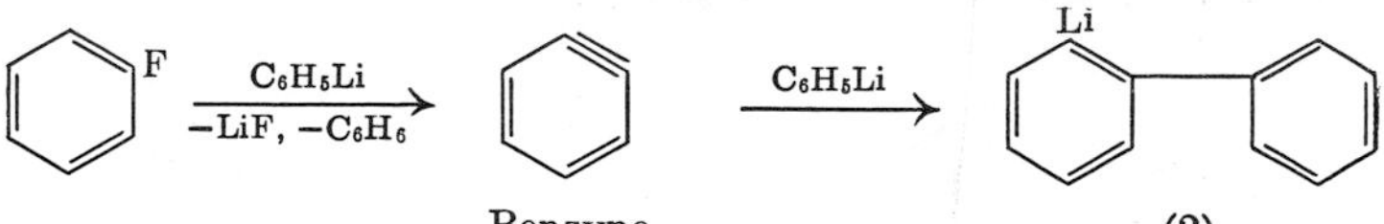

$$\underset{\text{(1)}}{\text{F}} \xrightarrow[\text{—LiF, —C}_6\text{H}_6]{\text{C}_6\text{H}_5\text{Li}} \underset{\text{Benzyne}}{\bigcirc} \xrightarrow{\text{C}_6\text{H}_5\text{Li}} \underset{\text{(2)}}{\text{Li}}$$

lithium adds to this nucleophilic intermediate to give the aryllithium (2). The first step finds analogy in the known behavior of vinylhalides:

$$\text{C}_6\text{H}_5\text{CH}{=}\text{CHX} + 2\ \text{C}_6\text{H}_5\text{Li} \rightarrow \text{C}_6\text{H}_5\text{C}{\equiv}\text{CLi} + 2\ \text{C}_6\text{H}_6 + \text{LiX}$$

Eleven years after Wittig's suggestion of the exciting benzyne postulate, J. D. Roberts (1953) independently arrived at the idea of the same intermediate from the finding that chlorobenzene-1-C^{14} reacts with potassium amide in liquid ammonia to give aniline-1-C^{14} and aniline-2-C^{14}. Roberts later (1955) pointed out

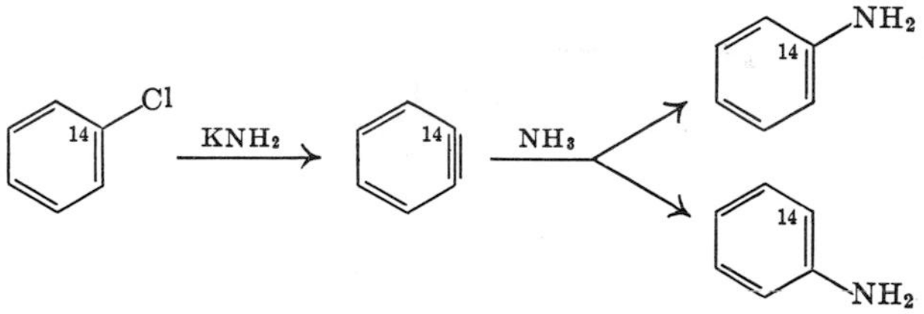

$$\underset{}{\bigcirc}\text{Cl} \xrightarrow{\text{KNH}_2} \underset{}{\bigcirc} \xrightarrow{\text{NH}_3} \begin{array}{c} \bigcirc\text{NH}_2 \\ + \\ \bigcirc\text{NH}_2 \end{array}$$

that the model of the electronic structure shows that ring strain is not excessive and is comparable to that in cyclopentene. Huisgen (1955) investigated the reaction of 1-fluoronaphthalene with phenyllithium, followed by carbonation, and isolated in about equal amounts 2-phenyl-1-naphthoic acid and 1-phenyl-2-naphthoic acid, easily separable because only the latter is esterified by the Fischer method. 2-Fluoronaphthalene

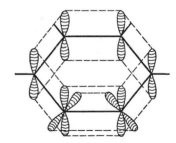

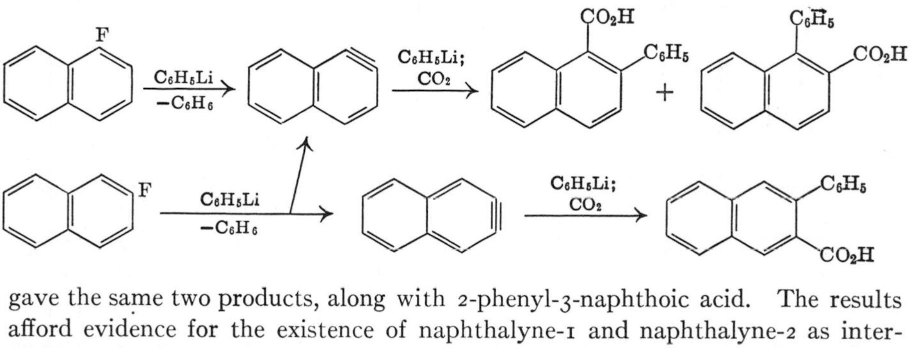

gave the same two products, along with 2-phenyl-3-naphthoic acid. The results afford evidence for the existence of naphthalyne-1 and naphthalyne-2 as intermediates.

Evidence for the existence of benzyne adduced by Wittig (1956) involves in part use of the trapping technique of generation of the intermediate in the presence of a diene. Thus a solution of *o*-fluorobromobenzene in furane when shaken with lithium amalgam (4 days) afforded a product (m.p. 56°) identified as 1,4-dihydro-

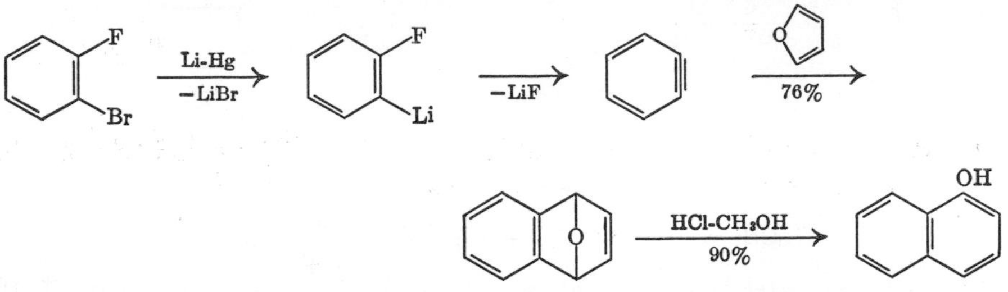

naphthalene-1,4-endoxide by acid hydrolysis to α-naphthol. A neat procedure for generation of benzyne is via the Grignard derivative formed by reaction of *o*-fluorobromobenzene in tetrahydrofurane solution. When this is done in the

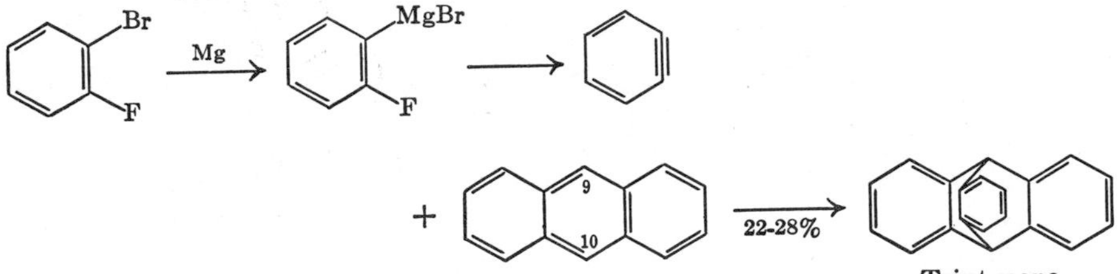

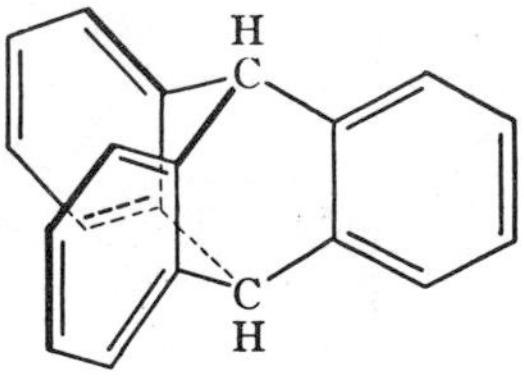

Triptycene
(colorless, m.p. 255°, unreactive)

presence of anthracene, addition occurs with the reactive 9,10-diene system and the product is triptycene (Wittig, *Org. Syn.*, 1959). This interesting hydrocarbon had been prepared previously by a six-step degradation of the anthracene–*p*-benzoquinone adduct (Bartlett, 1942). Generated in ether in the absence of a trapping agent, benzyne is converted into the dimer, diphenylene, and the trimer, triphenylene.

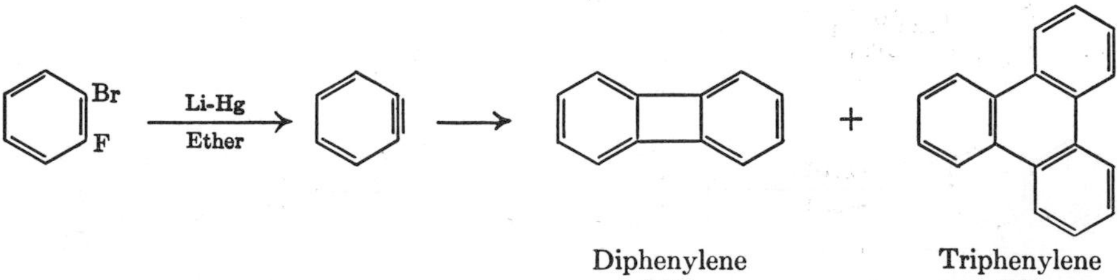

Diphenylene   **Triphenylene**
24%   3%

No benzyne has as yet been isolated, but study of the flash photolysis of benzenediazonium-2-carboxylate has afforded spectroscopic evidence of a short-lived intermediate to diphenylene tentatively identified as benzyne (Stiles,[1] 1960).

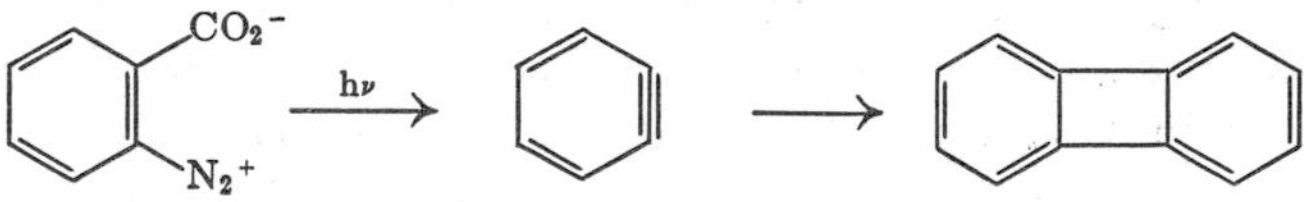

Benzynes have been suggested as intermediates in the halobenzene → phenol reaction. Thus in the reaction of o-chlorotoluene with 4 M sodium hydroxide at 340° nucleophilic attack of the benzyne in the two possible directions would

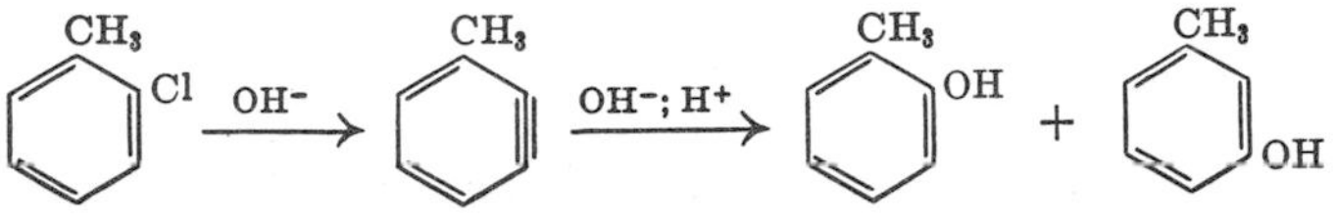

account for the formation of about equal parts of o- and m-cresol and no p-cresol (J. D. Roberts, 1957). However, benzyne does not appear to be involved in the Dow phenol process.[2] Catalytic amounts of cupric oxide added to the charge eventually produce in the iron reactor a lining of catalytically active copper. In such a reactor at a temperature of 300° the products are phenol and diphenyl ether, along with smaller amounts of o- and p-hydroxydiphenyl; these by-products are produced also from reaction of aqueous sodium phenoxide with chlorobenzene. In reactions conducted in a bomb of stainless steel, nickel, or silver, or in an iron bomb that has been incompletely copperized, products of rearrangement result, probably through a benzyne intermediate. Thus sodium carbonate solution hydrolyzes p-chlorodiphenyl in an iron reactor at 350° to a mixture of m- and p-hydroxydiphenyl; in a copper reactor no *meta* isomer is formed. The function of copper appears to be to accelerate ordinary nucleophilic displacement to a point where this reaction is faster than formation of a benzyne.

A general principle of synthesis involves creation of an intermediate benzyne having a nucleophilic center so located that it can add intramolecularly to the triple bond (J. F. Bunnett, 1961). An example is the synthesis of 3-acetyloxindole by reaction of o-acetoacetochloroanilide with potassium amide in liquid ammonia

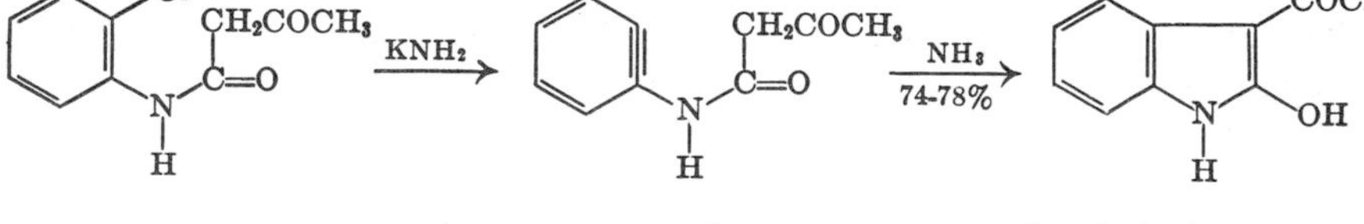

(ferric nitrate as catalyst). In another instance the o- and m-halo isomers gave the same product.

22.6   Halophenols. — Chlorination of phenol without solvent at temperatures from 40–155° affords mixtures of o- and p-chlorophenol in which the latter predominates. Phenol present in the reaction mixture can be removed,

---

[1] Martin Stiles, b. 1927 Huntington, West Va.; Ph.D. Harvard (Bartlett); Univ. Michigan

[2] Private communication from Edgar C. Britton, b. 1891 Rockville, Ind.; Ph.D. Michigan (Hale); Dow Chemical Co.

owing to the greater acidic strength of the chlorophenols, by extraction of the substitution products with 10% potassium carbonate solution from an ethereal solution, which retains the less acidic phenol. The mixture of chlorophenols is easily separated by fractionation, for the o- and p-isomers differ in boiling point by 41°. When chlorination is conducted in carbon tetrachloride solution at a low temperature, the more volatile *ortho* isomer can be obtained in 26% yield. Pure o- and p-chlorophenol, like the *meta* isomer, are best prepared from the corresponding chloroanilines by diazotization and hydrolysis. Monobromination of phenol at low temperatures results in almost exclusive *para* substitution; the *ortho* isomer is produced in appreciable amounts only at higher temperatures.

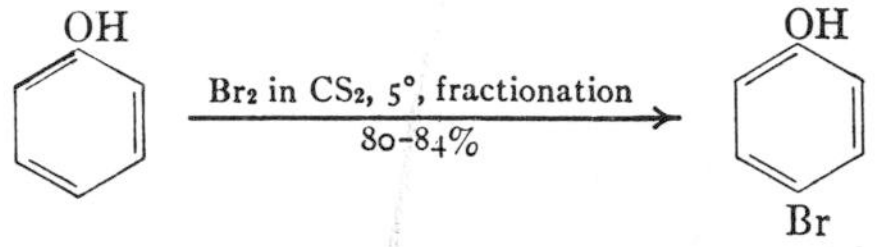

Thus in contrast with chlorination, bromination is satisfactory for preparation of the p-halo derivative. An indirect preparation of pure o-bromophenol is given in section 18.12. On treatment with a sufficient amount of chlorine or bromine, with or without solvent, phenol is converted into the 2,4,6-trihalo derivative. In analogy to the behavior of aniline, phenol is converted rapidly by bromine water into the sparingly soluble tribromo derivative. The reaction is employed for detection of phenol, since turbidity is discernible at dilutions as high as 1:100,000.

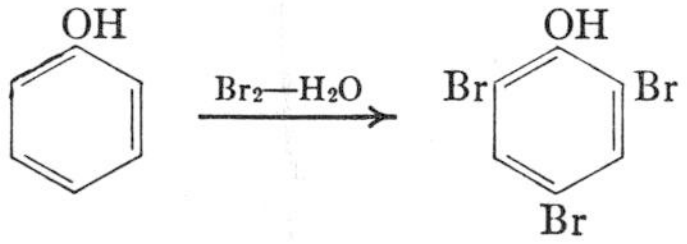

When bromine water is added slowly to a 0.1% solution of phenol in water and continued after precipitation of tribromophenol is complete, one more mole of bromine is absorbed with formation of "tribromophenol bromide" (Rudolf Benedikt; Vienna, 1879). The substance, which forms glistening yellow plates (m.p. 118°), was recognized from an infrared band at 5.99 μ and an ultraviolet band at 280 mμ ($\epsilon = 9,270$) to be the tetrabromodienone formulated (J. A. Price, 1955; compare 20.9).

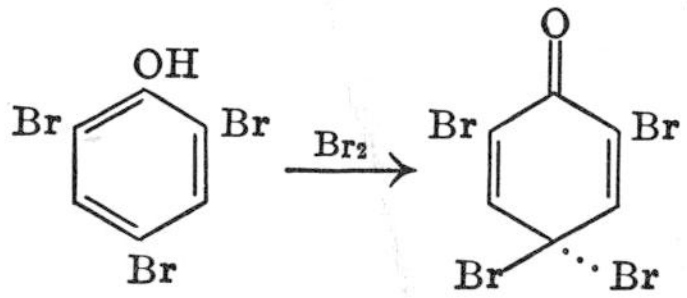

2,4-D, or (2,4-dichlorophenoxy)acetic acid, is a useful herbicide for weed control. It is made by reaction of 2,4-dichlorophenol with monochloroacetic acid in aqueous alkali. The acid is employed as an amine salt, for example, the ethanolamine salt, which is more soluble in water than the sodium salt. A small

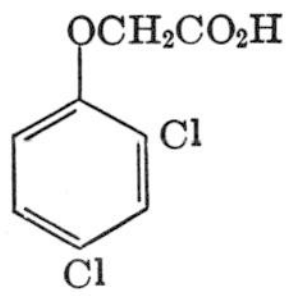

2,4-D    EDTA

amount of sequestering agent such as ethylenediamine tetraacetic acid tetrasodium salt is added to prevent complex formation in hard water (1 g. of EDTA binds 201 mg. of calcium carbonate).

22.7   **Nitrophenols.** — Nitration of phenol with dilute aqueous nitric acid gives a mixture of the *o*- and *p*-isomers, with some predominance of the former substance, and since a sharp separation can be made by steam distillation, both isomers are obtainable satisfactorily from the reaction mixture. *o*-Nitrophenol is readily volatile with steam and is obtained from the distillate in substantially pure form, whereas the nonvolatile *p*-isomer is retained in the distillation flask along with any dinitrophenols and other contaminants and requires more extensive purification. The steam volatility of *o*-nitrophenol, as that of *o*-nitroaniline, is attributed to the presence of a che- late ring. A method of preparing *p*-nitrophenol in better yield and subject to no contamination with the *ortho* isomer consists in oxidation of *p*-nitrosophenol with nitric acid. A satisfactory preparation of *m*-nitropheno

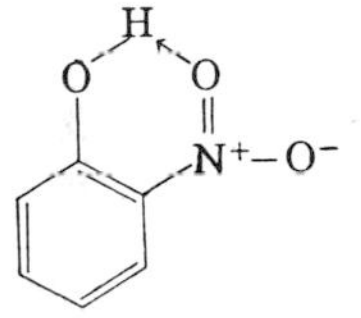

o-Nitrophenol

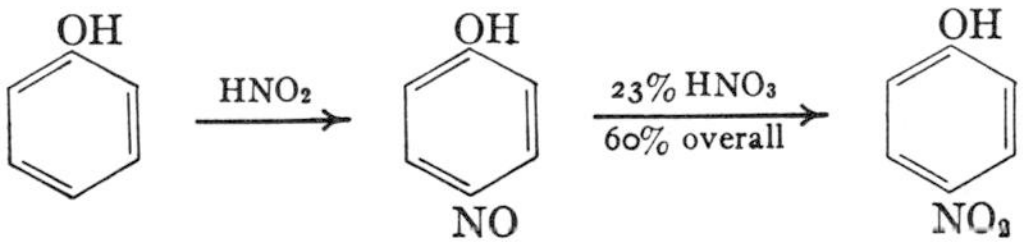

proceeds from *m*-nitroaniline by the diazo reaction. 2,4-Dinitrophenol is produced as an intermediate in the preparation of picric acid by nitration of chlorobenzene.

22.8   **Catechol.** — Catechol, or 1,2-dihydroxybenzene, occurs in many plants and is excreted in horse urine both as such and as a sulfate ester. Several methods are available for the preparation of this technically important compound. One is demethylation of the monomethyl ether guaiacol, obtainable from natural sources, accomplished either by heating the ether with aluminum chloride at 210° or by refluxing with 48% hydrobromic acid (85–87% yield). A technical process involves hydrolysis of either *o*-chlorophenol or *o*-dichlorobenzene with

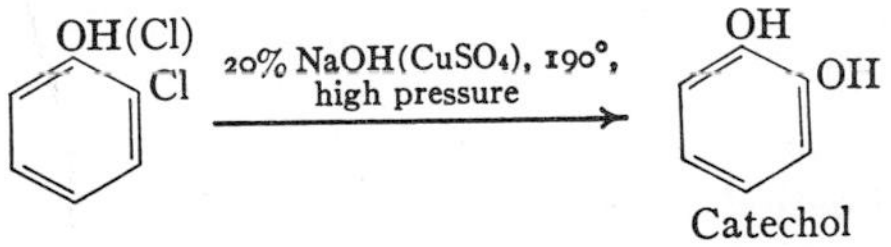

Catechol

aqueous alkali in the presence of a catalyst under forcing conditions. In another technical process, sodium phenol-2,4-disulfonate is fused with alkali under conditions so controlled that only the *ortho* sulfonate group is replaced by hydroxyl; the *para* sulfonate group is then removed by hydrolysis.   A further method by which

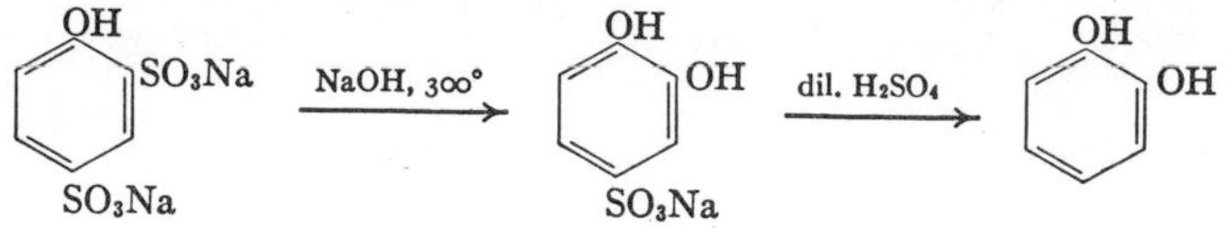

catechol can be obtained in moderate yield illustrates a reaction generally applicable to the *o*- and *p*-hydroxy derivatives of aromatic aldehydes and aceto compounds; this consists in oxidation with hydrogen peroxide in alkaline solution and results in replacement of the aldehydic or acetyl group by hydroxyl (Dakin reaction).   Evidence supports the reaction mechanism shown in the following formulation:

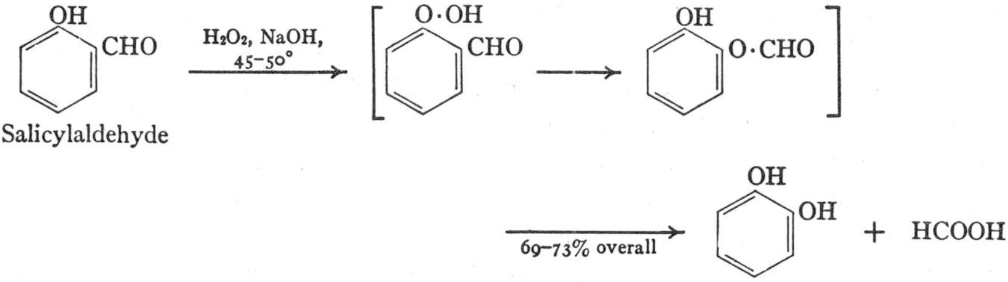

Catechol Ethers. — The monomethyl ether guaiacol. o-$C_6H_4(OH)OCH_3$ (Table 22.1), first obtained by distillation of the resin guaiacum, is prepared synthetically from *o*-anisidine by the diazo reaction.   The dimethyl ether veratrole, o-C_6H_4-$(OCH_3)_2$ (m.p. 22.5°, b.p. 207°), is obtainable from catechol in 95% yield by methylation with dimethyl sulfate and alkali.

22.9   **Resorcinol.** — The *m*-dihydroxy derivative of benzene, not found in nature, is prepared by alkali fusion of sodium *m*-benzenedisulfonate.
Resorcinol is highly reactive because of the reinforcing action of the two hydroxyl

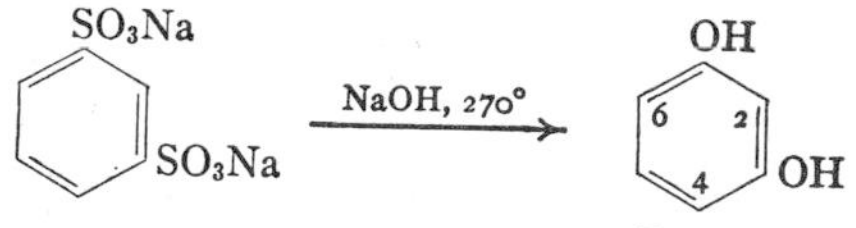

groups, and is substituted initially at the 4-position, *para* to one hydroxyl and *ortho* to the other.   The course of disubstitution is dependent on the reagent and on the conditions; specific procedures afford the 4,6-dichloro and the 2,4-dinitro derivatives.   Partial alkylation of a polyhydric phenol presents inevitable difficulties, and **resorcinol monomethyl ether** (liq., b.p. 244°) is obtained at best in 31% yield by heating resorcinol with methanol and potassium bisulfate in an autoclave at 165–170°.   The **dimethyl ether** boils at 217°.

22.10   **Hydroquinone.** — Hydroquinone occurs in certain plants as the glycoside arbutin, from which it is liberated on hydrolysis with emulsin or sulfuric acid.   A special method of preparation is oxidation of aniline, through a succession of intermediates leading to the yellow substance quinone, from which hydroquinone (colorless) is obtained on reduction.   The reduction is reversible,

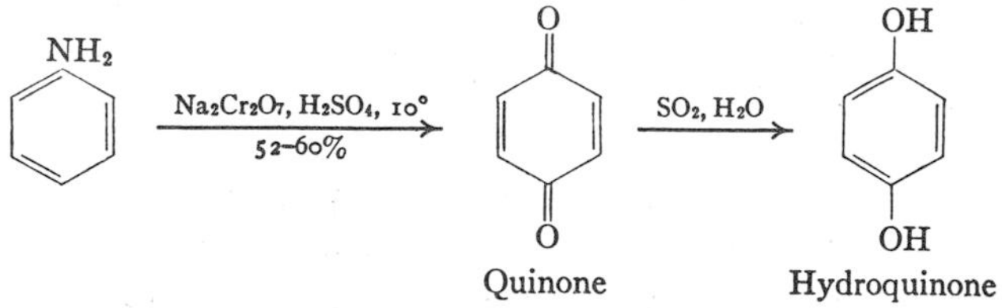

Quinone   Hydroquinone

and hydroquinone has reducing properties.   It is employed as a photographic developer because of its ability to reduce to metallic silver the silver subhalide resulting from exposure of silver halide emulsion to light.

Hydroquinone is the only compound of the benzene series known to enter into

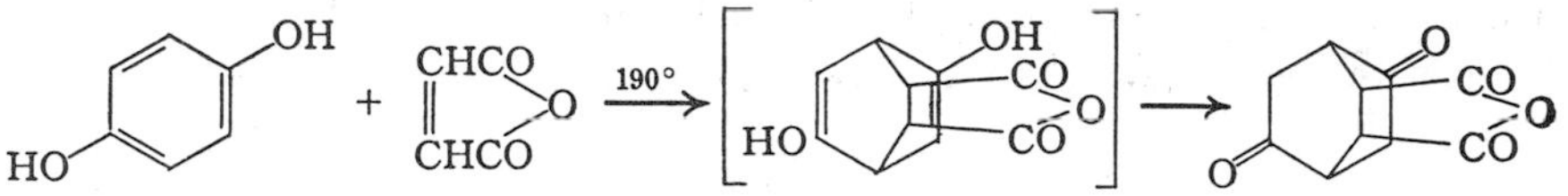

Diels-Alder addition with maleic anhydride (R. C. Cookson,[1] 1955).   The transient adduct ketonizes to a bridge-ring diketo anhydride.

Hydroquinone monomethyl ether, m.p. 53°, b.p. 243°; **dimethyl ether,** m.p. 56°, b.p. 213°.

22.11   **Pyrogallol** is produced technically from the natural product gallic acid by distillation from a mixture with pumice in an atmosphere of carbon dioxide.   Like other polyhydroxy acids, gallic acid undergoes decarboxylation more readily than ordinary aromatic carboxylic acids.   Pyrogallol has strong re-

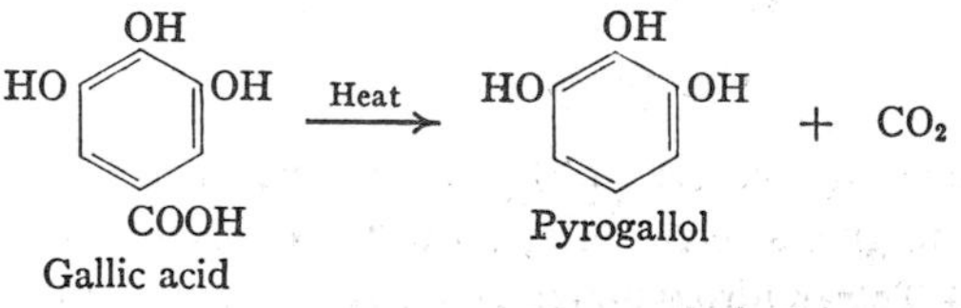

COOH   Pyrogallol
Gallic acid

ducing properties and is used as a photographic developer.   It is also employed in a strongly alkaline solution as an absorbent for oxygen in gas analysis.   **Pyrogallol 1,3-dimethyl ether** is obtained by methylation with methyl iodide in methanol solution in the presence of potassium hydroxide at 150–160°.

22.12   **Phloroglucinol,** or s-trihydroxybenzene, is an expensive chemical obtainable from s-triaminobenzene.   The amine is available as a reduction product of the corresponding trinitro compound, which in turn is prepared from TNT, and the intermediate 2,4,6-trinitrobenzoic acid is a point of departure for the preparation of phloroglucinol.   The reduction product of the trinitro compound when refluxed in a nearly neutral solution for a prolonged period undergoes

[1] Richard C. Cookson, b. 1922 near Hexham, England; Ph.D. Cambridge Univ. (F. G. Mann); Univ. Southampton

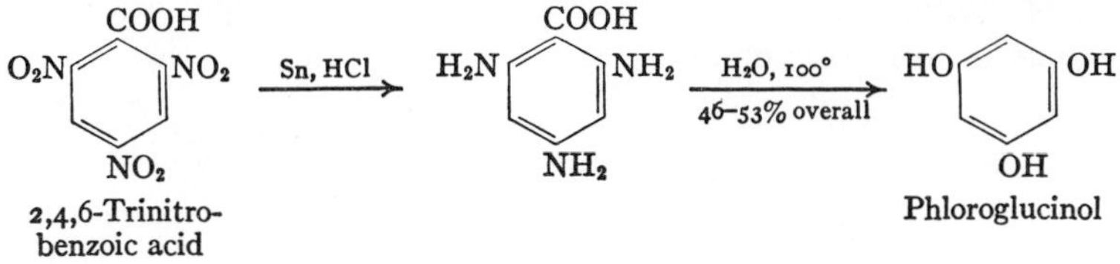

2,4,6-Trinitro-
benzoic acid

Phloroglucinol

hydrolysis of the amino groups to hydroxyl groups, and decarboxylation.   The ready replacement of amino groups by hydroxyl and the low-temperature decarboxylation are both reactions specific to the structures in question and are probably associated with the tendency of the symmetrical triol system to react in the triketo form.   Thus phloroglucinol reacts with hydroxylamine to form the trioxime of cyclohexane-1,3,5-trione.   Spectroscopic evidence indicates that the substance exists largely in the oxime form (R. H. Thompson,[1] 1956).   Phloroglucinol also adds hydrogen cyanide to form a red addition product convertible by dehydration and hydrolysis into 3,5-dihydroxybenzoic acid (W. T. Gradwell, 1956).   When refluxed with concentrated hydrochloric acid phloroglucinol is converted in good

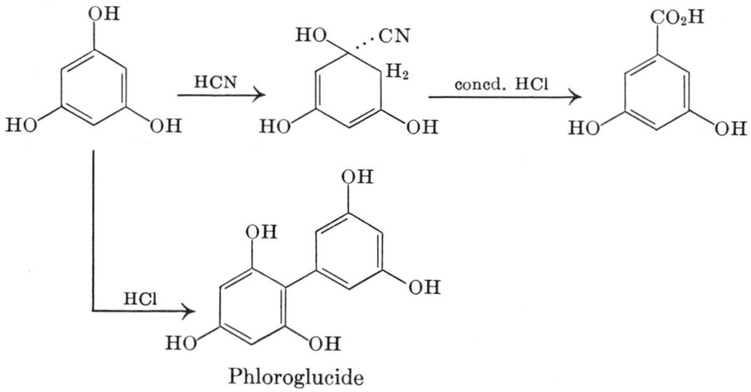

Phloroglucide

yield into the diphenyl derivative phloroglucide, distinguished from starting material by its failure to give a ferric chloride test (W. Riedl, 1955).

22.13   1,2,3,4-Tetrahydroxybenzene (Apionol, m.p. 161°) is best prepared by boiling 4-aminopyrogallol hydrochloride with water.   It dissolves in ferric chloride solution with a deep blue color which rapidly fades to red-brown; if ferrous ion is also present the blue color is stable (W. Mayer,[2] 1960).   Careful

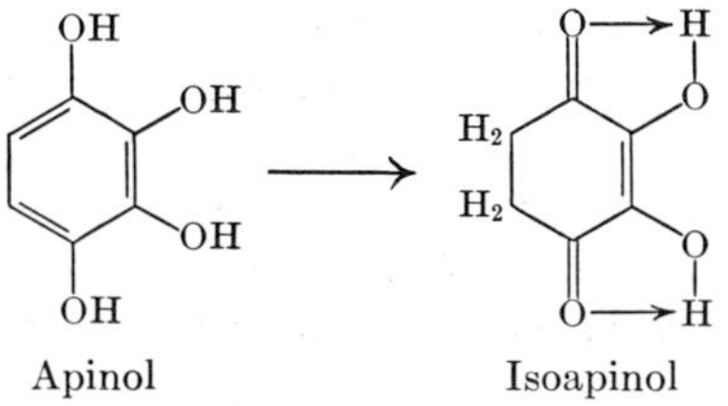

Apinol   Isoapinol

[1] Ronald Hunter Thompson, b. 1919 Darlington, England; Ph.D. and D.Sc. Leeds (F. M. Rowe); Univ. Aberdeen, Scotland
[2] Walter Mayer, b. 1915 Stockach; Ph.D. Heidelberg (O. Th. Schmidt); Univ. Heidelberg

acidification of an oxygen-free solution in alkali produces the isomeric diketonic form, which on sublimation in vacuum is only partially converted to the phenolic form.   The unusual stability is attributable to the presence of two strong hydrogen bonds.   The structure was established by methylation (CH_2N_2) and oxidation to 2,3-dimethoxy-1,4-benzoquinone.   Isoapionol condenses with phthalaldehyde to give 2,3-dihydroxyanthraquinone.

22.14   Hexahydroxybenzene and Oxidation Products. — It is interesting that glyoxal, the product of ozonization of benzene, apparently is able under appropriate conditions to undergo trimerization with reformation of the aromatic ring.   In the presence of strong alkali the dialdehyde disproportionates to glyoxalic acid: $OCHCHO + H_2O \rightarrow HOCH_2CO_2H$.   However, when air is passed into a carbonate-buffered aqueous solution, the aldehyde condenses to hexahydroxybenzene, which is oxidized to give the sodium salt of tetrahydroxyquinone (B. Homolka, Höchst Farbwerke, 1921).   In a procedure worked out by Sager[1] (1961), 30% glyoxal solution (Dow commercial grade) is added to an aqueous solu-

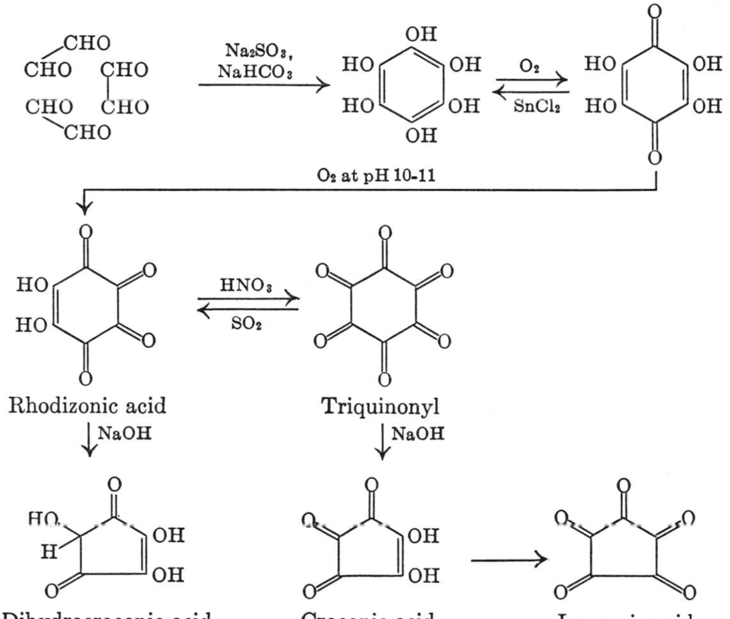

Rhodizonic acid   Triquinonyl

Dihydrocroconic acid   Croconic acid   Leuconic acid

tion of sodium sulfite and sodium bicarbonate and a brisk stream of air is drawn through the solution.   Greenish black crystals of the disodium salt of tetrahydroxyquinone separate, and acidification affords glistening black crystals of tetrahydroxyquinone in 8% yield.   Although the yield is low, the starting material is cheap and the process simple.   Reduction of tetrahydroxyquinone with stannous chloride–hydrochloric acid affords hexahydroxybenzene in yield of 75–78% (hexaacetate, m.p. 203°).   Further oxidation of tetrahydroxyquinone affords first rhodizonic acid, a colorless substance which forms a dark blue potassium salt and

[1] William F. Sager, b. 1918 Illinois; Ph.D. Harvard (Bartlett); George Washington Univ.

which condenses with only one equivalent of *o*-phenylenediamine. The product of exhaustive oxidation is triquinonyl, or hexaketocyclohexane, which is isolated as the colorless octahydrate. The reactions were described by R. Nietzki (Basel, 1885–90). On treatment with concentrated sodium hydroxide solution, rhodizonic acid and triquinonyl undergo benzilic acid-type rearrangement with conversion, respectively, to dihydrocroconic acid and croconic acid. Croconic acid, a triketo enediol, can be oxidized to pentaketocyclopentane, known as leuconic acid.

22.15   Aminophenols. — *o*-Aminophenol is prepared by reduction of *o*-nitrophenol, for example with sodium hydrosulfite ($Na_2S_2O_4$) in alkaline solution or with zinc dust and aqueous calcium chloride solution. The *m*-isomer, a dye intermediate, is produced technically by the following method:

Resorcinol   *m*-Aminophenol

p-Aminophenol is employed in production of dyes and as a photographic developer; it has strong reducing properties and is rapidly discolored in neutral or alkaline solution. Technical processes of preparation are reduction of *p*-nitrophenol with iron powder and dilute hydrochloric acid, and electrolytic reduction of nitrobenzene in sulfuric acid solution; the latter reaction proceeds through formation and rearrangement of phenylhydroxylamine. Convenient laboratory procedures for preparation of *p*-aminophenols from phenols are based on the reduction of the *p*-nitroso or *p*-sulfobenzeneazo derivatives resulting from nitrosation or coupling with diazotized sulfanilic acid. Typical N-substituted derivatives of *p*-aminophenol are obtainable by methods summarized as follows:

1. $p\text{-HOC}_6\text{H}_4\text{NH}_2 \cdot \text{HCl} + (\text{CH}_3\text{CO})_2\text{O} + \text{CH}_3\text{COONa} \xrightarrow{\text{aq. solution, 25°}} p\text{-HOC}_6\text{H}_4\text{NHCOCH}_3$
   p-Acetylaminophenol
   (m.p. 169°)

2. $p\text{-HOC}_6\text{H}_4\text{NH}_2 \xrightarrow{\text{C}_6\text{H}_5\text{CHO}} p\text{-HOC}_6\text{H}_4\text{N}{=}\text{CHC}_6\text{H}_5 \xrightarrow{\text{Zn, NaOH}} p\text{-HOC}_6\text{H}_4\text{NHCH}_2\text{C}_6\text{H}_5$
   p-Benzalaminophenol   *p*-Benzylaminophenol
   (m.p. 183°)   (m.p. 90°)

3. $p\text{-HOC}_6\text{H}_4\text{OH} + \text{C}_6\text{H}_5\text{NH}_2 \xrightarrow{\text{aq. CaCl}_2, 260°} p\text{-HOC}_6\text{H}_4\text{NHC}_6\text{H}_5$
   p-Hydroxydiphenylamine
   (m.p. 70°)

Selective acetylation of the amino group (1) is easily accomplished in aqueous solution. A solution of *p*-aminophenol hydrochloride in water is treated with one equivalent of acetic anhydride, followed at once by one equivalent of sodium acetate; the free amine is acetylated as it is liberated.

22.16   Alkylated Phenols. — **Carvacrol** and **thymol** occur in several essential oils and probably are transformation products of terpenoid constituents. The preparation of thymol from a typical terpene ketone by dehydrogenation with bromine has been recorded (22.2). A practicable synthesis of carvacrol consists in sulfonation of *p*-cymene (1-methyl-4-isopropylbenzene) and alkali fusion of the resulting 2-sulfonic acid. No route is open for introduction of a hydroxyl

Carvacrol Thymol

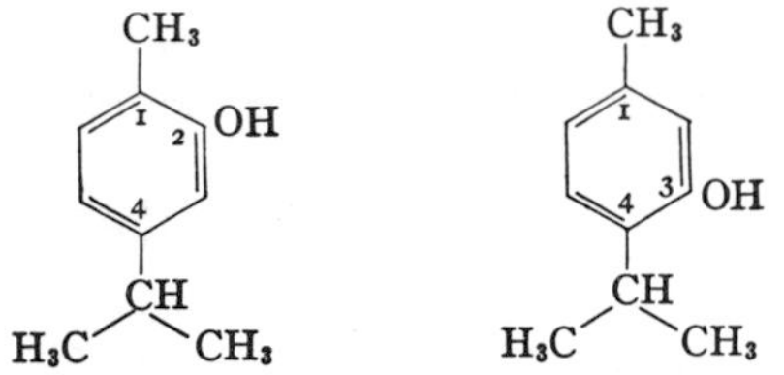

group at position 3, *ortho* to the more bulky isopropyl group, but the isomer thymol can be produced satisfactorily from natural sources. When either carvacrol or thymol is heated with phosphorus pentoxide, the isopropyl group is split off as propylene, and the nonvolatile residue is a phosphoric acid ester that on alkaline hydrolysis affords *o*-cresol in the first instance and *m*-cresol in the second. In various substitution reactions carvacrol and thymol are attacked almost exclusively in the position *para* to the hydroxyl group.

Anol is the *p*-α-propenyl derivative of phenol. It can be obtained from the naturally occurring allyl isomer chavicol by boiling with alkali, which causes the

Chavicol (b.p. 237°) Anol Anethole (m.p. 22.5°, b.p. 235°)

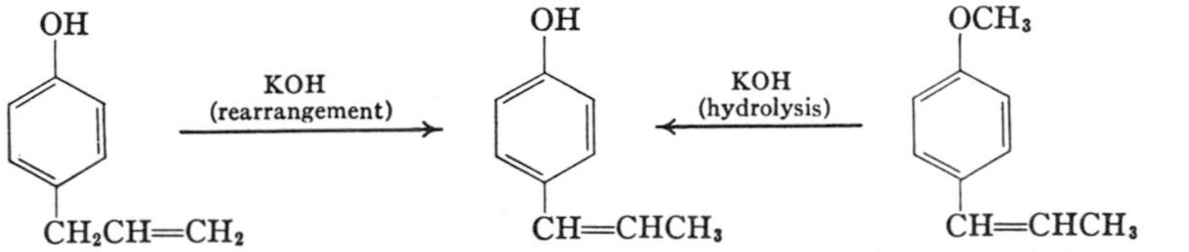

double bond to rearrange to a position conjugated with the ring. A more abundant source is alkali fusion of the methyl ether, **anethole**, one of the chief constituents of oil of aniseed.

Eugenol, or 2-methoxy-4-allylphenol, is a colorless liquid widely distributed among plants and obtainable in practical amounts from oil of cloves. It is isomerized by alkali to the α-propenyl isomer, **isoeugenol.**

Saligenin, *o*-$HOC_6H_4CH_2OH$, results from hydrolysis of salicin ($C_{13}H_{18}O_7$), a bitter glucoside found in the bark of willow and poplar trees and used to some extent in medicine as an antipyretic and a tonic.

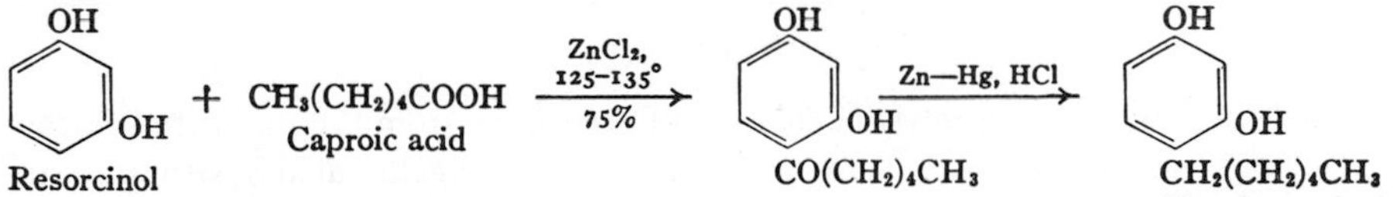

4-*n*-Hexylresorcinol, a synthetic disinfectant, is prepared by condensation of resorcinol with caproic acid in the presence of anhydrous zinc chloride. The con-

Resorcinol Caproic acid 4-*n*-Hexylresorcinol (m.p. 69°)

densation is a Friedel-Crafts type, but resorcinol is substituted with such ease that an acid, rather than an acid chloride, can be employed and the moderately active zinc chloride provides adequate catalysis. The completing step is reduction of the ketone by the Clemmensen method.

Mesitol (m.p. 68°), or 2,4,6-trimethylphenol, is best prepared by hydrolysis of the diazonium salt from mesidine.

o-**Alkylation.** — Ethyl Corporation operates an interesting process involving alkylation of phenol with an olefin in the presence of aluminum phenoxide as catalyst (A. J. Kolka, 1957). Isobutylene reacts particularly readily (100°, 245 p.s.i.) to give a product containing as much as 75% of 2,6-di-*t*-butylphenol (m.p. 37°) and 10–15% of *o*-*t*-butylphenol (m.p. −7°) and 2,4,6-tri-*t*-butylphenol (m.p. 131°). Propylene reacts somewhat less readily but at 200–210° and 30 atmospheres affords chiefly 2,6-diisopropylphenol (liq.) and a small amount of *o*-isopropylphenol (liq.). Alkylation with ethylene proceeds with difficulty even at 280°. Aniline can be alkylated in the presence of aluminum anilide, but the reactivity to olefins is the reverse of that in the alkylation of phenol. Thus ethylene reacts satisfactorily at 325° and 800 p.s.i. to produce 2-ethyl- and 2,6-diethylaniline, but propylene and isobutylene react only poorly. The preference for substitution of bulky alkyl groups into one or both *ortho* positions suggests that the reaction involves a cyclic transition state (2) analogous to one postulated for the Claisen rearrangement of phenol allyl ether (22.23). Ether formation, observed at lower temperatures,

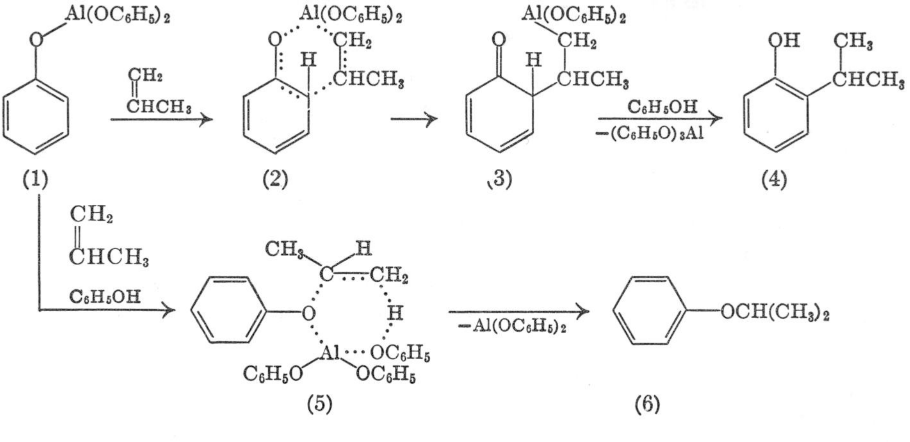

may involve transition state (5). The reactions are all reversible, and at high temperatures the hindered *o*-alkylphenols give way to the thermodynamically more stable *p*-products, available by allylic rearrangement of (3).

REACTIONS

22.17　　Tests. — Typical phenols are differentiated from the majority of other organic compounds by their characteristic weakly acidic nature, recognizable by ready solubility in alkali but not in sodium carbonate solution (exception: the more strongly acidic nitrophenols). Many phenols, like aliphatic enols, give rise to characteristic colors when treated with ferric chloride in very dilute aqueous or alcoholic solution as the result of complex formation (phenol, violet; cresols, blue; catechol, green; resorcinol, dark violet).

22.18   Substitutions. — The facility with which phenols undergo substitution is illustrated by the ready formation of the 2,4,6-tribromo derivative, by the diazo coupling reaction, and by nitrosation, preferentially in the *para* position, on interaction with nitrous acid at ice-bath temperature. A further instance of the substitution-facilitating influence of the hydroxyl group is the mercuration reaction, applicable specifically to phenols. Thus phenol reacts with mercuric

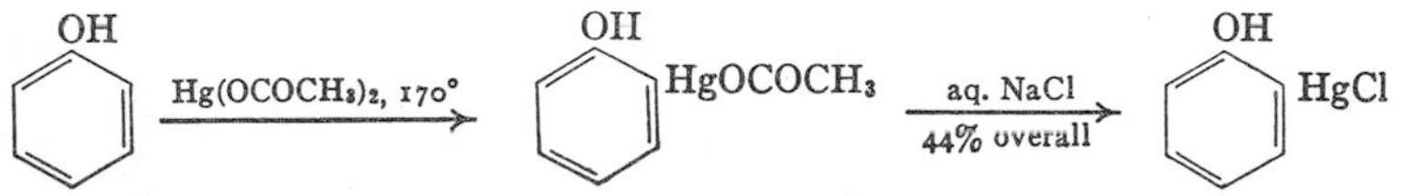

o-Chloromercuriphenol
(m.p. 152°)

acetate to give the *o*-acetoxymercuri derivative, which is convertible into the chloromercuri derivative by interaction with sodium chloride. The chlormercuri group is replaceable by iodine; for example *o*-chloromercuriphenol is converted by iodine in chloroform solution into *o*-iodophenol (m.p. 43°) in 63% yield. A few phenols have been shown to react with acetyl sulfur chloride (CH_3COSCl) in chloroform to give *o*- or *p*-derivatives, HOArSCOCH₃. 2-Naphthol gives the 1-derivative; 1-naphthol gives the 2,4-bis derivative (H. Böhme, 1959).

22.19   Friedel-Crafts Reaction. — The presence of a phenolic hydroxyl group alters the behavior in the Friedel-Crafts reaction, for phenol initially reacts with aluminum chloride with evolution of hydrogen chloride and production of a salt:

$$C_6H_5OH \; + \; AlCl_3 \; \longrightarrow \; C_6H_5OAlCl_2 \; + \; HCl$$

One equivalent of the reagent is thus consumed, and in order to promote condensation with an acid chloride or anhydride a suitable additional quantity of aluminum chloride must be used. Satisfactory acylations are sometimes accomplished by this procedure, but in other instances the results are unfavorable, sometimes because the metal halide group reduces the solubility in organic solvents to a point where the material is not easily brought into a state conducive to interaction. Two alternative procedures are available that avoid this difficulty, and usually are preferred to direct condensation. One is use of the methyl ether derivative, and the other is a modification of the general method known as the Fries reaction.

A phenol methyl ether enters into Friedel-Crafts reactions normally if the mixture is kept at a temperature low enough to avoid cleavage of the ether group by

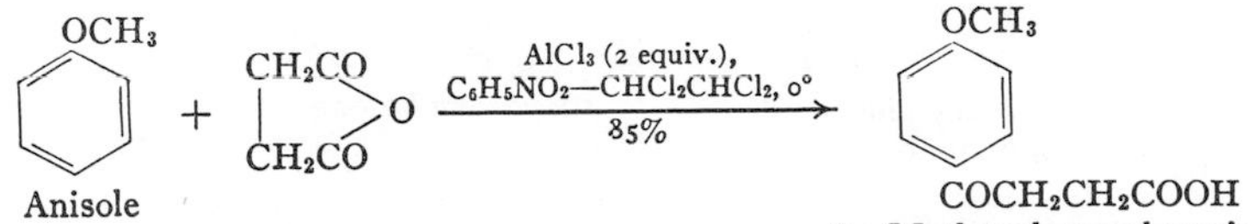

Anisole

COCH₂CH₂COOH
β-4-Methoxybenzoylpropionic
acid (m.p. 147°)

aluminum chloride.   In large-scale preparations, where uniform cooling may be difficult, some cleavage of the ether group may occur and the crude reaction product is remethylated prior to purification.   If the free phenol is ultimately required, the crude material can be treated with more aluminum chloride in a warm solution (80°) to complete demethylation.   The ether group forms a labile complex with aluminum chloride, and the reagent so bound is not restrained from exerting a catalytic function.   Thus in the example shown, the amount of catalyst used is that required for condensation of an anhydride with a hydrocarbon, and the same amount suffices for succinoylation of the diether veratrole (67% yield).

22.20   Fries Reaction. — Fries[1] discovered (1908) that an acyl derivative of a phenol when heated with aluminum chloride is converted into the isomeric *o*- or *p*-hydroxy ketone or more often into a mixture of both.   The material is present in the reaction mixture as the aluminum chloride salt, and the hydroxy compound is liberated on hydrolysis with ice and hydrochloric acid.   *m*-Hydroxy

$$C_6H_6OCOCH_3 \xrightarrow{\text{AlCl}_3(-\text{HCl})} CH_3COC_6H_4OAlCl_2 \longrightarrow CH_3COC_6H_4OH$$

Phenyl acetate   *o*- and *p*-Hydroxy-
                                                                        acetophenone

ketones have been observed very rarely as products of the Fries reaction, and the chief variation is in the ratio of the *ortho* and *para* isomers.   This ratio varies with the solvent and the amount of catalyst, and is influenced particularly by the temperature, as illustrated strikingly by the behavior of *m*-cresyl acetate, which can be converted into either of two products in good yield by adjustment of the temperature.   Although the temperature effect usually is not so pronounced as in this in-

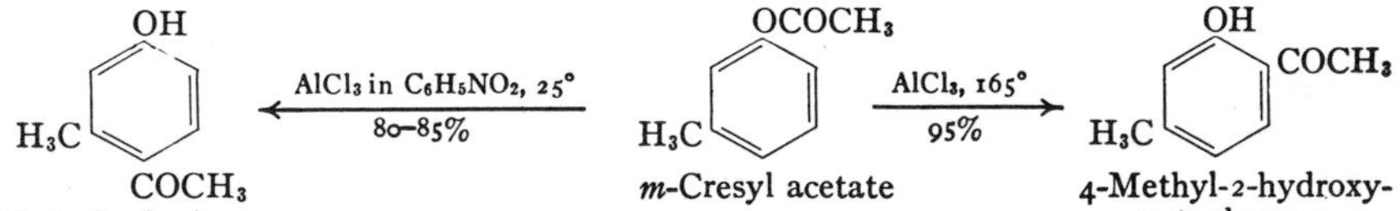

2-Methyl-4-hydroxy-
acetophenone
(m.p. 128°, b.p. 313°)

m-Cresyl acetate

4-Methyl-2-hydroxy-
acetophenone
(m.p. 21°, b.p. 245°)

stance, a similar effect is general, for a low temperature favors *para* substitution and a high temperature *ortho* substitution.   This orientation is just the opposite of the relationship encountered in Friedel-Crafts condensations with substituted hydrocarbons, where the extent of attack in a hindered *ortho* position decreases with

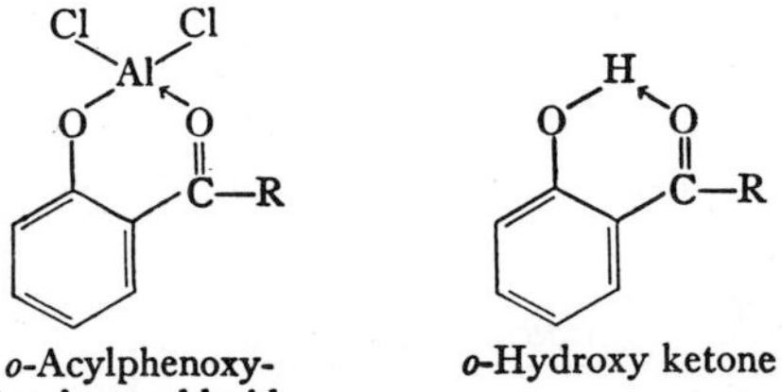

o-Acylphenoxy-
aluminum chloride

o-Hydroxy ketone

---

[1] Karl Fries, b. 1875 Kiedrich/Rhine, Germany; Ph.D. Marburg (Zincke); Univ. Marburg, Braunschweig

rise in temperature.   That the *o*-hydroxy ketone, in the form of the aluminum chloride complex, accumulates at a high temperature in preference to the *p*-isomer also contrasts with the rearrangement of heat-labile orthanilic acid to the more stable *para* isomer, sulfanilic acid.   Chelation in the aluminum chloride complex accounts for the phenomena.   Intramolecular bonding, with consequent stabilization, is possible only in the complex of an *ortho* isomer.   The bonding must be stronger in a metal complex than in a free *o*-acetophenol, and abundant evidence demonstrates such bonding.   Thus the boiling point of 4-methyl-2-hydroxyacetophenone is 68° below that of 2-methyl-4-hydroxyacetophenone, and *o*-heptanoylphenol boils at 135–140°/3 mm., whereas the *p*-isomer boils at 200–207°/4 mm. *o*-Hydroxy ketones are often volatile with steam whereas the *para* isomers are not, and the chelated derivatives are more soluble in ligroin than the hydroxylic isomers.

The Fries reaction probably involves initial intramolecular acylation in the unhindered *p*-position, and the product of low-temperature reaction is thus the nor-

(+ phenol)

mal product.   Rearrangement at a higher temperature then proceeds by reversal of the initial Friedel-Crafts substitution and resubstitution at the stabilized site. Evidence of reversibility is that 2-methyl-4-hydroxyacetophenone is cleaved by hot sulfuric acid or phosphoric acid to *m*-cresyl acetate.

The Fries reaction often offers a convenient route to both the *o*- and *p*-acyl derivatives of a phenol.   If both isomers are formed in appreciable amounts, separation of chelated and unchelated products often can be effected easily by distillation or steam distillation.   If the substances are of low volatility, the *para* isomer usually is a solid and can be separated by crystallization.   An example is the production of *o*- and *p*-hydroxypropiophenone from phenyl propionate, which can be obtained in a condition suitable for the reaction by heating equivalent quantities of phenol and propionyl chloride until the evolution of hydrogen chloride ceases.

OCOCH₂CH₃

Phenyl propionate

AlCl₃, 140–150°

OH

COCH₂CH₃
(45–50%)
p-Hydroxypropiophenone
(m.p. 148°)

+

OH
COCH₂CH₃

(32–35%)
o-Hydroxypropiophenone
(liq., b.p. 115°/15 mm.)

Aluminum chloride is then added, along with carbon disulfide, in which solvent the reaction is begun; after an initial evolution of hydrogen chloride has ceased, the solvent is removed by distillation and the mixture is heated to the required temperature.   After hydrolysis of the cooled mixture, the *p*-hydroxy ketone largely crystallizes and is purified by recrystallization, whereas the *o*-isomer is recovered from the oily residue by distillation.

22.21   Oxidation. — Phenols, like amines, are susceptible to attack by oxidizing agents, and the initial step consists in abstraction of the hydroxylic hydrogen atom with formation of a free radical with an odd electron on oxygen. Such radicals usually are so unstable and reactive that they undergo rapid transformation into secondary products, but certain hydroxy derivatives of phenanthrene afford radicals of stability comparable to triphenylmethyl (Goldschmidt,[1] 1922). Thus 9-chloro-10-phenanthrol, on oxidation with potassium ferricyanide in alkaline solution or with lead dioxide in organic solvents, gives a colored phenanthroxyl radical that slowly associates to a colorless dimeric form till equilibrium is reached; the monomer and dimer are present in about equal amounts at equilibrium in pyridine solution at room temperature. Reducing agents regenerate chlorophenanthrol. The 9-methoxyl, 9-ethoxyl, and 9-bromo derivatives of 10-

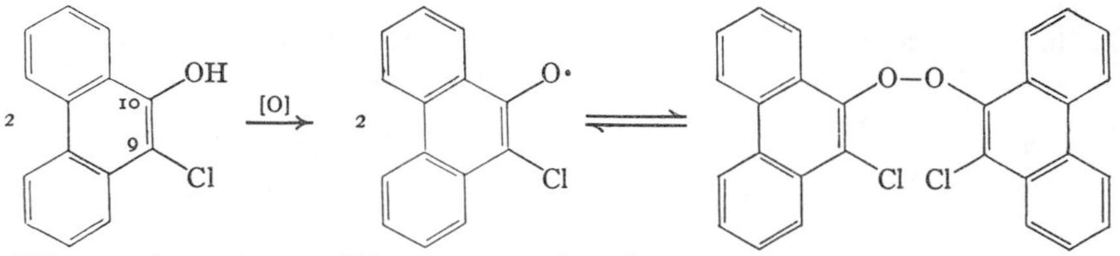

9-Chloro-10-phenanthrol   9-Chloro-10-phenanthroxyl   Dimer (peroxide)
        (m.p. 121°)   (deep blue-red)   (colorless, m.p. 125° dec.)

phenanthrol on oxidation also afford equilibrium mixtures containing radical forms, but the 9-acetoxy derivative is oxidized to a dimeric peroxide that is colorless in solution, as in the solid state, and shows no indication of dissociation.

E. Müller (1950–60) found that 2,4,6-tri-*t*-butylphenol when oxidized by shaking a benzene solution with an aqueous solution of potassium ferricyanide [potassium hexacyanoferrate (III)] affords a stable blue aroxyl radical of high oxidizing power. The substance is completely monomeric in the solid state as well as in a 0.1 N solution in benzene. It is very sensitive to oxygen. 2-Phenyl-4,6-di-*t*-butylphenol gives a radical (I) which is dissociated only to the extent of 13% in

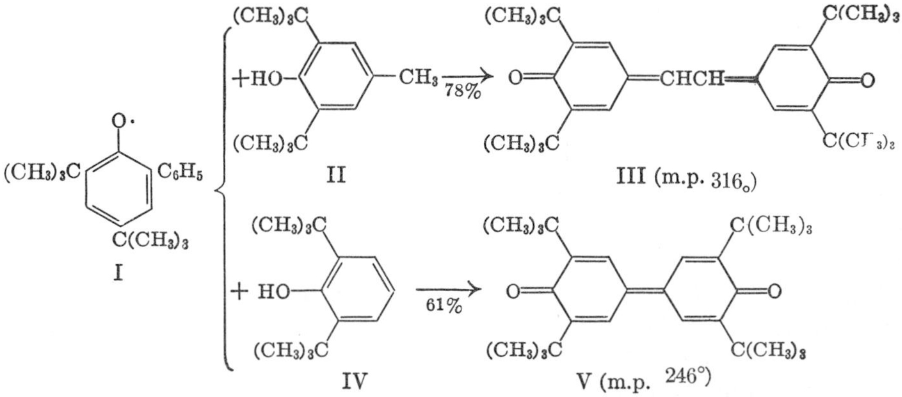

[1] Stefan Goldschmidt, b. 1889 Nürnberg, Germany; Ph.D. Munich (Dimroth); Univ. Karlsruhe, Munich

0.1 N solution in benzene but which is a potent oxidizing agent.   Thus it oxidizes the phenol II to the stilbenequinone III and it oxidizes 2,6-di-t-butylphenol (IV) to the diphenoquinone V.

A hindered phenol such 2,4,6-tri-t-butylphenol (VI) reacts with oxygen in alkaline solution at a low temperature to form the nonplanar hydroperoxide VII, in which the initial strain is relieved (G. G. Yohe, 1959; H. R. Gersmann, 1959).

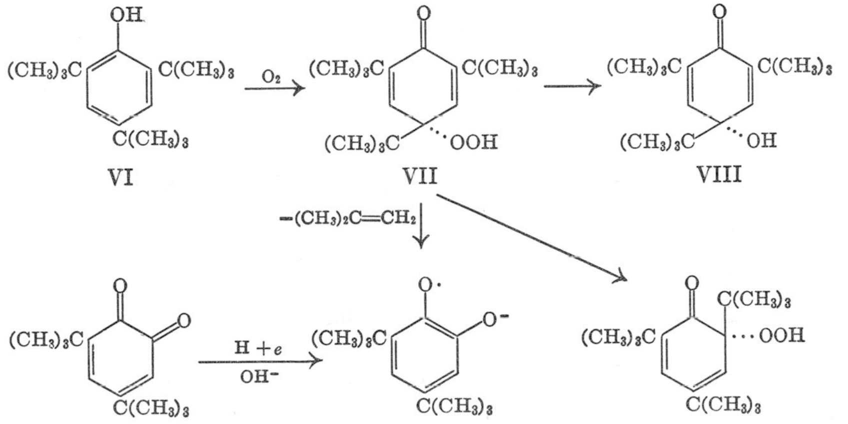

In the alkaline solution such a hydroperoxide can decompose to VIII, rearrange to XI, or suffer isobutene elimination with formation of a semiquinone anion X, characterized by the electron spin resonance spectrum and identical with the anion formed on reduction of the o-quinone IX (J. J. Conradi, 1960).

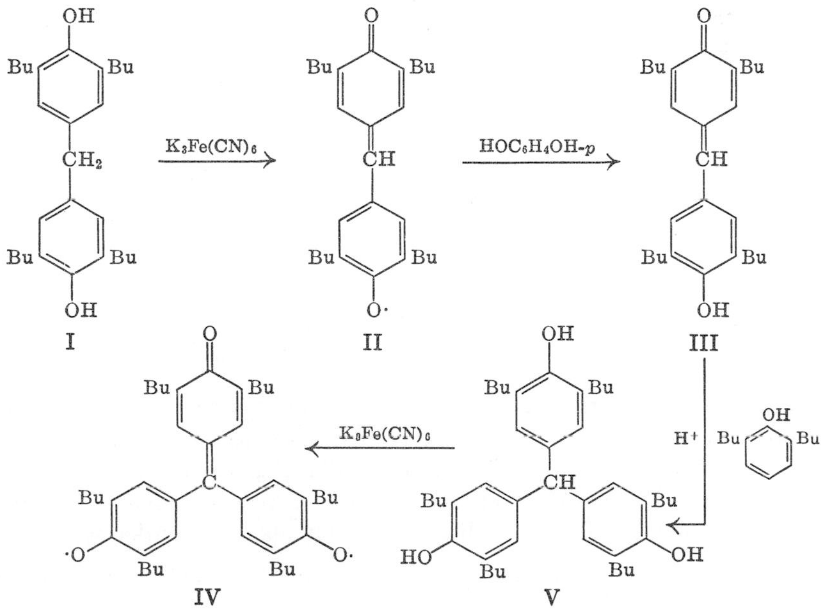

A stable aroxyl radical (II), which is unique in being unreactive to oxygen, results on oxidation of 3,3',5,5'-tetra-t-butyl-4,4'-dihydroxydiphenylmethane (I) with lead dioxide in ether (G. M. Coppinger,[1] 1957) or with alkaline ferricyanide (B. S. Joshi, 1957). The substance forms deep blue needles, m.p. 157°. Magnetic susceptibility measurements indicate the presence of one unpaired electron in the solid state, and the infrared spectrum contains a band at 1572 cm^{-1} (6.35 μ) characteristic of an oxygen radical. The blue substance is reduced by hydroquinone to the quinone methide III. Condensation of III with 2,6-di-t-butylphenol in H$_2$SO$_4$–HOAc gives the triphenylmethane V and the quinone methide derived from it by disproportionation with III; reduction of the mixture affords V (N. C. Yang, 1960). Potassium ferricyanide (2 equiv.) oxidizes V to the stable, deep purple diradical IV, λ 442 mμ (log ϵ 5.15). The radical contains two uncoupled electrons in the same π-electron system and may exist in a triplet ground state. The Chichibabin hydrocarbon (10.13) contains two uncoupled electrons in separate π-electron systems which are essentially independent of each other.

Even where neither a phenoxyl radical nor a peroxide has been isolated, the structure of a secondary product of oxidation sometimes is indicative of a radical intermediate, and apparently the phenoxyl radical can isomerize to a radical with the unpaired electron on a carbon in a position *ortho* or *para* to the oxygen atom. Thus β-naphthol is oxidized by ferric chloride in dilute aqueous solution to a substance, 2,2'-dihydroxydinaphthyl or di-β-naphthol, that corresponds in empirical

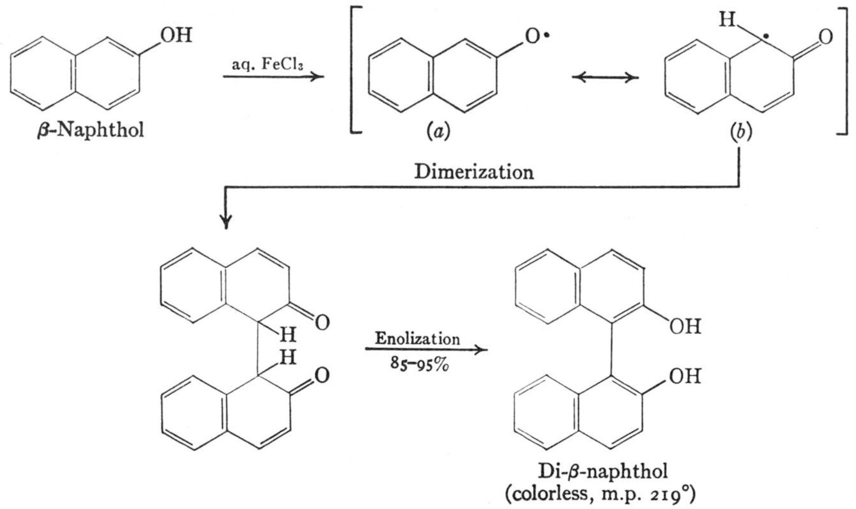

β-Naphthol

(a)   (b)

Dimerization

Enolization
85–95%

Di-β-naphthol
(colorless, m.p. 219°)

formula to the dimeric form of a radical but with a linkage between carbon rather than oxygen atoms. The formation is attributed to resonance between the initial naphthoxyl radical (a) and a carbon radical (b), dimerization of the latter radical, and enolization. An isomeric oxidation product, dehydro-β-naphthol, resulting in low yield from oxidation of β-naphthol in weakly alkaline solution with potas-

[1] G. M. Coppinger, b. 1923 Denver, Colo.; Ph.D. Rice Inst. (E. S. Lewis); Shell Development Co.

sium ferricyanide evidently arises by union of the naphthoxyl radical and the carbon radical, and enolization (Pummerer,[1] 1914). A reaction that probably pro-

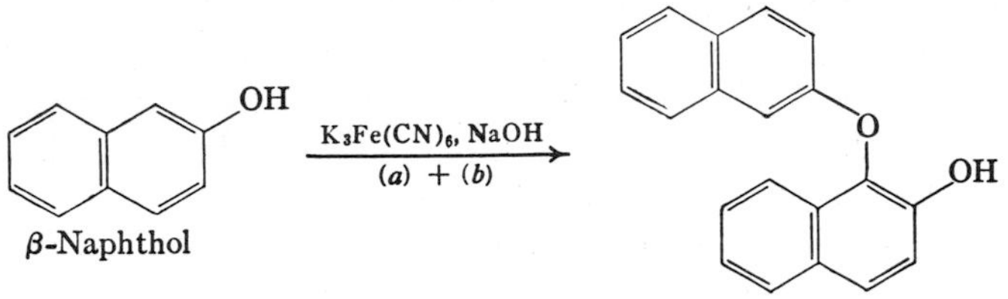

β-Naphthol

K₃Fe(CN)₆, NaOH
(a) + (b)

Dehydro-β-naphthol
(colorless, m.p. 196°)

ceeds through a radical with trivalent carbon in the *para* position is the oxidation of pyrogallol 1,3-dimethyl ether (Hofmann, 1878). The reaction product was

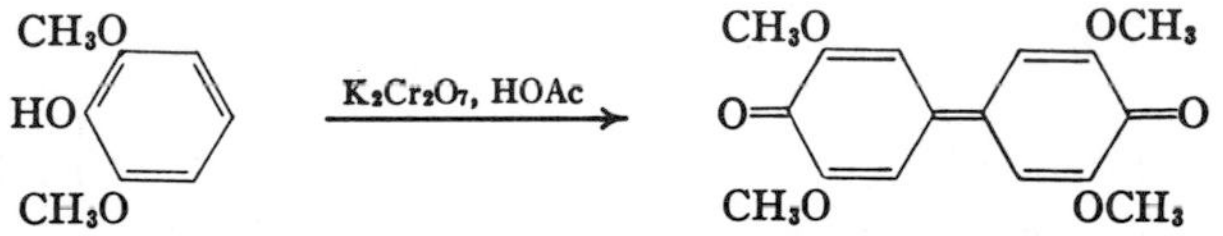

Pyrogallol 1,3-
dimethyl ether

K₂Cr₂O₇, HOAc

Cerulignone (cedriret, 3,5,3′,5′-
tetramethoxy-4,4′-diphenoquinone, blue)

first isolated as a blue pigment arising in the purification of acetic acid derived from beechwood by treatment with potassium dichromate, and accordingly was named cerulignone (L. *caeruleus*, sky blue, + *lignum*, wood, + quin<u>one</u>). The isolation of pyrogallol 1,3-dimethyl ether from beechwood tar suggested the oxidative reaction found applicable to the synthesis of the pigment. The deeply colored cerulignone is sparingly soluble in ordinary organic solvents and is best crystallized from phenol.

Investigations of Erdtman[2] and others have shown that dehydrogenative phenol coupling is a reaction of considerable biosynthetic importance. Thus the natural product magnolol has been prepared by dehydrogenation of chavicol with ferric

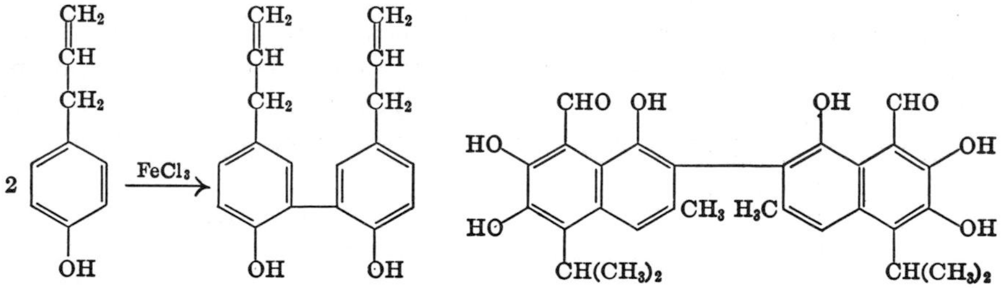

Chavicol   Magnolol   Gossypol

chloride. Gossypol, a yellow pigment isolated from cottonseed, was shown by R. Adams (1938) to be a symmetrically substituted 2,2′-di-(1-naphthol) derivative,

[1] Rudolf Pummerer, b. 1882 Wels, Austria; Ph.D. Munich (O. Dimroth); Univ. Karlsruhe, Munich

[2] Holger Erdtman, b. 1902 Ed, Sweden; Fil. dr. Stockholm (K. A. Vesterberg, H. von Euler-Chelpin); Royal Inst. Techn. Stockholm

which therefore probably arises by phenol coupling.   J. D. Edwards, Jr.[1] (1958) achieved the synthesis of the pigment starting with an oxidative coupling of 6,7-dimethoxy-3-methyl-5-isopropyl-1-naphthol, which was effected in quantitative yield by heating the substance above its melting point (130°).   Demethylation (BBr₃) gave apogossypol, in which the two formyl groups are missing, and this on reaction with N,N'-diphenylformamidine ($C_6H_5NHCH=NC_6H_5$) gave dianilinogossypol, which on hydrolysis afforded gossypol.

22.22   Condensation with Aldehydes. — Phenols condense readily with aliphatic and aromatic aldehydes to give initial products that arise from an aldol-like addition of the phenol molecule, at a reactive *o*- or *p*-position, to the carbonyl group of the aldehyde.   With adjustment of the proportion of the reac-

$$R-C\overset{H}{\underset{O}{\diagdown}} \ + \ H\cdot C_6H_4OH \ \longrightarrow \ R-\underset{\underset{OH}{|}}{CH}C_6H_4OH \ (o \ \text{and} \ p)$$

tants and the conditions, two molecules of phenol react with one of the aldehyde. The type of condensation lends itself to continuation, with the resulting production

$$HOC_6H_4\cdot H \ + \ RCH=O \ + \ H\cdot C_6H_4OH \ \longrightarrow \ HOC_6H_4-\underset{\underset{R}{|}}{CH}-C_6H_4OH$$

of polymeric products, and forms the basis for the preparation of phenol-formaldehyde plastics.

22.23   Claisen Rearrangement. — Working in his private laboratory at Godesberg on the Rhine after his retirement from a succession of professorships, Ludwig Claisen discovered (1912) that the allyl ether of ethyl acetoacetate on being heated rearranges to ethyl C-allylacetoacetate.   Saturated O-alkyl ethers

$$\underset{CH_3\overset{|}{C}=CHCO_2C_2H_5}{\overset{OCH_2CH=CH_2}{\big|}} \quad \xrightarrow[85\%]{200°} \quad \underset{CH_3\overset{||}{C}-\overset{|}{C}HCO_2C_2H_5}{\overset{O \quad CH_2CH=CH_2}{}}$$

are stable to heat.   Since phenol resembles the enolic form of acetoacetic ester in acidity and in the ability to couple with diazonium salts, Claisen examined phenol allyl ether and found that it rearranges smoothly at the boiling point and affords *o*-allylphenol in high yield.   The reaction proved to be generally applicable and

Phenol allyl ether   *o*-Allylphenol
    (b.p. 192°)   (b.p. 220°)

has found many useful applications.   Claisen's last paper, published (1926) four years before his death at the age of 79, was on the mechanism of the rearrangement

[1] J. D. Edwards, Jr., b. 1924 Alexandria, La.; Ph.D. Texas; Baylor Univ.; U. S. Vet. Admin. Hosp.; Clemson College; Monsanto Chem. Co.

which now bears his name.   Claisen's postulate, according to W. N. White (1961), "has been shown to be correct in all its details."

A clue to the mechanism emerged from the investigation of allyl ethers bearing an identifying substituent in the allyl group, for example I, in which the γ-carbon

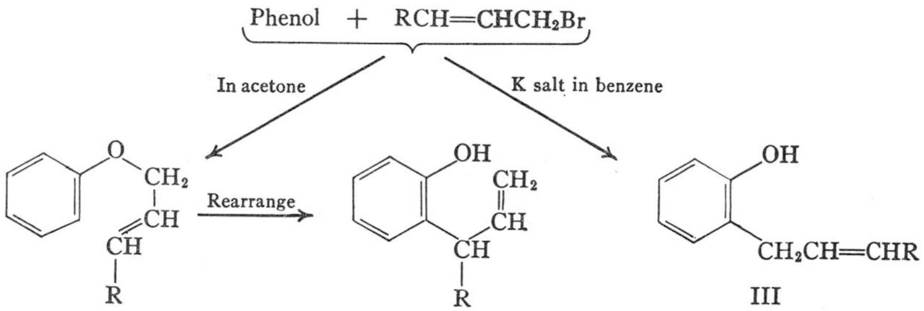

Phenol + $RCH=CHCH_2Br$

In acetone   K salt in benzene

Rearrange

I   II   III

carries an alkyl substituent.   The product of rearrangement is the α-substituted o-allylphenol II, not the γ-derivative III.   The reaction thus involves both a migration and an allylic rearrangement in the allyl group.   Claisen's procedures for preparing both isomers have proved to be generally applicable.   Allyl ethers required for rearrangement to II are prepared by reaction of allyl bromide with a solution of the phenol in acetone in the presence of potassium carbonate to neutralize the hydrogen bromide liberated (yield of phenol allyl ether, 86–97%).   On the other hand, the reaction of allyl bromide with a suspension of the anhydrous potassium salt of the phenol in benzene affords chiefly the product of C-allylation (III).   Acetone, a polar solvent, favors O-allylation, and nonpolar benzene favors C-allylation.

Since ethers having a free *ortho* position rearrange to o-allylphenols, and since the γ-carbon of the allyl group is the point of attachment, the reaction must proceed

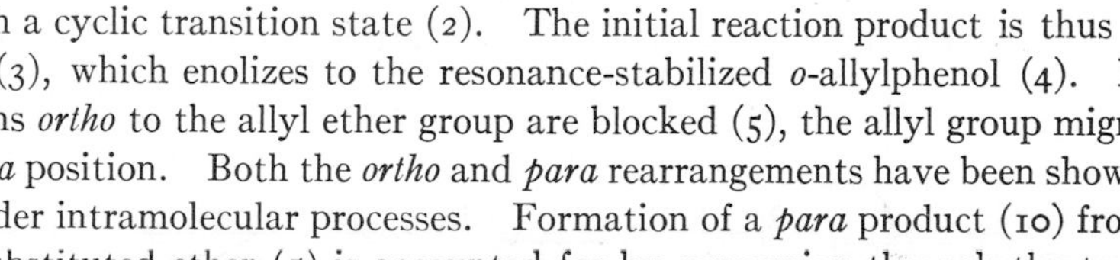

(1)   (2)   (3)   (4)

through a cyclic transition state (2).   The initial reaction product is thus the dienone (3), which enolizes to the resonance-stabilized o-allylphenol (4).   If both positions *ortho* to the allyl ether group are blocked (5), the allyl group migrates to the *para* position.   Both the *ortho* and *para* rearrangements have been shown to be first-order intramolecular processes.   Formation of a *para* product (10) from a di-*ortho*-substituted ether (5) is accounted for by conversion through the transition state (6) to the dienone (7), which cannot acquire stability by enolization and which therefore undergoes allylic rearrangement through (8) to the dienone (9), which on enolization affords the p-allylphenol (10).   Conroy[1] (1953) rearranged

[1] Harold Conroy, b. 1917 Hamden, Conn.; Ph.D. Harvard (Stork); Brandeis, Yale Univ.; Mellon Inst.

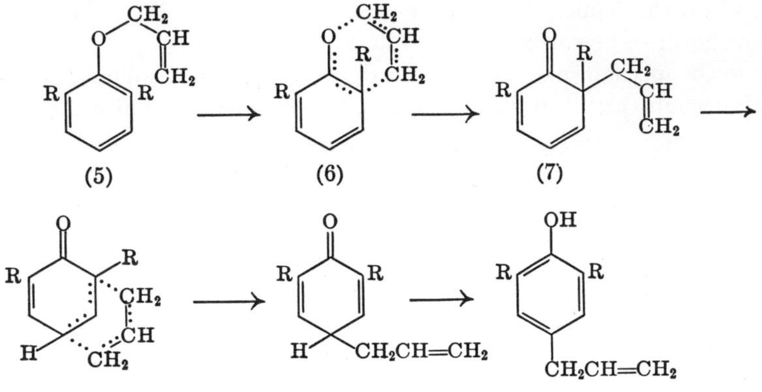

(5) → (6) → (7) →

(8) → (9) → (10)

the allyl ether of 2,6-dimethylphenol in the presence of maleic anhydride and isolated the adduct of the dienone (7), and Curtin[1] isolated the dienone itself by running the reaction of the phenol sodium salt with allyl bromide under Claisen conditions but at 15°. The intermediate rearranges on heating to a mixture of the *p*-substituted phenol (50%) and the allyl ether (28%).

Hurd[2] found (1938) that vinyl allyl ethers also rearrange. The products in this case are aldehydes, and here also the new carbon–carbon bond extends to the γ-carbon of the original allyl group. Burgstahler[3] extended the reaction to vinyl

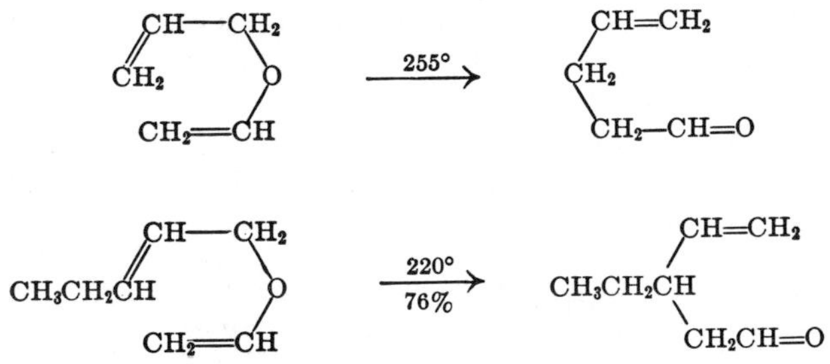

ethers of substituted allyl alcohols and found (1960) that both the *cis* vinyl ether I and the *trans* isomer on Claisen rearrangement give essentially only *trans* products (II). The observation implies that the geometry of the transition state is strongly influenced by factors relating to the stability of the product.

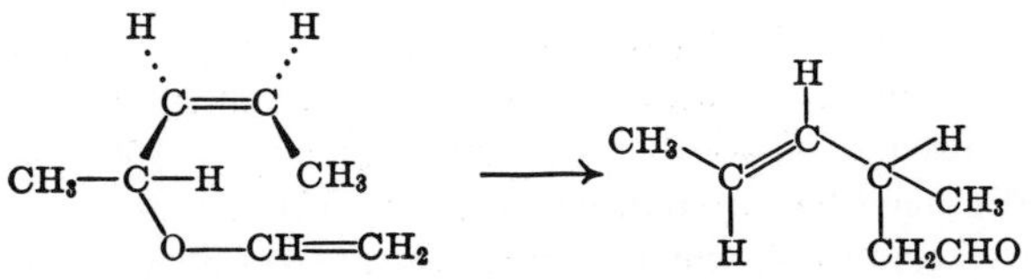

I → II

[1] David Y. Curtin, b. 1920 Philadelphia; Ph.D. Illinois (Price); Columbia Univ.; Univ. Illinois
[2] Charles D. Hurd, b. 1897 Utica, N. Y.; Ph.D. Princeton (L. W. Jones); Northwestern Univ.
[3] Albert W. Burgstahler, b. 1928 Grand Rapids, Mich.; Ph.D. Harvard (Stork); Univ. Kansas

Alexander[1] had made a preliminary study of the rearrangement of $(-)$-*trans*-α,γ-dimethylallyl phenyl ether (III) and obtained an optically active product. Burgstahler, on the basis of his findings, inferred that the orientation of the transition state is that suggested in IV, that the product has the *trans* configuration V, and that the configuration of the asymmetric center in V is enantiomeric to that in III.

III   IV   V

W. Gerrard[2] (1957) found that treatment of phenol allyl ether with boron trichloride at $-80°$ and hydrolysis of the product gives exclusively *o*-allylphenol.

22.24   Clathrates. — *o*-Thymotic acid (1) on dehydration affords *cis*-*o*-thymotide (2) and tri-*o*-thymotide (3; W. Baker, 1952). Tri-*o*-thymotide (3)

(1)   (2)   (3)

crystallizes from benzene, chloroform, or *n*-hexane in the form of very stable solvates from which the solvent is eliminated only by heating at 180° in vacuum.

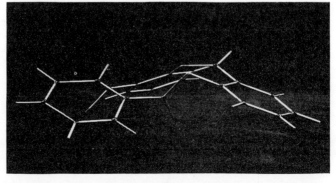

These complexes are known as clathrates (L. *clathri*, lattice); they are similar to the urea inclusion complexes (4.18) except that the host is a covalently bonded molecule with a hole in it. X-ray crystallographic examination of these clathrates revealed that enantiomorphous forms exist resembling three-bladed

[1] Elliot R. Alexander, 1920–1950; b. Kansas City, Mo.; Ph.D. Columbia (Cope); Univ. Illinois
[2] William Gerrard, b. 1900 Tyldesley, Lanchashire, England; Ph.D. London; Northern Polytechnic, London

propellors of opposite pitch, as is evident from the model of the ring system of the host component of one enantiomeric form of a complex (H. M. Powell,[1] 1952). Since racemization occurs rapidly in solution, addition of a (+)-seed crystal to a saturated solution causes eventual crystallization of the entire lot as the (+)-enantiomer. By this means an optically active compound is produced without use of an optically active resolving agent. When an adduct is formed from a guest solvent which is itself a racemic mixture, any one crystal will take in preferentially the (+) or (−) form of a solvent molecule according to the shape of its cavity; the volume available is sufficient for the excluded molecule but the configuration is wrong. *sec*-Butyl bromide was resolved by seeding a solution with a single crystal. The large (−) rotation of the resulting crystallizate due mainly to the tri-*o*-thymotide decays rapidly through racemization and leaves a smaller permanent (−) rotation due to the (−)-*sec*-butyl bromide.

PROBLEMS

1. Compare the effect of *o*-, *m*-, and *p*-nitro groups on the dissociation of phenol and of aniline (see Tables 21.1 and 22.1).
2. Summarize instances of the modification of physical properties attributable to chelation.
3. Outline a series of experiments by which saligenin (22.16) could be shown to contain one phenolic hydroxyl group and one alcoholic group.
4. Suggest a method for the synthesis of 4-ethylcatechol.
5. Outline the steps involved in the synthetic production from benzene of:
   (*a*) Anisole   (*d*) *p*-Aminophenol
   (*b*) Catechol   (*e*) 4-*n*-Hexylresorcinol
   (*c*) *o*-Aminophenol
6. Cite qualitative tests that would distinguish between the following compounds: $C_6H_5OCH_2COOH$, *p*-$CH_3COC_6H_4OH$, $C_6H_5OCOCH_3$, $C_6H_5COCH_2OH$.
7. Formulate syntheses of α- and of β-naphthol starting with benzene or anisole and succinic anhydride.
8. By what sequence of reactions could *p*-aminophenol be converted into 2-bromo-4-aminophenol?

[1] H. M. Powell, b. 1906 Coventry; F.R.S.; Oxford Univ.

Note on the Claisen rearrangement.—Commenting on the citation of his work on page 771, Dr. A. W. Burgstahler has called our attention to the communication by E. N. Marvell and J. L. Stephenson, *J. Org.*, **25**, 676 (1960), reporting more complete work on the same rearrangement. "The quasi-chair picture of IV proposed by Marvell is much preferred to this." Dr. Burgstahler notes also that our account omits reference to the C^{14} tracer work of H. Schmid reported in *Helv.*, **41**, 657 (1958) and earlier papers.

Chapter 23

ARYL HALIDES

23.1 **Properties.** — The more common aryl halides available for synthetic uses or as solvents are listed in Table 23.1. Methods of preparation are summarized in the following section.

TABLE 23.1. ARYL HALIDES

NAME	FORMULA	M.P., °C.	B.P., °C.
Fluorobenzene	C_6H_5F	-45	85
Chlorobenzene	C_6H_5Cl	-45	132
Bromobenzene	C_6H_5Br	-30.6	155.5
Iodobenzene	C_6H_5I	-29	188.5
o-Chlorotoluene	$o\text{-}CH_3C_6H_4Cl$	-36	159
m-Chlorotoluene	$m\text{-}CH_3C_6H_4Cl$	-48	162
p-Chlorotoluene	$p\text{-}CH_3C_6H_4Cl$	7	162
o-Bromotoluene	$o\text{-}CH_3C_6H_4Br$	-26	182
m-Bromotoluene	$m\text{-}CH_3C_6H_4Br$	-40	184
p-Bromotoluene	$p\text{-}CH_3C_6H_4Br$	28	184
o-Bromoanisole	$o\text{-}CH_3OC_6H_4Br$	liq.	222
p-Bromoanisole	$p\text{-}CH_3OC_6H_4Br$	11	223
p-Bromodimethylaniline	$p\text{-}(CH_3)_2NC_6H_4Br$	55	264
o-Dichlorobenzene	$C_6H_4Cl_2(1,2)$	liq.	179
p-Dichlorobenzene	$C_6H_4Cl_2(1,4)$	53	173
1,2,4-Trichlorobenzene	$C_6H_3Cl_3(1,2,4)$	17	213
1,2,3,4-Tetrachlorobenzene	$C_6H_2Cl_4(1,2,3,4)$	46	254
1,2,4,5-Tetrachlorobenzene	$C_6H_2Cl_4(1,2,4,5)$	138	245
Hexachlorobenzene	C_6Cl_6	228	332
p-Dibromobenzene	$p\text{-}C_6H_4Br_2$	89	218
o-Bromochlorobenzene	$C_6H_4ClBr(1,2)$	liq.	199
p-Bromochlorobenzene	$C_6H_4ClBr(1,4)$	67	196
o-Bromoiodobenzene	$C_6H_4BrI(1,2)$	liq.	257
p-Bromoiodobenzene	$C_6H_4BrI(1,4)$	92	252
o-Chloroiodobenzene	$C_6H_4ClI(1,2)$	liq.	235
p-Chloroiodobenzene	$C_6H_4ClI(1,4)$	57	227

23.2   **Preparation.** — The benzene nucleus is readily substituted by chlorine or bromine atoms on interaction with the halogens in the presence of ferric chloride or bromide, aluminum chloride, or iodine. The less reactive iodine does not give comparable substitutions because the equilibrium is unfavorable. The equilibrium can be displaced by conducting the reaction in the presence of

$$ArH \; + \; I_2 \; \rightleftharpoons \; ArI \; + \; HI$$

an oxidizing agent to destroy the hydrogen iodide. Iodic acid and mercuric oxide have been used, but nitric acid usually is preferred, as in the example

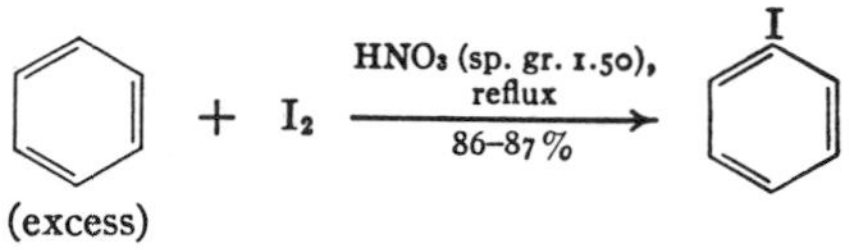

(excess)

Aryl iodides can also be prepared by reaction of an aryl Grignard reagent with diiodoacetylene (V. Franzen, 1954). At the end of the reaction the acetylenedi-

$$2C_6H_5MgBr \; + \; IC{\equiv}CI \rightarrow 2C_6H_5I \; + \; BrMgC{\equiv}CMgBr$$

magnesium bromide is hydrolyzed with dilute acid to acetylene; the iodide is isolated easily in yields up to 95%. An interesting procedure for iodination of

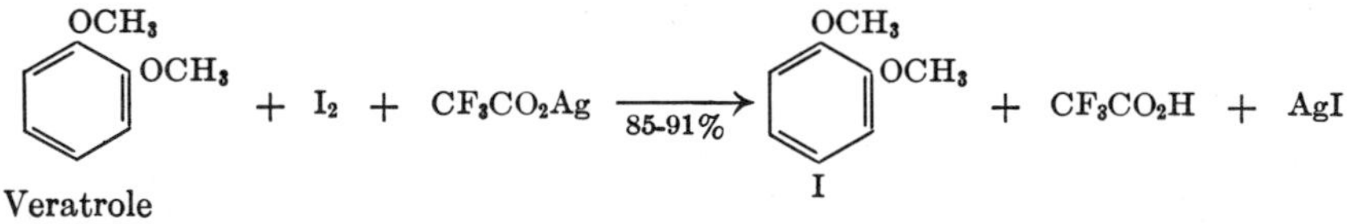

Veratrole

veratrole involves gradual addition of a suspension of iodine in chloroform to a mixture of veratrole and dry silver trifluoroacetate (D. E. Janssen, 1956). The reagent is made by adding trifluoroacetic acid to a suspension of precipitated, moist silver oxide and evaporating the filtered solution. Commercial silver acetate can be used, but the yield is then 75–80%. The reaction succeeds owing to the activating effect of the *p*-methoxyl group. Aniline affords *p*-iodoaniline on re-action with iodine in the presence of aqueous sodium bicarbonate. 2,4-Dinitro-iodobenzene is obtained in 65–71% yield by reaction of 2,4-dinitrochloroben-zene with sodium iodide in dimethylformamide (*Org. Syn.*, 1960).

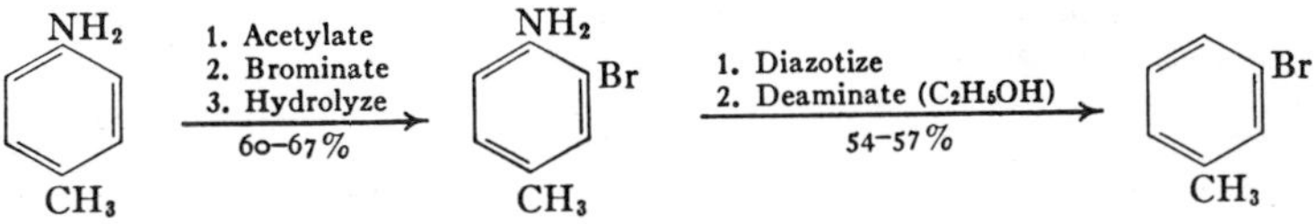

The Sandmeyer reaction is the standard preparative route to the chloro- and bromotoluenes. The total process for preparation of *m*-bromotoluene requires either the preparation of *m*-toluidine from *p*-toluidine or the alternative route from the same starting material as formulated. The Sandmeyer reaction affords the best route to *o*-bromochlorobenzene, to *o*- and *p*-bromoiodobenzene, and to the chloroiodobenzenes. The Schiemann reaction (21.25) is useful for the preparation of fluorobenzene (51–57 %), *o*- and *p*-bromofluorobenzene (about 70–80 %). Several *p*-dihalobenzenes can be obtained satisfactorily by direct halogenation; the *p*-isomers are formed as the chief products, along with smaller amounts of the *o*-dihalides, and since the symmetrically substituted *p*-isomers are all solids, in contrast with the companion substances, they can be purified by crystallization. *p*-Dibromobenzene has been obtained in yields of 61–71 % and 85 % by bromination of benzene with use of aluminum chloride or ferric bromide, respectively, and by similar processes chlorobenzene affords *p*-bromochlorobenzene in yields of 77 % and 88 %. The *p*-bromo derivatives of anisole and of dimethylaniline also can be made satisfactorily by direct bromination without catalyst. Dichlorination of benzene in the presence of aluminum chloride gives a preponderant amount of solid *p*-dichlorobenzene, employed as a moth repellant, and the liquid *o*-isomer, formed to the extent of about 30 %, is useful as a special solvent, for which purpose the presence of small amounts of the *m*- and *p*-isomers is not objectionable. A higher proportion of *o*-dichlorobenzene results from the use of ferric chloride as catalyst. Further chlorination gives chiefly 1,2,4-trichlorobenzene, which is also formed on treatment of the stereoisomeric benzene hexachlorides with alkali. The symmetrical 1,2,4,5-derivative is the principal product of tetrachlorination, and a fifth and sixth halogen can be introduced, though with increased difficulty (see p. 787).

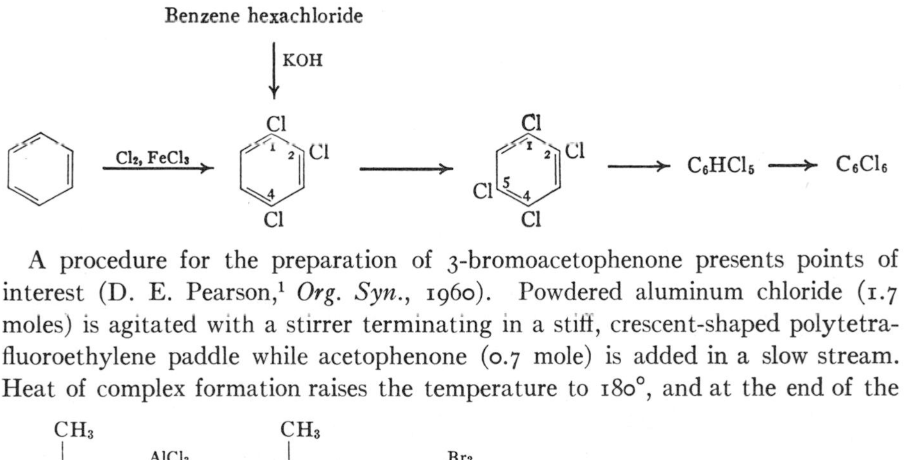

Benzene hexachloride

A procedure for the preparation of 3-bromoacetophenone presents points of interest (D. E. Pearson,[1] *Org. Syn.*, 1960). Powdered aluminum chloride (1.7 moles) is agitated with a stirrer terminating in a stiff, crescent-shaped polytetrafluoroethylene paddle while acetophenone (0.7 mole) is added in a slow stream. Heat of complex formation raises the temperature to 180°, and at the end of the

addition the mass becomes molten and is easily stirred. Bromine (0.8 mole) is then added at 80–85° and the mixture heated until it solidifies. The cooled cake is added in portions to ice–HCl; yield 70–75 %; m.p. 8°. Bromination of aceto-

[1] D. E. Pearson, b. 1914 Madison, Wis.; Ph.D. Illinois (Marvel); Vanderbilt Univ.

phenone in ether in the presence of a catalytic amount of aluminum chloride affords phenacyl bromide in 88–96% yield, but formation of the 1:1 complex without solvent blocks attack of the methyl group, probably because there is a positive charge close to the methyl group; the complex may have an eight-membered cyclic structure. The second mole of aluminum chloride specified in the procedure greatly increases the activity of the bromine through complex formation, $Br^+[AlCl_3Br]^-$.

Two other observations emphasize the importance of conditions in determining the direction of substitution. Bromination of 4,4'-dinitrodiphenylmethane proceeds slowly (7 days) in refluxing carbon tetrachloride (trace of I_2) to give di-p-nitrophenyldibromomethane in 41% yield, whereas bromination in sulfuric acid in the presence of silver ions (Ag_2SO_4) for 3 hrs. at room temperature affords the 2,2'-dibromo derivative in yield of 94% (J. H. Gorvin, 1955). Bromination of o-hydroxyacetophenone in anhydrous acetic acid gives the ω-bromo derivative, bromination in 80% acetic acid gives the 4-derivative (Ng. Ph. Buu-Hoï,[1] 1955). Higher ketones, for example 4-hydroxystearophenone and 2- and 4-acetyl-1-naphthol, undergo only nuclear bromination.

23.3   Side-Chain Halogenation. — In the presence of a Lewis acid catalyst, toluene reacts with chlorine or bromine to give about equal parts of the o- and p-halo derivatives. When the hydrocarbon is treated with either halogen at the reflux temperature in the absence of catalyst, preferably with exposure to light, the halogen attacks the methyl side chain rather than the ring with formation in succession of the mono-, di-, and trihalo derivatives. The reaction re-

Benzyl chloride   Benzal chloride   Benzotrichloride

sembles the chlorination of methane but proceeds more rapidly because of the activating effect of the phenyl group. Aromatic compounds with other alkyl side chains (except t-butyl) react similarly. A free radical mechanism is involved, as indicated by the fact that side-chain chlorination is favored by reaction in the vapor phase at 400–600° and by the observation that N-bromosuccinimide reacts with toluene in the presence of dibenzoyl peroxide to give benzyl bromide in 64% yield; in the absence of peroxide the predominant reaction is $para$ substitution. Kharasch discovered (1939) that side-chain chlorination can be accomplished with sulfuryl chloride in the presence of a peroxide. The peroxide-

$$C_6H_5CH_3 \ + \ SO_2Cl_2 \ \xrightarrow[\text{80\%}]{\text{Dibenzoyl peroxide, 15 min.}} \ C_6H_5CH_2Cl \ + \ SO_2 \ + \ HCl$$

catalyzed reaction proceeds rapidly in the dark, whereas in the absence of a peroxide the light-promoted reaction is complete only in seven hours.

[1] N. P. Buu-Hoï, b. 1915 Hué, Vietnam; Ph.D. Univ. Paris (Mme. Ramart-Lucas); Univ. Vietnam; Radium Inst., Univ. Paris; French National Center for Sci. Res.

TABLE 23.2. SIDE-CHAIN HALOGENATED DERIVATIVES OF TOLUENE

NAME	FORMULA	M.P., °C.	B.P., °C.
Benzyl chloride	$C_6H_5CH_2Cl$	liq.	179
Benzal chloride	$C_6H_5CHCl_2$	liq.	206
Benzotrichloride	$C_6H_5CCl_3$	−5	221
Benzyl bromide	$C_6H_5CH_2Br$	liq.	199
Benzyl iodide	$C_6H_5CH_2I$	24	98/11 mm.

t-Butyl hypochlorite is an efficient reagent for effecting free-radical chlorination under very mild conditions (C. Walling, 1960). Thus in the presence of azobisisobutyronitrile as initiator, the reaction with toluene at 40° affords benzyl chloride (84%), benzal chloride (4%), *t*-butyl alcohol (97%), and 1–3% each of chlorotoluenes, chloro-*t*-butyl alcohol, methyl chloride, and acetone.

$$(CH_3)_2\overset{\overset{CN}{|}}{C}N{=}N\overset{\overset{CN}{|}}{C}(CH_3)_2 \xrightarrow{-N_2} (CH_3)_2\overset{\overset{CN}{|}}{C}\cdot \xrightarrow[\text{(CH}_3)_3\text{C(CN)Cl}]{\text{(CH}_3)_3\text{COCl}}$$

$$(CH_3)_3CO\cdot \xrightarrow[-\text{(CH}_3)_3\text{COH}]{C_6H_5CH_3} C_6H_5\dot{C}H_2 \xrightarrow[-\text{(CH}_3)_3\text{CO}\cdot]{\text{(CH}_3)_3\text{COCl}} C_6H_5CH_2Cl$$

Ethylbenzene on bromination in sunlight at 0° gives first α-phenylethyl bromide ($C_6H_5CHBrCH_3$) and then α,α-dibromoethylbenzene ($C_6H_5CBr_2CH_3$). *n*-Propylbenzene reacts analogously. Bromination of ethylbenzene at the boiling point gives a mixture of α-phenylethyl bromide and styrene dibromide ($C_6H_5CHBrCH_2Br$). Chlorination of ethylbenzene in the cold under irradiation leads to α-phenylethyl chloride, but chlorination of boiling ethylbenzene in diffused daylight gives a mixture of the α- and β-chlorides and styrene dichloride.

The benzyl and benzal halides and benzotrihalides are all liquids (Table 23.2) with the exception of benzyl iodide, a low-melting solid that can be prepared from a mixture of benzyl chloride and potassium iodide in refluxing alcohol. The halides listed all undergo rapid hydrolysis in moist air, and they are potent lachrymators. Benzyl bromide and benzyl iodide cause a flow of tears, with painful swelling of the eyes, at concentrations of 0.004 mg. and 0.002 mg. per liter, respectively. ω-Chloroacetophenone (phenacyl chloride), $C_6H_5COCH_2Cl$ (m.p. 54°, b.p. 245°) is a still more powerful lachrymator, effective at a concentration of only 0.0003 mg. per liter, and has been used as a chemical warfare agent and in police work; it is dispersed by explosion in grenades, either in the solid form or in solution, and also by burning a mixture of the substance with black powder. The substance is made by chlorination of acetophenone in acetic acid solution.

The preparation of halides of the types $ArCHF_2$ and $ArCF_3$ can be accomplished by reaction of the corresponding aldehyde or acid with sulfur tetrafluoride (W. C. Smith,[1] 1960). The reaction with benzoic acid gives the acid fluoride at room temperature (1a) and benzotrifluoride at a higher temperature (1b). Benzaldehyde reacts to give benzal fluoride (2). The reaction is generally applicable in both the aliphatic and the aromatic series, and double or triple bonds

[1] William C. Smith, b. 1925 Geneva, N. Y.; Ph.D. Illinois (Audrieth); du Pont Co.

ia. $C_6H_5CO_2H$ + SF_4 $\longrightarrow$ C_6H_5COF + HF + SOF_2
ib. C_6H_5COF + SF_4 $\longrightarrow$ $C_6H_5CF_3$ + SOF_2
2. C_6H_5CHO + SF_4 $\longrightarrow$ $C_6H_5CHF_2$ + SOF_2

present are not affected. With carbon dioxide the reagent gives first carbonyl fluoride and then carbon tetrafluoride. The observation that carboxylic acids react much more readily than anhydrides suggested that the hydrogen fluoride formed in the initial step (1), accelerates the reaction, and indeed use of HF as catalyst raised the yield of difluorodiphenylmethane from benzophenone from 10 to 97%. The catalyst probably participates in formation of a cyclic transition state, as formulated. Even more potent catalysts are BF_3, AsF_3, PF_5, TiF_4.

$$Ar_2C{=}O \xrightarrow{SF_4} Ar_2C{-}OSF_3 \xrightarrow{HF}$$

$$Ar_2C \overset{O\cdots SF_2}{\underset{F\ \ F\cdots H}{|}} F \longrightarrow Ar_2CF_2 + O{=}SF_2 + HF$$

A disadvantage of sulfur tetrafluoride is that it requires pressure equipment constructed of fluorine-resistant alloy, but fortunately the same reactions can be conducted on a laboratory scale in glass, polyethylene, or metal containers by use of phenylsulfur trifluoride (W. A. Sheppard,[1] 1961). This reagent is prepared (3) by reaction of diphenyl disulfide with silver difluoride in Freon-113, b.p. 47° (1,1,2-trichloro-1,2,2,-trifluoroethane). The liquid reagent slowly attacks

3. $(C_6H_5S)_2$ + $6AgF_2$ $\xrightarrow[56-61\%]{}$ $2C_6H_5SF_3$ + $6AgF$
                                                        b.p. 48°/2.6 mm.

4. C_6H_5CHO + $C_6H_5SF_3$ $\xrightarrow[71-80\%]{}$ $C_6H_5CHF_2$ + C_6H_5SOF

glass but can be stored indefinitely in bottles of aluminum or of polytetrafluoro-ethylene resin (Teflon). Reaction of the reagent with benzaldehyde (4) is conducted in a glass flask connected to a dry distillation column and heated to 100°; the pressure is then reduced until the benzal fluoride distills (b.p. 45°/15 mm.). The second product, benzenesulfinyl fluoride, b.p. 60°/2.5 mm., is obtained in 82–89% yield.

23.4   Chloromethylation. — The chloromethyl group, $-CH_2Cl$, characteristic of benzyl chloride can be introduced directly by a process akin to the Friedel-Crafts reaction. This consists in interaction with formaldehyde and hydrogen chloride in the presence of a catalyst such as zinc chloride or aluminum chloride (Blanc reaction). Benzyl chloride, for example, can be prepared in good yield by passing hydrogen chloride gas into a suspension of paraformaldehyde and anhydrous zinc chloride in benzene. Paraformaldehyde undergoes depolymerization under the influence of hydrogen chloride, and in the presence of the catalyst benzene condenses with formaldehyde or the addition product with hydrogen chloride, $HOCH_2Cl$, with ultimate production of benzyl chloride. The procedure

[1] William A. Sheppard, b. 1928 Hamilton, Ontario; Ph.D. Mass. Inst. Tech. (Roberts, Swain); du Pont Co.

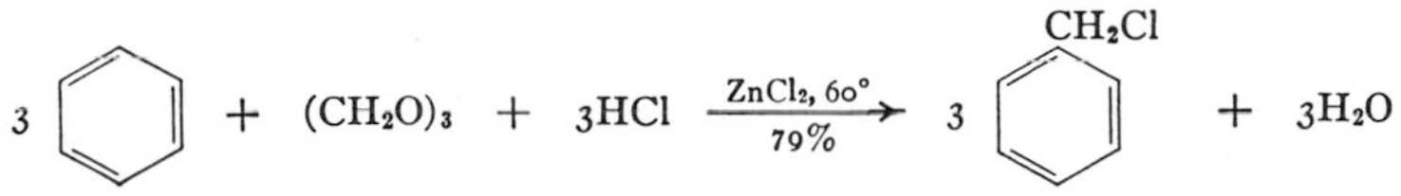

$$3 \; \bigcirc \; + \; (CH_2O)_3 \; + \; 3HCl \; \xrightarrow[79\%]{ZnCl_2, \, 60°} \; 3 \; \bigcirc^{CH_2Cl} \; + \; 3H_2O$$

(with some *p*-xylylene
dichloride, $ClCH_2C_6H_4CH_2Cl$,
m.p. 100°)

can be varied by replacing formaldehyde by methylal, $CH_2(OCH_3)_2$, or by chloro-methyl ether, produced as follows:

$$(CH_2O)_3 \; + \; 3 \, CH_3OH \; + \; 3 \, HCl \; \longrightarrow \; 3 \, CH_3OCH_2Cl \; + \; 3 \, H_2O$$

Zinc chloride is sometimes fused with a small quantity of aluminum chloride to increase the activity, or even replaced entirely by the more reactive reagent, and in other instances sufficient catalysis is obtained with a mineral acid alone, as in the preparation of 2-hydroxy-5-nitrobenzyl chloride.

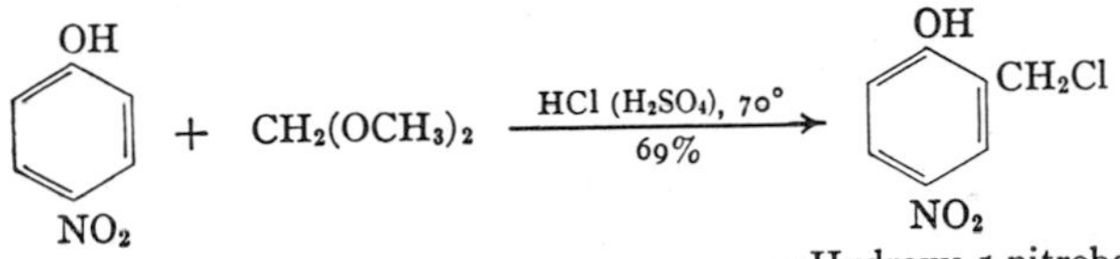

$$\overset{OH}{\underset{NO_2}{\bigcirc}} \; + \; CH_2(OCH_3)_2 \; \xrightarrow[69\%]{HCl \, (H_2SO_4), \, 70°} \; \overset{OH}{\underset{NO_2}{\bigcirc}}{}^{CH_2Cl}$$

2-Hydroxy-5-nitrobenzyl
chloride (m.p. 130°)

Chloromethylation is subject to most of the limitations and specific characteristics of the Friedel-Crafts alkylation reaction. The orientation is comparable, and some polysubstitution usually occurs; thus in the first example cited benzyl chloride is accompanied by the *p*-disubstitution product. Introduction of the chloromethyl group perhaps proceeds under milder conditions and more selectively than Friedel-Crafts alkylations, and the reaction, followed by reduction, has occasionally been employed in synthesis of the methyl derivatives: ArH → $ArCH_2Cl$ → $ArCH_3$; the reduction can be accomplished with zinc and acetic acid or with stannous chloride. The great value of the chloromethylation reaction, however, is that the products are reactive halides capable of being transformed into products of a variety of types: $ArCH_2OH$, $ArCH_2OCH_3$, $ArCH_2CN$, $ArCH_2$-COOH, $ArCH_2N(CH_3)_2$. One synthetic use is the introduction of an acid side chain required for formation of a new ring:

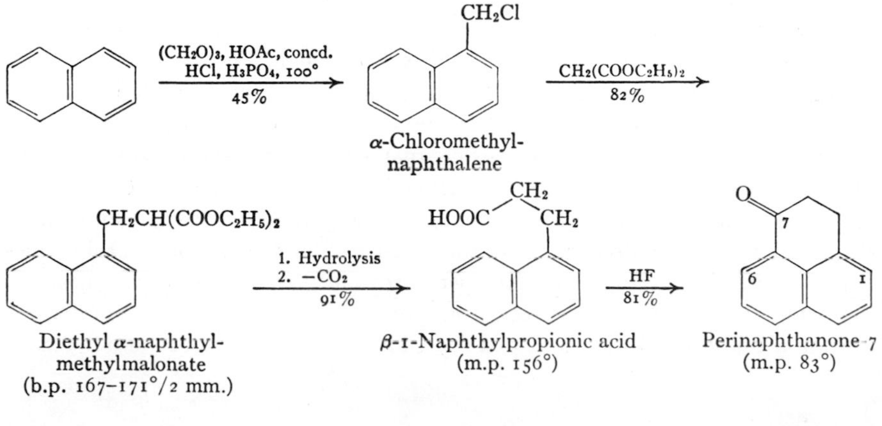

$$\bigcirc\bigcirc \; \xrightarrow[45\%]{\substack{(CH_2O)_3, \, HOAc, \, concd. \\ HCl, \, H_3PO_4, \, 100°}} \; \bigcirc\bigcirc^{CH_2Cl} \; \xrightarrow[82\%]{CH_2(COOC_2H_5)_2}$$

α-Chloromethyl-
naphthalene

$$\overset{CH_2CH(COOC_2H_5)_2}{\bigcirc\bigcirc} \; \xrightarrow[91\%]{\substack{1. \, Hydrolysis \\ 2. \, -CO_2}} \; \overset{HOOC^{CH_2}CH_2}{\bigcirc\bigcirc} \; \xrightarrow[81\%]{HF} \; \bigcirc\bigcirc\bigcirc$$

Diethyl α-naphthyl-
methylmalonate
(b.p. 167–171°/2 mm.)

β-1-Naphthylpropionic acid
(m.p. 156°)

Perinaphthanone-7
(m.p. 83°)

Acetaldehyde and some of the higher aldehydes have been used for production of compounds of the type ArCHClR, and an iodomethylation has been reported in one special instance.

23.5   **Reactivity.** — Compounds of the benzyl halide type show greatly enhanced reactivity as compared with alkyl halides, and are similar to allyl halides.   Activation in benzyl halides is attributed to formation of a carbonium ion with distribution of the positive charge between the *ortho* and *para* positions and the side chain.   Whereas substituted allyl halides invariably un-

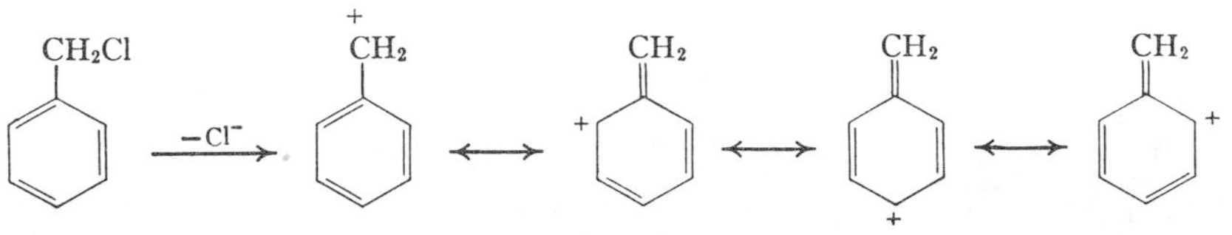

dergo some allylic rearrangement in replacement reactions [C_6H_5CH=$CHCH_2Br$ → $C_6H_5CH(OAc)CH$=CH_2 + normal product], the resonance structures of the benzyl ion that carry a charge in the nucleus do not play so prominent a role in determining the point of attack by reagents, for the usual products are those of the benzyl type: $C_6H_5CH_2A$.   However allylic rearrangements occur in some condensations of benzylmagnesium halides (Tiffeneau).   Thus the reaction of benzylmagnesium bromide with formaldehyde gives none of the normal product,

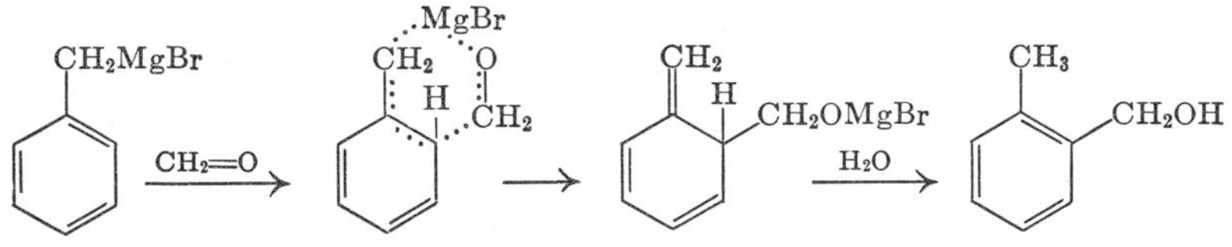

o-Tolylcarbinol

$C_6H_5CH_2CH_2OH$, but affords *o*-tolylcarbinol, probably through a cyclic transition state.   *o*-Tolyl derivatives resulting from allylic rearrangements are formed similarly in condensations of the same Grignard reagent with acid chlorides and anhydrides, but the normal benzyl derivatives are produced in reactions with ketones, carbon dioxide, and typical esters.   The greater disposition of comparable aliphatic systems to react in the abnormal sense is indicated by the observation that the Grignard reagent of cinnamyl chloride reacts chiefly to give products of the type $C_6H_5CH(A)CH$=CH_2, even with carbon dioxide (Gilman).

In contrast with benzyl halides, the ring-substituted halogen derivatives of benzene are markedly less reactive than the corresponding alkyl halides and are comparable to vinyl halides.   The inert character of the aryl and vinyl compounds is attributed to the opportunity for resonance in the halide molecules, rather than in a derived ion, with resulting shortening of the carbon–halogen bond distance and increased firmness of binding.   In the absence of labilizing groups, aryl halides are inert to alkalis except at high temperatures and pressures (chlorobenzene → phenol, 300°), and often can be freed from persistent impurities by steam distillation from a mixture with aqueous alkali.   Chloro- and bromobenzene differ from alkyl halides in being unattacked by silver hydroxide, alcoholic ammonia, or sodium ethoxide even at temperatures of 100–150°. The chief practical reactions involving the halogen atoms are those with specific metals and with cuprous cyanide, as detailed in the following section.

REACTIONS

23.6   **Types.** — Aryl halides generally enter into the **Wurtz-Fittig reaction** under influence of metallic sodium. Bromides and iodides also combine with magnesium in the presence of ether to give **Grignard reagents**; the reaction usually is initiated somewhat less readily than when an alkyl halide is used, but arylmagnesium bromides and iodides nevertheless are obtainable without difficulty and in good yield, and are of inestimable value in syntheses. There are few limitations beyond those encountered as well in the aliphatic series (incompatible groups), though the factor of steric hindrance sometimes is important. Thus a bromine atom flanked in both ortho positions by substituents, one of which is a chlorine atom, may react abnormally. However, o- and p-bromochlorobenzene afford mono-Grignard derivatives satisfactorily; the p-compound, p-ClC$_6$H$_4$MgBr, is characterized by a beautiful chemiluminescence of its solutions, observable in the dark and due to slow air oxidation. p-Bromodimethylaniline also yields a Grignard reagent, p-(CH$_3$)$_2$NC$_6$H$_4$MgBr. Aromatic chlorides are not reactive enough to form Grignard reagents by the ordinary procedure, but Gilman's entrainment method is often applicable: use of a mixture of the aryl chloride and ethyl bromide. The presence in the solution of ethylmagnesium bromide may be objectionable in reactions other than carbonation, but this difficulty is eliminated in the modified procedure of D. E. Pearson (1959) in which the entrainer is ethylene dibromide and the sole products are ArMgCl, CH$_2$=CH$_2$, and MgBr$_2$. The entrainer, which clears the surface of the metal and activates it, is added to a solution of the aryl halide and magnesium over a period of 12 hrs., or else a large excess is added rapidly. Yields, after carbonation, are: α-chloronaphthalene, 56%; p-bromodimethylaniline, 48%.

23.7   **Aryllithium Compounds.** — Either chloro- or bromobenzene, when treated in ethereal solution with two equivalents of freshly cut metallic lithium by the technique employed in preparing a Grignard reagent, reacts with the separation of lithium halide and production of phenyllithium. The organo-

$$C_6H_5Br(Cl) \ + \ 2Li \ \xrightarrow{\text{Ether}} \ C_6H_5Li \ + \ LiBr(Cl)$$
$$\text{Phenyllithium}$$

metallic compound is soluble in ether and is decomposed by water, alcohol, acids, or bases, for example:

$$C_6H_5Li \ + \ H_2O \ \rightarrow \ C_6H_6 \ + \ LiOH$$

Aryllithiums enter into the reactions characteristic of the corresponding Grignard reagents and significant differences exist only when two modes of reaction are open. Thus phenyllithium and phenylmagnesium bromide give different ratios of 1,2- to 1,4-addition in reactions with α,β-unsaturated ketones (12.27). When both reagents give the same product or products, the Grignard reagent usually has a slight advantage. Thus if a bromide can be secured as a synthetic intermediate, it is usually treated with magnesium rather than with lithium, whereas if only the chloride is available, it can be utilized through conversion into the aryllithium. Occasions arise where advantage can be taken of the gradation in reactivity. Thus in 1-chloro-8-bromonaphthalene the more reactive halogen can be replaced by methyl through the Grignard derivative, and the other one utilized in production of a lithium derivative that will link the aryl residue to another component:

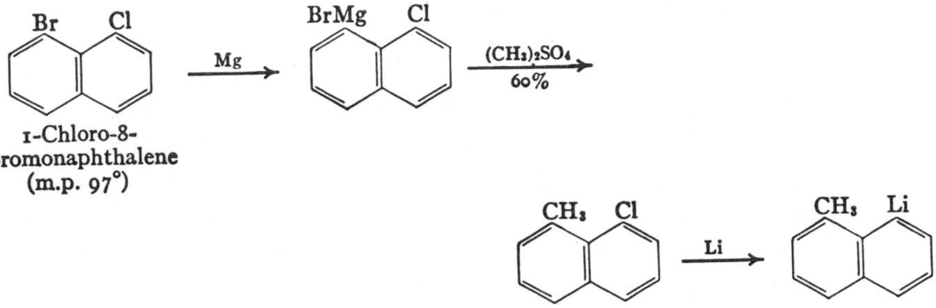

1-Chloro-8-bromonaphthalene
(m.p. 97°)

1-Chloro-8-methylnaphthalene
(m.p. 69°)

Reactions of phenyllithium with onium salts are of interest. The product of the reaction with tetramethylammonium bromide (1) is trimethylammonium

1. $(CH_3)_3N^+CH_3Br^-$ + C_6H_5Li $\longrightarrow$ $(CH_3)_3N^+$—CH_2^- + C_6H_6 + $LiBr$
2. $(C_6H_5)_3P^+CH_3Br^-$ + C_6H_5Li $\longrightarrow$ $(C_6H_5)_3P$=CH_2 + $LiBr$ + C_6H_6
3. $(C_6H_5)_4P^+I^-$ + C_6H_5Li $\longrightarrow$ $(C_6H_5)_5P$ + LiI

methylide (Wittig, 1947), and that formed on reaction with methyltriphenylphosphonium bromide (2) is triphenylphosphinemethylene, which reacts with carbonyl compounds with replacement of oxygen by methylene (13.2c). Tetraphenylphosphonium iodide, which·is typically ionic (m.p. about 340°), reacts (3) to give nonionic pentaphenylphosphorus (m.p. 124°, crystallizes from cyclohexane).

Aryllithiums are also available by **halogen-metal exchange** (Gilman, 1938; Wittig, 1940). For example, n-butyllithium reacts with α-naphthyl bromide to give α-naphthyllithium in high yield. The reaction is reversible and the position

$$n\text{-}C_4H_9Li \ + \ \alpha\text{-}C_{10}H_7Br \ \xrightarrow{\ 95\%\ } \ n\text{-}C_4H_9Br \ + \ C_{10}H_7Li$$

of equilibrium depends on the relative electron-attracting power of the two groups. Thus use of an aliphatic lithium component in combination with an aromatic halide favors exchange. The reaction is useful for the preparation of reactive organometallic derivatives not otherwise accessible. Thus no appreciable amounts of ArMgBr or ArLi derivatives are obtainable directly from 3-bromo-2,4,5-triphenylfurane (2) or from 2-bromo-3,4,6-triphenylpyridine (3), but the ArLi derivatives are prepared readily by exchange with n-butyllithium. The reaction is particularly useful for application to compounds having functional groups which interfere with direct reaction with magnesium or lithium. o-Bro-

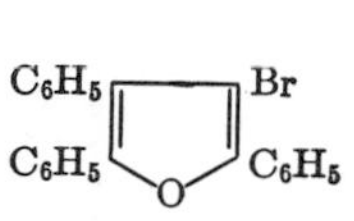

(2) 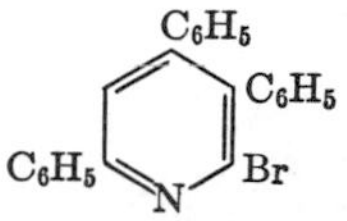   (3)

mophenol, for example, is convertible into salicylic acid by exchange with *n*-butyllithium and carbonation (4); similar transformations have been effected in

4.

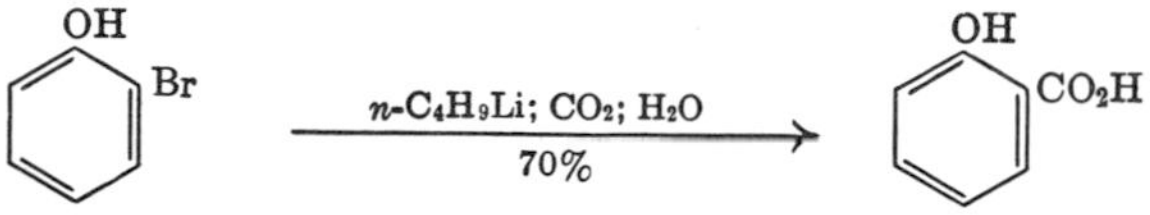

$$\xrightarrow[70\%]{n\text{-}C_4H_9Li;\ CO_2;\ H_2O}$$

satisfactory yield with *p*-bromoaniline, *p*-iodobenzoic acid, and α-bromopyridine.

Vinyllithium, a violently pyrophoric white solid which affords ethylene on hydrolysis, was prepared for the first time by D. Seyferth (1961). On reaction of phenyllithium with tetravinyllead in ether, tetraphenyllead (m.p. 230°) precipitates and the filtered solution contains vinyllithium. A second method in-

$$Pb(CH\!=\!CH_2)_4 + 4C_6H_5Li \rightarrow 4LiCH\!=\!CH_2 + Pb(C_6H_5)_4$$

$$Sn(CH\!=\!CH_2)_2 + 4Li \rightarrow 4LiCH\!=\!CH_2 + Sn$$

volves metal exchange between divinyltin and lithium; tin separates as a black precipitate and is the only by-product.

23.8   Metalation. — One type of metalation which can be effected with an alkyl- or aryllithium is replacement by lithium of a hydrogen atom activated by one or more aromatic rings (W. Schlenk and E. D. Bergmann, 1928). Examples are fluorene (5) and quinaldine (6). Gilman discovered (1934) that

5.

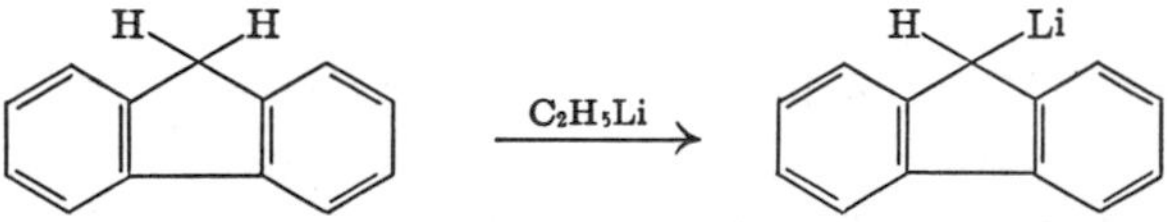

$$\xrightarrow{C_2H_5Li}$$

Fluorene   9-Fluorenyllithium

6.

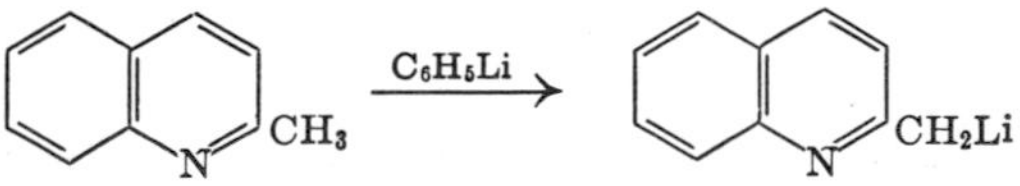

$$\xrightarrow{C_6H_5Li}$$

dibenzofurane (7), which contains no activated hydrogen, reacts with *n*-butyllithium in ether to yield the 1-lithium derivative, which on carbonation affords

7.

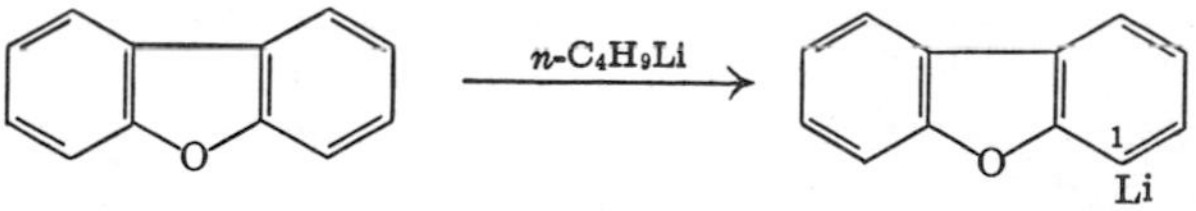

$$\xrightarrow{n\text{-}C_4H_9Li}$$

Dibenzofurane   1-Dibenzofuryliumlithium

the corresponding 1-acid in 76% yield. The reaction is an electrophilic substitution (R$^-$Li$^+$) and is facilitated by electron-releasing groups. Thus benzene itself

is not attacked, but anisole and resorcinol dimethyl ether on treatment with
n-butyllithium followed by carbonation afford *o*-methoxybenzoic acid (32%) and
2,6-dimethoxybenzoic acid (55%). On similar treatment, 1-methoxynaphtha-
lene yields 1-methoxy-2-naphthoic acid (25%) and 2-methoxynaphthalene yields
2-methoxy-3-naphthoic acid (50%). The *o,o*-metalation of resorcinol dimethyl
ether and the ready metalation of mesitylene with phenyllithium (8) show that
reaction can occur at highly hindered sites. Furthermore, mesityllithium

8.

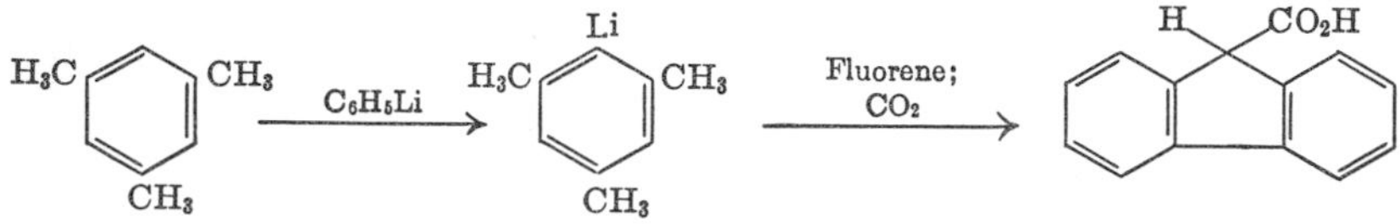

Mesitylene

metalates fluorene in satisfactory yield. Comparative experiments show that
phenyllithium is less effective as a metalating agent than *n*-butyllithium and
that *p*-anisyllithium is completely ineffective.

As in the examples cited, metalation of ethers usually gives *ortho* products un-
mixed with *meta* or *para* isomers. Dibenzothiophene (9) and 9-ethylcarbazole
(10) also are metalated (*n*-BuLi) *ortho* to the hetero atom. When the two com-

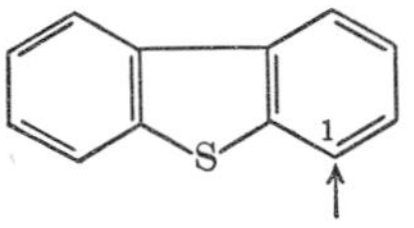

Dibenzothiophene
(9)

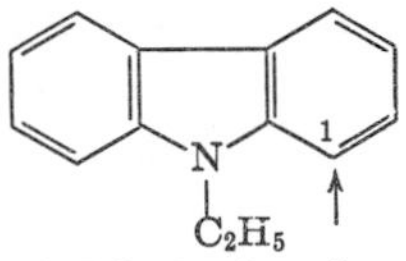

9-Ethylcarbazole
(10)

pounds are allowed to compete for one equivalent of *n*-butyllithium, only dibenzothiophene (9) is metalated. Also, the 1-Li derivative of (10) metalates (9)
but the 1-Li derivative of (9) is without action on (10). Various interpretations
of the mechanism of metalation have been advanced, but the problem is obscured
by the fact that *ortho* substitution is the usual but not the invariable rule. Thus
triphenylamine reacts with *n*-butyllithium to give the *m*-lithium derivative (11),

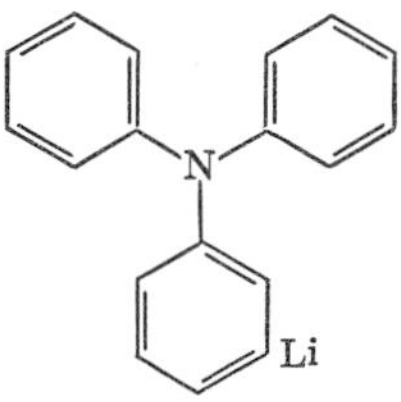

(11)

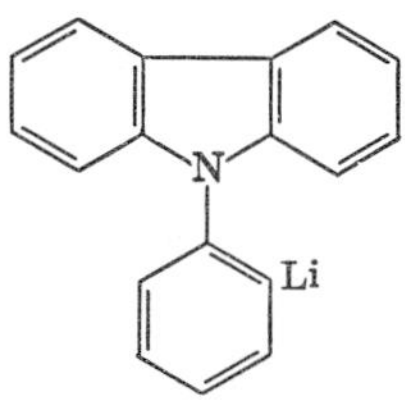

(12)

although the closely related 9-phenylcarbazole is metalated in the *ortho* position
of the 9-phenyl group (12). Triphenylarsine and triphenylphosphine also are
metalated anomalously in the *meta* position.

23.9 **Ullmann Reaction.** — The action of metallic sodium on an aryl halide results in formation of a certain amount of the expected diphenyl derivative, but the reaction does not proceed well and gives rise to several by-products. Thus p-bromotoluene on reaction with sodium gives a mixture containing the normal product, 4,4'-dimethyldiphenyl, together with 3,4'-dimethyldiphenyl, dibenzyl, and p-benzyltoluene. The by-products probably arise through isomerization of initially formed arylsodium (p-CH$_3$C$_6$H$_4$Na), with migration of the sodium to other positions in the ring and also into the side chain. Ullmann discovered that diphenyl derivatives can be prepared more satisfactorily by use of copper powder or copper bronze at an elevated temperature. The high-boiling iodobenzene affords diphenyl when refluxed with copper, but this parent hydrocarbon is made more easily by a method described earlier (18.3). The Ullmann reaction, however, is valuable for the synthesis of substituted diphenyls. The

2,2'-Dinitrodiphenyl
(m.p. 125°)

reaction is sometimes conducted in nitrobenzene solution, with suspended copper. A procedure recorded in *Organic Syntheses* for the preparation of 2,2'-dinitrodiphenyl from o-nitrochlorobenzene calls for use of specially prepared copper bronze and sand as a diluent to moderate the reaction. W. Davey (1948) obtained a slightly higher yield (65%) from o-nitroiodobenzene. P. H. Gore and G. K. Hughes (1959) precipitated copper powder by addition of zinc dust to a slightly acidified solution of copper sulfate and washed it with water and then with acetone. By gradually adding the dried (100°) copper to o-nitroiodobenzene at 190° and then raising the temperature to 240° they obtained 2,2'-dinitrodiphenyl in 96% yield.

A new method of aryl coupling consists in photolysis of an aromatic iodide in an aromatic solvent (N. Kharasch, 1961). Iodine is liberated with generation of the aryl radical, which attacks the solvent. Thus irradiation (at λ 253.7 mμ) of o-iodophenol in benzene (20 hrs., room temperature) affords o-hydroxydiphenyl in 60% yield. With toluene as the solvent, attack is at the op-positions. Photolysis of 4,4'-diiododiphenyl in benzene yields quaterphenyl.

23.10 **Conversion to Nitriles.** — Although alkyl halides react readily with potassium cyanide in aqueous alcohol, aryl halides are indifferent to this reagent. They do, however, afford nitriles on interaction with anhydrous cuprous cyanide in pyridine solution at somewhat elevated temperatures. Pyridine is required to promote reaction, perhaps because it not only dissolves the halide but forms a molecular complex with cuprous cyanide, which separates as a crystalline solid on mixing the reagents and dissolves on heating. The reagents are employed in a strictly anhydrous condition to obviate hydrolysis of the nitrile at the high temperature required. A little acetonitrile can be added to react with a trace of moisture. If the halide has a sufficiently high boiling point, a suitable reaction temperature can be obtained in an open flask, as in the following example:

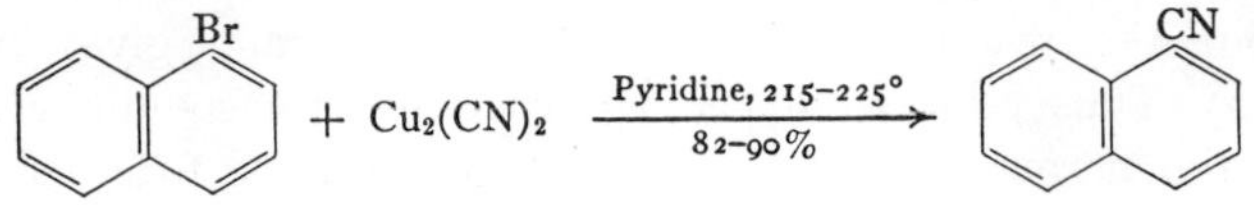

α-Bromonaphthalene   α-Naphthonitrile

When applied to a more volatile halide the reaction is conducted in a sealed tube or autoclave. Chlorides serve as satisfactorily as bromides, and the yield and purity of the products leave little to be desired.

POLYHALO DERIVATIVES

23.11   Insecticides Containing Halogen. — The remarkably active contact insecticide known as DDT (dichlorodiphenyltrichloroethane) was introduced in 1942 by the Swiss firm J. R. Geigy. The substance is prepared by condensation of chlorobenzene with chloral hydrate in the presence of sulfuric acid, based upon the original synthesis by F. Zeidler (1874). Various isomers

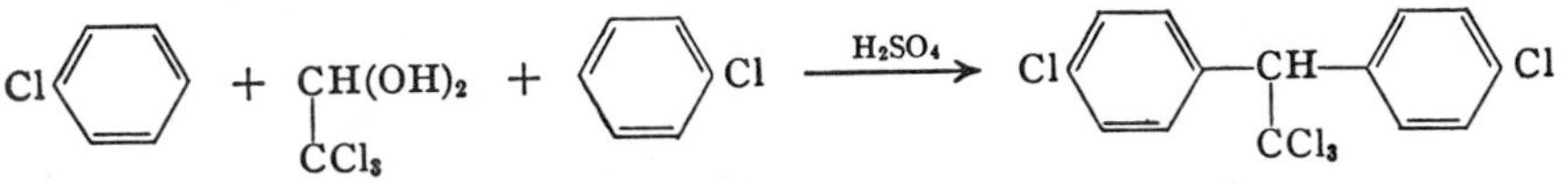

DDT(p,p', m.p. 109°)

are also formed, particularly o,p'-DDT, and technical preparations contain only about 70% of the p,p'-form, which is the most active isomer. The toxic effect may be due to combination of the action of the chlorobenzene unit (respiratory poison) with that of chloroform (lipid-soluble narcotic). DDT has shown spectacular success in control of diseases (typhus, malaria) that are transmitted by insect carriers. It is also used effectively in protecting agricultural crops against a variety of pests.

An insecticide of even simpler constitution was announced in 1945 by the Imperial Chemical Industries. It is one of six isomeric benzene hexachlorides produced by chlorination of benzene under illumination. The isomers are distinguished by the prefixes α, β, γ, etc. Only the γ-isomer (m.p. 111°) has insecticidal properties and it is a minor constituent of the mixture (10–12%). It is

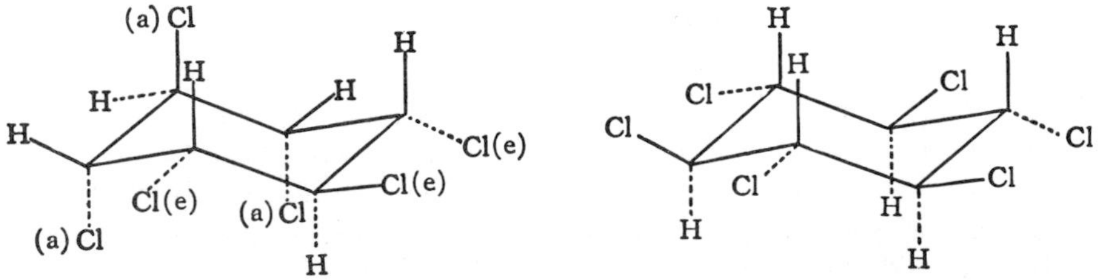

known as lindane (formerly gammexane) after T. van der Linden, who isolated the first four of nine possible isomers. Preparations sold for pharmaceutical purposes contain at least 99% of pure γ-isomer. The conformation established for the substance is shown in the formula. The β-form (m.p. 200°) is known from X-ray studies to have the centro-symmetric configuration. This isomer is capable of undergoing only *cis* elimination of hydrogen chloride, and it is dehydrohalogenated by sodium ethoxide at a rate 1/7000 to 1/24000 that of the other isomers, all of which can undergo *trans* elimination.

23.12   **Perhalobenzenes.** — Hexachlorobenzene (m.p. 231°, b.p. 326°) has been made by chlorination of phthalic acid, of tetrachloro-1,4-benzoquinone (chloranil), and of other compounds. A new process (F. Becke, 1958) utilizes the residual mixture of hexachlorocyclohexanes remaining from the production of lindane. The charge is put into an autoclave along with ampoules of sulfur trioxide, a 20-atmosphere pressure of nitrogen is applied, and the temperature is raised, when the ampoules break. After stirring at 250° for 10 hrs. the product is obtained in 87% yield. Hexabromobenzene (m.p. 326°) is obtained by the same method. Hexachlorobenzene is considerably more reactive than chlorobenzene, one chlorine atom being hydrolyzed by alkali at 135°. Pentachlorophenol (m.p. 191°), made in this way or by chlorination of phenol, is used in the form of the water-soluble sodium salt to prevent blueing of forest products, particularly in Finland. Other compounds used as germicides and fungicides are the sodium salts of 2,4,6-trichlorophenol (m.p. 69°) and *o*-phenylphenol (m.p. 57°).

In the reaction of hexachlorobenzene with the potassium salt of ethylmercaptan in methyl ethyl ketone, the halogen atoms are replaced two at a time (M. Kulka, 1959). By adjustment of the proportions of reagents and the reaction time it is possible to obtain either the bis-ethylthio derivative (II, 68% yield) or the tetrakis derivative (III, 50%). The structure of II was established by degradation to

chloranil. The reaction of equivalent amounts of I and KSC_2H_5 afforded none of the monoethylthio derivative; II was the major product formed.

Several processes are available for the production of hexafluorobenzene but the best, developed by Mlle. Y. Désirant (1955), consists in pyrolysis of tri-

$$CFBr_3 \xrightarrow[\text{Pt tube}]{630-640°} C_6F_6$$

bromofluoromethane (from CBr_4 and SbF_3). Since dichloroacetylene is known to trimerize to hexachlorobenzene, an acetylenic intermediate probably is involved, possibly through the sequence: $CFBr_3 \rightarrow :CFBr \rightarrow FC{\equiv}CF \rightarrow C_6F_6$.

The boiling point of hexafluorobenzene, 82°, is close to that of benzene and 150° below that of hexachlorobenzene. Other boiling points for comparison are: perfluoronaphthalene, 140°; naphthalene, 218°; C_6F_5OH, 143°; C_6H_5OH, 181°.

Hexafluorobenzene is sensitive to nucleophilic attack, but only in nonaqueous solvent. Thus unlike hexachlorobenzene it is resistant to aqueous alkali at atmospheric pressure. The perfluoro compound, however, reacts readily with sodium methoxide, and the ether formed can be cleaved with aluminum chloride. The phenol is obtained under milder conditions by heating hexafluorobenzene with potassium hydroxide in t-butyl alcohol (R. N. Haszeldine,[1] 1959). Pentafluorophenol (pK_a 5.5) is much more strongly acidic than phenol and slightly less acidic than pentachlorophenol (pK_a 5.3). Other reactions of hexafluorobenzene are shown in the formulation. Pentafluorothiophenol has been prepared by reaction

$$C_6F_6 \; + \; \begin{cases} NaOCH_3 \longrightarrow \quad C_6F_5OCH_3 \longrightarrow \quad C_6F_5OH \;(AlCl_3) \\ NaNH_2 \longrightarrow \quad C_6F_5NH_2 \\ Mg, \text{ ether} \longrightarrow \quad C_6F_5MgF \longrightarrow \quad C_6F_5CH_3 \;(CH_3I) \\ H_2\text{-}Pd \longrightarrow \quad C_6HF_5 \longrightarrow \quad C_6F_5SO_3H \;(H_2SO_4, SO_3) \\ CoCl_2 \longrightarrow \quad C_6F_5\text{---}C_6F_5 \end{cases}$$

of hexafluorobenzene with sodium hydrogen sulfide in boiling pyridine (P. Robson, 1960).

23.13   Polyvalent Iodine Compounds. — Aromatic iodides can form a variety of derived compounds containing polyvalent iodine, the first of which was discovered by Willgerodt[2] (1886). Iodobenzene reacts with chlorine to form **iodobenzene dichloride** (phenyl iodochloride), $C_6H_5ICl_2$, a yellow substance which is moderately soluble in chloroform or benzene and sparingly soluble in ether, and which when heated to 110–$120°$ decomposes abruptly, chiefly as follows: $C_6H_5ICl_2 \rightarrow p$-$ClC_6H_4I + HCl$. The dichloride can be prepared in 87–94% yield by chlorination of iodobenzene in cold chloroform solution, from which it separates in a crystalline condition. The dichloride is converted into **iodosobenzene** by alkali. The reaction is conducted by grinding the dichloride

$$C_6H_5ICl_2 \xrightarrow[60\text{-}62\%]{NaOH} C_6H_5IO$$

Iodobenzene   Iodosobenzene
dichloride

in a mortar with sodium carbonate and ice and stirring in the required amount of alkali. Iodosobenzene is an amorphous yellow solid, somewhat soluble in hot water or alcohol and sparingly soluble in ether; it decomposes explosively when heated to about $210°$. The substance is basic and is reconverted into iodobenzene dichloride by hydrochloric acid. Properties of these trivalent iodine compounds suggest a saltlike character, and consideration of the possible disposition of the electrons shows that one of the three linkages of the iodine atom must be polar. Iodosobenzene is structurally comparable to amine oxides (14.21), and the union between iodine and oxygen must involve transfer

$$C_6H_5 \overset{+}{:} \overset{-}{\underset{\cdot\cdot}{O}} : \quad \text{or} \quad C_6H_5 \overset{+}{I} \text{---} \overset{-}{O}$$
Iodosobenzene

[1] Robert N. Haszeldine, b. 1925 Manchester; D.Sc. Birmingham (W. N. Haworth); Sc.D. Cambridge (Eméleus); Univ. Cambridge, Manchester

[2] Conrad Willgerodt, 1841–1930; b. Braunschweig, Germany; Ph.D. Freiburg; Univ. Freiburg; *Ber.*, **64A**, 5 (1931)

of an electron from iodine to oxygen, with development of ionic charges and establishment of a pair of shared electrons. Iodobenzene dichloride can be considered as formed from the components by transfer of an electron from iodine to one of the chlorine atoms and sharing of electrons with the second atom. The salt of iodosobenzene and acetic acid, iodosobenzene diacetate (phenyl-

$$C_6H_5 : \overset{..}{\underset{..}{I}} : \quad \xrightarrow[\text{share}]{\text{transfer}} \quad \overset{..}{\underset{..}{Cl}} : \quad \longrightarrow \quad [C_6H_5 : \overset{..}{I} : Cl]^+ : \overset{..}{\underset{..}{Cl}} :^-$$

Iodobenzene dichloride

iodoso diacetate), $[C_6H_5IOCOCH_3]^+CH_3COO^-$ (m.p. 157°), is soluble in acetic acid or benzene, but insoluble in ether; it is prepared in 83–91% yield by oxidation of iodobenzene with peracetic acid (*Org. Syn.*, 1961) and can be purified by crystallization from benzene–petroleum ether. The substance is an oxidizing agent comparable to lead tetraacetate; for example, it cleaves *vic*-glycols in the same manner, though less rapidly (5.27).

The compounds mentioned above are not distinctive to the aromatic series, for aliphatic iodides also form iodoso and dichloride derivatives, but the products are much less stable. Iodosobenzene can be obtained as a solid, but is not stable and undergoes slow change on storage. The change, which can be brought about rapidly by heat, consists in disproportionation to iodobenzene and **iodoxybenzene,** a pentavalent iodine compound. Iodobenzene is removed as formed from the mixture by steam distillation. Iodoxybenzene is a colorless solid that

$$2\,C_6H_5\overset{+}{I}{-}\overset{-}{O} \xrightarrow[92-95\%]{\text{Steam distil}} C_6H_5\overset{+}{I}\underset{O}{\overset{\overset{-}{O}}{\diagdown}} + C_6H_5I$$

Iodosobenzene   Iodoxybenzene   Iodobenzene

melts with explosive decomposition at 237°; it is practically insoluble in benzene or acetone, and soluble in water to the extent of 12 g. per liter at 100°. An alternative method of preparation is oxidation of iodobenzene dichloride with sodium hypochlorite solution (87–92% yield).

A further compound containing trivalent iodine is **diphenyliodonium hydroxide,** a strongly basic substance resembling quaternary ammonium hydroxides; it is not stable in the solid state but can be prepared in aqueous solution by the action

$$C_6H_5\overset{+}{I}{-}\overset{-}{O} + C_6H_5\overset{+}{I}\underset{O}{\overset{\overset{-}{O}}{\diagdown}} + AgOH \longrightarrow [(C_6H_5)_2I]^+OH^- + AgIO_3$$

Iodosobenzene   Iodoxybenzene   Diphenyliodo-
                                         nium hydroxide

of silver hydroxide on a mixture of iodosobenzene and iodoxybenzene (Victor Meyer, 1894). The same substance results from interaction of iodosobenzene

$$C_6H_5\overset{+}{I}{-}\overset{-}{O} + C_6H_5MgBr \xrightarrow{(H_2O)} [(C_6H_5)_2I]^+OH^-$$

with phenylmagnesium bromide and hydrolysis. The iodide salt, diphenylio-donium iodide, $[(C_6H_5)_2I]^+I^-$, is a stable solid, m.p. 176°, dec.

Diphenyliodonium sulfate is obtainable by reaction of benzene with sodium iodate and sulfuric acid in acetic acid–acetic anhydride (I. Masson, 1937); the effective reagent may be iodyl sulfate, $(IO)_2SO_4$. Another method involves a

$$2C_6H_6 \xrightarrow[54\%]{NaIO_3,\ H_2SO_4,\ Ac_2O\ (0°)} C_6H_5I^+C_6H_5(HSO_4^-)$$

novel Friedel-Crafts type condensation of an iodoso compound with an aromatic compound (F. M. Beringer,[1] 1958–60). In the example formulated o-nitroiodoso-

$$o\text{-}NO_2C_6H_4I \xrightarrow[85\%]{Cl_2} o\text{-}NO_2C_6H_4ICl_2 \xrightarrow[91\%]{OH^-} o\text{-}NO_2C_6H_4I^+\!\!-\!O^-$$

$$o\text{-}NO_2C_6H_4I^+\!\!-\!O^- \ + \ C_6H_6 \ + \ H_2SO_4 \xrightarrow[75\%]{-H_2O} o\text{-}NO_2C_6H_4I^+C_6H_5(HSO_4^-)$$

benzene, prepared by chlorination of o-nitroiodobenzene and hydrolysis, is added to a stirred mixture of benzene and sulfuric acid at 5°; the product was isolated as phenyl-o-nitrophenyliodonium bromide. A particularly interesting reaction of this salt is condensation with the sodio derivative of ethyl oxalacetate. The

$$o\text{-}NO_2C_6H_4I^+C_6H_5(Br^-) \ + \ C_2H_5O_2C\overset{-}{C}H(Na^+)COCO_2C_2H_5 \xrightarrow{-C_6H_5I}$$

$$\overset{\displaystyle COCO_2C_2H_5}{\underset{\displaystyle o\text{-}NO_2C_6H_4\overset{|}{C}HCO_2C_2H_5}{}} \xrightarrow[79\%]{-CO} o\text{-}NO_2C_6H_4CH(CO_2C_2H_5)_2$$

intermediate o-nitrophenyloxalacetate loses carbon monoxide to form diethyl o-nitrophenylmalonate.

PROBLEMS

1. Indicate all the steps required for preparation of p-bromoiodobenzene from aniline.
2. What products would be expected to result from the action of alkali on the three products of side-chain chlorination of toluene?
3. (a) How could $p\text{-}CH_3C_6H_4CH_2OH$ be made in two steps from toluene? Would you antici-pate difficulty in securing a pure product?
   (b) Suggest a synthesis of pure p-methylbenzyl alcohol from p-bromochlorobenzene.
4. Suggest a method for the preparation of 2,5-dimethylbenzyl chloride.
5. How could you convert anisole into 2-amino-4-bromoanisole?
6. Suggest a method for removal of an aromatic bromine atom (replacement by hydrogen).
7. What alternative procedures are available for the conversion of m-xylene, through a mono-halo derivative, into 2,4-dimethylbenzoic acid?

[1] F. Marshall Beringer, b. 1920 New York; Ph.D Columbia (Doering); Polytechnic Inst., Brooklyn

Chapter 24

AROMATIC CARBOXYLIC ACIDS

24.1 **Properties.** — The monocarboxylic acid derivatives of the benzene series (Table 24.1) are all crystalline solids melting above 100°; derivatives of benzoic acid substituted in the p-position by methyl, halo, nitro, hydroxyl, methoxyl, or amino groups melt at a temperature in the neighborhood of 200°. As compared with aliphatic acids of similar molecular weight, the boiling points are slightly higher and the melting points very much higher. Benzoic acid is somewhat more acidic (pK_a 4.17) than acetic acid (pK_a 4.74), and nearly all the common substituents, other than the amino group, increase the acidic strength, particularly when in the o-position. A hydrophilic carboxyl group joined to the benzene ring tends to decrease solubility in hydrocarbons or ether and to produce some solubility in water; the monocarboxylic acids are only slightly soluble in cold water, and on the addition of sodium carbonate or bicarbonate characteristically pass into solution with liberation of carbon dioxide.

24.2 **Hammett Equation.** — L. P. Hammett defined (1940) a relationship between the effect of *meta* and *para* substituents on either rates of reaction or equilibrium constants which has been shown to apply to a large number of reactions. If reaction rates are being considered, for example for the hydrolysis of substituted benzyl chlorides, and if k^0 is the rate constant for benzyl chloride itself and k is that for a m- or p-substituted benzyl chloride, the Hammett equation takes the form (1), where ρ (rho) is a constant that depends on the

$$
\begin{aligned}
&\text{1.} && \log k - \log k^0 = \rho\sigma \\
&\text{2.} && pK - pK^0 = \rho\sigma \\
&\text{3.} && \sigma_m \text{ (or } \sigma_p) = pK_m \text{ (or } pK_p) - 4.17
\end{aligned}
$$

particular reaction in question and is independent of the substituent, and σ is a constant that characterizes the substituent and is independent of the nature of the reaction. If equilibrium constants are under consideration, for example

TABLE 24.1. MONOBASIC ACIDS

ACID	FORMULA	M.P., °C.	B.P., °C.	$pK_a^{25°}$
Benzoic	$C_6H_5CO_2H$	121.7	249	4.17
o-Toluic	o-$CH_3C_6H_4CO_2H$	104	259 $^{751\ mm.}$	3.89
m-Toluic	m-$CH_3C_6H_4CO_2H$	111	263	4.28
p-Toluic	p-$CH_3C_6H_4CO_2H$	180		4.35
o-Chlorobenzoic	o-$ClC_6H_4CO_2H$	141		2.89
m-Chlorobenzoic	m-$ClC_6H_4CO_2H$	158		3.82
p-Chlorobenzoic	p-$ClC_6H_4CO_2H$	243		4.03
o-Bromobenzoic	o-$BrC_6H_4CO_2H$	149		2.82
m-Bromobenzoic	m-$BrC_6H_4CO_2H$	155		3.85
p-Bromobenzoic	p-$BrC_6H_4CO_2H$	252		4.18
o-Nitrobenzoic	o-$NO_2 \cdot C_6H_4CO_2H$	148		2.21
m-Nitrobenzoic	m-$NO_2 \cdot C_6H_4CO_2H$	142		3.46
p-Nitrobenzoic	p-$NO_2 \cdot C_6H_4CO_2H$	240		3.40
3,5-Dinitrobenzoic	$3,5$-$(NO_2)_2 \cdot C_6H_3CO_2H$	205		2.80
Salicylic	o-$HOC_6H_4CO_2H$	159		3.00
m-Hydroxybenzoic	m-$HOC_6H_4CO_2H$	200		4.12
p-Hydroxybenzoic	p-$HOC_6H_4CO_2H$	215		4.54
Anisic	p-$CH_3OC_6H_4CO_2H$	184	277	4.49
Gallic	$3,4,5$-$(HO)_3C_6H_2CO_2H$	253 dec.		4.40
Syringic	4-(HO)-$3,5(CH_3O)_2C_6H_2CO_2H$	205		
Anthranilic	o-$NH_2 \cdot C_6H_4CO_2H$	145		5.00
m-Aminobenzoic	m-$NH_2 \cdot C_6H_4CO_2H$	174		4.82
p-Aminobenzoic	p-$NH_2 \cdot C_6H_4CO_2H$	187		4.92

ionization constants, the equation is (2). The ionization of benzoic acid is selected arbitrarily as the standard reaction of reference for which ρ is taken as unity. Hence the value of σ_m or σ_p is calculated from expression (3).

An *ortho* substituent may influence a functional group by a combination of inductive and resonance effects as further modified by steric effects or nonbonded interactions. Hammett's treatment simplifies the situation by considering only positions where steric effects are not operative. A *meta* substituent modifies rates or equilibria by pure induction; the effect of a *para* substituent is the result of resonance superimposed on a comparable inductive effect, and either the one or the other effect may play the dominant role (compare 17.4). Once σ values have been determined for a number of substituents for one reaction, these values can be used to obtain the constant ρ for another reaction. Rate or equilibrium constants are measured, the logarithms of the measured constants are plotted against the corresponding σ values, and the slope of the best straight line through the points of the plot is the ρ value for the reaction at hand; see compilation of constants by H. H. Jaffé, *Chem. Rev.*, **53,** 191 (1953). A new equation applicable to electrophilic aromatic substitutions has been advanced by J. R. Knowles, *et al.* (Oxford, 1960).

24.3   **General Methods of Preparation.** — One route to carboxylic acids is oxidation of carbon side chains or rings. Thus toluene yields benzoic acid, *m*- and *p*-xylene afford isophthalic and terephthalic acid, respectively, and mesitylene and durene are convertible into the corresponding polybasic acids. On a laboratory scale the polyalkyl compounds usually are oxidized most satisfactorily either with a dilute aqueous solution of potassium permanganate at the reflux temperature or with dilute nitric acid at an elevated temperature, attained in a sealed tube or autoclave. In technical operations the most economical process usually is chlorination and hydrolysis: $ArCH_3 \longrightarrow ArCCl_3 \longrightarrow ArCO_2H$ (see benzoic acid, below). Another degradative method of preparation is **hypohalite oxidation of aceto compounds**: $ArCOCH_3 \xrightarrow{HOCl} ArCOCCl_3 \xrightarrow{NaOH} ArCO_2H + CHCl_3$. The required methyl ketones are readily available by the Friedel-Crafts reaction, and the combination of this efficient condensation with the haloform reaction often offers an excellent method of introducing a carboxyl group. An advantage over the method of oxidation of alkyl derivatives is that the hypohalite reaction is more generally applicable because the reagent is not destructive to ring systems less resistant to oxidative attack than the isolated benzene nucleus. Thus β-methylnaphthalene is oxidized in the nucleus in preference to the methyl group, but the aceto derivative made by the Friedel-Crafts method undergoes hypochlorite oxidation readily:

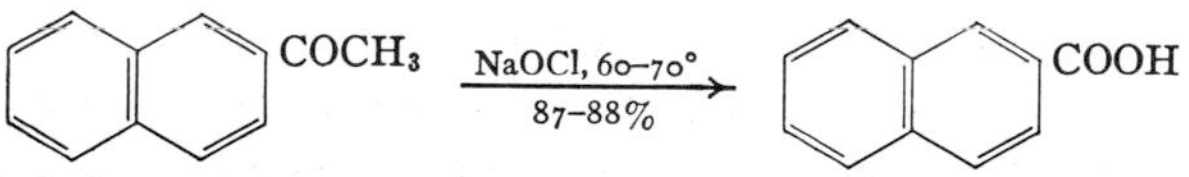

Methyl β-naphthyl ketone   β-Naphthoic acid

Study of the Kuhn-Roth oxidation of methylbenzenes shows that ring oxidation competes with side-chain oxidation, that the rate is a function of the σ-complex

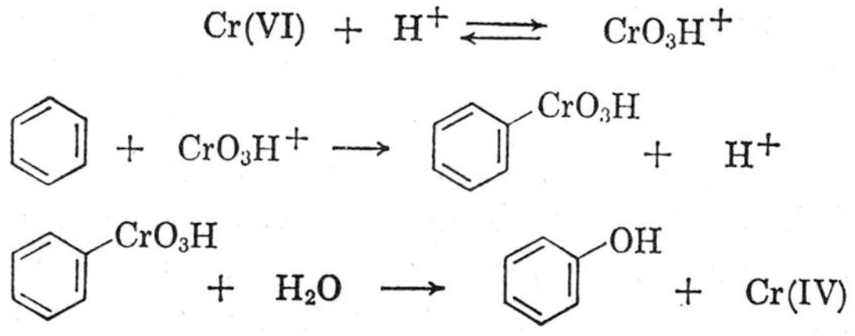

basicity of the hydrocarbon, and that oxidation occurs by electrophilic attack; the mechanism suggested postulates an intermediate phenol (S. G. Brandenberger, 1961).

Carboxylic acids are also prepared by **hydrolysis of nitriles,** available from aryl halides by reaction with cuprous cyanide and pyridine, from amines by diazotization and the Sandmeyer reaction (or from the less efficient fusion of sulfonates with potassium cyanide). A unique one-step synthesis of nitriles from aldehydes is illustrated by the reaction of N,N-dimethylaminobenzaldehyde with ammonium dibasic phosphate, nitropropane, and acetic acid with production of the nitrile in 77 % yield (H. M. Blatter, 1961). A further general method is **carbonation of Grignard reagents or aryllithiums.** For example carbonation of an ethereal solution of α-naphthylmagnesium bromide with carbon dioxide gas or with dry ice affords α-naphthoic acid in 70–85 % yield from the bromide. Mesitylenecarboxylic

TABLE 24.2.   DERIVATIVES OF BENZOIC ACID

NAME	FORMULA	M.P., °C.	B.P., °C.
Methyl benzoate	$C_6H_5COOCH_3$	liq.	199
Ethyl benzoate	$C_6H_5COOC_2H_5$	liq.	213
Phenyl benzoate	$C_6H_5COOC_6H_5$	71	314
Benzyl benzoate	$C_6H_5COOCH_2C_6H_5$	21	324
Benzoic anhydride	$(C_6H_5CO)_2O$	42	360
Benzoyl chloride	C_6H_5COCl	-1	197
Perbenzoic acid	C_6H_5COOOH	43	dec.
Dibenzoyl peroxide	$(C_6H_5COO)_2$	105 dec.	
Benzamide	$C_6H_5CONH_2$	130	
Benzanilide	$C_6H_5CONHC_6H_5$	163	$119^{10\,mm.}$
Benzhydrazide	$C_6H_5CONHNH_2$	112	

acid (m.p. 152°, pK$_a$ 4.43) can be prepared similarly, but the preparation of bromomesitylene requires treatment of the crude product with alkali and careful fractionation, and the overall yield (68%) is no better than that of a one-step process in which mesitylene is treated with oxalyl chloride and aluminum chloride in carbon disulfide (*Org. Syn.*, 1961). Carbon monoxide and hydrogen chloride are evolved, with production of the acid chloride complex, which is decomposed cautiously with ice and hydrochloric acid.

SPECIFIC ACIDS

24.4   **Benzoic Acid.** — The simplest acid of the series occurs in both the free and esterified condition in various plants, particularly resins and balsams, and early supplies were derived from hippuric acid of horse urine by acid or alkaline hydrolysis or by bacterial decomposition. The acid inhibits fermentation and decay of foodstuffs and has been used as a food preservative in the form of the sodium salt. Values for the solubility in various solvents at 17° are as follows (g. per 100 g.): water, 0.21; hexane, 0.94; benzene, 0.82; chloroform, 14.6; acetone, 28.6; ethanol, 29.4; methanol, 36.4. The acid is volatile with steam and easily sublimed. One method of technical production is hydrolysis of benzotrichloride with lime in the presence of iron powder as catalyst at

$$C_6H_5CCl_3 \longrightarrow [C_6H_5C(OH)Cl_2] \longrightarrow C_6H_5COCl \longrightarrow C_6H_5CO_2H$$

50°, followed by acidification. An alternative process that obviates contamination with chlorobenzoic acids is oxidation of toluene with manganese dioxide and sulfuric acid.

The methyl and ethyl esters of benzoic acid (Table 24.2) are prepared conveniently by the Fischer method (excess alcohol, mineral acid catalyst); they can be prepared also by heating potassium benzoate with the dialkyl sulfate at 205–210°. Phenyl benzoate is made by heating a mixture of benzoic acid and phenol with phosphorus oxychloride. The benzyl ester, which occurs in tuberose oil, can be prepared from benzoyl chloride and benzyl alcohol. Benzoic anhydride is prepared in 72-74% yield by fractional distillation of a mixture of benzoic acid and acetic anhydride containing a small amount of sirupy phosphoric acid. Dibenzoyl peroxide is made by stirring benzoyl chloride at 0° with a 5-7% solution of sodium peroxide, and the peroxide can be converted into perbenzoic acid by treatment with a solution of sodium methoxide in methanol at 0° (5.17). The amides listed in the table are prepared by the action of benzoyl chloride on the appropriate amine.

1,4-Dihydrobenzoic acid (m.p. 17°) is obtainable in high yield by reduction of benzoic acid with sodium in liquid ammonia in the presence of ethanol as a proton

source (M. E. Kuehne, 1959). o-Toluic acid and 3,4,5-trimethoxybenzoic acid likewise yield 1,4-dihydrides, but p-toluic acid and m-anisic acid yield mainly the tetrahydrobenzoic acids.

24.5   Phthalic Acid. — Phthalic acid is the normal oxidation product of o-xylene and other o-dialkylbenzenes. Naphthalene, abundantly available from coal tar, can be regarded as a benzene derivative with a carbon side ring fused to adjacent positions; it is readily oxidized and provides the chief source of the acid or of the anhydride, formed on heating. The bicyclic hydrocarbon is attacked easily by oxidizing agents under conditions to which benzene is resistant,

Naphthalene   Phthalic acid   Phthalic anhydride

and since the benzenoid reaction product is stabilized still further by two *meta* directing groups, there is no danger of overoxidation. The modern method is vapor-phase catalytic oxidation (H. D. Gibbs). Naphthalene vapor is passed with air over a catalyst at an elevated temperature at which the acid is cyclized to the anhydride, which sublimes into a condenser and is obtained very pure. Results of experiments approximating commercial conditions (R. N. Shreve, 1943) indicate that phthalic anhydride can be obtained in 76% yield from commercial naphthalene with vanadium pentoxide catalyst on silica gel at 460-480°. α-Naphthoquinone is a by-product.

Phthalic acid (pK$_a$ 3.0) melts with decomposition to the anhydride at temperatures ranging from 200° to 230°, depending on the rate of heating and the condition of the glass capillary surfaces. It is sparingly soluble in ether or chloroform and readily soluble in alcohol or water; 100 parts of water dissolve 0.77 part at 11.5° and 18 parts at 99°. The anhydride is very soluble in ether, melts sharply at 132°, and sublimes easily in long sparlike needles. A convenient qualitative test for phthalic anhydride consists in the formation of the dye fluorescein by fusion with resorcinol in the presence of sulfuric acid.

24.6   **Derivatives of Phthalic Acid and Phthalic Anhydride.** — The monomethyl ester of phthalic acid can be prepared in good yield by refluxing phthalic anhydride with methanol; the half-ester melts at 85°, and is slightly
less acidic (pK$_a$ 3.18) than the dibasic acid.   The **dimethyl ester** is a liquid,
b.p. 282°.   The normal acid chloride derivative, **phthaloyl chloride,** is made by
heating phthalic anhydride with phosphorus pentachloride and distilling the
product; when heated with aluminum chloride at 95° for a prolonged period, the

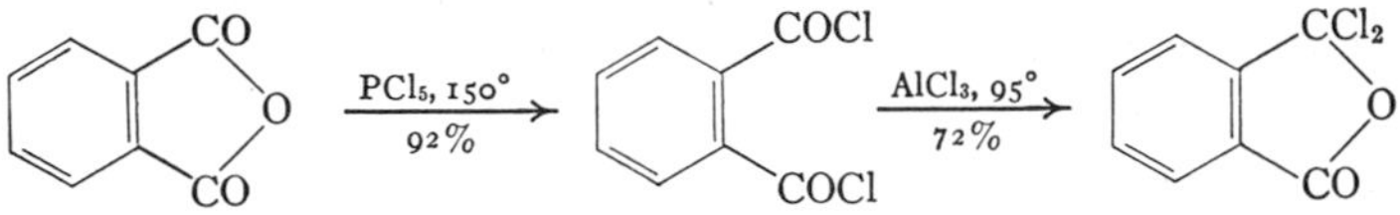

Phthaloyl chloride   as-Phthalyl chloride
(m.p. 16°, b.p. 277°)   (m.p. 89°)

normal chloride rearranges into the isomeric **as-phthalyl chloride,** a derivative of
phthalic anhydride in which one of the carbonyl oxygen atoms is replaced
by two chlorine atoms.   The equilibrium between the isomers is shifted in
favor of the noncyclic acid chloride at high temperatures, and hence as-phthalyl
chloride reverts to phthaloyl chloride on slow distillation in the absence of a catalyst.

Phthalimide, an important member of the series, is produced in industry by
saturating molten phthalic anhydride with dry ammonia and heating the mixture
to 170–240° under pressure.   The cyclic imide can be prepared on a laboratory

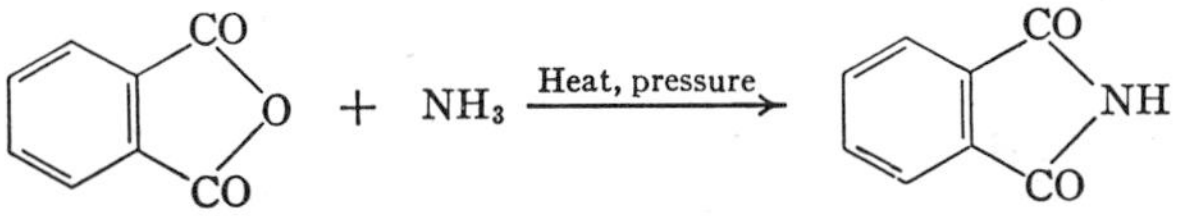

Phthalimide
(m.p. 234°)

scale in 95–97% yield by heating the anhydride with concentrated aqueous
ammonia solution and eventually raising the temperature to 300°.   The acidic
character of phthalimide (pK$_a$ 8.30) and the use of the potassium salt in the Gabriel synthesis of primary amines have
been mentioned.   By careful saponification the heterocyclic ring
can be opened without elimination of nitrogen; thus when a solution of phthalimide in 25% aqueous potassium hydroxide is

Phthalamidic acid

allowed to stand in the cold for one to two hours and acidified, the acid-amide,
phthalamidic acid, is produced.

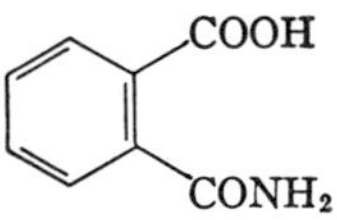

Phthalide, a γ-lactone, has been obtained by reduction of phthalic anhydride
by various methods.   A convenient laboratory procedure is reduction of phthalimide in aqueous sodium hydroxide solution with zinc dust activated with a small
amount of copper (deposited from copper sulfate solution) at 8°; yield 67–71%.
The preparation of monoperphthalic acid is described in section 5.17.

Diphthaloyl peroxide (1), obtainable in good yield by reaction of phthaloyl
chloride in ether with hydrogen peroxide and sodium carbonate, melts at 127°

Phthalide
(m.p. 74°, b.p. 228°/730 mm.)

Monoperphthalic acid
(m.p. 110° dec.)

and explodes violently at 130°. Investigations of F. D. Greene[1] (1956–60) have shown the reagent to be less prone than dibenzoyl peroxide to undergo unimolecular decomposition but to be surprisingly reactive to olefins. It reacts stereospecifically with *cis*-stilbene to give the cyclic phthalate (2), convertible by base to *meso*-stilbenediol and the lactonic ortho ester (3). *trans*-Stilbene gives the

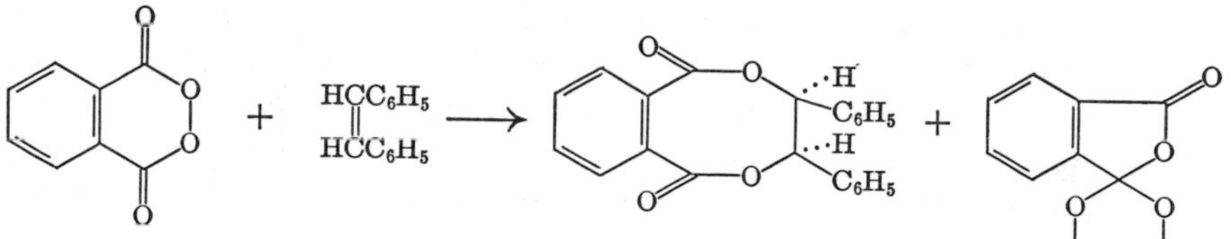

(1)
Diphthaloyl
peroxide

(2)

(3)

corresponding stereoisomers. With aliphatic olefins products of allylic oxidation are also formed. The data in the table show that the effect of structure on reactivity parallels that observed in epoxidation, dibromocarbene addition, and bromination.

RELATIVE REACTIVITY OF OLEFINS

OLEFIN	DIPHTHALOYL PEROXIDE	PERACETIC ACID	DIBROMO-CARBENE	BROMINE
1-Methylcyclopentene	31.3	17.2		
Trimethylethylene	9.4	9.6		1.04
trans-Stilbene	2.0			
cis-Stilbene	1.0			
Cyclohexene	1.0	1.0	1.0	
Styrene	0.3	0.09	1.0	0.34
1-Decene	0.02	0.04	0.18	0.20
Allylbenzene	0.01	0.2	0.05	
Diphenylacetylene	0.006			

F. Ramirez[2] (1961) has described a novel route to the cyclic diacyl peroxide (6) involving ozonolysis of the crystalline cyclic adduct (5) of phenanthrenequinone and trimethyl phosphite. Diphenoyl peroxide (6) can be preserved at room temperature but explodes at about 70° or on impact. It reacts with tri-

[1] Frederick D. Greene, b. 1927 Glen Ridge, N. J.; Ph.D. Harvard (Bartlett); Mass. Inst. Tech.
[2] Fausto Ramirez, b. 1923 Zulueta, Cuba; Ph.D. Michigan (Bachmann); Columbia Univ.; State Univ. New York

phenylphosphine to give diphenic anhydride and on iodometric assay it yields diphenic acid.

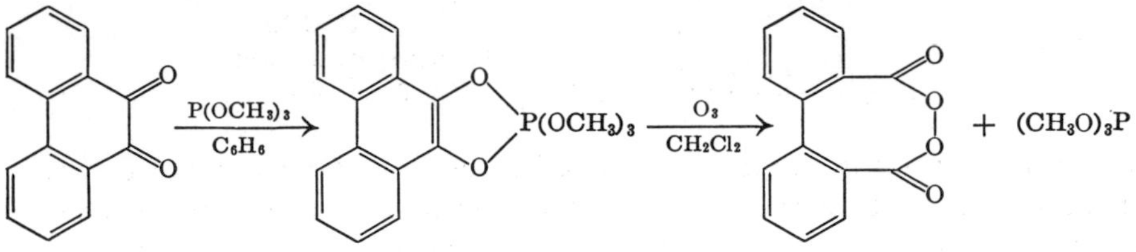

(4)   (5) M.p. 74°   (6)

24.7   **Anthranilic Acid.** — This *o*-amino derivative of benzoic acid is pre-
               pared in high yield by the action of sodium hypochlorite on phthal-
imide in alkaline solution at 80°; the ring is opened by hydrolysis and the phthalamidic acid formed undergoes the Hofmann reaction.   The amino acid is largely
precipitated on neutralization of the alkaline solution, and an additional amount
can be recovered as the copper salt.   **Methyl anthranilate,** found in oils extracted

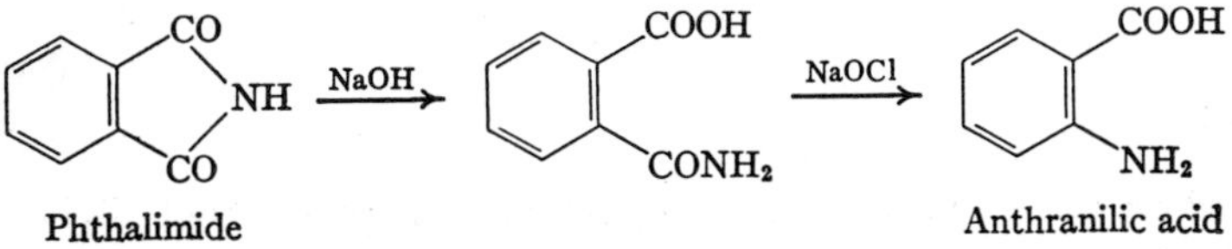

Phthalimide   Anthranilic acid

from jasmine and orange leaves, is obtained by esterification with methanol and
sulfuric acid as a crystalline solid of characteristic fragrance (m.p. 25°, b.p.
135°/15 mm.).

24.8   **Salicylic Acid.** — The *o*-hydroxy derivative of benzoic acid was
               obtained for the first time in 1838 by the action of alkali on the
corresponding aldehyde, probably as the result of disproportionation (Cannizzaro reaction).   In 1859 Kolbe discovered a method of preparation that, in
slightly modified form (Schmitt,[1] 1885), has made the substance available in
quantity at a low price.   In the technical process a solution of phenol in aqueous
alkali is evaporated to a dry powder, and the sodium phenolate is saturated with
carbon dioxide at 4–7 atmospheres pressure and heated to 125°; free salicylic
acid is liberated on acidification of an aqueous solution of the cooled melt and is
obtained in close to the theoretical amount.   A mechanism for the **Kolbe-Schmitt
reaction** similar to that postulated for *o*-alkylation of phenol (22.16) seems applicable.

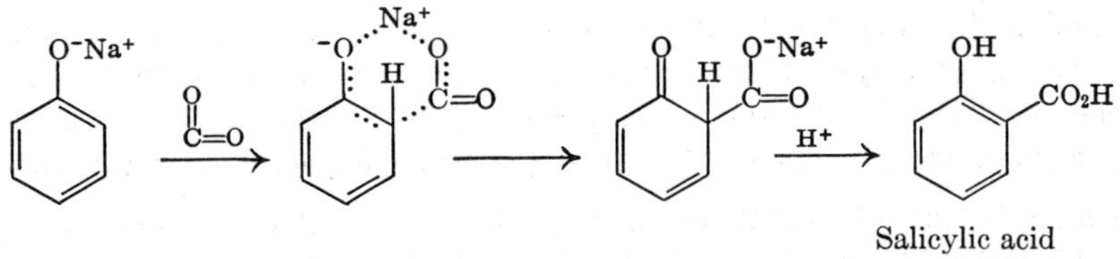

Salicylic acid

---

[1] Rudolf Schmitt, 1830–98; b. Wippershain, Germany; Ph.D. Marburg; Univ. Dresden

Removal of the elements of water from salicylic acid gives mixtures of di-, tri-, tetra- (1) and hexasalicylide in yields varying with the dehydrating agent and the experimental conditions (W. Baker and W. D. Ollis,[1] 1951). Dehydration of

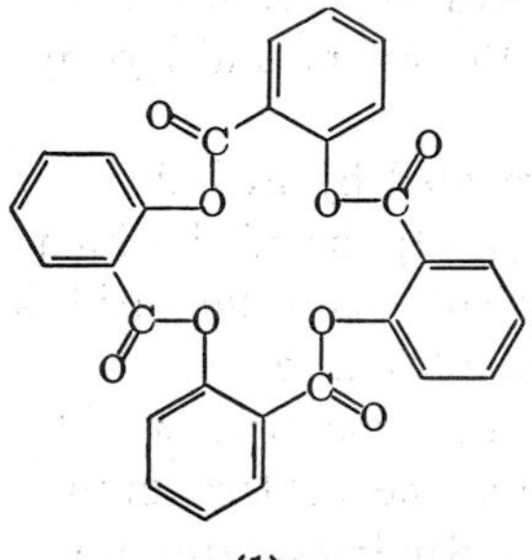

(1) 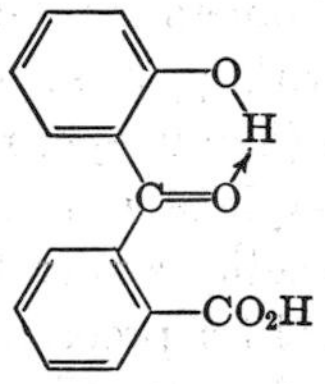   (2) 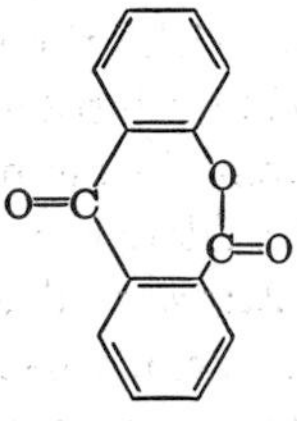   (3) 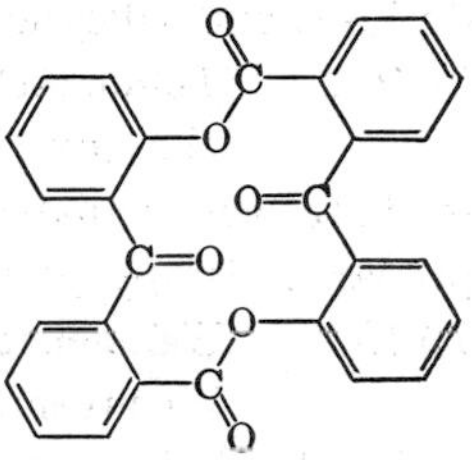   (4)

2-carboxy-2'-hydroxybenzophenone (2) with acetic anhydride gives the 7-membered lactone (3), whereas dehydration with phosphorus pentoxide or trifluoroacetic anhydride gives only the 14-membered lactide (4). Baker and Ollis suggest that hydrogen bonding in (2) inhibits lactonization but favors intermolecular lactide formation and that acetic anhydride produces the phenolic acetate which affords the lactone (3) by acyl exchange. Other dehydrating agents probably react first with the carboxyl group to give either a mixed anhydride or an acylium ion. 2-Carboxy-2'-hydroxydiphenylmethane, in which hydrogen bonding is impossible, gave only the 7-membered lactone.

Methyl salicylate occurs in many plants and was known first as the fragrant principle of wintergreen and called oil of wintergreen. It is one of three ester derivatives used in medicine, the others being **acetylsalicylic acid, or aspirin,** and the phenyl ester, **salol.** The methyl ester is prepared synthetically by Fischer esterification of salicylic acid. The acetyl derivative can be prepared efficiently by acetylation with acetic anhydride with sulfuric acid as catalyst. The name aspirin is from acetyl + spiraeic acid, an old name for salicylic acid. Salol is made by condensation of salicylic acid with phenol under the influence of phosphorus oxychloride. The application of these substances in medicine is based on the fact that salicylic acid itself produces a beneficial physiological response when absorbed through the intestinal membrane, but, being rather

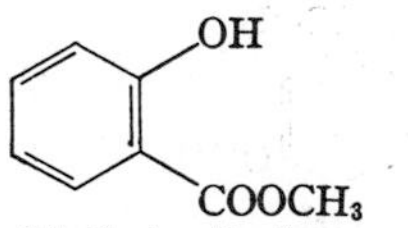

Methyl salicylate   Acetylsalicylic acid   Salol
(oil of wintergreen,   (aspirin, m.p. 137°,   (phenyl salicylate,
m.p. −8°, b.p. 223°)   pKₐ 3.48)   m.p. 43°)

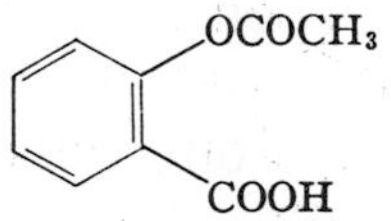

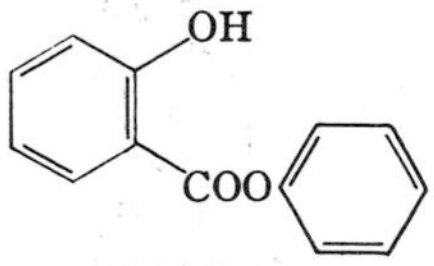

strongly acidic, is disagreeably irritating when taken by mouth. The irritating action is eliminated by esterification of the carboxyl group with either methanol

[1] W. David Ollis, b. 1924 Bristol; Ph.D. Bristol (W. Baker); Univ. Bristol

or phenol and also by acetylation, for the acetyl derivative is less acidic than the phenolic carboxylic acid. The three ester derivatives, methyl salicylate, aspirin, and salol, are not hydrolyzed to an appreciable extent on contact with the weakly acidic digestive fluids of the stomach, and pass through without harmful action; on discharge to the alkaline intestinal tract, however, the esters undergo hydrolysis, and salicylic acid is liberated.

24.9   Toluic Acids. — The three isomers can be prepared by hydrolysis of the corresponding nitriles with 75% sulfuric acid; the nitrile intermediates are available from the amines (Sandmeyer reaction). *m*-Toluic acid is prepared also by partial oxidation of *m*-xylene with dilute nitric acid.

24.10   Halobenzoic Acids. — The readily available anthranilic acid provides a convenient starting material for preparation of the *o*-chloro, bromo, and iodo derivatives of benzoic acid (diazotization and Sandmeyer reaction). Another method, applicable to the *o*- and *p*-chloro and bromo acids, is permanganate oxidation of the appropriate halogen derivative of toluene. Chlorination of benzoic acid at room temperature in the presence of ferric chloride gives *m*-chlorobenzoic acid as the chief product, along with the 2,5- and 3,4-dichloro derivatives. A technical process for production of 2,4-dichlorobenzoic acid is side-chain chlorination of 2,4-dichlorotoluene and hydrolysis.

24.11   Nitrobenzoic Acids. — The *ortho* and *para* isomers are made by oxidation of the nitrotoluenes with potassium permanganate or potassium dichromate. *m*-Nitrobenzoic acid is the chief product of nitration of benzoic acid and can be prepared also from benzotrichloride because of the *meta* directing effect of the trichloromethyl group and the susceptibility of the side-chain substituents to hydrolysis. Methyl *m*-nitrobenzoate (m.p. 78°) can be prepared in 81–85% yield by nitration of methyl benzoate with mixed acid, and alkaline hydrolysis affords the acid in 85–90% yield. 3,5-Dinitrobenzoic acid is prepared by nitration with mixed acid; 3,5-dinitrobenzoyl chloride (m.p. 74°) is useful as a reagent for conversion of alcohols into often sparingly soluble and high-melting esters.

24.12   Hydroxy and Methoxy Acids. — The ready preparation of salicylic acid by the Kolbe reaction has been described above. A route to *m*-hydroxybenzoic acid is fusion of sodium benzoic acid 3-sulfonate with sodium and potassium hydroxide at 220°. The *p*-methoxy derivative, anisic acid, is

COOH   COOH   COOH

OCH₃   OH   OH
Anisic acid   Gallic acid   Syringic acid

found in extracts of natural oils containing anethole, from which it probably arises by oxidation. Gallic acid, or 3,4,5-trihydroxybenzoic acid, results from fermentative cleavage of tannins, and is extracted by a process based on a method used by Scheele in 1786. The dimethyl ether, syringic acid, is also derived from natural sources. One gram of gallic acid dissolves in 87 ml. of water at 25°,

3 ml. of boiling water, 100 ml. of ether. The acid has reducing properties and the *n*-propyl ester (m.p. 150°) is used as an antioxidant for fats and oils. Gallic acid readily loses carbon dioxide on heating (pyrogallol). Decarboxylation at relatively low temperatures is a property characteristic of phenolic acids of *ortho* or *para* orientation of the two functional groups, but not of *m*-hydroxy

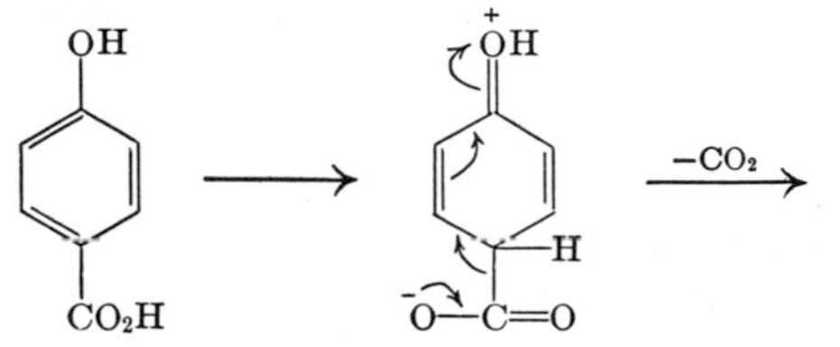

acids. A possible interpretation is that transfer of a proton from the carboxyl group to the ring is greatly facilitated by the hydroxyl group (resonance).

TANNINS AND RELATED PRODUCTS

24.13   Tannins, Ester Type. — A gall is a swelling or excrescence of tissues of a plant resulting from attack by certain parasitic insects. The insect punctures the bark or leaf and lays eggs in the wound, and the larva lives in and feeds on the gall produced. Galls on oak leaves resemble nuts and are called nutgalls. Extraction of nutgalls with water affords in about 50% yield an initially amorphous, strongly astringent substance known as a tannin, or tannic acid, because one distinctive property is the ability to tan hides. Hide contains the water-soluble protein gelatin, the main constituent of glue. A tannin renders gelatin (ox glue) insoluble and thereby converts hide to leather. Tannins are obtained also from dried and powdered leaves of sumac shrub, tea leaves, oak bark, horse chestnut, etc.

Many tannins are esters which on saponification yield gallic acid, and in some cases the sugar glucose. E. Fischer found that the characteristic component is often an ester formed from two molecules of gallic acid, a **depside** (Gr. *depsein*, to tan); if three or four units are involved, the substance is a tridepside or tetra-depside. The simplest depside was shown by synthesis to be *m*-digallic acid, in which the carboxyl group of one unit is esterified with a *meta* hydroxyl group of

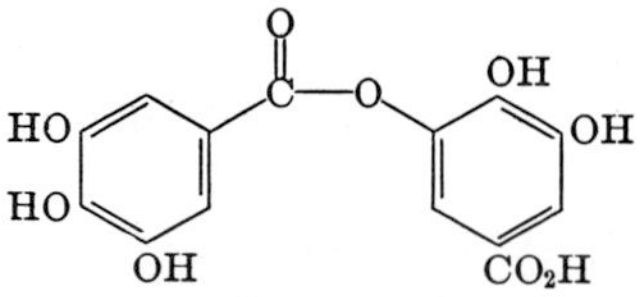

m-Digallic acid
(m.p. 295°)

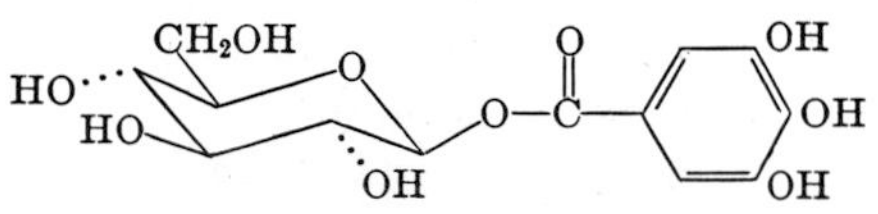

1-Galloyl-β-D-glucoside

another. The substance precipitates glue and thus has tanning properties. A tannin of Chinese rhubarb was shown by Fischer to be identical with synthetic 1-galloyl β-D-glucoside. The tannin of Chinese galls contains a mixture of esters in which all five hydroxyl groups are esterified with either gallic acid or *m*-digallic acid, or even with trigallic acid residues. On the average, each sugar molecule has nine gallic acid residues.

Erythrin ($C_{20}H_{22}O_{10}$), a colorless crystalline solid from certain lichens of the genus *Roccella*, was so named because it is capable of forming transformation prod-

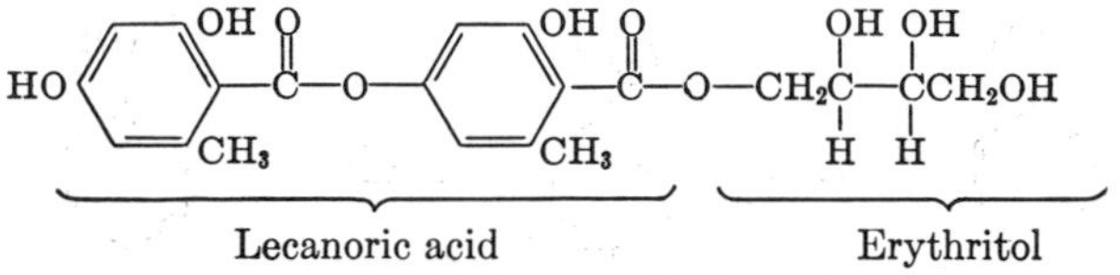

Lecanoric acid   Erythritol
Erythrin, m.p. 148°, α_D + 10.6°

ucts that are red (Gr. *erythros*, red). Gentle saponification splits erythrin into lecanoric acid (m.p. 166°) and a C_4-sugar alcohol which, because of this origin, was named erythritol (the sugar is erythrose). Lecanoric acid is a depside derived from orsellinic acid. Asahina[1] characterized as the tridepside of orsellinic acid the substance gyrophoric acid from *Gyrophora esculenta*, the edible rock-inhabiting manna lichen of Japan.

Chlorogenic acid (α_D −33° in water) is a depside made up from the α,β-unsaturated caffeic acid and quinic acid, a tetrahydroxycyclohexanecarboxylic acid found in cinchona bark along with quinine (Freudenberg, 1920). Chlorogenic

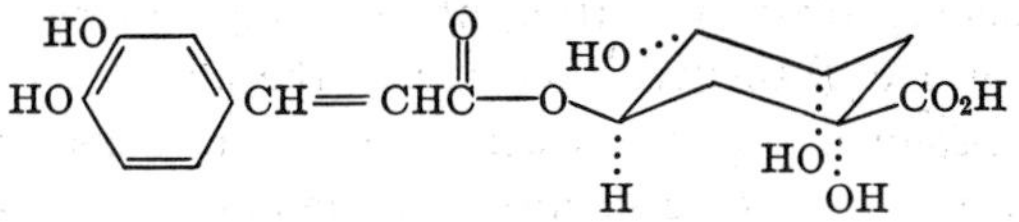

Chlorogenic acid

acid occurs in considerable quantities in the coffee bean as the potassium salt combined with one equivalent of caffeine.

Tannins of the gallic acid type are used in the manufacture of ink; they form colorless water-soluble ferrous salts which on air oxidation give black, insoluble ferric salts. A blue dye, which need not be light-fast, is added to make the ink initially visible. Tannin is used also in the application of certain basic dyes to cotton. Cloth impregnated with tannin is treated with antimonyl tartrate, which fixes the polyhydroxy acid to the fiber and so provides acidic groups capable of binding the dye. A binding link between cloth and dye is known as a mordant (L. *mordere*, to bite).

24.14   Tannins, Nonester Type. — Tannins of a second type contain phenolic nuclei joined by C—C or C—O—C links. Some belong to the widely distributed group of catechins, exemplified by *l*-epicatechin, obtained from *Acacia catechu* and tea-catechin II, isolated from green tea. These substances are penta- and hexahydroxyflavans, and each is the product of hydrogenation of an

[1] Yasuhiko Asahina, b. 1881 Tokyo; Ph.D. Tokyo (Z. Shimoyama); Univ. Tokyo; Introchem. Inst. Pharmacolog. Res. Found. Tokyo

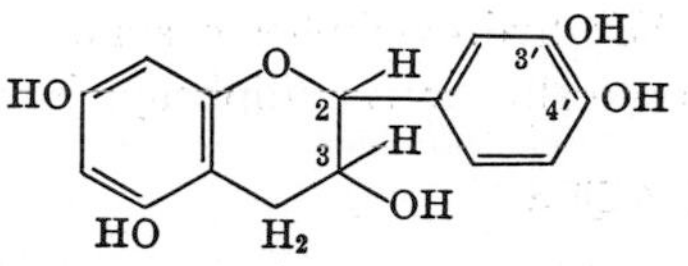

l-Epicatechin 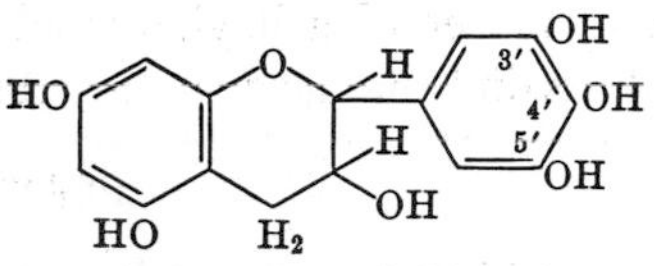   Tea-catechin II

anthocyanidin pigment.   l-Epicatechin and its 3-galloyl derivative are regular
constituents of tea leaves.   A group of lichen substances investigated by Asahina
and known as depsidones are exemplified by physodic acid and cetraric acid.

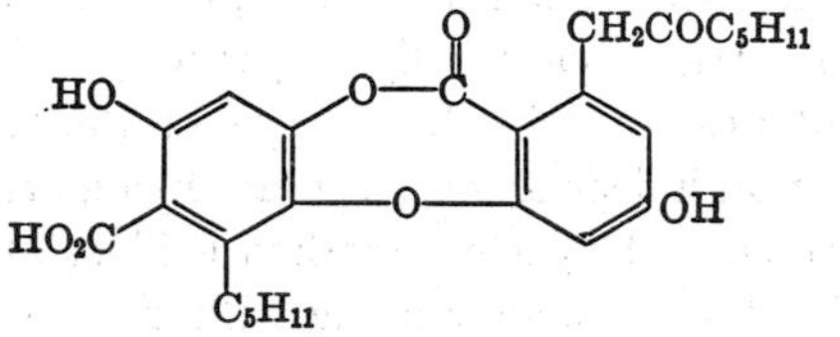

Physodic acid 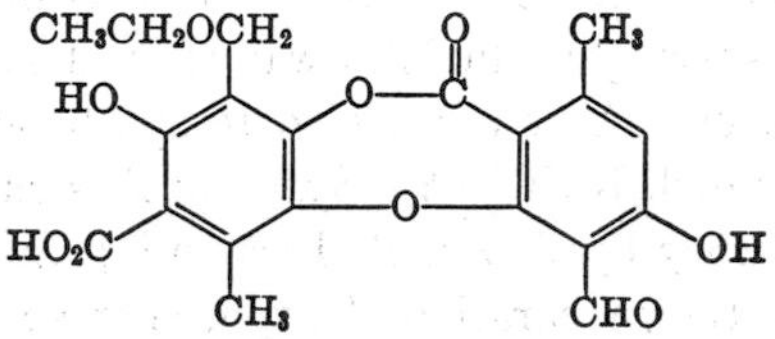   Cetraric acid

Ellagic acid, a constituent of many tannins, is a phenolic dilactone of quinonoid
bond structure.   It forms yellow-green needles from pyridine, melts above 360°,
is insoluble in ether, slightly soluble in water, and soluble in alkali with an intense
yellow color.   Ellagic acid dyes chromium-mordanted cotton a very light-fast

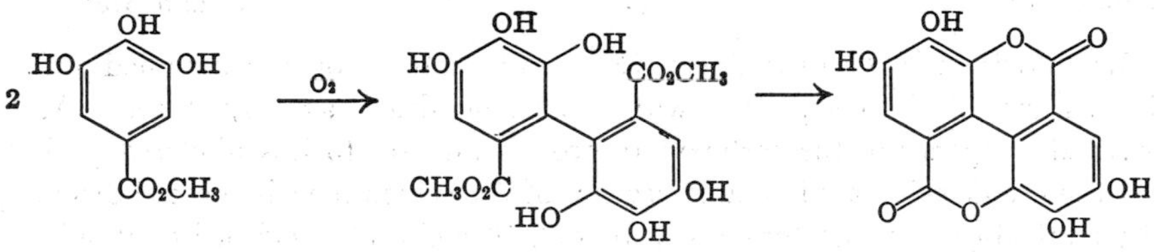

Ellagic acid

olive green.   Autoxidation of methyl gallate (but not the free acid) in $2\,N$ ammonia affords the dimethyl ester of hexahydroxydiphenic acid, which rapidly
undergoes intramolecular transesterification to ellagic acid.   The observation
suggested that ellagic acid arises in nature by oxidative coupling of gallic acid
esters, specifically, sugar gallates.   This inference was amply confirmed by work
of Schmidt,[1] who showed (1956) that a tannin corilagin, convertible into ellagic

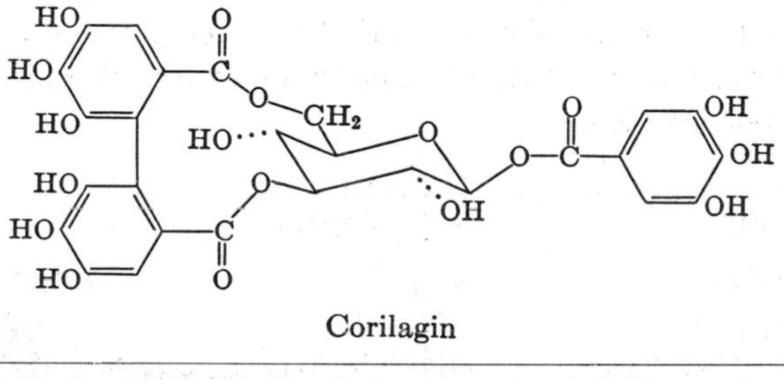

Corilagin

[1] Otto Th. Schmidt, b. 1894 Karlsruhe; Ph.D. Univ. Münich (Willstätter); Techn. Hochschule,
Karlsruhe; Univ. Heidelberg

acid, is a diester of galloylglucoside and hexahydroxydiphenic acid. The free hexahydroxydiphenic acid in this case is optically active (diphenyl isomerism).

POLYBASIC ACIDS

24.15   **Phthalic acid** has been produced for many years, as the anhydride, by vapor-phase catalytic air-oxidation of naphthalene from coal tar. With development of efficient processes from aromatization of the C_8-cut from petroleum and separation of the three xylenes (7.16), oxidation of the xylenes from this source has made phthalic acid, **isophthalic acid** (m.p. 348°), and **terephthalic acid** (sublimes at about 300°) available as petrochemicals. Terephthalic acid is sparingly soluble in water; the less symmetrical isomers dissolve readily in hot water. A new route to terephthalic acid described by B. Raecke of the firm Henkel, Berlin (*Org. Syn.*, 1960) is based upon independent observations reported in 1873 by V. von Richter and J. Wislicenus. The general method is illustrated by the preparation of naphthalene-2,6-dicarboxylic acid starting with 1,8-naph-

(1) m.p. 275°   (2)   (3) m.p. 313°

KOH-CH₃OH 88-92%   430°; HCl 57-61%

thalic anhydride (1, Coaltar Chem. Co.). The anhydride is saponified and the dipotassium salt is precipitated with methanol, dried, and pyrolyzed. At the elevated temperature the carboxylate groups migrate to less hindered positions and the product liberated on acidification of the cooled melt is the 2,6-diacid (3). The method can be used for conversion of either phthalic acid or isophthalic acid into terephthalic acid (90–95%); diphenyl-2,2'-dicarboxylic acid to the 4,4'-isomer; pyrrole-3,4-dicarboxylic acid to the 2,5-isomer; and pyridine-2,3-dicarboxylic acid to the 2,5-isomer. A related reaction is the thermal disproportionation of the potassium salt of an acid, for example, the conversion of potassium benzoate into dipotassium terephthalate and benzene. Other examples are: the three pyridinecarboxylic acids → pyridine-2,5-dicarboxylic acid (30–50%); 2-furoic acid → furane-2,5-dicarboxylic acid; quinoline-2-carboxylic acid → quinoline-2,4-dicarboxylic acid. In a kinetic study using C^{14}-tracers, Y. Ogata (1960) found that the conversion of phthalic to terephthalic acid is an intramolecular rearrangement and that the conversion of benzoic acid to terephthalic acid is a disproportionation.

Hemimellitic acid
(m.p. 190–197° dec.; anhydride, m.p. 196°; trimethyl ester, m.p. 102°)

Trimellitic acid
(m.p. 225–235° dec.; anhydride, m.p. 166°; trimethyl ester, liq.)

Trimesic acid
(m.p. 380°; trimethyl ester, m.p. 144°)

Characteristic properties of the three benzenetricarboxylic acids are indicated in the notations under the formulas. The first two acids of unsymmetrical structure are very soluble in water and are extracted from aqueous solution by ether or ethyl acetate only after several applications of fresh solvent or with a continuous extractor. The 1,2,3- and 1,2,4-acids yield anhydrides when heated, and melt with decomposition in ill-defined temperature ranges. The 1,2,3-isomer, hemimellitic acid, is prepared most conveniently by stepwise oxidation of acenaphthene from coal tar. Trimellitic acid (1,2,4) and trimesic acid (1,3,5) result from

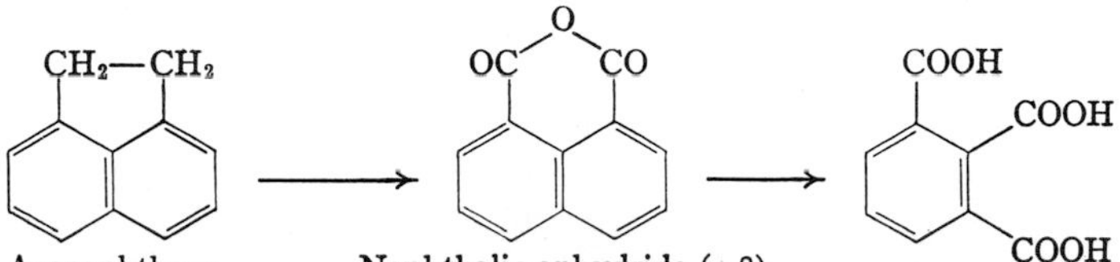

Acenaphthene   Naphthalic anhydride (1,8)   Hemimellitic acid

permanganate oxidation of the corresponding trimethylbenzenes, pseudocumene and mesitylene.

Prehnitic Acid (Benzene-1,2,3,4-tetracarboxylic Acid). — This acid is very soluble in water and is extracted with ether only slowly. It is best characterized as the crystalline tetramethyl ester, prepared with diazomethane; a remarkable property of this ester is that on exposure to light a purple color is acquired that disappears when the sample is either melted or recrystallized. On esterification with methanol and hydrogen chloride, the less hindered carboxyl groups in the 1- and 4-positions react preferentially to form the 1,4-dimethyl ester. The acid can be prepared by oxidation of prehnitene (Jacobsen reaction, 18.14) or of the indanedione intermediate in Buchta's synthesis of prehnitene (18.10). Another convenient route is permanganate oxidation of naphthalene-1,4-dicarboxylic

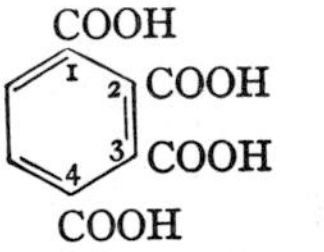

Prehnitic acid

(m.p. 241° dec.; dianhydride, m.p. 196°; tetramethyl ester, m.p. 133°; 1,4-dimethyl ester, m.p. 177°)

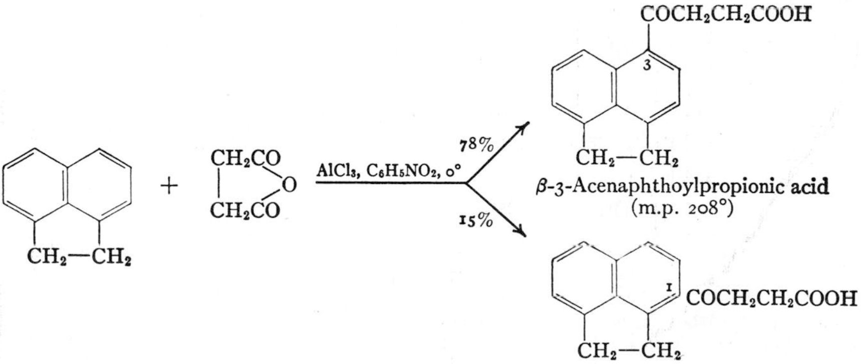

β-3-Acenaphthoylpropionic acid
(m.p. 208°)

β-1-Acenaphthoylpropionic acid
(m.p. 181°)

acid (33% yield); the starting material is obtained through a process involving 1,2- and 1,4-addition of sodium to naphthalene. A more readily available starting material is obtained by succinoylation of acenaphthene. The 3-acid is the chief product and can be isolated as the less soluble sodium salt; the solubility relationship is reversed in the methyl esters, and hence the 1-acid can be isolated easily by esterification of the material recovered from the mother liquor. Separation is not required, however, for both isomers are converted on permanganate oxidation into prehnitic acid (yield, 25%).

Mellophanic Acid (Benzene-1,2,3,5-tetracarboxylic Acid). — This substance has been isolated as a product of oxidation of a number of derivatives of benzene

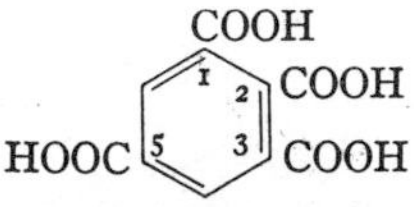

Mellophanic acid
(m.p. 260–265° dec.; tetramethyl ester, m.p. 111°)

and of polynuclear compounds, and identification of such degradation products, usually as the sharply melting esters, often constitutes evidence of structure. A comparison sample of mellophanic acid can be prepared conveniently by oxidation of mesitylenecarboxylic acid (from bromomesitylene) with nitric acid at 170–180°.

Pyromellitic Acid. — This symmetrically substituted tetrabasic acid can be made by oxidation of durene with nitric acid or by condensation of pseudocumene with acetyl chloride in the presence of aluminum chloride and oxidation of the resulting acetopseudocumene (2,4,5-trimethylacetophenone) with sodium hypobromite and then permanganate. The name is derived from the fact that the

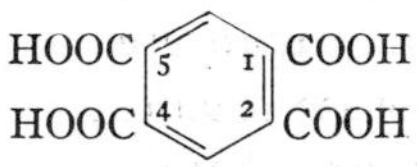

Pyromellitic acid
(m.p. 276° dec.; tetramethyl ester,
m.p. 141°; dianhydride, m.p. 286°)

substance is produced as the stable dianhydride when the hexabasic mellitic acid is strongly heated. Pyromellitic dianhydride forms 1:1 complexes with polymethylbenzenes and approaches tetracyanoethylene in strength as a π-acid (L. L. Ferstandig, 1961).

Benzenepentacarboxylic acid, obtained by the action of potassium permanganate on pentamethylbenzene, when heated above the melting point at reduced

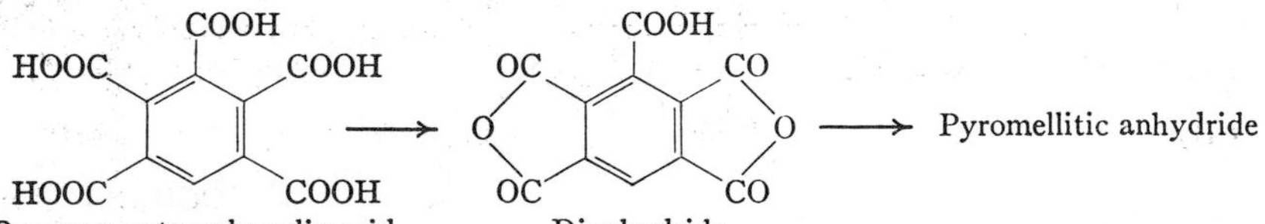

Benzenepentacarboxylic acid
(m.p. 238° dec.)

Dianhydride
(amorphous)

Pyromellitic anhydride

pressure gives a glassy dianhydride, which undergoes decarboxylation when heated at 270–300° and affords pyromellitic anhydride.

Mellitic Acid. — The hexabasic acid derives its name from the occurrence of the aluminum salt ($Al_2C_{12}O_{12} \cdot 18H_2O$) as the mineral mellite (honey-stone), found in brown coal. It results from oxidation of graphite or of hexamethylbenzene with permanganate or of wood charcoal with nitric acid (sp. gr. 1.5). A dianhydride melting with decomposition at about 300° has been produced by treatment with thionyl chloride, and probably has the free carboxyl groups in the 1,4-positions. When heated with acetyl chloride at 160° in a sealed tube, mellitic acid yields a stable trianhydride that sublimes when heated at 200° at 3–4 mm. pressure.

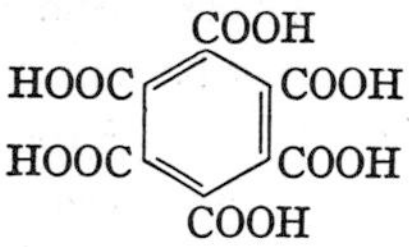

Mellitic acid
(m.p. in sealed tube 288°;
hexamethyl ester, m.p. 188°)

Diphenic Acid. — The preparation of this substance from anthranilic acid is described in section 21.27. Diphenic acid is also obtainable by the oxidation of phenanthrenequinone with hydrogen peroxide.

Diphenic acid can be converted into the anhydride by treatment with acetyl chloride or acetic anhydride, but it does not suffer dehydration on heating with

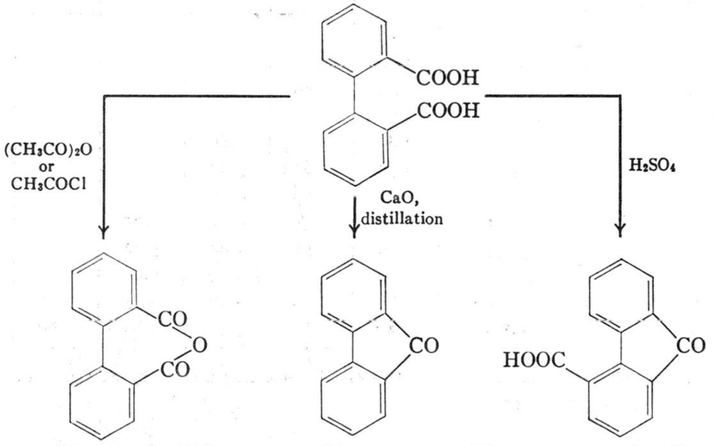

Diphenic anhydride
(m.p. 217°)

Fluorenone
(m.p. 84°, b.p. 341.5°)

Fluorenone-4-carboxylic acid
(m.p. 227°)

the readiness characteristic of polybasic acids containing carboxyl groups in adjacent positions in the same ring, where cyclization gives a five-membered rather than a seven-membered ring structure. Thus by careful heating diphenic acid can be sublimed (needles) without dehydration. Another transformation (see chart), accomplished by distillation with lime, results in closure of a five-membered ketonic ring by loss of carbon dioxide and production of fluorenone. A ring closure involving elimination of water between one of the carboxyl groups and an *ortho* position in the adjoining ring is brought about by treatment of diphenic acid with concentrated sulfuric acid (fluorenone-4-carboxylic acid).

Dissociation Constants of Polybasic Acids. — The constants of successive stages of dissociation of the polybasic carboxylic acids have been determined (W. R. Maxwell and J. R. Partington, 1937, Table 24.3). The acidic strength, as measured by pK_{a_1}, increases progressively with introduction of additional carboxyl groups, particularly into *ortho* or *vicinal* positions, and the relationship roughly parallels that in dibasic aliphatic acids, where enhanced acidic strength is associated with proximity of the functional groups. With increase in the number of nuclear carboxyl groups, separation of the last proton from the multiple-charged ion becomes increasingly difficult.

24.16 Aryl-Substituted Paraffinic Acids. — Acids having a phenyl group at the terminal position of an aliphatic chain, or ω-phenyl fatty acids, are useful synthetic intermediates; representatives are listed in Table 24.4 along with two frequently encountered unsaturated acids. **Phenylacetic acid** can be prepared from toluene through benzyl chloride, which reacts with sodium cyanide

TABLE 24.3. ACIDIC DISSOCIATION CONSTANTS[1]

ACID	POSITION OF CARBOXYL GROUPS	DISSOCIATION CONSTANTS					
		pK_{a_1}	pK_{a_2}	pK_{a_3}	pK_{a_4}	pK_{a_5}	pK_{a_6}
Benzoic	1	4.17					
Phthalic	1,2	3.00	5.28				
Isophthalic	1,3	3.28	4.46				
Terephthalic	1,4	(3.82)					
Hemimellitic	1,2,3	2.80	4.20	5.89			
Trimellitic	1,2,4	2.52	3.85	5.20			
Trimesic	1,3,5	3.12	3.89	4.70			
Prehnitic	1,2,3,4	2.06	3.25	4.72	6.21		
Mellophanic	1,2,3,5	2.38	3.51	4.44	5.82		
Pyromellitic	1,2,4,5	1.92	2.89	4.49	5.64		
Benzenepentacarboxylic	1,2,3,4,5	1.80	2.74	3.96	5.25	6.46	
Mellitic	1,2,3,4,5,6	1.40	2.19	3.31	4.80	5.89	6.96

[1] With the exception of the value given in parentheses, the constants are based on determinations at an ionic strength of 0.03.

TABLE 24.4. BENZENE DERIVATIVES WITH ACIDIC SIDE CHAINS

ACID	FORMULA	M.P., °C.	B.P., °C.	$pK_a^{25°}$
Phenylacetic	$C_6H_5CH_2CO_2H$	78	265	4.31
Hydrocinnamic	$C_6H_5CH_2CH_2CO_2H$	49	280	4.64
γ-Phenylbutyric	$C_6H_5CH_2CH_2CH_2CO_2H$	51	$171^{15mm.}$	
δ-Phenyl-*n*-valeric	$C_6H_5CH_2CH_2CH_2CH_2CO_2H$	61	$178^{13mm.}$	
ε-Phenyl-*n*-caproic	$C_6H_5CH_2CH_2CH_2CH_2CH_2CO_2H$		$208^{30mm.}$	
Cinnamic (*trans*)	$C_6H_5CH{=}CHCO_2H$	136		4.43
Phenylpropiolic	$C_6H_5C{\equiv}CCO_2H$	137		2.23
Homophthalic	$o\text{-}C_6H_4(COOH)CH_2CO_2H$	183		
o-Phenylenediacetic	$o\text{-}C_6H_4(CH_2CO_2H)_2$	150		3.96
m-Phenylenediacetic	$m\text{-}C_6H_4(CH_2CO_2H)_2$	170		
p-Phenylenediacetic	$p\text{-}C_6H_4(CH_2CO_2H)_2$	244		
o-Phenyleneacetic-β-propionic	$o\text{-}HOOCCH_2C_6H_4CH_2CH_2CO_2H$	139		

in aqueous alcohol to give benzyl cyanide in 80–90% yield; hydrolysis of the nitrile with dilute sulfuric acid then affords phenylacetic acid (80% yield). The acid is also produced in 90% yield by reduction of mandelic acid with potassium iodide, red phosphorus, and phosphoric acid. The next member of the series, β-phenyl-propionic acid, is known as **hydrocinnamic acid** because it is made most readily by reduction of its unsaturated derivative, cinnamic acid ($C_6H_5CH\!=\!CHCO_2H$), with sodium amalgam, by catalytic hydrogenation, or by electrolytic reduction. **Cinnamic acid** can be synthesized readily from benzaldehyde (13.6, 13.8, 13.16), and it is the chief constituent of the fragrant balsamic resin storax, formerly used as an expectorant and as incense; oriental and American storaxes contain 47–51% of free cinnamic acid and small amounts of styrene, $C_6H_5CH\!=\!CH_2$, the product of decarboxylation. Nuclear substituted derivatives of hydrocinnamic acid that are not obtainable in the manner described for the parent substance, because of unavailability of the aldehydic starting materials, sometimes can be prepared from benzyl halides by the malonic ester synthesis (23.4).

γ-**Phenylbutyric acid,** $C_6H_5CH_2CH_2CH_2COOH$, is prepared conveniently by the Friedel-Crafts succinoylation of benzene and Clemmensen reduction of the keto acid. The method is applicable to the preparation of many other γ-aryl-butyric acids, but where a particular orientation is not achievable by substitution, the intermediate keto acid required may be obtainable by a Grignard synthesis. The Stobbe reaction (13.12) affords γ-alkyl-γ-phenylbutyric acids. The

$$C_{14}H_9MgBr \quad + \quad \underset{CH_2CO}{\overset{CH_2CO}{\Big\rangle}}O \quad \xrightarrow{45\%} \quad C_{14}H_9COCH_2CH_2COOH$$

9-Phenanthrylmagnesium β-9-Phenanthroylpropionic
bromide   acid (m.p. 181°)

next homolog, **δ-phenyl-*n*-valeric acid,** has been made from cinnamaldehyde in three steps (the yields in the last two reactions are reported as practically quanti-

$$C_6H_5CH\!=\!CHCHO \;+\; CH_2(COOH)_2 \;\xrightarrow[70-80\%]{HOAc,\,95°}\; C_6H_5CH\!=\!CHCH\!=\!C(COOH)_2 \;\xrightarrow{H_2,\,Pd}$$

Cinnamaldehyde   Cinnamalmalonic acid
             (m.p. 208° dec.)

$$C_6H_5CH_2CH_2CH_2CH(COOH)_2 \;\xrightarrow{Heat\,(-CO_2)}\; C_6H_5CH_2CH_2CH_2CH_2COOH$$

ω-Phenyl-*n*-propylmalonic   δ-Phenyl-*n*-valeric acid
acid (m.p. 98°)

tative). ε-**Phenyl-*n*-caproic acid** has been made by reduction of the keto acid formed on chromic acid oxidation of the carbinol from phenylmagnesium bromide and cyclohexanone (8.29), by Friedel-Crafts condensation of adipic acid half ester half acid chloride with benzene and Clemmensen reduction, and by stepwise elaboration of the chain.

Homophthalic Acid. — This *o*-carboxy derivative of phenylacetic acid can be prepared from an intermediate nitrile available by a special reaction discovered by Wislicenus (1886). The nitrile is obtained by heating molten phthalide with potassium cyanide, followed by solution of the cooled melt in water and acidification, and it is then hydrolyzed with sulfuric acid. Homophthalic acid forms an anhydride (six-membered ring) on being heated or on treatment with acetyl chloride. The carboxyl group located in the side chain is more easily esterified

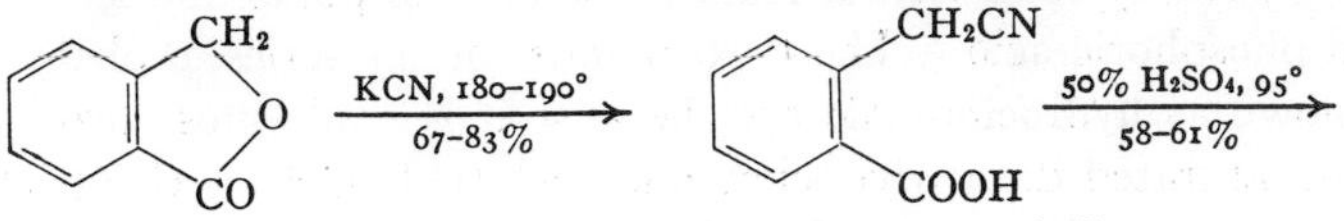

Phthalide

KCN, 180–190°
67–83%

o-Carboxyphenylacetonitrile
(m.p. 116° dec.)

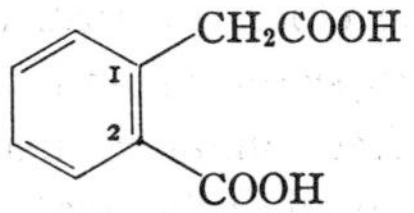

50% H₂SO₄, 95°
58–61%

Homophthalic acid
(m.p. 183° dec., pK$_{a1}$ 3.72, pK$_{a2}$ 6.05;
dimethyl ester, m.p. 42°; anhydride, m.p. 141°).

than that joined to the ring, for partial esterification with methanol and hydrogen chloride in the cold gives the ester $HOOCC_6H_4CH_2COOCH_3$ (homophthalic acid 1-methyl ester, m.p. 98°, pK$_a$ 4.12); the anhydride reacts with benzene in the presence of aluminum chloride to give desoxybenzoin-2′-carboxylic acid, C_6H_5-$COCH_2C_6H_4COOH$ (m.p. 170°).

o-Phenylenediacetic acid can be prepared from o-xylene by side-chain bromination and application of the nitrile synthesis (isolated as the ester). The next

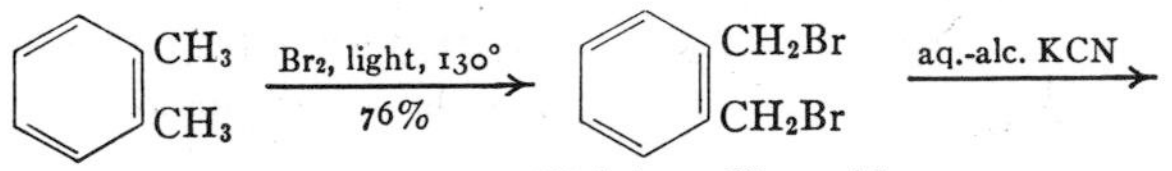

o-Xylylene dibromide
(m.p. 93°)

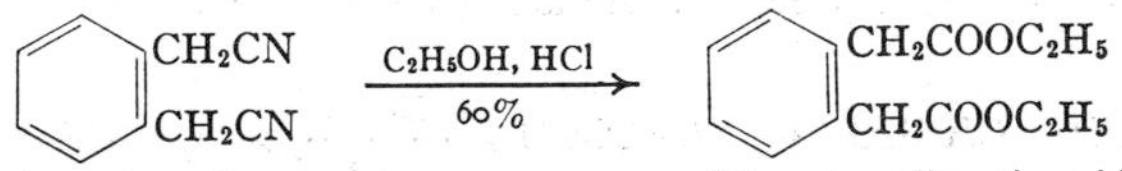

Br₂, light, 130°
76%

aq.-alc. KCN

o-Phenylenediaceto-
nitrile (m.p. 60°)

C₂H₅OH, HCl
60%

o-Phenylenediacetic acid
diethyl ester (b.p. 147°/2 mm.)

higher homolog of the o-series, **o-phenyleneacetic-β-propionic acid,** is readily available by a special reduction reaction similar to the conversion of salicylic acid into pimelic acid (15.22); a 1,4-addition of hydrogen yields an intermediate enol,

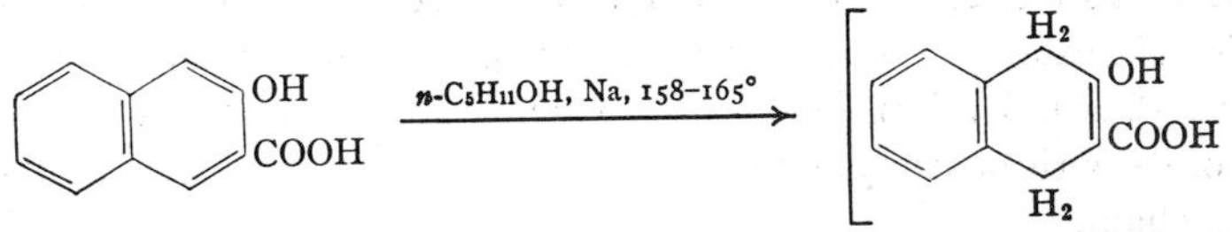

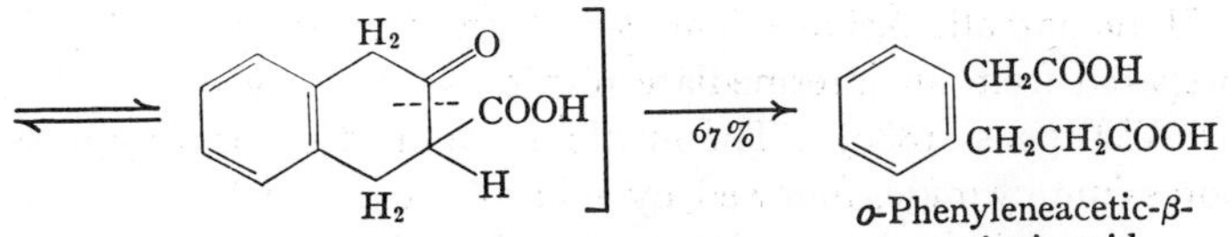

n-C₅H₁₁OH, Na, 158–165°

67%

o-Phenyleneacetic-β-
propionic acid

the tautomeric form of which is a β-keto acid susceptible to hydrolytic cleavage (reversal of the Dieckmann reaction).

24.17   Esterification of Aromatic Acids. — Among aliphatic carboxylic acids, those of primary structure (RCH_2CO_2H) are esterified readily with an alcohol and a mineral acid catalyst, whereas those in which the carboxyl group is joined to a quaternary carbon atom (R_3CCOOH) react sluggishly, probably because the alkyl groups dominate so much space in the neighborhood of the carboxyl group that they tend to block formation of an intermediate ionic addition complex. Still more striking instances of the suppression of catalyzed esterification are encountered in benzoic acid derivatives having substituents in the two *ortho* positions. The phenomenon was discovered and extensively investigated by Victor Meyer (1894), but isolated instances of a comparable blocking effect had been encountered earlier by Hofmann (1872), who observed that certain dialkylaniline derivatives having substituents *ortho* to the functional group are very resistant to the action of alkyl halides. Meyer investigated the response of aromatic acids to attempted esterification either by refluxing (3–5 hrs.) a solution in methanol containing 3% of hydrogen chloride (Fischer method) or by saturating a methanol solution of the acid with hydrogen chloride in the cold and allowing the solution to stand overnight. Benzoic acid and its *m*- and *p*-substituted derivatives afforded the methyl esters in about 90% yield by either method, but di-*o*-substituted acids formulated yielded little or no ester. If the two *ortho*

positions are blocked by nitro, chloro, or bromo substituents, no appreciable esterification results, even under forcing conditions, and if methyl, hydroxyl, or fluoro substituents occupy both positions flanking the carboxyl group, esterification proceeds to only a slight extent. A single *ortho* substituent exerts a significant blocking effect; for example, the *o*-hydroxyl group of salicylic acid has a retarding action such that the refluxing period adequate for esterification of benzoic acid must be extended about fivefold to produce methyl salicylate in practical quantity.

Esterification of *o*-disubstituted acids does not fail as the result of any instability of the reaction products, for the esters of mesitylenecarboxylic acid, 2,6-dibromobenzoic acid, and comparable acids can be prepared by the action of methyl iodide on the silver salt of the acids, by esterification with diazomethane, or by interaction of the acid chloride with the alcohol, and are very resistant to hydrolysis by acids or alkalis. Thus *ortho* substituents block hydrolysis of the esters just as they inhibit catalyzed esterification. Meyer introduced the term steric hindrance to describe the blocking effect, and suggested an association of the effectiveness of a given group in blocking esterification or hydrolysis with the relative size, as judged by the atomic weight. Thus an *o*-fluoro substituent exerts less hindrance than a chloro or bromo substituent, and hence the chemical nature of the substituent is not the controlling factor; groups of both the *ortho-para* and the *meta* directing type exert a hindering effect when adjacent to the carboxyl group. The resistance to esterification noted in mesitylenecarboxylic acid, $2,4,6\text{-}(CH_3)_3C_6H_2CO_2H$, disappears on separation of the carboxyl group from the ring, for mesityleneacetic acid, $2,4,6\text{-}(CH_3)_3C_6H_2CH_2COOH$, is esterified easily by the Fischer method. The influence of an *ortho* substituent, however, probably is the result of several factors, including the effective volume of the group, the effect of the substituent on the acidic dissociation constant, and the extent of coordination or chelation with the acidic group.

Newman (1941) discovered that $2,4,6$-trimethylbenzoic acid can be esterified by dissolving it in 100% sulfuric acid and pouring the solution into an alcohol; the reaction takes only a few minutes and the yields are excellent. Conversely, the ester is efficiently hydrolyzed by pouring a sulfuric acid solution into water. When treated in the same way, benzoic acid is not esterified and methyl benzoate is not hydrolyzed. According to Newman's interpretation, both the hindered and unhindered acid combine with a proton from sulfuric acid to form a conjugate

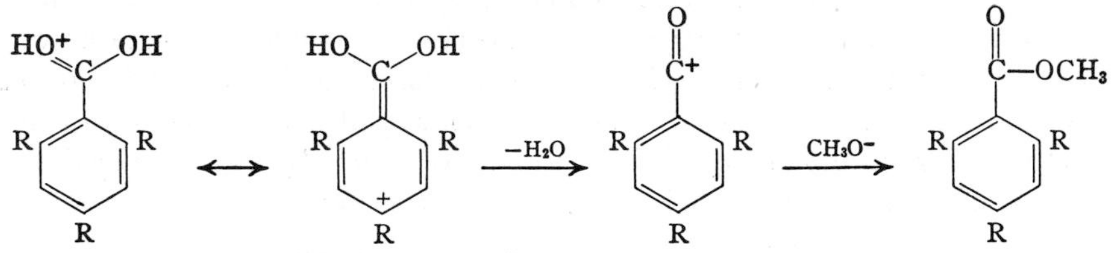

(With *o*-forms)

I   II   III   IV

acid (I), stabilized by resonance (II). The resonance structures, however, require coplanarity of all the carbon and oxygen atoms and, if R = methyl, interference between methyl and hydroxyl groups enhances the tendency for expulsion of water with formation of the positive acyl ion III, which can react with methanol to form the ester IV. In the absence of this steric factor (R = H), structures I and II are stable and have no tendency to lose water. The method of esterification is not successful with some esters, for example $2,4,6$-tribromobenzoic acid.

PROBLEMS

1. Suggest methods for the preparation of $2,4$- and $2,5$-dimethylbenzoic acid, starting with coal-tar hydrocarbons.
2. Indicate all the steps in the preparation of anthranilic acid from naphthalene.
3. Outline the steps in the preparation of *m*-toluic acid, starting with toluene.
4. Explain why polycarboxy derivatives of benzene are identified in the form of certain derivatives and not in the free form.
5. Suggest a scheme for the synthesis of $4,4'$-dibromodiphenic acid ($4,4'$-dibromodiphenyl-$2,2'$-dicarboxylic acid).
6. How could the following substances be synthesized:

    (a) γ-*p*-Tolylbutyric acid   (c) β-Tetralone (from one of
    (b) 1,5-Diphenylpentane   the acids of Table 24.4):

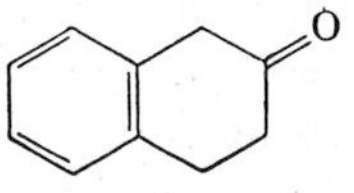

Chapter 25

AROMATIC ALDEHYDES AND KETONES

Aldehydes and ketones in which the carbonyl group is linked to an aromatic ring differ from aliphatic carbonyl compounds in relatively minor respects. The main interest in the chemistry of the aromatic derivatives are synthetic uses and methods employed for preparation. Ketones of the types ArCOR and ArCOAr′ are available by the Friedel-Crafts reaction, but several specific reactions are employed for production of aldehydes. In the following sections these methods are classified with respect to types of starting materials. Properties of the better known members are indicated in the tables and formula charts.

25.1   ALDEHYDES FROM ARYLMETHANES

$$(ArCH_3 \longrightarrow ArCHO)$$

Benzaldehyde. — Benzaldehyde occurs as the glycoside amygdalin, found in seed of bitter almonds. Amygdalin is a β-gentiobioside of mandelonitrile, $C_6H_5CH(CN)O—C_{12}H_{21}O_{10}$, and undergoes enzymic hydrolysis with liberation of benzaldehyde, hydrogen cyanide, and the sugar component. Because of this formerly utilized source of the liquid hydrolysis product of characteristic aromatic fragrance, benzaldehyde was known as oil of bitter almonds. Benzaldehyde is also the chief constituent of essential oils expressed from kernels of the peach, cherry, and other fruits.

The chief technical processes for production of benzaldehyde, required as an intermediate for dyes and other synthetic chemicals and in flavors and soap perfumes, utilize toluene as starting material. One efficient method of conversion into the aldehyde is side-chain chlorination in Pyrex glass or porcelain reactors (preferably with illumination), fractionation, and hydrolysis of the benzal chloride

TABLE 25.1.　MONOSUBSTITUTED DERIVATIVES OF BENZALDEHYDE

NAME	FORMULA	M.P., °C.	B.P., °C.
Benzaldehyde	C_6H_5CHO	liq.	179
m-Tolualdehyde	$m\text{-}CH_3C_6H_4CHO$	liq.	199
p-Tolualdehyde	$p\text{-}CH_3C_6H_4CHO$	liq.	204
o-Chlorobenzaldehyde	$o\text{-}ClC_6H_4CHO$	11	$208^{748\,mm.}$
p-Chlorobenzaldehyde	$p\text{-}ClC_6H_4CHO$	49	$213^{748\,mm.}$
o-Nitrobenzaldehyde	$o\text{-}NO_2 \cdot C_6H_4CHO$	44	
m-Nitrobenzaldehyde	$m\text{-}NO_2 \cdot C_6H_4CHO$	58	
p-Nitrobenzaldehyde	$p\text{-}NO_2 \cdot C_6H_4CHO$	106	
o-Aminobenzaldehyde	$o\text{-}NH_2 \cdot C_6H_4CHO$	40	
p-Aminobenzaldehyde	$p\text{-}NH_2 \cdot C_6H_4CHO$	71	
Salicylaldehyde	$o\text{-}HOC_6H_4CHO$	−7	197
m-Hydroxybenzaldehyde	$m\text{-}HOC_6H_4CHO$	108	
p-Hydroxybenzaldehyde	$p\text{-}HOC_6H_4CHO$	116	
o-Methoxybenzaldehyde	$o\text{-}CH_3OC_6H_4CHO$	3, 35	244
Anisaldehyde	$p\text{-}CH_3OC_6H_4CHO$	0	248
p-Dimethylaminobenzaldehyde	$p\text{-}(CH_3)_2NC_6H_4CHO$	75	

cut.　The hydrolysis is accomplished with water at 95–100° in the presence of iron powder or ferric benzoate as catalyst; lime is then added for neutralization and the

$$C_6H_5CH_3 \longrightarrow C_6H_5CHCl_2 \xrightarrow[76\%]{} C_6H_5CHO$$

benzaldehyde is steam distilled.　Benzoic acid usually appears as a by-product. Phosphorus pentachloride is sometimes used as catalyst for the side-chain chlorination; traces of iron (factory dust) or antimony (rubber stoppers and tubing) promote substitution in the ring, and commercial preparations of benzaldehyde from the chlorination process usually contain small amounts of chlorobenzaldehyde.　Such contamination is undesirable in material to be used in perfumery, and a premium is placed on alternative processes that afford chlorine-free benzaldehyde.　One method consists in partial oxidation of toluene with manganese dioxide in 65% sulfuric acid at 40° followed by steam distillation; the process can be operated to yield either benzaldehyde or benzoic acid as the chief product. Another is vapor-phase air oxidation of toluene with vanadium pentoxide catalyst.

2,6-Dichlorobenzaldehyde. — This aldehyde is produced technically for use in the synthesis of triphenylmethane dyes.　The process starting with o-nitrotoluene is interesting because it involves introduction of chlorine by three methods: catalytic nuclear halogenation, side-chain chlorination, and the Sandmeyer reaction.　Initial chlorination gives the 6- and 4-chloro derivatives in the ratio of about 2:1, and the former isomer can be isolated by fractional distillation in vacuum.　A noteworthy feature of the subsequent steps is that the di-o-substituted dichlorobenzal chloride is resistant to hydrolysis with water and iron, even under pressure or with potassium hydroxide, but can be hydrolyzed in moderate yield when warmed in sulfuric acid for twelve hours.

The chlorination and oxidation processes employed for preparation of benzaldehyde from toluene are used in isolated instances for laboratory-scale preparation of other aldehydes; *o*-nitro- and *o*-chlorotoluene have been converted into the corresponding aldehydes with 65% sulfuric acid and manganese dioxide; partial oxidation of *m*-xylene by this method gives *m*-tolualdehyde.

CH₃ — O₂N benzene ring — Cl₂(Fe–I₂), 50–60° / 37% → CH₃ O₂N benzene ring Cl — Fe, dil. HCl / 94% → CH₃ H₂N benzene ring Cl

o-Nitrotoluene   2-Nitro-6-chlorotoluene   6-Chloro-2-amino-
                          (m.p. 37°; with 4-isomer)   toluene (b.p. 245°)

1. Diazotize / 2. Cu₂Cl₂—HCl / 88% → CH₃ Cl benzene ring Cl — Cl₂, light (at b.p.) / 95% → CHCl₂ Cl benzene ring Cl — concd. H₂SO₄, 55° / 40% → CHO Cl benzene ring Cl

          2,6-Dichlorotoluene   2,6-Dichlorobenzal   2,6-Dichloro-
          (b.p. 198°)   chloride   benzaldehyde
                                                                   (m.p. 71°)

Other Procedures. — The transformation $ArCH_3 \rightarrow ArCHO$ can be accomplished also by the **Étard reaction** (1881). A solution of two equivalents of chromyl chloride (CrO_2Cl_2) in carbon disulfide is added cautiously to the hydrocarbon with control of the temperature to 25–45°. The red color of the reagent is discharged slowly and a chocolate-brown crystallizate separates consisting of a molecular complex containing two equivalents of the inorganic component. The dry solid on treatment with water decomposes to give the aldehyde and an aqueous solution containing chromic acid and chromic chloride, and the aldehyde must be removed rapidly by distillation or solvent extraction to avoid destruction. In-

$$ArCH_3 \ + \ 2\ CrO_2Cl_2 \ \longrightarrow \ ArCH_3 \cdot (CrO_2Cl_2)_2 \ \xrightarrow{H_2O} \ ArCHO$$

stances are reported where yields are as high as 70–80% when the reaction is conducted under closely defined conditions (*m*-tolualdehyde from *m*-xylene), but the results may be much poorer. The method has limited use.

Another method, which probably is more reliable and has given good service in several instances, is oxidation of the methyl derivative with anhydrous **chromic acid in acetic anhydride** solution; the aldehyde as it is formed is converted into its *gem*-diacetate, which is stable to oxidation. The diacetate is collected and

benzene ring CH₃ / Br — CrO₃, Ac₂O, HOAc, H₂SO₄, 5–10° → benzene ring CH(OCOCH₃)₂ / Br — HCl → benzene ring CHO / Br

o-Bromotoluene   *o*-Bromobenzaldehyde   *o*-Bromobenzaldehyde
                          diacetate (m.p. 72°)   (m.p. 22°, b.p. 230°)

purified and can be converted into the free aldehyde by acid hydrolysis. The over-all yield of *o*-bromobenzaldehyde is about 45%.

Conversion of 2,4-dinitrotoluene into the corresponding aldehyde represents a special case, for the nitro groups activate the methyl group sufficiently to permit condensation with *p*-nitroso-N,N-dimethylaniline. In a related reaction due to

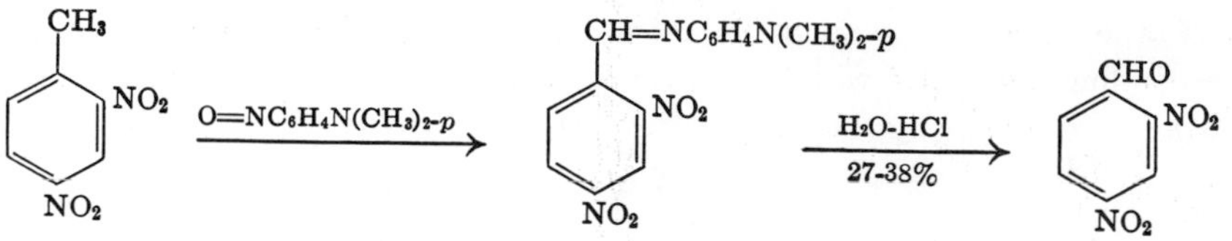

CH₃ structure with NO₂, NO₂ → (O=NC₆H₄N(CH₃)₂-p) → CH=NC₆H₄N(CH₃)₂-p structure with NO₂, NO₂ → (H₂O-HCl, 27-38%) → CHO structure with NO₂, NO₂

F. Ullmann (1904), the carbon atom required for the aldehyde group is introduced as formaldehyde. Cleavage of the Schiff base from N,N-dimethylaniline, formal-

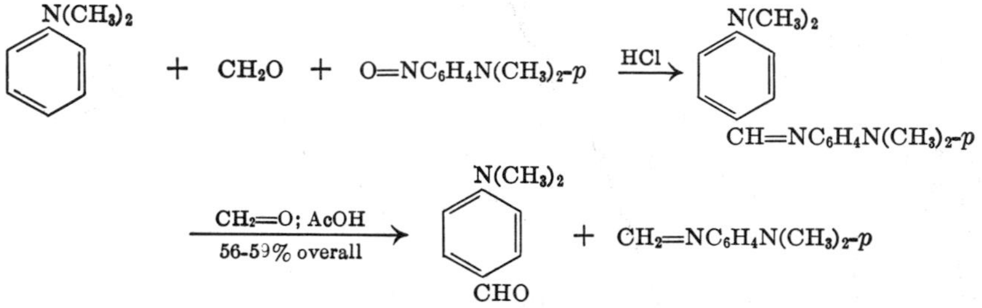

N(CH₃)₂ + CH₂O + O=NC₆H₄N(CH₃)₂-p →(HCl)→ N(CH₃)₂ / CH=NC₆H₄N(CH₃)₂-p

→(CH₂=O; AcOH, 56-59% overall)→ N(CH₃)₂ / CHO + CH₂=NC₆H₄N(CH₃)₂-p

M.p. 73°

dehyde, and p-nitroso-N,N-dimethylaniline is accomplished by reaction with more formaldehyde in the presence of acetic acid.

25.2   ALDEHYDES FROM ARYLMETHYL HALIDES

$$(ArCH_2Cl \longrightarrow ArCHO)$$

An early technical process for preparation of benzaldehyde consisted in heating **benzyl chloride with aqueous lead nitrate or copper nitrate.** The intermediate ester, $ArCH_2ONO_2$, may be attacked by base with abstraction of hydrogen and elimination of nitrite ion. The method has been employed somewhat for preparation of substituted benzaldehydes, for example the p-nitro compound; the starting material is produced along with the o-nitro isomer on nitration of benzyl chloride, and, being a solid, can be purified by crystallization. Another favorable

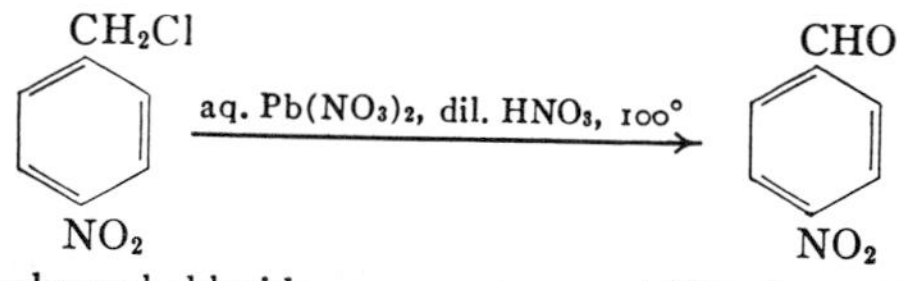

CH₂Cl structure with NO₂ →(aq. Pb(NO₃)₂, dil. HNO₃, 100°)→ CHO structure with NO₂

p-Nitrobenzyl chloride
(m.p. 72°)

p-Nitrobenzaldehyde

factor is that p-nitrobenzaldehyde is more resistant to oxidation than ordinary aldehydes, and withstands the prolonged heating required for complete reaction.

Sommelet Reaction. — M. Sommelet discovered (1913) that benzyl chloride is converted into benzaldehyde in good yield by reaction with hexamethylenetetramine (12.37), or hexamine, at the boiling point of an aqueous solvent, usually 60% ethanol or 50% acetic acid. The reaction is applicable to most benzyl-type halides but fails if the chloromethyl group is flanked by two o-methyl groups.

The present interpretation of the reaction is based upon a reinvestigation by S. J. Angyal (1949). In a nonaqueous medium benzyl chloride reacts with hexamine to form the quaternary salt, $[C_6H_5CH_2 \cdot C_6H_{12}N_4]^+Cl^-$, which on acid hydrolysis

$$
\begin{array}{ccc}
\text{CH}_2\text{Cl} & & \text{CHO} \\
\bigcirc & + \quad C_6H_{12}N_4 \quad \xrightarrow[\text{70-80\%}]{\text{60\% Alcohol}} & \bigcirc \\
\text{CH}_3 & \text{Hexamethylene-} & \text{CH}_3 \\
p\text{-Methylbenzyl} & \text{tetramine} & p\text{-Tolualdehyde} \\
\text{chloride} & &
\end{array}
$$

forms benzylamine hydrochloride. The hydrolysis is best effected with ethanol and concentrated hydrochloric acid, for the formaldehyde is then removed as the volatile diethyl formal. This process, the formation and hydrolysis of a hexaminium salt, is the **Delépine reaction** (M. Delépine,[1] 1895). The reaction is useful for the preparation of primary amines uncontaminated with secondary amines and is sometimes more convenient than the Gabriel synthesis. In the Sommelet reaction isolation of the intermediate hexaminium salt is not necessary but is sometimes desirable, for example for purification of starting material prepared by chloromethylation. Hexamine is required in the first phase of the Sommelet reaction for production of benzylamine, and it functions again in another way at a later stage. Benzylamine combines reversibly with formaldehyde present in the reaction mixture to form methylenebenzylamine (2) and, in the absence of hexamine, this substance enters into a disproportionation with benzyl-

$$
\begin{array}{ccccccc}
C_6H_5CH_2NH_2 & + & C_6H_5CH_2N{=}CH_2 & \rightleftharpoons & C_6H_5CH{=}NH & + & C_6H_5CH_2NHCH_3 \\
(1) & & (2) & & (3) & & (4)
\end{array}
$$
$$
\xrightarrow{\text{H}_2\text{O}} \quad C_6H_5CHO \quad + \quad NH_3
$$
$$
(5)
$$

amine with reduction of (2) to methylbenzylamine (4) and oxidation of (1) to the imine (3), which is hydrolyzed to give benzaldehyde in low yield. Addition of hexamine to the reaction mixture inhibits formation of methylbenzylamine (4), increases the yield of aldehyde, and leads to formation of methylamine. At the pH required for the Sommelet reaction (pH 3.0–6.5), hexamine reacts as the methylene derivative of ammonia, $CH_2{=}NH$, which accepts hydrogen from benzylamine and is reduced to methylamine. The fundamental process is thus:

$$
C_6H_5CH_2NH_2 \; + \; CH_2{=}NH \; + \; H_2O \; \longrightarrow \; C_6H_5CHO \; + \; NH_3 \; + \; CH_3NH_2
$$

The oxidation-reduction process resembles the Cannizzaro reaction (12.36) and probably proceeds by a similar hydride ion shift involving as acceptor the Schiff base conjugate acid.

$$
\begin{array}{ccccc}
C_6H_5\overset{\displaystyle H}{\underset{\displaystyle :NH_2}{CH}} \overset{\displaystyle CH_2}{\underset{\displaystyle (^+NH_2)}{}} & \longrightarrow & C_6H_5CH \atop {}^+NH_2 & + & CH_3 \atop NH_2
\end{array}
$$

In the related **Duff reaction** (J. C. Duff, 1932–52) a phenol is treated with

[1] Marcel Delépine, b. 1871 Saint-Martin le Gaillard; Ph.D. Paris (Berthelot); Collége de France; *J. Chem. Ed.*, **27**, 567 (1950)

hexamine in glyceroboric acid or acetic acid with the result that an aldehyde group is introduced in a position *ortho* to the hydroxyl group. The reaction appears to involve aminomethylation to the secondary amine $HOArCH_2NHCH_2ArOH$, followed by a Sommelet reaction. The reaction has been used extensively and successfully by Seshadri[1] in the flavone series (1939–50).

In the **Kröhnke reaction** (F. Kröhnke, 1936–39) a benzyl halide is converted into the pyridinium salt, which reacts with *p*-nitrosodimethylaniline to give a nitrone; this, in turn, gives an aldehyde on acid hydrolysis. The Kröhnke reaction is

$$C_6H_5CH_2Cl \xrightarrow{C_5H_5N} [C_6H_5CH_2N^+C_5H_5]Cl^- \xrightarrow{p\text{-}ONC_6H_4N(CH_3)_2}$$

$$C_6H_5CH{=}\overset{O^-}{\underset{|}{N^+}}C_6H_4N(CH_3)_2 \xrightarrow{H_2O\ (H^+)} RCHO$$

not suitable for the preparation of saturated aliphatic aldehydes but has useful applications for the preparation of aromatic, unsaturated, and α-keto aldehydes and also of dialdehydes and aromatic ketones. Since the reaction conditions are very mild, the method is particularly useful for the preparation of sensitive aldehydes.

The **Hass reaction** (H. B. Hass, 1949) consists in the preparation of an aldehyde by reaction of a benzyl halide with the sodio derivative of 2-nitropropane. The method is not suitable for the preparation of nitrobenzaldehydes and has been

$$o\text{-}CH_3C_6H_4CH_2Cl + [(CH_3)_2C{=}NO_2]^-Na^+ \xrightarrow[68\text{-}73\%]{} o\text{-}CH_3C_6H_4CHO +$$

$$(CH_3)_2C{=}NOH + NaCl$$

shown to fail with several polysubstituted aldehydes, but it has been applied with success to 1,4-polymethylenebenzenes (Blomquist, 1961).

A special reaction somewhat related to those discussed was discovered by C. Graebe's[2] student S. Racine (Geneva, 1887). Molten phthalide at 140° is treated with bromine vapor entrained by a stream of carbon dioxide. Hydrolysis of 2-bromophthalide with hot water affords phthalaldehydic acid. The bromination can also be done with N-bromosuccinimide in carbon tetrachloride. A phthalide

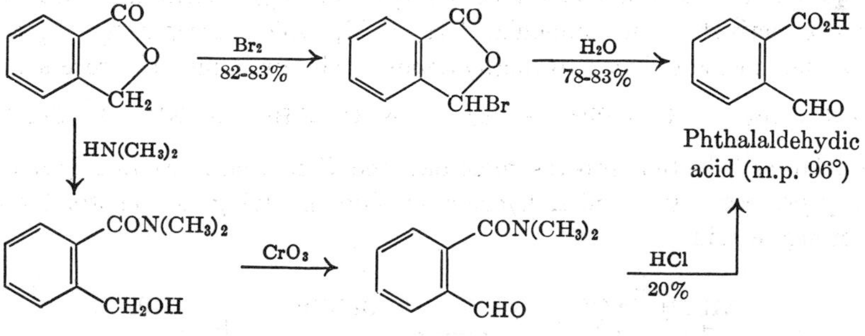

Phthalaldehydic acid (m.p. 96°)

[1] T. R. Seshadri, b. 1900 Kulittalai, Madras State, India; Ph.D. Manchester (R. Robinson; G. Barger); Research Inst., Coimbatore; Andhra Univ.; Delhi Univ.

[2] Carl Graebe, 1841–1927; b. Frankfurt, Germany; Ph.D. Heidelberg (Bunsen); Univ. Königsberg, Geneva; *Ber.*, **61A**, 9 (1928)

easily substituted in the nucleus can be converted to the dimethylamide, which is oxidized and hydrolyzed (J. Blair, 1955).

25.3   DIRECT FORMYLATION

$$(ArH \longrightarrow ArCHO)$$

Gattermann-Koch Synthesis (1897). — L. Gattermann and J. C. Koch devised a method for direct introduction of the formyl group (—CHO) by a process analogous to the Friedel-Crafts ketone synthesis utilizing a mixture of gaseous carbon monoxide and hydrogen chloride in the presence of a metal halide catalyst, usually a mixture of aluminum chloride and cuprous chloride. Formyl chloride may be a transient intermediate, but has not been isolated as such. Cuprous chloride probably functions as a catalyst because it can bind carbon monoxide in

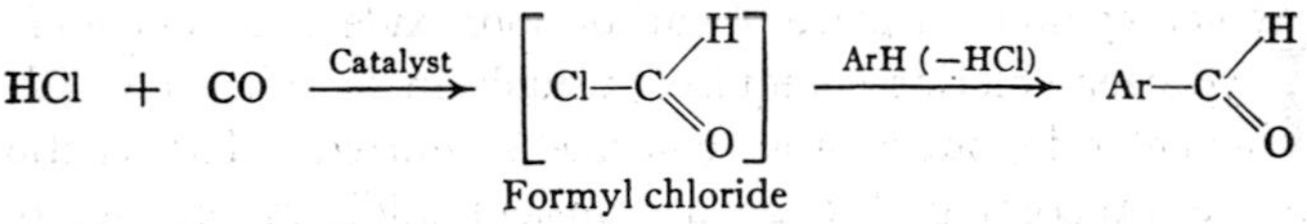

$$HCl + CO \xrightarrow{\text{Catalyst}} \left[Cl-C\begin{array}{c}H\\\diagup\\\diagdown\\O\end{array} \right] \xrightarrow{ArH\,(-HCl)} Ar-C\begin{array}{c}H\\\diagup\\\diagdown\\O\end{array}$$

Formyl chloride

the form of a labile molecular complex. In a typical example a suspension of anhydrous cuprous chloride and powdered aluminum chloride in dry toluene is stirred mechanically, and a stream of dry hydrogen chloride and carbon monoxide is passed into the mixture for several hours. The reaction mixture is decom

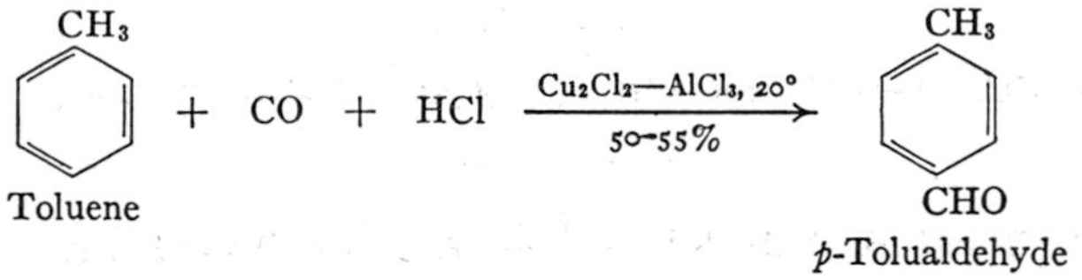

Toluene + CO + HCl $\xrightarrow[\text{50-55\%}]{Cu_2Cl_2-AlCl_3,\ 20°}$ *p*-Tolualdehyde (CHO)

posed with ice and steam distilled; the *p*-tolualdehyde formed is separated from unchanged toluene by distillation. The orientation and the limits of the reaction are much the same as in the Friedel-Crafts ketone synthesis, but yields are lower. Benzene does not react under ordinary conditions unless aluminum chloride is replaced by aluminum bromide, and has been used as a solvent for the reaction of other hydrocarbons.

In a newer variation of the Gattermann-Koch reaction the formylating agent is dichloromethyl methyl ether, prepared as in (1). The reactants are dissolved in methylene chloride or carbon disulfide and treated at 0° with a Friedel-Crafts

1. $HCOOCH_3 + PCl_5 \longrightarrow Cl_2CHOCH_3 + POCl_3$

2. $1,3,5-(CH_3)_3C_6H_3 + Cl_2CHOCH_3 \xrightarrow{TiCl_4} [ArCHCl(OCH_3)] \xrightarrow[58\%]{-CH_3Cl}$

$$2,4,6-(CH_3)_3C_6H_2CHO$$

catalyst (AlCl$_3$, TiCl$_4$, SnCl$_4$); the reaction (2) is complete in about 10 min. (A. Rieche, 1960).

Formyl fluoride (b.p. $-29°$) is now available by the reaction (3) of anhydrous hydrogen fluoride with the mixed anhydride of acetic and formic acids (G. A. Olah, 1960); when anhydrous hydrogen fluoride is added to acetic-formic anhydride at 0° and the formyl fluoride continuously removed from the mixture, acetyl fluoride is formed in only minor amounts. The reagent reacts with aromatic

3. $\overset{O}{\overset{\|}{HC}}-O\overset{O}{\overset{\|}{C}}CH_3 + 2HF \xrightarrow[61\%]{} \overset{O}{\overset{\|}{HC}}-F + CH_3COF + HCO_2H + CH_3CO_2H$

4. $ArH + HCOF \xrightarrow{BF_3} ArCHO + HF$

hydrocarbons in the presence of boron fluoride (or BCl_3) to give aldehydes in yields of 55–80% (4). The reagent reacts with alcohols and phenols in the presence of base to give formates.

Gattermann Synthesis (1907). — This variation consists in use of liquid anhydrous hydrogen cyanide in place of carbon monoxide as a source of the formyl substituent; hydrogen chloride is required, usually in combination with aluminum chloride or zinc chloride, but cuprous chloride is omitted. The reaction formerly was regarded as proceeding through a transient addition product of hydrogen cyanide and hydrogen chloride (formimino chloride, $ClCH=NH$), but now appears to follow a more complicated course. In the absence of the hydrocarbon component the other reagents combine to form a molecular complex, $AlCl_3 \cdot 2HCN \cdot HCl$, possibly by addition of the intermediate formimino chloride to hydrogen cyanide. The complex condenses with the hydrocarbon component

1. $HC\equiv N + HCl \longrightarrow [ClCH=NH] + HC\equiv N \xrightarrow{AlCl_3} ClCH=NCH=NH \cdot AlCl_3$

2. $ArH + ClCH=NCH=NH \cdot AlCl_3 \xrightarrow{-HCl} ArCH=NCH=NH \cdot AlCl_3$

3. $ArCH=NCH=NH \cdot AlCl_3 \xrightarrow{H_2O} ArCHO + 2NH_3 + HCOOH$

(2) with elimination of hydrogen chloride and formation of an arylmethylene-formamidine complex, which subsequently is hydrolyzed to the aldehyde (3). The Gattermann synthesis has been improved by use of special solvents, chlorobenzene, o-dichlorobenzene, and tetrachloroethane, and by conducting the reaction at temperatures of 60–100° instead of at 40°; a distinct simplification is use of sodium cyanide in place of the hazardous hydrogen cyanide. Thus a simple procedure consists in passing hydrogen chloride into a suspension of sodium cyanide and aluminum chloride in an excess of the hydrocarbon component. Yields of aldehydic derivatives of hydrocarbons by the best procedures are generally low, however (benzaldehyde, 11–39%; p-ethylbenzaldehyde, 22–27%; 9-anthraldehyde, 60%; mesitylaldehyde, 83%).

Condensation with hydrogen cyanide or a metal nitrile, unlike that with carbon monoxide, is applicable to phenols and phenol ethers, often with considerable success. Thus anisaldehyde is reported to be formed in nearly quantitative yield by the Gattermann synthesis. Aluminum chloride is required as catalyst in the case of phenol ethers and some phenols; the less potent zinc chloride is generally adequate for phenols. The procedure has been modified to advantage (R. Adams,

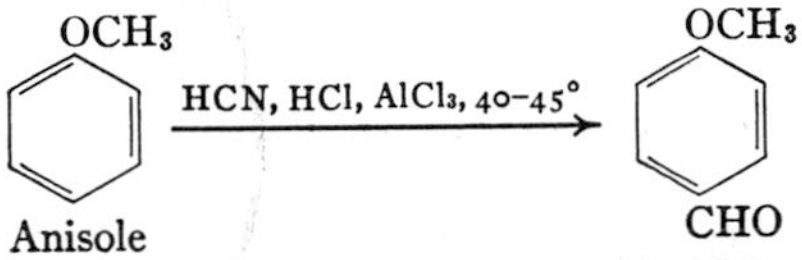

$$\text{Anisole} \xrightarrow[\text{HCN, HCl, AlCl}_3,\ 40-45°]{} \text{Anisaldehyde}$$

OCH₃ → OCH₃ / CHO

Anisole → Anisaldehyde

1923) by substitution of zinc cyanide for hydrogen cyanide and a metal halide. When hydrogen chloride is passed into a mixture of the phenol or phenol ether and zinc cyanide in absolute ether or benzene, it liberates the hydrogen cyanide required for condensation and produces zinc chloride as catalyst. The method is illustrated for the reaction of thymol.

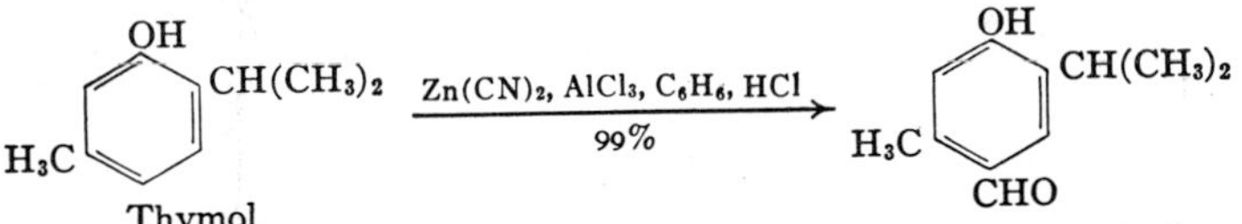

$$\text{Thymol} \xrightarrow[99\%]{\text{Zn(CN)}_2,\ \text{AlCl}_3,\ \text{C}_6\text{H}_6,\ \text{HCl}} \text{p-Thymol-aldehyde (m.p. 133°)}$$

Thymol → *p*-Thymol-aldehyde (m.p. 133°)

Formylation with Amide Derivatives. — By heating N-methylaniline with formic acid in toluene solution and displacing the equilibrium by slow distillation

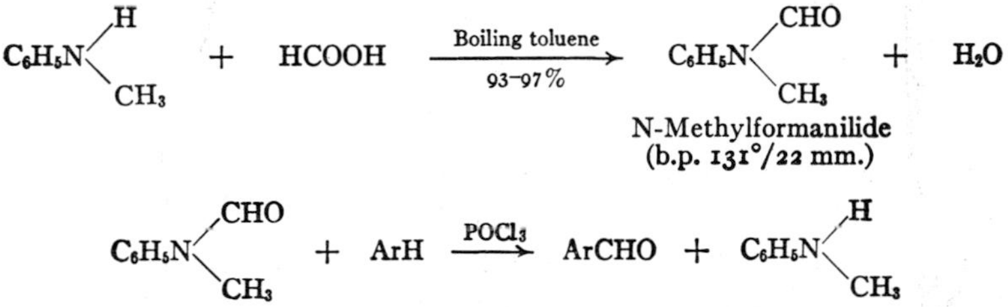

$$C_6H_5N\binom{H}{CH_3} + HCOOH \xrightarrow[93-97\%]{\text{Boiling toluene}} C_6H_5N\binom{CHO}{CH_3} + H_2O$$

N-Methylformanilide (b.p. 131°/22 mm.)

$$C_6H_5N\binom{CHO}{CH_3} + ArH \xrightarrow{POCl_3} ArCHO + C_6H_5N\binom{H}{CH_3}$$

of the water formed, the amine can be converted into N-methylformanilide. In the presence of phosphorus oxychloride, this substance acts as a formylating agent for aromatic compounds that possess a particularly reactive nuclear position. Anthracene is converted smoothly into an aldehyde, preferably in solution in *o*-dichlorobenzene, an effective inert solvent. If the hydrocarbon or other com-

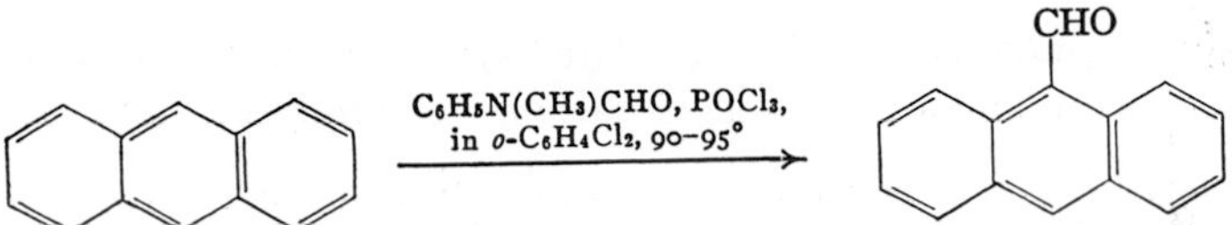

$$\text{Anthracene} \xrightarrow[\text{in } o\text{-C}_6\text{H}_4\text{Cl}_2,\ 90-95°]{C_6H_5N(CH_3)CHO,\ POCl_3,} \text{9-Anthraldehyde (m.p. 105°)}$$

Anthracene → 9-Anthraldehyde (m.p. 105°)

ponent is liquid at the required temperature, no solvent is needed. Although anthracene, pyrene, acenaphthene, and a few other highly reactive polynuclear hydrocarbons can be formylated by this method, the reaction is not applicable to benzene or naphthalene or to any but exceptional hydrocarbon derivatives of these two series (*e.g.*, acenaphthene). The reaction is applicable, usually with distinct success, to phenol ethers and to dialkylamines, which are formylated in an activated nuclear position *ortho* or *para* to the directing group. Thus 2-ethoxy-naphthalene reacts with N-methylformanilide and phosphorus oxychloride without solvent to give 2-ethoxy-1-naphthaldehyde (m.p. 112°), and dimethylaniline yields *p*-dimethylaminobenzaldehyde.

Dimethylformamide, $(CH_3)_2NCHO$, has been found useful for the formylation of reactive compounds such as N,N-dimethylaniline, pyrrole, and indole in the presence of phosphorus oxychloride as catalyst. The compounds mentioned are convertible by this method into the 4-, 2-, and 3-formyl derivatives in yields indicated. Dimethylformamide reacts exothermally with phosphorus oxychloride

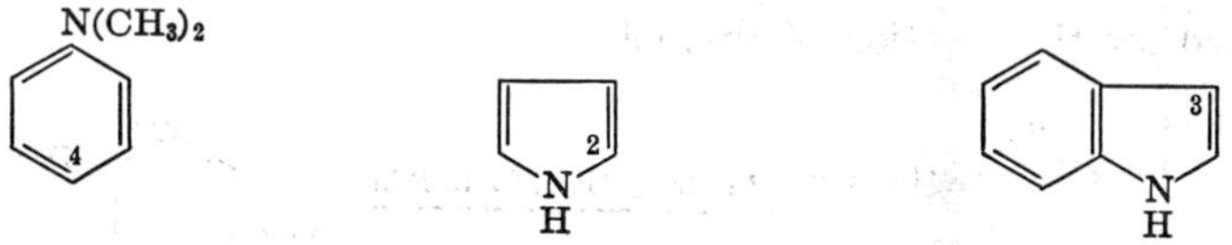

N,N-Dimethylaniline	Pyrrole	Indole
80-84%	78-79%	97%

Formylation

to form a complex which combines with the aromatic component to form another complex which yields the aldehyde on hydrolysis.

$$(CH_3)_2\overset{+}{N}{=}CHOPOCl_2(Cl^-) \xrightarrow{ArH} ArCH{<}\begin{matrix}OPOCl_2\\N^+H(CH_3)_2Cl^-\end{matrix} \xrightarrow{H_2O}$$

$$ArCH{=}O \ + \ HN(CH_3)_2 \ + \ H_3PO_4$$

Another route to aldehydes utilizes methylphenylcarbamyl chloride, prepared from N-methylaniline and phosgene (Weygand,[1] 1955). This reacts with aromatic hydrocarbons under Friedel-Crafts conditions to give the N-methylanilide of a carboxylic acid; this derivative is reducible to the aldehyde with lithium aluminum hydride.

$$C_6H_5N(CH_3)COCl \ + \ C_6H_5CH_3 \xrightarrow[53\%]{AlCl_3} C_6H_5N(CH_3)COC_6H_4CH_3\text{-}p \xrightarrow[60\%]{LiAlH_4}$$

$$CH_3C_6H_4CHO\text{-}p$$

H. C. Brown (1961) has described a related synthesis illustrated by the following example. Reaction of cyclopropane carbonyl chloride (1) with ethyleneimine

---

[1] Friedrich Weygand, b. 1911 Eichelsdorf, Germany; Ph.D. Frankfurt, Heidelberg (Kuhn), Oxford (Robinson); Univ. Heidelberg, Strasbourg, Tübingen, Techn. Univ. Berlin-Charlottenburg

$$\underset{(1)}{\underset{H_2C}{\overset{H_2C}{\diagdown}}\hspace{-4pt}CHCOCl} \;+\; \underset{(2)}{HN\hspace{-2pt}\underset{CH_2}{\overset{CH_2}{\diagup}}} \;\xrightarrow{Et_3N}\; \underset{(3)}{\underset{H_2C}{\overset{H_2C}{\diagdown}}\hspace{-4pt}CHCON\hspace{-2pt}\underset{CH_2}{\overset{CH_2}{\diagup}}} \;\xrightarrow{LiAlH_4}\; \underset{(4)}{\underset{H_2C}{\overset{H_2C}{\diagdown}}\hspace{-4pt}CHCHO}$$

(2) and triethylamine in ether at 0° gives a precipitate of the amine salt and a solution of the 1-acylaziridine (3), which reacts with lithium aluminum hydride to give, after hydrolysis, cyclopropanecarboxaldehyde (4) in 60% yield.

25.4　　ALDEHYDES FROM HALIDES, ACIDS, NITRILES

Mention has been made of the synthesis of aldehydes from a Grignard reagent and ethyl orthoformate (12.8; example: 9-phenanthraldehyde in 40–42% yield) and from acids by the reactions of Rosenmund (12.11) and Grundmann (12.12).

The **Sonn-Müller reaction** (1919) involves condensation of an acid chloride with aniline and conversion of the anilide with phosphorus pentachloride into an imino chloride, probably by enolization and replacement of the enolic hydroxyl group by chlorine. On reaction with anhydrous stannous chloride the halogen of the imino chloride is replaced by hydrogen with formation of an anil derivative that

$$\underset{\text{Acid chloride}}{ArCOCl} \;\xrightarrow{C_6H_5NH_2}\; \underset{\underset{\text{Anilide}}{\overset{\|}{O}}}{ArC-NHC_6H_5} \;\xrightarrow{PCl_5}$$

$$\underset{\underset{\text{Imino chloride}}{Cl}}{ArC=NC_6H_5} \;\xrightarrow{SnCl_2}\; \underset{\underset{\text{Anil}}{H}}{ArC=NC_6H_5} \;\xrightarrow{H_2O,\,-C_6H_5NH_2}\; \underset{\text{Aldehyde}}{ArCHO}$$

is cleaved on hydrolysis to the aldehyde and aniline. Isolation of the intermediates is not necessary. The 1-, 2-, 3-, and 9-aldehydes of phenanthrene have been prepared by this method with an average yield of 62% (typical yield by the Rosenmund reaction, 90%).

The **method of J. S. McFadyen and T. S. Stevens** (1936) involves conversion of an ester into a hydrazide, preparation of the benzenesulfonyl derivative, and decomposition with alkali. The method is applicable only to aromatic aldehydes

$$\mathbf{ArCOOC_2H_5} \;\xrightarrow{H_2NNH_2}\; \mathbf{ArCONHNH_2} \;\xrightarrow{C_6H_5SO_2Cl}$$
$$\mathbf{ArCONHNHSO_2C_6H_5} \;+\; \mathbf{KOH} \;\longrightarrow\; \mathbf{ArCHO} \;+\; \mathbf{N_2} \;+\; \mathbf{C_6H_5SO_2OK}$$

and even so gives variable results; yields, 40–85%.

The **H. Stephen reaction** (1925) is conducted by passing hydrogen chloride into a mixture of an aromatic nitrile and anhydrous stannous chloride in absolute ether; probably a transient imino chloride resulting from addition of hydrogen chloride to the nitrile group is the effective intermediate and gives rise to an aldimine complex that affords the aldehyde on hydrolysis. The results are highly

$$\underset{}{ArC\equiv N} \;\xrightarrow{HCl}\; \underset{\underset{}{Cl}}{ArC=NH} \;\xrightarrow{SnCl_2,\,HCl}\; \left[\underset{\underset{}{H}}{ArC=NH\cdot HCl}\right]_2 SnCl_4 \;\xrightarrow{H_2O}\; RCHO$$

variable, for though benzaldehyde and β-naphthaldehyde are obtained in good yield, the reaction fails in the attempted preparation of α-naphthaldehyde, and gives only negligible amounts of other aldehydes (o-tolualdehyde).   In the method of **B. O. Field** (1955) the acid chloride or methyl ester is reduced to the benzyl alcohol (LiAlH₄) and this is oxidized with dinitrogen tetroxide in chloroform at 0°.   As the reaction proceeds the green color due to dinitrogen trioxide deepens, and hence oxidation is attributed to homolytic attack of the ·NO₂ radical on the

$$2C_6H_5CH_2OH \xrightarrow{\ 4\ \cdot NO_2\ } 2C_6H_5CH(OH)NO_2 \ + \ H_2O \ + \ N_2O_3$$
$$\longrightarrow \ 2C_6H_5CH{=}O \ + \ H_2O \ + \ N_2O_3$$

α-carbon atom to give a nitro alcohol, which decomposes to the aldehyde.   Yields are over 90% regardless of the nature of the substituent groups or of the degree of hindrance.

25.5   OTHER ROUTES TO SUBSTITUTED BENZALDEHYDES

The many synthetic processes described in the preceding sections, and still others, do not exhaust the opportunity for practical preparation of aldehydes, for this functional group, though reactive, is sufficiently durable to withstand certain alterations at other positions.   Thus **m-nitrobenzaldehyde** can be prepared satisfactorily by nitration of benzaldehyde, and can be converted into **m-hydrobenzaldehyde** by reduction with stannous chloride and hydrochloric acid, diazotization without isolation of the amine or of the hydrochloride, and hydrolysis.   **o-Nitrobenzaldehyde,** a substance very useful in syntheses but difficultly attainable by any method, has been prepared not only from o-nitrotoluene (25.1) but by an interesting process starting with cinnamic acid, $C_6H_5CH{=}CHCOOH$.   This acid on nitration affords the o- and p-nitro compounds, separable by fractional crystallization.   The purified o-nitrocinnamic acid is then oxidized with permanganate at 0° in a dilute aqueous solution of the sodium salt covered with a layer of benzene and vigorously agitated.   The o-nitrobenzaldehyde produced passes into the benzene phase and is thereby protected from overoxidation; the yield is 50–53%.

Both **o- and p-aminobenzaldehyde** can be isolated as crystalline solids by reduction of the corresponding nitro compounds, but neutral solutions of the substances darken rapidly as the result of condensations involving the two functional groups. The m-isomer is known only in the form of aqueous solutions of the hydrochloride.

PHENOLIC ALDEHYDES

25.6   **Reimer[1]-Tiemann[2] Reaction** (1876). — Working in Hofmann's laboratory, Reimer performed an experiment to see if phenol could be substituted for aniline in Hofmann's isonitrile reaction, involving treatment with chloroform and alkali.[3]   Since the phenolic oxygen atom carries one hydrogen

[1] Carl Reimer, 1856–1921; b. Berlin; Ph.D. Berlin; indust. chem.

[2] Ferdinand Tiemann, 1848–99; b. Rübeland, Germany; Univ. Berlin; *Ber.*, **32**, 3239 (1899); **34**, 4403 (1901)

[3] Related by the late Arthur Michael

and not two, the idea was at the time far-fetched. Nevertheless a reaction occurred, and subsequent exploitation of the observation with the collaboration of Tiemann established the reaction as a generally applicable method for the preparation of phenolic aldehydes. Details of the present laboratory procedure are indicated in the formulation. At the end of the reaction the mixture is acidified and steam distilled; salicylaldehyde (chelated) passes into the distillate along with

Phenol   +   CHCl₃ $\xrightarrow[37-45\%]{\text{aq. NaOH, 65-70°}}$ Salicylaldehyde
(+ 8-11% of *p*-isomer)

a considerable amount of phenol, from which it can be separated through the bisulfite addition compound. From the residue not volatile with steam, the solid isomer *p*-hydroxybenzaldehyde is isolated by crystallization in quantity amounting to about one-fifth the weight of the salicylaldehyde. Although yields in the Reimer-Tiemann reaction are low, separation is efficient and the recovered phenol can be recycled.

In the modern view, the reactions of aniline and of phenol with chloroform and alkali have in common the possibility for generation of dichlorocarbene (J. Hine, 1950). According to the mechanism formulated, the key step is a nucleophilic attack of the phenoxide anion on dichlorocarbene. The reaction occurs only at

an alkalinity suitable for formation of the anion, and failure of phenol ethers and tertiary amines to react indicates that this anion is an essential intermediate. No satisfactory explanation has been advanced for the persistence of a considerable amount of unchanged phenol even though a large excess of chloroform is employed. A suggestion that phenol is bound as the diphenyl acetal, ArCH(OC₆H₅)₂, is discounted by further evidence (H. Wynberg, 1954). Carbon monoxide and formate are by-products of the reaction and arise by alkaline hydrolysis of chloroform in which formation of dichlorocarbene is the rate-controlling step. A kinetic study of the hydrolysis has shown that carbon monoxide is the primary product and yields formate in a subsequent slow reaction with hydroxide ions (E. A. Robinson, 1961). Dichlorocarbene reacts with water and not with hydroxide ions, and the following mechanism is suggested:

$$CCl_2 \xrightarrow{H_2O} H_2\overset{+}{O}-\overset{-}{C}Cl_2 \xrightarrow{-H^+} HO-\overset{-}{C}Cl_2 \xrightarrow{-Cl^-} HO-CCl \xrightarrow{-H^+, -Cl^-} CO$$

In the course of a research on "solid pseudocumidine" undertaken in 1884 in the Berlin laboratory at the suggestion of Hofmann, von Auwers applied the Reimer-Tiemann reaction to pseudocumenol and observed that the reaction proceeded poorly and gave at most only about 5% of the theoretical amount of the expected aldehyde, accompanied by some unchanged starting material. He noticed that a considerable amount of alkali-insoluble material is produced, from which he isolated a chlorine-containing by-product characterized by a striking tendency to form large crystals. The structure, established only several years later (1902), is that of a cyclic ketone with a dichloromethyl group linked to the *para* carbon atom along with the original methyl substituent, as shown in the formulation. The chlorine atoms in the ketonic by-product are not activated

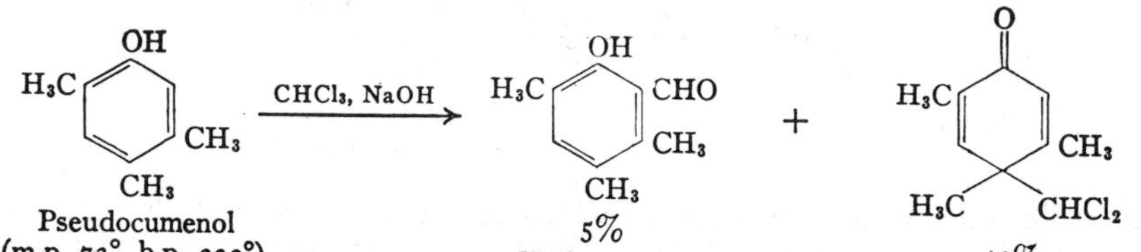

Pseudocumenol
(m.p. 73°, b.p. 232°)

CHCl₃, NaOH →

2-Hydroxy-3,5,6-
trimethylbenzaldehyde
(m.p. 106°)
5%

+

2,4,5-Trimethyl-4-dichloro-
methyl-Δ²,⁵-cyclohexadienone-1
(colorless, m.p. 96.5°)
42%

by adjacent unsaturation, as those of a compound of the benzal halide type are, and survival of the substance in the alkaline medium is understandable.

von Auwers found that comparable ketonic by-products are formed rather generally from phenols having alkyl groups in the *ortho* or *para* positions, but not from *m*-cresol, picric acid, or 2,4,6-tribromophenol. The isolation is accomplished by acidifying the reaction mixture, steam distilling the monomolecular products to effect separation from a certain amount of resinous material, extracting the phenolic aldehyde and starting material with alkali, and recovering the dichloro ketone from the neutral portion by crystallization. Both *o*- and *p*-cresol afford alkali-insoluble by-products, even though free positions *ortho* or *para* to the hydroxyl group are available for normal substitution. Yields and properties of the products resulting from *p*-cresol are indicated in the formulas. *o*-Cresol gives only about half as much of the ketonic by-product under optimum conditions.

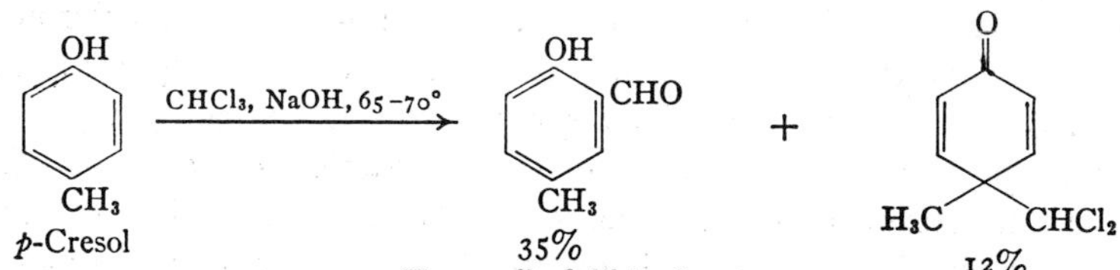

p-Cresol

CHCl₃, NaOH, 65-70° →

Homosalicylaldehyde
(m.p. 56°)
35%

+

4-Methyl-4-dichloro-
methyl-Δ²,⁵-cyclohexa-
dienone-1 (m.p. 55°)
12%

The yield of ketone is somewhat fortuitous and does not give an accurate index of the initial ratio of normal to abnormal substitution, for the dichloromethyl compounds differ considerably in their resistance to hydrolytic destruction in the alkaline medium. Test experiments have shown, for example, that the dichloro ketone from *o*-cresol is hydrolyzed by alkali more rapidly than the product from *p*-cresol. The ketone derived from pseudocumenol is particularly resistant to alkaline hydrolysis, probably because of the blocking effect of the methyl group *ortho* to the halogenated group.

The facts cited about the abnormal Reimer-Tiemann reaction support the mechanism ascribed to the normal reaction. Isolation of dichloromethyl derivatives in one reaction substantiates the postulated formation of similar intermediates in the other. An electron-releasing methyl group at an *ortho* or *para* position enhances the nucleophilicity at that position and hence favors reaction with dichlorocarbene. Electron-attracting halo and nitro substituents have the opposite effect.

The vulnerability of alkylated phenols to abnormal attack has been utilized in the preparation of compounds difficultly accessible by other syntheses. Thus Woodward (1940) employed the abnormal reaction for synthesis of a model compound containing an angular methyl group. The phenolic starting material *ar*-tetralol (*ar*- indicates that the substituent is in the aromatic and not the alicyclic

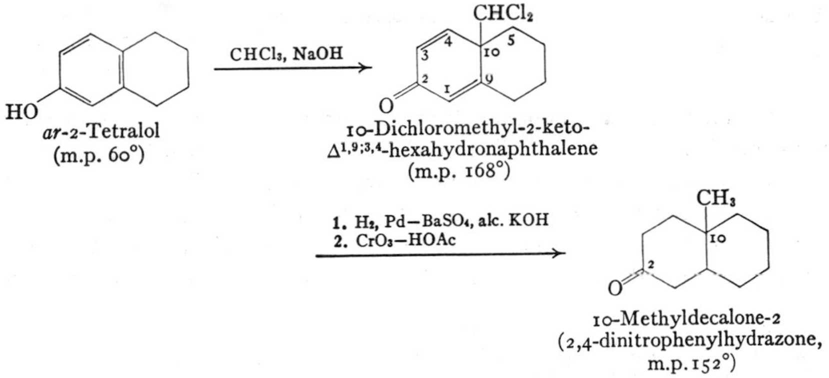
HO
ar-2-Tetralol
(m.p. 60°)
$CHCl_3$, NaOH
$CHCl_2$
4
5
3
10
2
1
9
O
10-Dichloromethyl-2-keto-
$\Delta^{1,9;3,4}$-hexahydronaphthalene
(m.p. 168°)
1. H_2, Pd—$BaSO_4$, alc. KOH
2. CrO_3—HOAc
CH_3
10
2
O
10-Methyldecalone-2
(2,4-dinitrophenylhydrazone,
m.p. 152°)

or *ac*-ring) reacts with chloroform in part to give an aldehyde and in part to give a dichloro ketone. The latter product on hydrogenation under drastic conditions suffers reduction of the three unsaturated centers and replacement of halogen by hydrogen, and the crude alcoholic product on oxidation gives a liquid ketone that has been isolated as the crystalline dinitrophenylhydrazone.

Salicylaldehyde forms colored chelate ring complexes with metal ions; the sodium salt is deep yellow. The complex cobaltous bis-salicylaldehydeethylenediimine (Salcomine), prepared by Pfeiffer in 1933, was investigated by Calvin (1946) for use in production of pure oxygen from air. The substance is capable of selectively absorbing 4.9% of its weight of oxygen from the air and then of

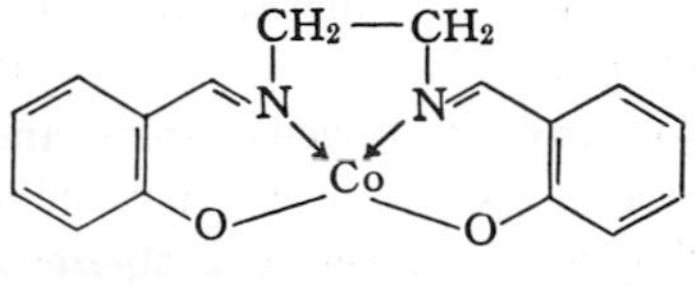
CH_2—CH_2
N
N
Co
O
O

Salcomine

evolving the pure gas when heated to 50–60°. Use of salicylal derivatives as gasoline additives for deactivation of metals has been mentioned (7.15).

The methyl ether of salicylaldehyde is prepared by alkylation with dimethyl sulfate. The methyl ether of *p*-hydroxybenzaldehyde, anisaldehyde, is made by gentle oxidation of aniseed oil, which is rich in anethole, p-$CH_3OC_6H_4CH$=$CHCH_3$, with potassium dichromate and 50% sulfuric acid.

25.7   Aldehydic Derivatives of Polyhydric Phenols. — Vanillin, a partially methylated aldehyde of the catechol series, is the fragrant constituent of vanilla bean, and occurs also in the sugar beet and in balsams and resins; it also is obtained as a by-product of the manufacture of cellulose pulp by the action of alkali on basic calcium lignosulfonate. It is an important component of artificial flavors. One synthetic process utilizes eugenol, available from essential oils.

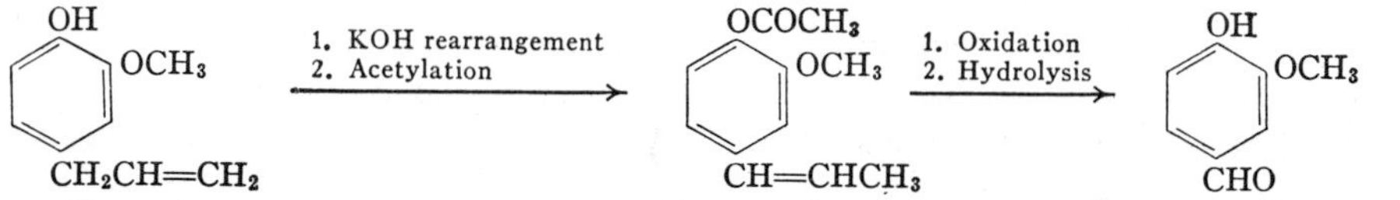

Eugenol → (1. KOH rearrangement, 2. Acetylation) → Isoeugenol acetate → (1. Oxidation, 2. Hydrolysis) → Vanillin (m.p. 81°, b.p. 285°, pK_a 5.32)

Under the influence of alcoholic alkali at 140° or of concentrated aqueous potassium hydroxide at 220°, the double bond of this allyl compound migrates to a position of conjugation with the ring and gives isoeugenol. This is acetylated to protect the phenolic group and oxidized under mild conditions (dichromate, electrochemical oxidation, ozone), when the double bond of the α-propenyl group is severed and an aldehyde group produced. A second process is application of

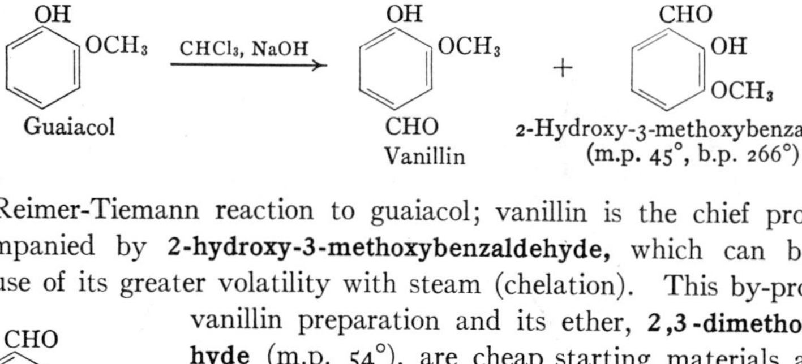

Guaiacol → (CHCl₃, NaOH) → Vanillin + 2-Hydroxy-3-methoxybenzaldehyde (m.p. 45°, b.p. 266°)

the Reimer-Tiemann reaction to guaiacol; vanillin is the chief product but is accompanied by **2-hydroxy-3-methoxybenzaldehyde,** which can be separated because of its greater volatility with steam (chelation). This by-product of the

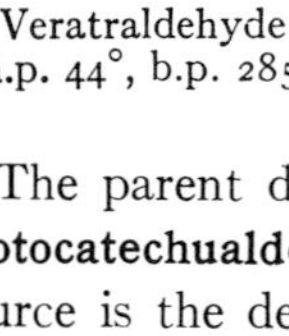

Veratraldehyde (m.p. 44°, b.p. 285°)

vanillin preparation and its ether, **2,3-dimethoxybenzaldehyde** (m.p. 54°), are cheap starting materials available for use in synthesis. Still more useful in synthesis is **veratraldehyde,** or 3,4-dimethoxybenzaldehyde, obtainable in 92–95% yield by methylation of vanillin with dimethyl sulfate; it can be synthesized by the Gattermann reaction from veratrole, hydrogen cyanide, and aluminum chloride.

The parent dihydroxy compound from which vanillin is derived is known as **protocatechualdehyde,** and its methylene ether is **piperonal,** for which a convenient source is the degradation of **safrole,** the methylene ether of 3,4-dihydroxyallyl-benzene. Safrole is the chief constituent of oil of sassafras, and is produced commercially from camphor oil. When heated with alkali it is converted by migration of the double bond into **isosafrole,** which on oxidation yields piperonal. Piperonal has an agreeable odor like that of heliotrope and is manufactured for

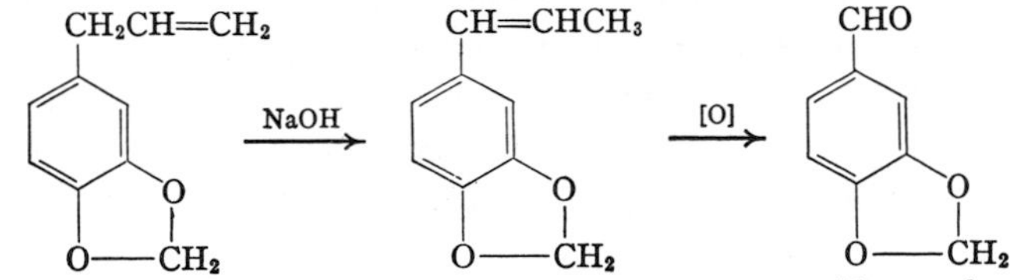

| Safrole | Isosafrole | Piperonal |
| (m.p. 11°, b.p. 233°) | (*cis*, b.p. 243°; *trans*, b.p. 248°) | (m.p. 37°, b.p. 263°) |

the perfume industry under the name heliotropine. This inexpensive aldehyde is a satisfactory starting material for preparation of protocatechualdehyde; a convenient procedure is indicated in the formulas.

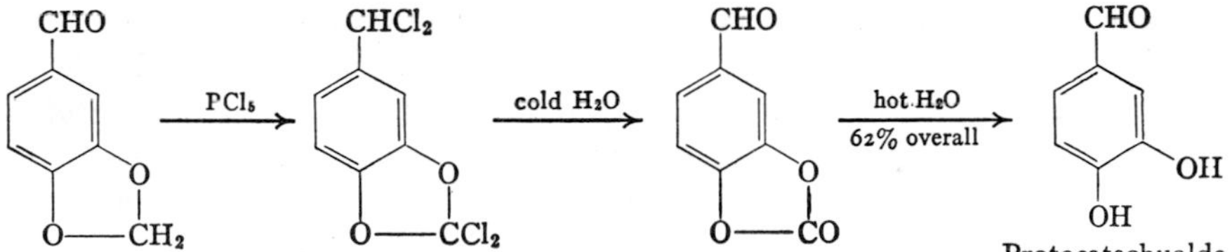

Piperonal

Protocatechualde-
hyde (m.p. 154°,
pK$_a$ 7.55)

β-Resorcylaldehyde and **gentisaldehyde** are fairly readily accessible formyl derivatives of resorcinol and hydroquinone, respectively. They have been synthesized by the Gattermann and the Reimer-Tiemann reactions; gentisaldehyde

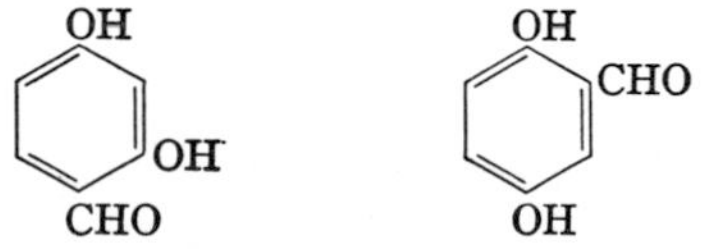

β-Resorcylaldehyde
(m.p. 136°)

Gentisaldehyde
(m.p. 99°)

can be prepared somewhat more satisfactorily by oxidation of salicylaldehyde with potassium persulfate in alkaline solution:

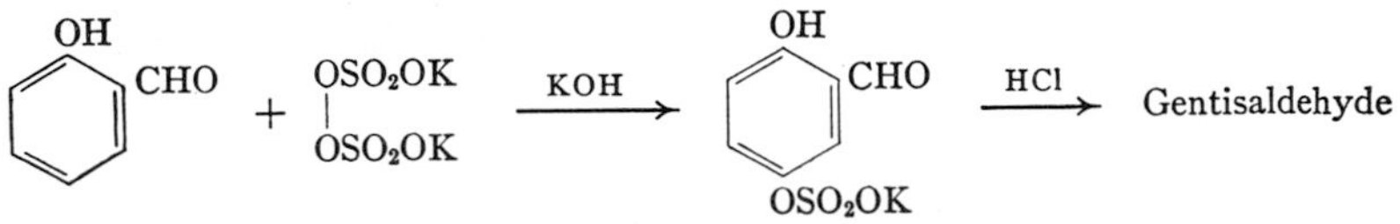

25.8 **PREPARATION OF KETONES**

Standard methods have been indicated for the preparation of ketones of types exemplified by:

Acetophenone, C$_6$H$_5$COCH$_3$ (m.p. 20°, b.p. 202°/749 mm.)

Propiophenone, $C_6H_5COCH_2CH_3$ (m.p. 21°, b.p. 218°)

Benzophenone, $C_6H_5COC_6H_5$ (stable form, m.p. 48°; labile form, m.p. 26°, b.p. 306°)

α,β-Unsaturated ketones are readily available from aldehydes by the Claisen-Schmidt condensation, and the preparation of cyclic ketones by intramolecular acylation is illustrated by the synthesis of α-tetralone and α-hydrindone (18.9). The aceto derivatives of resorcinol and pyrogallol of the structures shown can be

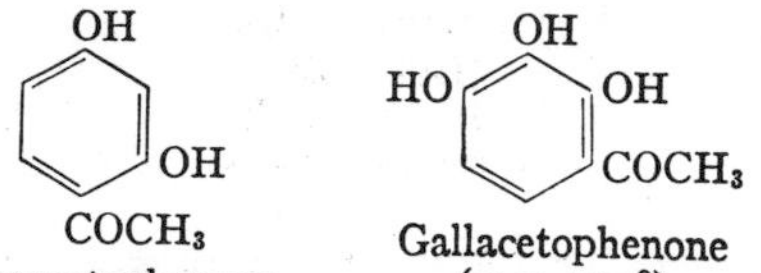

Resacetophenone
(m.p. 147°)

Gallacetophenone
(m.p. 173°)

made in about 60% yield by heating the phenolic component with acetic acid or acetic anhydride and fused zinc chloride in the temperature range 140–160°. n-Hexylresorcinol is prepared from a ketone made by a similar process.   The Fries reaction (22.20) is another practical method of preparing phenolic ketones; a further method is the **Hoesch**[1] **synthesis** (1915), which is essentially a modification of the Gattermann aldehyde synthesis and consists in the condensation of a phenol with acetonitrile and hydrogen chloride in the presence of zinc chloride or aluminum chloride as catalyst in solution in ether or chlorobenzene. The reaction is illustrated for the preparation of phloroacetophenone, a useful intermediate in the synthesis of naturally occurring flavone and flavonol pigments. Saturation of the ethereal solution of the phenol, acetonitrile, and zinc chloride

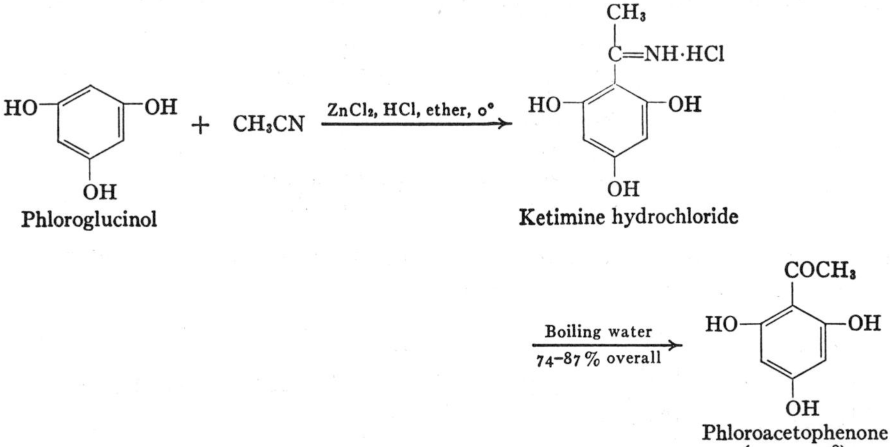

Phloroglucinol

Ketimine hydrochloride

Phloroacetophenone
(m.p. 219°)

with hydrogen chloride results in separation of a crystalline yellow precipitate of the ketimine hydrochloride, which is collected and hydrolyzed with boiling

[1] Kurt Hoesch, 1882–1932; b. Düren, Germany; Ph.D. Berlin (E. Fischer); Univ. Istanbul; *Ber.,* **66A,** 16 (1933)

water to the aceto compound.   The reaction proceeds well with many polyhydric
phenols and can be varied by use of trichloroacetonitrile (CCl_3CN), but it is not
applicable to phenol itself, for this substance is converted merely into an imido
ester, $C_6H_5OC(CH_3)\!\!=\!\!NH \cdot HCl$.

Diaryl ketones containing dialkylamino groups are useful intermediates in
synthesis of triphenylmethane dyes and are made by special condensations in the
activated nuclear positions of dimethyl- and diethylaniline. The important p,p'-
dimethylaminobenzophenone, or **Michler's ketone,** is prepared by interaction of

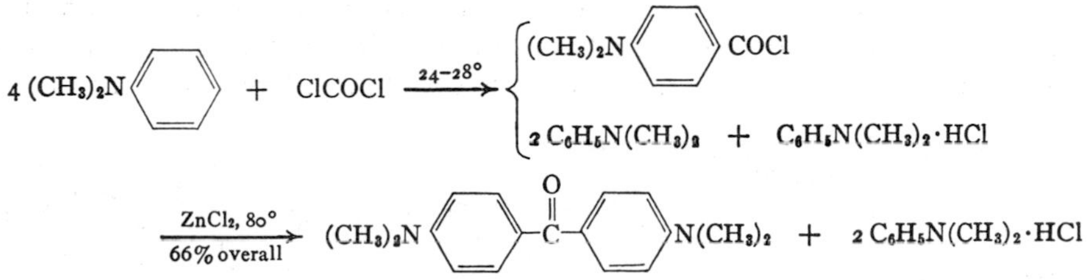

Michler's ketone
(m.p. $172°$)

dimethylaniline with phosgene in the ratio of four moles to one; the excess amine
binds the hydrogen chloride liberated.   The mixture is kept at a controlled temperature till the phosgene has been consumed and the —COCl radical introduced
into one equivalent of the amine; fused zinc chloride is then added, and the temperature is raised to effect further condensation.   The reaction mixture is poured
into water, and enough hydrochloric acid is added to keep the dimethylaniline
in solution; the precipitated Michler's ketone, being less basic, remains undissolved
and is collected. p-Dimethylaminobenzophenone can be prepared from dimethylaniline by reaction with benzanilide and phosphorus oxychloride. The
effective reagent probably is the imino chloride derived from the enolic form of
benzanilide (compare the Sonn-Müller reaction, 25.4):

$$C_6H_5CONHC_6H_5 \;\rightleftharpoons\; C_6H_5C(OH)\!\!=\!\!NC_6H_5 \;\longrightarrow\; C_6H_5CCl\!\!=\!\!NC_6H_5$$

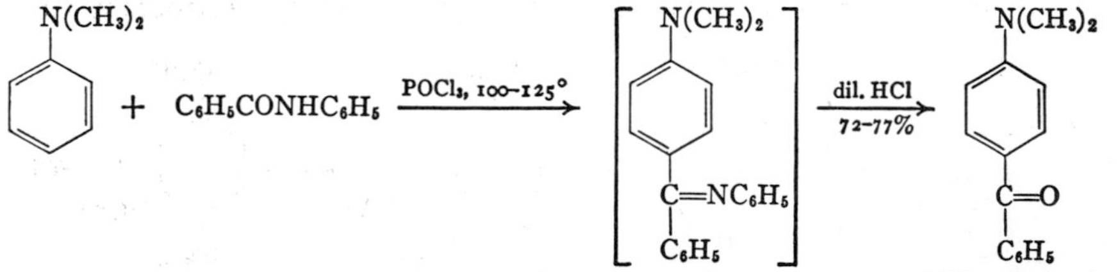

p-Dimethylamino-
benzophenone
(m.p. $90°$)

Methods available for the preparation of **α,β-unsaturated ketones** present
points of interest.   One is the **Darzens reaction** (1910), in which, for example,
addition of acetyl chloride to cyclohexene is effected at a low temperature in the
presence of aluminum chloride to give 1-acetyl-2-chlorocyclohexane, which on
dehydrohalogenation with dimethylaniline gives methyl cyclohexenyl ketone.

Wieland (1922) added benzoyl chloride to cyclohexene in this way and demonstrated that the addition product is convertible into Δ^1-tetrahydrobenzophenone, though in low yield, by treatment with aluminum chloride; the experiment was conducted with the object of substantiating the then current theory that Friedel-Crafts acylation proceeds by an addition-elimination mechanism. A new route to Δ^1-tetrahydrobenzophenones developed by E. A. Braude (1950) utilizes cyclohexenyllithium (1), readily obtainable by reaction with lithium in ether of adequately purified cyclohexenyl chloride. This reagent condenses readily with aldehydes, ketones, and with the lithium salts of carboxylic acids. Thus (1) with lithium m-methoxybenzoate gives 3'-methoxy-Δ^1-tetrahydrobenzophenone (2), which is cyclized to the hexahydrofluorenone (3) with a mixture of formic and phosphoric

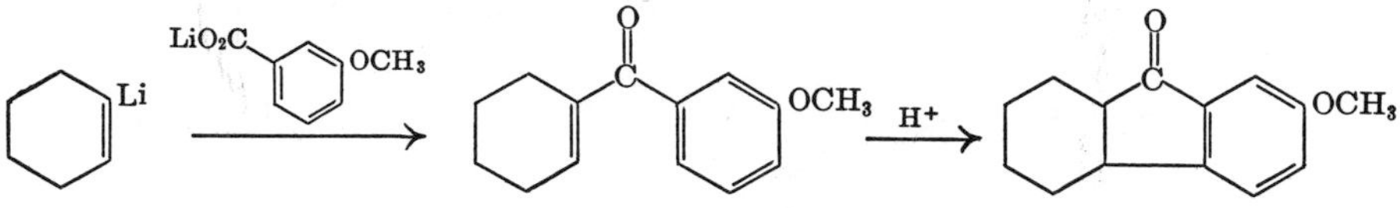

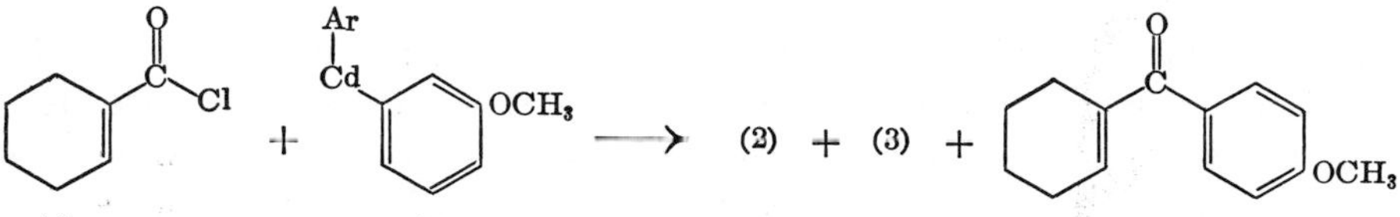

acids. W. G. Dauben (1959) explored the alternative route from cyclohexenyl-1-carbonyl chloride (4) and di-(m-methoxyphenyl)cadmium and obtained a mixture containing the normal product (2), the hydrofluorenone (3), and the p-methoxy ketone (6). The cadmium reagent (5) reacts normally with diacetyl, and hence rearrangement does not occur in its preparation. Acylation at a carbon atom adjacent to that originally occupied by the metal is accounted for by the following mechanism. Coordination of cadmium with the chlorine atom of the acid chloride with partial polarization of the C—Cl bond (7) is followed by electrophilic attack

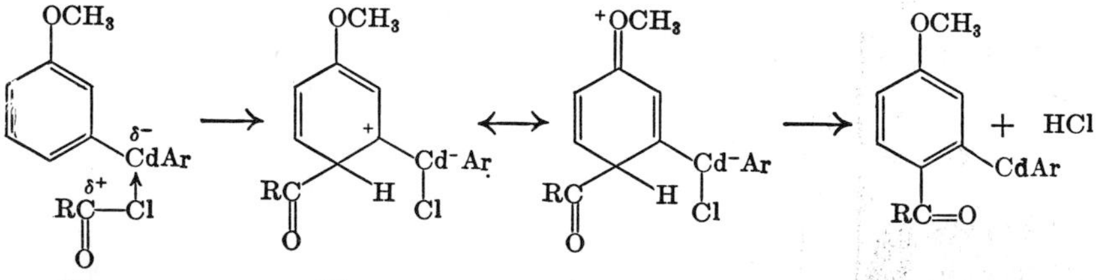

of the ring with production of the dipolar ion (8), stabilized particularly by resonance involving the methoxy group (9). Loss of hydrogen chloride to (10) and hydrolysis affords the *para* ketone (6).

o-Diacetylbenzene was not known until 1948, for all classical preparative routes tried proved unsuccessful. The best of several methods now available is that of S. Goldschmidt (1961). The reaction of *o*-phthalaldehyde with methylmagnesium bromide proceeds poorly in ether (39%) because of separation of the addition product, but with hot tetrahydrofurane as solvent the adduct remains in so-

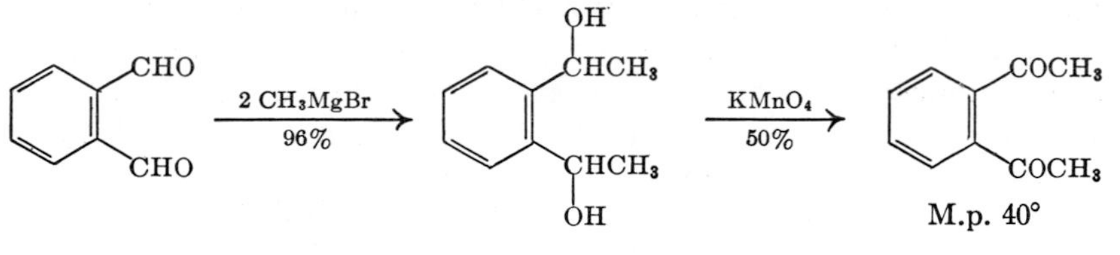

lution and the yield is high. Oxidation with permanganate in a solution buffered with magnesium nitrate gives o-diacetylbenzene. The substance stains the skin dark blue and condenses with amines and with amino acids to give deep colored products, but it is not so satisfactory as ninhydrin for paper chromatography of amino acids.

25.9   EXTENSION OF REACTIONS ALREADY CITED

Many of the reactions of carbonyl compounds are applicable in both the aliphatic and aromatic series and have already been described, but a few extensions specific to the aromatic series are of interest.   Thus Michael and Gabriel (1877) discovered that phthalic anhydride can function as the carbonyl component in the Perkin reaction.   The anhydride condenses with acetic anhydride in the presence of potassium acetate to give phthalylacetic acid.   This substance undergoes a number of inter-

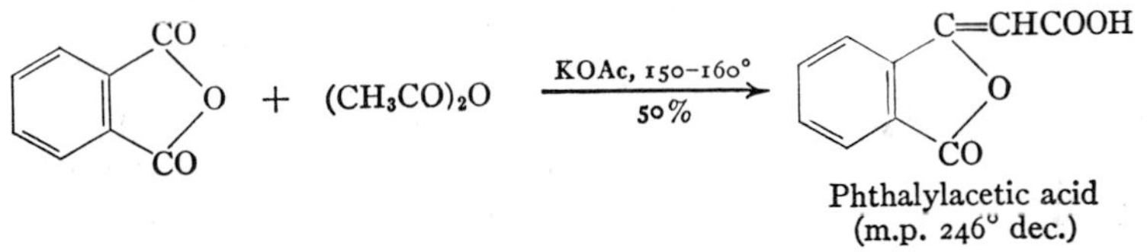

Phthalylacetic acid
(m.p. 246° dec.)

esting transformations, two of which are illustrated.   Cold aqueous alkali opens the lactone ring, and on careful acidification of the solution a keto dibasic acid sepa-

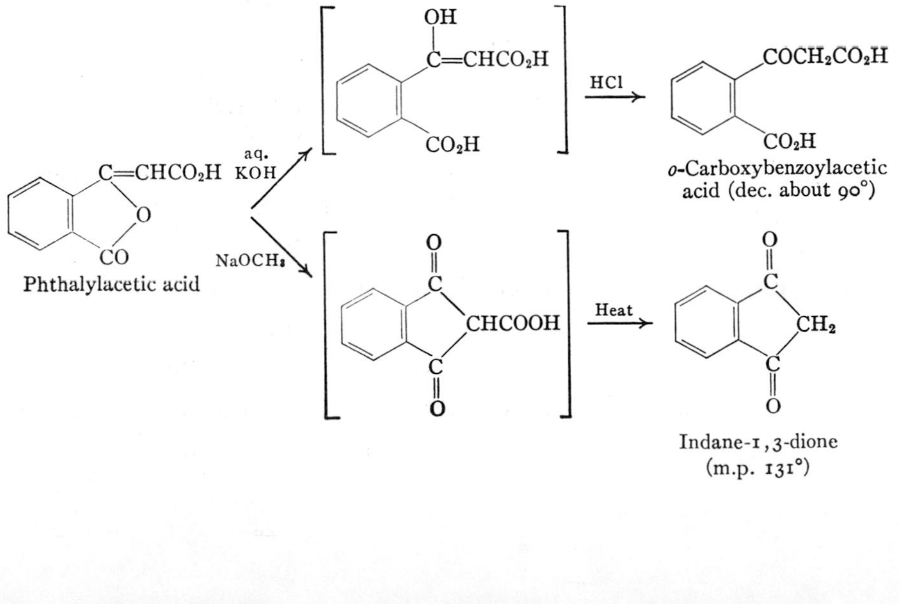

Phthalylacetic acid

o-Carboxybenzoylacetic acid (dec. about 90°)

Indane-1,3-dione
(m.p. 131°)

rates; this β-keto acid readily loses carbon dioxide when heated, and yields aceto-phenone-o-carboxylic acid, o-$C_6H_4(COCH_3)COOH$ (m.p. $115°$).

Ketones of the acetophenone type undergo ω-substitution (terminal) particularly readily because the methyl group is activated. As already noted (23.2), **phenacyl bromide,** or ω-bromoacetophenone, is prepared by bromination in ether in the presence of aluminum chloride. The product is a highly reactive,

$$C_6H_5COCH_3 \xrightarrow{\text{Br}_2(\text{AlCl}_3),\ \text{ether, o}°} C_6H_5COCH_2Br$$

Phenacyl bromide
(m.p. $51°$)

lachrymatory substance that reacts readily with liquid acids to give crystalline esters, and hence is used in identification of acids. Further side-chain halogenation can be accomplished; thus two molecular equivalents of bromine convert acetophenone (carbon disulfide or acetic acid solution) into **ω,ω-dibromaceto-phenone,** $C_6H_5COCHBr_2$, m.p. $37°$. This substance undergoes an interesting hydrolytic rearrangement with alkali; when shaken with 10% aqueous potassium hydroxide at room temperature, it slowly dissolves, and on acidification of the solution mandelic acid is liberated in good yield. The reaction is blocked by sub-

$$C_6H_5COCHBr_2 \xrightarrow{\text{10\% aq. KOH}} \underset{\text{Mandelic acid}}{\overset{\displaystyle C_6H_5CHCOOH}{\underset{OH}{|}}}$$

ω,ω-Dibromoacetophenone

stituents in both positions *ortho* to the acyl group, but otherwise is generally applicable; for example 2,4-dimethylacetophenone on dibromination and treatment of the crude product with alkali is converted in 61% yield into 2,4-dimethylmandelic acid (two polymorphic forms, m.p. $103°$ and $119°$). Trihalo derivatives of the type $C_6H_5COCX_3$ are intermediates in the conversion of acetophenone into benzoic acid by the action of sodium hypochlorite or hypobromite.

Another instance of attack of the activated methyl group of acetophenone is oxidation with selenium dioxide to the α-keto aldehyde phenylglyoxal:

COCH₃ →[SeO₂, aq. dioxane, 50–55° / 69–72%] COCHO

Phenylglyoxal
(b.p. $96°/25$ mm.)

Phenylglyoxal is also formed from phenacyl bromide, $C_6H_5COCH_2Br$, by simply dissolving the substance in dimethyl sulfoxide (N. Kornblum, 1957). The reac-

$$C_6H_5\overset{O}{\overset{\|}{C}}-CHBr_2 \xrightarrow{OH^-} C_6H_5\overset{O}{\overset{\|}{C}}-\overset{O}{\overset{\|}{C}}-H \xrightarrow{OH^-} C_6H_5\overset{O}{\overset{\|}{C}}-\overset{O^-}{\underset{OH}{\overset{|}{C}}}-H \longrightarrow$$

$$C_6H_5\overset{O^-}{\underset{H}{\overset{|}{C}}}-\overset{O}{\underset{OH}{\overset{\|}{C}}} \longrightarrow C_6H_5\overset{OH}{\underset{H}{\overset{|}{C}}}-\overset{O}{\underset{O^-}{\overset{\|}{C}}} \xrightarrow{H_2O} C_6H_5\overset{OH}{\underset{H}{\overset{|}{C}}}-\overset{O}{\underset{OH}{\overset{\|}{C}}} + OH^-$$

tion may involve O-alkylation and subsequent decomposition. Since phenyl-glyoxal on treatment with alkali affords mandelic acid, it is the evident intermediate in the formation of this acid from ω,ω-dibromoacetophenone. The reaction is a benzilic acid rearrangement (25.13) involving migration of hydrogen promoted by resonance stabilization in the mandelate anion.

Acetophenone undergoes self-aldolization in the presence of various catalysts, one of the best being aluminum t-butoxide. The name of the product, dypnone,

$$C_6H_5C{=}O \underset{CH_3}{|} + CH_3COC_6H_5 \xrightarrow[\substack{77-82\%}]{\substack{Al[OC(CH_3)_3]_3, \\ \text{xylene, } 133-137°}} C_6H_5C{=}CHCOC_6H_5 \underset{CH_3}{|}$$

Dypnone
(b.p. 150–155°/1 mm.)

is derived from the fact that acetophenone has soporific properties and has been known as hypnone; the condensation product is thus a di-hypnone. Formation of dypnone is analogous to the condensation of acetone to mesityl oxide. Acetophenone condenses to form s-triphenylbenzene when heated with hydrochloric acid in a sealed tube:

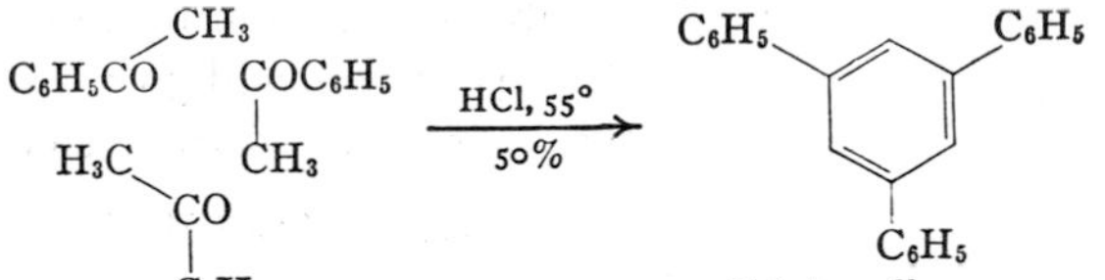

$$\begin{array}{c} \overset{CH_3}{\diagup} \\ C_6H_5CO \quad COC_6H_5 \\ H_3C \quad CH_3 \\ \diagdown CO \\ | \\ C_6H_5 \end{array} \xrightarrow[50\%]{HCl,\ 55°} \begin{array}{c} C_6H_5 \diagdown \quad \diagup C_6H_5 \\ \\ \\ C_6H_5 \end{array}$$

s-Triphenylbenzene
(m.p. 174.5°)

Aromatic ketones are reduced bimolecularly by metal combinations. Benzophenone, an α,β-unsaturated ketone, absorbs ultraviolet light and is thereby

$$2\,(C_6H_5)_2C{=}O + (CH_3)_2CHOH \xrightarrow[95\%]{Sunlight} \begin{array}{c} (C_6H_5)_2C{-}OH \\ | \\ (C_6H_5)_2C{-}OH \end{array} + \begin{array}{c} CH_3 \diagdown \\ C{=}O \\ CH_3 \diagup \end{array}$$

Benzopinacol
(m.p. 189°)

activated for reduction by isopropyl alcohol, as hydrogen donor. Thus exposure to sunlight of a solution of the ketone in this solvent results in production of benzopinacol in high yield. Benzopinacol rearranges under catalysis by a mineral acid or iodine to benzopinacolone.

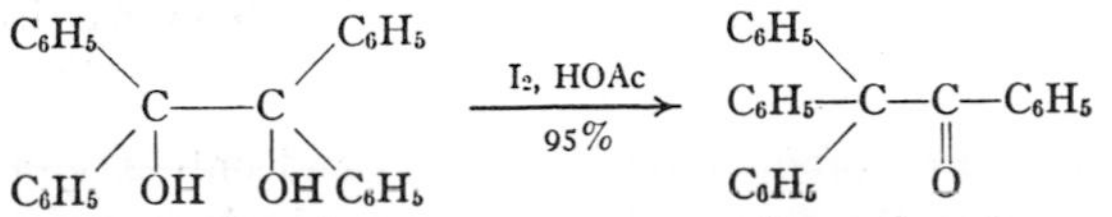

$$\begin{array}{c} C_6H_5 \diagdown \quad \diagup C_6H_5 \\ C{-}C \\ \diagup | \quad | \diagdown \\ C_6H_5 \ OH \ OH \ C_6H_5 \end{array} \xrightarrow[95\%]{I_2,\ HOAc} \begin{array}{c} C_6H_5 \diagdown \\ C_6H_5{-}C{-}C{-}C_6H_5 \\ \diagup \quad \| \\ C_6H_5 \quad O \end{array}$$

Benzopinacol   Benzopinacolone
(m.p. 180°)

P. T. Lansbury[1] (1961) discovered an interesting reaction of benzopinacolone in investigating, with success, the use of pyridine as solvent for lithium aluminum

[1] Peter T. Lansbury, b. 1913 Vienna, Austria; Ph.D. Northwestern (Letsinger); Univ. Buffalo

hydride reduction of ketones sparingly soluble in ether or tetrahydrofurane. In pyridine solution benzopinacolone suffers reductive cleavage to triphenylmethane and benzyl alcohol, rather than normal reduction. The phenomenon is at-

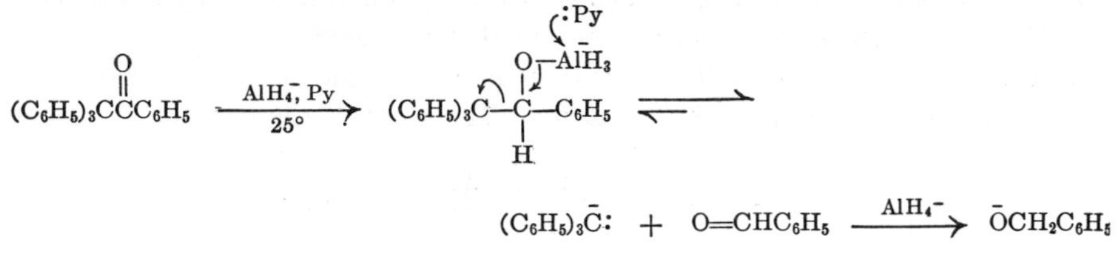

$$(C_6H_5)_3C\overset{O}{\overset{\|}{C}}C_6H_5 \xrightarrow[25°]{AlH_4^-,\ Py} (C_6H_5)_3C\overset{O-AlH_3}{\underset{H}{\overset{|}{\underset{|}{C}}}}C_6H_5 \ \rightleftharpoons \ \longrightarrow$$

$$(C_6H_5)_3\bar{C}: \ + \ O{=}CHC_6H_5 \xrightarrow{AlH_4^-} \bar{O}CH_2C_6H_5$$

tributed to the enhanced polarity of pyridine and its power to coordinate with Lewis acids. The triphenylmethide initially formed undergoes the usual carbanion reactions, e.g. carbonation, alkylation, deuterium exchange. Test tube demonstrations of carbanion reactions with triphenylmethide generated from either benzopinacolone or triphenylmethane with LiAlH$_4$ in pyridine provide impressive colors.

The Beckmann rearrangement is sometimes useful for the preparation of amines not available by nitration and reduction. Thus methyl dehydroabietate on nitration under very mild conditions gives only the 6,8-dinitro derivative. Friedel-Crafts acylation, however, stops at monosubstitution, and gives almost exclusively the 6-aceto derivative (with 3–4% of the 8-isomer). Rearrangement of the oxime

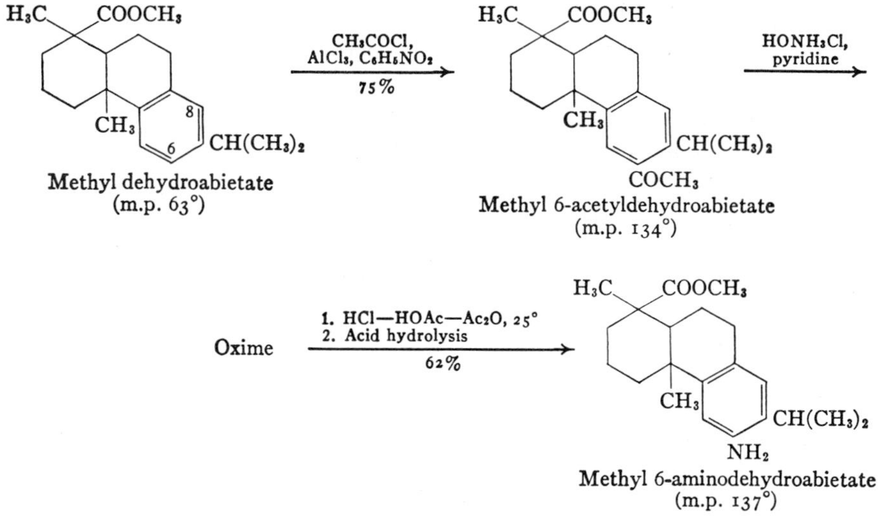

Methyl dehydroabietate
(m.p. 63°)

CH₃COCl, AlCl₃, C₆H₅NO₂
75%

Methyl 6-acetyldehydroabietate
(m.p. 134°)

HONH₂Cl, pyridine

Oxime
1. HCl—HOAc—Ac₂O, 25°
2. Acid hydrolysis
62%

Methyl 6-aminodehydroabietate
(m.p. 137°)

yields 88% of the desired product ArNHCOCH$_3$ and only 4% of the isomer Ar-CONHCH$_3$, and hence the 6-amine, obtained by hydrolysis with hydrochloric and acetic acid, can be produced in satisfactory overall yield.

One of the few deviations from normal behavior is that acetomesitylene, which has a highly hindered carbonyl group, does not add Grignard reagents but instead is converted into the magnesiohalide salt of the enolic form:

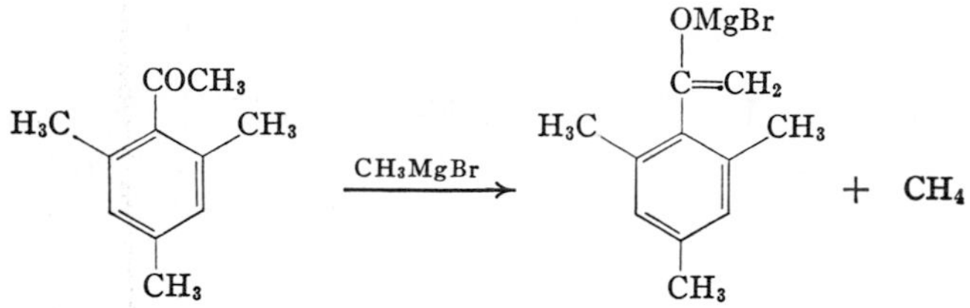

Acetomesitylene
(b.p. 236°)

OTHER REACTIONS

25.10   Autoxidation; Peroxides. — Benzaldehyde readily undergoes air oxidation to benzoic acid, particularly in the presence of minute traces of iron or on exposure to light, and the transformation is readily apparent because the aldehyde is a liquid and the acid, a solid.   If benzaldehyde is distilled through an air-cooled condenser and the hot liquid allowed to flow down the walls of a receiver in a thin film in contact with air, crystals of benzoic acid usually are visible in the film.   Thus distillation should be conducted with exclusion of air and the material stored in a completely filled brown bottle.

Autoxidation of benzaldehyde has the characteristics of a free radical chain reaction, for it is photocatalytic, subject to catalysis by traces of metal derivatives and to suppression by inhibitors.   H. L. J. Bächström (1934) concluded from results of physicochemical studies of the autoxidation that the reactive chain-propagating

1. $ArCH=O \xrightarrow{h\nu} Ar\dot{C}HO\cdot$

2. $Ar\dot{C}HO\cdot + ArCHO \rightarrow Ar\dot{C}=O + Ar\dot{C}HOH$

3. $Ar\dot{C}=O + O_2 \rightarrow ArC(=O)O-O\cdot$

4. $ArC(=O)O-O\cdot + ArCHO \rightarrow ArCO_3H + Ar\dot{C}=O$

5. $ArCO_3H + ArCHO \rightarrow 2ArCO_2H$

5a. $ArCO_3H + H_2O \rightarrow ArCO_2H + H_2O_2$

species is the benzoyl radical, produced photochemically (1 and 2) or otherwise, and which is assumed to combine with oxygen to form a perbenzoyl radical (3). This reacts with benzaldehyde with generation of the benzoyl radical and formation of perbenzoic acid (4), which either converts benzaldehyde into benzoic acid (5) or decomposes to benzoic acid (5a).   Perbenzoic acid indeed has been detected in autoxidized benzaldehyde.   The essential feature of the process is that a free-radical intermediate promotes the ultimate transformation and is regenerated in each cycle.   The chain mechanism explains the efficacy of antioxidants in inhibiting autoxidation at low concentrations.   Hydroquinone, which is easily oxidized, inhibits autoxidation of benzaldehyde at a concentration of only 0.001%, and it is commonly added to benzaldehyde for protection in storage; since the phenolic substance is nonvolatile, the protective action applies only to the liquid phase and not to a vapor space over the liquid.   The inhibitor molecules react with and destroy free-radical intermediates, each of which otherwise would initiate a chain process resulting in the conversion of hundreds of molecules of aldehyde into the acid.

By ozonization of triphenylethylene, Kohler and Richtmyer[1] (1930) obtained a crystalline product which they characterized as dimeric benzophenone peroxide by analytical data and by the observation that when heated with phosphorus

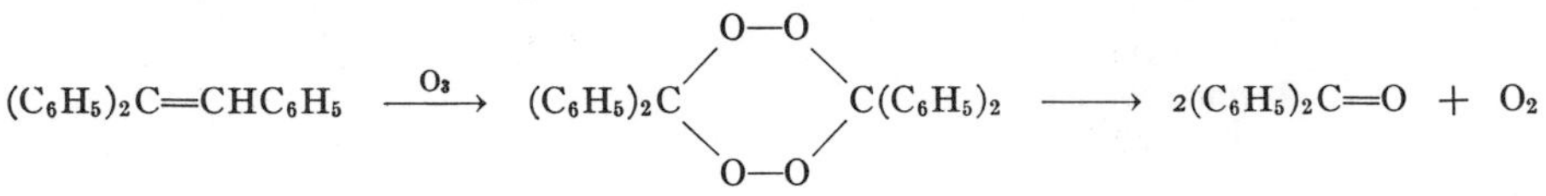

$$(C_6H_5)_2C = CHC_6H_5 \xrightarrow{O_3} (C_6H_5)_2C \underset{O-O}{\overset{O-O}{\diagup\diagdown}} C(C_6H_5)_2 \longrightarrow 2(C_6H_5)_2C = O + O_2$$

pentachloride it liberates chlorine and when heated by itself it passes quantitatively into benzophenone and oxygen. Intramolecular elimination of oxygen also occurs on thermal decomposition in solvents (D. H. Hey, 1960).

25.11 **Benzoin Condensation.** — Under the catalytic influence of an alkali cyanide in aqueous alcohol, benzaldehyde undergoes bimolecular condensation to the α-hydroxy ketone benzoin (87% yield). Cyanide ion is an indispensable catalyst and probably participates as shown. Discovery of the ben-

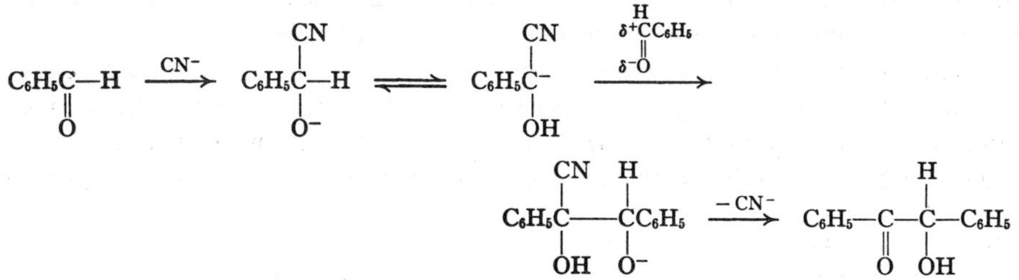

Benzoin (m.p. 134°)

zoin condensation resulted from the fortuitous circumstance that early workers purified crude "oil of bitter almonds" by washing with aqueous alkali to extract acids; the crude material from amygdalin contained hydrogen cyanide, and the sodium cyanide produced in the alkali wash catalyzed formation of benzoin (Wöhler and Liebig, 1832). Other aromatic aldehydes form benzoins (acyloins) under catalysis by cyanides. Treatment of a combination of two different aromatic aldehydes with a cyanide usually results in formation of chiefly one of the mixed acyloins, ArCHOHCOAr' and Ar'CHOHCOAr; mixed benzoins also are produced from a mixture of a benzoin, a substituted benzaldehyde, and a cyanide; the benzoin condensation is therefore reversible. The optically active l-benzoin (m.p. 132°, $[\alpha]_D^{12}$ −117.5°) has been synthesized from l-mandelamide and phenylmagnesium bromide (low yield), and found to undergo rapid racemization in alcoholic alkaline solution through tautomerism to the enediol $C_6H_5C(OH)=C(OH)C_6H_5$. The same phenomenon may be involved in the partial isomerization of the mixed benzoin benzoyl-p-anisylcarbinol to p-anisoylphenylcarbinol by cold alcoholic potassium hydroxide.

Formation of acyloins by the action of an alkali cyanide on an aldehyde is not

[1] Nelson K. Richtmyer, b. 1901 Cocksackie, N. Y.; Ph.D. Harvard (Kohler); Bryn Mawr College; National Institutes of Health

specific to aromatic aldehydes, but is seldom encountered in the aliphatic series because the basic reagent promotes the more rapid aldol condensation. However, enzymes can bring about the acyloin condensation of aliphatic aldehydes; for example under the influence of yeast enzymes acetaldehyde condenses to form acetoin (methylacetylcarbinol), $CH_3CHOHCOCH_3$ (m.p. 15°), and added benzaldehyde combines with acetaldehyde to form benzacetoin (phenylacetylcarbinol), $C_6H_5CHOHCOCH_3$ (liq., b.p. 207°).

Like the α-hydroxy ketones of the sugar series, benzoin reduces Fehling solution and forms a phenylosazone (m.p. 225°) with phenylhydrazine. A charac-

$$\begin{array}{c} C_6H_5C=O \\ | \\ C_6H_5CHOH \end{array} \xrightarrow{3C_6H_5NHNH_2} \begin{array}{c} C_6H_5C=NNHC_6H_5 \\ | \\ C_6H_5C=NNHC_6H_5 \\ \text{Phenylosazone} \end{array} + C_6H_5NH_2 + NH_3$$

teristic color reaction is observed on addition of aqueous alkali to a solution of benzoin in the presence of air (autoxidation). After a certain induction period the solution acquires a violet color, which disappears when the solution is oxygenated by shaking and reappears in the quiet state. The ultimate product is the α-diketone benzil, $C_6H_5COCOC_6H_5$, which itself is not colored by alkali but which apparently forms a colored complex with benzoin and alkali, as demonstrated by the appearance of the violet color when the three components are brought together in the absence of air. The colored substance, which is very sensitive to oxidation by air, probably is derived from the enediol form of benzoin and is regarded as a radical containing univalent oxygen (Weissberger; Michaelis, 1937).

25.12   Benzoin–Benzil Series. — The α-diketone benzil is obtained in high yield by oxidation of benzoin with nitric acid in acetic acid solution or with copper sulfate in aqueous pyridine. The yellow color of benzil is dis-

$$\begin{array}{c} C_6H_5CHCOC_6H_5 \\ | \\ OH \\ \textbf{Benzoin} \end{array} \xrightarrow[86\%]{\text{CuSO}_4,\ \text{aq. pyridine, 95°}} \begin{array}{c} C_6H_5COCOC_6H_5 \\ \textbf{Benzil} \\ \text{(yellow, m.p. 95°)} \end{array}$$

charged by a variety of oxidizing and reducing agents. Thus the diketone is oxidized to benzoic acid by hydrogen peroxide in warm acetic acid, and it is reduced to benzoin by stannous chloride in alcohol or by sodium hydrosulfite in aqueous alcohol. The reduction proceeds by 1,4-addition of hydrogen and ketonization of the initially formed enediol. Thiele (1899) established this mechanism

$$\begin{array}{c} O\ \ \ O \\ \| \ \ \| \\ C_6H_5-C-C-C_6H_5 \end{array} \xrightarrow{2\,H} \left[\begin{array}{c} OH\ \ OH \\ | \ \ \ \ | \\ C_6H_5-C=C-C_6H_5 \end{array} \right] \longrightarrow C_6H_5CHOHCOC_6H_5$$

by conducting the reduction in the presence of acetic anhydride and a catalyst in order that the alcoholic product would be acetylated as formed. Reductive acetylation with zinc dust and acetic anhydride containing a little hydrochloric

$$\begin{array}{c} C_6H_5C=O \\ | \\ C_6H_5C=O \end{array} \xrightarrow[\text{Zn(HCl)}]{(CH_3CO)_2O} \begin{array}{c} C_6H_5COCOCH_3 \\ | \\ C_6H_5COCOCH_3 \\ \text{M.p. 119°} \end{array} + \begin{array}{c} C_6H_5COCOCH_3 \\ \| \\ CH_3COOC-C_6H_5 \\ \text{M.p. 155°} \end{array}$$

acid gives a mixture from which about equal parts of the *cis* and *trans* diacetates can be isolated by crystallization. Benzoin can be converted by reduction into a number of products, some of which are indicated in the chart. Reduction with powdered tin and concentrated hydrochloric acid in ethanol affords desoxybenzoin in 80–84% yield (P. H. Carter, *Org. Syn.*, 1960). Reduction with sodium boro-

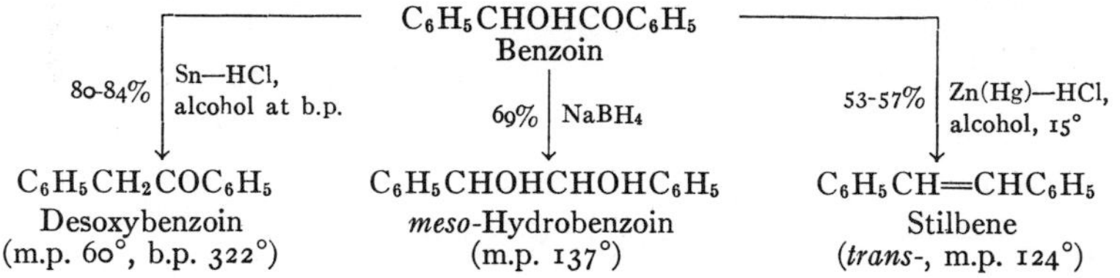

$$C_6H_5CHOHCOC_6H_5$$
Benzoin

| 80-84% | Sn—HCl, alcohol at b.p. | 69% NaBH$_4$ | 53-57% | Zn(Hg)—HCl, alcohol, 15° |

$C_6H_5CH_2COC_6H_5$
Desoxybenzoin
(m.p. 60°, b.p. 322°)

$C_6H_5CHOHCHOHC_6H_5$
meso-Hydrobenzoin
(m.p. 137°)

$C_6H_5CH{=}CHC_6H_5$
Stilbene
(*trans*-, m.p. 124°)

hydride gives mainly *meso*-hydrobenzoin (stilbenediol). The combination of amalgamated zinc and cold alcoholic hydrochloric acid eliminates both oxygen atoms and gives *trans*-stilbene, but a better route to this hydrocarbon is via desyl chloride (5.19)

Desoxybenzoin can be made also from phenylmagnesium bromide and benzyl cyanide or by the Friedel-Crafts reaction of phenylacetyl chloride with benzene (68–72% yield). The end product of the series, **dibenzyl** ($C_6H_5CH_2CH_2C_6H_5$, m.p. 52°), is produced by hydrogenation of benzil over nickel catalyst at 230° or by the action of sodium on benzyl chloride. A reaction of benzil generally characteristic of α-diketones is condensation with *o*-phenylenediamine with closure of an aromatic heterocyclic ring (pyrazine ring).

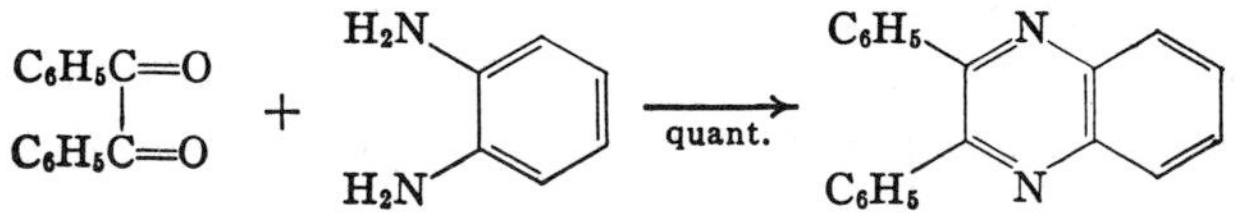

$$C_6H_5C{=}O$$
$$C_6H_5C{=}O$$
$+$ H_2N ... H_2N $\xrightarrow{\text{quant.}}$ C_6H_5 ... C_6H_5

2,3-Diphenylquinoxaline
(colorless, m.p. 126°)

25.13   Benzilic Acid Rearrangement. — When benzil is heated with 70% aqueous sodium hydroxide at 140°, or refluxed with alcoholic potassium hydroxide, it is converted in high yield to benzilic acid. The rearrangement

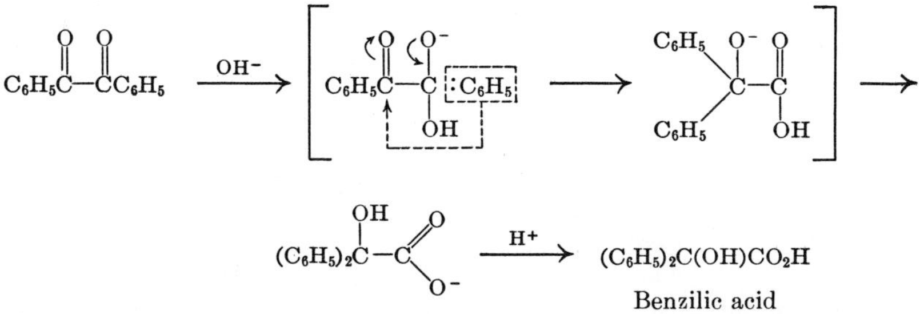

$$C_6H_5C-CC_6H_5 \xrightarrow{OH^-} \left[C_6H_5C-C{:}C_6H_5 \atop OH \longrightarrow C_6H_5 \atop C_6H_5 C-C \atop OH \right] \longrightarrow$$

$$(C_6H_5)_2C-C\,{\overset{OH}{\diagdown}}\overset{O}{\underset{O^-}{}} \xrightarrow{H^+} (C_6H_5)_2C(OH)CO_2H$$

Benzilic acid
M.p. 151°, pK$_a$ 3.04

is interpreted as initiated by a nucleophilic attack by hydroxide ion on a carbonyl carbon with formation of a hydrate anion that rearranges by migration of a phenyl group. The formation of the resonance-stabilized carboxylate group provides the driving force for the reaction. A preparative procedure that dispenses with isolation of benzil is to heat benzoin with sodium bromate and alkali at 85–90°; the diketone is produced in the mixture under conditions such that it rearranges as formed (84–90% yield). Benzilic acid is sensitive to oxidation in acid solution, for example with potassium dichromate and sulfuric acid, and yields benzophenone and carbon dioxide.

25.14 Willgerodt Reaction. — This reaction, discovered in 1887, is conducted by heating a ketone, for example $ArCOCH_3$, with an aqueous solution of yellow ammonium sulfide (sulfur dissolved in ammonium sulfide), and results in formation of an amide derivative of an arylacetic acid and in some reduction of the ketone. The dark reaction mixture usually is refluxed with alkali to effect

$$ArCOCH_3 + (NH_4)S_x \longrightarrow ArCH_2CONH_2 + ArCH_2CH_3$$

hydrolysis of the amide, and the arylacetic acid is recovered from the alkaline solution. Although the yields are not high, the process sometimes offers the most satisfactory route to an arylacetic acid, as in the preparation of 1-acenaphthylacetic acid from 1-acetoacenaphthene, a starting material made in 45% yield by acylation of the hydrocarbon with acetic acid and liquid hydrogen fluoride. The

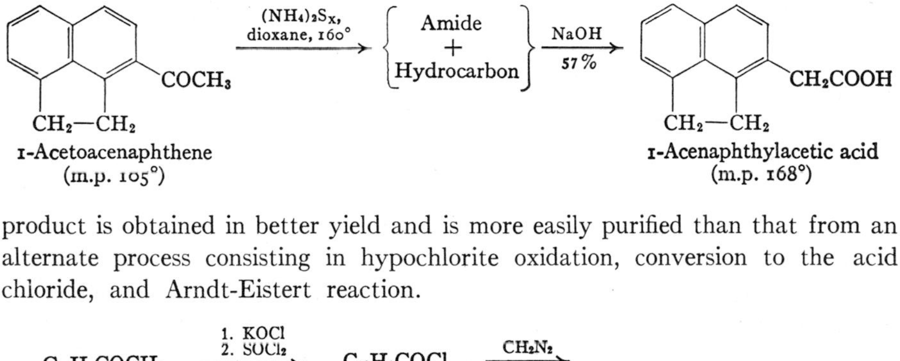

1-Acetoacenaphthene (m.p. 105°) 1-Acenaphthylacetic acid (m.p. 168°)

product is obtained in better yield and is more easily purified than that from an alternate process consisting in hypochlorite oxidation, conversion to the acid chloride, and Arndt-Eistert reaction.

$$\underset{\text{1-Acetoacenaphthene}}{C_{12}H_9COCH_3} \xrightarrow[78\%]{1.\ KOCl;\ 2.\ SOCl_2} C_{12}H_9COCl \xrightarrow{CH_2N_2}$$

$$\underset{\text{Diazo ketone}}{[C_{12}H_9COCHN_2]} \xrightarrow[64\%,\ \text{from acid chloride}]{Ag_2O,\ Na_2S_2O_3} \underset{\text{1-Acenaphthylacetic acid}}{C_{12}H_9CH_2COOH}$$

A modification of the Willgerodt reaction that simplifies the procedure by obviating the necessity of a sealed tube or autoclave consists in refluxing the ketone with a high-boiling amine and sulfur (Schwenk,[1] 1942). Morpholine, so named because of a relationship to an early erroneous partial formula suggested for morphine, is suitable and is made technically by dehydration of diethanolamine. The reaction is conducted in the absence of water, and the reaction product is not

[1] Erwin Schwenk, b. 1887 Prague, Czechoslovakia; Ph.D. Techn. Hochschule Vienna; Schering A. G. Berlin; Schering Corp. N. J.; Worcester Found. Exptl. Biol.

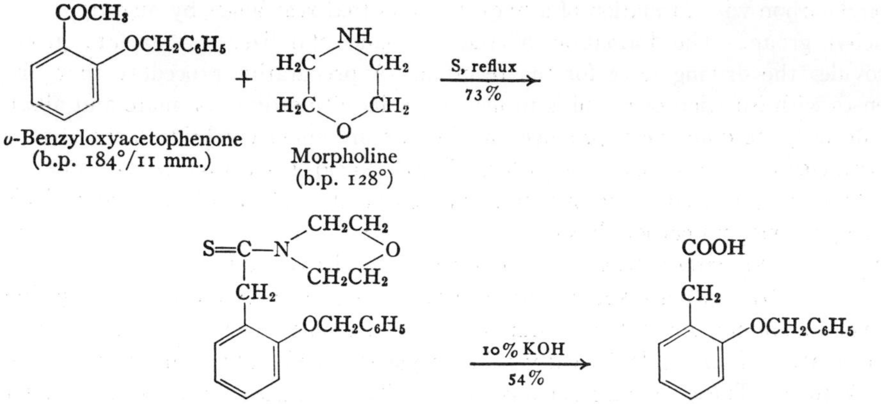

v-Benzyloxyacetophenone
(b.p. 184°/11 mm.)

Morpholine
(b.p. 128°)

o-Benzyloxyphenyl-
thioacetmorpholide
(m.p. 119°)

o-Benzyloxyphenylacetic acid
(m.p. 99°)

the amide but the thioamide; this, however, undergoes hydrolysis in the same manner to the arylacetic acid.

25.15   Synthesis of Amines from Ketones. — Several methods are available for the synthesis of compounds having an amino group in an alkyl side chain. One is oximation of a ketone and reduction; for example α-phenylethylamine can be made by reduction of acetophenone oxime with sodium and

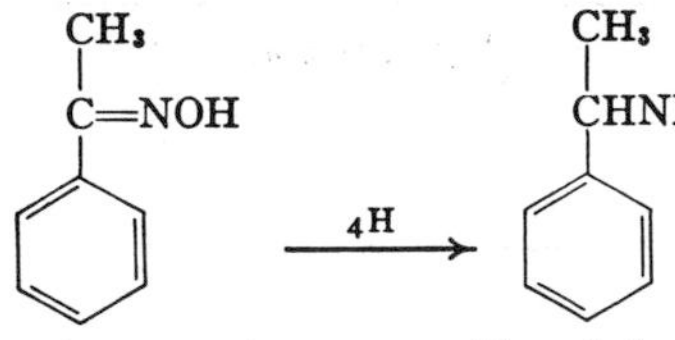

Acetophenone oxime

α-Phenylethylamine
(b.p. 186°)

absolute alcohol or with sodium amalgam. A more convenient preparation of the same compound is by the Leuckart reaction (14.8).

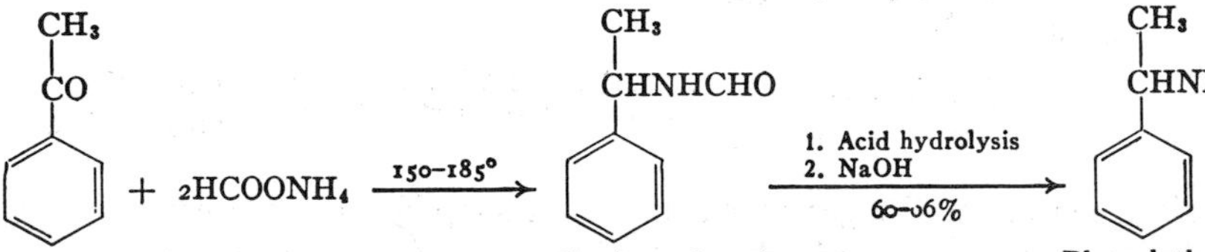

Crude α-phenyl-
ethylformamide

α-Phenylethylamine

In another method, a ketone of the type ArCOCH$_2$R, where R is alkyl or hydrogen, is condensed with a nitrous acid ester in the presence of sodium ethoxide (or hydrogen chloride) to an oximido ketone, ArCOCR=NOH (13.18). The reaction is comparable to a Claisen-Schmidt condensation. The oximido ketone yields a primary amino compound on reduction.

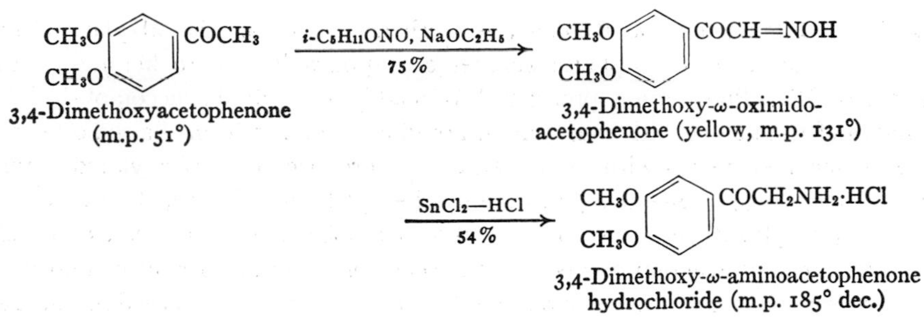

3,4-Dimethoxyacetophenone
(m.p. 51°)

3,4-Dimethoxy-ω-oximido-
acetophenone (yellow, m.p. 131°)

3,4-Dimethoxy-ω-aminoacetophenone
hydrochloride (m.p. 185° dec.)

The Mannich reaction (13.5) is useful for the preparation of ketonic amines of the type illustrated, for these on reduction afford physiologically active amino

$$C_6H_5COCH_3 + CH_2O + (CH_3)_2NH \cdot HCl \xrightarrow[60\%]{\text{Alcohol (reflux)}} C_6H_5COCH_2CH_2N(CH_3)_2 \cdot HCl$$

ω-Dimethylaminopropiophenone
hydrochloride (m.p. 156°)

alcohols of value in therapy. Amino alcohols of similar types are available also from oximido ketones by catalytic hydrogenation in an alcoholic solution containing hydrochloric acid (Hartung and Munch, 1929), as shown.

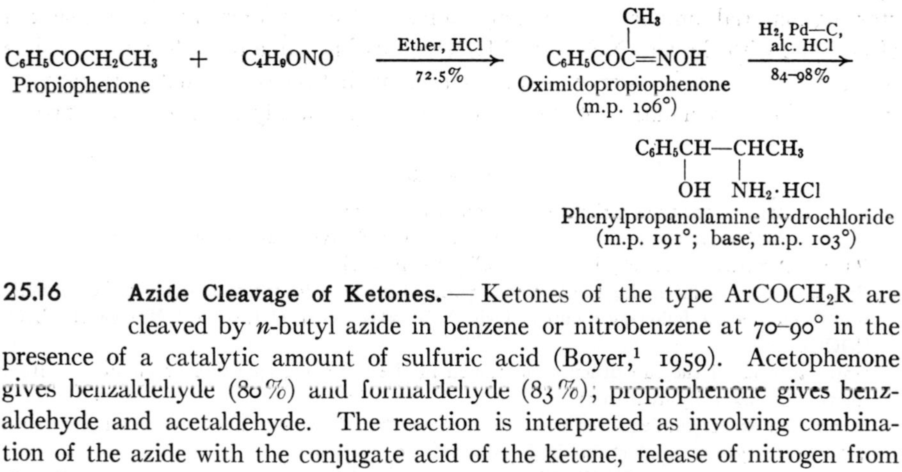

$$C_6H_5COCH_2CH_3 + C_4H_9ONO \xrightarrow[72.5\%]{\text{Ether, HCl}} \underset{\substack{\text{Oximidopropiophenone}\\ \text{(m.p. 106°)}}}{C_6H_5COC=NOH} \xrightarrow[84-98\%]{\substack{H_2, Pd-C,\\ \text{alc. HCl}}}$$

$$\underset{\substack{\text{Phenylpropanolamine hydrochloride}\\ \text{(m.p. 191°; base, m.p. 103°)}}}{C_6H_5CH-CHCH_3}$$
OH   NH₂·HCl

25.16   Azide Cleavage of Ketones. — Ketones of the type ArCOCH₂R are cleaved by n-butyl azide in benzene or nitrobenzene at 70–90° in the presence of a catalytic amount of sulfuric acid (Boyer,[1] 1959). Acetophenone gives benzaldehyde (80%) and formaldehyde (83%); propiophenone gives benzaldehyde and acetaldehyde. The reaction is interpreted as involving combination of the azide with the conjugate acid of the ketone, release of nitrogen from the diazonium cation with elimination of water, hydration, and cleavage.

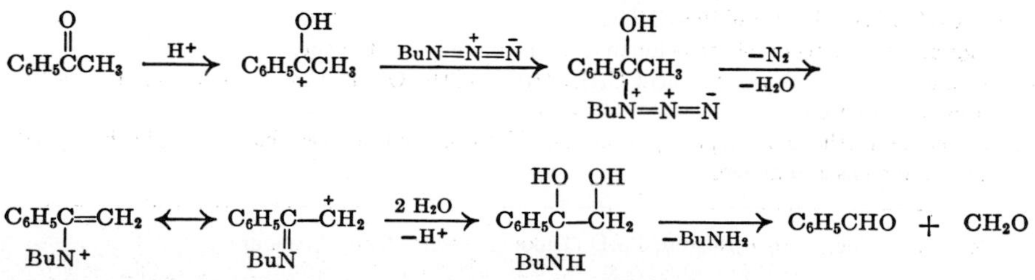

[1] Joseph H. Boyer, b. 1922 Otto, Ind.; Ph.D. Illinois (Leonard); Tulane Univ.

25.17　　　Phenylation of Ketones. — Methods used for the alkylation and acylation of aliphatic ketones are applicable also to ketones of the type ArCOR. Phenylation proceeds less readily but can be accomplished by reaction of the ketone with sodamide in liquid ammonia to form the sodio derivative, which then reacts with bromobenzene to produce the α-phenylated ketone (R. Levine,[1] 1959). Acetone gives methyl benzyl ketone (34%), diethyl ketone gives 2-phenylpentane-3-one (62%), and acetophenone gives desoxybenzoin (28%). Since no reaction occurs in the absence of sodamide, a reagent known to convert bromobenzene into benzyne, the reaction is regarded as proceeding through

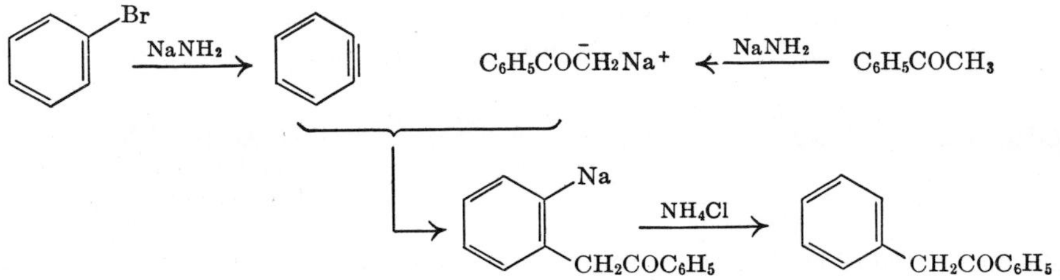

this intermediate. After a 10 min. reaction period the reaction mixture is quenched by addition of solid ammonium chloride and processed for recovery of product, starting material, aniline, and diphenylamine. The two amines arise by reaction of benzyne with the ions $\bar{N}H_2$ and $C_6H_5\bar{N}H$. By the same procedure it is possible to phenylate malonic ester with production of diethyl phenylmalonate in 51% yield. Direct phenylation of the ester had not previously been accomplished.

PROBLEMS

1. Suggest methods for the synthesis of the following aldehydes:
   (a) p-Bromobenzaldehyde　　　(c) 2,4-Dimethoxybenzaldehyde
   (b) 2,5-Dimethylbenzaldehyde　　(d) Terephthalaldehyde
2. Prepare a chart summarizing the principal methods available for introduction into the aromatic ring of each of the following groups: CH_3, NO_2, NH_2, SO_3H, OH, Cl, I, CN, COOH, CHO, $COCH_3$.
3. How can each of the substituents mentioned in the preceding question be eliminated from the ring (replaced by hydrogen)?
4. Would you expect condensation to occur between the following pairs of components? If so, indicate the type of catalyst required and write the reactions:
   (a) C_6H_5CHO + $CH_3CH_2CH_2CHO$
   (b) $C_6H_5CH{=}CHCHO$ + $C_6H_5COCH_3$
   (c) C_6H_5CHO + $CH_3CH{=}CHCHO$
5. Suggest a synthesis of o-bromocinnamic acid from o-bromotoluene.
6. Formulate a synthesis of the acid $C_6H_5CH(CH_3)CH_2COOH$ from acetophenone by the Reformatsky reaction.
7. Summarize methods of preparing aromatic aldehydes and ketones that are applicable specifically to phenols and amines.

---

[1] Robert Levine, b. 1919 Boston; Ph.D. Duke (Hauser); Univ. Pittsburgh

Chapter 26

QUINONES AND ARENONES

26.1   **Introduction.** — The generic name quinone is derived from the fact
that the first-known and commonest member of the series was discovered in Liebig's laboratory as a product of the oxidation of quinic acid with
manganese dioxide and sulfuric acid (Woskresensky, 1838).   Quinic acid, a constituent of cinchona bark and of the coffee bean, is a 1,3,4,5-tetrahydroxyhexa-
hydrobenzoic acid of the configuration shown, and its conversion into quinone in-

Quinic acid
(monohydrate, m.p. 162°, $[\alpha]_D^{15°} -44°$)

Quinone
(yellow, m.p. 116°)

volves dehydration, decarboxylation, and oxidation.   The yellow reaction product
is called quinone, or *p*-benzoquinone; the isomeric *o*-benzoquinone is known, but
meta quinones do not exist.

One characteristic of quinones is color, and a usual
differentiation between *para* and *ortho* quinones is
that most of the former are yellow and the majority
of the latter are orange or red.   Particularly beautiful color phenomena often are observed on dusting
a few crystals of a quinone on the surface of a dilute
aqueous solution of alkali or on a drop or two of con-

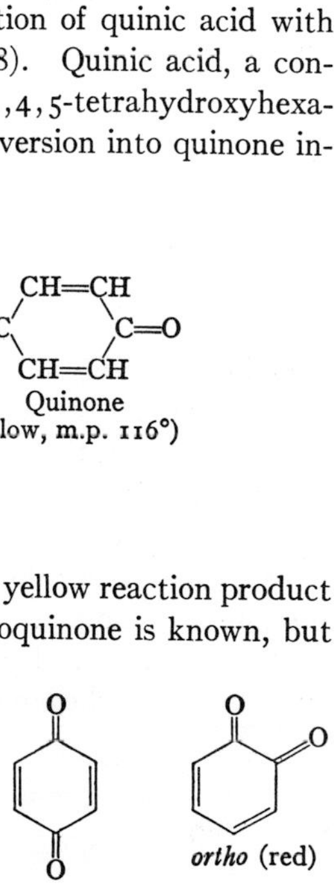

ortho (red)

para (yellow)

Benzoquinones

centrated sulfuric acid. Hydroxyquinones form intensely colored alkali salts, and quinones of all types form vividly colored oxonium salts in concentrated sulfuric acid. The quinone ring contains only two double bonds and is non-aromatic; quinones are analogous to open-chain α,β-unsaturated ketones but considerably more reactive. They are reduced by mild reagents to colorless hydroquinones.

26.2   **Quinone.** — Quinone is the end product of oxidation of aniline in sulfuric acid solution with manganese dioxide. An initially formed free radical condenses with aniline to form a succession of intensely colored dyes, which afford quinone by oxidation and hydrolysis. The crude product is vacuum distilled and reduced with iron to hydroquinone. Quinone is then produced by reoxidation.

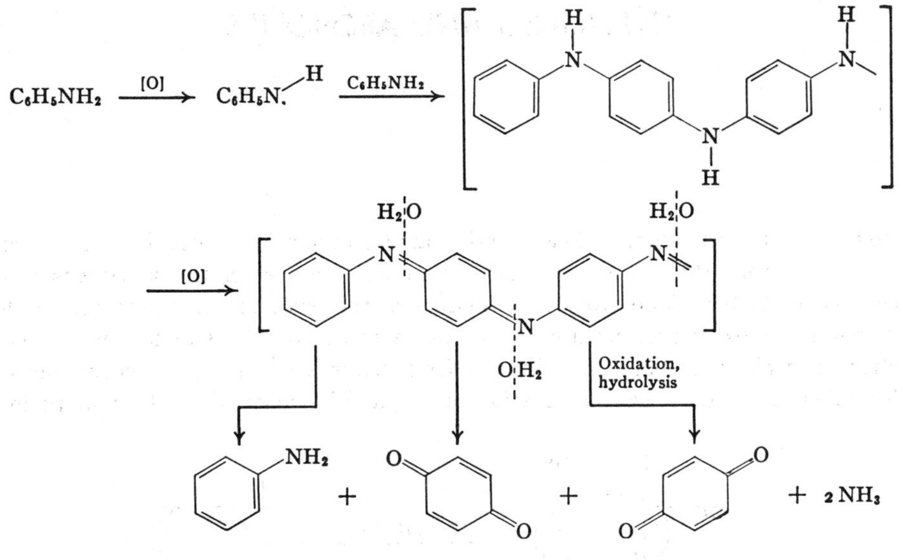

Quinone in the solid state has considerable vapor pressure, and when heated gently sublimes readily to form large yellow crystals. The substance has a characteristic pungent odor and causes sneezing, particularly in individuals subject to hay fever. It is attacked by aqueous alkali, with transient coloration, and is rapidly converted into a humuslike material. Quinone readily combines with proteins, probably by addition reactions involving free amino and sulfhydryl groups; it stains the skin and can be used for tanning leather. Quinone is polymerized by acids to a mixture of products, one of which has been identified as a trimer with an o-terphenyl skeleton (H. Erdtman, 1960).

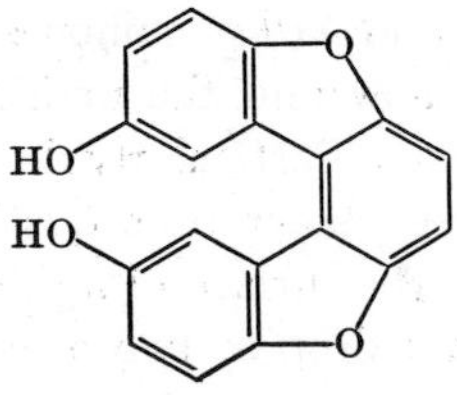

Quinhydrone. — When a yellow solution of quinone in alcohol is added to a colorless solution of hydroquinone in the same solvent, the color deepens to brown-red, and dark green crystals separate. The substance, quinhydrone (m.p. 171°), is a molecular complex composed of equimolecular amounts of quinone and hydro-quinone. It is much less soluble than either component, but dissociates to the components to a point of equilibrium.

26.3   Oxidation-Reduction Potentials. — The reduction of quinone to hydro-quinone in aqueous solution is a rapid, quantitative, and reversible process comparable to the reduction of ferric to ferrous ions and can be formulated as an electrochemical reaction. A platinum electrode introduced into a solution

containing quinone and hydroquinone at a fixed hydrogen-ion concentration acquires an electric potential which can be measured by making connection through a conducting liquid to a reference half-cell such as a calomel or hydrogen electrode. The electrode potential (E) of the organic half-cell is dependent on the concentrations of the species entering into equilibrium, namely quinone, hydroquinone, and hydrogen ions, in accordance with the equation:

$$E^{25°} = E_0 + 0.05912 \log [H^+] + 0.02956 \log \frac{[Quinone]}{[Hydroquinone]}$$

The quantity E_0 is a normal potential characteristic of a specific quinone-hydro-quinone system, and is defined as the potential of the half-cell when the hydrogen-ion concentration is unity and the concentration of the quinone, or oxidant, is equal to that of the hydroquinone, or reductant. Thus the second term in the right-hand side of the equation is reduced to zero if $[H^+] = 1$, and the third term disappears if [Quinone] = [Hydroquinone]. A method that ensures the latter condition consists in using quinhydrone for the measurement, for the complex dissociates to give equivalent amounts of the oxidant and reductant. The only variable then remaining is the hydrogen-ion concentration, which can be determined; but since the expression $0.05912 \log [H^+]$ is the potential of a hydrogen electrode (at 25°), a technique of measuring the normal potential is to make connection between a half-cell containing a solution of quinhydrone in a given buffer and a hydrogen electrode in the same buffer. The hydrogen-ion potential on the two sides is then the same, and since the concentration of quinone is equal to that of hydroquinone, the cell potential, or the potential difference between the two half-cells, is equal to the normal potential of the quinone-hydroquinone system. The value of the normal potential for the system from p-benzoquinone is 0.699 v. With this constant accurately known, the hydrogen-ion concentration of a given solution can be determined: quinhydrone is added to the solution, connection is made to a reference electrode, the potential (E) of the organic half-cell is measured, and the hydrogen-ion concentration is calculated from the expression: 0.05912 $\log [H^+] = E^{25°} - 0.699$.

In instances other than the specific one cited the normal potential can be determined by titrating potentiometrically either a solution of the quinone with a reducing agent or one of the hydroquinone with an oxidizing agent, for the mid-point of either titration curve corresponds to equivalence of oxidant and reductant. If a hydrogen electrode containing the same solution used to dissolve the organic reactants is used as the reference half-cell, normal potentials can be determined even in alcoholic solutions of unknown hydrogen-ion concentration, and hence quinones insoluble in water can be characterized. The normal potential provides a precise characterization of the oxidizing power of the quinone or, conversely, of the reducing intensity of the hydroquinone. Values for quinones derived from benzene and from some of the polynuclear hydrocarbons are shown (determinations at $25°$). Diphenoquinone, with the unsaturated conjugated quinonoid system extending throughout two rings, has a very high potential and is a powerful

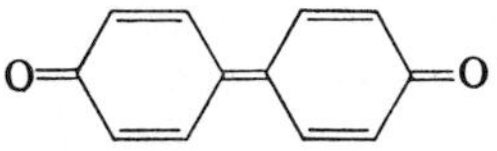

Diphenoquinone
$E_0^{alc.}$ 0.954 v.

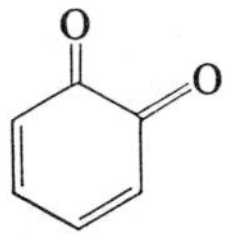

o-Benzoquinone
$E_0^{aq., 30°}$ 0.792 v.

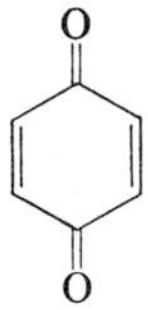

Quinone
$E_0^{aq.}$ 0.699 v.
$E_0^{alc.}$ 0.715 v.

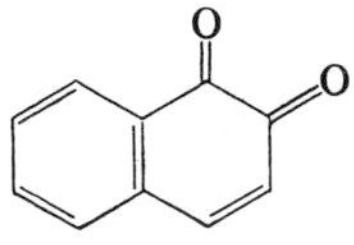

β-Naphthoquinone
$E_0^{aq.}$ 0.555 v.
$E_0^{alc.}$ 0.576 v.

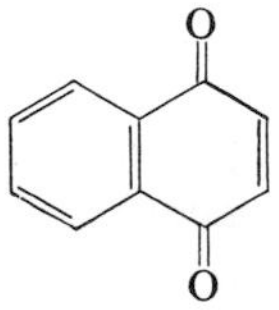

α-Naphthoquinone
$E_0^{aq.}$ 0.470 v.
$E_0^{alc.}$ 0.484 v.

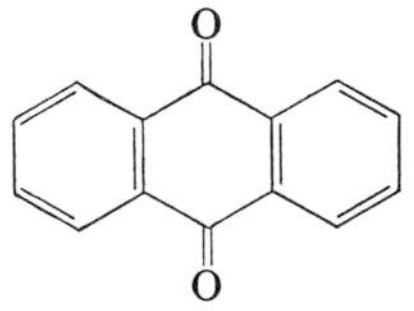

Anthraquinone
$E_0^{alc.}$ 0.154 v.

oxidizing agent. Since *ortho* quinones of the benzene and naphthalene series have potentials higher by 85–95 mv. than the isomeric *para* quinones, the former structure has a higher energy content than the latter. Comparison of benzoquinones with corresponding naphthoquinones indicates a regular difference in potential of 230–240 mv., which represents a diminished energy content of the bicyclic compounds. Stabilization attending fusion of a benzene ring to a double bond of either o- or p-benzoquinone can be attributed to the fact that the double bond is then incorporated in the aromatic nucleus and hence is relatively inert. In anthraquinone both the otherwise reactive quinonoid double bonds participate in benzenoid ring systems; hence the quinone has a low potential. Conversely, its reduction product, anthrahydroquinone, is a powerful reducing agent.

Substituent groups often exert a marked influence on the oxidation-reduction potential in either a positive or negative sense, as illustrated in Table 26.1 for a

TABLE 26.1   EFFECT OF 2-SUBSTITUENTS ON THE POTENTIAL
OF 1,4-NAPHTHOQUINONE

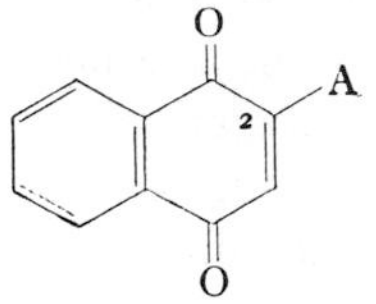

SUBSTITUENT	EFFECT, IN MV.	SUBSTITUENT	EFFECT, IN MV.
$NHCH_3$	−252	$NHCOCH_3$	−67
NH_2	−210	C_6H_5	−32
$N(CH_3)_2$	−181	$OCOCH_3$	−9
OH	−128	Cl	+24
OCH_3	−131	SO_3Na	+69
CH_3	−76	$SO_2C_6H_4CH_3$	+121

series of α-naphthoquinone derivatives (Fieser[1] and Fieser,[2] 1935). m-Directing groups, such as NO_2, CN, SO_2Ar, COAr, COOH, and SO_3H, as well as halogens, raise the potential of the parent quinone, whereas a potential-lowering effect is exerted by the following groups, arranged approximately in order of decreasing effectiveness: NHR, NH_2, $N(CH_3)_2$, OH, OR, CH_3, $NHCOCH_3$, C_6H_5, $OCOCH_3$. The relationships are those expected from the course of aromatic substitutions. Strongly unsaturated groups and halogen atoms are electron-attracting and tend

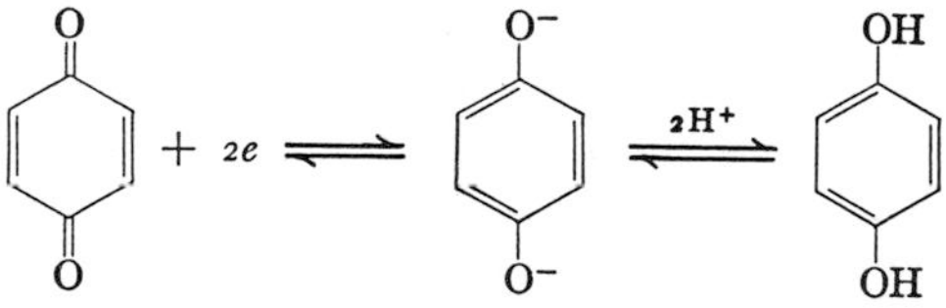

to increase the attractive power of the system terminating in the oxygen atoms for external electrons, the acquisition of which converts the quinone into the hydroquinone ion.   Combination of this ion with protons is a secondary process occur-

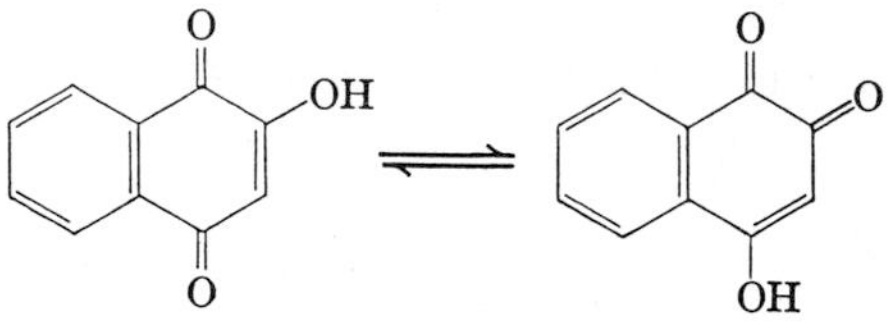

α-Form   β-Form
2-Hydroxy-1,4-naphthoquinone
(yellow, m.p. 192° dec., $E_0^{a|o.}$ 0.356 v., pK$_a$ 4.0)

[1] Louis F. Fieser, b. 1899 Columbus, Ohio; Ph.D. Harvard (Conant); Bryn Mawr College; Harvard Univ.

[2] Mary Fieser, b. 1909 Atchison, Kansas; stud. Bryn Mawr and Harvard (L. F. Fieser); Harvard Univ.

ring to an extent dependent on the acidity of the solution; if reduction is accomplished at a sufficiently high pH, no association occurs and electron transfer is the sole process involved. Amino, hydroxyl, alkyl, and other electron-repelling substituents decrease affinity for electrons and hence lower the potential.

Oxidation-reduction potential data are valuable in interpretation of the behavior of those hydroxy- and aminoquinones that can exist in tautomeric forms, for example 2-hydroxy-1,4-naphthoquinone. The tautomer of lower potential and consequent lower energy content must predominate in solutions, and a reliable estimate of relative potentials can be made from values found for the correspond-

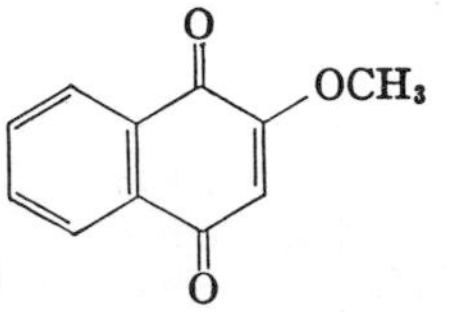

2-Methoxy-1,4-naphthoquinone   4-Methoxy-1,2-naphthoquinone
(yellow, m.p. 183.5°, $E_0^{alc.}$ 0.353 v.)   (orange-yellow, m.p. 190°, $E_0^{alc.}$ 0.433 v.)

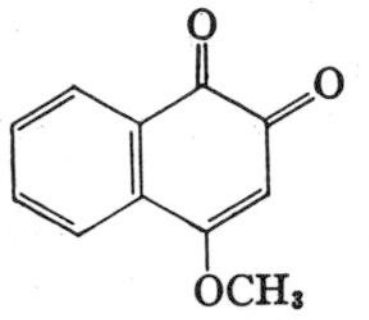

ing ethers, which are produced together in the reaction of the silver salt of the hydroxy compound with methyl iodide. The β-quinone ether has a potential higher by 80 mv. than the α-isomer, and a difference of similar magnitude must exist between the hydroxy compounds; hence the α-form is the more stable. The difference corresponds to a difference of 3.7 kcal. in the free energy of reduction. The relative abundance of the tautomers can be estimated from the following expression correlating the equilibrium constant ($K = [\alpha\text{-Form}]/[\beta\text{-Form}]$) with the oxidation-reduction potentials of the two forms (Fieser, 1928):

$$\log K^{25°} = \frac{E_0^{\beta\text{-Form}} - E_0^{\alpha\text{-Form}}}{0.02956}$$

If the difference in potential is 80 mv., only 0.2% of the β-form is present in the equilibrium mixture. The conclusion is supported by chemical evidence; for example, by the fact that esterification of the strongly acidic hydroxy compound with diazomethane gives 2-methoxy-1,4-naphthoquinone as the only isolated product (87% yield).

The aminoquinone 4-amino-1,2-naphthoquinone (Ia) offers the possibility of tautomerism to a hydroxyquinonimine (Ib). One tautomer has a basic substitu-

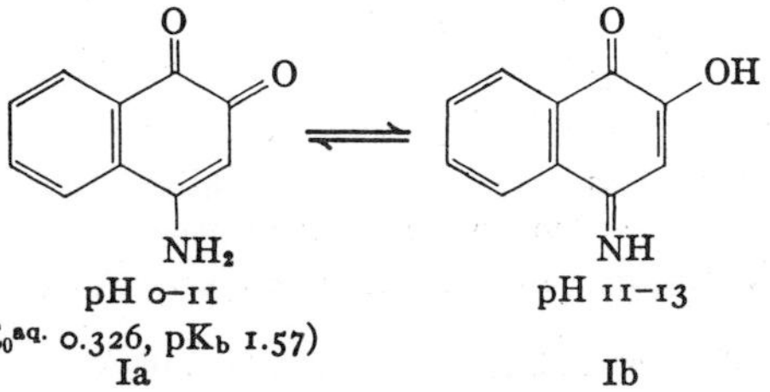

pH 0–11   pH 11–13
($E_0^{aq.}$ 0.326, pK$_b$ 1.57)
Ia   Ib

ent and the other an acidic group, and since the potential in a given solution is dependent on the nature and on the degree of ionization of functional groups of both the oxidant and the reductant, analysis of the variation of potential with hydrogen-ion concentration indicates which tautomer predominates. The substance exists exclusively in the aminoquinone form Ia in all pH regions except those of extreme alkalinity. Both tautomers participate in the equilibrium in a transition region (pH 10.4 to 11.5), but beyond this point the hydroxyquinonimine form Ib becomes the form of lower potential and hence the predominant tautomer. This tautomerism accounts for the fact that the substance dissolves freely in sodium hydroxide solution but, unlike hydroxynaphthoquinone, does not dissolve in sodium carbonate solution. The amino derivative of α-naphthoquinone, II, is found by potentiometric analysis to exist exclu-

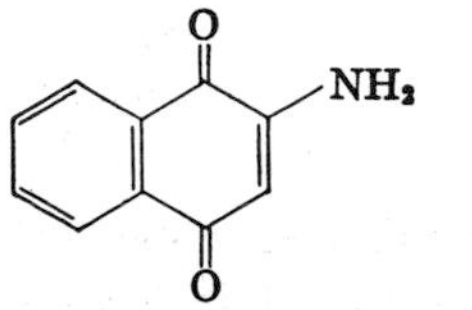

2-Amino-1,4-naphthoquinone, II
(red, m.p. 206°, E_0aq. 0.283 v., very weak base)

sively in the amino quinone form throughout the entire pH range; it does not dissolve even in strong alkali.

H. Musso found (1961) that in a given series, for example that of 1,4-benzoquinone and its methylated derivatives, the rate of catalytic hydrogenation over Pd—BaSO₄ in a given solvent, expressed as the logarithm of the half-time of reduction, is proportional to the oxidation-reduction potential.

In some cases the slope of a titration curve indicates that the oxidation or reduction involves two one-electron transfers (L. Michaelis,[1] 1931; B. Elema, Delft, 1931). The intermediate, known as a semiquinone, is characterized by its mag-

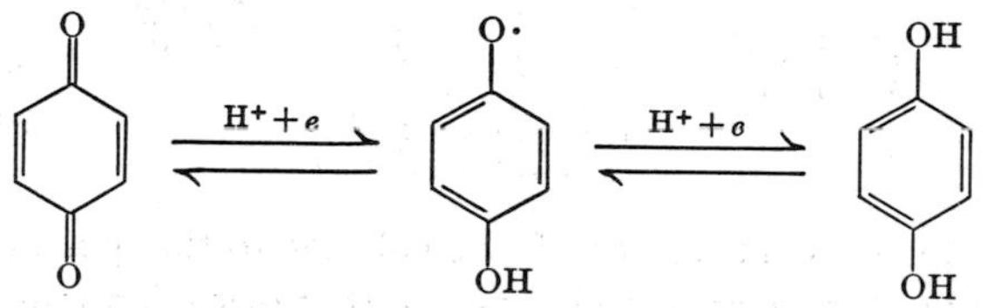

netic susceptibility as a radical containing an odd electron. The degree to which a reaction occurs as a one-electron transfer depends upon the pH, being favored in some cases by a low pH and in others by a high pH. The stability of the semiquinone depends upon the extent of resonance stabilization, and proof of the existence of such intermediates has been adduced with particularly stable radicals (22.21).

26.4   **Preparation.** — The general procedure for preparation of a quinone starts with a phenol or an amine, followed by introduction of either a hydroxyl or an amino group in an *ortho* or *para* position and oxidation of the intermediate in acid solution. The initial oxidation product of *p*-aminophenol, *p*-quinonimine, is extremely sensitive and has been isolated and characterized potentiometrically only by special techniques; even in an oxidation conducted at 0° in dilute acid solution, it is transient and undergoes hydrolysis to quinone.

---

[1] Leonor Michaelis, 1875–1949; b. Berlin, Germany; M.D. Berlin; Rockefeller Inst. Med. Res.

p-Phenylenediamine similarly is converted into quinone through the easily hydro-lyzed *p*-quinonediimine. The highly pigmented N-phenyl derivatives of quinoni-

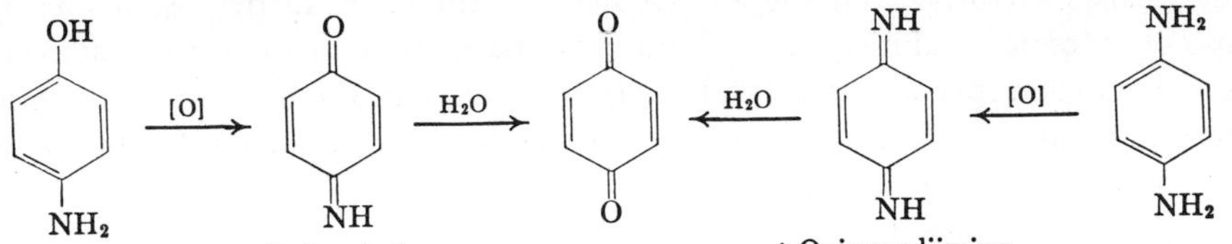

p-Quinonimine
($E_0^{alc.}$ 0.733 v.)

p-Quinonediimine
($E_0^{alc.}$ 0.783 v.)

mine and quinonediimine, indophenol and indamine, are relatively stable, crystal-lizable substances but they also can be hydrolyzed to quinone. One route to a bi-functional compound suitable for oxidation is illustrated by the preparation of β-naphthoquinone from β-naphthol. The naphthol is coupled in alkaline solution with diazotized sulfanilic acid, and the azo dye, Orange II, without being isolated is reduced with sodium hydrosulfite and the aminonaphthol is purified as the

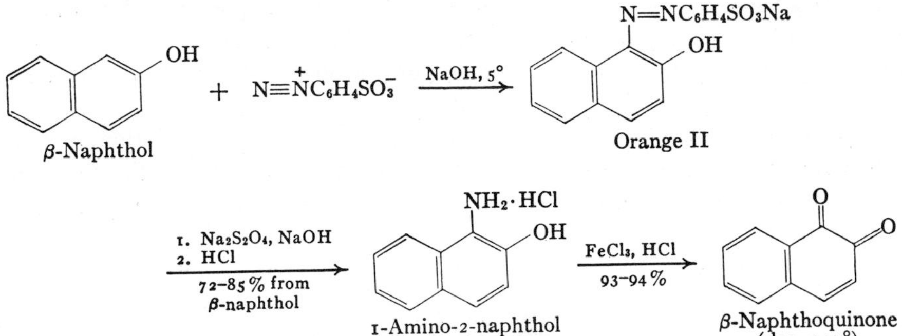

β-Naphthol

Orange II

1-Amino-2-naphthol
hydrochloride

β-Naphthoquinone
(dec. 147°)

hydrochloride, which is oxidized with ferric chloride to the quinone.

Some quinones are so reactive and sensitive that oxidation must be carried out under carefully controlled conditions. Investigators attempted without success to convert catechol into a quinone till Willstätter (1904), recognizing that *o*-benzo-quinone is extremely sensitive to water, devised a preparation that consists in oxi-dation in absolute ether solution with carefully dehydrated silver oxide in the presence of fused sodium sulfate to absorb the water formed:

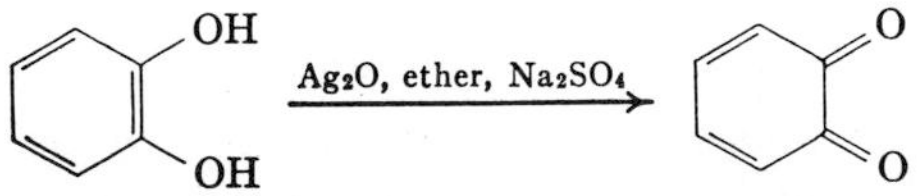

Diphenoquinone, stilbenequinone, and homostilbenequinone (red violet, m.p. >

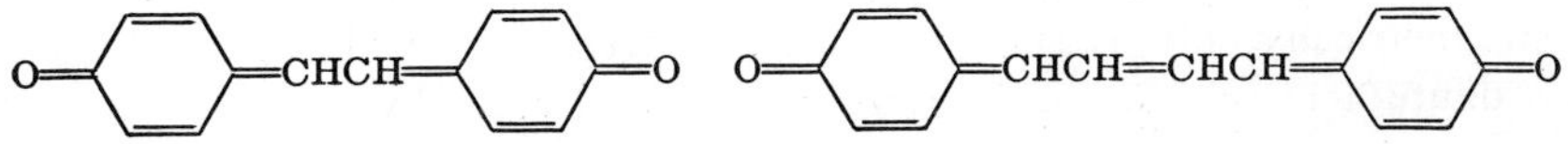

Stilbenequinone

Homostilbenequinone

400°; G. Dreyfahl, 1956) are all highly sensitive to moisture. β-Naphthoquinone is converted by strong mineral acid into a black dimer, and in weakly acidic aqueous solution it adds a mole of water.

2,3-Dichloro-1,4-naphthoquinone, used as a foliage fungicide, is made by chlorination of α-naphthoquinone. The starting material was formerly a by-product of the catalytic air oxidation of naphthalene to phthalic anhydride, but improvements in the process largely eliminated the by-product. Another catalyst (V_2O_4–V_2O_5) which gives naphthoquinone in improved yield is the basis of a process in which phthalic anhydride is the by-product.

Phenols can be oxidized to quinones, often in high yield, by means of potassium nitrosodisulfonate (H.-J. Teuber, 1952–54):

$$C_6H_5OH + 2(KSO_3)_2NO \rightarrow O{=}C_6H_4{=}O + (KSO_3)_2NOH + (KSO_3)_2NH$$

Phenol, 2,3-dimethylphenol, 2,3,5-trimethylphenol, and 2-hydroxydiphenyl give the corresponding p-quinones in yields of 75–88%. *Para* substituted phenols give *ortho* quinones: 3,4-dimethylphenol $\rightarrow$ 4,5-dimethyl-1,2-quinone (50%). 2,6-Xylenol is oxidized to m-xyloquinone in 77% yield by adding 85% hydrogen peroxide (10 ml.) all at once to a mixture of the phenol (10 g.) and trifluoroacetic acid (10 g.) in methylene chloride (50 ml.) at room temperature (R. D. Chambers, 1959). The trifluoroperacetic acid initially formed furnishes the strongly electrophilic OH^+; p-hydroxylation is followed by further oxidation of the hydroquinone.

One of two synthetic methods described by F. Weygand (1942, 1954) is illustrated by the reaction of o-phthalaldehyde with the glyoxal bisulfite addition product and potassium cyanide and sodium carbonate in aqueous dioxane to give isonaphthazarin. The other involves oxidation of an o-diacylbenzene with selenium dioxide in aqueous isopropanol, with formation of a 2-hydroxy-3-alkyl-1,4-naphthoquinone.

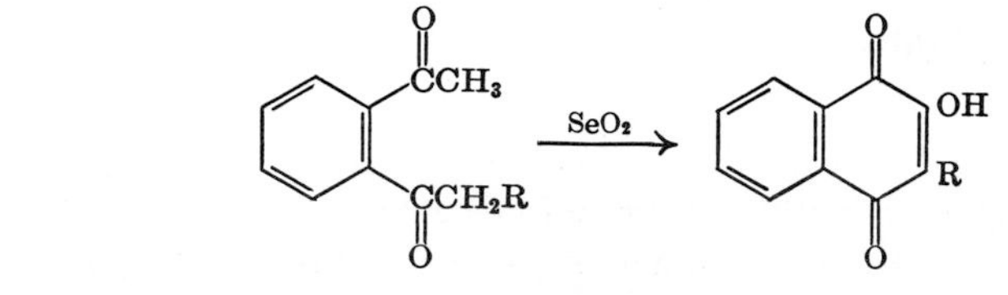

Isonaphthazarin

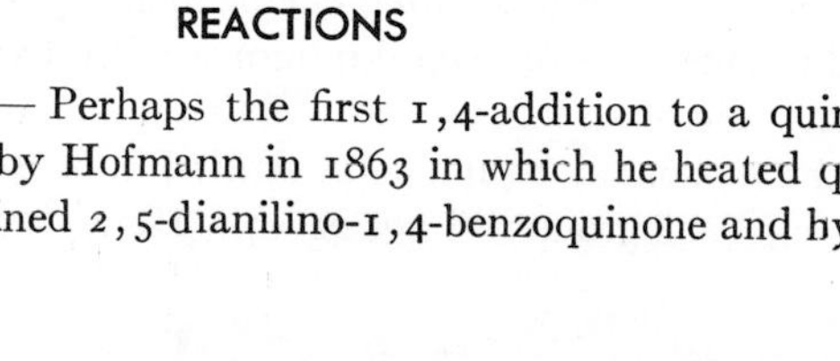

REACTIONS

26.5 **1,4-Additions.** — Perhaps the first 1,4-addition to a quinone was in an experiment by Hofmann in 1863 in which he heated quinone with aniline in alcohol and obtained 2,5-dianilino-1,4-benzoquinone and hydroquinone and thereby demonstrated that the addition is attended with oxidation-reduction equilibration of product with starting material. Aniline reacts with α-naphtho-

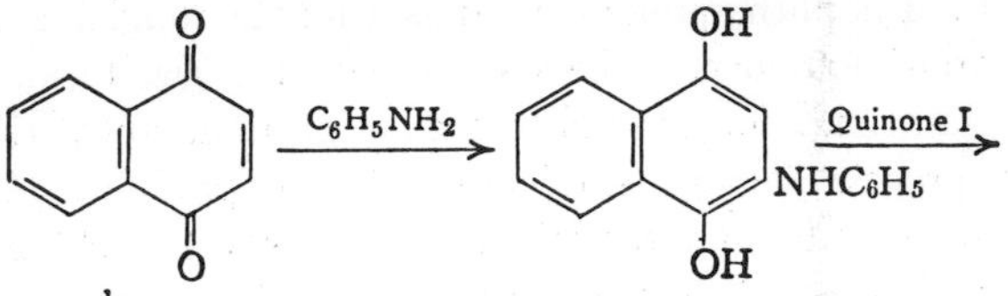

I, $E_o^{alc.}$ 0.484v.   II

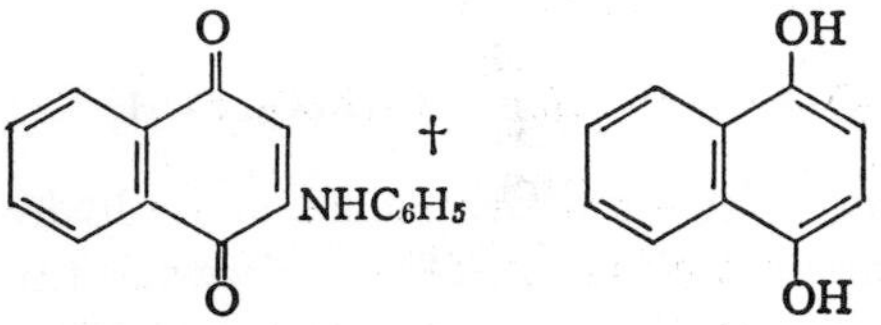

III, $E_o^{alc.}$ 0.286v.   IV

quinone (I) in alcoholic solution with prompt separation of red needles of 2-anilino-1,4-naphthoquinone (III), formed by oxidation of the initial product II by I. The potential of the substituted quinone is so far below that of the starting material that the reaction is practically complete; hence two moles of I are required to produce one of III. In bisulfite addition, the group introduced raises the potential and oxidation of the substituted product does not occur. The reaction is applicable to nitrosophenols, in equilibrium with quinone oximes, as in the standard preparation of 1,2-naphthoquinone-4-sulfonate. On oxidation of the amino-

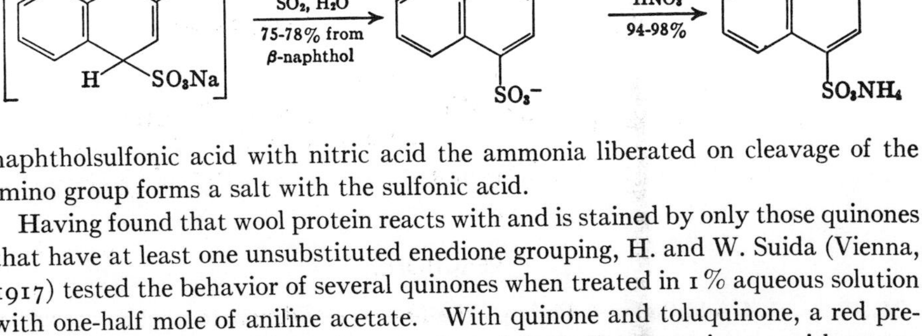

naphtholsulfonic acid with nitric acid the ammonia liberated on cleavage of the imino group forms a salt with the sulfonic acid.

Having found that wool protein reacts with and is stained by only those quinones that have at least one unsubstituted enedione grouping, H. and W. Suida (Vienna, 1917) tested the behavior of several quinones when treated in 1% aqueous solution with one-half mole of aniline acetate. With quinone and toluquinone, a red precipitate of the monoanilinoquinone separated immediately; quinones with no unsubstituted enedione group did not react. Hofmann's experiment illustrates the usual orientation in additions: the initially formed anilinoquinone reacts further to give the 2,5-dianilino compound. The reaction probably is a nucleophilic addition, as formulated. Quinone reacts similarly with methanol or ethanol in

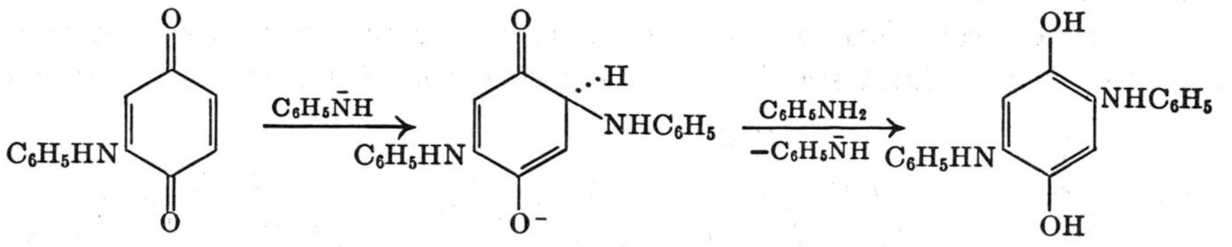

the presence of zinc chloride to give the 2,5-dialkoxyquinones and hydroquinone. 2-Chloro-1,4-benzoquinone reacts with dry hydrogen chloride in ether to give mixtures from which 2,3-, 2,5-, and 2,6-dichloroquinone have been isolated. Thiele and Meisenheimer (1900) found that quinone does not react with preformed hydro-

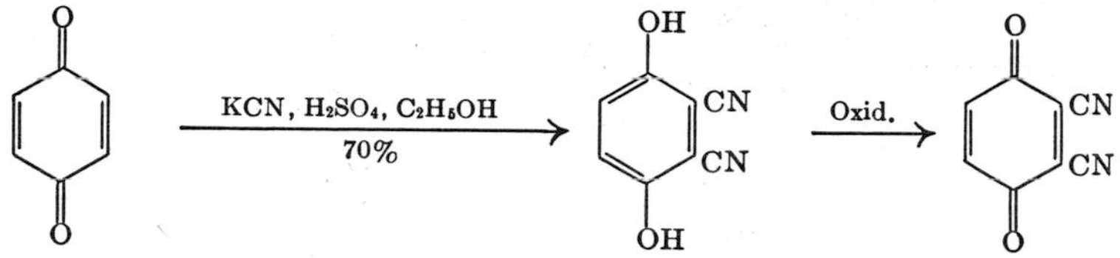

E_0 0.971v.

gen cyanide but that on addition of aqueous potassium cyanide solution to a solution of quinone and a little sulfuric acid in ethanol the color changes from brown to a fluorescent green and the product is 2,3-dicyanohydroquinone, as established by hydrolysis to 3,6-dihydroxyphthalimide (dil. H_2SO_4, 15 min.) and conversion of this substance to 2,5-dihydroxybenzoic acid (20% HCl, prolonged refluxing).

The **Thiele reaction** (1898), in which acetic anhydride is added to a quinone under catalysis by sulfuric acid or boron fluoride etherate with formation of the hydroxyhydroquinone triacetate, affords a route to hydroxyquinones. Thus the

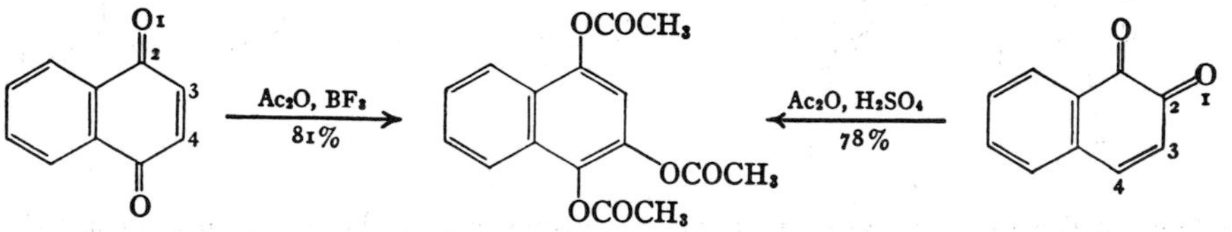

2-Hydroxy-1,4-naphthohydroquinone
triacetate (m.p. 136°)

common product from α- and β-naphthoquinone on alkaline hydrolysis and air oxidation gives 2-hydroxy-1,4-naphthoquinone. The Thiele reaction is blocked by a 2-methyl group in the *para* naphthoquinone but not by a 3-methyl group in the *ortho* isomer. In the benzoquinone series a 2-methoxyl or 2-methyl group directs the entering acetoxyl group to the 5-position. 2,6-Dimethyl-1,4-benzoquinone adds acetic anhydride in the presence of sulfuric acid as catalyst but not under the influence of boron fluoride etherate; the 2,5-dimethyl isomer is more reactive since it undergoes the Thiele reaction in the presence of the evidently less potent boron fluoride. Even with sulfuric acid as catalyst, no reaction occurs with 2,5- or 2,6-dimethoxy-1,4-benzoquinone or with the 2,6-dichloro or 2,3,5-trimethyl derivatives.

A possible mechanism for the reaction of toluquinone is protonation of the C_1-carbonyl group (2), formation of the carbonium ion (3), attack by acetate ion

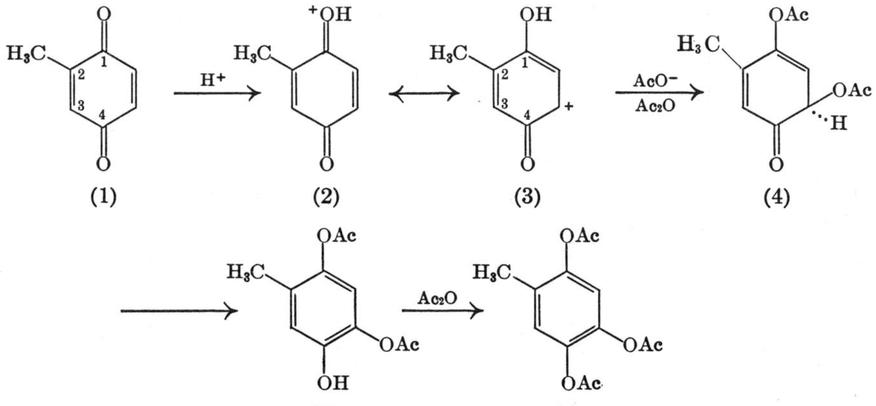

(1)   (2)   (3)   (4)

(5)   (6)

(4), and aromatization (5). The carbonium ion (3) is destabilized by the presence of a positively polarized carbonyl carbon adjacent to the carbon atom bearing the charge, but the 2-methyl group on a carbon atom conjugated with the carbonyl group tends by induction to decrease the polarization at C_4. Since a methyl group at C_3 instead of at C_2 would not similarly assist the reaction, the production of the 2,5-product is accounted for. 2,5-Dimethyl-1,4-benzoquinone can react via the ion (7), whereas with the less reactive 2,6-isomer the combined inductive

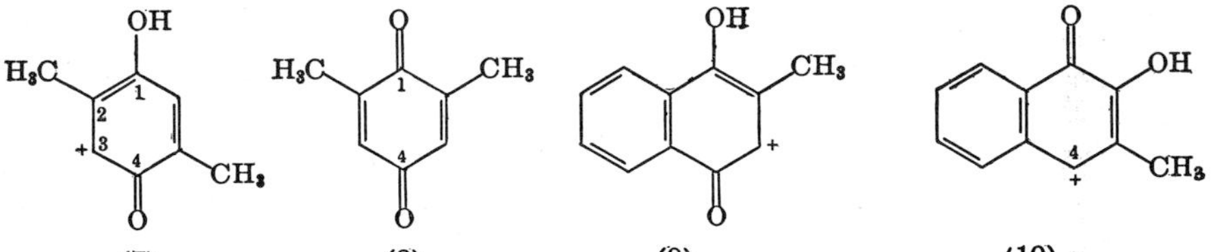

(7)   (8)   (9)   (10)

effects of the two methyl groups favor protonation of the 4-carbonyl group (8); the derived carbonium ion is sterically shielded from attack by a methyl group. In the 2,5-dimethoxy analog of (7) the reactivity is greatly decreased by stabilization of the charge by the methoxyl groups. That 2-methyl-1,4-naphthoquinone does not enter into the Thiele reaction is attributable to steric hindrance by the methyl group in the ion (9). In the ion (10) from 3-methyl-1,2-naphthoquinone, position 4 is also hindered, but a compensating feature of the structure is the separation of the charged carbon from the polarized carbonyl group.

1,4-Additions to benzo- and naphthoquinones occur with a number of other reagents of the HA type, including hydrogen cyanide, mercaptans, benzenesulfinic acid, benzene in the presence of aluminum chloride, malonic ester, cyanoacetic ester, and acetoacetic ester.   Grignard reagents react with substituted and un-substituted quinones to give mixtures of products of 1,4-addition, of addition to the carbonyl group, and of reduction.   A special case is the reaction with hydra-zoic acid (HN$_3$); an initial addition is followed by intramolecular oxidation-reduc-tion, with transference of the hydroquinone hydrogen atoms to the azido group, which suffers reductive cleavage:

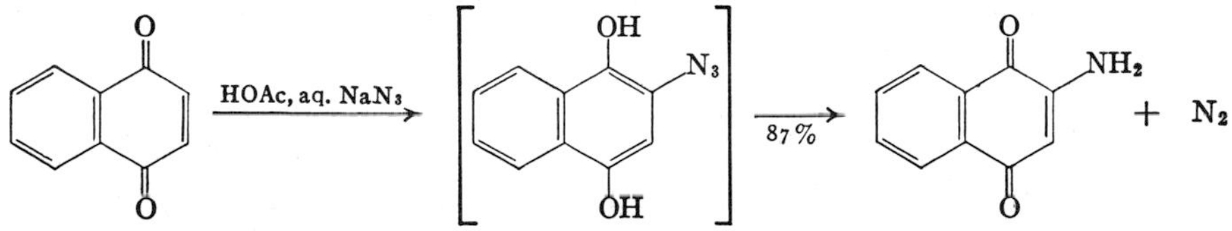

The reaction of the silver salt of 2-hydroxy-1,4-naphthoquinone with alkyl halides affords a 4-alkoxy-1,2-naphthoquinone along with the product of normal replacement (reaction of an ambident anion at the two possible sites).   The iso-mers are easily separated by extraction of the *ortho* quinone ether with aqueous

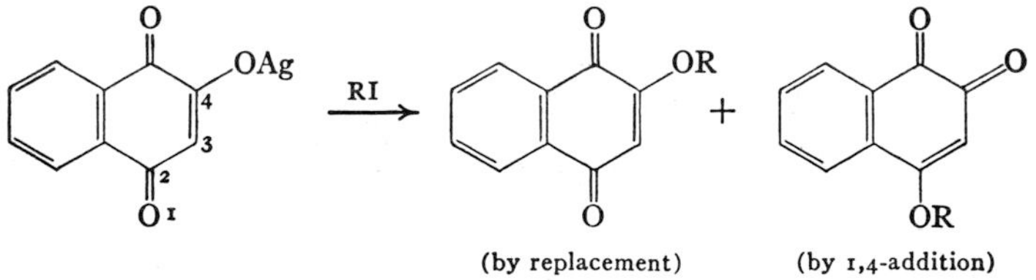

(by replacement)   (by 1,4-addition)

sodium bisulfite, which dissolves the substance as a labile addition complex that subsequently can be decomposed with acid or with sodium carbonate; the *para* quinone reacts with bisulfite only to a minor extent.   Hydroxynaphthoquinone is a stronger acid (pK$_a$ 4.0) than acetic acid and is readily esterified by the Fischer method.   The more stable methyl and ethyl *p*-quinone esters are the exclusive products and have the properties of esters.

Mercaptans react with quinones by addition and oxidation-reduction equi-librium to give thio-substituted quinones, and all free positions in the quinonoid ring are attacked.   Thus toluquinone reacts with thioglycolic acid (HSCH$_2$CO$_2$H) to give the trithioacetic acid derivative.   The reduced form of glutathione, GSH, adds readily in the same way.   The product is a conjugated tripeptide that differs

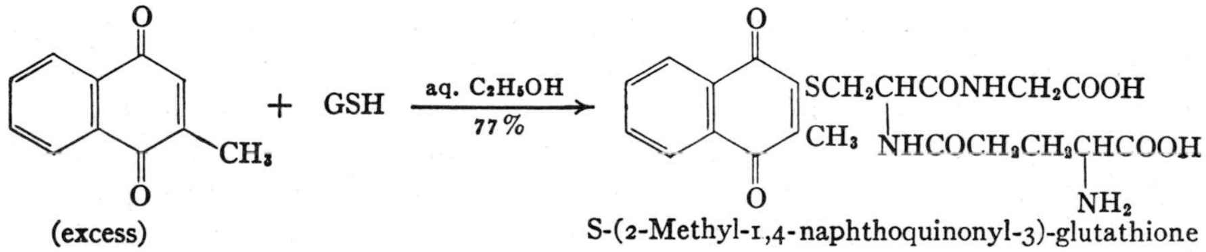

S-(2-Methyl-1,4-naphthoquinonyl-3)-glutathione

from glutathione in having in place of the sulfhydryl-disulfide system a quinonoid group capable of establishing an oxidoreduction system.   Proteins containing free sulfhydryl groups likewise form conjugates with methylnaphthoquinone, as established by the appearance of characteristic ultraviolet absorption bands that persist after repeated purification by precipitation with ammonium sulfate.

26.6   Displacements. — Nucleophilic displacements are exemplified by the behavior of chloranil, or tetrachloro-1,4-benzoquinone (m.p. 290°). In a technical process chloranil is obtained in 60% yield by passing chlorine into a stirred mixture of phenol and concentrated hydrochloric acid to produce 2,4,6-trichlorophenol; concentrated nitric acid then effects oxidation and further chlorination. Chloranil dissolves in aqueous alkali with a red color and acidification

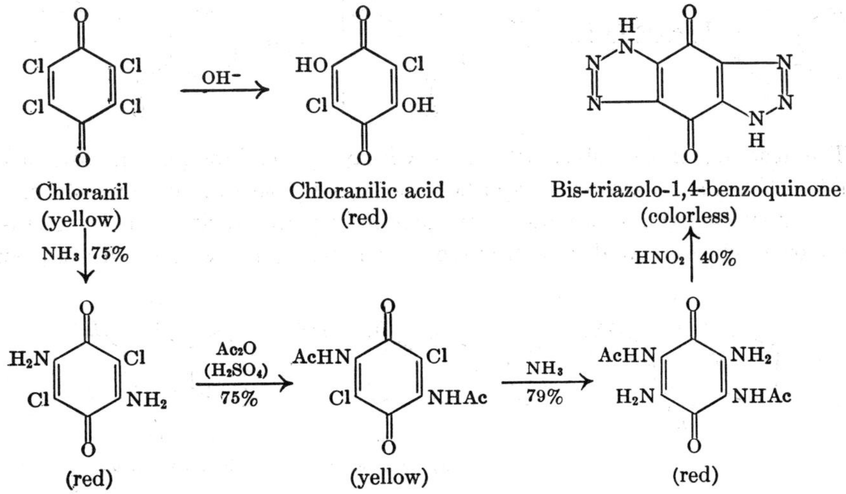

Chloranil   Chloranilic acid   Bis-triazolo-1,4-benzoquinone
(yellow)   (red)   (colorless)

NH₃ 75%   HNO₂ 40%

(red)   (yellow)   (red)

precipitates chloranilic acid. When dry ammonia is passed into a suspension of chloranil in boiling ethanol, the yellow crystals soon give place to deep red needles of 2,5-diamino-3,6-dichloro-1,4-benzoquinone. The two halogen atoms in this substance resist further displacement under forcing conditions, but displacement can be effected if the amino groups are first acetylated. Treatment of the resulting tetraaminoquinone diacetate with sodium nitrite in acetic acid gives bis-triazolo-1,4-benzoquinone monosodium salt (E. L. Martin, 1935). The quinone itself is colorless (!) and gives a yellow vat with alkaline sodium hydrosulfite.

Fluoranil (m.p. 179°) has been obtained in 25% yield by subliming chloranil from a mixture with calcium fluoride over potassium fluoride at 350° in a nitrogen atmosphere (K. Wallenfels,[1] 1957–60). The substance is very sensitive to hydroxylic solvents and is generally much more readily attacked by nucleophilic reagents than chloranil. Thus all four halogen atoms are replaceable by amino groups. The reaction with a primary or secondary amine can be controlled to give the 2,5-diamine which, on reaction with the same amine or with a different one, can be converted into a tetraamine. Tetraaminobenzoquinone is prepared most conveniently by reaction of fluoranil with potassium phthalimide and cleavage of the product with hydrazine. When chloranil is heated with anhydrous potas-

[1] Kurt Wallenfels, b. 1910 Marburg an der Lahn; Ph.D. Graz (A. Soltys); KWI Heidelberg; Univ. Freiburg

sium fluoride in methanol, the solution remains neutral and the product is 2,5-dichloro-3,6-dimethoxy-1,4-benzoquinone (formation of KCl and sparingly dissociated HF). Addition to a suspension of fluoranil in dioxane–water of $N/50$ sodium hydroxide affords trifluorohydroxybenzoquinone in 50% yield; when 4 N alkali is used the product is fluoranilic acid (57%). These nucleophilic displacements doubtless proceed through aronium-like anions, since an oxygen atom is

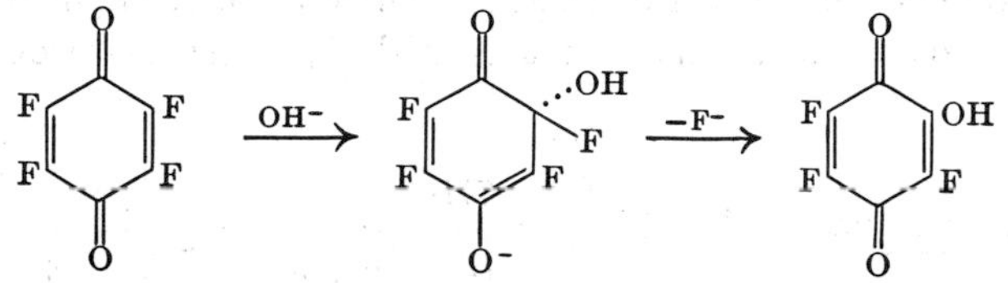

available for acceptance of the charge. A similar process accounts for the ready reaction of ammonium 1,2-naphthoquinone-4-sulfonate with aniline with displacement of the sulfonate group. The conversion of the sulfonate to 2-hydroxy-1,4-

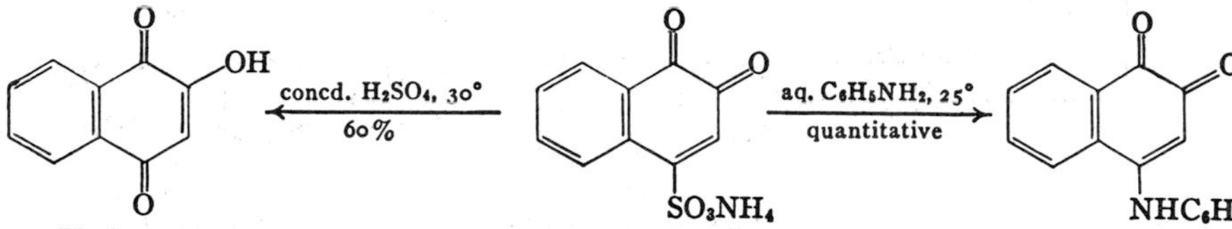

2-Hydroxy-1,4-naphthoquinone

concd. H_2SO_4, 30°
60%

aq. $C_6H_5NH_2$, 25°
quantitative

4-Anilino-1,2-naphthoquinone (red, dec. 260°)

naphthoquinone by reaction with sulfuric acid probably involves initial protonation and conversion to an aronium complex.

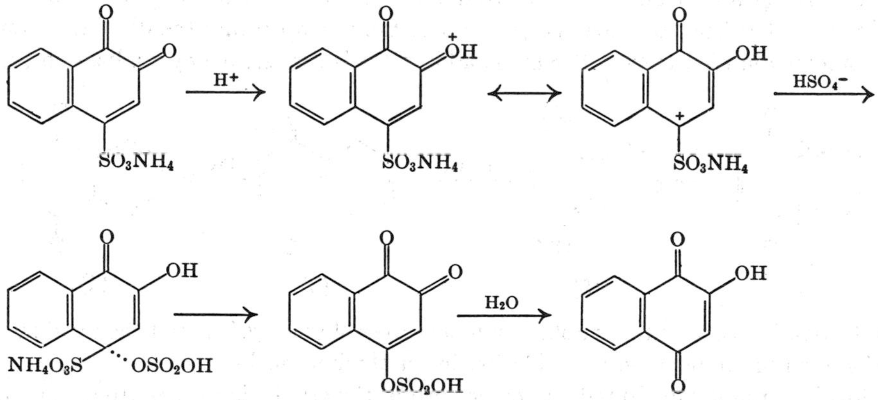

Cyananil (tetracyano-1,4-benzoquinone) is not available by the action of potassium cyanide on chloranil for the reaction stops with production of 2,3-dicyano-4,6-dichlorohydroquinone, as the potassium salt, and the halogen atoms of the corresponding quinone can not be displaced by cyano groups. Wallenfels (1961) synthesized cyananil hydroquinone from diethyl 2,5-dimethoxy-3,6-dibromo-terephthalate and oxidized it with oxides of nitrogen to the bright yellow, sparingly soluble quinone. The substance is a powerful oxidizing agent, for example, it attacks solvents such as ethanol and tetralin. It apparently is a stronger π-acid than tetracyanoethylene for it forms more deeply colored complexes with aromatic π-bases: benzene (deep red), xylene (violet), pyrene (blue-green).

26.7   Ethylenic Additions. — Methylnaphthoquinone forms a crystalline dibromide from which hydrogen bromide is easily eliminated with production of a bromoquinone, and it reacts with hydrogen peroxide under basic

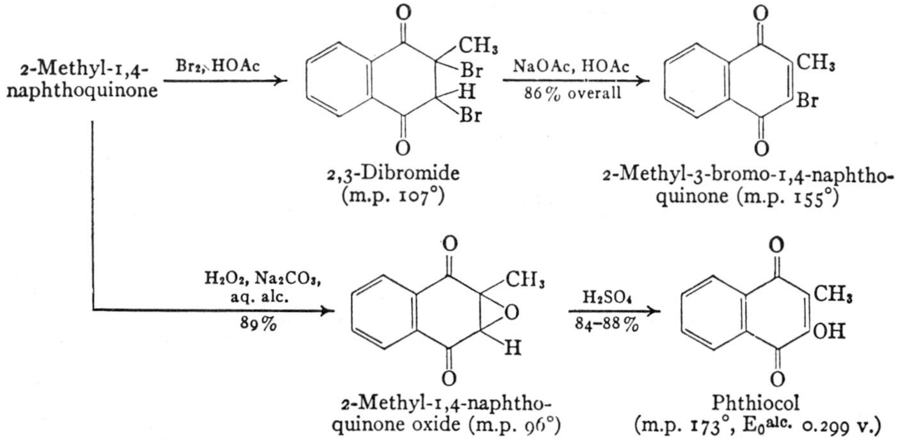

2-Methyl-1,4-naphthoquinone $\xrightarrow{\text{Br}_2,\ \text{HOAc}}$

2,3-Dibromide
(m.p. 107°)

$\xrightarrow[\text{86\% overall}]{\text{NaOAc, HOAc}}$

2-Methyl-3-bromo-1,4-naphthoquinone (m.p. 155°)

$\xrightarrow[\text{89\%}]{\text{H}_2\text{O}_2,\ \text{Na}_2\text{CO}_3,\ \text{aq. alc.}}$

2-Methyl-1,4-naphthoquinone oxide (m.p. 96°)

$\xrightarrow[\text{84–88\%}]{\text{H}_2\text{SO}_4}$

Phthiocol
(m.p. 173°, $E_0^{\text{alc.}}$ 0.299 v.)

catalysis to give an oxide. The oxide ring is easily opened by the action of concentrated sulfuric acid in the cold, and hence combination of the two reactions constitutes an efficient synthesis of phthiocol.

The Diels-Alder reaction of p-benzoquinone with butadiene to give the mono adduct (1) has been described (5.37); at a suitable temperature the di adduct can be prepared in high yield. The mono adduct (1) is convertible by enolization (2)

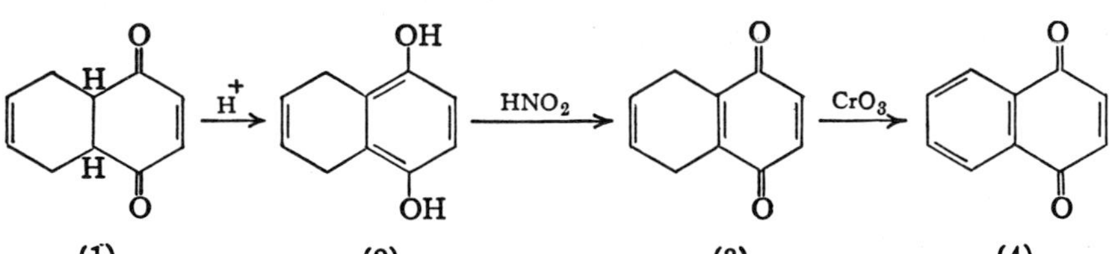

(1)   (2)   (3)   (4)

and oxidation (3, 4) into α-naphthoquinone (overall yield 76%), and the di adduct affords anthraquinone on air oxidation in an alkaline medium.

Methyl groups substituted on one or both of the ethylenic carbon atoms do not stop the reaction but necessitate a slight increase in the reaction temperature (A. M. Seligman,[1] 1934). Halogen substituents likewise fail to interfere with addition of a diene, and in the β-naphthoquinone series such substitution stabilizes the otherwise sensitive quinone ring (J. T. Dunn,[2] 1937). Thus 3-chloro-1,2-

[1] Arnold M. Seligman, b. 1912 St. Johnsbury, Vt.; M.D. Harvard; Sinai Hospital, Baltimore
[2] Jesse T. Dunn, b. 1910 Foraker, Okla.; Ph.D. Harvard (Fieser); Union Carbide Chemicals Co.

naphthoquinone can be employed in a Diels-Alder reaction, whereas the parent quinone is destroyed. The electron-attracting character of the halogen atom helps offset steric inhibition of addition. The powerfully electron-attracting substitu-

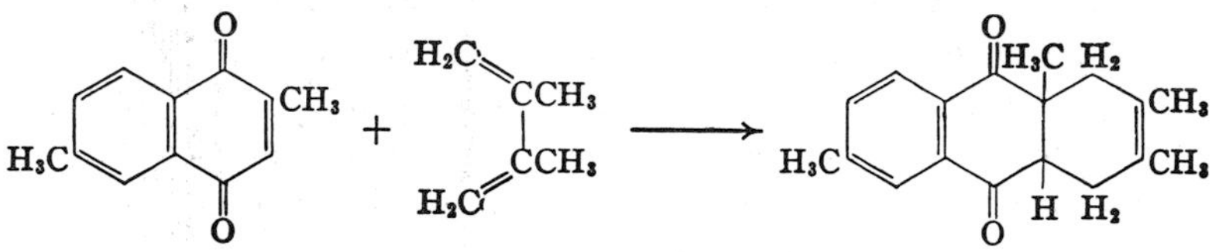

(colorless, m.p. 77°)

ents of 2,3-dicyano-1,4-benzoquinone so enhance the dienophilic character of the double bond to which they are attached that the diene 1'-acetoxyvinylcyclohexene (I) adds exclusively to the disubstituted enedione system of the quinone (II) to

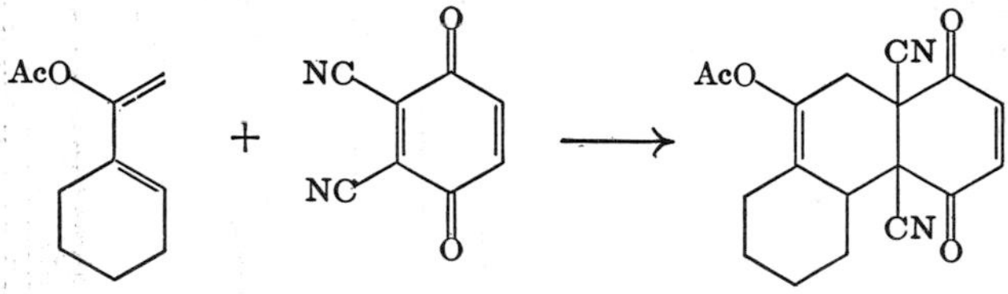

I   II   III

give the adduct III (M. F. Ansell, 1960). The dicyanoquinone is probably intermediate in strength as a π-acid between p-benzoquinone and tetracyanoethylene.

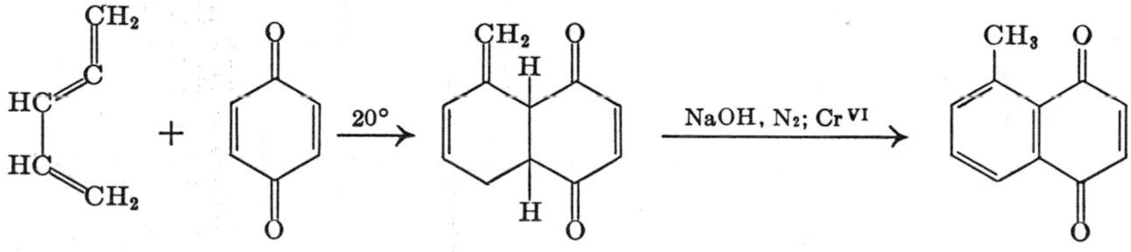

A novel synthesis of 5-methyl-1,4-naphthoquinone utilizes $\Delta^{1,2,4}$-pentatriene, a

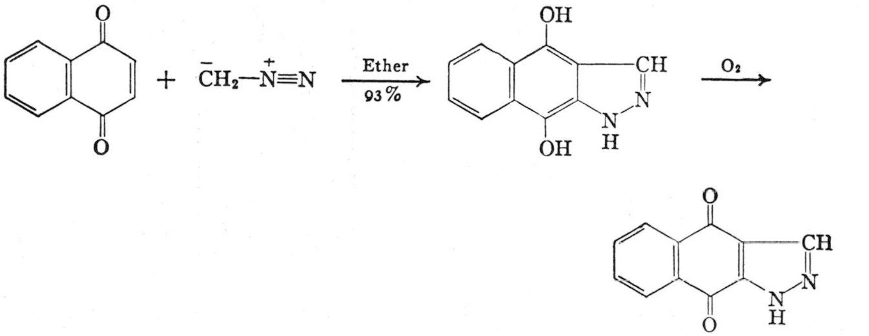

lin-Naphthindazole-4,9-quinone
(m.p. 349°, $E_0^{alc.}$ 0.154 v.)

readily available allene (E. R. H. Jones, 1960). Examples of the use of Diels-Alder reactions of quinones in synthesis have been cited (15.35).

Additions occur with unsaturated nitrogen compounds of the diazoalkane and aryl azide types. Diazomethane reacts with α-naphthoquinone to give a hydroquinone (alkali-soluble), which in the course of recrystallization is oxidized by air to the quinone (M. Fieser, 1931). The resulting product, *lin*-naphthindazole-4,9-quinone, has a potential practically identical with that of anthraquinone, which is evidence that the heterocyclic pyrazole ring is comparable in aromaticity to the benzene ring. Similar additions occur with phenyl azide and methyl azide to give further analogs of anthraquinone, obtained in either the oxidized or reduced form. Diphenyldiazomethane, prepared by oxidation of benzophenone

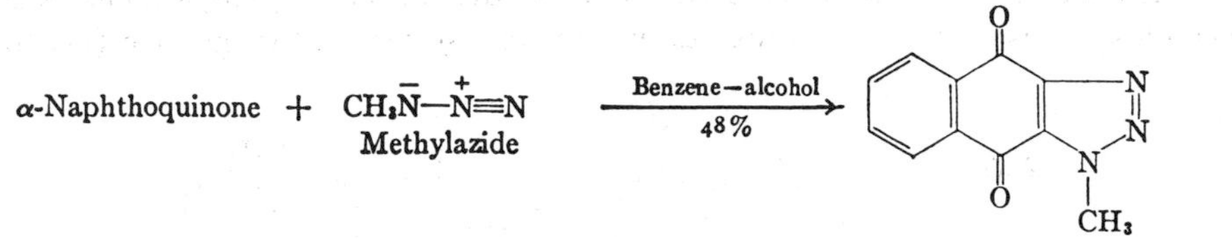

α-Naphthoquinone + CH₃N̄—N⁺≡N $\xrightarrow[\text{48\%}]{\text{Benzene—alcohol}}$
Methylazide

1-Methyl-*lin*-naphthotriazole-4,9-quinone (m.p. 250°, $E_0^{alc.}$ 0.256 v.)

hydrazone with mercuric oxide in petroleum ether, adds to α-naphthoquinone in the same manner to give a substituted hydroquinone. *o*-Quinones react with diphenyldiazomethane differently, for nitrogen is evolved and the quinone is converted into a methylene ether derivative of its hydroquinone (J. L. Hartwell,[1] 1935). Presumably diphenylcarbene is the reactive species.

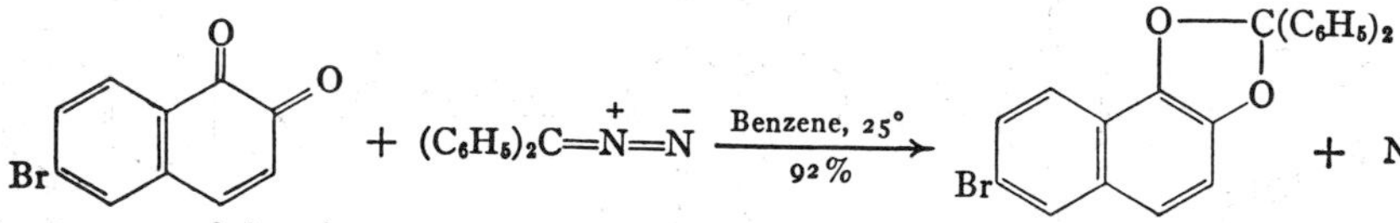

+ (C₆H₅)₂C=N⁺=N̄ $\xrightarrow[\text{92\%}]{\text{Benzene, 25°}}$ + N₂

6-Bromo-1,2-naphthoquinone
(orange-red, dec. 168°)

(colorless, m.p. 151°)

26.8   Substitutions. — In view of the sensitivity of quinones, it is not surprising that aromatic substitution reactions are applicable only rarely. The nitration of β-naphthoquinone is particularly remarkable because this quinone cannot be recrystallized without undergoing some decomposition and because in

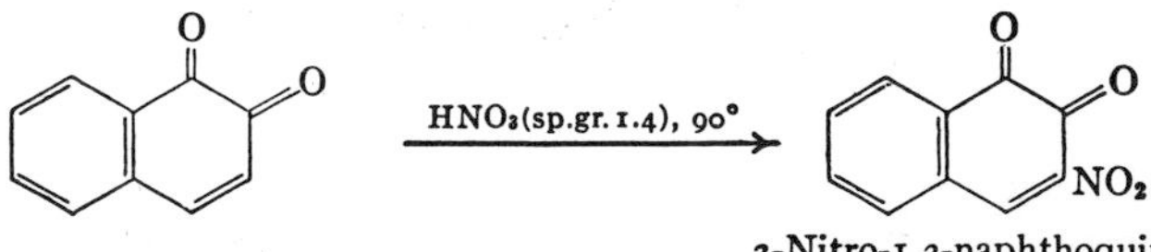

$\xrightarrow{\text{HNO}_3(\text{sp.gr. 1.4), 90°}}$

3-Nitro-1,2-naphthoquinone
(red, m.p. 158°)

aqueous solutions of hydrochloric or sulfuric acid it is converted into products of

---

[1] Jonathan L. Hartwell, b. 1906 Boston; Ph.D. Harvard (Fieser); National Cancer Inst.

dimerization and hydration, depending on the concentration. β-Naphthoquinone also can be brominated in the 3-position (67% yield). Addition rather than substitution of halogen occurs in the *para* quinone series.

Arylation of *p*-benzoquinone with benzenediazonium chloride in aqueous alcoholic solution weakly acidified with acetic acid had been demonstrated prior to Meerwein's generalization of the reaction (21.28). This free radical reaction af-

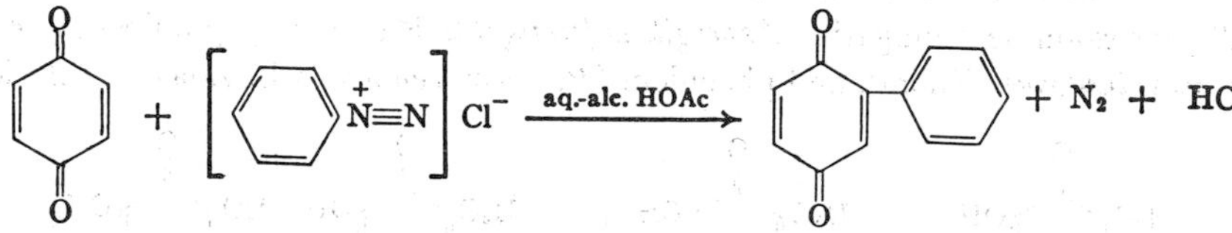

2-Phenyl-1,4-benzoquinone
(m.p. 114°, $E_0^{alc.}$ 0.694 v.)

fords, in succession, phenyl-, 2,5-diphenyl-, and triphenylquinone.

Another reaction that apparently proceeds by a free-radical mechanism is alkylation of the quinone ring with either an acyl peroxide or a lead tetraacylate (Fieser *et al.*, 1942). When a solution of 2-methyl-1,4-naphthoquinone in acetic acid is warmed with slightly more than one equivalent of acetyl peroxide or with 3–4 equivalents of lead tetraacetate, a brisk reaction ensues with evolution of gas, and the starting material is converted into the 2,3-dimethyl compound. In the

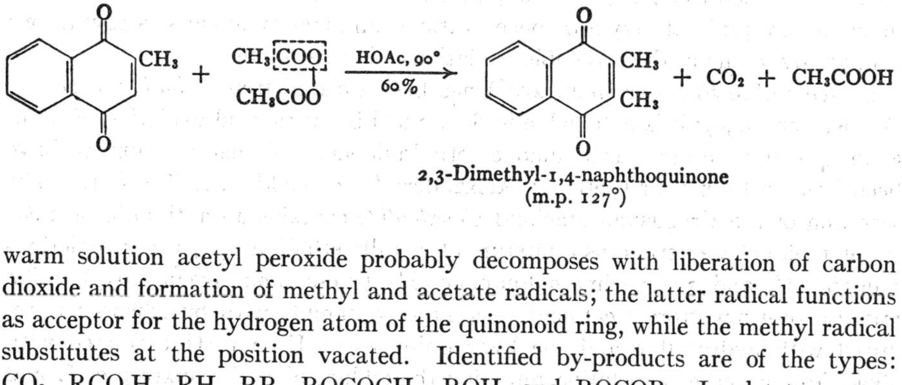

2,3-Dimethyl-1,4-naphthoquinone
(m.p. 127°)

warm solution acetyl peroxide probably decomposes with liberation of carbon dioxide and formation of methyl and acetate radicals; the latter radical functions as acceptor for the hydrogen atom of the quinonoid ring, while the methyl radical substitutes at the position vacated. Identified by-products are of the types: CO_2, RCO_2H, RH, RR, $ROCOCH_3$, ROH, and $ROCOR$. Lead tetraacetate perhaps undergoes decomposition in large part to the same reactive species:

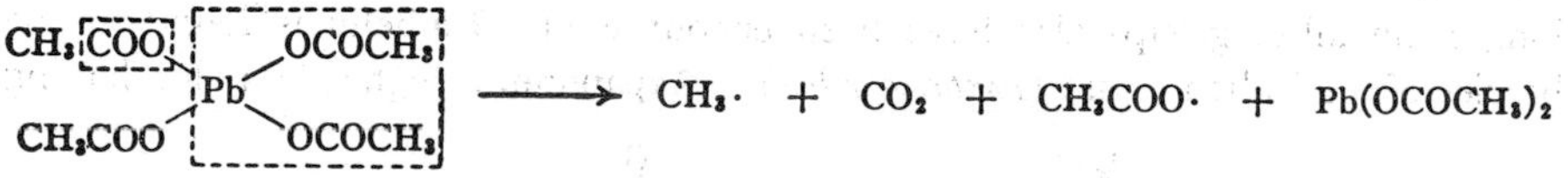

NATURALLY OCCURRING QUINONES

A considerable number of pigments characterized as quinones have been isolated from high and lower plants, and a few members of the series have been found in animal organisms. Some are dyes, some are growth factors, some are antibiotics, some catalyze respiratory processes, and some are respiration inhibitors. Although the following discussion is limited to benzo-, naphtho-, and phenanthrenequinones, many anthraquinones are produced by molds, and pigments from aphids have been characterized as perylenequinones.

26.9   Benzoquinones. — A number of mold pigments have been characterized as benzoquinones or dibenzoquinones (H. Raistrick, A. Oxford, 1938), for example, fumigatin (*Aspergillus fumigatus* Fresenius), spinulosin (*Penicillium spinulosum* Thom), and phoenicin (*P. phoeniceum* van Beyma). Isolation

Fumigatin   Spinulosin   Phoenicin
(brown, m.p. 116°)   (purple-bronze, m.p. 203°)   (yellow-brown, m.p. 231°)

of fumigatin hydroquinone along with the pigment under conditions indicative of the presence of both substances in the growing mold is regarded as an indication that the oxidation-reduction system functions in the metabolism of the organism. Spinulosin has been prepared from fumigatin by Thiele addition of acetic anhydride, hydrolysis of the resulting tetraacetate, and oxidation. Phoenicin increases the respiration of washed unpigmented cells of *Bacillus pyocyaneus* by as much as 200–300% at very low concentrations, and may function as a respiratory catalyst by virtue of the reversible oxidation-reduction system.

2,6-Dimethoxyquinone (m.p. 250°) has been isolated from *Adonis vernalis* L. (W. Karrer, 1930); it is obtainable in 80% yield by nitric acid oxidation of pyrogallol trimethyl ether. Toluquinone, ethylquinone, and methoxyquinone have been isolated from flour beetle (P. Alexander; A. R. Todd, J. R. Loconti). The secretion of the Uruguayan arachnid *Gonyleptide* contains an antibiotic pigment (C. Estable) characterized as a mixture of 2,3-dimethylquinone, I, 2,5-dimethylquinone, II, and 2,3,5-trimethylquinone, III (Fieser and Ardao, 1955). The mixture resulting from treatment of a 115-mg. sample with butadiene was reduced with hydrosulfite and the hydroquinones of II and III extracted with alkali from an ethereal solution retaining the adduct of I; the mixture of II and III on Thiele reaction (BF₃) and steam distillation afforded III in the distillate and the Thiele product from II in the residue. Hydroxybenzoquinones with long-chain alkyl groups also have been encountered. **Embelin** is found in the berries of an Indian shrub (*Embelia ribes*). **Rapanone,** a higher homolog having

Embelin   Rapanone
(orange-yellow, m.p. 142°)   (orange-yellow, m.p. 140°)

two additional methylene groups in the alkyl chain, occurs in *Rapanea Maximowiczii* and in *Oxalis purpurata* Jacq. Both have been synthesized by peroxide alkylation of 2,5-dihydroxyquinone. *p*-Benzoquinone itself has been isolated from two insect species (E. Lederer, 1957). An optically active antibiotic, **terreic acid,** has been identified as 2,3-epoxy-5-hydroxy-6-methyl-1,4-benzoquinone (J. C. Sheehan, 1958).

The pigment **perezone,** isolated from the root of various Mexican species of *Perezonia* in yields up to 3.6%, is a *p*-benzoquinone having a methyl, a hydroxyl, and a branched-chain unsaturated C$_8$-group (Kögl,[1] 1935). The structure is

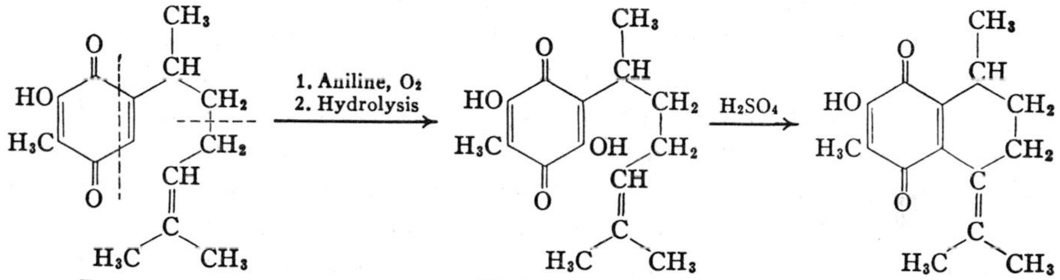

Perezone
(orange, m.p. 103°,
$[\alpha]_D^{20°} - 17°)$

Hydroxyperezone
(m.p. 130°)

Perezinone
(m.p. 145°)

divisible into isoprene units, as shown by the dotted lines, and it is thus a quinone of the sesquiterpene series. The free position in the quinone ring can be hydroxylated by formation and hydrolysis of the anilino derivative, and the hydroxy compound undergoes cyclodehydration under the influence of sulfuric acid to give perezinone.

26.10   **Fungus Pigments.** — The metabolism of parasitic fungi is fundamentally different from that of assimilating plants and the fungus pigments constitute a rather distinct chemical class. **Polyporic acid,** shown by degradation (Kögl, 1926) and synthesis (R. Adams, 1931) to be the 3,6-dihydroxy derivative of the diphenylquinone, has been extracted in yields as high as 18% of the dry weight of a fungus (*Polyporus nidulans* Pers.) found growing on diseased oak trees. Screening of New Zealand flora for antitumor agents revealed the fact that polyporic acid possesses this activity (B. F. Cain, 1961). **Atromentin,** a dihydroxy derivative of polyporic acid, is found in a fungus growing

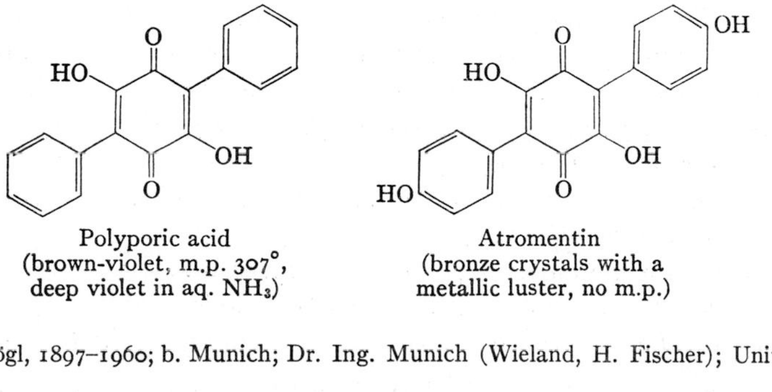

Polyporic acid
(brown-violet, m.p. 307°,
deep violet in aq. NH$_3$)

Atromentin
(bronze crystals with a
metallic luster, no m.p.)

[1] Fritz Kögl, 1897–1960; b. Munich; Dr. Ing. Munich (Wieland, H. Fischer); Univ. Utrecht, Netherlands

on old oak trunks (Kögl). More material is obtained by direct solvent extraction from the highly pigmented fungus collected in the autumn than from the superficially colored fresh fungus. The latter contains substantially the same total amount of material (2%) but the bulk of pigment is present in the reduced, or leuco, form. **Leucomelone,** isolated by M. Akagi (1941) from a black edible mushroom found in Japanese pine wood, differs from atromentin in having an additional hydroxyl group in the *meta* position of one of the phenyl groups. **Volucrisporin,** a new fungal pigment, has been shown to be 2,5-di-*m*-hydroxyphenyl-1,4-benzoquinone; the usual quinonoid hydroxyl groups are missing. The four pigments described yield *p*-terphenyl on zinc dust distillation.

Thelephoric acid was isolated in Kögl's laboratory in 1930 from fungi of several *Thelephora* species. Thirty years later the structure was established by Gripenberg[1] (1960), who isolated the pigment in 0.6% yield by acetone extraction of sporophores of *Hydnum suaveolens.* The substance crystallizes from pyridine in dark violet crystals; it dissolves in aqueous ammonia with a blue color. The structure was established from spectrographic evidence, by identification of *p*-terphenyl as a product of zinc dust distillation, and by synthesis from 3,4-dimethoxyphenol and chloranil. Potentiometric titration in dimethylsulfoxide

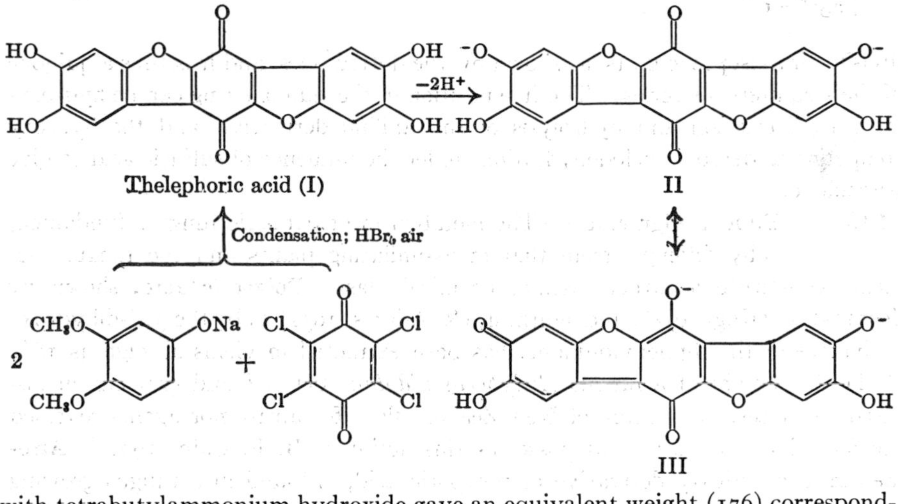

Thelephoric acid (I)   II

Condensation; HBr, air

2   III

with tetrabutylammonium hydroxide gave an equivalent weight (176) corresponding to two readily ionizable hydrogens, and comparison of the titration curves with those of reference substances showed that the substance is a slightly weaker acid than *o*-nitrophenol. The strong acidity of thelephoric acid is attributable to resonance in the anion among structures of types II and III. That the fungus pigment absorbs at a longer wave length (λ 450 mμ, Di) than similarly substituted 2,5-diphenyl-1,4-quinones is due to the fact that the benzene rings are forced into the plane of the quinone ring.

26.11   **α-Naphthoquinones.** — A yellow pigment **lawsone** is extracted from leaves of the tropical shrub henna (*Lawsonia inermis*), which is cultivated in Egypt. The substance is identical with synthetic 2-hydroxy-1,4-naph-

---

[1] Jarl Gripenberg, b. 1914 Helsingfors; Ph.D. Finland Inst. Techn.; Finland Inst. Techn.

thoquinone.   It dyes wool and silk an orange shade, and a paste made from powdered henna leaves and catechu has been used for tinting the hair red.   Mo-

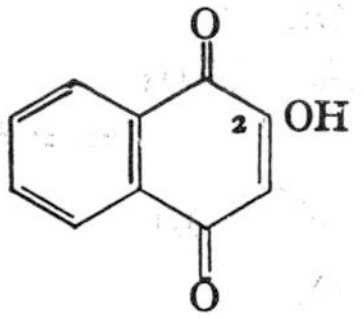

Lawsone

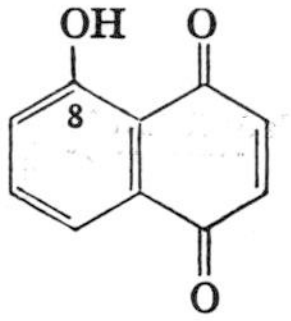

Juglone
(yellow-brown, m.p. 154°,
$E_0^{alc.}$ 0.447 v.)

hammed is said to have dyed his beard with henna.   The isomeric 8-hydroxy compound **juglone** is present in shells of unripe walnuts, largely as α-hydrojuglone, a hydrogen-bonded ketonic form of the normal hydroquinone.   The colorless hydro compound undergoes rapid oxidation on exposure to air and the resulting quinone stains the skin (addition of active groups of protein).   Juglone can be prepared in 15% yield by oxidation of 1,5-dihydroxynaphthalene with dichromate in aqueous sulfuric acid solution.

Two monohydroxy derivatives of 2-methyl-1,4-naphthoquinone have been isolated from natural sources.   **Plumbagin,** shown by synthesis to be the 5-hydroxy isomer, was known in a fairly pure form as early as 1828 and is the active principle of Chita, a drug of medicinal value obtained from Indian shrubs of various *Plumbago* species.   **Phthiocol,** or 2-hydroxy-3-methyl-1,4-naphthoquinone

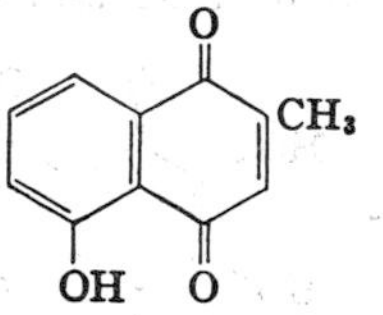

Plumbagin
(yellow, m.p. 79°)

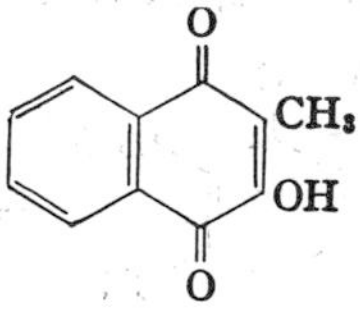

Phthiocol

(synthesis, 26.7), has been isolated from human tubercle bacilli (*Mycobacterium tuberculosis*), but probably is formed during the isolation process by degradation of a vitamin K factor during saponification with alcoholic potassium hydroxide.

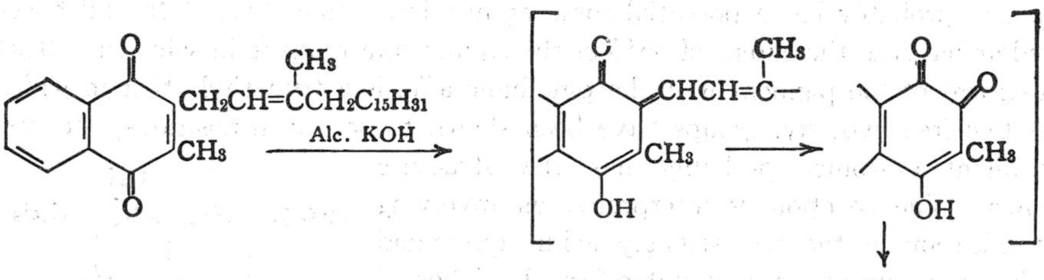

Vitamin K₁

Phthiocol

The related pigments **droserone** and **hydroxydroserone** are found under the outer covering of bulbous root growths of *Drosera whittakeri*, a plant of Australia (E. H. Rennie, 1887).   The more highly hydroxylated pigment has been characterized as 3,5,8-trihydroxy-2-methyl-1,4-naphthoquinone and synthesized by condensation of maleic anhydride with the hydroquinone component shown in the formulation (A. K. MacBeth and F. L. Winzor, 1936). The methoxyl group

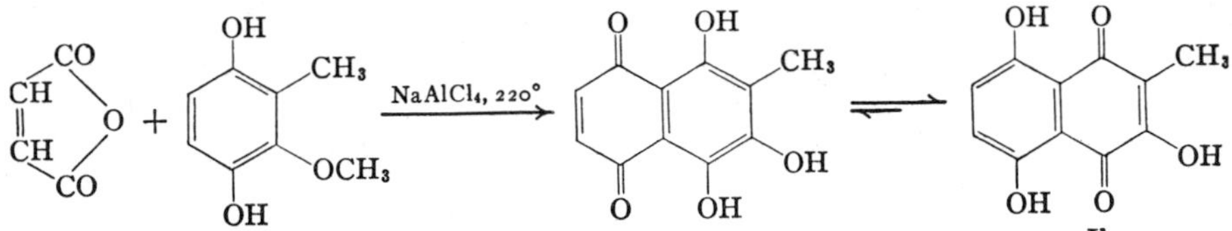

Ia

Hydroxydroserone
(red, m.p. 193°, E_0alc. 0.200 v.)

Ib

of the hydroquinone component is cleaved in the process. The initial reaction product Ia is less stable thermodynamically than the tautomeric form Ib, since methyl and hydroxyl groups have a much greater potential-lowering effect when attached to a quinonoid ring than when present in an adjacent benzenoid nucleus. Hydroxydroserone is thus assigned the structure Ib, which combines features of the structures of lawsone, juglone, plumbagin, and phthiocol. Droserone (yellow, m.p. 178°) lacks one of the two nonquinonoid hydroxyl groups of Ib and is 3,5-dihydroxy-2-methyl-1,4-naphthoquinone (R. H. Thomson, 1949).

26.12   Echinochrome A. — This pigment of sea urchin eggs (10 mg. per ovary) was characterized by R. Kuhn and K. Wallenfels (1939) as a pentahydroxyquinone derivative of β-ethyl- rather than β-methylnaphthalene, the parent hydrocarbon of the plant pigments cited above. Two tautomeric *para* quinone forms are possible, Ia and Ib, as well as several *ortho* quinone forms.

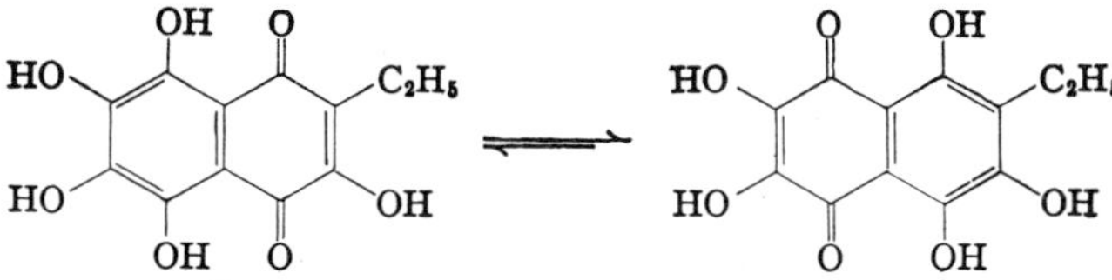

Ia   Ib

Echinochrome A
(red, m.p. 220° dec., E_0aq.,30° 0.080 v.)

Form Ib, with two effective potential-lowering hydroxyl groups in the quinone nucleus, probably has a potential some 25 mv. lower than that of Ia and hence predominates to the extent of 90% of the equilibrium mixture in solution. Brief treatment of the pigment with diazomethane affords a trimethyl ether in which the two free hydroxyl groups have been shown to occupy α-positions; the predominant tautomer probably has the structure shown. The reaction is interpreted as involving esterification of the two strongly acidic quinonoid hydroxyl groups of the more stable form Ib, followed by esterification of the acidic quinonoid hydroxyl group of the less abundant tautomeric form.

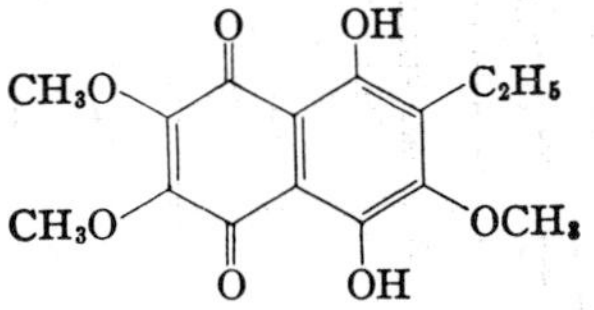

Echinochrome A trimethyl ether
(red, m.p. 130°)

Spinachrome E isolated by M. Yoshida (1959) from a sea urchin, has been identified as 2,3,5,7-tetrahydroxy-1,4-naphthoquinone (R. H. Thompson, 1961).

26.13   Lapachol. — Lapachol is a beautifully crystalline yellow coloring matter occurring in the grain of various woods, including Lapacho and Bethabarra, once imported to the United States (Philadelphia) from the west coast of Africa for the manufacture of high quality bows and fishing rods. The pigment forms a bright red, water-soluble sodium salt, and can be isolated by extraction of the ground wood with cold 1% sodium carbonate solution, precipitation, and extraction with ether. Elucidation of the structure and of a number of remarkable transformations was the theme of researches initiated by S. C. Hooker[1] in 1889–96 as a side problem while engaged as a sugar technologist, and completed in 1915–35 after his retirement. Hooker characterized the pigment as a 2-hydroxy-1,4-naphthoquinone having a C_5-isoprenoid side chain at position 3 (1896),

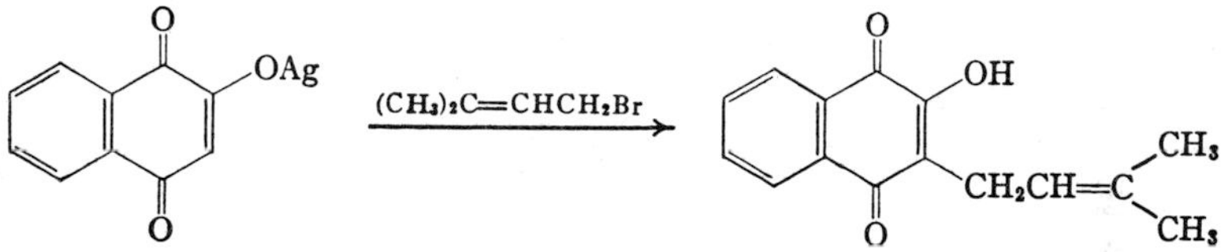

$(CH_3)_2C\!=\!CHCH_2Br$

Lapachol
(yellow, m.p. 140°, $E_0^{alc.}$ 0.287 v.)

and this structure was later confirmed by synthesis from the silver salt of 2-hydroxy-1,4-naphthoquinone (lawsone) and isoprene hydrobromide; whereas saturated alkyl halides give *ortho* and *para* quinone ethers, the more reactive allylic halides also give some of the product of C-alkylation. Lapachol can be converted quantitatively into either of two cyclic derivatives, α- and β-lapachone. The *ortho* quinone is distinguished by a more intense color, higher oxidation potential, and solubility in sodium bisulfite solution with formation of a colorless complex, from which the quinone can be regenerated by either sodium carbonate or a mineral acid. Hooker prepared β-lapachone by pouring a solution of lapachol

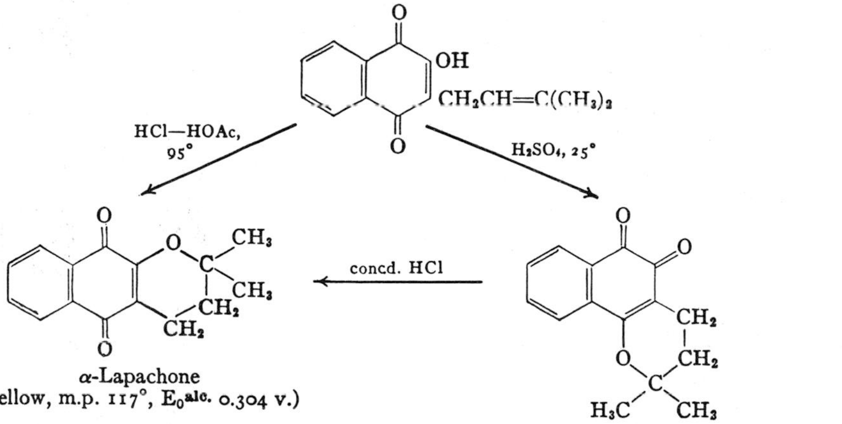

$CH_2CH\!=\!C(CH_3)_2$

HCl—HOAc, 95°

H_2SO_4, 25°

concd. HCl

α-Lapachone
(yellow, m.p. 117°, $E_0^{alc.}$ 0.304 v.)

β-Lapachone
(orange-red, m.p. 154°, $E_0^{alc.}$ 0.403 v.)

---

[1] Samuel C. Hooker, 1864–1935; b. Brenchley (Kent), England; Ph.D. Munich (Bamberger); Franklin Sugar Refining Co., Philadelphia; private laboratory, Brooklyn, N. Y.

in concentrated sulfuric acid into water, and he obtained α-lapachone by heating a solution of lapachol (2 g.) in acetic acid (20 ml.) and concentrated hydrochloric acid (5 ml.) and gradually adding water to cause separation of the yellow product in a crystalline condition. The yields are quantitative and each isomer is directly pure. M. G. Ettlinger (1950) measured the ionization constants in strongly acid solutions and found that β-lapachone is stronger as a base than α-lapachone by about two pK_a units. Thus although the α-isomer is the more stable of the unionized quinones, the β-isomer is the more stable of the two cations (two p-quinoid structures). In concentrated sulfuric acid the equilibrium favors the β-cation, and β-lapachone is precipitated on rapid dilution with water. In the

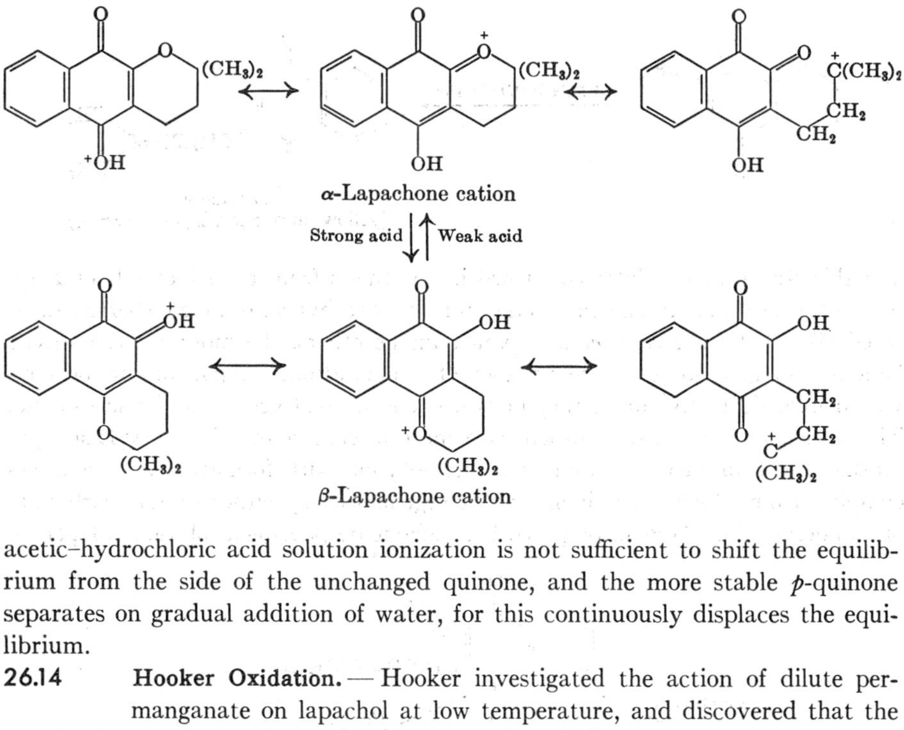

α-Lapachone cation

Strong acid ↓↑ Weak acid

β-Lapachone cation

acetic–hydrochloric acid solution ionization is not sufficient to shift the equilibrium from the side of the unchanged quinone, and the more stable p-quinone separates on gradual addition of water, for this continuously displaces the equilibrium.

26.14   Hooker Oxidation. — Hooker investigated the action of dilute permanganate on lapachol at low temperature, and discovered that the reaction leaves the double bond untouched and results in elimination of a methylene group from the side chain, as shown in the accompanying formulation. The oxida-

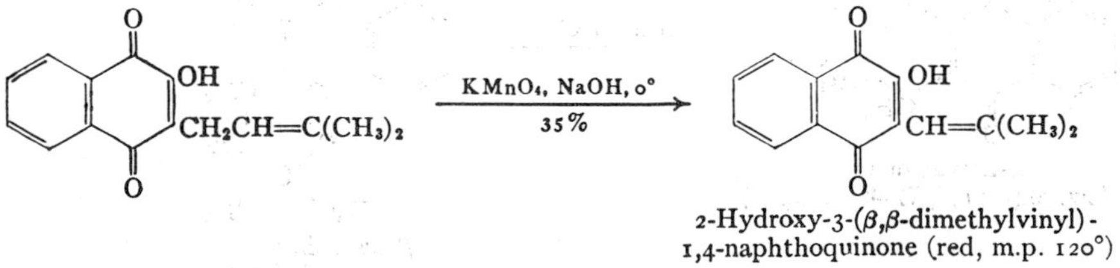

2-Hydroxy-3-(β,β-dimethylvinyl)-
1,4-naphthoquinone (red, m.p. 120°)

tion product has a red color ascribable to conjugation of the double bond in the side chain with the quinone nucleus. The reaction is generally applicable to alkyl and β-alkenyl derivatives of hydroxynaphthoquinone. The observation that the initial red color of the solution disappears during the oxidation and then reappears suggested that the quinone ring opens and then closes again in a different manner, and experiments with quinones having a marking substituent in the benzenoid ring established that the hydroxyl group changes place with the alkyl or alkenyl group in the course of the oxidation. The mechanism of the Hooker oxidation was finally elucidated by isolation and characterization of a colorless intermediate (Fieser and Fieser, 1948). The intermediates from a variety of quinones of type I are obtainable in 85–95% yield by the action of hydrogen peroxide in aqueous sodium carbonate–dioxane. The crystalline intermediate is

the dihydroxyindanonecarboxylic acid IV, probably formed by hydroxylation of the quinone double bond to form the trione hydrate II, and benzilic acid rearrangement of the hydrate anion III (compare 25.13). When oxidized with copper sulfate in an alkaline solution, the indanone reacts in the tautomeric ketol form V and affords the triketo acid VI, from which the bicyclic structure is restored by aldolization to VII. The last step was shown by Shemyakin,[1] Shchukina[2] et al. (1951) to be air oxidation of the α-hydroxy acid VII to VIII, the ketonic form of

[1] M. M. Shemyakin, b. 1908 Moscow; D.Sc. Moscow Univ.; State Inst. of Exptl. Med.; State Inst. Biol. and Med. Chem.; Inst. Chem. Natural Products, Moscow

[2] L. A. Shchukina, b. 1910 Samarkand; D.Sc. Moscow Mendeleev Inst. Chem. Techn.; State Inst. Biol. and Med. Chem., Moscow

the final product IX. Several trione hydrates analogous to II have been characterized; for example, chlorination of phthiocol in aqueous suspension yields the analog of II with chlorine as the second substituent at C_2. The configuration of the indanone IV was established in an investigation by Bader[1] (1951) of a reaction characteristic of hindered 2-hydroxy-3-alkyl-1,4-naphthoquinones, for example the cyclohexyl derivative X. When a solution of X in 5% alkali is

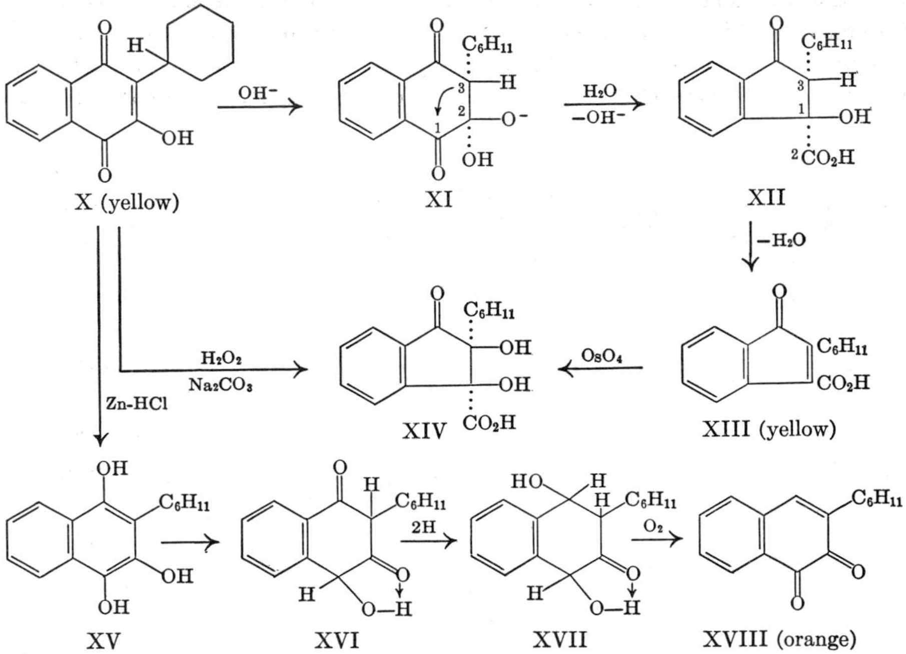

X (yellow)　　　　　　XI　　　　　　XII

XIV CO_2H　　　XIII (yellow)

XV　　　XVI　　　XVII　　　XVIII (orange)

heated on the steam bath the initially deep red solution becomes pure yellow in about 27 hrs. and acidification precipitates the yellow indenone acid XIII. When the reaction is done in a buffer at pH 9.2 the intermediate alcohol XII is isolable. This alcohol is formulated as being formed through the trione hydrate anion XI, which has the requirements for undergoing benzilic acid rearrangement to the indanone XII. A bulky alkyl substituent thus favors ring contraction because steric strain in the planar quinone anion is relieved by conversion to the nonplanar trione hydrate anion XI. Hydroxylation of the indenone acid XIII with osmium tetroxide and with alkaline peroxide gave the *cis* and *trans* diols, and the former (XIV) proved to be identical with the intermediate in the Hooker oxidation of X. Another reaction characteristic of 2-hydroxy-3-cyclohexyl-1,4-naphthoquinone (X) and other analogs with bulky alkyl groups is that Clemmensen reduction followed by air oxidation yields 3-cyclohexyl-1,2-naphthoquinone (XVIII). Evidently hindrance of the coplanar groups in the hydroquinone XV favors isomerization to the nonplanar diketone XVI, which is reduced at the unchelated carbonyl group to XVII; dehydration and enolization then gives the hydroquinone of XVIII.

[1] Alfred R. Bader, b. 1924 Vienna, Austria; Ph.D. Harvard (Fieser); Aldrich Chem. Co.

26.15   **Lomatiol.** — This pigment, discovered by Rennie (1895) and characterized by Hooker as the ω-hydroxy derivative of lapachol, is found as a yellow powder surrounding the nuclei of seeds of the Australian plant *Lomatia ilicifolia*. The structure and some reactions of the pigment are shown in the formulas. The product of cyclization with sulfuric acid is an *ortho* quinone formed as the result of an allylic shift of hydroxyl, as is evident from the structure of the hydroxy compound obtained by hydrolysis of the cyclic product with alkali. Another consequence of the presence of an allylic alcohol grouping is that catalytic hydrogenation affords not only the product of saturation of the double bond with hydrogen but also hydrolapachol.

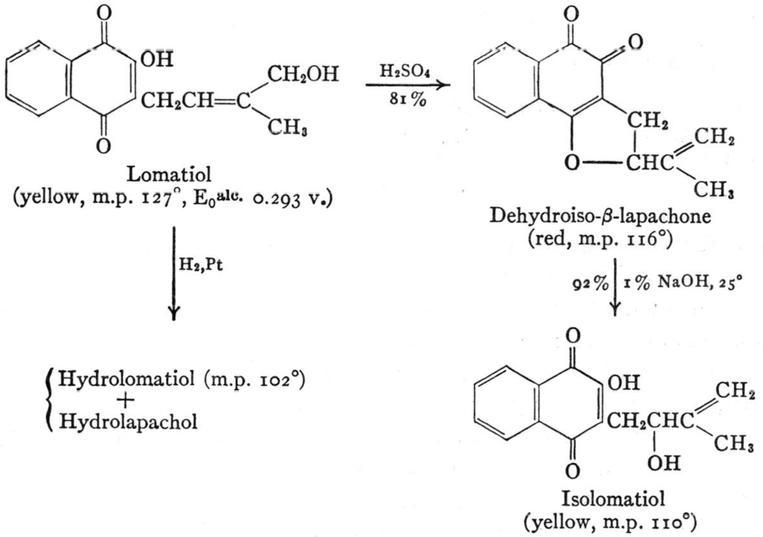

Lomatiol
(yellow, m.p. 127°, $E_0^{alc.}$ 0.293 v.)

Dehydroiso-β-lapachone
(red, m.p. 116°)

Hydrolomatiol (m.p. 102°)
+
Hydrolapachol

Isolomatiol
(yellow, m.p. 110°)

26.16   **Alkannin and Shikonin.** — **Alkannin,** a dark red pigment occurring as the angelic ester in the root of *Alkanna tinctoria* and employed to some extent as a mordant dye and indicator, was characterized by Brockmann[1] (1935) as a derivative of naphthazarin (5,8-dihydroxy-1,4-naphthoquinone) having as a substituent in the quinonoid ring an unsaturated side chain containing a secondary alcoholic group. The side chain contains a terminal isoprenoid unit and resembles the side chains of perezone and lapachol. The hydroxyl group in the α-position of the side chain is reactive and is easily eliminated by the action of 10% methyl alcoholic hydrogen chloride in the cold (or of hot 2 N alkali) with formation of a dienic system; this dehydration reaction eliminates the center of asymmetry responsible for the optical activity of the natural pigment. Etherification of the reactive hydroxyl group by the action of 2% methyl alcoholic hydrochloric acid in the cold is accompanied by racemization. On cyclization of the pigment with stannic chloride in benzene solution at room temperature the hydroxyl group is left intact and optical activity is retained. Dry distillation of either cycloalkannin

---

[1] Hans Brockmann, b. 1903 Altkloster, Germany; D.Sc. Halle (Abderhalden, Kuhn); Univ. Göttingen

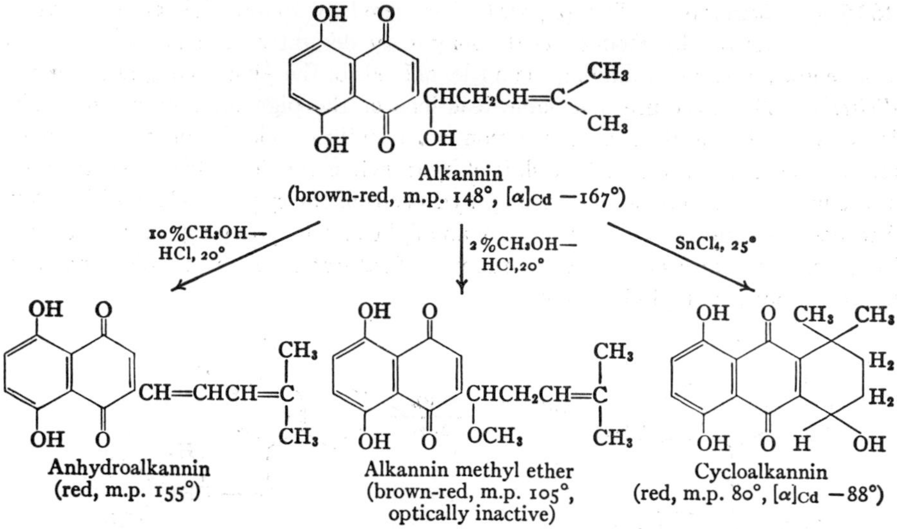

Alkannin
(brown-red, m.p. 148°, [α]cd −167°)

10%CH₃OH—
HCl, 20°

2%CH₃OH—
HCl,20°

SnCl₄, 25°

Anhydroalkannin
(red, m.p. 155°)

Alkannin methyl ether
(brown-red, m.p. 105°,
optically inactive)

Cycloalkannin
(red, m.p. 80°, [α]cd −88°)

or the original pigment results in loss of methane and water and formation of
1-methyl-5,8-dihydroxyanthraquinone (1-methylquinizarin, m.p. 247°), synthesized for comparison from naphthazarin diacetate and piperylene. The product
of hydrogenation of anhydroalkannin, 3-isohexylnaphthazarin (red, m.p. 98°),
occurs along with alkannin. Another red pigment of the same composition and
properties, shikonin (m.p. 147°), has been isolated from the root of the Japanese
plant shikone. Brockmann discovered that the pigment is the dextrorotatory
enantiomer of alkannin, for it yields an optically inactive methyl ether identical
with that obtained from the levorotatory pigment.

26.17   Dunnione is an orange-red pigment (m.p. 99°, [α]D + 310°) derived
from *Streptocarpus dunnii* Mast.; it occurs as a deposit on the 2-ft.
long leaves of the plant (0.5–2 g. per leaf). The structure shown (III) was deduced by J. R. Price and R. Robinson (1939), and racemic dunnione has been

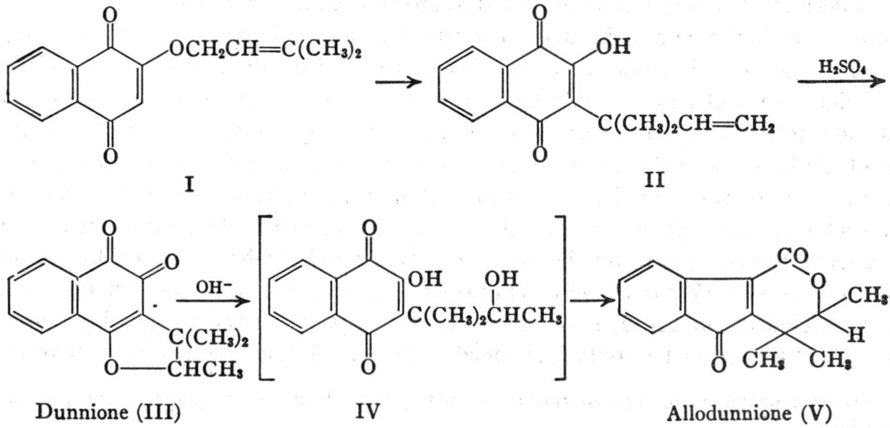

I

II

H₂SO₄

Dunnione (III)   IV   Allodunnione (V)

synthesized (R. G. Cooke, 1948) by Claisen rearrangement of 2-γ,γ-dimethyl-allyloxy-1,4-naphthoquinone (I) and ring closure. Dunnione (III) is isomerized by alkali to allodunnione (V); the hydroxy-*p*-quinone IV has a bulky substituent like 2-hydroxy-3-cyclohexyl-1,4-naphthoquinone (26.14), and hence can form a trione hydrate anion subject to benzilic acid rearrangement to the indenone hydroxy acid precursor of V.

26.18   Coenzyme Q. — Coenzyme Q is the term applied to a group of related quinones which are involved in the electron transport mechanism of oxidative phosphorylation. They are 2,3-dimethoxy-5-methylbenzoquinones with a side chain made up of varying numbers of isoprene units and are designated coenzymes Q_6, Q_7, Q_8, Q_9, and Q_{10}. Isolation was reported independently in

Coenzyme Q_{10}

1955–57 by R. L. Lester, F. L. Crane, and Y. Hatefi of the Wisconsin Institute of Enzyme Research (from beef mitochondria) and by R. A. Morton[1] *et al*. The groups of K. Folkers at Merck and of O. Isler at Hoffmann-La Roche participated in the work of structural elucidation and synthesis. The esterlike property of hydroxyquinone ethers (26.5) led to considerable confusion, for saponification of crude extract with ethanolic potassium hydroxide was attended with ester interchange with one or both methoxyl groups. The English and Swiss workers have used the name ubiquinone both to describe the group as a whole and for coenzyme Q_{10}; they isolated 37 g. of pure Q_{10} (m.p. 50°) from 750 kg. of pig heart. The Q coenzymes have been found in many species of animals, plants, and microorganisms but they are not ubiquitous. Usually a tissue in which a Q factor is absent (*e.g.* tubercle bacilli) contains a structurally related vitamin K.

26.19   Arenones. — Bamberger found (1901) that under controlled conditions of acid catalysis *p*-tolylhydroxylamine (1) can be rearranged to the dienone (2), known as *p*-tolylquinol. In a modern procedure the hydroxylamine is added to partially frozen dilute sulfuric acid and the mixture is shaken and allowed to come to room temperature; a complicated mixture results from which (2) is isolated by chromatography. The reaction is now regarded as involving an anionotropic intermolecular rearrangement (Hughes and Ingold, 1951). Bamberger obtained the *p*-quinol (2) also by oxidation of *p*-cresol with a peracid in neutral medium (1903). Extensive investigations of Wessely[2]

[1] Richard Alan Morton, b. 1899 Liverpool; Ph.D. and D.Sc. Liverpool (Baly, Heilbron); Univ. Liverpool

[2] Friederich Wessely, b. 1897 Kirchberg/Wagram, Austria; Ph.D. Vienna (Franke); Univ. Vienna

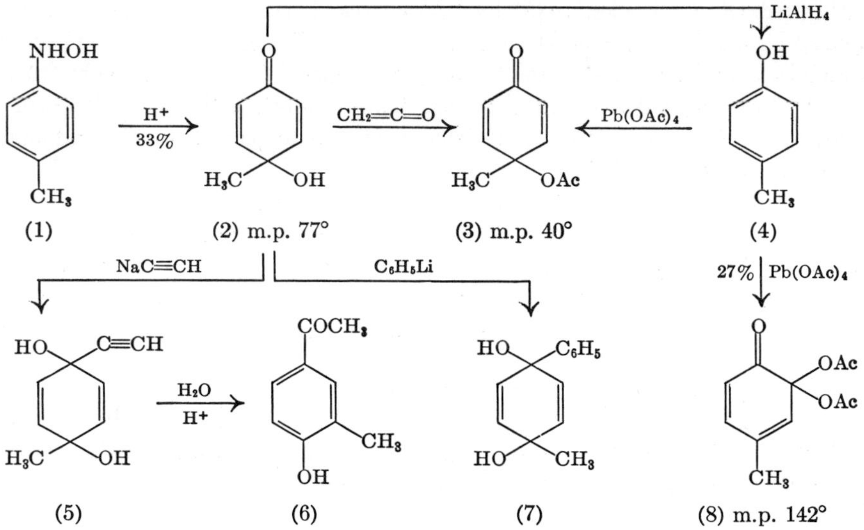

(1)   (2) m.p. 77°   (3) m.p. 40°   (4)

(5)   (6)   (7)   (8) m.p. 142°

(1950–60) have shown that both o- and p-quinol acetates are obtainable as the acetates by oxidation of phenols with lead tetraacetate. Thus oxidation of p-cresol (4) affords the o-quinol diacetate (8) in 27% yield and a smaller amount of the p-quinol acetate (3). Since the hydroxyl group of p-toluquinol is allylic, the tertiary alcohol is acylable, for example with 3,5-dinitrobenzoyl chloride in pyridine. The acetate is best prepared by reaction with ketene. Other transformation products are shown in formulas (5)–(7).

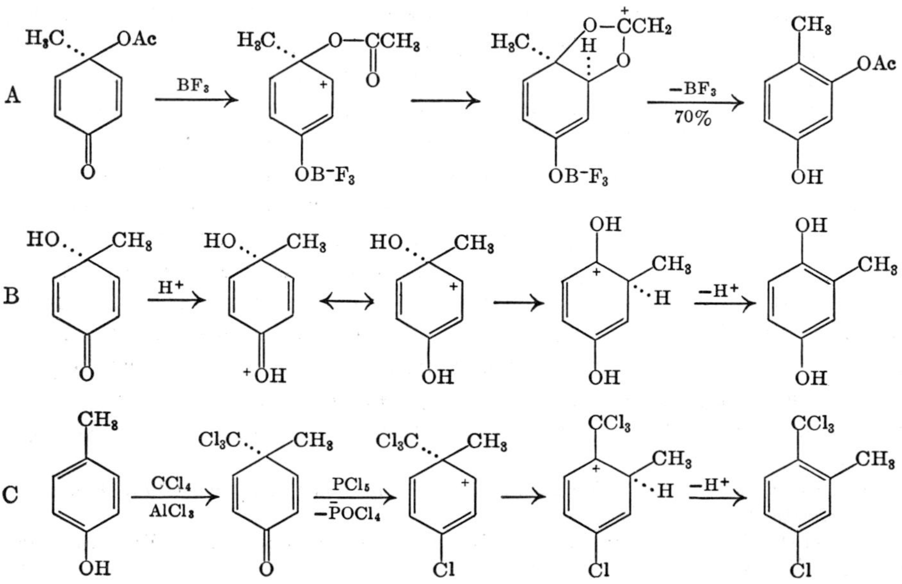

Goodwin[1] and Witkop[2] (1957), who are responsible for the yields cited in the above chart, interpret the rearrangement of p-toluquinol acetate to cresorcinol 2-acetate (A) under Thiele conditions as proceeding through cyclization of an intermediate aronium ion. Acid-catalyzed rearrangement of free p-toluquinol to p-toluhydroquinone (B) is interpreted as involving a 1,2-methyl shift in an aronium ion analogous to those postulated in the isomerization of the xylenes (18.8). The dienone formulated in C was prepared by Zincke (1906) in high yield by reaction of p-cresol with carbon tetrachloride in the presence of aluminum chloride, and its conversion to 2-trichloromethyl-5-chlorotoluene on reaction with phosphorus pentachloride was demonstrated by von Auwers (1912); an analogous 1,2-methyl shift accounts for the reaction.

Since the C-dienone is analogous to the p-quinols in structure and properties, as are the related dienones obtainable by the Reimer-Tiemann (25.6) and Claisen allylation (22.23) reactions, we suggest the name arenone for the compounds of all four classes; an arenone (o or p) is a dienone derivable from or convertible into an aryl hydroxy compound.

An interesting reaction of o-arenones is photochemical cleavage of an originally phenolic ring (Barton, 1960). Irradiation of 6-acetoxy-6-methyl-$\Delta^{2,4}$-cyclohexadienone (1) conducted in ether saturated with water as the nucleophilic agent affords the nonconjugated dienic acid (4) in 79% yield. The evidence indicates that the ring opens to give the cis-ketene (2), which rearranges to the $trans$-ketene (3), which in turn reacts with the nucleophile to form the product (4). Arenones with two acetoxyl groups at C_6 afford hitherto unknown ketene diacetates. Those having an additional methyl group at C_4 behave like the parent compound. Use of the stronger nucleophile aniline may lead to the amide of the nonconjugated acid (4) or may effect isomerization to the conjugated amide (5); use of cyclohexylamine favors the isomerized product. The only deviating behavior noted was with the arenone from mesitol (2,4,6-trimethyl-

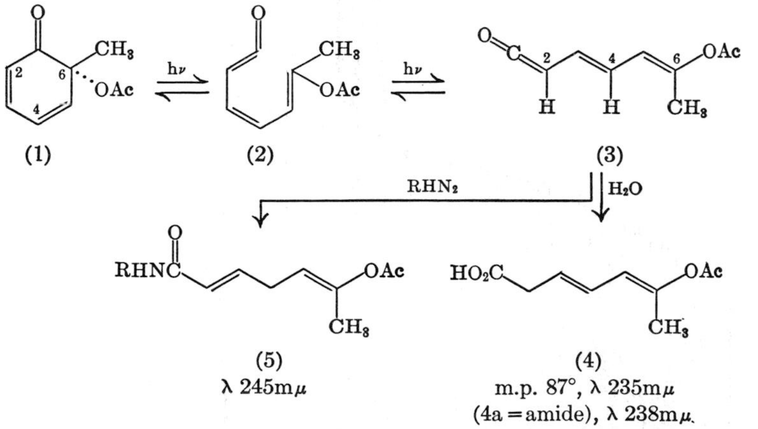

(1) (2) (3)

RHN₂ H₂O

(5)
λ 245mμ

(4)
m.p. 87°, λ 235mμ
(4a = amide), λ 238mμ.

---

[1] Sidney Goodwin, b. 1925 San Francisco; Ph.D. Harvard (Fieser); Nat. Heart Inst.; Univ. Calif. Santa Barbara

[2] Bernhard Witkop, b. 1917 Freiburg, Germany; Ph.D. Munich (Wieland); Nat. Heart Inst.

phenol). Fission occurred normally in the presence of cyclohexylamine to give the nonconjugated amide in 84% yield, but in the presence of water or aniline the chief reaction was aromatization to 3-acetoxymesitol, formed by a 1,2-shift of the acetoxyl group by a mechanism analogous to A, above. Inspection of the formula of the *trans*-ketene (3) shows that introduction of methyl groups at C_2 and C_4 sets up two destabilizing 1:3 interactions involving one of the two groups at C_6 (configuration unknown). Inhibition of the forward reaction increases the rate of the back reaction and the arenone undergoes the much slower reaction of aromatization.

Chapter 27

NAPHTHALENE

27.1   **Orientation of Derivatives.** — Naphthalene, the most abundant single constituent of coal tar, is important as a source of phthalic acid and anthranilic acid, which are intermediates to indigo, indanthrone, and triphenyl-methane dyes, and of an array of intermediates for azo dyes. Use of the hydrocarbon as a moth repellant and insecticide has fallen off with the introduction of *p*-dichlorobenzene. Liquid hydro derivatives of naphthalene (m.p. 80°) utilized in motor fuels and lubricants and as solvents are the 1,2,3,4-tetrahydride, tetralin, and the decahydride, decalin.

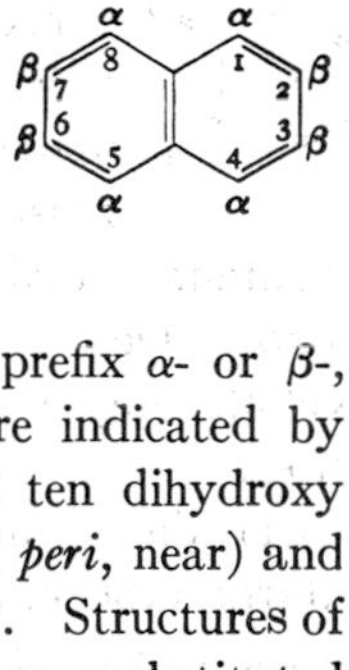

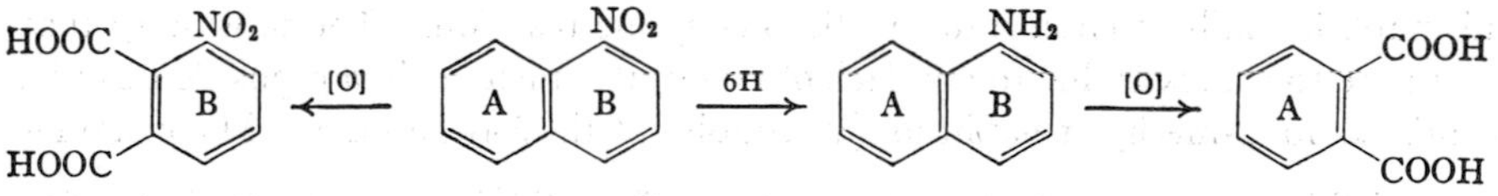

Monosubstituted naphthalenes usually are designated by the prefix α- or β-, while the positions of groups in polysubstituted derivatives are indicated by numbers. Ten isomeric disubstitution products are possible; all ten dihydroxy derivatives are known. 1,8-Derivatives are designated *peri-* (Gr. *peri*, near) and 2,6-derivatives are designated *amphi-* (Gr. *amph-*, on both sides). Structures of simple derivatives are established by oxidation to phthalic acid or a substituted phthalic acid. A nitro group stabilizes the ring to which it is attached, and hence the unsubstituted ring (A) of α-nitronaphthalene is degraded on oxidation and the product is 3-nitrophthalic acid. If the nitro compound is reduced, the substituted ring (B) becomes the more vulnerable center, and oxidation of α-naphthyl-amine yields phthalic acid. This sequence of reactions proves that naphthalene contains two fused benzene rings, for each ring is identified in a degradation product with carbon substituents in the *o*-positions. This structure was postulated by Erlenmeyer[1] in 1866 and proved by Graebe (1868), who applied the above principle in a more elaborate sequence involving chlorinated quinones. Structures of substances such as β-naphthol or β-ethylnaphthalene, which yield phthalic acid on drastic oxidation, are established by correlation with other derivatives that undergo degradation in the alternative direction. β-Ethylnaphthalene results from Clemmensen reduction of an aceto compound established as a β-derivative by oxidation to trimellitic acid (benzene-1,2,4-tricarboxylic acid). β-Naphthol can be correlated through β-naphthylamine with β-naphthoic acid, which also yields the 1,2,4-acid.

27.2   Bond Fixation. — Three resonance bond structures for naphthalene are possible, the symmetrical structure I and the two unsymmetrical, equivalent structures II and IIa. In formulations of the unsymmetrical structures, one of the two rings is indicated as quinonoid (q) because the arrangement

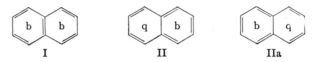

of double bonds corresponds to that of *o*-benzoquinone. Rings that correspond to the normal Kekulé benzene formula in containing three double bonds, in contrast with a quinonoid ring containing two, are described as normal benzenoid rings (b). Fries (1927), recognizing that quinonoid systems are more reactive, or less stable, than benzenoid systems, formulated a generalization known as the Fries rule, which states that the most stable form of a polynuclear hydrocarbon is that in which the maximum number of rings have the benzenoid arrangement of three double bonds. On this basis the symmetrical structure composed of two normal Kekulé rings would be expected to be more stable than the quinonoid structures.

Certain peculiarities in the reactions of β-naphthol and β-naphthylamine are interpretable only on the basis of the symmetrical formula. A striking difference in the two positions *ortho* to the functional group in these compounds was noted first by Marckwald (1893) and investigated extensively by Zincke,[2] Fries, and others. Whereas the 1-position exhibits functions normally associated with the *o*-position of an amine or a phenol, the 3-position does not. On reaction with a diazotized amine in alkaline solution, β-naphthol (III) couples exclusively at the 1-position in preference to the alternative position 3. The lack of reactivity at the 3-position is more apparent in the behavior of 1-methyl-2-naphthol (IV), for this naphthol fails to enter into the diazo coupling reaction. The possibility that resistance to attack is due to any lack of reactivity inherent in a β-position can be dismissed, for 4-methyl-1-naphthol (V) couples at the β-position 2. The behavior

[1] Emil Erlenmeyer, Jr., 1864–1921, b. Heidelberg; Ph.D. Göttingen; Univ. Strasbourg, Berlin; *Ber.*, **54A**, 107 (1921)

[2] Theodor Zincke, 1843–1928; b. Ulsen, Germany; Ph.D. Göttingen; Univ. Marburg; *Ber.*, **62A**, 17 (1929)

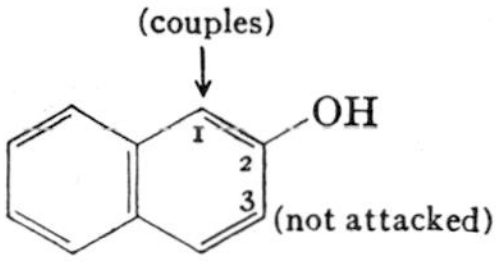

Response to diazotized amines

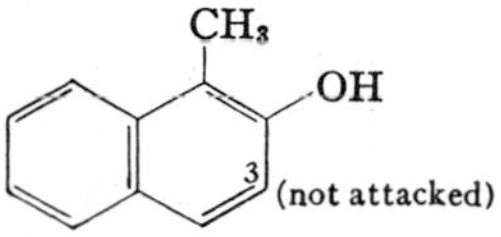

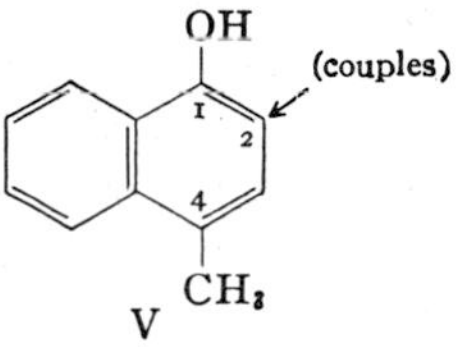

of IV is therefore anomalous, and one of the two positions adjacent to the hydroxylated carbon atom does not have the characteristics of a normal *ortho* position. An interpretation of this deviating behavior can be developed from the consideration that aliphatic enols having the grouping —CH=C(OH)— couple with diazotized amines to give azo compounds, —C(N=NAr)=C(OH)—, whereas alcohols with the grouping —CH$_2$—CH(OH)— do not. The diazo group evidently can attack a position connected to a hydroxylated carbon by a double bond, but not one joined by a single linkage. This relationship would indicate that in β-naphthol the 1- and 2-carbon atoms are connected by a double bond and the 2- and 3-carbon atoms by a single bond. Position 1 is therefore described as a normal *ortho* position because it is enolic, —$\overset{1}{C}$H=C(OH)—, whereas the 3-position, with the grouping =C(OH)—$\overset{3}{C}$H=, is nonenolic and hence abnormal. *p*-Coupling, as observed with α-naphthol, can be ascribed to attack at the end of a dienolic system: —CH=CHCH=C(OH)—.

The facts cited suggest that the bond structure of the naphthalene nucleus is not so mobile as that of benzene and that there is a relative fixation of bonds in at least that part of the molecule at which substitution occurs. Investigations of the properties of compounds hydroxylated in both rings have shown that the two rings have the same character (Lothrop,[1] 1935). 2,7-Dihydroxynaphthalene (VI) couples at positions 1 and 8, but if these positions are blocked by alkyl

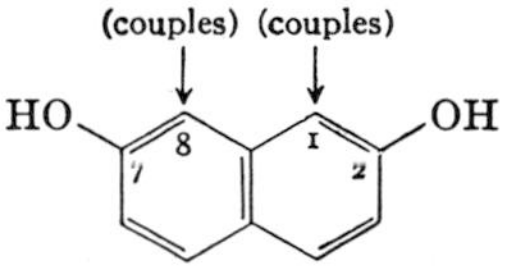

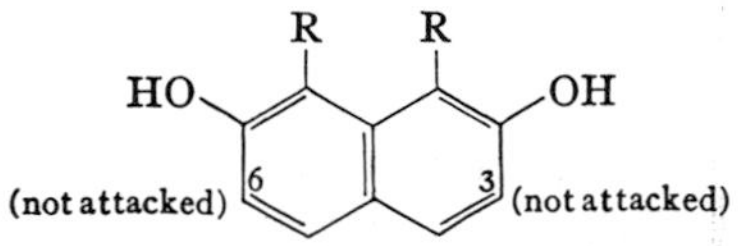

groups (VII), no coupling occurs. The observation is consistent with the symmetrical, but not the unsymmetrical formulation for naphthalene.

Analogous phenomena are encountered in other reactions. β-Naphthyl allyl

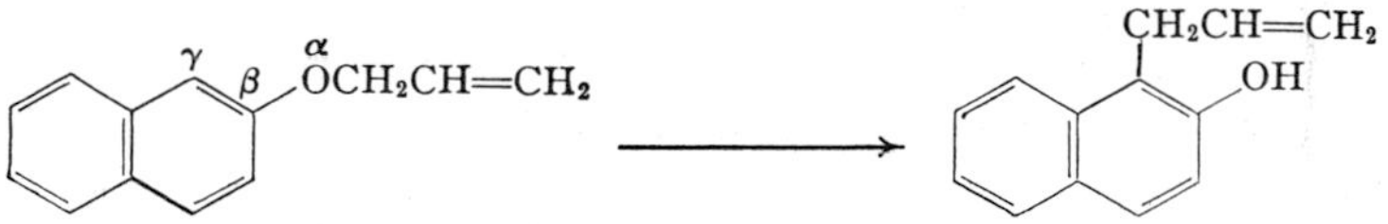

[1] Warren C. Lothrop, b. 1912 Brookline, Mass.; Ph.D. Harvard (Fieser); Trinity College: Williams College; A. D. Little, Inc.

ether (VIII) undergoes Claisen rearrangement when heated and affords 1-allyl-2-naphthol (IX), but when the 1-position is blocked by an alkyl group no rearrangement occurs. If the normal reaction is an α,γ-migration of the allyl group, the failure of the 1-substituted compounds to rearrange is an indication that the double bond normally present at the 1,2-position does not shift to the 2,3-position to form a second α,γ-system, even at the elevated reaction temperature, in an extent sufficient to allow the allyl group to migrate.

Another manifestation of enhanced 1,2-double bond character is the course of halogenation and nitration of β-naphthol and β-naphthylamine derivatives (Zincke, Fries), as illustrated in the following typical example. p-Cresol is easily chlorinated in both free o-positions, and the reaction sequence can be visualized as proceeding by substitution at an initial enolic position, progression of the double bonds to render the alternative o-position enolic, and further substitution at this site. Chlorination of β-naphthol follows a different course, for the initially formed 1-chloro derivative (X) can be converted by interaction with a second mole of chlorine (particularly in the presence of sodium acetate) into the keto dichloride

XI (1,1-dichloro-2-keto-1,2-dihydronaphthalene). Apparently there is in this case no bond migration to produce an enolic center at the 3-position, $-\underset{3}{C}(OH)=$ CH $-$, and chlorine attacks the perhaps less reactive system $-CCl=\underset{1}{C}(OH)-$ with introduction of a second halogen at the 1-position. The comparable ketonic

substances XII and XIII result from chlorination and nitration of 1-methyl-2-naphthol, and the mixed halogenide XIV has been prepared from both the 1-bromo and 1-chloro derivatives of β-naphthol.

X-ray and electron-diffraction analysis (Robertson, 1951) has confirmed chemical evidence. Whereas in benzene the C—C bond distances are all 1.40 Å, intermediate between aliphatic C—C (1.54 Å) and C=C (1.33 Å) bonds, the bond distances in naphthalene are not identical. The 1,2-bond distance is 1.36 Å, shorter than any other bond, and the 2,3-distance is 1.39 Å. That these distances do not correspond exactly to aliphatic double and single bonds indicates some resonance stabilization, and the chemical evidence requires only bond fixation in the part of the molecule undergoing substitution and is not incompatible with resonance stabilization in another part. Attack of a 1,8-dialkyl-2,7-dihydroxy-naphthalene (XV) by $C_6H_5N_2^+$, Cl^+, or other electrophilic agent requires a center of adequate electron density at an unsubstituted center, as in the *o*-quinonoid structure XVIII. That substitution does not occur at position 3 (or 6)

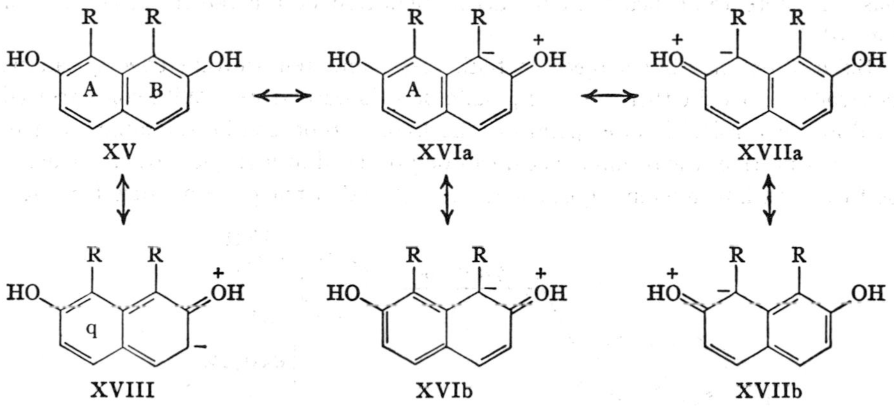

R   R
HO   OH
  A   B
XV

R   R
HO   −   + OH
  A
XVIa

R   R
HO   −   + OH
XVIIa

R   R
HO   + OH
  q   −
XVIII

R   R
HO   −   + OH
XVIb

R   R
+ HO   −   OH
XVIIb

means that structure XVIII (or its equivalent counterpart) is an excited structure that makes little contribution to the hybrid because of the high energy associated with the *o*-quinonoid arrangement of linkages.

27.3 **Substitutions.** — In reactions of the normal type represented by nitration and halogenation the more reactive *α*-positions of naphthalene are attacked almost exclusively, whereas reversible reactions subject to steric hindrance result in substitution in the less hindered *β*-position to an extent that increases with increasing reaction temperature but varies with the reagent and perhaps with the bulkiness of specific group complexes. Nitration, bromina-

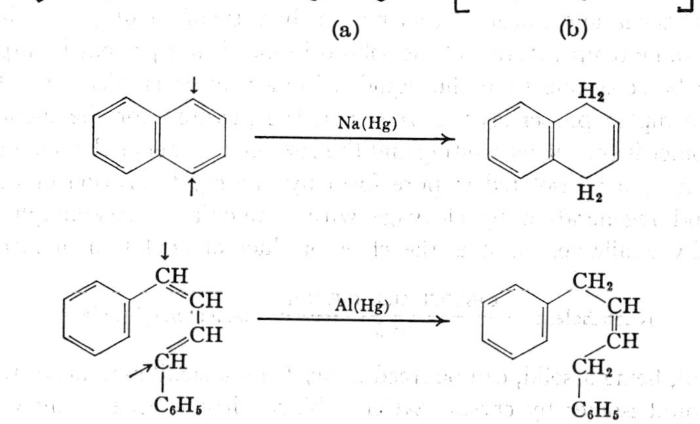

Br
Br_2

H   ··Br
+
(a)

+   H
··Br
(b)

H_2
Na(Hg)
H_2

CH
CH
CH
CH
C_6H_5
Al(Hg)

CH_2
CH
CH
CH_2
C_6H_5

tion, or chlorination of naphthalene affords exclusively α-substituted derivatives. This is due to the lower energy of the transition state leading to ion (a), which has one more resonance form for accommodation of the positive charge than ion (b).

Sulfonation, notably subject to both steric and temperature effects, can be controlled to yield either the α- or β-sulfonic acid derivative. With concentrated acid at a controlled low temperature, the hydrocarbon can be sulfonated largely in the α-position; the β-sulfonic acid can be produced in high yield by introducing sulfuric acid into molten naphthalene at 165° and stirring the mixture for a few

$$\text{Naphthalene} \xrightarrow[96\%]{100\% \text{ H}_2\text{SO}_4,\ 0\text{-}60°} \text{Naphthalene-}1\text{-SO}_3\text{H}$$

$$\xrightarrow[\text{H}_2\text{SO}_4,\ 180°]{}$$

$$\text{Naphthalene} \xrightarrow[85\%]{94\% \text{ H}_2\text{SO}_4,\ 165°} \text{Naphthalene-}2\text{-SO}_3\text{H}$$

minutes. Naphthalene-α-sulfonic acid when heated with sulfuric acid is transformed into the β-isomer, probably as the result of a reversal of the substitution followed by resulfonation.

The course of Friedel-Crafts acylations of naphthalene varies more with the nature of the reagent and solvent than with the temperature. The hydrocarbon is converted by acetyl chloride or acetic anhydride in carbon disulfide solution into

$$\text{Naphthalene} \xrightarrow{\text{CH}_3\text{COCl, AlCl}_3,\ \text{CS}_2,\ -15°} \alpha\text{-COCH}_3 \text{ deriv.} \quad + \quad \beta\text{-COCH}_3 \text{ deriv.}$$

3 parts	1 part
α-Acetonaphthalene	β-Acetonaphthalene
(liq., b.p. 302°;	(m.p. 56°, b.p. 302°;
picrate, m.p. 120°)	picrate, m.p. 85°)

a mixture of the α- and β-aceto derivatives in the ratio of about 3 : 1. The ketones boil at the same temperature and the solid β-isomer is not present in large enough amount to be separable from the liquid α-isomer by crystallization. However, the relationship in properties is reversed in the picrates, for the picrate of the liquid α-isomer is the higher melting and the less soluble; hence the more abundant liquid ketone can be isolated in pure form by one crystallization of the picrate mixture and regeneration by cleavage with ammonia. β-Acetonaphthalene is more readily available, for it is the chief product of acylation in nitrobenzene

$$\text{Naphthalene} \xrightarrow[90\%]{\text{CH}_3\text{COCl, AlCl}_3,\ \text{C}_6\text{H}_5\text{NO}_2} \beta\text{-Acetonaphthalene}$$

solution and, being a solid, can be freed easily from a small amount of the accompanying liquid isomer by crystallization. Since nitrobenzene is known to form molecular complexes with aluminum chloride and acid chlorides, the preferential β-substitution may be attributable to an avoidance of the hindered α-position by a bulky intermediate complex. Friedel-Crafts succinoylation of naphthalene proceeds most satisfactorily in nitrobenzene solution and affords a mixture of isomeric keto acids that can be separated by special procedures [crystallization of the β-isomer, esterification of the mother liquor material, distillation and hydrolysis (*Org. Syn.*, 1961); fractional precipitation from alkali]; the optimum yields are indicated in the formulation:

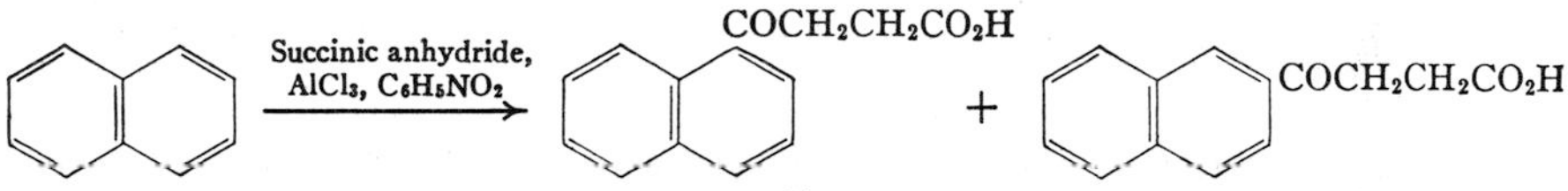

	36%	47%
	β-1-Naphthoylpropionic acid (m.p. 133°)	β-2-Naphthoylpropionic acid (m.p. 173°)

Friedel-Crafts substitution of an acyl group derived from an aromatic acid gives predominantly the α-isomer, and the course of the reaction is not greatly nfluenced by the solvent or temperature. Benzoylation is best accomplished by

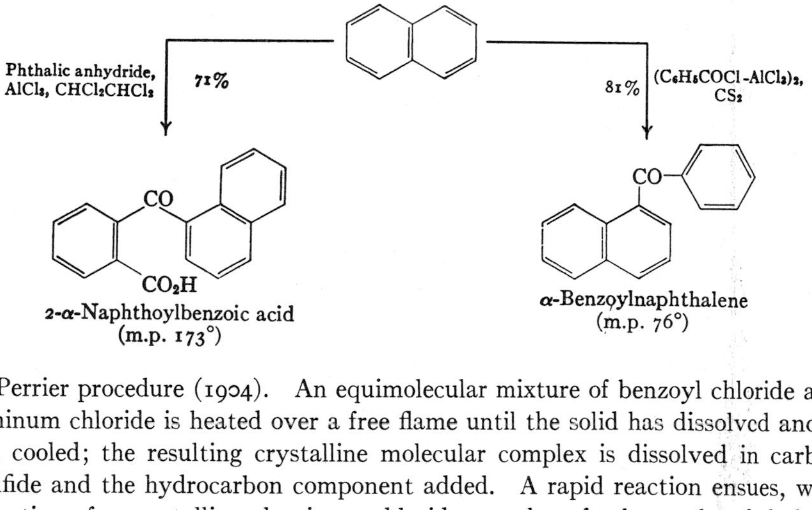

2-α-Naphthoylbenzoic acid
(m.p. 173°)

α-Benzoylnaphthalene
(m.p. 76°)

the Perrier procedure (1904). An equimolecular mixture of benzoyl chloride and aluminum chloride is heated over a free flame until the solid has dissolved and is then cooled; the resulting crystalline molecular complex is dissolved in carbon disulfide and the hydrocarbon component added. A rapid reaction ensues, with separation of a crystalline aluminum chloride complex of α-benzoylnaphthalene, from which the pure ketone is liberated on decomposition with water. Some β-benzoylnaphthalene (m.p. 82°) is produced but remains in the carbon disulfide mother liquor as a much more soluble complex. The method fails with *p*-methoxybenzoyl chloride because the 1:2 complex with this substance is too sparingly soluble in carbon disulfide to permit it to react. G. Baddeley noted (1949) that this solvent has a low dielectric constant (2.6), comparable to carbon tetrachloride (2.2), and found that solubility of the complex increases with increasing dielectric constant of the solvent: chloroform (5), tetrachloroethane (8.2), methylene chloride (10). Thus aluminum chloride (2 equiv.) dissolves in a solution of *p*-methoxybenzoyl chloride in methylene chloride to give a clear solution, and on addition of naphthalene a rapid reaction occurs giving 1-anisoylnaphthalene.

When a β-acyl derivative of naphthalene is required as a synthetic intermediate, advantage can be taken of the fact that the orientation of tetralin in the Friedel-Crafts reaction is exclusively at the unhindered β-position. The resulting ketonic product, for example I, can be dehydrogenated directly to the naphthalene

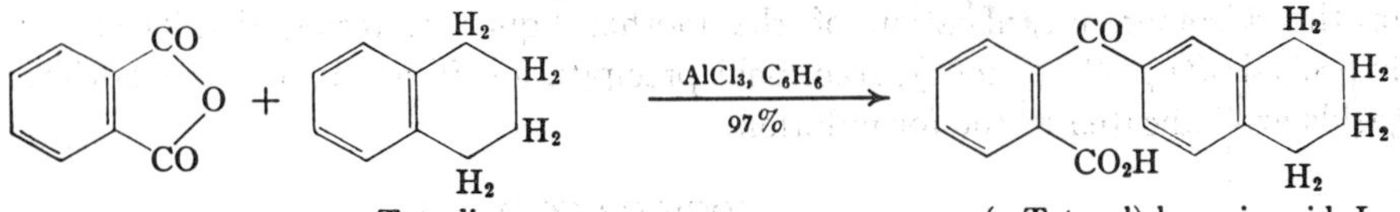

Tetralin   o-(2-Tetroyl)-benzoic acid, I
                                          (m.p. 155°)

derivative, or dehydrogenation can be accomplished at some later stage in the synthesis. The product of succinoylation, II, has been transformed into γ-2-naphthylbutyric acid (III) by heating the corresponding ester with palladium charcoal (Newman, 1943); the nucleus is dehydrogenated and the carbonyl group

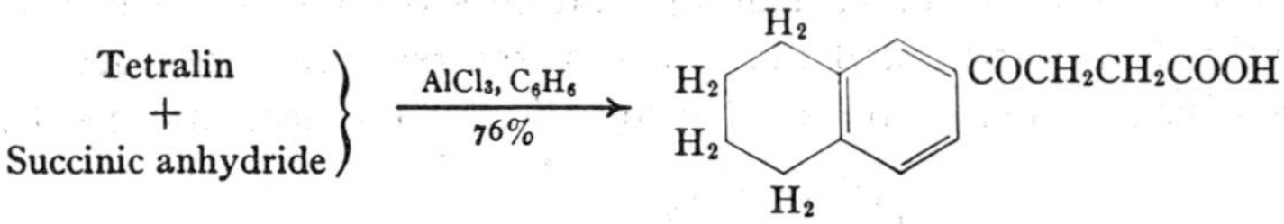

β-2-Tetroylpropionic acid, II

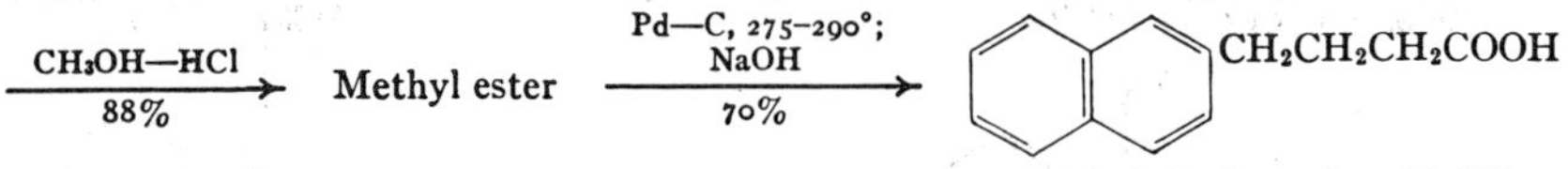

γ-2-Naphthylbutyric acid, III

adjacent to the aromatic ring is reduced to a methylene group. The intermediate III can be made by this method more efficiently than from naphthalene.

A. J. M. Wenham (1957) found that derivatives of β-naphthylpropionic acid carrying a methyl, ethyl, or isopropyl group at C_7 undergo *peri* ring closure to

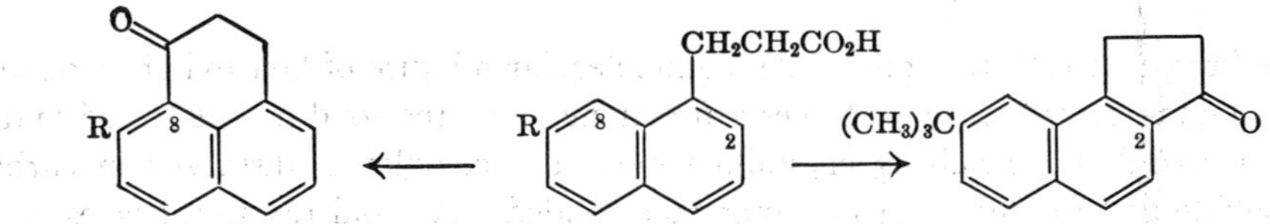

(1)   (2)   (3)
R=CH₃, C₂H₅, CH(CH₃)₂

perinaphthanones (1), whereas the 7-*t*-butyl derivative yields 2'-*t*-butyl-4,5-benzindane-1-one (3). The method of W. S. Johnson[1] (1945) proved of service for distinguishing between the two possible structures. The formyl derivative (5) of cyclohexanone reacts in acetic acid with hydroxylamine hydrochloride to give the neutral isoxazole (6), which is readily cleaved to the acidic β-ketonitrile (7). Cyclopentanone gives a formyl derivative (9) which reacts with hydrox-

---

[1] William S. Johnson, b. 1913 New Rochelle, N. Y.; Ph.D. Harvard (Fieser); Univ. Wisconsin; Stanford Univ.

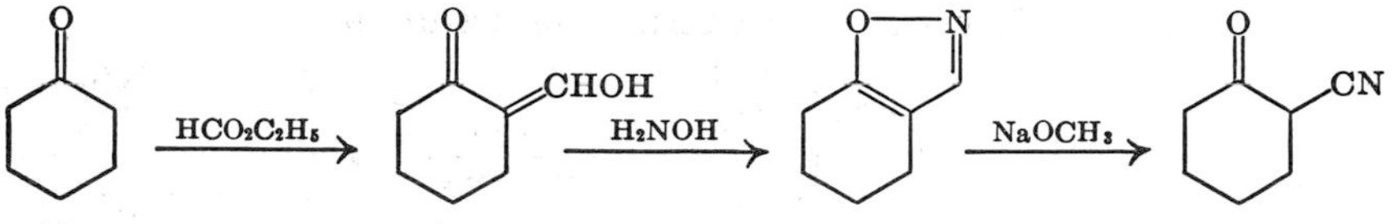

ylamine to give the colored, weakly acidic disubstituted hydroxylamine (10). The test is generally applicable to 5- and 6-ring ketones having one α-methylene group. The ketone (3) gave a deep red hydroxylamine derivative soluble in alcoholic alkali (not in aqueous alkali) to give a deep violet colored solution.

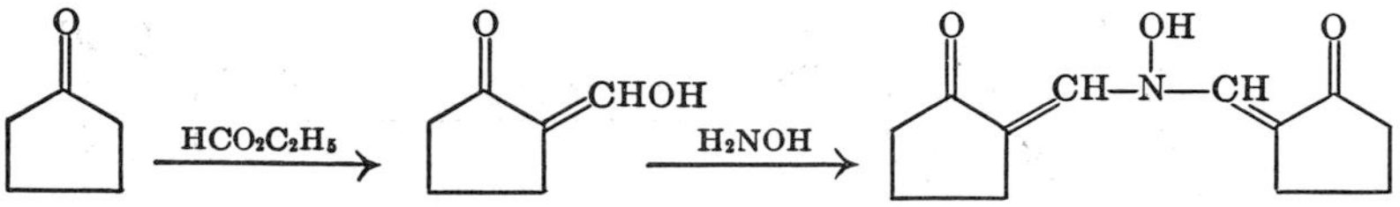

27.4   Monosubstitution Products. — The chief substitution reactions of naphthalene of practical value are summarized in Chart I, which also shows key transformation products of the resulting substances. Properties of the substances formulated and of a few additional members of the series are listed in Table 27.1.

Nitration of naphthalene must be conducted under controlled conditions to avoid formation of dinitro compounds, for the nitro group initially introduced into one ring has only a weak deactivating influence on the other nucleus. Naphthalene reacts much more readily than benzene, and best results are obtained with diluted mixed acid. In a procedure described by Fierz-David[1] and Blangey (1938), finely pulverized naphthalene (128 g.) is stirred into a mixture of 62% nitric acid (103 g.) and 80% sulfuric acid (300 g.), and the reaction conducted at 50–60° for seven hours. The crude material, which contains some unchanged hydrocarbon but only a trace of dinitro derivatives, can be reduced with iron powder and a mixture of water and concentrated hydrochloric acid (10:1) to α-naphthylamine in 77% overall yield from naphthalene.

Naphthalene is easily halogenated, for example by bromine in carbon tetrachloride solution at the reflux temperature (72–75% yield). Some dihalogenation invariably occurs, but dihalides can be eliminated by fractionation after the crude product has been warmed with powdered sodium hydroxide or steam distilled from an alkaline medium to destroy labile halo compounds. α-Bromonaphthalene readily forms a Grignard reagent, and carbonation of this derivative is the preferred method for preparation of α-naphthoic acid. A convenient preparation of α-naphthonitrile by refluxing α-bromonaphthalene in pyridine with cuprous cyanide has been described (23.10); the less expensive but lower boiling α-chloro compound can be employed with use of pressure equipment. The best route to β-naphthoic acid is hypochlorite oxidation of β-acetonaphthalene (24.3).

[1] Hans Eduard Fierz-David, 1882–1953; b. Zurich; Ph.D. London (Forster) and Zurich (on recommendation of Werner); ETH Zurich

CHART 1. NAPHTHALENE SUBSTITUTIONS

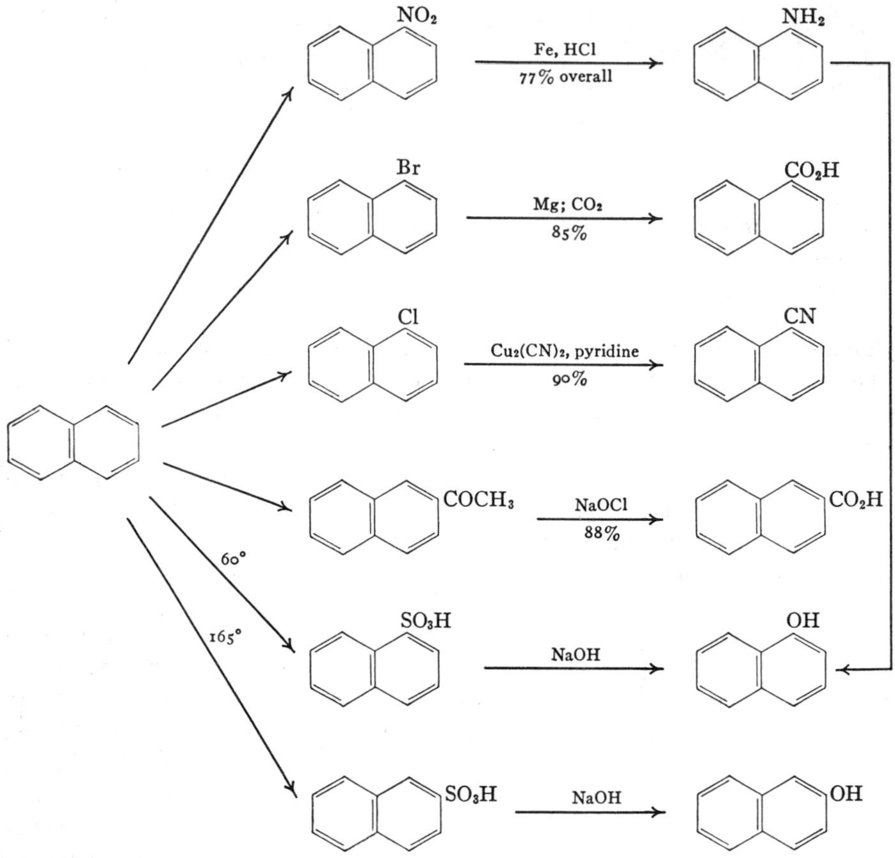

β-Naphthol is produced efficiently by alkali fusion of sodium naphthalene-β-sulfonate. The reaction can be conducted on a laboratory scale with 1 part of sodium hydroxide, mixed with 23% of water to lower the melting point, and 1.5 parts of the sulfonate; in the technical process the amount of sulfonate is increased to 2.8 parts. The sulfonate is added to the melt at 270–290°, and the temperature eventually is brought to 318°. The cooled melt is extracted with water, and the solution is acidified; the yield of β-naphthol, purified by distillation, is 84%. Economy in the technical process is achieved by adding the sodium sulfite-containing mother liquor from precipitation of the β-naphthol to the diluted sulfonation mixture in order to salt out sodium naphthalene-β-sulfonate; sulfur dioxide is liberated and is utilized to acidify the solution of the β-naphtholate melt. α-Naphthol can be prepared in a similar manner, but the product is not pure. A better process consists in hydrolysis of α-naphthylamine with 9.2% aqueous sulfuric acid at 200° and 14 atmospheres pressure; the product is pure and the yield 94–95%. The ready hydrolysis of the amine to the naphthol is a reaction seldom encountered in the benzene series but often applicable to amines of the more reactive naphthalene.

TABLE 27.1. MONOSUBSTITUTION PRODUCTS OF NAPHTHALENE

NAME	M.P., °C.	B.P., °C.	DISSOCIATION CONSTANT
Naphthalene-α-sulfonic acid (dihydrate)	90		
Naphthalene-β-sulfonic acid (monohydrate)	124		
α-Nitronaphthalene	61	304	
β-Nitronaphthalene	79		
α-Naphthylamine	49	301	pK_b 10.0
β-Naphthylamine	112	306	pK_b 9.3
α-Naphthol	94	280	pK_a 8.0
β-Naphthol	122	286	
α-Naphthoic acid	162		pK_a 3.7
β-Naphthoic acid	185		pK_a 4.15
α-Chloronaphthalene	liq.	259	
α-Bromonaphthalene	6.2	281	
β-Bromonaphthalene	59	282	
α-Naphthonitrile	37	299	
β-Naphthonitrile	66	306	

27.5   Bucherer Reaction. — β-Naphthylamine is prepared by a procedure developed by Bucherer[1] (1904), consisting in this instance in heating β-naphthol with aqueous ammonium sulfite or bisulfite. A sulfite solution is prepared by saturating concentrated ammonia solution with sulfur dioxide and adding an equal volume of concentrated ammonia solution; β-naphthol is added, and the charge is heated in an autoclave provided with a stirrer or a shaking

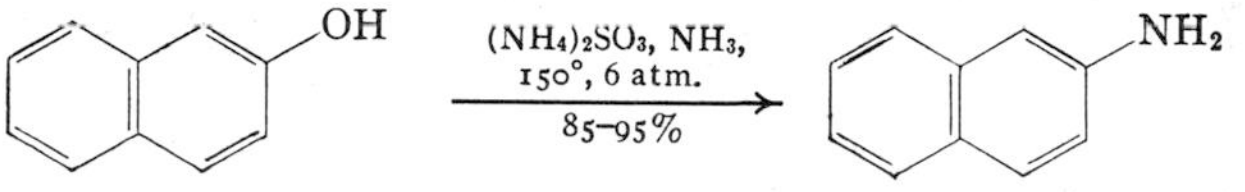

mechanism. The corresponding amine is obtained in excellent purity and high yield. Several comparable aminations have been realized in the naphthalene series, but the reaction requires a reactive aromatic nucleus and is not practicable for benzene derivatives other than particularly reactive polyhydroxy compounds such as resorcinol. Amination is reversible; for example, β-naphthylamine can be reconverted into β-naphthol by heating with aqueous sodium bisulfite solution and then adding alkali and boiling the solution until the ammonia is expelled. Both the amination and hydrolysis reactions are classified as Bucherer reactions.

Intermediate bisulfite addition products isolated initially were regarded as resulting from tautomerization of the naphthol or naphthylamine followed by addition of bisulfite to the carbonyl or ketimine group. However, investigations of A. Rieche and H. Seeboth (Berlin, 1960) have shown that the product of addition of sodium bisulfite to α-naphthol is sodium 1-tetralone-3-sulfonate (4),

[1] Hans Th. Bucherer, 1869–1949; b. Cologne, Germany; Ph.D. Leipzig (Wislicenus); Techn. Hochsch. Munich

which reacts with ammonia to give α-naphthylamine through the intermediate imine (5). The addition product (4) shows an infrared carbonyl band and reacts

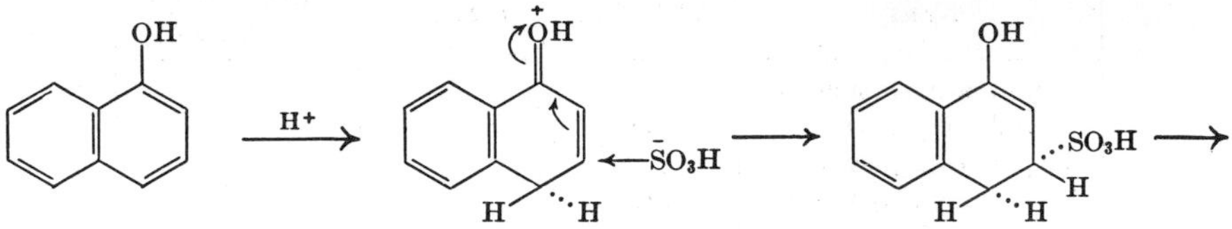

with carbonyl reagents, and the position of the sulfonate group was established by dehydrogenation to sodium 1-naphthol-3-sulfonate.

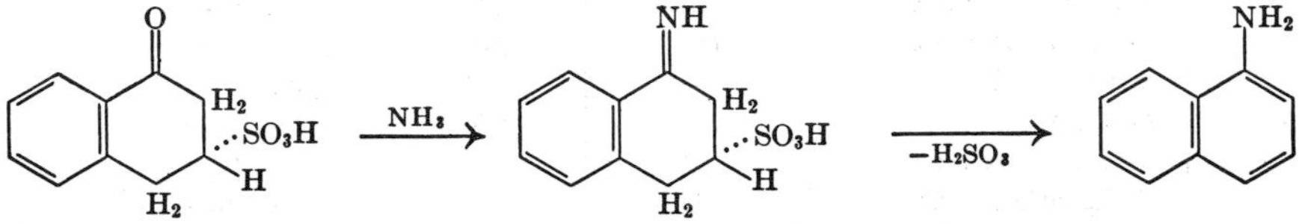

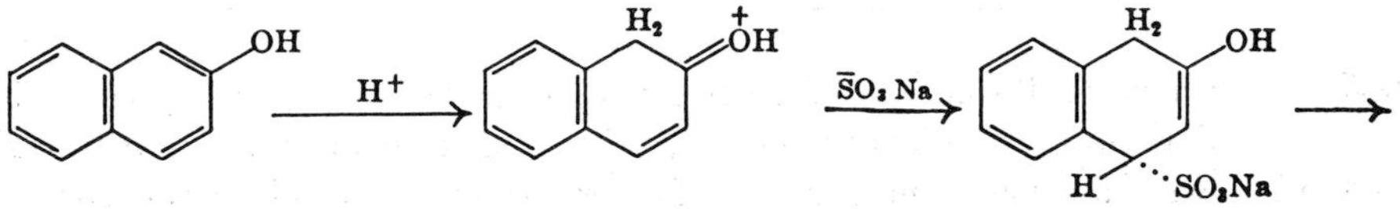

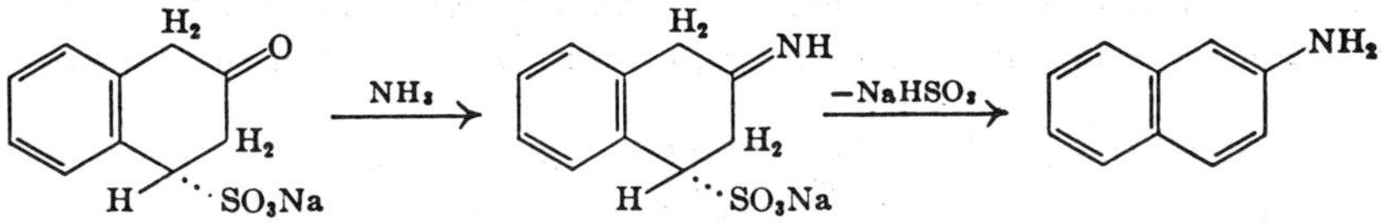

Other Derivatives. — The ready preparation of β-naphthylamine by the Bucherer reaction makes available substances otherwise difficultly accessible. Thus β-bromonaphthalene can be prepared in moderate yield by the Sandmeyer reaction, which likewise is employed for the preparation of β-naphthonitrile.

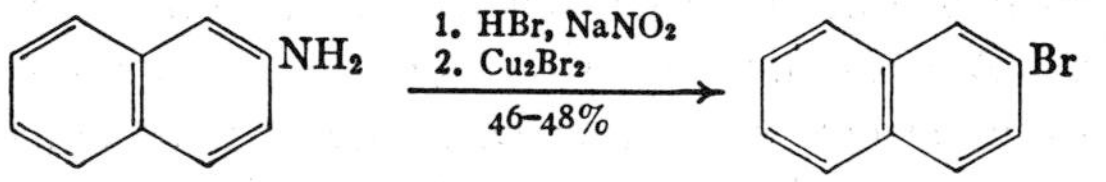

β-Nitronaphthalene is produced to a certain extent by the action of sodium nitrite on diazotized β-naphthylamine in the presence of cuprous hydroxide, but the process involves a time-consuming steam distillation of the difficultly volatile product, and the yield is only 10%.

27.6   Substitutions of Derivatives. — The course of substitution reactions of naphthalene derivatives is determined by a combination of factors. The group initially present exerts a directive influence, and either activates or deactivates the ring to which it is attached. α-Positions are, *per se*, more reactive than β-positions to normal substitutions or to sulfonations and Friedel-Crafts reactions conducted at low temperatures. In α-naphthol (I), the 4-position is particularly favored because it is a reactive α-position *para* to the powerfully activating hydroxyl group, and consequently it is the first point of attack. Dini-

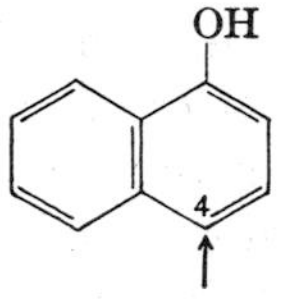

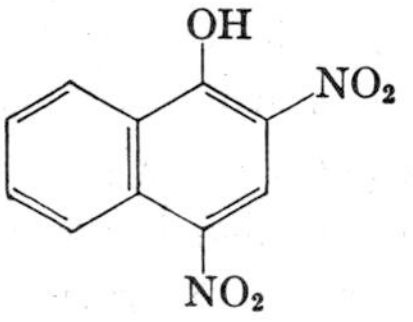

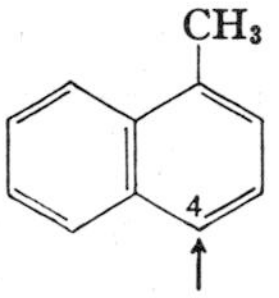

tration of α-naphthol is conducted, as in the preparation of picric acid, by conversion into the disulfonic acid and treatment of this derivative with nitric acid; the product is 2,4-dinitro-1-naphthol (II), or Martius Yellow, a dye. After introduction of one sulfonic acid or nitro group, the ring carrying the substituents is activated by the hydroxyl group and deactivated by the unsaturated, *meta* directing group, but the outcome of the reaction shows that the activating tendency predominates. In α-methylnaphthalene (III) the 4-position is also the preferential point of attack, for example in nitration or in low-temperature sulfonation (conducted with chlorosulfonic acid in carbon tetrachloride solution at 0°; 88% yield). Direct bromination affords chiefly 1-bromo-4-methylnaphthalene (m.p. 7°) in an impure condition and in low yield; the pure bromide is made more readily from the 4-sulfonate by the action of bromine in an aqueous solution of sodium bromide at 50° (yield 68%). α-Methylnaphthalene is substituted at the 4-position also in Friedel-Crafts acylations, even in nitrobenzene solution, which indicates that the *p*-directing effect of the methyl group overcomes the hindrance effect noted with naphthalene itself.

If one ring of the naphthalene nucleus carries a *m*-directing, deactivating group, a substituent tends to enter the other ring, preferentially at the more reactive α-position. Thus α-nitronaphthalene gives on nitration a mixture of the 1,5- and 1,8-dinitro compounds in which the latter predominates. The higher-melting 1,5-dinitronaphthalene is much less soluble than the isomer, and separation can be accomplished by crystallization from pyridine or by warming the

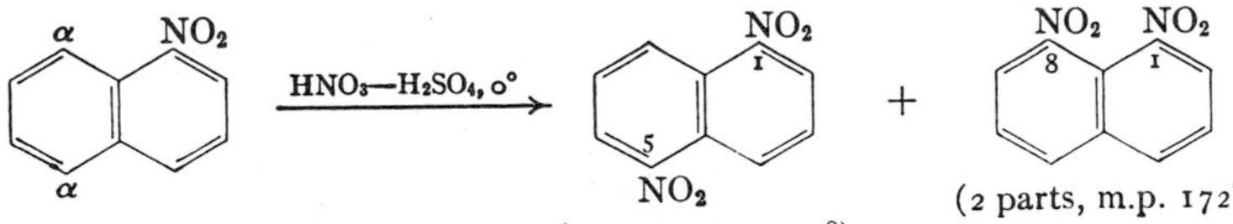

nitration mixture till the solid is dissolved and then allowing the 1,5-compound to crystallize. Another example of heteronuclear substitution is bromination of the rare β-nitronaphthalene, which affords 5-bromo-2-nitronaphthalene (m.p. 131°) as the chief product.

In β-naphthol, β-methoxynaphthalene, and β-methylnaphthalene, the point of first attack is the activated 1-position, which is the only available normal position *ortho* to the directing group. Thus β-naphthol couples exclusively at this position, β-ethoxynaphthalene on reaction with N-methylformanilide gives the 1-formyl derivative, and β-methylnaphthalene undergoes bromination and nitration at the 1-position. This position, however, though particularly reactive because of both the α- and the *o*-relationships, is flanked by a substituent on one side and by the adjacent ring on the other, and it is consequently hindered. In reactions subject to hindrance and to temperature effects, a 1-derivative is produced only as a transient phase, for under the usual operating conditions the substituent assumes a position in the second ring. Nitration of β-methylnaphthalene, which proceeds normally, may be contrasted to the sulfonation at only slightly elevated temperature, which affords the pure 6-sulfonic acid in high yield. Unhindered β-positions are available in the second ring at 6 and 7, but only the 6-position is

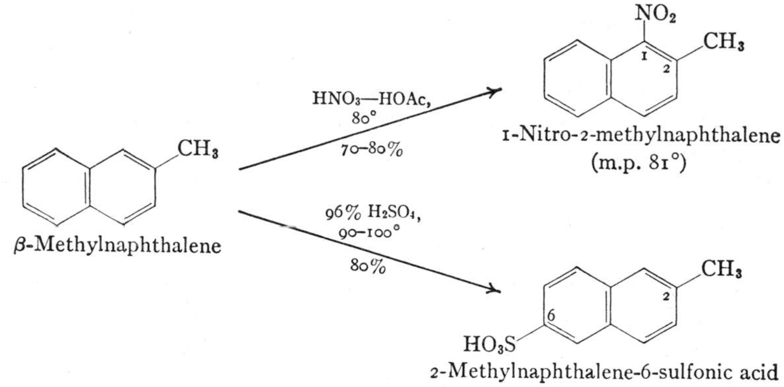

1-Nitro-2-methylnaphthalene
(m.p. 81°)

β-Methylnaphthalene

2-Methylnaphthalene-6-sulfonic acid

attacked. Since the same *amphi*-orientation applies to the thermal isomerization of naphthalene-1,8-dicarboxylic acid to the 2,6-diacid (24.15), the orientation is not dependent upon the chemical character of the group originally at $C_2(CH_3)$ or displaced to $C_2(CO_2H)$ but is determined by the steric factor. The superior stability of the 2,6- over the 2,7-disubstituted derivatives probably is due to their greater symmetry.

The behavior of 2,6-dimethylnaphthalene is interesting. On sulfonation in the cold the substance is attacked in an unhindered α-position to give the 8-sulfonic

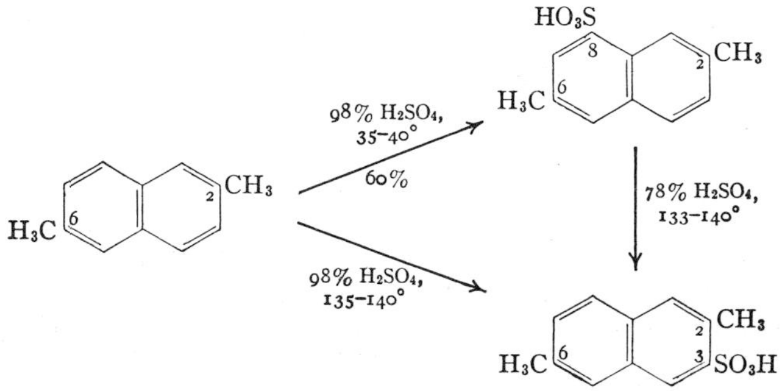

acid, which rearranges quantitatively when the sodium salt is heated with 78% sulfuric acid to give the β-substituted 3-sulfonate, the product of high-temperature sulfonation. The concentration of acid employed to effect the rearrangement is critical, for the sulfonate is hydrolyzed quantitatively to the hydrocarbon by 70% acid.

In Friedel-Crafts acylations, which also are subject to hindrance, β-methylnaphthalene is substituted in the 1-position in large part, though not exclusively, when the reaction is conducted with carbon disulfide or tetrachloroethane as solvent. In nitrobenzene solution β-methylnaphthalene is substituted principally in the 6-position (R. D. Haworth, 1932), as illustrated for the succinoylation reaction.

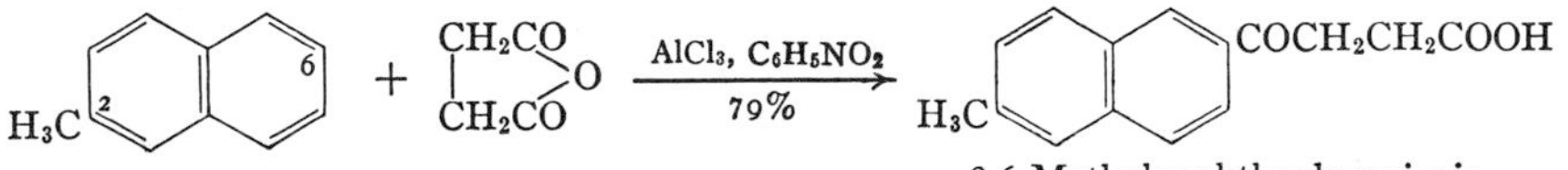

β-6-Methylnaphthoylpropionic
acid (m.p. 162°)

The 6-propionyl derivative (m.p. 62°) also is easily prepared (62% yield) by acylation in nitrobenzene solution. In general, 6-acylation in this solvent is a usual reaction of β-alkylnaphthalenes.

The 6-position is the favored point of secondary attack in substitutions of β-naphthol and analogous compounds. Dibromination of β-naphthol in acetic acid solution proceeds exothermally to give the 1,6-dibromo derivative, and the more reactive bromine atom at position 1 can be eliminated by adding tin and refluxing the mixture; reduction is accomplished by reaction of the metal with hydrogen bromide derived from the bromination step. Investigations of

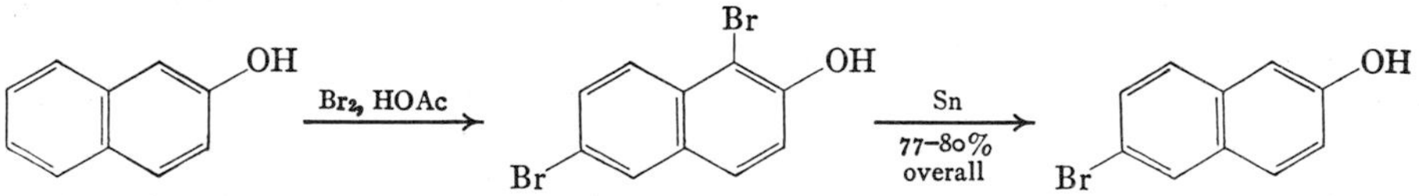

1,6-Dibromo-2-naphthol
(m.p. 106°)

6-Bromo-2-naphthol
(m.p. 129°)

the reaction by Zincke and by Fries have shown that the initially formed 1-bromo-2-naphthol reacts with bromine reversibly to form the 1,1-dibromo-2-keto compound, which can be isolated if sodium acetate is added to neutralize the hydrogen bromide. If the acid is not neutralized, as in the dibromination procedure cited, the equilibrium is shifted, and the material is converted irreversibly into the 1,6-dibromo derivative. A parallel reaction is conversion of acetyl β-naphthylamine into the 1,6-dibromo derivative, a substance useful as an intermediate to 1,6-dibromonaphthalene:

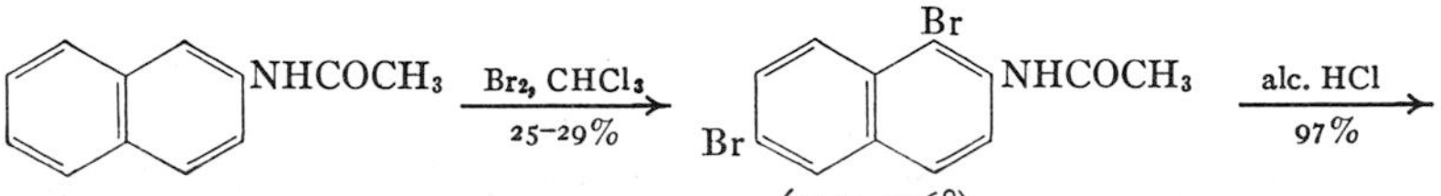

(m.p. 216°)

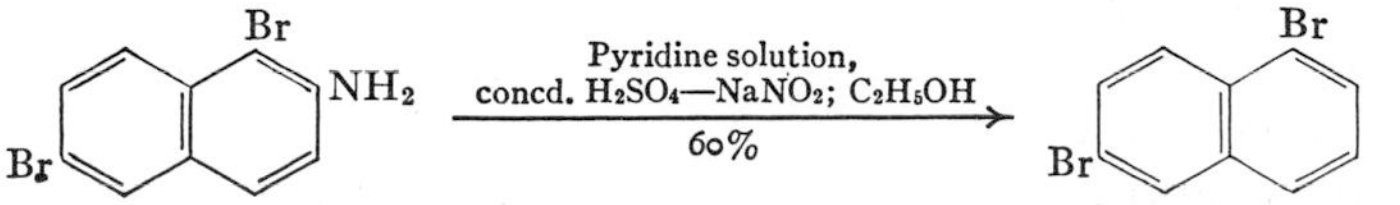

1,6-Dibromonaphthalene
(m.p. 57°)

In these substitutions attack by an electrophile at C_6 is attributable to a resonance structure with a negative charge at this position; position 7 is not similarly accessible.

The effect of hindrance in the Friedel-Crafts reaction is illustrated further by results of acetylation of β-methoxynaphthalene under different conditions. In carbon disulfide (or benzene) solution the chief product is the 1-aceto derivative;

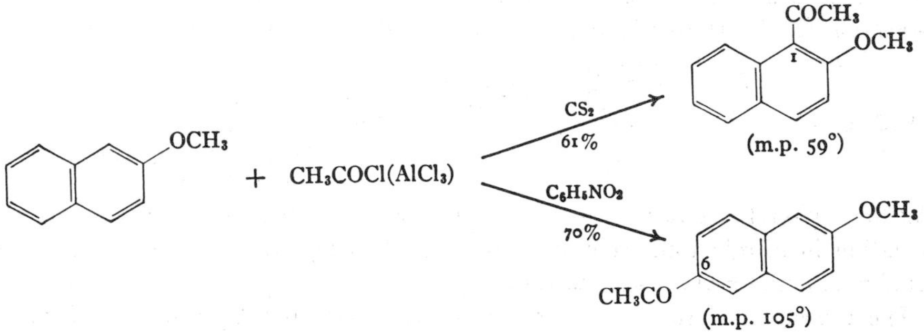

but when the reaction is conducted in nitrobenzene solution the 6-aceto derivative is produced in good yield.

27.7   Relative Reactivity of Naphthalene. — Substitutions generally proceed under milder conditions with naphthalene than with benzene, and a striking demonstration of the greater susceptibility of the bicyclic hydrocarbon to substitution is that in the Friedel-Crafts reaction of naphthalene with phthalic anhydride to form 2-α-naphthoylbenzoic acid, benzene can be used as solvent without interference with the reaction, for even though the monocyclic hydrocarbon is employed in large excess of naphthalene, very little o-benzoylbenzoic acid is formed. Naphthalene also shows greater reactivity in additions. It is reduced by sodium amalgam to the 1,4-dihydride, whereas benzene under the same conditions is unattacked. Naphthalene also is reducible to the tetrahydro stage (tetralin) with sodium and amyl alcohol, and the reaction stops abruptly at

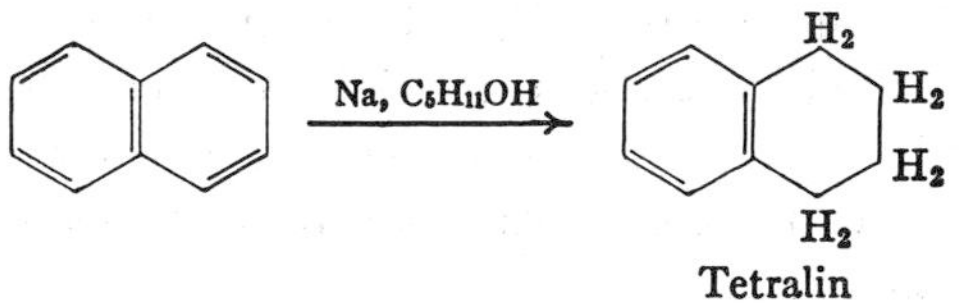

Tetralin

this stage because the benzenoid ring in the product is resistant to addition. Tetralin is prepared technically by partial catalytic hydrogenation.

A similar difference in reactivity is observable in oxidation reactions. Naphthalene is oxidized more readily, but a better criterion is the course of oxidation of the methyl derivatives of the two hydrocarbons. In toluene the methyl group is more susceptible to oxidation than the aromatic nucleus, for oxidation of the hydrocarbon affords benzoic acid in high yield. In the case of β-methylnaphthalene, the reactive α-positions in the nucleus appear more susceptible to oxidation than the methyl group, for oxidation with chromic acid under mild conditions affords chiefly 2-methyl-1,4-naphthoquinone. Naphthalene itself has been

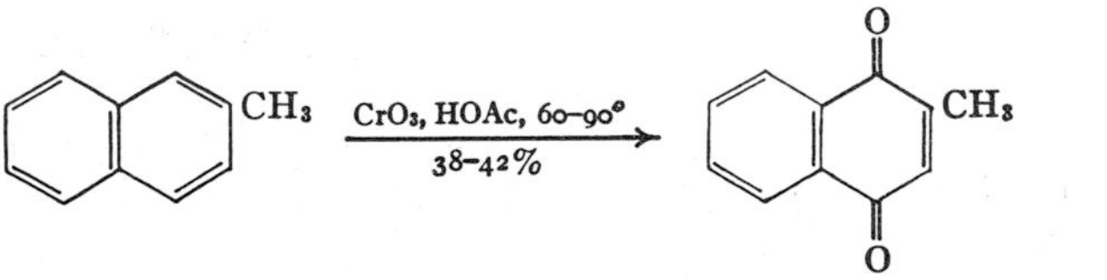

2-Methyl-1,4-naphthoquinone

converted by oxidation with chromic acid in acetic acid at a moderate temperature into α-naphthoquinone in 16% yield; the higher yield obtained with the β-methyl derivative can be attributed to the activating influence of the alkyl substituent on the adjacent α-position of the nucleus.

27.8   **Hydronaphthalenes.** — Naphthalene is reduced by sodium in boiling absolute ethanol to Δ^2-dialin, which is isomerized by boiling sodium ethoxide solution to the conjugated Δ^1-dialin, reducible with sodium and ethanol to tetralin. Addition of sodium to a solution of naphthalene in liquid ammonia,

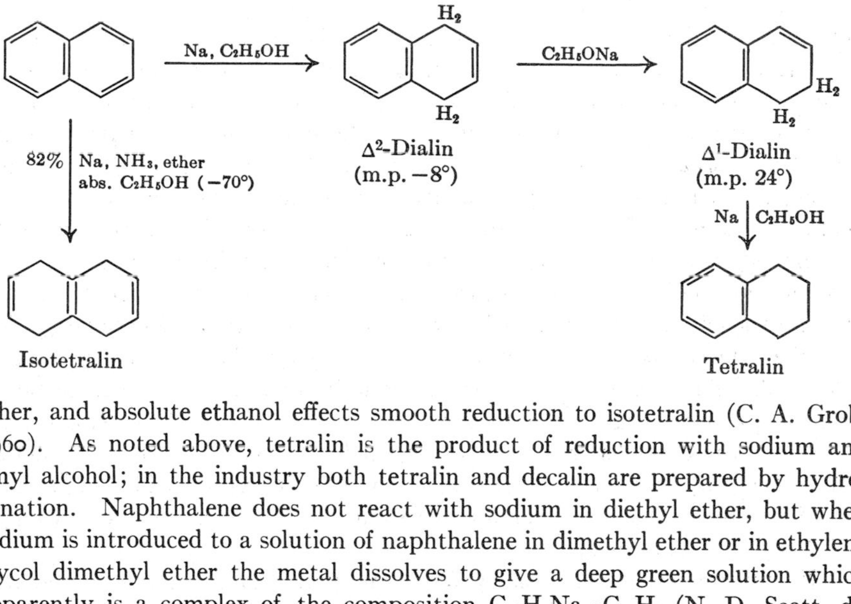

ether, and absolute ethanol effects smooth reduction to isotetralin (C. A. Grob, 1960). As noted above, tetralin is the product of reduction with sodium and amyl alcohol; in the industry both tetralin and decalin are prepared by hydrogenation. Naphthalene does not react with sodium in diethyl ether, but when sodium is introduced to a solution of naphthalene in dimethyl ether or in ethylene glycol dimethyl ether the metal dissolves to give a deep green solution which apparently is a complex of the composition $C_{10}H_8Na_2 \cdot C_{10}H_8$ (N. D. Scott, du Pont, 1936). The disodio derivative results from 1,2- and 1,4-addition, and the reaction stops when half the naphthalene has been utilized. By carbonation as the derivative is formed and at a rate just sufficient to keep the solution colorless, a crystalline mixture of Δ^1-dialin-3,4-dicarboxylic acid and Δ^2-dialin-1,4-dicarboxylic acids is obtained in 80% yield. The latter acid on oxidation with alkaline ferricyanide is converted smoothly into α-naphthoic acid [compare the last step in the synthesis of quinquephenyl (13.25) and oxidative decarboxylation (p. 577)].

The best route to Δ^9-octalin is reduction of naphthalene or tetralin with lithium in ethylamine (R. A. Benkeser,[1] 1955). The product is a mixture of Δ^9- and $\Delta^{1(9)}$-octalin in the ratio of 50:1, as determined by conversion to the crystalline

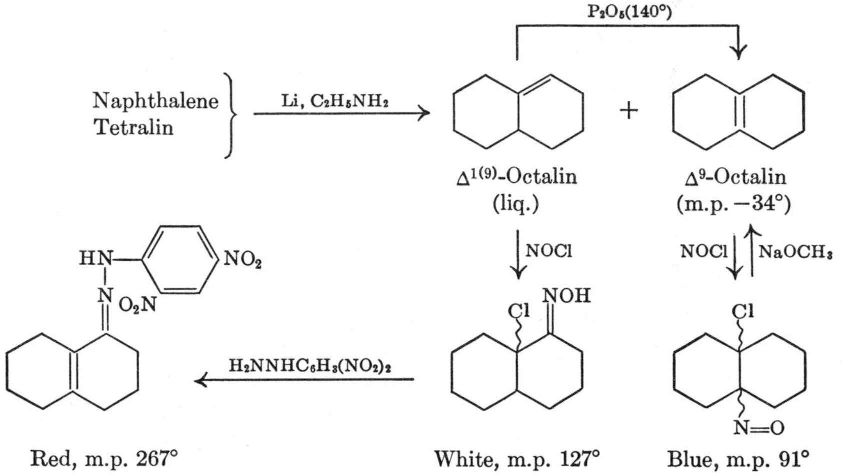

nitrosochloride derivatives (the wavy lines in the formulas indicate that the configurations are not known). The blue 9-chloro-10-nitrosodecalin is converted by sodium methoxide in methanol into pure Δ^9-octalin, as shown by the failure of the hydrocarbon to form an adduct with 2,4-dinitrobenzenesulfenyl chloride; $\Delta^{1(9)}$-octalin forms a yellow adduct, m.p. 143°. The white 9-chloro-1-oximino-decalin on reaction with 2,4-dinitrophenylhydrazine affords the derivative of 1-keto-Δ^9-octalin. The 50:1 mixture of Δ^9- and $\Delta^{1(9)}$-octalin when heated with phosphorus pentoxide affords a mixture in which the isomer ratio is 95:1. Lithium–amine reduction of ethylbenzene at the reflux temperature of ethylamine (17°) gave a mixture of 1-ethylcyclohexene (45%) and ethylcyclohexane (55%); when the reduction was carried out at −78°, 1-ethylcyclohexene was produced in 75% yield. The efficient conversion of aromatic hydrocarbons to monoolefins is regarded as involving 1,4-addition of the metal, reaction with solvent to form the 1,4-dihydride, isomerization to a conjugated diene, and further 1,4-reduction until ultimately a monoolefin is formed. In the Grob procedure for the preparation of isotetralin the conditions are such that the initial product of two 1,4-additions is not isomerized.

27.9   **Oxidation.** — P. S. Bailey[2] found (1957) that on ozonolysis in methanol at −70°, naphthalene absorbs two equivalents of reagent and affords in 85% yield a peroxidic ether derived from a dipolar precursor of the type postulated by Criegee (5.31). With catalysis by either acid or base, the substance undergoes hydrolytic rearrangement to phthalaldehydic acid. Ozonolysis of phenanthrene follows a similar course and affords a practical preparative route to two interesting compounds (P. S. Bailey, *Org. Syn.*, 1960). Prompt reduction

---

[1] Robert A. Benkeser, b. 1920 Cincinnati, Ohio; Ph.D. Iowa State College (Gilman); Purdue Univ.

[2] Philip S. Bailey, b. 1916 Chickasha, Okla.; Ph.D. Virginia (Lutz); Univ. Texas

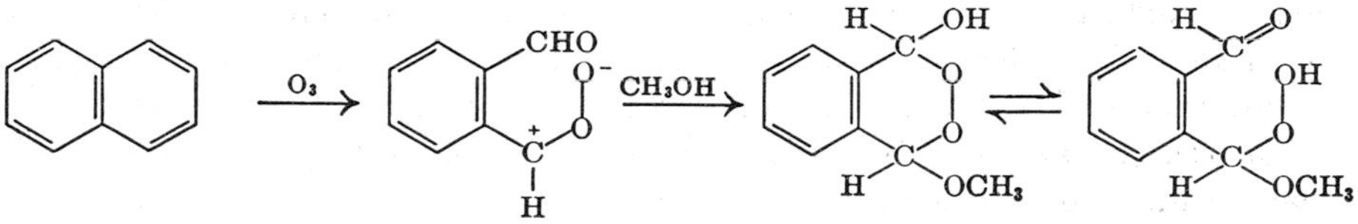

with sodium iodide of the product (2) of low-temperature ozonolysis affords diphenaldehyde (3). When the methanolic solution of (2) is let stand at room temperature and then cooled to 0°, the dimethoxy peroxide (4) separates in crystalline form. When refluxed with alcoholic alkali, this peroxide is converted in good yield into diphenaldehydic acid (5).

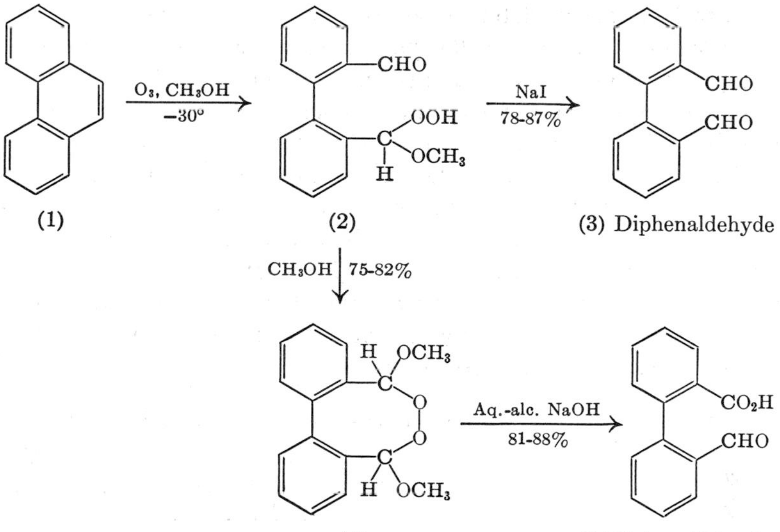

(1)   (2)   (3) Diphenaldehyde

(4)   (5) Diphenaldehydic acid

From urine of animals dosed with naphthalene, trans-3,4-dihydroxy-Δ¹-dialin (2) has been isolated in the dl-form (m.p. 100°; rats and rabbits) and in both optically active forms, m.p. 126°: rats, −159°; rabbits, +158° (E. Boyland,[1]

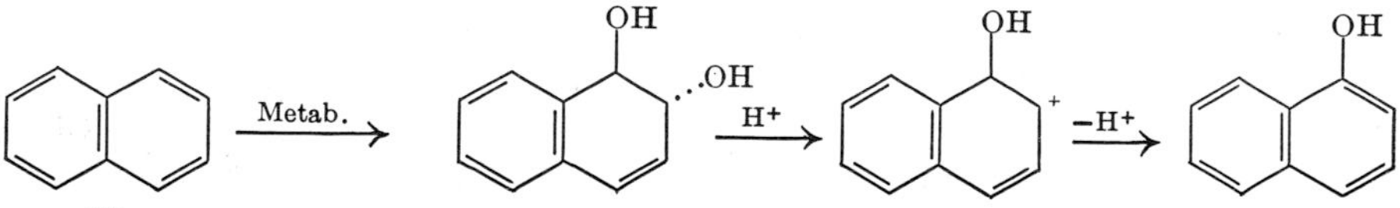

(1)   (2)   (3)   (4)

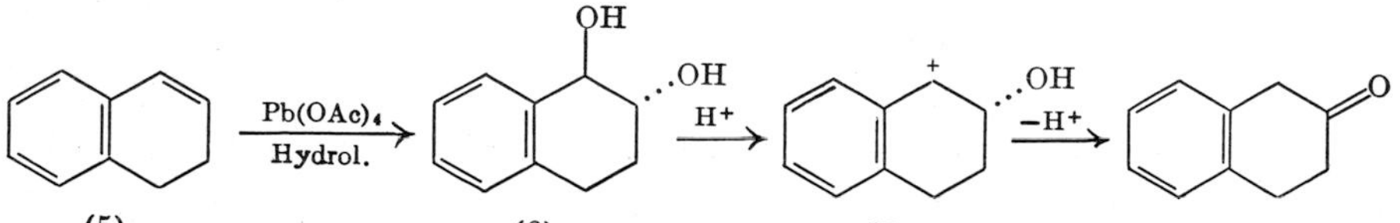

(5)   (6)   (7)   (8)

[1] Eric Boyland, b. 1905 Manchester; Ph.D. Manchester (Harden); Chester Beatty Res. Inst., Royal Cancer Hospital, London

1949). Reduction of 1,2-naphthoquinone with lithium aluminum hydride gives the *trans* diol, identical with the *dl*-metabolite. *cis*-1,2-Dihydroxytetralin results from hydroxylation of Δ¹-dialin with osmium tetroxide or permanganate (24% yield). *trans*-1,2-Dihydroxytetralin (6) is obtained by oxidation of Δ¹-dialin with lead tetraacetate and hydrolysis of the resulting diacetate. The behavior of the *trans* diols (2) and (6) on acid-catalyzed dehydration is interesting. The unsaturated diol (2) can form the carbonium ion (3) in which the charge is adjacent to the conjugated system, and the product is α-naphthol (4). The saturated diol (6) gives the similarly stabilized ion (7) and affords β-tetralone (8). The rate constant (k^{20}) for lead tetraacetate cleavage of the *trans* diol (6) is 2.0; for the *cis* isomer the constant is 40.

27.10   Azo Dye Intermediates. — Several sulfonic acid derivatives of α- and β-naphthol and α- and β-naphthylamine are valuable coupling components for production of azo dyes, and efficient methods have been developed in the industry for preparation of important members of the series. The following summary is based largely on an account by Fierz-David and Blangey (1938).

From α-Naphthylamine. — In analogy to the formation of sulfanilic acid, the acid sulfate of α-naphythlamine, when heated at diminished pressure for several hours, undergoes rearrangement to 1-naphthylamine-4-sulfonic acid, or **naphthionic acid (II).** By a reverse Bucherer reaction, that is, by heating the amine with aqueous sodium bisulfite and hydrolyzing the bisulfite-addition product with alkali, the substance can be converted in yield reported as quantitative into **1-naphthol-4-sulfonic acid, or Neville-Winter acid.**

CHART 2.   REARRANGEMENT OF α-NAPHTHYLAMINE ACID SULFATE

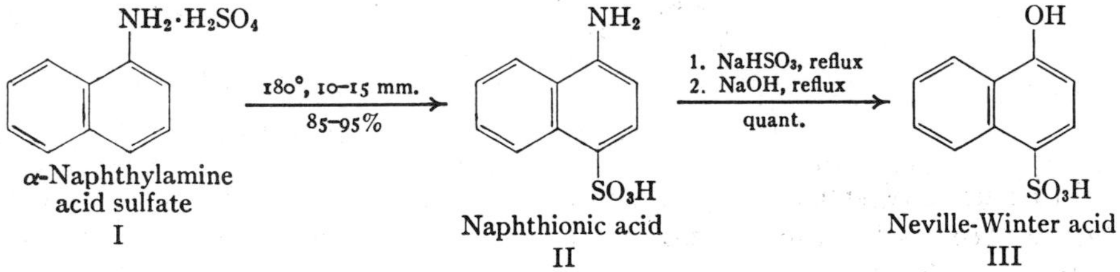

CHART 3.   SULFONATION OF β-NAPHTHOL

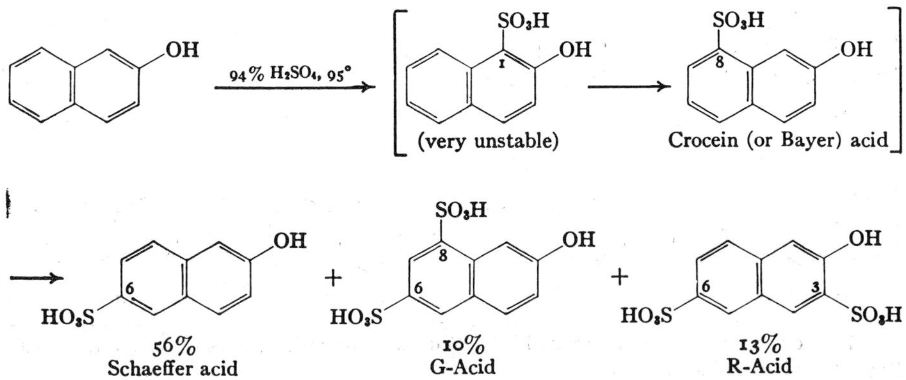

From β-Naphthol. — The chief products obtainable by sulfonation of β-naphthol are indicated in Chart 3. The initial product, as established in low-temperature sulfonations, is 2-naphthol-1-sulfonic acid; however, this is very unstable and rearranges to the 8-sulfonic acid, **crocein acid,** which can be prepared by operating at a low temperature, but which in the more useful sulfonation conducted at steam-bath temperature rearranges to the technically important **2-naphthol-6-sulfonic acid, or Schaeffer acid.** Although with proper control this acid is the chief product, it is accompanied by the 6,8- and 3,6-disulfonic acids, which are used as dye intermediates and are known as **G-acid** and **R-acid,** respectively, because of the yellowish ("gelb") and reddish colors of the derived azo dyes. The sulfonation mixture also contains small amounts of 2-naphthol-1,6-disulfonic acid and 2-naphthol-1,3,6-trisulfonic acid, but since these by-products have no technical value and complicate isolation of the main products, the sulfonation mixture is diluted with water and boiled to effect hydrolysis of the 1-sulfonic acid group. The mixture is then separated by virtue of the different solubilities of the metal salts, and the three important products, Schaeffer acid, G-acid, and R-acid, are obtained in a fairly pure state in the yields indicated. The procedure can be varied to make G-acid the principal product (87–93% yield) by increasing the amount and concentration of acid and by controlling the temperature to 60° to favor retention of the α-sulfonic acid group at the 8-position. Schaeffer acid on alkali fusion affords 2,6-dihydroxynaphthalene, m.p. 218° (51% yield).

When β-naphthol is sulfonated with sulfuric acid, even at room temperature, the initially formed 2-naphthol-1-sulfonic acid rearranges rapidly under hydrogen-ion catalysis. The rearrangement can be prevented by conducting the sulfonation with chlorosulfonic acid in a suspension in nitrobenzene at ice-bath temperature (Chart 4), and the 1-sulfonic acid, which can be isolated if desired as the pure

CHART 4. SULFONATION OF β-NAPHTHOL IN A NONAQUEOUS MEDIUM

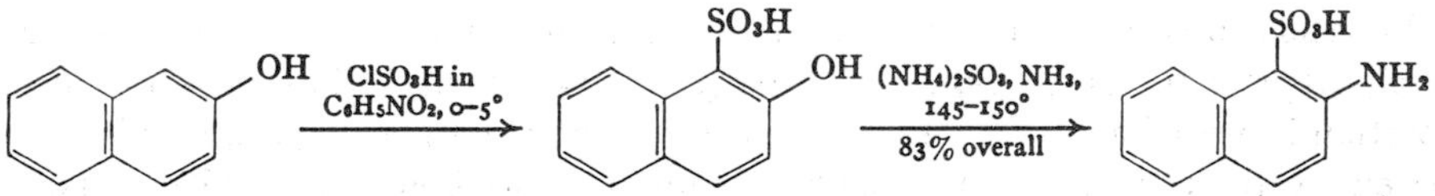

Tobias acid

sodium salt by extraction with water and addition of sodium chloride, is an intermediate in the production, by the Bucherer reaction, of the dye component **2-naphthylamine-1-sulfonic acid, or Tobias acid.**

From β-Naphthylamine. — Two useful dye intermediates, **γ-acid** and **J-acid,** are prepared in a sequence of reactions starting with the sulfonation of β-naphthylamine sulfate (I) with strong oleum (Chart 5). The amine is present as the ion, and the positively charged ammonium group deactivates the ring to which it is attached and hence largely diverts the entering groups into the other ring. With suitable adjustment of the conditions the main products are 2-naphthylamine-6,8-disulfonic acid (II) and 2-naphthylamine-1,5,7-trisulfonic acid (IV). The disulfonic acid is distinctly less soluble than the trisulfonic acid and is precipitated in a pure condition on suitable dilution of the reaction mixture with

CHART 5. γ-ACID AND J-ACID FROM β-NAPHTHYLAMINE SULFATE (I)

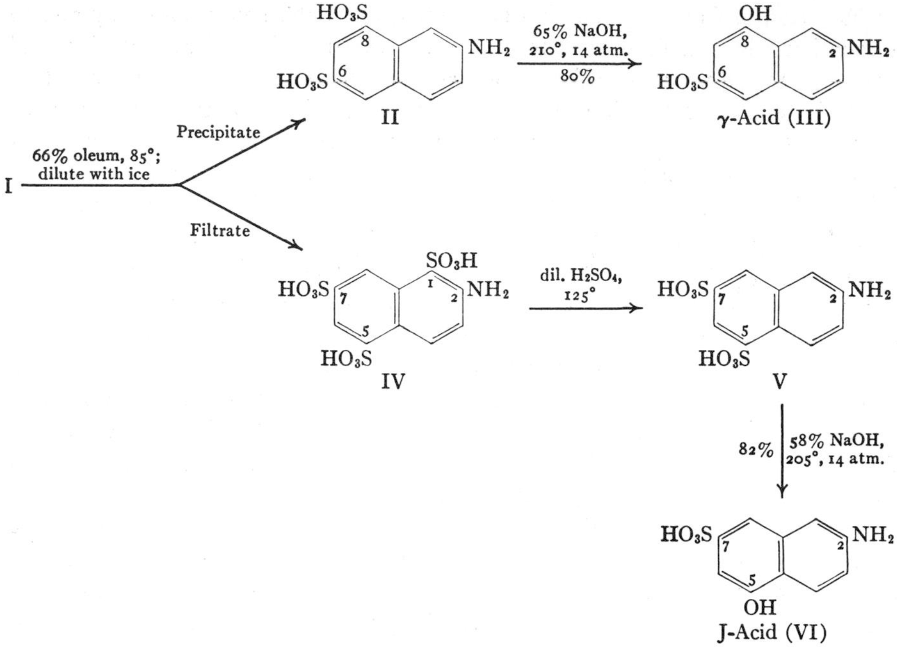

ice. The precipitated 2-naphthylamine-6,8-disulfonic acid on fusion with alkali under appropriate conditions is converted into γ-acid (III), since the sulfonic acid group at the α-position 8 is distinctly more reactive than that situated at the β-position 6. In technological terminology, γ-acid is described as aminonaphtholsulfonic acid-2,8,6; the functional groups are numbered in the order in which they are designated in the name. The mother liquor remaining from the diluted sulfonation mixture after collection of the precipitated 2,6,8-acid (II) contains 2-naphthylamine-1,5,7-trisulfonic acid (IV). When the dilute sulfuric acid solution is heated at 125°, the sulfonic acid group in the 1- or α-position is eliminated, with formation of 2-naphthylamine-5,7-disulfonic acid (V). Alkali fusion of V proceeds, as with the isomer II, by preferential attack of the α-sulfonic acid group, and 2-amino-5-naphthol-7-sulfonic acid, or J-acid, is produced in good yield.

From Naphthalene-β-Sulfonic Acid. — Mononitration of naphthalene-β-sulfonic acid (Chart 6) results in attack of the unsubstituted ring in the α-positions 5 and 8, and reduction of the product affords an easily separated mixture of **1-naphthylamine-6-sulfonic acid,** or **Cleve's acid,** and **1-naphthylamine-7-sulfonic acid** (or Cleve's acid-1,7). In the process starting with naphthalene, neither the β-sulfonic acid nor other intermediate is isolated. The hydrocarbon is sulfonated at 165° as described; the mixture is cooled, diluted with 85% sulfuric acid, and nitrated with 62% nitric acid, with reduction of the temperature to 15° as soon as the initially stiff mass becomes fluid enough to permit proper stirring. The mixture of nitronaphthalenesulfonic acids is reduced as the sodium salts with iron

CHART 6. CLEVE'S ACID-1,6 AND -1,7

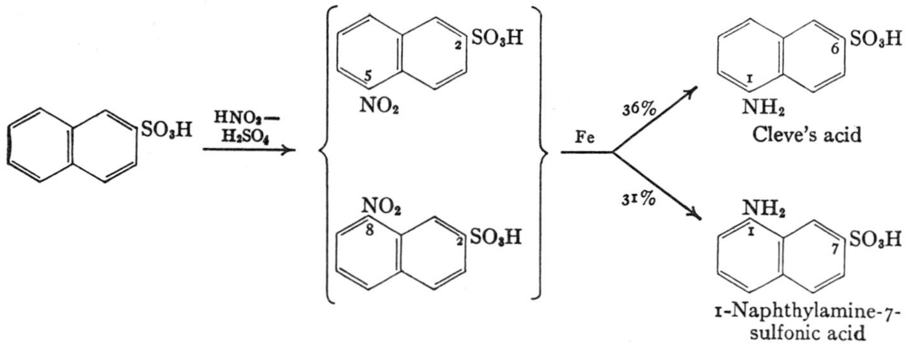

1-Naphthylamine-7-
sulfonic acid

powder and water weakly acidified with acetic and hydrochloric acid. 1-Naph-thylamine-7-sulfonic acid is separated by crystallization as the sparingly soluble sodium salt, and the 1,6- or Cleve's acid precipitates on acidification of the mother liquor. The two acids are valuable dye components; since they give azo dyes of practically identical color, they are often used in the form of the mixture. The yields of the separated acids indicated in Chart 6 are the overall yields from naphthalene.

H-Acid (V) and **chromotropic acid** (VI) can be made as alternative products of a sequence of reactions involving in the key step disulfonation of naphthalene-β-sulfonic acid (Chart 7). In analogy with the sulfonation of β-naphthylamine sulfate (see Chart 5), two sulfonic acid groups enter *meta* positions in the second ring on treatment of the monosulfonic acid (not isolated) with 60% oleum. On nitration of the resulting naphthalene-1,3,6-trisulfonic acid (II), substitution

CHART 7. H-ACID AND CHROMOTROPIC ACID

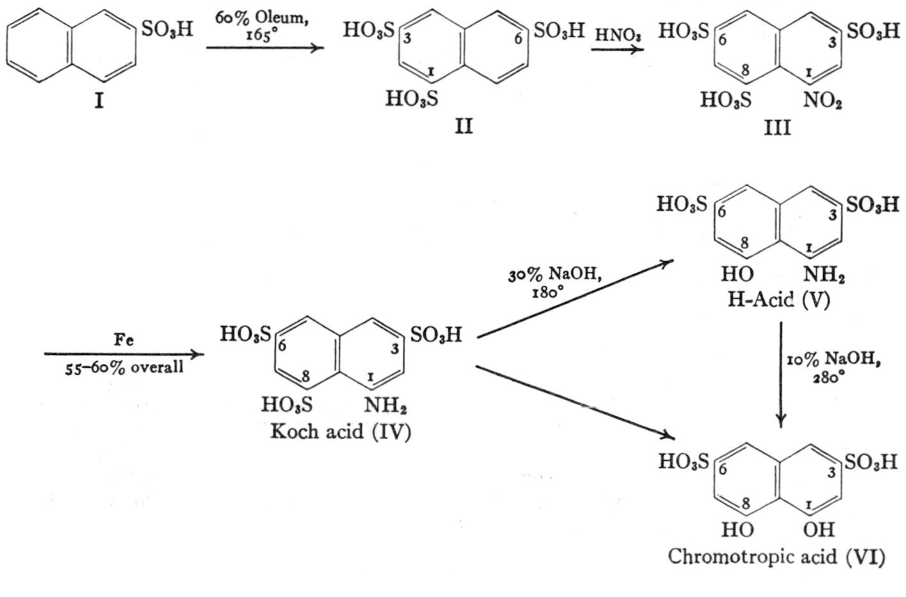

CHART 8. 1,8- AND 1,5-NAPHTHYLAMINESULFONIC ACIDS

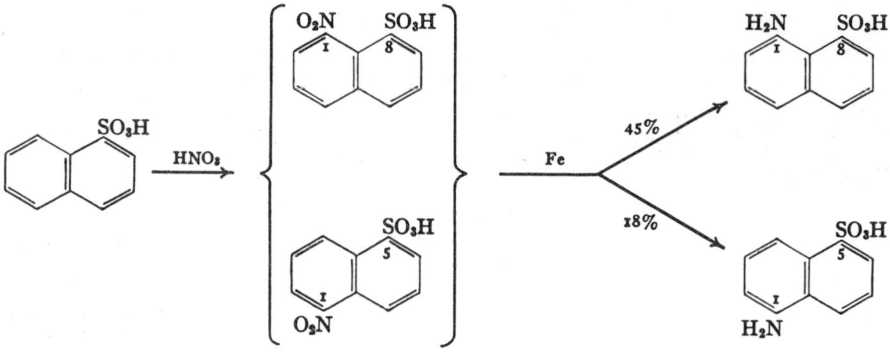

occurs in the only available position not *ortho* or *para* to one of the sulfonic acid groups to give III, which on reduction yields the corresponding amine, IV, **Koch acid.** Replacement of the α-sulfonic acid group at 8 to give H-acid (V, 1-amino-8-naphthol-3,6-disulfonic acid) is accomplished by fusion with weak alkali in an autoclave at a controlled temperature. The amino group is hydrolyzed at higher temperatures, and the process thus can be varied to afford 1,8-dihydroxynaphthalene-3,6-disulfonic acid, or chromotropic acid (VI).

Nitration of Naphthalene-α-Sulfonic Acid. — By a process analogous to the preparation of Cleve's acid (Chart 6), naphthalene-α-sulfonic acid resulting from low-temperature sulfonation is converted by nitration and reduction (Chart 8) into **1-naphthylamine-8-sulfonic acid (Peri acid)** and **1-naphthylamine-5-sulfonic acid.** The 1,8-acid, resulting as the chief product in 45% yield from naphthalene, is isolated by crystallization of the sodium salt; the 1,5-acid separates as the inner salt on acidification of the mother liquor.

1-Naphthylamine-8-sulfonic acid is utilized for the preparation of the further dye component **Chicago acid,** or **1-amino-8-naphthol-2,4-disulfonic acid** ("1,8, 2,4-acid"), by the process outlined in Chart 9.

CHART 9. CHICAGO ACID

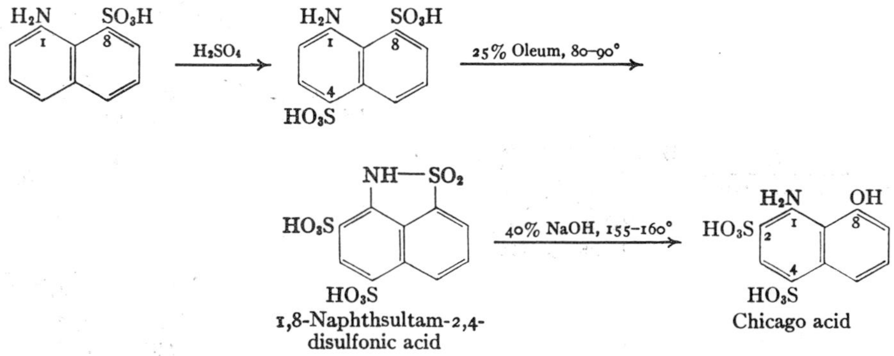

1,8-Naphthsultam-2,4-disulfonic acid

Chicago acid

PROBLEMS

1. Suggest methods for the preparation of each of the following compounds from an available monosubstitution product of naphthalene:
   (a) β-Benzoylnaphthalene
   (b) α-Naphthaldehyde
   (c) β-Iodonaphthalene
   (d) β-Isopropylnaphthalene

2. Indicate methods by which each of the following compounds can be prepared from β-naphthol:
   (a) 2,6-Dihydroxynaphthalene
   (b) 1-Amino-2-naphthol
   (c) 1-Nitroso-2-naphthol
   (d) 6-Ethyl-2-hydroxynaphthalene
   (e) 1-n-Propyl-2-naphthol

3. Give methods for the preparation of each of the following compounds from β-methylnaphthalene:
   (a) 1-Amino-2-methylnaphthalene
   (b) 2-Methylnaphthalene-6-carboxylic acid
   (c) 6-Methyl-2-naphthylamine

4. How could the following compounds be obtained starting with α-nitronaphthalene or its reduction product?
   (a) 1,5-Diaminonaphthalene
   (b) 1,3-Dibromonaphthalene
   (c) 2,4-Diamino-1-naphthol

5. Outline a synthesis of phenanthrene from naphthalene.

Chapter 28

NONBENZENOID AROMATICS AND PSEUDOAROMATICS

28.1 **Hückel Rule.** — In 1938 the German physical chemist Erich Hückel, noting that the carbon atoms of benzene are coplanar and that the number of π electrons (6) is represented by the expression 4n + 2, where n is an integral number, predicted that other monocyclic systems in which the π electron centers are arranged on a circle and which are capable of resonance should have aromatic properties if, and only if, the number of π electrons conforms to the pattern 4n + 2. Cyclooctatetraene contains 8 π electrons, and hence the pattern (6n + 2) is unfavorable for resonance stabilization and the molecule is tub-shaped (16.6). Since the Hückel rule applies only to structures in which all the atomic orbitals participating in the π electron system are peripheral ones, attempted application to condensed systems can be misleading. Thus the rule applies to naphthalene, but it does not fit the cases of the aromatic types acenaphthylene,

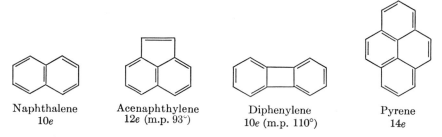

Naphthalene	Acenaphthylene	Diphenylene	Pyrene
10*e*	12*e* (m.p. 93°)	10*e* (m.p. 110°)	14*e*

diphenylene, or pyrene.

28.2 **Aromatic Anions.** — Thiophene, pyrrole, and furane derive aromaticity from the sextet of electrons composed of the four π electrons from the double bonds together with the unshared electron pair from the heterocyclic atom.　Cyclopentadiene is formally analogous to these heterocycles but, because of the lack of a lone electron pair, it is completely devoid of aromatic character. The cyclopentadienyl anion, however, displays the stability predicted by the Hückel rule, and indeed the hydrocarbon has been known since the work of Thiele in 1901 (13.19) to have an acidic hydrogen and to react with granular potassium to form potassium cyclopentadienylide, represented as five resonance structures (a), or in a cumulative formula (b) indicating that the charge is dis-

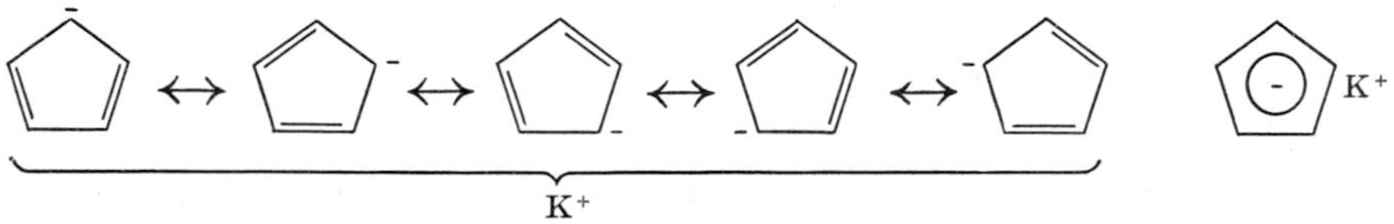

(a)　　　　　　　　　　　　　　　　　　　　　　　(b)

tributed over the five carbon atoms.　Grignard prepared the corresponding cyclopentadienylmagnesium bromide by reaction of the hydrocarbon with C_2H_5MgBr.　A group of highly ionic compounds now known is exemplified by pyridinium cyclopentadienylide (III), obtained by treating cyclopentadiene

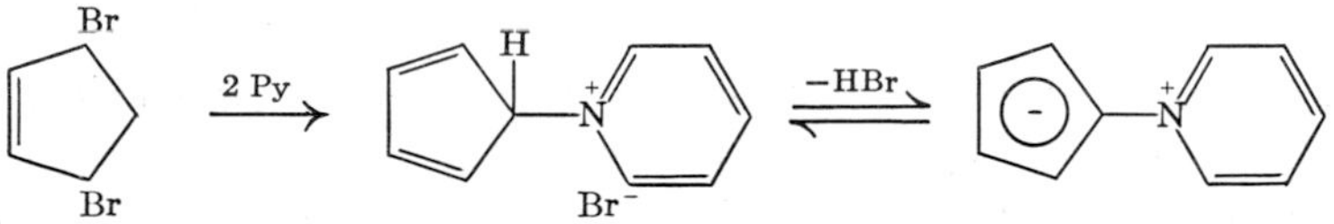

I　　　　　　　　　　　II　　　　　　　　　　　III

dibromide (I) with pyridine to yield cyclopentadienylpyridinium bromide (II), which loses hydrogen bromide readily (and reversibly) to form III (D. Lloyd, 1955).　Reaction of the dibromide I with trimethylamine and with triphenylphosphine gives the trimethylammonium and triphenylphosphonium ylides (F. Ramirez, 1957).　The ylide III is red brown, and its highly polar character is evident from a wide range in intensity and diversity of color in solution.　Significant in the same respect is the high dipole moment (7.0 D) of triphenylphosphonium cyclopentadienylide.

The fulvenes (13.19) form an interesting group of nonbenzenoid hydrocarbons of moderate aromaticity.　Thus 6,6-dimethylfulvene has a dipole moment of 1.48 D, the negative end being directed toward the ring (J. Thiec, 1956).　This property indicates a contribution of the ylide form, and indeed the fulvene has a

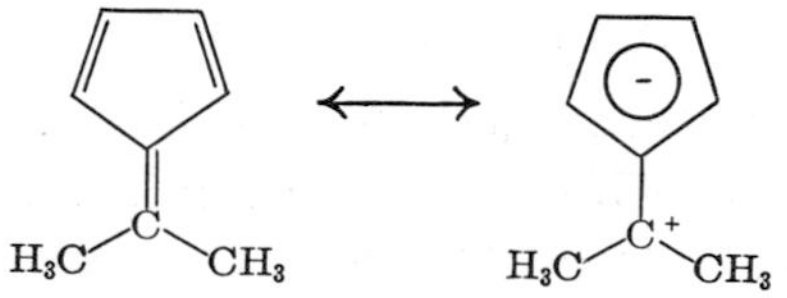

resonance energy of 11.9 kcal./mole (J. H. Day, 1957).　Hence the six π electrons become available in the five-membered ring because of the presence of the exocyclic double bond.　Doering (1953) prepared the related diazocyclopentadiene by treating cyclopentadienyllithium with *p*-toluenesulfonazide. In this remarkably

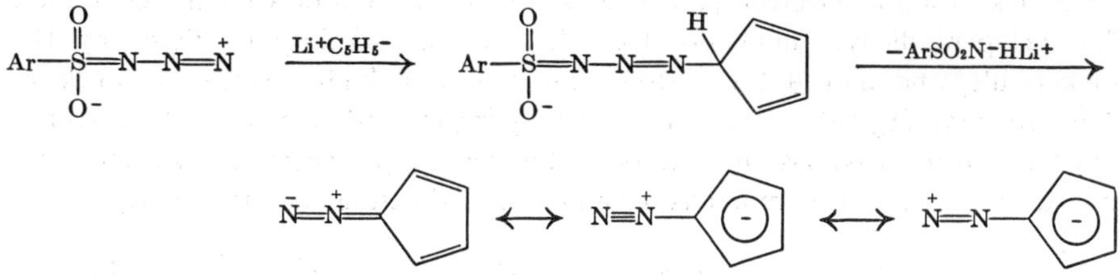

stable dark red compound (b.p. 53°/50 mm.) the positive charge is accommodated by the nitrogen atom.

The nonexistence of cyclopentadienone is attributable to the fact that the ylide structure is impossible, since oxygen is more negative than carbon. A related observation is that 2-cyclopentene-1,4-dione is completely ketonic; the enol form would be a hydroxycyclopentadienone (C. H. DePuy,[1] 1959). The yellow dione

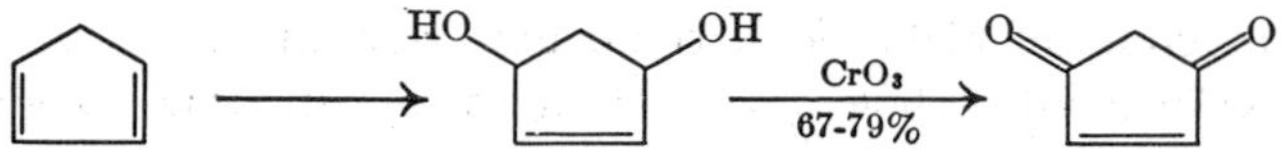

(with isomers)   M.p. 36°

is obtainable by oxidation of 2-cyclopentene-1,4-diol with chromic acid in a stirred mixture of dilute sulfuric acid and methylene chloride (*Org. Syn.*, 1961). A diol mixture prepared from cyclopentadiene via the monoepoxide on fractionation affords about 70% of 2-cyclopentene-1,4-diol and 30% of 3-cyclopentene-1,2-diol.

28.3   Ferrocene. — The most striking example of aromaticity in the five-membered ring is afforded by ferrocene (dicyclopentadienyliron). This stable, crystalline orange compound (m.p. 173°) was obtained by T. J. Kealy and P. L. Pauson[2] in 1951 as a product of the reaction of cyclopentadiene in ether with ethylmagnesium bromide and ferric chloride. The Grignard reagent reduces the ferric chloride to ferrous chloride and converts the hydrocarbon into cyclopentadienylmagnesium bromide and reaction takes place as in (1). A convenient procedure (2) utilizes diethylamine as base in the reaction between cyclopentadiene

1. $2 C_5H_5MgBr + FeCl_2 \longrightarrow Fe(C_5H_5)_2 + MgBr_2 + MgCl_2$
                                                    Ferrocene

2. $2 C_5H_6 + \frac{2}{3} FeCl_3 + \frac{1}{3} Fe + 2(C_2H_5)_2NH \xrightarrow[73-84\%]{} Fe(C_5H_5)_2 + 2(C_2H_5)_2NH \cdot HCl$

3. $2 C_5H_6 + 2 Fe(CO)_5 \xrightarrow{135°} (C_5H_5)_2Fe_2(CO)_4 \xrightarrow{250°} (C_5H_5)_2Fe$

4. $(C_5H_5)_2Fe_2(CO)_4 + 2 C_5H_5R \longrightarrow 2 C_5H_5FeC_5H_4R + 4 CO + H_2$

and ferrous chloride (G. Wilkinson, *Org. Syn.*). Another method involves heating cyclopentadiene with iron or an iron carbonyl, or passing a mixture of hydrocarbon and hydrogen over ferric oxide. The iron carbonyl method (3) can be conducted in two stages and has the advantage that the carbonyl intermediate

[1] Charles H. DePuy, b. 1927 Detroit; Ph.D. Yale (Doering); Iowa State College
[2] Peter L. Pauson, b. Bamberg, Germany; Ph.D. Sheffield (R. D. Haworth); Sheffield Univ.: Royal College Sci. and Techn., Glasgow

from cyclopentadiene can be heated with a substituted cyclopentadiene to effect the synthesis of an unsymmetrically substituted ferrocene (4).

The structure of ferrocene was deduced independently in 1952 by G. Wilkinson, R. B. Woodward, *et al.*, and by E. O. Fischer.[1] Two cyclopentadiene anions combine with the ferrous ion to form a completely covalent neutral molecule of double-cone structure. X-ray evidence shows that ferrocene is centrosymmetrical, with the two rings lying in parallel planes and with all carbon atoms equidistant from

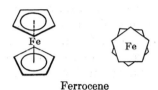

Ferrocene

the central iron atom. The compound is diamagnetic, has no dipole moment, and the infrared spectrum shows but a single C—H stretching band at 2075 cm^{-1}, which is within the range observed for C—H stretching bands in benzenoid compounds. Ferrocene is stable at a temperature of 400°; it is resistant to alkali and, in the absence of oxygen, it is resistant to acids. Acidic oxidizing agents convert the substance into the much less stable blue cation, $[Fe(C_5H_5)_2]^+$. Since ferrocene is volatile with steam, steam distillation affords a ready means of purification.

The chemical behavior of ferrocene characterizes the substance as more highly aromatic than benzene in the sense that it has a greater tendency to undergo electrophilic substitutions and a greater resistance to addition reactions. Substitutions include Friedel-Crafts acylation, sulfonation, mercuration, and metalation with butyllithium or phenylsodium. Ferrocene shows high reactivity also in free-radical arylation with diazonium salts. No nucleophilic substitutions have been reported. Reactivity of a high degree is demonstrated by the reaction of ferrocene with N-methylformanilide to give ferrocenecarboxaldehyde and with bis(dimethylamino)methane in the presence of phosphoric acid to form N,N-di-

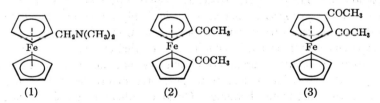

(1)   (2)   (3)

methylaminomethylferrocene (1), the methiodide of which is convertible by reaction with potassium cyanide into ferrocenylacetonitrile and by alkaline cleavage into hydroxymethylferrocene (C. R. Hauser, *Org. Syn.*, 1960). Friedel-Crafts acylations can be effected with mildly active catalysts (*e.g.* H_3PO_4). The reaction with acetyl chloride and excess aluminum chloride affords as the chief product 1,1'-diacetylferrocene (2); free rotation about the single bond excludes the existence of additional isomers of this type. The structure of the product was inferred

[1] Ernst Otto Fischer, b. 1918 Munich; Ph.D. Tech. Hochsch. Munich (W. Hieber); Munich

from the fact that hypohalite oxidation gives a ferrocenedicarboxylic acid of pK_{a_1} 6.5 and pK_{a_2} 7.6; the absence of a large spread between the constants shows that the two groups are not in the same ring. A. N. Nesmeyanov,[1] D. N. Kursanov, M. E. Volpin *et al.* (1956) supplied degradative proof of the structure assigned. Conversion to the diethyl derivative and hydrogenation under forcing conditions afforded ethylcyclopentane in over 50% yield. A small amount of an isomeric diacetylferrocene isolated by chromatography was characterized as the 1,2-derivative by the observation that the corresponding diacid forms a monomeric anhydride. The resistance of the five-membered rings of ferrocene to addition reactions is evident from the fact that with derivatives having attached phenyl groups or having benzene rings fused to the five-membered rings, the phenyl groups or fused rings can be hydrogenated without attack of the ferrocene system (E. O. Fischer, 1954).

A substituent in one ring of ferrocene seems capable of exerting a transannular activating or deactivating effect on substitution in the second ring. Thus Friedel-Crafts acylation with a mild catalyst (BF_3, $SnCl_4$, and especially H_3PO_4) stops with the introduction of one acyl group. Reaction with the potent reagent chlorosulfonic acid leads exclusively to monosulfonation.

The ease of oxidation of ferrocene prevents direct substitution by nitric acid or halogen. Ferrocenylamine (5) has been prepared by reaction of ferrocenyllithium (4) with O-benzylhydroxylamine (Kocheshkov reaction) and by Curtius degradation of ferrocenecarboxylic acid via the ester, hydrazide, azide, and benzylurethane (6). The amine (5) is very sensitive to air and heat, and attempts to effect

diazotization have failed. Haloferrocenes, available by reaction of a mercurated ferrocene with an appropriate halogen, are remarkably inert; thus they fail to form Grignard reagents or to react with copper in the Ullmann reaction.

The experiences with aromatic substitutions carried out with the dicyclopentadienyl derivatives of ruthenium and osmium show that the reactivity falls off progressively with increasing molecular weight, presumably because of increasing strength of the ring-metal bonding. Cyclopentadienylmagnesium tricarbonyl undergoes Friedel-Crafts acylation and alkylation and it is intermediate in reactivity between anisole and benzene, and thus is much less reactive than ferrocene. Ruthenocene (m.p. 200°) is prepared by addition of cyclopentadiene to a suspension of sodium in 1,2-dimethoxyethane (a good solvent for cyclopentadienyl sodium) until evolution of hydrogen has ceased, adding a mixture of ruthenium trichloride and ruthenium metal, and heating the mixture under nitrogen; yield 56–69% (*Org. Syn.*, 1961).

[1] A. N. Nesmeyanov, b. 1899 Moscow; D.Sci. Moscow; Moscow Univ.; Institute of Organic Chemistry, USSR Academy of Sciences

28.4   **The Tropylium Cation.** — The alkaloid atropine was so named because
it was isolated from *Atropa belladonna*. When the substance was
found to be an ester, the acidic and alcoholic products of hydrolysis were named
tropic acid and tropine. Eventually tropic acid was characterized as α-hydroxy-
methylphenylacetic acid, $C_6H_5CH(CH_2OH)CO_2H$ and tropine was found to be a
cycloheptanol having an N-methyl bridge, as shown in the formula. In one of
the early investigations of structure, G. Merling (1891) converted tropine by de-

Tropine   Tropilidene

hydration and two Hofmann degradations to an unsaturated hydrocarbon which
he named tropilidene. Merling regarded the substance as a methylenecyclo-
hexadiene, and he did not explore further his interesting observation that the liquid
dibromide, when heated, slowly loses hydrogen bromide with conversion in part
to benzyl bromide and in part to a crystalline, yellow, bromine-containing, ether-
insoluble solid.

Willstätter deduced the true structure of tropilidene in 1898 and synthesized
the hydrocarbon in 1901, but he gave no attention to the yellow, saltlike substance
and the problem went neglected for half a century. Finally, in 1954, Doering
recognized that tropilidene offered the opportunity for testing another prediction
of the Hückel rule. This rule had correctly predicted aromaticity in the cyclopentadiene anion; it predicts similar resonance stabilization in cycloheptatriene
cation, the tropylium ion. Addition to tropilidene of one mole of bromine gave a
liquid dibromide which when heated at 70° (1 mm., 9 hrs.) afforded a yellow sub-

Tropylium bromide

stance which forms yellow prisms (m.p. 203°) from ethanol. The substance is insoluble in ether but dissolves readily in water to give a solution from which silver
nitrate precipitates silver bromide; on hydrogenation it affords cycloheptane.
The properties clearly indicate that the substance is the salt, tropylium bromide.
The infrared spectrum shows only four bands of significant intensity, a simplicity
consistent with the highly symmetrical structure of the six π electron ion. M. M.
Shemyakin (1958) proved the equivalence of the seven carbon atoms. Tropilidene
labeled in the methylene group was prepared from benzene and $C^{14}H_2N_2$ by the
Buchner reaction and converted into labeled tropylium bromide. Reaction of this
salt with phenylmagnesium bromide gave labeled phenylcycloheptatriene, which
was oxidized with permanganate to benzoic acid. If the charge in the ion is completely delocalized, the activity of the benzoic acid should be 14.3% that of the
tropylium bromide; the value found was 13.4%.

A route to tropylium bromide described by M. J. S. Dewar[1] and R. Pettit (1956) involves Buchner reaction of benzene with ethyl diazoacetate, conversion of the ester to norcaradienecarboxazide (1), and decomposition of the substance in benzene to a mixture of norcaradienyl isocyanate (2, liquid) and a high-melting solid later shown (Doering, 1961) to be the urea (3). Both substances on treatment with hydrogen bromide yield tropylium bromide. Another method is by

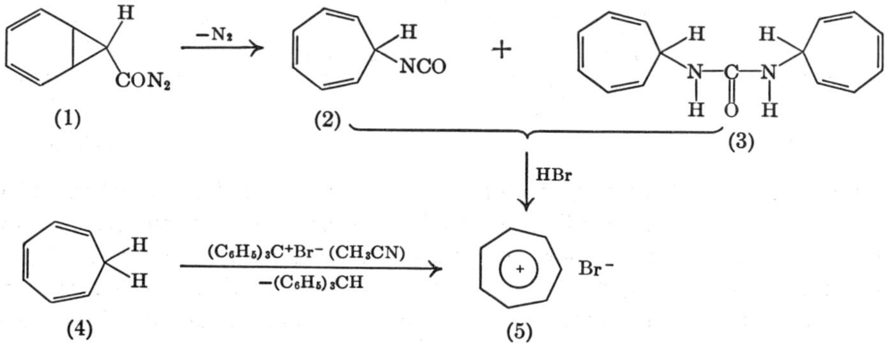

hydride abstraction from cycloheptatriene by reaction with a trityl salt in aceto-nitrile or liquid sulfur dioxide (H. J. Dauben, Jr., 1957).

G. L. Closs and L. E. Closs (1960) report the formation of tropylium chloride as a transient intermediate in the reaction of benzene with chlorocarbene, generated from methylene chloride and methyllithium. The chloronorcaradiene, if an

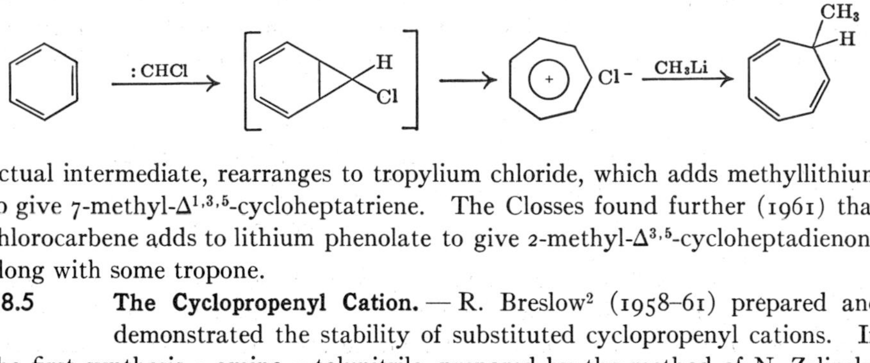

actual intermediate, rearranges to tropylium chloride, which adds methyllithium to give 7-methyl-$\Delta^{1,3,5}$-cycloheptatriene. The Closses found further (1961) that chlorocarbene adds to lithium phenolate to give 2-methyl-$\Delta^{3,5}$-cycloheptadienone along with some tropone.

28.5   The Cyclopropenyl Cation. — R. Breslow[2] (1958–61) prepared and demonstrated the stability of substituted cyclopropenyl cations. In the first synthesis α-amino-α-tolunitrile, prepared by the method of N. Zelinsky (1906), was converted into α-phenyldiazoacetonitrile, which on reaction with diphenylacetylene afforded 1,2,3-triphenylcyclopropenyl cyanide (overall yield 3%). This covalent compound on reaction with boron fluoride etherate containing a little water gave the triphenylcyclopropenyl hydroxylfluoroborate (actually a mixed salt), a high melting salt insoluble in ether. Reaction of this substance with methanol gave a covalent methyl ether, which on treatment with hydrogen

[1] Michael J. S. Dewar, b. 1918 Ahmednagar, India; D.Phil. Oxford (F. E. King); Queen Mary's College, Univ. London; Univ. Chicago

[2] Ronald Breslow, b. 1931 Rahway, N. J.; Ph.D. Harvard (Woodward); Columbia Univ.

bromide in ether gave another ether-insoluble salt (precipitation of AgBr, etc.).

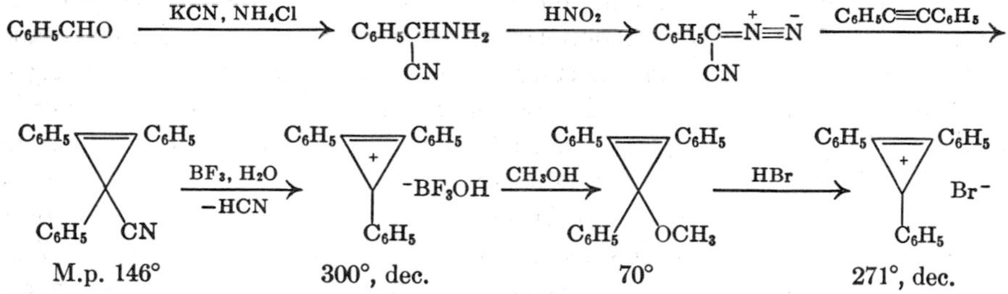

$$C_6H_5CHO \xrightarrow{KCN,\ NH_4Cl} \underset{CN}{C_6H_5CHNH_2} \xrightarrow{HNO_2} \underset{CN}{C_6H_5C}{=}\overset{+}{N}{\equiv}\overset{-}{N} \xrightarrow{C_6H_5C{\equiv}CC_6H_5}$$

| M.p. 146° | 300°, dec. | 70° | 271°, dec. |

Other stable salts prepared include one with only aliphatic substituents: 1,2-di-n-propylcyclopropenyl perchlorate.

28.6 Tropolones.

— Long-known members of this group include the mold product stipitatic acid, the alkaloid colchicine, and the pigment purpurogallin, a C_{11}-compound found in nature and obtainable by oxidation of pyrogallol. Each substance had been investigated extensively, but the structures were not known and no relationship between the three compounds was suspected. In 1945 Dewar in England, noting that cycloheptatrienolone should have aromatic properties since two equivalent Kekulé structures are possible, named this as yet unknown parent compound tropolone and suggested tropolone struc-

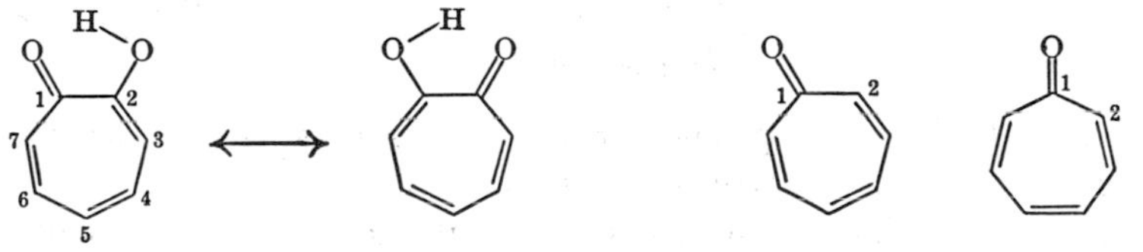

Tropolone   Tropone

tures for stipitatic acid and colchicine. Independently, Nozoe,[1] who had been working in Formosa on the essential oil of a local cedar, Taiwan Hinoki, isolated from the oil (1936) a phenol-like substance that forms a red complex iron salt and named it hinokitiol. By 1940 Nozoe had established that hinokitiol has an α-enolone structure in an unsaturated seven-membered ring and that it possesses a fair degree of aromatic character. Thus hinokitiol is 4-isopropyltropolone; the 3- and 5-isopropyl derivatives also have been isolated from natural sources.

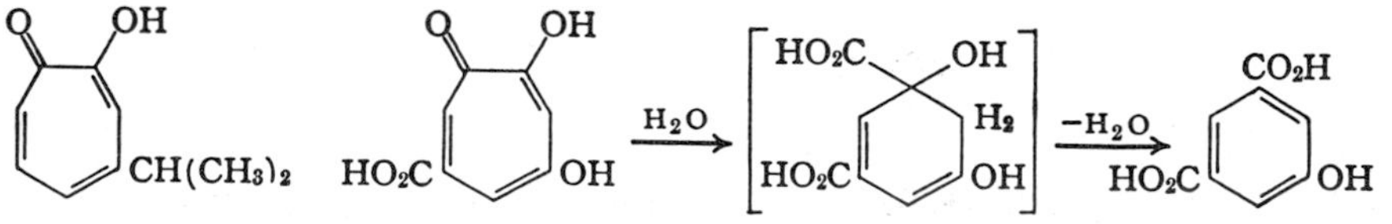

Hinokitiol   Stipitatic acid

Stipitatic acid is the 4-hydroxy-6-carboxy derivative of tropolone. Tropolones have phenolic properties (positive ferric chloride test) and have pK values close

[1] Tetsuo Nozoe, b. 1902 Sendai, Japan; D.Sc. Osaka Imperial Univ.; Tohoku Imperial Univ. (Formosa); Tohoku Univ., Sendai

to 7, intermediate between those for phenol and for acetic acid. They undergo substitution reactions with bromine and with nitric acid and couple with diazotized amines. The enolic hydroxyl group can be alkylated with ease (diazomethane), but acylation occurs with some difficulty. Tropolones are resistant to permanganate oxidation, they are not readily hydrogenated, and the ketonic character is masked, although after complete or partial hydrogenation the ketone group reacts normally. The probable explanation for the lack of ketonic properties, as well as for the acidity and resistance to acylation, is that a tropolone is a vinylog of a carboxyl group, the components being separated by a conjugated system. Another characteristic reaction is a benzilic acid type rearrangement induced by alkali at 300° and leading, in the case of stipitatic acid, to 5-hydroxyisophthalic acid.

Purpurogallin, which occurs in various galls, was prepared in 1869 by oxidation of pyrogallol; sodium iodate is the reagent of choice. Before 1945 the pigment had been investigated by many chemists, notably by A. G. Perkin and by Willstätter. No satisfactory structural formula had been advanced, although Perkin deduced the structure of the naphthalene derivative produced by alkaline re-

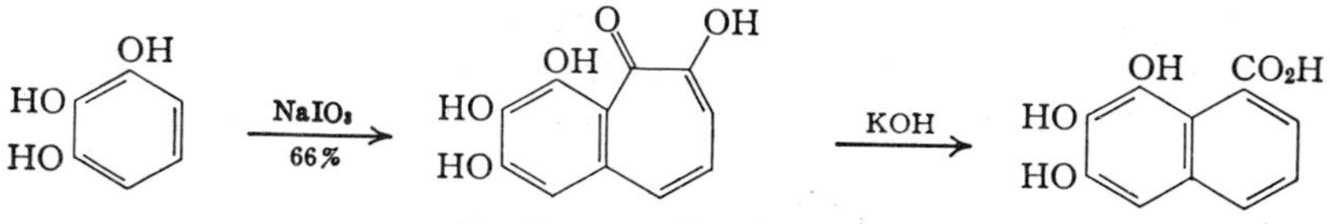

Purpurogallin

arrangement. The benzotropolone formula was suggested in 1948 by J. A. Barltrop and by R. D. Haworth[1] and confirmed by synthesis.

The alkaloid colchicine, which occurs in the autumn crocus has intrigued many investigators because of its biological activity. It is invaluable for treatment of

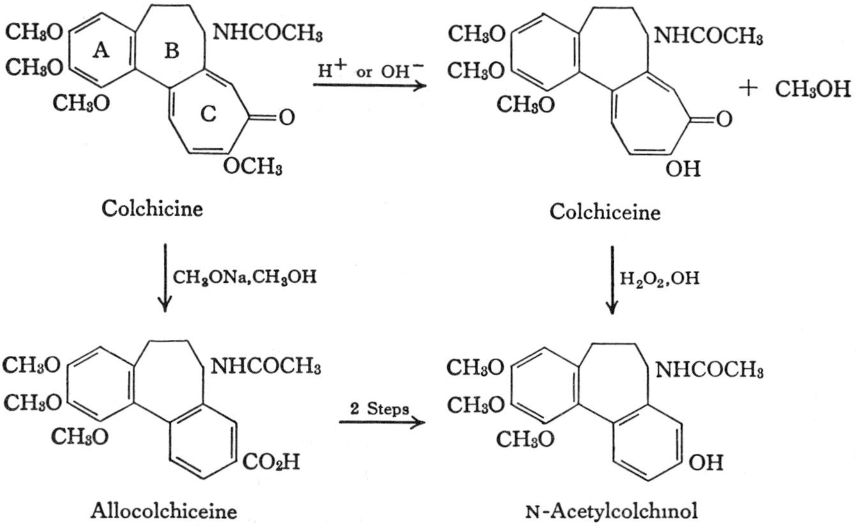

Colchicine

Colchiceine

Allocolchiceine

N-Acetylcolchinol

---

[1] Robert Downes Haworth, b. 1898 Cheadle (Cheshire); Ph.D. and D.Sc. Manchester (Lapworth, Perkin, Jr.); Sheffield Univ.

gout and it arrests cell division in both plant and animal cells. Early fundamental work by Windaus (1911–24) led to suggestion of a formula containing a
partially reduced phenanthrene ring system. Dewar (1945) suggested that one
of the end rings is a tropolone methyl ether, and this feature is incorporated in
the structure now known to be correct. In this the partly saturated central ring B
is also seven-membered. The enol methyl ether group is readily split by acid or
alkaline hydrolysis with formation of colchiceine, and experience with this reaction
led Zeisel to develop his method for methoxyl determination (8.37). The tropolone ring (C) readily rearranges to an aromatic ring. Colchicine undergoes
benzilic acid rearrangement to allocolchiceine, but colchiceine rearranges only in
the presence of an oxidizing agent; alkaline hydrogen peroxide leads to N-acetylcolchinol. The groups of Van Tamelen[1] and of Eschenmoser achieved the total
synthesis of colchicine in 1959–61.

Tropolone was at first thought to be a resonance hybrid of two hydrogen-bonded
structures, but X-ray studies of the hydrochloride and of the chelated copper

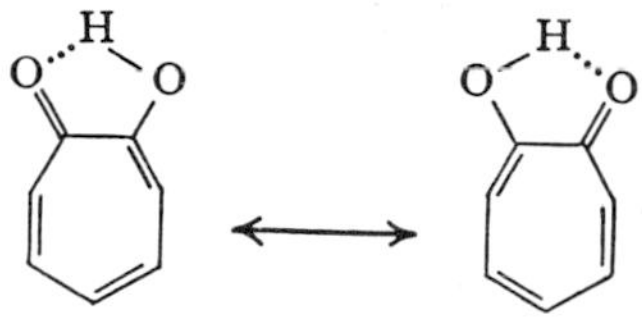

complex indicate that all seven carbon–carbon distances are the same (1.40 Å) and
correspond to the hybrid bonds of benzene. Recognition of the aromatic character
of the tropylium cation led to the view that the stability of the tropolone system
is associated with resonance structures of type (1). Thus one electron in the
seven π electron system of the carbon ring is taken up by oxygen to leave an
aromatic sextet. The resonance energy is 21 kcal./mole. Tropolone forms

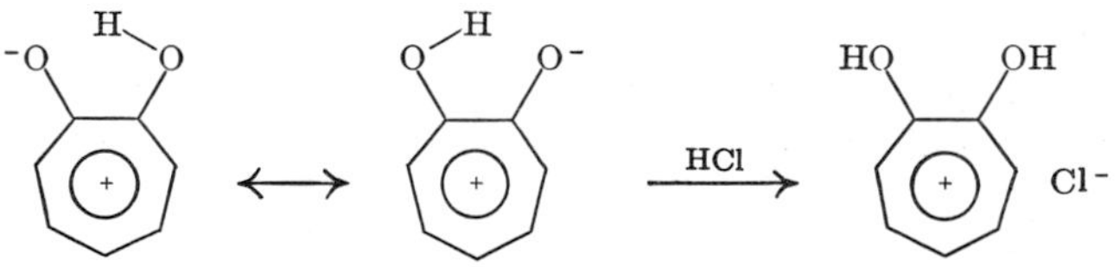

(1) Tropolone   Hydrochloride

conjugate cations in strong acid and forms molecular compounds such as picrates,
useful in separation and purification.

The contribution of resonance structures of the type bracketed accounts for a
tendency for electrophilic substitution to occur at positions 3, 5, and 7. Tropolone

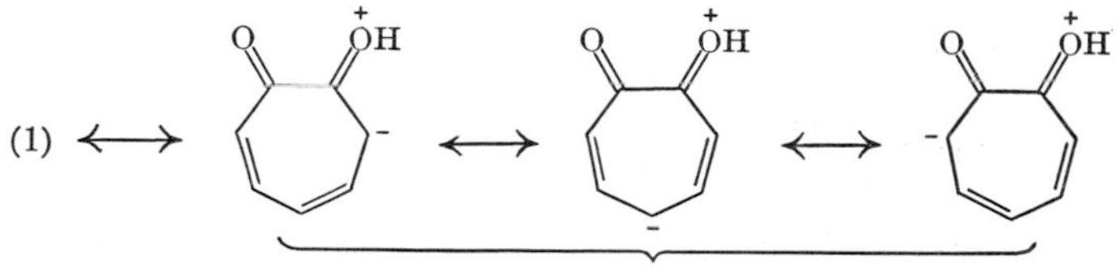

(1) $\longleftrightarrow$

resembles phenol in undergoing diazo coupling, nitrosation, nitration, halogena-

---

[1] Eugene E. Van Tamelen, b. 1925 Zeeland, Mich., Ph.D. Harvard (Stork); Univ. Wisconsin

tion, aminomethylation, Reimer-Tiemann reaction, Claisen rearrangement of the allyl ether, etc. Reactions such as sulfonation with sulfuric acid, Friedel-Crafts reactions, and Fries rearrangements are inapplicable because tropolone forms a conjugate acid in strong acid or a complex aluminum chloride salt. Added sulfuric acid accelerates the nitration of benzene but suppresses nitration of tropolone. Sulfonation is accomplished by use of sulfamic acid.

The first syntheses were of benzotropolones (Cook,[1] 1949; Tarbell,[2] 1950) and of purpurogallin (Haworth, 1950). The parent substance was synthesized in 1950–51 by four groups (Doering, Haworth, Cook, Nozoe). The syntheses are mainly of two types. One, chosen by Cook and by Nozoe, involves dehydrogenation of cycloheptane-1,2-diones and the main drawback is that these intermediates are not readily available. The dione required for synthesis of tropolone is

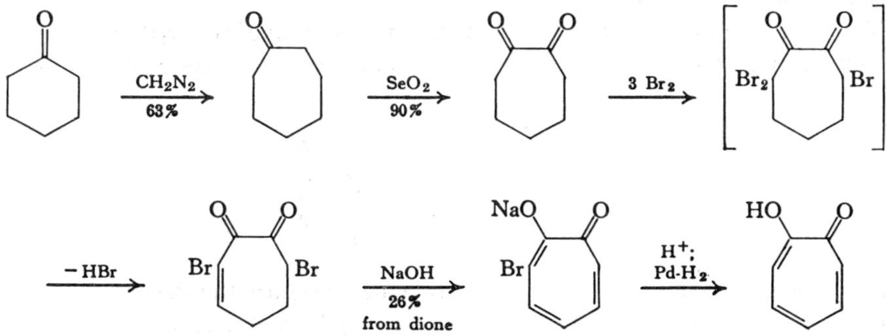

made by ring expansion of cyclohexanone with diazomethane and selenium dioxide oxidation of an activated methylene group. In the introduction of double bonds by bromination and dehydrobromination it is experimentally advantageous to introduce an extra atom of bromine, which is eliminated in a terminal step of hydrogenation.

A second general synthesis, developed principally by A. W. Johnson,[3] is exemplified by the synthesis of stipitatic acid from 1,2,4-trimethoxybenzene. The ring

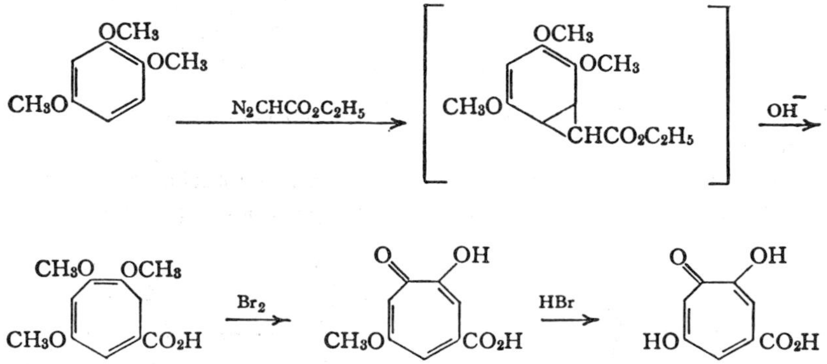

[1] James Wilfred Cook, b. 1900 London; Ph.D. and D.Sc. London (Barnett); London, Glasgow, Univ. Coll. of the South West (Exeter, Devon)

[2] D. Stanley Tarbell, b. 1913 Hancock, N. H.; Ph.D. Harvard (Bartlett); Univ. Rochester

[3] Alan Woodworth Johnson, b. 1917 South Shields, Co. Durham; M.A. Cambridge (Todd); Ph.D. London (Heilbron); Univ. Cambridge, Nottingham

is expanded by reaction with ethyl diazoacetate, which also provides the carboxyl function required. Treatment with alkali gives the trimethoxycycloheptatriene-carboxylic acid, which requires oxidation and demethylation to give the tropolone structure. Oxidation with bromine proved most satisfactory, and finally cleavage of the remaining enol ether group gave stipitatic acid (overall yield 4.5%).

A convenient route to tropolone itself is a three-step synthesis from cyclopentadiene and tetrafluoroethylene (J. J. Drysdale, du Pont, 1958). At 475° these reagents combine to give a mixture of products which rearrange on brief thermal

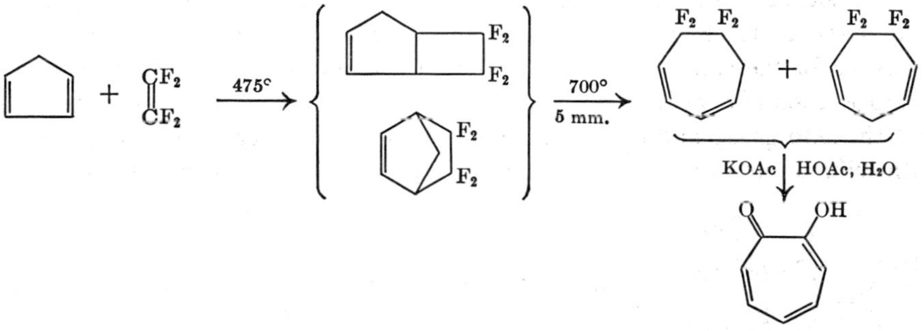

treatment to give a mixture of tetrafluorocycloheptadienes. Hydrolysis then affords tropolone in overall yield of 20%.

A novel synthesis of β-tropolone (5) from 3,4,5-trimethoxybenzoic acid involves conversion to the tosylate (3) and solvolysis with refluxing pyridine (O. L. Chapman,[1] 1961). The resulting mixture of 1,3-dimethoxycycloheptatrienes, of which

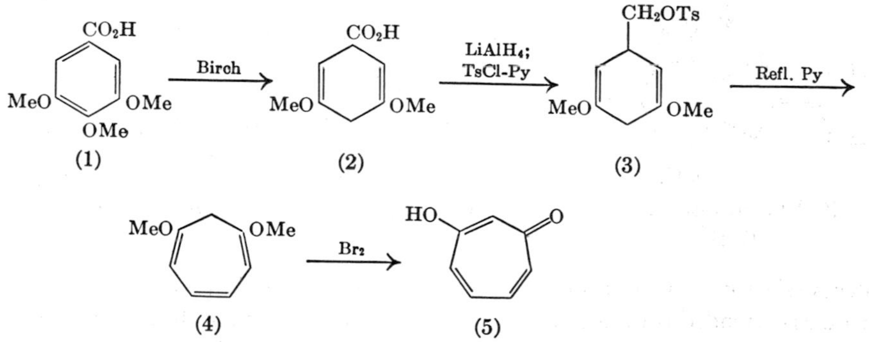

(4) is a component, on oxidation with bromine as in the A. W. Johnson synthesis affords β-tropolone in 28% overall yield.

28.7   Azulenes. — The generic name azulene was applied in 1864 to a group of blue substances present in essential oils or, more often, formed from a precursor on dehydrogenation or on dehydration-dehydrogenation of the oil. Some azulenogenic oils are recognized as such by the development of a blue, green, or violet color when tested with bromine in chloroform; some give colors on treatment with p-dimethylaminobenzaldehyde. Natural azulenes eventually were

[1] Orville L. Chapman, b. 1932 New London, Conn.; Ph.D. Cornell (Mcinwald); Iowa State Univ.

recognized as highly unsaturated C_{15}-hydrocarbons. From degradative experiments conducted in 1926, Ruzicka concluded that azulenes are related to sesquiterpenes, that is, C_{15}-isoprenoid alcohols, ketones, and hydrocarbons, and that they contain a then unknown unsaturated bicyclic system. A. St. Pfau and Pl. A. Plattner (1937) introduced two valuable techniques for purification: chromatography and conversion to crystalline picrates, which can be split by chromatography on alumina. These investigators deduced the structure of guaiazulene, the most abundantly available azulene from natural sources, and of vetivazulene. Some of the evidence is as follows. Vetivazulene (3) is derived from the optically active sesquiterpene precursor β-vetivone (1), the fragrant constituent of vetiver oil responsible for the value of this oil to the perfume industry. Palladium-catalyzed hydrogenation of β-vetivone in acetic acid effects saturation of both double bonds and the keto group and gives an alcohol mixture (2) which on dehydrogenation with sulfur affords vetivazulene. Hydrogenation of β-vetivone with Raney nickel

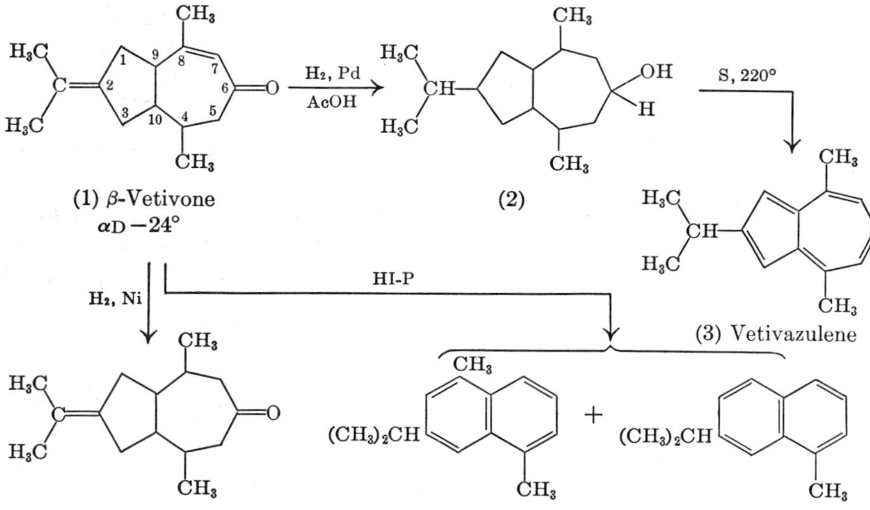

(1) β-Vetivone
αD $-24°$

(2)

(3) Vetivazulene

(4) Dihydrovetivone
αD $\pm 0°$

(5) Vetivalene

(6) Eudalene

effects selective reduction of the more reactive 7,8-double bond, and since the process is attended with loss of optical activity the structure of the dihydride must be symmetrical, as in (4). The structures conform to the isoprene rule and are not inconsistent with the production on high-temperature degradation of the naphthalene derivatives (5) and (6); the first arises through rearrangement and 1,2-methyl migration and the second by loss of the migrating methyl group.

Guaiol is a sesquiterpene alcohol found in the wood of *Guaiacum officinale* (Ruzicka, 1926). The product of dehydration, guaiene, on dehydrogenation with sulfur at a moderate temperature affords the blue guaiazulene; at the high temperature of a selenium dehydrogenation (350°) a methyl group of guaiazulene migrates from C_3 to C_2. Treatment of guaiol with hydriodic acid and red phos-

phorus affords guaiazulene, 1,4-dimethyl- and 1,4-dimethyl-6-isopropylnaph-
thalene. Deduction from these and other observations (and from the isoprene
rule) that the hydrocarbon is 3,8-dimethyl-5-isopropylazulene was confirmed by
synthesis.

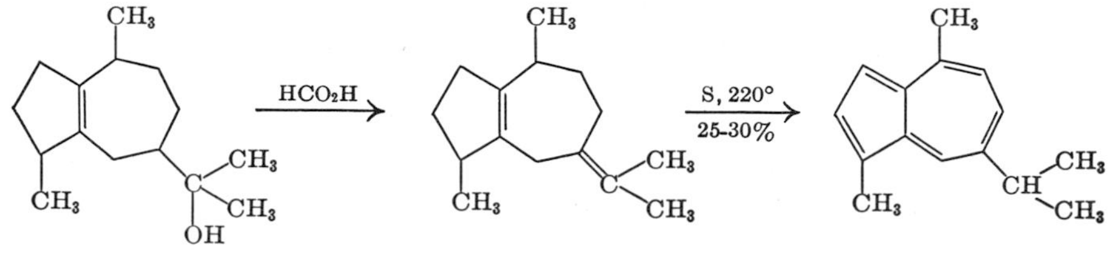

| Guaiol | Guaiene | Guaiazulene |

Plattner and St. Pfau (1937) synthesized azulene itself from Δ⁹-octalin as shown.
The crystalline blue solid has the same characteristic odor and crystalline form as

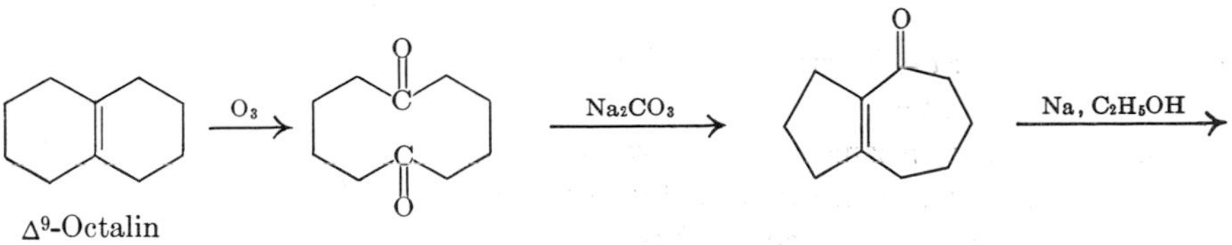

Δ⁹-Octalin

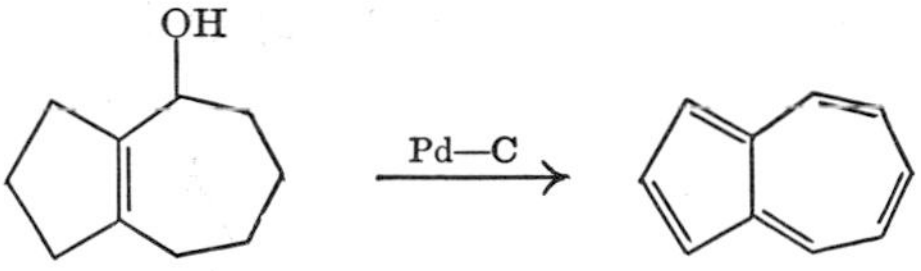

Azulene, m.p. 99°
λ 580, 633, 699 mμ

its isomer naphthalene, and it likewise forms complexes with picric acid and trinitrobenzene. When heated in vacuum at 350°, azulene rearranges almost quantitatively to the evidently more stable naphthalene. The resonance energy is
about 49 kcal., which is considerably below that of naphthalene (61 kcal.) but still
appreciable. The structures contributing most to stabilization are two Kekulé
structures (a, b) and two cumulative ionic structures (c, d). Azulene has a dipole

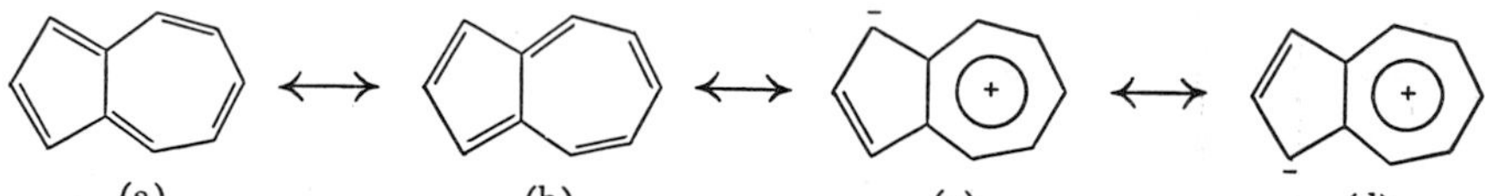

| (a) | (b) | (c) | (d) |

moment of 1.0 D, the positive end of which is directed to the seven-membered ring.
Dipole moments are characteristic of systems described by C. A. Coulson (1940)
as nonalternate. When the π electrons in naphthalene are labeled α and β in turn
to divide the centers into two sets, it is seen that every center of one set is adjacent
to a center of the other set; naphthalene is thus an alternate molecule, and it has

no dipole moment.   The alternate or nonalternate character of a molecule is not connected with its aromaticity.

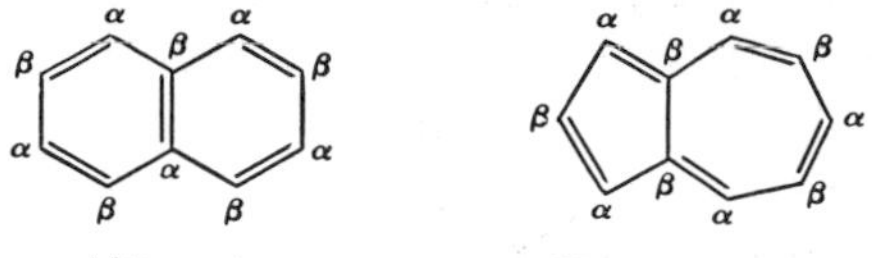

Alternate   Nonalternate

The azulenium cation is related to the tropylium cation and indeed shows similar, but less stability.   An azulene can be extracted from an organic solvent by

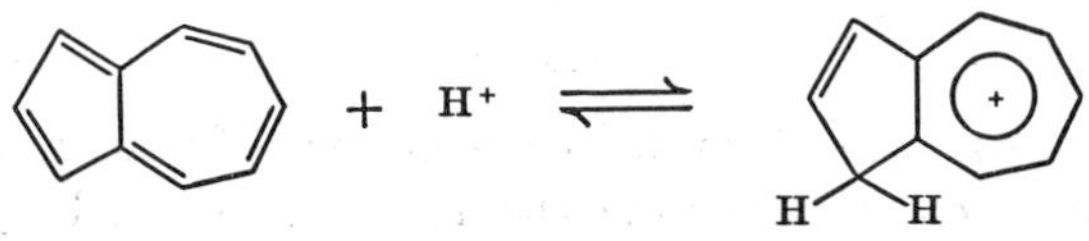

Azulenium ion

60% aqueous sulfuric acid with loss of the blue color; the hydrocarbon is recovered by dilution with water.

As expected from resonance structures (c) and (d), azulenes are particularly prone to electrophilic substitution and give 1-mono and 1,3-di derivatives (A. G. Anderson, Jr.,[1] 1950–53).   Thus on Friedel-Crafts acetylation azulene yields the 1-aceto and 1,3-diaceto derivatives; guaiazulene gives only 1-acetoguaiazulene.

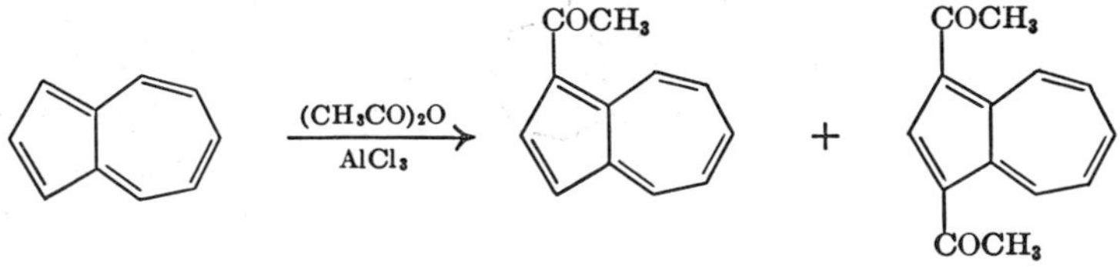

Nitration by the usual method fails but can be accomplished in some cases with tetranitromethane in pyridine; azulene affords the 1-nitro and 1,3-dinitro derivatives.   Azulene couples with diazotized aniline to give 1-benzeneazoazulene, which on reduction affords the highly unstable 1-aminoazulene.   Other azulenes couple except those in which positions 1 and 3 are blocked by substituents.   Azulenes form crystalline 1:1 π complexes with tetracyanoethylene (K. Hafner, 1960). When the blue complex from a 1-alkylazulene is heated in dimethylformamide, hydrogen cyanide is evolved and the solution turns red with formation of the 3-tricyanovinyl derivative.

One of a number of methods employed for the synthesis of azulene was applied first by Plattner (1941) to the synthesis of vetivazulene.   Buchner reaction of ethyl diazoacetate with the indane I is conducted at a temperature such that the norcaradiene II rearranges with ring expansion to the dicyclic ester III.   Saponification and dehydrogenation-decarboxylation completes the synthesis.   Variations in the procedure include catalysis of the Buchner reaction by ultraviolet irradiation

[1] Arthur G. Anderson, Jr., b. 1918 Sioux City, Iowa; Ph.D. Michigan; Univ. Washington, Seattle

and use of diazomethane in place of an ester. The method is limited to indanes symmetrically substituted in both rings or to those in which addition in all possible

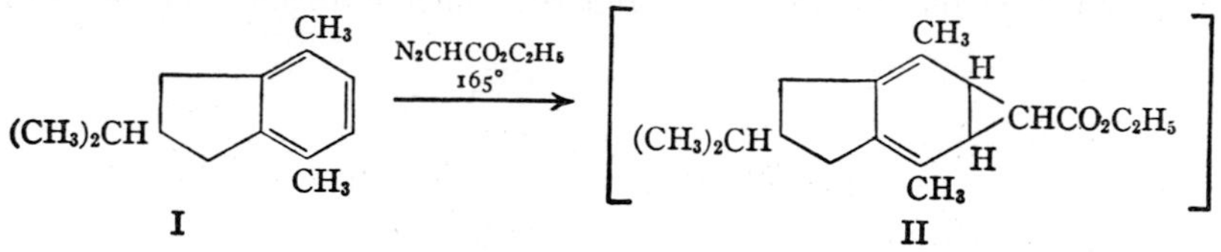

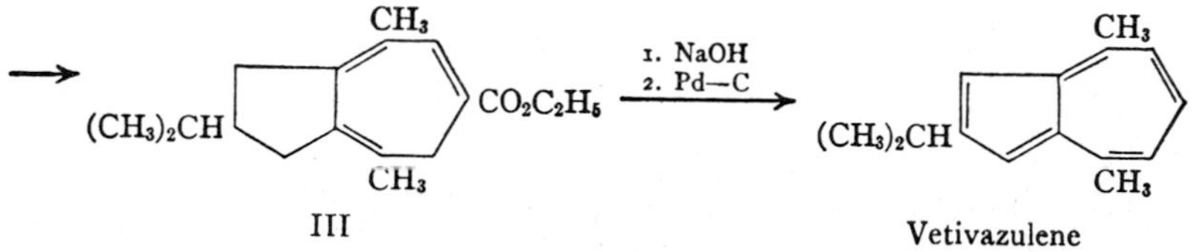

directions affords the same product. Production of isomer mixtures also limits syntheses involving ring expansion by Demjanov rearrangement and by methylene insertion in a cyclic ketone with diazomethane. Several syntheses are based on attachment of a seven-membered ring to a cyclopentane or of joining a five-membered ring to a cycloheptane, but all require many steps prior to dehydrogenation. All routes involving a terminal step of dehydrogenation suffer from low yields due to rearrangement to a naphthalene derivative or to isomerization or migration of alkyl groups. A new synthesis developed by K. Ziegler and K. Hafner (1955) avoids these difficulties. Azulene itself is obtained in high yield from a substance known as the Zincke base (2), a derivative of glutaconic dialdehyde readily prepared by reaction of 2,4-dinitrophenylpyridinium chloride with

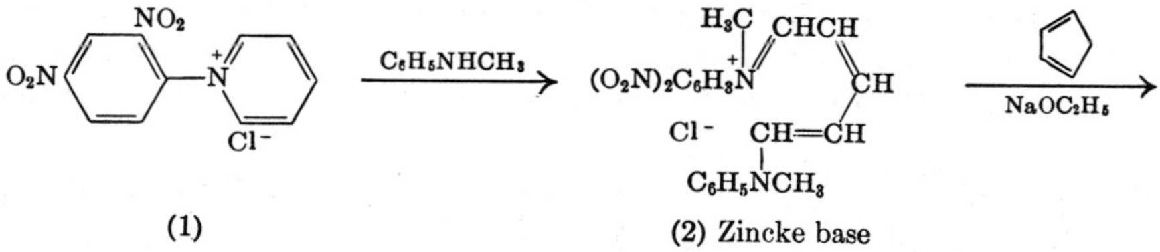

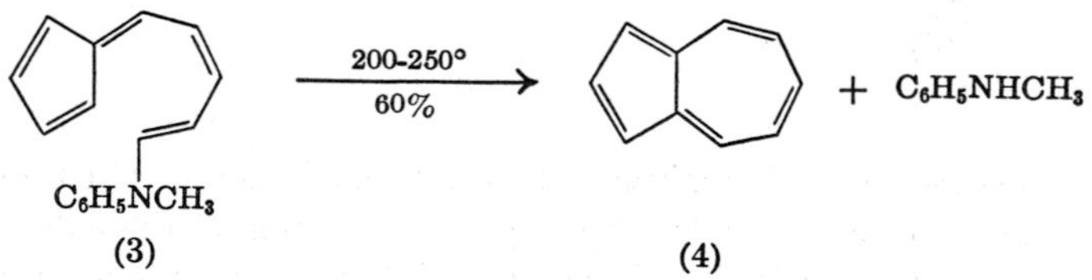

N-methylaniline. The Zincke base condenses with cyclopentadiene to give the fulvene (3), which is cyclized thermally to azulene with elimination of N-methylaniline. If a monosubstituted cyclopentadiene is used the product is a 1-substituted azulene. Substituted pyridines can be used to obtain azulenes substituted in the seven-membered ring. The unsaturated five-carbon system required for fusion to cyclopentadiene can be supplied also from a pyrylium salt, as in the synthesis of 4,6,8-trimethylazulene (*Org. Syn.*, 1961). 2,4,6-Trimethylpyrylium perchlorate, a colorless salt (dec. 200°) prepared from mesityl oxide, acetic anhydride, and 70% perchloric acid, is treated with a solution of sodium cyclopentadienylide in tetrahydrofurane, prepared under nitrogen. The solution ac-

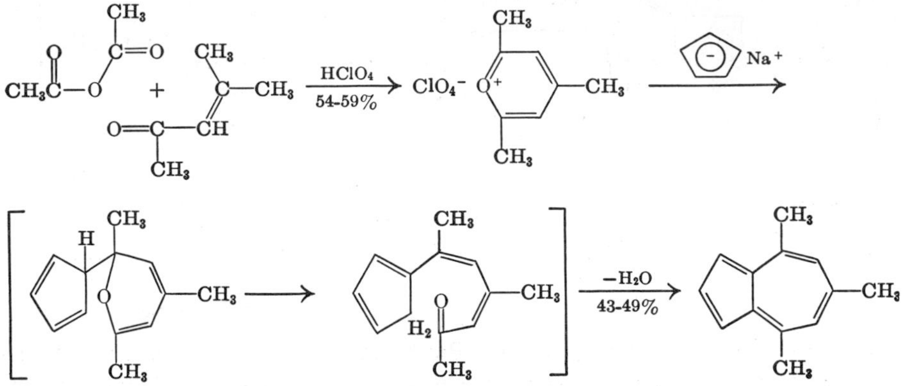

quires a violet color as the azulene system is produced by the succession of transformations indicated.

28.8   Diphenylene. — The earliest reported attempt (1893) to prepare this interesting hydrocarbon by the action of sodium on *o*-dibromobenzene afforded diphenyl as the only hydrocarbon. Several later attempts were reported as failures; others can now be recognized as failures in contradiction of the initial claims. Finally, in 1941 W. C. Lothrop at Trinity College achieved the synthesis of authentic diphenylene. Although the original route starting with *o*-nitrochlorobenzene and involving 2,2′-diaminodiphenyl as an intermediate afforded the hydrocarbon in overall yield of only 3%, improvements due to W. Baker (1954), R. B. Sandin[1] (1956), and Lothrop and Atkinson (1961) have shortened the synthesis and raised the overall yield to 20%. In the present process 2-aminodiphenyl

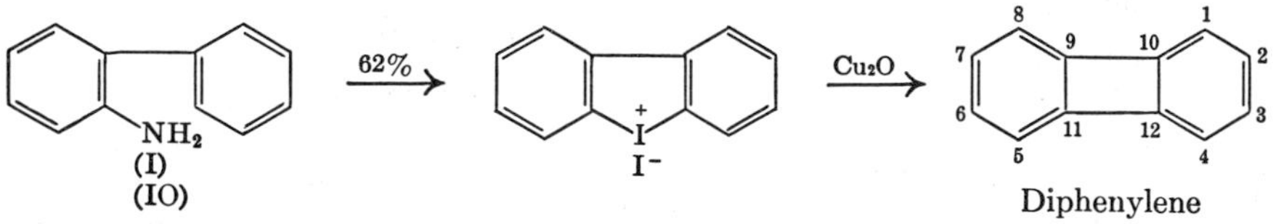

is converted via a diazonium salt into 2-iododiphenyl, which on oxidation with peracetic acid gives 2-iodosodiphenyl. Cyclization of the iodoso compound with sulfuric acid in acetic anhydride gives diphenyleneiodonium bisulfate (method of Beringer, 23.13), which is easily converted into the iodonium iodide. The final step is effected by heating this iodonium iodide with cuprous oxide in vacuum. Other routes are now known, but they are of less preparative value. Wittig's synthesis by dimerization of benzyne has been cited (22.5).

---

[1] Reuben B. Sandin, b. 1897 Forest Lake, Minn.; Ph.D. Chicago (Nicolet); Univ. Alberta, Canada

As evidence for the structure assigned, Lothrop cited analytical data, chromic acid oxidation of the hydrocarbon to phthalic acid, and reduction to diphenyl by hydrogenation over red-hot copper. He demonstrated that the molecule possesses at least one plane of symmetry by showing that 4,4'- and 5,5'-dimethyldiphenylene-2,2'-iodonium iodide yield the same hydrocarbon, namely, 2,7-dimethyldiphenylene. The remote possibility that the hydrocarbon was benzocyclooctatetraene was eliminated when this substance was synthesized. Electron diffraction measurements and X-ray analysis fully confirm the structure. Thus the average C–C distance in the six-membered rings is 1.39 Å and the C_9–C_{10} bond length is 1.52 Å (T. C. W. Mak, 1961).

Diphenylene is remarkably stable; it is not affected by boiling hydriodic acid, Clemmensen reduction, or hydrazine in the presence of palladium. Substitution reactions include nitration, sulfonation, mercuration, halogenation, acetoxylation, and the Friedel-Crafts reaction. By adjustment of the amounts of acetyl chloride and aluminum chloride, diphenylene can be converted into either 2-acetyl- or 2,6-diacetyldiphenylene in yield of 66%. Isomeric diacetyl derivatives are not

formed, even in traces; therefore the two six-membered rings do not behave as independent units but the substituent in 2-acetyldiphenylene directs the second substituent into the 6-position by a resonance effect involving both rings. 2-Mono and 2,6-di derivatives are formed in all the substitutions cited. That diphenylene behaves like a typical polycyclic hydrocarbon is further shown by the fact that it is stable at high temperatures, volatile with steam, sublimable, crystallizes from solvents readily in large crystals, and forms π complexes such as the scarlet picrate. The hydrocarbon is more basic than fluorene to tetracyanoethylene.

Molecular orbital theory suggests that structure (a) is a more accurate representation of the molecule than (b), that is, the 2,3-position has more double-bond character than the 1,2-position. Chemical evidence indeed points in this

(a)   (b)

direction: 2-acetylaminodiphenylene is brominated at the 3-position (W. Baker, 1958). The hydrocarbon thus is not primarily a cyclobutadiene derivative. However, the ultraviolet spectrum shows in addition to a high-intensity band at 235–260 mμ, corresponding to the lone intense band of diphenyl at 250 mμ, a band of lower intensity in the region 330–370 mμ probably attributable to some degree of resonance interaction between the two outer rings indicative of some cyclobutadienoid character in the central ring.

28.9   New Aromatic Types. — By reaction of hexafluorocyclobutene (1) with ethanolic potassium hydroxide to form the ether (2), followed by acid hydrolysis, Lacher[1] and Park[2] (1959) prepared the interesting diketocyclobutenediol (3). The substance, a white solid which decomposes at about 293°, is

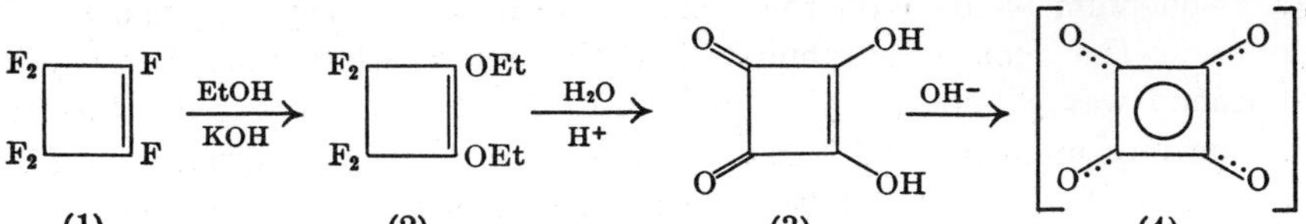

(1)   (2)   (3)   (4)

a dibasic acid almost as strong as sulfuric acid. It gives an intense purple color with ferric chloride and does not react with phenylhydrazine, since the carbonyl groups have the character of carboxylic carbonyl groups. The infrared spectrum shows strong hydrogen bonding and chelation. The anion is represented by the cumulative formula (4), in which all four oxygens become equivalent through resonance, since in the IR spectrum of the dipotassium salt the carbonyl absorption of the free acid at 5.5 μ gives place to an intense band at 6.5–6.75 μ characteristic of C—O vibration in acid salts.

Hirata[3] had suggested (1958) the analogous structure (5) for the dianion of croconic acid on infrared evidence, and West[4] (1960) found supporting evidence

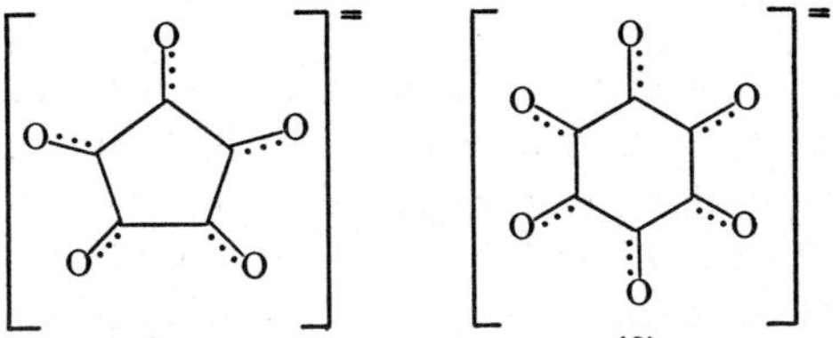

(5)   (6)

for this structure in the Raman spectrum. Infrared evidence points to structure (6) for the dianion of rhodizonic acid, but the deep orange color of the salts prevented determination of the Raman spectrum.

Stable nickel complexes of two novel types have been described (J. F. Tilney-Bassett, 1959; M. Dubeck, Ethyl Corp., 1960). One (II) results from reaction of nickelocene (I) with acetylene at 80° under pressure. The product, bis(cyclopentadienylnickel)-acetylene crystallizes from petroleum ether in light green

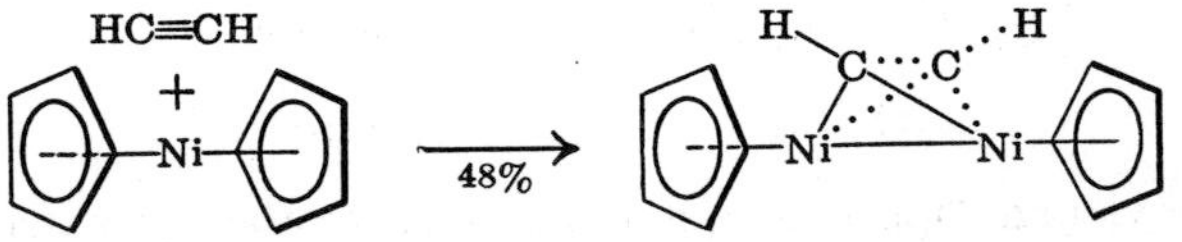

I   II

[1] John R. Lacher, b. 1911 Montrose, Colo.; Ph.D. Harvard (Kistiakowsky); Univ. Colorado
[2] J. D. Park, b. 1906 Honolulu, Hawaii; Ph.D. Ohio State; Univ. Colorado
[3] Yoshimasa Hirata, b. 1915 Yamaguchi, Japan; Ph.D. Nagoya; Nagoya Univ.
[4] Robert West, b. 1928 Caldwell, N. J.; Ph.D. Harvard (Rochow); Lehigh Univ.; Univ. Wisconsin

lustrous plates, m.p. 144°.   Since the substance is diamagnetic, the nickel probably has attained the rare gas electronic structure.   When dimethyl acetylenedicarboxylate is substituted for acetylene, the electron-withdrawing groups promote Diels-Alder addition to one of the cyclopentadienyl groups and the product
is an orange red complex (m.p. 84°) formulated as in III (Dubeck, 1960).   The

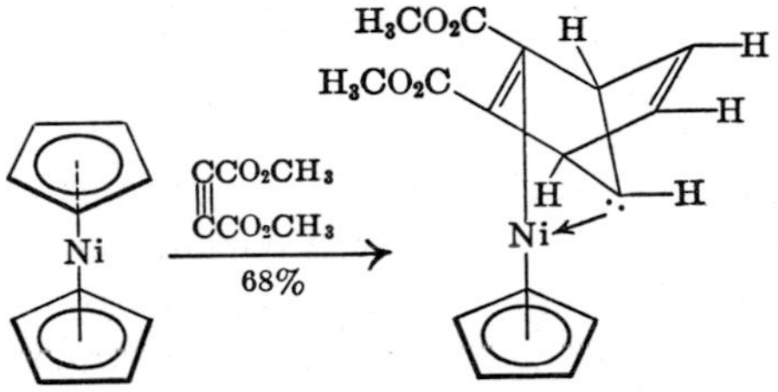

III

reaction is conducted in tetrahydrofurane at room temperature (60 hrs.).   Hydrogenation of III in tetrahydrofurane gives nickel, cyclopentane, and dimethyl
endo-cis-2,3-norbornanedicarboxylate.   The complex is diamagnetic and structure
III is supported by n.m.r. data.

PSEUDOAROMATICS

   Any completely conjugated carbocyclic system bears a formal resemblance to
benzene, and those that are so related but lack aromatic character are described
as pseudoaromatic.

28.10   Cyclobutadiene. — A few years before achieving the synthesis of cy-
            clooctatetraene, Willstätter (1905) attempted to make cyclobutadiene
by dehydrobromination of cyclobutene dibromide.   The dibromide on distillation

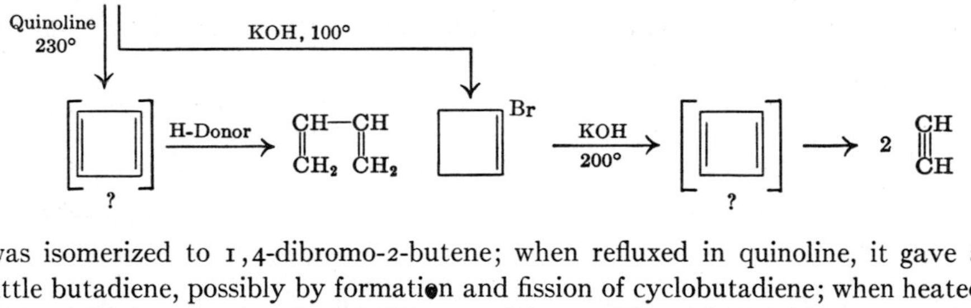

was isomerized to 1,4-dibromo-2-butene; when refluxed in quinoline, it gave a
little butadiene, possibly by formation and fission of cyclobutadiene; when heated
with alcoholic potassium hydroxide at 100° it gave the rather stable bromocyclobutene.   At a higher temperature this bromocyclobutene afforded acetylene as
the only volatile product, possibly via cyclobutadiene.   The experiments show
that cyclobutadiene, if indeed capable of existence, is very unstable at high
temperatures.

   Cyclobutadiene, with four π electrons, does not meet the requirement for stability of the Hückel rule.   According to the molecular orbital theory, the four

sigma bonds are bent and strained and the π electrons are localized either as two nonconjugated double bonds in a rectangular molecule (a) or in the next higher electronic state as a triplet in a square diradical (b). The hydrocarbon at best can be metastable.

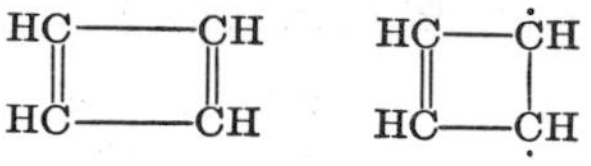

(a)   (b)

Cyclobutadiene has remained ellusive. E. R. Buchman[1] (1942–48) succeeded in preparing cyclobutane-*trans*-1,2-bis(trimethylammonium) hydroxide but found that on decomposition at temperatures varying from 250° to 420° it gave several products but no cyclobutadiene or compounds derived from it. C. D. Nenitzescu (1957) found that decomposition of cyclobutane-1,3-bis(trimethylammonium) hydroxide at 120° affords butadiene in 20% yield. Diels-Alder adducts from cyclooctatetraene, for example that (1) from dimethyl acetylenedicarboxylate, contain a cyclobutene ring and might yield cyclobutadiene on pyrolysis, but Nenitzescu *et al.* found that (1) gives only dimethyl phthalate and butadiene

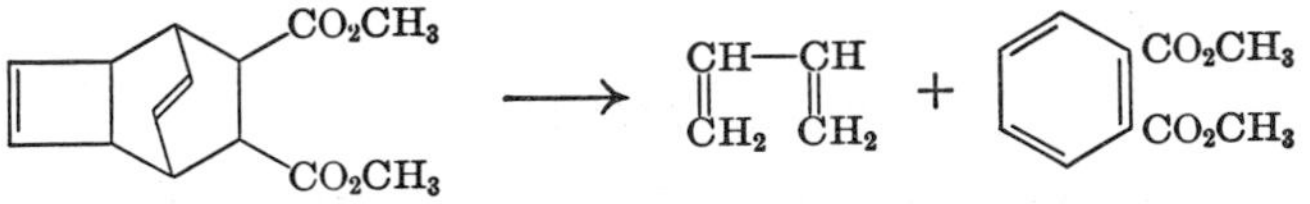

(15%), probably formed by reductive fission of cyclobutadiene. In 1959 Nenitzescu reported that 1,2,3,4-tetrabromocyclobutane, when treated with lithium amalgam followed by silver nitrate, gives a crystalline cyclobutadiene π complex of the formula $C_4H_4AgNO_3$, but the hydrocarbon was later recognized as a tricyclic dimer of cyclobutadiene (Nenitzescu, 1961).

Experiments with the hydrocarbons (1) and (2), which might undergo protofropic rearrangement to cyclobutadienes, have shown that such isomerizations do not in fact occur. 1,2-Dimethylenecyclobutane (1) was prepared by a double

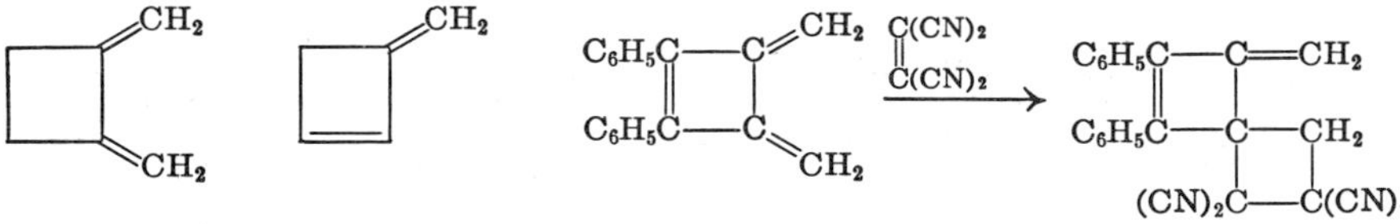

(1)   (2)   (3)   (4)

Hofmann elimination and also by dimerization of allene at 500° over glass beads (Blomquist, 1956). Another approach explored was the condensation of 3,4-diphenyl-1,2-dimethylenecyclobutene (3) with tetracyanoethylene. A normal Diels-Alder reaction would give a substituted cyclobutadiene; the actual adduct proved to be the spirane (4, Blomquist 1959). Criegee (1957) investigated the dehydrohalogenation of 3,4-dichloro-1,2,3,4-tetramethyl-1-cyclobutene (5) in the

[1] Edwin R. Buchman, b. 1904 Valley Falls, N. Y.; Ph.D. Frankfurt (von Braun), Columbia (R. R. Williams); Calif. Inst. Techn.

hope of isolating tetramethylcyclobutadiene (6), which should be more stable than the parent hydrocarbon.   Reaction of (5) with a variety of reagents afforded five stable products of dimerization of the cyclobutadiene (6).   Later (1959), reaction of the dichloride (5) with nickel carbonyl was found to afford a stable, colored, crystalline π complex with nickel chloride (7).

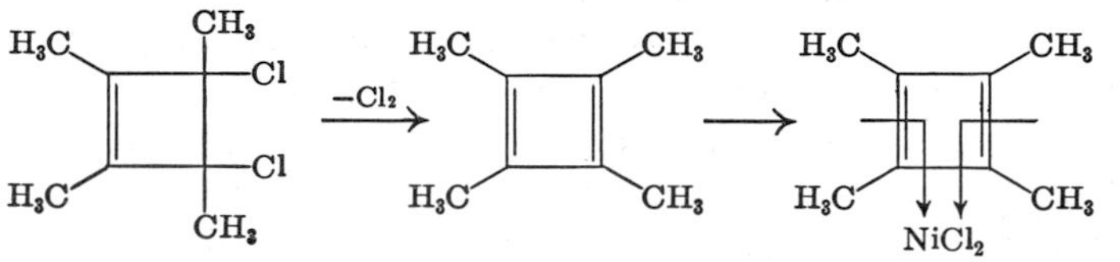

bromodimethyltin bromide II, which when heated with anhydrous nickel bromide in an inert solvent affords the complex III as black blue plates (H. H. Freedman, 1961).

A novel and high-yield route to the tetraphenylcyclobutadiene–nickel bromide complex (III) utilizes as starting material 1,1-dimethyl-2,3,4,5-tetraphenyl-stannole (I), available by reaction of dimethyltin dichloride with the organo-metallic product of dimerization of diphenylacetylene with lithium (F. C. Leavitt, 1960).   Reaction of the heterocycle I with bromine cleaves the ring to give the

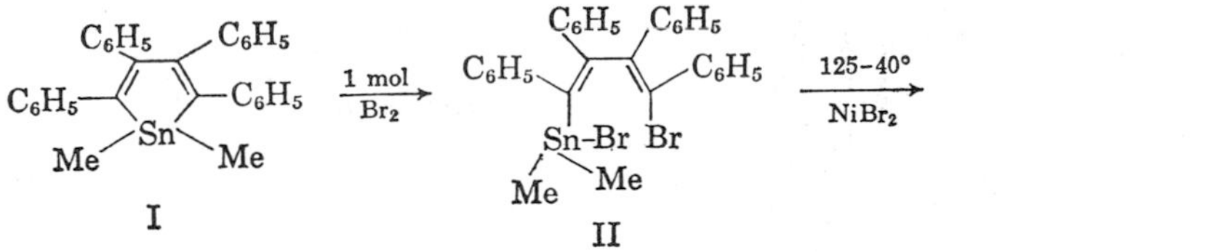

bromodimethyltin bromide II, which when heated with anhydrous nickel bromide in an inert solvent affords the complex III as black blue plates (H. H. Freedman, 1961).

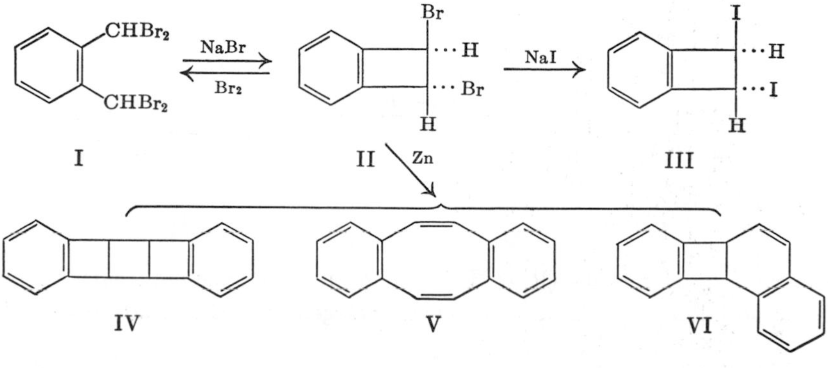

Following up an early observation by Thiele's student Hans Finkelstein (1910), Cava (1957–) found that o-xylylene tetrabromide (I) on reaction with sodium bromide affords a 1,2-dibromobenzocyclobutene which must have the *trans* configuration II, since the *cis* structure is sterically impossible.   Unlike usual benzyl halides, II is not easily solvolyzed; for example, it is stable to potassium acetate in refluxing acetic acid.   The dibromide reacts slowly with sodium iodide.   The product is the iodide III, which may well arise via benzocyclobutadiene.   Debromination with zinc gave the dimers IV, V, and VI, and the same products resulted on hydrogenolysis of the diiodide to benzocyclobutane, allylic bromination (NBS), and dehydrohalogenation.   Since the three hydrocarbons isolated are expected products of dimerization of benzocyclobutadiene, the result affords evidence of the transient existence of this substance.   Further evidence is supplied by trapping experiments with dienes and with dienophiles (Nenitzescu, 1957; Cava, 1959).

28.11   Pentalene and Heptalene.—Thus far all attempts to prepare hydrocarbons of the structures formulated have failed and no products suggestive of the existence of these substances as transient intermediates have been reported.   Hydrogenated pentalenes are fully resistant to dehydrogenation.

Pentalene   Heptalene

unknown

However, derivatives of 1,2,4,5-dibenzopentalene have been known for a long time (K. Brand, 1912–36).   Cyclization of α,β-diphenylsuccinic acid gives 9,11-diketodiphenylsuccindane (I), convertible by reaction with a Grignard reagent to a diol (II), which on dehydration yields an intensely colored 9,12-disubstituted diphenylsuccindadiene, or 1,2,4,5-dibenzopentalene (IV, R = CH₃).

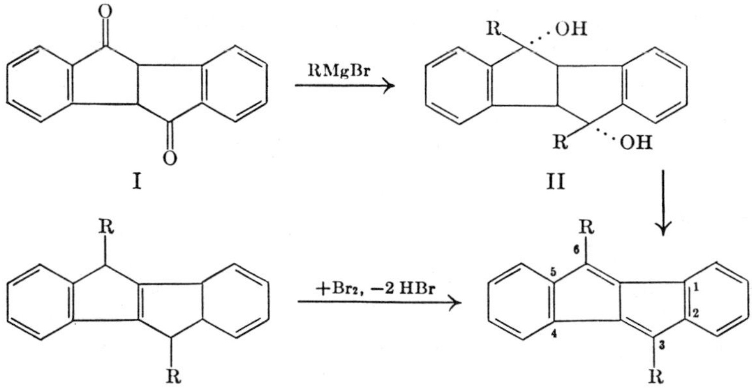

I   II

III (R = H)   IV

The parent hydrocarbon IV (R = H) has been prepared from diphenylsuccindene (III) by addition of bromine and dehydrohalogenation (Linstead, 1952).   Dibenzopentalene behaves as a conjugated diene, is very reactive to ozone and to hydrogenation, and the pentalene system shows no aromatic stability.

28.12   Cyclopolyenes.—Speculation on the possible stability of monocyclic, fully conjugated polyolefins higher than cyclooctatetraene suggested that the C_{10}, C_{12}, C_{14}, and C_{16} cyclopolyenes would be highly destabilized by steric clash between the internal hydrogen atoms. Furthermore, the opportunity for transannular cyclization during the construction of such rings might impose a limitation to synthesis, particularly by dehydrogenative routes. Even the C_{16} member might not approach coplanarity to an extent sufficient for much resonance stabilization. Thus W. Baker[1] and J. F. W. McOmie predicted that cyclooctadecanonaene should be the smallest member of the series likely to be stable and that it might show diminished unsaturation characteristic of aromatic compounds. This view was expressed in the body of the book "Non-Benzenoid Aromatic Compounds," and a note added in proof reported the synthesis of the C_{18} hydrocarbon by Sondheimer and his Israeli co-workers at the Weizmann Institute of Science. In the period 1957–61 this group achieved the synthesis of a number of cyclopolyenes and cyclopolyynes by a general method which will be illustrated for the case just cited. Oxidative coupling of hexadiyne-1,5 (I) with copper acetate in pyridine gives the trimeric hexayne II, along with the tetrameric and pentameric analogs. The cyclic hexayne II, which is unstable to heat but crystal-

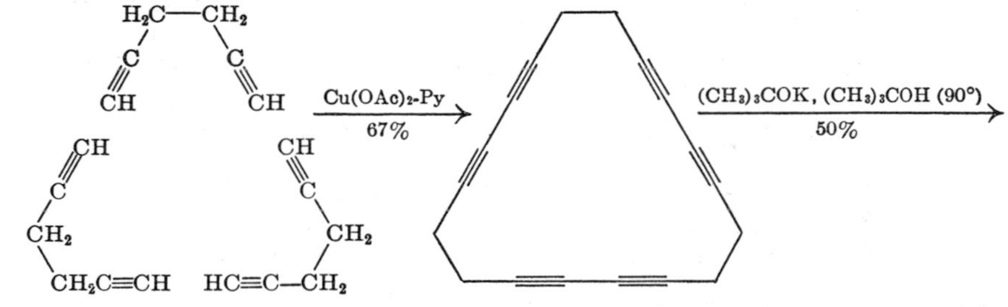

I   II

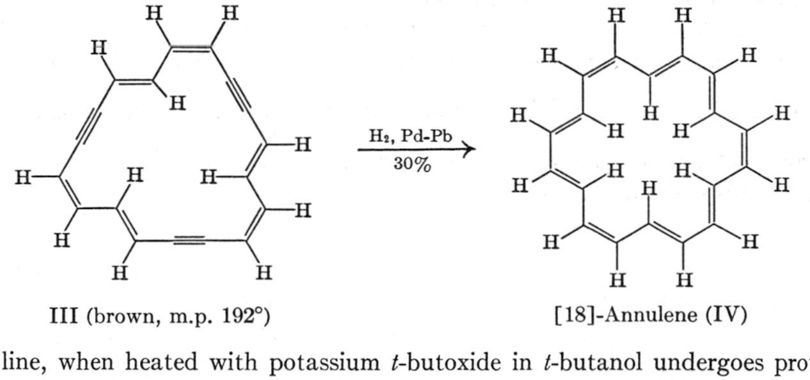

III (brown, m.p. 192°)   [18]-Annulene (IV)

line, when heated with potassium *t*-butoxide in *t*-butanol undergoes prototropic isomerization to the completely conjugated hexaenetriyne III, which is colored,

[1] Wilson Baker, b. 1900 Runcord, England; D.Sc. Manchester (Lapworth, Robinson); The University, Bristol

high melting, and stable enough to be kept for a few days. On hydrogenation over Lindlar catalyst it affords [18]-annulene (IV), the C_{18} vinylog of benzene and cyclooctatetraene. This hydrocarbon contains $(4n + 2)$ π electrons $(n = 4)$ and may be planar or near planar. The hydrocarbon is stable enough to be kept for a few days in light and air, but it is hydrogenated easily to the cycloalkane, and the system is definitely reactive. Evidence that the hydrocarbon is aromatic in the sense of being able to sustain an induced ring current is provided by the n.m.r. spectrum, which shows outer protons at 1.2 τ and inner protons at 11.8 τ. The analog of the formula $C_{30}H_{30}$ also conforms to the Hückel pattern for stability (30 π electrons, $n = 7$) and probably can exist in the planar configuration VI, but it is less stable than IV (too unstable for accurate analysis). The C_{14} analog (V, $4n + 2\pi$ electrons) may correspond to the periphery of pyrene, anthracene, or phenanthrene, but in any case the ring cannot be planar; the substance is

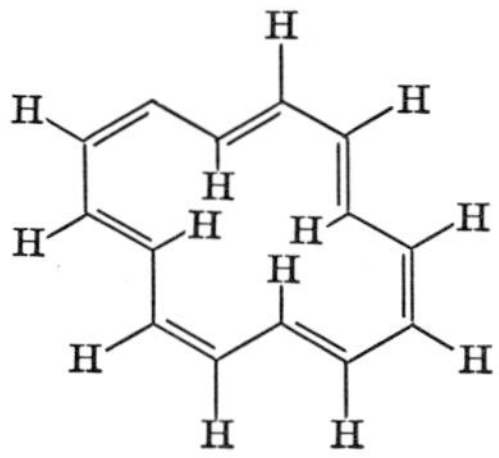

[14]-Annulene (V)
(dark brown, m.p. 135°)

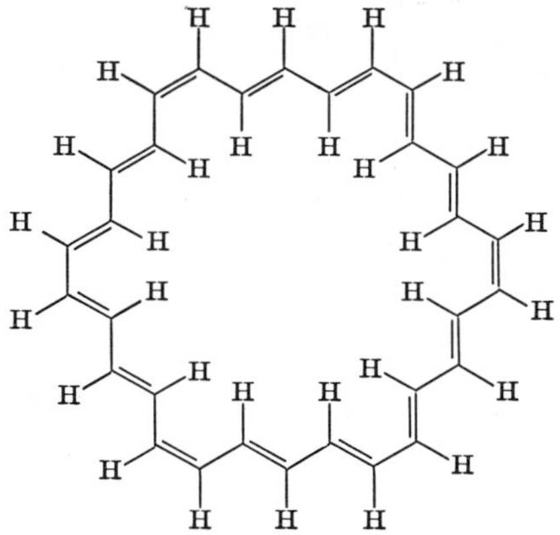

[30]-Annulene (VI)
(brown-red)

highly unstable. The Israeli synthesis provides a neat route to cycloalkanes, for example, the C_{40}, C_{45}, and C_{54} hydrocarbons. A new route explored successfully with linear models involves rearrangement of a 1,5-enyne with potassium t-butoxide to a conjugated polyene, probably via the allene (Sondheimer, 1961).

$$CH{\equiv}CCH_2CH_2CH{=}CH_2 \xrightarrow{(CH_3)_3COK} CH{=}C{=}CHCH_2CH{=}CH_2 \rightarrow H(CH{=}CH)_3H$$

Conjugated polyenes containing 3, 5, 6, 8, and 10 double bonds have been synthesized by this method.

Chapter 29

CARBOHYDRATES

29.1   Classification. — The name "hydrate de carbone" or carbohydrate was applied at an early date because the common C_6-sugars (hexoses) glucose and fructose have the empirical formula $C_6H_{12}O_6$, or $C_6(H_2O)_6$. These two hexoses are known as monosaccharides and are formed on acid-catalyzed hydrolysis of the disaccharide sucrose, the systematic name for cane sugar.

$$C_{12}H_{22}O_{11} \quad + \quad H_2O \quad \longrightarrow \quad C_6H_{12}O_6 \quad + \quad C_6H_{12}O_6$$

Sucrose		Glucose	Fructose
$[\alpha]_D +66.5°$		$[\alpha]_D +52°$	$[\alpha]_D -92°$

Sucrose is dextrorotatory, but the hexose mixture resulting on hydrolysis is levorotatory and is known as invert sugar. Honey is largely invert sugar, since bees contain an enzyme (invertase) capable of hydrolyzing sucrose. The two hexoses occur in many fruits (L. *fructus*, fruit). D-Glucose (Gr., *glykys*, sweet) is known also as grape sugar and as dextrose (D-fructose as levulose). Most natural monosaccharides are pentoses or hexoses, and most of them have a sweet taste. Of three disaccharides made up of two glucose units, maltose has to man only one third the sweetness of sucrose, cellobiose is indifferent, and gentiobiose is bitter. Di-, tri-, tetra-, penta-, and hexasaccharides occur in nature. Members of this group, containing up to 10–12 saccharide units, are called oligosaccharides (Gr., *oligo-*, few). The polysaccharides cellulose, starch, and glycogen contain thousands of glucose units linked together by oxygen bridges each of which on hydrolysis can liberate two hydroxyl groups; the formula is $(C_6H_{10}O_5)_n \cdot H_2O$ or, for practical purposes, $(C_6H_{10}O_5)_n$.

29.2   Glucose and Fructose. — The open-chain structures of these hexoses were inferred from a few simple observations. Both sugars reduce Fehling solution and hence are either aldehydes or acyloins. Kiliani[1] discovered

[1] Heinrich Kiliani, 1855–1945; b. Würzburg, Germany; Ph.D. Munich (Erlenmeyer); Freiburg; *Ber.*, **82A**, 1 (1949)

(1888) that both sugars add hydrogen cyanide, and on hydrolysis of the cyano-hydrins and reduction of the hexahydroxy acids with hydriodic acid and red

$$
\begin{array}{llll}
1 & CHO & CH_2CO_2H & 1 & CH_2OH & CH_3 \\
2 & HCOH & CH_2 & 2 & C=O & CHCO_2H \\
3 & HOCH & CH_2 & 3 & HOCH & CH_2 \\
4 & HCOH & CH_2 & 4 & HCOH & CH_2 \\
5 & HCOH & CH_2 & 5 & HCOH & CH_2 \\
6 & CH_2OH & CH_3 & 6 & CH_2OH & CH_3 \\
\end{array}
$$

1 CHO   →(Degrad.)   CH$_2$CO$_2$H   ...   D Glucose   ;   D-Fructose

phosphorus he obtained heptanoic acid from glucose and 2-methylhexanoic acid from fructose and thereby located the carbonyl group at C_1 in glucose and at C_2 in fructose. The formation of crystalline pentaacetates from both sugars established the presence in each of five hydroxyl groups, and the only stable structures are those in which one hydroxyl group is distributed on each of the five available carbon atoms. Emil Fischer's[1] classical deduction of the configurations will be described later; note that D-fructose corresponds to the stereochemical pattern of D-glucose in the centers of asymmetry at C_3, C_4, and C_5.

29.3   Pyranoses and Pyranosides. — D-Glucose reduces Fehling solution and adds hydrogen cyanide but, in contrast to ordinary aldehydes, it does not give the Schiff test.[2] Another peculiarity is that the sugar exhibits mutarotation. Glucose crystallizes from water as the monohydrate; anhydrous material crystallizes from methanol in what is now known as the α-form, m.p. 147° dec. One gram of this material dissolves in 1.1 ml. of water at 25°, in 0.178 ml. of water at 90°, and in 120 ml. of methanol at 20°; the substance is insoluble in ether, very slightly soluble in absolute ethanol, and soluble in hot pyridine or hot acetic acid. Measurements of freshly prepared solutions of the α-form in pure water and extrapolation to zero time indicate an initial specific rotation, αD, of +112°, with gradual decrease on standing to an equilibrium value of +52°. A trace of acid or base accelerates equilibration. Precipitation with ethanol, dehydration, and recrystallization from methanol leads to recovery of the α-form of initial αD +112°. In 1895 C. Tanret[3] devised a novel method of crystallization and discovered a new form of glucose, the β-form. He added a very concentrated aqueous solution of the ordinary (α) form in small portions to an

---

[1] For biography, see p. 78. For reminiscences of his son, see H. O. L. Fischer, *Ann. Rev. Biochem.*, **29**, 1 (1960)

[2] Abstraction of SO$_2$ from a colorless complex with leuco (reduced) magenta with liberation of the pink dye.

[3] Charles Tanret, 1847–1917; b. Joinville s. Marne; apothecary in Paris

evaporating dish maintained at 110° and as the water evaporated the β-form separated slowly as crystals. Later workers obtained the substance by crystallization of the α-form from hot acetic acid. A fresh solution of the β-form has a specific rotation of +19°, which increases on standing to the equilibrium value of +52°. The two forms are now known to be oxides (cyclic hemiacetals) of the structures and configurations shown. Since the six-membered oxide ring is present

```
   HCOH                    CH=O                    HOCH
   HCOH                    HCOH                    HCOH
  HOCH      O              HOCH                   HOCH      O
   HCOH         ⇌          HCOH         ⇌          HCOH
   HC                      HCOH                    HC
   CH₂OH                   CH₂OH                   CH₂OH

α-D-Glucopyranose                          β-D-Glucopyranose
       I                                           II
```

in pyrane, these cyclic sugars are called pyranoses; sugar oxides having a five-membered ring are called furanoses. In water solution the two oxides are interconvertible via the aldehydic form (or hydrate), which is present in trace amounts only. The reactions with Fehling solution and with hydrogen cyanide are irreversible under the conditions used and proceed through the aldehydic form, but the very low equilibrium concentration of this reactive species is unfavorable for reversible reaction with Schiff reagent. The two cyclic forms are epimeric at C_1 but, since the relationship between these mobile isomers is a special one, they are called anomers (gr. *ano-*, upper).

The stereochemistry of the pyranoses can be appreciated best from the conformational formulas Iα and IIβ. The chair form of preferential stability must

```
        CH₂OH                              CH₂OH
 HO···⟍    ⟍O            ⟶        HO···⟍     ⟍O
   HO⟍   ⟍   ⟍—H     37α:63β         HO⟍    ⟍    ⟍—OH
      :H    OH:                              OH:
      H     OH                               H
       Iα                                    IIβ
```

be that in which the large hydroxymethyl group assumes the equatorial orientation; since this is linked at C_5, all D-sugars conform to the same chair pattern. Note that β-D-glucopyranose, the sugar most widely distributed in nature, has the stable all-equatorial conformation. The α-form, in which the anomeric hydroxyl is axial, is destabilized by interaction of this hydroxyl group with two axial hydrogens. The equilibrium concentration, calculated from the specific rotations of the two pure forms and of the equilibrated solution, shows that the β-form is indeed the more stable isomer.

That the anomeric hydroxyl group of the α-form is *cis* to the 2-hydroxyl group was first deduced by Böeseken (15.10). Addition of the α-form to a solution of boric acid enhances the conductivity, which gradually decreases with time and reaches an equilibrium value; addition of the β-form results in a slow increase in conductivity.

In 1895 Emil Fischer refluxed D-glucose with methanolic hydrogen chloride in expectation of obtaining the dimethyl acetal: —CHO + $2HOCH_3$ → —CH($OCH_3)_2$. The crystalline reaction product was found to contain only one methoxyl group and eventually was characterized as the methyl ether of the α-oxide form of D-glucose. This anomeric ether of the α-pyranose is described as

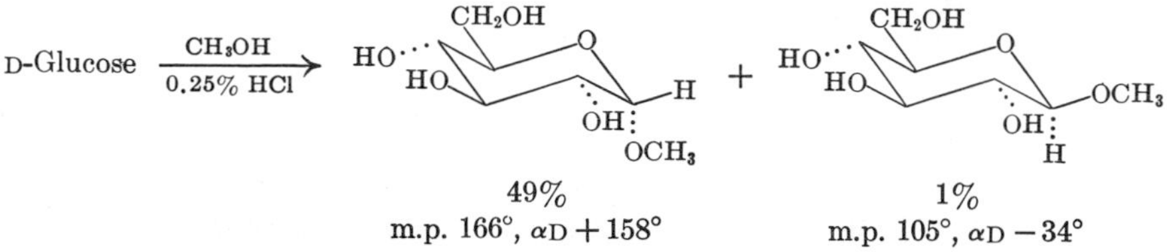

D-Glucose
CH₃OH
0.25% HCl
CH₂OH
HO
HO
O
H
OH
OCH₃
+
CH₂OH
HO
HO
O
OCH₃
OH
H
49%
m.p. 166°, αD +158°
1%
m.p. 105°, αD −34°

Methyl α- and β-D-glucopyranoside

a methyl pyranoside. A year later Alberda van Ekenstein isolated from the mother liquor the lower melting, levorotatory methyl β-D-glucopyranoside. In an improved procedure developed by B. Helferich[1] (*Org. Syn.*), a solution of D-glucose in methanol containing hydrogen chloride is refluxed for 72 hrs., cooled, and a first crop of methyl α-D-glucopyranoside is collected. Refluxing of the mother liquor again (72 hrs.) affords a second crop, and concentration affords a third crop. A small amount of the lower melting and more soluble methyl β-D-glucopyranoside can be isolated from the final mother liquor. Methyl furanosides are formed initially and are isolated most readily if milder conditions are employed. A better route to the β-isomer is by a reaction of a type used by Arthur Michael (1881) in the first synthesis of a naturally occurring mixed acetal of a sugar and a hydroxy component, a glycoside. Arbutin, from bearberry (*Arctostaphylos uva-ursi*), is the β-D-glucoside of hydroquinone. Michael synthesized the phenolic methyl ether of arbutin by condensation of the highly reactive cyclic chloride (1) with the potassium salt of hydroquinone monomethyl ether. The displace-

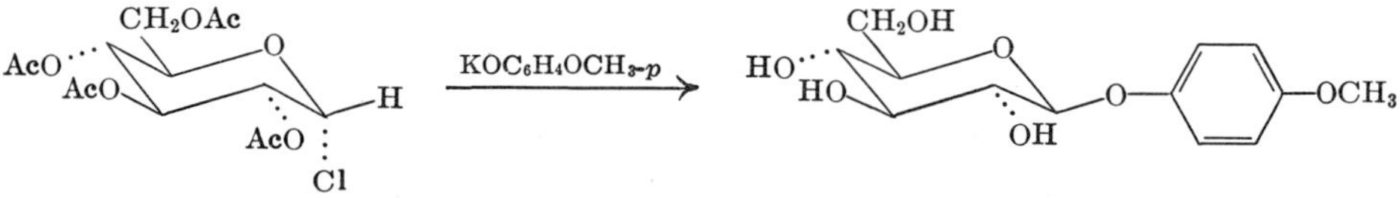

CH₂OAc
AcO
AcO
O
H
AcO
Cl
KOC₆H₄OCH₃-p
CH₂OH
HO
HO
O
O
OCH₃
OH

Tetra-O-acetyl-α-D-glucopyranosyl chloride (1)

Methylarbutin (2)

ment proceeds with Walden inversion. W. Koenigs and E. Knorr (1901) introduced a modified synthesis applicable to aliphatic alcohols as well as to phenols. Thus the tetraacetate (6) of methyl β-D-glucopyranoside is prepared by reaction

[1] Burckhardt Helferich, b. 1887 Greifswald; Ph.D. Berlin (E. Fischer); Univ. Berlin, Frankfurt, Greifswald, Leipzig, Bonn

of tetra-O-acetyl-α-D-glucopyranosyl bromide (5) with methanol in the presence of silver oxide. The bromide (5), like the chloride (1), is made by the action of

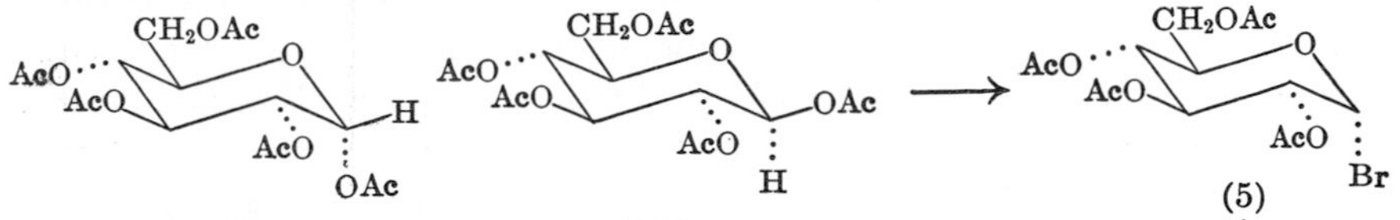

α (3)
D-Glucopyranose pentaacetate
M.p. 113°, αD + 105°

β (4)
M.p. 132°, αD + 5°

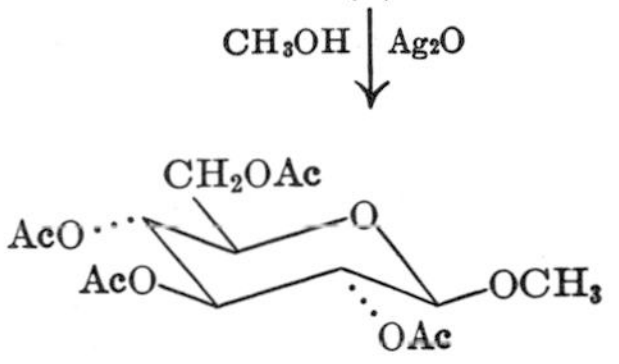

Methyl tetra-O-acetyl-
β-D-glucopyranoside (6)
M.p. 105°, αD − 27°

the halogen acid on β-D-glucopyranose pentaacetate (4, Walden inversion). The α-acetate (3) and the β-acetate (4) can both be made by acetylation of D-glucose, but the higher melting β-acetate is usually preferred. Since the equatorial β-D-sugar is acetylated more rapidly than the α-D-isomer, acetylation in hot acetic anhydride with sodium acetate as catalyst promotes rapid anomerization and selective acetylation of the β-D-sugar.

A new synthesis of α-glycosides utilizes the 1β-mesitoyl derivative (8), prepared by reaction of the α-bromide (7) with the silver salt of mesitylenecarboxylic acid (F. Micheel,[1] 1955). This hindered 1-O-acyl group is sufficiently resistant to weak base to permit deacetylation with methanol and a trace of sodium meth-

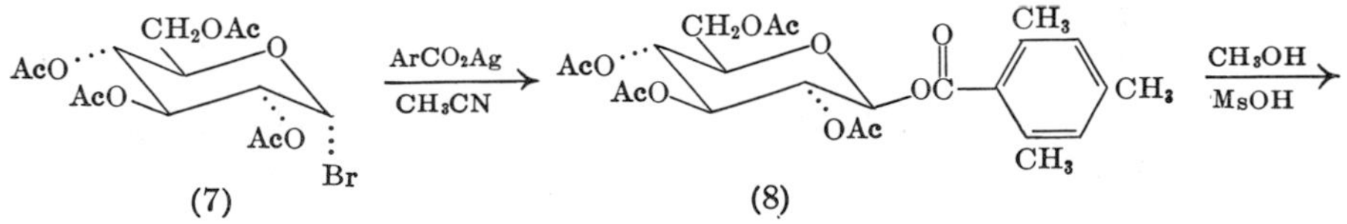

(7)

(8)

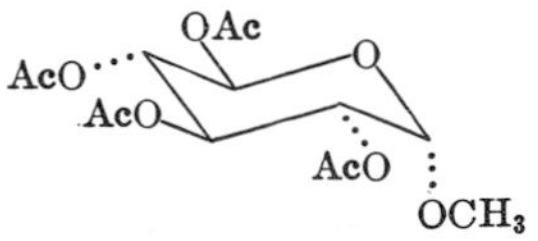

Methyl tetra-O-acetyl-α-D-glucopyranoside (9)
M.p. 102°, αD + 133°

oxide to 1-mesitoyl-β-D-glucose. Helferich found (1957, 1961) that when a solution of (8) in methanol is treated with methanesulfonic acid and let stand at room temperature the rotation gradually becomes strongly positive with formation in good yield of the methyl α-glucoside (9).

Methyl glycosides do not exhibit mutarotation, do not reduce Fehling solution,

[1] Fritz Micheel, b. 1900 Strasbourg/Uckermark; Ph.D. Berlin; Univ. Münster

and are unreactive to carbonyl reagents. They are stable to base but are hydrolyzed readily by a trace of acid. Fischer found that the enzyme maltase hydrolyzes methyl α-D-glucoside but not the β-anomer, and that the enzyme almond emulsin hydrolyzes methyl β-D-glucoside but not the α-isomer. Armstrong[1] (1903) followed the enzymic processes by polarimetric analysis and proved that the α- and β-D-glucosides yield α- and β-D-glucose, as had been expected from the optical rotations. The formation of methyl β-D-glucoside 3,4,6-triacetate (11) in nearly quantitative yield by reaction of the 1,2-epoxide (10) with methanol

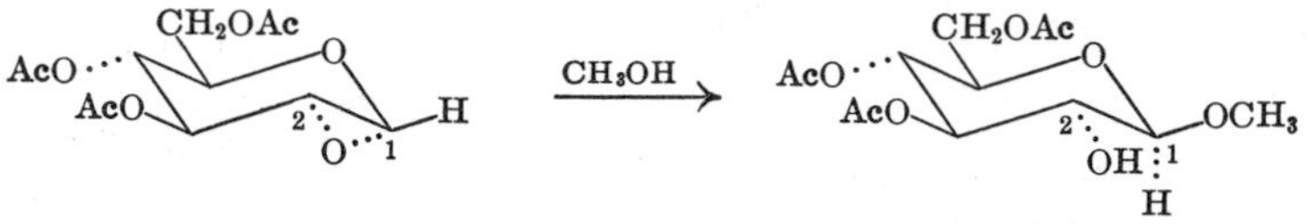

1,2-Anhydro-α-D-glucose (10)
3,4,6-triacetate

Methyl β-D-glucoside
3,4,6-triacetate (11)

at room temperature thus provides chemical confirmation of the configuration assigned to the D-glucopyranoses on physical evidence. Fission of the oxide bond extending to C_1 must be attended with Walden inversion, and hence the 1-methoxyl group is *trans* to the 2-hydroxyl group.

29.4   Determination of Ring Size. — Analogy with lactones led early sugar chemists to expect the stable sugar cyclic hemiacetals to contain five-membered rings (but see 15.34). However, investigations of Haworth[2] and Hirst[3] showed the stable D-glucosides to be pyranosides. This method of determining ring size as applied in the D-glucose series involves exhaustive methylation of a methyl D-glucoside such as (1), either with dimethyl sulfate and 30% sodium hydroxide (Haworth, 1915) or by repeated treatment with methyl iodide

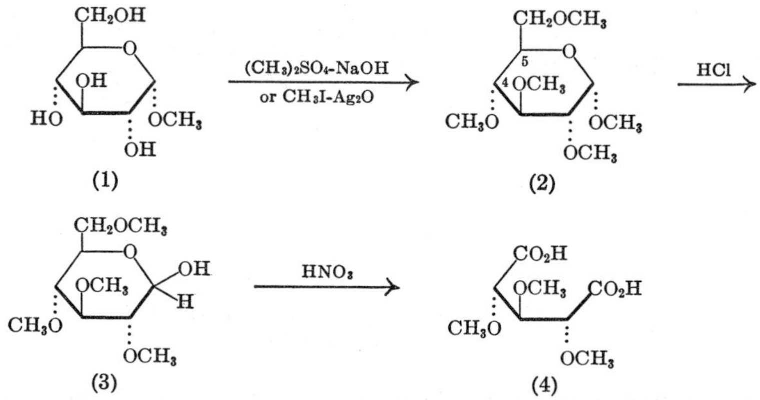

(1)   (2)

(3)   (4)

---

[1] Edward Frankland Armstrong, 1878–1945 (son of H. E. Armstrong); Dir. South Metropol. Gas Co., London; *Nature*, **157**, 154 (1946)

[2] Sir Norman Haworth, 1883–1950; b. Chorley, Lancashire; Ph.D. Göttingen (Wallach); D.Sc. Manchester (Perkin, Jr.); Univ. Birmingham; Nobel Prize 1937; *J. Chem. Soc.*, 2790 (1951)

[3] Edmund Langley Hirst, b. 1898; D.Sc. Birmingham (Haworth); Univ. Birmingham, Bristol, Edinburgh

and silver oxide (Purdie,[1] 1903),[2] hydrolysis of the pentamethyl ether (2) with dilute acid to liberate the anomeric hydroxyl group and produce a potential aldehyde (3), and oxidation.   Methyl α- and β-D-glucoside yield the same tetramethyl ether (3), which on oxidation yields tri-O-methylxyloglutaric acid (4). The oxide linkage thus extends to C_5, not to C_4.

A simple and elegant method of determining both the ring size of glycosides and the configurations at positions of glycosidic linkage developed by E. L. Jackson and C. S. Hudson (1936) involves oxidation with periodic acid in aqueous solution.   The pyranoside I consumes two moles of reagent and the furanoside III consumes one mole, and both substances afford the same dialdehyde II in high yield.   The oxidation eliminates three centers of asymmetry in I, and removes carbon atom 3 as formic acid; in III two centers of asymmetry are destroyed.   The method has provided direct proof that glycosides assigned to the α-D-hexose series on other evidence have the same configurations at C_1 and at

$$
\begin{array}{ccc}
\text{HCOCH}_3 & \text{HCOCH}_3 & \text{HCOCH}_3 \\
\text{HOCH} & \text{CHO} & \text{HOCH} \\
\text{HOCH} \quad\text{O} & \text{CHO} \quad\text{O} & \text{HCOH} \quad\text{O} \\
\text{HCOH} & \text{HC---} & \text{HC---} \\
\text{HC---} & \text{CH}_2\text{OH} & \text{CH}_2\text{OH} \\
\text{CH}_2\text{OH} & \text{(II)} & \text{Methyl }\alpha\text{-D-arabino-} \\
\text{Methyl }\alpha\text{-D-manno-} & & \text{furanoside (III)} \\
\text{pyranoside (I)} & &
\end{array}
$$

I $\xrightarrow[(-\text{HCO}_2\text{H})]{2\,\text{HIO}_4}$ II $\xleftarrow{\text{HIO}_4}$ III

II $\xrightarrow{\begin{array}{c}\text{Br}_2-\text{H}_2\text{O,}\\ \text{SrCO}_3\end{array}}$

$$
\begin{array}{cc}
& \text{HCOCH}_3 & \\
\text{Sr} \Big\langle & \begin{array}{c}\text{O---C==O}\\ \text{O---C==O}\end{array} \quad \text{O} & \\
& \text{HC---} & \\
& \text{CH}_2\text{OH} & \\
& \text{(IV)} &
\end{array}
$$

$$
\text{(IV)} \xrightarrow[\text{Br}_2-\text{H}_2\text{O}]{\text{Hydrol.,}}
\begin{array}{c}
\text{CO}_2\text{H} \quad\text{(V)}\\
\text{CO}_2\text{H}\\
+\\
\text{CO}_2\text{H}\\
\text{HCOH} \quad\text{(VI)}\\
\text{CH}_2\text{OH}
\end{array}
$$

C_5, for they all yield the dialdehyde II, in which these two asymmetric centers alone remain.   Oxidation of the dialdehyde with bromine water in the presence of a metal carbonate affords a dibasic acid easily isolated as the crystalline salt (IV), and this on hydrolysis and oxidation yields oxalic acid and D-glyceric acid

---

[1] Thomas Purdie, 1843–1916; b. Biggar, Scotland; Ph.D. Würzburg; St. Andrews Univ.

[2] Modifications include use of methyl iodide in dimethylformamide with silver oxide or barium oxide, dimethyl sulfate and anhydrous sodium hydroxide in tetrahydrofurane, methyl iodide and potassium in liquid ammonia. Each method has advantages in certain cases, but some require preliminary methylation according to Haworth to impart solubility in the organic solvent. Diazomethane catalyzed by boron fluoride offers promise for methylation of sugars (p. 307).

(VI). This sequence of reactions is the best method known of preparing optically pure glyceric and lactic acids.

29.5   **Furanosides.** — In his work on the methyl glucosides, Fischer obtained in addition to the two crystalline products a sirup which he described (1914) as a third isomer, γ-methylglucoside. Fischer felt that the γ-form must differ in ring size from the α- and β-isomers because it differed profoundly from these substances in properties: greater instability to acids, complete stability to maltase and to almond emulsin. The substance is a mixture of methyl α- and β-D-glucofuranosides. The ring size was established by Haworth (1927)

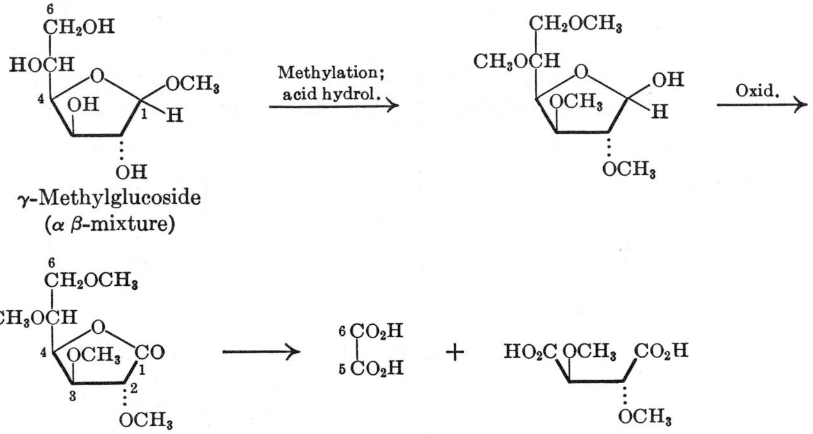

γ-Methylglucoside
(α β-mixture)

Di-O-methyl-L-threaric acid

by the methylation method. After methylation and acid hydrolysis, gentle oxidation gave a lactone which on nitric acid oxidation afforded the cleavage products formulated, showing that Fischer's product is a furanoside.

The crystalline ethyl D-furanosides VIII and IX were synthesized by Haworth (1929) in the following way. Sugars with *cis vic*-glycol groups react with acetone in the presence of an acid catalyst or a dehydrating agent (HCl, H_2SO_4, $ZnCl_2$, anhydrous $CuSO_4$, P_2O_5) to form mono- or diacetonides (isopropylidine derivatives) according to the structures. α-D-Galactose has one pair of *cis* hydroxyls at C_1 and C_2 and another at C_3 and C_4; hence it readily forms a diacetonide of pyranoside structure. α-D-Glucose has only one *cis vic*-glycol grouping in the pyranose form I, but has two in the furanose form II, and it reacts to give the 1,2;5,6-diacetonide III. The group in the 5,6-position is hydrolyzed about forty times as fast as that in the 1,2-position, and hydrolysis conducted with acetic acid affords the 1,2-monoacetonide, IV, which in turn can be converted by the action of phosgene in pyridine solution into the crystalline 1,2-acetonide-5,6-

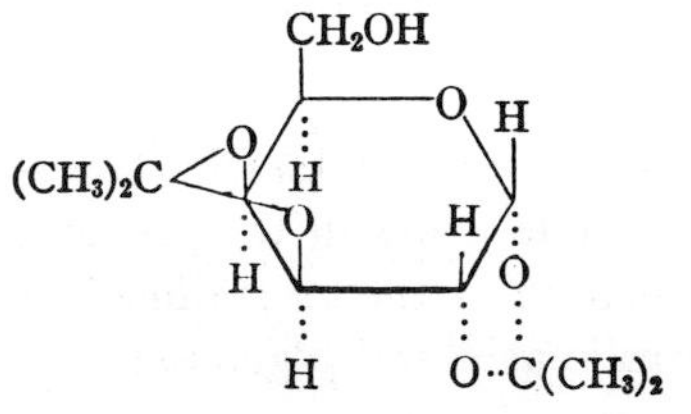

α-D-Galactose 1,2; 3,4-diacetonide

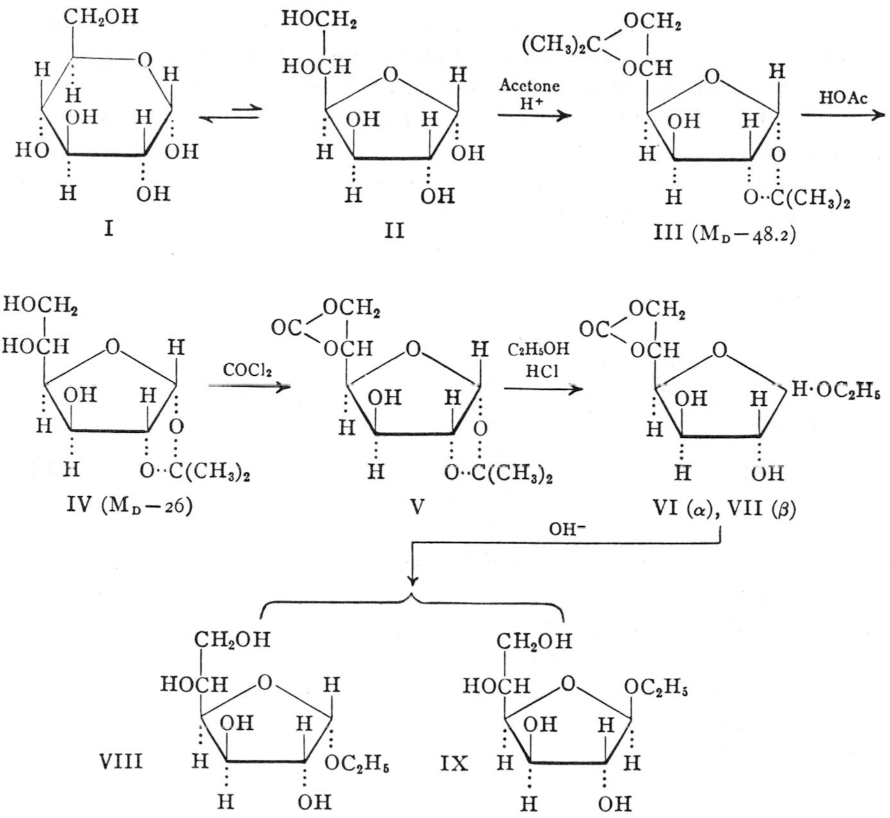

CH_2OH

H   O   H
H
OH   H
HO   OH
H   OH

I

$HOCH_2$
$HOCH$ O   H
OH   H
H   OH
H   OH

II

$(CH_3)_2C$
OCH_2
OCH O   H
OH   H
H   O
H $O\cdot\cdot C(CH_3)_2$

Acetone
H^+

III $(M_D - 48.2)$

HOAc →

$HOCH_2$
$HOCH$ O   H
OH   H
H   O
H $O\cdot\cdot C(CH_3)_2$

IV $(M_D - 26)$

$COCl_2$ →

OC
OCH_2
OCH O   H
OH   H
H   O
H $O\cdot\cdot C(CH_3)_2$

V

C_2H_5OH
HCl →

OC
OCH_2
OCH O
OH   H $H\cdot OC_2H_5$
H
H   OH

VI (α), **VII** (β)

OH^-

CH_2OH
$HOCH$ O   H
OH   H
VIII   H OC_2H_5
H   OH

Ethyl α-D-glucofuranoside
$M_D + 204$

CH_2OH
$HOCH$ O OC_2H_5
OH   H
IX   H   H
H   OH

Ethyl β-D-glucofuranoside
$M_D - 179$

carbonate V. A carbonate ordinarily is more stable to acid hydrolysis than an acetonide, and hydrolysis of V with dilute acid gives glucose-5,6-carbonate. Treatment of the acetonide-carbonate V with ethanol and hydrogen chloride removes acetone and simultaneously effects etherification to give a mixture of the α- and β-ethylfuranoside-carbonates, VI and VII, which can be separated by crystallization as such and as the diacetates. The acid-stable carbonate group as well as the acetyl groups are readily removed by basic hydrolysis to give the 1-epimeric ethyl-D-glucofuranosides, VIII and IX. In formula VIII the two-carbon side chain projects above the plane of the ring, *trans* to the C_1-OC_2H_5. Carbon atom 5 in the furanose structure (VIII) retains the original configuration of the pyranose form (I) or aldehydic form, and since C_5 is written below C_6, or in the reverse order of the usual projection formula, OH appears to the left and H to the right.

29.6   **Phenylosazones.** — Early progress in elucidation of sugar chemistry was handicapped by the difficulty of obtaining crystalline compounds, since sugars, especially when impure, tend to form sirups. One of the outstanding contributions of Fischer was introduction in 1884 of the use of phenylhydrazine, which reacts with many carbonyl compounds to give sparingly soluble and beautifully crystalline derivatives. Fischer's dissertation for the doctorate at Strasbourg under Baeyer ten years earlier had described the discovery, preparation, and uses of phenylhydrazine.[1] The reaction with sugars proceeded in an unexpected manner, since Fischer found that three equivalents of reagent are consumed and that the products, which he called osazones (-ose + hydrazone), contain two phenylhydrazine residues rather than one.   Three years later Fischer

$$
\begin{array}{cccc}
\text{CH}{=}\text{O} & & \text{CH}{=}\text{NNHC}_6\text{H}_5 & & \text{CH}_2\text{OH} \\
| & & | & & | \\
\text{HCOH} & & \text{C}{=}\text{NNHC}_6\text{H}_5 & & \text{C}{=}\text{O} \\
| & & | & & | \\
\text{HOCH} & \xrightarrow[-\text{C}_6\text{H}_5\text{NH}_2,\ \text{NH}_3]{3\text{C}_6\text{H}_5\text{NHNH}_2} & \text{HOCH} & \xleftarrow[-\text{C}_6\text{H}_5\text{NH}_2,\ \text{NH}_3]{3\text{C}_6\text{H}_5\text{NHNH}_2} & \text{HOCH} \\
| & & | & & | \\
\text{HCOH} & & \text{HCOH} & & \text{HCOH} \\
| & & | & & | \\
\text{HCOH} & & \text{HCOH} & & \text{HCOH} \\
| & & | & & | \\
\text{CH}_2\text{OH} & & \text{CH}_2\text{OH} & & \text{CH}_2\text{OH} \\
\text{D-Glucose} & & \text{D-Glucose phenyl-} & & \text{D-Fructose} \\
& & \text{osazone (m.p. 208°)} & &
\end{array}
$$

isolated the true phenylhydrazone of D-glucose, showed that it is an intermediate in the formation of the phenylosazone, and assumed that it is oxidized at C_2 by phenylhydrazine. His formula for the derivative accounts for the fact that D-glucose and D-fructose yield the same product, D-glucose phenylosazone. However, phenylhydrazine is not an oxidizing agent, and evidence presented by Weygand (1946) supports the following mechanism. The key step is a disproportionation of the phenylhydrazone (b) with migration of two hydrogen atoms from the secondary alcoholic group to the double bond, with formation of (c).

$$
\begin{array}{cccc}
\text{CHO} & & \text{CH}{=}\text{NNHC}_6\text{H}_5 & & \text{CH}_2\text{NHNHC}_6\text{H}_5 & \xrightarrow{\text{C}_6\text{H}_5\text{NHNH}_2} \\
| & \longrightarrow & | & \longrightarrow & | \\
\text{HCOH} & & \text{HCOH} & & \text{C}{=}\text{O} \\
| & & | & & | \\
(a) & & (b) & & (c)
\end{array}
$$

$$
\begin{array}{ccc}
\left[\begin{array}{c} \text{CH}_2\text{NHNHC}_6\text{H}_5 \\ | \\ \text{C}{=}\text{NNHC}_6\text{H}_5 \\ | \end{array}\right] & \longrightarrow & \left[\begin{array}{c} \text{CHNHNHC}_6\text{H}_5 \\ \| \\ \text{C}{-}\text{NHNHC}_6\text{H}_5 \\ | \end{array}\right] \xrightarrow{-\text{H}_2\text{NC}_6\text{H}_5} \\
(d) & & (e)
\end{array}
$$

$$
\left[\begin{array}{c} \text{CH}{=}\text{NH} \\ | \\ \text{C}{=}\text{NNHC}_6\text{H}_5 \\ | \end{array} \quad \text{or} \quad \begin{array}{c} \text{CH}{=}\text{NNHC}_6\text{H}_5 \\ | \\ \text{C}{=}\text{NH} \\ | \end{array}\right] \xrightarrow{\text{C}_6\text{H}_5\text{NHNH}_2} \begin{array}{c} \text{CH}{=}\text{NNHC}_6\text{H}_5 \\ | \\ \text{C}{=}\text{NNHC}_6\text{H}_5 \\ | \end{array} + \text{NH}_3
$$

$$
\quad\quad\quad\quad (f) \quad\quad\quad\quad\quad\quad (g) \quad\quad\quad\quad\quad\quad\quad\quad\quad \text{Osazone} \\
\quad\quad\quad\quad\quad\quad\quad\quad\quad\quad\quad\quad\quad\quad\quad\quad\quad\quad\quad\quad (h)
$$

M. Amadori observed transformations of this type with compounds of structures precluding osazone formation (Amadori rearrangement, 1925–29). The ketonic product (c) then condenses with phenylhydrazine to give (d), which by an allylic

[1] For twelve years following 1891, Fischer suffered from the insidious poisonous effects of phenylhydrazine, which even so, he later described as his "first and most lasting chemical love."

shift of hydrogen yields (*e*). A 1,4-elimination of aniline to give either (*f*) or (*g*), or both, is followed by condensation of the imine with phenylhydrazine to give the phenylosazone and ammonia.

Weygand's formulation does not explain why the reaction stops with introduction of two residues of phenylhydrazine. Why, for example, does not the phenylosazone (*h*) undergo a further intramolecular oxidation-reduction reaction involving the C_3-position? In the reaction of glucose with Fehling solution, an amount of reagent is consumed greatly beyond that calculated for oxidation of the aldehydic group, an indication that oxidation progresses down the chain through successively activated positions adjacent to a center of unsaturation.

A suggestion of ours (*Organic Chemistry*, 1944) that the phenylosazone is stabilized by chelation (I) is supported by chemical evidence adduced by L. Mester (Budapest, 1955). From an ultraviolet spectrographic study of model

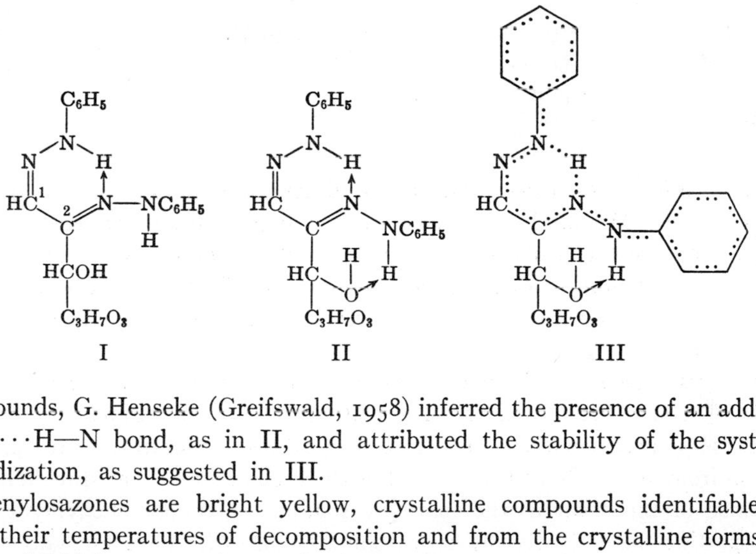

I II III

compounds, G. Henseke (Greifswald, 1958) inferred the presence of an additional $C—O \cdots H—N$ bond, as in II, and attributed the stability of the system to hybridization, as suggested in III.

Phenylosazones are bright yellow, crystalline compounds identifiable both from their temperatures of decomposition and from the crystalline forms. W. Otting (Heidelberg, 1961) examined the IR spectra of the phenylosazones of 17 sugars and found that spectroscopy is particularly well suited to characterization. That the solubility in water is markedly less than that of the sugar is understandable, for introduction of two phenylhydrazine residues into a hexose increases the molecular weight by 64%, and the derivative contains one less hydroxyl group and two hydrophobic phenyl groups. Thus an osazone, which is produced easily by brief warming of a solution containing the reagent, usually will separate from a dilute solution of an impure sugar. The phenylosotriazoles

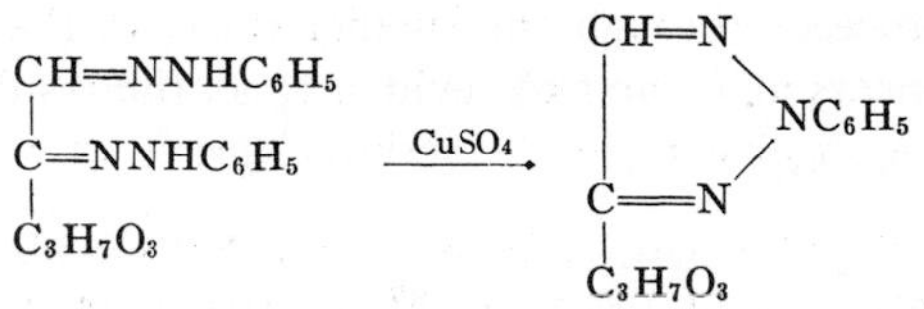

I IV

(IV), obtained by heating the phenylosazones with copper sulfate solution, are regarded as even more reliable for characterization.

29.7   D-Mannose. — In 1888, Fischer reduced D-glucose with sodium amalgam and obtained, in part, an alcohol which on oxidation afforded not D-glucose but a new aldohexose, which Fischer was able to isolate as the phenylhydrazone. The alcohol is mannitol, formed by partial epimerization of the aldose at C_2 in the alkaline solution prior to reduction. Note that the struc-

$$
\begin{array}{ccccccc}
\text{CHO} & & \text{CH}_2\text{OH} & & \text{CH=NNHC}_6\text{H}_5 & & \text{CHO} \\
| & & | & & | & & | \\
\text{HCOH} & & \text{HOCH} & & \text{HOCH} & & \text{HOCH} \\
| & & | & & | & & | \\
\text{HOCH} & \xrightarrow{\text{Na-Hg}} & \text{HOCH} & \xrightarrow[\substack{\text{1. dil. HNO}_3.\\ \text{2. C}_6\text{H}_5\text{NHNH}_2\\ \text{10\%}}]{} & \text{HOCH} & \xrightarrow[\text{80\%}]{\text{HCl}} & \text{HOCH} \\
| & & | & & | & & | \\
\text{HCOH} & & \text{HCOH} & & \text{HCOH} & & \text{HCOH} \\
| & & | & & | & & | \\
\text{HCOH} & & \text{HCOH} & & \text{HCOH} & & \text{HCOH} \\
| & & | & & | & & | \\
\text{CH}_2\text{OH} & & \text{CH}_2\text{OH} & & \text{CH}_2\text{OH} & & \text{CH}_2\text{OH} \\
\text{D-Glucose} & & \text{D-Mannitol} & & & & \text{D-Mannose} \\
& & \text{(m.p. 166°,} & & & & \\
& & \alpha\text{D} -0.5°) & & & &
\end{array}
$$

ture of D-mannitol is such that oxidation of either terminal alcoholic group gives the same aldose. Mannitol is highly crystalline, high melting, and less soluble in water than most sugar alcohols (100 g. of water dissolves 13.0 g. at 14°), and it was the first crystalline alditol to be isolated. M. Proust was the discoverer (1806); the source was the manna, or sweetish exudate, of the flowering ash *Fraxinus ornus.*

Many polysaccharides subsequently were found to afford D-mannose on hydrolysis. Fischer's "Anleitung zur Darstellung organischen Präparate" (1908) describes the preparation of the sugar by acid hydrolysis of scrap from the cutting of buttons from vegetable ivory, the seed of the tagua palm. The directions call for isolation of the sugar as the sparingly soluble D-mannose phenylhydrazone and for splitting the derivative by hydrazone-exchange with benzaldehyde.

Elucidation of the structure and configuration was a simple matter, for D-mannose phenylhydrazone on reaction with more phenylhydrazine gave D-glucose phenylosazone; the sugars are therefore 2-epimeric aldohexoses.

29.8   Lobry de Bruyn[1]-van Ekenstein[2] Rearrangement. — Fischer's discovery that reduction of glucose in an alkaline medium affords mannitol as one of the products is a consequence of a rearrangement of α-ketols in alkaline solution named for the Dutch discoverers. An aldose treated with base usually gives a mixture of the 2-epimer, the 2-ketose, and the original aldehyde. The isomerization proceeds through the enediol since, in the presence of heavy water, deuterium appears at C_1 and C_2, evidently as the result of exchange with the acidic enediol. A sugar carrying a methoxyl group at the 2-position is epi-

---

[1] C. A. Lobry de Bruyn, 1857–1904; b. Leedenwarden, Netherlands; Ph.D. Leiden; Univ. Amsterdam; *Ber.,* **37,** 4827 (1904); *J. Chem. Soc.,* **87,** 570 (1905); *Rec. trav.,* **24,** 223 (1905)

[2] W. Alberda van Ekenstein, 1858–1937; b. Gröningen, Netherlands; Univ. Amsterdam

$$
\begin{array}{c}
\text{CHO} \\
| \\
\text{HCOH} \\
|
\end{array}
$$

$$\Updownarrow$$

$$
\begin{array}{ccccc}
\text{CH}_2\text{OH} & & \overset{\text{H}}{\underset{|}{\text{C}}}-\text{OH} & & \text{CHO} \\
| & & \| & & | \\
\text{C}=\text{O} & \rightleftharpoons & \text{C}-\text{OH} & \rightleftharpoons & \text{HOCH} \\
| & & | & & |
\end{array}
$$

Enediol

merized by alkali at C_2 with deuterium exchange at this position. A possible path from an aldose to a ketose is nucleophilic attack by hydroxide ion to give an ionic intermediate in which hydrogen migrates with its electron pair; reversal of the process would give opportunity for epimerization at C_2.

$$
\begin{array}{c}
\text{H} \\
| \\
\text{C}=\text{O} \\
| \\
\text{H}-\text{C}-\text{OH} \\
|
\end{array}
\xrightarrow{\text{OH}^-}
\left[
\begin{array}{c}
\text{H} \\
| \\
\cdot\rightarrow\text{C}\overset{\curvearrowleft}{=}\text{O} \\
| \\
\boxed{\text{H}:}\text{C}\overset{\curvearrowleft}{-}\text{O}^- \\
|
\end{array}
\right]
\longrightarrow
\begin{array}{c}
\text{H} \\
| \\
\text{H}-\text{C}-\text{O}^- \\
| \\
\text{C}=\text{O} \\
|
\end{array}
\xrightarrow{\text{H}^+}
\begin{array}{c}
\text{CH}_2\text{OH} \\
| \\
\text{C}=\text{O} \\
|
\end{array}
$$

29.9   Synthesis. — The cyanohydrin reaction discovered by Kiliani is the classical method for increasing the chain length of an aldose.   Fischer found that two isomeric nitriles are formed; for example L-arabinose, a pentose obtained on hydrolysis of various plant gums, is converted into two epimers,

$$
\begin{array}{ccc}
\left[
\begin{array}{c}
\text{CN} \\
| \\
\text{HOCH} \\
| \\
\text{HCOH} \\
| \\
\text{HOCH} \\
| \\
\text{HOCH} \\
| \\
\text{CH}_2\text{OH}
\end{array}
\right]
&
\xrightarrow[\text{11–13\%}]{\text{Hydrol.}}
&
\begin{array}{c}
\text{COOH} \\
| \\
\text{HOCH} \\
| \\
\text{HCOH} \\
| \\
\text{HOCH} \\
| \\
\text{HOCH} \\
| \\
\text{CH}_2\text{OH}
\end{array} \\
& & \text{L-Gluconic acid}
\end{array}
$$

$$
\begin{array}{c}
\text{CHO} \\
| \\
\text{HCOH} \\
| \\
\text{HOCH} \\
| \\
\text{HOCH} \\
| \\
\text{CH}_2\text{OH} \\
\text{L-Arabinose}
\end{array}
\quad\xrightarrow{\text{HCN}}
$$

$$\Big\Updownarrow \text{Quinoline, 140°}$$

$$
\begin{array}{ccc}
\left[
\begin{array}{c}
\text{CN} \\
| \\
\text{HCOH} \\
| \\
\text{HCOH} \\
| \\
\text{HOCH} \\
| \\
\text{HOCH} \\
| \\
\text{CH}_2\text{OH}
\end{array}
\right]
&
\xrightarrow[\text{34\%}]{\text{Hydrol.}}
&
\begin{array}{c}
\text{COOH} \\
| \\
\text{HCOH} \\
| \\
\text{HCOH} \\
| \\
\text{HOCH} \\
| \\
\text{HOCH} \\
| \\
\text{CH}_2\text{OH}
\end{array} \\
& & \text{L-Mannonic acid}
\end{array}
$$

L-gluconic and L-mannonic acid.   Note that one cyanohydrin is favored over the other by a factor of about 3:1.

A sugar acid produced by the Kiliani reaction, for example L-gluconic acid, is transformed easily into the corresponding aldose by lactonization and reduction.

$$
\begin{array}{ccccc}
CO_2H & & C=O & & CH=O \\
HOCH & & HOCH & & HOCH \\
HCOH & \rightarrow & \mathrm{O}\;HCOH & \xrightarrow{\;NaBH_4\;} & HCOH \\
HOCH & & CH & & HOCH \\
HOCH & & HOCH & & HOCH \\
CH_2OH & & CH_2OH & & CH_2OH \\
\text{L-Gluconic} & & \text{L-Gluconolactone} & & \text{L-Glucose} \\
\text{acid} & & & &
\end{array}
$$

Kuhn and co-workers (1956–1961), in developing practical syntheses for all eight D-hexosamines (2-amino-2-desoxyhexoses), worked out a procedure for addition of ammonia and hydrogen cyanide to a pentose and hydrogenation of the resulting α-amino nitrile (2) in weakly acid solution.   The initial addition always gives a mixture of the 2-epimers, but these are formed in unequal amounts.   Thus the end products from D-arabinose (1) are D-glucosamine·HCl (3, yield 64%) and D-mannosamine·HCl (1%).   The major product invariably is that in which the

$$
\begin{array}{cccccccc}
 & & CN & & NH_2 & & CHO \\
CH=O & & HCNH_2 & & N\!\equiv\!C\!\diagup\!\overset{\displaystyle H}{C} & & HCNH_2\cdot HCl \\
HOCH & \xrightarrow{\;HCN,\;NH_3\;} & HOCH & = & H\!-\!\underset{O}{\,}\quad CH & \xrightarrow{\;H_2,\,Pt\;\; HCl\;} & HOCH \\
HCOH & & HCOH & & HCOH & & HCOH \\
HCOH & & HCOH & & HCOH & & HCOH \\
CH_2OH & & CH_2OH & & CH_2OH & & CH_2OH \\
(1) & & (2) & & (2a) & & (3)
\end{array}
$$

amino group is *trans* to the hydroxyl group at C_3, as in the example cited.   Other *trans/cis* ratios (yields) are 28/7, 38/8, 29/9.   The 2,3-*trans* epimer (2) is the major product expected either on application of the Prelog-Cram rule or on consideration that this epimer is stabilized by chelation (2a).   Although allosamine and talosamine are of the unfavorable 2,3-*cis* type and are formed in very low yield, R. Kuhn and J. C. Jochims found (1961) that these rare sugars can be prepared readily in pure form by application of the solubility-product principle defined by O. Dimroth (1910) for a solution saturated with two interconvertible compounds in contact with a solid phase initially containing only a small amount of one isomer.   An N-benzyl type substituent renders a hexosamine capable of epimerization and is easily eliminated by hydrogenolysis.   Thus condensation of D-ribose with 9-aminofluorene gives N-(fluorenyl-9)-D-ribosimine, which on reaction with hydrogen cyanide in ethanol affords a mixture rich in the ribosaminonitrile and containing only a little of the allosaminonitrile.   When a suspension of this mixture in isopropanol is stirred for 13 hrs. at 65° under nitrogen the solid phase, collected without cooling, is nearly pure N-(fluorenyl-9)-D-allosaminonitrile. Hydrogenation in dilute hydrochloric acid removes the fluorenyl group as fluorene and gives β-D-allosamine hydrochloride in overall yield of 53%.

29.10 Oxidation and Reduction. — When D-glucose is reduced by catalytic hydrogenation or electrolytically, the product is D-glucitol (m.p. 97°, αD −2°), known to the trade as sorbitol (L. *sorbum*, the fruit). Oxidation

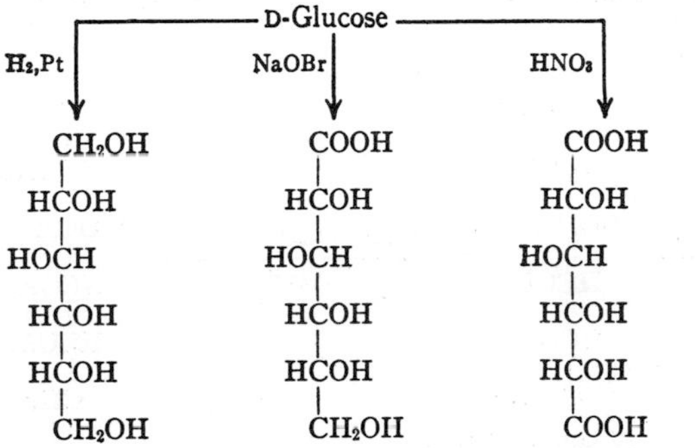

D-Glucitol D-Gluconic acid D-Glucosaccharic acid

with hypobromite attacks the aldehydic group and gives a monobasic aldonic acid, D-gluconic acid; nitric acid attacks both the aldehydic group and the primary alcoholic group to give the dibasic D-glucosaccharic acid (D-glucaric acid[1]).

For comparative tests of the reactivity of reducing sugars, once done with Fehling solution, the reagent of choice is Blue Tetrazolium: 3,3′-dianisole-bis [4,4′-(3,5-diphenyl)tetrazolium chloride]. When a 0.5% aqueous solution of the lemon yellow reagent is added with a trace of alkali to a 0.1 *N* solution of

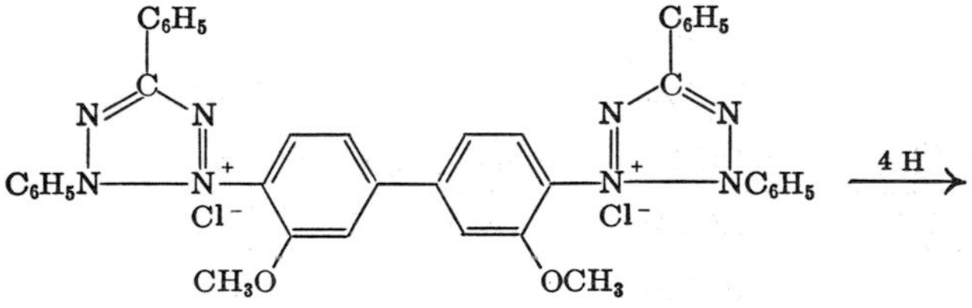

Blue tetrazolium

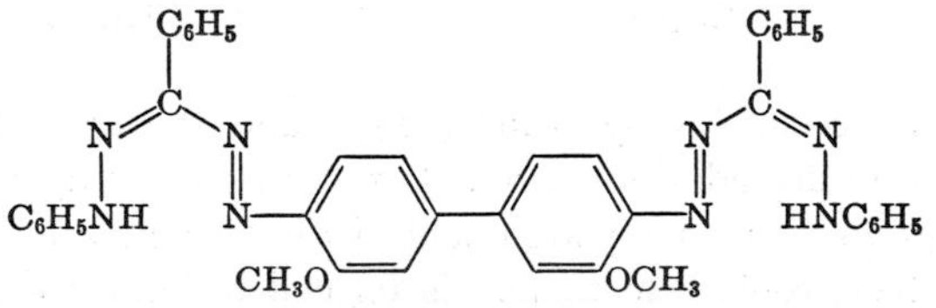

Diformazan pigment

glucose and the solution is warmed, a vivid color develops in a few minutes. This sensitive test for reducing sugars distinguishes between α-ketols and simple

[1] The IUPAC system uses glucaric, mannaric, galactaric, etc., also pentaric and tetraric; natural tartaric acid is L-threaric acid and the *meso* form is erythraric acid.

aldehydes. Thus the order of reactivity is as follows: fructose > glucose > lactose > maltose > n-butyraldehyde. The reagent is useful for detection of dehydrogenase in tissues, cells, and bacteria, for research in seed germination, and for determination of cortisone.

29.11 **Degradation.** — Four general methods of degradation are illustrated below for the conversion of D-glucose into D-arabinose. The first method (1) was developed by Wohl[1] (1893) and simplified (1a) by Zemplén[2] (1927),

1. Wohl degradation:

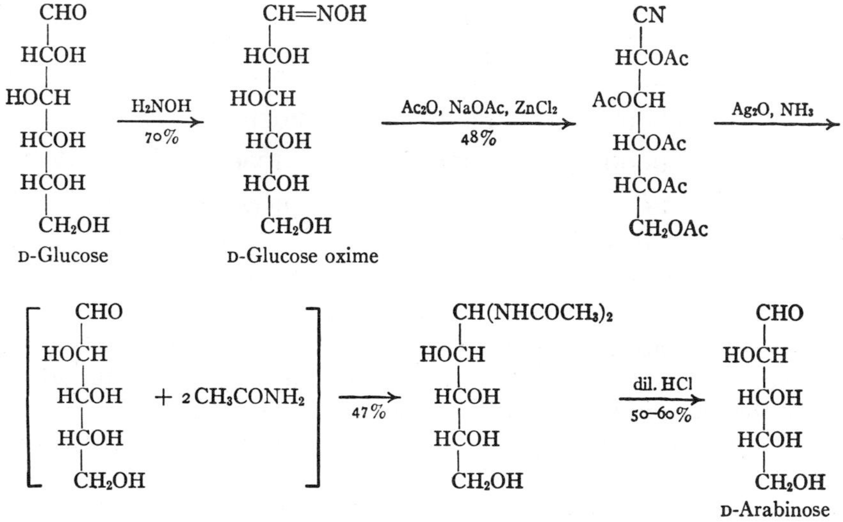

$$\begin{array}{c} CHO \\ | \\ HCOH \\ | \\ HOCH \\ | \\ HCOH \\ | \\ HCOH \\ | \\ CH_2OH \\ \text{D-Glucose} \end{array} \quad \xrightarrow[70\%]{H_2NOH} \quad \begin{array}{c} CH{=}NOH \\ | \\ HCOH \\ | \\ HOCH \\ | \\ HCOH \\ | \\ HCOH \\ | \\ CH_2OH \\ \text{D-Glucose oxime} \end{array} \quad \xrightarrow[48\%]{Ac_2O,\ NaOAc,\ ZnCl_2} \quad \begin{array}{c} CN \\ | \\ HCOAc \\ | \\ AcOCH \\ | \\ HCOAc \\ | \\ HCOAc \\ | \\ CH_2OAc \end{array} \quad \xrightarrow{Ag_2O,\ NH_3} $$

$$\left[\begin{array}{c} CHO \\ | \\ HOCH \\ | \\ HCOH \\ | \\ HCOH \\ | \\ CH_2OH \end{array} \ +\ 2\ CH_3CONH_2 \right] \quad \xrightarrow[47\%]{} \quad \begin{array}{c} CH(NHCOCH_3)_2 \\ | \\ HOCH \\ | \\ HCOH \\ | \\ HCOH \\ | \\ CH_2OH \end{array} \quad \xrightarrow[50-60\%]{dil.\ HCl} \quad \begin{array}{c} CHO \\ | \\ HOCH \\ | \\ HCOH \\ | \\ HCOH \\ | \\ CH_2OH \\ \text{D-Arabinose} \end{array}$$

1a. Zemplén simplification:

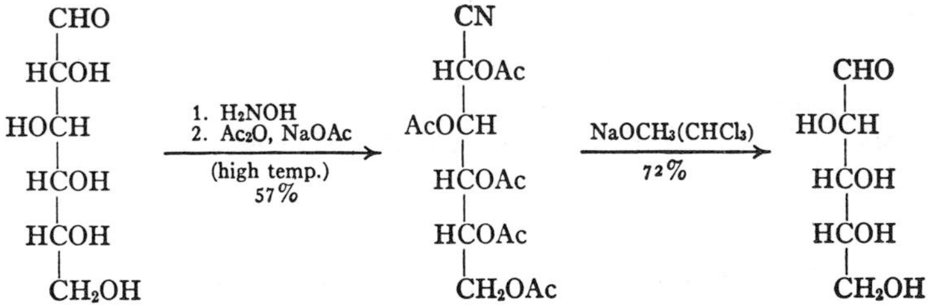

$$\begin{array}{c} CHO \\ | \\ HCOH \\ | \\ HOCH \\ | \\ HCOH \\ | \\ HCOH \\ | \\ CH_2OH \end{array} \quad \xrightarrow[\substack{(high\ temp.) \\ 57\%}]{\substack{1.\ H_2NOH \\ 2.\ Ac_2O,\ NaOAc}} \quad \begin{array}{c} CN \\ | \\ HCOAc \\ | \\ AcOCH \\ | \\ HCOAc \\ | \\ HCOAc \\ | \\ CH_2OAc \end{array} \quad \xrightarrow[72\%]{NaOCH_3(CHCl_3)} \quad \begin{array}{c} CHO \\ | \\ HOCH \\ | \\ HCOH \\ | \\ HCOH \\ | \\ CH_2OH \end{array}$$

the second (2) by Ruff[3] (1899), and the third (3) by Weerman (1917). The Wohl degradation represents reversal of the cyanohydrin synthesis. The nitrile group of the acetylated acid nitrile is eliminated by treatment with ammoniacal silver oxide. Acetamide is formed by ammonolysis of the acetate groups and

---

[1] Alfred Wohl, 1863–1933 Graudentz; Ph.D. Berlin (Hofmann); Univ. Danzig; *Nature*, **145**, 290 (1940)

[2] Geza Zemplén, 1883–1956; b. Trencsén, Hungary; Ph.D. Budapest; Univ. Budapest; *Adv. Corbohyd. Chem.*, **14**, 1 (1959)

[3] Otto Ruff, 1871–1939; b. Schwäbisch-Hall, Germany; Ph.D. Berlin (Piloty); Univ. Danzig, Breslau: *Ber.*, **73A**, 124 (1940)

reacts with the aldose to form the diacetamide derivative, which is hydrolyzed to the aldose. In the Zemplén modification the nitrile group is eliminated by treatment with sodium methoxide; the yield is more than twice that in the original procedure. The Ruff degradation consists in oxidation of an aldonic acid to a

2. Ruff degradation:

$$
\begin{array}{ccccc}
\text{CHO} & & \left[\text{COO}\right] & & \left[\text{COOH}\right] \\
\text{HCOH} & & \text{HCOH} & & \text{C=O} & \text{CHO} \\
\text{HOCH} & \xrightarrow[77\%]{\substack{\text{Electrolytic}\\\text{oxidation}}} & \text{HOCH} & \xrightarrow{\text{H}_2\text{O}_2,\,[\text{Fe(OAc)}_2]} & \text{HOCH} & \text{HOCH} \\
\text{HCOH} & & \text{HCOH} & & \text{HCOH} & \xrightarrow[25\%]{-\text{CO}_2} & \text{HCOH} \\
\text{HCOH} & & \text{HCOH} & \text{Ca} & \text{HCOH} & \text{HCOH} \\
\text{CH}_2\text{OH} & & \left[\text{CH}_2\text{OH}\right]_2 & & \left[\text{CH}_2\text{OH}\right] & \text{CH}_2\text{OH}
\end{array}
$$

Calcium D-gluconate

2-ketoaldonic acid (aldosulose), which yields the next-lower aldose by loss of carbon dioxide. The yield is poor owing to further degradation of the aldose. R. L. Whistler[1] (1959–61) improved the method by oxidizing glucose with 3 moles of hypochlorite at pH 11 to gluconic acid and oxidizing this with 1.4 moles

3. Weermann degradation:

$$
\begin{array}{ccccc}
\text{Calcium} & \xrightarrow{\text{HCl}} & \left[\begin{array}{c}\text{CO}\!-\!\\\text{HCOH}\\\text{HOCH}\\\text{HC}\!-\!\\\text{HCOH}\\\text{CH}_2\text{OH}\end{array}\right]\!\text{O} & \xrightarrow[80\%]{\text{NH}_3,\,\text{C}_2\text{H}_5\text{OH}} & \begin{array}{c}\text{CONH}_2\\\text{HCOH}\\\text{HOCH}\\\text{HCOH}\\\text{HCOH}\\\text{CH}_2\text{OH}\end{array} & \xrightarrow{\text{HOCl},\,\text{Na}_2\text{CO}_3} \\
\text{D-gluconate} & & \text{D-Gluconolactone} & & \text{D-Gluconamide}
\end{array}
$$

$$
\begin{array}{ccc}
\left[\begin{array}{c}\text{N=C=O}\\\text{HCOH}\\\text{HOCH}\\\text{HCOH}\\\text{HCOH}\\\text{CH}_2\text{OH}\end{array}\right] & \xrightarrow[49\%]{-\text{HNCO}} & \begin{array}{c}\text{CHO}\\\text{HOCH}\\\text{HCOH}\\\text{HCOH}\\\text{CH}_2\text{OH}\end{array}
\end{array}
$$

of reagent at pH 4.5–5. After treatment of the solution with anion and cation exchange resins, crystalline arabinose was obtained in 35% yield. The Weerman method involves degradation of the amide of a sugar acid by a variation of the Hofmann reaction with hypochlorous acid. Another degradation (F. Weygand, 1950) involves reaction of a sugar oxime in aqueous bicarbonate solution with 2,4-dinitrofluorobenzene; the oxime aryl ether produced decomposes to 2,4-dinitrophenol, the next lower aldose, and hydrogen cyanide (yields 50–60%):
—CHOHCH=NOC$_6$H$_3$(NO$_2$)$_2$ → —CH=O + HCN + HOC$_6$H$_3$(NO$_2$)$_2$.

[1] Roy L. Whistler, b. 1912 Morgantown, W. Va.; Ph.D. Ohio State (Hixon); Purdue Univ.

29.12   Configurations of Tetroses and Pentoses. — The configurations of the lower sugars are represented below with formulas in which a bar written to the right or left stands for a hydroxyl group. The configurations of the two D-tetroses, erythrose and threose, can be distinguished experimentally in a simple manner: nitric acid oxidation and examination of the resulting C_4-diacids for optical activity. The product from erythrose has a plane of symmetry and hence is optically inactive (mesotartaric acid); that from threose is not symmetrical and is optically active (L-tartaric acid). Two of the four D-pentoses, ribose and arabinose, are C_2-epimers related to erythrose in that they both yield

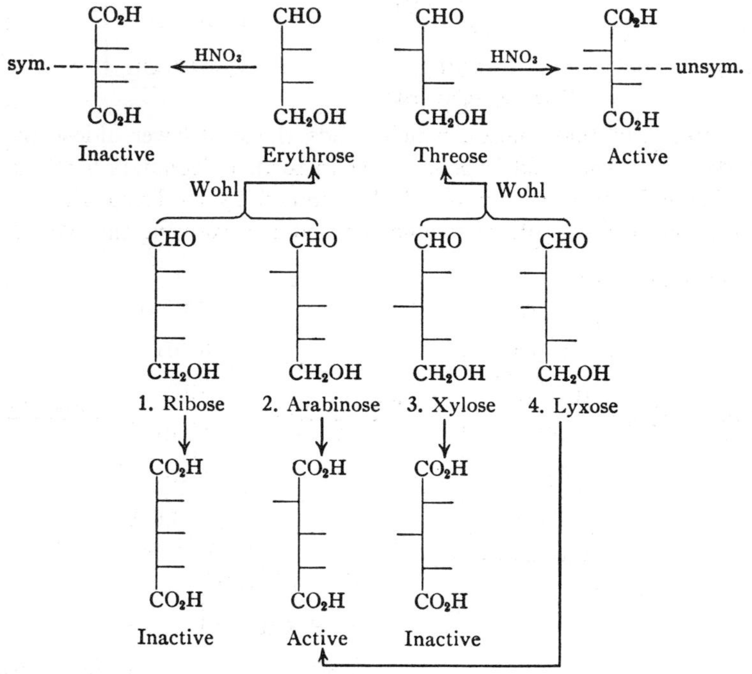

$$\text{sym.} \xleftarrow{\;HNO_3\;} \text{Erythrose} \qquad \text{Threose} \xrightarrow{\;HNO_3\;} \text{unsym.}$$

Inactive	Erythrose	Threose	Active

Wohl → Erythrose   Wohl → Threose

CHO	CHO	CHO	CHO
1. Ribose	2. Arabinose	3. Xylose	4. Lyxose

CO₂H	CO₂H	CO₂H	
Inactive	Active	Inactive	

this substance on Wohl degradation. Xylose and lyxose are related in the same way to threose. The C_5-diacids (saccharic acids) resulting on oxidation of the pentoses with nitric acid are characterized as follows: ribose gives an inactive acid and arabinose an active one; xylose gives a different inactive acid, while that from lyxose is active and if the formula is inverted this is seen to be identical with the acid from arabinose. If the configurations were unknown, they could be deduced as follows. Ribose can be assigned formula (1) because it is the only D-pentose which affords an inactive C_5-diacid and which on Wohl degradation and oxidation gives a likewise inactive C_4-diacid. Arabinose could be shown by phenylosazone formation to be the 2-epimer of ribose, and the configuration thus deduced. The 2-epimers xylose and lyxose are distinguished by the inactivity and activity of the respective C_5-diacids. The fact that arabinose and lyxose yield the same C_5-diacid provides confirmatory evidence.

29.13   Aldohexose Configurations. — An aid for remembering the names of the eight D-aldohexoses is: All Altruists Gladly Make Gum In Gallon Tanks. Construct eight outline formulas, and under each write the name of the sugar in the order suggested: Allose, Altrose, Glucose, Mannose, Gulose, Idose, Galactose, Talose. In the line corresponding to C_5, write a bar (or OH) to the right to signify that in each sugar (D-series) C_5-OH is to the right (and hydrogen to the left). In the line representing C_4, write four bars to the right and four to the left. At C_3 write OH twice to the right and twice to the left, and repeat the process; at C_2 write OH alternately to the right and to the left. The result is as shown.

CHO	CHO	CHO	CHO	CHO	CHO	CHO	CHO
CH₂OH	CH₂OH	CH₂OH	CH₂OH	CH₂OH	CH₂OH	CH₂OH	CH₂OH
I	II	III	IV	V	VI	VII	VIII
Allose	Altrose	Glucose	Mannose	Gulose	Idose	Galactose	Talose

The derivation automatically arranges the sugars in four pairs of 2-epimers, and it will be noted that on Wohl degradation the pair I–II yield ribose, III–IV arabinose, V–VI xylose, and VII–VIII lyxose. Configurations can be deduced from considerations like those cited above for the pentoses. Thus one of the eight D-aldohexoses is identified by the following observations: (a) the product of nitric acid oxidation is an optically inactive C_6-diacid; (b) the C_5-diacid resulting on Wohl degradation followed by nitric acid oxidation is optically active. Observation (a) shows that the sugar has the configuration I or VII, since these alone can give rise to C_6-diacids which are inactive. Of these two configurations, only VII can give an optically active C_5-diacid, and hence the sugar, galactose, is identified as having the configuration VII.

Steps by which the formula of D-glucose can be inferred are as follows. (a) Nitric acid oxidation of glucose gives an optically active C_6-dibasic acid; therefore glucose cannot have formula I or VII. (b) The active C_6-dibasic acid from D-glucose results also from oxidation of L-gulose, the formula for which is derivable by inverting III and interchanging the terminal groups, —CHO and —CH₂OH. In formulas IV and VI, however, similar changes do not result in a new structure and hence each sugar affords an active C_6-dibasic acid not obtainable from any other aldohexose; hence IV and VI are eliminated. (c) Wohl degradation of glucose followed by nitric acid oxidation gives an active C_5-dibasic acid; hence formulas II and V are eliminated. (d) Of the remaining formulas, III and VIII, III is correct because glucose gives a phenylosazone identical with that from IV (active C_6-acid) and different from that from VII (inactive C_6-acid).

All sixteen aldohexoses have been isolated or synthesized and their configurations established (twelve by Fischer). Only three occur commonly in nature: D-glucose, its 2-epimer D-mannose, and its 4-epimer D-galactose. The only other hexose widely distributed in nature is D-fructose. Strikingly enough, these are the only sugars that yeasts are able to ferment. Thus the 6-desoxyhexose[1] L-fucose is isolated from acid-hydrolyzed seaweed after fermentation with yeast to

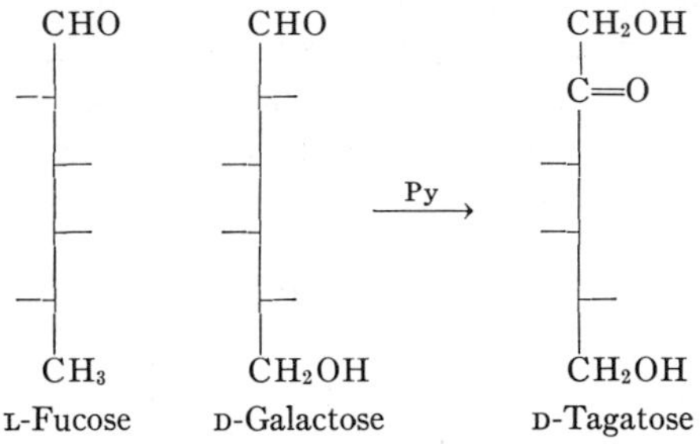

L-Fucose   D-Galactose   D-Tagatose

remove D-mannose and D-galactose. Another rare sugar, D-tagatose, was prepared by Lobry de Bruyn and Alberda van Ekenstein by isomerization of D-galactose with pyridine. P. F. Wily (Eli Lilly Co., 1958) isolated D-talose from the antibiotic hygromycin B after acid hydrolysis. Polysaccharides of agar-agar and of flaxseed mucilage on hydrolysis yield both L-galactose and DL-galactose.

29.14   Characterization of an Octulose. — A method of degradation that eliminates two carbon atoms at a time is based upon the fact that lead tetraacetate is selective for cleavage of the α-hydroxyhemiacetal group (A. S. Perlin and C. Brice, 1956). When a solution of D-glucose in a little water is taken up in acetic acid and treated with an acetic acid solution of two equivalents of lead tetraacetate, the sequence of events is as follows. Cleavage of the C_1–C_2 bond gives initially 4-O-formylarabinose (1), in which the formyl group may

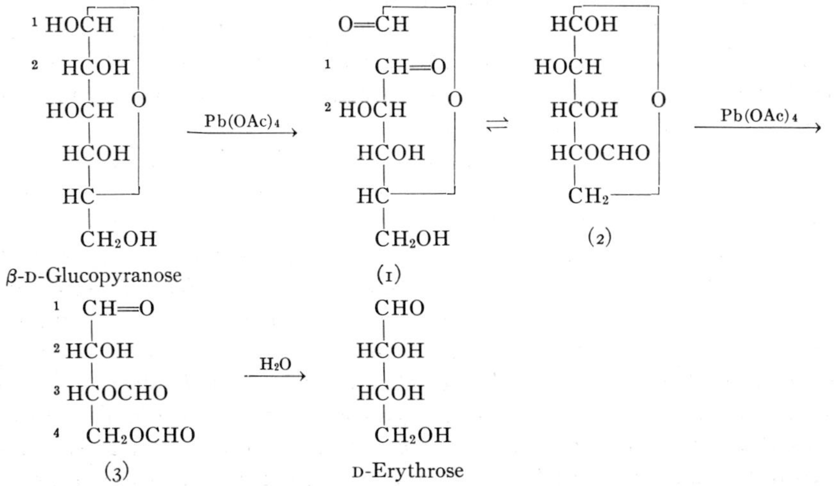

β-D-Glucopyranose   (1)

(3)   D-Erythrose

---

[1] Sugar chemists use the prefix deoxy-; steroid chemists use desoxy-. We prefer the form of stronger pronunciation and for uniformity have used it throughout this book.

migrate to C_3 via the orthoester. In any case, cyclization to the pyranose (2) is followed by a second cleavage to give 3,4-di-O-formyl D-erythrose (3, or the 2,3-diformate). Water alone hydrolyzes the ester to D-erythrose.

From 27 kg. of the fruit of a Californian avocado, A. J. Charlson and N. K. Richtmyer (1960) isolated as a sirup 1 g. of a new sugar characterized as its crystalline 2,5-dichlorophenylhydrazone as an octulose. The configuration (5) was established as follows. Oxidation with two equivalents of lead tetraacetate

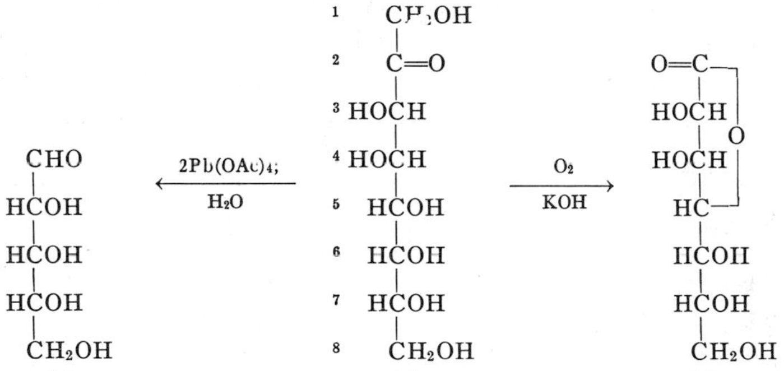

$$
\begin{array}{cc}
& 1 \quad CH_2OH \\
& 2 \quad C=O \qquad\qquad O=C \\
& 3 \quad HOCH \qquad\quad HOCH \\
CHO & 4 \quad HOCH \qquad\quad HOCH \;\;O \\
\xleftarrow[\;H_2O\;]{2Pb(OAc)_4;} \quad HCOH \\
HCOH & 5 \quad HCOH \xrightarrow[KOH]{O_2} HC \\
HCOH & 6 \quad HCOH \qquad\quad HCOH \\
HCOH & 7 \quad HCOH \qquad\quad HCOH \\
CH_2OH & 8 \quad CH_2OH \qquad\quad CH_2OH \\
(4) & (5) \qquad\qquad\quad (6)
\end{array}
$$

cleaved the 2,3-bond and the 3,4-bond and afforded D-ribose (4). Degradation of the octulose by passing oxygen into a cold solution in potassium hydroxide and acidification gave the known heptonic lactone (6), which reveals the full configuration as that shown in (5). The name D-*glycero*-D-*manno*-octulose defines the configurations at C_7 (C_2 in D-glyceraldehyde) and at C_3–C_6 (C_2–C_5 in D-mannose). The fruit of the avocado, a long known source of D-*manno*-heptulose and D-*glycero*-D-*galacto*-heptitol, was found also to contain D-*erythro*-D-*galacto*-octitol (m.p. 170°). D-*Glycero*-D-*galacto*-heptitol has been isolated also from the semicrystalline exudate of wounds in the bark of avocado trees (J. K. N. Jones, 1961).

29.15 Synthesis of D-Hexoses. — Early attempts to produce a hexose ($C_6H_{12}O_6$) by reaction of formaldehyde (CH_2O) with dilute alkali gave complex mixtures. Fischer (1887) developed a synthesis from glycerol in which the hexose chain is formed as the result of aldol addition of dihydroxyacetone, through the activated α-hydrogen atom, to the carbonyl group of glyceraldehyde. The reverse reaction later was found to be the first step in the fer-

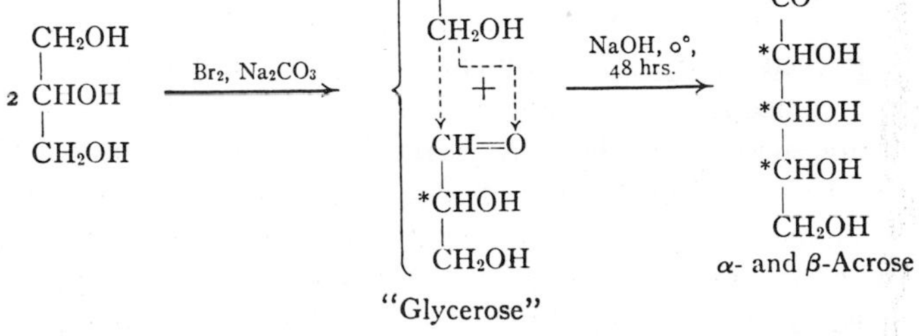

$$
\begin{array}{ccccc}
& & & CH_2OH & \\
& & & CO & CH_2OH \\
CH_2OH & & & CH_2OH & CO \\
| & \xrightarrow{Br_2,\,Na_2CO_3} & \left\{ \begin{array}{c} + \end{array} \right. & \xrightarrow[48\;hrs.]{NaOH,\,0°,} & *CHOH \\
2\;CHOH & & CH=O & & *CHOH \\
| & & *CHOH & & *CHOH \\
CH_2OH & & CH_2OH & & CH_2OH \\
& & \text{"Glycerose"} & & \alpha\text{- and }\beta\text{-Acrose}
\end{array}
$$

mentation of D-fructose to ethanol and carbon dioxide. The resulting ketohexose has three asymmetric carbon atoms, and hence eight optically active forms are possible. However, the aldehydic reaction component has an asymmetric carbon atom, and this exercises a control over the mode of addition to the carbonyl group. The glyceraldehyde involved in the synthesis is the *dl*-form, but because of the principle of asymmetric synthesis each enantiomer directs the aldol addition in a specific steric sense, with the result that only half of the theoretically possible isomers are produced. The synthesis thus affords two substances of different physical properties, α- and β-acrose, each of which consists of a *dl*-mixture of enantiomers. The overall yield of α-acrosazone is about 1.5%. In 1890 Fischer showed that α-acrose is DL-fructose by the following series of reactions:

$$
\begin{array}{cccccccc}
\text{CH}{=}\text{NNHC}_6\text{H}_5 & & \text{CHO} & & \text{CH}_2\text{OH} & & \text{CH}_2\text{OH} \\
| & & | & & | & & | \\
\text{C}{=}\text{NNHC}_6\text{H}_5 & \xrightarrow{2\,H_2O} & \text{C}{=}\text{O} & \xrightarrow{Zn-HCl} & \text{C}{=}\text{O} & \xrightarrow{Na(Hg)} & \text{CHOH} \\
| & & | & & | & & | \\
(\text{CHOH})_3 & & (\text{CHOH})_3 & & (\text{CHOH})_3 & & (\text{CHOH})_3 \\
| & & | & & | & & | \\
\text{CH}_2\text{OH} & & \text{CH}_2\text{OH} & & \text{CH}_2\text{OH} & & \text{CH}_2\text{OH} \\
\alpha\text{-Acrosazone} & & \alpha\text{-Acrosone} & & \alpha\text{-Acrose} & & \alpha\text{-Acritol}
\end{array}
$$

α-Acritol (0.2 g. from 1 kg. of glycerol) is identical with DL-mannitol, the reduction product of either DL-fructose or DL-mannose (in alkali solution, see 29.7), and hence α-acrose could be either of these DL-hexoses, but the second possibility is eliminated by the fact that DL-mannose forms a characteristic insoluble phenylhydrazone, a property that is not shown by α-acrose. Fischer first attempted to separate α-acrose by preferential fermentation with yeast, but the substance isolated from the unfermented residue proved to be the dextrorotatory enantiomer of natural fructose, namely L-fructose. Consequently, the ketohexose was

$$
\begin{array}{ccccccccc}
\text{CH}_2\text{OH} & & \text{CH}_2\text{OH} & & \text{CHO} & & \text{COOH} & & \\
| & & | & & | & & | & & \\
\text{C}{=}\text{O} & \xrightarrow{Na-Hg} & \text{CHOH} & \xrightarrow{HNO_3} & (\text{CHOH})_4 & \xrightarrow{Br_2-H_2O} & (\text{CHOH})_4 & \xrightarrow{Morphine} & \\
| & & | & & | & & | & & \\
(\text{CHOH})_3 & & (\text{CHOH})_3 & & \text{CH}_2\text{OH} & & \text{CH}_2\text{OH} & & \\
| & & | & & \text{DL-Mannose} & & \text{DL-Mannonic} & & \\
\text{CH}_2\text{OH} & & \text{CH}_2\text{OH} & & & & \text{acid} & & \\
\text{DL-Fructose} & & \text{DL-Mannitol} & & & & & & \\
(\alpha\text{-acrose}) & & & & & & & &
\end{array}
$$

$$
\left\{\begin{array}{l} d\text{-Morphine salt} \\ l\text{-Morphine salt} \end{array}\right\} \xrightarrow{\text{Fractional crystallization, NaOH}} \begin{array}{l} \text{D-Mannonic acid} \\ \text{L-Mannonic acid} \end{array}
$$

reduced to an alcohol and this was oxidized in two steps to DL-mannonic acid, which was resolved by fractional crystallization of the morphine salt to the optically active components. D-Mannonic acid was converted into the epimeric acid, D-gluconic acid, which has the stereochemical configuration of D-glucose, by a reaction discovered by Fischer in 1890, epimerization induced by heating in pyridine. Conversion of D-gluconic acid into D-glucose is accomplished by reduction of the readily formed γ-lactone. The first synthesis of a natural sugar was announced in the statement:[1] "One is now able to prepare grape sugar from

[1] E. Fischer, "Synthese des Traubenzuckers," *Ber.*, **23**, 799 (1890)

```
   COOH                      COOH                    CO─┐                   CHO
    |                         |                      |  |                    |
  HOCH                      HCOH                    HCOH |                  HCOH
    |                         |                      |  │O                   |
  HOCH    Pyridine, 140°    HOCH        HCl        HOCH │     Na─Hg        HOCH
    |     ───────────────>    |       ──────>       |  │     ──────>        |
  HCOH                      HCOH                    HC─┘                   HCOH
    |                         |                      |                      |
  HCOH                      HCOH                    HCOH                   HCOH
    |                         |                      |                      |
  CH₂OH                     CH₂OH                   CH₂OH                  CH₂OH
 D-Mannonic               D-Gluconic              γ-Lactone              D-Glucose
   acid                     acid
```

glycerol and even from formaldehyde." Synthesis of D-fructose was accomplished in the same year by the reactions shown.

```
   COOH                     CO─┐                    CHO
    |                        |  |                     |
  HOCH                     HOCH |                   HOCH
    |                        |  │O                    |
  HOCH        HCl          HOCH │      Na─Hg        HOCH        3 NH₂NHC₆H₅
    |       ──────>          |  │     ──────>         |         ─────────────>
  HCOH                      HC─┘                    HCOH
    |                        |                        |
  HCOH                     HCOH                     HCOH
    |                        |                        |
  CH₂OH                    CH₂OH                    CH₂OH
 D-Mannonic acid         γ-Lactone               D-Mannose
```

```
  CH=NNHC₆H₅                 CHO                    CH₂OH
    |                         |                      |
  C=NNHC₆H₅                  C=O                    C=O
    |                         |                      |
  HOCH          H₂O         HOCH       Zn─HOAc     HOCH
    |         ──────>         |       ──────>        |
  HCOH                      HCOH                   HCOH
    |                         |                      |
  HCOH                      HCOH                   HCOH
    |                         |                      |
  CH₂OH                     CH₂OH                  CH₂OH
 D-Glucosazone            Glucosone              D-Fructose
```

29.16   **Molecular Rotation Relationships.** — When an alcohol R_1R_2CHOH is to be compared in optical properties with its derivatives, for example the acetate, benzoate, or methyl ether, compensation for incidental variations in molecular weight is made by comparisons based on molecular rotation, M_D, calculated as follows:

$$M_D = \frac{[\alpha]_D \times \text{Mol. Wt.}}{100}$$

Thus for α-D-glucose: $[\alpha]_D^{20} = +112.2°$ (water solution; extrapolated to zero time) and $M_D = (+112.2 \times 180.16)/100 = +202.1$. Whereas sucrose octaacetate, $[\alpha]_D$ $+59.6°$ Chf (chloroform), differs considerably from sucrose octastearate, $[\alpha]_D$ $+16.6°$ Chf, in specific rotation, the molecular rotations, M_D $+404$ and $+411$, are the same within the limits of error of polarimetry (0.5° difference in $[\alpha]_D$ of the octastearate changes M_D by 12 units).

van't Hoff in 1898 deduced the principle that the molecular rotation of a compound containing several centers of asymmetry is the algebraic sum of the indi-

TABLE 29 1   COMPARISON OF SUGAR ANOMERS

SUGAR	M_D		$M_D^\alpha - M_D^\beta$
	α	β	
Glucopyranose type			
Glucose	$+202.1$	$+33.7$	$+168.4$
Galactose	$+271.5$	-95.1	$+176.4$
Lactose (disaccharide)	$+306.3$	$+119.5$	$+186.8$
Mannopyranose type			
Mannose	$+52.8$	-30.6	$+83.4$
Talose	$+122.5$	$+23.8$	$+98.7$
4-Glucomannose	$+53.0$	-22.0	$+75.0$

vidual rotatory contributions of the component rotatory centers, or rotophores. Since experimental data were not available for calculation of individual rotatory effects, the idea was illustrated by supposing the superposition of a molecule composed of $+A +B +C$ centers with one made up of $-A +B +C$ rotophores; since the fragment $+B +C$ is common to both molecules, the difference in M_D between them is $+2A$.   The **van't Hoff principle of additivity** thus is often described by the rather misleading designation "principle of optical superposition."

   This principle is the basis of **C. S. Hudson's first rule**, which states that the rotatory contribution of C_1 is affected to only a minor degree by rotation of the remainder of the molecule and that in the D series the more dextrorotatory anomer is always the α-form.   The data of Table 29.1 show that $M_D^\alpha - M_D^\beta$ is invariably positive but that the numerical values fall into two groups. The sugars in the first group differ in configuration at C_1 and at the nonadjacent center C_4, whereas those in the second group differ in configuration at each of the contiguous centers C_1 and C_2.   In the latter case each center exerts an as yet undeterminable vicinal effect on the rotatory contribution of the other.   Thus the difference in the averages ($+177$ and $+86$ units) affords an indication of the magnitude of the vicinal effect concerned.   The rule that an α-pyranose or pyranoside is distinctly more dextrorotatory than the β-anomer is generally applicable, for example, to the pentoses formulated, to the methyl D-fructopyranosides, and to the ethyl D-glucofuranosides formulated above (29.5).

   Hudson's **second rule** states that changes at the glycosidic carbon atom (C_1), for example the change from C_1-OH to C_1-OR, affect in only a minor degree rotation of the remainder of the molecule. That methyl α-D-glucoside is distinctly more dextrorotatory than α-D-glucose can be interpreted as meaning that the bulkier OCH_3 increases dissymmetry of C_1 and hence accentuates the dextrorotatory contribution of C_1. Methyl β-D-glucoside is correspondingly more levorotatory than the parent β-D-glucose (Table 29.2).   Increase in size of the

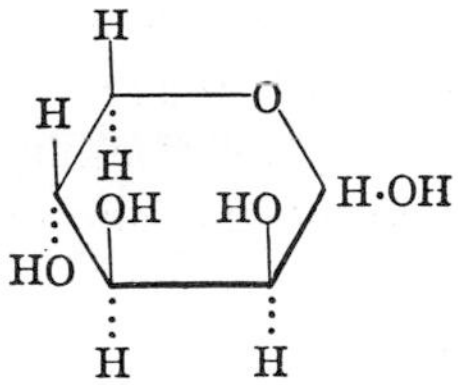

D-Lyxose
+ 117.4

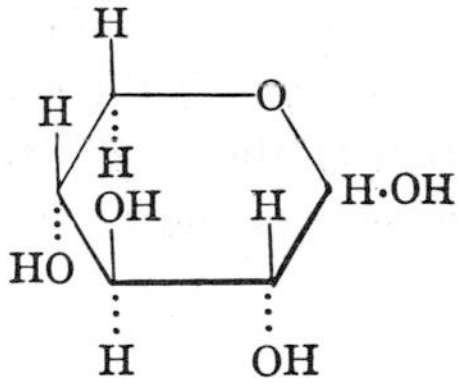

D-Xylose
+ 170.5

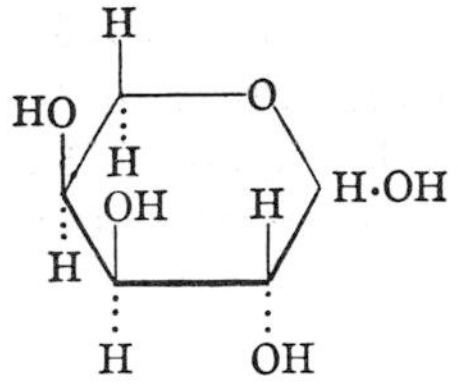

L-Arabinose
+ 170.5

$M_D^{\alpha} - M_D^{\beta}$

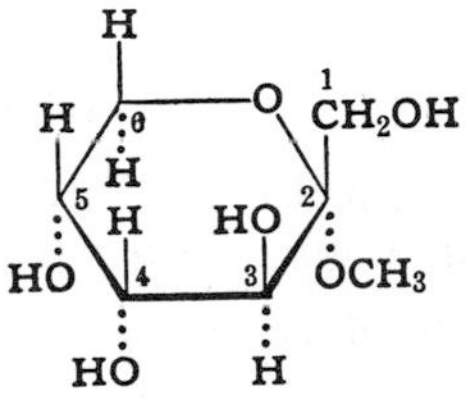

Methyl α-D-fructopyranoside
M_D + 85

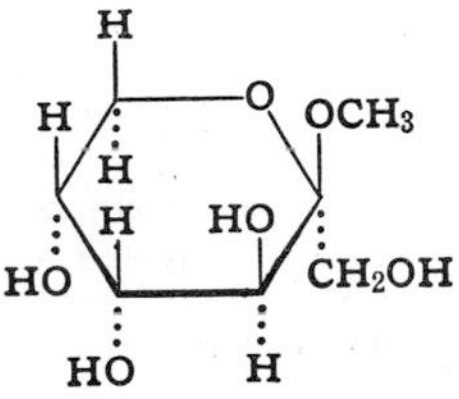

Methyl β-D-fructopyranoside
M_D − 334

alkyl group from methyl to benzyl results in progressive, smaller changes in the same direction. If the rotatory contribution of C_1 is +A in the α-form and −A in the β-form and the contribution of the rest of the molecule is B, then the sum of the rotations of any pair of 1-epimers should be a constant quantity, 2B. The data of Table 29.2 show that (M_D^{α} + M_D^{β}) is indeed substantially a constant; whereas M_D^{α} varies from +202 to +463, the sum of the molecular rotations deviates from the average of +240 to the extent of only ±15 (average).

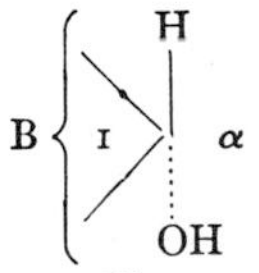

α-D-Glucose
M_D + 202.1

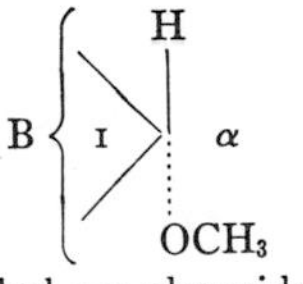

Methyl α-D-glucoside
M_D + 308.6

The relationship between an aldonic acid and its γ-lactone is described in the following rule formulated by Hudson (1910): a γ-lactone in which the oxide ring,

TABLE 29.2.　D-GLUCOPYRANOSIDES

C_1-SUBSTITUENT	M_D		
	1α	1β	SUM
OH (D-Glucose)	+ 202.1	+ 33.7	+ 235.8
OCH₃	+ 308.6	− 66.4	+ 242.2
OC₂H₅	+ 313.6	− 69.5	+ 244.1
OC₃H₇-n	+ 312.9	− 77.6	+ 235.3
OCH₂C₆H₅	+ 354.1	− 150.2	+ 203.9
OC₆H₅	+ 463.3	− 181.9	+ 281.4

as represented in the conventional projection formula, lies to the right is more dextrorotatory than the parent acid, and if the ring lies to the left the lactone is more levorotatory. An illustration of the rule is the contrasting relationships of D-gluconic acid and of D-talonic acid to their γ-lactones. Notice that the sugar

$$
\begin{array}{cc}
\text{COOH} & \text{C}=\text{O} \\
\text{HCOH} & \text{HCOH} \\
\text{HOCH} & \text{HOCH} \\
\text{HCOH(4)} & \text{HC} \\
\text{HCOH} & \text{HCOH} \\
\text{CH}_2\text{OH} & \text{CH}_2\text{OH} \\
M_D - 13.5 & M_D + 121.1
\end{array}
\qquad
\begin{array}{cc}
\text{COOH} & \text{C}=\text{O} \\
\text{HOCH} & \text{HOCH} \\
\text{HOCH} & \text{HOCH} \\
\text{(4)HOCH} & \text{CH} \\
\text{HCOH} & \text{HCOH} \\
\text{CH}_2\text{OH} & \text{CH}_2\text{OH} \\
M_D + 39.9 & M_D - 61.8
\end{array}
$$

D-Gluconic acid and γ-lactone   D-Talonic acid and γ-lactone

acids are weakly rotatory and that cyclization produces a large rotational shift; the geometry of the ring is thus the dominant factor. We suggest that the rule applies because lactones of the two types bear a quasi-enantiomeric relationship to one another, evident from models of γ-D-gluconolactone and γ-D-talonolactone.

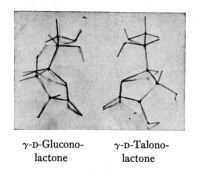

γ-D-Glucono-   γ-D-Talonolactone   lactone

The lactones are not true enantiomers, but differences in the substituents are relatively minor. Thus one lactone is dextrorotatory and the other levorotatory, if not to the same degree. D-Gluconic acid forms a less stable δ-lactone, which has

γ-D-Gluconolactone   δ-Gluconolactone
$M_D + 121$ $M_D + 118$

the same sign of rotation as the γ-lactone. Since in D-glucose the 4- and 5-hydroxyl groups have the same orientation, the two lactone rings have nearly the same geometry. The same situation exists in the following instances:

D-Mannonic acid: γ-lactone (M_D + 91.7); δ-lactone (M_D + 204.5)

L-Rhamnonic acid: γ-lactone (M_D − 63.6); δ-lactone (M_D − 162.0)

29.17   Disaccharides. — Three disaccharides occur commonly in nature, sucrose (cane sugar), lactose (milk sugar), and maltose, and the latter is found free only occasionally. Maltose and cellobiose are important disaccharides because they are products of hydrolysis of starch and cellulose, respectively. Disaccharides resemble monosaccharides in that they are very soluble in water. Sucrose is much less stable to acids than methyl glycosides and can be cleaved very readily to D-glucose and D-fructose by acid hydrolysis or by the enzyme invertase. Sucrose does not reduce Fehling solution or form derivatives with phenylhydrazine, and hence the two sugar units are linked through the glycosidic hydroxyl group of each sugar and contain no free or potential carbonyl groups. Unlike the majority of sugars, sucrose crystallizes readily, probably because it does not undergo mutarotation in solution. The ring structure of the two component units was established (Haworth, 1916) by hydrolyzing completely methylated sucrose (octamethyl ether). One product was the usual tetramethyl-D-glucose,

I Octa-O-methylsucrose   II (α,β)   III

but the other was a tetramethylfructose derivative unknown at the time. Its structure was not established until ten years later, when it was found to contain a furanose, or 2,5-oxide ring. No combined fructose has ever been found to have the more stable pyranoside structure. The glucose unit has the α-configuration, since sucrose is hydrolyzed by maltase (an α-D-glucosidase); the configuration of the fructose unit is β.

Sucrose has been an important foodstuff for centuries. Originally the only commercial source was the juice of sugar cane, a tropical plant native to India, which is now grown on plantations mainly in the West Indies, Java, the Philippines, and South America. The juice as obtained by pressing the crushed canes contains about 14% sucrose; the spent cane, bagasse, is used as fuel or as a source of cellulose. Lime is added to the extract to precipitate proteinic substances (defecation), and the clear juice drawn off after settling is evaporated in vacuum to a semisolid mass. The crystalline raw sugar is freed from mother liquor (blackstrap molasses) in centrifugal baskets. Raw sugar (95% sucrose) is colored and has a slight odor; it is purchased in this form by refineries. The usual purification consists in removal of odoriferous contaminants with steam, followed by filtration through columns of charcoal to remove colored contaminants. White crystalline sucrose of high purity is obtained by concentration in vacuum.

Approximately half of the sucrose produced throughout the world now comes from the sugar beet, which can be grown in temperate climates. Although the beet was shown to contain sucrose as early as 1747, commercial production from this source commenced some time later in France, when the industry was subsidized by the state as a result of the British blockade during the Napoleonic Wars. The sugar content of the beet has been steadily improved by cultivation and is about the same as that of sugar cane (16–20%), but the yield per acre is not so high as that from cane.

Lactose occurs in the milk of mammals; human milk contains 5–8%, cow's milk, 4–6%. It is produced commercially from the latter source as a by-product in the manufacture of cheese. Lactose is a reducing sugar, forms a phenyl osazone, and can be obtained in crystalline α- and β-forms, $[\alpha]_D$ +90° and $[\alpha]_D$ +35°. It is hydrolyzed by dilute mineral acid to D-glucose and D-galactose. Since the acid obtained on bromine oxidation of lactose is hydrolyzed to D-galactose and D-gluconic acid, the reducing group must be in the glucose unit, and hence lactose is a

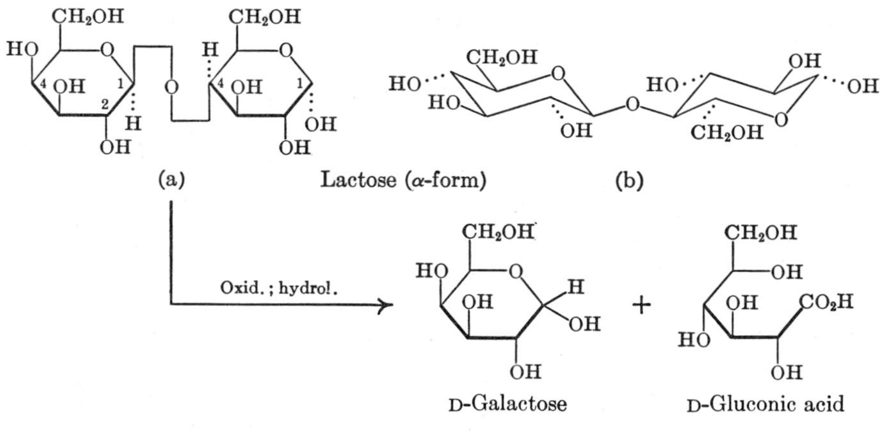

(a)   Lactose (α-form)   (b)

Oxid.; hydrol.

D-Galactose   D-Gluconic acid

galactoside and not a glucoside. Methylation and degradation showed the rings to be six-membered and the point of glycosidic linkage to the glucose unit to be at C_4. Since lactose is cleaved by β-D-galactosidase enzyme, the sugar is 4-O-β-D-galactopyranosyl-D-glucopyranose. One way of showing that the glycosidic 1β-linkage of the galactose unit is joined to an oppositely oriented linkage of glucose is with formula (a); another is to invert one of the units, as in the more realistic conformational formula (b).

Maltose is obtained in about 80% yield by enzymic (amylase) degradation of starch. Since the disaccharide yields only D-glucose on hydrolysis with acids or maltase, an α-D-glucosidase, it is evidently a glucose-α-D-glucoside. It is a reducing sugar, and hence contains one potential aldehydic group. Methylation studies established the structure as that of 4-O-α-D-glucopyranosyl-D-glucopyranose.

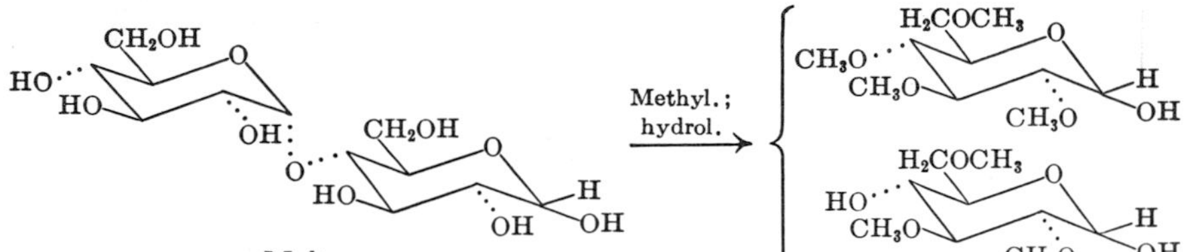

Maltose

Cellobiose can be obtained by partial hydrolysis of cellulose. It is a reducing sugar consisting of two glucose units, and since it is hydrolyzed by almond emulsin the substance is a glucose-β-D-glucoside. Methylation studies have shown that the linkage is 1,4'.

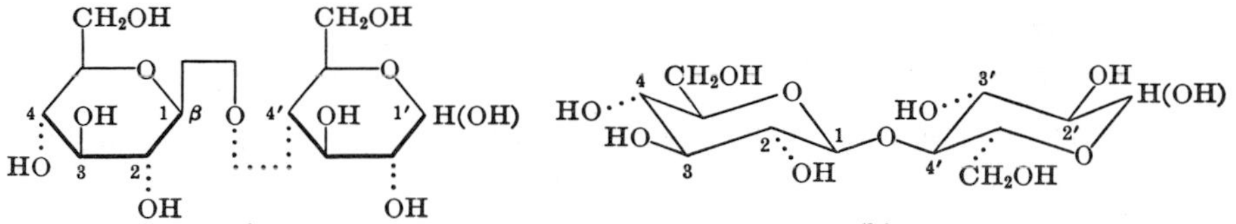

(a)   (b)
Cellobiose

29.18   Natural Glycosides. — Many natural phenolic substances occur in plants as glycosides, for example, arbutin and methylarbutin (29.3). In the animal organism phenolic substances are often detoxified by conjugation with glucuronic acid and excreted in the urine as water-soluble sodium salts (8.35). Triterpenoid (C_{30}) alcohols and steroid (C_{27}) alcohols form a group of plant glycosides known as saponins because they form a soapy lather in water; they have found some use as detergents, foaming agents in fire extinguishers, and fish poisons (fish are dazed but not rendered inedible). D-Glucose is the common sugar component, buᴛ D-galactosides, D-xylosides, and L-rhamnosides are frequently found. L-Rhamnose, a C-methylpentose or a 6-desoxyhexose, is liberated

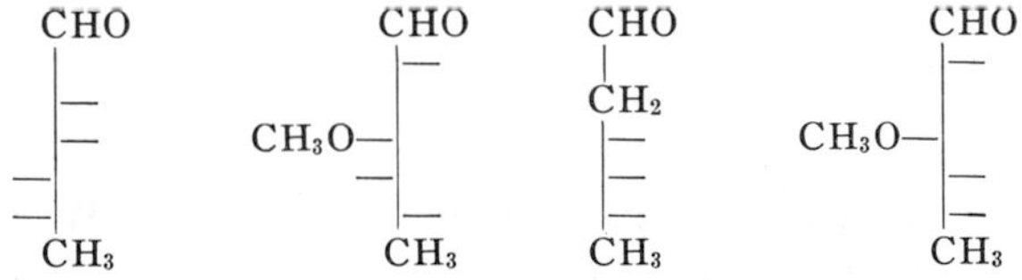

L-Rhamnose   D-Digitalose   D-Digitoxose   D-Thevetose

on hydrolysis of L-rhamnosides by a type-specific enzyme L-rhamnase. The steroid saponin digitonin (C_{56}) on hydrolysis yields digitogenin (C_{27}), two moles each of D-glucose and D-galactose, and one mole of D-xylose; the sugar linked to the aglycone is thus a pentoside. Cardiac-active principles once used as arrow poisons and now valued in therapy for beneficial stimulation of the diseased heart (*e.g.* digitalis) are glycosides of C_{23}-steroid alcohols containing an α,β-unsaturated lactone ring. Digitoxin, a constituent of digitalis, is made up of the aglycone digitoxigenin linked to a trisaccharide containing units of digitoxose. The maximal daily dose for digitalization is 0.3 mg. of the glycoside; the aglycone

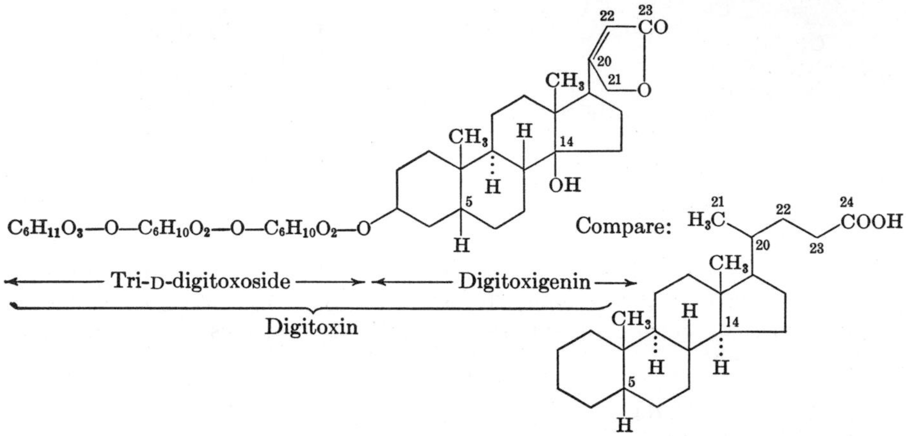

$C_6H_{11}O_3$—O—$C_6H_{10}O_2$—O—$C_6H_{10}O_2$—O

Compare:

←———— Tri-D-digitoxoside ————→ ←———— Digitoxigenin ————→

Digitoxin

Cholanic acid

has only low-order activity. Of the 20 sugars isolated as products of hydrolysis of plant heart poisons only three, D-glucose, L-rhamnose, and D-fucose have been isolated from other plant sources. Some of the rare sugars encountered are D-digitalose, a 6-desoxyhexose 3-O-methyl ether, D-digitoxose, a 2,6-didesoxy-hexose, D-thevetose, and L-thevetose. Glycosides of 2-desoxy sugars are split easily by acid hydrolysis, whereas those of 2-hydroxy sugars are split with difficulty. The resistance to hydrolysis is attributable to the inductive effect of a basic 2-oxygen function, since 2-amino-2-desoxy glycosides are even more resistant to acid hydrolysis; the positively charged nitrogen at C_2 shields the glycosidic center from approach of hydrions and retards hydrolysis.

Amygdalin is a glycoside in which the rare disaccharide gentiobiose is linked to D-(−) mandelonitrile. Isolated in 1830 from seeds of the bitter almond (*Prunus*

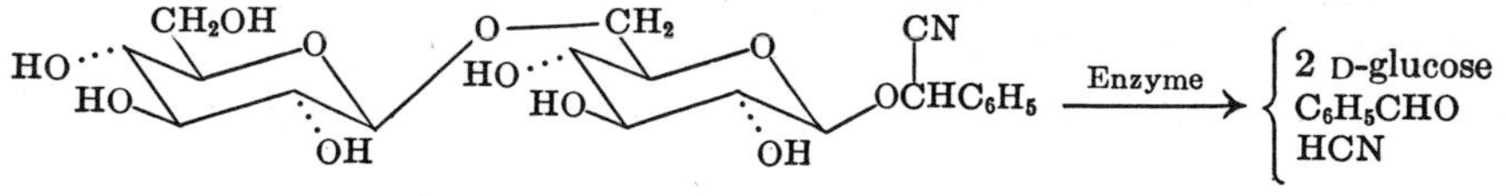

$\xrightarrow{\text{Enzyme}}$ 2 D-glucose / C_6H_5CHO / HCN

Amygdalin

amygdalis), amygdalin attracted the attention of Liebig and Wöhler, who found that the glycoside is split by almond emulsin to D-glucose and benzaldehyde with liberation of hydrogen cyanide. It is the best known of a group of cyanophoric glycosides. Gentiobiose, a disaccharide in which the 6-hydroxyl group of one unit is involved in the glycosidic link, is a component of a trisaccharide present in the root of the *Gentiana* and of the saffron pigment crocin.

Sinigrin is the simplest member of a group of glycosides which are cleaved by the enzyme myrosin, specific for this class, and which are not attacked by almond emulsin, rhamnase, or maltase. Sinigrin is a potassium salt which occurs in the seed of black mustard and horseradish. Under the influence of myrosin it is cleaved to D-glucose, mustard oil, or allylisothiocyanate, and potassium bisulfate. A structure proposed by J. Gadamer[1] in 1897 was accepted until 1956, when M. G. Ettlinger established the structure formulated and showed that the enzymic

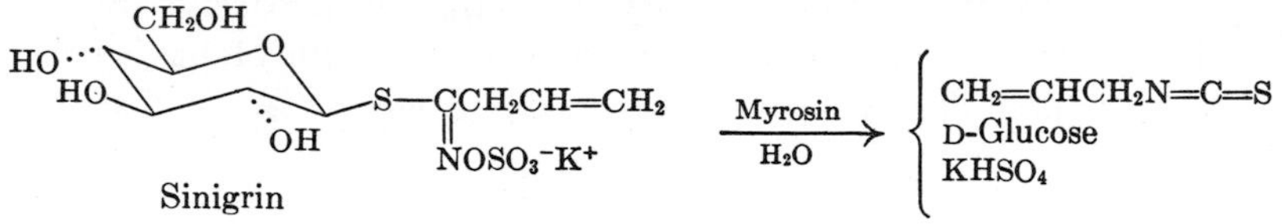

cleavage involves a rearrangement.   Alkaline hydrolysis of sinigrin affords 1-thio-β-D-glucopyranose; acid hydrolysis yields allylacetic acid and hydroxylamine.

29.19   Synthesis of Sucrose. — Several investigators attempted the synthesis of sucrose by condensation of the tetraacetyl derivatives of D-glucose and D-fructose.   As already noted, D-glucose is easily converted into the 2,3,4,6-tetra-O-acetyl derivative III, which has a free anomeric hydroxyl group, by the

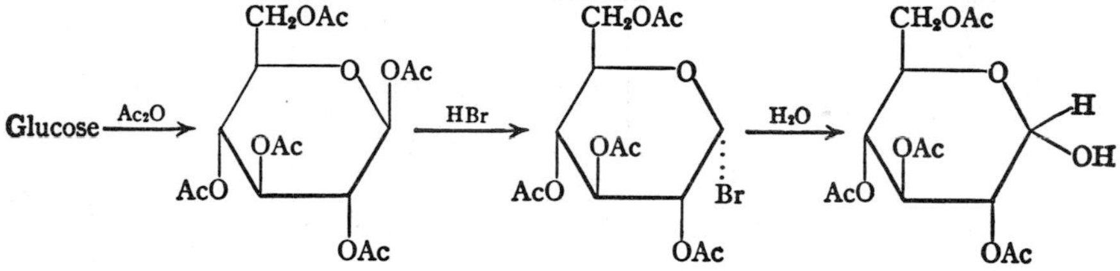

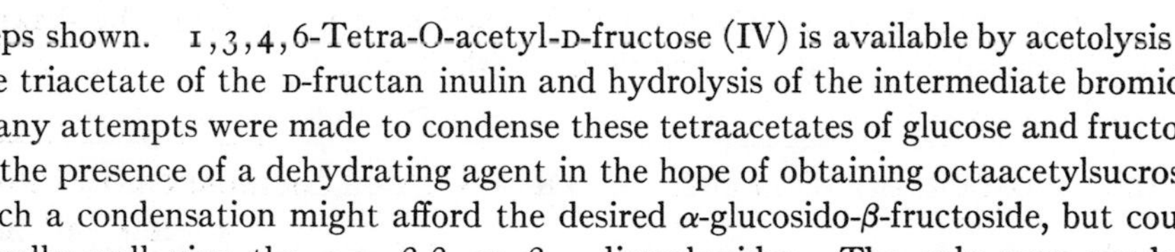

steps shown.   1,3,4,6-Tetra-O-acetyl-D-fructose (IV) is available by acetolysis of the triacetate of the D-fructan inulin and hydrolysis of the intermediate bromide. Many attempts were made to condense these tetraacetates of glucose and fructose in the presence of a dehydrating agent in the hope of obtaining octaacetylsucrose. Such a condensation might afford the desired α-glucosido-β-fructoside, but could equally well give the α-α, β-β, or β-α disaccharides.   The only pure product isolated was the octaacetate of the β-α isomer (isosucrose, J. C. Irvine, Univ. St. Andrews, 1929).

The synthetic objective was finally achieved by R. U. Lemieux[2] and G. Huber (1953) from consideration of the mechanism of replacement reactions.

The background for the work was a discovery by Percy Brigl (Tübingen, 1922)

---

[1] Johannes Georg Gadamer, 1867–1928; Ph.D. Marburg; Univ. Marburg
[2] Raymond U. Lemieux, b. 1920 Lac la Biche, Alberta, Canada; Ph.D. McGill (Purves); Saskatoon, Univ. Ottawa, Alberta, Canada

that β-D-glucose pentaacetate, I, reacts with phosphorus pentachloride to give a product, V, with chlorine at the anomeric position 1 and a trichloroacetoxy group at 2 derived from chlorination of the acetoxy group. By careful treatment at 0° with a limited amount of ammonia in dry ether, the trichloroacetyl group could be selectively eliminated as CCl_3CONH_2 to give the triacetate VI, having chlorine in the anomeric position, *trans* to a free hydroxyl group at C_2. On passing am-

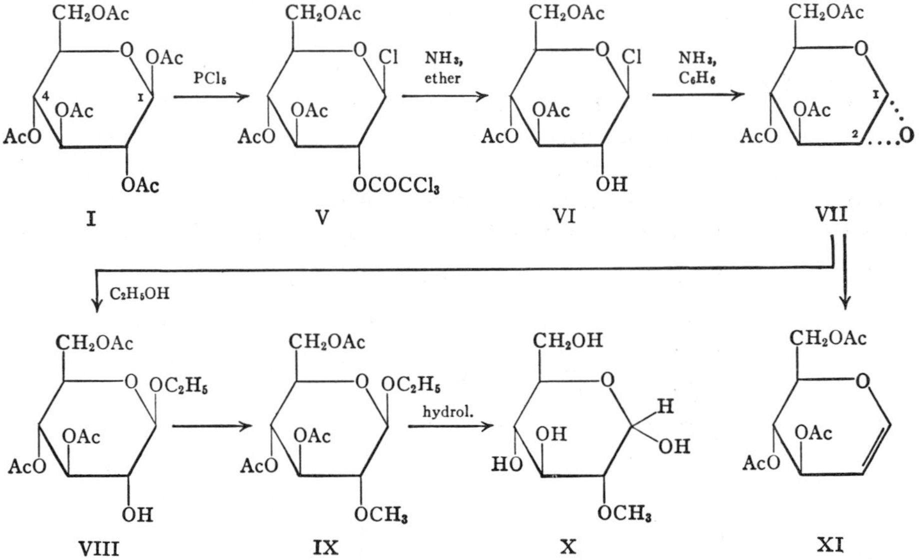

CH₂OAc structures with labels:

I   V   VI   VII

PCl₅ → ; NH₃, ether → ; NH₃, C₆H₆ →

OCOCCl₃ (V) ; OH (VI)

C₂H₅OH ↓

VIII   IX   X   XI

OC₂H₅ ; OC₂H₅ ; hydrol. ; OCH₃

monia into a suspension of VI in benzene for several days, Brigl observed gradual replacement of the original solid by ammonium chloride and from the solution isolated the crystalline oxide VII, resulting from *trans* elimination of HCl with inversion at C_1. The structure of this substance, later called the Brigl anhydride, was established by indirect conversion to a dichloride which was recognized as the *trans* 1,2-dichloride by its ready reaction with zinc dust to give crystalline D-glucal triacetate, XI, which Fischer had obtained in high yield (1914) by shaking an acetic acid solution of acetobromoglucose with zinc dust:

$$AcOCH_2CHCH(OAc)CH(OAc)CH(OAc)CHBr + 2H \longrightarrow AcOCH_2CHCH(OAc)CH(OAc)CH=CH$$
$$+ HBr + AcOH$$

Brigl found that the oxide ring of VII opens with unusual ease; for example, the substance reacts with ethanol at room temperature to give the β-glycoside VIII (all-equatorial). The direction of ring opening is understandable on the assumption that the reaction involves attack by $C_2H_5O^-$ at one of the two oxidic carbons; since C_1 is linked to the electronegative pyranoside oxygen, it is polarized more than C_2 in a sense that makes it the more inviting center. Confirmatory evidence of the structure assigned was adduced by W. J. Hickinbottom (Birmingham, 1928) by methylation of VIII (CH_3I, Ag_2O) to IX and hydrolysis to X, the structure of which follows from observation that it forms a phenylhydrazone but not a phenylosazone (an exception to the usual rule).

In 1950 both M. P. Bardolph and G. H. Coleman (State Univ. Iowa) and A. Dyverman and B. Lindberg (Roy. Techn. Inst., Stockholm) found that the Brigl

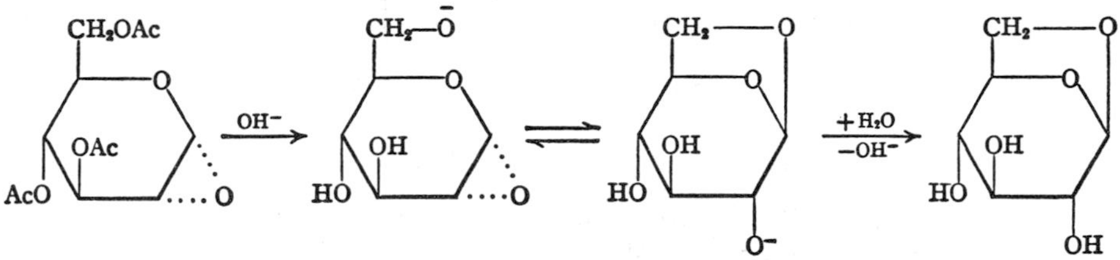

| VII | (a) | (b) | XII |

anhydride VII is converted very rapidly into levoglucosan, XII, a levorotatory anhydro sugar first prepared by Tanret (1894). Lemieux interpreted the alkaline rearrangement in terms of participation of the neighboring hydroxyl group at C_6: the anion (a) is formed to some extent in the alkaline medium and rearranges into the more stable anion (b), which affords levoglucosan (XII) with regeneration of hydroxide ion. Lemieux reasoned that the Brigl anhydride should be particularly prone to react in the half-chair conformation VIIa, in which the structure must be

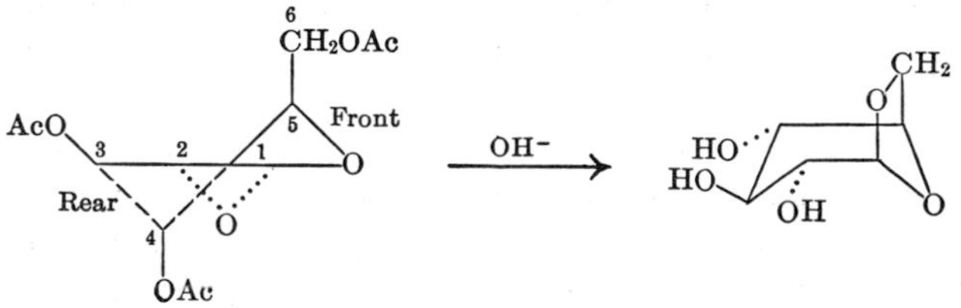

| VIIa | XIIa |

more strained than that of levoglucosan (XIIa); indeed heats of combustion are as follows (P. Karrer and W. Fioroni, 1923): Brigl anhydride, 4594.8 cal./g.; tri-O-acetyllevoglucosan, 4530.5 cal./g.

Brigl had found his anhydride to react with methanol to give methyl β-D-glucoside triacetate as the sole product, as shown by conversion to the known tetraacetate, whereas for coupling to D-fructose to produce sucrose formation of an α-glucoside link is required. However, Brigl obtained $\alpha\beta$-mixtures in some cases and found that phenol reacts chiefly to give the α-glucoside. Hickinbottom and later Hardegger (ETH Zurich, 1948) found that secondary alcohols of higher molecular weight (menthol, cholesterol) tend to give $\alpha\beta$-mixtures. Regarding a fructofuranose component in the same category, Lemieux reasoned that in a high-temperature condensation with this rather hindered alcohol opening of the oxide ring in the desired direction would involve neighboring group participation of the 6-acetoxy group, as in the alkaline isomerization to levoglucosan. The CH_2OAc group in VIIa, being axial, shields the approach of an external agent but is available for cyclization to the ion XIII on diaxial opening of the epoxide ring. The

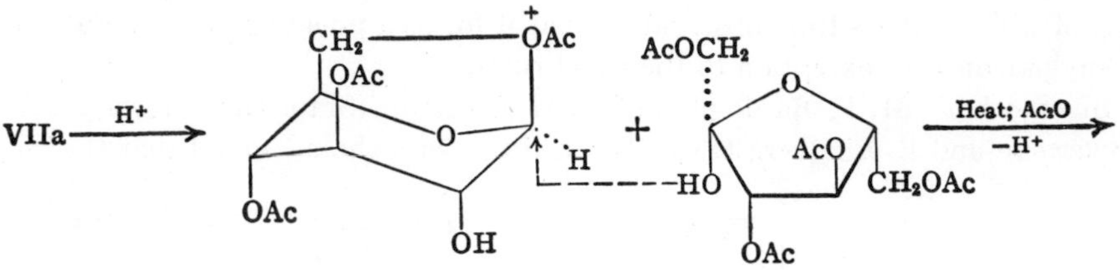

XIII   IV

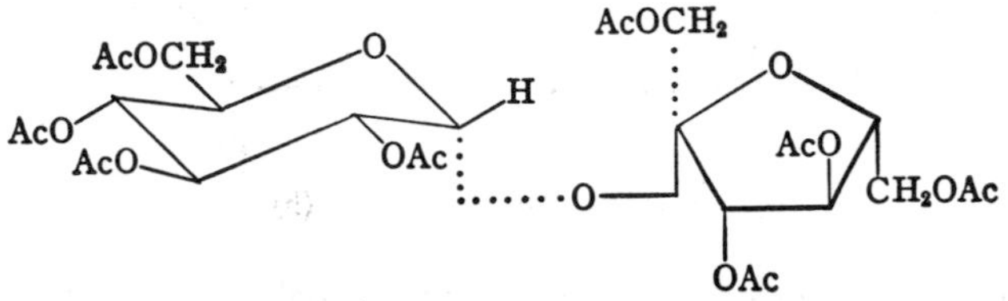

XIV

second component 1,3,4,6-tetra-O-acetyl-D-fructofuranose (IV) was thus expected to attack C_1 of the ion XIII with inversion to the desired configuration.
The components were heated in concentrated benzene solution in a sealed tube
in the range 80–120° for periods of 72–168 hrs. The yield, as determined by isotopic dilution analysis, was only 2–9%, but techniques of preparative paper
chromatography after deacetylation and of chromatography on Magnesol-Celite
after reacetylation enabled successful isolation of an octaacetate identical with
that (XIV) from sucrose.

29.20   Cellulose. — Cellulose, the most widely distributed skeletal polysaccharide, constitutes about half of the cell-wall material of wood and
other plant products. Cotton is almost pure cellulose, and together with bast
from flax is the preferred source of cellulose for use as fiber. Wood cellulose, the
raw material for the pulp and paper industry, occurs in association with hemicelluloses and with lignin, a nonpolysaccharide. Lignin is separated by treating
wood with sodium bisulfite to form lignosulfonates (sulfite process) or with sodium
hydroxide–sodium sulfide.

Isolation of cellobiose and cellotetraose as products of hydrolysis of cellulose
establishes the mode of linkage of the glucose units and hence the structure of the
polysaccharide. The molecular weight is in the range 300,000–500,000, corre-

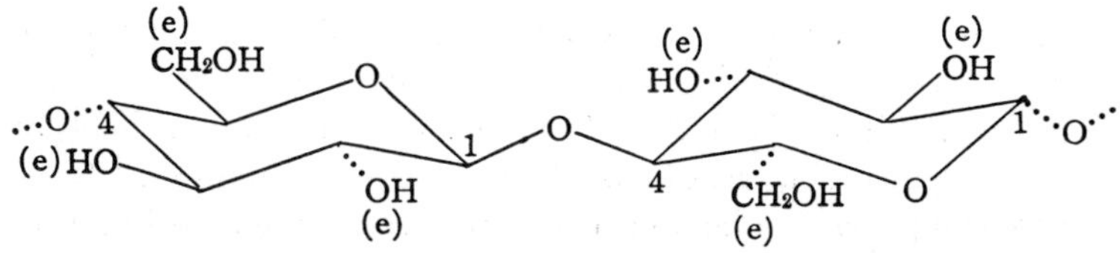

Cellulose, conformation

sponding to 3,000–5,000 C_6-units. X-ray data indicate that the length of a
unit cell along the chain axis (frequency period) is close to the value 10.25 Å
calculated for one cellobiose unit; consequently the chains must be nearly straight

with respect to the fiber axis. That fibers show crystalline regions is accounted for on the postulate of a crystalline supermolecular unit made up of bundles of parallel oriented chains (micelles). The width of a micellar unit is about 60 Å (100–200 cellulose chains); the length is at least 200 Å (200 glucose units). The remarkable mechanical strength and chemical stability are attributed to the micellar structure which, in turn, may be the result of the all-equatorial conformation of the cellulose molecule.

Man and other carnivorous animals are unable to utilize cellulose as food, since they lack enzymes required for hydrolysis. Many microorganisms, some protozoa, and the snail can decompose cellulose. Digestion of cellulose by ruminants (cud-chewing animals) is due to the presence of microorganisms within the specially constructed alimentary system.

29.21 Hemicelluloses. — Of several polysaccharides that occur in association with cellulose, two are pentosans; that is, they yield pentoses on hydrolysis. The more common one, xylan, is built from D-xylose units linked in the 1- and 4-positions: β-D-(1→4). It is closely related to polyglucuronic acid

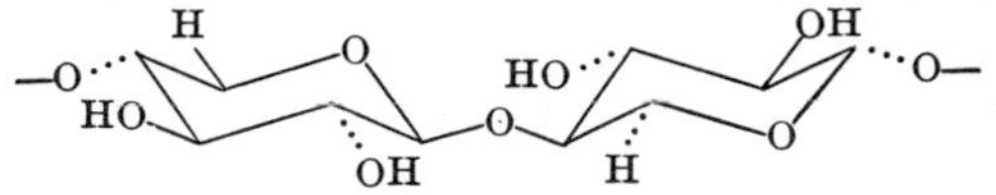

Xylan

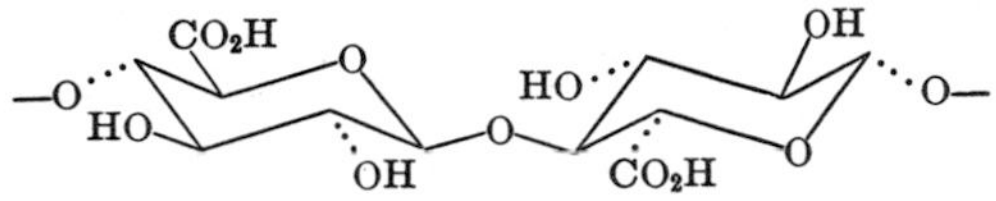

Polyglucuronic acid

with which it is associated in nature. The pentosans occur in large amounts (20–40%) in cereal straws and brans, and are used for the large-scale industrial preparation of furfural. The pentosans are hydrolyzed by sulfuric acid, which then dehydrates the liberated pentoses (12.15).

29.22 Starch. — Starch is the reserve carbohydrate in the majority of plants. It is hydrolyzed partially by the enzyme amylase to maltose, or completely by mineral acids to D-glucose, and evidently starch consists of chains composed of maltose units. Starch can be separated into two fractions by treatment with hot water: a soluble component known as amylose

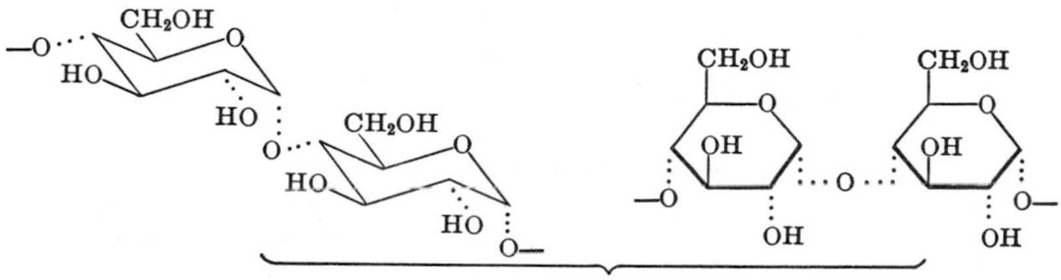

Starch

(10–20%) and an insoluble residue, amylopectin (80–90%). Both substances yield glucose or maltose on hydrolysis, but differ in several respects. Amylose gives a blue color on treatment with iodine, amylopectin a violet to red-violet color.

End-group methods of assay are important in determining if a polysaccharide consists essentially of one long-chain molecule or if it is branched. A method developed by Haworth (1932) involves acetylation of the polysaccharide to produce a more soluble acetyl derivative and exhaustive methylation of this derivative. Hydrolysis of a methylated poly-D-glucopyranose gives mainly 3,4,6-tri-O-methyl-D-glucose derived from the body of the chain, but careful fractionation may afford a little 2,3,4,6-tetra-O-methyl-D-glucose derived from a terminal group or groups. End-group assays of amylose indicate only one end group per molecule of a size in the range of molecular weight (10,000–50,000) found by osmotic pressure measurements. Amylose is thus a long-chain molecule structurally related to cellulose but differing from cellulose in conformation and stability.

A second method of end-group analysis depends upon periodic acid cleavage of *cis*-glycols (Jackson and Hudson, 29.4); if three or more contiguous hydroxyl groups are present, formic acid is liberated and can be determined by titration. Molecular weights of amylopectin samples are in the range 500,000–1,000,000, and since end-group assays by the periodate procedure indicate one end group for every 25–27 units, the structure must consist of branched chains. Hydrolysis of exhaustively methylated amylopectin furnishes small amounts of 2,3,4,6-tetra-O-methyl-D-glucose derived from end groups and of 2,3-di-O-methyl-D-glucose corresponding to branching points. Therefore the main chains are composed of D-glucose units joined by 1,4-links and the branches are joined to it by 1,6-links (see formula). Wolfrom (1950) confirmed this structure by partial acid hydrolysis of amylopectin and isolation of 6-O-α-D-glucopyranosyl-D-glucose (isomaltose).

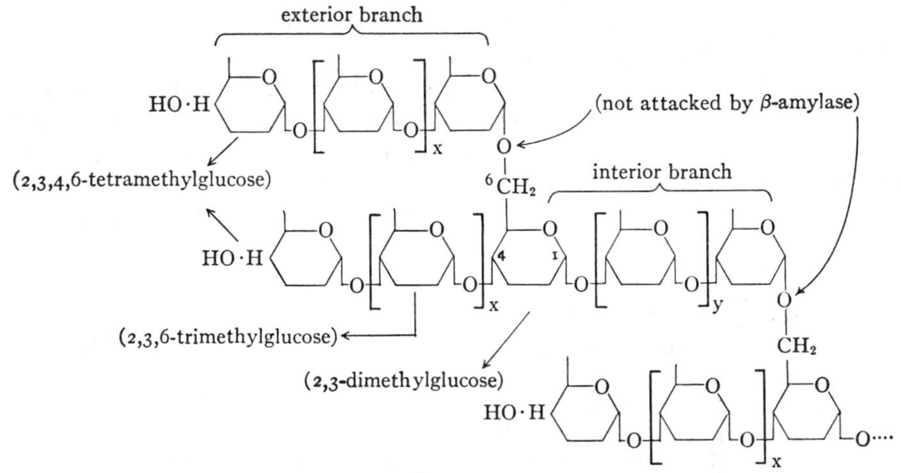

Amylopectin and glycogen (K. H. Meyer)

Further information was obtained from study of enzymic hydrolysis by amylose, which hydrolyzes amylose completely to maltose but degrades amylopectin to maltose only to the extent of 62%. The linkage between the 1-position of one unit and the 6-position of another offers a point of obstruction to enzymic hydrolysis and a resistant residue known as a limit dextrin is left, which corresponds to the interior of the molecule. It is estimated that exterior branches account for more than two-thirds of the molecule.

29.23   Glycogen. — Glycogen is the reserve carbohydrate of animals; it occurs particularly in liver and muscle. It gives a brown to violet color with iodine, resembling that of a limit dextrin. It is composed entirely of D-glucose units joined as in maltose, a product of enzymic hydrolysis; and the end-group method indicates one end group for every 12–18 glucose units. Glycogen is very similar to amylopectin, since methylated glycogen yields the same three methylated glucose derivatives as methylated amylopectin. One difference, indicated by an end-group content of 9% as compared with 5% for amylopectin, in that the degree of branching is about twice as great. Another is that the proportion of the molecule hydrolyzed by amylase is slightly smaller (55–60%).

29.24   Inulin. — A number of reserve carbohydrates of plants are composed almost entirely of D-fructofuranose units and are known as fructans. An example is inulin (29.19), the polysaccharide of the *Compositae* (dahlia, dandelion) and of the Jerusalem artichoke. It was originally believed to consist entirely of fructose units but more recent results (Hirst, 1950) have shown that glucose is a terminal unit of the chain as well as a minor constituent within the chain.

29.25   Ascorbic Acid (Vitamin C). — Scurvy, an ancient disease of mankind, is characterized particularly by a marked tendency to hemorrhage and by structural changes in the cartilage, bone, and teeth. Although the administration of fresh fruits was known since 1752 to decrease the high incidence associated with long sea voyages and abnormal living conditions, the disease was recognized as due to a deficiency of a specific dietary factor, vitamin C, only in 1917. The majority of mammals are not subject to the disease, but the guinea pig when restricted to a cereal diet develops a hemorrhagic condition very similar to scurvy and curable by administration of the same foods that have proved of value in treating scurvy. Isolation of a pure crystalline antiscorbutic substance from lemon juice was finally achieved in 1932 (King[1]), and the material was shortly identified as hexuronic acid, $C_6H_8O_6$, isolated four years earlier from fruits and vegetables by Szent-Györgyi. The substance was renamed ascorbic acid after its striking biological activity was demonstrated.

The most distinctive chemical property of ascorbic acid is its reducing action, manifested in reversible oxidation to a dehydro compound, $C_6H_6O_6$. The majority of chemical methods for determination of vitamin C are based on the ability of the substance to reduce colored dyes to the colorless, or leuco form. Dehydroascorbic acid is a neutral lactone, and the acidity of ascorbic acid is recognized as due not to a carboxyl group but to an enediol grouping (pK$_1$ 4.17; pK$_2$ 11.57).

[1] Charles G. King, b. 1896 Entiat, Wash.; Ph.D. Pittsburgh; Nutrition Foundation, New York

The structure was established in 1933. Observation that ozonization of the dimethyl ether II is attended with the uptake of two atoms of oxygen without producing two fragments established the presence in the molecule of a double

$$
\begin{array}{cccc}
1 & CO & CO & CO \\
2 & HOC & CH_3OC & CH_3OC \\
 & \| \quad O & \| \quad O & \| \quad O \\
3 & HOC & CH_3OC & CH_3OC \\
4 & HC & HC & HC \\
5 & HOCH & HOCH & CH_3OC \\
6 & CH_2OH & CH_2OH & CH_2OCH_3 \\
 & \text{L-Ascorbic acid (I)} & \text{II} & \text{III}
\end{array}
$$

$\xrightarrow{CH_2N_2}$ (from I to II)

$\xrightarrow[Ag_2O]{CH_3I,}$ (from II to III)

$\Bigg\Uparrow 2H$ (downward from I)

$\Bigg\downarrow O_3$ (downward from III)

$$
\begin{array}{ccc}
CO & CO & CONH_2 \quad (VI) \\
O=C & CH_3O_2C & CONH_2 \\
\quad\quad O & \quad\quad O & CONH_2 \\
O=C & CH_3O_2C & \\
HC & HC & HCOH \\
HOCH & CH_3OCH & CH_3OCH \quad (VII) \\
CH_2OH & CH_2OCH_3 & CH_2OCH_3 \\
\text{Dehydroascor-} & & \\
\text{bic acid (IV)} & \text{V} &
\end{array}
$$

$\xrightarrow{OH^-,\ NH_3}$ (from V to VI/VII)

bond and a ring (Micheel). Similar oxidative fission of the tetramethyl ether III (Haworth, Hirst) gave 3,4-dimethyl-L-threonamide (VII), whose configuration is established by conversion to D-(+)-tartaric acid. The first synthesis of L-ascorbic acid was announced almost simultaneously by Haworth and by Reichstein in 1933. The method has only historical interest because the starting material is the rare L-xylose. Present processes are modifications of a later synthesis of Reichstein, which starts with D-glucose. The sugar is converted into the alcohol, D-sorbitol, (D-glucitol) by catalytic (Cu-Cr) hydrogenation, and this on bacterial oxidation (*Acetobacter suboxydans*) yields the 2-ketohexose, L-sorbose, in which the configuration at C_5 (C_2 of glucose) is that of ascorbic acid. The next opera-tion, oxidation of the primary alcoholic group at C_1, requires protection of the four remaining alcoholic groups, which is accomplished by conversion to the diacetonide. In the pyranose form the sugar can form only a monoacetonide, and hence equilibration favors conversion to the more stable furanose diacetonide. After oxidation the diacetonide is hydrolyzed easily to the free acid, 2-keto-L-gulonic acid. The final steps consist in enolization and formation of the lactone ring. Synthetic ascorbic acid has been available since 1937 at a fraction of the cost of the natural product, which was marketed in 1934 at approximately $200 an ounce. Although acute scurvy is very rare, many humans suffer from a partial lack of the vitamin, resulting in abnormal tooth structure, anorexia, anemia, and predisposition to some infectious diseases. The healing of wounds and fractures has been shown to be hastened by administration of ascorbic acid. The minimal

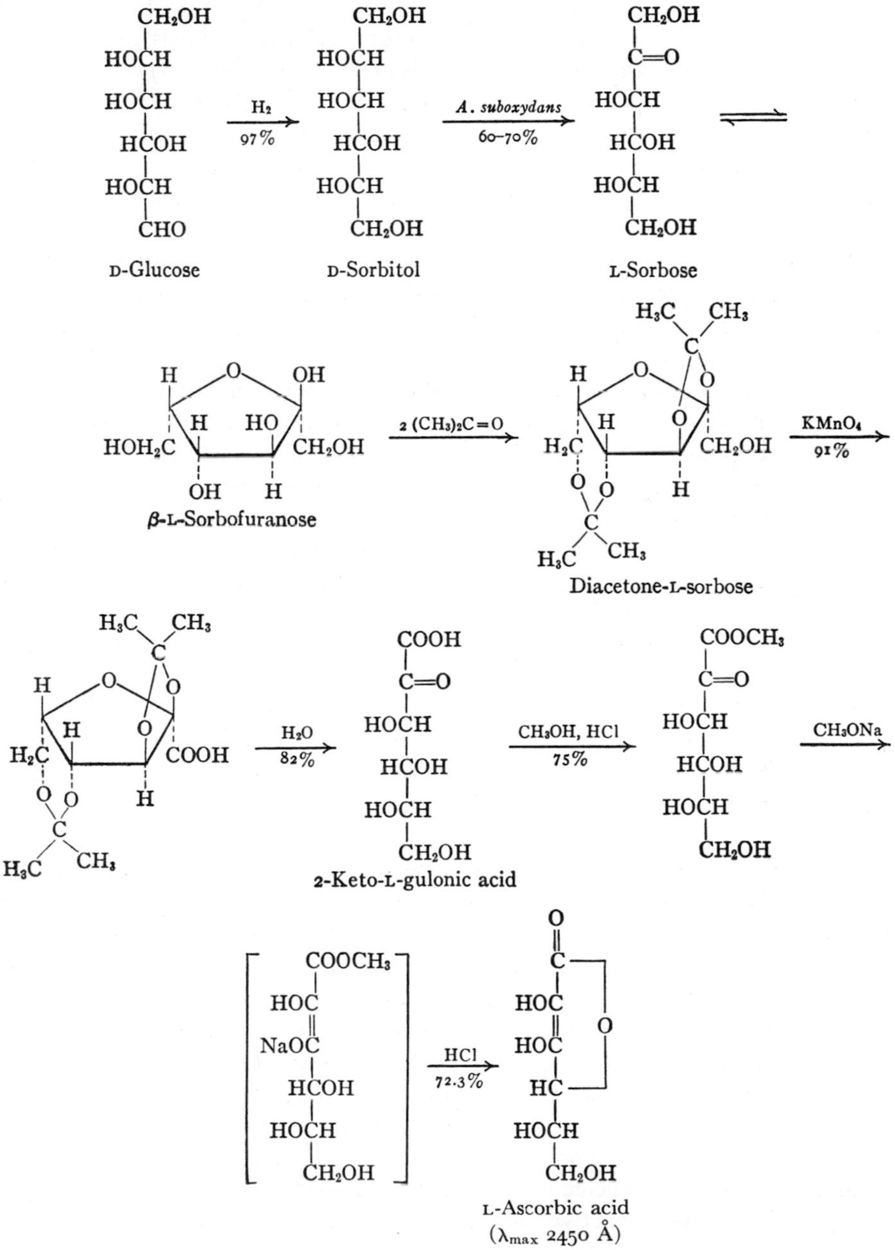
CH₂OH
HOCH
HOCH
HCOH
HOCH
CHO
D-Glucose
H₂
97%
D-Sorbitol
A. suboxydans
60–70%
L-Sorbose
β-L-Sorbofuranose
2 (CH₃)₂C=O
Diacetone-L-sorbose
KMnO₄
91%
H₂O
82%
2-Keto-L-gulonic acid
CH₃OH, HCl
75%
CH₃ONa
HCl
72.3%
L-Ascorbic acid
(λmax 2450 Å)

daily requirement for an adult is 30 mg., considerably higher than that of the majority of other factors, some of which are required in daily doses as low as 1–2 mg. (thiamine hydrochloride, riboflavin) or even 5–10 γ (vitamins D and B_{12}).

Although ascorbic acid occurs abundantly in fruits and vegetables, the content may be only slight in cooked, canned, or dried foods, since the vitamin is readily oxidized.

29.26   Inositols. — Before recognition (1901–12) that animals require vitamins from the diet for normal functioning, Liebig (1871) postulated that microorganisms require growth-accessory factors. Pasteur had been led from his experiments to assert (1860) that yeast can grow in media containing only sugar and nutrient salts, but Liebig found otherwise, and maintained that yeast requires some essential biological factor, supplied, for example, by addition of blood serum or juice of muscle. An active controversy raged for a time, and Pasteur was considered to have won the argument until 1901, when E. Wildiers obtained results that substantiated Liebig's position and introduced the term "bios" for the alcohol–water extracts of boiled yeast cells, beer wort, or commercial peptone that promoted normal functioning of yeast. Bios was separated in 1923 into bios I and bios II by precipitation of the former fraction with barium sulfate, and five years later the first pure crystalline substance from bios was obtained from the precipitated material and identified as inositol, which had been known for some time as a common constituent of plants and animals.

J. Scherer (1850), who first isolated inositol (m.p. 227°) from a mother liquor of the preparation of creatin and later found it in muscle tissue, developed a test specific to this substance and its isomers (but not to the monoethers). In a modified procedure (E. Salkowski, 1910), 0.1 mg. of inositol is treated with 1–2 drops of nitric acid (sp. gr. 1.2), a drop each of 10% $CaCl_2$ and 1–2% H_2PtCl_6 solutions are added, and the mixture is concentrated on a porcelain crucible cover. A brick-red color develops. L. Maquenne (1887) studied the oxidation of inositol with hot nitric acid, found that the chief products are tetrahydroxy-1,4-benzoquinone and rhodizonic acid, and deduced from the observation that inositol is a cyclohexanehexol. The Scherer test involves formation of the red calcium salt of rhodizonic acid.

In a paragraph in a paper on stereoisomers of camphor, L. Bouveault (1894) noted that inositol is one of nine possible isomers; seven nonresolvable or *meso* forms and a pair of optically active epimers. In 1928 S. Posternak[1] and his son Th. Posternak[2] initiated work on the stereochemistry with a study of phytin, the calcium-magnesium salt of the hexaphosphate ester of inositol which, like the free alcohol, is optically inactive. By interrupting the enzymic hydrolysis of the ester at various stages, they were able to isolate an optically active tetraphosphate, an optically active diphosphate, and an optically inactive monophosphate identical with one described by R. J. Anderson (1914). The inactivity of the monophosphate, they noted, rules out one of the possible configurations, namely one numbered and named by a scheme introduced by Maquenne as in (a) and (b). The existence of the optically active di- and tetraphosphates eliminates configuration

---

[1] Swigel Posternak, 1870–1932; b. Tirasapol (Russia); M.D. Paris; Institut Pasteur, Paris; Ciba Ltd., Basel; Laboratoire privé, Geneva

[2] Théodore Posternak, b. 1903 Paris; D.Sc. Univ. Geneva (S. Posternak); Univ. Lausanne, Basel, Geneva

(c). Later (1929), the Posternaks extended the evidence by isolation, as products of permanganate oxidation of inositol, of DL-glucosaccharic acid (DL-glucaric acid)

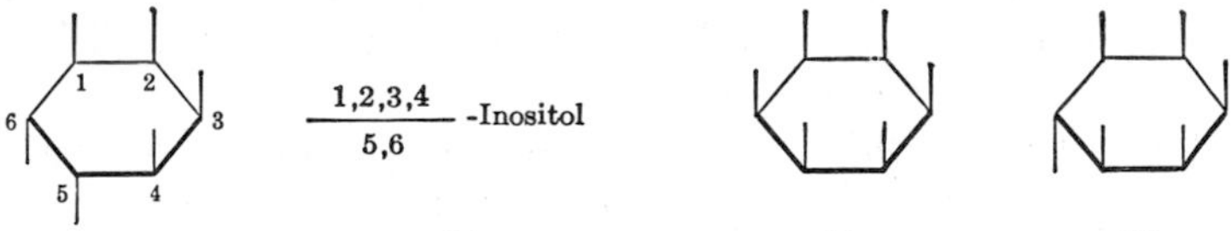

$$\text{(a)} \xrightarrow[5,6]{1,2,3,4} \text{-Inositol}$$

(a)   (b)   (c)   (d)

and an acid which E. Fischer regarded as DL-allosaccharic acid. A configuration deduced from this evidence was later withdrawn when Th. Posternak (1935) found that Fischer's diacid is, in fact, DL-talosaccharic acid. Correct identification of the two products of oxidation did not solve the problem of configuration. The formation of DL-glucosaccharic acid (1) and DL-talosaccharic acid (3) is consistent not only with configuration (2) but with that of another *meso*-form

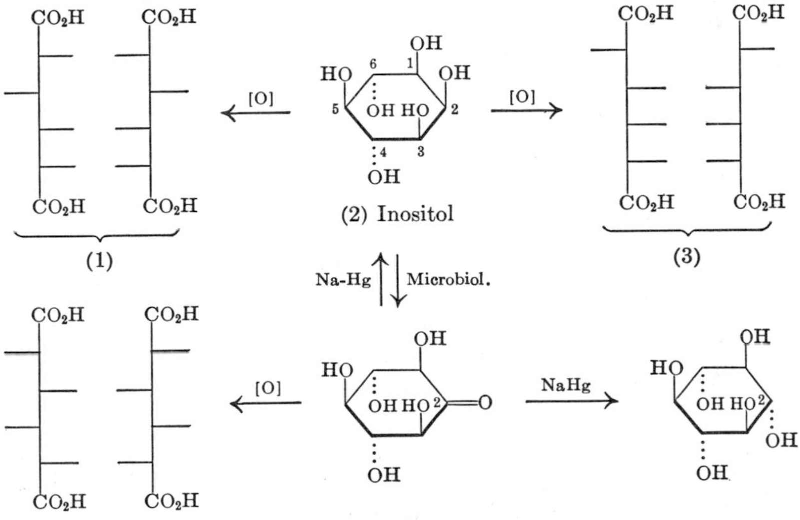

(1)   (2) Inositol   (3)

(4)   (5) Inosose-2   (6) Scyllitol

(d, above). However, Posternak (1942) found completing evidence in characterization of a ketone which Kluyver had obtained by microbiological oxidation (*Acetobacter suboxydans*) and which, for reasons stated below, we identify by the name inosose-2. A procedure worked out by Posternak (*Biochem. Preps.*) affords the ketone in 85% yield. The same product is formed in about half this yield on reaction of inositol with oxygen in the presence of platinum oxide (Kurt Heyns, 1953). Reduction of inosose-2 gave inositol and its 2-epimer, which proved to be identical with scyllitol (m.p. 348°), isolated from sharks, rays, and dogfish (Gr. *skylion*, dogfish). Permanganate oxidation of inosose-2 gave a product identified as DL-idosaccharic acid (4), a result consistent with (2) and (5) but not with the alternative *meso*-structure.

Note, in the conformational formula written below, that the stable form of inositol is that in which all hydroxyl groups but one are equatorial. That an axial hydroxyl group is the point of attack in this and other microbiological oxidations of cyclitols is an interesting instance of steric acceleration in the conversion of tetrahedral carbon to the trigonal state.

Gerda Dangschat (Berlin, 1942) obtained independent completing evidence of the configuration of inositol in the following manner. She refluxed inositol for several hours with acetone containing 10% each of zinc chloride and acetic acid, acetylated the product, and so obtained the 1,2-acetonide tetraacetate (7) and

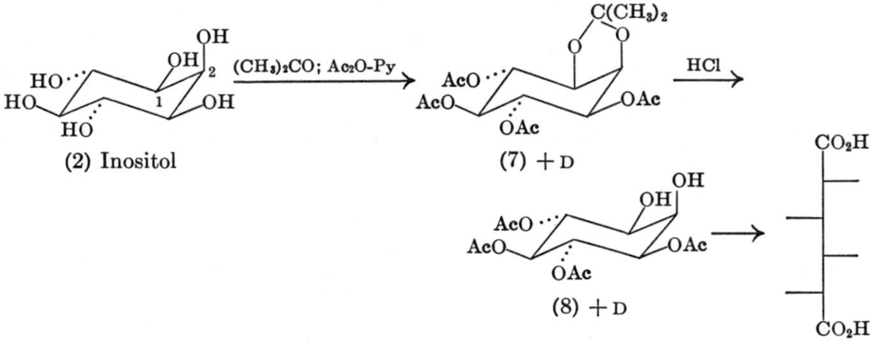

its enantiomer. Deacetylation with methanolic ammonia gave the free acetonide (m.p. 183°), characterized by its stability. Hydrolysis of the acetonide tetraacetate with dilute hydrochloric acid in acetone gave the free diol tetraacetate (8), which was indifferent to periodic acid in acetic acid but which was cleaved by lead tetraacetate in hot benzene. Oxidation of the resulting dialdehyde with peracetic acid and deacetylation gave DL-idosaccharic acid (9, and the enantiomer).

The optically active inositols occur as monomethyl ethers: pinitol (m.p. 187°, αD +65.5°), isolated from pine sugar (A. Girard, 1873); quebrachitol (m.p. 191°, αD −80°) first isolated from bark of the quebracho tree and most readily available from commercial latex concentrate from the rubber tree (*Hevea braziliensis*) (1 kg.→12 g.). Posternak (1936) established the configuration of (−)-inositol (3) by permanganate oxidation and identification of the two optically active saccharic acids formed. H. O. L. Fischer[1] (1952) characterized pinitol as the 5-methyl ether by a degradation of a diacetonide assumed to be that (5) involving the two *cis*-diol groups. Although the assumption was reasonable, S. J. Angyal (1953) proved it to be correct by converting (−)-inositol into the diacetonide (7) and degrading this by lead tetraacetate cleavage and Meerwein-Ponndorf reduction to L-mannitol diacetonide (6). Also, on partial methylation of (7) he obtained the monomethyl ether (8), which is the enantiomer of (5). The naturally

[1] Hermann O. L. Fischer, 1888–1960; b. Würzburg; Ph.D. Jena (Knorr, E. Fischer); Univ. Berlin, Basel, Toronto, Calif. (Berkeley)

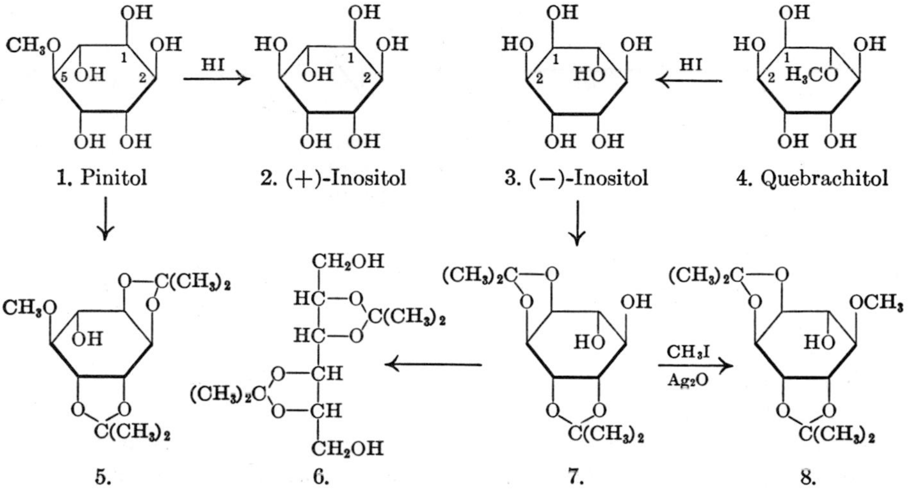

OH — CH₃O, OH (5 OH, 1, 2), OH OH

1. Pinitol

$\xrightarrow{HI}$

OH — HO, OH (OH, 1, 2), OH OH

2. (+)-Inositol

OH — HO, OH (2, 1, HO), OH OH

3. (−)-Inositol

$\xleftarrow{HI}$

OH — HO, OH (2 H₃CO, 1), OH OH

4. Quebrachitol

5.

6.

7.

CH₃I / Ag₂O

8.

occurring ethers (1) and (4) are not enantiomers but differ in the position of the methyl group.

The early name muscle sugar for the sweet tasting cyclitol gave way to inositol. On recognizing that the molecule has a plane of symmetry, the Posternaks described it as *meso*-inositol. H. A. Lardy (1951) raised the objection that the name does not distinguish between the other *meso* forms and proposed the name *myo*-inositol. This name is redundant (Gr. *inos*, muscle; *myo*-, of muscle), and the system requires memorization of a configuration for each prefix (*myo*-, *muco*-, *scyllo*-). We prefer the trivial name inositol, the numbering system arbitrarily employed by Posternak, use of the same numbers for keto derivatives, identification of an isomer where necessary as an epi- or polyepiinositol, and optional identification of a mirror-image form as an enantio form. Thus alternative names are as follows:

Scyllitol	2-Epiinositol
(+)-Inositol	Enantio-1-epiinositol
(−)-Inositol	1-Epiinositol

Maquenne's interesting observations on the oxidation of inositol with hot nitric acid prompted Posternak (1936) to explore the reaction under milder conditions, and he isolated in 10% yield (*Biochem. Preps.*) a superbly crystalline new ketone (m.p. 200°) of intense reducing power. Permanganate oxidation (1946) characterized the substance as a (±)-mixture of inosose-4 (II) and inosose-6 (III). Reduction of the mixture with sodium amalgam affords a mixture of inositol (I) and 6-epiinositol (IV), but hydrogenation affords 6-epiinositol as the sole product. This substance has two axial hydroxyl groups, and on microbiological oxidation one of these is attacked with production of pure (−)-inosose-6 (III). In his first investigation of the (±)-inosose obtained by nitric acid oxidation, Posternak encountered a remarkable reaction: transformation of the pentabenzoate by the action of pyridine or sodium acetate in hot acetic acid (5 min.) into 2,3,5-

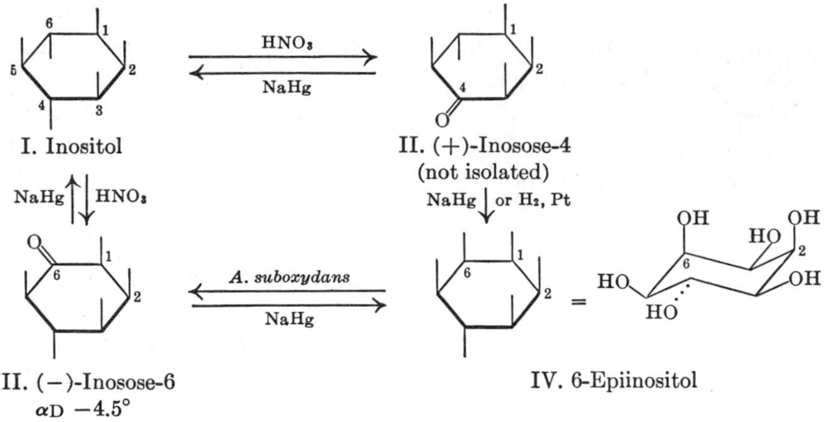

I. Inositol   II. (+)-Inosose-4
(not isolated)

III. (−)-Inosose-6   IV. 6-Epiinositol
αD −4.5°

tribenzoyloxyphenol. The pentaacetate on treatment with acetic anhydride and a basic catalyst is aromatized to 1,2,3,5-tetraacetoxybenzene. The pentaacetate

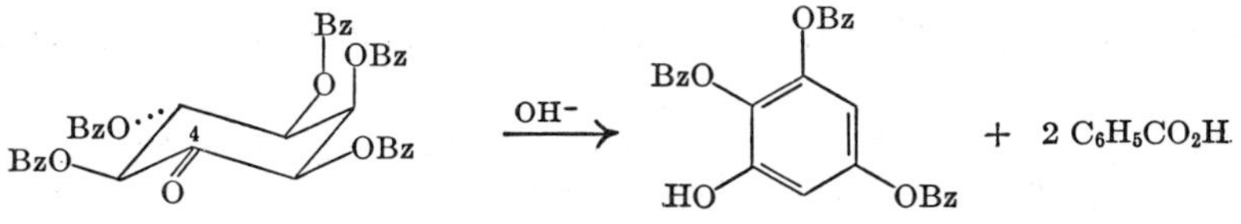

(+)-Isomer

of inosose-2 yields the same product. The reaction probably proceeds via tetra-acetoxycyclohexene-2-one-1 (Posternak, 1936; Angyal, 1959; Stanacev and Kates, 1961).

(±)-Inosose-4 forms a phenylhydrazone but forms a phenylosazone only with difficulty. Perhaps the rigid chair conformation stabilized by four equatorial hydroxyl groups restricts the plane of the C=N bond from becoming parallel to an HCOH group and this retards the Amadori hydrogen shift. Inosose-3 and inosose-5 have been described by E. Chargaff (1948) and by G. R. Allen, Jr. (1956). All the inoses in alkaline solution have intense reducing properties, attributed to an enediol form (Posternak, 1951; Heyns, 1953). They are more reactive in this respect than D-glucose and D-fructose and reduce Fehling solution instantly in the cold. Improved procedures and revised constants for a number of cyclitols are reported by N. Z. Stanacev and M. Kates (National Research Council, Canada, 1961).

29.27   Animal Polysaccharides. — Chitin is a polysaccharide that forms the hard shell of crustaceans and insects. Complete acid hydrolysis requires drastic conditions but affords nearly the theoretical amounts of acetic acid and D-glucosamine (2-amino-2-desoxy-D-glucose). Hydrolysis with an enzyme present in the intestine of the snail affords N-acetylglucosamine. Chitin is a linear polymer comparable to cellulose in structure and stability. The identity period along the fiber axis is 10.4 Å.

Hyaluronic acid is a related polysaccharide isolated first from vitreous humor (K. Meyer,[1] 1934) and later from synovial fluid (of joints), skin, and various

[1] Karl Meyer, b. 1899 Kerpen, Germany; M.D. Cologne, Ph.D. Berlin; College Phys. Surg., Columbia Univ.

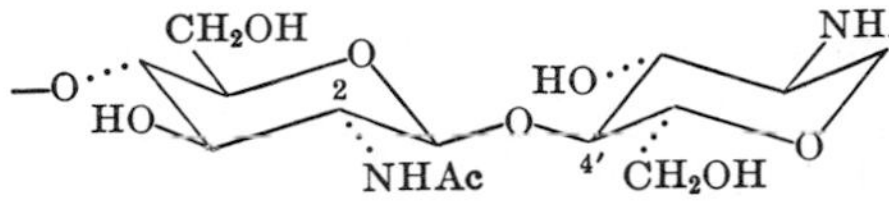

Chitin

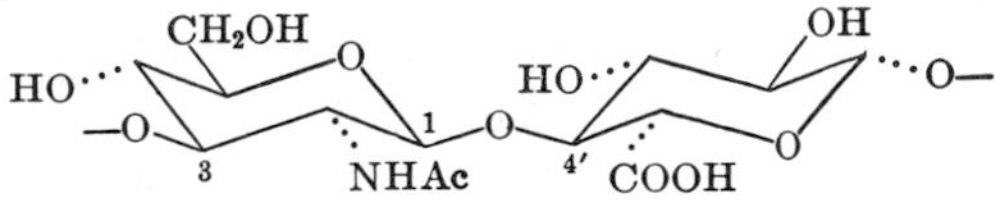

Hyaluronic acid

microorganisms. It is composed of N-acetyl-D-glucosamine and D-glucuronic acid units in equal or nearly equal amount. One glucosidic link probably extends from C_1 in the amino sugar to C_4 in the uronic acid; the other one involves C_1 in the acid and C_3 in the amino sugar. Solutions are highly viscous, and this property is the basis for the biological function as a lubricant. The hydrolytic enzyme hyaluronidase, which occurs in many bacteria, in snake venoms, bee stings, and in various animal tissues, particularly the testes, is called a spreading factor because it increases diffusion of toxins, drugs (and dyes) on intradermal injection. Hyaluronidase, which occurs in spermatazoa and is involved in the fertilization process, has many uses. In conjunction with intradermal administration of a large volume of fluid, it increases the rate of absorption of fluid by the tissue and thus prevents distention at the site of injection. When injected with a therapeutic agent, it enhances the effect.

Heparin, a polysaccharide present in various animal tissues, is characterized by a specific property of prolonging the clotting time of blood. It is used clinically in preventing formation of blood clots (thrombosis) after certain types of surgery. It is composed of equimolecular amounts of D-glucuronic acid and D-glucosamine. The amino group is sulfated and one hydroxyl group per C_{12} unit is sulfated. The structure is currently under investigation.

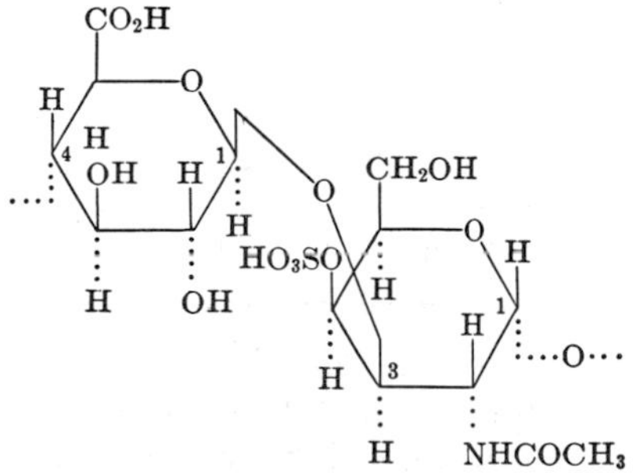

Chondroitin sulfate

Closely related complex polysaccharides known as **chondroitin sulfates** occur linked to protein in skeletal tissues, particularly cartilage. Gentle hydrolysis of chondroitin sulfate with oxalic acid splits off sulfuric acid and acetic acid and cleaves the polysaccharide chain to units of the disaccharide chondrosine, isolated as the crystalline ethyl ester hydrochloride. Chondrosine on further hydrolysis affords 2-amino-2-desoxy-D-galactose (chondrosamine) and D-glucuronic acid. The formula shown for the polysaccharide was established by K. Meyer (1954). A chondroitin sulfate isolated from umbilical cord is sulfated in the amino sugar residue at C_6 instead of C_4. The chondroitin sulfate from skin is structurally similar to that from cartilage except that L-iduronic acid replaces D-glucuronic acid.

29.28   **Immunologically Active Polysaccharides.** — A foreign protein (antigen) introduced into an animal stimulates production in the blood of substances (antibodies) that can combine with the antigen. The interaction may result in formation of a precipitate (precipitin reaction). Since the toxins, or poisonous secretions of several pathogenic organisms, have been identified as proteins, this antigen-antibody reaction is evidently the basis for immunity to specific diseases that an animal may acquire as a result of infection. The reaction is highly specific; for instance, the pneumococci belong to some forty serological types, and an animal that has acquired immunity to one type will usually not be immune to any other type. Landsteiner introduced the term hapten for the nonproteinoid portion of an antigen that determines the specificity of antigen to antibody. The antibodies (or antitoxins) are modified serum globulin.

In 1917 Dochez and Avery found that filtrates of cultures of pathogenic pneumococci contain a substance that precipitates with antiserum of the same serological type. Investigations of Heidelberger[1] have shown that these substances are polysaccharides and that the type specificity and virulence of the pneumococci are associated with the presence of the polysaccharide which is the main component of the capsule surrounding the organism. Avirulent pneumococci are not encapsulated. Proteins of the pathogenic pneumococci are serologically related throughout the entire group. The polysaccharide of type III pneumococcus (molecular weight about 150,000) consists of D-glucose and D-glucuronic acid in equimolecular amounts. It can be hydrolyzed to an aldobiuronic acid of which the probable structure is that of cellobiuronic acid. The serum of rabbits that have

Cellobiuronic acid

been immunized to type III pneumococcus will agglutinate (L. *agglutinare*, to glue) not only type III but also type VIII pneumococcus. This effect, which is known as an immunological cross reaction, is due to the fact that the capsular polysaccharides of the two types are related chemically. Type VIII polysaccharide is also composed of D-glucose and D-glucuronic acid, but the molar ratio is 7:2, whereas it is 1:1 in type III polysaccharide. The polysaccharide of type XIV pneumococcus contains N-acetyl-D-glucosamine and D-galactose in the molar ratio of 1:3. Fundamental work of Avery has shown that the type specificity of the pneumococcus is controlled by the particular nucleic acid of each type. Thus the nucleic acid of type III pneumococcus can induce type II pneumococcus to change into type III pneumococcus; that is, it controls production of the polysaccharide responsible for the type specificity. When the change is once induced, the nucleic acid is also reproduced in the course of cell division. Similar specifically active polysaccharides have been obtained from other pathogenic bacteria. The hapten of group A hemolytic streptococcus is composed of N-acetyl-D-glucosamine and D-glucuronic acid in equimolecular amounts. Two active polysaccharides of

[1] Michael Heidelberger, b. 1888 New York; Ph.D. Columbia (Bogert); College Phys. and Surg., Columbia Univ.; Inst. Microbiol., Rutgers Univ.

human tubercle bacillus are highly branched, high-molecular weight substances composed of four sugar units (Haworth, 1948). The antigens of several bacteria have been identified as complexes containing a polysaccharide and a protein, and carbohydrate-protein antigens have been synthesized whose specificity is determined by the pattern of the carbohydrate constituent.

Since cross reactivity depends upon structural similarity, immunological reactions are useful in investigation of structure. Thus M. L. Wolfrom (1947, 1952) isolated a galactan from residues of beef lung after separation from heparin and showed it to be composed in large part of D-galactose. M. Heidelberger found (1955) that the lung galactan gave a precipitate with the polysaccharide of type XIV pneumococcus, as expected, but that it also showed some cross precipitation with the polysaccharide of type II pneumococcus, known to be composed of L-rhamnose, D-glucose, and D-glucuronic acid. Paper chromatography then showed that the lung galactan was not homogeneous but was contaminated with an impurity containing D-glucuronic acid.

29.29 Photosynthesis.—The green plant synthesizes its complex organic constituents from carbon dioxide, as the only source of carbon, and from water and inorganic salts derived from the soil. The animal organism cannot initiate syntheses starting with such simple entities, and is dependent upon preformed organic materials supplied in the diet. Since fats and proteins of plants are apparently derived from carbohydrate precursors rather than the reverse, carbohydrates are the probable primary products of photosynthesis. The energy required for the overall process shown in the equation is supplied by the sun, but photosyn-

$$n\,CO_2 \ + \ n\,H_2O \ \underset{\text{Respiration}}{\overset{h\nu}{\rightleftarrows}} \ n\,O_2 \ + \ (CH_2O)_n$$

thesis is possible only in plants which contain pigments of a specific type capable of absorbing light. The commonest is the green pigment chlorophyll, which Willstätter showed (1906–14) to consist of the two pigments chlorophyll-a and chlorophyll-b; these differ in that the latter has a formyl group in ring II in place of a methyl group. They are dihydroporphyrins related to hemin but the metal is

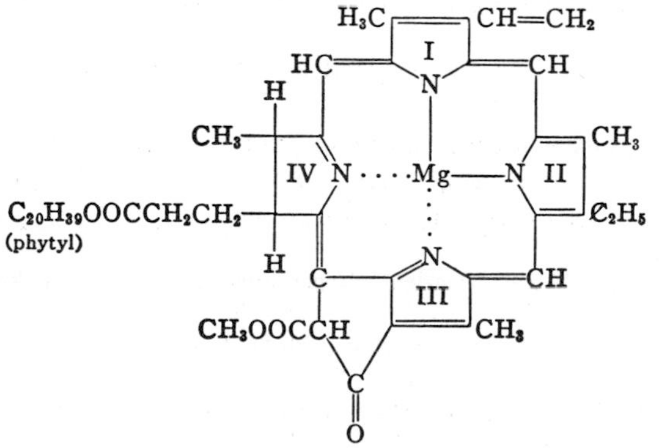

Chlorophyll-a (H. Fischer)

magnesium rather than iron, and one of the propionic acid groups is esterified with phytol.   In the plant the pigments are bound to protein.   The mechanism by which they function is not known, but maximal rate of photosynthesis is observed at a wave length corresponding to maximal absorption by chlorophyll.

The once-held belief that green plants alone are able to effect photosynthesis was questioned by Englemann (1883), who suspected that certain bacteria require light in order to assimilate carbon dioxide and thus are photosynthetic.   This view was strengthened by isolation from purple bacteria of the pigment bacteriochlorophyll, which differs from chlorophyll-a in having two dihydropyrrole rings instead of one, and in replacement of the vinyl group in ring I by an aceto group.   van Niel[1] (1941) investigated the metabolism of purple bacteria and found that they do require light for growth.   Thus *B.Thiorhodaceae* can grow on a medium containing an oxidizable inorganic sulfur compound and bicarbonate as the sole carbon source, but only when irradiated.   Typical equations that were verified are as follows:

$$2CO_2 \ + \ 4H_2O \ + \ H_2S \ \xrightarrow{h\nu} \ 2(CH_2O) \ + \ 2H_2O \ + \ H_2SO_4$$

$$CO_2 \ + \ 2H_2O \ + \ 2H_2SO_3 \ \xrightarrow{h\nu} \ (CH_2O) \ + \ H_2O \ + \ 2H_2SO_4$$

The essential step in these and similar processes is reduction of carbon dioxide by a hydrogen donor, H_2A, two moles of which are required:

$$CO_2 \ + \ 2H_2A \ \xrightarrow{h\nu} \ (CH_2O) \ + \ H_2O \ + \ 2A$$

This general equation was shown to be applicable to purple bacteria that require an organic substance as substrate (*Athiorhodadaceae*), when a strain was found that reduces one mole of carbon dioxide by oxidation of two moles of isopropyl alcohol:

$$CO_2 \ + \ 2(CH_3)_2CHOH \ \xrightarrow{h\nu} \ (CH_2O) \ + \ H_2O \ + \ 2(CH_3)_2CO$$

Ruben[2] and Kamen[3] (1941), using isotopically labeled water, H_2O^{18}, established that van Niel's general equation applies to photosynthesis in green plants.   In this case water functions as hydrogen donor, since the oxygen produced is isotopic:

$$CO_2 \ + \ 2H_2O^{18} \ \longrightarrow \ (CH_2O) \ + \ H_2O \ + \ O_2^{18}$$

Ruben also initiated experiments on the fixation of $C^{14}O_2$; the radioactive label has the advantage of ready detection.   He ruled out an early postulate that chlorophyll functions as acceptor for CO_2, and found that in the absence of light CO_2 is

[1] Cornelius B. van Niel, b. 1897 Haarlem, Netherlands; D.Sc. Delft; Hopkins Marine Station, Stanford Univ.

[2] Samuel Ruben, 1913–43; b. San Francisco; Ph.D. Univ. California, Berkeley (Latimer); Univ. California, Berkeley

[3] Martin D. Kamen, b. 1913 Toronto, Canada; Ph.D. Chicago (Harkins); Washington Univ., St. Louis; Brandeis Univ.

assimilated but not reduced. Hence the key photochemical reaction is reduction of CO_2 to (CH_2O), followed by conversion of (CH_2O) to specific stable compounds, in a sequence of steps investigated mainly by Calvin and by Gaffron.[1] The carbon of assimilated CO_2 is incorporated into a wide variety of cellular constituents, even during a period of exposure of only a few minutes, and hence identification of early products in the sequence is difficult. One expedient is to expose the plant to $C^{14}O_2$ for periods as short as 0.4–15 sec.; another is to conduct the experiments at low temperatures (2°). By these methods, and by extrapolation to zero time, Calvin established that the first stable derivative of assimilated $C^{14}O_2$ is phosphoglyceric acid, $(HO)_2OPOCH_2CH(OH)C^{14}O_2H$. In short-term experiments only the carboxyl group contains the label, but after longer exposure radiocarbon appears in the other two positions of the acid, and to the same extent. Other radiocarbon components detected in short-term experiments are dihydroxyacetone monophosphate, $HOCH_2COCH_2OPO(OH)_2$, glucose monophosphate, and fructose monophosphate. The two hexose monophosphates evidently arise from combination of two C_3 units related to glyceric acid, because the distribution of radioactivity agrees with that expected on this basis. The technique for experimental determination of distribution is illustrated for the case of D-glucose (H. G. Wood,[2] 1945). The microorganism *Lactobacillus casei* cleaves the 3–4 bond to form two

$$
\begin{array}{ccc}
\text{1 CHO} & & \text{1 CH}_3 \\
\text{2 CHOH} & & \text{2 CHOH} \\
\text{3 CHOH} & \xrightarrow[\text{casei}]{\textit{Lactobacillus}} & \text{3 COOH} \xrightarrow{\text{KMnO}_4} \\
\text{4 CHOH} & & \text{4 COOH} \\
\text{5 CHOH} & & \text{5 CHOH} \\
\text{6 CH}_2\text{OH} & & \text{6 CH}_3
\end{array}
$$

$$2\ CH_3CHO + 2\ \overset{3,4}{CO_2}$$

$$\xrightarrow[\text{NaOI}]{}\ 2\ \overset{1,6}{CHI_3} + 2\ \overset{2,5}{HCOOH}$$

molecules of lactic acid of the origin indicated. Oxidation of this acid gives carbon dioxide derived from C_3 and C_4, and haloform cleavage of the aldehyde gives fragments derived from the combinations C_1–C_6 and C_2–C_5.

The phosphoglyceric acid isolated from barley after exposure to $C^{14}O_2$ for 15 sec. has the following distribution of radiocarbon: C_1, 49%; C_2, 25%; C_3, 26%. The distribution of radiocarbon in the hexose monophosphates formed in the same experiment is: $C_1 + C_6$, 24%; $C_2 + C_5$, 26%; $C_3 + C_4$, 52%. Thus the central two carbon atoms of the chain contain twice as much label as the others and can be

[1] Hans Gaffron, b. 1902 Lima, Peru (German parentage); Ph.D. Berlin (Traube); Univ. Chicago

[2] Harland G. Wood, b. 1907 Delavan, Minn.; Ph.D. Iowa State Coll.; Nat. Res. Fell. Wisconsin; Iowa State Coll., Minnesota, Western Reserve Univ.

represented as C^{++}, in contrast to C^+. The condensation of the three-carbon units is thus as follows:

$$\overset{+}{C}\ \overset{+}{C}\ \overset{++}{C} + \overset{++}{C}\ \overset{+}{C}\ \overset{+}{C} \longrightarrow \overset{+}{C}\ \overset{+}{C}\ \overset{++}{C}\ \overset{++}{C}\ \overset{+}{C}\ \overset{+}{C},$$

or:

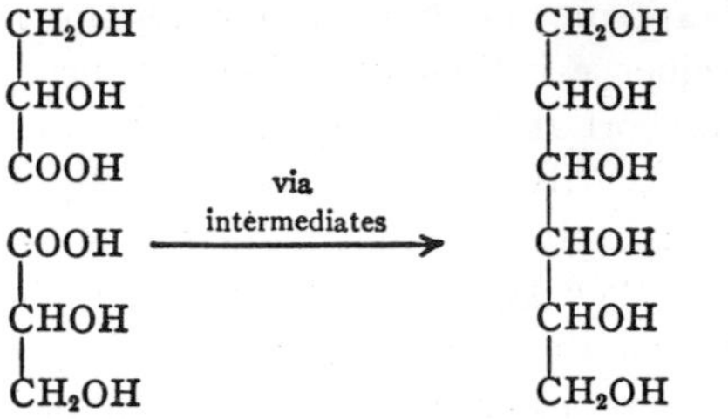

$$
\begin{array}{c}
CH_2OH \\
CHOH \\
COOH \\
COOH \\
CHOH \\
CH_2OH
\end{array}
\quad \xrightarrow[\text{intermediates}]{\text{via}} \quad
\begin{array}{c}
CH_2OH \\
CHOH \\
CHOH \\
CHOH \\
CHOH \\
CH_2OH
\end{array}
$$

(as phosphate)　　　　(as phosphate)

Other labeled compounds identified in short-term experiments are substances known to be involved in the metabolism of hexoses [Krebs cycle (31. 42)]: phosphoenolpyruvic acid, phosphoglycolic acid, malic acid, citric acid.

In addition to the two common D-hexose phosphates, two other D-sugars have been identified by paper chromatography as early products in photosynthesis. One is the monophosphate of the heptose sedoheptulose, previously known as a general but minor constituent of plants. The other is the 1,5-diphosphate ester

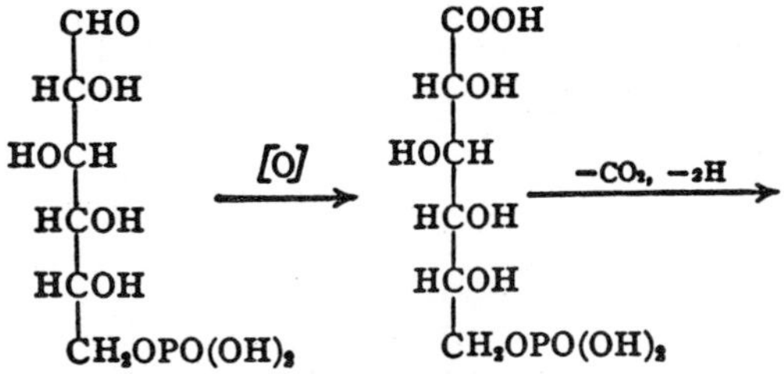

$$
\begin{array}{c}
CHO \\
HCOH \\
HOCH \\
HCOH \\
HCOH \\
CH_2OPO(OH)_2
\end{array}
\xrightarrow{[O]}
\begin{array}{c}
COOH \\
HCOH \\
HOCH \\
HCOH \\
HCOH \\
CH_2OPO(OH)_2
\end{array}
\xrightarrow{-CO_2,\ -2H}
$$

Glucose-6-　　　　6-Phospho-
phosphate　　　　gluconic acid

$$
\begin{array}{c}
CH_2OH \\
C=O \\
HCOH \\
HCOH \\
CH_2OPO(OH)_2
\end{array}
\rightleftharpoons
\begin{array}{c}
CHO \\
HCOH \\
HCOH \\
HCOH \\
CH_2OPO(OH)_2
\end{array}
$$

Ribulose-5-　　　　Ribose-5-
phosphate　　　　phosphate

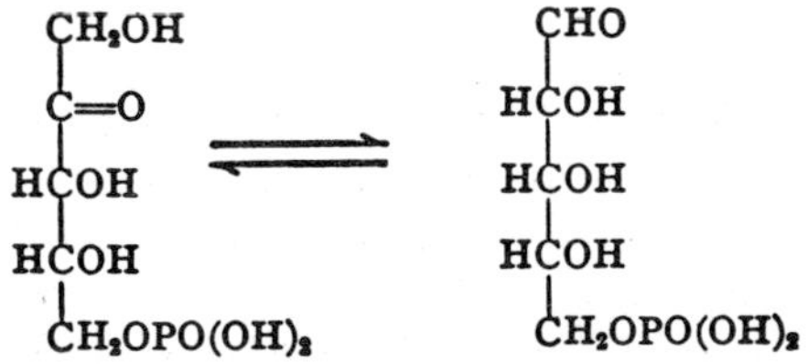

of a ketopentose, ribulose, which at the time of identification (1952) had not been known as a natural product. The sugar was later shown to be an oxidative metabolite of glucose in several microorganisms. An identified intermediate in the conversion is 6-phosphogluconic acid. Ribulose is related to the common natural aldopentose ribose in the same way that fructose is related to glucose, and indeed, in the presence of the enzyme phosphopentose isomerase, ribulose-5-phosphate is reversibly isomerized to ribose-5-phosphate. Sedoheptulose is also a 2-ketose, and is related to ribulose and ribose. The enzyme transketolase, isolated from plants in essentially pure form, can catalyze the reversible transformations formulated, in which a two-carbon fragment is transferred from a seven-carbon phos-

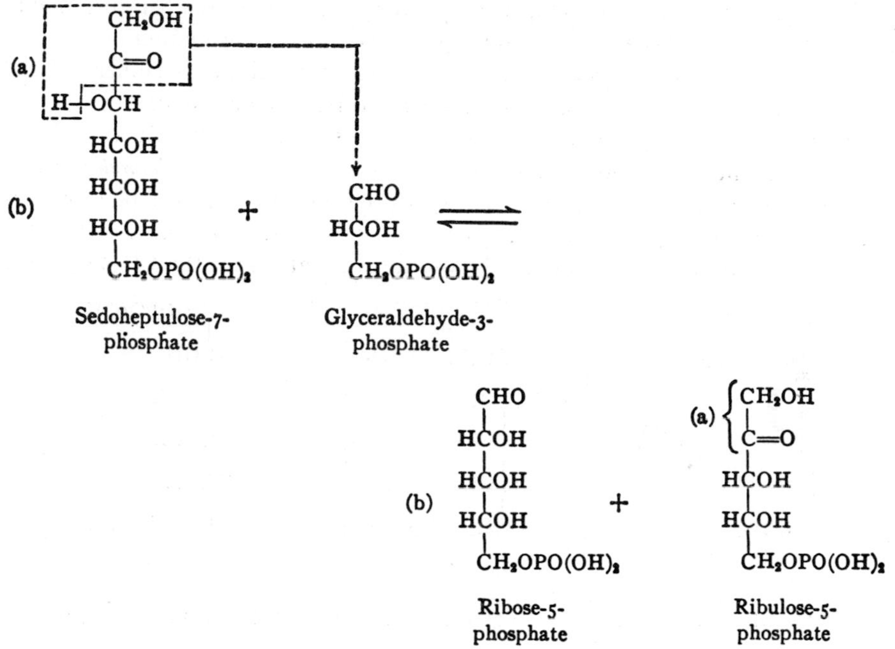

(a)
(b)

$$
\begin{array}{c}
\text{CH}_2\text{OH} \\
\text{C}{=}\text{O} \\
\text{H}{-}\text{OCH} \\
\text{HCOH} \\
\text{HCOH} \\
\text{HCOH} \\
\text{CH}_2\text{OPO(OH)}_2
\end{array}
\quad + \quad
\begin{array}{c}
\text{CHO} \\
\text{HCOH} \\
\text{CH}_2\text{OPO(OH)}_2
\end{array}
\rightleftharpoons
$$

Sedoheptulose-7-
phosphate

Glyceraldehyde-3-
phosphate

(b)
(a)

$$
\begin{array}{c}
\text{CHO} \\
\text{HCOH} \\
\text{HCOH} \\
\text{HCOH} \\
\text{CH}_2\text{OPO(OH)}_2
\end{array}
\quad + \quad
\begin{array}{c}
\text{CH}_2\text{OH} \\
\text{C}{=}\text{O} \\
\text{HCOH} \\
\text{HCOH} \\
\text{CH}_2\text{OPO(OH)}_2
\end{array}
$$

Ribose-5-
phosphate

Ribulose-5-
phosphate

phate to a three-carbon phosphate to produce two five-carbon phosphates. The same enzyme catalyzes interconversion of the phosphates of fructose (6-C) and glyceraldehyde (3-C) to those of erythrose (4-C) and ribulose (5-C).

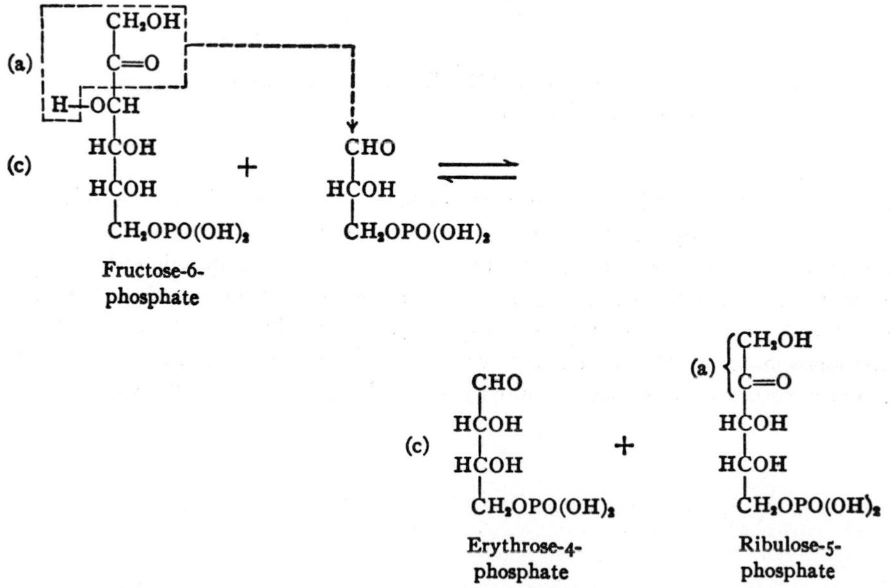

(a)
(c)

$$
\begin{array}{c}
\text{CH}_2\text{OH} \\
\text{C}{=}\text{O} \\
\text{H}{-}\text{OCH} \\
\text{HCOH} \\
\text{HCOH} \\
\text{CH}_2\text{OPO(OH)}_2
\end{array}
\quad + \quad
\begin{array}{c}
\text{CHO} \\
\text{HCOH} \\
\text{CH}_2\text{OPO(OH)}_2
\end{array}
\rightleftharpoons
$$

Fructose-6-
phosphate

(c)
(a)

$$
\begin{array}{c}
\text{CHO} \\
\text{HCOH} \\
\text{HCOH} \\
\text{CH}_2\text{OPO(OH)}_2
\end{array}
\quad + \quad
\begin{array}{c}
\text{CH}_2\text{OH} \\
\text{C}{=}\text{O} \\
\text{HCOH} \\
\text{HCOH} \\
\text{CH}_2\text{OPO(OH)}_2
\end{array}
$$

Erythrose-4-
phosphate

Ribulose-5-
phosphate

That the first recognized product of assimilation of CO_2 is a C_3-compound suggested that the CO_2-acceptor is a C_2-unit, which is continuously regenerated during photosynthesis. However, no evidence to support this hypothesis has been forthcoming. In a study of the effect of various external variables (temperature, light, partial pressure of CO_2 and O_2), Calvin found (1955) that formation of ribulose diphosphate and of phosphoglyceric acid are related in a reciprocal manner. Thus factors which suppress formation of ribulose diphosphate correspondingly increase production of phosphoglyceric acid, and vice versa. Other investigators have shown that addition of ribulose diphosphate to cell-free extracts of *Chlorella* (green algae) causes fixation in the dark of $C^{14}O_2$ into the carboxyl group of phosphoglyceric acid. Ribose-5-phosphate is also active in this respect, but other substrates are inactive. It thus appears that ribulose diphosphate (I) is the CO_2-acceptor.

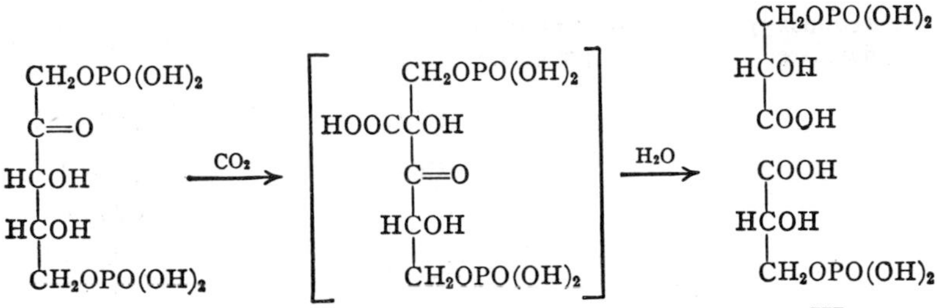

$$
\begin{array}{ccccc}
\begin{array}{c}
CH_2OPO(OH)_2 \\
| \\
C=O \\
| \\
HCOH \\
| \\
HCOH \\
| \\
CH_2OPO(OH)_2 \\
\mathbf{I}
\end{array}
& \xrightarrow{CO_2} &
\left[
\begin{array}{c}
CH_2OPO(OH)_2 \\
| \\
HOOCCOH \\
| \\
C=O \\
| \\
HCOH \\
| \\
CH_2OPO(OH)_2 \\
\mathbf{II}
\end{array}
\right]
& \xrightarrow{H_2O} &
\begin{array}{c}
CH_2OPO(OH)_2 \\
| \\
HCOH \\
| \\
COOH \\
\\
COOH \\
| \\
HCOH \\
| \\
CH_2OPO(OH)_2 \\
\mathbf{III}
\end{array}
\end{array}
$$

Calvin postulates that conversion to glycerophosphoric acid (III) proceeds through the branched intermediate II.

The CO_2-acceptor, ribulose diphosphate, must be regenerated in a cyclic process such as that outlined in the diagram; the actual pathway undoubtedly is more com-

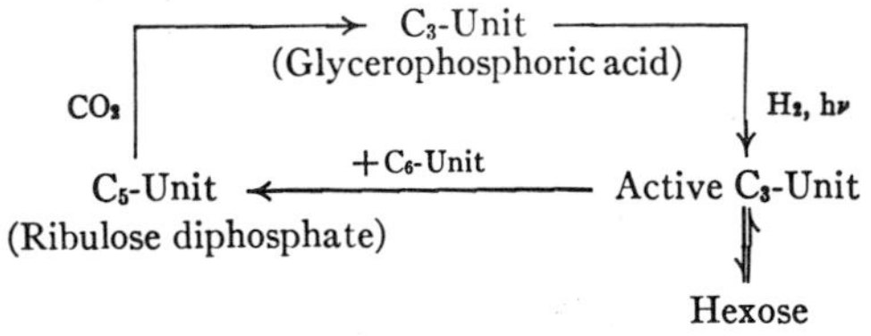

plex and may well involve the interconversions of C_5, C_3, and C_7 sugars indicated above. The initially formed C_3-unit appears to be glycerophosphoric acid, reduction of which with absorption of radiant energy gives a substance described as an active C_3-unit and defined as the precursor of the C_5-acceptor of CO_2. The photochemical reduction may afford phosphoglyceraldehyde and dihydroxyacetone monophosphate, which are known to condense to fructose diphosphate; combination of hexose with phosphoglyceraldehyde could then regenerate the C_5-unit.

Chapter 30

LIPIDS

30.1 **Neutral Fats.** — Members of this group of saponifiable lipids are glycerides of higher fatty acids, saturated and unsaturated. The most abundant saturated acids are the straight-chain even-carbon acids: caprylic (C_8), capric (C_{10}), lauric (C_{12}), myristic (C_{14}), palmitic (C_{16}), and stearic (C_{18}).[1] Melting points in this series (Table 30.1) range from $16.5°$ (C_8) to $70°$ (C_{18}). The common unsaturated acids are oleic, linoleic, and linolenic acids, which are the cis-Δ^9-, cis,cis-$\Delta^{9,12}$- and all cis-$\Delta^{9,12,15}$-dehydro derivatives of stearic acid. The

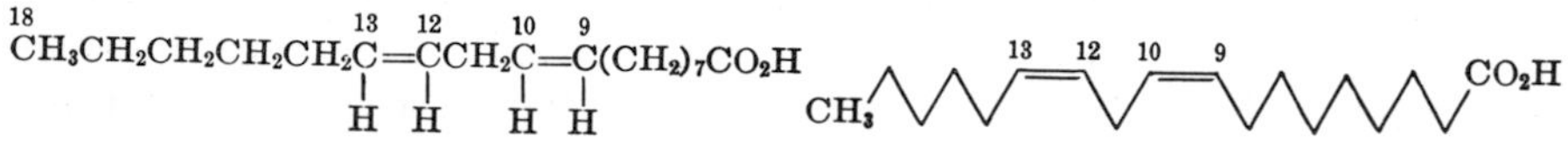

Linoleic acid (m.p. $-5°$)

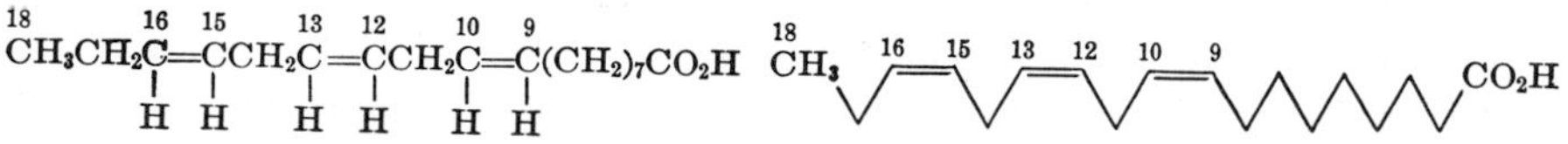

Linolenic acid (m.p. $-11°$)

unsaturated acids are liquids and yield solid stearic acid on hydrogenation. The synthetic saturated glycerides of C_{10} and higher acids are all solids: tricaprin melts at $31°$, trilaurin at $46°$, trimyristin at $59°$, tripalmitin at $60°$, and tristearin at $71°$. Mixtures of these glycerides are solids of intermediate melting range. The vegetable oils are liquid because of a high content of olefinic acid components. The degree of unsaturation of a fat determines uses to which it can be put: salad

[1] Names of the odd-numbered acids are: C_9, pelargonic acid; C_{11}, undecylic acid; C_{13}, tridecylic acid; C_{15}, pentadecylic acid; C_{17}, margaric acid; C_{19}, nondecylic acid.

TABLE 30.1. SATURATED FATTY ACIDS

ACID	No. OF C ATOMS	FORMULA	M.P., °C.	B.P., °C.
Butyric	4	$CH_3(CH_2)_2COOH$	-4.7	163
Isovaleric	5	$(CH_3)_2CHCH_2COOH$	-51	174
Caproic	6	$CH_3(CH_2)_4COOH$	-1.5	205
Caprylic	8	$CH_3(CH_2)_6COOH$	16.5	237
Capric	10	$CH_3(CH_2)_8COOH$	31.3	269
Lauric	12	$CH_3(CH_2)_{10}COOH$	43.6	102/1 mm.
Myristic	14	$CH_3(CH_2)_{12}COOH$	58.0	122/1 mm.
Palmitic	16	$CH_3(CH_2)_{14}COOH$	62.9	139/1 mm.
Stearic	18	$CH_3(CH_2)_{16}COOH$	69.9	160/1 mm.
Arachidic	20	$CH_3(CH_2)_{18}COOH$	75.2	205/1 mm.
Behenic	22	$CH_3(CH_2)_{20}COOH$	80.2	
Lignoceric	24	$CH_3(CH_2)_{22}COOH$	84.2	
Cerotic	26	$CH_3(CH_2)_{24}COOH$	87.7	

oil, cooking grease, soap or candle stock. Unsaturation is measured by the iodine value, the number of grams of iodine that combine with one hundred grams of fat. Test solutions employ iodine monochloride (ICl), iodine monobromide (IBr), or iodomercuric chloride (I_2HgCl_2), all of which are more reactive than iodine alone. The amount of fatty acid volatile with steam (C_{12} and less) is expressed as the Reichert-Meissl value. The melting range is described by citing the titer, defined as the temperature of initial solidification of a melt. The saponification value, expressed as the number of milligrams of potassium hydroxide required to hydrolyze one gram of fat, indicates the average molecular weight.

Analyses of common fats and oils are given in Table 30.2. Some fats contain glycerides of only three or four acids; butter contains fourteen, one of which is *n*-butyric acid.* Isobutyric acid, an odd-carbon branched-chain acid the carbon skeleton of which is that of isoprene, has been isolated from saponified dolphin and porpoise blubber oils (3.2 and 13.6%, respectively). The extent of unsaturation of a fat may be influenced markedly by the temperature at which biosynthesis occurs. Warm-blooded animals tend to produce solid fats that are fluid at, or only a little above, body temperature. Variation may occur in fats from different parts of the organism. Neat's-food oil, from the hoofs of cattle, has a higher iodine number than fats derived from other locations. A gradation is noted in the subcutaneous fat of the pig, the outer layers of which are progressively unsaturated. The striking influence of climate on the composition of linseed oil is shown by the following comparison: an iodine value of 190 has been reported for linseed oil from seed grown in the cold climate of Switzerland, and a value of 93 for oil from seed of the same stock grown in a Berlin greenhouse at a temperature of 25–30°. The degree of unsaturation is also dependent on the type of fat in the diet. The iodine value of lard of corn-fed hogs is 69–72, of peanut-fed hogs, 90–100.

* Butyric (3%), caproic (1.4%), caprylic (1.5%), capric (2.7%), lauric (3.7%), myristic (12.1%), palmitic (25.3%), stearic (9.2%), arachidic (1.3%), lauroleic (0.4%), myristoleic (1.6%), palmitoleic, (4.0%), oleic (29.6%), and linoleic (3.6%).

Since the principal unsaturated acyl components of fats are convertible to stearoyl groups by catalytic hydrogenation, unsaturation in a natural fat or oil can be reduced to any stage desired by hydrogenation (Ni catalyst). Since hydrogenation progressively raises the melting point, the process is described as hardening; abundant, highly unsaturated vegetable oils (peanut, cottonseed, soybean) are hardened by hydrogenation to more valuable products for use in making soap or to lard substitutes for use as cooking greases. Whale oil (iodine number 110–150) is partially hydrogenated to reduce the most highly reactive unsaturated centers and so eliminate odor and produce more stable oils for use as salad oil and in the compounding of cosmetics. Lard is often hydrogenated to improve keeping qualities, since development of rancidity is associated with unsaturation.

The acids of human depot fat are shown in Table 30.3; the composition is close to that of beef tallow and of lard. Unsaturated acids predominate over saturated acids in the ratio 3:2, and the most abundant single component is oleic acid. Considerable linoleic acid is also present. The tetraunsaturated C_{20}-component present in human fat in amounts of 0.3–1.0% is arachidonic acid, which deviates from the prevailing types both in carbon content and number of double bonds. The adrenal gland is the richest known source of arachidonic acid, which accounts

$$CH_3CH_2CH_2CH_2CH_2CH\overset{14}{=}CHCH_2CH\overset{11}{=}CHCH_2CH\overset{8}{=}CHCH_2CH\overset{5}{=}CHCH_2CH_2CH_2CO_2H$$

Arachidonic acid ($\Delta^{5,8,11,14}$)

for 22% of the fatty acids of the phosphatide fraction of beef adrenal glands. Arachidonic acid can be hydrogenated easily to the tetrahydro stage and affords 80–90% of the $\Delta^{5,14}$-dienic acid and 5–10% of the $\Delta^{8,14}$-dienic acid; the two double

TABLE 30.2.[1] ACID COMPOSITION OF FATS AND NONDRYING OILS

FAT OR OIL	IODINE VALUE	TITER OF ACIDS, °C.	FATTY ACIDS, %							
			Caprylic	Capric	Lauric	Myristic	Palmitic	Stearic	Oleic	Linoleic
Coconut	8–10	20–23	8.0	7.0	48.0	17.5	8.2	2.0	6.0	2.5
Babassu	12–16	23–24	6.5	2.7	45.8	19.9	6.9	....	18.1	....
Palm kernel	15–18	20–25	3.0	3.0	52.0	15.0	7.5	2.5	16.0	1.0
Palm	51–58	38–47	...	...	....	1.0	42.5	4.0	43.0	9.5
Olive	80–85	17–21	...	...	....	....	6.0	4.0	83.0	7.0
Castor [2]	81–89	3	...	...	....	....	....	0.3	8.0	3.6
Peanut [3]	85–90	28–32	...	...	....	....	7.0	5.0	60.0	21.0
Rape [4]	94–106	12–18	...	...	....	1.0	1.0	1.0	29.0	15.0
Beef tallow	32–47	37–47	...	...	....	2.0	32.5	14.5	48.3	2.7
Lard (leaf)	46–66	36–43	...	...	....	1.1	30.4	17.9	41.2	5.7
Whale blubber [5]	110–150	22–24	...	...	....	8.0	12 1	2.3	33.4	9.0

[1] Data of Werner G. Smith Company.
[2] Contains 87.8% ricinoleic acid.
[3] Contains 4.0% arachidic acid and 3.0% lignoceric acid.
[4] Contains 1.0% lignoceric acid and 50.0% erucic acid.
[5] Contains 1.5% of a C_{14}-monounsaturated acid, 15% palmitoleic acid, and 18.7% C_{20}- and C_{22}- highly unsaturated acids.

TABLE 30.3. PERCENT FATTY ACIDS IN HUMAN DEPOT FAT[*]

SATURATED				1 C=C			2 C=C	4 C=C
C_{12}	C_{14}	C_{16}	C_{18}	C_{14}	C_{16}	C_{18}	C_{18}	C_{20}
0.5	3.3	25.0	8.4	0.4	6.2	45.9	9.6	0.6

[*] Average analyses of five normal specimens reported by D. L. Cramer and J. B. Brown, 1943.

bonds in the central part of the molecule are thus the most susceptible to hydrogenation.

30.2   Isolation of Acids. — Whereas most fats are esters of glycerol with 3–14 different fatty acids, probably in a variety of combinations, the nutmeg (*Myristica fragrans*) contains a single ester, trimyristin, isolated by L. Playfair in Liebig's laboratory in 1841. Ether extraction of 1.5 kg. of crushed nutmegs and two crystallizations from ethanol affords 350 g. of nearly pure trimyristin (*Org. Syn.*); if commercial nutmeg butter is used, the saponification number should be checked to guard against a product adulterated with foreign fats.

Procedures of *Biochemical Preparations* illustrate some of the techniques of purification. Commercial **stearic acid** of 90% purity is crystallized from acetone at 20°, when unsaturated components are retained in the mother liquor (D. Swern[1]). Esterification and fractional vacuum distillation then affords the pure methyl ester, m.p. 39°. In the preparation of **oleic acid** (Swern), aqueous sodium hydroxide (at 30°) is added in portions to a vigorously stirred mixture of olive oil and ethanol preheated to 60°; the temperature rises to about 75° and saponification is soon complete. The crude acid is purified according to J. B. Brown.[2] Two crystallizations from acetone at −60° leave polyunsaturated acids in the mother liquor, and a further crystallization from acetone at −20° removes palmitic and stearic acid as a crystallizate. Distillation at 4 mm. gives oleic acid of 96–99% purity and leaves a residue of saturated components. For many years the procedure for the purification of **linoleic acid** involving conversion to the tetrabromide and debromination was regarded as reliable because the product has the expected iodine number. However, this material is now known to contain about 12% of geometrical or positional isomers. The currently preferred method for isolation of this *cis,cis*-dienic acid is based upon the finding that it does not form a stable urea inclusion complex (Swern). The acidic fraction obtained on saponification of safflower seed is added to a solution in methanol of an amount of urea sufficient to precipitate the saturated and monounsaturated acidic components. Fractionation of the material recovered from the mother liquor affords pure linoleic acid. **Methyl ricinoleate** obtained from castor oil by methanolysis ($NaOCH_3$)

[1] Daniel Swern, b. 1916 New York, N. Y.; Ph.D. Maryland (J. T. Scanlon); Eastern Utilization Research Branch, Philadelphia

[2] John Bernis Brown, b. 1893 Rock Falls, Ill.; Ph.D. Illinois (G. D. Beal); Ohio State Univ. College of Medicine

and fractional distillation is essentially pure, m.p. $-6°$, $\alpha_D + 5°$ (Swern). The polyunsaturated acids are so sensitive to autoxidation that they are always manipulated in an inert atmosphere. Thus chromatography of methyl esters on silica gel is done under nitrogen.

Several investigators, in analytical studies, have used a method of partition chromatography in which the stationary phase, medicinal paraffin, is held on kieselguhr made nonwetting by treatment with dichlorodimethylsilane and the mobile phase is a range of aqueous solutions containing from 40 to 90% acetone (see F. D. Gunstone, St. Andrews Univ., 1960). Acids in the range C_8–C_{24} can be separated.

30.3   **Olefinic Acids.** — Unsaturated acids with less than ten carbon atoms have not been observed in nature, and the C_{10}, C_{12}, and C_{14} acids occur only in traces in a few fats. Of the acids characterized (Table 30.4), the majority are in the C_{18} series. Palmitoleic acid (C_{16}) occurs in nearly all fats but is most abundant in those of marine origin. Gadoleic (C_{20}) and cetoleic acid (C_{22}) have

TABLE 30.4   UNSATURATED FATTY ACIDS

ACID	CARBON ATOMS	FORMULA	M.P., °C.
Δ^9-Decylenic	10	$CH_2{=}CH(CH_2)_7COOH$	
Stillingic	10	$CH_3(CH_2)_4CH{=}CHCH{=}CHCOOH$ (*cis, trans*)	
Δ^9-Dodecylenic	12	$CH_3CH_2CH{=}CH(CH_2)_7COOH$	
Palmitoleic	16	$CH_3(CH_2)_5CH{=}CH(CH_2)_7COOH$ (*cis*)	
Oleic	18	$CH_3(CH_2)_7CH{=}CH(CH_2)_7COOH$ (*cis*)	13, 16
Ricinoleic	18	$CH_3(CH_2)_5CH(OH)CH_2CH{=}CH(CH_2)_7COOH$ (*cis*)	50
Petroselinic	18	$CH_3(CH_2)_{10}CH{=}CH(CH_2)_4COOH$ (*cis*)	30
Vaccenic	18	$CH_3(CH_2)_5CH{=}CH(CH_2)_9COOH$ (*cis* and *trans*)	
Linoleic	18	$CH_3(CH_2)_4CH{=}CHCH_2CH{=}CH(CH_2)_7COOH$	-5
Linolenic	18	$CH_3CH_2CH{=}CHCH_2CH{=}CHCH_2CH{=}CH(CH_2)_7COOH$	-11
Eleostearic	18	$CH_3(CH_2)_3(CH{=}CH)_3(CH_2)_7COOH$ (*cis, trans, trans*)	49
Punicic	18	$CH_3(CH_2)_3(CH{=}CH)_3(CH_2)_7COOH$ (*cis, trans, cis*)	44
Licanic	18	$CH_3(CH_2)_3(CH{=}CH)_3(CH_2)_4CO(CH_2)_2COOH$	75
Parinaric	18	$CH_3CH_2(CH{=}CH)_4(CH_2)_7COOH$	86
Gadoleic	20	$CH_3(CH_2)_9CH{=}CH(CH_2)_7COOH$	
Arachidonic	20	$CH_3(CH_2)_4(CH{=}CHCH_2)_4(CH_2)_2COOH$	
5-Eicosenic (65%)[1]	20	$CH_3(CH_2)_{13}CH{=}CH(CH_2)_3COOH$ (*cis*)	
5-Docosenic (7%)[1]	22	$CH_3(CH_2)_{15}CH{=}CH(CH_2)_3COOH$ (*cis*)	
Cetoleic	22	$CH_3(CH_2)_9CH{=}CH(CH_2)_9COOH$	
Erucic (13%)[1]	22	$CH_3(CH_2)_7CH{=}CH(CH_2)_{11}COOH$ (*cis*)	33.5
5,13-Docosadienic (10%)[1]	22	$CH_3(CH_2)_7CH{=}CH(CH_2)_6CH{=}CH(CH_2)_3COOH$ (*cis, cis*)	
Selacholeic or nervonic	24	$CH_3(CH_2)_7CH{=}CH(CH_2)_{13}COOH$ (*cis*)	39

[1] Percent of total acids of Californian *Limnanthes douglasii* seed oil, as determined at the Northern Regional Research Laboratory (I. A. Wolff *et al.*, 1960–61).

been isolated only from fish oils. Erucic acid (C_{22}) occurs in large amounts in the seed oils of rape, mustard, wallflower, and nasturtium. It can be isolated easily from the last source (80% of total acids) by crystallization from alcohol–water.

When heated under helium at 200° in the presence of a catalytic amount of selenium, oleic acid is transformed into the *trans* isomer, elaidic acid. The con-

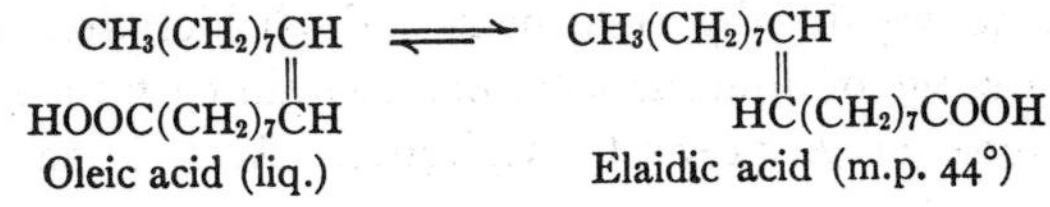

$$CH_3(CH_2)_7CH \rightleftharpoons CH_3(CH_2)_7CH$$
$$HOOC(CH_2)_7CH \qquad\qquad HC(CH_2)_7COOH$$

Oleic acid (liq.)   Elaidic acid (m.p. 44°)

version is an equilibrium process, and the same mixture, containing 66% of the *trans* form, is attained from either acid (M. Orchin,[1] 1957). The observation that the rate of isomerization increases with increasing initial selenium concentration (0.05 to 0.2%) suggests the formation of a π-complex between the olefinic substrate and the selenium, resulting in solution of the selenium. This complex appears to undergo both isomerization and irreversible conversion to a different species in which the selenium is catalytically inactive. The *trans, trans* isomer of linoleic acid is linelaidic acid; the *trans* isomer of erucic acid is brassidic acid.

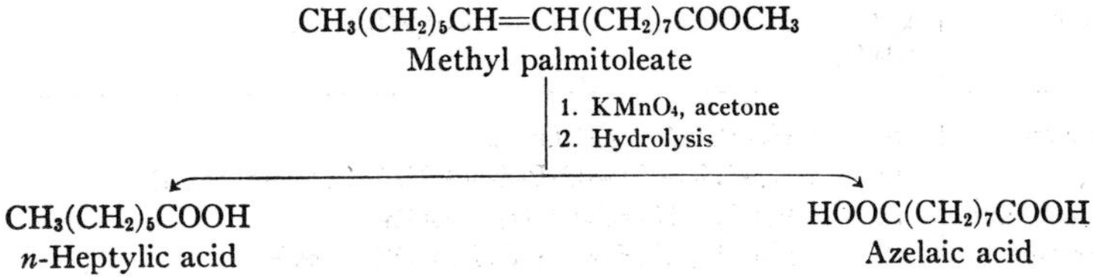

$$CH_3(CH_2)_5CH=CH(CH_2)_7COOCH_3$$
Methyl palmitoleate

1. $KMnO_4$, acetone
2. Hydrolysis

$CH_3(CH_2)_5COOH$ $HOOC(CH_2)_7COOH$
n-Heptylic acid   Azelaic acid

Elucidation of structure is done by oxidative fission and identification of the fragments. Oxidation of the methyl ester of a monoolefinic acid with perman-

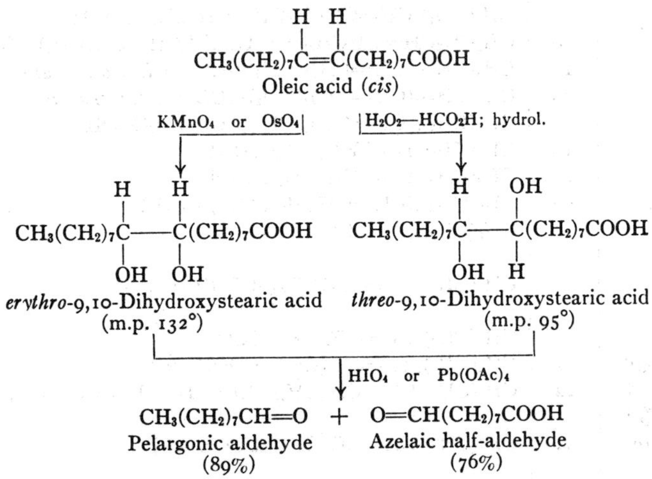

$$\underset{\text{Oleic acid }(cis)}{CH_3(CH_2)_7\overset{H}{C}=\overset{H}{C}(CH_2)_7COOH}$$

$KMnO_4$ or OsO_4 | | H_2O_2—HCO_2H; hydrol.

$$CH_3(CH_2)_7\underset{OH}{\overset{H}{C}}—\underset{OH}{\overset{H}{C}}(CH_2)_7COOH \qquad CH_3(CH_2)_7\underset{OH}{\overset{H}{C}}—\underset{H}{\overset{OH}{C}}(CH_2)_7COOH$$

erythro-9,10-Dihydroxystearic acid   *threo*-9,10-Dihydroxystearic acid
(m.p. 132°)   (m.p. 95°)

HIO_4 or $Pb(OAc)_4$

$$CH_3(CH_2)_7CH=O \; + \; O=CH(CH_2)_7COOH$$
Pelargonic aldehyde   Azelaic half-aldehyde
(89%)   (76%)

[1] Milton Orchin, b. 1914 Barnesboro, Pa.; Ph.D. Ohio State (Newman); U. S. Bur. Mines; Univ. Cincinnati

ganate in acetone affords a mixture of a monobasic and a dibasic acid from which the monobasic acid can be removed by extraction with petroleum ether (Hilditch,[1] 1925). The dibasic acid is always obtained in better yield (80–85%) than the monobasic acid (50–60%). In another procedure the double bond of an acid or ester is hydroxylated and the *vic*-glycol cleaved with lead tetraacetate or periodic acid. Ozonolysis is also useful (see p. 193). Acids with conjugated double bonds are conveniently characterized as the maleic anhydride adducts.

Many of the natural olefinic acids have been synthesized. One synthesis of vaccenic acid (F. M. Strong, 1948) involves in the first step condensation of the

$$CH_3(CH_2)_5C\equiv CNa + I(CH_2)_9Cl \xrightarrow[95\%]{NH_3} CH_3(CH_2)_5C\equiv C(CH_2)_9Cl \xrightarrow[85\%]{NaCN;\ KOH}$$

$$CH_3(CH_2)_5C\equiv C(CH_2)_9CO_2H \xrightarrow{Pd,\ H_2} CH_3(CH_2)_5\overset{H}{C}=\overset{H}{C}(CH_2)_9CO_2H$$

Vaccenic acid

$$CH_3(CH_2)_5\overset{H}{C}=\overset{H}{C}(CH_2)_7CO_2H + HO_2C(CH_2)_2CO_2CH_3 \xrightarrow{\quad} \Big\uparrow Electrol.\ (12\%)$$

sodio derivative of an alkyne with an α-iodo-ω-chloroalkane. The product is converted through the nitrile to the acetylenic acid, which is selectively hydrogenated to the *cis*-ethylenic acid. A second synthesis (R. P. Linstead, 1954) is by electrolysis of a mixture of palmitoleic acid with a large excess of methyl hydrogen succinate (followed by hydrolysis). A synthesis of linoleic acid described by R. A. Raphael[2] (1950) and improved by W. J. Gensler[3] also utilizes the convenient

$$CH_3(CH_2)_4C\equiv CCH_2Br + HC\equiv C(CH_2)_6Cl \xrightarrow{Cu_2Cl_2}$$
$$(1) \qquad\qquad\qquad (2)$$

$$CH_3(CH_2)_4C\equiv CCH_2C\equiv C(CH_2)_6Cl \xrightarrow{KI;\ Malonation}$$
$$(3)$$

$$CH_3(CH_2)_4C\equiv CCH_2C\equiv C(CH_2)_4CO_2H \xrightarrow{H_2,\ Pd}$$
$$(4)$$

$$CH_3(CH_2)_4\overset{H}{C}=\overset{H}{C}CH_2\overset{H}{C}=\overset{H}{C}(CH_2)_4CO_2H$$
Linoleic acid

acetylene approach. Raphael used the methanesulfonyl derivative in place of the bromide (1); Gensler found that the coupling of (1) with (2) is catalyzed by cuprous chloride.

30.4   Waxes. — Waxes differ from fats in that glycerol is replaced by a sterol or by higher even-numbered aliphatic alcohols from C_{16} to C_{36}. These often occur in excess of the acids, which are also even-numbered and range from C_{24} to C_{36}. Cerotic acid (L. *cera*, wax), a component of many waxes, is a

---

[1] Thomas Percy Hilditch, b. 1886 London; D.Sc. London (Collie, Smith, E. F. Armstrong); Univ. Liverpool

[2] Ralph A. Raphael, b. 1921 London; Ph.D. and D.Sc. London, Imperial College (Heilbron, E. R. H. Jones); Queen's Univ., Belfast; Univ. Glasgow

[3] Walter J. Gensler, b. 1917 Minneapolis, Minn.; Ph.D. Minnesota (Lauer); Boston Univ.

TABLE 30.5. ALCOHOLIC COMPONENTS OF WAXES

NAME	SOURCE	STRUCTURE	M.P., °C.
Cetyl alcohol	Sperm whale, porpoise	$CH_3(CH_2)_{14}CH_2OH$	49.3
n-Hexacosanol	Cocksfoot grass	$CH_3(CH_2)_{24}CH_2OH$	79.5
n-Octacosanol	Wheat	$CH_3(CH_2)_{26}CH_2OH$	83.4
n-Triacontanol	Lucerne leaf	$CH_3(CH_2)_{28}CH_2OH$	86.5
Cocceryl alcohol	Cochineal	$CH_3(CH_2)_{18}CO(CH_2)_{13}CH_2OH$	100.5
Oleyl alcohol	Sperm whale, porpoise	$CH_3(CH_2)_7CH=CH(CH_2)_7CH_2OH$	2

mixture of C_{24}, C_{26}, and C_{28} acids. Plant waxes also contain paraffin hydrocarbons. Several ketonic primary alcohols and some ketones have been isolated; e.g., palmitone, $CH_3(CH_2)_{14}CO(CH_2)_{14}CH_3$, and 10-hydroxypalmitone, $CH_3(CH_2)_{14}CO(CH_2)_5CHOH(CH_2)_8CH_3$, are found in sandalwood. It is extremely difficult to separate the individual alcohols, and Chibnall has shown that some of the alcohols claimed in the literature are in reality mixtures of even-numbered homologs. Occasionally only one alcohol is present, and its isolation in pure form is possible. Some of the identified alcohols are listed in Table 30.5.

30.5   Degras (Wool Fat). — Degras contains a minor amount of free acids (11%) and consists predominantly of esters of cholesterol, lanosterol, and three related C_{30} alcohols which, like lanosterol, are 4,4,14α-trimethylsterols.

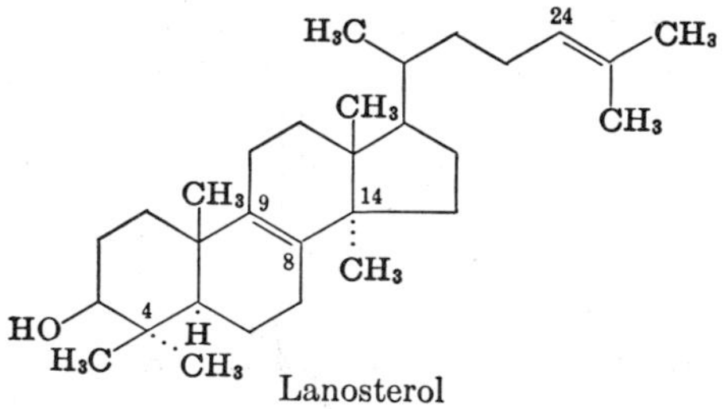

Lanosterol

Isolation and characterization of 32 acids from this source was accomplished by A. W. Weitkamp[1] (1945). He removed and discarded the free acids, saponified the esters, and fractionally distilled the methyl esters at 2 mm. pressure with a 44-in. column of an efficiency of 100 theoretical plates. Separation of binary mixtures was assisted by addition of a large volume of a uniformly boiling hydrocarbon oil carrier. The separated esters were saponified and the acids were all analyzed and the structures of the new ones elucidated. The acids fall into four groups: nine normal, even-carbon acids, C_{10} to C_{20}; optically active C_{14} and C_{18} α-hydroxy acids of the formula $CH_3(CH_2)_nCHOHCO_2H$; ten iso acids, $(CH_3)_2CH(CH_2)_nCO_2H$, C_{10} to C_{28}; eleven dextrorotatory odd-carbon anteiso acids, $CH_3CH_2CH(CH_3)(CH_2)_nCO_2H$, C_9 to C_{27} and C_{31}. A synthetic sample of one of the isoacids was available for comparison, but Weitkamp assigned struc-

[1] Alfred W. Weitkamp, b. 1909 Nickerson, Nebr.; Ph.D. Nebraska (C. S. Hamilton); Standard Oil Co. (Indiana)

tures to the other members of the series from determination of solidification point curves for binary mixtures of isoacids with n-acids. That a 1:1 mixture of the adjacent even-carbon natural acids (1) and (2) exhibits two transitions in the solidification diagram is attributed to intermolecular complex formation; one molecule fits the shape of the other. A normal acid (4) fits the shape of an isoacid (3) and gives rise to a two-transition solidification diagram only if the chain of the unbranched portion of the isoacid is the same as that of the normal acid. Structures assigned on this basis were later confirmed by synthesis. The anteiso series differs from the iso series in that the end group is sec-butyl instead of isopropyl. Binary solidification point curves with normal acids established the point of

branching, and the optical activity of the acids eliminated the only alternative structure, that with a terminal t-butyl group. The structures assigned were later confirmed by X-ray diffraction analysis and by synthesis (anodic coupling). The weakly dextrorotatory acids, of uniform molecular rotation, have been correlated with isoleucine and thus shown to belong to the L-series (L. Crombie, 1950).

$$
\begin{array}{cc}
\begin{array}{c}
CO_2H \\
| \\
(CH_2)_2 \\
| \\
H_3C-C-H \\
| \\
CH_2CH_3
\end{array}
&
\begin{array}{c}
CO_2H \\
| \\
H_2N-C-H \\
| \\
H_3C-C-H \\
| \\
CH_2CH_3 \\
\text{Isoleucine}
\end{array}
\end{array}
$$

30.6   **Drying Oils.** — Certain fatty oils possess the ability, when exposed on a surface to air, to form dry, tough, and durable films; 700–800 million pounds of drying oils are used each year in the United States, mainly in paints, which are drying oils with added pigments, and in varnishes, which differ from paints in containing resins. Oilcloth is made by applying several coats of linseed-oil paint to a woven canvas; linoleum is made by cementing cork particles with thickened linseed oil and rosin. The common drying oils are listed in Table 30.6; the first three are more properly known as semidrying oils, and are used only slightly in protective coatings. The main characteristic of drying oils is a high content of unsaturated fatty acids. Although linseed and perilla oils have particularly high iodine values, they contain isolated double bonds and do not dry so rapidly as oiticica and tung oils, in which the double bonds are conjugated.

$$CH_3(CH_2)_3\overset{13}{CH}=CHCH=\overset{11}{CHCH}=\overset{9}{CHCH_2}CH_2CH_2CH_2CH_2CH_2CH_2CO_2H$$
Eleostearic acid (tung oil)

$$CH_3(CH_2)_3\overset{13}{CH}=CHCH=\overset{11}{CHCH}=\overset{9}{CHCH_2}CH_2CH_2CH_2\overset{4}{C}OCH_2CH_2CO_2H$$
Licanic acid (oiticica oil)

TABLE 30.6.[1] DRYING OILS

Oil	Iodine value	Titer, °C.	Fatty acids, %						
			Palmitic	Stearic	Oleic	Linoleic	Linolenic	Licanic	Eleostearic
Cottonseed	103–111	32–38	21.0	2.0	33.0	43.5	....	....	....
Corn [2]	117–130	18–20	7.5	3.5	46.3	42.0	....	....	....
Soybean [2]	124–133	20–21	6.5	4.2	33.6	52.6	2.3	....	....
Oiticica	139–155	44–47	5.0	5.0	5.9	10.0	....	74.1	....
Tung	160–180	37–38	4.0	1.5	15.0	....	....	....	79.5
Linseed	170–185	19–21	5.0	3.5	5.0	61.5	25.0	....	....
Perilla	180–206	12–17	7.5	...	8.0	38.0	46.5	....	....

[1] Data of Werner G. Smith Company.
[2] Contains traces of arachidic and lignoceric acid.

The phenomenon of drying involves a process of oxidative polymerization. All unsaturated fatty acids and their glycerides are subject to air oxidation, the *cis* isomers being more susceptible than the *trans*. The reaction probably involves a chain reaction (4.16) leading to an unstable hydroperoxide, which decomposes to keto and hydroxyketo acids. An acid with an isolated double bond is attacked either at an allylic position (1) or at an unsaturated carbon atom (2) to give a radical; a conjugated system (3) is attacked more readily because the radical is more effectively stabilized by resonance.

Tung oil, once imported from China, is produced in Florida and currently costs $0.30/lb.; oiticica oil from Brazil costs $0.16/lb.; linseed oil, imported mainly from Argentina, costs $0.17/lb. Japanese perilla oil is comparable to linseed oil but is not imported by U. S. dealers. Raw (fresh) linseed oil dries only slowly, and use is recorded as early as A.D. 200 of the faster-drying boiled oil, made by heating linseed oil with lead oxide. Such an oil, however, is muddy owing to suspended insoluble lead salts; the driers in modern boiled oil are the soluble cobalt, manganese, and lead salts of linoleic, rosin, or naphthenic acids. The metal is the effective portion of the molecule; one part of cobalt is equivalent to eight parts of manganese or forty parts of lead. The drier can be incorporated at temperatures that do not induce decomposition of the oil. Application of heat promotes a chemical change; boiled oils are more viscous than raw oils, and eventually set to a gel if heating is prolonged. Bodying is also attained by blowing air at 120° through an oil in which the drier has been incorporated (blown oil). Stand oils are heat-bodied oils that do not contain driers.

30.7 **Soaps.** — Sodium salts are the most widely used soaps, but potassium soaps, which are softer and more soluble, serve special purposes (shaving cream, liquid soap). Natural or hardened fats are generally saponified with caustic soda, in slight excess of the theoretical amount, in an open kettle having at the bottom closed coils for indirect heating and perforated coils for direct heating through which steam can be passed at a rate to maintain agitation and ebullition. When the reaction is complete, salt is added to precipitate thick curds of the soap. The aqueous layer containing glycerol (sweet waters) is drawn off and concentrated to glycerol, which is refined by distillation in vacuum. In a process known as countercurrent hydrolysis (Ittner), advantage is taken of the fact that under pressure and at elevated temperatures water is soluble in fats to a considerable degree. Hot water is fed in near the top of the vessel and fat near the bottom. Split acids rise to the surface and are drawn off at the top, while glycerol is removed continuously in the water stream at the bottom. Hydrolysis proceeds substantially to completion and at a rapid rate even in the absence of a catalyst. Acids are obtained and are then saponified with soda ash, which costs about half as much as caustic soda. The crude curds contain glycerol, alkali, and salt; impurities are removed by boiling with sufficient water to form a homogeneous liquid, followed by reprecipitation of the soap with salt. In this way the soap is given several washings for recovery of glycerol and removal of impurities; then it is boiled with sufficient water to give a smooth mixture, which on standing separates into a homogeneous upper layer of kettle soap, and a diluted lye phase that contains nearly all the salt and excess alkali. Kettle soap contains 69–70% soap, 0.2–0.5% salt, and about 30% water; some is sold as such or after addition of perfume or dye for household purposes. Sand, sodium carbonate, and inert fillers are added for scouring soaps; cresol or other antiseptic for medicated soaps. Toilet soaps are made from kettle soap dried to a content of 85–90% and milled with perfume to thin shavings, which are then compacted in bars which are cut and pressed into cakes; transparent soaps are made by dissolving partly dried soap in alcohol. The specific gravity of ordinary soap is about 1.05, but by blowing air into hot molten kettle soap the specific gravity can be lowered to 0.8–0.9 (floating soap). In a newer process air is blown into dried soap chips at an elevated temperature, and the mass is then extruded.

Tallow (depot fat of cattle and sheep) is the most important soap stock. Soap made from tallow alone has excellent detergent and water-softening properties but must be used in hot water (tallow yields mainly C_{16} and C_{18} acids, whose soaps are only slightly soluble in water). The nut oils, coconut, babassu, and palm-kernel oil, are widely used in conjunction with tallow; their value lies in the high content of C_{12} and C_{14} acids, the soaps of which are firm and also readily soluble. Very unsaturated components cannot be used for soap since they are subject to oxidation.

Detergency is a complicated phenomenon. One important factor undoubtedly is the orientation of the molecules. I. Langmuir (1916–17) showed that a drop of fatty oil when placed on a clean surface of water spreads rapidly until it covers a definite area, when it spreads no farther. The area occupied by equivalent weights of homologous fatty acids from palmitic to cerotic is identical, though the depth of the film increases with increasing chain length. These films consist of monomolecular layers, in which the —COONa group is dipped in water and the hydrocarbon part directed away from water. This behavior is a property of substances that contain both a hydrophilic and a hydrophobic group, but the effect of each must be properly balanced or the molecule will be in one phase more than the other. Langmuir found that ricinoleic acid lies almost flat on the surface, an effect ascribable to the presence of a second hydrophilic group in the center of the molecule. Sodium ricinoleate is an inferior detergent. It is possible to build films in which monomolecular layers are superimposed, with the like groups adjacent to each other (Langmuir and K. B. Blodgett). If the carboxyl groups are directed outward in the last layer, the surface can be wetted by water but cannot if the hydrocarbon residues are outermost. The most striking characteristic of soap solutions is the reduction of surface tension (gas–liquid system) or of interfacial tension (liquid–liquid system). The surface tension of pure water is 73 dynes/cm.; that of solutions of sodium oleate or linoleate is about 25 dynes/cm.; of sodium laurate, myristate, and palmitate from 25 to 30 dynes/cm. Substances that lower surface or interfacial tension are known as surface-active compounds. These all contain a hydrophilic and a hydrophobic group, preferably at opposite ends of the molecule, which may be a long chain as in soap or a complicated ring system.

Satisfactory detergency is first noted with the laurates and myristates, which are often employed in soaps intended for use in sea water, since they are more soluble in salt solution than the higher soaps. Soaps of fatty acids above C_{22} are unsuitable, since they are practically insoluble in water at room temperature. Detergency generally consists in removal of oil or grease or of solid particles dispersed in oil, and photographic studies have shown that, in the initial stages, the oil is displaced from fiber by soap solution (wetting action) to form large globules that can be detached by jarring and finally dispersed (emulsified) in the aqueous solution. Emulsions consist of fine droplets of one liquid dispersed in an immiscible liquid. The particles are kept from coalescing by a protective film of an emulsifier. This stabilizing action can be correlated with surface activity and is shown by soaps and other polar-nonpolar compounds. Emulsifiers are almost always soluble in the external phase but insoluble in the dispersed liquid, and hence soaps show a detergent effect only when in solution. Foams are similar to emulsions except that gas is dispersed in a liquid, and these are also stabilized by surface-active compounds that lower surface tension at the gas–liquid interface.

30.8   Synthetic Surface-Active Compounds. — Soap is still the most widely used detergent, but it has definite limitations: it is unstable in acid solutions, and many of its salts are insoluble. In hard water, which contains calcium and magnesium ions, insoluble soaps are formed by metathesis. This reaction can be prevented by large amounts of tetrasodium pyrophosphate, sodium hexametaphosphate, or similar substances which are considered to function by forming water-soluble complexes with the objectionable metallic ions. The first synthetic compounds to compete with soap were developed about 1860, and are sulfonated (actually sulfated) oils made by treating unsaturated oils, mainly castor oil, with concentrated sulfuric acid. Sulfonated castor oil is known as Turkey-red oil (I), since it is most widely used as an assistant (wetting agent) in Turkey-red dyeing with ground madder root, which contains alizarin as the active principle. Turkey-red oil soaps are not particularly good detergents.

$$CH_3(CH_2)_5CHCH_2CH=CH(CH_2)_7COOH$$
$$\underset{OSO_3H}{|}$$

Turkey-red oil (I)

A group of detergents introduced in Germany about 1930 are sulfates of long-chain alcohols prepared by hydrogenation of fats. Compounds containing 10 to 14 carbon atoms are most useful and are prepared from nut oils. They are more

$$RCOOH \longrightarrow RCH_2OH \xrightarrow{O(SO_2ONa)_2} RCH_2OSO_2ONa$$

resistant to hard water, and since, unlike soap, they are salts of strong acids, they are more stable in solutions of low pH. The sodium salt of the monosulfate of a monoglyceride is an excellent nonsoapy detergent. Syntex M is a typical member of this class:

$$CH_2OCO(CH_2)_{10}CH_3$$
$$|$$
$$CHOH$$
$$|$$
$$CH_2OSO_2ONa$$

Sodium glyceryl monolaurate sulfate (Syntex M)

Sulfonates of succinic esters show pronounced wetting characteristics. In this case the solubilizing group is located near the center of the chain, as shown by formula II for a typical member of this class. The preparation involves reaction between the appropriate alcohol and maleic anhydride, followed by addition of sodium bisulfite. Alkylaryl sodium sulfonates of the type $R \cdot Ar \cdot SO_3Na$ are

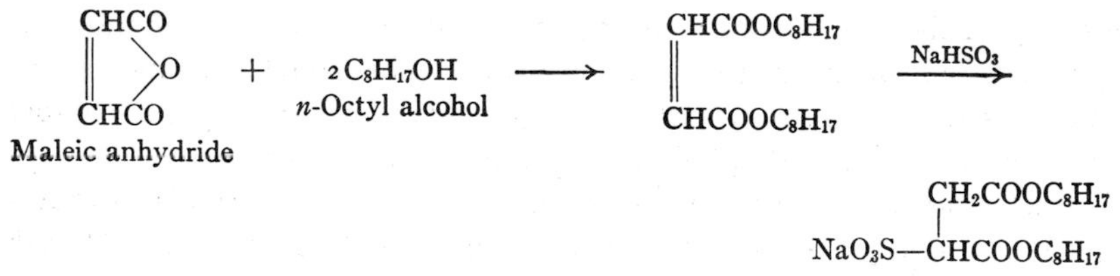

$$\underset{CHCO}{\overset{CHCO}{\big|\big|}}\!\!\!>\!\!O \quad + \quad 2\,C_8H_{17}OH \longrightarrow \underset{CHCOOC_8H_{17}}{\overset{CHCOOC_8H_{17}}{\big|\big|}} \xrightarrow{NaHSO_3}$$

Maleic anhydride n-Octyl alcohol

$$CH_2COOC_8H_{17}$$
$$|$$
$$NaO_3S-CHCOOC_8H_{17}$$

Dioctyl sodium sulfosuccinate (Aerosol OT)

II

produced in quantity and at a price that competes with soap, since the long-chain alkyl group is derived from petroleum. The manufacturing process involves chlorination of a kerosene fraction, condensation with an aromatic hydrocarbon, and sulfonation of the aromatic nucleus. Alkyl sulfonates, RSO_3Na, are made by alkaline hydrolysis of sulfonyl chlorides resulting from the action of sulfur dioxide and chlorine on petroleum hydrocarbons under illumination; optimum detergency is attained in the range C_{13}–C_{18}, and higher members are used in textile finishing.

Resistance to hard water is attained in another type of detergent by blocking the carboxyl group so that it is unable to react with metals. The earliest, the German product Igepon A, is sodium β-oleylethanesulfonate (III) and is made by esterification of oleic acid with isethionic acid, with subsequent saponification (neutralization). Igepon A is not stable in an alkaline medium owing to hydrolysis

$$CH_3(CH_2)_7CH=CH(CH_2)_7COOH \;+\; HOCH_2CH_2SO_3H \longrightarrow$$

Oleic acid	Isethionic acid

$$CH_3(CH_2)_7CH=CH(CH_2)_7COOCH_2CH_2SO_3Na$$

Igepon A (III)

at the ester grouping; the defect is corrected by use of an amide linkage, —CONH—, as in Igepon T (IV):

$$CH_3(CH_2)_7CH=CH(CH_2)_7COOH \;+\; CH_3NHCH_2CH_2SO_3H \longrightarrow$$

Oleic acid	N-Methyltaurine

$$CH_3(CH_2)_7CH=CH(CH_2)_7CO-N(CH_3)CH_2CH_2SO_3Na$$

Igepon T (IV)

In a third type of surface-active agent, the problem of precipitation of insoluble soaps in hard water is solved by use of nonionizing hydrophilic groups. One group is made by partially esterifying polyglycerol or pentaerythritol, $C(CH_2OH)_4$, with one molecule of a fatty acid. Polyglycerol is a condensation product of glycerol in which several molecules have been condensed to both open-chain

$$CH_2OHCHOHCH_2-O-CH_2CHOHCH_2OH$$

V

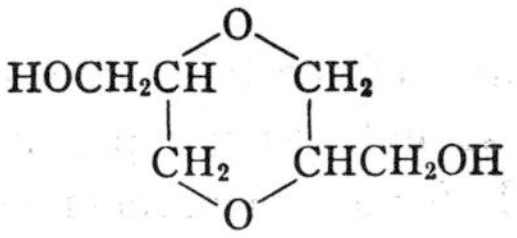

$$\begin{array}{c} O \\ HOCH_2CH \quad CH_2 \\ | \qquad\quad | \\ CH_2 \quad CHCH_2OH \\ O \end{array}$$

VI

and cyclic ethers of the types V and VI. Satisfactory detergents can be prepared by esterifying a polyglycerol corresponding to a pentaglycerol with one molecule of a fatty acid. In pentaerythritol monostearate and monolaurate the unesterified hydroxyl groups serve as the water-attracting groups; several are required because the hydroxyl group is less hydrophilic than sulfate, carboxyl, or sulfonate groups (listed in the approximate order of decreasing effectiveness). Similar surface-active agents are glycol esters of fatty acids, prepared by treating the acid with ethylene oxide. A third group is made by the following reactions:

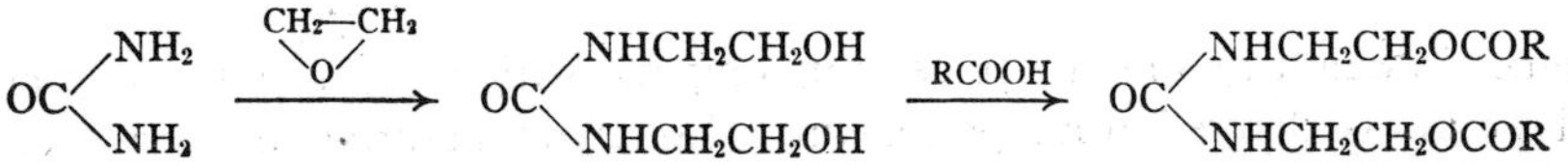

$$OC\begin{array}{c} NH_2 \\ NH_2 \end{array} \xrightarrow{CH_2-CH_2 \; (O)} OC\begin{array}{c} NHCH_2CH_2OH \\ NHCH_2CH_2OH \end{array} \xrightarrow{RCOOH} OC\begin{array}{c} NHCH_2CH_2OCOR \\ NHCH_2CH_2OCOR \end{array}$$

Substances of the ester type are not particularly good detergents but are useful wetting agents.

The triethanolamine salts of fatty acids are purely organic soaps. These are excellent emulsifiers and good dry-cleaning soaps, since they are soluble in organic solvents. Another interesting type is known as an invert soap or a cation-active compound (VII) since the organic part is positively charged, whereas in ordinary

$$\left[R_1{-}\overset{\overset{\displaystyle R_2}{|}}{\underset{\underset{\displaystyle R_3}{|}}{N^+}}{-}R_4 \right] Cl^-$$

VII

$$[C_{17}H_{33}CONHCH_2CH_2\overset{+}{N}(CH_3)_3]_2SO_4^=$$

VIII

soaps the organic part is negatively charged. Invert soaps cannot react with heavy-metal ions, which are similarly charged; they are used in neutral or acid solution. One alkyl group must be a long chain; the others can be methyl or ethyl. The Sapamines are prepared from a fatty acid and an unsymmetrical dialkyl-diamine, followed by alkylation. A typical Sapamine derived from oleic acid is shown in formula VIII. Invert soaps exhibit marked bactericidal activity (Zephiran), although their use is limited due to high toxicity. 1-Lauryl-3-ethyl-benzotriazolium bromide (IX) is particularly active; it kills Staphylococcus of several strains at a dilution of 1:600,000 (R. Kuhn).

IX

30.9   **Natural Acetylenic Acids.** — In 1892 Arnaud[1] investigated the seed fat of a species of *Picramnia tariri* from Guatemala and found it to consist essentially of the glyceride of a single fatty acid, which he named tariric acid. Unlike most glycerides, including synthetic tristearin and tripalmitin, tritaririn separates from a chilled ether solution in "magnificent crystals" (m.p. 47°). Arnaud established the formula $C_{18}H_{32}O_2$ for the acid (m.p. 50.5°), reported the preparation of a dibromide (m.p. 32°) and a tetrabromide (m.p. 125°), and then leisurely continued investigation of the structure. Since the technique of catalytic hydrogenation had not yet been developed, he tried various chemical reductions and in 1896 effected reduction by heating tariric acid with hydriodic acid and red phosphorus in a sealed tube at 210° for 10 hours. The product was stearic acid. Tariric acid is considerably higher melting than any known C_{18}-dienic acids, but the melting point is close to that of synthetic stearolic acid (m.p. 48°), now obtainable by dehydrobromination of methyl oleate dibromide

$$CH_3(CH_2)_7C{\equiv}C(CH_2)_7CO_2H$$
Stearolic acid

with sodamide in liquid ammonia (6.4). Since in this series absence of a depression in the melting point of a mixture is not conclusive evidence of identity, Arnaud compared the solubilities of a series of salts of the two acids and satisfied himself that they are different. In 1902 he reported that tariric acid on oxidation with

$$CH_3(CH_2)_{10}C{\equiv}C(CH_2)_4CO_2H \longrightarrow CH_3(CH_2)_{10}CO_2H \;+\; HO_2C(CH_2)_4CO_2H$$
Tariric acid   Lauric acid   Adipic acid

[1] Albert Arnaud, 1853–1915; b. Paris; Ph.D. Paris (Chevreul); Muséum National d'Histoire Naturelle

either alkaline permanganate or nitric acid affords adipic and lauric acids and therefore is the 6,7-acetylenic derivative of stearic acid.

The synthesis of tariric acid was accomplished by P. B. Lumb and J. C. Smith[1] (1952) as follows. The ester $CH_2=CH(CH_2)_8CO_2C_2H_5$ (pyrolysis of castor oil, 8.3) was hydrogenated (Raney Ni) and the saturated ester reduced (Na, C_2H_5OH) to the alcohol, which afforded the corresponding bromide. This was condensed

$$CH_3(CH_2)_{10}Br \xrightarrow{NaC\equiv CH} CH_3(CH_2)_{10}C\equiv CH \longrightarrow [CH_3(CH_2)_{10}C\equiv C]_2Hg$$

$$\xrightarrow{Li} CH_3(CH_2)_{10}C\equiv CLi \xrightarrow{ICH_2CH_2CH_2Cl} CH_3(CH_2)_{10}C\equiv CCH_2CH_2CH_2Cl$$

$$\xrightarrow{Na\overset{+}{C}H(CO_2C_2H_5)_2} CH_3(CH_2)_{10}C\equiv CCH_2CH_2CH_2CH(CO_2C_2H_5)_2 \xrightarrow[\text{2. Heat}]{\text{1. KOH}}$$

$$CH_3(CH_2)_{10}C\equiv C(CH_2)_4CO_2H \xrightarrow{H_2, Ni} CH_3(CH_2)_{10}\overset{H}{C}=\overset{H}{C}(CH_2)_4CO_2H$$
$$\text{Tariric acid} \qquad\qquad\qquad \text{Petroselinic acid}$$

with sodium acetylide to produce undecylacetylene. Attempts to convert this into a lithium derivative by a direct method were unsuccessful, but the derivative was obtained via the mercury derivative and condensed with 1-chloro-3-iodopropane (from $ClCH_2CH_2CH_2Cl$ and NaI in acetone). The resulting chloride was condensed with sodiomalonic ester, and saponification and decarboxylation gave material identical with natural tariric acid. Selective hydrogenation in a neutral aqueous solution of the sodium salt gave the corresponding *cis* ethylenic acid, identical with natural petroselinic acid.

The synthesis of erythrogenic acid (6.7) is one of many examples of the use of oxidative coupling of terminal acetylenes in the synthesis of diacetylenic acids related to the natural acetylenic hydrocarbons (6.21).

A most unusual unsaturated acid is mycomycin, an optically active antibiotic elaborated by the fungus *Norcardia acidophilis*. The substance was discovered in 1947 by E. A. Johnson and K. L. Burdon of the department of bacteriology, Baylor Medical School, who extracted filtered and acidified broth with hexane, and then found that extraction of the hexane solution with sodium phosphate buffer removed an acidic substance exhibiting absorption maxima at 267 and 281 mμ, which could be correlated with the microbiological activity. Extreme sensitivity to heat was evidenced by rapid loss of both ultraviolet absorption and antibiotic activity unless the concentrates were stored at dry ice temperature. Isolation of the pure substance and elucidation of its structure was accomplished in 1952–53 by W. D. Celmer[2] and I. A. Solomons. Concentration was effected by an eight-plate countercurrent distribution of a dilute solution of the antibiotic between chloroform and cold 2% pH 7.0 phosphate buffer, conducted in a nitrogen atmosphere. The antibiotic was finally obtained as white needles which exploded at about 75° in a capillary tube sealed with nitrogen. Repeated low-

[1] John Charles Smith, b. 1900 Wellington, New Zealand; Ph.D. Manchester (R. Robinson), D.Sc. Oxford; Oxford Univ.

[2] Walter D. Celmer, b. 1925 Plymouth, Penna.; Ph.D. Illinois (Carter); Pfizer and Co.

temperature recrystallization did not alter the ultraviolet spectrum or improve the stability.

Mycomycin is strongly levorotatory (αD $-130°$) and has the formula $C_{13}H_{10}O_2$. The two oxygen atoms are present in a carboxyl group, since the neutralization equivalent found (200) agreed with that calculated (198). On catalytic hydrogenation, 1.01 millimoles of substance (200 mg.) consumed 7.8 millimoles of hydrogen and afforded *n*-tridecanoic acid, $CH_3(CH_2)_{11}CO_2H$. In view of the extreme sensitivity of mycomycin, Celmer and Solomons undertook to isolate and characterize a transformation product, and found that when excess sodium hydroxide is added to mycomycin, the crystalline salt of an isomeric acid, isomycomycin, separates within a few minutes. This isomer also absorbs eight moles of hydrogen and yields *n*-tridecanoic acid and hence has the original straight chain of thirteen carbon atoms. However, it is optically inactive. Kuhn-Roth determination established that whereas mycomycin contains no C-methyl groups, one such group is present in isomycomycin. This can only be a terminal methyl group (C_{13}). The terminal part of the hydrocarbon chain in mycomycin was recognized as $HC{\equiv}C-$ from the observation that the methyl ester forms a silver derivative on treatment with alcoholic silver nitrate. Both acids show an infrared absorption band at 1730 cm^{-1} characteristic of nonconjugated acids and superposable with the carboxyl band of *n*-tridecanoic acid, and therefore contain the grouping $-CH_2CO_2H$. Isomycomycin, in contrast to mycomycin, reacts very readily with maleic anhydride to form a Diels-Alder adduct. This reaction provided evidence of the presence of a conjugated diene system, $C{=}C-C{=}C$, since addition to an eneyne system, $C{=}C-C{\equiv}C$, could afford only an excessively strained allene-containing ring.

Analysis of the infrared spectra and comparison with the spectra of matricaria methyl ester and other related or model compounds led to complete elucidation

$$\begin{array}{cc} H\ H & H\ H \\ CH_3C{=}CC{\equiv}CC{\equiv}CC{=}CCO_2CH_3 \end{array}$$
Matricaria methyl ester

of the complicated unsaturated systems of the two acids and of the stereochemistry. Thus the spectrum of mycomycin has characteristic bands at 3180, 2200, 1930 cm.$^{-1}$ attributable to $RC{\equiv}C-H$ (monosubstituted acetylene), to $RC{\equiv}CR$, and to the allene system (C_7-C_9), respectively. Fine structure spacing in the characteristic ultraviolet absorption bands showed that the mono and disubsti-

$$HC{\equiv}C-C{\equiv}C-CH{=}C{=}CH-\overset{H}{\underset{13\ 12\ 11\ 10\ 9\ 8\ 7\ 6\ 5}{C}}{=}\overset{H}{\underset{}{C}}-\overset{H}{\underset{3\ 2\ 1}{C}}{=}C-CH_2CO_2H \xrightarrow{OH^-}$$
Mycomycin

$$CH_3-C{\equiv}C-C{\equiv}C-C{\equiv}C-\overset{H}{\underset{13\ 12\ 11\ 10\ 9\ 8\ 7\ 6}{C}}{=}\overset{H}{\underset{}{C}}-\overset{H}{\underset{3\ 2\ 1}{C}}{=}C-CH_2CO_2H$$
Isomycomycin

tuted acetylenic bonds are conjugated (C_{10}–C_{13}). A 3,5-diene system was recognized in both isomers; the configurations, deducible from the infrared spectra, are: mycomycin, 3 (*trans*), 5 (*cis*); isomycomycin, 3 (*trans*), 5 (*trans*). *Trans, trans* dienes are known to undergo Diels-Alder addition much more readily than *trans, cis* dienes, but the failure of mycomycin to react with maleic anhydride could not be taken as evidence of its configuration because of the instability of the antibiotic.

The optical activity of mycomycin is accounted for by the presence of an unsymmetrically substituted allene grouping. The asymmetry is destroyed on isomerization with alkali to isomycomycin. This remarkable reaction involves an allene → acetylene isomerization, an acetylene migration, and a *trans, cis* to *trans, trans* isomerization.

Two similar highly unsaturated antibiotics isolated from fungus cultures, nemotinic acid and nemotin, have been characterized (E. R. H. Jones, 1955). The acid has a pair of conjugated acetylenic linkages and an asymmetrically

$$CH\equiv CC\equiv CCH=C=CHCH(OH)CH_2CH_2CO_2H$$
Nemotinic acid

substituted allene grouping and is optically active. Nemotin is the corresponding γ-lactone.

30.10   Bacterial Lipids. — Certain bacteria, including the infectious bacteria of tuberculosis and of leprosy, are called acid-fast because, although they are stained only with some difficulty by rosaniline, a basic triphenylmethane dye, they tenaciously retain dye once applied and, unlike other nonacid-fast bacteria, are not decolorized by vigorous washing with alcoholic acid. Both the slow penetration of dye and the fastness to acid are attributable to the presence of a characteristic fatty envelope. As part of a cooperative project sponsored by the American Tuberculosis Association, which involved culturing of human tubercle bacilli on the huge scale required for chemical investigation of different constituents, R. J. Anderson,[1] experienced in sterol chemistry, undertook investigation of the lipid components of the fatty capsules (1927). The nonsaponifiable fraction contained no sterols. The fatty acids present were found esterified not with glycerol, even though the organisms had been grown on a medium in which glycerol was the chief carbon source, but with the nonreducing α,α-disaccharide trehalose, previously isolated from ergot of rye and other fungi (hydrogen bonding probably forces one ring to lay over the other).

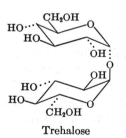
Trehalose

The fatty acid mixture resulting on saponification was unusual. Relatively large amounts of palmitic acid were present, but only traces of the usual C_{18} fatty acids. Instead, a number of unique acids are present. One, named tuberculostearic acid, was shown by various degradations to be 10-methylstearic acid. It is interesting that the branching methyl substituent lowers the melting point

[1] Rudolph J. Anderson, 1879–1960; b. Harna, Sweden; Ph.D. Cornell; Yale Univ.

from 70° (stearic) to 10–11°. Although the natural acid seemed to be optically inactive, Cason later suspected that the substance is one of a pair of epimers of very weak rotatory power, an inference established by synthesis of the (+) and (−) forms. Decanol-2 was resolved by reaction with phthalic anhydride and crystallization of the brucine salt of the resulting acid phthalate. Each active form of the alcohol was then put through the synthetic sequence shown. The

$$n\text{-}C_8H_{17}\overset{*}{C}HOH \longrightarrow RBr \longrightarrow RCH(CO_2C_2H_5)_2 \longrightarrow RCH_2CO_2H \longrightarrow$$
$$\underset{|}{\phantom{n\text{-}C_8H_{17}}}\underset{CH_3}{}$$
$$(ROH)$$

$$RCH_2CO_2C_2H_5 \longrightarrow RCH_2CH_2OH \longrightarrow RCH_2CH_2Br \xrightarrow{\overset{Mg;}{CdCl_2}}$$

$$n\text{-}C_8H_{17}CHCH_2CH_2CdCl \quad (+ \; ClC(CH_2)_5CO_2C_2H_5) \longrightarrow$$
$$\underset{CH_3}{\overset{|}{}} \qquad\qquad\qquad \overset{\parallel}{\underset{O}{}}$$

$$n\text{-}C_8H_{17}CHCH_2CH_2CO(CH_2)_5CO_2C_2H_5 \xrightarrow{\overset{Zn\text{-}HCl;}{NaOH}}$$
$$\underset{CH_3}{\overset{|}{}}$$

$$\overset{10}{CH_3CH_2CH_2CH_2CH_2CH_2CH_2\overset{|}{C}HCH_2CH_2CH_2CH_2CH_2CH_2CH_2CO_2H}$$
$$\underset{CH_3}{\overset{|}{}}$$

Tuberculostearic acid

very weakly rotatory active forms melt at 13° and the *dl*-form at 26°. A mixture of the natural acid with the (−) form melted at 11–12° and a mixture with the (+) form at 25°; tuberculostearic acid is thus identified as the (−)-epimer.

A second novel component isolated by Anderson (1929, 1936) was named phthioic acid and characterized as an acid of the probable formula $C_{26}H_{52}O_2$, m.p. 20°, α_D +12.6°. This substance attracted considerable interest because on interperitoneal injection into normal animals it produced typical tubercular lesions. Cason later (1951) made a careful distillation analysis of 24 g. of crude methyl ester obtained from Anderson. This was fractionally distilled at 2 mm. pressure through a 4-ft. column and 39 fractions were characterized as to boiling point, refractive index, optical activity, and ultraviolet absorption. The results suggested the presence of at least twelve compounds ranging in molecular weight from C_{23} to C_{31}. Constancy of all properties indicated that fractions 17–20 contained a single, pure ester component. The corresponding acid, named C_{27}-phthienoic acid, was assigned the formula $C_{27}H_{52}O_2$ and had the constants: m.p. 22° and 31° (polymorphic forms), α_D + 17.8°; $n_D^{25°}$ 1.4666; λ216 mμ; 4 methyl groups (Kuhn-Roth); methyl ester, m.p. 14°, 31°; α_D +14.7°; $n_D^{25°}$ 1.4666; λ218 mμ. The ultraviolet absorption is that characteristic of α,β-unsaturated acids, and Cason drew the further inference that the chromophoric system is α-substituted: $-CH{=}C(R)CO_2H$. C_{27}-Phthienoic acid proved comparable to Anderson's phthioic acid in capacity for producing tubercular lesions in test animals. Cason (1956) investigated the fatty acids of an avirulent (noninfectious) strain of tubercle bacilli and did not find C_{27}-phthienoic acid.

A different method of separation was employed in an independent investigation by Polgar[1] (1948–54) of lipid material (145 g.) prepared by the Glaxo Laboratories by extraction of 50 lbs. of steam-killed cells (*B. tuberculosis*, human type) in a Soxhlet apparatus with acetone (30 l.) and then with diisopropyl ether. Extensive processing afforded 2.6 g. of a solid product characterized as a mixture of a saturated acid and an unsaturated component which Polgar named mycolipenic acid. Since the pure acid was not isolated, comparison could not be made with Cason's acid. However, the saturated component present did not interfere with establishment of the structure of mycolipenic acid. Ozonization of the mixture gave pyruvic acid, consistent with the formulation as an α-methyl α,β-unsaturated acid. Permanganate oxidation of the methyl ester mixture left the saturated component unchanged and gave an acid II, characterized as an α-methyl acid by Barbier-Wieland degradation to the methyl ketone V (CHI$_3$ test) by the steps:

$$RCH(CH_3)CO_2CH_3 \ + \ 2\ C_6H_5MgBr \ \longrightarrow \ RCH(CH_3)C(OH)(C_6H_5)_2 \ \longrightarrow$$
$$RC(CH_3){=}C(C_6H_5)_2 \ \longrightarrow \ RC(CH_3){=}O.$$

The ketone V was isolated as a by-product of oxidation of I to II. The saturated acid II was converted through the α-bromo acid to the α,β-unsaturated acid III, which on oxidation (as ester) gave, in part, the optically inactive methyl ketone IV. The semicarbazone, m.p. 125°, did not depress the melting point of the semicarbazones of either n-C$_{18}$H$_{37}$COCH$_3$ or n-C$_{17}$H$_{35}$COCH$_3$, both of which melt at 126°, but X-ray crystallographic comparison established identity with the former. The structure I was later confirmed by synthesis and the synthetic

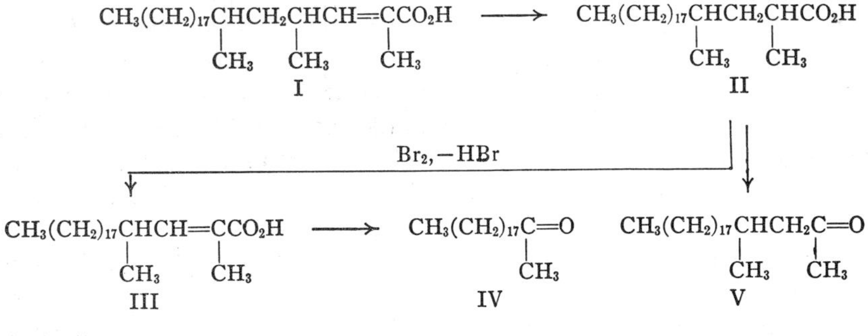

acid shown by infrared comparison to be identical with Cason's C$_{27}$-phthienoic acid (C. and J. Asselineau, S. Ställberg-Stenhagen, and E. Stenhagen, Göteborg, 1956).

It is of interest that chaulmoogra oil, a fatty acid glyceride, has been used for centuries in India and China for treatment of the two diseases caused by fat encapsulated, acid-fast bacteria, leprosy and tuberculosis. The oil is usually administered orally and, since it is irritating in large amounts, treatment must be

[1] Nicholas Polgar, b. 1904 Budapest; Ph.D. Vienna (Späth); D.Phil. Oxford (Robinson); Oxford Univ.

extended over years.　The glycerides are probably converted in the body to the free fatty acids, which are the active agents; the acids themselves are effective when administered in suitably dispersed form (in stearic acid).　Chaulmoogra oil

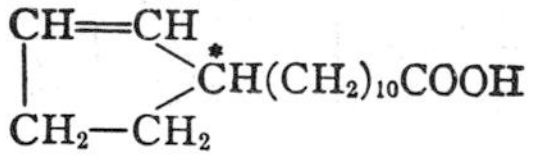

$$CH=\!\!=\!\!CH$$
$$| \qquad\!\! \overset{\textstyle *}{>}CH(CH_2)_{10}COOH$$
$$CH_2\!\!-\!\!CH_2$$

Hydnocarpic acid ($C_{16}H_{28}O_2$)
$[\alpha]_D + 68°$; m.p. 59–60°

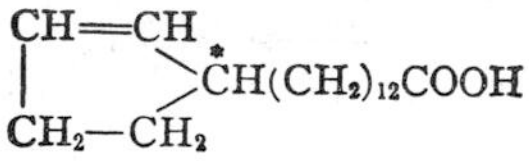

$$CH=\!\!=\!\!CH$$
$$| \qquad\!\! \overset{\textstyle *}{>}CH(CH_2)_{12}COOH$$
$$CH_2\!\!-\!\!CH_2$$

Chaulmoogric acid ($C_{18}H_{32}O_2$)
$[\alpha]_D + 56°$; m.p. 71°

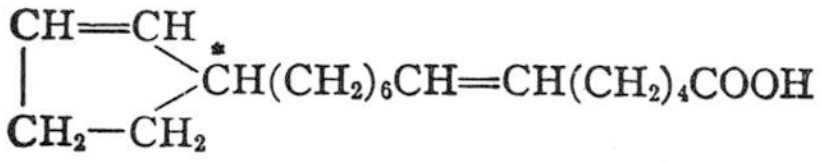

$$CH=\!\!=\!\!CH$$
$$| \qquad\!\! \overset{\textstyle *}{>}CH(CH_2)_6CH=\!\!=\!\!CH(CH_2)_4COOH$$
$$CH_2\!\!-\!\!CH_2$$

Gorlic acid ($C_{18}H_{30}O_2$)
$[\alpha]_D + 61°$; m.p. 6°

is the native name (East Indian) for the seed fat of *Hydnocarpus kurzii*.　Investigations by F. B. Power (Wellcome Chem. Res. Lab., London, 1904–07) and by R. L. Shriner[1] and R. Adams (1925) established the structures of the main acid components, hydnocarpic acid and chaulmoogric acid, of minor components having shorter side chains (n = 8, 6, 4), and of a dienic acid component, gorlic acid.　R. Adams synthesized a large number of analogous cyclopentane acids and branched chain acids and found that leprocidal activity *in vitro* parallels ability of the acids to depress surface tension; probably the antibacterial activity is a result of impairment of the fatty envelope of the bacilli.

The bacillus of diphtheria is related to those of tuberculosis and leprosy.　It is not acid fast, but has the related classification of Gram positive.　Hans C. J. Gram, a Danish physician, developed (1884) a technique for staining bacteria with the basic triphenylmethane dye gentian violet and iodine.　Cells that retain the dye after washing with alcohol or acetone are Gram positive, those that are decolorized are Gram negative.　Lederer[2] (1951–) found the lipids of *Mycobacterium tuberculosis* to contain a series of acid components of the type $RCHOHCHR'CO_2H$, called mycolic acids.　Two related acids were isolated from the lipids of *Corynebacterium diphtheria*.　One pure component acid, corynomycolenic acid (oil, $n_D^{25°}$ 1.4758; methyl ester, α_D +9°), was characterized by degradation as having the structure XII, shown below, which was confirmed by synthesis.　The key step required conversion of an acid, RCO_2H, into a β-keto ester of the type $RCOCHR'CO_2Et$, and this was accomplished by use of a neat synthetic method introduced by R. E. Bowman and W. D. Fordham (Birkbeck Coll., London, 1952).　An alkyl-substituted malonic ester (I) is saponified with exactly one equivalent of alcoholic potassium hydroxide to produce the half ester (II) and, for protection of the free acid group, this is condensed with dihydropyrane in benzene solution with *p*-toluenesulfonic acid as catalyst to give (III).　Condensation of the sodio derivative of (III) with an acid chloride gives (IV),

[1] Ralph L. Shriner, b. 1899 Iowa City; Ph.D. Illinois (R. Adams); N. Y. Expt. Sta., Illinois, State Univ. Iowa

[2] Edgar Lederer, b. 1908 Vienna; Ph.D. Vienna (Späth); Pasteur Institute; Sorbonne, Paris

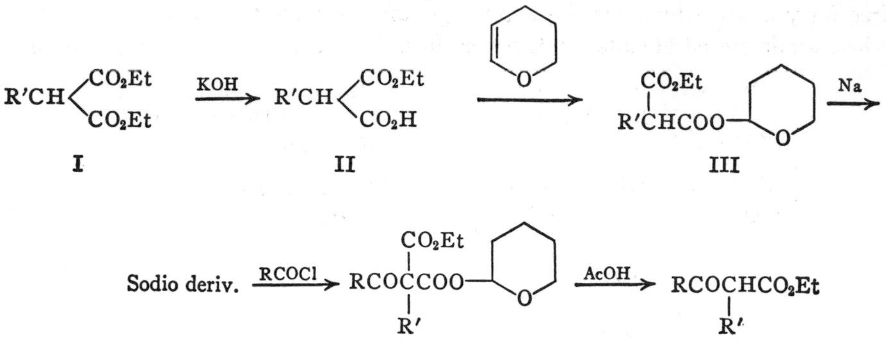

$$R'CH\begin{smallmatrix}CO_2Et\\CO_2Et\end{smallmatrix} \xrightarrow{KOH} R'CH\begin{smallmatrix}CO_2Et\\CO_2H\end{smallmatrix} \longrightarrow \begin{smallmatrix}CO_2Et\\R'CHCOO-\end{smallmatrix}\text{(pyran)} \xrightarrow{Na}$$

$$\text{I} \qquad\qquad \text{II} \qquad\qquad\qquad \text{III}$$

$$\text{Sodio deriv.} \xrightarrow{RCOCl} \begin{smallmatrix}CO_2Et\\RCOCCOO-\\R'\end{smallmatrix}\text{(pyran)} \xrightarrow{AcOH} \begin{smallmatrix}RCOCHCO_2Et\\R'\end{smallmatrix}$$

$$\text{IV} \qquad\qquad\qquad \text{V}$$

and when this is heated in a medium weakly acidified with acetic acid, dihydro-pyrane is eliminated, the carboxyl group liberated suffers decarboxylation, and the β-keto ester (V) is formed in good yield. For the synthesis of corynomycolenic acid (XII), Lederer and Julio Pudles (1954) employed the acid chloride of natural palmitoleic acid, $CH_3(CH_2)_5CH=CH(CH_2)_7CO_2H$, the C_{16} analog of oleic acid. Condensation of this acid chloride with the sodio derivative of VIII gave IX, converted on elimination of the protective group into X. Reduction of the keto group of X with sodium borohydride gave the alcohol XI. The product was puri-

$$n-C_{14}H_{29}Br \xrightarrow{NaCH(CO_2Et)_2} \begin{smallmatrix}CO_2Et\\CH\\C_{14}H_{29}\,CO_2Et\end{smallmatrix} \xrightarrow{KOH,\,H^+} \begin{smallmatrix}CO_2Et\\CH\\C_{14}H_{29}\,CO_2H\end{smallmatrix} \xrightarrow{\text{Dihydro-pyran, }H^+}$$

$$\text{VI} \qquad\qquad\qquad \text{VII}$$

$$\begin{smallmatrix}CO_2Et\\CHCOO-\\C_{14}H_{29}\end{smallmatrix}\text{(pyran)} \xrightarrow{Na,\,RCOCl} CH_3(CH_2)_5CH=CH(CH_2)_7\begin{smallmatrix}CO_2Et\\CCOO-\\O\,|\\C_{14}H_{29}\end{smallmatrix}\text{(pyran)} \xrightarrow{HOAc}$$

$$\text{VIII} \qquad\qquad\qquad\qquad \text{IX}$$

$$CH_3(CH_2)_5CH=CH(CH_2)_7\underset{\underset{C_{14}H_{29}}{|}}{\overset{\overset{O}{\|}}{C}}-CHCO_2Et \xrightarrow{NaBH_4} CH_3(CH_2)_5CH=CH(CH_2)_7\underset{\underset{OH}{|}}{CH}-\underset{\underset{C_{14}H_{29}}{|}}{C}HCO_2Et$$

$$\text{X} \qquad\qquad\qquad\qquad\qquad\qquad \text{XI}$$

$$\longrightarrow CH_3(CH_2)_5CH=CH(CH_2)_7\underset{\underset{HO}{|}}{CH}\underset{\underset{C_{14}H_{29}-n}{|}}{C}HCO_2H$$

$$\text{XII}$$

fied by saponification and chromatography of XII on alumina by elution with ether containing 3% of acetic acid. Reesterification (CH_2N_2) and further chro-matography gave the pure methyl ester of dl-corynomycolenic acid, identical in infrared spectrum with the ester of the natural acid.

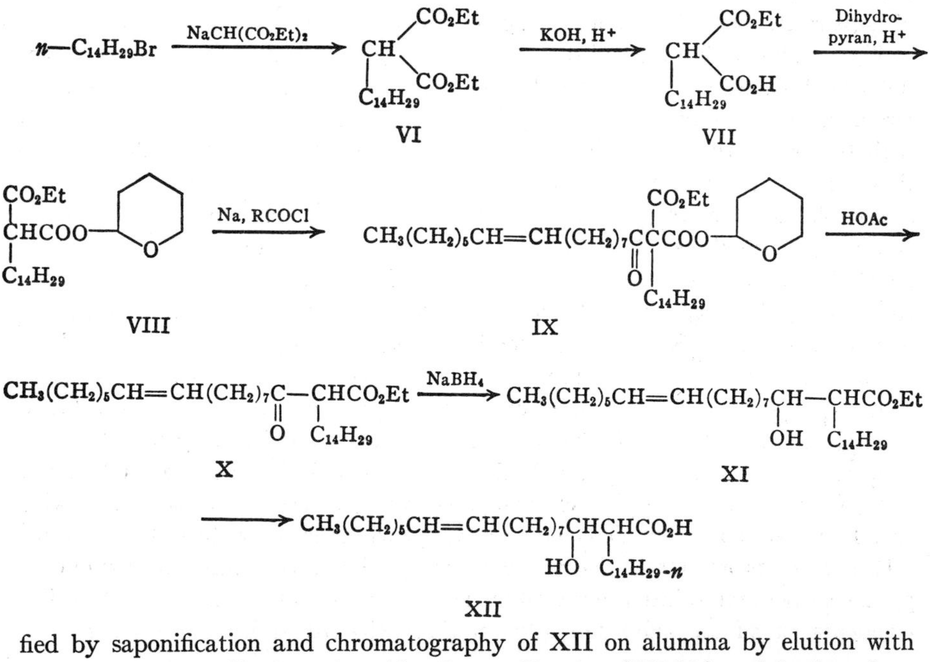

30.11 **Thioctic Acid.** — In a study of the nutritional requirements of the protozoan *Tetrahymena geleii*, G. W. Kidder (Amherst College) found liver extracts to contain a factor required for normal growth (1944–45). In view of its essentiality for protozoa, the unknown factor was named protogen. Later protogen was shown to possess biological activity corresponding to that of a factor named lipoic acid, which is required by various lactic acid-producing bacteria and shown also (1946–49) to be a cofactor in the oxidative decarboxylation of pyruvic acid:

$$CH_3COCO_2H \ + \ \tfrac{1}{2}O_2 \ \longrightarrow \ CH_3CO_2H \ + \ CO_2$$

α-Lipoic acid, now called thioctic acid, is released on hydrolysis of various tissues, but liver is the best source. The active principle was isolated from liver in 1951 in several laboratories. In one project, conducted jointly by groups at the University of Texas (chemical; L. J. Reed[1] *et al.*), the University of Illinois (bacteriological; I. C. Gunsalus[2] *et al.*), and the Eli Lilly research laboratory, ten tons of the water-insoluble residue of beef liver was processed. The assay procedure involved manometric determination of the carbon dioxide liberated on activation of pyruvate oxidation by resting *Streptococcus faecalis* cells. A 250-lb. batch of liver residue was hydrolyzed with 6 N sulfuric acid and the filtered hydrolyzate extracted with benzene, which afforded material of average activity of 150 units/ mg. The active material was then extracted into aqueous bicarbonate, and the extract acidified and extracted with benzene. The crude acidic material thus obtained was processed further in various ways. For example, a 12-g. sample having an activity of 1265 units/mg. was distributed between 2 liters each of benzene and 50% aqueous acetic acid in 10 separatory funnels (Craig countercurrent method). The benzene layers of funnels 7–9 yielded 5.0 g. of material having a potency of 2550 units/mg. This was esterified with diazomethane and the ester mixture chromatographed on alumina (benzene–*n*-heptane). Fractions 9–22 afforded a total of 196 mg. of material of activity in the range 18,000–40,000 units/mg., and when 136 mg. of this material was chromatographed further on Florisil 88% of the activity was concentrated into a series of fractions (18–28) affording 18.8 mg. of methyl thioctate of a potency of 172,000 units/mg. This ester mixture was shaken with 0.1 N potassium hydroxide under nitrogen for six hours and the acidic fraction on crystallization from ligroin afforded 10 mg. of pale yellow platelets of pure thioctic acid, m.p. 47.5°, αD +96.7° (2% in benzene), potency 250,000 units/mg. A total of 30 mg. of thioctic acid sufficed for determination of structure.

Analyses and molecular weight determinations of thioctic acid established the formula $C_8H_{14}O_2S_2$. A band in the infrared spectrum at 5.8μ is indicative of an aliphatic carboxyl group, and the pK_a value of 4.76 (cf. *n*-butyric acid, 4.82) indicates that polar or unsaturated groups are not α or β to the carboxyl group. Thioctic acid does not give a positive nitroprusside test for the thiol group (—SH),

[1] Lester J. Reed, b. 1925 New Orleans; Ph.D. Illinois (Fuson); Univ. Texas

[2] I. C. Gunsalus, b. 1912 Sully County, So. Dakota; Ph.D. Cornell (Sherman); Cornell; Merck and Co.; Univ. Illinois

but a polarographic study established that the sulfur is reducible at the dropping mercury electrode and therefore is present as a disulfide group. Desulfurization with Raney nickel converts thioctic acid into *n*-caprylic acid, $CH_3(CH_2)_6CO_2H$. Since thioctic acid does not contain a methyl group (Kuhn-Roth determination, absence of a striking infrared band at 3.37μ), one sulfur atom must be linked to the terminal carbon atom of the skeleton. These data suggest for the factor the three possible structures formulated. That the correct structure is the first was

$$
\begin{array}{ccc}
CH_2CH_2\overset{*}{C}H(CH_2)_4CO_2H & CH_2CH_2CH_2CH(CH_2)_3CO_2H & CH_2CH_2CH_2CH_2CH(CH_2)_2CO_2H \\
| \qquad | & | \qquad | & | \qquad | \\
S\text{——}S & S\text{———}S & S\text{————}S \\
\text{6-Thioctic acid} & \text{5-Thioctic acid} & \text{4-Thioctic acid}
\end{array}
$$

shown by synthesis in five laboratories (1952–55). The first syntheses gave *dl*-material, but identity could be inferred from characteristic physical and optical properties and from biological activity.

One synthesis (L. J. Reed, 1955) starts with addition of adipic acid half-ester acid chloride (1) to ethylene in the presence of aluminum chloride, and reduction of the keto ester (2) with sodium borohydride in ethanol to (3). The hydroxyl group was replaced by chlorine (4), and the two chlorines were converted into thiol groups through the dibenzylmercaptide (5). The C—S bonds in this derivative are activated by the phenyl groups and hence easily severed on reduction

$$
CH_2{=}CH_2 \ + \ Cl\overset{O}{\overset{\|}{C}}(CH_2)_4CO_2C_2H_5 \ \xrightarrow{AlCl_3} \ ClCH_2CH_2\overset{O}{\overset{\|}{C}}(CH_2)_4CO_2C_2H_5 \ \xrightarrow{NaBH_4}
$$
$$
(1) \hspace{4cm} (2)
$$

$$
ClCH_2CH_2\underset{\underset{OH}{|}}{CH}(CH_2)_4CO_2C_2H_5 \ \xrightarrow{SOCl_2} \ ClCH_2CH_2\underset{\underset{Cl}{|}}{CH}(CH_2)_4CO_2C_2H_5 \ \xrightarrow[KOH]{2\ C_6H_5CH_2SH}
$$
$$
(3) \hspace{4cm} (4)
$$

$$
C_6H_5CH_2SCH_2CH_2\underset{\underset{SCH_2C_6H_5}{|}}{CH}(CH_2)_4CO_2H \ \xrightarrow{Na,\ NH_3} \ CH_2CH_2\underset{\underset{SH}{|}}{CH}\underset{\underset{SH}{|}}{}(CH_2)_4CO_2H
$$
$$
(5) \hspace{4cm} (6)
$$

$$
\xrightarrow{O_2} \ \textit{dl}\text{-Thioctic acid (m.p. 62°)}
$$

with sodium in liquid ammonia to give the 6,8-dithiol (6), which on oxidation with oxygen in the presence of a trace of ferric chloride afforded *dl*-thioctic acid in 35% overall yield.

A synthesis developed by the Folkers[1] group introduced a resolution of the first intermediate and permitted preparation of the (+) and (−) forms. Addition of thiolacetic acid to the α,β-unsaturated acid group of I gave a *dl*-acid which was resolved with use of *d*- and *l*-ephedrine, $C_6H_5CH(OH)CH(CH_3)NHCH_3$.

---

[1] Karl Folkers, b. 1906 Decatur, Ill.; Ph.D. Wisconsin (Adkins); Merck and Co.

$$C_2H_5O_2C(CH_2)_4CH{=}CHCO_2H \xrightarrow{\text{CH}_3\text{COSH}} C_2H_5O_2C(CH_2)_4\overset{*}{C}HCH_2CO_2H \xrightarrow{\text{SOCl}_2}$$
$$\text{I} \qquad\qquad\qquad\qquad \underset{\underset{\text{SCOCH}_3}{|}}{} $$
$$\text{II}$$

$$\underset{\underset{\text{SCOCH}_3}{|}}{C_2H_5O_2C(CH_2)_4CHCH_2COCl} \xrightarrow[\text{2. NaOH}]{\text{1. NaBH}_4} \underset{\underset{\text{SH}}{|}}{HO_2C(CH_2)_4CHCH_2CH_2OH} \xrightarrow{\text{HBr}}$$
$$\text{III} \qquad\qquad\qquad\qquad\qquad \text{IV}$$

$$\underset{\underset{\text{SH}}{|}}{HO_2C(CH_2)_4CHCH_2CH_2Br} \xrightarrow{\text{S=C(NH}_2)_2} \underset{\underset{\text{SH}}{|}}{HO_2C(CH_2)_4CHCH_2CH_2}\underset{\underset{\text{NH}_2}{|}}{\overset{+}{S}C{=}NH_2Br^-}$$
$$\text{V} \qquad\qquad\qquad\qquad\qquad\qquad \text{VI}$$

$$\xrightarrow{\text{NaOH}} \quad \underset{\underset{\text{SH}\quad\text{SH}}{|\qquad|}}{HO_2C(CH_2)_4CHCH_2CH_2} \xrightarrow{\text{I}_2\cdot\text{KI}} \qquad \underset{S\diagdown_S}{}\!\diagup(CH_2)_4CO_2H$$
$$\text{VII } (+ \text{ NaBr } + \text{ H}_2\text{NC}{\equiv}\text{N}) \qquad\qquad\qquad \text{VIII}$$

Treatment of an ethereal solution of *dl*-II with *l*-ephedrine gave a crystalline salt of the (−)-form. Alternatively, addition of *d*-ephedrine to an ethereal solution of the *dl*-acid precipitated the crystalline salt of the (+)-form, corresponding, as was found, to natural thioctic acid. Each optically pure form of II was converted into the thioctic acid by the following steps. The carboxyl group was reduced via the acid chloride III, and hydrolysis gave IV. The alcoholic hydroxyl group was replaced by bromine, and V was condensed with thiourea to give the isothiuronium salt VI, which on hydrolysis eliminated cyanamide and afforded the dithiol derivative VII. Oxidation, conducted as described above or with iodine in potassium iodide, completed the synthesis. Of the two enantiomers, only the natural (+)-form has biological activity. *dl*-Thioctic acid has half the activity of the natural form.

30.12 Complex Lipids. — Whereas depot fats are mainly glycerides, tissues of brain and spinal cord contain complex structural units constructed from protein, cholesterol, and phospholipids of a type exemplified by the lecithins. A lecithin is a glyceride containing two, usually different, fatty acid ester groups (*e.g.* of stearic and oleic acid) and a phosphocholine group, which on saponifica-

$$\underset{\underset{\underset{\overset{\displaystyle\|}{O}}{\diagup}}{CH_2{-}O{-}P}\diagdown_{OCH_2CH_2\overset{+}{N}(CH_3)_3}}{\overset{\displaystyle CH_2OCOC_{17}H_{35}}{\overset{|}{\underset{|}{CHOCOC_{17}H_{33}}}}}^{O^-} \xrightarrow{\text{5 NaOH}} \left\{ \begin{array}{c} \text{Glycerol} \\ \text{Soap} \\ \text{Na}_3\text{PO}_4 \end{array} \right\} + [HOCH_2CH_2\overset{+}{N}(CH_3)_3]OH^-$$

Typical lecithin   Choline

tion affords inorganic phosphate and the quaternary base choline. A lecithin mixture was encountered first in egg yolk, hence the name (Gr. *lekithos*, yolk). The potency of the phospholipid as an emulsifying agent is evident from the fact that an egg yolk contains about 0.6% of cholesterol, a water-insoluble solid of m.p. 149°. The lecithin mixture extracted from egg yolk or soybean oil is a waxy, hygroscopic white mass which rapidly becomes yellow or brown in air. The acid components of soybean lecithin are: palmitic 11.7%, stearic 4%, palmitoleic 8.6%, oleic 9.8%, linoleic 55%, linolenic 4%, C_{20} to C_{22} (includes arachidonic), 5.5%.

E. Baer[1] (1950) devised a synthesis of α-lecithins of the natural L-configuration which involves phosphorylation of the free hydroxyl group of an L-α,β-diglyceride (I) with phenylphosphoryl dichloride to give a diacyl α-glycerylphenylphosphoryl chloride (II), which can react with the alcoholic group of choline chloride to form a phosphate diester (III). The protective phenyl group is removed by catalytic

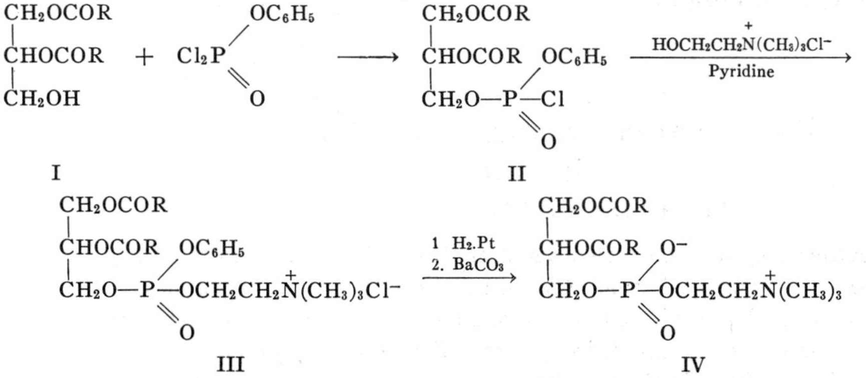

hydrogenation and the salt is hydrolyzed to the free lecithin. Synthetic L-α-(distearoyl)-lecithin proved to be identical with hydrogenated egg yolk lecithin, the acids of which are stearic and oleic acid; L-α-(dipalmitoyl)-lecithin is identical with a natural phosphatide of brain, lung, and spleen.

Hydrolysis of an α-lecithin gives rise to both α- and β-glycerophosphoric acids; the migration of the phosphoric acid residue probably occurs through an intermediate cyclic ortho ester (Posternak has demonstrated such a reaction in the

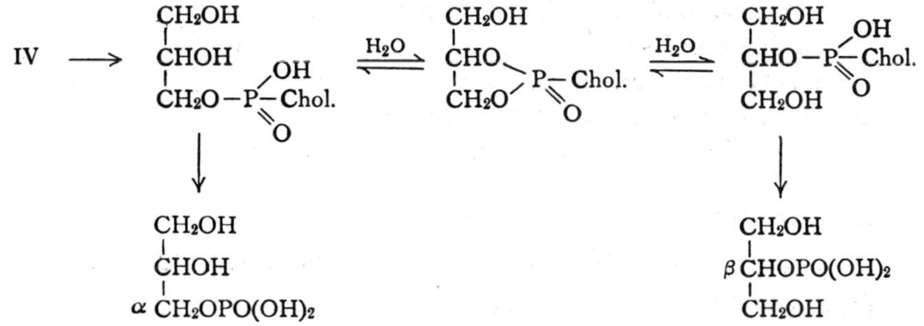

inositol series). Isolation of β-glycerophosphoric acid in early structural studies was taken as evidence of the existence of natural β-lecithins, but the facts just cited show this evidence to be invalid.

The cephalins (Gr. *kephale*, head; first isolated from brain tissue) are mixtures of phospholipids of three types. One (V) differs from a lecithin only in that the

[1] Erich Baer, b. 1900 Berlin; Ph.D. Berlin; Univ. Toronto

basic component is ethanolamine in place of choline; in a second the basic component is the amino acid serine. A phospholipid of a third type, unusual in that it

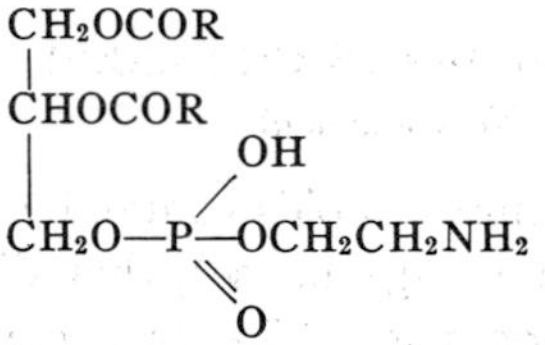

CH₂OCOR

CHOCOR
               OH

CH₂O—P—OCH₂CH₂NH₂

       O

V. α-Cephalin

CH₂OCOR

CHOCOR
               OH

CH₂O—P—OCH₂CHCO₂H

       O   NH₂

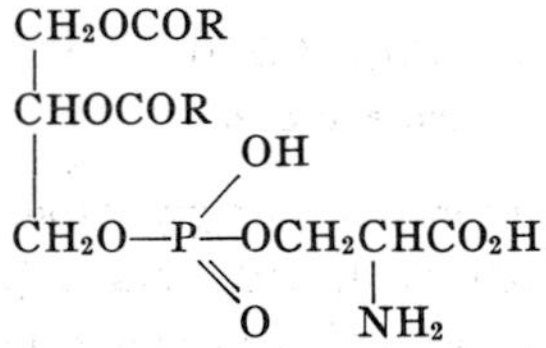

VI. Phosphatidylserine

contains no basic component, was isolated from brain by Folch[1] (1949) and characterized as comprised of fatty acid esters of a substance regarded as an inositol diphosphate. However, phosphate esters are now known to be so susceptible to acid-catalyzed phosphate migration that Folch's phosphate ester was probably a complex mixture. C. E. Ballou[2] (1961) submitted beef brain phospholipid to the gentler alkaline hydrolysis and obtained, along with inositol diphosphates, a considerable amount of triphosphates and some monophosphate.

Baer (1951) synthesized α-cephalins of type V by condensing the diacylphenylphosphoryl chloride II with N-carbobenzoxyethanolamine, $C_6H_5CH_2CONHCH_2$-CH_2OH, and removing the protective groups simultaneously by hydrogenation (overall yield 48–51%).

A number of phosphatides contain the base sphingosine (structure, Klenk,[3] 1931; Carter,[4] 1942). The fats containing this basic component are known as sphingolipids and are particularly prevalent in nerve tissue. The phosphosphingosides, or sphingomyelins (Gr. *sphingein*, to bind tight + Gr. *myelos*, marrow), are com-

CH₃(CH₂)₁₂CH=CHCHOHCH(NH₂)CH₂OH

Sphingosine

posed of a fatty acid, phosphoric acid, and both choline and sphingosine. Choline is linked as usual to phosphoric acid which, in turn, is esterified with the primary

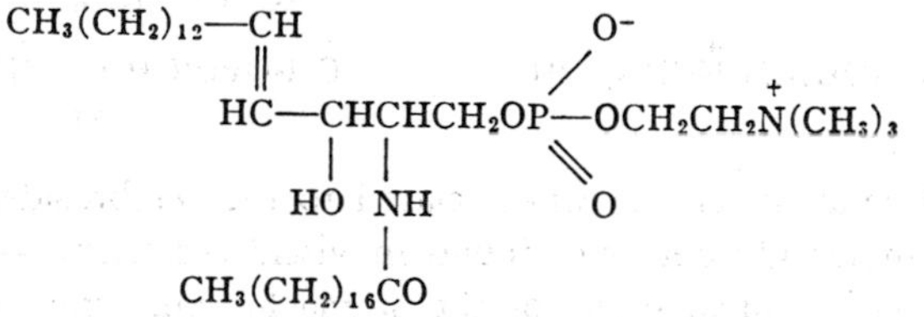

CH₃(CH₂)₁₂—CH   O⁻

HC—CHCHCH₂OP—OCH₂CH₂N⁺(CH₃)₃

HO   NH   O

CH₃(CH₂)₁₆CO

Sphingomyelin

alcoholic group of sphingosine; the double bond has the *trans* configuration (Stotz,[5]

---

[1] Jordi Folch (Folch-Pi), b. Barcelona, Spain; M.D. Barcelona; McLean Hospital, Belmont, Mass., and Harvard Univ.

[2] Clinton E. Ballou, b. 1923 King Hill, Idaho; Ph.D. Wisconsin (Link); Univ. Calif, Berkeley

[3] Ernst Klenk, b. 1896 Pfalzgrafenweiler, Germany; Ph.D. Tübingen; Univ. Cologne

[4] Herbert E. Carter, b. 1910 Mooresville, Ind.; Ph.D. Illinois (Marvel); Univ. Illinois

[5] Elmer H. Stotz, b. 1911, Boston; Ph.D. Harvard (Hastings); Univ. Rochester School of Med. Dent

1953–54). Only four acids have been isolated from hydrolyzates of sphingomyelins: lignoceric acid, palmitic acid, stearic acid, and nervonic (selacholeic) acid.

$$CH_3(CH_2)_{22}COOH \qquad\qquad CH_3(CH_2)_7CH=CH(CH_2)_{13}COOH$$

Lignoceric acid   Nervonic acid

The cerebrosides, or glycosphingosides, are complex lipids containing sphingosine, a fatty acid, and a sugar (either D-glucose or D-galactose); they differ from most complex lipids in containing no phosphoric acid. The probable arrange-

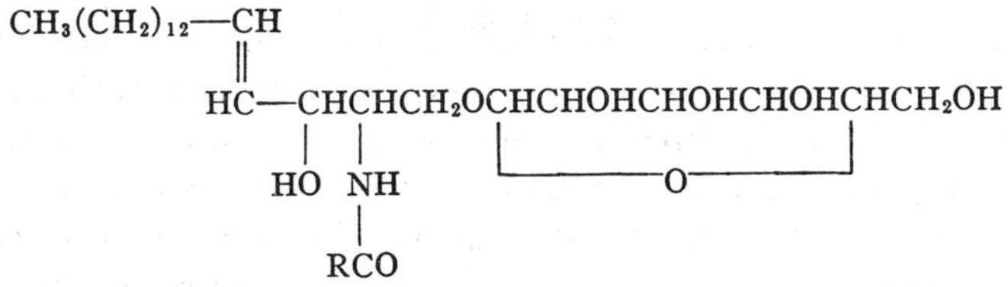

$$CH_3(CH_2)_{12}-CH$$
$$\|$$
$$HC-CHCHCH_2OCHCHOHCHOHCHOHCHCH_2OH$$
$$\quad| \;\;|$$
$$HO \;\; NH \qquad\qquad O$$
$$\quad\quad|$$
$$\quad\quad RCO$$

Cerebroside

ment of the component units is shown in the formula. Known acid constituents of cerebrosides are: lignoceric acid, α-hydroxylignoceric (cerebronic) acid, nervonic acid, and α-hydroxynervonic acid.

Plasmalogens, phospholipids which liberate a fatty aldehyde on hydrolysis, are found in mammalian tissue (R. Feulgen, 1939; S. J. Thannhauser, 1951) and, in remarkably homogeneous form, in sea anemone and sponges (W. Bergmann,[1] 1958, 1961). The phospholipid fraction of the common West Coast sea anemone consists of an N-palmityl type sphingomyelin (20 parts) and the plasmalogen I (1 part), an acetal. In the sponge *Speciospongia vesparia* the plasmalogen is the enol ether II.

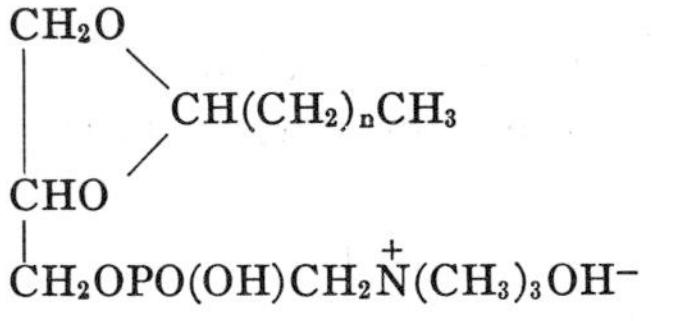

$$CH_2O$$
$$\quad\quad\diagdown$$
$$\quad\quad\quad CH(CH_2)_nCH_3$$
$$\quad\quad\diagup$$
$$CHO$$
$$\quad|$$
$$CH_2OPO(OH)CH_2\overset{+}{N}(CH_3)_3OH^-$$

I

$$CH_2OCH=CH(CH_2)_nCH_3$$
$$\quad|$$
$$CHOCO(CH_2)_nCH_3$$
$$\quad|$$
$$CH_2OPO(OH)CH_2\overset{+}{N}(CH_3)_3HO^-$$

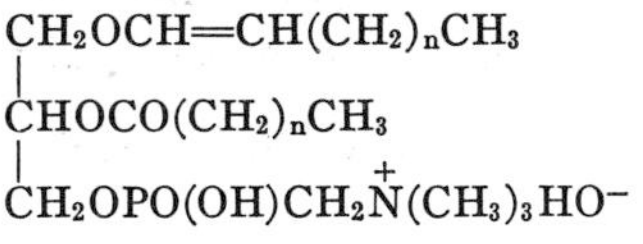

II

A group of compounds somewhat related to the cerebrosides are components of mucins, complex glycoproteins found in viscid secretions and tissues of man and animals, as in saliva, lining of the stomach, skin, gray matter within the brain or spinal cord (lipids of ganglia, gangliosides). They contain a fatty acid, sphingosine, hexose (both D-glucose and D-galactose), and neuraminic acid. Neuraminic acid is not known as such, but Klenk in 1941 isolated crystalline methoxyneuraminic acid after heating brain gangliosides with 5% methanolic hydrogen chloride (105°); in 1954 he isolated N-acetylneuraminic acid as a byproduct of the methanolysis of bovine subaxillary mucin. Degradative studies indicated that N-acetylneuraminic acid is a derivative of a nine-carbon sugar, a nonulose. Work of G. Blix (1956) suggested that the substance is a product of

---

[1] Werner Bergmann, 1904–59; b. Bielefeld, Germany; Ph.D. Göttingen (Windaus); Yale Univ.

aldol condensation of a hexosamine with pyruvic acid, and indeed degradation with nickel acetate in pyridine afforded, among other products, 2-acetamino-2-desoxy-D-glucose. The structure initially assigned was epimeric at C_5 with that

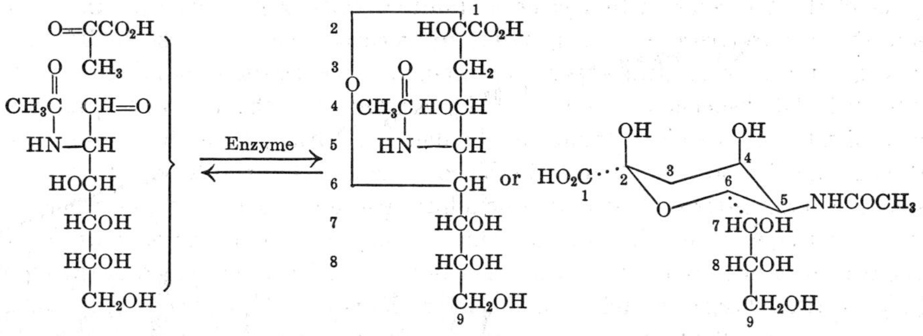

2-Acetylamido-
2-desoxy-D-mannose
                      β-D-(−)-N-Acetylneuraminic acid

formulated. However, S. Roseman (Univ. Michigan, 1958) found that the 2-acetamido-2-desoxy derivatives of D-glucose and D-mannose separately undergo epimerization under the conditions of the degradation and demonstrated that the D-glucose derivative isolated from the chemical degradation is an artifact. Thus enzymic degradation of N-acetylneuraminic acid gave 2-acetamido-2-desoxy-D-mannose; in the presence of pyruvic acid and an enzyme, 2-acetamido-2-desoxy-D-mannose, but not the D-glucose analog, can be incorporated into N-acetyl-neuramic acid. Note that the larger of the groups at C_2 is equatorial and that the large substituents at C_5 and C_6 are also equatorial.

30.13   **Nonsaponifiable Lipids.** — When brain tissue is saponified, the fats, proteins, phospholipids, and complex lipids are converted largely into water-soluble, ether-insoluble products, and extraction of the alkaline mixture with ether affords a nonsaponifiable lipid fraction consisting of cholesterol (structure and conformation, 5.12) and a few per cent of companion steroids. Cholesterol results from saponification and extraction of all body tissues, including blood, which normally contains about 200 mg. of total cholesterol per 100 ml. Some 27% of the blood cholesterol is present as such and the rest is esterified with C_{16} and C_{18} fatty acids. The total cholesterol in a man weighing 170 lbs. is about 250 g. It is derived in part by biosynthesis in the body and, in carniverous animals, from the diet. Saponification of ox bile, acidification, and solvent ex-

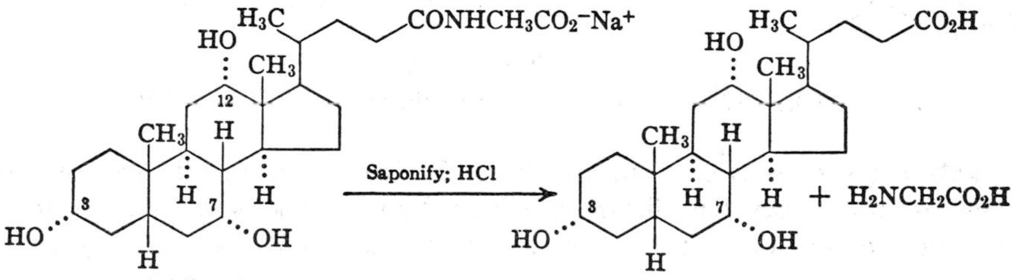

A bile salt   Cholic acid (bile acid)   Glycine

traction gives a mixture of bile acids of which the two most abundant constituents are cholic acid and desoxycholic acid (which lacks the 7α-hydroxyl group). These acids are present in bile as bile salts, which are the sodium salts of amide conjugates of the bile acids with glycine or taurine ($H_2NCH_2CH_2SO_3H$). In a bile salt the balance between the lipophilic hydrocarbon part and the hydrophilic ionic group is such that the salt is a surface-active agent capable of bringing lipids into colloidal dispersion in water. Bile secreted into the intestine emulsifies neutral fats and lipoidal vitamins of the diet and so facilitates their absorption through the intestinal wall into the blood stream. Isotope-tracer studies have shown that cholesterol is the biosynthetic precursor of the bile acids, as well as of steroid hormones, but bile normally contains only a trace of cholesterol. Some animals, including man, store a reserve of bile in a gall bladder joined to the liver (man, cattle, sheep) or built into the liver (shark), and sometimes gall stones appear in the gall bladder (man, cattle). These stones, weighing up to 78 g. (man), consist to the extent of about 80% of cholesterol.

Present in the body in trace amounts in comparison to cholesterol and the bile acids, are a number of steroid hormones which are secreted into the blood to control specific processes of growth essential to healthful functioning of the body. The testis produces the androgen testosterone (12.24); the ovary produces estradiol (15.35) and progesterone (15.35); the adrenal gland produces cortisol (8.23) and cortisone (15.35), as well as forty-one companion steroids. The nonsaponifiable lipid fraction from urine contains a shower of products of metabolism of the steroid hormones. The first known androgens and estrogens, androsterone and estrone, were isolated from urine; they are less active than the true hormones. In the first isolation of progesterone by A. Butenandt (1934), 625 kg. of ovarian tissue from 50,000 sows afforded 20 mg. of the pure hormone. A. Windaus (1935) identified vitamin D_3 as a product of irradiation of a sterol precursor which H.

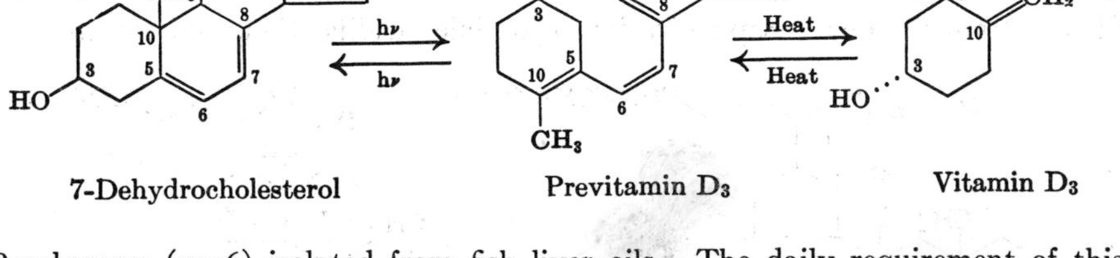

7-Dehydrocholesterol   Previtamin D_3 Vitamin D_3

Brockmann (1936) isolated from fish liver oils. The daily requirement of this vitamin is only 5γ per day; dietary deficiency leads to rickets, a disease characterized by softening of the bone. Work of L. Velluz and E. Havinga[1] (1949–60)

[1] Egbert Havinga, b. 1909 Amersfoort, The Netherlands; Ph.D. Utrecht (Kögl); Univ. Leyden

showed that irradiation of the provitamin 7-dehydrocholesterol opens ring **B** to give a previtamin which is isomerized thermally (50°) to the vitamin.

Another group of nonsaponifiable lipids which occur in trace amounts in specific tissues have in common the feature that the structures are divisible into isoprene units. Squalene, a C_{30} isoprenoid found in shark liver oil, contains six isoprene units joined thus: tail-head, t-h, t-t, h-t, h-t. The structural formula is derived easily by joining the units by 1,4-additions. Squalene belongs to a group known

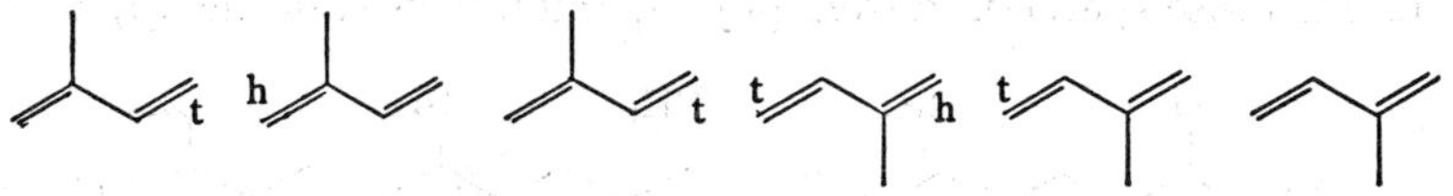

Isoprene units

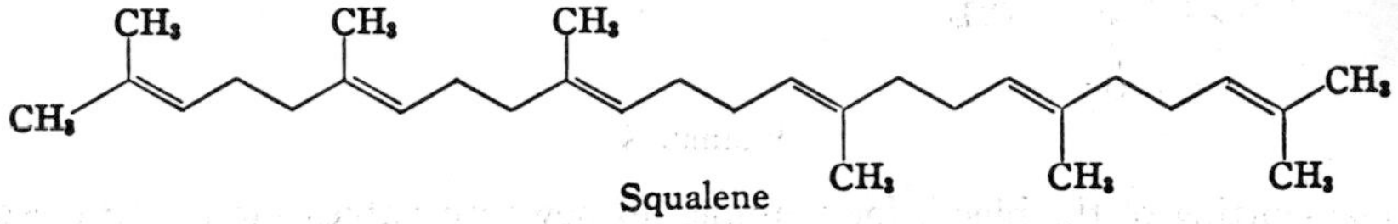

Squalene

as carotenoids, after the prominent member β-carotene, a pigment which occurs in the carrot, in green leaves, and in blood, and which owes its color (red, dilute solutions yellow) to the presence of eleven conjugated double bonds. β-Carotene, $C_{40}H_{56}$, is oxidized in the liver and suffers fission at its central link to produce vitamin A, $C_{20}H_{30}O$, a factor isolated from fish liver oils which plays a role in photoreception in the retina. It is a primary allylic alcohol derived from four isoprene units joined tail to head.

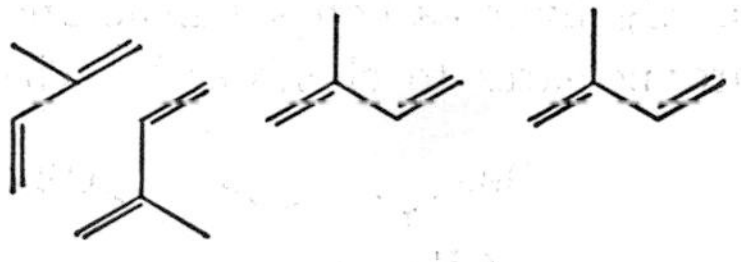

Isoprene units

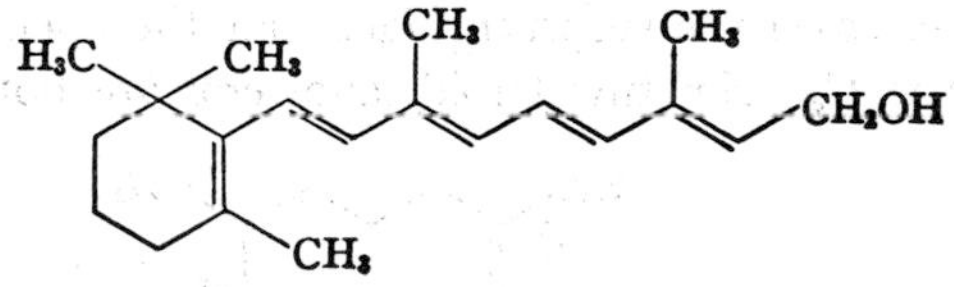

Vitamin A

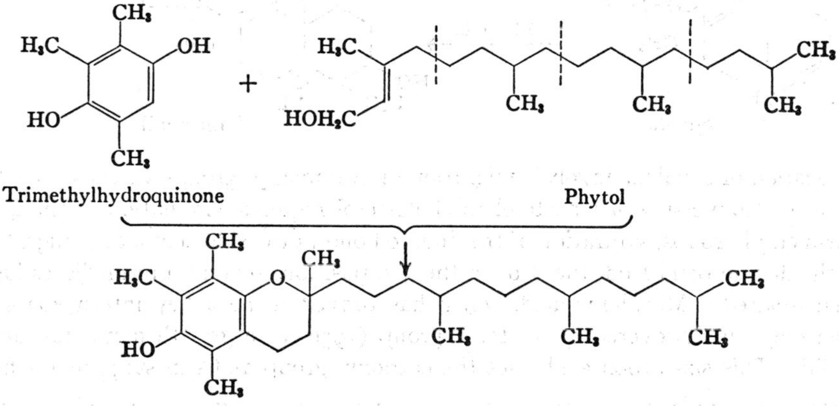

Trimethylhydroquinone   +   Phytol

α-Tocopherol

α-Tocopherol, a vitamin E factor which counteracts sterility in rats but which is not known to be essential to man, has been isolated from the nonsaponifiable lipid fractions of wheat germ oil and of liver. Synthesis is accomplished by condensation of trimethylhydroquinone with phytol, an allylic, isoprenoid alcohol ($C_{20}H_{40}O$) which is liberated on saponification of an ester grouping of chlorophyll (29.29).

Vitamin K_1 also contains a phytyl group, which in this case is linked to a quinone ring. It is likewise synthesized from phytol, and it is used in therapy to promote

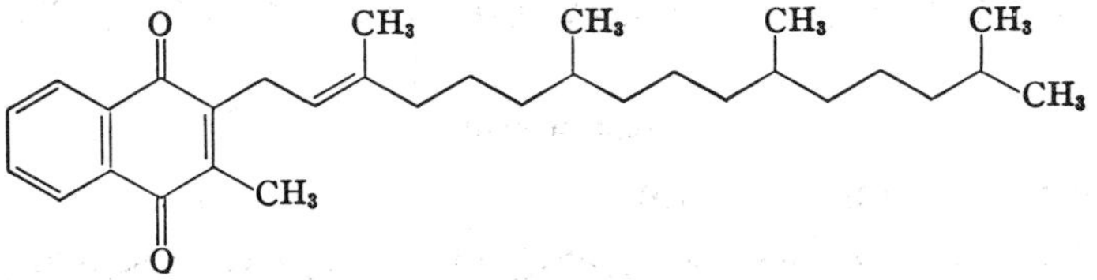

Vitamin K_1

normal clotting of the blood, for example, in newborn babies subject to bleeding to death from a pin prick because they have not yet acquired adequate antihemorrhagic factor from the diet. Operation for removal of a cancerous growth obstructing the flow of bile may be attended by dangerous bleeding because, in the absence of emulsifying bile salts, K_1 is not absorbed from the diet. The deficiency can now be corrected prior to operation by intravenous injection of a water-soluble derivative of synthetic vitamin K_1.

Investigations by K. Bloch[1] and by J. W. Cornforth and G. Popjak (1950–60) of the biosynthesis of cholesterol from $C^{14}H_3CO_2H$ and from $CH_3C^{14}O_2H$ have disclosed the surprising fact that the open-chain C_{30} hydrocarbon squalene and the C_{30} trimethylsteroid lanosterol are both intermediates to cholesterol. The

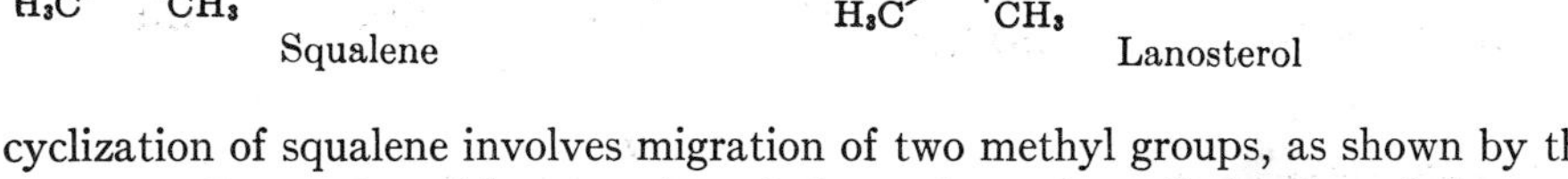

Squalene   Lanosterol

cyclization of squalene involves migration of two methyl groups, as shown by the arrows. Conversion of lanosterol to cholesterol requires elimination of the 4,4, 14α-methyl groups, saturation of the double bond in the side chain, and migration of the double bond from the 8,9- to the 5,6-position; several intermediates have been isolated. Mevalonic acid, which has proved to be a key intermediate to squalene, was discovered by a Merck group (1956) as a growth factor for lactobacilli. This six-carbon acid loses the carboxyl group at C_1 in supplying a five-

[1] Konrad E. Bloch, b. 1912 Neisse, Germany; Ph.D. Columbia (Schoenheimer); Univ. Chicago; Harvard Univ.

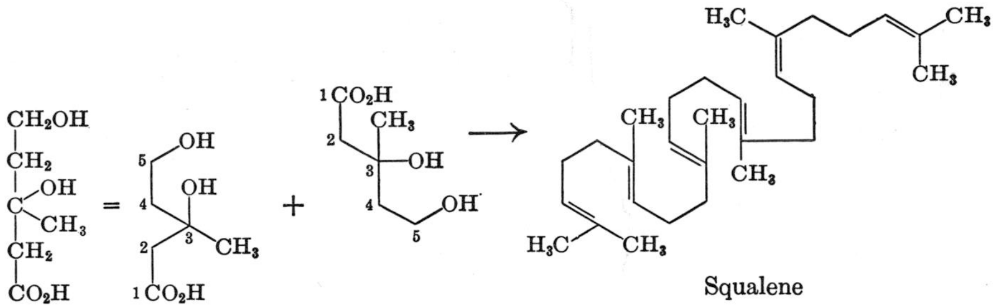

Mevalonic acid

Squalene

carbon unit for a condensation involving six units, which join together by a process shown in part in the formulation.

Chapter 31

PROTEINS

Proteins derive the name from their great importance in all forms of living matter (Gr. *proteios*, primary). The pronunciation is prō'tē·ĭn. Some serve as structural materials for animals, some transport fat in the blood stream, some are hormones, some are enzymes, one transports oxygen from the lungs to body tissues. Since they are all compounded from amino acids and yield mixtures of these acids on hydrolysis, we shall discuss first the chemistry of the building units.

31.1   Component Acids. — The twenty common acids from proteins (Table 31.1) are α-amino acids and in all of them except glycine the α-carbon atom is asymmetric. The first to be discovered was glycine. H. Braconnot (1820), investigating the hydrolysis of gelatin to see if this material, like cellulose, would yield a sugar, isolated a substance which he called glycine because it has a sweet taste (Gr. *glykys*, sweet). Eighteen years elapsed before the "sugar of gelatin" was found to contain nitrogen. Most of the other acids likewise were given names terminating with -ine (amine). Some of the names refer to structural correlations. Thus alanine is compounded from a̲ldehyde + ine with insertion of a̲n. Alanine and all the higher acids belong to the L-series. Threonine, named because of its relationship to D-threose, belongs to the L-series of amino acids and the D-series of sugars. Valine is a derivative of isov̲aleric acid, proline

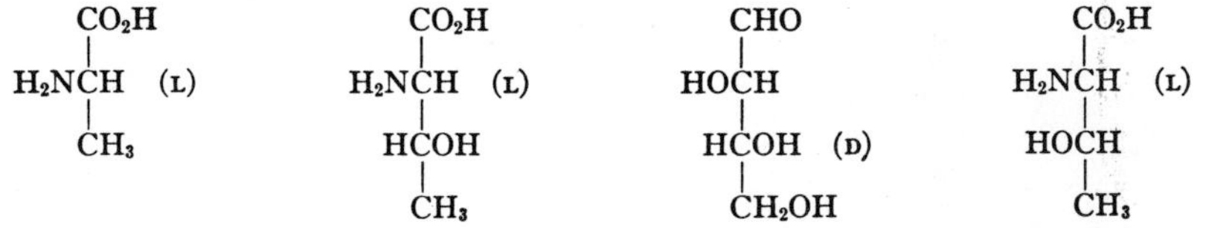

CO₂H	CO₂H	CHO	CO₂H
H₂NCH (L)	H₂NCH (L)	HOCH	H₂NCH (L)
CH₃	HCOH	HCOH (D)	HOCH
	CH₃	CH₂OH	CH₃
L-(+)-Alanine	L-(−)-Threonine (natural)	D-Threose	L-Allothreonine

TABLE 31.1. COMMON AMINO ACIDS FROM PROTEINS

NAME	SYMBOL	FORMULA	ISOELEC-TRIC POINT	Rf*
Glycine	Gly	$CH_2(NH_2)CO_2H$	5.97	0.41
Alanine	Ala	$CH_3CH(NH_2)CO_2H$	6.00	.60
Valine	Val	$(CH_3)_2CHCH(NH_2)CO_2H$	5.96	.78
Leucine	Leu	$(CH_3)_2CHCH_2CH(NH_2)CO_2H$	6.02	.84
Isoleucine	Ileu	$CH_3CH_2CH(CH_3)CH(NH_2)CO_2H$	5.98	.84
Phenylalanine	Phe	$C_6H_5CH_2CH(NH_2)CO_2H$	5.48	.85
Tyrosine	Tyr	$p\text{-}HOC_6H_4CH_2CH(NH_2)CO_2H$	5.66	.51
Proline	Pro	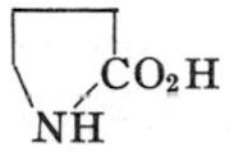	6.30	.88
Hydroxyproline	Hypro	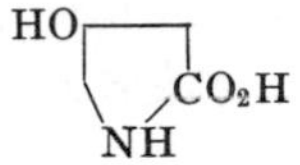	5.83	.63
Serine	Ser	$HOCH_2CH(NH_2)CO_2H$	5.68	.36
Threonine	Thr	$HOCH(CH_3)CH(NH_2)CO_2H$		.50
Cysteine	CySH	$HSCH_2CH(NH_2)CO_2H$	5.05	—
Cystine	CyS SCy	$[-SCH_2CH(NH_2)CO_2H]_2$	4.8	.03
Methionine	Met	$CH_3SCH_2CH_2CH(NH_2)CO_2H$	5.74	.81
Tryptophane	Try	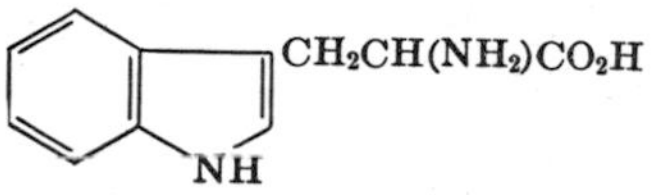	5.89	.75
Aspartic acid	Asp	$HO_2CCH_2CH(NH_2)CO_2H$	2.77	.19
Glutamic acid	Glu	$HO_2CCH_2CH_2CH(NH_2)CO_2H$	3.22	.31
Arginine	Arg		10.76	.89
Lysine	Lys	$H_2NCH_2CH_2CH_2CH_2CH(NH_2)CO_2H$	9.74	.81
Histidine	His	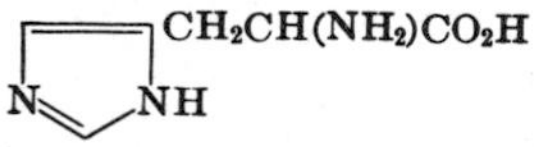	7.59	.69

* 77% Ethanol

is pyrrolidine-2-carboxylic acid. Leucine, $(CH_3)_2CHCH_2CH(NH_2)CO_2H$, is easily purified because it is much less soluble than the other neutral (dipolar) amino acids, and was so named (Gr. *leukos*, white) because at the time of its first isolation from muscle tissue (1820) whiteness apparently was a distinctive property of a chemical obtained from natural sources. Names of several acids are based upon the source of initial isolation. Thus the sparingly soluble disulfide cystine (Gr. *kystis*, bladder) was isolated first from urinary calculi (1810) and only later (1899) recognized as a constituent of proteins (*e.g.* hair). The disulfide on reduction affords two moles of cysteine, the β-sulfhydryl (or thiol) derivative

$$
\underset{\text{Cysteine}}{\underset{\overset{|}{NH_2}}{2 \ HSCH_2CHCO_2H}} \quad \underset{\overset{|}{H_2}}{\overset{[O]}{\rightleftarrows}} \quad \underset{\text{Cystine}}{\underset{\overset{|}{NH_2}}{\overset{\overset{NH_2}{|}}{SCH_2CHCO_2H}} \atop \underset{}{SCH_2CHCO_2H}} \quad \underset{\text{Methionine}}{\underset{\overset{|}{NH_2}}{CH_3SCH_2CH_2CHCO_2H}}
$$

of alanine. Methionine is the S-methyl ether of homocysteine; the name is compounded from m̲e̲t̲h̲yl + th̲i̲o̲- + i̲n̲e̲. Serine, the hydroxy analog to cysteine, is the most abundant constituent of silk̲ (L. *serieus*, silken) other than glycine and alanine. Tyrosine was obtained first from cheese (Gr. *tyros*, cheese). Tryptophane was isolated as a product of tryptic digestion, but the implication of the last syllable is not clear; -p̲h̲a̲n̲e̲ is a combining form used to denote one substance appearing to resemble another. Aspartic acid and glutamic acid occur in some

$$
\underset{\text{Aspartic acid}}{\underset{\overset{|}{NH_2}}{HO_2CCH_2CHCO_2H}} \qquad\qquad \underset{\text{Glutamic acid}}{\underset{\overset{|}{NH_2}}{HO_2CCH_2CH_2CHCO_2H}}
$$

$$
\underset{\text{Asparagine} = \text{Asp}(NH_2)}{H_2NCOCH_2CH(NH_2)CO_2H} \qquad \underset{\text{Glutamine} = \text{Glu}(NH_2)}{H_2NCOCH_2CH_2CH(NH_2)CO_2H}
$$

proteins as the amides, asparagine and glutamine. The names reflect isolation of asparagine from asparagus and of glutamine from gluten. Although glutamic acid is the α-amino derivative of glutaric acid, the name glutaric acid is derived from glutamic + tartaric acid. Three protein components have an excess of

$$
\underset{\text{Arginine}}{\underset{\overset{}{\underset{H_2N}{}}}{\overset{HN}{\diagdown}}\underset{\overset{|}{NH_2}}{C-N\overset{\delta}{C}H_2CH_2CH_2\overset{\alpha}{C}HCO_2H}} \qquad \underset{\text{Guanidine}}{\overset{HN}{\diagdown}\underset{H_2N\diagup}{}C-NH_2} \qquad \underset{\text{Lysine}}{\underset{\overset{|}{NH_2}}{\overset{\epsilon}{C}H_2CH_2CH_2CH_2\overset{\alpha}{C}HCO_2H} \atop \underset{\overset{|}{NH_2}}{}}
$$

basic over acidic groups. The most strongly basic one is arginine, α-amino-δ-guanidylvaleric acid; guanidine is the imino derivative of urea. The substance was first isolated as the silver salt (L. *argentum*, silver + i̲n̲e̲). Lysine, α,ϵ-diaminocaproic acid, was named as a product of hydroly̲sis (Gr. *lysis*, loosening).

The name of the rare protein component histidine is derived from the Greek *histion*, tissue; this amino acid contains the weakly basic imidazole ring.

Table 31.2 lists amino acids encountered as constituents of only one or two proteins or in nonproteinoid natural products. T. Viswanathe (1960) established that hydroxylysine is a constituent not only of collagen but also of trypsin and chymotrypsin.

The amino acids of the first group listed in Table 31.1 are typified by glycine. In an electric field glycine migrates to the cathode if the solution is acidic and to the anode if it is basic. At pH 5.97, the isoelectric point for this acid, glycine

TABLE 31.2. UNUSUAL AMINO ACIDS

NAME	FORMULA	SOURCE
β-Alanine	$H_2NCH_2CH_2COOH$	Pantothenic acid
α-Aminobutyric acid	$CH_3CH_2CH(NH_2)COOH$	*Corynebacterium diphtheriae*
γ-Aminobutyric acid	$H_2NCH_2CH_2CH_2COOH$	Bacteria, plants, yeast
α,ε-Diaminopimelic acid	$HOOCCH(NH_2)CH_2CH_2CH_2CH(NH_2)COOH$	*Coryn. dipth.*
Thyroxine	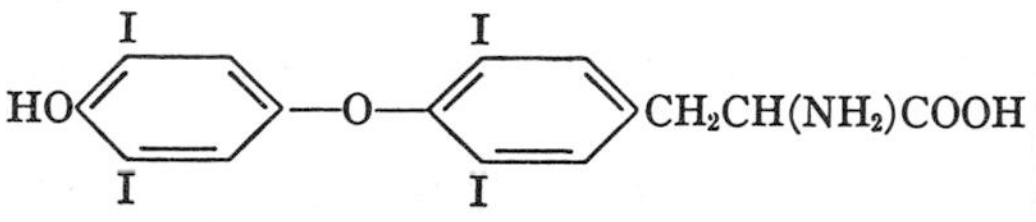	Thyroglobin
Diiodotyrosine	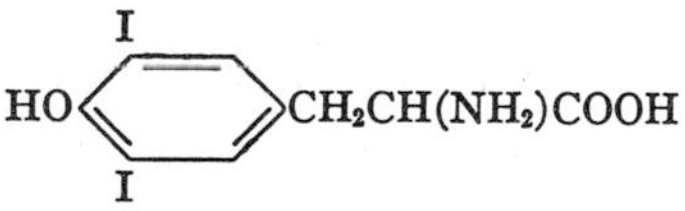	Thyroglobin
β-Thiolvaline	$(CH_3)_2C(SH)CH(NH_2)COOH$	Penicillins
Lanthionine	$S[CH_2CH(NH_2)COOH]_2$	Subtilin
Djenkolic acid	$CH_2[SCH_2CH(NH_2)COOH]_2$	Djenkel nuts
γ-Methyleneglutamic acid	$HOOCC(=CH_2)CH_2CH(NH_2)COOH$	Ground nut
α,γ-Diaminobutyric acid	$H_2NCH_2CH_2CH(NH_2)COOH$	Polymixins
Ornithine	$H_2NCH_2CH_2CH_2CH(NH_2)COOH$	Polypeptides
Hydroxylysine	$H_2NCH_2CH(OH)CH_2CH_2CH(NH_2)COOH$	Collagen
Citrulline	$H_2NCONHCH_2CH_2CH_2CH(NH_2)COOH$	Watermelon, cascin
Canavanine	$H_2NC(=NH)NHOCH_2CH_2CH(NH_2)COOH$	Soybean

does not migrate for it exists as the neutral dipolar ion. The ionic character of the neutral amino acids accounts for their relative infusibility, low volatility,

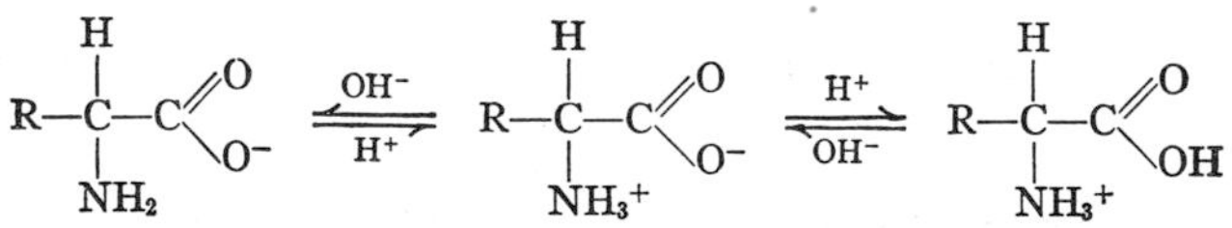

Dipolar ion

solubility in water, lack of solubility in ether, and sparing solubility in absolute ethanol. Isoelectric points of neutral amino acids are in the range 5–6.3, of acidic acids 2.8–3.2, and of basic acids 7.6–10.8.

Constants for both acidic and basic dissociation are expressed as the negative logarithm of a common acidity constant K. With acids, pK corresponds numerically with pK_a. With a basic substance such as methylamine the species $CH_3NH_3^+$ can dissociate to give a proton, and the acidity constant is defined by the expression (1) and correlated with pK_b as in (2), derived by application of the ionization constant of water. The curve obtained on titrating glycine with alkali and plotting points read on a pH meter shows two similar inflections: $pK_1 = 2.4$ and

$$(1) \quad K = \frac{[CH_3NH_2][H^+]}{[CH_3NH_3^+]}$$

$$(2) \quad pK = 14 - pK_b$$

$pK_2 = 9.8$; the first value refers to ionization of the carboxyl group and the second to that of the amino group. In a strongly acidic solution the substance is present as the positively charged ion (*a*). The positive charge tends to repel a proton from the carboxyl group and renders the species (*a*) much more strongly

$$\overset{+}{H_3N}CH_2COOH \underset{pK\ 2.4}{\overset{-H^+}{\rightleftharpoons}} \overset{+}{H_3N}CH_2COO^- \underset{pK\ 9.8}{\overset{-H^+}{\rightleftharpoons}} H_2NCH_2COO^-$$
$$\quad\ (a) \qquad\qquad\qquad (b) \qquad\qquad\qquad (c)$$

acidic than acetic acid (pK 4.76). The neutral dipolar ion (*b*) is thus formed at a lower pH than required to convert acetic acid into the acetate ion. The electrostatic effect must operate against loss of a second proton by ionization of the dipolar species to give (*c*). The fact that the value for pK_2 is less than that of methylamine (pK 10.6) can be attributed to the modifying effect of the adjacent carboxylate group, for glycine ethyl ester ($H_2NCH_2COOC_2H_5$), with which there is no electrostatic effect, is a still weaker base (pK 7.7).

The acidity constants of alanine, leucine, valine, and other monoamino monocarboxylic acids are very close to those of glycine. The dipeptide of glycine, glycylglycine, is weaker both as an acid and as a base, as seen from the constants

$$\overset{+}{H_3N}CH_2COOH \qquad\qquad \overset{+}{H_3N}CH_2CONHCH_2COOH$$
(pK₂ 9.8)   (pK₁ 2.4)   (pK₂ 8.2)   (pK₁ 3.1)
Glycine   Glycylglycine

written under the groups to which they refer; the change in each case can be ascribed to increased distance between functional groups and consequently weaker electrostatic effects. Typical pK values for acidic and basic amino acids are illustrated for aspartic acid and for lysine.

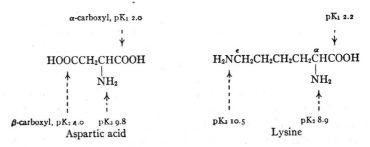

The properties of a protein are dependent upon both the electrical character and the solubilities of the component acids (Table 31.3). In the series glycine, alanine, valine, leucine, and isoleucine solubility in water decreases markedly with

TABLE 31.3. SOLUBILITIES

| ACID | MOL. WT. | G./100 ML.$^{25°}$ | | Rf |
		WATER	ABS. ETH-ANOL	
Glycine	75.07	25.0	0.06	0.41
Alanine	89.09	16.7		.61
Valine	117.15	8.8		.78
Leucine	131.17	2.4	0.07	.84
Isoleucine	131.17	4.1		.84
Proline	115.13	162	67	.88
Cystine	240.30	0.006		.03

increasing size of the alkyl group, as reflected in the molecular weight; isoleucine is nearly twice as soluble as leucine. Leucine, which contains the large, lipophilic isobutyl group, can be extracted with hot butanol from a mixture of this acid with glycine. For some unknown reason the cyclic structure of proline confers on the molecule extraordinary solubility in both water and ethanol, as compared with valine, which has nearly the same molecular weight. The solubility of cystine in water is abnormally low, probably because of chelation (p. 1023).

31.2   **Paper Chromatography.** — This technique, introduced by Martin[1] and Synge[2] in 1944 and now employed in all fields of chemistry, is particularly useful for identification of the components of mixtures of amino acids with di- and tripeptides produced by partial hydrolysis of a protein or a polypeptide. The components of a hydrolyzate are partitioned between water, adsorbed on cellulose and so held in a stationary phase, and an organic solvent (aqueous ethanol, butanol, phenol) which is caused to travel the length of the strip by either ascending or descending flow, a moving phase. The more lipophilic the component acid, the more it tends to travel with the organic solvent; the more hydrophilic, the greater is the tendency to be retained in the stationary water phase. Even homologs differing by a single methylene group travel at sufficiently different rates to be easily differentiated. At the end of the chromatogram the paper is dried and sprayed with ninhydrin to bring out spots revealing the positions of the component acids, since this reagent, indane-1,2,3-trione-2-hydrate, oxidizes amino acids to RCHO, NH$_3$, and CO$_2$ and affords a dihydride

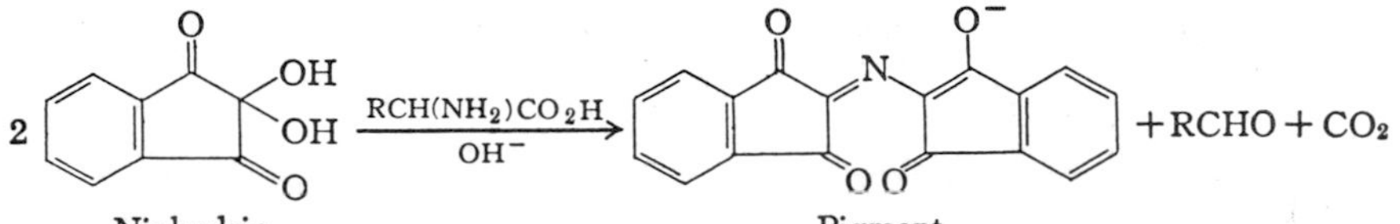

Ninhydrin   Pigment

---

[1] Arthur John Porter Martin, b. 1910; Nat. Inst. Med. Res., Mill Hill, London; Nobel Prize 1952

[2] Richard Lawrence Millington Synge, b. 1914, Liverpool; Ph.D. Cambridge (Pirie); Rowett Res. Inst., Bucksburn, Scotland; Nobel Prize 1952

that combines with the ammonia to produce a pigment.   The ratio of the distance travelled by the amino acid to the distance of solvent travel is the Rf value (rate of flow), a constant characteristic of the specific acid.   In an elaboration of the method the hydrolyzate is placed at the corner of a sheet of paper, a chromatogram is developed by allowing solvent to flow in the direction of the x-axis and then allowing another solvent to flow in the direction of the y-axis; a greater spread is thus achieved.

The Rf values given in Table 31.1 and plotted in the chart indicate the nature of the effect of specific groups on the hydrophilic-lipophilic balance of a protein.

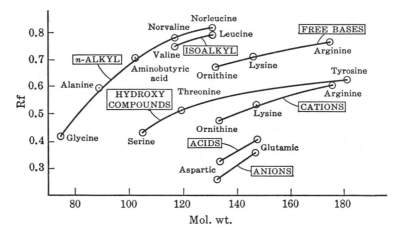

The chart shows that Rf increases with increasing molecular weight, is slightly higher for straight-chain than branched alkyl groups, and decreases with introduction of polar groups.

31.3   Rotatory Power. — That the amino acids from proteins all correspond in the configuration of the α-carbon atom was established by interconversions not involving the asymmetric center, effected mainly by the schools of E. Fischer, P. Karrer, and P. A. Levene (1907–30). Interestingly enough, one of two chemical correlations of the amino acids with the sugars involves deliberate use of a reaction at an asymmetric center.   Having established that S_N2 reactions invariably proceed with Walden inversion and that the reaction of a halogen compound with sodium azide can be controlled to insure bimolecular substitution, Hughes and Ingold (1937) converted D-lactic acid by the process formulated into

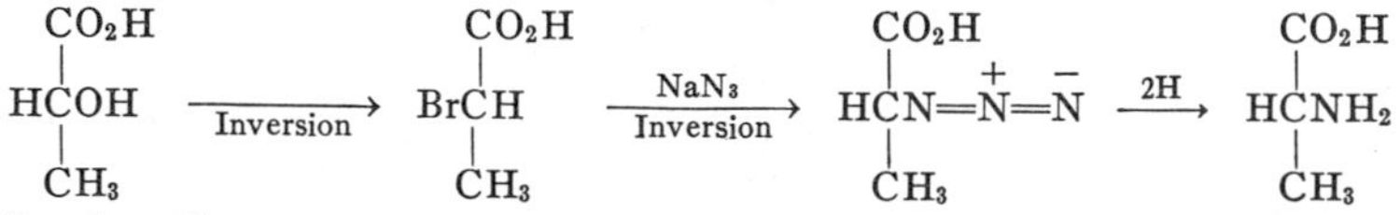

$$\begin{array}{cccc} CO_2H & CO_2H & CO_2H & CO_2H \\ | & | & | & | \\ HCOH & BrCH & HCN{=}\overset{+}{N}{=}\overset{-}{N} & HCNH_2 \\ | & | & | & | \\ CH_3 & CH_3 & CH_3 & CH_3 \\ \text{D-Lactic acid} & & & \text{D-Alanine} \end{array}$$

$$HCOH \xrightarrow[\text{Inversion}]{} BrCH \xrightarrow[\text{Inversion}]{NaN_3} HCN{=}N{=}N \xrightarrow{2H} HCNH_2$$

a product which proved to be unnatural alanine and thereby identified the natural acid as L-alanine.   Wolfrom (1949) achieved a correlation starting with D-glucosamine (2-amino-2-desoxy-D-glucose).   N-Acetyl-D-glucosamine was converted by reaction with ethyl mercaptan into the diethylthioketal, and the corresponding

pentaacetate I was desulfurized with Raney nickel to II.   The O-acetyl groups
were selectively removed by treatment with ammonia, and the resulting N-acetyl

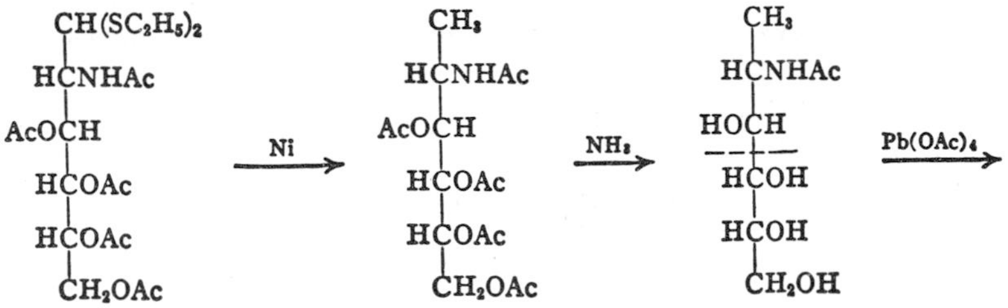

$$
\begin{array}{ccccc}
\text{CH(SC}_2\text{H}_5)_2 & & \text{CH}_3 & & \text{CH}_3 \\
\text{HCNHAc} & & \text{HCNHAc} & & \text{HCNHAc} \\
\text{AcOCH} & \xrightarrow{\text{Ni}} & \text{AcOCH} & \xrightarrow{\text{NH}_3} & \text{HOCH} & \xrightarrow{\text{Pb(OAc)}_4} \\
\text{HCOAc} & & \text{HCOAc} & & \text{HCOH} \\
\text{HCOAc} & & \text{HCOAc} & & \text{HCOH} \\
\text{CH}_2\text{OAc} & & \text{CH}_2\text{OAc} & & \text{CH}_2\text{OH} \\
\text{I} & & \text{II} & & \text{III}
\end{array}
$$

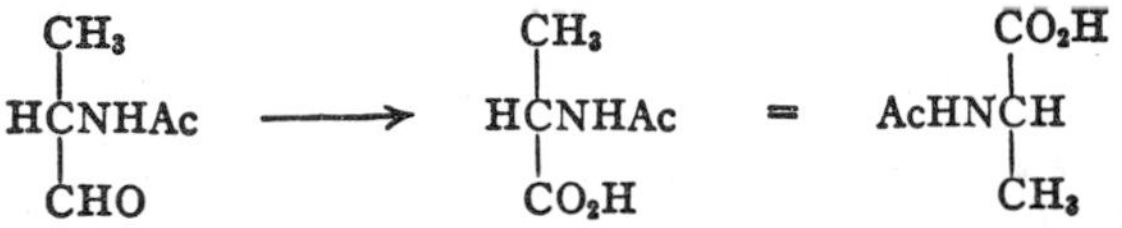

$$
\begin{array}{ccccc}
\text{CH}_3 & & \text{CH}_3 & & \text{CO}_2\text{H} \\
\text{HCNHAc} & \longrightarrow & \text{HCNHAc} & = & \text{AcHNCH} \\
\text{CHO} & & \text{CO}_2\text{H} & & \text{CH}_3 \\
\text{IV} & & \text{Va} & & \text{Vb}
\end{array}
$$

derivative III was oxidized with lead tetraacetate.   The aldehyde IV was oxidized directly with bromine water to the acid, of configuration shown in formula
Va = Vb.   Identity with the acetyl derivative of natural alanine established that
the latter belongs to the L-series.

The molecular rotations of the amino acids present points of interest.   Eleven
of the acids form a group of M_D ranging from -14 to $+22$.   In each of these
acids the side chain R is an alkyl group or an alkyl group containing oxygen or
nitrogen usually two or more carbon atoms removed from the center of asym-

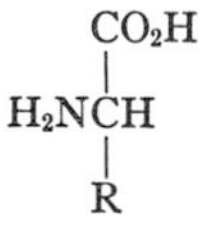

	ACID	R	M_D
	Alanine	$-CH_3$	$+2$
	α-Aminobutyric acid	$-CH_2CH_3$	$+8$
	Valine	$-CH(CH_3)_2$	$+7$
CO_2H	Leucine	$-CH_2CH(CH_3)_2$	-14
H_2NCH	Isoleucine	$-CH(CH_3)CH_2CH_3$	$+15$
R	Alloisoleucine	$-CH(CH_3)CH_2CH_3$	$+18$
	Aspartic acid	$-CH_2CO_2H$	$+6$
	Glutamic acid	$-CH_2CH_2CO_2H$	$+17$
	Ornithine	$-CH_2CH_2CH_2NH_2$	$+15$
	Lysine	$-CH_2CH_2CH_2CH_2NH_2$	$+21$
	Arginine	$-CH_2CH_2CH_2NHC(=NH)NH_2$	$+22$

metry.   The eleven acids of this group are only weakly rotatory, and under the
conditions specified all but leucine are dextrorotatory.   Cysteine, methionine,

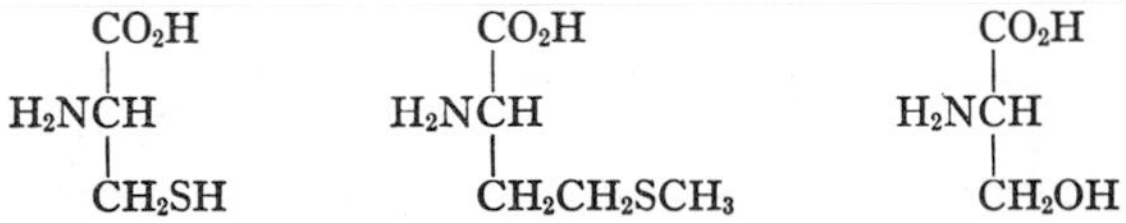

$$
\begin{array}{ccc}
\text{CO}_2\text{H} & \text{CO}_2\text{H} & \text{CO}_2\text{H} \\
\text{H}_2\text{NCH} & \text{H}_2\text{NCH} & \text{H}_2\text{NCH} \\
\text{CH}_2\text{SH} & \text{CH}_2\text{CH}_2\text{SCH}_3 & \text{CH}_2\text{OH} \\
\text{Cysteine} & \text{Methionine} & \text{Serine} \\
M_D-13 & M_D-12 & M_D-7
\end{array}
$$

and serine comprise a small group of weakly levorotatory acids having sulfur or oxygen substituents at the first or second carbon atom of the alkyl group.   A third group includes phenylalanine, histidine, and tryptophane, all of which have very nearly the same, rather pronounced levorotation.   The aromatic rings in

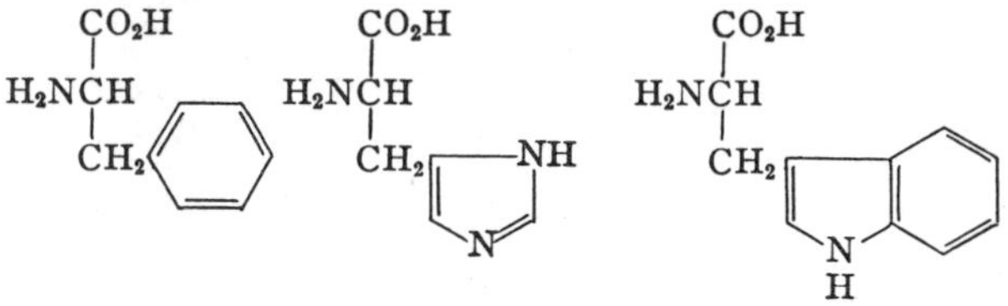

Phenylalanine   Histidine   Tryptophane
M_D-58 M_D-61 M_D-62

these substances, derived, respectively, from benzene, imidazole, and indole, are only one carbon atom removed from the center of asymmetry and exert an effect because they contain conjugated unsaturated systems that absorb light. Proline is more strongly rotatory than any of the natural acids of the above three groups. In this substance the asymmetric carbon atom is incorporated into a five-membered ring, and the case exemplifies a general rule that ring formation produces a marked enhancement of optical rotation.   Perhaps proline has more rotophoric power than a noncyclic analog because of the greater rigidity of the cyclic asymmetric system; a propeller made of soft rubber would have little of the thrust of

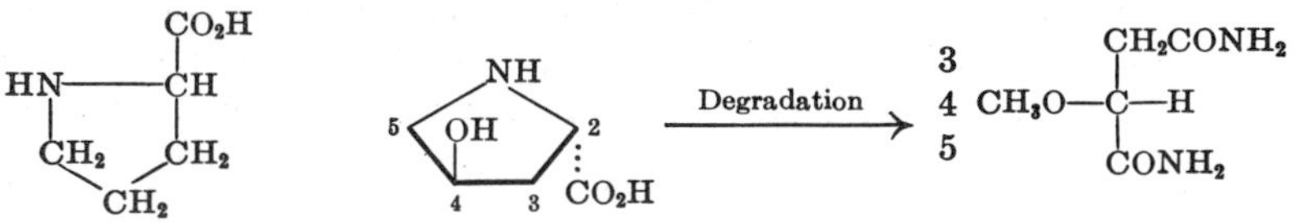

Proline   Hydroxyproline
M_D-98 M_D-100

one made of metal.   The configuration of hydroxyproline was established by C. S. Hudson and A. Neuberger (1950) by degradation to a known $(-)$-methoxy-succinic acid diamide.   The configuration at C_2 is the same as in proline and the other natural acids and the hydroxyl group is *trans* to the carboxyl group.

The strikingly high rotatory power of cystine ($M_D -662$) in contrast with its weakly rotatory reduction product cysteine ($M_D -13$) caught the attention of van't Hoff (1898), who cited the comparison under the heading "Remarkable Cases" and commented as follows: "The small rotation of cysteine ($\alpha_D -8°$) characteristic of the amino acids is maintained when the sulfhydryl hydrogen is replaced by phenyl, bromophenyl, or acetyl ($\alpha_D -7°$).   Upon oxidation to cystine, however, we get at once the enormous value of $\alpha_D -214°$."   In a paper published in 1950 in the *Recueil des travaux chimique des Pays-Bas*, one of us suggested that the anomalously high rotation is because in a neutral solution cystine exists in the chelated endocyclic ring structure I.   The tripeptide glutathione in the disulfide form is similar (II).   The idea is supported by the fact that cystine shows maximal rotatory power in the isoelectric region (M_{5641} -785 at pH 3–7) and that the rotation falls off in acidic or basic solution: M_{5641} -643 at pH 2;

$$
\begin{array}{cc}
\text{I} & \text{II}
\end{array}
$$

Structure I: HOC(=O→H)–NH, HCCH₂SSCH₂CH, HN–COH (O←H), forming a ring.

Structure II: HO₂CCH₂N·C(H)(=O→H)–N·COCH₂CH₂CHCO₂H (NH₂), HCCH₂SSCH₂CH, HO₂CCHCH₂CH₂C·N (NH₂, O), C·NHCH₂CO₂H (H←O).

-168 at pH 12.　F. Haurowitz[1] (1961) attributed large changes in α_D following performic acid cleavage of dithio bridges in proteins rich in cystine chiefly to destruction of the rigid, hydrogen-bonded structure of the cystinyl residues.

31.4　　Analysis. — A protein usually is hydrolyzed by refluxing it with hydrochloric acid (20%) or sulfuric acid (35%). Alkaline hydrolysis is attended with extensive racemization and is employed only for estimation of tryptophane and tyrosine, which are sensitive to mineral acids. Enzymic hydrolysis is slow and probably never complete, but it is nondestructive to sensitive primary products. If aspartic or glutamic acid is present in a protein as the monoamide, acid hydrolysis converts the amide nitrogen to ammonium chloride or sulfate. Kjeldahl determination gives the total nitrogen in the hydrolyzate and the proportion contributed by amide nitrogen is determined by alkalinization of an aliquot portion and distillation of the ammonia into standard acid. The quantity of ammonia parallels the amount of dicarboxylic acids. That the amide nitrogen is bound to the γ-carbonyl group of aspartic acid and the δ-carboxyl group of glutamic acid was established by isolation of asparagine and glutamine after enzymic hydrolysis of proteins. The primary amino content of a protein or a hydrolyzate is accurately determinable by the micromethod of D. D. Van Slyke (1911). An acid containing a primary amino group reacts with nitrous acid with quantitative evolution of nitrogen, which is determined manometrically. Both the α- and ϵ-amino groups of lysine are determinable as Van Slyke nitrogen; in arginine gas is evolved from the α-amino group but not from the guanidyl group. The —NH— groups of proline, tryptophane, and histidine liberate no nitrogen. Glutamine yields two moles of nitrogen. Use of the method is illustrated by a procedure for analysis of the portion of hydrolyzate that is precipitated by phosphotungstic acid. The precipitate contains the three basic amino acids, together with cystine, the amount of which can be calculated from the total nitrogen content of the precipitate (Kjeldahl) and the result of a sulfur determination. The arginine in the precipitate is determined by boiling a sample with sodium hydroxide, which splits off two of the four nitrogens as ammonia (from the guanidyl group). The histidine content can then be calculated from the above results and from the Van Slyke nitrogen content of the precipitate, since the

---

[1] Felix Haurowitz, b. 1896 Prague, Czechoslovakia; M.D. and Dr. ver. nat. Prague (R. von Zeynek); Univ. Istanbul; Indiana Univ.

amount of total nitrogen not accounted for in the nitrous acid reaction corresponds to the summation of three quarters of the arginine nitrogen, which is already known, and two thirds of the histidine nitrogen.

The β-hydroxy-α-amino acids serine and threonine can be determined by cleavage with periodic acid. The amount of ammonia liberated is a measure of the

$$\underset{\underset{\text{OH NH}_2}{|\quad|}}{\text{RCHCHCO}_2\text{H}} \xrightarrow{\text{HIO}_4} \text{RCHO} + \text{NH}_3 + \text{OCHCO}_2\text{H}$$

total amount of the two acids, and the amounts of the individual acids can be established by determination of the specific aldehydes formed, formaldehyde from serine and acetaldehyde from threonine. The cystine content can be determined from the depth of color developed on addition of sodium 1,2-naphthoquinone-4-sulfonate and sodium hydrosulfite (Sullivan reaction); p-dimethylaminobenzaldehyde (Ehrlich's reagent) is a specific color reagent for the indole nucleus of tryptophane.

31.5   Amino Acid Content of Proteins. — Since several proteins contain all twenty of the amino acids listed in Table 31.1, amino acid analysis of a protein hydrolyzate presented a challenging problem. Rittenberg[1] (1940) developed an isotope dilution method in which a labeled acid of known isotopic content, for example isotopic glutamic acid, is added in known amount to the mixture to be analyzed, and glutamic acid is then isolated by the usual procedure. Since the chemical properties of the natural acid and the labeled acid are the same, the isolated material is a representative sample of added acid and acid originally present; the percent recovery is thus unimportant. The amount of acid in the hydrolyzate is calculated from the isotopic analysis of the isolated acid. If the added isotopic synthetic acid is racemic, the hydrolyzate acid is racemized before isolation, or the pure L-form is separated from the isolated racemic acid. The degree of accuracy is independent of the method of isolation, the yield, and the concentration in the hydrolyzate. Snell[2] (1946) introduced a method of quantitative analysis by microbiological assay. A given microorganism requires certain amino acids for growth, and the rate of growth in a medium containing all but one of the essential acids provides an index of the amount of that component present in a test sample. Thus arginine in a hydrolyzate can be determined by the effect on growth of *Lactobacillus casei*; the concentration is determined by comparison with the effect of a standard sample at various concentrations. Chromatographic fractionation on starch columns (Moore[3] and Stein,[4] 1948) or on ion-exchange resins (Moore and Stein, 1951) has become the method of choice. A quantitative ion exchange procedure available on an automatic basis (1958) makes possible a complete amino acid analysis of a mixture containing only 10^{-7} mole of each component (18–24 hrs.).

[1] David Rittenberg, b. 1906 New York; Ph.D. Columbia (Urey); Dept. Biochem., College of Phys. and Surg., Columbia Univ.

[2] Esmond E. Snell, b. 1914 Salt Lake City; Ph.D. Wisconsin (Peterson); Univ. Wisconsin, Texas

[3] Stanford Moore, b. 1913 Chicago; Ph.D. Wisconsin; Rockefeller Inst.

[4] William H. Stein, b. 1911 New York; Ph.D. Columbia; Rockefeller Inst.

TABLE 31.4. AMINO ACID CONTENT OF PROTEINS

Amino Acids, g/100 g. Protein

Protein	Gly	Ala	Val	Leu	Ileu	Cys (Cys)$_2$	Met	Phe	Pro	Ser	Thr	Tyr	Try	Asp	Glu	Arg	Lys	His	Total,[a] g.
Fibroin (silk)	43.6	29.7	3.6	0.91	1.1	—	—	3.36	0.74	16.2	1.6	12.8	0	2.76	2.16	1.1	0.68	0.36	120.6
Keratin (wool)	6.53	4.14	4.54	11.3	—	11.9	0.7	3.65	9.5	10.01	6.42	4.65	1.8	7.2	14.1	10.4	2.76	1.1	110.8
Collagen	27.2	9.5	3.4	3.4	1.8	—	0.8	2.5	15.1	3.37	2.28	1.0	—	6.3	11.3	8.50	4.47	0.74	101.7[b]
Salmin (protamine)	2.95	1.12	3.14	0	1.64	—	—	—	5.80	9.1	—	—	—	—	—	85.2	—	—	108.9
Calf liver histone	5.07	6.94	3.22	5.21	20.5	7.11	4.43	4.08	4.04	4.71	4.80	3.30	—	5.71	4.30	17.4	10.23	2.69	102.2
Ribonuclease	1.3	—	7.3	3.1	3.1	1.86	5.2	3.6	3.6	12.0	9.0	7.93	—	14.2	13.0	5.16	10.4	4.22	106.3
Ovalbumin (hen)	3.05	6.72	7.05	9.2	7.0	—	3.21	7.66	3.6	8.15	4.03	3.68	1.20	9.30	16.50	5.72	6.30	2.35	108.6
β-Lactoglobulin	1.50	7.07	5.67	15.48	5.88	3.39	3.21	3.86	5.27	4.07	5.15	3.69	1.92	11.46	19.10	2.88	11.30	1.60	112.5
α-Casein	2.26	3.81	6.3	7.9	6.4	0.43	2.5	4.6	7.57	6.3	4.9	8.1	1.6	8.4	22.5	4.3	8.9	2.9	109.7
Hemoglobin (horse)	5.60	7.40	9.10	15.40	1.70	1.01	1.0	7.70	3.90	5.80	4.36	3.03	1.70	10.60	8.50	3.65	8.51	8.71	106.0
Serum albumin (human)	1.60	3.70	7.70	11.00	4.80	6.30	1.30	7.80	5.10	3.34	4.60	4.70	0.2	8.95	17.0	6.20	12.30	3.50	103.3
Fibrinogen	5.60	—	4.10	7.10	2.7	2.70	2.60	4.60	5.70	7.0	6.10	5.50	3.30	13.10	14.50	7.80	9.20	2.50	110.0
γ-Globulin	4.2	—	9.7	9.3	4.7	3.1	1.1	4.6	8.1	11.4	8.4	6.8	2.9	8.8	11.8	4.8	8.1	2.5	108.3
Edestin	—	4.31	6.5	7.5	2.8	1.43	2.4	5.45	4.25	6.30	3.85	4.34	1.48	12.0	20.7	16.7	2.4	2.5	106.8
Insulin (ox)	4.3	4.5	7.8	13.2	3.1	12.5	—	8.1	2.5	5.2	2.1	13.0	—	6.8	18.6	3.1	2.5	4.9	113.6
ACTH	8.0	—	3.4	7.8	—	7.2	1.9	4.0	8.2	6.0	3.2	2.4	—	6.7	15.6	8.7	5.0	1.3	92.5
Thyroglobulin[c] (ox)	3.7	7.4	1.45	12.80	—	3.60	1.30	6.68	—	10.80	—	3.12	2.08	—	—	12.72	3.42	2.23	71.3
Growth hormone (ox)	3.8	—	3.9	12.1	4.0	2.5	2.9	7.9	3.4	5.7	6.1	5.2	0.84	9.0	13.0	9.1	7.1	2.65	99.2

[a] Since water is incorporated into the molecules of the component acids, the theoretical totals vary from protein to protein and are all well over 100 g.

[b] Includes 14.0 g. of hydroxyproline and 1.1 g. of hydroxylysine.

[c] Contains also 0.21% thyroxine and 0.54% diiodotyrosine.

Gas chromatography of the aldehydes liberated on reaction with ninhydrin is limited to determination of neutral amino acids (I. R. Hunter, 1956; A. Zlatkis, 1960). Gas-liquid chromatographic separation of N-acetylamino acid amyl esters (*n*- and *iso*-) at relatively low temperatures (95–148°) has been used for analysis of hydrolyzates of small peptides eluted from paper chromatograms and offers promise for amino acid analysis of proteins (A. Meister, 1961).

Analyses of representative proteins are given in Table 31.4, inspection of which will show that protein type is not characterized by any particular amino acid pattern. The first three proteins listed, fibroin (silk), keratin (wool), and collagen (connective tissue), are of the fibrous, water-insoluble type, but they vary considerably in amino acid content. Thus the acidic acid constituents range from 5 to 21 g., the basic acids from 2 to 14 g., sulfur-containing acids from 0 to 13 g. hydroxy acids from 21 to 31 g., other neutral amino acids from 42 to 83 g. The amino acid pattern of water-soluble ovalbumin is comparable: basic 14.4 g., acidic 25.8 g., S-acids 7.1 g., hydroxy acids, 31.0 g., other neutral acids, 45.5 g. The last four proteins in the table are hormones, and again no particular amino acid pattern is discernible, except that thyroglobulin is the only protein containing iodinated amino acids. Insulin has a high content of cysteine-cystine, but so does keratin. It is known that the amino acid composition of a protein of highly specialized properties varies from species to species (*e.g.* insulin, M. Harfenist, 1953).

31.6   Essential Amino Acids. — In 1906 young rats fed on a diet containing zein (protein of corn) as the sole source of protein were found incapable of maintaining body weight. Zein lacks lysine and tryptophane, and addition of these acids to the diet permits normal growth. A nutritional study led W. C. Rose (1935) to discover threonine. A mixture of threonine and nineteen other pure amino acids supports growth of rats, but omission of threonine causes loss in body weight. Rose defined an essential amino acid as one that is not synthesized by an animal at a rate necessary for normal growth from materials ordinarily available. The eight amino acids essential to man (Table 31.5) are used as dietary supplements for protein-depleted patients; doses of 1–2 g. per day are recommended for the normal adult. Lysine added to wheat-based foods and to poultry feed improves growth and tissue synthesis.

Glutamic acid, nonessential but valued for enhancement of flavor (3.12), is manufactured by acid hydrolysis of vegetable proteins such as gluten and soybean cake. Protein sources are used also for production of phenylalanine (ovalbumin, zein) and arginine; the strongly basic acid is precipitated from gelatin hydrolyzate as the flavianate (2,4-dinitro-1-naphthol-7-sulfonate). Laboratory procedures (*Org. Syn., Biochem. Preps.*) are available for the preparation of cystine from horsehair (1 kg. → 50 g.), alanine and serine from degummed Japanese white silk,

TABLE 31.5.   ESSENTIAL AMINO ACIDS

Rat	Arg	His	Ileu	Leu	Lys	Met	Phe	Thr	Try	Val
Man			Ileu	Leu	Lys	Met	Phe	Thr	Try	Val

tryptophane (and tyrosine) from casein, and histidine and lysine (by separate processes) from commercial dried blood corpuscle paste. Lysine is precipitated from the hydrolyzate as the sparingly soluble monopicrate.

31.7 **Resolution of Synthetic Acids.** — Greenstein[1] developed a practical method for enzymic resolution of DL-acids. DL-Alanine, for example, is acetylated, and the DL-acetate is treated with a solution containing an enzyme capable of effecting deacetylation. The solution is easily prepared from fresh pork

$$
\underset{\substack{| \\ NH_2 \\ \text{DL-Alanine}}}{CH_3CHCO_2H} \longrightarrow \underset{\substack{| \\ NHCOCH_3 \\ \text{DL-Acetate}}}{CH_3CHCO_2H} \longrightarrow \underset{\substack{| \\ CH_3 \\ \text{L-Alanine} \\ \text{M.p. } 297° \\ \text{Insol. } C_2H_5OH}}{\overset{CO_2H}{\underset{|}{H_2NCH}}} + \underset{\substack{| \\ CH_3 \\ \text{Acetyl D-alanine} \\ \text{M.p. } 125° \\ \text{Sol. } C_2H_5OH}}{\overset{CO_2H}{\underset{|}{HCNHCOCH_3}}}
$$

kidneys. Slices are agitated with water in a Waring blender and the homogenate centrifuged. The clear supernatant liquid containing enzyme is decanted into a bag made from cellophane sausage casing, which is then soaked in running water overnight to remove soluble nonproteinoid kidney components by dialysis, and the residual enzyme solution after a second centrifugation is ready for use. The action on the DL-acetate is complete in about four hours. The enzyme acts preferentially on the natural acetate and the result is a mixture of natural L-alanine and acetyl D-alanine. The mixture is easily separated because free alanine is insoluble in ethanol and the acetyl derivative is soluble.

A second method is based upon deamination by an oxidase (Krebs, 1933). D-Oxidases occur widely and may serve for destruction or utilization of unnatural

$$
\underset{\substack{| \\ CO_2H}}{RCHNH_2} \underset{}{\overset{-2H}{\rightleftarrows}} \underset{\substack{| \\ CO_2H}}{RC=NH} \underset{NH_3}{\overset{H_2O}{\rightleftarrows}} \underset{\substack{| \\ CO_2H}}{RC=O}
$$

amino acids; L-oxidases are found mostly in snake venoms and certain molds Greenstein (1958) prepared a number of optically pure acids on a small scale by treatment of DL-acids with two enzymes. Rattlesnake venom L-amino acid oxidase afforded D-amino acids, and hog renal D-amino oxidase gave the L-isomers.

SYNTHESIS OF AMINO ACIDS

31.8 **α-Haloacid Synthesis.** — α-Halogenation of an acid and amination was the method employed in the first synthesis of an amino acid (glycine, Perkin and Duppa, 1858). The Gabriel synthesis gives better yields and purer products.

31.9 **Strecker[2] Synthesis** (1850). — When a cyanohydrin is formed in the presence of ammonia, addition occurs and the product is an aminonitrile, which affords an α-amino acid on hydrolysis. Fischer (1902) prepared

[1] Jesse P. Greenstein, 1902–59; b. 1902 New York; Ph.D. Brown (Mitchell); Nat. Cancer Inst.

[2] Adolph Strecker, 1822–71; assistant to Liebig at Tübingen

$$CH_3CHO \xrightarrow{NH_3,\ HCN} CH_3CHC\equiv N \xrightarrow{2\ H_2O} CH_3CHCOOH$$

Acetaldehyde $\quad\quad\quad$ | $\quad\quad\quad\quad\quad\quad$ |

$\quad\quad\quad\quad\quad\quad\quad\quad\quad$ NH_2 $\quad\quad\quad\quad\quad\quad$ NH_2

$\quad\quad\quad\quad\quad\quad\quad$ Aminonitrile $\quad\quad\quad\quad$ Alanine

serine by this method from the difficultly accessible and unstable glycolaldehyde (HOCH_2CHO). Later workers used ethoxyacetaldehyde, but the overall yield

$$C_2H_5OCH_2CH_2OH \xrightarrow[43\%]{Cu,\ 250-275°} C_2H_5OCH_2CHO \xrightarrow{NH_3,\ HCN} C_2H_5OCH_2CH(NH_2)CN \xrightarrow{HBr}$$

Ethylene glycol $\quad\quad\quad\quad\quad\quad$ Ethoxyacetaldehyde

monoethyl ether

$$HOCH_2CH(NH_2 \cdot HBr)COOH \longrightarrow HOCH_2CH(NH_2)COOH$$

$\quad\quad\quad\quad\quad\quad\quad\quad\quad\quad\quad\quad\quad\quad\quad\quad$ Serine

is only 40%. Bucherer improved the Strecker synthesis by treating the amino-nitrile with ammonium carbonate to form the hydantoin, which is hydrolyzed

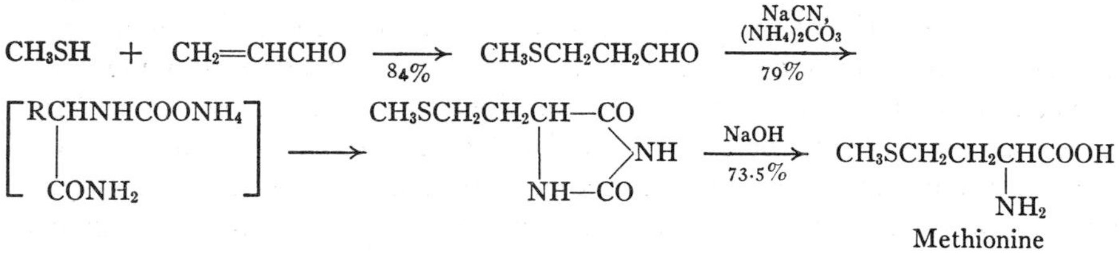

$$CH_3SH + CH_2=CHCHO \xrightarrow{84\%} CH_3SCH_2CH_2CHO \xrightarrow[79\%]{NaCN,\ (NH_4)_2CO_3}$$

$$\begin{bmatrix} RCHNHCOONH_4 \\ | \\ CONH_2 \end{bmatrix} \longrightarrow \begin{array}{c} CH_3SCH_2CH_2CH-CO \\ | \quad\quad\quad >NH \\ NH-CO \end{array} \xrightarrow[73.5\%]{NaOH} CH_3SCH_2CH_2CHCOOH$$

$\quad\quad\quad\quad\quad\quad\quad\quad\quad\quad\quad\quad\quad\quad\quad\quad\quad\quad\quad\quad\quad\quad\quad\quad\quad$ NH_2

$\quad\quad\quad\quad\quad\quad\quad\quad\quad\quad\quad\quad\quad\quad\quad\quad\quad\quad\quad\quad\quad\quad\quad\quad$ Methionine

readily to the amino acid. Tishler (1948) used the Bucherer modification for the synthesis of methionine from acrolein and doubled the yield.

31.10 **Malonic Ester Synthesis.** — The method is illustrated by Fischer's synthesis of leucine (1906). A combination of the malonic ester and phthalimide methods is exemplified by G. Barger's synthesis of methionine (1931). Acids which have been prepared in this way are Phe, Ser, Asp, Pro, Tyr, and

$$(CH_3)_2CHCH_2Br \xrightarrow[hydrol.]{NaCH(CO_2Et)_2:} (CH_3)_2CHCH_2CH(CO_2H)_2 \xrightarrow[heat]{Br_2;}$$

$$(CH_3)_2CHCH_2CHBrCO_2H \xrightarrow{NH_3} (CH_3)_2CHCH_2CH(NH_2)CO_2H$$

$\quad\quad\quad\quad\quad\quad\quad\quad\quad\quad\quad\quad\quad\quad\quad\quad\quad$ Leucine

$$H_2NCHCH_2CH_2SCH_3$$

$\quad\quad\quad$ |

$\quad\quad\quad$ CO_2H

$\quad\quad\quad$ Methionine

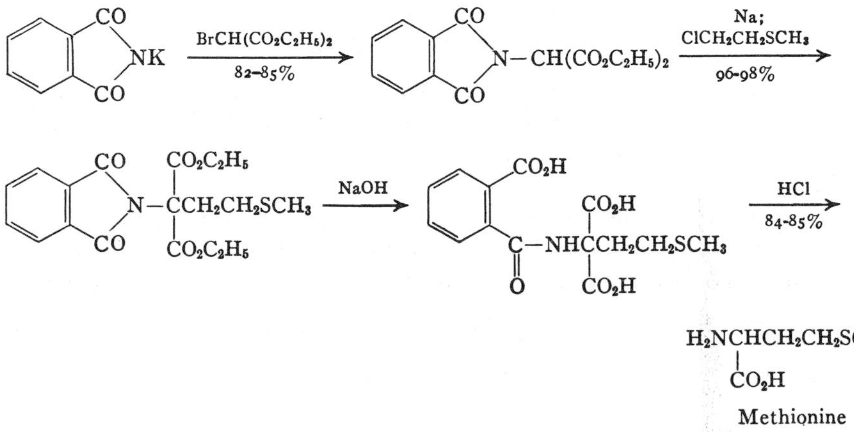

CyS-SCy. The acetamido and benzoylamido derivatives of malonic ester are useful synthetic intermediates. An improved procedure affording diethyl

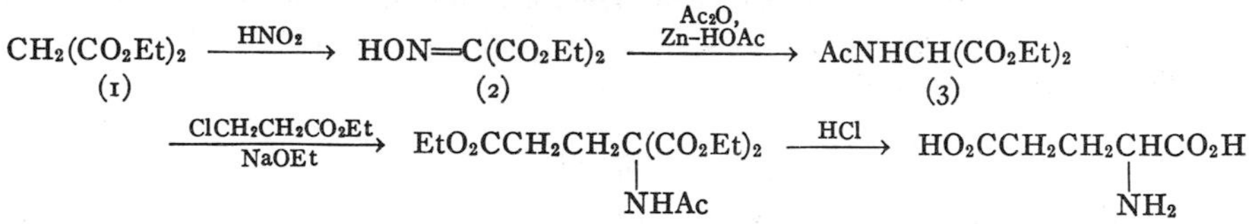

$$CH_2(CO_2Et)_2 \xrightarrow{HNO_2} HON{=}C(CO_2Et)_2 \xrightarrow[\text{Zn-HOAc}]{Ac_2O,} AcNHCH(CO_2Et)_2$$
$$\text{(1)} \qquad\qquad\qquad \text{(2)} \qquad\qquad\qquad\qquad \text{(3)}$$

$$\xrightarrow[\text{NaOEt}]{ClCH_2CH_2CO_2Et} \underset{\underset{NHAc}{|}}{EtO_2CCH_2CH_2C(CO_2Et)_2} \xrightarrow{HCl} \underset{\underset{NH_2}{|}}{HO_2CCH_2CH_2CHCO_2H}$$
$$\text{(4)} \qquad\qquad\qquad\qquad\qquad\qquad \text{(5) Glutamic acid}$$

acetamidomalonate (3) in 77–78% yield from malonic ester involves conversion to the isonitroso derivative (2), which is not isolated (E. E. Howe, Merck Co., *Org. Syn.* 1960). M. S. Dunn (1939) developed the method for the synthesis of glutamic acid (5). In a similar synthesis of tryptophane from indole (66% overall), alkylation is done with a tertiary amine containing a benzyl-type group.

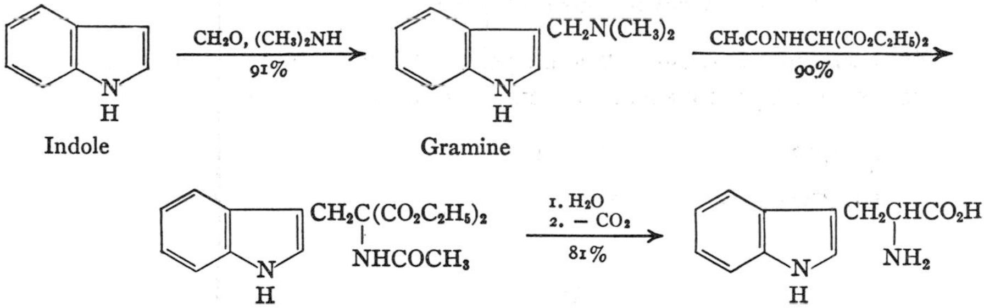

Indole → Gramine → Tryptophane

Curtius applied his azide degradation to the synthesis of glycine, alanine, valine, and phenylalanine.

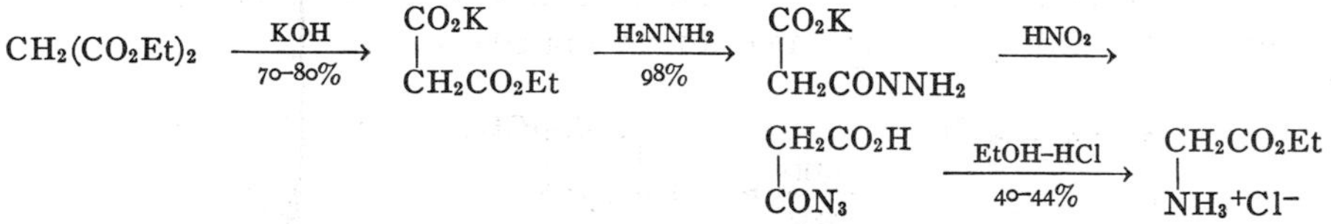

$$CH_2(CO_2Et)_2 \xrightarrow[70\text{–}80\%]{KOH} \underset{\underset{CH_2CO_2Et}{|}}{CO_2K} \xrightarrow[98\%]{H_2NNH_2} \underset{\underset{CH_2CONNH_2}{|}}{CO_2K} \xrightarrow{HNO_2}$$

$$\underset{\underset{CON_3}{|}}{CH_2CO_2H} \xrightarrow[40\text{–}44\%]{EtOH\text{–}HCl} \underset{\underset{NH_3{}^+Cl^-}{|}}{CH_2CO_2Et}$$

31.11 Aldehyde Condensations. — An amino acid having an aryl group (Phe, Tyr, Try) can be prepared by condensation of the appropriate

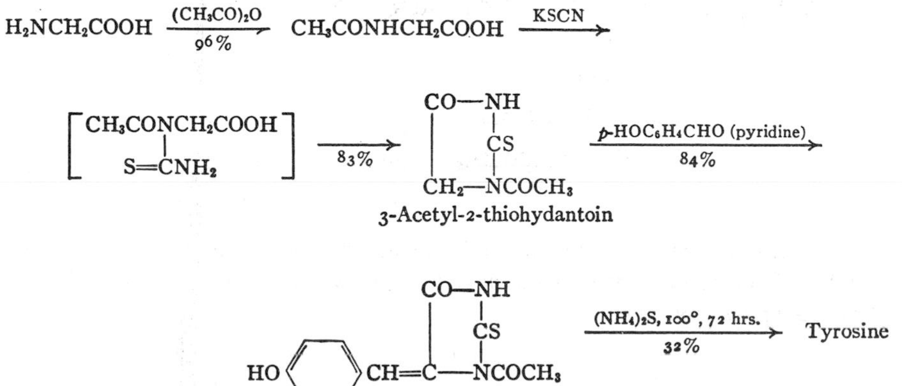

$$H_2NCH_2COOH \xrightarrow[96\%]{(CH_3CO)_2O} CH_3CONHCH_2COOH \xrightarrow{KSCN}$$

$$\left[\underset{\underset{S{=}CNH_2}{|}}{CH_3CONCH_2COOH} \right] \xrightarrow{83\%} \begin{array}{c} CO{-}NH \\ | \qquad | \\ \phantom{CH_2{-}}CS \\ | \qquad | \\ CH_2{-}NCOCH_3 \end{array} \xrightarrow[84\%]{p\text{-}HOC_6H_4CHO\ (pyridine)}$$
$$\text{3-Acetyl-2-thiohydantoin}$$

$$HO{-}\hexagon{-}CH{=}\underset{}{\overset{}{C}}\begin{array}{c} CO{-}NH \\ | \qquad | \\ \phantom{CH{=}C}CS \\ | \qquad | \\ {-}NCOCH_3 \end{array} \xrightarrow[32\%]{(NH_4)_2S,\ 100°,\ 72\ hrs.} \text{Tyrosine}$$

aromatic aldehyde with a hydantoin, or better with a thiohydantoin, as in the synthesis of tyrosine (1935) formulated. In place of a hydantoin, Dunn employed diketopiperazine, prepared from glycine ethyl ester (Fischer) or by heating glycine in the minimum quantity of water and glycerol at 170° for 4 hrs. (L. Balbiano, yield 50–60%).

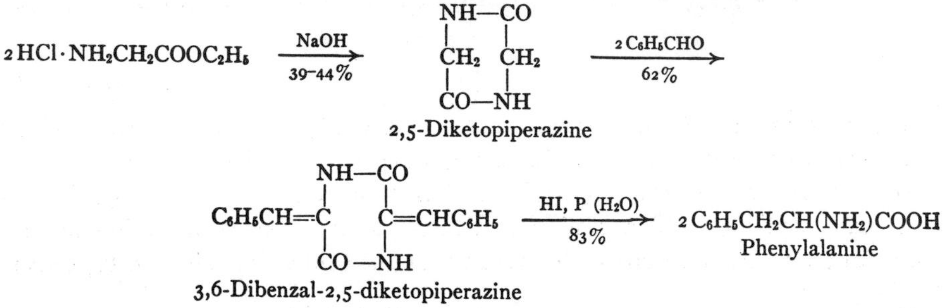

$$2\,HCl\cdot NH_2CH_2COOC_2H_5 \xrightarrow[39\text{-}44\%]{NaOH}$$

NH—CO
| |
CH₂ CH₂
| |
CO—NH

$$\xrightarrow[62\%]{2\,C_6H_5CHO}$$

2,5-Diketopiperazine

NH—CO
| |
C₆H₅CH=C C=CHC₆H₅
| |
CO—NH

$$\xrightarrow[83\%]{HI,\ P\ (H_2O)}\ 2\,C_6H_5CH_2CH(NH_2)COOH$$

Phenylalanine

3,6-Dibenzal-2,5-diketopiperazine

The azlactone synthesis of Erlenmeyer, Jr. (1883) consists in condensation of an aldehyde with hippuric acid and acetic anhydride to form an azlactone, which on

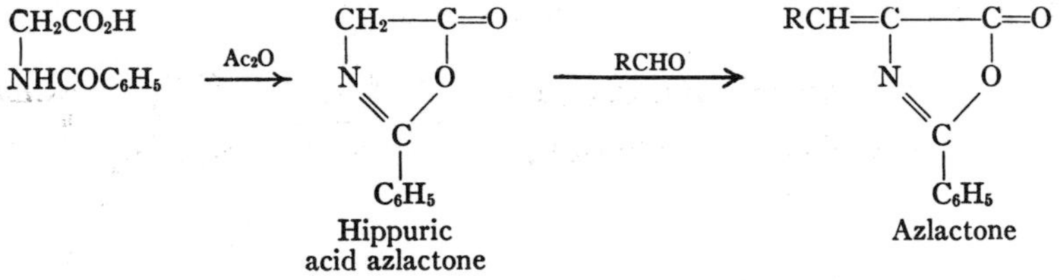

CH₂CO₂H
|
NHCOC₆H₅

$$\xrightarrow{Ac_2O}$$

CH₂——C=O
| |
N O
\\ /
C
|
C₆H₅
Hippuric
acid azlactone

$$\xrightarrow{RCHO}$$

RCH=C——C=O
| |
N O
\\ /
C
|
C₆H₅
Azlactone

reduction and hydrolysis yields an amino acid. Hippuric acid is first converted into its azlactone, which has a reactive methylene group available for condensation with the aldehyde to form an α,β-unsaturated azlactone.

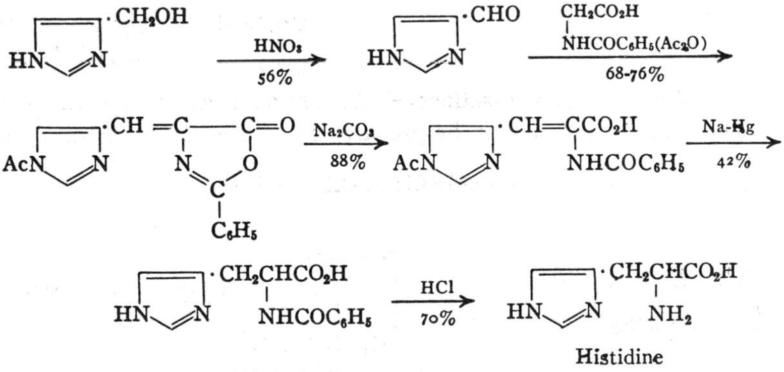

·CH₂OH
[imidazole] HN N

$$\xrightarrow[56\%]{HNO_3}$$

·CHO
[imidazole] HN N

$$\xrightarrow[68\text{-}76\%]{\begin{array}{c}CH_2CO_2H\\NHCOC_6H_5(Ac_2O)\end{array}}$$

·CH=C——C=O
[imidazole] AcN N, N O
\\ /
C
|
C₆H₅

$$\xrightarrow[88\%]{Na_2CO_3}$$

·CH=CCO₂H
[imidazole] AcN N, NHCOC₆H₅

$$\xrightarrow[42\%]{Na\text{-}Hg}$$

·CH₂CHCO₂H
[imidazole] HN N, NHCOC₆H₅

$$\xrightarrow[70\%]{HCl}$$

·CH₂CHCO₂H
[imidazole] HN N, NH₂

Histidine

The synthesis of histidine (1911) is shown in the formulation (11% overall yield). This method has been employed for the synthesis of Phe (39–43%), Leu, Try (10–17%), thyroxine.

An interesting variation involves condensation of the aldehyde with rhodanine, as illustrated for the synthesis of phenylalanine.

$$2NH_3 + S{=}C{=}S \longrightarrow \underset{\substack{\text{Ammonium}\\\text{dithiocarbamate}}}{NH_4S{-}\overset{\overset{\displaystyle NH_2}{|}}{C}{=}S} \xrightarrow{ClCH_2COONa} S{:}\overset{\overset{\displaystyle NH_2}{|}}{C}\diagdown\diagdown\overset{\overset{\displaystyle COONa}{|}}{CH_2} \xrightarrow{HCl}$$

$$\underset{\substack{\text{Rhodanine}\\\text{(60–66\% overall yield)}}}{S{:}\overset{\overset{\displaystyle NH{-}CO}{|\qquad|}}{C}\diagdown_S\diagup CH_2} + C_6H_5CHO \xrightarrow[90\%]{} S{:}\overset{\overset{\displaystyle NH{-}CO}{|\qquad|}}{C}\diagdown_S\diagup C{=}CHC_6H_5 \xrightarrow[77-84\%]{Ba(OH)_2}$$

$$\underset{\substack{\displaystyle |\\COOH}}{C_6H_5CH_2C{=}S} \xrightarrow[77\%]{NH_2OH} \underset{\substack{\displaystyle |\\COOH}}{C_6H_5CH_2C{=}NOH} \xrightarrow[(80-90\%)]{H_2(Na{-}Hg)} \underset{\substack{\displaystyle |\\COOH}}{C_6H_5CH_2CHNH_2}$$

31.12   **Special Methods.** — Serine is prepared most satisfactorily through the α-halo-β-hydroxy acid (H. E. Carter, 1936); the overall yield is 30–40%.

$$\underset{\text{Methyl acrylate}}{CH_2{=}CHCOOCH_3} \xrightarrow[CH_3OH]{Hg(OAc)_2} CH_3OCH_2CH(HgOAc)COOCH_3 \xrightarrow{KBr}$$

81–86% overall

$$CH_3OCH_2CH(HgBr)COOCH_3 \xrightarrow{Br_2} \underset{\substack{\text{Methyl } \alpha\text{-bromo-}\\\beta\text{-methoxypropionate}}}{CH_3OCH_2CHBrCOOCH_3} \xrightarrow{NaOH(H_2SO_4)}$$

$$CH_3OCH_2CHBrCOOH \xrightarrow{NH_3} CH_3OCH_2CH(NH_2)COOH \xrightarrow{HBr}$$

$$CH_2(OH)CH(NH_3Br)COOH \xrightarrow{NH_3} \underset{\text{Serine}}{CH_2(OH)CH(NH_2)COOH}$$

The classical threonine synthesis utilized similar reactions applied to crotonic acid. Most methods of making the intermediate α-bromo-β-methoxy-n-butyric acid give material that on amination affords chiefly allothreonine and at most 35% of threonine, as determined by microbiological assay. Tishler and co-workers

$$\underset{\text{Crotonic acid}}{\overset{\displaystyle HCCO_2H}{\underset{\displaystyle CH_3CH}{\|}}} \xrightarrow[(trans)]{Br_2,CH_3OH} \underset{\text{DL-Allo (chiefly)}}{\underbrace{\underset{\substack{\displaystyle |\\CH_3OCH\\\displaystyle |\\CH_3}}{BrCH} + \underset{\substack{\displaystyle |\\HCOCH_3\\\displaystyle |\\CH_3}}{\overset{\displaystyle CO_2H}{HCBr}}}} \xrightarrow[(\text{no inversion})]{\substack{NH_3;\\ \text{hydrol.}}} \underset{\text{(chiefly)}}{\text{DL-Allothreonine}}$$

$$\underset{\text{DL-Threonine (chiefly)}}{\underbrace{\underset{\substack{\displaystyle |\\CH_3OCH\\\displaystyle |\\CH_3}}{\overset{\displaystyle CONR_2}{BrCH}} + \underset{\substack{\displaystyle |\\HCOCH_3\\\displaystyle |\\CH_3}}{\overset{\displaystyle CONR_2}{HCBr}}}} \xrightarrow[(\text{inversion})]{\substack{NH_3;\\ \text{hydrol.}}} \underset{\text{(chiefly)}}{\text{DL-Threonine}}$$

(1949) found that amination of the bromomethoxy acid proceeds without inversion and that under most conditions the addition of hypobromite follows predominantly the *trans* course to give an intermediate of allothreo configuration. They then found that when the acid is converted into a tertiary amide and this is aminated, inversion occurs to a large extent; this sequence of reactions is one practical synthesis. Another, also developed by the Merck group, proceeds from acetoacetic ester (I) through its acetylamino derivative (III), which is hydro-

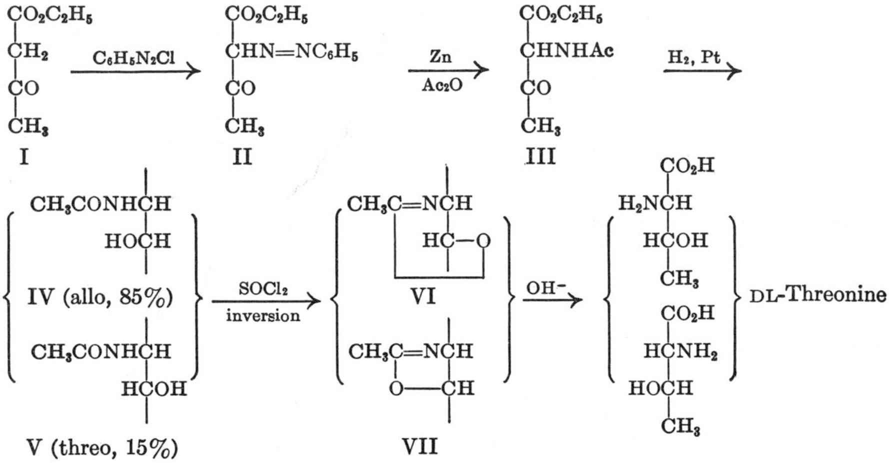

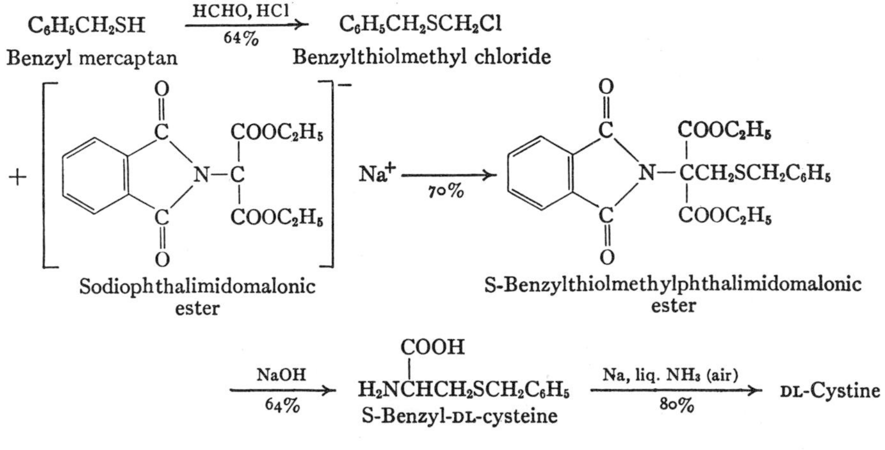

genated quantitatively in water solution to a mixture containing 85% of DL-acetylallothreonine (IV). The mixture, without being separated, is cyclized to a mixture of oxazolines; since both IV and V react with inversion, the oxazoline hydrolyzate is a mixture in which DL-threonine predominates in the ratio 85:15. On conversion into the sodium salt in alcohol the salt of the small amount of DL-allothreonine remains in solution, and the much less soluble salt of DL-threonine separates and affords the pure DL-acid in 57% overall yield. The oxazoline of allothreonine ester can be isomerized with a trace of alkali to the oxazoline of threonine (D. F. Elliot, 1948) and when this step is applied no separation is required and the yield is raised.

A first synthesis of L-cystine (Fischer, 1908) utilized L-serine as starting material. A synthesis by the phthalimidomalonic ester method is formulated (du Vigneaud, 1939).

Another synthetic route involves formation of the α-amino group by reduction of an α-oximido derivative (oxime). Thus Bouveault (1906) prepared isoleucine from the alkylacetoacetic ester I via the oxime II; the reaction with nitrosyl chloride is attended with acid cleavage. Later improvements include treatment

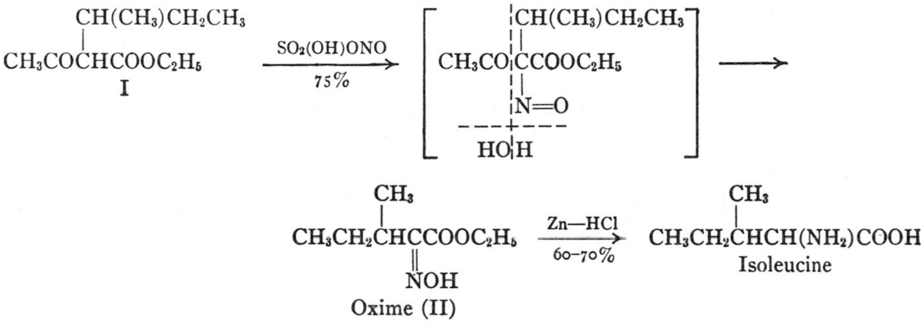

$$CH_3COCHCOOC_2H_5 \quad \xrightarrow[75\%]{SO_2(OH)ONO} \quad \left[CH_3CO\!-\!CCOOC_2H_5 \right] \longrightarrow$$

with CH(CH₃)CH₂CH₃ groups:

I ; intermediate with CH(CH₃)CH₂CH₃, N=O, HO|H

$$CH_3CH_2CHCCOOC_2H_5 \quad \xrightarrow[60\text{-}70\%]{Zn\text{--}HCl} \quad CH_3CH_2CHCH(NH_2)COOH$$

with CH₃ substituents; NOH

Oxime (II)   Isoleucine

of the substituted acetoacetic ester (type of I) with an alkyl nitrite (catalyst: H₂SO₄) and reduction by hydrogenation (Pd). Acids synthesized in this way include Ala, Norval, Norleu, Ileu, Asp, Phe, Glu, and Tyr.

One of several methods for the production of lysine utilizes commercial caprolactam (1) as starting material (M. Brenner, 1958). This is converted in two

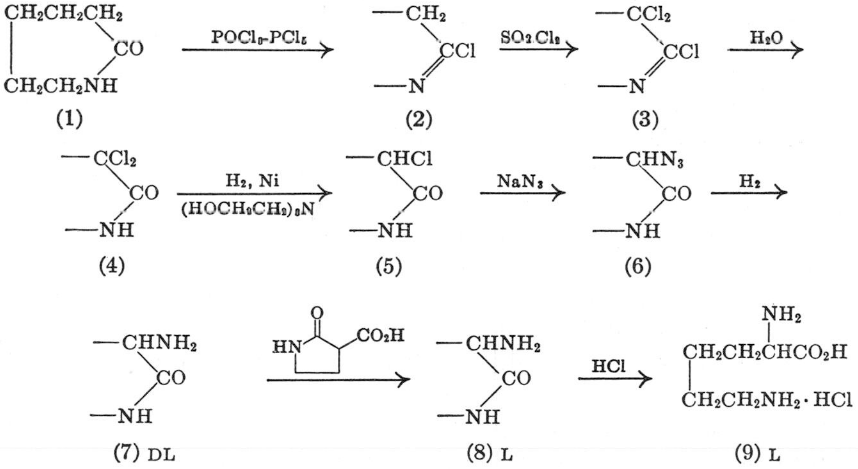

$$\begin{array}{ccc}
\text{CH}_2\text{CH}_2\text{CH}_2 & \xrightarrow{\text{POCl}_3\text{-PCl}_5} & -\text{CH}_2 \\
\quad\diagdown\text{CO} & & \quad\diagdown\text{CCl} \\
\text{CH}_2\text{CH}_2\text{NH} & & -\text{N}
\end{array}$$

(1) → (2) $\xrightarrow{SO_2Cl_2}$ (3) $\xrightarrow{H_2O}$

(2) —CCl₂ / —N ; (3) —CCl₂ / —N

(4) —CCl₂ / CO / —NH $\xrightarrow[(HOCH_2CH_2)_3N]{H_2, Ni}$ (5) —CHCl / CO / —NH $\xrightarrow{NaN_3}$ (6) —CHN₃ / CO / —NH $\xrightarrow{H_2}$

(7) DL —CHNH₂ / CO / —NH ; with HN–CO₂H (pyrrolidone) → (8) L —CHNH₂ / CO / —NH $\xrightarrow{HCl}$ (9) L

$$CH_2CH_2CHCO_2H$$ with NH₂; $$CH_2CH_2NH_2 \cdot HCl$$

stages of chlorination to the α,α-dichloroimide chloride (3), which is hydrolyzed by water to (4). Hydrogenation removes one chlorine atom (5) and the other is replaced smoothly by an azide group (6). Hydrogenation gives DL-α-amino-caprolactam (7), which is resolved with L-pyrrolidonecarboxylic acid, prepared from L-glutamic acid. By an ingenious scheme of crystallization, splitting with hydrochloric acid, racemization, and recycling, the DL-α-aminocaprolactam is converted into about equal parts of L-lysine monohydrochloride and DL-α-amino-caprolactam, with recovery of the L'-acid. DL-Lysine can be produced in overall yield of 50%.

PROTEIN TYPES

31.13   Fibrous Proteins. — This group includes fibroin (silk), collagen (connective tissue), and keratin (skin, hair, wool, horn, feathers, nails). They are all insoluble in water, but collagen on being boiled with water is converted into water-soluble gelatin. Fibroin and keratin are resistant to hydrolysis by water or by enzymes.

X-ray diffraction analysis (Meyer and Mark,[1] 1928) of fibroin reveals an identity period along the fiber axis apparently corresponding to recurring pairs of amino acids of analogous type. The protein is made up largely of four neutral amino acids, two with hydroxyl groups and two without, and an identity period of 7 Å may be due to a pair such as that formulated. The length of one amino acid unit

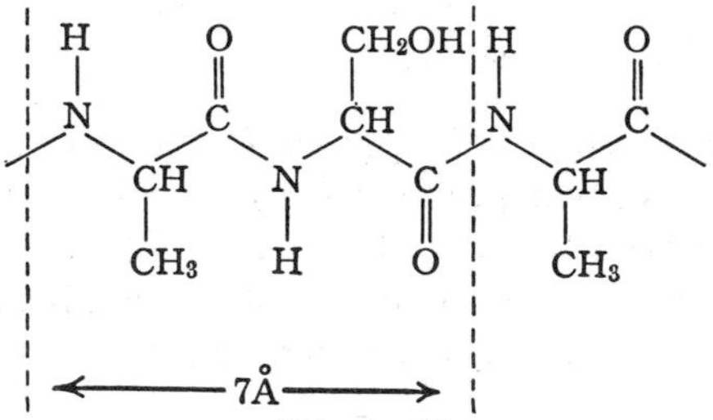

Fibroin (?)

is then half this amount, or 3.5 Å. The keratins of hair and wool possess elastic properties, believed from X-ray evidence to be because in the unstretched protein the polypeptide chain is folded over onto itself. Stretching unfolds the loops and gives a chain of amino acid units of identity period 3.3 Å, comparable to fibroin. Keratin is rich in cystine, which provides disulfide cross links between peptide chains. Wool can be modified, and hair curled, by reduction with a mercaptan to break some of the cross links and reoxidation to produce different cross links. The reduction, which in the case of hair-curling lotions is effected with thioglycolic acid, produces a denatured protein of less rigid structure permitting stretching and rearrangement of the molecule. The appearance and disappearance of sulf-hydryl groups can be followed by application of the nitroprusside test.

Collagen is unique in having an identity period of only 2.86 Å and also in containing considerably more proline and hydroxyproline than other proteins. Since the peptide links from these amino acids are incapable of forming hydrogen bonds with C=O groups of adjacent chains, collagen lacks the stability of fibrous proteins in which the chains are extensively hydrogen-bonded. Thus boiling with water

[1] Herman Mark, b. 1895 Vienna; Ph.D. Vienna; Polytechn. Inst. Brooklyn

disrupts such hydrogen bonds as are present in collagen and converts it into gelatin.

31.14   Globular Proteins. — Globular proteins are characterized by solubility in water or in water solutions of acids, bases, or salts. Examples are egg albumin, casein, and plasma proteins. Other globular proteins are: glutelins of cereal seeds (soluble in water only in presence of dilute acid or alkali); prolamines, for example zein from corn (insoluble in water or absolute ethanol but soluble in 80% ethanol). Histones and protamines are distinguished from other globular proteins by a high content of basic amino acids, as can be seen from the data of Table 31.4 for calf liver histone and for salmin, from salmon sperm. Protamines are found only in the ripe sperm of certain families of fish. They are of unusually low molecular weight, deficient in many amino acids, and so rich in arginine that they are the most strongly basic proteins known. Thus arginine accounts for 78% of the amino acids of salmin and the only other component acids are all neutral: Gly, Ala, Val, Ileu, Pro, Ser. This protein can be isolated by dialysis in a cellophane bag against 1 M HCl; the protamine is small enough to pass through the membrane.

The globular proteins are spherical in shape and seem to contain cross links formed by interactions between side chains. Some globular proteins containing an active prosthetic group are enzymes. Some, known as glucoproteins, contain a carbohydrate component. Hemoglobin is a protein conjugated with a ferroporphyrin. Myelin, a structural unit of nervous tissue, is a combination of protein, phospholipid, and cholesterol.

31.15   Plasma Proteins. — Centrifugation of blood that has been treated with citrate solution or with heparin to prevent clotting causes settling of the heavier red blood corpuscles and separation of a yellowish, opalescent supernatant liquid that constitutes blood plasma and is an approximately 7% solution of plasma proteins in water at a pH close to 7.0. If the plasma is siphoned off and the sludge of corpuscles stirred with a little ether, the ether reduces the surface tension of the liquid external to the cells but does not penetrate the cell membranes and hence does not alter the pressure within the cells, and the result is that the cells burst. Centrifugation, after hemolysis, causes the ruptured cell membranes to settle and gives a rich red solution of the globular protein hemoglobin.

Blood plasma, prepared by the procedure described, is a liquid slightly pigmented with carotinoids which contains the following proteins: albumins (soluble in 5% salt solution), lipoproteins, fibrinogen, prothrombin. Whole blood that is not protected as it is drawn clots on standing for a few minutes as the result of conversion of the soluble, globular fibrinogen, under the influence of prothrombin and calcium ion, into an insoluble, fibrous protein fibrin, strands of which form the enmeshing structure of the clot. Centrifugation of clotted blood gives a residual mixture of fibrin and red blood corpuscles and a supernatant solution known as blood serum. Serum differs from plasma in that it contains no fibrinogen. Vitamin K is an antihemorrhagic agent because it maintains an adequate concentration of prothrombin. Citrate and heparin prevent formation of blood clots by immobilizing calcium ions. Human blood drawn into a plastic bag for storage passes through a chamber containing an ion-exchange resin for removal of calcium ions. Early attempts to separate plasma proteins depended mainly on fractional precipitation with ammonium sulfate or with alcohol. Fibrinogen can be obtained fairly readily by salting-out techniques. Electrophoretic analysis of blood serum indicated the presence of four main fractions designated as albumin, α-, β- and γ-globulin. With further refinement of the technique it became clear that these fractions are not individual proteins but groups of proteins having similar rates of migration. Further advances made during World War II by E. J. Cohn[1] and J. T. Edsall[2] (Harvard Medical School) were prompted by the demand for large quantities of plasma preparations suitable for treatment of shock. Since the effect is due to maintenance of osmotic pressure by the serum proteins and since whole plasma contains proteolytic enzymes that eventually cause extensive degradation, the preparation of stable, solid protein fractions offers many advantages. The method developed at Harvard involves fractional precipitation with alcohol at low temperature and with suitable variation of the pH, and takes advantage of the marked influence of extremely low concentrations of salts on the solubility of proteins. In this manner five principal fractions are obtained, which are by no means homogeneous but which are suitable for clinical purposes and for further fractionation into individual components. One fraction consists mainly of albumin and is particularly effective against shock. Another fraction contains the γ-globulins, which include a large number of antibodies. These are proteins formed in the animal organism in response to the introduction of foreign proteins (antigens), for example those of various pathogenic organisms. This fraction has clinical use in providing temporary passive immunization to various diseases. About ten globulins, belonging to all three types, have been obtained as individual components. Two are lipoproteins, or perhaps different forms of the same lipoprotein. The blood lipoproteins are comprised of protein, phospholipid, cholesterol, and an amount of neutral fat which varies from a very low value to as much as 75%, and hence they may well serve for transport of fat.

31.16   Hemoglobin. — This is the protein responsible for transport of oxygen from the lungs to body tissues. The mechanism of animal respiration can be demonstrated with the solution of hemoglobin prepared as described: when the solution is shaken with oxygen it becomes bright red (arterial blood), and when it is evacuated at the suction pump it becomes bluish red (venous blood). Crystallization of the oxygenated form, oxyhemoglobin, is accomplished easily: the above solution is treated with a moderate amount of ethanol to decrease solubility and let stand at 0° for 2-3 weeks. Subsequent crystallizations require decreasing proportions of ethanol and less time. Values for the percentage composition vary slightly for different animal species; a typical empirical formula is as follows: $(C_{738}H_{1166}O_{208}N_{203}S_2Fe)_n$. Minimal molecular weights of 16,500-17,000 are indicated on the basis of the iron content. Since the ultracentrifuge values are four times this value, n evidently has a value of four. The transport of oxygen

---

[1] Edwin J. Cohn, 1892-1953; b. New York; Ph.D. Chicago (E. J. Henderson); Harvard Medical School

[2] John T. Edsall, b. 1902 Philadelphia; M.D. Harvard (E. J. Cohn); Harvard Univ.

is associated with the iron function.   One gram of hemoglobin combines with 1.35 ml. of oxygen (0°, 760 mm.), which corresponds to a ratio of one atom of iron to 1 molecule of oxygen.   The position of equilibrium is determined by the partial

$$\text{Hemoglobin} + 4O_2 \rightleftharpoons \text{Oxyhemoglobin}$$

pressure of oxygen.   Carbon monoxide is a poison because it combines readily with hemoglobin to form an addition compound more stable than oxyhemoglobin and prevents the protein from exerting its normal function of transporting oxygen. Chemical oxidizing agents convert hemoglobin (ferrohemoglobin) into the brownish-red substance methemoglobin (ferrihemoglobin), which cannot act as an oxygen carrier.

On careful hydrolysis with hydrochloric acid the protein is cleaved to two fragments: hemin (4%) and globin (96%).   Hemoglobin is then a conjugated protein; it is made up of the protein globin linked to a prosthetic group (Gr. *prosthetos*, put on), which contains the iron.

Globin belongs to the histone group of proteins, for it is soluble in dilute acid solutions (isoelectric point, pH 7.5).   About one fifth of the molecule consists of basic amino acids, of which lysine predominates; in most histones the preponderant constituent is arginine.   The amino acid analysis of horse globin is shown in Table 31.4.   The sulfur content (cystine) of the globins varies widely: horse hemoglobin, 0.39%; cat hemoglobin, 0.62%; fowl hemoglobin, 0.86%.   Hemoglobin A of normal adults, like horse hemoglobin, contains no isoleucine; whereas fetal hemoglobin (HbF) contains approximately eight units of this amino acid. Hemoglobin S, which occurs in the blood of victims of sickle cell anemia, a disease characterized by excessive destruction of erythrocytes, represents an inborn error in metabolism.   Hemoglobin S is considerably less soluble than hemoglobin A and the isoelectric point is sufficiently higher (by 0.2 pH unit) to permit electrophoretic separation of HbS and HbA.   However, the structural difference is limited to a single amino acid unit (Pauling, 1949).   Digestion of HbS with trypsin, which splits only lysine and arginine peptide bonds, gives a series of peptides all but one of which are identical, in electrophoretic and chromatographic behavior, with peptides from HbA.   One nonapeptide from HbS matches one from HbA except that a neutral valyl group replaces a negatively charged glutamyl group.   The far greater incidence of sickle cell anemia among Negroes of Central Africa as compared to Negroes of the United States is attributed to a marked resistance of victims of the disease to malarial infection, since erythrocytes containing HbS are less susceptible to invasion by malaria-inducing protozoa.

Hemin has the formula $C_{34}H_{32}O_4N_4FeCl$, and is a chloride derived from the parent compound heme, $C_{34}H_{32}O_4N_4FeOH$.   The hemin molecule presented a structure that was both unusual and elaborate, and the problem of elucidating the structure was solved eventually only as the result of exhaustive researches extending over a period of forty years (Nencki, Piloty, Küster, Willstätter, H. Fischer[1]).

---

[1] Hans Fischer, 1881–1945; b. Höchst/Main; Ph.D. Marburg (Zincke), M. D. Munich; Techn. Hochsch. Munich; Nobel Prize 1930

The four pyrrole rings of hemin are substituted with methyl, vinyl, and propionic acid groups and are bridged by unsaturated methine groups. The iron is bound

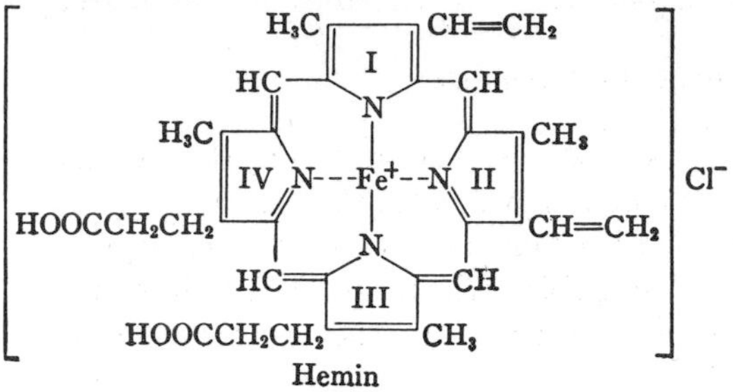

Hemin

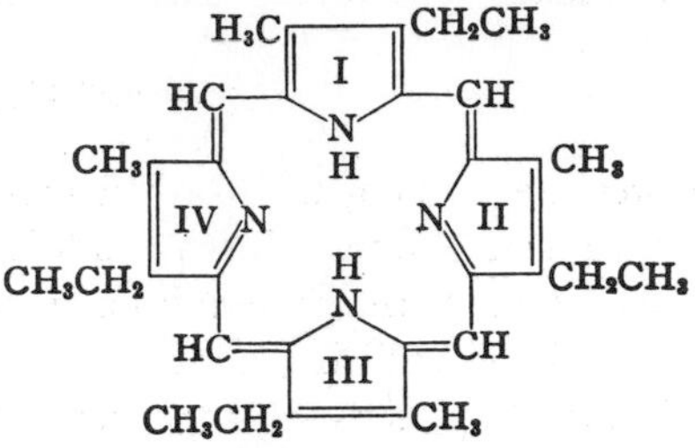

Etioporphyrin

to all four nitrogens, by either primary valences or coordinated links. Hemin (hemin chloride) on hydrolysis with dilute alkali affords the halogen-free hydroxide heme (hemin hydroxide). Methods are available for removal and reintroduction of the iron; iron-free substances having the characteristic system of four linked pyrrole rings are known as porphyrins and iron-containing derivatives as hemes. A key substance is etioporphyrin ($C_{32}H_{38}N_4$), obtained by degradation of hemin involving elimination of iron, decarboxylation, and reduction of the vinyl groups; it is a tetramethyltetraethylporphyrin. Isolation of the same etioporphyrin as a degradation product of chlorophyll established a close structural relationship between the leaf and blood pigments.

The first insight into the porphyrin structure resulted from development of degradative methods by which hemin could be broken into mixtures of smaller fragments that could be isolated and characterized. Thus drastic reduction with hydrogen iodide and red phosphorus gives a mixture of four pyrroles variously substituted with methyl and ethyl groups as shown in the formulas. Oxidative degradation also proved of value in providing the further fragment hematinic acid, a maleic imide derivative carrying a methyl and a propionic acid group as sub-

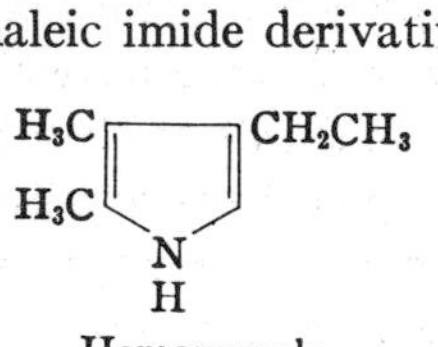

Hemopyrrole
(2,3-dimethyl-4-ethylpyrrole)

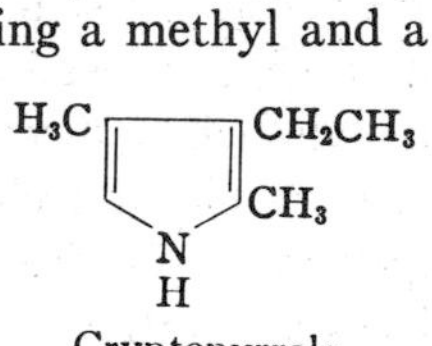

Cryptopyrrole
(2,4-dimethyl-3-ethylpyrrole)

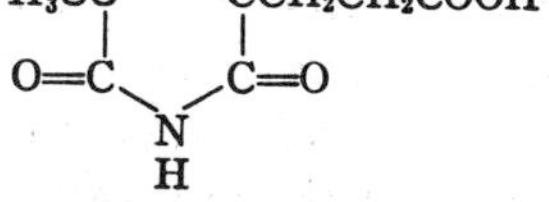

Hematinic acid

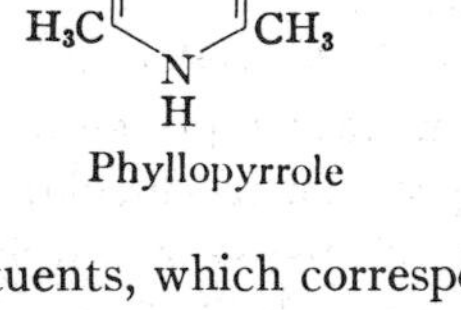

Phyllopyrrole

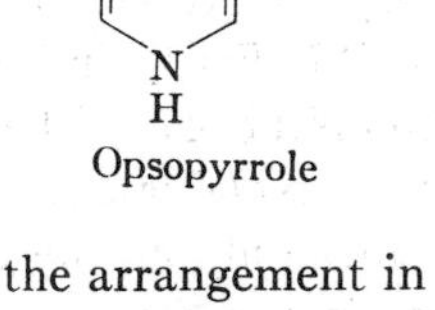

Opsopyrrole

stituents, which corresponds to the arrangement in two of the four original rings. Structures of the various fragments not only provided information concerning the substituents but gave a basis for the formulation of a working hypothesis concerning the character of the porphyrin system, and eventually it became feasible to approach the problem from the synthetic route. Attempts to link **pyrrole nuclei** together by synthesis derived assistance from the fact that **porphyrins exhibit very** characteristic line spectra observable with a simple visual instrument, and synthetic experiments initiated by Hans Fischer were rewarded with the discovery that the combination of four pyrrole rings, condensed with bridging methine groups to form a system of conjugated double bonds of no less than eighteen atoms, possesses such remarkable stability that it is formed, if in low yield, in unusual reactions consisting in condensation of even approximate moieties of the final molecule.

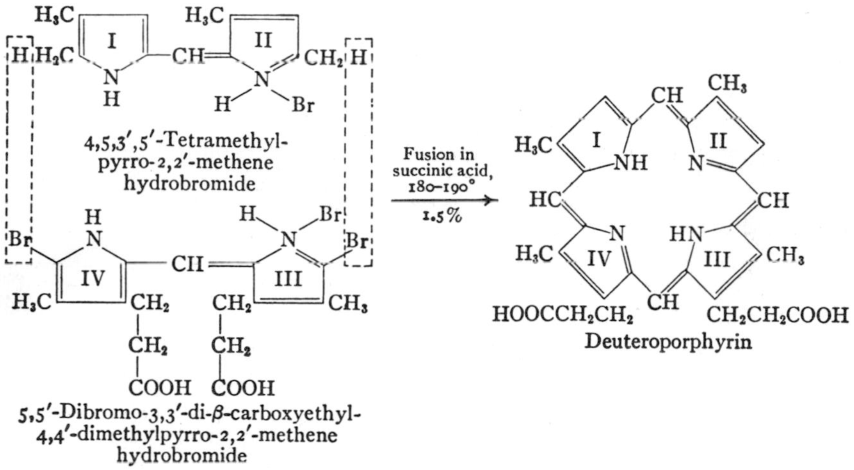

4,5,3',5'-Tetramethyl-
pyrro-2,2'-methene
hydrobromide

Fusion in
succinic acid,
180–190°
———→
1.5%

5,5'-Dibromo-3,3'-di-β-carboxyethyl-
4,4'-dimethylpyrro-2,2'-methene
hydrobromide

Deuteroporphyrin

Fischer achieved the synthesis of deuteroporphyrin in 1928 by the fusion of the two pyrromethane bases shown in the formulas. A porphyrin thus has aromatic character. Although the conjugated system is in part cross conjugated, 22 π electrons are available and the system conforms to the stable $4n + 2$ pattern (28.1). Elimination of two molecules of hydrogen bromide links the two parts by methylene bridges and must produce initially a dihydroporphyrin structure, but the tendency to form the unsaturated porphyrin structure evidently is so great that two hydrogen atoms are eliminated during the condensation (the nitrogen atoms are all present as quaternary salts).

Fisher's further researches culminated in 1930 in synthesis of hemin itself. The two free nuclear positions in deuteroporphyrin were substituted with acetyl groups by the action of acetic anhydride and stannic chloride, and the new substituents were transformed into vinyl groups by the sequence of reactions: $-COCH_3 \rightarrow -CH(OH)CH_3 \rightarrow -CH{=}CH_2$. Introduction of iron afforded hemin.

PEPTIDE SYNTHESIS

31.17   Early Methods. — The better of two routes to polypeptides investigated by Fischer (1901–03) involved condensation of an α-halo acid chloride with the ethyl ester of an amino acid or of the next lower polypeptide. The ester group can be saponified under mild conditions without attack of the peptide links and then the α-halo acid can be aminated (an ester group would also react). The sequence is then repeated. Fischer prepared the octadecapeptide leucyltriglycylleucyltriglycylleucyloctaglycylglycine by this method.

$$ClCH_2COCl + H_2NCH_2CO—NHCH_2COOC_2H_5 \xrightarrow{27\%}$$
Chloroacetyl chloride   Glycylglycine ester

$$ClCH_2CO—NHCH_2CO—NHCH_2COOC_2H_5 \xrightarrow[100\%]{NaOH}$$
Chloroacetylglycylglycine ester

$$ClCH_2CO—NHCH_2CO—NHCH_2COOH \xrightarrow{25\% NH_4OH} NH_2CH_2CO—NHCH_2CO—NHCH_2COOH$$
Chloroacetylglycylglycine   Diglycylglycine

31.18   Carbobenzoxy (Cb) Derivatives. — The next problem was to produce optically active peptides by linking the carboxyl group of a natural L-acid A with the amino group of an L-acid B, and to do this means had to be found for protecting the amino group of A during conversion to the acid chloride and coupling with B. Ordinary acyl groups are unsatisfactory, for hydrolytic

(a) $C_6H_5CH_2OH + ClCOCl \longrightarrow C_6H_5CH_2OCOCl + HCl$

(b) $C_6H_5CH_2OCOCl + H_2NR \xrightarrow{NaOH} C_6H_5CH_2OCONHR + NaCl + H_2O$

(c) 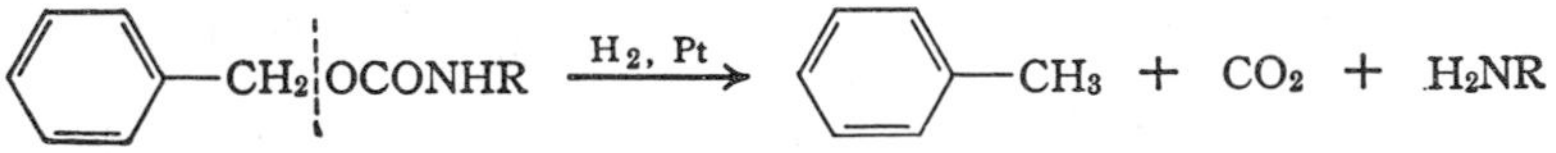   ⬡—CH₂|OCONHR $\xrightarrow{H_2, Pt}$ ⬡—CH₃ + CO₂ + H₂NR

removal of the protective group would split the peptide bond as well. Max Bergmann,[1] however, found (1932) a protective group that can be removed by hy-

$$HOOCCH_2CH_2CHCOOH \xrightarrow[90\%]{C_6H_5CH_2OCOCl(MgO)} HOOCCH_2CH_2CHCOOH \xrightarrow[84\%]{Ac_2O}$$ 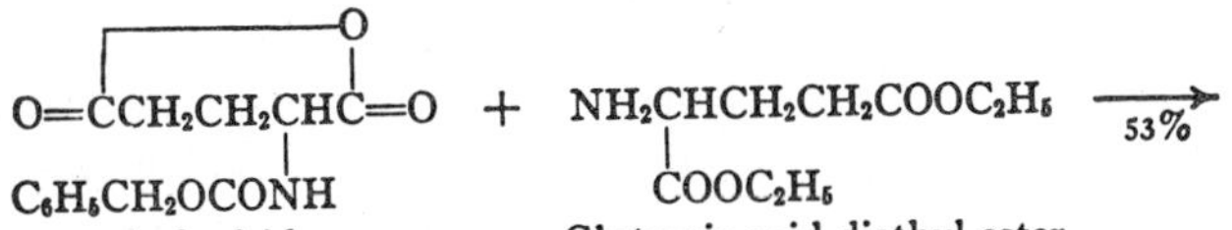
       | |
     NH₂   C₆H₅CH₂OCONH
L-Glutamic acid   Carbobenzoxy-L-glutamic acid

$$O=CCH_2CH_2CHC=O + NH_2CHCH_2CH_2COOC_2H_5 \xrightarrow{53\%}$$
     C₆H₅CH₂OCONH   COOC₂H₅
        Anhydride   Glutamic acid diethyl ester

$$HOOCCH_2CH_2CHCO—NHCHCH_2CH_2COOC_2H_5 \xrightarrow[80\%]{H_2O(NaOH)}$$
    C₆H₅CH₂OCONH   COOC₂H₅

$$HOOCCH_2CH_2CHCO—NHCHCH_2CH_2COOH \xrightarrow[quant.]{H_2(Pd)}$$
  C₆H₅CH₂OCONH   COOH
     Carbobenzoxy dipeptide

$$HOOCCH_2CH_2CHCO—NHCHCH_2CH_2COOH + C_6H_5CH_3 + CO_2$$
         NH₂   COOH
      L-Glutamyl-L-glutamic acid

---

[1] Max Bergmann, 1886–1944; Ph.D. Berlin, asst. to E. Fischer; from 1933, Rockefeller Inst.; *J. Chem. Soc.*, 716 (1945).

drogenation. Carbobenzoxy chloride, prepared from benzyl alcohol and phosgene (a), condenses with an amine, or with an amino acid or ester, to give the N-carbobenzoxy derivative (b). At an appropriate stage of synthesis the amino group can be liberated by hydrogenolysis of the activated C—O bond with formation of toluene and carbon dioxide. L-Glutamyl-L-glutamic acid was the first dipeptide to be synthesized by this method.

Hydrogenative cleavage of the carbobenzoxy derivative is not applicable to peptides containing sulfur, since even combined sulfur poisons the catalyst. In

$$\text{Cystine} \xrightarrow{\text{CbCl}} \begin{array}{c} \text{NHCb} \\ | \\ \text{SCH}_2\text{CHCO}_2\text{H} \\ | \\ \text{SCH}_2\text{CHCO}_2\text{H} \\ | \\ \text{NHCb} \end{array} \xrightarrow{\text{PCl}_5} \begin{array}{c} \text{NHCb} \\ | \\ \text{SCH}_2\text{CHCOCl} \\ | \\ \text{SCH}_2\text{CHCOCl} \\ | \\ \text{NHCb} \end{array} \xrightarrow[75\%]{\text{CH}_2(\text{NH}_2)\text{CO}_2\text{Et}}$$

$$\begin{array}{c} \text{NHCb} \\ | \\ \text{SCH}_2\text{CHCO—NHCH}_2\text{CO}_2\text{Et} \\ | \\ \text{SCH}_2\text{CHCO—NHCH}_2\text{CO}_2\text{Et} \\ | \\ \text{NHCb} \end{array} \xrightarrow[75\%]{\text{PH}_4\text{I}}$$

$$\begin{array}{c} \text{NH}_2 \cdot \text{HI} \\ | \\ \text{HSCH}_2\text{CHCO—NHCH}_2\text{CO}_2\text{Et} \end{array} \xrightarrow[58\%]{\overset{\overset{\text{O}}{\|}}{\text{ClCCH}_2\text{CH}_2}\overset{\text{NHCb}}{\underset{|}{\text{CHCO}_2\text{CH}_3}}}$$

$$\begin{array}{c} \text{NHCb} \\ | \\ \text{NH—COCH}_2\text{CH}_2\text{CHCO}_2\text{CH}_3 \\ | \\ \text{HSCH}_2\text{CHCO—NHCH}_2\text{CO}_2\text{H} \end{array} \xrightarrow[11\%]{\text{PH}_4\text{I}}$$

$$\begin{array}{c} \text{HO}_2\text{CCHCH}_2\text{CH}_2\text{CO—NHCHCO—NHCH}_2\text{CO}_2\text{H} \\ | \quad\quad\quad\quad\quad\quad\quad\quad | \\ \text{NH}_2 \quad\quad\quad\quad\quad\quad \text{CH}_2\text{SH} \end{array}$$

Glutathione (Glu-CySH-Gly)

this case reduction can be effected either with phosphonium iodide or with sodium in liquid ammonia, but yields are low: 11% and 27% respectively in the synthesis of glutathione (1933–36), a widely occurring tripeptide.

Another method for removal of the carbobenzoxy group involves brief treatment with hydrogen bromide in acetic acid; the hydrobromide of the peptide is formed and can be isolated by precipitation with ether:

$$\text{C}_6\text{H}_5\text{CH}_2\text{OCONHCHRCONHCHR}'\text{CO}_2\text{CH}_3 + \text{HBr} + \text{CH}_3\text{CO}_2\text{H} \rightarrow$$

$$\text{C}_6\text{H}_5\text{CH}_2\text{OCOCH}_3 \text{ (or C}_6\text{H}_5\text{CH}_2\text{Br)} + \overset{- \quad +}{\text{BrNH}_3\text{CHRCONHCHR}'\text{CO}_2\text{CH}_3}$$

In a method which affords the free amino acid or peptide, the reducing agent is triethylsilane (b.p. 107°). A mixture of the Cb-derivative (0.01 mole), triethylsilane (0.04 mole; preparation: F. C. Whitmore, 1947), triethylamine (4 drops), and PdCl$_2$ (50 mg.) is refluxed for 3 hrs., and the solution is filtered and diluted with methanol, which precipitates the amino acid or peptide (L. Birkofer, 1961). Yields are high, and an S-benzyl group is not disturbed.

$$\begin{array}{c} RCHCO_2H \\ | \\ HNCO_2CH_2C_6H_5 \end{array} \xrightarrow[-H_2]{Et_3SiH} \begin{array}{c} RCHCO_2SiEt_3 \\ | \\ HNCO_2CH_2C_6H_5 \end{array} \xrightarrow[-CO_2,C_6H_5CH_3]{Et_3SiH}$$

$$\begin{array}{c} RCHCO_2SiEt_3 \\ | \\ HNSiEt_3 \end{array} \xrightarrow{2CH_3OH} \begin{array}{c} RCHCO_2H \\ | \\ NH_2 \end{array} + \ 2Et_3SiOCH_3$$

Unwanted side reactions often encountered in the synthesis of peptides containing methionine are eliminated by temporary conversion of the thioether function of methionine into the sulfoxide at any stage of synthesis (B. Iselin, 1961). The sulfoxide oxygen is introduced without formation of a sulfone when hydrogen peroxide is used in small excess, and the oxygen is eliminated easily by reduction with thioglycolic acid. Whereas acid cleavage of carbobenzoxy-methionine peptides is attended with partial conversion to S-benzylhomocysteine, removal of the carbobenzoxy group from the corresponding sulfoxides proceeds smoothly on mild treatment with concentrated hydrochloric acid.

β-Aspartyl and γ-glutamyl peptides can be prepared by a modification illustrated in the simplest form in the synthesis of L-asparagine. From the anhydride of carbobenzoxy-L-aspartic acid or of carbobenzoxy-L-glutamic acid on treatment

$$HOOCCH_2CH(NH_2)COOH \longrightarrow O=CCH_2CHC=O \xrightarrow[85\%]{C_6H_5CH_2OH}$$
$$\underset{\text{L-Aspartic acid}}{} \qquad \underset{NHCOOCH_2C_6H_5}{\overset{\overset{\displaystyle O}{\rule{2cm}{0.4pt}}}{}}$$

$$\begin{array}{c} HOOCCH_2CHCOOCH_2C_6H_5 \\ | \\ NHCOOCH_2C_6H_5 \end{array} \xrightarrow[(quant.)]{PCl_5} \text{Acid chloride} \xrightarrow[55\%]{NH_3}$$

$$\begin{array}{c} NH_2COCH_2CHCOOCH_2C_6H_5 \\ | \\ NHCOOCH_2C_6H_5 \end{array} \xrightarrow[70\%]{H_2(Pd)} \begin{array}{c} NH_2COCH_2CH(NH_2)COOH \\ \text{L-Asparagine} \end{array}$$

with benzyl alcohol, only the α-ester is formed; the other carboxyl group is free and available for condensation.

31.19   Phthaloyl (Phth[1]) and Other Derivatives. — Of a number of other blocking groups proposed, the phthaloyl group has proved particularly useful (J. C. Sheehan, 1949; D. A. Kidd, 1949). The phthaloyl derivative is prepared by heating the amino acid with phthalic anhydride, and after the peptide bond is formed treatment with alcoholic hydrazine followed by hydrochloric acid effects cleavage of the protective group as phthalhydrazide and liberates the free amino group (A. R. Ing and R. H. F. Manske,[2] 1926). Cleavage of the phthaloyl derivative proceeds more readily than hydrogenolysis of the carbobenzoxy group, which sometimes requires several days. The dipeptide is obtained as the hydrochloride; the free amine can be liberated by passage over a basic ion-exchange resin. Glycyl-DL-phenylalanine and glycyl-L-cysteine have

---

[1] The symbol Ph is not recommended because of prior use to indicate phenyl. We prefer Cb to the longer Cbz, Cbo, or CBO. Abbreviations for the carbobenzoxy and phthaloyl derivatives based on the system of E. Brand (1951) are: Z-Ala, Phth-Ala.

[2] Richard H. F. Manske, b. 1901 Berlin; Ph.D. Manchester (Robinson, Lapworth), D.Sc. Manchester: Dominion Rubber Co., Canada

been prepared by this method in overall yields of 60–61%. Sheehan has also reported preparation from phthaloylglycyl chloride (I) and silver dibenzyl phos-

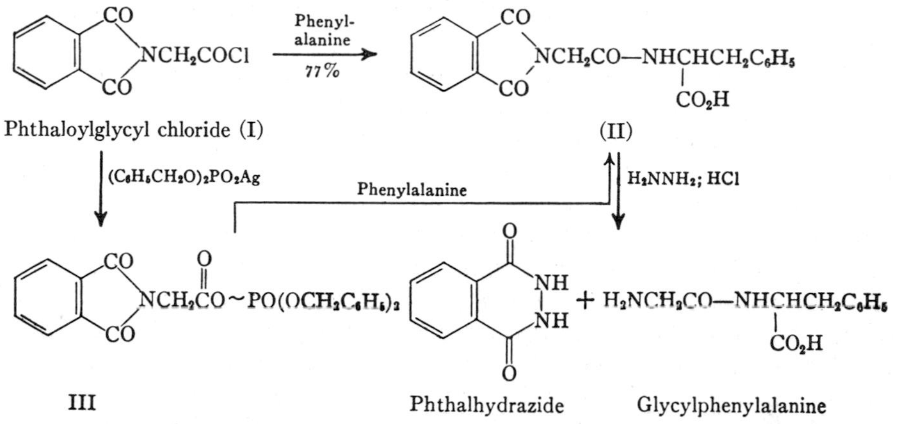

Phthaloylglycyl chloride (I)

(II)

III   Phthalhydrazide   Glycylphenylalanine

phate of the derivative III (91% yield), which contains an anhydrophosphate bond and in aqueous solution at pH 7.4 acylates phenylalanine to give II in good yield.

Preparation of the phthaloyl derivative of an optically active acid by fusion may be attended with racemization, but A. K. Bose (*Org. Syn.*, 1960) obtained the derivative of L-phenylalanine without racemization by refluxing a solution of the components in toluene containing a little triethylamine in a flask fitted with a water separator. A simpler method of considerable novelty is described by G. H. L. Nefkens[1] (1961). N-Carbethoxyphthalimide (1), prepared by reaction of ethyl chlorocarbonate in dimethylformamide with potassium phthalimide or with phthalimide and triethylamine, reacts with an amino ester in aqueous sodium

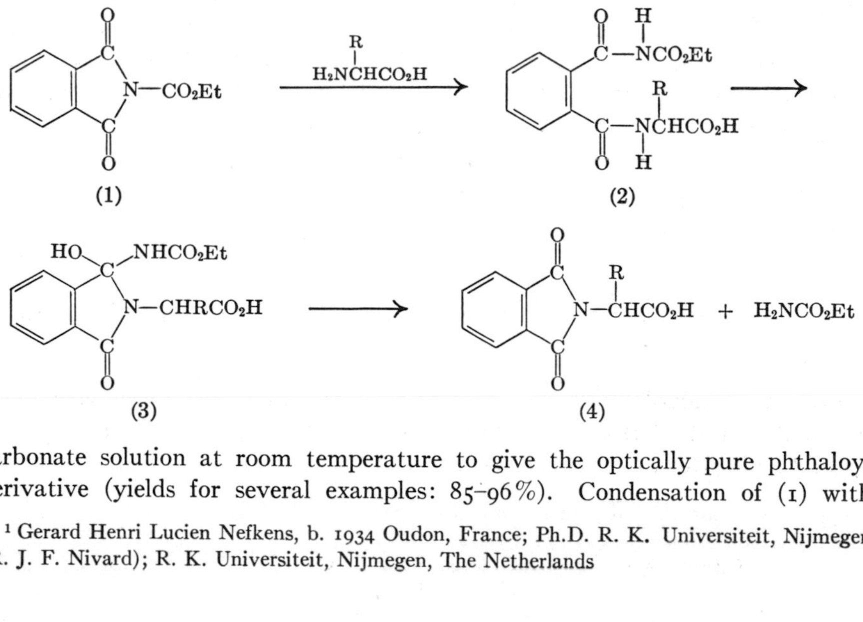

(1)   (2)

(3)   (4)

carbonate solution at room temperature to give the optically pure phthaloyl derivative (yields for several examples: 85–96%). Condensation of (1) with

[1] Gerard Henri Lucien Nefkens, b. 1934 Oudon, France; Ph.D. R. K. Universiteit, Nijmegen (R. J. F. Nivard); R. K. Universiteit, Nijmegen, The Netherlands

an amino acid is facilitated by the electron-attracting power of the carbamate residue. The condensation involves fission of the five-membered ring (2), reformation of this ring (3), and elimination of ethyl carbamate, which was shown to be a reaction product.

Other N-protected derivatives that have found some use are the formyl, *t*-butoxycarbonyl-, trifluoroacetyl-, tosyl-, *p*-nitrocarbobenzoxy-, cyclopentyloxy-carbonyl-, and phenoxycarbonylamino acids. Difficulties frequently encountered in obtaining the derivatives in crystalline form or in satisfactory yield are obviated by isolation of the derivative as the dicyclohexylammonium salt (E. Klieger, Schering AG, 1961). On addition of one equivalent of dicyclohexylamine to a solution of an N-protected derivative of any type, the salt usually crystallizes at once. After addition of ether, the salt is collected and washed with ether (58 examples). For the synthesis of peptides containing lysine, J. D. Ciperda (1961) immobilized the α-amino group by conversion of lysine to a copper complex to permit formation of N^{ϵ}-tosyllysine and then prepared N^{α}-carbobenzoxy-N^{ϵ}-tosyllysine. After construction of the first peptide link, the α-amino group can be liberated by hydrogenation without disturbance of the N^{ϵ}-tosyl group, which is left in place until the end of the synthesis and then removed by reduction with sodium in liquid ammonia.

31.20   Mixed Anhydride Synthesis. — This method was developed in 1950–51 by three independent groups: T. Wieland[1], R. A. Boissonnas,[2] and J. R. Vaughan (American Cyanamid Co.). The fundamental principle is that the mixed anhydride of a carboxylic acid with an alkyl acid carbonate ($HOCO_2R$) is an efficient reagent for acylation of amines. In the standard procedure the amino group of the amino acid is protected as the carbobenzoxy (Cb) or phthaloyl (Phth) derivative, which is treated in an inert solvent (tetrahydrofurane) with enough base (triethylamine) to form the salt and then with an alkylchlorocarbonate. The mixed anhydride produced need not be isolated, and on addition of an amino acid (usually as ester) carbon dioxide is formed and the N-substituted peptide ester is obtained, usually in excellent yield and optical purity. The ester group is eliminated by hydrolysis with dilute acid and the blocking group by an

$$\underset{NHCb}{RCHCO_2H} \xrightarrow{N(C_2H_5)_3} \underset{NHCb}{RCH\overset{-}{CO_2}\overset{+}{N}H(C_2H_5)_3} \xrightarrow[-(C_2H_5)_3\overset{+}{N}H\overset{-}{Cl}]{ClCO_2C_2H_5}$$

$$\underset{NHCb}{RC\overset{O}{\overset{\|}{H}C}-O-\overset{O}{\overset{\|}{C}}OC_2H_5} \xrightarrow{H_2NCHR'CO_2CH_3} \underset{NHCb}{RCHCONHCHR'CO_2CH_3} + CO_2 + C_2H_5OH$$

appropriate standard procedure. Methyl and ethyl esters have been commonly used, but *t*-butyl esters offer advantages since the *t*-butyl group can be removed by mild acid hydrolysis (G. W. Anderson, Lederle Laboratories, 1960).

[1] Theodor Wieland, b. 1913 Munich (son of H. Wieland); Ph.D. Munich (H. Wieland); Univ. Mainz, Frankfurt/Main

[2] Roger A. Boissonnas, b. 1921 Zurich; D.Sc. Geneva (K. H. Meyer); Univ. Geneva; Sandoz

31.21   Dehydration Methods. — Under this heading are listed peptide syntheses involving elimination of water between a protected amino acid or
peptide and an amino ester with use of a reagent that is converted into a hydrated
form.   G. W. Anderson[1] (1952) used tetraethyl pyrophosphite as the dehydrating
agent and water-miscible diethyl phosphite as solvent (1).   The reaction product
precipitates on addition of water.   J. C. Sheehan (1955–56) employed N,N'-

1. $CbNHCHRCO_2H + H_2NCHR'CO_2C_2H_5 + (C_2H_5O)_2POP(OC_2H_5)_2 \rightarrow$

$CbNHCHRCO—NHCHR'CO_2C_2H_5 + 2 (C_2H_5O)_2POH$

2. $PhthNCHRCO_2H + H_2NCHR'CO_2CH_3 + C_6H_{11}N=C=NC_6H_{11} \rightarrow$

$PhthNCHRCO—NHCHR'CO_2CH_3 + C_6H_{11}NHCONHC_6H_{11}$

dicyclohexylcarbodiimide (2) as the dehydrating agent and a solvent (tetrahydrofurane, acetonitrile, methylene chloride) in which the dicyclohexylurea
formed is insoluble.   Although alternative procedures are possible, the most
convenient one is to add the dehydrating agent to a mixture of the components
that are to be peptidized.

31.22   Activated Esters. — Whereas the methyl or ethyl ester of an N-
protected amino acid reacts only slowly with the free amino group of
a second component, a strongly electron-attracting group, for example that of a
p-nitrophenyl ester, facilitates nucleophilic attack by the amine and makes pep-
tidization practicable (1). p-Nitrophenyl esters are prepared in yield of 80–90 %

1. $CbNHCHRCO_2C_6H_4NO_2\text{-}p + H_2NCHR'CO_2Et \rightarrow$

$CbNHCHRCONHCHR'CO_2Et \xrightarrow[\text{HOAc}]{\text{HBr}} H_2NCHRCONHCHR'CO_2Et$

by adding one equivalent of dicyclohexylcarbodiimide to a solution of the N-
protected amino acid and p-nitrophenol in ethyl acetate (M. Bodanzsky and V. du
Vigneaud, 1959).   Thiophenyl esters (Th. Wieland, 1951) provide particularly
favorable activation (F. Weygand, 1960).   Cyanomethyl esters have been used
(R. Schwyzer, Ciba, Basel, 1955); they are prepared by reaction of the protected
amino acid with chloroacetonitrile and triethylamine and they react readily with

2. $CbNHCHRCO_2H + ClCH_2CN \xrightarrow{\text{Et}_3N} CbNHCHRCOOCH_2CN + Et_3NHCl$

$CbNHCHRCONHCHR'CO_2Et + m\text{-}HO_3SC_6H_4COCH_2CONHEt$

---

[1] George W. Anderson, b. 1913 Gainsville, Fla.; Ph.D. Florida (C. B. Pollard); Am. Cyanamid
Co.

amines at room temperature to form amides. An activated ester of novel type is obtained by treatment of a protected amino acid or peptide in acetonitrile or nitromethane with N-ethyl-5-phenylisoxazolium-3'-sulfonate; reaction with an amino acid ester affords the peptide derivative and a water-soluble by-product (R. B. Woodward, 1961). Another efficient method makes use of an interesting reaction of N-carbethoxyphthalimide (compare 31.19). When this urethane (1) is heated with one mole each of hydroxylamine and triethylamine in absolute ethanol, the

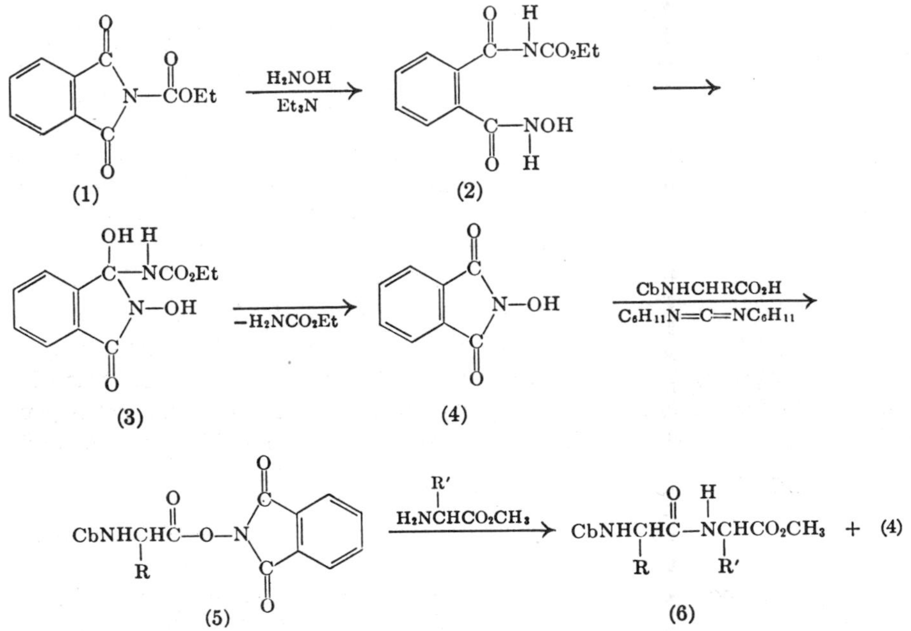

solution turns red with formation of the triethylammonium salt of N-hydroxyphthalimide (4), which separates, after acidification and dilution with water, in nearly colorless needles, m.p. 230° (G. H. L. Nefkens, 1960). Condensation of (4) with an N-protected amino acid in the presence of dicyclohexylcarbodiimide gives the activated ester (5), which reacts readily with an amino ester to give the protected dipeptide (6); the N-hydroxyphthalimide formed is removed by shaking with aqueous bicarbonate solution (Nefkens, 1961).

PROTEINS AND PEPTIDES

31.23 **Denaturation.** — A serious difficulty in the investigation of proteins is that most of them are extremely prone to undergo some form of alteration, described as denaturation. Almost all proteins (gelatin is an exception) are sensitive to heat, and the temperature coefficient of the reaction is remarkably high. Similar changes occur on treatment with acid or alkali, alcohol, acetone, urea, potassium iodide, trichloroacetic acid, tungstic acid, sulfosalicylic acid, ultraviolet light or X-rays, or even as the result of shaking or application of high pressure. The resultant changes are at least qualitatively if not entirely similar.

A denatured protein is always less soluble than the native form; any physiological activity originally associated with the substance is lost. Probably the ability to exist in crystalline form is lost, since no denatured protein has been crystallized. In many cases an increase in sulfhydryl groups accompanies the change, as in the reduction of keratin. The molecular weight is sometimes but not always affected. The hemocyanin of *Helix pomatia* shows a molecular weight at the isoelectric point of 6,740,000, but dissociates with change in pH into fragments that are progressively one half, one fourth, and one eighth the size of the original protein. The same effect has been observed on treatment with urea; for instance, hemoglobin is split into halves that are apparently identical, edestin into fourths. There are some indications that the number of acidic or basic groups is reduced upon denaturation, probably owing to intramolecular reaction.

Denaturation is a property unique to proteins and is not shown by other known macromolecules. Proteins vary widely in sensitivity; insulin, for example, is notable in its resistance to denaturation. Some proteins can revert more or less to the native form after removal of the denaturing agent.

31.24 Reactive Groups. — Proteins are characteristic amphoteric substances. In neutral solution both the basic and carboxyl groups are generally charged, corresponding to the dipolar ions of amino acids. At the isoelectric point dissociation as an acid is equal to that as a base, solubility is at a minimum, and rate of migration in an electric field is at a minimum. The formula for a heptapeptide (hypothetical) is written in the conventional way with the amino terminal group to the left and the carboxy terminal group to the right. The pK values show that the acidic groups in order of decreasing acidic strength

are: the terminal carboxyl group, the β- and γ-carboxyl groups of the two dibasic acid chains, the sulfhydryl and the phenolic hydroxyl groups. The order of decreasing basic strength is: the guanidyl group (Arg), the ε-amino group (Lys), and the imidazole ring (His).

31.25 Isolation and Purification. — Since most proteins are highly sensitive and occur as mixtures of closely related substances, isolation of homogeneous individual components in native form presents considerable difficulty. Since the solubility is usually at a minimum at the isoelectric point, and since there is often considerable spread in the pH of isoelectricity (Table 31.6), adjustment of the pH to a particular value may favor separation of one component of the mixture and retention of the others when either a salt or a water-miscible or-

TABLE 31.6 ISOELECTRIC POINTS OF VARIOUS PROTEINS (PH UNITS)

Casein	4.6
Egg albumin	4.84–4.90
Silk fibroin	2.0–2.4
Serum globulin	5.4–5.5
Gelatin	4.80–4.85
Insulin	5.30–5.35
Lactoglobulin	4.5–5.5
Hemoglobin	6.79–6.83
Serum albumin	4.88

ganic solvent such as ethanol is added in controlled amount. A method favored for slow addition of ammonium sulfate for isoelectric salting out of a protein is to rotate a cellophane bag of solid ammonium sulfate in the buffered protein solution; the electrolyte diffuses through the membrane and eventually causes precipitation of protein. If the precipitate, consisting of protein contaminated with the salt, is put in a bag and dialyzed against distilled water the ammonium sulfate is eliminated and the protein dissolves and can then be reprecipitated as before. Crystallization of proteins has been effected by suitable repetition of the process. An alternative method of effecting precipitation, and sometimes crystallization, is adjustment to the isoelectric point, addition of ethanol, and refrigeration.

31.26   Criteria of Purity. — The Swedish chemists The Svedberg[1] and Arne Tiselius[2] contributed importantly to the advancement of protein chemistry by developing analytical techniques uniquely suited to characterization of these macromolecular compounds. The ultracentrifuge method of Svedberg provides a means of determining molecular weight. When a protein solution contained in a small cell is spun at very high speeds, the protein moves to the outer edge because of the centrifugal force, to an extent dependent upon its molecular weight. Observations and photographs are made while the centrifuge is in operation through use of special optical systems. The molecular weight can be determined either from the sedimentation equilibrium or from the rate of sedimentation; although theoretically the first method is sounder, an excessive amount of time is required to establish equilibrium, and values obtained from the velocity determinations are considered more reliable. By use of the ultracentrifuge it is also possible to tell whether the molecules are all the same size and shape. The method developed by Tiselius (1937) is that of electrophoresis. In an electric field a protein moves at a rate determined by the size and shape of the molecule and by the number and kind of ionized groups. Material that appears homogeneous by the criterion of solubility may contain components that differ in rate of electrophoretic travel. Unfortunately the method is not applicable on a preparative scale. The pattern of countercurrent distribution provides a particularly rigid criterion of purity (Craig, see 31.29).

[1] The Svedberg, b. 1884 Gärleb; Univ. Uppsala; Nobel Prize 1926
[2] Arne Tiselius, b. 1902 Stockholm; Univ. Uppsala; Nobel Prize 1948

31.27   End Group Analysis. — The first insight into the amino acid sequence in proteins and polypeptides came from application of a method introduced by Sanger[1] (1945) for identification of the amino-terminal unit. The reagent which serves for labeling is 2,4-dinitrofluorobenzene, prepared by nitration of fluorobenzene (*Biochem. Preps.*). Condensation occurs under mild conditions to form a 2,4-dinitrophenyl protein; on acid hydrolysis the terminal amino acid is

$$\underset{\textstyle \overset{|}{\text{H}_2\text{NCHCO—protein}}}{\overset{\textstyle \text{R}}{}} \xrightarrow{(NO_2)_2C_6H_3F} \underset{\textstyle \overset{|}{(NO_2)_2C_6H_3\text{NHCHCO—protein}}}{\overset{\textstyle \text{R}}{}}$$

$$\xrightarrow{\text{hydrol.}} O_2N\!\!\left\langle\!\!\begin{array}{c}NO_2\\ \\ \end{array}\!\!\right\rangle\!\!-\!\!\underset{\textstyle \overset{|}{\text{NHCHCO}_2\text{H}}}{\overset{\textstyle \text{R}}{}} + \text{Amino acids}$$

liberated as the bright yellow 2,4-dinitrophenyl derivative, which is easily separated from the accompanying amino acid mixture and which can be identified by paper chromatography. A unit of lysine that is amino-terminal gives the α,ϵ-di derivative; one that is internal or carboxy-terminal gives the ϵ-mono derivative. The phenolic group of tyrosine and the imino group of histidine also react with the reagent but the derivatives are split on acid hydrolysis of the peptide links. For determination of the sequence within the chain, the protein is subjected to partial hydrolysis to give a mixture of di and tripeptides, whose structures can be investigated by end group analysis. If all possible dipeptides in the hydrolyzate can be characterized, a unique solution can be established for the sequence in the protein without further end-group assay.

One of the several other nitrofluoro derivatives suggested as amino acid reagents is 2,4-dinitro-5-fluoroaniline (E. D. Bergmann, 1961). The bathochromic effect of the amino group shifts the maximum from 350 mμ for the Sanger derivative to 405 mμ and permits diazotization and coupling to produce an azo dye.

A second method of end-group analysis introduced by P. Edman[2] in 1950 involves selective elimination of the amino-terminal group. Reaction of this group with phenylisothiocyanate (a) gives the phenylthiocarbamyl derivative (b), which

$$\underset{\textstyle (a)}{C_6H_5N{=}C{=}S} + \underset{\textstyle \overset{|}{R}}{\overset{\textstyle }{H_2NCHCO\text{—protein}}} \longrightarrow \text{protein—OC} \underset{\textstyle \overset{|}{R}}{\overset{\textstyle C_6H_5NHC{=}S}{\underset{\textstyle \overset{|}{CH}}{\overset{\textstyle |}{\diagdown NH}}}} \xrightarrow{HCl}$$

(b)

$$\underset{\textstyle \overset{|}{R}}{\overset{\textstyle C_6H_5N{-}{-}C{=}S}{\underset{\textstyle CH}{\overset{\textstyle |\qquad|}{OC\diagdown \, _{/}NH}}}} \xrightarrow{OH^-} \underset{\textstyle \overset{|}{R}}{\overset{\textstyle }{HO_2C\underset{\textstyle CH}{\diagdown \, _{/}NH_2}}}$$

(c)   (d)

[1] Frederick Sanger, b. 1918 Gloucestershire, England; Ph.D. Cambridge; Cambridge Univ.; Nobel Prize 1958

[2] Pehr Edman, b. 1916 Stockholm; M.D. Karolinska Inst. (E. Jorpes); Univ. Lund

is cleaved by hydrogen chloride to a phenylthiohydantoin (c). Finally, alkaline hydrolysis of (c) affords the free amino acid (d). In the cases in which peptides have been analyzed by both the Sanger and the Edman method, the same sequence has been deduced.

The Japanese chemist S. Akabori (1952) found a way of identifying the carboxy-terminal (C-terminal) group. The peptide or protein is heated with anhydrous hydrazine (10 hrs. at 105°), with transformation of all but the C-terminal acid into acid hydrazides, which are separated as the benzal derivatives from the now free C-terminal amino acid, as illustrated for Gly-Ala-Phe. Limited use has been

$$H_2NCH_2CO-NHCH(CH_3)CO-NHCH(C_6H_5)CO_2H$$

$$H_2NNH_2 \downarrow \text{ 10 hrs. at } 105°$$

$$H_2NCH_2CONHNH_2 \; + \; H_2NCH(CH_3)CONHNH_2 \; + \; H_2NCH(C_6H_5)CO_2H$$

$$\longrightarrow H_2NCH(R)CONHN{=}CHC_6H_5$$

made of an enzymic method. Carboxypeptidase sometimes releases the C-terminal amino acid, but only if certain environmental requirements are met.

31.28   Oxytocin, a Peptide Hormone. — The posterior pituitary gland elaborates several hormones, of which two have been isolated in pure form. One, oxytocin, stimulates the smooth muscle of the uterus; the other, vaso-pressin, is an antidiuretic hormone which exerts a pressor action. The two hormones are so similar in physical properties that for a time a single substance was thought to be responsible for both physiological actions. However, techniques of fractional precipitation, chromatography, and electrophoresis were all found to effect partial separation (1928–44). Then, by countercurrent distribution of a commercial extract having oxytocic activity of 20 units/mg., du Vigneaud[1] (1949) obtained essentially pure material of activity of 850 units/mg. Complete hy-drolysis and amino acid analysis of the hydrolyzate indicated the presence of eight different amino acids in equimolecular ratio, and the amount of ammonia liberated corresponded to three amide groupings of the type —$CONH_2$. The molecular weight was that of an octapeptide, and not a higher multiple. One of the eight units identified is cystine. In some proteins this disulfide unit binds peptide chains together and its severance by performic acid oxidation causes separation of the chains: $RS-SR' \xrightarrow{+OH} RSO_3H + HO_3SR'$. However, similar oxidation of the cystine unit of oxytocin gives material of molecular weight in the same range as oxytocin, and hence the disulfide unit must be part of a ring system.

The sequence of the eight amino acids in the cyclic peptide was established independently in 1953 by du Vigneaud and by Tuppy.[2] The two investigators arrived at the same conclusion from two sets of experimental evidence, both of which will be summarized. Tuppy first oxidized oxytocin with performic acid and submitted the oxidized peptide to partial hydrolysis with hydrochloric acid. The cystine unit gives rise to two oxidized amino acid units of the formula $HO_3SCH_2\cdot$

---

[1] Vincent du Vigneaud, b. 1901 Chicago; Ph.D. Rochester; Cornell Med. Coll.; Nobel Prize 1955

[2] Hans Tuppy, b. 1924 Vienna; Ph.D. Vienna (Späth, Wessely); Univ. Vienna

CH(NH$_2$)CO$_2$H, named cysteic acid, and designated by the symbol CySO$_3$H. Four dipeptides and two tripeptides were isolated, and most of the amino acid sequences were established by treatment of each peptide with 2,4-dinitrofluoro-benzene, hydrolysis, and chromatographic identification of the amino acid present as the DNPh derivative. When the sequence in a peptide is known, the symbols for the components are connected with a dash or dot; use of a comma means that the order is not known. The six peptides initially isolated by Tuppy from oxidized oxytocin are represented as follows:

I Asp—CySO$_3$H	IV Leu—Gly
II CySO$_3$H—Tyr	V CySO$_3$H—(Leu, Pro)
III Ileu—Glu	VI Tyr—(Glu, Ileu)

Since the tripeptide VI was characterized as having an amino-terminal tyrosine unit, the structure of the dipeptide III establishes for VI the structure Tyr—Ileu—Glu. The structure of dipeptide II establishes the further sequence CySO$_3$H—Tyr—Ileu—Glu. The tripeptide V is shown to have the order CySO$_3$H —Pro—Leu rather than the alternative order CySO$_3$H—Leu—Pro because in IV the carboxyl group of leucine is shown to be bound to the amino group of glycine, not of proline.

Tuppy then submitted oxidized oxytocin to partial hydrolysis by a crystalline proteinase isolated from *Bacillus subtilis* by Linderstrom-Lang[1] (1949) and obtained a basic product identified as glycine amide, H$_2$NCH$_2$CONH$_2$, symbol Gly(NH$_2$), and two acidic peptides. Each was hydrolyzed and the amino acids identified by chromatography, and each was treated with DNF and the end group determined. The first tetrapeptide, VII, corresponds to the above sequence:

VII CySO$_3$H—(Glu, Tyr, Ileu) VIII Asp—(CySO$_3$H, Leu, Pro)

CySO$_3$H—Tyr—Ileu—Glu. The second tetrapeptide, VIII, contains aspartic acid in addition to the acids of the tripeptide V, shown above to be CySO$_3$H —Pro—Leu, and therefore it is identified as Asp—CySO$_3$H—Pro—Leu. The glycine amide resulting from enzymic hydrolysis must be a terminal unit and the structure of dipeptide IV shows it to be linked to leucine. Thus the following carboxy-terminal sequence can be deduced:

—Asp—CySO$_3$H—Pro—Leu—Gly(NH$_2$).

The amino-terminal sequence must be that deduced above for VII, and hence the complete sequence of oxidized oxytocin is that formulated.

CySO$_3$H—Tyr—Ileu—Glu(NH$_2$)—Asp(NH$_2$)—CySO$_3$H—Pro—Leu—Gly(NH$_2$)
⌞------- proteinase --------⌟
Oxidized oxytocin

The linkages hydrolyzed by bacterial proteinase are indicated. The two additional amide groups are placed in the two available dibasic acid units. The two cysteic acid units in the oxidized peptide evidently arose by cleavage of the disulfide group of a cystine unit in a cyclic system, and hence oxytocin is:

[1] Kaj Linderstrom-Lang, 1896–1959; b. Copenhagen; Ph.D. Copenhagen (S. P. L. Sörensen); Carlsberg Laboratory, Copenhagen

$$\begin{array}{c} \text{Ileu}\text{------}\text{Tyr}\text{----------}\underset{|}{\text{CyS}} \\[2pt] \underset{\text{Oxytocin}}{\text{Glu(NH}_2)\text{---Asp(NH}_2)\text{---}\text{CyS---Pro---Leu---Gly}} \end{array}$$

The du Vigneaud group relied less on end-group analysis than on identification of the components of a large number of small peptides. They also investigated the reaction of oxidized oxytocin with bromine water, which cleaves the molecule into a heptapeptide and a brominated dipeptide. The smaller fragment was shown to have the structure formulated, indicative of the sequence CySO$_3$H—Tyr,

$$\underset{\text{NH}_2}{\overset{}{\text{HO}_3\text{SCH}_2\text{CHCO}}}\text{---}\underset{\text{CO}_2\text{H}}{\text{NHCHCH}_2}\overset{\text{Br}}{\underset{\text{Br}}{\bigcirc}}$$

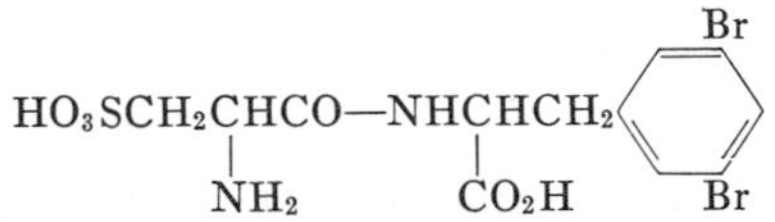

and the free amino group of the heptapeptide to which tyrosine was originally linked was found, on end-group analysis by the DNF method, to be that of an isoleucine residue, whence the sequence CySO$_3$H—Tyr—Ileu is established.

Of the thirteen peptides listed below, the first four were obtained by hydrolysis of the heptapeptide just mentioned. The next group resulted from hydrolysis of oxytocin. The neutral fraction was separated and treated with bromine water to oxidize cystine units to cysteic acid units and the resulting acidic peptides were separated from residual neutral peptides on an ion-exchange resin. The third

From the heptapeptide	1. Asp—CySO$_3$H
	2. CySO$_3$H, Pro
	3. CySO$_3$H, Pro, Leu
	4. CySO$_3$H, Pro, Leu, Gly
From oxytocin	5. Leu, Gly, Pro
	6. Tyr, CyS·SCy, Asp, Glu, Leu, Ileu
	7. Tyr, CyS·SCy, Asp, Glu
	8. CyS·SCy, Asp, Glu
	9. CySO$_3$H, Asp, Glu
From desulfurized oxytocin	10. Ala, Asp
	11. Ala, Asp, Glu
	12. Glu, Ileu
	13. Ala, Asp, Glu, Leu, Ileu

group of peptides resulted from hydrolysis of desulfurized oxytocin (Raney Ni), in which case an alanyl residue represents an original cysteinyl unit. The sequence was established in only one of the thirteen fragments; peptide 1 was shown by DNF analysis to be Asp—CySO$_3$H. This peptide is the equivalent of peptide 10 from desulfurized oxytocin. From the overlapping constituents of peptides 1–4, the following sequence can be deduced:

$$\text{Asp—CySO}_3\text{H—Pro—Leu—Gly.}$$

Peptide 5 is consistent with this sequence and evidently is Pro—Leu—Gly. Consideration of peptide 9 extends the sequence to:

$$\text{Glu—Asp—CySO}_3\text{H—Pro—Leu—Gly.}$$

Peptide 12 shows that the Glu unit is preceded by Ileu, and peptide 7 shows that

Tyr is linked to the second half of the cystine unit:

$$Tyr—CyS$$
$$Ileu—Glu—Asp—CyS—Pro—Leu—Gly.$$

This sequence, which is supported by the observation that only one of the cysteic acid units in oxidized oxytocin carries a free amino acid group (DNPh derivative), contains all eight amino acid units known to be present, and hence the Tyr and Ileu units must be joined together to form a cyclic pentapeptide system, a deduction confirmed by evidence presented above that bromine oxidation cleaves a Tyr—Ileu link. Further evidence was adduced by end-group analysis by the method of Edman. Oxidized oxytocin was degraded and after removal of the first amino-terminal unit the residual peptide was hydrolyzed and the component amino acids determined. The degradation was applied four times with the following results: the first Edman reaction removed cysteic acid, the second tyrosine, the third isoleucine, and the fourth glutamic acid.

The structure of the hormone was confirmed by a synthesis (du Vigneaud, 1954) involving coupling of the N-carbobenzoxy-S-benzyl dipeptide I with the heptapeptide triamide II by means of tetraethylpyrophosphite. On removal of the carbobenzoxy and benzyl groups protecting respectively the α-amino group of one cystein unit and the sulfhydryl groups of both units, the dithiol nonapeptide was produced and this on air oxidation was cyclized to oxytocin. Boissonnas (1955) synthesized the dithiol nonapeptide by a different route and likewise oxidized it to a cyclic octapeptide having the biological activity of oxytocin. Several other syntheses have since been reported.

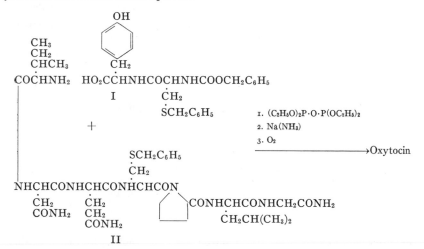

Insulin, Hormone of the Pancreas. — The pancreas is a large gland discharging into the intestine; when used as food it is called sweetbread. The gland secretes a proteinoid hormone, insulin, required for normal metabolism of carbohydrates. Deficiency of insulin leads to the disease diabetes mellitus, characterized by depletion of glycogen normally stored in liver and in muscle, increased blood glucose, and excretion in the urine of sugar and "acetone bodies," which are products of incomplete metabolic oxidation of sugars: aceto-acetic acid, acetone, β-hydroxybutyric acid. A procedure for preparation of concentrated active extracts of ox pancreas suitable for treatment of diabetic patients was developed in 1921 by Banting[1] and Macleod[2] by use of special techniques to protect the hormone from destruction by enzymes present in the gland. Crystalline insulin was isolated in 1926 by J. J. Abel by isoelectric precipitation and found to contain 0.52% zinc.

Insulin is highly aggregated in a 0.9% solution at pH 7, but in very dilute solutions at pH 2–3 dissociation is complete. Determinations of molecular weight by several physical methods indicated a value of 12,000, but application of a chemical method of determination showed this value to be in error. E. J. Harfenist and L. C. Craig first fractionated insulin by countercurrent distribution and obtained a preparation of partition curve approaching that ideal for a single solute. They then (1952) found conditions for partial reaction of the protein with dinitrofluoro-benzene, separated the products by partition chromatography, and from the extinction coefficient at 350 mμ of the mono-DNPh, and from the partition curves, arrived at a value for the molecular weight of 6,500. F. Sanger established the complete amino acid sequence by partial hydrolysis with chymotrypsin (1949–50) and found the theoretical molecular weight (5,734) to be close to the new experimental value. He found that the insulin molecule contains one peptide chain (A), in which the N-terminal group is glycine, and that A is bound by disulfide links to a second chain (B) with an N-terminal phenylalanine unit. Oxidation with performic acid cleaves the CyS—SCy binding links and gives two cysteinyl peptides. After determination of the sequence in each chain, the final problem was to discover which half-cystine units are joined together. Sanger solved this problem (1955) by partial hydrolysis of insulin under conditions such that the S—S links remain intact. The different cystine-peptides, without being separated

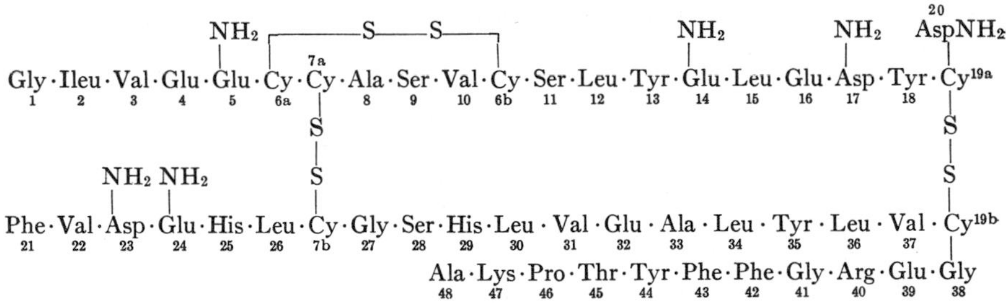

Insulin

from the other components, were fractionated from one another and then oxidized to cysteic peptides. The cysteic peptide of each fraction was then separated by ionophoresis and identified. The complete structure of the protein hormone was thereby elucidated.

[1] Sir Frederick G. Banting, 1891–1941; Univ. Toronto; Nobel Prize 1923
[2] John J. R. Macleod, 1877–1935; Univ. Toronto, Aberdeen; Nobel Prize 1923

Insulin is denatured and inactivated by alkali. The physiological activity is largely lost on complete acetylation and is partially restored on deacetylation. If only the amino groups are acetylated (ketene), no appreciable decrease in activity is observed; thus the phenolic hydroxyl groups are an important factor. Insulin loses its activity on reduction of the disulfide linkages by hydrogen sulfide, cysteine, or thioglycolic acid; approximately half of the activity is lost when only one or two disulfide groups have been reduced, and the only detectable chemical difference is the appearance of a few sulfhydryl groups. The activity is not restored on oxidation by the usual methods, and this observation is explained on the following basis:

$$\text{RS·SR'} \xrightarrow{\text{H}_2} \text{RSH} + \text{HSR'} \xrightarrow{\text{O}_2} \text{RS·SR} + \text{R'S·SR'}$$

31.30   Thyroglobulin. — The hormone of the thyroid gland, thyroglobulin, is a protein whose primary function is to increase the rate of metabolism (calorigenic action). The syndrome resulting from thyroglobulin deficiency is known as myxedema and is characterized by dry skin and swollen connective tissues. Dramatic cures are obtained on administration of the hormone. Congenital hypofunction results in cretinism (a specific mental deficiency), which can also be cured by the hormone if treatment is started early in life. The presence of iodine was detected in the thyroid gland in 1896, and at about this time an almost inactive iodine-containing amino acid, diiodotyrosine, was isolated from the coral *Gorgonia cavolini*. The successful isolation from the thyroid gland of the active substance thyroxine, which contains iodine, was accomplished in 1915 by E. C. Kendall. The synthesis was achieved in 1927 by C. R. Harington, who had proposed the correct formula the previous year. This amino acid accounts for about half the iodine content of the gland; the remainder is present as diiodotyrosine. Thyroxine is about 10,000 times as potent as diiodotyrosine, and on the basis of the iodine content is as active as thyroglobulin. Probably the organism is able to effect conjugation of thyroxine with a specific protein. In certain instances the gland enlarges (goiter), evidently in order to elaborate sufficient hormone, since the basal metabolism rate is normal. Administration of iodides for prevention of simple goiter is effective, and this fact, coupled with the close relationship among thyroxine and diiodotyrosine and tyrosine, indicates that the body probably synthesizes thyroxine from these latter substances.

Substances known as goitrogens interfere with the synthesis of thyroid hormone. Thiouracil and some of its derivatives are particularly effective, but

Thiouracil

other compounds containing the grouping—NHC(=S)NH— are active. The substances have clinical use in the treatment of hyperthyroidism.

31.31   β-Melanocyte-Stimulating Hormone. — C. H. Li[1] and his group in 1957 isolated this hormone from hog posterior pituitary glands, established the presence of 18 amino acid units (mol. wt. 2,177, isoelectric point 5.8), and determined the complete sequence shown. Free aspartic acid forms both

$$\text{H—Asp·Glu·Gly·Pro·Tyr·Lys·Met·Glu·His·Phe·Arg·Try·Gly·Ser·Pro·Pro·Lys·Asp—OH}$$
$$1\quad 2\quad 3\quad 4\quad 5\quad 6\quad 7\quad 8\quad 9\quad 10\quad 11\quad 12\quad 13\quad 14\quad 15\quad 16\quad 17\quad 18$$

terminal units (the Akabori degradation was done on a 3-mg. sample and Asp was identified as the DNPh-derivative). The hormone from beef pituitary (β_b-MSH) differs from that from hog (β-MSH) in replacement of the second amino acid (Glu) by serine. Synthetic β_b-MSH carrying six protective groups elicits activity in frog skin of 1.4×10^7 U/g. as compared to 1.2×10^9 U/g. for β_b-MSH (R. Schwyzer, Ciba-Basel, 1959). The synthetic 8–13 hexapeptide has an activity of only 2×10^5 U/g. (H. Koppeler, Ciba-Basel, 1961).

31.32   Pituitary Hormones. — Purified hormones of the posterior lobe act directly at the site of origin. Those of the anterior lobe are proteins that act indirectly at a distant site by stimulating other hormones in various endocrine glands. One is a hormone essential to growth; molecular weight, 49,000; isoelectric point, 6.85; amino acid content, Table 31.4 (last entry); properties of a globulin. Hormones of the anterior lobe include two which are necessary for proper functioning of the gonads, FSH (follicle-stimulating hormone) and ICSH (interstitial-cell stimulating hormone). Both are glucoproteins.

Particular interest attaches to the adrenocorticotropic hormone (ACTH), which is carried in the blood from the brain to the adrenal glands, where it stimulates production in the cortex of cortisol. Before cortisol became available in adequate amount by synthesis, ACTH found some use in medicine. It is used extensively in the treatment of ketosis in cattle. P. H. Bell[2] and his group isolated (1954) the 39-unit peptide β-corticotropin from hog ACTH and established the complete amino acid sequence (see formula). Results of partial hydrolysis

$$\text{Ser·Tyr·Ser·Met·Glu·His·Phe·Arg·Try·Gly·Lys·Pro·Val·Gly·Lys·Lys·Arg·Arg·Pro·}$$
$$1\quad 2\quad 3\quad 4\quad 5\quad 6\quad 7\quad 8\quad 9\quad 10\quad 11\quad 12\quad 13\quad 14\quad 15\quad 16\quad 17\quad 18\quad 19$$

$$\text{Val·Lys·Val·Tyr·Pro·Asp·Gly·Ala·Glu·Asp·Glu·Leu·Ala·Glu·(NH}_2\text{)·Ala·}$$
$$20\quad 21\quad 22\quad 23\quad 24\quad 25\quad 26\quad 27\quad 28\quad 29\quad 30\quad 31\quad 32\quad 33\qquad 34$$

$$\text{Phe·Pro·Leu·Glu·Phe}$$
$$35\quad 36\quad 37\quad 38\quad 39$$

$$\beta\text{-Corticotropin}$$

suggested (1956) that the biological activity resides in the first 24-unit part of the molecule, and it is now known that the active end stops with unit 23. The amino acid sequences determined for hormones of other sources by groups headed by W. F. White[3] (hog ACTH), C. H. Li (sheep ACTH), and A. B. Lerner[4] (human

---

[1] Choh Hao Li, b. 1913 Canton, China; Ph.D. Calif., Berkeley (T. D. Stewart); Univ. Calif., Berkeley

[2] Paul H. Bell, b. 1914 Cornerville, Ohio; Ph.D. Penn. State Univ.; Am. Cynamid Co.

[3] Wilfrid F. White, b. 1913 Chicago; M.S. Loyola; Armour Labs.

[4] Aaron Bunsen Lerner, b. 1920 Minneapolis; Ph.D. and M.D. Minnesota; Yale Univ.

ACTH) reveal that they differ from β-corticotropin only in the nonessential part of the molecule beyond unit 23.

It is noteworthy that the corticotropins have at least limited melanocyte-stimulating activity (3.7×10^7 U/g.) and that they contain an area of identity with β-melanocyte-stimulating hormone: the sequence Met·Glu·His·Phe·Arg·Try·Gly occurs in both (units 4–10 in the former and 7–13 in the latter). Initial synthetic experiments were encouraging. K. Hofmann and his group in 1959 synthesized a peptide corresponding to β-corticotropin in the first 13 units and it proved to be identical in biological activity with α-melanocyte-stimulating hormone, which darkens skin. This peptide showed very weak adrenal-stimulating activity, about one thousandth that of ACTH. Extension of the chain to 16-units (1960) did not increase the activity, but Li's group (later in 1960) found the 19-unit peptide to have about 30% the activity of ACTH. Finally, the Hofmann group (1961) extended the synthesis to the complete 23-unit structure present in β-corticotropin and found the synthetic peptide (mol. wt. 3,200) to have the complete biological activity of the natural hormone.

31.33   Peptides of Unusual Acid Components. — A variety of polypeptides isolated from bacteria and lower plants are characterized by the presence of an unusual amino acid as one or more of the constituents (Table 31.2), the D-isomer of one of the common amino acids, or a component which is not an amino acid.

Several closely related peptides possessing antibiotic properties have been isolated from a strain of soil microorganism, *Bacillus brevis* (Dubos,[1] 1940). They fall into two groups, the tyrocidines and the gramicidins, individual members of which have been isolated in relatively pure form by countercurrent distribution. The most extensively investigated member is gramicidin-S (S = Soviet; the substance was first described by Russian scientists), a cyclic decapeptide of the structure: cyclo-(L-Val-L-Orn-L-Leu-D-Phe-L-Pro)$_2$.

Bacitracin A, isolated from *B. subtilis* has been characterized by Craig (1955) as a cross-linked cyclic peptide made up of twelve amino acid units identified, after partial hydrolysis of the peptide and its DNPh derivative, by a combination of countercurrent distribution, paper chromatography, zone electrophoresis, and

Bacitracin A

ultimate analysis. Since the peptide gives cysteine on hydrolysis but contains only one atom of sulfur and gives a test for a thiol group only after reduction (SnCl$_2$), the sulfur must be present in an easily opened ring. Demonstration of the sequence Ileu—CySH—Leu in a hydrolyzate and characterization of a nine-

[1] René Dubos, b. 1901 Saint-Brice, France; Ph.D. Rutgers; Rockefeller Inst. Med. Res.

carbon product of oxidation and hydrolysis as having the UV absorption of a thiazole (aromatic) showed that bacitracin A contains a thiazoline ring (dihydro-aromatic) formed by loss of water from Ileu—CySH—Leu.

31.34   Conformation. — In 1951 L. Pauling and R. B. Corey[1] deduced a conformation for the polypeptide chain, particularly of fibrous proteins, which has since been supported by abundant evidence. Their reasoning was based in part upon interatomic distances accurately determined by X-ray analysis of simple peptides such as L-alanyl-L-alanine, data for which are shown in diagram (a). In consequence of resonance in the peptide group, the C—N

link is shortened, the C=O bond is lengthened, and the amide group is planar and *trans*. The hydrogen bond is a factor of considerable importance in determining conformational stability. X-ray evidence shows that in crystals of amino acids,

peptides, and proteins hydrogen atoms attached to nitrogen are almost without exception involved in the formation N—H···O=C hydrogen bonds (b). In almost all cases the distance between nitrogen and oxygen in this system is within 0.12 Å of 2.79 Å. Bonding also imposes near-linearity on the bonded system.

The conformation that best fits both sets of requirements is known as the α-helix; five other helical forms have been identified, but they lack the stability of the α-form. Since drawings and photographs of detailed models are difficult to follow, we present as an approximation a helix made from Dreiding models in which the nitrogen bonds have been flattened to better represent the near-linearity of the N—H···O bond and the *trans* orientation of the amide group (cylinder, o.d. 7.5 cm.). The helix of an L-peptide winds downwards to the left (N-terminus at the top); that of a D-peptide winds to the right. One complete turn in the helix includes 3.67 residues. The C=O groups point down and are bonded to N—H groups pointing up. Note that the bonding produces a series of chelate ring structures. Thus the hydrogen bonds between CO(1) and NH(3) and between CO(2) and NH(4) close a twelve-membered ring in which all the bonds but two are covalent. That helical proteins exhibit unusually high optical rotatory power can be attributed

[1] Robert B. Corey, b. 1897 Springfield, Mass.; Ph.D. Cornell (Dennis); Calif. Inst. Techn.

to the chelated ring structure. Denaturation, which disrupts the helical conformation and the chelate rings, is attended with a marked drop in rotation; the randomly coiled chains show only the low rotations characteristic of the component acids. The relationship between a native protein and its denatured form is similar to that between cystine and cysteine (31.3).

The helical structure applies to fibrous proteins of identity period of about 7 Å (fibroin). Proteins of folded structure (keratin) presumably are composed of extended chains held together by intermolecular hydrogen bonding. Globular proteins often contain segments in which the amino acids are arranged in a helical conformation, as well as nonhelical segments. Measurement of the helical content from the change in rotatory power on denaturation was applied first to polyamino acids (31.35) and later applied to proteins. A second method is based on the rate of exchange of secondary amide hydrogens by deuterium; exchange within the helical portion of the molecule is slower than in the randomly coiled segments (Blout,[1] 1953–61; Linderstrøm-Lang, 1955).

Linderstrøm-Lang suggested (1952) that protein structure can be examined at three levels; primary (amino acid sequence, *i.e.* structure), secondary (conformation), and tertiary. The tertiary structure refers to the manner in which a chain is folded and refolded to give the spherical shapes characteristic of globular proteins. Disulfide linkages play a major role in maintaining the tertiary structure. Study of tertiary structure of proteins by X-ray diffraction analysis has become known as molecular biology. The technique is illustrated by the work of J. C. Kendrew[2] on sperm-whale myoglobin (1958–60). This protein consists of 153 amino acid residues and contains a single heme prosthetic group. The method involves comparison of the X-ray pattern of crystalline myoglobin before and after introduction of a heavy atom by reaction of myoglobin with *p*-chloromercuribenzenesulfonic acid or with mercury diammine, or with both reagents.

Based on a resolution of 6 Å, Kendrew and coworkers were able to trace the polypeptide chain and to locate the heme group in the electron density map. The drawing shows a model (25 x 35 x 45 Å) in which the polypeptide chain is arranged in a highly irregular and complicated manner (the disc at the top is heme; the heme group is now known to be tilted in the direction opposite to that shown). The estimate that 70% of the chain is in the helical conformation is supported by results obtained by the deuterium-exchange method. Helen Scouloudi (1959) found from a two-dimensional Fourier projection of the unit cell of seal myoglobin that although the amino acid composition is entirely different from that of the sperm-whale protein the two myoglobins have essentially the same tertiary structure. M. F.

[1] Elkan R. Blout, b. 1919 New York; Ph.D. Columbia (Elderfield); Polaroid Corp.

[2] John C. Kendrew, b. 1917 Oxford, England; Ph.D. Cambridge; Cambridge Univ.

Perutz (1960) from a three-dimensional analysis of hemoglobin concluded that each of the four subunits of this molecule bears a close structural resemblance to myoglobin. By analysis of myoglobin at a resolution of 2 Å, which is not far short of atomic resolution, the Kendrew group (1961) have been able to deduce a part of the amino acid sequence of myoglobin.

31.35 **Polyamino Acids.** — This section is concerned mainly with synthetic polypeptides obtained by polymerization of an amino acid derivative or, in some cases, of two or more components. The acids themselves are not satisfactory monomers because of the dipolar ion character. Esters of glycine and of alanine have been polymerized, but the monomer now preferred is of a type known as a Leuchs anhydride (4). H. Leuchs (1906) prepared compounds of this type by reaction of an amino acid (1) with methyl chlorocarbonate to form the N-carbomethoxyamino acid (2); conversion to the acid chloride (3), and vacuum distillation, gives the anhydride (4) with elimination of methyl chloride.

$$H_2NCHRCO_2H \xrightarrow{ClCO_2CH_3} CH_3OCONHCHRCO_2H \xrightarrow{SOCl_2}$$

$$(1) \qquad\qquad\qquad\qquad\qquad (2)$$

$$\begin{matrix} RCHCOCl \\ | \\ HNCOOCH_3 \end{matrix} \xrightarrow[-CH_3Cl]{Dist.} \begin{matrix} RCHC{\Large<}^O_O \\ | \quad \\ HN-C{\Large<}^O_{\;} \end{matrix} \xrightarrow{-CO_2} \left[\begin{matrix} -NHCHCO- \\ | \\ R \end{matrix} \right]_n$$

$$(3) \qquad\qquad\qquad\qquad (4) \qquad\qquad\qquad (5)$$

$$(1) \xrightarrow{ClCOCl} ClCONHCHRCO_2H \xrightarrow{-HCl} O{=}C{=}NCHRCO_2H$$

In a newer procedure (F. Fuchs, 1922) the amino acid is treated with phosgene in toluene or dioxane. Leuchs noted that the anhydrides when treated with a trace of water lose carbon dioxide and form polymers, but the observation attracted little attention until E. Katchalski[1] and others initiated extensive investigations in the field. Poly-α-amino acids of high molecular weight have been prepared from Leuchs anhydrides of almost all the natural amino acids. Some copolymers have been prepared in which minor amino acid residues are distributed at random along a major polypeptide chain. Studies, particularly by P. Doty[2] and by E. R. Blout, have shown that synthetic polypeptides exist in solution either as α-helices or as randomly coiled chains, depending upon the conditions. The two forms are readily distinguishable by characteristic optical rotations. As with native and denatured proteins, randomly oriented synthetic polypeptides show only low rotations, but helical polypeptides have greatly enhanced rotatory power. The difference between helical conformations and random residues is particularly striking when evaluated by rotatory dispersion curves for the far ultraviolet; Blout (1961) reports rotations into the tens of thousands. The new machine for determining circular dichroism spectra (Roussel-Uclaf, 1961) should be particularly useful.

[1] Ephraim Katchalski, b. 1916 Bielsk, Russia; Ph.D. Hebrew Univ. (M. Frankel); Weizmann Institute of Science, Israel

[2] Paul Doty, b. 1920 Charleston, W. Va.; Ph.D. Columbia (J. Mayer); Harvard Univ.

One natural polyamino acid has been described. A polypeptide (mol. wt. 50,000) found in the capsules of *Bacillus anthraces*, *B. licheniformis*, and *B. subtilis* is composed exclusively of poly-D-glutamic acid. Unusual features are the stereochemical series and the fact that the glutamic acid residues are linked exclusively by γ-peptide bonds (J. Kovacs and U. Bruckner, 1951–53). The virulence of these bacilli may be associated with the fact that proteolytic enzymes are unable to attack the polypeptide. Synthetic poly-γ-D-glutamic acid is identical in properties with the natural product (U. Bruckner, 1955).

ENZYMES

31.36 **Discovery.** — In 1897 Buchner[1] was able to prepare a cell-free extract of yeast capable of transforming D-glucose into ethanol and carbon dioxide. The name enzyme is derived from this discovery (Gr. *en*, in; *zyme*, yeast); a specific catalyst is identified as an enzyme by the suffix -ase. Sumner[2] (1926) isolated a pure, crystalline enzyme for the first time and named it urease because it is specific to the substrate urea and catalyzes hydrolysis to carbon dioxide and ammonia. The number of enzymes now known in pure or nearly pure form is well in the hundreds. All are proteins, although some contain a nonprotein prosthetic group essential for activity. Enzymes of one type, hydrolases, contain nothing but protein and promote hydrolysis of proteins, glycosides, glycerides (lipase), esters (esterase), and phosphates. Enzymes involved in oxidation-reduction reactions contain a prosthetic group.

31.37 **Proteolytic Enzymes.** — Important enzymes of the digestive tract are pepsin (gastric juice), trypsin, chymotrypsin, and carboxypeptidase (pancreas). They usually are secreted as an inactive precursor (zymogen). The precursors pepsinogen, trypsinogen, and chymotrypsinogen have all been obtained pure. Activation consists in the release of small peptide fragments and is catalyzed by the active enzyme itself or by enterokinase, another enzyme present in the digestive tract. In the trypsinogen → trypsin conversion, the hexapeptide Val—(Asp)₄—Lys is released from the N-terminus with formation of Ileu as the new N-terminal group (H. Neurath,[3] 1955). Activation of other zymogens is more complex. Pioneering work of M. Bergmann (1937) on simple model peptides showed that enzymes preferentially split certain peptide bonds. Pepsin, trypsin, and chymotrypsin are known as endopeptidases because they attack central peptide bonds. Pepsin splits an amide bond derived from the amino group of phenylalanine or tyrosine, whereas chymotrypsin splits one derived from the carboxyl group of these aromatic acids. Trypsin splits amide bonds derived from the carboxyl group of the basic amino acids (Lys, Arg). These proteolytic enzymes also split esters of similar structural environment. In all cases only peptides derived from L-amino acids are affected.

The suggestion of Michaelis (1913) that enzyme-catalyzed reactions proceed

---

[1] Eduard Buchner, 1860–1917; b. Munich; Ph.D. Munich (Curtius); Univ. Breslau, Würzburg; Nobel Prize 1907

[2] James B. Sumner, 1887–1955; b. Canton, Mass.; Ph.D. Harvard (C. H. Fiske); N. Y. State Agr. College, Cornell Univ.; Nobel Prize 1946

[3] Hans Neurath, b. 1909 Vienna; Ph.D. Vienna (W. Pauli); Univ. Washington, Seattle

through an intermediate enzyme–substrate complex has been supported by all subsequent work, and considerable evidence shows that catalytic activity is limited to a small portion of the enzyme, the active site. Study of the potentialities as chemical warfare agents of organophosphorus compounds which poison enzymes suggested their use in locating active centers. A common reagent is diiosopropylphosphorofluoridate (DPF: "diisopropylfluorophosphate, DFP"),

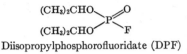

Diisopropylphosphorofluoridate (DPF)

which can be labeled with radioactive P^{32}. DPF poisons esterases and proteolytic enzymes by combination at or near the active center; it reacts with one mole of trypsin with liberation of HF and formation of inactive DP-trypsin (A. K. Balls,[1] 1952). Acid hydrolysis of DPF-treated enzymes in all cases gives phosphoserine, $(HO)_2P(O)OCH_2CH(NH_2)CO_2H$. Degradation of DP-chymotrypsin and isolation of peptides containing phosphoserine indicates that the sequences Asp-Ser-Gly-Glu-Ala-Val and Gly-Asp-Ser-Gly-Gly-Pro-Leu are involved in the active site. The sequence Gly-Asp-Ser-Gly occurs in both trypsin and chymotrypsin.

Trypsin and chymotrypsin appear to possess a second active site involving histidine. The second site is not adjacent to the first one, but the two are held in proximity by the helical conformation. Identification of histidine is based in part on the observation that variation of the rate of the enzymic reactions with pH corresponds to that expected for a strategically located weakly basic group of the character of histidine. Furthermore, imidazole itself catalyzes the hydrolysis of simple esters (T. C. Bruice[2] and G. L. Schmir, 1955–57; M. L. Bender, 1957). That the enzyme is 10^5 times more effective than imidazole finds a parallel in model experiments on the mutarotation of glucose, a reaction catalyzed by both acids and bases. o-Hydroxypyridine, which contains an acidic and a basic center, both relatively weak, is a much more effective catalyst than a combination of pyridine and phenol (G. Swain, 1952). In both o-hydroxypyridine and the proteolytic enzymes, the bifunctionality enhances catalytic activity because protons can be donated and removed simultaneously in a concerted reaction. The mode of action suggested for chymotrypsin by H. Neurath (1957) is as follows. Interaction between the hydroxyl group of serine and the imidazole ring of histidine (1) and withdrawal of a proton gives an activated complex (2) having an electrophilic and a nucleophilic center. Reaction with the peptide carbonyl group of a protein (3) gives an O-acyl derivative (4), which rearranges to the N-acyl derivative (5) in a fast step. The rate-controlling step (first order) is hydrolysis of (5) to the peptides (6) with regeneration of the activated complex (2).

A unit of cysteine rather than of histidine has been implicated in the activity of papain (E. L. Smith, 1954–58). For maximal proteolytic activity, the pure

---

[1] Arnold Kent Balls, b. 1891, Toronto; Ph.D. Columbia; Deutsch. Techn. Hochschule, Prague; Purdue Univ.

[2] Thomas C. Bruice, b. 1925 Los Angeles; Ph.D. Southern Calif. (N. Kharasch); Johns Hopkins Sch. Med.; Cornell Univ.

(crystalline) enzyme requires activation by a natural activator (probably gluta-thione) or by cysteine, H_2S, HCN, etc.   Treatment of a crystalline mercuric com-

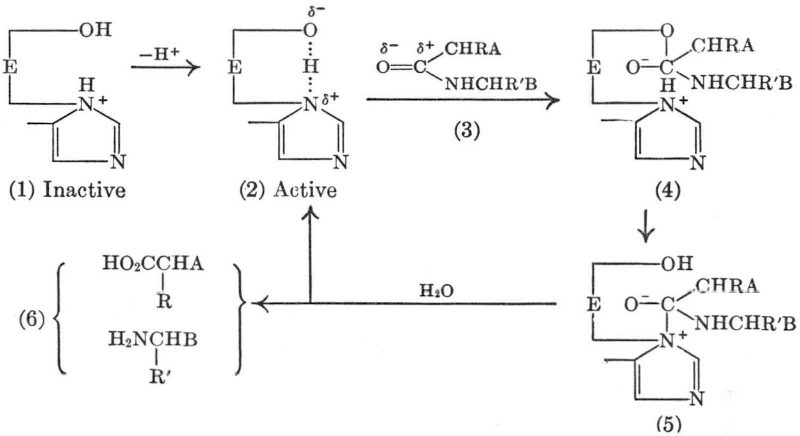

plex of papain with purified aminopeptidase removes about two thirds of the 180 amino acid residues originally present without loss of enzymic activity.   M. Berg-mann and H. Fraenkel-Conrat demonstrated (1937) that papain can catalyze the formation of a peptide bond, as well as its rupture.   In the example formulated,

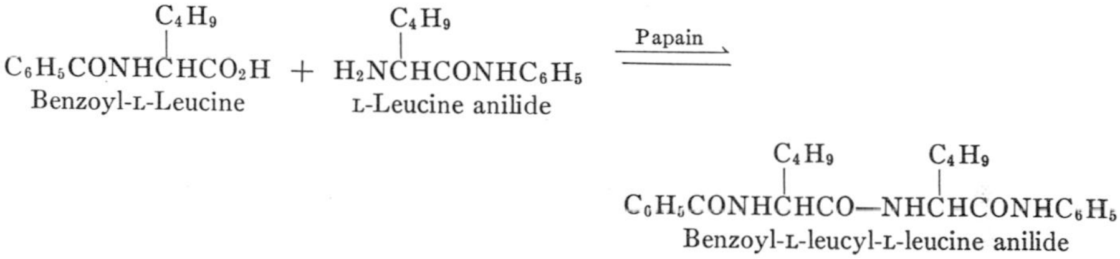

$$\underset{\text{Benzoyl-L-Leucine}}{C_6H_5CONH\overset{\overset{\displaystyle C_4H_9}{|}}{C}HCO_2H} + \underset{\text{L-Leucine anilide}}{H_2N\overset{\overset{\displaystyle C_4H_9}{|}}{C}HCONHC_6H_5} \xrightarrow{\text{Papain}}$$

$$\underset{\text{Benzoyl-L-leucyl-L-leucine anilide}}{C_6H_5CONH\overset{\overset{\displaystyle C_4H_9}{|}}{C}HCO-NH\overset{\overset{\displaystyle C_4H_9}{|}}{C}HCONHC_6H_5}$$

as well as in all other known examples of enzymic synthesis of peptides, the suc-cess of the synthesis is due to the fact that the peptide formed is less soluble than the components and separates from the reaction mixture with displacement of the equilibrium.   Ordinarily the equilibrium lies far to the side of hydrolysis (ca. 99%).   Peptide bond formation requires an estimated 2–4 kcal./mole.   Various ways have been suggested by which the unfavorable energy relationship might be overcome, but the main objection to the idea that proteinases also control syn-thesis is that these enzymes probably cannot control the amino acid sequence.

31.38   Structural Units of Prosthetic Groups. — The pyrimidine ring occurs as such in the prosthetic group of some enzymes, but more often it is fused to a second heterocyclic ring.   If this second ring is imidazole, the structural unit is purine.   In isoalloxazine, the basic unit of riboflavin, a reduced pyrimidine

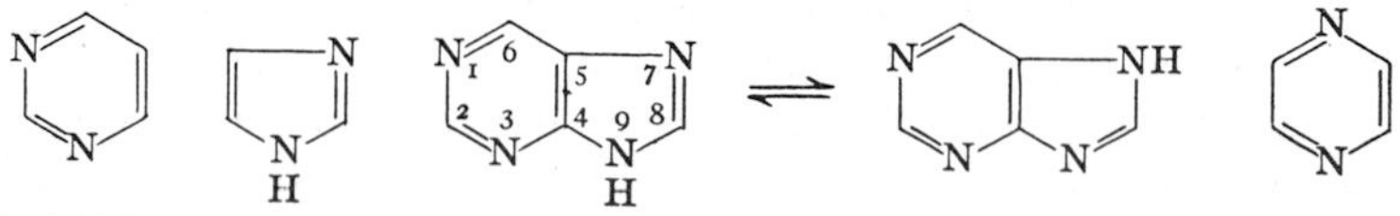

Pyrimidine Imidazole   Purine   Pyrazine

ring is fused to a pyrazine ring and this is fused to a benzene ring. The isoalloxazine structure is less aromatic and hence less stable than the alloxazine structure, and exists as such only when the central nitrogen at position 9 carries a carbon substituent in place of hydrogen. The chief basic constituent is adenine, or 6-aminopurine.

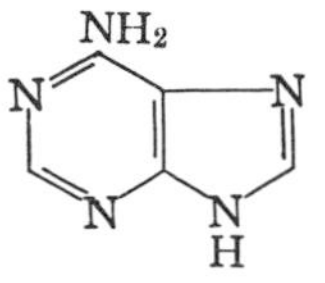

Adenine 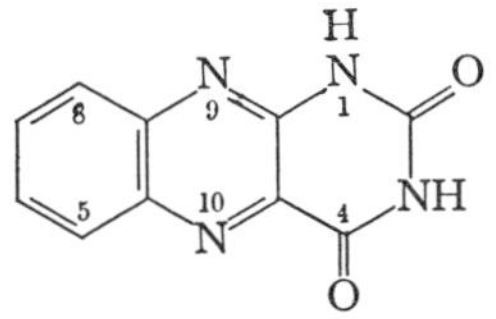   Alloxazine 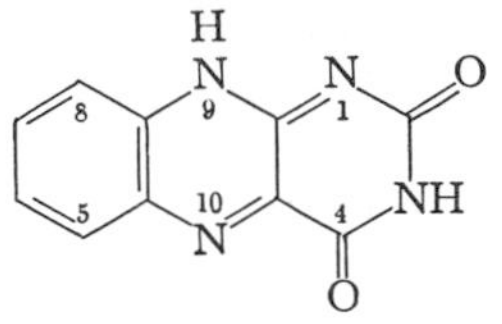   Isoalloxazine

A further component is the pentose D-ribose, which is combined with purines as β-D-ribofuranose. In riboflavin the reduction product ribitol is combined at position I with an isoalloxazine derivative.

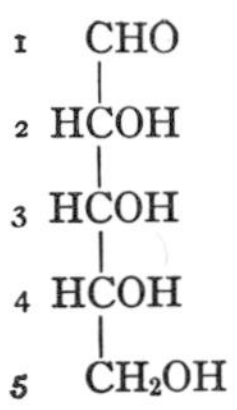

D-Ribose 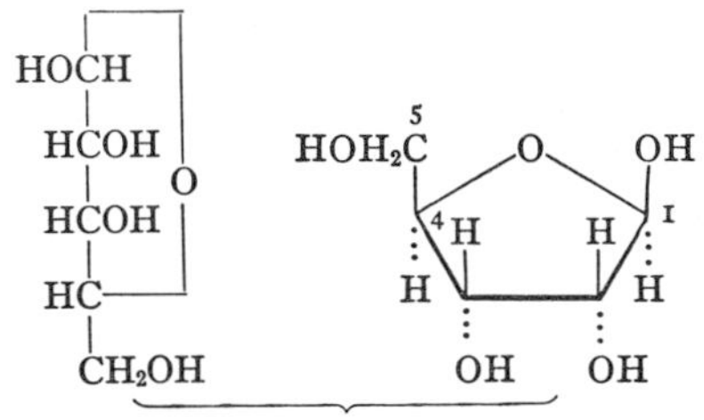   β-D-Ribofuranose 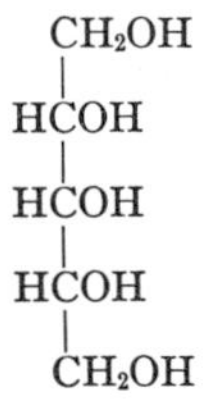   D-Ribitol

The formula of adenosine is derived by elimination of the elements of water between the I-hydroxyl group of β-D-ribofuranose and the 9-NH group of adenine.

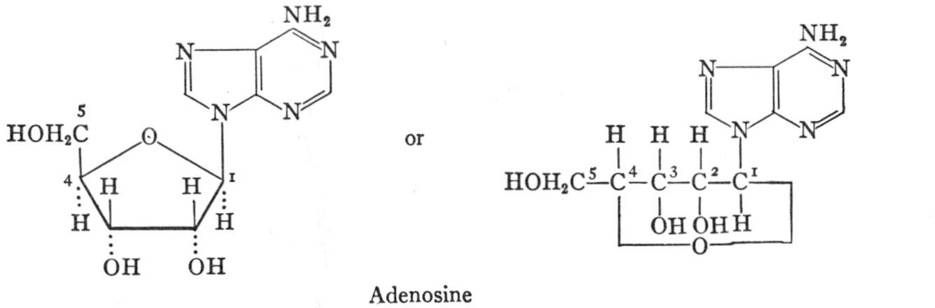

or

Adenosine

An adenylic acid contains one molecule of phosphoric acid esterified with adenosine and is an adenosine monophosphate (AMP). If a second molecule of phosphoric acid is condensed with the first in a pyrophosphate grouping, —OPO(OH)—OPO(OH)$_2$, the substance is an adenosine diphosphate (ADP). If a third molecule of the acid is condensed to give the grouping —OPO(OH)—OPO(OH)—OPO(OH)$_2$, the substance is an adenosine triphosphate (ATP). Adenosine is called a nucleoside; its phosphoric esters are called mono-, di-, and trinucleotides.

Although work on the synthesis of nucleotides is too extensive for adequate review here, some idea of the ingenious methods developed in this rapidly moving field may be conveyed by citation of three examples. One is Todd's synthesis of the coenzyme uridinediphosphoglucose (pp. 310–311); a second is Khorana's synthesis of coenzyme A (31.42); a third is a method capable of wide variation developed by Cramer[1] (1958–61) and illustrated below. The first step, an application of the W. Perkow reaction (1952–55), involves reaction of diethyl bromomalonate (1) with triethyl phosphite in ether to produce diethyl α-ethoxy-β-carbethoxyvinyl phosphate (2). This phosphoric acid triester is capable of

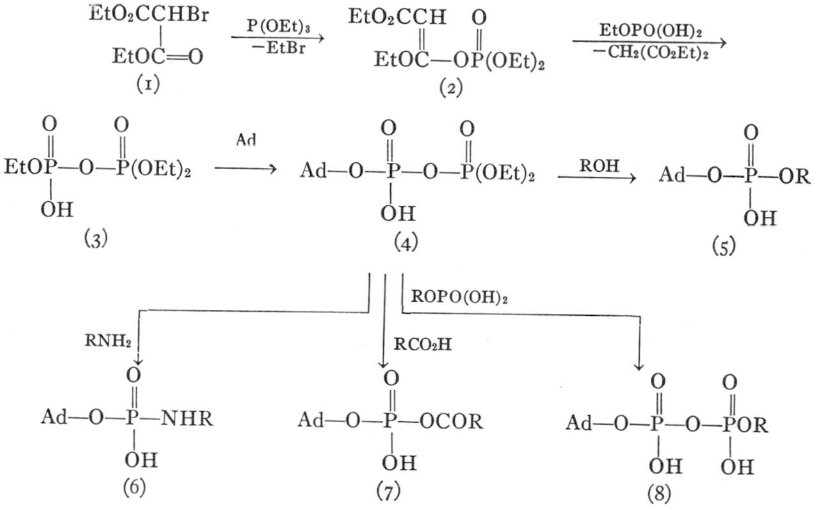

transferring the phosphoric acid diethyl ester residue to a monoethyl phosphate to give the triester (3), with liberation of malonic ester as the only by-product. The triester (3), in turn, reacts with adenosine-5′-phosphoric acid (abbreviation Ad) to give diethyl P¹-(adenosyl-5′)-P²-pyrophosphate (4), isolated as the stable sodium salt. This substance contains, and can transfer to a variety of acceptors, an activated adenosyl-5′-phosphoric acid residue, as illustrated by conversion to products (5)–(8). Another reagent of promise for selective phosphorylation is trichloroacetonitrile (Cramer, 1961).

31.39   **Oxidative (Respiratory) Enzymes.** — Enzymes that effect oxidation by transfer of hydrogen from the substrate directly to oxygen are known as oxidases. Tyrosinase is an enzyme of this type, which catalyzes air oxidation of tyrosine to the pigment melanin, a brownish pigment of the retina, skin, and hair of higher animals (except albinos); three intermediates have been identified (H. S. Raper, 1937).

Fully homogeneous tyrosinase (D. Kertesz, 1957) contains 0.20% copper, which appears to function as a prosthetic group. Thus chromatography of a preparation from mushroom gave material of lower copper content (0.06%) and greatly reduced activity (E. Frieden,[2] 1961). Others, dehydrogenases, transfer

[1] Friedrich Cramer, b. 1923 Breslau; Ph.D. Heidelberg (Freudenberg); Techn. Hochschule Darmstadt

[2] Earl Frieden, b. 1921 Norfolk, Va.: Ph.D. Southern Calif.; Florida State Univ.

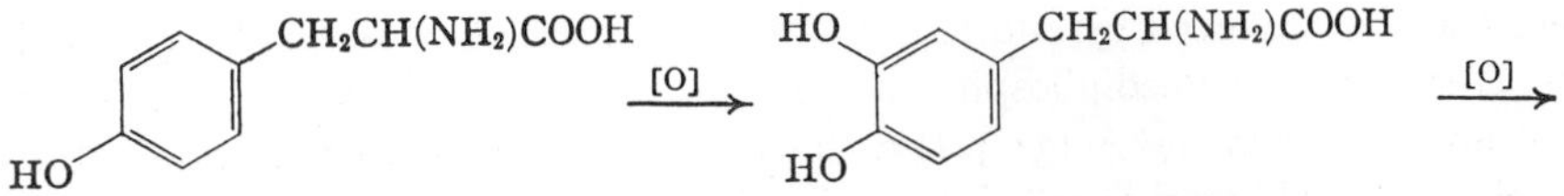

Tyrosine — 3,4-Dihydroxyphenylalanine 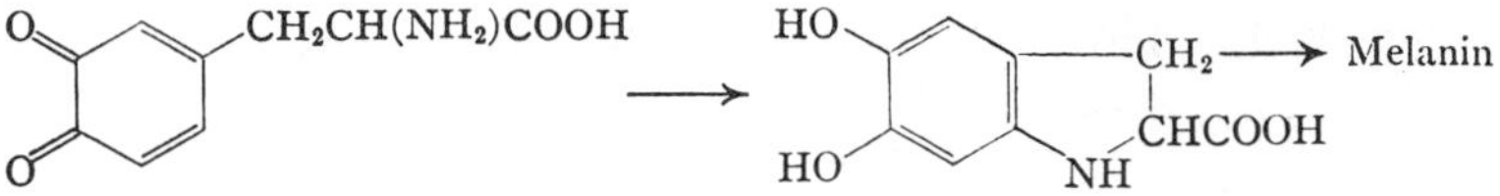 — Intermediate quinone — 5,6-Dihydroxydihydroindole-α-carboxylic acid — Melanin

hydrogen not to oxygen but to an acceptor enzyme or coenzyme. The term coenzyme is sometimes applied to a proteinoid enzyme necessary for activation of another proteinoid enzyme, but a prosthetic group without which a protein is inactive also is often described as a coenzyme. The donor enzyme requires an acceptor enzyme of specific oxidation-reduction potential and cannot function with another acceptor, even one with a closely related prosthetic group. A specific unit in the prosthetic group of each acceptor enzyme is responsible for the uptake of two hydrogen atoms. In some instances this unit is a nicotinamide group, and nicotinamide is an essential dietary constituent for many animals. This residue contributes a reversible oxidoreduction function:

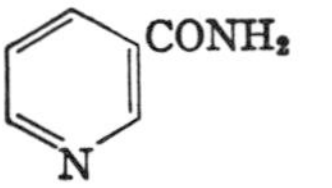

Nicotinamide

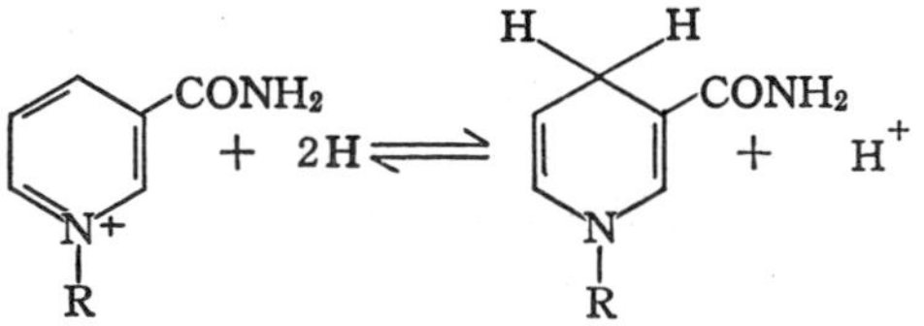

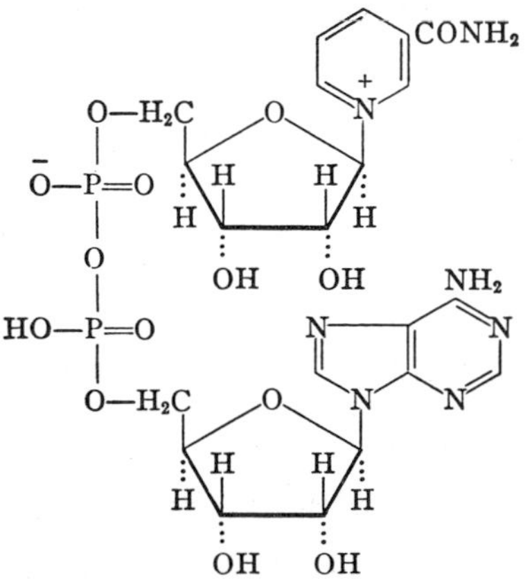

Diphosphopyridine nucleotide (DPN)

Two acceptor **pyridinoprotein enzymes** containing the nicotinamide unit were formerly called coenzyme I and coenzyme II. The structures of the prosthetic groups are now known and these groups are known as **diphosphopyridine nucleotide (DPN)** and **triphosphopyridine nucleotide (TPN).** The former is characteristic of the acceptor enzyme of yeast (coenzyme I) discovered by Harden[1] and Young in 1904 in their classical investigation of alcoholic fermentation. They separated yeast juice by dialysis into a protein and a nonprotein fraction

[1] Arthur Harden, 1865–1940; Univ. Manchester, Lister Inst., London; Nobel Prize 1929

(prosthetic group) and found that neither alone promotes fermentation but that ability to promote fermentation is restored by mixing the two solutions. The linkage between the protein and the prosthetic group is thus loose, and separation into the two fragments or recombination to the enzyme occurs readily. The structure of DPN was finally settled in 1942 through work of von Euler, Karrer, Schlenk, and Warburg. The complicated substance is composed of one molecule each of nicotinamide and of adenine, and two molecules each of D-ribose and of phosphoric acid, joined as shown in the formula. TPN contains one more molecule of phosphoric acid which is esterified with the hydroxyl group at position 2' in the ribose unit linked to adenine. Each of the two enzymes can accept two hydrogen atoms to form a dihydro derivative, which then can serve as hydrogen donor enzyme.

A representative of another important group of dehydrogenases known as flavoproteins is the yellow enzyme of yeast (Warburg[1] and Theorell,[2] 1934). The chromophoric group is riboflavin, and the prosthetic group is the 5'-phosphate ester, named flavin mononucleotide. Combination of the synthetic 5'-phosphate ester with the specific protein of yellow enzyme affords active flavoprotein (Kuhn, Karrer).

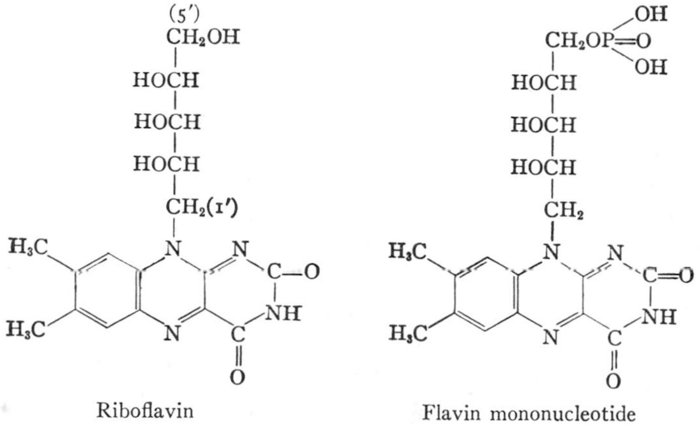

Riboflavin
(6,7-dimethyl-9-D-ribitylisoalloxazine)

Flavin mononucleotide
(riboflavin 5' phosphoric acid)

Riboflavin contains the isoalloxazine nucleus, and this grouping is responsible for the oxidation-reduction function; reduction involves 1,4-addition of hydrogen to the conjugated system:

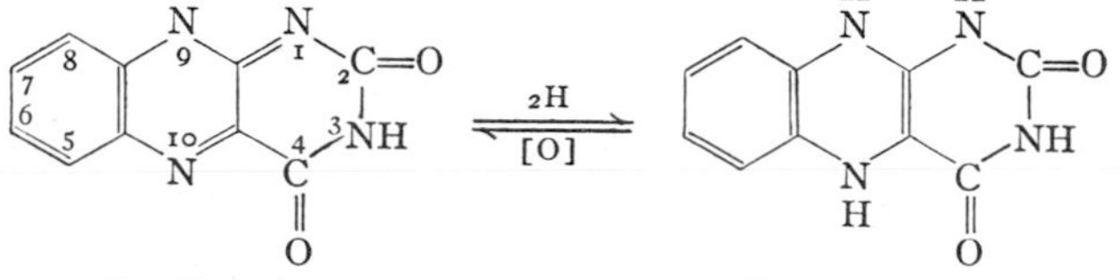

Isoalloxazine
(flavin, yellow)

Leuco compound
(colorless)

[1] Otto Warburg, b. 1883 Freiburg; Ph.D. Berlin and Heidelberg; Kaiser Wilhelm Inst., Berlin; Nobel Prize 1931

[2] Hugo Theorell, b. 1903 Linköping, Sweden; M.D. Stockholm; Stockholm; Nobel Prize 1955

Several other flavoproteins are similarly constituted. In one the prosthetic group is riboflavin adenine dinucleotide, in which riboflavin is linked at the 5′-position to a pyrophosphate group which, in turn, is linked at the 5-position in the riboside residue to adenosine.

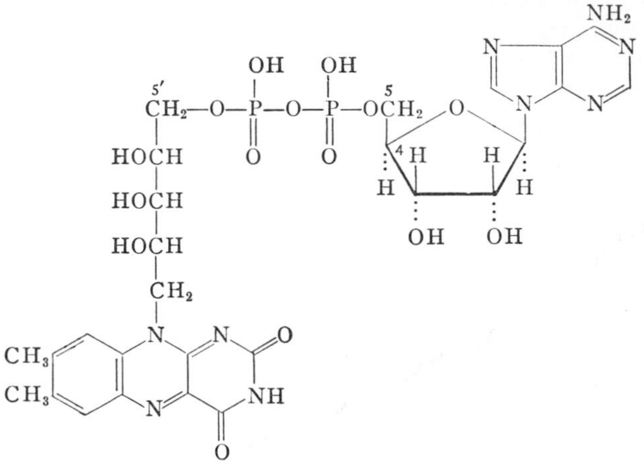

Riboflavin adenine dinucleotide

Another group of oxidases contain hemin or a closely related substance as the prosthetic group and are called **hemoproteins.** **Hemoglobin, catalase,** and **peroxidase** contain heme as the prosthetic group. In hemoglobin the iron is in the ferrous state, in catalase it is in the ferric state. **Cytochrome c** has a slightly different prosthetic group, the iron-free porphyrin of which, designated porphyrin c (Theorell) has been found to contain two residues of cysteine linked to two-carbon side chains that replace the vinyl groups in the porphyrin of heme. Cytochrome c functions as an electron transfer system by change of valency of the iron: $Fe^{+++} + e \rightleftharpoons Fe^{++}$. Tuppy (1954–55) degraded cytochrome c with proteolytic enzymes, separated the heme-containing peptides, and analyzed them for the amino acid sequence. The sequence established in the heme portion of the

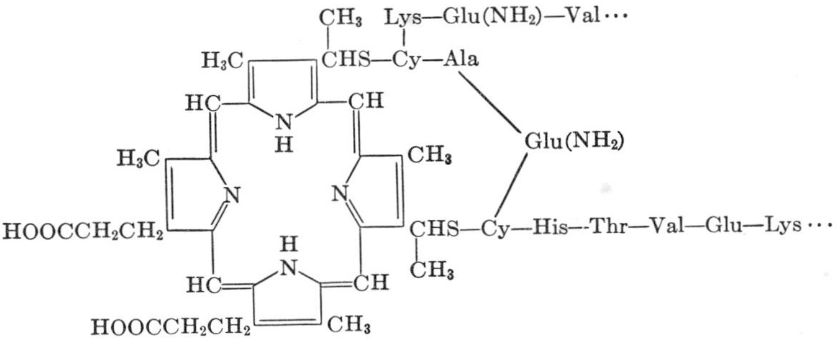

Hemopeptide from porphyrin c

molecule is shown in the formula.

In the living cell the transfer of hydrogen from a substrate to molecular oxygen proceeds through a series of coupled oxidation-reduction reactions involving enzymes of different types and of graded potential, such that the oxidation energy of oxygen is released in a series of graded steps. The coupled steps may be as follows:

Substrate–H_2 + DPN–protein → Substrate + H_2–DPN–protein

H_2–DPN–protein + Yellow enzyme → DPN–protein + Leuco yellow enzyme

Leuco yellow enzyme + Cytochrome → Yellow enzyme + H_2–Cytochrome

H_2–Cytochrome + ½ O_2 → Cytochrome + H_2O

A generalized representation of the energy relationships given in the chart includes approximate values of E_0, the oxidation-reduction potential in a solution of equimolecular amounts of oxidant and reductant. In spite of the large difference in

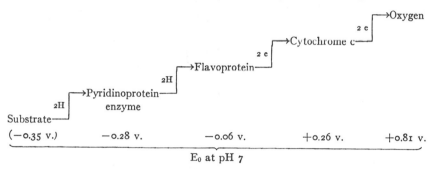

$$\text{Substrate} \xrightarrow{2H} \text{Pyridinoprotein enzyme} \xrightarrow{2H} \text{Flavoprotein} \xrightarrow{2e} \text{Cytochrome c} \xrightarrow{2e} \text{Oxygen}$$

(−0.35 v.)   −0.28 v.   −0.06 v.   +0.26 v.   +0.81 v.

E_0 at pH 7

potential between systems at the two ends of the respiratory chain, these systems are unable to interact with each other directly. The chart suggests the hypothesis that the initial changes occur by hydrogen transfer and the terminal changes by electron transfer.

31.40   Alcoholic Fermentation. — That enzymes catalyze numerous reactions other than those of the types discussed above is well illustrated in the elaborate sequence of steps involved in the fermentation of hexoses to

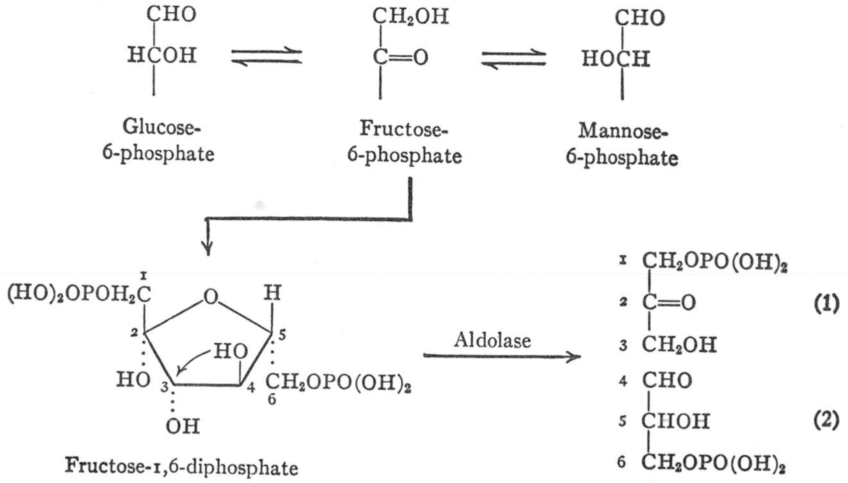

$$
\begin{array}{ccccc}
\text{CHO} & & \text{CH}_2\text{OH} & & \text{CHO} \\
| & & | & & | \\
\text{HCOH} & \rightleftharpoons & \text{C}{=}\text{O} & \rightleftharpoons & \text{HOCH} \\
| & & | & & | \\
\end{array}
$$

Glucose-6-phosphate   Fructose-6-phosphate   Mannose-6-phosphate

$$\text{Fructose-1,6-diphosphate} \xrightarrow{\text{Aldolase}}$$

1 $CH_2OPO(OH)_2$
2 $C{=}O$ (1)
3 CH_2OH
4 CHO
5 $CHOH$ (2)
6 $CH_2OPO(OH)_2$

ethanol and carbon dioxide. Key intermediates are D-fructose-6-phosphate and -1,6-diphosphate, formed from the sugar and a phosphate donor under the influence of an enzyme. Fission of fructose-1,6-diphosphate involves reverse aldolization by transfer of hydrogen from the C_4-hydroxyl to carbon atom 3 with formation of the fragments (1) and (2). Since the transfer occurs in a *trans*-glycol grouping and involves attack by hydrogen at the unshielded back side of C_3, it is not surprising that the enzymic cleavage is stereospecific. If either D-glucose or D-mannose is the substrate, it is converted into the 6-phosphate and this is isomerized by the enzyme isomerase to fructose-6-phosphate to a point of equilibrium. D-Galactose, which has the unfavorable 3,4-*cis* glycol grouping, is fermented at a rate substantially below the rate for glucose or mannose, and Leloir[1] established (1950) that fermentation of galactose requires initial epimerization at C_4 to give glucose. He isolated the enzyme responsible for the inversion and named the prosthetic group cogalactowaldenase. The name is now known to be incorrect

$$\text{CHCHOHCHOHCHCH}_2\text{OP}-\text{O}-\overset{\text{OH}}{\underset{\text{O}}{\text{P}}}-\text{OCHCHOHCHOHCHOHCHCH}_2\text{OH}$$

(ribose)   (diphosphate)   (glucose)

(uracil)

UDPG (uridinediphosphoglucose)

in a strict sense because inversion is accomplished by a process of dehydrogenation-hydrogenation. The name now used is UDPG (synthesis: pp. 310–311). The reaction UDPGluc → UDPGal requires DPN as cofactor.

The next stage of fermentation proceeds through glyceraldehyde 3-phosphate (2), into which dihydroxyacetone-1-phosphate (1) is converted by isomerase.

$$\begin{array}{ccccc}
\text{CH}=\text{O} & & \left[\begin{array}{c}\text{OH}\\ \text{CHOPO(OH)}_2\\ \text{CHOH}\\ \text{CH}_2\text{OPO(OH)}_2\end{array}\right] & & \overset{O}{\text{COPO(OH)}_2}\\
\text{CHOH} & \xrightarrow{\text{HOPO(OH)}_2} & & \xrightarrow[-\text{DPNH}]{\text{DPN}} & \text{CHOH}\\
\text{CH}_2\text{OPO(OH)}_2 & & & & \text{CH}_2\text{OPO(OH)}_2 \xrightarrow{\text{ADP}}\\
(2) & & (3) & & (4)
\end{array}$$

$$\begin{array}{cccc}
\text{CO}_2\text{H} & \text{CO}_2\text{H} & \text{CO}_2\text{H} & \text{CO}_2\text{H}\\
\text{CHOH} \longrightarrow & \text{CHOPO(OH)}_2 \longrightarrow & \text{CHOPO(OH)}_2 \xrightarrow[-\text{H}_2\text{O}]{\text{Enolase}} & \text{C}-\text{OPO(OH)}_2\\
\text{CH}_2\text{OPO(OH)}_2 & \text{CH}_2\text{OPO(OH)}_2 & \text{CH}_2\text{OH} & \text{CH}_2\\
(5) & (6) & (7) & (8)
\end{array}$$

$$\begin{array}{cccc}
& \text{CO}_2\text{H}\\
\xrightarrow{\text{ADP}} & \text{C}=\text{O} \xrightarrow[-\text{CO}_2]{\text{Carboxylase}} & \text{CH}=\text{O} \xrightarrow[-\text{DPN}]{\text{DPNH}} & \text{CH}_2\text{OH}\\
& \text{CH}_3 & \text{CH}_3 & \text{CH}_3\\
& (9) & (10) & (11)
\end{array}$$

[1] Luis F. Leloir, b. 1906 Paris (Argentine citizen); M.D. Buenos Aires; Buenos Aires

Nonenzymic addition of phosphoric acid to the carbonyl group (3) is followed by enzymic dehydrogenation by diphosphopyridine nucleotide (DPN), which is reduced to the dihydride (DPNH). 1,3-Diphosphoglyceric acid (4) transfers the anhydride 1-phosphate group to ADP, giving (5) and, under the influence of phosphoglyceromutase, 3-phosphoglyceric acid (5) is converted via the 2,3-diphosphate (6) into 2-phosphoglyceric acid (7). Elimination of water gives phosphoenol pyruvic acid (8), from which ADP eliminates the phosphate group to give pyruvic acid (9). Carboxylase effects decarboxylation to acetaldehyde, which in the final step is reduced by DPNH to ethanol.

A vast amount of experimental work contributed by many investigators established the sequence of steps outlined. Some intermediates were isolated by fixation methods (trapping). Acetaldehyde can be fixed as the bisulfite addition product or as the dimedone derivative, and glycerol rather than ethanol is then the main product. Pyruvic acid has been isolated by fixation with β-naphthylamine, with which it forms a derivative which is fermentable but isolable because of its sparing solubility. A further method of investigation is based upon the

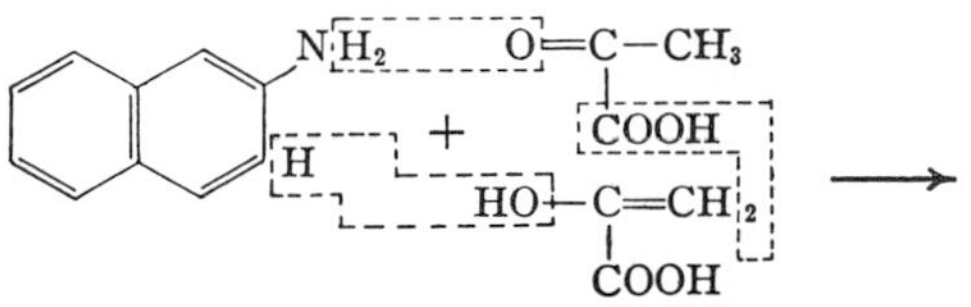

β-Naphthylamine   Pyruvic acid

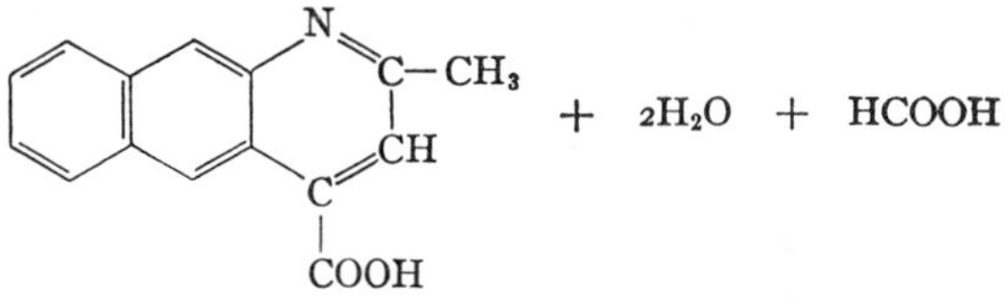

α-Methyl-β-naphthocinchonic acid

ability of certain chemicals to poison specific enzyme systems. When sodium fluoride is added to the fermentation, the enzyme enolase is poisoned, with the result that the phosphoglyceric acids accumulate and are not converted into phosphopyruvic acid. The addition of monoiodoacetic acid poisons DPN and thus inhibits reduction of acetaldehyde to alcohol by hydrogen transfer from DPNH.

Carboxylase of yeast was one of the first known enzymes (C. Neuberg,[1] 1911). The prosthetic group, cocarboxylase, has been isolated as the crystal-

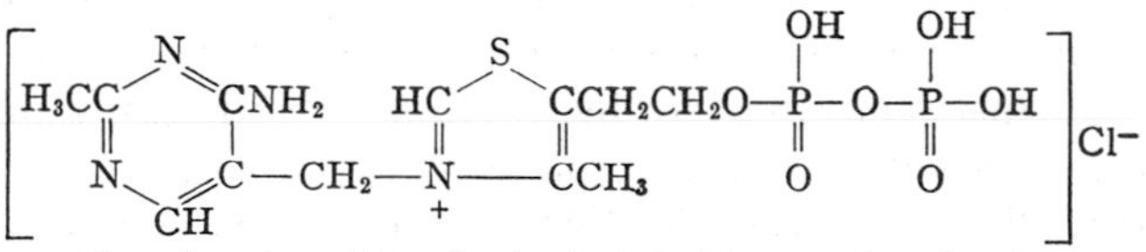

Cocarboxylase (thiamine hydrochloride pyrophosphate)

---

[1] Carl Neuberg, b. 1877 Hannover; Ph.D. Berlin (Wohl); Kaiser Wilhelm Inst.; New York Med. College

line hydrochloride and identified as the pyrophosphate ester of thiamine, or vitamin B_1 (K. Lohmann and P. Schuster, 1937). The enzyme requires the presence of a divalent ion for activity (Mg, Mn, Co, or Fe). Cocarboxylase is also a coenzyme for other reactions, for example the conversion of pyruvic acid to acetoin, $CH_3CHOHCOCH_3$. T. Ugai (1943) and S. Mizuhara (1951) found that thiamine itself can serve as catalyst for reactions catalyzed by cocarboxylase enzymes. The reactions are slower and the yields poor, but the reactions proceed under physiological conditions and serve as interesting models for the enzymic reactions. A. Breslow (1958–60) found that the hydrogen atom at C_2 in a thiazolium salt (1) is acidic (deuterium exchange) and that the resulting ylide (2) is analogous to the cyanide ion, a specific catalyst for the acyloin condensation, and on this basis formulated a reasonable mechanism for the acetoin synthesis.

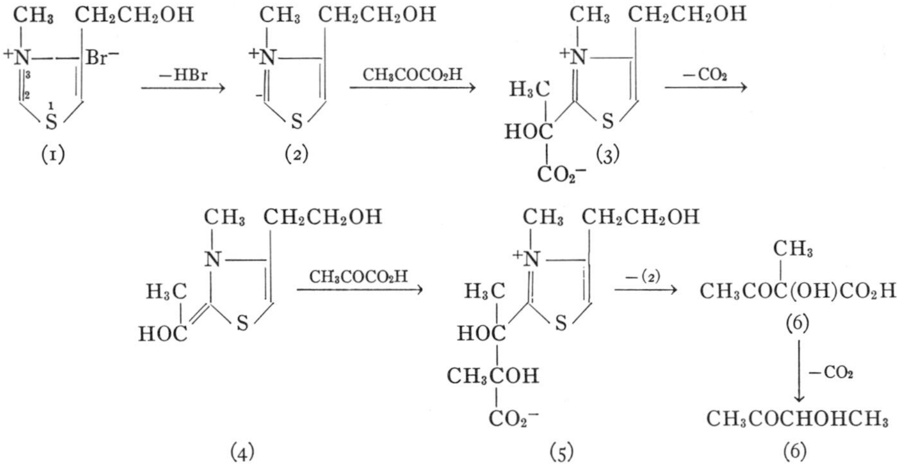

31.41 Specificity of Action.

In early work on the production of penicillin by the mold *Penicillium notatum* (1932–41), certain preparations were found to exert antibiotic activity only in the presence of glucose, whereas pure penicillin is active in the absence of glucose. The substance requiring glucose for antibiotic activity was isolated in nearly pure form in 1941 and named penicillin B, and later notatin. H. Raistrick obtained pure material in 1945. Actually notatin is an enzyme having the specific function of catalyzing the oxidation of glucose to gluconic acid and hydrogen peroxide, and the antibacterial action is due to the hydrogen peroxide produced. Notatin was thus recognized as identical with glucose oxidase, first obtained (crude) by D. Müller (1928–36) from *Aspergillis niger*. Further study, mainly by D. Keilin[1] (1948–52), showed that the enzyme, which is yellow, has an absorption spectrum suggesting that the coenzyme is flavin adenine dinucleotide, FAD. The isoalloxazine unit in this substance (lower left) is responsible for the oxidation-reduction function; acceptance of hydrogen by 1,4-addition to the conjugated system gives the dihydrocoenzyme

[1] David Keilin, b. Poland; Molteno Inst., Univ. Cambridge

FADH.   Other oxidative coenzymes have various other reducible groups in place of isoalloxazine.   The simplest proof that FAD is the specific coenzyme of glucose

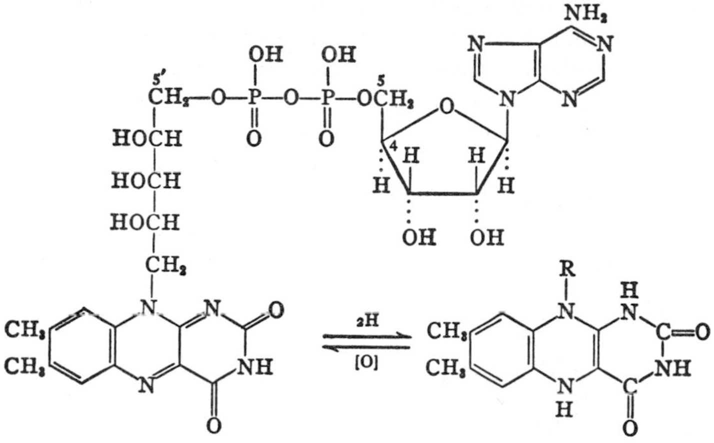

Flavin adenine
dinucleotide (FAD)   FADH

oxidase would be to split off the prosthetic group of the enzyme and obtain the native, inactive protein; restoration of activity on addition to the inactive protein of FAD would identify this as the specific coenzyme.   This standard method could not be used in the case at hand because the protein moiety of glucose oxidase was found to be denatured by all procedures that split off the coenzyme.   FAD was known to be the prosthetic group of another enzyme, D-amino acid oxidase, the inactive protein of which can be obtained without destruction.   Therefore a solution of glucose oxidase was boiled with water to denature the protein and liberate the coenzyme and the solution was added to the native protein of D-amino acid oxidase.   Restoration of ability to oxidize D-amino acids established that FAD is indeed the prosthetic group of both enzymes.

Keilin found that of some fifty sugars investigated, only glucose is attacked by the enzyme to any significant extent, and, more significantly, only the β-form of glucose (I).   The product of enzymic oxidation is δ-gluconolactone (II), which

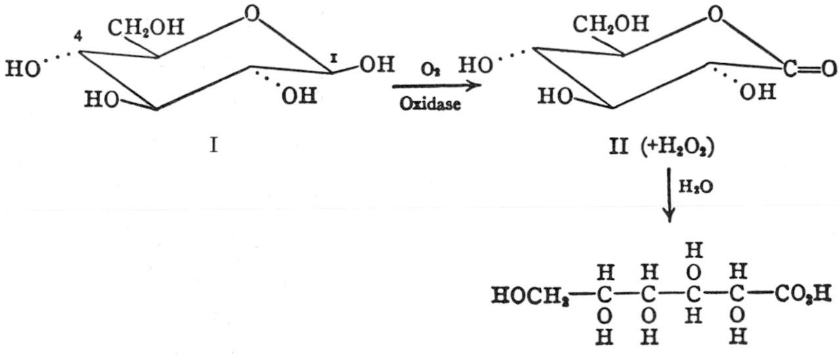

I   II (+H_2O_2)

III

then undergoes spontaneous nonenzymic hydrolysis to gluconic acid (III). β-D-Glucopyranose is also more susceptible than the α-form to chemical oxidation (bromine water, hypoiodous acid); it is oxidized 25–35 times more rapidly. In the enzymic oxidation, however, the relative rates are 100 to 0.6.

This and several related enzymic dehydrogenations involve direct transfer of hydrogen from substrate to coenzyme. It is not known whether the process involves transfer of hydride ion, or transfer of a hydrogen atom and an electron in separate steps. The transfer, at least in the cases examined, is stereospecific. An example is the reversible dehydrogenation of ethanol to acetaldehyde by the enzyme alcohol dehydrogenase, studied by B. Vennesland[1] and F. H. Westheimer (1954). The coenzyme of this protein is diphosphopyridine nucleotide, DPN.

Diphosphopyridine
nucleotide (DPN)

$+ CH_3CD_2OH \xrightleftharpoons{\text{Enzyme}}$

$+ CH_3CDO$

Reduced coenzyme

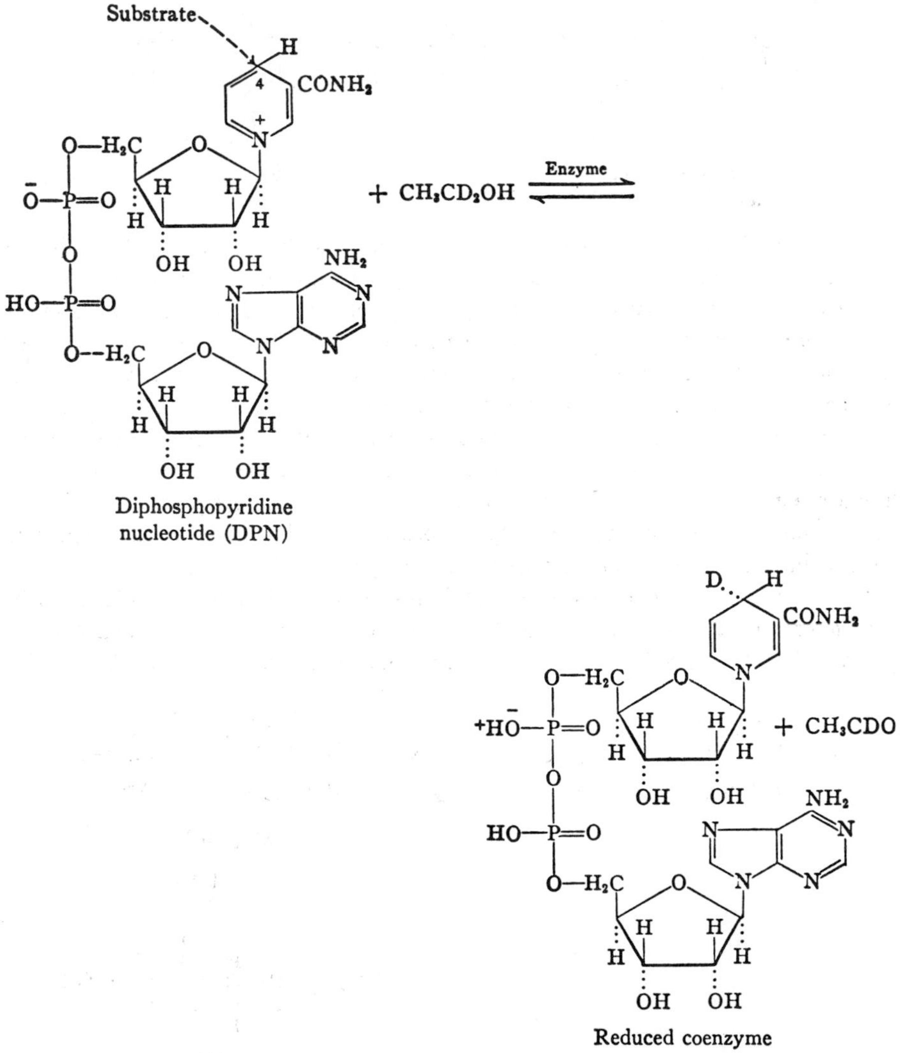

[1] Birgit Vennesland, b. 1913 Kristiansand, Norway; Ph.D. Chicago (Hanke); Univ. Chicago.

This substance contains a nicotinamide grouping responsible for the reversible oxidation-reduction function of the enzyme; a positive charge on the ring nitrogen is balanced by a negative charge on one of the two phosphate groups. When the enzyme reacts with dideuterioethanol, CH_3CD_2OH, a deuterium atom abstracted from the α-position of ethanol appears in nonionic form in the pyridine ring of the coenzyme and the hydroxylic hydrogen acquires the positive charge. On reversal of the reaction, that is enzymic oxidation of the reduced coenzyme with acetaldehyde, the coenzyme produced is completely free from isotopic label. In contrast, on chemical oxidation the product carries about half the deuterium initially present. Position 4 in the reduced coenzyme is asymmetric, and the formula shows one of two possible 4-epimers; the other would be represented with deuterium to the front and hydrogen to the rear. Asymmetry would not be possible in the absence of the amide group. Evidently chemical reduction gives nearly equal amounts of the two forms, with only a slight preference for one form because of the principle of asymmetric synthesis; on chemical oxidation of the reduced coenzyme formulated the product carries close to half the deuterium initially present. In contrast, enzymic reduction gives one specific epimer. Deuterium (or hydrogen in the general case) is transferred onto one specific side of the pyridine ring only, as shown schematically for back-side approach of substrate. In enzymic oxidation of the reduced coenzyme the stereochemical requirements are the same as in the reduction reaction.

The relationship of stereospecificity to the mechanism of enzymic action was first discussed by Fischer (1894), who said "To use a metaphor, I would say that enzyme and substrate must fit together like a lock and key." In modern terminology this concept is expressed as the idea of an intermediate activated complex between enzyme and substrate.

31.42   Coenzyme A. This substance is the prosthetic group of an enzyme first recognized as a catalyst required for biological acetylation (Lipmann,[1] 1947) and it was named accordingly (A = Acetylation). Investigations of structure (Lipmann, Lynen,[2] Baddiley[3]) established that coenzyme A is com-

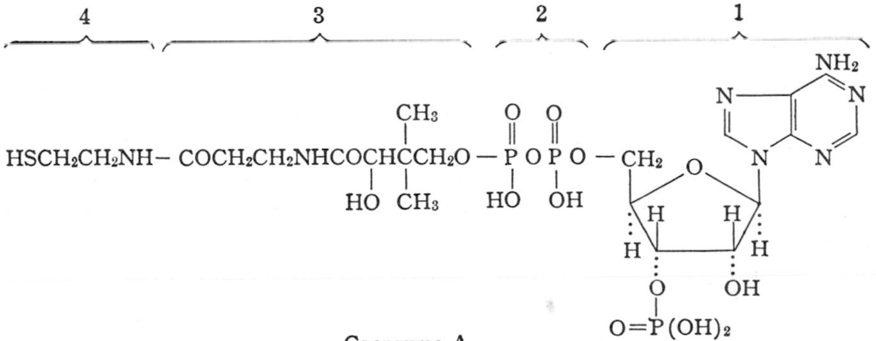

Coenzyme A

---

[1] Fritz Lipmann, b. 1899, Königsberg; Ph.D. Berlin; Rockefeller Inst., Mass. Gen. Hospital and Harvard Univ.; Rockefeller Inst.; Nobel Prize 1953

[2] Fedor Lynen, b. 1911 Munich; PhD. Munich (Wieland); Univ. Munich

[3] James Baddiley; b. 1918 Manchester; Ph.D. and D.Sc. Manchester (Todd); Univ. Durham

posed of an adenylic acid residue (1) linked through a pyrophosphate group (2) to pantothenic acid (3), which is joined by a peptide bond to β-mercaptoethanolamine (4). The difficult feat of structure elucidation was achieved by ingenious analytical, chemical, and enzymic work in a period (1948–1953) when preparations of the coenzyme were only 10–60% pure. The total synthesis of coenzyme A by H. G. Khorana (1961) brought to a close seven years of research in the development of methods for the synthesis of unsymmetrical pyrophosphates. The

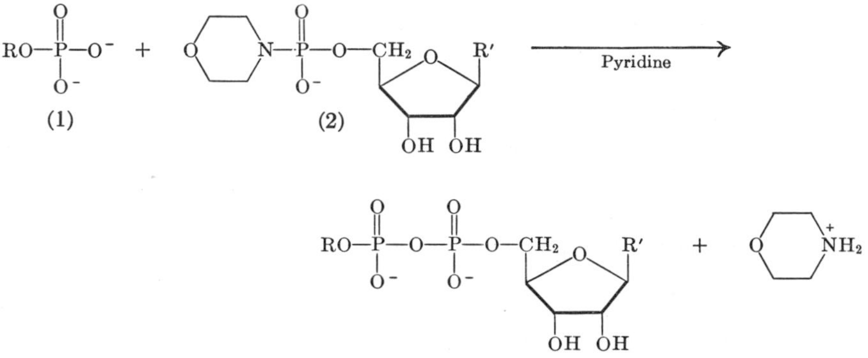

R = sugar, choline, etc.; R′ = purine, etc.

efficient method of coupling employed is formulated for a general case. The nucleoside-5′-phosphoromorpholidate (2) is obtainable in quantitative yield and offers the advantage over other derivatives of greater solubility and higher reactivity. It is prepared by reaction of the 5′-alcohol with the product of addition of morpholine to dicyclohexylcarbodiimide.

Coenzyme A occupies a central position as a mediator of all biosynthetic reactions proceeding through C_2 units. It is involved in carbohydrate metabolism in the following way. Hexose is degraded to pyruvic acid by the same steps that are involved in alcoholic fermentation, but in muscle tissue the pyruvic acid is in part reduced reversibly by an enzyme to lactic acid and in part oxidized with the following net result: $CH_3COCO_2H + 5/2\ O_2 \rightarrow 3\ CO_2 + 2\ H_2O$. Various observations suggested the participation of several intermediary metabolites. Szent-Györgyi[1] noted that addition of traces of either fumaric, succinic, malic, or oxalacetic acid greatly increases the rate of oxygen consumption by muscle tissue, and Krebs[2] noted the similar catalytic effect of α-ketoglutaric and citric acid. The suggestion that all these substances are participating metabolites eventually was firmly established. The first step was for long suspected of involving conversion of pyruvic acid to an "active acetate" unit, and work of F. Lipmann, F. Lynen, and S. Ochoa[3] (1951) identified this substance as acetyl coenzyme A. The reac-

[1] Albert Szent-Györgyi, b. 1893 Budapest; M.D. Budapest, Ph.D. Cambridge; Marine Biol. Lab., Woods Hole, Mass.; Nobel Prize 1937

[2] Hans Adolf Krebs, b. 1900 Hildesheim, Germany, Ph.D. Hamburg; Sheffield, Oxford Univ.; Nobel Prize 1953

[3] Severo Ochoa, b. 1905 Luarca, Spain; M.D. Madrid; Dept Biochem., New York Univ.; Nobel Prize 1959

tion is one of oxidative decarboxylation involving not only the enzyme itself (abbreviation: CoASH) but the following cofactors: cocarboxylase (decarboxylation), thioctic acid (activation), and DPN (hydrogen acceptor). Acetyl coenzyme

$$CH_3COCO_2H + CoASH + DPN \rightarrow CoASCOCH_3 + DPNH + CO_2$$

A then initiates a series of transformations deduced by Krebs (1940) and described as the Krebs cycle (see chart). Acetyl coenzyme A adds to the carbonyl group of

KREBS CYCLE

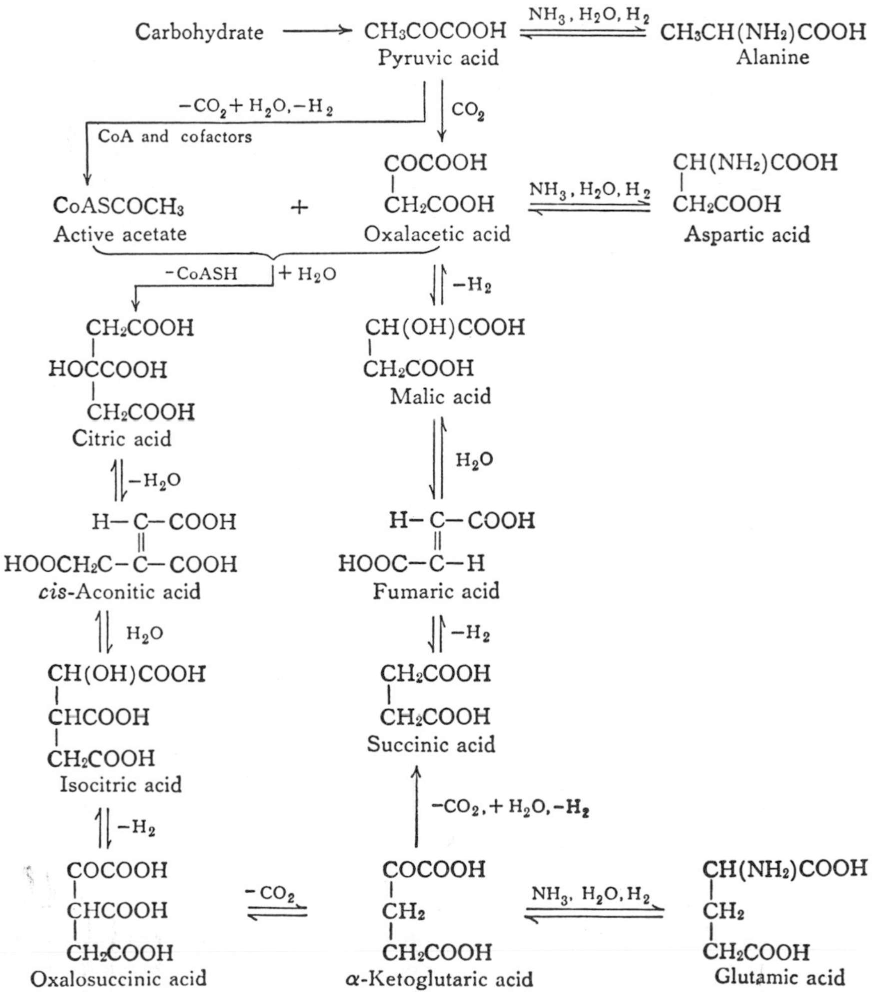

Carbohydrate $\longrightarrow$ CH₃COCOOH $\xrightarrow[]{NH_3, H_2O, H_2}$ CH₃CH(NH₂)COOH

              Pyruvic acid   Alanine

$-CO_2 + H_2O, -H_2$ | CO_2

CoA and cofactors

COCOOH   CH(NH₂)COOH
|
CoASCOCH₃   +   CH₂COOH $\xrightarrow[]{NH_3, H_2O, H_2}$ CH₂COOH

Active acetate   Oxalacetic acid   Aspartic acid

$-$ CoASH | $+ H_2O$ $-H_2$

CH₂COOH   CH(OH)COOH
|
HOCCOOH   CH₂COOH
|
CH₂COOH   Malic acid

Citric acid

$-H_2O$ H_2O

H$-$C$-$COOH   H$-$C$-$COOH
   || ||
HOOCH₂C$-$C$-$COOH   HOOC$-$C$-$H

cis-Aconitic acid   Fumaric acid

H_2O $-H_2$

CH(OH)COOH   CH₂COOH
|
CHCOOH   CH₂COOH
|
CH₂COOH   Succinic acid

Isocitric acid

$-H_2$ $-CO_2, + H_2O, -H_2$

COCOOH   COCOOH   CH(NH₂)COOH
| $-CO_2$ | NH_3, H_2O, H_2 |
CHCOOH $\rightleftharpoons$ CH₂ $\rightleftharpoons$ CH₂
| | |
CH₂COOH   CH₂COOH   CH₂COOH

Oxalosuccinic acid   α-Ketoglutaric acid   Glutamic acid

oxalacetic acid to give the CoA-derivative of citric acid, which is hydrolyzed to citric acid with regeneration of CoASH. The succeeding steps are mainly reversible and each is catalyzed by an enzyme. Citric acid is dehydrated to an unsaturated acid which adds water in the reverse sense to give isocitric acid. Dehydrogenation gives oxalosuccinic acid which, being a β-keto acid, readily loses carbon dioxide to form α-ketoglutaric acid. Oxidative decarboxylation then gives succinic acid, and the cycle is completed by dehydrogenation to fumaric acid, addition of water (malic acid), and dehydrogenation to oxalacetic acid. The net balance in the Krebs cycle is that the three moles of carbon dioxide formed by metabolic oxidation of pyruvic acid come from decarboxylation of three intermediates (pyruvic, oxalosuccinic, and α-ketoglutaric acid), and the 5/2 moles of oxygen expended are utilized for oxidation of five moles of hydrogen derived from five dehydrogenative steps.

Experiments with labeled intermediates for a time cast doubt on the participation of citric acid in the Krebs cycle. Since citric acid is symmetrical, a label appearing initially in the upper terminal carboxyl group ($C^{14}O_2H$) should be distributed equally between the two terminal carboxyl groups of the succeeding C_5-metabolites, including γ-ketoglutaric acid. On the contrary, the label was found to be exclusively in the carboxyl group eliminated on decarboxylation (as $C^{14}O_2$). A. G. Ogston (1948) questioned the interpretation and suggested that citric acid loses its symmetry when bound to the asymmetric enzyme surface at three points of attachment. If the transformation of citric acid to the unsymmetrical cis-aconitic acid involves attachment to the enzyme aconitase by three groups simultaneously, only one of the four faces of the now asymmetric tetrahedron of the central carbon atom can be accommodated by the enzyme, and one CH_2CO_2H group will be in a different relation to the enzyme than the other. The hypothesis was soon verified. V. R. Potter and C. Heidelberger[1] (1949) demonstrated the formation of isotopically asymmetric citric acid by rat liver homogenates, the fixation of $C^{14}O_2$ being as formulated.

$$CH_3COCO_2H + C^{14}O_2 \rightarrow \begin{array}{c} CH_2C^{14}O_2H \\ | \\ COCO_2H \end{array} \rightarrow \begin{array}{c} CH_2C^{14}O_2H \\ | \\ HOCCO_2H \\ | \\ CH_2CO_2H \end{array}$$

Three of the metabolites of the Krebs cycle, pyruvic, oxalacetic, and α-ketoglutaric acid, are α-keto acids which, by transamination, can afford the amino acids alanine, aspartic acid, and glutamic acid. These acids are not essential dietary constituents and evidently are synthesized from the intermediates of carbohydrate metabolism. The reverse process is demonstrated by the fact that alanine, aspartic acid, and glutamic acid, and only these amino acids, are oxidized rapidly in muscle.

Coenzyme A also plays a key role in biosynthesis of fatty acids, now known to follow the path formulated. The C—S linkage of the acetyl derivative of the coenzyme is very reactive, and the first step is condensation of two molecules of acetyl CoA (1) by elimination of CoASH (2) and formation of acetoacetyl CoA (3). Reduction of the carbonyl group (4), dehydration (5), and hydrogenation gives n-butyryl CoA (6). The cycle is repeated by condensation of (6) with another

[1] Charles Heidelberger, b. 1920 New York; Ph.D. Harvard (Fieser); Univ. Wisconsin

$$CH_3C-SCoA \ + \ H-CH_2CSCoA \ \rightleftharpoons \ HSCoA \ + \ CH_3C-CH_2CSCoA$$

$$\underbrace{\overset{\|}{O} \qquad\qquad\qquad \overset{\|}{O}}_{(1)} \qquad\qquad (2) \qquad\qquad\qquad \overset{\|}{O} \ \ \overset{\|}{O}}_{(3)}$$

$$\underset{(6)}{CH_3CH_2CH_2COSCoA} \ \overset{2\,H}{\rightleftharpoons} \ \underset{(5)}{CH_3CH=CHCOSCoA} \ \overset{H_2O}{\rightleftharpoons} \ \underset{(4)}{CH_3CH(OH)CH_2COSCoA} \ \overset{H_2}{\Updownarrow}$$

$$\overset{CH_3COSCoA}{\Updownarrow}$$

$$HSCoA \ + \ \underset{(7)}{CH_3CH_2CH_2COCH_2COSCoA} \ \rightleftharpoons \ Etc.$$

molecule of acetyl CoA to give (7), followed by reduction, dehydration, and hydrogenation with formation of a six-carbon acyl unit. In animals the cycle is repeated until full chain-length is reached, and it is now understandable why the chains are always normal and of even-carbon content. Some bacteria carry the cycle only to the butyric acid stage. In the normal organism intermediates in the cycle are all bound through the coenzyme to protein and are not isolable from the lipid fraction. In diabetes, however, metabolism is abnormal, and products of incomplete oxidation known as ketone bodies accumulate in the blood and urine (ketonuria). They include products from the cycle: acetoacetic acid (and its decomposition product acetone) and β-hydroxybutyric acid.

S. J. Wakil (1958) has shown that malonyl CoA is involved in the biosynthesis of fatty acids, possibly by condensation with acetyl CoA with release of one mole of CoA and formation of a C_5-intermediate which is reductively decarboxylated to butyryl CoA.

31.43   Other Enzymes. — Catalase, a hemoprotein containing four atoms of iron (ferric) per molecule, catalyzes decomposition of hydrogen peroxide but of no other peroxide: $2\,H_2O_2 \rightarrow 2\,H_2O + O_2$. It occurs almost universally and has the function of protecting the organism from hydrogen peroxide, formed on oxidation by various oxidases. The hemoprotein **peroxidase** catalyzes the oxidation of many phenols and aromatic amines. **Esterases** control formation and hydrolysis of esters of simple alcohols and acids; **lipases** are required in the case of glycerides of higher fatty acids. **Carbohydrases** catalyze splitting of the glycosidic linkages of simple glycosides and of polysaccharides.

The interconversions of α-amino and α-keto acids associated with the Krebs cycle exemplify reactions promoted by **transaminases.** Those specific to aspartic and glutamic acid contain pyridoxal phosphate or pyridoxamine phosphate as the prosthetic groups. Pyridoxal and pyridoxamine are derivatives of pyridoxine (vitamin B_6), in which a hydroxyl group replaces the amino group of pyridoxamine. The aldehyde and amine derivatives are interconvertible and are believed

Pyridoxal $\quad\underset{H_2O,\,[O]}{\overset{NH_3,\,H_2}{\rightleftharpoons}}\quad$ Pyridoxamine to function in the overall reaction as shown in the formulation (X = ring system of pyridoxine):

$$\underset{\underset{R}{|}}{\overset{\overset{COOH}{|}}{C}}=O + H_2NCH_2X \underset{-H_2O}{\rightleftharpoons} \underset{\underset{R}{|}}{\overset{\overset{COOH}{|}}{C}}=NCH_2X \rightleftharpoons \underset{\underset{R}{|}}{\overset{\overset{COOH}{|}}{C}}HN=CH \cdot X \underset{H_2O}{\rightleftharpoons} \underset{\underset{R}{|}}{\overset{\overset{COOH}{|}}{C}}HNH_2 + OHCX$$

E. E. Snell (see *Vitamins and Hormones*, 1958) has effected transaminations nonenzymically under the influence of pyridoxal phosphate and a polyvalent cation (Cu^{++}, Fe^{+++}, Al^{+++}) and has shown that a chelated Schiff base intermediate is involved.

NUCLEOPROTEINS

31.44   Ribonucleoproteins. — The proteinoid part of a nucleoprotein has the character of a protamine or histone, that is, it is rich in arginine and/or lysine and contains only a limited number of neutral amino acids and no sulfur, and the molecule is relatively small.   The strongly basic protein is bound to a nucleic acid, a strongly acidic substance of molecular complexity comparable to that of the apoprotein portion.   It is not known whether the two moieties are bound merely by salt formation or whether some covalent bonding is involved. The proteinoid part can be separated from the nucleic acid by the action of trypsin or, in some instances, by sodium chloride at a suitable concentration.   The residual nucleic acid consists of a chain of repeating units, each of which is built up from a sugar, phosphoric acid, and a purine or pyrimidine base.   The sugar is either

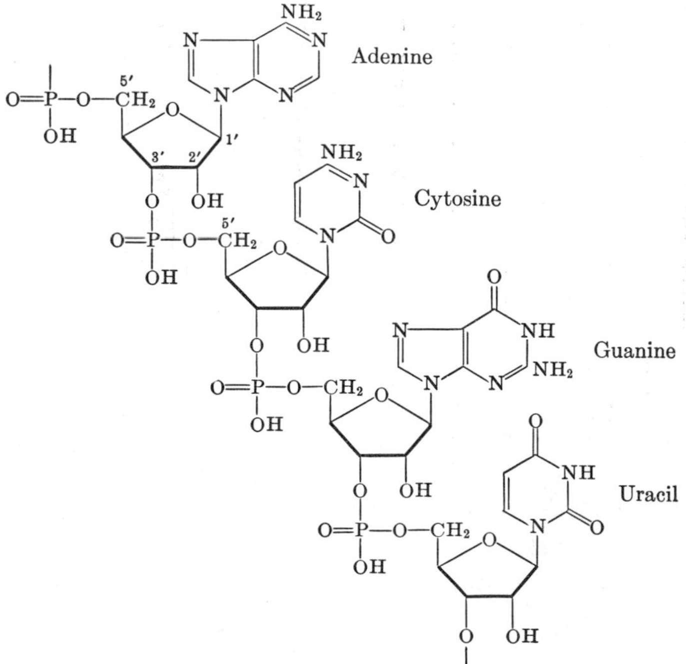

Ribonucleic acid (RNA)

D-ribose or 2-desoxy-D-ribose, and a given nucleic acid contains only one or the other, not both.   The protein of yeast affords a nucleic acid containing ribose, hence it is a ribonucleic acid (RNA).   This substance was the subject of a first series of extensive investigations conducted by P. A. Levene[1] and summarized in 1934.   Levene deduced the outline structure of this complex molecule, and A. Todd and others supplied further details.   The structure formulated for a four-unit section of the chain represents one possible sequence.   The backbone of the chain consists of four riboside units joined by phosphate ester groups extending from the 3'-oxygen of one unit to the 5'-oxygen of the next unit.   The 1'-β-glycosidic basic groups are in an alternating order: adenine and guanine are purines, cytosine and uracil are pyrimidines.   The particular tautomeric forms shown are those indicated by evidence of hydrogen bonding in the more fully characterized nucleic acids discussed in the next section.

Since the 5'-ester function is primary and the 3'-function secondary, acidic hydrolysis of RNA tends to split the 5'-ester groups preferentially to give four riboside-3'-phosphate glycosides known as nucleotides.   That containing adenine is yeast adenylic acid; alkaline hydrolysis of this nucleotide removes the 3'-phosphate group and gives the nucleoside adenosine, which is fully described as 9-β-D-ribo-

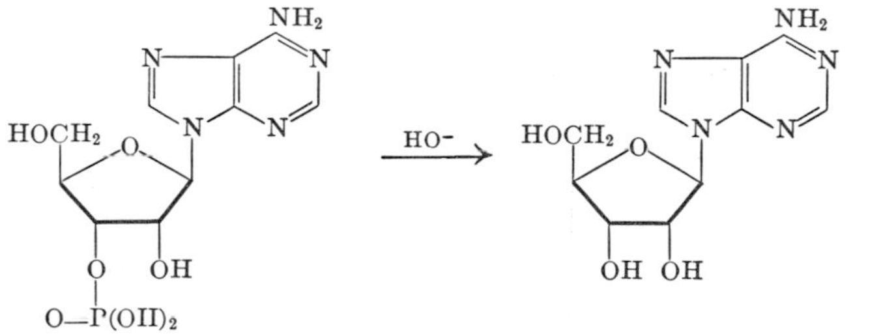

Yeast adenylic acid
(Nucleotide)

Adenosine
(Nucleoside)

furanosyladenine.   The other three nucleotides are guanylic acid, uridylic acid, and cytidylic acid; the nucleosides are guanosine, uridine, and cytidine.

Ribonucleic acids of three types have been isolated from cells.   They all conform to the same structural pattern and differ in minor degree in molecular weight or in the pattern of basic-group sequence.   Little information is as yet available about the conformation of the molecules.   Proteins appear to be synthesized in ribonucleoprotein particles in the cytoplasm (the protoplasm exclusive of the nucleus).   The RNA in these particles is described as ribosomal RNA to differentiate it from another type, transfer RNA, which has the function of bringing amino acids into the particles.   Since ribosomal RNA differs very little from transfer RNA, P. Doty (1961) has predicted the existence of a messenger RNA which carries a code determining the amino acid sequence in the proteins synthesized under the influence of ribosomal RNA.

[1] Phoebus A. Levene, 1869–1940; b. Russia; Ph.D. St. Petersburg; Rockefeller Inst.; *Science*, **92**, 392 (1940)

31.45   Desoxyribonucleoproteins. — Proteins containing desoxyribonucleic
              acid (DNA), desoxyribonucleoproteins, occur in the nuclei of cells
as major parts of the chromosome structure and are believed to be responsible
for genetic control of cellular reproduction and to be capable of self-reproduc-
tion.   They are viscous materials insoluble in physiological salt solution (0.15%)
but soluble in $1\,M$ salt solution.   The protein when precipitated is so viscous and
sticky that it can be collected by winding a strand on a stirring rod.   Procedures
for separation of DNA from the protein usually involve denaturation of the
protein, even though the binding is relatively weak.   The DNA content of the
protein (dry weight) is in the range 25–50%.

DNA differs structurally from RNA in two respects (see formula).   The pentose
is 2-desoxy-D-ribose and the uracil unit of RNA is, in DNA, replaced by thymine;

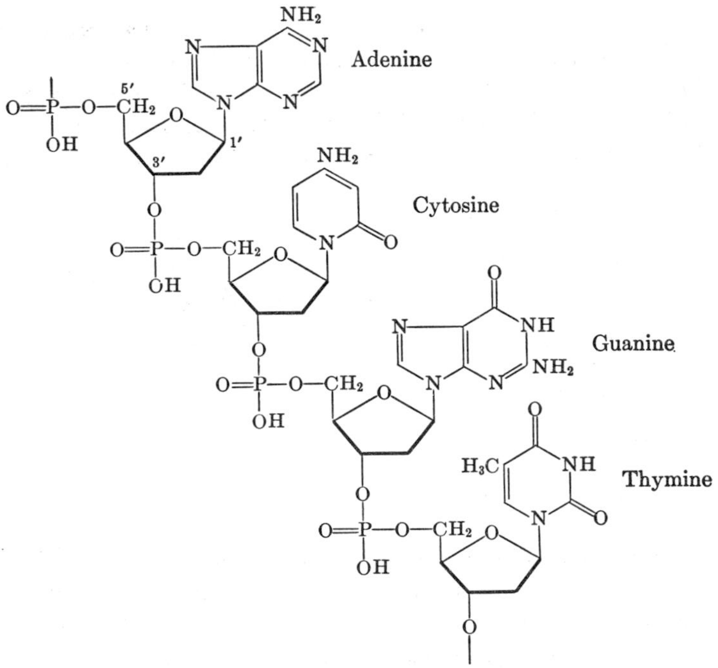

Desoxyribonucleic acid (DNA)

the desoxyriboside of thymine is called thymidine.

The nature of the DNA molecule is such that J. D. Watson[1] and F. H. C.
Crick[2] (1953) were able to deduce considerable information about the structure
and conformation from X-ray diffraction analysis.   Their conclusions are expressed in a model which shows two helical polynucleotide strands which are identical but which run in opposite directions.   Each twist of a chain includes about
ten nucleotide units.   The diameter of the cylinder is 20 Å.   It should be pointed

[1] James Dewey Watson, Ph.D. Indiana (Lulia); Harvard Univ.
[2] F. H. C. Crick, b. 1916 England; Ph.D. Cambridge, Cavendish Lab., Cambridge

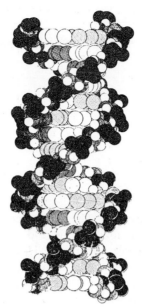

Watson-Krick Model of DNA

out that some of the sequences are still unknown and that the model is an idealized representation of a finding of major importance deduced from the X-ray evidence concerning hydrogen bonding in the molecule. The data disclose that the pyrimidine cytosine is hydrogen bonded to the purine guanine and that the pyrimidine thymine is bonded to the purine adenine, as shown in the diagram. The C-G

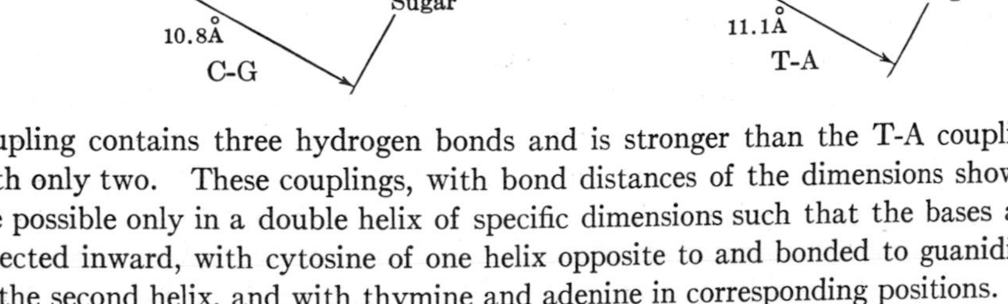

Cytosine ...... Guanine ...... C-G

Thymine ...... Adenine ...... T-A

coupling contains three hydrogen bonds and is stronger than the T-A coupling with only two. These couplings, with bond distances of the dimensions shown, are possible only in a double helix of specific dimensions such that the bases are directed inward, with cytosine of one helix opposite to and bonded to guanidine of the second helix, and with thymine and adenine in corresponding positions.

Chromatography, coupled with UV spectroscopic determination of the purine and pyrimidine bases, has facilitated precise study of the composition of hydrolyzates of desoxyribonucleic acids of various sources (E. Chargaff,[1] 1955). Some of

[1] Erwin Chargaff, b. 1905 Austria; Ph.D. Vienna (Feigl); College Phys. Surg., Columbia Univ.

TABLE 31. 7. MOLAR RATIO OF DNAs OF DIFFERENT ORIGIN

	ADENINE/ GUANINE	THYMINE/ CYTOSINE	ADENINE/ THYMINE	GUANINE/ CYTOSINE	PURINES/ PYRI- MIDINES
Man	1.56	1.75	1.00	1.00	1.0
Salmon	1.43	1.43	1.02	1.02	1.0
Wheat	1.22	1.18*	1.00	0.97*	1.0
Yeast	1.67	1.92	1.03	1.20	1.0
Bacillus coli K-12	1.05	0.95	1.09	0.99	1.0
Avian tubercle bacillus	0.4	0.4	1.09	1.08	1.1

* Includes cytosine plus methylcytosine.

the results are shown in Table 31.7. The equivalence of adenine and thymine, of guanine and cytosine, and of total purine and total pyrimidine, is a striking confirmation of the Watson-Crick deduction. However, the ratios A/G and T/C vary over a wide range and follow no as yet evident pattern, and the nucleotide sequence in the chains awaits elucidation. Discovery of a method, say of end-group analysis, is a challenging goal. Since DNA transmits hereditary properties from one generation to the next and is able to undergo self-duplication with great precision, it must be the carrier to RNA of the code for control of protein synthesis in the chromosomes. The sequence of genes is linear, and the nucleic acids are linear.

P. Doty and co-workers (1957–61) discovered a new line of investigation in the thermal denaturation of DNA in an aqueous solution of defined ionic strength and with concentrations of sodium and calcium ions sufficient to neutralize the charges on the phosphate ester groups. The helix-to-coil transition occurs in a narrow temperature range centering at 60° and is complete in a few minutes at 80°. Denaturation involves untwisting of the two helical strands. Depolymeriza-tion occurs to some extent, but determination of the molecular weight of quickly cooled aliquots and extrapolation to zero time indicates the expected drop by a factor of 2 (*E. coli* DNA of molecular weight 10,500,000 → denatured DNA, 5,000,000). Another criterion is optical activity. Rigidity resulting from hydro-gen bonding enhances rotophoric power in the helical form; furthermore, a strand coiled in one direction to the right reinforces the effect of a strand coiled in the opposite direction to the left. Thus denaturation is attended with a profound drop in specific rotation. Since rupture of hydrogen bonds eliminates inhibition of resonance, denaturation is attended with increase in absorbance at 260 mμ.

Particularly exciting is the discovery that the two disorganized, flexible strands of denatured DNA produced at 80° recombine when the solution is allowed to cool slowly below the transition temperature. That renatured DNA has the original double helical structure is evident from near identity in the various properties enumerated. The electron micrograph shows the characteristic 20-Å diameter cylinder characteristic of helical DNA. Furthermore, it is possible to build DNA hybrids, at least from two strains of bacteria that are genetically similar and of comparable molecular weight. If two bacteria have nearly the same genetic relation, segments of the two DNA chains must be identical and hence favorable for promoting partial hybridization. Since segments of DNA and RNA chains may correspond sufficiently well to fit into a double-helix conformation, the possibility exists for forming a code-carrying hybrid of DNA and RNA.

31.46 Muscle adenylic acid (isolation, G. Embden, 1927) is an isomer of yeast nucleic acid which yields adenosine on alkaline hydrolysis and therefore differs only in the position of the phosphoric acid residue. Since muscle adenylic acid, unlike yeast adenylic acid, is capable of forming a complex with boric acid, a property characteristic of *cis* glycols, the 2'- and 3'-hydroxyl groups must be free and the ester group is therefore at the 5'-position. This inference is supported by the synthesis of muscle adenylic acid (J. Baddiley and A. Todd, 1947).

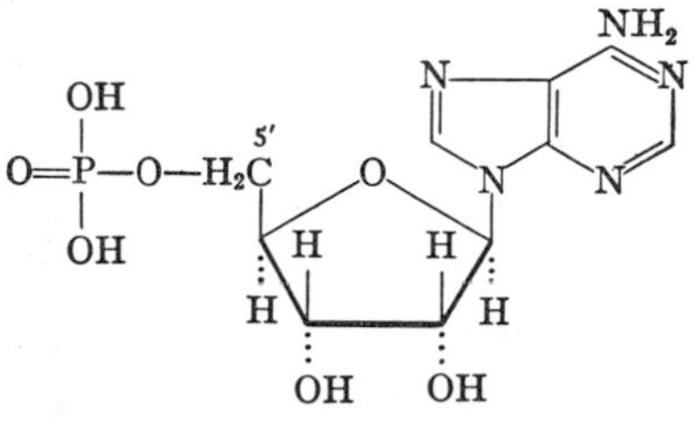

Muscle adenylic acid

31.47 Ribonuclease. — This protein was crystallized from bovine pancreas by M. Kunitz (1940). Ribonuclease hydrolyzes ribonucleotide linkages in which a pyrimidine nucleotide is esterified at the 3'-position. Since this enzyme contains 124 amino acid residues and the chain contains four disulfide linkages, elucidation of the complete primary structure by W. H. Stein and S. Moore (1960) represents a milestone in protein chemistry. The sequence was worked out in part with oxidized ribonuclease, which on enzymic cleavage gave 24 peptides of size suitable for sequence determination (chemical and enzymic methods). Finally, enzymic hydrolysis of the native protein, separation of the cystine-containing peptides, oxidation of these to cysteic peptides, and amino acid analysis of these fragments revealed the manner in which the eight half-cystine residues are

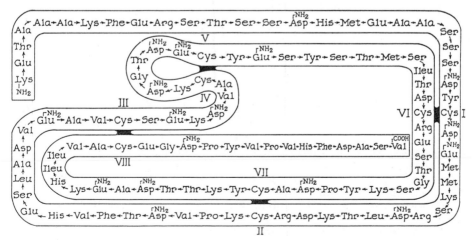

Ribonuclease

joined to one another. The diagram shows that the disulfide bridges hold the main chain in a series of folds and loops; the result is a molecule of considerable stability. Deuterium exchange experiments indicate a helical content of 41%.

31.48 **Virus Proteins.** — A virus is a submicroscopic infective agent that will pass through a filter (Berkefeld) capable of removing all known living cells. Viruses are capable of autocatalytic growth and multiplication in living tissues, and were once regarded as living organisms smaller than any known ones. One, tobacco mosaic virus, present in filtered juice of plants infected with a disease known as tobacco mosaic, was isolated by Stanley[1] (1935) in crystalline form and found to be a nucleoprotein. The molecular weight is unusually high (40 million); the nucleic acid portion amounts to about 6% of the total weight. The crystalline protein is highly infectious and its virus activity exactly parallels the range of pH stability. The substance is able to reproduce itself in the tobacco leaf, and amounts of 2–3 g. of virus protein have been isolated from plants inoculated with as little as 1 microgram of the protein. Since this pioneering work a number of other plant viruses have been isolated and shown to be nucleoproteins (examples: cucumber mosaic, tomato bushy stunt, potato x virus, tobacco ringspot).

Tobacco mosaic virus can be split into an inactive protein and a ribonucleic acid which retains about one hundredth the activity of the intact virus. The activity of the virus depends upon the nucleic acid component but the protein portion augments this activity to a considerable extent. The viral ribonucleic acid seems to resemble other RNAs in structure. It contains the usual four bases, but the content of cytidine is low and that of adenine is high. It appears to consist of a single unbranched chain of about 6,500 nucleotide units. The protein subunit of tobacco mosaic virus contains 158 amino acid residues. An American group (W. M. Stanley, 1960) and a German group (F. A. Anderer, Tübingen, 1960) have published complete, and nearly complete, amino acid sequences.

Some of the substances secreted by pathogenic organisms and responsible for the lethal effect have been obtained in pure form and characterized as proteins. These include diphtheria toxin and *Clostridium botulinum* type A and type B toxin. The substances are extremely toxic; 1 mg. of the botulinus A toxin is sufficient to kill 30 million mice. The molecular weight of this toxin is 900,000. The amino acid content reveals no clue to the physiological effect.

[1] Wendell M. Stanley, b. 1904 Ridgeville, Ind.; Ph.D. Illinois (R. Adams); Rockefeller Inst., Virus Lab., Univ. Calif., Berkeley; Nobel Prize 1946.

Biographies Omitted by Oversight

[1] Adolph von Baeyer, 1835–1917; b. Berlin; Univ. Strasbourg, Munich; Nobel Prize 1905; *J. Chem. Soc.*, **123**, 1520 (1923)

[2] Lyman C. Craig, b. 1906 Palmyra, Iowa; Ph.D. Iowa State College (Hixon); Rockefeller Institute for Medical Research

[3] Claude S. Hudson, 1881–1952; b. Atlanta; Ph.D. Princeton; U. S. Public Health Service; *J. Chem. Soc.*, *4042 (1954)*

[4] Heinrich Wieland, 1877–1957; b. Pforzheim, Germany; Ph.D. Munich (Thiele); Freiburg/Brg., Univ. Munich; Nobel Prize 1927; *Angew. Chem.*, **71**, 1 (1959)

Answers to Problems

ANSWERS TO PROBLEMS

1.

Hydrazine: H_2NNH_2. Formic acid: $H—\overset{\displaystyle OH}{\underset{|}{C}}=O$

2. CH_3CHBr_2 and $BrCH_2CH_2Br$; CH_3CBr_3 and $BrCH_2CHBr_2$

3. $H:\overset{H}{\underset{H}{\overset{..}{N}}}: + H:\overset{..}{\underset{..}{Cl}}: \rightarrow \left[H:\overset{H}{\underset{H}{\overset{+}{N}}}:H \right] \overset{..-}{:\overset{..}{Cl}}:$

4. $H:\overset{:Br:}{\underset{:Br:}{\overset{..}{C}}}:Br:$ $H:\overset{H}{\underset{H}{\overset{..}{C}}:\overset{..}{O}}:H$ $H:C::C:H$
(with H H below)

5. 65.47% C, 6.73% H

6. (a) $C_6H_6O_2$; (b) $C_{11}H_8O_3$

7. Possible formulas: $C_{10}H_{22}O$, $C_{14}H_8O_4$, $C_{21}H_{31}O_3N$, $C_{20}H_{32}OSN_2$

8. $C_5H_{12} = (CH_3)_4C$, b.p. $9.5°$

9. $C_{15}H_{14}O_3$ (lapachol, 26.13); 74.36% C, 5.82% H

10. $C_{31}H_{46}O_2$ (vitamin K_1, analysis at the Merck Research Laboratories of a sample isolated by L. F. Fieser)

11. $C_{18}H_{21}O_3N$ (codeine)

13. No; C_3H_7I could be either $CH_3CH_2CH_2I$ or CH_3CHICH_3.

14. $CH_3CH_2CH_2OH$, $CH_3CH(OH)CH_3$, $CH_3CH_2OCH_3$. The third formula is correct.

15. Optically active: (a), (d), (h)

16. Optically active

17. See section 3.9

CHAPTER 2. STRUCTURAL TYPES

1. Dibromoisobutanes:
$(CH_3)_2CHCHBr_2$ (1,1-),
$(CH_3)_2CBrCH_2Br$ (1,2-),
$BrCH_2CH(CH_3)CH_2Br$ (1,3-)
Dibromo-*n*-butanes:
$CH_3CH_2CH_2CHBr_2$ (1,1-),
$CH_3CH_2CHBrCH_2Br$ (1,2-),
$CH_3CHBrCH_2CH_2Br$ (1,3-),
$BrCH_2CH_2CH_2CH_2Br$ (1,4-),
$CH_3CH_2CBr_2CH_3$ (2,2-),
$CH_3CHBrCHBrCH_3$ (2,3-)

2. Dimethyl-*n*-butylmethane,
$(CH_3)_2CHCH_2CH_2CH_2CH_3$
Diisopropylmethane, $(CH_3)_2CHCH_2CH(CH_3)_2$
Methylethylisopropylmethane,
$(CH_3)_2CHCH(CH_3)CH_2CH_3$
Methylethyl-*n*-propylmethane,
$CH_3CH_2CH(CH_3)CH_2CH_2CH_3$
Trimethyl-*n*-propylmethane,
$(CH_3)_3CCH_2CH_2CH_3$

3.
(a) $CH_3CH_2CH_2CH_2CH_2CH_2CH_2CHClCH_2Br$
(b) $CH_3CH_2CH_2CH_2CHClCCl_2CH_3$
(c) $CH_3CH_2C(OH)(CH_3)_2$
(d) $(CH_3)_2CHCH(CH_3)_2$
(e) $(CH_3CH_2)_4C$

4. (a) Dichlorodifluoromethane
(b) Dimethyldiethylmethane
(c) Trimethyl-*n*-butylmethane
(d) Di-(*n*-propyl)-isopropylmethane

5. (a) 2,5-Dimethylheptane
(b) 2-Methylpropane
(c) 3-Methylhexane
(d) 2,5-Dimethyl-3-ethylhexane

6. 2,2-Dimethylhexane,
$CH_3CH_2CH_2CH_2C(CH_3)_3$
3,3-Dimethylhexane,
$CH_3CH_2CH_2C(CH_3)_2CH_2CH_3$
2,2,3-Trimethylpentane,
$CH_3CH_2CH(CH_3)C(CH_3)_3$
2,2,4-Trimethylpentane,
$(CH_3)_2CHCH_2C(CH_3)_3$

7. (a) Propanetriol-1,2,3
(b) 2,4-Dimethylhexanol-2
(c) 2,5-Dimethylheptene-3
(d) 4-Methylhexyne-1
(e) 2,5-Dimethylhexadiene-2,4
(f) 2-Methyl-3-isopropylhexene-5-ol-1
(g) 1,2-Dimethyl-4-ethylcyclohexane
(h) Cyclohexanedione-1,2

8. (a) $CH_3CH_2CH(CH_2CH_3)CH(CH_3)CH_2OH$
(b) $C_6H_5CH=CHCH=CHC_6H_5$
(c) $(CH_3)_2C=CHCH_3$
(d) $CH_3CH(OH)CH(OH)CH_3$
(e) $ClCH_2CH(CH_3)CH_2CH=CH_2$

9. 3-Methylhexanol-1
3-Methylhexanol-2
2-Ethylpentanol-1
3-Methylhexanol-3.
4-Methylhexanol-3
4-Methylhexanol-2
4-Methylhexanol-1

10. (a) $CH_3CH_2COOCH_3$
(b) $CH_3CH_2COOCH(CH_3)_2$

1089

(c) CH_3CH_2C with $=O$ and $\backslash Cl$ (acyl chloride structure)

(d) CH_3CH_2C with $=O$ and $\backslash O$, and CH_3CH_2C with $=O$ (anhydride structure)

11. There is no possibility for formation of a resonance stabilized anion.

12.

$$\begin{array}{ccc} \overset{-}{O} & O^- \\ \diagdown\diagup \\ C \\ \| \\ O \end{array} \longleftrightarrow \begin{array}{ccc} \overset{-}{O} & O \\ \diagdown\diagup \\ C \\ | \\ O^- \end{array} \longleftrightarrow \begin{array}{ccc} O & O^- \\ \diagdown\diagup \\ C \\ | \\ O^- \end{array}$$

13. $CH_3CH_2CH_2CH_2CH_2OH$
$CH_3CH_2CH_2CH(OH)CH_3$
$CH_3CH_2CH(OH)CH_2CH_3$
$CH_3CH_2CH(CH_3)CH_2OH$
$CH_3CH_2C(OH)(CH_3)_2$
$(CH_3)_2CHCH(OH)CH_3$
$(CH_3)_2CHCH_2CH_2OH$
$(CH_3)_3CCH_2OH$

14. Structure (a) is impossible. Bonds extending on opposite sides of the ring are in a line and the normal separation distance is about thrice the length of a hybrid aromatic bond. Structure (b) probably cannot exist for it would be under excessive strain, but the large-ring acetylene is a perfectly reasonable structure. Structure (d) would surely be under considerable strain; all attempts to prepare the hydrocarbon have failed.

CHAPTER 3.   STEREOCHEMISTRY

1.

COOH	COOH
HCCH₃	CH₃CH
HCBr	BrCH
COOH	COOH
I	**II**
COOH	COOH
HCCH₃	CH₃CH
BrCH	HCBr
COOH	COOH
III	**IV**

I is the enantiomer of II and is diastereoisomeric with III and IV; III and IV are enantiomers.

2. (a) 4; (b) 2; (c) 8; (d) 16
3. $CH_3CH_2CH(CH_3)COOH$
4. Monomethyl ester of mesotartaric acid
5. (a) d-, l-, dl-
(b) No stereoisomers
(c) cis and trans
(d) d-, l-, dl-
(e) d-, l-, dl-, d'-, l'-, d'l'-
(f) No stereoisomers
(g) d-, l-, dl-, meso-
(h) Eight optically active isomers; four dl-forms.

6. Partial epimerization at the asymmetric carbon atom adjacent to the carbonyl group (through enol form).

7. The 1,2-acid can exist in an optically inactive cis form and in d- and l-trans forms; the 1,3-acid can exist only in one cis and one trans form.

8. Menthol: 8 optically active forms possible.
9. It must be tetrahedral.
10. The fluorescent agent originally has the trans configuration but on absorption of light it may change in part to the cis form, which probably is less powerfully fluorescent.

11. Both forms are enolic; they are the hydroxy derivatives of maleic and fumaric acid:

HO—C—CO₂H	HO—C—CO₂H
‖	‖
H—C—CO₂H	HO₂C—C—H
m.p. 152°	m.p. 184°

12. Pairs (a), (c), and (d) are epimers. Pairs (a) and (c), but not (d), should be interconvertible through the common enols.

13. (a), Epimeric diastereoisomers, the first is optically active, the second inactive (meso); (b), identical; (c), structural isomers; (d), enantiomers, optically active; (e), diastereoisomers, optically active.

CHAPTER 4.   ALKANES

1. Most favorable: $n\text{-}C_{12}H_{25}CO_2K$ + $n\text{-}C_3H_7CO_2K$. Least favorable: $n\text{-}C_8H_{17}CO_2K$ + $n\text{-}C_7H_{15}CO_2K$ (see boiling points, p. 106).

2. The normal alkane formed could be removed from the mixture by conversion to the urea complex; the uncombined material would then contain only the two branched hydrocarbons.

3. The chloro and nitro substituents are electron-attracting and exert an inductive displacement of electrons favorable for separation of the hydroxylic hydrogen as a proton.

4. See text.

5. $(C_2H_5)_2Mg + CH_3OH \rightarrow$
$C_2H_6 + CH_3OMgC_2H_5$
$CH_3OMgC_2H_5 + CH_3OH \rightarrow$
$C_2H_6 + CH_3OMgOCH_3$

6. The sum of the bond energies of the prod-

ucts is 123 kcal.; that of the reactants is 114 kcal.

7. The experimental facts demonstrate that the initially formed species is a resonance hybrid: $C_6H_5CH=\overset{+}{C}HCH_2 \leftrightarrow$ $C_6H_5\overset{+}{C}H—CH=CH_2$.

8. The molecular weight is 61.04, and hence the boiling point of 102° means that the liquid is somewhat associated. The association probably is due to electrostatic attraction between semipolar bonds:

$$CH_3—\overset{\overset{O}{\|}}{\underset{+}{N}}—O^-$$

$$O^-—\overset{+}{\underset{\underset{O}{\|}}{N}}—CH_3$$

9. Tetranitromethane on explosion liberates six moles of gaseous products: $C(NO_2)_4 \rightarrow 2N_2 + CO_2 + 3O_2$. Nitromethane does not contain enough oxygen to convert all the carbon and hydrogen present into gaseous products, and the one nitrogen atom could give rise to only $\frac{1}{2} N_2$.

10. Sulfur has twice the atomic weight of oxygen.

CHAPTER 5. ALKENES

1. The α-ketol (b) is resistant to acid-catalyzed elimination but can be dehydrated over alumina. The relative ease of dehydration of the other compounds is (c) > (a) > (d).

2. (a) $(CH_3)_2C=CHCH_2CH_2Br$
(b) $CHCl=CCl_2$
(c) $BrCH_2C(Br)=CH_2$
(d) $[C_6H_5CH=C(Br)COOH] \rightarrow C_6H_5CH=CHBr + CO_2$

3.

$$CH_3CH_2CH=C=CH_2 \xrightarrow[-H_2O]{+OH^-}$$

$$CH_3CH_2CH=C=\overset{-}{C}H \leftrightarrow$$

$OH^- | -H_2O$ $CH_3CH_2\overset{-}{C}H—C\equiv CH$

$H_2O | -OH^-$

$$CH_3CH_2CH_2C\equiv CH$$
(Less stable)

$$CH_3CH_2\overset{-}{C}=C=CH_2$$
$\updownarrow$
$$CH_3CH_2\overset{-}{C}=C—\overset{-}{C}H_2 \xrightarrow[-OH^-]{H_2O}$$

$$CH_3CH_2C\equiv CCH_3$$
(More stable)

4. *trans*-Stilbene

5. (a) 5α-Chlorocholestane-3β,6β-diol
(b) Cholestane-3β,6β-diol

6. (a) $CH_3CHBrCHBrCH_2CH=CHBr$
(b) $(CH_3)_2CBrCHBrCH_2CH=CH_2$
(c) $CH_2=CHCOOCHBrCH_2Br$

7. The inductive effect of the electron-releasing methyl group tends to oppose separation of the electrophile OH^+.

8. $CH_3CH=C(R)CH_2R' \xrightarrow{H^+}$

$$CH_3CH_2\overset{+}{C}(R)CH_2R' \xrightarrow{-H^+}$$

$$CH_3CH_2C(R)=CHR'$$

9.

Vitamin A₂

The scheme of synthesis that comes to mind is allylic bromination of vitamin A₁ with N-bromosuccinimide, and dehydrohalogenation. The high reactivity of the allylic alcohol group, however, introduces a complication. The synthesis achieved by E. R. H. Jones in England in 1951 thus utilized vitamin A₁ acid, which has a carboxyl group in place of —CH₂OH; after allylic bromination and elimination of HBr, the synthesis was completed by the transformation —COOH → —CH₂OH by LiAlH₄ reduction.

10. (a) $C_6H_5CH_2CH_2CH=C(CH_3)_2$
(b) $CH_3CH=CHCH=CHCH_3$
(c)

(d)

(e)

11. (a) Wash with concentrated sulfuric acid and discard the lower layer of acid containing $ROSO_2OH$ formed by addition to the olefin.
(b) Same as in (a).
(c) Prepare the dibromide, separate it from n-hexane by fractionation, debrominate with zinc.

12. On drastic oxidation the first hydrocarbon gives a C₃-acid and a C₃-ketone and the second gives a C₂-acid and a C₄-ketone.

13. 1,4-Dimethylcyclopentadiene-1,3

14. Hexene-2
15. $CH_3CH_2C(CH_3){=}CH(CH_2)_2CH{=}$
$CHCH_2CH_3$
16. (a) 2 rings; (b) 4 rings

17. $CH_2CH_2CCH_2CH_2$
   | || |
   $CH_2CH_2CCH_2CH_2$

CHAPTER 6. ACETYLENIC AND RELATED COMPOUNDS

1. Bohlmann suggests:

$CH_3CHClCH{=}CHC{\equiv}CC{\equiv}CCH{=}$

$CHCHClCH_3 \xrightarrow{-HCl} CH_3CHClCH{=}$

$CHC{\equiv}CC{\equiv}CCH{=}C{=}CHCH_3 \rightarrow$

$CH_3CHClCH_2CH{=}CHC{\equiv}CC{\equiv}CC{\equiv}$

$CCH_3 \xrightarrow{-HCl} CH_3CH{=}CHCH{=}CHC{\equiv}$

$CC{\equiv}CC{\equiv}CCH_3$

2. (a) $ClCH_2C{\equiv}CCH_2Cl + 3NaNH_2 \rightarrow$

$NaC{\equiv}CC{\equiv}CH \xrightarrow{CH_3Br} CH_3C{\equiv}CC{\equiv}CH$

(b) $ClCH_2C{\equiv}CCH_2Cl + 4NaNH_2 \rightarrow$

$NaC{\equiv}CC{\equiv}CNa \xrightarrow{2CH_3Br} CH_3C{\equiv}CC{\equiv}$

CCH_3

(c) $CH_3C{\equiv}CC{\equiv}CH \xrightarrow{Cu^+ - O_2} CH_3C{\equiv}$

$CC{\equiv}CC{\equiv}CC{\equiv}CCH_3$

3. Progression of the double bond along the chain may proceed thus:

$CH_2{=}CH{-}CH_2{-} \overset{OH^-}{\rightleftharpoons} CH_2{=}CHCH{-}$

$\leftrightarrow \ \bar{C}H_2{-}CH{=}CH{-} \xrightarrow{H_2O} CH_3CH{=}$

$CH{-} + OH^-$

Formation in the terminal step of a resonance-stabilized α,β-unsaturated acid provides a driving force for displacement of a succession of equilibria.

4. $C_6H_5COCH_3 \xrightarrow{PCl_5} C_6H_5CCl_2CH_3 \xrightarrow{3NaNH_2}$

$C_6H_5C{\equiv}CNa \xrightarrow{HCl} C_6H_5C{\equiv}CH$

5. Conversion via the dibromide to acetylene-dicarboxylic acid and selective hydrogenation.
6.

$R{:}\ddot{C}{::}N{\vdots}{:}\underset{\cdot\cdot}{N}{\vdots} \longrightarrow R{:}\ddot{C}$

$R{:}C{::}N{\vdots}{:}\underset{\cdot\cdot}{N}{\vdots} \qquad\qquad R{:}\ddot{C}$

$+ \ 2{:}\underset{\cdot\cdot}{N}{:}N{:}$

7. $C_6H_5CH{=}CHCH{=}CHCO_2H$
8. See 11.29.

9. $CH_3CH_2CH_2I + NaC{\equiv}CH \rightarrow$

$CH_3CH_2CH_2C{\equiv}CH \xrightarrow{NaNH_2}$

$CH_3CH_2CH_2C{\equiv}CNa \xrightarrow{BrCH_2CH_2Cl}$

$CH_3CH_2CH_2C{\equiv}CCH_2CH_2CH_2Cl$

CHAPTER 8. ALCOHOLS

1. (a) 3-Methylpentene-2
(b) $(CH_3)_2C{=}CHCH_2CH(CH_3)_2$
(c) $(CH_3)_2C{=}CHCH_2CH_2OH$
(d) $CH_3CH_2CO_2H + O{=}C(CH_3)_2$ [initial dehydration to $CH_3CH_2CH{=}C(CH_3)_2$]
(e) Adipic aldehyde, $OHC(CH_2)_4CHO$
(f) $n\text{-}C_5H_{11}OCH_2CH_2OH$
(g) Ethanolamine, $HOCH_2CH_2NH_2$
2. (a) $CH_3CH_2CH_2MgBr + (CH_3)_2CO$
(b) $2CH_3CH_2CH_2MgBr + CH_3CO_2C_2H_5$
(c) $CH_3CH_2CH_2MgBr + CH_2O$
(d) $CH_3CH_2CH_2MgBr + $ ethylene oxide
(e) $CH_3CH_2CH_2MgBr + CH_3COCH_2CH_3$
3. (a) $(CH_3)_2CHMgBr + CH_2O$
(b) $(CH_3)_2CO + BrMgCH_2CH_3$
(c) $CH_3CH_2CO_2CH_3 + 2CH_3CH_2MgI$
(d) $CH_3CH_2CH_2MgBr + $ ethylene oxide
(e) $CH_3CH_2MgCl + OC(CH_3)_2$; dehydration
(f) $(CH_3)_2CHMgBr + $ ethylene oxide $\rightarrow$ $(CH_3)_2CHCH_2CH_2OH$;
$(CH_3)_2CHCH_2CH_2MgBr + CH_2O$; dehydration
(g) $(CH_3)_2CHMgI + OC(CH_3)_2$; dehydration
(h) $(CH_3)_2CO + CH_3MgCl$; dehydration; hydrogenation
(i) $CH_3CH_2CH_2MgBr + OC(CH_3)_2$; dehydration; hydrogenation
(j) $2(CH_3)_2CHMgBr + CH_3CO_2C_2H_5$; dehydration; hydrogenation
4. (a) $2CH_3CH_2CH_2MgBr + CH_3CH_2CO_2CH_3$; dehydration; hydrogenation
(b) $CH_2{=}CHCH_2MgBr + OC(CH_3)_2$; dehydration
(c) $(CH_3)_2CO + CH_3MgI \rightarrow (CH_3)_3COH$; $(CH_3)_3COH \rightarrow (CH_3)_3CBr \rightarrow (CH_3)_3CMgBr$; $(CH_3)_3CMgBr + CH_2O \rightarrow (CH_3)_3CCH_2OH$
5. (a) $(CH_3)_2CHCH_2MgCl + OC(CH_3)_2$; dehydration
(b) $CH_3CH_2CH(OH)CH_3 \rightarrow$ $CH_3CH_2COCH_3$; reaction with $CH_3CH_2CH_2MgBr$
(c) $(CH_3)_2CO + CH_3CH_2CH_2CH_2MgCl$; dehydration; hydrogenation
(d) $(CH_3)_3CMgCl + CH_3CH_2CHO$; conversion to $(CH_3)_3CCHBrCH_2CH_3$; formation of $RMgBr$; decomposition with water
6. $(CH_3)_2CHCH{=}CH_2$
7. $(CH_3)_2CHCHOHCH_3$
8. Cyclohexene $+ H_2O_2 \rightarrow$ cyclohexane-diol-1,2; glycol cleavage with HIO_4 gives the dialdehyde, $OHCCH_2CH_2CH_2CH_2CHO$, which on condensation with CH_3MgCl yields $CH_3CHOHCH_2CH_2CH_2CH_2CHOHCH_3$; dehydration affords

$CH_3CH=CHCH_2CH_2CH=CHCH_3$.

9. On dehydration to a diene, followed by chromic acid oxidation, the first diol would give a C_6-diketone and the second would give a C_6-diacid.

10. From ricinoleic acid by hydroxylation of the double bond (H_2O_2—HOAc) and reduction with $LiAlH_4$.

11. Rates of chromic acid oxidation in 90.9% acetic acid at 25° are:

11β-ol	60	1α-ol	13.0
6β-ol	36	7α-ol	12.3
4β-ol	35	3α-ol	3.0
2β-ol	20.0		

CHAPTER 10. HALIDES

1. (a) Treat stearyl alcohol with thionyl chloride and remove excess by evaporation in vacuum; or use PCl_5 and remove $POCl_3$ by distillation.
(b) Shake t-amyl alcohol with 36% hydrochloric acid in a separatory funnel; separate and wash the upper layer, dry, and distil.
(c) Treat the alcohol with PBr_3; decant the bromide from phosphorous acid.
(d) Heat the alcohol with constant-boiling hydriodic acid.

2. $d > b > a > c$

3. Positive: b, e, g

4. (a) $(CH_3)_2CHMgBr + BrCH_2CH=CH_2$
(b) $CH_2=CHCH_2Br + Br_2$
(c) $CH_2=CHCH_2Br + HBr$
(d) $CH_2BrCHBrCH_2Br$ (b) + alc. KOH

5. $CH_2=CHCHO$

6.

$$H:C::C:C:H \xrightarrow{\quad} $$

with :Br: above the middle carbon, H H H below, and −:Br: to the right

$$\overset{+}{H:C:}C:\overset{\cdot\cdot}{C}:H \longleftrightarrow H:\overset{+}{C}:C::C:H$$
H H H   H H H

(Note that the departing bromide ion takes along one electron that originally belonged to carbon, with the result that carbon is left with a positive charge.)

7. (a)

$$H:\overset{\cdot\cdot}{C} ::C: \overset{\cdot\cdot}{Br}: \longleftrightarrow H:C:C::\overset{+}{Br}:$$
H H   H H

(b) The initially uncharged bromine atom shares an additional pair of electrons with the adjacent carbon atom, and this atom in turn donates to the terminal carbon atom a pair of shared electrons in which each atom originally had an equal stake of one electron. Hence bromine, in effect, has donated one electron to the terminal carbon atom.
(c) The electron formulation of

$\overset{+}{C}H_2-CH=Br^-$ represents more electrons (10)

$$H:\overset{+}{C}:C::\overset{\cdot\cdot}{Br}:$$
H H

than bromine can accommodate.

8. The hydrocarbon exists as a diradical; a quinonoid structure is impossible.

CHAPTER 11. CARBOXYLIC ACIDS

1. Acidic strength increases in the order $CH_3CH_2CO_2H$, $HOCH_2CO_2H$, ICH_2CO_2H, $ClCH_2CO_2H$. The order of relative electronegativity, as indicated by the position in the periodic table, is: $C < O < I < Cl$.

2. The values of pK_{a2} for phthalic and isophthalic acid are 5.28 and 4.46.

3. (a) $CH_3CH(CH_3)CH_2CH_2 \cdot$
$C(CH_3)=CHCO_2H$. (b) $HO_2C(CH_2)_8CO_2H$.

4. (a) Grignard (KCN probably would eliminate HBr).
(b) Nitrile synthesis (the hydroxyl group would prevent formation of a Grignard reagent).

5. $CH_3CH_2OH \rightarrow CH_2=CH_2 \rightarrow BrCH_2CH_2Br \rightarrow NCCH_2CH_2CN \rightarrow HO_2CCH_2CH_2CO_2H$

6. By sodium hypochlorite oxidation.

7. Dissolve the mixture in ether, extract the acidic component with sodium bicarbonate solution, acidify the extract, extract with ether, dry the solution, and evaporate the solvent.

8. On chlorination in the presence of iodine as catalyst, (a) would give a monochloro derivative, (b) would give a dichloro derivative, and (c) would remain unchanged. Rates of esterification would also distinguish between the three acids.

9. (a) Fischer esterification with HCl, H_2SO_4, or BF_3 as catalyst.
(b) Diazomethane or silver salt method.
(c) Fischer esterification with BF_3 as catalyst (HCl or H_2SO_4 might add to the double bond).
(d) Reflux the n-propyl ester with excess methanol containing 3% sulfuric acid.

10.

$$\overset{:O:}{\underset{\parallel}{R-C}}-OH \xrightarrow{BF_3} \overset{:\overset{+}{O}:B^-F_3}{\underset{\parallel}{R-C}}-OH$$

$$\xrightarrow{HOCH_3} R-\overset{OH}{\underset{\overset{\cdot\cdot}{+O}:B^-F_3}{\underset{CH_3}{\mid}{C}-OH}} \xrightarrow{-H_2O}$$

$$R-\overset{O}{\underset{\underset{CH_3}{\overset{+}{O}:B^-F_3}}{\parallel}{C}} \xrightarrow{-BF_3} R-\overset{O}{\underset{\parallel}{C}}OCH_3$$

11. $(CH_3)_2CHCO_2H \rightarrow (CH_3)_2CHCOCl$ (reaction with $SOCl_2$); $(CH_3)_2CHCOCl + CH_3CdCl$

12. The order is as follows (rates relative to that of acetic acid):

Acid	Rate	Six-atoms	Substituents
(c)	0.01	6 H	1 α-R group
(e)	0.0033	3 C	2 α-R groups
(b)	0.00059	9 H	1 α-R group
(d)	0.00013	9 H	2 α-R groups
(a)	Too slow to measure	12 H	1 α-R group

13. $CH_3COOH + Br_2$ (I_2 catalyst) $\rightarrow$ $CH_2BrCOOH$; $CH_2BrCOOH + PCl_3 \rightarrow$ $CH_2BrCOCl$

14. Acetic acid and ethyl acetate.

15. Dehydration with acetic anhydride to succinic anhydride; action of boiling methanol on the anhydride to produce the half ester; reaction with thionyl chloride.

16. Replacement of hydrogen by acetyl involves a net gain of C_2H_2O, hence four hydroxyl groups must have been acetylated. The substance contains only four carbon atoms and each can carry only one hydroxyl group (gem-diols are unstable), hence the structure must be $HOCH_2CHOHCHOHCH_2OH$. Note that the structure $(HOCH_2)_3COH$ is ruled out because the tertiary alcoholic group would not be acylated on treatment with acetic anhydride.

17. Prepare the diester, $CH_3OCOCH_2COOCH_3$, and treat it with four moles of CH_3MgCl; dehydrate the diol, $(CH_3)_2C(OH)CH_2CH_2C(OH)(CH_3)_2$.

18. $RCOCl > (RCO)_2O > RCOOCH_3 > ROR$

19. (a) Conversion to capryl alcohol; hypochlorite oxidation. (b) Conversion to n-heptaldehyde; oxidation with dichromate solution.

CHAPTER 12. ALDEHYDES AND KETONES

1. Reaction with silver tosylate and oxidation with dimethyl sulfoxide.

2. (a) Oxidation with chromic acid
(b) Oxidation with chromic acid
(c) Grignard reaction of allylmagnesium bromide with acetaldehyde to give CH_2=$CHCH_2CH(OH)CH_3$; Oppenauer oxidation (chromic acid would attack the double bond).
(d) Hydroxylation of the double bond with H_2O_2 in acetic acid and cleavage of the glycol, $HOCH_2CHOH(CH_2)_8COOH$, with lead tetraacetate.
(e) Conversion to the acid chloride (e.g. with $SOCl_2$); Rosenmund reduction.

3. Cyclohexanone on nitric acid oxidation gives adipic acid, $HO_2C(CH_2)_4CO_2H$; pyrolysis of the calcium salt of this acid affords cyclopentanone. To effect the reverse transformation, oxidize cyclopentanone with nitric acid to glutaric acid, $HO_2C(CH_2)_3CO_2H$, reduce the diethyl ester with sodium and alcohol (Bouveault-Blanc method) to produce pentamethyleneglycol, $HO(CH_2)_5OH$, replace both hydroxyl groups by bromine, replace the bromine atoms by nitrile groups (aqueous-alcoholic KCN), hydrolyze to $HO_2C(CH_2)_5CO_2H$, pyrolyze the calcium salt of the diacid.

4. Aldehydes, but not ketones: give the Ag-mirror test and reduce Fehling solution, polymerize under acid catalysis or in aqueous solution, give a positive Schiff test; aldehydes with no α-hydrogen atom undergo the Cannizzaro reaction. Aldehydes react to a greater extent than ketones: with $NaHSO_3$, with HCN, and with alcohols (acetal formation).

5. Chloral is the most reactive of the compounds because it alone forms stable addition products with water and with hydroxylamine. The bisulfite reaction establishes the order acetaldehyde > acetone > diethyl ketone. The failure of diisopropyl ketone to add isopropylmagnesium bromide shows it to be the least reactive compound listed.

6. By reduction with aluminum isopropoxide and isopropyl alcohol (Meerwein-Ponndorf method).

7. (a) Cholestane-2β,3α-diol 2-acetate
(b) Cholestane-2β-ol

8. $(CH_3)_3CCH_2OH + (CH_3)_3CCO_2H$

9. Reformatsky reaction with ethyl α-bromoacetate and hydrolysis.

10. $CH_3COCH_2CH_2CHO + 2C_2H_5OH$ (dry HCl) $\rightarrow CH_3COCH_2CH_2CH(OC_2H_5)_2$; oxidation with alkaline hypochlorite to $HO_2CCH_2CH_2CH(OC_2H_5)_2$; hydrolysis of the acetal with dilute aqueous hydrochloric acid.

11. Reformatsky reaction with ethyl α-bromoacetate and hydrolysis.

12. Methyl ketones add $NaHSO_3$ and HCN; none of the esters add these reagents. Ketones react with hydrazine with replacement of the carbonyl oxygen, whereas an ester reacts with hydrazine to form a hydrazide ($RCONHNH_2$) in which the carbonyl group is still intact.

13. $(CH_3)_2CHCH(OH)CH_3$

14. $CH_3COCH_2CH_2CHO$

15. (a) $HOCH_2CH_2CN$ (compare action of RMgX on ethylene oxide and on carbonyl compounds).
(b) $CH_3COOC(CH_3)_3$

16. (a) Pyrolysis of $(CH_3CH_2COO)_2Ca$
(b) $CH_3CH_2CH_2MgBr + CH_3CH_2CHO$; oxidation of the resulting secondary alcohol
(c) Reaction of acetone with allylmagnesium bromide and acid catalyzed dehydration.

17. Vinylcyclopentane

18. The formation of a monoacetate indicates the presence of a primary or secondary alcoholic group; resistance to phenylhydrazine shows that the second oxygen atom is not present as a carbonyl group. The reaction with lead tetraacetate is evidently a glycol cleavage producing two carbonyl groups; since these are in the same molecule, III, the glycol group must be part of a ring. The positive Fehling test indicates that at least one carbonyl must be present as an aldehydic group, and the formation of iodoform reveals the

presence of a methyl ketone group. The acid $HOOC(CH_2)_4COOH$ must, then, have come from the keto aldehyde $CH_3CO(CH_2)_4$-CHO, and the glycol I must have the structure:

$$CH_3$$
$$|$$
$$CH_2CH_2COH$$
$$| \quad |$$
$$CH_2CH_2CHOH$$

19. Condensation with ethanedithiol and desulfurization with Raney Ni.

20. $C_6H_5CHOHCOOH$ (mandelic acid).

21. (a) $(CH_3)_2CHBr + Na^+[CH(CO_2C_2H_5)_2]^-$ $\rightarrow (CH_3)_2CHCH(CO_2C_2H_5)_2$; hydrolysis and decarboxylation

(b) $CH_3I + Na^+[CH(CO_2C_2H_5)_2]^- \rightarrow$ $CH_3CH(CO_2C_2H_5)_2$; conversion to sodio derivative; reaction with CH_3CH_2I; hydrolysis and decarboxylation.

(c) Condensation of $Br(CH_2)_4Br$ with two moles of sodiomalonic ester, etc.

22. The second compound, the C-acetyl derivative, has three carbonyl groups in a position to activate the central hydrogen atom and hence this substance exists to the greater extent in the enolic form.

CHAPTER 13. CONDENSATIONS

It is evident from the absorption spectrum that six of the eleven carbon atoms are present in a phenyl group. The formation of an evident O-diacetate shows that two hydroxyl groups are present. Reduction to a substance capable of forming a diazonium salt indicates the presence of a nitro substituent in the phenyl group. Absorption of three moles of hydrogen confirms this conclusion, for unsaturated nitrogen compounds other than nitro compounds do not require this much hydrogen for reduction.

One of the two products of alkaline hydrolysis, $C_2H_2O_2Cl_2$, is acidic and hence the only possible formula is $CHCl_2COOH$. The other product is basic, whereas chloramphenicol is not. Thus hydrolysis liberates an amino group and dichloroacetic acid, and hence chloramphenicol must contain the group $-NHCOCHCl_2$. This amide group, which would be inert to carbonyl reagents, accounts for one of the five oxygens, and one nitro and two hydroxyl groups account for the remainder. Oxidation with periodic acid to an aromatic aldehyde, $ArCHO$, formaldehyde, formic acid, and ammonia indicates the presence of a three carbon chain, $Ar-C-C-C$, containing two hydroxyl and one amino group, and these have to be distributed one to a carbon atom to account for the cleavage. Since chloramphenicol, which contains one $-NHCOCHCl_2$ and two free hydroxyl groups, is stable to periodic acid the distribution cannot be $ArCHOHCHOHCH_2NH_2$ or

$ArCHNH_2CHOHCH_2OH$ and can only be:

$$ArCHOH-CHNH_2-CH_2OH$$
$$\downarrow \quad (OH)_2 \quad \downarrow \quad (OH)_2 \quad \downarrow$$
$$ArCH(OH)_2 \quad CHNH_2(OH)_2 \quad CH_2(OH)_2$$
$$\downarrow \qquad \qquad \downarrow \qquad \qquad \downarrow$$
$$ArCHO \qquad HCOOH + NH_3 \quad CH_2O$$

The aldehyde, $C_7H_5O_3N$, must still carry the nitro group and hence is a nitrobenzaldehyde, $NO_2C_6H_4CHO$, identified as the *para* derivative. Chloramphenicol thus has the structure $p-NO_2C_6H_4CH(OH)CH(NHCOCHCl_2)\cdot CH_2OH$.

Chloramphenicol contains two asymmetric carbon atoms and could have the threo configuration I or the erythro configuration II. That I is probably correct was deduced by

$$CH_2OH$$
$$|$$
$$HCNHCOCHCl_2$$
$$HOCH$$

$$CH_2OH$$
$$|$$
$$HCNHCOCHCl_2$$
$$HCOH$$

$$NO_2 \qquad \qquad NO_2$$
$$I \qquad \qquad \qquad II$$

$$CH_3$$
$$|$$
$$HCNHCH_3$$
$$HOCH$$

$$CH_3$$
$$|$$
$$HCNHCH_3$$
$$HCOH$$

$$III \qquad \qquad \qquad IV$$

comparison of the antibiotic with ephedrine (IV), a plant product, and pseudoephedrine (III), and the corresponding nor derivatives (lacking the N-methyl group). Configurations in the ephedrine series were deduced by Freudenberg (1934) through correlation to mandelic acid and to alanine. Various salts of the C_9 base desacylchloramphenicol show shifts in molecular rotation corresponding to those of norpseudoephedrine, of threo configuration. The Geneva name for the antibiotic is $D(-)$-threo-2-dichloroacetamido-1-p-nitrophenylpropane-1,3-diol.

The first synthesis involved the steps shown in the formulation.

$$C_6H_5CHO + CH_2(NO_2)CH_2OH \xrightarrow{NaOCH_3}$$

$$C_6H_5CH(OH)CH(NO_2)CH_2OH \xrightarrow{H_2, Pd}$$

$$C_6H_5CH(OH)CH(NH_2)CH_2OH \xrightarrow{Ac_2O\text{-}Py}$$

$$C_6H_5CH(OAc)CH(NHAc)CH_2OAc \xrightarrow{HNO_3}$$

$$p\text{-}NO_2C_6H_4CH(OAc)CH(NHAc)CH_2OAc \xrightarrow{hydrol.}$$

$$p\text{-}NO_2C_6H_4CH(OH)CH(NH_2)CH_2OH \xrightarrow{Cl_2CHCO_2CH_3}$$
(resolved, D-form used)

$$p\text{-}NO_2C_6H_4CH(OH)CH(NHCOCHCl_2)CH_2OH$$

A second synthesis (L. L. Bambas, 1950) from p-nitroacetophenone involved conversion to p-nitrophenacyl bromide (V), reaction with an ammonia donor (hexamethylenetetramine) and hydrolysis of the product to the amino derivative VI. The N-acetyl derivative VII added to formaldehyde to give VIII. Usual methods for reduction of the carbonyl group would also reduce the nitro group, but the Meerwein-Ponndorf method has just the specificity required and afforded XIX. The preponderant reduction product proved to be the DL-threo base, the D-form of which could be resolved and converted into chloramphenicol.

$$p\text{-}NO_2C_6H_4COCH_2Br \xrightarrow{2\ steps}$$
$$V$$

$$p\text{-}NO_2C_6H_4COCH_2NH_2 \xrightarrow{Ac_2O}$$
$$VI$$

$$\overset{\displaystyle NHAc}{\underset{\displaystyle |}{p\text{-}NO_2C_6H_4COCH_2}}$$
$$VII$$

$$\xrightarrow{CH_2=O} \overset{\displaystyle NHAc}{\underset{\displaystyle \underset{\displaystyle O}{\underset{\displaystyle \|}{|}}}{p\text{-}NO_2C_6H_4CCHCH_2OH}}$$
$$VIII$$

$$\xrightarrow{Al[OCH(CH_3)_2]_3} \overset{\displaystyle H\ \ NH_2}{\underset{\displaystyle OH\ H}{\underset{\displaystyle |\ \ |}{p\text{-}NO_2C_6H_4C-C-CH_2OH}}}$$
XIX, main product

CHAPTER 14. AMINES

1. (a) Yes.
(b) Yes, the case is like that of a similarly substituted allene.

2. Weakly acidic: phthalimide (pK$_a$ 8.3), succinimide (pK$_a$ 10.5). Substantially neutral: acetamide, acetylmethylamine; inner salt: β-alanine. Feebly basic: urea. Basic: methylamine (pK$_b$ 3.4), tetramethylammonium hydroxide (pK$_b$ nearly zero).

3. (a) Treat with a little acetic anhydride, extract an ethereal solution of the resulting mixture with portions of dilute hydrochloric acid until no more amine is removed, neutralize the acid solution, extract with ether, distil the ether and then the triethylamine.
(b) Treat with NaNO$_2$ + HCl, extract an ethereal solution of the resulting mixture with dilute HCl to remove the triethylamine, heat the neutral fraction with HCl to hydrolyze the (CH$_3$CH$_2$)$_2$NNO, extract the acidic solution with ether, recover the diethylamine from the acid liquor by neutralization and ether extraction.
(c) Treat with benzenesulfonyl chloride, separate the alkali-soluble CH$_3$CH$_2$NHSO$_2$C$_6$H$_5$ from the alkali-insoluble (CH$_3$CH$_2$)$_2$NSO$_2$C$_6$H$_5$ and (CH$_3$CH$_2$)$_3$N, hydrolyze the alkali-soluble derivative.

4. (a) CH$_3$CH$_2$CH$_2$CH$_2$OH → CH$_3$CH$_2$CH$_2$CO$_2$H → chloride → amide → CH$_3$CH$_2$CH$_2$NH$_2$ (NaOBr).
(b) CH$_3$CH$_2$CH$_2$CH$_2$OH → bromide → nitrile → CH$_3$CH$_2$CH$_2$CH$_2$CH$_2$NH$_2$ (LiAlH$_4$).

5. CH$_3$CH$_2$CHOHCH$_3$ → CH$_3$CH$_2$COCH$_3$ → oxime → CH$_3$CH$_2$CHNH$_2$CH$_3$ (H$_2$, Pt).

6. The Gabriel synthesis would give a pure product, whereas reaction with ammonia would give some secondary amine. The route through the aldehyde and oxime suffers from some difficulty in avoiding overoxidation in the preparation of the aldehyde.

7. RCN → RCONH$_2$ → RCOOH.
RCOOH → RCOCl → RCONH$_2$ → RCN (Ac$_2$O). Yes, the reaction RCH=NOH → RC≡N is realizable (action of Ac$_2$O).

8. Exhaustive methylation, conversion to the quaternary ammonium hydroxide, and pyrolysis affords cyclohexene.

9. Yes, they both contain an electron sextet (they are described as isoelectronic):

$$\begin{array}{cc} R & R \\ \cdot\cdot & \cdot\cdot \\ R\!:\!B & R\!:\!C^+ \\ \cdot\cdot & \cdot\cdot \\ R & R \end{array}$$

10.

$$\underset{CH_2C}{\overset{CH_2C}{}}\!\!N^- \leftrightarrow \underset{CH_2C}{\overset{CH_2C}{}}\!\!N \leftrightarrow \underset{CH_2C}{\overset{CH_2C}{}}\!\!N$$

11. In an alkyl bromide (a) the bromine atom is described as negative because it separates with the pair of shared electrons and accepts a proton.

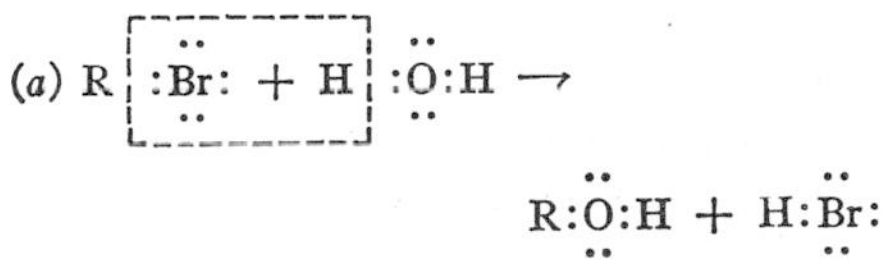

(a) R $\lceil$:Br: $+$ H $\rceil$:Ö:H $\longrightarrow$

R:Ö:H $+$ H:Br:

In N-bromosuccinimide (b) the two electron-attracting carbonyl groups prevent separation

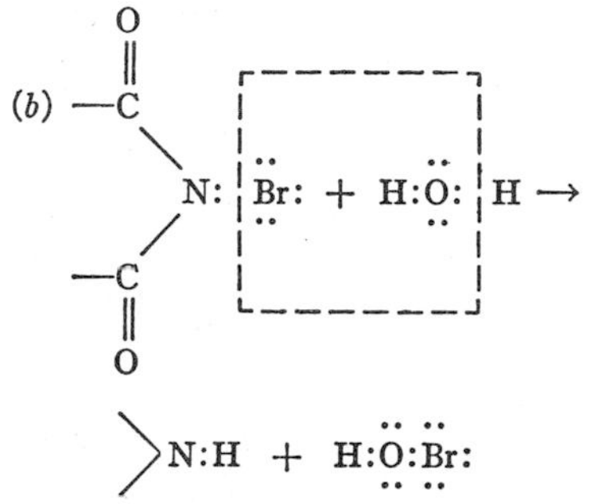

(b) —C (=O)
N: Br: $+$ H:Ö: H $\longrightarrow$
—C (=O)

$\rangle$N:H $+$ H:Ö:Br:

of the electron pair shared between nitrogen and bromine, and hence bromine departs with only an electron sextet and combines with hydroxide ion to form HOBr.

12. Cracking: methane (CH$_4$ → HC≡CH); alkanes (CH$_3$CH$_3$ → CH$_2$=CH$_2$); alkenes (CH$_3$CH$_2$CH=CH$_2$ → CH$_2$=CHCH=CH$_2$); aromatization (n-heptane → toluene). Thermal dehydration of alcohols over alumina. Alkenes from alkylsulfuric acids. Formation of calcium carbide (electric furnace). Pyrolysis of castor oil to n-heptaldehyde and undecylenic acid. Decarboxylation of formic acid at 160°. Thermal chlorination of propylene to allyl chloride (formed instead of the saturated addition product). Pyrolysis of acetone to ketene. Catalytic dehydrogenation of secondary alcohols to ketones. Thermal depolymerization of aldehyde polymers. Aldol → crotonaldehyde. Thermal decomposition of quaternary ammonium hydroxides

13. The chemical evidence does not distinguish between the structure shown and the alternative structure with the amino group at the

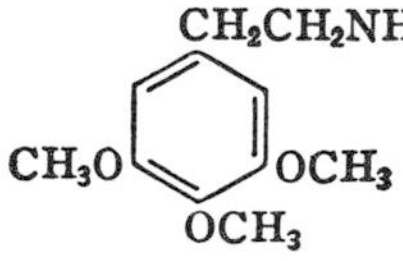

CH$_2$CH$_2$NH$_2$

CH$_3$O — OCH$_3$
OCH$_3$

Mescaline

α- rather than the β-position in the side chain, but a naturally occurring base of the latter structure would contain an asymmetric carbon atom and should be optically active. Synthesis: (CH$_3$O)$_3$C$_6$H$_2$CHO + CH$_3$NO$_2$ (OH⁻, heat) → (CH$_3$O)$_3$C$_6$H$_2$CH=CHNO$_2$ → (CH$_3$O)$_3$C$_6$H$_2$CH$_2$CH$_2$NH$_2$.

CHAPTER 15. RING FORMATION AND STABILITY

1. Pentene-2 and 1,2-dimethylcyclopropane would decolorize bromine solution whereas cyclopentane would not. Pentene-2, but not 1,2-dimethylcyclopropane, would give a test for unsaturation with permanganate.

2. In muscone the carbon atom carrying the methyl group is asymmetric because the part of the ring joined to it on one side contains a β-keto group and the part joined on the other side does not; reduction of the carbonyl group destroys the asymmetry.

3. Condensation of butadiene with maleic anhydride; saturation of the double bond by catalytic hydrogenation; hydrolysis of the anhydride group.

4. See pages 147, 221, 267, 268, 379, 406.

5. See C. R. Noller "Chemistry of Organic Compounds," p. 836 (Saunders, 1957), or E. R. Rodd, "Chemistry of Carbon Compounds," IIA, 61–62 (Elsevier, 1953).

6. CH$_2$=O + 2CH$_2$(CO$_2$C$_2$H$_5$)$_2$ → CH$_2$[CH(CO$_2$C$_2$H$_5$)$_2$]$_2$ (elimination of H$_2$O); hydrolysis to CH$_2$[CH(CO$_2$H)$_2$]$_2$; decarboxylation to CH$_2$(CH$_2$CO$_2$H)$_2$.

7. (a) O=C=C=C=O + 2H$_2$O → (HO)$_2$C=C=C(OH)$_2$ → HOOCCH$_2$COOH
(b) Malonamide: H$_2$NCOCH$_2$CONH$_2$

8. In trans-decalin the 1,2-interactions (2.49 Å) are 9β,1β; 1α,2α; 1β,2α; 1β,2β; 2α,3α; 2α,3β etc. The total number is 22, and at an energy equivalent of 1.07 kcal. per interaction the strain energy is 23.54 kcal./mole. Addition of sixteen 1:3 interactions (2.50 Å or 1.07 kcal.) gives a total strain energy of 40.2 kcal./mole. cis-Decalin contains twenty-five 1:2 interactions at a separation distance of 2.49 Å, nine 1.3 interactions (2.50 Å), and two transannular interactions: 1α,5α (2.0 Å); 3α,5α (1.8 Å). In all there are thirty-six interactions at an average distance of 2.46 Å, equivalent to 1.18 kcal., whence the total energy is 42.5 kcal./mole. The calculation shows the trans form to be more stable by 2.3 kcal./mole (found: 2.1).

9. In 9β-methyl-trans-decalin the methyl group is axial to both rings and hence its hydrogen atoms are repelled by interaction with the axial hydrogens in each ring. In the cis isomer the angular methyl group is axial to one ring but equatorial to the other, and hence the energy increase is only half as great. Hence the difference in energy is less than with the unsubstituted decalins.

CHAPTER 16. HISTORY OF THE BENZENE PROBLEM

1. The 1,3-dicarboxylic acid could be obtained by condensation of trimethylene dibromide with methylenebismalonic ester,

CH$_2$[CH(CO$_2$C$_2$H$_5$)$_2$]$_2$, followed by hydrolysis and decarboxylation of the tetrabasic acid. The ester (C$_2$H$_5$O$_2$C)$_2$CHCH$_2$CH$_2$CH(CO$_2$C$_2$H$_5$)$_2$, required for the synthesis of the 1,4-isomer, is obtainable by condensation of BrCH$_2$CH$_2$Br with two moles of sodiomalonic ester; the preparation of methylenebismalonic ester by condensation of formaldehyde with diethyl malonate is mentioned in answer 6, Chapt. 15.

2. Yes; 1,2,3-trimethylbenzene can afford two monosubstitution products, three are derivable from 1,2,4-trimethylbenzene, and one from the 1,3,5-isomer.

3. This numbering is required because a 1,2-di derivative would then give two substitution products (3- or 4-, 5- or 6-), the 1,3-isomer would afford three (2- or 4-, 5-, 6-), and the 1,4-isomer (fully symmetrical) only one.

4. The answer will be obvious from the formulas.

5. Nine geometrical isomers, two of which are optically active enantiomers (see 23.11, 29.6).

6. The molecular ratio of glyoxal to diacetyl to methylglyoxal should be 1:1:4.

CHAPTER 17. AROMATIC SUBSTITUTIONS

(a) 4-Nitro-1,3-dimethoxybenzene
(b) Substitution *ortho* to the acetylamino group (more potent)
(c) Substitution *ortho* to the methyl group (smaller)
(d) Substitution *ortho* to the methyl group and *meta* to —COCH$_3$
(e) Mild conditions: 2-nitrophenol-4-sulfonic acid; more drastic conditions: 2,4-dinitrophenol, picric acid
(f) 2,4,5-Trimethylacetophenone
(g) 2,4-Dichloronitrobenzene
(h) C$_6$H$_5$COCH$_2$C$_6$H$_4$(p)-COCH$_2$CH$_2$CO$_2$H
(i) o- and p-NO$_2$C$_6$H$_4$CH$_2$C$_6$H$_4$CO$_2$H(p)
(j) 4-ClC$_6$H$_4$CH$_2$C$_6$H$_4$CH$_3$-4'
(k) 4-Methyl-3'-nitro-4'-hydroxydiphenyl
(l) *m*-Nitro derivative
(m) *m*-Chloro derivative

CHAPTER 18. AROMATIC HYDROCARBONS

1. (a) Benzene, *t*-butyl chloride, with 0.4 mole AlCl$_3$.
(b) Condensation of *t*-butyl chloride with *t*-butylbenzene in the presence of BF$_3$ at 25°.

2. (CH$_3$)$_3$CCl + C$_6$H$_5$CH$_3$ (+ BF$_3$) → p-(CH$_3$)$_3$CC$_6$H$_4$CH$_3$; the *t*-butyl group is resistant to oxidation, and hence the hydrocarbon can be oxidized to the acid desired.

3. Isopropylbenzene could be obtained by Friedel-Crafts condensation of benzene with (CH$_3$)$_2$CHCl, CH$_3$CH$_2$CH$_2$Cl, CH$_3$CH=CH$_2$, or (CH$_3$)$_2$CHOH; condensation of (CH$_3$)$_2$CHC$_6$H$_5$ with CH$_3$COCl in the presence of AlCl$_3$ would give p-(CH$_3$)$_2$CHC$_6$H$_4$COCH$_3$, which could be converted by the haloform reaction with NaOCl into p-(CH$_3$)$_2$CHC$_6$H$_4$CO$_2$H (the usual

oxidizing agents would attack the isopropyl group).

4. (a) C$_6$H$_5$C(CH$_3$)$_3$
(b) p-(CH$_3$)$_2$CHC$_6$H$_4$CH$_2$CH$_3$
(c) 1,3,5-Triethylbenzene
(d) p-CH$_3$C$_6$H$_4$COCH$_3$

5. (a) CH$_3$CH$_2$CH$_2$COCl + C$_6$H$_6$ (AlCl$_3$) → CH$_3$CH$_2$CH$_2$COC$_6$H$_5$; Clemmensen or Wolff-Kishner reduction.
(b) CH$_3$CH$_2$CH$_2$CH$_2$Br + C$_6$H$_5$Br + 2Na
(c) C$_6$H$_5$CH=O + BrMgCH$_2$CH$_2$CH$_3$ (decompose reaction mixture with H$_2$O) → C$_6$H$_5$CH(OH)CH$_2$CH$_2$CH$_3$; dehydrate to C$_6$H$_5$CH=CHCH$_2$CH$_3$; hydrogenate.

6. Friedel-Crafts succinoylation of benzene → C$_6$H$_5$COCH$_2$CH$_2$CO$_2$H; Clemmensen reduction to C$_6$H$_5$CH$_2$CH$_2$CH$_2$CO$_2$H; cyclization to α-tetralone with HF (or by the action of AlCl$_3$ on the acid chloride); reaction with C$_6$H$_5$MgBr; dehydration of the resulting carbinol; dehydrogenation with Se (or S, or Pd—C).

7. 2,6-Dimethyl- and 1,2,6-trimethylnaphthalene

8. α-Tetralone

9. (a) Condense toluene with acetyl chloride (AlCl$_3$), brominate, condense the α-bromoketone with the sodio derivative of diethyl methylmalonate, and complete the steps for conversion via the tetralin derivative to the aromatic hydrocarbon.
(b) The only variation from (a) necessary is to condense toluene initially with propionyl chloride.

10. (a) Wurtz-Fittig reaction of α-bromonaphthalene with methyl bromide (+2Na); (b) conversion to α-naphthylmagnesium bromide and reaction of the latter with (CH$_3$)$_2$SO$_4$.

11. Condensation of cyclohexanone with C$_6$H$_5$MgBr to give 1-phenylcyclohexanol-1; dehydration to 1-phenylcyclohexene-1; permanganate oxidation to cleave the hydrocarbon at the position of the double bond to give C$_6$H$_5$CO(CH$_2$)$_4$CO$_2$H; Clemmensen or Wolff-Kishner reduction to C$_6$H$_5$(CH$_2$)$_5$CO$_2$H (see pages 299–300 for a shorter method).

CHAPTER 19. NITRO COMPOUNDS

1. (a) C$_6$H$_5$NH$_2$ → 2,4,6-tribromoaniline; oxidation with CF$_3$CO$_3$H.
(b) Acetylation; nitration to 2,4-dinitroacetanilide; hydrolysis; oxidation with CF$_3$CO$_3$H.

2. 1,2,3,5-Tetrachlorobenzene

3. (a) 5-Nitro-1-tetralone
(b) Mixture of 2,2'- 2,4'- 4,4'-derivatives
(c) 3-Chloro-4-methoxynitrobenzene

CHAPTER 21. ARYL AMINES

2. Oxidation of a primary amine can abstract a hydrogen atom from the amino group (transient free radical) and can also result in

attack at the reactive *p*-position (formation of quinone). Stabilization is achieved by salt formation (e.g. nitration in a solution in concentrated sulfuric acid), when the nitrogen function becomes ionic and weakly *meta* directing. Stabilization by formation of the N-acetyl derivative decreases the substitution-facilitating effect and makes possible the preparation of mono *o*- or *p*-derivatives.

3. Aniline sulfate → phenylsulfamic acid → orthanilic acid → sulfanilic acid. N-Methylaniline → N-nitroso derivative → *p*-nitroso-N-methylaniline. Benzenediazonium chloride + aniline → diazoaminobenzene → *p*-aminoazobenzene. Similar rearrangements: phenylhydroxylamine → *p*-aminophenol; hydrazobenzene → benzidine.

4. Brominate, hydrolyze to *p*-bromoaniline, diazotize, hydrolyze diazonium salt.

5. Diazotize, run Sandmeyer with $Cu_2(CN)_2$, hydrolyze the nitrile to 2-methylbenzoic acid, oxidize with permanganate in alkaline solution.

6. (a) Diazotize, Sandmeyer to give *p*-bromotoluene, oxidize.
(b) Diazotize, reduce with sodium sulfite.
(c) Brominate (*e.g.* with bromine water), with introduction of Br at both positions *ortho* to the amino group, diazotize, deaminate by reduction with H_3PO_2.
(d) Diazotize, run Gattermann condensation with toluene in the presence of copper powder.
(e) Acetylate, nitrate adjacent to the acetylamino group, deacetylate, diazotize, hydrolyze —N_2Cl to —OH, reduce the nitro group.
(f) Treat with benzenesulfonyl chloride to produce the Hinsberg derivative, methylate this in alkaline solution, and remove the benzenesulfonyl group by hydrolysis.

7. Make the N-nitroso derivative, rearrange to 4-nitroso-N-methylaniline, reduce.

8. (a) Diazotize *m*-nitroaniline, run a Sandmeyer reaction to form *m*-chloronitrobenzene, reduce.
(b) From *m*-toluidine (available from *p*-toluidine) by diazotization and hydrolysis.
(c) Convert *m*-nitroaniline into *m*-chloronitrobenzene as in (a), reduce, replace NH_2 by Br by the Sandmeyer method.

9. (a) From mesitylene by mononitration, reduction, diazotization, and hydrolysis.
(b) From *p*-xylene by nitration, reduction, diazotization, and Sandmeyer reaction with $Cu_2(CN)_2$. Another route: reaction of *p*-xylene with $CH_3COCl + AlCl_3$, hypochlorite oxidation to *p*-xylenecarboxylic acid, conversion through the acid chloride to the amide, dehydration with acetic anhydride. The route from *p*-xylene through the sulfonate to the nitrile would be limited by a poor yield.
(c) Monochlorination of *m*-xylene (or nitration, reduction, replacement of NH_2 by Cl) and oxidation.
(d) From *p*-xylene by sulfonation, alkali fusion, coupling with diazotized sulfanilic acid, and reduction.

(e) From toluene by Friedel-Crafts acetylation in the 4-position, nitration, and reduction.

1. A *meta* nitro group decreases pK_a of phenol by 2.0 units and increases pK_b of aniline by 1.9 units; for a *para* group the effects are −2.8 and +3.6 units. The *ortho* series is irregular: −2.8 units for phenol and +4.9 units for aniline.

2. Instances in this chapter: steam-volatility of *o*-nitrophenol; greater steam-volatility, lower boiling points, greater solubility in ligroin of *o*-hydroxyacetophenones as compared with *p*-isomers. Instances cited earlier: volatility of ethyl acetoacetate enol; separation of *o*-(chelated) from *p*-nitroaniline by steam distillation; chelation of *o*-hydroxy azo compounds accounts for insolubility in alkali, steam volatility, and low m.p. as compared with *p*-isomers.

3. Saligenin is not soluble in bicarbonate solution but dissolves in aqueous alkali and, unless the solution is very dilute, precipitates on acidification; hence at least one phenolic hydroxyl group is present. On treatment with HBr one hydroxyl group is replaced by bromine, and hence this must be an alcoholic and not a phenolic group.

4. Prepare the dimethyl ether (dimethyl sulfate and alkali) and condense it with $CH_3COCl + AlCl_3$. Reflux the product in benzene with $AlCl_3$ to remove the methoxyl groups, and reduce the ketonic group with amalgamated zinc and HCl.

5. (a) $C_6H_6 → C_6H_5SO_3H → C_6H_5SO_3Na → C_6H_5OH → C_6H_5OCH_3$ (dimethyl sulfate and alkali)
(b) $C_6H_5OH → 2,4$-disulfonate → catechol-4-sulfonate → catechol
(c) $C_6H_5OH → o,p$-$NO_2C_6H_4OH$; separate *o*-nitrophenol by steam distillation; reduce
(d) $C_6H_5OH + N_2{}^+C_6H_4SO_3{}^-(p)$ + alkali → $NaO_3SC_6H_4N{=}{=}NC_6H_4OH(p)$ → sulfanilic acid Na salt + *p*-aminophenol. (Alternatives: $C_6H_5OH → p$-nitrosophenol; reduction; $C_6H_5NO_2 → C_6H_5NHOH → p$-aminophenol.)
(e) Preparation and alkali fusion of *m*-benzenedisulfonic acid to give resorcinol; condensation with caproic acid $(ZnCl_2)$; Clemmensen reduction.

6. The acid is soluble in bicarbonate solution; the phenol is insoluble in bicarbonate but soluble in alkali solution; the ester is insoluble in cold alkali but dissolves when the mixture is warmed or allowed to stand; the last compound, a ketol, is neutral and nonhydrolyzable and it could be identified by formation of an osazone.

7. α-Naphthol: C_6H_6 + succinic anhydride $(+ AlCl_3) → C_6H_5COCH_2CH_2CO_2H$; reduce to $C_6H_5CH_2CH_2CH_2CO_2H$; cyclize with HF to α-tetralone, dehydrogenate. β-Naphthol: $CH_3OC_6H_5 → CH_3OC_6H_4COCH_2CH_2CO_2H →$

$CH_3OC_6H_4CH_2CH_2CH_2CO_2H \rightarrow$ 7-methoxy-1-tetralone (with HF); Clemmensen reduction of keto group; dehydrogenation; demethylation.

8. In either p-aminophenol or its diacetate the N-function has a stronger directive influence than the O-function. However, acetylation in aqueous solution gives p-HOC$_6$H$_4$NHCOCH$_3$, in which a free hydroxyl group competes for a substituting agent with the weaker acetylamino group. Hence controlled bromination gives 2-bromo-4-acetylaminophenol, which affords the desired product on hydrolysis.

CHAPTER 23. ARYL HALIDES

1. $C_6H_5NH_2 \rightarrow C_6H_5NHCOCH_3 \rightarrow$
p-BrC$_6$H$_4$NHCOCH$_3$ $\rightarrow$ p-BrC$_6$H$_4$NH$_2$ $\rightarrow$
p-BrC$_6$H$_4$N$^+$Cl$^-$($+$ KI) $\rightarrow$ p-BrC$_6$H$_4$I.

2. $C_6H_5CH_2Cl \rightarrow C_6H_5CH_2OH$.
$C_6H_5CHCl_2 \rightarrow [C_6H_5CH(OH)_2] \rightarrow$
C_6H_5CHO.
$C_6H_5CCl_3 \rightarrow [C_6H_5C(OH)Cl_2] \rightarrow$
$C_6H_5COCl] \rightarrow C_6H_5COOH$.

3. (a) $CH_3C_6H_5 + CH_2O + HCl(ZnCl_2) \rightarrow$
p-CH$_3$C$_6$H$_4$CH$_2$Cl; hydrolysis (expect mixture in which p-isomer predominates).
(b) p-ClC$_6$H$_4$Br $\rightarrow$ p-ClC$_6$H$_4$MgBr
$[+ (CH_3)_2SO_4] \rightarrow p$-ClC$_6H_4CH_3$ ($+$ 2 Li) $\rightarrow$
p-LiC$_6$H$_4$CH$_3$ ($+$ CH$_2$=O) $\rightarrow$
p-HOCH$_2$C$_6$H$_4$CH$_3$.

4. Chloromethylation of p-xylene.

5. $C_6H_5OCH_3 + Br_2 \rightarrow p$-BrC$_6H_4OCH_3$ $\rightarrow$
2-nitro-4-bromoanisole $\rightarrow$
2-amino-4-bromoanisole.

6. Conversion to the nitrile, hydrolysis, decarboxylation. Catalytic hydrogenation is also applicable.

7. Preparation of the 4-bromo derivative, formation and carbonation of the Grignard reagent; chlorination, formation and carbonation of the lithium derivative; conversion of either the bromide or chloride to the nitrile (cuprous cyanide in pyridine) and hydrolysis.

CHAPTER 24. AROMATIC CARBOXYLIC ACIDS

1. From m- and p-xylene by Friedel-Crafts acetylation and hypohalite oxidation.

2. Naphthalene $\rightarrow$ phthalic anhydride $\rightarrow$ phthalimide $\rightarrow$ phthalamidic acid $\rightarrow$ anthranilic acid.

3. Toluene nitrated and o- and p-isomers separated by fractionation; p-nitrotoluene $\rightarrow$ p-toluidine $\rightarrow$ N-acetyl-p-toluidine; bromination $ortho$ to acetylamino group, hydrolysis, diazotization, deamination to m-bromotoluene; preparation and carbonation of the Grignard reagent.

4. The esters melt at much lower temperatures and more sharply than the acids; a high melting acid often suffers decarboxylation or dehydration to an anhydride when heated.

5. In analogy with the behavior of acetanilide, the N-acetyl derivative of anthranilic acid would be expected on bromination to yield 2 - acetylamino - 5 - bromobenzoic acid. This could be deacetylated, diazotized, and the diazonium salt treated with Cu(NH$_3$)$_2$OH.

6. (a) Friedel-Crafts succinoylation of toluene and Clemmensen reduction.
(b) $C_6H_5(CH_2)_4COCl + C_6H_6$ (AlCl$_3$) $\rightarrow$
$C_6H_5(CH_2)_4COC_6H_5$; Clemmensen reduction $\rightarrow$ $C_6H_5(CH_2)_5C_6H_5$. The required δ-phenylvaleric acid is available from cinnamaldehyde and malonic acid or from phenylmagnesium bromide and cyclopentanone.
(c) Pyrolysis of the calcium salt of the diacid o-HO$_2$CCH$_2$C$_6$H$_4$CH$_2$CH$_2$CO$_2$H or Dieckmann condensation of the diester.

CHAPTER 25. AROMATIC ALDEHYDES AND KETONES

1. (a) Oxidation of p-bromotoluene (available from p-toluidine) with MnO$_2$—H$_2$SO$_4$.
(b) p-Xylene $+$ CO, HCl, ZnCl$_2$—Cu$_2$Cl$_2$ (Gattermann-Koch).
(c) Resorcinol dimethyl ether $+$ HCl, Zn(CN)$_2$ in ether (Gattermann-Adams).
(d) Side-chain bromination of p-xylene to p-Br$_2$CHC$_6$H$_4$CHBr$_2$ and hydrolysis.

2. The chart should include all methods specifically covered.

3. The groups CH$_3$, CN, CHO, and COCH$_3$ are ordinarily convertible to COOH, which can be eliminated by decarboxylation. The nitro group is convertible to NH$_2$, which can be eliminated by the deamination reaction. The SO$_3$H group can be removed by hydrolysis. The phenolic OH group can be eliminated by conversion to the diethyl phosphite and reduction with lithium in liquid ammonia. A halo substituent can be replaced by CN, the nitrile hydrolyzed, and the acid decarboxylated; an iodide can be reduced directly with HI; a bromo substituent is removable by catalytic hydrogenation.

4. (a) $C_6H_5CH=C(C_2H_5)CHO$ (10% alkali)
(b) $C_6H_5CH=CHCH=CHCOC_6H_5$ (10% alkali)
(c) $C_6H_5CH=CHCH=CHCHO$ (condensation in 70% alcohol with piperidine acetate as catalyst affords the phenylpentadienal in 50% yield).

5. Oxidation] with MnO$_2$—H$_2$SO$_4$ to o-bromobenzaldehyde; condensation of the aldehyde with (CH$_3$CO)$_2$O—CH$_3$CO$_2$Na or with CH$_2$(CO$_2$H)$_2$ in pyridine-piperdine.

6. $C_6H_5COCH_3 + BrCH_2CO_2C_2H_5 + Zn \rightarrow$
$C_6H_5C(OH)(CH_3)CH_2CO_2C_2H_5$; dehydration to $C_6H_5C(CH_3)=CHCO_2C_2H_5$ (or bond isomer); hydrogenation; hydrolysis.

7. Reimer-Tiemann synthesis of aldehydic phenols; Fries synthesis of ketonic phenols; acylation of resorcinol-type phenols (very reactive) with RCOOH $+$ ZnCl$_2$; condensation of dimethylaniline with phosgene to give Michler's ketone.

CHAPTER 27. NAPHTHALENE

1. (a) β-Acetonaphthalene → β-COOH → β-COCl; Friedel-Crafts condensation with benzene.

(b) α-Bromonaphthalene → α-MgBr → α-COOH → α-COCl → α-CHO (Rosenmund or Sonn-Müller reaction).

(c) Naphthalene-β-sulfonic acid → β-naphthol → β-naphthylamine → diazonium salt → β-iodonaphthalene (Sandmeyer).

(d) β-Acetonaphthalene + CH₃MgBr → β-C(OH)(CH₃)₂ → β-C(=CH₂)CH₃ → β-CH(CH₃)₂.

2. (a) Sulfonation to Schaeffer acid (27.10) and alkali fusion.

(b) See 26.4

(c) Nitrosation

(d) Methyl ether + CH₃COCl (AlCl₃ in C₆H₅NO₂) → 6-aceto-2-methoxynaphthalene; Clemmensen reduction and demethylation.

(e) Claisen rearrangement of β-naphthol allyl ether and hydrogenation of the double bond in the side chain.

3. (a) Nitration and reduction

(b) Friedel-Crafts reaction with acetyl chloride in nitrobenzene solution and hypochlorite oxidation of the 6-aceto derivative.

(c) Sulfonation to 2-methylnaphthalene-6-sulfonic acid, alkali fusion to the naphthol, Bucherer reaction with ammonium bisulfite.

4. (a) Nitration of α-nitronaphthalene gives a mixture from which the high-melting 1,5-dinitro compound is easily separated; this on reduction gives the 1,5-diamine.

(b) Dibromination of α-naphthylamine gives the 2,4-dibromo compound (compare dinitration of α-naphthol); this on diazotization and deamination gives 1,3-dibromonaphthalene.

(c) α-Naphthylamine → α-naphthol → 2,4-disulfonic acid → 2,4-dinitro-1-naphthol (Martius Yellow) → 2,4-diamino-1-naphthol.

5. Succinoylation of naphthalene gives a mixture of 1- and 2-naphthoylpropionic acids that need not be separated. Clemmensen reduction gives a mixture of two naphthylbutyric acids, each of which on cyclization with liquid HF yields a ketotetrahydrophenanthrene. Both isomers on reduction afford tetrahydrophenanthrene, and phenanthrene is obtained on dehydrogenation (Se or Pd—C).

AUTHOR INDEX

Biographies are indicated by boldface type.

SUBJECT INDEX

A

Acenaphthene, 641,* 649,† 694, 805

β-1(and 3)-Acenaphthoylpropionic acid, 805–806

1-Acenaphthylacetic acid, 841

Acenaphthylene, 904*

Acetal, 441*†

Acetaldehyde, 228,† 396,* 397,† 398†
  aldol condensation, 456
  derivatives, 433,* 434*
  polymers, 395, 397

Acetaldoxime, 432*†

Acetals, 441–442, 484–485

Acetamide, 381,* 519†

p-Acetaminophenol, 758

Acetanilide, 439, 506,† 634, 710,* 713, 714

Acethydrazide, 381*†

Acetic acid, 360,* 364†
  perdeutero, 566*

Acetic anhydride, 389*–390†

1-Acetoacenaphthene, 841

Acetoacetic acid, 581–582

Acetoacetic ester, see Ethyl acetoacetate

Acetoacetic ester synthesis, 445–448

o-Acetoacetochloranilide, 751

Acetoacetyl fluoride, 383*†–384

Acetoin, 839, 1072

Acetomesitylene, 836–837

1- and 6-Aceto-2-methoxynaphthalene, 894

α-Acetonaphthalene, 884

β-Acetonaphthalene, 884

Acetone, 127,† 396,* 398,† 402†
  cyanohydrin, 418
  diethyl acetal, 442*†
  dimethyl acetal, 372
  enol content, 409
  halogenation, 316
  pyrolysis, 389–390

Acetone bodies, 1054, 1079

Acetonides, 187–188, 554, 597–598, 936–937, 966–967, 970, 971

Acetonylacetone, 280

Acetophenone, 385,† 426, 429, 656,† 829*
  Mannich reaction, 463–464
  oxime, 439
  reactions, 647, 775–776, 835, 843, 844

Acetophenone-o-carboxyiic acid, 834

Acetoxime, 432

α-Acetoxyacrylonitrile, 406–407

γ-Acetoxybutyraldehyde, 404†

o-Acetoxymercuriphenol, 761

3-Acetoxymesitol, 878

6-Acetoxy-6-methyl-Δ^{2,4}-cyclohexadienone, 877

1′-Acetoxyvinylcyclohexene, 861

Acetylacetone, 396,* 472†
  cleavage, 451
  enol content, 409

Acetylbenzoyl, 480

Acetyl bromide, 382*

Acetyl chloride, 382*†

Acetyl coenzyme A, 1076–1079

N-Acetylcolchinol, 912–913

1-Acetylcyclohexene, 414†

Acetylene, 213–215,*† 219–220, 232–234
  dichloride, 226
  reactions, 200, 647, 648

Acetylene–allene rearrangement, 237–241

Acetylene-D$_2$, 648

Acetylenedicarboxylic acid, 98–99, 208,* 215†

Acetylferrocene, 908

Acetyl fluoride, 382*

Acetyl iodide, 382*

1-Acetyl-2-methylcyclohexane, 429

Acetyl β-naphthylamine, 893

3-Acetyloxindole, 751

Acetylsalicylic acid, 799–800

Acetyl sulfur chloride, 761

Acidity constant, 58–59

cis-Aconitic acid, Krebs cycle, 1077–1078

Acridine, 643*

α-Acritol, 950

Acrolein, 208,* 284,† 396,* 405,† 459†
  diethyl acetal, 405

Acrose, 949–950

α-Acrosone, 950

Acrylic acid, 154, 156, 360,* 573, 733

Acrylonitrile, 227,*† 478

ACTH, 1056–1057

Activation energy, 23–24

Activation by unsaturated group, 126–127, 128, 130, 131

Active amyl alcohol, see d-Amyl alcohol

Acyloin condensation, 582–583, 838–839

Acyloins, see α-Ketols

---

* Physical constants; † Preparation

1114

Hemopyrrole, 1038
n-Heneicosane, 106*
Henry reaction, 461
Hentriacontane, 110
Heparin, 973
  anticoagulant, 1035, 1036
n-Heptacontane, 106*
Heptacosane, occurrence, 110
n-Heptadecane, 106,* 404†
Heptadecylamine, 503†
n-Heptaldehyde, 267,† 268, 396*
n-Heptaldoxime, 505
Heptalene, 926
n-Heptane, 106,* 110, 121–122, 124,* 131–132
Heptanes, 42,* 43
o- and *p*-Heptanoylphenol, 763
Heptene-1, 135,* 342†
n-Heptyl alcohol, 268†
n-Heptylamine, 505†
n-Heptyl *n*-heptanoate, 374
n-Heptylic acid, 360,* 364,† 986
HET acid, 211
Heterocyclic rings, conformation, 578–579
Heterocyclophanes, 510
Hexabromobenzene, 787
Hexachloroacetone, 507
Hexachlorobenzene, 773,* 787
Hexachloroethane, 344,* 348†
n-Hexacontane, 106*
n-Hexacosanol, 988*
n-Hexadecane, 106,* 124*
n-Hexadecanol, 280†
Hexadecylsulfuric acid, 296
Hexadeuterobenzene, 648*†
Hexadiyne-1,5, 927
Hexaethylbenzene, 645,* 652, 672–673
  pi-base, 147
Hexaethylidenecyclohexane, 673
Hexafluorobenzene, 787–788
Hexafluorocyclobutene, 922
Hexahydroxybenzene, 757
n-Hexaldehyde, 401†
Hexamethylbenzene, 238,† 645,* 647–648,†
  651,† 694
  pi-base, 147
Hexamethylenediamine, 490*
Hexamethylene dibromide, 344*
Hexamethylenetetramine, 436–437, 816–817
n-Hexane, 41–42, 106,* 107, 111,† 124*
1,4-Hexanediol, 278†
1,6-Hexanediol, 265*
2,5-Hexanediol, 280†
Hexanes, 41–42
1,2,6-Hexanetriol, 265*
Hexanone-2 and -3, 396*

Hexaphenylbenzene, 648*†
Hexaphenylethane, 349–350
Hexatriene-1,3,5, 928
Hexene-1, 135*
cis-Δ³-Hexene-1-ol, 273†
Hexene-1-yne-5, 928
n-Hexyl alcohol, 265,* 270–271†
n-Hexylamine, 490,* 504†
n-Hexyl bromide, 339*
γ-*n*-Hexylparaconic acid, 466
4-*n*-Hexylresorcinol, 759–760
Hexyne-1, -2, and -3, 214*
H:H interaction energy, 559
Hinokitol, 911
Hinsberg test, 507
Hippuric acid, 2, 794
L-Histidine, 1015,* 1016, 1022,* 1025, 1026,
  1027,† 1030,† 1062–1063
Histones, 1025, 1035
Hoesch synthesis, 830–831
Hofmann degradation, 509–513
Hofmann elimination, 669
Hofmann-Löffler reaction, 516–517
Hofmann reaction, 499–501, 523
Hofmann rule, 510–511
Homolysis, 120–122, 123–124
Homolytic substitution, 637–638, 681, 863
Homophthalic acid, 808,* 809–810†
Homosalicylaldehyde, 826
Homostilbenequinone, 852–853
Hooker oxidation, 870–872
Huang-Minlon reduction, 438
  triethanolamine as solvent, 604
Hückel rule, 904
Hudson's rules, 952–955
Hund rule, 29–30
Hunsdiecker reaction, 340–341, 357, 522, 544
Hyaluronic acid, 972–973
Hyaluronidase, 973
Hydantoins, 1028, 1029
Hydnocarpic acid, 1001*
Hydracrylic acid, 573, 574
Hydration, alkenes, 172–173
  alkynes, 228–229
Hydrazides, 501, 502
Hydrazobenzene, 689, 691*†
Hydrazoic acid, 502, 503
Hydrindene, *see* Indane
α-Hydrindone, 658,*† 661
β-Hydrindone, 575
Hydrobenzoins, 323, 430, 840
Hydrocinnamic acid, 658, 808,* 809†
Hydroformylation, 404
Hydrogenation, alkenes, 176–182
  alkyl halides, 114

32.1

BOND DISTANCES (* DESIGNATES HYBRID BOND)

BOND	TYPE	DISTANCE, Å	BOND	TYPE	DISTANCE, Å
C—C	R—R	1.54	C—N	(CH₃)₃N	1.47
C—C	Ar—R	1.54	C—N	CH₃—NO₂	1.46
C—C	Cyclopropane	1.53	C—N*	Trinitrobenzene	1.4
C—C	CH₃CH=CHCH₃	1.54	C—N	H₂N—CHRCO₂H	1.47
C—C*	CH₃C≡N	1.49	C≡N	HC≡N	1.15
C—C*	CH₃C≡CCH₃	1.47	C⋯N⁺*	Diazomethane	1.34
C—C*	C₆H₅—C₆H₅	1.48			
C—C*	CH₂=CH—CH=CH₂	1.46	C⋯N⁺*	Urea	1.37
	(2,3-bond)		C⋯N*	Pyridine	1.37
C—C*	Furane (β,β-bond)	1.46	C—S	CH₃SCH₃	1.82
C—C*	Thiophene (β,β-bond)	1.44	C=S*	CS₂	1.54
C—C*	O=CH—CH=O	1.47	C—F	CH₃F	1.42
C—C*	N≡C—C≡N	1.37	C—F	CCl₂F₂	1.35
C—C*	HC≡C—C≡CH	1.36	C—Cl	CH₃Cl	1.77
C=C	R₂C=CR₂	1.33	C—Cl	(CH₃)₃CCl	1.78
C=C	CH₂=C=CH₂	1.31	C—Cl*	CH₂=CHCl	1.69
C⋯C*	Benzene	1.40	C—Cl*	C₆H₅Cl	1.70
C⋯C*	Naphthalene	1.36, 1.39	C—Cl	HC≡CCl	1.68
C≡C	RC≡CR	1.20	C—Cl	N≡CCl	1.67
C≡C	C₆H₅C≡CC₆H₅	1.19	C—Br	CH₃Br	1.91
C—H	CH₄	1.09	C—Br*	CH₂=CHBr	1.86
C—H	CH₂=CH₂	1.09	C—I	CHI₃	2.12
C—H*	HC≡CH	1.05	C—I*	CH₂=CHI	2.03
C—H*	HC≡N	1.05	O—H	H₂O	0.96
C—O	CH₃OCH₃	1.42	N—H	NH₃	1.01
C—O	CH₃—ONO₂	1.43	N—O	CH₃O—NO₂	1.36
C—O	Dioxan	1.46	N—N	Calculated	1.40
C=O	CH₂=O	1.21	N=N	C₆H₅N=NC₆H₅	1.23
C=O*	CCl₃CHO	1.15		(cis and trans)	
C=O*	Carbon dioxide	1.16	N≡N⁺*	Diazomethane	1.13
C⋯O⁻*	Carbonate ion	1.30	S—H	H₂S	1.35
:C=O:*	Carbon monoxide	1.13	S—S	CH₃SSCH₃	2.04
C=O*	Carbon suboxide	1.20			

BOND ENERGIES[a] (Kcal./mole)

BOND	IN	ENERGY	BOND	IN	ENERGY
C—H	R—H	87	O—H	H_2O	111
C—C	RCH_2—CH_2R'	59	O—O	H_2O_2	33
C=C	RCH=CHR'	100		O_2	96
C≡C	CH≡CH	194	N—H	NH_3	84
C—O	CH_3—OCH_3	74	N—N	H_2N—NH_2	32
C=O	CH_2=O	164	N=N	RN=NR'	100
	RCH=O	171	N≡N	N_2	226
	R_2C=O	174	N—F	NF_3	56
C—N	CH_3—NH_2	55	N—Cl	NCl_3	37
	CH_3—$NHCH_3$	53	S—H	H_2S	81
C=N	RN=CHR'	147	S—S	S_6	48
C≡N	HC≡N	207	S—Cl	S_2Cl_2	61
	RC≡N	213	S—Br	S_2Br_2	51
C—S	CH_3—SCH_3	52	F—F	F_2	37
C=S		114	Cl—Cl	Cl_2	58
C—Si	C—Si	66	Br—Br	Br_2	46
Si—Si	Si	50	I—I	I_2	36
C—F	CF_3—F	93	Cl—F	ClF	61
C—Cl	Cl_2CH—Cl	70	Cl—Br	BrCl	52
C—Br	Br_2CH—Br	58	I—Cl	ICl	50
C—I	I_2CH—I	43	I—Br	IBr	42
H—H	H_2	103	Li—Li	Li	26.5
H-Bond		2–10	Na—Na	Na	18
H—F	HF	135	K—K	K	13
H—Cl	HCl	103	Li—H	LiH	58.5
H—Br	HBr	87.5	Na—H	NaH	48
H—I	HI	71	K—H	KH	44

[a] Values from M. L. Huggins, Am. Soc., **75,** 4123 (1953), and L. Pauling, "The Nature of the Chemical Bond," 3rd Ed., Cornell Univ. Press, 1960.

RESONANCE ENERGIES[1] (kcal./mole)

COMPOUND	ENERGY	COMPOUND	ENERGY
Acetamide	17	Ethyl acetate	18
Acetic acid	14	Furane	22
Acetic anhydride	30	Indole	49
Acetophenone	37	Naphthalene	61
Aniline	40	Phenanthrene	92
Anthracene	84	Phenol	36
Azulene	37	Phenylacetylene	35
Benzene	36	Pyridine	43
Butadiene	3.5	Pyrrole	24.5
Carbon dioxide	27	Quinoline	69
Carbon monoxide	105	trans-Stilbene	78
Cyclohexadiene-1,3	1.8	Styrene	38
Cyclooctatetraene	6	Thiophene	28
Cyclopentadiene	2.9	Toluene	35
2,3-Dimethylbutadiene-1,3	2.9	1,3,5-Triphenylbenzene	150
Diphenyl	71.5	Tropolone	22

[1] Values largely from G. W. Wheland, "Resonance in Organic Chemistry," Wiley, 1955.

PROPERTIES OF SOLVENTS

SOLVENT	DIELECTRIC CONSTANT	SOLY. IN $H_2O^{20°}$, %	SOLVENT	DIELECTRIC CONSTANT	SOLY. IN $H_2O^{20°}$, %
HCN (liq.)	95	∝	Pyridine	12.5	∝
Water	81.1		Aniline	7.2	3.49
Formic acid	47.9	∝	Acetic acid	7.1	∝
Nitromethane	39.4	sl. sol.	Ethylamine	6.3	∝
Acetonitrile	38.8	∝	Chlorobenzene	5.9	insol.
Nitrobenzene	36.1	0.19	Chloroform	5.0	0.82
Methanol	33.7	∝	Ether	4.3	7.5
Ethanol	25.7	∝	Triethylamine	3.1	∝ < 19°
Ammonia (liq.)	21	∝	Dioxane	2.3	∝
Acetone	21.4	∝	Benzene	2.3	0.06
Acetic anhydride	20.5	12	Carbon tetrachloride	2.2	0.1
n-Butanol	17.8	8.3	Pentane	1.8	insol.

INDUCTIVE EFFECTS (ALIPHATIC SERIES)

Electron-attracting groups: $Cl > Br > I > OCH_3 > OH > C_6H_5 > CH=CH_2 > H$
Electron-releasing groups: $(CH_3)_3C > (CH_3)_2CH > CH_3CH_2 > CH_3 > H$

ELECTRONEGATIVITY VALUES

F	4.0	S	2.5	B	2.0
O	3.5	C	2.5	Sn	1.7
N	3.0	I	2.4	Al	1.5
Cl	3.0	P	2.1	Mg	1.2
Br	2.8	H	2.1	Na	0.9